Current Biography® Yearbook 2009

EDITOR
Clifford Thompson

SENIOR EDITORS
Miriam Helbok
Mari Rich

PRODUCTION EDITOR
Forrest Cole

ASSISTANT EDITOR
Bertha Muteba

CONTRIBUTING EDITOR
Kieran Dugan

COPY ASSISTANT
Jessica McHugh

STAFF WRITERS
Christopher Cullen
William Dvorak
Dmitry Kiper
Majid Mozaffari
Margaret E. Roush
Maria A. Suarez

CONTRIBUTING WRITERS
Terence J. Fitzgerald
Tracy O'Neill
Geoff Orens
Kenneth J. Partridge
Jamie E. Peck
Claire Stanford
Hope Tarullo

EDITORIAL ASSISTANT
Carolyn Ellis

THE H. W. WILSON COMPANY
NEW YORK DUBLIN

SEVENTIETH ANNUAL CUMULATION—2009

PRINTED IN THE UNITED STATES OF AMERICA

International Standard Serial No. (0084-9499)

International Standard Book No. – 978-0-8242-1104-2

Library of Congress Catalog Card No. (40-27432)

Table of Contents

In Memory

It is with sadness that we report the death of Kieran Dugan, who was an associate editor of *Current Biography* from 1964 to 1988 and served as our consulting editor, writing obituaries, until this year. Kieran crafted obituaries that not only succinctly summarized the facts of their subjects' lives but also illuminated their uniqueness and offered glimpses of the influences they had had on their societies and cultures. Kieran loved the job of researching and writing *Current Biography* obituaries, and—to use a cliché that in his case rings true—he put his heart and soul into all of them. We will miss Kieran greatly for his diligence and meticulousness, his warmth and good humor, and his fine writing.

His former wife, Sheila Dugan, has provided us with the following obituary, written to approximate Kieran's own style:

Kieran Dugan, June 27, 1925–April 26, 2009, a writer who brought his own concise style to *Current Biography* in the early 1960s and, after formally retiring and moving to Oregon, continued to write the publication's obituary section. He will be best remembered for his understated wit and outstanding memory.

Born Thomas Russell Dugan in Taunton, Massachusetts, he entered the Holy Cross religious order at Notre Dame, Indiana, in 1943, where, as Brother Kerran, he attended the University of Notre Dame and taught in its high-school system. During that time he began to hone his writing skills, producing many articles for Catholic magazines. Upon leaving the order, in 1951, he chose to keep the name under which he wrote, changing the spelling to "Kieran." Three years later, after furthering his education at Université d'Angers, in France, and Howard University, in Washington, D.C., he joined the staff of Dorothy Day's pacifist commune and newspaper, the *Catholic Worker*. He became an anti-war activist and worked with groups seeking racial equality. In 1958 he met and married the former Sheila Johnson. Although they eventually divorced, they remained lifelong friends. He is survived by his daughters and sons-in-law, Marianne Dugan and Michael Fields, Felicia and Tom Hazel, Ianthe Dugan, Elena Dugan and William Shaw, and Erika and Denny Gordon; his grandchildren, Selena Dugan-Fields, Sophie DiStefano, Trevor Williams, Caitlin Cooper, and Audrey Hazel; his brother, Edward Dugan, and sister, Carol Lucet; his former wife, Sheila Dugan; and his cat, Brandy. He was preceded in death by his grandson Evian DiStefano in 2006.

PREFACE

The aim of *Current Biography Yearbook 2009*, like that of the preceding volumes in this series of annual dictionaries of contemporary biography, now in its seventh decade of publication, is to provide reference librarians, students, and researchers with objective, accurate, and well-documented biographical articles about living leaders in all fields of human accomplishment. Whenever feasible, obituary notices appear for persons whose biographies have been published in *Current Biography.*

Current Biography Yearbook 2009 carries on the policy of including new and updated biographical profiles that supersede earlier articles. Profiles have been made as accurate and objective as possible through careful researching of newspapers, magazines, the World Wide Web, authoritative reference books, and news releases of both government and private agencies. Immediately after they are published in the 11 monthly issues, articles are submitted to biographees to give them an opportunity to suggest additions and corrections in time for publication of the *Current Biography Yearbook.* To take account of major changes in the careers of biographees, articles are revised before they are included in the yearbook.

Classification by Profession–2009 and *2001–2009 Index* are at the end of this volume. *Current Biography Cumulated Index 1940–2005* cumulates and supersedes all previous indexes.

For their assistance in preparing *Current Biography Yearbook 2009*, I thank the staff of *Current Biography* and also the staffs of the company's Computer and Manufacturing departments.

Current Biography welcomes comments and suggestions. Please send your comments to: The Editor, *Current Biography*, The H. W. Wilson Company, 950 University Ave., Bronx, NY 10452; fax: 718-590-4566; E-mail: cthompson@hwwilson.com.

Clifford Thompson

List of Biographical Sketches

Current Biography® Yearbook 2009

Koji Watanabe/Getty Images

Abrams, J.J.

June 27, 1966– Filmmaker; screenwriter; producer

Address: c/o William Morris Agency, One William Morris Pl., Beverly Hills, CA 90212

"A lot of people in Hollywood have one great idea, one great movie in them," Steven McPherson, the president of ABC Entertainment, told David Segal for the *Washington Post* (May 5, 2006). "J.J. [Abrams] gives you four great ideas over lunch. Plus he's talking about the soundtrack, the amusement ride, the video game. He thinks about the whole world of entertainment." Abrams came to prominence in the 1990s, as the screenwriter for the feature films *Regarding Henry* (1991), *Forever Young* (1992), and *Gone Fishin'* (1997). In the latter part of the decade and the early 2000s, he amassed television credits, as the writer and producer of three critically acclaimed shows: the coming-of-age drama *Felicity*, the spy thriller *Alias*, and the cult series *Lost*. In 2006 Abrams made his feature-film directorial debut with the third installment of the *Mission: Impossible* franchise. Recent projects include the 2009 adaptation for the silver screen of the *Star Trek* television series and the Fox science-fiction TV show *Fringe*.

Jeffrey Jacob Abrams was born on June 27, 1966 in New York City and grew up in Los Angeles, California. Both of his parents are television producers. His father, Gerald W. Abrams, a former retail commercial contractor, has earned Emmy Award nominations in the outstanding-miniseries category for *Family of Spies* (1990) and *Nuremburg* (2000), and his mother, Carol Abrams, a former lawyer, is the president of Let's Pretend Productions. "I became incredibly comfortable and familiar with that world, so it never felt like anything but second nature to be on a set. Even as a little kid, all I ever wanted to do was be one of those guys on any level," Abrams told Jake Coyle for the Associated Press (May 4, 2006). He began making 8-mm movies at age eight, after witnessing a special-effects shoot during a visit to the Universal Studios backlot with his grandfather. "I remember thinking, 'There is nothing in the world that's cooler than this,'' he recalled to Jacob Bernstein for *W* magazine (May 1, 2006). When Abrams accompanied his father to his office on the Paramount Pictures studio backlot, he would watch rehearsals for *Happy Days* and *Mork and Mindy*, among other television shows. "I would go and I would be so absolutely desperate to be on the floor and be working, doing something, it was like a physical pain, I so wanted to do it. And I didn't care what. I wanted to be there and do anything," Abrams told an interviewer for madeinatlantis.com.

Upon graduating in 1984 from Palisades Charter High School, in California, Abrams enrolled at Sarah Lawrence College, a small liberal-arts school in Bronxville, New York. During his senior year he and his classmate Jill Mazursky, the daughter of the director/producer Paul Mazursky, wrote a screenplay about an escaped criminal who impersonates the advertising executive whose wallet and keys he has found. Shortly after receiving his bachelor's degree, in 1988, the 22-year-old Abrams sold the screenplay to Touchstone Pictures. Two years later *Taking Care of Business*, a big-screen comedy directed by Arthur Hiller and starring James Belushi, was released. Though the film failed to achieve box-office success, it officially launched Abrams's filmmaking career.

Abrams's sophomore effort, *Regarding Henry* (1991), a dramatic film that he also co-produced, is about a ruthless, arrogant New York City lawyer (played by Harrison Ford) who undergoes a life change following a gunshot wound to the head. The film, directed by Mike Nichols, opened to mostly negative reviews. Kenneth Turan, writing for the *Los Angeles Times* (July 10, 1991), called the movie's script "fundamentally schematic and undemanding," while Jack Mathews described it as "contrived" in his review for New York *Newsday* (July 10, 1991). Abrams also wrote and co-produced *Forever Young* (1992), which starred Mel Gibson as a 1930s test pilot and grieving widower who submits to a cryogenics experiment and awakens decades later.

After serving as the producer of the romantic comedy *The Pallbearer* (1996), which was directed by his childhood friend Matt Reeves, Abrams collaborated with Jill Mazursky on the screenplay for the lighthearted, forgettable *Gone Fishin'* (1997), in which Danny Glover and Joe Pesci played two friends who embark on a disastrous fishing trip. Abrams had better box-office success with the Bruce Willis/Ben Affleck blockbuster *Armageddon* (1998), for which he co-wrote the screenplay, with Jonathan Hensleigh. The film, about a group of oil drillers who travel in space to intercept a giant asteroid before it destroys Earth, grossed more than $500 million domestically. Also in 1998 Abrams made his first foray into television, with *Felicity*, a drama he created and penned with Reeves. The two conceived the story as a feature film before deciding that it would work better on the small screen. Their script centered on the title character, a recent high-school graduate, played by Keri Russell, who forgoes college and medical school and instead follows her high-school crush to New York City. During the show's four-year run (1998–2002) on the WB network, *Felicity* earned a Golden Globe nomination for best television show (1999); the same year Russell won a Golden Globe Award for best performance by an actress in a TV series. Abrams also produced the 1999 independent film *The Suburbans*, a comedy.

Alias, Abrams's next television project, was conceived as an edgier version of the critically acclaimed *Felicity*. "In college there are no stakes. You are supposed to play around, fail classes, get drunk and so on. But there is nothing really at stake," Abrams told Donald Clarke for the *Irish Times* (May 5, 2006). "So, I suddenly thought: what if Felicity was a spy? What if a college student was also an agent?" The spy drama, which revolved around Sydney Bristow (played by Jennifer Garner), a secret agent for a classified division of the CIA, earned favorable reviews when it premiered, on ABC, on September 30, 2001. Miki Turner wrote for the *Fort Worth Star-Telegram* (September 30, 2001), "This series . . . is riveting from start to finish." Robert Bianco, writing for *USA Today* (September 28, 2001) added, "Hip, bright and done with a great deal of flair, *Alias* is like some candy-colored—and very violent—comic book come to life. Created and directed by *Felicity*'s J.J. Abrams, who was clearly looking for a change of pace, *Alias* exhibits an assured artistic style without crossing into the artsy/phony territory of NBC's *UC: Undercover*. *Alias* has no pretensions to anything but entertainment." Although *Alias* was not a huge ratings hit, the series earned a loyal cult following—particularly among the coveted 18–49 demographic—during its five seasons on the air. It also won several awards, including a best-actress Golden Globe for Garner in 2002.

In 2004 Lloyd Braun, then the chairman of ABC Entertainment, contacted Abrams about developing a fictional show modeled after the CBS reality show *Survivor*. "I thought if I were to do this, it would be far too weird and borderline sci-fi and he'd never want to do it. But his response was no, I love that idea," Abrams told Tony Horkins for the London *Guardian* (August 6, 2005). In one week Abrams wrote the outline for *Lost*, and over a 12-week period, he wrote, cast, and shot the show's two-part first episode, which was filmed in Hawaii at a cost of about $12 million—making it one of the most expensive pilots ever produced. Abrams thrived under the fast-paced shooting schedule. "That was an incredible challenge," he told Horkins. "Though the lack of development *was* one of the greatest assets for *Lost*—we didn't have time to second-guess what we were doing and sanitize it into a more middle-ground story." (Abrams's hectic schedule prevented him from accepting an invitation from the actor Tom Cruise to pen the screenplay for an adaptation of H. G. Wells's 1898 novel, *War of the Worlds*.)

Although Braun's approval of the pilot episode's multimillion-dollar budget presumably led to his firing, his decision proved to be wise. Premiering on September 22, 2004, *Lost* was a critical and ratings success, attracting an average of 16 million viewers per episode in its first year. In a review for the *Palm Beach (Florida) Post* (September 22, 2004), Kevin D. Thompson wrote, "Forty-eight plane crash survivors are stranded on a desert island that's probably not on any map. It's a mysterious desert island, where spine-tingling creature noises can be heard in the lush jungle. The 48 strangers are scared. They're hungry. They're confused. And they're not alone. That's the delicious premise for *Lost*, ABC's intriguing *Lord of the Flies*-like new series from J.J. Abrams." The series quickly amassed a loyal following for its continuing, mysterious plot line and technique of intercutting present-day scenes with flashback or flash-forward scenes regarding the characters' lives off the island. *Lost* won several industry accolades in 2005, most notably two Golden Globes, in the categories of outstanding directing and outstanding drama series, and a Writers Guild of America Award for outstanding achievement in writing for a television series (drama).

Also in 2005 Cruise contacted Abrams again and offered him the chance to direct the third installment of the *Mission: Impossible* franchise, in which Cruise stars as special agent Ethan Hunt. After being granted creative control, Abrams teamed up with his fellow *Alias* writers Alex Kurtzman and Roberto Orci and retooled the screenplay into a more character-driven story. "In the first two movies you've learned almost nothing about who the character is. That's not going to be the case with this movie," he explained to Laura Miller for the *New York Times* (November 21, 2004). *Mission:*

Impossible III, Abrams's feature-film directorial debut, opened on May 6, 2006. Two months later Abrams signed a five-year contract with Paramount Pictures and a six-year deal with Warner Bros.; the two contracts totaled more than $55 million. Also in 2006 Abrams served as an executive producer of the ABC dramas *What About Brian* and *Six Degrees*, which were both canceled in 2007.

For his next big-screen project, *Cloverfield*, Abrams collaborated with Reeves and Drew Goddard, a fellow writer on *Lost* and *Alias*, on the script about a monster terrorizing New York City. The screenplay was inspired by Abrams's visit with one of his sons to a store in Tokyo, Japan, that contained toys based on the classic 1950s fictional Japanese movie monster Godzilla. "I loved monster movies when I was a kid, and I had not seen a monster movie since then that made me feel anything, where I got that rush. I just desperately wanted to have that sensation," he told Mark Olsen for the *Los Angeles Times* (January 16, 2008). In his film Abrams included visual references to the September 11, 2001 terrorist attacks on the U.S., and he shot *Cloverfield* in cinema-verité style to give the appearance that the footage was being recorded on a handheld camera by one of the characters. During the marketing campaign for the film, Abrams kept the monster's identity a closely guarded secret. *Cloverfield* was released in the U.S. in January 2008 and grossed more than $170 million worldwide.

Also that year Abrams had success on the small screen, as the writer and producer for the Fox science-fiction series *Fringe*, which was renewed for a second season in May 2009—the same month that Abrams's next film, *Star Trek*, the 11th film installment in the science-fiction franchise, was released to overwhelmingly favorable reviews. "Summer officially hits warp speed with *Star Trek*, a burst of pure filmmaking exhilaration that manages to pay homage to the classic 1960s TV series and still boldly go where no man, William Shatner and Leonard Nimoy included, has gone before. I couldn't be more surprised," Peter Travers wrote for *Rolling Stone* (May 6, 2009). "After six TV series and 10 movies . . . the franchise has been milked so hard, it's a wonder the udders haven't dried up and disintegrated. So how does this newbie break the jinx? By plugging in livewire J.J. Abrams, a director of style and substance . . . who fuels this origin story with killer action, bracing wit and a sense of true discovery."

Abrams's next television project is a medical drama based on Jerome Groopman's book *The Anatomy of Hope: How People Prevail in the Face of Illness* (2003). He signed on as director and executive producer of the series, which was scheduled to air on HBO in 2009. Abrams will also produce the film "Morning Glory," starring Harrison Ford and Rachel McAdams; the fifth installment of the *Mission: Impossible* franchise (which he will also co-write); and a sequel to *Star Trek*.

Abrams lives in Pacific Palisades, California, with his wife, Katie McGrath, and their three children, Henry, Gracie, and August. An avid musician, Abrams composed and recorded the theme songs for *Alias* and *Lost*.

—M.E.R.

Suggested Reading: *Daily Record* p26 Jan. 23, 2008; *Irish Times* The Ticket p2 May 5, 2006; (London) *Daily Telegraph* Art p4 Apr. 29, 2006; (London) *Guardian* The Guide p4 Aug. 6, 2005; *New York Times* (on-line) Apr. 16, 2006; *Northern Echo* p14+ May 4, 2006; *Salon.com* Jan. 18, 2008; tvguide.com Aug. 11, 2006; *Washington Post* C p1+ May 5, 2006

Selected Films: as writer—*Taking Care of Business*, 1990; *Regarding Henry*, 1991; *Forever Young*, 1992; *Gone Fishin'*, 1997; *Armageddon*, 1998; *Joy Ride*, 2001; *Mission: Impossible III*, 2006; as producer—*Regarding Henry*, 1991; *Forever Young*, 1992; *The Pallbearer*, 1996; *The Suburbans*, 1999; *Joy Ride*, 2001; *Cloverfield*, 2008; *Star Trek*, 2009; as director—*Mission: Impossible III*, 2006; *Star Trek*, 2009

Selected Television Shows: as director and producer—*Anatomy of Hope*, 2009– ; as writer and producer—*Felicity*, 1998–2002; *Alias*, 2001–06; *Lost*, 2004–08; as producer—*What About Brian*, 2006-2007; *Six Degrees*, 2006–07; *Lost*, 2004–08

Adams, Ernie

1953(?)– Director of football research

Address: New England Patriots, One Patriot Pl., Foxborough, MA 02035

In football circles Ernie Adams, the director of football research for the New England Patriots, is regarded as a mysterious figure. No one with that title appears on the payroll of any other team in the National Football League (NFL), and many Patriots players and staff members profess not to know precisely what his job entails. According to the Patriots' on-line media guide, Adams handles the team's "computer analysis" and "statistical evaluation"; when Andy Cline, a reporter for the *Alumni Magazine* (Fall 2004) of the Phillips Academy, which Adams attended, asked him to describe his responsibilities, he replied, "Think of things to help us win." Adams's ideas have proved to be very helpful indeed: since his arrival, in 2000, the Patriots have been ranked among the most intelligent and disciplined teams in the league, and between 2001 and 2008, they played in five Super Bowls and won in four. Adams works closely with Bill Belichick, the Patriots' head coach, who is

New England Patriots

Ernie Adams

widely regarded as one of the greatest and most innovative coaches in the history of the NFL. During the football draft Adams provides Belichick with information about the players in the pick; before games he helps the coach come up with game plans designed with the opposing teams' particular strengths in mind; and during games he views the field from the press box and makes suggestions directly into Belichick's ear.

Adams and Belichick have been good friends since they met in 1970, at the Phillips Academy, a private secondary school where they both dreamed of becoming coaches of professional football teams. Except for two stints with Wall Street firms, Adams has been employed by NFL teams since his college graduation, in 1975. He served as an unpaid "graduate assistant" with the Patriots (1975–79), quarterback coach with the New York Giants (1979–85), and offensive coordinator with the Cleveland Browns (1991–96) before rejoining the Patriots in 2000. A football enthusiast since early childhood, he possesses knowledge of all aspects of the game that is arguably unrivaled by anyone in the league, as are his skills at analyzing live and recorded games, evaluating players' abilities, and applying his findings. "His ability to recall particular instances is the best I've ever seen," Bill Rees, then the San Francisco 49ers' director of player personnel (he now holds the same position with the Cleveland Browns), told Pete Thamel for the *New York Times* (January 16, 2004). "He could tell you a play from when he was at Northwestern [University] in 1974 that someone ran against him, the down and distance, the yardage and how they blocked it." As Belichick's right-hand man, Adams told Thamel, "I stick my finger in as many pies as possible. It's important that I don't have everyone in the organization thinking I'm in their way. If I come to a conclusion on something, I go to Bill and give it to him." He also said, "The reason we're successful here is everyone is on the same page. We sing from the same hymn, the same notes. No one deviates."

Ernest Adams was born in Brookline, Massachusetts, in about 1953 to Helen Adams, a schoolteacher, and her husband, a career navy officer. According to Wright Thompson, writing for the ESPN magazine *eTicket* (2008, on-line), his father "wasn't around much." As a child Adams was fascinated by naval tactics and football tactics and read whatever books he could find on those subjects. From kindergarten through eighth grade, he attended the Dexter School, a private boys' school in Brookline. He began playing football when he was in third grade; even then he understood that in order to win a game, many players must function in ways for which they will not get credit. Adams's favorite play, introduced to his team at his request, was one in which he served as a decoy so that an offensive lineman could receive the ball. As an adolescent and teenager, Adams read many additional books about football, even obscure texts, such as a primer of which there were probably only about 400 copies in print; called *Football Scouting Methods*, the primer was written by Steve Belichick, Bill's father, a former navy football coach. Adams also sent away for game films and built a large collection of them.

By the time Adams enrolled at Phillips Academy, a prestigious boarding school in Andover, Massachusetts, he had acquired an encyclopedic knowledge of football history, strategy, and tactics. While he became one of the best Latin scholars at the school (which is often referred to as Andover), it was obvious to many people that he was destined to become a football coach. "Andover is the kind of place, all those young men with all that talent and ambition, where everyone knows who is going to be who in later life . . . ," H. G. Bissinger, one of Adams's classmates at Andover, told David Halberstam, who included that quote in his book *The Education of a Coach* (2005), a biography of Bill Belichick. "Ernie was going to be the coach, he loved coaching, he was always doing Xs and Os." Adams played for the school's football team as a lineman and spent his free time in the library dissecting football plays, watching and analyzing televised games, and sneaking into Boston University's stadium to watch that school's football team practice. Adams also went to coaching clinics where most of the participants were at least 10 years his senior. His near-obsessive interest in football, along with his old-fashioned way of speaking and his quirky attire, which included high-top football cleats, earned him a reputation as an eccentric.

In the fall of 1970, during his senior year, Adams met Bill Belichick, who was completing a one-year pre-college program at Andover. Belichick, he discovered, was as passionate about football as he was. The two became close friends and spent many hours together watching football films and drawing the formations of famous football plays. That season the Andover team, for which both Adams and Belichick played (the latter as center), went undefeated. Adams devoted his senior thesis to an analysis of all of Andover's offensive plays during the season. One of the highlights of his senior year was a dinner to which Steve Belichick treated his son and Adams. Adams revealed to the elder Belichick his goal of becoming a football coach; Steve Belichick was struck by the young man's passion for and knowledge of the sport.

Adams enrolled at Northwestern University, in Chicago, Illinois, in 1971. As an undergraduate—with the help of a reference from Steve Belichick, who described him as "very, very smart," according to Halberstam—he secured a position as a manager for the school's football team. At the end of his freshman year, Adams sent the head coach, Alex Agase, a letter asking if he could help coach the Northwestern team the next season; he also included a lengthy discussion of the importance of "the drop-back quarterback movement in the T-formation football." (In T-formation football, three running backs line up in a row about five yards behind the quarterback, who is positioned behind the center, so that they form the shape of the letter T. In the drop-back quarterback movement—used mostly by professional teams, whose offensive strategies rely on passing to a greater extent than do college teams—the quarterback "drops back" behind the line of scrimmage before throwing.) Agase and his assistant coach, Jay Robertson, were impressed by what he wrote and even more so with Adams himself, whom they had not met until then. "He was eighteen, I think, and I still don't know what the bottom of his knowledge is, what it is that he doesn't know, because he knows so much," Robertson told Halberstam. "I was impressed by everything about him—his intelligence in all areas, his work ethic, and his innate decency." Adams was assigned the task of "breaking down" film for Northwestern: that is, watching a single football play dozens of times to determine precisely what each player on the field was doing at any particular moment and speculating as to why. Adams proved adept at analyzing the action during live as well as filmed games, and at 18 he was made a full-fledged scout for Northwestern. Adams became a de facto assistant coach, helping during practice sessions and guiding visiting high-school coaches on tours of Northwestern. He became so influential that in 1973, when Agase became the head coach at Purdue University, he asked Adams to leave school to become his assistant. Adams turned that offer down and graduated from Northwestern in 1975, with a B.A. degree in education.

In the spring of 1975, thanks to Robertson's intercession, Adams won a job interview with staff members of the New England Patriots. He overcame the disadvantage of his lack of college playing experience by displaying his expertise, enthusiasm, and initiative: in a single day he memorized the team's entire offensive playbook. Amazed, officials offered him an unpaid position as as a "graduate assistant." His duties included analyzing film for the Patriots and preparing scouting reports about the tactics of opposing teams. "Every Monday morning, I got the most thorough report that I have ever gotten from anybody in my whole career in football," the former Patriots coach Chuck Fairbanks told Bob Hohler for the *Boston Globe* (February 3, 2008). Adams also stood out because he had intellectual interests outside football, among them Latin and finance. (Every morning he committed to memory much of the information from his newspaper's stock-market pages.) Adams grew particularly close to Ray Perkins, the Patriots' receivers coach in 1976 and 1979, who regarded Adams as "a kind of football genius," as he told Halberstam. The Patriots posted winning records during each of the three seasons that Adams spent with the team in the 1970s; in 1976 and 1978 they placed first in their division.

When Perkins became the head coach of the New York Giants, in 1979, Adams was the first person he asked to join his coaching staff. At the age of 26, Adams became the Giants' quarterback coach, even though he had never played that position. That same year, in the opinion of various observers, he in effect launched the career of Bill Belichick, who had been working for the Denver Broncos, by persuading Perkins to hire him; Belichick accepted the post of special-teams coach. He and Adams often jogged together after practice while discussing strategy. In time Adams was promoted to director of pro personnel, with responsibilities including the assessment of talent on the Giants and other teams. He presented a game plan for each team the Giants played and, by observing the Giants at practice, tried to determine whether his plans had a chance of success. For four of the six seasons Adams spent with the Giants, the team struggled to post a winning record. In 1985 the team's new head coach, Bill Parcells, helped the Giants finish in first place in the American Football Conference (AFC) East Division. Still, Adams reportedly became frustrated in New York; in 1986 he resigned to take a lucrative job as a bond trader at the Wall Street firm Mabon, Nugent & Co.

In 1991, when Belichick took his first head-coaching job, with the Cleveland Browns, he immediately hired Adams as his offensive coordinator. The Browns had a complicated history. Since 1961, when the public-relations and television executive Art Modell had purchased the team and put many controversial changes into effect, the Browns had not once made it to a Super Bowl. At the end of the 1990 season, the team's win–loss record was 3–13. Hired with a five-year contract, Belichick developed, with Adams, a long-term plan to improve what had become an undisciplined and downtrodden team. The two became known for their ability to work steadily for hours on end. "During the season, we usually start around 7 in the morning and can go as late as midnight," Adams told a reporter for the *Columbus (Ohio) Dispatch* (December 26, 1994). "That's Monday through Thursday." As a behind-the-scenes strategist, Adams gained a reputation as mysterious; Modell famously offered $10,000 to anyone who could tell him precisely what Adams was doing to earn his salary. In 1996 Belichick was fired, after clashing with Modell and the media, failing to improve the Browns' record significantly, and making the unpopular decision to fire Cleveland's much-loved quarterback, Bernie Kosar, in 1993. Adams quit, again taking a highly paid job on Wall Street.

Belichick next took assistant-coaching jobs with the New England Patriots and then the New York Jets, both under Bill Parcells, each team's head coach. In February 2000, when Belichick became the head coach of the Patriots, Adams left his job in finance to join Belichick's coaching staff. "I'm not money-motivated," Adams told Hohler. "I don't look at life in terms of how many chips I can pile up. The important thing in life is to challenge yourself and enjoy what you're doing." The Patriots were considered weak in 2000; when the team's owner, Bob Kraft, asked Adams whether he thought the team would make the play-offs that season, Adams said no, according to Halberstam. That year the Patriots won five games and lost 11.

In the following off-season, Adams and Belichick acquired several new players in the 2001 draft, including the defensive tackle Richard Seymour and the offensive tackle Matt Light, and worked to build a club based on a philosophy of team-oriented, ego-free football. The backup quarterback Tom Brady, a late-round draft pick in 2000, became the team's starting quarterback when the former starter Drew Bledsoe was severely injured in a collision on September 23, 2001. Brady emerged as an outstanding talent, leading the team to a season record of 11–5. In the 2001 Super Bowl, the Patriots faced the St. Louis Rams, who had defeated the Patriots handily during the regular season and were widely favored to win. After poring over films of Rams' games, Adams concluded that the team's offense revolved around giving the ball to the team's strong running back/receiver, Marshall Faulk, at critical moments. On the plane ride to New Orleans, Louisiana, the week before the Super Bowl, Adams and Belichick (who had drawn the same conclusion) devised a strategy in which the Patriots' defense would hit Faulk during every play, even if he had not gotten the ball, in order to wear him down. The scheme worked. In Super Bowl XXXVI Faulk gained just 76 yards, and the Patriots won, 20–17, with a last-second field goal. After the victory, Belichick, aware that the win was more the result of strategy than sheer talent, hugged Adams and said, as quoted by Halberstam, "Can you believe we won the Superbowl against the Rams with this team?" The Patriots won the Super Bowl again in the 2003 season, against the Carolina Panthers, and in the following year, in a contest with the Philadelphia Eagles.

Adams has discovered ways to make improvements in areas designated by Belichick, often seeking out the latest thinking on strategies, leadership styles, and statistical analysis. When the Rutgers University statistics professor Harold Sackrowitz made public the results of a study that might help teams determine, for example, when a moment was right to try for a field goal, many NFL coaches consulted him, but none asked him as many questions as Adams. "He got to what was really important," Sackrowitz told Hohler. "He wanted to know where the gray areas were and where it was black and white." "With every team in the NFL working full time to study their opponents and prepare their teams to compete, the margins are small," Adams told Andy Cline, "and it is often the details and the subtleties that can give one team an edge."

Before the start of the 2007 season, the Patriots acquired several strong players, including the former Oakland Raiders receiver Randy Moss; some of them agreed to take significant pay cuts to join a team that had gained a reputation for the cohesion of its coaching staff and roster. The Patriots broke many records in 2007 and became the first NFL team to complete a season with a perfect record of 16–0. (In 1972 the Miami Dolphins had a perfect record, but at that time there were only 14 games in a season.) Then, on February 3, 2008, in Super Bowl XLII, the New York Giants won an upset victory, 17–14, over the Patriots. During the 2008 season the Patriots struggled more than they had the year before; Brady sustained a season-ending knee injury in the opening game, against the Kansas City Chiefs, and was replaced for the rest of the season by the second-stringer Matt Cassel. Despite a winning record of 11–5, the team failed to advance to the play-offs. In 2009 Brady returned as a starter; as of October 20, 2009 the Patriots were in first place in their division, with four wins and two losses.

On September 10, 2007, a day after a game between the Patriots and the Jets, the Patriots were accused of having videotaped the Jets' offensive signals from a sideline location. (It is permissible to view a team's signals from the press box or on the field, but recording signals during a game violates NFL rules.) An NFL investigation into "spygate," as the taping became known, revealed that the Patriots' coaching staff had been taping signals for most of Belichick's tenure with the team. In September 2006 the NFL vice president of football operations, Ray Anderson, had sent out a memo stating that coaches were prohibited from videotaping during games; Belichick maintained that he had misunderstood the rule. He claimed to have been acting in accordance with a certain NFL Constitution bylaw that prohibits a team from using videotaped information about an opponent in the same game in which it was collected, but not from videotaping signals in the first place or from using the information in future games. Though a number of observers came to Belichick's defense—in part because videotaping opponents' signals is widely practiced in the NFL—Belichick was fined $500,000, the greatest sum ever levied against an NFL coach. The Patriots were fined $250,000, and the team was prohibited from participating in the first round of the 2008 draft.

Further investigations, conducted by the NFL in May 2008 and including an interview with the former Patriots' video assistant Matt Walsh, revealed that the tapes of signals were not used during the Jets game itself but were given to Adams. Belichick told the CBS reporter Armen Keteyian (May 17, 2008) that Adams would often glean information from such tapes "as one part of a very broad—hundreds of things that are put into preparation and game-planning." The spring 2008 investigations turned up no evidence of wrongdoing for which the team had not already been fined. When a *Boston Globe* (February 23, 2008) reporter asked Adams whether he was surprised that the spygate controversy remained a "hot topic," he responded, "You guys need something to put in your papers. . . . I'm sure you guys will keep grinding it out."

Thamel reported that Adams wears oversize glasses and "look[s] more like a doctor or a dentist than a football coach." An intensely private man, Adams does not use a computer and rarely uses the phone. He relishes watching films in the solitude of his office, and when the Patriots moved into new offices, Adams traded his second chair for an extra bookshelf, to discourage visitors from staying very long. Adams lived with his mother in Brookline until her death, in 2004.

—M.E.R.

Suggested Reading: *Boston Globe* Sports p128 Jan. 30, 2004, D p8 Feb. 3, 2008, C p7 Feb. 23, 2008; *Columbus (Ohio) Dispatch* G p1 Dec. 26, 1994; *New York Times* D p7 Jan. 16, 2004; Phillips Academy *Alumni Magazine* p20+ Fall 2004

Adele

May 5, 1988– Singer; songwriter

Address: c/o September Management, 80 Chiswick High Rd., London W4 1SY, England

Dave Hogan/Getty Images

The British singer/songwriter Adele has often been compared to the legendary American vocalists Ella Fitzgerald and Etta James—whom she has cited as her two biggest influences—and to the award-winning British crooner Amy Winehouse. To many of her fans, however, Adele is "simply too magical to compare her to anyone," Matthew Chisling wrote for the All Music Guide (on-line). In February 2009, when she was three months short of 20, Adele won a Grammy Award for her debut album, *19*, and another for the single "Chasing Pavements"—in what a critic for *Maclean's* (March 23–30, 2009) termed "a rare triumph of talent over sales in the music industry." "Smashing" is the word a critic for *People* (June 23, 2008) chose to describe *19*, writing that it "seamlessly weaves R&B, pop, jazz, folk and blues into her own torchy tapestry. With a knockout voice that's rich and supple, robust and sultry, it's hard to believe that this singer-songwriter is barely out of her teens." Adele, widely quoted as saying that she has always liked to be the center of attention, Adele completed a rigorous course of study at a performing-arts high school in London, England. Recordings of several of her songs that she uploaded to her MySpace.com profile won her a contract in 2006 with the independent British label XL, whose roster also includes Radiohead, White Stripes, and M.I.A. In 2008 she was named the first recipient of the Brit Awards Critics' Choice Award. Several of Adele's singles became hits in her native land before the release of *19*. The album landed at the top spot on British charts as soon as it went on sale; in the U.S., where it was released five months later, it drew only moderate attention until October 18, 2008, when Adele performed on the TV show *Saturday Night Live*. Thanks to the appearance of the 2008 Republican vice-presidential nominee, Governor Sarah Palin of Alaska, on the same installment, the show attracted 17 million viewers—its biggest audience in years. Sales of *19* immediately jumped;

they received another huge boost after Adele's Grammy wins, and the record has achieved platinum status (selling more than a million copies). In early 2009 150 British music critics ranked Adele first in the BBC's "Sound of 2008" poll of most promising new music talent.

Adele Laurie Blue Adkins was born on May 5, 1988 in Tottenham, an area of North London, England, and spent her early years in Brixton, a multiethnic community in South London. Her mother, Penny, was an unmarried 18-year-old at the time of Adele's birth. Her father, a Welsh dockworker, took no part in her upbringing. To eke out a living, her mother worked odd jobs, among them freelance masseuse and furniture maker. "She's the most supportive mum ever," Adele told Hamish Bowles for *Vogue* (April 2009). "She's my best friend." Beginning at a very young age, Adele told Stuart Husband for the London *Sunday Telegraph* (April 27, 2008), she was fascinated by singers' voices: "I used to listen to how the tones would change from angry to excited to joyful to upset." She liked to sing for her mother and her mother's friends, sometimes imitating the styles of the Spice Girls, Gabrielle, and other pop acts. During Adele's childhood her mother married; her husband works for Wickes, a British home-improvement chain, and Adele has a half-brother. When Adele was 11 the family moved to West Norwood, a mostly residential section of South London. There, she attended a rough comprehensive school, where she was the only white student in most of her classes. Outside school she was exposed to R&B and hip-hop acts including Destiny's Child, Faith Evans, and P. Diddy.

When Adele was 14 her mother enrolled her at the tuition-free London School for the Performing Arts and Technology, an independent school funded by both the government and charitable donors. Known as the Brit School, it is the alma mater of many British recording artists, among them Amy Winehouse, Leona Lewis, Kate Nash, Katie Melua, Imogen Heap, and members of the indie pop bands the Feeling and the Kooks. In addition to taking courses in singing, as a student there Adele studied the guitar and learned how recording studios operate, how to interpret legal contracts, and other aspects of the music business. "I never got bored, so I was never getting in trouble," she told Hamish Bowles. "I'd always had a problem taking teachers seriously, whereas there, you wanted to listen to them because they'd all done it, practiced whatever subject they were teaching."

One day while browsing in a bargain bin at a local record shop, Adele came upon albums by the soul and jazz masters Etta James and Ella Fitzgerald. She bought them because the singers' photos on the covers—in particular, their hairdos and James's eye makeup—appealed to her. "Chart music was all I ever knew," she told Husband. "So when I listened to the Ettas and the Ellas, it sounds so cheesy, but it was like an awakening. I was like, oh, right, some people have proper longevity and are legends. I was so inspired that as a 15-year-old I was listening to music that had been made in the Forties. The idea that people might look back to my music in 50 years' time was a real spur" to her in aiming for a singing career. She told Hamish Bowles that hearing James and Fitzgerald sing "changed my life. It was so heartfelt compared with the music I'd been listening to." She began listening to recordings by other "old legends," as she thought of them: Roberta Flack, Diana Ross and the Supremes, and Johnny Cash.

During that period Adele lived next door to and frequently jammed with Shingai Shoniwa, the British vocalist and bassist for the indie rock band the Noisettes, who encouraged her to write her own songs. She received further support from a friend of her stepfather's, a music producer who was impressed by the skill with which she sang the Blondie song "Heart of Glass." With the producer's help she recorded a demo of her first song, "Hometown Glory," an ode to Tottenham that she wrote at age 16. One of Adele's friends then posted the song on the social networking site MySpace.com, where it drew a lot of attention. On Christmas Eve 2004 Adele launched her own MySpace page, as a way to gauge reactions to her songs.

One night after she graduated from the Brit School, in May 2006, Adele performed at the Troubadour, a small London club, as the opening act for her friend Jack Peñate. With seating for about 100 people, "the whole room was packed," Adele recalled to Bowles. When she began to sing, "the whole room was silent, and I saw these random girls just, like, crying. That was the time I was like, 'Oh, my God, this is amazing, can't live without it.' There's nothing more freeing than playing live, nothing." In November 2006, largely on the strength of three songs on her MySpace page, Nick Huggett, then the A&R (artist and repertoire) manager of XL Recordings, recruited Jonathan Dickins of September Management to be her manager and signed her to a contract for her first album.

In early 2007 Adele started performing at small pubs in North London. She then toured in the United Kingdom with the singers Jamie T., Raul Midon, Devendra Banhart, Amos Lee, and Keren Ann and the band Exist. That June she made her U.K. television debut on the popular BBC2 music program *Later . . . with Jools Holland*, on the same day that the major music stars Paul McCartney and Björk also appeared. Adele performed her song "Daydreamer," about a bisexual friend with whom she had fallen in love. The song later received a lot of airplay on BBC Radio 1. Writing for the London *Observer* (January 20, 2008), Casper Llewellyn Smith praised "the way she stretched the vowels" in her singing of "Daydreamer," as well as "her wonderful soulful phrasing [and] the sheer unadulterated pleasure of her voice." In October 2007 Adele released "Hometown Glory" as her debut single, on the Pacemaker Recordings label (founded by the British singer Jamie T, a friend of hers); the limited-edition, seven-inch vinyl also featured the song "Best for Last" on its B-side. According to Llewellyn Smith, "Daydreamer" proved that Adele is "a rare singer." That month she also embarked on her first U.K. headlining tour. Meanwhile, the British press had begun referring to her as "the new Amy Winehouse." (Winehouse's two dozen awards include five Grammys, won in 2007.)

In December 2007 some 1,000 music-industry insiders and critics named Adele the first recipient of the Critics' Choice Award; the newest of the so-called Brit Awards, it was introduced by the British Recording Industry Trust to recognize the most promising among the artists or groups poised to release their debut albums in 2008. At the Brit Awards ceremony, held in February 2009, Adele performed with Mark Ronson, one of the producers of *19* and a winner of the 2008 Brit Award for best British solo artist.

In Great Britain *19* was released on XL Recordings in January 2008. The 12 songs on *19*—including "Chasing Pavements," "Cold Shoulder," "Crazy for You," "Melt My Heart to Stone," "First Love," and a cover of Bob Dylan's "Make You Feel My Love"—are mostly about heartbreak, or, as Brett Johnson wrote for the Associated Press (2008, on-line), "the twisted emotions that spring from tainted love." The disk immediately resonated with British music fans and entered the U.K. charts at number one. "Chasing Pavements," which arrived on the U.K. singles charts at number two and remained there for three consecutive weeks, was inspired by Adele's discovery that her boyfriend had cheated on her. After pummeling him in a club late one night, she left the premises and began to run. "I was running down Oxford Street," she recalled to Melinda Newman for the *Washington Post* (February 1, 2009, on-line). "I get cabs everywhere, right? So for me to be running is a big thing; it's never going to happen again. And I thought 'What are you doing? You're just chasing a road.' And then I thought, 'Oh, chasing pavement. I like that,' and went home and wrote it." In the chorus she sings, "Should I give up, / Or should I just keep chasing pavements / Even if it leads nowhere? / Or would it be a waste / Even if I knew my place / Should I leave it there? / Should I give up, / Or should I just keep chasing pavements / Even if it leads nowhere?" Thanks in part to unexpected support from the hip-hop superstar Kanye West, who uploaded the video of "Chasing Pavements" onto his personal blog, the song remained in the United Kingdom's Top 10 for seven weeks.

After signing a U.S. deal involving a collaboration between Columbia Records and XL Recordings, Adele embarked on a short North American tour to promote *19*. The album was released in the U.S. in June 2008; produced by Ronson, Eg White, and Jim Abbiss, it was greeted enthusiastically, for the most part. Matthew Chisling wrote for the All Music Guide Web site, "Bluesy like it's no one's business yet voluptuously funky in a contemporary way, Adele rocks out *19* with a unique voice and gritty sound that dazzle endlessly. Synthesizing blues, jazz, folk, soul, and even electric pop, Adele mystifies through her mature songwriting skills and jaw-dropping arrangements. . . . This debut isn't an empty promise of a career; *19* is a fleshed-out stunning portrayal of a young woman with a talent beyond her years who deserves immense credit for a unique style that never fails. A beyond stellar debut in both quality and originality." Ron Hart, in a review for the Pop Matters Web site (July 1, 2008, on-line), proclaimed, "This is music . . . that clear blows the roof off any other blue-eyed R&B album that has come out of Great Britain since Macca [Paul McCartney] got down with Stevie Wonder [in 1982]." The critic for *Variety* (June 10, 2008, on-line), Phil Gallo, wrote that Adele has "an affinity for strains of soul music largely forgotten by U.S. artists. Her phrasing, for the most part, veers toward the softer R&B singers, a bit of Dionne Warwick, Minnie Ripperton and Dusty Springfield sharing a pot of tea in a plush and comfortable room. *19* is a most agreeable, soulful album. . . . Yes, Amy Winehouse comparisons are justified in spots. But whereas Winehouse, Kate Nash, Lily Allen, Joss Stone and Duffy are plowing single plots of R&B soil, Adele is taking a broader perspective, assimilating various predisco R&B styles to create a field with the potential to bear fruit for years to come." Earlier, Andy Gill, the chief rock critic for the London *Independent* (January 25, 2008, on-line), had offered a different perspective: "The iTunes/MySpace revolution has speeded up the pop process to such an extent that a new act barely has time to draw breath before being acclaimed in ever-growing hyperbole and seeing their debut album go straight to No 1. But, though superficially impressive, this is often disastrous for the artist's long-term prospects, destroying the vital growth period during which musicians develop their performing acumen, musical tastes, and the kind of world-view obtained only through years of hard knocks. Instead, artists are now catapulted up the pop mountainside and expected to grab hold of whatever outcrop is within their grasp, and grimly hold on for dear life. . . . Adele . . . is the latest recipient of this hype. Am I the only one to find something slightly sinister in the way we're being brow-beaten into unanimous acclaim for her modest talents?" Although he deemed *19* to be "a passably decent debut," he complained, "It's pretty much the same sort of shallow-but-showy vocal facility favoured by TV talent contests that's being praised, [Adele's] delivery sounding like a convenient blending of Winehouse's R&B chops with Nash's mockney mannerisms: interesting in small doses (notably 'Hometown Glory'), it becomes irritating over a full album. In sparse settings, as here, [Adele] struggles to sustain one's interest—a situation not helped by a narrow, youthful focus on romantic themes. There's a limit to the appeal of teenage crushes, brush-offs and frustrations, and Adele sails blithely beyond it."

To promote *19* in the U.S., Adele appeared on television on programs including *The Today Show, The Late Show with David Letterman*, and *The View*. The album debuted at number 56 on *Billboard*'s Top 200 album chart, and sales remained mediocre. Then Adele landed a coveted guest spot on the October 18, 2008 installment of *Saturday Night Live*. Buildup to that particular show grew enormous amid rumors, which turned out to be correct, that the Republican vice-presidential nominee, Sarah Palin, would make a guest appearance that night. (Contributing to viewers' heightened expectations were the half-dozen cameos on the show in which Tina Fey, a former *Saturday Night Live* writer and actress, had performed impressions of Palin.) That night Adele sang both "Chasing Pavements" and "Cold Shoulder," and in the following week, the popularity of *19* rose tremendously. As of mid-2009 it had sold upwards of 1,200,000 copies worldwide. In December 2008 Adele was nominated for four Grammy Awards: song of the year, record of the year, best new artist, and best female pop vocal performance; she won the last two, for *19* and "Chasing Pavements," respectively. At the awards ceremony, held in February 2009, she performed "Chasing Pavements" with the country musician Jennifer Nettles.

In the course of an extensive U.S. tour in June 2009, Adele performed with Chaka Khan and Janelle Monae in the Hollywood Bowl, in Los Angeles, California. The following September she performed with Jennifer Hudson, Jordin Sparks, Kelly Clarkson, Leona Lewis, and Miley Cyrus at the Brooklyn Academy of Music, in New York City, as part of a VH1 "Divas" concert that raised money for the Save the Music Foundation. Adele's sophomore album is scheduled to be released in 2010.

Adele has spoken openly about being overweight. "It doesn't bother me . . . ," she told Sylvia Patterson for the London *Observer* (January 27, 2008). "I'm very confident. Even when I read people saying horrible stuff about my weight. Until I start not liking my own body, until it gets in the way of my health or stops me having a boyfriend then I don't care. I'm fine. Since I was a teenager I've been a size 14 or 16, sometimes 18. And it's never been an issue in any of the relationships I've had." "Fans are encouraged that I'm not a size 0—that you don't have to look a certain way to do well," she told Hamish Bowles, whose article about her for *Vogue* was accompanied by photos of Adele by the celebrated portrait photographer Annie Liebovitz. Adele currently shares an apartment with her mother in the Battersea section of London.

—C.C.

Suggested Reading: *Baltimore Sun* (on-line) Jan. 15, 2009; blogcritics.org July 16, 2008; (London) *Observer* (on-line) Jan. 27, 2008; (London) *Sunday Express* p71 Jan. 6, 2008; (London) *Sunday Telegraph* p8+ Apr. 27, 2008; (Minneapolis, Minnesota) *Star Tribune* Jan. 20, 2009; *New York Times* AR p30 Dec. 28, 2008; *San Francisco Chronicle* (on-line) Jan. 29, 2009; *Vogue* p198+ Apr. 2009; *Washington Post* M p3 Feb. 1, 2009

Selected Recordings: *19*, 2008

Allen, Ray

July 20, 1975– Basketball player

Address: Boston Celtics, 226 Causeway St., Fourth Fl., Boston, MA 02114

While he has not attained superstar status, Ray Allen, a 12-year veteran guard of the National Basketball Association (NBA), has developed a reputation as one of the league's "pure" shooters—meaning that there is a deftness and smoothness to his shots. "He's among the league's most explosive players. His skill at dropping in floaters and finger rolls makes him more dangerous still. Give him a step and, with the most elegant of strokes, he'll bury a medium range jumper. Give him two steps and he'll hit the three pointer . . . ," L. Jon Wertheim wrote for *Sports Illustrated* (February 26, 2001). "It's not that he's elusive or shy—in fact, as far as star athletes go, he is uncommonly engaging and personable . . . ," he continued. "This prompts an obvious question: Why is Allen still on the B-list of NBA stars? . . . . A player this well-rounded and with this much charisma ought to be on the front lines of the league's marketing offensive, scooping up endorsements by the handful." As an undergraduate Allen helped the University of Connecticut's Huskies gain three consecutive Big East Conference regular-season titles while becoming the fourth-leading scorer in the school's history, with 1,922 points, and the school's single-season record holder for three-pointers scored (115). During his first 10 NBA seasons, Allen averaged 21.2 points per game for the Milwaukee Bucks and the Seattle SuperSonics. Traded to the Boston Celtics in 2007, Allen helped lead the team in 2008 to their 17th title and first NBA championship in more than 20 years.

Wortheim partly answered his own question about Allen when he wrote, "His enthusiasms and experiences are so disparate and often incongruous that no coherent profile emerges. Allen admits his interests are all over the map, but he figures it's because that's where he spent his childhood." The third of five children, Walter Ray Allen Jr. was born on July 20, 1975 to Walter and Flora Allen in Merced, California. His father was a welder and

Stephen Dunn/Getty Images

Ray Allen

machinist for the U.S. Air Force, and Allen spent his childhood living on military bases in the U.S. and abroad. "We moved around a lot, which is pretty natural when you're a military kid," he told Perry M. Lamek for *Milwaukee Magazine* (February 27, 2003). "We were in most places for about three years, then we'd have orders to go to another place. I was born in California, then we moved to Germany, then to Oklahoma, then to England, back to California and then to South Carolina." While in grade school Allen participated in sports, including baseball, football, and soccer, at the youth-activities centers on the various bases. At the age of about nine, he started playing basketball with his father and brother. His father first noticed Allen's talent for basketball when the boy was 12. "He was . . . playing in a tournament at Edwards [Air Force Base, in California's Mojave Desert]," Walter Allen told Pat McKenna in an interview posted on the Air Force Link Web site. "Ray was dribbling down the floor on a fast break, and he had a man wide open underneath the basket. I was thinking 'throw it, throw it,' but didn't know if he saw the man. All of [a] sudden, he fires this no-look pass downcourt for the score. I thought, 'Man, how'd he see that guy?' At that point, I knew." When Allen was 13 years old, he and his family transferred to Shaw Air Force Base, in South Carolina, where he honed his basketball skills at the base gym during pick-up games against former college and high-school players. (Allen often found ways to circumvent the gym's minimum age requirement of 16.) On the court he felt compelled to score five lay-up shots with each hand before leaving. During his youth and early adulthood, he hid that compulsion, later diagnosed as mild obsessive-compulsive disorder, from his family and friends. "I was almost embarrassed by it," he told Jackie MacMullan for the *Boston Globe* (April 20, 2008). "It was just always beating inside my brain when I was young and trying to make sense of who I was."

At age 15 Allen attended Hillcrest High School, in Dalzell, South Carolina, where he played on the varsity basketball team. As a junior he averaged 25.5 points and 11.5 rebounds per game. Allen, whose on-court performance earned him the high-school nickname "Candy Man," improved on those numbers during his final year of high school (1992–93), averaging 28.5 points and 13.5 rebounds while helping lead his team to a 27–4 record and a state championship title. After receiving scholarship offers from a number of top colleges, including the University of Kentucky, he decided to attend the University of Connecticut, in Storrs, where he played point guard for the Huskies men's basketball team, under head coach Jim Calhoun. Allen, a business-education major, struggled offensively in his rookie season (1993–94). Following a four-game scoring drought, during which he scored 32 percent from the field and had only nine field-goal attempts, Allen began toting a basketball with him everywhere he went, adopting a practice of the legendary Milwaukee Bucks player Oscar Robertson. "I wanted to be more familiar with the ball, more comfortable with it," he told Ken Davis for the *Hartford (Connecticut) Courant* (November 25, 1994). Allen regained his offensive stroke; at the end of the season, he averaged a team-leading 12.6 points and 4.6 rebounds in 34 regular-season games and also shot 40.2 percent from three-point range, earning Big-East All-Rookie Team honors. That same year he helped the Huskies win the Big East regular-season title. Allen attributed his first-year success to the greater emphasis on Huskies' forward Donyell Marshall, who planned to forgo his senior year to enter the 1994 National Basketball Association (NBA) Draft. "When I came in, I wasn't the focal point," Allen told Davis. "Donyell was. That's where I think I got my confidence, because a lot of people didn't pay attention to me."

Allen's offensive numbers improved during his sophomore season (1994–95)—his first year as a starter. He averaged 21.1 points, 6.8 rebounds, 2.3 assists, and 1.9 steals per game, helping the Huskies capture their second consecutive Big East regular-season championship and advance to the National Collegiate Athletic Association (NCAA) Tournament's Elite Eight. Next came Allen's breakthrough 1995–96 season, in which he established himself as one of college basketball's most dominant shooting guards by averaging 23.4 points, 6.5 rebounds, and 3.3 assists per game. At the 1996 Big East Championships, held at New York City's Madison Square Garden, Allen scored the dramatic game-winning shot to give the Huskies a one-point victory (75–74) over the Georgetown University Hoyas. "That was the best feeling I've ever had in basketball," he told Percy Allen for the *Seattle Times* (February 15, 2004). "Hitting the game-winning shot in the Garden is something that probably every kid dreams about." For his effort Allen was named to the All Big East First Team and the All-America First Team and also earned player-of-the-year honors from the Big East and United Press International (UPI).

At the end of his junior year, Allen announced that he was leaving the University of Connecticut to enter the 1996 NBA Draft, joining other top-ranked college players, including Allen Iverson, Kobe Bryant, Stephon Marbury, Marcus Camby, Shareef Abdur-Rahim, Antoine Walker, and Derek Fisher. Even as a team member for three years rather than four, Allen currently ranks as the Huskies' fourth all-time leading scorer (1,922 points) and also holds the single-season record for three-point shots made (115). (His number was retired in February 2007, as part of a halftime ceremony honoring the accomplishments of 13 former players and three former coaches. Prior to that he was named honorary captain of the 25-member UConn All-Century Basketball Team.)

In 1996 Allen was selected fifth overall by the Minnesota Timberwolves, who subsequently traded him, along with the center Andrew Lang, to the Milwaukee Bucks for the fourth pick, Marbury. The trade announcement elicited loud boos from Bucks' fans. "That was one of the most discouraging moments of my life, to know that I got booed," he told Jason Wilde for the *Wisconsin State Journal* (March 22, 1998). "I cried. I did, really. That whole night. . . . I've always gone to a place where people wanted me and I felt wanted. And that was the one time where I was like, 'If the people don't want me, then trade me.' My heart was broken. I didn't know what I should do. I talked to my parents and a couple of my friends, and I just decided to go out there and play and be myself. All I could do was try to keep a smile on my face and play like I played in college."

Allen had a strong debut season (1996–97), appearing in all 82 regular-season games and averaging 13.4 points—third-best on the team. He led the team in games started (81) as well as three-point percentage (.393) and free-throw shooting percentage (.823). Allen was selected to play in the NBA Rookie All-Star Game, in which he scored eight points. During that period he unexpectedly embarked on an acting career, after the film director Spike Lee, a famously avid New York Knicks fan, approached him about trying out for the starring role in *He Got Game*, about a promising basketball player and his estranged relationship with his father, a recently paroled convict (played by Denzel Washington). (Allen was among a group of young NBA players, including Marbury, Iverson, and Kevin Garnett, who were contacted about the part.) After a successful audition Allen underwent five weeks of intensive private training with an acting coach to prepare for the role. Allen's cinematic debut earned critical raves.

Prior to his sophomore NBA season (1997–98), Allen found himself tangentially involved in a controversy, following claims by John Lounsbury, a sports agent, that he had given thousands of dollars in cash and gifts to several UConn college players, among others, during the 1995–96—a violation of NCAA rules. Allen denied any wrongdoing and was never charged. Two of his former Huskies teammates, Kirk King and Ricky Moore, received suspensions; the University of Connecticut was stripped of its victories in the 1996 NCAA tournament and ordered to pay more than $90,000.

Although Allen averaged 19.5 points, 4.9 rebounds, and 4.3 assists per game in the 1997–98 season, the team, which finished with a 33–46 record, failed to make the play-offs for the second consecutive year. During the strike-shortened 1998–99 season—the result of the failure by NBA players and owners to reach a new collective-bargaining agreement—Allen played in all 50 regular-season games, posting an average of 17.1 points and 4.2 rebounds. His free-throw percentage (.903) was fourth-best in the league. With a record of 28 wins and 22 losses, the Bucks advanced to the NBA Playoffs, where they suffered a first-round defeat by the Indiana Pacers. In February 1999 Allen signed a six-year, $71 million contract extension with the Bucks, despite their struggles. "You can be on a winning team and you may not be content," he told Steve Aschburner for the Minneapolis *Star Tribune* (March 19, 2000). "I hope I'm an example in this league. . . . People said maybe I should go to L.A. if I want to do more movies. But I said why, when I made that one while I was with Milwaukee. It's all in the will of the man. If you really want to accomplish something, you can." The 23-year-old Allen negotiated directly with the team's owner, Herb Kohl, a U.S. senator, retaining the agent's standard 4 percent commission and instead hiring lawyers to examine the contract. In the 1999–2000 season Allen averaged 22.1 points, 4.4 rebounds, and 3.8 assists per game to help the Bucks earn their second consecutive NBA play-off berth. Allen was voted to his first All-Star Game and was a member of the 1999 U.S. Men's national team, which won a gold medal at the 2000 Summer Olympics, in Sydney, Australia. The following season (2000–01), for the fifth consecutive year, Allen appeared in every regular-season game, solidifying his reputation as one of the NBA's most durable players. Averaging 22 points per game, he also showed improvement in his rebounding numbers—from an average of 4.4 to 5.2 rebounds—and in his assists, from an average of 3.8 to 4.6. He also provided a powerful offensive complement to the guard Sam Cassell, who averaged 18.2 points per game, and the forward Glenn Robinson, who also finished the season with a 22-points-per-game average. Their combined efforts helped the Bucks (52–30) claim their first division title since 1986. The team advanced to the Eastern Conference finals, losing the deciding seventh game (108–91) to the Philadelphia 76ers, who advanced to the NBA finals against the Los Angeles Lakers, the eventual champions. In 18 play-off games Allen averaged a team-high 25.1 points, a career-best 6.0 assists, and 1.33 steals in 42.7 minutes per game. During the regular season Allen led the team in average number of minutes played (38.2); he also set career highs in field-goal percentage (.480) and average number of assists per game (4.6), steals per game (1.51), and rebounds per game (5.1). He made his second consecutive appearance at the All-Star Game; he also entered and won the event's three-point-shootout competition.

After narrowly missing the NBA finals in 2001, the Milwaukee Bucks (again led by Allen, Cassell, and Robinson) failed to advance to the play-offs during the 2001–02 season, losing 14 of the final 19 games and finishing with a disappointing 41–41 record. Allen averaged 21.8 points, 4.5 rebounds, and 3.9 assists per game. Despite being sidelined for nearly two weeks by tendinitis in his left knee, which ended his consecutive-games streak at 400, Allen achieved career-bests in three-point percentage (.434), three-pointers made (229) and attempted (528). He also led the league in three-point field goals made (229) and ranked number 10 in three-point percentage (.434). In the off-season Robinson was traded to the Atlanta Hawks for Toni Kukoc, Leon Smith, and a 2003 first-round draft pick. The Bucks continued to struggle during the first half of the 2002–03 season. Allen's field-goal-percentage numbers dropped, from .462 to .437; he also saw a drop in three-point percentage, from .434 to .395. In an interview for *Sports Illustrated*, the Milwaukee Bucks' coach, George Karl, criticized what he perceived as Allen's lack of killer instinct. "I call him Barbie Doll because he wants to be pretty. He's a great player, but he cares too much about having style, making highlights and being cool. Basketball isn't about being cool. It's a tough, competitive game, and to win you have to be mean, you have to be an assassin, and that's not Ray."

In February 2003 Allen was traded to the Seattle SuperSonics (now called the Oklahoma City Thunder). Appearing in 29 games Allen averaged 24.5 points, 5.6 rebounds, and 5.9 assists for the Sonics, who finished the season with a 40–42 record. (In 47 games with the Bucks that season, he had averaged 21.3 points, 4.6 rebounds, and 3.5 assists per game.)

In November 2003 Allen underwent arthroscopic surgery on his right ankle, causing him to miss the first 25 games of the season. Despite that setback he finished the season with solid numbers, averaging 23 points, 5.1 rebounds, and 4.8 assists per game. In 2004–05 he averaged 23.9 points (10th-best in the league) and 4.4 rebounds per game to help lead the Sonics to a 52–30 record and the Northwest Division title. The Sonics advanced to the Western Conference Semifinals, where they lost in six games to the San Antonio Spurs, the eventual champions. In the summer of 2005, Allen signed a five-year, $80 million contract to remain in Seattle. Additionally, Nate McMillan left the Sonics to become the head coach of the Portland Trailblazers. In the 2005–06 season, under head coaches Bob Weiss and Bob Hill, the Sonics finished with a 35–47 record and failed to earn a postseason berth. Allen, however, performed well, averaging 25.1 points per game—10th-best in the league for a second straight season. In July 2006 the franchise was sold to an Oklahoma City–based investment group. Allen's 2006–07 season was cut short after 55 games when he underwent surgery to remove bone spurs in both of his ankles. At the time he was averaging 26.4 points per game—a career high. Allen's tenure with the Sonics ended on June 28, 2007—NBA Draft day—when he was traded to the Boston Celtics, along with the Sonics draft pick Glen Davis, for Jeff Green, Wally Szczerbiak, and Delonte West. During his four seasons (2003–07) with the Sonics, Allen was the team's scoring leader and appeared in every All-Star Game. The Celtics made headlines again in July, with the acquisition of the power forward Kevin Garnett from the Minnesota Timberwolves, in exchange for the center Theo Ratliff, the guard Sebastian Telfair, and the forwards Al Jefferson, Ryan Gomes, and Gerald Green, as well as two first-round draft picks and a monetary settlement.

Following those deals the Celtics, who had finished last (24–58) in the Eastern Conference's Atlantic Division during the 2006–07 season, were instantly regarded as play-off contenders. However, many questioned whether the team's success would be hampered by a clash of egos involving Allen, Garnett, and the shooting guard Paul Pierce concerning playing time. "I've never been insecure," Allen was quoted as saying by Marc J. Spears in the *Boston Globe* (September 21, 2007). "I've never been the jealous type. I don't have a big ego. . . . We have to absolve ourselves of any animosity or any egos out there on the floor. If we win, everybody will ride together on whatever float it is on the championship parade." In his first season with the Celtics, Allen, who was still recovering from the surgery on both ankles, struggled with his perimeter shooting. He averaged 17.4 points and 3.1 assists per game in 73 regular-season appearances—his lowest scoring numbers since the 1998–99 season. He was the team's third-leading scorer, behind Pierce, who averaged 19.6 points, 5.1 rebounds, and 4.5 assists per game in 80 appearances, and Garnett, who averaged 18.8 points, 3.4 assists, and 9.2 rebounds per game in 71 appearances. However, Allen led the team in two categories: three-point percentage (.398) and free-throw percentage (.907). His offensive output helped propel the Celtics to a 66–16 record—a 42-game improvement over the previous season and the greatest single-season turnaround in NBA history—as well as the Atlantic Division title.

Allen struggled with consistency during the play-offs. In the first round of the Eastern Conference play-offs, he averaged more than 10 points in the first six games against the Atlanta Hawks but managed only seven points in the deciding game—a 99–65 victory for the Celtics. Allen's offensive struggles continued throughout the Eastern Conference semifinals against the Cleveland Cavaliers. He averaged only 9.3 points per game during the seven-game series, which the Celtics won, 4–2. With that victory the team advanced to the conference finals, against the Detroit Pistons. Allen regained his momentum, scoring more than 20 points in each of three games and helping his team eliminate the Pistons in six contests to advance to the NBA finals against the Los Angeles Lakers—the Celtics' first finals appearance since 1987. There, Allen continued his strong offense, averaging 20.3 points per game in the series. He tied a franchise record, scoring seven three-pointers in the championship-clinching Game Six victory (89–81), despite learning, just prior to Game Five, that one of his sons had been diagnosed with diabetes. Earlier that year he had also made his eighth NBA All-Star appearance, replacing Caron Butler. Allen, who has scored more than 15,000 points during his NBA career, is currently the second all-time leader in career three-point field goals in the league. He also ranks number eight all-time in the NBA in free-throw shooting percentage.

Although his production in the 2008–09 season was below his career averages in points, rebounds, and assists per game, Allen set personal bests in field-goal percentage (.480) and free-throw percentage (.952). In February 2009 he broke the Celtics' record for consecutive free-throws, with 72. (The previous record, 71, was set by Larry Bird.) That same month Allen made his ninth All-Star Game appearance, when he was called up to replace the injured Orlando Magic guard Jameer Nelson. In the play-offs that spring, after a miserable opening game against the Chicago Bulls, Allen scored 30 points in Game Two, including a game-winning three-pointer with two seconds left on the clock. While Allen and the Celtics moved on to the second round, they lost to the eventual finalists, the Magic, in seven games, due in part to the absence of Kevin Garnett, who was sidelined by injury. As Allen headed into the final year (2009–10) of his three-year contract, in which he stood to earn almost $20 million, observers speculated as to whether he would be offered an extension or would be traded. Allen's expressed preference was to finish his career in Boston.

Allen has garnered attention for his off-the-court philanthropic activities. He has established the Ray of Hope Foundation, which promotes community-based sports programs for young children. Additionally, he has served as a spokesman for junior NBA and WNBA organizations and for the Thurgood Marshall Scholarship Fund, a program that has provided millions of four-year grants to students attending dozens of traditionally African-American colleges. Allen's accolades include the Good Guy Award (2000–01, 2005) from the *Sporting News*, and the Joe Dumars Trophy (2003), also known as the NBA Sportsmanship Award. Allen lives with his wife, Shannon, and children, Walter Ray III, Walker Reese, and Tierra, his daughter from a previous relationship. In 2009 Allen was named to the board of trustees of the Joslin Diabetes Center. (His son Walker has Type 1 diabetes.)

—M.M.

Suggested Reading: *Boston Globe* (on-line) Oct. 10, 2007, Apr. 20, 2008; *Hartford (Connecticut) Courant* (on-line) Oct. 26, 1993, Apr. 8, 2007; *Milwaukee Magazine* (on-line) Feb. 27, 2003; *Sports Illustrated* (on-line) Mar. 4, 1996, p50 Feb. 26, 2001

Selected Books: *Ray of Hope: More Than Basketball and Money* (with Zach Burgess and Florence Allen), 1998

Sajjad Hussain/AFP/Getty Images

Ambani, Anil

June 4, 1959– Indian businessman

Address: Reliance Communications, Dhirubhai Ambani Knowledge City, Navi Mumbai 400 709, India

The business tycoon Anil Ambani and his close relatives are among the families who have come to embody India's bold and booming economy. The second-richest man in India, after his brother, and for a time the sixth-richest in the world, Ambani has become one of the country's top celebrities. "Think of Rockefeller, Bill Gates and Howard Hughes combined," Gunjan Bagla, the author of *Doing Business in 21st Century India* (2008), told Martin Zimmerman for the *Los Angeles Times*

(June 19, 2008). "That's how well the Ambani family name is known in India." Scion of the Reliance Group, India's largest private company—which, by some estimates, accounts for between 3 and 5 percent of the country's gross domestic product (GDP)—Anil Ambani was for over two decades the flamboyant and charismatic public face of the corporation. Started from scratch by his father, Dhirubhai Ambani, Reliance came to be a world leader in industries including textiles, oil and petrochemicals, energy, telecommunications, information technology, finance, and entertainment; it provided an ambitious entrepreneurial model to a new generation of millions of postcolonial middle-class Indians. "There is a mystical aura that surrounds . . . [the Reliance] empire, a Midas touch ensuring that virtually every project it launches turns to gold," Dilip Bobb and Malini Bhupta wrote for *India Today* (November 30, 2004). "The house that Dhirubhai Ambani built almost from nothing has gone on to become the darling of investors, an all-powerful entity that had, as its legend grew, the power to change governments and ministers. It is not just India's biggest private-sector entity but the burnished showpiece of Indian enterprise. No other private corporation has managed to straddle the old and the new economy with such awesome success. Reliance is, in almost every which way, a corporate fairy-tale."

After Dhirubhai Ambani's death, in 2002, his sons, Mukesh and Anil—much like the brothers in many fairy tales—engaged in a public feud and bitter power struggle over their father's empire, with "the distinction between afternoon soap and corporate drama often blurring," the journalist Govindraj Ethiraj wrote on his blog *DatelineBombay* (June 27, 2005). "Mukesh is a projects and technical man," a senior Reliance official told Ravi Velloor for the Singapore *Straits Times* (December 16, 2004). "Anil is fantastic at marketing and raising money. Together they were a fine pair as long as the father was alive." By virtue of a deal brokered by their mother in 2004, Mukesh retained the chairmanship of Reliance, along with its core industries in oil, petrochemicals, and textiles, while the communications, finance, entertainment, and energy divisions went to Anil, who left the parent company after playing a central role in its success for more than 20 years. Following the breakup, the brothers' individual wealth surged, thanks to the massive growth and strength of the Indian economy, favorable exchange rates, and perhaps in some measure, according to observers, because of their fierce competitiveness with each another. Anil Ambani's wealth rests chiefly with his majority stake in Reliance Communications, the country's largest telecommunications and mobile-services provider. A colorful socialite who hobnobs with Bollywood celebrities and politicians, he was voted MTV Youth Icon of the Year in 2003, a title usually reserved for movie and sports idols. He served in the Indian Parliament from 2004 until 2006. Ambani is famous for his aggressive business style, dealmaking prowess, and innovative approaches to marketing and finance. Along with his father, he has been credited with masterminding India's first major deals in international capital markets. The deterioration of the economy in 2008 severely affected the Ambani brothers. In March 2008, according to *Forbes*, Anil Ambani was the biggest single gainer of wealth among billionaires in the previous year. The following March *Forbes* described Ambani as the previous year's single largest loser: his fortune fell by over three-quarters, or $31.9 billion, to $10.1 billion, and he dropped from sixth place, in 2008, to 34th place, in 2009, on lists of the wealthiest people in the world.

Anil Ambani was born in India's financial center, Mumbai (formerly known as Bombay), to Dhirubhai Ambani and Kokilaben Ambani on June 4, 1959, the year after his father established the family company and two years after the birth of his brother, Mukesh. Ambani also has two sisters, Dipti and Nina. Very much like his father (he was his father's favorite child, according to some sources), Anil studied at the University of Bombay—now the University of Mumbai—where he received a B.S. degree. He then studied management at the distinguished Wharton Business School, a division of the University of Pennsylvania, in Philadelphia, earning an M.B.A. in 1983. By the time he returned to India, his father's business had grown into a major industrial conglomerate. Dhirubhai Ambani, born in Gujarat in 1932, came from a relatively humble background and was forced to drop out of school to work. At the age of 17, he went to Yemen, where he worked at a gas station for a while; after he returned to India, in 1958, he founded Reliance, an export and trading company. In 1966 he opened a textile mill, and in 1977, rather than having to rely on banks for funding, he took the company public—an unprecedented move for all but India's wealthiest entrepreneurs. His action enabled him to expand and greatly diversify Reliance and led to his recognition as a trailblazer in popularizing stock-market investments among India's growing middle class. The firm's enormous subsequent growth and the consistently rising shareholder earnings—it is said that one in every four Indians who own stock has shares in Reliance—catapulted the Ambanis to iconic status in the country and made their name almost synonymous with India's new booming economy.

Seen as part of a new wave of Indian entrepreneurs, the Ambanis have sometimes been criticized for their brashness and brazenness, especially in the political realm. Their favorable treatment from politicians received much negative attention during the so-called economic-liberalization period in the early 1990s, when they were awarded many licenses in areas including telecommunications and energy. In an article for the *Straits Times* (June 6, 2004), Pranay Gupte detailed the Ambanis' generous contributions to political campaigns and their cultivation of connections with policymakers. "The Ambanis are at the apex of an elite group in India known by the cognoscenti as the 'politico-industrial complex' . . . ," Gupte wrote. "While no Indian industrialist will acknowledge it, the contributions—some would say bribes—which these businessmen make to political parties, and to individual politicians and top bureaucrats, are extensive. . . . But, of course, the money is well spent: in exchange, the industrialists pretty much get what they want in terms of governmental concessions and favourable policy terms for their businesses." Gupte wrote that while the demands of a globalized economy and foreign investors were forcing the liberalization of the once insular Indian economy, "the influence of the politico-industrial complex is, if anything, increasing. Why? Because the cost of conducting elections and practising politics is rising dramatically. . . . Only the plutocrats of the politico-industrial complex are in a position to supply the vast wherewithal needed to grease the wheels of democracy." Some observers have linked Anil Ambani's brief foray into parliamentary politics to that phenomenon.

When Anil Ambani returned to India, in 1983, his father offered him advice. "You are entering India," his father said, as paraphrased by Anil in 2004, according to *Business Line* (March 28, 2004). "You need to Indianise your MBA. Learn about income-tax, sales tax and Parliament. If you don't get to know all these things, all your formal education is not going to help you." That year Anil Ambani joined Reliance as co-CEO. Mukesh Ambani, who had studied chemical engineering at the University of Bombay and earned an M.B.A. from Stanford University, in California, had come on board two years earlier; he led the company's expansion into the manufacture of polyester fibers and then into petrochemicals, oil, and natural gas and was given responsibility for large-scale project management. Anil was placed in charge of marketing, media and investor relations, and fund-raising and is credited with developing several financial innovations to raise billions of rupees (Indian currency) in foreign investment. In that respect—having been central to the success, growth, and particularly the diversification and reinvention of their company—the Ambani brothers are unlike many other scions of business and industry, who made or have made only small changes to the companies they inherited. By July 2002, when Dhirubhai Ambani died of a stroke, Reliance was a diversified conglomerate and an industry leader in textiles, petroleum, petrochemicals, power, telecommunications, information technology, and finance.

Because their father had not left a will, the Ambani brothers became joint managing directors of Reliance, with Mukesh taking the role of chairman and Anil that of vice chairman. Almost immediately, tensions between them began to surface, with observers noting that Mukesh, backed by the company's board, was increasingly asserting himself, while Anil was given lesser roles in some of Reliance's biggest projects and was almost completely excluded from its telecommunications arm, Reliance InfoComm. "The synergy between Anil and Mukesh has been the corporation's greatest asset," Dilip Bobb and Malini Bhupta wrote in late 2004. "It would be tragic if Reliance's biggest strength becomes its fatal weakness." In July 2004—the month the Reliance board voted to give ultimate decision-making powers to Mukesh—Anil Ambani, backed by the Samajwadi Party in Uttar Pradesh and with the help of Bollywood bigwigs as well as party leaders who were friends of his, won a nomination to the Indian Parliament's Upper House. His reasons for seeking that position were, perhaps, to regain power and leverage in the operation of Reliance, to win a bid to build a gas power plant in Uttar Pradesh Province (an undertaking that Mukesh vehemently opposed), and to take advantage of, and build on, his celebrity status. Mukesh was apparently incensed by that turn of events, because the regional Samajwadi Party had been critical of the ruling coalition, which included the National Indian Congress Party, led by Sonia Gandhi, which had traditionally supported the Reliance empire and had close ties to Mukesh. Uttar Pradesh is among India's most populous and poorest states (the majority of Samajwadi Party backers are people of low income—members of the lower castes), and during his campaign, which was successful, Anil promised residents that the proposed power plant would become a reality.

By June 2005 the conflict between the brothers had escalated beyond any hope of reconciliation, and Reliance's board had stripped Anil of most of his powers. At that point the brothers' mother, Kokilaben Ambani, stepped in to negotiate a truce. On June 18, 2005 Anil resigned from the Reliance board and was given control of three companies: Reliance Energy, under which he planned to build the gas power plant (the world's biggest) in Uttar Pradesh; Reliance Capital, a banking and financial powerhouse; and Reliance InfoComm, India's biggest telecom and mobile-phone-service provider. Those assets became part of Anil Ambani's new company, the Anil Dhirubhai Ambani Group (ADAG). Mukesh Ambani retained Reliance and took over Reliance Industries, whose oil-related operations have helped to make it India's biggest private-sector company. "Ironically, despite the bitter war, neither brother has got what he probably wanted most," a reporter wrote for *India Abroad* (July 1, 2005). "Anil, who along with Mukesh played an instrumental role in building Reliance Industries to the level it is today, finds himself out of the company. Mukesh, on the other hand, who saw Reliance InfoComm as his baby, was forced to part with it." The article noted that even though Mukesh's petrochemical giant enjoyed a virtual monopoly in India, "most industry observers believe the younger brother has gained more. . . . Investors and industry analysts may feel that he will have restricted cash flows in ADAG companies now that he is no more a part of Reliance Industries, but his capacity to raise capital is almost as legendary as his links with various industrialists, bankers and politicians are strong. Further Anil has a presence in three sectors which show huge promise for growth in years to come. In conclusion, this is not the end of the battle, but the commencement of a healthy rivalry." The Bombay Stock Exchange reacted immediately to news of the split; record levels of trading in the companies' stock produced immense profits for both brothers. According to observers, Anil Ambani's companies "soared": "investors seemed to be voting not only for the more forward-looking businesses that Anil Ambani will receive in the deal, but also for his more brash public persona," Saritha Rai wrote for the *New York Times* (June 21, 2005).

Both brothers began expanding energetically, with Anil overseeing the plans for the new gas plant and acquiring media entities and entertainment conglomerates and Mukesh building oil refineries and diversifying into agriculture. Anil's extensive investments in media and entertainment include his takeover of Adlabs, a Bollywood movie-production and -distribution company, which many regard as a stepping stone to the Hollywood market. Bollywood, the world's largest producer of films, has long been an insular industry, but now, with India emerging as an economic superpower and with the ambition of financiers such as Ambani, the industry is beginning to look abroad to capitalize on Hollywood's revenue potential. In September 2008 Ambani entered into talks to provide between half a billion and a billion U.S. dollars in financing to DreamWorks, which is headed by Steven Spielberg, Jeffrey Katzenberg, and David Geffen, to enable it to separate from Viacom, its parent company since 2006. The deal, including an initial investment of $825 million, was completed in the summer of 2009; Ambani now owns 50 percent of the shares in DreamWorks, which expects to produce half a dozen films a year. Reliance Big Entertainment, the entity overseeing those endeavors, is also in talks with several other Hollywood producers regarding the financing of films. "We see Reliance Big Entertainment [a division of Reliance Entertainment] as a global entertainment company, and Hollywood certainly presents a bigger and wider basket of opportunities," Reliance Entertainment's president, Rajesh Sawhney, told Subramaniam Sharma and Joseph Galante for Bloomberg News (June 18, 2008). Ambani, who has been linked with reports of the possible purchase of several high-profile European soccer clubs, has denied rumors that he may attempt to buy Newcastle United or another soccer team in the English Premier League.

Overall, 2008 was a disastrous year for Ambani, who, according to Luisa Kroll, writing for *Forbes* (December 22, 2008, on-line), lost more money than any other billionaire as a result of the financial crisis that struck most of the world's major economies. "Touted on the cover of our 2008 billionaires issue for having added $24 billion to his fortune in one year, Ambani has dropped $30 billion since then . . . more than anyone in the world. Stock of his telecom company dropped after his estranged brother helped scuttle a deal with African telecom MTN." Mukesh Ambani, too, suffered huge financial losses in 2008. Nevertheless, the brothers remain extremely wealthy.

In 2009 the Ambani brothers' public feud intensified, and Anil Ambani became the victim of what he alleged was an assassination attempt. In the spring of that year, a technician working on Ambani's private helicopter discovered pebbles and gravel in the engine; police investigators suggested that they had been placed there in an attempt at sabotage. Ambani charged that business rivals were trying to kill him. The technician, a key witness in the case, was later found dead amid suspicious circumstances, and the case remains unresolved. In October 2009 Ambani's battle with his brother over an energy deal reached the country's top court. Back in 2005, after the family business was split between them, Anil Ambani had signed a deal with Mukesh that the latter's company would sell to his brother's firm 28 million cubic meters of gas per day at a fixed price for 17 years. In the following years the price of gas rose, and by 2009 the fixed price was 44 percent below the government-set price. The deal was essential to the energy-providing projects Anil Ambani planned with Alliance Natural Resources, and observers predict that whoever loses the dispute will lose billions of dollars. The elder Ambani, backed by the government, pulled out of the agreement, claiming that it was not government-approved. Anil Ambani argued that for a country attempting to attract foreign investment by liberalizing its economy, the sanctity and transparency of contracts—as well as the eradication of government corruption—are essential. Before the Supreme Court hearings on the case, which were set to begin in late October 2009 and continue for several months, Anil Ambani publicly offered to make peace with his brother. Mukesh responded that the matter was a legal one and that his younger brother's public overtures were disingenuous.

Ambani is among his nation's foremost patrons of contemporary Indian art. A fixture in Bollywood glitterati circles, he counts among his closest friends the film superstar Amitabh Bachchan and the politician and Samajwadi Party leader Amar Singh. His wife, Tina Munim, was a famous Bollywood film star in the 1980s; she had mostly retired from acting when she married, in 1991. The couple have two sons, Anmol and Anshul. For many years, despite their feuds, he and his brother lived, along with their mother, wives, and children, in the same 18-story mansion in Mumbai, though on different floors. (Mukesh is currently building a 27-story home.) As a devout Hindu, Ambani is a vegetarian and a teetotaler. He became a self-proclaimed "fitness freak" after an investor allegedly implied in his presence that he was overweight. Since then he has run several marathons in Mumbai, inspiring the nickname "Marathon Man."

—M.M.

Suggested Reading: *Asiamoney* p7+ July 2005; *Far Eastern Economic Review* p48+ Jan./Feb. 2005; *Hindu* (on-line) Mar. 31, 2004; *India Abroad* July 1, 2005; *India Today* Nov. 30, 2004; *Los Angeles Times* June 19, 2008; *New York Times* B p3+ Oct. 20, 2009, (on-line) June 21, 2005; (Singapore) *Straits Times* June 6, 2004; Srinivas, Alam. *Storms in the Sea Wind: Ambani vs Ambani*, 2005

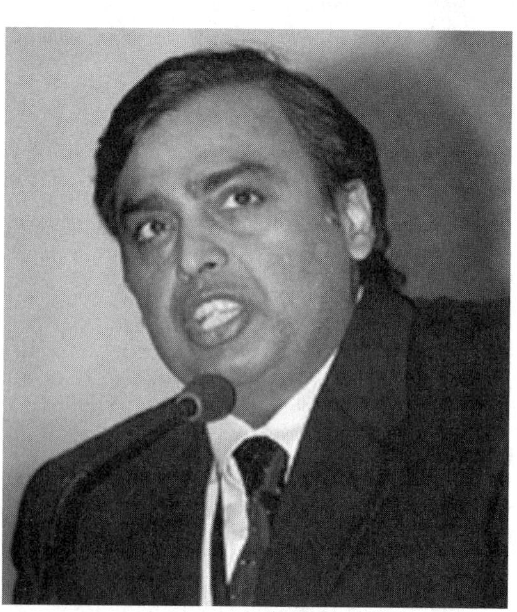

Sam Panthaky/AFP/Getty Images

Ambani, Mukesh

Apr. 19, 1957– Indian businessman

Address: Reliance Industries, Makers Chambers IV, 222 Nariman Point, Mumbai 400 021, India

India's wealthiest man is Mukesh Ambani, the chairman, managing director, and principal shareholder of the Reliance Group, his country's "biggest company by market value," Santanu Choudhury wrote for the *Wall Street Journal* (February 28, 2009). Ambani is famous for his extravagance—his private residence is a brand-new, 550-foot-high, 400,000-square-foot, 27-story edifice with space for upwards of 150 cars and a staff numbering more than 500—and he "isn't known for his charitable giving," according to Sheelah Kolhatkar, writing for the now-defunct *Portfolio.com* (November 2007). Nevertheless, he "isn't just trying to make money anymore," Nisid Hajari wrote for *Esquire* (October 2008). "He's aiming to remake India." A key part of that endeavor is connected with one of Reliance's dozens of subsidiaries—Reliance Retail, which buys produce directly from Indian farmers, thereby avoiding the centuries-old network of middlemen, who typically earn far more than the farmers. The average monthly income for farm households in India, according to the nation's government, as Tim Arango reported in the *New York Times* (June 29, 2008), is the equivalent of $50—less than the country's legal minimum wage. "A lot of us think the world is flat," Ambani said, as quoted by Sheelah Kolhatkar, referring to the global economy and the level playing field it will presumably offer. "I think the world is spiky . . . because 15 to 20 percent of people in the developing world live in plenty, while 80 percent live in scarcity. We have people who have to survive on $2 a day. . . . We cannot have islands of prosperity surrounded by oceans of poverty." While it remains to be seen whether Ambani's dreams of ending poverty in his native land will become a reality, there is no question that Reliance has helped to raise the standards of living of the many thousands of people whom it has employed. In addition, for most of the last three decades, the company has increased the incomes of its approximately three million stockholders—far more than the number of people who own shares in any other Indian firm. The principal division of the Reliance Group is Reliance Industries, the foremost manufacturer of polyester yarn and fabric and one of the top 10 producers of petrochemicals in the world. Reliance Industries exports commodities to more than 100 countries and in recent years has accounted for at least 3 percent of India's gross domestic product.

Reliance is one year younger than the 52-year-old Ambani. The company was founded in 1958 by his father, Dhirubhai Ambani, a high-school dropout who, with only enough cash to rent office space for two hours a day, began to buy and sell spices, rayon, and nylon. By the time Mukesh Ambani began working full-time for Reliance, the company had grown to include factories that manufactured polyester (a form of plastic), chemicals necessary to produce it, and a line of enormously popular polyester garments. Immediately demonstrating his superlative, hands-on organizational and managerial skills and capacity to keep track of myriad details, the 24-year-old Ambani took charge of the building of a factory, and in the following years, he oversaw the construction of many additional factories and the further diversification of Reliance's products. In the most ambitious of his projects, Mukesh Ambani supervised the construction of the Reliance oil refinery in Jamnagar, in the western Indian state of Gujarat; one of the largest such facilities on Earth, it began operating in 1999. After its massive expansion, completed in 2008, it became the most technologically advanced as well. Earlier, with the help of Ambani's brother, Anil, who is younger by two years and who joined the company in 1983, Reliance had branched successfully into the telecommunications, information technology, media, finance, and entertainment industries. The death of Dhirubhai Ambani, in 2002, without instructions regarding the disposition of his property, sparked a bitter power struggle between Mukesh and Anil Ambani that provided fodder for tabloids for many months. In June 2005, in a deal brokered by their mother, Mukesh was placed in charge of Reliance Industries and its subsidiaries Reliance Petroleum and Reliance Retail, among many others; Anil gained control of Reliance Energy, Reliance Capital, and Reliance InfoComm. Both brothers continued to prosper; in March 2008, according to *Forbes*, Mukesh's net worth totaled $43 billion, and Anil's, $42 billion. In the recent economic downturn, Mukesh's fortune has dropped to about $19.5 billion, and Anil's to an estimated $10.1 billion; the value of Reliance stock has declined by 40 percent. "All of us, in a sense, struggle continuously all the time, because we never get what we want," Mukesh told Anand Giridharadas for the *New York Times* (June 15, 2008). "The important thing which I've really learned is how do you [sic] not give up, because you never succeed in the first attempt."

The eldest of the four children of Dhirajlal Ambani ("Dhirubhai" is the nickname by which he became known) and his wife, the former Kokilaben Patel, Mukesh Dhirubhai Ambani was born on April 19, 1957 in Aden, Yemen. In addition to his brother, he has two sisters, Nina and Dipti (sometimes spelled "Deepti"). At the time of his birth, his father, then 25, was managing a gas station in Aden. In 1958 Dhirubhai Ambani returned to India with his family and settled in Mumbai, where, with an investment of $400, he launched Reliance Commercial Corp., to trade and export commodities. Mukesh Ambani and his siblings spent their early years in modest surroundings in the Bhuleshwar neighborhood of Mumbai. His family lived in a tiny apartment in a tenement complex whose residents had little privacy and enjoyed few luxuries. During his childhood half of Ambani's left pinky was accidentally severed when a door slammed shut on it.

In 1966 Dhirubhai Ambani, his two brothers, and one of his nephews, Rasikbhai Meswani, opened a textile mill in Naroda, in the western Indian state of Ahmedabad. Dhirubhai Ambani, the mastermind of the operation, adroitly got past the extremely cumbersome licensing requirements overseen by the huge bureaucracy set up as part of the national government's attempts (from 1947 to 1990) to maintain a planned economy. His ability to surmount the nearly endless red tape that stymied many other businessmen proved to be a major factor behind his success. (According to *The Polyester Prince: The Rise of Dhirubhai Ambani*, an unauthorized biography by Hamish McDonald, Dhirubhai sometimes used improper, unethical, ruthless, and even nefarious methods to achieve his goals. The book was banned in India.) Dhirubhai Ambani was also famous for his fierce determination to surpass others in sales and in the quality of his products. When wholesalers long associated with other suppliers refused to buy Reliance textiles, he went directly to retailers and built up a loyal clientele. In another bold business decision, Dhirubhai Ambani acquired from the American chemical company DuPont the technology necessary to begin producing high-quality polyester fabric and clothing, to which he affixed the label Vimal. Franchise retail outlets soon sprouted up throughout India and started selling Vimal textiles and products exclusively. Demand for Vimal items mushroomed, and in many areas they supplanted cotton goods, previously the universal favorite. Reliance now produces over one million tons of polyester each year. In addition to Vimal, its brand names include Harmony, Reance, RueRel, Recron, Relene, Repol, Reon, Relab, Reclair, and Koylene. The Naroda textile mill has grown into a huge, state-of-the-art complex that in 2007 was producing about 25 million yards of fabric sold domestically and internationally.

In the late 1960s, with Reliance growing ever more prosperous, Ambani's family moved into an upper-class Mumbai neighborhood. In interviews with Sucheta Dalal and Debashis Basu for *MoneyLife* magazine (January 17, 2007), as posted on ManagementParadise.com, Mukesh said, "My father never came to our school even once. Nevertheless, he was hugely interested in our all-round development." With that in mind, Dhirubhai Ambani devised a program to help Mukesh (and later his younger children) gain a comprehensive understanding of working-class life. He hired a tutor who came to their home every evening and spent two hours with Mukesh, playing hockey, soccer, and other games and traveling with him on buses and trains to various parts of Mumbai. For two weeks every year, Mukesh and the tutor would camp out in one or another of India's more than half a million villages. Far different from the pampering typically experienced by second-generation heirs, Ambani's on-the-ground education was "one of the best things that happened to me in my life," he told Anand Giridharadas. "We never studied. We went out . . . , and we said, 'This is what life looks like.'" In addition, he told Dalal and Basu, his father "shared with me his passion for business and entrepreneurship from every early on." In the 1970s Ambani attended St. Xavier High School, in Mumbai, and then enrolled at the Mumbai University Institute of Chemical Technology, where he majored in chemical engineering. As an undergraduate he worked every afternoon for his father's company. In 1977, eager to expand Reliance without having to borrow money from banks, Dhirubhai Ambani took Reliance public. The company's initial public offering lured 58,000 investors from all over India, helping to usher in an investment boom among India's middle class. (In some years Reliance had to hold its annual shareholder meetings in stadiums.) In 2008 one in four Indian investors reportedly had a stake in Reliance.

After his graduation from college, in 1979, Mukesh Ambani pursued an MBA at Stanford University, in California. In 1981,with six months left in his program, he returned to India to supervise the building of a huge polyester plant in Patalganga, a rural village; his father, he told Dalal and Basu, wanted to start construction immediately rather than wait for Ambani to earn the master's degree. During the construction Mukesh Ambani slept much of the time in a trailer at the site; he would watch training videos during his morning workout, then attend to every aspect of the project. "He's a guy who likes to get his hands dirty," a close friend of his told Giridharadas. The plant began operating on schedule, thus providing evidence of Ambani's ability to handle complex tasks with little or no help from his father. As his responsibilities at Reliance increased, he directed the creation of dozens of additional world-class facilities for the manufacture of terephthalic acid, monoethylene glycol, and other components of polyesters as well as other plastics, including high-density polyethylene. Meanwhile, in 1983 Anil Ambani had joined the company; his primary jobs included marketing, fund-raising, and media and investor relations.

In 1985 Rasikbhai Meswani, who had directly supervised Mukesh, died suddenly, and five months later, in 1986, Dhirubhai Ambani suffered a stroke that left him partially paralyzed. During their father's six-month recovery, Mukesh and Anil assumed greater control of Reliance's day-to-day operations. "There was no sense of panic," Mukesh told Dalal and Basu. "The whole picture was in my head. That was the strength of the open system." He was referring to an environment, common in the U.S. but unusual at that time in India, in which standard operating conditions and procedures had been recorded in detail. "Everyone was on the same page," Mukesh added, and Reliant was "not dependent on a few individuals."

In the 1990s Reliance continued to build new factories, and its revenues and profits increased apace. Meanwhile, Dhirubhai Ambani was taking steps to enter the petroleum business, which India's government had controlled domestically since the 1970s. During that decade, as a consequence of the Arab oil embargo and skyrocketing prices of fuel, India nationalized its divisions of international petroleum companies and imposed strict regulations on all aspects of the Indian oil industry, ranging from refining to distribution and pricing. The system worked until the early 1990s, when the biggest state-owned company, Oil and Natural Gas Corp. (ONGC), began to run out of money for exploration and the development of new oil fields. In 1997, Christopher Helman and Naazneen Karmali wrote for *Forbes* (May 8, 2006), "the government couldn't even pay ONGC for months of delivered crude [oil], forcing the company to default on loans." That year the Indian government announced that price controls for oil would be phased out by 2002. Anticipating that turn of events, ever ready to make use of loopholes in the law, and ever able to persuade government officials to smooth the way for their company (sometimes with bribes or other shady means, according to various sources), the Ambanis had made their move: in 1993 Reliance had made the largest public offering in India's history, with shares in its new division, Reliance Petroleum. By 1997 Mukesh Ambani was ready to launch one of the most ambitious construction projects in India's history: the building in Jamnagar of a refinery for crude oil that would be twice the size of any other refinery in India. Financing came partly from a $100 million, 100-year bond, sold on the U.S. market. (Reliance is one of only two dozen corporations, and the first in Asia, to be issued a bond of that magnitude in the U.S.) Commenting on Mukesh's philosophy and his refusal to listen to the naysayers who predicted that the Jamnagar project would never materialize, Yogesh Desai, a longtime Reliance executive, told Saritha Rai for the *New York Times* (June 4, 2004), "The approach was: 'There's no road? Let's build a road. There's no power? Let's build a power station. There's no port? Let's build a port.'" Saritha Rai quoted Arun Shourie, a journalist, former government minister, and onetime critic of Reliance, as saying that Dhirubhai Ambani and his sons were "to be thanked not once, but twice over. First, they set up world-class companies and facilities in spite of . . . regulations, and second, by exceeding the limits and restrictions, they created the case for scrapping those regulations. They made a case for reforms."

During construction of the Reliance crude-oil refinery—which was completed in only three years, an industry record—Ambani flew to Jamnagar from Mumbai four times a week to oversee all aspects of the work. A Bloomberg News reporter, in an article posted on *ExpressIndia.com* (April 26, 2005), learned from a Reliance executive that "Jamnagar is one of the few refineries in the world that can process very thick, high-sulfur grades of crude oil into pure, low-polluting gasoline and diesel fuel—the grades sold in California." In addition to the refinery itself (whose construction reportedly required 16 times as much steel as was used to build the Eiffel Tower), the site encompasses such amenities as a 1,600-acre parkland where antelopes and other wild creatures graze; a school; and a hospital for workers and their families. With the recent expansion of the refinery, its capacity rose to 1.24 million barrels a day.

By mid-2002, when Dhirubhai Ambani died of a stroke, Reliance had become an industry leader not only in textiles, petrochemicals, and petroleum, but also telecommunications, information technology, finance, and power. Dhirubhai did not leave a will or otherwise record his wishes for his sons' futures and that of Reliance. After his death the brothers became joint managing directors of Reliance, with Mukesh taking the position of chairman and Anil that of vice chairman. Within six months of their father's demise, "hints of a rift" between the brothers surfaced, according to the Bloomberg News reporter, evidence being the absence of one or the other brother at major Reliance events at which, in the past, both would have appeared. The conflict worsened in July 2004, when Reliance's board of directors voted to give Mukesh the power to make all decisions, including the right to overrule any of Anil's with which he disagreed. Mukesh's aversion toward Anil's increasing involvement in politics and friendships with entertainers widened the breach between them. The brothers' feud and struggle for power became matters of public discussion and daily-tabloid fodder. In June 2005, in a resolution engineered by Kokilaben Ambani, Mukesh and Anil's mother, the Reliance empire was split, with each brother to run different parts of the business independently. Mukesh Ambani gained control of Reliance Industries and its more than 70 subsidiaries, among them Reliance Petroleum, Reliance Jamnagar Infrastructure, Reliance Industrial Investment and Holdings, Reliance Exploration and Production, Reliance International Exploration and Production, Reliance Gas, Reliance Polymers, Reliance Polyolefins, Reliance Aromatics and Petrochemicals, Reliance Digital Media, and Reliance Infrastructure Management Services. Reliance Industries also has a controlling share of Indian Petrochemicals Corp. Ltd., India's second-largest petrochemicals company. The splitting of Reliance left control of Reliance InfoComm, one of Mukesh's pet projects, in Anil's purview. As of October 2009 the brothers were embroiled in a court battle regarding contracts for natural gas from a field in India whose reserves have been valued at more than $38 billion.

Earlier, the year 2006 saw the founding of Reliance Retail, whose subsidiaries include Reliance Fresh, Reliance Dairy Foods, Reliance Hypermart, Reliance Agri Products Distribution, and Reliance Food Processing Solutions. With those businesses Mukesh Ambani is attempting to revolutionize what he has often referred to as the "value chain in the foods business" in India—the way agricultural products are grown, marketed, delivered, and sold, not only to Indian consumers but to consumers globally—and to transform "the relationship between [India's] cities and the countryside," Dean Nelson wrote for the London *Times* (October 8, 2006, on-line). The vast majority of India's farmers do not have refrigerated trucks or facilities to store their produce; middlemen who own such trucks or warehouses buy the produce from farmers for a fraction of what farmers in other countries earn. Poorly maintained or unpaved roads make transport of produce to cities difficult and unreliable. An estimated 40 percent of India's produce rots without being sold, some of it while on its way to markets. According to Dean Nelson, "A network of local markets originally introduced to protect poor farmers from exploitation [are] now controlled by cartels of traders, bureaucrats, and moneylenders." Ambani is spending billions of dollars to construct distribution centers and retail outlets for farm products and other goods and to provide them with necessary sources of power, roads, and other infrastructure. He has bought a fleet of planes to transport produce to other countries. As part of the Indian government's program of special economic zones (SEZs), he is also building two small cities, one outside Mumbai and the other outside New Delhi, the nation's capital, to attract foreign investors and create jobs for some of the millions of young Indians who graduate from college each year without any prospects of finding suitable work. "Both agri-business and SEZs will make a sustainable return in the long run and we have a strong enough balance sheet to sustain these," Ambani told Sucheta Dalal and Debashis Basu. "At the end of the day, it will leave us with the satisfaction of having tried to show the way" — "to blaze a new trail or change the status quo."

"Despite all of his almost absurdly big plans, Ambani is anything but a publicity-seeking social climber," according to Sheelah Kolhatkar. "In fact, he's a semi-recluse: awkward, shy, a traditional Hindu who practices strict vegetarianism and abstains from drinking alcohol. With his mix of hubris, business savvy, and personal eccentricity, he may be a modern-day Howard Hughes." Like his father, he spends Sundays with his family. His wife, the former Nita Dalal, whom he married in 1985, is the president of the Dhirubhai Ambani Foundation and runs the Dhirubhai Ambani International School and the Kokilaben Dhirubhai Ambani Hospital and Medical Research Institute. The Ambanis have two sons, Akash and Anant, and a daughter, Isha. Ambani is the owner of the Mumbai Indians, a cricket team in the Indian Premier League.

—C.C.

Suggested Reading: *Chemical Week* Oct. 27, 2004; *Forbes* p114+ May 8, 2006; *India Today* p38+ Nov. 30, 2004; (London) *Times* (on-line) Oct. 8, 2006; *MoneyLife* (on-line) Jan. 17, 2007; *New York Times* W p1+ June 4, 2004, III p1+ June 15, 2008; *Portfolio.com* Nov. 2007; Reliance Industries Web site; *Time* (on-line) Feb. 16, 2004; McDonald, Hamish. *The Polyester Prince: The Rise of Dhirubhai Ambani*, 1999

Arenas, Gilbert

(ah-REE-nass)

Jan. 6, 1982– Basketball player

Address: Washington Wizards, 601 F St., N.W., Washington, DC 20002

"We are inspired by men who can survive at this level"—that of the National Basketball Association (NBA)—"and still play like kids," Myles Brown wrote for the basketball magazine *Slam* (October 8, 2008). "Men who dare to enjoy themselves amidst pressure that would grind mere mortals to dust.

Gregory Shamus/Getty Images

Gilbert Arenas

Men who remind us that though this may not be for kids, it is still just a game. Men like Gilbert Arenas." Arenas is a guard for the NBA's Washington Wizards. An excellent scorer, among the league's quickest and most difficult players to guard, and a genuine eccentric and comical nonconformist, Arenas surmounted a difficult early childhood and others' pessimism about his future to become one of the most popular players of his generation. "Arenas has three physical skills: quickness, strength, and endurance. He has the quickest first step in basketball. He explodes past any defender," Fred Barnes declared in an article for the *Washingtonian* (November 1, 2006). Similarly, Chuck Klosterman, writing for the *New York Times* sports magazine *Play* (March 4, 2007), noted that Arenas "has evolved into one of the least stoppable humans of the early 21st century. . . . The key is his rare combination of explosiveness and range: Arenas is fundamentally a slasher, but he regularly takes (and makes) shots from well beyond 25 feet. . . . More importantly, he loves shooting at meaningful moments. . . . He is devoid of fear."

A three-time All-Star, Arenas was drafted by the Golden State Warriors in 2001 and moved to Washington, D.C., two years later, after being named the NBA's most improved player. He has often been called a "shoot-first, pass-second" guard—a label that he has rejected, insisting that he is first and foremost a team player. His teammates' scoring statistics and his popularity, as well as his willingness to take a pay cut in order to help his franchise in its quest for a championship, provide strong evidence to back that contention. Arenas has inspired such nicknames as "Agent Zero," because since his undergraduate years he has worn a zero on his jersey, signifying the number of minutes unimpressed coaches told him he would play in college; "Hibachi," the term for a Japanese grill and a word he shouts out when shooting from long range in games—evidently his way of saying that he is "on fire"; and "Black President," a self-chosen moniker he vowed to drop after Barack Obama was elected president of the U.S., in 2008. Arenas is an intensely driven, competitive, and charismatic star whose unusual behavior, both on and off the court, has been called "Gilbertology." "Arenas is allegedly something of a crazy man," Klosterman wrote. "Virtually everything written about him mentions the litany of his mild eccentricities. . . . But Arenas is atypical, and here's why: unlike almost every other consciously nonconformist superstar, Arenas is never polarizing. Nobody hates him for being odd; his behavior has exclusively served to make him more beloved." Barnes wrote, "Arenas is an antidote to the self-centered superstar stereotype," and Mike Wise, in a profile entitled "The Psychic Scars That Shaped an NBA Star," published in the *Washington Post* (October 29, 2006), wrote, "In a league filled with huge personalities and oversize egos, Arenas stands apart." Arenas, in Wise's words, is "one of the league's most enigmatic figures, an idiosyncratic loner, a charmingly candid young man who freely admits he pushes away those who get close to him." For his part, Arenas told Wise, "Basketball is where I put all my pain and let it go. The court became my sanctuary, my outlet."

Gilbert Arenas was born on January 6, 1982 in Tampa, Florida. His father, also named Gilbert Arenas, had been a multi-sport star in high school; according to Wise, he had been known on the basketball courts of West Tampa as "Gil the Thrill." A few months before his girlfriend, Mary Francis Robinson, gave birth to their son, Arenas Sr. enrolled at a college near Miami, Florida, where one of his uncles coached and which had awarded him a scholarship. For several years Robinson, a drug addict, lived with the boy in Tampa in what Arenas Sr. described to Wise as a "rough" housing project. One day when young Gilbert was three, Robinson's mother told the boy's father in a phone call that she had abandoned the child. Gilbert Sr. then arranged to have the boy live with his parents, in Tampa; Fannie Lee Arenas, Gilbert Jr.'s paternal grandmother, served as his primary caregiver for the next few years. When Gilbert Arenas was seven, his father moved with him to Burbank, California, in hope of pursuing a career in acting. After a few nights in a car and several more at a YMCA, Gilbert Sr. got a job as a clerk, and the two moved into a low-to-middle-income apartment complex in nearby Van Nuys, a district of Los Angeles, which remained their home for about nine years. According to Gilbert Sr., his son's engaging personality endeared him to virtual strangers, who invariably wanted to help the two of them in one way or another. To this day father and son remain extremely close. Since childhood Gilbert Jr. has seen his mother only once, when she approached him outside the team bus when Golden State was playing in Miami; according to Wise, "Those who know him best say [that that] encounter with her . . . deeply traumatized him."

Arenas enrolled at Grant High School in Van Nuys and signed up for the junior varsity basketball team. According to Barnes, 10 minutes into his first practice, the team's coach, Howard Levine, pulled him aside and told him that he could make it to the NBA. Arenas went on to be named to the Los Angeles All-City team three years in row. By his senior year he was averaging 33 points per game. Nevertheless, to his dismay, few colleges showed any interest in him. He accepted the offer of the University of Arizona, where he chose the jersey number zero, as a reminder to detractors who told him he would play zero minutes in college and as a motivator for himself. As a freshman, according to Barnes, Arenas became a "gym rat" and a valuable starter on his team, the Wildcats. During his two years in college, he averaged 15.8 points per game, helping the squad reach the National Collegiate Athletic Association (NCAA) Championship finals in 2001. But he was not seen as a valuable prospect when he left college, at age 19, to enter the 2001 NBA draft. The problem, according to various sources, was that scouts could not place Arenas: he seemed to be neither a typical point guard, because of the "shoot first, pass second" label, nor a typical shooting guard, because, at six feet four inches, he is relatively short. Wally Walker, the general manager of the Seattle Supersonics, who passed on Arenas in the 2001 draft, later told Barnes,"No one was quite sure what his position was. It turned out he didn't need a position. He's just a guard." Similarly, Ernie Grunfeld, the president of the Washington Wizards, told Barnes, "His progress has been phenomenal. He's a modern-day point guard. If you look around the league, point guards are bigger scorers." He was not drafted until the second round, at number 31 overall. That experience reportedly left him in tears and led him to declare, according to Michael Lee in the *Washington Post* (April 24, 2005), "That's the worst mistake the NBA has made. I'm going to the gym right now." At that time, first-round draft picks were forced to sign four-year contracts at rookie salary levels, while second-rounders were exempt from that requirement. Arenas signed a two-year contract with the Golden State Warriors, betting that his value would only rise.

While his first NBA season was marred by injuries—he spent half of it on the disabled list—Arenas showed considerable potential. In his second year, 2002–03, he won the NBA's Most Improved Player Award, starting all 82 games and averaging 35 minutes and 18.3 points per game. After that breakout season Arenas became one of the league's most coveted free agents; he signed a lucrative contract, worth $65 million over six years, with the Washington Wizards. Thus, as Barnes pointed out, his selection in the second round turned out to be a financial coup. "It paid off so handsomely . . . ," Barnes wrote, "that what became known as the 'Arenas rule' allowing second-round picks to freely negotiate a contract was revoked by the NBA." Nevertheless, Arenas would continue to see the draft-day snub as a motivator: he still keeps a list of every player drafted ahead of him in 2001 and checks it periodically to cross off the names of those no longer playing at the top level.

While Arenas upped his scoring average to 19.6 points per game in his first year in Washington (2003–04), he played in only 55 games because of injuries, including a strained abdominal muscle. The following season Arenas averaged 25.5 points per game (the seventh-highest number in the NBA that year), joining his teammate Larry Hughes to give Washington the highest-scoring backcourt in the league and leading the team to its first play-offs since 1997. For his achievements that season, Arenas was selected to play in his first All-Star Game. He continued to improve in the 2005–06 season, putting up his best numbers to date: he posted an average of 29.3 points and just over two steals per game (fourth-highest in the league in both categories that year) while averaging 34 points per game in the play-offs and cementing his reputation for being able to make buzzer-beating shots. Nevertheless, Arenas was not selected for the All-Star Game (but played in it nonetheless, after Jermaine O'Neill dropped out, due to injury) and was passed up for the U.S.A. basketball team in the 2006 World Championships. Arenas has often mentioned those disappointments as having strengthened his determination.

The following season, 2006–07, Arenas averaged 28.4 points per game (third-highest in the NBA) and was voted a starter in the All-Star Game. In December 2006 he scored 60 points in a contest against the Los Angeles Lakers—a personal best and a Washington franchise record. He also began to achieve media-star status, stemming from his undiplomatic and outspoken umbrage at having been perennially underrated, overlooked, and dismissed as erratic and immature, as well as from his antics on and off the court and his hugely popular blog, launched in October 2006 on nba.com. In 2007–08 Arenas played in only a handful of games before being sidelined until the end of the season with a knee injury. Reemerging to help his team in the play-offs, Arenas was clearly suffering pain. During the summer of 2008, he opted out of the last year of his contract and renegotiated another one. He said that he would be willing to accept less money from Washington if doing so would help the franchise acquire the necessary players to win a championship and if the Wizards' executives would re-sign his teammate Antawn Jamison. After Jamison signed, Arenas agreed in July 2008 to a six-year, $111 million contract, roughly $16 million less than the team had originally offered him. The move garnered praise and admiration from observers and peers and endeared him even more to fans.

"I looked at it like this: There is nothing I can do for my family with $127 million that I can't do with $111 million," Arenas explained, as quoted by Ivan Carter in the *Washington Post* (July 4, 2008). "I mean, college is expensive but it ain't that dang expensive. Now, [the Wizards] have room to add a piece. There is a window of opportunity for us. Adding key pieces leads to championships and that's what we all want." Meanwhile, the knee injury that had troubled him several times and had required three surgeries kept him on the disabled list, forcing him to miss all but two games of the 2008–09 season; it caused concern in those who worried about his long-term durability.

After essentially missing two seasons, Arenas spent time working with Tim Grover, Michael Jordan's former trainer. In September 2009 he criticized the Washington Wizards organization for mishandling his rehabilitation. He appeared fully fit and ready for the start of the 2009–10 NBA season. Arenas has said that observers' reduced expectations of him and the criticism leveled at him for failing to live up to the promise reflected in the terms of his contract have served as motivators. "Since I got hurt, I'm back at ground zero. Now I've got to work myself back again," he told Mike Wise for the *Washington Post* (October 17, 2009). "The whole contract thing. Me being injured. It's like anything, the what-have-you-done-for-me-lately theme."

Although known and feared as one of the most dangerous offensive guards in the NBA, Arenas is perhaps just as famous for "Gilbertology," a term the Wizards' head coach, Eddie Jordan, coined to describe Arenas's antics and eccentricities. One site on the World Wide Web (gilbertology.net) is devoted to documenting that phenomenon. Among the many examples of his humorously unorthodox behavior (some of which he has dismissed as exaggerations or myths): while playing for Golden State, he is said to have once showered at halftime with his Golden State uniform and shoes on before scoring 24 points in the second half of a game. Arenas has also been known, after purchasing a new cell phone, to call himself repeatedly from another line in order to fill his voice mailbox, presumably to avoid receiving others' messages. According to gilbertology.net, his messages to himself are along the lines of "It's me," "This is Gilbert," "It's Gilbert." Arenas has a reputation for pulling pranks on teammates. As a rookie, for instance, he was made to bring doughnuts to practice for his veteran teammates—a service often demanded of new players. Taking exception to that demand, he is said on one occasion to have licked glazed doughnuts before presenting them, and on another to have sprinkled baby powder—which appeared to be confectioners' sugar—on the pastries. In one of his more notorious stunts, Arenas bet his teammate DeShawn Stevenson $20,000 that he could make more college-range three-point shots with one hand than Stevenson could make NBA-range three-pointers with two hands (the three-point line in college play is closer to the basket than that in the NBA). Arenas netted 73 of 100 attempts while Stevenson made only 68 of 96, albeit with Arenas apparently doing everything he could to distract Stevenson during the contest. Arenas explained his behavior on his blog: "So what if I cheated? It was mostly for bragging rights. . . . It wasn't that I cheated (of course I cheated). . . . It wasn't for the money. I'm not going to make him pay. . . . It's a moral victory more than anything."

Arenas is said to be fanatical about training; to improve his conditioning, he has installed in his home a hypobaric chamber, which simulates the air pressure at high altitudes. He is also something of a loner, rarely leaving his hotel room when the team is on the road; instead, he watches infomercials on TV and works out. When the team is in Washington, he stays home. "I have so much entertainment going on in my house that I don't need to go out," he told Tom Chiarella for *Esquire* (November 1, 2006). "I don't need to go to the movies if I own all these movies. I don't need to go out to a game because I've got all these video games. I don't have to leave my house to have a conversation because I just hop online and have fun with my friends, talk trash, and do whatever we're gonna do right there." His blog, which draws fans into his quirky world while keeping them at a distance, is the most popular Web log of any athlete in professional sports, according to the NBA. On his November 15, 2008 post, he wrote: "With Obama winning, I just had to blog again. . . . I gave my nickname up for Obama, he's the true black president now. . . . Now I really want to win a championship. When you win a championship you get invited to the White House, and I want to go to Obama's White House. . . . For our age group, it was important because with a black president, now you believe your parents when they were speaking to you saying, 'You can be anything you want to be.' At the time we thought it was crap, but now we believe that." Arenas has implied that his popularity stems in part from his view of himself as a simple entertainer in a field dominated by colossal egos. "Most of the stars, they're not entertainers," Arenas told Liz Robbins for the *New York Times* (January 5, 2007). "When I was growing up, that's what I loved about [Shaquille O'Neal]. I want to be like that, fun-loving. I think everyone takes things too serious. For some reason, I look around, it's like, we're not grateful for what we get and what we are." Klosterman wrote, "The N.B.A., like all sports leagues, thrives on control. Its culture is corporate and clinical. . . . As a business principle, control is what makes the N.B.A. a successful product. But it's those rare moments that cannot be controlled that make the game meaningful, and Arenas creates these moments all the time. He is always slightly beyond control, because it's impossible to control what you cannot understand." Klosterman identified Arenas's honesty as a major attraction for fans in the market-driven world of professional sports. For example, every time Arenas takes a free throw, he, like many other players, performs a specific pre-throw routine; unlike the others, though, he has acknowledged that he designed his gestures for fans to copy. "It's an honest explanation of his motives: he deliberately created a way to be idolized by strangers," Klosterman wrote. "Yet this is the kind of motivation athletes never admit to. Arenas's professional vanity is so straightforward it inevitably comes across as charming and childlike. Everyone in the N.B.A. dreams of playing in the All-Star Game, but very few openly lobby for the opportunity; in the 2003–4 season, Arenas traded two pairs of shoes and a jersey for a box of All-Star ballots and voted for himself 50,000 times."

In 2009 Arenas announced that he would be retiring the names "Hibachi" and "Agent Zero" and ending his blog. He claimed that the media had turned his candor—on the blog and elsewhere—against him. "Win," Arenas told Wise in their October 2009 conversation. "That's it. Win. The entertainer part of me, I gotta get rid of that. Or at least make it take a hiatus. I'm back to being strictly a basketball player now."

After the election of Barack Obama as the 44th president of the U.S., Dan Steinberg reported for the *Washington Post* (November 9, 2008, on-line), Arenas had an abbreviated version of Obama's slogan "Change we can believe in" and the numeral 44 tattooed on the fingers of his left hand. He also has extensive tattoos on his torso. In 2005 Arenas launched the Zer0 Two Her0 Foundation, which, according to its Web site, "helps promote the safety and well being of children by raising funds to support organizations that aid in the preservation of families through foster care, adoption, and child welfare services." Since 2006 he has contributed to Washington schools $100 for every point he scores on the court, and for several years he has held a Christmas party for 300 area children. He became a mentor to a boy named Andre McAllister soon after the youngster lost his family in a fire when he was 10, in 2004. Arenas secured a job for Andre as a Wizards ball-boy and has forged a friendship with him.

Arenas and his longtime girlfriend, Laura Govan, have a daughter, Izela, born in 2005, and a son, Alijah, born in 2007. The birth of their third child was expected in December 2009.

—M.M.

Suggested Reading: *Esquire* p170+ Nov. 1, 2006; *New York Times* (on-line) Jan. 5, 2007; *New York Times Play Magazine* (on-line) Mar. 4, 2007; *Slam* (on-line) Oct. 8, 2008; *Washington Post* A p1+ Apr. 24, 2005, A p1+ Oct. 29, 2006, E p1+ July 4, 2008; *Washingtonian* p92+ Nov. 2006

Aronofsky, Darren

Feb. 12, 1969– Filmmaker

Address: Creative Artists Agency, 162 Fifth Ave., Sixth Fl., New York, NY 10010

Stephen Lovekin/Getty Images

Since the release of *Pi* (1998), his first feature film, the director Darren Aronofsky has been compared to such masters of the form as David Lynch and Stanley Kubrick. Initially hailed as a wunderkind and praised for his fast-paced, "in-your-face" visual style and serious themes—drugs, addiction, the meaning of life, and the pursuit of knowledge—Aronofsky also has his fair share of detractors, which seems to be the way he likes it. He told Tasha Robinson for the *Onion* (November 21, 2006, on-line) that all of his films have been very divisive, adding, "I like films that make you feel in a strong way." His goal, from the start of his career, has been to make films that are original, complex, and challenging. Aronofsky gained fame with the release of his second film, *Requiem for a Dream* (2000).

Darren Aronofsky was born on February 12, 1969 in Brooklyn, New York. He grew up in the neighborhood of Manhattan Beach, a few miles from the Brighton Beach boardwalk and Coney Island roller coasters. (In several interviews Aronofsky has said that he wants to make movies that are "roller-coaster rides.") His parents, Abraham and Charlotte, were schoolteachers and still live in the neighborhood where the filmmaker spent his youth. "I was raised as a conservative Jew," he told

Jonathan Romney for the London *Guardian* (January 5, 1999). "I was bar mitzvahed and circumcised. But I was a rowdy skeptic kid who ran around cursing. I have a lot of respect for the Jewish religion, and the heritage and the culture, and I think it's definitely one way to reach spirituality, but there are other roads to get there." As a young boy Aronofsky spent his time taking black-and-white photographs and writing angst-filled prose. Over time, his interests broadened; at about 11 he began sneaking into the family's TV room after midnight to watch the often eerie tales featured on *The Twilight Zone*. As a student at Edward R. Murrow High School, Aronofsky would occasionally cheat or cut class; he told Scott Timberg for the *Dallas Observer* (April 19, 2001) that the only book he remembers reading during those years is Dostoyevsky's novel *Crime and Punishment*. One day during his senior year, he and a friend went to the local mall to see a mainstream Hollywood movie, which was sold out; instead, "I saw a poster with a goofy guy with a Brooklyn hat, went in, and it turned out to be [Spike Lee's independent film] *She's Gotta Have It*," Aronofsky told Timberg. "And I remember being just blown away. It spoke to me partly because I was from Brooklyn, and I really related to the hip-hop culture, but also the whole aesthetic of it was really refreshing." Lee's "guerrilla filmmaking" opened Aronofsky's eyes to a new kind of storytelling. Aronofsky would also, on occasion, take the subway to Manhattan and sneak into movies such as Kubrick's *A Clockwork Orange* and Lynch's *Eraserhead*. "They were films," he told Timberg, "you weren't supposed to see." Aronofsky has said that the stories on Bill Cosby's comedy albums of the 1960s were another influence on his work.

In 1987 Aronofsky enrolled at Harvard University, in Cambridge, Massachusetts. He initially majored in anthropology, later changing his focus to film. Aronofsky told Robinson about the Harvard film program: "It's mostly a documentary program. They were very, very free when I was down there, and they basically let you do what you wanted. For me, that's a very good environment. They give you the camera and a budget, and they say, 'Go have fun.' To me, that was great, because I was good at sort of putting together my own team and just going for it." At Harvard he met several of his future collaborators, including Sean Gullette, who would co-write and star in *Pi*. During his senior year at Harvard, Aronofsky became a Student Academy Awards national finalist for his film *Supermarket Sweep*. After graduating from Harvard he attended the American Film Institute, in Hollywood, where he earned an M.F.A. degree. There, as at Harvard, he met some of his future colleagues, including the producer Eric Watson and the director of photography Matthew Libatique. Aronofsky returned to New York in 1995.

Pi was shot in New York in 1996 for $60,000, most of which was raised via donations from Aronofsky's friends and family. A psychological thriller with science-fiction elements, *Pi* follows the life of a mentally unstable math genius, Max Cohen (played by Gullette), who is obsessed with order. Max constantly searches for patterns in the stock market; with the help of his computer, he eventually finds a 216-digit number whose significance, in his mind, ranges from the financial to the spiritual, and he finds himself pursued by both a powerful Wall Street firm and a group of Hasidic Jews who believe that the number sequence could help them decipher the Torah's "code of God." Shot in black and white, the film won the Director Prize at the 1998 Sundance Film Festival and brought praise from critics. "A Kafkaesque semi-science-fiction film without special effects, the work recalls early David Lynch in the impressionistic connections it makes between its assorted bizarre preoccupations—computer parts, ants, a disembodied brain, Orthodox Jews, physical torment, creative mania—as well as Stanley Kubrick in its expressive precision, technical virtuosity, intellectual range and dispassionate bemusement at the spectacle of intense human pursuit," Todd McCarthy wrote for *Variety* (June 22, 1998). "And unlike most American films, it is part of the grand historical tradition of works interested in the pursuit of knowledge and theories of existence." Romney complimented the film's cinematography: "Aronofsky does urban anxiety with rare vigor, in some of the best New York photography of recent years—cinematographer Matthew Libatique creates the old-style grimy, steamy Manhattan inferno that seems to have disappeared from cinéma since the city's big clean-up." Speaking to Romney, Aronofsky elaborated on what soon became known as his hip-hop technique: "There have been films about hip-hop, but not many hip-hop techniques used in film—the whole idea of visual sampling, repetition of beats and sounds." Aronofsky's style was also influenced by the *Sin City* comic-book series and the director Shinya Tsukamoto's surreal science-fiction *Tetsuo* films.

Aronofsky wanted *Pi* to be visually unlike anything that had been done before, and most critics felt that he achieved his aim; but some, while crediting Aronofsky for his original techniques and clever story, took issue with the film's aesthetic. "As smart as it is, *Pi* is awfully hard to watch," Stephen Holden wrote for the *New York Times* (April 3, 1998). "Filmed with hand-held cameras in splotchy black-and-white and crudely edited, it has the style and attitude of a no-budget midnight movie. Those very qualities are likely to give it a certain hip cachet among those who like their cinema technically raw and spontaneous. But with its ink-stained cinematography and jarring electronic score by Clint Mansell, *Pi* can be extremely grating." The film earned more than $3 million, which allowed Aronofsky to give his friends and family a return on their investments. He then signed a movie deal with Miramax Films.

Aronofsky's next film, *Requiem for a Dream* (2000), was based on a novel by Hubert Selby Jr. Aronofsky wrote the screenplay with Selby, who was also the author of *Last Exit to Brooklyn*, one of Aronofsky's favorite books. The film, a fast-paced drama, was more complex and mature than its gritty predecessor and had a substantially bigger budget, approximately $5 million. *Requiem* was praised for its visual, aural, and emotional intensity. The film revolves around the addiction-driven lives of Sara (Ellen Bursyn), her son, Harry (Jared Leto), and Harry's girlfriend (Jennifer Connelly) and friend (Marlon Wayans). Sara obsessively watches television while consuming diet pills and dreaming of being on her favorite show; Harry and his friend consume hard-core drugs (heroin and cocaine, among others) and aspire to become successful drug dealers; and the ambition of Harry's girlfriend, also an addict, is to open her own clothing-design store. As the film's title implies, the characters' dreams do not come true. "The filmmaker's effrontery is effectively a personal statement, a brand of dynamism that isn't just technique for its own explosive ends but rather is integral to the storytelling," Elvis Mitchell wrote for the *New York Times* (October 6, 2000). "The book is unremittingly grim, and the flashes of visual wit supplied by Mr. Aronofsky . . . are offputting because he is infatuated with the rot. By the end, he has made the movie bleaker than the original material. People may find it infuriating precisely because it's so intimidating, and it may leave you shaken. Be warned: it's a downer, and a knockout." While drugs play a key role in the film, *Requiem* is not simply a "drug movie" but a nuanced portrait of addiction, hopeless dreams, and ruined lives. "[Aronofsky] doesn't put a gloss on his characters' problems," Mitchell wrote. "Their drug gobbling is highlighted, accompanied by slurps, gulps and other loud noises that infantilize their appetites. For them, it's all sensation-seeking, and to a lesser extent it's the case with the movie as well. Instead of falling back on the cliché of junkies' vegetative states, Mr. Aronofsky races through their buzzes because he wants to show how quickly the time passes when they're high. And it explains why their lives are so empty when they're not consuming, which drug movies haven't made so clear before." The film's visual style, most critics agreed, complemented the story: Aronofsky used fish-eye lenses, quick cuts, split screens, and extreme close-ups, most notably of dilating pupils. The soundtrack, which combines electronic and classical music, was composed by Clint Mansell. In his review Mitchell also observed that Aronofsky "draws astonishing performances from his actors." Most critics agreed that the four principal actors were extremely convincing in their roles, and Burstyn received an Oscar nomination. Speaking about the film to Timberg, Aronofsky said, "I wanted to make a roller coaster ride. One that smashed into a brick wall."

Six years and many struggles preceded the release of Aronofsky's next film, *The Fountain*. The movie was originally budgeted for $70 million, more than 1,000 times what Aronofsky's debut film cost to make. "To convince Warner Bros. to give us the big budget to make this very experimental film, we knew we needed real stars," Ari Handel, a friend of Aronofsky's from Harvard and the co-writer of *The Fountain*, told Steve Silberman for *Wired* (November 2006). Brad Pitt, a fan of *Requiem*, signed on for *The Fountain* after reading the script, and Cate Blanchett was set to co-star in the film. The moviemakers built elaborate sets, assembled a 450-person crew (in Australia, where parts of the film were to be shot), and planned epic battle scenes. Then, in 2002, seven weeks before shooting was scheduled to begin, Pitt pulled out of the project, citing creative differences with Aronofsky (the actor had demanded many script changes); with the film's big star having left, others followed, and the project came to a halt. Stressed out, Aronofsky left for India and China, alone. He returned to the project in 2003. "I could feel that *The Fountain* was not out of my blood," he told Silberman. "And then I remembered: I don't have to write for the studio or Brad Pitt or any other movie star. I decided to start acting like an independent filmmaker again." Aronofsky revised the script and decided to make the film without computer-generated images, usually referred to as CGI. In the end *The Fountain* was made for half of its original budget and starred Hugh Jackman and Rachel Weisz, whom Aronofsky had been dating since 2001.

Released in 2006, *The Fountain* was Aronofsky's most ambitious and divisive film yet. Silberman called it "one of the most visually original and emotionally complex science fiction films in history." The film takes place in three time periods, set several hundred years apart, each with characters played by Jackman and Weisz. In 16th-century Spain, Queen Isabella sends the conquistador Tomas to the Mayan jungle in search of the Tree of Life. In 21st-century America, a research scientist named Tom is also on a mission—to cure his wife's cancer. Five hundred years in the future, Tom travels through space toward a golden nebula where he hopes his wife's soul will be reborn. "*The Fountain* dispenses with everyday assumptions about time, space and causality," A. O. Scott wrote for the *New York Times* (November 22, 2006), "and tries to replace the prose of narrative cinema with a poetic language of rhyming images and visual metaphors. I wish I could say it succeeded." Other reviews were less measured; Dana Stevens, for example, wrote for *Slate* (November 30, 2006), "*The Fountain* is the story of a gifted artist who dared to reach for the stars and paid for his ambition with a really stupid movie." Stevens went on to compare Aronofsky to Max Cohen, the troubled math genius in *Pi*: "With *The Fountain*, Aronofsky has become the hero of *Pi* without the desistance or the humility. He not only wants to ask the big questions, he tries to tie it all up with The Big Answer. And that's worse than bad metaphysics, it's bad filmmaking."

The film had been controversial ever since it was shown at the 2006 Venice International Film Festival. After the first screening, lovers and haters of the film alike voiced their opinions in the theater; two people got into a fistfight over the film and had to be pulled apart. "It's funny," Aronofsky told Michael Idov for *New York* (November 27, 2006), "how the same people who complain that Hollywood never does anything different attack when you do." Not everyone complained. Some critics praised the film, albeit with qualifications. "I'm as touched and charmed by its failures . . . as I am transfixed, at times, by its successful inventiveness and audacity . . . ," Lisa Schwarzbaum wrote for *Entertainment Weekly* (November 21, 2008, on-line). "It's an entirely mood-dependent experience enhanced by identification with romantic/spiritualistic/kabbalistic/journal-or-blog-keeping tendencies of one's own, and ruined by impatience." The film critic Roger Ebert, writing for the *Chicago Sun-Times* (September 13, 2007), admitted that the film is "not a great success" but gave Aronofsky the benefit of the doubt: "When a film telling three stories and spanning thousands of years has a running time of 96 minutes, scenes must have been cut out. There will someday be a Director's Cut of this movie, and that's the cut I want to see."

Aronofsky's latest film is *The Wrestler* (2008), a drama that centers on the life of a retired professional wrestler, Randy "The Ram" Robinson (played by Mickey Rourke), who wants to return to the ring to face a former rival. At the 2008 Venice International Film Festival, the film received the Golden Lion Award, the festival's highest honor. Critics have praised both the film and Rourke's performance, hailing it as a comeback for the actor. *The Wrestler* went into wide release in December 2008. "The movie has the simplicity and confidence of a Johnny Cash song," the film critic Mick LaSalle wrote for the *San Francisco Chronicle* (December 25, 2008)."We recognize all the shopworn elements, and yet the ballad still has the power to take audiences to a real emotional and philosophical place. To call *The Wrestler* a formula movie would be to misunderstand it. This is an homage to formula, a knowing treatment that's loving rather than cynical." A. O. Scott, writing for the *New York Times* (December 17, 2008, on-line), praised the director's technique: "Shooting his battered hero mainly in trudging, hand-held tracking shots, Mr. Aronofsky . . . makes a convincing show of brute realism." Aronofsky is set to direct a remake of *RoboCop*, the futuristic 1987 action film about a crime-fighter who is half-man, half-machine. The film is currently in development. His film *Black Swan*, a psychological thriller about a ballet dancer living in New York City, is currently in preproduction; it will star Natalie Portman and Mila Kunis.

Aronofsky is married to the Oscar-winning English actress Rachel Weisz, with whom he has a son, Henry, born on May 31, 2006. They reside in New York City.

—D.K.

Suggested Reading: *Dallas Observer* Apr. 19, 2001; (London) *Guardian* Jan. 5, 1999; *New York* p115+ Nov. 27, 2006; *New York Times* E p27 Oct. 6, 2000, E p13 Nov. 22, 2006; *Slate.com* Nov. 30, 2006; *Wired* (on-line) Nov. 2006;

Selected Films: *Pi*, 1998; *Requiem for a Dream*, 2000; *The Fountain*, 2006; *The Wrestler*, 2008

Alex Wong/Getty Images for Meet the Press

Axelrod, David

Feb. 22, 1955– White House senior adviser; political consultant

Address: The White House, 1600 Pennsylvania Ave., N.W., Washington, DC 20500

Before he became the top political adviser to Barack Obama, during Obama's 2004 bid for the U.S. Senate, David Axelrod was already known as one of the nation's preeminent political strategists and, according to many, the best political consultant in the Midwest. The president of the Chicago, Illinois–based company AKP&D Message and Media (formerly known as Axelrod and Associates), he began his career as a political reporter and columnist with the *Chicago Tribune*; he was then inspired to join the 1984 senatorial campaign of the socially liberal Paul Simon and went on to advise Harold Washington, the first (and, so far, only) African-American mayor of Chicago, during his 1987 reelection campaign. Many have credited his efforts to elect progressive and African-American candidates to public office in Chicago with helping to ease racial tensions in that city's political sphere. In the 1990s and 2000s, Axelrod emerged as a specialist in urban politics and contributed to Democratic victories in mayoral races across the country. In 2006 he was the chief strategist in the historic campaign that led Deval Patrick to become the first black governor of Massachusetts. Axelrod—whose work for candidates has included developing strategy and message, creating television and radio commercials, and dealing with the media—often ran campaigns that centered on office-seekers' biographies rather than specific issues, believing that the power and poignancy of their stories are what win votes. "What [Axelrod] brings to the table," the political strategist Donna Brazile told David Montgomery for the *Washington Post* (February 15, 2007, on-line), "is the ability to help a candidate not only find their voice but also their roots. Their soul. David understands how to push through all the paper to get to the person."

While Axelrod—known as "the Axe" by many of his opponents—is just as aggressive, cut-throat, and willing to use negative advertising as anyone else in his industry, his friends and colleagues have observed that he also possesses an uncommon idealism and sincere belief in the candidates he advises. "He's really sort of an innocent . . . ," Sam Smith, a retired *Chicago Tribune* sportswriter and a longtime friend of Axelrod's, told Robert G. Kaiser for the *Washington Post* (May 2, 2008). "He loves his candidates when he starts; he's usually let down when he finishes [a campaign]." While Axelrod has disputed the claim that he ends up disappointed by his candidates, he has admitted to being inspired by them, particularly Obama, whom he considers "a really special guy" and whose presidential candidacy, he has said, embodied idealism in the way that the 1960s candidacies of John F. and Robert F. Kennedy did. "You never want to compare yourself to an iconic figure like that, and Obama doesn't, but the spirit of possibility in difficult times is a powerful thing," Axelrod told Kaiser. "And I see that again." Following Obama's election to the presidency, Axelrod was tapped to be a White House senior adviser.

David M. Axelrod was born in New York City on February 22, 1955 to politically liberal Jewish parents. In the 1940s his mother, Myril, was a journalist with *PM*, a left-wing newspaper; she later ran focus groups for an advertising firm. His father, Joseph, was a psychologist. Axelrod's parents separated when he was five years old; they reunited but separated again three years later and divorced when he was 13. With his sister, Joan, Axelrod grew up on the Lower East Side of Manhattan, in New York City. In 1960 he witnessed a rally held there to support the presidential bid of John F. Kennedy, then a Democratic U.S. senator from Massachusetts. Axelrod has recalled being hoisted onto a mailbox to watch Kennedy deliver what he recognized even then as an important speech. "The crowd was chanting, and he was speaking, exhorting them," Axelrod told Patrick T. Reardon for the *Chicago Tribune* (June 24, 2007). "There was a sense that people could get together and make history." When he was nine Axelrod handed out leaflets supporting the former U.S. attorney general Robert F. Kennedy's campaign for the U.S. Senate, and at 10 he passed out literature for John V. Lindsay, who was running for mayor of New York as the candidate of both the Republican and Liberal parties. In 1968 Axelrod and a friend set up a card table at the Bronx Zoo to sell "Robert Kennedy for President" buttons and bumper stickers. Axelrod attended Stuyvesant High School, a highly selective public school.

In 1972 Axelrod enrolled at the University of Chicago, where he majored in political science. As a reporter for the daily campus paper, the *Chicago Maroon*, he specialized in the politics of Chicago's South Side, a poor area with a predominantly black population. He wrote a political column for one of the city's weeklies, the *Hyde Park Herald*, and contributed freelance articles to *Time* magazine. In May 1974 his father, while alone in his apartment, committed suicide. Axelrod, who was deeply affected by his father's death, told Reardon that his father "had a great sense of humor. We used to yell puns to each other. I'd like to think I inherited my sense of humor from him." One summer during his undergraduate years, he completed an internship at the *Chicago Tribune*. He so impressed the editors with his knowledge of politics that, upon his graduation from college, with a B.A. degree in 1977, the newspaper hired him as a full-time reporter; his beat encompassed "every manner of disaster, murder and mayhem," as he told Kaiser. "Little by little I got to know the city really well, and I fell in love with it." In 1979 Axelrod married Susan Landau; the two had met as members of a co-ed basketball league in Hyde Park. Two years later he became the youngest political writer and columnist in the *Tribune*'s history; later, he was named the paper's City Hall bureau chief.

As time went by, Axelrod started to feel the urge to become "one of the few people inside the room shaping the news," as he told Cheryl Lavin for the *Chicago Tribune* (March 25, 1992), "rather than one of the hundred people standing outside, waiting to hear what it was." In 1984, when the Democratic Illinois congressman Paul Simon, whom Axelrod had interviewed several times, asked him to join his campaign for a seat in the U.S. Senate against the three-term Republican incumbent Charles Percy, Axelrod quit his job at the *Tribune* to become Simon's communications director. Within weeks Simon had fired his campaign manager and promoted Axelrod—along with David Wilhelm (who later chaired the Democratic National Committee)—to run his campaign. Working 12- to 15-hour days, Axelrod crafted a message that portrayed Simon as decent and principled and Percy as out of touch with local issues. With his upset victory over Percy, Simon was one of only two Democrats to defeat an incumbent Republican senator that year. Wilhelm told Christopher Hayes for the *Nation* (February 6, 2007, on-line) that the naïveté and idealism he and Axelrod shared at that time contributed to their success. "We were too dumb to quit," Wilhelm said.

In 1984, with Forest Claypool, one of his deputies during Simon's campaign, Axelrod launched a political consulting firm, Axelrod and Associates. Two years later Axelrod was hired to manage the mayoral reelection campaign of Harold Washington. During his first term Washington, a Democrat, had dealt with a city council dominated by members of Chicago's political machine, made up largely of corrupt, nonprogressive Democrats. In what became known as the "council wars," the efforts of council members to undercut Washington's efforts at reform had resulted in racially charged disputes. Axelrod had been inspired by Washington's 1983 mayoral campaign, describing the candidate to Hayes as "the most kinetic campaigner and politician that I've ever met." The mayor was extremely popular among Chicago's African-American residents; Axelrod helped him increase his appeal to the city's liberal whites. In the Democratic primary Washington defeated former mayor Jane Byrne, whom he had unseated four years earlier, and in the general election, held in April 1987, he defeated Edward Vrdolyak, a onetime Democrat who ran on the Illinois Solidarity Party ticket. (Washington died of a heart attack seven months later.)

Many liberal reformers were surprised by some of the other Democratic politicians for whom Axelrod chose to work in his firm's early years. In 1989, for example, he worked on the mayoral campaign of the Democrat Richard M. Daley, the son of Chicago's former mayor Richard J. Daley, the latter of whom had led an extraordinarily powerful—and, according to some, corrupt and undemocratic—political machine in the city in the 1960s and 1970s and maintained an iron grip on party and civic affairs. After Richard M. Daley handily defeated Eugene Sawyer in the Democratic primary, Axelrod used Daley's enormous war chest to create a series of negative television and radio commercials directed at his lesser-funded opponents, Vrdolyak and Timothy Evans. In the general election Daley triumphed; he took office on April 24, 1989 and has been reelected five times, most recently in 2007. Axelrod has advised him on each of his reelection campaigns, and the two are close friends.

In 1992 Axelrod represented a number of incumbents in the national political arena as well as challengers to other incumbents; he therefore had to create campaigns defending the existing policies of some candidates and opposing those of others. He was the political strategist for the 16-term Democratic congressman Dan Rostenkowski, the son of a former Chicago ward boss, Joseph Rostenkowski, and for Al Hofeld, a millionaire personal-injury lawyer who was challenging the incumbent U.S. senator Alan J. Dixon of Illinois in the Democratic primary with a campaign promise to "break the rules" of Washington and fight to institute term limits. Axelrod's campaign for Hofeld was dubbed by Steve Neal, writing for the *Chicago Sun-Times* (March 15, 1992), as "the most vicious, negative, and mean-spirited assault in a statewide Illinois election in more than a decade." Accusing Dixon of being "paid by the taxpayers" but "owned by the special interests," Axelrod issued a series of ads and direct-mail items vividly pointing to Dixon's supposed corruption. One such piece read, as quoted by Neal, "Money-stained fingers smear fine crystal glasses. Fancy colognes mix with the odor of corruption. Expensively dressed diners can hardly control their obscene appetites for wealth and power." At one point Axelrod even remarked to a reporter for the *National Journal* that his former mentor Paul Simon, who had endorsed Dixon, was "an aspiring hack trapped in a reformer's body." Years later Axelrod told Reardon that that comment about Simon, who died in 2003, was the thing he regretted most in his political life. Ultimately Rostenkowski won his reelection bid, but Hofeld finished in third place behind Dixon and the winner, Carol Moseley-Braun.

Axelrod has defended his use of negative advertising. "Look, voters don't go into the voting booth saying, 'I love all these folks—who do I love the most?'" he told Lavin. "You have to draw distinctions between them. Negative advertising can be very effective." Axelrod has also been accused of being hypocritical, billing himself as a representative of the progressive wing of the Democratic Party while working for wealthy candidates who are considered part of the Democratic establishment. "In a primary, you fight to define your party. But I'm partisan; in a general election I support the Democratic candidate," he told Lavin. "And just because I work with a candidate doesn't mean I belong to them for life. If someone disappoints me, I move on."

Despite the criticism he has received, Axelrod earned a positive reputation among progressives for working successfully on the campaigns of Democratic African-American politicians, particularly mayors. He helped elect African-American mayors Michael R. White of Cleveland, Ohio, in 1990; Dennis Archer of Detroit, Michigan, in 1992; Anthony A. Williams of Washington, D.C., in 1998; Lee P. Brown of Houston, Texas, in 1998; and John F. Street of Philadelphia, Pennsylvania, in 2000 and 2004. "He understands the African American community must see themselves in the candidate," Brazile told Montgomery, "not just their successes, but also their struggle."

Axelrod created issue ads for Hillary Clinton during her successful 2000 campaign to become a U.S. senator from New York. In 2002 he worked as a media adviser for Rahm Emanuel, a former official in the administration of President Bill Clinton, in his campaign for a seat in the House of Representatives from Illinois. In 2004 Axelrod was a media consultant for the reelection campaign of Connecticut senator Christopher Dodd and for the presidential campaign of John Edwards, a former senator from North Carolina. Although many of the national candidates for whom he worked, including Bill Clinton, offered Axelrod staff positions after being elected, Axelrod declined the offers, preferring to remain with his family in Chicago—where, as he quipped to Montgomery, "at least they stab you in the front."

In 2002 Barack Obama, then an Illinois state senator, asked Axelrod for his advice about running for the U.S. Senate. The two had met in the early 1990s, when Obama, then a recent Harvard Law School graduate, was working as a civil rights attorney and coordinating voter-registration drives in Chicago's South Side neighborhoods. Though Axelrod had been asked to work for another candidate who was campaigning for the same Illinois Senate seat, he signed on to work with Obama. Impressed with what he saw as Obama's optimism and dynamism, Axelrod charged Obama only a small fee for his services, given that the state senator had very little money at the time. "My involvement was a leap of faith," Axelrod told Obama's biographer David Mendell, as quoted by Kaiser. "I thought that if I could help Barack Obama get to Washington, then I would have accomplished something great in my life." In Obama's 2004 campaign Axelrod highlighted the candidate's public service. He also ran an endorsement by the daughter of Paul Simon and an ad that linked Obama to the city's late, beloved mayor Harold Washington. Obama defeated six other Democratic candidates in the primary election, held in March 2004, earning over 50 percent of the vote. Obama's opponent in the general election, the Republican Jack Ryan, dropped out shortly after the primary, following a disclosure about his mistreatment of his ex-wife; Ryan was replaced by the black Republican Alan Keyes. In November 2004 Obama defeated Keyes, winning 70 percent of the vote.

In 2006 Axelrod oversaw the Democratic Congressional Campaign Committee's independent-expenditure media program, helping Democrats gain their first majorities in the Senate and House of Representatives since 1994. That year Axelrod was also the political strategist for Deval Patrick in his campaign for the governorship of Massachusetts. Patrick, an African-American who had worked as assistant U.S. attorney general for the Justice Department's civil rights division in the Clinton administration, was widely considered an underdog in the race. In a campaign that would become the model for Obama's 2008 presidential run, Axelrod projected an optimistic message of reform and pragmatism; Patrick's candidacy used a slogan that Axelrod would later adopt for Obama: "Yes. We. Can!" Patrick's campaign also focused on his inspiring life story—of having been born to a poor family on Chicago's South Side and worked his way up to attend Harvard University. After winning the Democratic nomination, in September 2006, Patrick won 56 percent of the vote in that November's four-way general election, becoming Massachusetts's first black governor and the second African-American elected governor in U.S. history.

Before Obama asked him, in the fall of 2006, to be the political strategist for his 2008 presidential campaign, Axelrod had been planning to take some time off, in part because a number of politicians for whom he had once worked were planning to run for president—including Hillary Clinton, Edwards, Dodd, and the former Iowa governor Tom Vilsack—and he was reluctant to campaign against a former client. Three weeks before Obama officially announced his candidacy, in a speech on February 10, 2007, Axelrod released on the Internet a five-minute video of footage related to Obama's unusual life story; the son of a Kenyan father and a white mother from Oklahoma, he was raised by his white grandparents in Hawaii, gave up a corporate job to work for years as a community organizer on the South Side of Chicago, then attended Harvard Law School, where he became the first black editor of the *Harvard Law Review*. Entering a Democratic primary race in which the well-connected and well-funded New York senator Hillary Clinton was the presumed winner almost from the outset, Obama criticized the "divisive" and unproductive politics that he said had come to dominate Washington; he adopted messages of "hope" and "change," of which Obama himself—as the potential first black president—became a symbol. Many have cited Axelrod's influence regarding some of Obama's most memorable speeches, including his response to an accusation made by Hillary Clinton during one debate that Obama had raised false hopes in the American electorate with his idealistic speeches. In a January 2008 speech, as quoted by Maria L. La Ganga in the *Baltimore Sun* (February 21, 2008), Obama responded to Clinton's statement by asking: "What does that mean, false hopes? How have we made progress in this country? Did John F. Kennedy look at the moon and say, 'Ah, thought so, too far. Reality check. Can't do it'?"

Axelrod used the Internet to organize a nationwide grassroots coalition, which raised an unprecedented amount of money, most of which came in donations of less than $100. In contrast to the strategy used by Clinton, who campaigned mainly in states that had a lot of delegates, Axelrod focused on those with lower delegate counts, among them Alaska, Idaho, Kansas, and North Dakota. After winning a surprising, decisive victory in the first contest, the Iowa caucuses, held on January 3, 2008, then losing to Clinton in the New Hampshire primary, on January 9, Obama won 11 contests in a row, gaining 200 delegates. Though Obama earned only slightly more delegates than Clinton in the 24 primary elections or caucuses held on February 5, 2008, also known as "Super Tuesday," it soon became clear that he had collected so many delegates that it was nearly impossible for Clinton to catch up, even after her March victories in the so-called "big states," Ohio, Texas, and Pennsylvania. After what became one of the lengthiest and most contentious presidential primary elections in history, Clinton conceded the contest to Obama on June 7, 2008, shortly after Obama secured the requisite 2,025 delegates. Obama's campaign has been called one of the best-organized and best-run in U.S. history. "Axelrod . . . seems to have a profound understanding of people's yearning for a politics that is somehow less petty and rancorous," Hayes wrote. "Together [he and Obama] have crafted a potent message that speaks to this." Axelrod insisted that if Obama were elected president the following November, he would not accept a position in the Obama White House; those who knew Axelrod well, however, questioned whether he would be able to resist being a part of such a historic administration.

In the general election Obama faced the Republican senator John McCain of Arizona, who, as a military veteran who had spent more than five years as a prisoner of war in North Vietnam, had a life story as compelling as Obama's. Obama's general-election campaign, which began months before his official nomination, in August 2008, was notable for its lack of negativity as well as its discipline and consistent message. In the summer of 2008, as McCain's approval ratings improved—especially in the weeks following his selection of the conservative Alaska governor Sarah Palin as his running mate, in late August—some Democrats called for Obama to step up his attacks on McCain. While Obama himself typically dismissed McCain's negative attacks, which became increasingly frequent and biting, Axelrod and Obama's communications director, Robert Gibbs, occasionally challenged them. On July 30, 2008 Axelrod criticized a particularly sensational McCain ad that compared Obama to such international celebrities as Britney Spears and Paris Hilton in terms of both his popularity and (the ad implied) his lack of substance and understanding of the American people. Axelrod told Andrea Mitchell for MSNBC: "The thing that is sad about [the ads] is that Senator McCain entered this campaign as someone who was going to elevate the debate and talk about the future, and that is the reputation he had. And instead, we get some very familiar tactics. And it makes you wonder who is running the campaign and who is making the decisions, who is behind all this."

Obama opted to forgo public campaign financing, which allowed him to raise a record-setting amount of money through his grassroots network of supporters. On November 4, 2008 he was elected the 44th president of the United States, with 365 electoral votes to McCain's 173. Obama named Axelrod his senior adviser on November 19, 2008. Since his inauguration, on January 20, 2009, the new president has moved quickly to fulfill a number of major campaign promises, among the most urgent the proposal for a stimulus package to help revitalize the nation's ailing economy; voting along party lines, the House approved the measure, which called for spending totaling $819 billion, on January 28, and the Senate followed suit on February 10.

In subsequent months Obama embarked on an ambitious agenda, which included reevaluating the country's strategies in Afghanistan and Iraq, establishing a new regulatory system for the banking industry, and overhauling the nation's health-care system. Regarding health-care reform in particular, Congress has become increasingly polarized, and Obama's approval rating has dropped. Many have already identified health-care reform as the most crucial issue of Obama's presidency. "To govern is to make choices, and to make choices is to make some unhappy," Axelrod said in an interview with Peter Baker for the *New York Times* (September 7, 2009, on-line). "[Obama] made some very tough decisions that pulled us away [from a long-term economic depression]. But he had to expend some political capital to do that. He's expending some capital to do something that's very important, which is to bring security and health care to people who don't have it."

Over the course of his career, Axelrod has tailored messages for more than 150 successful campaigns at the local, state, and national levels. Axelrod ran AKP&D with three partners, John Kupper, David Plouffe, and John Del Cecato; in addition, along with Kupper and Eric Sedler, he headed ASK Public Strategies, which works on behalf of companies and organizations to mount ad campaigns relating to specific issues. Axelrod no longer runs either company and is not listed as a partner on either of the groups' official Web sites. He has served as an adjunct professor of communications studies at Northwestern University and lectured on the subject of political media at Harvard University, the University of Chicago, and the University of Pennsylvania. He has often been a guest political analyst on network television programs as well as on National Public Radio.

Owing to his droopy mustache, comb-over, and often rumpled attire, Axelrod's appearance has been compared—by his own mother—to that of "an unmade bed." Axelrod and his wife, Susan, have three children—Lauren, Michael, and Ethan—who are now grown. Lauren, the couple's oldest child, has developmental disabilities associated with the chronic epileptic seizures from which she suffered throughout her childhood. In 1998 Susan Axelrod joined two other mothers to form Citizens United for Research in Epilepsy (CURE), a group that lobbies for increased funding to find a cure for the disease; according to the AKP&D Web Site, CURE has raised $9 million to date. Axelrod has brought many of his former clients, including Bill Clinton, Obama, and Edwards, to speak at the group's annual fund-raising events.

—M.E.R.

Suggested Reading: *Baltimore Sun* A p4 Feb. 21, 2008; *Chicago Sun-Times* p42 Mar. 15, 1992; *Chicago Tribune* Tempo p1 Mar. 25, 1992; *Chicago Tribune Magazine* (on-line) June 24, 2007; *Nation* (on-line) Feb. 6, 2007; *New York Times Magazine* p30+ Apr. 1, 2007; *Washington Post* (on-line) Feb. 15, 2007, May 2, 2008

Courtesy of Thomas Good/Next Left Notes

Ayers, William

Dec. 26, 1944– Educator; writer; activist

Address: University of Illinois, 1040 W. Harrison, M/C 147, Chicago, IL 60607

In 2008 William Ayers, who holds the title of distinguished professor of education at the University of Illinois at Chicago, found himself the subject of fierce debate among the principal players in the race for the U.S. presidency. Ayers was a founding member of the Weather Underground, which in the early 1970s claimed responsibility for dozens of nonfatal bombings—including those at the Pentagon and U.S. Capitol—meant to protest the U.S. war in Vietnam. After years as a fugitive, he turned himself in to authorities and later earned a doctorate in education; he has since focused on a career as a teacher, writer, and education reformer in the Chicago, Illinois, area. It was there that he became acquainted with Barack Obama, who would become the 2008 Democratic presidential nominee, when both served on the boards of philanthropic and education-reform groups. The campaign of the Republican nominee, John McCain, emphasized the Obama-Ayers link and implied that Obama thus had ties to terrorists, in an effort to sow doubts about the Democratic candidate's patriotism and commitment to American values.

In an interview with Terry Gross for the National Public Radio program *Fresh Air* (November 18, 2008), Ayers insisted that there were no hidden aspects of his relationship with Obama. He also sought to explain the Weather Underground's motivation for its actions of decades past: "The question facing us was, in a situation where the American people have come out against the war, the people of the world have been against the war for much longer, what do you do when 2,000 people a week are being murdered? How do you respond to that? And the question was answered in a variety of ways. Some people went into the Democratic Party and tried to build a peace wing. Some people left for Europe and Africa and said they had to leave the madness. Some people organized communes and alternative communities. Some people went into factories and organized the industrial working class. And we decided that we would try to create an organization that could survive what we thought of as kind of impending American fascism and take the war to the warmakers." Ayers told Gross that in his 2001 memoir, *Fugitive Days*, he described "two groups of young Americans, one group [the Weather Underground] despairing, a little bit off the tracks, also hopeful that things can change, entering into the Pentagon, finding a way to penetrate the Pentagon to put a small explosive device kind of in a restroom. . . . And then I describe another group of Americans [U.S. soldiers] also despairing, also a bit off the tracks, marching into a Vietnamese village and murdering everyone who is alive and everything that's alive—every animal, all the livestock—and then burning the buildings to the ground, destroying the village. And I raise the question, what is terrorism?"

William Charles Ayers was born on December 26, 1944 in Oak Park, Illinois. He grew up in Glen Ellyn, a wealthy suburb of Chicago, with three brothers, John, Richard (Rick), and Thomas Jr., and a sister, Catherine. Their mother, Mary (Andrew) Ayers, was a homemaker; their father, Thomas G. Ayers, was a businessman who later served as president, chief executive officer, and chairman of Commonwealth Edison Co., the largest electric utility in Illinois. (It is now a unit of the Chicago-based Exelon Corp.) William Ayers has often credited his father, who promoted racial equality and once acted as a mediator between Chicago mayor Richard J. Daley and the civil rights leader Martin Luther King Jr., for sparking his interest in social activism. A smart and lively child, Ayers attended public schools until his sophomore year of high school, when he transferred to the Lake Forest, Illinois, prep school Lake Forest Academy. There, he played football and was the school's lone member of the Young Socialists Association. After graduating, in 1963, he enrolled at the University of Michigan (UM) at Ann Arbor. During those years Ayers was a member of the Merchant Marine. Learning about the U.S. war in Vietnam, and having read the novelist Norman Mailer's accounts of combat, he had romantic ideas about armed conflict and considered enlisting to fight overseas. But then, as he recalled to Terry Gross, "I came back to Ann Arbor, and as luck would have it, I found myself drawn to a group of anti-war people." He joined Students for a Democratic Society (SDS), which staged nonviolent protests to try to achieve its main objectives: ending racial inequality and U.S. involvement in the Vietnam War. By the late 1960s SDS boasted a membership of more than 80,000 young people. Though some sources claim that Ayers dropped out of college to focus his attention on SDS, his résumé on the University of Illinois Web site indicates that he earned a B.A. degree in American studies from UM in 1968.

Ayers became increasingly involved in SDS and began organizing for the group. He burned his draft card and was arrested in 1965 during a sit-in at a draft-board facility. Shortly afterward he got his first teaching job, at Children's Community, a small alternative school in Ann Arbor. Part of the free-school movement, the school emphasized cooperation over competition in its educational approach, and his work there opened his eyes to what would later become his passion. "I found out I'm at my best with kids," he later said of the experience to Jon Anderson for the *Chicago Tribune* (July 8, 1993). Ayers soon became the director of the school, where he met Diana Oughton. The two began dating and attended SDS meetings together.

In 1967 Ayers met Bernardine Dohrn, a 25-year-old activist with a law degree from the University of Chicago. A charismatic speaker, Dohrn became an SDS spokesperson. Ayers became the leader of the Midwest faction of SDS and was elected national education secretary at SDS's last national convention, in June 1969. During that convention SDS began to splinter. One faction, including Ayers, Oughton, and Dohrn, called for the formation of a militant group called the Weathermen. (The name was inspired by the Bob Dylan song "Subterranean Homesick Blues": "You don't need a weatherman / to know which way the wind blows.") They believed peaceful protests were not effective and issued a call to "bring the war home" through violence. "We wanted the people in the government waging the war to feel a sense of fear, a sense of consequences," Ayers told Don Terry for the *Chicago Tribune Magazine* (September 16, 2001). "Not personal fear, but fear that they were unleashing something that could rise up and overwhelm them." The Weathermen caused a schism within SDS, which disbanded in 1970.

Meanwhile, the Weathermen's first public protest had occurred in October 1969. Outraged by the trial of eight men accused of plotting to disrupt the 1968 Democratic National Convention, the group organized hundreds to riot in Chicago over the course of three days that became known as the Days of Rage. Wearing helmets and leather gloves, the rioters charged through the city, smashing car and building windows and destroying police cars. Unlike many other members, Ayers was not arrested during the riots. In March 1970 three Weathermen members, including Oughton and Ayers's close friend Terry Robbins, died when a bomb they were making in a New York City townhouse accidentally detonated. Soon afterward about two dozen Weathermen, including Ayers and Dohrn, went into hiding. They moved constantly, to locations in 15 states, and frequently changed their identities. Ayers held a series of odd jobs, working as a baker or as a teacher at a day-care center, and began a romantic relationship with Dohrn.

Still passionate in their political beliefs, Ayers and his colleagues went on to form the Weather Underground. Between 1970 and 1974 the group was responsible for a series of bombings, including that of the New York City police headquarters in 1970, the U.S. Capitol in 1971, and a Pentagon bathroom in 1972. Ayers has said that the bombs were intended only to destroy property and that group members set off blasts late at night, after checking to make sure no one was around, to ensure that no one would be hurt. "There were tens of thousands of [acts of] vandalism and bombings and arsons at government targets, and the Weather Underground took credit for something like two dozen," Ayers told Terry Gross. "You know, it crossed certain lines of legality, of proprieties, maybe even of common sense. But it was not terror. It never targeted people, it never meant to hurt or injure anyone, and thank God it never did hurt or injure anyone." Others, however, dispute Ayers's claims. Todd Gitlin, a professor at New York University and former SDS member, told Don Terry that the Weather Underground members "wanted to be terrorists. They planned on being terrorists. Then their bomb blew up and killed several of them and they thought better of it. They were failed terrorists."

In the mid-1970s the Weather Underground disbanded when one faction wanted to join the Black Liberation Army and another, which included Ayers and Dohrn, wanted to turn themselves in to the authorities. Dohrn, by that time, had been placed on the FBI's Ten Most Wanted List. Ayers and Dohrn, now settled in New York but still in hiding, abandoned their militant activism and had two sons: Zayd, named in honor of the Black Panther leader Zayd Shakur, in 1977 and Malik, named in honor of the black nationalist Malcolm X, who named himself El-Hajj Malik El-Shabazz, in 1980. Realizing that their children would have a difficult life if they remained in hiding, the couple decided to turn themselves. Shortly after Malik's birth they negotiated their surrender with New York authorities. Charges related to their Weather Underground activities had been dropped in January 1974 due to government misconduct in the case. (Investigators had wiretapped phones without a court order.) Dohrn, however, still faced charges stemming from the Days of Rage riots for inciting mob action, fleeing prosecution, and kicking a police officer; she was fined $1,500 and placed on three years' probation. The next year she was sent to jail for seven months after refusing to cooperate with a grand jury investigating a bank robbery that had involved two former Weather Underground members, Kathy Boudin and David Gilbert, and had left three people dead. (Dohrn was not directly involved in the robbery but refused on principle to cooperate with authorities.) Ayers and Dohrn married that same year, while Dohrn was on furlough from prison, and together they adopted Chesa Boudin, the infant son of Boudin and Gilbert, both of whom had been sentenced for their involvement in the robbery. (Boudin was released in 2003. Gilbert is serving a sentence of 75 years to life.) When he was no longer a fugitive, Ayers resumed his close relationship with his family. "It's funny," he told Jon Anderson for the *Chicago Tribune* (July 8, 1993), "when we came out of hiding, the first thing my father said was, 'Your hair's a bit long.'" Ayers said to Jo Napolitano for the *Tribune* (June 12, 2007), "It was as if we were in the middle of a conversation and nothing much had changed."

In 1984 Ayers enrolled at Columbia University's Teachers College, in New York City. While there he was inspired by a course that introduced him to critical pedagogy, an approach to teaching that emphasizes the importance of social justice. Education reform soon became a passion for Ayers. He went on to receive two master's degrees in early-childhood education: the first in 1984 from Bank Street College, also in New York City, and the second from Columbia, in 1987, the year he also earned an Ed.D. degree in curriculum and instruction from that school. Shortly afterward Ayers and his family moved to Chicago; there, he became a professor of education at the University of Illinois, wrote, co-wrote, or edited books on education, and worked to reform the crowded, failing Chicago-area public schools. With Anne C. Hallett, then the executive director of the Cross City Campaign for Urban School Reform, he drafted a proposal on ways to improve the school system. They won funding from the Annenberg Foundation to form the Chicago Annenberg Challenge, a $49 million initiative aimed at having smaller class sizes and increased community involvement with schools. The Annenberg challenge funded projects in more than 210 area schools between 1995 and 2001.

In 1991, through the University of Illinois at Chicago (UIC), Ayers and Michael Klonsky founded the Small Schools Workshop, an organization that works to create small, innovative learning communities within public schools. Eight years later Ayers founded the Center for Youth and Society, which worked to improve the educational environments of young urban students of color. In 1997, in recognition of his efforts toward education reform, Ayers won Chicago's Citizen of the Year Award. Also in 1997 UIC named Ayers a senior university scholar, and in 1999 he became a distinguished professor of education. Praised by many for his work, Ayers has also attracted critics who dismiss his educational philosophy as a guise for left-wing radicalism. "Now, instead of planting bombs in bathrooms, he has been planting the seeds of resistance and rebellion in America's future teachers, who will then pass on the lessons to the students in their classrooms," Sol Stern, a senior fellow with the conservative Manhattan Institute, wrote for the urban-policy magazine *City Journal* (Summer 2006). "Teaching has always been, for me, linked to issues of social justice," Ayers explained to Marcia Froelke Coburn for *Chicago Magazine* (August 2001, on-line). "I've never considered it a neutral or passive profession." One of Ayers's colleagues at UIC, Pamela Quiroz, told the Associated Press (October 17, 2008, on-line) that Ayers "gives of himself greatly to his students. He gives of his time, his energies, his commitment. He is just a superb individual."

Ayers wrote a first-hand account of his activities with both the Weathermen and the Weather Underground in his memoir *Fugitive Days*. In what was certainly among the more unfortunately timed book releases in history, *Fugitive Days* was published in September 2001. Even more unfortunate was, as the *New Criterion* (October 2001) described it, a "long and flattering profile" of Ayers published on the front of the *New York Times*'s E section on the morning of the September 11 terrorist attacks. The feature, written by Dinitia Smith, began with a quote from Ayers: "I don't regret setting bombs. I feel we didn't do enough." (The September 16 edition of the *New York Times Magazine*, which had been sent to print before the attacks, featured yet another profile of Ayers.) The backlash from the article began immediately. The favorable reviews Ayers had received before the attacks (David Farber wrote for the *Chicago Tribune* [August 26, 2001] about the book, "For anyone who wants to think hard about the social conflagration the Vietnam War produced in the U.S., and more generally about a citizen's obligations in troubled times, Ayers' powerful, morally charged account of a life and a society in the political balance is provocative reading") gave way to scornful critiques that lambasted Ayers's unrepentant attitude toward his past. "I know that you can never control the timing of your appearances. But justifying violence on the most violent day in American history cannot be written off as Ayers's mere bad luck," Alan Wolfe wrote for the *Chronicle of Higher Education* (October 12, 2001). "On any day, his comments would have been remarkably insensitive to the victims of violent acts. On that particular day, they seemed like poetic justice, as if the gods had somehow conspired to remind Ayers of what any good weatherman could have predicted: When turbulence hits the atmosphere, there are no easy ways to control it." Beacon Press, the publisher of *Fugitive Days*, immediately canceled Ayers's promotional tour for the book. Ayers wrote a letter to the *New York Times*, published on September 16, which read in part, "I'm filled with horror and grief for those murdered and harmed [during the September 11 attacks], for their families and for all affected forever. *Fugitive Days*, the memoir I've written about my participation in the Weather Underground and the antiwar movement and the events of 30 years ago, is now receiving attention in a radically changed context. My book is a condemnation of terrorism in all its forms. We are witnessing crimes against humanity. The intent of my book was and is to understand, to tell the truth and to heal." Ayers's letter seemed only to fuel his critics' outrage. *Fugitive Days* was reprinted in 2003 with a new foreword and reissued in November 2008 following President Obama's election.

Ayers once again found himself in the national news when, during the 2008 presidential campaign season, his past connection to the Democratic candidate Barack Obama came to light. Another Democrat, Hillary Clinton, had raised the issue during the primaries, before Obama became his party's nominee; later, during a campaign event in Englewood, Colorado, on October 4, 2008, the Republican vice-presidential nominee, Sarah Palin, accused Obama of "palling around with terrorists." Obama and Ayers, who lived in the same Chicago neighborhood, had served together in two Chicago-based philanthropic groups and an education-reform group. (Obama chaired the Chicago Annenberg Challenge from 1995 to 1999.) Ayers had also held an event at his home to introduce Obama to community members during the politician's first run for public office, in the mid-1990s. According to both men, that was the extent of their relationship. The McCain-Palin ticket, however, tried to use Obama's connection with Ayers to tarnish his reputation and insinuate that the Democratic candidate secretly held radical if not anti-American beliefs. Ayers, who has said that he began receiving death threats shortly after his name was publicly linked to Obama's in that fashion, refused to be interviewed and made no public statements during the campaign. He said to Terry Gross, "I felt like . . . how does one enter into that discussion when the premises are so . . . profoundly dishonest that I didn't know where to get a purchase on the question? Just jumping into the conversation is jumping into a dishonesty that I didn't want to promote. So I decided that when they thrust microphones at me I would turn away, and I did." Following Obama's election, however, Ayers decried the GOP's use of his name to attack Obama. In an op-ed piece for the *New York Times* (December 6, 2008, on-line), Ayers wrote, "Now that the election is over, I want to say as plainly as I can that the character invented to serve this drama wasn't me, not even close. . . . For the past 40 years, I've been teaching and writing about the unique value and potential of every human life, and the need to realize that potential through education. I have regrets, of course—including mistakes of excess and failures of imagination, posturing and posing, inflated and heated rhetoric, blind sectarianism and a lot else. No one can reach my age with their eyes even partly open and not have hundreds of regrets. The responsibility for the risks we posed to others in some of our most extreme actions in those underground years never leaves my thoughts for long. . . . [Obama and I] didn't pal around, and I had nothing to do with his positions. I knew him as well as thousands of others did, and like millions of others, I wish I knew him better."

In addition to his memoir, Ayers is the author, co-author, or editor of several dozen books on education, including *The Good Preschool Teacher: Six Teachers Reflect on Their Lives* (1989), *To Become a Teacher: Making a Difference in Children's Lives* (1995), and *Zero Tolerance: Resisting the Drive for Punishment in Our Schools* (edited with Dohrn and Rick Ayers, 2001). In 1997 Ayers, along with his mentor, the educational philosopher Maxine Greene, persuaded Teachers College Press to publish a series of books on teaching social justice. As of October 2009 16 books in that series were in print; Ayers wrote, edited, or contributed to several of them. He also co-authored, with Dohrn, *Race Course: Against White Supremacy* (2009).

Ayers is currently a professor of curriculum and instruction at the University of Illinois. He is vice president of curriculum studies for the American Educational Research Association, a Washington, D.C.–based organization that seeks to advance educational research and its application. His wife, Bernardine Dohrn, is the director of, as well as an associate professor with, Northwestern University's Children and Family Justice Center. The couple reside in the Hyde Park neighborhood of Chicago. As for his radical past, while Ayers has never apologized for his actions, he told David Remnick for the *New Yorker* (November 4, 2008, on-line), "I wish I had been wiser. I wish I had been more effective, I wish I'd been more unifying, I wish I'd been more principled." He said to Terry Gross, "The fact is that [Weather Underground] didn't do enough, and we didn't do it well enough. . . . The proof of that is that the American war in Vietnam went on for a decade. Three million people or so were murdered needlessly, and the end came when the Vietnamese threw the Americans out." He added, "We were issuing a screaming response to murder and to terror. . . . I don't think everything that we did was brilliant. . . . But I don't think [our actions] can be conflated with terrorism nor should they be, and I think that I don't feel any real regret for taking action against this war."

—M.A.S.

Suggested Reading: billayers.org; *Chicago Tribune* Tempo p1 July 8, 1993; *Chicago Tribune Magazine* C p10 Sep. 16, 2001; *Education Week* p1 Oct. 15, 2008; *New York Times* E p1 Sep. 11, 2001, A p21 Dec. 6, 2008; *New Yorker* (on-line) Nov. 4, 2008

Selected Books: As author—*The Good Preschool Teacher: Six Teachers Reflect on Their Lives*, 1989; *To Become a Teacher: Making a Difference in Children's Lives*, 1995; *Teaching the Personal and the Political: Essays on Hope and Justice*, 2004; *Fugitive Days: A Memoir*, 2001, 2008; *Race Course: Against White Supremacy* (with Bernardine Dohrn), 2009; As editor—*A Simple Justice: The Challenge of Small Schools* (with Michael Klonsky and Gabrielle H. Lyon), 2000; *Zero Tolerance: Resisting the Drive for Punishment in Our Schools* (with Dohrn and Rick Ayers), 2001; *Pledging Allegiance: The Politics of Patriotism in America's Schools* (with Joel Westheimer), 2007

Courtesy of Firefox

Baker, Mitchell

June 7, 1957– Internet-company executive; lawyer

Address: Mozilla Corp., 1981 K Landings Dr., Mountain View, CA 94943-0801

"Meeting the needs of Web users worldwide" is the mission of the Mozilla Foundation, its chairwoman, Mitchell Baker, said in an interview with *Business Wire* (December 4, 2006). Mozilla is the nonprofit organization responsible for Firefox, the world's second-most-popular Internet browser. "By creating a choice in how people access and experience the Web, we have spurred a revival in the browser market and changed the way people interact with the Web for the better," Baker told the *Business Wire* interviewer. Since its introduction, in 2004, Firefox—an "open-source" program whose software code has been updated by some 200,000 unpaid volunteers around the world—has gained more than 15 percent of the Web-browsing market. While it runs a distant second to the industry leader, Microsoft's Internet Explorer, Firefox boasts what many users consider to be superior security protections and browsing capabilities.

Consisting of a nonprofit foundation and a for-profit subsidiary branch, Mozilla grew out of Netscape Communications, which, in 1994, introduced one of the world's first commercial Web browsers. Baker, who studied law, not computer science, joined Netscape that year as associate general counsel. In that capacity she wrote the Netscape and Mozilla Public Licenses, documents that made it possible for Mozilla products to blur the line between proprietary and open-source software. In 1999 Baker was named the head—or "chief lizard wrangler," the title she chose for herself—of the Mozilla project, an initiative aimed at creating an open-source Web browser to rival Internet Explorer and end Microsoft's domination of the field. (Under the terms of the licenses, Mozilla is allowed to trademark Firefox and retain ownership of certain sections of the software code.) "Baker and Mozilla are wrestling with new questions about the boundaries between communities and the corporation," Siobhan O'Mahony, a Harvard Business School assistant professor, told David H. Freedman for *Inc.* (February 2007, on-line). "She's creating a new management model based on engaging a business ecosystem." In 2003 Baker became president of the Mozilla Foundation, which was created after Mozilla's parent company, AOL, decided to leave the project. From 2005 to 2008 Baker served as chief executive officer of the for-profit Mozilla Corp., which uses its earnings—most of which come from incorporating search engines, such as Google, into the Firefox interface—to fund its nonprofit initiatives. Explaining Mozilla's "public-benefit mission," Baker told Roland Tellzen for the *Australian* (May 29, 2007), "The return on investment we are looking for is to move the needle on the quality of the Internet and individual life. We are not looking for financial return on investment."

"It would be easy to assume that leadership is less important in this sort of community-driven organization" than in a traditional business, David Freedman wrote. But in reality it is more important, according to Sandeep Krishnamurthy, an associate professor in the business-administration program at the University of Washington, who has studied Mozilla. "Someone has to take the lead and reach out to this large group of people to provide feedback and motivate them," Krishnamurthy told Freedman. He also said, "Just because it's open source doesn't mean it's open door. To get anywhere, you have to win the respect of an elite group of people who develop code." Mitchell's success in winning that respect, in Freedman's view, is especially noteworthy because, as he wrote, "it's estimated that less than 2 percent of the open-source community is female. Meanwhile, the percentage of respected open-source leaders who didn't get to their positions via daring feats of coding is probably just as small. To do that entirely through nontechnical management skills would be nearly unprecedented, to do it as a woman all the more so."

Siobhan O'Mahony told Freedman that Baker "listens, she debates, she changes her mind, she adapts, she allows herself to be convinced by outsiders"—and she does so in public, on her blog. In an entry posted on June 1, 2005, Baker wrote that most entrepreneurs have a "sense of possibilities" that drives them and that they want to make those possibilities a reality by "maintain[ing] control over all significant aspects of the project of the company." "My case is very much the opposite," she continued. "The actual technical direction is not my space." Nevertheless, she wrote, "there is of course a piece of the Mozilla project where I have a very strong sense of the possibilities and a determination to see things proceed in a way that makes sense to me. That area is the organizational structure of the project. How do we integrate the various constituencies? How do we organize ourselves? How do we provide enough structure to build top quality products and still provide room for individual initiative and serendipity? . . . How do we generate funds and remain true to our mission? How do we create an asset of great value, keep it vital and maintain it? These questions are only a part of the Mozilla project, and yet they provide *plenty* of challenges."

Winifred Mitchell Baker was born on June 7, 1957 in Berkeley, California. Little information about her early years is readily available to the public. She grew up in or near Berkeley and attended a public high school in Oakland. Along with 30 other students and one teacher in what she labeled on her blog, blog.lizardwrangler.com, an "experiment in educational alternatives amidst the general decline of Oakland public schools," she spent her senior year at the Oakland Zoo as an "escape route" to "avoid the last year of regular high school." (The Web site lizardwrangler.com is devoted solely to a report on the Mozilla project dated March 2002. Mozilla's Web sites are mozilla.org and mozillafoundation.org.) As an undergraduate at the University of California (UC) at Berkeley, Baker—who is fluent in Mandarin, the principal language spoken in mainland China—studied for one year at Peking University (now known as Beijing University), in Communist China. She graduated from UC–Berkeley, with an A.B. degree in Asian studies, in 1979. In the 1980s she entered the School of Law at UC–Berkeley, commonly referred to as Boalt Hall; she earned a J.D. degree in 1987.

On her blog Baker revealed that she started work at her first place of employment—a law firm—a week late, in order to "finish anti-rabies treatment in Katmandu," in Nepal, "after being bitten by a dog in Samye, Tibet." In 1990 she became an associate at Fenwick & West, a national law firm with offices in California, Washington State, and Idaho that specialized in technology and the life sciences. Baker remained with that practice until 1993, when she left to become an associate general counsel for the technology giant Sun Microsystems, based in Santa Clara, California. In 1994 she changed jobs again, to become associate general counsel for Netscape Communications. (Her starting date was moved back five weeks, so that she could recover from a case of malaria, contracted during a trip to some small Indonesian islands.) Netscape had created the Netscape Navigator, one of the first commercial Web browsers. Its browser dominated the market until Microsoft began bundling its browser, Internet Explorer, with its widely used Windows operating system. Netscape accused Microsoft of "illegal, monopolistic behavior," as Baker told Quentin Hardy in an interview for *Forbes* (October 29, 2007), and even though, in 1993, the U.S. Department of Justice deemed Microsoft's tactics illegal, the ruling was not enough to keep Netscape from losing market share and influence in the Web-browsing field. In 1998 Netscape made public its software code, hoping that an open-source browser—one designed with the help of unpaid experts—might be able to compete with Internet Explorer. The effort was called the Mozilla project. (According to some sources, the inspiration for its name was Netscape's Godzilla-like mascot; David H. Freedman reported that the name "supposedly was derived from" Mosaic killer, "Mosaic having been the first browser".)

Within a few years of her arrival at Netscape, Baker had decided that she wanted to change the course of her career. While she lacked a programming background, she had grown familiar with the process of software engineering. Indeed, the Netscape and Mozilla Public Licenses that she drew up provided evidence of her understanding and insights. "She had proved so adept at finding common ground in the often intensely conflicting needs and styles of her corporate employer, the tech-obsessed and sometimes militant open-source community, and the world of users," as David H. Freedman wrote, that in 1998 Netscape's chief executive officer, James Barksdale, suggested that she head the Mozilla project. "I went and talked to some of the key engineers, and they said, yes, we know you, we trust you, we think you know enough about the project to be a decent leader, and let's give it a try," she told Charlie Rose in an interview for *The Charlie Rose Show* (April 21, 2005). Baker accepted the offer, dubbing herself "chief lizard wrangler," a title that "captured the idea that there was some leadership in there and some general management, but that it wasn't at all like an employment setting," she told Rose.

In 1999 AOL purchased Netscape. About two years later Baker was one of roughly 1,200 AOL employees to be laid off. "I remain committed to the Mozilla project and to contributing in whatever ways I can," she wrote in a widely distributed online message, according to Client Server News (September 10, 2001). Baker continued to work for Netscape, but as a volunteer, and Mozilla pressed ahead. In 2002 she began drawing a paycheck again (though at a smaller salary than before), thanks to a grant from the Open Source Applications Foundation. By April of that year, more than 200,000 Internet users had downloaded a trial version of the Mozilla browser, which was largely created by two young programmers, Blake Ross and David Hyatt. Among the browser's special features was "tabbed browsing," which enabled users to view multiple Web pages in a single window. The Mozilla browser was also far more secure than Internet Explorer, whose users were grappling with irritating pop-up windows and crippling viruses. In late 2002 Mozilla released its new browser, christened Phoenix.

The following year AOL formally severed its ties with Mozilla and created the nonprofit Mozilla Foundation. (The company also donated $2 million and key portions of its software code.) Baker became head of the foundation, overseeing a staff of about 10 employees. As Mozilla readied the formal release of its browser that year, some experts doubted whether it would be possible to challenge Internet Explorer, which then controlled 95.4 percent of the market. "It's very unlikely that Mozilla is going to make any inroads at this point," Michael Gartenberg, a research director at Jupiter Research, told Matt Hicks for *eWeek* (October 13, 2003). In February 2004 Mozilla officially changed the name of its browser from Firebird, a name that was also being used by an open-source database project, to Firefox. ("Firefox" is an informal name for the red panda, a stylized image of which appears on the Mozilla Firefox logo.) On November 9, 2004, following a two-month preview in which more than eight million Internet users downloaded the free browser, Mozilla made Firefox version 1.0 available to the public. In addition to introducing tabbed browsing, the program blocked pop-up advertisements and offered "live bookmarks"—"a set of things you would want in a browser if you sat down and really thought about it," Baker explained to Hicks for *eWeek* (November 9, 2004). Baker told Hicks that Mozilla's goal was to have a 10 percent market share by 2005. Achieving that benchmark, she said, would force major companies to make their Web sites compatible with Firefox, effectively ending Microsoft's monopoly. "That's a large number of people and a large enough number of people that if you're running a Web site, you don't want to be turning away that number of people," she noted.

By November 25, 2004 Firefox had been downloaded by more than six million on-line users. By January 12, 2005 the browser had come to control 4.6 percent of the market, while Internet Explorer's share had fallen to 90.6 percent. "We're not out to get Microsoft," Baker told Steve Hamm for *BusinessWeek* (January 24, 2005), dismissing the idea that Mozilla's persistence was fueled by revenge. "Our goal is to offer people a better experience so the Web remains open and people actually have a choice." In August 2005 the Mozilla Foundation announced the creation of the for-profit Mozilla Corp., an entity designed to comply with federal tax laws and give the organization more opportunities to earn money. Mozilla had already been accepting money from Google Inc., which paid to have its search page programmed as Firefox's default homepage. "The Mozilla Corp. is not a typical commercial entity," Baker, who was named president of the corporation, told Matthew Fordahl for the Associated Press Financial Wire (August 3, 2005). "Rather it is dedicated to the public benefit goal at the heart of the Mozilla project, which is to keep the Internet open and available to everyone."

In December 2005, a week after Mozilla unveiled Firefox version 1.5, the *San Jose (California) Mercury News* reported that that browser's market share had risen to between 10 and 12 percent. In an interview with the *Economist* (December 17, 2005), Baker said that Mozilla was responsible for reinvigorating a form of technology that, during years of Microsoft dominance, had experienced little innovation. "The browser matters; it's the piece [of the Internet] that touches human beings," she said. "This area shouldn't be stagnant; it should be exciting." In March 2006 it was reported that Microsoft's forthcoming Internet Explorer 7 (IE 7) would include many of the features introduced by Firefox. "I think IE 7 represents a significant success for the Mozilla project in its own right," Baker told Kim Clark for *USNews.com* (March 6, 2006). "The fact that IE users will have the benefit of [those] things is part of our goal of making the Web better." In the same interview Baker explained that, unlike Wikipedia, the popular open-source Internet encyclopedia, Mozilla did not accept contributions from volunteers blindly. "It is a lot more disciplined than people think," she said. "We can tell you for any piece of code that is checked in, who checked it in, when it was checked in, what problem they thought they were solving, who looked at that piece of code and thought it was OK, how many revisions it had been through." She added that at least one paid staff member looked at each piece of code before it was checked in. In December 2006 the World Economic Forum placed Mozilla on its annual list of "Technical Pioneers."

In an interview with Noam Cohen for the *International Herald Tribune* (May 22, 2007), Baker estimated that between 75 million and 100 million people were using the browser. "That is 75 million decisions, somewhere around the world to put this piece of software on someone's machine," she said. Estimates placed Firefox's market share at 15 percent, and the Mozilla corporation posted revenues of more than $50 million in both 2005 and 2006. (Most of the money came from Google.) In the November 12, 2007 interview with Cohen, Baker called her $500,000 annual salary, which included an unspecified amount for benefits, "yet another example of Mozilla as a hybrid," referring to the way the company had succeeded in turning open-source software into a moneymaking product. Cohen wrote that, despite Mozilla's claim that it would use earnings to fund other open-source initiatives, the foundation had, in 2006, given less than $100,000 in grants. (Mozilla claimed it had awarded $287,000.) In January 2008 Baker stepped down as CEO of the Mozilla Corp., handing the reins to John Lilly, who had previously served as the firm's chief operating officer. At the time of Baker's departure, the Web-survey firm XiTiMonitor reported that Firefox enjoyed a 27.7 percent share of the European market and about 17 percent in the U.S. More than 1,000 volunteers had been instrumental in creating the latest version of Firefox, which was available in 37 languages. Baker stayed on as chairwoman and vowed to continue upholding Mozilla's core beliefs. "We could not operate without our community," she told John Markoff for the *International Herald Tribune* (January 9, 2008). "More money doesn't give you more opportunity." In February 2008 the Electronic Frontier Foundation presented Baker and Mozilla with one of its three annual Pioneer Awards.

On June 18, 2008 eight million users around the world downloaded Firefox3, a new version of the browser touted as being twice as fast as its predecessor. "We definitely knew that it would be millions, probably about 5 million," Baker told Cho Jin-seo in an interview for *Korea Times* (June 19, 2008). "We didn't think it could be this much." By the following day the total download count had increased to 10.7 million. While Firefox's popularity continued to grow, Baker contended that Mozilla was wary of becoming far bigger in the marketplace. "I think if you tossed a number like 80 percent around even inside Mozilla, some people would start to worry, because if we behaved poorly, it would affect the industry in bad ways," she told Jack Schofield in an interview for the London *Guardian* (February 28, 2008). "We want to show why having openness is useful, so the market share enables us to move the industry towards a better place. As a project we have values, and there's a core for whom Mozilla acting as a tyrant is no better or only slightly better than somebody else acting as a tyrant."

In a recent entry on her blog (February 6, 2009), Mitchell quoted a preliminary report in which the European Commission (E.C.) concluded that "Microsoft's tying of Internet Explorer to the Windows operating system harms competition between web browsers, undermines product innovation and ultimately reduces consumer choice." "I'll be paying close attention to the EC's activities, both personally and on behalf of Mozilla," she wrote. "Mozilla has enormous expertise in this area. . . . I'd like to offer Mozilla's expertise as a resource to the EC as it considers what an effective remedy would entail." She then invited the public to send her their ideas on the matter.

According to David H. Freedman, Baker "seems to have two different haircuts that face off on opposite sides of her head, unified only partially by a dose of red dye." In on-line discussions that are open to the public, Freedman wrote, Baker is "fond of tossing out what seem like contradictory ideas in quick succession." She is a skilled amateur trapeze artist. She is married to Casey Dunn, an open-source software developer. The couple live in Belmont, California, with their young son, Jarett.

—K.J.P.

Suggested Reading: *Australian* p7 May 29, 2007; blog.lizardwrangler.com; *BusinessWeek* p78 Jan. 24, 2005; *Economist* Dec. 17, 2005; *Forbes* p60 Oct. 29, 2007; *Inc.* (on-line) Feb. 2007; *International Herald Tribune* p16 May 22, 2007, p11 Jan. 9, 2008; *Korea Times* June 19, 2008; (London) *Guardian* p5 Feb. 28, 2008; (London) *Sunday Telegraph* p6 May 28, 2006

Banksy

July 28, 1973(?)– British graffiti artist

Address: Lazarides Gallery, 8 Greek St., London W1D 4DG, England

The street artist who calls himself Banksy became famous in the United Kingdom for his highly distinctive graffiti—stenciled spray-paintings that appeared with increasing frequency in the late 1990s and early 2000s on walls and the sides of buildings in Bristol and other British cities. Banksy's images and messages tend to be irreverent, antiestablishment commentaries on contemporary society and politics; they have been described as provocative, witty, comical, satirical, mischievous, and easily understandable. In a conversation with Ciar Byrne for the London *Independent* (November 1, 2007), Gareth Williams, the head of the Urban Art Department at the British auction house Bonhams, connected the appeal of Banksy's work to "the whole phenomenon that surrounds him—a relatively unknown graffiti artist from Bristol who has taken the art world by storm, but has done it on his own terms. Also because his images are so accessible, iconic, democratic and humorous, his work reaches people on a simple level." "He catches the feeling that something is wrong with modern life," James Button wrote for the Melbourne, Australia, *Age* (July 16, 2007). Among the most common of Banksy's subjects are rats, which are ubiquitous in cities and almost universally despised. "If you are dirty, insignificant and unloved then rats are the ultimate role model," Banksy wrote in his book *Wall and Piece* (2005). Technology, in particular the Internet, has contributed to Banksy's popularity: as of late February 2009, there were about 2,260,000 entries about him on Google, many accompanied by photographs of his graffiti and other paintings. Dubbed a "guerrilla artist" as well as a "people's artist," he has boosted his celebrity through public stunts—for example, affixing his works to the walls of major museums in London, New York, and Paris; stenciling the words "We're bored of fish" in the London Zoo's penguin enclosure; putting the words "Designated riot area" on the pedestal of the statue of Admiral Nelson in London's Trafalgar Square; stenciling "Mind the crap" on a step leading up to that city's Tate Gal-

Gareth Cattermole/Getty Images

Banksy's Kids on Guns *at the Andipa Gallery, London, England*

lery; and, on the Palestinian side of the highly controversial Israeli-built wall in the West Bank, painting "holes" through which bucolic scenes are visible.

In *Wall and Piece* Banksy wrote: "Graffiti is not the lowest form of art. Despite having to creep about at night and lie to your mum it's actually the most honest artform available. There is no elitism or hype, it exhibits on some of the best walls a town has to offer, and nobody is put off by the price of admission. . . . The people who run our cities don't understand graffiti because they think nothing has the right to exist unless it makes a profit. But if you just value money then your opinion is worthless. . . . The people who truly deface our neighbourhoods are the companies that scrawl their giant slogans across buildings and buses trying to make us feel inadequate unless we buy their stuff. They expect to be able to shout their message in your face from every available surface but you're never allowed to answer back. Well, they started this fight and the wall is the weapon of choice to hit them back." The outlaw and performative elements of graffiti are also important to Banksy. He told Rick Hewett for the London *Evening Standard* (October 23, 2003), "The adrenaline of the whole operation . . . well, what a buzz. Where's the excitement of sitting in a field painting horses and flowers? Art should have your pulse racing, your palms clammy with nerves and the excitement of creating something truly original in a dangerous environment."

Banksy's refusal to reveal his real name or any other information about himself, and his absence from exhibitions of his work, have drawn much attention in the media and helped to increase his prominence in the art world. Along with mainstream recognition, his paintings—occasionally removed from their original sites but more often created on paper or canvas in a studio—have commanded high prices in galleries and auction houses. In October 2006, for example, Banksy's cover art for the British band Blur's album *Think Tank* (2003)—a painting of an embracing couple wearing divers' helmets—sold at Bonhams for £62,400 ($105,905 at that time); in February 2007 an acrylic and spray-painted canvas called *Bombing Middle England*, which shows three elderly women bowling outdoors with spherical bombs ("bombing" is also a synonym for graffitiing), sold for £102,000 ($199,800) at Sotheby's; and two months later, also at Sotheby's, a self-portrait, in which Banksy's head was that of a chimpanzee, brought £198,000 ($393,604). "Before he became a cultural icon, these paintings were removed quickly" from public places, Clementine Ford wrote for the South Australia *Sunday Mail* (July 20, 2008). "Now they're featured in private collections, a statement in itself about how our society seeks to commodify everything of popularity, even if its central manifesto is anathema to it. . . . And herein lies the rub. Banksy has reached such phenomenal levels of fame and cultural value he has become a brand himself." Banksy's agent, and public face, is the London gallery owner Steve Lazarides, who specializes in what he calls "outsider art." In May 2009 several sources reported that an entity called Pest Control will authenticate works attributed to Banksy.

During an interview for an undated issue of *Swindle Magazine* (Issue 08), the artist Shepard Fairey asked Banksy how long he intended to remain anonymous. Banksy answered, "I have no interest in ever coming out. I figure there are enough self-opinionated [expletives] trying to get their ugly little faces in front of you as it is. You ask a lot of kids today what they want to be when they grow up, and they say, 'I want to be famous.' You ask them for what reason and they don't know or care. . . . I'm just trying to make the pictures look good; I'm not into trying to make myself look good. I'm not into fashion. The pictures generally look better than I do when we're out on the street together. Plus, I obviously have issues with the cops. And besides, it's a pretty safe bet that the reality of me would be a crushing disappointment to a couple of 15-year-old kids out there."

After a year-long investigation, Claudia Joseph reported in the London *Mail on Sunday* (July 13, 2008) that Banksy was born Robin Gunningham in Bristol on July 28, 1973 to Peter Gordon Gunningham, a contracts manager, and Pamela Ann Dawkin-Jones, a secretary. (Neither his parents nor his agent or anyone else has confirmed the accuracy of that identification.) According to Joseph, Banksy's father and mother (who are now separated or divorced) raised him and his older sister, Sarah, in a middle-class suburb of that city. According to Joseph, in the mid-1980s Banksy attended the Bristol Cathedral School, an exclusive private school. Former classmates of his told Joseph that they remembered him as having unusual artistic talent.

The practice of writing on walls in cities began thousands of years ago. The spray paintings we commonly refer to as modern graffiti originated in Philadelphia, Pennsylvania, in the 1960s, first in connection with territorial gang culture and then as a form of artistic expression. By the late 1970s and early 1980s, it had become a cultural phenomenon, inextricably linked to hip-hop culture. In 1983 the New York hip-hop group the Rock Steady Crew performed in London, England, and Paris, France, with graffiti artists in tow; they are said to have inspired a generation of European artists, including those in Bristol's vibrant underground. When Banksy was about 10, the 18-year-old Bristol-born artist and musician Robert del Naja (later, as a member of the band Massive Attack, known as 3D) began spray-painting graffiti on Bristol walls and streets. "I grew up seeing spray paint on the streets way before I ever saw it in a magazine or on a computer . . . ," Banksy told Shepard Fairey. "Graffiti was the thing we all loved at school—we all did it on the bus on the way home from school. Everyone was doing it." Banksy is said to have left school at 16 and immersed himself in Bristol's graffiti subculture. He has been quoted as saying that he was not adept at spray-painting freehand and worked very slowly, which increased his risks of getting caught in the act by police officers. (By his own account, he was arrested at least once, before he adopted the moniker Banksy.) His lack of skill and speed led him to develop his stenciling technique. He has named among his influences the groundbreaking French stencil artist Blek le Rat (whose real name is Xavier Prou); Gary Larson, the creator of *The Far Side* cartoons; and the magician and escapologist Harry Houdini.

In the latter half of the 1990s, Banksy honed his technique and developed a recognizable style; he also attracted a growing number of fans. He sold illustrated T-shirts and posters to concertgoers, especially aficionados of Britpop, an alternate form of rock popular in Great Britain during that decade. In 1998, for a "graffiti event" held in Bristol's Harbourside area, he painted an image of an operating room in which the "patient" was a twisted, bubble-lettered piece of calligraphy. His first formal show was held at a Bristol restaurant in 2000. The next year he began exhibiting his art at what was dubbed Santa's Ghetto, set up in a London art store. With a show called Turf War, which he set up in a London warehouse in July 2003, he drew the attention of people linked to the art-world establishment. The exhibit included live pigs and cows bearing spray-paintings on their bodies and a now-famous painting of a crowned, jewelry-laden monarch, her face that of a chimpanzee, set against an image of the Union Jack—a satirical portrait of Queen Elizabeth II, according to many sources.

That autumn Banksy painted a landscape in the style of the British artist John Constable (1776–1837) that included criss-crossing white and blue "Do not cross" police tape across the bottom; then, using a strong adhesive, he affixed his painting to a wall in the Tate Gallery, along with a small sign reading "Crimewatch UK has ruined the countryside for all of us." The signage continued, "This new acquisition is a beautiful example of the neo post-idiotic style. . . . It can be argued that defacing such an idyllic scene reflects the way our nation has been vandalised by its obsession with crime and paedophilia, where any visit to a secluded beauty spot now feels like it may result in being molested or finding discarded body parts." Banksy's painting was soon removed; later, the Tate bought it for its permanent collection. "This is how a lot of people see the world these days," Banksy said of that picture to Rick Hewett. "People don't see Constable's hay and rivers any more."

Many more such takeoffs of famous oil paintings comprised Banksy's exhibit Crude Oils—"a gallery of re-mixed masterpieces, vandalism and vermin," mounted in 2005 at 100 Westbourne Grove, a London venue. Dozens of brown rats roamed freely or lay dead within the exhibition space, having been deposited there as part of the show; visitors to the exhibition were permitted to view the paintings for only a few minutes, and each was required to sign a statement absolving the gallery of responsibility if he or she happened to slip on the rat droppings and sustain injury. The show included Banksy's rendition of Claude Monet's painting *Water Lily Pond and Japanese Bridge* in which two supermarket shopping carts lie upended in the water. In a variation on Edward Hopper's *Nighthawks*, three customers and a worker in a brightly lit urban diner stare at an overweight, barefoot man who stands defiantly outside, wearing nothing but undershorts bearing a Union Jack design; the man has thrown a chair and broken one of the diner's wraparound windows, which now has a jagged hole surrounded by cracks. Two of Banksy's paintings showed a haloed madonna and child; in one, the mother is listening through earpieces to an iPod, and in the other, the Christ child has explosives strapped around his chest.

In 2004 Banksy smuggled into the Natural History Museum of London and glued onto a wall a shadow box that contained a stuffed rat outfitted with sunglasses, a backpack, a flashlight, a microphone, and a miniature can of spray paint; the words "Our time will come" appeared behind it. Below, a sign stated that "an increase in junk food waste, ambient radiation and hardcore urban rap music" had led to the evolution of the species Banksus Militus Vandalus at an "unprecedented rate." "They are impervious to all modern methods of pest control and mark their territory with a series of elaborate signs," the text continued. "Professor B. Langford of University College London states 'You can laugh now . . . but one day they may be in charge.'" In New York in 2005, in a similar action, Banksy affixed works of his to walls in the Museum of Modern Art, the Metropolitan Museum of Art, the Brooklyn Museum of Art, and the Museum of Natural History. The piece that appeared in the last-named place, also in a shadow box, was a dead harlequin beetle to which Banksy had affixed tiny wings with American insignia and miniature missiles. In *Walls and Pieces*, Banksy wrote that the warrior beetle remained in place for 12 days. Also in 2005 Banksy traveled to the West Bank and stenciled nine paintings on the Palestinian side of the West Bank barrier—known as the "apartheid wall" among Palestinians and as the "security fence" among Israelis—that Israel has been constructing since 2002. "As a graffiti writer you have to make a pilgrimage to the biggest wall on earth at some point," he told a reporter for the European magazine *Zoo*, as quoted by Paul Valley in the London *Independent* (September 23, 2006). The West Bank wall, he added, is "the most politically unjust structure in the world today."

What has become one of Banksy's most famous paintings appeared in June 2006 on the wall of a birth-control and sexual-health clinic that stands opposite the offices of the Bristol city council. The trompe-l'oeil painting shows an open window that closely resembles real ones nearby. A man wearing a suit and tie is leaning out of the window, peering intently at the street; hovering behind him is a woman clad only in bra and panties, and outside, hanging from the window ledge by the fingertips of one hand, is a naked man. The city council placed the fate of the painting in the hands of the public, and 93 percent of approximately 1,000 voters requested that it remain in place. Also in 2006, in several British cities, Banksy and a few of his cohorts doctored the album covers on hundreds of copies of the debut CD by the celebrity Paris Hilton. Hilton was shown topless on some and with a dog's head on others; alongside her image were the song titles "Why Am I Famous?," "What Have I Done?," and "What Am I For?" Reportedly, the songs were recorded for a CD that Banksy substituted for the original disk, and, because the bar code on the cover was reproduced precisely, the hoax was not immediately detected. In September 2006 in the U.S., Banksy sneaked into Disneyland a blow-up doll dressed in the orange clothes and black hood of a Guantánamo Bay prisoner, and in Los Angeles he mounted a show entitled Barely Legal, at which several Hollywood stars bought some of his works. A live elephant in a cordoned-off part of the Barely Legal exhibit space, according to leaflets distributed at the show, represented global poverty—"the elephant in the room."

Back in the United Kingdom, Banksy was becoming what Ciar Byrne called "the darling of the collectors." His reputation increased considerably when the artist Damien Hirst included some of Banksy's pieces in an exhibit of his personal collection. "Everybody loves a maverick. The fact that Banksy was taken up so whole-heartedly by Damien Hirst has upped his market currency immeasurably," Louisa Buck, a reporter for *Art Newspaper*, told Ciar Byrne. In December 2007 Banksy returned to the West Bank, along with several other artists; during that visit he painted not on the Israeli-created wall but on the exteriors of small buildings. One picture showed a small girl in a pink dress frisking a soldier for weapons. In another a dove bearing an olive branch in its beak wears a bulletproof vest; a red target of the sort visible through a rifle sight appears over its heart.

One night in April 2008, in response to the installation in Great Britain of hundreds of thousands of closed-circuit television (CCTV) cameras for purposes of surveillance (as a means of catching lawbreakers, according to the government), Banksy scaled an iron fence, erected scaffolding opposite a CCTV camera, and painted a three-story-high image on the side of a building. In it a security guard watches a boy who, while perched atop a tall ladder, has painted the words "One Nation Under CCTV." Somehow Banksy completed the work without interference. In May 2008 Banksy hosted the Cans Festival, a celebration of graffiti in which dozens of artists painted on the walls of a London tunnel. During the three-day event, some 28,000 people came to view the paintings—considerably more than the number who visited a concurrent exhibition at the nearby Tate Modern (a division of the Tate Gallery).

In August 2008 Banksy produced a series of murals in New Orleans, Louisiana, to mark the third anniversary of Hurricane Katrina, which devastated a large portion of that city and other areas along the American Gulf Coast. Painted on walls of buildings abandoned in New Orleans after the storm and the flooding it caused, Banksy's pieces were said to be partly critiques aimed at the inadequate government response to the disaster and partly tributes to the resilience of many New Orleanians. Most of the pieces were quickly painted over. In October 2008 Banksy unveiled an exhibit in New York City, entitled the Village Pet Store and Charcoal Grill, featuring animatronic pets. In one piece a mother hen watched over her children—chicken nuggets—as they ate from a pack of barbeque sauce; in another, fish fingers swam in a water-filled tank. Those two works and about 100 others were on exhibit for three weeks beginning in June 2009 in Bristol's City Museum and Art Gallery. Called Banksy Versus the Bristol Museum, it was Banksy's biggest exhibition to date. The works included replicas, with various changes, of items in the museum's collection along with never-before-seen Banksy pieces. In an example of the former, a copy of Jean-Francois Millet's *The Gleaners*, one of the three women has stepped out of the painting and is seen sitting on the frame, smoking a cigarette. In an example of the latter, two starving children stand in a wasteland; one carries a bucket and wears a T-shirt bearing the words "I hate Mondays." In one animated sculpture, what looked from one side like a cheetah lounging in a tree was revealed on the other side as a fur coat; in another, a rabbit (a member of a species long used to test the properties of mascara and other eye makeup) files its nails while standing in front of a mirrored vanity crowded with containers of rouge and nail polish. "This is the first show I've ever done where taxpayers' money is being used to hang my pictures up rather than scrape them off," Banksy remarked, according to the *Bristol Evening Post* (June 13, 2009). In actuality, the *Post* reported, Banksy himself had funded the project, which he said was a tribute to his hometown. Free of charge, the show attracted huge crowds.

Although Banksy has consistently turned down lucrative work in commercial advertising, his financial success has drawn accusations that he has abandoned his principles. "Wait a minute. This guy is supposed to be an anarchist, a man of the street, an urban guerrilla—and he has a dealer? An agent? A spokesperson?" Richard Dorment complained in the London *Daily Telegraph* (May 6, 2008). Charlotte Higgins wrote for the London *Guardian* (November 2, 2007), "The work is so mainstream that there is actually a guidebook to it," and also in the *Daily Telegraph* (March 19, 2007), William Langley wondered about the "the state of [Banksy's] street cred": "Penury and failure are central to the whole business of outlaw artistry." An editorial in the Bristol *Evening Post* (November 9, 2007) maintained that countercultural icons are not supposed to be celebrated or encouraged by the establishment: "It's like the parent of an angry, rebellious teenager shouting through a slammed bedroom door 'turn that music up louder, love—I like it.'" For his part, Banksy confessed in an e-mail interview with Lauren Collins for the *New Yorker* (May 14, 2007) that he felt uncomfortable with all the success and attention; he also said, "I love the way capitalism finds a place—even for its enemies. It's definitely boom time in the discontent industry." Banksy's detractors include art critics who refuse to recognize what he produces as art and antigraffiti campaigners who condemn him as a vandal. In an article for the *Guardian* (July 15, 2006), the graffitist Edward Hammond argued that most of Banksy's work "is not even graffiti in the real sense, other than in the shared clothing of illegality. Banksy's black and white daubing is an art form in its own right, and although it falls under the umbrella of street art, it is actually a closer relative of stickering, fly posting and billboard advertising than of graffiti-writing. Unfortunately this is probably the least addressed issue arising from his work, partly because it suits Banksy to present himself as a graffiti writer to the liberal intelligentsia, whose favourite he is. His popularity, ironically, is due not to the intelligence and thoughtfulness of his work but to its contained simplicity, which contrasts so strongly with the often indecipherable writings adorning the streets and railways."

Reproductions of works by Banksy, accompanied by his texts, appear in the books *Banging Your Head Against a Brick Wall* (2001), *Existencilism* (2002), and *Cut It Out* (2004) as well as *Wall and Piece*. Banksy and his work are the subjects of Martin Bull's *Banksy Locations and Tours: A Collection of Graffiti Locations and Photographs in London* and Steve Wright's *Banksy's Bristol: Home Sweet Home*, both published in 2007.

—M.M.

Suggested Reading: (London) *Daily Mail* (on-line) June 13, 2008; (London) *Evening Standard* p28 Oct. 23, 2003; (London) *Guardian* p10 July 17, 2003; (London) *Inde-pendent* p44 Nov. 1, 2007; (London) *Mail on Sunday* p2 July 13, 2008; *New Yorker* p54+ May 14, 2007; *Swindle Magazine* (on-line) Issue 08; (South Australia) *Sunday Mail* p105 July 20, 2008; Bull, Martin. *Banksy Locations and Tours: A Collection of Graffiti Locations and Photographs in London*, 2007; Wright, Steve. *Banksy's Bristol: Home Sweet Home*, 2007

Selected Books: *Banging Your Head Against a Brick Wall*, 2001; *Existencilism*, 2002; *Cut It Out*, 2004; *Wall and Piece*, 2005

Barlow, Maude

May 24, 1947– Environmental activist; writer

Address: Council of Canadians, 251 Laurier Ave. W., Ottawa, Ontario K1P 5J6, Canada

"Water is the new oil . . . ," Maude Barlow told Katherine Monk for the *Montreal (Canada) Gazette* (January 25, 2008), adding, "The global water shortage means it is fast becoming a commodity . . . and one that corporate interests are realizing a profit on. Water has become a huge business, and it's increasingly being controlled by a very small number of corporations." Often referred to as "Canada's Ralph Nader," Barlow, a Canadian writer and political activist, has authored or co-authored 16 books on public policy and on issues involving the environment. Since the late 1990s she has been known particularly for her effort to achieve universal access to clean water, a mission summed up in her best-selling, widely translated 2002 book, *Blue Gold: The Fight to Stop the Corporate Theft of the World's Water*, written with Tony Clarke. One of her central arguments is that such access should be viewed as a basic human right rather than a commodity. Barlow explained to Monk, "In the years I've been traveling the world, water is where people draw the line. When people are denied water, they will put their lives on the line because they know without water, they are being sentenced to a slow and miserable death anyway." She followed up *Blue Gold* with *Blue Covenant: The Global Water Crisis and the Coming Battle for the Right to Water* (2008), and her work is a main focus of *Flow:*

Pam Woolridge, courtesy of the Council of Canadians
Maude Barlow

For Love of Water (2008), a documentary by the French filmmaker Irena Salina. Barlow is a founding board member and national chairperson of the Council of Canadians, Canada's largest public-advocacy organization, and the co-founder of the Blue Planet Project, a global initiative that works against the privatization and commodification of the world's water.

Maude Victoria Barlow was born on May 24, 1947 in Toronto, Ontario, Canada. Her mother, Flora, was a homemaker. Her father, William, who was a criminologist, perhaps created a model for Maude Barlow's own activism. According to the Web site of *Life and Times*, a television program of the Canadian Broadcasting Corp. (CBC), William Barlow—a "witness to wartime atrocities"—returned from military service determined to make a positive contribution to society and became a voice for prison reform in Canada. In the late 1960s Maude Barlow enrolled at Carleton University, in Ottawa, receiving her bachelor's degree in 1972. Later in the decade, according to the *Life and Times* Web site, she "was a nice middle-class" woman "who got caught up in the Canadian women's movement." As posted on the Web site of the publication *Canadian Geographic*, Barlow noted, "That work gave me a global perspective. I learned the responsibilities women had and how shortages of basic resources, like water, affected their lives." In 1980, after a five-year stint as vice president of the Ottawa-based Women Associates Consulting Inc., she began running the City of Ottawa's Office of Equal Opportunity for Women. In 1983 Canadian prime minister Pierre Trudeau asked her to work as a senior adviser for federal programs geared toward women's-equality issues.

In 1988 Barlow made a bid for political office, when she sought to represent the Ottawa Centre district in the Canadian House of Commons, but she lost to the Ottawa alderman Mac Harb. Barlow instead began heading the Council of Canadians, a citizens' advocacy group devoted to policy change on a number of issues, namely fair trade, public health care, and the right to water. That year saw the signing of the Canada–United States Free Trade Agreement, aimed at increasing trade between the two countries; Barlow emerged as one of its most outspoken critics, arguing that the agreement amounted to a form of political annexation by the U.S. that compromised Canada's sovereignty. In 1990 she published *Parcel of Rogues: How Free Trade Is Failing Canada*, which set out to explain why maintaining a nationalist government was preferable to placing trust in multinational corporations. She collaborated with Bruce Campbell on two more books on the subject, *Take Back the Nation* (1991) and *Take Back the Nation 2* (1993).

In 1994 Barlow tackled the Canadian education system in the controversial, best-selling book *Class Warfare: The Assault on Canada's Schools*. The book's premise is that business, political, and religious leaders had attacked the effectiveness of Canada's education system as a way to determine its agenda for their own ends. Co-authored with Heather-Jane Robertson, then the director of professional development services for the Canadian Teachers Federation, the book received generally favorable reviews. Alan Haskvitz, writing for *Canadian Social Studies* (Winter 1997), called *Class Warfare* "a study in applied propaganda" in which "there is little attempt to offer a balanced view"; he nonetheless judged it to be "an excellent book" that "can be used by student teachers, university instructors, and the general public." In 1995 Barlow collaborated with Bruce Campbell again for *Straight Through the Heart: How the Liberals Abandoned the Just Society*, which blamed the Canadian liberal government for contributing to the rise in poverty in Canada through its capitulation to the business sector. Barlow has written other books critiquing both Canadian and U.S. public policy, including *MAI: The Multilateral Agreement on Investment and the Threat to Canadian Sovereignty* (1997), co-authored with Tony Clarke.

As quoted on the *Canadian Geographic* Web site, Barlow explained, "The environment has always been a lens for understanding the issues that affect Canadians. It was natural to find common ground with environmentalists." In 2000 Barlow teamed up with one of Canada's most prominent environmentalists, Elizabeth May, for *Frederick Street: Life and Death on Canada's Love Canal*. The book chronicled the history of a steel plant in Sydney, Nova Scotia, which, since its opening, in 1899, had been responsible for widespread environmental destruction in local areas and caused health hazards to local residents. Parker Barss Donham commented for *Canadian Geographic* (May/June 2000) that "Barlow and May delineate the intricacies of steel-making and the insidious impact of polycyclic aromatic hydrocarbons with admirable clarity. They undertake some original, often touching social history of Whitney Pier's eclectic residents. They deftly skewer provincial health bureaucrats who did backflips to explain away epidemiological evidence of the plan's harm. . . . But they avert their critical gaze from the environmentalist side of the fight, glossing over the venomous bullying of eco-activist Bruno Marcocchio, reciting litanies of illness as if every conceivable ailment could be traced to the plant, and mocking suggestions that Sydney's high smoking rates and poor dietary habits might contribute to residents' health problems. The handful of federal and provincial officials who made sincere efforts to clean up the plant get short shrift. . . . As a result, *Frederick Street* fails to grapple with the tough problem at the heart of the Sydney Steel debacle: how to overcome Canada's entrenched habit of letting jobs trump public health and the environment."

Barlow next collaborated with Tony Clarke on two books: *Global Showdown: How the New Activists Are Fighting Global Corporate Rule* (2001) and *Blue Gold: The Fight to Stop the Corporate Theft of the World's Water* (2002). The latter, which has been printed in 16 languages and 47 countries around the world, earned widespread praise and is often referred to as Barlow's finest work. In researching the topic, she traveled around the world to gain a perspective on the importance of water. During one visit to a small Mexican town north of Tijuana, which was without running water and relied for survival on biweekly water deliveries, she was urged by one of her guides to gauge the level of local water pollution by dipping a pencil into the town's single stream. When she pulled the pencil out, all of its paint had been stripped away by the mix of raw sewage and chemical waste that had come from a local factory. She commented, as posted on the *Canadian Geographic* Web site, that "not a drop was wasted" from the clean-water deliveries. "They used it first for food, then washing and laundry, then for watering the animals and the garden. I live in an average Canadian house, and there are seven water outlets. It's something we all take for granted." Barlow and Clarke's main argument is that since the need for water supersedes many other human needs, access to clean water should be considered a basic right, and water should not be subject to privatization. Matthew Behrens, in a review for *Quill & Quire* (March 2002), called the book "a strong manifesto to save the planet's most precious resource—water—from becoming unusable in the next few decades." As posted on Amazon.com, a contributor for *Publishers Weekly* noted, "The authors cogently argue that water, a basic necessity, should be treated differently from other commodities and not placed into private hands. In the end, their argument becomes a screed against the power that multinationals wield in our economically liberalizing world: in free trade treaties, they argue, governments effectively yield control over water rights to corporations, with harmful consequences for both economic parity and nature. The authors are vague about what the average person can do to help stave off this crisis, but those concerned about the environment and about the costs of economic globalization will find much to get riled up about in this book."

Barlow followed up *Blue Gold* with two more critiques on public policy: *Profit Is Not the Cure: A Citizen's Guide to Saving Medicare* (2002) and *Too Close for Comfort: Canada's Future Within Fortress North America* (2005). In a review of the former, Rachel Rafelman wrote for *Quill & Quire* (November 2002), "While Barlow has produced a well-researched and clearly written study of a complicated issue, it's also entirely one-sided. It isn't that Barlow's numerous warnings about the continuing erosion of medical care and potential dangers of for-profit facilities are wrong. But we've heard most of them many times, along with the horror stories and the tales of hardhearted, greedy American HMOs. What we need now is a fresh practical perspective, some creative new ideas, and an open mind to all possible reforms." Barlow's latest work, *Blue Covenant: The Global Water Crisis and the Coming Battle for the Right to Water* (2007), picks up where *Blue Gold* left off in its call for clean water for all. The book also portrays the global water crisis as being closely linked to global warming. While noting that Barlow "covers familiar territory," Daniel Aldana Cohen wrote for the *Walrus* (December 2007), "*Blue Covenant*'s key contribution is its proposed solution: the eponymous three-part covenant of conservation, justice in North-South trade deals, and water democracy. To ensure the last, Barlow echoes calls for a UN treaty proclaiming water a human right, while asserting public needs over commercial interests. Her program flies in the face of free-market orthodoxy but is not without hope. One of her proposals is replacing private sector involvement in developing countries with a massive expansion of public enterprises. In the world of politics, Barlow notes, expertise is flowing north, but activists in the global South are forging idiosyncratic institutions at the municipal level, incorporating community participation and oversight. They could be on to something: figuring out how to keep common resources public without handing them over to the state." Cohen listed among the book's "shockers" that "one-tenth of the world's irrigated crops are watered with sewage, mostly untreated, that spews out of city pipes into adjacent fields."

Barlow is one of the central figures in the French filmmaker Irena Salina's documentary *Flow: For Love of Water* (2008), which opened at the Sundance Film Festival to rave reviews and focuses on many of the issues Barlow has long addressed. As did *An Inconvenient Truth* (2006), the Academy Award–winning documentary about Al Gore's fight to make global warming and its potentially calamitous effects a problem recognized throughout the world, *Flow* met with some skepticism. Dismissing the charge that she is creating fear needlessly, Barlow said to Monica Trauzzi in an interview for E&E-TV's program *OnPoint* (March 4, 2008, on-line), "We're going to add 3 billion people, at a modest estimate, to this planet by 2050 and many of those are in countries where they're developing and so their consumer patterns are dramatically rising. There's going to be a demand, and this is a U.N. statistic, for an 80% increase, just for food production, in water to feed those people. Nobody has any idea where it's going to come from."

Barlow has been married since July 1983 to Andrew Davis. The couple have two sons, Charles and William. Barlow is the recipient of six honorary doctorates from Canadian universities and won the 2005/2006 Lannan Cultural Freedom Fellowship Award and the 2005 Right Livelihood Award, often referred to as the "Alternative Nobel," for her work. In addition to her longstanding chairmanship of the Council of Canadians, she is a director of the International Forum on Globalization, a San Francisco, California–based think tank geared toward fighting economic globalization; a board member of Food & Water Watch, a Washington, D.C.–based consumer-rights group that fights for corporate and government accountability with regard to the production of safe, healthful food and public control of water sources; and a founding member of the European-based World Future Council, which works toward achieving environmentally and socially sustainable conditions worldwide. In 2007 Barlow was honored with a Lifetime Achievement Award at the Canadian Environment Awards ceremony, for her 25 years of advocacy for Canadian rights and sovereignty.

—C.C.

Suggested Reading: Council for Canadians Official Web site; *Montreal (Canada) Gazette* D p6 Jan. 25, 2008; (Toronto, Ontario, Canada) *Globe and Mail* p54 Mar. 28, 2008

Selected Books: *Parcel of Rogues: How Free Trade Is Failing Canada*, 1990; *Take Back the Nation* (with Bruce Campbell), 1991; *Take Back the Nation 2* (with Bruce Campbell), 1993; *Class Warfare: The Assault on Canada's Schools*, 1994; *Straight through the Heart* (with Bruce Campbell), 1995; *MAI: The Multilateral Agreement on Investment and the Threat to Canadian Sovereignty* (with Tony Clarke), 1997; *MAI: The Multilateral Agreement on Investment and the Threat to American Freedom* (with Tony Clarke), 1998; *The Fight of My Life: Confessions of an Unrepentant Canadian*, 1998; *Frederick Street: Life and Death on Canada's Love Canal* (with Elizabeth May), 2000; *Global Showdown: How the New Activists Are Fighting Global Corporate Rule* (with Tony Clarke), 2001; *Blue Gold: The Fight to Stop Corporate Theft of the World's Water* (with Tony Clarke), 2002; *Profit Is Not the Cure: A Citizen's Guide to Saving Medicare*, 2002; *Too Close for Comfort: Canada's Future Within Fortress North America*, 2005; *Blue Covenant: The Global Water Crisis and the Coming Battle for the Right to Water*, 2007

Bechdel, Alison

(BECK-dull)

Sep. 10, 1960– Cartoonist; graphic novelist

Address: c/o Houghton Mifflin Co., Trade Division, Adult Editorial, Eighth Fl., 222 Berkeley St., Boston, MA 02116

Since it debuted, in 1983, Alison Bechdel's comic strip, *Dykes to Watch Out For*—known casually as *DTWOF*—has become a cultural institution within the lesbian community. Syndicated in some 50 gay and alternative publications in the U.S., the strip examines the lives of several lesbian, bisexual, and transsexual characters. Louise Gray wrote for the London *Independent on Sunday* (October 19, 2003), "The sad fact remains: unless you're a lesbian . . . it's unlikely that you have heard of Bechdel. In which case, you are missing out on one of the most subtle comedies of modern manners to come along in the last two decades." While Gray's sentiments held true in 2003, in 2006 Bechdel's popularity began to expand far outside the gay and lesbian community, with the publication of her graphic memoir *Fun Home: A Family Tragicomic.* The memoir was a finalist for a National Book Critics Circle Award and the winner of an Eisner Award for best reality-based work. (The latter prize is named after the legendary cartoonist and graphic novelist Will Eisner.)

"I became a cartoonist somewhat by default because it was a medium that my hyper-artistic parents didn't know anything about. It was a way I could express myself creatively under their radar," Bechdel told Dave Weich in an interview posted on Powells.com (June 15, 2006). Bechdel's parents were high-school English teachers, and both were "into poetry and literature," she told Weich; in addition, her mother was a trained actress, and her father's avocations included interior design. For Alison, cartooning was a "way to do my own thing. . . . I don't perform well under a spotlight." Bechdel had an unusual childhood, at the center of which was her father—a part-time mortician who, as she later learned, had engaged in illicit affairs with teenage boys. Though Bechdel bonded to a degree with her father over literature, he remained emotionally detached from others throughout his

Courtesy of Alison Bechdel

Alison Bechdel

life, which ended in 1980 when he was hit by a truck. Though his death was ruled an accident, Bechdel has always suspected that he jumped in front of the truck intentionally.

Following college Bechdel began writing and drawing *DTWOF*. Often described as a lesbian soap opera, the comic strip showcases the lives of a group of characters from a range of racial, cultural, political, and economic backgrounds. The main character, Mo, is a radically liberal bookstore-clerk-turned-librarian. Other characters include Mo's partner, a college professor named Sydney; Clarice, an environmental lawyer, and her partner, Toni, an accountant; Clarice and Toni's son, Raffi; Lois, who dresses as a man; New Age practitioner Sparrow and her partner, Stuart; Janis, a transsexual adolescent formerly known as Jonas; and a right-wing conservative named Cynthia. *DTWOF* deals with the everyday events of their lives—romances, heartbreak, births, and deaths—as well as such topics as adoption, "coming out" to family members, sex and gender, and women's health issues. The left-leaning Bechdel often incorporates current events and political satire into the strips.

Some 20 years after her father's death, Bechdel decided to write a memoir. She chose the graphic-novel format because, as she said in an interview for Houghton Mifflin's press release for *Fun Home*, "You can do things in graphic storytelling that you can't do with words alone. . . . I can say two or three things at once, like following the main story and a footnote at the same time. I can use the words and pictures in unison, to say the same thing, or in counterpoint, harmonizing the two separate strands into a third level of meaning. And if I hit a wall with the text, the visuals would bail me out by presenting an unusual association or segue." *Fun Home* is a detailed, often humorous account of Bechdel's youth, chronicling such events as her first menstrual period and her first lesbian relationship. At its center is her relationship with her father. "In some ways I actually think of this book as a longitudinal, sociological study of two generations of gay people. . . . My dad came of age a decade before the Stonewall riots, that watershed moment of modern gay history. And I came of age a decade after. And it was extremely different," Bechdel told Liane Hansen for the National Public Radio program *Weekend Edition* (July 2, 2006). "It was extremely easy for me to [come out as a homosexual], when there was a whole movement out there. But for my dad it just wasn't possible. And so part of what I investigate in the book is, how much of that was his historical circumstances, how much of it was his character? If I had been born 25 years [earlier], would I have made similar decisions?" The critical attention *Fun Home* has received, while appreciated by the author, has been a surprise to her. "I have this devoted but rather circumscribed audience [for *DTWOF*]," Bechdel told Tom Beer for *Newsday* (July 2, 2006). "I didn't think a lot of people would see *Fun Home*. That's what enabled me to reveal such intimate information. But if I had known at the outset that it would get a review in the *New York Times Book Review* or that I'd be in *People* magazine, I wonder if I would have been so forthcoming. My obscurity was an asset."

Alison Bechdel was born to Bruce Allen Bechdel and the former Helen Fontana on September 10, 1960 in Lock Haven, Pennsylvania. Along with her two younger brothers, Christian and John, she grew up in Beech Creek, Pennsylvania, a small borough with a population of about 800 people, not far from Lock Haven, where her father was born and raised. In 1963, following the death of Alison Bechdel's paternal grandfather, Claude H. Bechdel, her father became the part-time director of, and mortician at, the Bechdel Funeral Home. Alison Bechdel's grandmother lived in private quarters at the funeral home, while Bechdel and her family lived in a nearby 4,000-square-foot, seven-bedroom Victorian house built in the 1880s. Bruce Bechdel was passionate about antiques and decorating, and he meticulously restored the house to its original condition, with custom-made reproduction wallpaper, gas chandeliers, and antiques. As a father, Bruce was distant, prone to fits of rage, and, Bechdel wrote in *Fun Home*, "treated his furniture like children, and his children like furniture."

In a house filled with literature and music (her mother played piano), Bechdel and her brothers were encouraged to explore creative pursuits. "I think I was drawn to cartooning because of the absence of color," she told Ginia Bellafante for the *New York Times* (August 3, 2006). "It was such a rejection of the environment I grew up in, and my father had no aesthetic criteria for judging it."

Throughout her childhood Bechdel was very much a tomboy and enjoyed dressing in her father's old clothing. That put her at odds with her father, who encouraged her to be more feminine. Bechdel has said that she first pondered her sexuality at age 13, after she stumbled across the word "lesbian" in a dictionary. It was not until her junior year of college, however, that she fully acknowledged her homosexuality. For two years Bechdel attended Simon's Rock College (now known as Bard College at Simon's Rock), in Great Barrington, Massachusetts. (Simon's Rock students typically enter the academically rigorous institution at age 15 or 16.) In 1979 she transferred to Oberlin College, in Ohio, where she studied art and art history. During her first year at Oberlin, Bechdel was browsing through a local bookstore when she discovered *Word Is Out: Stories of Some of Our Lives*, a 1978 book of interviews with gay and lesbian individuals. (The book was a companion volume to the landmark 1977 documentary of the same name.) After reading those interviews, Bechdel has said, she fully realized that she was a lesbian.

After earning her bachelor's degree, in 1981, Bechdel moved to New York City. She applied to various art schools for graduate study but was rejected by all of them. To make ends meet Bechdel worked at office jobs around the city. She wrote letters to a friend and began including in them small drawings, the first of which she titled "Marianne, dissatisfied with the morning brew: Dykes to Watch Out For, Plate No. 27." "I put a silly drawing of a lesbian in the margin [of the letter], a crazy naked woman about to throw a pot of coffee," Bechdel told Ng Yi-Sheng for the gay-interest Web site fridae.com (November 13, 2008). "I don't know where [the cartoon] came from, or why I titled [it] 'Dykes to Watch Out For, Plate No. 27.' But it seemed to beg for at least 26 more dykes, so I set about drawing the rest of them and never stopped."

Friends encouraged Bechdel to send her drawings to *WomaNews*, a now-defunct New York City–based feminist monthly. *WomaNews* published her first comic strip in 1983, and it was soon appearing in every issue. In its earliest incarnation, *DTWOF* did not feature recurring characters or a continuous plotline. Instead, it consisted of single self-contained anecdotes. In one of the most popular, a 1985 strip titled "The Rule," a woman explains her criteria for watching a film. "I only go to a movie if it satisfies three basic requirements," the character says to a friend. "One, it has to have at least two women in it. Who, two, talk to each other about, three, something besides a man."

DTWOF was syndicated in 1985 and was picked up by a small number of alternative newspapers with gay and lesbian readerships. At about that time Nancy K. Bereano, the founder of the lesbian/feminist independent publisher Firebrand Books, approached Bechdel about publishing a collection of her strips. The first collection, *Dykes to Watch Out For*, appeared in 1986. That same year, Bechdel and her girlfriend moved to Minneapolis, Minnesota, where Bechdel worked as a production manager at *Equal Time*, a now-defunct gay and lesbian newspaper. Bechdel began producing *DTWOF* strips biweekly, and in 1987 she began to write a continuous storyline, introducing Mo and the rest of the strip's regular characters. The rising popularity of *DTWOF* led Bechdel to quit her job at the newspaper in 1990 and dedicate herself to the comic strip full-time. (Later in the decade Universal Press Syndicate, the largest independent newspaper syndicate in the world, offered to carry *DTWOF*, on the condition that Bechdel alter the content and title to appeal to a more conservative audience. She declined.) Firebrand Books published several more collections of her strips, and three of them, *New, Improved! Dykes to Watch Out For* (1990), *Dykes to Watch Out For: The Sequel* (1992), and *Spawn of Dykes to Watch Out For* (1993), won the Lambda Literary Award for humor from the Lambda Literary Foundation, an organization for lesbian, gay, bisexual, and transgender (LGBT) writers and readers in the U.S.

In 1991 Bechdel moved to Vermont. Though her work was largely unnoticed outside the lesbian and gay communities, she won praise from fellow comic writers and critics. Harvey Pekar, best known for writing the autobiographical comic series *American Splendor* (which was made into a film in 2003), told Hillary Chute for the *Village Voice* (July 12, 2006), "As soon as I became aware of *Dykes to Watch Out For* in the mid '80s, I just thought Alison was head and shoulders above most people even in alternative comics." Lisa London, then the associate publisher of the Feminist Press at the City University of New York, wrote for the *Women's Review of Books* (December 2003), "Panel by panel, person by person, in chronicling the lives and loves of a group of friends, Bechdel has charted, and in some cases, propelled cultural and political shifts. [When I was] growing up, *Dykes to Watch Out For* was a vital cultural thread of lesbian subculture woven into my life, and helped to shape my identity as a third-wave feminist."

Bechdel continued to win Lambda Literary Awards for her work. Her 1998 illustrated memoir, *The Indelible Alison Bechdel: Confessions, Comix, and Miscellaneous Dykes to Watch Out For*, which chronicled her progression as a cartoonist, from her early childhood drawings to the development of *DTWOF*, won that year's Lambda Award in the lesbian biography/autobiography category. In 2003 her collection *Dykes and Sundry Other Carbon-Based Life-Forms to Watch Out For*, published by the LGBT publisher Alyson Books, won her another Lambda Award for humor.

After years of considering the idea of writing about her father and his sudden death, Bechdel began working on *Fun Home* in 1999. "I've wanted to tell this story since I was about 20," she told Margot Harrison for the Burlington, Vermont, newspaper *Seven Days* (May 31–June 7, 2006), "as soon as I had enough perspective on my father's death to see what a really excellent story it was. For a long time I thought I couldn't reveal this family secret. But something changed along the way . . . history changed, the cultural climate changed, and eventually it didn't seem like that earthshaking a thing to reveal, even for my family." The growing popularity of graphic novels also factored into her decision. "When I was 20, there wasn't such a thing as a graphic novel," she told Harrison. "So that was part of the evolution, too, finding a form for the story to take."

Bechdel's father died on July 2, 1980, when he was struck by a truck while standing along a highway. Bechdel believes that her father may well have jumped in front of the truck, committing suicide. In the months leading up to the incident, Bechdel had sent a letter to her parents proclaiming her lesbianism. Afterward, her father alluded to his own homosexuality, and her mother divulged to Bechdel that he had carried out affairs with various young men around town. "[My father] couldn't deny things anymore; he'd been holding everything in place until that moment. It was something I felt pretty immediately," Bechdel told Ginia Bellafante. She added that she thought it would be "ridiculous" and narcissistic to think that he committed suicide solely because she had revealed her lesbianism. Bechdel also cites her mother's request for a divorce weeks prior to her father's death as a possible factor.

Bechdel spent nearly seven years working on *Fun Home*. (The title refers to the abbreviated name her siblings gave the family's funeral home.) She researched diligently, combing through her childhood diaries, family photographs, public records, and her father's letters. Her mother, upon discovering that her daughter was working on the book, ceased talking about her late husband. Bechdel told Hillary Chute, "[My mother] felt quite betrayed. And justifiably so. Essentially I used information she had given me in confidence over the years." Although her mother has been unsettled by the publication of personal information about the family, Bechdel told Chute, "[My mother] also understands writing and the imperative of storytelling, and there's a way that she respects the project, despite her discomfort."

Literature was a major part of Bechdel's childhood, and *Fun Home* contains many literary references. Writings of Albert Camus, James Joyce, Marcel Proust, F. Scott Fitzgerald, and Colette, as well as the lives of the authors themselves, are referenced throughout the memoir. In an effort to make sense of her relationship with her father, Bechdel employed her father's favorite book, Joyce's *Ulysses*, as well as the tale of the mythological figures Icarus and Daedalus. (In the Greek myth, Daedalus builds wings for himself and his son, Icarus, so that they may escape Crete. Ignoring his father's advice, Icarus flies too close to the sun. His wings melt, and he drowns in the sea below. In her memoir Bechdel cast herself as Daedalus and her father as Icarus.) "Books were our bond, the one point where we connected," Bechdel told Tom Beer. "It was a substitute for intimate personal contact. Just the fact that I resort to describing my parents as fictional characters is an indication of how remote we all were. My dad to me is Jay Gatsby [from F. Scott Fitzgerald's *The Great Gatsby*], and my mother Isabel Archer from [Henry James's] *The Portrait of a Lady*."

Houghton Mifflin published *Fun Home*, its first graphic novel, in June 2006. The book received rave reviews. "More than the witty art, more than the mordant prose, it is . . . openness that distinguishes Bechdel's generous and intelligent work," Jennifer Reese wrote for *Entertainment Weekly* (June 2, 2006), which later named *Fun Home* the best nonfiction book of the year. "While *Fun Home* takes only a couple of hours to read, it has a depth and sweetness few can match at five times the length." "*Fun Home* must be the most ingeniously compact, hyper-verbose example of autobiography to have been produced," Sean Wilsey wrote for the *New York Times* (June 18, 2006). "It is a pioneering work, pushing two genres (comics and memoir) in multiple new directions, with panels that combine the detail and technical proficiency of [celebrated underground cartoonist] R. Crumb with a seriousness, emotional complexity and innovation completely its own." In a review for *Salon* (December 12, 2006, on-line), Laura Miller and Hillary Frey wrote, "*Fun Home* shimmers with regret, compassion, annoyance, frustration, pity and love—usually all at the same time and never without a pervasive, deeply literary irony about the near-impossible task of staying true to yourself, and to the people who made you who you are."

Fun Home became a best-seller and was named among the best books of the year by the London *Times*, Amazon.com, *Time*, *New York* magazine, *People*, the *New York Times*, and *Publishers Weekly*. In 2007 it won the Eisner Award for best reality-based work, the Gay & Lesbian Alliance Against Defamation (GLAAD) Media Award for outstanding comic book, the Stonewall Book Award for nonfiction, the Publishing Triangle's Judy Grahn Nonfiction Award, and the Lambda Literary Award for best lesbian memoir/biography. It was also a finalist for a National Book Critics Circle Award in the memoir/autobiography category. The Tony Award nominees Lisa Kron and Jeanine Teson recently penned an as-yet unproduced musical based on *Fun Home*.

On May 10, 2008 Bechdel announced on her blog that she would begin an official sabbatical from *Dykes to Watch Out For* with the publication of strip number 527, on May 14. The decision was made for financial reasons—in the post Bechdel acknowledged that income from the strip's publication had fallen over the past few years—as well as time constraints; she is currently working on her third graphic memoir, tentatively titled "Love Life: A Case Study." It will focus on her past romantic relationships, including her brief marriage to her longtime partner, Amy Rubin, in 2004. (The wedding took place in California before the state reversed its ruling on same-sex marriages.) Bechdel's relationship with Rubin later ended.

In November 2008, to commemorate the 25th anniversary of *DTWOF*, Houghton Mifflin published *The Essential Dykes to Watch Out For*, a collection that contains 390 of the series' 527 strips.

Bechdel lives in Bolton, Vermont, with her partner, Holly Rae Taylor. Taylor is the founder of Waste Free Living Inc., a Web-based business that promotes composting and sells environmentally friendly products. The couple have a cat named Dr. Winnicott.

—M.A.S.

Suggested Reading: (Burlington, Vermont) *Seven Days* A p32 May 31–June 7, 2006; (London) *Guardian* p10 Dec. 1, 2008; (London) *Independent on Sunday* p8 Oct. 19, 2003; *New York Times* F p7 Aug. 3, 2006, C p1 Dec. 3, 2008

Selected Comics Compilations: *Dykes to Watch Out For*, 1986; *More Dykes to Watch Out For*, 1988; *New, Improved! Dykes to Watch Out For*, 1990; *Dykes to Watch Out For: The Sequel*, 1992; *Spawn of Dykes to Watch Out For*, 1993; *Unnatural Dykes to Watch Out For*, 1995; *Hot, Throbbing Dykes to Watch Out For*, 1997; *Split-Level Dykes to Watch Out For*, 1998; *Post-Dykes to Watch Out For*, 2000; *Dykes and Sundry Other Carbon-Based Life-Forms to Watch Out For*, 2003; *Invasion of the Dykes to Watch Out For*, 2005; *The Essential Dykes to Watch Out For*, 2008

Selected Graphic Memoirs: *The Indelible Alison Bechdel: Confessions, Comix, and Miscellaneous Dykes to Watch Out For*, 1998; *Fun Home: A Family Tragicomic*, 2006

Courtesy of Dmitry Kiper

Beiser, Maya

Dec. 31, 1963– Cellist

Address: c/o Koch Entertainment, 740 Broadway, #7, New York, NY 10003

Maya Beiser is a classically trained cellist, but nobody with even a slight acquaintance with classical music would ever mistake her performance for a traditional one. Beiser attacks the cello the way Jimi Hendrix, Kurt Kobain, and Jimmy Page attacked the guitar—with attitude, playfulness, and rock-and-roll showmanship. Since an early age the Israeli-born cellist has sought in part to re-create pieces from the classical repertoire rather than reproduce them note-for-note to conform to traditional ideas of how they should sound. For the most part, though, she performs works by contemporary composers. Her concerts often include video projections, spoken-word poetry, prerecorded cello music, and elements of rock, electronica, minimalism, and Middle Eastern music. After receiving a master's degree in music in the United States, Beiser joined the avant-garde, New York City–based group Bang on a Can All-Stars, in 1992. A decade later, eager to become more involved in the creative process and gain more control in the projects in which she engaged, she embarked on a solo career. She has released four solo albums in addition to several in which she played with the All-Stars or others, and she has contributed to the soundtracks of three major motion pictures: Edward Zwick's *Blood Diamond* (2006), Denzel Washington's *The Great Debaters* (2007), and M. Night Shyamalan's *The Happening* (2008). Composers including Steve Reich, David Lang, Louis Andriessen, and Eve Beglarian have written pieces especially for her. In the last few years, in a consciously crosscultural approach, she has collaborated with composers, instrumentalists, and other artists from the Middle East, Europe, and the United States. She has perfomed with the Brooklyn Philharmonic, the Montreal Philharmonic, the St. Paul Chamber Orchestra, the Sydney Symphony, the China Philharmonic, and other ensembles and in countries including Japan, China, France, Taiwan, Spain, and Australia as well as the U.S. "I feel that my role right now is to do something big for the cello," she told an interviewer for the *Idaho Mountain Express* (February 16, 2005, on-line). "I want to change the image of the cello as this somber classical music instrument. And I've been doing it quite successfully."

The oldest of the four daughters of an Argentinean father and a French mother, Maya Beiser was born on December 31, 1963 in Gazit, a kibbutz in the Galilee region of northern Israel—"the most beautiful place, very close to the Jordan River," as she described it to *Current Biography*, the source of quotes for this article, unless otherwise indicated. Designed to be a sort of socialist utopia in which the individual is secondary to the group, a kibbutz is a settlement where up to a few hundred families live communally. The residents eat their meals together, share certain tasks, and support themselves through agriculture and other kibbutz-based endeavors, such as small factories. In Gazit, whose residents were mostly Jewish immigrants from Argentina, Beiser's father was in charge of a herd of cattle. Beiser considers the guiding philosophy of the kibbutz movement "a really beautiful idea," and she has fond memories of her childhood, but she has also recalled feeling socially and emotionally suffocated.

The kibbutz was very arts-oriented; from an early age children studied music, visual arts, and art history, and they were encouraged to be creative. When Beiser was six years old, her teachers discovered that she has perfect pitch—the ability to hear one note (played by itself) and identify it (as a B or a C, for example). Her father, who also had perfect pitch, loved music. For his first daughter, he played recordings of tangos, Argentinean folk music, and classical compositions, especially Haydn's two cello concertos, written in the 18th century. Her mother played recordings made by French musicians, among them the chanteuse Edith Piaf. The kibbutz was close to several Arab villages, and Beiser would hear the singing of the adhan (the Islamic call to prayer) five times a day.

When, at age eight, Beiser was offered her choice of string instruments to study, she picked the cello. "There was something about the *sound* of the cello," she has said. "I was drawn to it." She also said, "There was something about the 'everybody together' community in the kibbutz that just didn't fit my personality. I needed—and this is my analysis today—I needed something that would distinguish me and give me a really strong identity. I had all these things that were bursting to come out of me and I just needed that. There was something about the fact that the cello was big that attracted me, and the fact that nobody else played it. Everybody else played the violin."

At the age of 11, Beiser was noticed by a representative from the America-Israel Cultural Foundation, one of whose missions is to nurture talented Israeli children through adolescence. About a year later the organization's founder, the famed violinist Isaac Stern, became Beiser's mentor. He would give her lessons a few times a year and, most important, would offer advice. Beiser's parents did not push her to be a virtuoso; she was self-driven. "When I was twelve," she told Michael Ajzenstadt for the *Jerusalem Post* (June 9, 1997), "I knew that the cello would take me out of the kibbutz and would open doors for me worldwide." During those formative years Beiser displayed her desire to be distinctive not only by playing the cello but also by the way she played it. Her cello teacher would often tell her to tone down her personality in her playing and to imagine instead what the composer would have wanted. "The idea that there was just one truth never agreed with me," she said. When, at the age of 15, she was asked to perform one of Haydn's cello concertos at a major hall in Tel Aviv, Israel's second-largest city, it was expected that she would wear a proper evening dress. To Beiser that was an example of "the stiffness that exists in the classical music world." Although she wanted to wear pants and a shirt, her mother insisted that she wear a formal dress, and Beiser agreed to do so out of respect for her mother, who was very supportive of her music career. But she later realized that "all those codes about how you're supposed to look and how you're supposed to be" extend to how one is supposed to play. Such restrictions, she said, were "totally opposite to my personality."

After she completed her junior year of high school, Beiser left the kibbutz to serve in the Israeli army, as is required of all Israeli citizens, women as well as men. She did not face combat. Earlier, she had learned that the army's string quartet had an opening for a cellist. She auditioned for that position and was accepted into the quartet, whose members up to that time had all been men. During her two years in the army, she also attended Tel Aviv University, in Israel, where she studied music and took classes in literature, film, and philosophy. She graduated with a bachelor's degree in music in the spring of 1985.

By that fall Beiser had moved to the United States to continue her education, at the Yale School of Music, in New Haven, Connecticut. She studied there with several renowned musicians, among them the Brazilian-born cellist Aldo Parisot. After about a year she moved to New York City and commuted to Yale. Her desire to express herself more freely and make her playing more personal intensified. (Even before she came to the States, her musical interests and experiences outside concert halls were very diverse: She liked contemporary rock bands, including Nirvana and Nine Inch Nails, and such classic rock bands and musicians as Led Zeppelin and Jimi Hendrix; she also listened to Middle Eastern music.) Meanwhile, Beiser was becoming increasingly impatient with the expectations of classical-music concertgoers, who, she believes, have a fixed idea of what they want to hear: compositions of Bach must be played like this, those of Beethoven like that. She did not want to be an "interpreter"; rather, she wanted to be a "creator."

At Yale Beiser met the Dutch post-minimalist composer Louis Andriessen, who offered Beiser a musical challenge: to tackle his piece *La Voce*, which calls for the performer to recite a text by the Italian poet Cesare Pavese while playing the cello. "It just changed my life," Beiser recalled. "The idea that I can sing and play and that it's okay to do that. I discovered this whole other sound that I can do. After I started to work on that piece I realized that's what I want to do. I want to stop playing classical music altogether, move to New York, start collaborating with composers. I didn't know exactly where it was going to lead, but I knew I wanted to do more stuff in the nontraditional genres and the rock world." Isaac Stern and some of her teachers did not approve of her plans to incorporate nonclassical elements into her music. Speaking to Paul de Barros for the *Seattle Times* (November 17, 2006), Beiser explained, "The idea of using electronics, amplifying the cello, manipulating the cello sound with anything other than your own bow was not acceptable."

While at Yale Beiser also met the composers Julia Wolfe, David Lang, and Michael Gordon, who guided her further along an experimental path. In 1987 Wolfe, Lang, and Gordon founded Bang on a Can, a music collective and festival that debuted with a 12-hour music marathon at an art gallery in the SoHo district of New York City. "The founders saw that among young composers and all around the world there were powerful musical ideas, just starting to flow freely between categories, between minimalism and rock, between written and improvised music, between world music and noise, between live performance and electronica," the group's Web site explained in 2009. "Restlessly inventive musicians everywhere were pulling the barriers down—there needed to be a place where all the uncategorizable music could find a home." Beiser soon began to perform with Bang on a Can musicians. In 1992 Beiser and a few others among the festival's regulars formed a group, the Bang on a Can All-Stars, which performed and made recordings with an unusual combination of instruments: cello, electric guitar, double bass, clarinet, piano, and percussion. Also in 1992 Beiser gave her New York debut recital, at the 92nd Street YM-YWHA. With piano accompaniment, she performed pieces by Dmitri Shostakovich, David Lang, Witold Lutoslawski, Joaquín Nin, Leoš Janáček, and Claude Debussy. In a review for the *New York Times* (May 30, 1992), Bernard Holland wrote that Beiser seemed to have "aimed at touching just about every cello style in 20th century music."

In 1995 the Bang on a Can All-Stars released *Industry*, their first studio album. Wolfe, Lang, and Gordon each wrote a piece for the recording, and Louis Andriessen wrote two. The music showed pop and rock influences while also indicating that the band members still valued traditional composition techniques. The title track is a solo cello piece Gordon wrote for Beiser, in which the cello's sound is modified by a "tube screemer," for an effect like that of a wailing electric guitar. Writing for allmusic.com, Steward Mason described the album as "a piece of contemporary classical music that is neither pretentiously inaccessible nor a blatant attempt at reaching a mainstream audience." With time the All-Stars established an identity separate from that of the organization that had spawned their band. The members—Beiser, Robert Black, Lisa Moore, Steven Schick, Mark Stewart, and Evan Ziporyn—collaborated regularly and received a series of commissions from notable contemporary composers. In 1996 the group released their sophomore album, *Cheating, Lying, and Stealing*, which, like its predecessor, was marked by innovation and self-expression. The All-Stars' live shows were similarly diverse: in addition to original compositions by others, the All-Stars performed their own versions of songs by such groups or artists as Nirvana and the Brazilian jazz composer Hermeto Pascoal. In a conversation with the *San Francisco Chronicle* (October 20, 1998) music critic Joshua Kosman, Gordon expressed the view that the All-Stars were successful for two reasons: open-mindedness and outstanding musical abilities. "Speaking as a composer and not as artistic director of Bang on a Can," Gordon said, "I have to say that these are the six greatest musicians I've ever worked with." After almost a decade with the All-Stars, Beiser left the group. "There is a particular aesthetic" associated with them, she told Allan Kozinn for the *New York Times* (October 26, 2003). "At a certain point I felt too defined by what people heard me play with the group. Also, it's an electric ensemble, and I was frustrated with the way the cello sounded in it."

Meanwhile, Beiser had released two solo albums, *Oblivion* (1999) and *Kinship* (2000). Her next, *World to Come*, came out in 2003. On tour Beiser performed the third disk's 25-minute title piece, composed by David Lang after the September 11, 2001 terrorist attacks on New York, with the accompaniment of jumpy, buzzing, prerecorded cello tracks; projected on a screen behind her were black-and-white images of water, the sky, and abstract shapes. Another work she presented on stage, Steve Reich's *Cello Counterpoint*, included seven of her prerecorded cello tracks. In New York City on October 30, 2003, the cellist gave a sold-out concert as part of the inaugural season of Zankel Hall, Carnegie Hall's new auditorium. Her performance, Anthony Tommasini wrote for the *New York Times* (November 1, 2003), was "mesmerizing," and at the end of the concert, he reported, Beiser was "vigorously cheered by the packed house." By contrast, John Allison, a London *Times* (September 9, 2004) critic, found Beiser's performance at the 2004 Vale of Glamorgan Festival to be a disappointing mixture of "blandly amplified cello musings with navel-gazing video installations." For the most part, Allison wrote, the pieces were "all interchangeable, which suggests either that Beiser has become a one-trick player or that the composers are writing to order rather than from inspiration. Possibly both." But most reviewers have praised Beiser's performances as demonstrations of virtuosity and a powerful presence.

In 2006 Beiser released the three-track *Almost Human*. The album includes the 39-minute piece "I Am Writing to You from a Far-Off Country," whose title is that of a poem by the Belgian writer Henri Michaux. The poem, which consists of 12 letters in which a woman describes to an unidentified recipient the mysterious land in which she is traveling, had deeply impressed Beiser during her teenage years. Two decades later, on a commission from the Kennedy Center and the Washington Performing Arts Society, both in the nation's capital, she recruited the composer Eve Beglarian to create a score for an English translation of the poem (originally written in French) and the filmmaker Shirin Neshat to make a video to accompany both the words and the music. When "I Am Writing" is performed in concert, Beiser plays the cello while reciting the poem; she is accompanied by both recorded music and a mezzo-soprano singing a vocalise (a wordless melody), while images of desert and sea, videotaped in Israel, are projected.

Beiser has said that although she was not trying to make a political statement with the piece, her collaboration with Beglarian, a Christian of Armenian descent, and Neshat, a Muslim from Iran, clearly demonstrated the power of music to bring people from very different cultures together. Neshat told Kathryn Shattuck for the *New York Times* (March 9, 2006) that she had never collaborated with anyone from Israel before and was initially "wary" of working with Beiser. "We have in Iran in many ways been brainwashed since childhood about certain cultures and religions," Neshat said. "But. . . . These days more than ever, I feel that culture can be a tool of peace and mediation and negotiation and understanding." What Neshat learned from the hours she spent with Beiser was precisely what Beiser had hoped to convey to audiences: "We are connected to where we come from and that's important," Beiser told Shattuck, "but in the end we all transcend that if we let ourselves go into a deeper kind of place." Some critics completely dismissed "I Am Writing." A reviewer for the *Washington Post* (October 23, 2006), for example, who characterized Beiser as a "hot young cello diva of the avant-garde," found the music "self-important and drab" and the images "excruciatingly dull." Most critics, however, responded more positively. "Despite Beiser's lavish use of video, sampled and live voices, and electronic multitracks," Hedy Weiss wrote for the *Chicago Sun-Times* (December 4, 2006), "she never loses touch with the all-important human element of live music."

In 2008 Beiser created *Provenance*, a concert piece commissioned by Carnegie Hall and the New Haven–based International Festival of Arts & Ideas. For *Provenance* she recruited composers from Israel, Iran, Morocco, Palestine, Armenia, and the United States, with the goal of making a "social statement: we are all human beings." She added, "To me, music is the ultimate human expression." Together the musicians created 10 pieces, all of which feature a cellist and various guest musicians on percussion, electronic instruments, and such Middle Eastern instruments as the ney and the oud, which are similar to a flute and a lute, respectively. Beiser's theme was the existence from the ninth to the 15th centuries on the Iberian Peninsula (modern-day Spain and Portugal) of "the greatest peaceful agglomeration of cultures ever known in the post-literate world," according to her Web site. "The cultural richness of this time was so remarkable that historians speak of it as the 'Golden Age.' Even more remarkable than the flowering of art itself, was the confluence of cultures that produced it: under the rule of Islam, Moslems, Jews and Christians lived and worked together in relative harmony." Beiser's collaborative work embraces coexistence "not as an abstract ideal but as a creative necessity."

In addition to those already mentioned, Beiser has worked with composers, conductors, or instrumentalists including Brian Eno, Philip Glass, Tan Dun, Mark O'Connor, Anthony de Mare, Astor Piazzolla, and James Newton Howard. She hopes to add Tom Waits, Jimmy Page, and Radiohead's Johnny Greenwood to that list. Beiser reads voraciously, maintains a vegetarian diet, and practices yoga. She and her husband, a psychiatrist, live in New York City with their two children—Dorian and Aurielle.

—D.K.

Suggested Reading: *Chicago Sun-Times* p49 Dec. 4, 2006; *Idaho Mountain Express* (on-line) Feb. 16, 2005; *Jerusalem Post* Arts p5 June 9, 1997; *New York Times* p27 Oct. 26, 2003, E p3 Mar. 9, 2006

Selected Recordings: *Oblivion*, 1999; *Kinship*, 2000; *World to Come*, 2003; *Almost Human*, 2006

Bernstein, William J.

July 29, 1948– Financial theorist; historian; writer

Address: Efficient Frontier Advisors LLC, P.O. Box 237, Eastford, CT 06242

For thousands of years people have traded gold, silver, tin, and copper; grain, silk, wine, and horses; cloves, nutmeg, cinnamon, and pepper; cotton, incense, and opium; coffee, tea, and sugar; and much more. In his highly praised book *A Splendid Exchange: How Trade Shaped the World* (2008), William J. Bernstein, a financial expert (and neurologist by training), provided a detailed history of how trade has shaped and been shaped by the worlds of politics, religion, science, and social interaction. Starting with the trade of grain for

Courtesy of William Bernstein

William J. Bernstein

metals in Mesopotamia five thousand years ago, he went on to tell stories of the trade of Rome's gold and silver for the Middle East's myrrh and frankincense as well as the rise and spread of Islam and its various influences on trade—not only in the Middle East but also in Europe, Asia, and Africa. Bernstein also shared tales of trade and conquest revolving around Europe's desire for such rare and expensive spices as nutmeg, mace, and cloves in the first half of the second millennium; of how traders unintentionally helped spread the plague—by transporting rats that carried germ-ridden fleas—in the sixth century and again in the 14th, when the plague wiped out at least one-third of Europe's population; and of the dangerous missions of explorers such as Vasco da Gama of Portugal, whose expert navigational skills were matched only by his feelings of religious and ethnic superiority and his extreme cruelty. Bernstein dismissed many myths, such as the notion that colonists at the Boston Tea Party dumped tea in the harbor because they were protesting "taxation without representation": in fact, Boston tea dealers were protesting an act of the British Parliament that allowed the East India Co. to sell tea directly to North America, because, Bernstein wrote, they simply did not want to face competition in the tea trade. Bernstein also told the tale of the slave trade from Africa to the Americas, of the technological innovations of the 19th century, and of the increasing trade protectionism of the 20th century. A review in the *Economist* (July 19, 2008) concluded that the book is "a timely and readable reminder that the desire to trade is not only one of the oldest human instincts but also the cause of the most important developments in our shared history." In addition to *A Splendid Exchange*, Bernstein is the author of *The Birth of Plenty: How the Prosperity of the Modern World Was Created* (2004), as well as successful books on investment: *The Intelligent Asset Allocator* (2000) and *The Four Pillars of Investing* (2002). His most recent book is *The Investor's Manifesto: Preparing for Prosperity, Armageddon, and Everything in Between* (2009).

The second child of an attorney and a homemaker, William James Bernstein was born on July 29, 1948 and grew up in a modestly prosperous suburb of Philadelphia, Pennsylvania. He has said that he received an excellent education in high school, where he was interested in science, especially chemistry; he pursued that subject in college and graduate school, receiving a bachelor's degree from La Salle College, in Philadelphia, in 1969 and a Ph.D. from the University of California at Berkeley in 1972. But even before he earned his Ph.D., he changed his mind about his choice of career. "The physical sciences seemed a bit dry to me," he told *Current Biography*, the source of quotes for this article unless otherwise noted. "I wanted more human contact, I suppose. I didn't want to spend the rest of my life in the laboratory. I think I enjoyed the messier, more human side of medicine." Bernstein stayed in the Bay Area to study medicine at the University of California at San Francisco, where he received his M.D. in 1976. After a four-year residency in neurology at the University of California at Los Angeles, he moved to Coos Bay, Oregon, where, for the next 15 years or so, he was the only practicing neurologist.

Bernstein had chosen Coos Bay because he had always wanted to live in a small town, as well as in a place where his services would truly be needed—a desire he attributed to "misplaced, or perhaps well-placed, '60s idealism." He opened a private practice and treated neurological ailments, including seizures, headaches, Parkinson's disease, multiple sclerosis, and pinched nerves in the neck and back. As probably the only neurologist on the Oregon coast, he had fulfilled his goal of being needed, which put a great demand on his time: he was working with patients between 60 and 70 hours per week—"a full-and-a-half-time job," as he called it. After a decade he hired an associate and cut his hours to around 40 a week, so that he would have more time to spend with his family and pursue his other interests—namely, economics and finance.

Bernstein's quest to understand those subjects began with his desire to save money for retirement. Setting out to educate himself, in the early 1990s he collected financial data, created spreadsheets, and developed a methodology that other investors could also use. He included his findings in his first book, *The Intelligent Asset Allocator.* Despite the soundness of his advice—which was to invest not only in individual stocks and bonds but in a variety of markets—he could not interest publishers in a book about investing by a neurologist from a small town in Oregon. So in 1996 Bernstein posted the content of the book on his new Web site, efficientfrontier.com. After getting more and more readers—mostly economists, financial consultants, and business journalists—he was approached by McGraw-Hill, which published his book in 2000. It went on to sell an impressive 70,000 copies. With *The Intelligent Asset Allocator*, Bernstein had tried to write a book for the average investor; what he "actually didn't understand," he recalled, was that his book was better suited "for engineers and finance people. People really good at math."

Bernstein next set out to write an investment book more accessible to the general public. The result, *The Four Pillars of Investing*, sold well—around 90,000 English-language copies—and was translated into languages including Chinese and Japanese. The "four pillars" of investment offered by Bernstein were theory, history, psychology, and business. Bernstein's theory of investing is that it is important to mix assets in an investment portfolio, thereby minimizing risk. He gave the following analogy: A cake is made of sugar, flour, eggs, salt, and shortening but does not taste like any of those ingredients. Similarly, portfolios should not focus on one particular stock or another but should contain a mix of government bonds, big-name stocks, technology stocks, foreign stocks, and others. Secondly, Bernstein wrote, it is important to know the history of finance. The study of that history is not a "hard" science like physics or chemistry (in which the same conditions will always produce the same results), because the past rarely repeats itself; but we can still learn from it. With regard to psychology, Bernstein wrote that human instincts are usually counterproductive in investing, so it is important to identify and control them. People who own stocks, for example, tend to become overconfident and make irrational trades regularly. Finally, about the "pillar" of business, Bernstein wrote that stockbrokers and mutual-fund companies operate at "a level of educational, moral, and ethical imperatives that would be inconceivable in any other profession." For example, lawyers, bankers, doctors, and accountants have a legal responsibility toward their clients. Stockbrokers do not. That forthrightness on Bernstein's part led to his being quoted with increasing frequency in such publications as *Forbes* and the *Wall Street Journal*.

Bernstein's next book, *The Birth of Plenty: How the Prosperity of the Modern World Was Created*, marked a departure for him, in that it was a work of economic history. The idea for the book came about after Bernstein's wife brought home a copy of P. J. O'Rourke's *Eat the Rich* (1999), a mostly jocular book about the economic history of the world that nonetheless included well-researched passages. One in particular grabbed Bernstein's attention: O'Rourke, as Bernstein wrote in the preface to *The Birth of Plenty*, cited the work of an obscure Scottish economist, Angus Maddison, who argued that world economic growth started around the year 1820. "It took me a while to rustle up a copy of Maddison's summary work, *Monitoring the World Economy, 1820–1992*," Bernstein wrote. "The bound edition looks as dull and as daunting as the densest legal brief, but inside, Maddison's dry data lay out the greatest story ever told: the economic birth of the modern world." Bernstein soon became obsessed with the year 1820. "Why," he wrote in the preface, "did world economic growth, and the technologic progress underlying it, suddenly explode *when* it did?" To be sure, there were people who got rich before the early 19th century—mostly nobles, kings, aristocrats, and the occasional explorer—but there was not any consistent, systematic increase in wealth on a per capita basis. So, Bernstein wondered, what happened? In *The Birth of Plenty*, he attempted to uncover the cultural and economic factors that contributed to the spread of wealth: property rights, scientific rationalism, capital markets, and transportation and communication. The absence of those factors, he argued, is a recipe for stagnant growth, both economic and cultural. While various economists and financial experts praised the book, *The Birth of Plenty* was not reviewed by any influential U.S. or British publication.

That would not be true of Bernstein's next book, *A Splendid Exchange: How Trade Shaped the World*. In 2004, when Bernstein was contacted by an editor at Grove/Atlantic Press about writing a book on the history of world trade, he was initially reluctant to take on that project. "In the first place, I'm not interested," he told the editor. "In the second place, you got the wrong Bernstein. You want Peter Bernstein"—a famous economic historian. The editor replied that, in fact, he had approached Peter Bernstein, who was busy working on another project and had told the editor, "There is another Bernstein you should call who I think can do the job." William Bernstein said that he would think about the offer. He then went to talk to his wife about it. When he mentioned Grove/Atlantic Press, she asked, "Do you know who Grove/Atlantic Press is?" After Bernstein said that he did not, she explained that the house—then Grove Press—had published such important avant-garde works as Samuel Beckett's play *Waiting for Godot* and Henry Miller's novel *Tropic of Cancer*. The *Atlantic*, she continued, is the excellent monthly magazine that covers foreign affairs, politics, ideas, and culture. "That's Grove/Atlantic Press," she said. "If they want you to write a cookbook, you'll write a cookbook." Laughing as he recalled that conversation, Bernstein said, "Suddenly a history of world trade didn't sound so bad compared to a cookbook."

It took Bernstein three and a half years to write the book. One of the things he found most challenging and exciting about the project, and one of the reasons it became a critical success, was that to his knowledge no one had ever before written a history of world trade that spanned thousands of years, from the dawn of history to the modern era. *A Splendid Exchange* contains many historical facts, maps, and insights, but the book's most prominent feature is its many narratives of the lives and adventures of traders, merchants, businessmen, and explorers. One of Bernstein's favorite stories is that of Christopher Columbus, who knew that the world is round—as did most educated people at the end of the 15th century—but wanted it to be smaller than it actually is. The world is about 25,000 miles in circumference, and to one who knew that, the journey Columbus planned—from Spain to India—would have seemed impossible at the time. So Columbus accepted an estimate of the world's circumference, 17,000 miles, that was in line with his goal; his obstinacy and willful ignorance gave him the courage to sail west. He returned from his first trip with minerals he thought were gold (actually iron pyrite, or "fool's gold"), a substance he thought was cinnamon (in reality a different bark), and people he thought were Indians (Native Americans he and his crew had captured). Only by his third trip did it occur to him that perhaps the land he had visited was not the Indian subcontinent. In *A Splendid Exchange* Columbus is just one of many characters who set out to trade, buy, capture, enslave, and explore. The historian John Steele Gordon wrote for the *New York Times* (April 30, 2008) that Bernstein "makes clear in his entertaining and greatly enlightening book" that trade "has been a major force in driving the whole history of humankind."

The publication of Bernstein's book was followed months later by the worldwide economic crisis. "I had spent a large part of my reading life reading about events like this," Bernstein said, "and to see that kind of event play out in front of my eyes was just absolutely fascinating." He attributed the crisis to three causes: "People did not understand the credit market; in other words, they didn't understand how expandable the money supply was. The second thing that happened: financial innovation completely outran our ability to regulate it. Third thing: the libertarian right got control of our financial system: this concept that the market always gets things right and never makes mistakes and the government always makes mistakes." Watching the failure of banks and investment companies and the accompanying panic, uncertainty, and speculation, Bernstein said, he felt like "a geologist who studies volcanos—to have one blow up in your backyard is both horrifying and fascinating."

In addition to writing books, Bernstein operates the money-management firm Efficient Frontier Advisors, which he co-founded in 1998. According to Bernstein's Web site, efficientfrontier.com, the firm now handles approximately $140 million in investments. Bernstein said that his fifth book, *The Investor's Manifesto*, is an investment guide for a general readership, with even less math than *The Four Pillars of Investing*—almost none, in fact; the book was due to come out in November 2009. Another of his books, scheduled for publication in 2012, will be about the way communication technology has shaped the social and political world order throughout history—from the production of papyrus to the ubiquity of the Internet.

Bernstein lives with his wife, Jane, in Coos Bay.
—D.K.

Suggested Reading: *Economist* July 19, 2008; efficientfrontier.com; *Foreign Affairs* p126 May/June 2008; *Money* p94 Sep. 2003; *New York Times* E p4 Apr. 30, 2008;

Selected Books: *The Intelligent Asset Allocator*, 2000; *The Four Pillars of Investing: Lessons for Building a Winning Portfolio*, 2002; *The Birth of Plenty: How the Prosperity of the Modern World Was Created*, 2004; *A Splendid Exchange: How Trade Shaped the World*, 2008; *The Investor's Manifesto: Preparing for Prosperity, Armageddon, and Everything in Between*, 2009

Courtesy of the Office of Joseph Biden

Biden, Joseph R.

NOTE: An earlier article about Joseph R. Biden appeared in *Current Biography* in 1987.

Nov. 20, 1942– Vice president of the United States; former U.S. senator from Delaware (Democrat)

Address: The White House, 1600 Pennsylvania Ave., N.W., Washington, DC 20500

In 1973 Joseph R. Biden, a 30-year-old lawyer from Delaware, became one of the youngest U.S. senators in history. More than 30 years later—after several Senate terms and two unsuccessful presidential bids—Biden again made history, when he was elected vice president under Barack Obama, the first African-American to win the nation's highest office. As the longest-serving U.S. senator in Delaware's history and a member of both the Judiciary Committee and Foreign Relations Committee, Biden is one of the most experienced and knowledgeable politicians in the country, with a hand in some of the most important national and international affairs of the past three decades. He has been involved in campaign-finance reform, arms negotiations with leaders of the former Soviet Union, crime and civil rights legislation, hearings on controversial U.S. Supreme Court appointees, and debate over the war in Iraq. According to the 1992 edition of *Congressional Quarterly*'s *Politics in America*, "From the time Biden arrived in the Senate, he struck observers as a man destined for big things, with the talent and charisma to be an influential Democrat for decades to come. He is legend for his ability to move audiences with his powerful oration. Intelligent and perceptive, he can quickly grasp and convey the essence of complex issues. Personable and conciliatory, he can be adept at legislative negotiations."

Biden's age and impressive political résumé were key factors in his being chosen to run on the Democratic ticket with Obama, whose youth and lack of foreign-policy experience were seen by some as strikes against him. Biden's Irish-Catholic roots in the working-class cities of Scranton, Pennsylvania, and Wilmington, Delaware; his pro-choice stance and support for women's rights; and his struggle to overcome the deaths of his first wife and baby daughter in a car crash struck chords with large segments of the public. "Mostly, I think what attracted [Senator] Obama was Biden's wisdom," David Axelrod, a senior Obama campaign strategist and now senior White House adviser, said on ABC's *This Week*, as quoted by Jill Lawrence and Martha T. Moore for *USA Today* (August 24, 2008, on-line). "And not the kind of wisdom you get in Washington, D.C., but the kind of wisdom you get when you overcome adversity, tragedy in your life as he has; the kind of wisdom you get in the working-class communities of Scranton and Wilmington."

Biden's success has come despite his propensity for speaking his mind without first considering the ramifications, a trait that has sometimes led to controversy. One infamous example is when he referred to President George W. Bush as "brain dead." When met with an outcry by Republicans, Biden countered by reminding them that he had, on occasion, called his fellow Democrat Bill Clinton brain dead as well. Pennsylvania governor Edward Rendell told Lawrence and Moore, "It's pretty easy to fall in love with Joe Biden. Even his mistakes, you have a tendency to shake your head and say, 'But that's Joe.'"

Of largely Irish descent, Joseph Robinette Biden Jr. was born on November 20, 1942 in Scranton, Pennsylvania, one of the four children of Joseph Robinette and Jean (Finnegan) Biden. When Biden was 10 years old, the family moved to a working-class suburb of Wilmington, where his father managed a Chevrolet dealership. Biden attended St. Helena's Roman Catholic parochial school and Archmere Academy. His grandfather often discussed politics at family gatherings, sparking in Biden an interest in pursuing a political career. As a teenager he had a stutter. In his 2007 autobiography, *Promises to Keep: On Life and Politics*, he wrote, "Truth was, I didn't let the stutter get in the way of things that really mattered to me. . . . As much as I lacked confidence in my ability to communicate verbally, I always had confidence in my athletic ability. Sports was as natural to me as speaking was unnatural. And sports turned out to be my ticket to acceptance—and more." Biden, who was the leading scorer on the football team during his senior year in high school, worked hard to overcome his stutter, spending time reciting passages from books in front of a mirror. "I prayed that I would grow out of the stutter, but I wasn't going to leave this to chance," he wrote. "I was going to beat the stutter. And I went at it the only way I knew how: I worked like hell." By the time of Biden's high-school graduation, he had become a skilled-enough speaker to give the commencement address.

Biden attended the University of Delaware, in Newark, initially earning a B-minus grade-point average. At his father's urging Biden left the university's football team and began to apply himself to his studies. After graduating from the University of Delaware in 1965 with a B.A. degree in history and political science, Biden enrolled in law school at Syracuse University, in New York, an institution that he chose partly because his future wife, Neilia Hunter of Skaneateles, New York, whom he had met in the Bahamas during a spring break, was a student there. Biden told Howard Kurtz for the *Washington Post* (July 28, 1986) that he found law school to be "the biggest bore in the world" and recalled that he "almost flunked out" but that, thanks to "doing all-nighters all the time," he managed to earn his J.D. degree in 1968. He married Hunter in 1966, and the couple's first son, Joseph R. "Beau" Biden III, was born in 1969. Their daughter, Naomi, was born in 1970, and their son Robert Hunter in 1971.

After his admission to the Delaware bar, in 1968, Biden joined the firm Prickett, Ward, Burt & Sanders. The firm represented large insurance, railroad, construction, and oil companies, and many of the people Biden worked with were Republicans. In his autobiography he wrote, "I didn't tell them that I could never join a party that was headed by Richard Nixon or that I wasn't comfortable representing the firm's bread-and-butter clients, which were big corporations." Biden left to become a public defender in 1969, and, because that position was not full-time, he also worked at a firm known as Arensen & Balick. There, he learned criminal-defense law from the respected attorney Sid Balick, who also introduced Biden to the Democratic Forum, an organization that was trying to reform Delaware's Democratic Party. Biden became active in that group's meetings, later recalling in his autobiography, "I was practicing law I believed in, and I was getting involved in politics. I was right where I wanted to be." When a senior member of the forum asked Biden to run for New Castle County Council, he agreed. In 1970 Biden was elected to the council after campaigning door-to-door in a primarily Republican district. His easy victory surprised many, since Biden, who had taken part in antisegregation sit-ins at Wilmington's Towne Theatre during high school, had run on a liberal platform that included support for public housing in the suburbs.

Biden had long aspired to become a United States senator, and as a new councilman he began to make plans for seeking that office during the 1972 election. Despite his inexperience and youth, he encountered little resistance within his own party, since no other Democrat was eager to challenge the popular Republican incumbent, J. Caleb Boggs, whose two terms as senator had followed three terms as Delaware's at-large member of the House of Representatives and two as its governor. Biden's Senate campaign was a low-budget, family-centered operation. His sister, Valerie, acted as his campaign manager, her husband was budget director, and Biden's mother organized the many coffee hours that her son attended each week to increase his name recognition. Biden's younger brother, James, raised money, and teenage volunteers distributed campaign literature by hand in order to save the cost of postage. Biden received some financial assistance from the American Federation of Labor and Congress of Industrial Organizations (AFL-CIO) and the national Democratic Party.

Biden's campaign theme was summed up in brief radio spots that stressed public distrust of officeholders and candidates. "Politicians have done such a job on the people that the people don't believe them anymore, and I'd like a shot at changing that," he asserted in one message, quoted in a transcript of the National Public Radio (NPR) show *Day to Day* (October 8, 2007). He argued that for trust to be restored, politicians had to become more accountable, and he called for an end to the war in Vietnam, more equitable taxation, legislation on behalf of consumers and the environment, and greater expenditures for mass transit and health care. Biden trailed Boggs 47 percent to 19 percent in polls conducted early in August, but the two men were neck and neck by late October. On Election Day Biden won some 4,000 votes more than his opponent. That narrow victory made him the second-youngest person at that time voted into the Upper House of Congress; indeed, he did not reach the minimum age prescribed by the U.S. Constitution for service in the Senate—30—until several weeks after the election.

Shortly before Christmas in 1972, a personal tragedy almost ended Biden's public career. On December 18, in Hockessin, Delaware, the car in which his wife and children were bringing home a Christmas tree for the holiday celebration crashed into a tractor-trailer. Biden's wife and daughter were killed instantly, and his two sons, ages three and four, were critically injured. While his sons recovered in a Wilmington hospital, Biden, struggling to deal with his loss, forgot about politics and his upcoming role in the Senate. In his autobiography he wrote, "I began to understand how despair led people to just cash it in; how suicide wasn't just an option but a *rational* option. But I'd look at Beau and Hunter asleep and wonder what new terrors their own dreams held, and wonder who would explain to my sons my being gone, too. And I knew I had no choice but to fight to stay alive." During the weeks following the accident, Biden considered surrendering his newly won seat, but Senator Mike Mansfield of Montana, the Democratic leader, persuaded him to accept his duties. Biden agreed and took his oath of office from the hospital where his sons were recovering.

Biden, not wanting to uproot his sons once they were released from the hospital, decided to keep his home in Wilmington. His sister and brother-in-law moved into the house in order to help with their care, and Biden commuted back and forth to Washington, D.C. every day—almost two hours in each direction—so that he could be with them at night. (He continued to commute throughout his tenure in the Senate.) Unsure when he took office that he would be able to be both an effective senator and father, Biden believed that he might quit after six months. "They can always get another senator," but the children "can't get another father," Biden once said, as quoted in an on-line transcript of *CNN Presents* (October 18, 2008). Biden's fears proved to be unfounded; he not only finished his first term but went on to win six more.

Among the issues Biden first tackled as a senator was campaign-finance reform; he supported the passage of legislation in 1974 that provided full federal subsidies for federal general-election campaigns and placed a ceiling on campaign contributions and spending. In 1975 Biden shocked some observers when, despite his identification with the cause of civil rights, he broke from liberal ranks on the issue of school busing. In September of that year, Biden won Senate endorsement of an amendment that forbade the Department of Health, Education, and Welfare (now the Department of Health and Human Services) to require busing aimed at school desegregation except in compliance with a specific court order. In his autobiography Biden argued that "the actual effect of busing seemed diametrically opposed to its intent." He noted that desegregation had led to "white flight" and to schools with a disproportionate number of students of a single race. He wrote, "Busing was a liberal train wreck, and it was tearing people apart. The quality of the schools in and around Wilmington was already suffering, and they would never be the same. Teachers were going to be transferred without consultation to new school districts. In some instances they would be forced to take a pay cut. New Castle County had about two-thirds of the school age population of the state, and now every one of those children was going to be assigned to a new school on the basis of racial balance." Biden's stance was unpopular with his party, but it won the support of Republicans, and he beat James H. Baxter, a poultry farmer, to retain his seat in 1978.

A year earlier Biden had married Jill Tracy Jacobs, his current wife. Jacobs has a background in education; before Biden was elected vice president, she was a professor of English at Delaware Technical and Community College. The couple's daughter, Ashley, was born in 1981.

In 1979 Biden was chosen by President Jimmy Carter to lead a delegation of senators to Moscow, to engage in discussions with Soviet Union leaders over the second Strategic Arms Limitation Treaty (SALT II). Biden was able to persuade the Soviet premier, Aleksei Kosygin, to agree to modifications in the treaty, although it was never formally ratified by the U.S.

Biden's stance on abortion generated controversy during his second term when he said that he was opposed to federal funding for the procedure but supported the right of a woman to undergo it. In 1983 he voted against Senate endorsement of a constitutional amendment that would have allowed individual states to ban abortion. "It's the only consistent position intellectually, which is that if you say government should be out, then government should be out," he told Kurtz.

In 1984 Biden served as the Democratic floor manager for the passage of the Comprehensive Crime Control Act, which overhauled federal sentencing procedures and reduced disparities in punishments for those convicted of similar crimes. In that year's election Biden achieved an almost 50,000-vote victory over John M. Burris, a businessman and former Republican leader of the Delaware House of Representatives.

Biden emerged as one of the most visible critics of President Ronald Reagan. He opposed Reagan's efforts to reduce various benefits under the Social Security system, and he became the chief opponent of several administration appointees while serving on the Senate Judiciary Committee. (In 1981 Biden had become the ranking Democrat on the committee, a post he held until 1987, when he became chairman. He remained chairman until 1995, and then served again as ranking Democrat from 1995 to 1997.) In 1985, for example, Biden vehemently—though unsuccessfully—opposed the confirmation of Edwin Meese III as attorney general, asserting that Meese's conduct was "beneath the office," as quoted by Larry Margasak for the Associated Press (June 6, 1987). In the summer of 1985, Biden led the effort to block a promotion for William Bradford Reynolds, who had very narrowly interpreted his responsibilities as civil rights chief at the Justice Department, and in 1986 Biden was floor manager of the Democrats' almost successful effort to keep Daniel Manion, another controversial Reagan nominee, from being named a federal appellate judge. In July 1986 Biden (unsuccessfully) opposed the confirmation of Associate Justice William H. Rehnquist as chief justice of the United States Supreme Court. His questioning of Rehnquist—who had been a young Supreme Court clerk during the *Brown v. Board of Education* case, in which the Supreme Court struck down the legal rationale for segregation—was considered especially severe, as Biden pressed the nominee about how he would have ruled had he been a justice at the time. In 1987 Biden presided over the confirmation hearings of Reagan's nomination to the Supreme Court of Judge Robert H. Bork, who was eventually rejected by the Senate. Although he had been opposed to Bork's confirmation from the outset, Biden won praise for the fairness with which he conducted the proceedings. According to the 1992 edition of *Politics in America*, "He ably grilled Bork about the judge's controversial contention that the Constitution was silent about privacy rights, zeroing in for political effect on Bork's criticism of a 1965 case in which the court had cited privacy rights to strike down a state law making it a crime for married couples to use contraceptives."

Biden's most publicized clash with the Reagan administration took place in July 1986, after the president refused to support extensive economic sanctions against South Africa as a way to encourage that country's government to end the system of racial segregation known as apartheid. During testimony by Secretary of State George P. Shultz before the Foreign Relations Committee, Biden chided the administration for lacking "moral backbone," according to an Associated Press (July 23, 1986) transcript of the event.

In June 1987 Biden announced his candidacy for the 1988 Democratic presidential nomination. Appealing to the "baby boom" generation that grew up after World War II, he stressed a social agenda that addressed child welfare, the alleviation of poverty, and the battle against illegal drugs. He also supported a trade policy that would be neither protectionist nor completely free and opposed Reagan's so-called Star Wars missile-defense system. His campaign did not go smoothly; he increasingly came under fire following revelations that in a speech at the Iowa State Fair in August 1987, he had lifted a significant passage from a campaign advertisement by the British Labour Party leader Neil Kinnock. He was later criticized for using words from a speech made two decades earlier by Senator Robert F. Kennedy. It was also revealed that as a first-year law student he had once been disciplined for failing to properly cite a source in a paper, an omission perceived by some as plagiarism, and that in an appearance in New Hampshire in April 1987, he had greatly overstated his academic achievements. In his autobiography Biden explained that he had quoted Kinnock several times in previous speeches, and that he had simply forgotten to attribute the quote during his speech in Iowa. Nonetheless, he wrote that although he had never intentionally plagiarized, he took responsibility for his actions: "When I stopped trying to explain to everybody and thought it through, the blame totally fell on me. Maybe the reporters traveling with me had seen me credit Kinnock over and over, but it was Joe Biden who forgot to credit Kinnock at the State Fair Debate. . . . I was the one who thought it was good enough to just get by in law school. . . . What I said about my academic achievements was just faulty memory or lack of knowledge."

In September Biden announced his withdrawal from the presidential race. A few months later, on the night of the 1988 New Hampshire primary, he suffered a life-threatening aneurysm. He was rushed to the emergency room and eventually made a full recovery. Although his Senate seat was seen as vulnerable after the plagiarism stories broke, Biden's subsequent triumph over his medical difficulties helped rekindle support for him, and he defeated his Republican challenger, M. Jane Brady, with 63 percent of the vote in 1990. In 1991 he began teaching constitutional law as an adjunct professor at Widener University Law School, in Delaware.

Aside from his ardent opposition to Bork, Biden's leadership on the Judiciary Committee is best remembered for his handling of the hearings on the appointment of the conservative African-American Supreme Court justice Clarence Thomas, who was picked by President George H. W. Bush in 1991. When information was leaked alleging that Thomas had sexually harassed a former staff member, Anita Hill, Biden was criticized by Democrats and women's groups for failing to properly use that information to block Thomas's confirmation. Biden had, in fact, shared the information with his committee, but because Hill was initially reluctant to testify, it was decided that using the information against Thomas was unfair. While Biden opposed Thomas as a nominee, the judge was later confirmed, and today many accuse Biden of being intimidated by the racially charged nature of the hearings and of not being equal to the task. Susan Deller Ross, a Georgetown University law professor and expert in sex discrimination, told Kate Phillips for the *New York Times* (August 23, 2008, on-line), "I don't think he did well and he bears responsibility for Mr. Thomas being on the court." By contrast, in an op-ed essay for the *New York Times* (August 27, 2008), Jeffrey Rosen, a George Washington University law professor, wrote in defense of Biden that in the Thomas hearings, as in those for Bork, Biden had done "everything in his power to resist the collapse of boundaries between nominees' public and private lives." (Biden was also on the Judiciary Committee in 2005 and 2006 during the failed efforts to block the conservative judges John Roberts and Samuel Alito from sitting on the Supreme Court.)

While Biden's reputation had suffered with feminist observers during the Thomas matter, those detractors largely joined a chorus of others in praising him for authoring and pushing for the eventual passage of the Violence Against Women Act (VAWA), which was aimed at preventing violent crimes against women. Among other provisions, it defined certain cases of violence against women as hate crimes and, therefore, violations of civil rights. Although Biden and his staff had formulated the legislation in 1991, it was not signed into law until 1994 due to controversy over the ambiguity of the civil rights provision. The bill became law when it was made part of the Violent Crime Control and Law Enforcement Act (VCCLEA), which Biden sponsored and which became known as the "Biden Crime Bill." In his autobiography Biden wrote, "We decided that the VAWA would have a civil rights component . . . which permitted women to seek civil damages against their attackers in a federal court and gave them a purchase of power in the system. . . . Acknowledging that a woman's right to be safe from a gender-based attack was a 'civil right,' I believed, was critically important in changing the American consciousness." The VCCLEA, the largest crime bill in U.S. history, provided for 100,000 new police officers, more than $9 billion in prison funding, and about $6 billion in funding for crime-prevention programs. The bill also expanded the reach of the federal death penalty and increased penalties for drug trafficking, gang-related crime, the smuggling of illegal aliens, and other crimes.

In the mid-1990s Biden became one of the most vocal senators on the issue of violence in what had been the Federal Republic of Yugoslavia, where well-armed Serbs in Bosnia, with the support of neighboring Serbia, were routinely imprisoning, torturing, and killing Bosnian Muslims in a campaign of "ethnic cleansing." Biden repeatedly pushed for intervention by the U.S. government and grew increasingly frustrated when he found most of his colleagues unwilling to take action. In a poignant speech he gave in the Senate, quoted in his autobiography, he said, "In the twenty-three years I have been here, there is not another issue that has more upset me, frustrated me, and occasionally made me feel a sense of shame about what the West, what the democratic powers of the world are allowing to happen. . . . We have stood by—we, the world—and watched in the twilight moments of the twentieth century, something that no one thought would ever happen again in Europe." In 1995 the Dayton Peace Agreement forced Serbian military forces to withdraw from Bosnia, but Slobodan Milosevic, the president of Serbia, was left in charge. When Milosevic ordered the invasion of neighboring Kosovo in 1999, Biden, who had retained his seat by a comfortable margin in the 1996 election, pressed for action, introducing a bill that authorized President Bill Clinton to use any means necessary to stop Milosevic. That resulted in a North Atlantic Treaty Organization

(NATO) air-strike campaign that led to Milosevic's eventual surrender. Biden became the ranking Democrat on the Foreign Relations Committee in 1997 and chairman in 2001 and again in 2007. He has called for caution in dealing with Iran and supports unilateral negotiations with nuclear-armed North Korea. In 2006 Biden supported a controversial nuclear agreement with India that opponents argued would undermine nonproliferation efforts.

In addition to his advances in the area of foreign relations, Biden has earned recognition for his stance against harmful and illegal drugs. In 2003 he sponsored the Reducing Americans' Vulnerability to Ecstasy (RAVE) Act, which allowed for prison terms of up to nine years for club owners who host events at which the recreational drug known as ecstasy is used. The next year he successfully encouraged the Senate to pass a bill that criminalized steroid precursors including androstenedione, and he later threatened legislation to regulate drug use in professional baseball if the major-league teams did not take further action against offending players. As chairman of the Senate International Narcotics Control Caucus, he is credited with writing the legislation that created a national "drug czar," a position with oversight of U.S. drug policy.

After the September 11, 2001 terrorist attacks, which toppled the twin towers of the World Trade Center and destroyed a section of the Pentagon building, killing nearly 3,000 people, Biden supported the Bush administration's military campaign in Afghanistan, which was intended to dismantle the terrorist network Al Qaeda, the group linked to the attacks, and drive out the Taliban government, which had harbored the terrorists. Following initial success in Afghanistan, the administration began to push for similar action in Iraq, arguing that the country's leader, Saddam Hussein, had chemical and biological weapons and links to terrorists. When Bush asked the United Nations to fulfill its obligation to force Hussein to disarm—as per a resolution made after the Persian Gulf War in 1991—Biden publicly supported the president. In his autobiography he wrote, "If international law was to mean anything, then it was time for the United Nations to enforce the ten-year-old resolution that called for Iraq to disarm in a way that could be verified by U.N. inspectors." Biden did not support military action, however, unless Hussein refused to disarm. He called for hearings to explore the consequences of military action and, with the Republican senator Richard Lugar, drafted a resolution that would allow the president to resort to force only if Hussein did not cooperate. When the bill failed to make it out of the Foreign Relations Committee, Biden opted to vote for the 2002 resolution authorizing the war. After the U.S. invasion failed to uncover any so-called weapons of mass destruction, and the war in Iraq later resulted in an insurgency, the death of thousands of U.S. troops, and sectarian violence, Biden became a vocal critic of the conflict and the Bush administration. In his autobiography he argued that Bush "took us to war essentially alone, before it was necessary, on the heels of the biggest and most lopsided tax cut in history, with half the troops needed to succeed." Biden later opposed Bush's troop surge, in 2007.

In 2004 Biden campaigned for his friend John Kerry, a U.S. senator from Massachusetts and presidential hopeful, and was often mentioned in the news as a possible pick for secretary of state if Kerry won the presidency. When Kerry lost to George W. Bush, Biden decided he would run in 2008. In 2006 he began campaigning, with trips to New Hampshire and Iowa. His platform included opposition to the war in Iraq and the Bush administration's fiscal policies. However, his inclination for verbal gaffes brought him damaging criticism, especially after he was heard to remark, according to the 2008 *Almanac of American Politics*, "You cannot go to a 7-Eleven or a Dunkin' Donuts franchise unless you have a slight Indian accent." (He claimed that his remarks had been taken out of context.) After officially launching his presidential run in February 2007, he stirred up further controversy when he said of Obama, according to Massimo Calabresi in *Time* (August 23, 2008, on-line), "I mean, you got the first mainstream African-American who is articulate and bright and clean and a nice-looking guy." Calabresi wrote that Biden was "apparently oblivious to his implied slur of previous African-American politicians," and that although Obama did not take personal offense at the comment, "other prominent African-Americans and much of the Washington political class came down hard on Biden." Biden later apologized, and the furor died down.

Biden has a reputation for sometimes being overly analytical and long-winded. In defense of his style, he told Cris Barrish, Nicole Gaudino, and Ginger Gibson for the *Delaware News Journal* (August 23, 2008, on-line), "One of the reasons we're in trouble is [that in] the last eight to 12 years, both political parties have concluded you've got to be able to get your whole platform down to a bumper sticker. But things are much more complicated and serious than that. I'm going to treat the American people with respect. I'm going to give them my rationale. I'm not going to assume they can't understand it."

Despite praise for Biden from fellow senators and his lengthy credentials, he came in fifth in the Iowa primary and decided to drop his bid for the White House. In August 2008, after months of media speculation and a two-month search, Obama, by then the Democratic presidential nominee, announced that he had selected Biden as his running mate. The first official announcement came to supporters via a cell-phone text message issued by the campaign, and a rally was held that same day. According to Calabresi, "In the end, Obama picked him for the simplest of reasons: The six-term Senator from Delaware is strongest in areas where the freshman from Illinois is weakest. Biden's tenure in the Senate, his foreign policy expertise, his religion [Roman Catholic], and his suburban middle-class background, all fill gaps in Obama's own presidential profile." Other key factors were Biden's sway with white, blue-collar voters; his pro-union and moderate-to-liberal record; his Irish-American roots; and his potential influence on Pennsylvania voters as a former resident of the swing state. His penchant for passionate speech was also considered; Calabresi wrote, "Biden's biggest edge in the homestretch may have come, paradoxically, from his greatest liability: his personality. Obama is charismatic, but in tough political confrontations he can be cautious and reserved. A running mate who can add passion to the coming battles, Biden has a fire-in-the-belly quality Obama lacks."

At the Democratic National Convention in Denver, Colorado, Biden displayed his sense of humor, saying in his acceptance speech: "Let me make this pledge to you right here and now. For every American who is trying to do the right thing, for all those people in government who are honoring their pledge to uphold the law and respect our Constitution, no longer will the eight most dreaded words in the English language be: 'The vice president's office is on the phone.'" The quip, while seemingly lighthearted, was indicative of Biden's feelings about Dick Cheney, Bush's powerful vice president. "In some respects, Biden is the anti-Cheney," Michael Hirsh wrote for *Newsweek* (August 27, 2008, on-line). "He's a garrulous glad-hander while Cheney is reticent and secretive; he's a sunny champion of diplomatic engagement while the vice president is known for his dark, Hobbesian view of the world. Though he is not averse to the use of force—Biden was one of the first Dems to urge Bill Clinton to intervene in the Balkans in the early '90s—he could not be more different from Cheney in personality or global outlook."

During the months leading up to the general election, Biden was largely overshadowed by McCain's running mate, the Alaska governor, Sarah Palin—a new face in national politics—whose enthusiastic speeches and potential future role as the first female vice president generated major media coverage. On October 2, 2008 Biden faced Palin in the campaign's one vice-presidential debate, held at Washington University, in St. Louis, Missouri. During the debate Biden compared the policies of McCain to those of Bush, reinforcing a familiar-yet-effective motif of the Obama campaign. Palin, in turn, criticized Obama for not having a serious agenda for change and argued that his willingness to meet with rogue leaders without preconditions was dangerous. Biden argued that the various deregulation policies McCain had supported in the Senate were part of the cause of the ongoing financial crisis. At one point, discussing the death of his first wife and daughter, Biden's voice cracked and his eyes filled with tears. Palin did not acknowledge the emotional moment, continuing instead to press her talking points, and many observers opined that their behavior humanized Biden in the public's mind, while making Palin appear callous and robotic.

On November 4, 2008, in a historic victory, Obama was elected president and Biden vice president. The Obama-Biden ticket had secured 365 Electoral College votes over McCain-Palin's 173. It also had won 53 percent of the nation's popular vote to the Republicans' 46 percent.

While campaigning as the Democratic vice-presidential candidate, Biden also sought reelection to his Senate seat against the Republican Christine O'Donnell, a conservative activist and media pundit; he won with 65 percent of the vote. (Ruth Miner, Delaware's governor, named Edward "Ted" Kaufman, who had been Biden's chief of staff from 1973 to 1994, as Biden's successor.)

Biden and Obama were sworn in on January 20, 2009. The new administration has had to contend with several pressing issues. The U.S. is still engaged in war in Afghanistan and in the unpopular occupation of Iraq; the threat of terrorist attacks is still present; and the worst financial crisis since the Great Depression has made the economy the national issue of most concern to American citizens. Biden chose Ron Klain to be his vice-presidential chief of staff, a post Klain held under former vice president Al Gore. Biden also selected Jay Carney, the *Time* Washington bureau chief, to be his director of communications.

According to Mark Leibovich, writing for the *New York Times* (March 29, 2009, on-line), within the first few months of the new administration, Biden became a key source of advice for the president and "a useful contrarian in the course of decision-making." Obama told Leibovich, "There's, I think, an institutional barrier sometimes to truth-telling in front of the president. Joe is very good about sometimes articulating what's on other people's minds, or things that they've said in private conversations that people have been less willing to say in public. Joe, in that sense, can help stir the pot." Leibovich noted that Biden, while agreeing to be Obama's running mate, expressed his unwillingness to serve in a ceremonial rather than an active role as vice president. "I think he's playing the role as 'adviser in chief' that he has foreseen," Secretary of State Hillary Clinton told Leibovich, adding that Biden was "involved in the whole agenda of the president."

One of Biden's major assignments has been overseeing the distribution of the 2009 $787 billion economic stimulus package. Toward that end he has engaged in weekly conference calls with governors and mayors to get progress reports on how the money is being used. His Senate connections have benefited Obama: Biden was credited with helping obtain the final votes for the president's stimulus and budget bills and for helping to persuade Pennsylvania's senior senator, Arlen Specter, to switch his party affiliation to Democratic. Biden has traveled to Afghanistan and Iraq several times to discuss with local leaders the fragile security situations in both nations. In October

2009, after military officials urged the president to send more troops to Afghanistan, Biden argued against doing so and said that he favored maintaining the current number of troops—a stance also taken by many congressional Democrats. Biden has also been instrumental in garnering support for Obama's health-care reform bill among his former Senate colleagues, particularly those on the Finance Committee, who were drafting a bill for consideration by the full Senate.

As many predicted, in his new post Biden has made several remarks that have been labeled gaffes. In April 2009, with concern about the spread of the H1N1 flu virus mounting, Biden said on NBC's *Today Show* that he would tell his family not to fly on commercial airplanes or ride subways so as to avoid possible infection. Biden's alarmist statement contrasted with the Obama's administration's suggestions to avoid travel only with regard to Mexico (where dozens had fallen ill), and it angered the airline industry. The White House issued an apology and noted that Biden had not intended to make people fearful. In another instance, on July 25, 2009, during a meeting with reporters, Biden—who had returned days earlier from a visit to the nations of Georgia and Ukraine—made remarks about Russia that triggered angry responses from Russian spokespeople. "I think we vastly underestimate the hand that we hold" with regard to Russia, Biden said, as widely quoted on the Internet. "Russia has to make some very difficult, calculated decisions. They have a shrinking population base, they have a withering economy, they have a banking sector and structure that is not likely to be able to withstand the next 15 years, they're in a situation where the world is changing before them and they're clinging to something in the past that is not sustainable." The following day, on the NBC program *Meet the Press*, Secretary of State Clinton made an attempt to soften Biden's words, saying that Biden had not meant that the U.S. now had an upper hand in its relations with Russia. She also said that Russia was a "great power" and that, although the U.S. questioned some of Russia's policies, the Obama administration wants "a strong, peaceful and prosperous Russia." During a press conference held on July 27, the White House press secretary, Robert Gibbs, in response to a question about Biden's remarks, said, "I think the President and his team are enormously helped by the Vice President. . . . I think he's an enormous asset to the administration."

Upon taking office, Biden moved with his family into the official vice-presidential residence, in Washington, D.C. His wife, who has a doctoral degree in education, is an adjunct professor of English at Northern Virginia Community College. "I think it's very important she have and maintain her own life, her own identity," Biden said on ABC's *This Week* (December 20, 2008, on-line). His son Robert Hunter Biden is a lawyer and lobbyist in the nation's capital. His daughter, Ashley Biden, is a social worker with the Delaware Department of Children, Youth, and Families. His son Joseph Robinette "Beau" Biden III is Delaware's attorney general; a member of the Delaware National Guard, he served for one year in Iraq (October 2008–September 2009). He is widely expected to run for his father's Senate seat in a special election to be held in 2010. The vice president and his wife have five grandchildren.

—W.D.

Suggested Reading: Associated Press (on-line) July 23, 1986, June 6, 1987; CNN (on-line) Dec. 18, 2008; *New York Times* (on-line) Aug. 24, 2008, Aug. 25, 2008, Mar. 29, 2009; *Newsweek* (on-line) Aug. 27, 2008; *Time* (on-line) Aug. 23, 2008; *USA Today* (on-line) Aug. 24, 2008; *Washington Post* A p1 July 28, 1986, A p16 Sep. 20, 1987, (on-line) Oct. 2, 2009

Selected Books: *Promises to Keep: On Life and Politics*, 2007

Steven Henry/Getty Images

Blankenbuehler, Andy

Mar. 7, 1970– Choreographer; former dancer

Address: c/o Barlow Hartman Public Relations, 1560 Broadway, Suite 909, New York, NY 10036

When the choreographer Andy Blankenbuehler stood up to receive a Tony Award for his work on the successful hip-hop-salsa musical *In the Heights*, in 2008, he had $400 in his bank account and a hole in his sock. After the awards ceremony his schedule—and bank account—filled up quickly. Blankenbuehler started dancing on Broadway in 1992 in the musical *Guys and Dolls*; as a dancer he is most proud of his work in the musical *Fosse*, which ran from 1999 to 2001. After that show he began to focus on choreography full-time. His first Broadway show as a choreographer, *The Apple Tree*, opened in the winter of 2006 and closed a few months later. Around that time *In the Heights* opened Off-Broadway, moving a year later to Broadway, where it brought him the theater world's highest honor. "I have to try not to be cocky, but I had great confidence that I was going to win the Tony," Blankenbuehler told *Current Biography*, the source of quotes for this article, unless otherwise indicated. "And that's for several reasons: one, the show is vastly different than shows that have been out there for the longest time; and also I felt that if you can't win a Tony with *In the Heights*, how could you ever win a Tony? It provides opportunities that are just rare." He said on the subject of his career, "When I started dancing I didn't think of myself as an artist. I thought choreographers wore scarves around their necks and wore high boots and they were artistic and crazy. I'm not that way. I'm just a normal guy who likes to dance. But what I've realized since I started choreographing full-time is that the possibilities are literally limitless."

Andy Blankenbuehler was born on March 7, 1970 in Cincinnati, Ohio. His father worked in a bank and, in his spare time, acted and directed shows for the community theater. Blankenbuehler's mother put her teaching career aside to raise the couple's children—Andy and his two older sisters. The whole family was artistic. "We wouldn't necessarily go to the water park on Saturday," Blankenbuehler said. "We would go to an art museum." Blankenbuehler began taking dance classes at the age of three; his sisters were already taking classes at the same studio, which offered lessons in tap, ballet, and jazz dancing. Blankenbuehler was the only boy in the class and would be for the next 15 years. By his own admission, he was no prodigy—"When I was very young," he said, "I was a horrible dancer"—and much preferred soccer to dance. "When I started playing soccer, I had this enjoyment, I wanted to play soccer, I practiced after school," he said. "I don't remember feeling that way about dancing." As with his guitar lessons and art classes, he participated in dance but did not think about it very much.

By the time Blankenbuehler was 12, though, he had started to think more about dance, asking himself: Do I enjoy this? Am I good at it? Why am I the only boy here? That self-examination led to what Blankenbuehler called an "awkward stage of noncommitment" on his part. It also took place in a different era of dance in America, before teens idolized the dancers on contemporary reality-television shows such as *So You Think You Can Dance*; although the young Blankenbuehler admired the legendary American dancers Gene Kelly, Fred Astaire, and Gregory Hines and loved Michael Jackson's dance-heavy music videos, he recalled, "I didn't really have idols." "If I could have been a professional soccer player, I would have quit dancing," he continued. "But I've always had a realistic side in my head, and I knew I wasn't ever going to be a professional soccer player."

Over time Blankenbuehler realized that he was not only beginning to enjoy dancing but that he had the potential to be very good at it. And he decided to use to his advantage the fact that he was the only boy in his class. "I knew I could get the teacher's attention and improve more rapidly," he said. During his freshman year of high school, Blankenbuehler attended his school's production of the musical *Bye Bye Birdie*, a satirical look at 1950s America with an Elvis Presley–like main character. Up to that point Blankenbuehler had had no idea that he might be interested in such a show—but he loved it. The next time his high school put on a musical, *Godspell*, he was in the cast. "From that moment on," he recalled, "all I wanted to do was dance and theater."

Though he was smitten with dance, Blankenbuehler did not know what it would mean to pursue dancing as a career. Of the 1,200 boys in the school, Blankenbuehler was the only aspiring dancer; the school's career counselor had never given advice to anyone interested in that field. "I had this strange idea," Blankenbuehler said, "that I would go to school for architecture for six years and then dance after that." By the middle of his senior year of high school, he had scrapped his plans to study architecture, a decision that displeased his parents, and found a college—Southern Methodist University, in Dallas, Texas—with a jazz-dance department willing to take him on short notice. After completing his freshman year, he found a well-paying summer job at Walt Disney World, in Orlando, Florida: along with other youths, he danced in front of the castle in the Magic Kingdom. "We had these red costumes with Mickey Mouse on the front and the show was all about the characters—Mickey Mouse, Peter Pan—it was totally cheese-whiz fun. It was crazy, we would dance on the stage and there would be literally 10,000 people watching us." That summer Blankenbuehler accepted an offer to dance at Disneyland in Tokyo, Japan.

After eight months in Tokyo, Blankenbuehler moved back to the States. Instead of returning to college, he moved to New York City; then 20 years old, he realized that he no longer wanted to be in a liberal-arts college. "All I wanted to do was dance," he said. "All I wanted to do was train." Blankenbuehler had no personal or professional contacts in New York. "My first few months here I auditioned for everything that was there, I took three dance classes a day, I went home at night and stretched. I had no life. I had no friends. I didn't go out." Having earned a lot of money in Japan, he was able to live in New York for over six months without working a regular job, putting all of his time and energy into dancing. "So many dancers move to New York City, and they never get a cog in the wheel," he explained, "because as soon as they move here they're waiting tables all day, they're missing auditions, they're not taking dance classes—and their career goes by." Blankenbuehler's first break came with a production of the musical *A Chorus Line* at a dinner theater just north of New York City. The musical was directed and choreographed by Rob Marshall, who would go on to direct the film version of the musical *Chicago* in 2002. For years afterward Blankenbuehler continued his professional relationship with Marshall, which provided him with many business contacts—dancers, producers, and directors. To make money on the side, Blankenbuehler taught dance classes, in New York and elsewhere.

At the age of 21, while Blankenbuehler was in a production of *West Side Story*—which he considers "the greatest musical ever"—at the Paper Mill Playhouse, in New Jersey, he went to Manhattan to audition for the Broadway musical *The Most Happy Fella*. Even though he missed the audition because he was late, the choreographer let the young dancer audition privately. He got the part, but the *West Side Story* producers would not let him out of his contract. A week later he injured his knee while working on *West Side Story* and suddenly was out of two jobs. "That became a sort of a recurring theme for me in my career," he recalled. He received physical therapy for his knee and was unable to dance for the next four months. (Blankenbuehler has had several knee and back injuries since then.)

After recovering fully Blankenbuehler auditioned for the Broadway musical *Guys and Dolls*, a process he found memorable: 500 male dancers auditioned for the show in a single day, making for a scene unlike anything he had ever experienced. While Blankenbuehler did not pass that audition, he joined *Guys and Dolls* on its national tour six months later; he remained with it for a year and a half. After that the show's choreographer moved him to the Broadway production—his first. Then Blankenbuehler was injured again: five months into the run of the show, he damaged two disks in his spine. Eight months later he tried to dance as well as teach, which aggravated his injury. It took him a year and a half to recover.

In 1997, at the age of 27, Blankenbuehler returned to Broadway to dance in the musical *Steel Pier*. "The biggest event in my dancing career" up to that point, as he put it, came in 1999, when he danced in *Fosse*, a musical revue showcasing the choreography of the multiple Tony Award–winner Bob Fosse. "The things I was able to do on stage," Blankenbuehler said, "they were totally golden. And if my career ended there it would have been an amazing career. I felt like Superman. That's the thing about dancers, when you're on stage dancing you feel like nothing can touch you." In addition to giving him personal satisfaction, the show presented him with a professional opportunity. "It took me out of the chorus," Blankenbuehler, who had a few dance solos in the show, said. "People would see the show and they would get to know me as an individual." Ben Brantley, a theater critic for the *New York Times* (January 15, 1999), wrote that a dance sequence featuring Blankenbuehler in *Fosse* was "vibrantly performed."

Such recognition was important for Blankenbuehler for several reasons, one being that he had just started his choreography career. After performing in a few more musicals, including *Saturday Night Fever* and *Man of La Mancha*, Blankenbuehler became a full-time choreographer, less because of the injuries he had suffered as a dancer than out of dissatisfaction with the way dance was being used on Broadway: "The dance should touch people's lives," he said, "but a lot of times in Broadway theater the dance is just the sugar on top. I wanted to portray more important emotions [through dance], like the pain of losing somebody you love or the joy of having a child. Those kinds of things are hardly ever expressed through dance. What's expressed through dance is having the girl at the high school prom say 'Yes' or, you know, getting fired. So that made me feel, one, I want to change that, and two, I'm going to be bored if I go to work and do that every night." Although Blankenbuehler was at a high point of his career as a Broadway dancer, he was at the bottom as a choreographer. For years he had trouble making money, and his savings slowly dwindled; to supplement his income he taught dance classes. (His wife, who is not in show business, had a steady income.)

Then came an opportunity that would, within two years, bring him recognition and fame. In 2006, recovering from knee surgery and still struggling as a choreographer, Blankenbuehler began work on *In the Heights*, a new musical that mixed modern music—R&B, hip-hop, and Latin rhythms—with an old-fashioned story about the mostly Hispanic New York City neighborhood of Washington Heights. On finding out about the musical, Blankenbuehler wanted very much to choreograph it. One obstacle—that he knew nearly nothing about hip-hip or salsa dancing—surfaced during his first phone interview with one of the show's producers, who asked him directly: You don't do hip-hop or salsa, so why should we hire you? "I can tell the story," Blankenbuehler assured him. "Let me learn how to tell the story." While Blankenbuehler is primarily a jazz and tap dancer, he insisted that "my musicality was not dissimilar to hip-hop. It all makes sense to me. I wanted it to look like 2008. I didn't want it to look like 1998. I needed to be specific to the [latest] hip-hop vocabulary, so I needed to figure out what that was." He spent months studying hip-hip and salsa, watching videos, listening to music, visualizing dance steps, taking hip-hop dance classes, and trying out his choreography on himself and others. Meanwhile, he was also choreographing the Broadway show *The Apple Tree*, and his wife was pregnant with their first child.

Blankenbuehler has said that he is his own toughest critic. "The only thing I've been happy with" as a choreographer thus far, he said, "is *In the Heights.*" Blankenbuehler was not alone in liking *In the Heights*: most theater critics, too, expressed their enthusiasm for the show. "Coffee, light and sweet, is the fuel that keeps a busy world in motion in the new musical *In the Heights*, a singing mural of Latin-American life that often has the inspiriting flavor of a morning pick-me-up on a warm summer day," Charles Isherwood wrote for the *New York Times* (February 9, 2007). "Light and sweet are actually just the words to describe this amiable show, which boasts an infectious, bouncy Latin-pop score by a gifted young composer, Lin-Manuel Miranda, an unfortunately underspiced book by Quiara Alegria Hudes, and a stage full of energized, energetic performers you can't take your eyes off and won't want to." Calling Blankenbuehler's choreography "joyous," Isherwood wrote that it "synthesizes street styles and Broadway athleticism, showcasing the fabulously elastic bodies of the ensemble." The show had a five-month run and won several Off-Broadway honors, including the Lucille Lortel Award for Outstanding Musical (tying with *Spring Awakening*) and the Drama Desk Award for outstanding ensemble performance. Blankenbuehler won three honors for his choreography: the Lucille Lortel Award, the Outer Critics Circle Award, and the Drama Desk Award.

In early spring 2008 *In the Heights* opened at the 1,500-seat Richard Rodgers Theatre on Broadway. Once again the critics were enthralled, as were audiences. (The average audience for *In the Heights* was more diverse in age and ethnicity than that of almost any other show on Broadway at the time.) "What makes *In the Heights* so unique . . . is that despite the driving pulse of its Latin-American rhythms, blending hip-hop, rap, jazz, pop, salsa and merengue, this buoyant musical also nods reverently to the traditions of the show tune," David Rooney wrote for *Variety* (March 9, 2008). "From its catchy opening number, which tosses in references to Cole Porter and Billy Strayhorn while swiftly introducing a large gallery of key characters and placing them within a vividly drawn community, the musical's plucky marriage of youthful freshness and lovingly old-fashioned craft is hard to resist."

In its move from Off-Broadway to Broadway, the show literally grew, with the stage, set, cast, and orchestra all getting bigger; the music, direction, and choreography were all re-polished. "Director Thomas Kail and choreographer Andy Blankenbuehler take full advantage of the playing space," Rooney wrote, "smoothly weaving the action and dancing in and out of doorways, up and down stairs, and into every cubby hole, giving the show a vitality that seems more spontaneous than studied." That apparent spontaneity resulted from a lot of thought and planning: Blankenbuehler wanted his dancers, when they were on the stage, to look like "normal" people rather than dancers.

In May 2008 *In the Heights* was nominated for 13 Tony Awards, more than any other show that year. The following month it received four Tony Awards, most notably for best musical, best original score, and best choreography.

Since then Blankenbuehler has become an in-demand choreographer, with projects lined up until 2011. After *In the Heights* he worked on *9 to 5*, a musical written by Dolly Parton, which opened on Broadway in April 2009 and closed the following September. The musical was not a critical success. (The day before Blankenbuehler spoke to *Current Biography*, Parton dropped by his dance studio in Manhattan and signed the back of his piano: "I will always love you, Dolly Parton.") As of mid-October 2009, *In the Heights* was still on Broadway; a national tour of the show started in the fall of 2009.

Blankenbuehler lives with his wife, Elly, and son, Luca, on Manhattan's Upper West Side.

—D.K.

Suggested Reading: *Dance Magazine* p224+ Jan. 2007; *New York Times* E p2 Feb. 9, 2007, Mar. 10, 2008; *Variety* Mar. 9, 2008

Selected Performances: as dancer—*Guys and Dolls*, 1992–95; *Steel Pier*, 1997; *Fosse*, 1999–2001; *Saturday Night Fever*, 1999–2000; as choreographer—*The Apple Tree*, 2006–07; *In the Heights*, 2008– ; *9 to 5*, 2009

Bolt, Usain

(OO-sane)

Aug. 21, 1986– Runner

Address: c/o Pace Sports Management, 6 The Causeway, Teddington, Middlesex TW11 0HE, England

The world's fastest man is the Jamaican sprinter Usain Bolt, who on August 16, 2008, at the Summer Olympic Games, held in Beijing, China, set a record of 9.69 seconds in the 100-meter dash—a race considered to be the purest measure of athletic prowess among runners. Four days later, with a time of 19.30 seconds, Bolt set a world record in the 200-meter race, thus becoming the first person to break both the 100-meter and the 200-meter records at the same Olympics. Bolt's finishes in those races were remarkable in other ways as well: in the final stretch of the former, when he realized that he was far enough ahead to clinch the gold, he slowed down to express his excitement by spreading his arms and then thumping his chest with one hand, in what became an iconic image of that summer's Games. In the 200-meter contest, he crossed the finish line yards ahead of, and .66 seconds faster than, his nearest competitor—the biggest margin of

Jamie McDonald/Getty Images

Usain Bolt

victory in that race in Olympic history. Bolt earned a third gold medal at the 2008 Summer Games in the 400-meter (4 x 100-meter) relay, which he and his Jamaican teammates completed in 37.10 seconds, another world record. In August 2009 Bolt broke his own records again at the 2009 World Championships in Berlin, Germany, completing the 100-meter run in 9.58 seconds and the 200-meter race in 19.19 seconds. "In statistical terms alone, the impact made by Usain Bolt over the past two years is not only stunning but also unprecedented," Simon Turnbull wrote for the London *Independent* (October 7, 2009). "Since the start of the 2008 track season, the 23-year-old Jamaican has lowered the 100m world record from 9.74sec to 9.58sec and the 200m world record from 19.32sec to 19.19sec. In the sprinting game, where the margins are measured in hundredths of a second, these have been quantum leaps the like of which have never been seen before." Bolt, at six feet five inches, is the tallest man ever to reach the top level in sprinting. As analyses of his performances have shown, his comparatively slow starts are offset by the advantages of his stride, which is longer and more rapid than others'.

Bolt's joyfulness and exuberance at the finish line in Beijing in 2008 delighted Jamaicans and most others who watched him there; according to Jenny McAsey, writing for the *Australian* (August 22, 2008), Bolt "has the happy knack of being a showman without tipping over to show-off." "Bolt is, one fervently hopes, exactly what he appears—all wrong for short-track, physically lean and long where most are stubby and muscular; delightfully vain in a self-mocking way that makes it amusing rather than annoying . . . ," Rosie DiManno wrote for the *Toronto (Ontario, Canada) Star* (August 21, 2008. "[He] eschews all the finicky self-consciousness of elite athletes." In Jamaica Bolt is a national hero and has had songs written in his honor, not only because of his gold medals but also because he earned them as a representative of the island; lured with large scholarships or other financial incentives, many other Jamaican champions have represented other countries. Bolt is also revered because he has rejected the use of performance-enhancing drugs in a sport that has been marred by drug-related scandals for years. A world-champion runner since the age of 15, Bolt celebrated his 22d birthday at the 2008 Olympics. "I wouldn't say I'm a phenomenon," he said at a press conference held in Beijing on August 24, 2008, as Andrew Longmore reported for the London *Sunday Times* (August 24, 2008, on-line). "I'm probably just a great athlete."

Usain Bolt was born on August 21, 1986 in Trelawny, a rural Jamaican parish, to Jennifer and Wellesley Bolt, who ran a local grocery store. His mother told Dave Sheinin for the *Washington Post* (August 1, 2008) that she decided on her son's unusual name after a boy touched her pregnant belly and said that if the child was a boy, she should name him Usain. The Bolt family, which included Usain's brother and sister, lived in Sherwood Content, a "poor farming community," according to Bolt's aunt Lillian Bolt-Smith, as quoted in the *Jamaica Gleaner* (July 28, 2002). As a child Bolt enjoyed playing cricket and dreamed of becoming a cricketer. His unusual swiftness as a runner was apparent by the time he was 10, and by 12 he would regularly beat older children in races at his school, Waldensia Primary School. He apparently ran barefoot on grass tracks at the time, and another year passed before he got his first pair of running shoes.

Jamaica, whose population in 2008 was estimated to be 2.8 million, has produced a disproportionately large number of the world's best sprinters, both male and female. Of the several dozen gold medals Jamaicans have won at the Olympics through the years, nearly all have been in track and field. For more than a generation, the country's schools have focused on developing running skills in Jamaican youngsters. At William Knibb Memorial High School, in Trelawney, Bolt came under the tutelage of two coaches, Dwight Barnett and the former Olympic runner Pablo McNeil, who convinced him that his natural talent was for running rather than cricket. Bolt's abilities in the 100-, 200-, and 400-meter races amazed the men; in his first "proper" 100-meter run, Barnett told Owen Slot for the *Weekend Australian* (September 13, 2008), his time was "around 10.50 seconds. I actually think he could easily [have been] as good at 400 metres as the 100 metres, but he did not like the 400 metres. I seriously think he was afraid of working hard." McNeil told Daraine Luton for the *Jamaica Gleaner* (August 18, 2008) that "he was running some phenomenal times before he was even 15."

Bolt made his first major mark in 2002, when he became the youngest athlete to win the World Junior Championships, with a 200-meter run of 20.61 seconds. (The men's world-record holder then, the American Michael Johnson, was 20 when he began clocking such times). Meanwhile, Bolt was gaining a reputation for not taking himself too seriously; he routinely joked around and showed a lack of discipline in training, and he often played basketball, socialized in clubs, and ate fast food. His excellent performances in domestic and international competitions earned him the IAAF (International Association of Athletics Federations) Rising Star Award in 2002 and 2003.

Over the years Jamaica had lost many future track-and-field superstars to schools in the United States, Canada, and the United Kingdom. American universities offered Bolt, too, incentives to matriculate, but he turned them down. Eager to ensure that Bolt would remain in Jamaica, P. J. Patterson, who was then the nation's prime minister, arranged for him to receive the best possible training in high-quality facilities. With the help of the Jamaica Amateur Athletics Association and the High Performance Centre at the University of Technology, in Kingston, Jamaica's capital and largest city, Bolt was brought to Kingston to live and train. The long hours he devoted to his recreational activities began to frustrate some of his coaches, who thought he was relying too heavily on his natural talent during training, but many observers empathized with Bolt. Elton Tucker, the sports editor of the *Gleaner*, explained to Anna Kessel, writing for the London *Observer* (August 24, 2008), that Bolt was a "country boy." "When Bolt moved to Kingston he was looking at the bright lights—where he came from there were no street lights. Suddenly there was Burger King and KFC," Tucker said.

In 2004, guided by a new coach, Fitz Coleman, Bolt turned professional. In that year's Carifta Games (the Caribbean regional championships), held in Bermuda in April, he broke the 200-meter record with a time of 19.93 seconds. Later that year and the next, he was hampered by injuries; the most serious, involving a hamstring, led to his first-round exit at the 2004 Summer Olympics, in Athens, Greece. In 2005 Bolt again changed coaches, and it is widely recognized—and acknowledged by Bolt himself—that he has flourished under the strict guidance of Glen Mills, who had coached two Caribbean sprinting champions, Don Quarrie and Kim Collins. "I worried a little bit after two years of injuries," Bolt said, as quoted by the *China Daily* (August 22, 2008). "However, things changed dramatically when I joined up with Glen. He is like a father figure to me. He has never done me any wrong and he has always made the right decisions." In the final race of the 2005 World Championships in Athletics, held in Helsinki, Finland, Bolt suffered another injury and finished in last place.

Mills pushed Bolt to develop a strict work ethic. He told Bolt to begin training for the 400-meter race, which he felt was more appropriate for such a tall runner. Bolt's insistence on focusing on the 100- and 200-meter races led some to accuse him of being too lazy for the more grueling event. In time Mills and Bolt reached an agreement: if Bolt broke Quarrie's 36-year-old Jamaican national record (19.8 seconds) in the 200-meter, Mills would approve his running the flashier 100. At the Jamaican Championships in 2007, Bolt succeeded, completing the 200-meter race in 19.75 seconds. In July of that year, he ran his first professional 100-meter race, finishing in 10.03 seconds—an astonishingly good time. (The so-called 10-second barrier was not broken until 1968, when the American Jim Hines ran 100 meters in 9.9 seconds—a record that stood for 15 years. The fastest recorded time as of mid-2007 was 9.85 seconds, achieved by Olusoji Fasuba of Nigeria in 2006.)

Bolt spent the following winter training for the 100-meter race. In particular, he strived to increase the speed with which he left the starting block. Taller racers are naturally less explosive in their starts than their stockier peers, and Bolt strived to get bigger and stronger through weight training to reduce that handicap. On May 3, 2008, at the Jamaica Invitational in Kingston, he ran the 100-meters in 9.76 seconds, a personal best that was just .02 second slower than the world record, held by his compatriot Asafa Powell. On May 31, at the Reebok Grand Prix, on Randall's Island, in New York City, in only his fifth men's 100-meter race, Bolt broke the world record with a 9.72 run and claimed the title of world's fastest man. After the race he downplayed the significance of that record, telling reporters that only an Olympic gold medal or a world championship would constitute a lasting achievement.

With the Summer Olympics fast approaching, Mills and Bolt needed to develop a strategy as well as declare which races Bolt would compete in. "In Mills's eyes, if there was a double to be had, it would be the 200m and 400m, not the standard sprint combination of 100m and 200m," Andrew Longmore wrote for the London *Sunday Times* (August 24, 2008). "Mills was against Bolt's double until that night in Randall's Island when the world record was smashed. The profit motive dictated the future then, but the old threat remained. 'If you don't win the gold tonight,' Mills told Bolt before the 100m, 'I'll get you running the 400m.'" Bolt devoted some time to training for the 400-meter.

Shortly before the start of the Olympic Games, Bolt announced that he would be running in the 100-meter and 200-meter races. Scheduled to include the three fastest men ever known—Bolt, Powell, and the American world champion Tyson Gay—the 100-meter event was being touted as the biggest showdown in Olympic history. In the preliminary heats Bolt seemingly never ran at his maximum speed. Gay and Powell were still recovering from serious injuries, and in the final race, held on

August 16, 2008, Bolt crossed the finish line in 9.69 seconds, breaking the record he had set less than three months earlier. (During the Olympic trials Gay had had a 9.68-second run, but he was aided by a tail wind that measured twice the speed accepted for record-setting purposes.) "It was not [Bolt's record-setting] time, but the manner in which it was achieved, which astonished . . . ," Doug Gillon wrote for the Glasgow, Scotland, *Herald* (August 18, 2008). "Bolt's long levers are hard to unwind, and he was second [to] last out of the blocks, with a reaction time of 0.165. But by 30 metres he was up with everyone. Then at 50 metres, something even more extraordinary happened. He seemed to find a supercharger, and just ran away from the field. Finally something even more remarkable occurred. He stopped running at 82 metres and, lowering his hands and spreading his arms wide, he waved both arms up and down in unison. He seemed to be jogging the final seven strides, one shoe lace flapping as he slapped his heart with his right hand." Bolt won the 100-meter race by the largest margin—0.2 seconds—since Carl Lewis's victory in 1984. Although Jacques Rogge, the president of the International Olympic Committee, and some journalists criticized Bolt for what they viewed as unsportsmanlike showboating, virtually all racers and fans who expressed an opinion publicly found no fault with what they viewed as Bolt's genuinely playful reaction. "I'm just enjoying myself, that's pretty much it," Bolt declared, according to Andrew Longmore. "I think it makes the fans happy too because I'm showing my personality. People enjoy watching me so I'll stay the way I am." Bolt told reporters that on the morning of the race he had not eaten breakfast. "I woke up at 11 o'clock, sat around and watched TV, then had some chicken nuggets, slept for two hours, then went back and got some more nuggets," he said, as quoted by Rick Broadbent in the London *Times* (August 18, 2008). He also said that his hard work in improving his technique in the first 20 meters had paid off; at the Olympics, "I executed it right." Similarly, Paul Hallam, the Australian Commonwealth Games sprint coach, told Scott Gullan for the Australian *Herald Sun* (September 11, 2008, on-line) that, given his height, Bolt's "ability to get to 30m as fast as he can is just extraordinary. . . . That is probably the most impressive component of it all." Scientists at the University of Oslo, in Norway, estimated that had Bolt not slowed down to celebrate, he might have completed the race in 9.55 seconds, taking almost 0.2 seconds off the record.

At the 1996 Olympics the American sprinter Michael Johnson ran the 200-meter race in 19.32 seconds, a record that remained unbroken for 12 years. A few hours before the start of the 200-meter race in Beijing, on August 20, 2008, Johnson told George Vecsey for the *New York Times* (August 21, 2008), "I don't think [Bolt] will break it here, although I wouldn't be shocked at anything he did." In what Johnson, after the race, described to Vecsey as "the most impressive athletic performance I have ever seen in my life," Bolt, making an all-out effort, set a new world record of 19.30 seconds, despite the presence of a slight headwind. The next day the Jamaican 400-meter-relay team—Nesta Carter, Michael Frater, Asafa Powell, and Bolt (running the third leg of the race)—won that competition with another world record: 37.10 seconds, 0.3 seconds faster than the previous world record.

Bolt's victories gave the lie to the belief that, in general, a top racer must be short and stocky, with a low center of gravity. Analyses of his performances at the Games showed that he had averaged 41 strides over 100 meters—about four fewer than the five-foot 11-inch Tyson Gay's average. Using a nickname of Bolt's, Rosie DiManno offered the following explanation: "The Lightning Bolt is anything but, out of the blocks, with the seventh slowest reaction time in the 100 [at the Summer Games]. The high knee lift is also unusual for a sprinter. But he has extraordinary baseline velocity through the middle 40 of the race and an astonishing 'turnover rate'—one foot coming down, one foot going up, barely finishing one stride before starting the other, so that he's actually suspended in air for a nanosecond." A study done at the Kingston University of Technology, Neil Wilson wrote for the London *Daily Mail* (August 6, 2008), suggested that the "fast-twitch muscles" of 70 percent of Jamaicans contain a protein called Actinen A, which aids sprinters. Bolt's father told a reporter for Reuters (August 16, 2008) that his son's abilities stem from his consumption of the yams that are a staple in Trelawny and other parts of Jamaica.

Bolt's extraordinary abilities, persona, and rejection of lucrative offers from abroad from countries that wanted him to run under their flags have endeared him to his countrymen. That is one reason why Jamaican officials and many members of the public reacted with outrage to accusations that Bolt must have used performance-enhancing drugs at the Summer Games. The American athlete Carl Lewis, who won a total of nine Olympic gold medals between 1984 and 1996, told Arash Markazi for *Sports Illustrated* (September 11, 2008, on-line), "When people ask me about Bolt I say he could be the greatest athlete of all time. But for someone to run 10.03 one year and 9.69 the next, if you don't question that in a sport that has the reputation it has right now, you're a fool. Period." (Lewis failed several drugs tests during his track-and-field career but was never penalized.) The Jamaican team doctor Herb Lewis responded angrily to Carl Lewis's comment, describing it to Broadbent as "condescending crap." "[Americans] still think we don't know anything down in Jamaica," he said. Jeré Longman reported in the *New York Times* (April 11, 2009) that Teddy McCook, the general secretary of the Jamaican Olympic Committee, dismissed Carl Lewis as "an idiot." Bolt has never failed any of the dozens of drug tests he has undergone, and in his own defense, he has pointed to his consistently superior track record, with his times at 21 years of age only slightly better than those he posted at 15.

In April 2009 Bolt suffered minor injuries when he crashed his car while driving on the highway that connects Kingston to Montego Bay, Jamaica. The following month he set another world record, running the 150-meter street race at the Manchester Great City Games in 14.35 seconds. On August 16, 2009, exactly one year after his world-record performance in Beijing, Bolt broke his 100-meter record at the World Championships in Berlin, clocking a time of 9.58 seconds. More than a 10th of a second faster than the previous record, it was also the largest margin of improvement ever recorded in that race. A few days later Bolt broke his 200-meter record by a similarly impressive margin, finishing with a time of 19.19 seconds. Bolt later said that he had been working on improving his starting times and reaction times and said that those improvements were the main reasons for his faster runs. He also won a third gold medal in the 4x100-meter relay event with his Jamaican teammates. Observers pointed out the historical significance of Bolt's most recent achievements: he broke the records in the same Berlin stadium where, in 1936, in the face of Nazi propaganda about the racial superiority of whites, the African-American athlete Jesse Owens became a legend by winning four gold medals. At the end of the championship competition, the mayor of Berlin presented Bolt with a section of the demolished Berlin Wall and said, as quoted by an Associated Press (August 24, 2009) reporter, that the runner had demonstrated that "one can tear down walls that had been considered as insurmountable."

Bolt was a co-winner of the IAAF Athlete of the Year Award in 2008. In 2009 he became the youngest person to receive the Order of Jamaica, one of his country's highest honors. According to Longman and other sources, his goals include increasing the popularity of running among athletes and the public and earning $10 million a year through commercial endorsements, payments for promotional appearances at races and other events, and prize money. At present he represents the sporting-goods company Puma, Gatorade, and Digicel, a mobile-phone company. Before he left Beijing in 2008, Bolt donated $50,000 to aid children affected by the massive earthquake that devastated Sichuan Province the previous May. He has also donated generously to improve conditions for Jamaicans: after his Olympic triumph tap water and other amenities became available in Sherwood Content for the first time. Bolt loves his country's dancehall music and after some races has celebrated on the track by dancing the Gully Creeper. During his interview with Longman and other reporters from around the world, he said, "My main goal is to be a legend in my sport." Bolt lives in Kingston.

—M.M.

Suggested Reading: (Australia) *Herald Sun* Sports (on-line) Sep. 11, 2008; (London) *Sunday Times* (on-line) Sports Aug. 24, 2008; (London) *Times* p93 Sep. 13, 2008, (on-line) Aug 18, 2004; *New York Times* D p2 Aug. 28, 2008, Sports p1+ Apr. 12, 2009; *Runner's World* p78+ Dec. 2008; *Sports Illustrated* p64+ June 9, 2008, p98+ July 28, 2008, p58+ Aug. 25, 2008, p48+ Oct. 20 2008; *Toronto (Ontario, Canada) Star* A p1+ Aug. 21, 2008; *Washington Post* E p1+ Aug. 1, 2008

Ethan Miller/Getty Images

Boras, Scott

Nov. 2, 1952– Baseball agent

Address: Boras Corp., 18 Corporate Plaza Dr., Newport Beach, CA 92660

"The one thing I learned about my role in this business is that I am the person that must take the heat for what is perceived to be a negative influence on baseball," Scott Boras, a prominent and highly influential agent for Major League Baseball (MLB) players, told Bob Nightengale for the *Los Angeles Times* (February 22, 1993). "My job is to represent individuals and advise them, and fans on the whole do not have much empathy or care for someone who is responsible for making an athlete a multimillionaire." Boras, who specializes in contract negotiations for draftees and free agents, had brief careers as a minor-league player and then as a lawyer before he became an agent. In a highly unusual transaction in his maiden effort, in 1983, he gained the upper hand in bargaining with the New

York Yankees to secure for the pitcher Tim Belcher what was then an extraordinarily lucrative deal. According to Nightengale, Boras is "solely responsible for changing the fate of the amateur draft, and challenges the arbitration process more than any agent." Boras—whose fee is 5 percent of every contract's worth—has repeatedly raised the ante in what professional players are paid. In 2000 he negotiated Alex Rodriguez's record-breaking 10-year, $252 million contract with the Texas Rangers—about one-eighth of the total of approximately $2 billion in contracts he has won to date. Many baseball aficionados have denounced him as injurious to the sport, particularly to teams with relatively small budgets. Agents have accused him of stealing their clients, and team managers have complained that he exploits loopholes and claims during negotiations to have competing offers for his clients when none exist. "My only responsibility is to make sure my players play and play well, to provide them with the support they need to do that, and to make sure they receive whatever the market is, whether it's good or bad, up or down," he told Ross Newhan for the *Los Angeles Times* (April 8, 2001). "My job is to read and define the market, not create it, and if I'm considered to be someone who's destroying the game, then I pat myself on the back because I assume I'm also involved enough to take credit for the fact that the majority of franchises are doing very well." The Boras Corp., based in Newport Beach, California, has some 75 employees, including former major-league players, who—as Boras himself did for years—scout for potential new talent and compile extensive statistical and other information on clients, along with comparisons and predictions that cast them in the best possible light. Boras currently represents around 65 major-league players and an equal number of minor-league contenders.

Scott Dean Boras was born on November 2, 1952 in California and was raised in Elk Grove, near Sacramento, the state capital, on an 800-acre farm owned by his parents. While growing up he shared in the work of the farm, where his family raised dairy cattle and grew alfalfa and oat hay. At 5:00 a.m. he would milk cows; after school and during summers, while driving a tractor in the fields, he would listen to radio broadcasts of baseball games. "My whole day was motivated around making sure I got done at a quarter to five, so I could make that glorious ride to the ballpark," he told James C. McKinley Jr. for the *New York Times* (December 14, 2000).

On his high-school baseball team, Boras played center field. When he was a senior, in 1970, his skills as a hitter earned him a baseball scholarship to the University of the Pacific (known as Pacific), in Stockton, California, where he majored in chemistry. By his junior year he had been accepted into Pacific's graduate program in industrial pharmacology, and he began to work toward a doctorate while pursuing his undergraduate degree. He earned a B.A. in 1974 and a Ph.D. two years later. (He did not write a dissertation; instead, he took oral examinations about research he conducted on an antacid of his own formulation.) Meanwhile, he had served as the captain of the university's baseball team and harbored hopes of becoming a major-league baseball player. A collision with another player left him with ripped tendons in his knee only two weeks before the MLB draft. Nonetheless, in 1974 the St. Louis Cardinals signed him to play as an amateur free agent in its minor-league division. To fulfill his obligations to St. Louis, he would leave Pacific several weeks before the spring term ended and take his final exams under the supervision of the Cardinals' coaches Ken Boyer and Jack Krol. "I'd buy 'em two six-packs of beer and they would proctor my exams," he told Ben McGrath for the *New Yorker* (October 29, 2007). Boras also told McGrath that during that period, he felt uncomfortable when he studied in view of his teammates. "It was difficult, because you didn't want to be held out to be a college boy—that was not a good thing then," he recalled. "And so when I studied on the bus I'd cover up my neuropharmacology book in a men's magazine so that no one knew."

After he achieved the highest batting average among members of the Class A St. Petersburg Cardinals, Boras succeeded in negotiating a pay raise, by persuading Cardinals officials that he should earn more than the next-best hitter. He again emerged victorious in salary negotiations after he was traded to the Chicago Cubs, in 1977. "I told them, 'I'm going to have to consider leaving, because I can go out in the real world and make ten times what I can make playing baseball,'" he told McGrath. (According to baseball-almanac.com, the minimum starting salary for an MLB player in 1977 was $19,000, and the average salary was $76,066.) By Boras's own account, his weakened knee prevented him from playing a single game in 1978, and he gave up playing baseball. After his four seasons with the St. Louis and Chicago Cubs farm systems, during which he played mostly as an infielder, his batting average was .283 (or .274, according to some sources).

Boras next enrolled at the McGeorge School of Law at Pacific. In 1982 he earned a J.D. degree and joined Rooks, Pitts & Poust, a Chicago-based firm that specialized in cases of alleged medical malpractice. Boras and another attorney in the firm won one case when they convinced a jury that the misuse of medication by a doctor during a baby's delivery had damaged the brain of the child, who suffered from cerebral palsy. The child's parents received $3.8 million in damages, one-third of which was split between Boras and his colleague. The prospect of earning additional large sums as a medical-malpractice specialist held little appeal for Boras, however. He still felt strongly drawn to the world of baseball, and when he learned that baseball revenues had increased and salaries for amatuer draftees had not, he began to contemplate becoming an agent. In the summer of 1983, when

Boras found out that the Minnesota Twins had offered a $100,000 signing bonus to their first draft pick of the year, the pitcher Tim Belcher, a student at Mount Vernon Nazarene College, in Ohio, he told Belcher to reject it. That winter, in the 1984 supplemental draft, the New York Yankees signed Belcher for over $150,000. "In one swift stroke," Bryan Curtis wrote for *Slate* (May 9, 2001, on-line), "baseball's amateur draft went from the owners' cheapest and most reliable way to hoard talent to a system heavily tilted toward the players." According to Thomas Stinson, writing for the *Atlanta Journal-Constitution* (October 21, 2007), "signing bonuses rose 21 percent in 1984, and teams have ever since had to weigh Boras into the equation when figuring a draft pick's signability."

Boras was still working for Rooks, Pitts & Poust when, in 1985, his friend Mike Fischlin, who was then playing with the Cleveland Indians, recruited him to help represent the Oakland Athletics' relief pitcher Bill Caudill in negotiations with the Toronto Blue Jays. Boras won a five-year, $7.5 million contract for Caudill, the second-highest amount for a reliever at that time. The deal earned Boras a mention in *Sports Illustrated*, and soon afterward, with other players having asked him to represent them, Boras stopped practicing law.

By 1986 Boras had negotiated the first of many record-breaking deals for draftees—$210,000 from the Texas Rangers for Kevin Brown. He secured $235,000 for Andy Benes from the San Diego Padres in 1988; $1.01 million for Ben McDonald from the Baltimore Orioles in 1989; $1.2 million for Todd Van Poppel from the Oakland Athletics in 1990; and $1.55 million for Brien Taylor from the New York Yankees in 1991. By then Boras had become known for his unswayable resolve and hard-line negotiation tactics. Echoing complaints about him that were being bandied about, Chris Jenkins wrote for the *San Diego Union Tribune* (April 1, 1992) that Boras had become "the Lord of Leverage. . . . Denied playing time in the bigs, he's now playing hardball at the negotiating table, and he plays it so hard that it's been suggested he's taking out his vengeance on baseball." "I've heard people say that," Boras told Jenkins. "It's not true. I love the game." In December 1992 *Sporting News* named Boris the 26th-most-powerful figure in sports.

Criticism of Boras's tactics increased steadily. In 1993 Nightengale wrote, "According to an informal survey of general managers, he has surpassed everyone in his profession as the most hated player-agent in the business." Antipathy toward him mounted that winter, when the California Angels, unable or unwilling to agree to the figure that Boras demanded for Jim Abbott, felt compelled to trade that pitcher; the same thing happened to the Chicago Cubs, who lost the pitcher Greg Maddux to the free-agent market. Nightengale wrote, "Never in one winter has an agent drawn the wrath of so many in baseball"; he quoted the Angels' manager, Buck Rodgers, as saying, "I think Jim Abbott wanted to sign with us all along, and I hate to think we had to coddle up to his agent. . . . I don't want to be vindictive, but it's hard not to be vindictive." Boras told Nightengale that, in his opinion, the Angels' mistake was to try to deny Abbott what he deserved to earn. "I know baseball is a business, but what troubles me is that I still clearly believe the Angels would have been much better served economically and for the best interests for their club if they signed Jim Abbott," he said. "The best business decision was to pay Jim Abbott what he's worth."

In 1996 Boras, whom some have dubbed "Lord of the Loophole," exploited a provision (widely viewed as a loophole) in the amateur-draft rules that granted free agency to four of the top first-round draft picks. When the teams that had drafted the four failed to come up with contracts within 15 days, as required by MLB rules, Boras offered his services to the players—Matt White, Travis Lee, John Patterson, and Bobby Seay—and acquired million-dollar contracts with other teams for all of them. The next year Boras filed a petition with the MLB commissioner's office in an attempt to free J. D. Drew from the Philadelphia Phillies, again citing the Phillies' failure to adhere to the 15-day requirement. Boras threatened to pull Drew from the team if he was not given a $10 million (some sources say $11 million) contract. The Phillies drew the line at $3 million, and following Boras's advice, Drew played for the duration of the season with a team from the independent Northern League. The next season Drew reentered the draft and was signed for $8 million to the St. Louis Cardinals, a record for a draft player. The Phillies' general manager, Ed Wade, questioned Boras's tactics, telling Ross Newhan, "One of the principles we live by is you play by the rules or you work to exact change in the rules, but you don't spend your time trying to circumvent them or find loopholes. Scott uses any ammunition at his disposal to get his client what he wants and where he wants to be, and I think he went into the Drew negotiations with a hidden agenda. There was no way we could have signed him, no matter what we offered."

Among other notable achievements, in August 1997 Boras secured a five-year contract for $11.5 million a year with the Atlanta Braves for Greg Maddux, who became the highest-paid player in baseball at the time. In 1998 Boras persuaded the New York Yankees to give the center-fielder Bernie Williams $12.5 million a year for seven years, a total of $87.5 million. Not long afterward he negotiated a contract with the Los Angeles Dodgers for pitcher Kevin Brown for $15 million a year for seven years, $105 million in total.

In 2000 Boras negotiated the then-highest salary for a player in baseball history, when he won from the Texas Rangers a 10-year, $252 million contract for the shortstop Alex Rodriguez. "When Alex Rodriguez signed his contract," Boras told Newhan, "I'm praying that every mother tells her son, 'Get out that bat and ball.' I know fans are puzzled by that kind of money, but I also think people recognize that it's a healthy industry overall. A majority of people have said to me, 'If they're going to pay it, they must have it.'" Rodriguez's tenure with the Rangers ended in 2004, when the team traded him to the New York Yankees. Boras oversaw the terms of the trade, in which the Rangers agreed to pay $67 million of the $179 million left on Rodriguez's contract, with the Yankees picking up the remainder.

In a reportedly unique deal executed in 2005, Boras and the Cleveland Indians included clauses in the contract of Kevin Millwood according to which Millwood's salary would be reduced if he missed games due to injury. In the same year Boras engineered Johnny Damon's departure from the Boston Red Sox to the Yankees, with whom Damon signed a $52 million, four-year contract. Damon had been well-liked among Boston fans, and many expressed dismay when his move to the Yankees was announced. Damon and Boras maintained that the $27 million that Boston had offered was inadequate; Boras told Ronald Blum for the Associated Press Online (December 23, 2005) that the amount "was something that really changed [Damon's] feelings about Boston."

In 2007 Boras was dealt a blow when Rodriguez negotiated a new contract with the Yankees without him. After the team rejected as exhorbitant the $350 million over 10 years that Boras had asked for, Rodriguez, acting on his own behalf, settled for $275 million, also for 10 years. "What happened here was that [Boras's] bravado got the better of him," Andrew Zimbalist, a Smith College economics professor, told Bill Shaikin for the *Los Angeles Times* (November 15, 2007). "Instead of pushing the envelope, he jumped zip codes. That was out of all sense of proportion, out of the grasp of the reality of the underlying economics." For his part Rodriguez explained to the media that Boras, without his permission, had announced during Game Four of the World Series that Rodriguez would opt out of the final three years of the Rangers/Yankees trade deal to become a free agent. The ESPN Web site (December 17, 2007) quoted Rodriguez as having said in an interview for the television news show *60 Minutes*, "When I realized things were going haywire, at that point I said, 'Wait a minute, I've got to be accountable for my own life. This is not going the way I wanted it to go.' So I got behind the wheel." Boras did not comment on the matter in public. In *Variety* (December 17, 2007) Phil Gallo reported that Rodriguez had fired Boras and hired the former record-company executive Gus Oseary to replace him.

In October 2008 Boras won a $550,000 decision against a former client, Gary Sheffield of the Detroit Tigers. An arbitrator determined that Sheffield should have paid Boras that sum for work that enabled the player to become a free agent in 2004. In the 2008–09 off-season, Boras brokered 12 MLB deals. They included an eight-year, $180 million contract for the Yankees' first-baseman Mark Texeira, a four-year, $60 million contract for the Braves' pitcher Derek Lowe, and a two-year, $60 million contract for the Dodgers' left-fielder Manny Ramirez.

In June 2009 Boras publicly criticized the Detroit Tigers manager, Jim Leyland, for indefinitely benching one of his clients, Magglio Ordonez, to give him time to improve his flagging skills. Boras argued that Ordonez's batting average and RBI numbers, although down somewhat, were close to what they had been in past years. Leyland told the press, according to Chris Iott in the *Jackson (Michigan) Citizen Patriot* (June 21, 2009), "Scott Boras might be better off if he lets Magglio and myself handle this instead of him." In August 2009 Boras won a four-year, $15.67 million contract for the pitcher Stephen Strasburg of the Washington Nationals.

Boras lives in Newport Beach with his wife, Jeanette, and their children, Natalie, Shane, and Trent.

—W.D.

Suggested Reading: *LA Weekly* (on-line) May 22, 2007; *Los Angeles Times* C p1 Feb. 22, 1993; *Los Angeles Times Magazine* p12 Apr. 8, 2001; *New Yorker* (on-line) Oct. 26, 2007; *Sports Illustrated* (on-line) June 14, 1993

Bublé, Michael

(boo-BLAY)

Sep. 9, 1975– Singer

Address: c/o Reprise Records, 3300 Warner Blvd., Burbank, CA 91505

"These guys were triple threats," the Canadian singer Michael Bublé told Gioia Patton for *Today's Woman* (March 2008), describing the show-business legends he counts as his greatest influences: Bobby Darin, Dean Martin, Elvis Presley, Ray Charles, and Frank Sinatra, the artist to whom he is most often compared. "They could sing, dance and act. They were entertainers, and I believe that's a lost art now." Bublé has not only revived that art but turned it into big business, selling 15 million records since he released his self-titled major-label debut album, in 2003. Best known for his crooning style, affinity for jazz standards, and suave "Rat Pack" persona—qualities that have made him especially popular among women—he has also recorded swinging versions of contemporary rock and pop songs and written some of his own material. "It's okay to borrow things, to be influenced," he told Jonathon Gatehouse for *Maclean's* (August 27, 2007). "But just to rip it off, just to repeat it? I think I have a responsibility to move the music forward."

Jason Merritt/Getty Images

Michael Bublé

Despite a lack of radio airplay, *Michael Bublé* reached number 47 on the *Billboard* 200 album chart—a remarkable achievement for a jazz album—and the singer's next two studio albums, *It's Time* (2005) and *Call Me Irresponsible* (2007), fared even better, climbing to number seven and number one, respectively. His success came as something of a surprise to executives at his label, Warner Bros. Records, who were unsure if audiences would embrace his throwback style. Even David Foster, the producer and record executive who discovered the singer, was skeptical about Bublé's chances for success—but no longer. "Michael's going to have a 30-year career," Foster told Michael Posner for the Toronto, Canada, *Globe and Mail* (September 22, 2007). "Or longer. A lot of other singers have turned to this material because their careers were in trouble. But Michael has always been here. He's lived this music. For my taste, he's the greatest singer alive, if you want that sound." In October 2009 Bublé released his fourth studio album, *Crazy Love*, which debuted at number one on the *Billboard* 200 album chart.

Michael Steven Bublé was born on September 9, 1975 in Burnaby, a town just east of Vancouver, in the Canadian province of British Columbia. His mother, Amber, is a homemaker; his father, Lewis, is a salmon fisherman. He has two sisters, Crystal and Brandee. While Bublé grew up listening mostly to contemporary pop artists, such as Michael Jackson, from an early age he found himself drawn to jazz and swing music. "It's really weird. The first time I really heard anything in that genre was Bing Crosby's *White Christmas* album," he told Roger Bull for the *Florida Times-Union* (February 22, 2008). "Maybe because I really love that time of year, it really made some kind of connection with me and all the good feelings associated with it. And I loved the musicality of it." Over time he became even more enamored of the music of the 1940s and '50s, as his maternal grandfather, Mitch Santaga, would play him records by such artists as Sinatra, Darin, Vic Damone, Mel Tormé, and the Mills Brothers. "Grandpa got a real kick out of the fact that I liked the music so much," an article in the Ontario, Canada, *Orillia Packet & Times* (March 11, 2003) quoted him as saying. "We'd start singing at the dinner table together, like 'Everybody Loves Somebody Sometime.'" Perhaps because many of Bublé's family members also enjoyed singing, it was not until he was a teenager that his parents recognized his talent.

By the time he was 16, Bublé had begun performing in Vancouver-area nightclubs. Santaga, a plumber, would sometimes do work for club owners in exchange for bookings. "I think the most beautiful thing is I got the chance to fail over and over again and to learn my craft. I played for audiences that didn't necessarily come to see me," Bublé told Malcolm X Abram for the *Akron (Ohio) Beacon Journal* (April 16, 2008), recalling the years he spent singing in hotel bars, strip clubs, and even shopping malls. He added, "At some point when I was confident enough to take an audience like that and put them in my hand, I knew I was going to be good enough to have success at the next level." When he was 18 Bublé won a local talent contest, though he was disqualified when the organizer, Beverly Delich, discovered that he was underage. Delich did, however, sign Bublé up for the Canadian Youth Talent Search—which he won—and agreed to become his manager. Delich guided his career for seven years, as Bublé struggled to make a name for himself. "Bev was Michael's ticket out of Burnaby," the jazz musician and composer Gabriel Mark Hasselbach, a friend of Bublé's, told Posner. "She took that boy by the collar and dragged him to fame." Confident and ambitious, Bublé spent the latter half of the 1990s performing in nightclubs, playing Elvis Presley in the 1950s-themed stage musical *Red Rock Diner*, and singing in a revue called *Forever Swing*. During that period he released *BaBalu*, a CD he recorded at the Vancouver lounge of the same name.

Bublé's big break came in 2000, when Michael McSweeney, an assistant to former Canadian prime minister Brian Mulroney, saw him perform in Toronto. McSweeney was impressed and persuaded Mulroney—a music lover and amateur crooner—to hire Bublé to sing at his daughter Caroline's upcoming wedding. Bublé agreed to perform for free, since David Foster, the Warner Bros. producer known for his work with Barbra Streisand, Céline Dion, and Whitney Houston, was to be among the invited guests. Mulroney urged Foster to pay close attention to the singer. "Brian told me, 'You're not going to believe this kid,'" Foster told Kerry Gold for the *Pembroke (Ontario) Observer* (October 29, 2002). "And I'm thinking, 'This is the last thing I want to do at a wedding, is see some singer—a wedding singer.' But we were kind of transfixed." Though he was quick to recognize Bublé's talent, Foster was reluctant to offer the singer a recording contract. "His wedding performance was incredible," he told Posner. "But I just didn't know how you'd market that music." Delich next pitched Bublé to Bruce Allen, the Canadian manager behind superstars including Bryan Adams and Martina McBride, but he, too, hesitated to sign the performer. "I don't know what I'd do with him," Allen said.

Bublé and Delich refused to give up, and after moving to Los Angeles, California, they persuaded Foster to produce a demo recording. (Mulroney, still a champion of Bublé's singing, was also instrumental in changing Foster's mind.) While Foster told Delich that she would have to raise roughly $500,000 for the session, he eventually covered the expense himself. He played the finished recording for his fellow Warner Bros. executives, and soon afterward Bublé had a meeting with Tom Whalley, the chairman of Warner Music. As Delich recalled to Posner, Whalley asked Bublé, "Why should we do this? People will compare you to Sinatra and you're not Sinatra." Bublé's response was, "I don't want to be Sinatra. I'm not Sinatra. I've never wanted to be Sinatra. I want to be Michael Bublé." In less than a week he had secured a recording deal, and before long Allen took over as his manager. Out of gratitude for Delich's early support, Bublé has continued to pay her a "trailing royalty."

In February 2003 Foster's own label, 143 Records, a subsidiary of the Warner imprint Reprise, released Bublé's self-titled debut. Produced by Foster and executive-produced by the legendary Canadian singer Paul Anka, the album included standards, such as "Come Fly with Me," a song made popular by Frank Sinatra, as well as more contemporary fare, such as "Crazy Little Thing Called Love," by the rock band Queen. The album peaked at a comparatively high number 47 on the *Billboard* 200 chart, which pleased the label's executives, who had not expected sales of *Michael Bublé* to exceed 100,000 copies. In a review for the All Music Guide Web site, Aaron Latham called Bublé "someone who has learned the art of popular song and is creating his own colorful music from shades of the past." He added, "He sounds absolutely thrilled to be singing these songs, and that goes a long way in making *Michael Bublé* an exciting debut." Bublé promoted the collection by appearing on several TV programs, including *The Today Show* and *Live with Regis and Kelly*, and concertizing. While the album established him as a major star, Bublé has since dismissed it, echoing the criticisms made by the New York radio deejay Jonathan Schwartz. "It was a dopey mistake to bring Sinatra songs into the fold and mimic them," Schwartz told Craig Offman for *Time International* (June 2, 2003). "It doesn't really advance the story."

In 2003 the label DRG released *Totally Bublé*, containing songs performed by Bublé in the 2001 film *Totally Blonde*, in which he had played a nightclub singer. That November Bublé released an EP of Christmas music, *Let It Snow*, and in 2004 he released a live CD/DVD set, *Come Fly with Me*. That same year he won a Juno Award—the Canadian equivalent of a Grammy Award—for best new artist. By that time Bublé's success had taken him all over the world, and the constant touring took its toll on his relationship with his then-fiancée, Debbie Timuss. Bublé's romantic troubles factored heavily into the recording of his sophomore album, *It's Time*, which reached stores in February 2005. "The CD is intensely personal and more unfettered than the tightly controlled, super-slick stylings of his first CD," Ken MacQueen wrote for *Maclean's* (February 7, 2005). In terms of song selection, Bublé again supplemented standards with more modern material, including swinging versions of songs such as the Beatles' "Can't Buy Me Love." The album also featured "Home"—an "aching, lonely lament," according to MacQueen—which Bublé cowrote. "A few of those songs, I just stuck her outside the studio," Bublé told MacQueen, referring to Timuss, "and I sang to her." (The couple broke up in 2005, and that same year Bublé began dating the British actress Emily Blunt.) In a review for All Music Guide, Latham credited *It's Time* with proving that Bublé "is much more than a flavor-of-the-month celebrity. Like his debut, *It's Time* mines the rich history of pop music as Bublé applies his own technique to classic standards and incorporates his Rat Pack sound into modern pop songs." Latham added, "He sounds pure of voice and pure of heart. Those are rare commodities in the recorded world and they, along with Bublé's talent and vision, help to make *It's Time* a wonderful listening experience." The album reached number one on the *Billboard* Top Jazz Albums chart and number seven on the *Billboard* 200; it topped the charts in Italy, Japan, Canada, and Australia. While the album represented an artistic step forward, Bublé was not satisfied with every aspect of it; during the recording sessions he butted heads with Foster and grudgingly agreed to use the arrangement of "I've Got You Under My Skin" made famous by Sinatra.

In November 2005 Bublé released another live CD/DVD, *Caught in the Act*. In 2006 he won Juno Awards for pop album of the year, album of the year, artist of the year, and single of the year, the last of which he received for "Home." *It's Time* also earned a Grammy Award nomination for best traditional pop-vocal album; it lost to Tony Bennett's *The Art of Romance*. The following year Bublé earned a Grammy nomination for *Caught in the Act*. Prior to the February 2007 ceremony, he told the Canadian Press (January 31, 2007) that he would not attend, since "I'll lose. . . . They might as well have already scratched Tony Bennett's name into the damn thing." Bublé's remarks were reprinted around the world, and the singer later apologized, insisting that his attempt at humor had been misinterpreted. "That was horrible," he told Tiffany Bakker for the Perth, Australia, *Sunday Magazine* (May 6, 2007). "I think it's a lesson in stupidity for me, to realise that some people don't get that I was joking." In the end Bublé's statement proved prophetic, as Bennett's *Duets: An American Classic* won the Grammy.

On May 1, 2007 Bublé released his third album, *Call Me Irresponsible.* The collection once again included songs associated with Sinatra, but with the new arrangements for which Bublé had lobbied. "I've Got the World on a String" became "breezy" and "Sylvester-the-cat sibilant," according to Gatehouse, while "That's Life" was transformed into a gospel-rock number. The album also featured songs by artists as diverse as Eric Clapton, Leonard Cohen, and Willie Nelson. On his version of "Me and Mrs. Jones," a 1972 R&B hit for Billy Paul, Bublé sang a duet with Blunt. He said that the idea behind *Call Me Irresponsible* was "growth without alienation," as Foster and Allen realized that fans would likely be expecting another album of neo-swing tunes. After debuting at number two on the *Billboard* 200 chart, the album reached number one in its second week. The sales may have been bolstered by Bublé's high-profile appearances on *The Oprah Winfrey Show* and *American Idol.* "Michael Bublé's third studio album is the Big One, in which the Canadian singer and upscale heartthrob emerges as a thoroughly contemporary pop traditionalist," Stephen Holden wrote in a review for the *New York Times* (May 14, 2007). He added, "This time Mr. Bublé, an endearingly cocky performer who likes to play the clown onstage, slaps on the after-shave, straightens his tie and shines his shoes for a heavy date, perhaps a marriage proposal. . . . If purists object to Mr. Bublé's cottony vocals, imperfect enunciation and sometimes casual phrasing, this is how it's done nowadays. The prerock tradition has acquired so many layers of cultural implication that singers who take it too seriously tend to sound more like curators than entertainers. In this night at the museum, the fossils come alive."

Call Me Irresponsible earned Bublé his first Grammy Award, for best traditional pop vocal album. (He was also nominated for best male vocal performance, for the song "Everything.") Bublé has reportedly written dozens of songs, and his desire to record his own material has led to disagreements with Foster. "It's testy," Bublé told Posner, describing his relationship with Foster. "But it's wonderful. I have the greatest producer in the world. We're both very passionate. I know what I want a song to sound like, and he's the same, and sometimes those visions clash. But I wouldn't be able to make these songs as good without him." Bublé has also said that he would like to be known as more than just a retro jazz singer, and he acknowledges that many critics have dismissed his music as schmaltzy. "I was born in '75, not '25 or '35," he told Bernard Perusse for the *Montreal Gazette* (April 18, 2007, on-line). So "pop music has naturally influenced me. One of the big fights that my manager and I have had is, 'Stop putting me on the jazz shelf.' Put me on the pop shelf. I'm a pop singer. I sing pop standards."

Bublé has been accused of not having a "filter"; his comments about Tony Bennett and the Grammys were not the first to cause controversy. He has also been described as fiercely ambitious—but also as one who cares more about professional success than about material wealth. As of September 2007 he did not own a car, preferring to get around Vancouver on a Vespa motor scooter. (He and Blunt shared a home in Vancouver before splitting up, in July 2008.) He is generous with his family; in 2006 he gave his parents $1 million for Christmas. His sisters each received $50,000. "Why not?" he told Posner. "They helped me out for years when I was struggling." In the fall of 2008, Bublé embarked on a 12-city tour of the U.S.; signed on as an ambassador for Campaign for BC Children, run by Canada's BC Children's Hospital Foundation; and became a minority owner of a hockey team—the Vancouver Giants of the Western Hockey League.

In 2009 Bublé released his third live CD/DVD, *Michael Bublé Meets Madison Square Garden.* That October he released his fourth studio album, *Crazy Love*, whose title is the name of a 1970 song by Van Morrison. The album, which debuted at number one on the *Billboard* 200 album chart after selling upwards of 130,000 copies within its first week of release, featured a cover version of that song, as well as contemporary takes on other classics, among them Arthur Hamilton's "Cry Me a River," Arthur Freed's "All I Do Is Dream of You," and Hoagy Carmichael's "Stardust."

—K.J.P.

Suggested Reading: *Akron (Ohio) Beacon Journal* Apr. 16, 2008; *(Australia) Sunday Herald Sun* IE p5 May 4, 2008; *Maclean's* p46 Aug. 27, 2007; (Toronto, Canada) *Globe and Mail* R p8 Sep. 22, 2007;

Selected Recordings: *Babalu*, 2001; *Michael Bublé*, 2003; *It's Time*, 2005; *Call Me Irresponsible*, 2007; *Crazy Love*, 2009

Selected Live CD/DVD Compilations: *Come Fly with Me*, 2004; *Caught in the Act*, 2005; *Michael Bublé Meets Madison Square Garden*, 2009

Courtesy of Little, Brown & Co.

Buergenthal, Thomas

May 11, 1934– Judge on the International Court of Justice

Address: International Court of Justice, Peace Palace, Carnegieplein 2, 2517 KJ The Hague, The Netherlands

Thomas Buergenthal, a judge on the International Court of Justice, the primary judicial body of the United Nations, is a preeminent expert in international human-rights law, a field that emerged to address some of the most horrific events of the 20th century. A survivor of the Nazi Holocaust, he holds a noteworthy dual perspective—as both a sufferer and a protector. "My Holocaust experience has had a very substantial impact on the human being I have become, on my life as an international law professor, human rights lawyer and international judge," he wrote in his memoir, *Ein Glückskind* (published in English translation in 2009 as *A Lucky Child*). "It might seem obvious that my past would draw me to human rights and to international law, whether or not I knew it at the time. In any event, it equipped me to be a better human rights lawyer, if only because I understood, not only intellectually but also emotionally, what it is like to be a victim of human rights violations. I could, after all, feel it in my bones."

Buergenthal has thus devoted his career to ensuring justice for the victims of human-rights abuses as well as to setting firm precedents intended to deter future perpetrators. Nonetheless, "I am no Mother Teresa. I am a lawyer," he told Tracy Thompson for the *Washington Post* (April 7, 1993). "In this kind of work, the worst thing you can do is show your emotions. You achieve so much more if you view this almost as a doctor dealing with a diagnosis."

Thomas Buergenthal was born on May 11, 1934 in Lubochna, Czechoslovakia. (Lubochna is in the central portion of what is today Slovakia.) His father, Mundek, who had worked as a banker in Germany, had moved his wife, Gerda, and the rest of the family to that Czechoslovakian village soon after the Nazi Party came to power, in 1933. Mundek bought a small hotel to run, and the family enjoyed relative security until 1938, when Slovak soldiers who had sided with Adolf Hitler commandeered the hotel. Buergenthal recalled in an interview posted on the Web site of the United States Holocaust Memorial Museum (USHMM), "We fled to Zilina, a nearby city, and lived there until after I turned 5. Then, my father took us across the border into Poland. On September 1, 1939, we boarded a train heading for a boat that would take us to England. But the German army invaded Poland that day, and our train was bombed. We joined other refugees, and walked north to [the central Polish city of] Kielce." A Jewish ghetto was established in Kielce in early 1941, and when it was liquidated, in August 1942, the Buergenthal family was sent to a labor camp. When young Thomas saw workers separating children from their parents, he approached the camp's commander in desperation. "They had us lined up on the field [and] the German commander of the camp was standing in the middle making the decision who was going to live and who was going to die," he told the USHMM interviewer. "[I] went up to [him], and I said, in German . . . to let me live, because I could work. And . . . what I saw happen in camps a number of times was that they were somehow shocked to find that somebody who looked very much like their own children, who spoke the same language the way their own children would speak, was there. They had, I think they believed a lot of their own propaganda. And he looked at me and said in German, 'Well, let's see,' and let me go. The whole thing may have lasted two seconds. And that's how I stayed." Buergenthal was made the commander's errand boy. "Basically, my job consisted of sitting outside his door and doing chores that he needed to have done," he said in the USHMM interview. "The job had great advantages, because I could hear what was going on and could report back, and I could also alert people to his coming . . . because if people were seen not working, they would be beaten very badly."

In 1944 Buergenthal and his parents were moved to the notorious concentration camp in Auschwitz, Poland. By early 1945 the advancing Soviet army had forced the German forces in Auschwitz to flee, and Buergenthal was sent on the infamous death march from the camp. He ended up, without his parents, at the Sachsenhausen camp, in Germany. Buergenthal, one of the few children to survive the ordeal, recalled to the USHMM interviewer: "We were marched out—

children at the front. Day one was a 10-hour march and tiring; we began to lag. Stragglers were shot, so two boys and I devised a way to rest as we walked: We'd run to the front of the column, then walk slowly or stop until the rear of the column reached us. Then, we'd run ahead again." Buergenthal had two frostbitten toes amputated once he reached Sachsenhausen.

In April 1945, as the German army was nearing total defeat, the camp at Sachsenhausen was evacuated, and Buergenthal was left in the infirmary with the rest of the prisoners who could no longer walk without assistance. He told the museum interviewer, "Finally, I went out [on my crutch] to look, because [of] all this silence. . . . And the Germans had left. Eventually the gates swung open, and Russian troops came in. And they began ringing the camp bell to say that we were free." He continued, "I didn't have any sense of the tremendous joy that other people must have experienced. I was alone in many ways. I think if my parents had been there it would have been different."

Mistakenly thinking that Buergenthal was a Polish Christian child, because of the language skills he had picked up in Kielce, a group of Polish soldiers (then under Soviet command) took him in. They gave him clothing, a pony, and—to his extreme gratitude—adequate food for the first time in years. (So malnourished was Buergenthal during the war that for years afterward, he made it a habit to eat before any major event or undertaking, unable to assure himself that another meal would be forthcoming.) Eventually, one of the soldiers, himself Jewish, discovered Buergenthal's religious and cultural heritage and arranged for him to be taken to a Jewish orphanage in Poland. There, a counselor was arranging for children to be sent to Palestine, and Buergenthal added himself to the list. He was not sent immediately, however, because as a Holocaust survivor he was needed for radio and newsreel interviews about the camps. While he waited at the orphanage, his mother, who had survived the camps in Auschwitz, Ravensbrueck, and Dachau, was in the British Zone in Germany, frantically looking for him. (His father had been executed just three days before the end of the war.) With the help of her brother in the U.S., Buergenthal's mother learned of his whereabouts via the Jewish Agency for Palestine, and in December 1946 he made the arduous journey from Poland to the British Zone, where he was reunited with her at a railway station near her hometown of Goettingen, Germany.

The two settled in Goettingen, where Buergenthal attended school and began to the overcome the trauma of the war. "I saw the fact that I survived as a victory, that we had won over them," he told the museum interviewer. He felt a sense of justice when some of the Nazi war criminals were tried and sentenced at Nuremberg, during the latter half of the 1940s. "The first . . . English words that I remember [were] 'by hanging.' I remember listening to the radio when they announced the sentences. And we were . . . listening to that and with sort of . . . joy." Buergenthal confessed to Tracy Thompson that initially, he sometimes fantasized about mounting a machine gun on his apartment balcony and shooting the German people who walked by, but said that over time he rose above those impulses: "The sense of detachment I have is forced. It's not that I don't feel the emotions. . . . But I came to the conclusion early in life—when I was 17 or 18, I suppose—that the only way to prevent another outbreak, to break this cycle of violence, was to stop hating." He has steadfastly maintained that detachment, telling the USHMM interviewer, "I haven't read any books about the camps. I can't. I can't go to movies that show it. I never could."

On December 4, 1951, at the behest of his mother, who remained in Germany, Buergenthal, then 17 years old, embarked on a 10-day ocean voyage to New York City. When the captain of the USS *General Greely*, the troop ship on which he was traveling, needed someone to make announcements in various languages, Buergenthal volunteered for that duty. Although Buergenthal meant to stay in the U.S. for just a year, to study and broaden his horizons, he never returned to live in Germany. (His mother ultimately settled in Italy, and he remained close to her until her death, in 1991.)

One of Buergenthal's uncles had immigrated, penniless, to the U.S. during the Great Depression and was still struggling to get by, but he welcomed his nephew to his home in Paterson, New Jersey. Buergenthal quickly distinguished himself in his studies and won a scholarship to Bethany College, in West Virginia. He earned a bachelor's degree in 1957, the same year he received his American citizenship. He went on to New York University Law School, earning his J.D. degree in 1960, and then to Harvard Law School, in Cambridge, Massachusetts, where he earned an LL.M.(master's of law) degree in 1961 and an S.J.D. (doctor of juridical science) degree in 1968, specializing in international law. In 1962, while earning his doctoral degree, Buergenthal began teaching at the State University of New York (SUNY) School of Law, in Buffalo, remaining in that post until 1975. Beginning that year he taught international law at the University of Texas School of Law; in 1980 he moved on to become a dean and professor of international law at the American University College of Law, in Washington, D.C.

In 1985 Buergenthal became the director of the Human Rights Program at the Carter Center, founded by former U.S. president Jimmy Carter and his wife, Rosalynn. Buergenthal stayed at the Atlanta-based center—a humanitarian organization focused on resolving world conflicts, preventing disease, eradicating hunger, and alleviating human suffering—until 1989, when he assumed the directorship of the International Rule of Law Center at George Washington University Law School, in Washington, D.C. During Buergenthal's academic career, he authored several seminal texts on international human-rights law and served on numerous editorial boards, including those of the *American Journal of International Law*, the *Encyclopedia of Public International Law*, and the *Human Rights Law Journal*.

Beginning in the early 1970s, Buergenthal was also affiliated with a variety of international groups, including the United Nations Educational, Scientific and Cultural Organization (UNESCO), created by the U.N. in 1945 to build peace through education and collaboration and to promote respect for human rights and the rule of international law. (In 1978 Buergenthal received the UNESCO Human Rights Prize.) One of the most noteworthy positions he assumed was on the Inter-American Court of Human Rights, on which he served from 1979 until 1991. (In the mid-1980s he was its president.) The court, established to interpret and enforce the American Convention on Human Rights, provided several landmark rulings, such as when it awarded compensation to families of those "forcibly disappeared" in Honduras. The court's unprecedented decisions held dictators, governments, armies, and police forces accountable for their actions. "You had the feeling that you were laying the foundations and mechanism for dealing with violations of human rights," Buergenthal told Marilyn Henry for the *Jerusalem Post* (June 15, 1999). "It was something that had [previously] seemed impossible."

In 1992, along with former Colombian president Belisario Betancur and former Venezuelan foreign minister Reinaldo Figueredo, Buergenthal was appointed to the U.N. Truth Commission for El Salvador, investigating and documenting abuses that had occurred during that country's 12-year civil war, which raged from 1980 to 1992 and claimed an estimated 75,000 lives. After conducting more than 2,000 interviews within six months, the panel released its report in March 1993, concluding that while leftist rebels from the Farabundo Marti National Liberation Front had been responsible for the assassination of government officials and the killing of innocent civilians, the U.S.-backed right-wing government had been largely responsible for the carnage, including some outright massacres. In 1981, for example, in El Mozote, hundreds of peasants had been slaughtered by U.S.-trained forces. The commission also documented the targeted killing of government critics, outspoken advocates of democracy, union organizers, and priests. It was revealed that the administrations of Jimmy Carter, Ronald Reagan, and George H. W. Bush had provided more than a billion dollars in military assistance to the El Salvadoran government, with the violence reaching its peak under the Reagan administration, whose officials repeatedly covered up war crimes and discredited those who tried to expose them.

The commission, which recommended a 10-year ban on government positions for implicated El Salvadoran officials as well as the payment of reparations, was guided by two principles, Buergenthal explained to Tracy Thompson: "That without a credible accounting of the truth, national reconciliation is impossible [and that] individuals, even those caught up in the fury of civil war and the orders of superiors, are responsible for their actions." Buergenthal continued, "The response to our report by the [El Salvadoran] high command was not that we were wrong. They called us 'insolent.' There's something wonderful in that word. We were insolent because we dared to tell them what they had done."

During his USHMM interview, Buergenthal discussed the importance of truth commissions, which are investigative and documentary bodies rather than criminal tribunals. "You simply cannot try people for 40,000 rapes, for example," he said. "So the truth commission to me is critical for the . . . peaceful evolution of a country that has gone through terrible things like El Salvador and Guatemala or South Africa have gone through."

In 1996 U.S. president Bill Clinton appointed Buergenthal to the U.S. Holocaust Memorial Council, which oversees the USHMM. (Buergenthal had previously been appointed to the council by Jimmy Carter but had stepped down after a year to work on the Inter-American Court of Justice.) Buergenthal was also a member of the council's Committee on Conscience, a think tank dedicated to the study and prevention of genocide. He chaired the committee from 1997 to 1999. During his museum interview he said, "The Committee on Conscience was something that was very close to my heart. Because I feel very strongly that the Museum shouldn't be just a cemetery. The Museum has to be a living organism that tries to make sure that these things don't happen again. And that means also speaking out . . . where other crimes against humanity and genocide are being committed."

During the latter part of the 1990s, a group of Holocaust survivors and heirs of the victims launched a case against Swiss banks, which they claimed had hidden behind the country's financial-secrecy laws to withhold the assets that European Jews, fearing for their futures, had deposited in the 1930s and 1940s. After a long and bitter battle, the Swiss banks agreed to pay $1.25 billion. In 1999 Buergenthal was charged with heading a tribunal to arbitrate the claims and match claimants to accounts. Although it was a painstaking process, Buergenthal, aware of the larger human-rights implications of his work, told Marilyn Henry, "It might have an impact on how people react in the future in similar cases—in Kosovo, Bosnia [for instance]. They could realize that they might get you even 30 years from now, in one way or the other. It shows that these crimes, offenses, violations, debts are something that come to haunt those who committed them. At least that is my hope." Buergenthal told Henry that the tribunal sounded "a 'built-in warning' that there is no statute of limitations on human-rights violations."

In 2000 Buergenthal was elected by the U.N. General Assembly and the Security Council to serve as one of 15 judges on the International Court of Justice (ICJ), also known as the World Court, based in the Hague. ICJ judges are elected for nine-year terms and may serve a total of three terms. Buergenthal originally filled another judge's unexpired term; in 2006 he began a term that will end in 2015. Because the court can have only one judge at a time from any given country, no other U.S. national will sit on the court during his tenure. The court's mandate is to handle disputes between member states, as well as to render advisory opinions on legal issues brought by international organizations. "For an international lawyer like me, this is a dream court and a dream come true," Buergenthal said during his museum interview. "It's like being on the Supreme Court of the United States. This is the court that determines what is and what is not international law. [For] those of us who believe in international law and practice international law, this is the Mecca to which you look."

When Buergenthal began his work there, the ICJ was dealing with issues relating to the North Atlantic Treaty Organization (NATO) bombings of Kosovo and to claims by the Democratic Republic of Congo that neighboring countries were aiding insurgents in the country. In 2003 he was part of a unanimous ruling that the U.S. had violated an international treaty by not notifying some 50 Mexican citizens held on death row in American prisons that they had the right to seek legal help from their own government. While President George W. Bush was reportedly aggrieved by that ICJ ruling, he ordered state courts to comply with it. (In 2008 the U.S. Supreme Court decided that Bush had exceeded his executive authority in doing so, however, and ruled that international treaty did not supersede individual state law.)

In 2004 the ICJ dealt with a high-profile claim by Palestinians against Israel's building of a massive wall in the West Bank. Buergenthal was the only dissenting judge in a ruling that concluded that the structure—which is called a "security fence" by Israel and its supporters and an "apartheid wall" by others—is illegal. Although the ruling represented an important victory for the Palestinians, the Israelis had asserted from the outset that since the court's decision would be non-binding and that they could count on the U.S.'s veto power if needed in the Security Council, they would continue building the wall whatever the outcome.

Buergenthal agreed with the court's major conclusions in the case of the wall and said that, Israeli and American wishes notwithstanding, international law is, in fact, applicable to the Occupied Palestinian Territories. However, he insisted that the court had not adequately taken into account Israel's need for security against Palestinian attacks. His dissent disappointed many observers. Ian Williams wrote for the *Washington Report on Middle East Affairs* (September 2004), for example, "The opinion is indeed a triumphant vindication of the Palestinian use of international law to maintain their position. It should put the U.S. administration on the spot: is international law something that only applies to others, or does it apply across the board?" Buergenthal has himself pointed out that there is an interesting distinction between the way the U.S. views international justice and the ways that other nations do. Whereas those from other countries tend to believe that international entities are the best mechanism by which to address such large-scale crimes as war and genocide and often do not trust their own nations' institutions to carry out fair trials, Americans tend to support the opposite view.

Buergenthal believes that international human-rights law has evolved since the Nuremberg trials, citing that at Nuremberg, the judges were from the victor states, whereas recent tribunals on Rwanda and Kosovo, among other places, were established by the U.N. Security Council and consisted of judges selected internationally. "That's progress," he told the USHMM interviewer, "and in a sense it shows that it's not only one group of the international community but the entire international community which has an interest in [justice] and has a part in it."

Buergenthal has won dozens of legal and human-rights awards, including the Pro-Humanitas Prize from the Federal Republic of Germany (1978), a first-place book award from the Inter-American Bar Association for his volume *Protecting Human Rights in the Americas: Selected Problems* (1982), a Distinguished Service in Legal Education Award (1987), a Wolfgang G. Friedmann Memorial Award for Outstanding Achievement in International Law from Columbia University Law School (1989), a Harry Leroy Jones Award for Outstanding Achievements in Foreign and International Law from the Washington Foreign Law Society (1990), a Human Rights Prize from the Jacob Blaustein Institute for the Advancement of Human Rights (1997), a Goler T. Butcher Medal for Excellence in Human Rights (1997), a Manley O. Hudson Medal (2002) from the American Society of International Law, an Alumni Achievement Award from New York University Law School (2005), a Louis B. Sohn Award from the International Law Section of the American Bar Association (2006), an International Humanitarian Award for Advancing Global Justice from Case Western Reserve University Law School (2006), and a Justice Award from the Peter and Patricia Gruber Foundation (2008).

Now a grandfather, Buergenthal married his first wife, the former Dorothy Coleman, a fellow Bethany College student, while he was in law school. They had three sons: Robert, John, and Alan. That marriage ended in 1981, and two years later he married the former Peggy Bell, a translator of Peruvian-British descent whom he met while working in Costa Rica.

—M.M.

Suggested Reading: *Houston Chronicle* A p31 Sep. 20, 1992; *Jerusalem Post* Features p9 June 15, 1999; United States Holocaust Memorial Museum Web site; *Washington Post* D p1 Apr. 7, 1993; *Washington Report on Middle East Affairs* p8+ Sep. 2004; Buergenthal, Thomas. *A Lucky Child* (2009)

Selected Books: *A Lucky Child*, 2009

Scott Olson/Getty Images

Burris, Roland

Aug. 3, 1937– U.S. senator from Illinois (Democrat)

Address: 523 Dirksen Senate Office Bldg., Washington, DC 20510

A longtime presence in Illinois politics, Roland Burris, a former state comptroller (1979–91) and Illinois attorney general (1991–95), campaigned repeatedly for public office after he last held a government position—nearly 14 years ago. He made a bid for the U.S. Senate, ran for Chicago mayor, and campaigned three times to become governor, but he was unsuccessful in each race's Democratic primary. On January 15, 2009 the wait ended: Burris was sworn in as the junior U.S. senator from Illinois, following a contentious battle over the seat vacated by President Barack Obama.

When Obama became president-elect, in November 2008, the responsibility to fill the vacated U.S. Senate seat fell to Illinois's governor, Rod Blagojevich, who allegedly tried in effect to put the position up for sale. The two-term governor was indicted for criminal misconduct for that act and was ultimately impeached by the Illinois legislature. Nonetheless, three weeks after his arrest, the indomitable Blagojevich appointed Burris to the open post. That Burris would accept a position from the accused governor, particularly after he had failed several times to gain elective office on his own, triggered outrage from Illinois citizens, and Senate Democrats initially refused to acknowledge the appointment.

Burris's predecessor in the Senate—who went on to become the first black U.S. president—has been hailed as a progressive, cohesive figure "who could transcend race and focus instead on more universal issues of economic disparities and class," as Peter Wallsten put it for the *Los Angeles Times* (January 6, 2009, on-line). By contrast, Burris has often openly blamed Illinois's racial tensions for his not being elected to more government posts. While Burris, until recently, had a relatively clean record, he has not been hailed as an exceptional public servant. "His service as comptroller and later as attorney general was viewed as competent but unspectacular," Perry Bacon Jr. wrote for the *Washington Post* (January 7, 2009, on-line). Bacon paraphrased Don Rose, a Chicago political consultant and an acquaintance of Burris's since the 1960s, as saying that Burris "struggled in elections because of a flat speaking style and lack of charisma that prevented him not only from connecting with white voters but also from garnering the kind of support among African-Americans that he needed to win statewide, even though many black politicians have backed his campaigns, including Obama and the Rev. Jesse L. Jackson." A fierce champion of civil rights early in his career, driven by his firsthand experiences with racism as a child and as a student at Southern Illinois University in the 1950s, Burris (who often refers to himself in the third person) has since taken moderate stances on such issues as government spending and taxes. As quoted by Gilbert Cruz in *Time* (December 31, 2008, on-line), Jackson called Burris "a sturdy, non-flash bridge-builder."

The youngest of three children, Roland Wallace Burris was born on August 3, 1937 to Earl L. Burris and Emma M. Burris in Centralia, Illinois, where he grew up. In the early 1950s Earl Burris took part in a campaign to racially integrate a local pool, and on Memorial Day in 1953, Roland Burris was one of the first African-Americans to swim there. He has often cited that episode as a formative experience that led to his career in public service. Burris graduated from Centralia High School and then enrolled on a scholarship at Southern Illinois University at Carbondale, where he played football and received his bachelor's degree in political science in 1959. He then studied for a year at the University of Hamburg, in Germany, before entering law school at Howard University, in Washington, D.C.

After receiving his J.D. degree and passing the bar exam, in 1963, Burris became a national bank examiner for the U.S. Treasury Department's Office of the Comptroller of the Currency—the first African-American ever to do so. For nine years beginning in 1964, Burris was a vice president of the Continental Illinois National Bank.

In 1973 Illinois's governor, Daniel Walker—who was later convicted of fraud, perjury, and misapplication of funds—appointed Burris as director of the state Department of Central Management Services. (It was in that post, in which he served until 1977, that Burris first worked with the future governor Neil Hartigan.) Burris made a failed 1976 run for state comptroller, in which he was defeated by the former state superintendent of education Michael Bakalis (who won 72 percent of the vote to Burris's 28 percent). Then, in 1977, he became the national executive director of Operation PUSH (People United to Serve Humanity), an organization founded in the early 1970s by Jesse Jackson in order to increase employment among Chicago's African-Americans. The following year, when Bakalis gave up his seat to make a gubernatorial bid, Burris successfully ran for state comptroller, defeating the Republican John Castle and becoming the first African-American to hold a statewide position in Illinois. He was reelected in 1982 and 1986. During that time, in 1984, he made an unsuccessful bid for the Democratic nomination for a U.S. Senate seat, coming in a strong second behind Paul Simon (who ultimately won the seat) in a four-way Democratic primary.

During his tenure as comptroller, Illinois's chief fiscal officer, Burris created monthly "Burris Reports," receiving credit from politicians of all stripes for improving the state's method of financial reporting. For his work in keeping taxpayers informed about how their money was spent, in 1986 he was one of only three to be named an outstanding financial officer in the U.S. by *Crain's Chicago Business* magazine. Meanwhile, Burris became increasingly critical of the Republican governor James R. Thompson's fiscal policies, accusing him of spending too much on prisons and not enough on education. In 1990 Burris himself announced a bid for Illinois governor. He had said to Rob Karwath and Thomas Hardy, writing for the *Chicago Tribune* (January 6, 1989), "We have to put someone into office who really understands state finances. Illinois in 1990 will need a strong fiscal individual to run this state and try to straighten it out after 14 years of fiscal disaster with Gov. Thompson." Only 11 hours after proclaiming his intention to run, Burris withdrew from the gubernatorial race and ran instead for attorney general. Burris cited as the reason for his withdrawal the decision by the incumbent attorney general, Neil Hartigan, to run for the governorship. "There was a higher-ranking Democrat with a shot at it," Burris said, as quoted by Thomas Hardy, writing for the *Chicago Tribune* (November 25, 1992, on-line). "I did not want to create a divisive primary, and I put the party above my own ambition." Burris was elected attorney general, but Hartigan lost to the former Illinois secretary of state Jim Edgar. As attorney general Burris was responsible for all legal matters pertaining to the state and for supervising more than 500 lawyers.

In his last year as attorney general, in 1994, Burris ran for governor of Illinois, an office that had been claimed by Republican candidates for the previous 16 years. Burris was criticized in the primary for not pressing a 1990 case against the Democratic U.S. senator Carol Moseley-Braun, the Senate's first black female, who was accused of not paying state taxes on a monetary gift from her mother, who had inherited the money while living in a nursing home and receiving Medicaid. Burris began the race for the Democratic nomination with slightly more campaign funds than the ultimate victor in the primary, Comptroller Dawn Clark Netsch, but Netsch was able to double her funds through donations from her husband. (She lost the race to the incumbent, Edgar.)

Burris was next urged by black activists to run an aggressive campaign against the incumbent Chicago mayor, Richard M. Daley. Entering the mayoral race in 1995 as an Independent, Burris accused the mayor of corruption and of indifference toward Chicagoans. While Burris was a passionate candidate, his campaign was severely underfunded, a recurring problem in his attempts to win public office. He dismissed the disparity between his campaign war chest and Daley's, claiming that supportive constituents would guarantee his victory. "This is not an ordinary election," he said, as quoted by Al Podgorski and John H. White, writing for the *Chicago Sun-Times* (March 26, 1995). "When you have a crusade, you don't need money." Podgorski and White wrote, "Known for a more low-key style of campaigning during his successful runs for state comptroller and attorney general, Burris has sparred with Daley like a street fighter and delivered speeches like a Southern preacher." Still, Burris lost the election, with 38 percent of the vote.

While Burris faulted "downstate whites" for not supporting his campaign for mayor, he received more than half of his support from white voters in his 1998 bid for the Democratic gubernatorial nomination—his second attempt to become governor. He lacked sufficient funds for television ads, which his rivals ran continually. To his further detriment Burris ignited controversy in February, when he was seen on videotape giving a speech in which he referred to his opponents in the Democratic primary—Congressman Glenn Poshard, former U.S. associate attorney general John Schmidt, and former federal prosecutor Jim Burns—as "nonqualified white boys." Burris later apologized, saying that he had made the comment after someone suggested he pull out of the race to make the Democratic ticket more racially balanced. (At that time whites made up about 70 percent of Democratic voters.) Some Democratic Party leaders criticized Burris for disloyalty. "His running for mayor in 1995 very shortly after losing the primary for governor, running as an independent, that has cost him a lot in terms of friends and financial support," the chairman of the Illinois Democratic Party, Gary LaPaille, told Pam Belluck for the *New York Times* (March 13, 1998). Burris lost the primary to Poshard.

When Burris made his third and final run for governor, in 2002, some predicted that he would be more successful than in either of his previous runs. Ample exposure in Illinois state politics (his campaign motto was "A name you know, a name you trust") had afforded him name recognition, and, perhaps more importantly, a $1 million campaign donation—26 times the amount of funding he had in 1998—bought Burris necessary television exposure. In the primary he faced U.S. representative Rod Blagojevich of Illinois; the former Illinois comptroller Michael Bakalis, to whom Burris had lost in his first run for that office; and the former Chicago Public Schools CEO Paul Vallas. As in his previous runs for governor, Burris's platform consisted largely of promises to revive the state's education system, by lowering school property taxes and replacing the revenue with state funds, without raising taxes in general. Some decried his plans as being too vague. Burris lost the primary to Blagojevich, then endorsed his candidacy in the general election, in which Blagojevich defeated Jim Ryan.

In 2002 Burris founded Burris & Lebed Consulting, LLC, which concentrated on government representation, public relations, and political and corporate strategies; he served as chairman and chief executive officer until the company dissolved, in 2008. Burris has served as counsel to Gonzalez, Saggio & Harlan as well as the Peters Law Firm. He has also served on the Board of Inland Real Estate Corp.

Following his election as president, on November 4, 2008, Barack Obama resigned from his post as Illinois's junior senator. A day later Burris began openly campaigning for that seat. "I'd say if there hadn't been a Roland Burris, there would not have been a Carol Braun or a Barack Obama," Burris had told the Associated Press earlier in 2008, according to Perry Bacon Jr. "I had to lay the groundwork . . . to perform in a high, statewide office." The person responsible for choosing Obama's successor, Governor Blagojevich, came under attack for allegedly trying to sell the appointment in exchange for bribes and promises of important positions for him and his wife; he was later brought up on federal corruption charges. Thus when Blagojevich appointed Burris to fill Obama's seat, most saw the appointment as tainted—particularly since Burris, through personal donations through his consulting firm, had given more than $20,000 to Blagojevich's campaign fund, and Burris's business received about $300,000 in state contracts while Blagojevich was in office. Many were unable to fathom why Burris still wanted the appointment, which other candidates had shied away from after the governor was arrested. Senate Democrats signed a statement vowing not to seat anyone appointed by Blagojevich, whose choice of an African-American senator was seen as a cynical move: many thought Blagojevich sought to win favor among African-Americans and thus save his political career, while making Senate Democrats reluctant to reject the appointment.

On January 6, 2009, exactly two weeks before the presidential inauguration, the 71-year-old Burris appeared on Capitol Hill, prepared to fill Obama's shoes. He was turned away by the Senate's highest-ranking members, Majority Leader Harry Reid of Nevada and Assistant Majority Leader Dick Durbin of Illinois, who argued that Blagojevich's appointment was not valid unless the Illinois secretary of state, Jesse White, signed his appointment document; on December 30 White had refused to do so. Initially, Obama, who had supported Burris in his primary run for governor in 2002, agreed with the Senate's decision. According to Roger Simon, writing for the *Chicago Sun-Times* (January 11, 2009), Obama said, "Roland Burris is a good man and a fine public servant, but the Senate Democrats made it clear weeks ago that they cannot accept an appointment made by a governor who is accused of selling this very Senate seat. I agree with their decision." The day before he went to Washington, on January 5, Burris—in an attempt to persuade officials that he was fit to be seated—had filed an affidavit to the special Illinois House panel investigating Blagojevich. Burris claimed that he had first mentioned filling the Senate-seat vacancy during a December 26, 2008 meeting with Blagojevich's attorney Sam Adam Jr., who asked Burris if he was interested in the position. Then, on January 8, Burris appeared again before the Illinois House impeachment panel; this time he testified that while he had not offered Blagojevich anything in exchange for the Senate seat, he had suggested himself for the position months earlier to one of Blagojevich's advisers, Lon Monk, and that he had also asked whether Monk had clients he could refer to Burris's consulting and lobbying firm. Burris declared that he had not received business from Monk and did not know whether Monk had disclosed his interest in the Senate seat to Blagojevich. (When Burris was asked if he spoke with Blagojevich's brother, Robert, or other close associates of Blagojevich's, Burris acknowledged only talking to Monk.) Burris and his lawyers petitioned the Illinois Supreme Court to order White to sign the document; the court ruled on January 9—the day after the Illinois House voted to impeach Blagojevich—that White's signature was not needed to seat Burris. Instead, White produced a form certifying that the appointment document was valid. In a decision attributed to pressure from the incoming presidential administration, which argued that the conflict over the Senate seat would deflect attention from more important issues and that no legal basis existed for preventing Burris's appointment, Burris was sworn in on January 15. Like Obama before him, he is currently the only black person serving in the U.S. Senate.

After less than a month in office, on February 5, Burris quietly submitted another affidavit. In it, he gave details about funding requests that Robert Blagojevich had made to Burris on behalf of the ex-governor's campaign. Burris said that Robert had called him three times about fund-raising and that Burris had then mentioned his interest in the Senate seat. Burris also wrote in his statement, as quoted by John Chase and Rick Pearson in the *Chicago Tribune* (February 14, 2009, on-line). He continued: "I was asked to raise money by the governor's brother and made it unequivocally clear to him that it would be inappropriate and pose a major conflict because I was interested in the Senate vacancy. I did not donate or help raise a single dollar for the governor from those conversations and would never consider making a donation through a third party." The U.S. Senate is conducting an ethics probe, and the Sangamon County state attorney John Schmidt is investigating Burris for "vague and contradictory information he provided under oath to an Illinois House panel that put together the impeachment case that resulted in the ouster of [governor] Rod Blagojevich," Dave McKinney and Chris Fusco wrote for the *Chicago Sun-Times* (April 18, 2009, on-line). In a phone conversation between Robert Blagojevich and Burris that came to light in May 2009, Burris voiced his concern about appearances and the need for discretion, promised to donate to Rod Blagojevich, and asked for consideration in connection with the Senate appointment. In July 2009, perhaps in a bid to placate the Senate ethics panel then investigating him, Burris, who had in January declared his intention to run for reelection in 2010, announced that he would leave Congress after his current term. Nevertheless, the ethics committee continued to investigate him.

Burris sits on several Senate committees, including Veterans' Affairs, Armed Services, and Homeland Security and Governmental Affairs. He supports abortion rights, Obama's economic stimulus plan, the removal of U.S. combat troops from Iraq, and an increase in U.S. military personnel in Afghanistan.

Burris's record of memberships and awards reflects his long run in Illinois politics. For 17 consecutive years (1979–95) he was named among the 100 Most Influential Black Americans by *Ebony*; he was named one of the Top Three Government and Financial Officers in the Nation (1989) by *City and State* magazine; and he was cited as being among the Ten Most Distinguished Alumni (1997) of Southern Illinois University, Carbondale, where he has served as an adjunct professor in the Master of Public Administration Program. He holds honorary doctors of law degrees from the National Louis University, in Evanston, Illinois, and Tougaloo College, in Mississippi, and he has been a member or chair of organizations devoted to business, arts, gaming, mental health, and civil rights, among other concerns.

Burris and his wife, Berlean (Miller) Burris, a former university administrator, live in Chicago. The couple, who married in 1961, have two grown children, Rolanda and Roland II, and a grandson, Roland. In his free time Burris enjoys barbequing, shooting pool, playing tennis, and dancing. He had a granite mausoleum built for himself and his family in Chicago's Oak Woods Cemetery. Inscribed on one wall is a long list of his accomplishments, etched below the heading "Trail Blazer."

—J.M.

Suggested Reading: *Chicago Sun-Times* p18 Mar. 26, 1995; *Chicago Tribune* (on-line) Nov. 25, 1992; *Los Angeles Times* (on-line) Jan. 6, 2009; *New York Times* (on-line) Mar. 13, 1998; *Washington Post* (on-line) Jan. 7 2009

Otto Greule Jr./Getty Images

Cabrera, Miguel

Apr. 18, 1983– Baseball player

Address: Detroit Tigers, Comerica Park, 2100 Woodward Ave., Detroit, MI 48201

On July 20, 2003 20-year-old Miguel Cabrera had a memorable major-league debut, hitting a game-winning home run for the Florida Marlins against the Tampa Bay Devil Rays (now called the Tampa Bay Rays) in the bottom of the 11th inning. During the rest of the 2003 regular season, Cabrera's .268 batting average, 12 home runs, and 62 runs batted in (RBIs) helped the Marlins clinch a National League (NL) wildcard play-off berth. He was also instrumental in his team's postseason success, batting .333 with three home runs and six runs batted in, helping his team defeat the Chicago Cubs in the NL Championship Series and advance to the 2003 World Series, in which the Marlins pulled off a stunning six-game upset victory against the New York Yankees. Following his impressive rookie season, Cabrera was highly touted as one of baseball's top young prospects, for his offensive ability and his uncommon poise. Since then he has exceeded expectations, compiling impressive offensive numbers during his relatively short tenure in the major leagues and establishing himself as one of the sport's best hitters. Cabrera is the fourth player in Major League Baseball (MLB) history—behind Hank Greenberg, Alex Rodriguez, and Albert Pujols—to have 50 doubles and 25 home runs before turning 24 and is currently the sixth-youngest player ever to hit 100 home runs. He is also the third-youngest since 1920 to have three consecutive 100-RBI seasons. (Mel Ott and Ted Williams are the first two.) Cabrera has also been voted to the National League All-Star team four times (2004–07). After the 2007 season Cabrera made headlines when he was traded to the Detroit Tigers of the American League (AL). In his first season with the Tigers, he led the league in home runs.

Jose Miguel Torres Cabrera was born on April 18, 1983 in Maracay, a city about 50 miles west of Caracas, Venezuela. He hails from a family with a long baseball tradition. His parents met on the baseball field. His mother, Gregoria (Torres) Cabrera, is a former starting shortstop for Venezuela's national softball squad. His father, Miguel Cabrera, was an amateur player for the Venezuelan team; the team also included the future legendary Cincinnati Reds player Dave Concepcion as well as several of Cabrera's uncles, one of whom (David Torres) was a minor-league prospect for the St. Louis Cardinals who managed a baseball academy in Venezuela. As young as age three, Cabrera developed a passion for the game, often accompanying his mother to softball practice, and honed his batting skills by swinging broomsticks at bottle caps. As a five-year-old he would often climb over his backyard fence to watch games at the adjacent baseball field, Maracay Stadium (later renamed after his uncle). When Cabrera was four, his parents enrolled him at his uncle's baseball academy. The boy displayed a natural ability from the start. "From the time he was little you could see certain qualities. All you had to do was correct him. It was like he was born with a glove on his hand," his mother told Juan C. Rodriguez for the Fort Lauderdale, Florida, *Sun-Sentinel* (February 22, 2004). By age 10 Cabrera was playing in a national youth league, and he expressed to his father a desire to pursue a career in baseball. Although his parents were supportive, they insisted that he remain in school. "I told him, 'For every 100 kids who want to play baseball, three or four make it,'" Cabrera's father recalled to Kevin Baxter for the *Miami Herald* (April 4, 2004). "'And I don't want you to be one of those who has no future. In case something goes wrong, at least you can fall back on your studies.'"

Following his uncle's death, from a heart attack, the 15-year-old Cabrera was trained by his father. During that period Cabrera began attracting the attention of international scouts from several major-league teams, including the New York Yankees, the Minnesota Twins, and the Florida Marlins. However, MLB rules prohibited scouts from signing players younger than 16. On July 2, 1999, after turning 16, Cabrera—whose family had developed a good relationship with the scouts Al Avila and Louie Eljaua of the Marlins—signed as a shortstop with the team for $1.8 million, a record amount for a Venezuelan-born player. A month prior to the signing, Cabrera had married his high-school girlfriend, Rosangel.

After spending the summer with the Aragua Tigers in Venezuela's Professional Baseball League, Cabrera, who played shortstop, appeared in 57 games with the Gulf Coast League Marlins, hitting .260 and driving in 22 runs. Toward the end of the season, the Marlins promoted him to the Utica Blue Sox, the Marlins' single-A, minor-league club in the New York Penn League; in eight games with that team, he hit .250 and had six RBIs. Cabrera spent the 2001 season with the Kane County Cougars, the Marlins' single-A team in the Midwest League. In 110 games with the Cougars, Cabrera had a .268 batting average and 66 RBIs while also committing 32 fielding errors. On the strength of his offense, Cabrera was voted to the All-Star Futures Game, an exhibition game showcasing top minor-league prospects from the U.S. and around the world. Cabrera, who served as the designated hitter for the international team, was hitless in his two plate appearances. In 2002, following another summer playing for the Aragua Tigers, Cabrera was promoted to the Jupiter Hammerheads, the Marlins' advanced Class-A team in the Florida State League. Despite his superior ball-handling ability, Cabrera showed limited range at the shortshop position, due largely to his increasing weight and lack of physical conditioning. As a result he was moved to third base. Learning a new position did not slow Cabrera down offensively. In 124 games with the Hammerheads, he batted .274 with 75 RBIs and also committed fewer errors (17) in the field. Also that year, he made his second consecutive appearance at the Futures Games, during which he hit a pair of singles.

Cabrera started the 2003 season with the Carolina Mudcats, a double-A team in the Carolina League, before being called up to join the struggling major-league club in late June of that year. At the time Cabrera was hitting .365, with 10 home runs and 59 RBIs. Cabrera made his major-league debut on June 30, during an interleague game against the Tampa Bay Devil Rays. After failing to reach base in his first four at-bats, Cabrera launched a three-run, game-winning home run in the bottom of the 11th inning. Cabrera was the third-youngest MLB player since 1900 to hit a walk-off home run in his debut appearance. (Billy Parker of the Los Angeles Angels and Josh Bard of the Cleveland Indians are the first two.) In August Cabrera replaced starting third baseman Mike Lowell, who was sidelined with a broken left hand for the remainder of the regular season. Cabrera established himself as one of the Marlins' most lethal offensive weapons. In 55 regular-season games, he hit .268, with 12 home runs and 62 RBIs, helping the Marlins clinch the NL wild-card spot and advance to the NL Division Series (NLDS), in which Florida defeated the San Francisco Giants in four games. Cabrera hit .286 in the series and also drove in three runs. In the National League Championship Series against the Chicago Cubs, Cabrera continued his torrid hitting, posting a .333 batting average and driving in six runs. His offensive output helped propel the Marlins past the Cubs in six games. Playing in their first World Series since 1997, the Marlins faced the New York Yankees, the heavy favorites. Baseball observers praised Cabrera for the poise he demonstrated in the fourth game of the series, in which he belted a first-inning home run immediately following a knockdown pitch by Roger Clemens. Although Cabrera only hit .167 in the series, he managed to drive in three runs for his club, which went on to win the series in six games. Months later Cabrera and the Aragua Tigers were crowned champions of the Venezuelan Professional Baseball League; it was the team's first title in 28 years.

With the return of Lowell, Cabrera was moved to the outfield during the 2004 season. Despite another position change, Cabrera played well in his first full major-league season, hitting .294 in 160 games, and ended the season ranked among the top 10 in the National League in RBIs (112) and home runs (33). Cabrera, who also had 31 doubles and scored 101 runs, also made his first All-Star Game appearance. The Marlins, who finished the season with an 83–79 record, were third-place finishers in the NL East division and did not advance to the postseason. Cabrera had better success with the Aragua Tigers, who captured their second consecutive title that year. Cabrera posted similar offensive numbers during the 2005 season. In 158 games he had 33 runs, 116 RBIs, and 106 runs scored while batting .323 and committing only seven errors for the Marlins, who again finished third in their division. For the second straight year, Cabrera finished in the NL's top 10 in batting average and home runs. He was voted to his second consecutive All-Star Game and also won a Silver Slugger Award, as one of the NL's top offensive outfielders.

Despite another impressive season, Cabrera's attitude and work ethic came into question following a series of incidents during the final week of the 2005 season. He was benched for one game after failing to show up on time for a medical appointment. Less than a week later he received another one-game suspension after he was late to a game against the Atlanta Braves. Cabrera's teammates held a closed-door clubhouse meeting to address his behavior. Following the meeting Cabrera told a reporter that he had nothing to learn from the Marlins' veteran players.

Prior to the 2006 season, the Marlins decided not to re-sign several of the veterans, including Derrek Lee and Hee Seop Choi, in an effort to reduce their payroll. After two seasons in the outfield, Cabrera was named the team's starting third baseman and continued to thrive offensively, batting .339 (a club record) with 26 home runs, 50 doubles (another franchise record), and 114 RBIs. He made his third consecutive All-Star appearance and won a second consecutive Silver Slugger Award, as the top offensive third baseman. However, Cabrera continued to clash with his teammates. In July 2006 he and Scott Olsen were involved in a physical altercation. Olsen yelled at Cabrera for not making an easy fielding play, and the two traded punches in the dugout before being pulled apart by their teammates. In February 2007, after earning $472,000 in 2006, Cabrera won an arbitration hearing against the Marlins and was awarded $7.4 million for the 2007 season. The amount was $700,000 more than Marlins executives had offered. "You're talking about a guy who's up in the top of his class, and rightfully so compared himself to players who are right there as well," the Marlins' manager, Larry Beinfest, told Rodriguez for the *Sun-Sentinel* (February 18, 2007). "We felt our filing number was indicative of that. Obviously, the arbitrators thought otherwise. It was a lot of money either way for a great player." During most of the 2007 season, Cabrera was among MLB's leading players in the categories of batting average, home runs, and runs batted in—known in the major leagues as the Triple Crown. He ultimately failed to finish first in any of those categories, although his offensive numbers were impressive. He ended the season batting .320, with 34 home runs, 188 hits, 79 walks, 119 RBIs, and 91 runs scored in 157 games for the Marlins, who finished fifth in the division, while also making his fourth straight All-Star appearance. During the 2007 season Cabrera became the third-youngest player to drive in 500 career runs. His 119 RBIs also made him the third-youngest player to drive in at least 100 runs in four consecutive seasons.

Months after the season ended, Cabrera became the subject of trade rumors, and in December 2007 he and Willis were dealt to the Detroit Tigers in exchange for a pitcher, outfielder, backup catcher, and three minor-league pitching prospects. Cabrera signed an eight-year contract for $152.3 million. At the time of the trade, he was the franchise's second all-time leader in home runs (138) and third all-time leader in RBIs (523). Following the trade many baseball observers instantly regarded the Tigers—whose lineup also included Cabrera's fellow power hitters Magglio Ordonez, Placido Polanco, Curtis Granderson, Gary Sheffield, and Ivan Rodriguez—as being among the favorite teams to win the World Series. "Make no mistake, the Tigers are going for it all, and if you want to do that in the American League, you have to be willing to gamble," Tony DeMarco wrote for MSNBC.com (December 5, 2007). In 2008, his first season in a new league, with a new team, and at a new position—first base—Cabrera showed up for spring training in better shape. "It's just too hard to ignore when just four years ago, he was a svelte 20-year-old nicknamed H-O-F because he was so obviously Hall of Fame material, and this season he's more fit for the H-F-O acronym as a Heavy Former Outfielder," Israel Gutierrez had written for the *Miami Herald* (June 17, 2007). As the Tigers' cleanup hitter, Cabrera thrived in his new environment, hitting .292, with 36 doubles, 127 RBIs, 180 hits, and 85 runs scored. He also led the league in home runs, with 37—a career high. The Tigers finished second in their division, with an 88–74 record, but did not advance to the postseason.

Before the start of his second season with the Tigers, Cabrera played for the Venezuelan team in the World Baseball Classic. During the 2009 season he again proved to be the Tigers' most prolific slugger, batting .324 with 34 home runs and 103 RBIs—fourth-, sixth-, and eighth-best in the league, respectively. In August of that year, Cabrera reached a career milestone when he hit his 200th career home run in his 1,000th career game, becoming the fifth Venezuelan player in Major League Baseball history to do so. (Tony Armas, Bobby Abreu, Magglio Ordonez, and Andres Galarraga are the other four.) Though the Tigers led the AL Central Division for nearly the entire year and seemed almost certain to advance to the postseason, they lost 15 of their final 26 games and blew a three-game lead in the division with four games to play. As a result, the Tigers were forced to engage in a do-or-die tie-breaker game with the Minnesota Twins to determine the division winner. Cabrera hit a double and a two-run homer during the game, which the Tigers lost, 6–5, after 12 innings. Earlier, during the final weekend of the regular season, Cabrera was arrested in connection with an alcohol-related altercation with his wife. A day before the tie-breaker game against the Twins, he issued a public apology for his behavior, addressed to the Tigers organization, his teammates, and fans.

Cabrera lives in Birmingham, Michigan, with his wife, Rosangel, with whom he has a daughter, also named Rosangel. He is said to practice Catholicism and Santeria, an Afro-Cuban religion. He is known for his sense of humor; during his stint with the Marlins, Cabrera's teammates often referred to him by the nickname "Blue," a reference to a character in the film *Old School* (2003), one of Cabrera's favorite comedies.

—K.J.P.

Suggested Reading: *Baseball Digest* p23 Nov. 1, 2005; (Fort Lauderdale, Florida) *Sun-Sentinel* A p1 Oct. 21, 2003, C p1 Feb. 22, 2003; *Miami (Florida) Herald* FM p3 Apr. 4, 2004; *Palm Beach (Florida) Post* C p1 June 24, 2003, BB p1 Feb. 15, 2004

Alex Brandon/AP Photo

Cao, Anh "Joseph"

(gow)

Mar. 13, 1967– U.S. representative from Louisiana (Republican)

Address: 2113 Rayburn House Office Bldg., Washington, DC 20515

On December 6, 2008, in an election in Louisiana that had been postponed because of a hurricane named Gustav, Anh "Joseph" Cao became the first Vietnamese-American to win a seat in the United States Congress. The victory of Cao, a Republican, surprised Republicans and Democrats alike, because the area he represents, Louisiana's Second Congressional District—which encompasses nearly all of the city of New Orleans and several of its suburbs—has a greater percentage of registered Democrats than all but 28 of the nation's other 434 congressional districts. In fact, Cao is the first Republican to serve the residents of Louisiana's Second Congressional District in the U.S. House of Representatives since 1891. The 42-year-old Cao, who came to the U.S. when he was eight, emerged from relative obscurity in New Orleans in 2005, when he played a major role in helping many of the Vietnamese-Americans whose lives were severely disrupted by Hurricane Katrina. His principal opponent in the 2008 election was the incumbent, the Democrat William Jefferson, an African-American, who had completed nearly nine terms in the House. Jefferson had won reelection in 2006 despite the public disclosure that he was the target of an FBI investigation and that FBI agents had found in his freezer $90,000 in marked bills; he won the

2008 Democratic primary despite his indictment by a grand jury the previous year on charges of bribery and corruption. His popularity among African-Americans notwithstanding, only about 12 percent of registered black voters went to the polls on December 6; they were outnumbered by white voters who, partly to express their disapproval of Jefferson's alleged illegal activities, cast their ballots for Cao and provided him with a margin of victory of 2.7 percent. Cao is one of only four nonwhite Republicans in the 435-member House, which represents a nation that is about one-quarter nonwhite. During the two decades before he entered Congress, Cao was a Jesuit seminarian and missionary, a professor of philosophy, a community activist, and an immigration lawyer. Within the Republican Party he is considered a moderate. He is against abortion and believes that the health-care system should remain market-driven, but his views on other social and economic issues, which developed in part out of his work in grassroots advocacy on behalf of poor and immigrant communities, set him apart from the right-wing core of the Republican Party. "I can be conservative on some issues and liberal on others," he told David Freddoso for the *National Review* (December 5, 2008).

The fifth of eight children, Anh Cao was born on March 13, 1967 in Saigon (now Ho Chi Minh City), in what was then South Vietnam. He added "Joseph" to his name because of his feelings of kinship with the humble carpenter whom the Bible identifies as Jesus's earthly father. "I'm a worker; I'm a hard-working worker," Cao told Jonathan Tilove for the New Orleans *Times-Picayune* (December 11, 2008). The first eight years of Cao's life coincided with what many regard as the worst years of the Vietnam War. According to his official on-line campaign biography, Cao "can vividly remember bombs exploding next to his elementary school." His father was an officer in the army of South Vietnam, the U.S.'s ally in the war. In 1975, as Saigon was being taken over by North Vietnamese forces, his mother secured a place for the eight-year-old Cao and two of his siblings on a military transport plane ultimately bound for the U.S. "She shoved me along with a bunch of relatives," Cao told Adam Nossiter for the *New York Times* (December 8, 2008). In the newly reunited Vietnam, his father spent years in prison, while his mother raised her remaining children. The whole family was reunited in 1991 in the U.S. Meanwhile, Cao and two of his siblings lived for several years in the care of an uncle, moving from Indiana to Arkansas to Mississippi before settling in Houston, Texas, where Cao went to Jersey Village High School. Liz Halloran reported on National Public Radio (December 10, 2008) that Cao was deeply affected by a letter he received as a nine-year-old refugee in Goshen, Indiana, in which his father wrote, "Son, you have to study hard, work hard and give back to your community and your country."

Cao earned a B.S. in physics at Baylor University, a Baptist institution in Waco, Texas, in 1990. Cao is Roman Catholic, and after his graduation he became a Jesuit seminarian and missionary. Fluent in French and Spanish as well as Vietnamese and English, he ministered to the poor in Tijuana, Mexico, and in Vietnamese refugee camps in Hong Kong (then a British territory and now part of the People's Republic of China). "I saw extreme poverty and the need for social change," he told Halloran. "At that time, I saw the fastest way to achieve that change was through political activity." That realization, along with his desire to have a family of his own, led to his decision against taking vows for the priesthood. In the early 1990s he studied theology in New Orleans and philosophy at Fordham University, in New York City, where he earned a master's degree in 1995. He has said that he was particularly inspired by the theological and philosophical ideas of the 19th-century Russian writer Fyodor Dostoyevsky and the existentialist philosophy of the 20th-century French writer Albert Camus. In 1997 he joined the faculty of Loyola University, in New Orleans, and taught courses in philosophy and ethics. He earned a J.D. degree from Loyola in 2000 and then became a legal associate with the firm Waltzer and Associates, specializing in cases involving immigration law. Earlier, while teaching in the mid-1990s, Cao had volunteered with Boat People SOS (BPSOS), an organization that helped Vietnamese-Americans with a range of legal, social, and poverty-related problems; he served on the group's board of directors from 1996 to 2002. After a brief period at Waltzer and Associates, he joined BPSOS as in-house counsel and opened a BPSOS office in New Orleans to assist the estimated 20,000 Vietnamese-Americans living in the New Orleans metropolitan area. The first immigrants to come there from Vietnam had supported themselves in their native land as fishermen; the local Catholic parish in New Orleans, Mary Queen of Vietnam, had sponsored them in the U.S. and had steered them to inexpensive housing in the largely African-American eastern part of New Orleans and nearby suburbs. The Vietnamese immigrants and their descendants became "a largely invisible minority in a city dominated by the racial politics of black and white," Ylan Q. Mui wrote for the *Washington Post* (December 14, 2008). Concurrently, in 2002, Cao opened his own law office, which continues to operate.

Along with hundreds of thousands of others, Cao and his family fled New Orleans after Hurricane Katrina hit the Gulf Coast, in late August 2005. When the Caos returned, in September, they found that their East New Orleans home and Cao's law office had been destroyed. The next month Cao began rebuilding his house and office, a task that took a year and a half to complete. Unlike a significant number of African-Americans, who could not or would not return to New Orleans after the hurricane, an estimated 90 percent of Vietnamese-

Americans came back within two years. Many of them rebuilt their homes and reopened their businesses despite getting little or no help from government agencies. Cao emerged as a leader in dealing with bureaucrats on behalf of his community. "Before the storm, I guess you could call us libertarians," Vien Nguyen, the pastor of Mary Queen of Vietnam church, told Eric Tang for the *Huffington Post* (December 10, 2008, on-line). "Our attitude toward government was, 'you don't bother us, we won't bother you.' But Katrina changed all that. We had a responsibility to speak out." Both the church and Cao's law office became hubs of community activism, with Cao pushing for the restoration of telephone service and other utilities, preventing the dumping of hazardous Katrina-generated waste in a neighborhood landfill, and providing legal assistance to people whose insurance companies had turned down their claims or had not responded to messages. The church launched a rebuilding and development project, and Cao was named to the board that oversaw it. (Despite such efforts, East New Orleans's recovery from the devastation caused by Hurricane Katrina is still far from complete.) During that period Cao's name recognition in his community greatly increased.

In 2007 Cao—impelled partly by a sense of duty that he has attributed to his religious beliefs—ran as an Independent for a seat in the Louisiana State House of Representatives. Although he failed in that bid, he decided to enter the race for the seat in the U.S. House of Representatives for Louisiana's Second District, which had been held since 1991 by William Jefferson, a Democrat. In 2005 the FBI had begun to investigate charges that Jefferson had accepted bribes to help a high-tech American company get clients in Africa; in 2006 the House of Representatives voted to remove him from the Ways and Means Committee (he voluntarily stepped down from the only other committee on which he sat), and in June 2007 a grand jury indicted him on 16 counts of bribery and corruption. Although Jefferson maintained his innocence and retained the support of many of his constituents, Cao believed that because of the congressman's mounting legal troubles, his winning a 10th term could no longer be regarded as a foregone conclusion. Republican Party leaders considered Cao a long shot at best, however, and they did almost nothing to support his candidacy. No other Republicans threw their hats into the ring for Jefferson's seat, so there was no need for a Republican primary election. On the Democratic side, five people in addition to Jefferson were to be on the ballot on primary day, which was scheduled for September 6, 2008.

In his December 2008 conversation with David Freddoso, Cao spelled out his platform: "Reform—reform of the image of Louisiana, good government, and accountability. Also, I've campaigned on coastal restoration after the hurricanes, and health care. . . . The whole question of conservative and liberal is really not that relevant in this race. For me, the emphasis, again, is in the rebuilding, the progress in the second district, and that's what I've been emphasizing." Cao also expressed his desire to be a progressive voice in his party, particularly regarding immigration, an issue on which the GOP has generally emphasized the importance of making U.S. borders impregnable, supported the immediate deportation of illegal aliens without hearings, opposed measures that would enable illegal aliens to gain legal status, and remained silent on the difficulties that drove such people from their native lands or those that they endure in the U.S. "When minorities like me hear that negative message, we really have to think what's going through these people's minds," Cao told Liz Halloran for NPR. "Even though we need to have security and prevent illegal immigration, we don't have to express it negatively."

Meanwhile, because of Hurricane Gustav, the Democratic primary had been moved back, to October 4. In that election Jefferson won a plurality rather than a majority of the votes cast, which made necessary a runoff election in which Jefferson faced the second-place winner, Helena Moreno, a former TV newscaster. That contest took place on November 4, the national Election Day. On that day Jefferson was victorious, despite his indictment and the confiscation by FBI agents of $90,000 in marked bills stashed in his freezer; he was apparently aided by the larger-than-usual turnout of blacks in his district, some 75 percent of whom came to the polls to vote for Barack Obama, the Democratic presidential nominee. During the weeks before the December 6 election, Jefferson condemned Cao as an "opportunist"; he told Frank Donze for the *Times-Picayune* (December 2, 2008) that Republican Party "operatives are reaching out to individual Republicans to give money to this man who they don't even know. . . . Where [Cao] can get the money is where he runs, and that's what is happening now." For his part, Cao described Jefferson as a compromised candidate whose legal troubles were hurting his constituents. In addition to his losing his committee assignments, Cao told Freddoso, "he's been a very poor representative. For the last three and a half years, nothing has been done by him. He has put through exactly one bill in the last three and a half years, and it was a bill to change the name of a post office. If you're talking about effective representation—well, no. There has effectively been no representation of this district at all for three and a half years now." On the day of the election, fewer than 67,000 voters came to the polls (about 100,000 fewer than in November) to choose from among Jefferson, Cao, the Green Party candidate, Malik Rahim, and the Libertarian Party candidate, Gregory Kahn. With 49.54 percent of the vote to Jefferson's 46.83 percent, Cao was victorious. "If not for Gustav, we would have been swamped by African-American voters on Election Day [November 4], and I would still be ignored," Cao admitted to Halloran.

Almost immediately the Republican establishment in Washington, reeling from their losses of the White House and the Senate and their failure to regain a majority in the House, hailed Cao's improbable victory as a hopeful sign for the GOP. The House Republican leader, John Boehner of Ohio, released a memo entitled "The Future is Cao" (December 7, 2008, on-line), in which—notwithstanding his silence during Cao's campaign—he wrote, "The Cao victory is a symbol of what can be achieved when we think big, present a positive alternative, and work aggressively to earn the trust of the American people. . . . The Cao victory is a symbol of our future." In his talk with Halloran four days after the election, however, Cao said, "I'm a little bit mad at the Republican Party because they, like everybody else, ignored us until the very end—until they saw that we might actually win. The message was, Why waste our time?" He has also said, as quoted by Benjamin Sarlin in the *Daily Beast* (September 16, 2009, on-line), "I would hope that . . . if the future truly is Cao, then we have to be approachable to minorities. We have to be approachable to the average American family. We have to be approachable to the average American. Unfortunately, I don't believe our message has been that. It's been somewhat anti-immigrant, it's been oftentimes too pro-business and anti-family."

On his campaign Web site, Cao had listed as his priorities ethics reform; recovery from Hurricane Katrina; coastal restoration, in part for purposes of protection during hurricanes; redevelopment of the port of New Orleans; economic recovery, including job creation; health-care reform; education reform; preservation of wetlands; and reduction of wasteful spending by the federal government. Cao was assigned to the Transportation and Infrastructure Committee and the Committee on Homeland Security, and later in his first year, he was appointed in addition to the Oversight and Government Reform Committee. The primary task of the last-named committee is to oversee and investigate federal programs. "This Committee has been the driving force behind Congress' investigation into what went wrong at all levels of government during Hurricane Katrina," Cao said, as quoted in Congressional Documents and Publications (October 8, 2009). Very soon after his arrival in Washington, Cao began focusing on getting funds secured for the redevelopment of his district in New Orleans; he also continued to speak out against the government agencies that had failed his constituents after the storm. In a move that was unpopular with his heavily Democratic district, he opposed president Obama's economic stimulus package, arguing that it would provide too little help for his district. On the other hand, to date Cao has been called one of Obama's few reliable Republican supporters in the House. Despite being pressured by the increasingly partisan Republican leadership to vote against the president's policies, Cao has cited Obama's attention to the problems in New Orleans and his pledge to help rebuild it as the main reasons for his support for the White House on several key votes and issues. "In the last eight months, for example, we have been able to channel out over $1 billion in recovery money to help to rebuild schools, fire stations, hospitals and so on," he told Alex Witt on MSNBC (October 15, 2009, on-line). "So there has been tremendous movement in the district in regards to recovery and we are very gracious to the president." Skeptics, however, suggested that Cao's backing of Obama stemmed mostly from his weaknesses as a Republican representative of a Democratic district. "Cao's willingness to play ball with the White House has a lot to do with his status as the most vulnerable incumbent of any party in 2010," Sarlin wrote. Sarlin also noted that Cao, perhaps hoping to impress his African-American constituents, sought membership in the Congressional Black Caucus. (As of late October 2009, he had not been invited to join.) While some observers have written Cao off, predicting that he will not be reelected, he has surprised many with his fund-raising prowess, having raised $365,000 in the second quarter of 2009 alone.

Cao's wife, Hieu Phuong "Kate" Hoang, worked as a pharmacist at a Walgreens branch until her husband's election to Congress. The couple have two daughters, Sophia and Betsy.

—M.M.

Suggested Reading: *Huffington Post* (on-line) Dec. 10, 2008; josephcao.house.gov; NPR.org Dec. 10, 2008; *National Review* (on-line) Dec. 5, 2008; *New Orleans Times-Picayune* p1 Dec. 9, 2008, p1 Dec. 11, 2008; *New York Times* A p18 Dec. 8, 2008; *Washington Post* B p2 Dec. 14, 2008

Charney, Dov

(dohv)

Jan. 31, 1969– Founder and chief executive officer of American Apparel Inc.

Address: American Apparel, 747 Warehouse St., Los Angeles, CA 90021

"America doesn't need another faceless, institutional apparel company," Dov Charney once said, as quoted on the Web site Young Entrepreneur (March 11, 2008). "They need an apparel company that gets it and does it right." Charney is the founder, president, and chief executive officer of American Apparel, which makes and sells T-shirts and other products and operates the largest clothing factory in the United States. All of American Apparel's operations, from design to manufacturing to marketing and distribution, take place in Los Angeles, California—making the company highly unusual at a time when an estimated 95 percent of the

American Apparel via Getty Images

Dov Charney

clothing sold in the United States is made in other countries. Founded by Charney in 1998, American Apparel is also very unusual because its sewing-machine operators earn, on average, $12 an hour, or about $25,000 per year—$10,000 more per year than the newly established federal minimum wage and far more than is earned by the vast majority of people who sew in factories, not only overseas but in the U.S. as well. Moreover, American Apparel sewers earn additional pay for working more quickly than their peers in the company. In contrast to the lack of employee benefits and the inhumane conditions that have led many clothing factories the world over to be condemned as sweatshops, American Apparel provides clean, well-lit, well-ventilated work areas and a host of employee benefits: company-subsidized medical and dental insurance; paid vacation time; English- and Spanish-language classes; citizenship-preparation classes; and much more. Charney has worked for the reform of U.S. laws regarding immigration and has given his employees, most of whom are Mexican immigrants, time off to participate in marches calling for such reform. He has also tried to keep American Apparel's environmental footprint as small as possible—for example, by using a rooftop solar-energy-generating system to cut down on fossil-fuel consumption, buying increasing quantities of yarn made from organically grown cotton, and recycling fabric scraps. Unlike nearly all other clothing companies, which rely on professional models for their advertisements, American Apparel uses as clothing models company employees and men and women Charney happens to meet on the street or elsewhere, and he himself often photographs them for the firm's ads. "Most importantly," according to the American Apparel Web site, "we guarantee job security and full-time employment; this is an anomaly in the garment industry, which has historically been dominated by seasonal work."

Charney has said that while his decent treatment of workers, use of high-quality yarn and innovative knitting techniques, and rejection of outsourcing make American Apparel products more costly than comparable items sold elsewhere, his company's rapid growth and profits demonstrate the excellence of his business model. (American Apparel is the nation's third-largest manufacturer of T-shirts, after Hanes and Fruit of the Loom.) Total wholesale, retail, and on-line sales increased from $132 million in 2004 to $545 million in 2008. In the latter year about 80 additional American Apparel stores opened, bringing the total number of stores, since the opening of the first one, in 2003, to 129 in the U.S., 34 in Canada, and 64 in other countries. In 2008 retail sales brought in $341 million, an increase of 62 percent over the previous year; retail sales in the first quarter of 2009 were bigger than in the same quarter in 2008, but those in the third quarter were 15 percent smaller than in the third quarter of the previous year. Nevertheless, the current economic downturn has affected American Apparel's retail sales less than those of many other businesses, largely because the firm's customers are mainly young people whose buying power has remained more or less unchanged, since few of them own stocks, houses, or cars and few are parents. "They're willing to pay a little bit more for higher-quality nonsweatshop products," Todd Slater, an analyst with Lazard Capital Markets in New York, told Maya Meinert for the *Los Angeles Business Journal* (January 5, 2009, on-line). "The prices aren't egregious. What you lose on price you more than gain in cachet, quality and speed." By "speed," Slater was referring to the time lapse between the concept for and design of a garment and its arrival in stores: one week for an American Apparel product, thanks to vertical integration (a system in which all facets of the business are under the direct control of a firm's top management), in an industry in which the average is three months. Speed has enabled American Apparel to respond rapidly to changing trends in fashion and to offer garments that reflect current tastes yet are "basic enough [that] they don't quickly go out of style," in Meinert's words. Except on the label, none of the items in American Apparel's line display the company logo.

In December 2006 American Apparel announced its forthcoming merger with the investment company Endeavor Acquisition, in a deal that brought Charney $382.5 million; the agreement was completed a year later, and American Apparel went public. Since then its stock price has dropped more than 85 percent, in part because of the firm's large debt load and to some extent because of several controversies that have swirled around the firm for several years. Those controversies are related to its print ads, which have been described as bordering on the pornographic and as demeaning to women; the presence of illegal aliens in the company's workforce; allegedly unrealistic production goals and the stressful conditions that have resulted; and charges of antiunion activity by management. Charney's sexually provocative dress, speech, and behavior in the workplace have also been called into question; four of his former female employees have sued him, on the grounds that he sexually harassed them and created an atmosphere in which they felt unsafe. One of the four lawsuits was dismissed and two have been settled out of court; the fourth remains active. In May 2009 the company paid $5 million to the filmmaker and actor Woody Allen to settle a suit involving American Apparel billboard ads that used a still photo of Allen from one of his films (*Annie Hall*) without his permission.

Such difficulties notwithstanding, Charney was named the man of the year by *GQ* magazine in 2003 and by the Los Angeles Apparel Industry, Fashion Industries Guild in 2004. Also in 2004 he won the Grand All-Star Award from *Apparel* magazine and the Ernst & Young Entrepreneur of the Year Award. He earned the 2008 Michael Award as retailer of the year, joining such past recipients as Calvin Klein, Oscar de la Renta, and Tommy Hilfiger. In surveys conducted in 2007 by Outlaw Consulting and in 2008 by Brand Keys Inc. and the Intelligence Group, respectively, American Apparel was ranked second among trendsetting brands, second among the top retail apparel stores, and eighth among the most trusted retail brands in the U.S.

A self-described "Jewish hustler," Dov Charney was born on January 31, 1969 in Montreal, Quebec, Canada. He has one sister and one half-sister. Charney's mother, Sylvia Safdie, whose parents were descended from Syrian Jews, was born in Lebanon and lived in Israel before immigrating to Canada; she is a painter and sculptor whose work is included in dozens of public, private, and corporate collections in Canada and overseas. Charney's father, Morris Charney (whose given name is misspelled as "Maurice" in many sources), is a native of Canada and a self-employed architect. Charney's maternal uncle Moshe Safdie is also an architect; he has been celebrated worldwide since Habitat 67, a housing complex that he designed, was built in Montreal in conjunction with the 1967 World's Fair.

Charney grew up in Westmount, a Montreal suburb. He attended an alternative elementary school, the Fine Arts Core Education School, which, on his Web site, he described as "fantastic." One of his teachers, Jim Stiller, he wrote, "had a profound influence on me. It was from him that I shaped a lot of my thoughts about discrimination and why it has a negative force on humanity." The hyperactive Charney suffered from a severe learning disability and, by his own account, was "functionally illiterate" when he graduated from sixth grade. Nevertheless, at age 10 he began to publish his own newspaper, called *What's Up*; containing stories by friends and classmates and photos that he shot himself, it appeared sporadically, with paid advertising that Charney solicited, and sold for 20 cents. Within a year it had several hundred subscribers. Its contents, Rebecca Rosenberg wrote for the *Canadian Jewish News* (June 5, 1980), included articles about such "grownup" issues as child molestation and inflation. According to Rosenberg, at 11 Charney was already "an avid news devotee, reading the newspaper daily and delaying the family's supper until he [had] viewed the televised evening news." His mother often expressed her views about world events; she used to tell her son that the two most serious threats to humankind were nationalism and religion.

For five years starting in seventh grade, Charney attended St. George's School, in Montreal. There, Rodney Walker, an English teacher, tutored him daily until he mastered reading and writing; another teacher, Hyacinth Young, awakened in him an awareness of "alternative thinking about race and politics," in his words. He earned a diploma from St. George's after he completed 11th grade and then spent a year at Choate Rosemary Hall, a prestigious boarding school in Wallingford, Connecticut. After his Choate graduation, in 1987, he enrolled at Tufts University, in Boston, Massachusetts. His major was American studies.

As a child Charney had come to love aspects of the U.S. and some of its products. During visits to his grandmother in Florida, he would buy items not available where he lived—certain brands of sunglasses, for example—and then he would sell them to his classmates. One year he became obsessed with American-brand T-shirts, particularly the Hanes Beefy. "Those Hanes T-shirts made me feel like the man I wanted to be," he told Josh Sims for *easyJet Inflight* (May 2004). While in high school Charney began buying T-shirts in the U.S. and reselling them in Canada. At Tufts he and a dormitory mate, Eric Ribner, launched their own business, with $2,000 of Ribner's savings; they would buy T-shirts that were on sale at K-Mart and elsewhere, screen-print them, and sell them out of their room. Within weeks, according to Charney, they had made a substantial profit.

So enthralled was he with the business that in 1991, after his junior year at Tufts, Charney dropped out of college and, with a $10,000 loan from his father, moved to Columbia, South Carolina, to set up a T-shirt manufacturing company. He would buy yarn in lots of thousands of pounds and have it knitted into fabric, dyed, cut, and sewn. His label bore the words "American Heavy." On his Web site Charney wrote that several South Carolina businessmen generously shared their knowledge of the design and manufacture of T-shirts with him. "Without a doubt, it was in South Carolina that I became a T-shirt expert," he wrote, "and I think today I am one of the most well-educated T-shirt men in the country." Despite what he learned, American Heavy went bankrupt in 1995.

Charney spent the next couple of years traveling in the U.S., scrutinizing people's T-shirts and thinking about the T-shirt business.

In 1997 Charney settled in Los Angeles. Short of funds, for months he lived in a friend's apartment, sleeping on a couch. During that time he began networking with people in the fabric-knitting and -dyeing businesses and with sewing contractors, most of whom were Korean immigrants. With two Koreans, Sam Lim and Sam Kim, he launched American Apparel in 1998. Even before they became partners, he recalled on his Web site, "the Korean garment community was vigorously supportive of my work. . . . Many suppliers extended me credit even after I bounced so many checks on them and continuously failed to pay them on time." American Apparel began as a strictly wholesale operation, manufacturing T-shirts that sold for between $3 and $4 per shirt—about double the cost of competitors' shirts. The higher price was connected to the quality of the fabric Charney used—softer and with greater stretch, and therefore more expensive, than others' fabrics—and a new knitting technique. Charney was determined to make a T-shirt that would be more form-fitting than the boxy-looking T-shirts being made at that time. Instead of hiring professional models for fittings, he would ask women who worked at a nearby strip club to try on American Apparel shirts. Charney told a reporter for *Bobbin* (May 2001), "We're focused on quality. We want to be the Starbucks—the gourmet T-shirt maker. Not everybody needs Starbucks. . . . Some people just want the sixty-cents cup. But some people want the best coffee, and will pay $3, $4, $5 for it. We're looking for those people who want a better T-shirt."

Initially, Charney had some of his products manufactured in Mexico, but his conscience—and problems with quality and communication—ended that brief experiment with outsourcing. "It wasn't feel-good and it wasn't viable," he told Linda Baker for the *New York Times* (December 14, 2003). "You think it makes you proud to pay someone $40 a week to make shirts all day? I spend $40 on a drink." Since then all American Apparel products have been manufactured in Charney's Los Angeles factory; indeed, all of the activities associated with his business take place there or nearby in a process known as vertical integration, which Charney believes is more efficient as well as more ethical than the practice of outsourcing. When David Greenberg interviewed him for the *Los Angeles Business Journal* (May 31, 2004), Charney said that the cost of producing a T-shirt in his factory was about 55 cents. "You take [production] to China and maybe you can cut that down to five cents," he said. "However, being in China—the elongated supply chain, the different time zone, the language barrier, the fact that you can't supervise production in a way you ordinarily could, the extra time it takes to react to different impulses of demand, the fact that you can't do shorter runs—all of those things involve a cost. I believe that my intangible costs are lower than [those of] my competition."

In 2002, having concluded that his business needed better organization, Charney hired Martin Bailey, an apparel-industry veteran, as American Apparel's vice president of operations. Among his first innovations, Bailey divided cutters and sewers into groups, each of which became responsible for producing a single type of clothing; each group competed with other groups to meet self-determined production goals and thereby augment their members' incomes. Within a few months the number of garments manufactured each day had grown from 30,000 to 90,000, with salary increases reflecting that rise in productivity. Since 2007 Bailey has served as the chief manufacturing officer.

In 2003 the Union of Needlework, Industrial and Textile Employees (UNITE) attempted to unionize American Apparel. At that time the competition among sewers in the company's 800,000-square-foot, pink-brick factory in downtown Los Angeles, and the resulting pressured, stressful atmosphere, as well as what Christopher Palmeri, writing for *BusinessWeek* (June 27, 2005), described as the "sexually charged culture" that Charney allegedly encouraged there, became targets of attack. During a six-month investigation conducted for Know-More.org (August 22, 2006), Bernard Dolan, a co-founder of that site, heard contradictory accounts from Charney and UNITE representatives about the conflict that ensued. Charney, for his part, contended that UNITE, as a way of forcing him to sign a contract that would have imposed a union on the workers, had threatened to arrange agreements whereby suppliers and buyers would refuse to do business with his firm unless it was unionized. He argued that because of the well-documented corruption that had plagued the union, the requirement that members pay union dues, and the exemplary working conditions that already existed at American Apparel, a union would do his employees more harm than good. On the other side, UNITE representatives complained to Dolan that American Apparel personnel had repeatedly obstructed their efforts to communicate with workers about the benefits of unionization and that a memo to employees from Charney had contained a veiled threat that unionization might cause the firm to go bankrupt. In November 2003 UNITE filed a complaint against American Apparel with the National Labor Relations Board. The following January the firm reached a no-fault settlement with the board, and in May 2004, after the company posted notices in the factory regarding workers' rights to join a union and Charney's "neutrality" concerning unionization, the case was dismissed.

According to Andrew Ross Sorkin and Michael Barbaro, writing for the *New York Times* (December 18, 2006), Charney "has gained a reputation as the Hugh Hefner of retailing." He has become famous, or notorious, for working among employees in American Apparel briefs at times, talking about sex in language that is generally considered obscene, and engaging in consensual sexual relationships with many of his female workers. The four former employees who sued Charney for sexual harassment constitute a tiny percentage of American Apparel's workforce, which now numbers 10,000, and Charney has described them as "disgruntled" and as having been dismissed for poor performance. Nevertheless, newly hired men and women must sign a statement that reads, as quoted by Jamie Wolf in the *New York Times Magazine* (April 23, 2006), "American Apparel is in the business of designing and manufacturing sexually charged T-shirts and intimate apparel, and uses sexually charged visual and oral communications in its marketing and sales activities. Employees working in the design, sales, marketing and other creative areas of the company will come into contact with sexually charged language and visual images. This is a part of the job for employees working in these areas." Regarding the charges that American Apparel ads feature underage girls and soft-core pornography, Charney has insisted that none of the women pictured have been underage, that sexual innuendos have driven clothing ads since the 19th century, and that American Apparel ads are no more provocative than countless ads that run in mainstream periodicals. As to the accusation that many of his workers are illegal aliens, Charney has pointed out that every person he hires must present papers documenting his or her legal status. He has acknowledged, though, that forged documents are not difficult to obtain. He has spent thousands of dollars of his own money in attempts to obtain green cards for some of his workers. In the fall of 2009, however, American Apparel announced that 1,800 employees—roughly one-fourth of its workforce—would be let go, because a federal investigation had found problems with the identity documentation of those workers. Among the general public, some praised the federal government for exposing apparently illegal workers, while others maintained that the government should focus instead on the exploitation of illegal immigrants by their employers.

Writing for *Inc.* (September 2005), Josh Dean described Charney as "a tightly wound dervish of energy." Charney has told interviewers that he does not believe in monogamy or marriage. He lives in Los Angeles and maintains a corporate apartment in New York City.

—T.O.

Suggested Reading:American Apparel Web site; *BusinessWeek* p88+ June 27, 2005; *Canadian Jewish News* (on-line) June 5, 1980; Dov Charney Web site; *Economist* p55 Jan. 6, 2007; *Inc.* p124+ Sep. 2005; (London) *Independent* p24 Dec. 23, 2006; *Los Angeles Business Journal* (on-line) Jan. 5, 2009; *New York Times* III p4 Dec. 14, 2003, B p11 Nov. 23, 2004, IX p1+ July 10, 2005, C p1+ Dec. 19, 2006; *New York Times Magazine* p58+ Apr. 23, 2006; *New Yorker* p70+ Apr. 24, 2000

Chestnut, Cyrus

Jan. 17, 1963– Jazz pianist

Address: c/o Avenue Management Group, Suite 407, 250 W. 57th St., New York, NY 10019

The pianist Cyrus Chestnut has distinguished himself as a prolific, versatile, and in some ways iconoclastic musician, happily and fearlessly integrating several genres and influences. He is known particularly for his ability to play soulful, gospel-infused music, which he traces to his childhood performances in the Baptist church his parents attended; listeners have frequently said that Chestnut "takes the people to church" when he plays. Before becoming a jazz star in his own right, Chestnut worked as a sideman in groups led by Jon Hendricks, Terence Blanchard, Donald Harrison, Wynton Marsalis, and Betty Carter; he has referred to his tenure with Carter's group, in the early 1990s, as his most formative period. In leading his own groups, Chestnut has won the most praise for his work as part of a trio, backed by a bassist and drummer. "As a leader, Chestnut has . . . almost single-handedly in a jazz generation dominated by horn players, raised the profile of the jazz trio . . . ," Tim Blangger wrote for the Allentown, Pennsylvania, *Morning Call* (October 4, 1997). "He's got the full sound of one of the old stride piano players, that fullness of tone," the legendary vocalist Hendricks told Nia Ngina Meeks for the Norfolk *Virginian-Pilot* (May 16, 1998). The music professor and jazz historian Mark C. Gridley said to Meeks that Chestnut "has a pretty solid rhythmic feeling. If you closed your eyes and didn't know it, you'd be fairly convinced you were sitting in an inner city tavern in the late '50s. '60s." While Chestnut, for all of his varied influences, is seen primarily as a player of traditional jazz, he has claimed not to feel limited by any rules of the genre and has called his music "kaleidoscopic." He said on the TV program *Tavis Smiley* (March 29, 2007, on-line), "I've always liked to stretch the type of music, 'cause being a quote, unquote jazz musician, you're supposed to do just certain things. And honestly, to keep the true tradition—great jazz musicians such as Miles [Davis], he pushed the envelope." Nate Chinen wrote for the *New York Times* (July 8, 2006): "Chestnut is one of jazz's most convincing anachronisms. His brand of crisp articulation and blues-inflected harmony evokes another era. . . . But unlike the typical nostalgist, who pines for the past partly because of a queasy discomfort with the present, Mr. Chestnut appears comfortable with his placement in time."

Gabe Palacio/ImageDirect

Cyrus Chestnut

Cyrus Chestnut was born on January 17, 1963 in Baltimore, Maryland, the son of McDonald Chestnut, a retired postal worker, and Flossie Chestnut, a city social-services worker. He grew up in Baltimore's Govans neighborhood. When Chestnut was a small child, his father played the piano to try to lull his son to sleep; Chestnut became enamored of the instrument's sound, and soon he was trying to play the piano himself. While banging on the keys, as he told Bob Young for the *Boston Herald* (November 16, 1994), "I'd just scream and holler. After a while my parents realized that I wasn't going to stop. They said, 'Let's teach him a bit and maybe his banging will be a little more pleasant to the ear.'" When he was five his father began teaching him to play, and he later took lessons from others. At six Chestnut started playing piano at the Mount Calvary Star Baptist Church, where his father was the organist and his mother the choir director. He has said that his skill at improvising and integrating jazz and gospel grew out of his having to accompany spontaneous passages in music. "It was my job to figure out what they were doing, and to follow them [musically] no matter where they went. I had to play behind them," he told Blangger. At nine Chestnut began studying classical music at the Peabody Institute, in Baltimore. In addition to the gospel music that filled his home and church, Chestnut was exposed to the popular music played on the radio, by groups including the Jackson Five, Parliament, the Spinners, and the Four Tops. He also discovered jazz. "When I was nine, I took my own money down to the five and dime store and bought a record called *Thelonious Monk's Greatest Hits* for $1.99," Chestnut told Mark L. Small for *Berklee Today* (Spring 2001). "That had a large impact on me. I didn't know who [the jazz pianist and composer] Monk was when I bought it. I just saw the picture on the cover of a man sitting at the piano, and I wanted it." Still, in the ninth grade at North Harford High School, Chestnut was initially more interested in playing junior-varsity football than in playing music. That changed, as he told R. J. DeLuke for the All About Jazz Web site (February 11, 2008), when "the band director came up to me and said he wanted me to play in the jazz band. I didn't think twice about it."

In 1981 Chestnut enrolled at the Berklee College of Music, in Boston, Massachusetts, which has served as a training ground for many of the country's top jazz musicians. He excelled at Berklee, winning the Eubie Blake fellowship, the Quincy Jones scholarship, the Oscar Peterson scholarship, and the Basie Award. Unlike many of his peers, who left the school to take jobs with established bands after getting what has been called the "two year itch," Chestnut acted on his parents' advice to stay at Berklee, graduating in 1985. He then returned to Baltimore and found work playing on a Caribbean cruise whose performers also included the jazz greats Dizzy Gillespie, Joe Williams, Tommy Flanagan, Maxine Sullivan, and Gerry Mulligan. "That was quite an experience for a young musician, being able to hang out with all of those people," Chestnut told Jack Lloyd for the *Philadelphia Inquirer* (April 19, 1996). After he returned to Boston, Chestnut began playing at hotels and found out that Jon Hendricks was holding tryouts for his group. He auditioned successfully, staying with the band from 1986 to 1988 and moving to New York City. "I felt like the green boy with them," he told Small. "I'm glad that I had the good fortune of being exposed to some of the great jazz pioneers." He also benefited from the larger music scene in New York, telling DeLuke: "I loved it at the time. I was able to hang out with some of the greats, able to go to a club and see Cedar Walton hanging out. George Coleman. All the cats, they used to just come and hang out." He spent the years 1988 to 1991 working with groups led by talented artists of his generation, including the saxophonist Donald Harrison and the trumpeters Terence Blanchard and Wynton Marsalis.

According to Chestnut, his most important apprenticeship was under the great jazz singer Betty Carter. He has referred to the two years and three months he spent as her pianist (1991–93) as being like graduate school. Often compared to the legendary drummer Art Blakey for her ability to scout and mold the best young musicians around, Carter was known as an intimidating and demanding bandleader. Chestnut had met Carter when he was a student at Berklee; she had come without a pianist to give a talk and perform at the school, and the students assembled in the audience suggested that Chestnut was up to the job of accompanying her. "She invited me up, and I was shaking," Chestnut recalled to Small. "She called 'Body and Soul,' and I thought, great, I know this one. This is going to be fun. As I went to the piano she said, 'Play it in G.' I had always played it in C. When I sat down and couldn't think of what the first chord would be, Betty started singing the chords to me. Afterwards, I went backstage figuring I would apologize and take my whupping like a man. She gave me a hug and said it was wonderful. I learned a good lesson that day about being nervous. You have to find a way of channeling nervous energy so that it can be of benefit to you." Chestnut's tenure with Carter was pivotal for him, because she demanded that her band members take risks—to create, rather than re-create, the music they played. "She was the one who planted the seed in me to always try something different," the pianist told Peter Kirn for *Keyboard* (November 1, 2006). Another lesson Chestnut learned from Carter, as he said to DeLuke, was to "win people over with skill, not with gimmicks and tricks. She'd always say jazz is about finding out who you are. That takes work."

Meanwhile, Chestnut had stepped into the role of leader for several recordings, including *There's a Brighter Day Comin'*, a gospel album released in 1989. He followed that up with several albums he recorded as part of a trio: *The Nutman Speaks* and *The Nutman Speaks Again*, both released on the small Japanese label Alfa Jazz in 1992, and *Nut* (1992) and *Another Direction* (1993), released on Evidence, another small label. While those albums had shown that Chestnut could interpret standards intelligently as well as compose original music, their impact was limited by low distribution. In the early-to-mid-1990s, just as Chestnut began to wonder whether he would ever break through, major labels began to revive their long-neglected jazz subsidiaries by signing gifted young artists. While some of the "young lions," as they were often called, were signed in the early 1980s, that first wave had been "driven by marketing," Matt Pierson, a producer at Warner Bros. Records, told Jeff Levenson for *Billboard* (April 2, 1994). "It was an age trend"—that is, labels had signed up musicians based on their youth as much as their talent. The second wave, Pierson explained, was "music-driven. Labels are looking for artists who have their own voice, who have stories to tell, which is the way it should be." One night, as Chestnut was playing for Betty Carter at New York's famed club SOB's, an executive from Atlantic Records—which was launching its Atlantic Jazz subsidiary and was looking for talent—saw him play and asked Chestnut for a meeting. "Not long after [the meeting], I was at a pay phone at a subway stop in New York checking my phone messages," Chestnut told Small. "There was one . . . saying Atlantic wanted to sign me. I just started yelling and jumping up and down in the subway."

In 1993 Chestnut, then 30, signed with Atlantic, left Carter's group, and recorded *Revelation*, again as the leader of a trio, this one including Clarence Penn on drums and Christopher J. Tomas on bass. *Revelation* was a critical and commercial success, vastly exceeding expectations to become the year's best-selling jazz release, with the *Village Voice* and the *New York Times* calling it one of the best jazz albums of the year. Critics and fans praised the gospel and blues sensibilities evident on the albums's 11 tracks, all but two of which were composed by Chestnut. The pianist has since become most recognized for his live and recorded work in the trio format. "It puts me up on the front seat and it challenges me," Chestnut explained to DeLuke. "A lot of times people, I think, will think that the piano trio is just a little country club thing for background music. [But] the Oscar Peterson trio. . . . Ahmad Jamal's trio. . . . McCoy Tyner's trio and Herbie Hancock's trio, the Bill Evans trio—they were not trios to be in the background. If you were to run with a quartet, quintet, sextet, octet, or whatever, a lot of times the pianist goes into the role of accompaniment until it's his time to solo. But in a trio, you have the opportunity to design everything."

In 1994 Chestnut released *The Dark Before the Dawn* on Atlantic Records, with Steve Kirby on bass and Clarence Penn on drums. He followed up that well-received record the next year with *Earth Stories*, also on Atlantic, an album that showed growth, maturity, and versatility, in the opinions of critics, and that further showcased his writing skills: most of the tracks were original compositions. That same year, 1995, Chestnut recorded with the opera diva Kathleen Battle; their chemistry, owing in part to their shared church backgrounds, was so strong that Chestnut joined her on an extensive tour in 1995 and 1996. Also in 1996 Chestnut released an ambitious, gospel-influenced solo effort, *Blessed Quietness: A Collection of Hymns, Spirituals and Carols*. "Chestnut has taken a group of songs that already mean a great deal to the listener, and attempts to share what they mean to him," Jason R. Laipply wrote in a glowing review on the All About Jazz Web site (October 1, 1997). "Putting his faith, heritage, and musical talent on full display, Chestnut proves himself the type of musician who is unafraid to strive for direct communication. And with his unique arrangements of several of the pieces, he proves himself a man unafraid to push towards the new." Meanwhile, Chestnut continued to lend his skills as a sideman to several projects, including Kevin Mahogany's 1997 album *Another Time, Another Place* and James Carter's 1998 record *In Carterian Fashion*, to name just two of the numerous albums to which Chestnut has contributed in his career. He also performed live with several prestigious orchestras, including the St. Louis Symphony. He boosted his exposure in 1996 when he appeared briefly in Robert Altman's film *Kansas City*, as a prohibition-era stride pianist modeled on Count Basie. (He was also featured—as himself—in the related Altman documentary, *Jazz '34*.) In 1998 the pianist released *Cyrus Chestnut* on Atlantic, widely considered to be one of his best recordings. Working with the legendary Atlantic Records producer Ahmet Ertegun, Chestnut had the chance to perform with top names in contemporary jazz, including a trio boasting Ron Carter on bass and Billy Higgins on drums, supplemented by Joe Lovano and James Carter on saxophones and Anita Baker on vocals. Critics praised Chestnut for his intelligent and soulful compositions, again pointing to his ability to integrate blues and gospel seamlessly into a jazz setting.

In 2000 Atlantic approached Chestnut with a project they felt would be commercially successful and could lead to a crossover market. *A Charlie Brown Christmas* featured guest vocals from Vanessa Williams, Brian McKnight, the Manhattan Transfer, and the Boys' Choir of Harlem. The album was intended as both a commemoration of the 50th anniversary of Charles M. Schulz's comic strip, *Peanuts*, featuring Charlie Brown, and a reinterpretation of Vince Guaraldi's classic jazz album *A Charlie Brown Christmas*, whose music is featured on the beloved TV special of the same name, aired annually since 1965. Chestnut told DeLuke that he jumped at the opportunity to make the record because Guaraldi's Charlie Brown music "was really my first introduction to jazz. Because at the age of six or seven, watching the Charlie Brown cartoon, I was listening to the music of Vince Guaraldi." Chestnut also told Lisa Simeone for the National Public Radio Show *All Things Considered* (December 16, 2000) that when he was 16, he was asked to provide entertainment during the intermission at a high-school jazz-band contest. "I had just learned 'Linus and Lucy,' so after playing a few makeshift improvisations, I started playing 'Linus and Lucy.' The audience went wild. And through the rest of my high school days, I was known as the boy who could play Charlie Brown."

Returning to original compositions in 2001, Chestnut released *Soul Food*, featuring a strong trio with Christian McBride on bass and Lewis Nash on drums, supplemented with guest appearances by Marcus Printup, James Carter, Wycliffe Gordon, and Stefon Harris. The recording was included on *Down Beat* magazine's Best Records of 2002 list and made it to the Top 10 on the jazz charts. Chestnut told Steve Graybow for *Billboard* (October 20, 2001) that although he remains steeped in the jazz tradition, he was pleased that the album was not promoted exclusively as a traditional jazz recording, an approach record companies have often used as a marketing hook. "I don't want to be imprisoned by jazz history," he told Graybow. "I want to build upon history and move myself forward."

Despite the success of Chestnut's albums for Atlantic, in the early 2000s the major record labels "began a retreat from jazz," as Andrea Canter put it for JazzPolice.com (February 16, 2006), and Chestnut was dropped from the label. Before long Warner Bros. signed him and suggested that he make a gospel record. "The norm is to do a record stereotypical of that genre," Chestnut said, as quoted in a review of the resulting album, *You Are My Sunshine* (2003), on JazzWorld.com. "People say I have all these various influences in my music—classical, soul, gospel, jazz, etc. I've always been on this continuous journey to try to find ways of how to get all these various influences working together, not separately, but working as a 'collective roundtable' . . . I wrote some tunes for this album in an effort to show my intent to write and play that goes far beyond the nomenclature." Chestnut also said, as quoted by Makkada Selah in the *Miami Herald* (July 16, 2004), that he wanted to go beyond some of the enduring, limiting, and mutually exclusive notions associated, respectively, with jazz and religious music: "Jazz has been labeled secular, but it is both religious and secular. The spirituals on my CDs are as standard as any Cole Porter tune." While critics praised the album, Warner Bros. did not renew his contract.

In 2004 Chestnut collaborated with Ali Jackson, James Carter, and Reginald Veal on *Gold Sounds*, a jazz interpretation of the music of the 1970s funk group Parliament. In 2006 he released *Genuine Chestnut* on TelArc Records, a trio recording with Michael Hawkins on bass and Neal Smith on drums, which was hailed as another tour de force on which Chestnut fused the various genres he had explored throughout his career. "There's just no way not to like Cyrus Chestnut," Rick Anderson wrote in an AllMusic.com review. "His playing is robust but tasteful, and he plays ballads with a liquid fluency; his original compositions brim with good cheer; he favors middling tempos that neither tempt him to show off excessively nor to bog himself down in extended, self-indulgent elaboration. [*Genuine Chestnut*] showcases all of his strengths."

In 2007 Chestnut released *Cyrus Plays Elvis*, featuring his interpretation of Elvis Presley songs, on Koch Records. He had come up with the idea a couple of years earlier, while recording a version of Presley's "Love Me Tender" with a singer. Realizing that no one had ever done a jazz version of Presley's music, and coming to understand the blues and gospel influences that had informed it, Chestnut began studying Presley's work and reinterpreting it in front of live audiences in 2006. "The thing about all the stuff Elvis did is it's so well loved," he told DeLuke. "He is so well loved. If somebody's going to come in and do an interpretation of it, especially if you're going to bring it into the jazz world, the project couldn't be so space age—throwing in the kitchen sink, so to speak—putting in everything and trying to be just so hip that nobody actually really recognized what it was. On the flip side, it couldn't be just a basic cover, because it would just be corny and that wouldn't work either. So I had to find a happy medium. . . . [*Cyrus Plays Elvis*] goes in interesting directions. It was honest." In 2008 Chestnut released the album *Black Nile* on the Japanese label M&I.

In 2009 Chestnut, who continues to tour with his trio, released a solo album, *Spirit*, on the Jazz Legacy label. Recorded in 2008, the album features solo piano covers of jazz standards and pop songs from the 1970s as well as interpretations of classic hymns and gospel songs. "It's clearly a labor of love for the always impressive pianist, still an underrated player in the general scheme of things," Michael G. Nastos wrote in his review of *Spirit* for the All Music Guide (on-line).

Chestnut lived in Brooklyn, New York, until 2006, when he moved with his wife, Ellen, and daughter, Jazzmin, to Catonsville, Maryland. He can be found in church on Sundays, often playing the piano. "I love playing the piano . . . ," he told J. D. Considine for the *Baltimore Sun* (February 25, 1994). "I hope one day to really master it—but only five minutes before I die. Just let me get there five minutes before I get out of here, and then I'll be fine."

—M.M.

Suggested Reading: AllAboutJazz.com Feb. 11, 2008; (Allentown, Pennsylvania) *Morning Call* A p39 Oct. 4, 1997; *Berklee Today* Spring 2001; *Boston Herald* p46 Nov. 16, 1994; Jazzworld.com; *Keyboard* Vol. 32 p32 Nov. 1, 2006; (Norfolk) *Virginian-Pilot* E p5 May 16, 1998; *Washington Post* G p3 Apr. 3, 1994

Selected Recordings: *The Nutman Speaks*, 1992; *The Nutman Speaks Again*, 1992; *Nut*, 1992; *Another Direction*, 1993; *Revelation*, 1993; *The Dark Before the Dawn*, 1994; *Earth Stories*, 1995; *Blessed Quietness*, 1996; *Cyrus Chestnut*, 1998; *A Charlie Brown Christmas*, 2000; *Soul Food*, 2001; *You Are My Sunshine*, 2003; *Genuine Chestnut*, 2006, *Cyrus Plays Elvis*, 2007; *Black Nile*, 2008; *Spirit*, 2009

Scott Olson/Getty Images

Chu, Steven

Feb. 28, 1948– Secretary of the U.S. Department of Energy; physicist

Address: U.S. Dept. of Energy, 1000 Independence Ave., S.W., Washington, DC 20585

Steven Chu is considered one of the world's leading experts on climate change and the development of alternative, environmentally friendly sources of energy. He first garnered attention in 1997, when he was jointly awarded the Nobel Prize in Physics for his work in developing methods to cool atoms using laser light. In December 2008 U.S. President-elect Barack Obama nominated Chu for the post of secretary of energy. Confirmed by the U.S. Senate on January 20, 2009, he is the first person of Chinese descent to occupy the post.

The second of three sons, Chu was born on February 28, 1948 in St. Louis, Missouri. He came from a family that valued learning. "Education in my family was not merely emphasized, it was our raison d'etre," Chu wrote in an autobiographical essay posted on nobelprize.org. "Virtually all of our aunts and uncles had Ph.D.'s in science or engineering, and it was taken for granted that the next generation of Chus were to follow the family tradition." His father, Ju Chin Chu, earned a chemical-engineering degree from the Massachusetts Institute of Technology (MIT), in Cambridge, where his mother, Ching Chen Li, studied economics. His maternal grandfather had also received an advanced degree in civil engineering, from Cornell University, in Ithaca, New York. (Chu's parents had originally planned to return to China upon finishing college but decided to settle in the U.S., due to the political unrest in their native country.) His older brother, Gilbert Chu, is a professor at the Stanford University School of Medicine; his brother Morgan Chu is a nationally known trial lawyer.

By 1950 Chu and his family had moved to Garden City, on Long Island, New York; his father taught nearby, in the New York City borough of Brooklyn, at what is now the Polytechnic Institute of New York University. From an early age Chu enjoyed constructing things with his hands. "I would be given for Christmas a model set of airplanes or boats and things, and I loved to put them together. I would ask my parents for things like Erector Sets," he said in an interview posted on the University of California, Berkeley Web site. "In many respects, my brothers and I are very similar, but in that respect, I seemed to love mechanical things in a way that was certainly nurtured by my parents, in that they said, 'Okay, he wants to do these things. We'll buy toys like that for him.' But my other two brothers didn't seem to like that."

Chu first developed an interest in science during his senior year at Garden City High School, when he took two advanced-placement courses, in calculus and physics. As a result of his A-minus average—well below family expectations—Chu, whose older brother was attending Princeton University and whose two cousins had been accepted to Harvard University, was denied admission to several Ivy League universities and enrolled instead at the University of Rochester, earning a B.A. degree in mathematics and a B.S. degree in physics in 1970. He then attended graduate school at the University of California (UC) at Berkeley, with the intention of becoming a theoretical physicist, but he developed an interest in experimental physics after conducting a series of laser experiments, under the supervision of Eugene Commins, his mentor.

After receiving his Ph.D. degree in physics, in 1976, Chu remained at UC Berkeley as a postdoctoral fellow until 1978. That year he joined the technical staff at AT&T Bell Laboratories, in Holmdel, New Jersey, where he met his future collaborator Art Ashkin, who was credited with developing the world's first methods of trapping atoms with laser light. At that time Ashkin and a group of fellow Bell scientists conducted several experiments, in which they explored how to cool an object by directing a laser beam at it.

Five years later, after funding for Ashkin's experiments was cut, Chu was promoted to head of the lab's quantum-electronics research department and collaborated with Ashkin on a series of experiments that involved manipulating atoms at low temperatures. "The [conventional wisdom] was first, you hold onto an atom; then you get it cold; and then you can do what you want with it. I said, Well, what if you reversed it? What if you cooled down the atom first? Don't hold onto it, but maybe in the process of cooling it down, it's going to hang around for enough time that you can have a chance of grabbing onto it,'" he said during the interview posted on the UC Berkeley Web site. "And so [after] a little calculation I said, 'Holy smokes. This looks like it's going to work.'"

In 1987, after nine years at Bell Labs, Chu accepted a position as a physics professor at Stanford University, in California, where he continued his research in low-temperature physics. The laser techniques he developed to cool and trap atoms and molecules earned him the 1997 Nobel Prize in Physics, which he shared with Claude Cohen-Tannoudji and William D. Phillips. While at Stanford Chu also helped establish the school's Bio-X program, which assembles scientists from the physics, chemistry, biology, and engineering fields. Chu also had two stints as chair of the Physics Department (1990–93 and 1999–2001).

In 2004 Chu was appointed the director of the Lawrence Berkeley National Laboratory, a U.S. Department of Energy national lab located at UC Berkeley. Under Chu the lab became an important center of research into alternative energies, energy efficiency, biofuels, and climate change. An advocate of reducing greenhouse gases, Chu has warned about the dangers of climate change and global warming, which he predicts will lead, if unchecked, to water and food shortages, resource wars, and chronic displacement of the world's poorest people. (The rise in temperatures due to climate change can lead to variable rainfall patterns. In developing countries it has led to decreased rainfall levels, reducing the water supply and making it difficult for crops to grow. In other areas it has resulted in rising sea levels and increased flooding, which can destroy the quality of water and contribute to waterborne diseases.) With the aim of avoiding such outcomes, he established the Helios Project, a new facility dedicated to researching low-cost solar and other sustainable, alternative, and renewable energy solutions, including advanced biofuels and artificial photosynthesis. Listing the facility's accomplishments, Steven Mufson wrote for the *Washington Post* (December 12, 2008), "The laboratory's scientists, including 11 Nobel laureates, have altered yeast and bacteria into organisms that produce gasoline and diesel, improved techniques for converting switchgrass into the sugars needed to produce transportation fuel, and used nanotechnology to improve the efficiency of photovoltaic cells used in solar panels, among other projects." Additionally, Chu is the founder of the Energy Biosciences Institute.

On December 11, 2008 President-elect Barack Obama nominated Chu to be the next U.S. secretary of energy; he was confirmed on Janaury 20, 2009 and sworn in on the following day. In that post he is responsible for implementing Obama's ambitious energy policy, which includes plans to invest $150 million over the next 10 years to create five million new jobs and to produce one million electric cars by 2015, among other projects. Chu has been called "America's first clean-energy secretary," and his mission, as Michael Grunwald described it for *Time* (August 23, 2009), is "part green evangelism, part venture capitalism and part politics." Both scientists and environmentalists expressed enthusiasm for his appointment, especially because past energy secretaries have often been, in Grunwald's words, "political loyalists with little energy expertise." Obama and Chu have listed several priorities, including promoting and institutionalizing energy efficiency, investing in wind, solar, and other renewable forms of energy, and providing incentives for privately funded research and development aimed at ending the nation's dependence on fossil fuels and making meaningful progress in the struggle to curtail global warming and climate change.

Chu has admitted to being politically naïve and has expressed frustration at the obstacles seemingly inherent in the day-to-day functioning of the bureaucracy in Washington. Some environmentalists have expressed the fear that clean-energy legislation will take a back seat to economic problems and the need to reform the nation's health-care system. Nevertheless, both the president and Chu have argued that the production of clean energy and measures to reverse global warming can create jobs and wealth. Chu has expressed optimism that a bill that requires cuts in carbon emissions will soon be passed and that the administration will lead the way in the fight against climate change.

A member of the Copenhagen Climate Council and a former adviser to the directors of the National Institutes of Health and the National Nuclear Security Agency, Chu has written or co-written more than 200 scientific papers and holds 10 honorary degrees. From his first marriage, which ended in divorce, he has two sons, Michael and Geoffrey. From his marriage to the physicist Jean (Fetter) Chu, in 1997, he has a stepson and a stepdaughter. —M.M.

Suggested Reading: *American Scientist* p22+ Jan./Feb. 1998; *New York Times* (on-line) Dec. 5, 2008; *New York Times Magazine* p14 Apr. 19, 2009; *Rolling Stone* p58+ June 25, 2009; *Science* p1774+ Dec. 19, 2008; *Washington Post* (on-line) Dec. 12, 2008

Alex Wong/Getty Images

Clinton, Hillary Rodham

NOTE: Earlier articles about Hillary Rodham Clinton appeared in *Current Biography* in 1993 and 2002.

Oct. 26, 1947– Secretary of the U.S. Department of State; former U.S. senator; former First Lady

Address: U.S. Dept. of State, Washington, DC 20520

Not long after Hillary Rodham Clinton was elected to the U.S. Senate in November 2000, observers began openly speculating about the likelihood that she would, one day soon, launch a campaign to become a Democratic presidential nominee. There was something of an assumption among party insiders that if she did decide to run, the brilliant and highly motivated former First Lady, whose husband, Bill Clinton, served as president from 1993 to 2001, would have little trouble securing the Democratic nomination. During her first years in the Senate, Clinton earned the support of New Yorkers by championing causes relevant to her adopted state, and she also gained the respect of her colleagues by working with Republicans to pass commonly sought legislation and deferring to senior senators on certain matters. By January 2007, when she announced her bid to become the first female president in the nation's history, Clinton had become one of the Senate's most successful fund-raisers, a leader in the Democratic Party, and a vocal critic of the policies of President George W. Bush. Clinton remained, however, a polarizing figure in national politics—a reputation she acquired during her eight years as First Lady, when she wielded an unprecedented degree of influence in national policy and was investigated for her involvement in several scandals that plagued her husband's time in office.

In 2008 Clinton took part in one of the longest, most divisive campaigns in the history of Democratic primaries. Though Illinois senator Barack Obama ultimately secured the party's nomination and was elected the country's first African-American president in November of that year, Clinton's historic campaign is not likely to be forgotten anytime soon. She conceded the primary race on June 7, 2008, telling her supporters, "As we gather here today, the 50th woman to leave this Earth is orbiting overhead. If we can blast 50 women into space, we will someday launch a woman into the White House." She continued, referring to the fact that some 18 million people had voted for her in the primaries, "Although we weren't able to shatter that highest, hardest glass ceiling, this time, thanks to you, it has about 18 million cracks in it and the light is shining through like never before."

Contrary to the advice of many of her supporters, after her concession Clinton endorsed Obama and campaigned energetically on his behalf before the general election. While the two had clashed frequently during the primaries, when Obama became president-elect, he nominated Clinton as his secretary of state. Confirmed by the U.S. Senate on January 21, 2009, she is the highest-ranking official in Obama's Cabinet, with primary responsibilities in the area of foreign affairs.

Clinton was born Hillary Diane Rodham on October 26, 1947 in Chicago, Illinois, the oldest child and only daughter of Hugh E. Rodham, who owned a drapery-making business, and Dorothy Howell Rodham, a full-time homemaker. Hillary and her brothers, Hugh and Tony, grew up in Park Ridge,

Illinois, a middle-class suburb of Chicago to which the Rodhams moved when Hillary was four years old. Clinton's natural leadership abilities attracted lots of friends at Eugene Field Elementary School, Emerson Junior High, Maine East High School, and the newly built Maine South High School, to which she was transferred in her senior year. Always a high achiever, Clinton maintained good grades, earned Girl Scout merit badges and DAR (Daughters of the American Revolution) community-service awards, played the piano, engaged in sports, and worked as a lifeguard. She was a member of the debate team, a participant in student government, a National Merit Scholarship finalist, and a member of the National Honor Society. As a teenager, the socially conscious Clinton organized baby-sitting services for local migrant workers. Through a program run by her youth minister at the First United Methodist Church, the Reverend Don Jones, Clinton attended cultural events with black and Hispanic youths from Chicago's inner-city neighborhoods. In 1962 Jones took his students to listen to a speech by the civil rights leader Martin Luther King Jr., to whom the group was introduced backstage.

Early on in her life, Clinton was, like her parents, staunchly Republican, supporting Barry Goldwater in the presidential campaign of 1964. After graduating in 1965 from Maine South High School in the top 5 percent of her class, which voted her the student most likely to succeed, Clinton enrolled at the all-female Wellesley College, near Boston, Massachusetts, where she headed the local chapter of the Young Republicans. She was led slowly leftward in her politics by the political turbulence of the late 1960s. Clinton campaigned for the Democrat Eugene McCarthy for president in 1968, worked to enroll more black students at Wellesley, organized the school's first teach-ins on the Vietnam War (which turned into antiwar protests), and wrote her senior thesis on poverty and community development. In 1969 Clinton graduated from Wellesley with a B.A. degree with high honors in political science. As president of the student government, she delivered the school's first student commencement address, immediately following a speech by Senator Edward W. Brooke, a liberal Republican from Massachusetts. After shocking her audience by castigating Brooke for the irrelevance of his remarks, she spoke passionately about the attitudes and future of her graduating class. "We are, all of us, exploring a world that none of us understands and attempting to create within that uncertainty," she told her fellow seniors. "But there are some things we feel, feelings that our prevailing, acquisitive, and competitive corporate life, including, tragically, the universities, is not the way of life for us. We're searching for more immediate, ecstatic, and penetrating modes of living." Clinton's words and her photograph were published in *Life* magazine.

Clinton next enrolled at Yale Law School, in New Haven, Connecticut, where she served on the editorial board of the now-defunct *Yale Review of Law and Social Action*. In the summer of 1970, she worked for the civil rights lawyer and Yale alumna Marian Wright Edelman—the first black woman to pass the bar exam in Mississippi—at the Washington Research Project, a congressional lobbying and advocacy group that later became the Children's Defense Fund. In that position Clinton interviewed the families of migrant laborers and reported her findings to a Senate subcommittee headed by Walter F. Mondale of Minnesota. Back at Yale, scheduled to graduate in 1972, she prolonged her education for a year in order to work at Yale's Child Study Center, where she helped research a book by Anna Freud, Joseph Goldstein, and Albert Solnit entitled *Beyond the Best Interests of the Child* (1973). During her final year at Yale, Clinton also performed legal research for the Carnegie Council on Children, specializing in the rights of children to education and medical care.

Meanwhile, in her second year at Yale, Hillary Clinton had met her future husband, Bill Clinton, at the law library. Well matched in temperament and in their commitment to social justice, Hillary and Bill became inseparable. Having spent the previous year in Oxford, England, on a Rhodes Scholarship, Bill Clinton was then in his first year of law school. The couple spent the summer of 1972 in San Antonio, Texas, where Bill ran George S. McGovern's presidential campaign and Hillary registered Hispanic voters. They graduated, in the same class, in 1973.

For several months after her graduation, Hillary worked as a staff attorney for the Children's Defense Fund in Cambridge, Massachusetts, while Bill taught at the University of Arkansas School of Law in Fayetteville. They kept in touch by telephone and occasional visits. In January 1974 Hillary Clinton moved to Washington, D.C., at the behest of John Doar, the special counsel to the House Judiciary Committee, who was in charge of the committee's inquiry into the possible impeachment of President Richard Nixon. One of only three women on the staff of 43 lawyers, Clinton was put in charge of legal procedures. She impressed her peers with her objectivity and her ability to distinguish advocacy from judicial guidance. Her colleagues found her to be energetic, emotionally supportive, and cooperative. When the impeachment staff was disbanded following Nixon's resignation, on August 8, 1974, Clinton was deluged with offers of high-paying jobs at prestigious law firms on the East Coast and also received an invitation to return to her post at the Children's Defense Fund. To the dismay of her friends and family, she instead joined Bill on the faculty of the University of Arkansas School of Law.

In the summer of 1974, Bill Clinton launched what was ultimately an unsuccessful bid for a seat representing Arkansas's Third Congressional District, a Republican stronghold. Hillary worked as his unofficial campaign manager and also taught criminal law, ran a legal-services clinic, and took on prison projects and advocacy work in Fayetteville, a quiet college town in the Ozark Mountains.

In August 1975 Bill surprised Hillary with a house and a proposal of marriage. When they were wed, on October 11, 1975, Hillary retained her maiden name. After Bill Clinton was elected state attorney general, in 1976, he and Hillary moved to Little Rock, the state capital, where she taught law as an adjunct professor at the University of Arkansas and directed the school's legal-aid clinic. In 1977 President Jimmy Carter appointed her to the board of directors of the Legal Services Corp., a Washington-based organization that provides federal funds to legal-aid bureaus throughout the United States. In that same year she founded and presided over the Arkansas Advocates for Children and Families, a nonprofit legal-advocacy group aimed at identifying the problems facing low-income children. Also in 1977 she was among the first female associates hired by Rose Law Firm, an Arkansas practice that focuses on business transactions and litigation.

In 1978 Hillary campaigned for Bill in his first run for governor, and he defeated his Republican opponent, A. Lynn Lowe, by a margin of almost two to one. Hillary, who had recently been named to the board of directors of the Children's Defense Fund, continued to work at Rose Law Firm after the election, thus becoming Arkansas's first-ever working First Lady. Additionally, Bill appointed Hillary chairperson of the Rural Health Advisory Committee, whose members tackled the problems involved with providing health care in isolated areas. In 1980, the same year she was made a partner at Rose Law Firm, Hillary gave birth to Chelsea Victoria Clinton, who was named for Joni Mitchell's song "Chelsea Morning." Also that year, when Ronald Reagan swept Republicans into office in a national landslide, Bill lost the gubernatorial election to Republican Frank White. After extensive campaigning in the interim years, he was reelected to office in 1982. Hillary took her husband's name that year, as part of a comprehensive image makeover. (She also traded in her thick glasses for contact lenses, lightened and tamed her hair, lost 15 pounds, and began dressing more fashionably.)

Bill Clinton was reelected governor in 1984, 1986, 1988, and 1990. During that time Hillary served in appointed positions in her husband's administration and worked in various other positions of public service. She served, for example, on the Arkansas Education Standards Committee, sat on the board of directors of the Arkansas Children's Hospital, worked for the Southern Governors' Association Task Force on Infant Mortality, and organized the state's first neonatal care unit, along with a helicopter service to bring emergency care to people living in outlying rural areas. She also served for a time on the boards of directors of the retail giant Wal-Mart and the yogurt company TCBY, among other such firms, resigning from them when Bill's political aspirations made it necessary. In 1988 and 1991 Hillary was listed among the most influential lawyers in the United States by the *National Law Journal*, and in 1989 she was ranked among the best business-litigation attorneys in Arkansas.

In 1991 Bill Clinton launched his presidential campaign and took an early lead in the polls, but he soon became the target of a barrage of criticism, when Gennifer Flowers, a former lounge singer, alleged that she and Clinton had engaged in a 12-year affair. Insisting that the campaign directly address the uncomfortable issue, which threatened to derail her husband's campaign, Hillary Clinton was interviewed, alongside Bill, by the CBS News correspondent Steve Kroft on the television news magazine *60 Minutes* on Super Bowl Sunday in January 1992. That extraordinary event constituted most Americans' introduction to Hillary Clinton. Grilled about whether he had betrayed his wife, Bill admitted that he had "caused pain" in their marriage but refused to be more specific. Hillary put an end to that line of questioning when she said that the public should respect the "zone of privacy" that surrounds the way any two people deal with their marital problems. "We've gone further [in discussing an issue of this nature] than anybody we know of, and that's all we're going to say," she declared. When it was reported that Flowers had been paid for her story, the Clintons went on the offensive, transforming the issue from a near-certain liability into an attack on the failure of the press to enforce the standards of responsible journalism.

Subjected to more intense scrutiny than any previous presidential candidate's wife, Hillary Clinton learned the danger of providing the media with sound bites that could easily be taken out of context. In a notable example, her response to Democratic presidential candidate Jerry Brown's attack on her professional record—"Well, I suppose I could have stayed home and baked cookies and had teas, but what I decided to do was pursue my profession, which I entered before my husband was in public life"—was widely interpreted as an indication of arrogance, despite the fact that she went on to praise all the choices available to women. Despite such blunders, on Election Day 1992 Bill Clinton won the presidency.

Most of the negative publicity that Hillary Clinton attracted derived from anxiety about how much power she would wield if her husband were elected president and how she would transform the role of First Lady. Early in the campaign Bill Clinton had boasted that he and his wife represented a "buy one, get one free" package deal. Shortly after he became president, he named her to the unofficial post of leader of his Task Force on National Health Care Reform, whose 34 working groups and 500 employees worked in secrecy from January 25 to May 30, 1993 to come up with a viable way to tame the costs of the nation's health-care industry—$800 billion annually at that time—

while expanding services and coverage. After Bill Clinton unveiled his health-care package in a well-received speech to Congress, on September 22, 1993, Hillary Clinton, in an unprecedented demonstration of political clout for a First Lady, drummed up support for the legislation in testimony before two House committees. In defending the president's health plan, which he made the cornerstone of his domestic policy, she impressed members of both parties with her command of detail, her poise, and, by combining flattery with persuasion at every turn, her public-relations expertise. The Clintons' bold reform plan, which was debated for months after its unveiling, would have provided health insurance to all Americans, including the 37 million who were uninsured and the 22 million who were considered to be "underinsured" at that time. The Clintons argued that by cutting wasteful spending through government regulation, raising taxes on alcohol and tobacco, and injecting "managed competition" into the health-insurance market, their plan to overhaul the nation's health-care system, which represented 14 percent of the United States economy, was superior to alternative proposals.

The plan attracted strong criticism from several sides, including those who resented the fact that Hillary Clinton, who did not hold public office, had been placed in charge of putting forth the package. It also worried many Americans when President Clinton's secretary of health and human services, Donna E. Shalala, testified before the Senate Finance Committee that 40 percent of then-insured Americans would be charged more for their insurance under the plan. Furthermore, small-business organizations objected to the fact that the new legislation would require all employers to pay 80 percent of their employees' health-care premiums. Support for the plan petered out, and many Democrats blamed its lack of success on the methodology the Clintons had used in presenting and advocating for the bill. Hillary Clinton eventually placed most of the blame on herself. "I think I was naive and dumb, because my view was results speak for themselves," she told Marian Burros for the *New York Times*, as quoted in the Toronto *Globe and Mail* (January 11, 1995, on-line). "I regret very much that the efforts on health care were badly misunderstood, taken out of context and used politically against the administration. I take responsibility for that, and I'm sorry for that."

Hillary Clinton also became embroiled in several investigations that would plague the couple for most of Bill Clinton's tenure as president. Among the most significant of those was the complex and far-reaching legal case known as Whitewater, so-called because it centered on the commodity and real-estate investments the Clintons had made in the 1970s and 1980s that were related to the Whitewater Development Corp., which the Clintons had formed in 1979 with their friends James and Susan McDougal. The issue first surfaced during the 1992 presidential campaign, when the *New York Times* published a story suggesting that the McDougals had heavily financed the Clintons in the Whitewater Development Corp.'s investment of river real estate, in what was supposedly a 50-50 partnership. The article also stated that the Clintons had claimed tax deductions for interest payments on Whitewater, when those payments came from the Whitewater Corp. itself. The Clinton campaign responded by producing a report showing that the Clintons had made large investments in Whitewater with their own capital and had lost tens of thousands of dollars as a result. The controversy continued, however. In 1993, after Bill Clinton had been sworn in as president, the deputy White House counsel and Clinton legal associate Vincent Foster committed suicide; some wondered if he had been murdered (a theory that was later disproved) and whether or not legal documents regarding the Whitewater business had been removed from his briefcase before investigators appeared on the scene. (Foster had recently filed three years of tax returns pertaining to the Whitewater investment on the Clintons' behalf.) Reporters also uncovered the fact that Hillary Clinton had made a $1,000 commodities investment in 1978 that had returned $100,000 within 10 months, a surprisingly high figure given the relatively modest amount invested. In the face of growing concern over Whitewater legal matters, Hillary Clinton held a press conference on April 22, 1994, in which she stated that she alone had been responsible for the trades that had earned her $100,000. However, she later admitted that Jim Blair—a friend and the chief attorney for the poultry producer Tyson Foods, which is headquartered in Arkansas—had advised her. She also denied having had anything to do with Castle Grande, a fraudulent deal that was made by the Madison Guaranty Savings & Loan, run by James McDougal, and that ultimately cost the public $4 million. She stated at the time that one of her associates at the Rose legal offices had handled most of the work with Madison. That could not be independently verified, however, as her billing records had mysteriously disappeared. In May 1995 the U.S. Senate opened its own investigation of the Whitewater affair.

In January 1996 Hillary Clinton's legal billing records suddenly surfaced, casting doubt upon her veracity, as they showed that she had put in 60 hours of legal work for Madison over a 15-month period. In June 1996, after 13 months of investigation, the Senate Whitewater panel concluded its probe and issued reports whose contradictions occurred along party lines. The Republicans on the committee accused Hillary Clinton and several high-ranking Clinton administration officials of obstructing justice, declaring their belief that Hillary Clinton was responsible for the withholding of her Whitewater billing records. That report concluded that the First Lady had been aware of the Castle Grande scheme, having held 22 conversations related to Castle Grande during her work with Madison. The report also alleged that she was responsible for the removal of incriminating evidence from Vincent Foster's office and had instructed aides to thwart an official search. The Democrats on the Whitewater panel, however, stated that there was no evidence of any wrongdoing on the part of the Clintons and denounced the Republicans' report as the product of a politically inspired witch hunt. On September 20, 2000 Robert Ray, the third independent counsel for the Whitewater investigation, noted in his final report, as quoted by CNN.com (September 20, 2000, on-line), "This office has determined that the evidence was insufficient to prove to a jury beyond a reasonable doubt that either President or Mrs. Clinton knowingly participated in any criminal conduct . . . or knew of such conduct."

Meanwhile, a further source of difficulty for the First Lady was the Monica Lewinsky scandal, which was connected tangentially to the Whitewater investigation. The independent counsel Kenneth Starr, who had replaced Fiske on the Whitewater case, decided to investigate the possibility that Bill Clinton had had a sexual relationship with Monica Lewinsky, a former White House intern, and that the president had later urged her to lie about the affair in her affidavit for the Paula Jones case. (Paula Jones, a former Arkansas state employee, had brought suit against Bill Clinton, in which she accused him of sexual harassment.) On January 17, 1998 President Clinton gave his deposition in the Jones case, during which he denied that he had had an affair with Lewinsky. On January 21 the *Washington Post*, among other publications, broke the story and revealed the existence of secretly recorded audiotapes on which Lewinsky gave details of the alleged affair. While Bill Clinton continued making denials to the media and his Cabinet, Hillary Clinton appeared on several talk shows, declaring that the allegations were the product of a "right-wing conspiracy" to topple the administration. On February 11, 1998, as reported by CNN.com (February 11, 1998, on-line), she predicted that the charge would "slowly dissipate over time under the weight of its own insubstantiality." On August 17, 1998, however, after months of investigation, President Clinton testified before a grand jury that, while he had not engaged in witness tampering, he had been involved in a sexual relationship with Lewinsky; he repeated the admission in a televised address to the nation. On December 19, 1998 Clinton was impeached by the U.S. House of Representatives on charges of perjury and obstruction of justice (thus becoming only the second president, after Andrew Johnson in 1868, to be impeached); he was acquitted by the United States Senate the following February. In *Talk* magazine, according to the BBC (August 1, 1999, on-line), Hillary Clinton defended her husband, noting, "Everyone has some dysfunction in their families. You don't walk away if you love someone. You help the person." According to the First Lady, her husband was guilty of a "sin of weakness, not a sin of malice."

Despite the scandals Hillary Clinton continued to undertake causes involving aid to children and health-care reform. In May 1995 she persuaded the president to appoint an advisory committee on Persian Gulf War–related illnesses. In 1997 she played leading roles in both the White House Conference on Early Childhood Development and Learning and the White House Conference on Child Care. The latter played a major role in the development of the president's Children's Health Insurance Program. The First Lady was also active in helping to pass the Family and Medical Leave Act and the Adoption and Safe Family Act of 1997, the latter of which made for easier transitions for foster children moving to permanent homes and increased the number of adoptions. Beginning in 1995 Hillary Clinton wrote a weekly syndicated newspaper column that appeared in about 100 newspapers nationwide, called "Talking It Over," in which she shared observations she had made as First Lady. In 1996 Clinton published her first book, *It Takes a Village and Other Lessons Children Teach Us*, the proceeds from which went to children's hospitals. A best-seller, *It Takes a Village* focuses on the role that society can play in raising children.

The negative publicity Hillary Clinton received during the Whitewater investigation was largely offset by the Lewinsky scandal, by the end of which many Americans had come to view her sympathetically as the wronged wife who had nonetheless stood by her husband. In the summer of 1999, after U.S. senator Daniel Patrick Moynihan of New York announced that he would not run for another term, Hillary Clinton began to prepare a campaign to succeed him. Many observers predicted that she would be unable to rise above her scandal-tainted past, the fact that she was not from New York State, or the popularity of her likely opponent, New York City mayor Rudolph Giuliani. Clinton, however, studied the state and its politics and eventually gained the trust of New York residents by embarking on an extensive tour, traveling to remote parts of the state, listening to voters' concerns, and fielding their questions. In early January 2000 Hillary Clinton moved into a $1.7 million house in Chappaqua, in Westchester County, New York, to meet the residency requirements for running for office in New York State. On February 6 she officially announced her candidacy, marking the first time a First Lady had run for office. Calling herself a "new Democrat," she made improving education a major issue of her campaign and also promised legislation that would help boost the economy in Upstate New York. On May 16, 2000 she accepted the nomination of the New York State Democratic Party for United States senator.

Days later, Mayor Giuliani dropped out of the race to focus on his treatment for prostate cancer, and the New York congressman Rick Lazio emerged as the Republican Senate nominee. Lazio's constant attacks on Clinton's character ultimately backfired, and after earning 55 percent of the vote in the November 2000 election, Clinton was sworn in as a U.S. senator in January 2001.

Though many expected Clinton to cause a stir by immediately proposing legislation of national significance, the former First Lady spent the first few months of her Senate career focusing on topics of concern to New York State residents and deferring to ranking senators on more major issues. On February 13, 2001 she made her first address from the floor of the Senate, offering several moderate health-care initiatives. By mid-April she had introduced 10 bills, most of them part of an economic package for Upstate New York. In June 2001, taking her first stance on a major issue, she introduced legislation to ban racial profiling in routine police investigations and to end arrest quotas. By the end of 2001, she had introduced 70 pieces of legislation, among them bills to create a nursing corps, reduce arsenic levels in drinking water, and help people injured by landmines.

In the days following the terrorist attacks on the United States on September 11, 2001, Hillary Clinton, along with New York's senior senator, Charles E. Schumer, led the fight for the allocation of $20 billion in federal disaster aid for New York City. On October 11, 2002 Clinton—and 22 other Democrats—voted for the Senate resolution that gave President George W. Bush the authority to order U.S. armed forces to attack Iraq when he determined that such action was necessary. The vote aroused heated controversy regarding its constitutionality and its effect on international relations.

During her first term Clinton served on the Senate Budget Committee, the Senate Environment and Public Works Committee, the Senate Health, Education, Labor and Pensions Committee, and the Senate Armed Services Committee. She was soon being recognized as one of the Senate's most successful fund-raisers, hosting events for Democratic candidates at her Washington residence and supporting Democrats in races across the country through her political action committee (PAC). She was also influential in setting up a new liberal think tank called the Center for American Progress. In 2003 Clinton assumed the chairmanship of the Senate's Democratic Steering Committee, the group that sets the Democratic agenda, thus solidifying her place in the Senate's Democratic leadership. Many observers noted that her actions seemed to be aimed at setting the groundwork for a possible presidential run in 2004 or 2008.

In June 2003 Clinton published a best-selling autobiography, *Living History*, which focused on her eight years as First Lady. The volume received mixed reviews from critics, who took issue with what they saw as Clinton's lack of candor about controversial subjects, including the Lewinsky matter. "For all its traffic in intimate material—the scandals, the early-morning bedroom encounters, the self-doubts, *Living History* is not, finally, a recording of a life; it is a political act," Elizabeth Kolbert wrote for the *New Yorker* (October 12, 2003). "It offers an account of Clinton's actions that, however bowdlerized, she can refer back to if, as seems almost inevitable, questions about them arise on a future occasion." Indeed, most reviewers saw the book as an effort to set the record straight in preparation for a presidential campaign. A year later Bill Clinton published his best-selling, 1,000-page memoir, *My Life*. In it the former president admitted to marital infidelities and cast his wife as an innocent bystander in the Lewinsky affair and other scandals.

Reelected to the Senate by a wide margin in 2006, Clinton grew increasingly more outspoken in her criticism of the Bush administration's handling of the economy, the Iraq war, and domestic security. Encouraged by many of her Democratic colleagues as well as by her husband, on January 20, 2007 Clinton announced that she was forming an exploratory committee for a presidential run. In the beginning of the primary race, which initially included Joseph Biden, John Edwards, and Bill Richardson and four other Democratic candidates, there was an air of inevitability surrounding the notion that Clinton would become the party's nominee. For the first half of 2007, she was the uncontested frontrunner; she performed expertly in the Democratic debates and consistently led all of her opponents in polls. In October 2007 a national poll reported by Fox News (October 3, 2007, on-line) showed Clinton leading her closest competitor, the Illinois senator Barack Obama, who had risen to national fame with a landmark speech at the 2004 Democratic National Convention, by a margin of 33 points.

The ideologies and proposed policies of the two candidates, each of whom claimed among the most liberal voting records in the Senate, were quite similar. Their proposals differed most significantly, according to pundits, in the area of health care. Both Clinton's and Obama's plans included measures to make insurance more affordable for lower-income Americans, required private insurers to offer policies to everyone regardless of their medical history, and allowed people the choice to buy government-offered insurance. Clinton's plan, however, required everyone to buy insurance, while Obama's plan didn't. Though Obama argued that people would willingly purchase insurance if it were made affordable, Clinton pointed to evidence showing that a mandate was necessary for universal coverage to be achieved.

The two differed more widely in style and overall message. Obama's simple mantra of "change," his relative newness to the national political stage, and his impassioned speeches appealed to voters who disapproved of President George W. Bush and the overall course of the country. Clinton's campaign, headed by her chief strategist, Mark Penn, endeavored to portray Clinton as the more experienced and able candidate, while being careful not to align her with the policies and perspectives of the Bush administration.

On January 3, 2008 Obama won the Iowa caucuses, and Clinton came in third, behind John Edwards. Clinton was declared the "comeback kid" when she narrowly won New Hampshire's primary election, on January 8, 2008, a victory that some attributed to her unexpectedly emotional display of just a few days before, when her eyes welled up with tears and her voice cracked as she spoke to a group of supporters. That moment, replayed repeatedly on television and the Internet, was thought to have considerably softened Clinton's public image.

Problems with Clinton's campaign strategy became evident over the course of the next several contests. Her advisers had focused on winning the nation's largest and most populous states, which award the most pledged delegates. In doing so they had failed to organize effectively in smaller states. Overestimating Clinton's status as the frontrunner, the campaign had wrongly anticipated that she would be able to secure the nomination by February 5, 2008, the date known as Super Tuesday, when numerous states were to hold primary elections and 1,681 pledged delegates were at stake. On that date, though Clinton and Obama were essentially even in the popular vote, Obama secured 847 delegates to Clinton's 834. Because her campaign was unprepared, financially or logistically, to continue beyond February 5, Clinton was forced to lend the campaign $5 million of her own money. Meanwhile, the Obama campaign, which had anticipated a long race and had established a successful Internet-based fund-raising model, was drawing record-breaking donations. Clinton also made several top-level personnel changes, which, along with reports of campaign in-fighting, contributed to the public's perception of turmoil and disorganization. Obama's victory in the next several contests and the numerous endorsements that he had obtained from party leaders led some Democrats to call for Clinton to bow out of the race. Fear spread that the increasingly vitriolic primary would alienate undecided voters and cost the Democratic Party the general election.

Encouraged by her loyal supporters, however, Clinton campaigned throughout the spring. Obama and Clinton had each established distinct bases of support that remained relatively consistent throughout the race; in general, Obama's consisted of young voters, blacks, and college-educated whites, while Clinton's included women, the elderly, and blue-collar whites. Though Obama was clearly the frontrunner in the delegate count, the two were neck in neck in national polls. On March 4, 2008 Clinton pulled off impressive wins in Ohio and Texas, both by large margins. Appearing more resilient than she had for much of the campaign, she told a crowd in Ohio, as quoted by John Heilemann in *New York* magazine (June 23, 2008, online): "For everyone here in Ohio and across America who's ever been counted out but refused to be knocked out, and for everyone who has stumbled but stood right back up, and for everyone who works hard and never gives up, this one is for you." Clinton won nine of the last 15 contests, and during those final months, many observers noted that she came into her own as a candidate. "With that speech [in Ohio], Clinton had finally found a theme: the resilient fighter, the underdog, the victim," Heilemann noted. "Having abandoned her corporate, Establishment campaign, she seemed more liberated; she seemed intoxicated. Suddenly she was giving terrific, well-modulated Election Night speeches . . . that were every bit as good, in their way, as Obama's more-celebrated orations."

On June 3, 2008 Obama earned enough delegates to clinch his victory as the Democratic nominee, and Clinton delivered a speech in which she congratulated her opponent but did not concede the election. She finally did so four days later. Many observers wondered whether Clinton's fervent supporters, some of whom were so angry at their candidate's loss that they pledged to vote for the Republican John McCain, would ultimately transfer their support to Obama. Clinton urged them to switch their allegiance, saying, "The way to continue our fight now to accomplish the goals for which we stand is to take our energy, our passion, our strength and do all we can to help elect Barack Obama, the next president of the United States. . . . I endorse him and throw my full support behind him and I ask of you to join me in working as hard for Barack Obama as you have for me."

Some speculated that Clinton might be asked to join Obama as his vice-presidential pick, thereby uniting a party that had grown increasingly divided and possibly forming a stronger presidential ticket. In August, however, Obama announced that Joseph Biden would be his running mate. Despite that disappointment, Clinton, who was reportedly willing to consider the number-two spot on the ticket, continued to stump for her former rival. On August 26, 2008 Clinton delivered a speech at the Democratic National Convention, held in Denver, Colorado, in which she stated: "I haven't spent the past 35 years in the trenches advocating for children, campaigning for universal health care, helping parents balance work and family, and fighting for women's rights at home and around the world . . . to see another Republican in the White House squander the promise of our country and the hopes of our people. And you haven't worked so hard over the last 18 months, or endured the last eight years, to suffer through more failed leadership. No way. No how. No McCain. Barack Obama is my candidate. And he must be our President." She expressed no regrets about her long, ultimately unsuccessful race, saying, "For me, it's been a privilege to meet you in your homes, your workplaces, and your communities. Your stories reminded me every day that America's greatness is bound up in the lives of the American people—your hard work, your devotion to duty, your love for your children, and your determination to keep going, often in the face of enormous obstacles. You taught me so much, you made me laugh, and . . . you even made me cry. You allowed me to become part of your lives. And you became part of mine. . . . To my supporters, my champions . . . from the bottom of my heart: Thank you. You never gave in. You never gave up. And together we made history."

While Obama's groundbreaking campaign highlighted the issues of race and ethnicity in America, Clinton's equally groundbreaking attempt brought up issues of gender and sexism. One article, written by Robin Givhan for the *Washington Post* (July 20, 2007), was devoted to a lengthy analysis of Clinton's faintly visible cleavage during one Senate speech—a "small acknowledgement of sexuality and feminity," according to Givhan. Pundits regularly discussed the effect that Clinton's strength and ambition might have on male voters and often described her voice with such negative, female-associated terms as "nagging" and "shrill." Though she generally refrained from commenting on such issues during the campaign, Clinton told Heilemann, "The contrast between the [public's] outrage over anything concerning race compared to anything concerning gender was incredibly out of balance, I thought."

On December 1, 2008 President-elect Obama formally announced his choice of Clinton as secretary of state. Though Clinton has a shorter foreign-policy résumé than many of her predecessors in the post, her selection was widely praised by those who pointed to her substantial diplomatic skills as well as her vast understanding of global issues. Her detractors, however, warned of possible conflicts of interest, given that Bill Clinton is an in-demand public speaker whose clients include many prominent foreign figures and that his eponymous foundation has attracted wealthy foreign donors including Saudi Arabia's King Abdullah. Obama's transition team, widely acknowledged as one of the most effective in modern history, reached an agreement with the foundation, which released the names of its past donors and promised to report new contributors each year. The foundation also pledged to allow State Department ethics officials to examine any documents they desire. The foundation's Clinton Global Initiative program, which does humanitarian work, will be incorporated separately under the terms set forth by Obama's team and will no longer take money from foreign governments.

Confirmed by the Senate in a vote of 94–2, Clinton is charged with helping to mediate conflicts around the globe. During her Senate confirmation hearings, she stated her intention to make women's issues central to American foreign policy rather than "adjunct or auxiliary, or in any way lesser than all of the other issues we have to confront." Women's rights are among many issues she has addressed during her extensive travels as she has worked to establish a new direction in American foreign policy. She took her first trip as secretary of state in February 2009, visiting Japan, Indonesia, South Korea, and China; the following month she visited Mexico, where she discussed issues including border security and the illegal drug and arms trades. In August she embarked on a seven-nation tour of Africa during the eighth African Growth and Opportunities Act (AGOA) Forum, in Nairobi, Kenya. During her travels Clinton emphasized the Obama administration's commitment to encouraging development and democracy in other nations, criticized governmental corruption, and spoke out against the widespread abuse of women. Observers have noted that Clinton's international visits are distinctive in that she engages with people outside political and diplomatic circles; she often holds public roundtables and town-hall-style gatherings to hear the concerns of ordinary citizens.

Clinton faced a diplomatic crisis during the summer of 2009, when two American reporters on assignment in North Korea were arrested on charges including entering that country illegally and sentenced to 12 years of hard labor. The matter was made more delicate by North Korea's having recently flouted international law by testing several nuclear missiles. After weeks of efforts by the secretary of state, a diplomatic group led by former president Bill Clinton met with the North Korean president, Kim Jong Il; they succeeded in securing a "special pardon" from the North Korean government, and the journalists were released. In October 2009 Hillary Clinton visited Russia in an effort to obtain the country's support for a plan to confront Iran's alleged nuclear ambitions. Clinton faces challenges in redefining the U.S. diplomatic policy elsewhere in the world, including the Middle East, Afghanistan, and Pakistan.

Clinton, who lives in the nation's capital during the week, typically spends her weekends at the home she shares with Bill Clinton in Chappaqua, New York. The secretary of state loves art and sculpture and is a devout Methodist. The Clintons' daughter, Chelsea, studied history at Stanford University, in California, and earned a master's degree in international relations from the University of Oxford, in England. Now employed at a financial firm in New York City, she made many appearances during the presidential campaign in 2008, during which she called her mother her hero.

—G.O./M.E.R.

Suggested Reading: BBC (on-line) Aug. 1, 1999; CNN (on-line) Feb. 11, 1998, Sep. 20, 2000; *New York* (on-line) June 23, 2008; *New York Times* (on-line) Jan. 24, 2002, Aug. 27, 2008, Dec. 22, 2008, May 2, 2009, Aug. 23, 2009; *New Yorker* p63 Oct. 13, 2003; (Toronto) *Globe and Mail* (on-line) Jan. 11, 1995; *Vanity Fair* p90 July 2005

Selected Books: *It Takes a Village and Other Lessons Children Teach Us*, 1996; *Living History*, 2003

Cooper, Kyle

1963– Director of film-title sequences

Address: Prologue Films, 534 Victoria Ave., Venice, CA 90291

"My job is to make people in the theater feel like they don't want to be anywhere else," Kyle Cooper explained to Jennifer Vilaga for the magazine *Fast Company* (on-line), which named him among the 100 Most Creative People in Business for 2009. Cooper, who specializes in crafting the opening-credit segments of films, is considered to be the most influential designer of motion-picture title sequences since Saul Bass. Beginning his career at the design firm R/Greenberg Associates (RGA) in New York in the late 1980s, Cooper rose to prominence with his highly stylized opening-credit sequence for David Fincher's neo-noir thriller *Seven* (1995), which featured hand-scratched type and other disturbing imagery to evoke the workings of a serial killer's mind. The highly influential title sequence not only set the dark, gritty tone of the film but also helped usher in a renewed interest in motion-picture title design, an art form that was first revolutionized by Bass in the 1950s. On the strength of his work for *Seven*, in 1996 Cooper and his RGA colleagues Chip Houghton and Peter Frankfurt founded the design firm Imaginary Forces, which quickly became the hottest company of its kind in Hollywood. "*Seven* woke everyone up to the possibility of main title sequences again," Frankfurt told Adam Eeuwens for *Advertising Age's Creativity* (October 1, 1998). "*Seven* felt totally of the moment; this dark . . . thing that was 1995. That was the moment and it just clicked." At Imaginary Forces Cooper headed title-design teams responsible for the openings to such films as *Donnie Brasco* (1997), *The Mummy* (1999), *Arlington Road* (1999), and *Spider-Man* (2002), as well as projects ranging from the Netscape browser's comet-field logo to graphics for the televised Academy Awards presentation. Following in the tradition of MTV and the groundbreaking music publication *Ray Gun*, the hallmarks of Cooper's style included jagged typefaces, hyper-fast editing, and bizarre yet relevant imagery.

Wanting to spend more time involved in the creative process and less overseeing the work of others, Cooper left Imaginary Forces in 2003 to found the multimedia design firm Prologue Films. At that company he has continued to design highly acclaimed title sequences, including those for the films *Dawn of the Dead* (2004), *Spider-Man 2* (2004), *Wimbledon* (2004), *The New World* (2005), *Superman Returns* (2006), *Spider-Man 3* (2007), and *Tropic Thunder* (2008); the firm has also branched out into title designs for video games and television shows.

Kyle Cooper was born in 1963 into a devoutly Christian family. He grew up with his two brothers in the seaside town of Swampscott, north of Boston in Essex County, Massachusetts. At an early age Cooper developed a penchant for comic books. He followed the adventures of the Marvel Comics superheroes and read the horror stories in magazines such as *Tales from the Crypt*; he also devoured cult magazines including *Fangoria* and *Famous Monsters of Filmland*. In an interview posted on the Art of the Title Web site, Cooper recalled, "Growing up, my brother and I had 6,000 comics." He became enamored of the visuals in grisly films such as *The Exorcist* (1973) and *An American Werewolf in London* (1981), and he read the seminal *Monster Make-Up Handbook*, by the makeup artist Dick Smith, which featured step-by-step instructions on how to create the look of a cut throat and other grave wounds. Cooper's interest in the subject even led him to read medical journals. The knowledge he gained later informed his extremely detailed professional work. In the book *Kyle Cooper* (2003), Andrea Codrington wrote, "While Cooper's youthful emphasis on replicating the physical manifestations of the horror genre has been replaced over the years by a focus on its psychic machinations, this early obsession with flayed bodies and anatomical pathologies seems to have led to a desire to tear away at the surface of things—to reveal the metaphorical blood and guts that lie just beneath the skin of reality. In the same way that Alfred Hitchcock was known to set the most dastardly plots against the backdrop of national monuments such as Mt. Rushmore (*North by Northwest*) or the Golden Gate Bridge (*Vertigo*), Cooper repeatedly picks away at American icons, in order, more often than not, to reveal something sinister."

It has been noted that during his adolescence, Cooper once spent seven weeks using a pin to etch the details of a mutant creature's dragon-like scales onto a metal plate. Commenting on his somewhat obsessive attention to detail, he explained to Codrington, "It may be a faulty paradigm but I do respect things that are intricate. The dysfunction came from needing to create all these incredibly detailed drawings because my parents were getting divorced or . . . needing to make intricate edits because I was breaking up with a girlfriend or people were taking advantage of me." (Cooper, whose parents divorced when he was eight years old, was raised by his mother.) Codrington noted another of Cooper's youthful activities that prefigured his later work: he would look up words in the dictionary and draw the letters in ways that related to the words' meanings—"extinguish," for example, with the "u" upside-down, resembling a bucket pouring water.

Cooper attended the University of Massachusetts at Amherst, where he earned a B.F.A. degree in interior architecture. During that time, while on a trip to Bermuda, his mother was involved in a car accident and fell into a coma; she remained in that state for three years before dying. That traumatic event led Cooper to become a born-again Christian. It also led him to devote all of his energies to design. Cooper went on to earn an M.F.A. degree in

Courtesy of Kyle Cooper

Kyle Cooper

graphic design from the Yale School of Art, in New Haven, Connecticut, writing his master's thesis on the pioneering Russian filmmaker Sergei Eisenstein. At Yale Cooper studied independently with Paul Rand, under whom he created a series of posters that made use of close-together type and conceptual imagery. He has since called Rand his greatest mentor. Referring to the common misperception that Saul Bass holds that distinction, Cooper noted in an interview posted on the Thunder Chunky Web site, "I love *Walk On The Wild Side* [1962] and *Man with The Golden Arm* [1955]"—which both featured groundbreaking title sequences by Bass—"but I actually have gotten much more familiar with his work after I started doing [film work]. Paul Rand was my mentor and he and Saul Bass were often compared to each other. There is no question that Saul Bass is the father of film titles but Paul Rand was the father of American graphic design." With regard to motion-picture title sequences, Cooper has cited Stephen O. Frankfurt's opening to Robert Mulligan's film adaptation of *To Kill a Mockingbird* (1962) as his favorite.

Upon graduating from Yale, in 1988, Cooper went to work for R/Greenberg Associates (now known as R/GA), a New York City firm devoted to film and video design. He served as the main title designer for Martin Scorsese's "Life Lessons" segment of the film *New York Stories* (1989), which impressed Scorsese enough to ask him to create a concept for his next project, *Goodfellas* (1990). Cooper's concept was rejected in favor of one proposed by Bass and his wife, Elaine, which began a long partnership between the couple and Scorsese. "I was too busy trying to think of a metaphor for the film, when really he just needed a beginning," Cooper recalled to N'Gai Croal for *Newsweek* (November 24, 1997).

Though Cooper was passed up for that job, he quickly ascended the ranks at R/Greenberg, rising from intern to creative director of the company's Los Angeles office in just a few years. In the 1990s he worked on title segments for such directors as Brian De Palma, Chris Columbus, Rob Reiner, Abel Ferrara, Adrian Lyne, John McTiernan, Philip Kaufman, Roger Donaldson, Robert Redford, James Cameron, and Mike Nichols. Among the films for which Cooper designed title sequences during that time are *The Bonfire of the Vanities* (1990); *Home Alone* (1990); *Home Alone 2* (1992); *Body Snatchers* (1993); *Carlito's Way* (1993); *Indecent Proposal* (1993); *Last Action Hero* (1993); *Rising Sun* (1993); *The Getaway* (1994); *Quiz Show* (1994); *True Lies* (1994); *Wolf* (1994); and *The American President* (1995). He worked on the sequences mostly in collaboration with other designers, including Garson Yu, Bruce Schluter, Thomas Barham, Michael Riley, and Richard Greenberg.

In 1995 Cooper was commissioned by the director David Fincher to create the title segments for *Seven*, a thriller, starring Morgan Freeman, Brad Pitt, and Gwyneth Paltrow, about a series of ritualistic murders inspired by the Christian notion of the seven deadly sins (pride, envy, gluttony, lust, wrath, greed, and sloth). Fincher wanted to go against the stars' likable images; the director told Mark Caro for the *Chicago Tribune* (December 10, 1995), "I said we definitely want people who think they're going to see *Legends of the Fall* to know that they're in the wrong movie. People should realize they're in for some evil." (Codrington wrote that Cooper himself "believes strongly in the existence of evil as an active, supernatural force in the world" and quoted him as saying, "Why deny the existence of evil? Let's all look at it for what it is.") Embracing Fincher's idea, Cooper created a title sequence that took the point of view of the serial killer. The sequence played to an eerie remix of the Nine Inch Nails song "Closer" and featured type scratched onto film stock with a pin, tight shots of the killer's copiously detailed notebooks, and split-second images of the killer slicing off his own fingerprints with razor blades. Cooper explained to N'Gai Croal, "My idea was to shoot [the murderer] John Doe's fetishistic preparation for his life's work, this very complex crime." Steeping himself in the mood of the film, Cooper spent hours at a time in his basement looking for dead insects and other unpleasant items to add to the end-credit sequence. Directing the visuals behind the credits took eight days, two of which were spent shooting on a soundstage with hand models. Cooper told Croal that his work with Fincher "opened my eyes a lot. It marked a very crucial point in my life."

Cooper's painstaking style is also evident in his title sequence for the John Frankenheimer film *The Island of Dr. Moreau* (1996), based on the H. G. Wells science-fiction novel of the same name, about a scientist who attempts to convert animals into people. Cooper's sequence compressed 400 shots into a little over two and a half minutes. Embracing Frankenheimer's idea of creating titles that would evoke violence at the cellular level, Cooper interspered splintering typography with a dizzying mix of stock medical photography, digital illustrations, and computer-animated images of cells dividing and multiplying, to reflect the theme of the film. In Cooper's title work for *Twister* (1996), the words swirl together and away from one another in a way suggestive of a tornado; in his titles for *Spider-Man*, the words coalesce to resemble flies getting stuck in a spider's web.

Meanwhile, the credit work for *Seven,* which *Entertainment Weekly* called a "masterpiece of dementia" and the *New York Times Magazine* hailed as one of the most important design innovations of the 1990s, single-handedly ushered in a new era in film-title design and brought a renewed interest to the form. Propelled by that success and acclaim, Cooper left R/Greenberg Associates in 1996 to found the design firm Imaginary Forces with his R/GA colleagues Chip Houghton and Peter Frankfurt. Imaginary Forces quickly became the most in-demand design firm in Hollywood during the late 1990s. The acclaimed title sequences produced by the firm included those for *Nixon* (1995); *Ghosts of Mississippi* (1996); *Gotti* (1996); *White Squall* (1996); *Donnie Brasco* (1997); and *Dreamcatcher* (2003). In addition to film projects, Cooper and his team designed the comet logo for the Internet company Netscape and worked on graphics for the televised Academy Awards ceremony. In 2002 the company branched out into video games and designed title graphics for Hideo Kojima's *Metal Gear Solid 2*.

By the start of the new millennium, Imaginary Forces had grown to a 90-person team of designers and artists. Cooper, meanwhile, had developed a reputation as "the guy who makes title sequences better than the movie," Zach Snyder, the director of *Dawn of the Dead* (for which Cooper designed the title shots), noted to Jon M. Gibson for *Wired* (June 2004, on-line). In many reviews of the films Cooper has worked on, critics have gone out of their way to praise the credit sequences, even as they panned the films themselves. As noted by Codrington, the *New Yorker* reviewer Anthony Lane, in his review for *Mission: Impossible*, wrote that the credits were "so tense and sexy that you could leave the theater immediately afterward without suffering the letdown of the film itself." In another review, of *Donnie Brasco*, Lane wrote in the first line, "The most beautiful thing about *Donnie Brasco* is the opening title sequence. . . . No one has had eyes like that, not since El Greco stopped painting saints." The *New York Times* critic Janet Maslin also contributed to the trend of praising Cooper's title designs more than the movies they adorn. In her review for Rob Reiner's *Ghosts of Mississippi*, she commented on Cooper's "rousing, majestic montage" before concluding, "None of what follows matches the impact of this title sequence." Cooper explained in a 1998 interview posted on the Web zine *Feed* that praise focusing solely on his work is "the worst thing for me. As a graphic designer I have to solve [the director's] problem, and if I'm not listening to the director and not giving him something that works in the service of his movie that's not going to get me any work."

Imaginary Forces continued to prosper, allowing Cooper to take a one-year leave to make his directorial debut, with the movie *New Port South* (2001). Produced by John Hughes and written by his son, James Hughes, the dark teen drama centered on teenagers rebelling against a high school's policies. The film received only a limited release and did poorly at the box office, opening to mixed reviews before going to DVD in 2002. In the following year Cooper decided to leave Imaginary Forces, after his administrative responsibilities began to get in the way of his creative work. That year he founded the design firm Prologue Films. One of the company's first major motion-picture projects was a remake of George Romero's 1978 cult horror film *Dawn of the Dead.* Cooper continued to push the boundaries of his specialty by using real blood in the opening title sequence.

Among the other films for which Prologue has supplied title sequences are *Spider-Man 2*; *Wimbledon* (2004); *Zathura: A Space Adventure* (2005); *The New World* (2005); *Freedomland* (2006); *Superman Returns* (2006); *The Painted Veil* (2006); *Bridge to Terabithia* (2007); *Spider-Man 3* (2007); *Across the Universe* (2007); *Tropic Thunder* (2008); and *RocknRolla* (2008). Cooper's work will also be seen in Julie Taymor's version of *The Tempest*, due for release in 2010 or 2011. In contrast to Imaginary Forces, which dedicated most of its time to film projects, Prologue—based in Venice, California—handles commercials as well as feature films. The company has worked on national campaigns for companies such as Hewlett Packard and American Express. Prologue has also provided designs for the video games *Metal Gear Solid 3: Snake Eater* (2004) and *Metal Gear Solid 3: Subsistence* (2005).

Codrington wrote that Cooper "is a postmodern paradox. He is an iconoclast who loves what he transgresses, whether the tenets of modernist typography, the idea of apple-pie America or even the belief in an all-loving, all-powerful God. He is by nature betwixt and between, not quite fitting into the commercial world of Hollywood and not entirely at home in the realm of high-design discourse. He is a true-believing Christian whose oeuvre has often lingered on the sinister themes of murder and madness." Cooper lives in Los Angeles, California, with his wife, Kimberly, an operations director at Prologue. He has received numerous honors for his design work, including a gold medal and Best of Show Award for graphic design at the New York Art Directors Club Awards, four Art Director's Club Merit Awards, a gold medal at the International Film & Television Festival of New York, an Architectural Foundation of Los Angeles Award for design achievement, two *I.D. Magazine* Annual Design Review Awards, five AIGA (American Institute of Graphic Arts) Awards for Outstanding Examples of Communication Graphics, and a 1998 Emmy Award nomination for the main title sequence for the TNT network's *The George Wallace Story*. Cooper is currently a faculty member of the Art Center College of Design in Pasadena, California. He also serves as a guest lecturer at the Yale University School of Art and is a member of the Type Directors Club.

—C.C.

Suggested Reading: Art of the Title Sequence Web site; *Chicago Tribune* C p1 Dec. 10, 1995; *Los Angeles Times* F p8 Nov. 3, 1995; *New York Times* p61+ Dec. 13, 1998, B p9 Apr. 22, 2000; *Newsweek* p50D Nov. 24, 1997; *Wired* (on-line) June 2004; Codrington, Andrea. *Kyle Cooper*, 2003; Eskilson, Stephen J. *Graphic Design: A New History*, 2007

Selected Films: as title designer—*New York Stories*, 1989; *The Bonfire of the Vanities*, 1990; *Home Alone*, 1990; *Home Alone 2*, 1992; *Body Snatchers*, 1993; *Carlito's Way*, 1993; *Indecent Proposal*, 1993; *Last Action Hero*, 1993; *Rising Sun*, 1993; *The Getaway*, 1994; *Quiz Show*, 1994; *True Lies*, 1994; *Wolf*, 1994; *The American President*, 1995; *Seven*, 1995; *Nixon*, 1995; *The Island of Dr. Moreau*, 1996; *Twister*, 1996; *Ghosts of Mississippi*, 1996; *Gotti*, 1996; *White Squall*, 1996; *Donnie Brasco*, 1997; *The Mummy*, 1999; *Spider-Man*, 2002; *Dreamcatcher*, 2003; *Dawn of the Dead*, 2004; *Spider-Man 2*, 2004; *Wimbledon*, 2004; *Zathura: A Space Adventure*, 2005; *The New World*, 2005; *Freedomland*, 2006; *Superman Returns*, 2006; *The Painted Veil*, 2006; *Bridge to Terabithia*, 2007; *Spider-Man 3*, 2007; *Across the Universe*, 2007; *Tropic Thunder*, 2008; *RocknRolla*, 2008; as director—*New Port South*, 2001

Selected Video Games: *Metal Gear Solid 2*, 2002; *Metal Gear Solid 3: Snake Eater*, 2004; *Metal Gear Solid 3: Subsistence*, 2005

Daly, Carson

June 22, 1973– Television talk-show host

Address: c/o Endeavor Agency, 9601 Wilshire Blvd., Third Fl., Beverly Hills, CA 90212

Carson Daly might be said to have turned inoffensiveness into wealth. As the host of the late-night talk show *Last Call with Carson Daly*, which debuted on NBC in early 2002 and airs at 1:35 a.m. Eastern Standard Time, Daly interviews celebrities and hosts musical acts for an average of one million viewers—with a geniality that often gets him compared to Dick Clark. Like that iconic TV host, Daly was for years the host of a music program, emceeing *Total Request Live* from 1998 to 2003.

The second of two children, Carson Jones Daly was born on June 22, 1973 in Santa Monica, California. His father, Jim Daly, died of cancer of the bladder when Carson was six years old, and the boy was raised afterward by his mother, Pattie Daly Caruso, and stepfather, Richard Caruso, a golf-store owner and real-estate agent. (Pattie Daly later became the host of her own, local talk show.) Raised as a Catholic, Daly considered becoming a priest until his mother convinced him that he would want to have a family someday. His older sister, Quinn, described him as having been a sociable young man with many friends but also a late bloomer romantically, one who had trouble finding dates. "I was kind of a wimpy type, a mama's boy a little bit," Daly told Jason Lynch and Cynthia Wang for *People* (May 29, 2000).

Rob Loud/Getty Images

Daly also considered becoming a professional golfer. A capable player since age 13, he entered Loyola Marymount University, in Los Angeles, California, in 1992 on a partial golf scholarship, then left after one year to pursue a golf career full-time. But when his family friend Jimmy Kimmel, a radio and TV personality, helped him get an internship at the radio station KCMJ-FM in Palm Springs, Daly decided that he would like to go into broadcasting. He had long held an interest in the field, as evidenced by the make-believe radio shows he made with his sister beginning at age eight. Kimmel quickly saw potential in Daly, then 19, and invited him to be his on-air sidekick. A fairly innocent young man, Daly was a good foil for Kimmel's raunchy style. "He was extremely likable," Kimmel told Lynch and Wang. "I always told him, 'We've got to get you on MTV. It's the perfect place for you.'"

Daly quickly rose through the ranks of radio, getting three other jobs before winning a coveted spot as a deejay at the popular Los Angeles–based rock radio station KROQ-FM in 1996, at age 23. His work there got the attention of MTV executives, who, in 1998, invited him to host their new music-video program, *Total Request Live*. The program, often called *TRL*, was meant to draw teen and preteen viewers with its after-school time slot and by-request format. Fueled by the popularity of pop acts including Britney Spears and N' Sync, which it in turn helped to promote, the show quickly became the cable channel's most popular daily offering and an essential stop on the publicity circuit for anyone promoting an album geared toward young listeners. Geoff Mayfield of *Billboard* told Eric Messinger for the *New York Times* (April 2, 2000) that *TRL* was a key ingredient in selling "millions of records." *TRL* "is the thing—not the only thing but a key thing—that gets you from here to there," he said. Some admirers compared Daly to Dick Clark, the famous television host who introduced many rock acts to America via his long-running show *American Bandstand*.

"In contrast to some of the flamboyant celebrities that appear on *TRL* . . . ," Messinger wrote, "Daly comes across as just a regular guy. His banter is genial and lightly sarcastic. On the air, he is charmingly fidgety . . . he still doesn't quite seem to know what to do with his hands. But Daly doesn't want too much polish; he fashions himself a kind of uncelebrity celebrity." His on-air persona was parodied by the comedian Jimmy Fallon on *Saturday Night Live*; Fallon's impression began with the line, "Hi, I'm Carson Daly, and I'm totally average in every way!" Still, gentle mockery sometimes crept into Daly's demeanor. "It's never been something strategic or plotted with me, but I've started to see how it works," he told Messinger. "When I'm on the air, I'll often make a teen reference like, 'Oh, Justin is the cutest member of 'N Sync,' and kind of laugh, and you don't really know if I'm poking fun or taking it seriously." Though Daly was careful not to publicly state a dislike of any *TRL* acts, a friend of his told Messinger, "Let's just say that Carson isn't dancing around naked in his apartment to the Backstreet Boys."

As it grew more successful, *TRL* raised the ire of many cultural critics. Some criticized the music's homogeneity; fans requested the same videos so many times in a row that the show instituted a policy of retiring videos once they had been aired 65 times. The genres that the show stuck to—bubblegum pop, with some mainstream rock and hip-hop—were narrow and strictly commercial. "This stuff is all very simple—and music that is more grown-up or sophisticated has been pushed aside," Alan Light, the editor of *Spin*, told Messinger. In a long article for *Salon.com* (August 29, 2001), Sarah Kendzior painted *TRL* as representing a general societal obsession with fame, in that the show seemed to be, for the young people who attended tapings, less about music than about the experience of being on TV. "While older music fans profess outrage for MTV's blatant commercialism, the *TRL* audience blows off such concerns as irrelevant," Kendzior wrote. "The goal, obviously, is to get on TV. *TRL* may claim to mark a return to videos, but in the end it's just another reality series."

In 2000 Daly signed a contract that made him the program's executive producer and gave him license to develop shows for MTV and CBS, which were both owned by Viacom at the time. In 2002 Daly began hosting a late-night talk show on NBC, *Last Call with Carson Daly*. The show, which premiered a day late due to contract issues, received mixed reviews. "The show is not a radical move in late night, but it's appealing and sometimes unusual," Caryn James wrote for the *New York Times* (January 10, 2002). "The guest scheduled for tonight is the rap producer and sometime prison resident Suge Knight, not a guy who's likely to be making the rounds of talk shows. Guests like that should help *Last Call* and its pleasant host set themselves apart." James thought that Daly's "mix of soft friendliness with a touch of sardonic irreverence is appealing and adaptable to a wide range of guests. He looks like a teddy bear with a mischievous gleam in his eye." Writing for the *Los Angeles Times* (January 21, 2003) a year into the show's run, Scott Sandell was more negative: "Despite a year's worth of experience under his belt, Daly still struggles mightily to ask interesting questions." With a focus on musical guests, Daly's show has hosted the first network and/or U.S. appearances of bands including Panic! at the Disco, the Killers, Maroon 5, Jack Johnson, and Gavin DeGraw. Daly has also hosted more established acts, among them the rapper 50 Cent and the rock band Greenday, who performed their nine-minute song "Jesus of Suburbia" in its entirety.

In 2003 Daly became executive producer of his own company, Carson Daly Productions, as well as head of 456 Entertainment, a record label he co-founded with the record executive Jonathan Rifkind. "I always had a pretty good ear for a hit song," Daly told Tom Gliatto and Mark Dagostino for *People* (October 11, 2004). "The major companies don't give a [damn] about developing acts anymore. This is a true independent record company." Daly's label found some success with the British pop group Mis-teeq, which he discovered while vacationing in Saint-Tropez; their 2004 single "Scandalous" peaked at second place on the *Billboard* dance-singles sales chart and at number 35 on the *Billboard* "Hot 100" list. Meanwhile, late in

2003, after a year of flying back and forth between New York and Los Angeles to film both *TRL* and his NBC talk show, Daly left *TRL* and moved to Los Angeles. Talking with Mark Dagostino for *People* (November 25, 2006), Daly described filming *Last Call* in Los Angeles as being a drastic departure from making *TRL* in New York. "We shoot on the NBC lot, which is completely different from shooting on the *Saturday Night Live* set in New York," he said. "You're constantly reminded that you work in TV-land. You drive onto the lot and see people dressed like pilgrims, and the cast of *Days of Our Lives*, and all the big stars going into the *Tonight Show*." (With the recently introduced change in the show's format, many interviews take place away from the studio, mainly in settings in Los Angeles.) The move to Los Angeles coincided with Daly's decision to make changes in his personal life. After a high-profile relationship with the actress Jennifer Love Hewitt and another with the actress Tara Reid, which ended in a broken engagement, Daly was weary of being tabloid fodder. "I'm trying to re-enter the human race," he told Dagostino. "All of my rock 'n' roll living at MTV and my fast-paced public relationships—a lot of the press that people associated me with was tied in with all of that. And as I got a little bit older and moved on to NBC I thought, 'I've gotta grow up here.'"

As part of his effort to "grow up," Daly focused squarely on his work, developing a submission-based on-line program with NBC called *It's Your Show* in 2006. Each week Daly and his staff combed through viewer-submitted videos based on a given theme and awarded prize money for the best entries. Plans to develop a television version of the show never materialized. During the Writers Guild of America strike in 2007, Daly caught some criticism for being the first late-night talk-show host to return to the air without writers. He joined other personalities, such as Ellen DeGeneres, who broke picket lines to prevent their crews from being fired. "If I had not been back on the air tonight, 75 members of my loyal staff and crew were going to get laid off," he explained at the beginning of his show, as quoted by Brian Stelter in the *New York Times* (December 4, 2007). He described the "ultimatum" he received from NBC: "You either come back or they're laid off. I said, 'Let's turn the lights on, I'm gonna come back.' It's that simple."

In November 2008 Daly returned to New York to host the three-hour final installment of *TRL*, called "Total Finale Live." The program included performances by Beyoncé, 50 Cent, Fall Out Boy, the Backstreet Boys, Nelly, Snoop Dogg, and Ludacris. In addition to his regular series, Daly has hosted many TV specials over the course of his career, including *MTV New Year's Eve*, which he emceed for several consecutive years; *Manson TV* (1999), featuring the rocker Marilyn Manson; the *Miss Teen USA Pageant* on CBS (1999); *Britney Live* (2000); the *MTV Sports and Music Festival 5* (2001); and NBC's New Year's Eve prime-time special, which he also produced. Daly has also served as executive producer for programs including *TRL Super Bowl* (2001), *The 25 Hottest Stars under 25* (MTV, 2001), and the *Second Annual TRL Awards* (2004). For five years beginning in 2001, he hosted the radio show *Carson Daly's Most Requested*. Daly lives in Los Angeles with Siri Pinter, a writer's assistant for his late-night show, with whom he has a son, Jackson James Daly, born in March 2009.

—J.E.P.

Suggested Reading: imdb.com; *Los Angeles Times* E p9 Nov. 18, 2009; *New York Times* (online) Apr. 2, 2000; *People* p71 May 29, 2000, p85 Oct. 11, 2004

Selected Television Shows: *Total Request Live*, 1998–2003; *Last Call with Carson Daly*, 2002–

Chris McGrath/Getty Images

D'Antoni, Mike

May 8, 1951– Head coach of the New York Knicks

Address: New York Knicks, Madison Square Garden, Two Penn Plaza, New York, NY 10121-0091

Mike D'Antoni, who became the head coach of the the New York Knicks in 2008, has one of the most unusual backgrounds of any coach in the National Basketball Association (NBA). After struggling for playing time in four seasons with NBA teams in the 1970s, D'Antoni spent 20 years in Italy, where, as a player and then a coach, he achieved celebrity status. He was the star point guard for Olimpia Milano, which competes with teams from Italy and other European countries in many tournaments year-round; during his time with the team, it won five Italian League titles. When he played with the national Italian basketball team, it won two European championships. As a coach of Olimpia Milano and then Benetton Treviso, he led his squads to several Italian and European championships and earned plaudits from many notoriously hard-to-please European sports fans. In Europe D'Antoni, who now holds dual American-Italian citizenship, became an expert in European-style basketball; a looser game than its American counterpart, it relies more on teamwork and rapid passes and shots, rather than the one-on-one matchups and displays of brute force common in NBA games. When he became the head coach of the Phoenix Suns of the NBA, in 2004, D'Antoni introduced to his players European-style offense, which was dubbed "run-and-gun," "high octane," or "seven seconds or less" (referring to the preferred maximum time between getting the ball and taking a shot). D'Antoni coached the Suns to four winning seasons, and under his leadership they dominated the Western Conference and shone not only as one of the most dynamic but one of the most entertaining teams in NBA history. D'Antoni gained a reputation as one of the NBA's most innovative coaches and was voted 2006 Coach of the Year by a panel of sportswriters. In May 2008 he signed a four-year, $24 million contract with the Knicks, who had not made the play-offs since 2001 and had faced turmoil both on and off the court in recent years. "The only thing I can promise," D'Antoni told Frank Isola for the New York *Daily News* (May 14, 2008), "is that we're going to play hard and be exciting—put on your seat belt and let's go." After a series of roster changes, which freed up salary-cap space for future player acquisitions, the Knicks finished the 2008–09 season with a disappointing record of 32–50. D'Antoni told Howard Beck for the *New York Times* (April 16, 2009, on-line): "Going forward, we can get a lot better real quick. Just have to have a little patience. And we're going to get there."

The second of the four children (three sons and one daughter) of Lewis and Betty Jo D'Antoni, Michael Andrew D'Antoni was born on May 8, 1951 in Mullens, West Virginia, a mining town so tiny that it lacked a traffic light. D'Antoni has recalled his childhood as idyllic. "Everybody looked after everybody. You felt safe," he told Wayne Coffey for the New York *Daily News* (May 18, 2008). "You thought you could conquer the world, and everybody else thought you could conquer it, too." D'Antoni's father, the son of an Italian immigrant coal miner, was a high-school principal and the legendary head coach of his school's basketball team; from 1950 through 1956 he guided the team to a 171–11 record. D'Antoni's mother worked as an assistant county clerk. She was an activist in the local Democratic Party and encouraged her family to engage in spirited political debates at the dinner table. The D'Antonis competed fiercely at games including ping pong, Monopoly, Risk, gin rummy, and bridge and posted the results on their refrigerator. Mike D'Antoni took to basketball early on. Joe Hill, a Mullens barber, recalled to Coffey that the boy and his basketball were "inseparable" and that "he'd dribble the ball all the way into town, and right into the barber shop."

D'Antoni played point guard in high school and at Marshall University, in Huntington, West Virginia. By the time he graduated from college, in 1973, he averaged 15 points and eight assists per game. The school's assist leader, he racked up a total of 659 assists, still the second-highest in Marshall's history. He was selected 20th in the second round of the 1973 NBA draft by the Kansas City/Omaha Kings. That year the Kings finished in fourth place in the Midwest Division, with a record of 33–49. Although D'Antoni was named to the All-Rookie second team in his first year, he played in only nine games in his two seasons with the Kings before being let go. In 1975, a year before the American Basketball Association (ABA) merged with the NBA, D'Antoni played 50 games with the ABA's Spirit of St. Louis. Next, he played two games with the San Antonio Spurs before the team cut him, in 1976. The next year, with his future in the NBA highly uncertain, the 25-year-old accepted an offer to play for the Milan, Italy–based Olimpia Milano, a member of the nation's 14-team professional league. Promised a year's salary of $30,000 and a place to live rent-free, D'Antoni, who neither spoke nor understood Italian, moved to Italy.

At that time European basketball differed from the American version in several ways. European leagues were generally less athletically competitive (a difference that has since significantly narrowed). Also, since most Europeans had not engaged in informal street or playground basketball games as youngsters, they avoided physical one-on-one matchups and fouls. Instead, European basketball, like soccer, emphasized quick ball movement and open formations. Teams were limited to having no more than two foreign players; the foreigners were usually Americans, who were often expected to lead their teams. While American players in European leagues were blamed for their team's losses, they were also given credit for victories, thus attaining stardom much more easily than they might have in the NBA. Because of his ancestry, D'Antoni was not categorized as foreign, making him an especially attractive acquisition.

D'Antoni still harbored dreams of playing with the NBA. After one season with Olimpia Milano, he asked the Chicago Bulls' management to consider him for the team. He attended the Bulls' summer rookie and veteran camps, where he performed well. A coach advised him that if he played equally well in the Bulls' preseason games, he would probably make the team. Soon afterward he suffered a thigh injury, which kept him out of the Bulls' first four preseason games and led him to reconsider his aspirations. "The Italian team [was] calling me," he recalled to Sam Smith for the *Chicago Tribune* (May 27, 2005). "There's more money in Europe. I said to myself, 'You know what, I might play here six months and be done. I can go over there and play 20 years.' I didn't even call [the Bulls]. I just went and it was like, 'Where's Mike?'"

In his first few years in Milan, D'Antoni concentrated on learning Italian. "I had no car, no phone, no TV," he told Teri Thompson for the *Daily News* (May 11, 2008). "I read about a book a day. That's about 600 books, and a new world opened up to me." D'Antoni stood out as Milano's star point guard and was celebrated for his ball-handling, passing, and defensive skills. He adopted the European style of offense and was given a lot of freedom to make strategic decisions on the court. Because of his impressive ball-stealing abilities, he was nicknamed "Arsenio Lupin," after Arsène Lupin, the fictional gentleman thief created by the French writer Maurice Leblanc. "The atmosphere playing here after the NBA is like being in college again," D'Antoni told Phil Hersh for the *Chicago Tribune* (March 31, 1986). "All of a sudden I'm important, I'm the star." During his 12 years with Olimpia Milano, D'Antoni became the franchise's leading scorer and helped his team win five Italian League titles. He also helped the Italian national team capture two European championships. D'Antoni earned a six-figure income, married an American model, Laurel Leibel, whom he had met in Milan, and associated with people famous in the fashion industry, among them Benettons and Versaces. "I grew up in Italy," he told Liz Robbins for the *New York Times* (January 16, 2005). "It broadened my way of life, how you deal with players, how you communicate." "I learned the American outlook on life isn't the only one there is," he told Greg Sandoval for the *Washington Post* (December 18, 2004). When D'Antoni retired from active play, in 1990, he was voted the league's top point guard of all time.

That year D'Antoni took on the job of coaching Olimpia Milano, with a starting salary of $200,000. He became one of Italy's top coaches, winning 68 percent of his games and guiding his team to the play-offs in each of seven seasons. From 1990 to 1994 the team's overall record was 86–34; they earned league titles in 1991 and 1992 and a Korać Cup in 1993. During that period D'Antoni fine-tuned his conception of high-tempo and improvisational play. He used an offensive formation often called "small ball"; instead of relying on a "big man" power center, who in more-traditional offenses remained next to the basket for short shots or dunks, "small ball" used three guards and two forwards who could adjust to movements all over the court like "quick, athletic, interchangeable parts," as Bob Cohn later described it for the *Washington Times* (December 25, 2004). D'Antoni had to modify that strategy when, in 1995, he became the coach of the Benetton Treviso, a squad that included two seven-foot players, Denis Marconato and Roberto Chiacig, whose height and playing style did not mesh with D'Antoni's "small-ball" offense. From 1995 to 1997 D'Antoni led Benetton Treviso to a record of 62–22; the team won the Cup of Europe in 1995 and the league title in 1997. Named Coach of the Year in Italy twice, he was said to be one of the best coaches in the league's history.

In the spring of 1997, after 20 years in Europe, D'Antoni accepted the post of director of personnel in the office of the Denver Nuggets, an NBA team that had finished the 1996–97 season fifth out of seven teams in the Midwest Division, with a win–loss record of 21–61. Though it was widely predicted that their performance in the 1997–98 season would not be much better, D'Antoni was excited to return to the NBA. "When you're living in Europe, you think you're missing out on something over here," he told Skip Myslenski for the *Chicago Tribune* (March 4, 1998). "You know, the NBA's the best, so you always have a dream to go back and try to climb the mountain a little bit more." While scouting for talent D'Antoni soon discovered that he missed coaching. In November 1997 he considered accepting an offer of a $700,000 annual salary to coach the basketball team in Barcelona, Spain, before rejecting that in favor of serving as the assistant to the head coach of the Nuggets, Bill Hanzlik, for half that amount. He thereby got "a front-row seat to what might be the most horrible NBA story ever told," Ian Thomsen wrote for the *International Herald Tribune* (January 31, 1998), in reference to the Nuggets' 1997–98 season. The team finished with 71 losses and 11 wins, only two games better than the worst record in NBA history. D'Antoni told Myslenski that his friends in Europe joked, "We thought you'd set some records in the NBA. . . . We just didn't think it'd be this quick."

After the 1998 season Hanzlik was fired, and D'Antoni took over as the Nuggets' head coach. With the return of players who had recovered from injuries and the hiring of several new ones, D'Antoni had high hopes for the team's chances to make the play-offs. A players' union strike over the issue of salary caps delayed the season's start until February 1999; in the remaining weeks of the season, the Nuggets compiled a record of 14–36, not enough to make the play-offs. D'Antoni was fired shortly before the start of the 1999 season, a less-than-ideal time to look for another job. Greg Sandoval, paraphrasing D'Antoni, described that experience as "one of the worst times of his life."

D'Antoni held administrative positions with the Spurs and the Portland Trail Blazers before returning to Italy to coach Benetton Treviso in the 2001–02 season. That year he led the team to the Italian League championship. After that season he became an assistant to Frank Johnson, the head coach of the Phoenix Suns. In 2001–02 the Suns finished with a 44–38 record. In the first 21 games of 2002–03, the team lost 13 games, and Johnson was ousted. On December 10, 2003 D'Antoni was named the Suns' new head coach; he hired his older brother, Dan, as his assistant coach. Taking over the squad midseason, he led the Suns to a final record of 21–40. In February 2004 D'Antoni made the controversial decision to trade the Suns' point guard Stephen Marbury to the New York Knicks. In the off-season, using money that became available with Marbury's departure, the Suns acquired several young, quick players, including the forward Quentin Richardson from the Los Angeles Clippers and, most importantly, the point guard Steve Nash from the Dallas Mavericks, a player known for his skills with assists, three-point shots, and free throws as well as his speed on offense.

In the 2004–05 season, his first as the team's head coach, D'Antoni engineered the third biggest season-to-season turnaround in NBA history. He introduced a strategy that relied on quick ball movement and shots taken in seven seconds or less during an offensive possession. In the conviction that that "high-octane" offense could beat even the best defense, he allowed Nash, who became an invaluable asset, the freedom to call plays and run the offense as fast as he liked. By December Nash was averaging 12 assists per game and had emerged as a three-point threat. The Suns' unusual offense proved to be both highly entertaining and highly effective. Chuck Culpepper, writing for *Newsday* (March 6, 2005), labeled it "free-flowing" and "picturesque," and Cohn described the Suns as "a throwback bunch, employing a hurry-up pace reminiscent of the racehorse NBA days before banging and plodding became the prevailing style." The Suns finished the season with the best record in the NBA (62–20) and the highest-scoring offense. They also broke the single-season record for three-point shots, with 796. In May 2005 D'Antoni was named the Coach of the Year, and Nash was named the Most Valuable Player. "I don't think many coaches in the NBA had such long coaching careers in Europe . . . ," Nash told Bill Harris for the *Toronto Sun* (May 11, 2005). "You don't have to be an NBA lifer to be a terrific coach, and he proves it. He's not very conventional." In the postseason, for the first time since 1993, the Suns advanced to the Western Conference finals, where they faced the Spurs. After losing the first three games in the best-of-seven series, the Suns won the fourth game. They lost the fifth game, 101–95.

Over the next three seasons, D'Antoni captained the Suns to 54, 61, and 44 wins, respectively, and consecutive play-off spots. In 2006 the Suns became the first team in NBA history to lead the league in scoring as well as percentages in field goals, free throws, and three-point shots. Nash was again voted the league's MVP, and the Suns advanced to the Western Conference finals, where they lost to the Mavericks in six games. In the 2006–07 season, the Suns enjoyed franchise-record winning streaks of 17 and 15 games and earned their third straight Pacific Division title. In the play-offs the Suns faced the Spurs in the Western Conference semi-finals. The Spurs won two of the first three games. During Game Four two starting members of the Suns, Amare Stoudemire and Boris Diaw, were suspended after leaving the bench when the Spurs' Robert Horry blatantly fouled Nash. The Suns won that game, then lost the next two, in part due to the absence of Stoudemire and Diaw. In February 2008 the Suns traded Shawn Marion to the Miami Heat for the seven-foot one-inch power center Shaquille O'Neal, who epitomized the traditional NBA style of play. The Suns finished the season with a 55–27 record, placing them sixth in the Western Conference. In the first round of the 2008 play-offs, they lost in five games to the Spurs, marking the fourth time in six years that Phoenix had ended its season with a loss to San Antonio. The Suns' repeated failure to advance to the NBA finals led many to question the overall effectiveness of D'Antoni's offensive style.

At the end of the 2007–08 season, the Suns' president, Steve Kerr, privately asked D'Antoni to alter his coaching style and place a stronger emphasis on defense, a suggestion that D'Antoni reportedly rejected. At his request, D'Antoni was granted permission to interview with other teams, despite the two years left on his contract. In April the Knicks' head coach, Isiah Thomas, was fired, in the wake of much criticism of his decisions regarding trades and coaching and his being named in a sexual-harassment lawsuit. The following month D'Antoni accepted a four-year contract with the Knicks.

New York fans were hopeful that D'Antoni—and the newly hired general manager, Donnie Walsh—would breathe new life into a team that Shaun Powell characterized for *Newsday* (May 11, 2008) as "bad and boring. That's two strikes. They haven't mattered in this town for a long time, and at least now, they have a coach who knows how to make basketball fun." D'Antoni's reputation as laid-back and inattentive led some to wonder whether he would mesh well with the Knicks' roster of "misfits," as Powell described them, and whether he would prove too thin-skinned for the often critical New York City media. The NBA draft lottery in May 2008 gave the Knicks a sixth-round draft pick, which was lower than they had anticipated. The Knicks selected the 20-year-old Italian player Danilo Gallinari and later signed Chris Duhon, who would become the team's new starting point guard. In the fall of 2008, Walsh made a number of roster changes that were widely interpreted as efforts to free up salary-cap space; that, in turn, would allow him to make an offer to one of a number of high-level players—including the Cavaliers' Lebron James and the Heat's Dwyane Wade—who will become free agents in 2010. D'Antoni succeeded in leading a drama-free 2008–09 season but finished with a disappointing record, including only 32 wins, which was not good enough to make the play-offs.

In 2009 the Knicks traded three players—Tim Thomas, Jerome James, and Anthony Roberson—to the Chicago Bulls in exchange for the versatile point guard Larry Hughes, and traded Malik Rose to the Oklahoma City Thunder for Chris Wilcox.

While acknowledging that the many trades that season interfered with the team's ability to establish a rhythm, D'Antoni remained optimistic about the team's future. In the summer and fall of 2009, he and Walsh continued to tweak the Knicks' roster. D'Antoni expressed particular excitement about Danilo Gallinari, the six-foot 10-inch forward from Italy who was drafted by the Knicks in 2008 but spent most of that season recovering from a back injury. In interviews D'Antoni and Walsh stated their hope that Gallinari's skills would help the Knicks earn a spot in the play-offs. D'Antoni has reportedly changed the Knicks' home-game-day routine, eliminating the morning shoot-around session to allow the players extra time to rest and to end players' commutes to two places in one day. (The team's training center is in Westchester County, north of New York City; their home games are held at Madison Square Garden, in the city's borough of Manhattan.)

Since 2006 D'Antoni has been one of three assistant coaches for the USA Men's Basketball Senior National Team. He helped guide them to a gold medal at the 2007 FIBA (International Basketball Federation) Americas Championship and a bronze medal at the 2006 FIBA World Championship in Japan. In 2007 D'Antoni was selected to coach the NBA Western Conference squad in the All-Star Game and led them to a 155–114 victory. While in Italy D'Antoni co-wrote two books on basketball strategy: *Playmaker*, written with the former Olimpia Milano head coach Dan Peterson, and *Vivendo Giacando*, written with the Italian sportswriter Tullio Lauro. (Neither book was registered with the U.S. Library of Congress.) In 2008 the Euroleague named D'Antoni one of the "50 Greatest Contributors in Euroleague History." D'Antoni served as the assistant coach, under head coach Mike Krzyzewski, of the U.S. national basketball team in the 2008 Olympics held in Beijing, China; the U.S. team won the gold medal.

D'Antoni and his wife married in 1986. In 2008 the couple and their teenage son, Michael, moved from Scottsdale, Arizona, to the New York City area. In his Suns office, according to Greg Sandoval, he kept a sign on his wall that read in Italian, referring to chess pieces, "When the game is over, the kings and pawns go into the same box." "It keeps me grounded," D'Antoni said.

—M.E.R.

Suggested Reading: *Chicago Tribune* C p4+ Mar. 31, 1986, N p4 Mar. 4, 1998, C p2 May 27, 2005; (New York) *Daily News* p57 May 14, 2008, p82 May 18, 2008; *New York Times* VIII p2 Jan. 16, 2005; *Newsday* B p31 Mar. 6, 2005, B p3 May 11, 2008; *Toronto Sun* S p11 May 11, 2005; *Washington Post* D p1 Dec. 18, 2004; *Washington Times* C p1 Dec. 24, 2004

Dati, Rachida

Nov. 27, 1965– Former French minister of justice; member of the European Parliament

Address: 7ème arrondissement de Paris Mairie, 116 rue de Grenelle, 75007 Paris, France

Joel Saget/AFP/Getty Images

The rise of Rachida Dati to one of the highest posts in the French government—that of minister of justice—has elements of a fairy tale. A child of Muslim immigrants who came to France from North Africa, Dati had no material advantages while growing up, but she had intelligence, ambition, determination, and good looks, and she succeeded in becoming well educated. Thanks to improbable opportunities that she created for herself, she fared well in the corporate world before earning a degree in law, entering government service, and, in 2002, joining Nicolas Sarkozy, then French minister of the interior, as an adviser. In early 2007 Sarkozy, a frontrunner for the presidency, picked her to be his spokesperson. A few months later, after Sarkozy won that office, he appointed her to head the Ministry of Justice. To some she was a symbol of change—the first person of North African ancestry and the first female Muslim to become a member of the French cabinet; to others, she was a puppet whom Sarkozy could use to justify the introduction of laws some perceived as harsh, particularly with regard to immigrants. Her management style, widely described as abrasive, angered many Justice

Ministry employees and led several to quit in protest. The pregnancy of the unmarried Dati provoked wide speculation as to the identity of the father (which she has not revealed), and her behavior became a hot topic in France when she returned to work less than a week after her daughter's birth, in early January 2009. Shortly afterward President Sarkozy, who had reportedly decided that she was more of a hindrance to him than a help, forced her to resign from her post; she did so in June 2009. Soon afterward French citizens elected Dati to a seat in the European Parliament, an arm of the European Union. According to John Lichfield, writing for the London *Independent* (February 13, 2009), Dati "let it be known" that she has set her sights on winning the mayoralty of Paris in 2014.

Rachida Dati was born on November 27, 1965 in Saint-Rémy, France, to poor Muslim parents of North African origin. She was the second of 12 children (some sources say 11). Her father, Mbarak Dati, was a Moroccan bricklayer, one of the many Muslim migrant workers who settled in Europe after World War II. Her mother, Fatim-Zohra Dati, an Algerian, was illiterate. According to Jason Burke in the London *Observer* (September 7, 2008), Dati was raised on the outskirts of Chalon-sur-Saône, in central France, where the family lived in a government housing project. Her father's first construction job in France was at a Catholic convent school. At his request, the school's administrators permitted Rachida and her older sister, Malika, to attend classes there. "It was here that Dati forged her fierce will to succeed," Angelique Chrisafis wrote for the London *Guardian* (November 20, 2008). "Anything less than top of the class was seen as a failure." In addition, Chrisafis wrote, Dati would "help adults in her council block write letters and fill out forms, order children to stop playing and do homework: she would give presentations about Islam to her Catholic class." When Dati was in her early teens, her mother died. (Readily available sources do not reveal the cause of her mother's death.) By the age of 14, she was not only helping to care for her many siblings while going to school but was also earning money at part-time jobs: selling Avon cosmetics door-to-door, answering phones as a nighttime hospital receptionist, and working at a supermarket. She left the Catholic school at 16; she later earned a master's degree in economics after studying at the University of Burgundy, in Dijon, France, and then at the University of Paris.

In 1987, at the age of 21, Dati wrote to the Embassy of Algeria in Paris asking for an invitation to its Independence Day celebration and succeeded in getting one. At the event she secured an invitation to lunch from France's then–justice minister, Albin Chalandon. "Suddenly, this nimble little woman came walking straight toward me and told me about the difficulties in her life, that she was physically exhausted, and that she needed my help," Chalandon recalled 20 years later, speaking to Anita Elash for the Toronto *Globe and Mail* (June 16, 2007). "This was someone with a lot of nerve, very direct, very intelligent, and who knew what she wanted. And when I saw all that, I decided it would be interesting to help someone of North African origin get out of the suburbs." Soon afterward Dati got a job as an accountant with the oil company ELF-Aquitaine, where Chalandon had been a director.

One day several years later, at an awards ceremony, she told the prominent businessman Jean-Luc Lagardère that she had dreams of working for him. Lagardère hired her as an auditor at Matra (later renamed the Lagardère Group), the conglomerate that he headed. Matra financed Dati's next academic degree, an MBA from the prestigious HEC School of Management, in Paris (the acronym stands for Hautes Etudes Commerciales, or Higher Studies in Commerce), which she earned in around 1993. (Dati's entry in *Who's Who* does not mention that school or degree. Whether or not she received it provoked a short-lived controversy in 2007, after a few journalists examined her application to law school.) From 1993 to 1994 Dati worked at the European Bank for Reconstruction and Development, in London, in its archiving and records-management department. After that she worked for a year at Suez S.A., a multinational French corporation, as secretary general of its bureau of urban development. From 1995 to 1997 she served as the technical adviser at the legal-management division of the Ministry of Education.

Taking the advice of Simone Veil, a former French minister of health and a Holocaust survivor, Dati decided to win the credentials necessary to become a magistrate—in France, either a prosecutor or a judge. From 1997 to 1999 she attended the prestigious National College of Magistrates, where she received a law degree. After graduation she became a magistrate judge in Bobigny, a city near Paris.

After three years of service in the judicial system, Dati landed a job with Nicolas Sarkozy, who was then the minister of the interior, responsible for maintaining the internal security of France. (The Ministry of the Interior has virtually nothing in common with the American Department of the Interior.) How Dati, a woman with no political experience, became one of Sarkozy's assistants has—like much of her life story—taken on an aura of legend. Dati wrote Sarkozy a series of letters (most accounts say five) asking for a job. In one letter she congratulated him on his tough (albeit unpopular) stance on young criminals. In 2002 Sarkozy hired her as a policy adviser. "There's something in me that echoes with him, a mirror effect," Chrisafis quoted her as saying. "Like me, he can't bear to be humiliated." Chrisafis continued: "Both feel themselves to be outsiders, her because of her background, him because of the foreign-sounding Hungarian surname he says haunted him, and the fact that he didn't study in Paris's elite graduate schools. He also feels deeply self-conscious about his absent father following his parents' divorce when he was a child, which set him apart from his bourgeois peers in western Paris." Dati devoted much of her time to policies and activities dealing with juvenile delinquents.

In 2006 Dati officially joined Union for a Popular Movement (UPM), a relatively conservative political party of which Sarkozy was also a member. In January 2007 Sarkozy was chosen as the official UPM candidate for president of France. On the day his candidacy was announced, Sarkozy—thanks in part to a strong suggestion from his then-wife, Cecilia—appointed Dati as his spokesperson for the presidential campaign. In May Sarkozy won 53 percent of the vote to defeat his main opponent, the Socialist Party candidate, Ségolène Royal. When Sarkozy took office, 10 days after the election, he appointed Dati minister of justice.

Sarkozy's selection of Dati to head the Ministry of Justice was seen by some as a hopeful sign of better governmental relations with Muslims and a symbol of France's increasing tolerance of Muslims—and by others as a calculated and overtly political move. To some, it was all of those things. On the positive side, Dati was the first person of North African origin and the first Muslim woman to hold a major government position in France. (Women in France hold significantly fewer political positions of power than women in most other European countries and many developing countries.) The main cause of cynical interpretations of Dati's appointment stemmed from remarks Sarkozy made in 2005, when he used such terms as "scum" and "thugs" to refer to the immigrants and children of immigrants (many of whom were Muslims or of North African origin) who rioted in violent protests against their marginalization, unemployment, poverty, and what they viewed as unfair treatment by the police. The appointment of Dati, said Sarkozy's critics, was a way of mollifying Muslims, North Africans, and others who opposed his tough stance on crime. But it also heartened conservatives, since Dati's stance on crime is also tough. She has supported minimum sentences for young offenders, many of them immigrants and some as young as 12, and she has pressed for a way to keep dangerous criminals locked up even after they have served their terms.

Dati soon took on the task of reforming the French court system. "Unpopular as it may be, the reform makes sense," according to the *Economist* (December 8, 2007). "The geography of the French court system has not changed in nearly half a century, despite huge population shifts. In largely rural areas, there is a *tribunal de grande instance* (county court) for fewer than 150,000 people; in big cities, one such court serves over 550,000. In Lorraine in eastern France, ten magistrates' courts employ a full-time judge without the workload to justify it, and two have none at all. By contrast, some city courts have vast backlogs." Acknowledging those changes in the "judiciary map," Dati drew up plans to close 178 of the 473 magistrates' courts and 23 county courts and to reallocate staff. The many lawyers, judges, and others who opposed her actions pointed out that France has 20 million more people than it did 40 years ago.

In September 2008 the public learned that Dati, at age 42, was pregnant. She announced that she would keep the identity of the father of her child secret. "I have a complicated private life and I'm keeping it off limits to the press," she declared, as quoted by Steven Erlanger in the *New York Times* (September 4, 2008). Her unmarried state received scant coverage in the mainstream press in France, where currently more than 50 percent of all births are out of wedlock. But in French tabloids and on French blogs and other Web sites, articles and discussions, most based on gossip, appeared for days on end. Fascination with Dati's pregnancy was also evident in news reports and commentary printed and posted outside France. "We are all enjoying the guessing game, but all I know is that I am extremely pleased for her," Valérie Hoffenburg, a Paris city councilor and one of Dati's close friends, told William Langley for the London *Sunday Telegraph* (September 7, 2008). "She has wanted a child for a long time, and has had many disappointments and sometimes been brought very low, and I think it is courageous of her to become pregnant knowing that there will be all this publicity and curiosity about who the father is." Hoffenburg then added that Dati, who is a secular Muslim, "has been held up as a role model for Muslim girls, and now we have Muslims denouncing her. Most people in France aren't shocked by an unmarried minister getting pregnant. The only real protests have come from her own community, and that must be hard for her."

On January 2, 2009 the 43-year-old Dati gave birth to a girl, Zohra. Five days after the delivery, by caesarian section, Dati—looking slim and attractive, according to many press reports—returned to work. While some of her compatriots applauded her commitment and dedication to her job, country, and president, her decision to resume her professional life so soon after the birth led to an outcry from French men and women, ranging from women's-rights activists to pediatric experts to politicians (most of them male). Some accused her of setting a bad example for French women, by not spending sufficient time with her newborn and failing to take advantage of her allowed time off. (Actually, French law stipulates that while companies must grant women four months of paid maternity leave, the government is not bound to give cabinet ministers or elected officials paid or unpaid leave after births.) Others noted that on the day that Dati came back to work, President Sarkozy held a press conference to announce important judicial reforms and perhaps had made Dati feel compelled to be at his side at that moment. A writer for Agence France Presse (January 13, 2009, online) quoted Ségolène Royal, who had four children with her partner (whom she never married) and was pregnant during her service as France's environment minister in the early 1990s, as saying,

"Being back on the job only five days after a caesarian is too soon, there's no doubt about that. But this exceptional duty requires exceptional behaviour." Others expressed the view that Dati's action was a somewhat desperate act to keep her job. Some observers suspected that Sarkozy already had plans to remove her from his cabinet. In late January Charles Bremner, writing for the *Irish Independent* (January 24, 2009, on-line), and many other sources reported that Sarkozy had forced Dati to announce that she would run for a seat in the European Parliament that June and would leave her ministry job at that time. "Despite denials on all sides," John Lichfield wrote, "this amounted to a slow-motion dismissal" of Dati.

While few hard facts were discernible amid the abundance of rumors and speculation that surrounded Dati's fall from favor, most political insiders and analysts attributed the change in Dati's fortunes partly to her "imperious," "high-handed," "abrasive," and "overly aggressive" manner with staff members, as it was variously described, and her failure to discuss with them Sarkozy's changes to the judicial system, which as justice minister she was obliged to introduce. Nearly 50 Justice Ministry employees quit, according to some reports. Photo essays about Dati in fashion magazines along with her penchant for wearing very expensive clothing and jewelry in a time of recession also drew sharp criticism. "The trial of a brother for heroin trafficking was an excuse for more attacks," Jason Burke wrote. "The slightest gaffe is the pretext for editorials questioning her competence." Some political commentators believed that animosity between Dati and Sarkozy's second wife, the model and singer Carla Bruni, also contributed to Sarkozy's dissatisfaction with her. In October 2009 Dati's brother Jamal published a controversial book, *In the Shadow of Rachida*, that casts aspersions on Dati's behavior and alleged actions. "I've definitively cut myself off from my brother since he started this project," Dati told reporters, as quoted by Jack Bremer in the *First Post* (October 5, 2009, on-line), a British publication.

According to some sources, Sarkozy promised Dati that, once she began her service in the European Parliament, he would not stand in the way of her political ambitions. In addition to her membership in the Parliament, Dati is the mayor of the seventh arrondissement (district) in Paris, a mostly ceremonial position that she won in March 2008. In February 2009 she announced that she plans to run for mayor of Paris in 2014, when the second term of the current mayor will expire.

—D.K.

Suggested Reading: *Economist* Europe Dec. 8, 2007, Jan. 10, 2009; (London) *Guardian* p8 Nov. 20, 2008; (London) *Observer* Sep. 7, 2008; *U.S. News & World Report* p39+ Dec. 29, 2008

Davis, Artur

Oct. 9, 1967– U.S. representative from Alabama (Democrat)

Address: 208 Cannon House Office Bldg., Washington, DC 20515

"Too many of us, black and white, are teaching our children first and foremost about what separates us," Artur Davis said in 2002, shortly after he won his first election to represent Alabama's Seventh Congressional District, as quoted in the *Almanac of American Politics.* Since he entered the House of Representatives, Davis has become prominent as a member of a new wave of African-American politicians, for whom the struggle against racial discrimination has been superseded by the push for better schools, better and more widely available health care, and economic development that will lead to more and better-paying jobs. "If Obama is president, it will no longer be tenable to go to the white community and say you've been victimized," Davis told Matt Bai for the *New York Times Magazine* (August 10, 2008), three months before Barack Obama's victory in that year's presidential election—the first such victory by an African-American. "And I understand the poverty and the condition of black America and the 39 percent unemployment rate in some communities. I understand that. But if you go out to the country and say you've been victimized by the white community, while Barack Obama and Michelle and their kids are living in the White House, you will be shut off from having any influence." Raised by a single mother literally on the wrong side of the tracks in Montgomery, Alabama, Davis completed his undergraduate and law degrees at Harvard University. During the decade between his completion of law school and his swearing in as a congressman, he interned at a nonprofit legal organization, held the post of assistant U.S. attorney in a federal district court in Alabama, and maintained a private law practice. Stung by his defeat in his first bid for election to the House, against the veteran politician Earl Hilliard, he identified an issue—the Israeli-Palestinian controversy—on which the incumbent's stance displeased many supporters of Israel; by reaching those voters, most of whom lived in states other than Alabama, he raised far more in campaign contributions than his opponent and triumphed on Election Day 2002. In *Time* (September 1, 2008), Davis was listed among five up-and-coming Democrats whom the magazine identified as "hotshots to watch." According to many sources, Davis has set his sights on winning the governorship of Alabama in 2010.

Courtesy of the Office of Artur Davis

Artur Davis

"If you want an American bootstrap story, his is it," the political scientist Natalie Davis said of Artur Davis, as quoted by Jonetta Rose Barras for the *New Democrats Online* (April 15, 2003). Born in Montgomery on October 9, 1967, according to most accounts (only *Who's Who* has a different month—April), Artur Davis was raised by his mother and grandmother in a small house beside railroad tracks in the low-income, western part of that city. According to Phillip Rawls, a writer for the Associated Press (October 29, 2008, on-line), his father, a nurse, and his mother, a schoolteacher, divorced when he was very young. His father moved to California and seems to have been mostly or totally absent from Artur's life. "I was painfully shy as a child," Davis recalled to Rawls. His discomfort among his peers continued into high school. "I had a giant Afro way past the point where they were fashionable," he told Rawls. "I had glasses, which are fine when you are older, but they are not so great when you are 16 or 17." When not in school or at home, Davis stayed in the local public library, reading and learning. Davis attended Montgomery public schools, performing well enough at Jefferson Davis High School to gain admittance to Harvard University, in Cambridge, Massachusetts, through a scholarship. During the summer before his junior year, his mother received a foreclosure notice on their house, and she, Davis, and his grandmother lived in a "tiny motel room" for three weeks, as he recalled in the speech in which he seconded the nomination of Barack Obama as president at the 2008 Democratic National Convention, as transcribed for *Congressional Quarterly* (August 28, 2008). Davis graduated with a B.A. degree in government, magna cum laude, in 1990, and then enrolled at Harvard's law school. While there he befriended his fellow student Barack Obama, who had been elected editor in chief of the *Harvard Law Review*. The first time he heard Obama speak publicly, to other students in a Harvard classroom, he found his friend's words compelling. "He said we faced three challenges," Davis told Howard Fineman for *Newsweek* (February 25, 2008). "First: competence, which was expected. Second: excellence, which only some seek. Third: mastery, which very few ever tried for. It was a level of proficiency and skill so high it allowed you to do something better than anyone else. He urged us to seek that." While he was in law school, Davis served an internship with U.S. senator Howell Heflin, an Alabama Democrat. In 1993 Davis earned a J.D. degree, cum laude.

After he completed his formal education, Davis returned to the South and became an intern at the Southern Poverty Law Center, whose main office is in Montgomery. For one year he worked on matters concerned with civil rights, employment discrimination, and racial equality. He then clerked under U.S. District Court judge Myron H. Thompson, one of the first African-Americans appointed to the federal bench. In 1994 Davis became an assistant U.S. attorney with the United States District Court for the Middle District of Alabama, the federal trial court where Judge Thompson presided. During the next four years, he helped to prosecute civil and criminal cases involving white-collar offenders, drug dealers, and people accused of violent crimes. He often appeared on local television programs to comment on legal issues and cases, and his shyness faded away. Davis regarded his work as a public attorney as a springboard to elective office. "It gets you accustomed to making a case to a group of people, quickly and concisely," he told Michael Wilson for the *New York Times* (July 3, 2002). He told Phillips Rawls, "Being a lawyer and standing up and arguing in front of juries, that was probably the best political training I got."

In 1998 Davis left his government job to start a private practice in Birmingham that would focus on civil rights law. In 2000 he made an unsuccessful, poorly funded bid to unseat the four-term Democratic congressman Earl Hilliard, Alabama's first African-American representative in Congress since Reconstruction. For a brief time he provided political commentary on a local Fox television affiliate. In 2002 he tried again to win Hilliard's seat as the representative of Alabama's Seventh Congressional District, one of the poorest districts in the U.S., running a spirited primary campaign against the incumbent, who was 25 years his senior and whom he labeled a member of the old guard in politics—"a guy who saw himself principally as a spokesman for the community rather than as an actual legislator," as Matt Bai paraphrased Davis in the *New York Times Magazine* (August 6, 2008). "Earl Hilliard is where we came from, not where we are going, and it is time to bring him back home," Davis said during his campaign, according to K. Ter-rell Reed and Sonia Alleyne, writing for *Black Enterprise* (November 2002). For his part, Hilliard tried to plant doubts in his constituents' minds about Davis's commitment to the community, and he disparaged Davis's accomplishments as a government attorney. "The only thing he's done for black people is put them in jail," Hilliard declared, as quoted by Michael Wilson.

In addition to stirring up tension between generations of black politicians, the Hilliard-Davis race drew the attention of pro-Israel lobbying groups, which considered Hilliard to be weak in his support of Israel or partial to Palestinians in the decades-long Israeli-Palestinian conflict. Thanks to publicity within and outside Alabama generated by those groups, individuals and organizations sympathetic to their views contributed about $300,000 to Davis's war chest. John Nichols reported in the June 27, 2002 on-line issue of the *Nation* that, according to the Center for Responsive Politics, in total Davis raised $879,368—more than 10 times the amount he had collected two years earlier; according to the *National Journal* (July 9, 2002), 82 percent of contributions above $200 that came to Davis arrived from out of state, particularly from New York. Other sources reported that Davis secured $1 million, while Hilliard's 2002 total came to a little over $500,000. In the primary election, held on June 25, 2002, Davis beat Hilliard by a margin of 56 percent to 44 percent. In his interview with Michael Wilson, Davis downplayed his financial advantage in that contest. "All money enables you to do is communicate your message," he said. "If the message doesn't resonate, you lose." In the general election, held the following November, Davis trounced his only opponent, the Libertarian candidate, Lauren Orth McCay, winning 92 percent of the ballots cast.

Once in Congress, Davis quickly gained a reputation for practicing bipartisanship and what some have dubbed "postracial politics" (a label Davis does not embrace). A member of the centrist New Democrat Coalition, Davis has taken liberal stands on some issues and conservative positions on others. In a show of support for business and economic development, he promised to "reach out in an aggressive manner to the business community," as quoted by Alexandra Starr in *BusinessWeek* (July 15, 2002). He was also a champion of social programs that helped his constituents. In his first term he helped to restore previously cut funds to minority land-grant colleges such as Tuskegee University. He later led bipartisan efforts to restore funding to the HOPE VI program, which sought to renovate and improve public housing. "This project is a major step towards revitalizing the Ensley/Five Points West community," Davis said in a press release announcing the grant of $20 million to the housing program (June 4, 2004), referring to a section of Birmingham. "I am pleased that the administration has realized the value of this program and look forward to watching it come to fruition in the coming years." Davis also campaigned successfully for the passage of the Southern Empowerment and Economic Development Act, which authorized the creation of the Delta Black Belt Regional Authority to help residents of the Black Belt; a large area of the Deep South that is historically associated with slave labor in agriculture, the Black Belt is home to some of the nation's poorest citizens.

On another front, Davis attempted to promote much of the pro-Israel agenda that had been part of his campaign platform. Viewing Israel as an admirable democracy and U.S. ally surrounded by hostile forces, he co-sponsored several bills designed to impose harsher penalties on Israel's neighbors for showing aggression, such as the Syria Accountability Act, which imposed sanctions against the Syrian government for harboring terrorists. He also voted "yes" on the Solidarity with Israel Resolution and the "Iran Democracy" bill, both of which hinted that the use of U.S. force against countries including Iran and Syria would be justified if they did not meet certain standards of behavior. In 2003 he signed his name to a letter in which members of Congress stated that they were "deeply dismayed" at President George W. Bush's criticism of Israel's recent missile strike on a site in Gaza City where the Hamas leader Abdel Rantisi was believed to be; Israel's action, the letter maintained, "was clearly justified as an application of Israel's right to self defense," as quoted by Shirl McArthur in the *Washington Report on Middle East Affairs* (September 2003).

In the 2004 Democratic primary, Davis faced a challenge from Albert Turner Jr., whose father had been a civil rights leader and adviser to Martin Luther King Jr. Davis's status as an incumbent and his image as a practical, productive lawmaker enabled him to rebuff Turner's challenge and capture 88 percent of the vote. In the general election he defeated the Republican challenger—Steve Cameron, a musician—by a ratio of three votes to one. During the 109th Congress (2005–06), Davis was appointed to the House Committee on the Budget as well as the House Financial Services Committee and three of its five subcommittees: Housing and Community Opportunity; Capital Markets, Insurance, and Government Sponsored Enterprises; and Oversight and Investigations. He also began serving on the senior whip team of the Democratic Caucus and became a vice chair of the centrist New Democrat Coalition.

With the Republican congressman Chris Smith of New Jersey, Davis co-sponsored the Stem Cell Therapeutic & Research Act of 2005, which aimed to establish a national bank for the storage of blood from newborns' umbilical cords, which contains stem cells. President Bush signed the bill into law on December 20, 2005. "We and all the patients who will be helped applaud the efforts of Representatives Chris Smith and Artur Davis for their sponsorship of this bill," Robert L. Jones, the president of the New York Blood Center, said in a press release (December 20, 2005). "They both have been strong advocates in the fight to save lives through providing more and better cord blood transplants."

In 2006 Davis won the Democratic primary with almost 91 percent of the vote; in the general election he ran unopposed. During the 110th Congress he served on the influential Ways and Means Committee and two of its subcommittees—Social Security, and Income Security and Family Support. He was also appointed to the Judiciary Committee and three of its subcommittees: Constitution, Civil Rights, and Civil Liberties; Crime, Terrorism, and Homeland Security; and Immigration, Citizenship, Refugees, Border Security, and International Law. He also became a member of the House Majority Leader's Advisory Group and of the Steering and Policy Committee, which has the power to approve committee assignments and rules changes for the Democratic Caucus.

In Alabama Davis chaired the health-care subcommittee of Governor Bob Riley's Black Belt Action Commission, whose mission was to take steps to improve the quality of life in the Black Belt. In an effort to remedy an often overlooked problem, Davis initiated the Black Belt Eye Care Consortium, a network of organizations that would provide eye care without charge to underserved groups. "Proper eye care is a dire necessity for children and adults," Davis said in a press release on the commission's Web site. "I am very pleased that these groups have decided to work together to begin to deliver a sense of normalcy to the lives of adults and children who otherwise would struggle at the most basic tasks in life." Other programs headed by Davis's subcommittee include the Rural Alabama Diabetes and Glaucoma Initiative and the Community Care Network, the latter of which recently organized health fairs in the state's 12 Black Belt counties.

Despite his firsthand knowledge of lingering disparities between whites and blacks in wealth, health, and other areas, Davis has frequently noted the progress the U.S. has made with regard to racial equality. "Until our generation, it was assumed the highest we could aspire to was to be a member of the House," he told Howard Fineman. "Now that ceiling has been lifted." Davis was the first congressman from a state other than Illinois to endorse U.S. senator Barack Obama of Illinois in his quest for the presidency. He has come under fire for diverging from traditional liberal Democratic stances on such issues as abortion rights and gun control—for example, he voted for the Partial-Birth Abortion Ban Act of 2003, which criminalizes a rarely performed procedure, known medically as intact dilation and extraction (or evacuation), except in cases in which the life of the mother is threatened. Davis also voted for the Protection of Lawful Commerce in Arms Act of 2005, which prohibits people from bringing product-misuse lawsuits against gun manufacturers. In addition, he has been taken to task for straying from purely "black" issues too often. "Davis is one of those 'New Blacks' who are black in skin tone, but philosophically they are not," Hilliard said of him during the 2002 campaign, as quoted by Kay S. Hymowitz in the quarterly periodical *City Journal* (Winter 2007). Davis has countered that he believes traditional racial politics are neither helpful to minority constituents nor productive in the give-and-take required among members of Congress. He recalled to Hymowitz an instance in which one of his black constituents accused him of not putting black issues first. "I told him point-blank: What about my white colleague in the Third District who has a 35 percent black population? Do you want him to just represent white people? We're not going to win that game. We're the minority in most places." "In just my lifetime the meaning of leadership for African Americans has changed," he told Terrence Samuel for the *American Prospect* (September 2007). "When my mother came along you could teach, but you couldn't teach white children, you could lead, but you couldn't lead white people. This is a different space. Now you could live up to your potential. . . . I can't think of a single issue in American political life where you can still say 'This will exclusively affect blacks,' or 'This will only affect whites.'"

In press releases in late 2008, Davis described his efforts to promote the adoption of foster children whose care is supervised by Alabama government agencies (December 2, 2008); announced his creation of a judicial advisory committee to help him evaluate candidates for federal judgeships in Alabama and United States attorney positions (December 8, 2008); announced the launch of that committee's Web site (December 18, 2008); discussed his opposition to the federal bailout of the auto industry (December 10, 2008); informed his constituents of a meeting aimed to ensure that Alabama's most needed infrastructure projects are included in the forthcoming federal-stimulus package (December 15, 2008); and expressed his support for the continuation of tax incentives to spur business growth in so-called empowerment zones in Alabama's most depressed areas (December 16, 2008).

In early 2009 Davis announced that he would run for the governorship of Alabama in that state's general election in November 2010. His campaign officially began in June 2009, and in its first few months, observers gave Davis little chance of succeeding in the heavily white, mostly Republican state. "If elected, he would be the first black governor of a Deep South state since Reconstruction . . . ," Robbie Brown noted for the *New York Times* (June 5, 2009). "If Mr. Davis hopes to win, he must convince Alabamians that he is more than Mr. Obama with a Southern drawl—and far more centrist than the president. Mr. Obama lost Alabama by 21 percentage points to Senator John McCain." While some observers argued that Davis's bid was unwise and potentially damaging to both his career and Democrats in general, others maintained that Davis was determined to win and might continue to move to the right in relation to his national Democratic colleagues in order to appeal to his state's more conservative voters.

Davis lives in Birmingham and Washington, D.C. On January 1, 2009 he married Tara Johnson, an outreach coordinator with the Alabama Forestry Commission.

—J.E.P.

Suggested Reading: *American Prospect* p23 Sep. 2007; Associated Press (on-line) Oct. 29, 2008; *City Journal* p30 Winter 2007; Congressman Artur Davis's Web site; *New York Times Magazine* (on-line) July 3, 2002, Aug. 10, 2008; *Newsweek* p33 Feb. 25, 2008; *Almanac of American Politics 2006*

David Paul Morris/Getty Images

Doerr, John

(dore)

June 29, 1951– Venture capitalist; social and environmental activist

Address: Kleiner Perkins Caufield & Byers, 2750 Sand Hill Rd., Menlo Park, CA 94025

"I love helping people make a large-scale impact. I'm a networker, an organizer, an unbounded enthusiast and supporter of great entrepreneurs and leaders." That self-description by the venture capitalist John Doerr appeared in a Harvard Business School (HBS) booklet published in October 2008, when the school honored him with an Alumni Achievement Award. Since he joined the California venture-capital firm Kleiner Perkins Caufield & Byers (KPCB), in 1980, Doerr has handled investments in some of the most successful technological start-ups of the past three decades, among them Sun Microsystems, Netscape, Intuit, Compaq, Amazon.com, and Google. In *Forbes* (October 25, 1993), Nancy Rutter identified Doerr as "arguably the finest venture capitalist of his generation," while John Chambers, the chairman and chief executive officer of Cisco Systems, has described him as "the single best venture capitalist in the world," according to the HBS booklet. Doerr's importance and influence in the world of venture capital has been likened to that of Bill Gates, the co-founder of Microsoft, in the field of software. Dubbing him the "Johnny Appleseed" of venture capital, *Time Digital* (October 4, 1999) ranked Doerr number 17 on a list of the "50 most important people shaping technology," declaring, "In a world of Midas touches, . . . Doerr's handshake is the most golden."

Venture capitalists, Doerr explained in an interview with John Brockman for *Edge* (1996, on-line), "help assemble and then invest in a team of entrepreneurs or scientists. Usually the ventures are startups. Sometimes they're already going—I call those 'speedups.' . . . In the end, we're recruiters who pay you for the right to help build your team. You reward us with shares of stock. We both work like crazy to make the stock valuable." In an interview for the HBS *Bulletin* (December 1997, on-line), Doerr said that his firm looks for "five characteristics [that] distinguish outstanding ventures. Most ventures will have only two or three of these when they come to us, so we work with the team to add the missing elements. The characteristics are technical excellence; outstanding management; strategic focus on a large, rapidly growing market; and a set of financings reasonable for all parties. Fifth, and most important, is a tremendous sense of urgency. We want to back ventures that are the first or second entrants in their markets, so speeding the product to market in advance of the competition is absolutely crucial."

Doerr has attributed his success in part to the skills, knowledge, and insights of his KPCB partners—there were 30 as of October 2009—and the entrepreneurs they have helped to bankroll. He told Laura Rich for the *New York Times* (May 3, 2004), "I'm part of a firm with lots of prominent partners. One of the things that happened in the [dot-com] boom was too much attention was paid to venture capital and not enough to the entrepreneurs and innovators and scientists. And that is rightly where the action is." In recent years Doerr has become an energetic advocate for alternative energy. "The climate crisis is the most urgent problem facing our planet," he has said, as quoted in the HBS booklet. "It is critical that we accelerate the flow of investment into green technology." Doerr recruited former vice president Al Gore, a friend of his, who won the Nobel Peace Prize for his efforts to stop global warming, to join Kleiner Perkins' GreenTech Team, which focuses on investments in sustainable-energy and -fuel ventures. In 2009 Doerr was named to President Barack Obama's 15-member economic-recovery advisory board.

The eldest of five children, Louis John Doerr III was born on June 29, 1951 in St. Louis, Missouri, to Louis John Doerr Jr. and his wife, Rosemary. He grew up in a "tight-knit middle-class family," according to the HBS interviewer, and was "influenced by his entrepreneurial father"; indeed, in an autobiographical account for the book *Done Deals: Venture Capitalists Tell Their Stories* (2000), edited by Udayan Gupta, he referred to his father as his "hero." (On the KPCB Web site, he also named as his heroes his mother and two computer-company executives: Bill Joy, the co-founder of Sun Microsystems, who has been a KPCB partner since 2005, and William F. "Bill" Campbell, currently the chairman and CEO of Intuit.) "My parents worked hard to give all five of their children something that no one could take away—a great education," Doerr told the interviewer. He attended Chaminade College Preparatory School, a Catholic boys school in St. Louis. Following his graduation he enrolled at Rice University, in Houston, Texas, where he studied electrical engineering. During his sophomore year, with two friends, he started a graphics-software business, Warren Rowe and Associates. After earning a B.S. degree, in 1973, and an M.S. degree, also in electrical engineering, in 1974, Doerr sold his interest in the software company and moved to Cambridge, Massachusetts, to pursue an M.B.A. at the Harvard Business School. He was interested in starting his own business and spent his first summer away from Harvard in California, hoping to find work at a venture-capital firm. "Venture capital, I'd heard, had something to do with building new companies," Doerr told Gupta. "So I cold-called Silicon Valley's venture groups, hoping to apprentice myself to one." At that time venture-capital jobs were sparse. Instead, Doerr was hired for the summer by the up-and-coming Intel Corp., a maker of semiconductor chips that was headquartered in Santa Clara, California.

Founded six years earlier, Intel had introduced in April 1974 its 8080 microprocessor, an eight-bit central processing unit (CPU) that is now considered the first true general-purpose microprocessor. Doerr spent that summer with Andrew "Andy" Grove, an Intel executive, helping to train Intel's sales force in the U.S. and Europe. Gupta wrote that Grove, who had been with Intel virtually from its beginning, served as a mentor to Doerr. After that summer Doerr returned to Harvard, at the same time working for Intel as a field engineer. Intel assigned him to work with the Digital Equipment Corp. (DEC), in Maynard, Massachusetts, which manufactured minicomputers for engineers and scientists. (DEC was acquired in 1998 by Compaq, which merged with Hewlett-Packard in 2002.) Upon his graduation from Harvard, in 1976, Doerr moved to Santa Clara, where he joined Intel's engineering department and then its marketing department. He transferred to Intel's Chicago office to take a job in sales, then returned to Santa Clara to become Intel's marketing manager. In 1978 Doerr married Ann Howland, a Rice graduate who was working at Intel as a software engineer.

In 1980 Doerr left Intel to join KPCB—named for the partners Eugene Kleiner, Tom Perkins, Frank Caufield, and Brook Byers—in Palo Alto, California. He was initially reluctant to take the job. KPCB "wanted a gofer to help check out new business plans. I was still interested in someday starting a venture, but I wasn't so sure about venture capital," he wrote for *Done Deals*. When the four partners interviewed him, they "promised that if I worked for them, they would someday back me in starting a new venture." They did just that the following year, when Doerr and the computer scientist Carver Mead co-founded Silicon Compilers, a company specializing in the development of software that aids in the design and manufacture of computer chips. Silicon Compilers later merged with Silicon Design Labs and was bought by Mentor Graphics in the early 1990s.

Doerr became a full partner at KPCB in 1982. That year he advocated investment in Compaq, a fledgling computer company that had been founded earlier in the year by three former employees of the semiconductor manufacturer Texas Instruments. KPCB had already turned down a request for funds from Compaq, when the company sought to sell hard-disk drives for IBM desktop computers. After Compaq executives revised their business plans to focus on building the first transportable computer, Doerr persuaded his partners to invest. In its first year Compaq sold $110 million worth of portable computers. In 1986 Compaq appeared on the *Fortune* 500 list (*Fortune*'s annual ranking of the 500 largest corporations in the U.S.), sooner after its founding than any other firm at that time. By 1988 Compaq's total revenues since its launch totaled $1 billion, a figure it reached faster than any other start-up in history.

In 1990 Doerr was instrumental in KPCB's $4.7 million investment in Intuit Inc., a computer-software company responsible for the finance software Quicken and QuickBooks. Scott Cook, the founder of the seven-year-old Intuit, which was already enjoying moderate success, wanted additional support to strengthen the company's hold on the market. In 1993 KPCB, which received ownership of 12 percent of Intuit's stock for their investment, helped facilitate Intuit's merger with Chipsoft Inc., which marketed the tax-preparation software TurboTax. Six years later Doerr's 85,000 shares of Intuit were valued at $8.2 million.

In 1994 Doerr handled KPCB's investment in Netscape Communications, founded in April of that year by the entrepreneur Jim Clark and the software engineer Marc Andreessen as the Mosaic Communications Corp. Clark and Andreesen were marketing Mosaic, the first Internet browser, which Andreessen had created with Eric Bina. KPCB invested $5 million for a 25 percent stake in the company. In 1995, after Mosaic was renamed Netscape, the company went public. At the beginning of its first day of trading, its stock price was

$28; by the closing bell it had risen to $58. In time KPCB's investment in Netscape earned the partners a total of $400 million. (America Online purchased Netscape for $4.2 billion in 1998.) Among Doerr's other major success stories were KPCB's $8 million investment in Amazon.com in 1996, which netted $60 million for the firm when Amazon.com went public the following year, and their $12.5 million infusion of funds into Google in 2001, an investment whose worth in 2007 was $12 billion.

A few of Doerr's recommendations have not borne fruit. One of his most notable failures involved the Go Corp., founded in 1987 by Bill Joy, of Sun Microsystems, Robert Carr, of the Ashton-Tate Corp., and Mitchell Kapor and S. Jerrold Kaplan, both of the Lotus Development Corp. The four entrepreneurs wanted to develop a mobile computer controllable with a pen: the computer would recognize a user's handwriting and transfer the data over wireless networks as e-mail messages, voicemail, or faxes. With $30 million of venture capital, almost $5 million of it from KPCB, Go was among the most investment-heavy start-ups in history. Nevertheless, it failed, "but not for lack of vision or good corporate partners," Doerr wrote in *Done Deals*. "IBM, AT&T, and [KPCB] backed some of America's smartest, most passionate entrepreneurs who were convinced that pen computers were the next big thing. But our implementation was just wrong. We misread the market and picked the wrong price point, and the handwriting recognition was too ambitious." "If you're not failing once in a while, you're not venturing enough," Vern Raburn, the former chairman of the Paul Allen Group, a technology-management company, and the founder of the Eclipse Aviation Corp., told Daniel Lyons for *Computer Reseller News* (November 18, 1996). "In a way, you could say [Doerr] is the ultimate venture capitalist."

As a member of various boards of directors, Doerr has been associated with several companies whose officers were accused of insider trading and accounting fraud. (They include the real-estate company Homestore.com Inc., later known as Homestore Inc., and Martha Stewart Living Omnimedia Inc. Three of Homestore's executives pleaded guilty to securities fraud in connection with the company's accounting practices in 2002. Doerr, who sat on the board of Stewart's company from July 1999 to March 2002, was a defendant in a 2003 lawsuit brought by Stewart shareholders, but the charges against him were dropped.) Before the burst of the so-called dot-com bubble (the period between 1995 and 2001, when Internet-based companies flourished, leading to extraordinarily bullish stock markets), Doerr had often touted the Internet as the source of "the greatest legal creation of wealth in the history of the planet," in his words. He thus encouraged people to have a romanticized view of the investment world, according to the business and technology expert Paul Kedrosky, now a senior fellow at the Kauffman Foundation, which is devoted to entrepreneurship. Doerr "was a blue-eyed believer but his proclamations were so full of hyperbole that there was no good that could come of them . . . ," Kedrosky complained to Ariana Eunjung Cha for the *Washington Post* (November 13, 2002). "He made a lot of people lose a lot of money." Paul Saffo, a former director of the Institute for the Future, defended Doerr, telling Cha, "It is in the nature of technological innovations for inventors and the people closest to them to be excited by what they see. . . . That John Doerr's enthusiasm was infectious is not John Doerr's fault." Still, some critics say Doerr's practice of *keiretsu*, a Japanese term that refers to a network of firms that help each other by sharing financial and strategic information, helped cause the dangerous inflation of the dot-com bubble. "During the late 1990s," Cha wrote, "the Kleiner keiretsu companies, which included e-retailers, optical-networking toolmakers and software companies, would sometimes get their initial revenue from online ads, equipment and services they bought from each other. . . . The result, some critics say, was an artificial demand for the companies' products that was deceptive because it wouldn't have existed without the involvement of Kleiner partners."

In about 2005 Doerr began to urge his partners to invest in alternative-energy projects. "I worry that America will not be able to innovate fast enough in its policies and technologies to prevent the catastrophic, irreversible climate crisis," he told Erika Brown for *Forbes* (January 24, 2008, online). "I want Kleiner to make major, measurable contributions to solving global warming. It's the largest economic opportunity of the 21st century, and a moral imperative." The firm's dedication to the green movement prompted the 2000 U.S. Democratic presidential nominee and environmental activist Al Gore, who has been a friend of Doerr's for years, to join KPCB as a partner in 2007. In turn, Doerr joined the board of Gore and David Blood's London-based investment company Generation Investment Management. In an article about the cooperative efforts of Gore, Doerr, and Blood, Marc Gunther and Adam Lashinsky wrote for *Fortune* (November 26, 2007), "If Gore is the elder statesman of the group, Doerr is the salesman. Famous both for his boundless energy and his high-end hucksterism, at 56 he is wiry and birdlike in his tendency to flit from topic to topic. He specializes in making everyone around him believe as passionately about his current cause—first the PC, then the Internet, now the environment—as he does." As of January 2008 KPCB had invested in 26 energy-related companies. Doerr currently sits on the boards of several, among them Amyris, a renewable-products company that creates and markets biofuels and malaria drugs; Bloom Energy, which manufactures fuel cells; and Miasolé, a maker of solar panels.

Doerr is an activist in areas including education reform, elimination of global poverty, improvement of health care around the world, stem-cell research, and an increase in the number of women in leadership positions. In 1998, with Brook Byers and the social entrepreneur Kim Smith, he co-founded the NewSchools Venture Fund, whose mission is to promote innovation in the education of children in kindergarten through 12th grade. The fund supports both nonprofit and profit-making entities. Doerr co-chaired successful efforts to pass Propositions 39 and 71—on ballots statewide in California in 2000 and 2004, respectively—the first of which raised about $23 billion for public schools and the second of which authorized the allocation of $3 billion in state funds for stem-cell research. Until recently he was a board member of the Grameen Foundation, which to date, through microfinancing (loans ranging from less than $100 to a few hundred dollars in U.S. currency), has helped 45 million people who were living in poverty in 23 countries start and maintain their own businesses. He is currently on the board of trustees of the Aspen Institute, which strives "to foster values-based leadership . . . and to provide a neutral and balanced venue for discussing and acting on critical issues," according to its Web site. Doerr was influential in the creation of the Biomedical Advanced Research and Development Authority (BARDA), overseen by the assistant secretary for preparedness and response, within the U.S. Department of Health and Human Services; established by the Pandemic and All-Hazards Preparedness Act of 2006, BARDA works to prepare the U.S. to meet threats posed by potentially epidemic or pandemic infectious diseases, such as influenza, as well as chemical, radiological, and nuclear threats. He devoted time and energy to the passage in California of the Global Warming Solutions Act, which the state's governor, Arnold Schwarzenegger, signed into law in 2006. The first such legislation to go into effect in the U.S., it requires the total amount of greenhouse-gas emissions in California to drop to 1990 levels by 2020 and calls for penalties for noncompliance.

With his personal funds, Doerr invests in businesses devoted to genomics, advanced medical equipment, technologies to increase Internet bandwidth, and alternative energy. He sits on the boards of directors of companies including Amazon.com, Google, Bloom Energy, Navigenics, and Zazzle. A thin man with sandy blond hair and glasses, he has been described as energetic, charismatic, and affable. Every year since 2001 *Forbes* has listed him among the 400 richest people in the U.S., and for the past seven years, it has placed him among the top four on its "Midas" list, which recognizes "the top tech deal makers in the world." Doerr's honors include the 2007 Lifetime Achievement Award from the Lester Center for Entrepreneurship and Innovation at the University of California–Berkeley. In 1997 Doerr and his wife established the L. John and Ann H. Doerr chair in computational engineering at Rice University, a $1 million endowment that honors Ken Kennedy, a professor who encouraged them to meet. They live with their two adopted daughters—Mary, who is in her late teens, and Ester, an adolescent—in Woodside, California. Since 2000, when his wife was diagnosed with cancer, Doerr has made sure to be home for supper with his family at least 20 days of every month. His recreational activities include bicycling, hiking, skiing, traveling, and surfing the Web.

—M.A.S.

Suggested Reading: *Computer Reseller News* (online) Sep. 20, 1999; *Forbes* p105 Oct. 25, 1993; *Fortune* p82+ Nov. 26, 2007, p96 July 21, 2008; kpcb.com; *New York Times* C p1+ May 3, 2004; *Washington Post* A p1+ Nov. 13, 2002; Gupta, Udayan, ed. *Done Deals: Venture Capitalists Tell Their Stories*, 2000

Courtesy of the office of Shaun Donovan

Donovan, Shaun

Jan. 24, 1966– Secretary of the U.S. Department of Housing and Urban Development

Address: U.S. Dept. of Housing and Urban Development, 451 Seventh St., S.W., Washington, DC 20410

Shaun Donovan began serving as the commissioner of the New York City Department of Housing Preservation and Development (HPD) in 2004. He took a brief leave of absence in 2008 to advise the Democratic presidential candidate Barack Obama during his successful run. In December of that year, the president-elect chose Donovan to head the U.S. Department of Housing and Urban Development

(HUD). He was confirmed by the U.S. Senate on January 22, 2009 and sworn in on January 27.

Shaun L. Donovan was born on January 24, 1966 in New York City. As a young boy he became fascinated with building model cars and dreamed of being a car designer. After graduating, in 1983, from the prestigious Dalton School, located on Manhattan's Upper East Side, he enrolled at Harvard University, in Cambridge, Massachusetts, earning a B.A. degree in engineering in 1987. Donovan also pursued graduate studies at Harvard; in 1995 he obtained both an M.A. degree in architecture from the Graduate School of Design and a master's degree in public administration from the John F. Kennedy School of Government. Over the next three years, Donovan worked as an architect in Italy and New York City; he also had a stint with the Community Preservation Corp. (CPC), a New York City–based nonprofit lender and developer of affordable housing. During that period Donovan conducted research and wrote case studies for the Joint Center for Housing Studies at Harvard.

In 1998 Donovan began a three-year stint at HUD, serving first as a special assistant and then as the deputy assistant secretary for multifamily housing. He helped oversee the development and administration of privately owned, government-subsidized housing programs, which provided more than $9 billion annually to 1.7 million families. His duties included managing a portfolio of 30,000 multifamily properties with more than two million housing units. He was also named acting commissioner of the Federal Housing Administration (FHA) during the transition from Bill Clinton's administration to that of George W. Bush.

After leaving the federal government, Donovan served as a visiting scholar at New York University (NYU), from June 2001 to July 2002, conducting research on the preservation of federally assisted housing. While at NYU he also worked as a consultant for the Millennial Housing Commission, a panel created by Congress to address the need for affordable multifamily housing in the U.S. He then spent two years as a managing director at Prudential Mortgage Capital Co., where he was responsible for managing the company's portfolio of affordable loans, which totaled more than $1.5 billion in debt from a number of federal agencies, including the FHA and the Federal National Mortgage Association (also known as Fannie Mae), the nation's largest underwriter of home mortgages. (In 2000 Prudential had acquired the WMF Group, a financial-services firm and lender to FHA and Fannie Mae.)

In March 2004 New York mayor Michael Bloomberg appointed Donovan to head HPD, whose task involves "building more low- and moderate-income housing in New York City while navigating the web of interests, including landlords, developers and lenders, who all have a stake in the outcome," according to the *New York Times* (December 13, 2008). At that time the city was plagued by problems, including a growing population, rising land and construction costs, and a declining inventory of city-owned property. Another point of concern involved landlords, who were increasingly opting out of state and federal programs that had kept rents low.

During his tenure at the HPD, Donovan implemented Bloomberg's New Housing Marketplace Plan, a $7.5 billion affordable-housing plan—currently the largest in the nation—to build or renovate 165,000 units that would house up to 500,000 New York City residents by 2013. Donovan was credited as a pioneer for capitalizing on the strength of the real-estate market and finding innovative ways to finance low- and moderate-cost housing. He told Janny Scott for the *New York Times* (September 25, 2006, on-line): "There are groups that would argue that we should only work with nonprofits. I believe we should work with [for-profit companies, too]. Because at some fundamental level, I believe in competition. I believe that by having a broader pool available, having for-profits in the mix, we may get a lower price or be able to manage it more efficiently." Donovan further argued that affordable housing was not simply a moral issue but was central to the economic development of the city. "We must make sure we can continue to attract the low- and moderate-paid workers who fuel those economies," he told Matthew Schuerman for the *New York Observer* (August 13, 2007). "So this is a fundamental competitive issue for the city as well as being a social justice issue. If the city can't continue to attract and house—and it's really been people from all over the world—it's a real risk to our economy overall."

Donovan has successfully pushed for inclusionary zoning—a concept not previously embraced by the Bloomberg administration—as a viable strategy to achieve affordable-housing goals. He persuaded private real-estate developers to allocate part of their projects for lower-income housing, and in exchange the developers were permitted to build at a greater density. Additionally, Donovan was instrumental in the reform of the city's 421A tax-abatement provision, which offers tax breaks to developers who are willing to include affordable housing in upscale development projects. He was instrumental in establishing the New York City Acquisition Fund—$200 million that was financed by the city government and seven major foundations and financial companies—whose goal is to help small developers and nonprofit groups compete on private-land acquisitions. Donovan's efforts helped keep foreclosures on low- and moderate-income housing to a minimum, with just five foreclosures out of 17,000 participating homes.

Donovan was granted a leave of absence from his position as New York City's housing commissioner to serve as an adviser during Senator Barack Obama's successful presidential campaign in 2008. On December 13 of that year, Donovan was President-elect Obama's surprising choice to be the next HUD secretary. (A number of Latino groups had campaigned to have the mayor of Miami, Florida, Manny Diaz, a native of Cuba, nominated for the post.)

In his first several months in office, Donovan had to deal with consequences of the housing bubble that was generated during the George W. Bush administration, as well as the related economic recession of 2008 and 2009 and its devastating effects on the housing industry. (An estimated 3.5 million foreclosures were predicted to occur during the first year of the Obama administration.) Donovan has worked with several federal agencies on measures to limit foreclosures and with mortgage providers to renegotiate terms so as to allow many to keep their homes. He has also made considerable efforts to improve the operations of the housing-assistance program in New Orleans, Louisiana, where, four years after the devastation caused by Hurricane Katrina, many people still lack permanent dwellings. Most observers, however, agreed that given the scope of the recession—and particularly its effects on the housing market—as of late 2009 it was too early to evaluate Donovan's performance. He has come under some criticism for his longstanding cooperation with ACORN (the Association of Community Organizations for Reform Now), an organization dedicated to fighting poverty and pushing for a higher minimum wage, more affordable housing, and increased voter registration among the poor and lower middle class. Various conservative media outlets have accused the organization of being corrupt, and Donovan, who worked with ACORN extensively while he was New York City's top urban-development official, has been forced to distance himself from the group.

Donovan, a recipient of the 2008 Public Service Award from the New York Housing Conference and National Housing Conference, is married to Liza Gilbert, a landscape architect, with whom he has two children, Lucas and Milo.

—M.M.

Suggested Reading: *New York Observer* (on-line) Aug. 7, 2007; *New York Times* (on-line) Sep. 25, 2006, Dec. 13, 2008

Douthat, Ross

(DOW-thut)

Nov. 28, 1979– Writer; op-ed columnist for the New York Times

Address: New York Times, *1627 I St., N.W., Washington, DC 20006*

Courtesy of Ross Douthat

In April 2009 Ross Douthat left his position as a senior editor of the *Atlantic* to join the *New York Times* as an op-ed columnist. The 29-year-old Douthat, a social conservative, is the youngest regular *Times* op-ed writer since the newspaper launched that page, in 1970. In addition to his six-year tenure at the *Atlantic,* he has been a film critic for the conservative magazine *National Review* since 2005 and has written two books. *Privilege: Harvard and the Education of the Ruling Class* (2005) is an autobiographical account of his undergraduate years at Harvard University; *Grand New Party: How Republicans Can Win the Working Class and Save the American Dream* (2008), written with Reihan Salam, analyzes the history of the Republican Party and proposes policies that might make the GOP more appealing to working-class voters. Douthat has also written for the *Wall Street Journal*, the *Weekly Standard, Policy Review, GQ*, the *Claremont Review of Books, Slate,* and *Details.* When his *Atlantic* colleague Marc Ambinder learned that Douthat would be leaving the magazine for the *New York Times*, he described the move on his *Atlantic* blog (March 11, 2009) as "one step back for the *Atlantic*, but an order of magnitude forward for the country." Ambinder then described Douthat as a "late-twenties-year-old public intellectual with the sensibility of a 60-year eminence grise" and compared his range to that of the radical journalist Christopher Hitchens; his "pitch" to that of the British historian A. J. P. Taylor, if the liberal Taylor had been a conservative; his conscience to that of the Protestant theologian and "Christian realist" philosopher Reinhold Neibuhr; and his "intellectual honesty" to that of "his frequent sparring partner, Andrew Sullivan," a senior editor at the *Atlantic* since 2007. Since he joined the *New York Times*, Douthat has written pieces on topics including the fictionalized view of Catholic history and its role in modern America presented by Dan Brown in his best-selling novel *The Da Vinci Code*, the increased power of the Supreme Court and why he believes justices should have term limits, and the correlation between the current economic crisis in the U.S. and the recent election in Iran.

The first of the two children of Patricia Snow and Charles Douthat, Ross Gregory Douthat was born on November 28, 1979 in New Haven, Connecticut. He has a younger sister, Jeanne. His mother, a Yale University graduate, was primarily a homemaker for some years. She is now a writer; her essays have appeared in periodicals including *First Things*, published by the Institute on Religion and Public Life. Douthat's father is a partner in the New Haven law firm Jacob, Grudberg, Belt, Dow & Katz; he specializes in cases involving people seriously injured by medical malpractice and dangerous products and in workplace accidents. With his partner Jonathan Katz, Charles Douthat coauthored *Injury Claims in Connecticut*, a consumer's guide. Ross Douthat was raised in an affluent suburb of New Haven by parents who were social and political liberals. He told Terry Gross for the National Public Radio program *Fresh Air* (July 16, 2008), "When I was growing up, my earliest political memory is my mother dragging us out to a polling station and saying, 'I need to grab every woman by the lapels and tell them to vote for Geraldine Ferraro.'" (Ferraro was a U.S. congresswoman when, in 1984, she became the Democratic vice-presidential nominee; she was the first woman to join the presidential ticket of a major political party in the U.S.) Ross attended Episcopalian church services with his family until his parents became practicing Pentecostals. When he was a teenager, all the Douthats converted to Catholicism. Douthat told Gross that as a youth he was already a "contrarian" in his "fairly liberal" town, and, in addition, he believes that "a lot of my conservatism does grow out of sort of socially conservative convictions that are rooted in religious belief."

Douthat attended Hamden Hall, a private school in Hamden, Connecticut, where he and his friend Michael Barbaro, now a reporter for the *New York Times*, edited and wrote for the school's newspaper, the *Advent*, as well as anonymously for an underground paper called *La Verite@*. He also tried his hand at writing a science-fiction novel; he completed most or all of it, Barbaro told Sheelah Kolhatkar for the *New York Observer* (March 6, 2005). "I think he sent that around to publishers and was really, really crestfallen when that didn't get any response," Barbaro said. After his high-school graduation, Douthat enrolled at Harvard University, in Cambridge, Massachusetts. He considered a career in law before making the decision to pursue his passion for writing. In his years as an undergraduate, he contributed biweekly opinion columns to the *Harvard Crimson*, the daily campus newspaper, and edited the school's biweekly conservative student paper, the *Harvard Salient*. Douthat earned money during his first two summers at Harvard by writing for SparkNotes, a Web site that at that time offered free study guides of literature. The summer before his senior year, he interned at the *National Review* under the conservative icon William F. Buckley Jr., the founder and longtime editor in chief of the magazine, who at that time was an editor at large.

Douthat graduated magna cum laude from Harvard in 2002, with a B.A. degree in history and literature. In the fall of 2002, he began working as a researcher at the *Atlantic* (formerly the *Atlantic Monthly*), in Washington, D.C. He soon began to toy with the idea of writing a memoir about his experiences at Harvard. "It seemed like there hadn't been anything written in a long time about the undergraduate experience from an undergraduate perspective," he explained to Kolhatkar. He cited as a work that he admired on that subject—but that was not written from that perspective—an article called "The Organization Kid," which David Brooks wrote for the *Atlantic* (April 2001). For his article Brooks, then a senior editor at the *Weekly Standard*, interviewed undergraduates at Princeton University and "sort of tried to get the sense of the place," Douthat told Kolhatkar. "And then you have Tom Wolfe with [the 2004 novel] *I Am Charlotte Simmons*—a similar thing, you know: Older reporter goes and tries to be a fly on the wall at college, and so forth. Those were very good, but I felt like college from the point of view of the college student was fertile literary terrain." He wrote several chapters during his free time and, with the help of a literary agent, began submitting his work to publishing houses. Before long Douthat received a $120,000 advance from Hyperion Books.

Privilege: Harvard and the Education of the Ruling Class was published in March 2005. Called a "withering indictment of Harvard's institutional culture" by Bryce Christensen for *Booklist* (February 1, 2005), *Privilege* recounts Douthat's experiences at that elite school, focusing on issues of diversity, academic rigor, sex, and class. In two statements that sum up its theme, Douthat wrote in *Privilege*, "Harvard is a terrible mess of a place—an incubator for an American ruling class that is smug, self-congratulatory, and intellectually adrift," and "Meritocracy is the ideological veneer, but social and economic stratification are the reality." In an interview with Kathryn Jean Lopez for the *National Review* (May 26, 2005, on-line), Douthat said, "On the one hand, Harvard—like America—is a fantastically wealthy place, a pioneer in science, medicine and technology, and possessed of an enviable degree of power and influence. . . . It has many of early-21st century America's strengths—but many of the country's weaknesses as well. Its diversity is skin-deep: like the country as a whole, Harvard is actually getting more class-stratified, not less so, both within the school and in how well the student body reflects the broader society. Its scientific successes have been balanced by drift and even rot in the humanities, which mirror the larger rot in American popular culture; its formidable clout is undercut by a deep insecurity about its purpose and its founding ideals; and perhaps most importantly, its unprecedented wealth has too often fostered a spirit of materialism, greed, and success-at-all-costs."

Douthat has said that he was not a member of Harvard's privileged class because he did not attend any of the "right" private schools and was not one of the people who "lived in the right suburb, vacationed in the right windswept part of Long Island or Maine or Nantucket or the Vineyard," as he wrote in *Privilege*. In the book he criticized the school's relatively unchallenging courses, lack of economic diversity (according to Douthat around 70 percent of Harvard students have parents who earn more than $100,000 per year), and grade inflation, a trend that has occurred at many other colleges, too, in recent decades. In an article on the same topic that he wrote for the *Atlantic* (March 2005, on-line), Douthat cited statistics: "More than 90 percent of the [Harvard] class of 2001 had earned grade-point averages of B-minus or higher. Half of all the grades given the year before were [A's] or A-minuses; only six percent were C-pluses or lower. By way of comparison, in 1940 C-minus was the most common GPA at Harvard, and in 1955 just 15 percent of undergraduates had a GPA of B-plus or higher." Readers who enjoyed *Privilege* included William F. Buckley Jr., who characterized it in the *National Review* (March 28, 2005) as "a satisfying account of the Harvard experience." Less pleased was a writer for the *New Yorker* (April 11, 2005, on-line), who complained, "Douthat critiques his peers' sense of entitlement from the perspective of a cultural conservative, although his high moral tone is somewhat compromised by an eagerness to bolster this account of campus life with salacious anecdotes of debauchery, greed, and snobbery. Douthat skewers the political and sexual shenanigans of his classmates and provides a thoughtful analysis of the prevailing liberal politics of the campus. But his righteous indignation can seem misplaced, when so many of the injustices that exercise him are so petty. It's hard to get really upset about charges of button-stealing in a campus election." Stephen Metcalf, writing for *Slate* (March 10, 2005, on-line), also found fault with *Privilege*: "Nothing in Douthat's tone, an awkward mix of *Brideshead* elegy with the *National Review Online*, renders his anatomy of college life trustworthy. As with many a promising young fogy, no adults have interposed themselves between Douthat and his first book contract, and so he has been allowed to persist in the belief that sounding wearied and a little bored will aid him in sounding adult and worldly."

At the *Atlantic* Douthat worked his way up the ladder to reporter, blogger, associate editor, and, in 2006, senior editor. He wrote articles on such topics as the radio host Howard Stern's possible influence on undecided voters in the 2004 presidential election, religion in the U.S. and Europe, and the possible link between pornography and adultery. On his own time he co-authored, with the *Atlantic* editor Reihan Salam, *Grand New Party: How Republicans Can Win the Working Class and Save the American Dream* (2008). That book stemmed from an article that Douthat and Salam had written for the *Weekly Standard* (November 14, 2005) called "The Party of Sam's Club"; the title referred to the assertion in 2001 by the governor of Minnesota, the Republican Tim Pawlenty, that Republicans "need to be the party of Sam's Club, not just the country club." (Sam's Club, an arm of Wal-Mart, is a national chain of so-called warehouse retail clubs, through which, for a modest membership fee, consumers can buy products in bulk at lower prices than charged at ordinary stores.) In their article Douthat and Salam argued that the Republican Party must focus on issues of immediate concern to people in the working class. The writers suggested that Republican politicians put aside their small-government ideals to support child-rearing incentives, wage subsidies for the working poor, reform of the health-care industry, and other social measures that would help families and low-income Americans. "Many of the issues that the Republican party rode to power remain salient today, of course. The GOP doesn't need to rethink its support for a strong national defense, for instance, or its commitment to social conservatism," Douthat and Salam wrote. "But having risen to power at a time when most Americans were worried about losing their economic *freedom*, the party needs to adapt to a new reality—namely, that today, Americans are increasingly worried about their economic *security*—and reorient its agenda to address those concerns."

In *Grand New Party*, Douthat and Salam discussed the history of the Republican Party and expanded on the ideas set forth in their 2005 article. "The biggest challenge—and it's one [Salam and I] try and tackle in our book—is that the Republican Party has become a working class party, but it's become . . . largely a white working class party," Douthat told Terry Gross, "and the challenge for Republican politicians demographically over the next 20 to 30 years is to persuade Hispanic and also black American working class voters to vote the way white working class voters do right now, and that's a challenge I'm not sure the Republican Party is prepared to meet." The columnist David Brooks, for whom Salam worked for a while as a junior editor at the *New York Times*, wrote of the book for the *Times* (June 27, 2008), "There have been other outstanding books on how the GOP can rediscover its soul . . . , but if I could put one book on the desk of every Republican officeholder, *Grand New Party* would be it. You can discount my praise because of my friendship with the authors, but this is the best single roadmap of where the party should and is likely to head." Norman J. Ornstein, a political scientist and a resident scholar at the American Enterprise Institute, a conservative-leaning think tank, wrote in his review for the *New York Times* (June 29, 2008), "The core Republican and conservative establishment should read this book. Its members may hate activist government, or at least bow politically to the hatred, but Douthat and Salam make a strong case that a conservatism of reflexive tax cuts and sink-or-swim economics will never resonate with the huge core of voters who are spread thin [financially] and falling behind." Some reviewers, among them Daniel McCarthy, writing for the libertarian magazine *Reason* (November 1, 2008), criticized Douthat and Salam for failing to offer a clear definition of "working class," while others, such as Stephen Amidon, in a review for the *New York Observer* (June 20, 2008), contended that the authors' suggestions were far more likely to please Democrats, many of whom would be willing to spend even more than proposed for programs considered in *Grand New Party.* The book failed to capture a wide audience; according to Ira Boudway in *New York* (March 30, 2009), only 6,500 copies had been sold before that issue of the magazine reached newsstands. Douthat's *Atlantic* colleague Andrew Sullivan told Boudway that *Grand New Party* "put coalition politics before philosophical coherence, and that's why it failed, despite its many virtues, to impact the debate."

In March 2009 the *New York Times* announced that Douthat would succeed the *Weekly Standard* editor Bill Kristol as one of its op-ed columnists. Although his appointment has received praise from many members of the media (including some liberals), some left-leaning writers have criticized his views on hot-button issues. In 2001 he supported President George W. Bush's decision to invade Iraq, later writing for the *Harvard Salient* (February 14, 2002, on-line), "It goes without saying that [Saddam Hussein] . . . is busy trying to acquire a nuclear bomb, to supplement his extensive collection of biological and chemical weaponry." He criticized Islam, writing for the *Harvard Crimson* (October 22, 2001), "Where Christianity has a Christ who turns the other cheek and gives himself over to be crucified, Islam has a Prophet who makes war—in self-defense, arguably, but with a glad heart, a warlike spirit and a knowledge that Allah is on his side. . . . That spirit endures to this day. Just ask Osama bin Laden." On social issues Douthat has remained true to conservative Catholic ideals. He is strongly anti-abortion and opposes stem-cell research. In a post on his *Atlantic* blog (February 25, 2009), Douthat wrote, "I don't expect or want American social policy to reflect the Catholic Church's teaching on contraception, I don't have a problem with our public health services providing access to birth control. . . . But I also think that an awful lot of the policies liberals like to champion in this area—expanded public-school sex ed programs chief among them—don't deliver anything remotely like the benefits they promise. And I'm extremely wary of defining 'common ground' on abortion in terms that essentially require the pro-life movement to give up the store in the legal debate, in exchange for at best marginal returns where the abortion rate is concerned." Writing for the liberal magazine the *Nation* (April 6, 2009), Katha Pollitt expressed her opposition to Douthat's appointment: "Even for a blogo-pundit, Douthat seems unusually averse to engaging with women intellectually, even on perennial topics like abortion and birth control, where you'd think we'd bring something missing to the table—like an interest in our health, well-being, happiness, longevity, pleasure and ability to have some control over our lives."

In 2007 Douthat married Abigail Tucker, whom he met when both were students at Harvard. Tucker was a reporter for the *Baltimore Sun* before becoming a *Smithsonian* magazine staff writer. The couple live in Washington, D.C.

—M.A.S.

Suggested Reading: *New York Magazine* p9 Mar. 30, 2009; *New York Observer* p1+ Mar. 7, 2005; topics.nytimes.com; *Weekly Standard* Features Nov. 14, 2005; *Who's Who in America*

Selected Books: *Privilege: Harvard and the Education of the Ruling Class*, 2005; *Grand New Party: How Republicans Can Win the Working Class and Save the American Dream* (with Reihan Salam), 2008

Duncan, Arne

(AR-nee)

Nov. 6, 1964– Secretary of the U.S. Department of Education

Address: U.S. Dept. of Education, 400 Maryland Ave., S.W., Washington, DC 20202

For seven years beginning in 2001, Arne Duncan served as the chief executive officer of Chicago Public Schools (CPS), overseeing the nation's third-largest school system. In December 2008 he was nominated by President-elect Barack Obama to be the U.S. secretary of education. Confirmed by the U.S. Senate on January 20, 2009 and sworn in the next day, Duncan is only the second schools superintendent (the former Houston superintendent Rod Paige was the first) to become the nation's top educator.

Arne Duncan was born on November 6, 1964 to Susan Goodrich (Morton) and Starkey Davis Duncan in Chicago, Illinois. He hails from a family of educators. His father was a psychology professor at the University of Chicago, and his mother was the founding director of an after-school tutoring center for underprivileged minority adolescents in Chicago's South Side. As a youth Duncan developed a

Jonathan Ernst/Getty Images

Arne Duncan

passion for basketball and honed his skills in pick-up games. "I'd go out to play on the South Side and the West Side, where I was the only white kid," he told Grant Pick for an interview posted on the Catalyst Chicago Web site (June 2003). "There were so many great role models. I learned to judge character."

Duncan played basketball at the University of Chicago Laboratory Schools, one of the nation's top preparatory schools, where he served as team captain during his senior year. After graduating from high school, he studied sociology at Harvard University, in Cambridge, Massachusetts. As a freshman he played for the junior-varsity basketball team and was named the starting forward for the varsity squad during his sophomore year. Following his junior year Duncan, who finished among the team leaders in rebounds, assists, and scoring, took a yearlong leave of absence from school to conduct research for his thesis (entitled "The Values, Aspirations and Opportunities of the Urban Underclass"), which explored the difficulties that children face in inner-city neighborhoods. He spent the year in Chicago, where he served as a tutor for his mother's after-school program.

Upon returning to Harvard Duncan was named co-captain of the varsity basketball team. As a senior he was among the team leaders in scoring, steals, rebounds, assists, three-point shots, field-goal percentage, and free-throw percentage. He also earned first team Academic All-American honors. After graduating magna cum laude with a B.A. degree in sociology, in 1987, Duncan pursued a professional basketball career and spent the next four years (1987–91) playing for several now-defunct Australian professional and semiprofessional squads, including the Eastside Melbourne Spectres of the National Basketball League, the Launceston Ocelots, and the Devonport Warriors. At that time Duncan, who also worked with children who were wards of the state, met his future wife.

When Duncan returned to Chicago in 1992, his childhood friend John W. Rogers Jr. appointed him director of the Ariel Education Initiative, a non-profit mentoring and tutoring program designed to enhance educational opportunities for Chicago's inner-city youth. Duncan also helped establish the Ariel Elementary Community Academy, a small public school located on the South Side.

In 1998 Duncan joined the Chicago Public Schools—the country's third-largest school system, behind those of New York City and Los Angeles—and spent his first year overseeing the state magnet schools and programs. "I had spent a lot of time in the classrooms at Ariel," he told Pick. "Here were kids with high academic potential who weren't being asked to do homework. It broke my heart. Throughout my [experience with] my mother's program and at Ariel, the public schools had always been the enemy. I wanted to change that." In 1999 he began serving as the deputy chief of staff to CPS chief executive officer Paul Vallas, and two years later Chicago mayor Richard Daley ousted Vallas and named Duncan to succeed him. Duncan was viewed as an unlikely choice, due to his lack of an education degree or formal teaching experience.

As superintendent of Chicago Public Schools, Duncan implemented several controversial reforms. To raise the performance levels in the city's schools, which had consistently lagged behind the state average for seven years, Duncan shut down a number of underperforming schools and fired ineffective teachers. In 2004 he helped launch Renaissance 2010, Mayor Daley's bold program to close 60 public schools and replace them with new charter, contract, or small schools by 2010.

Duncan received criticism from the teachers' unions for supporting performance-based financial initiatives not only for teachers but for students as well. In September 2008 a privately funded program was launched in which students in 20 Chicago schools could earn $4,000 per year for achieving straight-A grades. "The majority of our students don't come from families with a lot of economic wealth," Duncan told the *Chicago Tribune* (September 11, 2008). "I'm always trying to level the playing field. . . . This is the kind of incentive that middle-class families have had for decades." In December of that year, his proposal to establish a public high school for gay, lesbian, and transgendered teens—which was ultimately turned down—also met with criticism.

Duncan's performance as CPS superintendent, though controversial, was effective. Under his command, 53 new public schools were established, including the thriving Dodge Renaissance Academy, a once-failing school that had been closed in 2002 and has been hailed as a model for teacher-training programs since it reopened in 2005. Additionally, the schools' graduation rate has increased by nearly 6 percent. Duncan is also credited with raising the percentage of elementary-school students whose perfomances meet the state standards from 38 percent to 65 percent, although high-school scores have remained a source of concern.

In addition, Duncan served as an education-policy adviser to Barack Obama, beginning when Obama was a state senator. The two met in the early 1990s through Craig Robinson, Obama's brother-in-law, and often played pickup basketball games. During Obama's 2008 presidential campaign, Duncan helped Obama draft an education platform that advocated investment in early-childhood education, emphasis on math and sciences, merit-based pay initiatives for teachers, and training and recruitment programs for principals.

At a press conference held at the Dodge Renaissance Academy on December 16, 2008, President-elect Obama nominated Duncan to be the next secretary of education. His selection was hailed by the leaders of two major teachers' unions: Randi Weingarten of the American Federation of Teachers and Jo Anderson of the Illinois Education Association.

Confirmed (along with five other Cabinet members) by the Senate in a unanimous vote, Duncan is responsible for overseeing the Department of Education, which allocates billions of dollars in federal funding and guides the country's schooling policies and standards. His primary challenge will be to address the shortcomings of the No Child Left Behind Act, the controversial federal policy passed in 2001 that requires poorly performing schools to track data on low-income and minority students and impose penalties on the schools if those pupils do not perform well. The law also offers pay incentives to effective teachers who help improve student achievement. As Karen Kingsbury wrote for *Time* (December 16, 2008, on-line), the legislation "has managed to rankle both Republicans (for interfering with state initiatives) and Democrats (for placing so much emphasis on standardized testing)." While Duncan supports No Child Left Behind's accountability requirements, he called for increased funding and emphasized the need to gain the support of both political parties in order to get meaningful reforms passed.

In his first year as education secretary, Duncan, along with Obama administration officials, created an incentive for states to engage actively in education reform through the Race to the Top fund, which consisted of $4.3 billion in grant money, awarded competitively to those states that demonstrated their commitment to effective—and measurable—reform. The incentives have been particularly beneficial to charter schools. Duncan also made progress in negotiating with skeptical teachers' unions with regard to performance standards.

Duncan was named citizen of the year by the City Club of Chicago in 2006. He and his wife, Karen, have two children, Claire and Ryan.

—M.M.

Suggested Reading: *Chicago Tribune* (on-line) Jan. 3, 2009; *New York Times* (on-line) Dec. 16, 2008; *Time* (on-line) Dec. 16, 2008

Eve Welch, courtesy of Denis Dutton

Dutton, Denis

Feb. 9, 1944– Philosopher

Address: Philosophy School of Humanities, University of Canterbury, Private Bag 4800, Christchurch 8140, New Zealand

During a national tour to promote his most recent book, *The Art Instinct: Beauty, Pleasure, & Human Evolution* (2009), Denis Dutton stopped in New York City to give lectures and interviews. One interview stood out, not because it was particularly illuminating (it was not), but because listeners found it very funny. Dutton—a philosopher whose area of expertise is art, aesthetics, and evolutionary psychology—was getting peppered with absurd questions on the TV show *The Colbert Report.* Not very many philosophers can pride themselves on having verbally sparred with Stephen Colbert, but Dutton is no ordinary philosopher. In addition to being a prolific writer and highly regarded professor at the University of Canterbury, in New Zealand, he is the founder and editor of Arts & Letters Daily (aldaily.com)—which at least one authoritative source, the London *Observer*, has called the world's best Web site. A random day's sample might include links to stories, essays, and articles about the life of Charlie Chaplin; the irreconcilable differences between science and religion; Leonardo da Vinci's tendency to procrastinate; theories on links between race and IQ; the deification of the writer Franz Kafka; high-tech warfare; a scholarly explanation of charisma; or dozens of other subjects. For his role in managing the site, Dutton was named by *Time* (October 28, 2005) as one of "the most influential media personalities in the world." The site is influential not only because it gets three million hits per month but also because many writers and editors view it as an endless source of story ideas.

Meanwhile, Dutton's book *The Art Instinct* has been widely praised as ambitious, insightful, and original. The renowned evolutionary psychologist Steven Pinker said, as quoted in the *Washington Post* (February 4, 2009), that Dutton's book "marks out the future of humanities—connecting aesthetics and criticism to an understanding of human nature from the cognitive and biological sciences." The book argues that art—from the most sophisticated Beethoven quartets and Picasso paintings to sitcoms and popular fiction—has its basis in Darwinian adaptation, particularly the adaptation of the human imagination. The arts are a cultural phenomenon, Dutton admits, but they are also, he maintains, rooted in human biology—the side of creativity explored in *The Art Instinct*. Dutton is the author of numerous essays and reviews; he edited the books *The Concept of Creativity in Science and Art* (with Michael Krausz, 1981) and *The Forger's Art: Forgery and the Philosophy of Art* (1983).

The son of William and Thelma Dutton, Denis Laurence Dutton was born on February 9, 1944 in Los Angeles, California. He grew up, along with two brothers and a sister, in the city's North Hollywood district. His parents met at Paramount Pictures, where they both worked in the 1930s. Around the time that Dutton was finishing his studies at North Hollywood High School, his parents opened Dutton's Books, which became one of the best-known independent bookstores in Los Angeles. Dutton spent a lot of time reading and browsing at the store. He also conducted his own chemistry experiments. "I was a tinkerer and an experimenter as a teenager," Dutton told *Current Biography*, the source of quotes for this article unless otherwise noted. During his high-school years, Dutton's main interests were building telescopes, photographing the stars, and visiting observatories with friends. The order and beauty he found in astronomy filled him with a philosophical wonderment.

No one kindled the young Dutton's curiosity as much as his father. William Dutton liked to ask "big" questions at the dinner table. "Ours was a household where there was a lot of talk, a lot of argument—about what I later recognized were philosophical questions," Dutton recalled. "Questions of value, of existence, of the place of culture in life and the arts." In one evening the family's conversation might range from a single work of art to the origins of the universe. "I learned from my parents the idea that there's nothing that's beyond questioning, whether it's politics, science, religion or the arts." Although he was too young to participate, he remembers his mother organizing a Great Books group to discuss John Stuart Mill's *On Liberty*. Together with his father, Dutton read popular books on the Big Bang theory and Albert Einstein's theory of relativity, and he discussed the books with his father and siblings. One day Dutton's father discussed the structure of the atom; using an analogy popular at the time, William Dutton compared the atom's nucleus to the sun and the electrons to planets orbiting the sun, then jokingly suggested, pointing to a chair, that perhaps every atom in the chair was a solar system with an orbiting Earth where people were living just like us. "It was all good, imaginative fun," Dutton recalled, "but for a child's mind it was extremely intriguing."

In the early 1960s Dutton began his college education as a chemistry major at the University of California, Santa Barbara (UCSB). After his first year he switched his major to philosophy. At the time the UCSB Philosophy Department's focus was that of Ludwig Wittgenstein, an early-20th-century Austrian-born philosopher whose work involved language, mathematics, and logic. The courses that most fascinated Dutton, however, were in the philosophy of art and aesthetics. "I was trying to figure out how works of art—literature, music, paintings—could produce such intense experiences in human beings," he said. Like most thinkers at the time, he regarded aesthetic pleasure and values as being determined by one's culture, but he also suspected that there was something innate and natural in people's aesthetic preferences.

After graduating from college, in 1966, Dutton joined the Peace Corps and went to India. He was a big fan of Indian music; upon arriving in India he took up the sitar. (He studied with Pandit Pandurang Parate, a student of the famed sitar player Ravi Shankar, who would go on to influence many 1960s rock bands, most notably the Beatles.) Dutton, along with other Peace Corps volunteers, taught local residents to grow mushrooms in air-conditioned underground rooms. "It was a great idea," Dutton said, "except the Indians in that area do not eat mushrooms. All the buildings are chicken coops now." But Dutton made at least one valuable contribution to those he was trying to serve. Before returning to the U.S., in 1968, he gave a Zenith transoceanic radio to an Indian couple he had befriended. (At the time India had strict regulations regarding imports and exports, so such a radio was rare and valuable.) The husband and wife worked in education and desperately wanted to open their own school, so they sold the portable radio for about 1,000 rupees—a lot of money at the time—and founded what they named Dutton's School. The school started off humbly, with a few students and instructors. It now has a staff of more than 50 teachers.

In the summer of 1968, Dutton arrived in New York City, where he enrolled in the graduate philosophy program at New York University. Because tuition at the university proved to be prohibitively expensive, he transferred after one year to his alma mater, UCSB. Although his studies were not concentrated on any one area of philosophy, his doctoral thesis focused on the relationship between art and anthropology, particularly the perceived problems of cross-cultural understanding. After graduating, in 1973, he accepted a teaching position at the University of Michigan at Dearborn, moving there with Margit, his wife of four years. "I made it my business to try to teach almost every philosophy course in the catalog . . . ," Dutton recalled. "What I tried to do was to sharpen my philosophical background simply by teaching as many different courses as I could. Specialization is sometimes a vice." Although Dutton now considers himself a specialist in aesthetics, the history of music, and applications of Darwinism, he nevertheless remains, to a degree, a generalist. During his time in Michigan, he founded the journal *Philosophy and Literature*, which is now published by John Hopkins University Press and edited by Dutton.

In 1984 Dutton, his wife, and their two young children moved to Christchurch, New Zealand, where Dutton had been offered a teaching position at the University of Canterbury. "The idea of living in New Zealand struck us as charming," Dutton recalled. While still in Michigan he and his wife checked out library books about New Zealand. "Little did we know, those books were 20 years old. We were expecting a country of sheep farmers and cricket players. Yes, there are enough of them here, but this land is rather varied in its offerings." At the university he now teaches both graduate and undergraduate courses on the philosophy of art.

By 1995 Dutton had been in academia for nearly three decades and had encountered much academic writing that he thought lacked depth and coherence. He had become particularly weary of "the obscurantism and the junk prose that characterize literary theory," as he put it. One evening he was sitting at home in his easy chair, "trying to untangle some essentially meaningless, indecipherable" essay, when he had the idea of holding a contest for such incoherence. That is how the Bad Writing Contest was born. Since the academics doing the writing would not—for obvious reasons—submit their own work, readers were asked to find what they thought to be "the ugliest, most stylistically awful" sentences in a recent academic article or book and submit them to Dutton's journal, *Philosophy and Literature*. (The contest was not open to submissions that parodied such writing, because, Dutton explained, the amount of unintentionally bad writing in academia made parody superfluous.) Judith Butler—a celebrated figure, professor of rhetoric and comparative literature at the University of California, Berkeley, and author of many books, including *Gender Trouble* (1990)—was the winner of the fourth annual Bad Writing Contest, in December 1998. The article from which the "bad" sentence was taken, titled "Further Reflections on the Conversations of Our Time," appeared in the journal *Diacritics*. After Dutton's journal pronounced Butler the winner, dozens of newspapers around the globe carried the story. Butler's "winning" sentence read: "The move from a structuralist account in which capital is understood to structure social relations in relatively homologous ways to a view of hegemony in which power relations are subject to repetition, convergence, and rearticulation brought the question of temporality into the thinking of structure, and marked a shift from a form of Althusserian theory that takes structural totalities as theoretical objects to one in which the insights into the contingent possibility of structure inaugurate a renewed conception of hegemony as bound up with the contingent sites and strategies of the rearticulation of power." After months of receiving press coverage, some of it harsh, Butler retaliated in an op-ed article for the *New York Times* (March 20, 1999), in which she defended her use of "difficult and demanding language" to communicate social criticism. Butler's article missed the point, according to Dutton. "Much of the writing in literary theory wasn't bad because the points it was trying to make were difficult," he explained, "but because the thesis of the writing was banal, and the only way to make it interesting was to make the style difficult." Dutton ended the contest in 1999, with some—mistakenly, according to Dutton—attributing his timing to Butler's essay. "It was ended because the point had been made and it was time-consuming to run it every year," Dutton said. "One could only read so much bad writing."

In October 1998, as the Internet "bubble" was growing, Dutton created Arts & Letters Daily, a Web site that would soon change what a great number of people—academics, philosophers, psychologists, scientists, businesspeople, university students, politicians, artists, and many others—read on-line. When the site was only three months old, the London *Observer*, in a widely quoted comment, called Arts & Letters Daily the best Web site in the world. The cluttered layout—like that of 18th-century British broadsheets—was not easy on the eyes, but people flocked to the site for its content: carefully selected links to essays, articles, book reviews, and op-eds about an extremely broad range of topics. "Arts & Letters Daily is designed to provoke curiosity and expand the interests of its readers," Dutton said. "The nicest e-mails I get are from people who say, 'I never thought I would be interested in that subject.'" The site was sparked when Dutton put together a list of academics' e-mail addresses, so that he could send colleagues links to on-line articles he found interesting or thought-provoking. "Searching for material to put on [a mass email], I inadvertently had become something of an expert on the availability of good reading available on the Internet."

By 2000 several companies were interested in purchasing the site. The parent company of the academic literary magazine *Lingua Franca* offered $500,000 for it—a staggering figure, considering that Dutton had started the Web site at a cost of about $300. After the sale Dutton stayed on as editor. As a result of the economic slowdown that occurred after the September 11, 2001 terrorist attacks on New York City, *Lingua Franca* lost its financial support and, in 2002, shut down Arts & Letters Daily without fulfilling its sale agreement with Dutton. Within a few weeks, however, the *Chronicle of Higher Education*, a widely circulated, widely respected academic publication, purchased the site through the New York bankruptcy court. Again, Dutton stayed on as editor. During 2002, when the site was receiving 1.5 million hits per month, Dutton was awarded the "People's Voice" Webby Award at a ceremony in San Francisco, California. More than 10 years after it was founded, the site receives three million hits each month. Like his tenure as a professor in Michigan, during which he taught nearly every philosophy class available, managing Arts & Letters has been a highly educational experience for Dutton. "I feel, as an editor, immensely broadened as a result of producing it on a daily basis for all these years," he said.

Dutton's goal of formulating a coherent theory that examines human artistic practices and preferences from an evolutionary standpoint—a project that had occupied him for 15 years—was realized with the publication of his book *The Art Instinct: Beauty, Pleasure, & Human Evolution* (2009) on the 200th anniversary of the birth of Charles Darwin. (Darwin, a 19th-century English naturalist, developed the theory that some members of a given species survive and procreate, and others do not, according to their varying characteristics; traits that help ensure survival are passed to subsequent generations in a process called natural selection. The process in which a species gradually changes is known as evolution.) Culture, Dutton reasoned, surely exerts a powerful influence on our behavior and our views on nearly everything, especially the arts. Still, he posed the question: if the concept of evolution is important to the understanding of our biological and psychological makeup—from our circulatory system and organs to our intellect and emotions—would it not help us to understand our feelings and preferences with regard to the arts? *The Art Instinct* delves deeply into another question: What effect has evolution had on the human use of, understanding of, and relationship to art? Biologists, neurologists, psychologists, and philosophers agree—if not on every detail, at least on the general premise—that evolution accounts for our desire for food and sex; as a result we also developed specific tastes—for example, for food that is fatty or sweet or for a mate who is physically attractive. (Men's preferences with regard to women's body types, for example, tend to correspond to waist-to-hip ratios that statistically indicate greater fertility.) The point is not that each innate preference is still relevant to our survival—it may not be. But the reason for the preference is relevant, because it sheds light on our choices.

Understanding the interests, preferences, and capacities of our ancestors from the Pleistocene period (1.8 million to 10,000 years ago) with regard to natural and sexual selection, Dutton wrote, is the key to understanding our innate preferences and emotions with regard to art. For example, in his book Dutton cited a cross-cultural study that found that people all over the world prefer the same general kind of pictorial representations: "a landscape with trees and open areas, water, human figures, and animals." Hundreds of generations ago, Dutton wrote, our ancestors most likely found such an actual landscape useful because it indicated safety and fertile soil. In other words, such a view created certain associations—and emotions—that were crucial to the survival of our ancestors; and although such landscapes no longer have the same use for most of us, we still have positive feelings about them because of the process of natural selection.

Sexual selection, Dutton argued, played a more significant role than natural selection with regard to evolution and the arts. A classic example used to distinguish the two phenomena involves the peacock. The male peacock's tail, from the point of view of natural selection, amounts to a major disadvantage: it is big, heavy, and hard to grow, and it allows the peacock's natural enemies to spot the bird very easily. What accounts for its continued existence? The peacock's tail, according to Darwin's theory of sexual selection, indicates the bird's fitness for survival. Just as a human female's waist-to-hip ratio indicates her fertility, a large, colorful tail indicates a healthy male peacock. There are two kinds of sexual selection: in one, members of the same sex compete against each other for a desirable mate; in the other, an individual attempts to attract and seduce a member of the opposite sex. To a degree, Dutton wrote, the development of art can be explained through an analogy to the second kind of sexual selection: the ability of our distant ancestors to create stories, music, paintings, anecdotes, and various beautiful objects was—and continues to be—an indication of emotional and intellectual fitness.

Dutton's observations and conclusions are descriptive rather than prescriptive. In other words, Dutton does not maintain that our natural drives and innate feelings are necessarily good and must be catered to. His investigations have been aimed at finding explanations, not to telling artists what kind of art to create. Our innate preferences, he wrote, need not control our tastes: "Once we understand and know an impulse, we can choose to go along with it or we can resist it." Just as our knowledge of our sexual and dietary preferences sheds light on our choices for food and a mate, Dutton wrote, our knowledge of our aesthetic preferences—admittedly much more complicated than our preferences for certain foods—sheds light on our relationships with various arts, from *The Simpsons* and *The Daily Show* to the works of Franz Schubert and Salvador Dali.

Reviews of *The Art Instinct* were generally positive. "Why do we create art and beauty?" Carlin Romano wrote for the *Philadelphia Inquirer* (January 25, 2009). "Dutton may be the best-equipped thinker in the world to explain." Romano went on to call the book "the most shrewd, precisely written and provocative study you'll find on its topic's place in human nature. . . . *The Art Instinct* is the experiment of a master, and future aestheticians, one suspects, will naturally need to adapt to it." One major review was largely negative. Jonah Lehrer wrote for the *Washington Post* (January 11, 2009), "[Dutton] argues that our desire for beauty is firmly grounded in evolution, a side effect of the struggle to survive and reproduce. In this sense, a cubist painting by Picasso is no more mysterious than the allure of a *Playboy* centerfold: Both are works of culture that attempt to sate a biological drive. . . . Like so many other aesthetic theories, Dutton's ideas are ultimately undone by what they can't explain. This is the irony of evolutionary aesthetics: Although it sets out to solve the mystery of art, to explain why people write poems and smear paint on canvases, it ends up affirming the mystery. The most exquisite stuff is what we can't explain. That's why we call it art." Anthony Gottlieb, writing for the *New York Times Book Review* (February 1, 2009), expressed a different view. He observed that because "we know so little about the environment of our Pleistocene ancestors," any hypothesis about what helped them survive is "bound to be highly speculative." That ought to be a problem for Dutton, Gottlieb wrote, "but I rather think it isn't." Gottlieb went on to write of Dutton: "His discussion of the arts and of our responses to them is uniformly insightful and penetrating."

Dutton was one of the founders in 1986 of the New Zealand Skeptics, an organization dedicated to examining paranormal claims and debunking what he calls "pseudoscience." In 2000, after heading the group for many years, he was awarded the Medal for Services to Science and Technology by the Royal Society of New Zealand.

Dutton has contributed essays to many books, including *Literature and the Question of Philosophy* (1987), *Encyclopedia of Hoaxes* (1994), *The Encyclopedia of Aesthetics* (1998), *The Dictionary of Art* (1998), *The Literary Animal* (2005), and *The Encyclopedia of American Art* (2009). He is on the editorial boards of publications including *Evolutionary Psychology*, *Contemporary Aesthetics*, and the *Journal of Comparative Literature and Aesthetics*.

Dutton is a vocal proponent of public radio. During his undergraduate days at UCSB, he became a radio announcer for the local classical-music station, KRCW, and later served as general manager of KCSB, the UCSB student station. In Michigan he worked for the radio station WQRS, and in New Zealand he was on the board of directors of Radio New Zealand, a public radio station.

Dutton lives in Christchurch, New Zealand, with his wife. The couple's daughter, Sonia, lives in New York; their son, Benjamin, lives in Sydney, Australia.

—D.K.

Suggested Reading: aldaily.com; denisdutton.com; *New York Times Book Review* p12 Feb. 1, 2009; *Philadelphia Inquirer* H p14 Jan. 25, 2009; *Washington Post* C p1 Feb. 4, 2009

Selected Books: *The Art Instinct: Beauty, Pleasure & Human Evolution*, 2009; as editor—*The Concept of Creativity in Science and Art* (with Michael Krausz), 1981; *The Forger's Art: Forgery and the Philosophy of Art*, 1983

Evan Agostini/Getty Images

El-Tahri, Jihan

1962(?)– Documentary filmmaker; writer; journalist

Address: Big Sister Productions, 4 rue Lacépède, 75005 Paris, France

Jihan El-Tahri is a documentary filmmaker whose award-winning work has been widely described as provocative, revealing, illuminating, and absorbing. Her films include *The House of Saud*, a look into the modern history of Saudi Arabia and its complex relationship with the United States; *Cuba: An African Odyssey*, an investigation of Cuba's crucial yet often-overlooked support for African liberation movements; and *Behind the Rainbow*, an examination of the evolution in South Africa of the once-outlawed African National Congress, which has been in power since 1994. Although her aims as a filmmaker include the demolishing of widely believed myths, and she has described herself as a "loose cannon political activist," as she said in an interview with Daniel Dercksen for the South Africa *Cape Argus* (November 29, 2008), El-Tahri also told Dercksen, "I never give a conclusion to any one of my films. Who am I to conclude? I get you to the point where I provide a key to understand all the different elements and then it's your job to think about it. I don't have answers—I want everybody else to help me find the answer." For a decade before she began writing, directing, and producing documentaries, El-Tahri worked as a journalist; she covered the Middle East and Africa for Reuters, the *Washington Post*, *U.S. News & World Report*, and other news organizations. By 1990 she had started making films for French television, and in 1995 she began making documentaries for the BBC (British Broadcasting Corp.). Valuable to varying degrees as primary historical sources, her heavily researched films offer compelling narratives, an abundance of information, and clear presentations of complex issues and events. El-Tahri has proved adept at unearthing archival images previously seen only by experts or collectors, and to a remarkable extent she has succeeded in filming unprecedented, extensive interviews with highly influential people.

The youngest of the three daughters of Egyptian parents, Jihan El-Tahri was born in Beirut, Lebanon, in about 1962. She prefers to identify herself as African; according to the London *Guardian* (April 28, 2004, on-line), she has dual Egyptian and French citizenship. Her father, Hamdy El-Tahri, was a diplomat, and her family moved often, to locations in Egypt, Panama (where her father was an ambassador), Lebanon, Finland, and England. According to a profile in *AME Info* (January 26, 2003, on-line) of Neveen El-Tahri, Jihan's eldest sister, Hamdy El-Tahri raised his daughters to be strong-minded and independent, and all have pursued careers (Neveen as a financial broker in Cairo, Egypt, and Nermeen as an executive for American Express in London, England). El-Tahri has said that she was drawn to politics from a young age, telling Joseph Fahim for the *Daily News Egypt* (February 22, 2007, on-line), "I've always been fascinated by decision making and how the world is run. Early on, I realized that even a herd of sheep has a leader. Politics is probably the only thing that makes me tick." El-Tahri did not want to attend any Egyptian university, where memorization was emphasized, she told Fahim. "I wanted to learn how to find answers for myself," she explained. She resolved to study at the American University in Cairo (AUC), she said, where teachers provided students with the tools "to ask the important questions that need to be asked"—what she described as the "American system" of instruction. Her father, however, opposed her decision to apply to the AUC, seeing its preponderance of brief certificate programs as an indication that a "real" education was not possible there. To impress upon him that she would not consider any other college, El-Tahri remained at home for one semester after she completed high school, "until my panicked father realized I was serious." El-Tahri earned a B.A. degree with honors in political science from AUC in 1984 and a master's degree in the same subject from that school in 1986.

From the mid-1980s to the mid-1990s, El-Tahri worked as a news correspondent, stringer, researcher, and producer, mostly in the Middle East and North Africa, for various media outlets: Reuters, *U.S. News & World Report*, the *Financial Times*, the London *Sunday Times*, and the *Washington Post*. "It was the best training anyone could ever get because they teach you to break down the information into the basic minimum and move on," she told Fahim. During that period she reported on events including the Iran–Iraq War; the Lebanese civil war; the move by the Palestine Liberation Organization (PLO), headed by Yasir Arafat, to Tunis, Tunisia, and Arafat's subsequent return to the Gaza Strip, which was then under Israeli control; Algerian elections and Islamic resistance movements in Algeria; the Madrid Conference of 1991; and the Persian Gulf War of 1990–91. While with the *Sunday Times*, El-Tahri felt frustrated, because coverage of the most significant regional events was invariably assigned to Marie Colvin, the "star reporter of the paper," she told Fahim. Rebuffed yet again when she asked to be sent to Algeria to cover an important conference, she went there on her own. Colvin never came, and El-Tahri landed an exclusive interview with Arafat. She sent the story to the *Sunday Times*, which published it with Colvin's byline. "I resigned on the spot," she recalled to Fahri. "It was a blessing in disguise because Patrick Tyler from the *Washington Post* offered me a job." El-Tahri said that the Western media's practice of miscrediting articles to Westerners remains common. "At the end of the day, I'm a female Arab Muslim working on their turf. . . . I've been asked many times to change my name."

The *Washington Post* sent El-Tahri to cover the PLO, whose leadership was then in exile in Tunisia. After being arrested several times in Tunis for reasons that were never explained to her, she decided to make France her base, while still covering the Middle East and North Africa. When war erupted in the Persian Gulf in 1990, *U.S. News & World Report* assigned her to report on it. Her experience there marked a turning point in her life. She told Dercksen, "I suddenly started wondering, 'Am I an Arab? Am I a Westerner because I've only been in the Arab world for six years of my life?' I reached the conclusion that fundamentally my identity is an African one." Moreover, disillusioned with what she saw as essentially propaganda in the mainstream Western media and the media's censorship of unwelcome news, she decided to quit journalism. Her reporting of the war earned her an international prize for diplomatic correspondence, which in turn led to a job with the French TV company CAPA (Chabalier Associates Press Agency) as a producer. To a large extent she abandoned journalism in favor of documentary filmmaking, which allowed her to delve far more deeply into her subjects and to concentrate on African issues. In a departure from that path, she co-wrote, with Edward T. Pound, a long article for *U.S. News & World Report* (October 31, 1994) about the use of sanctions as political tools; they wrote specifically about Libya, whose government, despite sanctions, refused to bring to justice the masterminds behind the bombing in 1988 of Pan Am Flight 103, which killed 270 people, including 189 Americans. "In Libya," they wrote, "economic sanctions imposed by the United Nations have hurt ordinary citizens but done little to moderate the country's outlaw behavior."

"The Gulf war was traumatizing for me and I decided that I'm not going to cover anything about the Middle East any more," El-Tahri told Fahim. Instead, she chose topics that challenged her precisely because she knew little or nothing about them. Her films from the mid-1990s include *Abortion in Ireland*; *The Spiral Tribe: Rave Parties in the UK*; *Organ Thieves* (about the thefts of human organs in Colombia); and *The Koran and the Kalashnikov*. El-Tahri produced the last-named documentary, which first aired in English in 2000; it included footage she had shot in 1992 of Al Qaeda camps in Sudan.

El-Tahri's book *The Seven Lives of Yasser Arafat*, written with the French journalist Christophe Boltanski, was published in 1997. As with most people whose political activities remained underground for long periods, much of Arafat's life had been kept secret and had become either the stuff of legend or fodder for demonization; El-Tahri and Boltanski's book was an attempt to separate fact from myth. The following year, along with the Israeli historian Ahron Bregman, she wrote and produced *Israel and the Arabs: The Fifty Years War*, a critically acclaimed, six-part documentary series for the BBC; a book adapted from that series, called *The Fifty Years War: Israel and the Arabs*, was published in 1999. "Working with Bregman wasn't easy because he's an academic," El-Tahri told Fahim. "We got into lots of fights but it was a great learning experience." Observers praised the series as eye-opening and as offering remarkably candid interviews with Arabs and Israelis, among them people who had seldom granted interviews and others who worked behind-the-scenes and had seldom been seen or heard in the print or broadcast media. The authors' "major contribution," Paul Lalor wrote in a book review for the *Times Higher Education Supplement* (May 15, 1998), "is that they help to demolish a number of myths and to bring already published information to a wider public via an entertaining and engaging writing style."

To make *L'Afrique en Morceaux: La Tragédie des Grands Lacs* (*The Tragedy of the Great Lakes*, 2001), which aired on Canal+, a French pay-TV channel, El-Tahri worked with Peter Chappell for three years. That film is about the short-lived peace that followed the death in 1997 of Mobutu Sese Seko, the longtime president and dictator of Zaire (formerly the Belgian Congo, now the Democratic Republic of the Congo), and the region's subsequent descent into years of brutal warfare involving forces from within and without. El-Tahri's next film, *The Price of Aid* (2003), is an examination of the politics of international food aid. Looking behind the generosity of rich nations to poorer ones, and focusing on a severe food shortage in Zambia and surrounding areas in 2002, the film revealed the aid industry to be one that sometimes takes advantage of crisis, creates the destructive conditions of chronic and self-reinforcing dependency, and serves commercial interests, creating new problems for the victims of famine. "While it is good for American agribusiness, it does not always benefit Africans and African agriculture . . . ," Patricia B. McGee wrote for *Educational Media Reviews Online* (February 11, 2005). "American food aid has at its heart the purpose of protecting the heavily subsidized American farmer." "*The Price of Aid* is a lucid examination of a very tangled, complex issue," McGee wrote. "El Tahri does a fine job of presenting the many voices and points of view within a clearly understandable framework." El-Tahri's documentary *The History of a Suicide: Pierre Bérégovoy*, about a French Socialist politician, also appeared in 2001; *Viewpoints on AIDS* aired the following year.

El-Tahri told Fahim that after the September 11, 2001 terrorist attacks on the United States, she had been interviewed many times for her opinions on what had occurred and on terrorism. She had also been asked to make a documentary about those subjects, but she had refused. Instead, she decided to research the history of Saudi Arabia, the native land of 15 of the 19 September 11 attackers. The documentary that emerged, *The House of Saud*, focuses on the secretive Saudi royal family. "Jihan spent considerable time gaining the trust of her interviewees," Martin Smith of the BBC said in an on-line question-and-answer session with *Washington Post* (February 9, 2005) readers. "It's a testament to her skill." The original version of *The House of Saud* is three hours long; although BBC executives hailed it, they had her cut it down to two one-hour programs. In response El-Tahri set up her own company, Big Sisters Productions, to gain more editorial control of future projects. The documentary for which El-Tahri is perhaps best known, *The House of Saud* aired in Great Britain in 2004 and in the U.S. the next year and was highly praised by viewers and critics in both places. Its examination of the ways in which the Al Sauds had maintained their grip on power and the family's relationship with the United States also sparked a great deal of controversy, not least because discussions of the American backing of the dictatorship for economic and geopolitically strategic reasons has long been taboo in both countries.

El-Tahri's next film, *Cuba: An African Odyssey* (2006), explores the rarely publicized story of how, after their success in ousting the dictatorship of Fulgencio Batista in 1959, Cuban revolutionaries under the leadership of Fidel Castro and Che Guevara gave critical military, tactical, and humanitarian support to emerging anticolonial movements in Africa, from the early 1960s to the late 1980s. The movie contains never-before-seen archival footage and extraordinarily candid interviews with the major players from various nations who helped shape the continent's modern history. South African legislators were so impressed with the film that the Parliamentary Millennium Programme (PMP), the Parliament's primary nation-building and heritage program, set up special screenings of the film to help educate the public about the role of people from nations in addition to South Africa in the country's liberation struggle. (That aspect of the solidarity movement is called internationalism.) The film starts with footage of Nelson Mandela, months after being released from prison, thanking Fidel Castro in Havana, Cuba's capital, for his crucial part in ending apartheid, the legal system whereby the black South African majority had long suffered the brutal oppression and racial segregation institutionalized by the white minority. Why, the film asks, did the revered Mandela choose Castro as the first foreign leader he visited after gaining his freedom, and why would he show such appreciation and respect to Castro, who had been denounced in the West as a vicious dictator? Over the following two hours, the film argues that in the midst of the brutal yet faltering colonial empires set up by Belgium and Portugal, an intractable white government in South Africa, the jockeying for power between the U.S. and the Soviet Union, as well as competing indigenous interests, Cuba was alone in responding to the call of liberation movements whose goal was self-determination. In the spirit of revolutionary internationalism, as the PMP statement put it, Castro saw "the struggle in Africa as an extension of his own." When the proxy war in Namibia between Cuba and South Africa reached a stalemate, in the late 1980s, Cuba agreed to leave the continent for good in exchange for the withdrawal of South African troops from Namibia and the release of political prisoners in South Africa. (Cuba's additional demand for the ending of apartheid was rejected.) Revelations offered in the film include the following: the head of the CIA in the Congo admitted that U.S. president Dwight D. Eisenhower had ordered the killing of the anticolonial hero Patrice Lumumba and had backed the coup led by Mobutu Sese Seko; American diplomats admitted to backing the apartheid government in South Africa, providing it with money and weapons in its fight against the Angolans and Cubans; and the head of Russian intelligence admitted that the Kremlin had no knowledge of Che Guevara's operations in the Congo and conceded that the decision to support African liberation movements was made not in Moscow, as Americans had been led to believe, but in Havana.

The subject of El-Tahri's next film, *Behind the Rainbow* (2008), is the change that the African National Congress underwent after it gained power in South Africa. "The ANC is the final liberation movement on the African continent to undergo the delicate transformation from an exiled revolutionary movement to a ruling party governing state institutions," she told Dercksen. El-Tahri told the South African newspaper *Sunday Independent* (November 30, 2008), "I started this film after the 2004 election because I realized that the coming phase was no longer about the struggle but about the future of this country. I wanted to witness first-hand this moment of transformation and the pains of dealing with the transforming of your struggle credentials into policies that fulfil the promise to the people. I am using the ANC to demonstrate a process that every country on the continent can identify with." The film, which was produced by El-Tahri and Steven Markovitz, took more than five years to make. Like *Cuba*, it includes rare archival images and interviews with political heavyweights. With the aim of telling the story of South African politics in the past several decades, it focuses on the relationship and rivalry between two freedom-seeking comrades turned rivals, Jacob Zuma and Thabo Mbeki. "After a lot of research, I found this amazing story of how they met in Swaziland and how a bond was created when they were forced to share a jail cell," El-Tahri told Tanya Farber for the *Cape Argus* (November 21, 2008). "It gives us an understanding of how brothers can part ways over political interests."

El-Tahri has said that the experience of making *Behind the Rainbow* was the most difficult she has had as a documentary filmmaker. "I never would have thought that it would be that hard . . . ," she told Dercksen. "As an Arab woman covering Saudi Arabia for four years, and the Congo during the Civil War with everybody hacking everybody else and you were stuck in the middle, I didn't think anything could have been more difficult, but South Africa was." For the first six months of her project, most of the major political figures refused to be interviewed. "The ANC is such a disciplined movement, and it's very difficult to engage on a level that isn't party disciplined," she told Dercksen. "It's very hard when the collective idea is that you shouldn't be speaking to someone." Another difficulty was adapting to the facts on the ground: after she had spent several years on the project, the principal figures' jobs changed unexpectedly, forcing El-Tahri to adapt to "history's unfolding," as she put it to Dercksen. In addition, she told Janet Smith for the *Cape Argus* (November 27, 2008), she had to whittle down a tremendous amount of footage. "This should be a five-hour film," she said. "It's history, it's politics. But I knew I had to have one narrative, not deal with 10. And the ANC is that narrative. Also, it had to remain a film, so it had to be entertaining." She told Farber that she could have made a commercially successful film in six months but instead chose to "place everything in its proper context and look at how things have evolved." In a review of *Behind the Rainbow* that could describe El-Tahri's entire body of work, Janet Smith wrote for the *Pretoria (South Africa) News* (November 22, 2008), "If we did not see, this film goes some way to opening our eyes. And that means that if we have forgotten, we must remember. And since the media largely concentrates on examining the day to day political strife, we could so rapidly allow the significance of the past to be excised. This film revives it. It lifts the layers of polish, the layers of dirt. It reveals the underneath, the many things we did not properly contemplate. Even though it has been nearly 15 years since the South African soul was shifted, we have had pitifully few conversations." Another critic, Phillip Altbeker, wrote for the South Africa *Weekender* (November 29, 2008) that the film gives viewers "the opportunity to examine and explain our political history and to see it in the light of comparable circumstances elsewhere on the continent without obvious prejudice."

El-Tahri is a member of the executive bureau of the Federation of Pan-African Cinema and secretary general of the Guild of African filmmakers in the Diaspora. Her honors include the French Figra d'Or Award (1995) for *The Koran and the Kalashnikov*; a British Television Award (1998) for *Israel and the Arabs*; a European Media Prize (2004) for *The Price of Aid*; and a Banff Festival Award (2005) for *The House of Saud*. *Cuba: An African Odyssey* received several honors: it was named best documentary at the 2007 Pan African Film Festival and best film directed by a woman of color at the 2007 African Diaspora Film Festival, and it won an Olivier Masson Prize at the 2006 Sunny Side of the Docs Festival; El-Tahri was named best director at the 2007 Vues D'Afrique Festival in Montreal, Canada. *Behind the Rainbow* was named best documentary at the 2009 Pan African Film Festival in Burkina Faso.

El-Tahri told Janet Smith for the *Cape Argus* that she usually works on several projects at once. She has two children, and her work, she told Smith, "takes a heavy toll." Speaking of her children, she said, "I think they'll understand more and more later on. When you have to do something you believe in, there's often a price to pay. But, of course, it has to be worth it." El-Tahri lives in France.

—M.M.

Suggested Reading: *Daily Star Egypt* (on-line) Feb. 22, 2007; *Pretoria (South Africa) News* p6 Nov. 22, 2008; (South Africa) *Cape Argus* p4 Nov. 27, 2008, p5 Nov. 29, 2008; (South Africa) *Sowetan* p19 Nov. 28, 2008

Selected Films: *Israel and the Arabs: The Fifty Years War* (with Arhon Bregman), 1998; *The Tragedy of the Great Lakes*, 2001; *The Price of Aid*, 2003; *The House of Saud*, 2004; *Cuba: An African Odyssey*, 2006; *Behind the Rainbow*, 2008

Elo, Jorma

(EL-oh, YOR-ma)

Aug. 30, 1961– Ballet dancer; choreographer

Address: Boston Ballet, 19 Clarendon St., Boston, MA 02116

In the past decade Jorma Elo has become one of the busiest choreographers in the ballet world. Trained in dance mostly in Finland, his native land, Elo turned professional at the age of 16, when he joined the Finnish National Ballet. He next performed with the Cullberg Ballet, a Swedish troupe, and then, for 14 years beginning in 1990, with the Nederlands Dans Theater (NDT), a Dutch company. "I loved doing classical work, but you have to have a wide range of technical abilities to be a really good classical dancer, and I lacked some of these abilities," he told Sheryl Flatow for *PlaybillArts.com* (October 17, 2006). "I knew I could never be a prince. So I wanted to try something else. I needed to develop." Elo was performing regularly with the NDT when, with the encouragement of its artistic director, Jiří Kylián, he tried his hand at choreography. Since 2000 he has created more than two dozen dances, among them *1st Flash* and *Plan to A*, for NDT; *Cut to Drive*, for the Norwegian National Ballet; *Happy Is Happy*, *Twisted Shadow*, and *Two Fast*, for the Finnish National Ballet; *Glow-Stop*, for American Ballet Theatre, in New York City; *Slice to Sharp*, for the New York City Ballet; and for the Boston Ballet, where he has served as resident choreographer since 2005, *Sharp Side of Dark*, *Plan to B*, *Carmen*, *Brake the Eyes*, *In on Blue*, and, most recently, *Le Sacre du Printemps*. Companies that have introduced new dances by Elo also include the Vienna Opera Ballet, in Austria; the Royal New Zealand Ballet; the Royal Ballet of Flanders, in Belgium; Basler Ballet, in Switzerland; the San Francisco Ballet, in California; and Hubbard Street Dance Chicago, in Illinois.

Influenced and inspired by the ideas of choreographers including Mats Ek, Ohad Naharin, Hans van Manen, Paul Lightfoot, and William Forsythe as well as Kylián, Elo's work "challenges dancers

Eric Antoniou, courtesy of American Ballet Theatre
Jorma Elo

and excites audiences with a high intensity fusion of classical and contemporary movement that is physically demanding to the extreme as it hurtles along at warp speed," according to Flatow. In the *Boston Globe* (February 25, 2007, on-line), Geoff Edgers wrote that Elo's choreography is distinguished by "traditional jumps and turns mixed with undulating hips, windmilling arms, and jerking, thrusting moves more likely to be seen in a modern dance piece." "Elo's works . . . unwind like gyroscopes spinning off their axes," Erica Orden wrote for the *New York Sun* (October 16, 2006). "His ballets are at once vigorous and elegant—carefully edited constructions of darting limbs and intricate, whippet-fast partnering sequences."

While Elo's choreography has pleased many critics and inspired standing ovations, some dance aficionados have condemned it in scathing terms. When Roslyn Sulcas, during an interview for the *New York Times* (October 15, 2006), mentioned complaints about his choreography for *Carmen*, Elo responded, "Are there rules we have to follow? Can somebody sue me?" He added, "I use classical technique, but I'm open to everything. There's all sorts of stuff you can't put in boxes. I'm just trying to ask some questions in each piece." "Choreography is basically problem-solving," he explained to Christopher Moore for the Christchurch, New Zealand, *Press* (February 27, 2008). "It never stops for me. I am constantly looking at areas in which a work can be improved. My mind is always attuned to making something better. Whether I succeed, I don't know, but I never feel that anything is complete."

Elo was born on August 30, 1961 in Helsinki, Finland. His father was a urologist; his mother, too, was a physician. As a boy he enjoyed playing ice hockey, often as his team's goaltender. At 12, following in his older sisters' footsteps, he enrolled in a ballet class, primarily because he hoped to become more flexible and agile on the ice. Within the next two years, he had abandoned hockey in favor of dance. In an interview for *Esquire* (November 6, 2008, on-line), he said that he had come to regard hockey and ballet "in much the same way: To get it right, you have to see how things will evolve, their patterns and their movements, before anybody else." But in the dance studio, he told Christopher Moore, he had also "discovered an environment where I could create something." He also told Moore, "I fell totally in love with the theatre from the moment I stepped into the Helsinki Opera House," where the Finnish National Ballet performs. At 14 Elo earned a dance scholarship to attend the Finnish National Ballet School. He next studied at the renowned Vaganova Ballet Academy, in St. Petersburg, Russia; graduates of the school, founded in 1738, include such towering dancers and/or choreographers as Mikhail Fokine, Vaslav Nijinsky, George Balanchine, Anna Pavlova, Rudolph Nureyev, and Mikhail Baryshnikov. At 16 Elo became a member of the Finnish National Ballet. "When I told my parents I was going to start dancing as a professional dancer, they thought it was a crazy idea . . . ," he told an interviewer for *Pasatiempo* (July 6, 2007), a magazine associated with the newspaper *Santa Fe New Mexican*. "They expected me to go to university and be a doctor, or something. I kind of had to prove in a way, I could do it."

Elo danced with the Finnish National Ballet for six years, beginning in 1978. During that time he also fulfilled nine months of military service, required of all Finnish male citizens. Military officials granted him special permission to perform at night. In 1984, feeling that he wanted a change, he joined the Cullberg Ballet, a modern-dance troupe based in Norborg, Sweden, near Stockholm. There, he worked with Mats Ek, a dancer and choreographer who in 1978 became the troupe's co–artistic director, with the company's founder, Birgit Cullberg. In 1985 Ek became artistic director. "There was so much creativity there," Elo told Roslyn Sulcas. "[Ek] had an amazing skill at making you use your body to create dramatic effect. It was like having a big magnifying glass on the process of creativity." In 1990 the Czech choreographer Jiří Kylián, then the artistic director of the NDT, based in The Hague, staged one of his works at the Cullberg Ballet. "[Kylián] had a completely different intensity to Mats," Elo told Sulcas. "He said very few but very well-chosen words. I thought, 'I'd love to work with this guy.'" Elo left Cullberg later that year to join the NDT, considered one of the world's foremost modern-dance companies. "At the Nederlands Dans Theater, everything was about making something new . . . trying a new angle," Elo told

Christopher Moore. "Kylián looked at every aspect of dance. He fed dancers' minds." Kylián advised his dancers to try their hands at choreography. Elo began by creating 10-minute pieces for the company's annual workshops. His friend Mikko Nissinen, who had studied with Elo at the Finnish National Ballet School, commissioned him to choreograph works for the Alberta Ballet, in Calgary, Alberta, Canada, where Nissinen was then the artistic director.

Elo's first piece for the Alberta Ballet, *Blank Snow,* was included in Nissinen's inaugural Festival of New Works, in October 2000. "In an evening of strong, entertaining choreography, *Blank Snow* . . . is this critic's pick," Faye Lippitt wrote for the *Calgary Herald* (October 28, 2000). "The choreography is superb and strong dancing by each performer becomes quite simply a celebration of bodies. Bursts of released longing mix with both agony and passion in this exploration of emotions. Marvelously simple lighting and props top off the dramatic effect of the piece." Elo's second piece, *L'Après Midi d'un Faune/Spectre de la Rose,* was a reworking of ballets choreographed by Nijinsky, in 1912, and Fokine, in 1911, respectively; Nijinsky danced in both premieres. Elo's version debuted during the Alberta Ballet's second Festival of New Works, in 2001. "It's a fascinating piece," Bob Clark wrote for the *Calgary Herald* (October 28, 2001). "The rooted movement of the five constantly grouping and re-grouping dancers achieves a sinuous and sculptural quality—and intimacy, too—through the ever-changing twining and untwining of limbs." Pamela Anthony, the reviewer for the *Edmonton (Alberta) Journal* (November 4, 2001), wrote, "Elo is prolific in his movement inventions, and the dance is dense with intricate, fluid motion. . . . The most challenging and complex choreography on the program, [the piece] provided a stunning illustration of the technical and artistic depths of this company."

Elo soon received commissions from other dance companies, including the Pennsylvania Ballet and the Finnish National Ballet. When Nissinen became artistic director of the Boston Ballet, in 2002, he again commissioned Elo to create dances for the troupe. *Sharp Side of Dark* (2002), set to Johann Sebastian Bach's *Goldberg Variations,* was the first of Elo's pieces to incorporate pointe work, which requires the dancer to remain on the tips of the toes with the aid of special ballet shoes. "I was thinking of a dancer's life," Elo told Christine Temin for the *Boston Globe* (September 15, 2002), "of how we're so focused on virtuosity that we don't see life from a broad point of view. At the same time, we're longing for what we're missing. . . . [The pointe work] relates to that original idea of concentration on virtuosity. Pointe work is the extreme of a ballet dancer's technique. It lifts the ballerina out of the real world." Elo's *Plan to B* premiered in 2004. Theodore Bale, writing for *Dance Magazine* (January 2006), described *Plan to B* as "a spectacle of ricochet lighting and solo virtuosity set to organ music by the [17th-century composer Heinrich] von Biber" that "quickly became Boston Ballet's new signature work and ticket to the future."

Meanwhile—because, by his own account, he loved to dance—Elo had continued to perform with the NDT. In 2004, at the age of 42, Elo left the company to dedicate himself to choreography. "Nederlands Dans Theater was great to me. They gave me lots of time off, but I was away more than I was there, and it wasn't fair to anyone," he told Roslyn Sulcas. "I've come late to . . . [choreographing] full time, which is probably why I often get described as a 'young' choreographer." In December 2005 Mikko Nissinen named Elo Boston Ballet's resident choreographer. "[Elo's] distinct movement vocabulary made him an obvious choice," Nissinen told Theodore Bale. "He really develops the dancers. Working with Jorma has pushed many of them to another level." Since he took the post, Elo has created four more dances for the company: *Carmen* (2006), based on the story by Prosper Mérimée that inspired the opera *Carmen,* by Georges Bizet; *Brake the Eyes* (2007); *In on Blue* (2008), and *Le Sacre du Printemps* (2009).

Often when Elo is choreographing for a particular company, he will observe the dancers to draw inspiration and try to take into account their individual dancing styles. While working on *Sharp Side of Dark* for the Boston Ballet, as he explained to Theodore Bale for the *Boston Herald* (September 17, 2002), "First I watched the dancers in class, and then in rehearsals" of William Forsythe's *In the Middle, Somewhat Elevated.* "And then I gave them some material, and was looking at how they were moving. . . . Of course, I was looking for some contrast in the way they approached the movement. Some people had more softness, and others were very direct. I wanted different dynamic approaches." Kevin McKenzie, artistic director of American Ballet Theatre, described to Roslyn Sulcas how Elo worked with his company for *Glow-Stop* (2006): "At the first rehearsal he came in and started doing a movement without saying anything. The dancers kind of looked at each other uncertainly and started to copy him. He is like a painter starting off with a blank canvas and sketching the work. Later he shades and colors the piece." Elo may choose music for a dance after he has choreographed some of it; for other dances, a particular piece of music sparks his creativity.

Elo's work has pleased many critics as well as lay audiences. In a review of Elo's *Slice to Sharp,* for example, which was choreographed for the New York City Ballet in 2006 and set to music by von Biber and Antonio Vivaldi, John Rockwell, the *New York Times* (June 19, 2006) critic, called the piece "an exhilarating exercise in flat-out virtuosity." He added, "This is dance as animalistic release, albeit with a breathless abandon that only supreme technicians could accomplish. With some of the company's brightest stars, the 24-minute *Slice to Sharp* provoked the loudest cheering and the longest string of curtain calls seen at the New York State Theater in some time." *Brake the Eyes*, set to music by Mozart, struck a reviewer for the Quincy, Massachusetts, *Patriot Ledger* (March 2, 2007) as "a stunner." "Elo has choreographed to each notation of the ever-changing music and sound score in fascinating ways, as if the various styles of contemporary moving have been mixed to a froth in a blender and spilled out under the stage lights," the *Patriot Ledger* writer declared. Reviewing a performance by the Colorado- and New Mexico–based Aspen Santa Fe Ballet of Elo's *1st Flash* (2003), the arts critic Sid Smith wrote for the *Chicago Tribune* (November 19, 2007), "Elo projects strange, wriggling, oddball modernity onto his pristine classical base. Here the graft is deeply personal, employing a score by that towering emblem of Elo's Finnish homeland: Jean Sibelius. The juxtaposition is startling but exquisite, Sibelius' sweet melodies in outright opposition to Elo's streetwise tics and mercilessly fast phrasing."

Not all critics are fans of Elo's work, however. Robert Johnson, for instance, wrote in his review of *Glow-Stop* for the Newark, New Jersey, *Star-Ledger* (October 23, 2006), "Like cheap gold paint, the novelty of Jorma Elo's choreography wears off quickly. . . . For those who saw Elo's *Slice to Sharp*, at New York City Ballet, or who have seen any contemporary ballet at all during the past five years, *Glow-Stop* holds no surprises. Fast and hyper-articulated, the piece offers a string of fashionable clichés." Sarah Kaufman, writing for the *Washington Post* (June 16, 2008), reported that *Brake the Eyes* "felt like an assault on the art form, peculiar and pointless." Upon the premiere by the Boston Ballet of *Le Sacre du Printemps*, in May 2009, Alan Helms wrote for the British publication *Ballet.co Magazine* (June 2009) that Elo is "currently much in demand, and though I generally [do not like] his work, audiences usually do, so mine is definitely a minority opinion. When I first saw Elo's work four years ago it had the attraction of novelty, but it quickly became so predictable that before the curtain rose on a new piece you knew exactly what you were about to see. And what you saw was an unparalleled ugliness of movement: dancers flatfooted and knock-kneed bending sharply from the waist and moving like spastic praying mantises to what Alastair Macaulay has aptly called an anti-ballet aesthetic. To my surprise, Elo's new *Sacre* contains passages of lovely classical ballet, which shows that he can do it if he wants but also emphasizes just how ugly the ugly parts are."

Elo has also designed costumes and lighting for his ballets and made background videos for some of them. "I'm interested in mixing media onstage," he told Christine Temin. "I make dance movies that tell stories. I find narrative easier to do with a camera, because I can edit." Elo's honors include the prize for choreography at the 2005 Helsinki International Ballet Competition. In 2006 he won both the $75,000 Prince Charitable Trusts Prize for his work *From All Sides*, created for Hubbard Street Dance Chicago, and the Choo-San Goh Choreographic Award, from the Choo-San Goh and H. Robert Magee Foundation. Also in 2006 *Pointe Magazine* named him a Dance VIP and *Dance Magazine* listed him among "25 to watch" in the dance world.

According to Roslyn Sulcas, Elo is "of medium height and has a dancer's trimly muscular body. . . . [He] looks like a boyish professor of architecture (complete with rectangular, heavy-rimmed glasses) and speaks fluent, lightly accented English." Elo has homes in Boston and the Netherlands. His longtime girlfriend, Nancy Euverink, is a former principal dancer with the NDT. She now stages ballets and occasionally works as Elo's assistant.

—M.A.S.

Suggested Reading: bostonballet.org; *Boston Herald* Arts & Life p45 Sep. 17, 2002; (Christchurch, New Zealand) *Press* Arts p1 Feb. 27, 2008; *Christian Science Monitor* p16 May 19, 2006; *Dance Magazine* p23 May 2006, p30 Apr. 2007; *New York Times* II p28 Oct. 15, 2006; *Santa Fe New Mexican* Pasatiempo p26 Feb. 10, 2006

Selected Ballets: as choreographer—*Blank Snow*, 2000; *L'Apres Midi d'un Faune/Spectre de la Rose*, 2001; *Twisted Shadow*, 2002; *Sharp Side of Dark*, 2002; *1st Flash*, 2003; *Plan to B*, 2004; *Carmen*, 2006; *Slice to Sharp*, 2006; *Glow-Stop*, 2006; *Brake the Eyes*, 2007; *C to C (Close to Chuck)*, 2007; *Plan to A*, 2008; *In on Blue*, 2008; *Le Sacre du Printemps*, 2009

Emanuel, Ari

Mar. 29, 1961– Talent agent

Address: William Morris Endeavor Entertainment, 1 William Morris Pl., Beverly Hills, CA 90212

"Call me Helen Keller, baby, because I'm a . . . miracle worker." Those brash words were spoken by the fictional Hollywood talent agent Ari Gold (played by Jeremy Piven) in an episode of HBO's acclaimed comedy series *Entourage*. The show, which is loosely based on the real-life escapades of the actor-producer Mark Wahlberg and his circle during his years as a struggling rapper-turned-actor, has consistently generated "water-cooler" buzz in Hollywood for its realistic portrayal of some of the entertainment industry's most infamous players. No character has drawn more attention than Piven's scene-stealing Gold, whose manic behavior and go-for-the-jugular attitude are modeled on those of the real-life agent Ari Emanu-

Kevin Winter/Getty Images

Ari Emanuel

el. Since 1995, when he and three associates left International Creative Management to form Endeavor Talent Agency, Emanuel has become one of the most visible and successful people in his field, "a volatile charmer with a streak of foot-tapping impatience," as Bernard Weinraub put it for the *New York Times* (August 2, 2004). He is certainly the most controversial: a fearless and calculating businessman, he has relentlessly bullied studio heads on behalf of his clients; publicly attacked Disney's former CEO, Michael Eisner, for trying to shelve Emanuel's client Michael Moore's controversial documentary *Fahrenheit 9/11* (2004) for political reasons; called for an industry-wide blacklisting of Mel Gibson in July 2006, after the actor-director made anti-Semitic remarks; and been the subject of scandalous stories told among Hollywood insiders. Leslie Moonves, the president and chief executive officer of CBS Corp., told Weinraub, "Ari is relentless. There's no more loyal a guy for his clients. He'll beg, borrow and steal to get his clients what he wants. He clearly loves this business. He loves the art of the deal." Aaron Sorkin, one of Emanuel's most loyal clients and the creator of the television drama *The West Wing*, said to Danielle Berrin for the *Jewish Journal* (November 6, 2008, on-line), "With Ari, it's all about the bottom line. In a business deal, he's going to try to kill for you, and it's just going to be about putting as much money in your pocket as he can, until you tell him that there's something else that's important to you." Among Endeavor's other well-known clients are the director Martin Scorsese; Larry David, co-creator of the sitcoms *Seinfeld* and *Curb Your Enthusiasm*; the talk-show host Conan O'Brien; and a "Who's Who" roster of A-list actors including Wahlberg, Robert DeNiro, Matt Damon, Ben Affleck, Christian Bale, Michael Douglas, Jude Law, Adam Sandler, Jennifer Lopez, Drew Barrymore, Jennifer Garner, Jessica Alba, and Reese Witherspoon. Following in the tradition of the maverick talent agent and Hollywood powerhouse Michael Ovitz, the former chairman of Creative Artists Agency (CAA), Emanuel has also helped Endeavor to branch into other areas, including advertising, communications technology, and publishing. Emanuel told Michael Cieply for the *New York Times* (July 27, 2008, on-line), "I feel like we're just getting started."

One of four children, Ariel Z. "Ari" Emanuel was born on March 29, 1961 in Chicago, Illinois, to an Israeli-born pediatrician, Benjamin M. Emanuel, and the American-born Marsha (Smulevitz) Emanuel, a civil rights activist who later became a psychiatric social worker. Emanuel's family has deep political roots. In the 1930s his paternal grandparents changed the family surname from Auerbach to Emanuel in honor of their son Emanuel, who was killed in the 1933 Arab insurrection in Palestine. In the 1940s his father was active in Irgun, the Zionist paramilitary organization headed by the future Israeli prime minister Menachem Begin. Emanuel's family immigrated to the U.S. from Israel in 1959, settling in Chicago. There, his father built a medical practice from the ground up, which included treating poor immigrants for free. (He later quit the American Medical Association over its position on national health care.) Emanuel and his two brothers, Ezekiel and Rahm, were raised in Wilmette, a lakeshore Chicago suburb. Ezekiel, a nationally renowned bioethicist and a leading opponent of state-assisted suicide, is a special adviser to the White House budget director and serves as chairman of the bioethics department of the Clinical Center at the National Institutes of Health (NIH). Rahm, President Barack Obama's chief of staff, served previously as a Democratic U.S. congressman from Illinois and a top adviser to President Bill Clinton. (*The West Wing* character Josh Lyman, played by Bradley Whitford, was modeled on Rahm.) Emanuel also has an adopted sister, Shoshana.

With his siblings Emanuel enjoyed a culturally rich upbringing. His mother, the onetime owner of a Chicago-area rock-and-roll club, ran a local branch of the Congress of Racial Equality (CORE) and frequently took Ari and his brothers in the 1960s to marches protesting the Vietnam War. Growing up, Ari learned from his parents to respect but question and challenge authority; during family dinners he was schooled in the art of arguing. He recalled to Weinraub, "There was never a time at the dinner table when politics didn't come up. We always argued. I suppose that affected the way I talk to people. It doesn't mean you don't like somebody."

As a boy Emanuel was diagnosed as dyslexic and hyperactive; his mother spent many hours teaching him to read. He told Susan Baer for the

Washingtonian (May 2008), "Teachers said I'd never graduate high school, let alone college." (In 2007 the Lab School of Washington and Baltimore presented Emanuel with an award recognizing achievers with learning disabilities.) Emanuel went on to attend New Trier West High School, in Winnetka, Illinois, one of the most competitive high schools in the country. After graduating, he attended Macalester College, in St. Paul, Minnesota. While there he became a roommate and friend of the actor and director Peter Berg, who has directed such films as *The Kingdom* (2007) and *Hancock* (2008). Berg later recalled to Scott Bowles for *USA Today* (September 26, 2007) that the two had so little money that "we couldn't afford beer. One of us would distract a woman at a bar by flirting with her while the other one stole her drink."

After graduating from Macalester, in 1983, Emanuel played on the professional racquetball circuit and lived for a time in Paris, France, where he cultivated a playboy lifestyle. He then moved to New York City, where he began working as an assistant to Robert Lantz, a veteran talent agent who has represented the likes of Milos Forman and others. "Nothing stopped him," Lantz recalled to Elisabeth Bumiller for the *New York Times* (June 15, 1997, on-line). Impressed with his tenacity, Lantz soon suggested that Emanuel move to Los Angeles, California. In 1987 Lantz helped him land a trainee position at CAA, then at its height under Michael Ovitz. Emanuel later told Weinraub that Lantz gave him four valuable pieces of advice: "You have to have taste, you have to be aggressive, you have to be fearless and you have to have the ability to sell."

Emanuel learned the ropes of the entertainment industry in CAA's mailroom. Frequently likened to military boot camps, talent agencies' mailrooms weed out entry-level employees; many wanting to break into the entertainment industry never make it past that first stage, in which cruel and demeaning treatment is not uncommon. Those who move beyond the mailroom normally become agents' assistants and then, sometimes, agents. Undaunted by that atmosphere, Emanuel enjoyed a meteoric rise to the top of the industry. From CAA he moved on to Inter Talent and then International Creative Management (ICM). A turning point in Emanuel's life came when he was accidentally hit by a car driven by an ICM client, leaving him with cracked ribs and a badly injured knee. The incident led him to rethink the direction of his life. He recalled to Bumiller, "I wasn't going to sit around and say my big book on my life when I'm 50 years old is C.A.A. or I.C.M. I'd shoot myself."

In a move reminiscent of Ovitz's break from the William Morris Agency, in 1975, when he and four other similarly disgruntled employees left the agency to form Creative Artists Agency, Emanuel and three other agents—David Greenblatt, Rick Rosen, and Tom Strickler—started plotting their departure from ICM to form an agency of their own. Not long afterward ICM executives learned about their plan through an employee who had caught an assistant taking files from the office after hours for one of the conspiring agents, and all four men were fired. Emanuel and his co-defectors officially launched Endeavor Talent Agency on March 30, 1995. Although ICM's chairman, Jeff Berg, threatened them with a lawsuit, no suit was filed. Upon receiving a vehement midnight phone call from Berg, Emanuel recalled to Bumiller, "I said, 'I don't work for you. Don't raise your voice at me.' And I hung up."

Endeavor's beginnings were modest. The agency was run from a small office above a restaurant in South Beverly Hills; nearly everyone on its small list of clients was a TV writer-producer—there were few filmmakers and no movie stars. Endeavor's clout in the talent-agent industry grew as more partners stepped aboard with prominent clients. In 1996 the company relocated to a high-rise building on Wilshire Boulevard, and three new partners, formerly with CAA, joined the operation: David Lonner, Doug Robinson, and Adam Venit. While Lonner helped bring in feature-film directors, a group that Endeavor had been lacking, Robinson and Venit represented actors including Lisa Kudrow, Hank Azaria, David Spade, and Adam Sandler. Over the next several years, as its client list expanded significantly, Endeavor became known for its take-no-prisoners attitude toward negotiating and innovative approach to the industry, which included a strong focus on up-and-coming filmmakers trying to establish themselves apart from the studios. In 2003 Emanuel commissioned the architect Neil Denari to design Endeavor's headquarters in Beverly Hills.

Another key development at Endeavor came in 2001, when the company acquired the agent Patrick Whitesell from CAA. Whitesell became a partner at Endeavor and brought on board such high-profile stars as Ben Affleck, Matt Damon, Jude Law, Hugh Jackman, and Christian Bale. Among the 200-plus people who have since chosen Endeavor to represent them are the actors Amy Adams, Jessica Alba, Javier Bardem, Steve Carell, Sacha Baron Cohen, Robert DeNiro, Michael Douglas, America Ferrera, James Franco, Jennifer Garner, Dustin Hoffman, Kate Hudson, Keira Knightley, Shia LaBeouf, Jennifer Lopez, Frances McDormand, Ellen Page, Robert Pattinson, Charlie Sheen, Tilda Swinton, Rachel Weisz, and Mark Wahlberg; the directors Peter Berg, Spike Lee, Shawn Levy, McG, Adam McKay, Michael Moore, and Martin Scorsese; and the writers Anthony Bozza, Bruno Heller, Andre Nemec, Stephanie Savage, and Mark Schwahn. Endeavor's television group has packaged hit series created by Larry David (*Curb Your Enthusiasm*), Tina Fey (*30 Rock*), Ricky Gervais (*The Office*), Seth McFarlane (*Family Guy*), Conan O'Brien (*Late Night with Conan O'Brien*), and Josh Schwartz (*The O.C.* and *Gossip Girl*)—all of whom are clients. The company has also been associated with some of the most commercially successful movies of the 2000s, including *Charlie's Angels* (2000), *Meet the Parents* (2000), *Little Miss Sun-*

shine (2006), *Night at the Museum* (2006), *The Departed* (2006), *Enchanted* (2007), and the groundbreaking documentaries *Fahrenheit 9/11* (2004) and Al Gore's *An Inconvenient Truth* (2006).

While Endeavor has grown into the second-most-powerful agency in Hollywood (behind CAA), it has been mired in several controversies over the years. In April 2002 a former Endeavor agent, Sandra Epstein, who at one time was the sole female among about a dozen agents, brought a sexual-harassment suit against the company. That led underwriters at Endeavor's insurer, Lloyd's of London, to cancel the agency's employment-practices policy, which spawned a countersuit by Endeavor. In court depositions and filings in the second suit, Epstein and other former Endeavor employees alleged that the agency was a haven for drug use, sexual trysts, bigotry, and homophobia. Emanuel was accused of allowing a friend to operate a pornographic Internet site out of the agency's offices, and one agent was said to have tried to make his assistants arrange his meetings with prostitutes. While the second suit was ultimately settled under undisclosed terms, Epstein settled her claims for $2.25 million. Currently, roughly half of Endeavor's 80 agents and a quarter of its partners are women. Also, similar to Ovitz's approach at CAA, Emanuel has fostered a collaborative work environment by encouraging interaction among departments, with television agents working alongside movie agents.

Emanuel again put Endeavor in hot water in 2004, when he publicly castigated Michael Eisner, then chairman of the Walt Disney Co., for trying to shelve Michael Moore's documentary *Fahrenheit 9/11*, which took a critical look at the presidency of George W. Bush and the so-called war on terrorism. Eisner had tried to block Miramax from distributing the documentary in fear that it would endanger tax breaks Disney received for its theme parks and hotels in Florida, where Bush's brother, Jeb, served as governor at the time. Miramax's former owners, the brothers Harvey and Bob Weinstein, later acquired the rights to the documentary, which was distributed by Lions Gate Films. *Fahrenheit 9/11* went on to win the Palm d'Or at the 2004 Cannes Film Festival, the festival's highest honor, and became the highest-grossing documentary of all time, with $220 million in sales worldwide. Weinraub quoted Michael Moore as saying, "We would not have gotten the release our film received without Ari's work. He took a big risk. He did something agents were not supposed to do when he went on the record. He broke one of the unwritten rules. He made sure the film wasn't shelved." Emanuel went on to make headlines again in July 2006, when he called for an industry-wide blacklisting of Mel Gibson after the actor-director made anti-Semitic remarks during a drunken tirade.

Emanuel's profile has risen dramatically since Endeavor packaged the HBO television series *Entourage*, which is based loosely on the life of Mark Wahlberg, his group of friends, and his manager/producer, Steve Levinson. Since it debuted, in 2004, the show has been considered "the most accurately nuanced satire of the entertainment industry since the 1992 HBO comedy series *The Larry Sanders Show*," Hilary De Vries wrote for the *New York Times* (September 5, 2005). While the show centers on a young A-list star named Vincent Chase (played by Adrian Grenier) and his friends, the character who has drawn the most attention is Vincent's agent, Ari Gold, who was modeled after Emanuel. On the show Gold is portrayed as an abrasive, fast-talking Hollywood superagent who pops Viagra and likes to "hug it out" with colleagues after screaming at them. Emanuel, who personally enlisted Jeremy Piven to portray Gold, has acknowledged that the character is in many ways similar to himself—but has said that he does not take Viagra or do a lot of hugging. Commenting on Piven's portrayal, which garnered three consecutive Emmy Awards (2006–08), Emanuel explained to Kim Masters for the *Los Angeles Times* (July 14, 2004), "There's absolutely times when I'm over the top. Not to the level that he is, [but] there are parts of the character that are me. People that know me—they know that I'm a character, but I'm not that character." He admitted to Weinraub that Gold is "a lot funnier than I am." The show's creator, Doug Ellin, has said that the character is actually a composite of two agents, Emanuel and Ellin's own agent, Jeff Jacobs of CAA. Both agents have signed releases waiving the right to sue. The sixth season of *Entourage* began in July 2009.

Endeavor enjoyed much success in 2007 and 2008. In 2007 Endeavor clients swept nominations in the adapted-screenplay category at the Academy Awards for films including *The Departed*, and in 2008 an independent study of the U.S. television market conducted by tvtracker.com placed Endeavor first among major agencies in almost every category. According to the study, Endeavor clients created or ran 51 percent of prime-time shows and packaged 58 percent of new dramas for the 2007–08 season, 31 percent of all new comedies, and 33 percent of all new reality/unscripted series. Endeavor, which generates approximately $100 million in revenue per year, has also expanded its services beyond entertainment. The agency's marketing division has worked with a number of corporate clients, including American Express, AT&T, AOL, and Revlon. Endeavor also has a commercial/voiceover division, which has partnered on campaigns with leading brands including Neutrogena, L'Oréal, and Mercedes-Benz, and a literary division that encompasses all aspects of the publishing industry.

In 2009, following months of discussion and rumors, William Morris and Endeavor agreed to merge as William Morris Endeavor Entertainment (WME Entertainment). James A. Wiatt, who was the chief executive of William Morris, was named chairman of the new company, and Emanuel was named co-chief executive, along with Endeavor's

Patrick Whitesell and William Morris's David Wirtschafter. The merger was largely driven by the economic downturn that began in 2008 and forced television companies and film studios to cut costs. WME Entertainment hopes to shift the balance of power from the studios back to the agencies and challenge CAA in the Hollywood pecking order. According to an article in the *New York Times* (June 10, 2009, on-line), "Even hardened observers of Hollywood's coarse ways were stunned when Mr. Emanuel and his colleagues dumped dozens of Morris agents and parted ways with Mr. Wiatt, who had since become the Morris chairman, less than a month after the merger was approved."

Emanuel and his wife, the former Sarah Addington, live with their three children in a $10 million home in Brentwood, in western Los Angeles. Emanuel has hosted numerous fund-raisers for the Democratic Party, including a $2,300-per-plate fund-raiser for Barack Obama at Emanuel's home in 2008. He is also known for his environmental activism and has led campaigns against gas-guzzling SUVs. Emanuel, who is known to start calling studio heads at 4 a.m. to lobby for his clients, was named one of the 50 smartest people in Hollywood by *Entertainment Weekly* in 2007.

—C.C.

Suggested Reading: *Entertainment Weekly* p25+ Dec. 7, 2007; *Jewish Journal* (on-line) Nov. 6, 2008; *Los Angeles Times* E p1 July 14, 2004; *New York Times* (on-line) June 15, 1997, E p1 Aug. 2, 2004, (on-line) July 27, 2008; *Washingtonian* p70+ May 2008

Saul Loeb/AFP/Getty Images

Emanuel, Rahm

NOTE: An earlier article about Rahm Emanuel appeared in *Current Biography* in 1998.

Nov. 29, 1959– White House chief of staff; former U.S. representative from Illinois (Democrat)

Address: The White House, 1600 Pennsylvania Ave., N.W., Washington, DC 20500

Rahm Emanuel, a onetime high-level staffer in the Bill Clinton White House and former U.S. congressman from Illinois, was appointed by President Barack Obama to be the chief of staff in his administration, and when Obama took office, on January 20, 2009, Emanuel became one of the most powerful men in Washington. Although the specific duties of individual White House chiefs of staff have varied from one administration to the next, Emanuel is largely responsible for overseeing the other staff members, managing Obama's schedule, and controlling access to the president. Emanuel has been involved in government for more than 20 years and is both admired and feared for his political savvy, sharp tongue, and dedication to his work. He attacks problems with a relentlessness that often gives others pause. The political strategist James Carville, in a widely quoted assessment, once said about the wiry, five-foot-eight Emanuel, "I have never seen that small a mass produce that much energy."

Although Emanuel's work as chief of staff is usually not visible to the general public, he has been influential in virtually all arenas of White House activity, among them the economy, foreign policy, and national security. He played a significant role in the negotiations that led to the Obama administration's $787 billion stimulus package; the development of a plan to expand access to community colleges; the addition of Turkey to Obama's list of countries to visit during his diplomatic trip to Europe; and discussions and decisions regarding Pakistan, Israel, Russia, and the wars in Iraq and Afghanistan. In October 2009 a group of writers for *GQ* magazine placed Emanuel at the top of its list of the 50 most powerful people in Washington, D.C., aside from the president, vice president, and First Lady. According to *GQ*, Emanuel "knows procedure, he's ruthlessly pragmatic about what is politically achievable, and he knows how and when to twist arms and call in the many favors he's owed. All of which has helped him wrangle fence-sitters when it came to ponying up for the stimulus package, negotiate with the Senate Finance Committee on health care, and keep the liberal and conservative elements of his own party in line."

Dynamism seems to run in Emanuel's family. His father, Benjamin Emanuel, a pediatrician, was born in Jerusalem and passed secret codes for Menachem Begin's underground Irgun movement during the decade before Israel became a state. His mother, Marsha, a psychiatric social worker, is an American-born Jew who lived in Israel for a time and later became active in the civil rights movement in the United States. The Emanuels raised three sons in the Chicago, Illinois, area. Rahm, the middle son, was born on November 29, 1959. (An adopted daughter, Shoshana, joined the family years later.) In an interview with Elisabeth Bumiller for the *New York Times Magazine* (June 15, 1997, on-line), Emanuel said that his parents "left an indelible print that they expected nothing but the best from us, and taught us to expect it from ourselves." The children were required to keep abreast of current events and politics, and they had to come to the dinner table each evening "prepared to do battle," as Emanuel put it. Every Sunday, the family went on an excursion to a cultural institution in Chicago, and every summer the boys were sent to camp in Israel. Rahm developed an enduring attachment to the Jewish state. When the 1991 Persian Gulf War broke out, he flew to Israel and spent time at an army base, working on tank and jeep brakes. (His volunteer stint has led to persistent, but mistaken, reports that he was a member of the Israeli Defense Force and that he holds Israeli, rather than American, citizenship.)

The Emanuel brothers have been the subject of many magazine and newspaper articles. The eldest, Ezekiel, known as Zeke, is a well-known oncologist and medical ethicist. The youngest son, Ariel, called Ari, is a Hollywood talent agent with his own firm. The brothers "understand and enjoy power," Bumiller wrote, "and know how using it behind the scenes can change the way people think, live, and die." (Ari is the model for the character Ari Gold on the HBO show *Entourage*, and Rahm was the model for the character Josh Lyman on *The West Wing*.) In February 2009 Ezekiel Emanuel was appointed to the Obama administration's Office of Management and Budget as a special adviser.

While the boys were growing up, their mother insisted that they take ballet lessons, and Rahm showed a special talent for dance. He was offered a scholarship to the Joffrey Ballet School but turned it down. "I was way too small to be anything major," he was quoted as saying in *People* (January 11, 1993), "and I have too much ego to be a secondary performer." But Emanuel continued to train even as an adult, and on one occasion, after a dance class, he ran into Bill and Hillary Clinton. "They were taking [their daughter] Chelsea to her dance class," he told the *People* interviewer, "and out comes their national finance director in his leotard and tights."

Emanuel attended Sarah Lawrence College, in Bronxville, New York, where he earned a B.A. degree in liberal arts in 1981. He first got involved in politics in 1980, during his senior year in college, when he worked on the congressional campaign of David Robinson, an Illinois Democrat. The candidate's campaign manager, David Wilhelm, was "stunned by Rahm," as he recalled to Lloyd Grove for the *Washington Post* (July 7, 1992, on-line). "He was our finance director, 19 or 20 years old, and when people would give $250, he would call back and say, 'That's not enough.'" Wilhelm also worked with Emanuel on Richard M. Daley's successful 1989 run for mayor of Chicago. "Rahm would literally stand on top of my desk and gesticulate wildly about what we needed to do for him," Wilhelm told Grove. Emanuel reportedly executed one of his most notorious political deeds in the mid-1980s, when he allegedly sent a pollster with whom he had had a disagreement a large, decomposing fish.

In between those two political campaigns, in 1985, Emanuel earned an M.A. degree in speech and communications from Northwestern University, in Evanston, Illinois. Four years later, after stints as the Midwest field director for the Democratic Congressional Campaign Committee and then as the committee's national campaign director, he set up his own political consulting firm. According to the *People* article, when David Wilhelm became Bill Clinton's campaign manager in 1991, his first order was "Get Rahm."

Immediately after being hired as Clinton's national finance director, in November 1991, Rahm began stepping on "more toes than he ever did dancing *The Nutcracker*," Grove wrote. He called the campaign's Little Rock, Arkansas, headquarters to say that he was arriving from Chicago on a Sunday and that he needed a lift from the airport, after which he wanted to meet his staff. He was told that while he would get a ride, none of the staffers worked on Sundays. "You do now," Emanuel replied. Shocked to discover that the campaign had only about $600,000 in the bank, he organized 26 fund-raising events between Thanksgiving and Christmas that netted more than $3 million. "The money was credibility," Emanuel told Roger Simon for the *New Republic* (February 3, 1997). "It showed that a governor from the state of Arkansas could play in the major leagues." (Having a large nest egg also helped Clinton weather the storm of bad publicity that erupted in February 1992 about his alleged extramarital affairs and draft evasion.) In Little Rock Emanuel worked with strategists including James Carville and George Stephanopoulos.

Emanuel decided to solicit money primarily through fund-raising events, rather than through the more popular (and expensive) method of direct mail. He convinced Clinton that if he made the time to show up at arranged events and shake hands, he could raise millions. Indeed, the campaign raised more money than any previous presidential run and did so without getting mired in any fund-raising scandals.

Following his 1992 victory Bill Clinton tapped Emanuel to organize the inaugural celebrations. Emanuel, working with a 300-member staff, successfully arranged five days of events, including almost a dozen balls, several concerts, and the opening of the White House to the general public. "This is like being the CEO of . . . 3,500 bar mitzvahs," he told Jill Abramson for the *Wall Street Journal* (January 4, 1993). After Clinton's inauguration Emanuel tried to settle into his new position as the president's political director, but his tenure was rocky. He clashed repeatedly with Susan Thomases, a close confidante of Hillary Rodham Clinton, who reportedly believed that Emanuel was the source of leaks that reflected badly on the White House. (He vigorously denied the charge.) In less than a year, Emanuel was demoted to director of special projects and was exiled to an office that he described, according to Bumiller, as "a White House closet with a Playskool phone." Leon Panetta, the White House chief of staff from 1994 to 1997, has said that Emanuel's problems stemmed from a clash of cultures between Chicagoans and Arkansans. "His style is direct," Panetta told William Neikirk for the *Chicago Tribune* (November 23, 1997). "He tells you what he thinks. . . . A lot of people don't like that."

Emanuel prepared himself for a comeback. The demotion reminded him of an incident he had experienced as a 17-year-old: while working at the fast-food chain Arby's, he sliced off half of the middle finger on his right hand and did not immediately seek medical attention. Instead, he went to his school prom. The injury led to gangrene, which spread up his arm. "I could have died," he told Neikirk. "I could have professionally had a major wreck. In both cases, life transformed itself. I think I grew out of the political one. I didn't slow down any, I kind of focused and became more determined, but I did become more measured."

Emanuel's first assignment as special-projects director was to help coordinate the White House's effort to get the North American Free Trade Agreement (NAFTA) through Congress. When the hotly debated legislation passed, in November 1993, Emanuel's influence within the administration began to rise. He turned his attention to other policy issues; determining the best way to approach them turned out to be one of his greatest strengths. Like some of Clinton's other advisers, he was convinced that the president ought to focus on matters of concern to middle-class Americans. Toward that end he "plunged into the crime issue in particular, seeking to strengthen Clinton's and the party's ties to the law-enforcement community and stealing an issue away from the Republicans," Neikirk noted. "From the Brady bill [screening handgun purchasers] to the assault-weapons ban to a law dealing with sexual offenders, Emanuel's hands were all over the issue." He was also a strong proponent of the welfare- and immigration-reform bills that many members of the liberal wing of the Democratic Party opposed.

In addition to developing domestic policies, an important part of Emanuel's White House service was to promote the president's agenda in the media. Many reporters acknowledged that Emanuel was smart and effective, but they complained that he was a shameless spin doctor. "I got along with him, but like everyone else who ever covered [the White House], I also hung up on him," David Lauter, a *Los Angeles Times* writer, told Bumiller. "He'll call you up and start spinning something about how this is the greatest thing that any president has done in the history of man." Asked by Neikirk if he was bothered that some people considered him "obnoxious and arrogant," Emanuel replied, "No. . . . Am I obnoxious? I am loud. Am I loyal? Absolutely. Every bit."

Emanuel, who was nicknamed "Rahmbo" because of his aggressiveness, intended to resign after Clinton's first term, but when the president offered him a promotion to senior presidential adviser and executive assistant to the chief of staff for policy, he agreed to stay. George Stephanopoulos had filled the position during Clinton's first term. Ensconced in Stephanopoulos's old office, Emanuel played a key role in helping to form the administration's domestic policy. He was one of the five or six most senior people in the White House and formed the president's circle of closest and most trusted advisers. Unlike the liberal Stephanopoulos, Emanuel was a centrist and proved influential in Clinton's emergence as a more pragmatic, middle-of-the-road executive. (Emanuel was also a central player in the administration's handling of allegations that Clinton had had a sexual relationship with Monica Lewinsky, a former White House intern.)

Emanuel described his dealings with Clinton to Neikirk as "very frank and honest. . . . We have a very solid friendship, a relationship, rather. When I leave here, I will probably use 'friendship.' When I'm here, 'relationship.'" Emanuel left the Clinton White House in October 1998. He and his wife, Amy Rule, did not want to raise their children in Washington, D.C., and Rahm was also, by many accounts, interested in finding a higher-paying job in the private sector, in order to ensure financial security for his family. They decided to return to Chicago and bought a home in the neighborhood of Ravenswood, on the north side of town. Emanuel soon began working as an investment banker with the firm Dresdner Kleinwort Wasserstein, a job he obtained through Bruce Wasserstein, a Wall Street figure who had raised a lot of money for Clinton. Although Emanuel had never before worked at a similar institution, he viewed mergers and acquisitions as being not very different from funding campaigns and getting legislation passed. "You bring people together. You keep them talking," he told a reporter for the *Chicago Reader* (February 15, 2002). "You learn when a no could really mean a yes." During his two and a half years with the firm, Emanuel reportedly earned more than $16 million.

In the winter of 2002, Emanuel decided to run for the congressional seat representing Illinois's Fifth District, which spans much of the North Side of Chicago, from Lake Michigan into the western suburbs, and includes the neighborhood of Ravenswood. "Most Chicago politicians push the notion that they're neighborhood guys," the *Chicago Reader* reporter wrote. "They point to the parks where they played, the high schools they graduated from. But Emanuel isn't a neighborhood guy." In his earlier years in Chicago, the reporter wrote, Emanuel never ran for office, never led a local grassroots movement, and never joined a community group. Besides those disadvantages, it was widely acknowledged that Emanuel needed to change his image as an arrogant, pushy political operative. "He had to show he cared," the *Chicago Reader* reporter opined, "not just in a grand public-policy sense, but in a personal way." Rahm started emphasizing his family's ties to Chicago: his uncle Les had been a Chicago police officer for more than 20 years, his grandparents had lived in the city, and his father had a practice there for a time. During interviews and press conferences, Emanuel became more patient and moderated his temper, but many political observers expressed skepticism. Still, Emanuel managed to gain public support and the endorsement of the AFL-CIO, the Chicago Teachers' Union, and, not surprisingly, Bill Clinton.

Emanuel was elected to Congress in 2002 with 67 percent of the vote, and two years later he was easily reelected with 76 percent of the vote. As a congressman, Emanuel supported stem-cell research, abortion rights, benefits for same-sex domestic partners, strong gun control, tax incentives for production and use of renewable energy, comprehensive immigration reform without amnesty, and a quick withdrawal from Iraq. In 2005 then–Minority Leader Nancy Pelosi, a Democrat from California, asked Emanuel to become head of the Democratic Congressional Campaign Committee, reasoning that as a powerful, goal-oriented, experienced politician, he could help Democrats gain House seats in the November 2006 election.

In the summer of 2006, Emanuel and another former Clinton staffer, Bruce Reed, published the book *The Plan: Big Ideas for America*, which a reviewer for the *Economist* (August 19, 2006) called "[an] answer to Mr. [Newt] Gingrich's *Contract with America*, the small-government manifesto that helped Republicans capture the House in 1994." The reviewer called the pair's plan "solid and mostly sensible" and noted that it called for insurers to encourage free physicals to prevent costly illnesses later, for teachers to be paid for performance, and for families whose annual gross incomes did not exceed $100,000 to pay no more than 10 percent in taxes.

The Democrats gained some 30 seats in the House that November, and much of the credit was given to Emanuel, whom Naftali Bendavid, in an article for the *Chicago Tribune* (November 12, 2006) headlined "The House that Rahm Built," called "a brutally effective taskmaster." Emanuel, Bendavid noted, "[remade] the Democratic Party in his own image. Democrats had never raised enough money. Emanuel . . . yelled at colleagues and threatened his candidates into generating an unprecedented amount of campaign cash. Democrats had a history of appeasing party constituencies. Emanuel tore up the old litmus tests on abortion and other issues. With techniques that would make a Big Ten football coach blush, he recruited candidates who could mount tough challenges in some of the reddest patches in America. Democrats had blanched at hardball. Emanuel . . . muscled weaker Democrats out of races in favor of stronger ones." Bendavid concluded, "The Republicans always had killers on their side, ruthless closers like Karl Rove, Tom DeLay and Lee Atwater, the late mudslinging mastermind credited with getting the first President Bush elected. In Emanuel, Democrats had their counterpart." (Helping the Democrats' cause were several ongoing sex and corruption scandals among Republicans and increasing voter dissatisfaction with the situation in Iraq.)

Despite his close ties to Bill and Hillary Clinton, Emanuel endorsed his fellow Chicagoan Obama in the 2008 Democratic presidential primaries, rather than the former First Lady. He had been, he quipped to many reporters, "hiding under my desk" for much of the primary season.

In November Emanuel was reelected to his congressional seat with 74 percent of the vote, and many political analysts believed he was on his way to becoming House Speaker. That changed, however, when Obama offered him the position of White House chief of staff. Because Emanuel and his wife have three children—Zachariah, Ilana, and Leah—he was torn about accepting so demanding and time-consuming a job. After taking a few days to mull over the offer, he accepted. As quoted in the *Huffington Post* (November 6, 2008, on-line), he released a statement addressed to the president-elect: "I know what a privilege it is to serve in the White House, and am humbled by the responsibility we owe the American people. I'm leaving a [congressional] job I love to join your White House for one simple reason—like the record amount of voters who cast their ballot over the last month, I want to do everything I can to help deliver the change America needs." He added, "I am grateful to the people of the Fifth Congressional District who sent me to work on their behalf. I was proud to serve on a leadership team with Speaker Pelosi, Majority Leader Steny Hoyer and Majority Whip Jim Clyburn. They have taught me invaluable lessons—even a few lessons in humility, believe it or not. I want to say a special word about my Republican colleagues, who serve with dignity, decency and a deep sense of patriotism. We often disagree, but I respect their motives. Now is a time for unity, and Mr. President-elect, I will do everything in my power to help you stitch together the frayed fabric of our politics, and help summon Americans of both parties to unite in common purpose."

Emanuel's appointment has caused some controversy. His management style, while unquestionably effective, has often been called into question. "We joke that someone should open a special trauma ward in Washington for people who've worked for Rahm," Jose Cerda, a fellow Clinton staffer, had told Joshua Green for *Rolling Stone* (October 20, 2005, on-line). Additionally, his strong support for Israel worries those who feel he might exert anti-Arab pressure on Obama. Emanuel's father added to those fears when he told a reporter for an Israeli newspaper, as quoted in the *New York Times* (November 13, 2008, on-line), "Obviously he'll influence the president to be pro-Israel. Why wouldn't he? What is he, an Arab? He's not going to be mopping floors at the White House." Emanuel quickly issued a formal apology and disavowed his father's remarks. Others' doubts notwithstanding, Obama has asserted that Emanuel was a wise pick. In an official press release, also quoted in the *Huffington Post* (November 6, 2008, on-line), the president-elect said, "The Chief of Staff is central to the ability of a President and Administration to accomplish an agenda. And no one I know is better at getting things done than Rahm Emanuel."

—D.K.

Suggested Reading: *Chicago Reader* p1+ Feb. 15, 2002; *Chicago Tribune* C p1 Nov. 9, 2003, C p1 Nov. 12, 2006, C p6 June 16, 2007; *Economist* Aug. 19, 2006; *New Republic* p17+ Feb. 3, 1997; *New York Times Magazine* p23+ June 15, 1997; *People* p71+ Jan. 11, 1993; *Slate* (on-line) Nov. 6, 2008; *Washington Post* (on-line) July 7, 1992

Brad Barket/Getty Images

Emin, Tracey

(EH-min)

July 3, 1963– Artist; writer; filmmaker

Address: c/o Saatchi Gallery, Duke of York's HQ, King's Road, London SW3 4SQ, England

Enthusiasm, admiration, wonder, empathy—such reactions have greeted the work of the British artist Tracey Emin, which has been described as painfully honest, deeply moving, captivating, and thought-provoking. Her creations have also been met with disgust, derision, shock, and condemnation, and they have been labeled shallow, puerile, crude, repellent, intolerably egocentric, and absurdly narcissistic. Like Damien Hirst and Rachel Whiteread, Emin is a prominent member of a group dubbed the Young British Artists in the early 1990s. Now in their 40s, they are distinguished in part by a "fascination with the real: with how real objects can be incorporated, modified, implied, whatever, in . . . art and made somehow unreal or hyper-real," Michael Kimmelman wrote for the *New York Times* (May 17, 1996). In a complimentary assessment of Emin's work, Adrian Searle wrote for the London *Guardian* (April 22, 2007), "As a storyteller [Emin is] superb. She lets us rummage through her life and aspirations, and into corners most of us keep well away from the public gaze. Is Emin an artist or an autobiographer? Either way, her only invention, and only subject, is herself. Such solipsism could be seen as self-indulgent, or brave, or silly. Perhaps it is all three. But whatever else the phenomenon of Tracey Emin entails, she has turned the details of her private life . . . into something like poetry, or theatre, or unalloyed confession. The best of her work is filled with pathos, humour, regret, pain, and forgiveness. Her vulnerability and her self-confidence—bordering on monomania—are of a piece. . . . The best thing about her work is the way she deals with what most of us would keep to ourselves." Matthew Collings, writing for the London *Independent* (March 25, 1997), also lauded Emin for "do[ing] something we'd almost forgotten art could do. She tells stories. Harrowing, heartbreaking, funny and ironic stories" that offer glimpses into "her struggle to escape the past through art." But Collings's opinion later changed radically; in a fiercely derogatory article, subtitled "Tracey Emin: Failure + Charisma = Success," for *Modern Painters* (November 2008), he wrote, "Historically, Tracey Emin's rise was a touch-and-go situation: you could laugh in embarrassment or ignore her or maybe embrace the madness—and the last one won. Between 1993, her first show at White Cube, and 1999, her Turner

Prize nomination, she took the artworld. After that, she took the world. . . . Art writers round the world who want to be thought of as informed tend to be admiring toward her. She is thought to have suffered in life and to have found ways to transform suffering into art. In England, knowledge of her greatness reaches far beyond the artworld: art writers in the UK national press at first combined sneering with sympathy and then gradually caved in. Now it's all-out fawning. She's a household name. Years ago, she could be mocked as a media tart and a hopeless exhibitionist (in the pathological sense), but now it's considered a great faux pas to come out with an opinion like this." In another, somewhat mixed appraisal, for *Tate Magazine* (September/October 2002), Melanie McGrath wrote, "I don't know whether Tracy Emin is a great artist. . . . At its best, Emin's art presents the world in ways you've always known about but never admitted, or you've never wanted to admit, or never perhaps until that moment articulated."

"I'm not stupid," Emin declared to Catherine Deveney for the *Living Scotsman* (July 13, 2008, on-line). "I don't go around throwing up and saying, 'This is art.' I went to art school for seven years. . . . I really know what I'm talking about. I'm a brilliant f***ing artist. If I wasn't, I wouldn't be having the level of success that I am." "Anyone who knows me knows that I am really sincere about my work," she told Karen Wright for *Modern Painters* (June 2005). Emin's work includes drawings (most of them monoprints), paintings, photographs, and embroidered and appliquéd fabric—many with text on them; sculptures in bronze and other materials; objects constructed with found materials; sentiments or ideas spelled out in neon lights; assemblages of her journals or other memorabilia or possessions; videos; and performances. Among her most famous pieces is *Everyone I Have Ever Slept With 1963–1995* (1995), a small, igloo-shaped tent whose inner walls displayed the names of Emin's bedmates since birth, including not only her sex partners but her maternal grandmother, brother, and two aborted fetuses—a work that the ad-agency mogul and art connoisseur Charles Saatchi bought from a dealer in 1997 for £40,000, equal to $65,520 then. Others among Emin's best-known works are *My Bed* (1999), a double bed (in which she had once remained for several days in a suicidal depression) with stained, bunched-up sheets, standing beside a small rug cluttered with dirty slippers, bloodied panties, used condoms, empty liquor bottles, cigarette butts, and other debris (purchased by Saatchi in 2000 for £200,000, the equivalent of about $303,200 then); *Roman Standard* (2005), a small bronze bird perched atop a 16-foot-tall pole that stands near the Anglican Cathedral in Liverpool, England (commissioned by the BBC for £60,000, or about $122,000); and *Keep Me Safe* (2007), those words written in neon lights, with glass shaped by a helper of Emin's (sold at a Sotheby's auction for a children's charity for £60,000, or about $119,500).

Emin's most attention-getting works also include her one-minute film *Homage to Edvard Munch and All My Dead Children* (1999), in which she is seen naked, screaming on a jetty near the summer house of Munch. (She has named that Norwegian painter and the Austrian painter Egon Schiele as two of her important early influences.) Others are *The Last Thing I Said to You Is Don't Leave Me Here, or The Hut* (1999), a small, dilapidated beach shack she once owned, exhibited along with two photos of a nude Emin inside the hut; *One Secret Is to Save Everything* (2007), a 21-by-14-foot white flag with those words, written in orange-red letters, superimposed on hand-embroidered, swimming sperm; and *Star Trek Voyager* (2007), an embroidered blanket (sold at an auction for £800,000, or $1,601,600, the proceeds donated to the Elton John AIDS Foundation). Richard Brooks reported for the London *Sunday Times* (May 3, 2009, on-line) that the nearly 200 pieces Emin has given to charities "had a combined estimated value of £10 million," or about $15 million, according to the artist herself.

In 2007 Emin represented Great Britain at the 52d Venice Biennale, in Italy. That year she was one of two artists named to the independent, privately funded Royal Academy of Arts; one of Britain's most influential arts institutions, the academy restricts its membership to 80 active artists. Works by Emin are in the permanent collections of museums including the Tate Museum, in London; the National Galleries of Scotland, in Edinburgh; the Frans Hals Museum, in Harlaam, the Netherlands; the Castello di Rivoli Museum of Contemporary Art, in Torino, Italy; and the Brooklyn Museum of Art, in New York City. Emin has participated in dozens of solo and group shows worldwide. Books about her include *Tracey Emin*, by Neal Brown (2006), and *Tracey Emin 20 Years* (2009), by Patrick Elliott. She is the author and illustrator of books including *Exploration of the Soul* (1994), *Absolute Tracey* (1998), *This Is Another Place* (2003), *Strangeland* (2005), *Tracey Emin: Works 1963–2006* (2006), *Tracey Emin: Borrowed Light* (2007), and *One Thousand Drawings* (2009). She has co-written other books, among them *The Art of Tracey Emin* (2002) and *Tracey Emin: You Left Me Breathing* (2008). She has also made one, poorly received feature film, *Top Spot* (2003), and several very short films, among them *Why I Never Became a Dancer* (1995), about her humiliating experience in adolescence at a disco-dance contest, when her performance prompted young men in the audience to shout "Slag, slag, slag"—British slang for "whore." Essays by Emin, headed "My Life in a Column," have appeared in the London *Independent* since 2005.

Along with her twin brother, Paul, Tracey Karima Emin was born out of wedlock on July 3, 1963 in Croydon, a borough of London, England. On their mother's side they have an older half-brother, Alan Cashin. Emin's father, Envar Emin, a Turkish Cypriot, was a real-estate developer and chef; one of his properties was the International Hotel in Margate, a seaside town and popular vacation spot in southeastern England, where Tracey and her brother grew up. Emin's mother, Pamela Cashin, an Englishwoman, worked in the hotel as a chambermaid and, at night, in a club as a waitress. Cashin told her daughter that she nearly underwent an abortion and would have done so if she had known that she was carrying twins. During Emin's early years her father would spend part of each week with Cashin and the twins and part with his wife and their children. He has said that he fathered 23 illegitimate children; Emin told Nigel Farmdale for the London *Telegraph* (October 30, 2002) that the total was probably 11. Emin's home life "seemed quite natural," she told Miranda Sawyer for the London *Guardian* (July 20, 1997). "I was brought up to be completely honest, to express how you feel emotionally, with dramatic scenes. Screwed-up but loving is the best way to describe our family." For years Emin's family lived in luxury in the International Hotel; after it failed, they moved into a nearby staff cottage. "Growing up by the seaside was a magical experience, especially back then, when the great British seaside was in its heyday," Emin told Charlotte Philby for the London *Independent* (August 1, 2009, on-line). In Margate's lido—a resort complex containing a swimming pool and other recreational facilities—and elsewhere in the town, "there was always something to do" with her brother and their friends, she said. Emin attended an Anglican church school and, for brief periods, Sunday school, gym and youth clubs, and a "Jesus art club," as she labeled it, and she was a member of the Girl Guides (similar to Girl Scouts in the U.S.).

At the age of 13, following a New Year's Eve party, in an incident she has recalled in her books and many interviews, Emin was raped by an "older boy," as Miranda Sawyer described him. "As upsetting and distressing as it was, and much as I didn't want it to happen, I went, 'Oh yeah, it's what happens,'" Emin told Sawyer. By her own account, during the next two years she had sex—occasionally against her will—with dozens of men. Her mother, who had known about but not reported the first rape, apparently was unaware of or unconcerned about Emin's promiscuity or the sexual abuse she suffered. Her mother raised no objections when, around that time, Emin dropped out of school; her brother, too, quit school, and for months the twins hung out together. At 15 Emin left Margate and settled in London, about 50 miles west, and began working at a shoe shop. At 17 she enrolled at the Medway College of Design, in Rochester, near London, where she studied fashion. There she met Billy Childish, a painter, musician, and poet, with whom she embarked on a tumultuous five-year affair. She remained at Medway for a year and a half. For a while afterward she took printmaking classes at the John Cass School of Art (now part of London Metropolitan University). Although she had never earned a secondary-school diploma, she was accepted at the Maidstone College of Art, a division of the University for the Creative Arts; she studied at the campus in Kent, between Margate and London, and earned a fine-arts degree in 1986. She next enrolled at the Royal College of Art, in London, which offers only graduate courses. In 1989 Emin completed a master's degree in painting there. At around the time she graduated, she fell into a severe depression, triggered, she has said, by an abortion. (She subsequently underwent a second abortion.) The depression led her to destroy—after she photographed them—all the paintings she had made while at the Royal College, and she did not paint for several years afterward. In her January 29, 2009 *Independent* column, she wrote, "When I first started becoming successful, I was filled with strange guilt and misunderstanding of myself. I felt that my abortions had somehow been a Faustian pact, and in return for my children's souls, I had been given my success. I am not a Catholic, but I have a profound belief in the soul. It's only now, now that I know that it will never be possible for me to have children, that the guilt has finally lifted. I give a lot out into the world, and I care and love for all that I create. It's a really big endeavour that extends much further than just the ego of myself."

Meanwhile, in 1993, in collaboration with Sarah Lucas—who, like Emin, was later to become a major figure among the Young British Artists—she opened a small store, called the Shop, in Bethnal Green, in London's East End. There, with Emin as the primary storekeeper, the women sold their own handiwork. Emin's included decorated T-shirts, découpage ashtrays, and small appliquéd blankets, among other items. At a party during that time, Emin met the wealthy, influential art dealer and agent Jay Jopling, the owner of the White Cube gallery, in London. Jopling already represented Antony Gormley and Damien Hirst, both of whom had won the prestigious Turner Prize (in 1994 and 1995, respectively), launched in 1984 "to celebrate new developments in contemporary art," according to the Web site of the Tate museums, which sponsor the prize. In 1994 Jopling invited Emin to exhibit at the White Cube. Titled My Major Retrospective, her show included an assemblage of personal artifacts, including old letters, the crumpled cigarette pack her uncle Colin had been holding when he was decapitated in a car accident, bloody tissue in a vial, and a hospital bracelet; photographs of her Royal College of Art paintings; and a quilt with the stitched names of relatives of hers and messages to them. "It was an intensely emotional exhibit, a blast of warm humanism in an art world that had got used to cool cerebralism as the norm," Matthew Collings wrote for the London *Independent* (March 25, 2007). "Not everyone liked it. When someone reveals so much about themselves so straightforwardly, it can be embarrassing. . . . [Emin had] become a brilliant observer and monitor of human feeling, an inspired tapper into the things that people really care about."

In 1994, chauffeured by her then-boyfriend, the art curator Carl Freedman (an early promoter of the Young British Artists and, later, a gallery owner), Emin embarked on an extensive reading tour in the U.S. Sitting on a chair bequeathed to her by her much-beloved, recently deceased maternal grandmother, she would read from her handwritten memoir *Exploration of the Soul*, much of which dealt with her sexual experiences. A photograph of her, seated with book in hand, in Monument Valley (which straddles Arizona and Utah), is in the permanent collection of the Tate, as is the chair, parts of which are covered with names and other text that Emin embroidered. The money she earned from the readings covered the costs of the trip. She and Freedman also vacationed together in Whitstable; Emin later had the beach hut that they used transported to London, where in 1999 it appeared in a group show at the Saatchi Gallery. In 2004 the hut was destroyed in a huge fire at a private warehouse in which Saatchi, other gallery owners, major museums, and the British royal family had stored artwork from their collections.

Among the dozens of other items that were incinerated in the fire was Emin's handmade tent, *Everyone I Have Ever Slept With 1963–1995*, which, along with *My Bed*, she considers one of her "seminal" pieces, she told Barry Didcock for the *Sunday Herald* (April 30, 2006), a Scottish paper. Reportedly constructed after Freedman challenged her to make something "totally outstanding," in Emin's words, the tent debuted in 1995 at the Freedman-curated show Minky Manky, at the South London Gallery. After removing their shoes, visitors to the show could crawl through the work, which was about the size of a two-person tent. "The tent really is a remarkable work," Matthew Collings wrote for the *Independent* (March 25, 1997). "Instead of merely sensational, the effect is rather intimate and loving." "You can have various emotions about such a piece . . . , but you have to conclude that it's doubtful whether anyone has conjured up quite such a singular project before," Richard Gott wrote for the London *Guardian* (April 5, 1997). The tent appeared in Sensation, an exhibit devoted to pieces in the collection of Charles Saatchi. The show—in particular, works by Chris Ofili and Marcus Harvey—drew intense criticism and controversy, along with huge crowds, during its run at the Royal Academy of Art, in London, in 1997, and later, in 1999–2000, after it traveled to the Brooklyn Museum of Art.

From 1995 to 1998 Emin ran a tiny storefront gallery in London. The Tracey Emin Museum, as she called it, was open for a few hours two days a week. For two weeks in 1996, she placed herself on exhibit in a small walled-in space within the Galleri Andreas Brädström, in Stockholm, Sweden. Through wide-angle lenses set in the walls, which made everything in the space look distorted and tiny, viewers could see Emin, completely naked, as she ate, slept, and—for the first time in years—painted at an easel. The enclosure was later removed, along with 14 paintings, 78 drawings, body prints, personal belongings, kitchen supplies, and other items; owned by Charles Saatchi, it is called *Exorcism of the Last Painting I Ever Made* and has been exhibited in its entirety as an installation.

In a notorious incident in December 1997, Emin appeared with a group of gallery owners and art experts on a TV show that aired immediately after that year's Turner Prize awards dinner. Seemingly drunk, she slurred her words, interrupted other guests, and cursed before she abruptly detached her microphone partway through the program and then "walked noisily out of the studio, her loud goodbyes greeted with relieved laughter," Clare Longrigg wrote for the *Guardian* (December 4, 1997). Emin later contended that prescription medication had affected her behavior that night.

With the inclusion of *My Bed* in the 1999 Turner Prize exhibition, Emin became an art superstar. "Steve McQueen was the eventual winner, but nobody remembers that because it was Emin who captured the real prize: a place in the national consciousness," Barry Didcock wrote. Like virtually all her work, *My Bed* stirred a broad array of reactions. Matthew Collings wrote for the London *Observer* (October 24, 1999), "The critical storm that blew up during the week over Tracey Emin's unmade bed, made into art, was about content not formal qualities. It was assumed it didn't have any formal qualities, only cheap shock content. But this is wrong. For one thing, it has a lovely rumpled whiteness. Yes, there was torture and anguish; these are part of what the bed is. . . . It's because she so blatantly shows it that people get incensed. It's a truthful bed. On the other hand, Emin might be a maximalist in the emotion league but she's surprisingly economical in the things she collects to suggest meanings." By contrast, Mark Lawson wrote for the *Guardian* (October 23, 1999), "There's something phenomenally self-indulgent about squalidity. As a lifestyle choice, it doesn't serve anyone but you—and maybe the roaches you brag about spotting as they scuttle across your kitchen floor. It's a weird breed of hedonism, a twisted debauchery, a strange machismo. . . . Still, Tracey Emin's turned squalor into an art form."

A 2001 show of Emin's at White Cube, called You Forgot to Kiss My Soul, provoked similarly disparate assessments. (The show shared the title of a work in neon, in which those words, in Emin's handwriting, were fashioned in glass by an assistant and enclosed in a neon valentine.) Those who admired the show included Richard Dorment, who wrote for the London *Daily Telegraph* (May 2, 2001), "As usual, everything is about Emin herself, but what is different is that now, at 37, she has reached a stage of maturity where she can draw on her own experience to make statements that feel more universal. She has used her imagination to give dramatic shape to autobiographical material: what we have now is a coherent artistic vision." Philip Hensher, writing for the *Independent* (April

27, 2001), felt otherwise: "A dullard might hit on an interesting concept by chance, but the likelihood that they will go on to explore that idea, or even fully understand the implications of their initial concept, is a fairly small one. That's pretty clearly what happened to Tracey Emin. Plenty of people . . . believe her to be a charlatan, and cite her insatiable enthusiasm for publicity in support of that view. I don't think that's true, since for a charlatan, one can have some grudging admiration. She's something much worse: she's just no good."

The neons, drawings, photographs, embroidered and appliquéd fabrics, writing, videos, and sculptures on exhibit in Emin's show This Is Another Place, at the Museum of Modern Art in Oxford, England, in 2002, led Charlotte Mullins to assert in a *Financial Times* (November 11, 2002) review that "the strength that lies behind all of Emin's successful work" is that the artist "speaks from her soul. . . . She might exorcise horrors and mistakes from her own past in her work, but in doing so she translates them into universal experiences." Her sometime admirer Adrian Searle, however, wrote for the *Guardian* (November 12, 2002), "To say that these wall-hangings and half-begun paintings and drawings and confessional writings are just so much awful logorrhea, as indulgent and incoherent as they are heartfelt and soul-baring, is to state the obvious. There doesn't seem to be any quality control here at all (or perhaps pain management?), let alone much sense of the distinction between private revelation and publicity. Some of it is difficult to take seriously on any level. . . . Emin's scrappy canvases and drawings done in a tired fuzzy line, her half-baked sentimentalizing and incoherent writings, have only one point: as evidence of her slog through life's brutalities." In her own defense, Emin told a reporter for the *Sydney (Australia) Morning Herald* (February 1, 2003), "My work is about communication. I think I communicate really easily and really quickly. You don't have to be a genius to understand it. And that's why I get slagged off by a lot of critics. . . . I'm taking their job away from them."

"Emin divides people like no other artist alive," Barry Didcock wrote. "She is hated and adored in equal measure." That division exists among readers of her books as well as viewers of her artworks. Regarding *Strangeland* (2005), for example, a collection of reminiscences and observations, Nicholas Lezard wrote for the *Guardian* (October 7, 2006), "*Strangeland* is necessary, and not just the latest instalment of [Emin's] artistic project. It has too many funny stories in it for that. Nor, by the same token, is it the product of a self-pitying publicity hound. Self-pitying is, strangely, the last thing Emin is. . . . *Strangeland* comes over as honest and extraordinary." But Alev Adil, writing for the *Independent* (October 14, 2005), complained, "As an 'autobiography,' *Strangeland* fails abysmally. Emin writes, in the conventional sense, very badly. . . . Emin's writing privileges authenticity over craft, choosing a clumsy and sensationalist exploration of victimhood."

In 2008 Emin organized the Royal Academy of Arts summer exhibition. The following year she had solo shows at the Schirn Kunsthalle, in Frankfurt, Germany; CAC Málaga (Centro de Arte Contemporáneo de Málaga), in Spain; the Museum of Art–Fort Lauderdale, in Florida; and the Scottish National Gallery of Modern Art, in Edinburgh. Other solo Emin shows were scheduled to open in 2009 at the Tate Modern, in October, and at the Lehmann Maupin Gallery, in New York City, in November.

Emin lives in a 450-year-old Huguenot house in the Spitalfields section of London. She has reluctantly accepted the probability that she will never become a mother. "As an older woman without children, society sees you as pretty redundant," she told Miranda Sawyer for the London *Mirror* (September 24, 2009, on-line). "Especially because you lose your looks. But you have to force yourself to think, 'Maybe the mirror's not so important.' Rather than thinking, 'I've got to get my breasts raised or get some Botox,' why not think, 'I'm going to learn French'? I learned to drive last year. It was the best thing I've ever done in my life. And now I'm going to learn how to speak French."

—T.O.

Suggested Reading: (Edinburgh, Scotland) *Living Scotsman* (on-line) July 13, 2008; (Glasgow, Scotland) *Sunday Herald* (on-line) Apr. 30, 2006; Lehmann Maupin Gallery (on-line); (London) *Church Times* (on-line) Dec. 1, 2006; (London) *Guardian* Observer Life p6 July 20, 1997; (London) *Mirror* (on-line) Sep. 24, 2009; Saatchi Gallery (on-line); *Tate Magazine* (on-line) Sep./Oct. 2002; tracey-emin.co.uk; Brown, Neal. *Tracey Emin*, 2006; Emin, Tracey. *Strangeland*, 2005; Emin, Tracey, and Freedman, Carl. *Tracey Emin*, 2006; Fortnum, Rebecca. *Contemporary British Women Artists: In Their Own Words*, 2007

Selected Artworks: *Illustrations from Memory*, 1994; *Family Suite*, 1994; *Everyone I Have Ever Slept With 1963–1995*, 1995; *Exorcism of the Last Painting I Ever Made*, 1996; *Sleep*, 1996; *Kiss Me Kiss Me Cover My Body in Love*, 1996; *CV C**t Vernacular*, 1997; *Just Remember How It Was*, 1998; *My Bed*, 1999; *The Last Thing I Said to You Is Don't Leave Me Here, or The Hut*, 1999; *I've Got It All*, 2000; *Blinding*, 2000; *You Forgot to Kiss My Soul*, 2001; *Take What the F**k You Like*, 2001; *To Meet My Past*, 2002; *Dolly*, 2002; *Roman Standard*, 2005; *Reincarnation*, 2005; *Keep Me Safe*, 2007; *One Secret Is to Save Everything*, 2007; *Star Trek Voyager*, 2007; *Suffer Love II*, 2009

Selected Films: *Why I Never Became a Dancer*, 1995; *Homage to Edvard Munch and All My Dead Children*, 1999; *Top Spot*, 2003

Selected Books: *Exploration of the Soul*, 1994; *Absolute Tracey*, 1998; *This Is Another Place*, 2003; *Strangeland*, 2005; *Tracey Emin: Works 1963–2006*, 2006; *Tracey Emin: Borrowed Light*, 2007; *One Thousand Drawings*, 2009; as co-author—*The Art of Tracey Emin* (with Chris Townsend and Mandy Merck), 2002; *Tracey Emin: You Left Me Breathing* (with Jennifer Doyle), 2008

Emmanuel Dunand/AFP/Getty Images

Favreau, Jon

(fav-ROH)

June 2, 1981– White House director of speechwriting

Address: The White House, 1600 Pennsylvania Ave., N.W., Washington, DC 20500

Jon Favreau, President Barack Obama's head speechwriter, has compared his job to that of a batting coach for Ted Williams, one of the greatest hitters in the history of Major League Baseball. The president, after all, is well known for his superlative skills as a writer and speaker; he has written two best-selling books, and the first speech he gave before a national audience—the keynote address at the 2004 Democratic National Convention, which he wrote by himself—was hailed as "magical," "electrifying," and "transformative," and it immediately made him a rising star in his party. Nevertheless, like all presidents since Calvin Coolidge, who served in the White House in the 1920s, Obama has a team of official speechwriters. Favreau, who assumed his post in 2009 when he was 27, is the second-youngest person ever to serve as a president's head speechwriter. (The first was James Fallows, who was two months younger than Favreau when he joined the administration of Jimmy Carter.) Favreau has worked for Obama since the latter entered the U.S. Senate, in 2005, and partly through extensive study of Obama's writings and speeches and memorization of large parts of both, he has become the president's "mind reader," in Obama's words. The goal of both men in writing a speech, Favreau has said, according to Mike Dorning in the *Chicago Tribune* (March 7, 2009, on-line), is to "tell a story. That's the most important part of every speech, more than any given line. Does it tell a story from beginning to end?" The president's longtime adviser David Axelrod said of Favreau to Dorning, "I call him Mozart because he's just this young creative genius" and because Favreau, like Obama, "think[s] in terms of the cadence of the words. Not just the meaning of the words but the cadence of the words, how they work together, how they sound together." Axelrod also told Dorning, "I've never worked for a politician who values words as much as the president does. The speechwriter is an unusually important person in the operation." "Barack trusts [Favreau]," Axelrod told Ashley Parker for the *New York Times* (January 20, 2009). "And Barack doesn't trust too many folks with that—the notion of surrendering that much authority over his own words." Favreau's experience in politics dates to his junior year in college, when he spent several months as an intern in the office of U.S. senator John Kerry of Massachusetts. During Kerry's run for the presidency as the Democratic nominee, in 2004, Favreau served as his deputy speechwriter. Stephanie E. Yuhl, a professor of history who taught Favreau during his college years, told Lisa D. Welsh for the Worcester, Massachusetts, *Telegram & Gazette* (January 20, 2009), "Jon has an extraordinary talent of taking very complex ideas and translating them into very accessible language so that everyone can formulate their own decision"—a talent that has been attributed to Obama as well. And like Obama, Favreau has a strong sense of social justice and responsibility to others. "He and Obama are a good fit," Yuhl said. "They have a very cooperative, fluid kind of writing and working relationship."

Jonathan Favreau was born on June 2, 1981 in Winchester, Massachusetts, to Mark Favreau, a high-tech consultant, and Lillian Favreau, a public-school teacher. With his younger brother, Andrew, he was raised in North Reading, a suburb of Boston, Massachusetts. (Favreau is not related to the screenwriter, actor, and director of the same name.) His mother told Mike Dorning that she has a recording of him as a two-year-old reciting, with minimal prompting, Clement Clarke Moore's poem "A Visit from St. Nicholas" (better known as "The Night Before Christmas"). According to his father, as quoted by Mike Cullity in the *Manchester (New*

Hampshire) Union Leader (January 18, 2009), "Jon always had an amazing way with the written word." During his middle-school years, Favreau attended a leadership seminar in the nation's capital with his best friend, Josh Porter. "He just loved the idea of how much power there is there," Porter told Dorning.

After he graduated from North Reading High School, Favreau studied political science at the College of the Holy Cross, a Jesuit liberal-arts university in Worcester, Massachusetts. The school urged and expected students to take action to further social justice and help others, and Favreau took that injunction much to heart. "He was one of those kids that comes along once in a while that sets the place on fire," Gary DeAngelis, the associate director of the Holy Cross Center for Interdisciplinary and Special Studies, told Thomas Caywood for the Worcester *Sunday Telegram* (January 27, 2008). Favreau devoted some of his time to the organization Habitat for Humanity, which builds houses for people in need, and to a program that arranges weekly visits with cancer patients. With the Student Programs for Urban Development (SPUD), he volunteered in 1999 and 2000 in the Welfare Solidarity project, which aimed to inform welfare recipients about their rights and benefits and assist them in other ways as well. In 2000 he was named the program's director and succeeded in securing additional funding for it. With the support of professors and Holy Cross administrators, who made participation a component of coursework, he increased student involvement in the project. In 2002 he became the head of another SPUD effort, the Main South Workforce Development Program, which aided unemployed members of the community with job placement and training. In his college years Favreau also served as the treasurer and debate-committee chair of the campus's chapter of College Democrats of America.

"During my first few years at Holy Cross, my experiences advocating for clients in the Worcester welfare office left me wondering why I would regularly encounter single, working mothers who could not afford food, housing, or medical care, despite the fact that they worked over forty hours a week," Favreau recalled in the speech he gave at his graduation as the valedictorian of his class, as quoted in the *Des Moines (Iowa) Register* (January 19, 2009, on-line). "If the idea was to get people off welfare rolls and into jobs, why were the jobs failing to provide even the most basic standard of living?" Seeking answers to those questions, and eager to "see firsthand how and why decisions concerning welfare and other issues important to me were being made," as he said in his speech, Favreau spent one semester of his junior year in Washington, D.C., as an intern for Senator John Kerry. He worked closely with David E. Wade, the senator's communications and press director, primarily compiling press clippings for use in drafting opinions and positions. Recognizing Favreau's talents, Wade gave him the opportunity to write as well. Wade told Caywood, "Sometimes you see interns who try to distinguish themselves by constantly talking. They want to show you and tell you how much they know. Or they ask you endlessly if your job is like [the television series] *The West Wing*. Jon just very quietly, determinedly put his head down and distinguished himself through his writing. . . . This was clearly a young man in a hurry who was going to be going places. I thought he represented the right cocktail for politics: creativity, an unrelenting work ethic, enormous drive and a complete lack of ego." An essay that Favreau wrote about his experiences in Washington won his college's award for best thesis of the year. He also won a $30,000 Harry S. Truman Scholarship, a federally funded grant awarded to college juniors for their leadership abilities and potential for achievement in public service. (That money, which Favreau has not yet used, was supposed to cover some of the costs of graduate school.) As an undergraduate Favreau served as the editor of the op-ed page of the campus newspaper, and he became a serious student of the piano. He earned a B.A. degree in 2003.

Immediately after his graduation Favreau moved to the nation's capital to take on the job of press assistant for John Kerry's 2004 presidential campaign. In addition to assembling print, audio, and Internet news clips for the campaign's senior staff members, he prepared talking points and suggested a "message of the day" for transmission to the media. As the Kerry campaign began to stumble, and speechwriters and others departed, Favreau was promoted to deputy speechwriter. According to Eli Saslow's profile of him for the *Washington Post* (December 18, 2008), some staffers had gotten hold of a copy of his Holy Cross commencement address and felt that it merited giving him an opportunity to write, particularly because Kerry's poor poll ratings were discouraging speechwriters from joining his campaign, and in any event, a lack of funds precluded an expansion of the staff.

Favreau met Barack Obama backstage at the 2004 Democratic National Convention, shortly before the then-little-known Illinois state senator was to deliver that year's keynote address. Favreau had been sent to tell Obama to remove a sentence that Kerry wanted to use in his own speech. Favreau recalled to Ashley Parker that Obama, who had been rehearsing his address, "kind of looked at me, kind of confused—like, 'Who is this kid?'" Obama did not delete the sentence—"There are no red states or blue states, there are only the United States of America"—and his speech immediately catapulted him into the front ranks of Democratic politicians nationwide. Kerry's electoral loss to the incumbent, the Republican George W. Bush, the following November capped a period of disillusionment for Favreau. "After the Kerry campaign, after all the backbiting and nastiness, my idealism and enthusiasm for politics was crushed," he told Richard Wolffe for *Newsweek* (January 6, 2008, online). "I was grateful for the experience I got, but it was such a difficult experience, along with losing, that I was done. It took Barack to rekindle that" idealism and enthusiasm. Favreau told Parker that, finding himself without a job and short of money, he took advantage of "all the happy-hour specials I could find in Washington."

Favreau's period of unemployment was brief: soon after the 2004 congressional elections, in which Obama won a seat in the U.S. Senate, Robert Gibbs, who had been Kerry's campaign press secretary and had become Obama's communications director, invited Favreau to meet with Obama about a possible speechwriting job. Thinking that he wanted to give politics "one more shot with someone I'm ideologically aligned with," as quoted by Mike Cullity, he talked with Obama in January 2005, on the day that Obama was sworn in. The two chatted about their experiences in social work and their thoughts on social justice, and Favreau discovered that he was "closely aligned" with what Obama believed, as he told Charles P. Pierce for the *Boston Globe Magazine* (December 21, 2008). Instead of questioning Favreau about his background, Obama asked him about his motivations and goals in the political arena and his theory of speechwriting. According to Wolffe, Favreau told Obama, "I have no theory. But when I saw you at the convention, you basically told a story about your life from beginning to end, and it was a story that fit with the larger American narrative. People applauded not because you wrote an applause line but because you touched something in the party and the country that people had not touched before. Democrats haven't had that in a long time." Favreau also told Obama, as quoted by Saslow, "A speech can broaden the circle of people who care about this stuff. How do you say to the average person that's been hurting: 'I hear you. I'm there. Even though you've been so disappointed and cynical about politics in the past, and with good reason, we can move in the right direction. Just give me a chance.'"

For the next two years, Favreau worked in Obama's office in Washington. Then he moved to Chicago, Illinois, to work on the senator's incipient presidential campaign. He memorized many of Obama's speeches and long sections of his books and made a concentrated study of his tone and cadence, in both written works and oral presentations, thereby "channeling" Obama, as he has put it. According to Saslow, Favreau "mastered Obama's writing style—short, elegant sentences—and internalized his boss's tendency toward reflection and ideological balance."

After Obama officially announced his candidacy for the presidency, in February 2007—in a speech that, according to Wolffe, the politician had written himself—Favreau moved to the Lincoln Park area of Chicago, where he shared a home with six other Obama staffers. Favreau became the head speechwriter of a youthful team that also included Adam Frankel and Ben Rhodes. Later, Sarah Hurwitz, a former speechwriter for President Bill Clinton, was added to the team. "We were always informal—that's Favs's style," Rhodes told Saslow, using the nickname by which Favreau's close friends and associates refer to him. "I don't think he ever scheduled a meeting where we all sat down at a table and said, 'Here's what we have to do this week.' And if he had, we probably would have laughed at him." That casual approach notwithstanding, during the many months of the campaign, Favreau would often wake up at 5:00 a.m. and not get to bed until 22 hours later, keeping himself going with espressos and energy drinks and playing a computer video game while on breaks. He has also admitted to several reporters that he became obsessed with opinion polls—his "daily crack," as he called them.

For inspiration as a speechwriter, Favreau has often looked to the past; he told Parker that he has read many written works and speeches by John F. Kennedy, former U.S. attorney general and senator Robert F. Kennedy, and Martin Luther King Jr. "Many Democratic candidates have attempted to evoke both John and Robert Kennedy, but Senator Obama seems to have had more success than most," Parker remarked. Favreau has also named as influential President Ronald Reagan's speechwriter Peggy Noonan (he particularly admires the speech Reagan gave at Pointe du Hoc, in France, to mark the 40th anniversary of D-Day), and Michael Gerson, who wrote for George W. Bush. During the campaign Favreau often appropriated lines from Obama's books and previous speeches. While some speeches were almost entirely the work of the candidate, for others Obama relied to varying degrees on his writers. Favreau described to Wolffe how he and Obama work together: "What I do is to sit with him for half an hour. He talks and I type everything he says. I reshape it, I write. He writes, he reshapes it. That's how we get a finished product. It's a great way to write speeches. A lot of times"—with other politicians—"you write something, you hand it in, it gets hacked by advisers, it gets to the candidate and then it gets sent back to you. This"—the method the president uses—"is a much more intimate way to work." At times Favreau would find his job daunting. "If you start thinking about what's at stake, it can get paralyzing," he told Saslow. Occasionally Obama would offer words of encouragement: according to Saslow, he would tell Favreau, for example, "Don't worry. I'm a writer, too, and I know that sometimes the muse hits you and sometimes it doesn't. We'll figure it out together."

Favreau has contributed significantly to some of Obama's most memorable campaign speeches. He wrote the line "You know, they said this day would never come," the first words Obama spoke when he addressed cheering supporters in Iowa on January 3, 2008, after he became the first person of color to emerge victorious from the Democratic presidential caucuses in that state, whose population is more than 90 percent white. Days later U.S. senator Hillary Clinton of New York, Obama's main rival among the Democratic candidates, accused Obama of lacking substance, saying, according to Ashley Parker, "You campaign in poetry, but you govern in prose." After Clinton won the New Hampshire primary, on January 9, Obama recycled the hopeful slogan of his 2004 senatorial campaign, "Yes, we can." While many have credited Favreau with those words, they are in fact Obama's, but Favreau is said to have been instrumental in the decision to use them again. In concluding his concession speech in New Hampshire, Obama introduced the slogan by saying, "When we have faced down impossible odds, when we've been told we're not ready or that we shouldn't try or that we can't, generations of Americans have responded with a simple creed that sums up the spirit of a people: Yes, we can. Yes, we can. Yes, we can." He then repeated the words in succeeding paragraphs nine times, as a concise way of demonstrating the determination of the nation's founders, slaves and abolitionists, immigrants, workers who unionized, women who fought for the right to vote, President Kennedy when he decided to send men to the moon, Martin Luther King Jr. in his struggle to achieve justice and equality for African-Americans, and his own supporters in the current campaign. He ended by saying, "Tonight, we will begin the next great chapter in the American story, with three words that will ring from coast to coast, from sea to shining sea: Yes, we can." "And at that moment, a mere presidential campaign was transformed into a movement, coalesced around three simple words," Mark Warren wrote for *Esquire* (December 3, 2008).

According to Saslow, Obama called Favreau on the night of Saturday, March 15, 2008 and told him that he would be giving a speech about race and religion the following Tuesday, in Philadelphia, Pennsylvania. The impetus for it was the furor that had erupted after the public learned that Jeremiah Wright, the pastor of the Chicago church that Obama had attended for many years, had used, in Obama's words in his speech, "incendiary language to express views that have the potential not only to widen the racial divide, but views that denigrate both the greatness and the goodness of our nation; that rightly offend white and black alike." Obama dictated his ideas over the phone for half an hour and told Favreau to organize and polish them. "It would have been a great speech right then," Favreau told Saslow. Entitled "A More Perfect Union," the speech went some distance to quiet the uproar and quell the doubts that many people felt about Obama's association with Wright. Obama himself told Favreau, according to Eli Saslow, "So, I think that worked." An editorial headed "Profiles in Courage" that appeared the following day in the *New York Times* (a newspaper that had endorsed Clinton in the Democratic primaries) agreed: "There are moments—increasingly rare in risk-abhorrent modern campaigns—when politicians are called upon to bare their fundamental beliefs. In the best of these moments, the speaker does not just salve the current political wound, but also illuminates larger, troubling issues that the nation is wrestling with. . . . Senator Barack Obama, who has not faced such tests of character this year, faced one on Tuesday. It is hard to imagine how he could have handled it better. . . . He put Mr. Wright, his beliefs and the reaction to them into the larger context of race relations with an honesty seldom heard in public life. . . . He not only cleared the air over a particular controversy—he raised the discussion to a higher plane."

For the speech with which Obama accepted his party's nomination at the 2008 Democratic National Convention, Favreau reportedly wrote a first draft that the senator rejected as too long and lacking in focus. Obama rewrote it and then gave it to Favreau to whittle down to an acceptable length. According to some sources, the two were editing it until a few hours before Obama delivered the 44-minute speech, in front of an estimated 84,000 people crowded onto Invesco Field at Mile High, a stadium in Denver, Colorado, on the night of August 8, 2008.

Favreau and his team prepared two speeches for Obama to use on the night of the general election—one in the event of victory and the other, defeat. They were told, according to Catherine Philp, writing for the London *Times* (November 29, 2008), to "figure out a good Lincoln quote to bring it all together." Favreau recommended the lines from Lincoln's first, 1861 inaugural address that signaled the president's graciousness and desire for bipartisanship: "We are not enemies, but friends. We must not be enemies. Though passion may have strained, it must not break our bonds of affection." Obama included the first and third sentences in his Election Night speech.

Favreau worked on the first draft of Obama's inauguration speech in a Washington Starbucks, according to Ed Pilkington in the London *Guardian* (January 20, 2009), and then it went back and forth between the president-elect and his speechwriter four or five times. As Favreau told Saslow, Obama had indicated that the vision and theme he wanted to convey should focus on "this moment that we're in, and the idea that America was founded on certain ideals that we need to take back." For the next several weeks, Favreau and his team engaged in research, studying periods of crisis in the nation's history, conducting interviews of Peggy Noonan and other speechwriters and David McCullough and other historians, and listening to past inaugural speeches. On January 20, 2009 a record-breaking crowd of well over a million people filled the National Mall, in Washington, D.C., to witness the nation's first African-American president deliver his inaugural address. Although the speech did not strike most listeners as destined for immortality, it was widely praised. "More novel than short story, more ballad than poem—writers agree that restraint and plain speaking were the qualities that distinguished President Obama's inaugural address," Susan Salter Reynolds wrote for the *Los Angeles Times* (January 21, 2009). "Long on plot

. . . , it did what literature does best: the backward glance, the standing on shoulders, the salute to ancestors and other sources of wisdom." The memoirist Patricia Hampl told Reynolds, "I was glad that he denied himself rhetorical flourishes and gave a speech as refined and restrained in its power so that political language itself was restored to its greatest value—saying what the speaker means." The speech struck the writer Mark Kurlansky, as he told Reynolds, as "the most sophisticated view of the world and our role in it of any inaugural address in history." In his *Washington Post* (January 21, 2009) column, Michael Gerson complained that the speech contained too many clichés and platitudes, but then he wrote, "[Obama] rooted his vision of social and economic restoration in the renewal of moral virtues—courage, honesty, fair play, loyalty, tolerance, patriotism and duty. He insisted on using the word 'virtue' and explained that such convictions are not merely useful but 'true.' This shows a deep understanding of America, which remains moral to its core—and a mature understanding of American leadership." *New York Times* editorial writers (January 21, 2009) wrote, "What was surprising about the speech was how much Mr. Obama dwelled on America's choices at this moment in history, rather than the momentousness of his ascension to the presidency."

Earlier, in December 2008, Favreau had drawn criticism from some women's organizations and right-wing pundits stemming from a photo of him that appeared on Facebook.com and then many other sites. The photo showed him at a party standing next to a cardboard figure of Hillary Clinton, his left hand groping her breast, while another, unnamed partygoer, wearing a shirt reading "Obama Staff," nuzzles her ear and offers her a bottle of beer. Favreau immediately apologized to both Clinton and Obama, and Clinton released a statement, as quoted in an opinion piece by Kathleen Parker in the *Washington Post* (December 13, 2008), stating, "Senator Clinton is pleased to learn of Jon's obvious interest in the State Department, and is currently reviewing his application."

Obama, who as president addresses the country every week on the radio and the Internet, has made several memorable speeches in his first year in office. Among them was one directed at the "Muslim world," entitled "A New Beginning" and delivered in Cairo, Egypt, in June 2009; another was about his plans for health-care reform (what many observers have called his "signature issue"), delivered to Congress in September 2009. Favreau, who continues to lead a group of a half-dozen speechwriters at the White House, received what seemed like criticism from William Safire, a Pulitzer Prize–winning columnist and former speechwriter for President Richard Nixon, who said in April 2009 that Favreau was receiving "too much publicity too soon," as quoted by Stephanie Green and Elizabeth Grover in the *Washington Times* (April 17, 2009). Safire added that a presidential speechwriter should have a "passion for anonymity." In reality, apart from a couple of romantic relationships that have generated some gossip, Favreau has remained relatively anonymous.

Favreau lives in the Dupont Circle district of Washington, D.C. Someday, he remarked to Saslow a few weeks after the November 2008 election, he may "write a screenplay, or maybe a fiction book based loosely on what all of this was like. You had a bunch of kids working on this campaign together, and it was such a mix of the serious and momentous and just the silly ways that we are. For people in my generation, it was an unbelievable way to grow up." Favreau told John Marchese for *Holy Cross Magazine* (Summer 2009), "What Obama has been able to do, both himself and the movement that he's created, is to inspire people in a fundamental way to want to participate again. That's been the best thing about working for him."

—M.M.

Suggested Reading: *Chicago Tribune* (on-line) Mar. 7, 2009; *Des Moines Register* (on-line) Jan. 19, 2009; *New York Times* (on-line) Jan. 20, 2008; *Newsweek* (on-line) Jan. 6, 2008; *Washington Post* A p1+ Dec. 18, 2008; (Worcester, Massachusetts) *Sunday Telegram* A p1+ Jan. 27, 2008

Gallagher, Ellen

1965– Artist

Address: c/o Gagosian Gallery, 555 W. 24th St., New York, NY 10011

"I don't quite fit in," the artist Ellen Gallagher told Julie L. Belcove for *W* magazine (March 1, 2001), "but I think that's a good thing." Since 1995, when her inclusion in the prestigious Whitney Biennial created a stir in the art world, Gallagher has won acclaim for both the technical skill evident in her paintings and collages and her work's subtle commentary on issues involving race. That subtlety is perhaps the aspect of her work that keeps her from "quite fitting in." Rather than exemplifying protest art, Gallagher's pieces invite a variety of interpretations, making her ideas hard to classify—just as her style is difficult to pin down, mixing, for example, abstract and representational elements. Her work has been exhibited in major galleries and museums, including the Whitney Museum, the Gagosian Gallery, and the Mary Boone Gallery, all in New York; the Anthony d'Offay Gallery, in London, England; the Galerie Max Hetzler, in Berlin, Germany; and the Institute of Contemporary Art in Boston, Massachusetts. Gallagher has "a great stamina for work," one of her friends, the writer and performer Anna Deavere Smith, said of her to Edward Lewine for the *New York Times* (January 23, 2005). "'But she isn't just ambitious. She's after

Nicole Bengiveno, *The New York Times*/Redux

Ellen Gallagher

something as an artist and is willing to take time to find it."

Ellen Gallagher was born in 1965 in Providence, Rhode Island. Her mother, an Irish-American, worked as a coordinator for the government-funded Head Start early-childhood-education program; her father, an African-American, was "a professional boxer but not a very good one," as she told Celia McGee for the *New York Times* (January 7, 1996). Although her parents never married and she was raised primarily by her mother, she maintained a close relationship with her paternal grandmother, an immigrant from Cape Verde, an island republic off the western coast of Africa. Gallagher, who attended prestigious private schools—including the Moses Brown school, in Providence—on scholarships, was never a distinguished student. Her mother, whom she described to Belcove as "a strong, complicated woman," did not push her to succeed; instead, Gallagher said, she experienced "a profound lack of guidance."

Gallagher enrolled at Oberlin College, in Oberlin, Ohio, when she was only 16, initially studying creative writing there. She dropped out to work as a commercial fisherman in Alaska. Tiring of that after a year, she returned to Oberlin, which seemed to her, after her time away, to be a "very small, contained universe," as she said to Belcove. Her body, muscular from manual labor, "revealed choices I had made in my life . . . ," she said. "I tried to pretend to be who I was before, but my body was telling the truth."

Deciding that she wanted to work with her hands, Gallagher left Oberlin for good, but not before participating in a semester-long oceanography program in which she studied tiny water snails called pteropods. "Their shells were incredibly beautiful and elaborate and I would study them under the microscope then draw them," she told Tim Teeman for the London *Times* (July 20, 2005). While Gallagher became "really connected" to the drawings, she did not decide immediately to attend art school; instead, after leaving Oberlin, she went to work as a carpenter in Seattle, Washington. "It never occurred to me then that I would be an artist," she told Belcove. "I thought I would be in some really menial labor job or some really tough physical work my whole life—and that seemed really scary to me."

In 1992 Gallagher enrolled at the School of the Museum of Fine Art in Boston. In Cambridge, just outside Boston, she joined a collective of African-American writers and artists called the Dark Room; she began to incorporate into her work her interest in the significance that race is given in America. In the summer of 1993, Gallagher studied at the Skowhegan School of Painting and Sculpture, in Maine, where she took classes with artists including Ann Hamilton, Peter Halley, and Kiki Smith, forming a lasting friendship with Smith.

Gallagher mounted her first solo show in 1992 at the Akin Gallery, in Boston. Her second took place in 1994, at the Mario Diacono Gallery, also in Boston. Gallagher's paintings, which appeared from afar to be minimalist abstractions, coalesced into more realistic—and sinister—images as the viewer moved closer, incorporating tiny drawings of bulging lips and eyeballs and other examples of racist caricature. Another notable element was the lined children's notebook paper on which the works were painted; the paper was attached to canvases. "This humble but evocative material injects a wry immediacy into Gallagher's works by summoning a state of childhood pre-literacy and powerlessness," Ann Wilson Lloyd wrote for *Art in America* (April 1, 1995). Other critics pointed out that the notebook paper could symbolize the way racism is learned, like math and reading, rather than inborn. Lloyd also made note of the paintings' tiny lips and eyes, writing, "These slight and simple markings suggest lurking narratives. *Decoy*, for instance, contains nine bale shapes, each made up of row upon row of pencil-drawn lips. Dotted here and there are pairs of painted eyes rolled comically heavenward in a minstrel-show parody. For all Gallagher's offhandedness, there's a haunting implication of violence in one messy, blotted patch where eyes and lips come together in a scramble."

In 1995 Klaus Kerstess, the curator of that year's Whitney Biennial, asked Gallagher to participate in that high-profile biannual New York group show. Having seen her work in a group exhibition at New York's Artists' Space, he was so taken with it that he visited her Boston studio. Already interested in including her paintings in the biennial, he became convinced once he saw her work in Boston. As quoted by Paul Goldberger in the *New York Times* (February 26, 1995), Gallagher told Kerstess about her work, "I started out by using more explicit minstrel images, but then I realized that I was more interested in the language. Humor in minstrelsy is linguistic, not slapstick, and I wanted to show that." She did so by including visual allusions to language, among them the lined paper and, perhaps, the lips. Although the Whitney Biennial is generally a crowded affair, Gallagher received some positive notice. "Gallagher . . . combines complex references in these cool, irony-tinged compositions and subsumes multiple cultural histories within her sly social commentary," Lloyd wrote. She also caught the eye of Mary Boone of the Mary Boone Gallery, who in 1996 offered the artist her first New York solo show. Gallagher mounted seven new works that further examined America's history of racial stereotypes. Those painting/collages, she told Celia McGee for the *New York Times* (January 7, 1996), "deal with the way experience gets worked into abstract yet readable signs." The U.S. chapter of the International Association of Art Critics named the exhibition the year's best by an emerging artist, and Gallagher's star continued to rise, despite her being seen only rarely on the New York art circuit. That changed in 1997, when Gallagher moved from the coastal town of Provincetown, Massachusetts, to New York City. She missed living by the sea; "the tide would sometimes swell up to my door and then go way back out, and I loved that feeling of uncontrolled nature, this place where there was no clearly defined inside or outside," she told Belcove. She enjoyed living in a major cultural center, however. "I'm here for the people, for the other artists," she said. "And I thought, as you get older, if you're not married and if you don't live in a city like this, it can be weird. You start to stand out, or you just become a character."

Gallagher mounted her second New York solo exhibition, in 1998, at the Gagosian Gallery, which shortly thereafter became her home gallery. The work she showed continued her previous motifs, but with some permutations. Roberta Smith wrote for the *New York Times* (March 20, 1998) that Gallagher "expand[ed] her rather simple strategy to include differences of gender and culture as well as race"—for example, one piece showed "a stemmed heart shape that is suggestively phallic and spadelike, and a fat, curvy S-shape." At the same time, Smith wrote, the artist seemed "to chafe at [the strategy's] limits. Her surfaces continue to bubble with tiny details that like radioactive particles have big, uncontrollable implications." Smith believed Gallagher had room for improvement but was doing important work nonetheless. "The problem in these works is that the close reading is often more exciting than the big picture," she wrote, "but they lay an important foundation in Ms. Gallagher's attempt to bridge the gap between the abstract and the social."

As Gallagher's work attracted more notice, it sparked many conversations about race. Although the work dealt with racial themes, it could not be fit neatly into the category of "activist art." "She's certainly talking about race, but not in a didactic way," Thyrza Nichols Goodeve, an art writer who contributed to the catalog for Gallagher's 2000 show at the Anthony d'Offay Gallery, in London, told Belcove. "She's creating a new vocabulary. She's using stereotypes—minstrel stereotypes—and taking them apart piece by piece." Others marveled at how seamlessly Gallagher merged the aesthetic concerns of her minimalist forebears, who included Agnes Martin, with her social commentary, not allowing the latter to dominate the former. "You can't separate the way it's painted from what she's talking about," Tom Finkelpearl, deputy director of the P.S.1 Contemporary Art Center, in New York, told Belcove. "They're about blackness," he said of a series of her paintings that were made partly with hand-cut pieces of rubber. "About the color black and the reflections off this black paint—and also about black culture, black hairstyles, black people in America."

That ability to work on multiple levels accounted in large part for the acclaim Gallagher's work received. "They can fade into a pleasant pattern. Or they can shock with the memory of the history they represent," Joanne Silver wrote for the *Boston Herald* (February 2, 1997) about Gallagher's paintings. "Gallagher achieves an elegant tension between the coolness of her Agnes Martin–like canvases and the heat of her emotional content. In so doing, she expands the possibilities of both minimalism and expressionism, and refuses to be pigeonholed." That was true of few of her contemporaries, and Gallagher found it daunting at times to be in a category more or less by herself. "Sometimes that's painful because I feel, damn, it's all on me," she told Belcove. Her uniqueness, however, served to increase her work's value, monetarily as well as artistically; by 2001 her paintings were valued at around $60,000 each.

In the fall of 2001, the Institute of Contemporary Art in New York mounted a 10-year retrospective of Gallagher's work, including the pieces in her latest series, titled Watery Ecstatic. In those works she included references to Herman Melville's racially symbolic novel *Moby-Dick* and to a mythical "black Atlantis" called Drexciya (said to be peopled by slaves thrown overboard during the Middle Passage, the route by which Africans were forcibly transported from their homeland to the Americas). She had presented similar works in Blubber, her show at the Gagosian Gallery, earlier that year. "Ms. Gallagher has always been good at raising complicated ideas, and she's getting better because she's starting to mess around with the Minimalism-plus-minstrel-show content of her somewhat pat and demure paintings of a few years back," Holland Cotter wrote for the *New York Times* (April 13, 2001) about the show at the Gagosian. "The new work is funnier and nastier and alludes to all kinds of unwieldy things, not least to that great erotic emblem of American whiteness and darkness, Melville's sperm-whale leviathan Moby-Dick." Also included in the 2001 retrospective were collages Gallagher made using ads for wigs. The ads, taken from magazines—including *Ebony*—dating from the 1930s to the 1970s, varied from overtly racist offers to "whiten" African-American customers to efforts toward empowering them: some of the wigs are Afros, seen in the 1970s as symbols of black pride and freedom. Gallagher told Belcove, "People forget or don't understand that these very complicated, destructive forms can also be embodied with a kind of power and assertiveness."

The following years saw many successful shows for Gallagher, including exhibitions at the Fruitmarker Gallery, in Edinburgh, Scotland, in 2004; the Gagosian Gallery, in 2004; the Freud Museum, in England (where she exhibited her works alongside objects that belonged to Sigmund Freud, the founder of the psychoanalytic approach to psychology), in 2005; the Whitney Museum, in 2005; and the Tate Liverpool, in England, in 2007. The last-named show featured more paintings in her Watery Ecstatic series. Coinciding with local events commemorating the 200th anniversary of England's abolition of slavery, Gallagher's exhibition was not officially linked to the bicentennial but nonetheless seemed a fitting accompaniment. The paintings continued her examination of the history of slavery via the mythical underwater land called Drexciya, presenting her basic themes in steadily evolving ways. One example of that evolution was the introduction of a peg-legged, wild-haired male character in the painting *Bird in Hand*, whom she described to Michael Glover for the London *Times* (April 18, 2007) as "a kind of evil doctor" who figures into "an origin myth of sorts" involving "the corruption of Darwinian thought" and the classification of people into artificial categories. Gallagher told Glover that she enjoyed improvising in that way, saying that her ideas were "like blues or hip-hop. You've got this original loop and then all these other rhythms that build off it. So that any time you come back to your loop it is always difficult, always displaced somehow, even though it is the same beat or phrase."

Gallagher has published six monographs of her work, with her 2001 volume, *Ellen Gallagher*, including an introductory essay by the cultural critic Greg Tate. In the fall of 2008, her work was shown in the group exhibit For What You Are About to Receive, the Gagosian Gallery's second—and her first—show in Moscow, Russia. The group exhibition featured the works of canonical modern artists such as Alexander Calder, Jeff Koons, Pablo Picasso, and Roy Lichtenstein alongside those of newer names, among them Tom Friedman and Gallagher. The show included her 1994 piece "Laugh Tracks." Writing for the *Boston Herald* (July 10, 1994), Mary Sherman had described the piece as "what look like children's writing tablets . . . pasted side-by-side onto a canvas" on which "crossing lines made up of circles filled with dots look like stitches, seemingly binding the pages together. This lacing effect and the breaks between the lined pages transform the work's spatial arrangement from a physical to a mental one, encouraging endless interpretations of the artist's intent." That piece seemed apt for inclusion in the 2008 show, which, according to a press release, sought to contrast "ways in which contemporary artists continue to investigate the twin pillars of twentieth century art: the readymade and pure abstraction, reflecting on the sublime through a self-conscious engagement with material and process."

Gallagher has won numerous awards, including the American Academy Award (1993), the Ann Gund fellowship (1993), the Provincetown Fine Arts Work Center fellowship (1995), and the Joan Mitchell fellowship (1997). She currently divides her time between New York City and Rotterdam, the Netherlands.

—J.E.P.

Suggested Reading: (London) *Times* Features p16 July 20, 2005; *New York Times* II p35 Jan. 7, 1996, (on-line) Jan. 23, 2005; *W* p495 Mar. 1, 2001

Selected Exhibitions: Blubber, 2001; eXelento, 2004; Works on Paper, 2005; For What You Are About to Receive, 2008

Gates, Robert M.

NOTE: Earlier articles about Robert M. Gates appeared in *Current Biography* in 1992 and 2007.

Sep. 25, 1943– Secretary of the U.S. Department of Defense

Address: Office of the Secretary of Defense, 1000 Defense Pentagon, Washington, DC 20301

Robert M. Gates "is not a man who reveals himself," Paul Burka wrote for *Texas Monthly* (November 2006). "He's all business, a man under total self-control. He doesn't fidget. He isn't a backslapper. He doesn't make small talk. He doesn't boast; neither does he engage in false modesty. He is a motivator, not a cheerleader. He is always polite. He wears an air of authority as if it were tailored by Brooks Brothers. He answers questions fully but volunteers little. Most of his laughter comes from a finely developed sense of irony. I would back him to the hilt in a no-limit poker game." Gates was in a sense backed in such a "game" by President George W. Bush, who appointed him secretary of defense in late 2006, thereby making him one of the most important participants in the high-stakes military operations the U.S. has undertaken in the Middle East in recent years. Gates continues in his post in the administration of President Barack Obama, making him the first U.S. secretary of defense in 60 years to stay on under a new commander in

Scott Olson/Getty Images

Robert M. Gates

chief—and the first ever to be retained by a new president not of the party of the outgoing administration.

A career intelligence analyst, Gates served as the 15th director of the Central Intelligence Agency (CIA) from 1991 to 1993 and then spent a number of years in academia, becoming, in 2002, Texas A&M University's 22d president, a position he held until being sworn in as the U.S.'s 22d secretary of defense. In the latter post he has proven much more popular at home and abroad than his immediate predecessor, Donald H. Rumsfeld, having emphasized diplomacy over force in dealing with foreign-policy problems and approached Democrats on Capitol Hill in a spirit of bipartisanship.

Robert Michael Gates was born on September 25, 1943 in Wichita, Kansas. His father sold wholesale auto parts for a living. Raised in a middle-class section of Wichita, Gates was, by all accounts, a model child—a straight-A student and an Eagle Scout. A voracious reader, he tutored underprivileged children in his spare time and took part in activities sponsored by local religious youth groups. After graduating from high school, Gates enrolled at the College of William and Mary, in Williamsburg, Virginia, as a premedical student, but he soon switched his major to history, concentrating on that of Western Europe. During his college days he worked part-time as a school-bus driver and developed the custom of teaching his riders German and Russian words and phrases. William and Mary granted Gates a B.A. degree with honors in 1965, also naming him the graduate "who has made the greatest contribution to his fellow man," as Dan Goodgame reported for *Time* (May 27, 1991). Gates went on to obtain an M.A. degree in history from Indiana University's Institute on Soviet and East European Studies—now called the Russian and East European Institute—in 1966. While studying at Indiana, Gates was invited by a CIA recruiter to come to Washington, D.C., for an interview. Although he later admitted that he accepted the invitation only for the free trip to Washington, when the agency offered him a position as an analyst, he accepted it. Working for the CIA did not exempt Gates from the draft, and he served in Vietnam from 1967 to 1969 as a commissioned officer in the Strategic Air Command before entering the CIA full-time.

After returning from Vietnam Gates became an intelligence analyst specializing in Soviet affairs and impressed his superiors with his ability to peruse enormous amounts of information quickly and to produce crisply written, coherent reports. In 1971 he was rewarded for his outstanding work with an assignment on the CIA's support staff at the initial negotiations between the United States and the Soviet Union on reducing strategic arms. Although he appeared to be on the fast track at the CIA, Gates was still considering a career as a history professor, and in his off-hours he studied for a doctorate in Russian and Soviet history at Georgetown University, in Washington, D.C. He even refused a CIA offer to finance his studies because he "didn't want to feel obligated to stay," as Goodgame reported, in case an attractive teaching position opened up. Gates received his Ph.D. from Georgetown in 1974, having submitted a 290-page dissertation on Soviet assessments of China that later became known as an authoritative text on Sino-Soviet relations.

That year Gates was assigned to the staff of the National Security Council, where he remained for the next five years, serving under Presidents Richard Nixon, Gerald R. Ford, and Jimmy Carter. By 1979 he longed to return to the CIA, confiding to colleagues that his ambition was to someday be director of the agency. In January 1980 he was reassigned to the CIA as national intelligence officer for the Soviet Union and executive assistant to the director, Stansfield Turner. In 1980 Carter lost the presidency to Ronald Reagan, who appointed a new CIA director, William J. Casey. Casey soon became a mentor for Gates, and promoted him to deputy director for intelligence in January 1982, passing over about 60 other senior-level candidates. In September 1983 Casey appointed Gates to the concurrent position of chairman of the National Intelligence Council, with responsibility for overseeing the preparation of all intelligence estimates. One factor in Gates's rapid rise to the top of the CIA was his expertise on the Soviet Union, which was the main focus of United States intelligence efforts in the Cold War–driven 1980s. Even after Mikhail Gorbachev's rise to power in the Soviet Union in 1985 and his introduction of glasnost, a policy of openness, shortly after that, Gates remained a strict cold warrior.

When Gates was promoted to deputy director of central intelligence, on April 18, 1986, succeeding the retiring John McMahon in the agency's number-two position, he received his first exposure to the operations side of espionage. Exactly eight months later, he was named acting director while Casey underwent surgery for the removal of a brain tumor. Casey resigned his post on January 29, 1987, and four days later Reagan nominated Gates to be his successor in what was expected to be a straightforward appointment. Evidence began to surface, however, that Gates had possibly been involved in the Iran-Contra affair—the administration's sale of arms to Iran, with funds illegally directed to anti-Communist rebels in Nicaragua. Republican senator William S. Cohen of Maine interrogated Gates at his confirmation hearing, accusing him of knowing more about the arms sales than he had admitted and describing him as "an ambitious young man, type-A personality, climbing the ladder of success," as Dusko Doder and Walter Pincus reported for the *Washington Post* (February 18, 1987). "You basically didn't want to rock the boat. You were not prepared to lay your career on the line over a matter you did not create. You didn't want to know about it." Gates conceded that he had not done enough to keep Congress fully informed of the administration's activities, but he refuted the charge that he had hesitated to step forward out of fear for his career. "Sycophants can only rise to a certain level," he responded in a rare show of emotion, Stephen Engelberg reported for the *New York Times* (February 19, 1987). "There is an ample supply of them in this town, and they only go so far. Senior officials understand that the most dangerous thing in the world is a yes man, and the people I have worked for felt the candor with which I apprised them was a valuable asset." With his chances for confirmation fading quickly, Gates withdrew his nomination on March 2, 1987. A day later Reagan nominated William H. Webster to be director of central intelligence; Webster was confirmed by the Senate on May 19. At Reagan's request Gates stayed on as deputy director of the agency. When Brent Scowcroft, Gates's former boss in the Ford administration, was named national security adviser by President-elect George H. W. Bush in December 1988, he arranged for Gates's appointment as his deputy.

On May 14, 1991 Gates got a rare second chance at his dream job when Bush named him to succeed Webster, who was retiring, as director of central intelligence. Although the Iran-Contra affair no longer dominated the headlines, Gates's peripheral role in it still posed a potential obstacle to his confirmation. He was also widely criticized for being too slow to anticipate the collapse of the Soviet Union. Gates's case was further weakened when Congressman Dave McCurdy of Oklahoma, the chairman of the House Intelligence Committee, recommended, on October 2, that Gates withdraw his nomination. Nevertheless, two weeks later, the committee, after hearing statements from members both in support of and in opposition to Gates, voted 11 to four to recommend his confirmation by the full Senate. On November 5 the Senate voted, 64 to 31, to confirm Gates, as 22 Democrats joined all 42 Republicans present in supporting him. Seven days later Gates was sworn in as the nation's 15th director of central intelligence. (At 48 he was the youngest person ever to assume that prestigious position, and he was the first CIA director to have risen through the agency's analytical branch, where raw intelligence is studied and interpreted, as distinct from the operational branch, which is responsible for the collection of intelligence.) Gates subsequently redirected the CIA's resources away from monitoring the former Soviet Union toward checking the spread of nuclear weapons in the Third World and combating the international drug trade.

Gates resigned from the CIA on January 20, 1993. For the next several years, he worked as a traveling academic, evaluating theses for the International Studies Program at the University of Washington and lecturing at a number of schools, including Harvard, Yale, Georgetown, and the College of William and Mary. He also published many articles on government and foreign policy and was a frequent contributor to the *New York Times*'s op-ed page. In 1996 Gates published a memoir of his time at the CIA, titled *From the Shadows: The Ultimate Insider's Story of Five Presidents and How They Won the Cold War*, to largely positive reviews. While its title seemed to promise a scandalous account, the book proved to be an analysis of policy—and a response to the longstanding criticisms of Gates's tough stance on the Soviet Union—rather than a confessional tell-all.

In 1999 Gates was appointed interim dean of the George Bush School of Government and Public Service at Texas A&M. Though he was initially reluctant to leave his home in Seattle, Washington, he and his wife began spending more and more time on the A&M campus. On August 1, 2002 Gates was appointed the university's 22d president. He explained his decision to take the post to the Associated Press (May 11, 2002): "If I could do one more public service, I should. And I couldn't think of a better place to do it than Texas A&M." During his tenure as president, Gates made marked progress in the school's "Vision 2020" plan, which seeks to turn A&M into one of the country's top 10 public universities by the year 2020.

Throughout his time at Texas A&M, Gates maintained a connection with national politics as a frequent guest on political talk shows. On the afternoon of the September 11, 2001 attacks on the World Trade Center, Gates defended the U.S. intelligence community to Paula Zahn for CNN News (September 11, 2001). "I think we have to bear in mind, even against the background of this catastrophe today, that the FBI and CIA have thwarted some very major terrorist operations against [the] United States in recent years," he said. "So they have had some very important successes and saved a lot of lives." In the years that followed, as the U.S. began its invasion of Iraq, Gates continued to appear frequently on the news-analysis circuit. He also began getting active politically again. In January 2004 he co-chaired a Council on Foreign Relations task force on U.S. involvement in Iran, a country with which the United States had not had diplomatic relations since 1979. The task force urged the U.S. to pursue diplomacy over force on the issue of Iran's nuclear weapons, suggesting that Iran be allowed to develop its nuclear program in exchange for committing to use that resource solely for peaceful ends.

In 2005 President George W. Bush offered Gates the newly created post of United States director of national intelligence (DNI). Despite a reluctance to return to Washington, D.C., Gates initially decided to accept the position, feeling that it was his duty to serve the U.S. in a time of war. He scheduled a press conference to announce his decision and wrote an e-mail message to the Texas A&M student body expressing his sadness over leaving the school. Then Gates changed his mind, electing to stay at A&M—because of how much he felt he could accomplish at the university and how little he felt he could accomplish as DNI. Even though he remained in Texas, Gates stayed active in the political sphere, and in 2006 Congress appointed him a member of the Iraq Study Group, also called the Baker-Hamilton Commission, a bipartisan panel formed to assess the situation in Iraq and make specific policy recommendations.

On November 8, 2006, one day after the Democrats succeeded in winning a majority in the House of Representatives and the Senate, Secretary of Defense Donald Rumsfeld resigned, and Bush nominated Gates to become the next defense secretary. Despite an intense love for his work at A&M and an aversion to returning to Washington, D.C., Gates—who was one of the most popular presidents in A&M's history—accepted Bush's nomination, citing a sense of duty. At an on-campus farewell rally, Gates told the A&M student body, as Matthew Watkins reported for the Bryan, Texas, *Eagle* (December 8, 2006, on-line), "A little less than a month ago, I was worried about beating the hell out of Nebraska. Now, I am worried about beating the hell out of Al Qaeda. I can't tell you how much you all mean to me and how big a part of my life you have become, and I will miss you forever." Most pundits praised Gates's nomination, calling him the "anti-Rumsfeld," because it was widely believed that he would be more pragmatic and more cautious than Rumsfeld regarding military interventions; more apt to hold officials responsible for military disasters, such as the torture of prisoners at Abu Ghraib prison, in Iraq; more realistic regarding events in Iraq and other troublespots; and not defensive, prickly, or confrontational in his dealings with the media or Congress. Gates won even greater approval for the honesty he displayed in his Senate confirmation hearing a few weeks later. When asked by Senator Carl Levin, a Democrat from Michigan, if he believed the United States was winning the war in Iraq, Gates responded with a simple "No, sir." His answer immediately became such big news that he felt the need to clarify his words a few hours later, saying instead, "We are not winning, but we are not losing." When asked if he thought it had been a good idea to invade Iraq, he answered, "I think it's too soon to tell," adding, "I suspect, in hindsight, some of the folks in the administration probably would not make the same decisions that they made." Despite such unexpectedly candid answers, Gates still underwent intense scrutiny from senators concerned that he would simply become a mouthpiece for the administration. Gates strongly asserted that he would act independently. "I am not giving up the presidency of Texas A&M, the job that I probably enjoyed more than any that I've ever had, making considerable personal financial sacrifice, and frankly, going through this process, to come back to Washington to be a bump on a log," Gates told Senator Edward M. Kennedy, as quoted on CNN's *The Situation Room* (December 5, 2006). He further stated, "If I am confirmed, I'll be independent. I intend to draw my own conclusions and I'll make my recommendations. . . . I can assure you that I don't owe anybody anything."

The 23 members of the Armed Services Committee voted unanimously to confirm Gates, and he was sworn in as the secretary of defense on December 18, 2006. During his speech at the swearing-in ceremony, Gates gave a measured analysis of the war in Iraq, refraining from making any concrete statements about plans. "All of us want to find a way to bring America's sons and daughters home again," he said, as quoted by *The World Today* (December 19, 2006), an ABC Australia program. "But as the President has made clear, we simply cannot afford to fail in the Middle East. Failure in Iraq at this juncture would be a calamity that would haunt our nation, impair our credibility and endanger Americans for decades to come." That same day the Pentagon released its quarterly report on the situation in Iraq, which Jim Miklaszewski described for NBC News (December 18, 2006) as its "most devastating" yet. The report stated that the past three months had seen the highest number of attacks by Iraqi insurgents on record, with both American and Iraqi casualties on the rise.

On December 21, 2006, three days after being sworn in, Gates went to Iraq to talk to the commanders and troops on the ground. At the beginning of 2007, he recommended increasing the U.S. Army's strength in Iraq by 65,000 troops; he later oversaw the addition of some 30,000 soldiers. In February of that year, Gates announced the firings of the secretary of the army, Francis J. Harvey, and the army 's surgeon general, Kevin C. Kiley, following the disclosure in a series of *Washington Post* articles of inadequate medical care, instances of outright neglect, nearly impossible-to-negotiate red tape, and crumbling facilities at the Walter Reed Army Medical Center, in the nation's capital, where many servicemen and -women wounded in Iraq or Afghanistan were brought for treatment. In March 2007, reversing one of Rumsfeld's policies, he met with the directors of U.S. intelligence agencies with the goal of easing tensions between the intelligence community and the Pentagon. His recommendation that month that the detention center at Guantánamo Bay, Cuba, be closed was batted down by Vice President Dick Cheney and President Bush's former chief political strategist, Karl Rove.

In an effort to maintain adequate numbers of troops in Iraq and Afghanistan, Gates announced in April 2007 that the tours of duty for most active army units would increase from 12 to 15 months and that soldiers would remain at home for one year between tours. "This policy is a difficult but necessary interim step," he said at a news conference, as quoted by David S. Cloud in the *New York Times* (April 12, 2007). "Our forces are stretched, there's no question about that." The following September Gates spoke before the Senate Appropriations Committee regarding the continued involvement of the U.S. in Iraq, suggesting that in the future American forces there would consist of five combat brigades serving as a "long-term presence." "When I speak of a long-term presence, I'm thinking of a very modest U.S. presence with no permanent bases, where we can continue to go after Al Qaeda in Iraq and help the Iraqi forces," he said, according to David S. Cloud in the *New York Times* (September 27, 2007). He also said that, besides the many billions of dollars needed for other war-related expenses, the Pentagon wanted $11 billion for 15,000 additional heavily armored vehicles, to protect American troops from the increasingly sophisticated roadside bombs planted by insurgents in Iraq. Gates has said that he writes personal letters of condolence to the families of all Americans killed in service there.

In April 2008 Gates gave a speech at West Point in which he emphasized the need for the branches of the U.S. military to "reexamine their culture and their way of doing business" and to "think outside the box in problem solving," as quoted by Thom Shanker in the *New York Times* (April 23, 2008). On the same day, in an address at the Maxwell Air Force Base, in Alabama, he gave an urgent call for the armed-service branches to increase the availability of surveillance aircraft in war zones, implicitly criticizing the air force, in particular, for not having done so. With that address, as Shanker observed, Gates "departed sharply" from the "tone of reconciliation" he had attempted to set between military officers and their civilian superiors. In June of that year, Gates came out in favor of extending to three years the tours of thousands of U.S. troops stationed in South Korea and allowing the troops' families to live with them there. The previous, 12-month tours reflected the view that South Korea continued to be a combat zone; in giving approval for a policy shift, Gates said, as quoted by Eric Schmitt in the *New York Times* (June 4, 2008), "I don't think anybody considers the Republic of Korea today a combat zone." Also that month Gates fired the two top leaders of the air force—its civilian secretary, Michael W. Wynne, and General T. Michael Moseley—following disclosures that the air force had twice failed to guard components of nuclear weapons adequately. In September Gates lent his support to plans to withdraw 8,000 U.S. troops from Iraq by early 2009, while warning of the need for caution in doing so. (General David H. Petraeus stated around that time that the number of daily attacks by insurgents in Iraq had fallen to 25 from a high of 180 in June 2007.)

In late November 2008, three weeks after he was elected president, Barack Obama announced that he would retain Gates as defense secretary. As reported by Peter Baker and Thom Shanker for the *New York Times* (November 26, 2008), some criticized the decision. An unnamed adviser to Obama said that keeping the defense secretary from a Republican administration made Democrats "look like they're too wimpy to be trusted" to run the military, while Loren B. Thompson, head of the research group Lexington Institute, said, "I really can't begin to understand from a political point of view how Barack Obama, a person who got the nomination because he ran against the Iraq war, can keep around the guy who's been in charge of it for the last two years." Offering a different perspective, another unnamed Obama adviser said, "From our point of view, it looks pretty damn good because of continuity and stability. And I don't think there are any ideological problems." In December Gates said that the Pentagon planned to send thousands of additional troops to Afghanistan as soon as the spring of 2009 to counter the threat posed in that country by the Taliban. In late January 2009 President Obama took steps long sought by Gates, signing executive orders to close the detention center at Guantánamo Bay within a year. As of late October 2009, however, its closing remained an elusive goal, largely because of the unwillingness of all 50 U.S. states to imprison any captives from Guantánamo within their borders.

In March 2009 Obama announced that the number of additional troops to be deployed to Afghanistan would be 21,000. (Later in the year an additional 13,000 support troops—engineers, military police, and medical personnel—were also sent to Afghanistan).That month Obama also announced that U.S. combat troops would withdraw from Iraq by August 2010, although up to 50,000 could remain behind as a transitional force. Gates, who had supported the Bush administration's withdrawal of 8,000 troops from the country in early 2009, defended Obama's strategy, appearing on NBC's *Meet the Press* to point out that the remaining troops would serve as "advisory and assistance brigades" to aid in the transition to Iraqi control, as Emily S. Rueb wrote for the *New York Times* (March 1, 2009, on-line). As of September 2009 4,000 U.S. troops were expected to return home by the end of the next month.

In May 2009 Gates requested the resignation of the top U.S. general in Afghanistan, David D. McKiernan. The request came in the face of significantly increasing violence in that country. Gates's recommendation to the president was that the veteran Special Operations commander Stanley A. McChrystal succeed McKiernan; McChrystal took over in June 2009 as commander of U.S. forces in Afghanistan. According to Ann Scott Tyson, writing for the *Washington Post* (May 12, 2009), the removal of McKiernan "is in keeping with Gates's style of demanding accountability by dismissing senior military and civilian officials for a host of problems, including nuclear weapons mismanagement and inadequate care for wounded troops."

Gates has opposed the setting of a deadline for an end to military action in Afghanistan, a measure some Democrats have sought. In a September 2009 interview on CNN's *State of the Union*, according to the *Lewiston (Idaho) Morning Tribune* (September 28, 2009), Gates said an early pullout could be perceived as a defeat. "The notion of timelines and exit strategies and so on, frankly, I think would all be a strategic mistake," he said. "The reality is, failure in Afghanistan would be a huge setback for the United States." Gates made the comments as Obama was reevaluating his administration's strategy in the war-torn country and awaiting the results of Afghanistan's November elections. (General McChrystal, meanwhile, requested 40,000 more U.S. troops in Afghanistan.)

In April 2009 Gates announced a potential 2010 Pentagon budget that reflected a shift in priorities at the Defense Department. He proposed terminating overly expensive and long-running projects in favor of investing further in programs to aid the military in its ongoing fight against terrorists. Among other reforms, Gates sought to phase out production of the Air Force's expensive F-22 fighter jet and to terminate plans for 28 presidential helicopters whose estimated cost would total more than $13 billion. The plans to phase out F-22 production frustrated members of Congress from states where the aircraft's parts are manufactured. Nonetheless, Congress passed the budget in October, with most of the Pentagon's recommendations intact, including the cap on F-22 production. The legislation also raised military pay and provided funding for mine-resistant vehicles above the Pentagon's recommendations. "Mr. Gates has emerged as the man in the middle between policies of the past he once championed and the revisions and reversals he is now carrying out . . . ," Peter Baker and Thomas Shanker wrote for the *New York Times* (September 22, 2009). "Along the way, Mr. Gates has become a White House favorite, both for his pragmatic style and his political value. With little national security experience of his own, Mr. Obama has leaned heavily on the holdover Pentagon chief for advice, aides said. And as a result, Mr. Gates has played a central role in reshaping national security policy."

Gates has been married for more than 40 years to the former Rebecca Wilkie, whom he met at Indiana University when they were dormitory counselors chaperoning a hayride together. They have two adult children, Eleanor and Bradley. Among the awards Gates has received are the Presidential Citizens Medal, the Intelligence Medal of Merit, and the Arthur S. Flemming Award, presented annually to the 10 most outstanding federal employees. Gates is a two-time recipient of the National Intelligence Distinguished Service Medal and a three-time recipient of the CIA's highest award, the Distinguished Intelligence Medal.

—C.S.

Suggested Reading: *Los Angeles Times* E p1 June 25, 1996, A p1 Dec. 4, 2006; *Texas Monthly* p154+ Nov. 2006; *Time* p18 Sep. 23, 1991

Selected Books: *From the Shadows: The Ultimate Insider's Story of Five Presidents and How They Won the Cold War*, 1996

Alex Wong/Getty Images

Geithner, Timothy F.

(GITE-ner)

Aug. 18, 1961– Secretary of the U.S. Department of the Treasury

Address: U.S. Dept. of the Treasury, 1500 Pennsylvania Ave., N.W., Washington, DC 20220

In November 2008 President-elect Barack Obama announced his selection of Timothy F. Geithner, the president and chief executive officer of the Federal Reserve Bank of New York since 2003, as his nominee for U.S. secretary of treasury. Confirmed by the U.S. Senate on January 26, 2009, Geithner is one of the youngest treasury secretaries in the history of the nation. He is currently grappling with the daunting task of steering the nation's economy through its worst crisis since the Great Depression. Despite the large amount of criticism that Geithner, to no one's surprise, has received since he assumed his new post, Obama has remained confident in his choice. The president emphasized the enormity of Geithner's job, saying, "There has never been a secretary of the treasury, except maybe Alexander Hamilton right after the Revolutionary War, who's had to deal with the multiplicity of issues that Secretary Geithner's having to deal with, all at the same time."

Timothy Franz Geithner was born on August 18, 1961 to Deborah and Peter Geithner in the New York City borough of Brooklyn. He is one of four children, with two brothers, David and Jonathan, and a sister, Sarah. His father worked as an official with the U.S. Agency for International Development (USAID) and held senior posts with the Ford Foundation; he currently serves as president of that foundation's alumni association. As a result of his father's early work, Geithner spent most of his childhood abroad in Zimbabwe (then called Rhodesia) and several Asian countries, including China, India, and Thailand. His mother was a piano teacher.

After attending elementary school in New Delhi, India, and graduating from the International School of Bangkok, in Thailand, Geithner followed in his father's footsteps, enrolling at Dartmouth College, in Hanover, New Hampshire, where he received a B.A. degree in government and Asian studies in 1983. While there he met Carole Sonnenfeld, his future wife. Two years later Geithner earned a master's degree in international economics and East Asian studies from the Johns Hopkins School of Advanced International Studies, in Washington, D.C.

From 1985 to 1988 Geithner worked at the New York City–based international consulting firm Kissinger Associates, helping the company's founder, the former secretary of state Henry Kissinger, conduct research for a book. Geithner then embarked on a 14-year stint at the U.S. Department of Treasury. As the assistant financial attaché at the U.S. Embassy in Tokyo, Japan, he was credited with persuading Japan to contribute $13 billion to the Persian Gulf War campaign and to negotiate a financial-services agreement with the U.S. He was also involved in negotiating a World Trade Organization (WTO) financial-services agreement on behalf of the U.S.

Geithner quickly rose through the treasury's ranks during the late 1990s, becoming the deputy assistant secretary for international monetary and financial policy (1995–96), the senior deputy assistant secretary for international affairs (1996–97), and the assistant secretary of the treasury for international affairs (1997–98). In 1998 Geithner was named the special assistant to Lawrence Summers, then the treasury undersecretary for international affairs. In that role he was instrumental in helping arrange $100 billion in rescue packages for Brazil and South Korea, which had been affected by the Asian financial crisis of the late 1990s. (The crisis was preceded by the collapse of the Thai currency, which led to the decrease of foreign investment in emerging market economies, including Russia and Brazil.)

In 2001, shortly after serving as a senior fellow in international economics at the Council on Foreign Relations, Geithner joined the International Monetary Fund (IMF), where he was appointed the director of the Policy Development and Review Department. Two years later Geithner succeeded William J. McDonough as president and CEO of the Federal Reserve Bank of New York, the largest of the Fed's 12 regional banks. His appointment surprised many in the financial-services industry due to his lack of commercial-banking experience. He was hailed, however, for his intellect and his extraordinary communication skills. During his five-year tenure at the New York Fed, Geithner acted as the vice chairman of the 12-member Federal Open Market Committee (FOMC), an arm of the Federal Reserve that is responsible for open-market operations, namely the purchase and sale of U.S. Treasury and federal agency securities.

In an effort to stabilize the credit market, which had been crippled by defaults in subprime mortgage loans and home foreclosures, Geithner was a chief negotiator in the sale of Bear Stearns, the country's fifth-largest investment bank, to JPMorgan Chase, in March 2008. Later that year he also helped orchestrate the federal government's $150 billion rescue package for American International Group (AIG), the largest insurance company in the U.S. In exchange, the government would retain an 80 percent stake in AIG. Geithner drew criticism, however, for his decision to force the investment bank Lehman Brothers to file for bankruptcy, a decision that many in the financial industry felt contributed to the developing global economic crisis.

After being rumored to be President-elect Barack Obama's nominee for treasury secretary, Geithner was officially nominated to the post in late November 2008. His nomination became controversial in mid-January 2009, when it was revealed that he had neglected to pay $34,000 in federal taxes in the early 2000s, during his tenure with the International Monetary Fund. Because the IMF is an international organization, it does not withhold money from its employees' pay for Social Security and Medicare; instead, it gives employees extra money so that they can pay the Internal Revenue Service (IRS) themselves. Told erroneously by his accountant that he was exempt from what amounted to a self-employment tax, Geithner kept the extra funds from the IMF. (He has since paid back the taxes, with interest.) Some argued that a nominee who could not keep track of his own finances should not be entrusted with those of the nation. Nonetheless, the Senate confirmed Geithner, by a vote of 60 to 34. In a press conference on February 10, 2009, Geithner announced an expansion of the bailout plan for the nation's beleaguered banking system, one that would attempt to raise up to $2 trillion from the U.S. treasury, the Federal Reserve, and private investors. In March Geithner was harshly criticized after it was revealed that American International Group (AIG), an insurance company that had received more than $170 billion in government bailout money, gave $165 million in bonuses to hundreds of its employees, including people whose activities had apparently contributed to the financial meltdown. Many members of Congress, as well as ordinary citizens, were outraged and questioned why Geithner had failed to stop AIG's payments. Geithner had spoken to AIG's chairman and chief executive officer, Edward Libby, about the bonuses prior to their distribution, but lawyers had advised the treasury secretary that the government could not override the contracts that AIG executives had signed in 2008 to guarantee the bonuses.

Geithner got a reprieve from the anger over the bonuses on March 23, 2009, when he publicly revealed the details of his bailout plan. The plan focused on drawing private investors into partnerships with a new federal entity that could help rid banks of an estimated $1 trillion in troubled assets that would otherwise hinder economic recovery. The plan was received positively among financial-industry professionals; some economists, though, expressed doubts about its effectiveness. In the months since it was implemented, stock prices have slowly risen, and in the third quarter (July–September) of 2009, the gross domestic product grew by 3.5 percent, its best performance in two years. Whether or not the bailout plan will ultimately succeed remains unknown, however.

In addition to working on the economic recovery, Geithner has been pushing for the passage of financial-reform legislation that would give new powers to regulators and the Federal Reserve to combat the kinds of risky behavior among the nation's major financial institutions that led to the meltdown in 2008. He revealed the details of the bill before the House Financial Services Committee on October 29, 2009.

Geithner and his wife have two children, Elise and Benjamin. During his free time Geithner enjoys fly-fishing, surfing, and playing tennis.

—M.A.S.

Suggested Reading: *Chicago Tribune* C p1 Nov. 22, 2008; *Los Angeles Times* A p1 Nov. 22, 2008; *New York Times* C p6 Oct. 16, 2003

Gibbs, Robert

Mar. 29, 1971– White House press secretary

Address: The White House, 1600 Pennsylvania Ave., N.W., Washington, DC 20500

Mandel Ngan/AFP/Getty Images

Linda Douglass, a member of Barack Obama's presidential-campaign staff, told Howard Kurtz for the *Washington Post* (November 12, 2008) that she and her fellow workers called Robert Gibbs "the Barack Whisperer"—a reference to the term "horse whisperer," a person who has an uncommon ability to understand the minds of horses. Gibbs "completely understands [Obama's] thinking and knows how Barack wants to come across," she explained. One of the president's close friends, Gibbs identified himself as a media specialist for his entry in *Who's Who in America*; he served as Obama's chief spokesperson before Election Day and was part of his close-knit inner circle of advisers, led by David Plouffe, the head of the campaign, and David Axelrod, its chief strategist. "Obama's operatives spoke with a single voice and a precise message and only when they wanted to," Mark Leibovich wrote for the *New York Times Magazine* (December 21, 2008, on-line). "They did it with a smile, not complaining—at least not publicly—about how the press was the enemy. And they did it using interactive tools that bred a feeling of real-time connectedness between campaign and voter." Following Obama's victory, the president-elect chose Gibbs for the post of White House press secretary, with responsibility for gathering information—about the president's schedule and the administration's official position on issues and events, for example—and transmitting that information to members of the media. The press secretary fields questions from the White House press corps during on-the-record briefings known as "press gaggles" and during formal, televised press conferences. Sometimes said to hold the "podium job," the press secretary is in effect the public face of the administration. "Gibbs is about to start a job that, like the presidency, seems to age its occupants disproportionately to the years they spend in the job," Leibovich wrote. "And it happens live and on C-Span." Leibovich described Gibbs as "affable" but as having "pit-bullish tendencies behind the scenes in defense of [Obama]." In his first months as press secretary, Gibbs, while addressing a host of complicated issues, established what many have described as a genial—even light-hearted—relationship with the press.

Robert L. Gibbs was born on March 29, 1971 in Auburn, Alabama, to Robert and Nancy Gibbs. Liberal Democrats, both of his parents were librarians at Auburn University. Nancy Gibbs is currently the acquisitions director for the libraries at Duke University, in North Carolina. Years ago, when her children were young and she would attend meetings of the local branch of the League of Women Voters or participate in voter-registration drives, she would take Bobby, as he was then called, and his younger brother, John, with her. As the boys matured, the family often engaged in heated political discussions at the dinner table.

At Auburn High School Gibbs played the saxophone in the band and was a goalkeeper on the soccer team. After his graduation, in 1989, he entered North Carolina State University, where he majored in political science. He also continued to play soccer, although, by his own admission, he was not one of the better players on the university's team. In 1991, as an undergraduate, Gibbs worked as an intern with the Democratic U.S. congressman Glen Browder, who represented Alabama's Third District. Browder soon recognized that Gibbs "was not just another college student looking to spend a few months in Washington," Phillip Rawls wrote for the Associated Press (November 7, 2008, on-line). "Robert had a special quality even back then," Browder told Rawls. "In retrospect, it was clear that Robert was destined to make his mark." In 1992, the year he earned a B.A. degree, with honors, Gibbs served as a volunteer with Bill Clinton's successful presidential campaign.

After Gibbs completed college Browder hired him as a full-time employee; for a time he held the title of executive assistant. Over the next several years, Gibbs handled a variety of duties for the congressman, and he observed firsthand how Browder conducted his reelection campaign in 1994. At that time, according to Browder, it was still unusual in southern states for white politicians to seek the support of African-Americans publicly. Instead, they engaged in what he described to Rawls as "stealth Reconstruction," attempting to win black support discreetly and without alienating white voters. As a witness to such tactics, Gibbs gained insight into the complicated issues surrounding race in the political sphere.

In 1996 Gibbs and another Browder aide, Shar Hendrick, left Washington to work in Alabama on the congressman's race for a seat in the U.S. Senate, which proved to be unsuccessful. The pair roomed together, and Hendrick has joked that while Gibbs has many skills and abilities, housekeeping is not among them.

In 1998 Gibbs served as the spokesperson for the Democratic U.S. senator Ernest Frederick "Fritz" Hollings of South Carolina, during Hollings's fifth, successful reelection campaign. In 2000 Gibbs acted as the spokesperson for the Michigan Democrat Debbie Stabenow during her victorious run for the U.S. Senate. While working with Stabenow Gibbs caught the attention of the Democratic political strategist Jim Jordan, who in 2002 hired Gibbs to work for the Democratic Senatorial Campaign Committee (DSCC), an organization devoted to electing Democrats to the U.S. Senate. At the DSCC Gibbs held the positions of communications director, political director, and, later, executive director. Jordan told Kurtz that Gibbs had "a strong personality [and] all the skills of a good flack. He knew how to move a negative story."

In 2003, when Jordan was hired to manage the 2004 presidential campaign of Democratic U.S. senator John Kerry of Massachusetts, he recruited Gibbs to serve as the campaign's national press secretary. In November 2003, as part of a broad plan to reorganize his foundering campaign, Kerry fired Jordan, and Gibbs quit in protest. Gibbs next worked for a brief period with a group called Americans for Jobs, Healthcare, and Progressive Values. In key primary states the group ran an aggressive ad campaign attacking another Democratic presidential hopeful, former governor Howard Dean of Vermont. One of its most controversial commercials showed an image of the Al Qaeda terrorist leader Osama bin Laden while a voiceover emphasized Dean's inexperience in military matters and foreign affairs. That ad was widely considered responsible for Dean's defeat. (Kerry ultimately secured the nomination but lost the general election to George W. Bush.) In some political circles Gibbs has been strongly criticized for his involvement in the 527 group.

After a brief period of unemployment, Gibbs heard from Jordan about a job opening with Obama's U.S. Senate campaign—that of communications director. When he met Obama, Gibbs knew little about him other than that he was a member of the Illinois state Senate. The two immediately felt drawn to each other, in part because of their shared love for sports, especially college football. Gibbs accepted the job, having "promised" himself that he would serve as spokesperson or communications director "only . . . for somebody I had a really good relationship with," as he recalled to a reporter for *Newsweek* (May 19, 2008, on-line).

At the 2004 Democratic National Convention, held in Boston, Massachusetts, Obama, then little-known outside Illinois, delivered the keynote address. The power of his words and his ability to connect with people of diverse backgrounds placed him overnight among the ranks of potential Democratic Party leaders. He was elected to the Senate by a wide margin, and Gibbs remained on his staff as communications director and close adviser. Gibbs was said to be among the first to recognize the freshman senator as a political phenomenon and to encourage him to capitalize on his popularity. Gibbs began laying the groundwork for a 2008 presidential bid by Obama. He worked particularly hard to dispel the criticisms of those who saw Obama as overly ambitious, given his inexperience in the national and international arenas.

On February 10, 2007 Obama delivered a speech in Springfield, Illinois, in which he officially threw his hat into the presidential ring. When he entered the race for the presidency, other competitors included U.S. senator Hillary Clinton of New York, a former First Lady, whom many already considered to be the frontrunner. Working with Plouffe and Axelrod, Gibbs was charged with overseeing communications strategy and operations. In that capacity he helped Obama control his tendency to give excessively detailed and complex answers and use too many polysyllabic words in debates and interviews; Gibbs also ensured that Obama made the many courtesy calls to local officials required during a national campaign. As the Democratic primary campaign progressed, Gibbs, Plouffe, and Axelrod became informal policy advisers as well.

Things did not always run smoothly, however, despite the closeness of the team. Gibbs became known, as Leibovich noted, for his "frustrating and at times harmful knack for going dark for long periods of time, ignoring urgent e-mail messages from reporters and co-workers." Gibbs also disliked supervising junior members of the communications staff, telling Leibovich, "It's not what I'm good at, not what I want to do." The situation improved considerably when Anita Dunn was hired as the communications team's director, in February 2008. For the duration of the campaign, Gibbs acted as chief spokesperson and often presented Obama's views to the press.

While reporters spoke highly of Gibbs's gregariousness and quick wit, they were often frustrated by his tight control over their access to Obama. One complained, according to Gabriel Sherman, writing for the *New Republic* (July 24, 2008, on-line), that Gibbs was a "communications director who doesn't communicate." David Mendell, a reporter and author of a book about Obama, *From Promise to Power* (2007), described Gibbs to Sherman as "Obama's hired gun, skillfully trained to shoot at reporters whose coverage was deemed unfair." Mendell explained, "If [Gibbs] feels you're necessary to achieve a campaign goal, he will give you access and allow you in. But, if he feels you're not going to be of help, he can just ignore you." In addition, Gibbs's temper sometimes flared, and he was known to verbally attack journalists whose articles he thought sullied Obama's image or message. "In hindsight, there are discussions that I had in the heat of the moment that if I had to do over again, [I] would do differently," Gibbs admitted to Kurtz. "I think you do better when you treat people with respect. There were a couple of times that I flew off the handle."

Overall, Obama's presidential campaign has been cited as one of the best-run in U.S. history, with much of its success credited to the mastery of new technology by Gibbs and his colleagues. The campaign committee amassed a vast database of e-mail addresses of Obama's supporters, which were used—along with Web sites, blogs, text messaging, and on-line videos—to communicate directly to voters. (The Web sites included fightthesmears.com, launched to combat misinformation or lies that were being spread about the candidate's religious beliefs and political goals.) The Gibbs/Axelrod/Plouffe team also ruled against some traditional ways of communicating with the media. Obama, for example, never visited with the editorial board of the *Washington Post*, as virtually all other presidential candidates in recent decades have done. Referring to a city and a town in Iowa, Gibbs said to Leibovich, "You could go to Cedar Rapids and Waterloo and understand that people aren't reading the *Washington Post*."

On June 3, 2008 Obama won enough delegates to secure the Democratic nomination. Three days later Gibbs came under considerable fire from the media, after reporters on a Chicago-bound plane ready for takeoff realized that, contrary to what they had been led to expect, Obama was not with them. (He had stayed in Washington to meet secretly with Hillary Clinton.) Finding himself subjected to the anger of a planeload of journalists was "maybe the toughest point that I had," as Gibbs recalled to Jake Tapper during an interview for ABC's *This Week* (December 27, 2008, on-line). The Washington, D.C., bureau chiefs of several news organizations sent letters to Gibbs and Plouffe, accusing them of intentionally misleading the reporters. "Most of the pictures in that event are with me holding my hands up," Gibbs told Tapper, "as if I'm . . . being in a sense, held hostage."

On October 8, 2008 Gibbs attracted an unusual amount of attention when he confronted Sean Hannity, the far-right-wing co-host of the Fox News television program *Hannity and Colmes*, regarding Hannity's repeated attacks on Obama for reportedly consorting with a "known terrorist," William "Bill" Ayers. Ayers, who has held the title of distinguished professor of education at the Chicago campus of the University of Illinois since 1999, was during his 20s a founding member of the Weathermen (later called the Weather Underground), a radical leftist organization responsible between 1970 and 1974 for several bombings and riots mounted to protest the Vietnam War and other examples of what they denounced as U.S. imperialism. For a while Obama and Ayers, both residents of Chicago, had sat on the boards of the same philanthropic and educational organizations, and Ayers had hosted a small party to support Obama's bid for a seat in the Illinois state Senate. Ignoring the fact that when Ayers was active with the Weathermen, Obama was eight years old, Hannity—and the Republican presidential nominee, U.S. senator John McCain of Arizona—implied that Obama's links to Ayers provided evidence that he was a radical leftist whose statements to the contrary were not to be believed. When Hannity asked Gibbs whether Obama, given his associatiion with Ayers, could be trusted to fight terrorism, Gibbs responded by noting that Hannity had recently had as a guest on his program Andy Martin, a notorious anti-Semite. Gibbs went on to read previous statements or remarks made by Martin, including one in which he called a judge a "slimy Jew." If Obama's acquaintance with Ayers indicated that he was a terrorist sympathizer, Gibbs pointed out, then Hannity's relationship with Martin must make Hannity an anti-Semite. The ensuing shouting match, which became a popular clip on the video-sharing Web site YouTube, helped to undermine McCain's efforts to cast doubts on Obama's patriotism. Gibbs told Howard Kurtz that he enjoys such occasions, which give him the chance to spar with reporters or commentators. "Anybody who does this [job] has to like a little of the back and forth," he said.

Four days after Obama's victory in his race against McCain, the president-elect announced that after his inauguration, on January 20, 2009, Gibbs would serve as White House press secretary—one of the most high-pressure and visible positions in any administration. A press secretary "can send markets crashing and troops in motion by one slip of the tongue," Axelrod remarked to Leibovich. Gibbs reports to Rahm Emanuel, the former Illinois congressman whom Obama appointed chief of staff. Ellen Moran is the director and Dan Pfeiffer the deputy director of the communications team.

Gibbs delivered his first official briefing on January 22, 2009. In responding to questions on topics including the economic recession, health-care reform, and the wars in Afghanistan and Iraq, Gibbs has established a reputation for injecting an element of humor into his briefings. According to an article in the on-line publication *Politico* (May 27, 2009), during Gibbs's first four months as press secretary, the briefing transcripts included more than 600 instances of laughter. (His predecessors, President George W. Bush's press secretaries Dana Perino, Scott McClellan, and the late Tony Snow, got 57, 66, and 217 laughs, respectively, during their first four months in the job.) While some have attributed the lightheartedness in the Obama pressroom to the newness of the administration, others have cited Gibbs's personality. Mark Knoller, a longtime journalist for CBS News who has covered the White House for decades, told *Politico*, "[Gibbs] is at ease at the lectern, understands the press and is willing to offer a quip at our expense or his own." When he heard about the laughter count, Gibbs was quoted as saying, "I have always hoped that we could do our important jobs and still have a little fun doing it."

In the fall of 2009, Gibbs and other senior administration officials, including Rahm Emanuel and David Axelrod, publicly expressed their dissatisfaction with the manner in which the cable network Fox News was reporting on the White House. Fox News broadcasts several shows hosted by far-right-wing commentators who not only invariably criticize the administration but who, according to many observers of other political persuasions, slant their coverage so as to demean it, in the process misleading the public or propagating out-and-out falsehoods. Asked by an ABC journalist whether the White House should weigh in on the standards of news organizations, Gibbs said, as quoted in the *New York Times* (October 20, 2009), "We render opinion based on some of their coverage and the fairness of their coverage." In late October, responding to Republicans' allegations that Obama was rewarding campaign donors with special privileges and visits to the White House, Gibbs announced that the administration would make public lists of visitors to the White House.

Taking a tongue-in-cheek pride in his southern heritage, Gibbs was a member of the organization Rednecks for Obama. In a closet in his office, which is only yards from the president's, he keeps an army flak jacket, left there in 1977 by Ron Nessen, President Gerald Ford's press secretary, reportedly to be worn as protection when members of the White House press corp launch verbal attacks at whoever occupies that office.

The 38-year-old Gibbs struck Leibovich as having "an ageless face—at once boyish and well worn—that could put him anywhere from 25 to 50." "Gibbs gained considerable weight during the campaign that he is trying to shed, and he has a habit—maybe unconscious—of running his hands up and down his paunch while he speaks," Leibovich continued. Obama told Leibovich, "The chronicle of his weight is a story unto itself." Gibbs lives in Alexandria, Virginia, with his wife, Mary Catherine, an attorney, and their son, Ethan, who was six years old in 2009.

—M.E.R.

Suggested Reading: Associated Press (on-line) Nov. 7, 2008; *New Republic* (on-line) July 24, 2008; *New York Times* (on-line) Oct. 20, 2009, Oct. 29, 2009; *New York Times Magazine* (on-line) Dec. 21, 2008; *Newsweek* (on-line) May 19, 2008; *Politico* (on-line) May 27, 2009; *Washington Post* A p1 Nov. 12, 2008

Gilbert and George

Artists

Proesch, Gilbert
Sep. 11, 1943–

Passmore, George
Jan. 8, 1942–

Address: Gilbert and George, 12 Fournier St., London E1 6QE, England

The artists known as Gilbert and George "have formed a unit of singular genius . . . perennially fusing art and life, abstraction and representation, morality and decadence with the greatest of ease and inventing new mediums as they go," Roberta Smith wrote for the *New York Times* (September 27, 1991). Born Gilbert Proesch, in Italy, and George Passmore, in England, the men have been working and living together for over four decades. Except when talking about their lives before they met, in 1967, Gilbert and George refer to themselves as one person, and rarely if ever have they appeared in public separately; "in adopting a collective name, the artists refused individualization and reinforced the point that their art is their life together," Ray Ann Lockard wrote for glbtq.com in 2002. Of working-class origins, each man studied art in a series of academic settings; at the last school that both attended, in England, they discovered that they held similar views about art. The subject of art, they declared, "must be the human condition . . . ," as quoted by Julie Razzanti and Céline Gimenez in an undated essay posted on the Web site of the University of Perpignan, in France. "The whole formal side of life—colours and forms—is there only to serve the subject and is of no importance in itself. We hate art for art's sake. We are totally opposed to it." Soon after they began to collaborate, Gilbert and George became performance artists. Their act *Singing Sculpture*, in which for four years they performed as "living sculptures" in many places in and outside of Great Britain, "established their reputation," according to the Web site of the Tate Modern, in London, England. Thereafter they expressed themselves in charcoal drawings, paint, handmade books, videos, and, increasingly, photos and photomontages; the montages, which they laboriously printed and colored by hand for many years, are now produced with their custom-made computer and state-of-the-art software.

In their work Gilbert and George have examined a multitude of subjects, among them aspects of their own physical, sexual, emotional, spiritual, and intellectual lives; feelings of hope, love, desire, humility, embarrassment, fear, disgust, and rage; religion, faith, and religious hypocrisy; urban life and the natural world; and aging, death, homosexuality, prostitution, alcoholism, individual identity, racial tensions, class differences, AIDS, and violence, including the terrorist bombings carried out in London on July 7, 2005. Notably absent from their work are images of females. The photos in their works are among the hundreds of thousands in their continually expanding collection of pictures they have taken within a few miles of their home; they obtain most of the printed texts used in their pictures from places in their London neighborhood, such as signs posted on lampposts or walls, graffiti, or the headline-bearing posters displayed outside newsdealers' shops. Between 1971 and 2005 the artists produced well over 1,000 works, many of them wall-size. "What makes their huge pictures so special is the way in which the grubby, disturbing, upsetting, defecatory subjects they represent are portrayed in the most fastidiously conceived and beautifully crafted manner," Jonathan Glancey wrote for the London *Independent* (August 26, 1995).

"We never argue," George told John Tusa for a BBC Radio interview (2002, on-line). "We don't believe in discussing or planning or in ideas. How we are as people when we go to the studio is how the pictures will be." That statement notwithstanding, in 1986 Gilbert and George spelled out their principles in a manifesto called "What Our Art Means." As posted on the Web site of Kunsthaus-Bregenz, an exhibition space in Austria, it begins with a section called "Art for All": "We want Our Art to speak across the barriers of knowledge directly to People about their life and not about their knowledge of art. The 20th century has been cursed with an art that cannot be understood. . . . We say that puzzling, obscure, and form-obsessed art is decadent and a cruel denial of the Life of People." In the next part, "Progress Through Friendship," they wrote, "Our Art is the friendship between the viewer and our pictures. Each picture speaks of a 'Particular View' which the viewer may consider in the light of his own life. The true function of Art is to bring about new understanding, progress and advancement." "True Art comes from three main life-forces," they declared in another section: "They are: the head, the soul, and the sex. In our life these forces are shaking and moving themselves into everchanging different arrangements. Each one of our pictures is a frozen representation of one of these 'arrangements.'" In their manifesto's conclusion they declared, "The content of mankind is our subject and our inspiration. . . . We want to find and accept all the good and bad in ourselves. Civilisation has always depended for advancement on the 'giving person.' We want to spill our blood, brains and seed in our life-search for new meanings and purpose to give to life." In addition, in a two-minute video, now posted on the Internet, Gilbert and George recited their personal 10 commandments, the sixth of which states, "Thou shalt not know exactly what they dost, but thou shalt do it." Others order them to "fight conformism," "be the messenger of freedoms," "make use of sex," "have a sense of purpose," "give thy love," and "give something back."

Adrian Dennis/AFP/Getty Images
Gilbert (left) and George

In recent years Gilbert and George have become best known for their boldly, flatly colored photomontages, some more than 30 feet in length, each including an overlying grid of black horizontal and vertical lines that divide the whole into upwards of 16 identical rectangles. Many of them contain religious imagery, often cruciform shapes, accompanied by profane texts and depictions of nudity or bodily fluids and excretions—in some pictures, hugely blown-up images of human turds or greatly magnified photomicrographs of blood, urine, tears, sweat, semen, or saliva. Virtually all include pictures of Gilbert and George's faces or other body parts, clothed or nude."For us, being naked in front of the public, we are trying to make ourselves vulnerable in front of the viewer," one of them said in 1997, as quoted by Robert Rosenblum in his book *Introducing Gilbert & George* (2004). "That is very important because art is based on making ourselves more vulnerable and opening up what is inside us." The artists have said that they want to "unshock" viewers, to enable them to openly accept intrinsic aspects of human existence—such as defecation—that are generally kept hidden and rarely depicted in art. At the same time, as Gilbert told Andrew Wilson for the *Journal of Contemporary Art* (Winter 1993), art "has to be shocking in the beginning because if it wouldn't be shocking, then it wouldn't be new." Some of their individual works or series have titles that are decidedly provocative, if not shocking: *Sh*t Faith* (1982); *Sperm Eaters* (1082); *Sh*tted* (1983); *Naked Sh*t Pictures* (1995); *Blood, Tears, Spunk, P*ss* (1996); *In the P*ss* (1997); and *Sonofagod Pictures: Was Jesus Heterosexual?* (2006).

In stark contrast to such bawdiness, scatalogy, and political incorrectness, in public Gilbert and George are invariably dressed in immaculate shirts, patterned ties, and nearly identical, conservatively tailored, three-button suits—the "responsibility suits of our art," as they call them. Though during interviews they sometimes use four-letter words, they display excellent manners, kindness, and congeniality, as well as purposefulness, seriousness, and empathy. "We don't think that we're free and we're helping the audience, we feel that together with the viewer we're doing it, we're walking down life's road hand in hand with the viewer," George told John Tusa. "We don't want people running away from our exhibition because they find it freaky or too unusual or not part of their world," he told Andrew Wilson. "We want to seduce the viewer into entering our friendly world, to discuss together with us." A quarter-century ago, in an observation echoed by many since then, John Russell described Gilbert and George for the *New York Times* (March 4, 1984) as "paragons of composure, models of circumspection, all-time prize winners in the courtesy stakes. In fact, they can be ranked as living sculptures that just happen not to have been cast in bronze." Russell added, "They have looked into themselves, fished out whatever lay deepest, and presented it to us in a direct and fearless way. What else are artists there for?"

Gilbert and George as "living sculptures" and their works on paper have been the subjects of hundreds of print and Internet articles and have been in group and solo shows ("solo" because the men are considered a single artist) in galleries and museums worldwide every year for more than four decades. In 1972, 1977, and 1982 they accepted invitations to participate in Documenta Kassel, a highly regarded exhibition of contemporary works held in Germany every five years. In 1980, an especially busy year, they had solo shows in galleries in Amsterdam, the Netherlands; Düsseldorf, Germany; Athens, Greece; New York City; London; and Paris, France. Also that year the Stedelijk Museum, in the Netherlands, arranged a Gilbert and George retrospective that traveled to four museums in 1981: the Kunsthalle in Düsseldorf; the Kunsthalle in Bern, Switzerland; the Georges Pompidou Centre, in Paris; and the Whitechapel Art Gallery, in London. In 2007 more than 200 of their works were displayed in a huge retrospective that filled all 18 rooms of one floor of the Tate Modern and part of another.

Although some critics and laypeople have criticized work of theirs as narcissistic, shallow, tiresomely repetitive, or sordid or condemned it as blasphemous, evil, vile, the products of demented or psychopathic minds, or a blatant con, reactions have more often been positive, though sometimes with reservations. In 1986 Gilbert and George won the Turner Prize, Great Britain's most prestigious honor for contemporary artists who are under 50 and working in the United Kingdom. In 2005 they represented Great Britain at the Venice Biennale, in Italy.

Gilbert was born Gilbert Proesch on September 11, 1943 in San Marino, a village in the Dolomite Alps, in northern Italy. "My family was pretty much a peasant family, up in the mountains and totally isolated," he told Wolf Jahn, the author of *The Art of Gilbert & George, or, An Aesthetic of Existence* (1989), for a 1999 interview that appeared in *Tate Etc.* (Issue 9, 2007). "I think that's very important. When you're isolated from life in the city, you're different. I've never lost that." Gilbert's first language was Ladino (which derives from Spanish and is spoken mainly by a dwindling number of Sephardic Jews). His family was Catholic, and he attended church every Sunday until his late teens. "I had quite a nice childhood," he told Jahn. His father, a woodcarver, taught him that craft, and at a young age Gilbert began to make wooden religious objects, such as pieces for nativity scenes; he later worked with marble, too. He also enjoyed drawing. The first art school he attended was in Wolkenstein, in the Dolomites. "I was the only person there from a different village, a different culture," he told Jahn. "So I already felt isolated . . . different." He next took art classes at a school in Hallein, Austria. Later in his teens he enrolled at the Academy of Fine Arts in Munich, Germany. According to Matthew Collings, writing for the London *Independent* (November 6, 1999), other students there bullied him mercilessly because of his strangeness: "His torments included being stripped naked, being hung upside down by his feet from a high window, and being packed into a trunk partly filled with wet clay." Gilbert's skills in sculpting, Collings reported, eventually brought him the respect and friendship of his tormentors. In 1967 he won acceptance to the three-year program in advanced sculpture at Central St. Martins College of Art and Design, a division of the University of Arts London, and he moved to England.

George was born George Passmore on January 8, 1942 in Plymouth, Devon, a county in England, and grew up in nearby Totnes. His only sibling, a brother, is a vicar in a Protestant church. His father abandoned the family at around the time of his birth; his mother, Hermione Ernestine, a waitress, was divorced several times and reportedly had a series of boyfriends. The family was extremely poor; their building had no heat or hot water, and tenants shared a toilet. "Nobody had a nice piece of furniture, or a radio that worked," George recalled to Jahn. George's mother, determined to improve her sons' lives, paid for elocution lessons for them, and she "worked like a dog," George said, so she could afford to buy gold-framed glasses for him, rather than have him wear the inexpensive ones supplied by the National Health Service. "We were never allowed to play outside with the other children," he told Jahn. "We were always separate in some way." George left school at 15 and found work in a shop. A painting of his called *The Estrangement*, depicting a family arguing, was included in a local exhibition. Soon afterward he won a grant to attend art classes at Dartington Hall, a school near Totnes supported by a private trust and known for its progressive philosophy of education. "He thought the school was wonderful; it seemed to represent an ideal society," Collings wrote. After three years of study there, George tried unsuccessfully to gain entrance to a teachers' college. He then hitchhiked to London, where he worked in a department store during the day and as a barman at night. For a year he took art classes at the Oxford School of Art. He was admitted into the advanced-sculpture program at Central St. Martins in 1965.

When Gilbert and George met at Central St. Martins, two years later, they became friends "immediately," George recalled to Jahn. The reason, Gilbert said, was that "George was the only one who accepted my pidgin English." Sources differ as to the precise sequence of events in Gilbert and George's lives and careers from then through the first half of the 1970s, but most agree on the essentials. The men soon discovered that they felt similarly dissatisfied with the approach to sculpture pervasive at St. Martins at that time. "The style of art that was current then was formalistic art, it was to do with color, shape, form, weight, and you discussed art in those terms, you never discussed feeling, meanings, sex, race, religion, money, none of those things came into the discussion about art," George, who completed the Central St. Martins course in 1968, told John Tusa. "It was just another language, the language of sculpture. And we thought that was wrong, because if you took those sculptures out of the building of St. Martins School of Art into the street they wouldn't address the issues that were inside of all the people on the street, they [the viewers] wouldn't even identify them as art." For their earliest collaborations Gilbert and George "made objects of our own and showed them together," Gilbert told Robert Rosenblum. Then, Gilbert told Rosenblum, "we realised we didn't need the objects any more. It was just us."

For *The Meal* (1969) the pair ate and chatted with the British artist David Hockney while invited guests looked on. For *Postal Sculptures* ("mail art"), which debuted around that time and continued for a half-dozen years, the men mailed in plain brown envelopes to well-known artists and others their neatly signed, hand-drawn double portraits of themselves, along with "very personal messages," as Gilbert told Jahn. Also during that period the men bought an 18th-century house (in which George had been a renter) in Spitalfields, a working-class neighborhood in London's East End. They still live in that house, which they spent years restoring themselves. They also purchased adjoining and nearby properties, where they built their studios.

Early on in their partnership, Gilbert and George tried largely in vain to gain acceptance of their photographic "magazine sculptures" in gallery exhibitions. One such piece, entitled *George the C*nt* *and Gilbert the Sh*t* (1969), contains a portrait of each artist with the respective four-letter word superimposed on it. "A preemptive strike on their critics," Regina Marler wrote for the *Advocate* (April 22, 2008), it was rejected by all but one gallery (Robert Fraser's, where the piece was on display for one afternoon only). Amazed and angered by the rejection of their work for the exhibition When Attitude Becomes Form: Live in Your Head, mounted at the Institute of Contemporary Arts in London in 1969, they came to the opening with painted faces and stood motionless until the show closed for the night. That act so impressed the contemporary-art dealer Konrad Fischer that soon afterward he exhibited them in the same poses at his gallery in Düsseldorf, Germany. Gilbert and George were recognized in a professional publication for the first time in October 1969, when an article about them by the Dutch artist Ger Van Elk was included in the British monthly *Museums Journal.* Also in 1969 they revealed some of their ideas in "The Laws of the Sculptors," in which they wrote, in part, as quoted by Michael Bracewell in the London *Independent* (May 27, 2001), "Always be smartly dressed, well-groomed, relaxed, friendly, polite, and in complete control," and "Make the world to believe in you and to pay heavily for this privilege," referring to the price they themselves would have to pay. "I think all honest artworks, or creative things, are destructive, in that they damage the creator in some way . . . ," George told Jahn."You f*ck yourself up in some way by doing pictures such as *Sh*tty Naked Human World,*" he added, referring to 1994 series that contains images of the artists naked and clothed alongside hugely enlarged photos of their feces. "We become a little bit damaged, sexually or psychologically or emotionally."

Meanwhile, for some time Gilbert and George, their faces and hands covered in metallic makeup, had taken their performance art to the streets of London, sometimes simply strolling and at other times standing under one stone arch or another while singing or lip-synching to "Underneath the Arches," a 1932 British music-hall song, by Flanagan and Allen, in which a tramp sings of sleeping and dreaming under a railroad bridge every night. Word of that act spread, and they began to perform at locations in England. Billing themselves "The Singing Sculpture," the bronze-visaged Gilbert and George, clad in identical suits, would stand on a table and sing or lip-synch, executing what Roberta Smith, in the *New York Times* (October 24, 2007), described as "gently robotic dance steps," while one of them held a cane and the other a glove; a tape recorder underneath their perch provided the music. When the tape ended "the artists exchanged cane and glove," Ray Anne Lockard wrote; "then one of them stepped down from the table, reset the equipment, and stepped back up." Ger van Elk arranged for Gilbert and George to perform on the steps of the Stedelijk Museum, and then Konrad Fischer brought them to the Kunsthalle Düsseldorf, where, for the first time, they performed nonstop for eight hours. The art dealer Ileana Sonnabend and the director of her gallery, Antonio Homem, saw their act in Brussels, Belgium. "We stood there for an hour totally mesmerized," Homem told Carol Vogel for the *New York Times* (April 4, 2005). Gilbert and George's performance at the opening of Sonnabend's New York gallery, in 1971, "had the art world talking," Roberta Smith wrote (October 24, 2007). Smith described the duo's reprisal of their performance 20 years later at the Sonnabend Gallery in New York City: "Less a performance than a performance of a performance, this ritual simultaneously widens the gap between the artists and their audience and creates an odd intimacy. After a while, they come to resemble objects at an exhibition, forming a temporary sculpture that happens to be living." In 1971 and 1991 the Sonnabend Gallery also showed the same 23 enormous Gilbert and George drawings, almost-life-size portrayals of the men standing stiffly in parklike settings, all the drawings "seem[ing] to have been rapidly filled in by a giant, impatient hand," in Smith's view. Spatterings of acid had made the paper look old. Titled as a series *The General Jungle,* the pieces were captioned with such titles as "We Feel Briefly, But Seriously, for Our Fellow Artist Men" and "Nothing Can Touch Us or Take Us Out of Ourselves, It Is a Sculpture." Gilbert and George's last performance piece, *Red Sculpture,* debuted in Tokyo, Japan, in 1975.

By that time Gilbert and George had turned to drawing, painting, photography, and video as ways of reaching bigger audiences. Often noted among their black-and-white photomontages from the early 1970s is *Smashed* (1973), which documents an evening in which both men got drunk on gin and tonics—as they did day and night for several years, by their own account. Containing blurry, off-center, or tilted images arranged in a seemingly haphazard fashion, the montage conveys the sensation of inebriation. In their 12-minute film *Gordon's Makes Us Drunk,* (1972), a well-dressed Gilbert and George sit on decorous upholstered chairs at a small table set in front of a large, sheer-curtained window, repeatedly pouring themselves drinks from a bottle of Gordon's gin whose label has their names imprinted on it; classical music plays on the soundtrack. "Their deadpan expressions and repeated declaration that 'Gordon's makes us very drunk' creates an absurd scene that ironically questions identity, nationality and 'good behaviour,'" according to the Tate Modern Web site. *Smashed* and *Gordon's Makes Us Drunk* were part of Gilbert and George's series *Drinking Sculptures.* "We could see that all the other artists were drinking, but during the day they painted a nice grey square with a yellow line down the side," George told Jahn. "We thought that was completely fake. Why shouldn't all of life come into your art? The artists drink, but they do sober pictures. So we did drinking sculptures, true to life."

In about 1975 Gilbert and George used colored paint—bright red and yellow—for the first time in their work. Later in that decade they began to paint their photographs, all of which they developed in their own darkroom, with a limited palette of additional bold colors. Their series of photomontages *Dirty Words Pictures* (1977) include their photos of street graffiti, mostly shot in London and mostly obscene. Writing for the London *Observer* (June 9, 2002), Tim Adams suggested that the pictures represented "an about-face in G&G's lock-stepped career: where previously they had been happy enough to toy with a private sort of frank absurdity, this work looks like a more earnest stab at social realism." In an essay included in Bart Moore-Gilbert's *The Challenge of the Arts in the 1970s: Cultural Closure?* (1994), Stuart Sillars wrote that as social commentary the series is "powerful, disturbing and, because of its use of immediately recognizable late-twentieth century images, accessible—even if, to many, it is also deeply offensive." *Prostitute Poof* (1977), *The Alcoholic* (1978), and others among their photomontages from that period feature pictures taken in their London neighborhood and some of its troubled, marginalized inhabitants. In the view of Paul Richard, writing for the *Washington Post* (February 26, 1984), in the photos of themselves in those works, they seem primarily to be "observers, witnesses, participants, never . . . haters."

An often-noted Gilbert and George photomontage series is the four-part *Death Hope Life Fear* (1984), each piece in which includes from two to 19 photos of young men along with photos of the artists. In *Life*, which is more than 14 feet high and eight feet wide, seven images of Gilbert and George, ranging from two feet to 12 feet tall, appear in the middle, one behind the other. Their poses resemble those of some images of Jesus or saints: in each, Gilbert or George stands with one arm extending diagonally toward the ground with the palm facing the viewer, while the other arm is raised, with elbow bent and the palm also visible. The extended right arm of the tallest George nearly touches the hand of a teenaged boy, standing at the left, while the extended left hand of the tallest Gilbert touches the head of a slightly younger boy, standing at the right. Four hugely magnified, dappled leaves point upward on either side of the men, while at the top there are two two-foot-wide eyes, with white eyelashes, black irises, and red lids. The word "LIFE" appears between the eyes. In each of the 25-piece series *Gingko* (2005), which Gilbert and George showed at that year's Venice Biennale, the artists included huge blowups of Chinese gingko leaves. The Tate Modern acquired one of those photomontages, the 54-panel *Fates*, which is about 25 feet long and 14 feet high.

In the summer of 2009, *The Jack Freak Pictures*, Gilbert and George's first show since their 2007 Tate Modern exhibition, was mounted at the White Cube in London. It consisted of 153 images—the most the artists had ever produced for one series. The images incorporated the British flag, urban elements, and religious iconography. The White Cube's Web site posted comments by the writer and cultural commentator Michael Bracewell, who described the new show as containing "among the most iconic, philosophically astute and visually violent works that Gilbert & George have ever created." In a review of the show for the London *Guardian* (July 9, 2009, on-line), Jonathan Jones wrote, "The Britain in these pictures is scared, maddened, exciting, graffitied. The freaks who walk its mean streets and spooky parks are G&G themselves, playing visual games that distort their faces into cyclopean monstrosities; they turn their bodies inside out, and put themselves in impossible places and postures. Sometimes it's just an eye, moist and staring, that catches your attention in a chaotic pulse of medals, flags and street names. Yet, for all the apparent chaos, these pictures create kaleidoscopic structures that suggest everything is connected."

Examples of the more controversial of Gilbert and George's works include the eight-feet-square *We* (1983). In it the artists, in their signature attire, are seen standing and squatting near a partial cross, outlined in red, in whose four vertical and horizontal arms appear hugely magnified photos of the shafts of penises. Another example is *Naked Sh*t* (1994), in which a naked Gilbert and George, facing the viewers and holding their unzipped trousers at thigh level, stand on either side of a human turd that is taller than they are and about as wide. As in all their photos, George wears eyeglasses, and both men wear wristwatches. In *Spunkland* (1997) the artists are again unclothed but seen from the back; they stand at the far left of the montage, holding hands and looking toward the right; the background consists of an enormous blowup of a photomicrograph of semen.

Gilbert and George wrote the screenplay and drew extremely detailed storyboards for their 69-minute documentary film *The World of Gilbert and George* (1981), which they also directed. "When the cameraman was next to us, we had to be able to tell him that we wanted something absolutely identical to the drawing," Gilbert told the French art and film critic François Jonquet, as quoted by Michael Bracewell in a review of the film posted on the Web site of Arts Council England in 2007, when the film was released on DVD. "Otherwise, we would have lost control. . . . And we always want to remain in control." "One of the great films about London," Bracewell wrote, it presents the artists' world as "a place where the local becomes universal—through the East End streets and their inhabitants, we are shown the common denominations of modern human existence, in all its quotidian banality and fathomless emotional energy." He also wrote, "There is nothing obscure or esoteric about this film of their 'world.' Rather, it has an urgency, drama and open-handedness which is richly generous to the viewer. There is humour, too . . . and a compassionate insight into the lives of ordinary citizens. It is a film which shows the capacity for boredom, passion, reverie, anger, fear, faith and love that exists within us all—the same epic sweep of feelings that are the subject of all the art that Gilbert & George have made over the last forty years."

Except for their height (George is several inches taller) and George's chainsmoking, Gilbert and George have erased whatever differences they may have had in their public personas. In the late 1960s George was married briefly; that union produced two children. Although in interviews they have steadfastly refused to discuss their sexual preferences, they are widely assumed to be a couple. The men have raised money for AIDS-related causes—they donated all the proceeds of one of their shows to AIDS organizations—and are said to be supportive of young artists. Their home, which has been described as extremely clean and neat, does not contain a kitchen; the men eat all of their meals out, usually in the same eateries every day. Among other collections, they own many children's books and religious and theosophical books. Described as workaholics, they have rarely taken vacations. On a long wall of one of their studios, they maintain an extremely detailed index of all their photographs; their photos of crosses, for example, number in the thousands and those of themselves in the tens of thousands, and their records list many subcategories of each subject. They store in boxes all their 35-millimeter negatives and a contact sheet developed from each roll of film. They also maintain an archive of their 1,200 newspaper posters. In conversations transcribed for and posted on the Tate Modern's Web site in 2007, Gilbert and George described their techniques for making photomontages.

—W.D.

Suggested Reading: *ArtForum* (on-line) Sep. 2001; London *Independent* (on-line) Nov. 6, 1999, Feb. 11, 2007; London *Telegraph* (on-line) Jan. 20, 2006; *New York Times* II p25 Mar. 4, 1984, E p1+ Aug. 4, 2005, (on-line) June 1, 1990; *Tate Etc.* Issue 9 Spring 2007; *Washington Post* K p1+ Feb. 26, 1984; Jahn, Wolf. *The Art of Gilbert & George, or, An Aesthetic of Existence*, 1989; Jonquet, François. *Intimate Conversations with François Jonquet / Gilbert & George*, 2004; Rosenblum, Robert. *Introducing Gilbert and George*, 2004

Selected Works: *Photo-piece*, 1971; *Smashed*, 1973; *Dirty Words Pictures*, 1977; *New Cosmological Pictures*, 1989; *New Democratic Pictures*, 1991; *Naked Sh*t Pictures*, 1994; *New Horny Pictures*, 2001; *Sonofagod Pictures: Was Jesus Heterosexual?*, 2005; *Gingko Pictures*, 2005; *The Jack Freak Pictures*, 2009

Gladstone, Brooke

Mar. 6, 1955– Radio journalist; co-host of On the Media

Address: WNYC Radio, 160 Varick St., New York, NY 10013

Brooke Gladstone is the managing editor and co-host, with Bob Garfield, of *On the Media*, a weekly National Public Radio (NPR) program that features analyses of all things media-related—issues such as free speech, privacy, spin, fairness, and the complex relationships among words, truth, and perception. Gladstone's pet peeve, she told *Current Biography*—the source of quotes for this article, unless otherwise noted—is "the tendency of reporters who are at pains to appear objective by indulging in something that we call 'false balance.' There aren't always two equal sides to a story." Citing global warming and the harmful effects of cigarettes as examples of issues without two equal sides, Gladstone said that the principle applies to political issues and any other source of debate for which the evidence on one side is overwhelming. "If you see a story for what it is, if you see the sky is blue, you don't need equal voice saying that the sky is green." While Gladstone does not believe in journalistic "objectivity," she does believe in fair-

Courtesy of Dmitry Kiper

ness, seeking to practice it on her show—on which a great variety of perspectives give the listeners a deep, nuanced understanding of complicated, often divisive, issues. Prior to joining *On the Media*, in 2001, Gladstone served successively as the senior editor of the NPR programs *Weekend Edition* and *All Things Considered*, the network's Moscow reporter, and an NPR media correspondent based in New York City.

Gladstone, the third of six children, was born on March 6, 1955 in Long Island, New York. "It was a fun, noisy childhood," Gladstone said. "A lot of loud, verbal kids competing with each other over the dinner table for attention. And generally it was kind of a free-for-all in that time." Although growing up on Long Island was "sometimes bone-crunchingly boring," the teenage Gladstone kept busy by reading books and taking trips with friends to New York City, where "we saw a lot of strange and frightening things in those days, but just thought that's how cities are," she said. "And it certainly didn't prevent us from coming back again and again. . . . It was the city of [the gritty Martin Scorsese film] *Taxi Driver*. I had a kid's sense that I was immortal anyway, so I never felt like anything bad would happen to me. I *loved* the city. . . . The city was a place where everything happened on the street. People selling scraps of poetry. People playing music on every corner. People selling their art. People selling clothes. There were endless amounts of things. There was a sense you'd walked into the world, out of your sheltered little noplace into the world of everyplace." Gladstone also had a passion for politics during her adolescence and early teens. At the age of 12, she went to New York City with a group of friends to collect cans and tins so they would have money to send to the people of Biafra, a secessionist state within Nigeria that was in turmoil in the late 1960s. She would even skip school to protest the war in Vietnam. But by 1973, after the Republican Richard Nixon had resoundingly defeated the Democrat George McGovern in the presidential election, Gladstone's interest in politics had started to wane. Because McGovern was ahead in the New York polls, Gladstone had assumed he would win. "Like I said, I was pretty stupid," she said, smiling. "After that point I became disenchanted with politics for a long time."

Reading was a more enduring interest for Gladstone. "I did have the quirky thing of becoming obsessed with particular writers," she said. "So I would set myself a goal—this summer I will read everything Dostoyevsky ever wrote, this summer I will read everything Aldous Huxley ever wrote. I became particularly obsessed with one Aldous Huxley novel, *Point Counter Point*, and I started collecting editions of it whenever I saw it. . . . It was supremely—and this may relate to my later life—comforting to see somebody who was so smart and so cynical." Gladstone was also developing an interest in theater; she acted in several community-theater productions on Long Island. Her intellectual leanings had an aesthetic counterpart: "Like all pretentiously bright kids of my generation, I was heavy into the Existentialists and wore black all the time."

The Gladstone family's financial troubles soon forced them to leave Long Island and sell their home. Gladstone's father had worked for his own father's wholesale-textile business, then gone back to school in the mid-1960s to become a stockbroker; then, in 1971, the nation's economy took a sharp turn for the worse. "The bottom dropped out," Brooke Gladstone recalled. "My parents kept us in the dark about how financially wiggy things were—until it became obvious to all of us. Certainly it became obvious when my father started driving a truck and then sold the house and moved us to Vermont." The family arrived in Morrisville, Vermont, before the start of Gladstone's senior year of high school. The public high school she attended had 60 seniors, which allowed her to "win awards that I never would have won in my much bigger class of 1,500 in Long Island. So that was fun."

After graduating from high school, Gladstone attended the University of Vermont, where she majored in theater and minored in the classics—Greek and Roman history and the Greek language, in which she "didn't do well." She also studied psychology and "a lot" of English. Because she spent so much time in the theater—acting, designing sets, and handling the lighting—she had little time for most of her other subjects. By the time she graduated, she had participated in 45 productions. (The musical *Candide* was one of her favorites. She loved to sing.) After finishing college Gladstone wanted to be a theater actor, or thought she did. "Maybe I used it as a default mode," Gladstone recalled, "because I didn't know what I was going to do." She took part in a few theater festivals and dinner-theater productions before her acting work tapered off; soon afterward she joined the food-service workforce. "And I have the hairnets and nametags to prove it, to quote *Wayne's World*," Gladstone said. "I was pretty lost for a while. It started to dawn on me that I didn't have the versatility or the intestinal fortitude to pursue an acting career."

Trying to escape her frustration, Gladstone left Vermont for Washington, D.C, where a friend of hers had an available bedroom in an apartment she was subletting. She got a job as a waitress in several restaurants and diners. One of her regular customers, named Fred, took an interest in her. One day in 1978, when she and Fred discussed the U.S. missile-defense system, it became apparent that Gladstone had an interest in the issue. "You should write about this," he told her. "He thought that I could write," Gladstone recalled. "He thought any smart person could write." Fred got her an assignment to write about the topic and provided her with research material and the phone numbers of several sources. A month later her story was published in *Inquiry*, a left-leaning libertarian magazine. Gladstone ended up marrying Fred—the journalist Fred Kaplan, who at the time was a correspondent for the *Boston Globe* and now writes for the on-line magazine *Slate*. After publishing her first article, Gladstone landed a few more writing gigs—writing pamphlets for the group Americans for SALT (Strategic Arms Limitation Treaty) and contributing articles to the trade-association magazine of the strip-mining industry—but could not find work as a journalist. Gladstone wanted to write for the State News Service wire, which would not give her even unpaid work.

After working at a bookstore for "a while," in 1981 Gladstone got a job at *Current*, a biweekly newsletter that covers the public-broadcasting industry. "This was a big time for me," she recalled, "because it was during NPR's big financial scandal, when there were $9 million that were basically squandered—not stolen, just sort of badly handled. And because *Current* was the only way the public broadcasting industry talked to itself, I was suddenly somebody that people wanted to talk to, like the *Philadelphia Inquirer*, *Washington Post*, even the [Senate] subcommittee people wanted to talk to me, because I had bunches of documents people had given me. I was sort of feared and sought after, and that was a very strange experience for somebody as young as I was. The vice presidents of NPR—there were a lot of them at that point—felt they had to talk to me, because if I said something bad then it would alienate them within the system." During her time at *Current*, Gladstone decided that she wanted to pursue journalism as a career. "That was where I was finally developing some skills. I was able to use writing, analysis, and a consciousness of the world around me, and apply it in a way that was satisfying. I did know then I was going to be a journalist." After three years at *Current*, Gladstone joined the staff of *Washington Weekly*, where she wrote the entertainment column and edited the back-page listings. The paper folded after a year.

One day, at an event at which the jazz great Dizzy Gillespie donated his trumpet to the Smithsonian Institution, Gladstone's husband happened to see Scott Simon, who knew Gladstone from the time she was at *Current* and he was covering public broadcasting at NPR. Simon told Kaplan about *Weekend Edition*, a new NPR show he was hosting; his editor, he said, had to take a few weeks off. "What's Brooke doing?" Simon asked Kaplan. At that point Gladstone had not done any radio work, and the only editing she had under her belt was for print publications, but she was intrigued by the idea. After contracting meningitis and spending nine days in the hospital, Gladstone took on what she thought would be a temporary gig at NPR. Then the editor whom she replaced decided to stay in California, and a career opportunity opened for Gladstone. The year was 1987; Gladstone stayed on as senior editor of *Weekend Edition* for three years, during which she received, in her capacity as editor, a Peabody Award and the Ohio State award. She then became the senior editor of NPR's *All Things Considered*, a daily show that combines news, commentary, interviews, and analysis. For her work as senior editor, she received the Overseas Press Club Award. "I think one reason I was a good editor—and I moved up quickly at NPR—was because I had a very acute sense of pacing," Gladstone said. "I could tell when things were dragging. I could tell when the ideas slip off the track or become muddied."

Gladstone's husband, who was working for the *Boston Globe* at the time, was expecting to be offered the position of Moscow, Russia, bureau chief for the paper. Gladstone was happy for her husband, but her excitement was qualified: "I said we couldn't go," she recalled, "unless I got this fellowship [a Knight Fellowship from Stanford University], because I didn't want to go [to Russia] and be one of those spouses who didn't know how to speak or how to report and didn't understand what I was doing. I said, 'If I get this fellowship, I will focus on all things Russian.' I already knew a lot of Russian literature, because I was really fond of it, but I didn't know much about Russian political theory, art, architecture, Russian Orthodoxy. I was the one who was really pushing Fred to apply for the bureau job. Both of our decisions were contingent on the other person getting what they wanted." What Gladstone remembers as "one of the greatest moments of our married life" occurred when her husband landed the Moscow bureau-chief position on the same day that she was awarded the fellowship. The *Globe* gave Kaplan a year to study, so the couple moved to Palo Alto, California, where they both attended Stanford University. A year, it turned out, was a short time in which to master a language as difficult as Russian. "My reading was never very good, and my writing was almost non-existent," Gladstone said. "But my speaking, I became functional and conversational. But I would always have a translator with me when I did an interview for NPR." The couple, along with their six-year-old twin girls, Sophie and Maxine, moved to Moscow in the summer of 1992, less than a year after the collapse of the Soviet Union.

For the next three years, Gladstone served as NPR's Moscow reporter, focusing mostly on cultural stories. "There was a great deal of tension . . . ," she said, recalling her first impression of Moscow. "But there was a crazy sense of possibility—a new country being created every day. One day, a great story: the legalization of homosexuality. Another day, a terrible story: people being killed for their apartments by the rising organized crime. Then there would be an amazing story, like rewriting the [Soviet era] history textbooks. And then there would be a terrible story about how inflation is turning everybody's pensions to valueless paper." Among other subjects, Gladstone reported on bathhouses, communist summer camps, and the 1993 insurgency on the part of the Russian Parliament, which saw "sniper fire crisscrossing the streets around the Russian white house." While "we couldn't always get in to see the bureaucracy," she found that there was "absolutely no hesitation on the part of ordinary people, business owners, even members of the government" to talk to an American journalist. One of Gladstone's favorite stories was about a man called Doctor Zolotov (*zoloto* is Russian for gold). Zolotov, Gladstone explained, was said to "induce orgasms in his female followers just through the power of his mind." That story, she said, was an example of how people "start looking for guidance and salvation" during uncertain times. That period was a very fertile one for journalism in Russia, as President Boris Yeltsin had allowed independent journalism to flourish. "There was no nervousness about speaking to Americans," she said, "except among people of organized crime. They weren't that receptive to media scrutiny—naturally." That did not stop Gladstone from filing stories about such people and their impact on the country. Those stories illustrated some of the moral gray areas in Russian life, including the ways in which business, government, and organized crime overlapped. "I talked to people who opened kiosks, and they said they preferred to deal with the mafia because the mafia had an interest in their success. But the constant fees that were being exacted by level upon level of government bureaucracy were driving them into bankruptcy, and the government didn't care; so if they paid off the mafia, the mafia would pay off the bureaucracy and protect them from this ever-changing constellation of fees. The official structures were in such disarray that, in some ways, the structures within organized crime were more dependable." Those conditions, Gladstone added, were "emblematic of the chaos all around us, which made it a fantastic story for a reporter who got to parachute into people's lives from time to time, live them for a matter of hours, or a matter of days, or even a matter of weeks, and hop out again. I mean, it's a lot easier to cover these things with a sense of fascination when you have nothing personally at stake." But over time Gladstone developed a connection to the turbulent country. So when, after three years, it came time to leave, "I felt like I was abandoning the friends that I had made and that I was abandoning a story that I had, over time, developed a stake in."

After returning to the U.S., Gladstone became NPR's media correspondent. She reported for WNYC, the network's New York City affiliate. She had mixed feelings about her beat. On the one hand, it allowed her the pleasure of covering nearly unbelievable events, including "one of my favorite stories that I've ever done: There was this one local gallery that was doing an exhibit of this guy who made blueprints of the houses of sitcom families. Then I found out that this guy had been obsessed with sitcoms as a kid in the early '60s. He would cut school and would draw Lucy's house, Mary Tyler Moore's house, and the place where the Addams Family lived, and the *Brady Bunch* house—in such detail. Eventually he figured out that these homes were not coherent—they were just sets—he created blueprints of how these places would be if they were laid out. This was before VCRs, so it was only from repeated viewing. He was socially dysfunctional. And when I talked to him, he told me he had been clean and sober from television for three years. That is a story that says so much about American culture—not that all of us are like that, but in this extreme example, in this story of an obsessive, is writ large the story of all of us. I got a lot of mail after that story." On the other hand, Gladstone admitted, during the five years that she covered the media, she grew tired of her job at times. "What I didn't like about the media beat at NPR was that I would be asked to do a three-and-a-half minute piece every time Tina Brown [who was then the editor of the *New Yorker*] passed wind (or so it seemed to me)," Gladstone wrote for transom.org, a Web site that covers public radio.

As someone who was "sick to death" of the media beat, Gladstone was reluctant to join National Public Radio's weekly magazine-style program *On the Media*. But Dean Cappello—*On the Media*'s executive producer and the vice president for programming and operations at WNYC, where the show was broadcast—wanted her help in reviving the show, which was understaffed, uneven in quality, and underfunded. Gladstone accepted the offer. "So, in the end, I thought if I'm going to cover media for the rest of my life, I might as well cover it the way I want." *On the Media*, with Gladstone as managing editor and co-host with Bob Garfield, relaunched in January 2001. "The program," Gladstone explained, "tries to function as an outsider's in into how the media are created, how stories are chosen, how things are presented. We also try and pick apart cultural trends that are reflected by the media. We also, especially in the last few years, have worked very hard to do stories on what we call 'the conditions that enable us to do journalism'—so we talk a great deal about First Amendment issues, secrecy issues, freedom of information issues, whistle-blower issues, privacy issues. All of these things that could impinge upon the free flow of information." *On the Media*, Gladstone said, also "holds up the mirror" to society by discussing the meanings, uses, and implications of frequently used words, such as "marriage," "pro-life," "elite," "recession," and "torture." In addition, the show has discussed, with the help of media experts and scientists, how people process information, especially when it contradicts their worldviews. "You have to trust your audience," Gladstone said. "You present the story as you see it, but you present it fairly, and you don't just present one side. That doesn't mean you create a false equivalency. And then you let your audience take this information in, and they may come to a different conclusion."

Even though Gladstone had been a journalist for nearly 20 years by the time the program relaunched, she felt—and still feels—like a bit of an outsider, "a mediator between the journalism world and the world of people who consume journalism." The paradox is that while, as a journalist, she often feels like an outsider, as a private person she craves a journalistic approach to life. For example, after the September 11, 2001 terrorist attacks on the U.S., *On the Media* had to go off the air for a week. "I found it excruciating that I couldn't report the story. I don't think I've ever gotten over it—not because I wanted to be on the air so much as that I can't process information that well anymore unless I'm interpreting it for people outside myself. It just goes in there in a congealed mass and I can't sort through the strands unless I have the assignment of making it understandable to somebody else. So in that sense, I feel like I have journalism now sort of worked into my bones and mutating my DNA somehow. . . . That's not about me identifying with a community (i.e. journalists) so much as it is about my way of dealing with the entire outside world of ideas and emotions."

Gladstone lives in Brooklyn, New York, with her husband. In addition to her work for NPR, she is currently writing a graphic novel, tentatively titled "The Influencing Machine," about media history, in collaboration with the artist Josh Neufeld. She is also a big fan of science fiction; her cell-phone ring tone is the theme from the TV series *Star Trek: The Next Generation*.

—D.K.

Suggested Reading: *On the Media* Web site; transom.org

Courtesy of Wycliffe Gordon

Gordon, Wycliffe

May 29, 1967– Jazz trombonist

Address: c/o Coup de Cone Music Inc., 126 W. 121st St., Suite 4, New York, NY 10027

Nicknamed "Pine Cone" by his peers for his rotund frame and Georgia roots, Wycliffe Gordon is a leading player of arguably the most overlooked instrument in jazz: the trombone. Widely regarded as the greatest trombonist working in jazz today, Gordon has drawn comparisons to such legendary players as Tommy Dorsey and J. J. Johnson. Gordon, who has performed with jazz luminaries including Dizzy Gillespie, Joe Henderson, Lionel Hampton, Tommy Flanagan, and Shirley Horn, established his reputation with his work alongside Wynton Marsalis, as a member of the Lincoln Center Jazz Orchestra (LCJO) and the Wynton Marsalis Septet. His playing displays a wide range of influences, from big band to swing to straight-ahead jazz to gospel. Ben Ratliff, a jazz critic for the *New York Times* (July 6, 2003), wrote that Gordon "can outperform nearly anyone playing jazz. He's masterful with mutes, but on the deeper levels of music-making, he has an amazing capacity for playing bravura passages quietly." Nate Chinen, writing for the same publication (January 19, 2007), called him "a superior technician with a gift for buoyant swing." Gordon has enjoyed a thriving solo career and gained a reputation as a skilled composer, arranger, performer, and jazz educator, as well as a multi-instrumentalist proficient on the didgeridoo, trumpet, tuba, and piano. His discography includes 13 solo albums and nine as co-leader of a band; he has also been a featured guest performer on numerous recordings with the Wynton Marsalis Septet, Lincoln Center Jazz Orchestra, and many other groups. In addition, Gordon has lent his musical talents to a variety of other projects, which include a reorchestration of the theme song for National Public Radio's popular news program *All Things Considered*; a musical tribute to Muhammad Ali, titled *I Saw the Light* (2004); and scores for classic silent films, among them D. W. Griffith's *Intolerance* (1916) and Oscar Micheaux's *Body and Soul* (1925). He received the Jazz Journalists Association Award for Trombonist of the Year in 2001 and 2002, the Jazz Journalists Association Critics' Choice Award in 2000, and a nomination for the Jazzpar Award in 2003. On the subject of the trombone's being one of the more underappreciated instruments in jazz, Gordon told Wayne Bledsoe for the Knoxville, Tennessee, *News Sentinel* (April 14, 2006), "The voice of the trombone is a force to be reckoned with. . . . I feel it can hold its own with the trumpet and saxophone. It just so happens that the trombone is the hardest to master."

Wycliffe Gordon was born on May 29, 1967 in Waynesboro, Georgia, a small town 30 miles south of Augusta. He was raised in a religious household; his introduction to music was through the gospel performed at Waynesboro's Springfield Baptist

Church. Gordon's late father, Lucius, was a classically trained pianist and the church's resident organist; his influence helped further spark Gordon's interest in music. His father "was always playing classical music at home," Gordon noted to Mike Hughes for the *Lansing State Journal* (November 10, 2004). Wanting at first to play drums, Gordon turned to the trombone after his older brother, Lucius Jr., began playing the instrument in his junior-high-school band. When the family got a trombone for Lucius Jr., "they took it out of the case, and it was shining and beautiful. I knew that's what I wanted," Gordon recalled to Hughes.

Gordon became interested in jazz at the age of 13, when his aunt gave the family a five-disc set of jazz recordings. The collection introduced him to the music of Louis Armstrong, Dizzy Gillespie, and Sonny Rollins as well as the big bands of the 1930s and 1940s. "I would just listen to that over and over," Gordon recalled to Wayne Bledsoe. "The one that really got me was Louis Armstrong's 'Keyhole Blues.'" His passion for jazz developed quickly, and he started playing the trombone in his high-school band. He has credited his high-school band director and his mother, Lena, with giving him the encouragement and support necessary to take his musical pursuits to the next level. He noted to T. Ballard Lesemann for the *Charleston City Paper* (May 20, 2009, on-line), "They made sure I was available to try out for all-county band, all-state band, the McDonald's All-American High School Band . . . they were always there to support me, and always told me I could do it, rather than what I couldn't do." While in high school he won awards for music.

Gordon enrolled at Florida's Agricultural and Mechanical University (Florida A&M), in Tallahassee, where he studied music. As a sophomore he caught the attention of a visitor to the school, the trumpeter Wynton Marsalis, who was leading a national revival of traditional or "straight-ahead" jazz. After hearing Gordon play, Marsalis introduced him to his pianist, Marcus Roberts; Gordon and Roberts went on to have several discussions. As time went on, though, Gordon found himself discouraged by jazz's lack of popularity, the Marsalis-led movement notwithstanding. Shortly after graduating, in 1989, he was working at a Pizza Hut restaurant, having more or less given up on music, when Marsalis invited him to join the Wynton Marsalis Septet. As posted on the University of Scranton Web site, Gordon recalled, "I didn't learn as much about the instrument until I started with Wynton. He introduced me to trombone players on the road, including cats with symphonies who came to concerts, and I picked up tips from them." He added, "Being in the band was like music heaven."

Along with the septet, Gordon joined the Lincoln Center Jazz Orchestra, also led by Marsalis, and David Ostwald's Gully Low Jazz Band. He played with the septet until it disbanded, in late 1994, and remained with the LCJO until 2002. Gordon contributed to Marsalis's celebrated band as both musician and composer. His albums with Marsalis's band include *Crescent City Christmas Card* (1989); the original soundtrack from the film *Tune In Tomorrow* (1989); *Blue Interlude* (1991); *Citi Movement* (1992); *In This House, On This Morning* (1992); *Joe Cool's Blues* (1994); *Big Train* (1999); *Live at the Village Vanguard* (1999); *Marciac Suite* (1999); and *Reeltime* (1999). He was also featured on recordings by the LCJO, including *Blood on the Fields* (1997) and *Jump Start & Jazz* (1997). During his time in both outfits, Gordon developed his melodic approach to playing and performed alongside some of jazz's greatest virtuosos. He also got his start in composing and was commissioned to reorchestrate the theme song for the popular National Public Radio show *All Things Considered* in 1993. (His is the third version of the theme, penned by Don Voegeli in 1976.)

For the 1996 album *Bone Structure*, Gordon served as co-leader with his fellow trombonist Ron Westray; the two performed 12 tunes they had written separately or together. The album also featured the work of Marcus Roberts, the bassist Reginald Veal, and the drummer Herlin Riley. In a review for the All Music Guide, Scott Yanlow wrote, "The music sometimes looks toward the swing tradition but also has some post bop and fairly free selections. The extroverted personalities (and occasional humor) of the co-leaders make this often-rambunctious set of strong interest." Gordon's next recording as bandleader, *Slidin' Home* (1999), displayed a variety of styles and influences, from big band to gospel. The album featured other top jazz performers, including Riley, the saxophonist Victor Goines, the pianist Eric Reed, and the bassist Rodney Whitaker. Commenting on the album's wide range of styles, Dave Nathan wrote for the All About Jazz Web site, "Gordon runs the gamut from blues to gospel, from swing to Latin, from classical sounding to bop, often employing more than one of these genres on the same tune." He added, "Gordon can swing, slide, and tongue with the trombone. . . . This is a very interesting, attention-keeping album and is highly recommended."

In 2000 Gordon was commissioned to write a score for Oscar Micheaux's *Body and Soul*, a silent film, starring Paul Robeson, about religion, duplicity, and small-town life in the 1920s-era South. (The film was sometimes screened with the accompaniment of jazz bands at the time of its initial release.) For the score, performed with the Lincoln Center Jazz Orchestra, Gordon drew on his southern roots, with nods to church music, work songs, and early jazz. The score included vocal arrangements sung by Gordon himself. Also in 2000 Gordon released the eclectic solo effort *The Search*, on the Nagel-Heyer label. That album showcased Gordon's proficiency on other instruments in addition to the trombone, such as the tuba and didgeridoo (a long wind instrument normally used in the playing of Australian aboriginal music), on songs including "Sign Me Up" and "Blues for Deac'n

Cone." In 2001 he released, on the Criss Cross label, *What You Dealin' With*, which was made up of four original compositions and six jazz standards by masters including Duke Ellington, John Coltrane, and Dizzy Gillespie. Among Gordon's albums released over the next couple of years were *We* (2002) and *The Joyride* (2003), both on the Nagel-Heyer label. On the former he collaborated with Eric Reed on jazz and gospel songs, and on the latter he sang and demonstrated his talents on trombone, tuba, trumpet, piano, and other instruments. In a review of *The Joyride*, Ben Ratliff wrote for the *New York Times* (July 6, 2003), "[Gordon] creates music so tight and light that it seems to float."

Other recordings that Gordon has released on the Criss Cross label include *United Soul Experience* (2002), *Dig This!!* (2003), *In the Cross* (2004), and *Cone's Coup* (2006). In 2006 he recorded *Standards Only*, for the Nagel-Heyer label. That year he also served as co-leader on the album *This Rhythm on My Mind* (2006), a BluesBack Records release that evoked the vocal styles of Louis Armstrong and Fats Waller. On the album Gordon served as co-leader with the acoustic bassist Jay Leonhart and was joined by the tenor saxmen Wayne Escoffery and Harry Allen and the percussionist Jim Saporito. In 2007 Gordon was commissioned by Harlem in the Himalayas Jazz Series, a project of the Jazz Museum in Harlem, to create a jazz score for D.W. Griffith's silent-film masterpiece *Intolerance*. Composing music for each of the film's four stories, he later recalled to Rom Scott for the *New York Amsterdam News* (February 22–28, 2007) that his work on that project "was the hardest I've played in some time." Two of Gordon's latest solo albums, *Boss Bones* and *You and I*, were released on the Criss Cross and BluesBack labels, respectively, in June 2008.

Gordon, who has five children, lives and works in New York City. He has taught at Michigan State University, the Juilliard School, and the University of North Carolina at Greensboro and currently teaches in the Jazz Arts Program at the Manhattan School of Music, in New York. Among jazz's most committed educators, Gordon has presented master classes, clinics, workshops, children's classes, and lectures in numerous venues around the world. He has been working on a collection of trombone quartets, trios, and duos, collectively titled "Trombone Majesty," and on a book on trombone methodology, titled "Basic Training, Exercises, and Suggested Studies," both of which were scheduled to appear in 2009. Gordon's *I Saw the Light*, a musical tribute to the boxer Muhammad Ali, commissioned and premiered by the Brass Band of Battle Creek in March 2004, was also scheduled for release on DVD in 2009. Gordon is the youngest member of the U.S. Statesmen of Jazz and serves as a musical ambassador for the U.S. State Department. His compositions have been performed in programs throughout the U.S. and abroad, including concert halls in New York City; Los Angeles, California; Aspen, Colorado; and cities in Germany, England, Finland, and Switzerland.

—C.C.

Suggested Reading: All About Jazz (on-line); (Des Moines, Iowa) *Register* O p4 Oct. 17, 2004; (Knoxville, Tennessee) *News Sentinel* p8 Apr. 14, 2006; *Lansing State Journal* D p1 Nov. 10, 2004; *New York Sun* p13 Jan. 26, 2007; University of Scranton Web site; Wycliffe Gordon Official Web site

Selected Recordings: with Wynton Marsalis Septet and Lincoln Center Jazz Orchestra—*Crescent City Christmas Card*, 1989; *Tune in Tomorrow* (motion picture soundtrack), 1989; *Blue Interlude*, 1991; *Citi Movement*, 1992; *In This House, On This Morning*, 1992; *Joe Cool's Blues*, 1994; *Blood on the Fields*, 1997; *Jump Start & Jazz*, 1997; *Big Train*, 1999; *Live at the Village Vanguard*, 1999: *Marcias Suite*, 1999; *Reeltime*, 1999; as solo artist and bandleader—*Bone Structure*, 1996; *Slidin' Home*, 1999; *The Gospel Truth*, 2000; *The Search*, 2000; *What You Dealin' With*, 2001; *We*, 2002; *United Soul Experience*, 2002; *The Joyride*, 2003; *Dig This!!*, 2003; *In the Cross*, 2004; *Cone's Coup*, 2006; *Standards Only*, 2006; *This Rhythm on My Mind*, 2006; *Boss Bones*, 2008; *You and I*, 2008

Gordon-Reed, Annette

Nov. 19, 1958– Historian; lawyer; writer; educator

Address: New York Law School, 57 Worth St., New York, NY 10013

In 2009 the historian, lawyer, and educator Annette Gordon-Reed won the Pulitzer Prize in history for her fourth book, *The Hemingses of Monticello: An American Family*. The book concerns Thomas Jefferson, the third president of the United States, Sally Hemings, his slave and mistress, and the children Hemings bore Jefferson—as well as Hemings's parents and siblings and the two surviving daughters from Jefferson's union with his wife, Martha, who was Sally Hemings's half-sister. In its examination of the complex familial relationships that existed between the Jeffersons and the Hemingses, Gordon-Reed's 800-page book also sheds light on the relationships between other blacks and whites and on the plantation system that thrived in the American South before the abolition of slavery. *The Hemingses of Monticello*, in the words of the National Book Award citation, is a "mesmerizing narrative" that offers "the steady accretion of convincing argument" and is "at once a painstaking history of slavery, an unflinching gaze at the ways

Courtesy of Annette Gordon-Reed

Annette Gordon-Reed

it has defined us, and a humane exploration of lives—grand and humble—that our 'peculiar institution' conjoined. . . . More than the story of Jefferson and Hemings, it is a deeply moral and keenly intelligent probe of the harsh yet all-too-human world they inhabited and the bloodline they shared." *The Hemingses of Monticello* was published 11 years after *Thomas Jefferson and Sally Hemings: An American Controversy*, Gordon-Reed's first book, which, in its preface, she described as "a critique of the defense that has been mounted to counter the notion of a Jefferson–Hemings liaison." In presenting her critique, Gordon-Reed made use of her skills as a lawyer to analyze an enormous quantity of evidence, much of it previously disregarded or interpreted from perspectives radically different from her own. "This story has totally taken over my life," she told Vicki Hambleton for *Footsteps* (on-line), a now-defunct magazine devoted to African-American heritage, after the publication of her first Jefferson/Hemings book. "It's amazing to me that something that I have been interested in since I was a kid should come to this, but it is wonderful." Gordon-Reed worked for a corporate law firm for three years in the 1980s, then as an attorney with the New York City Board of Correction for four years. She has taught at the New York Law School, in Manhattan, since 1992 and at the Newark, New Jersey, campus of Rutgers University since 2006. She co-wrote the award-winning *Vernon Can Read!* (2001), a memoir by Vernon Jordan, the onetime president of the National Urban League, prominent businessman, and adviser to President Bill Clinton, and she edited *Race on Trial: Law and Justice in American History* (2002), for which she wrote one chapter and the introduction.

Gordon-Reed's short biography of President Andrew Johnson, which she has referred to as a "side trip" from her main interests as a historian—Jefferson, slavery, and the newly independent United States—will be published in 2009. She is also working on another book about the Hemingses, a chronicle that will continue their story into the early 20th century. After that she intends to write a two- or three-volume biography of Jefferson. "I've thought for a long time that we are overdue for a complete overhaul," she commented to David Liebers for the History News Network (November 24, 2008, on-line)—an "overhaul" that will reflect what she and others have learned and deduced about his life and times, unhampered by the desire to present Jefferson as a godlike figure who would never have acted upon or even felt carnal desire for a woman of color. Any biography, she said in an interview conducted for Amazon.com, is "a combination of what people said about their lives, inferences from the actions they took, and a consideration of the context in which they were living. Some people have problems with the use of 'inferences.' I don't, so long as they are reasonable. In fact, I would trust the reasonable inferences from a person's repeated behavior through the years over what they say any day, because people can say anything."

Gordon-Reed was born Annette Gordon on November 19, 1958 and grew up in the small town of Conroe, Texas, about 50 miles north of Houston. Her father, Alfred Gordon Sr., owned a funeral parlor and a store; her mother, Bettye Jean Gordon, was a high-school English teacher. Segregation was a part of daily life in Conroe during her girlhood; at the local health clinic, for example, blacks and whites sat in separate waiting rooms, and in the movie theater, blacks were relegated to the balcony. Gordon-Reed told David Schulman for the public-radio program *Weekend America* (December 13, 2008, on-line) that although blacks and whites now mix freely in her hometown, and white grandmothers can be seen with their mixed-race grandchildren in the local Wal-Mart—a sight that "would have been unheard of back in the 60s and 70s"—the distribution of power and the economic divisions in the town "are pretty much the same." Gordon-Reed attended kindergarten in a segregated school. Then, at age six, she became the first African-American to be admitted to a previously all-white public elementary school. "I was a bit on display," she told Deborah Solomon for the *New York Times Magazine* (December 5, 2008). "I can remember adults looking into my classroom and thinking: See? The books have not exploded. There's nothing weird going on here." As a child Gordon-Reed was a voracious reader, and she especially loved history. She has traced her interest in Thomas Jefferson to a juvenile biography of him that she read as a third-grader. The book depicted Jefferson as a child and was narrated by a fictional slave, a boy his age; bosom buddies when the story begins, they drift apart as Jefferson turns toward intellectual pursuits. "It was my first take on how black people were presented in history books," Gordon-Reed told Daryl Royster Alexander for the *New York Times* (June 29, 1997), "and my first major annoyance at the way that black people were portrayed. Why did the slave have to be shown to be stupid and unimportant in order to make Jefferson look good?" The characterization of the black boy as "a person of no consequence and no curiosity," Gordon-Reed recalled to Patricia Cohen for the *New York Times* (September 19, 2008), further dismayed her because she regarded him as a "stand-in" for herself and feared that any of her white classmates who read the book would do so as well.

At 12 Gordon-Reed read the 1969 National Book Award winner, *White Over Black: American Attitudes Toward the Negro, 1550–1812* (1967), by the historian Winthrop D. Jordan. A chapter in the book about Jefferson and Hemings sparked her interest in their connection. Two years later, lying about her age, she joined the Book-of-the-Month Club and bought *Thomas Jefferson: An Intimate History* (1974), in which the historian Fawn Brodie wrote about Jefferson and Hemings's 38-year-long affair. Gordon-Reed was particularly intrigued by the contradictions evident in Jefferson's life and work. A book lover who was "curious about the world," as Gordon-Reed described him to Schulman, Jefferson was the principal author of the Declaration of Independence, which states that "all men are created equal"; yet, as was usual for landed gentry in Virginia at that time, he owned many slaves—about 100. He considered people of African descent mentally and physically inferior to whites, and for that reason he disapproved, at least publicly, of interracial unions. He also thought that freed blacks should be shipped back to Africa. (As Gordon-Reed later learned, he felt otherwise about Sally Hemings, her siblings, and her children.)

Gordon-Reed majored in history at Dartmouth College, in Hanover, New Hampshire. In classes about the history of the South and slavery in the U.S., she was the only black student. She earned a B.A. in 1981 and then entered Harvard Law School, in Cambridge, Massachusetts, where she was a staff member of the *Harvard Law Review*. While there she audited an undergraduate class about the Reconstruction era and again found herself surrounded solely by whites. She later learned that her black peers avoided courses in African-American history because many pre– or post–Civil War accounts by whites regarding blacks were colored by their writers' contempt for or condescension toward blacks, making them painful to read. After Gordon-Reed received a J.D. degree, in 1984, she was hired as an associate at Cahill Gordon & Reindel, a well-established New York City firm specializing in corporate law and litigation. Cahill actively sought to make its workforce racially and ethnically diverse, and its employees performed an unusual amount of pro-bono work. In 1987 Gordon-Reed left the private sector to serve as counsel to the New York City Board of Correction, a watchdog group that monitored conditions in the city's prisons. In that position she learned firsthand about racial biases that persist in the American criminal-justice system.

Such biases are the subject of the essays in the book *Race on Trial: Law and Justice in American History* (2002), which Gordon-Reed edited. *Race on Trial* contains 12 original essays by Gordon-Reed and 11 other professors of political science, history, and/or law, including "The Impact of the *Amistad* Case on Race and Law in America (1841)," by Howard Jones; "The Dred Scott Case (1857)," by Xi Wang; "Celia's Case (1857)," by Gordon-Reed; "Race, Identity, and the Law: *Plessy v. Ferguson* (1896)," by Thomas J. Davis; "Jack Johnson versus the American Racial Hierarchy (1913)," by Denise C. Morgan; and *Black and White: The O. J. Simpson Case* (1995), by Walter L. Hixson. In her introduction Gordon-Reed noted that Winthrop Jordan, in *White Over Black*, "wisely suggested caution when studying the operation of law—created, practiced, and administered as it is by elites—as a firm guidepost to what is actually going on in a culture. Legislation and the outcomes of legal cases tell us a lot but not everything about the way people in a given society think, thought, or, most important, actually behave." Nevertheless, she continued, legal cases—"trials in particular—provide critical insights into the values, mores, obsessions, and aspirations (lived up to and not) of members of the community at particular moments in history. It is with this knowledge that the essays in this volume use legal disputes in which the concept of race plays a central role to explore American attitudes . . . about the proper boundaries between the races."

Gordon-Reed's essay in *Race on Trial* is about a slave called Celia, whose master, a recently widowed grandfather, raped her on the day he bought her, when she was 14, and forced himself upon her repeatedly during the next five years, impregnating her at least twice. One day, at the urging of a male slave with whom she had become intimate, Celia attempted to repel her master's advances. When that failed, she struck him with a large stick; the second blow killed him, and she burned his body in her fireplace. The master's family requested that she be tried, and her lawyers—unusually for that time—mounted a carefully constructed defense. As Gordon-Reed wrote, "They relied on a Missouri statute that allowed 'any woman' to use deadly force to protect her honor. Celia's counsel argued that 'any woman' was meant to include slave women as well." Guided by the judge's bias—he invariably ruled in favor of the prosecution—the all-male jury rejected that argument and found her guilty, as did the Missouri Supreme Court when Celia's lawyers appealed the verdict. In concluding her essay, Gordon-Reed wrote, "Celia's story should be remembered . . . because it shows without equivocation the ultimate meaning of slavery in America. Celia's body, like that of all slaves, was a form of property. An appeal that rested on the value of her soul had no place in a legal system devoted to protecting the right of men like [her master] to enjoy their property as they saw fit. As history bears out, the law was simply not the vehicle for resolving the injustices made so clear by Celia's unhappy life."

Earlier, in 1991, years before *Race on Trial* was published, Gordon-Reed had left her job with the board of corrections. The next year she joined the faculty of the New York Law School, the second-oldest independent law school in the U.S., as a professor. During her 18 years at the school, Gordon-Reed has taught courses in American slavery and the law, American legal history, investigation in criminal cases, the legal profession, and property law. At Rutgers University she teaches undergraduate courses in the American republic and graduate courses in topics in American political and legal history.

Gordon-Reed's first book, *Thomas Jefferson and Sally Hemings: An American Controversy*, was published in 1997. In that work Gordon-Reed offered no definitive judgment as to whether Jefferson had had sexual relations and sired children with Sally Hemings, a house slave who became his mistress—or concubine, as her son Madison Hemings and others have labeled her, regarding that word as implying bondage as well as cohabitation. Instead, Gordon-Reed illuminated the ways in which historians had treated that matter, particularly the attempt by many of them to ignore or dismiss historical evidence that bears directly on the close connections between Jefferson and Hemings. Such evidence includes the recollections of Madison Hemings, which was published in 1873, and a written account by Israel Jefferson, a former slave at Monticello. In her book Gordon-Reed noted that shortly before Jefferson's wife, Martha, died, in 1782, when he was 39, he promised at her request never to remarry. He was not obliged to remain celibate, however. Sally Hemings, who was born in about 1773 to Martha's father, Thomas Wayles, and his slave Elizabeth "Betty" Hemings (whose father was white), reportedly resembled Martha strongly and was similarly beautiful. After Wayles's death, in 1773, Betty and some of her children, including Sally, came to Monticello, Jefferson's Virginia home, to live and work as slaves. During his years as the U.S. ambassador to France (1785–89), Jefferson brought not only his two surviving daughters to Paris with him but also Sally Hemings and her brother James, who trained as a chef there at Jefferson's expense. The first of Hemings's children, a boy who died soon after birth, when Sally was 17, and all of her subsequent children were conceived during periods when Hemings and Jefferson were together; seven-eighths white, all were said to look strikingly like Jefferson. All bore the names of people among Jefferson's family or friends; none were named for any of their Hemings antecedents. Moreover, like Jefferson, Sally's sons, Beverley, Madison, and Eston, all played the violin—Eston professionally—and all became skilled woodworkers; her daughter, Harriet, learned spinning and weaving. Gordon-Reed told the Amazon.com interviewer that "the Hemings children were trained to leave slavery without ever developing the sensibilities of servants." Furthermore, the few slaves whom Jefferson freed during his lifetime (among them Beverley and Harriet) or in his will (Madison and Eston) were all Hemingses. (After Jefferson's death Sally, with the permission of Jefferson's daughter Martha, left Monticello to live with Madison and Eston.) Jill Lepore, writing for the *New Yorker* (September 22, 2008), described *Thomas Jefferson and Sally Hemings: An American Controversy* as "as much a painstaking investigation of the documentary record as a devastating brief on standards of evidence in historical research."

During a conference held at the University of Virginia and Monticello in 1999, Gordon-Reed said, as quoted by Lepore, "It is true that we do not and will never have the details of what went on between Jefferson and Hemings and their children. This does not mean that we have nothing to go on. Perhaps the most persistent, and ultimately damaging, feature of the original debate over whether the relationship existed at all was the tight rein placed upon the historical imagination. One was simply not to let one's mind wander too freely over the matter. Brainstorming, drawing reasonable inferences from actions, attempting to piece together a plausible view of the matter were shunted into the category of illegitimate speculation, as grave an offense as outright lying."

In her preface to *Thomas Jefferson and Sally Hemings*, Gordon-Reed wrote, "It is not my goal to prove that the story [of their affair] is true or that it is false. I suspect that if that is ever done, it will be the result of the miracles of modern science and all the wonders of DNA research, and not because of any interpretation of documents and statements." In the November 5, 1998 issue of *Nature*, Eugene A. Foster, a pathologist, and two other scientists reported that analyses by British geneticists of DNA samples taken from a descendent of Eston Hemings (who took the surname Jefferson as an adult) and the descendants of Field Jefferson, a paternal uncle of Thomas Jefferson's, showed with more than 99 percent certainty that Eston was the president's son. "If people had accepted this story [decades ago], [Jefferson] would never have become an icon," Gordon-Reed said to Dinitia Smith and Nicholas Wade for the *New York Times* (November 1, 1998) after the new evidence became public. Referring to the scholars who had dismissed the possibility of Jefferson's fathering a child with Hemings, she continued, "All these historians did him a favor until we could get past our primitive racism. I don't think he would have been on Mount Rushmore or on the nickel. The personification of America can't live 38 years with a black woman." For Princeton University Press, Gordon-Reed is compiling a collection of Jefferson's writings about race.

When David Liebers asked her what drew her to write *The Hemingses of Monticello* (2008), Gordon-Reed responded, "While finishing my first book, it occurred to me that there was a lot of information about the Hemingses that could be put in narrative form. I thought it would be useful to tell the family story, as a story. Sally Hemings . . . has been seen as a symbol, or as a 'problem.' She has been divorced from her context. It's hard to get a handle on her without putting her in context, just as it is hard to get a handle on [Jefferson]'s life without putting him in his context as a slaveholder who had a particular relationship with this family." In carrying out her research for the book, she said, she discovered new material as well as material that had been "overlooked," and she "looked at things in a different way. For example, I traveled to London and to Preston, Lancashire to ferret out information about John Wayles, [Sally Hemings's] father and Jefferson's father-in-law. That's all new stuff. The section on France contains new information, along with material that has been there all along, but not looked at or treated as important. Then there are unpublished letters as well."

"Gordon-Reed's genius for reading nearly silent records makes this an extraordinary work," according to a review of *The Hemingses of Monticello* for *Publishers Weekly* (July 14, 2008, on-line). The reviewer also wrote, "This is a scholar's book: serious, thick, complex. It's also fascinating, wise and of the utmost importance. Gordon-Reed . . . brings to life the entire Hemings family and its tangled blood links with slave-holding Virginia whites over an entire century. Gordon-Reed never slips into cynicism about the author of the Declaration of Independence. Instead, she shows how his life was deeply affected by his slave kinspeople: his lover . . . and their children. Everyone comes vividly to life, as do the places, like Paris and Philadelphia, in which Jefferson, his daughters and some of his black family lived. So, too, do the complexities and varieties of slaves' lives and the nature of the choices they had to make—when they had the luxury of making a choice." In a critique for the *New York Review of Books* (October 9, 2008), the historians Edmund S. Morgan and Marie Morgan described *The Hemingses of Monticello* as "a brilliant book. It marks the author as one of the most astute, insightful, and forthright historians of this generation." Some interested parties, however, maintained that the DNA evidence does not prove that Jefferson fathered all seven of Hemings's children. In his review of *In Defense of Thomas Jefferson: The Sally Hemings Sex Scandal* (2009), by the historian and foreign-affairs specialist William G. Hyland Jr., for the *Wall Street Journal* (August 28, 2009), Thomas Lipscomb wrote: "[Hyland] concludes, emphatically, that the male Jefferson family member who fathered Eston Hemings could have been any one of at least seven males. There were, he notes, 'two dozen-plus Jefferson males (with DNA markers in common) roaming Virginia at the time.' The seven include Jefferson's younger brother, Randolph, who had already fathered slave children and who had been invited to Monticello nine months before Eston's birth. Mr. Hyland does not exclude Thomas Jefferson as a possible father of Eston. But he deplores the false assumption that today's limited DNA evidence can answer the question one way or another."

In addition to the Pulitzer Prize, *The Hemingses of Monticello* brought Gordon-Reed the 2008 National Book Award for nonfiction, the 2009 George Washington Book Prize, the 2009 Anisfield-Wolf Book Award, and the 2009 Frederick Douglass Book Prize.

Gordon-Reed has been married to Robert Raymond Reed, a New York City civil-court judge, since 1984. The couple, who live in New York City, have a daughter, Susan Jean Gordon Reed, and a son, Gordon Penn Reed. Gordon-Reed dedicated *The Hemingses of Monticello* to her husband and children.

—J.E.P.

Suggested Reading:*Footsteps Magazine* (on-line); History News Network (on-line) Nov. 24, 2008; *Library Journal* p138 Sep. 1, 2008; National Book Foundation Web site; New York Law School Web site; *Who's Who in America*

Selected Works: *Thomas Jefferson and Sally Hemings: An American Controversy*, 1997; *The Hemingses of Monticello: An American Family*, 2008; as co-author—*Vernon Can Read!* (with Vernon Jordan), 2001; as editor—*Race on Trial: Law and Justice in American History*, 2002

Greenwald, Julie

Sep. 30, 1969– Chairman and COO of Atlantic Records Group

Address: Atlantic Records, 1290 Ave. of the Americas, New York, NY 10104

In February 2009, after 17 years in the industry, the music executive Julie Greenwald was named chairman and chief operating officer (COO) of the Atlantic Records Group. Greenwald had never listened to hip-hop music when, in 1992, Lyor Cohen, then president of Def Jam Records, hired her as a temporary assistant. She soon fell in love with hip-hop and developed a passion for the music business. She set up Def Jam's marketing department and was instrumental in building the careers of LL Cool J, Jay-Z, and DMX. "Some people said rap was just a fad. We knew better," Greenwald told Barbara Kantrowitz and Holly Peterson for *Newsweek* (October 15, 2007). "It was us against the world and we were on the cusp of greatness. We hadn't yet become mainstream, but we were the most significant brand name in urban culture. I was working

Neilson Barnard/Getty Images

Julie Greenwald

with some of the greatest rappers ever." The rap artist and entrepreneur Sean "Diddy" Combs, whose Bad Boy Records label is distributed by Atlantic Records, told Karen Schoemer for *Elle* (July 2009) that Greenwald "grew up on tour buses with LL Cool J and Public Enemy and Run-DMC. She's one of the reasons why hip-hop is where it's at today. She's probably the coolest white Jewish girl in history." Greenwald next became the president of Island Records and executive vice president of the Island Def Jam Music Group. She oversaw Island Records' rock and pop division, helping to promote Kanye West, the Killers, Sum 41, Mariah Carey, and Bon Jovi. When she was named president of Atlantic Records, in 2004, she became one of the few women to head a major label. Since then Greenwald has advanced the careers of many additional top-selling artists, among them T.I., James Blunt, Lupe Fiasco, Jason Mraz, and Missy Elliott. Thanks in part to her foresight and marketing skills, within four years of her appointment, Atlantic had become the number-one-selling record label in the nation.

Various forms of music piracy, combined with the exponential growth of electronic downloading, has led to widespread fears that "the music business is over," Greenwald told Barbara Kantrowitz and Holly Peterson. On the contrary, she continued, "that couldn't be farther from the truth. We've just had to transform ourselves to meet the new ways people are experiencing music. Mobile, digital, songs on TV, strategic licensing—our tools have changed but our outcome is still the same. People will always buy great music and support their favorite artists." Greenwald has topped *Billboard*'s "Women in Music" list twice (2006 and 2008); been named among *Crain's New York Business*'s "40 Under 40" (2005) and "100 Most Influential Women in New York City Business" (2007); and been included among *Hollywood Reporter*'s "Top Women in Entertainment." Lyor Cohen, who now serves as vice chairman of the Warner Music Group and chairman and chief executive officer (CEO) of Warner's U.S. recorded-music division, told Steve Israel for the Middletown, New York, *Times Herald-Record* (December 16, 2007) that Greenwald's "work ethic and drive alone are enough to justify her rise to the top levels of the music industry, but it is her aggressive, cutting-edge approach to A&R [artists and repertoire], marketing and promotion that has kept her there."

The third of four sisters, Julie Ilana Greenwald was born on September 30, 1969. She and her siblings—Ellen, Jodi, and Seena—grew up in Wurtsboro, a village in the Catskill Mountains of New York. Her father, Dennis Greenwald, was a town supervisor and businessman; her mother, Elsa (Konigsberg) Greenwald, was heavily involved in community service and served as a town deputy supervisor. Her parents also owned and operated pharmacies in Wurtsboro and Middletown, New York. (Dennis Greenwald sold their remaining pharmacy in 2003, following the death of his wife in a car accident.) "My parents were very community-oriented," Greenwald told Barbara Kantrowitz and Holly Peterson. "I grew up volunteering at food drives, day camps and food shelters." Greenwald attended Monticello High School, in nearby Monticello, New York, graduating in 1987. She then enrolled at Tulane University, in New Orleans, Louisiana, where she studied English and political science. During those years she was a fan of rock bands, mainly 10,000 Maniacs and the Smiths. After obtaining a B.A. degree, in 1991, she spent a year teaching in the B. W. Cooper Apartments neighborhood of New Orleans as an employee of Teach for America, a nonprofit organization that hires recent college graduates and professionals to teach in urban and rural public schools, with the aim of expanding educational opportunities for underserved children. (At that time the B. W. Cooper Apartments, more commonly known as the Calliope Projects, were notorious for their high rates of violent crime and rampant drug dealing.)

With the intention of soon moving to Washington, D.C., to become an education lobbyist, Greenwald returned to New York for the summer when the school year ended in June 1992. She landed a temporary job as a personal assistant to Lyor Cohen, the president of Def Jam Recordings. Founded in the mid-1980s by the producer Rick Rubin and the entrepreneur Russell Simmons, Def Jam had by the early 1990s become the premier independent hip-hop label in the U.S.; its roster included such celebrated rap artists and groups as Run-DMC, the Beastie Boys, LL Cool J, and Public Enemy. In addition to her role as Cohen's assistant, Greenwald worked with Rush Management, the management division of Def Jam and its umbrella company,

Rush Associated Labels; she managed several groups, including A Tribe Called Quest, EPMD, and Brand Nubian.

Cohen soon moved Greenwald to Def Jam Recordings' promotions department, with the title of promotions coordinator. "I didn't know anything about record-company promotions . . . ," she admitted to Kantrowitz and Peterson. "I programmed the fax machine, created itineraries, launched concert events, anything I set my mind to. I would literally get locked in the office, working around the clock, plotting and scheming. It was the most amazing time of my life. I would dream up hundreds of ideas, some good, some bad, some laughed at, but always encouraged by Lyor. Ignorance was bliss, and my out-of-the-box thinking was rewarded with a huge promotion to start our own marketing department at Def Jam."

Greenwald abandoned her dream of becoming an education lobbyist and remained in New York City. "I loved my new life. I loved hip-hop and everything about it," she told Kantrowitz and Peterson. "I could be as creative as I wanted, writing ads for [the hip-hop magazine] *The Source,* treatments for music videos, multi-artist campaigns—the opportunities were endless. Def Jam was at the top of its game and I was one of the big players behind the scenes." Greenwald designated September through November 1994 the "Month of the Man" to promote the rappers Redman and Method Man. To gain wide acceptance for them and some of Def Jam's other hard-core rappers, she masterminded the 1998 national tour "Survival of the Illest," featuring DMX, Onyx, and the Def Squad. Rather than removing sexual, violent, and other possibly offensive material from the raps, she and her colleagues decided, "'We're bringing the streets back,'" as she told Karen Schoemer. "We came up with a campaign that let [consumers] know that we were dealing with the streets, with the danger, which was what made hip-hop so exciting." The tour generated sales of more than four million records. In 1998, the label's most profitable year up to that point, Def Jam garnered an estimated $176 million in sales and around $40 million in profits.

Earlier, in 1993, Russell Simmons had sold a 60 percent stake in Def Jam to the Universal Music Group, for $33 million. Six years later Universal paid $100 million for the remaining 40 percent. Greenwald, who had been given a stake in the label four years before, became a millionaire. Universal merged Def Jam with its labels Island Records and Mercury Records, creating the Island Def Jam Music Group (IDJ). Despite the merger, Def Jam and Island continued to operate as separate imprints under the IDJ umbrella. (Mercury was dismantled, and most of Mercury's artists were moved to Island.) Simmons retained his post as chairman of Def Jam, while Cohen became chairman and CEO of IDJ. Greenwald was named senior vice president of marketing for IDJ, with responsibility for the marketing of recordings of its entire roster of musicians; those included the popular rappers Jay-Z, DMX, and LL Cool J as well as Island's pop and rock acts—Bon Jovi, Sum 41, Nickelback, and Ryan Adams. Greenwald told Danielle Cantor for *Jewish Woman* magazine (Fall 2008) that for her, the changes were bittersweet. "I never wanted to sell Def Jam and I loved it being small and independent," she said. "But it allowed me to start a whole new chapter in my life with Island records, where I got into the rock world. I'd mastered everything there was to know about hip hop and now I had a chance to do something new—take the best of what I knew about urban music and apply it to the rock side."

In 2002 Greenwald was promoted to executive vice president of IDJ and president of Island Records. In a January 7, 2002 press release, Cohen described Greenwald as "one of the industry's most formidable music executives. She is a world-class marketer and developer of talent, and has written the rules for marketing in this industry. She is exceptionally gifted, excelling in both her creative instincts and extensive industry-wide relationships. Her well rounded understanding of the creative process is stellar, and she is an extraordinary problem solver and resourceful thinker."

Cohen left IDJ in January 2004 to become head of U.S. recorded music at the Warner Music Group, the parent company of Atlantic Records. Greenwald followed her mentor; she was named president of Atlantic two months later. Due to the consolidation of Warner's Atlantic and Elektra labels, as well as a drop in music-industry profits, one of her first tasks was to fire more than 150 people. "I came over eight months pregnant," she recalled to Karen Schoemer. "I ran around the company and had a month to interview as many people as possible, because I knew the date of my C-section. I was looking for people who weren't married to the old Atlantic. Because I was like, 'I am nothing of that. I am this new thing that grew up under this crazy man named Lyor Cohen, and I am a different type of animal.' I really needed people who were going to follow me." Greenwald also reduced the number of artists on the label by half and ended what she deemed frivolous spending, including the purchase of billboard space for ads. She applied cost-efficiency rules to herself: contrary to standard executive practice, she flies economy and rides the subway to work instead of taking taxis or using a car service.

Under Greenwald's leadership, along with that of Atlantic's chairman and CEO, Craig Kallman, Atlantic Records grew substantially. By 2006, the label, which had ranked 13th in market share (in terms of total units sold) in 2004, increased its market share by more than 14 percent and moved to third place among the nation's top-selling labels. Home to a diverse group of artists, Atlantic enjoyed success with Gnarls Barkley, T.I., James Blunt, Panic! at the Disco, Rob Thomas, and Death Cab for Cutie. Greenwald built up the label's urban-market share by signing such popular acts as Yung Joc, Cassie, Young Dro, and Danity Kane. "I love [working with] young artists—sitting down with them and figuring out their goals and objectives and fears, and how to help them achieve their dreams," she told Danielle Cantor. "The greatest thing in the world is to take a new artist and help them break into the masses. To see them change their life economically—buy themselves a home, buy their Mom a home. . . . To know that they trusted you with their livelihood and it paid off." On February 5, 2009 Kallman announced Greenwald's promotion to chairman and COO of Atlantic Records.

Atlantic Records ranked first in the nation in market share in 2008. It was also the first major record label to receive more than 50 percent of its U.S. music sales from digital products—for example, downloads on Apple's iTunes digital music store. Greenwald has been credited as one of the first music executives to embrace the digital age, selling to Sprint Nextel and other telecommunications companies the rights to use music by Atlantic artists as cellphone ring tones and using MySpace, Yahoo!, and other popular Web sites to promote artists. In Greenwald's view, the technological advances of the past few years have been both a blessing and a curse for the music industry. "It's been fantastic; we have a direct relationship with our consumers now. But it's also very problematic. It's too easy for people to download and share music now, so it perpetuates a crime that people don't think is a crime, and as a result a lot of people don't get paid," she told Cantor. "Parents teach kids not to steal— if a child walked into a store and stole a candy bar, a parent would be mortified—but now they buy a kid an iPod and don't ask where the music is coming from. It's stealing, and parents shouldn't look the other way." (Any downloading of sound recordings without permission from an artist or record label is illegal.)

Recently, Greenwald was a part of an industry coalition that successfully lobbied Apple Computer Inc. to raise the price of some music downloads on iTunes from $.99 to $1.29. The new, three-tiered price system, which places the cost of downloading more popular songs at $1.29 and less popular songs at either $.99 or $.69, officially went into effect in April 2009. Many music critics and consumers criticized the move as arising from simple greed. In light of the ongoing economic recession, Sean Daly wrote for the *St. Petersburg (Florida) Times* (April 8, 2009), "what other industry is raising prices these days?" Greenwald has been quick to defend the new pricing system, telling Karen Schoemer, "These writers are focusing on, 'Why are they going to $1.29?'. . . . My artist went into a studio and worked really hard to create something beautiful that you're going to buy for less money than a cup of coffee and have for a lifetime. . . . You think I'm getting rich off $1.29 today? Or my artist is?" (According to several sources, when Apple priced all iTunes song downloads at 99 cents, the company kept 29 cents of each sale and gave 70 cents to the labels. The labels then paid the artists, songwriters, and publishers associated with the song. Generally, an artist received between 10 cents and 20 cents per song.)

Described by Karen Schoemer as "petite and thin-framed" and as having "unruly auburn hair," Greenwald is known to pepper her speech with hip-hop slang. She is married to Lewis Largent, a former music executive who is now a stay-at-home father. The couple met in the mid-1990s, when Largent was the music director for the television network MTV. He worked with Greenwald to acquire an LL Cool J song for the 1996 *Beavis and Butt-head Do America* movie soundtrack. The couple live with their two children, a 10-year-old daughter, Tallulah ("Lulu"), and a five-year-old son, Eli, in the Tribeca neighborhood of Manhattan.

—M.A.S.

Suggested Reading: *Billboard* p25+ June 11, 2005, p30+ Sep. 2, 2006, p30 Oct. 14, 2006, p34 Oct. 13, 2007, p28 Nov. 1, 2008; *Crain's New York Business* p21 Jan. 31–Feb. 5, 2005, pW18 Oct. 7, 2007; *Elle* p122+ July 2009; *Jewish Woman Magazine* (on-line) Fall 2008; (Middletown, New York) *Times Herald-Record* (on-line) Dec. 16, 2007; *Newsweek* p48+ Oct. 15, 2007

Groban, Josh

Feb. 27, 1981– Singer

Address: c/o Luke Burland, Warner Bros. Records Publicity, 3300 Warner Blvd., Burbank, CA 91505

When he is performing at his peak, according to a writer for pbs.org, the singer Josh Groban displays a "spectacular voice that has the power of an operatic tenor but the romantic tenderness of a pop balladeer." In the decade since he launched his career, the 28-year-old Groban has sold more than 23 million albums; he has performed to standing-room-only audiences all over the world and has been featured on the PBS TV series *Great Performances* three times, the first when he was only 21. Groban is usually categorized as a baritone whose range encompasses notes more commonly associated with tenors. Although he has often been hailed as a semiclassical crossover star or as the most successful crossover artist the U.S. has ever produced, he does not fit the definition of "crossover artist"—a singer who achieves success in a genre different from the one in which he or she originally became recognized. That label has been applied to him partly because of the operatic quality of his voice and partly because his repertoire includes songs in Italian, French, and Spanish that are from operas or that many people associate with opera. In an interview with Scott Mervis for the *Pittsburgh (Pennsylvania) Post-Gazette* (August 4,

Dave Hogan/Getty Images

Josh Groban

2004), Groban himself described the songs he performs at his concerts or on his albums as "pop music with many different influences."

A protégé of the multi-Grammy Award–winning songwriter and producer David Foster, Groban came to public notice with his performances as a stand-in at the inauguration of California governor Gray Davis, in 1999; at a rehearsal for that year's Grammy Awards ceremony; and in 2001, as a last-minute replacement for an actor in an episode of the popular TV series *Ally McBeal*. Additional appearances on TV in 2002—on the newsmagazine *20/20*, *The Oprah Winfrey Show*, and the closing ceremony of the Winter Olympics—gave his career further boosts. They also propelled sales of his first album to double-platinum status that year. Groban's discography also includes four studio albums, four CD and DVD sets that contain live recordings, and a greatest-hits collection.

Some music critics have faulted Groban's style, describing it as kitschy or saccharine, and have dismissed the singer as an "adult-contemporary milquetoast," in the words of Simon Vozick-Levinson, writing for *Entertainment Weekly*'s blog "Popwatch" (December 19, 2007, on-line). But Groban has won legions of enthusiastic fans, not only with his abilities as a singer but also with the charm, friendliness, sense of humor, and willingness to poke fun at himself that he exhibits on stage. "Grobanites," as his most devoted fans are called, have launched some two dozen sites dedicated to "Grobania." Through membership fees and Internet sales of Josh Groban T-shirts, mugs, flip-flops, wallets, and other items, the organization Friends of Josh Groban (his official fan club) has raised more than $860,000 for the Josh Groban Foundation, which helps children in need worldwide.

Joshua Winslow Groban was born on February 27, 1981 in Los Angeles, California, to Jack and Melinda "Lindy" (Johnston) Groban. His father is the founder and owner of an executive-search firm; of Russian-Jewish ancestry, Jack Groban converted to Christianity when he married. Lindy Groban, whose forebears were from Norway, worked as an art teacher before becoming a homemaker; currently, she is an interior decorator. After Josh's brother, Christopher, was born, in 1985, the family moved from Malibu, California, to Los Angeles. Starting when he was young, Groban's parents often took him to concerts, operas, and musicals, the last of which he especially loved. According to David Hochman, writing for *In Style* (July 2008), he has played the piano since the age of three. For several years Groban attended the Bridges Academy, a sixth-through-12th-grade prep school in Studio City, California; he took academic classes until early afternoon and then attended school-sponsored theater classes. His first public performance came in the seventh grade, when, at the request of a teacher who had recognized his vocal talents, he sang George Gershwin's "'S Wonderful" at a school talent show. During his teens he learned how to play the guitar and drums and became interested in a range of musical genres, among them popular rock, rap, R&B, and, to a lesser extent, classical.

Groban next enrolled at the Los Angeles County High School for the Arts, with the intention of pursuing a career in musical theater. His parents supported his musical ambitions but "weren't pushy," he told Valerie Scher for the *San Diego (California) Union-Tribune* (April 6, 2007). He starred in school productions of musicals including *Fiddler on the Roof*, *Finian's Rainbow*, and his favorite, *Sweeney Todd*. He also took private voice lessons—his voice already had "a very mature timbre," he told Scher—and spent two summers studying voice at the highly respected Interlochen Center for the Arts, in Michigan. In late 1998 Groban's voice teacher at that time, Seth Riggs, sent to the Canadian-born producer David Foster a tape Groban had made. On the strength of that tape, Foster invited the 17-year-old singer to perform at the inauguration of Gray Davis as governor of California. At the swearing-in ceremony, held in early January 1999, Groban sang "All I Ask of You," from the Andrew Lloyd Webber musical *The Phantom of the Opera*. Several weeks later Foster engaged him as a stand-in for the Italian singer Andrea Bocelli at a rehearsal for the 1999 Grammy Awards ceremony, at which Bocelli was slated to sing with Céline Dion. After some hesitation because of his fear of failure, Groban agreed; at the practice session, he and Dion sang "The Prayer," by Foster and Carol Bayer Sager. "Céline had to take my hand a few times to keep me from shaking," he told Jon Bream for the Minneapolis, Minnesota, *Star Tribune* (February 6, 2004). "But it was exhilarating."

After his high-school graduation, in 1999, Groban enrolled in the musical-theater program at Carnegie Mellon University, in Pittsburgh, Pennsylvania. At Foster's urging he left the school after only one semester. "When David pulled me out of obscurity and took me out of college, he said, 'Look, you don't have to do musical theater,'" Groban recalled to Keith Spera for the New Orleans, Louisiana, *Times-Picayune* (March 11, 2005). "You don't have to play a character right now. You can play yourself. I want to make an album with your face and your name and your voice." In late 1999 Groban signed a recording contract with Foster's label, 143, a subsidiary of Warner Bros. Records. Earlier, Foster had begun to promote Groban by having him perform at benefits. At one of them Groban drew the attention of the television producer and writer David E. Kelley, who, with his wife, the actress Michelle Pfeiffer, co-hosted the event. The enthusiastic reaction of the audience, which included President Bill Clinton and Hillary Clinton, to Groban's performance led Kelley to offer him a guest spot in that season's last installment of one of Kelley's most popular TV series, *Ally McBeal*. Groban was slated to appear in a cameo role, but the arrest of the actor Robert Downey Jr., who played one of the main characters, forced Kelley and his team of writers into last-minute rewrites, and they gave Groban a major part. Groban portrayed a geeky high-school student named Malcolm Wyatt, who hires the show's title character (played by Calista Flockhart) to fill in as his prom date after his original date dumps him. During the episode, which aired on May 21, 2001, Groban sang "You're Still You," written by Linda Thompson (who was then Foster's wife) and Ennio Morricone. Within hours thousands of viewers sent e-mail messages to the station extolling Groban's performance.

That lucky break notwithstanding, sales of Groban's eponymous debut album, released in November 2001, remained modest for some months. The album received tepid critical reviews. William Ruhlmann, writing for the All Music Guide (online), described it as "an ersatz classical crossover record that won't fool the experts," but he added that the album was "enjoyable even if it doesn't live up to its pretensions." Then, on February 24, 2002, Groban performed "The Prayer," one of the songs from his album, with Charlotte Church at the closing ceremonies of that year's Winter Olympic Games, in Salt Lake City, Utah; afterward, thanks to the estimated worldwide audience of at least a billion people who watched that event on TV, Internet sales of *Josh Groban* increased significantly. Sales rose far more after his appearances on the *Today* show, the *Tonight Show*, *Good Morning America*, and, especially, in a 10-minute profile of Groban on the April 12, 2002 installment of the ABC-TV series *20/20*: within a week the album had jumped from number 121 to number 12 on the *Billboard* album chart. As of mid-2009 sales of *Josh Groban* totaled four million copies in the U.S. and more than 5.3 million copies in other countries. On July 11, 2002 Groban was a guest on *The Oprah Winfrey Show*, and the next month "To Where You Are" became the first of several of his singles to rank at the top of the "adult-contemporary" charts.

The video of a concert that Groban gave in Pasadena, California, in October 2002 aired soon afterward on the PBS television series *Great Performances*. The DVD of that show went on sale in December 2002, packaged in combination with *Josh Groban in Concert*, a CD of live Groban performances. The DVD also included footage of Groban singing duos or trios with others, among them Andrea Corr, Rhys Fulber, Lili Hayden, and Angie Stone, and glimpses of rehearsals shot by Groban's brother. The 13-track CD contained six of Groban's previously released songs; "Broken Vow," by Lara Fabian and Walter Afanasieff; "For Always," by Groban; and Groban's hit Christmas single "O Holy Night." Groban sang "O Holy Night" at the lighting of the Christmas tree at Rockefeller Center, in New York City, in early December of that year. The DVD/CD combo sold six million copies in 2003, making the DVD that year's top-selling long-form music video. Also in December 2002 Groban sang in Oslo, Norway, at the ceremony during which the Nobel Peace Prize was awarded to former U.S. president Jimmy Carter. On September 22, 2003 he performed in a one-night concert version of the unsuccessful 1988 Broadway musical *Chess*, mounted to benefit the Actors' Fund.

Groban's next studio album, *Closer*, was released in November 2003. Its 13 tracks included a cover of Secret Garden's "You Raise Me Up," which reached the top 10 on *Billboard*'s adult-contemporary chart and received a Grammy Award nomination for best male pop-vocal performance. The album also contained Groban's first contributions as a lyricist, for the songs "Per Te," "Never Let Go," "Remember When It Rained" (co-written by Eric Mouquet of the French electronic group Deep Forest), and "Mi Mancherai (Il Postino)," for the last of which he was accompanied by the violinist Joshua Bell. With sales of approximately 116,000 copies on its first day and 370,000 copies in its first week, *Closer* debuted at number four on the *Billboard* 200 album chart, then rose to first place nine weeks after its release; the album went on to sell more than five million copies. Most critics, however, greeted it with faint praise. In a representative mixed review, Scott D. Paulin wrote for *Entertainment Weekly* (November 14, 2003, online), "There's no doubt that the 22-year-old Groban can sing. His rich baritone raises the occasional goose pimples even on sentiment-resistant flesh. But he hasn't yet found the ideal direction in which to channel his undeniable talent. Though *Closer* is superior to his self-titled '01 debut, Groban still lacks the personality to transcend banal material, and all the bombastic production in the world can't win that battle for him."

"Groban is a highbrow heartthrob," Jon Bream wrote for the Minneapolis *Star Tribune* (February 6, 2004), five days after Groban performed "You

Raise Me Up" during the pregame events at Super Bowl XXXVIII, to honor the memory of the astronauts who lost their lives one year earlier, when the space shuttle *Columbia* broke apart during reentry. "He combines the striking voice of Andrea Bocelli with the boyish charm of John Mayer and the pleasing nerdiness and romantic sentimentality of Barry Manilow, all wrapped in a sheen of sophistication." Also in early 2004 Groban embarked on his first headlining tour, performing at sold-out venues all over the United States. During the international tour that followed, he performed some songs not included on his albums, among them his rendition of the hard-rock band Linkin Park's "My December." In May 2004, with an audience of 500,000 in attendance, Oprah Winfrey introduced Groban before his performance at the We Are the Future concert, held outdoors in Rome, Italy, to raise money for children in need. Later that year—by which time total sales of his recordings had reached eight million—Groban released another CD-plus-DVD set, *Live at the Greek*. The title refers to his summer 2004 concerts at the Greek Theatre in Los Angeles, California, which were taped and aired on another installment of PBS's *Great Performances* series. For one piece, "Canto Alla Vita," Groban played a drum solo; for "Remember When It Rained," he played the piano; and the banjo virtuoso Bela Fleck joined him for "Anna luce Del Sole."

Groban performed "Remember When It Rained," accompanied by a full orchestra, at the 2004 American Music Awards ceremony, where he received a nomination for favorite male artist in the pop category. His recording of "Believe" was incorporated into the soundtrack of the film fantasy *The Polar Express*, which was released during that year's Christmas season. "Believe" earned an Academy Award nomination for best song, and Groban performed it with Beyoncé at the 2005 Oscars ceremony.

In November 2006, after spending nearly two years on the road, Groban released his third studio album, *Awake*. Reflecting the effects of his experiences in South Africa in 2004, the album features collaborations with individuals and groups whom he met there: Herbie Hancock, Dave Matthews, Five for Fighting (born John Ondrasik), Imogen Heap, Vusi Mahlasela, and Ladysmith Black Mambazo. Groban co-wrote four tracks, including the melancholy "February Song." The album reached number two on the *Billboard* album chart and sold more than a million copies within a month of its release; it impressed critics favorably as well. Matt Collar, writing for the All Music Guide Web site, described *Awake* as "a grand collision of pop culture and co-opted classical themes from then and now" that "perfectly embodies everything that has made Groban so successful."

Groban spent most of 2007 and 2008 touring to promote *Awake*. In July 2007 he sang "All I Ask of You" with the British singer and actress Sarah Brightman at a benefit concert at Wembley Stadium, in London. A few months later he released his Christmas album, *Noel*, which contained duets with Brian McKnight ("Angels We Have Heard on High") and Faith Hill ("The First Noel"). *Noel* broke several Christmas-album records, selling more than 3.6 million copies within the first 11 weeks of its release. It became the first Christmas album ever to remain for four consecutive weeks at the top spot of the *Billboard* 200 album charts, breaking the three-week record set by Elvis Presley's *Elvis Christmas* in 1957, and it became the best-selling album of 2007 within 10 weeks of its release. It went on to sell a total of 4.6 million copies in the U.S. and more than five million copies elsewhere. The album earned a 2008 Juno Award for International Album of the Year. The year 2008 saw the release of *Awake Live*, another CD/DVD set, and Groban's greatest-hits album, *A Collection*, which, in addition to tracks from his previous albums, contained the song "Anthem," from *Chess*. In February 2008 Groban joined Andrea Bocelli in a performance of "The Prayer" at the Grammy Awards ceremony. A concert version of *Chess*, costarring Groban, Idina Menzel, and Adam Pascal, which was taped in May 2008 at the Royal Albert Hall, in London, aired on the June 17, 2009 installment of *Great Performances*. At "We Are One," a concert held on January 18, 2009 at the Lincoln Memorial in Washington, D.C., to celebrate the upcoming inauguration of Barack Obama as president of the U.S., Groban sang "My Country, 'Tis of Thee" (also called "America") with Heather Headley and the Washington Gay Men's Chorus. In June 2009 Groban released another live CD/DVD set, *Soundstage Presents: Josh Groban—An Evening in New York City*. The title refers to a 2008 concert he gave during the Jazz at Lincoln Center concert series in New York City, which was filmed for PBS's program *Soundstage*. In that show Groban performed some of his best-known hits, including "You Are Loved (Don't Give Up)" and "February Song." In September 2009 Groban played himself on the new musical-comedy television series *Glee*, in an episode entitled "Acafellas."

Groban lives in Malibu, California, with his Wheaten terrier, Sweeney. His visit with Nelson Mandela in 2004 inspired him to establish the Josh Groban Foundation. Groban has expressed his desire to work in musical theater someday. He told Peter Crawley for the *Irish Times* (April 12, 2003), "The combining of a great lyric with an amazing melody, a great book, amazing acting and storytelling can touch an audience like nothing else."

—C.C.

Suggested Reading: *Billboard* p1 Dec. 6, 2003; *Chicago Sun-Times* p1+ Nov. 16, 2003; (Cleveland, Ohio) *Plain Dealer* p36 Feb. 13, 2004; *InStyle* p164+ July 2008; *Interview* p140+ Mar. 2004; (Minneapolis, Minnesota) *Star Tribune* E p1+ Feb. 6, 2004; (New Orleans, Louisiana) *Times-Picayune* p22 Mar. 11, 2005; *New Republic* p21+ Mar. 7, 2005; *New York Times* p25 July 28, 2002

Selected Recordings—*Josh Groban*, 2001; *Closer*, 2003; *Awake*, 2006; *Noel*, 2007; *A Collection*, 2008

Selected Live CD/DVDs: *Josh Groban in Concert*, 2002; *Live at the Greek*, 2004; *Awake Live*, 2008; *Soundstage Presents: Josh Groban—An Evening in New York City*, 2009

Frazer Harrison/Getty Images

Guggenheim, Davis

Nov. 3, 1963– Filmmaker

Address: Electric Kinney Films, 1661 Lincoln Blvd., Suite 101, Santa Monica, CA 90404

"Documentaries have this unfortunate connection with activism. They can describe an issue or problem so vividly, and people can attach their agendas to them," the Academy Award–winning filmmaker Davis Guggenheim told Kevin Lally for *Film Journal International* (June 1, 2006). He added that his father, the celebrated documentarian Charles Guggenheim, "always felt that when [documentaries] get too close to a pamphlet, a political agenda, they lose what film does best, which is to tell stories. He always said that people invest in people. There are films that are tools for politics, and that's fine. But he was never interested in making those, and neither am I. I try to stay away from how [my films] will be used politically."

Guggenheim, who has directed and produced episodes of hit television series including *NYPD Blue*, *ER*, *Alias*, *24*, and *Deadwood*, is best known as the director, executive producer, and cinematographer of the 2006 documentary *An Inconvenient Truth*, about former vice president Al Gore's campaign to educate the public about global warming and climate change. Guggenheim's other documentaries include *The First Year* (2001), which follows a group of first-year teachers in Los Angeles, California, public schools, and *A Mother's Promise: Barack Obama Bio Film* (2008), a 10-minute work that premiered at the 2008 Democratic National Convention, where Obama accepted his party's nomination for the presidency. The director has also made two feature films, *Gossip* (2000) and *Gracie* (2007). Most recently he directed and produced *It Might Get Loud* (2008), a documentary that explores the history of the electric guitar and focuses on the careers of three prominent rock guitarists—Jimmy Page of Led Zeppelin, The Edge of U2, and Jack White of the White Stripes.

Philip Davis Guggenheim was born on November 3, 1963 in St. Louis, Missouri, to Marion Davis (Streett) Guggenheim and Charles Eli Guggenheim. His German-Jewish father—a distant relative of Solomon R. Guggenheim, the businessman and art collector for whom a famous modern-art museum in New York City is named—was a film director and producer. Charles Guggenheim is best remembered for his four Academy Award–winning documentaries: *Nine from Little Rock* (1964), about the desegregation of Little Rock Central High School, in 1957; *Robert Kennedy Remembered* (1968), about the U.S. attorney general and senator from New York; *The Johnstown Flood* (1989), which marked the 100th anniversary of the flood that killed more than 2,000 people in Johnstown, Pennsylvania, and resulted in the first major disaster-relief effort undertaken by the American Red Cross; and *A Time for Justice* (1994), which chronicled the civil rights movement. Charles Guggenheim was also the media director for four presidential campaigns, including Robert Kennedy's in 1968, and was a pioneer of political-campaign television commercials. "I grew up making films with my father—stringing cable for lights," Davis Guggenheim told Amy Wallace for *Los Angeles Magazine* (September 1, 2001). "My first memory is of getting on Bobby Kennedy's campaign plane." (Charles Guggenheim died in 2002 of pancreatic cancer.)

In 1965 Davis Guggenheim's family—which included his older brother, Jonathan, and older sister, Grace—moved from St. Louis to Washington, D.C. There, Davis was a student at Sidwell Friends, a private Quaker school. Though he struggled with dyslexia, he performed well enough in his studies to enroll at Brown University, in Providence, Rhode Island, where he studied American civilization. His senior thesis argued that Jewish movie directors had forsaken their heritage in order to be successful in Hollywood. (Though Guggenheim has Jewish ancestry, he was not raised with Jewish traditions.)

Upon graduating, in 1986, Guggenheim passed up his father's offer to work with him on films and moved to Los Angeles to start his own career in the entertainment industry. As he told Ann O'Neill for the *Los Angeles Times* (July 26, 2001), his goal was to make Hollywood movies and "live the good life." Guggenheim joined the production company Outlaw Productions and began to work on feature films. His first major job was as the production coordinator for Steven Soderbergh's 1989 drama, *Sex, Lies, and Videotape.* He was next an associate producer on the 1991 comedy *Don't Tell Mom the Babysitter's Dead* and co-produced the romantic comedy *The Opposite Sex and How to Live with Them* (1992).

Throughout the 1990s Guggenheim directed episodes of television series, among them *Party of Five, NYPD Blue*, and *ER*. In 1999 he teamed up with his father to make *The Art of Norton Simon*, a 30-minute documentary about the industrialist and art collector, commissioned by the Norton Simon Museum in Pasadena, California. Guggenheim's father produced the film, which was directed by Davis and narrated by the actor Gregory Peck. Davis Guggenheim later directed his first feature film, *Gossip* (2000). Starring James Marsden and Kate Hudson, the movie tells the story of three college students who, for a project, spread a piece of gossip—only to find the rumors getting out of control. In 2001 Guggenheim was an executive producer on *Training Day*, a crime thriller starring Denzel Washington and Ethan Hawke.

In 1994 Guggenheim had married the actress Elisabeth Shue, who is best known for her starring roles in the films *The Karate Kid* (1984), *Adventures in Babysitting* (1987), and *Back to the Future Part II* (1989). Although Guggenheim enjoyed working on Hollywood productions, his priorities began to change after the birth of his son, Miles William, in November 1997. In preparation for Miles's future, he began to research the public-school system in Los Angeles. As quoted on the PBS Web site for *The First Year* (2001), Guggenheim said, "Suddenly, I found myself a parent living in Los Angeles. I was starting to think about sending my children to school and I was faced with some difficult questions: Do I send them to a public school that is poorly funded and understaffed, or do I send them to an elite private school and turn my back on public education?" He was soon inspired to make a documentary about teachers in public schools. "I wanted to make a *Hoop Dreams* about education," he told Amy Wallace, referring to the 1994 documentary that followed two Chicago youths determined to become professional basketball players. "[I] wanted to find out about the job by following the natural route of the teacher."

In July 1999 Guggenheim and Shue were invited to accompany President Bill Clinton to the FIFA Women's World Cup soccer finals in Pasadena, California. There, Guggenheim met Barry Munitz, then president and CEO of the J. Paul Getty Trust. One of the wealthiest philanthropic organizations in the world, the Getty Trust supports visual arts, among other cultural endeavors. Munitz, interested in Guggenheim's idea for a documentary, decided to fund the project. Guggenheim was also able to secure funding from California State University, the state's leading teacher-training institution. (Munitz had served as chancellor and CEO of the California State University system in the 1990s.) In addition, Guggenheim enlisted the Academy Award–nominated documentary producer Julia Schachter and the producer Senain Kheshgi.

The resulting documentary, *The First Year*, follows five novice teachers starting out in a Los Angeles public-school district. "Documentaries about schools had often been made from the outside in, about politics and experts and the crumbling of the schools," Guggenheim told Bernard Weinraub for the *New York Times* (September 6, 2001). "What I wanted was an intensely personal story about people who teach. And in the process, hopefully we could change the way people think about education." The project cost nearly $1 million—a pittance by Hollywood standards—and was filmed over the course of 110 days starting in September 1999. Much of the footage was shot by Guggenheim himself, with a handheld digital video camera. "There is talk about how the digital age will change how feature films will be made. I didn't realize how it would impact the documentary world," he told an interviewer for the PBS Web site. "After a half an hour of shooting, the students forgot I was there. When I shot without a crew, I got to witness extraordinarily intimate moments that I couldn't have captured with a full crew." *The First Year* focuses on the teachers—whose pupils range from kindergarteners to high-schoolers—as they deal with struggling students, uncooperative parents, and apathetic administrators. The documentary aired on PBS television stations in September 2001. In her review for the *New York Times* [September 3, 2001], Julie Salamon wrote, "[Guggenheim] . . . takes an unvarnished approach that records without dramatic flourish the frustrations and rewards of teaching." *The First Year* won a prestigious George Foster Peabody Award in 2001. A shortened, 35-minute version of the documentary, entitled *Teach*, has been used as a recruitment tool to provide prospective teachers with a realistic look at the profession.

In the early 2000s Guggenheim returned to television series, directing episodes of *Alias* (2002), *24* (2002), *The Shield* (2003), and *Numb3rs* (2005). He also produced the first season, in addition to directing four episodes, of the critically acclaimed HBO series *Deadwood*. In his interview with Kevin Lally, Guggenheim confessed, "I have to work in television to pay my habit. I love documentaries, I would make them all the time if I could. There's nothing better. It's just the question of how do you sustain your family, how do you pay your mortgage." (In addition to their son, Guggenheim and his wife have two daughters: Stella, born in March 2001, and Agnes, born in June 2006.)

In 2005 the environmentalist Laurie David (the wife of the writer and actor Larry David) and producer Lawrence Bender approached Guggenheim about making a film on former vice president Al Gore's traveling slide-show presentation about global warming. (Global warming, an increase in the average temperature of the Earth's atmosphere, is believed by most scientists to be progressing at a rapid—and dangerous—rate due to the release of carbon dioxide and other pollutants into the air.) Since the 2000 presidential election, in which Gore won the popular vote by more than 500,000 ballots but lost the Electoral College vote—and the presidency—to George W. Bush (after the U.S. Supreme Court settled the controversial Florida vote recount), Gore has dedicated himself to educating others on the issues of global warming and climate change. "I didn't see how you could make a movie about a slide show," Guggenheim told Joseph V. Amodio for *Newsday* (May 22, 2006). After attending one of Gore's shows in Los Angeles, however, the filmmaker decided that Gore's presentation "was . . . so amazing, so powerful, that I had to find a way to make a movie about it." "[Gore] goes from city to city, rolling his bag through airports. And if a Kiwanis Club invites him, or a civic club, or a Republican group, he will go and give a slide show, for free. That's what he's decided to do with his life. . . . That's as compelling a character as I can imagine," Guggenheim told the *Boston Globe* (May 28, 2006).

Shot and edited in just six months, *An Inconvenient Truth* (co-produced by David and Bender) is structured around Gore's presentation and weaves in stories about his life and family. "Running for president, [Gore] was scrutinized a lot, and criticized for bringing up a lot of his personal stories—I think unfairly . . . ," Guggenheim told Kevin Lally. "I just felt so strongly that we'd have to understand him and why he's telling this story, why he believes it so deeply. If I could show that part of his story, people would connect to him, and then they'd connect to the issue." In his review of the film for *Salon.com* (May 24, 2006), Andrew O'Hehir wrote, "More than anything I've ever seen or read about Gore, *An Inconvenient Truth* brings this notoriously awkward politician into focus as a human being, both warm and guarded, intellectually curious but not especially introspective. Guggenheim gets Gore, for instance, to discuss the two central emotional events in his life: his sister's death from lung cancer, and the near-death of his son, who was run down by a car, at age 6, in 1989. In both instances, it's clear that Gore is being as emotionally open as he can, and that behind his stilted, almost clichéd language lies a universe of painful meaning."

An Inconvenient Truth premiered at the Sundance Film Festival in January 2006 and was released in theaters in New York City and Los Angeles on May 24. As of August 2009 it was the fifth-highest-grossing documentary made in the U.S. since 1982 (when records began being kept), with domestic box-office earnings of over $24.1 million. The documentary received widespread critical acclaim and won several awards, including the 2006 Los Angeles Film Critics Association Award for best documentary/nonfiction film, the 2006 National Board of Review Award for best documentary, the 2007 special award for best nonfiction film from the National Society of Film Critics, and the 2007 Academy Award for best documentary—features. Gore, who also wrote a companion book for the film, was awarded the Nobel Peace Prize in 2007 for his commitment to the issue of global climate change. Gore said in an interview with Claudia Feldman for the *Houston Chronicle* (June 5, 2006) that he has devoted "100 percent of the profits from the book and the movie to a new bipartisan educational campaign to further spread the message about global warming." (Though Guggenheim does not consider himself an environmentalist, since he made the film he has purchased a hybrid vehicle—which uses less of the type of fuel that produce pollutants—and outfitted his home with solar panels.)

In 2007 Guggenheim returned to feature films, directing and producing the sports drama *Gracie*, which is loosely based on the lives of his wife's family. Shue's younger brother, Andrew, conceived the idea for the film as a way to tell the story of their late brother, William. The captain of a high-school soccer team that won the New Jersey state championship, William died in an accident in 1988. After Andrew approached Guggenheim about directing the project, the filmmaker shifted the focus of the story to his wife, who, as the only daughter in a family with three sons, had excelled at sports in an effort to win attention from her father. (At nine Shue was the first girl in her area to play organized soccer on an all-boys team.) Shue has said that her athletic prowess got little notice from her father. She quit organized soccer at the age of 13.

Set in New Jersey in 1978, *Gracie* follows a 15-year-old named Gracie Bowen, played by Carly Schroeder, who is coping with the sudden death of her older brother by trying to take his place on the high-school boys' varsity soccer team. Shue portrayed Gracie's mother in the film and, along with her brothers Andrew and John, served as a producer. *Gracie* received mixed reviews. Michael Phillips wrote for the *Chicago Tribune* (June 1, 2007) that the film is "a predictable but nicely acted triumph of the soccer-phenom spirit."

Guggenheim's most recent film, the rock documentary *It Might Get Loud*, premiered at the September 2008 Toronto Film Festival in Canada before its limited theatrical release in the U.S., in August 2009. The film concentrates on the relationships of three guitarists to their instrument of choice. Each guitarist represents a different generation of rock and roll: Jimmy Page, of the legendary 1970s band Led Zeppelin; The Edge, of the Irish band U2, which achieved international celebrity in the 1980s; and Jack White, whose success with the

White Stripes since the late 1990s has led to his formation of two other bands, the Raconteurs and the Dead Weather.

Thomas Tull, the chairman and CEO of the independent production company Legendary Pictures and a longtime collector of guitars, approached Guggenheim with the idea for the film in 2007. "Thomas asked me to come to his office in Burbank [California]. . . . I get there and he launches into this passionate pitch about the electric guitar and how no film has ever captured what it is that makes the instrument so great . . . ," Guggenheim was quoted as saying in the press kit for *It Might Get Loud*. "Most Rock and Roll documentaries focus on car wrecks and overdoses; or they pontificate with sweeping generalities about how this guy was 'God' and how 'music was changed forever.'. . . Thomas and I didn't want any of that. We wanted to focus on story-telling and the path of the artist, we wanted to push deeper beneath the surface."

Over the course of a year and a half, Guggenheim interviewed the guitarists and filmed each going about his daily life; in the film the guitarists recall their childhood dreams of rock stardom and discuss the writing of some of their more famous songs. The culmination of the film is a jam session among the three musicians, who had not met one another prior to the making of the documentary. *It Might Get Loud* received mostly positive reviews, though some critics felt that the film lacked a clear purpose. "Everything in [*It Might Get Loud*] is interesting. . . . But it isn't assembled well," Wesley Morris wrote for the *Boston Globe* (August 28, 2009). "Once I figured out that the movie has nowhere to go with this trio—they don't write a song together or overthrow a dictator—I started to lose interest." The *New York Times* (August 14, 2009) critic A. O. Scott, however, praised Guggenheim's film, writing, "For rock geeks of any age or taste, the lore in this documentary will be catnip. But *It Might Get Loud* is more than a narrowly focused fan artifact. It gives those of us with tin ears and clumsy fingers a chance to linger in the presence of serious artists with formidable chops and big, if not always clearly expressed, ideas about what they do. And it will put you in the mood to listen."

Guggenheim is currently working on a documentary about American public-school systems. He lives in Venice, California, with his wife, son, and two daughters.

—M.A.S.

Suggested Reading: *Boston Globe* N p9 May 28, 2006; davisguggenheim.com; *Film Journal International* p16 June 1, 2006, p16 Aug. 1, 2009; *Los Angeles Magazine* p90 Sep. 1, 2001; *New York Times* E p1 Sep. 6, 2001; teachnow.org

Selected Documentaries: as director—*The Art of Norton Simon*, 1999; *A Mother's Promise: Barack Obama Bio Film*, 2008; as director and producer—*It Might Get Loud*, 2008; as director, cinematographer, and producer—*The First Year*, 2001; *Teach*, 2001; *An Inconvenient Truth*, 2006

Selected Feature Films: as director—*Gossip*, 2000; as director and producer—*Gracie*, 2007; as producer—*Don't Tell Mom the Babysitter's Dead*, 1991; *The Opposite Sex and How to Live with Them*, 1992; *Training Day*, 2001

Selected Television Series (Episodes): as director—*Party of Five*, 1994; *NYPD Blue*, 1995–96; *ER*, 1996; 24, 2002; *Alias*, 2002; *The Shield*, 2003; *Numb3rs*, 2005; *Melrose Place*, 2009; as director and producer—*Deadwood*, 2004

Amy Sussman/Getty Images

Gunn, Tim

July 29, 1953– Chief creative officer of Liz Claiborne Inc.; fashion consultant for the TV series Project Runway *and* Tim Gunn's Guide to Style*; educator*

Address: Liz Claiborne Inc., 1441 Broadway, New York, NY 10018

The fashion consultant, television personality, and educator Tim Gunn is a member of "that rare breed of reality-TV star who is entertaining without resorting to scathing remarks," Siobhan Duck wrote for the Melbourne, Australia, *Herald Sun* (May 14, 2008). Since its debut, in December 2004, Gunn has appeared on the cable-TV series *Project Runway* in the role of fashion expert, counselor, therapist, or "den father," to cite a few of the labels that have been applied to him. At the start of each season of *Project Runway*, 12 would-be designers vie for a prize of $100,000, to be used by the winner to launch his or her first commercial clothing collection. Every week each contestant must create a particular type of garment while following rules concerning materials, cost, and time constraints. The competitors, whose numbers dwindle with each passing week, are shown in the process of designing garments, acquiring the materials to make them, and constructing them, while Gunn expresses his positive or negative reactions to their work and makes suggestions, in a manner that is unfailingly gentlemanly and encouraging. Writing for the Washington, D.C.–based *Metro Weekly* (September 27, 2007, on-line), Randy Shulman described Gunn as "instructive, authoritative, and completely, utterly accessible. He doesn't just have charm, he is charm personified. Even when Gunn shows disdain over a particular fashion option, it's with a feather's touch." Shulman continued, "True, he can be harsh, but he's no Simon Cowell–like pitbull . . ."—a reference to the acid-tongued, insult-prone judge on the TV series *American Idol.* "Gunn clearly cares about his subjects." "I want each one of them to succeed," Gunn told Shulman. "I know that someone by definition will be [voted] out, but I want all of them to have the opportunity to succeed. Sometimes my words are a little strong. . . . It's tough love because I want them to know what's on my mind. And not necessarily to change what they're doing, because I have tremendous respect for their point of view. But faulty execution is another matter." "Tim Gunn is the fairy godfather we all wish we could have—nurturing but no-nonsense, seasoned but not over it, frank but fair," Dennis Hensley wrote for the *Advocate.com* (March 15, 2006), in an article about Gunn titled "The Sanest Man in Reality TV."

Gunn comes across as a superlative educator on *Project Runway* partly because, for most of his professional life, he *was* an educator—a college teacher and administrator. Trained in architectural drawing and sculpture, he taught a course in three-dimensional design for several years at his alma mater, the Corcoran School of Art and Design. He later taught the same subject at the Parsons School of Design (known since 2005 as Parsons the New School for Design), where he also served as an associate dean (1987–2000) and chair of the Department of Fashion Design (2000–2007). "My role in [*Project Runway*] is so much like what I do at Parsons day in and day out," he told Dennis Hensley. Gunn also appears on the TV series *Tim Gunn's Guide to Style*, which debuted in 2007 and is a spin-off from his book, *Tim Gunn: A Guide to Quality, Taste, & Style* (2007), co-written with Kate Moloney. In 2007 Gunn ended his 25-year tenure at Parsons to become chief creative officer of Liz Claiborne Inc., a New York–based fashion conglomerate that generates nearly $5 billion in annual sales.

The first of the two children of Nancy Comfort Gunn and George William Gunn, Timothy Mackenzie Gunn was born on July 29, 1953 in Washington, D.C., and grew up in the Cleveland Park section of that city. His father (who died in 1995) was a special agent and writer with the Federal Bureau of Investigation (FBI) and an assistant to its longtime director J. Edgar Hoover; after he retired from the FBI, he became an editor for *Reader's Digest* and a consultant to writers on such subjects as the FBI and crime. Gunn's mother helped set up the Central Intelligence Agency (CIA) library before devoting herself to homemaking. Gunn's sister, now Kim Gunn Gundy, is three years his junior. His mother taught her son and daughter housekeeping skills to ensure that they would always be able to take care of themselves.

Gunn has traced his interest in design to his early childhood; he enjoyed constructing grand buildings out of Lego and creating outfits for his toy soldiers and his sister's Barbie dolls. He told Vicki Hyman for the Newark, New Jersey, *Star-Ledger* (February 15, 2006), "I had a Barbie obsession. I was concerned with the whole Barbie lifestyle." He also read avidly and studied piano. "I was solitary, but I was never lonely," he told Beth Perry for *People* (May 14, 2007). He was also introverted, introspective, and extremely shy and suffered from a severe stutter, which led his peers to bully him and fling "horrible slurs" at him, as he recalled to Eric Wilson for the *New York Times* (April 12, 2007). He felt so miserable that during his adolescence and teens, he repeatedly transferred from one boarding or private school to another—a dozen altogether. Adding to his unhappiness was his conviction that his father disapproved of him. "He loved me, but I knew that I wasn't quite the son he wanted; he really wanted a football jock," he told Perry. In elementary school Gunn was always last to be chosen for teams, and he joined none of the neighborhood youth teams that his father coached; as a high-school student, he excelled only at swimming—"It was nice and clean and you didn't sweat," he joked to Vicki Hyman. His limited athletic skills were, he added, "the bane of my father's existence."

After graduating from high school, Gunn entered Yale University, in New Haven, Connecticut; he concentrated first on English literature and then on architecture. He later transferred to the Corcoran College of Art & Design, in Washington, D.C., where he focused on sculpture. He was inspired by the work of the 20th-century American sculptor Joseph Cornell, famous for his boxed, compartmentalized assemblages of found objects. Commenting on Cornell's influence, Gunn told Eric Wilson, "I thought there must be a way of synthesizing all the different parts of my life in my own way. I really think it was Cornell who caused me to have the confidence to say I'm going to be an artist." Gunn has credited his teachers at Corcoran with fostering his creative impulses. One of his professors, William Christenberry, remembered him as "one of the most dedicated, passionate students" he had ever taught, as quoted in a Corcoran press release (April 23, 2009, on-line). According to Wilson, Gunn had an epiphany regarding his future when a professional artist who was assessing some of his student pieces told him, "I'd rather look at the space this work displaces than look at this work." Gunn graduated from Corcoran in 1976 with a bachelor of fine arts degree.

Gunn spent the next several years building models for architectural firms. He then returned to Corcoran to take a job as assistant director of admissions and to teach a course in three-dimensional design. Before the first day of classes, he vomited in the school parking lot from nervousness, but he soon grew to love teaching and interacting with students, and "the element of surprise when they set about doing their project assignments thrilled him even more," Robbie Daw wrote for *Instinct Magazine* (November 1, 2006, on-line). In the early 1980s a love affair in Washington led Gunn to reject an offer to teach at Parsons; after the painful breakup of the six-year relationship, he accepted a second offer from the school, in 1983. As a member of Parsons's admissions-office staff, he interviewed prospective students and evaluated their portfolios. He also taught three-dimensional design. During that period, in an environment in which many were deeply interested in fashion-related matters, he learned a great deal about the fashion industry. In 1989 Gunn was appointed Parsons's associate dean of academic affairs. In that capacity he collaborated on modernizing various curriculums and strengthened Parsons's affiliations with schools overseas, in France, Japan, South Korea, and the Dominican Republic. He also served as the school's resident fashion expert and engaged in many interviews for the print and broadcast media.

In about 1999 Gunn headed a committee charged with finding a successor to the soon-to-retire Frank Rizzo, the chairman of Parsons's Department of Fashion Design. (The first of its kind in the U.S., it was founded in 1906.) After an extensive search Gunn himself was appointed to the post, even though, unlike Rizzo, who had made his name as a designer of bridal gowns, he had never designed any clothing or studied fashion design. Assessing the fashion-design curriculum from the perspective of a Parsons insider who was also a fashion-department outsider—but one well-versed in design—Gunn concluded that it needed a major overhaul. "This famous department, with all of its great graduates, was really suffering from atrophy," he told Robbie Daw, referring to such former students as Tom Ford, Donna Karan, Marc Jacobs, Isaac Mizrahi, Anna Sui, Alexander Wang, and Jason Wu. "It was so caught up in its own success that it was afraid to change the formula. Basically the curriculum had remained unchanged for 48 years."

Gunn assumed his new post in the fall of 2000. Among other changes, the curriculum he introduced emphasized critical thinking and a broader and deeper study of both fashion history and the commercial aspects of the fashion industry. In a step that proved to be controversial, Gunn moved from the senior year to the junior year a program in which students designed and constructed apparel under the guidance of noted fashion designers, in what were termed internships. Now, to fulfill the requirements of what would be analogous to senior theses at other colleges, seniors had to design and produce seasonal collections without the direct influence of highly opinionated, strong-minded guest mentors, in the hope that the students' own design sensibilities would be strengthened. As before, the best of those collections would be shown in an end-of-year exhibition and runway show at Parsons. Many of Gunn's colleagues at Parsons and some of the famous designers who had worked with Parsons students took a dim view of the junior year/senior year change; some designers told him that he was "driving the American fashion industry into the ground," he recalled during a talk at the 92nd Street YM-YWHA in 2008, as quoted on jezebel.com (March 12, 2008). Parsons administrators stood by Gunn, and their confidence in him bore fruit when, after the senior show mounted in the spring of 2002, Julie Gilhart, the women's-fashion director at Barneys New York, bought the entire collection designed jointly by Lazaro Hernandez and Jack McCollough, who chose their mother's maiden names, Proenza and Schouler, for their label. Proenza Schouler apparel is now sold in dozens of high-end retail stores worldwide.

In 2004, when Bravo executives asked Gunn to join in the creation of a reality show devoted to fashion design, the premise of such a show struck him as "terrible," as he recalled to Randy Shulman. But after several meetings with the executive producers of the proposed show, Gunn agreed to work as an off-camera consultant. For the next six months, he helped to pin down various details, including characteristics to look for in potential contestants and whether or not those chosen should sew their own creations or have others sew them. Before long the producers decided that Gunn's role should be expanded to that of an on-camera mentor who would critique the would-be designers' work and offer advice. *Project Runway* debuted on the Bravo cable network on December 1, 2004. While the show initially attracted few viewers, for the season-one finale, it drew an audience of 2.5 million, making it the highest-rated telecast in Bravo history up to the time. Meanwhile, Gunn's appearances on the show had made him a cultural icon. Gunn, who has admitted to appearing too stiff when the show debuted, quickly emerged as an endearing fashion adviser, and he has been widely credited—along with the show's host, the supermodel Heidi Klum—with contributing greatly to the series' success. Some of his pet phrases—"Make it work," "Carry on," and "This worries me"—have caught on with the public. He told a *Time* (November 5, 2007) interviewer that in the classroom he always used the directive "Make it work": "It came about from having students who are much more inclined to start a project over rather than accept the challenge and try to fix it," he explained. *Project Runway* has earned 12 Primetime Emmy nominations and a 2007 Peabody Award for excellence in television broadcasting. Unlike most reality shows, *Project Runway* has never been faulted for sensationalism, and it has been generally well-received by the fashion industry. It has also been credited with renewing interest in fashion-design education; since the show's inception, applications and enrollments have increased dramatically in schools that offer programs in design and other aspects of fashion. (Applications to Parsons have risen by 30 percent.) According to Vicki Hyman, *Project Runway* "is smarter than your average reality show. In a genre that esteems deceit and champions ego, *Project Runway* is about talent and vision, whether it's constructing a new outfit by deconstructing a contestant's own ensemble or assembling a garden party dress made entirely from leaves and buds. . . . There is some ego . . . and some apparent maneuvering to keep the more ratings-friendly personalities in play . . . but the silver-haired, Banana Republic–clad Gunn elevates the proceedings with his dry wit and candid, though rarely condescending commentary." On *Larry King Live* (September 2, 2006, on-line), Gunn told King, "Fashion is so fully embedded in our culture today that there are mythologies about it. And if anything, this show demystifies much of that and really makes fashion very, very accessible to the public at large." Designers whose appearances on the show launched their careers—even if they were not the winners—include Jay McCarroll, Kara Saun, Wendy Pepper, Chloe Dao, Santino Rice, Jeffrey Sebelia, Uli Herzner, Christian Siriano, Kelli Martin, and Leanne Marshall. *Project Runway* now airs on the Lifetime Television network. Its sixth season began in August 2009.

In 2007 Gunn left Parsons to take the job of chief creative officer of Liz Claiborne Inc., one of the nation's largest apparel companies. Claiborne's chief executive officer, William L. "Bill" McComb, created the position specifically for Gunn, who serves as a creative guide for the hundreds of employees who design for Claiborne brands—Kate Spade, Lucky Brand Jeans, Juicy Culture, Mexx, Liz Claiborne New York (in partnership with its creative director, Isaac Mizrahi), Axcess (sold only at Kohl's department stores), Claiborne by John Bartlett (a menswear collection), Kensie, and KensieGirl, among others. "The easiest thing in the world for me would have been to stay at Parsons," Gunn told Randy Shulman. "I was very comfortable there and very proud of my achievements. I loved my work. I really thought I would retire there."

Tim Gunn: A Guide to Quality, Taste, & Style (2007) was co-written by Kate Moloney, the assistant chairperson of Parsons's Department of Fashion Design. Penelope M. Carrington wrote for the Richmond, Virginia, *Times Dispatch* (June 24, 2007), "The book is conversational and full of Gunn's sharp-witted prose that endeared him to TV viewers. The book expounds on his trademark 'Make it work' phrase and is more introspective than other books that link fashion success to knowing your body type." The spin-off reality series *Tim Gunn's Guide to Style* premiered on the Bravo network in September 2007.

In 2009 Gunn was featured in the first issue of Marvel Comics' sartorially themed miniseries *Models Inc.*, which went on sale during New York's Fall Fashion Week. Gunn was portrayed as a crime fighter, dressed in an Iron Man suit, who teams up with several Marvel heroines to help solve a murder committed during Fashion Week. Gunn will also appear in a cameo in the movie *Sex and the City 2*, which will be released in 2010.

Gunn lives in a condominium on the Upper West Side of New York City, in a duplex that houses his 10,000 books. He enjoys walking in the city, watching TV, and playing cards and the board game Trivial Pursuit. Openly gay, he is currently single. "I'd have to give something up to have a relationship, and I don't want to," he told Beth Perry. "I'm having the best time of my life."

—C.C.

Suggested Reading: *Advocate.com* Mar. 15, 2006; corcoran.org; *Instinct* (on-line) Nov. 2006; *New York Times* G p1+ Apr. 12, 2007; (Newark, New Jersey) *Star-Ledger* p35 Feb. 15, 2006; *People* p113 May 14, 2007; (Washington, D.C.) *Metro Weekly* (on-line) Sep. 27, 2007; *Washington Post* H p1 Apr. 2, 2009

Selected Books: *Tim Gunn: A Guide to Quality, Taste, & Style* (with Kate Moloney), 2007

Selected Television Shows: *Project Runway*, 2004– ; *Tim Gunn's Guide to Style*, 2007–

Halladay, Roy

May 14, 1977– Baseball player

Address: Toronto Blue Jays, 1 Blue Jays Way, Rogers Centre, Toronto, Ontario, Canada 0N M5V 1J1

The Toronto Blue Jays' pitcher Roy Halladay, Alan Schwarz wrote for the *New York Times* (April 5, 2009), is "the kind of professional most young pitchers want to become." "While his peers consider him the game's best starting pitcher," Schwarz noted, "the public cannot instantly see why. While holding best-pitcher status in past years, Randy Johnson had his left-handed slingball, Pedro Martinez had that changeup and flair, Greg Maddux his stiletto control. Halladay is just really good at everything, a high, quiet plateau camouflaged by others' peaks and valleys. It is the difference between being great and [being] remarkable." Halladay joined the Blue Jays' organization imme-

Marc Serota/Getty Images

Roy Halladay

diately after his high-school graduation, in 1995. He made a big splash when, in his second appearance in Major League Baseball (MLB) as a starter, in 1998, he pitched a near no-hitter. Demoted to the minor leagues because of his egregiously poor performance in 2000, he undertook a rigorous training and fitness regimen and became a keen student of the mental aspects of the game. He returned to the Jays the next year with newfound control, outstanding game-management skills, and "an array of pitches with more plane changes than a platinum-level frequent flier," Michael Farber wrote for *Sports Illustrated* (April 16, 2007). "All his pitches start in the same place and end in a different place," the Yankees' first baseman Mark Teixeira told Schwarz. A six-time All-Star selection, Halladay pitched for more innings than any other player in the American League (AL) in 2002, 2003, and 2008, and he has pitched more complete games (46) than anyone else in the majors since 2002. In 2003 he won the AL Cy Young Award for best pitcher. As of the end of his 12th season with the Jays, in 2009, he had posted a career winning percentage of .661, which ranks among the top 15 winning percentages ever among pitchers. In 2009 a panel of 100 baseball experts, many of them members of the Baseball Hall of Fame and winners of prestigious prizes in the sport, ranked Halladay seventh among the *Sporting News*'s choices of the 50 greatest current players of the game.

The second of the three children of Linda and Harry Halladay Jr., Roy Halladay was born Harry Leroy Halladay III on May 14, 1977 in Denver, Colorado, and was raised in Arvada, a Denver suburb. He has two sisters, Merinda and Heather; he and Heather, who is four years his junior, have been very close since childhood. Halladay's family began calling him "Roy" early on; his current nickname, "Doc," refers to the 19th-century Western dentist turned gunfighter John Henry "Doc" Holliday. Halladay's father worked as a private pilot for Stearns-Rogers Engineering and then the cheesemaker LePrino Foods; his mother was a homemaker. "We never had problems with Roy . . . ," Linda Halladay told Bob Elliott for the *Toronto (Ontario, Canada) Sun* (May 20, 2006), as posted on slam.canoe.ca. "He grew up wanting to please people." Both of Halladay's parents instilled in him a strong work ethic. Halladay began playing catch with his father at the age of three and joined a T-ball team at five. His intensity and competitive nature soon set him apart from his peers.

At Arvada West High School, Halladay made all-conference teams in both basketball and baseball. Already taller than average, he excelled in basketball with his "ability to dunk over most opponents with relative ease," Jeff Blair wrote for the Toronto *Globe and Mail* (June 27, 2003, on-line). He shone even more on the baseball diamond, where, when he was not pitching, he played first base. His high-school coach, Jim Capra, told Paul Willis for the *Rocky Mountain News* (July 4, 2007), "His freshman year during tryouts, you could tell he was going to be real good. He was throwing 82–84 [miles per hour]. . . . He had good size and good character. He was a good hitter." Relying on an overpowering fastball, as a pitcher Halladay posted a career high-school record of 25–2, with an astonishing 0.55 earned-run average (ERA), while leading Arvada West to a state championship in 1994 and a second-place finish in 1995. He was also an All-Conference and All-State selection for three years and was named the league and state Most Valuable Player during his junior and senior seasons. His senior-year statistics were outstanding: he allowed only 24 hits and five earned runs in 63 innings, with 105 strikeouts. He was an academic standout as well, graduating with a 3.6 grade-point average. By that time Halladay had become one of the most heavily recruited pitchers in the U.S. He signed a letter of intent to attend the University of Arizona but then chose to forgo college to enter the MLB draft. In a deal orchestrated by his longtime mentor, the legendary Colorado pitching coach Robert "Bus" Campbell (whom he had known since the age of 11, thanks to a meeting his father arranged), the Toronto Blue Jays selected Halladay with the 17th pick in the 1995 amateur draft. The Blue Jays' deal also included an $850,000 signing bonus, $11,000 of which Halladay used to buy a wooden fence for his high school's outfield.

By the time he entered the Blue Jays' farm system, Halladay had reached his full height—six feet, six inches—and had added a devastating curveball to his pitching arsenal. In the summer of 1995, he reported to the Blue Jays' Rookie League team in Dunedin, Florida. In 1996 he was assigned to the advanced class-A affiliate in Dunedin. He was named to the Florida State League's All-Star team and was ranked by the magazine *Baseball America* as the best all-around player in the Jays' farm system. During his time in Dunedin, Halladay started experimenting with a changeup, which soon became one of his staple pitches. Halladay spent the first half of the 1997 season with the Knoxville Smokies of the Southern League, then the class-AA affiliate of the Jays. Although he performed poorly the Jays sent him to the class-AAA Syracuse Chiefs (later renamed the SkyChiefs) partway through that season, as his last stop in preparation for the majors.

Halladay made his major-league debut on September 20, 1998, in a game against the Tampa Bay Rays. At 21 he was the third-youngest pitcher ever to start for the Blue Jays. He pitched five innings and racked up five strikeouts, while allowing two earned runs and two walks. He earned a no-decision in a 7–5 win for Toronto. In his second career MLB start and first MLB win, Halladay recorded a near no-hitter: in a game against the Detroit Tigers on the final day of the 1998 regular season, after throwing 73 strikes and no walks in 94 pitches, with two outs in the ninth inning, he surrendered a home run to the outfielder Bobby Higginson. (In baseball history there have been only two no-hitters pitched on the final day of the regular season: a combined no-hitter by four Oakland Athletics pitchers in 1975 and a perfect game thrown by the California Angels pitcher Mike Witt in 1984.) Halladay's performance helped to secure him a permanent spot on the Blue Jays roster for the 1999 season. That year he started in 18 of the 36 games that he pitched and ended the season with a record of 8–7, with a 3.92 ERA. He also garnered his first save as a relief pitcher, in a game against the Twins, and scored a complete-game shutout in a contest with the Tigers. By then it had become evident that Halladay was a strong starter who could go the distance, and that keeping him in the bullpen half the time to protect his throwing arm, as the Blue Jays' management had done, had not been necessary.

In 2000 Halladay performed poorly. In 19 game appearances, 13 of them starts, at the beginning of the season, he compiled a 4–7 record and posted a 10.64 ERA. He also allowed 80 earned runs, 107 hits, and 42 walks in 67 $^{2}/_{3}$ innings, while opponents had a scorching .350 batting average against him. By that time opposing batters had caught on to his mostly conventional four-seam fastball, which normally reached 95 miles per hour but with little to no movement up, down, or sideways. He also had problems with his knuckle curve, a slight variation of the standard curveball that he had developed under the tutelage of Bus Campbell. Halladay's difficulties led the Blue Jays to send him back to the class-AAA Syracuse team, on which he continued to struggle. In the spring of 2001, the Blue Jays demoted Halladay to class-A Dunedin in the Florida State League. There, he began working with the Blue Jays' pitching specialist Mel Queen, who immediately ordered him to abandon the four-seam fastball. Queen then trained him to change his stance to the three-quarters position, so as to generate more movement; he had previously hurled the ball with a standard over-the-top motion. Halladay also sought the counsel of the sports psychologist Harvey A. Dorfman, whose book *The Mental Game of Baseball* (1989), co-written with Karl Kuehl, is widely considered to be the standard text on sports psychology. Halladay read that book and Dorfman's *The Mental ABC's of Pitching* (2000) and began a daily routine that included running, weight training, and figuring out Sudoku puzzles to sharpen his concentration. To further rid Halladay of bad habits and improve his frame of mind—he had been contemplating retiring from baseball—Dorfman persuaded him to move with his wife from Arvada to Florida. Halladay later recalled to Mike Klis, "Looking back, I really had no idea what I was doing. Even with the near no-hitter, I just reared back and fired. Just relied on stuff. I always had confidence, even when I was a young kid, and all the sudden I'd go out for my second full year in the big leagues and I was getting hit around. You lose that confidence, and it's amazing how fast things snowball on you when you don't know how to handle it."

During that period Halladay was transformed from a power pitcher into a finesse pitcher—one whose greatest strength is not speed but control and accuracy. He now had mastery in three types of fastballs (split-fingered and two-seam as well as an improved four-seam), two types of curveballs, and a changeup. His new stance enabled him to throw with more movement and deception. (For example, Halladay's two-seam fastball normally sinks to the right, and his four-seam fastball cuts away from batters.) In a matter of months, Halladay had earned promotions from class-AA Knoxville to class-AAA Syracuse before rejoining the Blue Jays' starting rotation in July 2001. In his first game after his return to MLB, against the Montreal Expos, in which he was given a no-decision, he struck out a then-career-high 10 batters. He finished the season with a 5–3 record and 3.16 ERA, while making 16 starts in 17 game appearances. Commenting on his turnaround, the Blue Jays' then–general manager, J. P. Ricciardi, told Jeff Blair, "What Roy did that year was save his career, nothing less."

In 2002 Halladay had a breakout season, compiling a 19–7 record. (His 19 wins were the most by a Blue Jays pitcher since David Wells, in 2000.) He posted a 2.93 ERA with 168 strikeouts in 239.1 innings, placing him fifth, sixth, and first in those categories, respectively, in the AL. He also played in an All-Star Game for the first time.

In 2003 Halladay led the majors and set a franchise record with 22 wins. He also led the AL in innings pitched (266) and tied for the league lead in games completed (nine), while posting a 3.25 ERA and a then-career-high 204 strikeouts, placing him fifth and third in the AL in those categories, respectively. One of his more remarkable achievements that season was allowing only 32 walks, which resulted in an astonishing ratio of strikeouts per walk of 6.38. He participated in his second consecutive All-Star Game and helped lead the Blue Jays to 86 wins (nine too few for a wild-card spot). At the end of the season, the *Sporting News* named Halladay the AL Pitcher of the Year, and he won the AL Cy Young Award, receiving 26 of 28 first-place votes.

Injuries plagued Halladay for most of the 2004 season. Shoulder tendinitis twice forced him to go on the disabled list. He pitched for only 133 innings—half as many as the year before—going 8–8 with a 4.20 ERA, giving up 39 walks. He later attributed his mediocre performance to a "tired throwing arm," which had been overworked from excessive conditioning during the preseason. The season ended even more poorly for the Blue Jays, who won only 67 games and lost 94. That year Halladay agreed to a five-year extension of his contract, closing the door on becoming a free agent after the next season. In 2005 he was selected for the AL All-Star team for the third time and posted a 12–4 record and a 2.41 ERA in 19 games. Then, on July 8, a week before the All-Star break, a line drive hit by the Texas Rangers' outfielder Kevin Mench slammed into his left leg, fracturing the tibia and keeping him out of play for the rest of the season. Nevertheless, he led the AL that year in complete games, with five. In the spring of 2006, Halladay signed a $40 million contract that would keep him in Toronto through the 2010 season.

Halladay had recovered fully by the start of the 2006 season. In 32 starts he posted a 16–5 record with a 3.18 ERA in 220 innings, second- and fourth-best in the league, respectively. He also finished second in the majors in winning percentage (.762) and tied for second in complete games (four) and was again named to the All-Star team. The Blue Jays improved their record to 87–75 but missed out on a wild-card berth once again. Halladay opened the 2007 season in top form and compiled a 4–0 record in April, for which he was named AL Pitcher of the Month. In May he underwent an appendectomy, returning to action two weeks later to record his 100th career victory, in a game against the Chicago White Sox. He compiled a 16–7 record for the season and led the majors in complete games (seven). He was also among the AL leaders in wins, winning percentage (.696), and innings pitched (225.1). One of his complete games that season included a 10-inning win against the Detroit Tigers, which further solidified his reputation as one of the most durable pitchers in the game. The Blue Jays, however, were plagued with injuries throughout the 2007 season and missed out on the play-offs again, finishing with 83 wins and 79 losses.

In 2008 Halladay had one of his best all-around seasons. He recorded 20 wins for the second time in his career and was named to the AL All-Star team for the fifth time. He also set a then–career high 206 strikeouts and led the league in innings pitched (246), complete games (nine), and shutouts (two). He allowed only 39 walks, making him only the second pitcher in MLB history to post 200 strikeouts and fewer than 40 walks in each of two seasons. Only Cliff Lee of the Indians, who posted 22 victories and a 2.54 ERA, bettered Halladay's record of 20 wins and 2.78 ERA in 2008. Halladay also finished second to Lee in the voting for that year's AL Cy Young Award. The Blue Jays finished the season fourth in their division, with an 86–76 record.

In 2009 Halladay appeared in his seventh straight opening-day start for the Blue Jays (a team record) and achieved his first win of the season, against the Detroit Tigers. Going into the All-Star break, he was among the league leaders in wins, innings pitched, complete games, and ERA, despite his spending two weeks on the disabled list with a strained groin muscle. He was the starting AL pitcher in the All-Star Game. While Halladay was the subject of numerous trade rumors going into the MLB trade deadline of July 31, he remained with the Blue Jays. Though he struggled during the month of August, in which he posted a 2–4 record and lost three consecutive games, he returned to form in September, pitching two consecutive complete-game shutouts. That month he recorded his second career one-hitter, when he shut out the New York Yankees, 6–0, in another complete game victory. In 32 starts he posted a 17–10 record with a 2.79 ERA in 239 innings, third- and second-best in the league, respectively. He also managed a league-low 39 walks and led the majors in complete games (nine) and shutouts (four). In addition, with 208 strikeouts, he surpassed his career-high total from the previous year, making him the only pitcher in Blue Jays history to record 200 or more strikeouts in three consecutive seasons. The Blue Jays again finished the season fourth in their division, with a 75–87 record. Halladay's contract with the team will end in 2010.

Halladay and his wife, Brandy, are members of the Mormon Church (formally, the Church of Jesus Christ of Latter-day Saints). The couple live in Odessa, Florida, with their two young sons, Braden and Ryan. Halladay and his wife are active supporters of the Jays Care Foundation, which helps children in need. Each year since 2005 they have paid for a private luxury suite in Rogers Centre, the Blue Jays' home stadium, for use by youngsters under treatment at the Hospital for Sick Children in Toronto, and on an occasional Sunday they join that day's young guests in the suite; they have also provided funds to improve facilities at the hospital. In 2008 Halladay was named the George Gross/*Toronto Sun* Sportsperson of the Year (named for the *Sun*'s first sports editor).

—C.C.

Suggested Reading: *Denver Post* C p1+ Aug. 17, 2003; *New York Times* p1 Apr. 5, 2009; *Rocky Mountain News* p8 July 4, 2007; *Sports Illustrated* p42+ Apr. 16, 2007; (Toronto, Ontario, Canada) *Globe and Mail* (on-line) June 27, 2003; *USA Today* (on-line) May 8, 2008

David Silverman/Getty Images

Hass, Amira

1956– Israeli journalist

Address: Ha'aretz, *21 Schocken St., Tel Aviv 61001, Israel*

"My task as a journalist is to monitor power," the Israeli reporter Amira Hass told Robert Fisk for the London *Independent* (August 26, 2001). "I'm called 'a correspondent on Palestinian affairs,' but it's more true to say that I'm an expert in Israeli occupation." Hass, who reports on Israeli-Palestinian issues for the liberal Israeli newspaper *Ha'aretz*, is known for being the only Jewish Israeli journalist to live in Gaza and, subsequently, the West Bank, which have been home to Palestinian refugees since 1948 and have been under Israeli military occupation since 1967. Having lived among the Palestinian populations since the Oslo Accords of the early 1990s, Hass has documented the Palestinians' daily lives and hardships in reports that regularly contradict official Israeli accounts. Joel Schalit wrote for the leftist American magazine *Tikkun* (June 30, 2004) that Hass's reporting is "stunningly clear, concise, and unabashedly moralistic," adding, "one cannot walk away from any of Hass' writings on the subject without having learned what it really feels like to live under Israeli military rule." For the last two decades, Hass has written about Israeli policies with regard to Jewish settlements in Gaza and the West Bank and the severe restrictions placed on Palestinians in the occupied territories. "In the end, my desire to live in Gaza stemmed neither from adventurism nor from insanity, but from that dread of being a bystander, from my need to understand, down to the last detail, a world that is, to the best of my political and historical comprehension, a profoundly Israeli creation," Hass wrote in her book *Drinking the Sea at Gaza*. "To me, Gaza embodies the entire saga of the Israeli-Palestinian conflict; it represents the central contradiction of the state of Israel—democracy for some, dispossession for others; it is our exposed nerve." Hass has often said that her decision to report on the plight of Palestinians was inspired largely by her mother's recollection of being marched to a Nazi concentration camp while German women looked on indifferently. "While most people go through life fearful of being victims," Michael Fox wrote for the *Jewish Bulletin* (July 26, 2002), "[Hass's] nightmare scenario is to be a bystander." In her column in *Ha'aretz* (August 30, 2006), Hass explained her work as stemming from a sense of responsibility: "As Jews we all enjoy the privilege Israel gives us, what makes us all collaborators. The question is what does every one of us do in an active and direct daily manner to minimize cooperation with a dispossessing, suppressing regime that never has its fill. Signing a petition and tutting will not do. Israel is a democracy for its Jews. We are not in danger of our lives, we will not be jailed in concentration camps, our livelihood will not be damaged and recreation in the countryside or abroad will not be denied to us. Therefore, the burden of collaboration and direct responsibility is immeasurably heavy." The American writer and activist Susan Sontag, in praise of *Drinking the Sea at Gaza* (as quoted on the publisher's Web site, semiotexte.com), wrote that "a particular debt of gratitude is owed to courageous Israeli Jews such as Amira Hass who have born witness to the increasingly cruel terms of Israeli military occupation and settler annexation. Amira Hass speaks on behalf of justice; in speaking of the sufferings and the rights of people in despair, she defends the true interests of Israel."

The history of the Jews and that of the Arab peoples date from Old Testament times. For many centuries the two groups lived in relative harmony. The radical change in their relations has been traced to the late 19th century, which marked the birth of Arab nationalism and the beginning of Zionism, a movement whose aim was the establishment of a Jewish national state in Palestine. The determination of the precise boundaries of Palestine, which passed from Turkish rule to British rule after World War I, is but one of the many immense, and so far insurmountable, problems underlying the almost unceasing conflict that has raged in the Middle East for many decades. Contributing to the complexities in the question of who owns what land in Palestine are significant differences among the parties to the conflict, not only in the interpretations of events and historical documents but also in the accounts of what precisely happened on countless occasions; thus, the histories of Palestine according to Arabs, on one side, and Jews, on the other, bear little resemblance to each other. Among the key documents whose meanings and intentions are in dispute are the Balfour Declaration of 1917, which stated that the British government "view[ed] with favour the establishment in Palestine of a national home for the Jewish people," and United Nations Resolution 181, by which the General Assembly in 1947 called for the partition of British-ruled Palestine into an Arab state and a Jewish state. Among the many crucial events whose chronologies in Jewish and Arab accounts differ markedly is the Six-Day War, in which, in June 1967, the Israeli army defeated the armies of Egypt, Jordan, and Syria. Moreover, neither Jews nor Arabs form a cohesive group; rather, each has always been represented by several or many factions, all of which have distinctive ideas and agendas. Virtually no descriptions of armed conflicts or other events in the Middle East, whether published or broadcast from Israel or its Arab neighbors or from the United States, Western Europe, or elsewhere, are received dispassionately by those favoring one side or another; almost invariably, they are viewed as biased, inaccurate, and incomplete. "The Israeli-Palestinian conflict is a war of dueling narratives about who is the aggressor, who is the victim and who is the rightful heir to the land . . . ," Marjorie Miller wrote for the *Los Angeles Times* (March 15, 2002). "Language is a weapon in all wars, and no less so in the Israeli-Palestinian conflict."

While Hass is not the only dissident Israeli journalist—Tom Segev and Gideon Levy, both of whom also write for *Ha'aretz*, are among several others—she has often been the only correspondent in the territories when they have been under siege. Through her proximity to the subjects of her reports, Hass has exposed the shortfalls of the Israeli-Palestinian peace process, portrayed oppressive conditions on the ground as being among the causes of continued violence, and served as one of the few links between two populations who often view each other with fear, hatred, and distrust. While she is seen by some as an embodiment of the Israeli national conscience, others have called her a traitor to Israel. Her reports have functioned as counter-narratives to the official versions of both the Israeli and Palestinian authorities, and she has been criticized and threatened by individuals on both sides of the region's political spectrum. While condemning the policies of the Israeli leadership, Hass has also contrasted the privileges of some members of the Palestinian Authority with the poverty of the people they represent, shone a light on corruption in the occupied territories, and been a harsh critic of various factions in the Palestinian leadership, seeing them as often more focused on controlling the people they claim to speak for than on freeing them. Contrary to some people's views about her, Hass believes in the right of Israel to exist. "If a State is not allowed to exist because of the injustices it placed on others then tell me one that has a right to exist," Hass told Catherine Taylor for the *Australian* (March 22, 2001). "I can see how lives were torn apart by the creation of Israel. As a result I live in a contradiction and I have no way to solve it. All I can do is look for ways to stop the injustice now."

Amira Hass was born in 1956 in West Jerusalem, the only child of Hannah Levy, who came from Sarajevo, in what was then Yugoslavia, and the Romanian-born Avraham Hass, Holocaust survivors who later became longtime members of the Israeli Communist Party. "There are three things I always knew about," Hass told Chris Kutschera for the *Middle East* (January 1, 2008), a monthly headquartered in London, England. "My name. . . . Then communism: all our friends were communist. For me the world was communist . . . And finally, the Holocaust: I do not know when I first heard about it, I always knew." Her mother had joined Marshal Tito's partisans against the German occupation of Yugoslavia. Forced to surrender to the Nazis, she survived nine months in 1944–45 in the Bergen-Belsen concentration camp, in Germany. While in captivity, at great peril to her own life, her mother wrote a diary of events in the camp (published in 1982 as *Inside Belsen*) and taught children there. "To her it was a way of fighting, for sure, to have these most forbidden activities," Hass told Harry Kreisler of the Institute of International Studies at the University of California–Berkeley, as part of the Conversations with History series (October 24, 2003, on-line). Hass's father, meanwhile, had survived three to four years under Romanian fascists in the Jewish ghetto in the Nazi-occupied Transnistria region of the Ukraine. Hass has described her parents' lives as containing contradictions after they arrived as refugees in Israel: having been oppressed in Europe, they felt they had found sanctuary in a country whose government oppressed others.

After the establishment of Israel, in 1948, hundreds of thousands of Palestinians fled the new state of their own accord or were forced from their homes and settled as refugees in both Gaza and the West Bank. After Israel annexed those territories (as well as the Sinai peninsula of Egypt and the Golan Heights of Syria) in the 1967 war, the Palestinian refugees came under direct Israeli military oversight. Following the first *intifada* (or uprising against the occupation) in the late 1980s and early 1990s, the Oslo Peace Accords, announced as a step toward Palestinian self-determination, were signed. Hass's work, documenting daily life in the occupied territories, began in earnest after the signing of the accords. As a child of Holocaust survivors, Hass told Sylvain Cypel for the London *Guardian Weekly* (January 3, 2001), "I have an aching sensitivity to any dehumanisation that is typical of some survivors' children." A legacy of being the child of refugees, she told Fox, is that she identifies "with what I call the permanent temporaries."

Hass attended the Hebrew University of Jerusalem and then Tel Aviv University, where she pursued a master's degree but became frustrated by her thesis subject, which focused on the history of Nazism and the reaction of the European left to the Holocaust. "When you go deeply into the history of Nazism you begin to wonder how humanity could have reached such a point," she told Taylor. "The subject became too autobiographical and I knew I could not go on." After traveling and working at jobs that included teaching and cleaning, she took advantage of a connection to get a copy-editing position at *Ha'aretz* in 1989. Later that year, when a violent revolution took place in Romania, Hass asked her new editors to send her there. (She had spent several months in Bucharest in the late 1970s.) Her editors agreed, and she covered the revolution for two weeks before returning to her copy-editing job in Israel. While still at *Ha'aretz,* desiring "something more meaningful in life," as she told Taylor, she volunteered for the group Workers' Hotline, helping Palestinian workers who had complaints against Israeli employers. Hass's work with that group coincided with the first Palestinian intifada, which lasted from 1987 to 1993. Her experience with Workers' Hotline proved formative for her, as previously Hass had felt that her anti-occupation activism could be confined to Israel and that she did not need to interact with the Palestinians or to see how they lived. "During the Gulf War, I reached Gaza under curfew—I'd gone to give Palestinians their checks from Israeli employers," she told Fisk. "That's when my romance with Gaza started. No Israeli journalist knew or covered Gaza."

Hass began writing articles regularly for *Ha'aretz* from the occupied territories in 1991. "My heart would break when I'd talk to old women who still had the keys to the homes they were forced to leave [in 1948]," she told Taylor. She began staying at the homes of friends, among them the Palestinian leader Haidar Abdel-Shafi, which was an important step in establishing trust with the people she was sent to cover. After the Oslo Peace Accords were signed, in 1993, *Ha'aretz* assigned her to cover Gaza full-time. Although her editors advised her against moving there, especially as a single woman, "I knew at once that I wanted to live there . . . ," she told Fisk. "I really wanted to taste what it means to live under occupation—what it is like to live under curfew, to live in fear of a soldier." While many Israelis questioned her desire to live among the Palestinians, Hass saw the move as a necessity. "I think it's so natural for a journalist to do so," she told Kreisler. "If I were asked to cover French affairs, I would go and live in Paris, and travel a lot in France, not write about France from Germany." Similarly, she told Taylor that "Israel's colonialist thinking had seeped so deeply into people's minds that it was accepted to write about Palestinians but not to live with them." Renting an apartment with roommates in the Rimal neighborhood, she stayed in Gaza for three years, filing reports that detailed what she saw as the failure of the peace process. "I referred to Israel's policies on the ground, which were at stark contrast with [the] concept of peace: such as settlements, such as the developing policy of closure, which is the Israeli version of the apartheid pass system," she said in 2004 in Stockholm, Sweden, in accepting an award for journalistic courage. Hass has described Gaza since 1993 as a cramped area that most have not been allowed to leave; where borders have been shut down for weeks at a time, with resulting damage to the fragile economy; and where people sometimes do not know from day to day whether their electricity, gas, medicine, food, or water will be cut off by a blockade that, she told *Democracy Now* (December 2, 2008), "reduces people's lives . . . to basic concern[s]. . . . People are still offended by the very need to be preoccupied all the time by those needs." In 1996 she published her first book, *Drinking the Sea at Gaza* (published in English in 1999), a chronicle of the daily lives of Gazans since the first intifada. In 1997 she relocated to Ramallah, in the West Bank, where she remains today and which she has called a "five-star prison" in comparison with Gaza. While the West Bank was generally much safer than Gaza, in 1998 Hass and a photographer—while reporting on an attack by Jewish settlers on Palestinian farmers in the West Bank—were shot at by the settlers. In 2003 Hass published *Reporting from Ramallah: An Israeli Journalist in an Occupied Land,* translated by Rachel Leah Jones, an anthology of selected *Ha'aretz* articles printed from 1997 to 2002. The book chronicles the breakdown of the peace process, which preceded the second intifada, also commonly referred to as the Al Aqsa Intifada.

During an interview with Amy Goodman for the radio program *Democracy Now!* (April 12, 2005), Hass said that in Israel and the occupied territories, "There are two sets of laws which apply to each separate people. There are two—there are privileges and rights for the one people, for the Israeli people, and mostly for the Jews among . . . the Israeli people, and there are restrictions and decrees and military laws which apply to the other people, to the Palestinians. The Palestinians, as a people, are divided into subgroups, something which is reminiscent also of South Africa under apartheid rule. You have the Palestinians, the Israeli Palestinians who are citizens, but . . . seventh-rate citizens. You have the Palestinians of Gaza, and you have the Palestinians of the West Bank, and now you have Palestinians in every different enclave. There are different restrictions and different decrees which apply to these different enclaves. . . . So all these subdivision[s] of the other people, which disconnects them, which fragments them as a people. And then you have one government, which is elected, which actually decides about the future of both peoples, the scope of development of both peoples, but it is being elected only by one people. For me, this is a form of apartheid, of demographic separation which is meant to improve the conditions and the well-being and the future of one people on the account of the other." While some point to the 2005 Israeli withdrawal from Gaza as a step toward a two-state solution to the region's conflict, Hass, who has since found it increasingly difficult to travel there, has written that Israel still controls and polices Gaza and that the territory effectively remains under occupation. At the same time, Hass has been documenting the expansion of colonial settlements in the West Bank, which, she has argued, furthers the fragmentation of the Palestinian population there.

Some have described Hass's writing style as both passionate and, at times, scientific and observational. She told Kreisler, "I'm trying to avoid slogans as much as possible, because I live in a society, both Israeli and Palestinian, that is really overcrowded with slogans and one-sentence exclamations. And . . . I'm appalled by it." Hass, who rejects the notion of journalistic objectivity, has famously said that the social role of the journalist is to monitor, and be skeptical of, those in power. She has said that with regard to the occupation, Israeli journalists, while ostensibly free of censorship, are still faced with a dilemma of having to monitor the powerful figures who ensure their privileges—resulting in a reluctance to challenge official versions of events. Hass has repeatedly expressed the fear that her work amounts to, as the saying goes, preaching to the converted. She told Angel Ricardo Martinez for the *Palestine Chronicle* (December 28, 2008, on-line), "It's not that there is official censorship, it's just that there is an unwillingness of most Israelis to know."

Hass, who was named a Press Freedom Hero by the International Press Institute in 2000, has received numerous awards for her reporting. In 2002 she won a Bruno Kreisky Human Rights Prize. The following year she won the UNESCO/Guillermo Cano World Press Freedom Prize, which honors people who have advanced the cause of freedom of expression in the world at great personal risk. The award is named for the Colombian journalist Guillermo Cano, who was murdered in the 1980s for his critical reporting on the country's drug cartels. In 2004 Hass received the first Anna Lindh Award, named for the murdered Swedish foreign minister and given in honor of those who have fought against prejudice and oppression. In 2009 Hass received a Lifetime Achievement Award from the International Women's Media Foundation. In introducing Hass at the award ceremony, the CNN reporter Christiane Amanpour described her as "one of the greatest truth-seekers of them all," according to a transcript posted on the Web site Democracy Now (October 21, 2009). "Some call her a traitor. It is uncomfortable to hear the truth; it's very uncomfortable to tell the truth. Some say that she is the only voice of truth in a polarized conflict. For twenty years, she's paid no attention to either of these camps, choosing instead to follow her own path. Amira knows . . . that dictators do not like journalists, but more than that, democracies often don't like journalists either." Hass, in her acceptance speech, called the award a recognition of her failure rather than success as a journalist. "It's not about achievement that we should be talking here, but about a failure," Hass said, according to the Democracy Now transcript. "It is the failure to make the Israeli and international public use and accept correct terms and words which reflect the reality, not the Orwellian Newspeak that has flourished since 1993 and has been cleverly dictated and disseminated by those with [vested] interests. The peace process terminology, which took reign, blurs the perception of real processes that are going on: a special Israeli blend of military occupation, colonialism, apartheid, Palestinian limited self-rule in enclaves, and a democracy for Jews."

Hass is the subject of a documentary, *Between the Lines*, directed by Yifat Kedar, as well as a play, *Wall Whispers*, by the French playwrights Ariel Cypel and Gael Chaillet. The latter, about the life of Palestinian prisoners in Israel, centered on the relationship between Hass and a prisoner. A young militant sentenced in 1990, at 23, to almost three decades in prison for throwing Molotov cocktails at Jews during the first intifada, Mahmud Al Safadi began to read Hass's columns while incarcerated and started writing letters to her. Soon they were speaking regularly on a smuggled mobile phone, and Hass began recording his descriptions of daily life behind bars in Israel. In 2006, after 17 years, he was released on parole. *Wall Whispers* was first produced in Paris in 2008 and is scheduled to be shown in Israel and the West Bank.

In the fall of 2008, Israeli authorities declared Gaza off-limits to journalists and closed its borders in response to rocket attacks from Hamas, the governing body in Gaza; the attacks, which killed three Israeli civilians, had followed an Israeli-imposed, several-months-long, intermittent blockade of funds, food, water, electricity, and aid. Despite the closing of the borders, Hass entered Gaza by boat with peace activists but was told by Hamas to leave on November 30, because they could no longer guarantee her safety. Upon her return to Israel, she was detained by Israeli authorities; *Ha'aretz* later secured her release. Subsequently, Israel launched an attack on Gaza, killing at least 1,300 people and injuring thousands more. Hass's *Ha'aretz* column on January 7, 2009, was entitled "Lucky My Parents Aren't Alive to See This." "Even before the language laundromat developed to its current sophistication," she wrote, "my parents were nauseated by phrases like the 'the war for peace in the Galilee' or 'disturbances of public order' when the public order was the occupation and the disturbance was resistance to it. When order is preventing the Palestinians from having what the Jews have a right to and demand. . . . Because of my parents' history they knew what it meant to close people behind barbed-wire fences in a small area. . . . How lucky it is that they are not alive to see how these incarcerated people are bombarded with all the glorious military technology of Israel and the United States."

In May 2009, according to *Ha'aretz* (May 12, 2009), Hass was again arrested by Israeli authorities upon exiting the Gaza Strip, "for violating a law which forbids residence in an enemy state." She was later released on bail.

Hass lives in Ramallah.

—M.M.

Suggested Reading: *Australian* M p13 Mar. 12, 2001; *Counterpunch* (on-line) June 28, 2004; *Democracy Now* (on-line) Apr. 12, 2008, Dec. 2, 2008; *Ha'aretz* (on-line) Aug. 30, 2006, Jan. 7, 2009; (London) *Independent* (on-line) Aug. 26, 2001; *Los Angeles Times* A p1 Mar. 15, 2002

Selected Books: *Drinking the Sea at Gaza: Days and Nights in a Land Under Siege*, 1999; *Reporting from Ramallah: An Israeli Journalist in an Occupied Land*, 2003

Brad Barket/Getty Images

Hathaway, Anne

Nov. 12, 1982– Actress

Address: Creative Artists Agency, 2000 Ave. of the Stars, Los Angeles, CA 90067

The actress Anne Hathaway emerged as a teen icon when, at 19, she starred in the popular fantasy film *The Princess Diaries* (2001), and she solidified her appeal as a bankable young star in the 2004 movies *Ella Enchanted* and *The Princess Diaries 2: Royal Engagement.* Concerned that she would be typecast if she continued to portray sweet, klutzy young women in family films, she fought to secure roles in more adult-themed projects; as Mal Vincent put it in the Norfolk *Virginian-Pilot* (January 13, 2006), "Now, she's accepting only roles that don't require her to wear a tiara." When she appeared as the emotionally disconnected wife of Jake Gyllenhaal's character in the award-winning 2006 film *Brokeback Mountain,* audiences and critics alike recognized her potential as a dramatic performer. She came into her own as the star of the 2006 fashion-industry satire *The Devil Wears Prada*, following up that hit film with the lead role in *Becoming Jane* and a major part, opposite Steve Carell, in the 2008 comedy *Get Smart.* She also won praise and a Golden Globe Award nomination for her role as a recovering addict in *Rachel Getting Married* (2008). On her ability to avoid typecasting, Hathaway told Vincent, "I had to find myself as a woman before I could leave those girl-finds-a-woman stories. I used to worry about the wrong things—like how I looked and things. Now, I worry only about the character."

Anne Jacqueline Hathaway was born on November 12, 1982 in Brooklyn, New York. Her father, Gerald, is a lawyer; her mother, Kate McCauley, is an actress who played the character Fantine in a national tour of the highly popular musical *Les Misérables*, based on the novel by Victor Hugo. When Hathaway was five years old, her family moved from Brooklyn to the New York suburb of Millburn, New Jersey. Hathaway developed a taste for acting at a young age. "The day we moved from Brooklyn, my parents gave my brother [Michael] and me a video camera and told us to keep busy by making a movie," she told Stephen Whitty for the Newark, New Jersey, *Star-Ledger* (April 11, 2004). She noted that in the resulting footage, "I'm 5 years old, sitting on this cocktail table in an empty room, improvising a 15-minute monologue about being on the beach with my cat, and acting my heart out."

When Hathaway was seven or eight, she traveled with her mother on the *Les Misérables* tour and was inspired to become an actress. Although her parents supported her decision, they encouraged her to wait until she was in her teens before going on auditions. "I was champing at the bit to start earlier, honestly, but my parents insisted the career aspect could wait," Hathaway told Whitty. "It sounds like such a cliché, but you can have a career at any age. You can't relive your childhood." Taking her parents' advice, she focused on common childhood activities, excelling at schoolwork and playing soccer. In middle school she began to act in local plays at the Paper Mill Playhouse in Millburn, and at 14 she had a starring role in Millburn High School's production of the musical comedy *Once Upon a Mattress.* She was the only teen accepted to study for six months with the prestigious Barrow Group, a theater company in the New York City borough of Manhattan. At 15 Hathaway went on her first audition for a commercial. "I'd take a train, go into the city and smile for a Cheez Whiz commercial," she told Jesse McKinley for the *New York Times* (February 18, 2002, on-line) of such experiences. "I really didn't find it fulfilling." Raised as a Roman Catholic, Hathaway also considered becoming a nun when she was 15. When she later learned that her older brother was gay, she decided against that path, given the church's stance against homosexuality. In addition to acting, Hathaway had a talent for singing; a soprano, she honed her voice through training with vocal coaches and choral groups, culminating in her performance in 1999 at New York's Carnegie Hall as a member of the All-Eastern United States High School Honors Chorus.

Three days after singing at Carnegie Hall, Hathaway auditioned successfully for a role on the Fox television network's family drama *Get Real*. In that series, which proved to be the 16-year-old actress's big break, she played Meghan Green, a high-school overachiever struggling to decide if she wants to attend college immediately after graduation. The show lasted for only one season but provided Hathaway with enough exposure to secure roles in other productions. She co-starred in the independent film *The Other Side of Heaven* (2001) and, on her way to New Zealand for the shoot, stopped in Los Angeles, California, to audition for a role in the Disney comedy *The Princess Diaries*. During the audition Hathaway accidentally fell off her chair, endearing her to the film's director, Garry Marshall, who had been looking for an actress capable of a comedic performance as a clumsy young woman. "She didn't have to act to play the klutzy princess. She is authentically awkward," Marshall told Vincent. "I'm a big, fat, sloppy, messy, get-in-the-dirt, rip-your-clothes-up kind of klutz," Hathaway told the *Grand Rapids (Michigan) Press* (August 13, 2004). "I knock over lamps. I have bruises in the oddest places."

The Princess Diaries was a box-office success. In the film, based on Meg Cabot's 2000 novel of the same name, Hathaway played Mia Thermopolis, a socially inept teenage girl who discovers that she is a princess and heir to the throne of the (fictional) European country Genovia. The film followed Mia's struggle to balance her normal high-school life with her training at the hands of the queen (played by the veteran actress Julie Andrews) to become a princess. Although many critics pointed out the film's teen-drama clichés, most found Hathaway's performance a standout. "If Andrews oozes regal poise and Hathaway radiates movie star allure—and they do—credit the actresses, not this flimsy fairy tale," Christine Dolen wrote for the *Miami Herald* (August 3, 2001, on-line). The film's popularity elevated Hathaway to teen-idol status; she was named one of the "25 Most Intriguing People" by *People* and appeared as a guest on MTV's music-video show *Total Request Live* and the TV comedy show *Politically Incorrect*. Due to her acting work, Hathaway missed her first semester at Vassar College, in Poughkeepsie, New York, where she worked toward a degree in English with a minor in women's studies. She transferred to New York University in 2005; she has yet to finish her degree.

The Other Side of Heaven, filmed before *The Princess Diaries* but not released until 2002, opened to mediocre reviews. The film chronicles the adventures of the real-life Mormon missionary John Groberg (played by Christopher Gorham), who leaves his home and his girlfriend, Jean (Hathaway), to operate a mission on a remote island. In the film Hathaway's performance took a backseat to Gorham's, and Scott Foundas wrote for *Variety* (January 27, 2002, on-line) that her role "consists of little more than occasional voiced-over readings of Jean's love letters." That year Hathaway also had a small role in the film adaptation of Charles Dickens's novel *Nicholas Nickelby*, which focuses on the adventures of the young title character, whose father has left the family penniless. The film won a Golden Globe nomination for best picture, which helped Hathaway gain further recognition.

Hathaway made her Broadway debut in 2002, appearing in the musical play *Carnival* as the orphan Lili. Many critics were taken with her singing and dancing; the theater critic Ben Brantley wrote for the *New York Times* (February 9, 2002, on-line) that her status as a novice helped to project the innocence of the character she portrayed: "Somehow [she] makes unspotted purity look like the latest fashion. This is essential, since the appeal of *Carnival*, a show of strangely polarized sensibilities, lies in the balance of a slightly smirky cynicism and the unquestioned innocence of its leading lady. Ms. Hathaway, best known for the *Cinderella* fantasy film *The Princess Diaries*, has a flutish, frill-free soprano that is the opposite of show-biz brass and a pretty, open face that looks as if it had never raised an eyebrow."

Hathaway returned to teen-fantasy fare with *Ella Enchanted*, a modern take on the Cinderella fairy tale. While the film received mixed reviews, several critics commended Hathaway's performance. David Rooney wrote for *Variety* (April 4, 2004, on-line), "While the mix is as uneven as the performance styles, the glue that holds the sweet teen-fantasy together is star Anne Hathaway, who continues to evolve into a luminous young lead." Writing for *TVguide.com* (2004), Angel Cohn noted that "Hathaway's infectious charm and easy chemistry with the attractive [Hugh] Dancy more than compensate for minor liabilities like the uneven tone director Tommy O'Haver establishes. Audiences, especially preteens, will be enchanted by Ella." Also that year Hathaway starred in *The Princess Diaries 2: Royal Engagement*. The film finds Mia, now a recent college graduate, searching for a husband so that she can assume the throne of Genovia. Most critics found *Royal Engagement* to be little more than a more elaborate version of the original film; Claudia Puig wrote for *USA Today* (August 10, 2004, on-line), "*The Royal Engagement* seeks to plump up its thin plot with sentimentality, trotting out many of the original cast members in an attempt to remind audiences of what they liked in the first place."

Although she was now a bankable star with a growing fan base, Hathaway was concerned about being typecast in teen and family fare. "I'm a 21-year-old in a G-rated movie," she told the *Grand Rapids Press*. "This isn't exactly the kind of artistic choices that I want to be making right now, but at the same time, I'm grateful to be able to make them." She said in an interview for the Web site iVillage, "By the end of *Princess Diaries 2*, I was ready to do something completely different. I got into this not to typecast myself. I got into it to be an actress, to scare the sh*t out of myself, and force myself into a place outside of my comfort zone."

With her next two films, Hathaway was successful in making a break from teen fare. The 2005 film *Havoc*, which went straight to DVD, found the actress playing an affluent Los Angeles teenager who flirts with a dangerous inner-city gang to escape her safe suburban lifestyle. Hathaway also appeared that year in the Ang Lee–directed critical and box-office success *Brokeback Mountain*. Starring Heath Ledger and Jake Gyllenhaal, the film explored the ill-fated romance of two male ranch hands who fall in love while working together in the mountains of Wyoming. Confronted by the antigay prejudices of the rural Midwest of the 1960s and 1970s, Ennis (Ledger) and Jack (Gyllenhaal) pursue their love affair in secret. In the film Hathaway played Lureen Newsome, the rodeo queen Jack marries in order to give the appearance of living a "normal" life. Michelle Williams played the wife of the Ledger character; Jack Garner wrote for the Rochester, New York, *Democrat and Chronicle* (January 6, 2006) that Hathaway and Williams were "excellent as the emotionally abandoned women." The film won four Golden Globe Awards, including best motion picture in the drama category, and was nominated for an Academy Award for best picture.

Hathaway returned to the screen as the star of the hit comedy *The Devil Wears Prada*. The film was directed by David Frankel and adapted from Lauren Weisberger's best-selling, same-titled book, a roman à clef rumored to be about Weisberger's tenure under Anna Wintour, the editor of the fashion magazine *Vogue*. In the film Hathaway played Andrea, the assistant of the cold-hearted fashion mogul Miranda (Meryl Streep), the editor of the fictional magazine *Runway*. While enduring Miranda's malicious barbs, Andrea finds herself becoming more like her reprehensible boss. Writing for *Variety* (June 22, 2006, on-line), Todd McCarthy observed, "Hathaway is fine as the smart but green young woman who finally becomes so good at her thankless job that she comes perilously close to going over to the 'dark side' [represented] by Miranda." Some felt that Hathaway was not the best choice for the role. David Edelstein wrote for *New York* (June 25, 2006, on-line), "It's bizarre when all the *Runway* employees wrinkle their noses at Andrea instead of realizing that, with her long legs and neck and skinny face and big, dark eyes, she's pure *Runway*. Hathaway overdoes the girlish wonderment and isn't up to her big, to-hell-with-the-devil scene, but she certainly carries off the clothes."

In 2007 Hathaway starred in *Becoming Jane*, based on the life of the English novelist Jane Austen. The film—which featured Hathaway as a young, yet-to-be published Austen—met with mixed reviews but was given credit for its imaginative interpretation of the novelist's early life. According to Kyle Smith, writing for the *New York Post* (August 3, 2007, on-line), "Instead of trying to make Austen's life entertaining by pretending it was just like her work . . . *Becoming Jane* has a more astute appreciation of how Austen, or any fiction writer, works. There's a bit of stealing from life, lots of exaggeration, some wish fulfillment, mix-and-match character assembly." Critical reaction to Hathaway's performance was varied. Claudia Puig wrote for *USA Today* (August 2, 2007, on-line), "Hathaway is terrific as Austen. Not only does she nail the British accent, but her subtle mannerisms and expressions speak volumes. She delivers the sparkling dialogue, by screenwriter Kevin Hood, with just the right nuance and verve." Others felt that she did not capture the essence of Austen; Richard Shickel wrote for *Time* (August 3, 2007, on-line), "Hathaway never makes us think the woman could write anything more complex than a diet book. The real novelist must have been, even at the tender age she is supposed to be in this film, a much more ferocious creature, determined to make her way as a writer, certain that love . . . must prove a distraction from writing."

Hathaway appeared alongside the comedic actor Steve Carell in the 2008 adventure comedy *Get Smart*, an adaptation of the 1960s television series of the same name. Playing the seductive Agent 99, she won some critics' praise for her gift for slapstick. Lisa Schwarzbaum wrote for *Entertainment Weekly* (June 20, 2008, on-line), "The unexpected star is Hathaway, looking cool as a runway model in the role originated by Barbara Feldon, lithe as a (pink) panther, and displaying great comic timing." Despite that film's top box-office rankings, the June arrest of the Italian real-estate developer Raffaello Follieri—with whom Hathaway was romantically involved from 2004 until June 2008—quickly overshadowed her performance in the film. Follieri was charged with multiple counts of fraud, conspiracy, and money laundering after posing as a Vatican official looking to sell church-owned real estate. The couple's subsequent breakup became fodder for the press, and in October 2008 Follieri was sentenced to four and a half years in prison (Hathaway was not charged with any crimes). Although she has not commented directly on Follieri during interviews, Hathaway told David Carr for the *New York Times* (January 4, 2009, on-line), "I have not made perfect choices by any stretch of the imagination, but I think by and large I've managed to avoid making foolish decisions. I've never lost custody of myself. I know who I am." Hathaway is currently dating the actor Adam Shulman.

In 2008 Hathaway appeared in Jonathan Demme's film *Rachel Getting Married* as Kym, a recovering drug addict who attends her sister's wedding and stirs up family tensions. The film received positive reviews from many critics, and Hathaway's performance was praised. Owen Gleiberman wrote for *Entertainment Weekly* (October 1, 2008, on-line), "The last actress you'd expect to see cast as a self-loathing, frayed-nerves drug casualty is a red-carpet blossom like Hathaway. Yet from the moment she shows up, her eyes peering with a junkie's paranoid radar from beneath her Louise Brooks-helmet-slashed-with-a-straight-razor hair, the actress wires you right into her rage and awareness. Kym is a walking disaster, but a disaster with feelers, and the effect she has upon her family is to electrify them with the dreaded truths she calls up. Hathaway is a revelation: She makes toxic narcissism mesmerizing, but she also gives Kym a desperate confessional ardor." For her role in the film, Hathaway was nominated for a Golden Globe Award. Rachel Abramowitz wrote for the *Los Angeles Times* (November 13, 2008, on-line) that Hathaway's involvement with Follieri and emotional performance in *Rachel Getting Married* was a "double whammy of on-screen and off-screen despair [that] has curiously combined to give Hathaway heft and maturity, making her more than just another pretty face."

In 2008 Hathaway also appeared in *Passengers* as a young therapist hired to counsel the survivors of a plane crash. When her new patients begin to disappear, Hathaway's character is forced to uncover the truth behind the crash. In a representative, unenthusiastic assessment, Stephen Holden wrote for the *New York Times* (October 25, 2008, on-line), "With her wide, frightened Judy Garland eyes, Ms. Hathaway lends *Passengers* a frisson of anxiety. But how much emotional zing can be extracted from lifeless dialogue whose sole purpose is patching together 100 minutes of clichés?"

In 2009 Hathaway appeared alongside Kate Hudson in the romantic comedy *Bride Wars*. The film centers on two best friends, played by Hudson and Hathaway, as they prepare for their weddings. Critics responded negatively to the movie. Nathan Rabin, for example, wrote for the *A.V. Club* (January 8, 2009, on-line), "After her revelatory performance in Jonathan Demme's *Rachel Getting Married*, Anne Hathaway will have a much harder time getting away with pandering dreck like *Bride Wars*, which takes the burgeoning Anne Hathaway wedding-movie subgenre from the sublime to the despicable. An air of cynical commercial calculation hangs over the film, which witlessly explores two preeminent American obsessions: planning and executing the perfect wedding, and winning at all costs." That year Hathaway also lent her voice to episodes of *The Simpsons* and *Family Guy* and appeared as Viola in the New York Shakespeare Festival summer production of *Twelfth Night*. After seeing her in that role, Charles Isherwood wrote for the *New York Times* (June 26, 2009, on-line), "Among the many pleasures of her performances is [their] effortless modesty. On screen or onstage Ms. Hathaway possesses the unmistakable glow of a natural star, but she dives smoothly and with obvious pleasure into the embrace of a cohesive ensemble cast."

Hathaway's upcoming films, scheduled for 2010 release, include the Tim Burton–directed version of *Alice in Wonderland*, which will also star Johnny Depp; the comedy *Valentine's Day*; and the drama *Love and Other Drugs*. She is also slated to play the singer and actress Judy Garland in adaptations for the stage and screen of Gerard Clarke's biography *Get Happy: The Life of Judy Garland*. She has been cast in additional films that were in development in late 2009: *The Opposite of Love*, *Get Smart 2*, *Tokyo Suckerpunch*, and *The Greatest Showman on Earth*.

Hathaway has said that she would like to perform in more stage roles, telling the Associated Press (June 27, 2006), "I don't feel comfortable doing movies. It's not what I trained to do. I trained to be a theater actress. You put me on a stage in front of 2,000 people, I know what to do. You put me in front of a camera, I'm like, 'Duh.' . . . Although I'm still terrified of it —and I freely admit that I am—I've kind of grown to love it, and it is its own art form." Hathaway, a vegetarian, lives in New York City.

—W.D.

Suggested Reading: *Entertainment Weekly* p28+ Sep. 26, 2008; *Grand Rapids (Michigan) Press* C p5 Aug. 13, 2004; *Harper's Bazaar* p130+ July 2007; (Newark, New Jersey) *Star-Ledger* p1 Apr. 11, 2004; *Newsweek* p56+ Sep. 29, 2008; (Norfolk, Virgina) *Virginian-Pilot* p69 Jan. 13, 2006; *Seventeen* p248+ Sep. 2001, p102+ Feb. 2003

Selected Films: *The Princess Diaries*, 2001; *The Other Side of Heaven*, 2002; *Nicholas Nickelby*, 2002; *Ella Enchanted*, 2004; *The Princess Diaries 2: Royal Engagement*, 2004; *Havoc*, 2005; *Brokeback Mountain*, 2005; *The Devil Wears Prada*, 2006; *Becoming Jane*, 2007; *Get Smart*, 2008; *Rachel Getting Married*, 2008; *Passengers*, 2008; *Bride Wars*, 2009

Higgs, Peter

May 29, 1929– Theoretical physicist; educator

Address: 2 Darnaway St., Edinburgh EH3 6BG, Scotland

As the Large Hadron Collider (LHC)—the world's largest and most powerful particle accelerator, or atom smasher—neared start-up in September 2008, the theories of the British physicist Peter

Fabrice Coffrini/AFP/Getty Images

Peter Higgs

Higgs drew a great deal of media attention. That is because the primary goal of those who designed the collider and the more than 100 nations that paid for its construction is to produce evidence that Higgs's theories—actually, hypotheses—are correct. A crucial portion of what is known as the standard model of particle theory, his hypotheses are expressed in mathematical terms; Higgs formulated them during the decade after he earned his doctoral degree, in 1954, in an attempt to answer two questions about the nature of the universe: why do some elementary, or fundamental, particles have mass while others do not, and how did those that have mass acquire it? The answers to those questions will shed light on what happened in the infinitesimally tiny fraction of a second following the Big Bang—the moment when, theoretically, the universe, including time as well as space and matter, came into existence, 10 billion to 20 billion years ago. Higgs has proposed that, in addition to the electromagnetic and gravitational fields (whose existence has been proved experimentally or through observation and can be expressed mathematically as well), there exists a mass-generating field that pervades the whole universe. Associated with that field, he has suggested, is a particle that generates mass; that particle was dubbed (not by Higgs) the Higgs boson. The validity of Higgs's equations and the others connected with the standard model depends upon the existence of that particle, but no one has ever detected its physical presence; that is because the only way of doing so is by means of a particle accelerator, and even the most powerful accelerators that have been operating in recent years are insufficiently powerful to detect it. Higgs and the many physicists who believe that Higgs's theories are correct hope that the LHC, near Geneva, Switzerland, will provide proof that the Higgs boson is real. In an interview with Richard Wilson for the London *Sunday Times* (June 15, 2008), the theoretical physicist John Ellis said, "All this is important because it tells us how the universe works. People have been trying to figure out how the universe works ever since they noticed that there is a universe out there. Without Peter's work, we wouldn't have theories that made any sense." In a video of Higgs posted on YouTube.com (2009), Higgs echoed Ellis's words; if the Higgs boson turns out to be a chimera, he said, a huge body of work in contemporary physics would have to be discarded as erroneous. "Detecting the Higgs boson would represent an enormous breakthrough in particle physics," Peter Rodgers, the editor of *Physics World*, declared in that publication (July 10, 2004, on-line). Proof of the boson's existence will require the painstaking analysis of an enormous amount of data produced by the LHC—as well as the repair of that machine: the collider, a project overseen by CERN, the European Organization for Nuclear Research, functioned for only two weeks before a series of technical problems forced it to be shut down. Operations were not expected to resume until the end of 2009 at the earliest. Some scientists predict that it could take years before the device can run at full strength.

Higgs taught at the University of Edinburgh, in Scotland, for 36 years, until his retirement, in 1996. In 2004, when Rodgers talked with him, he seemed "embarrassed by the fame that his eponymous boson has brought," as Rodgers wrote. "In conversation he talks about 'the so-called Higgs field' and the 'so-called Higgs model,' and is keen to give credit to a host of other physicists whose work has led to our current understanding of the generation of mass within the Standard Model"—physicists including Abdus Salam, Sheldon Glashow, Steven Weinberg, Philip Anderson, Jeffrey Goldstone, Yoichiro Nambu, François Englert, Robert Brout, Gerald Guralnik, Carl Hagen, and Tom Kibble. (Englert, Brout, Guralnik, Hagen, and Kibble are widely considered to be co-discoverers of the boson on which the Dutch theoretical physicist Gerardus 't Hooft conferred Higgs's name in 1971.) "I get very uneasy when people try to attach too much importance to me," he said to James Morgan for the Glasgow, Scotland, *Herald* (April 7, 2008). His modesty notwithstanding, Higgs has won or shared a bevy of honors, among them the Rutherford Medal (1984) and the Paul Dirac Medal (1997), both from the Institute of Physics, the main professional body for physicists in Great Britain and Ireland, for "outstanding contributions to theoretical (including mathematical and computational) physics," and the Wolf Foundation Prize in Physics (2004), considered among physicists second in prestige only to the Nobel Prize.

Peter Ware Higgs was born to Thomas Ware Higgs and Gertrude Maude Higgs on May 29, 1929 in Newcastle upon Tyne (commonly referred to simply as Newcastle), a city in northeastern England. His father's job, as a sound engineer for the British Broadcasting Corp. (BBC), forced the family to move repeatedly. For that reason Higgs missed some of his early schooling. As a youngster he developed asthma; after he suffered a bout of pneumonia, his mother home-schooled him for a while. "She was very motivated to push me," Higgs told Ian Sample for the London *Guardian* (November 17, 2007). "My father, I think he was just rather scared of children." When the BBC sent his father to work in Bedford, Higgs and his mother moved to Bristol, more than 100 miles distant, in the southwestern part of the country.

In Bristol Higgs attended Cotham Grammar School, where science was emphasized, and he excelled at math. The German air force's heavy bombings of Bristol during World War II sometimes interrupted his schooling, and he once broke his arm when he fell into a bomb crater near the school. Cotham was the alma mater of Paul Dirac (1902–84), a Nobel Prize–winning theoretical physicist who was a pioneer in the fields of quantum mechanics and quantum electrodynamics. Complex mathematical calculations, not physical experiments or observations, led Dirac to predict—correctly, as later discoveries proved—that for every subatomic particle, there exists a mirror twin, an antiparticle, with the same mass but opposite charge. Dirac's work inspired Higgs to study theoretical physics. "It's about understanding!" Higgs exclaimed to Sample. "Understanding the world!"

When he was 17 Higgs enrolled at the City of London School, an independent day school known both for its diverse student body and its strong science and mathematics curricula. During his high-school years (and later at college), he much preferred, and was far more skilled at, grappling with mathematical formulas than handling equipment and chemicals or other materials in science labs. Having accepted his parents' contention that Great Britain's most prestigious universities—Oxford and Cambridge—"were all very well for the children of the idle rich to go and waste their time and that of their tutors" and that "if you were serious about university, you went somewhere else," as he recalled to Sample, Higgs opted to attend King's College London, a division of the University of London. He earned a B.S. degree with first-class honors in physics in 1950 and an M.S. degree, also in physics, the following year. He worked toward his doctorate under the supervision of two theoretical chemists—Charles Coulson and H. Christopher Longuet-Higgins, a former student of Coulson's. Higgs was awarded a Ph.D. in 1954. His thesis was entitled "Some Problems in the Theory of Molecular Vibrations"—"work which signalled the start of his life-long interest in the application of the ideas of symmetry to physical systems," according to a 2008 profile of him on the Web site of the School of Physics and Astronomy of the University of Edinburgh. In particle physics, "symmetry" has special meanings. One of them is "invariance," the property of remaining unchanged when certain conditions change, among them time, orientation in space, charge (positive or negative), and parity.

For two years after he completed his graduate studies, Higgs worked at the University of Edinburgh. He had grown fond of Edinburgh during his youth, when he had hitchhiked to the Edinburgh Festival (the umbrella name for several cultural festivals that occur concurrently every summer). He spent the next year at University College London (part of the University of London) and the following year at Imperial College, also in London. From 1958 to 1960 he taught mathematics at University College London. He then returned to the University of Edinburgh, where he held the title of lecturer at the Tait Institute for Mathematical Physics for the next 10 years. He was promoted to reader (an academic position in Great Britain) in 1970 and named to a "personal chair" in theoretical physics in 1980.

Meanwhile, in addition to his classroom duties, Higgs had become fascinated with quantum field theory, which describes the characteristics and behavior of atoms and subatomic particles and the forces that act on them, and he began to contemplate the origins of mass. A fundamental concept of physics, mass is the amount of matter that makes up anything that has substance, everything from atoms to parts of atoms and congregations of atoms: gases, liquids, and solids, the last including everything from grains of sand, animals and plants, and manmade objects to meteors, planets, moons, and stars. In physics, mass is not the same as weight, which is a measurement of Earth's gravitational pull on anything that has mass; according to the physicist Albert Einstein's famous equation $E=mc^2$—where "E" represents energy, "m" is mass, and "c" is the speed of light (186,000 miles or just under 300,000 kilometers per second)—energy also has mass. In the first scientific description of mass, the British mathematician and physicist Isaac Newton (1642–1727) wrote about it in terms of the force needed to move and accelerate a stationary object. According to Ian Sample, for several centuries "scientists were happy to think of mass as something that simply existed," but in the 20th century, as more was learned about subatomic particles as well as the probable origins of the universe, they began to wonder where mass had come from.

Carried out mathematically rather than experimentally or through observation of astronomical phenomena, Higgs's work was based on research that other physicists had been conducting, some of it beginning in the 1950s. In the course of performing his calculations, Higgs manipulated equations of the physicists Abdus Salam and Sheldon Glashow. When he "added in his own field equations (and thus the Higgs bosons) to equations somewhat analogous to those of Salam or Glashow," Charles C. Mann wrote for *Smithsonian* (March 1, 1989), "he found that certain particles in the original equation behaved in an astonishing fashion. They began with zero mass and then mathematically 'ate up' other, unwanted particles in the field (ones that had made a mess of the mathematics in the theory he was investigating), emerging with mass." In interpreting that outcome, Higgs came up with the idea that at the moment the universe came into being, particles had no mass. Then, a minuscule fraction of a second later, as a result of what became known as the Higgs mechanism, an all-encompassing force field was formed and some particles acquired mass. In Sample's words, "Higgs's theory showed that mass was produced by a new type of field that clings to particles wherever they are, dragging on them and making them heavy. Some particles find the field more sticky than others. Particles of light are oblivious to it. Others have to wade through it like an elephant in tar. So, in theory, particles can weigh nothing, but as soon as they are in the field, they get heavy"—that is, they acquire mass and weight.

Discoveries in physics are often derived from analyses of broader phenomena. That was true of what Higgs has called his "one important idea," the crux of which came to him during a single weekend, as James Morgan reported, when he was thinking about the work of the physicist Jeffrey Goldstone. The first mention of his idea appeared in a communication published in *Physics Letters* (Volume 12, September 1964), a CERN journal, in which Higgs questioned conclusions drawn by Goldstone regarding "the nature of relativistic field theories with spontaneously broken symmetries," according to a brief biography of Goldstone on the Web site of the Massachusetts Institute of Technology, where he is now professor emeritus. Higgs's letter—before the age of the Internet, such letters were the fastest way for scientists to share their discoveries—attracted scant attention. Higgs next sent another letter to the same CERN publication, elaborating on his findings and noting the possibility of the existence of a never-before-described, massive boson, but it was rejected "on the grounds that it did not warrant rapid publication," according to an article entitled "A Brief History of the Higgs Mechanism" posted in 2008 on the Web site of the School of Physics and Astronomy at the University of Edinburgh.

Higgs then sent his second letter to *Physical Review Letters*, a publication of the American Physical Society, where its worthiness for publication was reviewed by Yoichiro Nambu, whose discovery of the mechanism of what is called spontaneous broken symmetry earned him the Nobel Prize in physics in 2008. Higgs's missive had reached *Physical Review Letters* on August 31, 1964, the same day that the journal had published, in its 13th volume, a paper on work (about which Higgs had been unaware) conducted by the Belgian physicists François Englert and Robert Brout, in which Englert and Brout, through very different calculations, had presented a hypothesis similar to his. At Nambu's request, Higgs added to his letter material about Englert and Brout's findings, after having discussed their work and that of others with two American particle physicists—Gerald Guralnik, of Brown University, and Carl R. Hagen, of the University of Rochester—and a Briton, Tom Kibble, of Imperial College London. Higgs's revised second letter, entitled "Broken Symmetries and the Masses of Gauge Bosons," as well as two letters by Guralnik, Hagen, and Kibble, appeared in a subsequent issue of Volume 13 of *Physical Review Letters* in 1964. "I don't know why I separated the work into two pieces," Higgs told Peter Rodgers for the London *Independent* (September 1, 2004). "Maybe if I had written it as one continuous paper, they would have rejected the lot."

Higgs's second paper sparked some discussion among physicists. On a lecture tour of the U.S. in the mid-1960s, Higgs talked about his hypotheses at universities including Harvard and at the Institute for Advanced Study, at Princeton. "I was facing audiences who at first thought I was a crackpot . . . ," he recalled to Rodgers. "They didn't realize that you could do something useful with the work." That realization came when Steven Weinberg and Abdus Salam used Higgs's equations to identify new particles, called W and Z, and demonstrated that those particles could combine two of the universe's four forces—the electromagnetic force and the weak force—into what was named the electroweak force. After Weinberg, Salam, and Glashow received the 1979 Nobel Prize in physics for their discoveries, "the Higgs boson became part of the furniture in particle physics," as Rodgers wrote.

If particle physics is thought of as a room, as in Rodgers's analogy, it is a room that in the 20th century grew increasingly crowded with furniture but still lacked some important pieces and failed to present a unified whole—a situation that was still true in early 2009. Scientists now know that every atom—the smallest particle whose composition can be changed by chemical means—has a nucleus composed of one or more protons orbited by one or more electrons, and that, except for one form (or isotope) of the hydrogen atom, every atom contains one or more neutrons. (Protons have a positive charge; electrons have a negative charge; and neutrons are either totally or virtually charge-free.) The nature of every chemical element on Earth—oxygen, nitrogen, carbon, gold, mercury, iodine, and uranium are among the 92 naturally occurring elements—is determined by the number of protons in their atoms. Electrons are elementary, or fundamental, particles—that is, they have no component parts and therefore cannot be subdivided; protons and neutrons are composed of other fundamental particles—quarks, which are 100 million times smaller than the average atom (whose diameter, in turn, is smaller than a billionth of a meter). Scientists have identified six kinds, or flavors, of quarks:

up, down, charmed, strange, top, and bottom. The top quark, which is the largest, is 4,400 times bigger than the smallest, the up quark; three of the quark types have an electric charge of +2/3 each, while the electric charge of each of the other three is –1/3. Every proton consists of one down quark and two up quarks; every neutron consists of one up quark and two down quarks. The other fundamental particle is the lepton. There are six types of leptons—the electron, the muon, and the tau particle, each of which has an associated neutrino. Furthermore, all fundamental particles can be categorized as either fermions or bosons, depending on their spin, a highly complex, intrinsic property associated with the angular momentum of the particle, and on their "quantum state," which in the theory of quantum mechanics is expressed in statistical, rather than absolute, terms. Bosons can co-exist with one another in the same state at the same time and location; fermions (which include quarks and leptons) cannot co-exist in the same state at the same time and location. Bosons may be fundamental particles or composite particles; the fundamental bosons are called gauge bosons (which include the photon, the fundamental unit of light and every other form of electromagnetic radiation; the W and Z particles; gluons; and, hypothetically, the Higgs boson). Scientists have further separated the approximately 200 known fundamental or composite particles into three families. Only those in the first family exist for more than a fraction of a second; they make up the atoms of matter that we are familiar with in our everyday lives. Evidence for those in the second and third families has come from experiments conducted in atom smashers. All particles composed of quarks are called hadrons—hence the name of the LHC. There are two types of hadrons: those containing three quarks, which are called baryons, and those containing one quark and one antiquark (one of the antiparticles predicted to exist by Paul Dirac), called mesons.

According to the standard model of particle theory, there are also four fundamental forces in nature: the electromagnetic force, which acts between atomic particles carrying an electrical charge; the strong nuclear force, which acts between quarks and holds atomic nuclei together; the weak nuclear force, which operates between leptons and is associated with particle emission and nuclear decay (the processes that provide the basis for carbon dating, by which geological ages or the ages of fossils or other ancient materials are estimated); and gravitation, which operates on cosmic levels. Each of the forces is "carried" to subatomic particles, atoms, or congregations of atoms by a particular "messenger" particle, also called a force carrier or mediator. The carrier of the electromagnetic force is the photon, which has no mass and no charge; the carrier of the strong nuclear force is the gluon, of which there are eight kinds, each of which has a large mass and what is called a "color" charge; the weak force has three carriers—the positive and negative W particles and the neutral Z particle, which have large mass; that of gravitation is the graviton, which has no charge and no mass (and exists only hypothetically; no physical evidence for it has been found). Carriers with no mass move at the speed of light and act over long distances; those with large mass move only over short distances and at less than the speed of light.

The existence of the Higgs mechanism, Higgs field, and Higgs boson provides the only plausible explanation in the standard model of particle theory for the existence of mass. According to John Ellis, in an article entitled "Into a New World of Physics and Symmetry," posted on-line in the magazine *Symmetry: Dimensions of Particle Physics* (August 2006), most theoretical and particle physicists (one notable exception is Stephen Hawking) feel confident that the LHC will provide proof of their existence. Under construction since 1994 at a cost of $8 billion, the LHC is located 300 to 570 feet below ground. The creation of some 10,000 scientists from many countries, it is far more powerful than what until now had been the world's most powerful atom smasher—the Tevatron collider at the Fermi National Accelerator Laboratory (Fermilab), near Chicago, Illinois. In a ring 17 miles long surrounded by thousands of supercooled magnets (their temperature is near absolute zero: –459.67 degrees Fahrenheit, –273.15 degrees Celsius) in the LHC, beams of protons moving in opposite directions at 99.999999 percent of the speed of light will collide, reproducing conditions similar to those immediately after the Big Bang. The LHC will be "the world's most powerful microscope," John Ellis wrote, "with a resolution thousands of times smaller than the diameter of a proton. The high energies and small distances accessible with the LHC will be similar to the conditions of the very early universe, shortly after the big bang, turning the collider into a telescope and a time machine that will reveal the physics that underlies the world around us." Those revelations may include evidence of new types of symmetries or of supersymmetry, which implies, as Brian Greene wrote for the *New York Times* (September 11, 2008), that "for every known species of particle (electrons, quarks, neutrinos, etc.)" there exists not only an antiparticle but "a partner species," or "sparticle"—selectrons, squarks, sneutrinos—or a fermion associated with every boson. The LHC may also produce never-before-seen particles and the answers to questions about the nature of dark matter, why there are so many different kinds of particles, why the number of particles in the universe is many magnitudes greater than the number of antiparticles, why the gravitational force is so much weaker than the other fundamental forces, and whether the universe contains dimensions other than the three we know.

Higgs's work is the subject of several books, among them *Reflections on the Higgs System* (1997), by Martinus Veltman; *Search for the Higgs Boson* (2006), edited by John V. Lee; *Perspectives on Higgs Physics* (2008), edited by Gordon L. Kane;

and *The Quantum Frontier: The Large Hadron Collider* (2009), by Don Lincoln. The title of another book, *The God Particle: If the Universe Is the Answer, What Is the Question?* (1993), by the Nobel Prize–winning experimental physicist Leon Lederman, led some people to refer to the Higgs boson as the God particle. "I wish [Lederman] hadn't done that," Higgs has said, as quoted by Richard Wilson. "I have to explain to people it was a joke. I'm an atheist, but playing around with names like that could be unnecessarily offensive to people who are religious."

Higgs will not be directly involved in the operation of the LHC or the analyses of the data that it produces. More than a decade before he retired, he had begun to decrease the amount of energy he devoted to research and focus more on teaching. He has attributed that change to problems in his personal life. "After the break-up of my marriage, I think I just lost touch with the things I should have been learning about just to follow up my own work. I couldn't keep up," he told a reporter for *Scotland on Sunday* (September 14, 2008). Higgs and his wife, an American linguist named Jo Ann (nicknamed Jodie), divorced in the early 1970s; the two had met in the 1950s when both were members of the Campaign for Nuclear Disarmament, a network of British organizations opposed to the spread of nuclear weapons. A fellow of the Royal Society and the Royal Society of Edinburgh, Higgs lives in Edinburgh. A shy man who treasures his privacy, he enjoys walking, listening to music, and swimming. He has two children—Chris, a computer scientist, and Jonny, a jazz musician—and is a grandfather.

—W.D.

Suggested Reading: (Glasgow, Scotland) *Herald* Features p13 Apr. 7, 2008; (London) *Guardian* p44 Nov. 17, 2007; (London) *Sunday Times* p11 June 15, 2008; *New Scientist* p44+ Sep. 13, 2008; *Scotland on Sunday* p19 Sep. 14, 2008

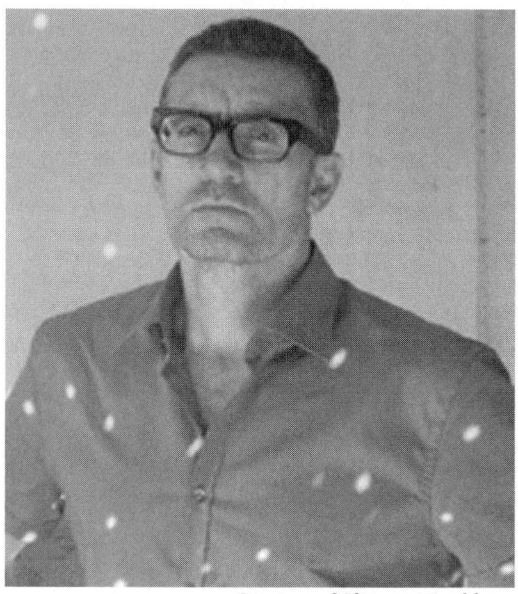

Courtesy of Thomas Hirschhorn

Hirschhorn, Thomas

1957– Installation artist

Address: c/o Barbara Gladstone Gallery, 515 W. 24th St., New York, NY 10011-1104

The Swiss-born conceptual artist Thomas Hirschhorn is on a mission to turn his creative energy into art—works that have stirred critics to describe them as provocative, disturbing, sick, farcical, or tragic. Hirschhorn's self-proclaimed emphasis on energy, as opposed to quality, is more than an aesthetic; it is a philosophy, one that he regards as the primary goal of his art, which is aimed at making viewers think. Hirschhorn uses such materials as cardboard, tape, and foil, not "because they are cheap, but because they are available, nonexclusive, and not intimidating," as he wrote in an e-mail interview with *Current Biography*, the source of quotes in this article, unless otherwise noted. He has often incorporated those materials into collages of photographs, books, printed texts, and videos. In the late 1990s he started to create large-scale collages that featured graphic images of war and turmoil but no specific messages or calls for action; rather, the artist hoped to inspire viewers to come up with their own interpretations of what they were seeing. Although Hirschhorn received a formal education in graphic design, he insists that it has had no measurable impact on him as an artist. "No training helps you make your work as an artist," he told Mark Rappolt in 2003 for *Tate Magazine* (now called *Tate Etc.*), published by the organization that manages the Tate museums, in London, England. "No training helps you to take decisions. No training helps you to make a choice. I decided to work as an artist because only as an artist can I be totally responsible for what I do. The decision to be an artist is the decision for freedom. Freedom is the condition of responsibility. To be an artist is not a question of form or content; it is a question of responsibility."

Thomas Hirschhorn was born in 1957 in Bern, Switzerland. (A few sources note May 16 as the date.) He was raised in Bern by his adoptive parents, an accountant and a homemaker. In his teens Hirschhorn was fascinated by the works of Kazimir Malevich, Alexander Rodchenko, and other Russian avant-garde artists. "I wanted to do work like them," he said. At the age of 21, he enrolled at the School of Graphic Design in Zurich, Switzerland, where he studied for five years, graduating in 1983. He later moved to Paris, France, where he was briefly associated with a workshop of communist graphic designers. "In the collective I realized I was not interested in doing [advertising or propaganda] even though I agreed with the human ideas," Hirschhorn told Alan G. Artner for the *Chicago Tribune* (February 6, 2000). "I didn't want to do work that was in the service of an ideology. So I had to make the choice to be an artist. I was always against it before, but it was an error of mine. It was a political error because I had felt an artist was somebody who didn't care about society. I was concerned with social ideas. That was always true. It's what for me makes the work. I cannot understand how an artist can work with no critical position."

By the mid-1990s Hirschhorn was making a name for himself in Europe, where his work was exhibited not only in museums and galleries but also in parks and other public spaces. He used inexpensive, familiar materials—cardboard, packing tape, aluminum foil, and inexpensive lumber—to create complex collages of books, photographs, printed materials, and videos. In his exhibition One Artwork: One Problem (1998), mounted at the Portikus gallery in Frankfurt, Germany, the artist intended to overwhelm the viewer with a large collage of newspaper and magazine clippings about many of the world's troublespots and problems—the conflicts in Kosovo, in the former Yugoslavia, and in the Middle East, for example. In another move that would develop into a Hirschhorn trademark, he attached two wings (that is, rooms) to the gallery, thereby expanding the space in a way he felt would best suit his purpose. "The title, *One Artwork, One Problem*, refers to the fact that each of the 'problems' is linked to a 'sculpture' via a network of veins made of aluminium foil," Verena Kuni wrote for *Frieze* magazine (March/April 1999). "The aesthetic of these cardboard forms (tightly covered with blue bin-bags) is suspiciously reminiscent of the public sculptures that populate parks and pedestrian areas all over postwar Europe. These were intended to honour democracy, rediscover pride, or express guilt-ridden dismay—whichever was appropriate. Hirschhorn's parodies seem to feed on the 'problems' through their foil extensions, as if through umbilical cords. The work of art as a vessel for all the thoughts we can't deal with?"

In 2000 Hirschhorn's Jumbo Spoons and Big Cake went on view at the Art Institute of Chicago, in Illinois, marking his first solo exhibition at a museum in the U.S. The exhibition featured a pink cake, 12 meters by 17 meters (about 39 feet by 57 feet) made out of cardboard and decorated with books on globalization, economics, and philosophy; photographs showing scenes of war, famine, and genocide; video monitors, some showing images of hardworking farmers and others showing gourmet chefs on a TV cooking show; and pieces of broken mirrors. Around the cake stood 12 cardboard, foil-wrapped spoons, each between eight and 12 feet high, meant to symbolize a failed utopian ideal (which was left to the viewer to identify). "I am interested in giving an image of the world like I feel it—in fragmentation," Hirschhorn told Artner. "The world is very, very complex, too complex for me, and I try to understand the complexity. My contribution as an artist is to link things together that I can't understand. I deal with contradictions, confusions. I try to give the world in my head a physical aspect in space. I know I have too much information [in each piece] but I will not make a selection. . . . You, the spectator, have to make such a judgment for yourself because I have not understood the whole. I've only understood what's important for me."

Most important to Hirschhorn are the ideas embedded in his art (as opposed to its perceived physical or aesthetic qualities) and its power to provoke thought, but not necessarily to inspire social or political action. One of his artistic guidelines is: Quality = No! Energy = Yes! "Energy is what really counts today," he said. "Energy is what I can reach. Energy is what I can struggle with. Energy is what owns the capacity to implicate the other. Energy is what possesses the faculty to cut an opening toward the non-exclusive public." He told Artner, "I am very optimistic about the human capacity to reflect. . . . Obviously, you have to look first, but then I want people to think about [what they've seen]. I believe in the spectator's capacity to reflect. It's the one thing that is human. That's why I give all this information."

Also in 2000 the exhibition World Airport, adapted from Hirschhorn's show at the 1999 Venice Biennale, in Italy, opened at the Renaissance Society, in Chicago. It featured an enormous runway with 24 large model airplanes that Hirschhorn had painted with real airline logos and national symbols. Near the planes were kiosks stocked with photographs and news clippings that told stories of corporate greed and regional conflicts. The show, which also included four altars each dedicated to a philosopher whose ideas had influenced Hirschhorn (he has named Baruch Spinoza, Gilles Deleuze, Félix Guattari, Friedrich Nietzsche, Antonio Gramsci, and George Bataille among his major influences), filled the entire space of the gallery—as has been true of many other Hirschhorn exhibits.

By the winter of 2000, Hirschhorn had begun to receive increasing recognition in the press and the art world; in December of that year, he attracted additional attention, when he was named the first winner of the Prix Marcel Duchamp, which the Association for the International Diffusion of French Art has awarded annually since then to pioneering contemporary artists living in France. He won approximately $30,000 in prize money and was honored with a show that ran for two months in 2001 at the Centre Pompidou, the best-known modern-art museum in Paris.

Meanwhile, Hirschhorn was continuing to express his views in novel ways. For the exhibition Laundrette, held in the Stephen Friedman Gallery in London in 2001, he created a brightly lit, vinyl-floored laundromat in which video screens in 16 foil-covered, cardboard-and-duct-tape models of washing machines showed raw images of war and death. "I am watching real-life executions and a dead face being peeled off a mutilated skull then replaced, again and again," Adrian Searle wrote for the London *Guardian* (July 3, 2001). "Rotted bodies pulled out of shallow graves, a severed head carried like a teapot through a house, a corpse anointed with quicklime. The dead grin back, in the video screens in the portals where the washing should be. This collision between knockabout display and absolute horror is more than bad taste. I find it appalling, terrible and deeply depressing, not least because I realize part of me is already inured to the shocking images. My eye scans the screen where people are being tied to a row of posts on some sunny African shoreline. The soldiers are nervous and excited. The officers swank about, issuing orders. The victims slump in the smoke as the shots ring out. I can't watch. I watch it again." The videos also contained a few common images: hands washing off a red substance that covers them and hands reaching for French fries covered in ketchup. Hirschhorn "tries to work with what he knows is too much unstable, indigestible stuff," Searle wrote. "But he is not, he insists, a chaotic artist; nor is he simply mirroring the chaos of the world, or playing a private language game. *Laundrette*—with its obvious references to ethnic cleansing and to washing the world's dirty linen—risks an insulting banality. But Hirschhorn's work is more complex and finely tuned than it looks. It has its own kind of rigour. It is farce and tragedy, all at once."

Few people took notice when, in 2003, Hirschhorn decided not to exhibit his work in Switzerland as long as the conservative, ultranationalist politician—and billionare industrialist—Christoph Blocher held the leadership position in the Swiss Parliament as the leader of the right-wing populist People's Party, which gained a majority of seats in 2003. That inattention ended the following year, when Hirschhorn's exhibition Swiss-Swiss Democracy opened at the Swiss Cultural Center in Paris. For that multimedia exhibit Hirschhorn painted graffiti on walls from which hung photographs, official documents, and newspaper clippings. The show included a one-hour lecture by the philosopher Marcus Steinweg, who collaborated with Hirschhorn on half a dozen map-like pieces; a daily newspaper published by Hirschhorn; and, most controversially, a play inspired by the story of the 14th-century Swiss folk hero William Tell. The play, adapted and directed by Gwenael Morin from Friedrich Schiller's version of the tale, questioned not only Switzerland's isolationism but also its commitment to democracy. Blocher, who had become the Swiss minister of justice and police early in 2004, "is not a dictator," Hirschhorn told Alan Riding for the *New York Times* (December 27, 2004), "but he legitimizes Swiss xenophobia, isolationism, nationalism; he legitimizes the feeling in Switzerland that all these foreigners want to come and take their money. He is a dangerous populist." Swiss conservatives' harsh criticism of Pro Helvetia, a Swiss-government-run cultural foundation (which owns the Swiss Cultural Center), for funding the Hirschhorn show led the nation's Parliament to cut Pro Helvetia's funding by nearly 3 percent, on the grounds that it had misused public money. Meanwhile, the exhibition attracted more than 30,000 visitors in eight weeks—a far greater number than the cultural center typically recorded.

Hirschhorn returned to New York City in 2006 to exhibit his new work, Superficial Engagement, at the Gladstone Gallery, where he had exhibited another installation four years earlier. Hirschhorn created four platforms—on which stood a monument, a mosque, a museum, and a morgue, respectively—each containing a collage of hundreds of wartime photos, shot in Iraq and Afghanistan, showing heads and limbs no longer connected to their owners; alongside those images were pictures of cheerful, 1960s geometric art. The show, Ken Johnson wrote for the *New York Times* (February 7, 2006), is "hands down the most disturbing and provocative art exhibition in town right now. . . . With this show Mr. Hirschhorn evidently decided to take off the gloves. He has crammed into the gallery a series of sculptural tableaus that resemble parade floats constructed by a gang of neo-punk high school anarchists. With mannequins studded with screws like African fetishes, fake coffins, video monitors, photocopied newspaper headlines and articles, Oriental carpets, hand-painted banners and photocopies of geometric artworks, the installation is almost overwhelmingly congested. But one element stands out clearly: thrusting at you from every direction are images copied from the Internet and other international news sources showing human bodies mangled, burned and dismembered by bombs in Iraq, Afghanistan and other theaters of war and terror." While the photos illustrated the effects of a U.S.-led war, for the most part they showed the corpses of Arabs rather than Americans, which, Jerry Saltz suggested in the *Village Voice* (February 7, 2006), might make them less horrifying to Americans. What sort of reaction would the artist have provoked, Saltz wondered, had he used images of the victims of the terrorist attacks in New York City in 2001 or in London in 2005? If he had done that, blame for the attacks would be reversed—pointed toward Muslim fundamentalists—and the detachment significantly reduced, or perhaps even missing.

The content of Hirschhorn's Universal Gym, mounted at the Gladstone Gallery in the spring of 2009, is distinctly different from that of Superficial Engagement and of most of Hirschhorn's other installations. Using his usual materials—wood, tape, and cardboard—Hirschhorn constructed models of machines for weight training, exercise balls, mats, free weights, and mirrors and also a few life-size mannequins with holes in their chests in the areas where their hearts should have been. The exhibit is "bland by the standards of his previous New York show," Roberta Smith wrote for the *New York Times* (March 27, 2009). Writing for *Time Out New York* (April 2, 2009), Joshua Mack agreed: the artist's ideas in Universal Gym are "simplistic and stale at best, especially given the wealth of art and political commentary parsing the same turf of late."

Hirschhorn's next U.S. exhibition, titled Abstract Resistance, will take place at the Walker Art Center, in Minneapolis, Minnesota, in 2010.

Hirschhorn lives in Paris.

—D.K.

Suggested Reading: frieze.com Mar./Apr. 1999; gladstonegallery.com; (London) *Guardian* p12 July 3, 2001; *New York Times* E p5 Feb. 7, 2006; tate.org.uk

Selected Exhibitions: One Artwork: One Problem, 1998; Jumbo Spoons and Big Cake, 2000; World Airport, 2000; Swiss-Swiss Democracy, 2004; Superficial Engagement, 2006; Universal Gym, 2009

Holder, Eric H. Jr.

Jan. 21, 1951– Attorney general of the United States

Address: U.S. Dept. of Justice, 950 Pennsylvania Ave., N.W., Washington, DC 20530-0001

On February 2, 2009, with 75 "yes" votes and 21 "no's" cast by those present on the floor of the United States Senate, Eric H. Holder Jr. was confirmed as the nation's 82d attorney general. He was sworn in on the same day, thus becoming the first African-American to head the U.S. Department of Justice (DOJ). "The confirmation of Eric Holder as our new Attorney General is a momentous day for the rule of law," Senator Russ Feingold, a Wisconsin Democrat, declared after the vote, as quoted by Stephen C. Webster on the Raw Story Media Web site (February 2, 2009). "During his confirmation hearings, Eric Holder clearly and unequivocally stated that no one, including the president, is above the law. Those were welcome words after eight years of Bush Administration policies that undermined our Constitution and damaged the integrity of the Department of Defense." Foremost among those policies, promulgated from 2001 to 2009 by Republican president George W. Bush and his vice president, Richard B. "Dick" Cheney, were those that had permitted the use of torture in interrogation of suspected terrorists or other detainees; the years-long holding at Guantánamo Bay, Cuba, of people who were described as enemy combatants but had not been charged with terrorist acts or any other crimes; the wiretapping of U.S. citizens and others without warrants; the rejection of DOJ job applicants deemed to be insufficiently supportive of President Bush and the Republican agenda; and the firing of nine federal prosecutors for what appeared to be partisan political reasons.

The office of attorney general was established not by the United States Constitution but by the Judiciary Act of 1789. As the head of the DOJ, Holder is considered the federal government's chief law enforcer. Some of the DOJ's 110,000 employees work in sections of the department that are relatively familiar to the public, including the Civil Rights Division; the Antitrust Division; the Federal Bureau of Investigation (FBI); the Bureau of Alcohol, Tobacco, Firearms, and Explosives; the Bureau of Prisons; the Drug Enforcement Division; and the United States Marshals Service. Other DOJ divisions are less well known: the Office on Violence Against Women; the Office of Dispute Resolution; the Tax Division; the U.S. Parole Commission; the Environment and Natural Resources Division; the Foreign Claims Settlement Commission; and many others. Holder has more than three decades of experience in law; "by all accounts," as Carrie Johnson wrote for the *Washington Post* (February 3, 2009, on-line), he is "among the most credentialed lawyers ever to become attorney general." He began his professional life as a federal trial attorney; after eight years at that job, he spent five years as an associate federal court judge, then four years as a United States attorney, another four as the deputy United States attorney general, and, most recently, eight years as an attorney for a private firm, Covington & Burling, where he dealt with "complex civil and criminal cases, domestic and international advisory matters and internal corporate investigations," according to the firm's Web site. When he greeted DOJ employees on his first day as attorney general, Holder said in part, as quoted on the DOJ Web site (February 3, 2003), "Citizens from across this nation look to us as the standard bearers of justice, fairness, and independence. At all times, and in all ways, we must demonstrate that we merit their confidence. We must fulfill our duties faithfully, and apply the law evenhandedly, without regard to politics, party or personal interest."

Eric Himpton Holder Jr. was born on January 21, 1951 in the New York City borough of the Bronx. His father was a real-estate agent who had emigrated from Barbados; his mother, Miriam (Yearwood)

Alex Wong/Getty Images

Eric H. Holder Jr.

Holder, was a telephone operator and church secretary whose parents were natives of the same Caribbean island, in the British West Indies. Holder and his younger brother, William, were raised in the New York City borough of Queens, in the neighborhood of East Elmhurst, where many people of West Indian descent lived. Holder attended regular classes in a Queens public school until the fourth grade, when he was placed in a program for intellectually gifted children. Thereafter, most of his schoolmates were white, and young Eric lost his closeness to his neighborhood peers. The high school he attended, Stuyvesant, is among the nation's most competitive public secondary schools; admission is based on results of an entrance exam. Holder commuted an hour and a half from his home to the school, which is in the borough of Manhattan, and one year he was the captain of its basketball team. He found his course work very demanding, and at home he spent much of his time studying. He attended Columbia University, also in Manhattan, his costs paid for in part by a New York State Regents Scholarship. As a freshman he played basketball with the college team. On Saturdays, according to biography.com (2008), he mentored children living in the low-income area surrounding Columbia, and he participated in civil rights activities. After he earned a B.A. degree, in American history, in 1973, he entered Columbia's law school. "The law inevitably is wound up with some great political movements, social movements," he told Javier C. Hernandez for the *New York Times* (November 30, 2008, on-line). "I wanted to be a part of that."

While at law school Holder clerked for attorneys at the National Association for the Advancement of Colored People (NAACP) Legal Defense Fund and at the DOJ's Criminal Division. After he earned a J.D. degree, in 1976, Holder was accepted in the U.S. attorney general's highly selective honors program for promising young attorneys. As a member of the department's newly formed Public Integrity Section, he investigated and prosecuted corruption by local, state, and federal officials. In cases he handled, the defendants included a Florida state treasurer, FBI agents, the U.S. ambassador to the Dominican Republic, a Philadelphia, Pennsylvania, judge, and an organized-crime boss.

In 1988 President Ronald Reagan nominated Holder as an associate judge on the Superior Court of the District of Columbia; he was confirmed by the U.S. Senate. He presided over hundreds of civil and criminal trials in his five years there. In 1993, when Bill Clinton was in the White House, the Senate confirmed Holder as the U.S. attorney for Washington, D.C., the largest such office in the country. During his four-year tenure in that position, Holder created a unit to more aggressively prosecute cases of domestic violence; pushed for more forceful enforcement of hate-crime laws; set up Operation Ceasefire, a program designed to lessen violent crime by reducing the number of guns in criminal hands; devised a strategy to get better results in cases involving abused children; and launched a project whereby members of communities and local government agencies worked with law-enforcement authorities to make neighborhoods safer.

In 1997 President Clinton appointed Holder to be the deputy to Attorney General Janet Reno; confirmed unanimously by the Senate, he became the highest-ranking African-American in law enforcement in the nation's history. In that position he oversaw civil and criminal litigation, enforcement, and administrative activities. He launched the Children Exposed to Violence Initiative, which aimed, as the president said, "to combat violence against children [and] to prevent children who are exposed to violence from being victimized a second time by the justice system," according to the *Weekly Compilation of Presidential Documents* (January 4, 1999). At Clinton's request Holder created Lawyers for One America, a program with both public and private components whose aim is to promote diversity within the legal profession and increase the quantity of pro bono work being performed nationally. In addition, Holder issued guidelines for handling health-care fraud, computer-related crimes, and software piracy. He also drew up what is now known as the Holder Memorandum, a guide to be used by the DOJ in determining whether to indict corporations or corporate employees suspected of illegal activities. A major factor to be considered was the degree to which corporate executives were "cooperating" with the DOJ in its investigations. "Put simply, the Holder Memo suggested that, by facilitating the ability of employees to continue working and to vigorously defend themselves, the company was demonstrating a noncooperative attitude that could get it indicted," Harvey Silvergate wrote for the *National Law Journal* (December 8, 2008, on-line). In Silvergate's opinion, the memo "was a serious affront to the basic adversarial and rights-driven structure of the American legal system." Aspects of Holder's memorandum were criticized in a case involving former employees of KPMG, a huge, international, Swiss-owned firm whose specialties include audits and tax preparation. To avoid being deemed "noncooperative," KPMG had refused to advance money for legal assistance to employees under investigation by the DOJ. The presiding judge in that case, Lewis A. Kaplan of the Southern District of New York, wrote in his decision (June 26, 2006), as quoted by Silvergate, that the government had "let its zeal get in the way of its judgment. It has violated the constitution it is sworn to defend."

From January 20 to February 2, 2001 Holder was the acting attorney general under President George W. Bush; he stepped down after the confirmation by the Senate of Attorney General John Ashcroft. After leaving his government post, Holder joined the law firm of Covington & Burling, which has five offices in the U.S. and three overseas. As a litigation partner, Holder represented major clients, among them the National Football League (NFL), Chiquita Brands International, and the pharmaceuticals company Merck. In May 2008 the *National Law Journal* named Holder among the 50 most influential minority lawyers in the U.S., and in the same month, *Legal Times* included his name in its list of the greatest Washington lawyers of the past 30 years.

In late 2007 Holder joined Barack Obama's presidential campaign as a senior legal adviser. He was a member of the committee that recommended Senator Joseph Biden of Delaware as Obama's running mate. On December 1, 2008 Obama nominated Holder for the post of U.S. attorney general. During Holder's confirmation hearings before the Senate Judiciary Committee, in January 2009, Republican members expressed their disapproval of his calls for stronger gun controls, such as requiring background checks for purchasers of guns at trade shows and licensing of all owners of handguns. They also tried in vain to extract from Holder a promise that he would not pursue prosecutions of anyone who used torture during interrogations at Guantánamo Bay or elsewhere as part of the Bush administration's "war on terror" or of anyone directly involved in warrantless surveillance operations; Senator Tom Coburn of Oklahoma cited Holder's stands on those issues as evidence that he was not fully committed to fighting terrorism. The most serious questions that arose during the hearings, however, involved Holder's role in several pardons granted by Bill Clinton on his last day in the White House. Most prominent—or notorious—among them was the president's pardon of the billionaire commodities trader Marc Rich. In 1983 Rich had fled to Switzerland after his indictment on multiple charges, including failure to pay millions of dollars in taxes—indeed, at that time it was the biggest tax-fraud case in American history—and illegally conducting business with Iran in 1979 and 1980. That pardon sparked an outcry from attorneys who had worked on the indictment against Rich; many columnists and others also condemned it, accusing Clinton of acting as he had because the scofflaw's former wife had contributed a lot of money to the Clinton Presidential Library, to be constructed in Little Rock, Arkansas. In the following weeks Holder had said that he had felt neutral about the pardon but somewhat "favorable" about its being granted; that he had not examined papers about the case in detail; and that his role in it had been peripheral. Investigations into the matter in 2001 and 2002 by the House Committee on Oversight and Government Reform, however, revealed that Holder, through a third party, had recommended a lawyer for Rich; that he had communicated with that lawyer at least a half-dozen times; and that he had not alerted prosecutors about the paperwork that the lawyer had submitted to the White House requesting a pardon. According to the report that the House committee made public in early 2002, Holder had played a major role and had been a "willing participant in the plan to keep the Justice Department from knowing about and opposing the pardon," as quoted by Alison Leigh Cowan in the *New York Times* (March 13, 2002). At his confirmation hearing Holder admitted that he had "made mistakes" in the Rich matter, primarily by not making sure that he was fully informed and by not consulting with other lawyers who had firsthand knowledge. The Judiciary Committee voted 17–2 in favor of his confirmation. In the full vote in the Senate, all 21 "no" votes were cast by Republicans, while 18 Republicans joined 57 Democrats to approve the nomination. Holder was sworn into office on February 2, 2009.

In his first major speech as attorney general, made on February 18, 2009 in honor of Black History Month, Holder surprised many when he expressed the view that the nation has yet to confront the issue of race openly and honestly. "Though this nation has proudly thought of itself as an ethnic melting pot, in things racial we have always been and continue to be, in too many ways, essentially a nation of cowards," he said, as quoted on the CNN Web site (February 19, 2009). Holder also criticized past discussions of race as "too simplistic and left to those on the extremes who are not hesitant to use these issues to advance nothing more than their own narrow self-interest."

On March 2, 2009 the Justice Department released internal memos and opinions in which Bush administration officials had offered parameters delineating the legal limits of government power in combating terrorism, including justification for that administration's practice of conducting searches without warrants in cases involving suspected terrorist activities. The following month, in response to requests made under the Freedom of Information Act, the Justice Department released four secret memos used by the Bush administration to provide a legal justification for interrogation tactics—among them waterboarding, head slapping, and the slamming of suspects into walls—that violated both domestic and international law. The American Civil Liberties Union, many Democrats, and others called on Holder to appoint an independent prosecutor to investigate the interrogations of terrorism suspects under the Bush administration. They did so despite President Obama's stated opinion that while criminal acts should be prosecuted, a broad inquiry that might distract his administration from present concerns should not take place. On August 24, 2009, after reviewing classified documents from the CIA and other sources, the Justice Department's Ethics Office announced its recommendation that several prisoner-abuse cases be reopened. On August 25, five years to the day after the CIA made public a report containing graphic accounts of interrogations in which Americans had used threats of violence and sexual assault, mock executions, and other unlawful tactics, Holder appointed the independent prosecutor John H. Durham to investigate the CIA's destruction of certain interrogation videotapes, in order to determine whether a full criminal investigation of such conduct was necessary. The CIA's 2004 report also described the ways in which the information obtained from the interrogations supposedly helped to derail terrorist plots. "As attorney general, my duty is to examine the facts and to follow the law," Holder said, as quoted in the *New York Times* (August 25, 2009). "Given all of the information currently available, it is clear to me that this review is the only responsible course of action for me to take."

Holder has also announced a number of broad changes in Justice Department policy, including reinstituting a ban on assault weapons, revitalizing the Justice Department's Civil Rights Division, which had been downsized during the Bush administration, and ceasing the Bush administration's policy of prosecuting distributors and purchasers of marijuana used for medical purposes in states where that practice is legal. In late October Holder announced that authorities had arrested 303 people and confiscated illegal drugs, weapons, and millions of dollars obtained through illegal activities linked to a major Mexican drug cartel.

In December 2004 Racine Tucker-Hamilton, of the George Washington University School of Business, interviewed Holder for a two-hour videotape for HistoryMakers, an archive of African-American oral histories. In February 1997 Holder was the keynote speaker at a Library of Congress celebration of African-American History Month; his address was titled "African American Civil Rights: A Reappraisal."

Holder and his wife, Sharon Malone, an obstetrician, have two daughters, Maya and Brooke, and one son, Eric.

—M.E.R.

Suggested Reading: *Congressional Quarterly Weekly Report* p1444 June 4, 1994; *New York Times* (on-line) Nov. 30, 2008, Dec. 2, 2008, Dec. 3, 2008, Feb. 3, 2009, Aug. 24, 2009, Aug. 25, 2009; *Slate* (on-line) Nov. 22, 2008; *Washington Post* (on-line) Feb. 3, 2009

Honderich, Ted

(HAHN-der-ik)

Jan. 30, 1933– Philosopher; educator

Address: 66 Muswell Hill Rd., London N10 3JR, England

The philosopher Ted Honderich is widely known for his writing and research on the subjects of determinism, consciousness, the justification for punishment, human equality, terrorism, democracy, and the tradition of conservatism. Honderich has been described as a "consequentialist" philosopher, for his belief that the appropriateness of actions is determined not by intentions but by consequences. Honderich has published dozens of academic papers and authored or edited more than 15 books on philosophy, including *A Theory of Determinism: The Mind, Neuroscience and Life-Hopes* (1988), an influential manifesto reconciling the seemingly contradictory ideas of determinism and free will, and the intimate autobiography *Philosopher: A Kind of Life* (2000). But it is Honderich's writing on such subjects as the rationale for political violence and the responsibility of individuals to resolve the world's inequalities that has drawn the most attention and ignited the most controversy. He received particularly widespread criticism, as well as accusations of anti-Semitism, for his book *After the Terror: A Manifesto* (2002), in which he asserted that the world's vast inequalities are the fault of privileged individuals in the Western world and that, given those inequalities, certain acts of politically motivated terrorism may be "morally justified." Honderich, a mischievous man who is "always up for a ruck," as John Crace put in the London *Guardian* (March 22, 2005), has defended his theories with colorful and often acerbic responses to his detractors. Writing for the London *Independent* (August 27, 1995), Ian Parker described Honderich as "witty, and passionate, and cruelly inclined to give his ideologic opponents all the intellectual space they might want, feigning

Courtesy of Ingrid Honderich

Ted Honderich

surprise that they then seem to have nothing sensible to say."

The youngest of six children, Edgar Dawn Ross Honderich was born on January 30, 1933 in Baden, in southwestern Ontario, Canada, a town that he described in his autobiography as "a filthy peasant village." His father, John William Honderich, was a German descendant of Mennonites; his mother, Rae Laura (Armstrong) Honderich, was a Scottish Calvinist. Robert Fulford wrote for the Canadian *National Post* (November 11, 2005, on-line) that Honderich's father, who took on several occupations unsuccessfully, "dreamed ineffectual dreams while his mother kept the family alive" by running Baden's telephone exchange. Honderich's father and grandfather were excommunicated from their church for visiting one of a different denomination. Perhaps in part for that reason, Honderich never had much interest in religion. Even as a child, "I could see that nothing in religion could possibly be true," he told Crace. With the family facing tough times during the Great Depression, Honderich's brother Beland—15 years his senior—left school after eighth grade to work as a correspondent for the *Kitchener Record*, a Canadian newspaper. Honderich attended high school at the Kitchener-Waterloo Collegiate Institute and then, at age 16, when his mother fell ill, moved to Toronto to live with siblings. He studied at the University of Toronto while working as a journalist at the *Toronto Star*, where Beland had become editor in chief; Honderich became editor of the *Star*'s literary page. Meanwhile, his first year at the university was disastrous, largely because he was distracted from his studies by the bohemian lifestyle that he encountered in the city. He also had dreams of being a playwright, possibly "another Arthur Miller," as Martin Levin reported for the Toronto *Globe and Mail* (March 17, 2001)—which, Levin wrote, "is why it took him seven years to graduate from university." Honderich graduated with B.A. degrees in philosophy and English literature in 1959. Eventually realizing that he had a desire to "get things of importance straight," as he told Levin, and deciding that that goal would be better pursued through logic than literature, he decided to further his study of philosophy.

In 1959 Honderich left Canada for England to pursue a graduate degree at University College London (UCL). One of his instructors was A. J. Ayer, an eminent British philosopher whom Honderich particularly admired. As a graduate student Honderich was proud to join the philosopher Bertrand Russell and other protesters in an antinuclear sit-in in Parliament Square in the early 1960s. He earned his Ph.D. degree in the philosophy of logic and the mind in 1968, meanwhile spending two years teaching at the University of Sussex. He then became, successively, a lecturer, reader, and professor at UCL. In 1988 he was named Grote professor of the philosophy of mind and logic, the position he held until his retirement, in 1998.

In Honderich's first book, *Punishment: The Supposed Justifications* (1969), he analyzed a number of traditional justifications of state-sanctioned punishment—reform, retribution, and deterrence—finding each one insufficient in that it does not aim at consequences that "maximize the equalization of happiness," or result in the greatest happiness for the greatest number of people. Honderich concluded that the best justification of punishment is "the reduction of distress at an economical rate" and "the avoidance of greater inequality," as Jonathan Glover put it in his review of the book, which is posted on Honderich's Web site. Representing the general critical response, Glover described Honderich's writing as "cumbersome and at times ungrammatical" and faulted the book for "the total absence of argument in support of Honderich's own views of justice as equality." Glover nonetheless called the work a "sane, thorough, and socially radical book." *Punishment* was published in five subsequent editions, most recently in a greatly revised version titled *Punishment, the Supposed Justifications Revisited* (2006). In 1976 Honderich published *Three Essays on Political Violence*, a collection of articles on the subjects of causation, determinism, justice, and various ideas explored by the 19th-century liberal British philosopher John Stuart Mill. The book was expanded and republished in 1989 under the title *Violence for Equality: Inquiries in Political Philosophy.*

A Theory of Determinism: The Mind, Neuroscience and Life-Hopes (1988), published shortly after Honderich's promotion to the Grote professorship, is considered his magnum opus. In it Honderich discussed determinism—the belief that every event, including each process of human cognition and decision-making, is causally determined by a chain of prior occurrences. The traditional philosophical question of determinism is whether or not it is compatible with the notion of free will. In general, the answer to that question depends on a person's definition of freedom. If freedom comprises "the idea of action as voluntary and unconstrained," in Honderich's words, as paraphrased by Justin Broackes in the London *Times* (June 5, 1988), then philosophers deem determinism and free will as compatible, because even if a given choice has been predetermined by a chain of events since the beginning of time, in most cases that choice is still voluntary, since no one else is forcing it to be made. However, if freedom is defined as "the idea of self lying outside the realm of cause and necessity," then the two are not thought to be compatible. Those two schools of thought are called, respectively, compatibilism and incompatibilism. The notion of incompatibilism is accompanied by questions of accountability. For instance, if individuals are not responsible for their actions, what are the implications for our ideas of love, morality, and society? Honderich asserted that both views—compatibilism and incompatibilism—are wrong, arguing instead for a mixture of the two, in which we both accept the existence of determinism as a force with major consequences for our lives and, as Mark Thornton, a philosopher at Victoria College, put it in his review for the *Toronto Star* (November 12, 1988), "affirm what can be retained in our present personal, moral and social attitudes alongside a belief in determinism." To illuminate his point, Honderich asked the question, "What but an uncaused and unsuperfluous self could rescue us from the situation in which our actions are simple products of our environments and the manifold of our dispositions?" Thornton concluded that Honderich's approach is "Incompatibilist about the past and Compatibilist about the future," adding, though, that that view failed to resolve "the traditional battles between Incompatibilists and Compatibilists." Honderich's practical approach to the question of determinism has been adopted by many philosophers. Honderich further discussed those ideas in the book *How Free Are You? The Determinism Problem*, published in 1993 and in an expanded version in 2002, and in the textbook *On Determinism and Freedom* (2005).

Honderich ventured into the realm of politics when he published *Conservatism* (1990), in which he analyzed and harshly criticized the conservative movements in both Britain and the United States. In each chapter Honderich attempted to discredit theories regarding often-discussed themes in conservative politics—such as human nature and freedom—advanced by conservative figures throughout history, from Edmund Burke, the 18th-century Anglo-Irish statesman and founder of Western conservatism, to Margaret Thatcher, who served as British prime minister from 1979 to 1990. Honderich's central argument was that the underlying principle tying all conservatism movements together is selfishness. What distinguishes conservatives from other political ideologues, Honderich argued, is not that they are selfish but that they "are nothing else." He added, as quoted by Conor Cruise O'Brien in the London *Times* (July 11, 1990), "Their selfishness is the rationale of their politics, and they have no other rationale. They stand without the support, the legitimation, of any recognisably moral principle." While many reviewers found Honderich's criticisms of conservatism thought-provoking, others interpreted the book as less a philosophically based analysis of conservatism than a partisan attack. O'Brien called the book "a competently conducted polemic against Conservatism," while Enoch Powell wrote in his review for the London *Independent* (July 1, 1990), "His book is the work of a virulent partisan who leaves no one guessing how he intends to vote, and hopes a majority will vote, at the next general election." A greatly revised edition of *Conservatism* was published in 2005 under the title *Conservatism: Burke, Nozick, Bush, Blair?*

Honderich edited the reference book *Oxford Companion to Philosophy* (1995) for "three reasons," as he told Parker. "First I thought it would increase my fame, second I thought I'd get a lot of money, and third I thought I could do it on the side. It is that third reason that really sticks in my mind. I cannot understand how people can make such amazing blunders. I spent two years, from dawn to dusk, from five in the morning to seven at night." The 1,000-page book contains nearly 2,000 entries by 249 contributors, including, in addition to biographies of major philosophers and definitions of terms, a number of "light-hearted" entries unrelated to philosophy; those were aimed at the average reader and intended, as Honderich wrote in the introduction, to satisfy "a curiosity owed just to a page that falls open." For example, an entry under the heading "tar-water" explains that the 18th-century British empiricist Bishop George Berkeley considered a mixture of tar and cold water to be an all-purpose medicine with extraordinary powers. While some found those playful entries charming, others found them distracting and unnecessary. Honderich's *Oxford Companion* was generally well received by his peers. An updated version, published in 2005, includes 300 additional entries, such as the words "ableism" ("It basically means being condescending to cripples," Honderich wrote) and "zombies."

Shortly after Honderich retired from his teaching position at University College London, in 1998, he began to write his autobiography, *Philosopher: A Kind of Life* (2001). In the book Honderich discussed the evolution of philosophy in the second half of the 20th century, while telling the story of his academic and personal lives. *Philosopher* is remarkably candid, revealing details, for instance, about his three failed marriages and numerous infidelities and other romantic exploits, including several with married women and his students;

Honderich refers to himself several times in the book as "a man of many women." While some readers took issue with what they saw as Honderich's pompous tone, many were impressed with his apparent honesty about the details of his life, both good and bad. "Honderich has been bravely honest about the limits of attempts at autobiographical honesty," Julian Baggini wrote for the London *Independent* (October 22, 2000). "And it is the book's dual nature, as an example of and reflection on the nature of biography, which contributes most to its success. Rarely does an autobiography make you question its author and, more importantly, your judgments on him to such a degree. Like good philosophy, it's unsettling and leaves you asking questions you hadn't even thought of when you first turned to page one."

Honderich generated controversy with his book *After the Terror: A Manifesto* (2002), which he was inspired to write after the September 11, 2001 attacks on the United States. Honderich argued that the world's inequalities—such as the imbalance of power and resources—are the root causes of much of the world's violence and terrorism. According to Honderich's reasoning, the acts of terrorists such as the 9/11 hijackers and Palestinian suicide bombers who attack Israelis may actually be "morally justified," if violence is the only way to draw attention to, and thereby remedy, inequality. Honderich further argued that the world's "haves," among them wealthy members of Western European and American societies who are unwilling to make sacrifices to close gaps of inequality, are partly responsible for the inequality and thus for much of the resulting terrorist violence. "We have done overwhelming wrong . . . in failing to help those Africans who lead bad lives. . . . [That is] as indubitable as sexually abusing a child," Honderich stated during a lecture at Brown University, as quoted by Sara Perkins for the *University Wire* (September 23, 2002). "We need to escape the illusion that to be ordinary is to be innocent." Honderich also devoted part of the book to countering common arguments in favor of the capitalist system, which he identifies as the underlying cause of the world's inequalities.

Honderich's book sparked outrage from those who questioned the reasoning behind his assertion that Westerners were responsible for the world's poverty and violence. Writing for the London *Sunday Telegraph* (September 8, 2002), Noel Malcolm called *After the Terror* "one of the worst books I have ever read," adding, "The key points of the argument are as follows. There is no real difference between an act of omission and an act of commission. This means that each time I fail to give money to Oxfam to save the lives of starving Africans—for example, each time I spend money on a holiday—I am responsible for killing people. Therefore we are all, in a real sense, murderers, and the West is collectively responsible for the elimination of human life on a colossal scale. (Western interventions to help starving Africans, such as the ill-fated American operation in Somalia, naturally pass unmentioned here.)" Others, such as the linguist and left-wing thinker Noam Chomsky, found the book both brave and provocative. "It guides the reader, lucidly and forcefully, from basic ideas about a good and decent life to contemplation of concrete and immediate issues that are or should be at the center of attention," Chomsky wrote, as quoted on Honderich's Web site. "It is a compelling and impressive contribution to thinking about problems that are complex, painful, and urgent."

Still others accused Honderich of anti-Semitism, citing his argument that Palestinian terrorists who murder Israeli civilians may have a moral right to do so. Honderich denied that charge, explaining that he had also written that Israelis may have a moral right to use violence to defend their land. The debate led to a series of public controversies. After the book's publication Honderich offered to give £5,000 of his book advance to Oxfam, a nongovernmental organization that works to fight global poverty and hunger, in an effort to demonstrate the sort of giving that he intended to encourage. In October 2002 the organization turned down Honderich's offer because of its association with a book that condoned violence. (A nonprofit organization, Medical Aid for Palestinians, or MAP, later accepted the money.) One well-publicized charge of anti-Semitism against Honderich came from Micha Brumlik, the director of a Holocaust education center and a Frankfurt University professor of science education, who in August 2003 wrote an open letter to Suhrkamp Verlag, the German company that published a German translation of Honderich's book, condemning the project. In response to the letter, which appeared in the German newspaper *Frankfurter Rundschau*, Suhrkamp Verlag pulled the book from publication. Honderich then wrote an angry letter to the newspaper and made appearances on German television news programs, in which he defended his book and called for Brumlik's dismissal. Although the controversy quieted somewhat when a Jewish publisher agreed to print Honderich's book, the philosopher's first lecture in Germany following the controversy brought protests from Palestinians, neo-Zionists, and neo-Nazis (who were protesting the views of the Zionists). Honderich reinforced his conclusion that violence is justified when committed in the name of the oppressed, writing in his 2003 essay "Terrorism for Humanity," as quoted by Richard Wolin in the *Chronicle for Higher Education* (October 24, 2003), "African terrorism against our rich countries would be right if it had a reasonable hope of success." That essay was published along with Honderich's other essays on the morality of political violence in the 2004 book *Terrorism for Humanity: Inquiries into Political Philosophy.*

In 2004 Honderich published *On Consciousness*, a book of collected papers detailing his theories on the nature of consciousness. Honderich divided prior schools of thought regarding consciousness between "physicalism," which identifies consciousness as a physical presence, and "spiritualism," which defines it as a mental quality and argues that human consciousness is limited by the extent to which the human mind can comprehend itself. Honderich concluded that neither school of thought had properly addressed the subject, arguing instead that consciousness is inextricably linked to existence; a person is conscious because that person is able to perceive the existence of the outside world. Honderich called that position "radical externalism." Honderich's book, and his related publication *Radical Externalism* (2006), elicited relatively little public reaction until 2007, when Colin McGinn, a fellow philosopher who holds the theory that the nature of consciousness—like some other areas of philosophical inquiry—is beyond the scope of understanding, wrote a scathing review of *On Consciousness* for the *Philosophical Review*. "This book runs the full gamut from the mediocre to the ludicrous to the merely bad," McGinn wrote, as quoted by Stuart Jeffries in the London *Guardian* (December 21, 2007). "It is painful to read, poorly thought out, and uninformed." McGinn also called the book "radically inconsistent" and Honderich's reasoning "shoddy, inept, and disastrous." The review sparked a feud between the two philosophers that played out largely over the Web. In an interview with Jeffries, Honderich suggested that McGinn's review was motivated by a personal matter involving a comment made decades earlier. "At UCL we had a jokey locker-room relationship. But then I made a misstep. I suggested to [McGinn] that his new girlfriend was not as plain as the old one, and I could see the blood drain out of his face," Honderich told Jeffries. "That was possibly the start of our frostiness." Honderich posted a lengthy defense of his theory on a well-known philosophy blog called Leiter Reports, which in turn elicited a response on the blog from McGinn. Appearing to take joy in such bickering, Honderich has posted on his Web site in their entirety that and other, similar exchanges between him and fellow philosophers.

In his most recent book, *Humanity, Terrorism, Terrorist War: Palestine, 9/11, Iraq, 7/7 . . .* (2006), Honderich revisited many subjects that he had addressed in *After the Terror*. He rejected a number of commonly accepted guiding principles of morality, such as international law, "just war theory," conservatism, liberalism, and notions of democracy and freedom. He also dismissed the notion that nonviolence has ever been used successfully as a political philosophy. In light of what he saw as the failure of all other guiding moral systems, Honderich suggested an altogether new "principle for humanity," according to which "we must actually take rational steps to the end of getting and keeping people out of bad lives"—with a "bad life" defined as one that lacks reasonable length, quality, freedom, or power. Honderich went on to apply that principle to various global conflicts and to discuss whether the acts of the aggressors were morally just, offering the by-then familiar conclusion that violence is morally justified only in cases in which it is the sole possible means of improving lives. As with others of his works, reviewers' responses ranged from praise to strong criticism. One of Honderich's essays was included in *Israel, Palestine and Terror* (2008), a book of essays that focus on the possible moral justifications of Palestinian terrorism, edited by Stephen Law. A staff reviewer from *Publishers Weekly* (May 5, 2008) criticized the collection for lacking a single Palestinian voice and including perspectives from very few Israelis—as well as for discussing the conflict in abstract terms. The reviewer wrote: "Such a conversation might be of interest in the halls of academia, but to the extent that it can be expected to contribute meaningfully to the real-life resolution of decades of conflict, this largely aloof and oddly bloodless effort fails to engage, even though the issues raised are urgent and go the heart of what drives Western foreign policy today."

In addition to his work at University College London, Honderich has been a visiting professor at Yale University, City University of New York, Brooklyn College, and the University of Lethbridge. From 1995 to 2005 he was the vice chairman, and since 2005 has been chairman, of the Royal Institute of Philosophy. He is a member of the Garrick Club, the Aristotelian Society, and the Mind Association. According to his Web site, Honderich is currently working on a book whose title will probably be "Actual Consciousness."

In 1995 Parker described Honderich as "a very social, funny man, with a taste for gossip and wine—and for waving at girls through the windows of fast-moving trains." Honderich has two grown children, Kiaran and John Ruan, from his second marriage; as he revealed in his autobiography, he also has a third child, whom he has never met. A British citizen for many years, Honderich lived in Hampstead, a suburb of London, England, for decades before moving to Somerset. He returned in 2007 to Hampstead, where he lives with his fourth wife, Ingrid Coggin Purkiss, the secretary of the Royal Institute of Philosophy. Under "recreations" on his curriculum vitae, Honderich lists "wine, old houses, hearing all of Trollope's novels being read aloud, some more than once, decent and inexpensive restaurants."

—M.E.R.

Suggested Reading: (London) *Evening Standard* p30+ Nov. 3, 2000; (London) *Guardian* p10 Aug. 26, 2006, p14 Dec. 21, 2007; (London) *Independent* Review p4 Aug. 27, 1995, Books p7 Sep. 16, 1995, Features p69 Oct. 22, 2000; (London) *Sunday Telegraph* Nov. 12, 2000; (London) *Times* July 11, 1990; Ted Honderich's Web Site; (Toronto, Ontario, Canada) *Globe and Mail* D p15 Mar. 17, 2001; *Toronto Star Magazine* p12 Nov. 12, 1988

Selected Books: As writer—*Punishment: The Supposed Justifications*, 1969, fourth edition 1989; *Three Essays on Political Violence*, 1976; *A Theory of Determinism: The Mind, Neuroscience and Life-Hopes*, 1988; *Conservatism*, 1990; *How Free Are You? The Determinism Problem*, 1993, 2002; *Philosopher: A Kind of Life*, 2001; *After the Terror: A Manifesto*, 2002; *On Political Means and Social Ends*, 2003; *Terrorism for Humanity: Inquiries in Political Philosophy*, 2004; *On Consciousness*, 2004; *On Determinism and Freedom*, 2005; *Conservatism: Burke, Nozick, Bush, Blair?*, 2005; *Punishment, the Supposed Justifications Revisited*, 2006; *Humanity, Terrorism, Terrorist War: Palestine, 9/11, Iraq, 7/7 . . .*, 2006; *Radical Externalism: Honderich's Theory of Consciousness Discussed*, 2006; as editor or co-editor—*Essays on Freedom of Action*, 1973; *Social Ends and Political Means*, 1976; *Philosophy As It Is*, 1979; *Philosophy Through Its Past*, 1984; *Morality and Objectivity*, 1985; *The Oxford Companion to Philosophy*, 1995, 2005

Iijima, Sumio

(ee-ee-jee-mah, soo-mee-oh)

May 2, 1939– Physicist; electron microscopist; educator

Address: NEC Corp., R&D Group, 34 Miyukigaoka, Tsukuba, Ibaraki 305-8501, Japan

On June 23, 1991, while examining minuscule crumbs of carbon with an electron microscope, the Japanese physicist Sumio Iijima discovered what, soon afterward, he dubbed carbon nanotubes. Iijima's description of his discovery, published in the November 7, 1991 issue of the journal *Nature*, gave a tremendous boost to the fledgling science of nanotechnology. Immediately, molecular manufacturing—the fabrication of microscopically small devices for use in medicine, communications, electronics, energy production, chemical processes, and other industries—moved significantly closer to reality, as did the possibility of "extending precise control of molecular structures to larger and larger scales," as K. Eric Drexler predicted in his book *Engines of Creation: The Coming Era of Nanotechnology* (1986). "The earthshaking insight of molecular nanotechnology is that, when we reach this scale, we can reverse direction and begin building up, making products by placing individual atoms and molecules exactly where we want them," Mike Treder wrote for the *Futurist* (January/February 2004). In addition, according to a writer for *Nature*'s on-line "Physics Portal" (2001), "as a tool to test quantum mechanics and model biological systems," among other areas of basic science, "nanotubes seem to have unlimited potential." For his discovery of carbon nanotubes and other contributions to science, Iijima has earned some 40 awards and honors from schools, organizations, and governments in Japan, China, European nations, and the U.S. He received his first prize—the Bertram Eugene Warren Diffraction Physics Award, from the American Crystallography Society—in 1976, when he was a postgraduate research associate at Arizona State University. Among those he has received in recent years are the John M. Cowley Medal, from the International Federation of Societies for Microscopy, in 2006; the Gregori Aminoff Prize in crystallography, from the Royal Swedish Academy of Sciences, in 2007; the award for technical scientific research from the Prince of Asturias Foundation, in Spain, in 2008; the "No Boundaries" Innovation Award, from the British weekly the *Economist*, in 2008; and admission to the Norwegian Academy of Science and Letters, in 2009, as a foreign member. Iijima was elected a foreign associate of the U.S. National Academy of Sciences in 2007.

Named in 1974, nanotechnology involves the study, formation, and manipulation of molecules or of bits of matter only a few molecules in width. The primary unit of measurement is the nanometer: one billionth of a meter (a meter being close to 3.281 feet, or a little over a yard). The nanometer is about 10 times the radius of a hydrogen atom (the smallest atom), or about the size of one carbon atom, or approximately 1/100,000th the width of a human hair. Carbon nanotubes are seamless tubes of carbon atoms joined in a honeycomb pattern; the tubes are at most a few nanometers in diameter and a few micrometers in length. (A micrometer is one-millionth of a meter.) While scientists have found tubular structures among a few minerals in their natural state, carbon nanotubes are manmade; none have ever been detected in the natural world. The carbon nanotubes that Iijima saw on that summer day in 1991 were not created intentionally; they came into being during experiments in which carbon rods were vaporized. The products of such vaporization—spheres whose surfaces are patterned like honeycombs—had drawn the attention of Iijima's colleagues in Japan, the U.S., and Great Britain. The spheres were "not interesting for a microscopist," however, Iijima told Dennis Normile for *Science* (November 18, 1994). Rather, what captivated Iijima were the whiskery structures that had appeared on the ends of the electrodes used in the vaporization process; they reminded him of the "whisker-like" structure of silver-bromide crystals, which he had studied a quarter-century earlier, while conducting research as a graduate student, as he told Irene M. Kunii for *BusinessWeek* (July 8, 2002), and the tubular structure of chrysotile asbestos, which he had examined when another researcher in his lab studied it in the 1960s. "When I saw carbon nanotubes under the electron microscope, my old experiences came immediately to mind and helped me to figure out what they were," he wrote for a Meijo University

Yoshikazu Tsuno/AFP/Getty Images

Sumio Iijima

Web site (nanocarb.meijo-u.ac.jp, 2007). His path as a researcher has also been influenced by his uncommon understanding of the nanoworld, which stems from skills in electron microscopy that are second to none.

Iijima's journey to success in science began in early childhood, when, "stated very simply, I loved nature," as he wrote in "About Myself," an on-line essay for the NEC Corp., in Tsukuba, Japan, where he has worked since 1987 as a senior principal researcher. "I learned many things from my experiences with nature," he wrote, "and I believe that this helped me to develop both sensitivity and insight." He also wrote, "The most important thing that I learned while in the U.S. was 'Don't do what others have done.'" Iijima "has a sense of what to look for, of what will give us the most interesting and most valuable information," Hiroyoshi Rangu (also known as Roy Lang), then the general manager of NEC's Fundamental Research Laboratories, told Normile. From 1998 to 2002, along with Christian Colliex of the French National Center for Scientific Research, Iijima co-directed research for the Nanotubulites Project, a joint venture of the International Cooperative Research Project and the Japan Science and Technology Agency. In his native land, in addition to his work with NEC, Iijima has been a professor in the Department of Materials Science and Engineering of Meijo University, in Nagoya, since 1998; the director of the Nanotube Research Center (also known as the Research Center for Advanced Carbon Materials) of the National Institute of Advanced Industrial Science and Technology, in Tsukuba, since 2001; project leader of the Carbon Nanotube Capacitor Development Project of NEDO (New Energy and Industrial Technology Development Organization) since 2006; and a distinguished invited university professor at Nagoya University since 2007. He has also held the post of dean of the Advanced Institute of Nanotechnology at Sungkyunkwan University, in Suwon, Gyeonggi-do, South Korea, since 2005. More than 482 papers published in scientific journals between 1966 and mid-2009 carry Iijima's name as author or co-author.

Sumio Iijima was born on May 2, 1939 to Fukumatsu and Take Iijima in Koshigaya, a town in the Saitama Prefecture of Japan. At the small primary school he attended—there were only three classes, with a total of 120 pupils—he had a fine science teacher "who influenced me very much," he told Irene M. Kunii. His primary interests were unrelated to book learning, though; as a boy, he recalled in his NEC essay, "I collected plants and insects, I fished, and I kept a menagerie of small animals, including pigeons, rabbits, snakes, frogs, and crabs." As a high-school student, he ranked in the "lower middle" of his class, because he did not study diligently. "You see, I had so many things to do," he explained to Kunii. "I loved sports, collecting minerals, and looking at the stars at night." He was also a member of his school's mountaineering and music clubs. Iijima failed his university entrance exams on his first try. He then spent a year learning to play the mandolin and preparing to retake the exams, which, much to his dislike, required much memorization. His retest mark was sufficient to gain him acceptance into the University of Electro-Communications in Tokyo. He concentrated in communications engineering until his final year, when he changed his major to chemistry. When he realized that he wanted to gain admission to a graduate school, he uncharacteristically applied himself to his studies wholeheartedly. He earned a B.S. degree in 1963 and then enrolled at the Graduate School of Physics at Tohoku University, in Sendai, Japan. "It just so happened that I was assigned to the laboratory of Professor Tadatoshi Hibi," a pioneer in the use of electron microscopy for research, he wrote in "About Myself." (Hibi had built Japan's first electron microscope, in 1936.) That assignment "determined the rest of my life," Iijima told Kunii. He recalled in his essay, "It wasn't that I had a particularly strong desire to do research with electron microscopes at the time, but I found that I was perfectly suited to research in this field." He also wrote that the change in the trajectory of his career, from physics to microscopy, and "the fact that I dove into new fields," were "a result of my determination to find something"—that is, something new to science. Iijima earned an M.S. degree in chemistry, in 1965, and a Ph.D. in solid-state physics, in 1968, from Tohoku University.

From 1968 to 1975 Iijima worked as a research associate at Tohoku's Research Institute for Scientific Measurements. Also during that time, for 12 years beginning in 1970, he engaged in research at the Center for Solid State Science at Arizona State

University, in Tempe, under the physicist John M. Cowley, another major figure in electron microscopy and crystallography. "It was great because I had complete freedom and a very good microscope," he told Kunii. Iijima constructed a more sophisticated electron microscope and became the first microscopist ever to capture an image of individual atoms (those of tungsten). Colleagues told him that he "had achieved the dream held by researchers since the invention of the electron microscope in 1932—that of actually seeing a single atom," he recalled in "About Myself." With Cowley, Iijima wrote a paper titled "Electron Microscopy of Atoms in Crystals," published in *Physics Today* (March 1977); according to its deck, "Now we can see atoms in crystals directly with electron microscopy, allowing us to determine structures of both ordered and disordered solids and to study the way atoms cluster around crystal defects." (Ordered solids, or crystals, have precise, regular patterns of atoms or molecules, called lattices; their lattices may have defects, but only very few, and far between. Disordered solids have random patterns or crystal lattices with many defects.) With Michael A. O'Keefe and Peter R. Buseck, members of the University of Arizona Departments of Chemistry and Geology, Iijima set out to expand the boundaries of what could be seen with electron microscopes, by improving their resolution. Their influential paper on their work appeared in *Nature* (July 27, 1978). The abstract read, "It is now possible to compute images of crystal structures corresponding to experimental images produced by using high-resolution transmission electron microscopy (HRTEM)," and it noted that the authors had used several minerals and a binary oxide in their investigations.

In 1979, as a visiting senior scientist, Iijima joined the Department of Metallurgy and Materials Science at Cambridge University, in England. While studying graphite, a form of carbon, Iijima noticed a previously undescribed spherical arrangement of carbon atoms. His article about it contained only a partial description of its structure. Six years later the British scientist Harold Kroto and the American scientists Robert Curl and Richard Smalley published in *Nature* (November 1985) a description of C_{60} (C is the symbol for carbon), in which carbon atoms are joined to form a ball. The men christened it buckminsterfullerene, because it reminded them of the geodesic dome designed by Buckminster Fuller. Iijima recognized buckminsterfullerene as the spherical structure he had seen years earlier. His second paper about the structure, "The 60-Carbon Cluster Has Been Revealed!," written at Smalley's request and published in the *Journal of Physical Chemistry* (Volume 91, 1987), provided corroborating evidence that a new form, or allotrope, of carbon had been discovered. (Kroto, Curl, and Smalley won the 1996 Nobel Prize in chemistry for their work.) Later, additional allotropes of carbon were found; they became known collectively as fullerenes (or, less commonly, buckyballs). Despite the efforts of many researchers, the anticipated practical applications of fullerenes have not yet materialized.

In the meantime, in 1982 Iijima had returned to Japan to become a group leader in the Hayashi Ultra-Fine Particle Project, an activity of the national Exploratory Research for Advanced Technology (ERATO) program. "My major task in this project was to develop a new high resolution electron microscope accessible for characterizing ultra-fine crystals without exposure to air," he wrote for nanocarb.meijo-u.ac.jp. With that tool he demonstrated, as he reported in the *Journal of Electron Microscopy* (December 1985), that ultrafine, crystalline particles of gold "move about like amoeba," in his words; both their external form and internal arrangements of atoms change continuously. He earned the 1985 Nishina Memorial Award for that finding.

In 1987 Iijima left the ERATO project and signed on as a senior principal researcher with the NEC Corp. He chose to enter the private sector for the first time, at the age of 48, partly because private facilities like NEC's "have unique materials produced using expensive equipment that cannot be made in universities, and I was sure that these materials would become the basis for exceptional research results using electron microscopes," he wrote in "About Me." In addition, NEC executives promised to give him the resources to build an ultrahigh-vacuum, high-resolution transmission electron microscope. He also liked NEC's style of management, which, he wrote, "was based on the approach of 'broad proliferation of science and technologies, and the creation of new value,' and of 'giving back to society.'"

Iijima was using not the ultrahigh-vacuum electron microscope but a standard electron microscope on June 23, 1991, when he obtained the clearest pictures yet of the structures that would come to be known as carbon nanotubes. His achievement was a combination of instinct, skill, and luck. "I emphasize that it was serendipity," Iijima told Dennis Normile, adding, "I have the best technique in microscopy." His paper about his findings, titled "Helical Microtubules of Graphitic Carbon," attracted worldwide attention among chemists, physicists, and others when it appeared in *Nature* (November 7, 1991). The first nanotubes that he detected had several concentric walls; in 1993 he discovered single-walled carbon nanotubes. In either case, because of their smallness, nanotubes "exhibit unique physical and chemical properties," as he wrote for nanocarb.meijo-u.ac.jp. "A single piece of single-wall carbon nanotube can be a transistor . . . ," he continued. "Many other industrial applications utilizing the unique properties of carbon nanotubes include the electron emitter source with high current density, highly conductive electrical wire, the high thermal conductor for the heat radiator, the probe needle for scanning probe microscopes, molecular sieves, gas absorbers, [and] carriers for drug delivery systems in nano-bio medicine." Nanotubes can be made to function either as metals or semiconductors and are the smallest known molecules to display metallic properties. The tubes' conductivity of electricity is higher than that of copper, and their conductivity of heat is higher than that of diamond (whose heat-conductivity ability is superior to that of tungsten, beryllium, aluminum, gold, copper, and silver). They are also extremely strong (reportedly, 50 times stronger than an equivalent piece of steel) and may be used to increase the strength of various materials. For example, some manufacturers of tennis rackets now incorporate carbon nanotubes in the yoke of the frame to strengthen it.

Iijima has published hundreds of papers describing his research on nanotubes. They cover subjects including nanotubes' growth and structural flexibility; their formation by such means as laser evaporation and hydrogen-arc discharge; responses of nanotube bundles to visible light; effects on them of oxygen, heat, and high pressure; techniques for opening and filling them; methods of mass-producing and purifying them; and methods of fabricating carbon-nanotube tips for use in scanning-probe microscopy or atomic-force microscopy. The titles of a handful of papers hint at the scope of Iijima's work: "A Simple Way to Chemically React Single-Wall Carbon Nanotubes with Organic Materials Using Ultrasonication" (*Nano Letters*, 2001); "Metal-Free Production of High-Quality Multi-Wall Carbon Nanotubes, in Which the Innermost Nanotubes Have a Diameter of 0.4nm [nanometers]" (*Chemical Physics Letters*, 2002); "Diameter Enlargement of Single-Wall Carbon Nanotubes by Oxidation" (*Journal of Physical Chemistry*, 2004); "Water-Assisted Highly Efficient Synthesis of Impurity-Free Single-Walled Carbon Nanotubes" (*Science*, 2004); "Synthesis of Single- and Double-Walled Carbon Nanotube Forests on Conducting Metal Foils" and "Metallic Wires of Lanthanum Atoms Inside Carbon Nanotubes" (*Journal of the American Chemical Society*, 2006 and 2008, respectively).

Iijima has also studied nanobeads and nanohorns, the latter of which resemble chubby, single-walled carbon nanotubes closed on one end with what looks like a cone-shaped cap (the horn); various sources describe them as resembling dahlias in shape. In an interview in Japanese on July 8, 2003 for nanonet.go.jp (posted in English on that site on July 22, 2004), Kuniko Ishiguro wrote that Iijima "now thinks that commercial applications of carbon nanohorns will be realized much earlier than those of carbon nanotubes." Iijima told Ishiguro, "People are exaggerating carbon nanotubes too much. However, I can say with confidence that carbon nanotubes have made great contributions to basic science." He also said, "I had conducted research using electron microscopy for 30 years before I discovered carbon nanotubes, so discovering them is just one of the results of my research based on electron microscopy." And he offered some advice to aspiring scientists: "When you do not have any clue as to how to start new research, you cannot rely on anyone but yourself. What you can rely on when you face a serious difficulty is nothing but your experience."

Iijima's name entered the *Guinness Book of World Records* in connection with a lecture he gave in May 1997 at the Friday Evening Discourse at the Royal Institution in London, England. Lectures at that event, which dates from 1825 and is open to the public, start promptly with the sound of a bell and must end—even if the speaker is in midsentence—when the bell rings again, precisely one hour later. Iijima ended his talk three seconds before the second bell rang.

Iijima's recreational interests include playing the flute, playing tennis, and skiing. He and his wife, Aida Nobuko, a professor of gerontological nursing at Nagoya University, married in 1968. The couple live in Nagoya and have two children, Masako and Arihiro.

—J.E.P.

Suggested Reading: Absolute Astronomy (on-line); aist.go.jp Feb. 2002; *BusinessWeek* (on-line) July 8, 2002; *Journal of Japanese Trade and Industry* Sep. 1, 2001; nanonet.go.jp July 22, 2004; *Science* p1182 Nov. 18, 1994; voyle.net; *Who's Who in America*

Inskeep, Steve

1968– Radio journalist; co-host of Morning Edition

Address: National Public Radio, 635 Massachusetts Ave., N.W., Washington, DC 20001

"I love a good story and I love to write," the radio journalist Steve Inskeep told an interviewer for WEKU.FM (on-line) several years ago. "When you're lucky, you can find a story that has many layers of meaning." Since 2004 Inskeep has been the co-host, with Renée Montagne, of *Morning Edition*, the most popular program on National Public Radio (NPR) and the most-listened-to radio news program in the U.S. Inskeep, who turned 40 in 2008, covered local sporting events for his high-school and college radio stations. He worked for local radio stations in New York City and New Jersey for six years before he joined NPR, in 1996, as a political reporter. Since then he has covered hundreds of domestic and international events and phenomena, ranging from American politics, national U.S. elections, the wars in Afghanistan and Iraq, and the aftermath of Hurricane Katrina, to the presence of rats in Washington, D.C., and a West Virginia town whose population is 11. He has conducted interviews with men and women whose names are familiar worldwide and also with peo-

Donald Baxter

Steve Inskeep

ple known only to a few, among them victims of disasters, both natural and manmade, blue-collar workers, school-board members, and the mother of a fallen soldier. "I'm not a celebrity," he said after the WEKU.FM interviewer remarked that he had joined the ranks of "a distinguished list of media celebrities from Indiana," among them Ernie Pyle, Jane Pauley, and David Letterman. "I'm a reporter. I'm a writer. Sometimes I get to talk to famous or powerful people, but I never forget that they are talking to me because they want to reach the 19 million people who listen to NPR." Inskeep's honors include the National Headliner Award (2003), bestowed by the Press Club of Atlantic City, New Jersey; the Alfred I. duPont–Columbia University Silver Baton Award (2004 and 2007), which he earned with other NPR reporters for their coverage of the war in Iraq; and the Robert F. Kennedy Journalism Award (2006), given by the Robert F. Kennedy Memorial, an organization whose mission is the promotion of human rights.

Steven Alan Inskeep was born in 1968 to Roland and Judith Inskeep in the suburban town of Carmel, Indiana, near Indianapolis. His father was the athletic director of a high school; his mother was an English teacher. As a teenager Inskeep served as a sports announcer for Carmel High School's radio station, WHJE. "I learned a lot of my radio that way," he told Tony Rehagen for *Indianapolis Monthly* (April 2005). "When you're live for huge chunks of time, it's entirely up to you to paint that picture and carry that broadcast and convey the excitement of what is in front of you. If you screw up, you can screw up monstrously, and that was a great experience." As an example of such a mishap, Inskeep recalled to Rehagen that once, while he was providing commentary for a basketball game, the station's main power cord became disconnected. Unaware that the backup system had come on, he "let out a string of obscenities, many of which went out over the air." A National Merit scholar in his senior year of high school, Inskeep attended Morehead State University, in Morehead, Kentucky, on a full academic scholarship. He has described his years there as the beginning of his engagement with the larger world.

As an undergraduate Inskeep volunteered at Morehead's campus radio station, WMKY. For a small salary he worked at WMOR, a local Morehead radio station, where he gave running commentary at athletic competitions involving Rowan County, Kentucky, high-school teams. "We'd travel around to all these schools out in the hills and different places," Inskeep said about WMOR assignments to Marie Bouvier for *Kentucky Monthly* (February 2004). "We got to travel to all these old gymnasiums that were built by the WPA [Work Progress Administration, a Depression-era federal government program] in 1935 and sit in some seat where you can only see maybe two-thirds of the court. You'd kind of have to guess at what was happening in the other third." During that period Inskeep began listening to NPR broadcasts. "Sometimes I arrived [back at college] after staying up all night or sleeping only a couple of hours . . . ," he told Bouvier. "At 8 a.m., I put Scott Simon's outstanding *Weekend Edition* on the air, which meant that I was a captive audience, hearing it from beginning to end. That's how I learned to appreciate public radio."

After he graduated from college, with a B.A. degree, magna cum laude, in 1990, Inskeep moved to New York City. He worked there as an anchor and reporter for several radio stations, including WOR-AM, and wrote for various publications as a freelancer. He also took courses at Hunter College, a division of the City University of New York. Next, in 1992, he moved to New Jersey to take a job as news director at WBGO-FM, an NPR-affiliated radio station, based in Newark, that specializes in jazz standards. During his tenure there WBGO won several awards for its coverage of local news regarding poverty and crime. Inskeep married in 1993.

In 1996 NPR hired Inskeep as a political reporter, and he and his wife settled in Washington, D.C. For his first assignment he traveled to New Hampshire to cover that year's presidential primary elections. Since then, his job has taken him all over the world. In 1999 Inskeep received a Pew Fellowship in International Journalism, which is awarded to journalists in mid-career. As a fellow, he attended seminars and participated in discussion groups at the Paul H. Nitze School of Advanced International Studies, a division of Johns Hopkins University, before and after he spent five weeks in Colombia. There, he investigated the role of right-wing factions in the ongoing armed conflicts among guerrilla and paramilitary groups and other opponents of the Colombian government. When he returned to

NPR, he was named the organization's Pentagon correspondent. Among other events, he reported on the bombing of Kosovo, in the former Yugoslavia, by NATO (North Atlantic Treaty Organization) troops, to stop Serbian forces' campaign of violence against ethnic Albanians.

Inskeep left the Pentagon post in 2000 to cover that year's U.S. presidential race, in which the principal candidates were Vice President Al Gore, the Democratic nominee; Governor George W. Bush of Texas, the Republican nominee; and the social activist Ralph Nader, who ran as the Green Party's nominee and who, in the views of some people, won a crucial number of votes that otherwise would have been cast for Gore. In particular, Inskeep followed the campaign of Bush and attended the Republican National Convention, held that year in Philadelphia, Pennsylvania. On the Web site Reclaim the Media (November 15, 2003), Jonathan Lawson complained that Inskeep—in keeping with the "less edgy," "more conservative," and more risk-averse character that separated the NPR of earlier years from its 2000 incarnation—remained inside the convention center, "lamenting in detail that nothing newsworthy appeared to be happening there," instead of reporting from outside the building, where "Philadelphia police were beating and mauling protesters." On Election Day, November 7, 2000, Inskeep reported live from Bush's headquarters, in Texas, and he continued to do so for 20 straight hours, into November 8, when the results of the balloting in Florida remained in doubt. He subsequently reported on the controversy surrounding the election results in four of Florida's southern counties and on the U.S. Supreme Court's 5–4 decision, announced on December 12, 2000, that the recount of votes in those counties must end. Inskeep was present when officials in Tallahassee, Florida, certified that the state's electoral votes would go to Bush, thus giving him the presidency.

The next year Inskeep reported from Afghanistan on the early days of the U.S.–British invasion there, which was launched on October 7, 2001 in an attempt to capture Osama bin Laden, the leader of the terrorist organization Al Qaeda, and to destroy the Taliban, the Sunni Islamist group who then ruled Afghanistan and were believed to have aided Al Qaeda in the September 11, 2001 attacks on the U.S. "After Sept. 11, it was important to me to do that," Inskeep told Bouvier. "A lot of people felt like they had this horrible situation that their country was facing and they were looking for something to do. This was some small thing that I could do, to go and try to help people stay informed." Inskeep provided accounts of the war as it developed, and he later did the same in Iraq, after the U.S. invaded that country, in March 2003. In addition to reports on fighting and the activities of the U.S. military, he described the struggles of ordinary citizens to survive in war zones; later he also reported on efforts to democratize Iraq and such subjects as corruption among police officers in Baghdad, the Iraqi capital. "I think one thing to bear in mind is how people manage to go on with their lives under the most horrible of conditions," he told the WEKU-FM interviewer. "One remarkable thing about Afghanistan was that trucks drove over the blasted-out roads, past gunmen and robbers, and delivered goods to the cities, where you could buy food, and gasoline, and cassette tapes, and other items. Everything was destroyed and yet, in the cities anyway, society more or less functioned. People clearly were suffering but they had adapted to a degree that would have seemed impossible had I not seen it." Inskeep also traveled to Pakistan to keep NPR listeners abreast of important happenings there, such as the capture by Central Intelligence Agency (CIA) operatives of Abu Zubaydah, a senior member of Al Qaeda, in March 2002. Inskeep's schedule was often grueling. "One of the most interesting schedules I ever had was from November 2001 to April 2002," he told the WEKU-FM reporter. "I'd spend 35 or 40 days in Asia, working every waking hour of every day; then I'd fly home for a couple of weeks, and do absolutely nothing except spend time with my wife and sleep; then they'd send me back. I liked working hard, because I felt like the story was important to tell, and I also really liked not working at all."

In October 2002 Inskeep accepted the position of weekend host of NPR's late-afternoon series, *All Things Considered*. Public radio's longest-running national program and its second-most-popular show, *All Things Considered* offers up-to-the-minute news, updates on top news stories, features, interviews, and arts-related reviews. "We have tried over the last year to get better and better at really digging for something unique," Inskeep told Bouvier in 2004. "So when you turn on the radio on a Saturday or Sunday, you'll hear the latest news, and you'll also hear something extra. You'll hear a story that we've dug up that you won't hear anywhere else. Or a perspective on a story that you've been hearing about all week, but we'll find one more thing that's worth saying about it."

In April 2004 NPR executives, apparently in an attempt to attract more listeners to *Morning Edition*, announced that Bob Edwards's nearly 25-year-long stint as the program's host was ending. The next month, in what was termed a temporary move, Inskeep and Renée Montagne took Edwards's place, and in December of the same year, their posts became permanent.

In the aftermath of Hurricane Katrina, which struck the Gulf Coast of the U.S. in late August 2005, Inskeep hosted *Morning Edition* from New Orleans, Louisiana, talking to a wide variety of experts and survivors to convey some of the economic, social, and psychological effects of the disaster. Nearly a year later he returned to New Orleans to report on the hurricane's lasting consequences and ongoing relief and reconstruction efforts. He included vignettes that revealed ways in which people coped in the devastated city, which still lacked many amenities deemed necessities by contemporary urbanites. In the segment "A Day in the Life of New Orleans," broadcast on *Morning Edition* on August 11, 2006, Inskeep spoke with a food vendor who no longer had a bed, a man who was rebuilding his home, a young couple who were preparing to get married, a woman who had relocated to Houston, Texas, and Mark Schleifstein, a reporter with the New Orleans *Times-Picayune*, whose own house had been flooded. Schleifstein—a co-author of *Path of Destruction: The Devastation of New Orleans and the Coming Age of Superstorms*—took Inskeep to a huge drawbridge from which they could see a large swath of the city and the extent of the destruction. "From horizon to horizon, you see this city's uneven struggle to come back," Inskeep said in his broadcast, for which he had begun his investigations just after midnight. "Neighborhood by neighborhood, street by street, every wrecked home has a story." According to Mary Blue, a professor of communications at Tulane University, in New Orleans, NPR had continued to report on conditions in post-Katrina New Orleans "longer than anybody else nationally except maybe the *New York Times*," as she told Drew Lindsay for the *Washingtonian* (March 2007).

For NPR's series "The Price of Oil," about oil-related conflicts in Nigeria, Inskeep interviewed, among others, a freed hostage, the manager of a natural-gas plant, the director of Nigeria's Economic and Financial Crimes Commission, a native king, the leader of a separatist militia, a spokesman for Nigeria's president, and a woman whose child had been killed during fighting. He interspersed in his reports verbal snapshots of the daily activities of ordinary Nigerians. Once, Inskeep and his crew were arrested by unidentified gunmen outside an oil plant owned by Royal Dutch Shell and forced to surrender their tape. (They handed over one that was blank.) On another day an armed policeman jumped into Inskeep's car and demanded money. Audio recordings of those incidents were included in NPR broadcasts. "Our Nigerian companions persuaded them to let us go, but for many Nigerians, this is the face of the government that controls so much of their country's treasure," he said in his August 26, 2005 report, as quoted on NPR on-line. "The Price of Oil" earned Inskeep the 2006 Robert F. Kennedy Journalism Award.

Inskeep edited and can be heard on the audio compilation *NPR Driveway Moments: All About Animals: Radio Stories That Won't Let You Go* (2007). ("Driveway moments" refers to occasions on which a driver has arrived at his or her destination while an NPR animal story is on the air and remains in the car until the story ends.) Inskeep appeared in the televised documentary *Without Fear or Favor: The Best in Broadcast Journalism* (2004).

Inskeep and his wife, the former Carolee Gabel, live in the northwest section of Washington, D.C., with their daughter, Ava, who was born in 2005. Carolee Inskeep is a genealogy expert and the author of reference books about the New York Foundling Hospital, the Children's Aid Society, and New York City cemeteries. The Inskeeps do not own a car. For years one of their main leisure-time activities was their do-it-yourself renovation of their old house. Steve Inskeep enjoys reading, watching movies, and listening to old jazz and blues, alternative country music, and Bruce Springsteen albums. He told Tony Rehagen, "I'm perfectly willing to spend five minutes going all the way down the [radio] dial to avoid commercials."

—J.E.P.

Suggested Reading: *Indianapolis Monthly* p12 Apr. 2005; *Kentucky Monthly* p12 Feb. 2004; NPR.org; WEKU.FM (on-line)

Andrew H. Walker/Getty Images for Hugo Boss

Jacir, Emily

(JAH-ser)

1970– Artist

Address: c/o Alexander and Bonin, 132 10th Ave., New York, NY 10011

In the past decade Emily Jacir, a Palestinian-American, has become one of the most highly regarded of contemporary artists. Deeply political, she uses a variety of mediums—photography, sculpture, video, drawings, and performance—to address issues that have affected the Palestinian community, such as displacement from their homes in Israel, human-rights abuses, and restricted movement within the Israeli-occupied Palestinian territories, the Gaza Strip and West Bank. Her works include *Memorial to 418 Palestinian Vil-*

lages Which Were Destroyed, Depopulated and Occupied by Israel in 1948, a refugee tent covered with the names of Palestinian villages that were destroyed during the Arab-Israeli War; *Crossing Surda (A Record of Going to and from Work)*, a film chronicling Jacir's daily journey through checkpoints in the West Bank; and *Material for a Film*, a collection of documents, photographs, and other materials examining the assassination of the Palestinian intellectual Wael Zuaiter by Israeli intelligence agents in 1972. The artist's work has angered members of Israeli groups, who criticize Jacir for presenting only one side of the enormously complex Israeli-Palestinian conflict. Jacir, however, believes that her work helps to give a voice to the Palestinian people. "Our narrative, our story is absent from history books," she told an interviewer for the Web site of the Institute for Middle East Understanding (IMEU) in 2008. "When I made *Memorial to 418 Palestinian Villages Which Were Destroyed, Depopulated and Occupied by Israel in 1948* I chose [to write the village names in] English not only because the piece was made with 140 people in New York but because I wanted people to be able to read the names and say them out loud and question why they had not heard them before and why that history is not in their books."

Jacir's work has been featured in several biennials, including the 2003 Istanbul Biennale, in Turkey; the 2005 Sharjah Biennial, in the United Arab Emirates; the 2006 Sydney Biennale, in Australia; and the 2007 Venice Biennale, in Italy. She is the recipient of the 2007 Golden Lion Award, the 2007 Prince Claus Award, and the 2008 Hugo Boss Prize, one of the most prestigious honors in the contemporary art world. Most recently Jacir, who divides her time between the U.S. and the Palestinian territories, was short-listed for the 2009 Deutsche Börse Photography Prize.

Jacir was born into a Palestinian family in 1970. Though her birthplace is most often cited as Bethlehem, in the West Bank, other sources claim that it was elsewhere, reporting it variously as Chicago, Illinois; Baghdad, Iraq; and Houston, Texas. Jacir seems intent on keeping her origins shrouded in mystery; when asked by Michael Z. Wise for the *New York Times* (February 1, 2009) where she was born, she replied, "No comment." Her father, Yusuf Nasri Suleiman Jacir, who was born and raised in Bethlehem, is descended from a once wealthy and well-known family. In 1910 his grandfather, Suleiman Jacir, built Jacir Palace with the hope that his and his brothers' families would live together in the large house. The family lost their fortune, as well as the palace, in the 1930s, and the former Jacir Palace is now the largest hotel in Bethlehem.

When Emily Jacir was a young girl, her family, including her younger sister, Annemarie, moved to Saudi Arabia. There, her mother became the first teacher of Arabic at the American School in Riyadh. At 14 Jacir left her family to attend high school in Rome, Italy. She knew at an early age that she wanted to become an artist. When she was growing up in Saudi Arabia, whose society was particularly repressive with regard to women, "art was the one place where I could speak," she explained to the IMEU interviewer. Her parents, however, worried that their daughter's desire to become an artist would be dangerous, even deadly. (In retaliation for the 1972 Olympic Games massacre in Munich, Germany, during which 11 Israeli athletes and coaches were killed by the Palestinian militant group Black September, a number of Palestinian artists and intellectuals, with sometimes doubtful connections to the murders, were imprisoned, deported, or killed by Israeli agents during the 1970s and '80s.) Discussing her decision to focus her art on the plight of her people, Jacir said, "[Palestinians] are probably amongst the most discussed, yet most misrepresented people in the world. We are constantly dissected by foreign 'experts.' People have no problem claiming agency to speak on our behalf." Following high school Jacir moved to the U.S. to attend college. She received her B.A. degree in fine art from the University of Dallas, in Irving, Texas, in 1992, and went on to earn her M.F.A. degree from Memphis College of Art, in Tennessee, in 1994, the same year she received the Presidential Purchase Award from the school.

Jacir produced her first major work in 1998, while a resident at the Cité Internationale des Arts in Paris, France. For the work, titled *Change/Exchange*, Jacir traded $100 in U.S. currency for French francs, losing a bit of her money due to the exchange rate. She then exchanged the francs for American dollars and continued to trade the money back and forth until she was left with a few coins that could no longer be converted. For the exhibit she framed 60 photographs of the currency and exchange booths, along with the receipts of each transaction. "[*Change/Exchange*] might be read as an empiricization of the metaphysics of travel, since Jacir plays with travel's curious economy—the floating daily exchange rates, the loss or gain of hours crossing time zones—while also suggesting a race against mortality itself, the frantic struggle to preserve eroding value," Tom Vanderbilt wrote for *Artforum International* (February 1, 2004). Jacir next delved into her past to create *From Paris to Riyadh (Drawings for My Mother)*, first exhibited in 2000. During Jacir's childhood, whenever her family returned to Saudi Arabia from a trip abroad, her mother used markers to cover the exposed skin of models featured in their newly acquired fashion magazines. (Otherwise, airport censors would confiscate them.) For her project Jacir collected copies of *Vogue* magazine and drew clothing, reminiscent of the clothes made for paper dolls, on each photograph of otherwise scantily dressed models. Jacir has said that the piece is as much a criticism of Saudi Arabia's oppression of women as of the objectification of women in other countries.

Jacir moved to New York City in 1998. She participated in the Whitney Museum of American Art's Independent Study Program (1998–99), the Lower Manhattan Cultural Council's Studio Residency Program (1999–2000), and the National and International Studio Program at P.S. 1 Contemporary Arts Center (2000–01). During her residency at P.S. 1, Jacir created *Memorial to 418 Palestinian Villages Which Were Destroyed, Depopulated and Occupied by Israel in 1948.* Though Jacir had intended to do all of the sewing for the tent herself, it turned out to be an overwhelming task, and she soon sought help. Friends and strangers alike visited her studio every day and night to lend a hand. "Eventually the piece took on a new, more social dimension," the artist and writer John Menick wrote for his Web site, johnmenick.com (July 1, 2008, on-line). "On some nights, over a dozen people would participate in order to sew the letters. A few of those who showed up wanted to find the villages where their families came from; several people learned of the expulsion for the first time. Palestinians, Israelis, Americans, Egyptians, Syrians, Yemenis, Spaniards, and others sewed, told stories, joked, and gossiped." (More than 700,000 Palestinians fled or were forced out of their villages by Israeli forces during the creation of the state of Israel and the Arab-Israeli War that followed, in 1948.) *Memorial to 418 Palestinian Villages,* which was not finished at the time of its unveiling, was included in P.S. 1's May 2001 exhibition. Next to the tent Jacir displayed a record book in which she logged the names of people who had helped with the sewing. The work has since been acquired by the National Museum of Contemporary Art in Athens, Greece. It remains unfinished, with many of the village names simply penciled on the tent; Jacir has said that its incompleteness reflects the ongoing nature of the Palestinian people's struggle. In 2002 Jacir created and co-curated the first Palestine International Video Festival, held in Ramallah, Palestine.

For *Where We Come From* (2001–03), Jacir asked 27 Palestinians living away from the West Bank and Gaza and unable to return to those territories, "If I could do something for you, anywhere in Palestine, what would it be?" Jacir, who is able to move freely in and around the territories with her U.S. passport, fulfilled their wishes, which included eating one person's favorite food, placing flowers on a mother's grave, saying a prayer at a certain mosque, and playing soccer with neighborhood children. The exhibit comprised photographs documenting the events and texts explaining why the people she had interviewed were unable to perform the acts themselves. "The work is so personal and autobiographical in the sense that it is coming from my experience of spending my whole life going back and forth between Palestine and other parts of the world," Jacir told Chris Shull for the *Wichita (Kansas) Eagle* (January 16, 2005). "I am always taking things back and forth for other people. Because I have been going back and forth continuously my whole life, I have seen the deliberate fragmentation of our lands and the isolation of our people from each other by the Israelis."

Where We Come From, which was displayed at the Ulrich Museum of Art at Wichita State University, in Kansas, also became Jacir's first solo exhibit in New York, when it was shown as part of the 2004 Whitney Biennial at the Whitney Museum of American Art. Blake Gopnik wrote about the exhibit for the *Washington Post* (March 14, 2004), "Jacir's project bears eloquent witness to the effects that strife and politics can have on the most basic aspects of people's lives." Holland Cotter raved for the *New York Times* (May 9, 2003), "An art of cool Conceptual surfaces and ardent, intimate gestures, intensely political and beyond polemic, it adds up to one of the most moving gallery exhibitions I've encountered this season." The exhibit was protested by Israeli groups in New York and Kansas who felt that their side of the conflict was not represented fairly. Ted Bonin, of the New York gallery Alexander and Bonin, which represents Jacir, defended the piece, telling Chris Shull, "[Jacir's] work is not, in any way, propaganda. *Where We Come From* is a good example of how she presents the desires and losses of a group of people. It does not make a declaration of what has or should happen but rather draws our attention to human needs and conditions."

Jacir also created a 130-minute film, *Crossing Surda (A Record of Going to and from Work)* (2002–03), often paired with *Where We Come From* at exhibitions. Jacir conceived the work after she had been mistreated and threatened by an Israeli soldier while trying to film her feet at a West Bank checkpoint. She then hid a camera in her purse, filming through a hole in it, to document her daily travels over an eight-day period through the checkpoints between her home in Ramallah, in the West Bank, to Birzeit University, where she was teaching at the time. For another of her video installations, *From Texas With Love* (2003), Jacir asked Palestinians what music they would listen to if they were able to drive for an hour unrestricted by the checkpoints and roadblocks common in their homeland. Jacir compiled the songs, which ranged from traditional Arab music to American pop tunes, onto a soundtrack and paired it with film shot during a drive she had taken through Texas.

Jacir's 2005 gallery show Accumulations featured two new pieces by the artist. The first, *Inbox,* consisted of more than 40 small paintings depicting e-mail messages Jacir had received since 1998. (For the oil-on-wood paintings, each the size of a standard, 8 1/2-by-11-inch sheet of paper, Jacir painstakingly painted each letter of the messages, complete with dates, underlined links, and ads.) The e-mails chronicle the communication among a group of friends and among members of Palestinian/Arab-American communities; they include correspondence about the September 11, 2001 terrorist attacks on the U.S. and the resulting hate crimes against Arab-Americans. Also included in the show was *Ramallah/New York* (2005), a two-channel (or split-screen) video displaying footage taken of Palestinian businesses, including hair salons, delis, and coffeehouses, in both of the title cities. As the images run side by side, it is often hard to tell which footage was taken where.

One of Jacir's most lauded works has been *Material for a Film* (2005–), which tells the story of the assassination of the Palestinian poet and writer Wael Zuaiter. In 1972 Zuaiter was shot in Rome, Italy, by Israeli agents who alleged that he was linked to the massacre of Israeli athletes by Black September. (Zuaiter's supporters maintain that there is no evidence that he was involved with the Munich massacre.) His was the first in a series of assassinations of prominent Palestinian figures by Israeli agents that occurred during the early 1970s. "Since I was a teenager I have been haunted by the Mossad massacres of Palestinian intellectuals, poets and politicians," Jacir told Michael Z. Wise. "Back in 1998 I began collecting as much information as I could on the Palestinians who were murdered on European soil. Initially my plan was to make a project about all of them. The more I researched, however, the more compelled I became with Wael's story in and of itself. . . . I felt connected to him in that I lived in Rome and had moved there from the gulf as he did. He was also a pioneer in trying to tell our story to the outside world. Wael Zuaiter was a poet and a translator who despised all forms of violence." Inspired by a chapter in the 1979 book *For a Palestinian: A Memorial to Wael Zuaiter*, edited by Zuaiter's longtime companion, Janet Venn-Brown, Jacir decided to collect material in order to make a film about Zuaiter's life. She traveled to Rome, talking to Zuaiter's family and friends and even forming a friendship with Venn-Brown.

In 2005 Jacir used some of the material she had collected over the years to create an exhibit. *Material for a Film* includes photographs of Zuaiter, letters he wrote, photographs of the covers of books he had kept in his library, a recording of Gustav Mahler's Ninth Symphony (a favorite work of Zuaiter's), and a clip of the 1963 film *The Pink Panther*, in which Zuaiter made a brief appearance as an extra. Jacir also included photos she had taken of places Zuaiter frequented in Rome, as well as written accounts of her travels and of her encounters with people who had known the writer. After Jacir was invited to display her work at the 2006 Sydney Biennale, she learned to shoot a .22 caliber pistol, the same kind of weapon that had been used to kill Zuaiter. She then added a separate piece to the exhibit, *Material for a Film (Performance)*, which consisted of a room of shelves filled with 1,000 small, white books, each of which had been shot by Jacir. "This [performance] piece is based on one element of Wael's story that I discovered during my research, which was that he was killed by 12 bullets at close range to his body, but there was a 13th bullet which struck his copy of *A Thousand and One Nights*. Wael's dream had been to translate *A Thousand and One Nights* directly from Arabic into Italian . . . ," Jacir explained to Wise. "The books [I shot] were white, and they were blank and symbolized the thousands of stories that have not been written and will not be written." (Although there have been Italian translations of *A Thousand and One Nights* from other languages, there has not yet been a translation directly from Arabic to Italian.)

Material for a Film was later featured in the 2007 Venice Biennale. At the biennale Jacir won the prestigious Golden Lion Award, presented to artists under 40. In 2007 she was also presented with the Prince Claus Award from the Prince Claus Fund for Culture and Development in Amsterdam, the Netherlands. According to the organization's Web site, Jacir received the award "for the quality of her intensely evocative artworks that transcend the national framework and resonate with exiles around the world, for her resistance to injustice, and for her attempts through cultural actions to heal the wounds of conflict." Jacir's work on *Material for a Film* earned her a nomination for the 2009 Deutsche Börse Photography Prize.

In November 2008 Jacir was selected to receive the prestigious Hugo Boss Prize from a shortlist of finalists that included Christoph Büchel, Patty Chang, Sam Durant, Joachim Koester, and Roman Signer. The biennial award, established by the German fashion house Hugo Boss and the Solomon R. Guggenheim Foundation, recognizes significant achievements in contemporary art and carries a $100,000 prize. In their statement, the jury, which consists of museum directors and curators from around the world, said of their selection, "Emily Jacir's rigorous conceptual practice—comprising photography, video, performance, and installation-based work—bears witness to a culture torn by war and displacement. As a member of the Palestinian diaspora, she comments on issues of mobility (or the lack thereof), border crises, and historical amnesia through projects that unearth individual narratives and collective experiences. Jacir combines the roles of archivist, activist, and poet to create poignant and memorable works of art that are at once intensely personal and deeply political. It is the refined sophistication of Jacir's art and the relevance of her concerns—both global and local—in a time of war, transnationalism, and mass migration that led us to award her the 2008 Hugo Boss Prize."

Jacir lives and works in Ramallah and New York City. Since 2007 she has been a full-time digital-video instructor at the International Academy of Art Palestine, in Ramallah. Her sister is a filmmaker.

—M.A.S.

Suggested Reading: (Abu Dhabi, United Arab Emirates) *National* (on-line) July 10, 2008; alexanderandbonin.com; *Art Monthly* p22+ Apr. 1, 2009; *Electronic Intifada* (on-line) Dec. 15, 2006, Dec. 15, 2008; Institute for Middle East

Understanding (on-line); *New York Times* AR p28 Feb. 1, 2009, C p29 Feb. 13, 2009

Selected Works: *Change/Exchange*, 1998; *From Paris to Riyadh (Drawings for My Mother)*, 2000; *Memorial to 418 Palestinian Villages Which Were Destroyed, Depopulated and Occupied by Israel in 1948*, 2001; *Where We Come From*, 2001–03; *Crossing Surda (A Record of Going to and from Work)*, 2002–03; *From Texas with Love*, 2003; *Inbox*, 2005; *Ramallah/New York*, 2005; *Material for a Film*, 2005

Selected Monographs: *belongings*, 2003; *Emily Jacir*, 2008

Keith Heller, courtesy of Vintage Books

Jamison, Kay Redfield

June 22, 1946– Psychologist; educator; writer

Address: Meyer 2-181, The Johns Hopkins Hospital, 600 N. Wolf St., Baltimore, MD 21287

"I was used to my mind being my best friend; of carrying on endless conversations within my head; of having a built-in source of laughter or analytic thought to rescue me from boring or painful surroundings," the clinical psychologist Kay Redfield Jamison wrote in *An Unquiet Mind: A Memoir of Moods and Madness* (1995), about her struggles with manic depression. "I counted on my mind's acuity, interest, and loyalty as a matter of course. Now, all of a sudden, my mind had turned on me." Manic depression, also called bipolar disorder, is a widely misunderstood mental illness affecting some two million people in the United States. It is characterized by cycles of extreme moods, from "high," manic periods of extraordinary elation, energy, and rapid-fire thought processes, to "low," depressed periods, marked by such disabling symptoms as persistent sadness, greatly decreased energy, and a loss of interest in life. Often, the "high" and "low" periods overlap. Although she had experienced depression since childhood and mania since her mid-teens, Jamison was not diagnosed with manic depression until age 26, during her graduate studies in psychology at the University of California at Los Angeles (UCLA). While working to understand her illness and struggling to comply with her prescribed medical regimen—daily doses of lithium, a mood-stabilizing drug—Jamison became one of the world's foremost experts on manic depression. In 1978 she founded UCLA's mood-disorders clinic, which she ran for the next decade. She has held the title of professor of psychiatry at Johns Hopkins University School of Medicine since 1987. With Frederick K. Goodwin, a professor of psychiatry at George Washington University, she co-wrote the definitive scholarly text on the disorder, *Manic-Depressive Illness* (1990). Her next book was the controversial *Touched with Fire: Manic Depressive Illness and the Artistic Temperament* (1993), which offered reasons for the prevalence of mental illness in artistic and high-achieving individuals. With the publication of the best-selling and critically acclaimed *An Unquiet Mind*, Jamison gained nationwide attention. *Night Falls Fast: Understanding Suicide* (1999) is Jamison's comprehensive resource on suicide and its relationship to mental illness; her book *Exuberance: The Passion for Life* (2004) sheds light on what life is like for a person with an "exuberant temperament." Jamison's unusual perspective on mental illness, that of someone with both personal experience and medical expertise, has made her a popular speaker. Since she revealed publicly her history as a manic depressive, she has dedicated her career to reducing the stigma attached to mental illness and suicide. Her memoir *Nothing Was the Same* was published in September 2009.

The youngest of three children—she has a sister and a brother—Jamison was born on June 22, 1946. She also has a half-sister. Her father, Marshall Jamison, was a meteorologist and an officer in the U.S. Air Force; her mother, Dell Temple Jamison, was a teacher. While Jamison has recalled her father as being "gregarious," he also suffered from manic depression, a hereditary disorder, and experienced fits of deep depression and mania throughout Jamison's childhood. Jamison's half-sister, Danica, has been diagnosed with the same condition. Throughout high school Jamison was often moody and was given to long bouts of depression. As she recalled in *Night Falls Fast*, she began to consider suicide; she would fantasize about throwing herself down a flight of stairs, and she studied morning traffic patterns in her neighborhood to determine the best time to jump in front of a truck. At 16 Jamison experienced the highs of mania for the first time. "I raced about like a crazed weasel, bubbling with plans and enthusiasms, immersed in sports, and staying up all night, night after night, out with friends, reading everything that wasn't nailed down, filling manuscript books with poems and fragments of plays, and making expansive, completely unrealistic, plans for my future . . . ," she wrote in *An Unquiet Mind*. "I felt great. Not just great, I felt *really* great."

An excellent student, Jamison earned her B.A. and M.A. degrees in psychology in 1971 from UCLA, where she was a National Science Foundation research fellow and a John F. Kennedy scholar. She remained at UCLA to pursue a doctorate in psychology, which she earned in 1975; meanwhile, the previous year, she had begun teaching at UCLA. While pursuing her doctoral degree, she spent a year studying zoology and neurophysiology at the University of St. Andrews, in Scotland; she has described that time as an "Indian summer" of her life, one of the longest periods in which she experienced no psychological disturbances. With that exception, throughout her 20s Jamison's condition worsened, and her highs and lows became more intense. In 1974, while working as an adjunct professor of psychiatry at UCLA, she experienced a major psychotic breakdown, in which she hallucinated, spent far too much money, and humiliated herself in front of her peers, giving in to inappropriate impulses and speaking illogically and overexcitedly. She was admitted to a hospital, where doctors diagnosed her with manic depression and prescribed lithium. She responded well to the treatment, but when she began to feel better, she stopped taking her medication—not because of the side effects she had experienced, as she explained in *An Unquiet Mind*, but because she was afraid to lose the feeling of exhilaration and the heightened creativity that had accompanied her manic states; as she put it, she had become "addicted to the highs": "I could fly through star fields and slide along the rings of Saturn," she wrote. Because she did not take her medication, she entered a period of severe depression at age 28 and then ingested an overdose of lithium, in a failed attempt at suicide. That event marked a turning point in her life. She recognized that she needed lithium to function, and she committed herself to the study of manic depression and other mood disorders.

While conducting her postdoctoral research at UCLA, Jamison founded the school's affective-disorders clinic, in 1978, and became its director. In that position she treated many patients who suffered from manic depression. In 1987 she left UCLA and joined the faculty of the Johns Hopkins University Medical School. In 1990 Jamison co-wrote *Manic-Depressive Illness* with the psychiatrist Frederick K. Goodwin, who later (1992–94) directed the National Institute of Mental Health and hosted (1998–2008) the National Public Radio series *The Infinite Mind*. The culmination of about 10 years of research, the book discusses historical and contemporary treatments for manic depression and includes accounts of the highly varied experiences of sufferers of the disease. Named the best medical book of the year by the Association of American Publishers, it became known as the definitive textbook on manic depression. In 2007 Jamison and Goodwin published a second edition of their textbook, *Manic Depressive Illness: Bipolar Disorders and Recurrent Depression*, a 1,262-page compendium of medical knowledge about bipolar disorder.

For her book *Touched with Fire: Manic-Depressive Illness and the Artistic Temperament* (1993), Jamison drew on research that she had conducted while at Oxford University, in England, in 1989, while she was on a sabbatical leave from UCLA. For that work she surveyed culturally influential and creative Britons, including renowned artists, poets, and playwrights, with the goal of determining their mental states. While major depression affects between 5 and 15 percent of the general population in Great Britain at some point in their lives, Jamison found that about 38 percent of those in her sample had been treated for some kind of affective illness, a mental disorder that has a consistent, pervasive effect on a person's thoughts, emotions, and behaviors. Rates of such mood disorders were highest among playwrights and poets—63 percent and over 50 percent of them, respectively, reported having experienced depression or having been treated for mood disorders. In *Touched with Fire*, Jamison used scientific studies and personal accounts, in the forms of diaries, essays, poems, and other writings, to analyze the mental states of artists and writers including Robert Lowell, Gerard Manley Hopkins, and Lord Byron, all of whom suffered from bipolar disorder. Jamison described the discovery that, particularly during the manic stages of bipolar disorder, which bring periods of unusually creative thought processes and elevated energy levels, the chemistry of the brain is altered. *Touched with Fire* was met with great interest and acclaim and, from some, the criticism that the book glorified mental illness. "It's a fact that a disproportionate number of artists appear to have the disease compared with the general population," Jamison told Anastasia Toufexis for *Time* (September 11, 1995). Pointing out the way in which her findings were being misconstrued, Jamison went on to explain that she was in no way trying to show an inextricable link between mental illness and creativity. "You don't have to have manic depression to be creative. In fact, most creative people don't."

Jamison's next published work, *An Unquiet Mind: A Memoir of Moods and Madness* (1995), is both a detailed clinical analysis of manic depression and a candid first-person account of her agonizing battle with the illness. In it Jamison explained that while symptoms of manic depression vary among individuals, in the early stages of the disease they often include poor performance in school and excessive use of alcohol or drugs, and they often remain undetected or misunderstood; in young children, the malady is frequently confused with attention-deficit/hyperactivity disorder. When left untreated, manic depression usually worsens, as episodes of mania and depression become more severe. Jamison explained that while manic depression is highly treatable—80 percent of its victims respond well to medication—manic depressives are notorious for their inconsistent compliance with recommended drug regimens or their refusal to take any medicine. In Jamison's case, while she tried to reconcile her image of herself with the evidence of her affliction, she resisted turning her back on her exhilarating periods of mania. While Jamison has often insisted that manic depression has no redeeming features, she has also acknowledged that, were it not for her disease, "I would not have accomplished the same things." Although an article in which Jamison had revealed her problem had appeared in the *Washington Post* shortly before the publication of *An Unquiet Mind*, very few of Jamison's colleagues had known, until the book was reviewed and became the focus of news stories, that she suffered from manic depression. While most of her co-workers continued to treat her with respect, she was occasionally subjected to patronizing comments and sometimes heard people express doubts about her ability to handle her job. Taking all those things into account, Jamison gave up her practice at Johns Hopkins but continued to teach there.

Listed among *New York Times* best-sellers for five months, *An Unquiet Mind* drew rave reviews, as well as more than 10,000 letters of thanks from readers. "*An Unquiet Mind* is an honest and beautifully written book about a life-destroying illness experienced by both clinician and patient . . . ," K. D. Hopkins wrote for the *Lancet* (August 3, 1996). "[Jamison] has opened a door through which we can take a look—if we want—providing a remarkably honest, but at times frightening, account of this condition." Those who found fault in her efforts to destigmatize the illness included Peter Kramer, a psychiatrist and author of the bestseller *Listening to Prozac* (1993), who, in an article for the *New York Times* (April 7, 1996), described Jamison's book and other recent first-person accounts of mood disorders as "autopathographies." While acknowledging that such books helped to combat the stigma associated with mental disease, Kramer suggested that the book's publishers exploited the writers, who in turn manipulated readers, for entertainment purposes. Jamison dismissed Kramer's and other, similar criticisms as "ridiculous."

Following the publication of *An Unquiet Mind*, Jamison embarked on a speaking tour devoted to the topic of manic depression, schizophrenia, and other mental illnesses. In light of the frequent emergence of such disorders in early adulthood, she gave talks at many colleges and universities. As Jamison explained in her lectures, the stressful habits and lifestyles of many undergraduates, who have poor diets, lack sufficient sleep, and indulge or overindulge in alcohol and drugs, often trigger first episodes of mental illness. Jamison encouraged students to be vigilant for symptoms of depression and mania and to seek treatment as soon as possible. "These are such important years of life," Jamison said, as quoted in the Bergen County, New Jersey, *Record* (May 19, 1997). "To lose them to this intermittent illness, it's so unnecessary."

Jamison told one audience of her experiences with depression, as quoted by Thrity Umrigar in the *Akron (Ohio) Beacon Journal* (May 25, 1999), "I nearly died from it. It is total, complete despair, a sense of futility, marked by an emotional shutting down." At the end of her talks, Jamison was often approached by people who had lost a mentally ill friend or relative to suicide. Some of those who had died had "made serious attempts on their lives" before they succeeded in killing themselves, "and their parents had no idea," Jamison explained to Patricia Meisol for the *Baltimore Sun* (December 12, 1999). "Something about the sheer numbers hit me." They also inspired her to research and write her next book, *Night Falls Fast: Understanding Suicide* (1999), which explores the psychological, physiological, and other aspects of suicide through accounts of suicides and suicide attempts, including her own. *Night Falls Fast* "is at once the most relentless and the most sympathetic book she has produced, written with an edifying urgency that surpasses her previous volumes," Andrew Solomon wrote in a review for the *New York Times* (October 24, 1999). In it Jamison argued that suicide has been largely mischaracterized or even ignored by the medical establishment, romanticized by the media, and stigmatized by a society—that of the U.S.—that is uncomfortable with mental illness. She maintained that suicide's link to mental distress rather than physical problems (which can contribute to despair) should not lead medical practitioners and public-health officials to separate it from other kinds of illnesses. Rather, it should be considered the result of real illness and recognized as a virtual epidemic. As of 1999, the year that *Night Falls Fast* was published, about 31,000 Americans died by their own hands every year—the equivalent of one every 17 minutes. Suicide was the third-leading cause of death among adolescents in the U.S. and the second-leading cause among college students. "Where is the public concern and outrage?" Jamison wrote in the epilogue to *Night Falls Fast*, as quoted by Meg Kissinger in the *Milwaukee (Wisconsin) Journal Sentinel* (November 7, 1999). Countering the common perception that many suicides occur for no discernible reason, Jamison contended that the road to suicide is actually "well marked" and predictable. She cited studies suggesting that 90 to 95 percent of all suicides can be attributed to mental illnesses—bipolar disorder, depression, schizophrenia—that can be diagnosed and treated. In part because of her own experience, she supports the use of drug therapy in conjunction with psychotherapy. She also advocates the passage of laws that would decrease the accessibility of guns, which are used in 60 percent of suicides in the U.S. She encourages parents to talk to their children about depression and thinks that universities should take steps to try to prevent suicides.

In her 2004 book, *Exuberance: The Passion for Life*, Jamison expressed the view that neither science nor society has placed enough value on exuberance, which Jamison loosely defined as "an abounding, ebullient, effervescent emotion. It is kinetic and unrestrained, joyful, irrepressible." "I've always been interested in highly energized and higher mood states . . . ," she told Marina Pisano for the *San Antonio Express-News* (September 13, 2005). "I'm interested in what's a normal mood and what's an exceptionally productive creative mood—what are the layers of it but also what's the overlap with psychopathologies." Jamison wrote that about one in 10 individuals is born with an exuberant temperament. She offered examples of exuberant individuals from the past, among them the environmentalist John Muir, who founded the Sierra Club; the showman P. T. Barnum, who founded the Barnum and Bailey Circus; the politicians Theodore Roosevelt and Winston Churchill; and the photographer Wilson Bentley, who captured on film the images of more than 5,000 snowflakes to prove that no two are alike. Jamison also analyzed such fictional characters as Tigger, from the Winnie-the-Pooh books, and the dog Snoopy, from the *Peanuts* comic strip, who, according to Jamison, has "an extraordinary capacity for celebration." In each profile Jamison described discoveries or other results of unusual degrees of curiosity, energy, creativity, and passion. She also discussed hypomania, a milder form of the "high" experienced by people with manic depression, and noted that in some people, exuberance can lead to a dangerous lack of judgment and even—as in the case of Churchill—bouts of deep depression.

The *Washington Post*, the *Seattle Times*, and the *San Francisco Chronicle* selected *Exuberance* as one of the best books of 2004, and *Discover* magazine selected it as one of the best science books of the year. Most reviewers called Jamison's subject matter unique and her writing style captivating. Jacob Stockinger, in an assessment for the Madison, Wisconsin, *Capital Times* (January 14, 2005), called *Exuberance* "a fascinating and inspiring book that, one hopes, will serve as the opening shot in a campaign to explore our positive and constructive moods that, when closely looked at, yield their own mysteries and wonders." Some others criticized her account as vague. In a review for the *New York Times* (December 5, 2004), for instance, Daphne Merkin wrote that Jamison's book "is marked by a besetting critical haziness, blurring terms of definition that should be rigorous and shrugging off qualifications that need to be more thoroughly addressed."

Jamison believes that education is the key to changing the cultural perception of mental illness. She commended David Satcher, the U.S. surgeon general under President Bill Clinton, when, in 1999—for the first time—his office published a report on mental illness. She also praised the Republican U.S. senator Gordon Smith of Oregon, who, after the suicide of his son Garrett, sponsored a bill (signed into law by President George W. Bush in 2004) providing funding to colleges, universities, and American Indian organizations for suicide education and prevention. At Harvard University, Jamison and another mental-health professional set up the Vincent Prize, which finances proposals for projects on changing attitudes and increasing awareness of mental illness on the campus; the first prize was awarded in 2000. In 2001 Jamison received a MacArthur Fellowship, also known as a "genius grant," which includes a no-strings-attached $500,000 award distributed over five years. Jamison told Lisa Allen-Agostini for the *Washington Post* (October 24, 2001) that she planned to use the grant to establish programs similar to Harvard's at other universities. A supporter of genetic research into mental illness, Jamison was a member, in 2005, of the first National Advisory Council for Human Genome Research, a federally chartered committee that advises the National Human Genome Research Institute, a branch of the National Institutes of Health that works to improve health through genetic research. She is currently the senior scientific consultant to the Dana Foundation and chair of the Genome Action Coalition. Still, as she recently told Karen R. Long for the *Cleveland Plain Dealer* (March 16, 2008), Jamison believes that the public-health community is not doing "nearly enough" to address mental illness and suicide.

Jamison's memoir *Nothing Was the Same* (2009) focuses on her relationship with her late husband, Richard Wyatt, who overcame childhood dyslexia and went on to become the chief of the neuropsychiatry branch at the National Institute of Mental Health and a pioneer in schizophrenia research; Wyatt died in 2002 from lung cancer. Throughout the book, which delves into Jamison and Wyatt's shared research and their struggles with mental illness and cancer, respectively, Jamison draws comparisons between grief and madness. "The great gift that Jamison offers here, beyond her honesty and the beauty of her writing, is perspective: a clear-eyed view of illness and death, sanity and insanity, love and grief . . . ," Reeve Lindbergh wrote in her glowing review for the *Washington Post* (September 6, 2009, on-line). "Once again, Jamison seems to be telling the truth, no matter how difficult it may be, in a way that avoids self-pity and inspires courage. To write the truth with such passion and grace is remarkable enough. To do this in loving memory of a partner is tribute indeed."

In addition to the MacArthur Fellowship, Jamison's many honors include the National Mental Association's William Styron Award, the American Suicide Foundation Research Award, the Community Mental Health Leadership Award, the Endowment Award from the Massachusetts Genetics Hospital/Harvard Medical School, the Fawcett Humanitarian Award from the National Depressive and Manic-Depressive Association, the Steven V. Logan Award for Research into Brain Disorders from the National Mental Health Association, the Falcone Prize for Research in Affective Illness from the National Alliance for Research on Schizophrenia and Depression, and the Yale University McGovern Award for excellence in medical communication. She has been named a "hero of medicine" by *Time* and was one of five people profiled in the 1999 public-television series *Great Minds of Medicine*. Jamison was a distinguished lecturer at Harvard University in 2002 and the Litchfield lecturer at the University of Oxford in 2003. She has written and produced a series of award-winning public television specials about manic depression and the arts.

Described by Meisol as "animated and friendly, a thin, tousled blond [who] wears a large smile often painted coral," Jamison is currently a tenured professor of psychology at the Johns Hopkins University School of Medicine. She is also an honorary professor of English at the University of St. Andrews, where she teaches undergraduates for three weeks every fall. Her first marriage ended in divorce. From her eight-year marriage to Richard Wyatt, she has two stepsons, Christopher and Justin, and a stepdaughter, Elizabeth.

—M.E.R.

Suggested Reading: *Akron Beacon Journal* C p1+ May 25, 1999; *Baltimore Sun* F p3 Dec. 12, 1999; *Capital Times* A p9 Jan. 14, 2005; *Milwaukee Journal Sentinel* Lifestyle p1 Nov. 6, 1999; *New York Times* (on-line) Apr. 7, 1996; *New York Times Book Review* p13 Oct. 24, 1999, p56 Dec. 5, 2004; *San Antonio Express-News* C p1+ Sep. 13, 2005; *Time* p83 Sep. 11, 1995; *Washington Post* C p1+ Oct. 24, 2001

Selected Books: *Manic-Depressive Illness*, 1990, 2007; *Touched with Fire: Manic-Depressive Illness and the Artistic Temperament*, 1993; *An Unquiet Mind: A Memoir of Moods and Madness*, 1995; *Night Falls Fast: Understanding Suicide*, 1999; *Exuberance: The Passion for Life*, 2004; *Nothing Was the Same*, 2009

Jarrett, Valerie

Nov. 14, 1956– White House senior adviser; real-estate developer; lawyer; former Chicago government official

Address: The White House, 1600 Pennsylvania Ave., Washington, DC 20500

Saul Loeb/AFP/Getty Images

"Every successful politician, monarch or business tycoon needs someone like [Valerie] Jarrett," Don Terry wrote for the *Chicago Tribune* (July 27, 2008), "a straight-talking, fiercely loyal, well-connected, discreet, disciplined, protective confidant/friend/sounding board/surrogate sibling who has known the candidate since before he or she became the next big thing." Valerie Jarrett—a lawyer, real-estate developer, former member of the Chicago, Illinois, city government, and one-time chairman of the Chicago Stock Exchange—was a senior adviser to Barack Obama in his campaign for the U.S. presidency, and, with John Podesta, she co-chaired Obama's transition team, which smoothed the handover of power from the administration of President George W. Bush to that of the new chief executive. In the White House she serves as senior adviser to the president for intergovernmental relations and public engagement. A resident of Chicago since early childhood, Jarrett has also been a close friend of Barack Obama and his wife, Michelle, since before their marriage. In the summer of 1991, when Jarrett was the commissioner of the Chicago Department of Economic Development and Planning, Michelle Obama, then surnamed Robinson, applied for a job in the office of Chicago's mayor, Richard M. Daley, and Jarrett interviewed her. After Jarrett offered her the job, Robinson asked her to have dinner with her and Barack

Obama, who was then a community organizer in Chicago and Robinson's fiancé, so that all of them could discuss the position. Barack Obama "was worried about the same things that I worried about when Daley first got elected," Jarrett told Michelle Cottle for the *New Republic* (August 27, 2008). "Would [the mayor] be sufficiently progressive? Would Michelle get caught up in the Democratic machine? . . . If she disagreed with something the mayor wanted to do, would she be forced to do it?" At the end of the evening, Jarrett asked Obama if her responses to his questions had been satisfactory—if she had "passed the test." "Yeah, you passed the test," Obama said, smiling, as quoted in the *Chicago Tribune* (April 22, 2007). Jarrett and the Obamas have maintained a close personal and professional relationship ever since. Michelle Obama left the mayor's office in 1993 to work under Jarrett in the Department of Economic Development and Planning. Later, Michelle Obama worked at the University of Chicago and the school's medical center during Jarrett's tenure on both boards. At the start of Barack Obama's political career, Jarrett, a third-generation member of Chicago's black community leaders, introduced him to people of influence in that city and helped him organize fundraisers. During his campaign for a seat in the U.S. Senate, in 2004, Obama named Jarrett his financial adviser, and in February 2007, when he announced his candidacy for president, he appointed Jarrett as his senior adviser. Don Terry described Jarrett as "the other side of Obama's brain," and Michelle Cottle, in a profile of her for the *New Republic* (August 27, 2008), wrote that Jarrett is "an extension of the candidate. She is Obama's eyes and ears at meetings and events. When she speaks, it is in his voice." "I trust her completely," Obama has said of her, as quoted by Terry.

Characterized by Terry as "soft-spoken" but "steely willed," Jarrett served as the chair of the Chicago Transit Authority (CTA) from 1995 to 2003, when she left the public sector to join the Habitat Co., a Chicago-based real-estate company charged with overseeing the construction and management of Chicago's public housing. She held the titles of executive vice president and managing director of Habitat until 2007, when she was promoted to chief executive officer. One of her missions in that capacity was to integrate greater numbers of public-housing units in white or mixed neighborhoods, to end the de facto segregation of most low-income or welfare-dependent black Chicagoans, who live in virtually all-black public housing in virtually all-black neighborhoods. "Like Obama, she does not seek to fight the system so much as infiltrate it, scale it, and make it work for her," Cottle wrote. "It is a quieter, less dramatic form of activism that can cause friction with some of Jarrett's more traditional liberal allies—much the way Obama's post-racial positioning has raised eyebrows among older-generation black leaders. . . . For Jarrett, however, unifying people behind the system rather than against it has become something of an art form."

The only child of James Bowman and the former Barbara Taylor, Jarrett was born Valerie Bowman on November 14, 1956 in Shiraz, Iran, where her mother and father were working. Her parents are both internationally known experts—her mother in early childhood development and her father in hematology and pathology. Barbara Bowman was a co-founder, in 1966, of the Chicago School for Early Childhood Education (now known as the Erikson Institute) and currently serves as chief officer of the Chicago Public Schools' Office of Early Childhood Education. James Bowman, a physician, was the first African-American to be accepted into a residency program at St. Luke's Hospital in Chicago, in 1947, and before he retired he taught in the Departments of Pathology and Medicine at the College of Medicine at the University of Chicago. Both of Jarrett's parents have earned many honors. Jarrett's great-grandfather Robert Robinson Taylor was the first African-American to graduate from the Massachusetts Institute of Technology and was among the first to earn accreditation as an architect. Jarrett's maternal grandfather, Robert Rochon Taylor, was a Chicago community leader and onetime member of the board of the Chicago Housing Authority (CHA); what was once the world's largest public-housing development, the Robert Taylor Homes, was named for him. (The last of its 28 buildings was demolished in 2007.) Vernon Jordan, a onetime executive director of the United Negro College Fund, former president of the National Urban League, and close adviser to President Bill Clinton, is one of her great-uncles.

In Iran Jarrett and her parents lived near a local hospital in a community of Americans and Iranians. Its residents included participants in a program in which physicians and agricultural experts from the U.S. helped developing countries' health and farming efforts. "I remember how welcoming everyone was to the many Americans who were there," Jarrett told Terry. "We were viewed by the Iranians as Americans—not black Americans—so I had no awareness of race until we returned to the United States." In 1962 the Jarretts moved to London, England, where they lived for a year while Jarrett's father studied genetics. In 1963 they returned to the States and settled in the Hyde Park neighborhood of Chicago. Young Valerie attended a local elementary school until fourth grade, when she transferred to the University of Chicago Laboratory School. She spent the last two years of high school (1972–74) as a boarding student at the Northfield Mount Hermon School, a preparatory school in Massachusetts.

Jarrett graduated from Stanford University, in California, in 1978 with a B.A. degree in psychology. In 1981 she received a J.D. degree from the University of Michigan Law School and took a job at Pope, Ballard, Shepard & Fowle, a corporate law firm in Chicago, where she specialized in commercial real-estate law. She worked there for three years before moving to the firm of Sonnenschein, Carlin, Nath & Rosenthal. In 1983 she married a physician, William Robert Jarrett, a son of the pioneering Chicago journalist, television talk-show host, and radio commentator Vernon Jarrett, and within two years the couple became the parents of a daughter. By 1987 Jarrett had separated from her husband; they divorced the next year. (William Jarrett died in 1993.) Determined to pursue a career that she would find more meaningful, Jarrett consulted her friend Elvin Charity, a lawyer, who told her about his positive experience working in the city's legal department under Mayor Harold Washington. An outsider to Chicago's Democratic political machine, Washington, who took office in 1984, was the city's first African-American mayor. His election had largely been the result of the registration and mobilization of a record number of African-Americans and liberal whites.

Jarrett went to work in the office of the Chicago corporation counsel (which handles civil cases involving the city) in 1987, at the beginning of Washington's second term. In November of that year, Washington died of a heart attack. His successor, Eugene Sawyer, who was also black, was chosen by members of the city council and served as mayor for two years. In 1989 Richard M. Daley, the son of Richard J. Daley—the well-known (some would say notorious) boss of Chicago's Democratic political machine in the 1950s, '60s, and '70s—defeated Sawyer in the Democratic primary and went on to be elected Chicago's mayor. Many liberal idealists who had taken government jobs under Washington left the mayor's office, fearing that Daley would abandon the reforms that Washington had planned. Determined to maintain her progressive perspective and retain a chance to improve conditions in the city in a hands-on fashion, Jarrett stayed with the Daley administration. She soon became one of the mayor's most trusted advisers. In June 1991 she was promoted to deputy chief of staff. In that position she became skilled at negotiating the divides between competing interest groups.

In October 1991 Jarrett was named commissioner of the recently created Department of Economic Development and Planning. In a position that Steven R. Strahler, writing for *Crain's Chicago Business* (September 11, 1995), characterized as "the nearly indispensable bridge between go-go developers, slow-go community organizers and no-go preservationists," Jarrett was charged with renewing the city's efforts to facilitate industrial development in Chicago by means of financial and other incentives—a responsibility that, in the past, was widely thought to have been mishandled. Jarrett focused her efforts on bringing small and medium-size businesses to Chicago, attracting them not only with promises of tax credits but also by locating sites for development and pushing for improvements in infrastructure. Jarrett described her approach to the job to Alf Siewers for the *Chicago Sun-Times* (February 9, 1993) as "community-driven"; she also sought community input on questions such as the appropriate businesses for particular areas, and she worked to create public–private partnerships. She made it her business to visit communities to observe the progress being made. Paul Vallas, the city's budget director at the time, described Jarrett to Terry as "tough as nails [and always] one of the smartest, if not the smartest person in the room in terms of judgment, in terms of knowledge." By September 1993 the efforts of Jarrett and her staff had helped to keep thousands of jobs in Chicago, at companies including Tootsie Roll Industries; Luster Products Inc.; Bankers Life and Casualty Co.; Culinary Foods and Convention Exhibits Inc.; Chas. Levy Circulating Co.; Marshall Field's warehouse division; and Moo and Oink, a popular South Side meat retailer. In an article for *Crain's Chicago Business* (March 28, 1994), Mark Veverka named other large retailers with plans for development in Chicago, among them Kmart, Home Depot, Target, Menard, and Wal-Mart.

In 1995 Jarrett resigned from the Department of Economic Development and Planning and accepted a position as the executive vice president and managing director of the Habitat Co., a for-profit Chicago-based real-estate company that was commissioned by the city in 1987 to oversee all of Chicago's public housing. She also became the board chairman of the Chicago Transit Authority, a part-time job. At that time the CTA was facing problems including a budget deficit and low ridership. One way in which Jarrett cut costs was to end the use of city resources by many CTA attorneys who were practicing law privately on the side. Under Jarrett the CTA increased security in rail cars and buses and purchased new fleets of buses and subway cars. To stay in touch with the Chicago community, Jarrett oversaw a telephone hotline, organized annual public hearings, and regularly conducted customer surveys. At public lectures she often emphasized the importance of embracing Chicago's diversity. "Our philosophy and our vision and our mandate are to make sure our workforce and the resources we spend are allocated in a way which represents the diversity of our service area," she told a writer for the *Chicago Defender* (May 25, 2002). Under Jarrett fares remained relatively low, service was improved on half of the bus routes and all of the rail routes, and ridership increased annually for five years in a row (1997 through 2001). Jarrett announced her resignation from the CTA on April 1, 2003 but remained active in the position until the following August.

At the Habitat Co. Jarrett faced other problems. Habitat had been charged with overseeing the construction and management of public housing in Chicago as a result of a lawsuit known as the Gautreaux case, filed in 1966. In 1976 the case reached the U.S. Supreme Court, which ruled that the Chicago Housing Authority had for years located public housing in predominantly or almost completely black neighborhoods but none in white neighborhoods and had limited the number of blacks permitted to live in mixed-neighborhood projects. As a result the city had become increasingly racially segregated and public housing concentrated in low-income, high-crime African-American neighborhoods. Earlier, to remedy that situation, in 1969 a federal judge had ordered the CHA to replace the old public-housing projects—many of which were tall towers that held hundreds of apartments—with mixed-income housing on sites scattered throughout the city, especially in mostly white neighborhoods. The CHA had never taken the required steps, however. In 1987 a federal judge appointed the Habitat Co. to manage the construction of public housing under the scattered-site plan. Rather than attempt to construct tall buildings that contained only public-housing units, Habitat aimed to build townhouses having both government-subsidized and market-rate apartments. In order to integrate low-income residents into the surrounding community, Jarrett limited the number of government-subsidized units to one third of the total in the townhouses. That policy angered many low-income residents and housing advocates, who wanted the majority of units to be set aside for the poor. "We looked for a balance, with the goal being a healthy community, and we were extremely cognizant and mindful of not wanting to recreate horizontally what we had torn down vertically," Jarrett told Jason Grotto and Laurie Cohen for the *Chicago Tribune* (July 6, 2008).

Despite Jarrett's passionate commitment to the project, Habitat has encountered many difficulties in its attempts to remake Chicago's public-housing system. Some resident-advocacy groups have accused the CHA and Habitat of allowing the deterioration of properties they are managing so that those buildings can be condemned and the sites redeveloped. Since 1987 more than 13,000 public-housing units have been demolished to make room for new developments, which have taken years to build; in the meantime, many people have been forced to move into temporary housing, which has not been easy to find. Other problems have included missed construction deadlines, culture clashes between new residents and their communities, and a lack of meaningful integration. Despite Jarrett's efforts, most of the new mixed-housing projects have been built in predominantly black neighborhoods. In addition, in 2006 the renovation of the subsidized-housing-project Grove Parc Plaza was removed from Habitat's purview after it deteriorated so badly that federal inspectors rated conditions as 11 on a 100-point scale. Jarrett, who became CEO of the Habitat Co. in 2007, was pleased with much of the progress, while admitting that it had been slower than anticipated. "In the end," she told Terry, "I think some things take time because they should."

Also in 2007 Barack Obama announced his candidacy for the Democratic nomination for president of the United States. Obama had served as an Illinois state senator from 1997 to 2004 and as a U.S. senator since 2005. In his campaign for the U.S. Senate seat, Jarrett had served as Obama's finance chair. In his quest for the presidency, Obama gave Jarrett the official title of senior campaign adviser. Jarrett "participates in every conversation we have in the campaign," Obama told Terry. "She is involved in broad strategic decisions about our message and how we approach the campaign, and she's involved in the details of managing the organization. She's really a great utility player." One of Jarrett's responsibilities was to help improve Obama's standing among African-Americans. Early in the campaign Obama trailed one of his Democratic opponents, New York senator Hillary Clinton, in polls among African-American voters. Additionally, many black leaders were reportedly hesitant to support Obama because, unlike some African-American politicians, he avoided engaging in explicit discussions of race, opting for what many called a postracial attitude, in which he emphasized the shared concerns of all Americans and encouraged cooperation rather than confrontation. Obama's biracial background and Ivy-league education also led some to accuse him of not being "black enough." Jarrett assembled a task force to reach out to black leaders. Her well-known record as a Chicagoan as well as her ability to reduce discord among groups with divergent interests helped her gain for Obama the support of both traditional and nontraditional black leaders. "Part of what moved me from, 'Who is Barack Obama and what is he really about?' to 'Yes, this is a guy who can help make changes even if we're not on the same page in terms of style and approach'—a lot of that came from talking to her," the clergyman and political activist Al Sharpton told Cottle. "Sometimes I've called into the campaign with an issue I thought was upsetting . . . [and] she's so calm herself that you find yourself fighting to stay calm as well, trying to even out your tone."

Later in the campaign, in March 2008, excerpts of what were judged to be anti-American and anti-white statements in sermons by Obama's longtime pastor, Jeremiah Wright, became headline news; Obama was accused of harboring such attitudes himself and faulted for not distancing himself from Wright. When Obama convened his top advisers to decide how to handle the issue, Jarrett encouraged him to follow his gut and confront the issue of race head-on. "I knew that because of Barack's life experiences and many of our conversations, he had given a great deal of thought to the topic of race," Jarrett told Terry. "He had mentioned earlier in the campaign that he thought he could provide a framework for a conversation about race in a way that could bring the American people together and heal so many wounds. My advice was to seize this opportunity, speak honestly, directly from his heart, and I had every confidence that his message would resonate broadly with the American people." Acting on that advice, Obama addressed the controversy about Reverend Wright in a speech, entitled "A More Perfect Union," that he gave at the National Convention Center in Philadelphia, Pennsylvania, on March 18, 2008. Although his words did not completely quell the uproar surrounding Reverend Wright's remarks, it effectively communicated Obama's complex perspective on the role of race in the U.S., and it was generally well-received. Jarrett "is always very insistent on me trusting my instincts," Obama told Terry. "One of the dangers in running for high office is you get so much chatter in your ear that you stop listening to yourself."

On June 2, 2008 Obama earned the necessary number of pledged delegates to secure the Democratic presidential nomination. During the next five months, Jarrett served as one of Obama's closest advisers, frequently accompanying him on the campaign trail and serving as a liaison with both African-American leaders and business leaders. On the night of the general election, November 4, she appeared on television to respond to minute-by-minute reports of results of the ballot counting. After Obama's victory the president-elect assigned Jarrett to lead his transition team, along with John Podesta, President Clinton's last chief of staff, and Peter M. Rouse, Obama's chief of staff when he was a U.S. senator. In the months leading up to the election, Democratic Party leaders had discussed the possibility of Jarrett's filling the Senate seat vacated if Obama won the presidency, a notion that gained support from quarters of the Democratic Party over the following months. A few days before the election she discussed her future with the Obamas; later, she told Robert Draper for the *New York Times* (July 26, 2009, on-line) that Michelle Obama was adamant that Jarrett work in the White House. "You have to understand," Jarrett said. "This is right before the election. We're all really nervous. We knew by that point that chances are he's gonna win. [Michelle Obama is] about to embark on this entirely new episode in her life. And her attitude was like: 'You've come all this way, and you thought this was a good idea, and now you're gonna bail on me? No way!'"

Ultimately both the president and the First Lady decided that Jarrett's guidance was indispensable. On November 15, 2008 President Obama announced that Jarrett would serve in the White House as a senior adviser and an assistant to the president for intergovernmental relations and public liaison. Jarrett's official duties in the latter role include acting as a liaison between the White House and state and local officials and the White House and the public. In May 2009 Obama announced that the Office of Public Liaison would be renamed the Office of Public Engagement and, along with the Office of Intergovernmental Affairs, would engage more actively with ordinary Americans. Jarrett has been particularly helpful in reaching out to the segments of the population whom she courted during the campaign: minorities and business leaders. She also regularly accompanies the president and the First Lady to events and meetings; in September 2009, for example, she flew with Obama to Copenhagen, Denmark, to lobby for Chicago, Illinois's bid to host the 2016 Olympics. That same month she was sent by the White House to visit the Dalai Lama, in Dharamsala, India, along with Maria Otero, an undersecretary of state for global affairs; the visit was meant to convey the president's respect for the Dalai Lama despite Obama's decision not to meet with him during the religious leader's October visit to the States. Jarrett's role as both a close friend and senior adviser to the Obamas is unique and reportedly has led to minor clashes with other senior staff members. When Draper asked the president whether he consults with Jarrett on every decision he makes, Obama replied: "Yep. Absolutely."

From 2004 to 2006 Jarrett chaired the Chicago Stock Exchange. As of mid-January 2009, she served on the board of directors of the USG Corp., the Metropolitan Planning Council of Chicago, and the Local Initiative Support Corp., which operates nationally. She became a member of the board of trustees of the University of Chicago in 2001 and vice chair of the school's hospital board in 2002. When the name of the latter board was changed, to University of Chicago Medical Center board, in 2006, Jarrett was named its chair; at the same time she became vice chair of the university's board of trustees. She was also a trustee of Chicago's Museum of Science and Industry and has served on the boards of directors of Navigant Consulting Inc., RREEF America II, the Joyce Foundation, and the Federal Reserve Bank of Chicago. She was the vice chair of the Chicago 2016 Olympic Committee until late 2008. Jarrett lives in the Kenwood section of Chicago, just north of Hyde Park, where the Obama family maintains a residence. She also has an apartment in Washington, D.C. Her daughter, Laura, is a student at Harvard Law School. In 2008 *Newsweek* listed Valerie Jarrett among the "global elite."

—M.E.R.

Suggested Reading: *Chicago Defender* p24 May 25, 2002; *Chicago Tribune* Metro p1+ Aug. 22, 2003, State and Regional News Apr. 22, 2007, p22 July 6, 2008; *Chicago Tribune Magazine* p8+ July 27, 2008; *Crain's Chicago Business* p3 Mar. 28, 1994, p4 Sep. 11, 1995, p39 Oct. 6, 2008; *New Republic* p14+ Aug. 27, 2008; *New York Times* p1+ Nov. 24, 2008, (on-line) July 26, 2009; *Vogue* p336+ Oct. 2008; *Who's Who in America*

Jarvis, Jeff

July 15, 1954– New-media consultant; writer; educator

Address: City University of New York, Graduate School of Journalism, 219 W. 40th St., New York, NY 10018

"Jeff Jarvis is the very model of a modern new-media guru," Ron Rosenbaum wrote for *Slate.com*

Sean Gallup/Getty Images for Burda Media

Jeff Jarvis

(November 12, 2008). "If you work in media, you probably know his work. If you consume media, you probably should. He's one of the leading Web futurists, one of the few new-media consultant types who came over from old media." For the first two decades of his professional life, Jarvis was a full-time print journalist: he worked variously as a researcher, columnist, critic, editor, and assistant publisher at the *Chicago Tribune*, the *San Francisco Examiner*, *People* magazine, the New York *Daily News*, *TV Guide*, and *Entertainment Weekly*, the last of which he founded. In the mid-1990s he became the president and creative director at Advance.net, the arm of Advance Publications that oversaw its Internet activities, where he managed the expansion of the company's newspapers to the Web. Jarvis's desire to share his thoughts and feelings about his experience in Lower Manhattan on September 11, 2001, when Al Qaeda terrorists attacked the World Trade Center, led him to start his own blog, called buzzmachine.com. He has described the comments and discussions prompted by his and others' blog entries, and the entries posted in response, as part of an evolving process—one whose value and importance are greater than those of the information and opinions conveyed day to day. Jarvis has become a highly sought-after adviser and speaker on journalism and the new media. He serves as a consultant to the New York Times Co. regarding its subsidiary About.com; an associate professor at the Graduate School of Journalism at the City University of New York; and a columnist for the London *Guardian*.

In his articles and blog entries, Jarvis has placed the blame for newspapers' decline in readership and profitability largely on journalists. "It is our fault that we did not see the change coming soon enough and ready our craft for the transition," Jarvis wrote for his blog (October 8, 2008). "It is our fault that we did not see and exploit—hell, we resisted—all the opportunities new media and new relationships with the public presented. It is our fault that we did not give adequate stewardship to journalism and left the business to the business people. It is our fault that we lost readers and squandered trust. It is our fault that we sat back and expected to be supported in the manner to which we had become accustomed by some unknown princely patron." Not surprisingly, some journalists have rejected his argument, in whole or in part. According to Ron Rosenbaum, for example, "Firing people on the writing side because of the incompetence of the business side is a long tradition in the media business." Rosenbaum also contended that Jarvis's "pretensions to guru-hood" are not backed up by enough original, substantive ideas. Nevertheless, he described Jarvis as being "among the most rational of the new thinkers." In his first book, *What Would Google Do?* (2009), Jarvis argued that Google's reliance on innovation, collaboration, and experimentation should become a new model not only for newspapers but for book publishers, car manufacturers, hospitals, universities, airlines, and movie studios.

The second of two children, Jeffrey A. Jarvis was born on July 15, 1954 in Oak Park, Illinois. His sister, Cynthia A. "Cindy" Jarvis, is the minister of a Presbyterian church in Philadelphia, Pennsylvania. His mother stopped working to raise her children. His father's job, as an electronics salesman, required a series of moves to locations in Iowa, Illinois, New York, and New Jersey. For that reason Jarvis attended four elementary schools and four high schools in succession. He studied philosophy and political science at a California college, with the goal of becoming a lawyer, but after a year he abandoned that plan. "I wouldn't be able to say, 'Yes, your honor,'" he told *Current Biography*, the source of all quotes for this article unless otherwise noted. "I looked around and wondered, 'What the heck could I do?' I had been on the high school and college papers for years and decided I enjoy doing that." He next enrolled at Medill, Northwestern University's school of journalism, in Chicago, Illinois. Jarvis graduated from Northwestern after three years, in 1974.

After he earned his bachelor's degree, Jarvis got a job on the midnight shift of the *Chicago Tribune* as a rewrite person—someone who records the news reports called in by journalists in the field, taking down and organizing the most important information. Next to the typewriter on his desk stood a machine that, at that time, seemed foreign to many reporters and almost frightening to some: a personal computer. Jarvis used the computer to record the stories called in. Because typing them was much faster than writing them by hand, he had time to edit them as well. Within a year, at the age of 21, he had been promoted to assistant city editor. As one of the very few people in the newsroom who knew how to use computers, he started training others on the staff in their use.

After two years with the *Chicago Tribune*, Jarvis returned to California, where he was hired as the Sunday news editor at the *San Francisco Examiner*. A caption that he wrote soon after his arrival particularly pleased the paper's publisher, who promoted him to gossip columnist—a position newly created to provide competition for the popular gossip column in the *Examiner*'s chief rival, the *San Francisco Chronicle*. Jarvis could never obtain what he described as the "juiciest" gossip, because he did not know celebrities or anybody else who would provide such material. Instead, he usually wrote about politics and local happenings. He would frequently criticize then–San Francisco mayor Dianne Feinstein in terms that the publisher would often tell him to soften. He could not tolerate the publisher's intervention, so in 1981 he left the *Examiner* and moved to New York City.

In New York he found a job at *People* magazine as a rewrite person. After a few years he was promoted to television critic. "I didn't know what the hell I was doing," he said. "But I loved it." One day, just as he was about to go on the air on a CBS morning show to talk about TV ratings, the show's producer told him that he expected Jarvis to say that "the American people have taste." "I would *never* say that," Jarvis replied. The producer countered, "But you've said that the shows at the top of the ratings are good and the shows at the bottom are not. Then aren't you saying that American people have taste?" After a few moments' thought, Jarvis agreed. He regards that conversation as a life-changing moment, because "it taught me to be a populist. It taught me to have faith in the people. It taught me that when given a choice, people will gravitate toward the good stuff"—though there are always exceptions. Jarvis introduced a grading system, A through F, for the programs he reviewed for *People*. His fellow critics at other publications disapproved of it, because, they believed, readers would skip reviews of programs with low grades. Jarvis would counter that people are busy and should not have to waste time reading about shows that are not worth watching, but that a review graded "F" would draw their attention because it would probably be entertaining.

While at *People* Jarvis came up with an idea for a new magazine, to be called *Entertainment Weekly*. Six years passed before Time Warner, which owns *People*, approved it. With Jarvis as the founding managing editor, the first issue of *Entertainment Weekly*, with an image of the singer k. d. lang on its cover, went on sale in February 1990. Jarvis remained at that job for only half a year, because of what, in an interview with a *USA Today* (June 12, 1990) reporter, he described as "creative differences over the direction of the magazine." Time Warner, for example, criticized the first issue's cover photo, maintaining that Jarvis should have picked a far better-known entertainer. But the publisher had failed to inform him that the magazine was going to be sold primarily at newsstands rather than through subscriptions, Jarvis said, and initial newsstand sales were extremely low.

Jarvis next worked for a year and a half for the New York *Daily News*, as the Sunday editor and associate publisher. He then joined *TV Guide* as a TV critic. For the most part he worked from home, watching tapes of TV shows that came in the mail and then writing reviews. "A critic should basically start by liking what they're covering," he said. "If you have a TV critic who thinks all TV is crap, that's no service to the reader. A critic should start with the assumption [that TV is] basically good"—an assumption that Jarvis made.

Jarvis left *TV Guide* in 1994 to take on a managerial and consulting role, as the president and creative director of Advance.net, the on-line arm of Advance Publications, which at the time owned Condé Nast. (Condé Nast publishes two dozen magazines and newspapers in 29 markets and, at that time, owned the book publisher Random House.) The year 1994 marked an "incredibly important moment" in Internet history, according to Jarvis, because that is when the first commercial browser, Netscape, made its debut. Its arrival transformed the publishing industry in two ways: first, Internet links—direct connections from one Web site to others—"changed the essential economics of media." Thus, instead of striving to include content that might appeal to the greatest number of people, a publication could concentrate on what it did best and link to the rest. Second, Netscape and other browsers eventually allowed anyone to create content on-line—initially only text, but later photos, videos, and audio material as well. Instead of being merely passive media consumers, people could also be active media creators. At Advance, Jarvis was responsible for technological matters and the content of the company's newspaper and magazine Web sites. "We were creating sites from scratch," he recalled. "A lot of newspapers were trying to recreate the newspaper on-line. They had a pride in the product they put out." But focusing on content was misguided, in Jarvis's opinion; content has value, but "the real value" is the community—the people who connect through any particular site.

On the morning of September 11, 2001, Jarvis, as usual, took a New Jersey PATH train to New York City. His train arrived in Lower Manhattan just as Al Qaeda terrorists flew the first plane into the south tower of the World Trade Center, at 8:46 a.m. At that moment Jarvis was still below ground, in the train station, unaware of what had happened. He took an escalator onto another underground platform, where he and a few others discovered not the usual hustle and bustle but an eerie silence and women's shoes strewn everywhere on the floor. (When those who had arrived on the previous train heard about the attack, they had discarded their high heels and other shoes not designed for running and fled as fast as they could.)

As soon as Jarvis emerged onto the street, a policewoman yelled to him, "Run! Run!" He ran across the street, where he began talking to people and writing down his observations. He was there when the second set of hijackers flew their plane into the north tower. When the first tower started to collapse, Jarvis was only a block away. Along with everybody else he ran, his vision becoming clouded by the dust that had billowed during the collapse. When he reached his Condé Nast office, a few miles north, he called in reports to several Advance-owned local newspapers.

Days later, feeling that he wanted to communicate more about what he had witnessed and experienced, Jarvis started his blog, buzzmachine.com. He soon linked up with two bloggers in Los Angeles, California, who had happened upon it. "That was another *ding!*" Jarvis said, snapping his fingers. "That's when I saw the power of the link. I got to know these people [the Los Angeles bloggers] and did business with them later on, all because of the link." The realization of blogging's potential ended any thoughts Jarvis had had about shutting down buzzmachine.com after a few weeks. After several months of blogging about 9/11, he shifted his focus to the subject that is his specialty—the media. "Journalists, the straight-news reporters, often have problems writing in a voice because we are told not to," he said. "But having been a columnist, I already had the obnoxious habit of using the first person and writing in my own perspective. But it was not a column. It was a conversation. And I had to learn that." On buzzmachine.com Jarvis writes primarily about the media, journalism education, free speech, technology, and, to a lesser extent, politics.

On June 21, 2005 Jarvis posted what is still one of his most influential entries. Titled "Dell lies. Dell sucks," it conveyed his irritation and frustration with the deficiencies of his Dell laptop and the company's customer service. The entry drew responses from thousands of like-minded consumers. Two months later Jarvis returned his Dell computer, bought a Mac, and, on his blog, wrote an open letter to Dell's founder and chief executive officer, Michael Dell, inviting him or a Dell representative to "join the conversation your customers are having without you," so as to improve Dell products and service. The following year Dell did just that. For an article he wrote for *BusinessWeek* (October 29, 2007) two years after the blog post, Jarvis conducted a cordial interview with Michael Dell and wrote that the company and its customers are "collaborating on new forms of content and marketing." As of late 2009 Jarvis's June 21, 2005 post appeared in the top 10 Google search results for "Dell sucks."

Since 2006 Jarvis has written a biweekly column for the London *Guardian* about the subjects he discusses on his blog. In his September 1, 2008 *Guardian* column, he criticized the 15,000 journalists—and the publications that employed them—who covered the national Democratic and Republican presidential conventions. "Nothing happens at the conventions," Jarvis wrote. "They are carefully staged spin theater. . . . The attention given to the conventions and campaigns is symptomatic of a worse journalistic disease: we over-cover politics and under-cover the actions of our governments. We over-cover politicians and under-cover the lives and needs of citizens." That criticism relates to one change that Jarvis believes the Internet has made in journalism. Like it or not, Jarvis has argued, it is no longer necessary for newspapers and magazines to be "all things to all people." For example, not every newspaper in America needs to report on the latest golf tournament: the Internet makes it possible for anyone to read about it in the *New York Times*, in an on-line golf magazine, or on a golf Web site. Instead, according to Jarvis, each publication should figure out what makes it special and what it alone can provide. When a small local newspaper dedicates space to something that is plentifully available in bigger—and perhaps better—publications, it leaves out news or reports more essential to its community.

Jarvis opened his August 18, 2008 *Guardian* column with the provocative question, "Do we need editors?" In other words, in the age of new media, are editors "a luxury that we can do without"? Not quite, he wrote. There is still a role for editors, but it has changed: "As news becomes collaborative, editors will need to assemble networks from among staff and the public; that makes them community organizers. I also believe editors should play educator, helping to improve the work of the network." In large part because of new technologies, non-journalists can perform what Jarvis calls "acts of journalism"—for example, taking digital photos at the sites of disasters or analyzing on-line government reports. It is part of the new responsibilities of editors to collaborate with and, in some cases, train such contributors, Jarvis believes.

Jarvis also believes that there is still a role for professional journalists. Otherwise, he asks rhetorically, why would he be teaching journalism? In 2006 Jarvis joined the newly founded Graduate School of Journalism at the City University of New York (CUNY), as an associate professor and director of the Interactive Journalism program. He teaches a course entitled "Entrepreneurial Journalism," in which students aim to create sustainable journalistic businesses. On his blog Jarvis has often expressed his views about the journalism school's programs, events, and approach to teaching. Jarvis's entries and readers' responses to his ideas about where journalism is heading became the rough draft of his first book, *What Would Google Do?* (2009). (The title is a play on the question "What would Jesus do?," often used by groups that want to insert Christian values into individuals' choices and national policy.) The book, Bruce Manuel wrote for the *San Jose (California) Mercury News* (March 13, 2009), "makes a provocative case for why Google ought to become a new model for not just business but the wider culture too." Jarvis also cited Amazon.com, Craigslist, Twitter, and Facebook as useful models, but found none to be the equal of Google, whose innovative ideas and business practices, including collaboration with customers, have made its continuing growth possible. Jarvis argued that practically all businesses—media, advertising, energy, real estate, health care, education, automobile manufacturers—should emulate Google. "I sat in Detroit some time ago and suggested heresy: I urged the car people to open up their design process and make it both transparent and collaborative," Jarvis wrote in an excerpt from his book that appeared in *BusinessWeek* (February 9, 2009). "Car companies have no good way to listen to customers' ideas. If they had opened up, years before, I would have been among the legions who'd have gladly told them to invest 39 cents for a plug-in car radio so we could connect our iPods. . . . What if just one model from one brand were opened up to collaborative design? I don't suggest that design should be a democracy. But shouldn't design at least be a conversation?" As for newspapers, ideally, each "will be more of a network with a smaller staff of reporters and editors still providing essential news and recouping value for that," Jarvis wrote. "Paper 2.0"—the future newspaper—"will work with and support collections of bloggers, entrepreneurs, citizens, and communities that gather and share news. . . . It could be bigger than papers have been in years, reaching deeper into communities, having more of an impact, and adding more value." Despite the serious financial hardships many newspapers and magazines are now experiencing, "journalism will survive," Jarvis told *Current Biography.* "I'm an optimist to a fault." Jarvis has contributed articles to publications including *BusinessWeek*, *Advertising Age*, *Newsday*, the *New York Post*, *Rolling Stone*, the *Nation*, and the *Huffington Post.*

In August 2009 Jarvis announced on his blog that he had been diagnosed with prostate cancer. Afterward, in an unusually forthcoming, unsentimental way, he wrote about the surgery he underwent in September and its effects. The surgery was successful, and Jarvis was expected to make a full recovery.

Jarvis and his wife, Tammy, live in New Jersey with their two children, Jake and Julia, both of whom are very tech-savvy.

—D.K.

Suggested Reading: CUNY Graduate School of Journalism Web site; jeffjarvis.com; *San Jose (California) Mercury News* Technology Mar. 13, 2009; *Slate.com* Nov. 12, 2008; *Washington Post* (on-line) Apr. 19, 2009

Selected Books: *What Would Google Do?*, 2009

Jealous, Benjamin Todd

Jan. 18, 1973– President of the NAACP

Address: NAACP National Headquarters, 4805 Mt. Hope Dr., Baltimore, MD 21215

Jeffrey MacMillan, courtesy of the NAACP

In September 2008 Benjamin Todd Jealous, a former newspaper-industry executive, activist, and Rhodes scholar, was sworn in as president of the National Association for the Advancement of Colored People (NAACP), the oldest and most prominent civil rights organization in the United States. In assuming his post Jealous became, at 35, the youngest president in the organization's 100-year history. (The NAACP was founded in 1909 by W.E.B. DuBois, Ida B. Wells-Barnett, and others, largely as a response to the widespread lynching of African-Americans. Today it boasts roughly half a million members in hundreds of branches.) While his election rankled some NAACP board members who saw him as inexperienced—he was chosen the previous May in a divisive 34–21 vote—Jealous brought a fresh voice to an organization that has sought to regain the relevance it enjoyed during the height of the civil rights era, nearly a half-century ago, when African-Americans struggled successfully for integration and voting rights. "He's a young man with great training," Amos C. Brown, an NAACP board member, told Sumathi Reddy for the *Baltimore Sun* (September 28, 2008). "He's had experience in various areas, and coupling that experience with the needs of the NAACP, I think we'll have the best of both worlds in moving forward." Prior to his arrival at the NAACP, Jealous served as president of the Rosenberg Foundation, a private institution devoted to civil and human rights advocacy. He has also served as director of the U.S. Human Rights Program at Amnesty International and as executive director of the National Newspaper Publishers Association (NNPA). Many hope that Jealous's youth will help to draw a new generation of supporters to the NAACP. Commenting on his leadership style, Jealous, a fifth-generation NAACP member, explained to Hazel Trice Edney for the *New York Beacon* (May 22–28, 2008), "I'm a team player. I believe that in order to lead in the game, you've got to be completely in the game, that in order to have people to follow you, they need to know that you're willing to follow them. This isn't a new industry to me if you will. This is the family, the movement that I was raised in. So, I expect to have nothing but success."

Benjamin Todd Jealous was born on January 18, 1973 in Pacific Grove, a coastal town in Monterey County, California, known for its liberal politics. His mother, Ann Todd Jealous, an African-American psychotherapist, had met his father, Fred Jealous, a white education administrator, while teaching junior high school in her hometown of Baltimore. (As a boy Jealous spent his summers with his grandmother there.) Both of Jealous's parents had participated in Baltimore's desegregation movement during the 1960s. Jealous became conscious of his mixed race at a young age. He explained to Reddy, "The issue of race was always there. When your mom's black and your dad's white and it's the 1970s, it's in your face all the time. . . . I can remember getting into a fight with a kid . . . because he said I was rich because I had a nanny. He assumed the black woman [Jealous's mother] who picked me up every day was my nanny." Jealous's awareness of race, and his parents' backgrounds in activism, led him to become socially conscious early on. When he was in first grade, he complained to his school librarian about the scarcity of books on African-Americans. At seven he told his family of his desire to become a civil rights lawyer.

Jealous attended York School, a private Episcopal institution in Monterey, where he developed a passion for learning about history and economics. When he was 14, after accompanying his father to an event promoting the civil rights activist Jesse Jackson's candidacy for president, Jealous organized a youth voter-registration drive. His efforts contributed to Jackson's strong showing in Monterey County. "I was raised by my parents in a community during a time when social justice issues were taken very seriously," Jealous recalled to Sylvia Moore for the *Monterey County Herald* (February 10, 2003). "I believe there's no better way to spend one's life working to make this world better than when you found it than serving others." Also during his high-school years, he spent a semester in Washington, D.C., working for two U.S. congressional Democrats from California—as a page for Leon Panetta and an intern for Sam Farr.

In 1990 Jealous graduated from York and enrolled at Columbia University, in New York City. As an undergraduate he co-founded a group that provided low-income housing and free child care to residents in the largely black community of Harlem. That helped catch the attention of the NAACP Legal Defense Fund, which hired him to organize Harlem citizens to oppose the closure of a local hospital. Jealous's outspokenness got him suspended from Columbia for a semester, after he staged a student protest to stop the university from turning the Audubon Ballroom—where the black nationalist leader Malcolm X was assassinated, in 1965—into a biomedical research center. In response, Jealous decided to leave the university for good. (Columbia later reached a compromise with local community groups, agreeing to restore a portion of the original façade of the ballroom and to build a museum inside honoring Malcolm X; the museum opened in 2005.) "[Jealous's] leadership qualities have always stood out," Judith Russell, who taught and advised Jealous at Columbia, recalled to Reddy. "Not in an impulsive or rowdy or boisterous way. He just has a quality for measured evaluation, and he has a lot of passion."

Upon leaving Columbia Jealous moved to Mississippi to work for the American Federation of Labor and Congress of Industrial Organizations (AFL-CIO). While there, he helped organize a campaign to stop the state from closing two historically black universities, Alcorn State and Mississippi Valley State. He also opposed efforts to convert another school into a prison. Jealous, who received death threats for his work, noted to Sylvia Moore, "I was a bit of a controversial person in the state. There aren't very many light-skinned black people in [Mississippi]. I was often referred to as 'high-yellow carpetbagger from New York City.'" Despite such challenges, Jealous remained in Mississippi, where he entered the field of journalism. Initially applying for a graphic-designer position at the *Jackson Advocate*, an African-American weekly newspaper, Jealous soon became a reporter at the urging of the paper's publisher. He wrote a series of articles about alleged corruption at the Mississippi State Penitentiary in Parchman; state and federal investigations were conducted as a result. Another story he wrote, about a black farmer wrongfully accused of arson, led to the farmer's acquittal. Jealous later became the paper's managing editor.

Returning to Columbia to complete his studies, Jealous graduated with a degree in political science in 1997. He then attended Oxford University, in England, on a Rhodes scholarship—becoming, in the process, the only person from Monterey County ever to do so—and earned a degree in comparative social research. In 1999 he returned to the United States to become the executive director of the National Newspaper Publishers Association, a federation of more than 200 black-community newspapers. During his three-year tenure in that position, he tripled the organization's budget and staff and initiated changes that helped usher the NNPA into the information age. In addition, he introduced training programs that helped improve the professional skills of NNPA journalists and pressed reporters to serve their communities by writing about important matters regarding race, including prisoners' rights and the plight of black farmers. Hazel Trice Edney, the first female Washington correspondent in the NNPA and now the editor in chief of the group, explained to Sumathi Reddy, "[Jealous] is a person who is able to . . . get people to come together even though they might not necessarily agree to come together for the cause of justice. His heart is really toward human and civil rights in America. It's not a job for him. It really is a mission."

In 2002 Jealous left the NNPA to join the human rights advocacy group Amnesty International, where he headed the U.S. human rights program. While there he successfully lobbied for federal legislation against prison rape, rallied public opposition to racial profiling in the wake of the September 11, 2001 terrorist attacks, and called for a halt to the widespread sentencing of adolescents to life in prison without the possibility of parole. In 2004 he served as the lead author on a report entitled "Threat and Humiliation: Racial Profiling, Domestic Security, and Human Rights in the United States," which garnered national and international media attention upon its publication. The 50-page report, based on a series of hearings on discrimination across the nation and a yearlong analysis of racial-profiling practices by law-enforcement officials, argued that racial profiling ultimately undermines national security. As noted by a writer for the *New York Beacon* (September 22, 2004), the report stated, "Prior to 9/11, racial profiling was frequently referred to as 'driving while black.' Now, the practice can be more accurately characterized as driving, flying, walking, worshipping, shopping, or staying at home while Black, Brown, Red, Yellow, Muslim, or of Middle-Eastern appearance." Jealous noted to the same writer, "During our research, we collected testimony from Native Americans who were profiled going to and from religious ceremonies, Hispanics who were profiled while in the sanctity of their homes, African Americans who were profiled walking down the street, and a Boy Scout, who happens to be Muslim, constantly being subjected to airport searches. Racial profiling is so pervasive and widely accepted that it has become a corrosive acid on this nation's spirit of unity."

In 2005 Jealous became president of the California-based Rosenberg Foundation, a private grantmaking organization that supports civil and human rights advocacy. He succeeded the organization's longtime president Kirke Wilson, who retired that February after 31 years at the helm. As president Jealous was in frequent contact with some of the state's most powerful philanthropists and corporate donors. He expanded the foundation's support of groups working to create greater employment opportunities for ex-prisoners and to make new businesses in the Bay Area more resident-conscious.

Jealous's reputation caught the attention of the NAACP's search committee, which had formed shortly after its president, Bruce Gordon, resigned unexpectedly in March 2007, after 19 months on the job. When Gordon, an African-American business executive and former high-ranking official in the telecommunications company Verizon, was unanimously selected to head the NAACP, in June 2005, he had expressed excitement and optimism about moving the organization in a new direction. (Gordon's appointment was regarded as highly unusual at the time, since most of the group's past presidents had been prominent figures in politics, religion, or the civil rights movement before holding the office.) However, his efforts to steer the group toward more humanitarian endeavors, rather than focusing solely on civil rights advocacy, met with resistance from board members, who were also dissatisfied with Gordon's level of fundraising. Internal squabbles eventually resulted in his early exit.

After Dennis Hayes, the NAACP general counsel, stepped in as interim president and CEO, the group's officers began an intensive search for their next leader. They hoped to find a person who could bring new life to an organization that had seen waning influence and a steep decline in membership over the years. A search committee submitted to a three-member executive committee the names of Jealous and two other candidates drawn from a pool of roughly 200: the Reverand Frederick Haynes, a pastor based in Dallas, Texas, and Alvin Brown, a former White House adviser. Despite the efforts of board members in the weeks leading up to the selection to change the standard selection process, so that they could interview all three finalists, the executive committee unanimously selected Jealous in May 2008 over the other two candidates. The final vote, however, revealed division within the board, with 34 in favor of Jealous's appointment and 21 opposed; several sources reported that "no one clapped or celebrated" after the meeting. Some NAACP board members from the West Coast, who were unable to attend the meeting in Baltimore, also complained about not being told that they could have voted by phone. Speaking in support of Jealous, Julian Bond, chairman of the NAACP board, explained to Brennen Jensen for the *Chronicle of Philanthropy* (May 29, 2008), "Mr. Jealous was the only one of the candidates we saw who has spent his entire professional life working on the issues we work on. He is philosophically attuned to who we are and what we do. . . . He has spent almost all of his life in the nonprofit world, and in most of those positions he has shown a proven ability to raise money from a variety of sources: foundations, corporate donors, and individuals. We think he can do that for us."

In September 2008 Jealous was officially sworn in as president. In the process he became, at 35, the youngest leader in the NAACP's 100-year history. Jealous made fund-raising his main priority and called on the network of foundation leaders with whom he had forged relationships. He also worked to recruit more NAACP members, particularly among those between the ages of 20 and 50, and led efforts to strengthen the organization's on-line presence, which has included building a database for tracking acts of racial discrimination and hate crimes. In addition, he launched an aggressive civil rights agenda and a campaign to reshape the national office to make it more effective in helping local chapters. "This is the century when white people will become a minority in this country," Jealous said, as noted by a writer for the *Californian* (May 19, 2008). "What that means is right now, we need to have a clear picture of where we're headed and work together diligently with Latinos, Native Americans, Asians and progressive white groups as if our collective future depends on it. I'm committed to that."

Following the presidential election on November 4, 2008, in which Barack Obama became the first African-American to win the nation's highest office, Jealous—who had led vigorous efforts to ensure a high voter turnout among African-Americans—wrote in an article for *U.S. News & World Report* (November 6, 2008, on-line), "A moment 232 years in the making—from the end of chattel slavery to today—we are witness to the most inclusive election enjoyed by the largest, best-informed, motivated electorate in our nation's history. Consider that some African-American precincts saw the number of registered voters swell to 95 percent of those eligible. In some locations, more than 90 percent of those registered actually voted, many for the first time and others for the first time in years. They turned out because it finally mattered. . . . As we bask in the glow of Obama's stunning victory, the battles are still many. Racial and gender-based discrimination continue to warp our housing, employment, and credit markets. Nearly 50 million Americans are without health insurance. Foreclosures spiral upward. Racial profiling persists. No Child Left Behind has abandoned hundreds of thousands of children in underfunded schools. Wars rage on two fronts. Still, we have proof through the night that an engaged, inspired nation can come together across racial, cultural, and generational boundaries to bring about change. Real change can happen as we harness the energy that enables us to achieve the extraordinary, even as we fight for simple justice and basic opportunities. These things can propel us forward as we step out into the dawn's early light."

Since the inauguration of Obama as president, on January 20, 2009, Jealous and the NAACP have urged the White House and Congress to allocate more federal funding for education. They have also focused on matters related to the economic crisis that began in the fall of 2008. Among other actions, they called for the establishment of a nine-month moratorium on foreclosures and worked to ensure that President Obama's $787 billion stimulus package was distributed equitably.

The NAACP became heavily involved in the internationally publicized matter of the arrest, on July 16, 2009, of the Harvard professor and prominent African-American literary critic Henry Louis Gates Jr. Gates was arrested for disorderly conduct at his own home in Cambridge, Massachusetts, after his confrontation with a local police officer, James Crowley. Crowley had responded to a 911 call from one of Gates's neighbors, who had noticed two men trying to force open Gates's front door and feared that a burglary might occur. One of the men was Gates, and the other was the driver of the car that had just brought Gates from the airport; the neighbor had not recognized Gates, who had enlisted the driver to help him open the door, which was stuck shut. When Crowley followed Gates into his kitchen, Gates showed him his driver's license and a Harvard identification card as proof of his legal residence in the house. Later Crowley and Gates offered different accounts of the heated conversation that ensued and what happened next, when Gates stepped onto his porch. The arrest and the photo of Gates in handcuffs that appeared in many newspapers sparked widespread discussion of whether events might have progressed differently if Gates were white and whether the professor had been a victim of racial profiling. (Crowley had taught a course on racial profiling, and how to avoid it, to other Cambridge police officers for several years.) On July 22, 2009 President Obama, a close friend of Gates's, declared during a nationally televised, primetime press conference that Crowley had acted "stupidly," a remark that angered Crowley's many supporters. In response to the incident, the NAACP began working closely with police departments across the country to address the issue of racial profiling; it has also called for passage of the End Racial Profiling Act, which was introduced in Congress by Representative John Conyers Jr. of Michigan in 2007. In an interview with Deborah Solomon for the *New York Times Magazine* (July 30, 2009), Jealous said, "Racial profiling is a constant drumbeat in this country. It's a form of humiliation that strikes lightning on a daily basis, and that is part of what Professor Gates was responding to. It's hard to be in your house, told you're a burglary suspect and then when you are no longer a suspect, told you are the problem." On July 30, 2009 Gates, Crowley, President Obama, and Vice President Joseph R. Biden discussed the incident outdoors at the White House while having beers. (The meeting has been widely referred to as the White House "beer summit.")

Jealous lives in Alameda, California, with his wife, Lia Epperson, a professor of constitutional law at Santa Clara University and a civil rights attorney with the NAACP Legal Defense and Educational Fund. The couple have a daughter, Morgan.

Jealous is a board member of the California Council for the Humanities, PowerPAC, the Association of Black Foundation Executives, and the Asia Society.

—C.C.

Suggested Reading: *Baltimore Sun* A p1 May 18, 2008, B p1 Sep. 28, 2008; (Monterey, California) *County Herald* B p1 Feb. 10, 2003; National Association for the Advancement of Colored People Official Web site; *Philadelphia Tribune* A p10 May 20, 2008; (Salinas, California) *Californian* p1 May 19, 2008; *U.S. News & World Report* (on-line) Nov. 6, 2008

Attila Kisbenedek/AFP/Getty Images

Jean, Michaëlle

(zhon, mee-kah-el)

Sep. 6, 1957– Governor general of Canada; broadcast journalist

Address: Rideau Hall, 1 Sussex Dr., Ottawa ON K1A 0A1, Canada

When she was named governor general of Canada, in 2005, at the age of 47, Michaëlle Jean became one of the youngest people—and the first black person—ever named to the vice-regal post. "I have come a long way," she said at a news conference covered by the *Nelson (British Columbia) Daily News* (August 5, 2005). "My ancestors were slaves, they fought for freedom. I was born in Haiti, the poorest country in our hemisphere. I am a daughter of exiles driven from their home by a dictatorial regime." Indeed, from her youth in Haiti, spent under the thumb of François Duvalier, to her later success as a host on Radio-Canada, a television news reporter for the Canadian Broadcasting Corp. (CBC), and a documentary filmmaker, Jean's ascent is undeniably inspiring. Her unexpected appointment to the governor-general post initially caused some rumblings of disapproval, however, when allegations emerged that she had supported the Quebec sovereignty movement, whose members have sought independence for the francophone province. Although she has denied ties to the movement, those allegations, as well as her frequent outspokenness, have made her a controversial figure in Canadian politics.

As governor general, Jean is the representative in Canada of the queen of England. (Since the Canada Act of 1982 was implemented, Canada has been a fully sovereign state, with the ability to amend its own constitution; Queen Elizabeth II nonetheless remains Canada's official head of state.) Although the governor general operates independently of the British government, the queen, as explained on the official Web site of the British monarchy, "maintains direct contact with the Governor-General, although she delegates executive power to the Governor-General in virtually every respect." The governor general is appointed by the British monarch on the recommendation of Canada's prime minister. The duties of the post include summoning, opening, and ending sessions of Parliament; reading prepared speeches; giving "royal assent" to legislation passed by the Canadian House of Commons and the Senate; signing state documents; dissolving Parliament for elections; swearing in government officials; and representing Canada abroad. Since she took office, on September 27, 2005, Jean has been active as Canada's international representative, traveling to Europe, Africa, and Afghanistan, and has committed herself to bridging the cultural divide between English- and French-speaking Canadians.

Michaëlle Jean was born on September 6, 1957 in the Haitian capital of Port-au-Prince and spent her first 11 years in Bois Verna, a middle-class neighborhood. Her father, Roger, was the principal and a philosophy teacher at a prestigious Protestant preparatory school, and her mother, Luce, stayed at home to care for Michaëlle and her younger sister, Nadège. As a young child Jean was educated at home because her parents did not want her to be forced to pledge allegiance to Duvalier, as children at the local schools were required to do. Known as "Papa Doc," Duvalier rose to power in 1957 with army backing and, through his secret police force—the ruthless Tonton Macoutes—ruled the country with an iron fist until his death, in 1971; his son, Jean-Claude, immediately succeeded him. In 1965 Jean's father was arrested and tortured by Duvalier's police force, and the Jean family waited for several days before he was returned. Fearing for his life, Roger Jean used underground connections to escape to Canada, in 1967.

When violence under the regime escalated a year later, the rest of the family followed. "I remember my last day in my native land," Jean wrote in the preface to her book *Tout quitter pour la liberté* (*Leaving Everything for Freedom*), as quoted by Kate Jaimet and Neco Cockburn for the *Ottawa Citizen* (September 26, 2005). "The day of uprooting seemed to us the Day of Judgment. The day that we buried our old life. The day that we escaped from the usurping men who guarded our land like a prison. The day that we flew in an airplane toward the unknown." The family arrived in Thetford Mines, an asbestos-mining town south of Quebec City, where Roger Jean had found a job at a local college. Jean recalled in her book, "I remember the February night, so dark and so icy, when we arrived at [the airport in] Dorval, my mother, my sister and I, to join my father. . . . I don't remember the questions of the immigration officer, but I remember how I trembled at the sight of his uniform and the tone of suspicion in his voice. Was this a new torturer? I remember the soft replies of my mother, bewildered and exhausted, who only wanted to save her children and keep them safe and sound."

Once settled in Thetford Mines, Jean faced new challenges. As part of a very small black population in the town, she frequently heard racial taunts directed at her as she walked to the local school. Meanwhile, her parents' marriage began to dissolve; her father, apparently affected by the torture he had endured, had grown violent toward Jean's mother. As a result Luce Jean soon moved with her daughters to the city of Montreal, where she struggled to put the girls through school. (In 2003, after being out of touch for many years, Jean and her father re-established contact.) Jean and her mother and sister lived in a basement apartment, and Luce worked at a clothing factory and later as a night orderly in a psychiatric hospital. Despite the hard times, Jean managed to make friends in the new city and excelled in her classes. She graduated from the Marguerite-de-Lajemmerais girls' school and the CEGEP de Rosemont (a post-secondary school) and enrolled at the University of Montreal, earning an undergraduate degree in Spanish and Italian. Jean returned to the university to pursue a master's degree in comparative literature and obtained scholarships to study at the University of Perouse, in France, in 1982; the University of Florence, in Italy, in 1984; and the Catholic University of Milan, also in Italy, in 1985. When not studying overseas she lived in Montreal and volunteered at Auberge Transition, a shelter for battered women. She went on to volunteer at other shelters and later sat on the executive board of a shelter network. (She did not complete her master's degree.)

A meeting with Ghila Sroka, an ambitious doctoral student, helped give direction to Jean's career. Sroka had recently started a feminist journal called *Paroles Métèques* and was interested in visiting Haiti to conduct interviews for an article. She asked Jean for assistance, and in 1986 the two left for Haiti. There, Jean was able to employ her native Creole to conduct interviews and translate them into French. Her work with the journal eventually caught the eyes of a producer for the National Film Board of Canada, who hired her to work as a researcher and interviewer in Haiti for a film about the 1987 elections there, which followed the previous year's ouster of Jean-Claude Duvalier. The documentary was later shown on *Le Point*, a newsmagazine program on Radio-Canada Television. Radio-Canada officials were impressed with Jean and hired her in 1988 to host the news show *Actuel*, making her the first black person on French television news in Canada. She later hosted *Virages*, from 1991 to 1992, and *Le Point*, from 1992 to 1995. She initially faced skepticism from some colleagues. In an interview with the magazine *Chatelaine*, quoted by Jaimet and Cockburn, she said, "People I worked with said: She was hired by affirmative action, because she's young and pretty and black. She's never done television before and she's going to fall on her face." Jean also noted, "The pressure was incredible. I worked like crazy, knowing I didn't dare to make a mistake. I was trapped. I knew I was kind of a pilot project, and that if I failed, the door would close."

Jean met her husband, the filmmaker Jean-Daniel Lafond, while working at Radio-Canada; the two married in 1992. Lafond, a native of France who had moved to Canada in 1974, had asked for Jean's assistance on a documentary he was making about the Martinique poet Aimé Césaire. When they journeyed to Haiti to conduct research, they formed a connection. "When I saw this man tread on the soil of my childhood with such delicacy, and welcome my country, it's as though he was welcoming me," she told *Chatelaine*. "With him, I had a real dialogue." The two also formed a professional bond, and Jean has since worked with her husband on several of his documentary projects, including *Tropique Nord* (*Tropic North*, 1994), which chronicles the black experience in Quebec; the award-winning *Haiti dans tous nos rêves* (*Haiti in All Our Dreams*, 1995); and *L'Heure de Cuba* (*Last Call for Cuba*, 1999), a film about the 40th anniversary of the Cuban revolution.

In 1995 Jean took a position at Réseau de l'information (RDI), a Canadian French-language news channel run by CBC-Radio Canada, where she served as both a host and reporter on shows including *Le Monde ce soir*, *L'Édition Québécoise*, *Horizons francophones*, *Le Journal RDI*, and *RDI à l'écoute*. She also hosted specials, including a debate about the Catholic Church called *Le Pape en France* and a program on pedophilia entitled *L'Enfance volée*. She hosted shows aired in English Canadian markets as well, including the CBC Newsworld documentary shows *The Passionate Eye* and *Rough Cuts*, both in 1999. In 2004, by then a fixture on Quebec news, Jean was given her own RDI show, *Michaëlle*.

In August 2005 Prime Minister Paul Martin announced Jean's appointment as governor general. Canada's first governor general of Caribbean origin, she was preceded by two others with journalism backgrounds—Romeo Leblanc and Adrienne Clarkson. The term of office, which is not fixed by law, has generally lasted for five years. "I want this office to continue to have life to it and connect with people from all walks of life, all backgrounds and circumstances," Jean said at the August news conference in Ottawa, as quoted by Sandra Cordon for the *Pembroke Observer* (August 5, 2005). While many praised Jean's appointment, others were skeptical; she had no record of public service, and the choice of Jean was perceived by some as a move by Martin to garner support for his Liberal Party in Quebec, the province where Jean had lived. The biggest challenge to Jean's appointment, however, was the claim that she and her husband had ties to Quebec separatists. An article in the publication *Le Québécois* reported that in Lafond's 1991 documentary, *La Manière nègre*, Jean was heard saying while participating in a toast with sovereigntist hardliners, "You don't give independence, you take it." The news sparked controversy and debate. "I want to tell you unequivocally that both [Lafond] and I are proud to be Canadian and that we have the greatest respect for the institutions of our country," Jean declared in a statement released the next day, as quoted by Jack Aubry in the *Ottawa Citizen* (August 18, 2005). "We are fully committed to Canada. I would not have accepted this position otherwise." Although the statement satisfied some, others remained suspicious of Jean, and a poll in late August revealed that public support for her had dropped by 20 percent. In response to the poll, Montreal's Haitian community rallied behind the governor general–designate with special church services that brought out 300 supporters. Two days before Jean took office, she also renounced her French citizenship, which she had been granted upon marrying Lafond. That act quelled minor controversy over her dual citizenship.

Jean was sworn in on September 27, 2005 and delivered a speech that Elizabeth Thompson described for the *Montreal Gazette* (September 28, 2005) as one that "[set] aside the usual patriotic platitudes" and "was both passionate and surprisingly political, sending a clear message that she intends to be an activist vice-regent." During the speech she spoke of aiding youth and the disadvantaged and expressed her hopes for a unified Canada, imploring the audience to look past the division between English and French Canadians. "The time of the 'two solitudes' that for too long described the character of this country is past," she said, as quoted by Thompson. "The narrow notion of 'every person for himself' does not belong in today's world." Jean has since made it her stated mission to bridge the French-English divide in Canada, a goal symbolized in the words *Briser les solitudes* (Breaking down the solitudes), visible on the coat of arms she chose.

In her first few months in office, Jean traveled to several Canadian provinces, and in 2006 she embarked on an international tour. She visited Africa that year, highlighting Canada's commitment to assisting the struggling countries of that continent. The media noted that she was personally affected by observing the remaining signs of the former slave trade there. "[Enslaved Africans were] stripped of themselves, of their language, their name, their memory, their history, of their basic dignity as women and men, and were reduced to slavery and deported to the Americas," she said in a speech quoted by Alexander Penetta in the *Vancouver Sun* (November 21, 2006). "This trip is especially meaningful and emotional for me. And I am delighted that my first state visits have brought me to this continent—to which I feel forever bound by history, by heart and by blood." In March 2007 Jean visited Afghanistan to show support for the Afghan people and the Canadian troops fighting there as part of the multinational antiterrorism effort. She planned the visit for March 8—International Women's Day—to emphasize her concern for the treatment of women in that country, where religious fundamentalism has severely limited the rights of females. According to a press release on the governor general's Web site (March 8, 2007, on-line), she said, "The women of Afghanistan may face the most unbearable conditions, but they never stop fighting for survival. Of course, we, the rest of the women around the world, took too long to hear the cries of our Afghan sisters, but I am here to tell them that they are no longer alone. And neither are the people of Afghanistan."

Although the role of governor general is largely symbolic (political power is exercised by the prime minister), Jean has nonetheless been visibly active since she assumed office. She has even been criticized for "wading uncommonly deep in political territory," as Chantal Hebert wrote for the *Toronto Star* (September 27, 2006). At a 2007 event celebrating the 25th anniversary of the Canadian Charter of Rights and Freedoms, for example, a speech given by Jean was perceived by some to be a subtle stab at the government's decision to end the Courts Challenges Program, which allocated money to nonprofit groups to use in legal challenges against the government. "That is a constitutional no-no, obviously," Robert Finch, chairman of the Monarchist League of Canada, told Campbell Clark for the Toronto, Canada, *Globe and Mail* (April 25, 2007). "You can't have a Governor-General making speeches that run contrary to government policy of the day."

In 2005 Jean offended several politicians with a joke she made at a National Press Gallery dinner, an event at which politicians and reporters poke fun at themselves. While discussing André Boisclair, then a contender for the leadership position in the separatist Parti Québécois, she made a reference to his admitted cocaine use. Some, including Jean's sister, deemed the joke inappropriate. She has also fallen into disfavor with separatists for criticizing them; in September 2006 she drew fire for saying publicly that residents of Quebec "are sometimes very disconnected from the rest of Canada," according to the *Globe and Mail* (September 25, 2006). She later explained that she meant that all Canadians were disconnected from other parts of the country, and that she was attempting to point out that citizens should take an interest in provinces beyond their own. An editorial in the *Toronto Sun* (September 27, 2006) agreed with her, saying, "The idea of encouraging Canadians to get to know their whole country—and each other—better is an altogether healthy and sensible one, and fully appropriate for the Governor General."

In October 2008 the Conservative Party politician Stephen Harper was reelected prime minister; his party, though, failed to win a majority of seats in the Canadian Parliament. In December 2008 Harper's administration announced plans to cut public subsidies for political parties, angering opposition parties in Parliament whose existence depended on them. That move, along with several other unpopular proposals, led three of the opposition parties—the Liberals, the New Democrats, and the Bloc Québécois—to form a majority coalition and schedule for December 8 a vote of no-confidence in Harper. Harper persuaded Jean to shut down the Parliament (called "prorogue," that function is one of Jean's powers as the queen's representative); all parliamentary activities stopped until January 26, 2009, and Harper thus avoided the no-confidence vote. According to a profile of Harper on the *New York Times* Web site, prorogues "are not unprecedented"—they are "used routinely to break off sessions [of Parliament], for elections, for example. But this is the first time any members could recall the maneuver being used in the midst of a political crisis." The crisis passed after Harper unveiled a new budget "promising tens of billions of dollars in new spending, much of it in areas like housing that the party had never previously championed," according to the *Times* profile. With the Liberal Party's support of the budget, the three-party coalition opposing Harper disbanded, and Parliament passed the budget on February 3, 2009.

In May 2009 Jean took part in a traditional Inuit meal in the Nunavut, a federal territory, where she helped skin a seal and consumed a slice of its heart. The feast occurred not long after the European Union (E.U.) voted to impose a ban on seal products (the ban contained limited exemptions for Inuit in Canada and Greenland), and Jean won praise from Canadian Inuit leaders, who expressed their appreciation for her support for their traditional culture and food. Nonetheless, the E.U. and several animal-rights groups criticized the governor general for her actions. When asked if her actions constituted a message to Europe, Jean responded, "Take from that what you will," according to the CBC (May 26, 2009, on-line).

In June 2009 the public learned that Jean will officially open the 2010 Winter Olympics in Vancouver. She will also lead the Vancouver 2010 Olympic Truce, a program created by the Vancouver Organizing Committee for the 2010 Olympic and Paralympic Winter Games; according to the committee's Web site, the program aims to "encourage individuals to create everyday peace at home, schools, work, and in the community, based on the belief that lasting peace starts at the local level." In October Jean riled Canada's monarchists when she referred to herself in a speech as Canada's "head of state," even though the governor general is officially designated as the "Queen's representative in Canada." Officials at Rideau Hall (the official residence of the governor general) noted that the governor general carries out the duties of head of state as the queen's representative, an explanation that drew further criticism from the Monarchist League of Canada. Later in the month, in another speech, Jean referred to herself only as the governor general, and her official Web site, www.gg.ca, no longer refers to the governor general as "head of state."

Jean's honors include the Amnesty International Journalism Award in 1995 for a 15-part series on women; the 1994 Anik Prize for reporting; the French Médaillée de l'Ordre des Chevaliers de La Pléiade des Parlementaires de la Francophonie in 2003 for her contributions to francophone culture; and the 2000 Galaxi Award for best information-program host. In 2000 she also accepted the Raymond-Charrette Award for the quality of her French in broadcast journalism.

Jean and Lafond have an adopted daughter, Marie-Eden, who is the first child to live at Rideau Hall since the family of Edward Schreyer resided there, in the early 1980s. The family also includes Lafond's two daughters from a previous marriage, as well as his two grandchildren.

—W.D.

Suggested Reading: *Canadian Encyclopedia* (online); cbc.ca May 26, 2009; gg.ca; *Ottawa Citizen* A p1 Sep. 26, 2005; (Toronto, Canada) *Globe and Mail* A p1 Aug. 5, 2005; *Vancouver Sun* A p15 Nov. 21, 2006

Selected Television Shows: *Virages*, 1991–92; *Le Point*, 1992–95; L'Édition Québécoise, 1995; *Le Monde ce soir*, 1995; *Le Journal RDI*, 1995; *Grand Reportages*, 1995; *Rough Cuts*, 1999; *The Passionate Eye*, 1999; *Michaëlle*, 2004

Johnson, Simon

Jan. 16, 1963– Former chief economist for the International Monetary Fund; educator; founder of the Baseline Scenario blog

Address: MIT Sloan School of Management, 50 Memorial Dr., Cambridge, MA 02142

Simon Johnson—a British-born professor at the Massachusetts Institute of Technology (MIT), former chief economist for the International Monetary

Michael Spilotro/IMF/Getty Images

Simon Johnson

Fund (IMF), and founder of the popular blog the Baseline Scenario—has acquired a celebrity status unusual for anyone in his field. "The global economic crisis has produced far more villains than heroes among the economic experts in academia, journalism and business," Tim Fernholz wrote in an article entitled "The Unlikely Revolutionary" for *American Prospect* (April 22, 2009, on-line). "Nonetheless, a few outspoken economists have become central to the national conversation. . . . None, though, have created such a stir as Simon Johnson." Johnson's fame has spread in large part because of his widely read and cited blog, which carries the tagline: "What happened to the global economy and what we can do about it."

In the Baseline Scenario Johnson offers an accessible and highly critical analysis of the crisis, which he views as the result of the unchecked empowerment of the U.S.'s financial oligarchy. One of his central arguments has been that over the past several decades, the financial elite on Wall Street have grown disproportionately wealthy and powerful, co-opting the political process through personal connections, the revolving door between government and the financial sector, and the practices of financing political campaigns and lobbying. In order to truly reform and revitalize the economic system, Johnson believes, financiers' damaging hold on the political process must be broken. "Economists don't usually talk like that about policy making unless they're in political economy departments," Martin Wolf, a former World Bank economist who is now the chief economics commentator at the London *Financial Times*, told Fernholz. "That might change the way the debate goes and might delegitimize, if [Johnson] is successful, some of the policies promoted by the banking system and indeed the current administration."

Johnson has been so influential, in part, because he is neither a leftist nor a populist—he is instead a mainstream insider, a policy expert with years of experience. "No other economist of Johnson's credentials has stepped forward to call the United States a financier-run oligarchy," Fernholz wrote. "It's a charge that's attracted a lot of attention coming from an MIT professor and former chief economist at the International Monetary Fund, an institution that is normally a bête noire of the left." Johnson, who has increasingly been called upon to defend himself against charges of extremism and sensationalism, told Fernholz, "I'm not a populist. . . . I'm interesting to people on the left in part because I really am a very centrist-type character who is completely agreeing with, and in fact going further than, many left-type people."

Johnson's experiences at the IMF, working with post–Cold War Eastern European countries as well as nations in East Asia, Africa, and Latin America, have led him to conclude, as he wrote for the *Atlantic*, that the U.S. now resembles an emerging-market banana republic, hijacked by the wealthy. He has contended that if the crisis had originated in any other country, there would be no doubt as to the prescriptions needed: for the government to take insolvent banks into receivership, dismantle them, and implement a heavily regulated financial sector small enough to control. Unlike other countries, however, the U.S. effectively controls the IMF and World Bank, since it is their dominant shareholder. Johnson has pointed out that the U.S. remains wealthy enough to avoid needing loans or aid from those institutions, and the members of the country's financial ruling class are powerful enough to dictate not only the laws that regulate—or deregulate—their behavior but also to direct the national discourse, immediately disqualifying as radical or potentially disastrous any approach that might be detrimental to them. "This is about power, and this is about telling the financial sector that they do not run this country," Johnson told Terry Gross on the National Public Radio (NPR) program *Fresh Air* (April 15, 2009, on-line). "The country is run by people who have been elected to run the country, and having the financial sector build up massive vulnerabilities, create enormous dangers, generate big, big costs for the taxpayer and then walk away as if nothing had happened . . . that to my mind is not acceptable."

Like some of his colleagues, Johnson has maintained that the Barack Obama administration is too deferential to financial interests and has acquiesced to them by socializing losses and privatizing gains. In searching for solutions, Johnson believes, the president should look not only to President Franklin D. Roosevelt's New Deal but also to President Theodore Roosevelt's trust-busting. "The Quiet Coup," an article Johnson wrote for the *Atlantic* (May 2009, on-line), summarized many of the arguments he had put forward in the Baseline

Scenario in the preceding months and concluded, "Anything that is too big to fail is too big to exist." "Few magazine articles in recent memory have excited as much econo-blogospheric commentary as . . . Simon Johnson's 'The Quiet Coup,'" Andrew Leonard wrote for the on-line magazine *Salon* (March 31, 2009). "For good reason: Johnson's elucidation of how four decades of deregulatory ideology placed the interests of Wall Street 'oligarchs' above the interests of the general public is magisterial and convincing."

Simon Johnson was born on January 16, 1963 in Great Britain. He studied economics and politics at the University of Oxford, graduating with a B.A. degree in 1984. Two years later he earned a master's degree in economics from the University of Manchester. Johnson then moved to Boston, Massachusetts, and studied at MIT, receiving a Ph.D. degree in 1989. He next embarked on a career that has included academic appointments, stints as a consultant for various economic think tanks, and work in the private sector, in addition to his tenure at the IMF.

As an assistant professor of economics at Duke University's Fuqua School of Business, in Durham, North Carolina, during the early 1990s, Johnson focused on the causes of economic crises, corporate-governance issues, and the centrality of property rights in private-sector growth, among other issues. He also studied Eastern European countries that had just emerged from communist rule and were undergoing intense shock therapy—the overnight replacement of a controlled, centralized ecomony with a free-market system. Johnson managed the Fuqua School of Business Center for Manager Development, a research center in St. Petersburg, Russia, and spent much of his time tracking economic development in the former USSR. In 1995 Johnson co-authored the book *Starting Over in Eastern Europe: Entrepreneurship and Economic Renewal*, which stressed the importance of the private sector in Eastern Europe's post–Cold War economic recovery and examined Poland's prosperity following the application of shock therapy. In the book's foreword, Jeffrey Sachs, the American economist who is credited with much of the groundwork for shock therapy, called the book, as quoted by Dave Savona in *International Business* (July 1995), an "incomparable record of the early years of Poland's economic reform." While Gross Domestic Product (GDP) growth and other measures of economic well-being have been impressive, Savona maintained, "watching unemployment figures climb steadily from 0.3 percent all the way to the 16 percent range speaks volumes as to just how painful shock therapy can be."

In addition to his academic work, beginning in the early 1990s Johnson worked as a policy adviser in emerging and developing markets for the IMF, an institution whose origins can be traced back to World War II. With the U.S. emerging from that conflict as the dominant economic and political power in the world, its leaders set out to institutionalize the rebuilding of postwar Europe in order to prevent another Great Depression, stop the advance of communism, and open the continent's markets to trade. The IMF was established as a financial-oversight organization focused on maintaining the stability of the global economy; it was also heavily involved in development and aid issues. Some of its critics have seen the organization as being under the control of the U.S.—essentially as an arm of that country's Treasury Department, advancing its ideology and interests. When countries saddled with insurmountable debt and bankruptcy came to the IMF for aid—particularly during the tenures of U.S. president Ronald Reagan and British prime minister Margaret Thatcher and then in the aftermath of the fall of communism—the organization promoted what has come to be known by some critics as the Washington Consensus: an ideological economic policy that advocates free-market fundamentalism, small government, fewer social programs, deregulation, privatization, unrestricted movement of capital, and lower taxes. Typically, according to those critics, the experiments with shock therapy in post–Cold War Eastern Europe and in Latin America, while advancing the interests of international corporations and foreign investors, did little to help the underprivileged people of those countries. "One thing you learn rather quickly when working at the International Monetary Fund is that no one is ever very happy to see you," Johnson, who ultimately rose to the rank of chief economist at the organization, wrote in his *Atlantic* article. "Typically, your 'clients' come in only after private capital has abandoned them, after regional trading-bloc partners have been unable to throw a strong enough lifeline, after last-ditch attempts to borrow from powerful friends like China or the European Union have fallen through. You're never at the top of anyone's dance card. The reason, of course, is that the IMF specializes in telling its clients what they don't want to hear. I should know; I pressed painful changes on many foreign officials during my time there. . . . And I felt the effects of IMF pressure, at least indirectly, when I worked with governments in Eastern Europe as they struggled after 1989, and with the private sector in Asia and Latin America during the crises of the late 1990s and early 2000s." In exchange for the badly needed loans, the IMF imposed major structural changes on the countries' economies. As Johnson wrote in his controversial *Atlantic* article comparing the current U.S. to an emerging market, "The biggest obstacle to recovery is almost invariably the politics of countries in crisis. Typically, these countries are in a desperate economic situation for one simple reason—the powerful elites within them overreached in good times and took too many risks." He continued, "Emerging-market governments and their private-sector allies commonly form a tight-knit—and, most of the time, genteel—oligarchy, running the country rather like a profit-seeking company in which they are the controlling shareholders. . . .

Squeezing the oligarchs, though, is seldom the strategy of choice among emerging-market governments. Quite the contrary: at the outset of the crisis, the oligarchs are usually among the first to get extra help from the government. . . . From long years of experience, the IMF staff knows its program will succeed—stabilizing the economy and enabling growth—only if at least some of the powerful oligarchs who did so much to create the underlying problems take a hit. This is the problem of all emerging markets."

While at the IMF Johnson held other positions. In 2000 and 2001, for example, he served on the U.S. Securities and Exchange Commission's Advisory Committee on Market Information, and his strong recommendation for enhanced market regulations was included in the published findings of the committee. He has also been a fellow of the Center for Economic and Policy Research, established in 1999, and he has been an affiliate scholar at the Bureau for Research and Economic Analysis of Development (BREAD). He has served on the Advisory Group at the Center for Global Development and on the advisory board of Duke's Center for the Advancement of Social Entrepreneurship, in Poland, as well as being a research fellow at the Asian Institute for Corporate Governance at Korea University. At the Washington-based Center for Global Development, Johnson co-chaired a task force on Latin American economic reforms. Johnson also served on the global advisory board of Endeavor, a group that supports entrepreneurship in emerging markets in Latin America, the Middle East, and Africa, and he worked as a global-strategy consultant to the Brattle Group, which provides regulatory and economic expertise to the private sector. In 2006 Johnson became a visiting fellow at the Peterson Institute for International Economics, a research organization focused on global economic policy issues, and in 2008 he became a senior fellow.

Concurrently, Johnson taught at various institutions, and since 2004 he has held the position of Ronald A. Kurtz professor of entrepreneurship at MIT's Sloan School of Management. At MIT he co-founded the university's Global Entrepreneurship Laboratory, through which students collaborate with the heads of start-up businesses worldwide.

After working as an assistant director in the IMF's research department from 2004 to 2006, Johnson was named the organization's chief economist and director of the research department in early 2007. He took a leave of absence from MIT to fill the post. He has said that he had an epiphany upon becoming head economist, and he soon began warning that a "perfect storm" was looming. Although he had pushed market liberalization on developing countries for years, "now [since the economic crisis began], that's not my view," he told Fernholz. "We should go back and look at everything, and wonder . . . if anybody has the regulatory structures able to withstand what happens when you liberalize." He conceded, however, "You can say, look, that Simon has a hammer and everything's a nail. Maybe I'm wrong; maybe the banking system isn't too big, too powerful, or fundamentally bad for us."

In May 2008 Johnson announced that he would be leaving the IMF the following September to devote more time to research and teaching. (Some observers theorized about another motivation: a week earlier the IMF had announced that a significant number of its employees had applied for buyout packages in response to the fund's plan to slash its budget and cut jobs.) As the economic crisis came to a head in the fall of 2008, Johnson began to make public pronouncements with increasing frequency—on blogs, on the radio (particularly NPR's *Planet Money*), and in the op-ed pages of major newspapers.

In September 2008, along with James Kwak, Johnson co-founded the Baseline Scenario, a blog dedicated to elucidating, analyzing, and proposing solutions to issues related to the current economic situation. (Peter Boone of the London School of Economics also contributes to the blog.) "We believe that everyone should be able to understand how the financial crisis came about, what it means for all of us, and what our options are for getting out of it," the authors wrote.

The ideas expressed in the Baseline Scenario quickly gained currency. As Robert Teitelman wrote for TheDeal.com (March 20, 2009), Johnson and Kwak have employed "every channel available to them to transmit and amplify their positions." They send out e-mail alerts for breaking news and are linked to dozens of other widely read blogs and respected institutions. (In August 2009 Johnson began contributing a weekly post to the *New York Times*'s Economix blog.) They have also used the social-networking and micro-blogging tool Twitter, and Johnson has continued to appear on such traditional media outlets as NPR's *Fresh Air* and, on TV, the *Bill Moyers Journal*. Johnson's effort to inform the discussion about the economy "is working pretty well if Johnson's increasing ubiquity is any measure," Teitelman wrote.

While some activist groups have been inspired at least in part by Johnson, he has also had his share of critics. Many on the left are skeptical that an IMF economist whose free-market ideology greatly aided Wall Street could suddenly experience such an about-face. Many on the right have been equally skeptical. "Simon's account is based on a very simple, and I believe misguided, theory of politics and economics," the Harvard economist Dani Rodrik wrote on his own blog, according to Leonard. "It is an odd marriage of populist and technocratic visions. Countries fail because political elites always end up in bed with economic elites. The solution, apparently, is to let the technocrats (read the IMF) run your affairs. Among the many lessons from the crisis we should have learned is that economists and policy advisors need greater humility. Too many of us thought we had the right model when it turned out that we didn't. We pushed certain policies with much greater confidence than we should have. . . . Do we really want to exhibit the same self-confidence and assurance now, as we struggle to devise solutions to the crisis caused by our own hubris?"

Johnson's most vociferous detractors use the words "socialism" and "nationalization" to discredit his ideas. "You know, this socialism discussion is a complete red herring," Johnson told Gross on *Fresh Air* (March 3, 2009). "My view is the offense against American capitalism was committed by the big banks who brought us to this point: Their mismanagement, their compensation schemes, their . . . attitude towards the public."

In opinion pieces published in major newspapers including the *New York Times* and the London *Sunday Times* in 2009, Johnson—often in collaboration with Peter Boone—continued to question the U.S. government's response to the financial crisis. In several articles in the fall, he warned that because regulators and bankers had essentially learned nothing from the recession and bankers had gone unpunished, the failure of the government or any other entities to introduce meaningful regulations and reforms was paving the way for future meltdowns. "This policy of responding to bursting bubbles, rather than using regulation to deflate them before they start growing, has become the standard procedure of most central banks," Johnson and Boone wrote for the Sunday *Times* (September 13, 2009). In a *New York Times* (September 20, 2009) op-ed piece, the pair wrote, "The details of who makes which crazy loans to whom will no doubt be different from what they were from 2002 to 2007, but the basic structure of incentives in the system is unchanged."

Johnson's papers have been published in the *American Economic Review*, the *Journal of Political Economy*, the *Quarterly Journal of Economics*, and the *Journal of Finance*, among others. He sits on the editorial board of several publications, including the *Journal of Financial Economics*, the *Review of Economics and Statistics*, and the *Journal of Comparative Economics*.

In late April 2009 Johnson was named an adviser to the Congressional Budget Office, a nonpartisan agency that examines legislation affecting the federal budget. He continues to research and teach at MIT while overseeing his blog.

—M.M.

Suggested Reading: *American Prospect* (on-line) Apr. 22, 2009; *Atlantic* (on-line) May 2009; *International Business* p77 July 1995; *Irish Times* Finance p7 Apr. 17, 2009; *Salon* (on-line) Mar. 31, 2009

Selected Books: *Starting Over in Eastern Europe: Entrepreneurship and Economic Renewal* (with Gary W. Loveman), 1995

Jolly, Alison

May 9, 1937– Primatologist; writer; lecturer

Address: The Old Brewery House, 32 Southover High St., Lewes BN7 1HX, England

Alison Jolly is a zoologist, renowned author, and pioneer in the study of primate behavior and the evolution of social intelligence. More specifically, she is the world's leading authority on lemurs—furry primates that are native only to Madagascar, the world's fourth-largest island, in the Indian Ocean, about 185 miles off the coast of southeastern Africa. As members of the prosimian family, lemurs are the most primitive of all primates. In other parts of the world, over the course of millions of years, natural selection led lemurs' ancestors to be displaced by larger primates, such as monkeys and apes. The lemurs on Madagascar, however, were safe from competition and predators and thus differentiated into 12 species and more than 40 subspecies (more than a dozen of which are known only from fossils). Lemurs range in size from the six-inch mouse lemur—the world's smallest primate—to the endangered indri, which resembles a three-foot long, black-and-white teddy bear. Fossil evidence indicates that lemurs reached Madagascar—possibly by rafting—after the island broke away from Africa, about 100 million years ago. Because it was so isolated, Madagascar became what Jolly described in her conversation with Michele Landsberg for the *Toronto Star* (January 5, 1991) as an "alternate world," in which thousands of unique animal, plant, and insect species evolved separately from those on the rest of the planet. Lemurs are the closest living approximations of the ancient ancestors of all modern primates—including humans—which makes them valuable subjects for scientists studying human ancestry. They can provide "a clue to the moment when our own ancestors began to specialize in monkey sociability and monkey cleverness," Jolly wrote, as quoted by Eric Eckholm in the *New York Times* (June 16, 1987). In addition to lemurs, approximately 98 percent of the island's palm-tree species, 80 percent of its flowering plants, and more than 95 percent of its reptiles are found nowhere else in the world.

Since she first visited Madagascar (known geopolitically as the Republic of Madagascar), in 1962, Jolly has written dozens of scientific articles and authored or edited nine books on lemurs, Madagascar, and the evolution of cognition in primates. Among Jolly's main arguments is that cooperation and social interaction are the foundations of intelligence and cognition in animals. Her research in Madagascar has drawn the attention of internation-

Courtesy of Houghton-Mifflin

Alison Jolly

al agencies, which are now cooperating with the Malagasy (pronounced "Malagash") government in long-term plans to address the environmental threats that face Madagascar. Such threats are caused by overpopulation and the farming practices of the impoverished Malagasy people, which include cutting and burning down forests—the natural habitat of lemurs—to clear land for crops and grazing cattle. The conditions there constitute "a tragedy without villains," Jolly wrote of the environmental crisis in Madagascar, in an essay that was published in the photographer Frans Lanting's 1990 book, *Madagascar, A World Out of Time*. Because of the island's rich biological diversity, scientists have identified Madagascar as an environment as crucial to the world's ecosystem as South America's Amazon rainforests.

The only child of Morris G. Bishop and Alison K. Bishop, Alison Jolly was born on May 9, 1937 in Ithaca, New York, where her father was a professor at Cornell University. Her interest in animals began with her experience of owning several cats as a child. If she had not been drawn to study lemurs, she told Anusha Shrivastava for the *Wire* (March 20, 2004, on-line), she might have made gorillas the focus of her research, "because their calm intelligence makes them very therapeutic companions." She earned a B.A. degree from Cornell University in 1958 and her Ph.D. degree in zoology from Yale University, in New Haven, Connecticut, in 1962. It was while researching sponges at Yale that Jolly had begun to yearn for a more exciting research subject; she settled on the topic of lemurs in Madagascar, visiting that country for the first time shortly after completing her dissertation on those primates. She stayed on the estate of the powerful de Heaulme family, descendants of the aristocratic French colonizers of Madagascar, who had ruled the island for decades during the 19th century. On the estate the de Heaulmes maintain an area of about 650 acres, known as the Berenty Reserve, which consists of forests of ancient tamarind trees as well as "spiny forests," which are desert-like ecosystems that host a wide array of animals and spiny plants, such as cacti, and are unique to Madagascar. The reserve is home to six or so species of lemur, 103 bird species, and the largest colony of Madagascar fruit bats. While at Berenty, Jolly focused her studies on the ring-tailed lemur, a species known for its gregariousness and unusually long black-and-white striped tail. The Berenty Reserve—and the ring-tailed lemur—would become the focuses of Jolly's studies for the next 40 years. At the time of Jolly's initial visit, the plantation was also the home of many members of the Tandroy, tribes of native Malagasy people who arrived about 1,000 years ago from mainland Africa. The Tandroy live in traditional villages on the property and work in the de Heaulme family's fields of sisal, a plant fiber used in rope-making, in a system reminiscent of feudalism.

From 1963 to 1965 Jolly served as a research associate at the New York Zoological Society, headquartered in the Bronx Zoo, in New York City. Around that time she married an Englishman, moved to England, and started a family, which would come to include four children. Unable to travel to Madagascar with young children, Jolly began writing a book on her observations at Berenty—"in frustration at not doing more fieldwork," as she told Frank Diller for *American Scientist* (2004, on-line). In 1966 she published *Lemur Behavior: A Madagascar Field Study*, in which she argued that intelligence in both male and female primates is a consequence of social relationships, not a byproduct of using tools, as scientists had long thought. Jolly's arguments served as the foundation for what would become known as the "social intelligence hypothesis," a widely influential theory that was later applied to animals other than primates. Another of Jolly's early discoveries was that, contrary to the theories advanced by (predominantly male) scientists for years, communities of lemurs were not male-dominated in the way that other primate communities appeared to be. Rather, Jolly observed, female lemurs take precedence in the feeding order, a practice that protects the health of females, who can give birth to only one baby a year. Those two findings by Jolly initiated major paradigm shifts in primatology.

Jolly was a research associate at Cambridge University, in England, from 1966 to 1968, and held the same position at the University of Sussex from 1971 to 1981. As her children grew older she often returned to Madagascar to observe the lemurs and conduct studies; since 1990 she has returned every year for the lemurs' "birth period," in September and October. In 1972 she published the textbook *The Evolution of Primate Behavior*, which was immediately acknowledged as one of the most important works in primatology up to that time; it remains a benchmark in the field. In 1976 Jolly edited, along with Jerome S. Bruner and Kathy Sylva, the biology textbook *Play: Its Role in Development and Evolution.* Four years later Jolly published *A World Like Our Own: Man and Nature in Madagascar*, which she followed with *Madagascar* (part of a series called *Key Environments*), co-edited with Philippe Oberle and Roland Albignac.

In 1987 Jolly became a visiting lecturer at Princeton University, in New Jersey. By then she had gained an international reputation as an authority on lemurs; her work had opened the gates for researchers and tourists to visit and learn about Madagascar to an extent they never had before. While studying at the Berenty Reserve, Jolly gave tours and allowed visitors to participate in her research. Jolly and other researchers, including Russell A. Mittermeier, then the director of both the World Wildlife Fund's primate program and the Primate Specialist Group, an arm of an organization now known as the IUCN-World Conservation Union, aimed to bring attention to the rapid deterioration of the natural habitats of Madagascar's plants and animals. (Around that time a World Bank report identified Madagascar as the most eroded place on earth, due in part to the sparse distribution of trees, which exacerbated the problems caused by deforestation.) Jolly and Mittermeier predicted, as quoted by Henry Mitchell for the *Washington Post* (November 28, 1986), that if significant action was not taken, the island's "biological richness" could disappear within the next 15 years. "A very great deal can be saved," Jolly told Mitchell, "once people decide it is really worth saving. The tragic thing is we do not know the value of life forms that may be casually destroyed before we even understand them."

In 1986 French biologists captured three specimens of a species of lemur that was long thought to be extinct or confined to a small area of northeastern Madagascar: the aye-aye. The species was the sole surviving member of its family; the larger relatives, the Daubentonia robusta, had become extinct on Madagascar approximately 1,500 years earlier. The aye-aye is a medium-sized lemur with black fur, bat-like ears, large incisors, a large, bushy tail, and third and fourth fingers that are significantly longer than its other fingers. "Aye-ayes are really weird," Jolly told told Jeffrey Cohn for *BioScience* (November 1, 1993). "They don't fit our idea of what animals are. They are put together with things no one animal should have." The aye-aye's long fingers are used in ways similar to the way a woodpecker uses its beak—to tap the trunks of trees or vines in order to locate hollow areas where larvae may be hiding, then scoop them out. The native Malagasy people have long thought the presence of an aye-aye to be a bad omen, representing impending death. Jolly wrote in a 1988 article that appeared in *National Geographic*, as quoted by the *San Diego Union-Tribune* (August 19, 1988), "In much of the country tradition decrees that [the aye-aye] be slain on sight, lest it uncrook its skeleton finger to point out a victim for death." That belief has over time likely contributed—though not as much as other factors—to the dwindling population of aye-ayes. After the French biologists' discovery, a few aye-ayes were kept in captivity, where scientists conducted research into their biology and behavior, while a number of zoos and research facilities around the world launched collaborative captive-breeding programs for aye-ayes. The animals have since been sighted in more places on Madagascar than most other lemurs. "Aye-ayes are becoming a symbol of wildlife conservation in Madagascar," Jolly told Cohn. "They are not just another animal trying to make a living. It is a very exciting animal for scientists and ordinary people. It can be a flagship species for lemur conservation."

Along with the British researcher John Mack, Jolly contributed essays to *Madagascar, A World Out of Time*, Frans Lanting's book of photographs of Madagascar's people and wildlife. "Alison Jolly's articles and books about Madagascar are written with poetic intensity and an explorer's immediacy," Michele Landsberg wrote. "She can make you hold your breath when she describes her first sighting of the ghostly, mysterious little aye-aye." Among the subjects of Jolly's essays are the plight of Malagasy villagers, who, out of desperation, cut and burn forests to clear land for crops and livestock. In one essay she expressed both concern for the island's deteriorating ecosystem and sympathy for the people there. "Extraordinary for an impassioned ecologist," Landsberg wrote of Jolly's essay, "Alison writes with sensitivity and respect about the Malagasy villagers, despite their destruction of the rain forests."

In 1999 Jolly published *Lucy's Legacy: Sex and Intelligence in Human Evolution*, a book that explores the way in which cooperation among primates has shaped their minds and social patterns. The book takes its name from that given to the ancient hominid whose partial skeleton was discovered in Ethiopia by Donald Johanson and Tom Gray in 1974. The book covers four major areas: the general history of evolution; primate behavior; the evolution of human cognition; and the ways in which humans have created culture. To demonstrate her assertion that, throughout evolution, cooperation underpins much of human cognition and behavior, Jolly provided a number of examples of complex ways that animals work together. For instance, the male of a certain kind of African tick secretes a protein that blocks the host's immune system so that a nearby female tick can consume more blood. Jolly pointed out that in primates, sexual favors are the foundation of many successful alliances. She asserted, however, that female primates do not play—and have never played—simple, submissive roles; they do not, for example, merely use sex to buy protection from males. Rather, females give birth to a male's young—thereby passing his genes to the next generation—in exchange for the males' "egalitarian, energetic investment" in family life. Jolly also showed that throughout evolutionary history, mothers have been helped with child-rearing, and that there is no evolutionary basis for monogamous relationships. Jolly's focus on cooperation between the sexes deconstructs both the popular male-centered portrait of the evolution of sexuality—which positions the male as dominant actor—as well as the revisionist perspective of evolution, which focuses only on the female. "Her book is full of wry, ironic humour, as well as knowledgeable remarks about the way science works," Adrian Barnett wrote for the *New Scientist* (December 18, 1999). A reviewer for the London *Guardian* (April 22, 2000) criticized the book for its lack of scientific specificity but also predicted that it would be highly enjoyable for the average reader. "This is not what anyone would call headline science," the reviewer wrote; "it's just well-written, witty, thought-provoking and full of fascinating detail. You don't learn from it how to do primatology, but you do learn what sort of primate you are, which is, for most people, more valuable."

In her 2004 book, *Lords and Lemurs: Mad Scientists, Kings with Spears, and the Survival of Diversity in Madagascar*, Jolly wrote about the primates of Madagascar, the scientists who study the island, and the country's history, politics, and native population. She used specific examples from her own experiences at the Berenty Reserve to explain the history of French colonization that lies behind the complicated political relationships between the de Heaulme family and the Tandroy tribe members who live and work on their land. As Jolly explained in her book, Henry de Heaulme bought land bit by bit to found Berenty in 1936 and opened up a sisal plant, where he employed members of the local Tandroy tribes. The de Heaulme family protected the Tandroys when the French crushed the Madagasy people's fight for independence in 1947, so that they could continue to work on his farm. When sisal became unprofitable, Berenty became a destination for researchers and ecotourists. Jolly described Madagascar as a world in which people, the economy, and the natural world all support one another. "In the year 2000 Berenty and its lemurs are still flourishing because the de Heaulme family are still here," Jolly wrote, as quoted by Peter Rowe in the *San Diego Union-Tribune* (May 2, 2004). "And vice versa. Forest and family saved each other." Jolly also described in great detail the culture of the female-dominated ring-tailed lemur communities that she has spent decades studying. Giving the lemurs such names as "Cream Puff," Jolly told of the soap opera–like feuds that take place among the powerful bands of females. The writer Dale Peterson described the book as a "bright and loving story of a strange land, and a special people, and a few exotic tribes of primates and primate watchers," as quoted on the publisher Houghton Mifflin's Web site. Rowe, however, criticized the book for attempting to cover too much ground at once. "I had a swell time traveling with Alison Jolly," he wrote, "but, on returning home, wasn't sure what I had seen."

Jolly has written two illustrated children's books: *Ako the Aye-Aye* (2005), a story about a forest in Madagascar and its inhabitants, and *Bitika the Mouse Lemur* (2007). Both books are designed to teach the importance of science and conservation. "It is heart-warming to have a tiny animal alert the world to a large conservation issue," Lee Durrell, of Durrell Wildlife Conservation Trust, wrote in a review of *Bitika the Mouse Lemur* that was posted on amazon.com. "The charming 'Bitika' will draw much-needed attention to the exquisite, but heretofore neglected, western forests and wetlands of Madagascar and their rare and unusual inhabitants." Jolly co-edited, with Robert W. Sussman, Naoki Koyama, and Hantanarina Rasamimanana, *Ringtailed Lemur Biology: Lemur Catta in Madagascar* (2006).

Since 2000 Jolly has held the position of visiting scientist in the Department of Biology and Environmental Science at the University of Sussex. She has delivered numerous lectures and continues to conduct research on lemurs in Madagascar; she has been credited with enormous contributions to the study of evolution and to the environmental conservation effort in Madagascar. In June 2006 a new species of mouse lemur was discovered in the Madagascar provinces of Mananjary and Kianjavato. The lemur, which is reddish-brown with a white patch on its nose and a gray belly, was named Microcebus jollyae, to honor Jolly's research. The Oxford Brookes University has established the Alison Jolly Prize, which honors outstanding performance in the university's primate-conservation course.

In 1991 Landsberg wrote that Jolly "has the calm, blue-eyed gaze of a genuine American aristocrat." From 1992 to 1996 she served as the president of the International Primatological Society; she has been named an Officer of the National Order of Madagascar. She has four grown children—Margaretta, Susan, Arthur, and Richard—with her husband, Richard Jolly, a British economist, formerly a deputy executive director of the United Nations Children's Fund (UNICEF), and currently an honorary professor and research associate at the Institute of Development Studies at the University of Sussex. Many have credited Jolly as an inspiration to female scientists who wish to raise children while pursuing academic careers. "She wouldn't be as original and perceptive a scientist if she weren't a mother," Landsberg wrote, "[and] she might not have raised such interesting children if she hadn't always had her suitcases packed for Madagascar."

—M.E.R.

Suggested Reading: *BioScience* p668 Nov. 1, 1993; (London) *Guardian* p10 Apr. 22, 2000; (London) *Times Higher Education Supplement* p32 Apr. 22, 2005; *New Scientist* p5050 Dec. 19, 1999; *New York Times* C p1 June 16, 1987; *San Diego Union-Tribune* p8 May 2, 2004; *Toronto Star* J p1 Jan. 5, 1991; *Washington Post* A p1 Nov. 28, 1986

Selected Books: as writer—*Lemur Behavior: A Madagascar Field Study*, 1966; *The Evolution of Primate Behavior*, 1972; *A World Like Our Own: Man and Nature in Madagascar*, 1980; *Lucy's Legacy: Sex and Intelligence in Human Evolution*, 1999; *Lords and Lemurs: Mad Scientists, Kings with Spears, and the Survival of Diversity in Madagascar*, 2004; *Ako the Aye-Aye*, 2005; *Bitika the Mouse Lemur*, 2007; as co-editor—*Play: Its Role in Development and Evolution*, 1976; *Madagascar: Key Environments Series*, 1980

Courtesy of Tayari Jones

Jones, Tayari

(tee-AH-ree)

Nov. 30, 1970– Writer

Address: Rutgers/Newark Dept. of English, Hill Hall, Rm. 504, 360 Dr. Martin Luther King Jr. Blvd., Newark, NJ 07102-1801

"There are gushers and ekers," the novelist, short-story writer, and blogger Tayari Jones said to Richard Nilsen for the *Arizona Republic* (July 7, 2003), referring to different kinds of writers. "I am a gusher." In the last few years, Jones has "gushed" two critically acclaimed novels: *Leaving Atlanta* (2002), whose coming-of-age story is set in the era of the infamous murders of children in Atlanta, Georgia, from 1979 to 1981; and *The Untelling* (2005), about a young woman trying to cope with her tragic past, her current life in a decaying Atlanta neighborhood, and a painful secret. *Leaving Atlanta* won the 2003 Zora Neale Hurston/Richard Wright Foundation Legacy Award for Debut Fiction and was named as one of the best novels of 2002 by the *Atlanta Journal-Constitution* and *Washington Post*. *The Untelling* received the Lillian C. Smith Award for New Voices from the Southern Regional Council and the University of Georgia Libraries in 2005. Proclaimed by the *Atlanta Journal-Constitution* as "one of the best writers of her generation," Jones has woven elements of her own life into particular moments in history to address issues of human nature, society, and African-American tradition and experience. Her writing focuses largely on the urban centers of the American South, where she grew up. Jones explained to Nilsen, "Novels provide for a culture what a photo album does for a family; it is a freeze frame for history and lives." While recognizing the significance of race in African-American life, Jones has refused to define characters solely, or even chiefly, by their color. She explained to Nilsen, "I've come to see how I am a 'raced' person in this society. But I write about being Black the way Woody Allen writes about Jewish New Yorkers. I always write starting with my characters' humanity. I'm not commenting on race or oppression. I don't want everyone to be the same." Explaining that she wishes to represent life as she has never seen it portrayed in books, she added, "I want to fill in that gap." In 2008 Jones received a no-strings-attached $50,000 grant from the United States Artists Foundation. She maintains the blog tayarijones.com.

Tayari Jones was born on November 30, 1970 in Atlanta. (Her name, she has told interviewers, is a Swahili word meaning "she is prepared.") Her father, now retired, was a political scientist and professor at Atlanta University; her mother also taught at the college level and is now an economist at Alabama A&M University, in Hunstville. Her older brother, Patrice Lumumba Jones (named after her father's hero, the African leader Patrice Lumumba), is three years her senior. With the exception of a year her family spent in Nigeria, in West Africa, Jones was reared in southwest Atlanta. "I never met a White person until I was 20," she told Nilsen. "We had a complete community, Black lawyers, Black dentists, Black doctors." Jones developed a passion for writing at an early age; while she was a student at Oglethorpe Elementary School, she began crafting fiction about her friends' lives.

In 1979, shortly before the start of Jones's fifth-grade year, two local African-American boys were abducted and killed—the first of more than two dozen such killings that occurred from 1979 to 1981 and that became known as the Atlanta child murders. (An African-American man, Wayne Williams, was later convicted of two of the killings.) The murders had a profound and lasting effect on Jones's family, life, and work. "My lexicon was constantly growing with the frightening terms . . . pronounced each night on the evening news: asphyxia, decomposition, ligature . . . ," Jones wrote in an essay for the *Atlanta Journal-Constitution* (May 22, 2005). "My capable, sensible mother was preoccupied with the safety of her own children, and of the other kids in our school. . . . Once my father pointed out that the ornamental bars on our windows would prevent my abduction in my sleep, I was able to rest easily. But I doubt that he ever did." Jones's father helped search for victims, who included two of Jones's school mates.

Jones went on to attend Benjamin Mays High School in southwest Atlanta, known for its excellent science and math program and its gifted students. She came to feel like an outcast among those students, as science turned out not to be her strength; she once nearly destroyed her parents' basement in an experiment having to do with acid rain. Jones was ready to leave the school when a teacher persuaded her to take part in a statewide writing competition for high-school students sponsored by the nearby Pace Academy, in Buckhead, Georgia. Jones's story, "The Pursuit of Michael Thomas," an autobiographical tale about high-school love, took first prize. At the award ceremony Jones was asked to read from her work, which is how she discovered that authors give public readings.

After graduating from Benjamin Mays, in 1987, Jones enrolled in the writing program at Spelman College, a four-year liberal-arts women's school in Atlanta. There, she studied with the writer Pearl Cleage, who went on to publish one of Jones's first stories, "Eugenics," in a magazine she edited called *Catalyst*. During her time at Spelman, Jones was the victim of a carjacking. She told Nilsen, "He held a gun to my head. Every cliché you hear turned out to be true: I could feel the cold steel. My heart pounded. I couldn't get the keys out to give him. He pulled the trigger and the gun went click. He freaked out and ran away. It undermined my sense of personal security for a long time." Another traumatic episode in Jones's life also took place during her college years. One day the fourth-grade boy she tutored was a few minutes late for his appointment, and Jones was so frantic that she became physically ill. She told her dorm mates what was happening; some were unconcerned, while others became as nervous as Jones. After finding out that the boy was safe, "I realized that all of us who panicked shared a common terror: We had all grown up in Atlanta," Jones wrote for the *Journal-Constitution*. "We all knew that a little boy unaccounted for constituted an emergency. It was then that I knew that if I ever became a writer, I would write a novel about those of us who were children in Atlanta. I would put on paper this memory that we never spoke aloud but carried with us in our bones." Jones graduated magna cum laude from Spelman, earning a bachelor's degree in English in 1991. She next entered a graduate program at the University of Iowa, where she completed her master's degree in English in 1994 and worked for a time toward a doctorate.

A turning point in Jones's life occurred at a writing conference in Portland, Oregon, where she met the author Jewell Parker Rhodes. Jones "literally ran into" Rhodes, as she told Lindy Washburn for the Bergen County, New Jersey, *Record* (January 4, 2004). "She was 4-foot-10, and I'm 5-foot-10, and I knocked her over." Rhodes, who had remembered reading Jones's story "Eugenics," invited her to pursue a master of fine arts degree at Arizona State University (ASU), where Rhodes headed the creative-writing program. Drawn to the prospect of working on her own fiction rather than continuing to study the literary canon, Jones quickly accepted the offer, leaving the University of Iowa. Rhodes helped secure a scholarship for her and became her mentor, noting to Nilsen, "It takes a special kind of person to take you up on it. Tayari is one of those artists who make the choices and take the risks needed to achieve their dreams." Jones earned her M.F.A. degree from Arizona State in 2000. While there she had begun working on the manuscript that would become *Leaving Atlanta*. "When I sat down to write my very first novel—'my baby,' I call it—the project felt more like an urgent matter of truth-telling rather than the academic task of 'filling in the gaps of history,' which is often seen as the 'work' of the African-American writer," she wrote for *State Department Documents and Publications* (February 6, 2009).

Leaving Atlanta was published in 2002. That coming-of-age novel, set during the era of Atlanta's child murders, has three parts, each told from the perspective of a different fifth-grader. One of them is LaTasha Baxter, a high-spirited middle-class girl who struggles to fit in with the popular crowd at school; another is Rodney Green, an unhappy boy whom LaTasha describes as "the weirdest kid in class" and who acts out his frustration at being unable to please his demanding parents; and the third is Octavia Fuller, an extremely bright and confident social outcast referred to by peers as "the Watusi" because of her dark complexion. Commenting on *Leaving Atlanta*, Jones noted for her Web site: "This novel is my way of documenting a particular moment in history. It is a love letter to my generation and also an effort to remember my own childhood. To remind myself and my readers what it was like to [be] eleven and at the mercy of the world. And despite the obvious darkness of the time period, I also wanted to remember all that is sweet about girlhood, to recall all the moments that make a person smile and feel optimistic."

Leaving Atlanta received unanimous praise from critics. VeTalle Fusilier, assessing the novel for *Black Issues Book Review* (August 31, 2002), wrote, "Jones . . . reminds us of how unnerved black children remain growing up amid the racism, ignorance, and violence often perpetuated by police, apathetic teachers, and even family. *Leaving Atlanta* gently describes, through these children, their frustration and despair, with a measure of humor and love. Jones explores the pride and prejudices within the African-American community: skin color, hair envy, wealth and poverty, without apology or judgment." Michael Skube commented for the *Washington Post* (August 18, 2002), "Jones's prose too often is that of someone fresh out of a creative-writing program, and her word choice can be peculiar (I don't know when I've heard a fifth-grader, suburban or inner-city, use 'litigious' or speak casually of 'vichyssoise'). But when she sets the similes aside and simply narrates . . . she conveys powerfully the loneliness of a child no one knew." Roishina Clay noted for the *Mississippi Clarion-Leader* (September 1, 2002), "[Jones] has the magic of hypnotizing the reader with her words in showing that this story could only come from a child." *Leaving Atlanta* received many awards, including the 2003 Zora Neale Hurston/Richard Wright Foundation Legacy Award for Debut Fiction. It was named novel of the year by *Atlanta* magazine and best southern novel of the year by *Creative Loafing Atlanta* and was listed as one of the best novels of 2002 by the *Journal-Constitution* and the *Washington Post.*

Jones's second novel, *The Untelling*, published in 2005, tells the story of a young Atlanta woman, Aria Jackson, who struggles to overcome the loss of her father and younger sister in a car accident that took place during her childhood. Aria tries to patch up her relationship with her mother, who has become addicted to drugs; meanwhile, just as she meets the man of her dreams, she finds out that she is infertile, a discovery she keeps to herself. While working at a local literacy center, Aria becomes envious of a teen who is pregnant with her second child. Commenting on Aria's predicament, Jones told Kerry Lengel for the *Arizona Republic* (May 17, 2005), "The reason people tell big lies is because the truth . . . may well devastate what they've made for themselves. I think it's kind of dishonest the way television works, where a person takes a risk or tells the truth and they're rewarded by everything working out. But the reason people don't do the right thing is because there are consequences to doing the right thing."

Like Jones's first novel, *The Untelling* garnered high praise from critics. Carrie Brown wrote in a review for the *Washington Post* (April 17, 2005), "This might be a disappointing premise for a novel, too small to engage our sensibilities in any significant way, too confined to its small, solipsistic corner of the universe. But *The Untelling* widens and deepens as it goes, becoming not just the story of one woman's regret—but a shrewd and knowing portrait of poverty, racism and the hopelessness of the oppressed and the unlucky. In the end, it is very much about what human beings do when the world turns its back on them." In 2005 *The Untelling* received the Lillian C. Smith Award for New Voices from the Southern Regional Council and the University of Georgia Libraries.

Over the last several years, Jones has dedicated much of her time to her blog, tayarijones.com, which features book reviews, event announcements, writing advice, literary recommendations, and musings on a wide range of subjects. Following the inauguration of Barack Obama as the 44th president of the United States, in January 2009, she posted a blog entry that addressed the importance of Obama's often-repeated call for change. Jones wrote, referring to the celebrations of Obama's ascendance to the White House, "We are going to have to chill with some of the boogie-oogie-oogie and start thinking about the change we want in the world. Yesterday, I was in a store and an older black man said to me, 'Obama has done his job just by getting elected. That's all I need. To see him in the White House with his wife, and those pretty babies. That's all I need.' All around him, people nodded in agreement. . . . Well, that's not all I need and it's not all America needs. . . . As writers, we all dream of losing the day job and doing our writing full time. But can we ever do it as long as health insurance remains tied to employment? Even if you could make enough from your writing to pay your bills, you probably wouldn't make enough to take care of your health. . . . 46 million Americans are without health insurance. This must be our top priority when we think about Change."

Jones lives in northern New Jersey. She is currently an assistant professor in the graduate creative-writing program at Rutgers University, Newark, where she has taught since 2007. Jones has also taught at Prairie View A&M University, East Tennessee State University, the University of Illinois, and George Washington University. She has received grants and fellowships from institutions including the Illinois Arts Council, the Bread Loaf Writers Conference, the Corporation of Yaddo, the MacDowell Colony, the Arizona Commission on the Arts, and Le Chateau de Lavigny International Writers Colony, in Switzerland.

—C.C.

Suggested Reading: *Arizona Republic* E p3 Sep. 19, 2002, E p1 July 7, 2003, E p1 May 17, 2005; *Atlanta Journal-Constitution* p3 Oct. 3, 2002; (Bergen County, New Jersey) *Record* E p1 Jan. 4, 2004; tayarijones.com

Selected Books: *Leaving Atlanta*, 2002; *The Untelling*, 2005

Vince Bucci/Getty Images

Jones, Van

1968– Lawyer; writer; civil rights and environmental activist

Address: c/o All-American Speakers Bureau, 4717 Knights Arm Dr., Durham, NC 27707-9089

Van Jones is "the Martin Luther King of the green-jobs movement," Gary Kaplan, the executive director of a job-training agency in Boston, Massachusetts, told Elizabeth Kolbert for the *New Yorker* (January 12, 2009). From September 2007 to March 2009 Jones, an attorney, writer, and activist, served as the founding president of Green for All, a national environmental-justice organization "dedicated to building an inclusive green economy strong enough to lift people out of poverty," as stated on the organization's Web site. Through Green for All Jones worked with activists, organizations, policymakers, and business, labor, and community leaders to establish programs to train low-income and minority members of society for "green-collar jobs"—blue-collar jobs that are environmentally sound. As a result of Jones's work, in 2007 Oakland, California, became the first city in the nation to fund the creation of a Green Job Corps, which trains unemployed city residents for jobs connected with building a "green" economy.

Jones's founding of Green for All and his work toward environmental justice grew out of his earlier social-justice efforts. In 1995 he established the Bay Area Police Watch to monitor the conduct of officers in Oakland and San Francisco, California. The following year he renamed the organization the Ella Baker Center for Human Rights, broadened its mission to include all civil rights issues, and began focusing on steering urban youth away from negative influences in their communities and toward education and good jobs. While working at the Ella Baker Center, Jones began to view environmental degradation and urban poverty as interconnected problems. Although environmentalist movements have traditionally been dominated by whites and white-collar workers, many studies had shown that pollution and environmental degradation disproportionately affect low-income members of society, particularly urban blacks; those groups suffer more than others from pollution-induced ailments, including cancer and asthma, often live in neighborhoods that are near power plants, factories, sewage-treatment facilities, or garbage-disposal sites, and often lack access to parks, sources of healthful foods, and job opportunities. Those groups are also less likely to be concerned with or able to afford environmental innovations (energy-efficient light bulbs or solar panels, for example). In October 2008 Jones published *The Green Collar Economy: How One Solution Can Fix Our Two Biggest Problems*, which became a *New York Times* best-seller.

In March 2009 Jones was tapped to join the administration of President Barack Obama as a special adviser on the White House's Council on Environmental Quality. In that position—which he called that of a "green-jobs handyman"—he was charged with developing policy recommendations to help create clean-energy jobs. A few months into his tenure, Jones came under attack from congressional Republicans and conservative pundits for his controversial past associations and statements. In particular, they pointed to his past support for Marxist groups and his disparaging comments about congressional Republicans, which they characterized as "extremist," "coarse," and "incendiary." On September 6, 2009 Jones announced that despite having been "inundated with calls from across the political spectrum urging me to stay and fight," he was resigning from his White House post to avoid becoming a distraction to the Obama administration. According to the Web site VanJones.net, the environmental proposals supported by Jones while he worked in the White House "are in various stages of review and implementation."

Anthony "Van" Jones and his twin sister, Angela, were born in 1968 in Jackson, Tennessee, a small town about 90 miles east of Memphis. His father was the principal of a junior high school, and his mother was a high-school teacher. His grandfather was the leader of the local Methodist Episcopal Church, and Jones often accompanied him to religious conferences. Jones told Kolbert that as a child he was "bookish and bizarre," and his sister added that Jones was "the stereotypical geek—he just kind of lived up in his head a lot." As a boy, when Jones received action figures of Luke Skywalker and Han Solo, characters from the *Star Wars* films, he played with them by pretending that they were running for public office. After graduating from high school, Jones enrolled at the University of Tennessee at Martin. He changed his name the first day of his freshman year, having decided that "Anthony Jones" was too dull. He chose the first name "Van" because "it has a little touch of nobility, but at the same time, it's not overboard," as he told Kolbert. Hoping to become a journalist, Jones majored in communications and political science. During his time at the university, Jones founded several student newspapers, with the goal of building a network of black college students in Tennessee. According to the Web site of Ashoka, an organization devoted to what it calls social entrepreneurship, Jones's college journalism work "took him to Louisiana, where he saw racism and poverty as he had never seen before. He knew then that, to achieve the kind of change he wanted, he would have to be more than a writer." Additionally, internships at a few newspapers convinced him that a career in journalism was not for him. After graduating, in 1990, and serving an internship with the Tennessee state legislature, he enrolled at Yale Law School, in New Haven, Connecticut.

During his years at Yale, Jones witnessed events that helped to shape his worldview and further spurred him to activism. In March 1991, during his second semester, he was particularly disturbed by the infamous police beating of Rodney King, an African-American who, while intoxicated, was pulled over for speeding by Los Angeles police officers. When he resisted arrest, the officers violently subdued him, first with a Taser and then with repeated baton beatings. A bystander captured the event on video camera, and a portion of the footage was broadcast nationally. Jones had taken a semester off from law school and was working as an intern for the Lawyers' Committee for Civil Rights (LCCR) in San Francisco when, in April 1992, a jury whose members included no blacks acquitted the four officers charged with police brutality in the King case. The acquittal sparked widespread outrage, leading to a week of violence and mayhem that became known as the Los Angeles Riots of 1992. Jones, who observed those events for the LCCR, was arrested during the riots, along with many other young men, most of them members of minority groups. His arrest incident underscored for him that African-American men were often victims of wrongful arrest and police abuse. Jones had witnessed similar injustices in New Haven. "I was seeing kids at Yale do drugs and talk about it openly, and have nothing happen to them, or, if anything, get sent to rehab," Jones told Kolbert. "And then I was seeing kids three blocks away, in the housing projects, doing the same drugs, in smaller amounts, go to prison."

After graduating from law school, Jones moved to San Francisco, where in 1995 he founded the Bay Area Police Watch. That group used computer software in an attempt to track unjust practices on the part of officers and precincts and make the information available to lawyers, watchdog groups, and the media. Jones's organization soon received up to 15 complaints per day on its police-misconduct hotline, from residents of San Francisco and neighboring Oakland. In 1996 the Bay Area Police Watch expanded its focus to become a civil rights organization, renamed the Ella Baker Center for Human Rights, in honor of the activist who had pressured the national Democratic Party to confront racial discrimination and, in 1957, helped found the Southern Christian Leadership Conference. One of the center's main goals was to help youths avoid prison and secure good jobs. Through news conferences and sit-ins or other public demonstrations, the center also worked to publicize and protest police and government violations of civil rights.

The first major case the center took on was that of Aaron Williams, a young black man who on June 4, 1995 was arrested for burglary after a violent struggle with San Francisco officers and died while in police custody. Reading a news account of the incident, Jones noticed the name of one of the officers involved in it: Marc Andaya. "At the time I read that story, I had a file several inches thick sitting in my cabinet on Marc Andaya," he told Ken Garcia for the *San Francisco Chronicle* (March 12, 1998), "and when I saw his name in connection with the Aaron Williams death, I made a commitment to myself that I was not going to rest until people knew about this police officer and his record." In 1984 Andaya had shot to death a person whom Jones described to Garcia as a "mentally ill, unarmed black man"; the following year Andaya had been suspended for 30 days for choking a handcuffed suspect; and in 1993 the Oakland Police Citizens Review Board judged that Andaya had used excessive force and racial slurs against an African-American suspect. He had been hired by the San Francisco Police Department in 1994. At the Police Commission disciplinary hearing concerning Williams's death, several witnesses testified to having seen Andaya kick Williams in the head after he was subdued. The charges of police brutality were dismissed, however, when a medical examiner concluded that Williams, a crack-cocaine abuser, had died not from the beating he received from officers but from a heart attack triggered by drugs. Thanks to Jones's efforts to publicize Andaya's record, pressure mounted, mainly from the African-American community, to oust the officer. In 1997 Andaya was fired for lying on his police application about his previous record. For his advocacy work, Jones was honored with a Next Generation Leadership Fellowship from the Rockefeller Foundation and a Reebok Human Rights Award.

In another major accomplishment, the Ella Baker Center prevented an expansion of California's sprawling juvenile-incarceration system. In 2000 Jones learned about a state plan to construct a 540-bed juvenile-detention center in Alameda County, which would have been one of the largest facilities of its kind in the nation. Though the project was presented to the public as a way to improve conditions for young offenders, he saw it as a step that would inevitably lead to many more black teenagers' being incarcerated. Jones began a campaign to stop the construction of the center, using the tag line, "Stop the Superjail." He organized demonstrations involving local teenagers, and the public-awareness campaign worked: in 2003 the construction plans for the center were halted.

For Jones, that triumph was tarnished by what he feared was the selfishness of his motivation for community activism. "I certainly wasn't motivated only by love for the people," he told Kolbert. "I was trying to find some kind of community, or some sense of belonging, or some sense of redemption through heroic deeds. I wasn't being honest with myself about it, and it all just proved to be incredibly fragile." One day Jones attended a lecture at a San Francisco bookstore by Julia "Butterfly" Hill, the environmental activist best known for living in the canopy of a 600-year-old California redwood tree, from December 1997 to December 1999, to prevent Pacific Lumber Co. loggers from cutting it down. Hill saved the tree and later founded a nonprofit organization called Circle of Life. "There was no guarantee she was going to win . . . ," Jones told Kolbert. "I was always looking for clever things I could game out, and she just stepped out on faith, and did it. . . . I wanted to do my work like she had done her work." Jones was also amazed that Hill had felt no bitterness toward those who had opposed her efforts. Jones and Hill became friends and, realizing that they shared similar goals, began delivering lectures together. Hill told Kolbert about Jones, "We fit together like pieces of a puzzle. I brought the piece that we are not separate from this planet. His piece was we need to uplift everyone." "We could see underneath all of it was the idea of disposability," Jones told Kolbert. "The idea that you've got disposable people, a disposable planet."

Jones suggested that the Ella Baker Center work to link civil rights and environmentalism, which he saw as related issues. By involving the poor and minorities—the groups most affected by pollution, excluded from the benefits of technological advances, and in need of jobs—in the environmental movement and training them for jobs "greening" the infrastructure of the U.S., Jones believed that he could address three societal problems at once: poverty, racial inequality, and environmental degradation. His plan was to create a Green Job Corps in Oakland that would train poor and underserved city residents for such jobs as weatherizing buildings and constructing and installing solar panels. Though Jones's suggestion to expand the scope of the Ella Baker Center was not popular among the group's board members, who deemed it unrealistic, he began speaking to environmental organizations and applying for grant money to bring green jobs to Oakland. In 2004 Jones received $215,000 from the New York–based Nathan Cummings Foundation, which he used to fund organizational meetings and retreats. Jones was disappointed, however, when no jobs resulted from all his planning. He applied for and received another $215,000 grant from the foundation, which he again spent on planning meetings and research. Feeling as though he had wasted time and money, Jones realized that changing public policy was the only way he was going to bring green jobs to Oakland.

In February 2007 Jones was invited to a roundtable discussion of global climate change hosted by one of San Francisco's representatives in Congress, House Speaker Nancy Pelosi. Because the invitation specified that each guest was to deliver a brief self-introduction, Jones tried to be as succinct as possible, but as other invitees stood up and introduced themselves with lengthy speeches describing their work and goals, Jones realized he had missed an opportunity to articulate his vision. When Pelosi asked for questions at the end of the meeting, after which there was to be a press conference, Jones said, as quoted by Derrick Z. Jackson in the *Boston Globe* (September 29, 2007), "My question is, at the press conference, will you say four words?" He asked Pelosi to say the words, "Clean Energy Jobs Bill." Jones then launched into an engaging oration, asking Pelosi and all of the invitees to support the passage of a bill to provide funding for the creation of jobs that would contribute to a clean-energy economy. At the press conference Pelosi commended Jones's idea and stated that everyone at the roundtable meeting had agreed that a clean-energy jobs bill should be introduced in Congress.

Pelosi's endorsement inspired local and national support for bills that linked the creation of jobs for minorities with the quest for a green economy. Jones helped form the Oakland Apollo Alliance, a coalition of labor unions and environmentalists that seeks green-collar jobs in Oakland. In June 2007 Oakland became the first city in the nation to pass a law creating a Green Job Corps, a program geared toward building a green economy. The Oakland city government provided $250,000 to the Green Job Corps to create a program to train unemployed residents for jobs in such areas as solar energy, organic food, and wind power. They were also trained to bring existing buildings up to the energy-efficiency standards required by California state law. The first class of 40 graduated from the program in 2007. Jones sees those jobs as valuable because they rely on local labor and, therefore, cannot be outsourced. "You can't take a building you want to weatherize, put it on a ship to China and then have them do it and send it back . . . ," Jones told Thomas L. Friedman for the *New York Times* (October 17, 2007). "Those green-collar jobs can provide a pathway out of poverty for someone who has not gone to college." Also in June 2007 then–U.S. representative Hilda Solis of California (now the U.S. secretary of labor) introduced a measure authorizing the U.S. Department of Labor to spend $125 million to train low-income workers for green jobs. The bill, called the Green Jobs Act, was put under the umbrella of the Energy Independence and Security Act, approved by Congress and signed into law by President George W. Bush in December 2007. While Bush's 2009 budget proposal not only lacked funds for the act but also cut or eliminated money allocated for a range of existing job-training programs, the economic stimulus package passed by Congress in early 2009 and the budget proposed by President Obama in late February set aside billions of dollars for greening the economy.

In September 2007, while remaining the president of the Ella Baker Center, Jones founded Green for All, a national organization aimed at promoting green jobs and environmental justice. He partnered with other organizations with similar goals, including the New York City–based environmental-justice organization Sustainable South Bronx and the American Council on Renewable Energy (ACORE); he delivered many lectures throughout the U.S. to raise public awareness of the potential for green-collar jobs to transform the economy. Jones advocated banning the construction of new coal plants, establishing a national Clean Energy Corps, creating incentives to trade in traditional cars for hybrid cars, and establishing a loan program for "emergency efficiency measures." In October 2008 Jones published *The Green Collar Economy: How One Solution Can Fix Our Two Biggest Problems*, which makes the case for improving the failing U.S. economy and a damaged environment by investing in green-collar jobs. The book became a *New York Times* best-seller and was generally praised, though some critics contrasted Jones's considerable gifts as a public speaker with his workmanlike prose.

Many have questioned the premise of Jones's argument that combating climate change is a good way to lift people out of poverty. For instance, some economists have expressed doubts that the alternative-energy industry would provide more jobs than the number that would be lost in industries such as coal-mining; others question whether a green economy would succeed in providing permanent jobs for the chronically unemployed, a historically difficult task. Matthew Kahn, an economics professor at the Institute of the Environment of the University of California at Los Angeles (UCLA), is among those who have asked whether environmentally oriented public-works programs would be any better run than their traditional counterparts, which have often proven to be inefficient. According to Jones, the way to avoid such pitfalls is to make sure the plan pursues both goals: providing jobs for the poor and creating a greener society. "You can pass all the bills you want to; you can appropriate all the bills you want to," Jones told Kolbert. "You can even start retrofitting buildings. But if I go there and the people who are doing the retrofits are just the people who used to have the jobs anyway, and they're mostly all one color and mostly all one kind of people, then I'm not going to be satisfied."

Jones's ideas soon received support from many Democratic legislators, including Senate majority leader Harry Reid; several dozen governors; and more than 900 U.S. mayors, who expressed their support by signing the U.S. Conference of Mayors' Climate Protection Agreement. In Barack Obama's first months in the White House, the president expressed his support for the allocation of $15 billion per year on renewable energy, weatherization for low-income housing, and carbon-capture and -storage projects. In March 2009 Obama hired Jones as a special adviser for green jobs, enterprise, and innovation in the White House's Council on Environmental Quality. (That month Phaedra Ellis-Lamkins became the chief executive officer of Green for All.) During the six months he held his position in the administration, Jones focused on improving the energy efficiency of Americans' homes. According to VanJones.net, "Toward this end, he led a 12-Department inter-agency process, which designed proposals to weatherize and retrofit millions of American homes, including by leveraging private capital." Jones also headed an interagency group to help Democrats better implement the stimulus programs contained in the American Recovery and Reinvestment Act of February 2009; he worked to tailor the stimulus programs to address the needs of minorities and rural Americans.

Jones had been with the Obama White House for only a few months when he came under attack by conservative pundits, especially the Fox News analyst Glenn Beck, and several congressional Republicans, regarding several of his past associations and statements. Jones was criticized for signing a 2004 petition, sponsored by the controversial 9/11 Truth Movement, calling for an investigation into the actions of President George W. Bush with respect to the September 11, 2001 terrorist attacks; for using a derogatory word to describe congressional Republicans during a speech he delivered a month before he was appointed to his federal position; and for his association in the 1990s with a neo-Marxist organization called Standing Together to Organize a Revolutionary Movement. In the summer of 2009, Color of Change, an Internet-based advocacy organization that Jones co-founded in 2005 with James Rucker, formerly of MoveOn.org, initiated a boycott of Glenn Beck's show after Beck accused Obama of harboring a "deep-seated hatred for white people"; the boycott resulted in several companies' pulling ads from his show. In response to the boycott, Beck stepped up his criticisms, calling on Jones to resign. Congressional Republicans followed suit; Representative Mike Pence of Indiana was widely quoted as calling for Jones's resignation because "his extremist views and coarse rhetoric have no place in this administration or the public debate." As criticism from the right heightened, Jones defended his record and apologized for some of his past statements.

On September 6, 2009 Jones announced his resignation. "On the eve of historic fights for health care and clean energy, opponents of reform have mounted a vicious smear campaign against me," he said in a statement, as quoted on KTVU.com (September 6, 2009). "They are using lies and distortions to distract and divide." Jones stated, however, that he did not want the administration's efforts to defend his record to interfere with the president's agenda. That sentiment was echoed by the White House press secretary Robert Gibbs, who stated, "What Van Jones decided was that the agenda of this president was bigger than any one individual." The seeming reluctance of the administration to defend Jones angered many of Jones's supporters, who thought that his resignation served to legitimize what they called the false and distorted claims advanced by conservatives. "The Obama Administration should have acted like the victors they are and made sure Van Jones stayed just where he was," John McWhorter wrote for the *New Republic* (September 7, 2009, on-line). "I understand that Obama can't rule as the outright lefty many of his fans would prefer. But Jones' presence was a laudable representation of progressivism in the Administration. . . . If the Obama folks are going to throw even people like this off the train just because some silly people make some silly noises, then the bloom really is off the rose." Since he left the administration, Jones has reportedly been working in an office lent to him by the progressive Washington, D.C., think tank the Center for American Progress, where he previously served as a senior fellow; he does not have a salaried position there.

Jones has served on the boards of organizations including the National Apollo Alliance, Social Venture Network, Rainforest Action Network, Bioneers, and Circle of Life. His honors include the International Ashoka Fellowship, the World Economic Forum's Young Global Leader Award, the Paul Wellstone Award from the progressive think tank Campaign for America's Future, the Aspen Institute Energy and Environment Award in the category of individual thought leadership, and the Hubert H. Humphrey Civil Rights Award.

Jones is "tall and imposing, with a shaved head and a patchy goatee," Kolbert wrote. "He wears rimless glasses and favors dark clothing." A talented public speaker, Jones is known for his ability to relate to audiences ranging from unemployed urban youth to business and political leaders. "Green values are very consistent with African and indigenous values in the first place," he told Alwin Jones for *Black Enterprise* (May 2008). "Western society is coming back around to values that were and are a part of our core, our heritage, our history. We shouldn't think about it as jumping on a white bandwagon because it's our bandwagon in the first place." Jones lives in Oakland with his wife, Jana Carter, an employment lawyer, and their two young sons.

—M.E.R.

Suggested Reading: *Black Enterprise* p51 May 2008; *In These Times* p45 Jan. 2009; *New Republic* (on-line) Sep. 7, 2009; *New York Times* A p27 Oct. 17, 2007, (on-line) Mar. 10, 2009; *New Yorker* p22 Jan. 12, 2009; *San Francisco Chronicle* B p1 Oct. 27, 2008, (on-line) Mar. 10, 2009; VanJones.net

Selected Books: *The Green Collar Economy: How One Solution Can Fix Our Two Biggest Problems*, 2008

Courtesy of Michael Kamber

Kamber, Michael

Sep. 24, 1963– Photojournalist

Address: New York Times, *Photo Dept., 229 W. 43d St., New York, NY 10036*

Michael Kamber stands out even among the world's best photojournalists, not only because he has been nominated for the Pulitzer Prize three times—once for reporting and twice for photography—but also because he is one of the few photojournalists who also write full-length articles, some of which have appeared on the front page of the *New York Times*. In the last 20 years, he has reported from Haiti, Pakistan, Afghanistan, Mexico, Iraq, Israel, Somalia, Sudan, Kenya, Liberia, and the Ivory Coast. Before he decided to dedicate himself fully to photography, Kamber—who is mostly self-taught—worked as a mechanic and construction worker and attended art school for a year. Since September 2003, the beginning of his career as a foreign correspondent for the *Times*, Kamber has been embedded with U.S. Army forces in Iraq 30 to 40 times (he has lost count), occasionally for as long as a month. He has gone with the troops into streets, houses, military vehicles, and battlefields, documenting the soldiers' emotions, injuries, and deaths. In addition to taking photos and writing stories, he has narrated photo slideshows and shot video footage for the *Times* Web site. "Most [military] units want Americans to know what's going on . . . and they want the press coverage, because they feel like they're there fighting this war and nobody's paying attention, and they want people to know what they're going through," Kamber told *Current Biography*, the source of quotes for this article, unless otherwise noted. But he also acknowledged that many soldiers are "very suspicious" of the *New York Times*. The soldiers are "mostly working class, conservative guys from the South," he said. "They watch Fox News and they think the *New York Times* is the party organ of the Communist Party, and they'll tell you that." During one period of being embedded with a unit in Mosul, in northern Iraq, Kamber and a few other reporters received an impromptu talk from a sergeant major who, while casually holding a gun, told them, "I don't like the media. I don't trust the media. I'm tired of hearing negative stories. I want to see some positive stories." Kamber is used to such sentiments. But he also hears encouraging comments, such as, "I know you don't have to be here. We appreciate you risking your life to be out here with us." Whenever soldiers or commanders engage him in conversation, Kamber explains that the *Times* does not tell him which kinds of stories or photos to submit—that he merely reports what he sees. "There's good days and bad days," he said, "and everything in between."

Michael Kamber was born in Brunswick, Maine, on September 24, 1963. His parents, who were divorced, moved around a lot, and Kamber lived alternately with his father, a professor of foreign languages, and his mother, who was a photojournalist for a few years in the late 1960s; by the time he was 16, he had lived in New Jersey, New York, and Ohio. But he would always return to Maine. His mother's photos stayed at her apartment, and Kamber, especially when he was growing up, would often take them from her cabinets and examine them closely. He recalled one series of photographs that depicted a mental institution in Maine where patients were chained to the floor and forced to endure other forms of terrible treatment. After the photos were published in the *Maine Times*, the state began investigating the institution. "She did a couple of big exposés," Kamber said of his mother. "That kind of stayed with me as I grew up. It kind of gave me the idea of journalism and photography."

Kamber got his first camera at age 12 and began taking pictures of urban and natural landscapes. Two years later he built a darkroom. Although his parents did not discourage him from pursuing his passion, they did not really encourage him, either. Other adults simply told him that it was unrealistic to think he could make a living as a photographer. His peers had a different attitude. "My childhood friends knew me as a photographer," Kamber said. He admired the work of Edward Weston and Ansel Adams. At that time he was not consciously interested in photojournalism or even in photographing people; though he did not realize it, some of the shots he admired were outstanding works of photojournalism, including pictures documenting the civil rights struggle and the war in Vietnam.

Kamber had another passion: like many high-school students in Maine, he was obsessed with cars, and he loved to drag race in his '67 Ford Mustang. When he was 16 he moved to Asbury Park, New Jersey (a town made famous by Bruce Springsteen's 1973 debut album), where he continued his high-school education and worked as a mechanic part-time. Asbury Park was a "depressed town," Kamber said. "It was falling apart. A lot of vacant storefronts. And the guys I worked with were miserable." Whatever college plans Kamber may have had were put on hold after the owner of the body shop told him, "I'll train you as a master re-builder if you hold off on college for a year. I'll give you a raise and promote you." Kamber agreed, working as a mechanic until he was 22, when he decided to give college a try.

Kamber moved to New York City in 1985 and enrolled at the Parsons School of Design, where he studied photography, with a focus on photojournalism. Within a year he ran out of money and dropped out. Although he continued taking photos and trying to get them published, he made most of his money as a construction worker. New York in the late 1980s saw a lot of crime, poverty, political demonstrations, drug activity, and racial tension; on nights and weekends, when he was not doing construction work, Kamber would go out with his camera to document those events and phenomena.

Around 1987 an editor of a small magazine in Boston, *Z*, said that he would publish Kamber's photos if Kamber wrote the story to accompany them. Kamber agreed; he had liked writing in high school and felt equal to the challenge. "I basically faked my way though it," he said. "I just copied the *New York Times* style." The editor liked Kamber's story and asked him to write another article with his next batch of photos.

Also in 1987 Kamber and a fellow photographer—both of them young, ambitious, and desiring an extraordinary experience—decided to go to Haiti in time for the election that was about to take place there. (From 1957 to 1986 the Duvalier family ruled the country as brutal dictators. By early 1986, when Jean-Claude Duvalier was ousted, the country was in turmoil: street violence and other signs of unrest were ubiquitous.) Until then Kamber had never traveled outside the U.S. "It's a shock," Kamber said of his first impressions of Haiti. "People are living in mud huts, scrounging for food—no signs of modern life. And the violence! It's an eye-opener when you first go. I'm not sure that I had ever seen a dead person before, and there were just bodies on the street." The government's military leaders did not want the election to proceed because they saw democracy as a threat. As a result Election Day brought a great deal of violence. "They killed little kids," Kamber recalled. "Young girls hacked to death with machetes." On the morning of the election, Kamber was walking along a street when he saw a corpse. After staring at it, astonished, he reached for his camera and started taking photos. "I didn't really understand the danger," he said. Taking his time and oblivious to his surroundings, he initially did not notice "a car full of guys with guns" pull up next to him. The men stuck their guns out of the car window as if to shoot him, then talked among themselves and drove away. "A bunch of other journalists were shot that day," Kamber recalled. "I don't know why they didn't shoot me."

Upon his return to New York, Kamber sold some of his photographs to *Z* and another small publication. He went back to taking photos of street life, and soon wire services such as Reuters and the Associated Press started buying his photos. His goal was to break into the *Village Voice*, the nation's largest alternative weekly newspaper. He eventually started freelancing for the *Voice*, taking pictures mostly of the city's immigrants, political protests, and the homeless. The grittiness Kamber captured in his photos was also a reality in his neighborhood, the city's South Bronx area, which was very poor, violent, and drug-infested, and Kamber photographed everything he could. "Not that it was all negative," he said. "Some of it was positive. I used to photograph on Sunday mornings. Girls would be going to church in white dresses. There was a lot of nice stuff, too." The South Bronx was, and remains, heavily Hispanic, and Kamber picked up conversational Spanish—which came in handy a few years later.

Kamber quit his construction job in 1990 to dedicate himself to photography full-time. He continued freelancing for the *Village Voice*, and to supplement his income, he did commercial photography—portraits, ads, and coverage of various events and government-sponsored projects. While his financial situation improved, by 1998 he had had enough of such work and wanted to leave the U.S. for a while. In part because he had a cousin who worked in Mexico City, Mexico, Kamber went there and started taking photos for the *Village Voice* and various Web sites. He reported on poverty, politics, bullfighting, and almost anything else he encountered. While in Mexico Kamber became more and more interested in the villages that men had left to work in the United States. Through some research he found Zapotitlán, a village of mostly women and children (the men were working in the Bronx and sending money home). Kamber moved to Zapotitlán, where every day for two months he talked to the villagers about their lives. "People lived in huts made out of kindling wood," he recalled, "and once people started sending back thousands and thousands of dollars from the U.S., it completely transformed life there. New houses were going up every day." (The new houses were built by poor Mexican men from farther south who had not immigrated to New York.)

After leaving the village Kamber spent two months on the U.S.-Mexico border. He would tag along with Mexican men as they tried to cross the border illegally. Sometimes the men would get turned away, but they would try again. Back in New York Kamber spent time with Mexican immigrants. His three-part story of Mexicans' lives in Zapotitlán, on the U.S.–Mexico border, and in New York, for which he took the photos and wrote the text, ran in the *Village Voice* in 2001 and later earned him the Columbia University Graduate School of Journalism Mike Berger Award.

A few weeks after the September 11, 2001 terrorist attacks on the U.S., the *Village Voice* sent Kamber to write and take photos in Pakistan; that country borders Afghanistan, which had given refuge to Al Qaeda, the group that had planned the attacks. It turned out to be a "rough trip," Kamber said. He did not have a satellite phone or enough money for transportation and local guides. His situation might have been easier if he had had months to write one long story, but he was expected to send back photos and a story every week. In Pakistan Kamber experienced not only violence and political instability but fervent anti-Americanism. He also fell ill, losing 30 pounds because of intestinal problems. Worst of all, some of his colleagues were killed.

The most high-profile piece Kamber filed from Pakistan was a cover story for the *Village Voice* (October 16, 2001) with the headline "Why They Hate Us." He had spent weeks talking to Pakistanis of many tribal, religious, and economic backgrounds about their opinions of the United States and of the 2001 terrorist attacks. Speaking about U.S.–Pakistani relations "with a mixture of sadness and hostility," the Pakistanis complained about what they considered to be insufficient support of Pakistan's battles with India (primarily in the Kashmir region); what they saw as unfair sanctions imposed by the U.S. on Pakistan in 1998, after the country's nuclear tests; and what they viewed as unconditional U.S. support for Israel. "To me, the [attack on New York's World Trade Center] seems the design of the Jewish lobby," one aged mullah told Kamber. "The Jewish lobby wants to pit Islam against Christianity. American Jews want to remove the Taliban from Afghanistan, because the Taliban are the true representative of Islam. They did this as an excuse. How do you explain the 5,000 Jews that worked at the World Trade Center that called [in] sick that day?" With regard to the latter claim, the mullah said that he believed it to be true because he had read it in "many newspapers." In his article Kamber wrote that the mullah's views may have seemed extreme to Western readers but were not seen that way in Pakistan. "And his criticism of Israel and American Jews," Kamber wrote, "is echoed all over Pakistan in only slightly more reserved tones."

Kamber and his journalist companions spent three months in Pakistan trying to get into Afghanistan. Eventually they managed to hire drivers. After crossing the border Kamber noticed armed men on the road waving at his car, telling him to stop. His driver slowed down, pretending that he was about to stop, and then quickly took off, raising a large cloud of dust. "I looked back as we drove," Kamber recalled, "and there was unbelievable dust there, so it was very hard to see. I saw them run out and point their weapons, but they didn't shoot. Maybe they heard the other car coming." Behind Kamber was a car with four journalists—Spanish, Italian, Australian, and Afghan. After they stopped at the ad hoc checkpoint, they were all shot.

By his own account, Kamber has gotten used to being in such situations, which he described as triggering "pure fear." Yet he acknowledged that he experiences "a rush" afterward. "People shooting guns at you, that's exciting," he said, lightly laughing, adding that when he survives a brush with death, he "appreciates life a bit more." But sometimes, he said, he becomes inured to the danger, fear, and excitement. "Maybe I'm not as exhilarated as I used to be. I just find it fearful and not fun."

After the *Wall Street Journal* reporter Daniel Pearl—who was known by his captors to be Jewish—was murdered by terrorists in Pakistan after being taken hostage, Kamber wrote a short piece for the *Jewish Journal* (March 14, 2002) in which he recounted his own experience in Pakistan: "I returned in December from reporting for the *Village Voice* from Pakistan, exhausted from being stoned, punched and chased by Islamic fundamentalists. I was burned out—and burned literally—from being pushed into one too many burning George Bush effigies, weary from having to repeatedly explain that Americans do not hate Muslims, and that 'no, it's not true that we enjoy seeing dead Afghan children on television.'" He then discussed his experience of being identified as an American: "Word spread that a Westerner was in the crowd and people became agitated; stones and fists flew my way before my hosts pulled me to safety. These were times you wanted to crawl out of your skin, pretend you were someone else. I tried to buy a fake passport that listed my citizenship as Canadian. Journalists routinely lied when asked if they were American. Guides and interpreters introduced their American clients as Swiss or French." Kamber, whose father is Jewish, always denied any Jewish heritage when asked about it in Pakistan. "To admit to being Jewish in such a climate would have been unthinkable," he wrote. "On occasion, people asked me point-blank if I was Jewish. I denied it, listing instead my polyglot background."

In addition to his work for the *Village Voice*, Kamber started freelancing for the *New York Times*'s Metro section. In late 2002 the *Times* asked Kamber to go to West Africa as a full-time photographer. Since he was not married and his daughter was no longer a child, and he had no other commitments holding him back, in January 2003 he traveled to the Ivory Coast. The *Times* editors "wanted stories about things that are good, about peace, about what's successful," he recalled. "But when we [he and another *Times* reporter] got there, there were all these wars raging, so inevitably I just photographed the wars." Kamber and his colleague, based in the Ivory Coast, also reported from Liberia, Congo, and Nigeria. Kamber spent a few weeks at each location, often interviewing and photographing fighters on the front lines. He was frequently in dangerous situations but avoided getting shot by taking photos from behind concrete walls and staying close to the ground. Some of the journalists he was with—writers and photographers for other major publications and news services—did get hurt, and some were killed. Kamber and the French photojournalist Patrick Robert covered an intense battle between government troops and rebels in Liberia; Kamber and Robert followed the government troops over a bridge on an offensive as hundreds of soldiers were firing automatic rifles and rocket-propelled grenades. Kamber was taking photos from behind a concrete wall when he noticed Robert running out to the street to get a better photographic angle. Robert was immediately shot in the abdomen. Kamber and his fellow journalists ran out and dragged Robert behind the concrete wall. After trying to stop the bleeding, they carried him across the bridge, which was "hard when you're under that much gunfire," Kamber casually admitted. They eventually got a truck and took him to a hospital. Robert survived but lost a lot of blood and a kidney.

Kamber returned to New York in August 2003. A month later, on the strength of the photographic skill and ability to navigate war zones he had demonstrated in Africa, the *Times* sent him to Iraq. (He has been primarily a war and armed-conflict photographer ever since.) In the fall of 2003, a few months after the U.S. invasion, Baghdad, Iraq's capital, was still relatively peaceful. "We would walk downtown and have a kabob," Kamber recalled. "People would say hello to you on the street." After three months in Iraq, Kamber returned to New York. Since then he has gone back to Iraq many times and has also reported from Israel, Haiti, and Africa, witnessing many scenes of violence and cruelty. On the one hand, he suggested, those experiences can have a demoralizing effect. "You realize that man's capacity for violence is just extraordinary," he said. "Once the social strictures break down, people just go crazy; they just begin raping, pillaging, and looting as quickly as they can." On the other hand, Kamber found that in desperate times, some people go out of their way to help others, even people they do not know. He recalled seeing an old woman, lying in a hospital bed in Haiti, who sold her jewelry so that the man in the next bed—a stranger—could get money for lifesaving medicine.

Kamber reported from Israel and Gaza (the Palestinian territory to the south) for a few months in 2006. He found his stay there frustrating; although he faced less physical danger than he had in war zones, he also had to endure a lot of control and manipulation of the media from both sides of the region's conflict—the Israeli army, as representative of the nation's government, and the sociopolitical Palestinian organization Hamas. "Both sides were experts at dealing with the media," Kamber said. "I felt like it was very hard to get anything real." The Israeli army and Hamas would each stage photo ops to look like news events, he said. Kamber offered an example from each side. In 2006 a colleague of his took photos of Israeli soldiers walking out of Lebanon just as the sun was coming up, carrying one lightly wounded soldier while singing a patriotic song. (The army would leak such locations to photographers ahead of time so the photographers would know where to set up their equipment.) Kamber was immediately skeptical of the scene, because the army normally transports wounded soldiers via helicopter. "So rather than airlift him out in a chopper, they carry him out for the cameras," he said, because such an image is "very dramatic." That photo, taken by one of Kamber's colleagues, ran on the front page of the *New York Times*. In Gaza, a Hamas member would bring Kamber to a house, gather many insurgents, and have them stand with guns, wearing masks, chanting slogans in front of a flag. "It's a set-up. It's like a photo shoot," Kamber said. "But if you want to be out on the street photographing what's really going on, it's difficult."

It was also difficult to do so in Iraq, where the U.S. military started to impose stricter media control as the war progressed. During one period of being embedded with troops, after Kamber took a photo of a wounded American soldier, a high-ranking public-affairs officer told the *Times* that it could not publish the photo; regulations for embedded photojournalists allowed the publication of photos of "identifiable" wounded Americans only with the soldiers' written permission. Because the soldier whom Kamber had photographed was temporarily blinded and immediately airlifted to Germany, he could not sign the permission form. Kamber argued that the soldier should not have been required to sign the form to begin with, since he was not identifiable in the photo—his face was bandaged. The military countered that because the faces of several noninjured soldiers and unit patches were visible in the photo, the injured soldier could be identified. Despite the Pentagon's objections, the *Times*, confident of its legal right to do so, published the photo. Kamber believes that the military's policies and American publications' self-censorship prevent the public from seeing much of the harsh reality in Iraq. "If you finance a war with your taxes and reelect a president who supports the war," Kamber said, "then you should have to look at that war once in a while. People want to vote for it, to send 18-year-old kids off, and then go about their lives as if there's nothing happening. . . . If you don't want to look at [war photographs], then maybe you should think about whether or not you want to continue [the war], because there's 27 million Iraqis that have to look at the war every day, and there's upwards of one million American soldiers that have to look at it every day."

Kamber's stories and photos from Iraq show all aspects of the war: soldiers smoking during downtime, perspiring in military vehicles in 125-degree heat, caring for their wounded, crying over killed or badly injured fellow soldiers, and fighting. Kamber has also shown the Iraqi side of the conflict: mothers and fathers grieving for children lost in the war, desperate Iraqi refugees trying to get into Syria, children hiding from exploding missiles, and other scenes of chaos, destruction, and confusion. There were also instances when Iraqis and Americans made contact in peaceful ways, such as when U.S. troops conducted "knock and talks," to get to know their neighborhoods: soldiers would knock on doors at random and politely ask to be let in, not as part of a search but to chat or drink tea.

Spending a lot of time with a unit gave Kamber an insight into soldiers' thoughts and feelings. After spending a few weeks with the 82d Airborne Division, which he called "a very hard-core, elite unit," he learned that nearly everyone in the unit was against the Iraq war. "They were completely disillusioned," he said. Many of them were on their third tours in Iraq and did not see any progress in the war effort; they also did not trust the Iraqi army, which they saw as often sabotaging, rather than contributing to, their missions. After the soldiers told Kamber, off the record, that they had lost faith in the war effort, Kamber told their commander that he wanted to write a story about the subject. The commander agreed, and the story ran on the front page of the *New York Times* in May 2007. Whenever Kamber returned to the U.S., he found it frustrating that much of the truth of the war was unknown to or ignored by the public. "You see these American soldiers put their lives on the line, going through these incredibly difficult things, seeing their friends killed, just doing the hardest job imaginable, and you come back home and nobody's paying any attention."

Two weeks after his interview with *Current Biography*, in March 2009, the *New York Times* sent Kamber to Somalia and then Pakistan and Afghanistan. He spends about nine months of each year on assignment abroad.

—D.K.

Suggested Reading: *Digital Journalist* (on-line) July 2007; *Jewish Journal* (on-line) Mar. 14, 2002; kamberphoto.com; *Village Voice* p36+ Oct. 16, 2001

Jason Merritt/Getty Images

Kennedy, Kathleen

June 5, 1953– Film producer

Address: Kennedy/Marshall Co., 619 Arizona Ave., Santa Monica, CA 90401

While shooting the blockbuster 1981 adventure film *Raiders of the Lost Ark*, Steven Spielberg asked his assistant, Kathleen Kennedy, to serve as producer for his next project. That film turned out to be *E.T.: The Extra-Terrestrial*, a story about a lovable space alien who comes to Earth and befriends a group of children. A box-office smash that reigned for over a decade as the highest-grossing movie of all time, *E.T.* was released through Amblin Entertainment, the production company that Kennedy, Spielberg, and Frank Marshall—whom Kennedy would later marry—formed in 1982. Kennedy and Marshall broke from Spielberg and started their own company a decade later, but not before helping Amblin to produce some of the biggest hits of the 1980s and '90s, including the *Back to the Future* trilogy, *Indiana Jones and the Temple of Doom*, and *Who Framed Roger Rabbit?* Leaving Amblin with Spielberg's blessing, Kennedy went on to produce the director's critically acclaimed *Schindler's List*, released in 1993, and his wildly popular *Jurassic Park* films. In all Kennedy has produced more than 60 films, with her other notable credits including the action blockbusters *Congo* and *Twister*; the Academy Award best-picture nominees *The Color Purple*, *The Sixth Sense*, *Seabiscuit*, and *Munich*; and *The Bridges of Madison County*, a love story directed by Clint Eastwood. She has also shown a willingness to make smaller, less commercial films; in 2007 she produced two art-house French-language movies, *The Diving Bell and the Butterfly* and *Persepolis*. In an interview with Michael Sragow for the *Baltimore Sun* (July 3, 2005), the producer Rick McCallum said that Kennedy "is truly one of the very few people in the business who can do it all—set up and manage the day-to-day production on her own and enjoy and relish every challenge and obstacle." Walter Parkes, an executive with the film studio DreamWorks, told Jerry Roberts for *Variety* (June 12, 1998), "There are producers who are good creatively and at developing scripts. Then there are producers who know how this town works. There are also producers who know how to make a movie. Kathy is one of the two or three producers I've ever known who can excel at doing all of those jobs." "I enjoy the process of organizing things and opening a script and saying, 'My god, how are we going to do that?'" Kennedy told Jamie Portman for the Ontario, Canada, *Pembroke Observer* (July 11, 2001). "I enjoy breaking it down and beginning the process of analyzing how we're going to execute it." Among Kennedy's recent projects was *The Curious Case of Benjamin Button* (2008).

Kathleen Kennedy was born on June 5, 1953 in Berkeley, California. (Some sources have the date as January 1, 1954.) She spent much of her childhood in Weaverville, a small town. A standout athlete, she was the quarterback of her school's football team in sixth, seventh, and eighth grades, often practicing with her identical twin sister, who played wide receiver. Kennedy also excelled at baseball, basketball, skiing, and soccer. "Sports teaches you to understand the meaning of a team," she told Sragow. "You need to be able to work with everybody; you don't have to be their best friend. You can experience the fun of competition and driving toward a common goal without pushing to bond in some major way with each individual on a project." Though those skills would later prove useful in the film industry, Kennedy initially had no interest in show business. "I didn't grow up thinking I wanted to be a film producer or even really knowing that much about movies, because where I lived they had only one movie house with only one movie a month," she told Jessie Horsting for *Fantastic Films* (September 1984). When Kennedy was 13 the family moved to Redding, California, a slightly larger town, where, she told Horsting, she discovered "that people actually made careers out of making movies."

After graduating from Shasta High School, in Redding, Kennedy enrolled at San Diego State University, where she planned to study nursing. "I decided I wanted to have a profession where I could travel anywhere in the world," she told Sragow. She was not sure she wanted to be a nurse, though, and she studied a wide range of subjects, hoping to find one that interested her. Eventually she took a broadcasting course and became involved with the campus's Public Broadcasting Service affiliate. "I'd found something that I loved enormously and was pretty good at," she said. "I suppose I was always attracted to the producing function—trying to put things together and make things happen." Kennedy also took a sociology course that allowed her to make a documentary film about prisons. "Those two experiences made me start looking at 'the media' as something I wanted to pursue, even though at that time I still hadn't really considered moviemaking as a career," she told Horsting.

In 1972, before she graduated from college, Kennedy got a job at the television station KCST, San Diego's NBC affiliate. In the five years she spent at the station, she had an opportunity to perform a number of tasks, including operating cameras at professional baseball and football games, editing videos, and producing a local talk show, *You're On*. "It was terrific," she told Horsting. "Practically every year I was doing something different, so it gave me a nice overview of the broadcasting business in general." She might have stayed in the television industry if, in 1977, she had not gone to see Spielberg's science-fiction film *Close Encounters of the Third Kind*. Kennedy was "so completely blown away that I felt I needed to participate in some way in creating something like that," she told Sragow. After seeing the movie she started looking for a way to get into the film business, and she learned from a friend, Mary Ellen Trainor, that Spielberg was in need of a production assistant for his next film, *1941*. "They might think you're overqualified, so say you just graduated from college," Trainor told Kennedy before her interview. Whether or not because of that advice, Kennedy got the job.

"At first I didn't do anything directly related with the movie," Kennedy told Horsting, describing her first couple of weeks of work on *1941*. She worked mostly in the office and had little interaction with Spielberg, until about three weeks into the project, when the director asked her to visit his house and help organize his handwritten production notes and sketches. Kennedy, who lacked skill as a typist, took Spielberg's notes back to the office, where she organized them into books. "He went on and on about these books; it was an incredible bonding experience," she told Sragow. Spielberg was so impressed with Kennedy's work that he hired her as his assistant. He also asked her to be his associate on his next film, *Raiders of the Lost Ark*, which introduced the character Indiana Jones, a globe-trotting, pistol-packing archaeologist. One of her preproduction duties was to build model trucks for use in planning the film's chase scene, and she and the producer Frank Marshall spent one Thanksgiving break gluing together plastic vehicles. "I found it incredibly frustrating; he was having a blast," she told Sragow. Kennedy and Marshall soon developed a close friendship, and by the time production work ended on *Raiders of the Lost Ark*, the two were dating. The couple kept the romance secret, however, as Marshall did not want Kennedy to face accusations that her success was due to her relationship with him.

Kennedy joined the producers of *Raiders* on location and learned a great deal about the moviemaking process. Spielberg then asked her to produce his next project. That film, *E.T.: The Extra-Terrestrial*, was released under the banner of Amblin Entertainment, the production company founded by Spielberg, Kennedy, and Marshall. At Spielberg's suggestion, the trio created the company at the end of the summer of 1982—the year that both *E.T.* and *Poltergeist*, another Kennedy-Marshall collaboration and box-office hit, were released. "I associate-produced *Poltergeist* and Frank was the production executive on *E.T.*," Kennedy told Horsting. "Frank and I work together on everything, so titles become relatively insignificant."

Kennedy earned another associate-producer credit on *Twilight Zone: The Movie* (1983), and the following year she served as executive producer on two blockbusters, *Gremlins* and *Indiana Jones and the Temple of Doom*. For *Gremlins* Kennedy and Spielberg, who served as co–executive producer, were responsible for putting the story in place; hiring the director (Joe Dante); striking a deal with Warner Bros., the film studio; and supervising the shoot. For *Indiana Jones* Kennedy traveled to Sri Lanka, where the crew shot for three weeks. "Steven relied heavily on her," Harrison Ford, who played Indiana Jones, told Jerry Roberts. "She was always a calming influence and an entertaining presence." He added, "The Indiana Jones movies were very different and full of logistical problems with huge crews but often tight budgets. Much of the maintenance and the control were in the hands of Kathy and Frank. With all they had to do, they always managed to make the sets a pleasant atmosphere."

In 1985 Kennedy was the executive producer for two more highly successful films, *The Goonies* and *Back to the Future*. She also produced *The Color Purple*, which she urged Spielberg to direct, even though it was unlike anything he had done in the past; the film was based on Alice Walker's novel about the self-realization of a poor black woman in the Depression-era Deep South. "I would tell him, 'someone on the outside might not bring you this, but I know it's got elements you'd be attracted to and you'd make a really wonderful movie from it,'" Kennedy told Sragow. The film received an Oscar nomination for best picture. (It lost to *Out of Africa*.)

Two years later Kennedy persuaded Spielberg to take on another project of a sort he did not usually work on: *Empire of the Sun*, adapted from J. G. Ballard's novel about a young English boy confined in a Japanese prisoner-of-war camp. In the process of making the film, Kennedy and Marshall spent more than a year negotiating with the Chinese government, since the film's opening sequences were to be set in Shanghai. Kennedy told Jim Schembri for the *Age* (July 18, 1995) that *Empire of the Sun* "was one of my personal favorites," adding that financially, "it was the least successful picture we've ever made. It was basically a disaster."

Kennedy and Marshall married in 1987. The following year Kennedy served as co–executive producer on *The Land Before Time*, an animated movie about dinosaurs, and executive producer on *Who Framed Roger Rabbit?*, which featured a groundbreaking mix of animation and live action. That film grossed more than $650 million worldwide. In 1989 Kennedy served as executive producer for *Back to the Future, Part II*, the second film about the time-traveling teenager played by Michael J. Fox, and the following year she executive-produced the final installment of the trilogy. In 1990 she also produced *Arachnophobia* and executive-produced *Gremlins 2: The New Batch*, *Always*, and *Joe Versus the Volcano*, the last of which starred Tom Hanks and Meg Ryan. (While a producer has a hands-on role in the moviemaking process, an executive producer is concerned with the business and legal sides of making films.)

In 1992, as Spielberg was in the process of forming the studio DreamWorks with David Geffen and Jeffrey Katzenberg, Kennedy and her husband decided to break from the director and form their own company, Kennedy/Marshall. Soon afterward the couple signed a three-year, nonexclusive deal with Paramount Pictures. "We wanted to have a family," Kennedy, now the mother of two girls, told Rebecca Winters Keegan for *Time* (November 12, 2007). "We didn't want to become movie moguls and move into being executives within a company. We like making movies." The split from Spielberg was amicable, and in 1993, the same year that Kennedy/Marshall launched its first film, the plane-crash-survival drama *Alive*, Kennedy produced Spielberg's blockbuster *Jurassic Park*, about an amusement park that is home to cloned dinosaurs—which soon run amok. The filmmakers used newly emerging digital technology to create the images of the dinosaurs. "What Kathy did from a production point of view helped bring digital filmmaking of age with *Jurassic Park*," Jim Morris, president of the movie special-effects company Industrial Light & Magic, told Roberts. "She had the vision to embrace the technology that solved a myriad of problems. Her role in that was significant. I can't say enough good things about her. She's the role model."

That same year Kennedy served as executive producer for Spielberg's movie *Schindler's List*, a drama about Oskar Schindler, a German businessman who saved more than 1,000 Jews from being killed at Auschwitz, a Nazi concentration camp. In preparation for the film, Kennedy visited Auschwitz, later telling Army Archerd for *Variety* (October 22, 1993) that her trip "was one of the most moving experiences of my life." The film received rave reviews and won the Academy Award for best picture. "*Schindler's List* brings a pre-eminent pop mastermind [Spielberg] together with a story that demands the deepest reserves of courage and passion," Janet Maslin wrote for the *New York Times* (December 15, 1993). "Rising brilliantly to the challenge of this material and displaying an electrifying creative intelligence, Mr. Spielberg has made sure that neither he nor the Holocaust will ever be thought of in the same way again."

In 1994 Kennedy was the executive producer for *The Flintstones*, an adaptation of the popular TV cartoon series, and producer for *Milk Money*, starring Melanie Griffith. The following year she produced *The Bridges of Madison County*, based on the Robert James Waller novel of the same name. Kennedy bought the rights to the best-selling if critically reviled book before it was published, believing that the story—which centers on a rural Iowa woman's extramarital affair with a photographer—would make excellent source material for a film. "I thought it tapped into something very interesting," she told Bob Strauss for the *Los Angeles Daily News*, as printed in the Baltimore *Sun* (June 25, 1995). "I'm not going to get into what I liked or disliked, but the core of it spoke to something that I thought a lot of women think about, which is how women have a complicated, societal responsibility to family and children." Amblin Entertainment, Kennedy's former company, was originally slated to make the film, but Universal Studios, with which Amblin often worked, opted out of the project. Kennedy successfully lobbied Warner Bros. to sign on for the film. When it came time to choose a director, the studio was presented with an unlikely choice, as Clint Eastwood, an actor then best known for hard-edged Westerns, expressed interest. "Very early on, Clint came to us and said, 'I love this book; I know what it is,' and he absolutely, passionately connected to the book and wanted to commit," Kennedy told Strauss. "Needless to say, when somebody of that stature comes to you with that degree of passion, you pay attention. Even though there's been a fair amount of publicity about certain directors that have come and gone, and everybody, whether they were in the movie business or not, was trying to cast this book and had ideas of who should be in it, Clint's feeling was right from the beginning." Eastwood also starred—opposite Meryl Streep—in the movie, which critics deemed far superior to the novel.

At the other end of the spectrum, in terms of both theme and critical reception, 1995 also saw the release of the action film *Congo*, an adaptation of a novel by Michael Crichton, the writer behind *Jurassic Park*. Despite bad reviews, *Congo* enjoyed the biggest opening weekend of any film that year, earning $24.6 million at the box office. Kennedy, who served as producer, had originally wanted to shoot the film in the same central-African jungle used as the location for *Gorillas in the Mist*, but tribal warfare in Burundi made it necessary to find a new place to film. The filmmakers eventually settled on Costa Rica, where constant rainfall proved a challenge. "We kept laughing and saying: 'Well, what do you expect? It's a rain forest,'" Kennedy told Strauss. "But if that was the dry season, I'd hate to think what the wet season's like." Marshall directed the film, marking his second outing at the helm of a picture. (*Arachnophobia* was the first.)

"It's easier to say, 'No, we can't do that,' to Steven Spielberg than it is to say it to Frank," Kennedy said. "I think everybody can imagine, on some level, that you go through a certain adjustment when you're producing for your husband." "When I'm unsure about things, I really trust her judgment," Marshall told Strauss. "She's very good with the script and story side of things." In December 1995 Kennedy and Marshall signed a nonexclusive three-year deal with Walt Disney Pictures.

In 1996 Kennedy produced *Twister*, a box-office smash about a pair of storm chasers. While some critics dismissed the film as mindless entertainment, others enjoyed the special effects. "Another theme park ride of a movie without an ounce of emotional credibility to it, *Twister* succeeds on its own terms by taking the audience somewhere it has never been before: into a tornado's funnel," Todd McCarthy wrote for *Variety* (May 10, 1996). The following year Kennedy served as executive producer of Spielberg's *The Lost World*, the sequel to *Jurassic Park*. The film was a runaway success, earning a record $92.7 million in its opening weekend. *The Lost World* featured more sophisticated special effects than its predecessor, and thanks to computer animation, as well as old-fashioned animatronics, 10 species of dinosaurs roared across the big screen. "Steven has the privilege and the prerogative to come up with any insane idea he wants and it's up to us to figure out if it's possible, or to offer alternatives," Kennedy told Judy Gerstel for the *Toronto Star* (May 16, 1997). Critics were split in their responses to *The Lost World*, with some insisting that the movie was more concerned with special effects than events or characters.

Kennedy's next major film was *The Sixth Sense* (1999). Written and directed by the then-unknown filmmaker M. Night Shyamalan, the picture starred Haley Joel Osment as a young boy with the ability to see the spirits of dead people. While a number of producers had vied for Shyamalan's script, he chose Kennedy/Marshall because he had been a fan of the films *Raiders of the Lost Ark* and *E.T.* since childhood. While *The Sixth Sense* received mixed reviews, many critics saw it as having unusual emotional resonance for a summer thriller. "Writer/director M. Night Shyamalan knows how to build atmosphere—this is clear," Desson Howe wrote for the *Washington Post* (August 6, 1999). "And he does it painstakingly, brick by brick. By the end of the picture, a very powerful design becomes clear, with a twist that will put your head in a swirl." The film earned an Academy Award nomination for best picture. (It lost to *American Beauty*, which was produced by Bruce Cohen, who is godfather to one of Kennedy's daughters.)

In 1999 Kennedy also produced *Snow Falling on Cedars*, a film adapted from a novel by David Guterson about a murder trial and an ill-fated interracial romance, set against the backdrops of World War II and Japanese-internment camps in the U.S. Critics were less than enthusiastic about the film, which starred Ethan Hawke, and much to Kennedy's disappointment, it flopped at the box office. "The film never got a chance," Marshall told Akin Ojumu for the London *Observer* (April 23, 2000). "It didn't catch on in the first weekend and so it didn't stay long enough in the cinemas. These days it's like an election. You know the morning after whether you've won or not." Expressing a different view, Stephen Holden wrote in an assessment of the film for the *New York Times* (December 22, 1999), "Frame by frame the movie . . . isn't just a series of shots but a sequence of exquisitely balanced photographic compositions. The piling on of so much visual beauty, however, only contributes to the sense of the movie as a frozen artifact cut off from the real world and designed to be viewed from behind a glass casement. There's a lesson here about the aesthetics of mass-audience movies. Pretty pictures, as nice as they may be, are finally no substitute for a living, breathing screenplay."

In 2001 Kennedy was named interim president of the Producers Guild of America (PGA). Upon assuming the post, she vowed to help put a stop to studios' practice of giving undeserved production credits on films. "Everyone with the various guilds is questioning fair work for fair credit, the producers included," Kennedy, who several years earlier had formed the Producers Credit Board, told Greg Hernandez for the *Hollywood Reporter* (March 28, 2001). "Our hope in the next year by working with the [Alliance of Motion Picture and Television Producers] is to arrive at simple solutions to a simple problem by implementing an arbitration board similar to that of the Writers Guild model for the determination of producing credits." Several years later the Academy of Motion Picture Arts and Sciences adopted the PGA's criteria for determining producers' eligibility for Oscars.

Also in 2001 Kennedy produced *Artificial Intelligence: AI*, a Pinocchio-like science-fiction epic starring Osment as a sentient boy robot who goes to live with a couple whose son lies comatose. Spielberg directed the film after the death of a fellow filmmaker, the legendary Stanley Kubrick, who had spent more than a decade developing the project. Reviews were mostly positive; many critics felt that Spielberg's usually sunny directorial sensibility mixed well with Kubrick's darker visions. In 2001 Kennedy also produced *Jurassic Park III*, a film that, like its predecessor, was dismissed by many critics.

In 2002 Kennedy served as executive producer on another Shyamalan film, *Signs*. The following year she produced *Seabiscuit*, a drama about the rider (played by Tobey Maguire) and owner (Jeff Bridges) of a Depression-era racehorse. The film was nominated for seven Academy Awards, including best picture. (It lost to *The Lord of the Rings: The Return of the King*.) Kennedy followed *Seabiscuit* with a pair of high-profile 2005 films: *War of the Worlds*, an action picture starring Tom Cruise, and *Munich*, Spielberg's film about terrorism at the 1972 Olympic Games. *Munich* was nominated for five Academy Awards, losing to *Crash* in the best-picture category.

Kennedy spent 2007 producing a pair of uncharacteristically small films. The French-language film *The Diving Bell and the Butterfly* was based on a memoir by the magazine editor Jean-Dominique Bauby. Bauby, who was left completely paralyzed after a stroke, wrote the book by composing prose in his mind, memorizing it, and then communicating the words by blinking his left eye as an assistant reached the needed letter in a recital of the alphabet. Kennedy had hoped that the actor Johnny Depp would play the lead role in an English-language film version of the book, but Depp passed on the project, leading the producer to seek funds for a French-language film—which the film's director, Julian Schnabel, wanted. Kennedy told Anne Thompson for *Variety* (December 10–16, 2007) that she "reacted to the emotional impact" of the story. The film received rave reviews. The critic David Denby wrote for the *New Yorker* (December 3, 2007) that it featured "some of the freest and most creative uses of the camera and some of the most daring, cruel, and heartbreaking emotional explorations that have appeared in recent movies." Kennedy's other 2007 project, the black-and-white animated film *Persepolis*, was based on a graphic novel by Marjane Satrapi about Satrapi's childhood in Iran; Kennedy was intrigued by the artist's unique drawing style. Like *The Diving Bell*, *Persepolis* earned mostly positive reviews. In a critique for the *New York Times* (December 25, 2007), the critic A. O. Scott wrote that the film "is frequently somber, but it is also whimsical and daring, a perfect expression of the imagination's resistance to the literal-minded and the power-mad, who insist that the world can be seen only in black and white."

Kennedy's 2008 projects included the belated fourth installment of the Indiana Jones series, *Indiana Jones and the Kingdom of the Crystal Skull*, and *The Curious Case of Benjamin Button*. The latter film, directed by David Fincher and starring Brad Pitt and Cate Blanchett, focuses on a character who begins life looking like an old man and grows younger in appearance. The film proved to be a critical success. For her work on *Benjamin Button*, Kennedy was nominated as producer of the year by the Producers Guild of America. Kennedy will produce an upcoming Clint Eastwood–directed thriller called *Hereafter* and Steven Spielberg's next project, *The Adventures of Tintin: The Secret of the Unicorn*, a 3-D film based on the comic-book character created by the Belgian artist and writer Georges Remi, who used the pen name Hergé.

Kennedy regularly mentors young people who are interested in forging careers in the motion-picture industry. She has been involved with Communities in Schools/the L.A. Mentoring Partnership since the early 1980s. Robert Arias, the organization's president, told Andra R. Vaucher for the *Hollywood Reporter* (November 2, 1999), "Kathleen has been a guardian angel for mentoring in Los Angeles and the state of California through her deeds and her generosity."

—K.J.P.

Suggested Reading: *Baltimore Sun* F p1 July 3, 2005; imdb.com; *Time* p8 Nov. 12, 2007; *Variety* Special Section/Hall of Fame June 12, 1998, p16 Dec. 10–16, 2007

Selected Films: *E.T.: The Extra-Terrestrial*, 1982; *Poltergeist*, 1982; *Twilight Zone: The Movie*, 1983; *Indiana Jones and the Temple of Doom*, 1984; *Gremlins*, 1984; *The Goonies*, 1985; *Back to the Future*, 1985; *The Color Purple*, 1985; *Empire of the Sun*, 1987; *The Land Before Time*, 1988; *Who Framed Roger Rabbit?*, 1988; *Back to the Future, Part II*, 1989; *Arachnophobia*, 1990; *Gremlins 2: The New Batch*, 1990; *Always*, 1990; *Joe Versus the Volcano*, 1990; *Alive*, 1993; *Jurassic Park*, 1993; *Schindler's List*, 1993; *The Flintstones*, 1994; *Milk Money*, 1994; *The Bridges of Madison County*, 1995; *Congo*, 1995; *Twister*, 1996; *The Lost World: Jurassic Park*, 1997; *The Sixth Sense*, 1999; *Snow Falling on Cedars*, 1999; *Artificial Intelligence: AI*, 2001; *Jurassic Park III*, 2001; *Signs*, 2002; *Seabiscuit*, 2003; *War of the Worlds*, 2005; *Munich*, 2005; *The Diving Bell and the Butterfly*, 2007; *Persepolis*, 2007; *Indiana Jones and the Kingdom of the Crystal Skull*, 2008; *The Curious Case of Benjamin Button*, 2008

Kerlikowske, R. Gil

(ker-lih-KOW-skee)

Nov. 23, 1949– Director of the U.S. Office of National Drug Control Policy

Address: Office of National Drug Control Policy, Executive Office of the President, Washington, DC 20503

On May 7, 2009 R. Gil Kerlikowske was sworn in as the director of the U.S. Office of National Drug Control Policy (ONDCP)—or drug czar, as he is known colloquially. Established in 1988 as an arm of the government's executive branch, the ONDCP oversees the nation's policies regarding outlawed drugs; it strives to reduce the manufacture, trafficking, and use of such drugs, the misuse of prescription drugs, and the crime and health problems associated with illegal drug use. "With escalating violence along our Southwest border and far too many suffering from the disease of addiction here at home, never has it been more important to have a national drug control strategy guided by sound principles of public safety and public health," President Barack Obama stated on March 11, 2009, as quoted in the White House press release that announced his nomination of Kerlikowske to lead the ONDCP. "Gil Kerlikowske has the expertise, the experience, and the sound judgment to lead our national efforts against drug trafficking and use." The Obama administration also announced that the job

Chris Kleponis/AFP/Getty Images

R. Gil Kerlikowske

of ONDCP director would no longer be a Cabinet-level position, as it was during the tenures of Kerlikowske's five predecessors; nevertheless, according to a White House official, Kerlikowske will have "full access and a direct line to the president and vice president," David Stout wrote for the *New York Times* (March 11, 2009, on-line).

Kerlikowske has spent more than four decades in law enforcement. He began to prepare for his profession as a teenager, with a part-time job in his local police precinct. He earned bachelor's and master's degrees in law enforcement and supplemented his education in that field with courses at an FBI school and Harvard University. For 15 years he worked for the St. Petersburg, Florida, police department, starting as a patrol officer and leaving as a commander. He headed the police departments of four cities—two of them small (Port St. Lucie and Fort Pierce, in Florida) and two large (Buffalo, New York, and Seattle, Washington). In each of those cities, the crime rate declined during his years as chief of police. Much of his success has been attributed to his promotion of what is known as community policing; his modernization of the departments; his advocacy of greater use by police of Taser stun guns and similar devices and less reliance on lethal weapons; and his efforts toward fostering better relations among racial groups, both within the ranks of the police and in interactions between the police and members of their communities. Those who know him through his work have also praised his personal qualities: he has been described as thoughtful, kind, and uncommonly organized.

In the March 11, 2009 press release, the Miami, Florida, chief of police, John Timoney, described Kerlikowske as "the perfect person" for the job of ONDCP director. "With his years of experience as a police chief he knows that enforcement alone will not solve the nation's drug problem. It also requires prevention through education. With his background and temperament he will bring great credibility to the bully pulpit." Kerlikowske himself was quoted as saying, "The success of our efforts to reduce the flow of drugs is largely dependent on our ability to reduce demand for them. . . . Our nation's drug problem is one of human suffering, and as a police officer but also in my own family, I have experienced firsthand the effects that drugs can have on our youth, our families and our communities." Kerlikowske was referring to his estranged stepson, Jeffrey, who had been arrested twice for possession and distribution of marijuana and had served time in prison for assault with a deadly weapon; he is currently in prison because of a parole violation.

Those directly involved in matters under the purview of the ONDCP, ranging from public prosecutors to drug counselors to members of organizations fighting to legalize marijuana, have expressed the view that Kerlikowske will devote more of his efforts to prevention and treatment than did his immediate predecessor, John P. Walters, an appointee of President George W. Bush. As Seattle's police chief Kerlikowske opposed a 2003 measure, approved by voters, whose aim was to make arrests for marijuana possession the police department's lowest priority, but he noted that the department already considered marijuana possession a low priority. He also supported needle-exchange programs and rehabilitation in lieu of jail time for low-level drug offenders, and he did not protest Washington State laws that decriminalized the use of marijuana for medical purposes. In an interview conducted a few days after his swearing-in as director, Kerlikowske said that the Obama administration would no longer describe the activities of the ONDCP as a "war on drugs." "Regardless of how you try to explain to people it's a 'war on drugs' or a 'war on a product,' people see a war as a war on them," he said, as Gary Fields reported for the *Wall Street Journal* (May 14, 2008, on-line). "We're not at war with people in this country."

Richard Guilford Kerlikowske was born on November 23, 1949 in Fort Myers, Florida. He was raised by his stepfather, Thomas W. Shands, a circuit-court judge, and his mother, Norma Shands, a secretary at the local courthouse. His biological father was an alcoholic; little else has been made public about him. Trips to the courthouse during Kerlikowske's childhood sparked his interest in law enforcement. While attending Fort Myers High School, he worked part-time at the local police precinct, photographing crime scenes and fingerprinting people under arrest. "From the time I was small, I was fascinated by police work and law enforcement," he told Jack Reed for the *St. Petersburg*

(Florida) Times (November 30, 1992). "I've never [wavered] from what I wanted to do." After completing high school Kerlikowske enrolled at St. Petersburg Junior College (now St. Petersburg College), in Florida, where he studied law enforcement. He also volunteered as a police cadet. After he was drafted into the army, in 1970, he left college and spent the next two years stationed in Washington, D.C., as a military police officer. At the end of his tour of duty, he received a U.S. Army Presidential Service Medal.

In 1972 Kerlikowske got married and adopted his wife's two-year-old son. The couple, who later had a daughter together, settled in St. Petersburg, where Kerlikowske joined the city's police force. During the next 15 years, he worked his way up the ranks from patrol officer, to narcotics agent, to hostage negotiator, to lieutenant in charge of criminal investigations, to commander. Concurrently, Kerlikowske earned both B.S. and M.S. degrees in criminal justice from the University of South Florida in Tampa, in 1975 and 1978, respectively. In 1984, with a yearlong fellowship, he attended the National Executive Institute at the Federal Bureau of Investigation (FBI) Academy, located on the U.S. Marine Corps Base in Quantico, Virginia. Kerlikowske also attended the Executive Session on Policing and Public Safety at Harvard University's Kennedy School of Government, in Cambridge, Massachusetts.

In April 1987 Kerlikowske left St. Petersburg to become the police chief of Port St. Lucie, Florida, a small city (its population was 68,000 then) with a low crime rate. During his tenure he doubled the number of officers, from 42 to more than 80. Kerlikowske was hailed by Port St. Lucie residents for modernizing and improving the department. In 1989, however, he was given a vote of no confidence by the local police union. The vote was said to have stemmed from Kerlikowske's efforts to prohibit officers from taking their patrol cars home, among other unpopular measures. "I received a lot of positive support from the community. . . . It sets the tone that you are going to make decisions based on what's right for the community," Kerlikowske later told a *Fort Pierce Tribune* (January 16, 1994) reporter. The president of the police union later apologized for holding the no-confidence vote.

In January 1990 Kerlikowske became the police chief in nearby Fort Pierce. Though the population of Fort Pierce was about half that of Port St. Lucie, it had persistent drug problems and a high crime rate. (In 1988 there were 28 homicides in Fort Pierce, four in Port St. Lucie, and 30 in Buffalo, New York, a city with 10 times Fort Pierce's population.) Thanks in large part to Kerlikowske's community policing efforts, the city's homicide rate decreased 60.8 percent between 1989 and 1994. The aim of community policing is to build trust between the public and the police by encouraging people to voice their concerns, acting on those concerns, and tackling crime-related problems plaguing neighborhoods by identifying and addressing their root causes. "The closer the police officer is to the community the more trust there is and the more information there is . . . ," Kerlikowske told a *Fort Pierce Tribune* (January 16, 1994) reporter. "Victims that were reluctant to call now call, victims that were reluctant to follow through with prosecution will now follow through with prosecution. The officer gets more information." "Law enforcement does not have all the answers," he told Jane Kwiatkowski for the *Buffalo News* (January 24, 1994). "Even though we may have better equipment and more people, we may not do a better job. People [in the community] must take responsibility." Kerlikowske was also respected for his ability to combat racism within both the police department and Fort Pierce. He actively reached out to members of minority groups and increased the number of nonwhites in the police department.

While in Fort Pierce Kerlikowske made a failed attempt to win the post of police chief in St. Petersburg. In December 1993 he was hired as the police commissioner of the 933-member Buffalo, New York, police department; he assumed the post the following January. Kerlikowske was the first commissioner from outside the department in more than 30 years, and many Buffalo residents doubted that he could shrink the city's crime rate, which at that time was among the highest in the U.S. (It had jumped almost 50 percent since 1988—more than twice as much as the nationwide average.) He proved them wrong, however; during his four-and-a-half-year tenure, violent crime in Buffalo decreased by 38 percent—far more than the average decrease recorded in other U.S. cities in the 1990s. His accomplishment was linked to his steps toward modernization: he had computers installed in patrol cars, supplied bulletproof vests (previously, officers had to buy their own) and new guns, consolidated precincts, and increased officer training. He set up a telephone-reporting system for nonemergency calls, so that officers could concentrate on handling more serious matters; had pay phones removed or modified to thwart drug deals (cell phones were still uncommon then); and, with the help of housing inspectors, demolished or boarded up abandoned houses being used by criminals. He placed more officers on the streets and hired social workers to help troubled teenagers and counselors to help victims of domestic abuse. To raise standards within the department, he introduced random drug testing of officers and supported an FBI investigation of the narcotics division to weed out corruption. Rather than accepting applicants with only a high-school diploma, he required them to have completed at least two years of college. He also initiated regular communication with police departments in suburbs of Buffalo and with Rochester, the state's third-largest city, "to see how they do things," as he told Donn Esmonde for the *Buffalo News* (July 18, 1998). Joseph Riga, Buffalo's homicide chief at the time, told Esmonde, "We went from carbon paper to computers. [Kerlikowske] brought us out of the dark ages in equipment and training."

In Buffalo, too, Kerlikowske developed strong ties in the community. "Sometimes you get a commissioner you can't touch and can't see. That wasn't him," Laura Jackson, a Buffalo community activist, told Ray Rivera for the *Seattle Times* (July 12, 2000). "There was no time we could not call him that he did not respond. You could see his humanness even in his job." Kerlikowske worked with the city's minority groups and regularly attended community meetings in an effort to better serve and inform the public. "I want to educate the public about its role and about what police can and can't do," he told Gregory C. Racz for the *Buffalo News* (July 16, 1995). "Neighborhood watch and crime prevention steps have far more to do with crime reduction than 911 or the police. And anybody expecting miraculous, instantaneous change is going to be disappointed. Quick change is not lasting." Though he was criticized for spending too much time in Washington, D.C., his visits to legislators helped Buffalo: he secured $7 million in federal grants for the city's police department.

In 1998 President Bill Clinton appointed Kerlikowske to the position of deputy director of the Office of Community Oriented Policing Services (COPS). An arm of the Department of Justice, COPS seeks to advance the practice of community policing and provides grants to law-enforcement agencies to hire and train community-policing professionals and develop innovative policing strategies. For two years Kerlikowske oversaw communities' use of federal grants, to make sure they were in compliance with government requirements and rules. During that time he developed a relationship with Eric Holder, then the deputy attorney general and currently, under President Obama, the nation's attorney general. In 2000 Kerlikowske was short-listed for police-chief positions in Memphis, Tennessee, and Seattle. In July he accepted the offer of Seattle's mayor, Paul Schell, to head the city's 1,261-member police department. "I realize, more than ever, that leading a police department to improve the quality of life and provide a safer community is what motivates me," Kerlikowske told Ray Rivera. "The experience in Washington [D.C.] has been worthwhile and fills a void in my background, but is not something I want to end my career doing."

Kerlikowske was sworn in as Seattle's 47th police chief on August 14, 2000. He became embroiled in controversy in February 2001, when riots that broke out during a Madri Gras celebration resulted in the death of one man and injuries to 70 other people. Kerlikowske, who had ordered his officers to keep on the sidelines as the rioting erupted, was blamed for not taking action against the crowd, in which many had been inebriated. In defense of his actions and those of his officers, he maintained that police interference would have worsened the situation. One Seattle police officer, Eric Michl, explained to Alex Tizon for the *Seattle Times* (August 12, 2001), "Had we gone into that mess to stop it, it would have been very, very bad. There would have been seriously injured or dead cops, suspects or both. And with so many of the suspects being black, a lot of controversy would have followed." An investigation conducted by the police union concluded that police commanders had been wrong not to interfere. Kerlikowske impressed many critics when he publicly apologized for his mishandling of the incident.

Kerlikowske was further criticized in January 2002 when he reprimanded an officer who had been cleared of an accusation that his behavior toward a group of Asian-American teenagers had been based on racial profiling. Since the chief had failed to discipline any of the commanders on duty during the 2001 Mardi Gras celebration, union members complained that his system of discipline was unfair. In balloting held in March 2002, 88 percent of the city's police-union members expressed their lack of confidence in Kerlikowske. "The vote of no confidence in Chief Kerlikowske is not because he's not competent, he's very competent . . . ," Edward Tully, a retired FBI agent who at the time headed the Major Cities Chiefs Association, told Lewis Kamb, Mike Barber, and Hector Castro for the *Seattle Post-Intelligencer* (March 29, 2002). "Obviously, the Seattle police officers are not a happy lot and this is one of the few ways they have to demonstrate it." Tully added, "Kerlikowske's pretty good. He's one of the better, brighter chiefs of police in the United States. . . . [The vote] should be perceived as a tactic. It doesn't have that much to do with him personally."

Despite those controversies, Kerlikowske strengthened Seattle's police department. When he left the job, the city's crime rate stood at its lowest level in 40 years. Some of his accomplishments include his creation in 2002 of the Seattle Police Foundation, which has since raised over $1 million for training, technology, and equipment. The foundation set up a statewide database with which officers can access the records of and receive alerts about armed career criminals, and it provided officers with alternatives to lethal force, such as Taser devices. By 2004 Kerlikowske had turned down offers to run police departments in San Francisco, California, and Boston, Massachusetts. He was nominated for the 2004 *Seattle Post-Intelligencer* Jefferson Award for his leadership and compassion in preventing youth crime and violence; in 2006 he received the James V. Cotter Award from the Commission on Accreditation for Law Enforcement Agencies (CALEA) for leading three police agencies (those of Port St. Lucie, Fort Pierce, and Seattle) to achieve national accreditation. Kerlikowske was an adjunct professor at Seattle University, where he taught courses in law enforcement, and he served on the board of directors for the Washington State Criminal Justice Training Center.

Only one member of the U.S. Senate opposed Kerlikowske's confirmation as director of the ONDCP. Kerlikowske assumed the office on May 7, 2009, nearly 40 years to the day after President Richard Nixon, at a press conference, described drug abuse as "public enemy number one" and declared a "war on drugs." President Obama, according to Tim Dickinson, writing for *Rolling Stone* (June 25, 2009), has called the war on drugs an "utter failure." "It now appears that drugs have won," Nicholas D. Kristof wrote in his op-ed column for the *New York Times* (June 14, 2009), noting that in those 40 years, the number of people imprisoned for drug offenses has jumped by more than 1,200 percent, to 500,000, with the result that "the United States now incarcerates people at a rate nearly five times the world average"; the prices of illegal drugs have risen, enriching and impowering drug lords, smaller-scale criminals, and terrorist groups; and of the estimated trillion dollars spent so far in enforcing drug laws, only a small fraction has been devoted to treatment and rehabilitation—an unjustifiable squandering of resources, in Kristof's view.

On June 24, 2009 the U.N. Office on Drugs and Crime made public its 2009 *World Drug Report*, which, in a reversal of previous policy, recommended the decriminalization of drugs. In response to the publication of the report, Kerlikowske declared, in a statement posted on the ONDCP Web site that day, "We are moving away from divisive 'drug war' rhetoric and focusing on employing all the tools at our disposal to get help to those who need it. . . . My top priority is to intensify efforts to reduce the demand for drugs which fuels crime and violence around the world. . . . The earlier we can intervene to get people help, the better—that's why prevention through schools and the media, and screening for substance abuse problems in a wide variety of health care settings is so vital. We will be expanding these existing efforts and working to ensure drug abuse treatment services are incorporated into our national health care reform process. These efforts will include expanded work to address the abuse of pharmaceutical drugs, a problem of increasing concern within the United States." Kerlikowske also emphasized the importance of providing "evidence-based treatment" for drug offenders; reducing drug trafficking and commerce in weapons associated with drug trafficking, in partnership with the governments of nations including Mexico, Colombia, Peru, and Afghanistan; and sharing with other governments the findings of research funded by the National Institute of Drug Abuse. In his remarks Kerlikowske did not talk about the possibility of decriminalizing the use of illegal drugs. Both he and President Obama have specifically rejected proposals to decriminalize the production, sale, and use of marijuana, but the Obama administration has ended law-enforcement officers' raids on medical facilities that distribute marijuana to patients for the control of pain and nausea.

In 1990 the Police Executive Research Forum (PERF) honored Kerlikowske with the Gary Hayes National Memorial Award for Innovation in Policing. He served as PERF's president between 1996 and 1998 and as president of the Major Cities Chiefs Association in 2009. Kerlikowske's first marriage ended in divorce. According to David Saltonstall, writing for the New York *Daily News* (March 13, 2009, on-line), Kerlikowske told another *Daily News* reporter a month earlier that he had not seen or spoken to his adopted son for "well over a decade." In 1995 Kerlikowske married Anna Laszlo. As of mid-2009 Laszlo was the director of research, evaluation, and training for Circle Solutions Inc., "an employee-owned professional services firm providing products and services in support of healthier, safer people and communities," according to its Web site. Kerlikowske is a voracious reader. He and Laszlo enjoy running, bicycling, playing tennis, and attending performances of musicals. They have memorized most of the songs written by the composer Richard Rodgers and the lyricist Oscar Hammerstein. On February 23, 2005 Kerlikowske performed at the 5th Avenue Theatre, in Seattle, as the baton-twirling policeman in a stage production of *Singin' in the Rain*. His daughter, Kim, and her husband are the parents of Kerlikowske's three grandchildren.

—M.A.S.

Suggested Reading: *Buffalo (New York) News* Local Jan. 24, 1994, E p1 July 16, 1995; *Fort Pierce (Florida) Tribune* (on-line) Feb. 11, 2009; Office of National Drug Control Policy Web site; *Seattle Times* A p1+ July 12, 2000; *Seattle Post-Intelligencer* A p1+ Feb. 11, 2009; *St. Petersburg (Florida) Times* p1+ Nov. 30, 1992; *Washington Post* A p3 Mar. 24, 2009

Kilar, Jason

(KYE-lahr)

Apr. 26, 1971– CEO of Hulu

Address: Hulu, 12312 W. Olympic Blvd., Los Angeles, CA 90064

"When cable [television] eventually dies, websites like Hulu will be held responsible," a writer for *Time* (November 10, 2008) declared, referring to the on-line video site that is headed by Jason Kilar. Developed jointly by NBC Universal Inc. and the News Corp., Hulu.com debuted on March 12, 2008, and it ranked fourth on *Time*'s list of the 50 best inventions of that year. The site offers, at no cost to consumers, full-length episodes of 1,700 network television shows, ranging from *The Mary Tyler Show* and *Buffy the Vampire Slayer* to *Biography*, *Nova*, and *NBC News Specials*, and more than 400 feature films. Hulu users can stream the videos di-

Neilson Barnard/Getty Images

Jason Kilar

rectly through the Web site, eliminating the need to download programs or plug-ins. Although the shows are interrupted by commercials—the source of Hulu's revenues—there are far fewer commercial breaks than ordinarily occur on television. Kilar, who worked for Disney and Amazon.com after he earned a graduate degree in business, became the chief executive officer of Hulu in 2007. Since then Hulu's roster of content providers has grown to more than 150 and its advertisers to more than 250, among them such corporate giants as American Express, McDonald's, Intel, Johnson & Johnson, and Cisco. As of September 2009 Hulu was the fourth-most-popular video-streaming Web site in the U.S., with 38.5 million individual viewers and 488 million video streams recorded the previous month. Hulu's successful launch and its rapid growth have been attributed in large part to Kilar's foresight and business savvy. Kilar was chosen as one of *Entertainment Weekly*'s "25 Smartest People in TV" in December 2008, and he was named among *TV Week*'s "12 to Watch" in February 2009.

One of the six children of Lance and Maureen (Blake) Kilar, Jason Kilar was born on April 26, 1971 in Pittsburgh, Pennsylvania. His father was an engineer with the Westinghouse Electric Co. Kilar grew up in Murrysville, outside Pittsburgh. He attended the University of North Carolina (UNC) at Chapel Hill, where he was elected to the Phi Beta Kappa honor society and graduated in 1993 with two bachelor's degrees, a B.S. in business administration and a B.A. in mass communication. That year Kilar was hired as an analyst for Disney Design & Development, a division of the Walt Disney Co. For two years he worked in the strategy and marketing groups that handled the Disney Vacation Club. He continued his studies at the Harvard Business School, in Cambridge, Massachusetts, earning an M.B.A. degree in 1997.

Early that same year Kilar joined Amazon.com, the Seattle, Washington–based electronic-commerce company founded in 1994 by Jeff Bezos. His title at Amazon, which was then almost exclusively a seller of books, was product manager. "When I first came to Amazon . . . , it was a private company, and the future was uncertain. But I was very impressed with the quality of the people," Kilar said in an interview for the Web site of UNC–Chapel Hill Kenan-Flagler Business School. "Bezos held the quality bar extremely high in terms of the team he assembled. It's a company that's very much a meritocracy. You run as fast as you can, and you'll be rewarded accordingly. Responsibility at Amazon is accorded simply on your results and your ability to perform. That's very satisfying." Kilar added, referring to the site of the Wright brothers' first successful airplane flight, that part of what attracted him to Amazon was that "the opportunity [was] so immense," like "the Kitty Hawk era in terms of e-commerce."

Rising through the ranks, Kilar developed the business plan for Amazon's expansion into sales of videos and DVDs, in 1998. That new business generated hundreds of millions of dollars in revenues, and Amazon has since grown into one of the world's largest retailers of those items as well as books. In 2001 Kilar was promoted to general manager and vice president of Amazon's North American media businesses, which included the books, music, video, and DVD divisions. Two years later he was named senior vice president of worldwide application software, a position that placed him in charge of Amazon's Marketplace business (through which a customer can buy new and used items from a third party, either a retailer or an individual) and the applications used on Amazon's global Web sites (which include software that suggests products to a user based on his or her personal profile and purchase history). Reporting directly to Jeff Bezos, Kilar oversaw a large group of technologists whose task was to make sure Amazon was user-friendly. He left Amazon in early 2006.

In 2007 network television companies began searching for ways to provide profit-generating content on-line and also prevent the piracy of their programs. CBS invested in the start-up Internet video service Joost (which has thus far failed to capture a large number of Web users, because it requires the viewer to download a player onto his or her computer). Viacom, which owns MTV and Comedy Central, invested in Joost as well as in Google, the latter of which had just bought YouTube, the nation's most popular video-sharing site; Disney, the owner of ABC, provided videos on its own Web site. News Corp., which owns the Fox Entertainment Group, and NBC Universal, which is owned by the General Electric Co., teamed up to create an entirely new Internet video service. The two companies publicly announced their intentions in March 2007. Providence Equity Partners, a private equity fund whose specialty is the media, invested in the venture, and Yahoo!, AOL, MSN, and MySpace soon came on board as distribution partners. Having decided that their fledgling company, called NewSite, needed a chief executive officer with experience in Internet commerce rather than television, News Corp., NBC Universal, and Providence Equity Partners chose Kilar to direct it. "Jason's product and consumer expertise in the world of e-commerce is arguably unrivaled in this business and gives him a great insight into what it takes to create a superior user interface," Peter Chernin, the president and chief operating officer of News Corp., stated in a press release, as reported by *Business Wire* (June 28, 2007, on-line). "We already have access to world-class content and near ubiquitous distribution, and the next step is marrying it with the features and tools that will help define the ideal user experience for video content on the web. We think Jason is the ideal person to lead that effort."

Kilar took command of the Los Angeles–based venture in early July 2007. Drawing on the contacts he had made during his time in Seattle, he hired 28-year-old Eric Feng, a former Microsoft engineer, as the chief technology officer. Feng and his team were charged with developing the Web site and video player. Kilar worked on acquiring television series and films, not only from NBC, Fox, and their affiliated channels but also from other companies, including the film studios Lionsgate and Warner Bros. He persuaded them to become partners in the venture by emphasizing that through the Internet, their audiences would undoubtedly become much broader. Kilar suggested to Frank Rose for *Wired* (October 2008) that if he imagined himself as a network executive, "and I told you here was a tool that enabled your content to be shared, to be forwarded, to make your audience your most powerful marketing vehicle—it would be music to your ears, right? This is a tectonic shift, and what it does is allow network heads to find the audience they always should have had but couldn't reach."

Hulu, as NewSite was now called, officially launched on March 12, 2008. Earlier, in 2007, according to the Marketing Pilgrim and other Web sites, Kilar had explained why he and his colleagues had chosen the new name: "Objectively, Hulu is short, easy to spell, easy to pronounce, and rhymes with itself. Subjectively, Hulu strikes us as an inherently fun name, one that captures the spirit of the service we're building. Our hope is that Hulu will embody our (admittedly ambitious) never-ending mission, which is to help you find and enjoy the world's premier content when, where and how you want it." The day after Hulu's debut, Kilar explained in a Hulu blog that contrary to outsiders' claims that the name meant "snoring" in one of China's languages or "cease and desist" in Swahili, in Mandarin (the official language of mainland China), "Hulu has two interesting meanings, each highly relevant to our mission. The primary meaning interested us because it is used in an ancient Chinese proverb that describes the Hulu as the holder of precious things. It literally translates to 'gourd,' and in ancient times, the Hulu was hollowed out and used to hold precious things. The secondary meaning is 'interactive recording.' We saw both definitions as appropriate bookends and highly relevant to the mission of Hulu."

When it began, Hulu offered about 250 television shows and 100 movies. The site, as described by Chuck Salter for *Fast Company* (February 11, 2009, on-line), "features a larger screen and high-resolution video designed to showcase the content the networks and studios have spent millions of dollars writing, filming, and editing. There's no player to download—the video plays instantly in a Web browser. And the site is clutter-free, avoiding what Kilar calls the 'Tokyo at night' look of sites packed with blinking links." The site also makes it possible for users to embed clips from Hulu's library on their own Web sites. Kilar said, as quoted by Michael Learmonth in *Advertising Age* (November 17, 2008), "Also, my mother had to be proficient in [navigating the Web site] in 15 seconds or less with no help from me."

Hulu's large library, as well as the site's easy-to-use, sleek design, soon silenced critics who had doubted that the venture would find an audience. Indeed, its audience grew steadily in 2008. In October of that year, Hulu registered 24 million unique viewers (that is, its shows were downloaded on 24 million computers), nearly double the number of viewers the previous month. The boost was attributable in part to the site's enormously popular *Saturday Night Live* clips in which Tina Fey offered impressions of the 2008 Republican vice-presidential candidate, Governor Sarah Palin of Alaska. Hulu was also helped by Joss Whedon's three-part musical *Dr. Horrible's Sing-Along Blog*, starring Neil Patrick Harris, which was distributed exclusively by Hulu and became the fifth-most-watched viral video (a video clip that gains widespread popularity through Internet sharing) of 2008. Within six months of its premiere, Hulu had become the sixth-most-popular video Web site in the U.S., with 142 million video streams per month. "It is very understandable that so many journalists and respected bloggers felt that Hulu would have a very difficult time gaining traction," Kilar told Stephen J. Dubner, the co-author of the *New York Times*'s "Freakonomics" blog (May 13, 2009). "It is far more common for start-ups to fail, even without taking into account the unique dynamics that surrounded Hulu in the early days. . . . The Hulu team would be the first to say that we're very much the recipients of good timing and good fortune. . . . Hulu's original business plan did not include phrases like 'and then Tina Fey will impersonate Sarah Palin and an online sensation will ensue.' We're ever thankful for the wondrous and at times wacky things that helped get Hulu to this early point."

By the end of 2008, Hulu ranked third on the *Fast Company* 50, a list of "enterprises that will redefine our future and point the way to a better tomorrow"; it also was *PCWorld*'s "number one product of the year," was named "Web site of the year" by the Associated Press, and was heralded as the "best new way to watch TV" by *BusinessWeek* and *New York* magazines. "In the Wild West that is online video," Jake Coyle wrote for the Associated Press (December 19, 2008), "Hulu.com has proven to be a trailblazing answer to how professional content can thrive on the web." Though Hulu continues to trail the nation's largest video Web site, YouTube, in viewership by a wide margin, it has attracted far more advertisers. (The two sites are often cited as competitors, though YouTube specializes in user-generated content, movie and television clips, and music videos.) Among the advantages Hulu offers to advertisers is a way of targeting viewers by permitting them to choose a specific commercial; Nissan, for example, allowed viewers to choose an ad for an SUV, a coupe, or a sedan, depending on their preference. Another format, aimed at film studios, allows viewers to view an entire television show without commercials as long as they watch a movie trailer first. "One ad agency executive told me that he'd been waiting for this for 10 years," Kilar told Michael Schneider for *Daily Variety* (March 11, 2008).

In January 2009, according to the digital-marketing research firm comScore (March 4, 2009, on-line), Hulu ranked sixth among on-line firms in number of videos watched (250.5 million, or 1.7 percent of the total viewed on the Internet), behind Google sites, Fox Interactive Media, Yahoo! sites, Microsoft sites, and AOL, and it recorded 24.5 million unique viewers. Hulu's rapid growth was attributed to word of mouth until February 2009, when the company began to air advertisements on television. Featuring one or another actor or actress, among them Alec Baldwin, Seth McFarlane, Denis Leary, and Eliza Dusku, the ads mocked television's reputation as intellectually stultifying, with the slogan "Hulu: an evil plot to destroy the world. Enjoy." By the end of March 2009, Andy Fixmer reported for Bloomberg.com (April 28, 2009), Hulu ranked third among most-watched Internet video sites, with 380 million videos viewed in March. On April 30, 2009 Hulu announced a deal with Disney/ABC that has added several ABC series and ABC Family series to its library. As part of the agreement, Disney acquired a 27 percent stake in Hulu. (CBS is now the only major television network that is not signed with Hulu.) According to Screen Digest, which analyzes aspects of the media, Hulu is expected to generate $175 million in ad revenues in 2009, two and a half times the $70 million it earned in 2008.

One of the often repeated complaints about Hulu is that it is available only to viewers in the U.S. Licensing and copyright issues have slowed the Web site's expansion overseas, but Kilar assured the *New Zealand Herald* (May 21, 2008), "I personally would be very disappointed if we don't bring Hulu out in the next several years to countries around the globe."

Recently, there has been a lot of speculation that Hulu may require subscription fees for its content. Some reports suggest that in 2010, the Web site will begin charging users for new shows, while shows that were previously posted to the site will remain free. Chase Carey, the deputy chairman of the News Corp., which is a part-owner of Hulu, addressed the issue during a recent conference. "I think a free model is a very difficult way to capture the value of our content," he said, as quoted by Brian Morrissey for *AdWeek* (October 22, 2009, online). "I think what we need to do is deliver that content to consumers in a way where they will appreciate the value." He added, "We continue to believe that the ad-supported free service is the one that resonates with the largest group of users and any possible new business models would serve to complement our existing offering. There are no details or time lines to share regarding our future product road map."

Kilar and his wife have two children. Most of his consumption of TV shows takes place via his computer. One exception is sports, especially UNC basketball games, which he enjoys watching on his plasma television.

—M.A.S.

Suggested Reading: *Fast Company* (on-line) Feb. 11, 2009; hulu.com; *New York Times* C p1+ Oct. 29, 2007; UNC Kenan-Flagler Business School Web site (2009); *Wired* p136 Oct. 2008

Kimmel, Jimmy

Nov. 13, 1967– Host of Jimmy Kimmel Live; *comedian*

Address: Jimmy Kimmel Live, *6834 Hollywood Blvd., Los Angeles, CA 90028*

The comedian Jimmy Kimmel, the host and executive producer of ABC's popular late-night television talk show, *Jimmy Kimmel Live*, has long been known for his "guy's guy" persona and irreverent sense of humor. As a youth growing up in Las Vegas, Nevada, Kimmel became enamored of *Late Night with David Letterman*, which began airing on NBC in 1982, when he was 14, and he dreamed of one day enjoying a career similar to that of its host. Having learned that Letterman had started his career in radio, he got a job at a college radio station while still in high school. In the 1990s Kimmel made a name for himself on radio stations including KROQ in Los Angeles, California, where he was known as "The Sports Guy." He moved to television as the co-host of Comedy Central's critically acclaimed game show *Win Ben Stein's Money*. He

Kevin Winter/Getty Images

Jimmy Kimmel

next became the co-creator and co-host of the raunchy comedy program *The Man Show*, which celebrated stereotypical loutish male behavior and tastes. Kimmel later co-created and co-produced *Crank Yankers*, the popular Comedy Central show in which puppets act out real prank phone calls. In 2002 Kimmel was tapped to host ABC's late-night talk show, to replace *Politically Incorrect with Bill Maher*. *Jimmy Kimmel Live* premiered on January 26, 2003, after Super Bowl XXXVII. While retaining his regular-guy charm, he has successfully translated the comic style that he fine-tuned on *The Man Show*—described as "sophomoric," "immature," "gross-out," and "frat-guy humor"—into one acceptable to more-mainstream audiences. His "low-brow style of humor," Thomas Tennant wrote for About.com, "can be wickedly funny and good-natured." Currently, ABC promotes Kimmel as "the king of late-night cool," and his show, now in its fifth season, draws close to two million viewers each night.

The first of the three children of Jim and Joan Kimmel, James Christian Kimmel was born on November 13, 1967 in the New York City borough of Brooklyn. His father, a skilled bowler who dropped out of high school to earn money as a bowling hustler, met Kimmel's mother at a bowling alley. He later joined the U.S. Army and, after his military discharge, worked as both a short-order cook and an Equitable Insurance agent; according to some sources, he also worked for IBM. Kimmel's brother, Jonathan, is a television writer and producer. When Jimmy was nine years old, his family, which includes his sister, Jill, moved to Las Vegas, where his maternal grandparents, his uncle Frank Potenza, and his cousin Sal Iacono had recently moved. A Roman Catholic, he served as an altar boy for seven years. He told Bill Zehme for *Playboy* (December 2007) that he became "obsessed" with the snarky comedian and interviewer David Letterman and watched Letterman's show every weeknight. "The license plate on my first car was L8NITE," he recalled to Zehme. "For my 18th birthday my mom decorated the cake with the old NBC *Late Night with David Letterman* logo, and I posed for the picture with a big Dave-like cigar in my mouth." He told Kevin Cook for *Playboy* (February 2003), "You know how in high school, some guys play football and some are good students? I was the obsessed-with-Letterman guy." Kimmel also came to admire the comedy of the "shock jock" radio personality Howard Stern, after listening to a tape of Stern's show that his uncle had mailed to him.

Kimmel was a student at Ed W. Clark High School, in Las Vegas, when he got his first radio job, at the University of Nevada–Las Vegas (UNLV) station. After his high-school graduation, he attended UNLV for about one year before dropping out and enrolling at Arizona State University at Tucson. There he met Gina Maddy, whom he married two years later, when he was 20 years old. In 1989 he left college without earning a degree, to take a job with the morning radio program *The Me and Him Show*, on KZOK in Seattle, Washington. Kimmel and his on-air partner, Kent Voss, stayed at KZOK for 10 months before they were fired. Kimmel told Cook that he was ousted because he called his boss's idea for a new show "the stupidest idea I ever heard." He moved with his wife back to his parents' home in Las Vegas until, nine months later, he joined Voss and Voss's friend Mike Elliott, to serve as a producer and on-air personality for a morning radio show in Tampa Bay, Florida. Kimmel honed an irreverent on-air shtick that included live prank phone calls. After 10 months he and Voss were dismissed from that job as well. "People laugh about how I kept getting fired," Kimmel told Cook, "but it wasn't funny at the time. I was shocked and felt worthless." In the early 1990s Kimmel worked at a radio station in Tucson and had his own show on KCMJ-FM in Palm Springs, California, where Carson Daly (who later made a name for himself as an MTV video jockey and as the host of NBC's *Last Call with Carson Daly*) interned with him for a while. Kimmel also became the father of two children.

In 1994 Kimmel landed a job as a writer and sports commentator on the radio program *Kevin and Bean*, which aired on the popular Los Angeles modern-rock station KROQ. He adopted the moniker "Jimmy the Sports Guy" and injected humor into his sports commentaries. At KROQ he met Adam Carolla, a co-host with Drew Pinsky of the station's sex-and-relationship call-in show, *Loveline*. He and Carolla became close friends. In 1996 the two collaborated on a three-minute soap-opera parody, "The Cabbisons," that ran briefly as a segment on *Kevin and Bean* one morning each week.

"It's a parody of all sitcoms," Kimmel told Carrie Borziollo for *Billboard* (March 2, 1996). "I write it and make it as bad as possible and put in many unfunny lines and really bad laugh tracks." Kimmel went on: "My philosophy on radio is that you can't guess what people will think is funny. You can only do what you think is funny."

During the five years that he worked at KROQ, Kimmel took steps toward building a television career. In 1997 he began co-hosting Comedy Central's game show *Win Ben Stein's Money*, along with Stein, an attorney, former White House speechwriter, and actor known for his monotone and deadpan humor. On that show three guests competed to win $5,000, supposedly taken from Ben Stein's earnings, by correctly answering a series of questions. (A disclaimer that aired at the end of each installment explained that the prize money came out of the show's budget; any money left over after each season's finale was given to Stein.) Kimmel served as the wisecracking sidekick to the patrician Stein. Known for its irreverent tone and risqué humor, *Win Ben Stein's Money* won six daytime Emmy Awards, including one shared by Kimmel and Stein, in 1999, for outstanding game-show host. Around that time Kimmel began appearing as a guest host on *Fox NFL Sunday*, the pregame show for Fox's Sunday broadcast of National Football League games. In that role he became known for his smart-aleck remarks and for poking fun at the show's regular hosts, Terry Bradshaw, Cris Collinsworth, and Howie Long. His regular appearances on *Fox NFL Sunday* continued until 2003.

Concurrently, in 1999, Kimmel, Carolla, and the producer Daniel Kellison came up with the idea for *The Man Show*, a tongue-in-cheek comedy program geared toward young men and what were identified as their main interests—breasts, beer, masturbation, and farts. ABC commissioned the pilot but turned it down, deeming its contents too crude; Comedy Central accepted it. *The Man Show* debuted in June 1999, in the time slot following the popular and similarly raunchy animated-cartoon comedy *South Park*. One of the series' signature elements was the "Juggy Squad," the group of buxom female models who danced around the audience in revealing outfits at various moments throughout the show. Along similar lines, the closing credits for every episode included footage of young, bikini-clad women jumping on trampolines. Other segments included "Household Hints from Adult Film Stars," in which actors and actresses offered innuendo-laced advice; sing-along drinking songs performed by Bill "The Fox" Foser, who could drink two beers in less than two seconds; and Kimmel and Carolla's man-on-the-street antics. The first installment of *The Man Show* garnered the highest ratings ever for a Comedy Central premiere. Despite drawing criticism for its adolescent humor, the show became popular, mostly with male audiences. Kimmel and Carolla described *The Man Show* to a *Playboy* (August 1999) interviewer as a response to the many successful talk shows that catered to female audiences—Oprah Winfrey's and Rosie O'Donnell's, for example—and to the increasing "feminization" of men. "Our show is about what is true and what isn't," Kimmel told the interviewer. "It's no bullsh*t. I mean, *Baywatch, VIP* . . . they pretend to have a plot in all that stuff. We are not pretending; we have girls jumping on trampolines. That's as honest as it gets. We like to watch girls on trampolines." After Kimmel and Carolla left the program, in 2003, *The Man Show* aired for one more season, with Joe Rogan and Doug Stanhope as co-hosts. Drastically diminished audiences led to its cancellation, in 2004.

Meanwhile, in 2002, Kimmel, Carolla, and Kellison had founded a company, Jackhole Productions, and created another show for Comedy Central, called *Crank Yankers*. Developed largely because of Kimmel's love of prank phone calls, the show featured puppets mouthing and reenacting recordings of actual prank calls made by Kimmel and Carolla. Celebrity guests included Andy Dick, Bobcat Goldthwait, David Alan Grier, Seth McFarlane, Kevin Nealon, Sarah Silverman, Eminem, and Snoop Dogg; members of Kimmel's family also made appearances. In a time-consuming, labor-intensive process, each installment of *Crank Yankers* required preparing for and making the calls, obtaining release forms, constructing whatever new puppets were needed, and shooting and editing the puppet scenes. Kimmel and Carolla selected the best out of the 1,000 or so prank calls recorded for each season. *Crank Yankers*, which premiered in 2002, became the second-highest-rated show on Comedy Central, behind *South Park*. It was cancelled in 2005. In 2007 new episodes ran briefly on the MTV2 network; currently, MTV2 broadcasts reruns of the show.

Also in 2002 ABC offered Kimmel his own late-night talk show to replace the political-roundtable talk show *Politically Incorrect with Bill Maher*, which had been cancelled in July of that year. "It was so fast," Kimmel told Lynette Rice for *Entertainment Weekly* (November 28, 2003). "Suddenly I was on a plane to New York, and they were telling me things like 'This has to be a home run. There are a billion dollars of advertising at stake.' I was like, 'I'm hoping for a double. Would everyone be happy with a double?' And they're like, 'No.'" *Jimmy Kimmel Live* was modeled on CBS's *Late Show with David Letterman* and NBC's *Tonight Show with Jay Leno*: Kimmel was to sit behind a desk, recite an opening monologue, banter with celebrity guests, and take part in onstage and prerecorded segments. Unlike its competitors, it would be aired live before a studio audience.

Jimmy Kimmel Live debuted on January 26, 2003, in a special Sunday broadcast following ABC's airing of Super Bowl XXXVII, in an effort to draw a large audience. The show immediately experienced several problems. "It took just 10 minutes for the show to spiral out of control," Rice wrote. "An outdoor concert by Coldplay snarled traffic and enraged nearby businesses, while the plan to serve alcohol to the studio audience turned sour when a woman vomited off camera." Writing for *Time International* (February 10, 2003), James Poniewozik noted that the show's guests that night, among them the actor George Clooney, appeared uncomfortable with Kimmel's "tasteless jokes." Airing after Ted Koppel's news program, *Nightline, Jimmy Kimmel Live* received low ratings in its first season and was panned by critics. After 10 months its ratings lagged well behind those of its late-night competitors. Kimmel had trouble attracting celebrities to serve as guests, and ABC affiliate channels began to pull the show from the air and replace it with reruns of other shows. Kimmel grew frustrated and anxious. In early 2004 ABC's chairman, Lloyd Braun, one of Kimmel's biggest supporters, left the network—or was ousted, according to many reports. "It was definitely scary to lose Lloyd," Kimmel told Paige Albiniak for *Broadcasting & Cable* (June 28, 2004). Nevertheless, Albiniak wrote, ABC continued to support Kimmel and remained committed to improving the show's ratings. In early 2004 *Jimmy Kimmel Live* ended live broadcasts; according to the show's Web site, it is taped at 7:45 p.m. Pacific time and airs the same day. (All other late-night shows are recorded in the afternoon.)

On June 8, 2004 Kimmel joined the ABC sportscaster Mike Tirico to offer commentary during Game Two of the five-game National Basketball Association finals, which pitted the Los Angeles Lakers against the Detroit Pistons. At halftime Kimmel remarked, as quoted by Albiniak, "I realize that they're going to burn the city of Detroit down if the Pistons win, and it's not worth it." Tirico, who was then a Michigan resident, immediately objected to Kimmel's comment, and ABC received calls and e-mail messages from viewers condemning his words. ABC cancelled the June 9 installment of *Jimmy Kimmel Live*, and that day Kimmel issued through the network a written apology that read, according to *USA Today* (June 10, 2004, on-line), "What I said about Pistons fans during halftime was a joke, nothing more. If I offended anyone, I'm sorry. Clearly, over the past 10 years, we in L.A. have taken a commanding lead in postgame riots. If the Lakers win, I plan to overturn my own car." That statement, in turn, was criticized as a tasteless joke, and on June 10 Kimmel offered a second apology, distributed by ABC's publicity department, which read, as quoted in *USA Today*, "When you're 2,000 miles away from a city you've never lived in, it's hard to understand the sadness people feel from something that happened in their town—even if it happened many years ago. It was never my intention to cause anyone pain. I was trying to make a joke and I'm sorry it resulted in anything other than laughter."

Despite the difficulties Kimmel and *Jimmy Kimmel Live* experienced during the show's first season, it was renewed for a second. The 2005–06 season witnessed a 17 percent jump in its ratings among adults ages 18–49 and a 6 percent increase in overall ratings. After Jill Leiderman, a former producer for *The Late Show with David Letterman*, was hired as executive producer, in April 2006, she helped to reinvent the show, tailoring its humor to appeal to a broader audience. Critics and viewers responded favorably, and the show has continued to gain popularity. By March 2008 Kimmel's audience had reached just under two million viewers.

Kimmel's boyhood friend Cleto Escobedo III, a saxophonist and singer, leads Cleto and the Cletones, the *Jimmy Kimmel Live* band; Cleto Escobedo Jr., also a saxophonist, is a member of the band, too. (Father and son both had successful careers as musicians before joining Kimmel's show.) Kimmel's uncle Frank Potenza, Frank's former wife, Concetta (nicknamed Chippy), and Kimmel's cousins Micki and Sal have also appeared regularly, and his parents have been guests from time to time. Some of the popular recurring segments on *Jimmy Kimmel Live* include "This Week in Unnecessary Censorship," in which Kimmel presents a television clip in which an innocuous word or words have been bleeped, suggesting falsely that the material is scandalous. In another segment, "Uncle Frank and Aunt Chippy's Adventures," Kimmel's aunt and uncle paint nude models, take classes in self-defense, or engage in other potentially funny or ridiculous activities. Kimmel's daughter, Katherine (called Katie), and son, Kevin, both of whom are teenagers, have also appeared on *Jimmy Kimmel Live*; years ago they were occasionally seen on *The Man Show* and were heard making phone calls on *Crank Yankers*. Another segment featured the comedian Andy Milanokis; Kimmel later served as an executive producer of *The Andy Milanokis Show*, which ran on MTV in 2005–06.

In September 2008 Kimmel hosted an ABC special featuring celebrities including Ryan Seacrest, Tracy Morgan, Salma Hayek, Michael Phelps, Kobe Bryant, William Shatner, and Rachael Ray. Observers noted that the network's selection of Kimmel to host the show demonstrated its commitment to allowing his late-night show to continue. (Some people had speculated that Kimmel was to be replaced by Jay Leno.) In May 2009 Kimmel delivered what Dave Itzkoff, writing for the *New York Times* (May 19, 2009, on-line), described as a "withering, blistering monologue" at ABC's upfront presentation, in which potential advertisers watch samples of the next season's shows. In the much-talked-about monologue, Kimmel said in part, as quoted by Itzkoff, "Let's get real here. Let's get Dr. Phil-real here. These new fall shows? We're going to cancel 90 percent of them. Maybe more." Referring to advertisers' efforts to have their products appear on sets or as part of story lines, he said: "Next year on *Grey's Anatomy*, your product could kill Dr. Izzie. It just depends on how much you want to pay." According to an ABC press release, the total number of viewers of *Jimmy Kimmel Live*, and, in particular, the total number of viewers ages 18 to 49, was greater during the 2009 February/March "Sweeps" period than in the same period in 2008. In at least five consecutive weeks during the summer of 2009, the show garnered higher ratings than its time-slot competitor, NBC's *Late Night with Jimmy Fallon*, which premiered in March.

Kimmel's marriage ended in divorce, in 2003, after more than a year of separation. Kimmel and the comedian Sarah Silverman became romantically involved in about 2002. Kimmel became a topic in Silverman's stand-up routines, and Silverman was a frequent guest on Kimmel's show. During the show's fifth-anniversary special, on January 26, 2008, Silverman presented Kimmel with a satirical music video in which she "confessed" to having had an affair with the actor Matt Damon. The video was replayed millions of times on the Internet and brought Kimmel's show nationwide attention. (In September 2008 Silverman's video earned a Creative Arts Primetime Emmy in the category of outstanding original music and lyrics.) Kimmel responded on February 24, 2008 with a similar, star-studded music video, in which he confessed to having had an affair with the actor Ben Affleck, a longtime friend of Damon's. The following July representatives of both Kimmel and Silverman confirmed that the pair had broken up. Kimmel and Silverman reunited later in 2008 and split up again in early 2009.

Zehme described Kimmel as "a man of considerable heart and generosity who loves much, loves enthusiastically and loves nothing more than the ever fertile prospect of Good Times—the two hopeful words he reflexively employs most often in life, especially during awkward conversations, in dashed e-mail sign-offs and when nothing else interesting comes to mind." Kimmel lives in Los Angeles, less than a mile from the home of his ex-wife and children. He enjoys cooking, golfing, watching sports, and hosting large gatherings than often center on football games viewed on his big-screen television.

—M.E.R.

Suggested Reading: *Entertainment Weekly* p47 Nov. 28, 2003; *Esquire* p86 Jan. 1, 2007; *In Style* p524 Oct. 2006; *Interview* p120+ Oct. 1, 2003; *Playboy* p97+ Aug. 1999, p59+ Feb. 2003, p139+ Dec. 2007; *Ross Reports Television & Film* p5+ Jan. 1, 2005; *Time International* p45 Feb. 10, 2003

Selected Television Shows: as writer, actor, and producer—*The Man Show*, 1999–2003; *Crank Yankers*, 2002–05; *Jimmy Kimmel Live*, 2003– ; as co-host—*Win Ben Stein's Money*, 1997–2002; as producer—*The Andy Milanokis Show*, 2005–06

Selected Films: *Down to You*, 2000; *Road Trip*, 2000; *Donner*, 2001; *Like Mike*, 2002; *Garfield*, 2004

Knox, Simmie

Aug. 18, 1935– Portrait artist

Address: Knox's Portraits and Fine Arts, 13801 Ivywood Ln., Silver Spring, MD 20901

The artist Simmie Knox has painted portraits of some of the most influential and prominent figures in modern America. His subjects have included the U.S. Supreme Court justices Thurgood Marshall and Ruth Bader Ginsburg, the boxing champion Muhammad Ali, and the baseball Hall of Famer Hank Aaron. The highlight of his career thus far came in 2001, when he became the first African-American artist to be commissioned to paint an official presidential portrait. His portraits of former president Bill Clinton and Hillary Rodham Clinton were unveiled in 2004.

Knox, who grew up in Alabama in a poor family of sharecroppers, went on to study at the Tyler School of Art at Temple University and taught art for 18 years in schools in Pennsylvania, Delaware, Maryland, and Washington, D.C. He nonetheless describes himself often as a "self-taught" portrait artist. "When I graduated from Tyler, I was an abstract painter. At that time, abstract painting was in vogue," he explained to James Auer for the *Milwaukee Journal Sentinel* (June 16, 2004). "I'd had no classes in figure painting. I had to read some books and just kind of practice. I'd been taught elements of design and principles of composition, and this, coupled with my skill at drawing, enabled me to train myself to do the figure." Knox has said that he switched to portraits because he found them to be far more challenging than abstract art. "You have to get the exact likeness of a person you're striving to please, whereas in an abstract, things just happen. This requires a [certain] skill. The older I get, [the more] I realize that I have a special skill. I'm blessed," he told Betsy Peoples for the *Crisis* magazine (May/June 2002).

In the early 1980s Knox's family sold his art at a local public market in Washington. He has often credited the comedian Bill Cosby with helping to raise his profile in the city's art community. After a meeting in 1983, Cosby commissioned Knox to paint portraits of his family members and referred the artist to his friends. Elaine Bachmann, curator of the Maryland Commission on Artistic Property, said to Tamela Wallace for the Annapolis, Maryland, *Capital* (February 28, 2005), "Simmie Knox's portraits will emerge as some of the most insightful images of public servants. His work has the realism of photography, but clearly shows the hand of the artist. . . . Knox's portraits . . . have a timeless quality that places him within the great tradition of American portraiture." After almost three dec-

Courtesy of Simmie Knox

Simmie Knox

ades as a portrait artist, Knox remains passionate about his work. "I can look at something and render it just the way I see it," he told Foster Klug for the Associated Press (June 18, 2004). "That's a rush you never get tired of."

Simmie Lee Knox Jr. was born on August 18, 1935 in Aliceville, Alabama, the only child of Simmie Knox Sr., who worked as a carpenter and mechanic, and Amelia Knox. When Knox was three his parents divorced, and his father sent him to Leroy, Alabama, to live with his grandfather and a paternal aunt. Knox's father lived and worked in another city while young Knox was put to work on the family farm. "We worked, literally, from sunup 'til sundown, in the field. Whatever there was to be done. You didn't go to school. You worked on the farm," he told Peter Jennings on the ABC program *World News Tonight* (June 18, 2004, on-line). When Knox was nine he moved to Mobile, Alabama, to live with his father and stepmother, Lucille. Enrolled at Most Pure Heart of Mary, a Catholic grade school, Knox attended class seven days a week, making up for the schooling he had missed. He showed an interest in drawing at a young age and would often draw humorous versions of comic-book characters to amuse family members.

Knox's first love as a child, however, was playing baseball. He would spend his afternoons playing with neighborhood children, who included the future baseball legend Hank Aaron. One day, when Knox was in fourth grade, he was struck in the eye by a ball and taken to a doctor. "That ended my baseball career," he told Russell Nichols for the *Birmingham (Alabama) News* (June 27, 2004). His eye took over a year to heal, and his doctor suggested taking up a hobby that would help his eye regain the ability to focus. The nuns at the Heart of Mary School noticed Knox's artistic talent and encouraged him to draw. In the 1940s South he was banned from art classes due to his race; the nuns instead arranged informal Saturday-morning art lessons with a mail carrier.

Knox graduated from Central High School in 1956 and, unable to pay for college, enlisted in the U.S. Army. After his discharge he enrolled at Delaware State College, in Dover, attending classes in the morning and working at a textile mill in nearby Milford during the afternoon. Though he enjoyed drawing, Knox did not consider art a viable career option, so he majored in biology. While his work in that subject was less than stellar, the accurate drawings of animals and plants he made to accompany his written work led some of his professors to suggest that he take art classes.

Having grown up in the segregated South, where African-Americans were forced to use bathrooms and water fountains separate from those of the white population, Knox struggled with questions about his identity throughout his adolescence and beyond. His first attempts at portrait work, in the early 1960s, were a series of self-portraits in which he tried to express his internalized anger and confusion. Knox soon discovered that he had found his true passion, as well as an identity, in art.

Deciding that he wanted to become an art teacher, Knox transferred to the University of Delaware, in Newark, in 1963 to major in art education. Shortly after receiving his bachelor's degree, in 1967, he moved to Philadelphia, Pennsylvania, and began teaching in public schools. At night Knox attended art classes at the Tyler School of Art at Temple University. Although he had become interested in portraits, the faculty, who at the time considered representational art to be outdated, encouraged him to focus on abstract art. "You'd bring a figure painting into class, they'd laugh at you: 'What are you bringing that junk in here for?' So I said, 'I got to get with the program,'" he told Foster Klug. At the Tyler School Knox painted large-scale abstract works, which he later credited with helping him to perfect his portraits. "It forced me to really take a thorough look at the elements of design, which is very fundamental to making anything visual," he explained to Voice of America News (March 10, 2005, on-line). He received his bachelor of fine arts degree in 1970. In the following year he exhibited some of his abstract artwork at the Thirty-Second Biennial of Contemporary American Painting at the Corcoran Gallery of Art, in Washington, D.C., alongside work by the celebrated artists Roy Lichtenstein and Philip Pearlstein. In 1972 Knox earned his master of fine arts degree from the Tyler School.

Knox moved to the Washington, D.C., area and began teaching at Bowie State College, now known as Bowie State University, in Prince George's County, Maryland. "Art is a fantastic way of building character," he told Daniel Connolly for the Associated Press (November 4, 2005, on-line). "It's a fantastic way of teaching confidence. And once [the students] get that feeling of confidence they will excel and they can take on anything." In those years Knox dabbled in portraits, producing one of Martin Luther King Jr. in 1974 and one of Frederick Douglass (now a part of the Smithsonian's Museum of African Art collection) in 1975, while continuing to paint abstracts as well as still-lifes. Knox served as the director of the National Museum of African Art in downtown Washington in 1974 and left Bowie State in 1975 to teach art at the Duke Ellington School of the Arts, in Washington. The school did not renew his contract, and in 1980 he was without a job. He began to devote himself entirely to portraits and found a renewed love for the art form.

During that period Knox, his wife, Roberta, and their two young children, Amelia and Zachary, lived in a two-bedroom apartment in the Adams Morgan neighborhood of Washington. (He has another daughter, Sheri, born in 1961, from a previous marriage, to Marceline Ward.) One bedroom was transformed into Knox's studio, and the family leased a small space at the city's Eastern Market on the weekends to sell his paintings. In 1983 David Driskell, an artist and art historian, introduced Knox to Bill Cosby, who was then looking to hire a portrait artist. "Back in 1983, the Cosbys asked me to seek a person who could render a likeness of them," Driskell, who has served as curator of the Cosby Collection of Fine Art, told Betsy Peoples. "I knew of Knox's work. I saw the competency of his work and his technical ability—he's able to render an excellent likeness. [Knox's] art just isn't a form of realism, but it imprints a certain kind of feel; you see the character of an individual."

The meeting proved to be a turning point in Knox's career. Cosby commissioned the painter for 12 portraits of his family members over the course of eight years. Soon afterward Knox began receiving more commissions, including those for portraits of Dorothy Height, then the president of the National Council of Negro Women, and Supreme Court justice Thurgood Marshall, both in 1989. With his portrait of Marshall, Knox became the first African-American commissioned to paint an official portrait of a Supreme Court justice. Knox soon became a locally known and respected artist. Among his more famous subjects are the writer Alex Haley (1977), former New York City mayor David Dinkins (1993), Muhammad Ali (1995), Bishop John T. Walker (1995), Hank Aaron (1996), and the historian John Hope Franklin (1996).

Knox's realistic portraits are filled with detail and evoke their subjects' personalities. Betty C. Monkman, the chief White House curator during the Clinton administration, told Lynette Clemetson for the *New York Times* (June 15, 2004), "He paints beautiful faces that really say something to you." "Every face is different, and that's what I love about it," Knox told Kathy Adams for the Wilmington, Delaware, *News Journal* (June 7, 2007). "I don't think I've ever seen anything more fascinating than the face, the human face—it's the joy and the sorrow and the pain, and whatever is going on with the person you can read it in their face." As for his technique, Knox has said that he likes to meet his subjects in person (or, in the case of subjects who are deceased, their surviving relatives) and get a feel for their personalities. He starts his portraits by working on the subjects' eyes. "[The eyes] say more about a person than anything else," Knox explained to Betsy Peoples. "I like for my subject to have eye contact with the viewer. I like for the eyes to follow you. I want people to be able to say, 'I don't know that person, but I would like to meet them.'" Though Knox is an artist, he is attuned to the business side of his profession—particularly customer satisfaction. "I remind myself, I'm in a service capacity," he told Steve Inskeep for the National Public Radio program *Morning Edition* (June 14, 2004). "You know, you have to please your clients because you live and die on your reputation and, in fact, I get all of my work by word of mouth, so I try and be sure that when I let it go, it's what they would like to see." Although he claims not to take artistic liberties, he also believes that touching up subjects' features is sometimes warranted. "If you have to strengthen some things, you do. Sometimes you can leave out a few lines, you're trying to show a person at their best," he told Kathy Adams.

In 2001 Knox was selected to paint President Bill Clinton's official presidential portrait. President Clinton chose the painter, shortly before leaving office, once he had viewed Knox's portfolio and spoken to Supreme Court justice Ruth Bader Ginsburg, who loved the portrait Knox had painted of her the previous year. "It is rare in life that realization exceeds high expectation," Ginsburg told Betsy Peoples. "Viewing Simmie Knox's portrait of me was one of those rare occasions." Knox has said that he felt a connection with the former president, who also grew up in a poor southern family, and told David Hammer for the Associated Press (June 11, 2004, on-line), "I think that's why he has the compassion he has. He knows how it feels to have lived a certain life and to have been deprived of things. I knew the day [Clinton] came into office, if I ever have the chance to paint a president I think this is the one. Somehow I felt that." Even so, Knox was still in awe of the situation. "My mind hasn't completely wrapped around it yet," he told Hammer. "Just imagine: I was born in 1935 in Aliceville, Alabama, a sharecropper, and now I'm painting the president. Can you imagine that?" In preparation for the portrait, Knox visited the White House five times to discuss poses as well as sketch and take photos of President Clinton. A traditional sitting for the portrait was not possible because of Clinton's schedule, so Knox painted mostly from photographs. ("How are you going to tell a president that he's got to sit down for two hours for weeks in the same clothes?" Knox asked Russell Nichols.) After viewing the painter's mockups of her husband's portrait, then–First Lady Hillary

Rodham Clinton asked Knox to paint her official portrait as well. Although it is common for official portraits of presidents and First Ladies to be unveiled at the same time, it is rare for both to be done by the same artist.

Knox's work was unveiled before the Clintons, President George W. Bush, and First Lady Laura Bush in the East Room of the White House on June 14, 2004. His 48-by-58-inch, oil-on-linen portrait of the former president depicted Clinton in a dark blue suit, standing before his desk in the Oval Office, one hand in his pocket, the other resting on the table beside him. It is the first presidential portrait to include the American flag and also features Clinton's military-medallion collection, as he had requested. Senator Clinton's 36-by-48-inch portrait is not only the first to depict a broadly smiling First Lady, but also the first to show a First Lady wearing a pantsuit. The portrait also features a copy of Senator Clinton's best-selling book *It Takes a Village* (1996) placed on a table beside her. At the ceremony she remarked, in a widely quoted statement, "One thing that has never been said about either my husband or I . . . is that we are patient people. . . . And Simmie was more than understanding as he worked with us over the last several years. I'm very grateful to him, not only for his artistry, but for his humanity."

Knox, who enjoys listening to jazz while he paints, now works in a converted garage outside his four-bedroom home in Silver Spring, Maryland. While a student in Delaware, he sold his art pieces for $5 to $10 each; his portraits, which are always done in oil on oil-primed linen, now command prices starting at $20,000. At 74 Knox is grateful for his continued success and hopes he will be able to do what he loves for years to come. "It's been like having to run a marathon and having to run it uphill all the way," he told Kathy Adams. "Today, it's still uphill. The shoes are a little better. The food's a little better. The bills are paid now." His most recent commissions have included portraits of South Carolina congressman Joseph Rainey, the first African-American to serve in Congress, for the U.S. Capitol, in Washington, D.C. (2005); the media mogul Oprah Winfrey for Morehouse College, in Atlanta, Georgia; and the philanthropist James H. Gilliam Jr. for St. Johns College in Annapolis, Maryland (2008). Knox was also asked in 2006 to sculpt a bronze bust of the late Morgan State University music director Nathan M. Carter Jr. for the university. About that project, his first commissioned sculpture since the 1970s, he told Gadi Dechter for the *Baltimore Sun* (January 7, 2007), "I was glad to be able to reconnect with sculpture, something that I have wanted to do for years." Knox has said that he hopes to paint a portrait of the Nobel Prize winner and former South African president Nelson Mandela.

—M.A.S.

Suggested Reading: Associated Press On-line June 18, 2004; *Birmingham (Alabama) News* June 27, 2004; *Christian Science Monitor* Arts & Leisure p13 June 22, 2001; *Crisis* p45 May/June 2002; *New York Times* A p20 June 15, 2004; SimmieKnox.com; *Washington Post* C p1 June 16, 2004; *(Wilmington, Delaware) News Journal* A p1 June 7, 2007

Kevin Winter/Getty Images

LaBeouf, Shia

(la-BUFF, SHY-uh)

June 11, 1986– Actor

Address: c/o Beverly Hecht Agency, 3500 W. Olive St., Suite 1180, Burbank, CA 91505

"In an age when potential action heroes seem to be either rugged '80s relics like [Harrison] Ford and Sylvester Stallone or sensitive thespians willing to double up on their bench presses like Tobey Maguire and Orlando Bloom, [Shia] LaBeouf is that rarest of screen creatures, the scrappy kid next door," Rebecca Winters Keegan wrote for *Time* (July 5, 2007, on-line). The filmmaker Steven Spielberg, who directed LaBeouf in *Indiana Jones and the Kingdom of the Crystal Skull*, told Keegan, "Shia is within everyone's reach. He's every mother's son, every father's spitting image, every young kid's best pal and every girl's possible dream." In a similar assessment, the film critic Claudia Puig wrote for *USA Today* (April 12, 2007, on-line), "Shia LaBeouf is the kind of youthful everyman who brings to mind a young Jimmy Stewart. He has an ease on camera and a low-key sense of humor that makes him likable and relatable." LaBeouf's skills as an actor have been linked to his highly unconventional upbringing, by parents whose way of life harked back to the 1960s counterculture: his mother and father rejected salaried jobs and lived from hand to mouth; passed the hat at street performances; and, in his father's case, alternately succumbed to and battled drug addiction. LaBeouf, who turned 23 this past June, started performing by himself in coffee shops and a comedy club when he was 10. At 12 he secured an agent and got work in commercials and occasional television shows. At 14 he won a leading role as one of the title characters in the Disney TV series *Even Stevens.* He has since starred in films including *Holes, Disturbia, Transformers, Transformers: Revenge of the Fallen, Indiana Jones and the Kingdom of the Crystal Skull,* and *Eagle Eye.* With very few exceptions critics have greeted his performances with high praise. D. J. Caruso, the director of *Disturbia* (2007), which was filmed when LaBeouf was 20, told Barry Koltnow for the *Orange County (California) Register* (April 13, 2007, online), "When you look into his eyes, you can see an old soul. There is a lot of depth there because of his background, and that sets him apart from other actors of his generation."

The only child of Jeffrey Craig LaBeouf and Shayna Saide LaBeouf, Shia Saide LaBeouf was born on June 11, 1986 in Echo Park, a section of Los Angeles, California; he grew up in that neighborhood, which was largely Latino at that time and also had a fair number of artist residents. LaBeouf was named for his maternal grandfather, a Holocaust survivor who performed comedy routines at Jewish resorts in the so-called Borscht Belt, a vacation area in the Catskill Mountains, in New York State. His paternal grandmother reportedly associated with Allen Ginsberg and other Beat poets. LaBeouf described his parents to Keegan as "old hippies. They're not really worker bees. They're artists who just didn't have enough bureaucrat in them to get it all wrapped up in a nice little package to be able to feed to the American public." His mother, who is Jewish, studied modern dance until an injury forced her to give up that pursuit; afterward, she became a visual artist and jewelry maker. His father, who is of Louisiana Cajun descent, was a veteran of the Vietnam War. During his son's childhood he struggled with heroin addiction and had difficulty holding onto jobs; sometimes he would work as a clown or a mime. He also sold illegal drugs. "He was tough as nails and a different breed of man," LaBeouf told Koltnow. In an interview with Shannon Harvey for the Perth, Australia, *Sunday Times* (April 14, 2007, on-line), LaBeouf said, "It was a bad life. We were broke, really broke." Sometimes, in order to make ends meet, the family performed on the street. When LaBeouf was a toddler, his father stole a housekeeping cart from a hotel and set it up with hot dogs and buns; then, with the three of them dressed as clowns, the family would perform in a local park. "I hated selling hot dogs. I hated dressing up in clown," LaBeouf told Keegan. "But the minute somebody would buy into my thing and buy a hot dog from my family because of my shtick, my parents would look at me like, 'All right, man.' Besides performing, I've never had that validation from anything else I've ever done in my life."

By his own account, when LaBeouf was 10 he began smoking cigarettes, including marijuana cigarettes his father rolled. He also watched action films starring Steve McQueen and accompanied his father to Rolling Stones concerts and meetings of people who, like his father, were trying to give up their addictions. "When you're 10 years old and watch your father going through heroin withdrawals, you grow up real fast," he told Koltnow. "You become the parent in the relationship. But I must give him credit because he always told me that he didn't want me to be like him." That year LaBeouf's parents divorced; afterward, he lived with his mother, who eked out a living by selling her homemade jewelry on the street.

LaBeouf attended the 32nd Street/USC Visual and Performing Arts Magnet School, on the campus of the University of Southern California, in Los Angeles. Inspired by a schoolmate who had a role in the CBS family drama *Dr. Quinn, Medicine Woman,* he resolved to become a performer. His schoolmate, he explained to Keegan, "had all the stuff I wanted, materially. When you're in school, if you've got the new Filas [sports shoes] on, no one's gonna punch you that day." He began performing comedy in coffee shops, and after awhile he talked his way into a standup gig at the Ice House, a comedy club in Pasadena, a short distance from Los Angeles. Wearing overalls and his hair in a bowl cut, LaBeouf attempted to shock his audience with obscene jokes about adolescent sexuality. "My thing was the 50-year-old mouth on the 10-year-old body," LaBeouf told Keegan. "Sometimes I would bomb. I'd talk about personal stuff and instead of laughing, people would look at me like, 'Oh, man, I'm so sorry.'" Eager to make more money and gain greater attention, LaBeouf set about securing an agent. "I went to the Yellow Pages, called up an agent and pretended to be a manager called Howie Blowfish," he told Harvey. "I said I had this great client named Shia, and that he should come in for meetings and auditions. The agent knew I was a kid, but she said she'd never had a kid try to sell himself and that I should come in." The agent, Teresa Dahlquist, who had bought the Beverly Hecht Agency a few years earlier, signed him on. (As posted on the agency's Web site, Shayna LaBeouf stated that she brought Shia to Dahlquist, who she knew "was the best agent in town.") Dahlquist, who still represents LaBeouf, paid for headshots, transportation to and from auditions, and, when necessary, the LaBeoufs' rent.

LaBeouf soon got jobs in commercials. He broke into film in 1998, with small roles in *The Christmas Path* and *Monkey Business*; he also appeared in the made-for-television children's movie *Breakfast with Einstein* and the sitcom *Jesse*. He had a minor role in 1999 in an episode of the sitcom *Suddenly Susan* and appearances in the series *Touched by An Angel* and *The X-Files*. By that time he had become a student at Alexander Hamilton High School, in Los Angeles. Also in 1999 he landed a major role, in a new Disney Channel show called *Even Stevens*. He was cast as Louis Stevens, a geeky middle-school student and the rambunctious brother of Ren, a subdued, overachieving older sister, played by Christy Carlson Romano. The series, which premiered a few days after LaBeouf's 14th birthday, became popular with preteen and teenage audiences, and LaBeouf was hailed for his work in it. Carole Horst wrote for *Variety* (June 19– 25, 2000) that LaBeouf and Romano "should start plotting the rest of their careers, as these two young thesps bring polish and excellent timing to the material." LaBeouf won a Daytime Emmy Award for his portrayal of Louis in 2002, a year before the show went off the air. During its run, because he was a minor, he had needed an adult to accompany him to the set and remain there while he worked, and Disney had paid his father a weekly salary to serve in that capacity. "For three years we lived in a motel, and that's when we started to get our relationship back on track," LaBeouf told a reporter for the Perth, Australia, *Sunday Times* (May 7, 2008). "In a very real sense this business gave me my father back and I'll always be grateful for that." In 2003 LaBeouf appeared in *The Even Stevens Movie*. Earlier, in 2002, he had appeared as a mentally disabled child in the Disney Channel's family movie *Tru Confessions*.

In 2003, the year he graduated from high school, LaBeouf starred in the Disney film *Holes*, whose screenplay was Louis Sachar's adaptation of his award-winning 1998 same-titled novel for young people. LaBeouf portrayed the palindromically named Stanley Yelnats IV, a teenager sent to a desert boot camp after being wrongly accused of theft. Every day he and the other campers are forced to dig deep holes, leading him to suspect that the villainous camp warden (played by Sigourney Weaver) is searching for something that she knows has been hidden there. When Yelnats discovers a treasure chest that bears the name of his great-great-grandfather and is rightfully his, the warden and her sadistic assistant (Jon Voight) attempt to keep it. The film, which examined greed, racism, friendship, and the importance of holding onto dreams, was generally praised and brought LaBeouf both excellent reviews and much attention in the film industry. "Mr. LaBeouf, with his soft face and curly hair, rises to the challenge of depicting a coddled, sensitive young man who must prove his toughness without sacrificing his decency," A. O. Scott wrote for the *New York Times* (June 12, 2003). *Holes* brought LaBeouf close to Voight, who encouraged him to view acting as more than just a way to earn money. "He became my mentor," LaBeouf told Koltnow. "He took me under his wing at the exact time that I needed some serious adult guidance."

Also in 2003 LaBeouf had small roles in the action comedy *Charlie's Angels: Full Throttle* and the widely panned comedy *Dumb and Dumberer: When Harry Met Lloyd*. In the same year he starred in *The Battle of Shaker Heights*, which aired on TV during the second season of HBO's *Project Greenlight*, a reality series that documented the work of amateur filmmakers. Written by Erica Beeney and directed by Kyle Rankin and Efram Potelle, *The Battle of Shaker Heights* got a lukewarm critical reception, but LaBeouf's performance, as a teenage war reenactor bent on defeating the local bully through military tactics, was praised. The documentary showed that he maintained a professional demeanor despite the first-time filmmakers' difficulties. "Accustomed to hanging out with creative, chaotic grownups, LaBeouf came off as a charmer, a good sport, and one of the smarter people on set," Keegan wrote. In 2004, with his friend Lorenzo Eduardo, he wrote, directed, and produced the wordless, six-minute film *Let's Love Hate*. Also that year LaBeouf had a small role alongside Will Smith in the futuristic thriller *I, Robot*, followed by a similar part the next year, opposite Keanu Reeves, in the action/horror film *Constantine*.

In the biographical movie *The Greatest Game Ever Played* (2005), LaBeouf was seen as the amateur golfer Francis Ouimet, who beat top players in the 1913 U.S. Open. "As Ouimet, the always-terrific Shia LaBeouf is an oasis of depth in a film that otherwise can't pass up a sports-film cliché," Keith Phipps wrote for the *A.V. Club* (September 28, 2005, on-line). LaBeouf lent his voice to the character Asbel in the dubbed English version of Hayao Miyazaki's animated film *Nausicaä of the Valley of the Wind* (1984). He next appeared as the younger self of Dito Montiel, the character played by Robert Downey Jr., in the semiautobiographical coming-of-age drama *A Guide to Recognizing Your Saints* (2006), which Montiel wrote and directed. Before LaBeouf and Montiel met, LaBeouf's association with Disney productions led Montiel, like many others, to doubt that he was capable of the gritty performance the role demanded. "Immediately I said I'd like to come in and read [at an audition], they said 'No, no, no, he's the Disney kid,'" LaBeouf recalled to Neala Johnson for the Melbourne, Australia, *Herald Sun* (April 12, 2007, on-line). "It worked against me. But there's nothing I can do about that other than change people's opinion when I come in and read." Montiel's film was a critical success, while the response to LaBeouf's performance was mixed. Praise came from A. O. Scott, who wrote for the *New York Times* (September 29, 2006), "The casting of these two itchy, inventive actors [LaBeouf and Downey] in a single role is nothing short of revelatory. . . . Mr. LaBeouf has a watchful, excited demeanor, and his character, miserable as he sometimes is, is also curious and adventurous, savoring the funny, strange and beautiful things the world throws in front of him." By contrast, Robert Khoeler wrote for *Variety* (January 22, 2006, on-line), "If there's a casting hiccup, it's LaBeouf in effect playing a young Robert Downey Jr. Appearing more baby faced than streetwise, LaBeouf seems wrong for the role." *A Guide to Recognizing Your Saints* helped LaBeouf separate himself from the Disney image. "Disney is great," he told Neala Johnson, "it's been great to me and many other actors, it's a great place to cultivate your skills. But it can be debilitating because it's very one-notey, it doesn't stray, its goal is to create children-friendly entertainment. And a lot of 20-year-olds don't live children-friendly lives."

In the reality-based *Bobby* (2006), written and directed by Emilio Estevez, LaBeouf portrayed a drug-addled member of the campaign staff of U.S. senator Robert F. Kennedy of New York during his run for the Democratic presidential nomination in 1968, which ended with Kennedy's assassination. LaBeouf and the other actors in the film, among them Martin Sheen (Estevez's father), Harry Belafonte, Sharon Stone, Laurence Fishburne, and Demi Moore, were nominated for a Screen Actors Guild Award in the category "outstanding performance by a cast in a motion picture." Steven Spielberg, who had been impressed with LaBeouf's work in *Holes*, was instrumental in having him cast as the hero in LaBeouf's next film, the teen thriller *Disturbia* (2007). Executive-produced by Spielberg and directed by D. J. Caruso, *Disturbia* was a new version of Alfred Hitchcock's classic suspense film *Rear Window* (1954), starring James Stewart as a reporter whose broken leg has kept him housebound. LaBeouf played Kale Brecht, a teenager who, while confined to his room, takes to spying on his neighbors. After observing evidence of a murder in a nearby house, Kale becomes entangled in a game of cat and mouse with the killer. While the film received mixed reviews, most critics agreed that LaBeouf excelled in his role.

In *Transformers*, which grew out of a popular 1980s cartoon series, LaBeouf was cast as Sam Witwicky, who is unwittingly swept up in a war between opposing forces of robotic creatures that can change into technological devices—such as automobiles—to avoid detection on Earth. The main features of the film, directed by Michael Bay, were its special effects. "Alone among the human characters in *Transformers*, Witwicky makes an impression," Chris Kaltenbach wrote for the *Baltimore Sun* (July 2, 2007, on-line). "In part, that's because he's given all the best lines. But mostly, the credit goes to LaBeouf's spirited performance. Historically, director Bay has never paid much attention to his actors, and it shows; to say most of them sleepwalk through their performances would be to shortchange somnambulists everywhere. But LaBeouf, bless him, forces life into Witwicky, refusing to let us pin him down or to let the movie's relentless action overwhelm him."

LaBeouf played Mutt Williams, the rebellious sidekick of Indiana Jones (Harrison Ford) in *Indiana Jones and the Kingdom of the Crystal Skull* (2008), the fourth installment of the Indiana Jones series, which was launched in 1981. According to Kenneth Turan, writing for the *Los Angeles Times* (May 19, 2008, on-line), the film introduced Mutt "as a total copy of Marlon Brando on a motorcycle in *The Wild One*," adding, "LaBeouf doesn't seem completely comfortable in his disaffected teen role, a part that does not play to the innate likability that is one of his strengths." Others found LaBeouf's character more appealing and thought that he and Ford were perfectly paired. Michael Sragow, for example, wrote for the *Baltimore Sun* (May 29, 2008, on-line), "LaBeouf suffuses the young and restless Mutt with a ripe avidity that recalls 1950s idols like Tony Curtis as much as it does James Dean. . . . LaBeouf and Ford have ideal chemistry: Ford snarls with the experience of age, LaBeouf glitters with the fool's immortality of youth."

In September 2008 LaBeouf appeared in the thriller *Eagle Eye*. In the film, which received mixed reviews, he played a slacker who finds himself caught up with a stranger in a series of mysterious and sinister events. His next motion picture, *Transformers: Revenge of the Fallen*, debuted in 2009 to predominantly negative reviews, with critics taking Bay, its director, to task for placing greater emphasis on special effects and pyrotechnics than on acting. Ray Bennet wrote for the *Hollywood Reporter* (June 15, 2009, on-line), "LaBeouf gets little chance to show what charm he might have," and Carrie Rickey wrote for the *Philadelphia Inquirer* (June 23, 2009, on-line), "*Transformers 2* morphs from teen adventure into lumbering war movie. Bay and his screenwriters squander their human capital in order to show us scenes of 20-ton toys crushing 10-ton toys." Later in 2009 LaBeouf appeared in *New York, I Love You*, a film comprised of vignettes set in New York City. Around that time he also began work on Oliver Stone's *Wall Street 2: Money Never Sleeps*, a sequel to Stone's well-received *Wall Street* (1987). *Wall Street 2* will star Michael Douglas as the greedy financier Gordon Gekko and LaBeouf as a young stockbroker engaged to Gekko's daughter. In 2009 LaBeouf also directed a music video for "I Never Knew You," a single by the rapper Cage. He has been cast in a third *Transformers* film and an adaptation of John Grisham's novel *The Associate*.

Earlier, in November 2007, LaBeouf was arrested in the early morning hours for trespassing in a Walgreens store in Chicago, Illinois, before it opened and after refusing a security guard's orders to leave. The guard claimed LaBeouf was intoxicated, but Walgreens declined to press charges. In July 2008 LaBeouf's pickup truck collided with another vehicle at an intersection in Los Angeles. The actor suffered a broken hand and his passenger, the actress Isabel Lucas, received minor injuries. He was arrested on suspicion of drunk driving and, although police later stated that the driver of the other vehicle was at fault for running a red light, LaBeouf's license was suspended for a year because he refused to take a breathalyzer test. His injury was written into the storyline for *Transformers: Revenge of the Fallen*, but it forced him to abandon what would have been his next project, *Dark Fields*.

A tattoo on LaBeouf's right wrist reads "1986–2004." The actor told Keegan that it represents his childhood: "I've been working since I was 10; 2004 is when I decided I became an adult." LaBeouf was accepted to Yale University but has never enrolled there. Although he has told interviewers that he abstains from hard partying, LaBeouf admitted to a writer for *Details* (September 2008) that he had a drinking problem. As of May 2009 he was attending Alcoholics Anonymous meetings. LaBeouf lives in Burbank, California.

—W.D.

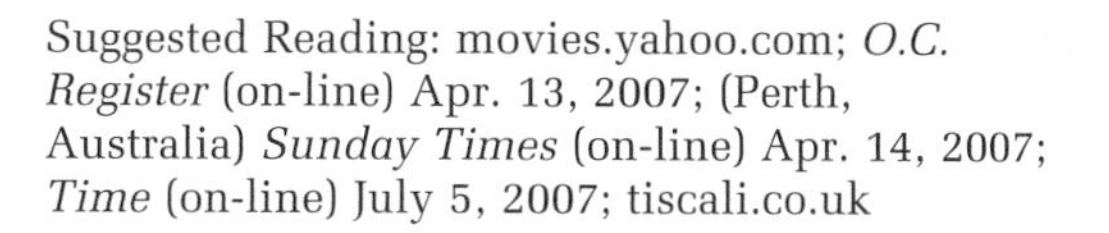

Suggested Reading: movies.yahoo.com; *O.C. Register* (on-line) Apr. 13, 2007; (Perth, Australia) *Sunday Times* (on-line) Apr. 14, 2007; *Time* (on-line) July 5, 2007; tiscali.co.uk

Selected Films: *The Even Stevens Movie*, 2003; *Holes*, 2003; *The Battle of Shaker Heights*, 2003; *I, Robot*, 2004; *Constantine*, 2005; *The Greatest Game Ever Played*, 2005; *A Guide to Recognizing Your Saints*, 2006; *Bobby*, 2006; *Disturbia*, 2007; *Transformers*, 2007; *Indiana Jones and the Kingdom of the Crystal Skull*, 2008; *Transformers: Revenge of the Fallen*, 2009; *New York, I Love You*, 2009

Selected Television Shows: *Even Stevens*, 1999–2003; *Project Greenlight 2*, 2003

Courtesy of the office of Ray LaHood

LaHood, Ray

Dec. 6, 1945– Secretary of the U.S. Department of Transportation; former U.S. representative from Illinois (Republican)

Address: U.S. Dept. of Transportation, 1200 New Jersey Ave., S.E., Washington, DC 20590

On January 3, 2009, the last day of the 110th Congress, Ray LaHood ended his seventh term as the representative of Illinois's 18th Congressional District and relinquished his seat in the House, as he had announced in July 2007 that he would do. The 63-year-old LaHood has not retired, however, as had been his intention: in December 2008 then-President-elect Barack Obama nominated him to be the next secretary of the U.S. Department of Transportation. On January 22, 2009 the Senate Commerce and Transportation Committee confirmed his nomination, and on January 26 he was sworn in. LaHood and U.S. senator Judd Gregg of New Hampshire, whom Obama tapped to head the Department of Commerce, were the only Republicans nominated by the president to serve in his Cabinet. (Gregg withdrew his nomination in February. Obama's next choice for commerce secretary, Gary Locke, who currently holds that position, is a Democrat. Secretary of Defense Robert M. Gates, a registered Independent who has identified himself as a Republican, is a holdover from the previous administration, that of George W. Bush.) When he entered Congress, in 1995, LaHood—whose previous jobs include teacher, city planner, and member of the Illinois state legislature—succeeded Robert H. "Bob" Michel, for whom he had worked for 12 of Michel's 38 years as a representative. In the House LaHood became known for thinking independently, treating others fairly, fostering friendly relations, and promoting bipartisanship. When Republicans held a majority in the House, LaHood, thanks to his reputation for evenhandedness and his solid knowledge of parliamentary procedure, often presided over House sessions as a temporary replacement (officially, Speaker pro tempore, or "for the time being") for the House Speakers—Newt Gingrich, in the 104th and 105th Congresses, and Dennis Hastert, in the 106th through 109th. Those qualities also led to LaHood's presiding over part of the impeachment proceedings against President Bill Clinton, in 1998. "More than once" during the impeachment debate, as Democratic representative Anna Eshoo of California told John Hughes and Julianna Goldman for Bloomberg.com (December 28, 2008), "the entire House stood up and applauded how he comported himself in the chair." In a speech on the floor of the House in October, then-congressman Rahm Emanuel of Illinois, with whom LaHood worked closely, said that the framers of the Constitution might have had someone like LaHood "in their mind's eye" when they "thought of a member of Congress," as quoted by Michael A. Fletcher and Philip Rucker in the *Washington Post* (December 18, 2008). "He is an individual who, while firm in his principles, [is] very flexible about his opinions," Emanuel added. In his new post LaHood has focused on Obama's economic-recovery projects related to transportation and the president's push for "livable communities," high-speed rail, and a reduction of automobile emissions and oil dependence.

Raymond H. LaHood was born into a Maronite Catholic family on December 6, 1945 in Peoria, Illinois, where hundreds of immigrants from Lebanon, including at least one of his grandparents, settled in the early 1900s. His parents, Edward and Mary (Vogel) LaHood, managed a restaurant and tavern. LaHood was raised in the East Bluff, a blue-collar neighborhood in Peoria, where he attended St. Bernard's Grade School. He graduated from the Spalding Institute, a Catholic High School in Peoria. He then enrolled at Canton Junior College (now called Spoon River College), in Canton, Illinois, and later transferred to Bradley University, in Peoria, where he majored in sociology and education. He got married in 1967 and had become the father of his first two children by the time he earned a B.S. degree, in 1971. He next taught social studies at the junior-high-school level and, concurrently, served as a director of the Rock Island County Youth Services Bureau, a delinquency-prevention agency. From 1974 to 1977 he worked as a chief planner for the Bi-State Metropolitan Planning Commission (now the Bi-State Regional Commission), which addresses matters concerning both Iowa and Illinois.

For five years beginning in 1977, LaHood was the district representative for Thomas "Tom" Railsback, a Republican from Illinois's 19th Congressional District. "That's a very big job, because that person has to deal with all of the people in the district," Railsback told Brandy Donaldson for the Quad-Cities, Illinois, *Dispatch-Argus* (December 29, 2008, on-line). "He's your spokesman and your communicator. Ray came in and had this shaggy hair. But he was very articulate, very positive. After meeting with him for 15 or 20 minutes, I thought, 'This guy is great.' So I brought him into congressional politics and service."

In May 1982 LaHood was appointed to fill the seat in the Illinois State House of Representatives vacated by Ben Polk, who had resigned. After serving the remainder of Polk's term, LaHood ran to retain the seat; he lost by a narrow margin to another Republican, Bob DeJaegher. In 1983 LaHood was hired as an aide to the veteran U.S. representative and Peoria native Bob Michel, who represented Illinois's 18th Congressional District (which contains 11 of the counties of the district that Abraham Lincoln represented in Congress); at that time Michel was the House minority leader. In 1990 LaHood became Michel's chief of staff. When Michel retired, in 1994, LaHood made a successful bid to succeed him; in a contest against the Democrat G. Douglas Stephens (who had previously lost two races against Michel), LaHood captured 60 percent of the votes. In his most recent reelection, in 2006, he won more than 67 percent of the ballots cast.

LaHood was one of only three Republicans (the others were incumbents) who did not sign the Contract with America. Written a few weeks before the November 1994 election, with much of it taken verbatim from President Ronald Reagan's 1985 State of the Union Address, the contract (referred to by some of its opponents as the Contract on America) was presented as the Republicans' promise to the American people to pass, within 100 days of Congress's opening day in 1995, legislation aimed at shrinking the federal government, lowering taxes, limiting the role of the United Nations in U.S. foreign policy, and reforming welfare, among other goals. In other areas in which he broke with his party's stance, in October 2001 LaHood was one of only three House Republicans to vote against the Patriot Act, an antiterrorism bill whose provisions many critics viewed as violations of civil liberties. (Five years later, however, he voted in favor of renewing the act.) In 2007 he and 10 other Republicans visited the White House to warn President George W. Bush that the war in Iraq was becoming increasing unpopular among members of the American public. In matters in which LaHood adhered to the GOP line, he voted to prohibit the noncitizen children of illegal immigrants from attending public schools, to lift the ban on private ownership of certain types of assault weapons, and to weaken certain Clean Water Act regulations, among other stands.

During his years in Congress, LaHood served on the House Agriculture Committee and introduced legislation supporting the expansion of ethanol production in Illinois. As a member of the Appropriations Committee, he was credited with securing funding for highway-improvement and airport-expansion projects. LaHood opposed striker-replacement legislation, which would allow employers to hire replacement workers when their employees go on strike, and he opposed the deployment of U.S. troops to Kosovo, a disputed region in what was once Yugoslavia, as part of a 1990s U.N. peacekeeping mission. He has introduced legislation to abolish the Electoral College and was outspoken in denouncing the racial profiling of Arab-Americans.

In Congress LaHood developed a reputation as a centrist, publicly criticizing as well as praising Republicans and Democrats alike. He fostered strong relationships with members of both parties, among them two Democratic legislators from Illinois: then-congressman Rahm Emanuel and then-U.S. senator Barack Obama. Making it his mission "to restore civility to Capitol Hill," as Kathy Kiely wrote for *USA Today* (December 18, 2008), he helped to organize a series of bipartisan retreats; one, held in March 1997, drew more than 200 Democratic and Republican members of the House and people in their families. With Emanuel, he regularly invited groups of six Democratic and six Republican representatives to have a meal together, "to bridge the partisan divide," in Kiely's words.

In July 2007 LaHood announced that he would retire from Congress at the end of his seventh term. Then, a few weeks after Obama's victory in the presidential election, Obama chose him to be the next U.S. secretary of transportation. Some critics of LaHood's appointment complained that he lacked the administrative experience necessary to oversee a complex Cabinet-level department. Although LaHood supported several measures aimed at preserving the Illinois River and enhancing or expanding two national wildlife refuges in his home state, other detractors worried that LaHood's largely conservative voting record on environmental issues gave little hope that he would push for "green" solutions to transportation-related problems, and that his close ties with certain corporations would place consumers at a disadvantage. Most prominent among those firms is Caterpillar, a Fortune-100 company that is headquartered in Peoria; though it is commonly associated most closely with the production of tractors, Caterpillar is also "the world's leading manufacturer of construction and mining equipment, diesel and natural gas engines and industrial gas turbines," according to its Web site. Despite such criticism, on January 22, 2009 the U.S. Senate approved LaHood's nomination by voice vote, and he was sworn in the next day.

The Department of Transportation (DOT) employs almost 60,000 people and oversees 11 agencies: the Federal Aviation, Federal Highway, Federal Transit, and Maritime Administrations; the Federal Railroad Administration, which deals with railway safety, and the Surface Transportation Board, which judicially settles railroad rate and service issues (and certain rate matters involving trucking and moving companies, intercity passenger buses, and ocean-shipping companies); the Federal Motor Carrier Safety Administration, which deals with the safety of large trucks and buses; the Pipeline and Hazardous Materials Safety Administration; the National Highway Traffic Safety Administration, which monitors safety issues involving light trucks and passenger cars; the Saint Lawrence Seaway Development Corp.; and the Research and Innovative Technology Administration. In addition, the DOT, like all Cabinet-level departments, has an Office of Inspector General, whose responsibility is to ensure that all divisions act lawfully.

As DOT secretary LaHood plays a major role in the Obama administration's proposed massive public-works projects, part of the $787 billion stimulus package (officially, the Economic Recovery and Reinvestment Act) that the president signed into law in February 2009. The projects were designed both to stimulate the economy, providing thousands of jobs, and repair the nation's badly deteriorating roads, bridges, and other aspects of infrastructure. Decisions emanating from his department also affect the way in which the Chrysler and Ford corporations spend the billions of dollars in federal bailout funds recently lent to them. In addition, LaHood's agenda includes trying to improve the badly strained labor-management relations at the Federal Aviation Administration (FAA), modernizing the air-traffic-control system, and ameliorating congestion in and around airports.

LaHood oversees a $70 billion budget, $48 billion in funds from the stimulus package, and $61.5 billion authorized by the extension, in July 2009, of the so-called highway bill, which funds transportation projects. Aside from steering recovery money into highway and bridge projects, LaHood has approved investments in mass transit and airports and $8 billion for high-speed rail. He is in favor of creating "livable communities" in which residents walk, ride bicycles, and use public transit instead of driving; he told Amanda Ruggeri for *U.S. News.com* (June 12, 2009), "This is a transformational president, and the department is following the president's lead. People haven't really been thinking about these things. They have been thinking about how to build roads, how to build interstates, how to build bridges. People now are thinking differently about where they want to live, how they want to live, and how they want to be able to get around their communities." The DOT is actively pushing for passage of the Clean Energy Jobs and American Power Act, sponsored by Democratic U.S. senator John Kerry of Massachusetts.

In July and August 2009, the DOT oversaw the $3 billion "Cash for Clunkers" program—officially, the Consumer Assistance to Recycle and Save (CARS) program—which allowed owners of "gas guzzlers" (cars that use gasoline inefficiently) to turn in their vehicles for $3,500–$4,500 vouchers to be used to purchase more fuel-efficient cars. The program boosted auto sales, and some auto factories that had closed reopened to replenish shrinking inventories. The White House estimated that the purchases of some 690,000 cars by those who took advantage of the vouchers would boost the economy by .3 to .4 percent in the third quarter of the year and would save or create 42,000 jobs.

The Ray and Kathy LaHood Scholarship for the Study of American Government is awarded annually to a junior at Bradley College, LaHood's alma mater. In 2001 LaHood won the Frank Bellrose Illinois River Valley Conservation Award from the Illinois chapter of the Nature Conservancy; in 2005 he earned the Charles B. Shuman Distinguished Service Award from the Illinois Farm Bureau. He has also received four honorary degrees from Illinois institutions. LaHood and his wife, Kathy, have two sons, Darin and Sam; two daughters, Amy and Sara; and seven grandchildren. Darin LaHood, an attorney, has served as a federal prosecutor and an assistant Illinois state prosecutor. Sam LaHood, who has a master's degree in Middle Eastern studies from American University in Lebanon, is employed by the Office of Strategic Communications and Planning in the U.S. State Department's Bureau of Public Affairs. Amy LaHood is a physician.

—W.D.

Suggested Reading: *Chicago Tribune* (on-line) Dec. 18, 2008; fastlane.dot.gov; *New York Times* (on-line) Dec. 17, 2008; *USA Today* (on-line) Dec. 18, 2008

Don MacKinnon/Getty Images

Layton, Jack

July 18, 1950– Canadian politician; leader of the New Democratic Party

Address: House of Commons, Ottawa, Ontario K1A OA6, Canada

Since 2003 Jack Layton, one of Canada's best-known politicians, has been the leader of one of that country's four main political parties, the left-leaning New Democratic Party. The social-democratic NDP, sometimes described as "the moral conscience of Canada," has traditionally been seen more as a minority party in opposition to the country's two major parties—the Liberals and the Conservatives—than as a governing body in its own right. (The NDP has only slightly fewer seats in Canada's Parliament than the Bloc Québécois.) For instance, many Canadians agree that without the NDP in opposition, universal access to health care and education might no longer exist in the country; Layton has famously and repeatedly portrayed the party as advocating policies from "the kitchen table, not the boardroom table." Layton first made his name as an outspoken left-wing activist and municipal politician in Toronto, Ontario, in the 1980s and 1990s. Perceived initially as a brash and uncompromising socialist with a penchant for grandstanding, he gradually came to be seen as a skillful, media-savvy politician and power broker able to take advantage of flexible alliances in order to achieve the goals of his party. In 2005, for example, Layton offered political support to the then-governing but badly ailing Liberal government in exchange for greater funding of education, affordable housing, programs aimed at energy efficiency, and other NDP causes. (At times his support of coalitions in exchange for policy changes has angered some of the stauncher socialist members of the NDP.) More recently, he has focused on changing his party from one of opposition to one that can genuinely contest for power. "There are some people who think that if you win seats, you must've done something wrong," he told Aaron Wherry for *Maclean's* magazine (September 8–15, 2008). "You must have betrayed some principle. The most principled person wouldn't win any seats. Well, I'm not that kind of leader. . . . Winning seats, I thought that was the purpose." Layton, who had virtually no national profile when he ran for the position of NDP leader in 2003, was seen as a gamble for a party that had been almost completely decimated in the 1990s and early 2000s. Under his leadership, however, the NDP has doubled its support and consistently improved its position in Parliament, coming close to the numbers it boasted at its peak, in the 1980s.

The NDP was created in the early 1960s to advocate for agrarian, labor-union, working-class, and social-justice causes. Its first major contribution to public life—the championing of universal public health care—came under its first, charismatic leader, the Reverend Tommy Douglas, premier of Saskatchewan. Over the years, and especially at the height of its popularity, under Ed Broadbent, from 1975 to 1989, the party broadened its constituency to include New Left concerns, including the environmental, feminist, gay-rights, antiglobalization, and peace movements. After the party's popularity dipped in the 1990s, along with that of many other social-democratic movements in the West, the NDP began to be pulled in different directions, between labor-union and New Left inclinations on the one hand, and pragmatic calls for a shift to the center, in the manner of U.S. Democrats and U.K. New Labor politicians, on the other. Layton, as Margaret Wente explained for the Toronto *Globe and Mail* (June 12, 2004), was voted leader of the party at that uncertain juncture: "The NDP has three distinctly different constituencies. One is the Prairie heartland, where Tommy Douglas invented medicare. One is the world of labour unions and the working man. And one is Latteland, where socially conscious urbanites dream of a greener, gentler world. A good NDP leader needs to straddle all three. But most of all, he needs to make the party sexy again." In the view of many, Layton did exactly that, bringing a contagious and seemingly boundless energy to his campaigns. In his run for his party's leadership, Layton addressed what he called the prevailing but misleading notion that radical ideas cannot be implemented efficiently. He said, as quoted by Doug Ward for the *Vancouver Sun* (July 27, 2002), "Some people say to me: 'Are you left or are you pragmatic?' I say that's a false dichotomy."

The eldest of Doris and Robert Layton's four children, Jack Layton was born on July 18, 1950 in Montreal, Quebec, and raised in nearby Hudson, a prosperous anglophone enclave in Canada's francophone province. Much has been made of his family background, which features a long line of Canadian politicians. His mother is a descendant of one of the fathers of the Canadian Confederation, William Steeves. It has been said that Layton inherited his activist streak—as well as his flair for the dramatic—from his great-grandfather Philip Layton. A British immigrant, Philip Layton had been blinded in his youth and founded the Montreal Association for the Blind, which later became the Canadian National Institute for the Blind; his actions led to the creation of one of the country's first social programs, after he spearheaded a campaign for disability pensions during the Great Depression—and threatened to show up outside the Parliament building with hordes of blind people if the measure was not adopted. Layton is said to have inherited his political skill from his father and paternal grandfather. That grandfather, Gilbert Layton, a cabinet minister in Maurice Duplessis's Union Nationale government in Quebec, was an ardent antifascist who resigned in 1939 over the government's opposition to conscription in World War II. Jack Layton's father, an engineer who reportedly had a hand in building Canada's first hybrid car, was an activist in the Liberal Party in the 1960s and 1970s; after shifting rightward to join the Conservatives in the 1980s, he was elected to Parliament in 1984, serving in the cabinet of Conservative prime minister Brian Mulroney.

As John Geddes wrote in an in-depth profile of Jack Layton for *Maclean's* (December 5, 2005), "His boyhood and youth seem defined by the cliches of two eras: an idyllic 1950s small-town nurturing, followed by an exhilarating 1960s campus-activist coming-of-age." A top student and popular varsity athlete whom friends described as being rebellious and able to inspire others, Layton was president of his high-school student council and was highly involved in community service. He once led an ultimately unsuccessful campaign to have a youth center built in Hudson. "At one point Jack thought he might go in the ministry," his mother told Kathleen Harris for the *London (Ontario) Free Press* (June 6, 2004). "Then he thought he might go to Africa with the Peace Corps." Upon graduating, in 1967—after writing for his high-school yearbook that he would become prime minister someday—he traveled to the west coast of Canada with his friend Bert Markgraf to attend a national youth parliament. The two hitchhiked back across the country in what both would describe as a formative experience. "We were very earnest. . . . We stayed up all night discussing all kinds of philosophical things, a lot of existentialist things—at least as far as we could at 17," Markgraf told Geddes. "That was our centennial project, to get to know Canada," he told Hubert Bauch for the *Montreal Gazette* (June 13, 2004).

Layton then studied political science at McGill University, in Montreal, where he supported the Liberal Party before turning further leftward. As Graham Fraser pointed out in the *Toronto Star* (January 26, 2003), "Layton identifies his involvement in politics with some key events in recent Quebec history." As with many of his contemporaries in the late 1960s, Layton took part in university sit-ins and campaigned for a variety of causes, including affordable housing. His most important intellectual and political mentor at McGill was the renowned political philosopher Charles Taylor, who had run unsuccessfully for Parliament in 1968 as an NDP candidate. As a Liberal Layton had met several candidates at the party's leadership convention in 1970, including Pierre Laporte, who was kidnapped and murdered by radical Quebec separatists later that year in what came to be known as the October Crisis. (James Cross, a British trade commissioner, had been kidnapped earlier.) When the Liberal government of Prime Minister Pierre Trudeau, in response, introduced the War Measures Act, Tommy Douglas's NDP was the only political party to oppose the act, on the grounds of its threat to civil liberties. The NDP's stance inspired Layton to join the party in 1971.

Layton had graduated from McGill with a B.A. degree in 1970 and had moved to Toronto to pursue master's and Ph.D. degrees in political science at York University. He has said that he got "hooked" on politics in 1972, when he worked on the successful campaign of Michael Goldrick, his professor of urban studies at York, who was running for Toronto city council. In the same election David Crombie, a professor of urban politics at Ryerson University, in Toronto, was elected mayor, and Layton was hired to fill his teaching position. Layton spent the next decade teaching political science, municipal politics, sociology, and urban and environmental studies at Ryerson, York University, and the University of Toronto, while getting more involved in municipal politics and activism. He was also completing his Ph.D. thesis, a study of how countries have addressed the international flow of capital, entitled "Capital and the Canadian State: Foreign Investment Policy, 1957–1982." Layton was awarded a doctorate in 1983. He has written books on homelessness—proposing a subsidized national housing policy—and on environmental politics and green energy. In *Speaking*

Out: Ideas That Work for Canadians (2004), Layton outlined the development and trajectory of his political views and the mix of idealism and pragmatism in his strategies.

In 1982 Layton was elected to the Toronto city council as the running mate of former mayor John Sewell, who became an alderman. For the next three years, he was known as Sewell's understudy. Layton quickly got a reputation as a scruffy, outspoken left-wing council member, often seen wearing blue jeans and riding his bicycle; his actions, some felt, got attention but often fell short of accomplishing their stated goals. Layton opposed the building of the Skydome Stadium (to house the Toronto Blue Jays of Major League Baseball) as well as the city's Olympic bid, arguing that they would be a waste of public funds. He wore a black gag to protest other politicians' ignoring his opposition to what he denounced as an exploitative government deal with the Shell Oil Co. in Nigeria. His profile on the CBC (Canadian Broadcasting Corp.) Web site notes that Layton alternately "threatened and cajoled his way into getting official sanction for such things as curbside recycling, bike lanes and a downtown windmill."

Layton has said that he experienced an epiphany in 1985, when he decided to shift his focus from merely criticizing policies to offering solutions to problems. "I realized I was in the process of being typecast," he told Fraser. "I decided, 'We're going to switch from opposition to proposition.'" That year he was elected chairman of Toronto's board of health and "went on a rampage of proposition," as he recalled to Fraser, introducing an extensive plan to fight AIDS and restrictions on smoking in the workplace. In 1988 Layton and his left-leaning allies won control of the Toronto city council. By the time of the 1991 mayoral election, he had adopted a new suit-and-tie image, as part of his effort to show that he was serious enough for the post. Due in part to the unpopularity of the NDP leadership of Ontario, which was blamed—unfairly or not—for failing to respond effectively to a profound recession, Layton was soundly defeated in the mayoral election by June Rowlands. After that loss Layton continued teaching and also spent a few years in the private sector, founding the Green Catalyst Group, an environmental consulting firm that outlined sustainable policies for energy conservation. In 1993, in a campaign he later admitted to knowing he could not win, he ran unsuccessfully for the federal Parliament as an NDP candidate in the Toronto riding (or district) of Rosedale. The following year he returned to municipal politics, where he would slowly gain a larger national profile for his work with—and later stewardship of—the Federation of Canadian Municipalities; he became known for pressing progressive urban causes. In 1997 he ran again as an NDP candidate in the federal elections, this time to represent what is now called the Toronto-Danforth constituency; he was beaten by the Liberal member of Parliament (MP) Dennis Mills.

In 2003, with the NDP suffering a crisis of direction, a lack of appeal among voters, and a decade's steady erosion of its support base, Layton decided to seek the post of national leader. Countering critics who pointed to his lack of experience and qualifications, particularly when it came to national issues, he campaigned as a badly needed fresh face. Layton persuaded several influential voices to back him, including those of the popular band the Bare Naked Ladies, who played at some of his rallies, and, perhaps more importantly, the former NDP leaders Audrey McLaughlin and Ed Broadbent. In an opinion piece for the *Globe and Mail* (November 28, 2002) entitled "Why I Am Supporting Jack Layton," Broadbent, who was easily the most popular living NDP figure, wrote, "I want a revival of progressive politics in Canada and a rejuvenated NDP. Jack Layton is crucial to both. Once, pressure from the left on Canada's all-things-to-all-people parties (Liberals and Conservatives) brought us pensions, health care and progressive taxation. . . . We desperately need to restore a commitment to the public good after a decade of attempts to assess all political projects by the market criteria of profitability. We need to get excited about politics again. . . . It is true that millions of Canadians hold social democratic values on public health care, a fair distribution of wealth and measures to protect our air and water. . . . Having the right policies is important. But it's not enough. Any good intellectual can win the debate. More is needed from a political leader. He or she must have substance—and must, through language, attitude and approach, get the people's interest in that substance. . . . More than any other candidate, Jack Layton has demonstrated that he would be this kind of leader." Layton was elected head of the party on January 25, 2003, defeating NDP members of Parliament Bill Blaikie and Lorne Nystrom on the first ballot. Layton, who did not have a seat in the federal Parliament, refused to run in a by-election or try to unseat another MP in a "safe seat," instead appointing Blaikie as the NDP's interim parliamentary leader and vowing to win the 2004 election for Parliament against Mills in the Toronto-Danforth riding. Still, Layton managed to stay in the media spotlight, usually attacking the Liberal Party as having shifted rightward (making it, according to Layton, indistinguishable from the Conservative Party) during its virtually uncontested decade in power. By the end of 2003, enthusiasts were pointing to a considerable increase in NDP support, which they attributed in large part to the "Layton effect" as well as Liberal Party "fatigue" among voters and the effective collapse of the Conservative groups, the Canadian Alliance and the Progressive Conservatives (which later united as the Conservative Party of Canada).

Layton entered the 2004 election campaign as both national party leader and parliamentary candidate, outlining his priorities as including increased funding for cities, opposition to the privatization of health care, proportional representation in Parliament, support of the international Kyoto environmental agreement, and investment in development in Afghanistan rather than participation in the U.S.-led war there. Some of Layton's statements proved controversial, including those he made during a heated tirade in which he accused Prime Minister Paul Martin of killing the homeless with his policies; a few miscues he made in discussing the hot-button issue of separatism in Quebec also caused some to call him a political novice. Nonetheless, the elections in June 2004 were considered a partial success. The party claimed 15 percent of the popular vote—its highest percentage since the late 1980s—but gained only five seats in Parliament (claiming less than a 6 percent share of the power), less than half of what Layton had predicted. Many observers said that NDP supporters had been scared in the end into voting for the Liberal Party, in order to avoid a Conservative victory. Again complaining about a lack of proportional representation, Layton noted that while the NDP had won almost half a million more votes than the Bloc Québécois, they gained 35 fewer seats in Parliament than their French-Canadian rivals. Layton managed to squeak into Parliament, narrowly beating Mills in Toronto-Danforth. (Layton's wife, Olivia Chow, failed to win in the Toronto riding where she ran.)

The Liberals remained in power but had been reduced to a minority government—that is, they had more seats than any other party but fewer than the others combined, making them vulnerable. When a scandal involving Liberal Party corruption broke out in the winter of 2004–05, the Conservatives and the Bloc Québécois saw an opportunity and called for a vote of no confidence, which would lead to new elections. It was at that point, most observers agreed, that Layton emerged as an effective politician and a credible national leader. In return for his party's essential support in propping up the Liberal government, Layton asked the prime minister for major concessions: to cancel $4.6 billion in corporate tax cuts and increase funding for affordable housing, education, public transit, environmental and energy-efficiency programs, international aid, and social programs in Canada. Many called the 2005 federal budget "the NDP budget," as Layton achieved many of his party's stated goals. "Not bad for a guy who commands only the fourth party in the House, a mere 18 MPs out of 308," Geddes wrote. At the end of 2005, when the scandal further damaged the Liberal Party, Layton offered continued backing in exchange for several more concessions, including a ban on private health care. When his proposals were rejected, Layton backed the opposition parties in calling for a no-confidence vote, which led to the 2006 federal elections. In that campaign Layton appeared more polished than in his 2004 race, sticking to talking points. He focused attacks on the Liberals, arguing that "Canadians have a third choice," noting that the NDP was the only party to safeguard health care, and pointing to his success in changing the previous budget; he asked Liberals to "lend us your vote and we'll earn it next time round." The Liberals had been intensifying a campaign of strategic voting, arguing that all progressives should vote for them to avoid a Conservative victory, and were even able to persuade the Canadian Auto Workers head, Buzz Hargrove, to campaign for them, landing a major symbolic blow against the NDP. Even so, the NDP won 10 more seats in Parliament, bringing their total to 29 (still well behind the other three main parties, with the Conservatives winning a minority government).

Layton, who had presided over a virtual renaissance of the party, boasted almost unanimous support later that year in the NDP leadership vote. On the other hand, he was facing considerable criticism, with many liberal and progressive Canadians blaming him directly for the Conservative victory; in some increasingly loud circles, Layton's shrewd politicking was being seen more as a naked desire for power than an effective way to secure his party's goals. "The New Democrats' 29 MPs now hold the balance of power, meaning they can stop the other opposition parties from defeating [Stephen] Harper's [Conservative] government," Frances Russell wrote for the *Winnipeg Free Press* (January 10, 2007). "Beginning with the last election, the NDP and the Conservatives have been, well, indecently cosy." For example, Layton offered his support to the minority Conservative government in exchange for concessions on the environment. Without much of a mandate in its minority-leadership role, the Conservative government called an early election for October 2008, to try to better its position. In the campaign, which climaxed as the country and the world were on the verge of a major financial crisis, Layton proposed redirecting the more than $50 billion corporate tax cut put forward by the Conservatives toward a national child-care policy and a child-benefit rebate for families, among other core goals of the NDP. "What we've seen on Wall Street this week is what happens when the rich and powerful are allowed to do whatever they want with other people's money," Layton said, as quoted by Mike Blanchfield and Juliet O'Neill in the *Edmonton Journal* (September 29, 2008). "Can we afford to let Stephen Harper take us down that George Bush road?" In fact, many observers noted that Layton seemed to be emulating the rhetoric successfully employed by Barack Obama, the U.S. Democratic presidential nominee at the time. While Layton responded that working people in both countries were merely facing similar issues, he attended the U.S. Democratic National Convention in Denver, Colorado, and his campaign officials admitted that he was benefiting from comparisons to the charismatic Obama. (Others sneered at the comparison. In a blog post Bob Rae, a former NDP provincial leader of Ontario who had turned to the Liberal Party, wrote, "Jack Layton thinks he's Obama. What a joke. He's Ralph Nader." He was referring to the progressive U.S. presidential candidate whom many saw as the spoiler in the 2000 race, in which the Democrat Al Gore lost to the Republican George W. Bush.)

Layton signaled a change in goals in the 2008 election. For the first time he stated publicly that he was running for the post of prime minister (or at least leader of the opposition). "For decades, the NDP has debated about whether we're running for government or running to be a strong third party or the principled party in the House of Commons, and I think [Layton] has decided since the last election that, 'By golly, we're going to run for government and let the chips fall where they may,'" Dick Proctor, Layton's former chief of staff, told Mike Desouza for Canwest News Service (October 12, 2008). "I think that was a bold decision, and probably, in the long term, the right decision." On October 14, 2008 the NDP gained another eight seats, bringing their total to 37. It remains the country's fourth-largest party, though not far behind the Bloc Québécois. Within weeks of the elections, the opposition parties were calling for still another vote of no confidence, proposing a coalition government between the Liberals and the NDP and supported by the bloc.

In December 2008 Governor General Michaëlle Jean granted a request by the Conservative leadership to prorogue Parliament—and thus delay a no-confidence motion—until the end of January. In the interim, the Liberals had a leadership change, with the new head of the party, Michael Ignatieff, deciding to side with, and thus save, the Conservatives—and distance himself from the coalition. In the summer of 2009, at the NDP federal policy convention, Layton received another significant vote of confidence from his party and went essentially unchallenged as its leader. In September, in what some observers called a reversal on the part of both Liberals and New Democrats, the Liberals announced that they would end their support of the minority Conservative government and put forward a motion of no-confidence, forcing a new election. In response, Layton announced that he would support the Conservatives and prevent an election in exchange for $1 billion allocated to unemployment benefits for those hardest hit by the global economic recession of 2008–09. To some, that move was another example of Layton's pragmatism: again presenting his smaller party as the indispensable power broker between the two major parties, with each having to court and make concessions to the NDP in order to gain the upper hand against the other. "When . . . Michael Ignatieff announced earlier this month that he would end his support for Harper's minority government, my party saw an opening to help the thousands of Canadians who are counting on us. Harper can't govern alone," Layton wrote in an op-ed piece for the *Toronto Star* (September 27, 2009). "We told him he needed to reach out or he'd have to call an election. He did reach out. The $1 billion he is proposing to spend on improving EI [Employment Insurance] benefits isn't enough, of course. Too many unemployed won't benefit from these changes. . . . For us, though, the real question is how to use political leverage responsibly when you have it." While his critics lashed out at what they called his hypocritical opportunism, Layton argued that he could not ignore the opportunity to push through legislation that was at least a "step in the right direction," and that the NDP was supporting unemployment benefits, not the Conservative government.

Layton married his first wife, his high-school sweetheart, Sally Halford, in 1969. Although the marriage, which produced two children, Sarah and Michael, ended in 1983, they remain close. In 1988 Layton married then–Toronto school-board trustee Olivia Chow. Over the years he and Chow have become one of Canada's best-known political couples; currently, both are federal MPs representing Toronto ridings. "We are the political partnership," Layton told Fraser. "No one has more influence on the way I think and work than Olivia. We have almost never had even an argument." He and Chow live with Chow's mother and their cat, George, in the Chinatown section of Trinity-Spadina, the riding that Chow represents.

—M.M.

Suggested Reading: *Maclean's* p20 Dec. 5, 2005, p28 Sep. 29, 2008; *Maple Leaf Web* (on-line) Nov. 22, 2007; (Toronto, Canada) *Globe and Mail* A p21 Nov. 28, 2002, A p27 June 12, 2004; *Toronto Star* A p7 Jan. 26, 2003

Selected Books: *Homelessness: How to End the National Crisis*, 2000; *Speaking Out: Ideas That Work for Canadians*, 2004

Lee, Cliff

Aug. 30, 1978– Baseball player

Address: Philadelphia Phillies, Citizens Bank Park, 1 Citizens Bank Way, Philadelphia, PA 19148-5249

It was not for nothing that the Major League Baseball player Cliff Lee won the 2008 American League (AL) Comeback Player of the Year Award. In 2007, while with the Cleveland Indians, the pitcher—whose accuracy does not always match his formidable power—had an injury-plagued season that was spent partly in the minors, ended with a win–loss record of 5–8, and once saw him booed off the mound. The following year, demonstrating his often-cited ability to overcome pressure, he pitched well enough to win the AL Cy Young Award. Though he struggled somewhat in the first weeks of the 2009 season, many observers blamed his mediocre win–loss record (4–8 as of early July) on the Indians' lack of offensive support. On June 14, 2009 he had a strong showing when he held the St. Louis Cardinals to eight hitless innings, helping

Jared Wickerham/Getty Images

Cliff Lee

the Indians to a shut-out victory (3–0) and marking the longest no-hit performance of his career. On July 29, 2009 Lee was traded to the Philadelphia Phillies, and he has went on to help lead that team to its second World Series berth in two years; the Phillies lost to the New York Yankees. In the series opener, on October 28, 2009, Lee pitched for the entire game and allowed no earned runs, leading the Phillies to beat the Yankees, 6–1. With that game Lee became the first pitcher since the Pittsburgh Pirates' Deacon Phillippe in Game One of the 1903 World Series to pitch a complete World Series game with 10 or more strikeouts and no walks. Throughout the postseason observers were impressed with the performance by Lee, who allowed just two earned runs in 33 1/3 innings in his first four play-off starts and appeared remarkably composed—even casual—on the mound. Writing for the *New York Times* (October 30, 2009, on-line) after the Phillies' victory in Game One, Lynn Zinser observed: "It was possible to stumble into Game 1 of the World Series and believe the Phillies' Cliff Lee was pitching a game in May. Against a beer league team. He shrugged. He caught a pop-up while rolling his eyes. He never once stopped chewing his gum, even while snaring a line drive behind his back. He did everything but yawn and check his text messages."

One of the three children of Steve Lee, a firefighter, and Sharon Lee, Clifton Phifer Lee was born on August 30, 1978 in Benton, Arkansas, a suburb of Little Rock. He has a sister, Cara, and an older brother, Chad. Doug Crise reported for the *Arkansas Democrat-Gazette* (June 8, 2008) that Lee's father "raised his boy to be polite and respectful and to value people over games and superlatives." Still, Steve Lee told Crise, Cliff Lee does not "put up with much nonsense. . . . He's pretty low-key. He gives you one warning. When he tells you that's enough, that's enough." As a pitcher playing Little League baseball, Lee won recognition for his strength before he developed control of his pitches. "He was always the guy who threw hardest in Little League," Mark Balisterri, Lee's baseball coach at Benton High School, told Crise. "You always said, gosh, if he could just throw strikes he could be dominating." His control improved toward the end of his junior year of high school.

After graduating, in 1997, Lee was chosen in the eighth round of the amateur draft by the Florida Marlins, but he instead decided to attend and play baseball at Meridian Community College, in Mississippi. In 1998, after he had been there a year, the Baltimore Orioles attempted to draft Lee, but he turned down that offer as well. After graduating from junior college, in 1999, he enrolled at the University of Arkansas and pitched for their team, the Razorbacks. In 65 innings Lee had a record of four wins and three losses and an earned-run average (ERA) of 4.45. ("ERA" refers to the average number of earned runs, or runs scored by opposing batters without the aid of field errors, per nine innings pitched.) He threw 77 strikeouts and held opposing batters to a .208 batting average. After the 2000 season Lee accepted an offer from the Montreal Expos after being selected in the draft's fourth round. His college play, he hold Rick Fires for the *Arkansas Democrat-Gazette* (June 6, 2000), "helped prepare me to where I think it's time."

Lee was sent first to play for Montreal's Class-A farm team, the Cape Fear Crocs, in the South Atlantic League, where he went 1–4 in 11 starts. In 2001 he spent his first full professional season with Montreal's single-A team in the Florida State League, the Jupiter Hammerheads, winning six games and losing seven but giving up only 78 hits in 109.2 innings pitched with 129 strikeouts, which was the third-best total in the league. His average of 10.53 strikeouts per nine innings put him in first place in that category among the league's starters. Lee spent the first three months of 2002 with Montreal's double-A team, the Harrisburg Senators, where his numbers improved: in 15 starts he went 7–2, led the league with 105 strikeouts, and maintained a 3.23 ERA, which was seventh-best in the league. In May he was named minor-league player of the month. On June 27, 2002 Lee, along with the Expos' shortstop Brandon Phillips and outfielder Grady Sizemore, was traded to the Cleveland Indians in exchange for Bartolo Colón and Tim Drew. The trade was seen as an attempt by the Indians to fill their roster with young talent. Lee's stellar performance with the Senators earned him a spot in the Class AA All-Star Game, played on July 10 in Norwich, Connecticut.

Joining the Indians in late June, Lee began playing with their Class AA team, the Akron Aeros. In 16.2 innings, Lee allowed only 11 hits and led the

Eastern League with 18 strikeouts. In mid-July he was promoted to Cleveland's triple-A team, the Buffalo Bisons. Lee made his major-league debut with the Indians in a game against the Minnesota Twins on September 16, 2002. Though he allowed just two hits and one earned run in over five innings, the Indians suffered from a weak offensive performance, and the Twins won the game, 5–0, clinching first place in the American League Central Division. Despite the loss, Cleveland's interim manager, Joel Skinner, was reportedly pleased with Lee's ability to place his fastball over different areas of the plate. Lee made his second and final 2002 start on September 21 in an away game against the Kansas City Royals, allowing one run and four hits in five innings. In light of his fine performances in those two starts, Lee was named the fifth-best prospect in the Indians organization by the magazine *Baseball America*.

During the team's winter workouts in the months that followed the 2002 season, Lee strained one of his lower abdominal muscles. When the pain did not subside after a week's rest, he was placed on the disabled list for 60 days, beginning on March 29, 2003. Because of his injury, he stayed in extended spring training for most of April and May, before reporting to Cleveland's Class A team in Kinston, North Carolina, on May 29. In June he split his time between the double-A Akron Aeros and the Bisons. Brought up to pitch for the Indians in a game against the Royals on June 30, Lee threw for six scoreless innings and secured his first major-league win. Though he had hoped the performance would earn him a permanent spot on Cleveland's pitching rotation, he was sent back to Buffalo the same day. He was brought back to pitch for the Indians on August 16 and started seven more games during that month. At the season's end, at the request of the Indians' management, Lee underwent surgery for a hernia, which he had suffered in junior high school and had never had surgically repaired—and which was thought to be the cause of his abdominal pain. After the surgery, on October 8, 2003, Lee was unable to work out for six weeks.

Lee's performance in spring training in 2004 led to his becoming the third starting pitcher on the Indians' roster. Early in the season he began to establish himself as a young talent on the mound and became known for his well-placed fastball. He also proved his ability to pitch through difficult situations. For example, he was able to maintain his focus and throw strikes even after a disappointing walk. "There's no quit in that guy . . . ," the pitching coach Carl Willis told Scott Priestle for the *Columbus Dispatch* (May 30, 2004), after a game against the Oakland Athletics, in which Lee walked five batters but managed to throw eight strikeouts, a career high, contributing to the Indians' ninth-inning win. "He has a history of problems with pitch counts because of the walks," Willis said. "But he's getting closer to the zone. He's getting more refined with his control." Lee's main weakness, his occasional loss of control, got him into trouble when he faced the famed Cincinnati Reds slugger Ken Griffey Jr., in Griffey's second at-bat in a game on June 13, 2004. In his first at-bat, in the third inning, Griffey had hit a home run off Lee, increasing Griffey's career home-run total to 499 and setting the stage for a possible 500th. Lee had pitched inconsistently in the game; he had allowed seven runs on six hits and walked four batters in just 3 2/3 innings. When Griffey stepped to the plate for the second time that game, Lee pitched a wild fastball that sailed over the batter's head and hit the backstop. Perceiving Lee's inaccurate pitch as an attempt to hit Griffey, the plate umpire, Matt Hollowell, ejected Lee without a warning, making for Lee's shortest-ever starting appearance. Lee did not argue with the umpire but contended that he had not meant to hit Griffey. (The Indians won the game, 10–8.) On June 19, 2004 Bob Watson, the vice president of Major League Baseball (MLB) on-field operations, penalized Lee for the wild pitch with a $1,000 fine and a six-game suspension. At first Lee appealed the decision, but he gave up that effort at the request of Cleveland's manager, Eric Wedge, so that the pitching rotation would not have to be adjusted, which might have been necessary if Lee had delayed the suspension with his appeal.

Lee embarked on a five-game winning streak from June 18 to July 16, 2004, giving him an impressive record of 10–1, which was at the time the best of the Indians' starting five pitchers. Lee's pitches became inconsistent near the end of July, however, and stayed that way through September, as he lost seven straight contests. His bad streak began on July 21, against the Chicago White Sox, when he allowed seven runs and nine hits in four innings in what culminated in a 14–0 loss. In his next start, against the Detroit Tigers on July 26, 2004, Lee was pulled from the mound after just two-thirds of an inning, having allowed six runs and six hits. Lee became so frustrated during an August 2, 2004 game against the Toronto Blue Jays, after having given up nine hits in $4^1/_3$ innings, that he threw his hat and glove into the stands when the game ended in a 6–1 loss for the Indians. By September the Indians had been dubbed "Team Streak," because of their alternating series of wins and losses, and Lee, who had posted a 1–6 record and a ghastly 9.69 ERA in the second half of the season, became known as "Kid Streak"—or, as Paul Hoynes put it for the Cleveland *Plain Dealer* (September 3, 2004), "the ultimate hot-and-cold pitcher."

The 2005 and 2006 seasons were far more successful for Lee. By July 18, 2005 Lee led the Indians' pitching squad with 10 wins and just four losses. By August 21 he had improved those marks to 13–4. In great contrast to his reputation from the previous season, by September—as the Indians drew closer to the New York Yankees in the race for the wild-card spot in the play-offs—Lee's pitching became known for its consistency. He attributed his improvement to his ability to focus on a few key ideas. "When I pitch, I keep it as simple as possible. I try not to let the other team score," Lee told Priestle for the *Columbus Dispatch* (September 7, 2005). "I try not to walk guys. I throw strikes and let them put the ball in play. That's really all I'm thinking about: Locate my pitches, don't walk guys, don't let them score." Finishing the 2005 season with 18 wins and five losses and a 3.79 ERA, Lee was the winningest left-handed pitcher in the American League and the first Cleveland pitcher since Bob Feller in 1951 to lead that league in winning percentage. He also came in fourth place for the Cy Young Award, an honor, voted on by the Baseball Writers Association of America, that recognizes the best pitcher in each major league. (The winner was the Los Angeles Angels' Bartolo Colón.) The Indians finished the 2005 season with a record of 93–69, falling just short of the American League wild-card spot, which went to the Boston Red Sox.

In the 2006 season, with 33 starts and 200 innings pitched, Lee had a record of 14–11. Though Lee's ERA rose to 4.40 by season's end, he managed to hold opposing batters to an average of .278. David Sabino wrote for *Sports Illustrated* (March 20, 2006), "Lee has an odd arm angle, making his pitches hard to pick up, and he's not afraid to challenge hitters." As quoted by Sabino, Wedge described Lee's pitching as "sneaky, aggressive, and very smart." On August 8, 2006 Lee signed a contract extension with the Indians through 2009, which included the possibility for him to stay until 2010.

Lee had plans to expand his range and experiment with a new arsenal of pitches during the spring training before the 2007 season. But in the first few weeks of training, Lee again strained his abdominal muscle. The injury led to him to miss virtually all of spring training and begin the 2007 season on the disabled list. He pitched for the Class A Kinston team before spending time in extended spring training in Winter Haven, Florida, and throwing for the Class AAA Bisons through mid-April. He returned to Cleveland's starting rotation in May 2007, but after he won his first two starts, his record went sharply downhill. Observers noted that Lee had great difficulty in controlling the speed and placement of his pitches, resulting in his throwing fastballs across the middle of the plate, among the easiest pitches to hit. On May 23, 2007, in an away game against the Royals, opposing batters hit a career-high eight runs off Lee. That loss was followed by a four-game Indians' losing streak. On July 21, 2007, in an away game against the Texas Rangers, Lee argued from the mound with the Indians' catcher Victor Martinez after giving up five runs on six hits in the game's first inning. The two argued again in the third inning, when Lee hit the Rangers batter Sammy Sosa in the head with a fastball. Sosa, who had been honored before the game by family, friends, and politicians from his native Dominican Republic for hitting his 600th home run on July 20, 2007, was forced to sit out the rest of the game. Though Lee contended that he had not intended to hit Sosa, Martinez reportedly thought that Lee had not shown enough remorse for the dangerous pitch. Though Lee recovered from his pitching troubles to throw five scoreless innings, the altercations between Lee and Martinez led to a 25-minute private team meeting in the locker room following the game. Lee hit his low point in the 2007 season in a home game against the Red Sox on July 26, when he allowed eight runs to score in just four innings. When he was pulled from the game, after the fourth inning, the home crowd booed and jeered at him. The loss capped a four-game losing streak in which Lee allowed 26 earned runs and 32 hits in 20 innings. When Lee telephoned Wedge that night to discuss the loss, Wedge informed him that he was being sent down to the Class AAA league for the rest of the season. After the Indians finished first in their division and earned a spot in the play-offs, Lee learned that he would also be left off the Indians' play-off roster and replaced by the left-handed pitchers Aaron Laffey and Jeremy Sowers. "Obviously I wasn't happy," Lee told Jodie Valade for the *Plain Dealer* (May 18, 2008). "I didn't want to go to Buffalo. But the team was trying to play in the play-offs. And that's the honest thing—if you're not getting the job done, there's someone else behind you. That's how it should go." In Lee's absence the Indians defeated the Yankees in the American League Division Series and went 3–1 against the Red Sox in the American League Championship Series before losing three straight games to the Red Sox, who became that year's World Series champions.

Despite his recently signed contract, in the off-season sports analysts predicted that Lee would be traded. The pitchers who had replaced him, Sowers and Laffey, had performed well, and because each had spent less than two years in the major leagues, their lower salaries would save the Indians money. Despite trade rumors that linked Lee to several other teams, the Indians' management expressed confidence in Lee. "His stuff is still there," Cleveland's general manager, Mark Shapiro, told Hoynes. "His competitiveness is still present. I still feel he can be a 200-inning pitcher again and a valuable contributor to our staff."

Lee was not traded, but he had to work hard to earn back his spot on the Indians' five-pitcher starting rotation. He began a streak of remarkable pitching that continued throughout the season. When he earned his sixth straight win, on May 7, he became the first Indians pitcher to do so since Greg Swindell, in 1988. At that point Lee's strikeout-to-walk ratio peaked at an astonishing 11–1. "More than any time in his career, when he goes out and falls behind in the count or doesn't execute a pitch, he's able to take a step back, slow things down, get back together and execute the next pitch . . . ," Willis told Valade. "He has much better focus." Lee was voted to play for the American League team in the All-Star Game, held at New York's Yankee Stadium. The Boston Red Sox manager, Terry Francona, who had been selected to manage the American League squad, chose Lee to be the team's starting pitcher. Lee finished the season with an astounding 22–3 record and won both the AL Cy Young Award and the AL Comeback Player of the Year Award.

Lee made 22 appearances in the 2009 season as a member of the Indians. He amassed a record of 7–9, with 107 strikeouts, and an ERA of 3.14—less impressive figures than those of the year before. On July 29, 2009, two days before the trade deadline, the Indians traded Lee, along with the outfielder Ben Francisco, to the Philadelphia Phillies, the reigning World Series champions, in exchange for the pitchers Jason Knapp and Carlos Carrasco (both minor-league prospects), the catcher Lou Marson, and the shortstop Jason Donald. The trade was characterized by the Indians' management as part of an effort to make room in the team's budget for future acquisitions and to rebuild its roster for 2010 and beyond. On July 31, 2009, in his first appearance on the mound with the Phillies, Lee pitched a complete game, in a 5–1 victory over the San Francisco Giants. He went on to pitch a total of 79.2 innings with the Phillies in the 2009 season, amassing a 7–4 record, 74 strikeouts, and a 3.39 ERA. Lee's efforts helped lead the Phillies to finish the season with record of 93–69, the best in the National League East. The team defeated the Colorado Rockies and the Los Angeles Dodgers in the play-offs to advance to the World Series for the second year in a row. The Phillies' manager, Charlie Manuel, named Lee as the team's starting pitcher in Game One of the series, after Lee's wins in his two play-off appearances. In that game, on October 28, 2009, Lee put on a stunning performance, allowing no earned runs and racking up 10 strikeouts and zero walks, helping his team secure the 6–1 win. The Phillies went on to lose the next three games of the series, with final scores of 3–1, 8–6, and 7–4. Lee returned to the mound as the Phillies' starting pitcher for Game Five, which was held in Philadelphia's Citizens Bank Park, on November 2. On the mound Lee exhibited what Tyler Kepner, writing for the *New York Times* (November 3, 2009), described as "the rapid pace he had set while mastering the Yankees in Game 1" as he "cruised through the middle innings." Lee held the Yankees to just two runs in the first seven innings, as the Phillies' offense scored eight, establishing a six-run lead. In the eighth inning, however, the Yankees managed three hits off Lee, each of which resulted in a run scored, and Lee was replaced by Ryan Madsen, who held the Yankees to one more run and closed Game Five with an 8–6 victory. In Game Six the Yankees defeated the Phillies, 7–3, and claimed victory in the 2009 World Series. Lee was one of only two pitchers (the other was Roy Halladay of the Toronto Blue Jays) in the major leagues who managed to defeat the Yankees three times during the 2009 season. On November 5 it was reported that the Phillies were discussing the possibility of signing Lee, who is on contract with the team for $9 million through the 2010 season, to a longer-term contract.

An avid hunter and fisherman, Lee makes his off-season home in Benton, Arkansas, with his wife, Kristen, his son, Jaxon, born in 2001, and his daughter, Maci, born in 2003. When Jaxon was four months old, he was diagnosed with leukemia; he underwent chemotherapy and a stem-cell transplant before the cancer went into remission. Maci was born three months premature. Given those problems, which coincided with the first few years of Lee's professional career, the athlete and his wife have been able to keep his professional struggles in perspective. Referring to Lee's temporary demotion to the minor leagues in 2007, Kristen told Mel Antonen for *USA Today* (May 29, 2008) that the children's troubles "brought us back to reality and helped us remember what is really important. The season wasn't all that bad. We know what real struggles are when you have a child that almost dies of leukemia. [Lee] wasn't pitching well, but compared to everything else, it was minor." Lee was nominated by his team in 2005 for the John Hancock Roberto Clemente Award, in recognition of his community service. Lee runs a free baseball clinic for children at Cleveland State University; he also contributes his efforts to the Providence House, the Grand Slam Literacy Program, and other local charities. He and his wife were honorary chairs of the Light the Night Walk, held in Jacobs Field on September 17, 2006, to raise funds for cancer research and patient services for the Leukemia & Lymphoma Society.

—M.E.R.

Suggested Reading: (Cleveland) *Plain Dealer* Sports D p1 Sep. 16, 2002, D p1 Sep. 3, 2004, D p1 Dec. 5, 2007, C p1 May 18, 2008, D p1 July 15, 2008; *Columbus Dispatch* Sports E p7 May 30, 2004, D p1 Sep. 7, 2005; (Little Rock) *Arkansas Democrat-Gazette* Sports June 8, 2008; *New York Times* (on-line) Oct. 28, 2009, Oct. 30, 2009, Nov. 3, 2009; *USA Today* Sports C p4 May 20, 2008

Leo, Melissa

Sep. 14, 1960– Actress

Address: c/o Agency for the Performing Arts, 9200 Sunset Blvd., Suite 900, Los Angeles, CA 90069-3604

In the majority of her film and television roles, Melissa Leo, a celebrated character actress, has played strong women who adapt to difficult situations. Although Leo has been acting professionally since the mid-1980s, it was not until she portrayed the Baltimore police sergeant Kay Howard on the se-

Kevork Djansezian/Getty Images

Melissa Leo

ries *Homicide: Life on the Street*, from 1993 to 1997, that audiences began to take note of her talent. While most female television characters (even those in such gritty professions as law enforcement) were unrealistically manicured, coiffed, and garbed in designer fashions, Leo refused to portray Howard in that way. "The makeup-free, no-nonsense actress played Howard as a no-nonsense, makeup-free woman during her four years on *Homicide*," Tamara Ikenberg wrote for the *Dallas Morning News* (June 5, 1998). Leo's take on the detective—sensible, competent, plainly dressed—instantly made Howard a role model and icon for the show's small but devoted fan base.

Despite her character's popularity, in 1997 Leo was fired from the show, and more conventionally attractive actresses were added to the cast. She returned to appearing in supporting roles, mostly in independent films and television series. Leo reemerged in 2003 with a high-visibility supporting role in the film *21 Grams*, and in 2008 she had her first starring role, in the independent hit *Frozen River*, playing a downtrodden woman whose resolve to escape poverty leads her to take part in an illegal smuggling operation. The movie won the Grand Jury Prize for best drama at the Sundance Film Festival, and the universal praise lavished on Leo's performance has attracted increased interest from casting agents.

Melissa Chessington Leo was born on September 14, 1960 in New York City. Her father, Arnold, was an editor who later in life turned to commercial fishing, and her mother, Peggy, worked as a teacher. When she was very young, her mother enrolled her in the Peter Schumann Bread and Puppet Theater Workshop, one of the oldest nonprofit theatrical companies in the country. "Peter would teach us to not just manipulate the puppet but to be the puppet. It freed the inhibited child that I was," Leo told a reporter for *Vanity Fair* (February 11, 2009, on-line). "I found there was a space and a people that I knew and felt comfortable with, inside the darkened theater. And I learned, slowly, what it is to be an actor and how an actor can be employed and all of those things."

When Leo was nine her parents divorced, and she moved with her mother and older brother, Erik, to the town of Putney, Vermont. She continued her training as an actress under Arthur Lithgow, the actor John Lithgow's father, at the Brattleboro Center for the Performing Arts. Five years later Leo's family moved to London, England, where Peggy found a job supervising American students studying abroad. In London Leo enrolled in theater classes, and when Peggy was ready to return to the U.S. a year later, Leo asked if she could stay behind to continue her studies. Her mother granted her permission and helped her rent a flat. "People say, 'Did you leave home?'" Leo told Pam Lambert and Sarah Skolnik for *People* (December 4, 1995). "No, home left me."

Leo returned to the U.S. in 1980 and began attending classes on the Purchase campus of the State University of New York (SUNY). She dropped out of school during her junior year and moved to New York City in search of work. She found a job as a waitress and started to audition, unsuccessfully, for television and film roles. Leo tried out for a part in the film *Razor's Edge* (1984), and while she did not get the role, the picture's lead actor, Bill Murray, was impressed by her performance. "[Murray] told me: 'Wow, you got something. If you want to do this, go do it,'" Leo recalled to Rebecca Rothbaum for the *Poughkeepsie (New York) Journal* (January 25, 2004). "I took it to heart and quit my waitressing job that afternoon."

In 1984 Leo won a role on *All My Children*, a popular soap opera that has been broadcast on the ABC network since 1970. (She beat out the now-famed actress Julia Roberts for the part.) Although her character, Linda Warner, was on the show for only a few episodes, Leo's visibility increased, and she began to get work more frequently. In 1985 she appeared in the semi-confessional comedy *Always*, directed by Henry Jaglom, an independent filmmaker with whom she continues to work. (*Always* was released on video under the title *Always, But Not Forever.*) That year she also had a role in an episode of the crime series *The Equalizer* and appeared in the film *Streetwalkin'* as a runaway teen who becomes a prostitute in New York City's then-seedy Times Square.

Over the next few years, Leo took on numerous minor roles. She appeared in the horror film *Deadtime Stories* in 1986, an episode of the cop drama *Miami Vice* in 1988, and the television action film *Nasty Boys* in 1989. From 1989 to 1990 she played the character Emma Shannon in *The Young Riders*, a show based on the exploits of the Pony Express, a 19th-century mail service. In 1992 Leo appeared in Jaglom's dramatic film *Venice/Venice*, and in 1993 she had a role in the Western drama *The Ballad of Little Jo*.

That year Leo became a regular cast member on the critically acclaimed NBC crime series *Homicide: Life on the Street*. From 1993 to 1997 Leo portrayed Detective Sergeant Kay Howard, a tough, hard-working homicide investigator. Based on the former *Baltimore Sun* journalist David Simon's nonfiction book *Homicide: A Year on the Killing Streets* (1991), the show focused on the daily lives and challenging investigations of Howard and the other officers on the streets of crime-ridden Baltimore, Maryland.

Leo played the only female member of the show's homicide unit, and her portrayal was praised by both critics and fans for its realism. Tim Goodman wrote for the *Hamilton (Ontario, Canada) Spectator* (February 8, 1997), "This is the perfect example of what other women on cop shows could only hope to be. Howard knows it's a man's world in the department, but uses that to motivate herself to new heights. She keeps her personal life out of the office as much as possible. She's not always invited into the boys' club, but keeps knocking on the door." Alan Sepinwall wrote for the Cleveland, Ohio, *Plain Dealer* (June 15, 1997), "Leo was a breath of fresh air when *Homicide* debuted in the spring of 1993. Then-Detective Howard was not only a believable cop who wasn't sleeping with any of her male colleagues, but she was actually the best detective in the homicide unit." Sepinwall continued, "She was tough, she was smart, and, thanks to Leo's insistence that a real cop wouldn't waste time in the morning trying to look like a fashion model . . . she had an interesting look all her own: almost no makeup, a wardrobe of bargain-basement men's sports coats and ties, and a shock of curly red hair that made her still seem feminine without sacrificing her credibility as 'one of the guys.'" Lon Grahnke wrote for the *Chicago Sun-Times* (August 13, 1995), "Brilliantly played by Melissa Leo, Baltimore detective Kay Howard is television's finest female cop."

Leo told Tamara Ikenberg that she took cues from real-life female homicide detectives to develop the character. "There are very few female homicide detectives," she observed. "There are some, and they are very particular women. They are bright women. They are deeply involved in their work. They are not vain women. They are not concerned about what the fellas think." She told Scott Tobias for the *A.V. Club* (July 31, 2008, on-line), "It's not that I don't like wearing dresses, because geez, I'm a girl, and I love to put a dress on from time to time. But I went to [the producers] when we first started, and I . . . said, 'Okay, you take me into court, I'll put a skirt on, but you can't show up to work in a homicide unit in skirts and heels. You've gotta have trousers on.'" While Leo became inextricably linked to the role of Howard, she told Lambert and Skolnik that she was unlike her character in many ways. "I don't slow down at [a car] accident," she said. "I don't like to look at the horror that's in the world."

While *Homicide: Life on the Street* aired, Leo also appeared in other projects, including two episodes of the TV miniseries *Scarlett* (1994) and Jaglom's film *Last Summer in the Hamptons* (1995). In 1997 NBC removed Leo from the show. Although network executives never fully explained their reasons, Leo has discussed her guesses with reporters. Explaining that she felt that the show's writers were trying to make her conform to the standards of conventional female television roles, she told Ikenberg, "I won't ever know what the truth is. . . . I staunchly maintained the original premise, and they thought that I was being difficult." She later told Scott Tobias, "There had never been Kay Howard on TV before she was on TV, and you see her all over the place now. Aspects of Kay Howard. Her hair, her pants, her suits, all of it. As a matter of fact, there are several movie-star actors who are doing television shows now. And those characters—and the actors and the producers are aware of this—are going after something that got my ass fired." (In 2000, however, Leo reprised the role of Howard in *Homicide: The Movie*.)

In 1999 Leo appeared alongside Rosie Perez in *The 24 Hour Woman*, and in 2000 she starred in the film comedy/drama *Fear of Fiction*. In the latter movie she played a novelist who embarks on a road trip to get over a bout of writer's block. The film as a whole received lukewarm reviews, but Leo's performance garnered praise. Bob Campbell wrote for the Newhouse News Service (July 12, 2000), "Better known for her *Homicide: Life on the Street* TV stint than her scattershot movie roles, the flinty, flame-haired actress unsentimentally sketches a hard-edged New York novelist in rebellious flight from herself."

In 2003 Leo appeared in the director Alejandro González Iñárritu's *21 Grams*, which followed the struggles of three characters brought together by a tragic car accident. The picture was generally well-received by critics. Lee Ann Gilan wrote for the *Halifax (Nova Scotia) Daily News* (November 27, 2003), "It's a rather silly movie-of-the-week-style story transformed into something much more moving," and Elvis Mitchell wrote for the *New York Times* (October 12, 2003): "The depths of intimacy that . . . Iñárritu plumbs here are so rarely touched by filmmakers that *21 Grams* is tantamount to the discovery of a new country."

In the film Leo played the supporting role of Marianne Jordan, the wife of Jack Jordan, a deeply troubled man played by Benicio Del Toro. Although Marianne was not a main character, critics praised Leo's poignant performance. Mitchell wrote, "As Jack's wife, Melissa Leo makes her relationship to a man given to tremendous and simultaneous hostility and remorse so real it's absorbing and painful to watch." Charles Britton Valenzuela wrote for the Torrance, California, *Daily Breeze* (November 21, 2003), "It's a terrific performance for someone who is best known for her TV work . . . and if she doesn't get a supporting actress nomination, there's no justice in the world." Focus Features, the film's U.S. distributor, mounted a campaign to win Leo an Academy Award nomination, and although those efforts proved futile, Leo was named the runner-up in the best-supporting-actress category by the Los Angeles Film Critics Association.

Between 2004 and 2007 Leo took on numerous roles in films and television shows, including an episode of the popular TV drama *CSI: Crime Scene Investigation*, in 2004, and three episodes of the acclaimed series *The L Word*, in 2005. She had a role in the Western film *The Three Burials of Melquiades Estrada* (2005), directed by Tommy Lee Jones, and appeared in Jaglom's *Hollywood Dreams* (2006). In 2007 Leo was featured in the family drama *Black Irish* and appeared alongside Billy Bob Thornton in the comedy *Mr. Woodcock*, a box-office disappointment.

In 2008 Leo starred in the independent film *Frozen River*, the first feature by the director Courtney Hunt. In the film, which won the Grand Jury Prize for best drama at the Sundance Film Festival, Leo played Ray Eddy, an upstate New York resident who assists a Native American woman (Misty Upham) in smuggling illegal immigrants into the U.S. from Canada. Ray, a poverty-stricken mother of two, reluctantly agrees to the illegal operation as a means to secure a much-needed down payment on a new trailer. The movie was widely praised for its verisimilitude. "There's a moment in the film, a small moment, when Ray has to give her sons lunch money because they're off to school," Leo told Tobias. "I remember growing up in Vermont, and I was on a meal plan myself up there, and with my meal-plan ticket and $.50, I could get my lunch. But I had to have that $.50. . . . If I had information that I could bring to the film, or if I could imagine myself in a situation I may have been in, I would bring that to the table."

Reviews of the film were almost entirely positive. "The biggest thrill for many fans will be watching Ms. Leo perform with enough room to explore one of the complicated, surprising women she's so good at sketching in smaller roles," Karen Durbin wrote for the *New York Times* (July 27, 2008). "Ray is vulnerable to life's punches, but she's no sentimental construct. For one thing she's a bigot, though not overtly—at least toward most of the people she and [her smuggling partner] Lila shovel into the trunk of her car. But she's furious at having to transport a Pakistani couple she suspects of being Muslim terrorists and soothes her conscience by treating them horribly. At the same time she embodies the almost invisible heroism of someone continually pecked at by poverty. She not only keeps going, but her dogged problem-solving concentration also makes it clear that the thought of quitting doesn't enter her mind." Robert Koehler wrote for *Variety* (January 20, 2008, on-line), "No trendsetter or breakthrough, this [film] is more than anything else a welcome chance for the fine actor Melissa Leo to finally dominate a film in a terrific and affecting lead role." He continued, "The movie . . . belongs to Leo, a [thespian] of considerable flinty character and honesty who brings all of her reserves to bear on a big, complex role. Unafraid to show herself weathered by the cold, harsh elements and never working to make [audiences] love her, Leo builds the kind of [performance] that invites concentration, and then high respect." Leo was nominated for an Academy Award as best actress for her role in *Frozen River* but lost to Kate Winslet, who had played an illiterate concentration-camp guard in *The Reader*.

In 2008 Leo could also be seen in an episode of the popular TV show *Law & Order*; the big-screen thriller *The Alphabet Killer*, which starred Eliza Dushku and Timothy Hutton; *Santa Mesa*, a movie about the plight of a Filipino orphan; the basketball picture *Ball Don't Lie*, which featured the rapper Ludacris; *Lullaby*, a film about kidnapping and the drug trade, set in South Africa; and *This Is a Story About Ted and Alice*, a short master's-thesis film by a Columbia University student. The next year Leo appeared in independent films including *Stephanie's Image*, *True Adolescents*, *Don McKay*, *Greta*, and *Dear Lemon Lima*. She also had a part in Kirk Jones's *Everybody's Fine*, a remake of Giuseppe Tornatore's *Stanno Tutti Bene* (1990); starring Robert De Niro, it was scheduled for release in December 2009.

Leo currently has several projects in various stages of development, most of them small, independent films. In 2010, however, she will appear with Sarah Michelle Gellar in the relatively large-budget film *Veronika Decides to Die*, whose protagonist, a young woman confined to a mental institution after a failed suicide attempt, regains her will to live.

Leo told Tobias that she was "perfectly comfortable" with being labeled a character actress. "I've always been somebody who is much more invested in who I am playing than how they look," she noted.

Leo lives in Ulster County, New York, and has a son, John, whose father is the actor John Heard. In 1997 Heard was sentenced to 18 months probation and ordered to seek psychological treatment after he was convicted of harassing Leo by phone and trespassing on her property.

—W.D.

Suggested Reading: *A.V. Club* (on-line) July 31, 2008; (Cleveland) *Plain Dealer* p121 June 15, 1997; *Dallas Morning News* C p3 June 5, 1998; *Hamilton (Ontario, Canada) Spectator* W p16 Feb. 8, 1997; *New York Times* Arts p7 July 27, 2008; *People* p101 Dec. 4, 1995; *Poughkeepsie (New York) Journal* D p1 Jan. 25, 2004

Selected Films: *Always*, 1985; *Street Streetwalkin'*, 1985; *Deadtime Stories*, 1986; *Venice/Venice*, 1992; *The Ballad of Little Jo*,

1993; *Last Summer in the Hamptons*, 1994; *The 24 Hour Woman*, 1999; *Homicide: The Movie*, 2000; *Fear of Fiction*, 2000; *21 Grams*, 2003; *The Three Burials of Melquiades Estrada*, 2005; *Hollywood Dreams*, 2006; *Black Irish*, 2007; *Mr. Woodcock*, 2007; *Frozen River*, 2008; *The Alphabet Killer*, 2008; *Santa Mesa*, 2008; *Ball Don't Lie*, 2008; *Lullaby*, 2008; *This Is a Story About Ted and Alice*, 2008; *Stephanie's Image*, 2009; *True Adolescents*, 2009; *Don McKay*, 2009; *Greta*, 2009; *Dear Lemon Lima*, 2009

Selected Television Shows: *All My Children*, 1984–85; *The Young Riders*, 1989–90; *Homicide: Life on the Streets*, 1993–97; *The L Word*, 2005

Courtesy of Rodolfo Llinás

Llinás, Rodolfo R.

(yee-NAHS)

Dec. 16, 1934– Neurophysiologist; educator; writer

Address: New York University Dept. of Physiology and Neuroscience, 550 First Ave., New York, NY 10016

"Groups of neurons, millions strong, act like little hearts beating all on their own. It's like a Riverdance performance." That description of neurons came from Rodolfo Llinás, the chairman of the Department of Neuroscience and Physiology at the New York University (NYU) School of Medicine, during an interview with Sandra Blakeslee for the *New York Times* (December 2, 2008). Also called nerve cells, neurons are cells in the brain, spinal cord, and other parts of a vertebrate's nervous system; they process and transmit information by electrochemical signaling, in a manner that Llinás, in that interview, was likening to traditional Irish step dancing. Elaborating on that analogy, he said, "Some cells are tapping in harmony and some are silent, creating myriads of patterns that represent the properties of the external world. Cells with the same rhythm form circuits to bind information in time. Such coherent activity allows you to see and hear, to be alert and able to think." Llinás is an expert on the electrophysiology of the brain—the way the brain carries out its jobs by means of electrochemical activity. At the beginning of his career, in the early 1960s, he worked at the Australian National University with the Nobel Prize–winning neuroscientist John C. Eccles and other members of the first team to construct a physiological chart of an entire region of the brain—the outer layer of the cerebellum, known as the cerebellar cortex. Later, successively, between 1965 and 1976, he joined the faculties of the University of Minnesota; the American Medical Association Institute of Biomedical Research; Northwestern University; Wayne State University; the University of Illinois; the University of Iowa; and New York University, where since 1976 he has been the chairman of the Department of Physiology and Neuroscience and is in addition the Thomas and Suzanne Murphy professor of neuroscience.

The brain is the most complex organ in the human body and the most "expensive" in terms of energy. At about three pounds, it constitutes about 1/50th of body mass but consumes 25 percent of the energy resources. The different parts of the brain communicate with one another by firing electrochemical signals from one neuron to another in neural chains. A neuron is composed of a cell body, or soma, a long arm known as an axon, which conducts electrochemical signals to the cell body, and branched projections known as dendrites. A neuron's action is either excitatory, meaning that it passes a signal to the next neuron, or inhibitory, meaning that it stops a signal. Each signal begins with an electrical event, when ions (charged molecules) generate a so-called action potential; that triggers chemical events involving synapses, the gaps that exist between neurons. The presynaptic ending at one end of a synapse contains neurotransmitters, mitochondria, and other so-called organelles; the postsynaptic ending at the other end of the synapse contains receptor sites for neurotransmitters. The brain is divided into sections according to function. The cerebral cortex, as part of the thalamocortical loop, is the central processor and is responsible for consciousness, memory, language, and reasoning. The brainstem consists of the hindbrain and the midbrain and acts as a relay center for such involuntary activities as the beating of the heart and breathing. The cerebellum (Latin for "little brain") plays a major role in the integration of sensory perception and motor control. It receives information, in the form of electrochemical signals, from other parts of the brain through input fibers. The job of the cerebellar cortex, the outer layer of the cerebellum, is to modulate the information it receives from clusters of neurons within the cerebellum, known as deep nucleii, and transmit the information to other parts of the brain, by way of climbing fibers. Those fibers wrap around Purkinje neurons in the cerebellum, causing them to fire. Other structures involved in the process of sensory integration include the inferior olivary bodies, or olives, and the thalamus. The two olives (often referred to in singular form, as the IO), located in the brain stem, also transmit information to the cerebellum through mossy and climbing fibers. The thalamus, located just above the brainstem, relays information from the cerebellum to the cerebral cortex.

Llinás's research has helped to elucidate the electrophysiological activities that link the cerebellum to other parts of the brain. One of his most controversial findings threw into question the generally accepted notion that neurons do not act independently but only react to stimuli. Also a matter of dispute is his theory that the IO and the thalamus are constantly communicating with other parts the brain via oscillations. Llinás has found evidence suggesting that, when those oscillations occur at high or regular frequencies, a person's motor and cognitive skills indicate that he or she is fully awake and functioning at a high level. The thalamus enters into low-frequency oscillation after a person has been awake and active for many hours, and he or she falls asleep. Llinás believes that when abnormal rhythms—called thalamocortical dysrhythmias—link certain parts of the brain, a variety of maladies may result: Parkinson's disease, epilepsy, depression, chronic pain, tinnitus, obsessive-compulsive disorders, and some symptoms of schizophrenia. Llinás has suggested treating those disorders with deep brain stimulation (DBS), in which pinpointed parts of the brain are stimulated with a few volts of electricity through implanted electrodes. DBS has been used with notable success in some victims of Parkinson's disease; it has also been used successfully to treat some victims of movement disorders or intractable depression, and it is currently being tested on people suffering from one or another of dozens of other disorders. Among his other achievements, Llinás discovered in mammalian neurons what are called dendrite calcium spikes ("spikes" in the sense of a sudden burst of activity) and dendritic inhibition, and he has shown the existence of presynaptic calcium current in giant squids. An essay by Llinás about his life and work is included in the series *The History of Neuroscience in Autobiography* (Volume 5, 2006); as of mid-2009 that essay was posted on the Web site of the Society for Neuroscience.

Rodolfo Riascos Llinás was born to Jorge Enrique Llinás and Bertha Riascos Llinás on December 16, 1934 in Bogotá, Colombia. His father, a thoracic surgeon; his paternal grandfather, a psychiatrist; and an uncle were all professors at the National University School of Medicine in Bogotá. "From very early on," Llinás told Philip J. Hilts for the *New York Times* (May 27, 1997, on-line), "I was thinking and talking about the mind, because that is what the subject was in our house." For a year when he was four, Llinás lived with his grandfather. One day Llinás witnessed a client of his grandfather's collapse in an epileptic seizure in his grandfather's waiting room; later, he asked his grandfather why a person would behave like that. His grandfather explained that the man did not want to flail about; rather, his brain was controlling his actions. "He doesn't want to," Llinás thought, as he recalled to Hilts. "How can he do something he doesn't want to? Such an incredible event!" Llinás told Hilts, "I began to wonder, when I move, how do I know whether I want to or not?" When he posed such questions to his grandfather, the older man acknowledged that he could not explain how the brain worked. Back at his parents' home, Llinás began to conduct experiments in the basement; for example, he would attach electrodes to mice and rats and observe what happened. "My mother kept after me, to make sure I was not unkind," he told Hilts, "but there it is, I was already started."

In 1952 Llinás earned a B.S. degree in general studies (equivalent to a high-school diploma in the U.S.) from Gimnasio Moderno, a private school in Bogotá where, he wrote in his autobiographical essay, he learned "intellectual rigor." At age 17 he enrolled in a combined undergraduate/graduate medical program at the Pontificia Universidad Javeriana, in Bogotá. As he had planned to do for years, he focused on nervous-system physiology.

During his undergraduate years Llinás met the neurosurgeon Walter R. Hess, a pioneer in hypothalamic electrical stimulation—the use of electrodes to stimulate the hypothalamus, the part of the brain that, among other functions, regulates the automatic nervous system. During visits to Hess's laboratory in Switzerland in 1954 and 1956, Llinás assisted in experiments that showed that electrical stimulation of specific areas of cats' brains could induce behavior typical of that species. An electrical signal imparted to a cat at rest, for example, could cause the animal to leap up with an arched back and erect fur, as if it had been threatened. Back in Bogotá he was unable to replicate such experiments for his thesis because he lacked the proper equipment and set-up—and even Bogotá's stray cats, he has recalled, proved to be uncooperative. Instead, he earned a doctoral degree with a dissertation about circuit analysis of the visual system, a more theoretical subject. He was awarded an M.D. degree in 1959.

Llinás then traveled to the U.S. to study neurosurgery. He took courses at the Massachusetts Institute of Technology (MIT), in Cambridge, and conducted research at Massachusetts General Hospital (MGH), in Boston. He was disappointed to discover that "for the most part, and rightly so," the MGH neurosurgeons "were more interested in saving lives than in figuring out how the brain works," he wrote in his autobiographical essay. After a year and a half at MIT, he left for the University of Minnesota, supported by a grant from the National Institutes of Health (NIH). In Minnesota, under the supervision of the electrophysiologist Carlo Terzuolo, he studied the electrical properties of motor neurons (or motoneurons), which originate in the spinal column and affect the movement of muscles. "I was basically left on my own," he wrote in his essay. "I would report to [Terzuolo] once a week. I cannot overstate the importance of having had Carlo be as tough as nails concerning science and as hands-off as he was during this time." Within about a year and a half, Llinás and Terzuolo had made several significant discoveries concerning inhibitory responses in the brain. One was that an inhibitory response could take place at either the level of the cell body or on a dendrite. The finding regarding dendritic inhibition was particularly controversial, because it countered the assumption that motoneuron electrical activity was driven exclusively by synaptic input directly into the soma. In general scientists had dismissed the notion that synapses could occur by way of a dendrite.

Llinás and Terzuolo presented their findings about dendritic inhibition at the 1962 International Physiological Conference, in Amsterdam, the Netherlands. Following the presentation Llinás was approached by the renowned neuroscientist John C. Eccles, who told him that he and Terzuolo were "clearly wrong," as Llinás wrote; nevertheless, Eccles invited him to work in his laboratory in Canberra, Australia. Llinás spent the next two years in Canberra, collaborating with Eccles and another researcher, Kazuo Sasaki, in an investigation of the physiology of the cerebellar cortex. Shortly after Llinás began his research there, in 1963, Eccles was awarded the Nobel Prize for physiology or medicine, in conjunction with Andrew Huxley and Alan Hodgkin, for his work on synapses. Eccles's team of researchers spent years mapping the synaptic interactions that occurred in the cerebellar cortex and characterizing them as either excitatory or inhibitory. Among their most surprising findings was that the climbing fibers elicited huge synaptic electrical potentials that were activated by a single input fiber, rather than the summation of many fibers acting in unison, which was formerly thought to be the case. By 1966 Llinás and his colleagues had completely mapped the cerebellar cortex, making it the first region of the brain to be physiologically charted. The group's findings were published in several papers in the *Journal of Physiology* and the *Journal of Experimental Brain Research*, as well as in two articles for *Nature*. They were also presented at the International Physiological Congress in Tokyo, Japan. Llinás completed a second dissertation on the functioning of the cerebellar cortex and earned a second Ph.D., in 1966, from Australian National University.

Meanwhile, around that time Llinás had met Gillian Kimber, who was finishing her Ph.D. at the university on the philosophy of mind and shared his ideas about the mind. Llinás and Kimber married in December 1965 and then moved to Minneapolis, Minnesota, where Llinás became an associate professor of physiology at the University of Minnesota. In 1966, under the auspices of the American Medical Association Education and Research Foundation (AMA/ERF), Llinás joined Eccles at the newly established Institute for Biomedical Research (IBR) at the University of Chicago. There, until 1970, Llinás and a team of postdoctoral fellows investigated the physiology and anatomy of the cerebellum in various species. Llinás and his colleagues studied the cerebellums of vertebrates including frogs, fish, reptiles, birds, and mammals. Among Llinás's conclusions was that although the cerebellum is more complex in higher animals, it nonetheless has evolved to function in a similar way in many vertebrates.

In 1968 Eccles left the AMA/ERF, and Llinás became the IBR's director of neurobiology. About a year and a half after that, to the great outrage of the scientific community, the AMA decided to close down the institute. Shortly before the closing Llinás hosted an international symposium on the evolution and development of the cerebellum; the significant findings presented there were published in 1969 in a book that he edited. In 1970 Llinás and his research group, with whom he had worked for five years, relocated to the University of Iowa, in Iowa City. In an effort to stay connected to two Chicago institutions—the University of Illinois and Northwestern University, with which he had become affiliated—Llinás and two of his research partners obtained pilot's licenses, bought a small plane, and sometimes flew there from Iowa.

Continuing their research of comparative cerebellar physiology, Llinás and his co-workers focused on the IO, which share information with the cerebellum and help control voluntary body movements. Over the next 10 years, Llinás conducted research and wrote papers on neuronal networks and their relationships to the IO. Challenging the accepted dogma that dendritic spikes—the rapid firing of electrical current in dendrites—could be triggered only by sodium currents, Llinás proved that spikes in Purkinje cell dendrites were calcium-current dependent. Llinás recalled in his autobiographical essay that when he presented that unexpected finding at a conference, a onetime friend of his, Rafael Lorente de Nó, declared in front of the large audience, "Do you really believe that those are calcium spikes? Well, you are wrong." Lorente de Nó later declared to Llinás in a letter: "You have either lost your mind or your honesty." As many studies by other scientists as well as Llinás have since shown, it was Lorente de Nó who was in the wrong.

In 1976 Llinás accepted a position as the chairman of the Department of Physiology and Biophysics at the New York University School of Medicine.

His continuing research found that IO neurons were electrically coupled. Some years later, in collaboration with Yosef Yarom, he discovered slow, self-generated sinusoidal voltage changes in IO neurons—dubbed "subthreshold oscillation." That finding was so surprising that, again, some of Llinás's peers suggested that there was a flaw in his research. In his studies Llinás used harmaline, a hallucinogenic drug known to cause tremors and impaired coordination in humans and other animals. Working with brain slices, he introduced harmaline to the IO and observed an increase in currents sent to the thalamus. Then Eric J. Lang, one of Llinás's doctoral students, discovered that damage to cerebellar nuclei generated an increase in the coupling of the IO neurons, as Llinás had theorized in the 1970s. That finding was in complete disagreement with the accepted theory—that the cerebellum was the center for motor learning—and emphasized motor timing as the main role of the cerebellum.

In the 1980s Llinás began to suspect that the relationship between the IO and the thalamus might be one of the most important in the brain. He discovered that the neurons from both the thalamus, the major entry point into the cerebral cortex, and the IO exhibited low-threshold spikes. When the thalamus's neurons were hyperpolarized—or separated—they, like the IO, entered a state of subthreshold oscillation. Further research suggested that high-frequency activity, called "gamma," in both the cerebral cortex and the thalamus corresponded with high-level cognitive functioning, and that low-frequency activity in those regions corresponded with states of sleep or motor malfunction. In the conviction that thalamocortical oscillations were responsible for sleep/wake cycles, the dream state, and humans' moment-to-moment internal perception of the world, in the 1980s Llinás began to test his theories on the human brain by means of magnetoencephalography (MEG), a then-new imaging technique used to measure magnetic fields produced by electrical activity in the brain. His studies supported his earlier findings of a correlation between cognition and the brain's electrical activity, suggesting that "different cognitive events can be related to specific electrical events at brain level," as Llinás wrote in his autobiographical essay.

In the 1990s Llinás began working with Daniel Jeanmonod, professor of neurosurgery at the University of Zurich, in Switzerland, who had come to the same conclusions he had regarding low-threshold thalamic oscillation. Both concluded that the symptoms of Parkinson's disease—including impaired motor skills and speech—were likely related to low-frequency oscillation of the thalamus. In studies of patients with various brain diseases, Llinás and his colleagues noticed that specific regions of their thalamuses were disconnected from parts of the cerebral cortex, resulting in abnormally low oscillations, as if those regions of the brain were asleep. Llinás and Jeanmonod came up with the hypothesis that many neurological and psychiatric diseases originate when different parts of the thalamus or the cortex begin to exhibit abnormally low frequency of oscillation. They theorized that, in addition to Parkinson's disease, disorders including petit-mal epilepsy, seemingly irreversible depression, phantom-limb disorders (in which people with amputated limbs, hands, or feet experience pain where those parts of their bodies used to be), chronic pain, tinnitus, obsessive-compulsive disorders, and some aspects of schizophrenia are caused by a disconnection between parts of the thalamus and the cortex that leads to a long-term state of thalamocortical dysrhythmia. Llinás also speculated that the disorders might be treated by implanting electrodes into the thalamus to break the abnormal oscillation patterns. (For some years electrodes have been used to treat Parkinson's-disease victims who have not responded to drug therapy.)

In 1999 Llinás and Jeanmonod and three other scientists presented their hypothesis in a paper, "Thalamocortical Dysrhythmia: A Neurological and Neuropsychiatric Syndrome Characterized by Magnetoencephalography," published in the *Proceedings of the National Academy of Sciences* (Volume 96, Number 26, 1999). "This work is very important," Edward Jones, the president of the Society for Neuroscience and the director of the Center for Neuroscience at the University of California, told Sandra Blakeslee for the *New York Times* (October 26, 1999). "What makes it so compelling is that it doesn't come completely out of left field. It builds on a body of work that's been growing for some time. Everyone will say wow, yes!" Since then many neurosurgeons have successfully treated other neurologic and psychiatric disorders by implanting electrodes into the cortex or thalamus and stimulating carefully located parts of them. As of December 2008 some 40,000 people around the world had been treated, mostly for movement disorders. The treatment is currently being applied to patients with schizophrenia, epilepsy, Tourette's syndrome, dystonia, chronic pain, depression, phantom pain, and traumatic brain injuries. Llinás has noted that even if the treatments alleviate the symptoms of those disorders, they should not be regarded as cures; moreover, they sometimes produce unwanted side effects (which subside when the electrodes are removed). In *Science* (March 20, 2009) Miguel A. L. Nicolelis, a neuroscientist at Duke University, presented the results of a study showing that stimulating the spinal cords of rodents suffering from Parkinson's disease with a mild electrical charge reduced the severity of the their worst symptoms. Nicolelis suggested that the therapy could present a safer alternative to deep-brain stimulation for treating humans suffering from Parkinson's disease. Llinas, who was not involved in the study, told Sandra Blakeslee for the *New York Times* (March 20, 2009, on-line) that the treatment "makes good sense." He added, "How successfully it will translate to humans is an important issue. The human spinal cord is much more complex than the rodent counterpart, and long-term stimulation might result in nasty secondary effects."

On another front, with the goal of understanding the biophysics and molecular biology of synaptic transmission, Llinás has spent summers since 1962 at the Marine Biological Laboratory (MBL) at Woods Hole, Massachusetts, studying transmissions in the giant-squid synapse. That species is particularly useful, because its axons and synapses are far larger than those of humans and have been the focus of many successful studies concerning the mechanisms with which nerve cells communicate with each other. Llinás's book *The Squid Giant Synapse: A Model for Chemical Transmission* was published in 1999. Llinás is also the author of *I of the Vortex: From Neurons to Self* (2002), about the evolution and development of consciousness from scientific and philosophical points of view.

In the 1980s Llinás, the physiologist and biologist Frank M. Sulzman, and the neurophysiologist James Wallace "Wally" Wolfe proposed to NASA that a shuttle flight be devoted to the study of the nervous system in microgravity. The result was the NeuroLab, a 16-day mission, completed in April and May 1998, in which seven astronauts studied the effects of weightlessness on the nervous system and sleep and breathing in rats, fish, snails, and crickets as well as in themselves.

Llinás's "most striking feature, besides his easy smile," Hilts wrote, "is his head of white hair." His favorite writers include Fyodor Dostoyevsky, Guy de Maupassant, and Gabriel García Márquez, a friend of his. Llinás and his wife live in New York City. They have two sons: Rafael, a neurologist, and Alexander, an ophthalmologist.

—M.E.R.

Suggested Reading: *New York Times* D p2 Dec. 2, 2008, (on-line) May 27, 1997, Oct. 26, 1999, Mar. 20, 2009; *U.S. News & World Report* p68+ Jan. 3–10, 2000; Squire, Larry R. *The History of Neuroscience in Autobiography* Vol. 5, 2006; *Who's Who in America*

Selected Books: *Thalamic Oscillations and Signaling* (with Mircea Steriade and Edward G. Jones), 1990; *The Squid Giant Synapse: A Model for Chemical Transmission,* 1999; *I of the Vortex,* 2002; as editor—*Neurobiology of Cerebellar Evolution and Development: Proceedings of the First International Symposium of the Institute for Biomedical Research, American Medical Association/Education & Research Foundation,* 1969; *The Mind-Brain Continuum: Sensory Processes* (with Patricia S. Churchland), 1996; *The Workings of the Brain: Development, Memory, and Perception: Readings from* Scientific American *Magazine,* 1990

M.I.A.

July 17, 1975– Musician; visual artist; fashion designer

Address: c/o Interscope Records, 2220 Colorado Ave., Santa Monica, CA 90404

"I've got the bombs to make you blow, I got the beats to make it bang," M.I.A. sings on "Pull Up the People," from her 2005 debut album, *Arular.* Since the release of that record, the London-born Sri Lankan M.I.A.—who began her career as a visual artist—has emerged as a uniquely multicultural musician who complements her political and social commentary with danceable, often funky, beats. With the release of her 2008 single "Paper Planes," found on her sophomore album, *Kala* (2007), M.I.A. became a dominant force in the American music industry; the song was played continuously on radio stations across the nation and earned the musician her first Grammy Award nomination, in 2009. She was also nominated for the 2009 Academy Award for best original song for her collaboration with the Indian composer A. R. Rahman on "O . . . Saya," a song from the 2008 film *Slumdog Millionaire.*

The singer's stage name, M.I.A., besides being a play on her nickname, Maya, stands for both "missing in Acton"—a reference to the London suburb where she once lived—and "missing in action." The daughter of a member of the Tamil separatist movement, M.I.A. spent much of her childhood in Sri Lanka. (The separatist movement seeks to create an independent Tamil state in northern Sri Lanka. The Sinhalese, who are primarily Buddhists, are the country's majority ethnic group, making up about 74 percent of the population, while the mostly Hindu Tamils comprise about 9 percent; Tamils have long accused the Sinhalese of discrimination, and tension between the two groups, which had grown in the 1970s, sparked a civil war in 1983. The fighting between the Sri Lankan government and the Tamil separatists, led by the Liberation Tigers of Tamil Eelam, or LTTE—referred to in the West as the Tamil Tigers—continued for 26 years, until May 2009, when the nation's military defeated the LTTE. It is estimated that the war claimed between 80,000 and 100,000 lives.) M.I.A. witnessed violence and death at a young age. Her family escaped to England when she was around 11 years old, and though she was removed from the violence that had plagued her earlier childhood, M.I.A.'s struggles continued in the notoriously racist part of London in which she grew up. She channeled her frustration through vi-

Andrew H. Walker/Getty Images for Moet & Chandon
M.I.A.

sual art and later through music. "For years when I moved to England, I was so embarrassed about being Sri Lankan and never talked about it," she told Susan Carpenter for the *Los Angeles Times* (February 20, 2005). "The reason I started talking about my life is because I'd gone out thinking I was British for so long, I felt I owed it to inform myself on what was happening to the people I left behind. On a personal level, I feel guilty that I got away and so many kids didn't."

M.I.A.'s genre-melding sound has been a favorite of critics and independent-music fans since 2003, when her song "Galang" became an underground hit in the U.K. Referring to M.I.A.'s songs as "multicultural mashups," Richard Harrington wrote for the *Washington Post* (September 16, 2005) that her music is "a pastiche of hip-hop, electro, Jamaican dancehall, reggaeton, garage rock, Brazilian baile funk, grime, Bollywood bhangra and video game soundtracks." Greg Kot noted for the *Chicago Tribune* (April 3, 2005) that M.I.A.'s lyrics on her early recordings, such as "Galang," were "unconventional, a patchwork of street slang, nursery rhymes, political commentary and feel-good gibberish."

After M.I.A.'s familial connection to the Tamil separatist movement came to light, the artist was repeatedly questioned about her ties to what many countries consider a terrorist organization. (The movement is said to be the first to use suicide bombers.) Her lyrics are known to reference acts of violence, and her artwork often depicts guns, bombs, and tigers. (Though some have argued that the image of a tiger represents the Tamil population as a whole, the tiger has also become known as a symbol of the militant movement.) While M.I.A. has vehemently denied supporting terrorists of any kind, she has acknowledged that the subject is complex. "I wanted [*Arular*] to be about how confusing it is to talk about things as a civilian when you are caught up in something like [a civil war]," M.I.A. told Ben Sisario for the *New York Times* (August 19, 2007). "You can never say good and evil, and 'We'll fight the axis of evil,' because it's a confused line. Eighty percent of that argument is actually gray matter." "I don't want to represent what I've been through in a negative, victimized light," M.I.A. told Joan Anderman for the *Boston Globe* (March 13, 2005). "I want it to be fun because there is beauty in it, and that's really all I was interested in. I'm proud of being a refugee, which makes people uncomfortable. It's important to point out the good things that come from the outside, from the margins."

M.I.A. was born Mathangi Arulpragasam on July 17, 1975 in the Hounslow suburb of London, England. Her parents, ethnic Tamils, had had an arranged marriage in their native Sri Lanka and moved to London in 1971, when her father, A. R. Arulpragasam, found work as an engineer. When M.I.A. was six months old, her family returned to Sri Lanka. Her father had become involved in the Tamil separatist movement and helped found the Eelam Revolutionary Organization of Students (EROS), the first militant Tamil separatist group, in 1975. It is said that he trained with Palestinian militants in Lebanon in 1976; adopting the nom de guerre Arular, he became increasingly active in EROS and left M.I.A.'s mother, Kala, a seamstress, to raise and care for M.I.A., her older sister, Kali, and younger brother, Sugu. Arular's involvement with EROS made him a target of the Sri Lankan Army, and he rarely made contact with his family. On the rare occasions when he visited, M.I.A. and her siblings were told that he was an uncle in order to protect his identity. Even so, violence was still very much a part of M.I.A.'s childhood. "Although [my father] didn't live with us or spend any time with us, we suffered all the consequences of having him as a dad," M.I.A. told Hattie Collins for the London *Guardian* (August 18, 2007, on-line). "Our houses would get extra bombed and the people in our neighbourhood would get extra tortured and the army would come round and beat my mum up. All for this mythical dad figure that I never had." (Though Arular was an active member of the now-defunct EROS for many years, he never joined the LTTE. He is now a writer.)

Hoping to escape the violence, Kala moved her children to Jaffna, a Tamil-dominated city in Sri Lanka's Northern Province. In 1983 the fighting between the Sinhalese and Tamil separatists erupted into a civil war. Bullets and bombs became a part of daily life—aerial bombing on the part of the government wrecked a school M.I.A. attended—and M.I.A. and her family, without her father, sought refuge in Madras, India. They struggled in their new home, however: Kali became ill with typhoid fever, and the family suffered from malnourishment. An uncle, growing concerned for the family, moved them back to Jaffna. In 1986 M.I.A., her mother, and her siblings were able to flee Sri Lanka and settle in London as refugees.

M.I.A.'s family was placed in a poverty-stricken housing project in the South London town of Mitcham. As one of the area's few Asians, M.I.A. experienced persistent racism. She was placed in special-education classes to learn English, supplementing her lessons by watching TV and listening to the radio. She also discovered hip-hop. (As a young child she had listened to Bollywood tunes, Michael Jackson songs, and little other music; Harrington reported that when she arrived in England, M.I.A. "knew only four words in English, two of them 'Michael Jackson.'") "Where I lived [in England]," she told Harrington, "there was one black family and they lived next door to us. And they had a kid who listened to hip-hop all the time with his mates. It was a bit rowdy, a bit dangerous, listening to unknown music, but eventually I wanted to hang out, and that's how I learned hip-hop." Though M.I.A. grew to admire such groups as Public Enemy and N.W.A., she did not consider becoming a musician for some years. Instead, she focused on visual art as a means to express herself. "Coming from Sri Lanka, you can become so addicted to drama that when things are great you don't know how to deal with it," M.I.A. explained to Rashod D. Ollison for the *Baltimore Sun* (September 15, 2005). "It's like looking for trouble. In art, you look for a world where you can tap that without getting in jail."

Following high school M.I.A. studied fine art, film, and video at the Central St. Martins College of Art and Design, in London. During the late 1990s and early 2000s, she began to exhibit her artwork. (At her first show she sold all of her paintings.) Her art consisted largely of stencil graffiti depicting images from her childhood in Sri Lanka—palm trees, tigers, hand grenades, helicopters, and tanks—all in neon-bright colors. Her work was shortlisted in 2002 for the inaugural Alternative Turner Prize, a response to the famed Turner Prize, an annual visual-art award that recognizes contemporary British artists. (The Alternative Turner Prize seeks to recognize young British artists, ages 13 to 25, in a wider range of artistic mediums.) Earlier, M.I.A.'s art had caught the attention of Justine Frischmann, the lead singer and guitarist of the English band Elastica, who commissioned the young artist to design the cover of the band's second (and final) album, *The Menace* (2000). That year M.I.A. also directed the band's music video for their single "Mad Dog God Dam." The following year Elastica asked her to record their North American tour for a documentary. While on the road with the band, M.I.A. became close friends with their opening act, the Toronto electronica musician Peaches, who introduced M.I.A. to the Roland MC-505 Groovebox, a sequencing machine with which a user can program and arrange drum beats and other synthesized sounds. Peaches encouraged M.I.A. to experiment with the machine, and the artist returned to London with a newfound passion.

M.I.A. used a Groovebox, a four-track recorder, and a microphone to record her music. She initially hired other women to sing her lyrics but, unhappy with the results, decided to use her own vocals instead. By 2003 M.I.A. had produced her own six-song demo tape. One of the songs, "Galang," only the second song she had ever written, became enormously popular on Internet file-sharing Web sites. The independent label Showbiz Records made 500 CDs of the song, which was soon heard in dance clubs across the United Kingdom. "Galang" (the word means "go on" in Jamaican patois) is an infectious, slang-filled dance tune that blends elements from Indian pop, Jamaican dancehall, and American gangsta rap. *Rolling Stone* named "Galang" one of the year's best singles, and M.I.A. was soon signed to the British label XL Recordings. The music video for "Galang" was harshly criticized for showing M.I.A. dancing with images of tanks, fighter jets, and bombs in the background. The filmmaker Ruben Fleischer, who directed the video, told Robert Wheaton for *PopMatters* (May 6, 2005, on-line) that in his view, "the [principal] idea behind M.I.A.'s artwork is to have pretty heavy/political ideas, but to present them in a poppy candy-coated wrapper. So someone might buy her painting because it is pretty to the eye, and not necessarily consider that it is a rebellious image that she is presenting. However, after they've had it for a while, they might start to think—why do I have a pink tank on my wall?"

Though M.I.A.'s debut album was originally to be released in September 2004, legal issues regarding songs she had sampled delayed its sale by six months. As a way to promote the album, M.I.A. teamed up with the songwriter American DJ Diplo to produce the mixed tape *Piracy Funds Terrorism Volume 1*, which featured vocal tracks from M.I.A.'s coming debut together with samples of other songs, including "Walk Like an Egyptian" by the Bangles and "Push It" by Salt-n-Pepa. Starting in December 2004 the tapes were distributed for free during many of M.I.A.'s live shows.

M.I.A. next signed a distribution deal with the American label Interscope Records, and *Arular* was released in the U.S. in March 2005. (It went on sale in the U.K. a month later.) M.I.A. had titled her debut album after her father "because my mom, she raised me and all she ever said was, you know, 'Your father, he's ruined your life and all he gave you was his name, you know?' And then eventually I was, like, OK, fine. If that's all he gave me, then I'm going to use it," she told Christian Bordal for the National Public Radio program *Day to Day* (March 17, 2005, on-line). Upon reading about M.I.A. in the *Sri Lankan Times* newspaper, Arular contacted his daughter for the first time since 1990, sending her an e-mail message that read, "I'm very proud of you, but you have to change the name of the album." M.I.A. did not change the title. "What can you do?" she asked Richard Harrington.

"There's many things I'm not pleased about that he's done, so hey . . ." (M.I.A. remains out of contact with her father.)

Arular was a critical success and peaked at number three on the U.S. *Billboard* Top Electronic Albums chart. It was shortlisted for the 2005 Nationwide Mercury Prize, a prestigious award recognizing the year's best album by a U.K. artist, and both *Spin* and *URB* magazines named M.I.A. artist of the year. Controversy soon arose, however, regarding M.I.A.'s link to the Tamil separatist movement. The music video for her second single, "Sunshowers," was banned from the music-video channel MTV for lyrics that referenced the Palestine Liberation Organization (PLO), which has been classified as a terrorist organization by the U.S. government. "You wanna go? You wanna winna war? Like PLO I don't surrendo," M.I.A. sang. She told Robert Wheaton, "There's so much confusion about what I stand for and what I'm saying that that's the whole point: there *have* to be discussions; there *has* to be people talking, and there has to be young people talking about politics if they want. They have to have a chance to hear different opinions. And that's really what it's about." M.I.A.'s songs generally deal with war, refugees, and immigration, and she hopes that her music will start conversations that could lead people to form new ideas about (or a better understanding of) those issues. For example, M.I.A., having grown up seeing combatants and victims on both sides of the Sri Lankan civil war, questions the way in which some nations are quick to label certain groups or people "terrorists" before understanding their causes.

In 2006 U.S. immigration officials denied M.I.A. a work visa. She was forced to abandon her plans of recording her sophomore album, *Kala*, with the Grammy Award–winning American producer Timbaland. Instead she traveled the world, visiting India, Jamaica, Trinidad, and Australia, finding inspiration in local music scenes and recording bits of her album along the way. "The resulting songs feel airborne and deliberately rootless," Ben Sisario wrote. "The enormous drums of [the song] 'Boyz,' for example, were recorded in India, but the rest of the song—a Bollywood-tinged club banger about the rowdy, war-starting sex—was made in Trinidad. 'World Town' rewrites a Baltimore hip-hop anthem for a violent third-world ghetto; the dizzyingly abstract percussion loop of 'BirdFlu' is spiked with Indian dhol drums and chicken squawks." *Kala*, named in honor of her mother, was released in August 2007. (M.I.A. was granted a visa in 2007 and went to the U.S.)

Once again M.I.A. received favorable reviews. *Rolling Stone* and *Blender* both named *Kala* the best album of 2007, and in Canada the singer was nominated for two Independent Music Awards, for International Album of the Year and International Artist of the Year, in 2008. The album's first single, "Boyz," peaked at number three on the U.S. *Billboard* Hot Dance Singles Sales chart and was number nine on *Rolling Stone*'s list of the 100 best songs of 2007. However, it was the song "Paper Planes" that secured M.I.A.'s popularity in the U.S. In his description of the song, Darryl Sterdan wrote for the *Calgary (Alberta) Sun* (August 19, 2007), "M.I.A. adds reggae-style vocals—along with finger snaps and yes, gunshots—to a lazy Afro-Caribbean cooler built atop The Clash's 'Straight to Hell.'"

In his review of her second album, J. Freedom du Lac wrote for the *Washington Post* (August 21, 2007), "If M.I.A. felt any pressure, externally or otherwise, to craft an album with crossover potential, it doesn't show on *Kala*. Assembled by M.I.A. and a forward-thinking team of producers . . . the tracks often seem more like rhythm-based sound collages than songs, eschewing pop conventions—melody, for instance—for something more primal and visceral. Still, the songs jump out of the headphones, exploding with verve." Du Lac called the album "outrageously good." Though it was released as *Kala*'s third single in early 2008, "Paper Planes" did not become a commercial success until June, when it was used in a trailer for the Judd Apatow movie comedy *Pineapple Express*. The song reached number one on the U.S. *Billboard* Dance Sales chart and number four on the U.S. *Billboard* Hot 100. It was nominated for the 2009 Grammy Award for Record of the Year and was featured in the Oscar-winning film *Slumdog Millionaire* (2008). Typically for M.I.A.'s work, "Paper Planes" is a mellow pop tune on the surface but offers social commentary—in this case, on immigrant stereotypes. She told Alex Wagner for *Fader* (August 7, 2007, on-line), "People don't really feel like immigrants or refugees contribute to culture in any way. That they're just leeches that suck from whatever. So in the song I say, 'All I wanna do is [sound of gun shooting and reloading, cash register opening] and take your money.' I did it in sound effects. It's up to you how you want to interpret. America is so obsessed with money, I'm sure they'll get it."

Around the time "Paper Planes" was appearing on the music charts, M.I.A. discovered that she was pregnant by her fiancé, Benjamin Brewer. (Brewer is the singer and guitarist for the New York City rock band the Exit. He is also a son of Warner Music Group's CEO, Edgar Bronfman Jr.) On February 8, 2009 M.I.A. surprised many by appearing at the 51st Grammy Awards ceremony in Los Angeles, California, on her due date. With the American rappers Jay-Z, Kanye West, Lil Wayne, and T.I., she performed "Swagga Like Us," a popular song by T.I. and Jay-Z that sampled "Paper Planes." "Swagga Like Us" went on to win the Grammy for best rap song. M.I.A. gave birth to her son, Ikhyd Edgar Arular Bronfman, three days later.

In May 2009 M.I.A.'s name appeared on *Time* magazine's annual list of the world's 100 most influential people. The next month she won the 2009 BET Award for best female hip-hop artist. M.I.A. recently started her own record label, the Interscope imprint N.E.E.T., which stands for Not in Education, Employment or Training; she has signed the Baltimore rapper Rye Rye. The first album released on N.E.E.T. was the *Slumdog Millionaire* soundtrack, in December 2008. M.I.A. also has her own fashion line, Okley Run, with items of clothing available for purchase on her Web site. She lives in New York City, in the Bedford Stuyvesant neighborhood of Brooklyn. In a post to her Web site announcing the birth of her son, M.I.A. wrote that she is working on new songs as well as planning tour dates for 2010.

—M.A.S.

Suggested Reading: *Boston Globe* N p1 Mar. 13, 2005; *Fader* (on-line) Aug. 7, 2007; miauk.com; (Montreal, Canada) *Gazette* D p1 May 21, 2005; *New York Times* AR p20 Aug. 19, 2007; *SF Weekly* Music Mar. 9, 2005; *Washington Post* T p6 Sep. 16, 2005

Selected Recordings: *Piracy Funds Terrorism Volume 1*, 2004; *Arular*, 2005; *Kala*, 2007

Frederick M. Brown/Getty Images

Maddow, Rachel

Apr. 1, 1973– Television and radio host

Address: Air America Radio, 641 Sixth Ave., Fourth Fl., New York, NY 10011

Rachel Maddow, the host of the popular MSNBC program *The Rachel Maddow Show* and the Air America Media radio show of the same name, is an unusual cable-news personality in several ways. In a format that often lends itself to combativeness, with programs sometimes degenerating into shouting matches, the left-leaning Maddow tempers her wit with civility and a down-to-earth demeanor. And Maddow, a six-foot-tall former Rhodes scholar, is not only a woman in a male-dominated area of television, but the first openly lesbian host of a national prime-time news broadcast. *The Rachel Maddow Show* had its first MSNBC telecast in September 2008, in the period leading up to that year's presidential election; the timing of its debut, and a time slot following that of the popular MSNBC show *Countdown with Keith Olbermann*, helped Maddow's program achieve very high ratings very quickly. While her viewership has declined somewhat since the election, the program still has an enviable number of watchers—including much-sought-after 25-to-54-year-olds. Julia Baird wrote for *Newsweek* (December 1, 2008), "Maddow seems to have genuinely charmed younger viewers, a Twitter-savvy, podcasting generation that has hankered for someone more like them and delights in her use of 'duh,' her obvious intelligence and authenticity, and her ability to be both idealistic and skeptical about politics. She eschews vanity and insists she won't stop dressing 'like a 13-year-old boy' when she can."

One of two children, Rachel Anne Maddow was born on April 1, 1973 in Castro Valley, California, to Elaine Maddow, a school administrator, and Bob Maddow, a lawyer. Her parents told Baird that Maddow was a serious-minded child who rarely uttered baby talk and began reading the newspaper by the age of four. Maddow told Baird that she had political leanings even as a young girl, recalling her negative reaction to watching the Republican soon-to-be president Ronald Reagan on television during the 1980 campaign season, when she was only seven. "All I remember is the feeling of dislike," she said. "Maybe I have reverse-engineered it into my memory." Maddow's interest in media was partially influenced by her father, who had a habit of following sports events by watching television and listening to a transistor radio—at the same time. "He wanted to listen to the radio sound . . . and [watch] the TV with the sound off, even when they were out of sync," she told Robert Sullivan for *Vogue* (January 2009). "And I thought, Oh, right, radio is harder. He's getting a higher-level audio experience from people who know you can't see the picture. I also just thought, like, Oh, my dad's awesome; he has higher standards." Maddow's father served as a U.S. Air Force captain during the Vietnam War. Maddow herself has a strong interest in national security and defense policy. "I'm a national security liberal, which I tell people because it's meant to sound absurd," she told Jacques Steinberg for the *New York Times* (July 17, 2008). "I'm all about counterterrorism. I'm all about the G.I. Bill."

While attending Castro Valley High School, Maddow took to sports, participating in swimming, basketball, and volleyball. She had aspirations of becoming an Olympic athlete before a series of injuries dashed her hopes. She told Sullivan, referring to characters in John Hughes's 1985 film *The Breakfast Club*, "I was a cross between the jock and the antisocial girl who bit people. . . . I wanted to be the outsider so bad. But I was the jock and that bad-hair girl." In 1987 Maddow, who had not yet come out as gay, volunteered to work at an AIDS services center in nearby San Francisco. "I had a very acute sense that something was happening to 'my' people even before I knew I was gay," she told Louise France for the London *Guardian* (February 8, 2009, on-line). "I was very moved by what was going on. Growing up in the Bay Area as a gay kid was devastating. It defined the world in a very serious way for me, in a life-or-death sort of way. I had a lot of older friends and many of them died. There was a sense of: look, your life is happening now. This may be all you get."

After high school Maddow attended Stanford University, in California, graduating with a degree in public policy in 1994. Roger Noll, a onetime director of the public-policy program at Stanford, told Jessica Pressler for *New York* magazine (November 10, 2008), "She was a brilliant student, one of those that only come around every few years or so." Maddow wrote her undergraduate thesis on the change in societal perceptions of AIDS victims, and one Stanford professor, Debra Satz, told Pressler, "I still send students to that thesis as a model." As a 17-year-old freshman at Stanford, Maddow came out as a lesbian, in a way that was, by her own admission, confrontational: she made posters about her sexuality and placed them in the bathroom of her dorm. "I didn't want any drama," she told Baird. "I didn't want any personal touchy-feely BS from anybody. I just wanted to get it over, and make a joke about it, and move on." (After someone anonymously mailed Maddow's parents a student-newspaper account of their daughter's announcement, Bob and Elaine Maddow were stunned but, ultimately, supportive.)

After graduating from Stanford Maddow worked in San Francisco for a year with the AIDS-awareness organization ACT UP and the AIDS Legal Referral Panel. She also focused her activism efforts on prison reform for AIDS patients. She then received a John Gardner Fellowship and a Rhodes Scholarship, which allowed her to attend Oxford University, in England, to pursue a doctorate in political science. She was the first openly gay American to win a Rhodes scholarship. After a few months at Oxford, feeling out of her element and wanting a break from her studies, Maddow moved out of her Oxford apartment and into a rent-free part of a basement in London, where she worked as the general manager of an organization called the AIDS Treatment Project. She soon moved back to the U.S., where she settled in western Massachusetts to finish her dissertation. She took up a number of odd jobs to support herself, working as a landscaper, unloading trucks, and cleaning barrels at a coffee-bean factory.

While working at a friend's coffee shop in Northampton, Massachusetts, Maddow heard a radio announcement about open auditions for the on-air sidekick to a local radio personality, Dave Brinnel, the host of *Dave in the Morning*, on WRNX-FM. Maddow went into the station on a whim, won the audition, and spent the next few years on the show reading the day's news and setting up punch lines for Brinnel's jokes. "She was one of the wittiest, smartest people I've ever met," Brinnel told Pressler. In 2001 Maddow left *Dave in the Morning* to finish her doctorate, which focused on AIDS victims in prison. She then returned to the show, staying until 2004. From 2002 to 2004 she also hosted the radio show *Big Breakfast*, on WRSI, in Northampton.

In 2004 Maddow was tapped to host a show called *Unfiltered*, with the *Daily Show*'s co-creator Lizz Winstead and the rapper Chuck D, on the recently launched progressive radio network Air America (now Air America Media). The show was cancelled a year later. Maddow then got her own Air America program, *The Rachel Maddow Show*. The show, which premiered on April 14, 2005, proved to be popular; Maddow quickly began to build her reputation as a liberal through the show's content, taking on many of the day's issues with a tone similar to the one she would later bring to her MSNBC show. Her Air America program included interviews with journalists and politicians as well as segments such as "Ask Dr. Maddow," in which the host would address listeners' questions on various topics. The time slot for *The Rachel Maddow Show* was eventually increased from one hour to two; the program aired from 5 a.m. to 6 a.m. and then moved to a more prominent position in the morning time slot before its switch to evenings. From March 10, 2008 to September 5, 2008 the show ran for three hours, then returned to the two-hour format when Maddow began hosting her MSNBC show. As of mid-2009 the show's content consisted primarily of the audio portion of the previous night's MSNBC broadcast. Currently, the radio show airs on weekday mornings on Air America affiliates. It is also available on XM Satellite Radio and the Air America Web site.

In 2005 Maddow successfully auditioned for the MSNBC show *Tucker*, to provide left-leaning opposition to the program's conservative host, Tucker Carlson. *Tucker*'s producer, Bill Wolff, told Pressler, "She was unbelievably prepared. And she just killed [Carlson]." Aside from her regular spot on *Tucker*, Maddow spent the next three years serving as a guest commentator on other MSNBC shows and was seen frequently on CNN's *Paula Zahn Now*. By 2006 she was a regular guest and political analyst on both MSNBC and CNN; in 2008 she signed an exclusive agreement with MSNBC. That year *Tucker* was cancelled, and Maddow began to appear regularly on *Countdown with Keith Olbermann*. She also became a regular panelist on *Race for the White House* and took over hosting duties when the show's regular host, David Gregory, was absent. On occasion Olbermann asked Maddow to serve as the guest host for his show, as he felt that she shared his political and social views. In July 2008 Maddow hosted Olbermann's show for eight nights while he was on vacation. Maddow had filled in for Olbermann before, but never for so long; she was greeted with positive reviews and speculation about the possibility of her getting her own show on MSNBC. While hosting the show Maddow echoed Olbermann's sharp criticism of conservative figures. On a July 7 installment, for example, she criticized U.S. senator John McCain of Arizona, the soon-to-be Republican nominee for president, for saying that the U.S. economy was "slowing." Maddow said, "Slowing, senator? Try grinding to a halt."

In August 2008 it was announced that a new show hosted by Maddow would replace Dan Abrams's *Verdict* in the 9 p.m. Eastern Standard Time (EST) slot, immediately following *Countdown with Keith Olbermann. The Rachel Maddow Show* premiered on September 8 and surpassed the ratings of *Countdown* to become MSNBC's highest-rated evening program. By December 2008 the show had more than doubled the ratings of *Verdict*, with 1.9 million total viewers. It also fared better in the ratings than the popular CNN show *Larry King Live*, winning more viewers in the coveted 25-to-54 age range for 27 out of 44 nights. In her first six weeks of hosting her show, Maddow was also able to retain more than 90 percent of Olbermann's audience—an impressive feat for a new host. Much of her success has been credited to her welcoming demeanor and avoidance of the aggressive tone that has dominated cable news in the past few years. Unlike the hosts of other fast-paced cable-news shows, Maddow prefers to host only one guest at a time, to avoid the shouting matches that often erupt when personalities clash. With the latter scenario, "you're essentially watching for the kinetic activity of the fight rather than listening to what anybody says about the issue," she told Pressler. "And I think what people end up cheering for is winning, you know, rather than getting something out of it. I think there's more intelligent ways to entertain people." Alessandra Stanley wrote for the *New York Times* (September 25, 2008, on-line), "Ms. Maddow's deep, modulated voice is reassuringly calm after so much shrill emotionalism and catfights among the channel's aging, white male divas."

The Rachel Maddow Show features a combination of hard news analysis and lighter segments. The segment "Ms. Information" contains news stories that Maddow feels have been underreported by the press; "GOP in Exile" covers the Republican Party; and "Just Enough" covers pop-culture and entertainment news. Maddow's opinions and commentary are showcased in "Rachel Re," in which the host offers viewers a comprehensive discussion of a given topic; and the segment "Cocktail Moment" finds Maddow relating a bit of interesting or little-known nonessential information. *The Rachel Maddow Show* debuted during the months leading up to the historic 2008 presidential election. As a result, Maddow got the benefit of a large television-news audience and was able to establish her show's tone and her own views through discussion and criticism of the candidates. France wrote, "In the same way that [the conservative pundit] Ann Coulter emerged as the public face of the Bush era, Maddow swiftly emerged as the go-to media figure in the most picked-over election in American history." In the show's debut installment, Maddow introduced her biting sarcasm when she questioned the nature of the references to God in public-policy speeches given by the Republican vice-presidential nominee, Alaska governor Sarah Palin. Referring to a quote in which Palin suggested that God supported her proposal for an oil pipeline, Maddow said, "God's will is the pipeline? . . . Palin was also in church on August 17th, just three weeks ago, the day Jews for Jesus founder, David Brickner, gave a guest sermon in which he said the deaths of Israelis killed by a terrorist who commandeered a bulldozer were the result of, quote, 'God's judgment of unbelief against the Jews.' Governor Palin did not get up and walk out . . . she listened to the assertion that God uses terrorism to express judgment against Jews for not believing in Christ. So, on the one hand, we got some extreme inflammatory religious views, on the other hand, we got assertions that God's will is being done through Governor Palin's chosen public policies. I'm worried."

Although Maddow appeared to support Obama during the election (she aired her interview with him on the October 30, 2008 installment of her show), she has since been critical of some of his decisions. She found fault with his choice of Reverend Rick Warren, who has condemned homosexual behavior, to give the invocation at the presidential inauguration; she even dedicated a segment of her television show on December 18, 2008 to the matter. Maddow has also criticized the Obama administration for failing to repeal the government's controversial policy of "Don't ask, don't tell," which is spelled out in 1994 legislation authorizing spending for defense and forbids any homosexual person in the armed services from revealing his or her sexual orientation. In May 2009 Maddow aired several segments in which she interviewed U.S. servicemen who had been discharged from the military because they were gay.

Maddow is known for welcoming right-wing pundits to her shows and, despite the ensuing debates, treating them fairly. The controversial, conservative pundit and onetime presidential candidate Pat Buchanan is a frequent guest on her MSNBC show, appearing on the semi-regular segment "It's Pat" (whose title is possibly a reference to an old *Saturday Night Live* segment about a gender-neutral character, according to Pressler—a reference she felt certain was lost on Buchanan). Although Buchanan's 1992 "culture-war" speech, which focused in part on what he saw as the threat posed by the gay-rights movement, helped to galvanize Maddow's activism, the two have never traded insults on the show. "Even though I can be harsh in my criticism and I can be strong in my beliefs, I try not to be mean," Maddow told Pressler. "And I don't have a very high tolerance for other people who are cruel or personally insulting in a way that I think is meant to humiliate people."

Just as unusual as the civility Maddow brings to her job are her casual displays of erudition. "Ever heard of something called Dada?" she said during an October 2008 installment of her program, referring to an early-20th-century cultural movement. "Deliberately being irrational, rejecting standard assumptions about beauty or organization or logic. . . . Why am I trying to explain Dadaism on a cable news show thirteen days from this big, giant, historic, crazy, important election that we're about to have? Because that's what I found myself Googling today, in search of a way to make sense of the latest McCain-Palin campaign ad!" Pressler noted that Maddow's explaining Dadaism on her show was "something of a challenge considering she only [had] about twelve seconds. . . . It's hard to imagine many other cable news hosts going down that particular rabbit hole. . . . But then again, Rachel Maddow is not like other cable news hosts."

Maddow has received criticism for hosting what has been called a partisan cable news show. Just prior to the debut of Maddow's MSNBC show, Sacha Zimmerman wrote for the *New Republic* Web site (August 20, 2008), "I really like Maddow and have found her thoroughly compelling throughout this latest campaign season, but I am not so thrilled about this trend toward partisan networks and news. By all means we should have progressive and conservative commentators and analysts, but is there no room for argument between the two? Where have all the iconoclasts gone? With this split in the networks and a near perfect red-blue divide nationwide, it seems that we are more and more retreating to our comfortable trenches and refusing to acknowledge anything but spite, paranoia, and conspiracy theory when it comes to the other side. And, since cable news is not exactly renowned for its nuance or intellectual rigor, knee-jerk reactions can pass for smart commentary. I think Maddow will be a wonderful host (and God knows MSNBC could use a smart woman), but how exciting is it really if she is just preaching to the choir?" Baird observed that the popularity of Maddow's show has led her to become more visibly left-leaning, writing, "While she has long had the reputation of being the liberal whom conservatives like, some now say she's biased and theatrical." Maddow, however, has argued that she is not a hard-line liberal and is willing to challenge the views of any politician she disagrees with—Democrat or Republican. "My job of asking questions and being critical doesn't stop depending on who is in the White House," she told the *Austin (Texas) American-Statesman* (April 27, 2009). Maddow's ratings saw a drop in March 2009 from 1.9 million viewers during the leadup to the presidential election to 1.1 million in March 2009. Some have attributed that drop to the fact that Maddow now hosts a left-leaning show in the time of a liberal presidential administration, and there is thus little conflict to keep viewers interested. Maddow told the *American-Statesman* that her focus is not on numbers. "My main concern is keeping the quality of the show high," she said. "We don't debate the ratings very much." In 2009 Maddow's show was nominated for a Television Critics Association Award in the category of outstanding achievement in news and information. That year Maddow was listed on the *Advocate*'s "Forty Under 40" list of gay media professionals and on *Out*'s "Power 50" list.

Maddow's partner is Susan Mikula, a photographer and artist. Maddow and Mikula live in a house in Cummington, Massachusetts; Maddow stays in an apartment in Manhattan during the week to prepare and film her shows. She is writing a book for the Crown Publishing Group about the changing role of the military.

—W.D.

Suggested Reading: *New York* p30+ Nov. 10, 2008; *New York Times* E p3 July 17, 2008; *Newsweek* p55 Dec. 1, 2008; *Vogue* p128 Jan. 2009

Selected Television Shows: as guest host and contributor—*Race for the White House*, 2008; *Countdown with Keith Olbermann*, 2008; as host—*The Rachel Maddow Show*, 2008–

Selected Radio Shows: as co-host—*Unfiltered*, 2004–05; as host—*The Rachel Maddow Show*, 2005–

Mam, Somaly

(MAHM)

1970(?)– Human-rights activist

Address: Somaly Mam Foundation, P.O. Box 1272, Wheat Ridge, CO 80034

Somaly Mam is an advocate for victims of sex trafficking, the worldwide, illegal industry that reaps billions of dollars for exploiters who force men, women, and children to perform sex acts for very little or no money. The sex-trafficking industry thrives in impoverished cities, where job opportunities are scarce and government and many law-enforcement officials are corrupt; it is most common in Southeast Asian countries, particularly Cambodia, Vietnam, Laos, and Thailand. Mam is the co-founder of the organization Agir pour les Femmes en Situation Precaire (AFESIP), which translates as Acting for Women in Distressing Cir-

Amy Sussman/Getty Images

Somaly Mam

cumstances, based in Phnom Penh, Cambodia; she also founded the United States–based Somaly Mam Foundation. Both organizations aim to rescue and rehabilitate victims of human trafficking and raise awareness of the growing global problem of sexual slavery. Mam, a former sex worker herself, was born into a rural tribe in Cambodia in the early 1970s, during the height of the oppressive Khmer Rouge regime, led by the violent dictator Pol Pot. The regime imposed a radical form of agrarian communism under which the population was forced to work on collective farms and elsewhere; the Khmer Rouge tried systematically to eliminate every person thought to be involved in free-market activities, including professionals, college graduates, urban residents, and many others. Mam wrote in her memoir, *The Road of Lost Innocence*, that during that brutal period in Cambodia's history, children were "a kind of domestic livestock," and there was "only one law for women: silence before rape and silence after." Abandoned at a young age, Mam was raised by a cruel man who sold her when she was 14 years old to an abusive husband, who in turn sold her to a brothel in Phnom Penh when she was 16. There, she was forced to have sex with numerous men each night and was beaten if she resisted. After escaping from the brothel four years later, she married a French aid worker and moved to France. She later returned to Cambodia and, in 1996, founded AFESIP, which has rescued and rehabilitated more than 4,000 former sex-trafficking victims. Mam, who has put herself in great danger for her cause, and whose 14-year-old daughter was briefly kidnapped by traffickers in 2006 in retaliation for her work, has received many international awards, including the Roland Berger Human Dignity Award, presented to her in November 2008. Mam wrote in her memoir, as quoted by Claire Armitstead in the London *Guardian* (February 9, 2008): "People ask me how I can bear to keep doing what I do. I'll tell you. It's the evil that was done to me that propels me on. Is there any other way to exorcise it?"

Somaly Mam does not know exactly how old she is but estimates her birth year to be 1970 or 1971. She was born a member of the Phnong tribe, in Mondulkiri, a province in eastern Cambodia known for its mountains, dense forests, and waterfalls. The farming-based tribe was so remote that it had no schools or doctors and did not even use money. Because the tribe seemed to live collectively and was untouched by Western habits, it was not targeted by Pol Pot's regime. Mam lived with her parents and grandmother before she was abandoned at a young age. In her book Mam pondered the possible reasons for her parents' absence, taking into account the violence and chaos that ravaged the country during the Pol Pot regime: "Perhaps they were seeking a better life, or perhaps they were forced to leave. . . . There are many reasons why my parents might have left the forest." She spent years living on her own, foraging for wild fruits in the forest and seeking shelter with neighbors. When Mam was about 10 years old, a man claiming to be her grandfather took her in. He forced her to become his servant, regularly beat her, and, when she was 12 years old, accepted money from an older man in exchange for permitting the man to have sex with her. During that time Mam met and befriended a local teacher, who tried to offer the young girl comfort but was powerless to protect her. Mam, having no name that she was aware of, took the woman's name, Somaly Mam, as her own. When Mam was 14 years old, the man who claimed to be her grandfather sold her to another man, who married her. He too was cruel; he would get drunk, then beat and rape her. Sometimes he fired bullets at her, narrowly missing her head and feet.

When Mam was 16 years old, her husband sold her to a brothel in the Cambodian capital, Phnom Penh. Told by her captors that she needed to work to pay off her "grandfather's debts," Mam was sometimes forced to have sex with a half-dozen men in one night. Today, although prostitution is officially illegal in Cambodia—one of Southeast Asia's poorest countries—most brothels in Phnom Penh, a center of trafficking activity, operate in the open. The sex industry is generally tolerated by government and law-enforcement officials, in part because of the perceived economic benefits reaped from "sex tourism," which include bribes of local authorities. Many sex workers are sold into slavery by their husbands or parents for the equivalent of as little as $10; others join the brothels with the false hope that they might earn enough money to escape their impoverished surroundings. Their pimps—who are often women—take most of their earnings, leaving them with a meager salary of about $15 per month. Women are often beaten, tortured, or even murdered if they refuse customers. Brothel owners often give the women amphetamines or other drugs, so that they will form addictions, making them less likely to try to leave their circumstances. There is high demand for young girls (some are as young as five years old) in part because of a cultural belief that sex with a virgin is beneficial; many people even believe that the act destroys HIV, the virus that causes AIDS. Sexually transmitted diseases are rampant in brothels; an estimated 29 percent of sex workers have HIV.

If Mam refused to have sex, she was beaten or subjected to torture that involved such things as snakes or maggots. "I never thought, just lived hour by hour," Mam said to Bruce Finley for the *Denver Post* (April 6, 2008), describing her psychological state in the brothel. "I played with nothing. In my head: nothing. It was dark, dark, dark. I never trusted people. . . . I was dead." Mam remained at the brothel for four years. Over that time she felt her spirit break and even tried to commit suicide. A turning point in her life came when she saw the pimp who ran the brothel murder one of Mam's best friends, a woman named Srymom, for refusing a customer. Realizing that she needed to escape and help others, too, Mam stole the keys to the brothel door and helped two newcomers to get away. (For that she was beaten and her skin was burned with a car battery.) Mam befriended one of her customers (or "Johns"), a European aid worker named Dietrich, who was not violent with her and eventually gave her enough money to buy her way out of slavery. (According to some sources, Mam was set free when she became too old to attract customers as a prostitute.) In her memoir Mam recalled showering for the first time in her life, in Dietrich's hotel room. "He . . . turned on a shiny thing, like a snake, and it flashed to life, spitting at me," she wrote, as quoted by Paula Bock for the *Seattle Times* (September 16, 2008). "That was the first time I ever used proper soap, and I remember how good it smelled, like a flower."

After escaping the brothel, in 1991, Mam worked as a midwife at Cambodia's Choup District Hospital. That year she began dating a French relief worker, Pierre Legros. The two married in 1993 and moved to France. Mam recalled in her book being initially terrified by aspects of the modern world, such as airplanes and the tall buildings in cities. She was also surprised by the love and respect she received from her husband and was perplexed when he encouraged her to spend her time doing whatever she wanted. Mam attended school and earned money by cleaning houses and hotels. She later worked as the director of personnel at a restaurant and as a social worker at a retirement home. During that time Mam and Legros had three children. In 1995 Mam returned to Cambodia with her husband and began working for the Swedish nongovernmental organization (NGO) Médecins Sans Frontières (Doctors without Borders), a group that provides medical care to people in war-torn regions of developing countries.

In 1996 Mam and Legros founded Agir pour les Femmes en Situation Precaire to help prostitutes and other trafficking victims escape brothels and make the transition to self-sufficiency. The organization also works to improve the conditions in brothels. Mam became the group's president and worked at its headquarters, in Phnom Penh. At its main refuge, located in the countryside about three hours outside the city, Mam provides girls and women who have been rescued from brothels with free medical care and access to education. Many of the rescued girls have undergone such intense physical and psychological trauma that they require extensive medical and psychiatric care; for the many infected with HIV, Mam tries to make their lives as comfortable as possible. The refuge also provides the women with training, in weaving, sewing, and hairdressing, in an effort to build their confidence and skills. "If girls have financial independence, they can say no to the brothels," Mam explained to Susan Dominus for *Glamour* (December 2008). "So we have a hairdressing shop and sewing machines for them to learn skills." After the girls and women are rehabilitated, Mam and her colleagues typically return them to their families—but only if it appears that they will not be sold back to the brothels or return there on their own. Mam explained that many women return to brothels because they do not feel that they have other options. "Sometimes the women themselves, they think that it is normal that they have been sold in a brothel," she told David Montgomery for the *Washington Post* (September 22, 2008). "It's like me. Before, I think it's normal that I have been sold. . . . I never knew that I had rights." The brothel owners allow Mam's staff to visit the brothels because they bring condoms, soap, toothpaste, and other supplies related to hygiene; they also teach the women safe-sex practices. As the organization's mission became known, its reach expanded to Laos, Vietnam, and Thailand. In 1998 Mam founded AFESIP International, with additional bureaus in France and Switzerland. Also in 1998 she was made a member of the jury that judged performers at the First International Festival of Solidarity of the European Commission, held in Spain. That year, in addition, she was given Spain's Prince of Asturias Award as well as the Premio Principe de Asturias-Cooperacion Internacional, which honors contributions to mutual understanding or fraternity among peoples. In 1999 she was elected president of the Confederation of Women's Organizations in the Association of Southeast Asian Nations (ASEAN).

Mam's work is dangerous, and it is not unusual for her and her staff to receive death threats. In 2004 Mam worked with police to launch a raid of a hotel that ran one of Phnom Penh's biggest brothels, where about 200 women were held. A few days later a mob of men broke into Mam's refuge and took away 90 of the women and girls who were staying there; Mam never saw any of them again. Around that time a friend in France telephoned

Mam and urged her to flee Cambodia, because of the danger she was clearly in, but she refused to leave. Instead, Mam spent three days recording her life's story on cassettes, to ensure that someone would know about it in the event that she was silenced. She sent the tapes to a friend in France, who passed them on to a ghostwriter. Mam's story was thus published in France in 2005 under the title *Le Silence de l'innocence*, which was translated into English by Lisa Appignanesi as *The Road of Lost Innocence* (2008). The book's first half is devoted to the story of Mam's life; the second half focuses on the women and girls she cares for and the broader issues of sexual slavery and human trafficking. One of her observations is that the "moral bankruptcy" that exists within present-day Cambodia is linked to the violence and chaos the country experienced under Pol Pot. During the Khmer Rouge regime, she wrote, "people detached themselves from all kind of human feeling, because feeling meant pain. They learned not to trust their neighbors, their family, their own children." The memoir, which has appeared in many languages, was acclaimed by reviewers for its "matter-of-fact storytelling, which is strengthened by Mam's detachment and humility," as Charmaine Chan wrote for the *South China Morning Post* (September 28, 2008). A reviewer for the Irish *Sunday Business Post* (January 27, 2008) wrote that although Mam "is not a naturally gifted writer," the memoir "is a corrective for anybody who might somehow think there is anything consensual about foreign prostitution."

Mam's work received mainstream attention in August 2006, when the French journalist Marianne Pearl published an article in *Glamour*, as part of a year-long series dedicated to discovering "who changes the world and how." (Pearl is the widow of the journalist Daniel Pearl, who was kidnapped, held captive, and killed by Islamic militants in Pakistan in 2002.) When Pearl met with Mam in Cambodia, in May 2006, Mam's 14-year-old daughter, Ning, had been missing for 24 hours. Two days later police discovered Ning in Battambang, a province near the border of Thailand, known as a human-trafficking hub. She had been kidnapped, drugged, and raped, likely in retaliation for Mam's work. Pearl's article, which included painful stories of women in brothels and in Mam's refuge, shone a media spotlight on the atrocities of sexual slavery in Southeast Asia. Mam was named one of *Glamour*'s 2006 Women of the Year and was honored at a ceremony held at New York City's Carnegie Hall. During that visit Mam met with philanthropy-minded celebrities, including the actress Susan Sarandon, to seek help with fund-raising. (In October 2009 Sarandon received the first Somaly Mam Voices for Change Award, for her advocacy work on behalf of victims of human trafficking. The advisory board for the Somaly Mam Foundation also includes the actor Ron Livingston, the actresses Daryl Hannah and Laurie Holden, and the model Petra Nemcova.)

In 2008 Mam was contacted by two U.S. Air Force Academy cadets, Nic Lumpp and Jared Greenberg, who, after learning about human trafficking, had resolved to fight it. After visiting Mam's operation in Cambodia, they worked with her to found a U.S.-based group to stop human trafficking. The Somaly Mam Foundation, located in Denver, Colorado, is a nonprofit organization that raises money to dissuade foreign "sex tourists" from entering Southeast Asia and to fund continued rescue-and-rehabilitation efforts for girls and women at shelters in Cambodia and neighboring countries. The organization's current goals for Mam's three centers in Cambodia include providing micro-financing opportunities to newly released victims who want to start their own businesses and, in collaboration with Regis University in Denver, Colorado, creating a program to teach English as a second language. As of April 2009 the organization's Tom Dy Center contained a child-care house, to provide care for the young children of residents who were taking part in rehabilitation and vocational training. As of April 2008 the group had raised $400,000 from celebrities and corporations, including LexisNexis, which has taken up Mam's cause as part of its philanthropic support of "rule-of-law" projects. "We need the United States. Americans are more active," Mam told Finley. "Cambodia's own efforts to combat the sex trade have been crippled by corruption of police and courts." In March 2009 a group of 25 took part in Futures '09 Cycling Challenge, a 500-kilometer bike tour through Cambodia, to raise awareness and money for the Somaly Mam Foundation. According to the group's Web site, the event succeeded in raising $79,562. In June 2009 the Somaly Mam Foundation graduated its first class from its Voices for Change program, which trains survivors of slavery to become activists for the foundation. That same month the AFESIP Cambodia welcomed Carol Rodley, the U.S. ambassador to Cambodia, who visited the Siem Reap center. In August 2009 the Siem Reap center also hosted a U.S. delegation, which included Robin J. Lerner, the counsel to the Senate Committee on Foreign Relations, and Janice V. Kaguyutan, the senior counsel to the Senate Committee on Health, Education, Labor and Pensions, among others.

Mam continues to be honored for her work. In April 2008 she received the World's Children's Prize, established by the Swedish NGO Children's World and awarded by a jury of former child soldiers, street children, bonded workers, and refugees from 17 countries. Mam was also the winner of the 2008 Global Friends' Award, which is determined by a worldwide vote among some 6.6 million children. In November 2008 Mam was the recipient of the first Roland Berger Human Dignity Award, from the Munich, Germany–based Roland Berger Foundation, which documents human trafficking and slavery around the world. That award included a grant worth 1 million euros (the equivalent of about $1.3 million). For years Mam has lobbied U.S. lawmakers to pass stronger legislation against human trafficking. In December 2008 President George W. Bush signed such a bill—sponsored by New York congresswoman Carolyn B. Maloney, who chairs the Congressional Human Trafficking Caucus—into law. Among other functions, it increases penalties against traffickers, expands protections for trafficking victims and their families, requires that the Department of Justice develop a new state-level law to investigate and prosecute cases of human trafficking, authorizes increased assistance for victims, and establishes a presidential award for extraordinary anti-trafficking efforts. In December 2008 Mam was named one of *Time* magazine's people of the year, and in April 2009 the editors included her on the magazine's list of the 100 most influential people.

Mam is still haunted by memories of her past. She has difficulty sleeping, showers repeatedly every day, and wears copious amounts of perfume in an effort to forget the smells of the brothel. Though many have called her beautiful—"outshin[ing] supermodels at foundation fundraisers," according to Paula Bock—Mam wrote in her book, "I still feel that I'm dirty and that I carry bad luck." She finds solace in her ability to help and comfort the girls and women at her refuges. "I'm not sure what being happy really means," Mam told Pearl. "But when I cuddle with the girls, giving them the love I never received, then I do feel happy." Mam is constantly in danger of retaliation from the powerful forces she is fighting. Though she has been offered safe haven in other countries, Mam has refused to leave Cambodia. She wrote in her book, as quoted by Catherine Price for *Salon.com* (September 23, 2008): "I don't feel like I can change the world. . . . I don't even try. I only want to change this small life that I see standing in front of me, which is suffering. I want to change this small real thing that is the destiny of one little girl. And then another, and another, because if I didn't, I wouldn't be able to live with myself or sleep at night." Mam and Legros divorced several years ago.

—M.E.R.

Suggested Reading: *Denver Post* B p3 Apr. 6, 2008; *Glamour* (on-line) Aug. 1, 2006; (London) *Guardian* p9 Feb. 9, 2008; Salon.com Sep. 23, 2008; *Seattle Times* D p3 Sep. 16, 2008; *Washington Post* C p1 Sep. 22, 2008

Selected Books: *The Road of Lost Innocence*, 2008

Martin, Demetri

May 25, 1973– Comedian; writer; actor

Address: c/o Comedy Central, 1775 Broadway, New York, NY 10019

"With his anorexic build, boyish face and mop of hair . . . Demetri Martin looks like he should be playing hackeysack on some college green. Instead, he's poised to become comedy's next superstar," Neal Justin wrote in a profile of the rising comedian for the Minneapolis, Minnesota, *Star Tribune* (February 8, 2009). Nearly devoid of references to politics or pop culture, Martin's humor is based on wordplay and offbeat observations that follow their own, highly unusual logic. Martin first received national exposure in 2005, as one of the correspondents on the satiric news program *The Daily Show*, which airs on the cable network Comedy Central; his humor struck a chord with younger audiences, and he was tapped to host his own weekly half-hour sketch-variety program. Since its February 2009 debut, *Important Things with Demetri Martin* has earned critical and commercial success, drawing an average of 2.3 million viewers a week during its first season, making it Comedy Central's most-viewed new program since *Chappelle's Show*, in 2003. *Important Things* has since been renewed for a second season.

Kevin Winter/Getty Images

Demetrios Evan Martin was born on May 25, 1973 to Lillian Martin, a nutritionist at a nursing home, and Dean Martin, a Greek Orthodox priest, in New York City. (Orthodox priests are permitted to marry before they are ordained.) His parents, who raised their three children in Toms River,

New Jersey, also spent several summers managing Shorty's Shish-Kabob, a family-owned concession stand, located near the Jersey Shore. They later bought the Sand Castle Diner in Toms River, where Demetri Martin reluctantly performed busboy duties and often spent his free time with his head buried in puzzle books, absorbed by the various mathematical or linguistic challenges. That planted the seed for what would later become Martin's trademark comedy style. "I think I like one-liners and shorter jokes because they're like little puzzles," Martin told Vanessa Farquaharson for the Ontario, Canada, *National Post* (July 19, 2006). "They can encapsulate a larger idea, and instead of a solution, there's a punchline. . . . Later I started to realize a thread—the economy of words, or of images that simplify things appealed to me a lot." His other childhood pursuits included breakdancing, skateboarding, and playing basketball.

While growing up Martin served as an altar boy at his father's parish. He has credited his father, who was a fan of the comedian Bill Cosby, the comedically gifted actor Peter Sellers, and the NBC sketch-comedy series *Saturday Night Live*, as an early influence. "His sermons, in retrospect, I realize, they were like 20-minute sets . . . anecdotal, very personal and just really funny," Martin told Terry Gross during a September 24, 2007 interview for the National Public Radio (NPR) program *Fresh Air*. He continued: "There were no notes. He didn't read his sermon or have this big prepared thing. He'd have a couple of ideas jotted down on an envelope or something I'd see up there on the pulpit. And then he would just go."

After being elected president of his sixth- and eighth-grade classes, Martin developed an interest in law. He remained actively involved in student government at Toms River North High School, where he was voted student-council president during his senior year. By then he had also been elected president of the Greek Orthodox Youth Association's New Jersey chapter. While in high school he attended a stand-up comedy performance by Steven Wright, whose trademark deadpan humor and wry wordplay made an immediate—and lasting—impression on Martin.

Martin completed high school in 1991, then studied history at Yale University, in New Haven, Connecticut, where he served on the Yale College Council, ran a soup kitchen, and started a youth group with a local Greek Orthodox church. During his junior year Martin began writing a lengthy palindromic poem, "Dammit, I'm Mad," which consisted of more than 200 words. (Palindromes are words or sentences that read the same backward and forward.)

At about that time Martin also experienced a life-changing event—his father's death, from cancer, at the age of 46. At the funeral Martin had a profound realization about the fleetingness of life. While the unexpected death led many members of his family to seek psychological counseling, Martin did not. "That was the puzzle-solver in me," he told Aidan Smith for *Scotland on Sunday* (August 17, 2003). "I wanted to work it out for myself."

Martin earned his bachelor's degree in 1995, then received a full scholarship to attend the New York University (NYU) School of Law. He also became engaged to his high-school sweetheart, Jen, who together with Martin had been voted "most likely to succeed" by their classmates; Jen planned to become a doctor. During his first year of law school, Martin began to seriously reconsider his career path. "I realized, 'Oh my God. This is not for me. I can't believe I made such a miscalculation. I'm bored . . .,'" he told Alan Sepinwall for the Newark, New Jersey, *Star-Ledger* (February 10, 2009). "And I didn't know what to do. . . . My whole identity was based on the idea that I was going to be this guy." Bored and restless, Martin devoted himself more fully to his extracurricular activities, which included painting and drawing. In the spring of 1997, near the end of his second year of law school, the 24-year-old Martin decided to leave NYU and embark on a career in comedy. By then he was married, and his wife, like Martin's own family, thought he was making a big mistake. "And strangely I found my family's disapproval a kind of freedom," Martin said to Stephanie Merritt for the London *Observer* (October 12, 2003). "For the first time I realized how much of what I did was to feel I was a success in other people's terms." (He and his wife divorced in the late 1990s.)

After leaving NYU Martin held a series of odd jobs, including stints as a freelance worker for an advertising agency and as an intern with *The Daily Show*, which was then hosted by the comedian Craig Kilborn. In July 1997 Martin made his stand-up debut during an open-mic night at a New York City comedy club, where the audience laughed at half of his dozen jokes. "I was thrilled," he recalled to Anthony Weiss for the *Yale Alumni Magazine* (January/February 2008). "I left the stage thinking, 'Oh man, I'm a comedian.'" (One of the jokes he told that night remained in his act for years afterward: "I was riding an escalator and I tripped. I fell down the stairs for an hour and a half.") Martin was not as successful the next night. "I get on stage, do the same set," he continued. "Silence. Bombed, just died. I was shocked. I leave the stage, sweating, thinking, 'What happened?' The next day I get back to the *Daily Show* and they say, 'How'd it go?' I say, 'I bombed.' And they said, 'Now you're a comedian.'"

During the early part of the next decade, the young comic started to garner attention. In 2000 Martin was invited to appear on *Late Night with Conan O'Brien*, and the following year he was a featured comic on the Comedy Central series *Premium Blend*, a showcase for promising stand-up comedians. Martin's big break came in the summer of 2001, when he performed at the Just for Laughs festival in Montreal, Canada, which was attended by several TV network executives. Martin recalled to Adam Sternbergh for *New York* (February 16, 2009) about the festival, "People would do these sets that were like, 'My mom is such a character! And my neighbor . . .' so the executives in the audience could say, 'Yes, we can see your show. It's your mom, and your neighbor, and you?' But my set was just one-liners." Nonetheless, shortly afterward Martin signed a one-year development deal with NBC to star in a sitcom and flew to Los Angeles, California, to film the pilot episode, which he had also co-written. After NBC executives failed to greenlight the series, in which his character lives next door to a single mother, Martin returned to New York City, where he continued to hone his stand-up routine. To connect with his audience in a deeper, more personal way, Martin decided to create his own one-man show. He not only wrote jokes but drew charts and painted posters; he also learned to sew so he could make his own costumes, taught himself to play guitar, piano, and harmonica so he could accompany his jokes with music, and sprinkled the show generously with anagrams, palindromes, and other kinds of wordplay.

In 2002 Martin premiered his well-received one-man show, entitled *If I . . .*, which featured his now-celebrated palindromic poem "Dammit, I'm Mad." "I looked up 'if' in the dictionary, and there were five different meanings of the word if, and that's my show—explaining how they apply to my life and my future. That's generally where it came from. It's an honest show and kind of a confessional," he told the *Yale Daily News* (September 5, 2003). The show premiered at Manhattan's Upright Citizens Brigade Theatre; Martin later performed it at comedy venues around the world, including the Aspen Comedy Festival, in Colorado, where he won the Jury Prize (2003), and the Edinburgh Fringe Festival, in Scotland, where he received the Perrier Comedy Award (2003), becoming only the second American to win that prestigious honor. (Rich Hall won it in 1981.) His one-person show was adapted into a nearly hour-long special that aired on British television in January 2004.

Following his performance in Edinburgh, Martin was contacted by the renowned filmmaker Woody Allen to audition for the lead role in his movie *Melinda, Melinda* (2004)—a part that eventually went to Will Ferrell. From 2003 to 2004 Martin was a member of *Late Night with Conan O'Brien*'s writing staff, which earned a 2004 Emmy Award nomination, in the category of outstanding writing for a variety, music, or comedy program, and won a 2005 Writers Guild of America (WGA) Award, in the category of comedy/variety (including talk) series. After his writing stint had ended, he returned to the show over the next several years as a guest comedian.

Also in 2004 Martin was featured on *Comedy Central Presents*, a half-hour special during which he performed traditional comedy, used humorous drawings as visual aids, and told jokes while strumming his guitar. Martin also continued to perform stand-up in front of live audiences. Other projects that year included the comedic short *12:21*, for which he served as star and screenwriter, and *Spiral Bound*, another one-man show that touched upon personal topics, such as his family, his decision to leave law school, and the breakup of his marriage. The editors of *Entertainment Weekly* included Martin in their 2004 list of the 25 funniest people in America.

In November 2005, following appearances on the late-night series *Last Call with Carson Daly* and *The Late Late Show with Craig Ferguson*, Martin rejoined *The Daily Show* (now called *The Daily Show with Jon Stewart*) as the program's senior youth correspondent. In that role Martin hosted a segment called "Trendspotting," during which he mocked various trends among young people, including hookah lounges, the Xbox 360 video-game console, and the social-networking site MySpace.com. Martin, who does not keep up with politics or pop culture, found it difficult to blend his idiosyncratic, observational humor with that of the news-parody series, which features commentary on current events, politics, and pop culture. "I am typically not that relevant as a performer," Martin told Adam Sternbergh. "Political stuff is not a good fit for me. I like to daydream."

Elaborating on his approach to comedy, Martin explained to Sean O'Neal for the *A.V. Club* (November 29, 2006, on-line), "Usually, I walk around and think about things. When I come across a thought that makes me laugh, I write it down. Then, at night, I say the thought to people through a microphone. I don't think about politics or pop culture much, so those thoughts don't often make it to the microphone." The following are a few of the comedian's one-liners: *I was in this building and there's a door, and on the door it said, "This door must remain closed at all times." I was like, dude, you're thinking of a wall. . . . I'm going to open a store called Chasm. We're going to be just like the Gap, but way bigger. . . . I went into a store and the saleslady said, "If you need anything, I'm Jill." And I said, "Wow, I've never met anyone with a conditional identity before." . . . I was walking down the street and this guy waved at me. Then he said, "I'm sorry. I thought you were somebody else." And I said, "I am."*

In September 2006 Martin released his debut comedy album, *These Are Jokes*. His one-man show *Dr. Earnest Parrot Presents Demetri Martin* received the prize for best show at the 2006 Melbourne International Comedy Festival. After hosting his final "Trendspotting" segment, in November 2006, Martin returned to *The Daily Show* the following year. From March 2007 to February 2008, he appeared as a senior youth correspondent for another recurring segment, called "Professional Important News with Demetri Martin." In October 2007 Comedy Central executives announced that Martin would follow in the footsteps of Stephen Colbert, another former correspondent of *The Daily Show*, and headline his own series.

In February 2009 *Important Things with Demetri Martin* debuted on Comedy Central. The show mixes stand-up, quirky songs, anagrams, charts, animation, and sketches, most of which feature Martin. In a review for the Associated Press (February 5, 2009), Frazier Moore wrote, "As he proves anew in *Important Things with Demetri Martin*, this important rising comic has a gift for the shrewd but daydreamy. His material tingles with random micro-truths, each observation a dotty shared discovery with his audience." In one sketch, "Time Gigolo," Martin played a shady janitor who uses a time machine to pursue his romantic interests in different centuries. In another sketch his character got into a shouting match with another man over a parking spot; the action was frequently paused so that on-screen captions could convey the thoughts of the two angry men, making the skit appear somewhat cartoonish. Matthew Gilbert wrote for the *Boston Globe* (February 11, 2009), "*Important Things* is packaged with an extreme consciousness of language, which is Martin's trademark and what distinguishes him from other slacker comics." In June 2009 Comedy Central's president, Lauren Corrao, announced that the series had been renewed for a second season. (The first season was scheduled to begin airing in the U.K. in the fall of 2009.)

Martin has also launched an acting career. After supporting roles in the comedies *The Rocker* (2008) and *Paper Heart* (2009) and a guest turn in the HBO series *The Flight of the Conchords*, Martin made his leading-man debut in *Taking Woodstock* (2009), in which he played Elliot Tiber, the gay-rights activist who helped organize the 1969 music festival. He has several other projects in various stages of completion, including the films "Moon People" and "Will," both co-written by Martin.

Martin has appeared in several on-line comedic shorts promoting Microsoft's Windows Vista operating system. Additionally, he has been featured in music videos for the Fountains of Wayne single "Someone to Love" and the rock band Travis's song "Selfish Jean." He lives in New York City.

—D.K.

Suggested Reading: *Believer* (on-line) Feb. 2006; *Hartford (Connecticut) Courant* (on-line) Aug. 9, 2009; *Interview* (on-line) Mar. 1, 2005; (London) *Independent* (on-line) Aug. 17, 2004, Aug. 25, 2004; *New York Times* (on-line) Feb. 4, 2009; *Oakland (California) Tribune* (on-line) Feb. 10, 2009

Selected Television Shows: *Late Night with Conan O'Brien* (as writer), 2003–04; *The Daily Show with Jon Stewart*, 2005–08; *Important Things with Demetri Martin*, 2009–

Selected Films: *The Rocker*, 2008; *Paper Heart*, 2009; *Taking Woodstock*, 2009

Martin, Roland S.

Nov. 14, 1968– Journalist; commentator

Address: TV One Cable Network, Creators Syndicate, 5777 W. Century Blvd., Suite 700, Los Angeles, CA 90045

Frederick M. Brown/Getty Images for NAACP

"I represent the post–civil rights movement," the columnist, CNN commentator, and author Roland S. Martin told the *Chicago Reader* (September 17, 2004). "I have no living memory of Martin Luther King, of the civil rights movement, of actual marches." Accordingly, Martin—who has worked for or headed a dizzying variety of publications and Web sites—does not adhere to black orthodoxy, or dogma of any other sort, in his public views. For example, while his past support for some Republicans might lead observers to label him a conservative, he has also criticized both the Catholic Church and the black clergy for what he calls their inadequate response to the AIDS crisis. The only consistent element in his views is the forthright way that he airs them. Martin told a reporter for eurweb.com (March 12, 2009), "I get stopped by African Americans, by whites, by Hispanics, Democrats and Republicans who all say the same thing: 'Thank you for being real. Even if I disagree with you, I'm going to get somebody who's going to say it unapologetic, and is not going to compromise.'"

Before he became a regular and prominent presence on CNN, in the mid-2000s, Martin held positions including reporter for the *Austin American-Statesman* and the *Fort Worth Star-Telegram*, radio host in Dallas, Texas, managing editor of the *Houston Defender*, editor of BlackAmericaWeb.com, editor of the *Chicago Defender*, editor at *Savoy*, and blogger for *Essence* magazine—occupying some posts simultaneously. He also provides commentary for the radio program *The Tom Joyner Show*. His mother, Emelda Martin, told David Barron for the *Houston Chronicle* (March 7, 2009), "The drive he has is overwhelming to me. Some people just have that in them. They don't have time to get discouraged." "I've never wanted to allow the limits of any medium to dictate whether I had any power. . . . I am a hybrid," Martin said to Barron. "Call me what you want . . . but I am a true 21st-century multimedia, multi-platform journalist. There is no box you can put me in, and if you put me in a box, I will kill you to try to get out of it." Chuck Smith, Martin's former boss at KKDA radio station in Dallas, commented to Johnathon E. Briggs and Rob Kaiser for the *Chicago Tribune* (September 26, 2004), "One of the things that [Martin] has is a very great interest in himself. That's what egotistical people do, and I don't mean that in a negative way. If you're going to change stuff, you have to have some sense that you're right and you have some higher cause." For his part, Martin told Barron, "I don't have doubts. I don't wonder if things are going to work. As long as I am my own authentic self, that's all I focus on. Nobody who has ever hired me would have hired me if I gave the impression that I was going to fail. I have literally talked myself into jobs on the sole basis of 'I will do this.' And I see the looks on the faces of people asking how I will do this, and my deal is, 'Just watch me.'"

Roland Sebastian Martin was born on November 14, 1968 in Houston, Texas, to Reginald and Emelda Martin. His father worked for Amtrak and his mother for an insurance company; both were committed community organizers in the Clinton Park neighborhood of Houston. Reginald Martin also devoured newspaper and television news, and Roland Martin has traced his own interest in journalism to his father's influence. In the mid-1980s Martin attended Jack Yates High School in Houston, a magnet school specializing in communications. "Roland knew who he was. He knew the innermost part of his being," Mary Waites, one of Martin's teachers at Yates, told Barron. "He was persistent and always thought he was the best. You always knew he was there. There was a large bank of brilliant students who were as smart as he was, so he didn't always win. But he saw what it took to win, and you could bet your money that the next time, he would win. He learned by tripping and losing opportunities, and his willingness to pick himself up and press on is to his credit."

Martin started working and interning at television, radio, and newspaper outlets while still in school, demonstrating an interest in acquiring skills in multiple mediums. According to Barron, he was also an expert networker from an early age and, at Yates, "loved nothing more than to grill visiting dignitaries and then chat them up as he escorted them to the next class, leaving them, he hoped, with a name and an impression they would remember down the line." Martin, who maintains close ties to the school, told Barron, "I would not be where I am at this age had I not gone to Yates. Everything I'm dong right now was planted, was fertilized, was encouraged based upon what happened at Yates. Everything."

After graduating from Yates, in 1987, Martin enrolled as a journalism student at Texas A&M University, in College Station, on an academic scholarship. Some considered that choice an odd one; Texas A&M was not known for either its journalism program or the diversity of its student body. "A lot of people ask me all the time, 'Man, how in the world did a black guy from Houston decide to go to Texas A&M'," Martin said in a speech. The occasion was his induction into the university's Journalism Hall of Honor. He added, as quoted by Steve Fullhart on the Web site of KBTX News, a Texas television station (October 12, 2008), "I said, 'Because of what it stood for and what it represented.' . . . I want people to look at the reality that you can be an African American student, you can be Hispanic, you can come to this school and not play football or basketball." While at the university Martin interned at KBTX-TV and at a local radio station. During that time he persuaded the former Texas secretary of state George Strake, whom he had met at Yates, to fund his trip to the 1989 convention of the National Association of Black Journalists. There, Martin has recalled, he made some of the most important connections of his professional life. "Nearly every job I've ever gotten is a result of the relationships that came out of that first [NABJ] convention," he told Barron.

After graduating from Texas A&M with a degree in journalism, in 1991, Martin found work as a county, government, and neighborhood news reporter at the *Austin American-Statesman*. Even in that entry-level reporter's position, he covered the 1992 Republican National Convention and reported on the aftermath of Hurricane Andrew. In 1993 he moved on to the *Fort Worth Star-Telegram*. In addition to reporting on city hall, he wrote sports and general-news pieces, covering the deadly 1993 encounter between FBI agents and members of the Branch Davidian religious cult near Waco, Texas, as well as the 1995 Oklahoma City bombing. For his reporting on the latter story, he was given an award from the Texas Associated Press Managing Editors group. Stan Jones, one of Martin's editors at the *Star-Telegram*, described him to Al Brumley for the *Dallas Morning News* (October 7, 1995) as "one of the most energetic guys that I've ever come across. His positive attitude is just almost overwhelming, to the point that he will infect you."

According to Barron, Martin left both the *Statesman* and the *Star-Telegram* "because he was not advancing quickly enough to suit his rate of ambition." In 1995 Martin moved to KRLD, an all-news radio station in Dallas, where he spent a brief stint as a morning reporter, before moving on to station KKDA, also called Soul 73, which catered primarily to African-American audiences. Earlier, he had been offered a talk show on KKDA, but his superiors at the *Star-Telegram* would not allow him to accept it; then, in the summer of 1995, after the news director of the station resigned, KKDA offered the position to Martin. While some felt that Martin, at 26, was too young to lead a newsroom, he jumped at the opportunity. "Clearly, it was a hell of an opportunity to be a news director," he told Brumley months later. "I felt I had a vision of the direction we could go in. And it's always been a goal of mine to be in management." As news director, editor, and morning anchor at KKDA, Martin broke the story of the drug-possession charges against the Dallas Cowboys star football player Michael Irvin. For his sports reporting, Martin—by most accounts a demanding boss in his three years at the station—won a 1997 award from the National Association of Black Journalists.

After leaving KKDA, in 1998, Martin took on jobs at publications serving mainly African-American readerships. He worked as managing editor of the *Dallas Weekly* before returning to Houston to become managing editor of the weekly *Houston Defender*, the first place he had ever interned. Next came a trying period for Martin: in 1999, while in the process of divorcing his wife, he returned to Dallas for a job that fell through. In mid-2000, while he was covering the Democratic National Convention, in Los Angeles, California, Martin suffered a ruptured appendix, and the resulting medical costs forced him to file for bankruptcy.

Bouncing back, in 2001 Martin became the first editor of BlackAmericaWeb.com, a site launched as an information hub and community portal by the popular radio talk-show host Tom Joyner, whom he had met at the 1989 NABJ Conference. Martin, who set up the Dallas-based Romar Media Group to handle his many projects, also worked as a news correspondent for the American Urban Radio Network and as a sports reporter for a Washington, D.C., radio station. In 2002 he started writing a regular news column that was picked up and distributed to various papers across the U.S. by the Creators Syndicate. In one of his columns, after it became clear that then–U.S. senator Barack Obama was very likely to run for president, Martin wrote about the African-American community's need to rise above what he saw as its self-defeating tendency to demand that successful African-Americans prove their "blackness." "One of the insidious rituals any high-profile African American must endure in order to establish his or her credibility with some other African Americans is [to] show that they are 'down with the brothers and the sisters,'" Martin wrote in a column posted on the Creators Syndicate Web site (January 26, 2007). "We have reached the day when black folks are going to have to quit forcing others to pass a black test to establish their worthiness. Every black person in America doesn't have a 'hood' experience. . . . Segregation no longer limits where we live, work and play. So if Jim Crow is dead, why do we allow the system to continue to pervade our minds? The day has come when we judge a black man or woman for who they are, where they stand on issues and what they believe in. If Obama offers a political agenda that speaks to the needs of African Americans, good. If he chooses to offer one that is broad and more universal, that doesn't make him any less of an African American. . . . There is too much work to be done to raise the collective black community in the areas of education, economics and healthcare. And worrying about whether Obama or anyone else is black enough to do so should not be a part of the dialogue."

Also in 2002 Martin became news editor at the newly established, short-lived *Savoy* magazine, an African-American lifestyle publication based in New York. Keith Clinkscales, *Savoy*'s owner, described Martin, who worked for him until 2004, as a confrontational but professional editor. "He clashed in the spirit of bettering the work, in his opinion," Clinkscales told Briggs and Kaiser. "He was the kind of guy you could have a clash with and go out and have a drink with afterwards." In 2003 Martin left BlackAmericaWeb and, under the Romar Group, purchased the *Dallas–Fort Worth Heritage*—a faltering Christian monthly newspaper with a circulation of 28,000—for $75,000. The purchase represented Martin's first major business investment; as owner and publisher he aimed to revitalize the paper but was forced to shut it down after a year due to lack of interest among advertisers.

That experience would prove useful nonetheless: Martin left Texas for Illinois in the summer of 2004, when he was hired as a consultant by the *Chicago Defender*, historically one of the largest and most influential black newspapers in the country but one that had fallen on hard times. Soon he succeeded the editor. First published by Robert S. Abbott in 1905, the daily paper, focusing on the South Side of Chicago, is known for playing an important role in covering and supporting the civil rights movement. Its circulation had dwindled from 250,000 at its height to under 20,000. Martin reintroduced editorial standards at the paper, where there had come to be virtually no editing—in the process clashing with staff, many of whom either quit or were fired. He also expanded local coverage, to appeal to a wider readership, changed the paper's look, added auto and business sections, and revamped the Web site. In May 2005 the paper celebrated its centennial. According to Briggs and Kaiser, most observers felt that the paper would, "like nearly all of the country's 200 black newspapers," be forced to become a weekly. Under Martin's leadership, the paper remained a daily, although it continued to struggle; in December 2008, about a year after Martin had left, the paper announced that it would be publishing weekly.

In August 2004 Martin made national headlines when, at a conference held in Washington, D.C., by Unity: Journalists of Color, he questioned then–President George W. Bush on the subject of college-admissions policies. Bush, who had come out against what he referred to as "quotas" that benefited minority or other students in the admissions process, had been admitted to Yale University as a "legacy" student, because his father, President George H. W. Bush, had attended the school. Martin asked Bush why, if he opposed affirmative action, he had never spoken out against legacy policies, which give advantages to the children of alumni. As quoted in FDCH Political Transcripts (August 6, 2004), Martin asked the president, "If you say it's a matter of merit and not race, shouldn't colleges also get rid of legacy? Because that's not based upon merit. That's based upon if my daddy or my granddaddy went to my college." Pressed by Martin, Bush agreed that colleges should discontinue legacy-based admissions.

Martin had already had limited national exposure when he made his first appearance on CNN, in 2002. Beginning in 2004 he made more frequent guest appearances on the cable-TV news channel. On CNN Martin usually commented on issues affecting the African-American community; for example, as quoted in a CNN transcript (October 3, 2003, on-line), Kyra Phillips asked him about the potential tensions between Hispanics and blacks in the U.S., to which he responded: "This is one of the things I've covered for the last 12 to 13 years. And what you see is a fight as it relates to who is going to be the dominant minority group. Right now, Hispanics as a whole outnumber African-Americans. . . . You have African-Americans, namely activist[s], who feel as if Hispanics did not put in the sweat, blood and tears for a lot of the rights that folks are taking advantage of today. So then you have Hispanics who are saying that wait a minute, we fought the same fights, we have some of the same grievances. And because our numbers are now increasing, we have a right for a fair share in elected offices, in contracts and other forms of assistance across the country."

In 2005 Martin began a three-year stint as the host of a three-hour weekday talk-radio show on Chicago's WVON. After stepping down from his role at the *Defender*, in 2007, he began working as a commentator and documentary producer at TV One, a cable-TV network offering programming mainly for African-American audiences, and signed on as a regular contributor to CNN, with plans to develop his own show in the future. While moonlighting as a special correspondent for *Essence* magazine with a bimonthly column and a blog, Martin hosted a series on CNN entitled *What Would Jesus Really Do?* As the 2008 presidential-election season intensified, he began focusing almost exclusively on politics. His respective interviews with the candidate Barack Obama and with his wife, Michelle Obama, both won awards. Martin was an increasingly visible Chicago-based member of the CNN panel of pundits, getting increased airtime in 2008. In April 2009, when Campbell Brown, host of CNN's primetime show *No Bias, No Bull*, went on maternity leave, Martin was asked to fill in for her. CNN also announced that it was developing a weekend program around Martin, which was expected to debut after Brown returned to her on-air duties.

Brown returned from maternity leave in early June 2009 to replace Martin, but he did not immediately launch a weekend show of his own on CNN. Instead, in September 2009, while continuing to work as a commentator for CNN, Martin began broadcasting *Washington Watch*, an hour-long Sunday public-affairs program on TV One. The show, advertised as a *Meet the Press*–style program with a focus on African-American issues, features interviews with government and administration officials, policy makers, journalists, experts, and newsmakers and is seen as a response to the well-documented lack of racial and ethnic diversity on network shows, especially in weekend programming. "I am reminded of the founders of the first black newspaper in America, *Freedom's Journal*, who wrote in their lead editorial in 1827, 'We wish to plead our own cause; too long have others spoken for us,'" Martin told Othor Cain for the *Mississippi Link* (October 1, 2009). "The same applies today. The voices of African American elected officials, policy makers, [analysts] and journalists are important, and need to be a part of the discussion on a weekly basis, and on most Sunday morning shows, they are not."

Also in 2009 Martin left his radio show at WVON to join the hugely popular *Tom Joyner Morning Show* as a senior analyst and commentator. The show is the country's top-rated nationally syndicated "urban" radio program, boasting between eight million and 10 million listeners.

Martin is the author of two books: *Speak, Brother! A Black Man's View of America* (2002) and *Listening to the Spirit Within: 50 Perspectives on Faith* (2007), a collection of his columns on religious issues, both published by Romar. Martin has long been interested in religious issues, and in 2008 he earned a master's degree in Christian communications from Louisiana Baptist University. Recently, in one of his on-line columns for CNN (March 18, 2009), Martin strongly criticized Pope Benedict XVI and the African-American religious community, accusing them of "ignorance of reality" in their stances on HIV/AIDS. He charged that the black church, "primarily because of its opposition to homosexuality, has abdicated its responsibility and totally disregarded the human toll that HIV/AIDS has had on the members it largely serves." He also faulted the Catholic Church for its opposition to the use of condoms and other forms of birth control, writing, "For the church to continue to ignore the definitive research that condoms play a huge role in decreasing the spread of HIV/AIDS and other sexually transmitted diseases is mind-boggling." Martin has made the argument that while he has strong views, he is not biased, partisan, or dogmatic and is particularly opposed to being "pigeonholed," especially in politics. "I voted for George H. Bush. I voted for his son when he was Governor in Texas," Martin told the reporter for eurweb.com. "I've voted for Democrats. I've voted for Republicans. I've voted for white folks, black folks, Hispanics, women. I look at the individual and what they have to say and the policies that I'm concerned about." After supporting Obama for president in the 2008 election, for instance, Martin criticized his performance in office, as well as that of Democrats in general. In an on-line CNN commentary (March 11, 2009) about many Democrats' opposition to a voucher system that would allow lower-income students to attend private schools, he wrote, "I would have more confidence if President Obama and members of Congress truly walked the walk and sent their kids to public schools. If they have so much faith in them turning around with reform, entrust their own children to public education. . . . If it's good enough for yours, then surely it's good enough for mine. But preaching to the rest of us about the virtues of a public education, then sending your own children to private school and denying the use of vouchers so others can do the same, is frankly hypocritical."

Martin has won several journalistic awards, including the Edward R. Murrow Award from the Radio-Television News Directors Association, a 2008 NAACP Image Award for best interview for "In Conversation: The Senator Barack Obama Interview," a 2009 NAACP Image Award for best interview for "In Conversation: The Michelle Obama Interview," and a 2008 President's Award from the National Association of Black Journalists. In August 2009 Martin was elected secretary of the National Association of Black Journalists, and in October 2009 he was named Broadcaster of the Year by Rainbow PUSH, an organization headed by the civil rights activist Jesse Jackson that is dedicated to addressing civil rights and social-justice issues. *Ebony* magazine named him one of the 150 Most Influential African-Americans in 2008, and the British publication *Daily Telegraph* named him one of the top 50 political pundits. In 2008 he was inducted into the Texas A&M University Journalism Hall of Honor; upon receiving the award, he announced a donation of $10,000 to the program.

Martin, whose plans include starting another media company, has been married since 2001 to the Reverend Jacquie Hood Martin. His wife, who previously served at a Houston church and is now the dean of Kennedy King College, in Chicago, is the author of *Fulfilled! The Art and Joy of Balanced Living*. The couple have homes in Dallas and Chicago.

—M.M.

Suggested Reading: *Chicago Reader* p4 Sep. 17, 2004; *Chicago Tribune* C p1 Sep. 26, 2004; CNN (on-line) Mar. 18, 2009; *Dallas Morning News* C p1 Oct. 7, 1995; *Houston Chronicle* p8 Mar. 8, 2009

Selected Books: *Speak, Brother! A Black Man's View of America*, 2002; *Listening to the Spirit Within: 50 Perspectives on Faith*, 2007

Mashouf, Manny

June 6, 1938– Founder and chairman of bebe Stores Inc.

Address: bebe Stores Inc., 400 Valley Dr., Brisbane, CA 94005

The founder, chairman, and former president of bebe Stores Inc., Manny Mashouf, has emphasized both sex appeal and functionality in clothing offered by bebe (pronounced "beebee" and spelled by the company with a lowercase "b"). "Sexiness is part of our look," Mashouf told Mary Gottschalk for the *San Jose Mercury News* (October 12, 1998). "If we provide suits without that element, we'd look like [the clothing stores] Talbot's and Ann Taylor. And who needs another one of those?" Bebe became both popular and notorious in the mid-1990s for manufacturing and selling "impossibly short" skirts, as Gottschalk put it, and other items of apparel that proved highly popular among young, fashion-oriented women. Gabrielle Saveri wrote for *BusinessWeek* (May 31, 1999) that "the stores' reputation for sexy, trendy clothing at mall prices has spawned a growing fan club among its target audience of women in their 20s and 30s, including actresses." In 2008 the company launched a lingerie line and a collection of lower-priced clothing aimed at a younger clientele. The next year it introduced a new fragrance and announced a forthcoming line of shoes. As a result of such innovations, the Brisbane, California–based company has grown significantly since Mashouf opened the first few stores in San Francisco in the 1970s; at the end of 2009, bebe operated 307 retail stores internationally, including 215 bebe stores; 33 2b bebe outlets; one bebe accessories store; and 61 bebe Sports stores, the last of which were scheduled to be replaced by new stores offering streetwear. The new outlets were to be called PH8 (pronounced "fate"). Since 1989 bebe has been vertically integrated—that is, all aspects of the business are under the direct control of the management, including the manufacture of the materials used to produce its products. Mashouf has designed clothing himself, including many items that became instantly popular and made bebe a fixture in most major shopping districts and malls in the United States.

Timothy Norris/Getty Images for IMG

Manny Mashouf

Manoucher "Manny" Mashouf was born in Iran on June 6, 1938 and spent his early years in the country's capital city, Tehran. In an interview with Mikael Jehanno for savoirmag.com, he described his family as "fashion-conscious." He recalled that because of the predominantly Muslim country's strictly observed custom requiring a female to be accompanied in public by a male, "I was dragged on by my sister, sometimes against my own wishes, and often found myself in fabric and tailor shops at a very young age," as he told Jehanno. "Even though I resented it at the time, it somehow left a deep impression on my brain." His family later immigrated to the United States, where Mashouf attended San Francisco State University, earning a B.A. degree in political science in 1966. He told Jehanno that he was the most fashion-savvy member of the school's student body. "Whatever I was wearing seemed to become a trend," he said.

After graduating, Mashouf, having supported himself in college by working in restaurants, took over a steak house in San Francisco, which he renamed Barbary Coast. His business later expanded to include three other locations in the area. Nonetheless, he told Jehanno, "My heart was not into it. I would constantly go shopping for men's clothes for myself and women's for my girlfriends. I quickly noticed there was a gap, a void, in women's fashion at the time." In 1971 he opened a clothing store, Caspian Corner, on San Francisco's Polk Street. "My first inclination was to make men's clothing in the basement of the store," Mashouf told Joanna Ramey for *Women's Wear Daily* (November 29, 2006). "I bought three machines, hired a master tailor and patternmaker. Then I realized by the time I'd make enough clothing to fill the store, it would be out of fashion." He thus began to sell established brand-name clothing instead. When Mashouf opened another store on Union Street, in 1977, he dubbed it "bebe," as an homage to the famous first words of a soliloquy from William Shakespeare's *Hamlet*, "To be or not to be."

With bebe Mashouf hoped to profit by specializing in clothing for trend-following women in their 20s and 30s, saying to Jehanno, "There was nothing between junior and missy styles, nothing like what you would call now 'contemporary women's fashion.' I remember going from one showroom to another in New York, San Francisco and Los Angeles, and here and there, I found items that would fit these proverbial characteristics, but never all under one roof. A customer was being ignored." Between 1977 and 1989 Mashouf opened five bebe stores in the Northwest. While enjoying moderate success, Mashouf found it difficult to compete with large department stores. "Every time I would discover a [clothing] line or bring something new, they would come into the stores, pick up the labels and kill the business for me," he told Jehanno. As a result, Mashouf decided in 1989 to manufacture the company's apparel in-house, designing the earliest bebe originals himself. Vertical integration benefited bebe by allowing the company to control production costs; Mashouf and his fellow designers were able to monitor clothing items from the initial design stages to completion, making for consistent quality. Mashouf told Jehanno that the success of the earliest original designs was "enough to put bebe on the map."

In 1990, in a successful attempt to bolster bebe's image, Mashouf began to offer up-and-coming Hollywood actresses free clothing in exchange for appearing in the company's advertisements; among the actresses was Charlize Theron, who later won an Oscar for her role in the film *Monster*. Mashouf also announced that year that the company would expand to 20 new stores nationwide by 1993. By 1991 there were eight bebe stores in California, and the company was generating $8 million in total sales annually. In September of that year, bebe began to open stores in Southern California, featuring both original bebe clothing and that of Southern California designers including Helios, Nina K., Van Buren, Holly Sharp, and Leslie Hamel. Much of the bebe clothing was designed by Mashouf, in collaboration with his wife, Neda, and the company's buyer, Renee Bell.

By 1995 the company had 61 stores in malls and street-front locations in a number of states, including Illinois, Arizona, Florida, South Carolina, and New York as well as California and states in the Northwest; there were three boutiques in New York City. That year Mashouf announced that the company had generated sales of $65 million. The first appearance of bebe clothing on prime-time television occurred in 1995, worn by the actress Heather Locklear on the popular Fox network soap opera *Melrose Place*. That visibility helped increase the association of bebe clothing with female celebrities. Locklear's attire on the show consisted of tailored suits and miniskirts, a look that became known as "the Melrose suit," and bebe, according to Gottschalk, "was on the lips of the fashion savvy as the source." The year 1998 saw the company's initial public offering (IPO), which raised enough money to underwrite the opening of more retail stores and fund the later development of such bebe products as foot and eyewear. Also that year bebe expanded beyond U.S. borders, opening a store in Mexico City, Mexico.

In February 1999 the company unveiled plans for stores in the United Kingdom, Canada, and Israel. Later in the year it announced that it would open outlets in Singapore, the United Arab Emirates, Kuwait, Bahrain, Qatar, Oman, and Saudi Arabia as well. By that time bebe's list of celebrity clientele had grown to include the actresses Brooke Shields, Calista Flockhart, Ashley Judd, and Cameron Diaz and the pop megastar Madonna. Those names pushed bebe's popularity to new heights; in 1997, for example, $300 bebe tweed suits sold out within a week in New York after Shields wore one during an episode of the sitcom *Suddenly Susan*. More recently bebe featured the actress Rebecca Romijn as the "face" of its summer and fall 2007 lines, and the actress Eva Longoria was featured in the bebe Sport campaign for spring and summer 2007 as well as summer and fall 2008. In 2009 the company returned to using fashion models for its ad campaigns—Anne Marie Van Dijk in the spring and Diana Moldovan that summer.

In January 1999 bebe's vertical-production model met with a challenge when a style of pants with three-quarter-length legs, known as capris, sold out quickly at bebe stores; through the Los Angeles factory that had produced bebe suits, however, the company was able to supply enough capris to keep up with demand. That year *Forbes* ranked bebe as number two on its list of "200 Best Small Companies." Much of bebe's success is the result of a rapid manufacturing-and-delivery system that has enabled the company to bring high-demand products to the retail floor quickly. Most of the production is done through contracts with factories in San Francisco and Los Angeles, with a smaller portion in Canada, Europe, and Asia; a system of testing and, when necessary, reordering allows for quality control.

By August 2000 bebe had 126 retail stores, but it was reported that same-store sales had fallen, and by the end of June, sales were down to $54.1 million from $54.2 million the year before. ("Same-store sales" refers to sales at stores open for a year or more.) The company's stock had also fallen sharply, from about $50 in 1999 to $10. Blair Lambert, then the chief financial officer (CFO) of bebe, told Matthew Swibel for the Santa Clara Valley *Business Journal* (August 11, 2000) that the cause of the slip was that bebe had not "focused enough on fashion" that year. Some, however, felt that investors who had grown accustomed to bebe's higher-than-average earnings had exaggerated the significance of the lower numbers. Two of bebe's high-level employees, Heather Vandenberghe, the marketing director, and Gregory Scott, the merchandising vice president, had left the company earlier in the year. Bebesport, a store launched by the company in Minneapolis, Minnesota, in 1999 to carry sportswear, was also "not performing to expectations," as Mashouf told Swibel. Mashouf stepped down from his position as president of bebe in 2000, and John Parros, formerly a vice president at Saks Inc., joined bebe as president and chief operating officer. Parros resigned from his post in 2002; Walter Parks, the company's chief financial officer, took on the additional duties of chief operating officer in 2006. Mashouf continued on as chairman and chief executive. Gregory Scott currently serves as chief executive officer.

In 2002 bebe filed a suit against May Department Stores of St. Louis, Missouri, alleging that the department giant's apparel line, "be," was a trademark infringement. Bebe claimed that May's brand trademark, font style, and apparel were so similar to bebe's that they confused customers. Bebe sought a preliminary injunction against May Department Stores, and on October 21 United States District Judge Catherine D. Perry of the Eastern Division of the Eastern District of Missouri granted the injunction, writing, as quoted by *Business Wire* (October 23, 2002), "If the injunction is not granted, bebe stands to lose the goodwill and customer base it has grown through investment in advertising and through savvy marketing and the provision of a good quality product to its customers over the last 26 years. Bebe does just this one thing, and it has done it very well over the last 26 years, and it stands to lose it all if May is not enjoined." Mashouf was pleased, saying, according to *Business Wire*, "This injunction not only protects our rights, but safeguards our customers from devious corporate greed. We have spent 26 years establishing a brand that people equate with high fashion and high quality. For a giant retailer such as May Company with its hundreds of stores, billions of dollars in sales and unlimited resources to misappropriate bebe's reputation to enrich its bottom line is disgraceful. We are glad the judge recognized this plot and put a stop to it." In December of that year, May Department Stores was barred entirely by a federal appeals court from using "be" as the name for its clothing line. In November bebe had reported that same-store sales had declined, and Mashouf told *Women's Wear Daily* (December 24, 2002), "This clearly shows that any success May stores had with this line is because our customers associated it with bebe."

In 2005 bebe opened Neda, a store featuring accessories, handbags, and shoes, in San Francisco. The concept was Neda Mashouf's. Mashouf and his wife also donated $10 million to San Francisco State University that year for a new building and performance space to be dubbed the Mashouf Creative Arts Center. In 2007, following her divorce from Mashouf, Neda resigned from the company, and the Neda store was renamed bebe Accessories.

Meanwhile, by 2006 bebe had 228 stores, and Mashouf's family, holding 73 percent of the company's outstanding stock shares, was ranked at number 242 on the *Forbes* "400 Richest Americans" list. A new line of limited-edition luxury apparel, Collection bebe, was introduced at Los Angeles Fashion Week that year. In 2007 Mashouf and his family were ranked at number 754 on the *Forbes* world billionaires list. That year he took a 60 percent stake in a London, England–based clothing and accessories label, Biba International Ltd.; Mashouf also sits on Biba's board of directors. In December 2008 bebe partnered with Robin Antin of the pop group the Pussycat Dolls to launch a line of lingerie called "Shhh." According to a press release available on businesswire.com (December 2, 2008), the line "features nautical looks, animal prints, rock-and-roll styles, and frills. It covers every cut from boy shorts to micro-minis to delicate tops and bottoms."

Although bebe's net sales and income decreased during the fiscal year that began in 2008 due to underperforming stores and store closures, the company continued to offer new products. In August 2009 bebe launched a new fragrance, which went on sale in all its U.S. stores. PH8 stores, which offer streetwear, replaced bebe Sports stores in November 2009. "We believe that the conversion to PH8 is relevant and timely, especially now, when the market is flat and economy-conscious consumers are looking for new ideas and innovations," Mashouf said in a bebe press release, according to Reuters Business Wire (July 14, 2009, on-line). The company also announced plans for a new shoe collection, to be unveiled in the spring of 2010.

Mashouf is the father of Paul Mashouf, formerly the vice president of manufacturing and sourcing for bebe Sport, and Karim Mashouf, who serves bebe as an independent contractor; he is also the uncle of Hamid Mashouf, bebe's vice president of information systems and technology. Mashouf told Ramey that success had not altered his personality: "I don't think money will ever change me, no matter how much it is. I'm still the same person I was . . . when I was in college."

—W.D.

Suggested Reading: *Apparel Industry Magazine* p44 Apr. 1, 1999; *Business Wire* Oct. 23, 2002; *San Jose Mercury News* C p3 Oct.12, 1998; *Women's Wear Daily* p9 Nov. 29, 2006

McAdams, Rachel

Nov. 17, 1978(?)– Actress

Address: c/o Gersh Agency, 232 N. Canon Dr., Beverly Hills, CA 90210

Alberto E. Rodriguez/Getty Images

In the mid-2000s, when the actress Rachel McAdams appeared in a string of critically acclaimed hit movies, including *Mean Girls*, *The Notebook*, *Wedding Crashers*, and *Red Eye*, *Entertainment Weekly* and *Newsweek* dubbed her Hollywood's next "It girl" and "the next Julia Roberts." Since then McAdams has delivered on the promise of those films, with well-received performances in such movies as *Married Life*, *The Lucky Ones*, *State of Play*, and *The Time Traveler's Wife*. Often noted for her good looks and natural charisma, she has also won praise for her ability to perform in a variety of genres, from dark to screwball comedy, romance to psychological thriller. Growing up in a Canadian city, she received training in classical theater as a child and graduated from college before landing her first big Hollywood role, opposite Rob Schneider, in the comedy *The Hot Chick* (2002). Although her films have varied nearly as much as her hair color, McAdams—a self-described "hopeless romantic"—has admitted that there is one element, transcending genre, that she looks for in movie scripts. "I'd like to dabble in every genre. But I rarely enjoy a film that doesn't have some kind of love story to it," she told Bob Strauss for the Toronto, Canada, *Globe and Mail* (March 17, 2008). "It doesn't have to be the focus and it doesn't have to be sweeping or typical. But when love isn't involved, I'm not as interested."

The oldest of three children, Rachel McAdams was born on November 17, 1978 (many sources say October 7, 1976) in London, Ontario, about 120 miles southwest of Toronto. She has described her parents—Sandy, a nurse, and Lance, a truck driver—as being very supportive of her. As a child McAdams played volleyball and soccer and was a competitive figure skater. Showing an early interest in acting, she coordinated performances with her younger siblings for her parents in the family's backyard. During her elementary-school years, McAdams joined the Original Kids' Theatre Company, taking classes during the academic year and attending the program's summer camp. She felt embarrassed that she was inexperienced compared with many of her peers. "I was with these 8-year-olds who were going to be Broadway stars, singing at the top of their lungs, dancing since they were 2," McAdams recalled to Robert Abele for the *Los Angeles Times* (May 8, 2005). "I was so clumsy I would just go home and cry." McAdams eventually found confidence and inspiration through performing in Shakespeare plays at the camp.

In high school, unlike the character she portrayed in *Mean Girls*, McAdams was nearer to the bottom of her school's social hierarchy. "I think shyness was my problem," she told Judy Bachrach for *Allure* (November 2005). "I was nervous about approaching people. Therefore I became unapproachable." She found her niche in high-school theater productions and won an award for her performance in the student-written play *I Live in a Little Town*. McAdams had planned to pursue "cultural studies" in college until a high-school theater teacher persuaded her to focus on theater. She attended York College in Toronto, graduating with a B.F.A. degree with honors in 2001. One of her professors there, David Rotenberg, recalled to Shanda Deziel for *Maclean's* (July 18, 2005) that at first McAdams was "shy, but sort of had a twinkle." He added, "By the time she got to me in the fourth year, she was landed, she had feet." That year he gave her one of the lead roles in the school's production of Frank Wedekind's *Lulu*. "It was fascinating to watch the agents watch her, their eyes rolling back into their heads," Rotenberg said of their reaction to her performance. "They came chasing me after the first act." For McAdams the theater program relaxed its rules against taking outside acting jobs; earlier, she had violated the rules by appearing in the Disney TV show *The Famous Jett Jackson* and shooting a pilot for an MTV television series that was never picked up.

McAdams began her career with small roles in several films, among them *Guilty by Association* (2002), *My Name Is Tanino* (2002), and the Canadian movie *Perfect Pie* (2002). Her first major movie role was as a popular cheerleader who inadvertently switches bodies with a middle-aged man (Rob Schneider) in the poorly reviewed *The Hot Chick*. She next snagged a role on the Canadian television series *Slings & Arrows*, about a theater company performing Shakespeare plays. For her portrayal of the character Kate McNab, who appeared in episodes from 2003 to 2005, McAdams was honored with a Canadian Gemini Award.

McAdams rose to Hollywood stardom in 2004, the year she had leading roles in two very different box-office hits, *Mean Girls* and *The Notebook*. Directed by Mark Waters, *Mean Girls* follows Cady Heron (Lindsay Lohan), a very smart, formerly homeschooled girl who enters high school's vicious social hierarchy, at the top of which is a group of popular girls known as "the Plastics." The group is headed by McAdams's character, Regina George, a beautiful, cruel social tyrant and "queen bee," who befriends and then turns on Cady. McAdams claimed to have modeled her character after Alec Baldwin's in the 1992 film *Glengarry Glen Ross*. "It's fun to be mean!" she told Jay Boyar for the Biloxi, Mississippi, *Sun Herald* (July 8, 2004). "I know that sounds so horrible . . . but I really wanted to explore her as a sociopath."

McAdams made the transition from comedy to romance with *The Notebook*. Directed by Nick Cassavetes and adapted from the same-titled 1996 novel by Nicholas Sparks, *The Notebook* is the 1940s-era story of Allie Hamilton (McAdams), a privileged southern belle who falls in love with a lumber-mill worker (Ryan Gosling) but then loses him. She later falls for an equally kind, upper-class man (James Marsden), whom her family considers to be a more suitable mate for her. To prepare for the role, McAdams read widely about the attitudes of rich southern women and spent several weeks, along with Gosling, exploring southern culture. She also took classes in ballet, tennis, and etiquette and interviewed several debutantes. McAdams was attracted to the film because of her emotional reaction to its unabashedly romantic story. (The day after getting cast, she "devoured" Sparks's book.) Critics took note of the film's performances, with Abele writing, "McAdams' expressive beauty moved thrillingly between rapture and heartbreak." At the 2005 MTV Movie Awards ceremony, McAdams and Gosling, who is also from London, Ontario, shared the prize for "best kiss" for a scene in *The Notebook*; while accepting the award, the pair, who had for months been denying rumors of an off-screen romance, reenacted their passionate kiss. Shortly afterward they confirmed their romantic relationship. McAdams also took home the MTV prize for best breakthrough performance for her role in *Mean Girls*.

In 2005 McAdams solidified her place as a Hollywood star. In that year's comedy *Wedding Crashers*, about two friends (Owen Wilson and Vince Vaughn) who make a hobby of crashing weddings and seducing female guests, McAdams played Claire, the daughter of a diplomat (Christopher Walken), with whom Wilson's character falls in love. The role gave McAdams the opportunity to improvise with her three comedic co-stars. "I was really excited about watching these guys," she told Hugh Hart for the *Philadelphia Inquirer* (April 14, 2005). "They kept lobbing the curveballs and I appreciate that because when you keep things spontaneous, it just makes for better acting." *Wedding Crashers* was immensely successful, grossing over

$209 million in the U.S. In his review for *Rolling Stone* (July 14, 2005, on-line), Peter Travers wrote, "McAdams is a showstopping beauty with the talent to bend a laugh line to do her will."

That same year McAdams expanded her range when she starred opposite Cillian Murphy in Wes Craven's *Red Eye*, a psychological thriller about a woman who finds herself seated next to a terrorist on a plane. McAdams, who did not ride in an airplane until she was 22 years old, told Jamie Portman for the Montreal *Gazette* (August 17, 2005) that she was attracted to the film's premise. "It struck me as an incredible acting challenge to have to sit in one spot and be held hostage without letting anyone else know what is going on. It's a pretty dire situation." Although the thriller genre was new territory for her, both the film and McAdams's performance earned a warm critical reception. Writing for the *Chicago Sun-Times* (August 19, 2005), Roger Ebert found her work "convincing because she keeps it at ground level; thrillers are invitations to overact, but she remains plausible even when the action ratchets up around her." McAdams next appeared in the comedy *The Family Stone* (2005), as the daughter in a family that aims to foil the marriage plans of the son, Everett (Dermot Mulroney), and his fiancée, Meredith (Sarah Jessica Parker). Diane Keaton played the mother of McAdams's character. "I went to the set when I wasn't needed just to watch [Keaton] work," McAdams told Louis B. Hobson for the Manitoba *Winnipeg Sun* (August 13, 2005). "It's awe-inspiring. It was like sitting in on a master class in acting." In 2005 McAdams won a Hollywood Breakthrough Award at the Hollywood Film Festival.

With several successful movies under her belt, McAdams reportedly turned down roles in a few high-profile films, including *Mission: Impossible III* (2006), *Casino Royale* (2006), and *The Devil Wears Prada* (2006), deciding instead to spend a year with her family and friends and choose her next role carefully. That role came in *Married Life* (2007), a dark comedy set in the 1940s, which features both romance and murder. She played the beautiful peroxide-blond Kay, with whom the middle-aged Harry (Chris Cooper) has fallen in love and begun an affair. Instead of disclosing the painful truth to his wife, Pat (Patricia Clarkson), he decides to spare Pat emotionally—by killing her. All the while, Harry's friend Richard (Pierce Brosnan) also pursues Kay. The film's director, Ira Sachs, was impressed with the depth of McAdams's portrayal. "Rachel is extremely ambitious with the emotional life of her characters," he told Strauss. "There's also this emotional level that I think she has as an actress which is just beneath the surface. It's something that the audience wants more of, and on that level, she really understands the nature of what it is to be a movie star, which is to provide something but, also, to hold something back."

McAdams covered new ground with her next film, Neil Burger's *The Lucky Ones* (2008), the story of three soldiers returning home from the Iraq war. For the *New York Times* (September 26, 2008, on-line), Laura Kern wrote that McAdams was "luminous as always" in her role as the physically wounded Colee Dunn, who has a "determinedly sunny outlook on life."

In *State of Play*, a thriller inspired by the same-titled BBC series, McAdams played Della Frye, a young newspaper blogger who helps her coworker, the reporter Cal McAffrey (Russell Crowe), investigate the murder of a mistress of a congressman (Ben Affleck). Released in April 2009, the film received generally positive reviews and earned over $37 million in U.S. box offices. Later that year McAdams starred in the romantic drama *The Time Traveler's Wife*, adapted from the novel by Audrey Niffenegger. In that film McAdams played Claire, the love interest of Henry DeTample (Eric Bana), a librarian with a gene that causes him to travel inadvertently through time. Though many reviewers credited McAdams and Bana with sincere and effortful performances, the film was generally derided for its convoluted plot and for being "dull and sappy," in the words of Claudia Puig, a reviewer for *USA Today* (August 13, 2008, on-line). McAdams was cast in the Guy Ritchie–directed film *Sherlock Holmes*, as the love interest and rival of the famous fictional detective (played by Robert Downey Jr.); the picture was slated to premiere in late 2009. In 2010 she was to appear opposite Harrison Ford in *Morning Glory*, a comedy about a morning-news program.

McAdams has avoided the pitfalls—such as drug or alcohol abuse—that have tarnished the reputations of many of her peers. She is usually reticent about personal matters, including her two-year romance with Gosling (the pair reportedly broke up in 2007). McAdams maintains her home in Toronto, where she likes to ride her bicycle, watch movies, garden, cook, and play ultimate Frisbee. "I just think it's helpful in terms of maintaining some kind of normalcy and balance," she told Gayle MacDonald for the *Globe and Mail* (July 7, 2004) about her choice not to live in Los Angeles. "This is where my family and friends are. It's just home. I feel very Canadian. I just can't leave it."

—M.E.R.

Suggested Reading: *Allure* p189 Nov. 2005; (Biloxi, Mississippi) *Sun Herald* M p9 July 8, 2004; *Los Angeles Times* E p22 May 8, 2005; *Maclean's* p45 July 18, 2005; (Montreal, Canada) *Gazette* D p5 Aug. 17, 2005; (Toronto, Canada) *Globe and Mail* R p1 Mar. 17, 2008;

Selected Films: *Guilt by Association*, 2002; *My Name is Tanino*, 2002; *Perfect Pie*, 2002; *The Hot Chick*, 2002; *Mean Girls*, 2004; *The Notebook*, 2004; *Wedding Crashers*, 2005; *Red Eye*, 2005; *The Family Stone*, 2005; *Married Life*, 2007; *The Lucky Ones*, 2008; *The Time Traveler's Wife*, 2009; *State of Play*, 2009; *Sherlock Holmes*, 2009

Selected Television Shows: *The Famous Jett Jackson*, 2001; *Earth: Final Conflict*, 2002, *Slings & Arrows*, 2003–05

McChrystal, Stanley

Aug. 14, 1954– U.S. Army general; commander of U.S. forces in Afghanistan

Address: U.S. Central Command, 7115 S. Boundary Blvd., MacDill AFB, FL 33608

The September 11, 2001 terrorist attacks on New York City and Washington, D.C., preceded the U.S.'s entry into two wars. Later that year President George W. Bush ordered the invasion of Afghanistan, where the terrorists, members of the group Al Qaeda, had trained and found a haven; he also ordered the invasion of Iraq, in March 2003, based on the stated belief—later proved erroneous—that that country was stockpiling so-called weapons of mass destruction. (Some administration officials suggested that there was a connection between Iraq and Al Qaeda, a theory that was also later discredited.) After initial success in Afghanistan, where U.S. forces drove the Islamic fundamentalist group known as the Taliban from power, the military's focus was mainly on Iraq, even as the Taliban and its allies regrouped and posed a steadily increasing threat. With his election to the presidency, in 2008, Barack Obama promised to reduce the level of U.S. troops in Iraq and concentrate more heavily on Afghanistan, which has seen an increase in violence in the past year. His choice to lead U.S. forces in that country, announced in May 2009, was the U.S. Army general Stanley McChrystal.

In his position as commander of both the International Security Assistance Force (ISAF) and the U.S. Forces Afghanistan (USFOR-A), McChrystal replaced David McKiernan, a shakeup indicating that the U.S. was in need of new solutions to the growing problems in Afghanistan. McChrystal, a former Green Beret commander and Army Ranger, is known for having transformed the military's Joint Special Operations Command (JSOC) into an elite counterterrorism force responsible for capturing the deposed Iraqi president, Saddam Hussein, and killing a high-level Al Qaeda agent, Abu Musab al-Zarqawi, among other operations. According to the BBC News Web site (May 11, 2009, online), McKiernan's "removal from command in Afghanistan suggests President Obama does not believe Gen McKiernan is 'the guy' to turn around the coalition's deteriorating military position in central Asia. He clearly believes that Gen McChrystal's special ops tactics are more likely to get the job done." McChrystal has also been praised for pushing the traditionally secretive JSOC to work with the FBI and CIA. Henry Crumpton, a CIA official, told Elisabeth Bumiller and Mark Mazzetti for the *New York Times* (May 13, 2009) that McChrystal "knows intelligence, he knows covert action and he knows the value of partnerships."

McChrystal graduated from the U.S. Military Academy at West Point in 1976 and worked his way through the army's ranks, becoming a Green Beret, Army Ranger, and Special Operations commander. He served in Saudi Arabia during the Persian Gulf War in 1991 and was posted in Afghanistan as chief of staff of military operations in 2001 and 2002. He served at the Pentagon as vice director of operations for the Joint Staff from 2002 to 2003 and was then appointed commander of the JSOC. When he was confirmed as commander of forces in Afghanistan, in June 2009, he was promoted from lieutenant general (or three-star general) to full (four-star) general. Although he gives few interviews and was unknown to the general public until the assassination of al-Zarqawi, in 2006, McChrystal is highly praised in the military community. "He's lanky, smart, tough, a sneaky stealth soldier," the retired major general William Nash told Bumiller and Mazzetti. "He's got all the Special Ops attributes, plus an intellect." Despite such praise, McChrystal is also something of a controversial figure. JSOC officers serving under him have been disciplined for prisoner abuse, and although later cleared of wrongdoing, he was the subject of an investigation after one of his units provided false information about the shooting death of Corporal Patrick Tillman in 2004.

In September 2009 McChrystal requested an additional 40,000 U.S. troops in Afghanistan (62,000 were stationed there at that time), citing the danger of failure if more forces were not committed within the next year. His request reinforced the perception that achieving a stable Afghanistan was becoming increasingly elusive, and it renewed debate within the Obama administration and the U.S. Congress as to the necessity of further troop commitments and what might constitute "success" in Afghanistan.

The fourth of six children, Stanley A. McChrystal was born on August 14, 1954 into a military family. His siblings, four brothers and a sister, have all either served in or married into the military. His father, Herbert J. McChrystal Jr., was a two-star (or major) general who served in Germany during the U.S. occupation that followed World War II. He also later served at the Pentagon. McChrystal told Peter Spiegel for the *Wall Street Journal* (June 12, 2009, on-line), "When I was young, I admired my dad a lot, and when people would ask me what I wanted to do I'd say I wanted to be in the Army. I don't ever remember making a decision to go into the Army. It was just something I expected myself to do, although I never got any pressure or encouragement from my dad."

McChrystal graduated with a B.S. degree from West Point, in New York, in 1976. That June he was promoted to the rank of second lieutenant, and from November 1976 to February 1978 he served at Fort Bragg, North Carolina, as weapons platoon

Scott Davis, courtesy of the United States Army

Stanley McChrystal

leader for C Company, 1st Battalion, 504th Parachute Infantry Regiment, 82d Airborne Division. Promoted to first lieutenant in 1978, he served as rifle platoon leader from February until July of that year. He was executive officer from July to November, then enrolled in the Special Forces Officer Course at the Special Forces School at Fort Bragg, completing his course work in April 1979. Then, until 1980, he commanded a Green Beret team. The Green Berets, officially known as the United States Army Special Forces, are devoted to waging "unconventional warfare." McChrystal told Spiegel that he had wanted to command a Green Beret team since he learned about their actions in the war in Vietnam, in which his father and brother served: "That seemed to me—off by yourself requiring a lot of judgment, initiative from young leaders—something I would find interesting and challenging."

After commanding the Green Beret team, McChrystal achieved the rank of captain and studied at the Infantry Officer Advanced Course at the U.S. Army Infantry School in Fort Benning, Georgia, until February 1981. That month he arrived in South Korea to take up a post in intelligence and operations for the United Nations Command Support Group. In March 1982 he left for Fort Stewart, Georgia, where he served, for A Company, as a training officer in the Directorate of Plans and Training. In November 1982 he moved to A Company's 3rd Battalion, 19th Infantry, 24th Infantry Division (Mechanized) at Fort Stewart, where he served as commander. He held that post until September 1984, when he became an operations officer. From September 1985 to January 1986, he served at Fort Benning as liaison officer for the 3rd Battalion, 75th Ranger Regiment. He told Spiegel, "The Rangers were much better resourced, much better equipped in every way" than conventional forces. "They were a unit that was very based on discipline. I liked the direct action part of it; I liked the ethos of the unit. It just became a comfortable fit for me." He decided to remain with the Rangers instead of returning to the conventional forces. "I got a lot of advice not to do it," he told Spiegel. "I had some very close friends and respected people who said, you've already been in the Rangers, you've commanded a battalion already, go on and grow up. That was really tough. I waited literally until the last day to tell them whether I wanted to be considered [as a candidate to return to the Rangers as a battalion commander]." McChrystal became the commander of A Company, 75th Ranger Regiment, in January 1986, returned to his former post as liaison officer with the Rangers in May 1987, and then became the operations officer in April 1988. In June 1987 he was made a major.

For a year beginning in June 1989, McChrystal attended the Naval War College in Newport, Rhode Island, where he took the Command and Staff course. During the subsequent Persian Gulf War, he was deployed to Saudi Arabia as an Army Special Operations action officer. He became a lieutenant colonel in 1992. From April 1993 to November 1994, he commanded the 2nd Battalion, 504th Parachute Infantry Regiment, 82d Airborne Division, at Fort Bragg. He then commanded the 2nd Battalion, 75th Ranger Regiment, at Fort Lewis, Washington, from November 1994 to June 1996. He became a full colonel in September 1996 and, for a year, from June 1996 to June 1997, was a senior service college fellow at the John F. Kennedy School of Government, at Harvard University, in Cambridge, Massachusetts. He then became commander of the 75th Ranger Regiment, at Fort Benning, from June 1997 to August 1999. He was a military fellow at the Council on Foreign Relations, in New York City, from August 1999 to June 2000.

Between June 2000 and June 2001 McChrystal was assistant division commander for the 82d Airborne Division at Fort Bragg. He was made a brigadier (one-star) general in January 2001 and was also part of a joint assignment as commander of the Combined Joint Task Force at Camp Doha, in Kuwait. From June 2001 to July 2002 he was chief of staff of the XVIII Airborne Corps and also served as chief of staff for Combined Joint Task Force 180. In July 2002 he became vice director for operations of the Joint Staff, which assists the chairman of the Joint Chiefs of Staff. He held that post, based in Washington, D.C., until September 2003. He then became commanding general of the JSOC, based at Fort Bragg, serving in that capacity from September 2003 to June 2008. During his tenure in that position, McChrystal spent little of his time at Fort Bragg; most of it was devoted to directing counterterrorism efforts in Iraq and Afghanistan. In that period he received two promotions, to major general in 2004 and lieutenant general in 2006. He became the director of the Joint Staff in August 2008.

During his five years as commander of the JSOC, McChrystal was, as an article on the *Washington Times* Web site (October 2, 2006) put it, "Defense Secretary Donald H. Rumsfeld's chief terrorist pursuer in Iraq and Afghanistan." In those years McChrystal was responsible for hunting down numerous terrorists through so-called "direct action" forces, or SMUs (Special Mission Units). Among other actions, his JSOC forces captured the deposed Iraqi president, Saddam Hussein, in 2003 and killed Abu Musab al-Zarqawi, a high-level Al Qaeda operative, in 2006. McChrystal's team successfully located al-Zarqawi and enabled the air strike that killed him; the *Washington Times* article noted that McChrystal was "so personally involved in the hunt that he went with his men to the bombed-out hut near Baqouba [Afghanistan] to make sure they got their man. A source close to the special-operations community said Gen. McChrystal's eyes-on identification is representative of the three-star general's hands-on approach." McChrystal told Spiegel, "Counterterrorism, effective counterterrorism, is about networking. It's about building a really effective network so you can gather information and then you can act on it rapidly and precisely. Counterinsurgency still requires the ability to build a network, gather information, understand what you're trying to do. . . . The thing I believe in most is understanding what you're trying to do and the effects of what you do."

Some have credited the JSOC under McChrystal—rather than the troop "surge" that President Bush implemented in 2007—with the progress in winning Iraq over from insurgent forces. In 2003 the JSOC was given greater autonomy from U.S. Special Operations Command, and McChrystal wasted no time in transforming it into an elite terrorist-hunting force. Tim Heffernan wrote for *Esquire* (May 19, 2009, on-line) that JSOC "became a focused and highly active machine" that "accomplished a great deal." Heffernan wrote that in addition to capturing Hussein and killing al-Zarqawi, McChrystal's revamped JSOC captured and killed "dozens, if not hundreds, of others: the bombers, bomb-makers, spies, spotters, and assassins who created and sustained the bloody street war against U.S. soldiers and Iraqi civilians."

McChrystal's forces located Hussein and al-Zarqawi with help from various "intel groups"—intelligence officers from the CIA, FBI, and Defense Intelligence Agency. The covert activities of the JSOC have long been kept under wraps, and many details of McChrystal's career, including his time leading the JSOC, are classified. Making several references and comparisons to the *Star Wars* films, Michael Hirsh and John Barry wrote for *Newsweek* (June 26, 2006, on-line) that the "JSOC is part of what Vice President Dick Cheney was referring to when he said America would have to 'work the dark side' after 9/11. To many critics, the veep's remark back in 2001 fostered his rep as the Darth Vader of the war on terror and presaged bad things to come, like the interrogation abuses at Abu Ghraib and Guantánamo Bay. But America also has its share of Jedi Knights who are fighting in what Cheney calls 'the shadows.' And McChrystal, an affable but tough Army Ranger, and the Delta Force and other elite teams he commands are among them." For many years the Pentagon would not acknowledge the existence of JSOC. As Bumiller and Mazzetti wrote, "When McChrystal took over the Joint Special Operations Command in 2003, he inherited an insular, shadowy commando force with a reputation for spurning partnerships with other military and intelligence organizations." In fact, McChrystal's name was not widely known to the public until 2006, when President Bush announced publicly that it was McChrystal's teams that had found al-Zarqawi.

JSOC's clandestine activities have sparked much criticism. In 2004 a task force overseen by McChrystal converted one of Hussein's bases into a top-secret detention center known as the Black Room, which was part of a larger site called Camp Nama. Prisoners there were beaten, shot at with paintball guns, and treated to other forms of physical and mental abuse. According to Heffernan, at least three prisoner deaths occurred at the detention center; at least 34 of the soldiers who abused prisoners were later punished. Though McChrystal has denied being present for or authorizing any form of torture or abuse, Heffernan noted that "whether or not he was present during the actual abuse—and it seems unlikely that he would need or want to put himself in that exposed position—as commander of JSOC, Stanley McChrystal oversaw them." According to an editorial in the *New York Times* (June 1, 2009, on-line), "Special Operations task forces operated in secret, outside the normal military chain of command and with minimal legal accountability . . . [and] General McChrystal's command substantially overlaps this troubled period. . . . While there is no suggestion that General McChrystal was personally involved in any misconduct, he has a clear responsibility to illuminate what went wrong, what if anything was done to stop these horrors, and what he intends to do to ensure that they are not repeated under his command in Afghanistan." McChrystal was also investigated for his actions in the aftermath of the 2004 shooting death of the army corporal and former National Football League (NFL) player Patrick Tillman. Although Tillman had been killed by friendly fire, Tillman's unit, which was under McChrystal's command, asserted that the death was due to enemy fire, and McChrystal signed off on a commendation letter containing the false information. Several inquiries took place after the truth came out, and McChrystal was later cleared of any misconduct, since he was found to have had no reason to question the information in the letter and because he had later alerted his superiors to evidence of misinformation.

McChrystal's appointment as commander of both the ISAF and USFOR-A was announced by Defense Secretary Robert Gates in May 2009 and confirmed by the Senate on June 10. He replaced General David D. McKiernan, who had held the posts for less than a year. The Obama administration selected McChrystal in an attempt to find a different approach to the war in Afghanistan, which was launched by President Bush in late 2001, following attacks on the U.S. by Al Qaeda terrorists who had trained and found a haven in Afghanistan; though the U.S. and its allies initially succeeded in driving out the Taliban, the Islamic fundamentalist group that had ruled the country, the U.S. war effort had grown increasingly challenging in the months prior to McChrystal's appointment. Fred Kaplan wrote for *Slate.com* (May 11, 2009), "McKiernan's ouster signals a dramatic shift in U.S. strategy for the war in Afghanistan. . . . An intellectual battle is now raging within the Army between an 'old guard' that thinks about war in conventional, force-on-force terms and a 'new guard' that focuses more on 'asymmetric conflicts' and counterinsurgency. McKiernan is an excellent general in the old mold. McChrystal . . . is an excellent general in the new mold." McChrystal formally assumed command of U.S. and NATO forces in Afghanistan on June 15, during one of the most violent periods of the eight-year-old war. In the first week of June, for example, U.S. and NATO forces suffered more than 400 attacks by insurgents, eight times the number recorded in January 2004. In addition to the attacks, the U.S. forces were also criticized for the large number of civilian casualties that resulted from counterinsurgency efforts. Speaking at the headquarters of NATO's International Security Assistance Force, McChrystal said, as quoted by Laura King in the *Los Angeles Times* (June 16, 2009), "The Afghan people are at the center of our mission—in reality, they are our mission. We must protect them from violence, whatever its nature."

In Afghanistan McChrystal has been working to win the trust of the civilian population and avoid the use of aggressive military force as much as possible. According to Evan Thomas, writing for *Newsweek* (September 26, 2009, on-line), the general has asked ISAF personnel to obey local driving laws (previously, troops routinely broke speed limits and forced other vehicles off the roads), instructed his officers to think twice about opening fire on any target, and asked officers not to call in airstrikes or support fire unless necessary for self-defense. There have been fewer civilian casualties as a result, according to Thomas.

Despite his efforts, McChrystal has had little success in Afghanistan since June. Dexter Filkins wrote for the *New York Times* (October 18, 2009, on-line), "Success takes time, but how much time does Stanley McChrystal have? The war in Afghanistan is now in its ninth year. The Taliban, measured by the number of their attacks, are stronger than at any time since the Americans toppled their government at the end of 2001. American soldiers and Marines are dying at a faster rate than ever before. Polls in the United States show that opposition to the war is growing steadily." Adding to the challenge is the widespread fraud that has taken place, mostly by supporters of the U.S.-backed president, Hamid Karzai, during the 2009 presidential race. The vote count, which resulted in Karzai's reelection, was deemed invalid; a new election, between Karzai and his main competitor, Abdullah Abdullah, was scheduled to take place on November 7, 2009. Before the election could take place, however, Karzai was declared the winner by default, after his opponent withdrew from the race—reportedly because he believed that the new election, too, would be tainted by fraud.

On August 30, 2009 McChrystal submitted to Defense Secretary Robert Gates a report in which he warned that without additional troops and a comprehensive counterinsurgency strategy, the U.S. would lose the war in Afghanistan. The next month McChrystal specified that 40,000 additional troops were necessary. His request became a major political issue when Obama and many congressional Democrats expressed reluctance to commit more troops. The administration was still debating McChrystal's request in late October, which had by then turned into the deadliest month yet for Americans in Afghanistan, with 55 killed, mostly by roadside bombs. "The magnitude of the choice presented by McChrystal, and now facing President Obama, is difficult to overstate," Filkins wrote. "For what McChrystal is proposing is not a temporary, Iraq-style surge—a rapid influx of American troops followed by a withdrawal. McChrystal's plan is a blueprint for an extensive American commitment to build a modern state in Afghanistan, where one has never existed, and to bring order to a place famous for the empires it has exhausted. Even under the best of circumstances, this effort would most likely last many more years, cost hundreds of billions of dollars and entail the deaths of many more American women and men."

McChrystal is in command of the largest international force ever to serve in Afghanistan. As of September 2009 it numbered 109,000 men and women, with 62,000 U.S. troops and 39,000 troops from 41 other countries.

McChrystal's military decorations include the Defense Distinguished Service Medal, the Legion of Merit with two Oak Leaf Clusters, the Bronze Star, and the Army Commendation Medal. He is known for his asceticism and physical endurance; he sleeps for only a few hours a night, eats only one meal a day (to avoid lethargy), and keeps in shape through rigorous exercise. In 2000, when he was a fellow at the Council on Foreign Relations, he ran 12 miles every day from his home in Brooklyn to the council offices. Leslie H. Gelb, the president emeritus of the council, told Bumiller and Mazzetti, "If you asked me the first thing that comes to mind about General McChrystal, I think of no body fat." McChrystal is also known for his commitment to his fellow soldiers. In 1994 18 of his troops were killed when an F-16 jet crashed into a parked cargo plane at Pope Air Force Base, in North Carolina.

McChrystal and his wife, Annie, attended the funeral and memorial service for each victim. "That was real moral courage," Dan McNeill, McChrystal's commander at the time, told Mark Thompson for *Time* (July 10, 2009). "I don't know if I could have done that."

—W.D.

Suggested Reading:*Esquire* (on-line) May 19, 2009; *Los Angeles Times* A p17 June 16, 2009; *New York Times* (on-line) Oct. 2, 2006, May 13, 2009, Oct. 13, 2009; npr.org July 2, 2009

Bruce Glikas/Getty Images

McClinton, Marion

1954(?)– Playwright; theatrical director; actor

Address: c/o Bret Adams Ltd., 448 W. 44th St., New York, NY 10036

In spite of the racial qualifier, Marion McClinton does not mind being described as one of the best black stage directors in the United States. "I'm up there in very good company," he told Elaine Dutka for the *Los Angeles Times* (September 10, 2000). "My mom is black. I don't view myself as a second-class citizen. And I want people to know who I am." McClinton's reputation rests heavily on his direction of nine of the 10 plays in August Wilson's monumental chronicle of the experience of African-Americans in each decade of the 20th century, works whose characters, with a few exceptions, live in the Hill District of Pittsburgh, Pennsylvania: *Gem of the Ocean* (set in 1904); *Joe Turner's Come and Gone* (set in 1911); *Ma Rainey's Black Bottom* (1927); *The Piano Lesson* (1936); *Seven Guitars* (1948); *Fences* (1957); *Two Trains Running* (1969); *Jitney* (1977); and *King Hedley II* (1985), the last of which earned a Tony Award nomination for McClinton in 2001, when it ran on Broadway. (The final play in Wilson's cycle, *Radio Golf*, which is set in 1997, premiered five months before Wilson's death, in 2005; McClinton has not yet directed a production of it.) The distinctive vision displayed in McClinton's staging of *The Piano Lesson* in 1993 greatly impressed Wilson, who for many years was a mentor, inspirer, and close friend of McClinton's as well as a frequent collaborator. "It blew me away," Wilson told Don Shewey for the *New York Times* (April 29, 2001, on-line). "I saw a director who was willing to try very bold things." Speaking of McClinton during rehearsals of the Broadway production of *King Hedley II*, Wilson commented to Shewey, "I honestly don't know anyone more passionate than he is about the theater." In 2000 McClinton won an Obie Award for his direction of *Jitney* Off-Broadway, at the Second Stage Theatre. He has also directed in many other prestigious theaters, among them the Joseph Papp Public Theatre, in New York City; the Goodman Theatre, in Chicago, Illinois; the Mark Taper Forum, in Los Angeles, California; the Yale Repertory Theatre, in New Haven, Connecticut; the Guthrie Theater, in Minneapolis, Minnesota; and the Royal National Theatre, in London, England.

McClinton has also directed plays by other contemporary black writers, among them Kia Corthron (*Breath, Boom*), Cheryl L. West (*Jar the Floor*), Aishah Rahman (*Unfinished Women Cry in No Man's Land While a Bird Dies in a Gilded Cage*), Keith Glover (*Thunder Knocking on the Door* and *Dancing on Moonlight*), Eugene Lee (*East Texas Hot Links*), Michael Henry Brown (*Generations of the Dead in the Abyss of Coney Island Madness*), Oyamo (*I Am a Man*), Jerome Hairston (*Live from the Edge of Oblivion*), and the Nigerian Nobel Prize winner Wole Soyinka (*Death and the King's Horseman*). In addition, he has written seven plays—*Walkers, Who Causes the Darkness?, Stones and Bones, Police Boys, The Ghosts of Summer, Enlightenments on an Enchanted Island*, and *Hunters of the Soul*—all of which have been presented either in regional or Off-Broadway theaters or in staged readings at drama workshops. A resident of St. Paul, Minnesota, since his birth, McClinton has been a member of the Penumbra Theatre Company, based in that city, for three decades. He holds the title of associate artist–director/playwright at Baltimore's Center Stage, the state theater of Maryland. Although he never attracted much notice as an actor, he has found performing onstage to be more rewarding in some ways than directing and playwrighting. "The lights go out, and it's just you and the audience," he told Dutka. "Writing is so private. And while directing pays the bills, it's hard being the captain of the ship—particularly when the waters are rough."

Marion Isaac McClinton was born in St. Paul in about 1954. He grew up in that city's Selby-Dole neighborhood, an area he described to Elaine Dutka as "tough but beautiful." Because he suffered from severe asthma throughout his childhood, he avoided playing outdoors; as one alternative, he developed an interest in old movies. One weekend before his adolescence, he watched three films starring the actor Marlon Brando: *On the Waterfront*, *A Streetcar Named Desire*, and *The Wild One*. "After having grown up watching movies with John Wayne, who was John Wayne in every movie, this Brando guy was something else," McClinton told Shewey. "What he did was exciting, it was real." The 1963 film *Lilies of the Field*, starring Sydney Poitier, also made a powerful impression on him. McClinton decided that he wanted to be a Hollywood actor, director, and writer—a triple threat, like Orson Welles. That remained his goal even after he saw a mounting of the play *The Great White Hope*, by Howard Sackler, a fictionalized account of events in the life of the champion boxer Jack Johnson. The production "floored me with the power of theater," he told Shewey. (In his conversation with Dutka, he traced his passion for theater to his seeing a production of Shakespeare's *Julius Caesar* at the Guthrie Theater, in Minneapolis, when he was in eighth grade; before that, he recalled to Dutka, the only other live performance he had seen was a touring company's production of the musical *Funny Girl*.)

When McClinton was 13 his parents divorced; thereafter, he was raised by his mother, Lenora. "She was tenacious, indefatigable—the only person who ever scared me," he told Dutka. McClinton attended Catholic schools, including, briefly, the College of St. Thomas (now the University of St. Thomas), in St. Paul. He left that school in 1973, "by mutual agreement" with administrators, as he told Dominic P. Papatola for the St. Paul *Pioneer Press* (May 23, 2008), and enrolled at the University of Minnesota. He dropped out at the age of 21 and then entered a period of heavy drinking and drug use. During that time he took on what turned out to be a decade-long job as a counselor to troubled teenagers in public high schools. In 1976 he successfully auditioned for a role in a local production of Joseph A. Walker's drama *The River Niger*. "*Niger* turned things around for me," he told Dutka. "I became part of a world in which I was accepted." "It kept me sane. It kept me focused," he recalled in an interview with N. Graham Nesmith for *American Theatre* (May 1, 1993).

McClinton soon joined the newly formed Penumbra Theatre Company, a black troupe in St. Paul. "Our style of acting was based on rhythm," he told Shewey, comparing Penumbra's "bebop" feel to the "rock-and-roll" sensibility of the famed Steppenwolf Theatre Company, in Chicago, Illinois. At a poetry reading in about 1978, McClinton met August Wilson, who was then beginning his career as a playwright. In a conversation with J. Wynn Rousuck for the *Baltimore Sun* (January 3, 1999), Wilson recalled, "We had a nice poetry reading here and then someone with a saxophone, in a tuxedo, jumps up on the bar and starts reciting some stuff." That "someone" was McClinton, who read aloud a short story by Alice Walker (the saxophone serving as a prop). Before long McClinton became convinced that Wilson was on the verge of greatness. "I remember saying, 'Hey, this guy can write,'" he told Mike Steele for the Minneapolis *Star Tribune* (February 27, 1998). "He was taking naturalism and stretching it, giving it music and poetry." He added, "It was because of August I decided to start writing myself." In 1979 Wilson wrote *Jitney*, a play that McClinton admired so highly that he tried to pitch it to theaters in the Twin Cities, Minneapolis and St. Paul. Every theater turned him down, and it was not until 1982 that *Jitney* premiered (at the Allegheny Repertory Theatre, in Pittsburgh, Pennsylvania).

In the meantime McClinton had continued to act, as a member of both Penumbra and Mixed Blood, another local troupe. In 1981 he made his directorial debut, at the Park Square Theater, in St. Paul, with a production of Samuel Beckett's *Waiting for Godot*. "I was petrified, but I learned a valuable lesson: If you cast very, very well, the actors will cover your shortcomings as a director," he told Steele. "They can make you look like an Einstein of the theater." His experience with *Waiting for Godot* led him to consider himself a director and think about creative ways he might bring plays to the stage. "I was rooted in naturalistic theater up until then," he told Steele. "I had to learn how to stretch beyond that, past what I knew, to open my own imagination and to follow the play."

In 1981, at the Penumbra Theatre, McClinton was cast as the narrator in *Black Bart and the Sacred Hills*, the first of August Wilson's plays to reach the stage. He directed Charles Fuller's *Zooman and the Sign* at the Penumbra in 1982. Three years later he portrayed the alcoholic character Fielding in Penumbra's staging of Wilson's *Jitney*. Set in 1977 in a dilapidated storefront from which unlicensed cabs are dispatched, the drama was part of what would become a 10-play series, known as the Pittsburgh Cycle and, more recently, published in a boxed set, the Century Cycle. At around that time McClinton began writing plays himself. The first, the two-character drama *Walkers*, is about a seemingly upstanding black detective, Walker Gillette Walker, who suddenly kills nine people, among them members of his family. Immediately after the murders he loses his memories of both the homicides and everything else in his past. During sessions with a police psychiatrist, he remembers many painful incidents from his early years, involving rape, incest, and murder. *Walkers* debuted in 1989 at the Hudson Guild Theater, Off-Broadway, with McClinton as director. Stephen Holden, who reviewed the production for the *New York Times* (April 16, 1989), described the play as "enraged but exasperatingly sketchy" and wrote that it "tackles so many serious themes that only a four-hour epic tragedy could begin to develop them into a cohesive dramatic tapestry. Racism, black self-hatred and inherited patterns of family violence are only the three most obvious issues among those raised by the play. . . . Instead of creating a sprawling family history, the playwright has telescoped a story with overtones of Greek tragedy into a two-hour psychological mystery that makes a lot of noise but conveys little emotional resonance." The New York *Newsday* (April 12, 1989) reviewer, Leo Seligsohn, expressed similar complaints. "Ultimately, the painful emergence of Walker's self-awareness becomes a metaphor for heightening black consciousness in general. Unfortunately, the trip down memory lane involves too much heavy baggage. . . . Awkward dialogue stymies the playwright's efforts to link the mass murderer to his troubled past and lost African heritage. Explaining Walker on several levels has the paradoxical effect of turning him into a one-dimensional dispenser of rhetoric."

McClinton followed *Walkers* with *Who Causes the Darkness?* (1991), which he described to Dutka as being, like its predecessor, about the "difficulty of surviving when society denies one's humanity." His next drama was *Police Boys*, about a group of black police officers and their efforts to combat gang violence. The play debuted at the Center Stage in Baltimore in 1992, with McClinton directing, and opened in New York City three years later, with Donald Douglas at the helm. It earned mixed reviews, some of which echoed the criticisms that had greeted *Walkers*. Lloyd Rose, who described *Police Boys* for the *Washington Post* (April 6, 1992) as "heartfelt, at times wrenchingly so," and McClinton's direction as "melodramatic but vivid," felt that the play was "overwrought." "McClinton has enough energy to power three plays, and he pours it into his characters: They're going off in all directions . . . ," Rose wrote. "It's all too much, and yet you can feel the playwright's concern boiling in this excess—the mistakes aren't lazy or foolish, they spring from an extreme of passion." In an assessment for the *New York Times* (May 15, 1995), Vincent Canby wrote, "McClinton's *Police Boys* seems like the work of a very ambitious playwright who, having no clearly defined goal, has lost his way in magic realism, apocalyptic melodrama and the urban jungle of his own words. . . . *Police Boys* is shapeless, its unchanneled anger having little emotional or intellectual force." Such negative views notwithstanding, the National Arts Club, in New York City, awarded McClinton its Kesselring Prize, which recognizes promising new playwrights, and some critics dubbed him the "next August Wilson." McClinton's drama *Stones and Bones* earned the Heideman Award when it was produced, under his direction, at the Humana Festival of New American Plays, in Louisville, Kentucky, in 1994.

Earlier, in 1993, McClinton had made his debut as the director of a Wilson play: the Pulitzer Prize–winning *The Piano Lesson*, whose plot hinges on the fate of a piano that, before the emancipation of slaves in the U.S., was sold in exchange for the children of a slave. The piano is now owned jointly by two of the slave's descendants: Berniece Charles and her brother, Boy Willie. Yearning to buy the land in Mississippi on which he has toiled as a sharecropper for many years, Boy Willie journeys 1,800 miles to Berniece's house in Pittsburgh to implore her to sell the piano, but she fiercely refuses to part with it. In addition to revealing family dynamics, their heated discussions offer conflicting views about slavery's legacy. The play contains mystical elements as well. *The Piano Lesson* had premiered in 1987 at the Yale Repertory Theatre under the direction of Lloyd Richards (the theater's artistic director and the dean of the Yale School of Drama). McClinton, who staged the play at the Penumbra Theatre, told Shewey, "I'd taken some liberties with the play"—in terms of set design and use of music, for example—"and I was petrified that [Wilson] would hate it." McClinton was in New York City on the night that Wilson first saw the Penumbra production. When he knew that the last act would be over, he called an associate in St. Paul from his hotel room and learned that Wilson had "loved" it. "He was on his feet clapping at the end, came up onstage with the actors, took us out, told us it was the best production he'd ever seen," his informant said, as McClinton told Shewey. In a conversation with Shewey, Wilson noted approvingly that with *The Piano Lesson*, McClinton had had the confidence to take risks. "Most directors don't trust themselves," he said. "Instead of coming up with a concept for the play, they would just duplicate Lloyd's production." By contrast, in the case of his interpretation of Wilson's *Two Trains Running* at the Center Stage in Baltimore in 1994, McClinton later questioned the success of his efforts to make the play more exciting. "Working with August directly, I realized that sometimes your improvements aren't improvements, they're a contradiction of what he's saying," he told Shewey. "So what I've learned is: follow the text."

Since 1996 McClinton has directed at least a dozen productions of *Jitney*, in the U.S. and England. According to Christopher Rawson, writing for the *Pittsburgh Post-Gazette* (November 23, 1998), one of them represented *Jitney*'s "true professional premiere": a 1996 mounting at the Pittsburgh Public Theater, for which Wilson had expanded the original version of the play from 90 minutes to two hours. When the Huntington Theatre Company, in Boston, mounted *Jitney* under McClinton's direction, the play ran for an additional half-hour. After the curtain came down at the matinee performance Rawson attended, the audience gave the cast and crew a standing ovation. Ben Brantley, who wrote a review for the *New York Times* (April 16, 2000) of McClinton's new staging of *Jitney* at the Second Stage Theater, described the production as "thoroughly engrossing." "Under Mr. McClinton's sensitive and democratic direction, which treats all the performers equally as both soloists and members of a chorus, *Jitney* holds its audience in charmed captivity for its two and a half hours. . . . Mr. Wilson, Mr. McClinton and their excellent band of actors make us feel that we have known these people . . . for most of our lives." Brad Bradley, in an assessment for CurtainUp.com of the April 25, 2000 performance of *Jitney* at the Second Stage , wrote that McClinton's "tight production provides appropriate pacing to insure that the characterizations are powerful, and even touching in certain moments." The London *Independent* (October 21, 2001) critic Kate Bassett described the production presented at the Royal National Theatre as "one of 2001's theatrical high points" and wrote, "Wilson's early play, performed by a superb visiting US ensemble under director Marion McClinton, is a funny, heart-rending and morally knotting portrait of black guys scraping [out] a living."

Earlier, in 1999, at the Pittsburgh Public Theatre, McClinton had guided the premiere production of *King Hedley II*, a finalist for that year's Pulitzer Prize in drama. "It's operatic, Greek in size and structure," he told Dutka, describing the story, which centers on an ex-convict's search for redemption. "[Wilson is] wrestling with something huge this time." He also said, "I consider August one of the three most important American playwrights, along with Tennessee Williams and Eugene O'Neill. When it's your watch, you have to safeguard that legacy. I don't feel intimidated by that prospect, but I do take it very seriously." Also in 1999, Off-Broadway, McClinton directed Cheryl L. West's *Jar the Floor*, about four generations of African-American women. Despite rave reviews, the play failed to make the transition to Broadway. "There's a sector that believes that black plays don't work on Broadway unless there's singing and dancing," McClinton told Shewey. "Sometimes I believe that's a self-fulfilling prophecy."

King Hedley II, however, was brought to Broadway, in 2001, under McClinton's direction. In a *New York Times* (May 2, 2001, on-line) review of that production, the theater critic Ben Brantley wrote, "However flawed *Hedley* may be in its particulars, it has a collective ferocity and passion rarely found in new plays today." He went on to praise McClinton for doing an "admirable job of sustaining a melodic fluidness." McClinton earned a Tony Award nomination for his efforts. Also in 2001 he directed *Breath, Boom*, by Kia Corthron. In a review for the *New York Times* (June 11, 2001), Bruce Weber wrote that the show was "forcefully directed," and he commended McClinton for giving it an "everyday rhythm," which he felt kept the hardships faced by the 16-year-old female protagonist, a gang member, from becoming overwhelming. In 2003 McClinton returned to Broadway to direct a revival of Wilson's *Ma Rainey's Black Bottom* starring Charles Dutton and Whoopi Goldberg. During rehearsals three actors quit, and he himself was hospitalized because of dangerously low blood-potassium levels. In a review of the show for the *New York Times* (February 7, 2003, on-line), Ben Brantley referred to additional pre-opening-night problems, writing, "Plagued during rehearsals by highly public arguments among its creative and managerial teams, this *Ma Rainey* . . . rarely gets past the level of an orchestra still tentatively tuning up. . . . While the innate tragic grandeur and gritty, stinging humor of this story of racial exploitation and musicians at loggerheads can be discerned in fitful flashes, the production never achieves the rushing momentum required to capture Mr. Wilson's astonishing feel for the convergence of character and cultural destiny."

In 2004 McClinton was slated to direct a Broadway revival of Lorraine Hansberry's *Raisin in the Sun*, but when its producers expressed their desire to cast the comedian Martin Lawrence and the pop singer Janet Jackson in lead roles, he dropped out, believing that decisions were being made with ticket sales, not artistic integrity, in mind. In February 2004 McClinton directed *Drowning Crow*, a play by Regina Taylor that was inspired by Anton Chekhov's *The Seagull*. Later that year McClinton, who suffers from diabetes, fell ill and had to withdraw from directing the premiere of Wilson's *Gem of the Ocean*, which was to open at the Huntington Theatre, in Boston, Massachusetts.

In 2006 McClinton led a production of Dael Orlandersmith's *Yellowman*, a 2002 finalist for the Pulitzer Prize, at the Guthrie Dowling Studio, in Minneapolis. He remained in the Twin Cities to direct a 2007 production of Samm-Art Williams's play *Home*. "This is where the work gets done," he told Rohan Preston for the *Star Tribune* (October 5, 2007). "London and New York have the glamour and money. But when you are working on Broadway, you are as much a director as a manager solving people's problems. Here, I get to concentrate on the art, without distractions. Of course, I would be lying if I said I ain't missing the pay." Another reason for McClinton's desire to stay in the Minneapolis–St. Paul area, where he lives, was that after years of touring with Wilson's plays, he wanted to spend more time with his son, Jesse, who was nearing his high-school graduation. "I feel like I've missed so much of my son's growing up, he's almost out the door now," he told Preston. "I don't want to miss any more of it." In 2008 he directed *Bud, Not Buddy*, adapted by Reginald Andre Jackson from the same-named young-adult novel (1999), by Christopher Paul Curtis, that McClinton had once read to Jesse. That directing job took on special meaning, he told Preston for the *Star Tribune* (June 18, 2008), because "it's a way of saying goodbye to my son." In May 2008 McClinton directed Eisa Davis's *Bulrusher*, another Pulitzer Prize finalist, at the Pillsbury House, a small theater in St. Paul. Asked by Papatola why a director of his renown would choose to work in such a low-profile theater, McClinton responded, "There aren't finer actors anywhere else in the country, and there aren't people I trust more."

In May 2009 McClinton directed, Off-Broadway, Carlyle Brown's play *Pure Confidence*, which is set in the 1860s and 1870s. Centered on the life of an enslaved horse jockey and his relationship with his master's house slave, *Pure Confidence* was a hit with most audiences and critics. McClinton was praised for carefully controlling the play's dramatic tempo.

McClinton's honors include a half-dozen grants and fellowships, among them an Amblin Commission Grant from Playwrights Horizons. He is married to Jan Mandell, a public-high-school drama teacher. Mandell directs the Central Touring Theater Company, which mounts productions of student-created plays in Minnesota and nearby states. She is the co-author of the book *Acting, Learning, and Change: Creating Original Plays with Adolescents.* In 2007 she earned an Ambassador Award from the Saint Paul Foundation for her achievements in teaching multiculturalism through the dramatic arts. The couple's son, Jesse Mandell-McClinton, who was born in about 1990, has performed for several years as a student at Circus Juventas, a St. Paul performing-arts circus school for young people. He is also a pianist and composer.

—K.J.P.

Suggested Reading: *Boston Herald* Arts & Life p52 May 18, 2000; *Los Angeles Times* Calendar p68 Sep. 10, 2000; (Minneapolis, Minnesota) *Star Tribune* E p1 Feb. 27, 1998; *New York Times* II p7 Apr. 29, 2001, (on-line) June 3, 2001; (St. Paul, Minnesota) *Pioneer Press* May 23, 2008; *Village Voice* p74 May 1, 2001

Selected Plays: as actor—*Black Bart and the Sacred Hills*, 1981; as director—*Waiting for Godot*, 1981; *Zooman and the Sign*, 1982; *A Soldier's Play*, 1985; *Generations of the Unfinished Women Cry in No Man's Land While a Bird Dies in a Gilded Cage*, 1990; *Generations of the Dead in the Abyss of Coney Island Madness*, 1991; *King of the Kosher Grocers*, 1992; *The Piano Lesson*, 1993; *Live from the Edge of Oblivion*, 1993; *I Am a Man*, 1994; *Two Trains Running*, 1994; *East Texas Hot Links*, 1994; *A Midsummer Night's Dream*, 1995; *Dancing on the Moonlight*, 1995; *Fences*, 1996; *Jitney*, 1996, 1998, 1999, 2000; *Thunder Knocking on the Door*, 1997, 1998; *Seven Guitars*, 1997; *Splash Hatch on the E Going Down*, 1997–98; *Death and the King's Horseman*, 1998; *Les Blancs*, 1998; *King Hedley II*, 1999, 2000, 2001; *Jar the Floor*, 1999; *Yellowman*, 1999; *Ma Rainey's Black Bottom*, 2003; *Drowning Crow*, 2004; *Yellowman*, 2006; *Home*, 2007; *Bud, Not Buddy*, 2008; *Bulrusher*, 2008; *Pure Confidence*, 2009; as playwright—*Walkers*, 1989; *Who Causes the Darkness?*, 1991; *Police Boys*, 1992; *Stones and Bones*, 1994; *Hunters of the Soul*, 1994; *The Ghosts of Summer*, 1996

McCullough, Gary E.

(mih-KUL-uh)

Nov. 29, 1958– President and chief executive officer of Career Education Corp.

Address: Career Education Corp., 2895 Greenspoint Pkwy., Suite 600, Hoffman Estates, IL 60169

Gary E. McCullough is the president and chief executive officer of the Career Education Corp. (CEC), which owns for-profit vocational and postsecondary schools on 85 campuses in the United States, Great Britain, France, Italy, the United Arab Emirates, and cyberspace. In a press release (March 6, 2007, on-line) announcing his appointment, the company described him as "a highly experienced operations and brand-management executive." For two decades after he entered the corporate world, in 1987, McCullough oversaw aspects of the manufacture, marketing, and sale of tangible commodities, during his 13 years (1987–2000) at Procter & Gamble; three as a William Wrigley Jr. Co. senior vice president (2000–03); and four as the president of the Ross Products Division of Abbott Laboratories (2003–07). At CEC McCullough is responsible for the marketing and sale of an intangible product—education. The "brands" in his purview include American InterContinental University; Briarcliffe College; Colorado Technical University; the International Academy of Design & Technology; Le Cordon Bleu Schools of North America; International Academy of Design & Technology; and Sanford-Brown College or Institute, each of which has two or more campuses (in the case of Sanford-Brown, more than two dozen). About 430,000 people have graduated from CEC schools since the company was founded, in 1994. Currently, about 95,000 students are enrolled, one-third of them at American InterContinental University Online or Colorado Technical University Online.

When McCullough joined CEC, the company was grappling with serious problems on several fronts: it was being investigated by the U.S. Department of Justice and the Securities and Exchange Commission; the CBS newsmagazine *60 Minutes* had recently broadcast a segment presenting CEC in a highly unfavorable light; a half-dozen former students had brought lawsuits against it; and the value of the company's stock had dropped substantially from its one-time high. In addition, soon after McCullough assumed leadership of CEC, a long article appeared in the *San Francisco Weekly* (June 6, 2007) cataloging complaints about its adminis-

Courtesy of Wright State University

Gary E. McCullough

tration and classes. Less than two years later, Sonia Alleyne, Annya M. Lott, and Brittany Hutson wrote for *Black Enterprise* (February 2009), "McCullough has led CEC through substantial challenges, focusing on building a foundation for growth through improved organizational effectiveness and efficiency." At the 2009 William Blair & Co. Growth Stock Conference, McCullough said, as quoted on the FD (Fair Disclosure) Wire (June 10, 2009, on-line), "We've spent time over the last two years really positioning our organization to go forward. We had to move through a number of issues in the organization, but largely, the heavy lifting of the things that we had to do are behind us." He also said, "Our goal is by 2010 . . . to make sure that we're in a position that we're delivering sustainable, predictable growth going forward and that we have sustainable double-digit margins, which is not where we started our journey in 2007." In an interview with Adam Bryant for the *New York Times* (August 8, 2009, on-line), McCullough declared, "I will outwork, and have over the course of my career, about anybody. If you're clear about what you want, if you're strong, if you're resilient, if you're well prepared and you're willing to work—I mean really work—then good things can happen."

Gary E. McCullough was born on November 29, 1958 and raised in Fort Knox, Kentucky. His father, a career U.S. Army officer, was a strict disciplinarian. Once, on the grounds that Gary's grades were too low, his father refused to allow him to join his eighth-grade basketball team and demanded that he return his uniform. "I was crushed," McCullough told Steven R. Strahler for *Crain's Chicago Business* (January 21, 2008, on-line). "There were certain things that could get you into the club"—that is, make you popular—"and taking back your uniform was not one of them." Similarly, when, as a senior in high school, McCullough was drafted to play shortstop for the Cincinnati Reds baseball organization, his father refused to allow him to accept the position, because he did not want his son to pursue a career in sports. "I was angry. I wondered awhile if I could have made it" in baseball, McCullough told Strahler. "But life's turned out pretty well. I'm no longer wistful about the whole thing."

McCullough earned a B.S. degree in business at Wright State University, in Dayton, Ohio, in 1981. He then enlisted in the military, serving as a U.S. Army Ranger for five years. He told Adam Bryant that he learned an important lesson in leadership during one of his commanding general's visits to the platoon of privates whom McCullough supervised. The day was cold and rainy, and the ground was saturated from a week of rain, making conditions difficult and unpleasant for vehicle drivers. When the general questioned one driver about the day's exercise, the man said, "It stinks," explaining that he thought such weather was unsuitable for the exercise. "What can I do to make it better for you?" the general asked. "Sir, I sure could use a Snickers bar," the private answered. A few days later a box of Snickers chocolate bars arrived, enough for the whole platoon. "We would've followed that general anywhere," McCullough told Bryant. "It was a very small thing, and he didn't need to do it, but it impressed upon me that small gestures are hugely important"—"little things like saying 'please' and 'thank you'—just the basic respect that people are due, or sending personal notes. I spend a lot of time sending personal notes." McCullough was discharged from the army in 1986 with the rank of captain and a medal for meritorious service. In 1987 he earned an M.B.A. degree from the Kellogg School of Management at Northwestern University, in Evanston, Illinois.

That year McCullough joined Procter & Gamble (P&G), a Fortune 500 company headquartered in Cincinnati, Ohio. Founded in 1837, P&G manufactures many consumer goods in two dozen categories. Thanks in part to extensive advertising, many of P&G's products are widely known: Charmin toilet paper, Bounty paper towels, Pampers disposable diapers, Old Spice deodorant, Clairol hair dyes, Ivory soap, Crest toothpaste, Pepto-Bismol anti-nausea medication, and Gillette shavers, to name a few; other P&G products are sold only outside the U.S. For years McCullough made known his desire to become a brand manager in the soaps-and-detergents division but was repeatedly rebuffed, "because of his race, he suspected," Strahler wrote. "Everybody was promoted ahead of me," McCullough told Strahler. "I was never asked to play golf. I wasn't invited to people's homes." (When Strahler tried to discuss McCullough's experience with P&G representatives, he was told only that *Black Enterprise* had named the company one of the nation's 40 best in terms of ethnic and racial diversity of employees.) McCullough told Bryant, "I believed early in my career that if I just worked hard, put my head down and did my job, everyone would notice and good things would happen. And in fact, that's not true, necessarily. You can do your job and you can toil along in anonymity without anybody noticing for a real long time. . . . I would attribute part of that to the fact that I just wasn't very savvy politically."

McCullough acquired that practical know-how in 1995 under the tutelage of Edwin H. "Ed" Rigaud, an African-American who was then a vice president and 30-year veteran of P&G. According to Strahler, McCullough created a business plan that "streamlined the product portfolio and focused on high-volume customers"; the plan so impressed P&G executives that they promoted him to marketing director of laundry and cleaning products for Venezuela in December 1995. In September 1996 he was named marketing director of P&G's drink Sunny Delight. In December 1998 he became the general manager of P&G's North American home-care division, a position he held until March 2000.

Later in 2000 McCullough left P&G to join the Chicago, Illinois–based William Wrigley Jr. Co. (better known simply as Wrigley) as a senior vice president for North, Central, and South America. Founded in 1891, Wrigley is the world's largest manufacturer of chewing gum (bearing brand names including Juicy Fruit, Wrigley's Spearmint, Orbit, and Freedent); its product line also includes Life Savers and Altoids. According to the company's Web site, Wrigley gum and candies are sold in 180 countries—nearly every nation in the world. McCullough supervised 3,300 employees and a $1.2 billion product portfolio (that is, an array of products whose sales totaled that amount in one year). He succeeded in making Orbit the top-selling gum in the U.S., and he helped to boost sales of several other products, among them Big Red, Eclipse, and Juicy Fruit chewing gum. Under McCullough's leadership Wrigley's share of the gum market in the Americas grew from 47.5 percent to 58.4 percent in three years.

In 2003 McCullough changed jobs again, to become the senior vice president of the Ross Products Division of Abbott Laboratories. The division, now called Abbott Nutrition and based in Columbus, Ohio, is a leading provider of infant and adult nutritional products. Well known among them are Similac, for infants; Ensure, for adults; and Glucerna, for diabetics. All three products are available in various formulations for infants or adults with particular problems—for example, infants with fat intolerance or protein sensitivity, and adults diagnosed with HIV/AIDS or kidney disease. In his new post McCullough oversaw 5,300 employees and roughly $2.6 billion in annual sales. He reorganized Ross's departments and sales force and hired managers who had worked at such successful firms as the Coca-Cola Co. and the Campbell Soup Co. He then focused on new ways of marketing Abbott's products, because "where Ross has failed historically is their products have looked too much like medicine," Bruce Cohen, a consumer-goods analyst at Kurt Salmon Associates, told Tom Matthews for the *Columbus (Ohio) Dispatch* (January 23, 2005). "We've got wonderful strengths," McCullough told Matthews. "We have terrific brands and unbelievable science. But we have to be innovative. Each of our brands will have to have something new or different to survive in the marketplace." In addition to repackaging, McCullough negotiated some profitable acquisitions, including the purchase for $320 million of Experimental Applied Sciences, the makers of the health and fitness products Myoplex and Body for Life. Within a year of his arrival at Ross, the company's annual sales reached a record $2.3 billion—9 percent more than in the previous 12 months. During his three years with the company, McCullough saw annual sales increase a total of 23 percent.

In 2006 a recruiter contacted McCullough regarding the positions of president and CEO at CEC, whose headquarters are in Hoffman Estates, Illinois, about 20 miles northwest of Chicago. CEC was founded in 1994 by John M. Larson, an expert in for-profit vocational and higher education. Larson's strategy, the Web site Funding Universe explained, was to buy established schools and then improve their facilities and course offerings, with the goal of making them more profitable. "The company limited its acquisitions to schools that offered training in fields in which there was a strong continuing demand for workers, and which attracted motivated students," Funding Universe reported. Currently, those fields include business and management, visual and interior design, communications, information technology, computer science, game design, cooking and baking, hospitality and restaurant management, health science, criminal justice, and public administration. Some schools offer only diplomas or certificates; others offer associate degrees; still others offer bachelor's, master's, and doctoral degrees. Certificates, diplomas, or degrees are given only in the fields mentioned. (Thus, a student cannot major in, say, history, English literature, physics, or psychology at any CEC school.) The cost of an associate degree at a CEC school is far greater than the average cost at nonprofit colleges. In addition, four-year colleges do not accept the credits of those who have earned associate degrees at CEC schools.

CEC became a publicly traded company in 1998. Initially, the firm attracted the interest of Wall Street investors, but enthusiasm quickly dissipated when it was revealed that the company was under investigation by the Securities and Exchange Commission (SEC) regarding alleged financial-aid irregularities and exaggerated statements regarding enrollment; in addition, shareholders and students had filed lawsuits alleging that the company had falsified student records to enhance its job-placement and enrollment statistics. In 2006 a dissatisfied shareholder attempted without success to unseat Larson. In August 2006 the company's share price plummeted after it announced weak earnings. Larson resigned six weeks later.

When McCullough received the call from the recruiter, CEC was still under investigation by the SEC. (The commission never prosecuted the company and ended its probe in 2008.) The company had also received negative press in 2005 when the CBS investigative journalism show *60 Minutes* aired a report on the inability of top graduates at some CEC schools to find jobs in their fields. McCullough accepted the job offer despite the corporation's troubled recent history. He became president, chief executive officer, and a member of the board of directors in March 2007, filling in the seat on the board left vacant after Larson's resigntion.

During his first few months at CEC, McCullough replaced managers with executives with whom he had worked in the past. He cut the $250 million marketing budget and used the freed funds to improve the company's top five schools. In 2008 CEC underwent a major restructuring to eradicate marketing and operating inefficiencies and eliminate redundant positions. "We are transforming the culture of the organization to one that is more focused on student outcomes," McCullough said, as quoted in *Computer Technology Journal* (February 11, 2008).

Despite McCullough's efforts, he faced uphill battles in 2007 and 2008. In 2007 CEC closed three out of 11 schools it had tried unsuccessfully to sell. On June 6, 2007 the *San Francisco Weekly* published an article in which the author, Eliza Strickland, described deceptive tactics that CEC admissions personnel used to lure prospective students to register at the California Culinary Academy, one of CEC's schools; Strickland also recounted the unsuccessful efforts of many students to find any but the lowest-paying jobs in restaurants and the crushing debts they had been left with after leaving the school. In 2008 enrollment at CEC schools dropped significantly, as a growing credit crisis made it more difficult for students to obtain loans. According to H. Lee Murphy, writing for *Crain's Chicago Business* (September 15, 2008, on-line), investors, who had been surprised by CEC's choice of McCullough, a consumer-products marketer, to head the company, did not feel reassured by the steps McCullough had taken to increase the company's profits. By April 2009, however, business analysts had begun to advise investors that the outlook for CEC had brightened. Although McCullough was planning to shut down eight more schools, Brandon Dobell of the investment firm William Blair & Co. told Murphy for *Crain's Chicago Business* (April 30, 2009, on-line) that he felt optimistic that CEC's revenues would rise by 1 percent in 2009, to $1.73 billion, and possibly by 11 percent in 2010, to $1.93 billion. As Murphy wrote, Dobell predicted that "more school closings will keep full-year earnings down, falling 16% to 56 cents a share in 2009. But profits will triple in 2010 to $1.68 a share." "The potential for upside in both student enrollments and profit margins at Career Education is quite high," Dobell said to Murphy.

Among other positive changes since McCullough's arrival at CEC, as of June 2009 employee turnover had dropped from an annual rate of 50 percent to about 35 percent, and the admissions process was generating fewer problems. McCullough had also begun to invest in areas showing signs of growth, among them the company's health-care programs and on-line curricula.

In 2005 *Black Enterprise Magazine* named McCullough among the 75 most powerful African-Americans in business, and in 2009 the magazine listed him among the top 100 in that group. According to *Forbes.com* (2009), in 2008 his salary was $800,000. McCullough and his wife, Kimberley, have two sons and a daughter and live in Oak Park, Illinois.

—W.D.

Suggested Reading: AllBusiness.com Mar. 6, 2007; Career Education Corp. Web site; *Columbus (Ohio) Dispatch* G p1+ Jan. 23, 2005; *Crain's Chicago Business* (on-line) Dec. 5, 2005, Jan. 21, 2008; *New York Times* Business p2 Aug. 8, 2009; *Seeking Alpha* (on-line) May 7, 2009

McGill, Anthony

July 17, 1979– Clarinetist

Address: The Metropolitan Opera, Lincoln Center, New York, NY 10023

On January 20, 2009 the clarinetist Anthony McGill took part in history when he performed as part of a pickup classical-music quartet at the inaugural ceremony of the 44th U.S. president, Barack Obama. The performance, held on the steps of the U.S. Capitol, was part of an event that drew a record 1.8 million people and was televised internationally, marking a high point in the then-29-year-old McGill's career. "It's the most wonderful opportunity, obviously, I've ever gotten in my life," he told Daniel J. Wakin for the *New York Times* (January 19, 2009). "It's just great to be part of something like this, as a person, as an American, as a musician." The classical quartet was the first to perform at a presidential inauguration, and its makeup was a testament to both skill and diversity—in addition to McGill, an African-American from Chicago, Illinois, the group consisted of the world-renowned Chinese-American cellist Yo-Yo Ma, the acclaimed Israeli-American violinist Itzhak Perlman, and the Venezuelan-born pianist Gabriela Montero. The song, "Air and Simple Gifts," was arranged by the American composer John Williams and performed immediately before Obama was sworn into office, at noon.

Win McNamee/Getty Images

Anthony McGill

McGill is one of two principal clarinetists (the other is Stephen Williamson) in the Metropolitan Opera Orchestra of New York City, and in the past eight years he has earned respect as a soloist and chamber musician. Before joining the Met Orchestra, in 2004, he was the associate principal and E-flat clarinetist in the Cincinnati Symphony Orchestra, his first job after graduating, in 2000, from the Curtis Institute of Music, in Philadelphia, Pennsylvania. Wakin wrote that although McGill "is not a world-famous soloist like Mr. Perlman or Mr. Ma . . . he has quietly come to be recognized among colleagues for his sensitive playing and refined musicianship." Classical-music critics have often praised his playing as warm and highly expressive. Reviewing a recital, Peter Dobrin wrote for the *Philadelphia Inquirer* (November 8, 2005), "There's something so charmingly old-world about Anthony McGill's tone, so message-from-another-era, that his recital . . . could have been accompanied by the atmospheric crackling of 78 r.p.m. black shellac."

In addition to calling Chicago home, McGill has inspired comparisons to Obama—the first African-American president—for other reasons. Barry Elmore, the founder of the Chicago Teen Ensemble and one of McGill's former teachers, told Jason George for the *Chicago Tribune* (January 20, 2009, on-line) that McGill and the president have "both worked hard all their lives" and "achieved much in their life over a short time." George wrote, "Like Obama, McGill often operated in circles where there were few fellow African-Americans—a fact that McGill said he tried to ignore." McGill told him, "As Obama says he did, I tried to just work hard when I was the only black person in the room; that's the important thing. It wasn't any odd-man out type of focus. You've got to have your eye on the goal, not on your idea of the barrier."

Anthony McGill was born on July 17, 1979 in Chicago. His mother, Ira, is a former dance therapist and art teacher who recently began an acting career. His father, Demarre McGill Sr., is a retired deputy commissioner with the Chicago Fire Department. McGill was raised in the middle-class Chatham neighborhood, on the South Side of Chicago, and showed a penchant for music at a young age. He was influenced by his older brother, Demarre Jr. (now the principal flutist of the San Diego Symphony), who would rise at 6 a.m. daily to practice playing his flute. "He was obsessed," McGill told Janelle Gelfand for the *Cincinnati Enquirer* (January 21, 2001, on-line). "I realized there was some kind of passion behind it." Demarre Sr. told Jason George, "My wife and I don't play any instruments but we wanted to expose our kids to everything: art, tennis, tae kwon do—the goal was to keep them busy. They just showed an uncanny ability to pick up music concepts."

In 1988 McGill was given the option of playing one of several instruments when officials from the MERIT (Music Education Reaching Instrumental Talents) program, which provides music lessons in Chicago-area public schools, arrived in his class at Poe Classical Elementary School, in the city's Pullman neighborhood. "I wanted to play a saxophone, but it was too big for me," McGill told Gelfand. "So I picked the clarinet. My dad was there, and he's like, OK we can do this. We went to a music store and rented the clarinet." Although learning the instrument was a challenge, McGill felt connected to it from the beginning. "It was a gradual process," he explained to Gelfand. "I didn't wake up one day and go, 'Eureka! I've got it.' But from the start, I felt like I really liked it."

When he was only 11, McGill joined the Chicago Youth Symphony, becoming its youngest member. Also at 11 he was awarded a scholarship to the eight-week summer camp of the Interlochen Arts Academy, in Michigan. There, he became principal clarinetist for the intermediate orchestra, a position that reinforced his passion for music. He told Gelfand, "I thought, maybe this is something I'm decent at. It's the first time I ever got those chills running down my back." When McGill was 12 his teacher in the MERIT program informed Alice Pfaelzer, the program's co-founder, that McGill had absorbed all that the teacher had to impart. Pfaelzer then took McGill to audition for the Chicago Symphony Orchestra's principal clarinetist, Larry Combs. Pfaelzer told Gelfand that McGill "played a little bit of the [Aaron] Copland Clarinet Concerto, and Larry was blown away." Combs took McGill on as a student.

In Chicago McGill attended the Whitney M. Young Magnet High School—First Lady Michelle Obama's alma mater—before becoming a full-time boarding student at the Interlochen Academy. After high school he attended the Curtis Institute of

Music, a competitive music school that his brother also attended. At the school McGill's teachers quickly recognized his ability. His clarinet instructor Donald Montanaro told Gelfand, "When I heard him play, I saw that he has natural gifts for music and a natural agility for the clarinet. The other thing that I always look for is intelligence. . . . From the outset I have felt he had all those gifts." McGill's playing style was influenced by his schooling. Gelfand wrote, "Curtis is one of the few schools that cultivates a specific style of wind playing, as well as the plush string sound identified with the Philadelphia Orchestra." "Anthony's playing is a good example of what I try to teach," Montanaro told Gelfand. "I like a bel canto—singing—style on the clarinet. I concentrate on expressiveness, tone quality, smooth playing, and homogeneity of sound." Even before his graduation from the Curtis Institute of Music, McGill gave a number of noteworthy performances. In 1998 he played with his brother and the pianist Grace Hsaio-Chung as part of a concert series held in Akron, Ohio, at the E. J. Thomas Hall. As an undergraduate McGill also performed with Music from Marlboro and the New York String Orchestra, both of which took him to New York City's famed Carnegie Hall.

McGill graduated from the Curtis Institute in 2000. That year—after only three auditions with other orchestras—he joined the Cincinnati Symphony Orchestra as associate principal clarinetist, beating out about 70 other clarinetists for the position and becoming only the third African-American in 105 years to be hired by the orchestra. He also became the sixth clarinetist in history to win the $15,000 Avery Fisher Career Grant, awarded by the Avery Fisher Artist Program. In December 2000 he played in the Ravinia Festival's Rising Star Series, held outside Chicago. His early performances with the Cincinnati orchestra and as a guest clarinetist were met with praise. Assessing a 2001 performance with the Baltimore Symphony Orchestra, Tim Smith wrote for the *Baltimore Sun* (June 25, 2001) that McGill's "finely polished technique, limpid tone and unfailingly eloquent phrasing caught the work's charm and poetic soul in equal measure." McGill's playing of a Copland concerto in 2004 with the Baltimore Symphony Orchestra was praised by Tom Huizenga, who wrote for the *Washington Post* (March 8, 2004) that "McGill made the music his own. Like a singer, he shaped each phrase as if the notes were written just for him. The piece was actually composed for Benny Goodman, but McGill's interpretation was far more expressive than Goodman's own rigid recording. . . . In the cadenza, linking the melancholy and jazzy movements, McGill swaggered, splashing Copland's notes like bright flecks of paint."

In 2004, after four years with the Cincinnati Symphony Orchestra, McGill joined New York's Metropolitan Opera Orchestra as principal clarinetist. Since then he has solidified his reputation as a distinguished solo, chamber, and orchestral musician. Reviewing a 2005 Curtis Institute of Music alumni recital series, Dobrin wrote, "McGill is mellow through and through. In André Messager's 'Solo de concours' especially, his sense of sound was highly polished, thoroughly refined. The way he matched pianist Reiko Uchida, note for plummy note, was an exercise in absolute sensitivity (not to mention dead-on intonation). What exactly is old-world about his sound is hard to pin down. But you hear this approach in early orchestral recordings and film scores. It has something to do with warmth."

As a member of the Metropolitan Opera Orchestra, McGill plays regularly in Carnegie Hall's Isaac Stern Auditorium and in the Zankel and Weill Halls with the Met Chamber Ensemble. He has performed at the Marlboro Music Festival, in Vermont; the Sarasota Festival, in Florida; La Musica International Chamber Music Festival, also in Sarasota; the Tanglewood Music Festival, in Lenox, Massachusetts; the Grand Teton Music Festival, in Jackson Hole, Wyoming; the Martha's Vineyard Chamber Music Festival, in Massachusetts; the Great Lakes Chamber Music Festival, in Southfield, Michigan; and the Bridgehampton Chamber Festival, in New York. He has appeared as a soloist with the symphony orchestras of Baltimore; New Jersey; and Hilton Head Island, in South Carolina. He has performed with the Guarneri, Tokyo, Shanghai, Miami, Brentano, Miro, Avalon, and Daedalus string quartets and at New York City's Lincoln Center as a member of Chamber Music Society Two. McGill has also toured Europe and Japan as part of a chamber ensemble that included the pianist Mitsuko Uchida and members of the Brentano String Quartet, and he is a member of the chamber-music group the Schumann Trio, whose other members are the violist Michael Tree and the pianist Anna Polonsky. McGill has been featured on National Public Radio's *Performance Today* and *St. Paul Sunday*, on the children's television show *Mr. Roger's Neighborhood*, and on *The Met: Live in HD* broadcasts from the Metropolitan Opera.

In December 2008 McGill received a call from Yo-Yo Ma's office, inviting him to join Ma for an upcoming performance. "The first call came out of the blue," McGill told Wynn Delacoma for the *Chicago Sun-Times* (January 18, 2009, on-line). "When Yo-Yo's manager called back and told me what the concert would be"—a performance at the presidential inauguration of Barack Obama—"at first I thought it was a joke." McGill had collaborated with Ma on a performance of Olivier Messiaen's "Quatuor pour la Fin du Temps" ("Quartet for the End of Time") in Japan eight years earlier, and Ma recalled McGill's performance when he was selecting musicians for the inaugural quartet. Ma told Wakin, "I was so struck just by [McGill's] artistry. I thought, 'Oh my gosh, I really want to play with him again.'" The quartet was rounded out by Itzhak Perlman on violin and Gabriela Montero on piano, with music by the Academy Award–winner John

Williams, best known for his soundtracks for popular films including *Jaws* (1975), *Star Wars* (1977), *E.T.* (1982), *Jurassic Park* (1993), and *Schindler's List* (1993). Williams's composition, "Air and Simple Gifts," was based on "Simple Gifts," a Shaker hymn written in the mid-1800s by Joseph Brackett and adopted in 1944 by the influential American composer Aaron Copland as part of his orchestral suite *Appalachian Spring*. Obama had asked Ma and Perlman to choose a composition and select musicians to accompany them; the two then asked Williams to provide original music. Aware that Obama enjoyed Copland's work, they chose the Shaker hymn as the centerpiece of the performance, with Williams providing musical bookends. "We wanted something that could reference America, the president-elect's fondness for Copland, something that's both uplifting and solemn, that traverses time but is also quintessentially American," Ma told Wakin. (As Jon Burlingame noted for *Variety* [January 15, 2009], with the performance of that piece, "a 56-year-old musical injustice [was] rectified"—a reference to the fact that a piece Copland had written for the 1953 inauguration of Dwight Eisenhower, "Lincoln's Portrait," was pulled at the last minute when a congressman from Illinois voiced concern over the composer's political leanings. That decision reflected the climate of anti-Communist hysteria created largely by the Wisconsin senator Joseph McCarthy, in which actors, musicians, and many other public figures were accused of having Communist ties. McCarthy was later censured by the U.S. Senate for his actions.)

On January 20, 2009, immediately prior to Obama's swearing-in as president, the quartet played the five-minute "Air and Simple Gifts" in front of 1.8 million people. Because of the cold weather, the musicians played—without amplification—along with a track they had recorded two days earlier. Ma told Wakin for the *New York Times* (January 22, 2009) that doing so was necessary because the cold could have led to broken piano strings, cracked instruments, or tuning problems. "It would have been a disaster if we had done it any other way," he said. "This occasion's got to be perfect. You can't have any slip-ups." Martin Steinberg, observing the performance for the Associated Press (January 20, 2009), wrote, "This warm melodic air—evoking a musical image of bald eagles soaring over America's terrain—cut through the chill of the 28-degree temperature that forced Montero to wear gloves. . . . In the face of the awesome tasks facing Obama, Williams' arrangement of the song conveys a joyous romp filled with confidence and hope."

According to a September 2009 post on his blog, McGill is working on a solo album. The next month he released an Apple iPhone/iTouch downloadable application called Clarinet in Reach, designed for clarinetists. The program includes fingering charts, instructional videos, and audio files; it was part of a collection of musical applications provided by the organization Music in Reach.

Along with his brother, McGill is among only a handful of African-American principal wind players in major orchestras. Wakin noted in his January 19, 2009 article that that is "a distinction noteworthy in a field with far fewer people of color than other areas of American life." While McGill has acknowledged the efforts of musicians who came before him to integrate orchestras racially, his primary interest is in music itself. He told Wakin, "If you're a musician, you play music."

—W.D.

Suggested Reading: anthonymcgill.com; *Chicago Tribune* (on-line) Jan. 20, 2009; *Cincinnati Enquirer* E p1 Jan. 21, 2001; *New York Times* (on-line) Jan. 19, 2009

Courtesy of NASA

McKay, Christopher P.

1954(?)– Planetary scientist; astrobiologist; astrogeophysicist

Address: NASA Ames Research Center, MS 2402, Moffett Field, CA 94035

"Life can be in places and do things you can't imagine," the planetary scientist Christopher P. McKay said to Michael Tennesen for *Discover* (July 1989). One of McKay's goals is the formulation of a precise definition of life, one that "can guide a search for life outside Earth," as he wrote for *PLoS Biology* (September 14, 2004, on-line). "With only one example of life—life on Earth—it is not all that surprising that we do not have a fundamental understanding of what life is," he noted. "We don't know which features of Earth life are essential and which are just accidents of history." McKay launched his career at the Space Science Division of the Ames Research Center, an arm of the National Aeronautics and Space Administration (NASA), in 1982, the year he earned his doctoral degree, and he has worked there ever since. His specialties are astrobiology, the study of life in the universe, and astrogeophysics, the study of the physical processes that occur on planets other than Earth and those of the solar system's many moons. His main research interests include the origins of life on Earth and how it evolved; the possible existence of life on Mars when the solar system was much younger; and the properties of highly unusual microbial species called extremophiles, which flourish in earthly environments that are extraordinarily harsh and would quickly kill other creatures: places that are extremely cold, hot, dry, acidic, alkaline, salty, or radioactive, for example, or that appear to be devoid of nourishment.

The air on Mars, the fourth planet from the sun (Earth is third), is mostly carbon dioxide, and it is less than one percent as dense as the air on Earth; in addition, for much of the Martian year, the surface of the planet is frozen, its temperature far below zero. Such an environment would not be conducive to survival for the vast majority of living organisms found on Earth. Mars does not appear to harbor living organisms, but the discovery a few decades ago of extremophiles has led scientists to hypothesize that billions of years ago, the red planet, as it is called (Mars looks reddish in the night sky), might have hosted organisms impervious to conditions that are intolerably harsh for most forms of life on Earth. To understand how extremophiles survive, and how similarly hardy organisms on Mars might have survived, McKay has studied various extremophile species in their Mars-like natural habitats, including the driest desert on Earth (the Atacama, in Chile) and the coldest places on Earth (parts of Siberia, in Russia; the Canadian Arctic; and Antarctica). McKay is a leading proponent of a process known as terraforming: altering an environment, in this case that of Mars, so that it can sustain life. McKay believes that warming Mars and changing the density and composition of its air could restore its biosphere. "Mars lived fast, died young and left a beautiful body," he said during the seven-part "Great Terraforming Debate," posted on *Astrobiology Magazine* (June 14, 2004, on-line), a NASA publication. "We could . . . just ignore it, or we could do something better and bring it back to life. Mars is beautiful the way it is, but I think it would be even better if we could restore the biosphere that it once had. . . . In other words, give Mars back its heartbeat." McKay also said in that debate, "I'm not proposing to send life from Earth there. That's only the last resort. If Mars has no genome, then we could share ours with it. But I personally think that a Mars full of Martians is much more interesting than Mars full of Earthlings."

McKay is also an expert on Titan, the largest of the many moons of the planet Saturn, and he has worked with scientists on the building of, and interpretation of data from, the Cassini-Huygens probe, which passed through Titan's atmosphere in early 2005. For the past five years, he has participated in NASA's Robotic Lunar Exploration Program, which aims to put astronauts on Earth's moon by 2020. He is also a co-investigator on two NASA projects: the first, the Phoenix Mars Mission, landed an instrument-laden robotic spacecraft on the surface of Mars in 2008 and, three months later, found evidence of frozen water there. The second, the Mars Science Laboratory Rover Mission, is slated for a launch in 2011. The rover will explore its surroundings to determine whether the environment was once hospitable to microbial life. "I'm primarily interested in this work because I think one of the primary questions is, 'Are we alone?,'" McKay told Rosanne Spector for the *Chicago Tribune* (July 7, 1991). "And for me, 'we' is anything living. . . . We're all related to the same primordial mother."

Christopher P. McKay was born in about 1954 and raised in Florida. He has recalled playing in orange groves with his sister and seven brothers. His interest in science dates from his childhood. "I got a chemistry set one Christmas, and I read a lot of science books," he told Pamela S. Turner for her book *Life on Earth—and Beyond: An Astrobiologist's Quest* (2008). He was also mechanically inclined; after he acquired his own motorcycle, he completely disassembled it, removing every bolt and even taking apart each gasket, and then reconstructed it. McKay told an interviewer for spiked-online.com that the late-1960s TV series *Star Trek* inspired him, because it propounded the idea that "science could lead to a positive future and that there were great things still to do—great voyages of discovery waiting to be made. I was determined to help make that future real, and to participate in those great discoveries. It was all too easy to be disenchanted with science, at a time when the future looked grim and science was often blamed. Science had given us atomic weapons, chemical pollution and dwindling ozone. Science was not the hero of the bright new future, it was the villain. But *Star Trek* imagined that the future could be bright—that science and technology could be used to create a positive and humane future." In high school McKay enrolled in every science course available to him, and physics proved to be his favorite. "In physics there were just a few basic concepts you could apply over and over again," he told Turner. "But I hated marine biology. There were too many facts you had to memorize, like the name of this or that squid."

After high school McKay attended Florida Atlantic University (FAU), which has campuses in Boca Raton, Fort Lauderdale, and five other locations. He majored in physics and mechanical engineering. By chance he found a neglected telescope in a laboratory closet; after he repaired it, he took up stargazing. While at FAU, using instructions in books, he built his own telescope. "I was amazed you could take sand and two pieces of glass and make all the lenses you need for a telescope," he recalled to Turner. McKay earned a bachelor's degree in 1976.

That year McKay enrolled in the graduate program in astrophysics at the University of Colorado (CU) at Boulder, a school prominent in that field. The year 1976 also marked the end of the voyage of the NASA spacecraft *Viking 2* to Mars. The orbiters of that craft and its sister craft, *Viking 1* (which had arrived at its destination in 1975), sent back to Earth thousands of photographs of Mars's surface, and they transmitted to Earth the information gathered by the two *Viking* landers, whose instruments examined materials on the surface of Mars and gases in its air. The photos showed canyons, volcanoes, and craters, while the equipment on the landers detected molecules of carbon dioxide (CO_2,) water (H_2O), and nitrogen (N_2) in the atmosphere but no evidence of organic molecules (which, on Earth, contain carbon–hydrogen bonds and are present in all living organisms). "The results were most mysterious to me," McKay said, as quoted on a NASA Web site. "Here was a planet with all the elements needed to support life (CO_2, H_2O, N_2) present in its atmosphere, with evidence of liquid water in the past and yet there was no sign of life. It seems like Mars had 'the lights on but nobody home.' I slowly became more and more interested in life and how it originates, survives, and changes a planet." He has traced his fascination with astrobiology to the *Vikings*' discoveries.

McKay soon met other CU–Boulder students who shared his interest in the Martian landscape and atmosphere. They agreed that NASA should consider terraforming Mars and sending astronauts to the planet to explore it firsthand, and they decided to petition CU–Boulder administrators to offer a course to examine that idea. Inspired by the book *Project Icarus* (1968), whose authors, students at the Massachusetts Institute of Technology (MIT), described a class at MIT devoted to the feasibility of deflecting an asteroid on a collision course with Earth, McKay spearheaded the initiative and helped to organize the course. "Due to bureaucratic issues, which I no longer remember, I was actually listed as the instructor of this class," he said during an interview posted on the Web site of the Mars Society, "and at the first class meeting we had more than 20 students. In addition to terraforming Mars we also considered human exploration as a step toward terraforming." Some of the students—whom a journalist dubbed the "Mars underground"—organized a conference to discuss the possibility of sending humans to Mars. Called "The Case for Mars" and held in 1981, the conference was a great success. "We were stunned so many people came," McKay told Turner. "We had real scientists come, people from NASA." *Case for Mars* (1984), edited by Penelope J. Boston, contains papers presented at the conference. In the next decade and a half, five more "Case for Mars" conferences were held.

Earlier, in the summer of 1980, McKay had worked as a NASA planetary-biology intern at the Ames Research Center, at Moffett Field, in Sunnyvale, California. He was guided by James B. "Jim" Pollack, a world-renowned planetary scientist, and became acquainted with Imre Friedmann, a Florida State University biologist who also worked at Ames and whose interests included astrobiology and extremophiles. Through Friedmann, McKay joined a team of scientists associated with Florida State University's Cryptoendolithic Microbial Ecology Research Project. The scientists were studying microbes in the Dry Valleys of Antarctica, a region with unusual biological, chemical, and physical characteristics. McKay's job was to build sensors that monitored rock formations' temperature, light, moisture, and other features. His work involving microbes that flourished in an environment usually described as hostile to life led him to think about the possibility that living organisms might live or have lived in an environment even more extreme: that of Mars. When the internship ended McKay returned to CU–Boulder and completed his dissertation. Entitled "Photochemical-Thermal Model of Hydrogen and Oxygen in the Summer Mesosphere and Implications for Noctilucent Cloud Formation," it was about the formation of a type of cloud that has been detected only in the mesosphere (the third of the five layers of Earth's atmosphere), about 30 to 50 miles above Earth's surface. McKay earned a Ph.D. in astrogeophysics in 1982, and that year he joined the Ames Center as a full-time research scientist.

In collaboration with the biologist Robert Wharton, McKay began to study the mechanisms through which microorganisms survive in frozen Arctic lakes; working with Wharton, he became a research diver for NASA's Antarctic Lakes Project. One of the project's main goals was to identify the chemical "signatures" left by dead microorganisms embedded in sediment (particles of matter that have been carried by water and then deposited), the longer-term aim of which was to develop a means for future NASA explorations of Mars to find evidence of life there—not existing life, as had been attempted earlier, but extinct forms of life. From 1990 to 1991 McKay was a member of a team looking for frozen bacteria in Siberia. The scientists dug 150 feet into the arctic permafrost—permanently frozen soil, sediment, and rock—and removed chunks of material to test for life. They discovered bacteria that could be revived after having remained in a frozen state for three million years. "It may be possible that bacteria frozen into the permafrost at the Martian south pole may be viable," McKay later said, as quoted by Vincent Kiernan in *New Scientist* (March 5, 1994).

In an article titled "Making Mars Habitable," published in *Nature* (August 8, 1991), McKay, Owen B. Toon, and James F. Kasting discussed the possibility of terraforming the red planet. The scientists suggested that "planetary engineering" could alter Mars's environment to make it hospitable to humans. Paraphrasing their argument, Robert Cooke wrote for *Newsday* (August 8, 1991), "Terraforming the planet breaks down naturally into two steps: warming the planet, and altering its chemical state. Warming could be linked to an artificial greenhouse effect. If the temperature of the Martian surface were increased, say, by warming the poles with giant mirrors, or by spreading black soot over the polar caps, or by introducing greenhouse gases, then the amount of carbon dioxide and water vapor in the atmosphere would also increase."

McKay was a member of the National Geographic Society's expedition to the Gobi Desert of Mongolia in 1991–92 and of the NASA/United States Geographical Survey Expedition into the Lechuguilla Cave in Carlsbad Caverns National Park, in New Mexico, in 1994–95. The cave—the fifth-longest on Earth and the deepest in the continental U.S.—is of particular interest because, in the absence of any outside sources of energy, virtually no plants or fungi live there (except near the entrance); the bacteria that live in the cave thrive on sulfur, iron, and manganese—three of the 10 most abundant elements in Martian soil. "On Mars, if life has survived it has to be deep underground," McKay told Eduardo Montes for the Associated Press (April 18, 1994). McKay joined the 1995–96 McGill University expedition to Axel Heiberg Island, in the Canadian Arctic, and the 1994, 1995, and 1997 NASA expeditions to the Atacama Desert. Because of its extreme dryness, the Atacama Desert resembles Mars more closely than any other locality on Earth. On parts of the Atacama, no rain has ever been recorded; parts of it harbor virtually no life, and in others, the scant flora and fauna—most species of which live nowhere else in the world—exhibit highly unusual survival mechanisms. In 2005, by means of a mobile robot of the sort that could be used on Mars, McKay and his coworkers detected microbes in the soil of Atacama.

In 1998, at Pavilion Lake, in British Columbia, Canada, McKay and another NASA team studied rocklike mounds known as microbialites: assemblages of microbes and sedimentary particles and chemicals. Most of the few microbialites that have been discovered on Earth are fossilized forms of the widespread accretions of once-living organisms and inorganic materials that thrived on Earth one billion to two billion years ago. By studying the Pavilion Lake's modern-day analogues of those ancient specimens, scientists may be able to figure out ways to recognize microbial fossils on Mars. McKay and seven of his colleagues described their studies of Pavilion Lake microbialites in the October 5, 2000 issue of *Nature*.

In 2003, at a meeting of the American Astronomical Society's Division for Planetary Sciences, McKay presented a paper in which he proposed that billions of years ago, a "second genesis" had occurred on Mars, in which life forms whose proteins, DNA, and genes were vastly different from those that evolved on Earth had developed. In 2004 he participated in the Astrobiology Science Conference, organized by *Astrobiology Magazine*, the SciFi Museum in Seattle, Washington, and Breakpoint Media. During the conference he discussed the ethical implications of altering Mars, taking the view that humans have an obligation to restore Mars to its formerly hospitable state—even if terraforming the planet for human habitation is unlikely to happen anytime soon. "Human beings are a particular subset of life that require particular conditions," McKay said, as quoted by *Space Daily* (June 18, 2004). "And it turns out oxygen in particular is very hard to make on Mars. That is, I think, beyond our technological horizons—it's a long time in the future. But warming Mars up, and restoring its thick carbon dioxide atmosphere, restoring its habitable state, is possible." Arguing that Mars was once a living planet, McKay said, "We see that distinction for the first time when we look beyond the Earth, when we look at the moon. There's nature; there's no life. When we look at Mars, we also see nature, probably no life. It's different from the moon, and we lack the word that distinguishes between something that's dead, and something that was never alive. The moon was never alive. Mars is dead. The question in my mind is—should we bring it back to life? Well, I vote for life." McKay also advocates allowing any life found on Mars to exist without human interference. He told Jim Gilchrist for the *Scotsman* (August 3, 2001), "We should be intellectually prepared to face this issue and to defer to the indigenous Martians—however microscopic—and even assist them in regaining biological control of their planet. We will be the better for this, in both ethical and scientific terms." McKay has written or co-written articles about ethical issues regarding Mars for publications including *Scientific American* (December 1990), the *Journal of the Irish Colleges of Physicians and Surgeons* (Volume 22, Number 1, 1993), and the *Planetary Report* (July/August 2001); his essay "Does Mars Have Rights? An Approach to the Environmental Ethics of Planetary Engineering" is included in the book *Moral Expertise: Studies in Practical and Professional Ethics* (1990), edited by Don MacNiven.

McKay has been involved with research regarding Earth's moon since 2004, when NASA announced that it had assigned management of its Robotic Lunar Exploration Program to the Ames Research Center. Components of the program are the design and construction of a new spaceship, a voyage of astronauts to the moon by 2020, and the construction of a NASA base on the moon. "An exploration science program with a sustained human presence on the moon gives us the opportunity to conduct fundamental science in lunar geology, history of the solar system, physics, and the biological response to partial (Earth) gravity," McKay told *Space Daily* (November 21, 2005).

McKay has proposed sending seeds to Mars and Earth's moon to test plants' responses to conditions on those bodies. A robotic lander would transport seeds from the plant *Arabidopsis thaliana* (a member of the mustard family, which includes cabbages and radishes, that is often used in plant research) in a growth module (a miniature greenhouse). Soil from the Martian or lunar surface would then be added, and instruments in the module would monitor the plants' progress. The seeds would have been genetically modified so that the plants would glow in different colors if they were suffering in particular ways, to alert those monitoring them of trouble. McKay and the University of Florida plant biologist Robert Ferl presented those proposals at a meeting of lunar scientists held at the Ames Center in July 2008. McKay told Richard Macery for the Sydney (Australia) *Morning Herald* (April 6, 2002) that a plant growing on the moon or on Mars would be both "a true biological pioneer" and a "powerful symbol of the long-term vision of life expanding beyond the Earth."

McKay has edited or co-edited several books; the most recent is *Comets and the Origin and Evolution of Life* (2006). He sits on the board of the nonprofit Planetary Society, whose members include astronauts, scientists, engineers, and lay space enthusiasts. The society's mission is to advance the human understanding of space. McKay serves on the U.S. Committee for the International Permafrost Association and as an assistant editor of the journal *Planetary and Space Science.* He has won the Kuiper Award, from the Division of Planetary Sciences of the American Astronomical Society, and the Ames Honor Award, from NASA.

—W.D.

Suggested Reading: Mars Society (on-line) June 2000; *Scotsman* p4 Aug. 3, 2001; *Space Daily* June 18, 2004; Space Science and Astrobiology Division, NASA Ames Research Center (on-line); Turner, Pamela S. *Life on Earth—and Beyond: An Astrobiologist's Quest*, 2008

Selected Books: as editor or co-editor—*Case for Mars II*, 1985; *From Antarctica to Outer Space: Life in Isolation and Confinement* (with Albert A. Harrison and Yvonne A. Clearwater), 1991; *Comets and the Origin of Life* (with Paul J. Thomas and Christopher F. Chyba), 1996; *Earth's Climate: The Ocean-atmosphere Interaction: from Basin to Global Scales* (with Chunzai Wang, Mark A. S. McMenamin, and Linda Sohl), 2004; *Comets and the Origin and Evolution of Life* (with Paul J. Thomas, Roland D. Hicks, and Christopher F. Chyba), 2006

McLachlin, Beverley

Sep. 7, 1943– Chief justice of the Supreme Court of Canada

Address: Supreme Court of Canada, 301 Wellington St., Ottawa, Ontario K1A OJ1, Canada

Courtesy of Gervásio Baptista/ABR

"The fact that I am in this seat today is more than anything else a testament to the justice of Canadian society—a society where people without money or connections or the usual gender for a certain job will be allowed to do it, and having done it, will be allowed to succeed." Those words, quoted in the *Hamilton (Ontario, Canada) Spectator* (January 19, 2000), were spoken by Beverley McLachlin in 2000, when she became the first woman to be named chief justice of the Supreme Court of Canada. A lawyer and university professor before she became a Vancouver County Court judge in the province of British Columbia, in 1981, McLachlin has served on every level of the Canadian court system. In 1989 then–Prime Minister Brian Mulroney named her to the Supreme Court, making her, at the age of 45, one of the youngest appointees in that court's history. "When I was sworn in at the Supreme Court of Canada, the leader of the Law Society of British Columbia . . . amused everyone by saying that I made it through the court system faster than most cases," she told the New York University School of Law professor Joseph H. H. Weiler in an interview available on the school's Web site (March 29, 2004). By all accounts down-to-earth, McLachlin—who often refers to herself as a "farm girl" from Alberta, Canada—is the first woman to be a full professor on the University of British Columbia faculty of law; the first woman appointed to the British Columbia Court of Appeal; the first woman to be chief justice of the British Columbia Supreme Court; and the third woman to sit on the federal Supreme Court. "She is somebody who does not and will not be fit into preconceived stereotypes," Errol Mendes, a law professor and director of the Human Rights Centre at the University of Ottawa, told Kirk Makin for the Toronto, Canada, *Globe and Mail* (November 4, 1999). "With the Supreme Court being the final arbiter on so many fundamental issues facing the country, it needs someone like that as its head who resists being classified into artificial categories." According to C. Lynn Smith, who wrote an essay on McLachlin for the book *Women in Law: a Bio-Bibliographical Sourcebook* (1996), edited by Rebecca Mae Salokar and Mary L. Volcansek, McLachlin "has written some of the most significant judgments in Canadian law. . . . Her influence stems from the strength of her judicial approach, which combines rigorous analysis and logic with open-mindedness and an understanding of the social context in which legal problems are embedded, and from her enormous productivity."

McLachlin is known for her ability to write clear, concise judgments as well as for her prolific writing output. She has been called a libertarian, in the sense that she is seen as a strong defender of individual rights and freedoms. An independent thinker, she has often been a dissenter in court decisions, unafraid to take unpopular positions and make controversial judgments, such as a 1991 decision striking down parts of the "rape-shield law" and thus allowing a woman's sexual history to be used as evidence in a sexual-assault case, or a 1992 decision striking down a "hate" law that prohibited the "spread of false news," which had been used to convict Holocaust deniers. On the other hand, she has been described as a strong defender of rights for minorities and the disadvantaged, including women, indigenous peoples, and gays. "To perform their modern role well, judges must be sensitive to a broad range of social concerns," McLachlin wrote in "The Role of Judges in Modern Commonwealth Society," published in *Law Quarterly Review* (1994), as quoted by Smith. "They must possess a keen appreciation of the importance of individual and group interests and rights. And they must be in touch with the society in which they work, understanding its values and tensions. The ivory tower no longer suffices as the residence of choice for judges."

McLachlin assumed leadership of the court at a significant moment in its history, after it had sustained years of political attacks from conservative critics who called it overly intrusive and activist. After the country's constitution was amended in 1982 to include the liberal Charter of Rights and Freedoms, the court, first under Chief Justice Brian Dickson and then under his immediate successor, Antonio Lamer, was seen by some as pushing the limits of judicial powers to interpret the charter as a vehicle for social change, especially with regard to such hot-button social issues as abortion, gay rights, aboriginal treaties, minority rights, and the rights of the accused. By contrast, as Christopher Manfredi, a political scientist at McGill University, told Julian Beltrame for *Maclean's* (May 20, 2002), "McLachlin's agenda is protecting and preserving the court's reputation from political attack." Makin noted for the *Globe and Mail* (January 8, 2005) that McLachlin "moved on several fronts to enhance the court's credibility, beginning with the size and scope of its rulings. A bench once known for issuing rambling treatises was soon issuing short, crisp opinions that left less room for misinterpretation." Eugene Meehan, who was then president of the Canadian Bar Association, told Bruce Wallace for *Maclean's* (November 15, 1999) about McLachlin, "Though quiet and quietly spoken, she has a fire for the law that'd burn through the pouring rain."

One of five children in what she described to Weiler as a "happy and very busy family," McLachlin was born Beverley Gietz on September 7, 1943 in Pincher Creek, a small farming town in southwestern Alberta, about 200 kilometers (about 124 miles) from Calgary—and just north of the Montana border. Her parents, Ernest Gietz and Eleanora Kruschell, were ranchers who also had a lumber business. "We didn't have much money," she said, as quoted by David R. Calhoun in *Encyclopedia Britannica* (on-line). "We struggled, but we lived on land we loved and, like so many Canadian farm families, we did whatever was required to make a living from it." As a result, she told Weiler, she developed "a strong sense of a connection between people and place. Understanding that is important to the law." McLachlin has often attributed her work ethic and practicality to her modest farming roots and has said that she developed her intellectual curiosity and passion for reading and learning with the help of a small, community-run library. Another factor that shaped McLachlin's outlook was that Pincher Creek was near both Christian and aboriginal communities. "I remember being confronted with human rights issues even when they weren't a big thing, back in the 1950s," she told an interviewer for the Web site of the Canadian Council on Learning (April 3, 2008).

After she enrolled at the University of Alberta, in Edmonton, in 1960, McLachlin studied modern languages and thought about becoming a journalist before switching her major to philosophy. "It helped me learn to order my ideas better, because philosophy is insistent on approaching things in an analytical, logical way," she told Susan Harada for an extensive profile of her in the *Walrus* magazine (May 2009, on-line). "You have to be able to defend or analytically attack a position, and you have to be able to set out either process in clear terms that other people can understand." She earned a B.A. degree with honors in 1965 and was set to begin graduate work in philosophy at Cornell University, but over the summer she began to second-guess her decision. "I thought that perhaps I would like to do something a little more hands-on, a little more involved with people and society . . . ," she told Weiler. "I sent a letter into the [University of Alberta] law school just asking for information about applying. . . . The dean wrote back to me and said, 'You are admitted.' It was a much simpler world in those days." McLachlin received a master's degree in legal philosophy at the same time that she earned her law degree, writing a thesis titled "The Roles of Rules in the Concept of Law." She graduated from the University of Alberta in 1968, winning the gold medal as top student.

McLachlin was called to the Alberta bar in 1969 and to the British Columbia bar in 1971. She practiced litigation with Wood, Moir, Hyde and Ross in Edmonton from 1969 to 1971, when she moved with her husband, Roderick "Rory" McLachlin, a biologist, to Fort St. John, British Columbia, where she joined the firm of Thomas, Herdy, Mitchell & Co. for a year. In 1972 the couple moved to Vancouver, where she practiced law with Bull, Housser, and Tupper until 1975. That year she began lecturing as an associate professor of law at the University of British Columbia, in the areas of evidence, civil litigation, and creditors' remedies. She stayed there for five years and had earned full professorship and tenure when, in 1981, she was appointed as a judge on the County Court of Vancouver, beginning what Harada called a "meteoric rise [that] attracted national attention." McLachlin told Weiler, "I think I got carried along in this huge *crise de conscience*—'we have no women judges, what are we going to do about it?' And there was one that looked not too bad so they pushed me up very quickly." She spent roughly three months on the County Court before moving that same year up to the Supreme Court of British Columbia, on which she served for four years as a trial judge. In 1985 she was appointed to the Court of Appeal of British Columbia, where she spent three years before returning to the Supreme Court of British Columbia as chief justice, in 1988. Shortly after that appointment her husband died of throat cancer. About six months into her tenure as head of the British Columbia Supreme Court, a vacancy opened up on the Supreme Court of Canada, and on March 30, 1989 Prime Minister Brian Mulroney, who wanted a candidate from the western provinces to fill the post, appointed her to the top court in the country. At 45, she was one of the youngest Supreme Court justices in Canada's history and only the third female judge on the nine-person court (along with Bertha Wilson and Claire L'Heureux-Dubé).

On Chief Justice Antonio Lamer's court (1990–2000), McLachlin quickly proved to be an independent thinker who expressed herself clearly and strongly supported individual freedoms and equal rights. She was also seen as a frequent dissenter from the majority who was unafraid to make controversial—and often unpopular—rulings. In 1990, for example, she wrote a strong dissent in the landmark case against James Keegstra, a high-school teacher who had told his students that the Holocaust had not occurred. While the majority ruled that, because Keegstra was in effect a hate-monger, he was not entitled to constitutional free-speech protections, McLachlin argued that the law targeting hate propaganda was vague and overly broad and could potentially be used in the future to target reasonable speech. "Attempts to confine the guarantee of free expression only to content which is judged to possess redeeming value or to accord with the accepted values strike at the very essence of the value of freedom, reducing the realm of protected discussion to that which is comfortable and compatible with current conceptions," McLachlin wrote for herself and the other three dissenters, as quoted by Don Butler in the *Ottawa Citizen* (February 28, 2009). In 1991 she made another controversial ruling when she wrote for the majority in *R v. Seaboyer*, striking down the "rape-shield" law, which had restricted the amount of evidence about the victim's sexual past that could be admitted in a rape case. Although her decision infuriated feminists, who accused her of betraying women, McLachlin felt that the law excluded even potentially relevant evidence about a given victim's sexual past and thus denied the accused a fair trial. While she defended her position, she told Julian Beltrame for *Maclean's* (May 20, 2002) that it was "not easy finding oneself criticized for betraying the cause." She did, on the other hand, dissent against the majority—and in favor of women's rights—in other landmark cases; in one, the court found that child-care costs are not tax-deductible, and in another it ruled against a mother's attempt to avoid paying taxes on child-support payments. McLachlin has said that perhaps the most difficult yet rewarding case she has worked on was the one resulting in the unanimous 1998 ruling on whether the francophone province of Quebec could secede from Canada. While the constitution did not address the issue directly, it implied that such action was unlawful. In order to avoid dividing the country further, however, the judges cited principles of democracy not explicitly referred to in the constitution in ruling that Quebec could secede, but only if a majority of people in the province voted to do so in a referendum. Other important decisions included one in which she wrote the unanimous opinion that the justice system was plagued by racism and that greater screening of jurors was needed to exclude the prejudiced.

By the time Chief Justice Lamer announced his retirement, in 1999, conservative critics were charging that the court had become activist and politicized and were calling for reform. Thus Prime Minister Jean Chrétien made a popular decision when he named McLachlin as the 17th chief justice of the Supreme Court, with her gender, her background in western Canada (where conservatives enjoyed their biggest base), and her reputation for moderation making her the top candidate. The mandatory age for her retirement from the Supreme Court is 75. In assuming her post, on January 7, 2000, McLachlin listed her main priorities, which included reaching out to and educating the public about the role of the court, building consensus among the justices, and engaging in a "dialogue" with Parliament—in order to calm the debate and end the damaging accusation of politicization and activism without compromising the court's role as an important institution in a democratic society.

McLachlin's court developed a reputation as being more centrist, cautious, pragmatic, and difficult to pin down ideologically than her predecessors', and, according to Beltrame, "more deferential to Parliament and less open to charges of judicial activism." Beltrame added that McLachlin's "influence in terms of getting unanimity is already being noted. That may sound dull, even typically Canadian in the quest of a consensus in the middle, but it also suggests McLachlin could be coaxing the court back in line with public opinion. And that could, in a quiet way, be a notable legacy in its own right." Calls for reform of the court have generally subsided during McLachlin's tenure. That is in part because her predecessors' tenures coincided with the years after the Charter of Rights and Freedoms was adopted, a period in which many cases involved controversial social issues. During McLachlin's tenure as chief justice, as the court has already dealt with some of the most contentious issues, the types of cases have been somewhat different, involving, for example, issues related to technology. The McLachlin court has had to adjudicate terrorism laws, however, and in 2009 McLachlin made headlines when she spoke out against what she saw as the excesses of some government counterterrorism policies. "The fear and anger that terrorism produces may cause leaders to make war on targets that may or may not be connected with the terrorist incident," she told the Ottawa Women's Canadian Club, as quoted by Janice Tibbetts for the Canwest News Service (September 22, 2009). "Or perhaps it may lead governments to curtail civil liberties and seek recourse in tactics they might otherwise deplore . . . that may not, in the clearer light of retrospect, be necessary or defensible."

Earlier, in 2007, the McLachlin Court entered controversial territory, when it overturned an Ontario Court of Appeal decision that had thrown out the convictions of two men found with loaded handguns outside a strip club. In 1999, responding to a call about men with guns in the parking lot of the club, police had set up a roadblock to stop people from leaving the premises. When Wendell Clayton and Troy Farmer were stopped, and loaded guns were found in their car, they were arrested. Each man was convicted of unlawfully carrying a concealed weapon and possessing a loaded and prohibited firearm. But since their car did not fit the description given in the call to police, and since the roadblock was deemed unjustified because the situation was not seen as one of imminent danger, an Ontario Court of Appeal overturned the convictions and acquitted the men, arguing that the police had gone beyond their legal powers and had infringed on citizens' rights. In a decision that some critics saw as broadening police powers to conduct random searches and spot checks at the expense of individual liberties, the McLachlin Court unanimously restored the convictions, saying that the roadblock was an adequate response to a serious threat to public safety. Although all nine judges agreed that the convictions should be restored, there were differences of opinion among them. Six judges, including McLachlin, argued that the police conduct should be seen in context, and that the officers responded to a legitimate threat to public safety in a "fast-paced situation." The three other judges made the argument that the officers' actions constituted a "justifiable infringement" on the charter.

Still, McLachlin remains overall a staunch defender of the charter and of its progressive role in society. In a speech in Halifax in 2003, as quoted by the *Globe and Mail* (March 7, 2003), McLachlin shared her thoughts on the role of the law in society: "Canada's record on the treatment of Aboriginal Peoples, racial minorities and women—not to mention gays and lesbians—teaches us that notwithstanding our nation's foundation in the ethic of tolerance and accommodation, we are not immune from the evils of exclusionary thinking. . . . Since the Second World War and the international acknowledgement of the equal worth of all and the concomitant right to equal treatment, Canada has moved more quickly than many other countries to a more inclusionary, respectful model of society. The law, while not the entire answer, has played a pivotal role in this progression. . . . The adoption of the Charter of Rights and Freedoms in 1982 elevated the basic human rights, aboriginal rights and equality to the status of supreme law, against which all government actions and legislation must be assessed. The Charter stands as Canada's ultimate expression of our commitment to freedom and human dignity. . . . Yet the Charter is more than a litigation tool or a lawyer's text. A glance at our newspapers shows the extent to which the Charter, and the values and principles it embodies, have been internalized by Canadians. . . . Inclusion and equality cannot be achieved by mere rights. But when the rights reflect a nation's values and are accepted as a means of brokering our differences and finding accommodation, they take on profound importance."

McLachlin has been awarded numerous honorary degrees and distinctions, which include being named commander of the French Legion of Honor. She has co-written two books on legal procedure and has also written two unpublished novels (according to Beltrame, one is a mystery novel, the other a work of historical fiction). She is married to Frank McArdle, a lawyer and the former executive director of the Canadian Institute for Advanced Legal Studies. McLachlin has a son, Angus, from her first marriage.

—M.M.

Suggested Reading: *Hamilton (Ontario, Canada) Spectator* A p13 Jan. 19, 2000; *Maclean's* p28 May 20, 2002; New York University School of Law Web site Mar. 29, 2004; (Toronto, Canada) *Globe and Mail* A p1 Nov. 4, 1999, (on-line) Jan. 8, 2005; *Walrus* (on-line) May 2009; Salokar, Rebecca Mae, and Mary L. Volcansek. *Women in Law: a Bio-Bibliographical Sourcebook*, 1996

Andrew H. Walker/Getty Images

Meyers, Seth

Dec. 28, 1973– Comic actor; television scriptwriter

Address: Saturday Night Live, *30 Rockefeller Plaza, New York, NY 10112*

The current head writer for NBC's long-running sketch-comedy series *Saturday Night Live* (*SNL*), Seth Meyers is better known for his impressions on the show of John Kerry, Michael Caine, Ryan Seacrest, Anderson Cooper, Carrot Top, Prince Charles, Sean Penn, and other famous people. Since 2006 he has been head writer and anchor of *SNL*'s popular Weekend Update segment—alongside his good friend Amy Poehler and, since Poehler left the show, in late 2008, as a solo act. Meyers, now in his ninth season with *SNL*, has been a force behind the show's resurgence as a major late-night television draw. In 2008 he guided the show through one of the most talked-about periods in its 34-year history, which owed much to that year's presidential campaigns. Drawing heavily on a colorful cast of real-life political figures, the show's fall 2008 installments were highlighted by the *SNL* alumna and former head writer Tina Fey's dead-on impressions of the Republican vice-presidential nominee, Sarah Palin. (Palin herself made a guest appearance on the show several weeks prior to the November election.) Thanks to the Palin sketches, all but one of them written by Meyers, and other high-profile guest appearances—by the likes of the Olympic gold-medalist Michael Phelps and the Republican presidential nominee, John McCain—*Saturday Night Live* enjoyed its highest ratings in years, with viewership up as much as 46 percent from a year earlier. The fall of 2008 saw the airing of an unprecedented 10 shows in eight weeks, which helped create what pundits cited as "the *SNL* effect": according to the national public-opinion survey FirstView, 10 percent of voters were influenced by *SNL* skits. Meyers explained to Maureen Ryan for the *Chicago Tribune* (October 18, 2008), "People love elections because they're contests. I don't know if you've noticed—on TV now, there's lots of contests." He added, "We're sort of the *Meet the Press* of comedy shows; we sort of wrap up the week's events." In addition to his work on *SNL*, Meyers has ventured into the film world: in 2006 he appeared in Paul Weitz's *American Dreamz*, a satire of both the television show *American Idol* and the George W. Bush administration, and in 2008 he starred alongside Brendan Fraser in the 3-D film *Journey to the Center of the Earth*, inspired by Jules Verne's classic 19th-century novel of the same name. A writer observed for *Salon.com* (November 20, 2008), "Boy, does Seth Meyers set our inner geek aflame. Toothy and slightly gangly, he looks—and sounds, when his voice cracks—like that funny but shy kid in high school we secretly crushed on and now wonder about, wishing we had crashed his Dungeons & Dragons club or sidled up to him at a school dance, complimenting him on his skinny tie or yellow high tops. . . . As a performer, he's not the alpha dog of *SNL* stars past, but he has an endearing, crafted wit. . . . And on a show of often oversize personalities, he's the low-key presence that grounds it all, the guy we ultimately want to laugh along with."

Seth Adam Meyers was born on December 28, 1973 in Bedford, New Hampshire, to Larry Meyers, a business executive, and Hilary Meyers, a high-school French teacher. His younger brother, Josh, has been a regular cast member on Fox's television sketch-comedy series *MADtv* and played a recurring character on the sitcom *That 70s Show*. "I was in no way a high school stud," Meyers recalled to Alison Prato for *Page Six* (December 14, 2008, on-line), published by the *New York Post*. "But from a young age, I realized being able to make people laugh was a valuable tool." In an article for the *Boston Globe* (January 25, 2004), Janice Page noted about Meyers and his fellow New England natives and *SNL* performers Poehler and Rachel Dratch that they were not class clowns as much as "the kids at the back of the class muttering witty asides." Meyers told Page, "I think all of us have a sharper humor that comes from commenting on what's happening rather than being the actual happening. It's that sort of wry New England sense of pointing out anyone who's trying to make a big deal of himself." After graduating from West High School, in Manchester, New Hampshire, in 1992, Meyers enrolled at Northwestern University, in Evanston, Illinois, where he majored in film. As a senior he joined the school's improvisational-comedy group, the Mee-Ow Show, which was founded by Paul Warshauer and Josh Lazar in 1974 and whose past members include the former *SNL* alums Ana Gasteyer and Julia Louis-Dreyfus. After graduating Meyers performed with I.O. Chicago (formerly known as Improv Olympic), where many *SNL* cast members and writers have gotten their starts, honing his skills with the improv team Preponderate.

In 1997 Meyers and his friend and Northwestern schoolmate Peter Grosz joined Boom Chicago, an English-language sketch-and-improv ensemble based in Amsterdam, in the Netherlands. Grosz noted to Nina Metz for the *Chicago Tribune* (October 22, 2006), "We were like the two funny people in our pledge class. [Meyers is] a really smart guy, so if he has any flaw in the world of comedy, it's that he gets impatient if something isn't really funny. He knows how funny things can be; I could hand him a sketch and he could make it better in two seconds." In Amsterdam Meyers and a fellow comic, Jill Benjamin, began working on a partly improvised, partly scripted two-person comedy show called Pick-ups and Hiccups, which they staged five nights a week in a 200-seat Amsterdam theater and also performed in Scotland, England, and the U.S. During the 2000 Chicago Improv Festival, the show caught the attention of an *SNL* casting agent, Ayala Cohen. Meyers recalled to Metz that at the time Cohen "was visiting family in Chicago, and her sister suggested they go see the show. So it just goes to show how much luck has to do with it." He was invited to New York for a tryout and was hired after a protracted audition process, later noting to John Clayton for the Manchester *Union Leader* (November 26, 2001), "The biggest mistake you can make is to get a job on *Saturday Night Live* and say 'I made it!' You just took on the hardest job of your life and you can't look at it as some kind of culmination. You have to focus on the work."

Joining the *SNL* cast in 2001, Meyers made his first notable appearance on Weekend Update in a sketch that poked fun at the travails of being a Boston Red Sox baseball fan. He attributed the New York Yankees' struggles against the Arizona Diamondbacks in that year's World Series to the fact that the Yankees had the support of the seemingly luckless Red Sox fans. "If Boston rooted for gravity, we'd all be floating three inches off the ground," he said in the sketch, which aired in the wake of the September 11 terrorist attacks and on the eve of the seventh and deciding game of the World Series, won by the Diamondbacks. He added, referring to the then–U.S. secretary of defense, "Right now, Donald Rumsfeld is in West Roxbury, Massachusetts, trying to convince eight guys named Murph to root for the Taliban." During his first several seasons on the show, Meyers became known for a number of recurring roles. He played half of a sleazy British gossip-reporting team, opposite Poehler, in the "Spy Glass" sketches, about a tabloid-television show similar to *Access Hollywood*. Another recurring sketch, "Jarret's Room," about a Webcast hosted by two perennially stoned Hampshire College students (played by Jimmy Fallon and Horatio Sanz), featured Meyers as DJ Jonathan Feinstein, a student posing as a British disc jockey. In "Top O' the Morning," a sketch about an Irish morning talk show set in a bar, he played William Fitzpatrick, opposite Fallon as Patrick Fitzwilliam, and in "Pranksters," he was seen as the host of a practical joke–themed television show. In addition to the characters he created, most notably a workplace-insult king called the Zinger, Meyers also became known for his impressions of celebrities including Michael Caine, Anderson Cooper, Carrot Top, Prince Charles, Ryan Seacrest, Sean Penn, Stone Phillips, Tobey Maguire, Peyton Manning, Wade Robson, and Kevin Federline.

Meyers became a regular cast member on *SNL* in 2003. The following year he won rave reviews for his uncanny portrayal of U.S. senator John Kerry of Massachusetts for the show's satire of the 2004 presidential campaigns. Meyers noted to Virginia Rohan for the Bergen County, New Jersey, *Record* (October 25, 2004), "The thing I found is, [Kerry] started using his hands a lot. . . . It was like somebody told him, 'Look, you need to be animated,' and so he went, 'I'm going to move my hands more,' and nobody told him that his hand should actually correspond to what he was saying." In 2004 Meyers also landed small parts in three little-noticed big-screen releases: *See This Movie*, about a group of inept film-school graduates who enter the Montreal World Film Festival—without a movie; *Maestro*, about a bowling-alley attendant who dreams of conducting a timeless piece of music; and *Thunder Road*, about a Cub Scout who competes with his overzealous father at the scouts' annual Pinewood Derby.

As Meyers's profile on *SNL* grew, he began to get parts in more mainstream projects. In 2006 he won a role in Chris Weitz's *American Dreamz*, whose all-star cast included Hugh Grant, Dennis Quaid, Marcia Gay Harden, Willem Dafoe, Mandy Moore, and Chris Klein. That year he was promoted to co–head writer on *SNL*, with Tina Fey and Andrew Steele, after spending the previous year as a writing supervisor. When Fey left *SNL* to develop her semiautobiographical sitcom *30 Rock*, Meyers was named head writer as well as Fey's replacement as co-host of Weekend Update, alongside Poehler.

Since he took over two of the show's most important responsibilities—heading the writing staff and anchoring Weekend Update—Meyers has been a leading figure in *SNL*'s revival. Riding on the coattails of the 2008 presidential campaigns, the show's 34th season got off to a scorching start. The season premiere featured the swimmer and Olympic gold-medalist Michael Phelps as host and the rapper Lil Wayne as the musical guest; its most attention-grabbing segment, however, was "A Nonpartisan Message from Governor Sarah Palin and Senator Hillary Clinton," the sketch that debuted Tina Fey's now-legendary Palin impression. In it, Palin and Clinton discussed their differing views on sexism, the election, and other topics. The sketch received positive reviews from critics and has since become one of the most talked-about satirical pieces in *SNL* history. Marc Berman, who writes about Nielsen ratings for the trade journal *Mediaweek*, noted to Maureen Ryan that Fey's impressions of Palin "single-handedly lifted the show to water-cooler status." (Meyers wrote all but one of the Palin sketches.)

On three Thursdays in October 2008, *SNL* aired prime-time half-hour installments entitled *Saturday Night Live "Weekend Update" Thursday*, which focused on the election. That month the show drew its highest ratings in more than 14 years when the real Sarah Palin appeared, in an installment hosted by Josh Brolin (who portrayed George W. Bush in Oliver Stone's 2008 film, *W.*); that installment, which also featured cameos by Stone, Fey, Mark Wahlberg, and Alec Baldwin, drew 17 million viewers during its first half-hour. "I don't think we'd have the same heat if Mitt Romney had been picked as the vice presidential nominee," Meyers quipped to Ryan. *SNL* continued its hot streak in November, when John McCain and his wife, Cindy, appeared as themselves in one installment. (That night also marked Fey's last appearance as Palin; she has since retired her impression of the Alaska governor.) *SNL*'s ratings cooled after the election, but the show maintained a higher viewership in 2009 than in recent seasons. (Although *Saturday Night Live* enjoyed one of the most successful runs in its history in 2008, Meyers and his team of writers did not end the year without controversy. In December New York governor David Paterson, who has partial sight in one eye and none in the other, lambasted an *SNL* skit that mocked his blindness. Spokespersons for NBC refused to comment on the matter.)

On September 26, 2009 the 35th season of *SNL* began. With the actress Megan Fox serving as host and the rock group U2 as the musical guests, the show drew lower ratings than the previous season's premiere installment but topped the numbers for 2007. Fox's appearance on the show was overshadowed by a gaffe made by one of *SNL*'s newest cast members, Jenny Slate, who accidentally said the "f word" during a sketch. Slate's blunder led to speculation that she would be fired, but NBC representatives quickly dismissed such conjectures and announced that she would keep her job. (Several *SNL* cast members were fired after a similar incident in 1981.) *SNL*'s 35th season also saw the return of *Saturday Night Live "Weekend Update" Thursday*. Three prime-time half-hour installments aired during the fall of 2009, and another six were scheduled to air in 2010. Meyers has continued to serve as head writer for both the spin-off series and the main show.

Meyers lives in New York. He is an avid fan of the Boston Red Sox and the Pittsburgh Steelers football team. In addition to *SNL*, he has made several guest appearances on television and won the third season of the Bravo network's *Celebrity Poker Showdown*; he donated the $100,000 prize to the Boston-based Jimmy Fund, which supports research at the Dana-Farber Cancer Institute. In 2008 Meyers appeared in the 3-D film *Journey to the Center of the Earth*, with Brendan Fraser and Anita Briem, and in a cameo as a drunk man in the comedy *Nick and Norah's Infinite Playlist*, which starred Michael Cera and Kat Dennings. He appeared with other *SNL* performers in the film comedy *Spring Breakdown* in 2009 and is currently writing and set to star in an *SNL* sketch-turned-feature-film called *Key Party*.

—C.C.

Suggested Reading: *Chicago Tribune* C p13 Oct. 22, 2006, C p4 Oct. 18, 2008; (Manchester, New Hampshire) *Union Leader* A p1 Nov. 26, 2001; New Hampshire state Web site; *New York Post Page Six* (on-line) Dec. 14, 2008; *Saturday Night Live* Web site

Selected Television Shows: *Spin City*, 2001; *Saturday Night Live*, 2001– ; Selected Films: *See This Movie*, 2004; *Maestro*, 2004; *Thunder Road*, 2004; *Perception*, 2005; *American Dreamz*, 2006; *Journey to the Center of the Earth*, 2008; *Nick and Norah's Infinite Playlist*, 2008

Miasha

(me-AH-shah)

Feb. 17, 1981– Writer

Address: c/o Touchstone/Fireside, 1230 Ave. of the Americas, 11th Fl., New York, NY 10020-1513

Since 2006 the African-American writer Miasha has penned a series of novels—*Secret Society*, *Diary of a Mistress*, *Mommy's Angel*, *Sistah for Sale*, *Never Enough*, and, most recently, *Chaser*—depicting the sexual escapades of African-American characters, often set against the backdrop of an inner-city neighborhood rampant with drugs and violence. A rising star in the popular genre of urban fiction (also called street lit and

Courtesy of Miasha

Miasha

ghetto fiction), Miasha has drawn inspiration for her writing from her own experiences. "Being born in the era of crack-cocaine and having grown up in an environment surrounded by drug dealers and users, I've witnessed a lot that people may find shocking," she said in an interview for *Urban Magazine* in 2006, after her first book was published. "But to me it's just life—it's just the way it is. So when I write that's what I deliver. I deliver life as I know it, and it just happens to be shocking." According to Bliss Broyard, writing for *Elle* (July 2009), Miasha—whose novels have found a receptive audience among African-American readers—has sold a total of about 200,000 copies of her books.

Miasha Latima Nicole Rinehart was born on February 17, 1981 to Yolanda Joy Rinehart and Cecil Alex Thomas in Philadelphia, Pennsylvania. By the time Miasha was five, her parents, both drug addicts, had split up, and she was living with her mother, who had started smoking crack and keeping company with drug dealers, addicts, and prostitutes, all of whom were frequent visitors to her home. ("Crack" is the street name given to cocaine that has been processed to make rock crystals; when heated it produces vapors.) When Miasha was six her mother abandoned the family, shortly after having her fifth child, who was born addicted to drugs and taken away from her by social-service agencies. Miasha went to live with her then-sober father at his mother's house, just across the street. Her grandmother was a stabilizing force until Miasha was nine, when her grandmother died from cancer and her father resumed taking drugs, turning their home into a haven for addicts.

At age 12 Miasha was taken away from her father and placed in the custody of an aunt. During that time she started keeping a journal—the blank book was a gift from another aunt—and began to write poetry as a way of expressing herself. "Writing allowed me to get out all the pain and emotion of what I was going through, without embarrassment or judgment," Miasha told Broyard. The summer after seventh grade, she was profoundly affected by the murders of five teenage friends—all low-level crack dealers. "I couldn't just assume that my siblings and I would live until we were old. Any one of us could've been killed," she explained to Broyard. The following year she was contacted by her mother, who she learned had given birth to three more children in the previous seven years; all three had been taken away by social-service agencies. (After struggling with addiction for years, Miasha's parents are currently sober, and she has said that she enjoys a close relationship with each of them.)

After completing high school Miasha enrolled at Temple University, in Philadelphia, with an eye toward pursuing filmmaking. "I wanted to be the female Spike Lee when I enrolled in college, but I didn't want to limit myself to just film so I majored in communications as a whole and took classes on just about every subject it had to offer. But at the time film was my main focus," Miasha told *Current Biography*. While attending college Miasha honed her writing skills at the now-defunct local music magazine *Rhythm & Beats*, interviewing several musicians, including the singer Deborah Cox and the R&B duo Floetry, for the publication and supervising its fashion department. Miasha also worked with the promotional team at the hip-hop/R&B independent label Global Recording Group, first as a model and then as a product manager for the group 5 Grand, one of the label's artists.

Miasha next decided to pursue a career in advertising copywriting. She was motivated to become a novelist, however, after listening to the commencement address given by the best-selling author Karen E. Quinones Miller at her May 2003 graduation. "She delivered a speech about how she had written a book, self-published it and sold so many copies on her own that major publishing houses fought to offer her a deal," Miasha wrote on MySpace.com. "I sat amongst my graduating class fully alert and attentive. It was as if Karen was talking directly to me, telling me to bypass trying to get a job in advertising copywriting and follow my true passion of becoming an author. I was unquestionably inspired and two months after graduation I began writing my first novel, *Secret Society*."

Secret Society centers on Celess and Tina, best friends who use their beauty and wiles to trick men into spending their money on them. In a surprise twist the protagonists are revealed to be men masquerading as women. After completing the novel, in only three months, the first-time novelist contacted Quinones Miller by e-mail and requested advice on how to get published. "She simply told me to let self-publishing be my last resort and that

I should first seek a publishing deal," Miasha revealed on MySpace. "I took her advice and researched the ways to go about submitting a manuscript." She sent a query letter, a synopsis, and the first three chapters of the book to Teri Woods Publishing. Woods, an author and the founder of the eponymous publishing firm, which specializes in urban fiction, offered to buy the rights to Miasha's manuscript for *Secret Society*. Woods also presented her with a five-book deal that was contingent upon Miasha's penning a second novel. After Miasha had finished writing *Diary of a Mistress*—and before she had signed a contract with Woods—she again sought advice from Quinones Miller, who referred Miasha to her literary agent, Liza Dawson. After reading Miasha's manuscripts Dawson offered to become her agent. "I accepted and the next thing I knew, I had three major publishing houses interested in signing me," Miasha wrote on MySpace. "Simon and Schuster was the highest bidder offering a six-figure advance and a two-book deal—far exceeding my expectations as a new, unpublished author. I was in awe."

Published in March 2006, *Secret Society* got a mixed reaction. Although several reviewers agreed that the book lacked depth, they found the overall story fascinating. "Miasha's narrative has few developed scenes. . . . But beneath the litany of shopping and screwing, lying and dodging, the tension bubbles—Tina and Celess know they're playing a dangerous game," according to *Publishers Weekly* (January 2, 2006). "Scandalous and engrossing, this debut from Miasha . . . shows her to be a writer to watch." Equally complimentary was Lillian Lewis, who wrote for *Booklist* (February 1, 2006) that *Secret Society* is "an absorbing tale." An assessment for *Kirkus Reviews* (February 1, 2006) described *Secret Society* as a "glib debut with a truly astonishing twist" and also referred to the novel as "thin and glitzy, but bizarrely affecting in its way."

Urban fiction is generally characterized by explicit depictions of drug use, violence, and sexual promiscuity in inner-city neighborhoods. Written largely by and for African-Americans, urban fiction is usually—and purposely—peppered with spelling and grammatical errors to reflect language used on the streets. Novels in the genre first appeared on bookshelves in the 1970s; they have experienced a resurgence in recent years. According to Nielsen BookScan, urban fiction jumped from representing 0.2 percent of adult fiction book sales (or 4,000 copies sold) in 2005 to 4 percent (or 82,000 copies) in 2007. Sessalee Hensley, a fiction buyer for the book retail chain Barnes & Noble, told Broyard that in roughly 125 of the 777 Barnes & Noble stores located in the U.S., urban fiction not only outsells African-American literary classics, which include novels by Ralph Ellison, Zora Neale Hurston, and Alice Walker, but also works of popular fiction including Dan Brown's *The Da Vinci Code*. Urban fiction's newfound popularity has ignited controversy, however, especially among African-American literary authors. Although the genre's success in encouraging reading among urban African-American teenagers has been applauded, writers and publishers of urban fiction have been criticized for portraying a glamorized version of street life and perpetuating stereotypes. In an October 3, 2007 e-mail message circulated on-line, Terry McMillan, the best-selling author of *Waiting to Exhale*, *How Stella Got Her Groove Back*, and other novels, condemned works of urban fiction as "exploitative, destructive, racist, egregious, sexist, base, tacky, poorly written, unedited, degrading books." Miasha and other "street-lit" writers have countered that they are writing about the worlds in which they grew up and that their aim is often to spotlight the dangers and hardships of street life. "[Critics of the genre] are not going to tell me that where I'm from and what I've been through is not worth reading," another urban-fiction author, Toy Styles, told Broyard.

Miasha's second novel, *Diary of a Mistress*, which was published five months after *Secret Society*, tells the story of Monica and Carlos, a seemingly happy couple whose 10-year marriage is threatened when Angela, a woman claiming to be Carlos's mistress, sends Monica a diary filled with the details of their affair. "With *Diary of a Mistress*, I wanted to break the cliché that all men are dogs. I wanted to tell the other side of the story," Miasha told *Urban-Reviews.com* (2006, on-line). "There are good men out there, but for every good man there [are] about ten women trying to get him, even if he is taken. I've experienced this in my own relationship and my trust was often tested, so the idea for this novel pretty much derived from some personal situations." Following the publication of her first two books, Miasha embarked on a 15-city book tour.

Published in June 2007, *Mommy's Angel*, Miasha's third book, chronicles the struggles of 15-year-old Angel from Brooklyn, New York, who is forced to support her two younger siblings financially following the drive-by shooting death of her older brother, which plunges their grief-stricken mother into heroin addiction. The desperate teen becomes a stripper, then seriously considers entering prostitution when the strip club is shut down after a police raid. *Mommy's Angel* became an *Essence* magazine best-seller, and for her effort Miasha was nominated in the category of breakout author of the year at the 2007 African American Literary Awards. Also that year she established the Ask Miasha Foundation, a nonprofit organization that works to assist underprivileged youth and uplift impoverished communities.

For her next novel, *Sistah for Sale*, Miasha focused on the illegal sex-slave industry, one of the world's fastest-growing—but least-talked-about—enterprises. "I found out that there was more money involved in human trafficking than in drugs and firearms trafficking. You constantly hear about the war against drugs or even firearms, but the sex trade . . . you never hear about it," she told an interviewer for Sixshot.com. *Sistah for Sale*, which was published in March 2008, follows Sienna, an orphan who has grown up in Miami's sex-slave industry, as she attempts to free herself from a life of prostitution. "I wanted [Sienna] to have the power within to bring a stop to what was going on," Miasha told Sixshot.com. "A lot of movies, documentaries, or situations that deal with the sex slave industry—you get a third party who comes in and brings the bad guy down, and rescues the women or the victims. I wanted to give that power to the main character because once she found her will then she made the way." A reviewer for the *Michigan Citizen* (May 4–10, 2008) declared that Miasha's "skill is negligible," called *Sistah for Sale* a "mediocre effort," and added that the book "is good to read as a two part cautionary tale, what not to do and what not to write."

Never Enough, Miasha's fifth novel, was published in July 2008. The follow-up to *Secret Society*, *Never Enough* revisits Celess, now a successful model and rising talent in the entertainment industry whose career is jeopardized by the discovery that she has undergone gender-reassignment surgery. Calling Miasha "the new princess of urban literature," a critic for *Michigan Citizen* (July 20–26, 2008) praised *Never Enough* as "fascinating and interesting from beginning to end" and "definitely Miasha's best thus far."

Also in 2008 *Secret Society: The Stage Play*, an adaptation of Miasha's first novel, made its debut in Philadelphia. The theatrical project was produced by Fifth Avenue Productions, an entertainment company Miasha co-founded with her husband, Rich Coleman, to expand the author's reach into film, music, publishing, television, and theater. Explaining her move into theater, the author told *Current Biography*, "My ultimate goal was to have my books become movies." She added, referring to Tyler Perry, who in recent years has successfully adapted his urban-themed plays for television and film, "Being in the industry during the Tyler Perry movement, I felt like a stage play would be more feasible for me to produce myself and then make the jump to movies following the success of the play. I felt like it was a way to take matters into my own hands." The production's three-day run attracted more than 1,000 theatergoers. The play was staged in May 2009 at the University of Pennsylvania's Irvine Auditorium and in August 2009 at the Woodruff Arts Center in Atlanta, Georgia.

Miasha's latest book, *Chaser*, which was published in July 2009, centers on Leah, a young woman who is determined to end her relationship with the greedy and manipulative Kenny. After Leah becomes the fall guy for one of Kenny's scams, she decides to turn police informant and finds her life in danger.

The author is currently starting work on her seventh novel, which is tentatively titled "Til Death." Scheduled for publication in 2010, the book will continue the story of Celess. Miasha is also working on developing her own publishing company and has also established the Better World Mentorship program for young girls.

Since June 14, 2003 Miasha has been married to Rich Coleman, whom she met in 1996. Coleman runs a tow-truck business and sells real estate when not accompanying his wife on book tours. The couple have two young sons, Amir PJ and Ace Nasir, and divide their time between homes in Atlanta and Philadelphia.

—M.A.S.

Suggested Reading: *Elle* p126+ July 2009; Miasha.com; SixShot.com (on-line) Apr. 30, 2008; *Vibe* (on-line) July 11, 2006

Selected Books: *Secret Society*, 2006; *Diary of a Mistress*, 2006; *Mommy's Angel*, 2007; *Sistah for Sale*, 2008; *Never Enough*, 2008; *Chaser*, 2009

Mark Mainz/Getty Images

Millan, Cesar

Aug. 27, 1969– Dog trainer; television personality

Address: Cesar Millan Inc., 1033 N. Hollywood Way, Suite F, Burbank, CA 91505

"When I was 13, I said, 'I want to be the best dog trainer in the world,'" Cesar Millan told Norma Meyer for the Copley News Service (October 17, 2004). Despite having had no formal training, Millan—if not universally acknowledged as the world's best dog trainer—is perhaps the best-known. His reality-television show, *The Dog Whisperer*, broadcast on the National Geographic Channel, has become a global phenomenon, currently airing in 55 countries, including Australia, Spain, Sweden, and the United Kingdom. In the U.S. some 11 million viewers tune in to the show, and Millan is the owner of a renowned dog-psychology center in Los Angeles, California. Although some critics have denounced Millan's physical and psychological techniques as inhumane, his talent for turning aggressive and disobedient dogs into submissive pets has won him legions of fans, particularly among Hollywood celebrities. With Melissa Jo Peltier he has written four how-to books for dog owners.

Cesar Millan was born on August 27, 1969 to Felipe Millan Guillen and Maria Teresa Favela de Millan in Culiacan, a city in the state of Sinaloa, Mexico. His father worked as a government photographer, and his mother was a seamstress. To provide Millan and his sister with better educational opportunities, his parents moved the family to Mazatlán, the second-largest city in Mexico, when Millan was seven years old. There, they enrolled him in a judo class, and by his early teens he had won several local championships.

Millan credits his love of dogs to the summers he spent working on his grandfather's farm in Ixpalino, Mexico. "My grandfather was one of many workers and ranch families in Mexico who earned a meager income working parcels of land rented from the richer families. On every farm in the area including his, there were working dogs," Millan wrote for his official Web site."Through observing my grandfather's behavior with the pack on the farm, I learned much of what I apply in my work with dogs today. Other families found entertainment in watching the dogs fight for dominance, but my grandfather never allowed this. He always made sure that the dogs knew who was in charge: the humans." Millan's fascination with canines grew after his parents purchased the family's first television set; he became an avid watcher of the television shows *Lassie* and *The Adventures of Rin Tin Tin*, whose main characters were dogs. Millan later found work at a veterinarian's office. His fondness for dogs caused him to be teased by the neighborhood children, who called him the Spanish equivalent of "dog boy."

Millan was determined to become the world's best professional dog trainer. Although he did not speak a word of English, his "goal was always Hollywood," as he told Edward Wyatt for the *New York Times* (May 23, 2006). "Where I'm from, the only thing you hear is Hollywood and Disneyland. You don't hear Texas, you don't hear Ohio, you don't even hear New York. My target was Hollywood because that was the only thing I knew." At age 21 Millan paid $100 to a "coyote," or smuggler, who successfully guided him through brush to cross—illegally—from Tijuana, Mexico, into San Diego, California. There, Millan spent a month living on the street before landing a job at a dog-grooming parlor. He was paid a 50 percent commission and slept in a back room of the salon. Customers soon noticed that he had a natural talent for calming dogs. "My knack for dealing with even the most hard-to-handle dogs became apparent to clients, who started to ask me for help with their dogs' behavior problems," he wrote for his official Web site.

Over the next few years, Millan saved some money and moved to Los Angeles, where he met and married Ilusion Wilson. He found work at a dog-training school, where one of the customers, the owner of a limousine business, hired him to clean his vehicles. Millan also launched his own business. "While I was washing limousines, the owner let me train his friend's dogs on my breaks. I started walking dogs too and working with Rottweilers," he told Mimi Avis for the *Los Angeles Times* (October 18, 2004). "I had to do that because I couldn't just be around people. I'm used to being around dogs." Millan's clientele quickly grew, and he became a fixture in Los Angeles neighborhoods. "I'd take out 30 dogs, all walking behind me, and people would stop and stare as I'd go through Beverly Hills with rottweilers and pit bulls," he told Lucy Cavendish for the London *Telegraph* (March 3, 2008). "I'd take them for four-hour walks and charge $10, and their owners were amazed when I'd bring back calm, contented dogs."

Millan's reputation spread through word of mouth. In 1994 the actress Jada Pinkett Smith and her husband, the film actor Will Smith, hired him to tame their family's Rottweiler guard dogs, in exchange for English-language lessons. With the help of Pinkett Smith, Millan landed other celebrity clients. In the late 1990s Millan came up with the idea of expanding his enterprise beyond dog-training. He viewed himself as more of a dog therapist than a dog trainer. "Dog training is one human, one dog—obeying commands like sit and fetch," he told Sanjiv Bhattacharya for the *Ottawa Citizen* (March 25, 2007). "Dog psychology is about retraining the dogs to a pack mentality"—that is, accepting that dogs are not human and treating them accordingly. Dog owners, Millan insists, need to be leaders of the "pack," which can be achieved by maintaining a "calm and assertive" manner; that approach, Millan says, will lead dogs to be obedient, "calm and submissive."

In 1997 Millan and his wife established the Dog Psychology Center, on a two-acre property in the inner-city neighborhood of South Central Los Angeles. (Since 2007 the center has been housed on a 42-acre property in Santa Clarita, California.) From the late 1990s to the early 2000s, the facility has handled the dogs of such celebrities as the film director Ridley Scott and the actress/model Rebecca Romijn-Stamos as well as shelter animals whose bad behavior makes them hard to place with owners. After being profiled in a *Los Angeles Times* article (September 25, 2002), Millan was contacted by several television producers about developing a reality television show that would showcase his abilities with canines. Millan partnered with the producing team of Sheila Possner and Kay Sumner, who successfully pitched the show to executives at the National Geographic Channel (NGC). *The Dog Whisperer* debuted in September 2004 and was an immediate hit, despite a lack of marketing. "The network was only promoting primetime shows, and we weren't a primetime show. However, it slowly started gaining [momentum]," Ilusion told Vitisia Paynich for *Electronic Retailer Magazine* (October 2006). "People started watching it and the ratings were going up slowly and steadily." On the show, cameras follow Millan as he visits dog owners who are in desperate need of help with their pets. Calmly but assertively, Millan "rehabilitates" difficult-to-care-for dogs. After the series' debut, Millan was hired by a roster of high-profile celebrities—among them the best-selling author Deepak Chopra, the actor Nicolas Cage, and the actresses Scarlett Johansson and Hilary Duff—some of whom appeared on his show. The program's ratings skyrocketed after Millan appeared on an installment of the *Oprah Winfrey Show*, in which he helped the talk-show host learn to manage Sophie, one of her cocker spaniels.

In 2005, following the show's first-season success, NGC expanded *The Dog Whisperer* from a half-hour to an hour and moved the program to a primetime slot. That same year Millan and his wife formed a joint venture with two production companies, Emery/Sumner Productions and MPH Entertainment, to form Cesar Millan Inc., which developed program-related products, including instructional DVDs, such as the *Mastering Leadership* series, and accessories, such as the high-selling Illusion dog-training collar. Millan has also co-written, with Melissa Jo Peltier, a series of books, including the *New York Times* best-seller *Cesar's Way: The Natural, Everyday Guide to Understanding and Correcting Common Dog Problems* (2006) and *Be the Pack Leader: Use Cesar's Way to Transform Your Dog . . . and Your Life* (2008). In 2007 Millan and his wife established a foundation to provide U.S.-based animal shelters with financial and rehabilitation assistance. *The Dog Whisperer* has received two Emmy Award nominations (2006–07) in the category of outstanding reality program.

As the show gained national attention, so did Millan's dog-training methods, including his use of choke collars and leash corrections as well as his practice of forcing the canines into submissive postures. Those techniques have drawn criticism from some animal-behavior experts, who believe they are outdated and ineffective. In an op-ed piece for the *New York Times* (August 31, 2006), Mark Derr, the author of *A Dog's History of America: How Our Best Friend Explored, Conquered and Settled a Continent* (2004), wrote, "While Mr. Millan rejects hitting and yelling at dogs during training, his confrontational methods include physical and psychological intimidation, like finger jabs, choke collars, extended sessions on a treadmill and what is called flooding, or overwhelming the animal with the thing it fears. Compared with some training devices still in use—whips and cattle prods, for example—these are mild, but combined with a lack of positive reinforcement or rewards, they place Mr. Millan firmly in a long tradition of punitive dog trainers." Stephen Zawistowski, a spokesman for the American Society for the Prevention of Cruelty to Animals (ASPCA), told Sharon L. Peters for *USA Today* (May 30, 2007) that he was "disappointed that while we have made enormous advances in our understanding of the science, [*The Dog Whisperer*] presents out-of-date techniques. It's not necessary to physically manhandle a dog." Other organizations, among them the American Humane Association, the International Association of Animal Behavior Consultants, and the Animal Behavior Society, have also expressed opposition to Millan's methods. In Millan's defense, Martin Deeley, the co-founder of the International Association of Canine Professionals, which inducted Millan as an honorary member in 2006, explained to Peters, "It must be remembered that [he] is dealing with serious-problem dogs."

Although initially upset by the criticism, Millan is undeterred by it. "I'm the last hope for the people I work with," he told Maria Eftimiades for *People* (January 22, 2007). "In the hands of other professionals, these dogs would be put down or on medication." In an interview with Bhattacharya, which took place a few months after the *People* interview, Millan had some sharp words for his critics: "They don't watch all the episodes, these positive reinforcement people. They're just focusing on a few small incidents. And most of them don't truly understand a pack. I don't think they can walk 50 dogs at once. They don't tell the truth, which is that they're jealous. They wish they had what I got. But God bless them, I hope they find balance in their lives." Millan was the subject of a 2006 lawsuit filed by the television producer Flody Suarez, who claimed that his Labrador retriever was injured at the Dog Psychology Center. A private settlement was reached on March 29, 2007.

The controversy does not appear to have hurt the appeal of *The Dog Whisperer*, which is currently in its sixth season on the National Geographic Channel. In September 2008 the series broadcast its 100th episode, and in 2009, for the first time in the program's history, Millan will start shooting episodes overseas. Millan has premiered a new line of pet-care products on the QVC Channel, and he has also partnered with Petco to produce a line of pet food and supplies. Millan published *A Member of the Family: Cesar Millan's Guide to a Lifetime of Fulfillment with Your Dog* in 2008 and *How to Raise the Perfect Dog: Through Puppyhood and Beyond* in 2009. Also in 2009 he launched *Cesar's Way*, a magazine for dog owners. He and his work were parodied on an episode of the Comedy Central cartoon series *South Park*.

Millan received a 2005 Genesis Award commendation from the Humane Society for his work involving the rehabilitation of shelter animals. He lives in Los Angeles with his wife and two sons,

Andre and Calvin. In 2009 he became an American citizen.

—D.K.

Suggested Reading: *Electronic Retailer Magazine* (on-line) Oct. 2006; *Los Angeles Times* E p1 Oct. 18, 2004; *New York Times* E p1 May 23, 2006, A p25 Aug. 31, 2006; *Ottawa (Canada) Citizen* B p4 Mar. 25, 2007

Selected Books: with Melissa Jo Peltier—*Cesar's Way: The Natural, Everyday Guide to Understanding and Correcting Common Dog Problems*, 2006; *Be The Pack Leader: Use Cesar's Way to Transform Your Dog . . . and Your Life*, 2008; *A Member of the Family: Cesar Millan's Guide to a Lifetime of Fulfillment with Your Dog*, 2008; *How to Raise the Perfect Dog: Through Puppyhood and Beyond*, 2009

Selected Television: *The Dog Whisperer with Cesar Millan*, 2004–

Courtesy of Leonard Mlodinow

Mlodinow, Leonard

(MLAH-dih-now)

Nov. 26, 1954– Physicist; writer; educator

Address: Caltech, Mail Code 21676, Pasadena, CA 91125

As a postgraduate student in theoretical physics at the California Institute of Technology (Caltech) in 1981, Leonard Mlodinow was assigned an office next to that of Richard Feynman, the winner of the 1965 Nobel Prize in physics. Mlodinow formed a close friendship with Feynman, who was famous not only for his brilliance as a scientist but for his determination and ability to make complex theories and phenomena understandable even for those attending freshman courses in physics. He was also renowned for his sense of humor and pursuit of fun. Mlodinow's placement in an office adjoining Feynman's, which led to many wide-ranging conversations with Feynman that indelibly affected his life, was a chance event—of the sort that Mlodinow wrote about in his most recent book, *The Drunkard's Walk: How Randomness Rules Our Lives* (2008). In that work of popular science and in his others—*Euclid's Window* (2001), *Feynman's Rainbow* (2003), and *A Briefer History of Time* (2005), the last of which he wrote with Stephen Hawking—Mlodinow explained complicated concepts in physics and math in ways that reviewers have described as both entertaining and comprehensible for the average reader. In addition to his books, which also include two volumes in a series for adolescents, and his several years of research in theoretical physics, Mlodinow's résumé lists his work as a Hollywood scriptwriter, a designer of computer games, an executive with the publisher Scholastic Inc., and, since 2005, a lecturer at Caltech. In a conversation with Carl Bialik for the *Wall Street Journal* (April 30, 2008, on-line) about *The Drunkard's Walk* and the element of randomness that touches the lives of everyone, Mlodinow said, "I don't mourn the role of luck, I celebrate it. All else [being] equal, it is a lot more fun not knowing how your book will do, or how your life will turn out, than it would be if everything could be determined by a logical calculation. Moreover, the fact that luck matters means you can help yourself by being persistent. A failure doesn't mean you are unworthy, nor does it preclude success on the next try. As Thomas J. Watson, the highly successful IBM pioneer, said, 'If you want to succeed, double your failure rate.'"

Leonard David Mlodinow was born in Chicago, Illinois, on November 26, 1954. He has two brothers. Both of his parents were survivors of the Holocaust. His father, Simon Mlodinow, became a leader in the Jewish underground in Czestochowa, Poland, before being transported in 1944 to the Buchenwald concentration camp, in Germany; there, his first wife and their two children were killed. Improbably, his life was spared after he stole a loaf of bread: when camp guards threatened to shoot him and his fellow prisoners if the thief did not confess, he stepped forward, assuming that he would be shot sooner or later anyway. Instead, the camp baker made him his assistant. When Buchenwald was liberated, by U.S. Army troops in 1945, Simon Mlodinow weighed only 80 pounds. In 1948, in New York City, he met his second wife, Mlodinow's mother, Irene, who had been imprisoned in a Nazi labor camp in Poland during World War II.

As a third-grader Leonard Mlodinow began to write short stories—his first, about dinosaurs, earned hearty praise from the school librarian—and he enjoyed producing works in that genre through high school. As a youngster he liked to read science fiction and play with a chemistry set in his family's basement. In eighth grade, he told an interviewer for Powells.com, he "obsessed" over a book entitled *Non-Euclidean Geometry*, and in high school a book called *Qualitative Analysis and Electrolytic Solutions* "fascinated" him. With the encouragement of his high-school chemistry teacher, he set up his own little lab in a corner of a classroom.

In 1972 Mlodinow enrolled at Brandeis University, in Waltham, Massachusetts, with the intention of preparing for a career as a chemist. In October 1973 he left college for several months, after a coalition of Arab states led by Egypt and Syria attacked Israel in what became known as the Yom Kippur War (also called the Ramadan War, the October War, and the fourth Arab-Israeli War). Mlodinow went to Israel to work on a kibbutz, an agriculturally based settlement where Jewish families live communally. At night he read the only English-language books he could find in the kibbutz library: works by Richard Feynman. Their contents sparked his interest in physics and physics-related math, which he found far more intriguing than pure math or the math used by chemists, and after he returned to Brandeis, in 1974, he switched his major to math and physics. His course load was double that of most other students. "I didn't do this to try to break records," he told Seth Roberts, a professor emeritus of psychology at the University of California–Berkeley, as posted on Roberts's blog (January 29–30, 2009); "I was tremendously interested in things and if I saw a course I liked I wanted to take it. I was like the . . . kid in a candy store stuffing his face. I was stuffing my face with knowledge." Mlodinow graduated from Brandeis, in 1976, not only with a dual bachelor's degree but also with a master's degree in physics. (Had he taken one more chemistry course, he could have had a triple major.)

Mlodinow next pursued a doctorate in theoretical physics at the University of California at Berkeley. His adviser there was Eyvind Wichmann, a physicist who specialized in axiomatic quantum field theory, an area of quantum mechanics whose practitioners aim to formulate axioms, or rules, to explain phenomena occurring between physical entities at the scale of atomic or subatomic particles. For his doctoral research Mlodinow worked with the physicist Nikos Papanicolaou on a subject that he described on his Web site as "more practical [than Wichmann's work], at least if you are a physicist." He and Papanicolaou, in his words, "developed a new approximation method in which you solve a problem in infinite dimensions, and then calculate corrections to account for the fact that we live in only three." With a dissertation entitled "The Large N Expansion in Quantum Mechanics," Mlodinow earned a Ph.D. in 1981.

That year, largely on the strength of his much-lauded dissertation, Mlodinow received a faculty fellowship at Caltech that allowed him to conduct research in a topic of his own choosing; unlike many fellows, he was not obligated to teach. Mlodinow's office was between those of Feynman and Murray Gell-Mann, both of whom had won the Nobel Prize in physics (the latter in 1969). Mlodinow felt uncomfortable while at Caltech, because he feared that he would never again produce any work of the caliber of his dissertation and no longer felt sure about his research interests. Nevertheless, he developed a close friendship with Feynman, who at the time was undergoing treatment for cancer, and the two engaged in lengthy conversations, a number of which Mlodinow tape-recorded. Transcriptions of some of their chats appear in Mlodinow's book *Feynman's Rainbow: A Search for Beauty in Physics and in Life* (2003), about his postgraduate experience at Caltech. In a review for *Scotland on Sunday* (June 29, 2003), that publication's literary editor, the theoretical physicist Andrew Crumey, described *Feynman's Rainbow* as "highly enjoyable." "Physics is sketched as lightly here as the personalities . . . ," he wrote. "The book is more concerned with the process of creation and discovery than with the intricacies of particle theory, making ideal reading for anyone wanting to savour the scientific lifestyle and mind-set without getting bogged down in technicalities." The medical and health writer Sally Squires wrote in her critique for the *Washington Post* (August 17, 2003), "Where [the book] succeeds best is in explaining the theories, from quantum electrodynamics to string theory." She complained that Mlodinow "can be maddeningly whiny and self-centered."

Meanwhile, after his year at Caltech, Mlodinow had won an Alexander von Humboldt fellowship, awarded by the Humboldt Foundation, a German organization that recognizes promising young scientists and enables them to do research in Germany. Mlodinow worked at the Max Planck Institute for Physics and Astrophysics, in Munich, where he investigated quantum field theory as it applied to dielectrics, or substances that do not conduct electricity.

In 1985 Mlodinow was "bitten by the Hollywood bug," as he put it on his Caltech Web site. Encouraged by Feynman to pursue his writing aspirations, and having written a screenplay already, Mlodinow moved to Los Angeles. Six months later, with only $110 left of his savings, he sold his first script. He subsequently wrote for television series including *Night Court, MacGyver, Hunter, O'Hara, The New Adam 12, It's Garry Shandling's Show, Grand, What's Happening Now!!, Nine to Five*, and *Star Trek: The Next Generation*, for the last of which he also worked as a story editor. In 1993 Mlodinow entered the computer-gaming field. In a collaboration with Steven Spielberg, Robin Williams, and the Walt Disney Co., he became the designer, producer, and executive producer of several prize-winning games.

In 1997 Mlodinow settled in New York City, where until 2003 he served as the vice president for software development at Scholastic Inc., which publishes books, CDs, and DVDs for youngsters; he also held the title of vice president and publisher for math education. Mlodinow launched Scholastic's children's-games arm and helped develop it into one of the top five such divisions in the United States. On his own time he began to write books on popular science.

The first of those books, *Euclid's Window: The Story of Geometry from Parallel Lines to Hyperspace*, was published in 2001. In it Mlodinow presented an overview of the evolution of geometry by describing five major "revolutions" in the field and the men responsible for them. The first was Euclid, a Greek mathematician who lived two or three centuries before the Christian era. In the first six of the 13 books that comprise his *Elements*—the whole of which is considered the most influential textbook of all time—Euclid offered the first known systematic discussion of plane geometry (which involves shapes on a two-dimensional surface) and introduced the deductive method of mathematical proof. Mlodinow next focused on René Descartes, the 17th-century French philosopher and mathematician who invented the coordinate graphing system, which uses two perpendicular axes—the horizontal x axis and the vertical y axis—to describe the position of any point or the perimeter of any geometric figure. Mlodinow's third mathematician, the German genius Carl Friedrich Gauss (1777–1855), realized that Euclid's fifth postulate—that through any point external to a given line, only one line can be drawn parallel to the given line (an idea that seems obvious in everyday life, a common example being railroad tracks)—cannot be deduced from his other postulates. Mlodinow then offered a chapter about the physicist Albert Einstein, whose astounding insights in his General Theory of Relativity forever changed physicists' and cosmologists' ideas about the universe. Space and time, according to Einstein, are parts of a single entity, called spacetime, which is curved and thus cannot be described by means of Euclidean geometry. Mlodinow's last subject was the contemporary theoretical physicist Edward Witten, a major figure in superstring theory, which, in mathematical terms, models all particles and forces in nature as minuscule, densely curled, vibrating strings. Superstring theory is thought by many in the scientific community to be a possible model for the development of a unified theory for all of physics.

In an enthusiastic review of *Euclid's Window* for *New Scientist* (May 12, 2001), Ian Stewart wrote, "Mlodinow attempts the difficult task of presenting geometry as a core activity in mathematics, science and human culture, and pulls it off brilliantly. . . . *Euclid's Window* is a remarkably painless way to discover just how central geometric thinking has been to human culture." "The book is ideal for victims of early specialization in the humanities," Edward Skidelsky declared in his assessment for the London *Daily Telegraph* (February 2, 2002). "Mlodinow has a talent for lively and clear exposition. I understood—or at least I had the vivid illusion of understanding—non-Euclidean geometry." At the same time, Skidelsky found fault with Mlodinow's "unfortunate habit . . . of trying to compensate for the inherent abstractness of his subject with the occasional 'human touch.' The results are excruciating. His humour is of the geeky, bow-tie variety."

In 2005 Mlodinow collaborated with the renowned British theoretical physicist and cosmologist Stephen Hawking to revise Hawking's book *A Brief History of Time* (1988), which, despite being a best-seller that has sold 10 million copies, was widely acknowledged to be largely incomprehensible to most readers. (Hawking, who has suffered for four decades from amyotrophic lateral sclerosis, commonly called Lou Gehrig's disease, cannot move or speak; he communicates by means of a voice synthesizer, which he activates by blinking.) In *A Briefer History of Time*, Mlodinow and Hawking covered the same material—the origin of the universe (and of time), its composition and behavior, and where it might be headed—and discussed some of the results of the last two decades of discoveries in cosmology and astrophysics. According to Michelle Presser, writing about *A Briefer History of Time* for *Scientific American* (August 2008), "Hawking received many requests for a version that would make his discussion of deep questions about the universe more accessible. This book does that. Hawking and Mlodinow . . . proceed by small and careful steps from the early history of astronomy to today's efforts to construct a grand unified theory of the universe." A reviewer for *Publishers Weekly*, quoted on Amazon.com, wrote, "Hawking and Mlodinow provide one of the most lucid discussions of this complex topic ever written for a general audience."

In *The Drunkard's Walk: How Randomness Rules Our Lives* (2008), Mlodinow attempted to weave neatly into one account "three areas that are historically not that smoothly tied together—probability, statistics and the random processes," he explained to Seth Roberts. The theme of the book is that, as can be shown mathematically, chance has a far greater effect on the world than most people realize, and success is often the result more of luck than of expertise. "A path punctuated by random impacts and unintended consequences is the path of many successful people . . . ," Mlodinow wrote in the book. "In fact, it is more the rule than the exception." Through discussions of the work of such 18th- and 19th-century mathematicians as Daniel Bernoulli, Pierre-Simon LaPlace, and Blaise Pascal and analyses of ordinary events, Mlodinow showed that the laws of probability and the phenomenon of randomness contradict many widely held assumptions. As an example, he cited the experience of Sherry Lansing, for some years the chief executive officer of Paramount Pictures, whose string of blockbuster movies—*Forrest Gump, Braveheart,* and *Titanic*—led people to hail her as a genius and to expect her success to continue. But the statistical rule known as the law of regression to the mean made that unlikely to happen. According to that law, if someone performs significantly better than expected several times in a row, that person's next performance will be closer to average. Paramount's next few films proved to be box-office disappointments, and Lansing was subjected to harsh criticism. The law of regression also explains why a gambler's chances of winning large sums decrease the longer he or she continues to place bets, and why no mutual fund has consistently surpassed others in generating profits. That is because no one can predict with 100 percent certainty the success or failure of any particular film or any particular athletic competition, horse race, election, or anything else in which factors beyond the control of humans play a part. Despite the mathematical support for his explanations, Mlodinow told John Allemang for the Toronto, Canada, *Globe and Mail* (July 5, 2008), "People have a hard time buying my arguments when I try to convince them."

The Drunkard's Walk reached number 10 on the *New York Times* best-seller list in August 2008, and it has been widely praised. Writing for the London *Guardian* (July 12, 2008), Tim Radford described its appeal: "Most of us don't want to know about quantum mechanics, even if we do want to know why the universe is as it is. But we all want to know what follows when we take a chance on love, the lottery or a smear test for cancer. . . . Our lives may be shaped by chance, but they are enriched by awareness—just the sort of awareness that this fascinating book will give you." In June 2009 *The Drunkard's Walk* was shortlisted for the Royal Society Prize for Science Books, which celebrates the best science writing for a general adult readership published in the previous year.

Mlodinow's essays on randomness and probability have been published in various newspapers and magazines. In an article for the *New York Times* (June 15, 2009, on-line), Mlodinow discussed humans' desire to feel in control in light of the present economic recession. He wrote that his mother, unlike the average American, has not felt bothered by the recession, because "her early experiences of utter powerlessness" during World War II "taught her to give herself up to what she calls fate. Understanding my own need for control—and exactly why I cannot have it—I now take comfort in letting go of the illusion, and accepting that despite all my efforts and planning some aspects of my future are beyond my sphere of influence."

With Matt Costello, Mlodinow has written two books for adolescents in a series called The Kids of Einstein Elementary: *The Last Dinosaur* and *Titanic Cat,* both published in 2004. With Stephen Hawking and three others, he co-wrote the film *Beyond the Horizon,* which was to be released in I-MAX theaters in 2009. According to Mlodinow's Web site, the film follows a reporter who, in a diversion from her usual beat, religion, embarks on a "whirlwind journey through time and space, where deep space images explode onto the big screen and where the 'Big Questions' are answered" during an interview with Stephen Hawking. Due to appear in 2010 is a Random House audio-book, entitled *The Grand Design,* which Mlodinow and Hawking co-wrote. Mlodinow currently teaches a course at Caltech, "Introduction to Probability, Statistics, and Random Processes," which, as he wrote for his Web site, "explores the theory of random processes, with an emphasis on understanding its application in experimental science, engineering, and popular culture."

Mlodinow was injured when, while he was standing on the street beside the World Trade Center on September 11, 2001, terrorists flew a plane into the North Tower. The trauma suffered by one of his children, who was attending a kindergarten class minutes away from the center that day, led to his and his ex-wife's move from New York City to South Pasadena, California. With his ex-wife, he shares custody of his sons, Alexei and Nicholai.

—M.E.R.

Suggested Reading:Leonard Mlodinow's Caltech Web site; (London) *Daily Telegraph* p4 Feb. 2, 2002; *New York Times* BR p14 June 18, 2008, (on-line) June 15, 2009; *Scotland on Sunday* p4 June 29, 2003; Seth Roberts's blog Jan. 29–30, 2009; (Toronto, Canada) *Globe and Mail* F p7 July 5, 2008; *Wall Street Journal* (on-line) Apr. 30, 2008; *Washington Post* T p13 Aug. 17, 2003; *Washington Post Book World* p5 June 18, 2001

Selected Books: *Euclid's Window: The Story of Geometry from Parallel Lines to Hyperspace,* 2001; *Feynman's Rainbow: A Search for Beauty in Physics and in Life,* 2003; *A Briefer History of Time* (with Stephen Hawking), 2005; *The Drunkard's Walk: How Randomness Rules Our Lives,* 2008

Selected Television Shows: As writer: *Night Court,* 1984; *MacGyver,* 1987; *Star Trek: The Next Generation,* 1989; *Hunter,* 1989; *Adam 12,* 1990

Selected Films: as co-writer: *Beyond the Horizon,* 2009

©NPR, by Sandy Huffaker

Montagne, Renee

(mon-TANE)

1950(?)– Radio journalist; co-host of Morning Edition

Address: NPR West, 9909 Jefferson Blvd., Culver City, CA 90232-3505

For over two decades Renee Montagne's voice has been a familiar one to National Pubic Radio (NPR) listeners. In 2004 she was selected as co-host, along with Steve Inskeep, of one of NPR's most popular shows, *Morning Edition*—a live, two-hour morning news program with a daily audience of 13 million. Montagne began her work for NPR in the early 1980s, serving as co-host of the network's program *All Things Considered* for two years beginning in 1987. She has since filed thousands of stories—interviewing such prominent guests as the musician Paul McCartney and the novelist Kurt Vonnegut and reporting on topics including the release of Nelson Mandela from prison in South Africa; the funeral of Pope John Paul II in Italy; the complex social and political circumstances in Afghanistan, following the September 11, 2001 terrorist attacks on New York City and Washington, D.C., and the U.S. invasion later that year; and Afghanistan's 2009 presidential election.

The second of the three children of Ellene and Arthur "Bud" Montagne, Renee Montagne was born in about 1950 in California. Her father, a Marine Corps officer who attained the rank of major, witnessed the attack on Pearl Harbor, in 1941. A civil and aerospace engineer, Arthur Montagne retired from the military when his daughter was eight years old; afterward, with his family in tow, he moved to various places—including Arizona and Hawaii—where he had found work. (Montagne's mother was fond of moving to new locales.) Interviewed for the book *Public Radio: Behind the Voices* (2006), by Lisa A. Phillips, Montagne said on the subject of the frequent moves, "I made friends easily, so I never felt weird when I moved into a new classroom. You know, hi! Here I am!" Montagne had a close relationship with her father, whom she described to Phillips as a "real feminist." She added, "I would ask him a question about something, and we'd sit up until one in the morning talking about it. And he knew everything. I mean he knew—not everything, but he knew a lot about the world and knew things with great detail and he was pretty much always right, as best as I've been able to tell." As a girl Montagne did not listen to the radio a great deal. She excelled at writing and also enjoyed math and science; she considered becoming a physician.

Montagne enrolled at the University of California at Berkeley, where she graduated Phi Beta Kappa with a B.A. degree in English. During her years there she befriended two women who would go on to be famous writers, Ntozake Shange and Jessica Hagedorn. Both had radio shows on KPOO, a volunteer-run radio station in the San Francisco Bay Area, which was known as "Poor People's Radio" and as a "third-world" station. (According to the station's Web site, "KPOO's ongoing mission has been to open the airwaves to the disenfranchised and underserved.") Montagne obtained a radio license so that she could perform duties on Shange's music program, *The Original Aboriginal Dancing Girl*. Montagne was "the odd man out" at the station, "not being black or brown or Asian," she told Phillips. When others at the station suggested that she start a news department there, Montagne became news director and host of a program called *Women's Voices*. "Thank God none of it is on tape, none of it," she said for Phillips's book. "There were people there getting serious, going to journalism school. And I was just trying to do something fun and creative."

Montagne began contributing stories on a freelance basis to Pacific News Service, a nonprofit media organization that runs a wire service and produces documentary films with a focus on people it calls "marginalized" members of American society, among them immigrants, minorities, young people, and the elderly. On the advice of Hagedorn, who was having a play produced in New York City, Montagne moved there herself in 1980. With what Phillips called an "I'll-do-anything" attitude, Montagne filed stories for NPR for $30 each, rarely if ever turning down work; she also worked for the Canadian Broadcasting Corp. In the mid-1980s Montagne traveled to South Africa, which was still under the racial caste system called apartheid. Reporting from there with no expense account for housing, she was unable to stay in upscale areas with other correspondents; instead, she found quarters in racially mixed areas that bucked the country's segregation laws. The friends she made there offered her insights into the ways that the antiapartheid movement was changing life in the country. "It was intense and dangerous stuff," she said to Phillips. "But I always had the theory that I was always better off to go alone. And that I would be protected, basically."

Also in the 1980s Montagne became the health and science correspondent for *All Things Considered*, which at the time was NPR's most popular show. One day in December 1986 Montagne got a call from the Washington, D.C., headquarters of NPR and was asked to guest-host *All Things Considered* on Christmas Eve. She enjoyed doing so, even though the assignment was different from her previous work. "My entire experience as a journalist has been as a reporter," Montagne told Brian G. Bourke for the Syracuse, New York, *Post-Standard* (April 26, 1987). "I'm just not used to being part of the interview as the anchor has to be. As a reporter I am used to taking myself out of the story." NPR officials were in search of new anchors for *All Things Considered*, whose highly regarded co-hosts, Susan Stamberg and Noah Adams, had left the show. Montagne applied successfully to co-host the show with Robert Siegel. She held that post for two years, by the end of which her confinement to the studio—where she conducted long-distance interviews—had made her restless. "I was like, this is my life?" she recalled to Phillips. "I never meet anyone, I never see them, I never make eye contact."

In 1990 Montagne returned to South Africa to cover the release from prison of Nelson Mandela. (A political prisoner since 1962, Mandela had seen his reputation as a civil rights and antiapartheid leader grow steadily during his imprisonment. Released on February 11, 1990, he embarked on a world tour, making stops in major cities throughout North America and Europe, where he was welcomed as a hero.) Montagne reported from South Africa for NPR for three years. She returned there in April 1994 for the presidential election, won by Mandela; for their coverage of the election, Montagne and a team of other NPR reporters received the prestigious Alfred I. duPont–Columbia University Award. Reflecting on her time in the country—where she covered riots, elections, and the people of South Africa—Montagne told Jayette Bolinski for the Springfield, Illinois, *State Journal-Register* (November 16, 2001), "It was an intense and exciting time." Throughout the late 1990s Montagne reported for NPR in the U.S. and occasionally served as a guest co-host of *Morning Edition*.

After the September 11, 2001 terrorist attacks, Montagne went to Afghanistan, where Al Qaeda, the group responsible for the attacks, had established a base of operations. She traveled throughout the country, interviewing people ranging from farmers to mullahs to warlords, and even Hamid Karzai, after his election as president in December 2004. She covered a great variety of topics, including the popularity of an Afghani soap opera; the challenges for Americans living in Afghanistan; the dangers faced by foreign journalists there; the fighting in eastern Afghanistan between the U.S. Army and the forces of the country's Muslim fundamentalist Taliban regime; and the new Afghan government's uncertain grip on the country, following the U.S.'s toppling of the Taliban.

As of March 2004 Bob Edwards had been the sole host of *Morning Edition* for 24 years. NPR then reassigned Edwards to a reporting position and named Montagne and Steve Inskeep *Morning Edition*'s interim hosts; in December of that year, they took over their duties permanently, with Montagne based on the West Coast and Inskeep in Washington, D.C. Tens of thousands of calls, letters, and e-mail messages poured in from Edwards's fans in protest, but NPR executives felt that the two-host format would bring new energy and rigor to the broadcast; while it was unusual for Edwards to leave the studio for a story, for example, Montagne and Inskeep had often reported from afar. (In April 2005, for example, Montagne went to Rome, Italy, to cover the funeral of Pope John Paul II.) NPR officials also reasoned that two hosts on opposite coasts would bring to the show a greater variety of experience and perspective—and more West Coast coverage. Montagne, for example, reported on the likelihood that a tsunami would strike the West Coast, a story that might not have been covered otherwise.

Although Montagne and Inskeep became interim hosts in the spring of 2004, "the seeds of a bicoastally hosted *Morning Edition*," Susan Carpenter wrote for the *Los Angeles Times* (December 4, 2004), "date back further, to Sept. 11, 2001, which prompted the need for continuous news coverage." *Morning Edition*'s executive producer, Ellen McDonnell, told Carpenter, "When *Morning Edition* started, it was a studio show, a two-hour show. It was dusted off a little bit as it went west with big changes if needed, but most of the changes were minor. With 9/11, the listeners turned to us to know the latest information, and so that started a cycle of news that I don't think has let up." Three years after taking over as hosts, Montagne and Inskeep had established a large following. After only a year the show gained about 800,000 new listeners, and by 2007 the show had 13 million listeners in total. "Now here we are, three years later," Sam McManis wrote for the *Sacramento Bee* (May 22, 2007), "and you hardly hear a peep of protest about the *Morning Edition* lineup. Edwards, certainly, still has his supporters, who can listen to his show on XM satellite radio. But it's widely believed—especially in this space—that *Morning Edition* is a better, newsier, more nimble and relevant program with Renee Montagne and Steve Inskeep as co-hosts." Whereas Montagne had felt restless interviewing guests from the studio as the co-host of *All Things Considered*, her attitude about that kind of interviewing "shifted," as Phillips wrote; she feels a greater connection to her guests than before. She told Phillips, "I feel like when I hear guests in my ears, it's like a phone call. You know how in a phone call, you can feel like they're right there?" "To the listener . . . the show flows smoothly," Sam McManis wrote. "In fact, Montagne says, people often are surprised to learn the hosts are situated 3,000 miles apart."

As a correspondent for *Morning Edition*, Montagne has interviewed many very famous people, including writers and musicians. One of her favorite interviews, she told Susan Whitall for the *Detroit News* (May 8, 2008), was with the former Beatle Paul McCartney, in November 2002. The following year, on September 10, 2003, Montagne interviewed Kurt Vonnegut, the celebrated author of many novels, including *Slaughterhouse Five*. In the interview Vonnegut shared with Montagne his experience of being a prisoner of war in Dresden, Germany, during the Allied firebombing of the city toward the end of World War II. Vonnegut told Montagne, "The whole city was burned down, and it was a British atrocity . . . they came in and set the whole town on fire with a new kind of incendiary bomb. And so everything organic, except my little POW group"—who were deep underground, in the meat locker of a slaughterhouse—"was consumed by fire. And it was a military experiment to find out if you could burn a whole city down by scattering incendiaries all over it. . . . Finally they gave up this procedure because it was too slow and, of course, the city was starting to smell pretty bad. They sent in guys with flame-throwers." Earlier in the interview he said, "It was pure nonsense, the pointless destruction of that city." Of the many interviews Montagne has conducted, she has found politicians to be the most difficult subjects, because, as she told Whitall, "they're too on message."

In 2006 Montagne was honored by the Overseas Press Club for her coverage of Afghanistan. In late July 2009 she left her NPR West studio to do on-location reporting from that country, where she covered the upcoming presidential election, in which there were nearly 40 candidates. In addition to gathering the opinions of average Afghanis, Montagne spoke with the two top challengers to Afghan president Hamid Karzai—Ashraf Ghani and Abdullah Abdullah—as well as several lesser-known challengers. Amid charges of election fraud, Karzai won reelection. On *Morning Edition* Montagne has said that according to U.N. observers, there is "convincing evidence" of such fraud. Montagne also spoke with U.S. government and army officials about the ongoing U.S. military campaign in Afghanistan as well as the U.S. government's efforts to eliminate, or reduce, the cultivation of opium-poppy seeds—a key ingredient in heroin as well as opium—which are said to provide a steady monetary stream to terrorist organizations.

Montagne's workday—at NPR West's headquarters, in Culver City, California—begins at around 11 p.m., Monday through Friday, when she starts her writing and research. The show goes live at 2:00 a.m. (5:00 a.m. on the East Coast.) Montagne leaves the studio at about 11:00 a.m. and typically goes to bed at three in the afternoon. Phillips wrote about interviewing the journalist, "Montagne's manner is bubbly and effusive. . . . She speaks fast, her stories full of little digressions and retakes. She'll interrupt one flow of thought with another in her eagerness to get all the details in and express what she wants to say more effectively. The experience of interviewing her was like reading the edited manuscript of a great short story, full of cross outs and notes scribbled in between the lines and down the margins." Montagne, who is single, lives in Santa Monica, California.

—D.K.

Suggested Reading: Current.org Dec. 13, 2004; *Los Angeles Times* E p1 Dec. 4, 2004; npr.org; *Sacramento Bee* E p1 May 22, 2007; Phillips, Lisa A. *Public Radio: Behind the Voices*, 2006

Courtesy of Central Asia Institute

Mortenson, Greg

Dec. 27, 1957– Humanitarian; co-founder and director of the Central Asia Institute and Pennies for Peace; writer

Address: Central Asia Institute, P.O. Box 7209, Bozeman, MT 59771

A wrong turn that Greg Mortenson took in 1992, at the age of 34—while descending K2, the second-highest peak on Earth—led to a radical change in the direction of his life. Within months of his experience on the mountain, he had abandoned his career as an emergency-room and trauma nurse and taken the first steps toward what became his new profession—that of co-founder and director of the Central Asia Institute (CAI). Since 1996 the CAI has raised money for and/or completed the construction of approximately 130 schools serving tens of thousands of children, most of them in poverty-stricken Muslim villages in remote parts of northern Pakistan and Afghanistan. The CAI has also funded and overseen other community-based projects in those areas as well as in Kyrgyzstan and Mongolia, primarily with the aim of educating girls and women and shrinking the influence of the fundamentalist religious organization known as the Taliban.

For six years beginning in 1996, the Taliban, whose members belong to the Sunni branch of Islam, ruled most of Afghanistan, albeit unofficially; it was ousted from power by U.S.-led forces, who invaded in late 2001 in response to the September 11 terrorist attacks on the U.S. The Taliban has since regained strongholds in Afghanistan and taken over parts of Pakistan, all the while ruthlessly attempting to expunge Western culture from the region. One of the Taliban's principal beliefs is that no female should be formally educated; during the years that the group virtually ruled Afghanistan, it outlawed the schooling of girls and women, and in the past few years, members of the Taliban have destroyed hundreds of schools, including boys' schools that did not adhere to a strict Sunni Muslim curriculum. Mortenson firmly believes that the only way to defeat the Taliban in the long run, and in the process change the societies in which it flourishes, is through the widespread education of girls in schools whose curricula include the promotion of basic human rights (as spelled out, for example, in the United Nations' Universal Declaration of Human Rights). Women educated along those lines, Mortenson contends, would not willingly agree to their sons' becoming suicide bombers, as the mothers of many Taliban bombers have, and they would not support their attacking others simply because of religious differences. Mortenson's ideas are based both on his observations during many visits to Afghanistan and Pakistan and on research showing that educating girls to at least the fifth-grade level leads to measurable improvements in the standard of living of the societies in which those girls become adults.

Mortenson's life and work are the subjects of the award-winning book *Three Cups of Tea* (2006), co-written by David Oliver Relin, which as of October 25, 2009 had been on the *New York Times* paperbacks best-seller list for 141 weeks. Mortenson "has become a legend in the [Afghanistan–Pakistan border] region, his picture sometimes dangling like a talisman from rearview mirrors," and he "has done more to advance U.S. interests in the region than the entire military and foreign policy apparatus of the administration" of President George W. Bush, Nicholas Kristof wrote in his *New York Times* (July 13, 2008) column. "Mortenson's efforts remind us what the essence of the 'war on terrorism' is about," another *Times* columnist, Thomas L. Friedman, wrote for the July 19, 2009 edition of that paper, after witnessing Mortenson and Mike Mullen, the chairman of the Joint Chiefs of Staff, celebrate the opening of a new school in Afghanistan earlier that week. "It's about the war of ideas within Islam—a war between religious zealots who glorify martyrdom and want to keep Islam untouched by modernity and isolated from other faiths, with its women disempowered, and those who want to embrace modernity, open Islam to new ideas and empower Muslim women as much as men. America's invasions of Iraq and Afghanistan were, in part, an effort to create the space for the Muslim progressives to fight and win so that the real engine of change, something that takes nine months and 21 years to produce—a new generation—can be educated and raised differently."

Mortenson's honors include the Golden Piton Award for humanitarian effort, from *Climbing* magazine (2003), the Free Spirit Award, from the National Press Club (2004), and the Dayton Literary Peace Prize (2007). He has also received honorary doctoral degrees from 10 colleges and universities.

Of Norwegian ancestry, Greg Mortenson was born on December 27, 1957 in St. Cloud, Minnesota, the oldest child and only boy among the four children of Irvin "Dempsey" Mortenson and Jerene Mortenson. He has two married sisters, Kari and Sonja. His third sister, Christa, who was 11 years his junior, became mentally disabled and epileptic after she was stricken with meningitis in early childhood; a severe attack of epilepsy ended her life in 1992. When Greg was three months old, his parents settled in the part of East Africa now known as Tanzania, where they had taken teaching jobs. The family lived in a village on the remote Usambara Mountains and later in Moshi, a town at the base of Mount Kilimanjaro, Africa's tallest mountain. Mortenson's parents were Lutheran missionaries who "wore their faith lightly," in his words, and were more interested in helping to improve education and health care among the local people than in proselytizing. Mortenson's father spent a decade raising funds to establish the nation's first teaching hospital, the Kilimanjaro Christian Medical Centre, which opened in 1971. In 1969 Jerene Mortenson founded the Moshi International School, which currently has 300 students from more than 28 countries. Early on Greg Mortenson displayed sympathy for the poor and disadvantaged. His mother recalled to Karin Ronnow for the *Bozeman (Montana) Daily Chronicle* (October 7, 2007) that one day when Greg was a toddler, she found him outside their house, chatting with an old beggar and handing the man cookies from a jar. The little boy "didn't just give him something, they were talking," she said. "And that just sums up how Greg has been all his life." Mortenson learned to speak Swahili and grew up without television.

At age 11 he climbed to the summit of Mount Kilimanjaro with his father. Though the exertion and thin air made him sick—"I was gagging and puking all the way to the top," he told Terry Gross for the National Public Radio series *Fresh Air* (February 7, 2002, on-line)—the experience sparked in him a passion for mountaineering.

When Greg was 15 the Mortensons returned to the U.S. and settled in St. Paul, Minnesota. In Ramsey High School, in Roseville, a St. Paul suburb, Greg felt like an outsider and was subjected to taunts and ridicule from his peers. He played football and was adept at languages, math, and science. Heeding the advice of his parents, he enlisted in the U.S. Army four days after his graduation, to help pay for college. (The army paid monthly education benefits to eligible veterans.) For two years beginning in 1975, Mortenson served as a field medic in Bamberg, Germany; in his leisure time he traveled to other cities in Europe. He earned the Army Commendation Medal for his prowess in evacuating soldiers in a live-fire exercise. In 1977 he enrolled at Concordia College, in Moorhead, Minnesota, on a football scholarship; during his two years there, his team won the National Association of Intercollegiate Athletics Division II football championship. He left Concordia to attend the University of South Dakota (USD) at Vermillion. Soon afterward his father was diagnosed with cancer. Every other weekend until his father's death, in mid-1981, Mortenson drove to his parents' home to help care for him; the round-trip commute took 12 hours. Mortenson earned a B.A. degree in chemistry and an associate's degree in nursing in 1983. He next worked as an emergency-room nurse in South Dakota hospitals, in places including the Pine Ridge Indian Reservation. He moved to Indianapolis, Indiana, in 1985, and the next year he entered a master's-degree program in medical neuroscience at the University of Indiana Medical School, with the goal of finding a cure for epilepsy; after realizing that he did not want to devote the years to that pursuit that it would probably entail, he left the school, without earning the degree. For much of 1988 he lived in Minnesota with his sister Christa, with whom he had always remained close. Then he moved to San Francisco, California, where he worked as a trauma nurse and spent his free time mountaineering.

Christa's death, on the morning of her 23d birthday, devastated Mortenson. Seeking to honor her memory, he joined a 12-person expedition to climb K2, which lies within the Karakoram Mountains on the border of Pakistan and China; at 28,251 feet, K2 is less than 800 feet shorter than Earth's highest peak, Mount Everest. Mortenson hoped to leave Christa's amber necklace at the summit of K2, which is notorious for the fearsome hazards it presents to climbers; nearly one in four people have reportedly died in the attempt to conquer it. (Five members of Mortenson's expedition did not survive the climb.) Mortenson spent nearly four months on K2 and had come within 2,000 feet of the top when he lost his way and was forced to turn back. (That mishap occurred after he became separated from his climbing partner; Mortenson had helped another member of his party who had become incapacitated from altitude sickness.) By chance he wandered into Korphe, a tiny, impoverished Pakistani farming village 10,000 feet above sea level in the Karakorams. By that time Mortenson weighed 30 pounds less than he had before the climb, and he felt sick as well as overwhelmingly disheartened by his failure to achieve his goal; he was also bedraggled and filthy, having not showered for many weeks. Haji Ali, the chief of Korphe, and other peasants helped the physically and mentally exhausted Mortenson recuperate in their homes. Mortenson was amazed by their generosity and the strenuousness of the work that enabled them to live in such a difficult environment. He was also saddened by their extreme poverty: they suffered malnutrition, a high rate of infant mortality, chronic infections, and other problems linked to a poor diet and lack of access to modern methods of medicine and hygiene. During his three weeks in Korphe, Mortenson made use of his nursing skills to set broken bones and stitch wounds, and he supplied aspirin and antibiotics to grateful villagers, who took to calling him "Dr. Greg."

Korphe was too poor to build a school or hire a full-time teacher, not least because corrupt local officials regularly pocketed government money allocated for education. Nevertheless, whenever possible, children gathered in the open air to study—even on days when frost covered the ground—with or without the help of a part-time instructor. When Mortenson saw children working on arithmetic by marking the earth with sticks or writing on slates with mud, he felt as if his "heart was being torn out," he told David Relin. "There was a fierceness in their desire to learn, despite how mightily everything was stacked against them, that reminded me of Christa. I knew I had to do something." Mortenson impulsively promised Haji Ali that he would come back and build a school in Korphe.

Back home in California in late 1993, Mortenson set about raising the $12,000 he and village leaders had estimated it would cost to build a five-room schoolhouse for 100 students up to the fifth-grade level. To save money he sold most of his possessions and gave up his apartment, living out of his car for a while. Using a rented typewriter, he painstakingly typed a few letters asking for contributions. Then, by chance, a Pakistani shopkeeper taught him how to use a computer, and he quickly printed 580 letters and sent them to people he knew and wealthy celebrities. Among his few responses was only one from a famous person: a check for $100 from the NBC broadcast journalist Tom Brokaw, a fellow USD graduate. Soon afterward, at the suggestion of his mother, he gave a talk about his project to pupils at the Westside Elementary School in River Falls, Wisconsin, where his mother was the principal. He later received

$623.45 in pennies from the children. (Pennies for Peace, which he founded in 1995, grew out of that experience; it is now an arm of CAI.) Thanks to a doctor at the hospital where he was working, a story about him and his project was published in the newsletter of the American Himalayan Foundation in 1994. The article attracted the attention of the Swiss-born Silicon Valley inventor and entrepreneur Jean Hoerni, an avid mountaineer who had climbed in the Karakorams. Hoerni sent Mortenson a check for $12,000, along with a note reading, "Don't screw up."

In the fall of 1994, Mortenson returned to Pakistan to fulfill his promise, only to discover that before the school could be built, a bridge would have to be erected over the nearby Braldu River, so that the materials and equipment necessary for construction could be transported to the town. (The existing bridge, made of yak hair, was not strong enough for that purpose.) Mortenson flew back to California, secured funding for the bridge from Hoerni, and then returned to Korphe. Built with local labor, the 282-foot suspension bridge was completed in eight weeks. Meanwhile, realizing the importance of forming personal relationships and respecting local Pakistani mores, Mortenson had learned the language (a dialect of Urdu) spoken in Baltistan, that area of Pakistan. He worked to familiarize himself with the local culture and began to pray in the Islamic tradition.

During a trip back to the States in 1995, Mortenson attended a benefit dinner for the American Himalayan Foundation with Hoerni. There, he met Tara Bishop, the daughter of Barry Bishop, a National Geographic Society photographer who had climbed Mount Everest; Mortenson and Tara married six days later. Around that time Hoerni offered to donate $1 million to endow a nonprofit organization that would be set up to fund projects in Pakistan and Afghanistan. Mortenson became the director of that organization, the Central Asia Institute; his office was in the basement of the house he and Bishop had moved into. Hoerni saw a photo of the school, construction of which was completed in late 1996, shortly before his death, in January 1997. His will included provisions pertaining to CAI's endowment. The school admitted its first students in mid-1997; Mortenson, his wife, and their six-month-old daughter, Amira, attended the opening. In the next few years, with funding from the CAI, Mortenson and the residents of other impoverished villages were able to work more quickly to address the needs of youngsters and women in the region. By 1999 the CAI had undertaken the building of 11 schools, the installations of six potable-water systems, and the establishment of two women's vocational-training centers, and had launched a series of environmental-education workshops for teachers.

Though Mortenson's work was not politically motivated, it had significant political implications in the turbulent regions in which he was working. After the Soviet Union lost control of Afghanistan, in 1989, the Taliban began to recruit members from among the poor and uneducated mountain villagers in Afghanistan and near its border with Pakistan, attracting them with the promise of jobs. In 1996, when the Taliban in effect gained control of Afghanistan, females were banned from attending school and hundreds of radical Islamic religious schools, called madrassas, were opened. Mortenson came to see education as the key to providing children with the possibility of bettering their lives, improving societies as a whole, and preventing terrorism. "I've learned that terror doesn't happen because some group of people somewhere like Pakistan or Afghanistan simply decide to hate us," Mortenson told members of Congress, as quoted by Richard A. Kauffman in the *Christian Century* (July 29, 2008). "It happens because children aren't being offered a bright enough future that they have a reason to choose life over death." Moreover, he concluded that educating girls is even more important than educating boys, in part because whereas young men often leave their villages and move to larger towns and cities once they finish school, women tend to stay in their communities and use their knowledge to improve the quality of life there. In addition, Mortenson has pointed out, the Koran stipulates that men must ask permission from their mothers before they can engage in jihad, whether militant or not. ("Jihad," which means "struggle" in Arabic, refers both to an individual's attempts to live according to the tenets of Islam and to an individual's or group's efforts to spread Islam to nonbelievers and increase the amount of territory ruled by Muslims. In the West "jihad" is usually interpreted to mean "holy war.") "When women have an education they're much less likely to condone their sons getting into violence," Mortenson told Sue Corbett for the *Miami (Florida) Herald* (January 24, 2009).

Earlier, in the midst of construction of the school in Korphe, Mortenson's activities had provoked suspicion among local Pakistani village leaders and mullahs (men educated in Islamic law and theology), who feared that he intended to incite youngsters to challenge Islamic traditions. In August 1996 Mortenson was kidnapped while traveling in Peshawar, a city in Pakistan's mountainous Waziristan region, on the Afghan border. During the eight days that he was held prisoner, he earned his kidnappers' trust by showing respect for Islamic culture: he requested a Koran and a translator, prayed, and told his captors that his wife was pregnant with his firstborn son. (Mortenson knew that to them, a firstborn son was considered more important than a daughter.) When he was released (he had been used as a bargaining chip in a tribal dispute), his kidnappers gave him a handful of coins to help fund his school-building efforts.

Mortenson has also been the target of two fatwas (rulings by Muslim scholars or clerics that hold the weight of official law) to prevent him from building schools; one came from Shiite and the other from Sunni scholars, and both were retracted after pressure by locals. The first was issued in 1997 by a local official who objected to Mortenson's efforts to educate Pakistani girls. In response to that fatwa, Mortenson contacted the Pakistani Shiite Islamic leader Said Abas Resvi and appealed to the Supreme Islamic Council, in Kholm, Iran. During the next year or so, the council dispatched "spies" to CAI's school sites to determine the extent of Western influence in the curriculum and to ask questions about Mortenson's intentions and behavior while he was working in Pakistan: Did he drink alcohol? Did he seduce Muslim women? The answers to those and other questions were no. In April 1998 the council sent word to Mortenson that they had ruled that his work "follows the highest principles of Islam" and granted him their permission to continue it. After earning that judgment the CAI received an increase in proposals from local village leaders to build schools for both boys and girls.

On September 11, 2001 Mortenson was in a village near the Pakistan–Afghanistan border, opening a new school. He learned about the attacks on the World Trade Center and Washington, D.C., about eight hours after they occurred. "Immediately . . . there was an outpouring of sympathy," he told Terry Gross. "I met with Islamic leaders in prayer sessions and they, without exception, told me that this was not in accordance with Islam and that these were terrorists. Village army commanders, village chiefs, children, women—they embraced me. . . . What I saw and felt over the next two months certainly didn't reflect what I saw in the press when I came back here to the States." When Mortenson returned to Montana, he received hate mail accusing him of "helping the enemy" and wishing for his "painful death." Speaking of those who made such accusations, Mortenson told Stephanie Yap for the *Singapore Strait Times* (January 27, 2008), "They are ignorant and they don't understand complex issues. Terrorism is based on fear, peace is based on hope. The real enemy, really, is ignorance."

An article about Mortenson in *Parade* magazine (April 6, 2003) by David Oliver Relin, a journalist who had traveled with him, brought a lot of attention to the CAI. Donations increased manyfold, and Mortenson, now seen as someone with a unique perspective on conditions in Afghanistan and Pakistan, was invited to testify before lawmakers on Capitol Hill and military planners at the Pentagon. He presented his case for investing in education in the region rather than depending solely or mostly on military strategies. Mary Bono Clark, a Republican congresswoman from California, became one of his most vocal supporters. Mortenson has also argued in favor of forthrightly acknowledging the thousands of civilian casualties that have resulted from American military activities in Pakistan and Afghanistan and compensating the victims and their families. "By disavowing or denying the casualties," Mortenson told Gross, "what's happened has caused a schism and put up a wall instead of a bridge between us and the people there."

Three Cups of Tea, told from Relin's perspective, was subtitled (despite Mortenson's strong objections) *One Man's Mission to Fight Terrorism One School at a Time* when it was published in hardcover, in 2006. The title refers to traditions in Korphe and other parts of northeastern Pakistan that Haji Ali had described to Mortenson: "Here, we drink three cups of tea to do business," he said. "The first you are a stranger, the second you become a friend, and the third, you join our family, and for our family we are prepared to do anything—even die." The book sold sluggishly until the paperback edition arrived, the following year, with the subtitle Mortenson preferred: *One Man's Mission to Promote Peace One School at a Time.* The book appeared on the *New York Times* paperbacks best-seller list on February 17, 2007 and has remained there ever since. *Three Cups of Tea* was named *Time*'s Asia Book of the Year in 2006 and the Pacific Northwest Booksellers Association Nonfiction Book of the Year in 2007, and it won the 2007 Kiriyama Prize for nonfiction, from the organization Pacific Rim Voices, among several other awards. A picture book based on *Three Cups of Tea*, called *Listen to the Wind*, and a young-readers' version of *Three Cups of Tea*, adapted by Sarah Thomson from the original book, were published in 2009. The latter contains a foreword by the celebrated primatologist, conservationist, and United Nations messenger for peace Jane Goodall and a section in which Mortenson's daughter, Amira, answered questions about herself and her experiences during trips with her father to Afghanistan and Pakistan. Amira and her father have occasionally given talks together about CAI and its offshoot, Pennies for Peace, which by 2008 had raised about $30,000 from children in 3,000 schools to support CAI's work. In March 2009 Mortenson received Pakistan's highest civil award, the Sitara-e-Pakistan (Star of Pakistan) Award, for his humanitarian efforts. A follow-up to *Three Cups of Tea*, entitled *Stones into Schools: Promoting Peace with Books, Not Bombs, in Afghanistan and Pakistan*, was scheduled for publication in December 2009. For that book, which will recount Mortenson's ongoing efforts in Afghanistan and Pakistan, he worked with ghostwriters. (His relationship with his previous co-author, David Oliver Relin, reportedly ended unamicably.)

Mortenson, whom Nicholas Kristof described as a "frumpy, genial man," is, "by his own admission, chronically disorganized and awkward in front of crowds," Simon Houpt wrote for the Toronto, Canada, *Globe and Mail* (March 21, 2009). Scrupulously careful and thrifty with CAI's funds, Mortenson hires CAI staff reluctantly. CAI's board of directors is made up entirely of educators who have traveled or lived in Pakistan and/or Afghanistan. No volunteers work for CAI, mainly for security reasons but also because Mortenson is wary of the motives of would-be volunteers. (Many people, he has found, want only to experience something new for two or three months.) Mortenson is often away from his family for as many as six months at a time. His permanent home and office are in Bozeman, Montana, where he lives with his wife, daughter, and son, Khyber (named after Pakistan's Khyber Pass), who was born in 2000.

—M.E.R.

Suggested Reading: *Bozeman (Montana) Daily Chronicle* (on-line) Apr. 13, 2009; Central Asia Institute Web site; *Christian Century* p35 July 29, 2008; *Fresh Air* (on-line) Feb. 7, 2002; *Good Housekeeping* p142+ June 2009; *Miami Herald* E p6 Jan. 24, 2009; (Toronto, Canada) *Globe and Mail* R p9 Mar. 21, 2009; *Washington Post* C p12 Feb. 11, 2009; Mortenson, Greg, and David Oliver Relin. *Three Cups of Tea*, 2006

Selected Books: *Three Cups of Tea: One Man's Mission to Promote Peace One School at a Time* (with David Oliver Relin), 2006; *Stones into Schools: Promoting Peace with Books, Not Bombs, in Afghanistan and Pakistan*, 2009

Mousavi, Mir Hossein

Sep. 29, 1941– Former prime minister of Iran; presidential candidate

Address: Iranian Academy of Arts, 23 Bouzarjmehr Alley, Lozman-ul-Doleh Adham Alley, S. Palestine St., Tehran, Iran

The Iranian politician Mir Hossein Mousavi first rose to prominence in the early 1980s, as prime minister during the tumultuous early years of Iran's revolutionary Islamic Republic. After spending the 1990s and 2000s largely out of the public eye, he was thrust in 2009 into the center of one of the fiercest power struggles in the republic's 30-year history, which saw him defeated by the hard-line incumbent president, Mahmoud Ahmadinejad, in what many observers called a fraudulent election. As a candidate Mousavi was seen as a less-than-charismatic, moderate technocrat who favored social liberalization in the areas of women's rights and press freedoms, détente with the West, and improved economic management; he was perceived by many Iranians as representing the political change they desired, while his impeccable credentials as a veteran of the revolution were thought to make him less threatening to the status quo than other candidates. Maziar Bahari noted in *Newsweek* (June 1, 2009) before the election that there was a "chasm between what [Mousavi's] supporters expect from him and what he can actually deliver"; a grassroots embrace of his candidacy demonstrated that large segments of the population were hungry for a return to the potential for reform embodied by the presidency of Mousavi's ally, Mohammad Khatami, from 1997 to 2005. "The fact that this was a stolen election is not in doubt at all . . . ," Gary Sick, a scholar and adviser to several U.S. administrations on Iranian affairs, told Bernard Gwertzman for the Web site of the Council on Foreign Relations (June 14, 2009). "I really do see this as a kind of historic turning point. . . . Basically it means that Iran is moving from what had been a decent experiment of being an Islamic Republic to being a totalitarian dictatorship. Now it isn't at that point yet but it is a step in that direction."

A follower of Ayatollah Khomeini, the leader of the 1979 revolution in Iran, Mousavi changed jobs during that time from editor of one of the state's most important media organs, the Islamic Republican Party's official newspaper, to foreign minister and then prime minister—all within a couple of turbulent years. He held the latter post from 1981 to 1989 and is generally remembered as a competent manager who instituted important if drastic programs that helped Iran become economically self-reliant and weather the devastating eight-year war with Iraq as well as crippling sanctions imposed by Western nations. After Khomeini's death, Mousavi was marginalized in the new power structure, and the position of prime minister was abolished, with Mousavi ostensibly retreating from politics for the next two decades and concentrating on painting and running the Iranian Academy of Arts. But as Mustapha Fahs wrote for *Al Majalla* (April 8, 2009), "At every turning point in Iranian politics, the name of Mousavi jumps to the fore." In almost every presidential election since 1989, Mousavi's name has been near the top of the lists of potential candidates to represent moderate or reformist factions. On each occasion prior to 2009, he refused to run, instead working as an adviser to Khatami and others. Some attributed his refusal to his intense rivalry with the country's ultimate authority, the successor to Khomeini—Supreme Leader Ali Khamenei. (In the 1980s, when Mousavi was prime minister, he and Khamenei, then the president, were often at odds.) But Mousavi has said that he felt compelled to enter the 2009 presidential race, given what he felt was President Ahmadinejad's mismanagement of the economy and his counterproductive, inflammatory rhetoric with regard to foreign policy. The race was historic, not least because of the participation of Mousavi's wife (in a country where "first ladies" have rarely been seen or heard), the outspoken Zahra Rahnavard, herself a well-known political figure in Iran, whom many found to be more inspirational and charismatic than her husband. And what has been called the "stolen election" of June 12, 2009, which sparked the biggest street protests in the country since the 1979 revolution and exposed divisions among the ruling elite as well as the citizenry, may also prove to be a catalyst for change in Iran, according to observers.

Majid Saeedi/Getty Images

Mir Hossein Mousavi

Mousavi exceeded many people's expectations when he sided with those protesting the election results, openly defying the country's supreme leader. "[His supporters] are well aware of . . . Mousavi's flaws, past and present," Hamid Dabashi, a professor of Iranian studies at Columbia University, told the *New York Times* (June 23, 2009). He added, however, that for many Iranians, "the very figure of Mousavi has become, it seems to me, a collective construction of their desires for a peaceful, nonviolent attainment of civil and women's rights." An Iran analyst, Karim Sadjadpour, explained in an interview for National Public Radio (June 23, 2009) that the preelection Mousavi, who sought change within the system and ran as an anti-Ahmadinejad—not anti-establishment—candidate, was very different from the postelection Mousavi. Sadjadpour described a "symbiotic relationship" after the election "between Mousavi and the crowds, and the scale of the crowds and the defiance of the crowds allows Mousavi the political capital to remain defiant vis-à-vis the supreme leader. And Mousavi's defiance—he said, I'm not going to back down. I'm not going to concede my rights. I'm ready to become a martyr—has energized the crowds as well."

Mir Hossein Mousavi was born on September 29, 1941 in Khameneh, a small town in the province of East Azerbaijan. (Khamenei is from the same town.) Mousavi's father was an Azeri tea merchant, according to Mehrzad Boroujerdi, writing for *Foreign Policy* magazine (May 2009, on-line). Mousavi moved to Tehran in the early 1960s and studied architectural engineering and urban development at the National University (now called Shahid Beheshti University), graduating with a master's degree in architecture in 1969. (He later studied traditional Islamic architecture.) In the following years Mousavi worked as an architect and engineer for private companies and founded the Samarghand Co., a design and construction firm; he was also a lecturer and then assistant professor at the National University from 1974 to 1977. At the same time Mousavi was a member of underground resistance groups that opposed the dictatorship of the U.S.-backed monarch, the Shah of Iran, Mohammad Reza Pahlavi; Mousavi's activities led to his arrest in 1974. The revolution culminating in the overthrow of the Shah, led by Ayatollah Khomeini in the late 1970s, encompassed a wide range of constituencies, including leftists, business elites, Islamists, and many others. According to Amir Taheri, writing for the *National Review* (May 25, 2009), after "a brief flirtation with Marxism in the 1960s, [Mousavi] joined the thousands of educated middle-class Iranians who believed that only Islam could unite the people in a bid to destroy the country's ancient monarchic system."

Following the 1979 revolution, Mousavi's rise within the new state apparatus was meteoric. When Ayatollah Beheshti, one of the leaders of the revolution, founded the Islamic Republican Party (IRP), which would dominate the Iranian political scene in the next decade, Mousavi joined him and was quickly recognized as one of the party's most influential figures. He was named editor in chief of *Jomhouri-e Eslami* ("Islamic Republic"), the party's official mouthpiece, a post he held from 1979 to 1981, and was highly involved in formulating the party's political strategy. In 1981 Mousavi was named Iran's foreign minister, a high-profile post in which he represented Iran abroad in the wake of the American-hostage crisis. (For 444 days beginning in November 1979, 52 Americans were held in captivity in Iran.)

Meanwhile, following border disputes between Iran and Iraq, the Iraqi leader Saddam Hussein, armed and financed by the West, had attacked Iran in 1980, sparking a devastating eight-year war. An internal power struggle was also underway in Iran. In late June 1981 the president, Abolhassan Bani-Sadr, was ousted; days later terrorists attacked the IRP headquarters and its leaders, killing dozens, including Beheshti, and in late August both the president and the prime minister were assassinated. In the ensuing chaotic months, Ali Khamenei was elected president and became responsible for appointing a prime minister. His first choice, the conservative Ali Akbar Velayati, was rejected by the Parliament. In November 1981 Khamenei named the 40-year-old Mousavi, who was favored by Khomeini, as the Islamic Republic's fifth prime minister in just over two years. Over the next eight years, an enduring rivalry developed between the president and the prime minister. Khamenei, as a conservative, felt that Mousavi was too left-leaning, and he also resented Khomeini's support of Mousavi.

Mousavi assembled young and capable cabinet ministers in his two terms as prime minister, placating the Islamic right wing with several appointments but also choosing leftists including Mohammad Khatami (as minister of culture), who would go on to become a charismatic reformist president in the late 1990s and would remain a political ally. Mousavi's tenure as prime minister, which coincided with the Iran-Iraq war, lowered oil revenues, and harsh sanctions imposed by Western nations, is probably best remembered for his strong management of the economy. Rationing but evenly distributing food and other essential items, as well as taking other austerity measures, Mousavi steered Iran through a painful period from which it emerged debt-free and relatively stable. Nonetheless, Mousavi had many critics, including human-rights advocates who pointed to him as a central figure in the so-called Cultural Revolution that took place in the 1980s, during which those who opposed the new government's hard-line ideology were mercilessly purged. (While Mousavi's positions as head propagandist at the state paper, foreign minister, and prime minister clearly gave him influence, he was not in charge of the branches of state that dealt directly, and often brutally, with political prisoners.)

After Khomeini died, in 1989, the speaker of Parliament, Hashemi Rafsanjani—in a power play backed by right-wing clerics—engineered a constitutional coup in which Khamenei was made supreme leader and Rafsanjani became president. Together, the two marginalized the Islamic left in Parliament and elsewhere, including Mousavi, whose post was abolished, with the president absorbing the powers and duties of the prime minister. Mousavi then distanced himself, at least publicly, from the halls of power, focusing on abstract painting, calligraphy, architecture, teaching, and working for various cultural institutions. "He was really tired," Mohsen Aminzadeh, co-chair of Mousavi's presidential campaign, told Bahari. "He didn't even want to talk politics." Mousavi's abstract paintings have been exhibited publicly. A relative of his who was interviewed by Robert Worth for the *New York Times* (June 18, 2009) said that Mousavi's architectural influences include the Italian Renzo Piano and that Mousavi took "some elements of modern Japanese architecture, and American postmodern, and then [put] them in the context of Iranian architecture." In the late 1990s Mousavi designed the building that houses the Iranian Academy of the Arts in Tehran and became the group's president and editor of its quarterly publication *Khiyal* ("Imagination"), earning a reputation as a defender of artistic freedom and expression. In 1996 he became a member of the Supreme Council for Cultural Revolution in Iran, a body that ensures that cultural, artistic, and academic policies and works do not conflict with the state's Islamic values; he was seen by artists and filmmakers as a moderating force on the conservative council. Beginning in 1989 he was a member of the Expediency Council, whose role was to arbitrate in disputes between the elected Parliament and the largely unelected and ultraconservative supervisory body, the Council of Guardians, members of which are selected by the supreme leader. Mousavi was also an adviser to the two-term presidents Rafsanjani and Khatami.

In 2005, at the end of Khatami's second term, reformists urged Mousavi to run for the presidency. He refused, and instead Mehdi Karroubi ran as a reformist. Karroubi complained of electoral fraud after losing to the hard-line mayor of Tehran, Mahmoud Ahmadinejad, a member of the Revolutionary Guard establishment who campaigned on a populist platform of redistribution of wealth as well as social conservatism. Ahmadinejad spent much of his first term scrapping previous long-term economic plans and trying to push through populist economic policies. His practice of giving cash handouts to poorer constituencies, which wasted revenues from inflated oil prices during the war with Iraq launched under President George W. Bush and which could have been spent on badly needed development and infrastructure projects, added to the burdens brought by the international financial crisis in 2008. By the spring of 2009, Iran was facing massive inflation and unemployment. Ahmadinejad's first term also saw a strict monitoring of social behavior and a crackdown on media organizations that had grown under the Khatami administration. Ahmadinejad also emerged as a vocal antagonist of the West.

Khatami claimed that in the run-up to the 2009 presidential election, he asked Mousavi—a well-known reformist who nonetheless did not provoke the fear of drastic change in the establishment, as Khatami did—to run; the response, Khatami, said, was an unqualified no. The charismatic Khatami, helped by growing popular discontent with Ahmadinejad, then put his name forward. Almost immediately Khamenei expressed his disapproval, and Khatami began receiving death threats. In March Mousavi entered the race, saying that he felt compelled to run because of what he called Ahmadinejad's incompetence, mismanagement, and extremism. Khatami immediately withdrew, later telling Bahari, "Mr. Mousavi is the best candidate. He can prepare an environment in which people like us can act as reformers." In support of his candidacy, Mousavi launched a newspaper, *Kalameh Sabz* ("Green Word"), with the goal of publicizing his positions, given that most of the young voting population had little memory of him as a leader. The campaign adopted the color green; people began referring to Mousavi's following as the "green wave." After the vetting process by the Guardian Council, four candidates emerged in the race, each of them regime insiders heavily invested in the maintaining of the Islamic Republic. Ahmadinejad and Mousavi were joined by Mohsen Rezai and Mehdi Karroubi. Mousavi ran as an independent candidate, calling himself a "reformist principalist" and a "reformist who refers to the principles of the revolution," essentially trying to convince people that he was committed to the establishment of the Islamic Republic while seeking to bridge the gap between reformists and conservatives—a difficult task, and one that opened him up to charges of vague double-talk and lack of sincerity from all sides. His platform offered a critique of and alternative to Ahmadinejad's economic, domestic, social, and foreign policies. With regard to the economy, he relied on his reputation for steering Iran through the difficult years of the 1980s and promised to fight corruption, implement increased transparency in contracts, and move away from an oil-based economy and from what he called Ahmadinejad's "alms-based economy." On social issues he called for freedom of expression, vowing to amend the constitution to remove the ban on private ownership of media. Mousavi also called for the transfer of control over law-enforcement forces from the unelected supreme leader to the president, so that the police would represent and be accountable to the people. Greatly aided by the outsized personality of his wife, a university professor and author, he guaranteed that he would review all laws that discriminate against women. In the crucial area of foreign policy, he railed against Ahmadinejad and explicitly and repeatedly used the term "détente" when discussing relations with the West.

As the campaign progressed Mousavi began to gain increasing backing from large segments of the population as well as some key elements of the leadership, including the wealthy and powerful Rafsanjani. While few doubted that Khamenei supported Ahmadinejad, some segments of the incumbent's erstwhile power base, the military and the Revolutionary Guard, were seemingly defecting to Mousavi's camp in an open sign that they were unhappy with the president's policies. Mousavi also received almost across-the-board support from the country's intellectual and artistic communities. Toward the end of the race, in June 2009, Mousavi's campaign, aided by massive rallies drawing 10s of thousands, began to pick up energy and momentum. In response Mousavi began intensifying his call for more reforms. According to Bahari, a government poll suggested that 16 million to 18 million people intended to vote for Mousavi, compared to six million to eight million for Ahmadinejad, essentially guaranteeing a Mousavi victory. Robert Dreyfuss wrote for the *Dreyfuss Report* (June 8, 2009), "A year ago, when I visited Tehran in advance of the parliamentary elections, there was apathy. Voters then were convinced that their votes didn't matter, and that not voting was the best way to protest the current state of affairs. No longer."

On Election Day, June 12, 2009, a massive, record turnout of over 85 percent of voters suggested that Mousavi would be victorious. But within a couple of hours after the polls closed, the Interior Ministry, supervised by the Council of Guardians, with both composed of conservative Ahmadinejad supporters, announced a landslide victory for the incumbent, with Ahmadinejad getting 63 percent of the vote to Mousavi's 34 percent. Along with the two other losing candidates, Mousavi—whose headquarters had been ransacked—immediately rejected the results. He called for new elections and wrote an open letter, as quoted at Tehranbureau.com (June 13, 2009): "I object fully to the . . . obvious and abundant deviations from law on the day of election and alert people to not surrender to this dangerous plot. Dishonesty and corruption of officials as we have seen will only result in weakening the pillars of the Islamic Republic of Iran and empowers lies and dictatorships." Over the weekend mass demonstrations began to rock the country's major cities, and dozens of well-known reformists were arrested. On June 15 a defiant Mousavi appeared at a rally of millions of people, the most since the 1979 revolution, but that evening pro-government militias responded, killing several people and injuring dozens. In response, Mousavi called for people to protest the deaths in peaceful demonstrations. Khamenei, meanwhile, publicly supported the results of the election and ominously warned that demonstrators would be punished.

Following the election Mousavi seemed to be a changed man, caught up in a wave of popular protest. "Mousavi has become the public face of the movement," Robert Worth wrote. "But he is in some ways an accidental leader, a moderate figure anointed at the last minute to represent a popular upwelling against the presidency of Mahmoud Ahmadinejad. He is far from being a liberal in the Western sense, and it is not yet clear how far he will be willing to go in defending the broad democratic hopes he has come to embody. [He] is an insider who has moved toward opposition, and his motives for doing so remain murky. . . . The steadiness he has shown since the election results were announced . . . has helped solidify his role as a leader and has heartened his followers. . . . For a long time, he was compared unfavorably to Mohammad Khatami, the charismatic reformist cleric who was president from 1997 to 2005. But many now say that during the recent protests, Mr. Mousavi held firm against the government in ways Mr. Khatami never would have." If Mousavi had been seen as a poor man's Khatami who was too dull and unthreatening to worry hard-liners, the decision to let him run instead of Khatami seemed to have backfired. In a speech he gave at a large mourning rally in Tehran on June 18, as quoted in the London *Guardian* (June 18, 2009, on-line), Mousavi appeared to be undeterred: "I have come . . . to defend the rights of the nation. . . . I have come to be accountable to you my people. . . . We are Muslims: what is happening in the Iranian government is a sin."

On the following day, June 19, Khamenei gave a speech at Tehran University's Friday prayer ceremony in which he signaled unqualified support for Ahmadinejad as well as a violent crackdown on any form of dissent and opposition. He gave an ultimatum to the leaders of the opposition, saying that he would hold them personally responsible for the actions of their followers. Almost immediately crowds began calling for the end of his rule, marking the first time they had dared defy the leader publicly. By June 25 Mousavi's newspaper had been shut down, and most of its journalists, as well as most prominent reformers and members of Mousavi's campaign, had been imprisoned. Mousavi, suspected to be under house arrest, issued a defiant attack on the supreme leader, saying that Khamenei had broken with tradition by openly taking sides in a political matter; he added that his own supporters simply wanted their votes counted. "The recent pressure on me is aimed at making me withdraw from my stance of annulling the election," Mousavi said, as quoted in the *Guardian* (June 25, 2009). "Given the current situation, the government will face a crisis of political legitimacy." Under increasing repression from the authorities, Mousavi's supporters, who began to find it difficult to organize en masse without the risk of bloodshed, began considering new tactics for peaceful resistance, including civil disobedience, strikes, and the formation of a new political opposition movement, the Green Path of Hope, established by Mousavi. On August 5, 2009 Ahmadinejad was sworn in to a second term.

In the months following the election, dozens more citizens and opposition leaders were arrested in a coordinated crackdown and tried on charges of conspiring with external forces to foment a "velvet revolution." Hardliners (including leaders of the Revolutionary Guard, who had benefited from Ahmadinejad's tenure) publicly called for Mousavi's arrest on several occasions. While he was not imprisoned in those first few months, reports indicated that he was living under conditions of virtual house arrest, though he continued to make regular statements questioning the legitimacy of the government and calling both for the peoples' votes to be counted honestly and for respect for the rule of law and democracy. While some of his critics called Mousavi weak, other commentators indicated that while he and Khatami had remained quieter than the outspoken dissident clerics Karroubi and Ayatollah Montazeri, the Iranian opposition movement had developed what might prove to be an effective strategy: that of relying less on charismatic leaders (who could be arrested or co-opted) and instead on a more decentralized grassroots movement, which would be harder to identify and neutralize.

Mousavi married Zahra Rahnavard in 1969. The couple have three daughters.

—M.M.

Suggested Reading: *Al Majalla* (on-line) Apr. 8, 2009; *Foreign Policy* (on-line) June 2009; (London) *Guardian* (on-line) June 18, 2009; National Public Radio (on-line) June 23, 2009; *New York Times* (on-line) June 18, 2009; *New Yorker* (on-line) June 13, 2009; *Newsweek* (on-line) June 1, 2009, June 20, 2009; Tehranbureau.com May 5, 2009

Napolitano, Janet

NOTE: An earlier article about Janet Napolitano appeared in *Current Biography* in 2004.

(nah-pahl-ih-TAHN-oh)

Nov. 29, 1957– Secretary of the U.S. Department of Homeland Security; former governor of Arizona (Democrat)

Address: U.S. Dept. of Homeland Security, 3801 Nebraska Ave., N.W., Washington, DC 20528

A former United States attorney, Janet Napolitano was in the middle of her second term as governor of Arizona when President-elect Barack Obama tapped her to head the U.S. Department of Homeland Security (DHS). Napolitano, a Democrat, was sworn in as the third secretary of homeland security on January 21, 2009, a day after her confirmation by the U.S. Senate in a unanimous vote that also approved the appointments of five other Cabinet members. Established in 2003, in the wake of the September 11, 2001 terrorist attacks on the United States, DHS is the third-largest federal agency, after the Departments of Defense and Veterans Affairs. It works toward preventing such attacks (however and wherever in the U.S. they may be carried out); preparing for responses to such attacks if they occur; responding to natural disasters, including destructive hurricanes and floods; and protecting the nation's coastal and inland borders, not only from attacks but also from infiltration by illegal immigrants or visitors or illegal materials. The department is the umbrella for the Federal Emergency Management Agency, the U.S. Coast Guard, the U.S. Secret Service, the Transportation Security Administration, and the agencies whose formal names are U.S. Immigration and Customs Enforcement and U.S. Customs and Border Protection. An editorial in the *New York Times* (December 1, 2008) about Obama's selection of Napolitano to head DHS made an oblique reference to her predecessors in that position—Tom Ridge, whose system of color-coded alerts to possible terrorist threats was widely ridiculed, and Michael Chertoff, whose delayed and inadequate response to the disaster caused by Hurricane Katrina was widely denounced. "Lucky country. Poor Arizona," the editors wrote. "It would be a relief to see the job go

Alex Wong/Getty Images

Janet Napolitano

to someone with a solid understanding of immigration and all its complexities and political traps. As governor of a border state, Ms. Napolitano knows the landscape intimately. She has a cool head and a proven willingness to pursue policies that conform to reality, rather than the other way around." The first woman to chair the National Governors Association, Napolitano was instrumental in creating the governors' Public Safety Task Force and their Homeland Security Advisors Council. In 2005 *Time* magazine named her one of the five best governors in the U.S. In a comment posted on the Web site of the University of Virginia School of Law (March 20, 2003), Richard Merrill, a former dean, described Napolitano, an alumna, as "the epitome of what it means to be a public servant as a lawyer."

The first of the three children of Leonard M. Napolitano and the former Jane Winer, Janet Ann Napolitano was born on November 29, 1957 in New York City. Her brother, Leonard Jr., is a researcher and administrator at Sandia National Laboratories; her sister, Nancy, is an audiologist. Her father, a professor of anatomy who studied lipids, is a dean emeritus of the University of New Mexico College of Medicine. Napolitano and her siblings were raised in Pittsburgh, Pennsylvania, and later in Albuquerque, New Mexico. "I have no complaints about my childhood at all," Napolitano told Amy Silverman for the *Phoenix (Arizona) New Times* (October 22, 1998). "I had a great time." In Albuquerque she attended Comanche Elementary School, Madison Middle School, and Sandia High School. As a junior at Sandia, she participated in the New Mexico's Girls State program, an activity, sponsored nationwide by the women's arm of the American Legion, that aims to give girls a taste of leadership in government through role-playing; Napolitano won election to the post of lieutenant governor. She also edited the student newspaper and played the guitar and the clarinet, the latter as a member of the school band. "I was your basic overachieving high school student," she told Kate Nash for the *Albuquerque Tribune* (November 4, 2002, on-line). At her graduation, in 1975, she earned an award as the most accomplished musician in her class.

Napolitano attended Santa Clara University, in California, where she majored in political science. She spent one term studying in London, England. During her third year she won a Harry S. Truman Scholarship, awarded to juniors who intend to pursue graduate degrees and careers in public service. In 1979 she earned a B.S. degree summa cum laude from Santa Clara and became the school's first female valedictorian. She also gained membership in the honor societies Phi Beta Kappa and Alpha Sigma Nu. That year, thanks to her father's acquaintance with U.S. senator Pete V. Domenici of New Mexico, she secured an internship as an analyst with the Senate Budget Committee. Among other tasks, she helped to project the possible long-term costs to the U.S. government of the so-called Chrysler bailout—the government's loan of $1.5 billion to the auto manufacturer Chrysler in 1979–80, to save the company from bankruptcy.

In 1980 Napolitano entered the University of Virginia (UVA) School of Law, in Charlottesville. While there, she held a Hardy Cross Dillard Fellowship, for excellence in legal research and writing. She also won election to the Raven Society, the university's most prestigious honor society. Napolitano received a J.D. degree in 1983. She then moved to Phoenix, Arizona, to work for Judge Mary M. Schroeder of the U.S. Ninth Circuit Court of Appeals. Napolitano became a member of the Arizona bar in 1984. That year she left her job with Judge Schroeder after being recruited by the Phoenix law firm of Lewis and Roca, where she specialized in commercial and appellate litigation. In her first year at the firm, she worked with John P. Frank, an esteemed legal scholar who had argued many desegregation cases in the 1950s. Frank, who often worked pro bono, represented Ernesto Miranda in the landmark 1966 Supreme Court case *Miranda vs. Arizona*. Napolitano became a partner in Lewis and Roca in 1989. On her own time during the next year, she traveled in Eastern Europe with a delegation from a national teachers' organization and advised high-school instructors on ways to teach the skills necessary for maintaining a representative democracy.

In 1991 Napolitano served with Frank as co-counsel to Anita F. Hill, a professor of law at the University of Oklahoma, when the U.S. Senate Judiciary Committee questioned Hill regarding charges she had made concerning Clarence Thomas, whom President George H. W. Bush had nominated to succeed the retiring Thurgood Marshall on the U.S. Supreme Court. Through a leak to the press, the committee had learned that before the hearings, Hill had told FBI investigators that during her stint as one of Thomas's staff attorneys at the U.S. Department of Education and the Equal Employment Opportunity Commission in the early 1980s, Thomas had sexually harassed her. The committee had closed the hearings after voting 13–1 in favor of sending Thomas's nomination to the full Senate without a recommendation, then reopened them, to question both Hill and Thomas about Hill's accusations. During those special hearings, held on October 11, 12, and 13, 1991 and televised nationally, Frank advised Hill while Napolitano helped to line up and work with Susan Hoerchner, a California judge, and other witnesses who testified on Hill's behalf. The hearings ended when Thomas, after declaring that he had been subjected to a "high-tech lynching for uppity blacks," announced that he would not submit to any more questioning. On October 15 the Senate confirmed Thomas by a vote of 52–48. The special hearings left Napolitano with feelings of disillusionment and dismay. As she told Amy Silverman, "I'm a very big believer in . . . fair process. And I thought the process used by the Senate was terrible. It was terrible for everyone involved. It was terrible for Anita Hill, it was terrible for Clarence Thomas, and I thought the Senate looked very, very bad. It was a real eye-opening experience for me."

In July 1993 Napolitano learned from U.S. senator Dennis DeConcini of Arizona that President Bill Clinton wanted to nominate her for the post of U.S. attorney for the District of Arizona. She admitted to Silverman that when DeConcini phoned her with that news, "I really didn't know what a U.S. attorney did." After researching the post, she accepted the nomination, then began working as the acting U.S. attorney. During the hearings the Senate Judiciary Committee held to consider her nomination, in September 1993, several Republican senators contended that she was unfit for the job because she had improperly interrupted Susan Hoerchner during the Clarence Thomas hearings in an attempt to coach her. Napolitano vehemently denied that accusation and refused to answer questions about her conversations with Hoerchner, citing attorney-client privilege. On September 30 the Judiciary Committee voted 12–6 to confirm Napolitano, but her Republican detractors blocked the nomination from coming to the floor of the Senate. Several journalists later reported that a Judiciary Committee staff member, not Napolitano, had interrupted Hoerchner. On November 19, 1993, after a vote that ended a Republican filibuster, the Senate confirmed Napolitano.

Napolitano's responsibilities as a U.S. attorney included the prosecution of criminal cases brought by the federal government, the prosecution or defense of civil cases in which the U.S. government was either the plaintiff or the defendant, and the collection of debts owed to the federal government that could not be collected in any other way. Cases involving drug trafficking, gang-related violence on Indian reservations, hate crimes, and white-collar scams made up much of her workload. According to the *Rotarizonian* (October 23, 1998, online), under her leadership her office prosecuted more than 6,000 crimes, "more than any other federal prosecutor in Arizona history." Her achievements also included the procurement of $65 million in federal funds to enable Arizona cities to hire additional police officers. In addition, Napolitano helped the FBI to set up an office in Kingman, Arizona, and investigate the activities of Timothy J. McVeigh in Kingman in the months before he bombed the Alfred P. Murrah Federal Building, in Oklahoma City, Oklahoma, on April 19, 1995. (In June 1997 McVeigh was convicted of that crime, which killed 168 people and severely injured many more; he was executed four years later.)

In November 1997 Napolitano resigned from her job and announced that she would seek the Democratic nomination for attorney general of Arizona. After running unopposed in the Democratic primary, she faced the Republican Tom McGovern, who had served briefly as a special assistant to the state attorney general. With the notable exception of abortion—Napolitano was pro-choice, believed that so-called partial-birth abortions should be legal, and opposed the requirement that parents be notified when minors sought abortions; McGovern opposed those positions—the two candidates agreed on most issues. During their campaigns Napolitano, who is unmarried, rarely veered from remarks about the issues or her professional experience, while McGovern, who has three children, often spoke about his family. On Election Day, November 3, 1998, Napolitano emerged victorious, with 50.4 percent of the vote to McGovern's 47.5 percent. (The Libertarian candidate captured the remainder.) She was the first woman to serve as Arizona's attorney general. No other state had ever filled so many of its highest positions with women; besides Napolitano (the only Democrat), the group included Governor Jane Dee Hull, Secretary of State Betsey Bayless, Treasurer Carol Springer, and Superintendent of Public Instruction Lisa Graham Keegan. Collectively, they were nicknamed the "Fab Five" by the media.

As attorney general Napolitano distinguished herself as an advocate for children, women, senior citizens, and the environment. Her position enabled her "to do good things," as she told the UVA law school interviewer. For example, she said, the damages paid by shoe manufacturers whom she successfully sued for price fixing enabled the state "to keep women's shelters open and add beds." Among Napolitano's most significant accomplishments was the reduction of the backlog of unresolved child-abuse cases from 6,000 to fewer than 900. Among other actions, she created an Office for Women as an arm of the attorney general's department. She filed a consumer-fraud lawsuit against QwestCommunications International, accusing the company of placing unauthorized charges on consumers' bills and engaging in false and misleading advertising, which resulted in the firm's refunding some $721,000 to Arizonans. Napolitano also aggressively prosecuted con artists who preyed on the elderly, and she set up a unit to investigate Internet users' exploitation of children and others through an array of enticements and scams. After three police officers died and another was injured in explosions of Ford Crown Victoria sedans, which the Phoenix Police Department used, she exacted an agreement from Ford to install shields around the vehicles' fuel tanks. By the time she left the attorney general's office, Napolitano had argued cases before the U.S. Supreme Court, at The Hague, and in "virtually every federal circuit court in the country," as the UVA interviewer put it. Earlier, in 2000, Napolitano had been diagnosed with breast cancer and had undergone a mastectomy.

On January 15, 2002 Napolitano announced her candidacy for the governorship of Arizona; the incumbent, Hull, a Republican who had served the remainder of Governor Fife Symington's second term after his conviction on charges of bank fraud and who had won election to a full term in 1997, was barred by law from seeking another term. Running against three others in the Democratic primary, Napolitano secured the nomination with about 57 percent of the total vote. In the general election she faced (in addition to eight minor-party candidates who stood little chance of winning) the Republican Matt Salmon, a former U.S. congressman and former Arizona state senator. In a bitterly fought race that centered on Arizona's looming $1 billion budget deficit, Salmon branded Napolitano a "tax and spend liberal" while Napolitano derided Salmon's promise not to raise taxes and his assurances that he would personally attract a half-million new jobs to the state. Napolitano opted to depend entirely on public funds for her campaign; Salmon chose to rely on private contributions and spent a significant portion of his time trying to raise money. When the November 5, 2002 ballots were counted, Napolitano's tally came to 566,284 (46.2 percent of the total), only 11,819 more than Salmon's 554,465 (45.2 percent).

In an *Online NewsHour* discussion on January 3, 2003, three days before she was sworn in as governor, Napolitano noted that the financial woes Arizona was then suffering were being compounded by population growth. "With basically the same revenues we had in 1999, I have 300,000 more people on Medicaid, 100,000 more children in school and 5,000 more inmates in prison," she pointed out. In June 2003, although both the 30-seat State Senate and the 60-seat State House had Republican majorities, she and the legislature agreed upon a budget for fiscal year 2004 with which she felt largely satisfied (thanks in part to the governor's right to make line-item vetoes). Although it exceeded the previous year's total by $400 million, it called for no new taxes and no substantive cuts in essential services.

In Napolitano's January 12, 2004 State of the State Address, she declared that the budget deficit had shrunk by two-thirds and announced that through a new process called Efficiency Review, state employees had started to find ways to save millions of dollars. She herself had already saved about $800,000 by closing the Governor's Office for Excellence in Government. "Excellence in government should be the norm," she said, according to the New Democrats Web site. Among other accomplishments in 2003, she cited the introduction of the CoppeRx Card, which enabled all Arizonans eligible for Medicare to buy prescription drugs at discounts greater than those offered through the far more complicated, newly launched federal program. The state agency responsible for investigating child abuse had received increased funding, as had schools, shelters, and drug-addiction programs. In 2003 Arizona became the first state to complete a comprehensive homeland-security plan, and it began setting up a 211 phone system (similar to the 911 system for summoning police or fire fighters) for providing information during emergencies.

In addition to her duties as governor, Napolitano was proving to be a rising star in the Democratic Party. As Arizona's attorney general she had given a rousing speech at the 2000 Democratic National Convention, a few weeks after her mastectomy and despite being in pain. In the weeks leading up to the 2004 presidential debates between President George W. Bush and Senator John Kerry, Napolitano (who had been discussed as a possible Kerry running mate) was one of the Democratic Party luminaries entrusted to negotiate the terms of the debates, which took place in September and October.

Napolitano's first term was widely considered a success, and in 2005 the editors of *Time* named Napolitano one of the five best governors in the country. They cited her successful handling of Arizona's budget crisis, writing, "Now Arizona's economy is booming, with a projected budget surplus of more than $300 million and 4 percent job growth, the second highest in the nation after Nevada." They also praised her centrist handling of Arizona's immigration issues. As governor of a border state that is home to such extreme anti-immigrant groups as the Minutemen, Napolitano—who won a second term in 2006 by beating her opponent, Len Munsil, by a margin of nearly two to one—was often a crucial voice of moderation. She vetoed bills that would have denied United States citizenship to children born to illegal immigrants, required the police to arrest illegal immigrants for trespassing, and made English the official language of the state. However, she opposed amnesty for undocumented workers and the businesses employing them; in 2007, during her second term, for example, she signed a bill that called for revoking the licenses of businesses that are caught more than once knowingly employing illegal immigrants. Napolitano was the first governor to call for the National Guard to help protect her state's border at federal expense, but she was not a proponent of building border fences. "You show me a 50-foot wall," she said, according to David Savage in the *Los Angeles Times* (November 23, 2008), "and I'll show you a 51-foot ladder."

Napolitano's nomination as secretary of the Department of Homeland Security drew criticism from leaders on both sides of the immigration debate. Conservatives complained that she was not tough enough regarding illegal immigration, while other groups, including the Mexican American Legal Defense and Education Fund, complained that her positions were overly punitive. "Arizona has become one of the worst states for immigrants in this country," John Trasvina, president and general counsel of the fund, told Savage. "I would say her record fits the state of Arizona, and we look forward to a different focus when she reaches Washington."

In February 2009, within weeks of being sworn in as homeland-security secretary, Napolitano ordered a reevaluation of the federal government's biggest program—as it existed under then–President George W. Bush—for testing the nation's ability to respond to acts of terrorism. One of the more significant changes Napolitano planned to carry out called for more collaboration with local governments in planning for natural disasters and terrorist attacks. The following month Napolitano announced that the federal government would increase security at the 2,000-mile U.S.–Mexico border by sending 460 additional agents to strengthen border-patrol units and by making use of additional search tools, among them new canine teams and mobile X-ray units. (The stepped-up level of security sprang from the concern that drug-fueled violence in Mexico near the border might spill over into Arizona, Texas, and other states.) In August Napolitano launched an effort to enforce immigration laws more widely. The Obama administration, Julia Preston wrote for the *New York Times* (August 4, 2009), "undertook audits of employee paperwork at hundreds of businesses, expanded a program to verify worker immigration status that has been widely criticized as flawed, bolstered a program of cooperation between federal and local law enforcement agencies, and rejected proposals for legally binding rules governing conditions in immigration detention centers." In October Napolitano announced that the White House was considering converting hotels and nursing homes into immigration detention centers, on the grounds that the estimated 90 percent of detained illegal immigrants who are nonviolent offenders do not need to be held in prison-like buildings.

From 2006 to 2007 Napolitano chaired the National Governors Association, and she sat on the executive committee of the Democratic Governors Association. Her many honors include the Anti-Defamation League's Leader of Distinction Award (2000), the Woodrow Wilson Award for Public Service (2006), and the Americans for the Arts National Award for State Leadership (2007).

In her leisure time Napolitano enjoys whitewater rafting and hiking, especially in Arizona's Sandia and Superstition Mountains. She has climbed in the Himalayas and scaled Mount Kilimanjaro, in Tanzania. Her other hobbies include reading, watching movies and spectator sports, and spending time with her relatives.

—H.T./J.E.P.

Suggested Reading: *Albuquerque Tribune* (online) Nov. 4, 2002; *Arizona Republic* B p9 Aug. 2, 2002; Associated Press State & Local Wire June 20, 2003; *Los Angeles Times* A p17 Nov. 23, 2008, A p12 Dec. 3, 2008; *New York Times* (online) Dec. 1, 2008; *Washington Post* A p19 Dec. 2, 2008; *Who's Who in America*

Stephen Shugerman/Getty Images

Nas

(nahz)

Sep. 14, 1973– Rap musician; actor

Address: c/o Def Jam Recordings, 825 Eighth Ave., New York, NY 10019

Since his recording debut, in the early 1990s, Nas has risen to become one of the most influential and respected rappers in the industry. Though he has often struggled to reach the bar he set for himself with his first solo album, *Illmatic* (1994), the Queens, New York, rapper has since released some of the genre's most heralded albums of recent memory, including *It Was Written* (1996), *God's Son* (2002), *Street's Disciple* (2004), and his untitled 2008 recording. In 2006 the cable channel MTV ranked Nas number five on its list of the "10 Greatest MCs of all time," and the Grammy Award–nominated rapper Slick Rick provided a testimonial for the MTV Web site, saying, "[Nas] comes with emotions, he speaks on positivity. . . . There aren't too many rappers who can compete with him."

Nas's father, the jazz musician Olu Dara, fostered his interest in music early on. "If it wasn't for my pops makin' music, I wouldn't be makin' music," Nas told Shawn Edwards for the Kansas City, Missouri, *Pitch Weekly* (June 6, 2002). "He brought me onstage when I was about four or five. . . . So I've always had an understanding of the power of words and what my voice represents."

Nas is also well-known for his longtime feud with the Brooklyn, New York–born rapper Jay-Z. Following the 1997 murder of the famed New York City rapper Notorious B.I.G. (also known as Biggie Smalls), Nas and Jay-Z became rivals for the unofficial title of New York's top rapper. For years the two included on their albums insults targeted at each other. Their feud ended in 2005, much to the surprise of their fans, and Nas signed with Jay-Z's label Def Jam Recordings the following year. Later acknowledging his respect for Nas, Jay-Z told Toure for BET News, as quoted in the *Washington Afro-American* (March 17, 2006), "[*Illmatic*] was a great album. It was one of the most important albums in hip-hop history."

The older of two boys, Nas was born Nasir bin Olu Dara Jones on September 14, 1973 in Long Island City, Queens, New York. ("Nasir" is an Arabic name meaning "helper" or "protector," while "bin" means "son of.") Nas hails from a long line of musicians. His father, a cornetist and trumpeter, performed with Art Blakey's Jazz Messengers during the 1970s. Olu Dara's father and grandfather were both singers, and his great-uncles were members of the Rabbit Foot Company minstrel and variety troupe, alongside the legendary blues singers Ma Rainey and Bessie Smith. Dara was born Charles Jones III in Natchez, Mississippi, and adopted his current name, which means "God is good" in the West African language of Yoruba, when he was 23. Dara, who has performed on Nas's albums, leads the Okra Orchestra and Natchezsippi Dance Band.

Nas grew up in Long Island City's Queensbridge Houses, the largest public-housing development in the United States. Dara exposed his son to music at a young age. Nas's parents divorced when he was 12 years old, and he and his brother, Jabari—now known in hip-hop circles as Jungle—lived with their mother, Fannie Ann Jones, who worked for the U.S. Postal Service. In the 1980s Nas developed a passion for the hip-hop music of the era. The Queensbridge Houses complex is known as a hotbed for hip-hop talent, producing such legends as Marley Marl and MC Shan as well as Nas.

Although Nas hoped ultimately to get into the music business, he noticed his peers making quick money on the streets by selling drugs, and for that and other reasons, he decided to drop out of school in the ninth grade (some sources say eighth grade). "If it was up to me, I would have gone to college, but school wasn't what I wanted it to be. I hate to sound corny, but there's a problem between a lot of teachers and black boys. They don't understand our attitudes at an early age. They treat us like violent animals and throw us in special classes where we can't develop ourselves as people," Nas told Cheo Hodari Coker for the *Los Angeles Times* (August 11, 1996). "But even if you get through that, you still have to deal with society. As a young black man, sometimes you think the whole world is against you, and ignorant people—some teachers especially—will feed that to you. You need people feeding you motivation." When he was 18 his hustling days came to an abrupt end, after his best friend, William "Ill Will" Graham, was murdered. Graham's death convinced Nas that "there was no love on the street," as he recalled to Coker. "At that moment, I knew either I was going down or music was going to save me. I believe God came to me through the music, and he came right on time." (Nas, who has a tattoo dedicated to his friend on his left arm, later named his recording label Ill Will.)

Nas's first recorded work came in 1991, on the hip-hop group Main Source's debut album, *Breaking Atoms*; then known as Nasty Nas, he performed a verse on the track "Live at the Barbecue." MC Serch, formerly of the hip-hop group 3rd Bass, approached Nas soon afterward about contributing to the soundtrack for the 1992 film *Zebrahead*. For that album Nas recorded his first solo song, "Halftime." Serch, impressed with Nas, featured the young rapper on "Back to the Grill" on his solo album *Return of the Product*, released in 1992. Nas soon caught the attention of executives at Columbia Records and was signed to the label that same year.

Nas's debut album, *Illmatic*, was released in 1994. Named in honor of his slain friend, the album featured songs including "N.Y. State of Mind," in which Nas raps over a jazzy piano loop about life in his tough neighborhood, and the Q-Tip–produced "One Love," written as a series of letters to friends in prison: "So stay civilized, time flies / Though incarcerated your mind (dies) / I hate it when your mum cries / It kinda wants to make me murder . . ." Nas's father made an appearance, playing trumpet at the end of the track "Life's a Bi**h." The album received rave reviews. The *Source* awarded *Illmatic* five (out of five) microphones, an extremely rare rating from the magazine for any album, even more so for a debut record. The magazine's reviewer Shortie wrote (April 1994), "I must maintain that this is one of the best hip-hop albums I have ever heard. . . . Your mind races to keep up with Nas's [lyrics], while your body dips to the beat." Giving the album four out of five stars in *Rolling Stone* (1994, on-line), Toure declared Nas a new member of "the elite group of MCs" with "sharp articulation, finely detailed lyrics and a controlled tone reminiscent of [the rapper] Rakim." Toure also wrote that the album is "like a rose stretching up between cracks in the sidewalk, calling attention to its beauty, calling attention to the lack of it everywhere else."

In spite of its critical praise, the album failed to achieve substantial commercial success. After peaking at number 12 on the *Billboard* 200 chart in May and selling 59,000 copies in its first week, *Illmatic*'s sales soon dropped. It was not until two years later, in January 1996, that sales of the album rose to more than 500,000 copies, and it was certified gold by the Recording Industry Association of America (RIAA). (At the time of the album's release, the rap scene was dominated by West Coast artists and G-funk, a highly synthesized style of hip-hop that uses funk music and slow beats. In retrospect, many music critics have acknowledged that *Illmatic* both redefined and led the resurgence of East Coast hip-hop, placing a renewed focus on lyricism and vocal delivery.) *Illmatic* has since become one of the most popular hip-hop albums in history and is often cited as one of the most influential.

Nas's sophomore album, *It Was Written* (1996), shot to the top of the *Billboard* charts, selling more than three million copies, and was certified platinum. The album's hit single, "If I Ruled the World (Imagine That)," featured vocals by the future Grammy Award–winner Lauryn Hill, then a member of the acclaimed hip-hop group the Fugees.The album received mixed reviews, however. Dimitri Ehrlich gave the album an A– in *Entertainment Weekly* (July 26, 1996, on-line), writing, "Nas' delivery on *It Was Written* is disjointed, but his concerns are straightforward. On 'Street Dreams' he details how coke has ravaged his neighborhood, and on 'Black Girl Lost' he sympathizes with the struggle of African-American women without sounding self-consciously PC. Humor disguises the grim subject matter while Nas' eye for minutiae lends credibility and urgency to his hip-hop short stories." In *Rolling Stone* (September 19, 1996, on-line), Mark Coleman wrote, "Gang Starr's DJ Premier lays down a spooky, jazz-fusion groove on 'I Gave You Power,' and this time, Nas responds with a mind-blowing sustained metaphor, speaking as the voice of a gun. This extraordinary view of casual violence measures the exact dimensions of a vicious circle: 'I might have took your first child, scarred your life, crippled your style / I gave you power / I made you buck wild.'" Despite such praise Coleman awarded the album only two out of five stars, lamenting, "*It Was Written* proves that [Nas] . . . possesses a phenomenal way with words and some savvy musical sense. It's a pity that he doesn't put his verbal dexterity and powers of observation to better use."

Nas next became a member of the ill-fated group the Firm, with the rappers AZ, Foxy Brown, and Nature. Signed to Dr. Dre's Aftermath Entertainment label, the Firm released a self-titled 1997 album so critically and commercially disappointing that the group promptly split up. Two years later Nas released *I Am . . .*, his third studio album, which debuted at the top spot on the *Billboard* charts, selling more than 470,000 copies in its first week. The album was later certified platinum twice over. Although criticized for its commercial nature, it received generally good reviews. Later in 1999 Nas released *Nastradamus*, the rapper's first album under his newly established Ill Will Records imprint. Regarded as one of his most unpopular albums, *Nastradamus* was generally panned as uninspired and clichéd. His next release, *Stillmatic* (2001), fared much better. Though a number of critics felt that Nas was still not performing up to his potential, he received another five microphones from the *Source*. Rating the album a seven out of 10, Alex Needham wrote for *NME* (January 11, 2002, on-line), "Lyrically, Nas is pretty much back on form." Within a year *Stillmatic* had sold more than 1.7 million copies.

In 2001 the rivalry between Jay-Z and Nas, which had been brewing throughout the late 1990s following Jay-Z's unauthorized sampling of Nas's "The World Is Yours" on his 1996 song "Dead Presidents," escalated with the release of Jay-Z's *Blueprint*. On the album's song "Takeover," Jay-Z ridicules Nas for being unable to record an album that lives up to his debut (*Illmatic*) and questions Nas's "street cred." The song sparked a series of back-and-forth "diss" songs, including Nas's "Ether" on *Stillmatic*, Jay-Z's "Blueprint 2" on *The Blueprint 2: The Gift & the Curse* (2002), and radio freestyles from both rappers. The highly publicized feud gradually cooled off and was declared officially over when, on October 27, 2005, Jay-Z invited Nas to perform a few songs with him during a concert in East Rutherford, New Jersey. The following year Nas left Columbia Records to sign with Jay-Z's Def Jam Recordings. Referring to the feud between the rappers Tupac Shakur and Notorious B.I.G., which ended with both men murdered in 1996 and 1997, respectively, Jay-Z told Steve Jones for *USA Today* (January 25, 2006), "Everybody talks about Big and Pac and how that ended. [Nas and I] talked about showing a different side and what it would mean to the culture of hip-hop. It was bigger than just us and our trivial little beefs." Nas told Gail Mitchell for *Billboard* (February 4, 2006), "It was time for [the feud] to go in a direction that benefits the people who live for and love hip-hop. Our whole point is to move hip-hop to a much bigger level."

Nas's mother died of breast cancer in 2002. "That really pushed me forward," the rapper told Mike Osegueda for the *Fresno (California) Bee* (November 12, 2004). "Losing her was a thing that really made me look around and really not want to take another day for granted." His 2002 release, *God's Son*, reflected Nas's more emotionally open, mature side. Many of the songs refer to his mother, and the track "Dance" was written for her: "I'm thankful, to ever know a women so real / I pray when I marry my wife'll have one of your skills / But mom you could never be replaced / I'd give my life up / Just to see you one more day / To have . . . / One more dance with you mama."

The singles from *God's Son* enjoyed substantial commercial success. "I Can," a song set to the melody of Beethoven's "Für Elise," warns children of the dangers of drugs, sexual exploitation, gangs, and racism. In "Made You Look," which features samples from the Incredible Bongo Band's cover of "Apache," Nas boasts about his rapping prowess; in the chorus he raps, "They shootin'!—Aw made you look / You a slave to a page in my rhyme book / Gettin' big money, playboy your time's up / Where them gangstas at? / Where them dimes at?" Ethan Brown reviewed *God's Son* positively for *New York* magazine (December 16, 2002), writing, "Here, Nas is so fierce, so plainspoken, so lean with words, that he demolishes not just the oeuvre of our ruling rappers . . . and recalls the music's lyrical champs like Rakim, he even brings to mind hip-hop progenitors like Muhammad Ali in the 'Rumble in the Jungle' era."

Nas collaborated with his father, Olu Dara, for the first single from his two-disc release *Street's Disciple* (2004). The bluesy "Bridging the Gap" features Dara singing the song's hook while Nas raps about the foundations of black music. Nas reflected on the history of black music, rapping, "The blues came from gospel, gospel from blues / Slaves are harmonizin' them ahs and oohs / Old school, new school, know school rules / All these years I been voicin' my blues / I'm a artist from the start, Hip-Hop guided my heart." Nas has said that he considers "Bridging the Gap" his greatest song.

In 2006 Nas released his eighth studio album, *Hip-Hop Is Dead*, on the Def Jam label. His first single, the album's title track, criticizes the influx of rap artists ignorant of hip-hop's roots as well as the commercialization of the genre. When asked about the title of his album and first single, Nas told Ryan Dombal for *Pitchfork* (December 6, 2006, on-line), "To me, hip-hop's been dead for years . . . . With that being said, then, the object of the game now is to make money off of exploiting it. That's what it's all about—get this money. That's basically what I'm saying." Produced by Dr. Dre, Kanye West, and will.i.am, the album received favorable reviews.

Nas's most recent solo album, *Untitled*, sparked controversy even before it reached stores, when news spread that Nas was planning to title the album "Nigger." Several public figures and organizations, including the NAACP, publicly condemned the rapper for using a term so hurtful and derogatory to the African-American population. Nas said in response that he merely wanted the title to reflect the album's content, which focuses largely on the plight of black men in America. Even so, the rapper abandoned the title before the record's release, in July 2008; the record is untitled. "It got to the point where people were too concerned about the title," Nas told Joseph Barracato for the *New York Post* (July 13, 2008). "I didn't want them to miss the messages in it. But to be honest, I really believe my fans will always know what the real title of this album is and what to call it." Despite the controversy, or perhaps because of it, the album sold 186,600 copies in its first week.

An avid reader, Nas enjoys writing short stories; he also paints. In 1998 he made his acting debut, starring alongside the rapper DMX in Hype Williams's urban film drama *Belly*. (Nas also helped write the script.) While the film was praised for its visual style, it suffered from a weak plot. Nas also had starring roles in the 2001 action film *Ticker*, which co-starred Steven Seagal, Tom Sizemore, and Dennis Hopper, and the 2001 drama *Sacred Is the Flesh*, which Nas also co-wrote. It was rumored that he was to portray the rapper Kool G. Rap in "Vapors," a biographical film about the legendary Juice Crew hip-hop group. As of late 2009 financing for the film had not materialized. Nas has said that he enjoys acting and hopes to get the opportunity to do more of it.

Nas married the R&B singer Kelis (Rogers) in a small ceremony in Atlanta, Georgia, on July 28, 2003. In April 2009, when Kelis was seven months pregnant with the couple's first child, she filed for divorce. Citing irreconcilable differences, she took Nas to court to receive monetary support. Their son, Knight, was born on July 22, 2009. The following day a judge ordered Nas to pay his ex-wife nearly $40,000 per month in spousal and child support. Nas has a 15-year-old daughter, Destiny, from a previous relationship with Carmen Bryan. His next album, "Distant Relatives," a collaboration with the reggae artist and producer Damian Marley, was to be released in late 2009.

—M.A.S.

Suggested Reading: defjam.com; (Kansas City, Missouri) *Pitch Weekly* Music June 6, 2002; *Los Angeles Times* p62 Aug. 11, 1996, E p51 Dec. 5, 2004; (Minneapolis, Minnesota) *Star Tribune* E p1 Sep. 5, 2008; *New York Times* II p42 Oct. 6, 1996, II p35 Dec. 5, 2004;

Selected Recordings: *Illmatic*, 1994; *It Was Written*, 1996; *The Firm: The Album* (with The Firm), 1997; *I Am . . .* , 1999; *Nastradamus*, 1999; *Stillmatic*, 2001; *God's Son*, 2002; *Street's Disciple*, 2004; *Hip Hop Is Dead*, 2006; *Greatest Hits*, 2007; *Untitled*, 2008; *Distant Relatives* (with Damian Marley), 2009

Selected Films: as actor and screenwriter—*Belly*, 1998; *Sacred Is the Flesh*, 2001; as actor—*Ticker*, 2001

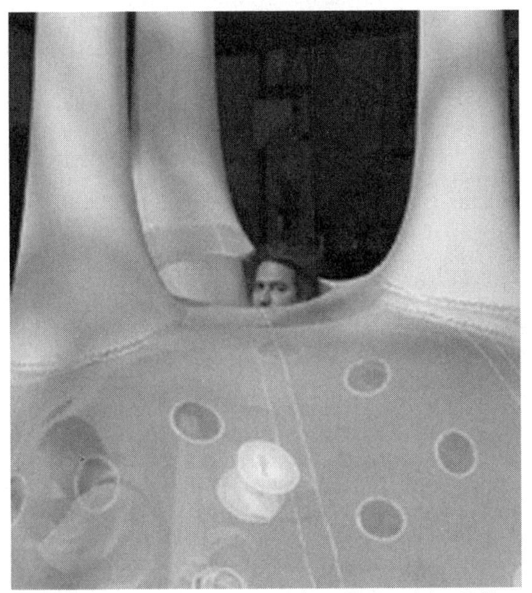

Giorgio Benni, courtesy of Tanya Bonakder Gallery

Neto, Ernesto

(NET-oh)

1964– Sculptor; installation artist

Address: Gentil Carioca, Rua Goncalves ledo 17, Sobrado, Centro Rio de Janeiro, RJ, Brasil CEP 20060-020

The Brazilian artist Ernesto Neto creates organic-looking sculptures that are intended to provide his viewers with intensely sensuous experiences. Most of his works are made from large swaths of Lycra or nylon; some are stretched taut so that they resemble a kind of skin, while others, hanging from ceilings, are filled with materials ranging from Styrofoam balls to lead pellets to aromatic spices that viewers can smell while walking through the exhibit. Defying the conventional rules of art exhibits, the sculptures are meant to be touched; viewers can even take off their shoes and walk inside Neto's largest room-sized installations. Glenn McNatt, writing for the *Baltimore Sun* (February 18, 2001), compared the experience of walking through one of Neto's works, *Sister Naves*, to that of being inside another person's body—being "a drop of blood flowing through a vein or a child enclosed within the womb." Others have seen in his work elements suggestive of a futuristic or otherworldly environment. Dobrila Denegri, a curator for the Museo d'Arte Contemporanea Roma, told Dan Horch for *Art Info* (May 16, 2008, on-line), "Neto is one of the few artists who both engage the viewer's imagination and offer a polysensorial experience. His immersive environments, his architectural and sculptural habitats, create a zone where organic and artificial are blurred, and categories like body and mind, sense and intellect, creation and decay are in constant flux." Some of Neto's best-known works are the large, chamber-like Lycra sculptures in his series of *naves*—"nave" being Portuguese for "ship"—the first of which, *Navedenga*, Neto created in 1998. The Rio de Janeiro–based artist, who has been creating his unique sculptures since the mid-1990s, received worldwide attention when he represented Brazil at the 2001 Venice Biennale. His work has been shown in solo and group exhibitions across Europe, the United States, Latin America, and Asia. In June 2009 Neto presented the largest installation of his career, entitled *Anthropodino*, at New York City's Park Avenue Armory. For the *New York Times* (May 15, 2009), Ken Johnson described the work, which encourages viewer participation, as "a spectacular installation of gauzy Lycra fabric, dangling pods, dinosaurish wooden bones and cavernous interiors." Neto told a writer for the *Economist* (September 9, 2006), "All my work is about our connection to the world, it is about relationships, about union. The skin is the end of yourself and the beginning of the other. It is the place of encounter. I want people to see my sculpture through their pores, as well as their eyes, to feel it with all their senses."

Ernesto Neto was born in 1964 in Rio de Janeiro, Brazil's second-largest city. His father was a building engineer. During Neto's childhood, in the 1970s, "the whole city was one big construction site," he told Horch. "Today whenever I hear or even smell construction, it brings me back to my childhood." When Neto was a boy his mother was a seamstress and a student of design. Neto intended to study engineering in college but dropped out after a semester, having failed the program's entrance examination. (One source says that he was not admitted to the school.) He then became immersed in the study of astronomy, envisioning a career as a scientist. "In my country to be an artist means that your father thinks you've gone crazy and your mother thinks that you're never going to make any money," he told Lynn Cline for the Santa Fe *New Mexican* (March 31, 2000). Nonetheless, after learning from a girlfriend about a sculpture class being offered at the Escola de Artes Visuais do Parque Lage, one of the country's top art schools, he enrolled at the school and began studying sculpture. "I started to work with clay and I realized, hey, this is what I want to do with my life," Neto told Cline. "I don't want to be an engineer or an astronomer. So I began to study everything I could about art."

Neto's earliest pieces involved what Horch described as "geometrically shaped iron slabs connected by a ligature." Neto developed a penchant for juxtaposing hard and soft materials, using, for instance, nylon stockings to hold metal plates together. For his sculpture *BarBall* (1987), Neto leaned heavy iron rods against soft rubber balls. He also began to experiment with different visual effects by filling stockings with lead ball bearings and other materials, such as Styrofoam balls and spices, to enhance the viewers' sensory experience. "When you put sand with stockings, there's a relationship there that transforms, making a new body out of two separate ones," Neto told Cline. "One thing can change another thing and there's always a duality. A stocking, for example, is not a stocking anymore when you put it with sand. It's become something else—something that moves, something that you want to touch." While he was still a student, his work was accepted for an exhibition of new artists at the now-closed gallery Petite Galerie in Rio. His first solo show followed in 1988. "I first saw Neto's work in 1989 . . . ," a São Paulo gallery owner, Márcia Forces, who represents Neto in his native country, told Horch. "All the elements that were to define his future body of work were already there: the preeminent organic form combined with a precise geometry, the concept of the work of art as a living organism, the use of gravity, the concern for balance and the soft, ordinary materials."

Neto has named as influences the Russian Constructivist and American Minimalist art movements. He is perhaps most influenced by the 1960s Brazilian neo-concretist movement, which represented a reaction to the mathematical certainty that characterized the previous artistic movement in Brazil, known as concrete art. Brazilian neo-concretists focused on subjective, symbolic, and organic means of expression and included artists such as Hélio Oiticica, Amilcar de Castro, and Lygia Clark. In his interview with Bill Arning for *Bomb Magazine* (Winter 2000, on-line), Neto pointed out one significant difference between his work and that of those 1960s Brazilian artists, who worked during a period of intense political turmoil and violence in the country, when limits on freedom of speech made it necessary for artists to communicate any subversive messages implicitly rather than explicitly. "Their works almost always have some form of cultural commentary hidden inside them," Neto explained to Arning. "I do not need to hide the concepts behind my work, the intellectual structures. In fact, it's the opposite: I want to show everything, everything is transparent. I open the pot and make everything as visible as possible for a big diverse audience."

One of Neto's early pieces was *Colonia* (1989), a 20-foot-long installation that consisted of nylon stockings, of various colors and sizes, containing small lead pellets and hung so that they expanded and spread out when they reached the ground. For *Grupolipo* (1990), another early sculpture, Neto filled stockings with Styrofoam beads to create "knee-high funguslike forms," as Alisa Tager described them for *Art in America* (July 1, 1994). These were situated among a dozen irregular white cylinders, each of which held a cluster of lead pellets packed into a crevice at the top, making "a small forest," according to Tager. Tager noted that both works "seemed emphatically corporeal, even erotic, as the low blobs merged and the open lips of the stocking tops rolled back to reveal the thousands of dense pellets within." Tager described Neto as one of many young Brazilian artists—including Leda Catunda, Edgar de Souza, and Nina Moraes—who "refer to the body without being directly figurative and are formally nonspecific without being wholly abstract. Notions of transformation or transfiguration permeate their works as they associate objects to invent anomalous forms and bizarre imagery recalling limbs, innards, skins and skeletons."

By the mid-1990s Neto's sensuous sculptures and installations had been shown in solo exhibitions. They had also appeared in group shows at galleries in New York City; Miami, Florida; Sydney, Australia; Wales; Berlin, Germany; London, England; and Madrid, Spain. He created a series of seven photographs, entitled *M.E.D.I.T.* (1994), which depicted Neto's face being distorted as it was bound progressively tighter with thread. (*Medit* means "to go forth in meditation," and the initials stand for a Spanish phrase that translates as "spiritual metamorphosis of the topological unconscious.") In the penultimate image a pair of scissors appears, which cuts him free in the final shot. Neto came up with the idea for the piece when one evening, on a whim, he picked up a spool of string and began wrapping it around his face. "That girl that I was with got scared," he told Arning. "I went to the mirror to see what was scaring her, but to me it looked beautiful."

Neto's first New York solo show, in 1997, at the Tanya Bonakdar Gallery, included his trademark pieces: organically and sensuously shaped sculptures. Among the works selected for the show were those with the titles *Piff, Paff, Poff, Puff; Piff Piff;* and *Puff Puff.* Those were small Lycra sacks filled with colorful, pungent substances, such as coriander and chili powder, that were hung from the ceiling, to create various compositions of form, color, and scent. Two years later Neto presented his work at the same New York gallery in a show called Navedenga and the Ovaloids. Sylvie Fortin, a writer for *Parachute: Contemporary Art Magazine* (April 1, 1999), observed that Neto appeared to be "working around the same principles" as in his 1997 show, "but in reverse. Suspension and weightlessness now replace impact and gravity. Penetration replaces spillage. The olfactory has given way to touch and proprioception." Neto's sculpture *Glop* (1998) is an elliptically shaped Lycra stocking filled with Styrofoam pellets and blood-colored red pepper. Neto's Ovaloid series (1998) included four white Lycra stockings filled with Styrofoam. Fortin noted that that piece "played wonderful tricks on perception, fully enlisting the body through touch and sending the mind through an interpretation frenzy. . . . Touching their surface evoked the touch of living flesh: the pressure of the hand unexpectedly met with the reverse pressure of the work in a sensual accommodation." The show also featured *Nave-*

denga (1998), a sculpture that became one of Neto's best-known works. (Its title is a combination of the Portuguese words *nave*, which means "ship," and *denga*, which translates to "womb," and is meant to refer to the concept of "female sexual internal space.") The piece was a large floating Lycra chamber stretched between the floor and ceiling and weighted down by Lycra sandbags. Viewers were encouraged to remove their shoes and enter an opening in the chamber, where they encountered a droplet-like form dangling above a nodular shape in the center of the floor. Fortin wrote that the act of walking into the chamber produced "a heightened sense of embodiment, of one's relationship to and impact on the work, and of the complete interdependence between the work and the viewer's experience. As one's presence literally gave shape to the piece, its floor stretching underfoot, its walls reconfigured by touch, one gained a heightened awareness of the productive process of experiencing art."

As one of 41 artists from 22 countries—and one of only two Latin Americans—who presented work at the 1999 Carnegie International, held in Pittsburgh, Pennsylvania, Neto produced *Nude Plasmic*, a large translucent sculpture containing beanbags, holes, and paths that viewers could enter and walk through. In 2000 his work gained significant attention at an important group show in Rio, entitled The Education of the Five Senses, which also featured work by Fernanda Gomes and Valeska Soares. The same year he was commissioned to create an original work for the Wexner Center, in Columbus, Ohio. The artist was inspired when he noticed the city's replica of Christopher Columbus's ship *Santa Maria* docked on the Olentangy River. In response Neto constructed *Sister Naves*, a large installation intended to represent the *Santa Maria*'s sister vessels, the *Nina* and the *Pinta*. Viewers could touch and walk through or around the two Lycra structures, which were 20 feet long and connected by a corridor. Neto produced many more sculptures as part of his *nave* series, among them *Nave Nove*, which premiered in 2000 at the Dundee Contemporary Arts Museum of Scotland, and *Flying Group Nave*, which is owned by collectors in Seattle, Washington.

At the Baltimore Museum of Art show BodySpace, in early 2001, Neto presented works including *O Habitat* (1999), *Sister Naves*, and *Globiobabel Nudelione Landmoonaia* (2000). "This is a startling, slightly disconcerting experience, one that is sharpened, moreover, by the pungent odor of cloves that suffuses the space and by the consciousness that one is fully visible to people standing outside in the gallery," McNatt wrote about being inside *Sister Naves*. "One has the oddly disorienting sense of occupying an intensely private space that is nevertheless completely accessible to public view." Neto represented Brazil at the 2001 Venice Biennale, a major contemporary art exhibition. His room-sized sculpture *O Bicho* was, according to Cynthia Rose, writing for the *Seattle Weekly* (August 23, 2001), a "powerful, seductive work." The sculpture received a lot of press coverage and was one of the event's most popular pieces.

Many critics noted that Neto's 2002 45-by-15-foot structure, *The Dangerous Logic of Wooing*, which opened at the Smithsonian Institution's Hirshhorn Museum, in Washington, D.C., represented an evolution of sorts. Devoid of the "olfactory stimulation" of his other pieces, the installation was designed to be touched as well as seen. It was composed of two large, abstract Lycra structures hanging from the ceiling, above the viewers' heads, with various parts filled with Styrofoam balls and rice, drooping to form different shapes. At first glance the shapes resembled "a group of cow udders or oddly shaped sausage casings," as Carl Hartman described them for the Associated Press (March 21, 2002). Gradually, viewers realized that the two structures were meant to represent abstract male and female figures. A writer for the *Washington (D.C.) City Paper* (March 29, 2002–April 4, 2002) described the experience of viewing the work: "You start picking the massive forms apart, uncovering symmetries in what once seemed chaotic, tallying masses and counterweights, cataloging the openings where rice and Styrofoam made their entrance, all now twisted shut like the necks of half-inflated balloons. . . . Finally, that *Star Trek* moment arrives when what you have been puzzling over is revealed, its extent understood; and what you thought was a dead planetoid, an abandoned starship, a mindless field of energy reawakens into sentience, emerging as a life form heretofore unknown. Here are two large bodies, male and female, intimately close but distinct and unlinked."

Neto produced *Just Like Drops in Time, Nothing* (2002) during an artistic residency at the University of Newcastle, in England, where he was assisted in its construction by a team of students. The work consisted of nylon droplets full of ground cumin stretching downward from a canopy. While conceding that the piece was alluring and stimulating—and revealed "an intuitive grasp of physics, space and materials"—Benjamin Genocchio, a writer for the *Australian* (August 16, 2002), noted "an odd passivity" in the work in its similarity to Neto's other pieces. "I get the sense Neto has run out of things to do with stockings and spices, and is dreaming up increasingly complicated combinations for the sake of novelty." In contrast, Neto's piece *Three Religions, No God and the Children*, presented at the Los Angeles Museum of Contemporary Art (MOCA), in 2003, consisted of three large Lycra pyramids woven together and stretched over a puzzle-piece–shaped green foam "island" on the floor. The work included Lycra sacks of spices hanging from the ceiling, openings where viewers could enter, and "toys" scattered on the foam flooring for viewers to touch and play with. Neto purchased many of the materials from stores in Los Angeles including Bed, Bath and Beyond and the drug store Rexall. The MOCA associate curator Alma Ruiz told Lisa Rosen for the *Los Angeles*

Times (October 1, 2003), "[Neto] creates what he calls a contemplative atmospheric space in which you can get in touch with yourself but also establish relationships with other people in the space, even people you don't know."

In 2006 Neto created a new piece called *The Malmo Experience*—an enormous "organic labyrinth" of fabrics and shapes—as part of an overview of his career at the gallery Malmö Konsthall, in Sweden. That year Neto's pieces were also shown at the Carnegie Museum of Art's Forum Gallery, along with work by another artist, in an exhibition called Forum 57: Luisa Lambri and Ernesto Neto. In 2006 he presented his piece *Leviathan* at a show at the Panthéon in Paris, France. The work's title refers to Thomas Hobbes's seminal work of political philosophy, in which he compared the interrelated parts of the political state to those of a person. Neto's piece, which the *Economist* described as "a tropical dreamscape," was particularly noted for its contrast to the exhibition space: the Panthéon, originally a church, was commissioned by Louis XV and contains the graves of great European thinkers, among them Voltaire and Rousseau. "Developed societies are too purely visual . . . ," Neto told the *Economist.* "My work is atmospheric and intuitive. We have to feel our way through situations—to swing a little—otherwise we're going to crash." In 2007 Neto presented a large work, called *Mother body emotional densities / for alive temple time baby son*, at the Museum of Contemporary Art San Diego. It was composed of "long stretches" of Lycra that "soar like cathedral arches, and its long 'limbs,' which encase aromatic spices, closely allude to the human form," as Robert L. Pincus wrote for the *San Diego Union-Tribune* (January 19, 2007).

Anthropodino, Neto's largest installation to date, opened in June 2009 in New York City's Park Avenue Armory, in a 55,000-square-foot, 80-foot-high space called the Wade Thompson Drill Hall. Construction of the piece, which was financed with a Rockefeller grant, required heavy machinery and a team of workers as well as 1,800 pounds of spices and hundreds of yards of Lycra. Randy Kennedy, writing for the *New York Times* (May 13, 2009), likened the enormous interactive installation to "a superfine spider web, laden with egg sacks, that has drifted down onto the skeleton of a forgotten species of dinosaur shaped like a cephalopod." *Anthropodino* consisted of huge, wooden rib-like structures wrapped in translucent pale cloth, from which extended blue- and pink-tinted tunnels and a separate space where viewers could relax on a large purple pillow or dive into a pool of balls. Additionally, Lycra tubes holding quantities of spices dangled from the ceiling. Writing for the *New York Times* (May 15, 2009), Ken Johnson observed an "Oedipal—or pre-Oedipal—erotic dimension" to the installation, owing to its "culinary aroma" and the use of sheer fabric, which recalls nylon stockings. Comparing the sculpture to work by the surrealist painter Joan Miró and the innovative architect Antonio Gaudí, Johnson concluded, "For all its aesthetic and art historical sophistication, there is a certain innocence about Neto's work. Demons may be lurking under the armory floor, but they aren't allowed into the sweetness and light of his protective, matriarchal utopia."

Described by Ula Ilnytzky for the Associated Press (May 18, 2009) as "an affable man with a full head of curls and a stream-of-conscious way of speaking in his heavily accented English," Neto lives and works in Rio de Janeiro. In his studio, located in a three-story former printer's shop, Neto stores hundreds if not thousands of yards of fabric. He employs two full-time seamstresses, who call in their sisters, grandmothers, daughters, and cousins to help out when Neto needs a large piece sewn. For his largest pieces, Neto does not complete the final design until it is displayed publicly. "I love the tension. It's like being a tightrope walker," he told Pincus for the *Union-Tribune* (January 7, 2007). "I think in life we need to have this kind of risk. The situation of these pieces very much involves a lot of tension. That is part of the pleasure of doing them." Neto owns an art gallery in Rio, called Gentil Carioca, which he founded with his fellow artists Laura Lima and Márcio Botner. A lover of drink and dance, Neto throws a New Year's Eve party every year on Brazil's Ipanema Beach. He has two young children with his wife, whom he married inside one of his sculptures.

—M.E.R.

Suggested Reading: *Art in America* p44+ July 1, 1994; *Art Info* (on-line) May 16, 2008; *Australian* Features p17 Aug. 16, 2002; *Baltimore Sun* Arts & Society F p6 Feb. 18, 2001; *Los Angeles Times* E p1 Oct. 1, 2003; *New York Times* C p1 May 13, 2009, C p26 May 15, 2009; *Parachute: Contemporary Art Magazine* p58+ Apr. 1, 1999; *San Diego Union-Tribune* Lifestyle E p3 Jan. 9, 2007; *Santa Fe New Mexican* p26 Mar. 31, 2000; *Seattle Weekly* Art p94 Aug. 23, 2001

Selected Works: *Colonia*, 1989; *Grupolipo*, 1990; *Glop*, 1998; *Navedenga*, 1998; *The Dangerous Logic of Wooing*, 2002; *The Malmo Experience*, 2006; *Anthropodino*, 2009

Nixon, Marni

Feb. 22, 1930– Singer; dubber; actress; educator

Address: c/o Harden/Curtis, 850 Seventh Ave., New York, NY 10019

Although her name and face are not familiar to most filmgoers, the voice of Marni Nixon is well known among fans of movie musicals and their soundtrack albums. A classically trained soprano and violinist, Nixon provided the singing voices of

Courtesy of Marni Nixon

Marni Nixon

Deborah Kerr, in the role of the very proper British governess Anna Leonowens, in *The King and I* (1956); Natalie Wood, as the Puerto Rican–American teenager Maria, in *West Side Story* (1961); and Audrey Hepburn, as the Cockney flower-seller turned grand dame Eliza Doolittle, in *My Fair Lady* (1964)—three of the most famous characters and movie musicals in cinema history. Labeled "Hollywood's vocal doppelgänger of choice" by Sam Sutherland, writing for Amazon.com, and "the queen of the dubbers" by the musicologist and musical-theater historian Kurt Gänzl, Nixon has perfect pitch, extraordinary skill at sight-reading musical scores, and the ability to mimic perfectly actresses' voices and enunciation and their characters' accented English. Because of the secrecy about her roles that her contracts obligated her to maintain, however, her name never appeared among the credits that moviegoers saw, and she has received no royalties for most of her work as a Hollywood dubber, or ghost singer. Despite her success in that field, she became disenchanted with the film industry and left to pursue a singing career as a soloist. "It got so I'd lent my voice to so many others that I felt it no longer belonged to me. It was eerie, I had lost part of myself," she told Albin Krebs and Robert Thomas for the *New York Times* (March 26, 1981). In a rare return to dubbing, she provided the singing voice for Grandmother Fa in the Disney animated feature *Mulan* (1998).

Now 79, Nixon has worked virtually nonstop since early childhood. As a youngster she appeared in bit parts or as an extra in dozens of films and performed with local orchestras and choral groups. She has sung in operas by composers including Mozart, Verdi, Puccini, Offenbach, Richard Strauss, Arnold Schoenberg, and Francis Poulenc, performing for radio and TV programs and with such companies as the Seattle Opera, in Washington State, and the San Francisco Opera and the Los Angeles Opera, in California. She has appeared in concert under such esteemed orchestra conductors as Leopold Stokowski, Bruno Walter, Otto Klemperer, and Zubin Mehta and such composer/conductors as Igor Stravinsky, William Walton, and Leonard Bernstein. She has appeared in singing and nonsinging roles on and Off-Broadway, in regional theater, and on TV; as the host of the Seattle children's TV series *Boomerang*, she won four local Emmy Awards.

As a soloist or with others, Nixon has recorded two dozen albums, among them *Walt Disney's Story and Songs from Mary Poppins* (1964), *Marni Nixon: Songs of Love and Parting* (1974), and *Marni Nixon Sings Gershwin* (1993). She was twice nominated for a Grammy Award, in the category of best classical performance—vocal soloist, for her albums *The Cabaret Songs of Arnold Schoenberg and Nine Early Songs* (1975) and *Aaron Copland: Eight Poems of Emily Dickinson* (1986). Her voice has also been heard on many radio and TV commercials. For four decades she has worked as a vocal and dialect coach, both privately and as a member of the faculty of several schools, and she has conducted many master classes. Her memoir, *I Could Have Sung All Night*, written with Stephen Cole, was published in 2006. In 2007 she was a co-winner of the VERA (Voice Education Research Awareness) Award, from the Voice Foundation, for her "contribution to the field of voice communication."

Of Scottish and German descent, Nixon was born Margaret Nixon McEathron to Charles Nixon McEathron and Margaret Elsa (Wittke) McEathron on February 22, 1930 in Altadena, California, a suburb of Los Angeles. Her mother nicknamed her Marni, by combining parts of her first and middle names. Nixon has two older sisters, Donyll and Adair, and a younger sister, Ariel (called Midge). Her father was a talented singer, and during the early years of her parents' marriage, he toured with trios and quartets. His wife encouraged him to continue his career in singing, but he disliked constant traveling and decided to take a job, in 1927, with the General Motors Co. in Los Angeles. Nixon has been singing since she was a baby; her parents told her that for a few weeks when she was about one and a half years old, she used to wake up after midnight and sing in her crib until she fell back to sleep. At the age of four, she saw a performance by Karl Moldrem's Hollywood Baby Orchestra (whose members were as young as two); afterward, at her request, her parents bought her a child-size violin. After only four violin lessons she joined Moldrem's orchestra. Moldrem soon found that she had perfect pitch, and he would often ask her to sing to provide examples for the other children. As a five-and-a-half-year-old violinist, Nixon joined the City Schools Youth Orchestra, in Altadena, with which her older sisters played. Her mother, father, and younger sister also played instruments, and the whole family would give concerts for neighbors on a platform built for that purpose in their living room. "Life in our household was strict," Nixon wrote in her memoir. "Mother ruled the roost with her Germanic perfectionism and our achievement was glorified." She also wrote that once, after she had accidentally lost her way while walking home from kindergarten, her mother screamed at her, "Either you're perfect, Marni, or you're nothing!"

Nixon made her debut on the silver screen in 1937, in a feature film whose script called for a young, redheaded violinist to play in the background. For the next decade she appeared in minor roles or as an extra in more than 50 films, including *The Great Waltz* (1938), *The Grapes of Wrath* (1940), *Babes on Broadway* (1942), *The Bachelor and the Bobby-Soxer* (1947), and *In the Good Old Summertime* (1949). She also had a recurring role as Angelica Abernathy in several of the "Lum and Abner" films of the 1940s (spin-offs from the radio series originated by Chester Lauck and Norris Goff, whose characters were named Columbus "Lum" Edwards and Abner Peabody, respectively), starting with *The Bashful Bachelor* in 1942. By that time Nixon had been taking singing lessons for years; the money she earned from her jobs in cinema and from babysitting helped pay for them. Her parents paid the balance, and once, when they had no extra money, her mother sold her diamond engagement ring so that Nixon could continue with her lessons.

In 1946 Nixon placed second in a singing competition judged by the celebrated choral director Roger Wagner (one of several competitions in which she placed at or near the top). At Wagner's invitation she joined his newly formed Los Angeles Concert Youth Chorus. The following year, now named the Los Angeles Concert Chorale—commonly referred to as the Roger Wagner Chorale—it turned professional. The group performed regularly with the Los Angeles Philharmonic Orchestra. Nixon became close friends with another chorus member, the future opera star Marilyn Horne (who later wrote the foreword to Nixon's memoir).

While a student at Susan Miller Dorsey High School, in Los Angeles, Nixon worked as a messenger girl at MGM Studios, delivering mail and giving guided tours. In 1947 she graduated from high school and entered Los Angeles City College, where she majored in music (but did not earn a degree). (Bennington College, in Vermont, had accepted her, but her mother had refused to let her enroll there.) One of her professors, Hugo Strelitzer, expanded her knowledge of opera and introduced her to leider, or art songs, written by 16th- and 17th-century French and Italian composers and 19th-century German composers. She took piano lessons with Leonard Stein, a teacher recommended by Strelitzer, but soon quit because she disliked practicing. "Now when my students and I anguish that I'm not a better pianist, I could kick myself for being so foolhardy and arrogant," she wrote in her memoir. "I should have taken the time to learn to play well."

Also in 1947 Nixon sang at the Hollywood Bowl in a performance of Carl Orff's *Carmina Burana*, with Leopold Stokowski conducting the Philadelphia Orchestra, and she participated in a performance of Mozart's Requiem with the Los Angeles Philharmonic, under the direction of Alfred Wallenstein. That year she won her first leading stage role, as the title character in a new musical, *Oh, Susanna*, mounted at the Pasadena Playhouse, in California. In addition, she took on her first ghosting job, as the singing voice of the child star Margaret O'Brien in *Big City* (1948). She dubbed for O'Brien again in *The Secret Garden* (1949). In 1948 she appeared in a production of Richard Strauss's opera *Elektra*, and around that time she debuted on CBS radio, singing a medley of songs by Jerome Kern on a program called *Tomorrow Calling*. Years later she recorded the album *Marni Nixon Sings Classic Kern* (1988).

Meanwhile, Nixon had become involved in musical activities in college. Her performances on campus and ability to sight-read complex scores led the composer Ernst Krenek to recruit her to sing one of his pieces at a chamber-music series at the college in 1948. Krenek was among many Jewish artists, musicians, writers, and others who had emigrated from European nations in the 1930s to escape the Nazis and had settled in Southern California, and thanks to him, Nixon began to attend informal concerts, called "Evenings on the Roof," at which she met other talented emigrés as well as native-born American musicians. Her participation in a performance of Stravinsky's cantata *Les Noces* at one of those concerts led to her professional and personal association with Stravinsky and his wife; to prepare for studio recordings of works by the composer, she often rehearsed in the Stravinskys' home.

On May 22, 1950 Nixon married the Austrian-born emigré and composer Ernest Gold, whose credits include the scores for the films *The Defiant Ones*, *On the Beach*, *Exodus*, and *It's a Mad, Mad, Mad, Mad World*. Later that year Nixon, whose greatest ambition had been to become a great opera singer, "made a major professional mistake," as she wrote in her memoir: after she auditioned for the New York City Opera's forthcoming production of Mozart's *The Magic Flute*, she turned down the role that she was offered—that of the Queen of the Night—because she regarded it as "totally pyrotechnic." "In retrospect," she wrote, "I realize that if I had accepted the role it might have led to others in the company and I probably would have come to New York and based my career on the East Coast, which might have afforded me more opportunities in the opera world."

Nixon gave birth to her first child in 1951 and her second in 1953. Juggling her career with her responsibilities as a homemaker, she continued to perform in "Evenings on the Roof" concerts and with the Roger Wagner Chorale. In a job that required her to mimic Marilyn Monroe's "breathy, sexy sound," in her words, she dubbed the second half of the line "But square cut or pear shape, these rocks don't lose their shape" in the song "Diamonds Are a Girl's Best Friend," from *Gentlemen Prefer Blondes* (1953); the notes accompanying those words were too high for Monroe, who starred in the film.

In 1955 Nixon landed her first major ghosting job, for the film version of the Richard Rodgers and Oscar Hammerstein musical *The King and I*, originally staged in 1951 with Gertrude Lawrence as Anna. (Nixon replaced a dubber, not named in her memoir, who had suddenly died.) The contracts offered to her by the film studio now known as 20th Century Fox and with Capitol Records, which later released the film's soundtrack, specified that she would receive a single payment but no royalties and no credits, either in the film or on the record jacket. "I was torn," she recalled in her memoir, "but the studio had made the choice very clear: either I do the job anonymously, with no credit at all, or walk away." Eager to work on such a high-profile project, as well as with the actress Deborah Kerr, Nixon signed the contracts. The recording process involved extremely close cooperation between Kerr and Nixon. "Whenever there was a song to be sung in a scene, I would get up and stand next to [Kerr] and watch her while she sang and she would watch me while I sang," Nixon told Jeff Lunden for the National Public Radio program *Weekend Edition Sunday* (September 3, 2006, on-line). "After we recorded that song, she would have to go to the filming of it and mouth to that performance. So she had to be very aware of what she was going to do and how she was going to sing the song ahead of time." "The challenge [for me] was singing in a voice that was consistent with the sound of [Kerr's] speaking voice," Nixon told Frank Magiera for the Worcester, Massachusetts, *Telegram & Gazette* (July 10, 1997). "You must imagine the conformation of the resonance that you hear coming out of [singers'] mouths; how to manufacture that within your own vocalism and not destroy yourself and still incorporate that as part of your own voice."

Studio executives ordered Nixon to keep her role in *The King and I* a secret. Though dubbing was a well-known practice within the film industry, many moviegoers were unaware of it. "Nowadays people accept stuntmen, doubles, all that," Nixon told a Minneapolis, Minnesota, *Star Tribune* (February 17, 2008) reporter. "But in those days, it was considered a detriment if people found out." Kerr, bound by no such constraints, revealed Nixon's role to reporters. "The first interview she gave with [the *New York Post*] columnist Earl Wilson was headlined 'Deborah Tells a Secret,'" Nixon told Frank Rizzo for the *Hartford (Connecticut) Courant* (July 5, 1997). "Of course, she said I just did the high notes, but she did mention me by name and said that I was dubbing her voice." In a representative, highly enthusiastic review of *The King and I* for the *New York Times* (June 29, 1956), Bosley Crowther wrote, "The voice of Marni Nixon adds a thrilling lyricism to [Kerr's] songs." Nixon dubbed Kerr's singing voice again in the romantic drama *An Affair to Remember* (1957), co-starring Cary Grant, in which Kerr played a lounge singer. Although Nixon received neither screen credit nor royalties, her name appeared on the back cover of the soundtrack album to that motion picture. In 1960, in her first appearance on screen as an adult, Nixon sang in the chorus in the film version of Cole Porter and Abe Burrows's 1953 stage musical, *Can-Can*.

Nixon was recruited to dub the singing voice of Natalie Wood in the film version of the theatrical musical *West Side Story* (1961), with music by Leonard Bernstein and lyrics by Stephen Sondheim, based on ideas of the choreographer Jerome Robbins and Shakespeare's *Romeo and Juliet*. Wood, who played the female lead, Maria (a role originated on the stage in 1957 by Carol Lawrence), worked on the project without knowing that her songs would be dubbed; indeed, according to Nixon, the film crew led Wood to believe that her own singing would be heard by moviegoers. After the shooting Nixon had to synchronize her singing precisely to the movements of Wood's lips and her facial expressions in the songs "Tonight" (and the "Tonight" quintet), "I Feel Pretty," "One Hand, One Heart," "Somewhere," and "I Have a Love." "That's a much more difficult process" than the one she and Kerr had used, she told the *Star Tribune* interviewer. Although Nixon was again sworn to secrecy, and her name did not appear among the credits in the film, she instructed her new agent to fight for her fair share of the royalties from the soundtrack album. That battle ended when Leonard Bernstein agreed to give to Nixon a quarter of one percent of his own royalties—"not a negligible amount," in Nixon's words: the album remained on the *Billboard* pop chart for 198 weeks—in the top spot for 54—and by 1986 it had sold more than three million copies. It also won the 1961 Grammy Award in the category "best soundtrack album—original cast." (Bernstein and Nixon's agreement applied only to long-playing records; Nixon has received no royalties from sales of the *West Side Story* CD.) Nixon's third child was born in 1962.

For *My Fair Lady*, her next major feature film, Nixon dubbed the singing of Audrey Hepburn. (Julie Andrews, who had played the lead when Alan Jay Lerner and Frederick Loewe's *My Fair Lady* opened on Broadway, in 1956, had not yet appeared on the big screen, and the producers of the film wanted the name of a female superstar on movie marquees.) Hepburn had demonstrated her ability to sing in the films *Funny Face* (1957) and *Breakfast at Tiffany's* (1961), but the role of Eliza

Doolittle required a voice more powerful and higher-pitched than hers. "Audrey, of course, wanted to do it all," Nixon wrote in her memoir, "but realized that I might have to supplement some of the higher notes and sing some of the longer-lined, more lyrical phrases." When Hepburn learned that all but one of the songs would be recorded in Nixon's voice, Nixon told Frank Rizzo, "she stomped out of the studio without saying a word. The next day she came back and apologized for her 'wicked' behavior." The knowledge that her singing was dubbed led to much criticism of Hepburn immediately after the release of *My Fair Lady*, at the end of 1964; the movie won eight Oscars (including one for the male lead, Rex Harrison) and many others awards, but Hepburn earned none. Earlier that year Nixon had provided the singing voices for the trio of animated geese in the "Jolly Holiday" sequence in the film *Mary Poppins* (in which Julie Andrews starred and for which she earned the Academy Award for best actress). In *The Sound of Music* (1965), in which Andrews also starred, Nixon was cast in the small part of a nun, Sister Sophia.

Later in the 1960s Nixon performed with the celebrated showman and pianist Liberace in Las Vegas, Nevada, and toured with the Danish-born pianist and comedian Victor Borge. In 1971, two years after her divorce from Gold, Nixon remarried and moved to Seattle to sing with the Seattle Opera. She appeared in productions mounted in local theaters and also gave concerts. During the late 1970s and early 1980s, Nixon hosted *Boomerang*, a local children's program for the Seattle TV channel KOMO 4. After the show's cancellation, reruns of its 169 episodes aired on local television for 25 years. Nixon earned four Northwest Chapter Emmy Awards for her work on the series.

In the early 1980s Nixon moved to New York City. In 1983 she starred alongside the singers Margaret Whiting and Cissy Houston in the Off-Broadway musical *Taking My Turn*, for which she earned a 1984 Drama Desk Award for outstanding featured actress in a musical. On Broadway she originated the roles of Sadie McKibben in *Opal* (1992) and Aunt Kate in *James Joyce's The Dead* (1999–2000). She also appeared in Broadway revivals of *Follies* (2001) and *Nine* (2003). In 2007 she appeared as Professor Henry Higgins's mother, a nonsinging role, in a concert performance of *My Fair Lady* with the New York Philharmonic at Lincoln Center, in New York City.

Earlier, Nixon underwent treatment for breast cancer in 1985 and again in 2000, after a recurrence. She has been married to her third husband, the jazz flutist Al Block, since 1983. Her second marriage, to Lajos Frederick Fenster, a physician, ended in divorce in 1975 after four years. From her first marriage she has one son, Andrew Gold, a musician and producer; two daughters—Martha Gold Carr, a psychologist, and Melani Gold Friedman, a singer and songwriter; and six grandchildren.

Since 1999 Nixon has given many performances of her one-woman show, *Marni Nixon: The Voice of Hollywood*. "I show some stills from the films I dubbed, tell some stories, sing a few things and answer questions about my life," she told Frank J. Prial for the *New York Times* (March 6, 2007). "People always love to ask me questions. And why not? I've had a really fantastic life."

—M.A.S.

Suggested Reading: AllMusicGuide.com; *New York Times* E p3 Mar. 6, 2007; *Opera News* p42+ Apr. 2004, p30+ Oct. 2004; *Philadelphia Inquirer* H p1 Mar. 9, 2008; *Playbill* (on-line) Jan. 4, 2000; *Time* p81+ Feb. 7 1964; Nixon, Marni, with Stephen Cole. *I Could Have Sung All Night*, 2006

Selected Films: as singing voice—*Big City*, 1948; *The Secret Garden*, 1949; *Dakota Lil*, 1950; *Gentlemen Prefer Blondes*, 1953; *Dementia*, 1955; *The King and I*, 1956; *An Affair to Remember*, 1957; *West Side Story*, 1961; *My Fair Lady*, 1964; *Mulan*, 1998; as actress—*The Bashful Bachelor*, 1942; *The Sound of Music*, 1965; *I Think I Do*, 1997

Selected Operas: *Carmina Burana*, 1947

Selected Plays: *Taking My Turn*, 1983; *Opal*, 1992, *James Joyce's The Dead*, 1999–2000; *Marni Nixon: The Voice of Hollywood*, 1999– ; *Follies*, 2001; *Nine*, 2003; *My Fair Lady*, 2007

Selected Television Shows: as host—*Boomerang*, 1975–1980

Selected Recordings: *Walt Disney's Story and Songs from Mary Poppins*, 1964; *Marni Nixon: Songs of Love and Parting*, 1974; *The Cabaret Songs of Arnold Schoenberg and Nine Early Songs*, 1975; *Marni Nixon Sings Gershwin*, 1985; *Aaron Copland: Eight Poems of Emily Dickinson*, 1986; *Marni Nixon Sings Classic Kern*, 1988; *Opal: The Complete Score*, 2000

Selected Books: *I Could Have Sung All Night* (with Stephen Cole), 2006

Northrop, Peggy

Aug. 6, 1954– Magazine editor

Address: Reader's Digest, *Reader's Digest Rd., Pleasantville, NY 10570-7000*

Three of the first four issues of *Reader's Digest* published in the U.S. entirely under the guidance of Peggy Northrop, its newest editor, earned that venerable monthly a 2009 National Magazine Award for general excellence. When, on April 30, 2009,

Mark Mainz/Getty Images

Peggy Northrop

the American Society of Magazine Editors (ASME) announced the winner in that category for magazines with circulations of two million or more, *Reader's Digest* was in its 88th year, and Northrop had been at its helm for just under a year and a half. "*Reader's Digest* has reinvented itself with fresh design, imaginative and timely feature stories and an engaging contemporary voice," ASME noted in a press release. "Articles about ordinary people overcoming extraordinary obstacles, useful and accessible service pieces on health and personal finance, and delightful humor columns make *Reader's Digest* not only a good companion but also a great escape." Worldwide, 50 other editions of *Reader's Digest*, each with its own editor and contents aimed at a particular geographic audience, are published in 22 languages in more than 60 countries, bringing its total readership to about 80 million. Since November 2007 Northrop has also held the positions of global editor in chief of *Reader's Digest* and editor in chief of the Readers Digest Association Inc., the latter of which also publishes books and more than 90 other periodicals.

Northrop was exposed to publishing and journalism firsthand from an early age: her father coowned a regional Pennsylvania daily, the *Observer-Reporter*. In the last three decades, she has held editorial positions at periodicals including the *San Francisco Examiner*, *Vogue*, *Glamour*, *Mirabella*, *Redbook*, *Real Simple*, *Organic Style*, and *More*. "I always think about my next job as 'this is it,'" she told Michael Bradwell for the *Observer-Reporter* (December 17, 2007, on-line). Northrop arrived at *Reader's Digest* in November 2007, after a determined effort by Mary Berner, the president and chief executive officer of the Reader's Digest Association, to lure her from *More*. "Peggy has a remarkable track record of editorial successes and circulation growth," Berner noted, according to Bradwell. Northrop told Bradwell, "What I think I do well is figure out what a magazine stands for."

With more than eight million copies of each issue of the U.S. edition reaching an estimated 40 million people, *Reader's Digest* is the largest-circulation general-interest magazine in the nation. "*Reader's Digest* is an American institution," James Doran wrote for the London *Times* (November 17, 2006, on-line) about the magazine, which for the most part offers abbreviated versions of articles from other publications. In Northrop's view, it is "the only magazine that can truly aspire to being America's magazine," as she put it to Bradwell. Northrop's outstanding editorial skills notwithstanding, in August 2009, in what its parent company described as a "prearranged move" and Northrop likened to "refinancing a house mortgage," *Reader's Digest* filed for bankruptcy. Nevertheless, "we are quite healthy," Northrop told Joyce Gannon for the *Pittsburgh Post-Gazette* (September 9, 2009). Northrop insisted that the idea of *Reader's Digest*'s founders, Lila Acheson Wallace and DeWitt Wallace, to provide condensations of longer articles published elsewhere is "still a valid one. No one has the time to read everything." "Reading the news today is like sipping from a fire hose," she told Andrew Vanacore for the Associated Press (September 7, 2009), referring to the immense amount of reportage available to the public from myriad print, broadcast, and Internet sources. "It's really an opportunity for us to do what we've always done, which is getting to the heart of what people want to know."

The daughter of Rose and John L. S. Northrop, Peggy Northrop was born on August 6, 1954. Her father and his brother William were the publishers of the *Observer-Reporter*, a newspaper for residents of Washington, Pennsylvania, where she grew up, and other towns in and around Washington and Greene Counties, in the southwestern part of the state. The newspaper, descended from a weekly launched in 1808, was bought by her paternal great-grandfather at the beginning of the 20th century and has remained in her family's hands ever since; her brother, Thomas Northrop, is currently the *Observer-Reporter*'s president and publisher, and Peggy Northrop sits on its board of directors. As a child she printed a newspaper, called the *Redstone Weekly*, for people in her neighborhood. Her first paying job, she told Joyce Gannon, was with the *Observer-Reporter*; among other tasks, she sold subscriptions, recorded wedding announcements, and wrote short articles. A self-described "late bloomer," she attended three colleges—among them Kenyon College, in Gambier, Ohio, and the American University in Beirut, Lebanon—and lived briefly in Israel before graduating from the University of California–Berkeley with a B.A. degree in anthropology, in 1980. Anthropology, which includes the study of human cultures, "prepared me for looking at the way people look at the world"—a useful skill for a writer and editor, she told Michael Bradwell.

After college Northrop remained in California, to take a job as a reporter for an arts and literature magazine, the *Berkeley Monthly*, in San Francisco. Next, for three years, she edited the *San Francisco Examiner's* Sunday magazine. Later in the 1980s she worked in the editorial departments of a series of women's magazines based in Sausalito, California. In 1990 she moved to New York City to become the health and fitness editor of *Vogue*, a women's fashion and beauty magazine published by Condé Nast. She was *Vogue*'s senior health editor when the organization Boycott Anorexic Marketing accused that magazine of including advertising with photos of models whose extreme thinness promoted unhealthy body images in girls and young women. While conceding that advertising in women's magazines sometimes reflected sexist stereotypes, Northrop told Stuart Elliott for the *New York Times* (April 26, 1994), "I find this a very difficult issue. The idea that body image is somehow set by the media is a provocative one, but I don't know of any good research to back that up." Northrop questioned the validity of belief that, as she put it, "women are so utterly victimized by the way they are portrayed that they go on a diet, starve themselves and become sick."

Northrop left *Vogue* to serve as the health editor of *Mirabella*, a fashion magazine geared toward women 40 years of age or older; it was launched in 1988 by Grace Mirabella, after she was fired as *Vogue*'s editor. In 1995 Northrop took a new job, as deputy editor for health-related articles for *Glamour*, a magazine known for its focus on fashion and beauty. She and the other senior editors resolved to include in the magazine substantive stories on current issues of interest to women. For example, in 1996 Northrop worked with the writers Leslie Laurence and Tessa DeCarlo on a pair of stories about managed health care. "In the first piece, we assembled overwhelming evidence that managed care affected women more often and in more ways than men," Northrop told Jeff Gremillion for *Media Week* (May 5, 1997). For the second article, Northrop explained, "we sent [DeCarlo] out to look at not just how lawyers are suing managed-care providers to get women the care that they need but also how women were going to their employers to get their health plans to change to cover reproductive services—how women were going to the press in some cases." Northrop told Gremillion, "*Glamour* really is a news magazine for women. *Glamour* takes a political stance in the world. It's unabashedly feminist. It is a very satisfying place to do serious work."

Next, in late 1998, Northrop became the executive editor of the women's magazine *Redbook*, published by Hearst. She left that magazine shortly after being passed over for the position of editor in chief, in the summer of 2001. In November 2001 Northrop was hired as the deputy editor of the magazine *Real Simple*, published by Time Inc. Like *O*, Oprah Winfrey's magazine, and *Martha Stewart Living*, *Real Simple* is devoted to topics including home design, cooking, motherhood, and social issues. *Real Simple* advocated "a simplified but sophisticated lifestyle," Carole Nicksin wrote for *HFN* (January 7, 2002). The magazine had "a shaky launch," Northrop told Nicksin, when it debuted, in 2000. "The magazine looked great from the start, but it was not connecting with its audience," she said. "But it's found both its voice and its audience. And right now"—that is, in the weeks following the September 11, 2001 terrorist attacks on the U.S.—"people want to be home and connecting with their home and family, which is what we're all about." One difference between *Real Simple* and Winfrey's and Stewart's publications was that it lacked what Northrop dubbed "a celebrity guru" as a symbol. Indeed, unlike most women's magazines, *Real Simple* rarely included articles about celebrities, because Northrop and her fellow editors had concluded that many magazine readers had tired of such pieces. They also insisted that *Real Simple* look uncluttered and sophisticated, to attract college-educated readers with higher-than-average incomes. "What's new about it is the women we reach expect their magazine to be beautiful," Northrop told Nicksin. She also said that she and her colleagues made an effort to appeal to readers on a higher intellectual and emotional level than traditional women's magazines: "I know for so many readers picking up a women's service magazine, it reflects this vision of American womanhood that a lot of women don't want to participate in. I know I don't want to participate in it. [We offer] service with soul, not service because your house needs to be clean for the neighbors." During Northrop's tenure at *Real Simple*, newsstand sales steadily increased; in February 2002 the magazine's circulation reached 900,000.

The following month Northrop left *Real Simple* to become editor in chief of *Organic Style*, the brainchild of Maria Rodale, the vice chairwoman of the Rodale Co. and a granddaughter of the company founder, J. I. Rodale, an early exponent of organic farming. The magazine was aimed at women who wanted to dress and furnish their homes stylishly with products that were "ecofriendly"—that is, that caused the least damage to the environment. In the few months since the publication of its first issue, in September 2001, two editors in chief had preceded Northrop at the magazine. "Any launch is risky," Northrop told Keith J. Kelly for the *New York Post* (March 13, 2002). "It doesn't scare me. I've worked with a lot of strong-willed editors. . . . Editorially, I don't think [*Organic Style*] is as coherent as it needs to be." Asked to articulate her vision for the magazine, Northrop explained to Kelly, "I did the hippie thing in California in the 70s—I don't want to go back there. . . . I want a magazine to show me the best life I can have." Northrop was credited with making *Organ-*

ic Style livelier during her two years with that magazine. She added investigative pieces, such as an article in the March 2004 issue about schools that were exposed to nearby toxic-waste sites and what steps residents in those areas could take to clean their environments; another, in the July/August 2004 issue, ranked the water quality of 25 U.S. cities. Northrop also doubled the number of photo shoots and devoted more spreads to photos of ordinary women. For the first time, in April 2004, the image of a celebrity appeared on the cover: that of the singer/songwriter Alanis Morissette, who in 2003 was a winner of the EMA (Environmental Media Association) Missions in Music Award, for publicly opposing drilling for oil in the Arctic National Wildlife Refuge, among other activities. During Northrop's tenure *Organic Style*'s circulation rose from 400,000 to 750,000, and its frequency of publication increased from six to 10 times per year. In 2003 *MIN (Media Industry Newsletter*) named Northrop to its annual list of 21 Most Intriguing People.

In 2004 Northrop left *Organic Style* to become the editor in chief of *More*, a magazine directed at women 40 and over. Introduced by the Meredith Corp. in 1998, *More* had seen its circulation grow steadily over the years, while its newsstand sales—a figure considered to be an indicator of a publication's vitality—had not. When Northrop joined the magazine, its newsstand sales had been around 113,000 for three years; its overall circulation was 950,000. Northrop aimed to narrow the magazine's focus to better serve the more than 40 million women in the U.S. who had been largely ignored by advertisers and magazines for years, even those, like *Mirabella* and *Lear's*, that were geared to women 40 and over. "I always thought those magazines were aimed at a woman who defined herself primarily as a career woman," Northrop told Nat Ives for *Advertising Age* (October 23, 2006). "At the time, that was a smaller crowd, and advertisers weren't interested." She also said, "Readers in general are looking for specifically targeted magazines that reflect them and are relentlessly focused on them. . . . [Women past their 30s] feel somehow the culture is ignoring the power and money they have." "I think 40 is still a huge milestone for women," Northrop told Rene Syler for the CBS News program *The Early Show* (November 29, 2004). "I mean, 40 might be the new 20, or maybe it's 50 is the new 30, but it's still a huge mental milestone for women. And I think as you become more competent in your life, and especially if you have kids and your kids have gotten a little bit older, you think, 'Well, what happened to the fun in my life?'" Northrop spearheaded an extensive redesign and added sections on health, finance, and work. In the first half of 2005, paid circulation for *More* increased by 9.3 percent over that of the same period a year earlier, to 1.05 million; newsstand sales rose 14.1 percent, and the number of advertising pages, through September 2005, rose 14.5 percent.

The most dramatic increase in *More*'s newsstand sales began in July 2005, when Northrop rejected a proposed cover line that conveyed a traditional anti-aging message in favor of one that read "Energy, Confidence, Attitude: The New Look of 40+." "You were supposed to write 'Lose 10 Pounds in 10 Minutes' kinds of cover lines," she explained to Ives. In the first half of 2006, newsstand sales of each issue averaged 148,600, up 25.1 percent from the same period in 2005. In addition, *More* began to sponsor events, including the *More* Marathon and the *More* Model Search. *More* won *Folio*'s Gold Prize for redesign in 2005, was named the 2006 Magazine of the Year by *Advertising Age*, appeared on *Adweek*'s "Hot List" for both 2006 and 2007, and was nominated for a National Magazine Award for general excellence. In 2006 Northrop was named as one of the "Women Who Get It Right" by the National Breast Cancer Coalition.

The widespread perception that *Reader's Digest* had "lost its relevance" and represented a "tired old culture," Northrop told Rebecca L. Fox for *mediabistro.com* (August 5, 2009), led some of her friends and family members to question her decision to leave *More*, where she had been so happy, to become the editor of *Reader's Digest*. For some years subscriptions and newsstand sales of *Reader's Digest* had been decreasing; the 2005 and 2006 fiscal years had ended with net losses. In March 2007 an investor group led by Ripplewood Holdings bought the magazine. But those problems and criticisms contributed to the appeal of the new job for Northrop. "That's what motivates me—the bigger the challenge, the more attracted I am to it," she told Fox. She also said, "I thought I had a pretty good shot of making [*Reader's Digest*] relevant to a new audience." In an attempt to reverse the decline of *Reader's Digest* in popularity and income, Northrop replaced about a quarter of its staff, in some cases with people with whom she had worked at *Real Simple*, *Organic Style*, and *More*. The typeface of the logo and the look of the cover were modernized, and new sections were added. Nevertheless, while Northrop's peers applauded such changes, as the magazine's receipt of the 2009 ASME award indicates, readership and advertising revenue continued to drop, in part because of the worldwide recession that began in the fall of 2008. Bob Van Voris and Christopher Scinta reported for Bloomberg.com (August 24, 2009) that the desire of Reader's Digest Association executives to reduce the corporation's $2.2 billion in debt by 75 percent led them to file for bankruptcy in late August 2009. Ripplewood Holdings and others who bought the magazine are expected to lose their investments, according to Van Voris and Scinta, and J. P. Morgan Chase and other lenders will gain control of the company. To aid in its recovery, Northrop and her colleagues have reduced from 12 to 10 the number of yearly issues of *Reader's Digest* and are engaged in a major overhaul of the magazine's Web site. Her aim, she told Fox, is to "leverag[e] all the assets we have so we can slice and dice them in new ways."

Northrop lives in a 150-year-old townhouse in the New York City borough of Brooklyn with her husband, Sean Elder, a writer. The couple have one daughter, Franny, whom they adopted in Paraguay in 1994, when she was a few months old. Elder also has a daughter from an earlier marriage. Northrop is a voracious reader of print and electronic periodicals and books. She is the vice president of the ASME board of directors. In addition, she sits on the advisory board of a local community group, Develop Don't Destroy Brooklyn, and is an active supporter of the international humanitarian organization CARE. In an interview posted on the ASME Web site (June 9, 2009), Northrop said that she wished that when she began her career in editing, someone had advised her, "You can never be too bold," and she offered another piece of advice: "Keep your ears open, you'll learn something."

—M.E.R.

Suggested Reading: *Advertising Age* S p4 Oct. 23, 2006; ASME Web site (June 9, 2009); *Crain's New York Business* p3 Dec. 20, 2004; *Media Week* May 5, 1997, Feb. 9, 2004; *mediabistro.com* Aug. 5, 2009; *New York Post* p30 Mar. 13, 2002; *New York Times* D p18 Apr. 26, 1994; *PR Newswire* Nov. 9, 2007; *Reader's Digest* Web site; (Washington County, Pennsylvania) *Observer-Reporter* (on-line) Dec. 17, 2007

Aude Guerrucci-Pool/Getty Images

Obama, Barack

NOTE: An earlier article about Barack Obama appeared in *Current Biography* in 2005.

(oh-BAHM-uh, ba-RAHK)

Aug. 4, 1961– President of the United States; former U.S. senator from Illinois (Democrat)

Address: The White House, 1600 Pennsylvania Ave., N.W., Washington, DC 20500

"If there is anyone out there who still doubts that America is a place where all things are possible; who still wonders if the dream of our founders is alive in our time; who still questions the power of our democracy, tonight is your answer," Democratic U.S. senator Barack Obama of Illinois said to a crowd of 125,000 supporters in Grant Park, in Chicago, on November 4, 2008, shortly after he was pronounced the winner of the 2008 presidential election—and became the first African-American to claim the nation's highest office. Obama handily defeated the Republican nominee, John McCain, the senior U.S. senator from Arizona, with 365 electoral votes to McCain's 173, and 69,456,897 popular votes (52.9 percent of the total) to 59,934,786 (45.7 percent) for his GOP opponent. He was the first Democrat to win more than 50 percent of the popular vote since Jimmy Carter, who secured 50.1 percent in 1976. Obama and his vice-presidential pick, Senator Joseph R. Biden of Delaware, won majorities in six of what were considered battleground states—Ohio, Pennsylvania, Indiana, Florida, North Carolina, and Virginia—the last of which had not voted for a Democratic presidential candidate since 1964. With Obama's victory, and a significant number of Democratic wins in the House and Senate, on January 20, 2009, when Obama took the presidential oath of office, all three branches of the federal government returned to Democratic control for the first time since 1994.

Obama worked as a community organizer, taught courses in constitutional law, practiced civil rights law, and served as an Illinois state senator before he was elected to the U.S. Senate, and he has written a memoir that, along with one of his other two books, became a best-seller. During much of his presidential campaign, he went against the political grain by focusing on his ideas and positions rather than attacking the Republican nominee, although he expressed many criticisms of the policies and actions of the administration of the incumbent, Republican president, George W. Bush. He and his advisers took full advantage of the Internet to organize existing voters and register new ones—young people and people of color in particular—and used the Web to raise a record-breaking amount of money for his campaign from an unprecedented number of individual contributors. With his slogans—"Change We Can Believe In" and

"Yes We Can"—Obama worked to instill a feeling of hope in the electorate at a time when a severe economic recession, prolonged wars in Afghanistan and Iraq, serious damage to the U.S.'s image overseas, and dire warnings about global warming had weakened morale and confidence among many Americans. That hope, and extraordinary excitement about his victory among large segments of the population in and beyond the U.S., led well over a million people to stand in freezing temperatures on the National Mall to witness Obama's swearing-in as the 44th president of the United States.

"That we are in the midst of crisis is now well understood . . . ," President Obama said in his inaugural address. "The challenges we face are real. They are serious and they are many. They will not be met easily or in a short span of time. But know this America: They will be met." Obama also said, "On this day, we gather because we have chosen hope over fear, unity of purpose over conflict and discord. On this day, we come to proclaim an end to the petty grievances and false promises, the recriminations and worn-out dogmas that for far too long have strangled our politics. We remain a young nation. But in the words of Scripture, the time has come to set aside childish things. The time has come to reaffirm our enduring spirit; to choose our better history; to carry forward that precious gift, that noble idea passed on from generation to generation: the God-given promise that all are equal, all are free, and all deserve a chance to pursue their full measure of happiness. In reaffirming the greatness of our nation we understand that greatness is never a given. It must be earned. . . . Everywhere we look, there is work to be done. The state of our economy calls for action, bold and swift. And we will act, not only to create new jobs, but to lay a new foundation for growth. We will build the roads and bridges, the electric grids and digital lines that feed our commerce and bind us together. We'll restore science to its rightful place, and wield technology's wonders to raise health care's quality and lower its cost. We will harness the sun and the winds and the soil to fuel our cars and run our factories. And we will transform our schools and colleges and universities to meet the demands of a new age. All this we can do. All this we will do. Now, there are some who question the scale of our ambitions, who suggest that our system cannot tolerate too many big plans. Their memories are short, for they have forgotten what this country has already done, what free men and women can achieve when imagination is joined to common purpose, and necessity to courage. What the cynics fail to understand is that the ground has shifted beneath them, that the stale political arguments that have consumed us for so long no longer apply. The question we ask today is not whether our government is too big or too small, but whether it works—whether it helps families find jobs at a decent wage, care they can afford, a retirement that is dignified. Where the answer is yes, we intend to move forward. Where the answer is no, programs will end. And those of us who manage the public's dollars will be held to account, to spend wisely, reform bad habits, and do our business in the light of day, because only then can we restore the vital trust between a people and their government."

In concluding his address, Obama said, "Let us mark this day with remembrance of who we are and how far we have traveled. In the year of America's birth, in the coldest of months, a small band of patriots huddled by dying campfires on the shores of an icy river. The capital was abandoned. The enemy was advancing. The snow was stained with blood. At the moment when the outcome of our revolution was most in doubt, the father of our nation ordered these words to be read to the people: 'Let it be told to the future world . . . that in the depth of winter, when nothing but hope and virtue could survive . . . that the city and the country, alarmed at one common danger, came forth to meet [it].' America: In the face of our common dangers, in this winter of our hardship, let us remember these timeless words. With hope and virtue, let us brave once more the icy currents, and endure what storms may come. Let it be said by our children's children that when we were tested we refused to let this journey end, that we did not turn back nor did we falter; and with eyes fixed on the horizon and God's grace upon us, we carried forth that great gift of freedom and delivered it safely to future generations."

Within days of his entering the White House, Obama signed executive orders that called for the closing of the Guantánamo Bay prison camp within a year; banned torture in interrogations of prisoners and ordered that only techniques described in the *Army Field Manual* may be used in handling suspected terrorists or prisoners of war; prohibited the practice of so-called extraordinary rendition, in which suspected terrorists were sent for interrogation in Syria or other countries known to condone torture; froze the pay of senior White House staff members earning more than $100,000 annually; imposed rules regarding lobbyists that were far stricter than existing regulations; and reversed several policies put in place during the Bush administration that discouraged labor-union activities and "tilted toward employers," in the words of David Stout, writing for the *New York Times* (January 30, 2009). Obama also reinstated a policy in effect during the administration of President Bill Clinton, whereby the U.S. would continue to help fund international family-planning agencies deemed worthy of support and would not withhold financial aid from such groups, as did the Bush administration, solely on the grounds that they provided information about or performed abortions. On January 29, 2009 Obama signed the so-called Lilly Ledbetter law, which removes certain barriers to women seeking to challenge pay discrimination where they work. One day earlier the House of Representatives had approved the president's $819 billion economic recovery plan. (Although Obama had gone to Capitol Hill the previous day to convince Republican lawmakers of its benefits, no GOP representatives voted for it.) On February 4 the president signed a bill that expanded the State Children's Health Insurance Program (known as S-CHIP), to cover, by 2013, an additional four million children who are uninsured; the measure continued coverage for seven million young people. In his first interview for an overseas news outlet, Obama told an interviewer for Al-Arabiya, a Dubai-based television-news service, as quoted by marketwatch.com (January 26, 2009), "My job to the Muslim world is to communicate that the Americans are not your enemy. We sometimes make mistakes. . . . But if you look at the track record . . . America was not born as a colonial power, and that the same respect and partnership that America had with the Muslim world as recently as 20 or 30 years ago, there's no reason why we can't restore that." In October 2009, in a controversial development, Obama received the Nobel Peace Prize.

Barack Hussein Obama was born on August 4, 1961 in Honolulu, Hawaii. He was named for his father, who was born in the town of Alego, Kenya, on the shore of Lake Victoria. A member of the Luo tribe—a nomadic people who had originated in the Sudan along the White Nile and migrated to Kenya—the elder Obama proved to be a gifted student. He won a scholarship to study in Nairobi, Kenya's capital, before being selected for a government sponsorship to go, in 1959 at age 23, to study econometrics at the University of Hawaii. The school's first African student, he established himself among its intellectual and social leaders, serving as the first president of the International Students Association, which he helped organize, and graduating at the top of his class in only three years. In 1959 he took a Russian class, in which he met an 18-year-old, white, Kansas-born anthropology major, Stanley Ann Dunham, known as Ann. The two married in 1960.

The elder Barack Obama received a scholarship to pursue a Ph.D. at Harvard University, in Cambridge, Massachusetts; the scholarship covered only his own expenses, however, and he left Hawaii alone when his son was two. He and his wife later divorced, and young Barack would see his father only once more, at age 10. When the younger Obama was six, his mother remarried; her second husband, named Lolo, was an Indonesian-born fellow student of hers at the University of Hawaii. The family moved to Jakarta, the capital city of Indonesia, where Obama's half-sister Maya was born. Ann taught English to Indonesian businessmen at the U.S. Embassy, while Lolo ascended from government surveyor to executive with an American oil company. When Ann and Lolo's relationship—which eventually ended in divorce—began to deteriorate, Ann sent Obama to Honolulu to live with her parents, who enrolled him in the prestigious Punahau Academy, a college-preparatory school attended by children of the islands' elite.

One of only a handful of black students in the academy, Obama grew more conscious of issues regarding race and identity. While his skin color and hair texture set him apart from most of his schoolmates, his home life made him socially, if not economically, similar to them, as he had been raised by a white mother and grandparents in a middle-class environment. He sought black role models from among the men he played basketball with on the local public courts and his grandfather's poker buddies. "I learned to slip back and forth between my black and white worlds, understanding that each possessed its own language and customs and structures of meaning, convinced that with a bit of translation on my part the two worlds would eventually cohere," Obama wrote in his memoir, *Dreams from My Father: A Story of Race and Inheritance*, published in 1995 and in a modified edition in 2004. In that book he recalled becoming unpleasantly aware that his race affected the way others responded to him: "The feeling that something wasn't quite right stayed with me, a warning that sounded whenever a white girl mentioned in the middle of conversation how much she liked Stevie Wonder; or when a woman in the supermarket asked me if I played basketball; or when the school principal told me I was cool. I did like Stevie Wonder, I did love basketball, and I tried my best to be cool at all times. So why did such comments always set me on edge?" "I engaged in self-destructive behavior," he told Sandy Banks for the *Los Angeles Times* (March 13, 2005). "Sometimes I lashed out at white people and sometimes I lashed out at black people."

Amid his confusion Obama experimented with drugs and alcohol and let his grades slip. He nonetheless graduated with his peers from Punahau, in 1979, and later that year he enrolled at Occidental College, in Los Angeles, California. After two years he transferred to Columbia University, in New York City, to study political science with a specialization in international relations. "Mostly, my years at Columbia were an intense period of study," Obama told Shira Boss-Bicak for *Columbia College Today* (January 2005). "When I transferred, I decided to buckle down and get serious. I spent a lot of time in the library. I didn't socialize that much. I was like a monk." One morning during his first semester at Columbia, in November 1982, he received a call from Nairobi, informing him that his father had been killed in a car accident. "At the time of his death, my father remained a myth to me, both more and less than a man," he wrote in his memoir. (Obama's mother died of ovarian cancer in 1995.)

In the period leading up to his graduation from Columbia, in 1983, Obama had sought work as a community organizer, writing letters of application to progressive grassroots organizations across the nation. His letters went unanswered, however, so he took a job as a research analyst for a financial consulting company. He was soon promoted to financial writer. "I had my own office, my own secretary, money in the bank," Obama wrote in *Dreams from My Father*. "Sometimes, coming out of an interview with Japanese financiers or German bond traders, I would catch my reflection in the elevator doors—see myself in a suit and tie, a briefcase in my hand—and for a split second I would imagine myself as a captain of industry, barking out orders, closing the deal, before I remembered who it was I had told myself I wanted to be and felt pangs of guilt for my lack of resolve." He ultimately quit his job and worked on a campaign to promote recycling in New York City, while sending out a second round of letters in search of community work. He eventually landed a job with the Developing Communities Project, a nonprofit coalition of secular and church groups on the South Side of Chicago. For three years he canvassed door-to-door and met with local business and political leaders in efforts to save manufacturing jobs, launch job-training programs, and improve city services in South Side housing projects.

During Obama's time in Chicago, his older half-sister Auma, the child of his father's first marriage (to a Kenyan woman) and one of seven half-siblings with whom he shares a father, came to the United States for an extended visit, during which she told Obama some of the details of their father's life. In the mid-1980s, when Obama was working as a community organizer and preparing to attend law school, he traveled to Kenya to see his father's homeland. "There, he managed to fully embrace a heritage and a family he'd never fully known and come to terms with his father, whom he'd long regarded as an august foreign prince, but now realized was a human being burdened by his own illusions and vulnerabilities," the lawyer and novelist Scott Turow, who is a friend and political supporter of Obama, wrote for *Salon* (March 30, 2004, online).

In 1988 Obama entered Harvard Law School, where he gained national attention in 1990 as the first African-American to be elected president (analogous to editor in chief) of the *Harvard Law Review*, the nation's most prestigious academic law journal. He earned his J.D. degree, magna cum laude, in 1991. While in law school Obama worked as a summer associate at Sidley Austin, a Chicago firm; Michelle Robinson, an associate attorney who had graduated from Harvard Law the year before, supervised him. Although she was hesitant to date someone with whom she was working, Obama eventually persuaded her to join him for a movie. The pair married in 1992. After Michelle Obama spoke at the 2008 Democratic National Convention, giving a speech almost universally praised for its warmth and eloquence, her husband commented, "Now you know why I asked her out so many times—you want a persistent president."

In 1992 Obama led a voter-registration drive that added approximately 150,000 new people to Chicago's voter rolls and helped Bill Clinton, the Democratic candidate, win Illinois in that year's presidential election. Obama turned down an offer to clerk for Abner Mikva, then chief judge of the U.S. Court of Appeals for the Washington, D.C., circuit, to accept a position at the Chicago firm of Miner, Barnhill & Galland. There, he focused on civil rights law, representing victims of housing and employment discrimination and working on behalf of voters' rights. Shortly thereafter he began lecturing part-time on constitutional law at the University of Chicago Law School. "Teaching keeps you sharp," Obama told William Finnegan for the *New Yorker* (May 31, 2004). "The great thing about teaching constitutional law is that all the tough questions land in your lap: abortion, gay rights, affirmative action. And you need to be able to argue both sides. I have to be able to argue the other side as well as [the Supreme Court justice Antonin] Scalia does. I think that's good for one's politics."

In 1996 the Illinois Democrat Alice Palmer decided to give up her seat in the Illinois state Senate to run for Congress. Seeing an opportunity, Obama, who harbored political ambitions, sought and secured Palmer's blessing to run for her seat, which represents Chicago's 13th District, covering the South Side, Hyde Park, and the University of Chicago. Palmer lost her bid for Congress and asked Obama to step aside so that she could run for reelection in the state Senate, but Obama refused and, without a Republican opponent, easily won the election. He quickly gained a reputation as an effective legislator, skilled at working with the Republican majority. He sponsored and passed a bill requiring Illinois to share its data on its welfare program with researchers, and he helped to push through the first campaign-finance-reform legislation to pass in his state in a quarter-century.

In 1999 Obama suffered two major political setbacks. The first involved a year-end vote on a controversial gun-control bill that was coming to the floor of the Senate. The bill, forged in a bipartisan coalition between Chicago's Democratic mayor, Richard M. Daley, and the Republican Illinois governor, George Ryan, faced intense opposition from the National Rifle Association (NRA), one of the nation's most powerful lobbies, and state Senate Republicans. Obama, who supported the measure, was visiting his extended family in Hawaii. Despite pleas to return, he was absent for the vote. The bill was defeated, and the local press and his Senate colleagues excoriated Obama. Around the same time, Obama made an ill-advised run for the U.S. House of Representatives, against fellow Democrat Bobby Rush. Obama thought Rush was an ineffectual lawmaker, but the four-term representative and former leader of the local Black Panther Party was very popular. In the 2000 Democratic primary, Rush defeated Obama by a two-to-one margin.

Obama bounced back emphatically in the following years. When Democrats took control of the Illinois state Senate in 2003, he successfully ushered 26 bills through the Legislature, including a large tax credit for the working poor and expanded health-care benefits for uninsured children and adults. Perhaps his greatest achievements were in criminal-justice reform. He co-sponsored landmark legislation to curtail racial profiling by requiring all police departments to record the race of every person stopped for questioning. He also sponsored a bill that made Illinois the first state to require its police to videotape interrogations in capital crime cases. Obama gained support from the police and state prosecutors by arguing that videotaping would cut down not only on coerced confessions but also on claims of police brutality. In addition, the videos are admissible in court, thus facilitating prosecutions.

Obama entered the 2004 race to become the junior U.S. senator from Illinois as one of several Democratic contenders. His popularity grew as he successfully spread his populist message to a base beyond Chicago, and he was soon the second-place favorite behind Blair Hull, a well-liked and wealthy businessman. Hull consistently held the lead for much of the race, but as the primary neared, a revelation that he had abused his ex-wife during their marriage caused his campaign to crumble. Obama went on to win the Democratic nomination, capturing 53 percent of the vote, in March 2004. He faced Republican Alan Keyes, a former United Nations ambassador and presidential candidate, in the general election. Obama's campaign built so comfortable a lead in the polls that he was able to take time to stump for Democratic candidates in Wisconsin, Colorado, South Carolina, and other states, thus increasing his national profile and garnering favor among fellow Democrats. He was selected to give the keynote speech at the 2004 Democratic National Convention, held in July in Boston, Massachusetts. (The decision met with curiosity by national politicians who knew little about him.)

The defining characteristic of the contentious 2004 presidential campaign had been—and continued to be—the division between so-called "Red" and "Blue" America: red being the pundits' blanket signifier for the allegedly Republican, conservative, and religious denizens of southern and midwestern states, and blue connoting the supposedly Democratic, liberal, secular population of the Northeast and West Coast. Amid this talk of red and blue, Obama delivered a message of shared values that crossed all color lines, racial and electoral. "Now even as we speak, there are those who are preparing to divide us, the spin masters, the negative ad peddlers who embrace the politics of anything goes," he declared to an energized crowd. "Well, I say to them tonight, there is not a liberal America and a conservative America—there is the United States of America. There is not a Black America and a White America and Latin America and Asian America—there's the United States of America. . . . We worship an awesome God in the Blue States, and we don't like federal agents poking around in our libraries in the Red States. We coach Little League in the Blue States and yes, we've got some gay friends in the Red States. There are patriots who opposed the war in Iraq and there are patriots who supported the war in Iraq. . . . In the end, that's what this election is about. Do we participate in a politics of cynicism or do we participate in a politics of hope?"

Obama's speech immediately made him the political equivalent of a rock star. That November, carried on a wave of good will and media attention, Obama went on to trounce Keyes, with 70 percent of the vote, to become the first male African-American Democrat (and the fifth African-American) to serve in the U.S. Senate. Assuming office in January 2005, Obama kept a low profile and focused on learning the procedures of the Senate and carefully choosing his public appearances. (Despite his attempts to stay out of the spotlight, that year he won the NAACP Image Award and the Newsmaker of the Year Award from the National Newspaper Publishers Association, and he was named one of *Time*'s most influential people of the year.) Obama was appointed to three top Senate panels: the Committee on Environment and Public Works, which provides oversight of the Department of Transportation and the Environmental Protection Agency (EPA); the Committee on Veterans Affairs, which has jurisdiction over compensation, pensions, and medical treatment for veterans of the U.S. military; and the Committee on Foreign Relations, which has responsibility for some aspects of U.S. foreign policy. Obama contributed to several key debates before the Senate in the 109th Congress and showed an independent streak that sometimes defied party lines. Stating that President George W. Bush should be allowed some latitude in the appointment of his Cabinet, Obama voted yes regarding the confirmation of Condoleezza Rice as secretary of state. However, he registered a minority vote of no in the confirmation of Alberto Gonzales as U.S. attorney general; as White House counsel, Gonzales had been responsible for setting guidelines for the treatment of suspected terrorists held in U.S. military prisons—directives seen by many as overly harsh and therefore illegal.

In late August 2004 Obama made his first trip overseas as a U.S. senator, accompanying the chairman of the Senate Committee on Foreign Relations, Richard Lugar of Indiana, to Russia, Ukraine, and Azerbaijan. On August 30, 2005, as a result of that mission, the U.S. and Ukraine signed an agreement placing safeguards on the storage or transport of potentially lethal pathogens and other such materials, the existence of which dated back to Soviet-era biological-weapons programs.

In the introduction to *Dreams from My Father*, Obama wrote, "The opportunity to write [this book] first arose while I was still in law school, after my election as the first black president of the Harvard Law Review. . . . A few publishers called, and I, imagining myself to have something original to say about the current state of race relations, agreed to take off a year after graduation and put my thoughts to paper." His memoir received middling reviews when it was published and quickly fell out of print. However, following his electrifying Democratic National Convention address and the attendant upswing in public interest in Obama, copies of the memoir began appearing on the Internet auction site e-Bay, where they sold for several hundred dollars each. The memoir was then reissued in paperback, with an updated preface and a copy of the convention speech in the back. (The book was otherwise unchanged.) In February 2005 Obama signed a $1.9 million, three-book deal with Random House. His second book, *The Audacity of Hope: Thoughts on Reclaiming the American Dream*, was published in 2006. While his first book focuses on his childhood and struggles with race, his second delves into his political career and beliefs. His third book, *Change We Can Believe In: Barack Obama's Plan to Renew America's Promise*, was published in September 2008. His first two volumes have been fixtures on the *New York Times* best-seller list, and Obama won two Grammy Awards for best spoken-word album, in 2006 and 2008, for his recordings of them.

The media soon began to speculate on a possible Obama run for the U.S. presidency. He had already become a favorite among many political insiders. (In 2005 he won a poll conducted by the Washington, D.C., magazine *National Journal* in which members of Congress, many lobbyists, and other movers and shakers in the world of politics were asked which politician had the greatest potential to become president in 20 years.) Thanks in part to *The Audacity of Hope*, his national status continued to rise in 2006, as he made appearances on television programs including *Oprah* and *Larry King Live*. Tickets for his book-tour appearances sold out within minutes in such big cities as Seattle, Boston, and Philadelphia. The columnist David Brooks, known for his conservative slant, wrote a commentary in the *New York Times* (October 19, 2006) titled "Run, Barack, Run." "I should note that I disagree with many of Obama's notions and could well end up agreeing more with one of his opponents," Brooks wrote. "But anyone who's observed him closely can see that Obama is a new kind of politician. As [Joe] Klein [of *Time*] once observed, he's that rarest of creatures: a megahyped phenomenon that lives up to the hype. It may not be personally convenient for him, but the times will never again so completely require the gifts that he possesses. Whether you're liberal or conservative, you should hope Barack Obama runs for president." Days later Obama was featured in the cover story, titled "Why Barack Obama Could Be the Next President," of the October 23, 2006 issue of *Time*. For the remainder of 2006, however, Obama focused his attention on that year's Senate elections, traveling the country to help raise funds and campaign for Democrats.

After months of mounting rumors and speculation, Obama formed a presidential exploratory committee in January 2007. The following month, in Springfield, Illinois (where Abraham Lincoln lived from 1837 to 1861), he officially announced his candidacy for the U.S. presidency. During the Springfield speech he introduced his campaign's overall theme of change: "For the last six years we've been told that our mounting debts don't matter, we've been told that the anxiety Americans feel about rising health care costs and stagnant wages are an illusion, we've been told that climate change is a hoax, and that tough talk and an ill-conceived war can replace diplomacy, and strategy, and foresight. And when all else fails, when [Hurricane] Katrina happens, or the death toll in Iraq mounts, we've been told that our crises are somebody else's fault. We're distracted from our real failures, and told to blame the other party, or gay people, or immigrants. And as people have looked away in disillusionment and frustration, we know what's filled the void. The cynics, and the lobbyists, and the special interests who've turned our government into a game only they can afford to play. They write the checks and you get stuck with the bills, they get the access while you get to write a letter, they think they own this government, but we're here today to take it back. The time for that politics is over. It's time to turn the page." Obama's entry into the presidential primaries placed him among several Democrats vying for the nomination, including U.S. senator and former First Lady Hillary Rodham Clinton, Senator Biden, and former North Carolina senator and 2004 Democratic vice-presidential nominee John Edwards.

From the start of his campaign, Obama's limited political experience was called into question. The Democratic Illinois state senator Ray Miller, for example, said to Gilbert Price for the Columbus, Ohio, *Call & Post* (February 15–21, 2007), "[Obama] has only been a member of the United States senate for two years. I'm not aware of any significant accomplishments he's had in his two years. Quite frankly, that is not my standard for pursuing the presidency of the United States. We don't have a lot to measure him by at this point." By contrast, another Democratic Illinois state senator, Donne Trotter, argued that Obama's intellect was more than sufficient to qualify him. "[Obama] is a reader, a learner of different approaches and philosophies. He has the brainpower to absorb the facts . . . and make good decisions," he told Judy Keen for *USA Today* (January 17, 2007, on-line). David Axelrod, Obama's political strategist and media adviser, told Keen, "Campaigns themselves are a gantlet in which you get tested. People get to see how you handle pressure and how you react to complicated questions. It's an imperfect and sometimes maddening system, but at the end of the day it works, because you have to be tough and smart and skilled to survive that process."

The Democratic primaries became increasingly heated as the year progressed. Clinton had been the favorite before Obama entered the race, and soon the two were in a head-to-head battle for what was bound to be, in either case, a history-making nomination. By the end of Super Tuesday, February 5,

2008, the day on which 22 states (and American Samoa) held their Democratic presidential primaries, Obama led the race with 847 delegates. Clinton, with 834 delegates, had narrowly won the popular vote, 46 to 45 percent. Amid accusations that the mainstream media had been soft in their coverage of Obama, Clinton's campaign began to focus on Obama's character. In March 2008 footage surfaced showing Obama's former pastor and spiritual mentor, Jeremiah Wright Jr., giving sermons at Chicago's Trinity United Church of Christ. (The source was reportedly not connected to the Clinton campaign.) In those sermons Wright proclaimed his disgust with the U.S. government for mistreating minorities; he accused those in power of purposefully flooding black neighborhoods with drugs and suggested that the country's international policies and activities were to blame for the 9/11 terrorist attacks. The sermons immediately sparked controversy; Clinton used the opportunity to question Obama's integrity. Shortly after the footage began to air on national news programs, Obama condemned Wright's remarks and delivered an impassioned speech on the topic of race in America. "As imperfect as [Wright] may be, he has been like family to me. He strengthened my faith, officiated [at] my wedding, and baptized my children. . . . I can no more disown him than I can disown the black community," Obama said in Philadelphia on March 18, 2008. "The profound mistake of Reverend Wright's sermons is not that he spoke about racism in our society. It's that he spoke as if our society was static; as if no progress has been made. . . . But what we know—what we have seen—is that America can change. That is the true genius of this nation." He added, "I would not be running for President if I didn't believe with all my heart that this is what the vast majority of Americans want for this country. This union may never be perfect, but generation after generation has shown that it can always be perfected."

The speech, titled "A More Perfect Union," received widespread praise, and as the months passed, Obama began to widen his lead. On June 3, 2008, the day of the final primaries, in South Dakota and Montana, he garnered 60 superdelegate endorsements. Obama ultimately accumulated 2,154 delegate votes, enough to become the presumptive Democratic nominee and the first major-party African-American presidential nominee in U.S. history. A few days later Clinton suspended her campaign and announced her support of her former rival.

Though many Clinton supporters hoped that Obama would choose Clinton as his vice-presidential running mate, Obama decided instead to pick a politician with more experience in international as well as national affairs, in hopes of silencing or at least muting those who complained that he was seriously deficient in those areas. He chose Joe Biden, a devout Roman Catholic raised in a working-class family. Biden had been a member of the U.S. Senate since 1973 and had chaired the Senate Committee on Foreign Relations, and he was widely recognized for his expertise on foreign policy and national-security issues. He was also known, however, for his tendency to be long-winded and for his verbal gaffes, which had become somewhat legendary on Capitol Hill. (In February 2007, for example, when he had thrown his own hat into the presidential ring, he had said of Obama, "I mean, you got the first mainstream African-American who is articulate and bright and clean and a nice-looking guy." Though, by his own account, Biden had not meant to offend African-Americans and later apologized to Obama, the remark is said to have soured his chances to become the Democratic nominee.)

Obama officially accepted the Democratic presidential nomination at the 2008 Democratic National Convention, held in Denver, Colorado. Senator John McCain, who was nominated soon afterward at that year's Republican National Convention, was a former navy pilot who had been held prisoner for over five years during the Vietnam War and had been elected to the Senate in 1987. A self-described "maverick," McCain became known for dissenting from his Republican colleagues on several important issues and working with Democrats more closely than many of his GOP colleagues to pass legislation. Though he had become popular with people across the political spectrum, his age (72) and past, serious health problems became matters of concern during the race. (His win would have made him the oldest person ever elected to a first term as president.) For his running mate McCain chose Sarah Palin, the governor of Alaska since 2007, who had previously served as chairperson of the Alaska Oil and Gas Conservation Commission and as mayor of her hometown, Wasilla, Alaska. Outside Alaska, Palin was virtually unknown. As the first female Republican vice-presidential nominee, she soon became a focal point in the presidential race. Though she brought youth and excitement to the Republican ticket, inquiries into her political past and family life raised questions about the campaign's vetting process and, by extension, about McCain's judgment. (The public soon learned, for example, that her unwed, teenage daughter was pregnant, and allegations surfaced that Palin had used her influence as governor to get her former brother-in-law fired from his job as an Alaska state trooper.)

The McCain campaign tried to capitalize on the public's uncertainty about Obama's history, character, religion, friends, and experience. During the Republican National Convention, Palin, touting her tenure in Wasilla and sarcastically casting aspersions on Obama's work at the community level, said, "I guess a small-town mayor is sort of like a community organizer, except that you have actual responsibilities." While the line got a laugh from party loyalists, it did no lasting harm to Obama, who has often said that his work on Chicago's South Side taught him many of the skills he would need later and also broadened his understanding of the problems of working-class people. More damaging to him was his rivals' repeated insinuations about his connection to William Ayers, which had first been mentioned during the Democratic primary campaign. Ayers was a founding member of the Weather Underground, a militant activist group seeking to end U.S. involvement in the Vietnam War in the late 1960s and early '70s. Underground members had been responsible for several bombings, including explosions at the Pentagon and the U.S. Capitol. Obama and Ayers lived in the same Chicago neighborhood and had served on several boards together. Ayers had also hosted a gathering at his home to introduce Obama to community members during his first run for political office. Although Ayers had long ago become a respected member of the Chicago community and an honored professor of education at the University of Illinois, his activities with the Underground—which dated from when Obama was a young child—led Palin, during an Englewood, Colorado, event on October 4, 2008, to accuse Obama of "palling around with terrorists." Obama dismissed the accusation at a campaign stop in Chillicothe, Ohio, on October 10, saying, "Nothing's easier than riling up a crowd by stoking anger and division, but that's not what we need now in the United States. The American people aren't looking for someone who can divide this country, they're looking for somebody who will lead this country. Now more than ever it is time to put country ahead of politics." (Following the election, Ayers spoke out about the accusations, writing for the December 6, 2008 edition of the *New York Times*, "[Obama and I] didn't pal around, and I had nothing to do with his positions. I knew him as well as thousands of others did, and like millions of others, I wish I knew him better.")

Obama's campaign, for the most part, limited attacks on McCain to his stance on political issues and his voting record. It focused on policies Obama sought to implement as president: tax cuts for middle-class Americans, reform of the health-care system, emphasis on renewable energy, fiscal discipline, and the withdrawal of troops from Iraq.

After three televised presidential debates, polls showed Obama pulling into the lead. He received endorsements from many celebrities and major newspapers, including the *Washington Post*, the *Los Angeles Times*, and the *Chicago Tribune*, the last of which had never before endorsed a Democrat for president. "Many Americans say they're uneasy about Obama. He's pretty new to them," the editors of the *Chicago Tribune* wrote (October 19, 2008). "We can provide some assurance. We have known Obama since he entered politics a dozen years ago. We have watched him, worked with him, argued with him as he rose from an effective state senator to an inspiring U.S. senator to the Democratic Party's nominee for president. We have tremendous confidence in his intellectual rigor, his moral compass and his ability to make sound, thoughtful, careful decisions. He is ready." In its endorsement, the *Washington Post* (October 17, 2008) explained, "The choice is made easy in part by Mr. McCain's disappointing campaign, above all his irresponsible selection of a running mate who is not ready to be president. It is made easy in larger part, though, because of our admiration for Mr. Obama and the impressive qualities he has shown during this long race. Yes, we have reservations and concerns, almost inevitably, given Mr. Obama's relatively brief experience in national politics. But we also have enormous hopes." Obama even gained the support of such well-known Republicans as former secretary of state Colin Powell, who, in endorsing him on the October 19, 2008 edition of the TV show *Meet the Press* (October 19, 2008), called him "a transformational figure."

Obama's presidential campaign has been described as arguably the best-organized in recent history. Reflecting his experiences as a community organizer, his campaign workers set up "Camp Obama" events—training courses for volunteers, lasting several days, about the political process and organizational techniques. Unlike most other campaigns, Obama's focused on recruiting college students and young adults. Hans Riemer, Obama's national youth-vote director, told David Shaper for National Public Radio (June 13, 2007, on-line), "Historically, campaigns have looked at young people as the hardest demographics to mobilize. In reality, if you know what you're doing, they can be one of the easiest to mobilize." (On Election Day, according to exit polls, some 66 percent of voters ages 18 to 29 cast their ballots for Obama.) Also, Obama used the Internet skillfully to rally voters. His presence on social networking Web sites, including Facebook and MySpace as well as the video-sharing site YouTube, helped spread his message, as did the My.BarackObama.com Web site launched by his campaign, with the help of Facebook's co-founder Chris Hughes. "From controlling the canvassing operations to corralling e-mail lists, organizing meetings and overseeing national phone drives, Obama's web network is the most ambitious, and apparently successful, internet campaign effort in any presidential race in the web's short history," Sarah Lai Stirland wrote for *Wired* (March 3, 2008, on-line). In October 2008 Obama and his team won *Advertising Age*'s Marketer of the Year Award.

Obama was also an extraordinarily successful fund-raiser. McCain's campaign, which opted for public financing, was thus barred from accepting private donations after his official nomination and was limited to about $84 million in U.S. Treasury funding; Obama's campaign managers, however, decided to forgo public financing and continue raising money as they had during the primaries. Obama was the first presidential candidate from a major party to decline public financing since 1976, when the public-financing system was launched. (McCain later criticized Obama for that decision, pointing out that the year before he had said that he would accept public financing.) By Election

Day, thanks in large part to millions of individual small donations, the Obama campaign had accumulated a reported $770 million. Obama spent a record $240 million on television advertisements, including a half-hour, prime-time infomercial broadcast during the final week of the campaign.

Two weeks before the election, Obama left the campaign trail for two days to fly to Hawaii to visit his maternal grandmother, Madelyn Dunham, who was losing her battle against ovarian cancer. In his speech at the Democratic convention on August 28, 2008, Obama had expressed his love and admiration for her. "[My grandmother's] the one who taught me about hard work," he said. "She's the one who put off buying a new car or a new dress for herself so that I could have a better life. She poured everything she had into me." Dunham voted for her grandson by absentee ballot. She died two days later, on November 2, 2008.

Obama's election to the presidency sparked jubilation all over the nation as well as around the world. Mwai Kibaki, the president of Kenya, declared November 6 a national holiday in honor of Obama's victory. The president of France, Nicolas Sarkozy, said about it, according to BBC News (November 5, 2009, on-line), "At a time when we must face huge challenges together, [Obama's] election has raised enormous hope in France, in Europe and beyond. France and Europe . . . will find a new energy to work with America to preserve peace and world prosperity."

After his election Obama quickly named his choices for his Cabinet. Most were confirmed without controversy by the Senate. Exceptions included New Mexico governor Bill Richardson, Obama's first choice for commerce secretary, who withdrew his name from consideration, citing a probe into allegations that his administration had given contracts to a political donor; Timothy F. Geithner, who was sworn in as treasury secretary despite having failed to pay $34,000 in federal taxes (which he later paid with interest); and Tom Daschle, whose own tax issues led him to withdraw his name from consideration for the post of health-and-human-services secretary. The Daschle episode, in particular, led to accusations that Obama had gone back on his pledge to apply strict ethical rules to appointments in his administration, especially when it was revealed that Obama had urged Daschle to seek confirmation in spite of the tax situation. Obama quickly admitted that he and others involved in the process had "screwed up."

Meanwhile, Obama and his team worked to come up with detailed solutions to some of the nation's economic problems. On December 6, 2008 Obama announced his plans for a public-works program, the largest since President Dwight D. Eisenhower signed the legislation that launched the federal interstate-highway system, in 1956. Obama's program, which would create millions of new jobs, seeks to make public buildings more energy efficient, repair the nation's highways and bridges, and modernize classrooms and hospitals. The program was part of Obama's larger economic-stimulus package, passed by the House on January 28 and by the Senate on February 10.

In his first months in office, Obama concentrated on boosting the U.S. economy and creating jobs. As of the end of October 2009, the overall effect of the administration's stimulus plan remained unclear; although the nation's gross domestic product (GDP) grew by 3.5 percent during the third quarter—July through September—of 2009, its best performance in two years, some economists maintained that the recession was far worse than the administration had anticipated and that the stimulus would not accomplish its aims.

Obama also focused on health-care reform. His promise to pass health-care legislation by the end of 2009 has been complicated by the actions of Republicans and a few Democrats who have balked at his call for an affordable, government-run insurance option for Americans who lack employer-provided insurance. An onslaught of conservative opposition to the health-care legislation during the summer of 2009 prompted the president to defend his plan against false claims, including the assertion that mandatory end-of-life counseling (by "death panels") would deny health care to sick senior citizens and children with birth defects. Some Republicans also accused Obama of starting down the slippery slope toward a socialist government. Health-care experts, even those who did not support the proposed plan, denied such allegations. In August 2009, while the health-care debate was raging in the media, Obama's approval ratings sank to 50 percent for the first time during his presidency.

On other fronts, shortly after he took office, Obama lifted the ban on most stem-cell research, imposed by George W. Bush, and has repeatedly addressed the issue of global warming. Obama has worked to make his administration more transparent to the public and has banned members of his administration from receiving gifts from lobbyists. He has increased the nation's military involvement in Afghanistan; in the fall of 2009, he grappled with the request by General Stanley McChrystal, the commander of the International Security Assistance Force and of U.S. forces in Afghanistan, for 40,000 additional troops to ensure "success" in Afghanistan.

On October 28, 2009 Obama signed into law a bill that expanded the definition of federal hate crimes to include those committed against individuals based on sexual orientation or gender identity. The law was hailed by gay-rights activists, who at the same time have harshly criticized the president for his failure to act on his promise to abolish the "Don't Ask, Don't Tell" policy, which bars from military service homosexuals who reveal that they are gay. The following day Nancy Pelosi, the Speaker of the House, introduced the Affordable Health Care for America Act, a bill crafted by House Democrats that would provide insurance to 36 million uninsured Americans by 2019. Obama praised the bill, calling it "a historic step forward."

The Affordable Health Care for America Act, along with an alternate health-care-reform bill crafted by Senate Democrats, were expected to reach the House and Senate for votes by the end of 2009.

The Obama family, which includes 10-year-old Malia and seven-year-old Natasha (known as Sasha), did not relocate to Washington, D.C., during Barack Obama's years in the U.S. Senate. Instead, as a senator Obama rented a small apartment there and on weekends flew to Chicago, where the Obamas lived in the Hyde Park neighborhood. Michelle Obama left her job, as vice president of community and external affairs at the University of Chicago Medical Center, to help campaign during her husband's run for the presidency. She said that as First Lady she hoped to be an advocate for the nation's working women and military families. Her top priority, however, would be to continue to raise Malia and Sasha. "Our girls are the center of Barack's and my world," she wrote for *U.S. News & World Report* (October 27, 2008). "They're the reason he is running for president—to make the world a better place for them and for all children." Michelle Obama's mother also moved into the White House.

—T.J.F./M.A.S.

Suggested Reading: *Chicago Tribune* C p1 Mar. 20, 2005, C p37 Oct. 19, 2008, (on-line) Dec. 5, 2008; *Columbia College Today* p14+ Jan. 2005; *Ebony* p196 Nov. 2004, p16 Nov. 2008; *New Republic* p21 May 31, 2004; *New York Times* A p21 Dec. 6, 2008, A p1+ Nov. 5, 2008, A p1+ Jan. 21, 2009; *New Yorker* p32+ May 31, 2004; *Newsweek* p74 Dec. 27, 2004; *Salon* (on-line) Mar. 30, 2004; *Time* p74 Nov. 15, 2004, (on-line) Aug. 23, 2008; *Washington Monthly* (on-line) Nov. 2004; *Washington Post* C p1 Feb. 24, 2005, A p1 Oct. 17, 2008; whitehouse.gov

Selected Books: *Dreams from My Father: A Story of Race and Inheritance*, 1995; The *Audacity of Hope: Thoughts on Reclaiming the American Dream*, 2006; *Change We Can Believe In: Barack Obama's Plan to Renew America's Promise*, 2008

O'Brien, Soledad

Sep. 19, 1966– TV news anchor; producer; reporter

Address: CNN, One CNN Ctr., Atlanta, GA 30348

Tasos Katopodis/Getty Images for National Urban League

In 1988, as a 21-year-old college student, the television news anchor, producer, and reporter Soledad O'Brien interned at a Boston TV station, WBZ. "Within a day at WBZ, I knew exactly what I wanted to do with the rest of my life," O'Brien told Robin Finn for the *New York Times* (June 26, 2003), explaining that she "loved the immediacy and the sense of urgency" that prevailed in the studio. O'Brien has worked in television ever since. Her two years as co-host of the Discovery Channel program *The Know Zone* in the early 1990s gave her national exposure for the first time. Her next job, as host of MSNBC's hour-long daily show *The Site* from early 1996 to late 1997, brought her national celebrity. She anchored NBC's *Weekend Today* from 1999 to 2003 and then co-anchored CNN's *American Morning*. Her on-the-scene reports at sites including Indonesia in the aftermath of the tsunami in 2004 and New Orleans, Louisiana, in the days after Hurricane Katrina struck, in 2005, earned her the first annual Goodermote Humanitarian Award from the Johns Hopkins Bloomberg School of Public Health. "O'Brien has shown the world tragedies of human conflict, natural disasters, chronic and infectious diseases," Michael J. Klag, dean of the Bloomberg School of Public Health, said, as quoted on the school's Web site (November 18, 2008). "In addition to focusing attention on the people impacted, she has shed a light on how humanitarian efforts can help alleviate suffering and where current efforts have fallen short." Since 2007 O'Brien has served as an anchor and special correspondent for CNN's Special Investigations Unit (SIU) and also as a political correspondent; she reported extensively during the 2008 presidential campaign. Her SIU credits include the documentaries *Children of the Storm* (2007), about teenage survivors of Hurricane Katrina, and the series *Black in America* (2008) and *Black in America 2* (2009), about the lives of African-American men, women, young people, and families and how circumstances have changed for them in the 40 years since the assassination of the civil rights leader Martin Luther King Jr. In 2008 her work inspired Community Voices—Healthcare for the Underserved and the Morehouse School of Medicine to create the Soledad O'Brien Freedom's Voice Award, which honors people recognized as outstanding catalysts for social change. John E. Maupin, the president of the school, presented O'Brien herself with the first of those awards; noting her "courage, integrity, and excellence," Maupin said, according to Melanie K. Hoffman in *Jet* (January 28, 2008), "O'Brien's accomplishments in her field, her commitment to cover stories that might otherwise go untold, and her steadfast willingness to be a voice for those in our society who are unseen and unheard set a high standard."

The fifth of Edward and Estella O'Brien's six children, Maria de la Soledad O'Brien was born on September 19, 1966 in Smithtown, Long Island, New York. Her father, an Australian of Irish descent, is a professor emeritus of mechanical engineering at the State University of New York at Stony Brook; her mother, who is of Afro-Cuban descent, taught high-school English and French. Because laws in Maryland, where they met, forbade interracial marriage, the couple married in Washington, D.C., in 1959. O'Brien was raised in a tight-knit family in the St. James area of Smithtown with her sisters, Maria, Cecilia, and Estela, her older brother, Tony, and younger brother, Orestes. Her parents, devout Catholics, emphasized the importance of kindness as well as academic achievement. O'Brien told Patricia Sheridan for the *Pittsburgh Post-Gazette* (July 21, 2008), "Growing up I always identified as being a light-skinned black girl. I consider myself black because historically people who are part black are black. . . . In this country just because your dad's white doesn't make you white." O'Brien graduated from Smithtown High School East in 1984 and then enrolled at Harvard University, in Cambridge, Massachusetts. Her siblings all graduated from Harvard and pursued graduate degrees in law or medicine. "It's less about the O'Briens are geniuses . . . and more about . . . role modeling," O'Brien told Kam Williams for *Newsblaze.com* (July 6, 2009). Her sister Maria, she said, served as that role model: Maria "demystified [Harvard] for the rest of us, and made it feel readily achievable." O'Brien was a pre-med major until she realized that she "didn't like the science part of medicine, but the people part," as she told Sara Glassman for the Minneapolis, Minnesota, *Star Tribune* (March 26, 2006), and switched her major to English and American literature.

During her senior year O'Brien landed an internship at WBZ-TV, an NBC affiliate in Boston, Massachusetts, where her first tasks were removing staples from bulletin boards and getting coffee; later she served as a researcher for the station's medical reporter. "Every job I had I enjoyed, even when I was fetching coffee," she told Glassman. "I liked being surrounded by the chaos and confusion." She volunteered for projects at the station as often as possible, and she soon learned that she could earn extra money if her voice was heard—or, even better, her face was seen—in any broadcast. She also worked part-time at radio station KISS-FM in Boston, where she secured assignments as a producer and reporter for the station's medical talk shows, *Second Opinion* and *Health Week in Review*.

O'Brien was still at Harvard when WBZ-TV offered her a full-time position as an associate producer and news writer for *Eyewitness News First Edition*, and she quit school to pursue a career in journalism. In 1991 she moved to the New York City headquarters of WBZ's parent company, NBC, where she worked as a researcher and field producer for *Nightly News* and *Today* under Robert Bazell, NBC's chief health and science correspondent. She has often said that in her early years on television, many people advised her to change her name, on the grounds that it was too confusing, or told her that she looked too ethnic, not ethnic enough, or not dark enough to join the ranks of black reporters. In 1993 she began a three-year stint with NBC's San Francisco affiliate KRON-TV, first as a local news reporter, then as East Bay bureau chief. The year 1993 also marked the first of her two years as co-host of the nationally televised Discovery Channel program *The Know Zone*, which presented science and technology issues in layperson's terms. The show earned her a local Emmy Award in 1995.

O'Brien's Discovery Channel job led directly in late 1996 to her next, as host of MSNBC's hour-long daily show *The Site*, which was devoted to discussions of the Internet, a then-emerging technology. O'Brien had lobbied for the host's position, promoting herself as a technology novice who would be able to make that subject accessible for average viewers. Based in San Francisco, *The Site* aired nightly and won two Emmys, while O'Brien earned such sobriquets as "Goddess to the Geeks" and "TV's Cyberbabe." One particularly popular segment featured O'Brien explaining the basics of creating a Web page. "The secret of Soledad's success," David Futrelle wrote for *Salon.com* (January 24, 1997), is that "while pretending to no great technical knowledge herself, she treats techheads with a certain respect (though not reverence); she cajoles them into opening up, and reins them in when they begin to babble. *The Site* allows geeks (and the somewhat geeky) to present their best face to the world."

In the fall of 1997, MSNBC executives decided to devote the fledgling network to round-the-clock hard news, and *The Site* was cancelled. O'Brien was named the main anchor for MSNBC's *Morning Blend*, a two-hour news and talk show broadcast on Saturdays and Sundays. While she anchored

Morning Blend (until 1999), O'Brien was still under contract to NBC News. Seen as a rising star at NBC, she began to appear as a regular contributor and occasional guest host on *The News with Brian Williams* and *Weekend Today*. In 1999 she was named permanent co-anchor (along with David Bloom) of *Weekend Today*; the weekend edition of the weekday-morning news show *Today*, it offered news, interviews, and segments devoted to culture, health, finance, and stories of human interest. At the same time O'Brien contributed reports to *Today* and to *NBC Nightly News*, on such events as the visit of Pope John Paul II to Cuba in 1998 (during which O'Brien met with relatives of her mother's there); the murder in 1999 of 12 students and one teacher at Columbine High School, in Colorado, by two students who then killed themselves; the death of John F. Kennedy Jr., his wife, and one of her sisters in the crash of the plane he was piloting, in 1999; the disintegration of the space shuttle *Columbia* during its reentry from space, in 2003, which killed all of its seven astronauts; and the U.S.–led invasion of Iraq in 2003. Earlier, in 2000, O'Brien, who had married in 1995, went on maternity leave; she gave birth in October of that year and returned to work the following December. During her leave she completed her bachelor's degree in English and American literature at Harvard.

In April 2003 David Bloom died suddenly of a pulmonary embolism while reporting from Iraq. Three months later O'Brien left NBC to join CNN as a co-anchor, with Bill Hemmer, of the network's morning news show, *American Morning*. O'Brien has said that she had felt limited at NBC, and though her CNN audience was far smaller, the prospect of covering hard news led her to make the job change. "It's so much more interesting to me to show up in cargo pants and boots and sleep on the floor of an RV and be knee deep in a story," she told Diane Clehane for *mediabistro.com* (December 19, 2006). "It's so much easier for me as a reporter than doing cooking or fashion segments. As a reporter, you're much more fulfilled."

In 2004 O'Brien reported from Asia on the consequences of the tsunami that killed an estimated 230,000 people on December 26 of that year; triggered by a magnitude 9.1–9.3 earthquake on the floor of the Indian Ocean, the tsunami inundated coastal areas of a dozen countries, most devastatingly in India, Sri Lanka, Thailand, and Indonesia. Eight months later she reported on the aftermath of another catastrophe—Hurricane Katrina, which struck the southern coast of the U.S. on August 28, 2005. In New Orleans breaches in floodwalls and levees caused massive flooding in 80 percent of the city. Thousands of people unable to leave the area—most of them poor African-Americans—took shelter in the Louisiana Superdome and Morial Convention Center, only to find themselves without water, food, sanitary facilities, medical assistance, or protection from hoodlums for four days or more. O'Brien was the first TV reporter to confront Michael Brown, the director of the Federal Emergency Management Agency (FEMA), regarding eyewitness accounts of the conditions in the Superdome and Convention Center and the suffering of thousands of additional New Orleanians stranded on rooftops or elsewhere. According to a CNN transcript of the interview (September 2, 2005, on-line), O'Brien, reacting to Brown's claim that he had been unaware of the unfolding humanitarian crisis due to a delay in the relaying of information, said to him: "How is it possible that we're getting better intel than you're getting? . . . I don't understand how FEMA cannot have this information. . . . FEMA has been on the ground for four days, going into the fifth day. Why no massive airdrop of food and water? In Banda Aceh, in Indonesia, they got food dropped two days after the tsunami struck. . . . Do you look at the pictures that are coming out of New Orleans? . . . And do you say, I'm proud of the job that FEMA is doing on the ground there in a tough situation? . . . Or do you look at these pictures and you say, this is a mess and we've dropped the ball; we didn't do what we should [have] done." She told Diane Clehane that she regarded that interview as her best on-air work to date: "It captured a lot of the disbelief that a lot of people were feeling—Stop spinning us about how great the efforts are going when we can clearly see . . . it's not going so well." CNN won a George Foster Peabody Award for its Hurricane Katrina coverage and an Alfred I. duPont Award for its reports on the tsunami.

Since then O'Brien has returned to New Orleans several times to report on how residents are coping; she has said that she feels it is her duty and finds it to be therapeutic. With the filmmaker Spike Lee, O'Brien co-produced the documentary *Children of the Storm*, which aired on CNN on August 29, 2007. In thinking about the best way to show the effects of Hurricane Katrina on people's lives two years after the disaster, O'Brien told Dave Walker for the New Orleans *Times-Picayune* (August 28, 2007, on-line), "You just can't go back and stand in front of collapsed buildings and stand in front of a levee and do it again. We might be doing that for the next 10 to 15 years. How are we going to tell the story in a way that's going to capture people and make them understand what the progress is or isn't? We just decided to hand out cameras to young people. I, literally one night, woke up in the middle of the night and said to my husband, 'Oh my God, I've got it. We can hand out cameras.'" *Children of the Storm* presented footage shot by four teenage survivors of Hurricane Katrina with video cameras given to them by Lee; the teenagers showed how they and members of their families were struggling in reduced circumstances, and they expressed their hopes for continuing their educations. In a postscript to their videos, three the four disclosed that they were now enrolled at colleges; the fourth was in high school and was also studying theater at the New Orleans Center for the Arts.

O'Brien worked on *Children of the Storm* (and another follow-up of events in New Orleans that aired in 2008) as an anchor and special correspondent for CNN's new Special Investigations Unit; she had left *American Morning* in the spring of 2007 to take on those jobs and also to serve as a reporter for *Anderson Cooper 360* and other CNN news programs. Less than a week after her move, O'Brien flew to Blacksburg, Virginia, where a mass shooting had occurred on April 16 at Virginia Polytechnic Institute and State University, known informally as Virginia Tech. The killer, a Virginia Tech undergraduate with a history of severe emotional problems, fatally shot 27 students and five faculty members and wounded 17 others before turning his gun on himself. *Massacre at Virginia Tech*, the hour-long SIU report that O'Brien anchored, aired on April 29, 2007.

In January 2008 CNN aired the documentary *MLK: The Words That Changed a Nation*. For that program O'Brien and her colleagues drew from handwritten sermons and other writings by Martin Luther King Jr. that had been made available for the first time by the Woodruff Library at Morehouse College, in Atlanta, Georgia, King's alma mater, which maintains a King archive. Also in 2008 O'Brien anchored *Black in America*, a six-hour CNN special that aired in three two-hour segments, on April 3, June 23, and June 24, 2008. The first segment, subtitled *Eyewitness to Murder*, was about the assassination of King, in 1968. The second was subtitled *Black Men in America*, and the third, *Black Women and Family*. Each part attracted from 13 million to 16 million viewers, making the series one of the highest-rated programs in CNN's history. The series presented a cross-section of African-Americans and tried to illuminate how the lives of blacks in the U.S. had changed since King's death; it offered information about single and two-parent households, the continuing disparities between blacks and whites regarding life expectancy, education levels, and income, and the effects of HIV/AIDS, from which blacks in the U.S. suffer disproportionately. "There are so many stories to be told and in the media, there are only three stories told; we hear a lot about rappers, we hear a lot about ballers, and occasionally exceptional people [such as] Condoleezza Rice," O'Brien told Marcus Vanderberg for BET.com (July 28, 2008). "You don't get the nuance from the community and that's what we really tried to do." "What we ended up seeing," she told Patricia Sheridan, "was the sense that there are two black Americas. One black America is doing very well. There's another black America that is incredibly poor. The gap between those two is getting bigger."

O'Brien achieved one of her goals in producing *Black in America*—to "get a conversation going" about race, she told Wendy L. Wilson for *Essence* (July 22, 2009, on-line). The series sparked widespread discussion, along with a great deal of criticism, with many African-Americans charging that the series' portrayal of blacks was simplistic and unrepresentative and reinforced old stereotypes. Such complaints, O'Brien told Vanderberg, were "fair," because "you can't tell the story of a people, even in our 40-year view that we had, in four hours." She told Wilson, "There are people who wrote in and said, well Soledad isn't Black enough to tell these stories. At first I thought, that is the dumbest thing I have ever heard. No one says Christiane [Amanpour] isn't Chinese enough to do a story on China. . . . But on the other hand, if your job is to begin a conversation, that's an interesting and relevant question."

O'Brien initiated the production of the two-part series *Black in America 2* partly in response to viewers who had watched *Black in America* and complained that the series had not offered practical suggestions for improving one's lot in life. The first part, which aired on July 22, 2009, focused on the "anatomy of success," O'Brien told Williams, as illuminated in the careers of such well-known figures as the actress Cicely Tyson, the former U.S. secretary of state and U.S. Army general Colin Powell, the writer Maya Angelou, the singer John Legend, the actor and filmmaker Tyler Perry, and the multimillionaire entrepreneurs Michael and Steven Roberts. In the same documentary O'Brien also included material about a program designed to help couples in troubled marriages, breast-cancer patients, and former prisoners. The second part, which aired the next day, was devoted to potential black leaders; it documented the experience of 30 "at-risk" teenagers from the Bushwick section of Brooklyn, in New York City, who, supported by Malaak Compton-Rock's program Journey for Change, worked with HIV-infected orphans and other people in need in South Africa. In complimentary reviews of the series, David Hinckley wrote for the New York *Daily News* (July 22, 2009, on-line), "Good journalism is snapshots of life, and *Black in America 2* has some strong pictures," and Michael Langston Moore wrote for the *examiner.com* (July 24, 2009), "What CNN successfully did with *Black in America 2*, and failed to accomplish with . . . *Black in America*, was to turn a negative situation into an empowering inspiration. While there are certainly many ills that afflict the black community, *Black in America 2* depicted people who were headstrong and adamant about overcoming their obstacles. . . . This series helped humanize African-Americans a bit more to the mainstream audience." By contrast, Neil Genzlinger, who assessed *Black in America 2* for the *New York Times* (July 22, 2009), criticized it as a "skim-the-surface program." "Not that the initiatives Ms. O'Brien spotlights aren't worthy," he wrote. "But Ms. O'Brien undercuts any heft this and other segments might build up by shamelessly injecting herself into the proceedings." He also declared, "The 'Black in America' concept needs to be put out of its misery. When poor urban children are crammed under the same umbrella as rich debutantes, as they are here, it's a good sign that you have an artificial construct. Being black, or anything else, in America is far more complicated than one demographic characteristic." CNN planned to broadcast another series, *Latina in America*, in October 2009.

O'Brien's honors include the Mickey Leland Humanitarian Award, from the National Association of Minorities in Cable (2006); a Gracie Allen Award, from the Foundation of American Women in Radio and Television (2007); and the NAACP President's Award (2007). O'Brien and her husband, Bradley Raymond, an investment banker, live in a loft in New York City with their daughters, Sofia, nine, and Cecilia, seven, and twin sons, Jackson and Charlie, who are five.

—M.M.

Suggested Reading: 43things.com July 22, 2008; CNN.com; *Hispanic* p30 June 2001, p18+ June/July 2005; *mediabistro.com* Dec. 19, 2006; *Newsblaze.com* July 6, 2009; *New York Times* C p3 July 22, 2009; *Pittsburgh Post-Gazette* C p1+ July 21, 2008; *Washington Post* B p1+ June 10, 1997; *Working Mother* p21+ Nov. 2006; Riley, Sam G. *African-Americans in the Media Today*, 2007; *Who's Who in America*

Selected Radio Shows: *Second Opinion, Health Week in Review* (KISS-FM), 1987–88

Selected Television Shows: *The Know Zone* (Discovery Channel), 1993–95; *The Site* (MSNBC), 1996–97; *Morning Blend*, (MSNBC), 1997–99; *Weekend Today, Today Show, Nightly News* (NBC), 1999–2003; *American Morning* (CNN), 2003–07; Special Investigations Unit (CNN), 2007–

Stephen Dunn/Getty Images

Ochocinco, Chad

Jan. 9, 1978– Football player

Address: Cincinnati Bengals, One Paul Brown Stadium, Cincinnati, OH 45202

In the late spring of 2009, the Cincinnati Bengals wide receiver Chad Ochocinco—formerly Chad Johnson—broke an uncharacteristic silence. He publicly expressed regret for his comparatively poor play in the 2008 National Football League (NFL) season, which saw him post some of the lowest numbers for touchdowns and receiving yards in his eight-year career—totals far below those that made him a Pro Bowl player for several consecutive years. He promised better performance in the 2009 season, as well as a return to the antics that had long made him both a fan favorite and a target of criticism: bold predictions of wins, taunts of opposing defensive squads, and spectacular end-zone celebrations of his touchdowns. Ochocinco "walks, talks and acts like the dangerous, trash-talking wide receiver, yet unlike other members of the club he doesn't speak critically about his teammates or call out his quarterback . . . ," Karl Taro Greenfeld noted for *Sports Illustrated* (October 30, 2006). The difference between Ochocinco and other trash-talkers, Greenfeld added, "is that Chad is so . . . likable." The 2008 season "was very humbling for me; it was an embarrassment . . . ," Ochocinco said, as quoted by James Walker on ESPN.com (June 3, 2009). He added, however, perhaps signaling a return to his old form, "Words cannot describe the type of shape I'm in right now. Words cannot describe the type of season I'm going to have. I'm telling you ahead of time."

Ochocinco was born Chad Johnson on January 9, 1978 and spent his early years in Miami, Florida. When he was five years old, his mother, Paula Johnson, moved to California along with Ochocinco's younger brother, Chauncey. She left Ochocinco in the care of his maternal grandmother, Bessie Flowers, a schoolteacher who lived in Liberty City, a Miami neighborhood. As quoted by Greenfeld, Paula Johnson told Paul Daugherty for the book *Chad: I Can't Be Stopped* (2006), "Two kids out of wedlock. That's not me. I just couldn't get it together. I do regret leaving him. But I did the right thing." Ochocinco reportedly has had very little contact with his father, Sam Brown Sr., throughout his life. As a boy Ochocinco spent most of his free time in the street, playing football, basketball, and soccer. He had a lot of unfocused energy; one day when he was 10, he crashed Flowers's car into her front gate while going—so he later claimed—to get it washed. "Boy cannot sit still," Flowers mused to Greenfeld. "Has no attention span. Never did." Flowers drove her grandson to North Miami Beach Elementary School, and then later to Coral Gables High and Miami Beach High, outside Liberty City, in order to provide him with a better education than he would have received in the schools closer to home. But "he could not stay in class . . . ," she told Greenfeld. "The school would call me and say, 'Where's Chad?' I'd have to get in the car and drive over there and find him myself." Sometimes Chad had joined other students' physical-education classes; once she found him helping painters who were touching up the front of the school. "I'm very smart, trust me," Ochocinco told Nate Penn for men.style.com (2007). "But I did horrible in school." Ochocinco played football at Miami Beach High School, from which he graduated only after taking night summer-school classes.

In 1996 Ochocinco attended Langston University, in Oklahoma, where he was expelled (some sources say cut from the football team) for fighting before he could play his first football game. His grandmother immediately sent him to live with his mother, in Los Angeles, California. There, he was able to practice football with his cousin, the NFL wide receiver Keyshawn Johnson. One day in the summer of 1997, Ochocinco came upon a football practice at nearby Santa Monica College, and though he was not on the team, he joined in the drills. "I just started running pass routes," Ochocinco told Penn. "I wasn't signed up or anything. I just showed up out of nowhere." The team's receivers' coach, Charles Collins, recognized his talent. "There was something about him," Collins told Greenfeld. "You could see that he was passionate about football. He was sloppy, wild—but he could run." Ochocinco enrolled at Santa Monica in 1997 and played football there that year but lost his eligibility due to poor academic performance. He worked throughout 1998 to improve his grades while training six days a week with Collins, who became a father figure to Ochocinco. The work paid off; he became eligible to play again. In the total of 20 games he played at Santa Monica—in both the 1997 and 1999 seasons—Ochocinco caught 120 passes for 2,100 yards and scored 23 touchdowns.

After his 1999 season at Santa Monica, Ochocinco received offers from more-prestigious college-football programs, including those at UCLA, USC, San Diego State University, and Oregon State University; he chose Oregon State because he admired the head coach, Dennis Erickson. The summer before the 2000 season, which was the last year of Ochocinco's college eligibility, he worked hard to make up six classes at Santa Monica College so that he would be able to play for a team in the National Collegiate Athletic Association (NCAA). As a result he did not attend regular practices until three weeks before the season opener; he almost decided to quit the team, due to homesickness and the fact that he was fourth in the team's depth chart. Collins reportedly flew to Oregon to persuade Ochocinco to stay. In early games, when he was still unfamiliar with the Oregon team's plays and signals, Ochocinco's fellow wide receiver (and future Cincinnati Bengals teammate) T. J. Houshmandzadeh helped him out. Ochocinco finished the 2000 season with an average of 21.8 yards per catch, a total of 37 catches, 806 total yards, and eight touchdowns, helping lead the Oregon Beavers to an 11–1 season and the fourth slot in the polls. Ochocinco scored a noteworthy 74-yard touchdown, dubbed the "bomb that broke the Irish," in Oregon's 2000 Fiesta Bowl win against Notre Dame. He also set a school record that season with a 97-yard touchdown reception in a game against Stanford University.

Heading into the NFL Scouting Combine—a yearly weeklong event in which college football players perform mental and physical tests before NFL coaches, general managers, and scouts—Ochocinco was predicted to be the NFL's first-round draft pick. His fun-loving ways got the better of him, however. "After yelling out jokes during other players' 40 yard dashes, [Ochocinco], wearing a gaudy, all-yellow outfit, slipped at the start and finished in a mediocre 4.57 seconds," Michael Silver reported for *Sports Illustrated* (September 5, 2005). Ochocinco was picked 36th in the second round by the Cincinnati Bengals, who chose Houshmandzadeh in the final round. The Bengals were, to say the least, a struggling franchise; occasionally referred to as the "Bungles," they had not had a winning record in 11 years. Ochocinco was nonetheless pleased to have been chosen by the team. "I thought it was great," he told Ian Aldrich for *Cincinnati Magazine* (January 2006). "I didn't want to go to a team that was winning. I wanted to be somewhere I could establish myself and help my team get to where we are now." Although Ochocinco started only three games and missed four games in 2001 after fracturing his left clavicle in a mid-October game, he finished the season with 329 receiving yards (the third-highest number on the team), averaged 11.8 yards per carry (a figure just under that of the team's starting halfback, Corey Dillon), and scored one touchdown. The Bengals finished the season with six wins and 10 losses.

In 2002 Ochocinco truly began to shine as a playmaker. He led the team in receptions (69) and yards per catch (16.9). The number of total yards he earned (1,166) was fifth-highest in team history at the time and continues to be the highest number of yards scored by a first- or second-year Bengal. Ochocinco also tied the club record with five 100-yards-receiving games, three of them consecutive. He was instrumental in the Bengals' setting a team record for pass completions, with 350 for the season. Unfortunately, in 2002 the Bengals set some other records, too, posting their worst season in franchise history, with just two wins and 14 losses.

They had problems with their quarterback, who was benched mid-season, and with their defense, which allowed the second-highest number of points in club history (456). At the end of the year, the head coach, Dick LeBeau, was replaced by Marvin Lewis, the defensive coach for the 2001 Super Bowl winners, the Baltimore Ravens. The Bengals also acquired the quarterback Carson Palmer from Southern California in the first round of the draft.

In the thick of the Bengals' frustration in 2002, Ochocinco emerged as a confident, comical, and cocky voice of optimism in the media. In an interview shortly before the Bengals' eighth game of the season, against the Houston Texans, on November 3, Ochocinco "guaranteed" a victory for the hapless Bengals. Though that outcome seemed unlikely, the Bengals won decisively, by a score of 38–3. Two weeks later Ochocinco told journalists that he guaranteed a second win, against the Cleveland Browns, on November 14. "I'm guaranteeing because we look good at what we're doing," Ochocinco told Ken Gordon for the *Columbus Dispatch* (November 14, 2002). Despite his team's dismal record, Ochocinco declared: "There are no teams that can stop us right now. When we're clicking and everything is going right, we look good." Although the Bengals lost to the Browns, 27–20, Ochocinco's spirited challenges brought attention from opposing teams, fans, and the media to a team that was otherwise frustrated.

Midway through the 2003 season, the Bengals had four wins and five losses, their best record since their last play-off season, in 1990. Ochocinco, now the starting wide-out, was one of the team's most consistent and acrobatic playmakers. Just before the team's seventh game, Ochocinco made another confident "guarantee" that the Bengals would win against the then-undefeated Kansas City Chiefs. Coach Lewis and several other Bengals players publicly expressed frustration with Ochocinco's outspokenness. But the Bengals won, 24–19, with Ochocinco scoring the first touchdown of the game, catching a 50-yard bomb from Palmer. The victory, which confirmed the Bengals as leaders in the American Football Conference (AFC) North, was exhilarating for the team, coach, and city residents, all of whom had longed for a consequential win. The Bengals finished the 2003 season with a much-improved record of 8–8, good for second in the AFC North. That season Ochocinco had 90 catches and a career-high of 10 touchdowns, and he led the AFC with 1,335 receiving yards. He accompanied the tackle Willie Anderson to his first Pro Bowl game, in Hawaii, where he caught a 90-yard pass in the first quarter, the third-longest in Pro Bowl history. That season Ochocinco signed a contract extension with the Bengals through 2009, happily telling Mark Curnutte for the *Cincinnati Enquirer* (November 13, 2003), "I want to stay in Cincinnati until I'm 40."

That year Ochocinco also solidified his reputation as a sort of class clown of the NFL. In 2003 he was one of the league's most often-fined players, penalized more than $70,000 for his elaborate touchdown celebrations and wardrobe offenses. One of his most notable celebrations took place during a late-season home game against the San Francisco 49ers, in which Ochocinco followed up a touchdown by fishing out a sign he had hidden in a snow bank and revealing its hand-written text to the cameras: "Dear NFL, Please don't fine me again!!!!! Merry Christmas." He was fined $10,000 for the stunt. That year the replica of his jersey became one the league's top five sellers, and he signed an endorsement deal with the athletic shoe and apparel company Reebok. He also became one of the most sought-after players for interviews. About his touchdown celebrations and other antics, Ochocinco told Greenfeld, "It's just me being me. It just comes out. Spontaneous. But you know what? I have to do it. The whole team feeds on me. They know if 85 is up, then it's gonna be a good day." Ochocinco has often verbally challenged the cornerbacks he will face in upcoming games. He told Peter King for *Sports Illustrated* (October 13, 2003), "When the corners are doing their drills before the game, I tell them, 'Man, your hips are too slow,' or 'That'll never work today.' Sometimes they talk back."

Before a 2004 game against the Cleveland Browns, Ochocinco sent bottles of the digestive medicine Pepto Bismol to members of that team's defensive squad, with a note reading, "They'll be sick to their stomachs after trying to cover me." The game was a disappointing one for Ochocinco, who caught only three passes and dropped three others. He redeemed himself the next week, helping the Bengals defeat the Denver Broncos, 23–10. Ochocinco caught seven passes for 149 yards, including two receptions for 50-yard gains. In 2004, working with the new starting quarterback, Carson Palmer, for the first 13 games (before Palmer suffered a knee injury), Ochocinco maintained his high numbers while facing double coverage most of the time; once again he led the AFC in receiving yards (1,274), caught 95 passes (third-most in the NFL), and scored nine touchdowns, making the Pro Bowl for the second straight year. The Bengals finished the season with another 8–8 record.

The Bengals' 2005 season was triumphant in many ways, bringing their first winning record, division title, and play-off spot since 1990. Ochocinco had a career-high 97 catches and yet again topped the AFC in receiving yards, with 286 more than his nearest competitor, Marvin Harrison of the Indianapolis Colts. In a November game against the Colts, he broke his game record for receiving yards, with 189 in eight passes. In a December game against Detroit, Ochocinco caught a career-high 11 passes. He was selected for the Pro Bowl for the third year in a row, along with Palmer. By season's end Ochocinco and Palmer had helped the Bengals to finish fourth in the league in scoring.

In 2005 Ochocinco outdid himself with touchdown celebrations and other shenanigans. He hung in his locker a laminated chart that read, referring to his jersey number, "Who Can Cover 85 in 2005?"—complete with a space for the name of each cornerback he would face in upcoming games. After each game he ceremoniously checked "yes" or "no" (usually, it was a "no"), often before a crowd of journalists. "Off the record," Ochocinco told the press, as quoted by John Mullin in the *Chicago Tribune* (September 22, 2005), "from a personal standpoint, we all know I'm not coverable. We all know that." Ochocinco's touchdown celebrations seemed to become more inventive with every game. After scoring on September 25, 2005 against the Chicago Bears, Ochocinco performed his own version of Irish step-dancing. Against the Jacksonville Jaguars he pretended to perform CPR on the football. Against the Indianapolis Colts he darted off the field to a cheerleader, before whom he bent down on one knee and pretended to propose marriage. And on November 27, 2005 Ochocinco was fined $5,000 when, after a touchdown, he picked up one of the pylons (the-out-of-bounds markers in the end zone) and used it to "putt" the football as if it were a golf ball, following up that motion with a Tiger Woods–style fist pump. "Fans pay to come to the games, just like when they go to the movies, and I'm determined to give them their money's worth," Ochocinco told Silver. Penn wrote, "His humor has an artlessness, an unexpected sweetness, that makes him seem at times like a character in a kids' cartoon."

In the weeks preceding Ochocinco's first-ever postseason game, at the request his coach, Ochocinco did not speak to the media; he became known as "Silent Chad." That home game, played on January 8, 2006, was a frustrating experience for the Bengals, especially Ochocinco. On the Bengals' second offensive play of the game, Palmer reinjured his knee, ending his season. The backup quarterback, Jon Kitna, steered the team to 10–0 and 17–7 leads before Pittsburgh scored 24 unanswered points to win the game, 31–17. Ochocinco faced double and even triple coverage, catching just four passes for 59 yards. There were reports that Ochocinco, while being hydrated through an IV at halftime, expressed anger at his coaches regarding the strategy of using him to draw coverage from others. "In the biggest game of our careers, you can't get your best player the ball?" he said to Penn over a year after the game. "The plan was not to utilize me. The plan was to allow them to do what they did to me and just use everyone else. I go back to that moment in Pittsburgh and they're giving me an IV and I'm thinking about Santa Monica. You know how hard I worked to get to this point? That's why I blew up like that."

Ochocinco began the 2006 season with a new look—a dyed-blonde mohawk and detachable gold front teeth—but the same attitude. On August 6, 2006 Daugherty's biography of Ochocinco, *Chad: I Can't Be Stopped*, was published by Orange Frazer Press. Despite requests from Lewis and other coaches that Ochocinco tone down his public persona, and in the face of new NFL restrictions on touchdown celebrations (use of the football or other props was no longer allowed), Ochocinco promised fans that he would find ways to entertain them. Ostensibly in recognition of Hispanic Heritage Month, the wide receiver informed journalists that his last name was no longer Johnson but "Ocho Cinco" (Spanish for "eight five," for 85, his jersey number) and requested that they refer to him accordingly in their stories. He went so far as to put "Ocho Cinco" on the back of his jersey during the practice before a game against the Atlanta Falcons, for which he was fined $5,000.

Ochocinco posted impressive numbers in the 2006 season. He set the Bengals' single-game record for receiving yards (260) on November 12, in a contest against the San Diego Chargers. When he caught for an additional 190 yards in the next game, against the New Orleans Saints, Ochocinco set a new NFL record for receiving yards in back-to-back games (450). He also made history by becoming the first player to win four consecutive receiving-yards titles in the AFC and won a spot in the Pro Bowl for the fourth year in a row. As a team, though, after looking promising in the first half of the season, the Bengals lost their last three regular-season games, the final one against the Pittsburgh Steelers—squandering their play-off chances. They finished the season 8–8.

Ochocinco continued to keep an upbeat attitude during the first half of the 2007 season, with sensational plays and creative celebrations. After his first touchdown of the season, at home against the Baltimore Ravens, a teammate draped over his shoulders a custom-made jacket resembling one worn by Hall of Fame inductees, the back of which read: "Future H.O.F. 20??" (The number and question marks referred to the as-yet-unknown year of his assumed induction.) After scoring against the Cleveland Browns, Ochocinco jumped into a rowdy section of the Cleveland stadium known as the "Dawg Pound," where he was doused with beer. "How do you rein him in? Do we tell him not to score touchdowns?" Lewis asked in an interview with José Miguel Romero for the *Seattle Times* (September 20, 2007). "We want him to score touchdowns and have the opportunity to celebrate, so I hope he gets a lot of dancing in the end zone or whatever he feels is his motive deal this week." The Bengals, as it turned out, would have little cause for celebration, as they spiraled toward their first losing record since 2002.

In light of the Bengals' losses, some suggested that Ochocinco's antics were acts of selfishness that distracted the team. "You've got to be selfish," Ochocinco told Mark Gaughan for the *Buffalo (New York) News* (November 4, 2007). "You know what I don't like and I don't understand? Who made that word a bad word? It don't matter what position you play, you've got to be selfish at what you do. You have to want it! You have to." Ochocinco earned his first-ever AFC Player of the Week award from the NFL for his efforts in the Bengals' 35–6 victory over the Tennessee Titans on November 25, a game in which Ochocinco made three touchdown catches, set a personal single-game record of 12 catches for 103 yards, and set the team's record for career receptions. After having gone weeks without scoring a touchdown, Ochocinco celebrated by grabbing a sideline camera and swirling it in the direction of where he had scored, a stunt that drew a fine, a 15-yard penalty, and even more public criticism. Feeling unfairly judged by the media, he declined interviews for most of the rest of the season. As he approached the Bengals' final 2007 game, against the 1–14 Miami Dolphins, in his home town of Miami, Ochocinco told Ben Volin for the *Palm Beach Post* (December 27, 2007, on-line), "It's just been a very hurtful year for me. All I want to do is win, and people are taking the way I play the game and approach the game as a negative and trying to twist it into the reason why we're not being successful." The Bengals' record for the season was 7–9. Ochocinco was selected as a replacement player in that season's Pro Bowl. Afterward he legally changed his last name.

Ochocinco and the Bengals both had a dismal season in 2008. The team's record by year's end was 4–11–1, and Ochocinco had career lows in touchdowns (four), receptions (53), and yards (540). For months in the following off-season, the receiver—who generally relishes interviews—gave none. That changed in June, when he spoke publicly about his disappointing season, explained that he simply had not prepared properly to play in 2008, and expressed optimism with regard to 2009. "I need the fans to embrace me. I know people are mad at me," he told Geoff Hobson for an article posted on the Cincinnati Bengals Web site (June 8, 2009). "If they embrace me, I can spread my wings and be myself. . . . I've seriously been working out. Hunger has created a monster in a positive way." He noted that he had received encouragement from the actor and filmmaker Denzel Washington during halftime at a Los Angeles Lakers basketball game. "Denzel told me, 'Go back to being Chad. People want to see that swagger. The Chad that's always smiling and wanting to be the best. Have fun.'"

On August 20, 2009, in a preseason game against the New England Patriots, Ochocinco demonstrated his diverse talents, serving as the team's replacement kicker for the injured starter Shayne Graham. The extra point he successfully kicked following a touchdown allowed the Bengals to win, 7–6. "Everyone has to remember, I've always said that soccer is my No. 1 sport," Ochocinco said, as quoted in the *New York Times* (August 21, 2009). "I think [the Brazilian soccer player] Ronaldinho would be proud of me right now." Many football aficionados were surprised by the Bengals' 4–2 record in the first six weeks of the 2009 season—the best among teams in the AFC North. For his part, Ochocinco had notched 29 receptions, 455 receiving yards, and three touchdowns. He had also resumed his spirited outspokenness, often communicating with other players and the general public by means of the social-networking and "micro-blogging" device Twitter. (He has almost 300,000 "followers.") In October 2009 Rock Software Inc., a company founded by the Bengals quarterback Jordan Palmer (the younger brother of the Bengals' starter Carson Palmer) and two of his childhood friends, released a new iPhone application that allows fans to follow Ochocinco's daily activities, view photos and videos of him, read his messages, and ask his advice on dating or other issues.

Ochocinco has four children—three daughters and a son—who live with their mother. He rarely sees his children. "I put everything into football, dude, studying long hours. I'm ridiculous with it," Ochocinco told Penn. "I wish I could put the same energy into them [his children]." He said to Greenfeld, "I don't think I'm the father I need to be right now. It doesn't really bother me that much because once I'm done, I'll have all the time in the world with them. I've lost a little time. I know I'm missing something valuable—valuable moments in their life." Ochocinco participates in various events to raise money for the nonprofit organization Feed the Children, which delivers food, medicine, clothing, and other necessities to children and families in need around the world. Ochocinco lives in Cincinnati and spends much of his time in Miami.

—M.E.R.

Suggested Reading: *Cincinnati Magazine* p68 Jan. 2006; ESPN.com Oct. 19, 2009, Oct. 20, 2009; *Gentlemen's Quarterly* p122 Nov. 2007; *Sports Illustrated* p64 Sep. 5, 2005, p58 Oct. 30, 2006; Daugherty, Paul. *Chad: I Can't Be Stopped*, 2006

Odierno, Ray

1954– U.S. Army general; commander of multinational forces in Iraq

Address: The Pentagon, Washington, DC 20310

In March 2003 the U.S. invaded Iraq and overthrew its leader, Saddam Hussein, for the ostensible purpose of ridding that nation of so-called weapons of mass destruction—none of which were found there. Several years into the U.S. occupation, Iraq was a hotbed of violence, perpetrated by opposing groups within the country as well as members of the terrorist group Al Qaeda. As the U.S. weighed the option of withdrawing troops and turning over patrolling duties to Iraqi forces, General Ray Odierno, then the second-highest-ranking American military officer in Iraq, successfully advocated a different strategy: increasing, rather than decreas-

Alex Wong/Getty Images

Ray Odierno

ing, the number of U.S. troops there. The resulting 2007 troop "surge" has been credited with bringing relative calm to the region.

Earlier, at the beginning of the war, Odierno's old-style, aggressive military tactics had generated criticism and, according to some detailed reports, served to fuel violence on the part of Iraqi insurgents bent on sabotaging the country's new, fragile government. But in his second tour of duty in Iraq, which began in 2006, Odierno has softened his approach to fighting terrorism in the region, devoting more time and energy to communicating with Iraqis. "The real key," he told Babak Dehghanpisheh for *Newsweek* (February 25, 2008), "is getting into the population." In September 2008 Odierno became the highest-ranking U.S. military officer in Iraq, succeeding General David H. Petraeus as commander of multinational forces there.

The son of Raymond J. and Helen Odierno, Raymond T. Odierno was born in 1954 in Rockaway, New Jersey. His father had been an army sergeant during World War II, and Odierno decided to follow in his footsteps. After graduating from Morris Hills High School, in Rockaway, in 1972, he attended the U.S. Military Academy at West Point, in New York State, where he played tight end on the football team and received a B.S. degree in engineering in 1976. He went on to earn two master's degrees: an M.S. in nuclear-effects engineering from North Carolina State University, in Raleigh, and an M.A. in national security and strategy from the U.S. Naval War College, in Newport, Rhode Island. Starting in 1986 he ascended the ranks of the U.S. Army, with assignments as a nuclear research officer (1986–87), commander of the Second Battalion, Eighth Field Artillery, Seventh Infantry Division (1992–94), and commander of the artillery division at Fort Hood, Texas (1995–97). During Operation Desert Storm, in 1991, in which U.S.-led forces drove Iraqi troops from Kuwait, he served as a brigade executive officer. From October 2001 to March 2004, Odierno commanded the Fourth Infantry Division at Fort Hood. In 2003 he led that division in Iraq as part of the U.S.-driven invasion. His unit was stationed in the unstable Sunni Triangle, a strategically significant, volatile region that includes Baghdad, the Iraqi capital, and areas north and west of the city. One of his unit's most publicized achievements was the capture of former Iraqi president Saddam Hussein, who had been in hiding from U.S. forces. Odierno told various news organizations that the moment was a "major psychological and operational defeat" for the insurgents.

Although Odierno's unit gained a lot of publicity for the capture of Hussein, the event was not a major strategic victory in the war. Furthermore, the Fourth Infantry Division engaged in rough, questionable tactics, such as kicking in doors of ordinary Iraqis and rounding up thousands of Iraqi military-age males, seemingly indiscriminately, as suspected insurgents—leading to overcrowding of military prisons, including the now-infamous Abu Ghraib facility. At the time, in 2003, little if any such information was reported in the U.S. media, and public sentiment favored the war effort. Two years later, however, after support for the war had started to wane, more reports of misconduct emerged. For his part Odierno dismissed as anecdotal and exaggerated any allegations that his unit engaged in rough—and possibly illegal—tactics. However, a December 2003 report by the U.S. Army stated that the Fourth Infantry Division had indeed rounded up military-age males indiscriminately. On the one hand, Odierno was not the only military leader in Iraq to engage in those kinds of tactics; on the other, his methods were called into question on strategic as well as ethical grounds. Stuart Herrington, a retired colonel and intelligence officer, concluded that such practices by U.S. commanders early in the Iraq war "effectively made them recruiters for the insurgency," according to Thomas E. Ricks in the *Washington Post* (February 8, 2009), who wrote that Herrington "was especially bothered by the actions of Odierno's division." As quoted by Ricks, Herrington wrote in the 2003 report, "Some divisions are conducting operations with rigorous detention criteria, while some—the 4th ID is the negative example—are sweeping up large numbers of people and dumping them at the door of Abu Ghraib."

When Odierno's first tour of duty in Iraq was over, in March 2004, his son's was just beginning. Anthony Odierno, a 2001 West Point graduate, was the only one of the general's three children to have entered the military. Months after Anthony's deployment, Odierno, who was with his wife at the time, received a phone call from his friend Major General Peter Chiarelli, who reported that Anthony was seriously hurt: a rocket-propelled grenade had hit the Humvee in which he was riding and all but severed his left arm. Anthony, who was later awarded the Bronze Star, had to undergo surgery in which his arm was amputated.

In 2004 Odierno was promoted to assistant to the chairman of the Joint Chiefs of Staff and as senior military adviser to Secretary of State Condoleezza Rice, whom he accompanied on international visits. Odierno returned to Iraq in May 2006, this time as commander of multinational forces in Operation Freedom, the second-highest U.S. military leader in the country after George W. Casey, the commander of all multinational forces in Iraq. Odierno's approach to his work this time was very different: heavy-handed tactics were mostly replaced by strategic thinking and an appreciation for the nuances of counterinsurgency warfare. Journalists and authors would point repeatedly to Odierno's "evolution." One cause of that evolution was the maiming of his son in Iraq. That incident "didn't affect me as a military officer. . . . It affected me as a person . . . ," Odierno told Ricks. "I feel an obligation to mothers and fathers. I understand [their feelings] better because [Anthony's injury] happened to me." Another cause of the shift in his thinking was the realization that a more nuanced, thoughtful approach was necessary for victory. "You now have different groups . . . trying to vie for power within Iraq," Odierno told Michael Hastings, Michael Hirsh, and Richard Wolffe for *Newsweek* (January 8, 2007). (After the general election of December 2005, a new Iraqi government took power in May 2006. Regardless, tensions between the two main religious groups in Iraq—Sunnis and Shiites—continued to intensify, especially after February of that year, when Al Qaeda allegedly bombed the al-Askari Mosque, in Samarra, Iraq, one of the holiest sites for Shiites.) Odierno told Hastings, Hirsh, and Wolffe, "That's what makes this extremely more complex than this has been in the past. It's not simply Sunni insurgents or Al Qaeda that we're fighting anymore—fighting is the wrong term—we're trying to influence [Iraqis] to operate within the confines of the government." A year later, at the beginning of 2008, Odierno was asked by Babak Dehghanpisheh whether he "struggle[d] with the idea of talking to your enemies." Odierno said that he did, adding: "But as we secured areas, they became more willing to cooperate with us and turn against Al Qaeda. I realized that many of these people were fighting against us for survival. It wasn't really because they were insurgents. It wasn't really because they were ideologically against the government or against progress. They were just trying to survive. And as I talked to them and listened, I realized there was a sincerity. And slowly we saw the effects: increased security, reduction in attacks. So it made me feel much more comfortable."

Along with a new understanding of the situation on the ground in Iraq came Odierno's realization that the U.S. strategy there—as dictated by President George W. Bush and Defense Secretary Donald H. Rumsfeld—was misguided. As a result, the situation in Iraq, Odierno told Ricks, was "fairly desperate." The Bush/Rumsfeld strategy was to start reducing the number of American soldiers in Iraq by the following year, 2007. Odierno was supposed to oversee the gradual transfer of U.S. forces from all major cities to big bases near roads leading to major metropolitan areas, which would ideally enable the Iraqi security forces to take over urban fighting and policing. The goal of the plan, which involved hurried training of Iraqis, was the eventual transfer of power from U.S. troops to Iraqi security forces. The plan also called for an increased U.S. troop presence at Iraq's borders in order to minimize outside influence, notably from Iran. (More soldiers at the border, however, would mean fewer in cities.)

Odierno opposed every aspect of the plan. He thought that the Iraqi security forces were not ready to take over the bulk of urban military operations and policing and that a hurried transfer of power would only worsen an already bad situation. Because, in his view, the bulk of the American force was needed where it mattered most—in big cities—cutting the number of U.S. troops was out of the question. In fact, he thought, *more* troops were needed. That line of thinking put him and a small group of others in direct conflict with many active military and political leaders in the upper echelons, including General Casey. But the retired general Jack Keane, who remained very influential, took Odierno's view; at Keane's urging Odierno asked for five brigades, in order to deploy more troops to cities and establish smaller outposts elsewhere—slowing, rather than accelerating, the handover of duties to Iraqi forces. Casey offered Odierno two brigades, but no more. Odierno knew that would not be enough, so he decided to sidestep Casey and the Pentagon and, with Keane's help, go directly to the White House. President Bush, however, was reluctant to commit more troops.

As that debate was going on, in the fall of 2006, the congressional midterm election campaigns were in full swing. On Election Day Democrats gained enough seats in the House and Senate to take charge of Congress, the following January, for the first time since the mid-1990s; their victory was attributed largely to voter dissatisfaction with the course of the war in Iraq. Almost immediately Rumsfeld resigned as defense secretary, and Bush named as his successor Robert M. Gates, formerly the director of the Central Intelligence Agency (CIA). Gates was not pleased with the progress in Iraq. Soon after his meeting with Odierno and Casey, he approved the five additional brigades, approximately 20,000 troops. (Eventually, about half would be stationed in Baghdad, the other half in surrounding areas.) The troop increase became known as "the surge"—announced to the nation by President Bush in a live television address in January 2007. That month Bush also chose David H. Petraeus as Casey's successor in Iraq. "If Petraeus

. . . was the public face of the troop buildup, he was only its adoptive parent," Ricks wrote. "It was Odierno . . . who was the surge's true father."

The surge began in January, with the deployment of one brigade. Subsequently, one brigade was deployed every month until May. Throughout the early months of 2007, there was no consistent decline in violence. As summer passed, however, the violence started to decrease, and the surge appeared to be working, due in part to Odierno's new, less-aggressive tactics. As various war correspondents and other knowledgeable journalists pointed out, there were also other significant factors in the reduction of bloodshed: the Shiite leader Moqtada al-Sadr declared a ceasefire; Shiite militias had, for the most part, achieved their goal of controlling Baghdad; and the Iraqi government absorbed some Sunni insurgents into the military and offered others vocational training—which had the effect, more or less, of paying them to stop fighting. (Although those combined factors led to less fighting in Iraq, they did not lead to any real political stability.)

In September 2008 General Odierno became the commander of multinational forces in Iraq, the position previously held by General Petraeus (who is currently the U.S. commander of all Middle East forces). One of Odierno's tasks was to advise the president on troop numbers. Odierno kept his post even after a new president—Barack Obama—came into office, in January 2009. Obama's plan called for a pullout of U.S. forces from Iraqi cities by June 30, 2009; the end of U.S. combat operations by August 2010; and the departure of the remaining 50,000 troops by the end of 2011. Although the level of violence in the first few months of 2009 was significantly lower than it had been in 2006, Odierno emphasized that true stability was necessary before a massive pullout. "We've learned a lesson here over the last several years," Odierno told Jane Arraf for the *Christian Science Monitor* (April 2, 2009), "that you have to clear an area, you have to have the force to hold it, and you have to allow the community then to rebuild itself. . . . If you rush your way through that, then the community will fall back into an insecure state." In late June Odierno said that he believed Iraqi police and military units could function in cities without the help of U.S. forces, which at that time were pulling out of Iraqi cities and being stationed in bases nearby. American forces, Odierno has said, could be called upon by the Iraqi military or police force if their assistance is needed in the cities. As of September there were still approximately 130,000 U.S. soldiers in Iraq. An incident that month underscored the continued unrest there: during a visit by Vice President Joseph R. Biden to Baghdad, four mortar shells landed in the city's heavily militarized Green Zone, killing at least two Iraqis and wounding several others. The previous month a bomb attack killed at least 132 people and damaged two government buildings. Odierno nonetheless announced in late September 2009 that he could decrease U.S. forces in Iraq to 50,000 troops by the fall of 2010, provided that the country's January 2010 elections proceeded in an orderly way.

The six-foot five-inch, 245-pound Odierno, who has a shaved head, has been described variously as "hulking" and "towering." Ricks reported that while Petraeus is "cool to the point of being remote," Odierno "is emotional, the type of general who will bear-hug a colonel having a hard day." He has received many awards and honors, including the Army Distinguished Service Medal, the Legion of Merit with five oak-leaf clusters, and the Meritorious Service Medal with three oak-leaf clusters. In addition to Anthony, Odierno and his wife, Linda, have two other children, Kathrin and Michael.

—D.K.

Suggested Reading: mnf-iraq.com; *Newsweek* p26 Jan. 8, 2007; *New York Times* A p10 June 29, 2009; *Washington Post* A p1 Feb. 8, 2009

Stephen Dunn/Getty Images

Odom, Lamar

Nov. 6, 1979– Basketball player

Address: Los Angeles Lakers, 555 N. Nash St., El Segundo, CA 90245

Lamar Odom, the versatile power forward for the Los Angeles Lakers of the National Basketball Association (NBA), traveled a long road to reach his full potential as an athlete. He was deemed the best basketball prospect to come out of New York State since Kareem Abdul-Jabbar—before a series of bad decisions, injuries, and tragedies prevented him from fulfilling expectations during his first several seasons in the league. The number-one-ranked High School All-American by the end of his junior year, Odom neglected his schoolwork to the point of nearly ruining his chance at a college career. In July 1997, after announcing that spring that he would play for the University of Nevada–Las Vegas (UNLV), Odom became embroiled in controversy after *Sports Illustrated* published a story that questioned the validity of his score on the ACT college-entrance test. Rejected by UNLV, he enrolled as a nonmatriculating student at the University of Rhode Island (URI), where over the next year and a half he earned the credits necessary to restore his National Collegiate Athletic Association (NCAA) eligibility. As a freshman at URI, Odom was named the Atlantic-10 Conference Rookie of the Year. That year he turned pro and, at the age of 19, was selected by the Los Angeles Clippers in the 1999 NBA draft. His solid play and impressive statistics got him named to the NBA All-Rookie First Team in 2000. During the next season he put up even better numbers, but then, within eight months, he was hampered by injuries and slapped with two suspensions for drug use, beginning a two-year period of inefficient play that led the Clippers to put him up as a free agent. "I was as lost as lost could be," Odom said about those years, according to a writer for the *Providence (Rhode Island) Journal-Bulletin* (June 4, 2008).

Under Pat Riley of the Miami Heat, who acquired Odom during the summer of 2003, the talented but immature player found the structure he had lacked. Odom started 80 games in the 2003–04 season to help lead the Heat to the play-offs and inspiring *Basketball Digest* to name him the 2004 Comeback Player of the Year. Prior to the start of the 2004–05 season, Odom was involved in a multiplayer trade that sent him to the Los Angeles Lakers. In his first year with that team, he had trouble establishing chemistry with superstar Kobe Bryant, then suffered a season-ending shoulder injury. Since the Lakers hired Coach Phil Jackson, in 2005, Odom has come into his own as one of the best players in the league. Under Jackson's triangle offense, he is able to control the flow and tempo of the game as a point forward—a big man with shooting range and rebounding strength who can bring the ball up the court like a point guard. In 2007–08 Odom put together one of his finest all-around seasons to date and was a pivotal figure in taking the Lakers to the 2008 NBA championship, which they lost to the Boston Celtics. He was moved to the bench and served as the Lakers' sixth man during the 2008–09 season, in which he helped lead the team to their first NBA championship in seven years. Commenting on his sometimes supporting role with the Lakers, Odom explained to Broderick Turner for the Riverside, California, *Press Enterprise* (April 20, 2008), "When a guy is getting 20 points, it's like, 'Oh, he's a great player, or he's a great scorer.' . . . I don't really approach the game like that. And I think some people like to criticize that."

Lamar Joseph Odom was born on November 6, 1979 in Jamaica, in the New York City borough of Queens. His mother, Cathy Mercer (some sources have spelled her first name with a "K"), worked for the New York City Department of Transportation before becoming a corrections officer at Rikers Island; his father, Joseph, was a disabled war veteran who became a drug addict and deserted the family when Odom was six. Odom's mother raised him in South Ozone Park, a tough Queens neighborhood. Odom took to basketball early on, learning the intricacies of the sport in pickup games at the courts in nearby Lincoln Park. His mother, diagnosed with colon cancer, died when he was 12 years old; afterward, Odom found an escape from his grief in playing basketball.

Odom was immediately placed in the care of his grandmother, Mildred Mercer, who reared him in a small row house in South Ozone Park. Sharing living quarters with his uncle, two cousins, and their children, he slept on the sofa. His grandmother, who had worked as a nurse and then gone back to school for a college degree after her children were grown, became another major influence in Odom's life, often emphasizing to him the importance of academics. During that time, though, basketball was Odom's main focus. He played in the CYO (Catholic Youth Organization) program at St. Benedict Joseph grammar school, in Richmond Hill, Queens, traveling with the team within the five boroughs and playing against such future NBA stars as Rafer "Skip" Alston (who would become his Miami Heat teammate) and Stephon Marbury. He then attended Christ the King Regional High School, a Catholic school in Middle Village, Queens.

During his high-school career, Odom emerged as one of the most celebrated basketball talents in New York State history. Not exceptionally tall as a freshman—he stood just over six feet—Odom overcame opponents through strategy, which immediately caught the attention of the school's varsity head coach, Bob Oliva. That summer, after earning a spot on Oliva's squad, he had a growth spurt of seven inches, which helped transform him from a skilled basketball player into a potential superstar. Now six feet nine inches tall (he would grow one more inch), with a seven-foot wingspan, he displayed unusual ball-handling skills and passing ability for someone his size, allowing him to play effectively at all five positions: point guard, guard, forward, power forward, and center. In his sophomore year many began comparing him to the Los Angeles Lakers' legendary Hall of Famer Magic Johnson, a six-foot-nine point guard whose command of the basketball court has rarely been matched. That year Odom helped lead Christ the King to New York's 1995 Catholic High School Athletic Association (CHSAA) title, after scoring a record-tying 36 points in the New York City championship game. In the state championship Christ the King lost to Marbury's school, Abraham Lincoln.

During his junior year Odom continued to dominate on the basketball court and was named the City and Queens Player of the Year, after averaging 17 points, 11 rebounds, six assists, and four blocks per game. That year his team entered the CHSAA play-offs undefeated but was edged out by Rice in the championship game, 64–63. (Odom missed a potential game-winning jumper at the buzzer.) He entered his senior year as one of the top recruits in the nation and was courted by some of the country's leading college-basketball programs. Meanwhile, however, he was neglecting his studies; after failing two classes, he was prevented from playing, which threatened his college eligibility. Then he failed his college-entrance exam. Commenting on his poor academic performance, Oliva told the *Providence Journal-Bulletin* reporter, "Lamar knows the difference between doing things the right way and not doing things the right way. He was just lazy. Like a lot of kids, he didn't like to go to school. He was always looking for the easy way, and outside of here he wasn't pushed." Oliva added that Odom was nonetheless well-behaved and popular among students and teachers alike.

Odom transferred to Redemption Christian Academy, in Troy, New York, and then to St. Thomas Aquinas Prep, in New Britain, Connecticut, where he finished his senior year; *Parade* magazine named him Player of the Year, and he made the *USA Today* All-USA First Team. The basketball coach at St. Thomas Aquinas, Jerry DeGregorio, whom Odom had met at a summer basketball camp, became a father figure for the young man, inviting Odom to live at his home for a time and helping him to focus on improving his grades. After regaining his academic standing, Odom played in the McDonald's All-American Game and Magic's Roundball Classic, and he announced his plans to play at UNLV. Then, that summer, *Sports Illustrated* broke a story that questioned the validity of Odom's score (22) on the ACT college-entrance test. Less than a month after he had moved to Las Vegas and days after the story broke, Odom was arrested for soliciting a prostitute, and UNLV asked him to leave.

Odom next entertained several offers, including a $1 million contract to play in Europe and $100,000 to compete in the Continental Basketball Association (CBA), before becoming a nonmatriculating student at URI and playing for the Rams, under Jim Harrick, their head coach. DeGregorio became the team's assistant coach. By that time Odom had patched up his relationship with his father, who with the help of the G.I. Bill paid the first year's tuition, room, and board for Odom. Odom sat out the 1997–98 basketball season while trying to earn the 24 credits necessary to restore his athletic eligibility, but his attempt was half-hearted, and he left the school just before his first-semester finals. He was then given yet another chance, after Harrick persuaded three of his four teachers to give Odom incompletes and allow him to make up the work in summer school. Under the watchful eye of DeGregorio, who steered him to counseling and away from bad influences, Odom fulfilled his course requirements. At the time he noted to Dick Weiss for the New York *Daily News* (November 11, 1998, on-line), "It was like a huge weight had come off my chest. This has been the longest year-and-a-half of my life. Now, I'm finally starting to feel like I did before my junior year at Christ the King."

That November Odom silenced his detractors in his college-basketball debut, against Texas Christian University, barely missing a triple-double with 19 points, 14 rebounds, and nine assists. He planted the game-winning basket with 5.4 seconds remaining to give URI the 87–85 victory. In the first nine games of that season, he led his team in scoring, rebounding, and assists. Other highlights during the season included scoring a career-high 28 points in a game against St. Joseph's and making 11 assists against George Washington. After ending the regular season with an average of 17.6 points, 9.4 rebounds, and 3.8 assists per game, he won First Team All-Atlantic 10 honors and was named the conference Rookie of the Year. In the Atlantic 10 tournament he nailed another dramatic three-pointer at the buzzer to give Rhode Island a 62–59 victory over Temple and the conference title, as well as a spot in the NCAA tournament. He scored 16 points and grabbed 12 rebounds for the Rams in their first-round game against North Carolina–Charlotte, but Rhode Island lost in overtime, 81–70.

After that loss there was much media speculation that Odom would move to the NBA. In 1999, at age 19, he was selected as the fourth-overall pick by the Los Angeles Clippers and signed a four-year, $11.4 million contract. On November 2, 1999 Odom made his NBA debut in a game against the Seattle Supersonics, scoring an astounding 30 points, with 12 rebounds, three assists, two steals, and two blocks in 44 minutes. (The Clippers nonetheless lost the game, 104–92.) Odom was named the NBA Rookie of the Month for November, and in a December game against the Golden State Warriors, he posted 22 points, 11 rebounds, a career-high seven blocks, and two steals. In January 2000 he averaged 19.1 points, 9.1 rebounds, and 3.6 assists, while posting a 47 percent field-goal percentage. During the season he scored in double-digits in 67 of 76 games played and finished in a tie for fourth place in the NBA in triple-doubles, with three. Though he sustained several injuries and missed five games, he averaged 16.6 points, 7.8 rebounds, 4.2 assists, 1.2 steals, 1.3 blocks, and 36.4 minutes in 70 starts. The Clippers, though, finished the season with a disastrous 15–67 record, which resulted in dramatic personnel shifts in the off-season.

With the addition of the Clippers' head coach, Alvin Gentry, and rookies Darius Miles, Keyon Dooling, and Quentin Richardson, along with the release of veterans Maurice Taylor and Derek Anderson, Odom emerged as the team's de facto leader. During the first two months of the 2000–01 season, he established himself as one of the most talented players in the league, and many began hailing him as the next Magic Johnson. Meanwhile, he was helping to turn the Clippers into a play-off contender. Then, in March, Odom was suspended for five games after testing positive for marijuana. Returning to competition, he put up some of the best numbers of his career, with three triple-doubles over nine days. The Clippers went on to win 10 of their final 11 home games and improved their regular-season record to 31–51. Meanwhile, by season's end, Odom had increased his numbers in virtually every statistical category, averaging 17.2 points, 7.8 rebounds, 5.2 assists, 1.61 blocks, and 37.3 minutes in 76 games.

Odom tested positive for marijuana again in December 2001, which resulted in an eight-game suspension. In a tearful press conference, he owned up to his lapse in judgment, saying, as quoted by John Nadel for the Associated Press (November 7, 2001, on-line), "I made the mistake once, now it's twice. . . . I know I can get through it, I'm strong enough. Nothing I can say is going to make people believe me, I've just got to do it." The Clippers suffered in Odom's absence, which was longer than expected: just after returning from the team's suspended list, he missed 45 more games due to a sprained ligament in his right wrist. Odom appeared in only 29 games that season, and the Clippers missed the play-offs again, with a 39–43 record. Many placed the blame on Odom, whose scoring and rebound averages had dropped to 13.1 and 6.1, respectively. During that time Odom had emotional support from DeGregorio, who had joined the franchise as director of player development.

In the 2002–03 campaign Odom appeared in fewer than 50 games for the second year in a row, missing 33 due to injury. The Clippers finished with a 27–55 record, one of the worst in all of sports. Following that season the Clippers released Odom. In the summer of 2003, he was signed by the Miami Heat in a six-year, $65 million deal. Pat Riley, who had stepped down as the team's head coach immediately before the 2003–04 season (he was replaced by Stan Van Gundy) in order to focus on his duties as general manager, took on the role of mentor to Odom. At Riley's suggestion Odom made the move from small forward to power forward. He started each of the 80 games in which he appeared and emerged as one of the most versatile players in the league. He was the Heat's high scorer in 25 games and averaged 17.1 points, 9.7 rebounds, 4.1 assists, 1.06 steals, 0.89 blocks, and a team-high 37.5 minutes for the season. Although Miami got off to a slow start, they won 17 of their last 21 games to finish at 42–40, which was good enough to make the play-offs. After defeating the New Orleans Hornets in seven games in the first round, they faced the Indiana Pacers in the Eastern Conference semifinals, losing the series in six games. Keith Loria, writing for *Basketball Digest* (July–August 2004), called Odom's successful season "one of the more shocking developments of 2003–04" and described Odom as having "regained the form that made him a lottery pick in 1999." That summer *Basketball Digest* named Odom the 2004 NBA Comeback Player of the Year.

In the off-season Odom was involved in a trade that sent him, Caron Butler, Brian Grant, and a draft pick to the Los Angeles Lakers for Shaquille O'Neal. He later commented to Rich Hammond for the *San Gabriel Valley (California) Tribune* (November 1, 2004), "I've changed, in a good way. I'm much more mature. I left L.A. as an 'old boy' and came back as a young man. It was my journey, the journey that the Lord put me on." That summer Odom was named as a replacement, along with former teammate Dwyane Wade, on the U.S. Olympic basketball team, which captured the bronze medal. During the 2004–05 NBA season, Odom was largely called upon to support the play of the superstar guard Kobe Bryant. Odom averaged a double-double for the season, scoring 15.2 points per game and grabbing 10.2 rebounds per game, but was unable to establish chemistry with Bryant, who proved unwilling to share the ball. In addition, in the power-forward position, Odom usually found himself up against players who were heavier and/or taller than him. As a result, his body took a beating most nights, and he missed the last 17 games of the season, after tearing the labrum in his left shoulder in a game against Indiana. The Lakers finished with an embarrassing 34–48 record; they missed the play-offs for only the fourth time in franchise history.

After undergoing surgery in the off-season, Odom returned to a revamped Lakers squad that saw the return of former coach Phil Jackson. By means of Jackson's triangle offense, Odom put up career-high numbers during the 2005–06 season, in field-goal percentage (.481), three-point field-goal percentage (.372), and minutes per game (40.3), while averaging 14.8 points, 9.2 rebounds, and 5.5 assists. (He was the only player to average more than 14 points, nine boards, and five assists per game.) Odom was a pivotal figure in preparing Los Angeles for the postseason, in which they were eliminated in the first round by the Phoenix Suns, after letting a three-games-to-one lead slip away. That summer Odom suffered a personal tragedy: while he was attending the funeral of an aunt in New York, his six-and-a-half-month-old son, Jayden, suffocated in his crib—three years to the day after Odom's grandmother died. Too distraught to return to basketball, Odom withdrew for a time from most of his family and friends and spent the summer in New York.

Odom was plagued with injuries during the 2006–07 campaign, missing 21 games with a sprained right knee and then another five late in the season with a torn left shoulder. He still put up solid numbers in the 56 games in which he appeared, averaging 15.9 points, 9.8 rebounds, and 4.8 assists. The Lakers faced the Suns in the play-offs again but lost in five games; Odom, by contrast, shone in the series, averaging 19.4 points, 13.0 rebounds, and 2.2 assists in 38.4 minutes. In 2007–08 he enjoyed one of his best all-around seasons to date and complemented Kobe Bryant's play in much the way perfected by the Chicago Bulls' Scottie Pippen in relation to Michael Jordan. His teammate Derek Fisher told Broderick Turner, "Lamar is a guy who is the consummate team player. He has arguably as many or more skills as anybody on our team. But I don't think he has the same interest in being The Guy. Lamar thinks about basketball as a team game." Thanks to the key addition of center Pau Gasol from the Memphis Grizzlies in a midseason trade, Odom finished the year with averages of 14.2 points, 10.6 rebounds, and 3.5 assists per game. With Gasol's arrival, Odom became the third (and sometimes fourth) option on offense, a role that improved his quality of play, as his game had sometimes suffered under the pressure of being the number-two man behind Bryant. Odom was instrumental in the Lakers' NBA championship run, but his numbers were comparatively low in the finals: an average of 13.5 points, nine rebounds, and three assists per game. The Boston Celtics took the series in six games.

With the return of the Lakers' starting center Andrew Bynum, who missed the final 46 games of the 2007–08 season after he had knee surgery, Odom reluctantly accepted the role of the team's sixth man for the 2008–09 season. He averaged 11.3 points, 8.2 rebounds, and 2.6 assists in 78 games that year. Odom returned to the starting lineup in early February due to another injury suffered by Bynum. In the 2009 postseason he made an impressive showing in another Lakers championship run, averaging 12.3 points, 9.1 rebounds, 1.8 assists, and 1.4 blocks in 23 games. That June he helped lead the Lakers to their 15th NBA championship and first title in seven years, when the team defeated the Orlando Magic in the 2009 NBA finals in five games. Odom became a free agent during the 2009 off-season; although he was vigorously courted by the Miami Heat, he signed a four-year, $33 million deal with the Lakers that July.

In 2006 Odom launched a clothing line called Son of Man, a collection of T-shirts and jeans emblazoned with images of Jesus and other biblical figures. According to his Web site, the clothing line is connected with his record label, Rich Soil Entertainment, whose "flagship artist" is the rapper Ali Vegas. "For years I've been seeing my young brothers wearing *Scarface* T-shirts, John Gotti T-shirts, Rick James T-shirts," Odom told Sam Alipour for ESPN Page 2 (on-line). "We don't have any icons or idols to look up to, just rappers and professional athletes. Before us, it was pimps and drug dealers. Remember when Jay-Z wore a Che Guevara T-shirt? Nobody knew who Che was. Then Jay-Z wears it, and it's everywhere. That's what I'm trying to do with this. My Man [Jesus] don't get his props and he's the biggest icon in the world."

On September 27, 2009 Odom married the reality-television personality Khloe Kardashian. The couple live in Los Angeles, California. Odom has a daughter, Destiny, and son, Lamar Jr., from his earlier relationship with Liza Morales.

—C.C.

Suggested Reading: *Los Angeles Times* D p2 Mar. 14, 2007; NBA Official Web site; (New York) *Daily News* Nov. 11, 1998; (New York) *Newsday* A p40 Mar. 13, 1999; *New York Times* p2+ Dec. 31, 2006, D p3 May 20, 2008; *Providence (Rhode Island) Journal-Bulletin* A p1 Mar. 13, 1999, p1 June 4, 2008; *Riverside (California) Press Enterprise* C p1+ Oct. 20, 2004, C p1 Apr. 20, 2008; *San Gabriel Valley (California) Tribune* Nov. 1, 2004; *Village Voice* p198 Feb. 22, 2000

Courtesy of the University of Pennsylvania

Offit, Paul A.

Mar. 27, 1951– Immunologist; pediatrician; writer; educator

Address: Children's Hospital of Philadelphia, 34th St. and Civic Center Blvd., Philadelphia, PA 19104

In recent years, in addition to many honors, the pediatrician, educator, author, and longtime biomedical researcher Paul A. Offit has received hate mail and death threats. He has drawn such attacks because of his leading role in a fierce controversy regarding the causes of autism. Offit is an outspoken advocate of immunization in early childhood against measles, diphtheria, polio, hepatitis B, and several other diseases, considering it to be crucial to maintaining the health of children; in journal articles, op-ed pieces, books, lectures, and media interviews, he has unequivocally rejected the claim that vaccinations in the early months and years of life have caused the apparent increase in the incidence of autism among American youngsters. In his latest book, *Autism's False Prophets: Bad Science, Risky Medicine, and the Search for a Cure* (2008), he argued that no credible evidence has been found to link immunization with autism. Most of those who have threatened or criticized Offit are parents of children diagnosed with autism who believe that Offit's close ties to the pharmaceutical industry (in particular, Merck & Co.), and the financial gains that he made from his co-discovery of a vaccine (RotaTeq, which protects against a virus that causes gastroenteritis), have led him to ignore or dismiss studies that show a cause-and-effect relationship between immunization and autism. "What I've learned in all this is to stick to the truth, talk about the science," Offit told Claudia Kalb for *Newsweek* (November 3, 2008). "It's not about me, it's about the data."

Offit has taught for three decades at the University of Pennsylvania School of Medicine (Penn Medicine), in Philadelphia, where he currently holds the titles of professor of pediatrics and Maurice R. Hilleman professor of vaccinology. (His book *Vaccinated: One Man's Quest to Defeat the World's Deadliest Diseases*, published in 2007, is about Hilleman, a pioneer in the development of vaccines that protect against measles; rubella, also called German measles; meningitis; pneumonia; hepatitis A and B; and other diseases.) At the Children's Hospital of Philadelphia (CHOP), Offit has served as the chief of the Division of Infectious Diseases since 1992 and director of the Vaccine Education Center since its founding, in 2000. Since 1987 he has also taught at the Wistar Institute of Anatomy and Biology, in Philadelphia. Offit's research, conducted between 1982 and 2005 at Wistar and CHOP, was funded by the National Institutes of Health, the World Health Organization, the Infectious Disease Society of America, Penn Medicine, CHOP, and several private companies, among them Merck, Pfizer Laboratories, and Pasteur-Merieux Serums & Vaccins. Offit closed his research lab in 2005 to concentrate on his writing and to run the Vaccine Education Center. The value of his work was recognized with the Lederle Young Investigator Award in Vaccine Development, in 1988, and the Jonas Salk Bronze Medal from the Association for Professionals in Infection Control and Epidemiology, in 2006, among many other honors.

The U.S. Centers for Disease Control and Prevention (CDC), the American Academy of Pediatrics (AAP), the Advisory Committee on Immunization Practices (ACIP), and the American Academy of Family Physicians (AAFP) recommend that between birth and the age of 18 months, children get a total of 20 inoculations, to protect against hepatitis B, diphtheria, tetanus, pertussis (whooping cough), influenza, polio, pneumonia, and gastroenteritis. All of the vaccines are given in a series of two or more doses at different ages; the hepatitis B vaccine, for example, is given at birth and at age one to two months, while the combined vaccine for diphtheria, tetanus, and pertussis is administered at ages two months, four months, and six months. Symptoms of autism—a neurological disorder that manifests itself within the first three years of life—often appear at around the time of one inoculation or another. (Symptoms include, but are not limited to, mild to severe difficulties in social interaction and language development; hypersensitivity or hyposensitivity to touch, light, and sound; repetitive behaviors such as hand flapping for hours on end; and ritualized activities such as insisting that different foods placed on a plate do not touch one another, and then eating each of the foods in an unchanging order.) Many parents of autistic children have come to the conclusion that if their children's symptoms appeared soon after vaccinations, the vaccinations must have caused the autism. A number of organizations—Vaccination Liberation, Vaccination Information & Choice Network, Safe Minds, and Generation Rescue—have worked to propagate that view. Contributing to their belief is that scientists have not identified a clear cause of autism. Evidence indicates that in some cases, there is a genetic component: in a pair of identical twins, whose genes are virtually the same, if one twin has autism, about nine times out of 10 the other twin is also autistic. Among nonidentical, or fraternal, twins, whose genes are not identical, the chances are less than one in 10 that if one twin is autistic, the other will be, too, as holds true among siblings in general. Scientists are also investigating whether chemicals in the environment can trigger autism. Experts disagree about whether the increase in autism in recent years is real or simply reflects changing ideas about what constitutes abnormal behavior: behavior that might have been considered eccentric or antisocial 10 or 20 years ago might now be classified as a symptom of autism. Moreover, physicians have widened the diagnosis of autism to include "autism-spectrum disorder," also called pervasive developmental disorder, which automatically increased the population so diagnosed.

The term "autism" was coined in 1943 by Leo Kanner, an American psychiatrist. The theory that autism results from inadequate mothering held sway for years; before it was thoroughly debunked, some women were vilified as "refrigerator mothers," for their supposed coldness toward their autistic children. In the scientific literature, the suggestion that a connection exists between vaccination and autism first appeared in the British medical journal *Lancet* (February 28, 1998), in a paper co-authored by the British gastroenterologist Andrew Wakefield and a dozen other researchers. The paper claimed that a genetic component (RNA) from the measles virus had been found in the intestines of 12 autistic children who began to suffer from a bowel disorder after inoculation with the measles/mumps/rubella (MMR) vaccine (which had been introduced in Great Britain in 1988). The publicity surrounding Wakefield's paper led to a precipitous drop in MMR vaccinations in Great Britain, with outbreaks of measles occurring in subsequent years. (Whereas 56 cases of measles were recorded in England and Wales in 1998, there were 1,348 in 2008, with two deaths.) In February 2004, in an editors' statement, the *Lancet* reported the discovery that while Wakefield had been conducting his research, he had also been "gathering information for lawyers representing parents who suspected their children had developed autism because of the vaccine," as Anahad O'Connor wrote for the *New York Times* (March 4, 2004)—a conflict of interest that he had not disclosed. Then, in its March 6, 2004 issue, the *Lancet* published a statement, signed by 10 of the co-authors of the February 28, 1998 paper, that repudiated its conclusion: "We wish to make it clear that in this paper no causal link was established between MMR vaccine and autism as the data were insufficient." In May 2004 the Institute of Medicine, an arm of the National Academy of Sciences in the U.S., reported that an extensive evaluation by a committee of experts of many scientific studies conducted worldwide had turned up "no convincing evidence that vaccines cause autism," as Sandra Blakeslee wrote for the *New York Times* (May 19, 2004). Blakeslee also reported that "in particular, no link was found" between autism and the MMR vaccine or vaccines containing the antifungal compound thimerosal, which is used as a preservative. (Some who have linked inoculations with autism have identified thimerosal as the causative agent.) In the February 9, 2009 issue of the London *Sunday Times*, Brian Deer reported that in an extensive investigation, he had found evidence that Wakefield had fabricated medical data and other information contained in his February 1998 *Lancet* paper. No researchers have ever succeeded in replicating the results of Wakefield's study.

In the 20th century the inoculation of all babies with the smallpox vaccine wiped out that disease in the U.S. (and nearly everywhere else on Earth). As health professionals universally agree, the benefits of inoculation overwhelmingly outweigh the minuscule risks associated with vaccines. (No vaccine is 100 percent risk-free. About one in every 600,000 people inoculated with the hepatitis B vaccine, for example, suffers a serious allergic reaction called anaphylaxis, but no deaths have been reported among them. By contrast, thousands of people, including children, die from hepatitis B infection every year.) As the Vaccine Education Center explains on its Web site, every year before the discovery and introduction of the other vaccines now in use, the polio virus would paralyze 10,000 youngsters; rubella in women in the first trimester of pregnancy would result in such birth defects as blindness, deafness, and malformed hearts as well as mental retardation in some 20,000 newborns. Measles killed about 3,000 of its four million juvenile victims, and diphtheria between 13,000 and 15,000. Thousands of other infants and children died of whooping cough, and influenza caused meningitis in 15,000 children, "leaving many with permanent brain damage." As Offit has pointed out, only the smallpox virus is believed to have been totally eradicated in the U.S. Viruses and bacteria that cause the other diseases preventable by vaccines still exist and may be brought into the U.S. by travelers as well. Nonvaccinated children are at risk for contracting those diseases and might then spread them to infants who have not yet been vaccinated or to children in whom the vaccines have lost their potency (many require booster shots) or are not 100 percent effective.

Offit has often warned that if parents of autistic children win court cases against pharmaceutical companies who produce and market vaccines, there will be little incentive for such firms to continue to conduct research into new or more-effective vaccines or to sell vaccines. That is what happened a half-century ago, as he explained in his book *The Cutter Incident: How America's First Polio Vaccine Led to Today's Growing Vaccine Crisis* (2005). In 1955, when more than 20 companies were manufacturing five vaccines, a polio vaccine made by Cutter Laboratories led to the paralysis of 56 children and the deaths of five others. In its manufacturing process, Cutter had followed safety measures required by the government rather than the protocols established by the vaccine's creator, Jonas Salk. For that reason it failed to detect a live strain of the polio virus present in the vaccine. Cutter was sued, and a jury found the company liable for the children's deaths, even though, according to the law, it had not acted negligently. The jury's decision, Offit told John Fischman for *USNews.com* (October 11, 2005), "meant vaccine makers could be sued for any harm. And juries who don't understand science, and who don't understand the difference between causality and coincidence, award giant sums of money. That scares companies away from making vaccines." For example, Offit told Fischman, "Group B strep infections—the leading bacterial killer of newborns—could be prevented with a vaccine for pregnant women. We have the technology to do it. But nobody is willing to risk lawsuits from women with babies born with unrelated birth defects." Moreover, as a result of the lawsuit against Cutter, Offit noted, there are now only four pharmaceutical companies manufacturing the vaccines recommended for children, and each of the necessary vaccines is produced by only one of those four—an inherently dangerous state of affairs, and one that has led to shortages of the flu and pneumonia vaccines in recent years.

In the U.S. since 1986, lawsuits involving vaccines have been tried in special courts set up by the federal government's National Vaccine Injury Compensation Program, which also established a vaccine-injury fund to compensate those determined in court to have been harmed by vaccines. In an op-ed piece for the *New York Times* (March 31, 2008) entitled "Inoculated Against Facts," Offit wrote, "If, at a trial in a special court, a preponderance of scientific evidence suggested that a vaccine caused [a disease or illness], a family would be compensated quickly, generously and fairly. . . . The system worked fine until a few years ago, when vaccine court judges turned their back on science by dropping preponderance of evidence as a standard. Now, petitioners need merely propose a biologically plausible mechanism by which a vaccine might cause harm—even if their explanation contradicts published studies." In a 2006 case, he wrote, Dorothy Werderitsch prevailed when she claimed that an inoculation with a hepatitis B vaccine had "triggered an autoimmune response in her brain that led to multiple sclerosis," although "two large studies had clearly shown that the hepatitis B vaccine could neither cause nor exacerbate multiple sclerosis." The victors in another case, in 2008, Jon and Terry Poling, maintained that five inoculations against nine diseases that their daughter, Hannah, had received at age 19 months had triggered the onset of autism. Hannah suffers from a mitochondrial disorder, which diminishes the ability of her cells to process nutrients; some of the symptoms of that disorder resemble those of autism. Researchers have shown that "multiple vaccines do not overwhelm or weaken the immune system," Offit wrote, and he quoted the neurologist Salvatore DiMauro, an expert on mitochondrial disorders, as saying that "there is no evidence" that children who suffer from them "are worsened by vaccines."

In his op-ed piece, Offit expressed his concern that the decision in the Poling case might lead more parents to refuse inoculations for their children, divert funding from research into causes and cures for autism to more studies on possible links between autism and vaccines, and weaken pharmaceutical companies' commitment to vaccine production. Offit's concerns were greatly lessened on February 13, 2009, when judges in three of the special courts set up by the federal program ruled in test cases (three among some 5,000 awaiting trial) that vaccines do not cause autism. One judge ruled that the MMR vaccine cannot be tied to autism, and a second ruled that thimerosal present in other vaccines (before the year 2000) did not cause the MMR vaccine (which never contained thimerosal) to trigger autism; the question of whether thimerosal in vaccines in earlier years can be linked to autism will be taken up in another trial. (Thimerosal has not been added to any vaccines except the influenza vaccine for more than a decade.) "This is a real victory for children and a great day for science," Offit declared, as quoted widely on the Internet immediately after the decisions were made public. "I hope that [the judge's] decision will finally put parents' fears to rest and that we can once again concentrate on protecting children from the resurgence of deadly vaccine-preventable diseases such as measles and whooping cough."

Paul Allan Offit was born on March 27, 1951 in Baltimore, Maryland. When he was five he underwent surgery to correct a clubfoot (a birth defect); he spent three weeks recovering in a hospital polio ward, an experience that affected him deeply. "It caused me to see children as very vulnerable and helpless and, I think, drove me through the 25 years of the development of the rotavirus vaccine," he told Kalb. Also highly influential in his choice of career were his readings in the history of epidemics and pandemics. On his Web site, paul-offit.com, he mentioned a form of influenza, dubbed the Spanish flu, that in 1918–19 took the lives of between 20 million and 40 million people worldwide (more than were killed during World War I), including about 675,000 in the U.S. Offit attended Tufts University, in Medford, Massachusetts, where he earned a B.S. degree in psychology in 1973. He then enrolled at the University of Maryland School of Medicine, in Baltimore, graduating with an M.D. degree in 1977. He completed his internship and residency in pediatrics at CHOP (1977–80). One night, as a senior resident on call, he tried in vain to save the life of a nine-month-old boy who had been admitted with symptoms of a gastrointestinal disorder that proved to be the result of a rotavirus infection. Until that tragedy he had been unaware of the potential deadliness of such viruses, which can cause fatal dehydration in a matter of hours. The baby's death triggered his thinking about the possibility of discovering a vaccine to prevent rotavirus infections.

From 1980 to 1982 Offit was a fellow in infectious diseases at CHOP. During that time, in a joint effort supported by CHOP and the Wistar Institute of Anatomy and Biology, an independent, nonprofit biomedical research facility in Philadelphia, he began working with H. Fred Clark, an immunologist who has a degree in veterinary medicine, and Stanley A. Plotkin, a pediatrician with expertise in virology and microbiology, whose vaccine against German measles had been licensed by the federal government in 1979. Their mission was to develop a vaccine against the rotavirus. In children, rotavirus gastroenteritis is the most common cause of diarrhea, which in turn causes dehydration; dehydration can lead to the depletion of electrolytes (among them sodium and potassium), which are vital for the proper functioning of cells and organs; if not stopped and reversed, dehydration can result in death. Rotavirus gastroenteritis looks somewhat like an orange stuck all over with cloves, but one that is only about 70 billionths of a meter in diameter; it was identified by means of an electron microscope in 1973. Researchers believe that nearly all children contract rotavirus infections at least once in their first five years. In the U.S. the virus is responsible for severe illness in several million children and the hospitalizations of roughly 60,000 of them every year; about three dozen of its juvenile victims die. In wide parts of developing countries, where clean drinking water and proper medical care are not available, the virus kills at least 600,000 children a year.

With Clark and Plotkin, Offit labored for about 25 years to develop an effective rotavirus vaccine. In a description of their research on the Penn Medicine Web site, Offit wrote that in the course of their work, they "studied the genetics of rotavirus virulence, rotavirus neutralization phenotype and protein-specificities of rotavirus-specific cytotoxic T lymphocytes as a prelude to making a bovine-human reassortant rotavirus vaccine." (The bovine-human reassortant rotavirus resulted from combining and manipulating rotaviruses involved in attacks of human gastroenteritis with rotaviruses connected to bovine gastroenteritis.) In the April 1995 issue of the *Pediatric Infectious Disease Journal*, Offit, Clark, and six of their colleagues reported that in a trial involving 325 babies that was supported by Merck and the NIH's National Institute of Allergy and Infectious Diseases, their vaccine had been highly effective in preventing illness from one strain of rotavirus. In 2006, after the completion of trials involving thousands of additional babies, the federal Food and Drug Administration (FDA) approved RotaTeq. The American Academy of Pediatrics and the U.S. Centers for Disease Control and Prevention recommend that babies get immunized with the rotavirus vaccine in three stages, at two months, four months, and six months. Since its introduction the rate of rotavirus infection among children in the U.S. has reportedly dropped by more than 50 percent. (A similar vaccine created by other researchers with a rhesus-monkey rotavirus, which had also received FDA approval, was withdrawn from the market by its manufacturer, Wyeth, in 1999, after 20 out of about one million babies inoculated with it suffered bowel obstructions or twisting of their intestines.)

Offit taught as a member of the Department of Pediatrics of the University of Pennsylvania School of Medicine from 1982 to 1985; concurrently, he engaged in research at the Wistar Institute. From 1985 to 1987 he was a research associate with the Department of Medical Microbiology of the Stanford University School of Medicine, in California, and in 1986–87 he was a clinical assistant professor with the Division of Pediatric Infectious Diseases there. He has taught and conducted research at Penn Medicine since 1987 and at Wistar since 1991. At CHOP, he has served as the chief of the Section of Infectious Diseases and the chairman of the Drug Use Evaluation Committee since 1992 and as chairman of the Therapeutic Standards Committee since 1994. Currently, he directs the Vaccine Education Center at CHOP, which produces educational materials for parents and health-care professionals, and co-directs CHOP's Rotavirus Vaccine Program. He teaches courses in pediatric infectious diseases; mechanisms of infection; microbiology; immunobiology; and immunotherapeutics (in which genes are manipulated to produce proteins that act like vaccines).

Offit's books *Vaccines: What Every Parent Should Know* and *Breaking the Antibiotic Habit: A Parent's Guide to Coughs, Colds, Ear Infections, and Sore Throats* were published in 1998 and 1999, respectively. His next volume, *The Vaccine Handbook: A Practical Guide for Clinicians* (2003), is for physicians. Fearing for his safety, he did not tour to promote *Autism's False Prophets*, which was published in September 2008. In the *Wall Street Journal* (September 23, 2008, on-line), Linda Seebach described the book as "an invaluable chronicle that relates some of the many ways in which the vulnerabilities of anxious parents have been exploited." "Opponents of vaccines have taken the autism story hostage," Offit said to McNeil. "They don't speak for all parents of autistic kids, they use fringe scientists and celebrities, they've set up cottage industries of false hope, and they're hurting kids. Parents pay out of their pockets for dangerous treatments, they take out second mortgages to buy hyperbaric oxygen chambers. It's just unconscionable."

In 2009, when U.S. health officials encouraged people to get vaccinated against the H1N1 flu virus, also known as the swine-flu virus, many expressed doubts about the safety of the vaccine. Offit attempted to allay these fears in an op-ed piece for the *New York Times* (October 11, 2009), in which he debunked myths about the vaccine, explaining that it was manufactured in the same way as seasonal flu vaccines and was similarly safe.

McNeil described Offit as "mild, funny and somewhat rumpled." Offit's wife, Bonnie L. Fass-Offit, is a pediatrician who practices privately and is an attending physician at CHOP. The couple live near Philadelphia with their two teenage children.

—W.D.

Suggested Reading: *New York Times* D p1+ Jan. 13, 2009, (on-line) Oct. 11, 2009; *Newsweek* p62+ Nov. 3, 2008; paul-offit.com; *Philadelphia Inquirer* (on-line) Sep. 17, 2008; *USNews* (on-line) Oct. 11, 2005; Vaccine Education Center Web site

Selected Books: *Vaccines: What Every Parent Should Know* (with Louis M. Bell), 1998; *Breaking the Antibiotic Habit: A Parent's Guide to Coughs, Colds, Ear Infections, and Sore Throats* (with Louis M. Bell and Bonnie Fass-Offit) 1999; *The Vaccine Handbook: A Practical Guide for Clinicians* (with Gary S. Marshall, Penelope H. Dennehy, and David P. Greenberg), 2003; *The Cutter Incident: How America's First Polio Vaccine Led to Today's Growing Vaccine Crisis*, 2005; *Vaccinated: One Man's Quest to Defeat the World's Deadliest Diseases*, 2007; *Autism's False Prophets: Bad Science, Risky Medicine, and the Search for a Cure*, 2008

Frederick M. Brown/Getty Images

Olbermann, Keith

Jan. 27, 1959– News anchor and commentator; sportscaster; writer

Address: MSNBC Cable LLC, 1 MSNBC Plaza, Secaucus, NJ 07094

"You need to make a newscast that looks like life," the news analyst and sportscaster Keith Olbermann told a reporter for CBS News (February 25, 2007, on-line). "Very serious, very angry, very stupid, very silly, very snarky—very much about pop culture." Olbermann began to work in broadcasting more than 30 years ago, when he gave play-by-play radio commentary during his high-school hockey team's games. Two years after his college graduation, when he made his debut on television, Stan Isaacs wrote for the *Washington Post* (June 14, 1981), "Young, bright, brash Olbermann stands out in an industry where so many of the sportscasters seem to be pale, inadequate copies of pale inadequate name announcers." Among many sports fans Olbermann is best remembered as the wisecracking co-host, from 1992 to 1997 with Dan Patrick, of the ESPN program *SportsCenter*. For the past six years, he has attracted much attention as the host of the TV show *Countdown with Keith Olbermann*, broadcast weeknights on MSNBC. For several months after the program's debut, in 2003, he presented straight news. Then, spurred by comments made by then–U.S. defense secretary Donald Rumsfeld about opponents to the war in Iraq—comments that struck him as highly offensive and antithetical to democratic principles—Olbermann began to include statements of opinion in each day's broadcast, often speaking with a vehemence rare among newscasters. Indeed, the deck of Mark Binelli's profile of him for *Rolling Stone* (March 8, 2007, on-line), entitled "The Most Honest Man in News," read "Keith Olbermann is mad as hell—and unlike Rush Limbaugh, he's not faking it"; the deck of a profile of him for the *New Yorker* (June 23, 2008), by Peter J. Boyer, entitled "One Angry Man," read "Is Keith Olbermann changing TV news?" "I'm not in a state of perpetual outrage," Olbermann told Mark Binelli. "But I don't think I've ever taken a position on the air that I didn't feel strongly about. What I do is not some kind of performance designed to create an image for myself, or to create false anger in people." Referring to the talk-show host Bill O'Reilly, he continued, "The difference between me and O'Reilly is, I will shout 'Fire!' in a crowded theater if there's a fire. I think Bill would shout 'Fire!' in a crowded theater to hear the sound of his own voice."

In "Keith Olbermann Unbound," an article for LarryFlynt.com (May 3, 2007), Danny Schechter rued the absence in "the hyper-commercialized, dumbed-down 'wasteland' of contemporary network TV news" of journalists of the stature of Edward R. Murrow; in the 1950s, Schechter explained, Murrow had "dared" to expose on CBS-TV the ruthless behavior of the Republican U.S. senator Joseph McCarthy of Wisconsin, who exploited Americans' fear of communism and accused various public figures in government and the arts of being members of the Communist Party. "Who among today's blow-dried anchors and reporters would have had the *cajones* to take on blustering blowhard McCarthy?" Schechter continued. He then declared, "One candidate has emerged from the media pack to reinvigorate the fourth estate," and he quoted the liberal radio host Stephanie Miller as saying, "Keith Olbermann is, quite simply, the Edward R. Murrow of our time"—an opinion disputed, not surprisingly, by many political conservatives and others.

Keith Olbermann was born in New York City on January 27, 1959 to Theodore Olbermann, an architect, and Marie Olbermann, a preschool teacher. He and his younger sister, Jenna, grew up in Hastings-on-Hudson, a town in Westchester County, which borders New York City. His father hated sports; his mother was a devoted New York Yankees fan, and she and Keith would often attend games together. Young Olbermann fell in love with the sport and began collecting baseball cards at the age of four; he is now considered an expert among collectors and is a consultant to Topps, a major manufacturer of baseball cards. He regularly listened to radio broadcasts of games at night and "became a fan of the announcers, as much as of the players," he told the CBS News reporter. When he watched televised games, he would turn the sound down and provide his own commentary. Olbermann also recorded the details of each game, noting the score, the number of pitches thrown per batter, and the weather. He was 14 when his first book, *The Major League Coaches: 1921–1973*, was published, by Card Memorabilia Associates.

In his book *The Worst Person in the World: And 202 Strong Contenders* (2006), Olbermann named "three of the great influences" of his "late childhood": the comedians and satirists George Carlin, Bob Elliott, and Ray Goulding. "Each," he wrote—"Carlin in his remarkable solo career and Bob & Ray in their nonpareil tandem work—was a social commentator." In 1974, with Bob and Ray's permission, the 15-year-old Olbermann visited the pair in their radio studio. Years later he heard a skit in which Bob & Ray talked about an "ominous" character named the W.P.I.T.W.—the Worst Person in the World—which later spawned the segment with that name in Olbermann's current show as well as the title of the book.

An extremely bright boy, Olbermann skipped first grade, entering second grade when he was five. Advised that he "might be better served by a private education," as Peter J. Boyer wrote for the *New Yorker* (June 23, 2008), his parents enrolled him at the Hackley School, a private college-preparatory school in Tarrytown, New York, a short distance from Hastings-on-Hudson. The school had its own radio station, where Olbermann learned about broadcasting firsthand. After he graduated from Hackley, at 16, he enrolled at Cornell University, in Ithaca, New York. He spent much of his time working at the college radio station, WVBR, becoming its manager at 18. After earning a B.S. degree in communication arts, in 1979, he got a job as a sports reporter for the United Press International (UPI) Radio Network in New York City. While with UPI he became known for counting the number of times athletes said "you know" during interviews. He next worked for two other radio stations, WNEW-AM (1980–83) and RKO Radio (1980–82); concurrently, in 1981, he served as a national sports anchor and reporter for CNN's New York bureau.

Three years later Olbermann became a reporter for the WCVB television station in Boston, Massachusetts. After six months the management ousted him, because they did not like his habit of poking fun at local sports teams. In his own defense, Olbermann told Steve Weinstein for the *Los Angeles Times* (January 22, 1989), "I suppose that if all you did was humor—people falling down, blood-and-guts cartoon video—then the sportscast would be a danger to the newscast. But as long as you cover the industry, report the scores and maintain a context of being journalistically sound, I don't think you have to be a full-time journalist. Sports is an aspect of life that is sometimes poignant, sometimes sad, sometimes inspiring and sometimes it's funny. For years growing up watching sportscasters read off the scores, I never saw that. Then I read Jim Bouton's *Ball Four* and it was a revelation. These were human beings, they weren't bubblegum cards. They were people who did stupid things and played pranks and spit on each other's birthday cakes."

Olbermann next moved to Los Angeles, California, where, from 1985 until 1991, he had jobs as a sports anchor and commentator for television and radio stations. Toward the end of that period, he held the title of sports director at KCBS. During that time Olbermann won 11 Golden Mike Awards, from the Radio and Television News Association of Southern California, for best sportscaster and best sportscast, and three Sportscaster of the Year Awards from the Associated Press–California. After some time, however, he grew unhappy with the atmosphere in Los Angeles. "My sports reports were perceived purely as an obstacle to getting more news about Madonna," Olbermann told a reporter for *Sports Illustrated* (December 21, 1992), referring to the celebrity singer. In 1992 he signed with ESPN and moved to Bristol, Connecticut, where the network had set up its headquarters. He became the weekend co-host of ESPN Sports Radio (1992–93) and the co-anchor and co-host (1992–97) of *SportsCenter ESPN*, a daily television-news show that within months of his arrival had become enormously popular among sports aficionados.

In the opinions of many critics and sports fans, Olbermann's reportage and commentary on *SportsCenter* with his co-host, Dan Patrick, reached the pinnacle of televised sports news. Olbermann, with his quick wit, and Patrick, with his wry humor, displayed exceptional chemistry as they mocked what struck them as ridiculous aspects of the sports world. Rudy Martzke, writing for *USA Today* (February 12, 2003), described Olbermann and Patrick as "the best cable news studio team in history." In *Sports Illustrated* (May 28, 2001), Chris Ballard declared that Olbermann and Patrick's reign as "tag-team partners" was "as good as sports news will ever be, an acerbic nightly ride through the backwoods of the box scores." Expressing the view that Olbermann and Patrick had "infused sports reporting with a late-night blend of Letterman-like loopiness and Koppel-esque smarts" (references to the talk-show host David Letterman and to Ted Koppel, then the anchor of the ABC program *Nightline*), *People* magazine included them on its 1996 list of the "40 Most Fascinating People on TV." In 1993 Olbermann was assigned to co-anchor a show on ESPN2, a channel geared toward a younger, hipper audience. His stint with the show, *SportsNight*, was short-lived, and the next year he returned to his co-hosting gig on *SportsCenter*. "I don't know nothin' 'bout sports, but even I picked up on Olbermann's variation on Lettermanesque sarcasm when he cohosted ESPN's *SportsCenter*," Ken Tucker wrote for *Entertainment Weekly* (October 17, 1997, on-line). "[Olbermann's] an agreeable odd duck, with the eyes and voice of [1950s and 60s television personality] Steve Allen but a wiseacre intelligence all his own."

Recalling his collaboration with Olbermann, Patrick told Binelli, "Keith had this knack for pissing people off. He pissed me off a lot. But at the end of the day, he'd make great TV. He could be upset about the littlest thing, or fighting management about something, but I think he worked better if he had a pebble in his shoe. I don't know if he sought out controversy or things that might bother him for that reason. But if he was agitated or uncomfortable, I always knew he'd be great."

Although Olbermann remained with *SportsCenter* for another three years, until 1997, he soon had reservations about his decision to resume his job there. "When you're actually on the air, and doing what you have sort of trained your entire career to do, obviously that part is exhilarating, but there were some drawbacks to it," he told the CBS News reporter. "One of them being, 'When are we going to talk about something besides sports?'" He also felt unhappy about working in Connecticut. In 1980 the six-foot-three Olbermann had hit his head while leaping into a subway car in New York City. The impact permanently impaired his equilibrium, and today, if he moves at speeds above 15 miles per hour, he loses his depth perception; for that reason he stopped driving. Although his condition had never been a problem in New York City, it became an inconvenient handicap in suburban Bristol. When he left ESPN, in 1997, Olbermann "didn't burn bridges here—he napalmed them," Mike Soltys, who was then the network's director of communications, told a *USA Today* reporter in 2001, as quoted on many Web sites.

Later in 1997 Olbermann signed with NBC to become a news anchor with MSNBC in Secaucus, New Jersey—a much shorter commute from Manhattan. *The Big Show with Keith Olbermann*, a weeknight news program devoted to events of the day and interviews with people deemed newsworthy, began airing on October 1, 1997. Olbermann also anchored for NBC Sports, hosting broadcasts of Major League Baseball's All-Star Game and the World Series and contributing to pregame coverage of the Super Bowl. In 1998 Olbermann became increasingly frustrated with the content of *The Big Show*, as it morphed into *White House in Crisis*—its new name—and began to focus solely on the scandal involving President Bill Clinton's sexual relationship with the former White House intern Monica Lewinsky. "I started missing sports," Olbermann told Steve Rushin for *Sports Illustrated* (November 23, 1998). "And I don't know why, because I very much wanted to get out of sports. Now I very much want to get back in. Last summer I would do five to six hours of research a week for a little 400-word column on baseball history in the back of *Sports Illustrated*. That probably should have been a hint." Olbermann voiced his dissatisfaction with his MSNBC show in the commencement address he delivered at Cornell University in 1998, in which he complained that its exhaustive coverage of the Clinton-Lewinsky story highlighted its lack of a "moral force." He also said, "While I'm having the dry heaves in the bathroom because my moral sensor is going off I'm so seduced by these ratings that I go along with them when they say do this not just one hour a night, but two." Those remarks, not surprisingly, displeased MSNBC executives. Olbermann's last show on MSNBC aired on December 4, 1998. Before the end of that year, he joined Fox Sports Net as an anchor and senior correspondent. (Fox Sports paid at least $1 million to buy out the two years remaining on his contract with MSNBC.) "I hope he's not insulted by this analogy, but I think Michael Jordan had to quit basketball to see that he loved it," Olbermann told Rushin.

At Fox Sports Net Olbermann taped 10 shows a week for the television program *National Sports Report*; he also wrote an Internet column, provided radio commentary, and hosted the TV show *Saturday Baseball*. His departure from Fox, in May 2001, reportedly stemmed from his failure to reach an agreement with the network on a new contract. Later, Fox's owner, Rupert Murdoch, told Peter J. Boyle for the *New Yorker* (June 23, 2008), "I fired [Olbermann]. He's crazy." Olbermann has since explained the events leading up to his leaving Fox. As he wrote in a May 29, 2008 e-mail message to the Media Bistro blog TVNewser, he had learned that Murdoch was thinking of selling the Los Angeles Dodgers baseball team in April 2001. After verifying the story, Olbermann decided to consult Murdoch's public-relations representative before reporting it on the air. "I said, in short, this is your candy store, if you don't want me to run this, I'm not running it, and I'm not leaking it, but at minimum you should know the story's out there. And the guy's answer was, thanks for thinking of us, here's our official denial, please report it and whatever your sources tell you, just please make clear that none of your sources are within the company." Olbermann explained parenthetically, "Baseball was, and is, extremely touchy about when a team is, or isn't, 'officially' for sale, and woe betide the owner who makes a deal before the 'officially' kicks in." "So I ran the Dodgers-Are-Unofficially-For-Sale story . . . ," he continued. "And two weeks later, the day before the annual Fox Baseball Meeting convened in L.A., my agent was suddenly notified 'he's no longer the host for baseball.' . . . A day or two later it was 'come in and clean out your office.' And a day or so after that I got a call from a friend who's a prominent [TV] sports beat writer, and he says, I'm hearing Rupert Murdoch just found out about your Dodgers story and personally ordered you fired."

Olbermann wrote for the on-line publication *Salon.com* for a year before MSNBC executives asked him to return. *Countdown with Keith Olbermann* began airing on March 31, 2003. On it Olbermann presents news items in ascending order, from what he considers to be the least important to the most important, or "biggest," news of the day. The media columnist Phil Rosenthal wrote for the *Chicago Sun-Times* (June 26, 2003), "*Countdown* flows from funny to poignant in connecting the seemingly random dots of a day's events, important and trivial, steadfastly clinging to basic tenets about what is and isn't news without being bound to traditional approaches. It informs but knows it must entertain to survive."

Originally intended to be a hard-news program, *Countdown with Keith Olbermann* changed significantly in August 2003, after Defense Secretary Donald Rumsfeld compared Americans who opposed the war in Iraq to appeasers of the German Nazi government during the 1930s. Olbermann was outraged not only about Rumsfeld's remark but about the failure of "constitutional-scholar conservatives" to declare Rumsfeld "a danger to the democracy. Not to the Democrats or Republicans but to the democracy," as he recalled to Stephen Rodrick for *New York* (April 16, 2007). "Then I thought, 'Oh, yeah, I have a newscast, don't I? I have editorial latitude, don't I?'" His next show, which aired on August 30, 2006, featured a six-minute segment—the first of his "Special Comments"—in which he lambasted Rumsfeld's comparison. Thereafter the show took on a liberal slant, with Olbermann regularly blasting the administration of President George W. Bush for what he considered its misdeeds. On his September 5, 2006 broadcast, for example, Olbermann responded to President Bush's claim that the terrorist leader Osama bin Laden was seeking to use the American media to turn the nation against its government: "Make no mistake here—the intent of that [claim] is to get us to confuse the psychotic scheming of an international terrorist with that familiar bogeyman of the right, the quote media unquote." On January 11, 2007, after President Bush had called for an increase in troops in Iraq, Olbermann called the idea "absurd" and said, "Mr. Bush, the question is no longer 'What are you thinking?' but rather 'Are you thinking at all?'. . . Our military, Mr. Bush, is already stretched so thin by this bogus adventure in Iraq that even a majority of serving personnel are willing to tell pollsters that they are dissatisfied with your prosecution of the war." In his "Worst Person in the World" segment, Olbermann often named the right-wing television host Bill O'Reilly, citing an O'Reilly quote that he regarded as false or outrageous. In turn, O'Reilly criticized Olbermann's bosses and even led a campaign against General Electric, the parent company of MSNBC. The constant bickering between the two hosts became so intense in 2009 that G.E.'s chairman, Jeffrey Immelt, and Rupert Murdoch, the CEO and chairman of FOX News's parent company, the News Corp., struck a deal that spring that appeared to put an end to the feud. A couple of months later, however, the two television hosts resumed their attacks. *Countdown*'s ratings have soared, arguably as a result of the ongoing feud, and it is MSNBC's most-watched show.

Though he has been called a liberal icon, Olbermann has maintained that he is critical of all politicians. "We in the media were guilty of assuming our government wouldn't lie to get us into war. We were largely exploited because we gave them the benefit of the doubt after 9/11 . . . ," he told Rodrick. "If the Democrats continue to drag their feet on what the country surely wants, which is non-escalation, I'll go after them in the same terms: 'Why are you not listening? Who do you think you answer to?'" The founder and editor in chief of the *Huffington Post*, Arianna Huffington, told Mark Binelli, "Keith's importance, to me, is as a truth teller. I think the way he's been represented—as leaning to the left or catering to the anti-Bush crowd—minimizes what he has done, which is to ignore the traditional journalistic view of the anchor as referee and stop pretending there are two sides to every issue. That's not how it is. Sometimes the truth is on one side." Stephen Spruiell, writing for the conservative publication *National Review* (November 6, 2006), rejected that view: "In the three and a half years since Olbermann took over as the host of *Countdown*, he has fully abandoned his stated goal of anchoring a sober news broadcast and become instead a shameless presenter of opinion as fact." Also among the show's detractors are those who dislike Olbermann's demeanor, which they view as smug. Others have charged that Olbermann selects guests who agree with him, thereby closing avenues of debate. The television critic Howard Rosenburg, for example, wrote for the *Los Angeles Times* (June 7, 2008), "Olbermann delights in mocking [Bill] O'Reilly. . . . But at least O'Reilly invites dissenters to his lair . . . whereas *Countdown* is more or less an echo chamber in which Olbermann and like-minded bobbleheads nod at each other." In February 2007 NBC extended through 2011 Olbermann's contract for *Countdown with Keith Olbermann*.

In his book *ESPN: The Uncensored History* (2002), the sportswriter Mike Freeman recounted instances of Olbermann's insensitive or hurtful behavior toward others at ESPN during the time he had co-hosted *SportsCenter*. Olbermann, who before he read Freeman's book had been unaware of how some of his colleagues had reacted to what he said or did, apologized in an article for *Salon.com* (November 18, 2002) called "Mea Culpa." In it he attributed his offensive actions or utterances to having "lived much of my life assuming much of the responsibility around me and developing a dread of being blamed for things going wrong. Moreover, deep down inside I've always believed that everybody around me was qualified and competent, and I wasn't, and that some day I'd be found out. If you think that way, when somebody messes up, you can't imagine that it just 'happened.' Since they're so much better than you are, how could they not complete a task successfully? They have to be not trying hard enough. . . . You suspend—no, let's be exact about this, *I* suspended—the whole human part of the equation. It never occurred to me that most of the problems were the result of mere *events*."

From 2005 to 2007 Olbermann provided sports commentary for ESPN Radio, working in New York City rather than Connecticut. He has served as the co-host of the NBC show *Football Night in America* since 2007. Olbermann has written articles for publications including the *New York Times, Playboy, Sports Illustrated,* and *Time.* With Dan Patrick, he wrote *The Big Show: Inside ESPN's SportsCenter* (1997); as sole author, he wrote *The Worst Person In the World: And 202 Strong Contenders* (2006), and *Truth and Consequences: Special Comments on the Bush Administration's War on American Values* (2007), a compilation of "Special Comments" from *Countdown.* Since April 2009 Olbermann has served as an at-large columnist for MLB Advanced Media (MLBAM), the interactive media and Internet company of Major League Baseball. Olbermann writes thrice-weekly columns on his "Baseball Nerd" blog, maintained by MLBAM, and has donated all of his MLBAM pay to charitable organizations.

Olbermann "has a long, sober face and trim hair that's going gray," Mark Binelli wrote in 2007. "With his glasses, he looks like a Fifties newsman—Clark Kent behind an anchor's desk—while his stentorian delivery can sound almost self-consciously retro, the sort of voice (of God or your high school principal) mocked nightly by Stephen Colbert." While having lunch with Binelli at a restaurant, he spoke "with a similar fastidiousness, never dropping his precise broadcasting-school enunciation." Olbermann lives in New York City with Katy Tur, his girlfriend since 2006.

—M.A.S.

Suggested Reading: *American Journalism Review* p42 Sep. 1997; *Los Angeles Times* E p1 June 7, 2008; msnbc.com; *New York* (on-line) Apr. 16, 2007; *New Yorker* p28 June 23, 2008; *People* p117 May 19, 1997; *Tampa (Florida) Tribune* Sports p1 Apr. 25, 2000

Selected Books: *The Major League Coaches: 1921-1973*, 1973; *The Big Show: Inside ESPN's SportsCenter* (with Dan Patrick), 1997; *The Worst Person in the World: And 202 Strong Contenders*, 2006; *Truth and Consequences: Special Comments on the Bush Administration's War on American Values*, 2007

Selected Television Shows: as host—*The Big Show with Keith Olbermann*, 1997–98; *The Keith Olbermann Evening News*, 2000–01; *Countdown with Keith Olbermann*, 2003–; as co-host—*SportsCenter ESPN*, 1992–97; *SportsNight*, 1993–94; *Football Night in America*, 2007–; as anchor—*National Sports Report*, 1999–2000

Oliver, Pam

Mar. 10, 1961– Sportscaster

Address: Fox Sports, 10201 W. Pico Blvd., Los Angeles, CA 90035

In the male-dominated field of broadcast sports journalism, Pam Oliver has distinguished herself as "uber-tough and not to be trifled with," according to a writer for *GQ* (September 2008)—and also as outstandingly professional and as having a vast knowledge and understanding of sports. In interviewing athletes and others, "you have to really work to find something beyond the obvious which means beyond what the play-by-play and the analyst would talk about," Oliver told Melody K. Hoffman for *Jet* (May 26, 2008). "That's your challenge. That's where your relationships with people come from. . . . I'm not comfortable if I haven't read almost every clip, every bio. That helps you when you're meeting someone for the first time." Oliver's career in broadcast journalism began 25 years ago, soon after she graduated from college. In 1992, after she had worked for eight years as a news reporter, her employer at that time, WTVT-TV, in Tampa, Florida, granted her wish to cover sports. The next year she was hired by ESPN; in 1995 she joined Fox Sports as a sideline reporter during National Football League (NFL) games. Commenting on the difficulty of landing a job as a broadcast journalist in New York, Los Angeles, or any other major media market, she told Gary Haber for the *Tampa Tribune*

Al Messerschmidt/Getty Images

(November 19, 2000), "You can have the plan of all plans, but it doesn't always work out that way. The minute I stopped looking down the road, things started to happen." She added, "It wasn't one of those things that happened overnight. It took a lot of hard work, patience, and diligence." Oliver has anchored Fox's *Southern Sports Report* and *South-*

ern Sports Tonight and contributed to the pregame show *Fox NFL Sunday* as a feature reporter. In 2005 she joined Turner Network Television (TNT) as a sideline reporter for its coverage of National Basketball Association (NBA) play-offs and finals. "She is a fearless interviewer," David Hill, the chairman and chief executive officer of Fox Sports, told Ernie Suggs for the *Tallahassee Democrat* (September 11, 2002). The quality that Hill called "fearless" has been labeled by others as "brash," "aggressive," and "uncompromising"—a characteristic that, whatever its name, has led Oliver to criticize teams and individual players on the air for insufficient effort and to engage in squabbles with some NFL superstars. Nevertheless, Hill said, "she has a way of making talent relax when they are talking to her. She has a wonderful way of putting people at ease." Ray Buchanan, a Fox Sports Radio broadcaster and retired NFL defensive back, one of several players-turned-broadcasters whom Oliver has mentored, told Ernie Suggs, "Pam is good at her job. She knows what she is talking about. She has helped to open a lot of doors and set a good example for females that want to get into sports journalism."

The youngest of the three daughters of John Oliver, a master sergeant in the U.S. Air Force, and Mary Oliver, a homemaker, Pamela Donielle Oliver was born on March 10, 1961 in Dallas, Texas. During her early years her family lived wherever her father was stationed—mostly in Dallas but also at locations in Florida, Michigan, California, and Washington State. On November 22, 1963, when she was two and a half, she drank some of her mother's hair dye, thinking that it was a milkshake. Her mother took her to the emergency room of Parkland Hospital, in Dallas, moments before President John F. Kennedy was brought there after being fatally shot. "I feel I have a connection" to that event, Oliver told Ray Buck for the Fort Worth, Texas, *Star-Telegram* (April 28, 2008). "I really think what happened that day somehow planted my desire to be in TV news." In one track meet held at the elementary school she attended, in the Arlington Park section of Dallas, she won three races. She often watched sports on television with her father, who had played football in college and as an air-force officer.

During her high-school years, Oliver's family moved to Niceville, Florida, a few miles from Eglin Air Force Base. She attended the predominantly white Niceville High School, where she lettered in basketball, tennis, and track. Unlike her sisters, who got married shortly after they completed high school, Oliver was determined to attend college. Thanks to her ability as a runner, she earned track scholarships from several colleges. While many of her classmates enrolled at Florida State University, she accepted a track scholarship from Florida Agricultural and Mechanical University (Florida A&M, also referred to as FAMU), a historically black college in Tallahassee, the state capital. "I needed a genuine black experience," she told Ernie Suggs. "I hadn't had the experience of being with black people." Most of the other students at Florida A&M had grown up in black communities, and Oliver's way of speaking and her worldview differed from theirs—so much so that she had difficulty relating to her classmates and feared that they did not accept her. With time she became adept in social situations on campus and comfortable with other students. A star on the school's track team, she was an All-American in the 400-meter and mile relay events. She set a school record in the 400-meter event (which still stood as of 2005), and her relay team helped bring home Florida A&M's first national track championship. As a journalism major Oliver honed her skills in writing and interviewing. In her senior year she qualified for the Olympic trials in track but gave up the sport at the end of the school year, because the demands of track had come to seem too onerous. "It all felt like a job," she told Suggs. "I was over it, because it was all-consuming." She earned a B.S. degree in broadcast journalism in 1984.

As a new college graduate, Oliver landed a 20-hour-a-week, unpaid internship at a Tallahassee television station, where she worked as a community-affairs reporter. She also worked part-time at the makeup counter at a local J. C. Penney store. She next was hired as a news reporter at WALB-TV, in Albany, Georgia, after hearing from a Florida A&M teacher about an opening there. Following her stint in Georgia, she worked successively at WAAY-TV, in Huntsville, Alabama; WIVB-TV, in Buffalo, New York; KHOU-TV, in Houston, Texas; and WTVT-TV, in Tampa. In total she spent eight years reporting on the news and serving as a news anchor, "but not by choice," she noted to Suggs; whenever she had expressed to higher-ups her desire to cover sporting events, she had been rebuffed. "I mainly assumed it was because I was a woman," she told Suggs. "But I eagerly took news jobs, and it was a really great experience." During her time as a news reporter and anchor, Oliver often worked nights and developed sports stories on her own on the side. In about 1992 she secured a transfer to the sports department of WTVT-TV—a move that some of her colleagues disparaged as a step down but which she regarded as "a natural extension of what I've always been interested in," she told Bill Fleischman for the Philadelphia *Daily News* (January 16, 2004). She also liked the predictability of her working hours as a sports reporter; unlike news reporting, sports journalism seldom involves unanticipated, sudden events that require being on the job far longer than usual. Oliver's good looks and broadcasting skills soon caught the attention of executives at ESPN, and in 1993 that national cable sports network hired her as a sportscaster. "They loved the fact that I had a news background," she told Suggs. "In news, you really are trained to cut through the bull crap. You know how to get the answers and avoid the clichés and crap. I covered a lot of politicians during my news days."

In 1995 Oliver left ESPN to offer sideline reporting during NFL games for Fox Sports. She currently serves as *Fox NFL Sunday*'s features and sideline reporter and contributes to both pregame and postgame shows. On game day she teams up with Fox's announcers Joe Buck and Troy Aikman, usually reporting from the sidelines during telecasts of New York Giants games. She has also covered the Super Bowl and served as an anchor for Fox's Atlanta-based shows *Southern Sports Report* and *Southern Sports Tonight*. In 2005 Oliver joined Turner Network Television (TNT) as a sideline reporter for the NBA. Now in her fourth season with TNT, she switches from the NFL to the NBA during the latter's play-offs and finals. One of only three female African-American sideline reporters who cover the NBA—the others are Lisa Salters and Cheryl Miller—she is known for her professionalism and class and for not drawing attention to herself. "You have to remember what you are there for," she told Suggs. "You have an audience that expects you to be a certain way. It is not a black-white thing. But where is it written that you can't have a good time? You can do both and be professional." Oliver reportedly prepares and writes all of her own scripts, which is highly unusual for a sportscaster of her stature. Her feature stories typically include subjects beyond the realms of football and basketball. According to Bill Fleischman, many NFL players have called Oliver their favorite interviewer, and some have asked their teams' public-relations directors to alert them ahead of time if she will be conducting interviews. "The players said that if they'd known Pam was coming in, they would have dolled themselves up a lot more," Ed Goren, the president of Fox Sports, told Fleischman.

Oliver has won the respect of NFL players and coaches, despite an aversion to sugarcoating that has sometimes led her to be unusually blunt. During a game between the New York Giants and the Green Bay Packers in September 2007, for example, she criticized the Giants' defense for lack of effort. Writing for the New York *Daily News* (September 18, 2007), Bob Raissman quoted her as saying, "I have not seen any kind of emotion, or any kind of leadership. Usually guys like Antonio Pierce, Michael Strahan are up trying to fire the guys up, but these guys have just been dead all day." "As Oliver spoke, Fox presented visual evidence . . . ," Raissman wrote. "Cameras panned the Giants' bench. Each and every member of the defensive unit wore a blank expression. They all looked lost. Oliver's 'dead' reference was kind. Those defensive faces had the look of quitters." Some have accused Oliver of casting them in a bad light. That happened in 2004, after Oliver reported during an October game between the Cowboys and the Green Bay Packers that the wide receiver Keyshawn Johnson had had a heated exchange with his team's assistant coach Sean Payton. On his weekly show, *Taking It to the House*, broadcast on Sirius Satellite Radio, Johnson accused Oliver of fabricating her account and said, "I almost wanted to get on a plane, find where she is at, and sit her down and spank her with a ruler really, really hard, because it makes no sense," as quoted on nbcsports.msnbc.com (November 2, 2004). According to many articles posted on the Internet, Oliver told a *Dallas Morning News* reporter, "My job is to report what I see. I do not make stories up. . . . Keyshawn is having a complete denial of reality." She also said that she would "punch him in the face" if he approached her with a ruler in his hand. Another much-publicized incident involving Oliver occurred in December 2007, when the Philadelphia Eagles quarterback Donovan McNabb denied controversial statements that Oliver had attributed to him during a pregame interview. According to Oliver, McNabb told her that he was unhappy on the team and believed his days with the Eagles were numbered. As reported by the *GQ* writer, Oliver responded to his denials by saying that her on-air remarks were "on-my-mother's-grave-accurate." She added, "McNabb questioned my integrity. As far as I'm concerned, I'm done with him."

Oliver has said that more often than not, female sports journalists are not considered the equals of their male counterparts simply because they are women, and that being a woman is a greater handicap than being an African-American. She told Michel Martin, who interviewed her for the National Public Radio program *News and Notes* (February 2, 2007), "For whatever reason, people still don't get it. It's just difficult for the guy next to you on the plane to process why you would be up to your eyeballs in all these football notes without you either being a wife [of a player] or cheerleader. So, I find it more maddening. . . . Comments that I get from people most often have to do with me being female. [They ask,] Do you really know; do people tell you what to say—I mean, those are insulting things. . . . I sort of laugh at it, but generally, I get mad about it, and so I would definitely say, from a female aspect, I get more interesting comments than as a black woman."

To maintain her body heat while reporting outdoors in subzero temperatures for hours at a stretch, Oliver wears a half-dozen layers of clothing over a layer of petroleum jelly. She has suffered from migraine headaches for many years; according to the Web site of the Black Women's Health Imperative, with which she is associated, she is working with that organization and as a representative of the pharmaceutical company GlaxoSmithKline "to educate black women about migraine." Oliver and her husband, Alvin Whitney, a freelance sports producer, live in Atlanta, Georgia. In 2004 she was honored with the Outstanding Woman in Journalism Award from *Ebony* magazine. A member of Florida A&M's Sports Hall of Fame, she returns to her alma mater periodically to serve as a journalist-in-residence.

—C.C.

Suggested Reading: (Fort Worth, Texas) *Star-Telegram* D p9 Apr. 28, 2008; *GQ* p292 Sep. 2008; *Jet* p53 May 26, 2008; (Philadelphia, Pennsylvania) *Daily News* E p40 Jan. 16, 2004; *Tallahassee (Florida) Democrat* C p1 Sep. 11, 2002; *Washington Post* A p1+ Jan. 31, 2009

Vince Bucci/Getty Images

O'Neill, Joseph

Feb. 23, 1964– Writer; lawyer

Address: c/o Pantheon Books, 1745 Broadway, New York, NY 10019

Joseph O'Neill, a lawyer turned writer, has received lavish praise for his novel *Netherland*, published by Pantheon Books in 2008. Set mostly in New York City in the aftermath of the September 11, 2001 terrorist attacks, *Netherland* is narrated by Hans van den Broek, a Dutch-born banker. His British wife, Rachel, returns to London with their young son after the attacks, leaving Hans alone and depressed. To cheer himself up, Hans joins a cricket team that consists mainly of immigrants from the West Indies. He soon forms a friendship with Chuck Ramkissoon, a Trinidadian whose great ambition is to build a cricket stadium on an abandoned airfield in Brooklyn. After Hans rejoins his family in London, he learns that Chuck's body has been found in a polluted city canal. "In recounting the story of Hans and Chuck, Mr. O'Neill . . . does a magical job of conjuring up the many New Yorks Hans gets to know," Michiko Kakutani wrote in her review for the *New York Times* (May 16, 2008). "He captures the city's myriad moods, its anomalous neighborhoods jostling up against one another, its cacophony and stillness, its strivers, seekers, scam artists and scoundrels. He takes us to Queens and Brooklyn, and gives us glimpses of the lives of immigrants from the West Indies, the Middle East, Africa and Russia. . . . Most memorably, he gives us New York as a place where the unlikeliest of people can become friends and change one another's lives, a place where immigrants like Chuck can nurture—and potentially lose—their dreams, and where others like Hans can find the promise of renewal." *Netherland* appeared on the *New York Times* list of the 10 best books of the year, and it was long-listed for the Man Booker Prize. In 2009 it won the PEN/Faulkner Award for fiction and the Kerry Group Irish Fiction Award. When David Leonhardt interviewed Barack Obama for the *New York Times* (April 28, 2009) and asked whether he was reading "anything good," the president "said he had become sick enough of briefing books to begin reading a novel in the evenings." That novel was *Netherland*.

A native of Ireland who was raised in the Netherlands and attended college in England, O'Neill spent a dozen years in Great Britain and the U.S. as a lawyer before devoting himself full-time, for seven years, to writing *Netherland*. He has lived in New York City since 1998 and, while retaining his Irish citizenship, became a naturalized U.S. citizen in 2007. His first two novels, *This Is the Life* and *The Breezes*, received scant notice. His third book, the nonfictional *Blood-Dark Track: A Family History*, about the imprisonment of his maternal and paternal grandfathers during World War II, was a *New York Times* Notable Book in 2002, and Caroline Walsh, the literary editor of the *Irish Times* (December 1, 2001), named it among her favorite books of the year.

The son of an Irish father and a Turkish mother, Joseph O'Neill was born in Cork, Republic of Ireland, on February 23, 1964. He has two sisters and one brother. During O'Neill's early years his father's job, as a builder of oil refineries, took the family to countries including Mozambique, South Africa, Iran, and Turkey. By the time O'Neill was six, the family had settled in the Netherlands, where he attended international schools. O'Neill spent the next 11 years in The Hague, the nation's third-largest city. At 17 he enrolled at Girton College, Cambridge University, in England, where he studied law. He decided against a literature major because, although he had always wanted to be a writer, he "did not wish to enter into a compulsory professionalized relationship with literature," as he told *Current Biography*, and felt that for him, writing could be no more than "hobbyistic."

Starting in 1987 O'Neill practiced law full-time in London. As a barrister, he worked in the Temple, part of the Inns of Court—centuries-old spaces for offices and courtrooms; he specialized in business law. In his spare time he wrote a novel, *This Is the Life*. Published in 1991, it is about a law student, James Jones, and his idolization of a famous international lawyer named Michael Donovan. After being mesmerized by what he views as Donovan's perfect life, Jones comes to realize that all is not as it seems. Calling the novel a "first-rate first effort," a *Publishers Weekly* (1991, on-line) reviewer wrote that "in terms of its plot and O'Neill's delicate treatment of its themes," *This Is the Life* was reminiscent of H. F. Saint's book *Memoirs of an Invisible Man*. O'Neill's novel struck the *Kirkus Reviews* (1991, on-line) critic as "witty and perceptive—but too drawn out, too carefully crafted, and too repetitive to really stun. Promise, but without pizazz." The editor who worked with him on *This Is the Life*, Sally Singer, became his wife in 1994. O'Neill's second novel, *The Breezes*, was published the next year. A dark comedy, the book follows a family as they deal with a series of misfortunes and tragedies.

O'Neill and his wife moved to New York City in 1998, after Singer, who had worked for the *London Review of Books* and *British Vogue*, accepted a job offer from American *Elle* magazine. The couple rented a suite at the famed Chelsea Hotel, in the Chelsea neighborhood of Manhattan. Their first son, Malachy, was born in 1999, the same year Singer began working for American *Vogue*. O'Neill continued to practice law.

Blood-Dark Track: A Family History was published in 2001. In that book O'Neill offered accounts of the lives of his Irish, paternal grandfather, James O'Neill, who died in 1974, and his Turkish, maternal grandfather, Joseph Dakad, who died before Joseph O'Neill's birth. Both men were imprisoned by the British during World War II—O'Neill in Ireland, for his membership in the Irish Republican Army, and Dakad in Palestine, on suspicion of being a spy for Germany. *Blood-Dark Track* received mainly favorable reviews, with most critics noting O'Neill's superior research abilities. "There is a sub-genre of historical writing . . . in which a family's life is transformed by the investigation of historical events in which earlier generations were implicated . . . ," Dina Rabinovitch wrote for the London *Independent* (February 15, 2001), in one of the few negative assessments of the book. "What's disappointing about [*Blood-Dark Track*] is the extent to which O'Neill's investigation fails to make any impact on his own life or on the lives of his living relatives. His research, while extensive, seems haphazard, and the style obscures the narrative. The stories lie inert across the generations." In the *New York Times* (February 17, 2002), Colin Harrison praised the book, writing, "*Blood-Dark Track* . . . is an enormously intelligent plunge into the World War II era that involves, among other elements, an unsolved 65-year-old murder, a rusted pistol, clandestine train travel and assignations in the dark. O'Neill . . . adeptly makes scene and character where otherwise there might be only chronology, but he also draws on his experience as a lawyer for insight into the Realpolitik of armies, embassies, prisons and families—or anywhere else men and power inevitably collide." *Blood-Dark Track* was long-listed for the BBC's Samuel Johnson Prize for Non-Fiction.

During that period O'Neill, struggling to reach a decision about his career path, consulted a psychologist. "So I went to see this guy, who knows all about life's forks, and I said, 'I have this really difficult problem. On the one hand, there's the bar, years of experience, my income and my family, maybe I should support my family. Then there's the writing . . . ,'" O'Neill recalled to Andrew Anthony for the London *Observer* (September 7, 2008). "He said, 'Yes I see that is a difficult problem. Tell me, what do you want to do?' I said, 'Well, of course I want to be a writer.' And he said: 'Well, there you are.' Nobody had authorised me [to become a full-time writer], because I was, and I am, a sort of conventional soul. I felt it was self-indulgent, but as [the psychologist] well understood . . . the price you pay for not doing what you want to do is incalculable." In 2001 O'Neill gave up his law career and dedicated himself to writing.

O'Neill knew that he wanted to write a story about cricket set in New York City. An avid batsman, he had played cricket as a teenager and as an undergraduate. After his move to New York, he had joined the Staten Island Cricket Club. After five years of writing, he began to despair of ever completing his book and considered giving up. But he pressed on and incorporated into his tale the events of the September 11, 2001 terrorist attacks. "After 9/11, the whole notion of writing about New York cricket, in which I knew there was a book somewhere, became fused with what had happened to New York City," he explained to Belinda McKeon for the *Irish Times* (June 7, 2008). "And the meaning of the cricket began to change until I began to see cricket as a kind of metaphor for that which is not seen by America. And obviously, that is part of the challenge that faces Americans now, the problem of the extent to which they are able to see the world and the world is able to see them, and the terms on which they are able to do that." O'Neill worked for another two years before he deemed his novel to be complete. His wife suggested the title *Netherland*, as an alternative to the author's tentative choice, "The Brooklyn Dream Game."

Dwight Garner wrote in his critique of *Netherland* for the *New York Times Book Review* (May 18, 2008), "O'Neill writes beautifully about what it sometimes felt like in the months after 9/11, when you couldn't attend a dinner party unless you were intellectually armed for hours of bitter debate." He then quoted a passage from the book: "For those under the age of 45 it seemed that world events had finally contrived a meaningful test of their capacity for conscientious political thought. Many of my acquaintances, I realized, had passed the last decade or two in a state of intellectual and psychic yearning for such a moment—or, if they hadn't, were able to quickly assemble an expert arguer's arsenal of thrusts and statistics and ripostes and gambits and examples and salient facts and rhetorical maneuvers. I, however, was almost completely caught out." On the subject of politics, O'Neill told Katie Bacon for the *Atlantic Monthly* (May 6, 2008, on-line), "It's very sad to say that, after having lived ten years in America, it increasingly dawns on you how politically undereducated people in this country are. It's a very dangerous thing, especially in combination with the power that the government has. I say this even though I've become anti-anti-American—one does when one starts to live here. . . . I really do feel that Hans's political limitations are reflective of limitations in American culture generally."

Many critics have noted similarities between *Netherland* and F. Scott Fitzgerald's classic novel *The Great Gatsby*, among them the authors' take on the American dream and the parallels between the ambitious dreamer Chuck Ramkissoon and Fitzgerald's Jay Gatsby. "It was unintentional. I was about three-quarters of the way through the book when I realised my plot was Gatsby's plot," O'Neill told Ed Caesar for the London *Sunday Times* (June 1, 2008). "But then there are only about three plots in the world, anyway. Now when I think about the relationship of *Netherland* to *Gatsby*—a book I love—I would say it's a farewell to *Gatsby*. Because the premise of *Gatsby* is that America is this exclusive, privileged land of opportunity. And that is not the case any more. In the globalised economy, the great narrative of the American dream has been dissipated." In his review of the book for the *New Yorker* (May 26, 2008), James Wood wrote, "The simplicity of the writing [in *Netherland*] and the choosing of a frozen racial emblem echo [those of works by] V. S. Naipaul, that Trinidadian Indian, and, if *Netherland* pays homage to *The Great Gatsby*, it is also in some kind of knowing relationship with [Naipaul's novel] *A House for Mr. Biswas*. These are large interlocutors, but *Netherland* has an ideological intricacy, a deep human wisdom, and prose grand enough to dare the comparison."

In July 2008 *Netherland* was long-listed for that year's Man Booker Prize, an annual literary prize awarded to the best full-length novel, written in the English language, by a citizen of either the British Commonwealth of Nations or Ireland. It was absent from the short list, which was announced the following September. Nevertheless, O'Neill felt grateful for the attention and praise he received. "All my [previous] books were out of print when *Netherland* was bought so I was practically dead and buried as a writer," he told Tom Leonard for the London *Daily Telegraph* (February 7, 2009). Thanks to the rave reviews he received from such prominent publications as the *New York Times* and the *New Yorker*, he said, "My life changed in the space of four days. It was amazing."

The film rights to *Netherland* are owned by Oprah Winfrey's company, Harpo Films. In October 2009 it was reported that the Oscar-winning director Sam Mendes planned to make an adaptation of the book for the silver screen. Mendes has asked the playwright Christopher Hampton, who adapted Ian McEwan's novel *Atonement* for the 2007 same-named film, to write the screenplay.

O'Neill has written literary and cultural criticism for publications including *New York* and, most frequently, the *Atlantic Monthly*. His wife is *Vogue*'s fashion news and features director. The couple's three sons, Malachy, Pascal, and Oscar, range in age from six to nine. Except for a few months in 2003, when they owned a home in Brooklyn, the O'Neills have lived in the Chelsea Hotel. An article about their living quarters and their affection for the Chelsea and its other inhabitants appeared in the *New York Times* (May 19, 2005). The O'Neills also own the studio in which O'Neill writes, in the Greenwich Village section of New York City.

—M.A.S.

Suggested Reading: *Atlantic Monthly* (on-line) May 6, 2008; (London) *Daily Telegraph* p15 Feb. 7, 2009; (London) *Observer* (on-line) Sep. 7, 2008; (London) *Times* p9 Oct. 11, 2008; *New York Times* F p9 May 19, 2005; *New Yorker* p80+ May 26, 2008

Selected Books: *This Is the Life*, 1991; *The Breezes*, 1995; *Blood-Dark Track: A Family History*, 2001; *Netherland*, 2008

Otis, Clarence Jr.

Apr. 11, 1956– Chairman and CEO of Darden Restaurants Inc.

Address: P.O. Box 593330, Orlando, FL 32859-3330

Many people who have never heard of Darden Restaurants Inc. have eaten at one or another of the company's 1,700 restaurants, which bear the names Red Lobster, Olive Garden, LongHorn Steakhouse, the Capital Grille, Bahama Breeze, and Seasons 52. Unlike fast-food outlets, the restaurants in those chains provide full service, complete with waiters or waitresses and menus with a wide variety of items. Clarence Otis Jr. is the chairman and chief executive officer (CEO) of Darden, which is headquartered in Orlando, Florida. In July 2008, in its annual report, Darden—a holding company whose subsidiaries operate its restaurants—described itself as the largest company-owned and -operated full-service restaurant business in the world. Darden and its founder, William H. "Bill" Darden, are acknowledged to be among the pioneers of what is known as casual dining. Otis arrived at Darden as treasurer in 1995, some 27 years after Bill Darden opened the first Red Lobster restaurant.

Courtesy of Darden Restaurants

Clarence Otis Jr.

Raised in a poor, high-crime area of Los Angeles, California, Otis earned undergraduate and law degrees with the help of scholarships. For 15 years beginning in 1980, he worked as a lawyer and then as an investment banker. When he rose to the top executive post at Darden, in 2004, only six other African-Americans headed Fortune 500 companies. In a brief essay for *BusinessWeek* (August 20, 2007), he wrote, "I always believed major companies had significant leverage and that they could make profound differences. So if you had the ability to shape the direction of a major company, then you could make a social difference." In an interview with Adam Bryant for the *New York Times* (June 7, 2009), Otis said, "Leaders really think about others first. They think about the people who are on the team, trying to help them get the job done. They think about the people who they're trying to do a job for. . . . You think last about 'what does this mean for me?'"

The oldest of the four children of Clarence Otis Sr. and his wife, the former Calanthus Hall, Clarence Otis Jr. was born on April 11, 1956 in Vicksburg, Mississippi. Along with two brothers and a sister, he was raised in Watts, a poor, black section of Los Angeles. His father was a janitor employed by the city. His mother, a homemaker, took an active role in the Otis children's education, volunteering at their schools, attending meetings of each school's parent-teacher association, and making sure her sons and daughter did their homework carefully. "Would Clarence have turned out as good as he did, a straight arrow, without his mother? I don't know. I doubt it," Felix Grossman, a lawyer who served as a recruiter for Williams College, and who met Otis as a teenager, conjectured to Sarah Hale Meitner for the *Orlando (Florida) Sentinel* (December 26, 2004). Around the time Otis started school, he developed a love for reading. He would go to the local library a few times a month and check out a big stack of books. By the time he started high school, he had read most of the biographies and novels in the library.

Otis also experienced the Watts riots of August 1965. The riots were triggered by a traffic arrest that inflamed years of growing animosity, fear, and rage that residents of Watts felt toward the virtually all-white police force; the fights, arson, and looting that continued for six days resulted in more than 30 deaths and 1,000 injuries, nearly 4,000 arrests, and the destruction of vehicles and hundreds of stores and other buildings. "I can still see the National Guard, with bayonets at the end of their rifles," Otis wrote in his *BusinessWeek* essay. Even on ordinary days Watts was plagued by gang activity, drug peddling, shootings, and other forms of violence as well as stop-and-frisk searches and other tension-filled encounters with police officers; as a teenager Otis himself was once "pulled over by the police, guns drawn, [and] told to get on the ground," he recalled for *BusinessWeek*. He always tried to avoid danger or potential trouble, however, and he became adept at dealing with many sorts of people. Thanks to his father he observed firsthand some of the radical differences between Watts and wealthy neighborhoods: on weekends Clarence Sr. would often take his wife and children for a drive to see the beautifully maintained houses, manicured yards, and clean sidewalks of Beverly Hills and experience the atmosphere of calm that prevailed there. "Those drives showed me how the other half lived," Otis told Bruce Horovitz for *USA Today* (November 27, 2006). "They made me believe another life was possible."

The summer before his senior year at the David Starr Jordan High School, in Watts, Otis fractured his hip. He spent the next few months bedbound in a body sling. Determined not to fall behind in his schoolwork, he studied, got tutoring, completed homework assignments, and took tests, and he graduated with his class, in 1973. He accepted a scholarship to Williams College, a private liberal-arts school in northeastern Massachusetts, where he concentrated in economics and political science. In his senior year Otis won the school's prize for political-science writing. He graduated magna cum laude with a B.A. degree in 1977; he was also elected to the honor society Phi Beta Kappa. By then he had developed an interest in law, and, again with the help of a scholarship, he enrolled at the Stanford Law School, in California. To cover his expenses he worked as a waiter. He earned a J.D. degree in 1980. He told Adam Bryant that what had prepared him "the most" for his career in management were his experiences as an actor in student plays in high school, college, and law school, "and even for a couple of years after law school," because in each production the cast had to function as a team: "I would say that probably is the starkest lesson in how reliant you are on others, because you're there in front of an audience. It's all live, and everybody's got to know their lines and know their cues and know their movement, and so you're totally dependent on people doing that."

After he graduated from Stanford, Otis moved to New York City, where for four years he practiced law, specializing in securities litigation and mergers and acquisitions. His first employer was the firm Donovan Leisure Newton & Irvine; the second was Gordon, Hurwitz, Butowsky, Weitzen, Shalov & Wein. Having found that he was more fascinated by finance than law, in about 1984 he joined the investment-banking firm Kidder, Peabody, & Co. (now defunct), where he served as a vice president. In 1987 he left that company to become a vice president at another investment firm, First Boston Corp., where his work involved real estate. In 1990 he changed jobs again, moving to Giebert Municipal Capital as a managing director; his focus there was public and government finance, which concerns the collection of taxes and uses of tax monies. Then, in 1991, he joined the Chemical Banking Corp. (now J.P. Morgan Chase & Co.), a holding company for Chemical Bank, first as a vice president and then as managing director of public finance. During his four years with Chemical, Otis contributed to "the turnaround of the company's struggling public-finance division," according to various sources, and he reinforced his reputation as an astute leader.

In 1995 a recruiter from Darden tapped Otis for a newly created job at the company—that of treasurer. During his interviews with Darden representatives, Otis wrote for *BusinessWeek*, "I felt, here's an organization that is pretty multidimensional compared to Wall Street. I liked the mass appeal of the brands, the fact that they really were pervasive. And you've got this broad employee base that was diverse in every respect, in an industry where folks can really go from entry level to the top. And it was an organization that was earnest. It had a humility that I was comfortable with." Earnestness and humility were said to be traits that characterized Bill Darden, who opened his first eatery in Georgia in 1938, when he was 19 years old. It was a tiny luncheonette called the Green Frog, whose motto was "Service with a hop." In subsequent years Darden became the owner or part-owner of 20 Howard Johnson's franchises and a seafood restaurant in Orlando, among other properties. The first Red Lobster opened in Lakeland, Florida, in January 1968. Darden insisted that no more than 10 minutes elapse between the time customers placed their orders and the time their food reached their tables, and on each table he left a card on which customers could assess the Red Lobster's service and food. Immediately, "the response was so overwhelming that even Darden and his investor partners had to work full shifts just to get the food out," Bill Carlino wrote for *Nation's Restaurant News* (February 1996).

In 1970, after two additional Red Lobster restaurants had opened and two more were under construction, the food giant General Mills bought the chain; as a General Mills employee, Darden supervised the chain and set up a Red Lobster headquarters in Orlando. Thanks to financing from General Mills, the business expanded enormously: within a decade some 260 Red Lobster restaurants were operating. The first Olive Garden restaurant opened in 1982. In a profile of Red Lobster for the *New York Times* (April 23, 1989) when the chain had 513 restaurants, Douglas C. McGill wrote that its success could be attributed to various factors, among them its emphasis on friendly, helpful service and comprehensive training of new waiters and waitresses; its frequent surveys of customers, awareness of trends, and rapid responses to changes in customers' preferences; a customized computer system that enabled management to keep track of every order in every restaurant and thus see which items were selling well or poorly; and a worldwide system for purchasing seafood from thousands of fishing operations, large and small. "We believe there is a science to running dinner-house restaurants," Joe R. Lee, then the president of General Mills restaurants, told McGill. "We believe there is a science to determining consumer needs, and a science to answering those needs, in a disciplined manner, on a massive scale." Lee, a protégé of Bill Darden, had begun his career with Darden Restaurants as the manager of the first Red Lobster restaurant. "Experts in the industry largely credit Mr. Lee with providing the vision that has guided Red Lobster's growth," McGill wrote.

When Bill Darden died, in 1994, there were 675 Red Lobsters and 458 Olive Gardens. That year General Mills began the process of divesting itself of Darden Restaurants; it was the anticipation that the company would become independent of General Mills that led to the creation of the treasurer post. Otis was present at the New York Stock Exchange when, on May 30, 1995, Darden became a publicly traded firm. Otis remained treasurer until, two years later, he was named senior vice president of investor relations. In 1998 he became senior vice president of finances, and in 1999 he was promoted to chief financial officer. Beginning in 2002, he took on the post of president of Smokey Bones Barbeque & Grill, a chain launched in 1999. In December 2004 Otis was appointed Darden's CEO. Otis succeeded Joe R. Lee, who had retired.

In his interview with Adam Bryant, Otis identified Lee as the person who "reinforced" the philosophies of management and service that have guided him at Darden. As an example of Lee's wisdom and humanity, Otis told Bryant that on September 11, 2001, after they learned about the terrorist attacks in New York City and Washington, D.C., "we had an all-employee meeting, and Joe started to talk. One of the first things he said was, 'We are trying to understand where all our people are who are traveling.' The second thing he said was: 'We've got a lot of Muslim teammates . . . who are going to be under a lot of stress during this period. And so, we need to make sure we're attentive to that.' And that was pretty powerful. Of all the things you could focus on that morning, he thought about the people who were on the road and then our Muslim colleagues." In speeches and interviews Otis has also cited curiosity—the desire to seek out truths that are not immediately obvious—as one the most essential characteristics of a leader.

In November 2005 Otis assumed the chairmanship of Darden Restaurants Inc., while remaining CEO. Noteworthy events since then include Darden's acquisition in 2007 of Rare Hospitality International, which owned the 288 restaurants in the LongHorn Steakhouse chain and the 29 restaurants in the Capital Grille chain. In the same year Darden sold the Smokey Bones chain. Despite the economic recession that began in the U.S. in December 2007, Darden as a whole has continued to prosper. In a report filed with the Securities and Exchange Commission in March 2009, the company reported that sales for the nine months that ended on February 22, 2009 totaled $5.24 billion, up from $4.80 billion during the corresponding nine months one year earlier. In a striking indication that Darden has fared better than many other firms during the current economic downturn, the company was ranked 374th on the 2009 Fortune 500 list of the nation's largest businesses, with annual sales of $6.747 billion and a profit of $377.2 million; on the 2008 Fortune 500 list, the company ranked 415th, with annual sales of $5.925 billion and a profit of $201.4 million. In mid-2009 Darden operated 1,773 restaurants. There were Darden restaurants in every state except Alaska; 35 were in Canada. In the year ending May 31, 2009, the chains served 380 million meals. Darden also owns one specialty restaurant: the Old Grist Mill Tavern, in Seekonk, Massachusetts, which has operated since 1745. According to Chuck Salter, writing for *Fast Company* (July 1, 2009), in its most recent fiscal year (which ended on May 31, 2009), Darden was the 29th-largest employer in the U.S., in terms of the number of people on its payrolls. (In 2009 the number totaled 180,000.)

Otis sits on the boards of directors of Verizon Communications, the apparel giant VF Corp., and nonprofit organizations including Enterprise Florida; he is a member of the Executive Leadership Council and a trustee of Williams College. He has been married since 1983 to Jacqueline Bradley, who has a master's degree in business from Columbia University; Bradley is a former vice chairperson of the Greater Orlando Aviation Authority, which manages Orlando International Airport, and is the secretary of the Florida Council on Arts and Culture. Otis and Bradley own one of the most extensive collections of African-American art in the U.S.; the couple are listed among the nation's 100 top collectors of art of any kind. The paperback book *Crossing the Line: African American Artists in the Jacqueline Bradley and Clarence Otis, Jr. Collection*, edited by E. Luanne McKinnon, was published by Rollins College in 2007; it contains introductions by both Otis and Bradley. The Otis-Bradley Fund provides grants through the Community Foundation, which seeks to address central Florida's most pressing needs. Otis and his wife have three children.

—D.K.

Suggested Reading: *Black Enterprise* p28 Nov. 2004, p114 Feb. 2005; *BusinessWeek* p54+ Aug. 20, 2007; *Fast Company* July 1, 2009; *New York Times* Business p2 June 7, 2009, (on-line) Feb. 10, 2007; *Orlando (Florida) Sentinel* A p1 Dec. 26, 2004; *USA Today* B p1 Nov. 27, 2006

Whitney Curtis/Getty Images

Palin, Sarah

Feb. 11, 1964– Former governor of Alaska (Republican); former vice-presidential candidate

Address: c/o Author Mail, Seventh Fl., HarperCollins Publishers, 10 E. 53d St., New York, NY 10022

Sarah Palin burst onto the national scene in late August 2008, when U.S. senator John McCain of Arizona chose her as his running mate for the 2008 presidential election, making her the first female Republican vice-presidential nominee in U.S. history. A newcomer to national politics, Palin had been governor of Alaska for less than one four-year term and was virtually unknown outside her home state. Calling her "the running mate who can best help me shake up Washington," McCain cited

Palin's moral character and record as a reformer as factors that led him to select her. By picking Palin, a woman and a social conservative, over more widely predicted choices, who included Senator Joseph Lieberman of Connecticut and former Massachusetts governor Mitt Romney, McCain also hoped to shore up support from the religious right wing of the Republican Party and possibly win over those female supporters of New York senator Hillary Clinton who were still disappointed over Clinton's loss to Barack Obama in the race for the Democratic presidential nomination. McCain accomplished only the former goal, as Palin's stances on such issues as abortion rights, gun control, and the environment were vastly different from Clinton's. On the campaign trail Palin electrified Republican crowds with her dynamic speaking style and "down-home" persona. Over the course of the campaign, however, she developed an uncomfortable relationship with the media. She granted few interviews, and those she gave—such as a three-part interview with the CBS News anchor Katie Couric—did little to reassure the public as to her readiness to take over the presidency; Christopher Beam wrote for Slate.com (September 25, 2005) that in those interviews Palin "looked like a high-schooler trying to B.S. her way through a book report." That perception persisted despite her better-than-expected performance in her vice-presidential debate with Senator Joe Biden. Additionally, she was accused of being overly harsh and divisive in her attacks against Obama and the Democratic Party. After McCain's defeat, many Republicans blamed Palin for the ticket's failure, and anonymous McCain staff members leaked to the media embarrassing reports about Palin, which she called "evil" and "mean-spirited," according to William Yardley and Michael Cooper, writing for the *New York Times* (November 8, 2008). In July 2009, two and a half years into her first term as governor of Alaska, Palin shocked conservatives and liberals alike when she announced her resignation. She cited the many ethics complaints filed against her since the presidential election as distractions that compromised her ability to govern. (All of the complaints were later dismissed.) Many observers have speculated that Palin is gearing up to run in the 2012 presidential election, a theory she has neither confirmed nor denied.

Born in Idaho and raised in Alaska, Palin has been highly opinionated and driven to succeed from a young age. In 1992, after graduating from the University of Idaho and working briefly in media, she began her political career with a successful run for a seat on the city council of Wasilla, Alaska. She served on the council until 1996, when she was elected mayor, following a campaign against the three-term incumbent, John Stein, in which she introduced issues such as abortion and gun rights into a race that had not traditionally involved such hot-button topics. Palin served two terms as mayor before campaigning successfully to become Alaska's first female governor, in 2006. Described by the then–Wasilla mayor, Dianne M. Keller, as "a P.T.A. mom who got involved," according to William Yardley, writing for the *New York Times* (August 30, 2008), Palin was known while in office for her ability to balance her responsibilities as a mother of five children with her political career. Many have also remarked upon her Teflon-like quality; she has emerged from several political scandals relatively unscathed.

Palin was born Sarah Louise Heath in Sandpoint, Idaho, on February 11, 1964, the third of four children. Her parents, Chuck and Sally Heath, both worked as public-school teachers. Before Palin's first birthday, her family moved to Skagway, Alaska, where her father continued teaching and her mother worked as a school secretary. The family moved several times within the state before settling in the Anchorage suburb of Wasilla, which at the time had a population of barely 400. Chuck Heath often took on extra jobs to make ends meet, working alternately as a hunting and fishing guide and bartender and, briefly, as an Alaska Railroad employee. The Palin family was passionate about exploring the outdoors, counting hiking, hunting, and fishing among their favorite pastimes (and, in the case of hunting and fishing, subsistence measures). "Dad never stopped lining up new adventures for us," Palin's brother, Chuck Jr., told Kaylene Johnson for her book *Sarah: How a Hockey Mom Turned Alaska's Political Establishment Upside Down* (2008). Palin reportedly shot a rabbit for the first time at age 10 and has continued to hunt game animals since then. "We could literally go hunting out our back door," Chuck Jr. told Johnson.

"The rest of the kids, I could force them to do something," Chuck Heath Sr. told Johnson. "But with Sarah, there was no way. From a young age she had a mind of her own. Once she made up her mind, she didn't change it." During her high-school basketball career, her aggressiveness on the court earned her the nickname "Sarah Barracuda." Not a standout player initially, Palin worked hard to improve at the sport; by her senior year she was co-captain of the varsity team and had a starting position as point guard, and she led her team to victory in the 1982 Alaska state championship. She was also head of her school's chapter of the Fellowship of Christian Athletes. "She was always a leader and led by example," her teammate Amy Backus told the Associated Press (October 8, 2008). "She always worked very hard, whether it was at practice or a game."

The Heath children had to be resourceful when it came to funding their college educations. In a successful effort to earn scholarship money, Palin entered and won the Miss Wasilla beauty pageant. Later, in 1984, she finished third in the Miss Alaska pageant, which also brought her scholarship money. Palin took a circuitous route to earning her college degree, studying at Hawaii Pacific University, North Idaho College, the University of Idaho, and Matanuska-Susitna College and changing her major several times before returning to the University of Idaho, where she graduated in 1987 with a B.A. degree in journalism and a minor in political science.

Following her graduation from college, Palin worked as a television sportscaster for KTUU and KTVA in Anchorage and also reported on sports for the *Mat-Su Valley Frontiersman*, which serves Anchorage and its suburbs. In 1992 she entered politics with a successful run for a seat on the city council of Wasilla. A suburb of Anchorage with about 5,000 residents at the time, Wasilla is known for political conservatism and a strong libertarian streak. She won two terms, serving until 1996, when she decided to run for mayor.

Palin ran against the three-term incumbent, John C. Stein, on a platform of reducing taxes and eliminating wasteful spending. Additionally, in a departure from the tone of past municipal elections, Palin injected social issues into the race, and the state Republican party made the unprecedented move of running advertisements on her behalf. "Sarah comes in with all this ideological stuff, and I was like, 'Whoa,'" Stein told William Yardley for the *New York Times* (September 3, 2008, on-line). "But that got her elected: abortion, gun rights, term limits and the religious born-again thing. I'm not a churchgoing guy, and that was another issue: 'We will have our first Christian mayor.' . . . The point was that she was a born-again Christian." Palin won the election with 617 votes to Stein's 413.

As mayor Palin oversaw the police force—which comprised 25 officers—and public-works projects, and she held the tie-breaking vote for decisions made by the six-member city council. In her first term she lowered property taxes, improved roads and sewers, and increased funds to the police department; she also blocked the construction of a new library and city hall and cut funds to the town's museum, whose staff resigned in protest. Although she was extremely popular with citizens, she drew criticism for seeking the resignations of Wasilla's top officials in what the *Anchorage Daily News* (November 26, 1996) called a "loyalty test," seen by some as an attempt to oust individuals hired by Stein. Many also complained about her ordering city officials not to talk to the press without first consulting the mayor's office. She defended her practices as an effort to find out who in the Wasilla government supported her and who did not. "Wasilla is moving forward in a positive direction," she told the *Anchorage Daily News*. "This is the time for the department heads to let me know if they plan to move forward or if it's time for a change." Palin forced the town's city planner and public-works director from their jobs and fired the police chief, who unsuccessfully filed a wrongful-termination suit. Speaking about Palin's first year as mayor, Victoria Naegele, then the managing editor of the *Frontiersman*, told William Yardley for the *New York Times* (September 3, 2008, on-line), "It was just things you don't ever associate with a small town. It was like we were warped into real politics instead of just 'Do you like Joe or Mary for the job?'" Another controversy occurred when Wasilla's librarian, Mary Ellen Emmons, accused Palin of pressuring her to remove books Palin deemed inappropriate from the library. Emmons told Rindo White for the *Anchorage Daily News* (September 4, 2008) that Palin asked her on several occasions if she would be amenable to removing books if the need should arise, and Emmons responded negatively. Several months later Palin attempted to fire Emmons for reasons she claimed were unrelated to the book-purging issue, but popular community support for Emmons kept her from following through with the firing.

In Palin's reelection bid, in 1999, she again defeated Stein, 826 votes to 255. In her second term as mayor, her main area of focus was the construction of the Wasilla Multi-Use Sports Complex, a $14.7 million project funded by a .5 percent sales-tax increase. The complex was built on time and within budget and became popular with the town's citizens. However, an as-yet-unresolved lawsuit concerning ownership of the site has cost the city an additional $1.3 million because Palin did not obtain proper titles to the land before construction began. In her second term she also won a grant to build a police-dispatch center, increased spending on street and water-system improvements, and joined with nearby towns in hiring a lobbying firm to obtain more federal funds for Wasilla. Palin's tenure as mayor was limited by law to two terms.

After leaving office, Palin sought the Republican nomination for lieutenant governor of Alaska, losing by fewer than 2,000 votes in a campaign that greatly increased her name recognition in the state. The newly elected Republican governor, Frank Murkowski, subsequently appointed her to the Alaska Oil and Gas Conservation Commission. She became the commission's chair in 2003 as well as its ethics supervisor. She resigned in January 2004, frustrated over ethics violations on the part of another member of the commission, Randy Ruedrich, who was also the head of Alaska's Republican Party. The investigation into his actions became public shortly thereafter, and Palin filed a formal complaint against him. He paid the state a $12,000 civil fine, admitted to wrongdoing, and resigned from his job. Those developments helped earn Palin a reputation as a reformer, which she used to her advantage in her 2006 bid for governor. She ran on an anti-corruption platform, painting the incumbent, Murkowski, as a "good ol' boy" out of touch with voters. She also exhibited a great deal of charisma, giving spirited speeches, and her growing young family and telegenic looks were factors in her favor. Opponents accused her of getting by on likability alone. "She wouldn't have articulated one coherent policy and people would just be fawning all over her . . . ," Andrew Halcro, a Republican who ran against her for governor, told Yardley (August 30, 2008). "It was, like, this isn't about policy or Alaska issues, this is about people's most basic instincts: 'I like you, and you make me feel good.'"

Palin defeated Murkowski in the Republican primary and went on to beat the Democratic candidate, Tony Knowles, in the general election, becoming the state's first female governor—and, at 42, the youngest governor in Alaska's history.

As governor, Palin put much focus on mining Alaska's natural resources. To that end she introduced Alaska's Gasline Inducement Act, aimed at the construction of a pipeline connecting natural-gas reserves in northern Alaska to the lower 48 states as well as Canada. The bill passed in the state legislature on May 11, 2008. Despite her popularity, environmental advocates have criticized Palin for her stances on measures designed to protect the state's wildlife. In the belief that they would hurt business, she has opposed measures that would protect endangered animals including salmon, polar bears, wolves, and beluga whales. Perhaps her most controversial position has been that in favor of drilling for oil and gas in the Arctic National Wildlife Refuge. "We are ready for that gas to be tapped so we can fill a natural gas pipeline," Palin said in her State of the State Address in January 2007, as quoted by ontheissues.org. "I promise to vigorously defend Alaska's rights, as resource owners, to develop and receive appropriate value for our resources." That stance pleased oil and gas companies, as Palin placed few restrictions on where they could drill. The companies were less pleased, however, when Palin increased taxes on gas profits from 22.5 percent to 25 percent after a spike in gas prices. The tax increase generated an estimated $6 billion in additional revenue for the state, some of it given to citizens to help compensate them for some of the highest gas prices in the nation. (Each year every person who has lived in Alaska for at least 12 months—including children—receives a dividend from the Alaska Permanent Fund, which profits from investments of proceeds from sales of petroleum and other minerals. The amount of the dividend is usually about $1,000. In 2008 it was $3,269.)

In the summer of 2008, Palin found herself at the center of a controversy referred to in the media as "troopergate." In July 2008 Palin fired Alaska's commissioner of public safety, Walt Monegan, stating several reasons, including her contention that he "did not turn out to be a team player on budgeting issues," as quoted by Sean Cockerham for the *Anchorage Daily News* (August 14, 2008, on-line). Monegan then accused Palin and her husband of having previously and unsuccessfully put pressure on him to fire the Alaska state trooper Mike Wooten, who was recently divorced from one of Palin's sisters and engaged in a bitter child-custody battle with her; Wooten was alleged to have threatened the Palin family prior to Sarah Palin's election as governor. Alaska legislators appointed Stephen Branchflower, an independent investigator, to look into the case.

The "troopergate" investigation was still underway in late August 2008, when the presumptive Republican presidential nominee, John McCain, announced Palin as his choice for a running mate. Though Branchflower released a report in October stating that Palin had violated the Alaska Executive Branch Ethics Act, the McCain campaign was more or less successful at sidestepping the issue. "Palin has a way of transcending the obstacles that come her way, gently bypassing possible scandals with apparent ease and little damage to her sky-high approval ratings in Alaska," David Gargill wrote for the British newspaper the *National* (October 3, 2008, on-line). "Troopergate' . . . would likely have felled a lesser personality, but Palin seems to have evaded censure, particularly now that the McCain campaign has devoted its substantial resources to quashing the investigation." The news that Palin's teenage daughter Bristol had conceived a child out of wedlock, which became public knowledge shortly after Palin was announced as McCain's running mate, had a similarly negligible effect on the campaign.

According to Jill Hazelbacker, a spokeswoman for the McCain campaign, McCain had first met Palin at the National Governors Association meeting in Washington, D.C., in February 2008 and had come away "extraordinarily impressed," as reported by the *Wall Street Journal* (August 29, 2008). In August he invited her for a meeting with him in Arizona, at the end of which he offered her the spot on the ticket. "She's exactly who this country needs to help me fight the same old Washington politics of me first and country second," McCain said, according to *CNN* (August 30, 2008, on-line). "She's got the grit, integrity, good sense and fierce devotion to the common good that is exactly what we need in Washington today."

Palin's acceptance speech at the Republican National Convention set the tone for her vice-presidential campaign. In folksy language she painted herself as a reformer and Washington outsider whose small-town ways and commitment to her family (she repeatedly referred to herself as a "hockey mom") reflected the values of the majority of Americans. As quoted on CNN, she spoke of her husband, Todd Palin, affectionately referred to in Alaska as the "first dude": "He's a lifelong commercial fisherman and a production operator in the oil fields of Alaska's North Slope, and a proud member of the United Steel Workers' Union. And Todd is a world champion snow machine racer. . . . We met in high school. And two decades and five children later, he's still my guy." She referred to her five children, Track, Bristol, Willow, Piper, and Trig, noting the fact that her older son, Track, was about to be deployed to serve in the Iraq war and that her younger son, Trig, born in April 2008, has special needs. "To the families of special-needs children all across this country . . . ," she said, "I pledge to you that, if we're elected, you will have a friend and advocate in the White House." In the speech Palin also began her harsh attacks on the Democratic nominee, then–U.S. senator Barack Obama of Illinois. Referring to Obama's background as a community organizer and to her tenure as Wasilla's mayor, she said, "I guess a small-town mayor is sort of like a community organizer, except that you have actual responsibilities."

In the following weeks Palin proved to be a polarizing figure. Her status as a born-again Christian and her strong stances against abortion, same-sex marriage, gun control, and environmental protection earned her praise from the religious right wing of the Republican Party, which had previously been lukewarm toward McCain, but it alarmed many Independents and moderate Republicans, whose votes McCain would need in order to win the election. Despite her claim to be a successor to Hillary Clinton—the first woman to run a viable candidacy for the U.S. presidency—by virtue of her vice-presidential run, Palin fared much worse with female voters than with their male counterparts, and the National Organization for Women endorsed Obama, making it clear that being a woman was not enough to gain their support. Many viewed her selection as a cynical ploy to garner the votes of women disappointed in Clinton's loss to Obama in the contest for the Democratic nomination.

In addition to criticism from feminists, Palin weathered many other political attacks during the campaign. Though Obama rarely criticized her directly, others took her to task for making misleading statements about her record as a crusader against "pork barrel" spending. The best-known of those statements was her claim to have killed an expensive and wasteful bridge-construction project in Alaska. "I told the Congress, 'thanks but no thanks on that bridge to nowhere,'" she repeated in speeches across the country. Echoing others, Howard Kurtz, writing for the *Washington Post* (September 8, 2008), called Palin's boast a "whopper." "She endorsed the remote project while running for governor in 2006, claimed to be an opponent only after Congress killed its funding the next year, and has used the $223 million provided for it for other state ventures," Kurtz wrote. "Far from being an opponent of earmarks, Palin hired lobbyists to try to capture more federal funding."

The "bridge-to-nowhere" controversy was only the beginning of Palin's troubled relationship with the media. Journalists criticized the McCain campaign for sheltering her from questions and Palin herself for granting few interviews; meanwhile, the campaign criticized the media for what they saw as unfair coverage of topics that should be off-limits, such as Bristol Palin's pregnancy. The interviews Palin gave tended to go badly; in a three-part segment with Katie Couric of CBS, for example, the governor appeared not fully informed and unprepared and often spoke in rambling, confusing sentences. As time wore on, even some conservatives questioned her readiness to step into the presidency if the then-72-year-old McCain should die or become incapacitated while serving as president. Some even called on Palin to step down. "I think she has pretty thoroughly—and probably irretrievably—proven that she is not up to the job of being president of the United States," David Frum, a conservative columnist and former speechwriter for President George W. Bush, told Adam Nagourney for the *New York Times* (September 30, 2008). Palin was an easy target for satire, with the comic actress Tina Fey appearing on *Saturday Night Live* to perform dead-on parodies of her, sometimes repeating the governor's words verbatim. In an effort to beef up Palin's foreign-policy credentials, McCain had her meet with several foreign leaders at the United Nations, and over the course of the campaign she was coached extensively on international relations. (Palin first obtained a passport, and traveled outside North America, in 2007.)

Many predicted that Palin would perform poorly in her vice-presidential debate with the six-term U.S. senator Joe Biden of Delaware. In the event, she engaged in spirited exchanges with Biden, making statements that sometimes meandered off-track but contained few glaring mistakes. Patrick Healy, writing for the *New York Times* (October 2, 2008), noted her "folksy manner" and "carefully scripted talking points" and concluded that she had "exceeded expectations." "She succeeded by not failing in any obvious way," he wrote. Many felt that Biden had done a better job of discussing policy, and journalists and bloggers were quick to point out mistakes Palin had made, such as referring to the top U.S. commander in Afghanistan, General David D. McKiernan, as "General McClellan." Many also noted that she failed to answer some questions completely. "Ms. Palin . . . tended to seize on a single point or phrase of Mr. Biden or the moderator, Gwen Ifill of PBS, and veer off on her own direction in her 90-second answer," Healy wrote. "Asked whether the poor economy would cause Mr. McCain to cut his spending plans, Ms. Palin picked up on Mr. Biden's discussion of energy to criticize Mr. Obama's positions on energy and talk about her fights against oil companies in Alaska."

As Election Day neared, Palin grew increasingly vicious in her attacks on Obama, famously accusing him of "palling around with terrorists," a reference to his acquaintance with William Ayers; a member of the Weather Underground, a radical antiwar group, in the early 1970s, Ayers was indicted for conspiracy to bomb government buildings. (Obama worked with Ayers, who is now a professor of education, on several panels on education reform in Chicago, Illinois, in the 1990s.) While the charges did little political damage to Obama, they contributed to a growing sense that McCain and Palin were running a campaign based mainly on negative attacks. Palin was also criticized for making little attempt to control the behavior of her supporters at rallies, some of whom shouted threats against Obama or displayed racist symbols. (Obama was the first African-American major-party presidential nominee in U.S. history.) Palin defended her negative tactics at a rally in Carson, California, saying, as reported by Nicholas Johnston for the Bloomberg News Service (October 6, 2008), "There does come a time when you have to take the gloves off and that time is right now."

Obama won the presidential election on November 4, 2008, with 365 electoral votes to McCain's 173. As McCain took the stage to make his concession speech, Palin, standing nearby, was visibly emotional. Pundits began post-election analysis immediately, with many Republicans pointing fingers at Palin for bringing down the campaign. One widely cited misstep was the decision to spend $150,000 from the Republican National Committee on clothing, shoes, and accessories for public appearances by Palin and her family, which was at odds with Palin's efforts to portray herself as a small-town "everywoman." Also following the election, anonymous McCain campaign aides passed on to the press unflattering reports about Palin, including claims that she was often ill-tempered and unwilling to prepare for interviews; that she believed Africa to be a country, not a continent comprising many nations; and that she could not name the countries participating in NAFTA, the North American Free Trade Agreement. Palin addressed those claims upon returning to Alaska, saying that the aides had lied and taken her words out of context. "It's mean-spirited, it's immature, it's unprofessional, and those guys are jerks," she said, as quoted by William Yardley and Michael Cooper.

Palin received a hero's welcome upon her return to Alaska. According to Michael Cooper and Liz Robbins, writing for the *New York Times* (November 13, 2008), she downplayed her own celebrity and ambitions while addressing the Republican Governors Association meeting, held in Miami, Florida, in November 2008, about the future of the party. "We are the minority party. Let us resolve not to be the negative party," she said. "Let us build our case with actions, not just with words." On January 27, 2009 Palin launched a political action committee, SarahPAC, to raise money for Republican candidates who share her beliefs and goals. SarahPAC raised more than $730,000 during its first five months of operation.

When Palin resumed her gubernatorial duties, she faced a deficit in the state budget, caused by a significant drop in the price of petroleum. (The 2009 dividend for Alaskan citizens was only $1,305 per person, less than half of the amount they received the year before.) In February 2009 Alaskan officials found that Palin owed back taxes on nearly $18,000 in expenses she had charged the state for living in her home outside Anchorage instead of the governor's house in the state capital. Palin agreed to pay the taxes, as well as $7,000 to reimburse the state for trips taken by her children. In the months following her return, Palin introduced little legislation—12 bills, only one of which became law. In addition, her nomination for state attorney general in April was rejected. Alaskan officials have said that many state legislators had become disenchanted with Palin during the 2008 presidential campaign. In an interview with Jay Newton-Small for *Time* (July 6, 2009, on-line), Alaska state representative Harry Crawford, a Democrat, recalled that Palin had been much more bipartisan back in 2006, working with Democrats on such issues as ethics reform and on legislation that prevented oil companies from profiting at the expense of ordinary Alaskans. "With Sarah, we [Alaskan Democrats] were able to do things that we'd been trying to do for 25 years. Everything she can point to in terms of achievements was done with nearly uniform Democrat[ic] votes and just a smattering of Republican votes," Crawford said. Palin's performance during the 2008 presidential campaign, most notably her inflammatory charges against Obama, alienated her Democratic allies in Alaska. Her approval ratings among Alaskans dropped, to percentages in the mid-50s, and various groups lodged a total of 15 ethics complaints against her. (Though Palin was later exonerated in all cases, she was obligated by Alaskan law to use her own money to defend herself; the inquiries resulted in more than $500,000 in legal fees for her.)

Moreover, the governor had become fodder for tabloids after Levi Johnston, the 18-year-old father of Bristol Palin's son, Tripp Easton Mitchell Johnston (born on December 27, 2008), began speaking to the press. He discussed his strained relationship with the Palin family since his split from Bristol, in March 2009. (During the presidential campaign Johnston and Bristol had repeatedly said that they were planning to marry.) Johnston, claiming to have been prevented often from seeing his son, has charged that Palin wanted to adopt her daughter's baby in an effort to hide Bristol's pregnancy; that Palin and her husband have discussed divorce; and that Palin has been largely absent from her children's lives. Palin has dismissed Johnston's allegations as "mean spirited, malicious and untrue."

On July 3, 2009, stunning both her critics and her supporters, Palin announced that she would resign the governorship by the end of the month. In a speech that she gave outside her home in Wasilla, Palin said, "As I thought about this announcement that I wouldn't run for re-election and what it means for Alaska, I thought about how much fun some governors have as lame ducks. . . . And then I thought—that's what's wrong—many just accept that lame duck status, hit the road, draw the paycheck, and 'milk it.' I'm not putting Alaska through that—I promised efficiencies and effectiveness. That's not how I am wired. I am not wired to operate under the same old 'politics as usual.'" The announcement confounded members of the media, who wondered what her true motivation had been and suggested that her decision could mark either her exit from politics or the start of a campaign for the White House in 2012. State officials have said that the ethics investigations had hampered her ability to do her job and played a major role in her decision to quit. Palin chose Lieutenant Governor Sean Parnell to finish out her term; he was sworn in as governor on July 26.

Palin recently signed with the Washington Speakers Bureau and has received hundreds of speaking invitations. She has also finished writing (with the help of a ghostwriter, Lynn Vincent) a memoir, *Going Rogue: An American Life*. Palin received a $1.25 million advance for the book from HarperCollins, which was scheduled to publish it on November 17, 2009.

—J.E.P.

Suggested Reading: *New York Times* (on-line) Sep. 2, 2008, Nov. 7, 2008, Aug. 30, 2008; *Salon.com* Sep. 11, 2008; Johnson, Kaylene. *Sarah: How a Hockey Mom Turned Alaska's Political Establishment Upside Down*, 2008; Palin, Sarah. *Going Rogue: An American Life*, 2009

Selected Books: *Going Rogue: An American Life*, 2009

Doug Pensinger/Getty Images

Paul, Chris

May 6, 1985– Basketball player

Address: New Orleans Hornets, 1250 Poydras St., 19th Fl., New Orleans, LA 70113

Chris Paul is one of professional basketball's fastest-rising stars. Paul was a standout player during his last two years of high school in North Carolina; from 2003 to 2005 he achieved national recognition in college as a member of the Wake Forest University Demon Deacons. In the latter year he was drafted by the New Orleans Hornets of the National Basketball Association (NBA), and he has since established himself as one of the league's leading point guards. In only four seasons he has become the face of his team, and his skills on the court have been praised by long-established players and sports journalists. "Paul possesses the perfect combination of passing touch, a scorer's skills, and the speed needed to play tight D[efense]," Sean Gregory wrote for *Time* (July 22, 2008, on-line). Some have credited Paul with reviving interest in his team and its home city, New Orleans, after the city was devastated by flooding in the wake of Hurricane Katrina, in 2005. "Chris Paul is the best point guard since Magic Johnson . . . ," Sam Baldwin wrote for the *Mother Jones* Web site (April 5, 2009). "Great basketball players are celebrated for their ability to elevate the players around them, well, Paul is so good he elevates his teammates, elevates the coach, the owner, the fans, hell he's trying to save the world. He has already been widely credited with saving the NBA in New Orleans, and for some time he has been the face of recovery in New Orleans." At six feet Paul is one of the shortest players in the NBA, leading some to call him the league's "best little man." Paul's personal coach, Idan Ravin, told Dave McMenamin for the NBA Web site (May 9, 2008), "I think it's the esoteric things that make him really special. At the end of the day, everybody in the NBA can go right, they can go left, they can shoot a jump shot, I mean everybody has a certain threshold of talent. But what makes him so special is his incredible tenacity and love for the game. It's not like this cliché, 'We work hard.' Everybody says they work hard. But it's the efficiency and . . . the smarts in which he maximizes his time. He's super. He's tenacious. He doesn't back down."

Christopher Emmanuel Paul was born on May 6, 1985 in Lewisville, North Carolina. His father, Charles, works as a builder of surveillance equipment, and his mother, Robin, is a longtime employee of a bank. Paul has an older brother, Charles, known as C.J. The boys' father, a sports fan, encouraged his sons to take up athletics when they were very young. When Paul was three his father purchased toy basketball hoops for the boys to use in the basement. Paul was also close to his maternal grandfather, Nathaniel "Papa Chilly" Jones, who was the owner of Jones Chevron, in nearby Winston-Salem, North Carolina, the first service station in the state to be owned by an African-American. Paul and his brother frequently spent time with Jones, working at the station—changing oil filters or washing car windshields—during summers. Jones believed his grandsons would become top basketball players and always supported them at school games. "Everybody knows Michael Jordan was the best player ever to play the game," Paul told Bob Lipper for the Richmond, Virginia, *Times Dispatch* (March 2, 2004). "But if you asked my grandfather, me and my brother were the two best ever to play basketball. I know he had more confidence in me than I have in myself." C.J. Paul told Barry Svrluga for the *Washington Post* (January 29, 2004) that his grandfather was "such a great guy, never mean. He would do work for people, and people would say they didn't have money now, and he'd say, 'Y'all go on. Pay me when you can.' He'd do anything for anybody." When C.J. left for college, Paul and Jones grew even closer. "My granddad was my best friend," Paul told Jenni Carlson for the *Oklahoman* (January 25, 2006).

Before entering high school Paul played on a Little League football team as a quarterback, running back, and linebacker. Although Paul hoped to make the varsity basketball team during his freshman year at West Forsyth High School, in Clemmons, North Carolina, he found a spot only on the junior-varsity team. By his junior year, however, having vastly improved his skills—and grown to almost six feet tall—he made the varsity squad. He then led the West Forsyth Titans to a 26–4 record and to the state 4-A championship semifinals. He averaged 25 points, 5.3 assists, and 4.4 steals per game and was named the 2002 Central Piedmont 4-A Player of the Year. He was also a member of the Amateur Athletic Union (AAU) and led his AAU team, Kappa Magic, to the U-17 National Championship, where he was selected as the tournament's most valuable player (MVP). In 2002 he was an Associated Press second team All-State selection. Paul was also highly motivated in other aspects of his high-school life—he was junior- and senior-class president, homecoming king, and an honors student.

In November 2002 Paul signed a letter of intent with Wake Forest University, in Winston-Salem, North Carolina, to play for the school's basketball team, the Demon Deacons. Nathaniel Jones, a fan of the Demon Deacons who was proud of his grandson's accomplishment, would not have the opportunity to cheer Paul on at the games: on November 15, 2002, a week before Paul was to start his senior basketball season at West Forsyth, Jones was beaten and robbed by a group of teenagers while unloading groceries in front of his home. As a result of the attack, Jones died from cardiac arrhythmia. Paul's brother broke the news to him. "It was weird, because just the day before, I was talking to [Jones] about plans for that weekend," Paul told Svrluga. "We knew what we were going to do, who we were going to be with. It was a very emotional time, a very emotional time." The loss of his grandfather left Paul distraught, and he was unsure if he could play in the season opener scheduled for the day after his grandfather's funeral. "We had prayed about it, and he told us he might not be able to play," Paul's mother told Svrluga. "We talked about it, and we said, 'Chris, you need to do what you think is best. But you know your Papa would want you to play.' It was hard on him, because he lost his best friend." A talk with his aunt Rhonda led Paul to consider playing. She suggested that as a tribute to his grandfather, he try to shoot 61 points—one for each year of his grandfather's life. Paul, whose highest number of points scored in a single game up to that time was 39, was initially reluctant to try; in an interview with Robin Roberts for the ABC show *Good Morning America* (December 30, 2002, on-line), he said, "I just thought to myself, you know, that would be lovely. And I just thought to myself, 'Ain't no way I can do that.'" Despite his doubts Paul decided to try his best to honor his grandfather by playing in the game. He asked his coach to keep him in the game for the entire night, and although he kept his goal of scoring 61 points mostly to himself, rumors were floating around the gym about his intentions. "We didn't know about it," his mother told Svrluga. "But then, the children in the stands, they started counting. They kept telling us how many he had to go." Paul missed only eight of his 34 shots that night, reaching 32 points in the first half of the game and reaching 61 with two minutes left on the clock. Although he had enough time to try to score 67 points and break the state record, he intentionally missed a subsequent free-throw shot. He told Roberts that he "didn't think anything about [breaking the record]. That had no meaning to me. It was all in honor of my granddad." In his *Good Morning America* interview he recalled that after realizing he had met his goal, "I laid there for a second and was just overwhelmed. . . . It felt like I could have just died and went to Heaven right there."

By the end of his senior year, Paul had averaged 30.8 points, eight assists, six steals, and five rebounds per game. He led the Titans to the Class 4-A Eastern Regional Final and a 27–3 record. He was selected as the *Parade* High School All-American and was named to *USA Today's* All–USA high-school second team; he also became the Associated Press's pick for North Carolina High School Player of the Year and for its All-State selection, and the *Charlotte Observer* named him North Carolina's "Mr. Basketball." Paul played in the North Carolina East-West All-Star Game in Greensboro and was ranked as the country's ninth-best high-school prospect and as the top point guard prospect by the recruiter's handbook, *PrepStars*. In the summer of 2003, Paul was a McDonald's High School All-American, racked up 10 assists in the McDonald's High School All-America Game, and won the contest's sportsmanship award. He also played in the USA Basketball Men's Youth Development Festival, achieving the festival's record for most steals—14—by an East team member.

When Paul entered Wake Forest as a point guard in the 2003–04 season, his skills perfectly complemented those of his fellow Demon Deacons. He lived up to his reputation when, during an early game against the Indiana Hoosiers at the Atlantic Coast Conference (ACC) Big Ten Challenge, he posted 20 points and eight assists, leading to a 100–67 victory. He soon developed a rapport with his teammate Justin Gray, and the two became a formidable guard duo. During the Demon Deacons' ACC schedule, Paul led a 119–114 victory against the University of North Carolina, defeated Duke University by racking up 19 points in the game's second half, and trumped the University of Maryland with 30 points. He led the team with 183 assists, 84 steals, a .465 three-point field-goal percentage, and 150 free throws. He broke five Wake Forest freshman records—for free throws, three-point percentage, free-throw percentage, assists, and steals. Paul was named ACC Rookie of the Year and voted to the ACC all-defensive and all-freshman teams. He was also named by *College Insider*, the *Sporting News*, *Basketball Times*, and the sportscaster Dick Vitale as the nation's top freshman college basketball player.

In his sophomore season Paul helped lead the Demon Deacons to 12 wins in its first 13 games. During the team's final regular-season game, he hit North Carolina State player Julius Hodge in the stomach with a closed fist and was removed from the game briefly; he pleaded ignorance about what he had done before admitting his guilt. As a result of the incident, he was suspended from his team in the first-round games of the ACC Tournament. In the second round Paul was responsible for scoring 22 points in 44 minutes against the West Virginia University Mountaineers. (The Demon Deacons lost the game nonetheless.) Wake Forest ended the season with a 27–6 record. By the end of his two seasons with the Demon Deacons, Paul had helped lead the team to 48 victories, two National Collegiate Athletic Association (NCAA) Tournaments, and a Sweet 16 appearance. After his sophomore season he was a consensus first-team All-American and a finalist for several player-of-the-year awards. His college-career free-throw percentage of .838 ranks fifth-highest in the school's history, and his career three-point percentage of .469 is good for second-highest. He also ranks seventh of all time at Wake Forest with 395 career assists and seventh with 160 steals. He finished his career at the school with 948 career points.

Deciding to leave college for the pros, Paul was selected by the New Orleans Hornets as the fourth overall pick in the first round of the 2005 NBA draft. Only 20 when the 2005–06 season began, Paul nonetheless earned a starter position. His team, having won only 18 out of 64 games the previous season, was hardly considered among the best in the league, but with Paul's help they ended the year with 38 wins. Paul was named NBA Rookie of the Year and averaged 16.1 points and 7.8 assists per game. During that season the Hornets played only three games in New Orleans as a result of the destruction wrought by Hurricane Katrina, which had struck the U.S. Gulf Coast region in late August. The majority of the Hornets' games were held in Oklahoma City, as they would be the next season. Paul told Nebojsa Petrovacki for HoopsHype.com (November 18, 2006) that his success in his first NBA season was due to a supportive team and coach. "I think it was just my teammates," he said. "They and the coaching staff had the ultimate confidence in me and they allowed me to play. They really gave me a lot of advice, gave me the ball and let me go." Paul played on the U.S. Men's National Basketball Team in the 2006 FIBA World Championships. His total of 44 assists and his per-game average, 4.9, were records for U.S. players in the world championships, and the U.S. men's team won the bronze medal. In the 2006–07 season Paul posted even better numbers: his points average went up to 17.3, and his assists average reached 8.9. He was plagued by injuries, however, and had to sit out 18 games. The Hornets fared better than they had the prior season, achieving a total of 39 wins.

The Hornets returned to New Orleans for the 2007–08 season, winning the Southwest Division title and finishing the regular season with 56 wins, the second-best in the NBA. Paul's skills were invaluable to the team: he led the NBA with 11.6 assists and 2.7 steals per game. His scoring average reached 21.1 points, and he was selected for the All-Star Game along with his teammate David West. In the Western Conference the Hornets beat the Dallas Mavericks, with Paul scoring 24 points in the second half of Game One to lead his team to a 104–92 victory. In Game Two he set a team playoff record with 17 assists, and in Game Five he had 24 points, 15 assists, and 11 rebounds. The team lost to the San Antonio Spurs in the semifinals. Paul was also a member of the U.S. men's basketball team for the 2008 Beijing Olympics. The national team, which had won only a bronze medal in the Olympics four years earlier, claimed the gold medal after defeating Spain, 118 to 107. Paul signed a three-year contract extension with the Hornets before the 2008–09 season. In March 2009 Hornets officials released a video called *CP3 for MVP*, hoping to encourage the NBA to pick Paul as the year's MVP. (LeBron James got the honor.) Paul was also named Western Conference Player of the Month.

The 2008–09 season was one of Paul's best to date, even though the Hornets won fewer games and failed to repeat as Southwest Division champions. During the season Paul increased his scoring average yet again, leading his team with 22.8 points per game. He also saw increased per-game numbers in other categories, with 5.5 rebounds, 2.8 steals, a 50.3 field-goal percentage, and an 86.8 free-throw percentage. He ranked first in the NBA with an average of 11 assists per game and returned to the All-Star Game as a starter.

Paul has been with his girlfriend, Jada Crawley, since he attended Wake Forest University. Their son, Christopher Emmanuel Paul II, was born in May 2009. Paul's brother, a vocal presence at Hornets games, works as his business manager and lives next door to him in a condominium in New Orleans. Off the court Paul is an avid 10-pin bowler and is a spokesman for the United States Bowling Congress. His endorsement deals include those with the makers of Jordan Brand shoes, Right Guard deodorant, and Vitamin Water. Paul's signature shoe, the Jordan CP3, available through Nike, features the number 61 in honor of his grandfather. Paul's organization, the CP3 Foundation, hosts the annual Chris Paul's Winston-Salem, a series of events that raise money for charity. The foundation has also established the Nathaniel Jones Scholarship Fund, which enables a Forsyth County student to attend Wake Forest University.

—W.D.

Suggested Reading:chrispaul3.com; *Oklahoman* A p1 Jan. 25, 2006; *Richmond (Virginia) Times Dispatch* E p1 Mar. 2, 2004; *Washington Post* D p1 Jan. 29, 2004

Jimmy Ryan, courtesy of Max Jazz

Pelt, Jeremy

Nov. 4, 1976– Jazz trumpeter

Address: c/o Phairelady Management Services, 20 W. 20th St. #2, New York, NY 10011

The veteran jazz critic Nat Hentoff has been quoted widely as writing for the *Wall Street Journal*, "It is the beat of Jeremy Pelt's heart that underscores the future of jazz." A sophisticated trumpet player from a young age, Pelt began performing in the famed Mingus Big Band in 1999, just a year after finishing college. He then made a name for himself in collaborations with such contemporary jazz stars as Roy Hargrove, Ravi Coltrane, Greg Osby, and Cassandra Wilson. In 2002 Pelt made his debut as a bandleader with his first solo album, *Profile*, a collection of mostly original tunes that was hailed as a boundary-pushing entrée into post-bop jazz. His third album, *Close to My Heart* (2003), featured Pelt's takes on jazz standards by masters including Duke Ellington and Charles Mingus, while his fourth, *Identity* (2005), showcased his continued experimentation, and his fifth, *Shock Value: Live at Smoke* (2007), showed his range, with an electric, rock-influenced sound. Pelt's most recent album, *November* (2008), has been hailed as representing another step in his progression as an artist. C. Michael Bailey wrote for the Web site All About Jazz (July 20, 2008) that the album is "a fully realized post-bop suite. . . . Pelt's compositions are all tightly angular and anxious, both probing and airy. His trumpet is tart and sweet, the tone very much his own." Pelt was named Rising Star on the Trumpet five years in a row by *Down Beat* magazine and was nominated as "best emerging jazz star" by the Jazz Journalists' Association in 2005.

Jeremy Pelt was born on November 4, 1976 in California. He began playing the trumpet in elementary school, focusing mainly on classical music. When he entered high school and found that his school lacked an orchestra, he joined the jazz band, whose director introduced him to the music he would grow to love. "That is kind of how the ball got rolling," Pelt told R. J. Deluke for the Albany, New York, *Times Union* (June 24, 2004). "I met my teacher, and he hipped me to jazz. Being the curious person that I was, I really wanted to investigate all the songs that we were playing, such as 'So What' and 'My Little Suede Shoes.'" At a time when most of his peers were listening to pop and hip-hop, Pelt immersed himself in the music of the trumpeters Miles Davis, Lee Morgan, and Freddie Hubbard.

Following his graduation from high school, Pelt attended the Berklee College of Music, in Boston, Massachusetts. In addition to loving jazz, he was an avid fan of film music. He and a trumpet-playing friend "were big John Williams fans," he told Deluke, referring to the composer of music for *Star Wars*, *Raiders of the Lost Ark*, and many other movies. "Every film that came out, we would get the soundtrack and listen to it." Pelt studied jazz improvisation and film scoring while playing with various jazz groups around the Boston area. He graduated in 1998 with a B.A. in professional music.

Having made many valuable connections at Berklee, Pelt moved to New York City to take on the challenging task of becoming a full-time musician. "There weren't many places to play the kind of jazz that we wanted to play, which was loud and exciting," he told Deluke of his experiences in Boston. "A lot of gigs you would get as a student would be society gigs, or part of cover bands, stuff like that." Once in New York he served as a sideman in the bands of several older musicians he admired, including the drummers Lewis Nash and Louis Hayes and the bassist Lonnie Plaxico. He also earned a chair in the Ralph Peterson quintet, playing on the albums *The Art of War* (2001) and *Subliminal Seduction* (2002).

In addition to small ensembles, Pelt has played in several big bands, most notably those of Frank Foster and Charles Mingus (the latter of which performs and reinterprets the music of the bassist and composer Mingus under the direction of his widow, Sue). He first took an interest in the Mingus band when a friend who was a member, his fellow trumpeter Philip Harper, invited him to sit in on their sessions. "I'd be down there every week, like a little lap dog at the side of the stage, hungry to sit in and impress Sue Mingus, who would be in the back," he recalled to Deluke. "I met her a couple times; she'd add you to the list, but whether you'd get the call is another thing." Pelt did indeed receive a call from Mingus, joined the band in 1999, and was a featured soloist on their 2005 album, *I Am Three*. Pelt has also played at various times in bands led by Ravi Coltrane, Cassandra Wilson, and Greg Osby.

In search of more experience playing traditional jazz, Pelt performed in the band led by the Grammy Award–winning saxophonist Frank Foster, who had joined the Count Basie Orchestra in 1953 and, following Basie's death, led it from 1986 to 1995. "That's the foundation of my training right there," Pelt told David Adler for *Down Beat* (February 2003). "The Mingus band is fun, but it's raw, and you're not concentrating too much on reading. So when you play with a more traditional band . . . it will kick your a**." Pelt has also played with the Village Vanguard Orchestra, the Duke Ellington Big Band, and the Roy Hargrove Big Band.

Pelt formed his own quintet and released his first album as a bandleader in 2002. Widely hailed as a promising debut, *Profile* featured mostly original songs composed and performed by Pelt on trumpet, with Robert Glasper on piano, Gerald Cannon on bass, Ralph Peterson on drums, and Jimmy Greene on tenor saxophone. "In addition to his formidable trumpet chops, Pelt displays a mature and engaging compositional voice," David Adler wrote for allmusic.com. "On 'Pieces of a Dream' and the bright bossa 'We Share a Moon,' he builds forms around unexpected rhythmic contours, pushing himself and the band well beyond the safe zone. . . . Cannon and Peterson, the session's veterans, provide a robust rhythmic engine without overshadowing Pelt's precocious musicianship."

Pelt's subsequent recordings exhibited a mastery that many critics found remarkable in such a young player. His sophomore album, *Insight* (2003), was heavily influenced by hard bop, a genre of jazz with a strong percussive element and blues influence. "I love that style so much . . . ," Pelt wrote in the album's liner notes, as quoted by Chris Searle for the *Morning Star* (October 15, 2003), a British publication. "I'm always trying to figure out how to add to it and move forward." "There is nothing imitative or merely nostalgic about Pelt's playing," Searle wrote. "It draws on the achievements of the great Jazz Messenger horns like Lee Morgan or Freddie Hubbard, but creates a sound that is scintillatingly new. . . . A poignantly lyrical 'I Wish You Love' makes it seem that the mouthpiece is only brushing Pelt's lips, so soft and balladic is his sound. . . . A mesmerising version of Herbie Hancock's 'Madness' with curvaceous solos by [saxophonists Greene and Myron Walden] is another powerful track, building *Insight* as an hour of understanding that this genre still has many roads to travel."

Close to My Heart (2003) featured Pelt leading a somewhat expanded band that included cello, viola, violin, and guitar—in addition to the usual drums, bass, piano, and trumpet—in standards by masters including Mingus and Duke Ellington. Pelt's goal, as stated in the liner notes, was "to try and define a voice within my compositions, as well as establish a firm musical direction." "Pelt opens with a melody statement on Charles Mingus' 'Weird Nightmare' that does justice to the title and hews to the theme through a harmonically bold improvisation," Ted Panken wrote for *Down Beat* (January 2004). "Pelt sustains the mood of burnished daring through a session comprising less-traveled compositions and romance-oriented standards that aren't in the fake books." Francis Davis, writing for the *Village Voice* (August 24, 2004), however, was more ambivalent. "Things go wrong right away with Charles Mingus's 'Weird Nightmare,' one of five tracks where a string quartet arranged by David O'Rourke enfolds Pelt and the first-call rhythm section of Mulgrew Miller, Peter Washington, and Lewis Nash in perfumed gauze," Davis complained. Still, he allowed that "Pelt bows to no one in speed or dexterity" and that he had "depth of emotion on ballads . . . to spare."

In 2004 Pelt took time off from recording to tour as part of the drummer Louis Hayes's band. He returned to the studio in 2005 to record *Identity*, which represented another major step in his musical evolution. With some of its tunes strongly influenced by Miles Davis and the 1970s jazz-rock fusion he pioneered, *Identity* was Pelt's first album to use electric instruments. "Featuring 10 original compositions by Pelt, the disc also showcases his growing confidence as an improviser and skill as a bandleader," Terry Perkins wrote for the *St. Louis Post-Dispatch* (March 8, 2007).

Identity continued themes that Pelt had begun exploring in 2004, around the time that the composer/trumpeter Dave Douglas invited Pelt to play a double bill with him at the jazz and avant-garde music venue Tonic, in New York. Pelt surprised Douglas by offering to play with a fusion-influenced band he had put together, called Noise (later renamed Wired). "It was a shock when Jeremy told me what he wanted to do," Douglas recalled to Jennifer Odell for *Down Beat* (June 2007). "I see someone who's coming up playing traditional music of the 1940s, '50s and '60s and making a sharp turn." Despite his initial surprise, he welcomed Pelt's new band onto the bill. "Not only was I listening to Billie Holiday and Dinah Washington, but I also used to listen to Jimi Hendrix," Pelt explained to Odell. "I can listen to all of that and now it's like I have an opportunity to adapt all these influences to my own creation. So why not do it?"

That performance was the first of many for Noise. Pelt recorded a live album, *Shock Value: Live at Smoke*, featuring the band's set at the iconic Harlem jazz club of the title, in 2007. Audience reactions were mixed; though some embraced the new sound, others wanted Pelt to play more standards, such as those on *Close to My Heart*. "We were rocking out and they were just looking at me," he recalled to Odell. "You could tell they didn't appreciate it. They didn't like it one bit." Even so, critics and friends admired Pelt's spirit of adventure. "A lot of people have the perception that if you take a bold step, you're undoing everything you've done before," Douglas told Odell. "I don't see that happening to Jeremy. He wants to take a step forward." "For sure, a bit of it sounds like an exercise in style," Ben Ratliff wrote for the *New York Times* (October 28, 2007), "but there's art here too. The constant volume and droning resonance of the band drive the players to focus and intensify their work, to make it matter; everyone's playing, especially Mr. Pelt's, is wise and serious."

November (2008) continued Pelt's negotiation between tradition and innovation. Nate Chinen wrote for the *New York Times* (July 20, 2008), "*November* . . . occasionally owes a surface debt to the music of Wayne Shorter, around 1965: the searching harmonies and streamlined pulse are there, as is Mr. Shorter's instrumental timbre, thanks to the tenor saxophonist J. D. Allen." Chinen also, though, emphasized the album's ability to evade "its own retro impulse." "Mr. Pelt plays brilliantly, with warmth and depth," Chinen wrote. "He makes each of his nine compositions feel like a personal discovery." Michael Bailey, in his assessment for allaboutjazz.com, drew an even more direct line between Pelt and his forebears: "In the same way that Roy Hargrove's *Earfood* (2008) updated Lee Morgan's *Cornbread* (1965), so Jeremy Pelt's *November* updates Miles Davis' *Miles Smiles* (1966). If creativity and art can be evaluated on both the vertical and horizontal, Morgan's and Davis' offerings represent horizontal progressions of the art of jazz into new areas, where Hargrove's and Pelt's are vertical elaborations of those previous collections."

In 2007 Pelt was asked to co-curate the Festival of New Trumpet Music, a not-for-profit event held yearly in New York City, showcasing the best up-and-coming jazz trumpeters, and he was a curator and board member of the 2008 festival. He continues to play with a variety of groups, including Wired and several other, more traditional ensembles. "I look for anything that's a learning experience and a challenging experience," Pelt told Deluke. "I don't really like to deal with titles—'mainstream' and this and that." According to his Web site, his next album, *Men of Honor*, was to be released in January 2010. Pelt lives in New York City.

—J.E.P.

Suggested Reading: (Albany, New York) *Times Union* P p24 June 24, 2004; *Down Beat* p26 Feb. 2003, p8 June 2007; peltjazz.com

Selected Recordings: *Profile*, 2002; *Insight*, 2003; *Close to My Heart*, 2003; *Identity*, 2005; *Shock Value: Live at Smoke*, 2007; *November*, 2008

Pennington, Chad

June 26, 1976– Football player

Address: Miami Dolphins, 7500 S.W. 30th St., Davie, FL 33314

"The beauty of being a quarterback is that we're all different," Chad Pennington, whose National Football League (NFL) career is now in its 10th year, told Jeff Darlington for the *Miami Herald* (December 24, 2008). "There's not a picture-perfect model." Pennington, a quarterback with the New York Jets from 2000 to 2008 and with the Miami Dolphins since then, differs from the vast majority of his peers in an unusual respect: he has a photographic memory, and since his youth he has regarded his brain as his greatest asset on the football field. Although, with the exception of his accuracy as a passer, his physical abilities have never been better than average, his analytical and decision-making skills during games are widely recognized as remarkable. "I've always had to find facets of the game that I could use to my advantage instead of my arm," he told Rachel Nichols for the *Washington Post* (January 8, 2003). Pennington has also had to overcome serious injuries: he underwent two operations less than a year apart, in 2004 and 2005, for tears to the rotator cuff in his throwing shoulder; his recovery from the second surgery may have marked the first time that two such injuries, or even one, did not end a quarterback's career.

The son of a high-school football coach, Pennington joined the Jets after an illustrious four years with the Thundering Herd, the football team of Marshall University, in West Virginia. In 2002, when he became the Jets' starting quarterback, he ended the season with a 104.2 quarterback rating—better than any other NFL passer that year and a Jets record. The terms of the contract he signed with the Jets in 2004 provide evidence of his value to the team: it was worth $64.2 million over seven years, more than had ever been earned by a Jets player up to that time. For most of the 2005 season, he was on the injured list, and the Jets lost 12 of their 16 games. His exemplary performance in

Marc Serota/Getty Images

Chad Pennington

2006 led the Associated Press to name him the NFL Comeback Player of the Year. Pennington lost the starter position in 2007 because of the effects of another injury. He was poised to return to that role when Brett Favre, having decided to end his retirement, joined the team, on August 7, 2008, and that same day Pennington was ousted. The next day the Miami Dolphins signed him on. The Dolphins, who had won only one of their 16 games in 2007, made an historic turnaround in 2008, winning 11 games and losing five, and Pennington had his finest season to date. The team's new head coach, Tony Sparano, told Steven Wine for the Associated Press (December 4, 2008), "I've been in this league now for 10 years, and I have never seen it done, not like that." Pennington, he added, is "like the pied piper. He's just saying, 'This is what we're doing,' and [his teammates] look forward to doing it." Pennington told Damon Hack for *Sports Illustrated* (September 15, 2008), "I think as human beings and as athletes, all we can ask for is a chance and a glimmer of hope. You can look at [moving to a new team] as a challenge or an obstacle. To me there's no greater feeling than walking into that huddle, looking your teammates in the eyes, calling a play and walking to the line of scrimmage together, ready to execute."

The older of two children, James Chadwick Pennington was born on June 26, 1976 in Knoxville, Tennessee. His sister, Andrea, is about four years his junior. His mother, Denise, teaches ninth-grade English at the Webb School; his father, Elwood, who played football and basketball as an undergraduate, taught physical education and coached football at the high-school level. (He never coached his son, though.) Pennington developed a passion for football as a child; he often accompanied his father to high-school football practices and would try to sneak into the team's offensive huddle. By the time he entered kindergarten, he had begun devising game plans. When he was eight he started watching films of games with his father; the two would spend hours analyzing plays. Pennington attended Halls Elementary and Middle Schools, in Knoxville, before he enrolled at the Webb School, where, according to Dave Link, writing for knoxnews.com (July 13, 2007), he repeated the eighth grade. At Webb, a private Knoxville secondary school known for its academic rigor, he played football and basketball and ran track. Although he lettered three times in basketball, he set his sights on getting a college football scholarship. As the quarterback of a team that favored running over passing, however, he was given only limited opportunities to showcase his talent for deducing opposing teams' defensive schemes, and he generated little interest in college scouts. During his senior year Pennington was recruited by only two Division I-AA schools, Middle Tennessee State University and the University of Tennessee at Chattanooga, both of which he turned down. Then, at a summer football camp held at Marshall University, a Division I-AA school in Huntington, West Virginia, he impressed the head coach, Jim Donnan, and won admission with a scholarship.

Marshall University was struck by tragedy in 1970, when a plane crash took the lives of its entire football team and coaching staff. Under Donnan in the 1990s, the Thundering Herd had grown into a football juggernaut; the team won a national title in 1992. When Pennington arrived at Marshall, in 1995, he was expected to be a fourth-string quarterback and redshirted. Early in his freshman year, however, the team's starter Larry Harris and his backup Mark Zban suffered season-ending injuries, and Pennington became the starting quarterback. Marshall won 10 of 11 games that season and cruised into the I-AA play-offs. Pennington finished the season with 2,445 yards, 15 touchdowns, and a passer rating of 125.4, ranking him second overall in the Southern Conference and earning him the title Freshman of the Year. In 1996 Donnan left Marshall; he was replaced by Bob Pruett, a Marshall alumnus and former University of Florida assistant coach. Pruett demoted Pennington in favor of Eric Kresser, a senior, who had transferred from Florida. "Competitively, you're ready to fight, no doubt about it, but that's where my experience when I was younger helped me," Pennington told Rachel Nichols. "You have to understand that I would see my father coach on Sundays, and on Mondays he would be mowing the field. So you see those types of sacrifices, you learn early." That year, with the help of a new wide receiver, Randy Moss, the Thundering Herd won another national championship, and Marshall's team was promoted to Division I-A and moved to the Mid-American Conference (MAC). Pennington reassumed his starting duties in 1997. That season he set conference records, with 3,480 passing yards and 39 touchdowns. The Thundering Herd ended the season as the loser in the inaugural Motor City Bowl, won by the University of Mississippi. At the end of his junior year, Pennington won the Cam Henderson Award as Marshall's student-athlete of the year. Despite losing Moss to the NFL, Marshall had even greater success in 1998, losing only one game and winning 12 and also winning the inaugural MAC championship game, against the University of Toledo. Pennington led the MAC in nearly every passing category, including yards (3,419), touchdowns (24), and passer rating (146.2). After taking home their second straight MAC title, Marshall returned to the Motor City Bowl, where the team celebrated a 48–29 victory over the University of Louisville. Pennington, who threw for 411 yards and four touchdowns, was named the game's Most Valuable Player (MVP).

By his senior season Pennington had become recognized as one of the nation's best college quarterbacks. That year he led Marshall to a 12–0 record and a third consecutive MAC championship, which helped them break into the Top 20 nationally, as ranked in a poll of sportswriters. In the Motor City Bowl, Marshall routed Brigham Young University, 21–3. Pennington ended the year with 4,006 yards and 38 touchdowns and was named the MAC Offensive Player of the Year. He finished fifth in the Heisman Trophy voting that year and was a finalist for the Davey O'Brien National Quarterback Award and the Johnny Unitas Golden Arm Award. In 1999 he graduated, with a 3.83 grade-point average and a B.A. degree in broadcast journalism. He was a finalist for a Rhodes scholarship.

Despite his impressive college résumé, Pennington—with his only-average arm strength and less-than-average speed—knew that many doubted that he was physically gifted enough to play for the NFL. For that reason he chose to play in the Senior Bowl, an annual exhibition game, to improve his chances in the draft. At that game, held on January 22, 2000, Pennington impressed coaches with his uncommon skill at reading opposing defensive schemes and his readiness to take charge in a huddle. In that year's draft the New York Jets selected him in the first round, as the 18th overall pick.

In his first two seasons in the NFL, Pennington appeared in only three games, completing only 12 of 25 pass attempts for 159 yards and two touchdowns. During that time he acted as an understudy to the Jets' veteran starting quarterback Vinny Testaverde and spent many hours in the film room studying footwork drills and play-calling exercises. "Since Day One when he arrived with the Jets, he prepared like he was the starter all along; he learned as much as he could," Testaverde told Rachel Nichols. Pennington stole a security code to gain access to the Jets' practice facility, in order to study film very early in the morning, and he brought his Jets playbook on his honeymoon, in March 2001. Once, he became dehydrated after practicing too strenuously and had to be rushed to a hospital. His hard work paid off: in the 2002 season, after the team lost four of their first five games, he was named the Jets' starting quarterback. His first start came in a home game against the Kansas City Chiefs. Though the Jets lost, 29–25, Pennington completed 22 of 29 passes for 239 yards and two touchdowns. The following week he led the Jets to victory over the Minnesota Vikings, passing for more than 300 yards and posting a quarterback rating of 124.7. He went on to lead the Jets to a 9–7 record and an American Football Conference (AFC) East Division championship. He finished the season with 3,120 passing yards, 22 touchdowns, and a 68.9 completion percentage; he led all NFL passers with a 104.2 quarterback rating, a Jets record. In the postseason he steered the Jets to a first-round 41–0 blowout of the Indianapolis Colts, after throwing three touchdown passes and posting an astonishing 142 passer rating. The next week, in the divisional play-offs, the Jets lost to the eventual AFC champions, the Oakland Raiders.

Pennington was forced to miss the first six games of the 2003 campaign because of an injury in his nonthrowing hand. In his first five games after his return, he quickly reestablished himself as the league's most efficient quarterback, with 10 touchdowns and only four interceptions. He ended the year with 2,139 yards passing, 13 touchdowns, and an 82.9 quarterback rating; the Jets' record was 6–10. The next year the team won six of their first seven games. Pennington, who had signed a seven-year contract worth $64.2 million (more than had ever been offered to any other Jets player), continued his efficient play during those games, throwing eight touchdowns with only two interceptions. A strain in a rotator cuff suffered during a game against the Buffalo Bills in early November forced him to miss three games. After engineering a rout of the Houston Texans in the first game after his return, he struggled for much of the rest of the season, because his shoulder had not fully healed. Nevertheless, many in the notoriously critical New York media faulted him for not delivering when it most mattered. The Jets' 10–6 record that season earned them a wild-card berth in the play-offs. Meanwhile, Pennington had finished the year with 2,673 yards, 16 touchdowns, and a 91 quarterback rating. In the postseason he orchestrated a 20–17 overtime win against the AFC West champions, the San Diego Chargers. In that game Pennington completed 23 of 33 passes for 279 yards and two touchdowns. The Jets went on to suffer an overtime loss to the Pittsburgh Steelers in the divisional play-off round. The Jets struggled offensively for most of the game, but the defense and special teams (offensive and defensive units that are on the field during kickoffs, free kicks, punts, and field-goal and extra-point attempts) helped the team rally from a 10–0 hole by scoring 17 unanswered points, only to lose after the kicker Doug Brien botched two crucial game-winning field goals.

During the off-season Pennington underwent surgery on his right shoulder. The damage was found to be more severe than had been believed: he had suffered a substantial tear in his right rotator cuff, and a large bone spur was detected. Pennington performed poorly in his first two games of the 2005 season. The following week he suffered yet another injury, in a game against the Jacksonville Jaguars. He briefly left the game, then came back to play after Testaverde was injured, and he almost led the Jets to victory despite not throwing well. Tests later indicated that he had suffered another tear in his rotator cuff, making further play impossible. That October Pennington underwent surgery again. His absence was clearly felt by the Jets, who lost 12 of 16 games that season. During the off-season Pennington engaged in an intensive rehabilitation program to strengthen his shoulder and arm. He and the Jets negotiated a new contract, in which he agreed to a significant pay cut in return for the promise that he would return as the starter and could earn additional money through various means.

Defying odds, Pennington returned to form in 2006. He threw for a career-high 3,352 passing yards and 17 touchdowns and started all 16 games. He led the Jets to 10 wins and a wild-card berth. Although the Jets lost to the Patriots in the first round of the play-offs, 37–17, Pennington was named the Associated Press NFL Comeback Player of the Year. During the opening game of the 2007 season, against the New England Patriots, he sprained his ankle—which apparently pleased fans: many cheered as he was led from the field. "When you get to this level, [fans] are really not for you," he remarked to Ohm Youngmisuk for the New York *Daily News* (December 28, 2008). "It is all about what is in the now. You not only learn a lot about yourself in that situation, people learn a lot about you and how you handle a situation like that and how do you change." Pennington missed the next game, then returned in the season's third week and led the Jets to a 31–28 victory over the Miami Dolphins, throwing two touchdowns and running for a third. The Jets lost the next five games, during which, because of his limited mobility—he was still suffering from the sprain—he threw many needless turnovers. When the team's record stood at 1–7, the Jets' head coach, Eric Mangini, benched Pennington in favor of the second-year backup Kellen Clemens. The Jets won only three more games before the season's end. Pennington finished with 1,765 yards, 10 touchdowns, nine interceptions, and a passer rating of 86.1.

In February 2008 Pennington hired a team of experts—a physical therapist, a nutritionist, a chiropractor, an acupuncturist, a massage therapist, and a mental-conditioning coach—who, along with his trainer, came up with a fitness regimen for him. Pennington added 15 pounds of muscle, increasing his weight from 217 to 232 pounds, and lowered his body fat by 6 percent. He also strengthened his arm sufficiently to be able to throw as far as he had as a rookie—63 yards (considered average by NFL-quarterback standards). At the training camp that summer, Mangini announced that Pennington and Clemens would have to compete for the starting-quarterback position. Pennington was winning in that contest when, on August 7, 2008, the Jets acquired the celebrated quarterback Brett Favre from the Green Bay Packers. (The Packers had agreed to take Favre back only if he would serve as a backup, an offer he had rejected.) Pennington was released later that day. A day later the Miami Dolphins signed him to a two-year, $11.5 million deal. The Dolphins had posted a record of 1–15 in 2007, a league and franchise worst. The owners then hired Bill Parcells, the legendary two-time Super Bowl–winning coach, as executive vice president of football operations. Parcells fired the team's first-year head coach, Cam Cameron, and general manager, Randy Mueller, and replaced them with his former Dallas Cowboy protégés Tony Sparano and Jeff Ireland, respectively. He also hired some 20 little-known free agents and released the defensive veterans Zach Thomas and Jason Taylor.

Under Parcells, Sparano, and Ireland, Pennington anchored one of the most unlikely turnarounds in NFL history. After dropping their first two games, on September 21, 2008 the Dolphins defeated the New England Patriots, 38–13, thus ending the Patriots' NFL-record winning streak of 21 consecutive games. The September 21 game marked the first in which the Dolphins implemented the now–widely copied "wildcat" offense, in which the running back assumes the quarterback position and the quarterback the flanker position. Pennington next led the Dolphins to a 17–10 victory over the San Diego Chargers. The Dolphins won nine of their last 12 games, leading them to an 11–5 record, their first play-off berth since 2001, and their first AFC East Championship since 2000. The 10-win improvement marked the greatest turnaround by a 1–15 team in NFL history and tied the greatest turnaround of all time, by the Indianapolis Colts, who went from 3–13 in 1998 to 13–3 in 1999. The Dolphins achieved most of their victories by seven or fewer points; their low turnover margin, 13, was best in the NFL that year, and with the New York Giants, they tied for an NFL record for fewest turnovers in a 16-game season. Pennington's teammates dubbed him "Coach Pennington" for his relentless efforts, which included holding private weekly strategy meetings with the Dolphins' wide receivers and offensive linemen. Pennington finished with a career-high 3,653 yards, 19 touchdowns, and only seven interceptions, while leading the NFL with a 67.4 completion percentage and finishing second in the league with a passer rating of 97.4. He became the first Dolphins quarterback since Dan Marino to throw for 3,500 yards, and he set team records in completion percentage and quarterback rating. He earned his second Associated Press NFL Comeback Player of the Year Award and finished second, to the Colts' Peyton Manning, in the MVP voting.

In January 2009, in the first round of the playoffs, the Dolphins were defeated by the Baltimore Ravens, 27–9. After that game, in which Pennington threw an uncharacteristic four interceptions, Sparano put to rest any speculation as to the identity of the Dolphins' starting quarterback in 2009. "I told Chad Pennington that he's my guy and that I believe in him," he told Tim Smith for the New York *Daily News* (January 5, 2009). "I can't thank him enough for what he's done for us."

Pennington's 2009 season was prematurely cut short after he suffered yet another injury to his right shoulder, in a game against the San Diego Chargers during the third week. Shortly after that game, he underwent surgery to repair a tear in the shoulder capsule. While the surgery revealed that the injury was not as severe as had initially been feared, Pennington's future with the Dolphins remained uncertain; plans were afoot to make his replacement, Chad Henne, a second-year player from the University of Michigan, the starter for the 2010 season. In addition, Pennington's contract will expire after the 2009 season. Pennington's influence on Henne, however, is already evident: Henne has begun to hold weekly strategy meetings with the team's wide receivers and offensive linemen.

Every July for some years, Pennington has shared his expertise at a camp for aspiring young quarterbacks and receivers at the Webb School. He married his college sweetheart, Robin Hampton, in 2001. The couple's sons Cole and Luke were five and three years old, respectively, in late July 2009; their third son, Gage, was born in March 2009. In 2003 Pennington and his wife founded the 1st and 10 Foundation, dedicated to building stronger communities in West Virginia, Tennessee, and the New York metropolitan area. To date it has donated over $500,000 to various organizations. The Penningtons live in the Fort Lauderdale area of Florida.

—C.C.

Suggested Reading: Associated Press Dec. 4, 2008; jockbio.com 2008; *Miami Herald* D p1 Aug. 14, 2008, A p1 Dec. 24, 2008, D p1 Dec. 25, 2008; (New York) *Daily News* p32 Dec. 28, 2008, p48 Jan. 5, 2009; *Newsday* C p17+ Oct. 6, 2002; *New York Times* D p1 Sep. 8, 2006, B p11+ Dec. 23, 2008; *Sports Illustrated* p52+ Oct. 25, 2004, p38+ Sep. 15, 2008; *Washington Post* D p1+ Jan. 8, 2003

Plouffe, David

(pluff)

May 27, 1967– Political consultant

Address: AKP&D Message and Media, 730 N. Franklin, Suite 404, Chicago, IL 60610

The night Barack Obama won the presidential election (November 4, 2008), he gave special thanks during his victory speech to "the unsung hero" of his campaign. This man, continued Obama, built the best political campaign "in the history of the United States of America." He was referring to David Plouffe, who for two years managed Obama's presidential campaign. Although he played a crucial role in doing what many thought was impossible—getting a relatively young, little known, mixed-race candidate elected to the highest office in the United States—David Plouffe is still not a household name. That is no accident. His relative anonymity was part of his campaign strategy: the focus, he insisted, must be on the candidate and on the message.

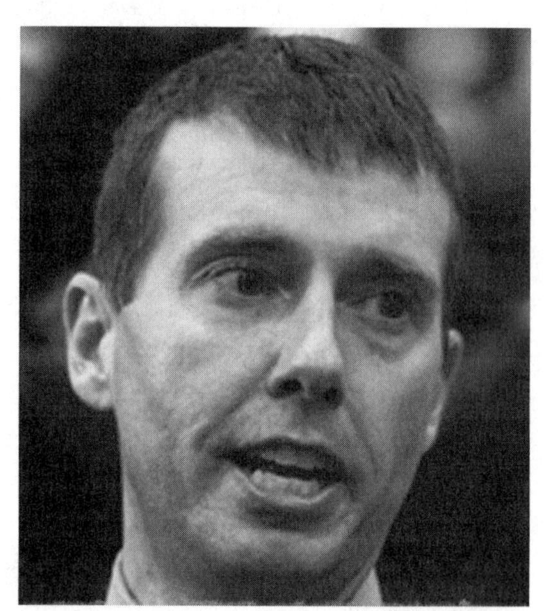

Chip Somodevilla/Getty Images

Plouffe has been working behind the scenes in the political arena for more than 20 years, since the summer following his junior year of college. He helped to manage several U.S. House and Senate campaigns, for Democratic legislators including Tom Harkin, John Olver, Robert G. "Bob" Torricelli, and Richard "Dick" Gephardt, before he undertook what was by far his biggest and most ambitious project. That job began in January 2007, when Obama, then a U.S. senator from Illinois, announced that he was a candidate for president. As Obama's campaign manager, Plouffe was ultimately responsible for the allocation of more than $750 million (nearly $1 billion, according to some sources) in campaign funds, the activities of millions of volunteers, and the work of more than 5,000 paid staff members, who dealt with the press, research, technology, outreach (on the ground and via the Web), scheduling, advertising, and many other aspects of the operation. His in-depth knowledge of the country's voters and obsessive attention to detail helped lead Obama to victory.

A few weeks before Obama was sworn in as president, he vacationed with his family in Hawaii and spoke to very few reporters. Among those few was Lisa Taddeo, who was writing a profile of Plouffe for *Esquire* (March 1, 2009). During Obama's conversation with Taddeo, he waxed lyrical about his campaign manager: "If you just look at the mechanics of our campaign, how we raised money, how we turned out votes, how we managed the caucus process—all these pieces were incredibly complex, and we had to build it from scratch. . . . I'm not sure there's anybody [else] who could have done it." Then Obama added: "David is a very unassuming guy. He's not flashy. He's not loud. He doesn't wear his brilliance on his sleeve. He's not trying to impress people. But what I think people miss with David is how tough he is—somebody who's very confident about what he knows, and he's able to stand his ground when he thinks he's right."

The third of the five children of James and Frances Plouffe, David Plouffe was born in Wilmington, Delaware, on May 27, 1967. According to whorunsgov.com, he grew up in a working-class family. After graduating from high school, in 1985, he enrolled at the University of Delaware, as a political-science major. According to the *Esquire* profile, during his college years Plouffe spent far more time hanging out with his friends and drinking beer than he did studying. He was also an enthusiastic fan of baseball. He dropped out of college in 1988. "He told me he was more interested in practical politics," James J. Magee, one of his professors, told the whorunsgov.com reporter.

Plouffe's affinity for the Democratic Party led him to seek work connected with politics. He landed his first such job in the summer of 1988, as one of 25 young aides hired by the political strategist Joe Hansen to work on the U.S. Senate campaign of Samuel S. Beard. According to Taddeo, "In two weeks Plouffe became the boss of them all." "Plouffe outperformed everybody, by every metric," Hansen told her. In 1990 Plouffe was hired as the deputy field director for the reelection campaign of U.S. senator Tom Harkin of Iowa—"a job that was better than mine," Hansen told Taddeo, "so realize that in one cycle it went from me supervising him to him supervising me."

Two years later Plouffe served as the Iowa state field director for Harkin's presidential run, which ended when Bill Clinton, then the governor of Arkansas, won the primaries. During that campaign Plouffe learned a lot more about Iowa's geography, the characteristics of the various segments of its population (especially farmers), and procedural rules regarding the Iowa caucuses, which since 1972 have been scheduled earlier than any other state's primary. Plouffe's experiences in Iowa paid off in January 2008, when his strategy enabled Obama to win the Iowa caucuses—an unexpected outcome that boosted Obama's national profile significantly. Later in 1992 Plouffe managed the successful reelection campaign of the freshman congressman John W. Olver of Massachusetts. His next several campaign jobs were also on the East Coast.

In 1994 Attorney General Charles M. Oberly of Delaware hired Plouffe to direct his campaign for a seat in the U.S. Senate. Oberly was the underdog: he was up against a four-term incumbent, the Republican William V. Roth Jr. That year, in a perceived rejection of the policies of President Clinton and his Democratic supporters in the House and Senate, the Republican Party gained control of both houses of Congress for the first time in four decades. Oberly lost the election, but in light of the Democrats' trouncing nationally, he got a relatively large portion of the vote—42 percent. He also ended his run with leftover campaign funds, which he donated to charity. In 1996 Plouffe served as manager for the senatorial campaign of Congressman Bob Torricelli of New Jersey. Torricelli and his Republican opponent, another New Jersey congressman, Richard A. "Dick" Zimmer, sought to fill the seat of Senator Bill Bradley, a Democrat, who had announced that he would be leaving the Senate. In a bitter race, Torricelli painted Zimmer, a moderate Republican, as an extreme right-winger and repeatedly denounced him for voting to cut funds from federal programs for education. He also attacked Zimmer for his support of the Contract with America, the GOP's promise to the American people to pass, within 100 days of Congress's opening day in 1995, legislation aimed at shrinking the federal government, lowering taxes, and reforming welfare, among other provisions. Torricelli, who raised twice as much for his war chest as did Zimmer, won the election, with 53 percent of the vote. Twelve years later, at the beginning of the 2008 presidential race, U.S. senator Hillary Clinton of New York—Obama's chief rival for the Democratic nomination—asked Torricelli whether Plouffe was good at his job. Speaking about that conversation to Peter Nicholas of the *Los Angeles Times* (July 8, 2008), Torricelli simply said, "I warned her."

From 1997 to 1998 Plouffe served as deputy chief of staff to Congressman Dick Gephardt of Missouri. He took on the role of senior strategist for Gephardt's 2004 bid for the Democratic presidential nomination, which the legislator lost to U.S. senator John Kerry of Massachusetts. From 1999 to 2000 Plouffe served as executive director of the Democratic Congressional Campaign Committee (DCCC). During that time he helped raise $95 million for House races—a record sum. He also made a remark that, in retrospect, was prescient: "I'm not sure that the Internet is the place that swing voters will turn to get information," he was quoted as saying in the *National Journal* (March 16, 2000). "But we think that candidates should be prepared for that to happen."

In 2000 Plouffe joined Axelrod & Associates, a firm headed by the expert political strategist David Axelrod. When Plouffe became a partner with the firm, four years later, Axelrod & Associates changed its name to AKP&D Message & Media (the "P" stands for Plouffe; "K" and "D" are John Kupper and John Del Cecato, respectively). Also in 2004 the firm ran Obama's victorious campaign for the U.S. Senate. In that election's seven-candidate Democratic primary, in March, Obama got 53 percent of the vote, which brought him a lot of attention. And in June of that year he got even more attention when he delivered an anti-partisanship speech at the Democratic National Convention. After the speech Obama's Republican opponent withdrew from the Senate race; his replacement, Alan Keyes, was not thought to present a serious challenge. Obama won that election, in November, with 70 percent of the vote. In 2006 Plouffe and Axelrod worked on Duval Patrick's successful campaign for governor of Massachusetts. In a four-way race, Patrick received 56 percent of the ballots, becoming only the second elected black governor in U.S. history.

AKP&D's next assignment was Obama's presidential campaign. As early as 2006 rumors had started to circulate that Obama might be considering a run for the presidency. Plouffe had no doubts about Obama's qualifications, but he wondered whether the senator was ready to assume the huge demands and burdens of campaigning for national office. "My sense is we had this conversation about whether he was going to run or not," Plouffe told Lloyd Grove for the now-defunct *Portfolio* (December 11, 2008), "and I had a pretty high degree of confidence that he had the intellect and the character and temperament to be a very good president. The bigger question was, could he be a good presidential candidate, because that's the horse of a different color—the grueling nature of it. He hadn't spent any time in Iowa, New Hampshire, didn't have a fundraising base. He had young kids—he wouldn't see them very often. Those are the big questions. Could he transact this brutal obstacle course at the presidential campaign?" In December 2006, at a strategy session with Obama and several of Obama's closest advisers, Plouffe laid out his state-by-state campaign strategy. The team began to implement it soon afterward.

In its initial phase the campaign was a small operation; Plouffe had virtually no money and a staff of only five people. In April, with the first primaries nine months away, Plouffe hired Jeff Berman, a former strategist for Gephardt whom Noam Scheiber, writing for the *New Republic* (May 7, 2008), called "probably the party's most respected authority on the dark art of delegate math"—voter analyses that seek to predict which states, counties, and age groups are important in light of the number of delegates likely to vote for a given candidate. By October Plouffe had organized "ground operations"—staff and volunteers—in heavily Republican states, among them Kansas and Colorado. One of his principal aims was to win in those and other states and in election districts where he believed that Hillary Clinton would not make a major effort to achieve victory.

Plouffe employed many strategies, using election math, volunteers, and technology in unprecedented ways. According to the *Esquire* profile, he divided the United States into 16 separate campaign regions with "a different strategy for each battleground state—and gave each its own ground crew and press office." In addition, Obama's team compiled approximately 13 million e-mail addresses and four million cellphone numbers, and they assigned tasks to two million volunteers (half of whom had never before been involved in politics). Plouffe emphasized to Taddeo that it would be a mistake to attribute Obama's success mainly to the use of new technology: also essential to Obama's victory were contacts that staff and volunteers made with voters on the phone and in person—what is commonly referred to as "fieldwork." Plouffe's frugality, too, made a crucial difference. In the *Los Angeles Times*, Nicholas wrote that although the Obama campaign was "one of the best-funded in history, Plouffe is famously tight." Cab rides, for example, were not reimbursed; staff members had to take public transportation. They were also asked to "double up" when staying in hotels. Nicholas reported that Plouffe's thriftiness inspired Axelrod to make up a joke: "Wave your hand under the automatic towel dispensers in the restrooms at campaign headquarters and a towel comes out. Wave your hand a second time and a message pops up: 'See Plouffe.'" By avoiding unnecessary spending, the Obama campaign had more money for advertising.

One of Plouffe's "most underappreciated accomplishments" of the election, in Scheiber's words, began with a color-coded spreadsheet that delineated the Democratic race for the nomination state-by-state. After more than two dozen state primaries, the overall result of which was widely judged to be inconclusive, the spreadsheet became public, in what at first seemed to be an unauthorized leak. In retrospect, though, many political observers suggested that the leak had been *made* to look unauthorized. In any event, the spreadsheet's appearance in one publication after another served its purpose: Plouffe wanted the press to cover what he thought was the real story—that despite Clinton's name recognition and greater experience, Obama, as determined by a very sophisticated analysis of data, was beating her. Obama then went on a roll, winning 11 primaries in succession by February 21. At that point, Scheiber wrote, the Obama campaign "was dropping spreadsheets like a nightclub drops fliers," and they had become "a sophisticated form of spin."

The next turning point, and what Plouffe in several interviews called "my biggest mistake" of the campaign, came in March, during the Ohio and Texas primaries. Obama lost both primaries to Clinton, and the campaign went on for another three months. By April eight Democratic primaries remained, in North Carolina, West Virginia, Montana, Puerto Rico, Kentucky, Oregon, Indiana, and South Dakota; in order to secure the Democratic nomination, Clinton would have to win a great majority of the popular vote, something that Plouffe insisted was highly unlikely. Throughout the year it was at times debatable who had the momentum, Clinton or Obama, but numbers, Plouffe said to the press, were hard to argue with. "He's fascinated by numbers," Bill Carrick, a Democratic consultant who worked with Plouffe during his time at the DCCC, told John McCormick for the *Chicago Tribune* (June 9, 2008). "He just has an insatiable appetite for this stuff and he could keep all of it in his head." After losing the Pennsylvania primary, Obama won in North Carolina and came close to victory in Indiana, losing with 49 percent of the vote to Clinton's 51. Then Obama went on to win in Oregon and Montana and lose in West Virginia, South Dakota, and Kentucky. Clinton's victories in the last three states, however, were not enough to give her a sufficient number of delegates to assure her victory, and on June 7 she officially ended her candidacy. After clinching the nomination, Obama gave a speech in which he expressed his gratitude to Plouffe: "Thank you to our campaign manager David Plouffe, who never gets any credit, but who has built the best political organization in the country."

After the summer of 2008, Obama's battle with the Republican Party nominee, U.S. senator John McCain of Arizona, became more intense. During that time Plouffe focused his efforts on winning in states, such as Montana and Colorado, where many thought a Democrat should not even try. Plouffe, with the political machine he had been running for nearly two years, continued to employ the state-by-state strategy that had proven so effective against Clinton; meanwhile, perhaps as part of his determination to spotlight his candidate rather than himself, he appears to have gone even further behind the scenes during the general-election campaign. Still, Ryan Lizza reported for the *New Yorker* (November 17, 2008) that in September 2008 Plouffe asked the campaign's budget chief, Jim Messina, if $7 million could be allotted for a 30-minute infomercial to air a week before Election Day. The resulting TV spot attracted an estimated 33 million viewers. In it, Obama presented his plans for rejuvenating the economy and withdrawing U.S. troops from Iraq; the infomercial also featured stories of families from swing states, including Ohio, and endorsements from notable supporters, among them New Mexico governor Bill Richardson. Although McCain won in some traditionally Republican states—Utah, North Dakota, and Texas—he lost in such important party strongholds as Florida, Virginia, Nevada, and Colorado. On the evening of November 4, 2008, Obama was declared the winner of the presidential race.

After Obama's victory, Mike Allen reported for Politico.com (December 5, 2008), more than 18 publishers approached Plouffe and expressed an interest in the book he is writing about the campaign; he accepted a seven-figure offer from Viking. The book's working title is "The Audacity to Win: The Inside Story and Lessons of Barack Obama's Historic Victory"—a reference to the title of Obama's book *The Audacity of Hope*. According to Allen, "The Obama campaign was a billion-dollar business, and Plouffe plans to write about the use of technology, grassroots organizing, crisis management, use of the Web, public relations and personnel." Plouffe has also had many corporate consulting offers. Represented by the Washington Speakers Bureau, he has given many talks about the Obama campaign and what can be learned from it. He has said that he plans to use the 13 million e-mail addresses gathered during Obama's campaign to advocate for the president's policies.

Plouffe declined to join the Obama administration because, he said, he wanted to spend more time with his family. He is married to Olivia Morgan, who was an adviser to Gray Davis, the governor of California from 1999 to 2003, and served as a spokesperson for the DCCC. Plouffe and his wife have two children—a son, born in 2005, and a daughter, born two days after the 2008 presidential election. According to the *Falmouth (Massachusetts) News* (March 31, 2009), the couple recently bought a home in Woods Hole, Massachusetts.

—D.K.

Suggested Reading: akpdmedia.com; *Chicago Tribune* C p1+ June 9, 2008; *Esquire* p122+ Mar. 1, 2009; *New Republic* p8 May 7, 2008; *New York Times* P p1+ Nov. 5, 2008; whorunsgov.com; (Wilmington, Delaware) *News Journal* (on-line) June 11, 2008, Aug. 25, 2008

Prodigy

Music group

Howlett, Liam
Aug. 21, 1971– Lyricist; musician; producer

Reality, Maxim
Mar. 21, 1967– MC; vocalist

Flint, Keith
Sep. 17, 1969– Dancer; vocalist

Address: Cooking Vinyl, P.O. Box 1845, London W3 0ZA, England

The British band the Prodigy "can fairly be described as the techno equivalent of [the rock bands] U2 or Oasis," David Pollock declared in the London *Independent* (December 10, 2008, on-line);

Courtesy of the Prodigy

The Prodigy (left to right): Keith Flint, Liam Howlett, Maxim Reality

"the perfectly timed half-step they tread outside the pace of what's fashionable is just enough to ease them into the realm of the timeless rather than the overtly dated." The Prodigy was founded as a one-man act by the lyricist/musician/producer Liam Howlett in about 1989, when he was 18. Howlett, who got his start as a breakdancer and a deejay at raves in Essex, England, was soon joined by the dancer/vocalist Keith Flint and the MC/vocalist Maxim Reality; another dancer/keyboardist, Leeroy Thornhill, was a member from 1990 to 2000. Howlett leads the Prodigy, and his is the only name that has appeared on the group's record contracts. Arguably the most influential of the electronic dance bands that emerged in Great Britain in the 1990s, the Prodigy was largely responsible for awakening interest in that genre in U.S. audiences.

The Prodigy's first album, *Experience* (1992), is regarded as a classic by cognoscenti of electronic dance music. The next, *Music for the Jilted Generation* (1994), "broke free of *Experience*'s rave conventions into a style that was entirely the Prodigy's own," Alex Petridis wrote for the London *Guardian* (August 1, 2008, on-line); with it, the band "reinvent[ed] themselves as parent-scaring anti-establishment figures." "None of their peers came up with anything like" the "gripping blend of distorted guitar, thumping warp-speed techno, drum'n'bass breakbeats and rasping flute" that the Prodigy offered in their second disc, Petridis wrote. "Indeed, the sense of audacity that marks out the album's highlights quickly became the Prodigy's trademark." The group's third album, *Fat of the Land* (1997), became the first recording of electronic dance music to debut at number one on the *Billboard* 200 chart; it debuted at the top spot in 22 other countries as well and sold 8.5 million copies worldwide, and its singles "Firestarter," "Breathe," and the controversial "Smack My Bitch Up" were chart toppers, too. In 2002, after seven years of being on the road together, the Prodigy took a break from touring. Although the band remained intact, Flint and Maxim (as he is commonly known) were not included in the Prodigy's next album, *Always Outnumbered, Never Outgunned* (2004). In 2005 the group resumed giving performances, in support of their compilation album, *Their Law: The Singles 1990–2005*. Tickets to the dozens of concerts scheduled for the arena tour the Prodigy launched in late 2008 sold out in one hour. Reporting on one of those concerts, presented in Sheffield, England, a couple of months before their latest album, *Invaders Must Die* (2009), went on sale, Dave Simpson wrote for the *Guardian* (December 16, 2008, on-line), "It's incredible that such preposterous anarchy on stage can produce such a thrilling, even dangerous racket. The Prodigy haven't changed—they've just turned everything up and added enough new cusses to run up a national debt at the swear box. The new material returns to their mid-90s trademark of making a simple and ostensibly meaningless slogan seem terribly important and threatening." *Invaders Must Die* was released on the Prodigy's own, new label, Cooking Vinyl. As of mid-2009 the Prodigy's five albums had sold a total of over 16 million copies worldwide, more than those of any other dance-music act. "For a band who started out being thought of as a novelty," John Robinson wrote for the *Guardian* (April 4, 2009, on-line), "the Prodigy have proved to endure remarkably well."

Liam Paul Howlett was born on August 21, 1971 in Cressing, in Essex, a county that borders Greater London in southeastern England. His father, who ran a grouting-implement factory, started him on piano lessons when he was very young. As a preadolescent Howlett became drawn to ska, hip-hop, and other music with a raw, dance-oriented edge; his favorite band was the Specials, whom he discovered on a British ska compilation album that his father bought for him. By the time he reached high school, Howlett had become drawn to hip-hop and its culture. The seminal hip-hop film *Beat Street* (1984) introduced him to the music of artists including Grandmaster Flash and Afrika Bambaataa. At 14 Howlett began mixing songs he recorded from the radio by using the pause button on his cassette player. Soon afterward he bought a set of turntables. He also learned how to breakdance, then formed a breakdancing crew, the Pure City Breakers. His talent as a deejay earned him both first- and third-place honors at a deejay-tape competition that he had entered under two aliases. Commenting on hip-hop's influence on him, Howlett told Chris Heath for *Rolling Stone* (August 21, 1997, on-line), "It wasn't just the music. It felt real. It felt like it was from the street. I knew that it was a ghetto thing. I knew it was somewhere I could never go, so it was special. It was the fact that no one else liked it. It felt like it was my own thing. Once I got it loud up in my room, nothing else mattered."

While he was a high-school student, at Alex Hunter Humanities College, in Essex (in Great Britain, secondary-level schools are sometimes called colleges), Howlett deejayed with a hip-hop band called Cut 2 Kill. Because he was white, other hip-hop bands viewed Cut 2 Kill as outsiders; once, a rival group robbed them at knifepoint. Howlett left the band in about 1988, when his bandmates used his demos to get a record deal that excluded him. Convinced "that there was no room for white people" in hip-hop, as he told a writer for *Spin* (September 1997, on-line), he abandoned that genre. Howlett then got a job at a London-based graphic-design magazine called *Metropolitan*. (Easily available sources do not reveal whether he earned a diploma from his school.) While listening to pirate radio stations at work, he heard about the burgeoning British rave scene. Shortly after he attended a rave for the first time, in 1989, at the age of 17, Howlett started deejaying at a popular rave haunt called the Barn, in the town of Braintree, Essex, and at other rave parties. He soon became a fixture on the scene and began to introduce original material that he created at his home studio under the moniker the Prodigy. Some sources have inaccurately linked that name to the brand of Moog synthesizer that he used; rather, he chose it because he wanted a name that sounded "grand," as he recalled to a writer for *Q* (December 1997, on-line). "When I first thought of the name, obviously I didn't consider it could be four people," he said. "It was just me, faceless in my bedroom, writing music: the prodigy."

Howlett's skills won him a strong following at the Barn. Two of his most avid fans were Keith Flint (born on September 17, 1969 in Chelmsford, Essex, England) and Leeroy Thornhill (born on October 8, 1968). With the idea of building the Prodigy into a more prominent act, Flint and Thornhill offered to perform as stage dancers during Howlett's live sets. Howlett accepted their proposal and then decided to add an MC who would serve as the group's frontman. The band chose the reggae vocalist Maxim Reality (born Keith "Keeti" Palmer, the youngest of seven children, on March 21, 1967 in Peterborough, Cambridgeshire, England), who had been recommended to them by their soon-to-be manager, known only as Ziggy. Emulating an older brother, Maxim had begun working as an MC at 14. Commenting on his move from reggae to dance music, he recalled to the *Spin* writer, "In them days, to be a good MC, you had to write lyrics every day. I found the dance scene easy to MC to because there wasn't any lyrical foundation. Lyrics are just fillers. The last thing people want is to hear you talking about life and politics. In a way, it took a bit away from me; the lyrics I used to write were quite deep—politics, old age, everyday life. My lyric style was . . . reality. That's where the name 'Maxim Reality' came from."

Now a quartet, the Prodigy performed on the United Kingdom club circuit for several months. (A female vocalist known as Sharky also appeared with them briefly.) At around that time Howlett secured a deal with XL Recordings; his was the only name on the contract (as it has been on all of Prodigy's succeeding contracts with record companies). The Prodigy's first single, "What Evil Lurks," was released in 1991; it sold around 7,000 copies. The group's second single, "Charly," which sampled the meow of a cat from a popular series of short TV films for children about public safety, reached number three on the British singles chart and helped increase recognition of the Prodigy on the rave circuit. The electronic-dance monthly *Mixmag* (August 1992) later criticized "Charly" for inspiring a slew of copycat singles that sampled children's-television themes; called "toytown techno," such music was condemned as sacrilege by enthusiasts of breakbeat hardcore. (Hardcore was the musical genre most commonly associated with the British rave scene; it was characterized by the combination of four-to-the-floor rhythms, played in 4/4 time, with rapid-fire polyrhythmic breakbeats.) The magazine further blamed the group for ushering in rave's supposed downfall and for "turning dance music from an ultra-cool and wildly subversive folk devil into a national laughing stock"—"an opinion widely shared by the club cognoscenti," Alexis Petridis wrote for the London *Guardian* (August 24, 2004, on-line). Such criticism notwithstanding, the Prodigy's third single, "Everybody in the Place," reached the second spot on the U.K. charts.

In 1992 the Prodigy released their debut album, *Experience*, which entered the British charts at number 12 and sold more than 200,000 copies in Great Britain. In a review that appeared years later in the All Music Guide (on-line), John Bush wrote, "One of the few noncompilation rave albums of any worth, *Experience* balances a supply of top-this siren whistles and chipmunk divas with Liam Howlett's surprising flair for constructing track after track of intense breakbeat techno. Almost every song sounds like a potential chart-topper (circa 1992, of course) while the true singles 'Your Love,' 'Charly,' 'Music Reach,' and 'Out of Space' add that extra bit of energy to the fray. More than just a relic of the rave experience, *Experience* shows the Prodigy near the peak of their game from the get-go."

The Prodigy's 79-minute second album, *Music for the Jilted Generation* (1994), was inspired by the British Parliament's passage of the Criminal Justice and Public Order Act of 1994, a complex, wide-ranging piece of legislation that criminalized aspects of raves. Unlike *Experience*, which was largely made up of hyperfast breakbeats and helium-induced vocals, *Music for the Jilted Generation* experimented with various styles—ambient, industrial, funk, and rap; it relied more on slower tempos with harder-sounding beats and incorporated hallucinatory whooshing effects and the sounds of shattering glass. One of its singles, the multilayered, mid-tempo "Poison," featured Maxim growling a voodoo-like chant ("I got the poison / I got the remedy / I got the pulsating rhythmical remedy"); another, "Their Law," opened with a sample from the 1977 movie *Smokey and the Bandit* ("What we're dealing with here is a total lack of respect for the law"), which led to a grinding guitar riff that gave way to an anarchic chorus ("F*** 'em and their law"), sung by the former Pop Will Eat Itself frontman Clint Mansell. *Music for the Jilted Generation* received widespread praise from critics and was nominated for a Mercury Music Prize (now known as the Barclaycard Mercury Prize), bestowed annually to the best album from the United Kingdom or Ireland. Paul Evans later wrote for *Rolling Stone* (February 2, 1998, on-line), "A soundtrack for those British rave hordes who dodge Tory truncheons, *Music for the Jilted Generation* thrills initiates with a political buzz Americans might miss. But the Prodigy's hard-core techno generates universal dance fever. Mastermind Liam Howlett mixes relentless jungle grooves that add guitars to the keyboard shudder 'Voodoo People' and then turn spacey on 'The Heat (The Energy).' 'No Good (Start the Dance),' with ecstatic vocal snippets, is as heady an anthem as any in a genre that exults in billboard statements; more ambitious is 'The Narcotic Suite.' The latter begins in woozy ganjaland and climaxes in an acid swirl, an echoing voice intoning, 'My mind is glowing.' Truly trippy." John Bush, in the All Music Guide, called the album "pure sonic terrorism," adding, "*Music for the Jilted Generation* employs the same rave energy that charged . . . *Experience* . . . up the charts in Britain, but yokes it to a cause other than massive drug intake. Compared to [the Prodigy's] previous work, the sound is grubbier and less reliant on samples; the effect moved the Prodigy away from the American-influenced rave and acid house of the past and toward a uniquely British vision of breakbeat techno that was increasingly allied to the limey invention of drum'n'bass."

While electronic dance music was enjoying mainstream popularity in Europe, it appeared to have little appeal to Americans; although *Music for the Jilted Generation* reached number one on British album charts, in the U.S. it sold poorly, peaking at 198 on the *Billboard* 200 album chart. Determined to reach a much bigger audience, the Prodigy began to present themselves as a "hard dance band" and to perform at rock festivals in the U.S. and other sites overseas. "Making people dance when they're out of their heads on ecstasy wasn't really that much of a challenge," Howlett told Ben Thompson for the London *Independent* (June 29, 1997), referring to the rave scene. He added, "There was no one on the dance scene who could create the energy on stage that a rock band did."

The Prodigy's reputation as a live act was strengthened with their performance in June 1995 at the Glastonbury Festival, in Pilton, England—one of the world's largest outdoor music and performing-arts festivals. Over the next 12 months, the band toured other parts of Europe, Australia, and the U.S. March 1996 saw the release of "Firestarter," a paroxysmal dance track that sampled two grunge acts, the Breeders and the Art of Noise. "Firestarter," in which Flint provided punk-style vocals, became the Prodigy's first major international hit and immediately shot to number one on the U.K. singles chart. The accompanying video, in which Flint looked like a cross between the Sex Pistols' Johnny Rotten and the monstrous clown from Stephen King's *It*, went into heavy rotation in the U.S. on the music channel MTV. That, in turn, helped another single, "Breathe," to become a bestseller. A major bidding war among U.S. music labels ensued; it ended when the Prodigy signed a contract with Maverick Records, a subsidiary of Warner Bros.

In June 1997 the Prodigy released *Fat of the Land*. (The band's name appears on that album as simply Prodigy.) With sales of more than 200,000 copies in the U.S. in its first week in stores, the album debuted at number one on the *Billboard* 200 album chart—an extremely rare feat for an electronic-dance-music disk. *Fat of the Land*, which debuted at number one in 22 other countries as well, offered simplified melodies, sparser sampling, and Flint's snarling punk-like vocals. Many critics hailed the album as a masterpiece. In a representative assessment, Barney Hoskyns, writing for *Rolling Stone* (July 1997), began with a take on electronic dance music in general: "Rarely has a pop trend so shamelessly been spoon-fed to America as the catch-all genre dubbed 'electronica.' Rarely, indeed, has the music industry tried so hard to convince us that the Next Big Thing is in fact a done deal—that another wave of English boys holds the future in its hands and we'd better get used to it. . . . Lately, dissenting voices have questioned the wisdom of the electronica hype. America, they argue, will never embrace the underground subculture of techno." Hoskyns continued, "Enter the Prodigy . . . and their bullishly titled third album, *Fat of the Land*. To say that the Prodigy aren't self-effacing synth nerds would be a comical understatement. To suggest that they are the Sex Pistols of techno would not even be such an exaggeration. What the Prodigy have done, quite simply, is to drag techno out of the communal nirvana of the rave and turn it into outlandish punk theater—and they've done it brilliantly. . . . *Fat of the Land* is a thrilling, intoxicating nightmare of a record, an energy flash of supernova proportions." One of the tracks, "Smack My Bitch Up," whose lyrics consisted solely of the lines "Change my pitch up / Smack my bitch up," angered women's organizations; the accompanying video, shot from the point of view of a person (revealed at the end to be a woman) taking drugs and drinking at clubs before picking up a lap dancer and having sex with her, generated far more controversy.

Thornhill left the Prodigy in 2000, because of trouble with his legs and the desire to pursue a solo career. (He has since performed with the band occasionally but never rejoined it.) The group's single "Baby's Got a Temper" (2002) launched what the British critic Louis Pattison, writing for Amazon.com, described as a "disastrous" comeback campaign that "found the band stagnant and on the verge of self-parody." Although Flint and Maxim remained members of the band, neither contributed to the Prodigy's next album, *Always Outnumbered, Never Outgunned* (2004). (The title was inspired by that of Walter Mosley's 1997 novel, *Always Outnumbered, Always Outgunned.*) The decision to make the recording without Flint and Maxim was Howlett's, who felt that as a threesome the band was in a rut. "Success and happiness makes you lazy and slows you down," he commented to Angus Batey for the *Guardian* (February 6, 2009). Maxim concurred, telling Batey, "We toured for almost seven years straight, and we were in each other's space for so long we needed to get away from that and have some different thoughts." Being cut off from the Prodigy troubled Flint, however; he told Batey, "I had no creative outlet at all. It really screwed me up, and I screwed myself up. I'm quite self-destructive." (In an example of his self-destructiveness, he had what he termed "quite a bad accident" while racing with a motorcycle team.)

Performers who contributed to *Always Outnumbered, Never Outgunned* included Liam Gallagher (Oasis's frontman), Kool Keith, Juliette Lewis, Twista, and the Ping Pong Bitches. Critical reception to the album was decidedly mixed—it earned an eight out of 10 from the *Drowned in Sound* (August 25, 2004, on-line) reviewer, four out of five from a London *Observer* (July 18, 2004) critic, and two out of five stars from the *Guardian* (August 20, 2004) and *Rolling Stone* (September 20, 2004). Nevertheless, on the U.K. album charts, the album reached number one, where it remained for one week only.

Howlett, Flint, and Maxim joined to record the Prodigy's fifth studio album, *Invaders Must Die* (2009). The album's singles, including "Omen" and "Warrior's Dance," marked a return to the band's rave roots. *Invaders Must Die* debuted at the top spot on the U.K. album charts. Between the beginning of January and the end of August 2009, the Prodigy performed at more than 80 sold-out concerts, in Singapore and cities in Great Britain, Ireland, the European continent, the U.S., Puerto Rico, Australia, New Zealand, and Japan. The group planned to tour in support of the album through March 2010.

In 2002 Howlett married the British singer Natalie Appleton, a member of the British-Canadian all-female pop group All Saints. Appleton's sister Nicole, a member of the same band, is married to Liam Gallagher. Howlett and his wife have a son, Ace Billy, born in 2004; Appleton also has a teenage daughter, Rachel, from her first marriage. In their house, outside Chelmsford, England—where their neighbors include Flint and his wife—Howlett has a state-of-the-art recording studio. Maxim and his wife have two sons and a daughter.

—C.C.

Suggested Reading: *Kerrang* (on-line) June 1997; (London) *Guardian* (on-line) Aug. 20, 2004, Feb. 9, 2009; *Mixmag* (on-line) Aug. 1992; *Rolling Stone* (on-line) Aug. 21, 1997; *Spin* (on-line) Sep. 1997; XLR8R Web site; Reynolds, Simon. *Generation Ecstasy: Into the World of Techno and Rave Culture*, 1999

Selected Recordings: *Experience*, 1992; *Music for the Jilted Generation*, 1994; *Fat of the Land*, 1997; *Always Outnumbered, Never Outgunned*, 2004; *Invaders Must Die*, 2009; EPs—*What Evil Lurks*, 1991; *Baby's Got a Temper*, 2002; compilations—*The Dirtchamber Sessions Volume One*, 1999; *Their Law: The Singles 1990–2005*, 2005

Rahman, A. R.

Jan. 6, 1966– Composer for films

Address: Panchathan Record Inn / A.M. Studios, No. 23, Dr. Subbaraya Nagar, 5th St., Swamiar Madam, Kidambakkam, Chennai 24, India

More likely than not, fans of movies made in India "need no introduction" to the composer A. R. Rahman, Richard Corliss wrote for *Time* (January 1, 2005, on-line). "Like Gershwin, Puccini or Lennon-McCartney, the name stands for melody, quality, energy, instant hummability—a sound both personal and universal, devouring older forms and transforming them into something gorgeously new." Since 1992 Rahman has scored and written songs for more than 100 films, including Mani Ratnam's *Roja* (1992) and *Dil Se . . .* (1998), Deepa Mehta's *Fire* (1996), *Earth* (1998), and *Water* (2005), Subhash Ghai's *Taal* (1999), and Danny Boyle's *Slumdog Millionaire* (2008). Rahman is "a composer every focused director loves to work with," Mani Ratnam told Arthur J. Pais for *India Abroad* (February 13, 2009). "He never sits down thinking, let me make a hit tune. Rather, he wants to know what exactly the director wants to do."

The 43-year-old Rahman—dubbed by Corliss in *Time* (May 3, 2004) the "Mozart of Madras," a reference to his hometown—has been credited with revolutionizing film music in his country. Trained in classical Western techniques and long familiar with a bevy of traditional folk instruments from India and elsewhere, he acquired hands-on knowledge of the electronic synthesizer as a child and be-

STR/AFP/Getty Images

A.R. Rahman

came a working musician in adolescence. Uncommonly experimental and innovative, "he shifted things from a simple East–West mode to a multicultural, global mode, where India and its regional musics are part of a palette of sound from around the world," David Novak, an ethnomusicologist at Columbia University's Heyman Center for the Humanities, in New York City, told Ben Sisario for the *New York Times* (February 21, 2009). "Before the advent of Rahman it took . . . 100 violin strings playing plaintively to augur an impending romance [in an Indian film], and a whole orchestra working together swept up emotions," B. S. Prakash wrote for *India Abroad* (July 14, 2006). "Rahman . . . changed that. He made street sounds respectable, made you listen to a single beat, say of rice husk being pounded, to natural sounds of daily implements and more." Rahman has won many awards in India, and his work for *Slumdog Millionaire* earned him two Academy Awards, for best score and best song.

Rahman was born A. S. Dileep Kumar on January 6, 1966 in Chennai (long known in the West as Madras), India's fourth-largest city and the capital of Tamil Nadu, one of India's 28 states. He was the second of the four children of R. K. Sekhar and his wife, Kasturi Sekhar, ethnic Tamils whose religion was Hinduism. Rahman has three sisters: Kanchana, Bala (now called Talat), and Israth. His mother was a homemaker, his father a well-known music arranger and composer in Malayalam cinema. (India is home to the most prolific film industry in the world, producing nearly 1,000 films a year. In a large portion of those films, the actors speak Hindi, which, with English, is considered one of the country's official languages; in other motion pictures, the characters speak one of the other 17 languages named in the Indian constitution, among them Tamil, Kannada, Telugu, Malayalam, Marathi, Bengali, Punjabi, and Urdu. Though many Westerners use the term "Bollywood" to refer to all Indian films, it actually applies only to the country's Mumbai-based Hindi-language film industry.)

Rahman's exposure to music began at birth, and he started piano lessons at the age of four. Nevertheless, he "was not crazy about music" and thought of it solely as "a means of earning bread and butter," he recalled to Shoma A. Chatterji for the Indian *Statesman* (January 31, 2009, on-line); he was far more interested in technology. His attitude toward music changed when his father brought home a synthesizer, "one of the very first in film circles then, from Singapore . . . ," he told Chatterji. "I could not take my eyes off the synthesizer. It was like a forbidden toy. I would spend hours experimenting with it. It has remained my favourite instrument because it was the ideal combination of music and technology."

After suffering from an unidentified illness for years, Rahman's father died when Rahman was nine. Left with no money and without a marketable skill, his mother began to rent out her late husband's instruments. "It was a difficult period. We had nobody to look after us . . . ," Rahman told interviewers for the *Hindustan Times* (July 22, 2006, on-line). "We had no support. Dad's family seemed to have vanished into thin air. It was lonely and sad. But Ma was optimistic." Urged by his mother to help the family by earning money as a musician, by age 11 Rahman had joined the troupe of the film composer Ilaiyaraaja as a keyboard player and computer programmer. Rahman graduated from high school, but because of his family's financial situation, he had to abandon his dream of attending college and becoming a software engineer. "I had to make a choice," he told reporters for the *Hindustan Times*. "I couldn't manage academics and earn a livelihood. Between the two, it was clear what I had to do. I was the only breadwinner in my family." In 1982 he changed his name to Allah Rakha Rahman, because, he told the *Hindustan Times* interviewers, his birth name "brought back very bad memories. It just didn't suit me." At around the same time, his mother changed her name to Kareema Begum.

Rahman continued to work as a keyboardist with Ilaiyaraaja's ensemble and others, among them those of the composers and music directors M. S. Viswanathan and Ramesh Naidu, the celebrated tabla player Zakir Hussain, and the violinist Kunnakudi Vaidyanathan. He also performed with such local rock bands as Magic, Fusion, and Nemesis Avenue. In 1987 Rahman began to compose music for radio and television commercials. His tunes for jingles for Tata Tea, Leo Coffee, and the watchmaker Titan Industries became very popular. At around that time Rahman won a scholarship to Trinity College of Music in London, England. As a participant in a distance-learning program, he studied Western classical music in Chennai.

In 1988 Rahman's family converted to Islam. According to some sources, their decision stemmed from their association with a Sufi Muslim mystic whose prayers they credited with restoring one of Rahman's sisters to health, after she had fallen severely ill; other sources reported that the mystic helped everybody in the family to accept the hardships of their lives with greater equanimity. When the *Hindustan Times* interviewers asked Rahman about his family's conversion, he said, "It wasn't that one day I suddenly got up and said, 'hey, let's convert.' It was a gradual progression and came naturally. I embraced Sufi Islam. For me it wasn't a religion but a belief. It was spiritualism. It healed me and gave me peace."

Starting in the early 1990s, Rahman built a recording studio in his home in Chennai. Originally called Panchathan Record Inn and recently renamed A.M. Studios, it has become one of the most technologically advanced recording sites in Asia.

A chat Rahman had with the Tamil director Mani Ratnam at a party led to his first job for cinema: composing the score and six songs, among them "Chinna Chinna Aasai," for *Roja* (*The Rose*). The hesitation he felt about taking on the project ended when Ratnam promised him full creative control. Released in 1992, *Roja* is about an Indian woman whose lover is abducted by Pakistani terrorists. The words to the songs were written in the Tamil language by the poet and lyricist Vairamuthu. Unlike most Tamil film music at the time, Rahman's compositions were layered and complex and included instruments—synthesizers and guitars, for example—seldom used in Indian productions. Also very unusually, Rahman encouraged the musicians to improvise. In 2005 Richard Corliss chose *Roja*'s soundtrack as one of *Time* magazine's 10 best of all time. "The songs and score for *Roja* . . . [are] possibly [Rahman's] best and most consistent work to date," Soutik Biswas wrote for the BBC News (February 23, 2009, on-line). "Working with a number of vocalists, the film's music showcases his talents—fusing flutes, synthesisers and traditional melody to a reggae backbeat and a rolling bass line. Sometimes it felt like listening to The Wailers—Bob Marley's iconic reggae band—playing to Indian vocals." Rahman won India's 1993 National Film Award for best music director, becoming the first composer to win that prize in a cinematic debut. He also received the 1993 Tamil Nadu State Film Award and the 1993 Filmfare Award for best music director. He became a household name in India with his scores for Ratnam's *Bombay* (1995), Ram Gopal Varma's *Rangeela* (1995), his first Hindi film, *Dil Se . . .* (1998), and *Taal* (1999).

Most of Rahman's work has been for films in the Tamil, Hindi, and Telugu languages. He picks his projects carefully, and, unlike some of Bollywood's most prolific composers, who score up to 150 movies a year, he composes at a deliberate pace. "Rather than making money, I believe in making people happy; all other things are secondary," he told S. R. Ashok Kummar for the Chennai *Hindu* (1993, on-line). "That is why I am not interested in a lot of movies but only in one at a time. . . . I have evolved a technique which requires a lot of time. Other music directors record a song in seven or eight hours. But I am different. We do a basic sitting and we record it. We record the voice and I add instrument by instrument to improve the quality." After Rahman takes on a new project, he told *Rolling Stone India* (June 2008, on-line), "There is always this question: 'How can I do this best?' I've never ever thought, let me just do a fast job. But I have never looked at music in any other way. Whatever goes out of my studio is precious."

Rahman's "Chaiyya Chaiyya," a song from the *Dil Se . . .* soundtrack, was a major hit: according to a BBC worldwide music poll involving 155 countries, it was ranked ninth out of 7,000 nominated songs. In addition, it is said to have prompted the famous musical-theater composer Andrew Lloyd Webber to collaborate with Rahman. In 2000 Lloyd Webber asked Rahman to compose the score for *Bombay Dreams*, a musical that Lloyd Webber was to produce. (It was the first musical that he produced for which he did not also compose.) Lloyd Webber told Matt Wolf for the Associated Press (June 17, 2002, on-line) that with *Bombay Dreams* he looked forward to introducing to the London theatergoing public "a superb melodist"—Rahman—"who's got a real idea of drama." The lavish, $7 million *Bombay Dreams*, with book by Meera Syal and lyrics by Don Black, debuted in a West End theater in London on June 19, 2002. A tale of a young slum-dweller who aspires to become a Bollywood star, it included the song "Shakalaka Baby," which gained great popularity; the highly praised ballad "The Journey Home"; and more than a dozen other songs, among them "Happy Ending," "How Many Stars," "Like an Eagle," and "Salaam Bombay." Despite mixed reviews, it was nominated for the 2003 Laurence Olivier Award for best new musical and enjoyed a two-year run in London, in part because of the interest it aroused in the city's large number of immigrants from the Indian subcontinent (about 12 percent of the population). A significantly changed version of *Bombay Dreams*, with some of Rahman's songs deleted and new ones added, ran for eight months on Broadway, in New York City, in 2004. In a lukewarm review of that $14 million production for the *New York Times* (April 30, 2004), Ben Brantley wrote, "The songs by A R Rahman . . . are now performed by a 19-member orchestra, nearly twice the size of that in London, and they have seemingly been rearranged (by Paul Bogaev and Christopher Nightingale) to please the ears of Americans accustomed to Top 40 fare, sacrificing some of the beguiling intricacy the music had in London."

In 2004 Rahman began working with the Finnish folk band Värttinä to compose music for a stage adaptation of J. R. R. Tolkien's *Lord of the Rings* trilogy. The show debuted in 2006 in Toronto, Ontario, Canada, and ran there for six months. Rahman, Värttinä, and Christopher Nightingale, who served as musical supervisor, were nominated for the Toronto Alliance for the Performing Arts 2006 Dora Mavor Moore Award for outstanding musical direction. *The Lord of the Rings* opened in London in June 2007. In a representative review of the British mounting, a critic for the London *Times* (June 20, 2007), after noting that "almost everything that was wrong" in the Canadian mounting "has been put right" for the British run, wrote, "The music . . . , airy and earthy by turns, carries and intensifies the story's swell of feeling." In a poll conducted in late 2008 by the British theater Web site Dress Circle, *The Lord of the Rings* ranked seventh on a list of the 10 "greatest musicals of the last 30 years."

Rahman wrote the score for Ping He's Hong Kong–made action film *Warriors of Heaven and Earth* (2003), Jag Mundhra's motion picture *Provoked: A True Story* (2006), filmed in India and England, and Shekhar Kapur's historical drama *Elizabeth: The Golden Age* (2007), starring Cate Blanchett and filmed in Great Britain, France, and Germany. Indian-made films for which he won one or more awards include *Rangeela* (1995), *Minsaara Kanavu* (1997), *Taal* (1999), *Lagaan: Once Upon a Time in India* (2001), *Saathiya* (2002), *The Legend of Bhagat Singh* (2002), *Kannathil Muthamittal* (2002), *Swades: We, the People* (2004), *Rang De Basanti* (2006), *Guru* (2007), *Jodhaa Akbar* (2008), and *Jaane Tu . . . Ya Jaane Na* (2008).

Slumdog Millionaire is about a poor Indian boy who, as an adult, competes on a universally watched TV quiz show in an attempt to find his lost love. In agreeing to write the score for the film, Rahman had to turn down the opportunity to work once again with the Indian director Ashutosh Gowariker, the director of *Lagaan* and *Jodhaa Akbar*. "I was hooked by the way Danny [Boyle] had directed [*Slumdog Millionaire*]," he told Arthur J. Pais for *India Abroad* (January 23, 2009). "I wanted to be a part of the film. In my career, I have taken up many films which were out of the box. And I thought this was one such project." Boyle, whose directorial credits also include *Trainspotting*, *A Life Less Ordinary*, *28 Days Later . . .*, and *Millions*, has avoided using sentimental music in his films; he asked Rahman for an edgy, loud, and vibrant score. Rahman worked with the Sri Lanka–born British musician M.I.A. and several popular Indian artists, including Ila Arun and Sukhwinder Singh, to produce a fast-paced, pulse-pounding blend of old and contemporary Indian music and hip-hop. "In the West, we are afraid of using music that loudly announces the emotions," Boyle told Pais. "In India, they are not afraid of using music that is loud and melodious at the same time. Rahman's work has elevated the film immensely." *Slumdog Millionaire* won the 2009 Academy Award for best motion picture, and Rahman received many honors for his score and/or songs, including two Academy Awards; a British Academy of Film and Television Arts (BAFTA) Award; a Golden Globe; and awards from the Broadcast Film Critics Association, the Chicago Film Critics Association, and the International Press Academy. Rahman was included on *Fast Company*'s list of the 100 most creative people in business and *Time*'s list of the world's 100 most influential people. On June 30, 2009, by invitation, he joined the Academy of Motion Picture Arts and Sciences. His most recent film scores were heard in the American romantic comedy *Couples Retreat* (2009) and the science-fiction action film *Endhiran* (2009).

"After a point of time, when you get success and fame, money and everything, the purpose of life has to be redefined," Rahman told Lauren Streib for *Forbes* (January 6, 2009, on-line). "For me, I think that purpose is to build bridges. Artists can do that very easily, more than politicians." In 2004 Rahman was appointed global ambassador of the World Health Organization's Stop TB Partnership. He established the A. R. Rahman Foundation to work to eradicate hunger and poverty through education. In 2008 he and the musician T. Selva Kumar (also identified as a music programmer whose surname is spelled Selvakumar) set up the KM Music Conservatory, which offers courses in Indian and Western music, voice lessons, and training in a dozen Western instruments to people of any age. "Music as a profession needs to be recognised here like law, medicine or engineering," Rahman told the *Times of India*, as reported by Mahathi R Arjun (February 24, 2009, on-line). He added, "I would love to see an orchestra like the London Philharmonic or the New York Philharmonic right here in Chennai."

Rahman has been described as unusually self-effacing. He and his wife, Saira Banu, have been married since 1995. The couple live in Chennai with their two daughters, Khatija and Rahima, and their son, Ameen.

—M.A.S.

Suggested Reading: ARRahman.com; *Hindustan Times* (on-line) Apr. 22, 2006; (Indian) *Statesman* (on-line) Jan. 31, 2009; (New York) *India Abroad* M p2 Feb. 13, 2009; *Time* (on-line) Jan. 1, 2005

Selected Film Scores and Soundtracks: *Roja*, 1992; *Rangeela*, 1995; *Bombay*, 1995; *Fire*, 1996; *Minsaara Kanavu*, 1997; *Dil Se . . .*, 1998; *Earth*, 1998; *Taal*, 1999; *Lagaan: Once Upon a Time in India*, 2001; *Saathiya*, 2002; *The Legend of Bhagat Singh*, 2002; *Kannathil Muthamittal*, 2002; *Warriors of Heaven and Earth*, 2003; *Swades: We, the People*, 2004; *Water*, 2005; *Rang De Basanti*, 2006; *Provoked: A True Story*, 2006; *Elizabeth: The Golden Age*, 2007; *Guru*, 2007; *Jodhaa Akbar*, 2008; *Jaane Tu . . . Ya Jaane Na*,

2008; *Slumdog Millionaire*, 2008; *Couples Retreat*, 2009; *Endhiran*, 2009

Selected Recordings: *Vande Mataram*, 1997; *Live*, 2000; *Live in Dubai*, 2004

Selected Stage Musicals: *Bombay Dreams*, 2002; *The Lord of the Rings*, 2006

Doug Benc/Getty Images

Ramirez, Hanley

(ruh-MEER-ez)

Dec. 23, 1983– Baseball player

Address: Florida Marlins, Dolphin Stadium, 2267 Dan Marino Blvd., Miami, FL 33056

The Florida Marlins' shortstop Hanley Ramirez has often been called a "five-tool" player, a term used to describe those who excel at running, throwing, fielding, hitting for average (that is, getting on first base), and hitting for power (reaching second or third base). One of the top all-around offensive players in Major League Baseball (MLB), Ramirez began to develop his athletic talents in the Dominican Republic at the age of four, and at 16 he signed a $55,000, five-year contract with a Boston Red Sox minor-league team. "Before I signed I didn't know they paid you for playing baseball," he told Kevin Baxter for the *Miami Herald* (March 2, 2006). "I played because I loved it. It was incredible when they told me they were going to sign me and they were going to give me money." In the minors Ramirez quickly caught the eye of baseball insiders and fans. He was named the Red Sox organization's number-one prospect by *American Baseball* in both 2004 and 2005, and many believed he was being groomed to join that American League team by 2006. But after he played two major-league games with the Red Sox in 2005, its management traded him to the National League's Marlins. He has now completed four major-league seasons with the Marlins, compiling a solid .316 batting average, with 470 runs, 170 doubles, 22 triples, 103 home runs, 313 runs batted in (RBIs), 164 stolen bases, and a .531 slugging percentage. (In determining the slugging percentage, the player's total number of points is divided by the number of at-bats, with a single rating one point, a double two points, a triple three points, and a home run four points.) Ramirez, who wears the number two in honor of his idol, the New York Yankees' shortstop Derek Jeter, was named the National League Rookie of the Year in 2006 and the Marlins' Most Valuable Player three consecutive times (2007–09), and he was the starting shortstop and leadoff hitter for the National League All-Star team in both 2008 and 2009. Ramirez became the first Marlins player to capture the National League batting title when he finished the 2009 season with the league's highest batting average (.342).

Although his defensive game is relatively weak, Ramirez has drawn plaudits from some of baseball's most accomplished players. José Reyes, the All-Star New York Mets shortstop, told Matt Baker for the Fort Lauderdale, Florida, *Sun-Sentinel* (May 27, 2007), "When I play against him, I see a kid who has a lot of talent, a kid who's working hard and trying to learn. He plays the game with passion. He plays the game hard. He plays the game the right way." Larry Bowa, a Los Angeles Dodgers coach and former five-time All-Star shortstop, told Joe Capozzi for the *Palm Beach (Florida) Post* (March 30, 2008) that Ramirez is "right up there with the best, if he's not the best. Put it this way: Nobody's better. There might be some guys tied. This guy does it all." The Hall of Fame shortstop Cal Ripken Jr. told Capozzi that Ramirez "has the whole package: power, speed—something I never had—and great range and instincts at shortstop. . . . He is only 24 years old and he is still growing stronger and getting more familiar with the league. He is very exciting." During the 2006 MLB winter meetings, held in Lake Buena Vista, Florida, in early December, the Cincinnati Reds' right fielder and 10-time Golden Glove winner Ken Griffey Jr., who ranks sixth in MLB history in number of home runs, told reporters that Ramirez would be his first pick if he were starting a franchise. "Ramirez is virtually anonymous to the casual fan," Scott Priestle wrote for the *Columbus (Ohio) Dispatch* (May 18, 2008). "But die-hards and fantasy players know him well, as do scouts, players and executives across the league. He has as complete a collection of skills as any player in the game." For his part, Ramirez told Clark Spencer for the *Miami Herald* (February 20, 2008), "It's about the team. It's not Hanley. It's the Marlins."

Hanley Ramirez was born on December 23, 1983 in Samana, Dominican Republic, to Toribio and Isabel Ramirez. He has two half-sisters and a half-brother. His father, an auto mechanic, owned a local garage; his mother was a homemaker. One of his great-grandmothers was born in the U.S., and as a child he absorbed some English by listening to his grandfather. Ramirez started playing baseball at age four and won his first trophy a year later, after leading his Little League team in home runs, with a total of at least six. Recognizing his love for baseball and his outstanding talents, his parents—who had little interest in baseball and had dreamed of his becoming an engineer—supported him by accompanying him to and from games, watching him play, and buying him gloves, bats, and balls; they believed, as Ramirez's father told Kevin Baxter, that "if a person likes something, they can be successful at it." Ramirez attended Adbentista High School and excelled on the school's baseball team. Levy Ochoa, a scout for the Boston Red Sox, noticed him and in July 2000 successfully recruited him for one of the team's minor-league affiliates. "The best day of my life was the day I signed with the Red Sox because it was the team I always dreamed of playing with," Ramirez told Stan Grossfeld for the *Boston Globe* (December 17, 2004). Ramirez participated in spring training in Boston, Massachusetts.

In 2001 Ramirez played for Boston's rookie-level Dominican Summer League affiliate, DS Red Sox, in the Dominican capital, Santo Domingo, and compiled a .345 batting average, with five home runs and 34 RBIs in 54 games. The following year he made his U.S. minor-league debut with the rookie-level Gulf Coast League Red Sox in Fort Myers, Florida. He was promoted on August 10, 2002 to the single-A Lowell Spinners team in Lowell, Massachusetts, and finished his rookie season with a batting average of .352 with 46 runs, 20 doubles, five triples, seven home runs, and 45 RBIs in 67 games—statistics that earned him the title of Lowell's Player of the Year. He was named the New York–Penn Leagues' Player of the Week (August 13–19, 2002) after hitting .548 in seven games and won the Red Sox minor-league player of the month award for August, during which he hit .383 in 25 games. He led the league with a .555 slugging percentage and was selected for the postseason Gulf Coast League All-Star team. Some members of the press and others touted him as the Red Sox organization's best prospect. Then, in October 2002, during Boston's Fall Instructional League, Ramirez cursed an assistant trainer and was sent back to the Dominican Republic temporarily. "I used to think I was hot," he later admitted to Kevin Thomas for the *Portland (Maine) Press Herald* (February 27, 2005). In Santo Domingo he strived to improve his skills at the Red Sox Dominican Baseball Academy.

Back in the U.S. Ramirez spent the 111-game 2003 season with the single-A Augusta GreenJackets, in Georgia. By the season's end he ranked second among Red Sox players for bases stolen (36); his batting average was .272, with 69 runs, eight home runs, 50 RBIs, 24 doubles, and three triples. He got into trouble again in May 2004, when he made an obscene gesture toward his team's dugout; he was suspended from the field for 10 days. "I learned from that," he told Steven Krasner for the *Providence (Rhode Island) Journal* (February 28, 2005). "You have to grow up. When you get to the big leagues, you're not a baby anymore. You have to be a man." Ramirez spent the off-season in Santo Domingo, playing for the Licey Tigers, a Dominican Winter League team. He also worked to improve his English.

In the January 7, 2004 on-line edition of the twice-monthly periodical *Baseball America*, Jim Callis ranked Ramirez first among the Red Sox's top prospects; citing his "quick hands" and "pitch recognition beyond his years," he wrote that Ramirez was "the best athlete and fastest baserunner, and has the strongest infield arm in the Red Sox system." Ramirez started the 2004 season with the single-A Sarasota Red Sox, in Florida, and won the title of SaraSox Player of the Year; he was also chosen as a mid-season All-Star for the West Division squad. He hit .310, with a home run, 24 RBIs, eight doubles, four triples, and 12 stolen bases in 62 games before he suffered a hairline fracture in his left wrist as the result of falling while running bases on May 1. Placed on the disabled list, he played with the Gulf Coast Red Sox while he recuperated. After rejoining Sarasota on June 30 and hitting .360 in 29 games, he was promoted in August to the double-A Portland Sea Dogs in Maine; in 12 games he posted a .512 slugging percentage and hit .310, with five home runs, 15 RBIs, and 12 stolen bases. The news in December 2004 that Boston had signed the shortstop Edgar Renteria to a four-year contract ended speculation that Ramirez would join the team roster by 2006 and fueled talk that the 20-year-old might be assigned another position.

In 2005 *Baseball America* again picked Ramirez as the top prospect in the Red Sox organization as well as the number 10 prospect in all of minor-league baseball. Ramirez played in 122 games with the Portland Sea Dogs during the 2005 season, batting .271, with six home runs and 52 RBIs. Once again he led the Red Sox minor league in stolen bases, with 26. Portland was the 2005 Eastern League's North Division champion, and Ramirez played in both the Eastern League All-Star Game and the All-Star Futures Game.

Ramirez made his major-league debut with the Red Sox on September 20, 2005. During that game, against the Tampa Bay Devil Rays (now called the Rays), he was called in as a defensive replacement in the seventh inning. His only other appearance with the Red Sox occurred on October 2, in a game against the New York Yankees. Ramirez returned to the Dominican Republic soon afterward to play with the Licey Tigers, helping the team win the Caribbean World Series. On November 24, 2005 the

Red Sox traded Ramirez and three minor-league pitchers to the Marlins in exchange for the third-baseman Mike Lowell and two pitchers, Josh Beckett and Guillermo Mota. Ramirez admitted to Dom Amore for the *Hartford (Connecticut) Courant* (August 12, 2007), "I was down at first when I was traded from Boston but this was my chance to play every day in the major leagues, so I wasn't down after I came [to Florida]." He felt welcomed in Florida and quickly became the team's top prospect for the starting-shortstop position. He debuted in that spot at the start of the 2006 season.

Ramirez experienced a slump in June, in which he batted .126, but he finished the season with a .292 batting average, 119 runs, 46 doubles, 11 triples, 17 home runs, 59 RBIs, and 51 stolen bases. That year he had the highest batting average of any qualifying rookie in MLB and set a club rookie record for runs, the most by a National League rookie since 1964 and the most by a major-league rookie since the Seattle Mariners' Ichiro Suzuki in 2001. Ramirez also became the fifth major-league player since 1900 to hit more than 45 doubles and steal more than 50 bases in a single season and the first National League rookie to score more than 110 runs and steal more than 50 bases in a single season. He is only the second National League rookie to hit 17 home runs in a season while playing more than 100 games as a shortstop. Ramirez's batting average of .341 during the final two months of the season led the Baseball Writers' Association of America to name him National League Rookie of the Year. Joe Girardi, the Marlins' manager in 2006, told Clark Spencer for the *Miami Herald* (November 14, 2006) that he was "not surprised" that the writers' association had honored Ramirez. "He's a special player. He has a knack for scoring runs and making things happen. I think the sky's the limit for this kid."

In 2007 Ramirez made 24 fielding errors, more than any other National League shortstop that season, but his offensive game continued to improve: his batting average rose to .332 (a tie with two other players and the third-highest in the league), 212 hits (second-highest in the league), 125 runs, 48 doubles, 29 home runs, 81 RBIs, 51 stolen bases (third-highest), and a slugging percentage of .562. He missed four games during the season after he dislocated a shoulder on July 22. The injury had not healed when he returned to play, and he had to keep it iced virtually all the time; during the off-season he underwent surgery to repair it. Nevertheless, Ramirez was named the Marlins' Most Valuable Player by the Southern Florida chapter of the Baseball Writers' Association of America. In March 2008 Ramirez renewed his contract with the Marlins; with a $37,000 pay raise, his annual salary reached $439,000.

Fans, players, coaches, and managers chose Ramirez to play in the 2008 All-Star Game. Having received 2.3 million votes from fans in the balloting for starting shortstop, Ramirez won that position on the National League All-Star team. He was also the leadoff hitter in the game, which took place on July 15 at Yankee Stadium, in the Bronx, New York. In a conversation with Mike Berardino for the Fort Lauderdale, Florida, *Sun-Sentinel* (July 7, 2008), Ramirez recalled that he has been watching the All-Star Games every year since he was five. "Everybody in the Dominican watched it . . . ," he said. "My people are going to be watching me." Indeed, although in the U.S. he is not famous, in his native land he is a star.

As the 2008 season approached, Ramirez was determined to perform outstandingly. "Everybody can have one good year," he told Clark Spencer for the *Miami Herald* (March 7, 2008). "I've got to prove I can do it again." By the season's end Ramirez had racked up a .301 batting average, 125 runs, 34 doubles, 33 home runs, 67 RBIs, and 35 stolen bases. In November he received the Louisville Slugger 2008 Silver Slugger Award for National League shortstops. The award, whose winner is selected by MLB coaches and managers, recognizes each season's best offensive players at each position in both the American and National Leagues. Earlier that year, in May, Ramirez had signed a $70 million contract extension through 2014 with the Marlins. He told Joe Capozzi for the *Palm Beach (Florida) Post* (March 3, 2008) that he had no desire to leave the team. "I just want to stay here for my career. . . . I think they treat me good from the bottom all the way to the top. I feel comfortable here."

In March 2009 Ramirez played with the Dominican Republic team during the World Baseball Classic. (The team lost during the first round of games.) For his fourth season with the Marlins, Ramirez moved from leadoff hitter to the third spot in the team's batting lineup, a position he relished. "All the good hitters, they're hitting third, fourth or fifth. I want to be around those guys," he told Joe Frisaro for MLB.com (February 26, 2009). The change proved fruitful: Ramirez ended the 2009 season with a .342 batting average, 101 runs, 42 doubles, 24 home runs, 106 RBIs, and a .543 slugging percentage. He was once again voted the Marlins' Most Valuable Player and won the Louisville Slugger 2009 National League Silver Bat Award. "I don't really take him for granted. . . . There is really nothing he can't do," Larry Beinfest, the president of baseball operations for the Marlins, told Joe Frisaro for MLB.com (October 4, 2009). "He can do it all. So when he does something, you just say, 'That's Hanley being Hanley.' But that doesn't mean he's not being appreciated. He just had another great year."

Ramirez told Juan C. Rodriguez for the *Sun-Sentinel* (February 25, 2007) that when he "made it to the big leagues," he "treated everybody the same if not better." "I told him you have to be humble with people and be decent," his mother told the same reporter. "That's the main thing. He's always had his fans and he signs [autographs], talks to people. Humility and decency are beautiful things. We're all human and you can't think yourself superior to another."

Ramirez and his wife, Elisabeth, maintain homes in both the Dominican Republic and Florida. The couple have two young sons, Hanley Jr. (born in 2004) and Hansel (born in 2007). The six-foot three-inch, 225-pound Ramirez enjoys shooting pool and playing video games.

—M.A.S.

Suggested Reading: *Boston Globe* D p1 Dec. 17, 2004; *Columbus (Ohio) Dispatch* C p6 May 18, 2008; HanleyRamirez.com; *Palm Beach (Florida) Post* p3 Mar. 30, 2008; *Portland (Maine) Press Herald* D p1 Feb. 27, 2005; (San Francisco, California) *Bohemio News* S p14 June 29, 2007; *Sports Illustrated* p54 May 7, 2007

Roger Kisby/Getty Images

Rock, Pete

June 21, 1970– Record producer; deejay

Address: c/o Nature Sounds, 109 S. Fifth St., Brooklyn, NY 11211

Among the many producers of hip-hop music since its inception, in the 1970s, Pete Rock is widely recognized as one of the most innovative and influential. Rock is a member of the second wave of hip-hop artists, who came of age during the decade beginning in the mid-1980s—hip-hop's "golden era." Like a significant number of other hip-hop masters, he grew up in Mount Vernon, a New York City suburb, where he learned the art and craft of the deejay. "I'm a DJ first before production and a lot of cats don't realize that being a DJ makes you a producer," he told Stephanie St. James for hiphop-elements.com (January 6, 2008). While the seminal duo Pete Rock and C.L. Smooth made three highly praised recordings during its brief existence (1991–94), Rock is probably more famous for his contributions as "the king of the remix"—work that was crucial in defining the bass-heavy, sample-infused early-to-mid-1990s East Coast hip-hop sound. His jazz- and soul-soaked instrumental compositions provided the sonic backdrop for many classics of the era, among them his and C.L. Smooth's "They Reminisce Over You (T.R.O.Y.)," "Shut 'Em Down," by Public Enemy, "The World Is Yours," by Nas, and "Down with the King," by Run-D.M.C. His work has often been cited to refute charges that hip-hop music is not a creative art; according to his admirers, witnessing Rock mix and scratch records or come up with an entirely original sound from 10 disparate and obscure samples on his SP-1200 sampler or more state-of-the-art equipment is no different from watching a skilled musician play an instrument. Bill Murphy wrote for *Remix* (June 1, 2004) that "what set him apart from the rest was his refined taste for complex horn and string arrangements, as well as his uncanny ability to unearth that rare, essential break." Rock "revolutionized rap production through groundbreaking studio wizardry," according to the Web site of the record label Okayplayer. "He made remixes matter more than the original songs. He established ad-libs as a standard recording asset. He introduced dramatic, forceful horns to rap's sonic discussion." He also initiated the tradition of adding intros and interludes to his recordings, making them sound more like exclusive deejay mix tapes than vehicles for commercial hits.

For *PopMatters* (June 27, 2003), Mark Anthony Neal wrote that "the so-called hip-hop/jazz hybrid" associated with Rock "never really took the hip-hop mainstream to the heights of improvisational genius." Nevertheless, as Neal pointed out, in the liner notes to *The Best of Pete Rock & C.L. Smooth: Good Life* (2003), the hip-hop specialist Charlie Braxton compared Rock and two other renowned hip-hop producers/deejays to three legendary jazz saxophonists. Marley Marl, one of Rock's mentors, Braxton wrote, "would be analogous to [Coleman] Hawkins, because he single-handedly changed the way we listen to hip-hop by popularizing the use of sampled drum tracks," while DJ Premier "would be akin to Charlie Parker, because of the way he chops up multiple samples to form his own rhythms and complex melodies." Braxton likened Rock to the intellectually curious, inventive, and nimble John Coltrane, because Rock has "dared to dig deeper into the musical lexicon to bring new excogitation to hip-hop"—that is, a new understanding and conception of and insight into the genre. While Rock's impressive portfolio has earned him the respect of critics, fans, and his peers, his music has rarely crossed over to the mainstream. In an interview with Andrew Friedman for *Guitar Center* (April 11, 2008, on-line), Rock advised aspiring producers "to have passion for what you do. . . . You gotta love what you're doing with your heart and soul."

A son of immigrants from Jamaica, Pete Rock was born Peter Phillips on June 21, 1970 in the New York City borough of the Bronx. During various periods he has called himself Soul Brother Number One, Chocolate Boy Wonder, and the Creator. When he was about seven, he and his family moved to Mount Vernon, a suburb of the city adjacent to the northeast Bronx. Rock has two brothers, two sisters, and two paternal half-sisters. His younger brother, Gregory, raps as Grap Luva, and his older cousin Dwight Myers as Heavy D; Heavy D's brother Floyd was a disc jockey whose group was named the Classic Rock Crew. Rock's father was a part-time disc jockey; the owner of upwards of 50,000 reggae, soul, jazz, hip-hop, and other vinyl recordings, he played a major role in Rock's musical development. In an interview with Andrew Mason for the magazine *Wax Poetics* (Issue 7, Winter 2004), Rock said that he has traced his interest in sound to a day when he was three years old: "My father was playing records and the music just did something to me. It made me want to dance, it made me want to hear more." "I used to play my father's 45's, stuff like James Brown, when he wasn't home," he told a reporter for the *Michigan Citizen* (November 7, 1992). "I'd always get in trouble because he had the stuff in a certain way, so when he came home, he'd know I messed with it." His father, he said, taught him "all about" music: composers, instrumentalists, vocalists, disc jockeys, the recording industry, the proper way to clean and store records, and how to listen to music and identify "catchy basslines and memorable drum patters," as he told an interviewer for okayplayer.com. He often watched his father spin reggae and soul records at matches of a Bronx cricket club named Wembley.

Rock told Mason that one day when he was about seven, he experimented with his cousin Floyd's equipment when Floyd was not home. "He came in and busted me, got mad at me, but I was so anxious to learn how to scratch that he showed me how . . . ," he said. "By watching him I learned why you needed two copies. You had to keep the beat going, you had to be quick on your hands." Rock began buying his own records with money he earned from a job as a paperboy. By the time he entered high school, he had started deejaying at parties and was making mixes, using the pause button on his cassette tape recorder in a rudimentary sample setup. He also owned two turntables, a mixer, and a tape deck. "If you're doing parties it's important that you know how to keep the crowd dancing," he told Mason. "To be a real DJ you need to know how to blend, scratch, and know what records to put on at what time." Rock would take his beats to another Mount Vernon resident, DJ Eddie F (Edward Ferrell, later a member of Heavy D and The Boyz), who was so impressed that he taught the 14-year-old Rock how to use the SP-1200, a beat, sample, and looping machine with which Rock became expert. "I studied that manual inside and out," Rock recalled, as quoted on okayplayer.com. "I did not come outside for a long time—for a couple of years." "Just as the Stradivarius or the Fender Stratocaster were standard-bearers by which other instruments were judged, the SP-1200 quickly became the tool of choice for East Coast beat-makers during rap's so-called 'Golden Age,' . . . ," Ben Detrick wrote for the *Village Voice* (November 6, 2007). "The machine rose to such prominence that its strengths and weaknesses sculpted an entire era of music: The crunchy digitized drums, choppy segmented samples, and murky filtered basslines that characterize the vintage New York sound are all mechanisms of the machine." Rock revolutionized the techniques of filtering (isolating the desired sound, usually a bassline, by muffling everything else), chopping (cutting samples into segments), and layering (using several samples at a time), to create sophisticated, textured soundscapes.

In 1986 Heavy D won a recording contract and began working with the groundbreaking producers Howie T (born Christian Howard) and Marley Marl (born Marlon Williams). Rock closely observed some of their recording sessions. By age 17 or so, he had started to assist with production on albums by Heavy D and by the short-lived group Groove B Chill. His influences, in addition to Marley Marl, included such successful deejays as Red Alert, Afrika Bambaataa, Mr. Magic, Chuck Chillout, Africa Islam, Jazzy Jay, Grand Wizard Theodore, Flash, and DST.

Rock got his first big break in 1987, when he was invited to deejay on Marley Marl's pioneering radio show *In Control* on WBLS-FM in New York, after the regular deejay, Kevvy Kev, was injured in a car accident. Referred to on the show as the man "puttin' in work," Rock soon made a name for himself as a skillful innovator, with a sound and style of his own. Meanwhile, he had forged a partnership with his friend Corey Penn, who renamed himself C.L. Smooth. "His voice was so distinctive," Rock told Mason. "He sounded like no one out there . . . and that's what attracted me. I thought, let's see what we can do." After recording and sending out dozens of demos, Rock and C.L. Smooth were signed by Elektra, in 1991. Their first record, a six-song EP titled *All Souled Out*, "officially introduced Pete Rock & C.L. Smooth to the hip-hop listening community, and it is hard to imagine a stronger or more confident introduction," Stanton Swihart wrote for the All Music Guide (on-line). "Pete Rock's unmatched production sound is already in place, fully-formed, drenched in obscure soul music samples and rumbling, cavernous bass. Characterized by his trademark sonic signature, muted and phased trumpet, and flute loops, the songs sound regal with endless depth. . . . Of course, C.L. Smooth's lyrics have just as much to do with that regal quality. . . . Bypassing the normal rap self-involvements, Smooth instead opts to make moral arguments and ask intellectual questions of the urban community, in essence holding a mirror up to that community without ever devolving into didacticism or soap-box judgment. He is decidedly tough-minded but also sympathetic. Standouts include both versions of 'Good Life,' the irresistible 'Go with the Flow,' and the anthemic title track, with rapid-fire rhyming from Smooth and a perfectly funky organ riff, but the whole EP is essential."

Also in 1991, acting on the conviction that "the original way of doing a remix was about changing the whole beat altogether, to make something hotter than the original," as he told Bill Murphy, Rock produced the remix of Public Enemy's song "Shut 'Em Down." According to Murphy, "Rock's horn-heavy, stupefyingly funky remix almost single-handedly secured his place in the pantheon." Named the best remix of all time in *Ego Trip's Book of Rap Lists* (1999), by Sacha Jenkins and others, the song hugely boosted Rock's reputation, and he found himself much-sought-after as a producer. Six months later, in 1992, Rock & C.L. Smooth released their first full-length album, *Mecca and the Soul Brother*. "*Mecca* is a hip-hop classic . . . ," Sabrina Miller wrote for the *St. Petersburg (Florida) Times* (August 14, 1992). "Each song tells a story. The soul-inspired music creates a lush, dramatic feel. It's not clichéd or misdirected, it's just the truth." A *Michigan Citizen* (November 7, 1992) critic described the album as "at once streetwise and effortlessly complex, brimming with an intricate, wide-ranging and highly developed musical talent," while Mark Anthony Neal characterized it as "one of the most finely crafted hip-hop recordings ever" and expressed his admiration for the "interludes, where Pete Rock offered snippets of the classic jazz that he was listening to—like Cannonball Adderley, Eddie Harris, and Les McCann." A dozen years later Richard Harrington wrote for the *Washington Post* (August 27, 2004), "The album derived its power from Rock's distinctive production techniques, a spare meld of rock-solid drums and cymbals beats, cavernous bass and taut horn loops." The lead single, "They Reminisce Over You (T.R.O.Y.)," honors the memory of Troy Dixon, who as a member of Heavy D & The Boys was known as Trouble T-Roy. That song "is on a very short list of the most exquisite hip-hop recordings ever," Neal wrote; Harrington pronounced the song to be "one of the most moving tracks in the genre's history." In his interview with Mason, Rock identified the track "Straighten It Out" as his "signature sound." In "Straighten It Out," Neal wrote, Rock and C.L. Smooth "defend the practice of sampling—an art-form (yes, I called it that) that has often been portrayed as a form of theft in its own right," and they reminded listeners that "that practice of sampling (in its most creative forms . . .) is not simply about appropriating, but reconstructing."

In the first half of the 1990s, in addition to his work with C.L. Smooth, Rock's name was associated with a significant number of commercially successful songs, as a producer and a remixer. Among many other hit songs, he produced EPMD's "Rampage" (remix); Brand Nubian's "Slow Down" (remix); Run-D.M.C.'s "Down with the King" (which, by his own account, Rock produced in the same sessions as he did the remix of House of Pain's "Jump Around"); Naughty by Nature's "Hip Hop Hooray" (remix); Nas's "The World Is Yours"; and Das EFX's "Jussumen" (remix). He also created the original beats for A Tribe Called Quest's "Jazz (We've Got)" and (although he was never officially credited) the Notorious B.I.G.'s smash hit "Juicy." In 1994 Rock and C.L. Smooth released their second full-length album, *The Main Ingredient*. Reviewers agreed that it was another tour de force. "In characteristic Pete Rock fashion, all of the sharp edges have been sanded down, leaving a vibrant and completely lush musical backdrop which seems to have a dreamy nostalgia about it," Stanton Swihart wrote for the All Music Guide. "Old '60s and '70s soul, soul-jazz, and funk samples abound, and the music is dotted with gauzy keyboard washes, hugely echoed bass-drum kicks, milky basslines, and muted horn loops, almost sounding like they are emanating out of water." Soon after *The Main Ingredient* went on sale, Rock and C.L. Smooth ended their partnership, for reasons that remain unclear. "It was a lot of record company madness, and there were a lot of things going down as far as money was concerned," Rock told Russell Myrie for the *Village Voice* (March 14, 2004). "At the time, we were so young and we weren't on top of our business. We only cared about the music. That costs you."

Rock next formed INI (pronounced "I and I" and sometimes spelled "Ini"), with Grap Luva, Rob-O (Robert Odindo), Rass (Rahsaan T. Rousseau), and Marco Polo (Marco Paolo Bruno). The group released the 12-inch single "Fakin' Jax" (1996), the lyrics of which were said to be intended as a putdown of C.L. Smooth. Elektra shelved INI's full-length album, *Center of Attention*, because, according to Rock, Sylvia Rhone, the chairman and CEO of Elektra Entertainment at that time, made demands that were unacceptable to him. "It was all about her changing everything around," Rock told Mason. "She wanted to change my whole sound. When she said, 'You gotta make a beat like Puffy,' I just knew it wasn't going to work out." Widely considered to be an underground gem, *Center of Attention* was heavily bootlegged; in 2003 it was released on Barely Breaking Even (BBE), a British label. With the rapper Deda (Nick Dida), Rock recorded *The Original Baby Pa*; Elektra shelved that album, too, and it remained in limbo until 2003, when BBE issued it as a double album with INI's *Center of Attention*.

In 1998 Loud Records, with which Rock had signed a one-album contract, released his critically acclaimed *Soul Survivor*. The guest vocalists who contributed to that album included C.L Smooth and, for the track "Tha Game," Raekwon (also known as Raekwon the Chef, born Corey Woods) and Ghostface Killah (Dennis Coles) of the Wu-Tang Clan, and Prodigy (Albert Johnson) of Mobb Deep. "Tha Game" showed that while Rock had remained true to his style, he had also updated it and evolved as a producer. The collaborations with Raekwon, Ghostface Killah, and other members of the Wu-Tang Clan proved to be a natural fit, and Rock has worked with them a number of times since then.

In 2001 Rock released on the BBE label a laid-back instrumental album, *PeteStrumentals*, which was lauded as another sophisticated, innovative record. "The relaxed moods and sampladelic strings and delays make it sound almost as if Rock decided to merge his soulful style with abstract down-tempo breaks," Markkus Rovito wrote for *Remix* (November 2001). "The album possesses an up-to-the-minute vibe even though most of the tracks are leftover, unreleased efforts from earlier in Rock's career—some tracks date back seven to ten years. That makes *PeteStrumentals* a testament to just how classic and far ahead of its time Rock's music actually is."

In 2003 Rock set aside his SP-1200 to begin working with the MPC-2000, whose sound was thinner and cleaner than that produced by the SP and offered far more than the 1200's 10-second sampling time. The next year he released *Soul Survivor II* on BBE. He has claimed that BBE never paid him in full for that album and that the label released his next album, *Surviving Elements*—a collection of leftover beats—without his permission. After signing with another label, Nature Sounds, he released *NY's Finest* (2008), a compilation of some of the hundreds of beats he had produced since 2001, with guest artists including the Roots, Little Brother, Lords of the Underground, Max B, Green Lantern, Papoose, Rell, and Doo Wop. "Unlike *PeteStrumentals*, made entirely with his prized SP-1200, this release strays from filtered, ethereal washes and aims for a pristine, distinctly MPC sound," Will Johnson wrote for *Remix* (February 1, 2008), referring to equipment made by Akai, a Japanese firm.

Rock oversaw, arranged, and mixed the album *Jay Stay Paid*, which was released on Nature Sounds in the summer of 2009. The record is a 25-track collection of previously unreleased material produced by the late Jay Dee (also known as Jay Dilla, born James Yancey). The talented and prolific Jay Dee, who died of lupus in 2006 at the age of 32, had along with 9th Wonder and many other producers been a disciple and admirer of Pete Rock. *Jay Stay Paid* was executive-produced by Yancey's mother, Maureen "Ma Dukes" Yancey, and Rock came on board as musical supervisor. "This album combines what [Jay Dee] did in the beginning of his career, what he did in some of our early hospital stays, which was very deep, and some stuff pulled from old disks and DATs," Rock said, as quoted by Clyde Smith on the Web site ProHipHop.com (May 24, 2009). "It's mind blowing. . . . This is like the missing links to Dilla's legacy." Presented in the form of a radio show on an imaginary station, with Rock as the deejay, the highly praised compilation consists mostly of instrumentals but also includes several noteworthy guest appearances from rappers with whom Jay Dee worked. "These reconstructed, reassembled beats . . . vividly show off how left-field [Jay Dee] was willing to get in the service of finding new ways to make a beat knock," Nate Patrin wrote for the music Web site *Pitchfork.com* (June 2, 2009). "You can consider this the most heartfelt eulogy Pete Rock's had a hand in since 'They Reminisce Over You (T.R.O.Y.).'"

In his conversation with Andrew Friedman, Rock said that he devotes a lot of time to staying current in his field: "I just listen to what's going on around me. Going out to the clubs, doing my homework, seeing what the people are going crazy for and so forth." Several times a week, or sometimes even daily, he goes "crate digging"—browsing through boxes of old records in music stores, searching for something that makes him think "I gotta make this when I get home," as he told Friedman. In one scene in Jeremy Weisman's documentary film *Deep Crates 2* (2007), which focuses on a dozen influential beat makers in hip-hop, Rock said, "It's real important that I study the players, the orchestrators. That's how you get sharper, with digging, like if you read and study these players, then the names stick in your head and when you look at records and you see their name on it, you're like, ok, that might be something that I wanna get."

Rock performs regularly as a deejay and also works in his basement recording studio. He plays both bass and keyboards. In his home in Rockland County, New York, he maintains a collection of upwards of 80,000 vinyl records.

—M.M.

Suggested Reading: hhnlive.com Jan 6, 2008; okayplayer.com ; *Pop Matters* (on-line) June 27, 2003; *Remix* p27 June 1, 2004; *Village Voice* (on-line) Nov. 6, 2007; *Washington Post* T p6 Aug. 27, 2004; *Wax Poetics* Issue 7, Winter 2004

Selected Recordings: *All Souled Out*, 1991; *Mecca and The Soul Brother*, 1992; *The Main Ingredient*, 1994; *Soul Survivor*, 1998; *PeteStrumentals*, 2001; *Lost & Found: Underground Hip Hop Soul Classics*, 2003; *Soul Survivor II*, 2004; *NY's Finest*, 2008; *Jay Stay Paid*, 2009

Al Bello/Getty Images

Rodriguez, Ivan

(EE-vahn)

Nov. 30, 1971– Baseball player

Address: The Ivan "Pudge" Rodriguez Foundation, 1000 Ballpark Way, Suite 306, Arlington, TX 76011

Ivan Rodriguez, known as "Pudge" for his stocky physique, is rivaled only by Johnny Bench as the greatest catcher ever to play baseball. He is tied with Bench for most All-Star Game appearances (14) by a catcher, holds the record for most Gold Gloves (13) won by a catcher, and recently passed Carlton Fisk's major-league record for most games caught, with 2,227. He also holds an impressive career batting average of .299. Known for his powerful arm, quick release, and signature snap throws, Rodriguez emerged in the 1990s as the most dangerous defensive catcher in the majors, posting a nearly 50 percent success rate in throwing out would-be base-stealers—the highest career mark since at least 1989, when the statistic began to be recorded. He quickly proved himself to be an excellent hitting catcher as well, batting .300 or better in eight straight seasons, from 1995 to 2002. In 1999 Rodriguez won the American League (AL) Most Valuable Player (MVP) Award after hitting .332 with 35 home runs and 113 runs batted in (RBIs), becoming the first catcher to win the award since Thurman Munson of the New York Yankees in 1976. His home-run total that year was then a record by an AL catcher, and he became the first catcher in league history with 30 homers, 100 RBIs, and 100 runs scored in a single season, as well as the only catcher in history to amass more than 20 home runs and 20 stolen bases (25) in a single season. In 2001 the Yankees' then-manager, Joe Torre, now the manager of the Los Angeles Dodgers, told Simon Gonzalez for *Baseball Digest* (July 2001, online) about Rodriguez, "He's the best. Johnny Bench was that one catcher who used to get all that recognition. But Ivan, he's done it batting average–wise, power-wise, and you change your whole offensive scheme when he's the catcher whether you're going to steal a lot because he's dominant in that area. It's very unusual to be a catcher and be that effective both offensively and defensively."

Over the course of his career, Rodriguez has played for the Texas Rangers, the Florida Marlins, the Detroit Tigers, the Yankees, and the Houston Astros; he is currently with the Rangers again. He helped lead the Marlins to their second World Series title, in 2003, and was responsible for ushering in a baseball renaissance in Detroit, whose squad was runner-up in the World Series in 2006. A product of the steroid era, Rodriguez has seen his reputation tarnished somewhat by allegations of steroid use (which he has vehemently denied) and has sometimes been criticized for selfishness. He is still regarded by peers, however, as one of the game's greatest-ever all-around players. The Los Angeles Dodgers catcher Brad Ausmus told Larry Lage for the Associated Press (March 29, 2004), "He's the best catcher, in terms of being able to be productive offensively and defensively, that has ever played this game in my opinion. And really, there's not a lot of guys at any position that have done what he has at the plate and in the field."

Ivan Rodriguez was born on November 30, 1971 in Manatí, Puerto Rico, about 30 miles west of the capital, San Juan; he was raised in the nearby barrio of Algarrobo, in the hills of the town of Vegas Baja. His father, Juan, worked as an electrician for a U.S.-based construction company, and his mother, Eva, was a second-grade teacher who later became a school principal. Rodriguez began playing baseball at an early age with his older brother, Jose, using a stick and wad of tape as a makeshift bat and ball. As a child he played ball with several future major-leaguers, including Ricky Otero and Juan González. (González, his chief rival when he was growing up, would later become his teammate on the Texas Rangers.) Originally a pitcher, Rodriguez switched to the catcher position after both his father and his Little League coach realized that his hard, fast pitches were intimidating the other children. Rodriguez has credited his father as a major influence in his development as a baseball player. The athlete attended Lino Padron Rivera High School, in Vegas Baja, where he quickly caught the eye of the famed scout Luis Rosa, who was known for signing other big-league stars, including Roberto and Sandy Alomar Jr. Rosa recalled to a writer for the *Puerto Rico Herald* (March 30, 2001, online), "Pudge was hard-nosed, even then. He showed leadership at 16 that I'd seen in few kids. He knew where he was going."

In July 1988, at 16, Rodriguez signed a contract with the Texas Rangers as a non-drafted free agent. On June 20, 1991, having spent less than three years in the minors, Rodriguez made his major-league debut for the Rangers in a game against the Chicago White Sox. At 19 years and seven months, he became the youngest player in the majors and the third-youngest player in franchise history. His age notwithstanding, Rodriguez quickly established himself as both an offensive and defensive threat. He was selected unanimously as the Rangers' Rookie of the Year and finished fourth in the American League Rookie of the Year voting, after ranking third among AL rookies in batting average (.264) and making an even bigger impact on the defensive side, throwing out a league-best 48.6 percent of runners trying to steal. Rodriguez was the youngest player in the majors the following season as well, starting 112 games behind the plate and batting .260, third best among AL catchers. That year he earned his first-ever All-Star selection as a reserve player and won a Gold Glove as best defensive catcher in the league. That began a string of what would become 10 straight All-Star selections and a record 10 straight Gold Gloves. During that off-season he played in the Puerto Rican Winter League and batted .262 in 17 games.

Over the course of the next several seasons, Rodriguez's offensive output began to rival his performance on defense. During the 1993 season he posted the fourth-best batting average among regular AL backstops (.273), finished fifth in RBIs (66), and tied for fifth in homers (10), while tying a team record for consecutive hits, after getting eight straight hits over two games against the Kansas City Royals. Rodriguez played the final month of the regular season in the Puerto Rican Winter League, where he batted .325 with 14 RBIs in 21 regular-season games. He was named to the league's All-Star team and was also its Most Valuable Player. The strike-shortened 1994 season was a breakout year for Rodriguez, who led the AL in batting average among catchers (.298). That year he placed high on his team in many other statistics, coming in second in batting average, tying for third in doubles (19), and ranking fourth in hits (108), total bases (177), runs (56), games (99), at bats (363), walks (31), and homers (16). Rodriguez's homer total was then a team record for catchers. A highlight came late in the season, when he caught a perfect game thrown by the Rangers' pitcher Kenny Rogers. He went on to play in the Puerto Rican Winter League but was forced to miss most of the season after suffering a severe knee injury.

Rodriguez was named the Rangers' Player of the Year for the 1995 season, after leading the team in batting, total bases, and doubles, at .303, 221, and 32, respectively. He also posted his first career two-homer game that season, hitting both off the perennial All-Star pitcher Roger Clemens in a contest against the Boston Red Sox. The following season Rodriguez finished third in the league in doubles (47), fourth in at bats (639), seventh in hits (192), tied for eighth in multi-hit games (55), and 12th in runs (116), while leading the Rangers in doubles, at bats, hits, and runs scored. He also set the all-time major-league record for doubles by a catcher, with 44 (getting three more as designated hitter), and set the big-league record for at bats by a catcher, with 639, surpassing Johnny Bench's record of 621 in 1974. Rodriguez's play over the next two seasons was equally stellar. In 1997 he led all AL catchers in batting average (.313), hits (187), and runs (98) and finished second to the Cleveland Indians' Sandy Alomar in home runs (20), RBIs (77), and doubles (34). That year he became the fourth Ranger in history to appear on the cover of *Sports Illustrated* and won the AL Silver Slugger Award. In 1998 Rodriguez led the Rangers with a .321 batting average, which ranked him eighth in the AL, and posted career highs in home runs (21) and RBIs (91). He also had 75 multi-hit games and 186 hits, good for seventh and ninth in the majors, respectively. The Rangers won the AL West Division title in 1996 and 1998 but lost in the first round of the play-offs to the eventual World Series champions, the New York Yankees, on each occasion.

In 1999 Rodriguez not only recorded the best season of his major-league career but also had arguably the greatest all-around offensive output by a catcher in major-league history. That season he posted a career-best batting average of .332 with 199 hits—also a career high—in 144 games and set a new single-season record for home runs by a catcher, with 35. (The Atlanta Braves' Javy Lopez broke the record in 2003, when he hit 43 home runs.) Rodriguez became the first catcher in major-league history with at least 30 home runs, 100 RBIs (113), and 100 runs scored (116) and the first catcher in history to hit 20 or more home runs and steal 20 or more bases in a season. His total of 25 stolen bases that year was fifth-most among catchers in the history of the league. On defense Rodriguez continued his dominance behind the plate, throwing out a league-best 54.2 percent of all runners attempting to steal. At the end of the season, he was named the Most Valuable Player of the American League, becoming only the ninth catcher in baseball history to garner the award and the first to win it since the Yankees' Thurman Munson, in 1976. He also added a sixth Silver Slugger Award and his eighth Gold Glove and was named by *Baseball Digest* the Major League Player of the Year. Rodriguez led the Rangers to another AL West Division title, but they lost to the Yankees in the first round of the play-offs—for the third time in four years.

In a game against the Anaheim Angels in July 2000, shortly after he had garnered the most votes in fan balloting for that year's All-Star Game, Rodriguez was attempting to throw out a runner stealing second base when the slugger Mo Vaughn's bat smashed into—and broke—his thumb. Rodriguez had surgery on his thumb the next day, which forced him to miss the rest of the season. At season's end he still ranked second on his team in homers (27) and RBIs (83) and had a career-high .347

average. Rodriguez returned to the starting lineup the following spring, when Puerto Rico hosted baseball's opening-day game between the Rangers and Toronto Blue Jays. That year he made his 10th consecutive All-Star Game appearance and tied Bench's record for Gold Gloves won by a catcher (10). (Bench holds the all-time record for consecutive All-Star Game appearances by a catcher, with 13.) Rodriguez appeared in only 111 games due to injuries to his heel and knee; he batted .308 with 25 home runs and 65 RBIs.

The year 2002 saw Rodriguez's first stint with the Rangers come to an end. He finished seventh in the league in batting, with a .314 average—his eighth straight season with a batting average of .300 or better—and hit 19 home runs with 60 RBIs. He was plagued by injuries again that year and appeared in just 108 games due to recurring back problems. After the 2002 season Rodriguez's contract with the Rangers ran out, and he became a free agent. During the off-season he signed a one-year, $10 million deal with the Florida Marlins. The Marlins, who had won the World Series (in 1997) more quickly after their founding than any other franchise in baseball history, had become perennial losers following the dismantling of their championship squad by their then-owner, H. Wayne Huizenga. When Rodriguez arrived the team had just closed out their fifth consecutive losing season, their ninth in 10 years. Rodriguez, by that point a major-league veteran, immediately stepped in to lead and motivate the young Marlins squad. During the 2003 season he set Marlins single-season records for a catcher, with a .297 batting average and 85 RBIs in 144 regular-season games. He also hit 16 home runs and threw out 32.2 percent of runners trying to steal, good for third-best among National League (NL) catchers. Rodriguez helped the Marlins reach the postseason for only the second time in franchise history. In the NL Division Series, the Marlins defeated the San Francisco Giants three games to one. Rodriguez batted .353 in the series and drove in all four runs in the Marlins' 4–3 victory over the Giants in Game Three, which included a two-run homer in the first inning and a game-winning, two-run single in the 11th inning. The following day he helped the Marlins clinch the series by holding onto the ball during a dramatic game-ending collision at home plate with the Giants' J. T. Snow. Rodriguez was then named the MVP of the National League Championship Series (NLCS), after helping the Marlins come back from a three-games-to-one deficit against the Chicago Cubs. In that series he batted .321 with two homers and a record 10 RBIs. The Marlins then defeated the heavily favored New York Yankees in six games to take home their second World Series title, with Rodriguez batting .273. In 17 postseason games he hit .313 with three homers, 17 RBIs, 10 runs, and five doubles.

In February 2004 Rodriguez shocked many in baseball by signing a four-year, $40 million contract with the Detroit Tigers, who had lost an American League–record 119 games during the 2003 season (one short of baseball's post-1900 record for futility, set by the 1962 New York Mets). The Tigers had lost more games over the previous 10 seasons than any other team in the major leagues, with their last winning season in 1993 and last play-off appearance in 1987. Some questioned Detroit's decision to hire Rodriguez, who had suffered from back problems during the last several seasons and who, at 32, was considered to be past his prime. Rodriguez himself received criticism for being more concerned with his own statistics and salary than with his team. For his part, he told Matt Markey for the *Toledo (Ohio) Blade* (April 4, 2004) about the Tigers, "I felt like this was a team that was committed to turning things around and winning, and a team that really wanted me to be a part of that." The Tigers had lost over a million paying ticket holders since the opening of the $300 million Comerica Park, in 2000; upon Rodriguez's signing, ticket sales immediately skyrocketed, and attendance rose by 32.4 percent. Rodriguez went on to have another outstanding season, leading the majors in batting going into the All-Star break, with a .373 average. He led All-Star balloting among catchers, earning his 11th All-Star selection and 10th as a starting player, joining Bench and Mike Piazza as the only Major League Baseball catchers to start 10 or more All-Star Games. He was also named the AL Player of the Month in June after posting a .500 batting average, becoming the first player since 2002 to do so over the course of a month. He finished the season with a .334 batting average, which was the highest average by a Detroit player since Alan Trammell hit .343 in 1987, the fourth-highest among career catchers in baseball history, and the fourth-best in the AL that year. Rodriguez also added 19 homers and 86 RBIs and recorded the 2,000th hit of his career in a game against the Chicago White Sox. In addition, he received his 11th Gold Glove Award as the American League's best defensive catcher and his seventh Silver Slugger Award. The Tigers, meanwhile, enjoyed a 29-game improvement over the previous season and finished with a 72–90 record. Rodriguez explained to Bill Jauss for the *Chicago Tribune* (July 25, 2004), "I work hard and take care of myself. Good things happen when you do that."

In 2005 Rodriguez underwent an off-season conditioning program. As a result he arrived at spring training 20 pounds lighter than he had been the previous year. That happened at roughly the same time that his former Rangers teammate Jose Canseco published a tell-all book, titled *Juiced: Wild Times, Rampant 'Roids, Smash Hits & How Baseball Got Big* (2005), which identified Rodriguez and some of Canseco's other former teammates as steroid users. While other players mentioned in the book, among them Mark McGwire, Jason Giambi, Rafael Palmeiro, and Juan González, have all been linked elsewhere to steroid use, Rodriguez has repeatedly denied using performance-enhancing drugs. The controversy cast a shadow over the veteran catcher's play for the remainder of the season. Despite being the sole player from the Tigers named to the AL All-Star team that year, Rodriguez struggled during the last two months of the season and finished with a sub-par batting average of .276, his lowest since the 1993 season. He saw his other numbers drop as well, hitting just 14 homers with 50 RBIs and posting a league-low on-base percentage of .290, thanks to drawing only 11 walks in 504 at bats. (Despite posting consistently high offensive numbers, Rodriguez has accrued low walk totals throughout his career due to his tendency to swing at every hittable pitch and get to base with hits.) During the season Rodriguez developed an adversarial relationship with the Tigers' manager, Alan Trammell, who was fired by season's end; he also—uncharacteristically—drew a four-game suspension for bumping a home-plate umpire. His on-field troubles would later be attributed to a bitter divorce from his wife, Maribel, whom he had married on the day of his Major League debut, in 1991.

Rodriguez bounced back in 2006 to have another All-Star season. The Tigers brought in the veteran manager Jim Leyland, whose strong leadership quickly changed the culture of the club. Returning to form on the defensive side that year, Rodriguez bested all other major-league catchers by throwing out 45.7 percent of base runners attempting to steal. He also led all AL catchers with a .998 fielding percentage (tied for best in the majors) and committed only two errors, which helped him earn his record 12th Gold Glove Award. He was selected to the All-Star squad for the 13th time in his career and was voted by the fans as the starter behind the plate for the 11th time. Rodriguez finished the regular season with a .300 batting average, 13 home runs, and 69 RBIs in 136 games. On the strength of a talented young pitching staff who posted a major league–best 3.84 earned-run average (ERA), the Tigers had their first winning season in 13 years and first play-off berth in nearly two decades. After beating the heavily favored Yankees in the AL Division Series, three games to one, the Tigers swept the Oakland Athletics to advance to the World Series, where they lost to the St. Louis Cardinals in five games. Rodriguez struggled throughout the postseason, which included a 0-for-23 hitting slump, but the season was regarded as a success for the Tigers, who opted to retain Rodriguez through at least the 2008 season. Jim Leyland said to a writer for the *Windsor (Ontario, Canada) Star* (February 20, 2007), "Pudge plays hurt, he plays hard and he plays to beat the other team. What else can a manager ask for?"

In 2007 Rodriguez made his 14th career All-Star appearance and was named the starter for the 12th time in his career. He batted .281 and belted 11 home runs, marking his 15th consecutive season with 10 or more homers. Rodriguez also reached two career milestones that year, as he became the first catcher in history to record 12,000 putouts and only the fourth player in history to catch at least 2,000 games. He struggled defensively, however, and runners trying to steal against him had a 71.2 percent success rate. The Tigers finished second in the AL Central Division, with a record of 88–74, marking their second consecutive winning season, but missed the play-offs when the Yankees clinched the wild-card spot.

Rodriguez split the 2008 season between the Tigers and Yankees. He hit a solid .295 with five home runs and 32 RBIs in 82 games with the Tigers before a midseason trade sent him to the Yankees for the relief pitcher Kyle Farnsworth. The Yankees, who were vying for a play-off spot, had lost their starting All-Star catcher Jorge Posada to injury early in the season and had used the backup catcher Jose Molina as his replacement prior to the trade. Rodriguez's half-season with the Yankees proved to be a disappointment; he hit just .219 in 33 games and threw out only seven of 27 runners. He was released at the end of the season, as the Yankees missed the play-offs for the first time since 1995. After going through the off-season without signing with a team, Rodriguez signed a one-year, $1.5 million contract with the Houston Astros two weeks before the start of the 2009 season. He played in 93 games for the Astros that season and batted .251 with eight home runs and 34 RBIs. During that time he reached two career milestones: in May he hit his 300th career home run, on a pitch from the Chicago Cubs' Rich Harden, and in June he passed Carlton Fisk for most games caught, with 2,227. In August 2009 Rodriguez was traded back to the Texas Rangers. The Rangers, who were in play-off contention at the time, had lost their backup catcher Jarrod Saltalamacchia to injury that month. Acting as the backup to the team's starting catcher Taylor Teagarden, Rodriguez batted .245 with two home runs and 13 RBIs in 28 games. The Rangers finished second in the AL West Division but missed the play-offs when the Boston Red Sox clinched the wild-card spot.

Rodriguez's primary residence is in Miami, Florida. He has three children: Ivan Dereck, Amanda Christine, and Ivanna Sofia. In 1993 Rodriguez and his then-wife founded the Ivan "Pudge" Rodriguez Foundation, which helps families with children who are battling cancer in Puerto Rico, Dallas, and Fort Worth, Texas. He has also donated thousands of dollars to numerous other causes, including $25,000 to assist victims of Hurricane George in Puerto Rico in 1998 and $20,000 to the victims of the World Trade Center attacks in 2001. In addition, Rodriguez has donated extensively to the Make-A-Wish Foundation.

—C.C.

Suggested Reading: *Baseball Digest* (on-line) July 2001, p52+ Dec. 1, 2004; *Chicago Tribune* C p9 July 25, 2004; *Detroit Free Press* E p1+ Apr. 5, 2004, p1 July 31, 2008; Ivan "Pudge" Rodriguez Foundation Official Web site; mlb.com; *Puerto Rico Herald* (on-line) Mar. 30, 2001; (Toledo, Ohio) *Blade* D p1 Apr. 4, 2004, C p1 Mar. 27, 2005

Ross, Jerilyn

Dec. 20, 1946– Psychotherapist; founder and director of the Ross Center for Anxiety and Related Disorders

Address: Ross Center for Anxiety and Related Disorders, 5225 Wisconsin Ave., N.W., Suite 400, Washington, DC 20015

Jerilyn Ross is a psychotherapist specializing in the treatment of anxiety disorders, the most common type of mental illness in the United States. According to the National Institute of Mental Health (2008, on-line), in any given year at least 18 percent of people 18 years of age or older in the U.S., or about 40 million people, suffer from at least one of the currently recognized anxiety disorders. The best-known among them are post-traumatic stress disorder, obsessive-compulsive disorder, and panic disorder, the last of which is associated with phobias: aerophobia (fear of flying), claustrophobia (fear of being trapped in a small space), and carcinophobia (fear of getting cancer), to name three of hundreds. "There are as many different kinds of phobias as there are different kinds of people," Ross wrote for the chapter "Phobias and Fears" in *The Doctors Book of Home Remedies* (2002). When Ross was in her 20s, she herself suffered from crippling phobias and panic attacks. After her successful treatment, with cognitive-behavioral therapy, she left her job as a schoolteacher to pursue a career as a mental-health therapist. In 1980 she co-founded the Phobia Society of America (renamed the Anxiety Disorders Association of America in 1990) and has served as president of the organization since 1987. She is also the director of the Ross Center for Anxiety and Related Disorders, which she established in 1991. Her first book, *Triumph Over Fear: A Book of Help and Hope for People with Anxiety, Panic Attacks, and Phobias*, was published in 1994. The big increase in the number of people who began to suffer from anxiety disorders after the September 11, 2001 terrorist attacks in the U.S. led Ross to create a self-help treatment kit, called Freedom from Anxiety. Growing fears related to the effects of the recession that began in 2008 and unceasing news reports about environmental degradation, global warming, and terrorism inspired her to write, with Robin Cantor-Cooke, her second book, *One Less Thing to Worry About: Uncommon Wisdom for Coping with Common Anxieties* (2009).

The daughter of Raymond Ross and the former Carolyn Karmitz, Jerilyn Ross was born on December 20, 1946 in the New York City borough of the Bronx. She has one brother, Richard. Ross, who is Jewish, has said that she was predisposed to anxiety from an early age. For years she feared school; to keep her mother from leaving her in the schoolyard one morning, she pulled so hard on her mother's skirt that it fell to the ground. Ross graduated with a B.A. degree from the State University of New York (SUNY) in Cortland in 1968. She then moved to the New York City borough of Manhattan, where she took a job as a math teacher in the city's public-school system. Ross had a panic attack for the first time at age 25: while dancing at a party held on the rooftop terrace of a 20-story building in Salzburg, Austria, where she was traveling with a friend, she suddenly felt a powerful urge to jump off the roof. That urge sparked a full-blown panic attack. "A bolt of terror shot through her," Marcia Barinaga wrote for the *Los Angeles Times* (November 2, 1987). "With pounding heart, she dove through the crowd to the elevator so she could get to the ground floor and safety." After Ross returned to New York, she felt terrified whenever she was on the 10th floor or higher in any building; even the thought of being so high made her anxious. For five years, with great difficulty in a city with thousands of high-rise buildings, she avoided situations that required her to be that far from ground level. She told Ena Naunton for the *Chicago Tribune* (December 16, 1987) that the phobia "came to affect every aspect of my life and who my friends were. Whenever I met someone new, I would find out first what floor they lived on. I became a very good cook, because I always entertained at my house." Like all phobias, Ross's was irrational; riding on a ski lift never made her feel anxious, and in buildings there was no reason why her anxiety should arise on the 10th floor rather than the ninth. Ross has often explained that her fear was not connected to heights per se but to the feelings that she feared would be triggered by heights. "It's a fear that while I'm up in this building, I'm suddenly gonna panic, I'm gonna lose control, I'm gonna jump out the window, I'm gonna pass out," she explained to Jane Clayson, who interviewed her on the CBS News program *The Early Show* (January 30, 2001, on-line). "If it makes sense, it's not a phobia."

In the early 1970s Ross pursued a master's degree in psychology at the New School for Social Research (now known simply as the New School), in New York City. She also began to look for another job. During that period she became so anxious that she could not bring herself to show up at some job interviews. Her boyfriend at the time, a psychiatrist, suggested that she seek therapy. By chance, she read a magazine article that described a treatment program for phobia sufferers being conducted at Roosevelt Hospital, in New York City. "I couldn't believe that there was somebody else on this planet who felt the way I did," she told Naunton. At that time the medical community knew very little about phobias and other anxiety disorders; the most common phobias, social phobia (extreme anxiety arising in social situations) and agoraphobia (fear of any environments outside one's home), had not even been named. The conventional treatment for such fears was psychoanalysis, a years-long form of talk therapy whose aim is to reveal the subconscious causes of a patient's problems or symptoms. Though such therapy some-

Clay Blackmore, courtesy of Jerilyn Ross

Jerilyn Ross

times helped patients understand the origins of their fears, it seldom helped them change their behavior or led them to feel differently. The Roosevelt Hospital Phobia Program offered a treatment, called cognitive-behavioral therapy (CBT), which uses specific procedures to change emotions, behaviors, and thought processes so as to achieve a stated goal. It is based on the conviction that if those changes occur, underlying causes become inconsequential. Dating from the 1920s, CBT began to be widely applied in the latter half of the 20th century. In the cases of phobias and anxiety disorders, the treatment typically involves gradually introducing a patient to the objects or situations that induce anxiety and teaching him or her to manage that anxiety by such means as slow, steady breathing or conscious mental distractions (counting backward from 300 by threes, for example). The treatment worked for Ross; though being on the 10th floor or higher still causes her to feel anxious, she now has the tools to keep her anxiety under control. Her experience in Roosevelt Hospital's phobia program awakened in Ross the determination to help others who suffered from anxiety disorders.

Ross completed her M.A. degree in 1975 and left the New York City school system two years later. In 1978 she joined the staff of the Center for Behavioral Medicine, in Rockville, Maryland, a Washington, D.C., suburb, as a senior clinical associate. The head of the center, Robert L. DuPont, a psychiatrist, and his colleagues had adopted the same sort of cognitive-behavioral therapy that Ross had undergone in New York. Their plan to open a clinic in which people with anxiety disorders would receive such treatment came to fruition in 1981, when DuPont, Ross, and others co-founded the Phobia Program of Washington. The program existed independently of any medical institution, because clinics and hospitals in the area were unwilling to fund CBT treatment. Modeled on others of its kind elsewhere in the country, the program provided individual therapy and group therapy for patients who shared similar phobias; the groups met regularly in DuPont's basement. In 1979 the Phobia Program of Washington opened a facility in Bethesda, Maryland. Ross explained to Christina Breda Antoniades for the *Washington Post* (August 10, 2008) that patients undergoing CBT are taught to replace the false messages they tell themselves, such as, "I can't do it, I'm going to pass out, I'm going to die," with statements such as, "My heart is pounding because I'm anxious," to enable them to accept and cope with the feelings they are experiencing. Ross said that she often suggests that patients envision their fear as an ocean wave: "If you fight it, you end up drinking it. I use the concept of just floating over it."

In 1980 Ross, DuPont, and a number of others founded the Phobia Society of America (PSA), to help people beset by irrational and debilitating fears. Around that time anxiety disorders were receiving increasing attention from the medical community. In 1980, for the first time, the American Psychiatric Association included in the latest edition of its *Diagnostic and Statistical Manual of Mental Disorders* (the "bible" used to diagnose mental illnesses) descriptions of anxiety disorders. In 2008 the National Institute of Mental Health's list of anxiety disorders included specific phobias, agoraphobia, social phobia, obsessive-compulsive disorder, post-traumatic stress disorder, generalized anxiety disorder, and panic disorder. Specific phobias are the most common. There are many such phobias, each linked to a particular thing (spiders, feathers, or thunder, for example) or situation (crossing a bridge, hearing a particular sound, or being in a dark hallway); in the mind of the phobic person, those things or situations pose imminent danger and arouse extreme, persistent fear, and they are strenuously avoided. Those suffering from agoraphobia are fearful of public places; many never leave their homes. Victims of social phobia, or social-anxiety disorder, cannot tolerate being with other people, especially in situations in which others might scrutinize them or judge them. People afflicted with obsessive-compulsive disorder continually repeat particular actions (washing their hands, checking that stove knobs are turned off) or are plagued by repeated, intrusive, anxiety-producing thoughts. Post-traumatic stress disorder strikes some victims of physical violence (rape, wartime combat), natural disasters, or other highly traumatic events. Those suffering from generalized anxiety disorder are chronically worried, anxious, or tense without any apparent precipitating factor. In those with phobias, exposure to the feared object or situation may cause a panic attack—"a discreet episode where suddenly someone is flooded with intense feelings of terror . . . ," as Ross explained in an on-line chat sponsored by *USAWeekend.com* (October 2, 2006). "The person experiences both physical and psychological sensations, such as pounding heart, sweaty palms, tightness in chest, dizziness, nausea, trembling, shaking, sometimes feeling 'spacey' and an overwhelming sense of dread." People who suffer from panic disorder typically experience panic attacks with no warning, in situations that previously never aroused any anxiety in them. Although they know that the situations are not inherently dangerous, they immediately develop phobias regarding those situations. That is what happened to Ross on the rooftop in Austria. A phobia, Ross explained in *The Doctors Book of Home Remedies*, is "a fear of one's own impulses. It's a fear of having a panic attack and losing control. Basically it's a fear of one's own self and loss of control." Although many people use the words "stress" and "anxiety" interchangeably, they are not the same. Stress is the body's physical response to what is viewed as a threat; anxiety is a person's reaction to the stress. "Some level of anxiety helps warn us when there's danger or motivates us to behave in a certain way. It's healthy," Ross told Antoniades. "The thing that separates an anxiety disorder from normal anxiety is that a disorder is always irrational, and the person is aware that their anxiety is irrational." By definition, anxiety disorders disrupt a person's normal life.

From 1985 to 1991 Ross served as associate director at the Roundhouse Square Psychiatric Center, in Alexandria, Virginia. In 1987 she succeeded DuPont as president of the Phobia Society of America, which by then consisted of about 6,000 members, including medical-health professionals and those suffering from phobias. In that position she delivered lectures and granted interviews, in an effort to reduce the stigma of anxiety disorders. In her talks she often recounted her own experiences with phobia. Beginning in 1987 Ross also hosted a weekly radio talk show, focusing on phobias and anxiety disorders, on the D.C.-based WRC Radio. That year the members of the PSA testified before a congressional committee on the seriousness and prevalence of anxiety disorders. In 1990, the year the PSA was renamed the Anxiety Disorders Association of America, the Food and Drug Administration (FDA) approved the use of Xanax (known generically as alprazalam), the first drug to treat panic disorder. Other medications to treat the disorder have since earned FDA approval. In many cases treatment for victims of anxiety disorders includes both CBT and medication.

In 1991 Ross founded the Ross Center for Anxiety and Related Disorders, in Washington, D.C., an outpatient treatment center that provides short-term treatment for anxiety disorders. According to the Ross Center Web site, the center's therapists offer information about the psychological and physiological causes of the conditions and teach techniques to reduce the emotional and physical symptoms of anxiety, guiding patients to recognize and change harmful thoughts and behavior. The therapy involves the gradual, step-by-step exposure of a patient to an anxiety-inducing thing or situation. For example, to help a person who has a severe fear of riding in an elevator, Ross might press the elevator button while the patient holds her hand. At later sessions the patient presses the button, then rides the elevator for one floor, and later, multiple floors. Speaking of the patient, Ross explained to Stephanie Stoughton for the Associated Press State & Local Wire (September 22, 2008), "You want to do [the activity] to the point that you're bored." During the "exposure therapy" sessions, patients rate their anxiety level on a scale of zero (no anxiety) to 10 (overwhelming panic). "The goal is to stay in the situation long enough to see that the feelings will pass," Ross told Antoniades. "You never want to leave a situation when your anxiety is above a five," because doing so reinforces the fear. The person's confidence grows along with the realization that the worst-case scenario he or she imagined has never occurred. "The scale doesn't go to 11," Ross told Antoniades. "Once you reach a panic attack, it doesn't get worse. And it doesn't go on forever. It's a huge relief for most people to discover that." When phobias involve overseas travel, cross-country driving, or other activities that make exposure therapy impractical, Ross and her colleagues use what is called "interoceptive exposure": replicating the physical symptoms, such as shortness of breath or dizziness, that the client has experienced during anxiety attacks, thus forcing him or her to deal with those feared sensations. The goal, Ross told Barbara Mathias for the *Washington Post* (June 30, 1994), is to help the phobic to relinquish "imaginary games of the future," or "the malignant disease of 'what ifs.'" The center also offers treatment programs for children and adolescents and an intensive, accelerated treatment program for people who do not live within easy traveling distance of the center.

Ross's first book, *Triumph Over Fear: A Book of Help and Hope for People with Anxiety, Panic Attacks, and Phobias*, contains accounts of patients who suffered from anxiety disorders and overcame them. Thanks to treatment one of Ross's patients, whose diagnosis was agoraphobia, became able to leave her home after 30 years indoors. The book describes research, therapies, self-help tools to manage anxiety, and advice on interacting with others who exhibit behavior associated with anxiety disorders.

During interviews on television and radio in the wake of the September 11, 2001 terrorist attacks, Ross offered advice regarding how to cope with fears and anxiety related to terrorism. She suggested that people try to express their emotions openly, avoid making major life changes, participate in activities that foster a sense of control, and focus on the positive aspects of daily life. That same year Ross produced a comprehensive self-help program for sufferers of anxiety disorders. Called Freedom from Anxiety, it includes 16 audio sessions, a one-hour video showing Ross working with clients, a workbook, and other materials, and it can be purchased through the Ross Center's Web site.

In 2004 Ross received the American Psychiatric Association's Award for Patient Advocacy. Playing the piano is one of her favorite stress-relieving activities. She also enjoys skiing, boating, and adventure travel. In 1997 she married Ronald Cohen, a real-estate developer. From his previous marriage, which ended with the death of his wife, Cohen has three children and several grandchildren. The couple live in Bethesda, Maryland.

—M.E.R.

Suggested Reading: Associated Press State & Local Wire Sep. 22, 2008; *Los Angeles Times* Metro p2 Nov. 2, 1987; *National Women's Health Report* p1+ Feb. 1, 2008; *Washington Post* C p5 June 30, 1994, B p1+ Feb. 14, 1998, F p1 Jan. 23, 2007, N p1 Aug. 10, 2008

Selected Books: *Triumph Over Fear: A Book of Help and Hope for People with Anxiety, Panic Attacks, and Phobias*, 1994; *One Less Thing to Worry About: Uncommon Wisdom for Coping with Common Anxieties* (with Robin Cantor-Cooke), 2009; as contributor—*The Doctors Book of Home Remedies*, 2002

Frederick M. Brown/Getty Images

Saakashvili, Mikheil

(sah-kahsh-VIH-leh)

Dec. 21, 1967– President of Georgia

Address: Office of the President, 7 Ingorokva St., 380034 Tbilisi, Georgia

The attempts by Mikheil Saakashvili, the president of Georgia, to westernize his country and resist the influence of Russia—the former Soviet republic of which Georgia was a satellite—have earned support from those who view him as a beacon of democracy in a formerly troubled region and opposition from those who believe he has a dangerous authoritarian streak. "He is really quite complex," a European former ambassador to Georgia told Quentin Peel for the *Irish Times* (August 16, 2008). "He is very intelligent, very thoughtful, and sometimes trips upon his own complex thought processes. . . . He wants the system to be democratic. But personally his instinct is strongly autocratic." Saakashvili became a national icon when he led protestors into the Georgian Parliament building during the 2003 "Rose Revolution" to demand the resignation of the country's then-president, the former Soviet foreign minister Eduard Shevardnadze. Shevardnadze stepped down, and Saakashvili, elected president the following year, implemented sweeping reforms that reduced government corruption, brought the country economic prosperity, and strengthened its ties to the West. However, his dramatic crackdown on a 2007 protest against his vigorous push for reform threw Saakashvili's reputation as a democratic reformer to the wind. When Russia and Georgia entered into armed conflict over the separatist Georgian territory of South Ossetia, in August 2008, some accused Saakashvili of provoking the Russians as a way to gain further western support. (A European Union–commissioned report released in September 2009 blamed Georgian forces for attacking the Russians first.) During the conflict Georgia lost the territories at stake—South Ossetia and Abkhazia, both sympathetic to Russia—and again Saakashvili's actions were questioned. "What is the future for Saakashvili?" Sozar Subari, Georgia's ombudsman for human rights, asked Ellen Barry for the *New York Times* (December 31, 2008, on-line). "He started the war, he lost the war, he lost the territories. There is a crisis. There is no investment in Georgia. The situation is getting worse and worse. If there is no change, he will leave Georgia as the president who lost everything."

Mikheil "Misha" Saakashvili was born on December 21, 1967 in Tbilisi, the capital and largest city of Georgia. (Georgia is located on the southern side of the Caucasus Mountains, between the Caspian Sea and the Black Sea. Taken over by Russia in the 19th century, Georgia maintained its own culture, language, and church—the Georgian Orthodox Church—and declared its independence following the Russian Revolution of 1917, only to give way to Soviet invasion four years later. Georgia regained autonomy when the Soviet Union dissolved, in 1991.) Saakashvili's father, Nikoloz Saakashvili, is a physician and the director of a physical-therapy and hydrotherapy center. His mother, Giuli Alasania, is a professor of Georgian history at Tbilisi State University. Saakashvili's parents divorced when he was three, and he grew up in a crowded apartment with his mother, her parents, and her grandparents. His mother told Wendell Steavenson for the *New Yorker* (December 15, 2008, on-line) that as a young boy, her son received "a lot of attention, and everyone somehow contributed to raising him." Although the members of his family were well-educated and held professional positions, they were not among the upper ranks of Soviet society, and his early years were informed by his family's humble standing. "I remember my grandfather had a special coupon from some institute he lectured in," Saakashvili told Steavenson. "Once a year we could go and receive two Finnish sausages, five or six specialty sprats from Latvia, Finnish chocolate, and sometimes, if we were very lucky, a box of red caviar. It was a very humiliating experience. You had to stand in long lines in some basement of the Communist Party headquarters or whatever, and we were standing there together—these professors together with the drivers of heads of departments of the Communist Party." Due to such experiences he began to distrust his country's government; he told Steavenson, "I grew up with the idea, like all my generation, that the West was an absolute paradise and that we lived in an absolute hell. That was the identity of my generation."

After he graduated, with honors, from Tbilisi Secondary School N51, in 1984, Saakashvili attended the Kiev University Institute of International Relations, a prestigious school in Ukraine, then also part of the Soviet Union. He earned his undergraduate degree from the institute in 1987, then pursued a law degree at the Strasbourg Human Rights International Institute, in France. There, he met his future wife, Sandra Roelofs, who is Dutch.

In the early 1990s Saakashvili established himself as an important broker in negotiations among Georgian ethnic groups struggling for power after the fall of the Soviet Union. In 1992 he worked for the Norwegian Institute of Human Rights, through which he organized a peace conference that led to a ceasefire between Georgia and South Ossetia, which had been fighting a civil war since the early 1990s. In 1992 and 1993 he worked for the Human Rights Committee of Georgia and arranged prisoner exchanges between Georgia and separatists in the Abkhazia region, who defeated the Georgian forces. He did the same for the Armenians and Azeris, who had fought for control of Nagorno-Karabakh, a breakaway region of Azerbaijan.

Soon afterward Saakashvili left Georgia for the U.S., where he earned a degree in international law at Columbia University, in New York City, in 1995. He soon landed a job practicing commercial law at the New York firm of Patterson, Belknap, Webb & Tyler LLP; his wife also found a job at a law firm. The next year Saakashvili began working toward a Ph.D. in law at George Washington University, in Washington, D.C. He was then visited by Zurab Zhvania, a reformer who belonged to Shevardnadze's Citizens' Union Party. Zhvania invited him to join the government of Georgia. Saakashvili agreed, abandoning his studies and leaving the U.S., where his experiences had "made him a profound admirer of the American system . . . and laid the foundations for a whirlwind career in Georgian politics," according to Peel.

Saakashvili was elected to Georgia's Parliament in 1995 and became chair of the Parliamentary Committee on Constitutional, Legal Issues, and Legal Affairs. With the committee he worked toward several legal and judicial reforms, including merit-based selection of judges, a process in which candidates underwent hearings supervised by representatives from the American Bar Association (ABA). He also worked to push for transparency in the courts. Saakashvili's reform work made him a highly visible and popular political figure in Georgia, and in 1998 his party elected him as leader of its parliamentary delegation. In 1999 he ran to represent Vake, a district of Tbilisi. "I was running against the very corrupt head of tax inspection," he told Steavenson. "We thought I would easily win because I am young, modern, et cetera, et cetera. But we did some polls and saw he was ahead by a very large margin. So that was the first real election campaign in Georgia. The first billboards, the first negative ads—the first real political ads on TV. It was really a classical Western political campaign. And I won by fifty votes."

In October 2000 Shevardnadze appointed Saakashvili to be Georgia's minister of justice. Seven of eight political parties in the otherwise deeply divided Parliament supported his appointment. In his new post he continued his assault on government corruption while cultivating a populist image, walking or taking public transportation to work and soliciting the opinions of ordinary citizens on the street. One day, growing frustrated with the government's seeming unwillingness to prosecute corruption cases, Saakashvili famously burst into a cabinet meeting followed by a television-news crew and displayed photos of dachas (Russian vacation homes) he claimed some of the cabinet members had obtained through illicit land transactions. According to Steavenson, "This move—audacious, self-righteous, and media-savvy—became a template for his future."

In September 2001 Saakashvili resigned as minister of justice. He also resigned from the Citizen's Union Party and was reelected as an Independent to represent the Vake District. Before the year was over, he had formed his own party, the United National Movement, on an anticorruption platform. Saakashvili later resigned from his seat in Parliament and ran successfully for a seat on the Tbilisi city council. With the campaign slogan "Tbilisi without Shevardnadze," he was elected council chair. From 2002 to 2003 he worked to improve city services.

Amending his slogan to "Georgia without Shevardnadze," in 2003 Saakashvili ran again for Parliament. Although analysts had predicted that Saakashvili's party would triumph, official totals after the election had Shevardnadze's coalition in the lead, prompting speculation that the election had been rigged—suspicions further fueled by reports of ballot stuffing and intimidation of election officials. Saakashvili and other politicians organized nonviolent demonstrations; continuing for 19 days and drawing more than 40,000 people, the protests became known as the Rose Revolution. On November 23, during a parliamentary meeting on the election results, Saakashvili and several other politicians entered the chamber and disrupted a speech given by Shevardnadze. Holding a rose—a symbol of peace—Saakashvili demanded Shevardnadze's resignation. He was removed from the room, but the throng of protestors outside quickly entered, and Shevardnadze and the other legislators fled. Shevardnadze resigned from his post the next day after meeting with Saakashvili and other members of the opposition. Saakashvili told Ken Stier for *Newsweek* (December 8, 2003, on-line) that he had had no detailed plan when he entered the Parliament building, knowing only that he and his supporters "had to somehow enter Parliament to kick them out. Definitely, we were afraid all the way through. If they had seen our fear, they would have gotten really nasty, really aggressive." He added, "To the superficial observer, it looked like a music festival, but it was not. It was very close to violence. It could have gone very, very badly. When we went into the Parliament, there were a lot of armed people there."

In January 2004 presidential elections were held, and Saakashvili won in a landslide, with 96 percent of the vote. Europe's youngest president, he told the media that he would model his presidency on the careers of current and historical figures, including U.S. president John F. Kennedy and U.S. senator John McCain, as well as the medieval Georgian king David the Builder. As president Saakashvili pushed for Georgia to become a member of the North Atlantic Treaty Organization (NATO), along with the U.S. and its mostly European allies. (As of October 2009 NATO officials were waiting for Georgia to implement further reforms before they consider granting the country membership.) In 2005 Saakashvili was visited by President George W. Bush, who offered U.S. support in the form of training for Georgian troops and a $300 million grant from a program intended to foster democracy in other countries. Saakashvili's first months as president saw a cut in tax rates, an increase in government revenues, a decrease in crime attributed to Saakashvili's decision to replace a large portion of the police force, and the public arrests of ministers linked to corruption. By 2007 the country's gross domestic product was growing by more than 12 percent, foreign investors were plentiful, and infrastructure was greatly improved. The president's zeal to change the country also led, however, to some criticism that his impatience for results often caused him to embrace undemocratic means. Saakashvili's westernization of the country also alienated citizens. Peel wrote, "In the process [of reforming], he has lost support among the Georgian population, including many from the older generation, roughly thrust aside by the westernised young bankers and consultants who came home to help the transformation. Saakashvili wanted to do it all at once—revolutionise the economy, and reintegrate the country. It was not to be done."

Discontent over aspects of Saakashvili's presidency erupted into full-scale protests in November 2007, with 50,000 citizens demonstrating in the streets. Saakashvili ordered police to disperse dozens of protestors who had gathered at the Parliament building; when others took their places, urged on by a television broadcast, police used tear gas and rubber bullets on the crowd and later shut down the TV station. Saakashvili declared a 10-day state of emergency in which he banned protests, which he blamed on a Russian-supported scheme to undermine his presidency. The European Union and NATO criticized him, some comparing his methods to those of Russia's leader, Vladimir Putin. Under pressure, Saakashvili moved the 2008 presidential election forward, from the fall to January, thus allowing for a referendum on his presidency and a chance for the opposition to make its case. In a speech to the nation, quoted by Clifford Levy in the *New York Times* (November 15, 2007, on-line), Saakashvili said, "Before anyone starts discussing which eccentric, authoritarian or, what is more, dictatorial ruler the Georgian president resembles, I would like to remind you that I am the president of Georgia who is reducing his own first presidential term of his own free will. And I am resorting to what is unprecedented in our region and in most of the world's countries." At the end of 2007, Saakashvili campaigned for reelection, promising to combat poverty and unemployment. He won the election with 53 percent of the vote, with his closest rival, Levan Gachechiladze, receiving 25 percent. While some observers accused the government of rigging the election, others argued that the election had been democratic. Saakashvili was sworn in for his second term on January 20. At his inauguration he said, according to several sources, "This election proved that our democracy is blossoming, and that we can build democratic institutions that will endure far longer than any single individual."

In March 2008 President Bush endorsed Georgia's request to join NATO. Although Saakashvili hoped that the prospect of Georgian membership in the alliance would deter Russian threats against Georgia, it appeared to increase tensions between the two nations, and in August 2008 an armed conflict erupted. Although the 2009 European Union report placed blame on Georgian forces for provoking the Russians, Georgia continues to hold Russia responsible for the conflict. The Georgian government argued that it had sent forces to the South Ossetian city of Tskhinvali after receiving reports that Russian military forces were preparing to invade. There were also skirmishes between South Ossetian and Georgian forces leading up to the conflict. "We wanted to stop the Russian troops before they could reach Georgian villages," Saakashvili told *Spiegel* (September 15, 2008, on-line). "When our tanks moved toward Tskhinvali, the Russians bombed the city. They were the ones—not us—who reduced Tskhinvali to rubble." The Russian government claimed that its movements into South Ossetia were not an invasion but merely part of an agreed-upon rotation and replenishment of Russian peacekeeping forces.

The conflict, which lasted for five days, began on August 7, when Georgia launched an artillery attack on Tskhinvali. Russia responded with a large military presence that drove back Georgian forces and led Georgian civilians to flee South Ossetia by the thousands, and Russia was able to seize South Ossetia and Abkhazia. Amnesty International released a report after the fighting that accused both countries of allowing missiles to hit civilian areas. Hundreds of people, many of them civilians, died in the conflict, and hundreds of thousands were at least temporarily displaced. On August 16 French diplomats helped broker a ceasefire.

Although Saakashvili had the support of the West as the conflict raged, he was later blamed by many for provoking Russia, and within a few weeks opinion was turning against him. The Organization for Security and Cooperation in Europe (OSCE) and NATO began to question whether Georgia had initiated the conflict, and independent investigations, such as one reported in a *New York Times* story on November 7, cast doubts on Georgia's account of the conflict. Positions in the U.S. also shifted; according to *Spiegel*, "Even Washington is beginning to suspect that Saakashvili, a friend and ally, could in fact be a gambler—someone who triggered the bloody five-day war and then told the West bold-faced lies." Saakashvili denied accusations of purposely starting the conflict, and the Georgian government released intercepted Russian phone messages that it has cited as proof that Russian forces moved into Georgia early on August 7. In September 2009 the European Union made public a report that dismissed the Georgian president's claims that he was responding to a Russian invasion when he ordered the artillery assault on Tskhinvali. It also accused both nations of human-rights violations and of sharing equal responsibility for the years of tension that led to the war. Although the Georgian forces were defeated, Saakashvili saw the conflict as a step forward in ridding his part of the world of the "Russian influence," as he put it to Steavenson. "If anyone had any illusions that we could get rid of two centuries of Russian influence in one week, that would have been a big mistake, but we are on the way," he said. "This is the beginning of the end for them in this region."

The fighting with Russia left Georgia with a ruined infrastructure and closed transportation routes. Adding to the country's challenges was its economy, which has suffered as a result of the global financial crisis. In October 2008 Saakashvili began to change the makeup of his cabinet, first replacing Prime Minister Lado Gurgenidze with Grigol Mgaloblishvili, Georgia's former ambassador to Turkey. In a statement quoted by Ellen Barry in the *New York Times* (October 28, 2008, on-line), Saakashvili said that a new government team was necessary to respond to the threat posed by Russia, which was building up its forces in South Ossetia and Abkhazia. "Existential threat hangs over Georgia like a Damocles' sword," he said. "New radical democratic reforms and liberalization are the only response to the challenge—I do not have any other recipe to offer to the new government." In December he announced that he would introduce constitutional changes that would expand the power of the Georgian legislature and weaken those of the president. Despite that move Saakashvili still faced opposition from many in his country; in early January 2009 the Conservative Party of Georgia issued a statement asking international organizations to investigate the January 5, 2008 presidential elections.

On April 9, 2009 tens of thousands of Georgians marched to the Parliament building to demand that Saakashvili resign or be forced out of office. The protestors were spurred to some extent by Levan Gachechiladze's brother, Giorgi, who had been televised for several hours a day in a fake jail cell on a cable show called *Cell No. 5*, which had "rivet[ed]" residents of Tbilisi, Clifford Levy wrote for the *New York Times* (April 10, 2009). Vowing to remain in the "jail" until Saakashvili left his post, Giorgi Gachechiladze repeatedly lashed out at the president as a tyrant who had reneged on his promises to rule democratically and who botched the management of the armed conflict with Russia. During the protest on April 9, Levan Gachechiladze declared, as Levy reported for the *Times* (April 9, 2009, on-line), "We are here because there is no other way to do this. We need to stay here until the end. [Saakashvili] must go!" Despite the size of the demonstration, it was "not at all clear that there is widespread public support for Mr. Saakashvili's resignation," Levy wrote in his dispatch from Tbilisi. In July 2009 Saakashvili proposed new democratic reforms, promising to limit presidential powers, create direct mayoral elections and a new electoral code, and assist an opposition cable channel to broadcast nationally. Despite those proposals the opposition continued to call for Saakashvili's resignation. However, as of October 2009 Saakashvili remained popular among Georgians, according to public-opinion polls.

The six-foot four-inch Saakashvili has been described as hypertalkative and restless. He and his wife and their two sons, Eduard and Nikoloz, live in Tbilisi. Addressing accusations that he is overly impulsive and authoritarian, he told Steavenson that his governing style is akin to those of some American leaders. "With Americans, you can be yourself, and they accept you," he said. " I've never heard from Americans that I'm hotheaded, bossy. From Europe, I've heard a lot of this. Because, for them, in some cases, in Europe spontaneity looks like a dangerous thing." According to many Internet sources, the American actor Andy Garcia has been cast as Saakashvili in a Hollywood film about the Georgia-Russia conflict. Directed by Renny Harlin and reportedly taking an anti-war stance, the movie was scheduled to be released in 2010.
—W.D.

Suggested Reading: *Irish Times* p9 Aug. 16, 2008; *New York Times* (on-line) Nov. 15, 2007; *New Yorker* p64 Dec. 15, 2008; *Newsweek* (on-line) Dec. 8, 2003; *Spiegel* (on-line) Sep. 15, 2008

Paul J. Richards/AFP/Getty Images

Salazar, Ken

Mar. 2, 1955– Secretary of the U.S. Department of the Interior; former U.S. senator from Colorado (Democrat)

Address: U.S. Dept. of the Interior, Mail Stop 7229, 1849 C St., N.W., Washington, DC 20240

On January 22, 2009, his second day as secretary of the U.S. Department of the Interior (DOI), Ken Salazar—a former U.S. senator from Colorado and Colorado attorney general—gave a speech to thousands of DOI employees, carried to most of them via satellite; in it he vowed to maintain ethical standards in the agency, which in recent years has been rife with scandals, become known for mismanagement, and gotten derailed from its missions by politicians and workers who appeared to be concerned mainly with self-aggrandizement. "I want to transform this Department from what is perceived as the Department of the West to the Department of all of America . . . ," he said, according to a DOI news release (January 22, 2009, online). "We will follow the law, we will hold people accountable, and we will expect to be held accountable. We will not tolerate the types of lapses that detract and distract from good honest service to the American people that this department does every day."

The Department of the Interior manages over one-fifth of the nation's land—more than 500 million acres, or nearly 760,000 square miles—as well as hundreds of dams and reservoirs and 1.76 billion acres (275 million square miles) under water, off the Outer Continental Shelf. It oversees the Bureau of Indian Affairs; the National Park Service; the Fish and Wildlife Service; the Bureau of Land Management; the Bureau of Reclamation; the U.S. Geological Survey; the Minerals Management Service; and the Office of Surface Mining Reclamation and Enforcement. Its purview ranges from operating schools for children on Indian reservations to maintaining national parks, monuments, seashores, and recreational sites; protecting and improving habitats for endangered species and other wildlife; checking water quality at thousands of sites; conducting biological, geological, and other research; producing more than 55,000 different maps; and monitoring the production of natural gas, oil, coal, and other sources of energy on federal lands. In his January 22 speech to DOI employees, Salazar said that he intended to work closely with the Departments of Energy and Commerce on energy issues, not only in such traditional areas as oil and gas leasing and offshore drilling but regarding the development of renewable and clean sources of energy.

One of the five sons and three daughters of Henry and Emma Salazar, Kenneth Lee Salazar was born on March 2, 1955 in Alamosa, Colorado. His older brother John has represented one of Colorado's seven congressional districts in the House since 2004. During World War II his father was a staff sergeant in the U.S. Army, and his mother worked for the U.S. War Department (as the Department of Defense was then called). Salazar has identified himself as a fifth-generation Coloradan and 12th-generation North American. Ancestors of his helped to found the city of Santa Fe, New Mexico, at the beginning of the 1600s, before settling in the San Luis Valley, which extends from southern Colorado to northern New Mexico. There, he and his siblings grew up on a remote ranch, with no electricity, running water, or telephone. Salazar has said that he learned how to use a gun as a preschooler, to scare off predators when he guarded his family's sheep.

After graduating from Centauri High School, in Conejos County, in 1973, Salazar attended Colorado College, in Colorado Springs, earning a B.A. degree in political science in 1977. (All of his brothers and sisters, too, are college graduates.) Four years later he received a J.D. degree from the University of Michigan School of Law. From 1981 to 1986 Salazar practiced environmental law and law dealing with water issues at Sherman & Howard, a private Denver, Colorado–based firm. In 1987 he was named the chief legal counsel for Colorado governor Roy Romer. Three years later Salazar was promoted to executive director of the Colorado Department of Natural Resources, a position he retained until 1994. In that post he co-wrote and helped pass a state constitutional amendment that created Great Outdoors Colorado, which uses lottery proceeds to fund one of the country's biggest land-conservation programs. He chaired Great Outdoors Colorado in 1993 and 1994.

In 1994 Salazar returned to private practice in Denver, as a director of the law firm Parcel, Mauro, Hultin & Spaanstra. Four years later he reentered government, narrowly defeating John Suthers in the race for Colorado attorney general. He was reelected in 2002. As attorney general Salazar toughened the state's sex-offender rules, addressed youth and family violence, and enforced environmental- and consumer-protection laws. His accomplishments include the establishment of the first-ever Colorado Attorney General Fugitive Prosecutions Unit, the first-ever Gang Prosecution Unit, and an Environmental Crimes Unit. He also served as the chair of the state's Peace Officers Standards and Training Board and on the Conference of Western Attorneys General, the Colorado Water Conservation Board, and selection committees for the United States attorney in Colorado and federal district court judges.

In 2004 Salazar successfully ran for a seat in the U.S. Senate, narrowly defeating the Republican Pete Coors, a Coors Brewing Co. executive. He served on three committees—Energy and Natural Resources; Veterans Affairs; and Agriculture, Nutrition, and Forestry—and on special committees on ethics and aging. As a senator Salazar advocated the use of clean and renewable energy; he sponsored the National Energy Policy Act of 2005, a bipartisan bill that aimed to decrease the country's dependence on foreign oil. A key supporter of wildlife conservation, Salazar sponsored legislation to ban drilling and protect endangered species on the Roan Plateau and the Wyoming Range. (He later backed a compromise allowing drilling for natural gas on limited parts of the Roan Plateau, which many environmentalists opposed.) Salazar also sponsored legislation to establish the Dominguez-Escalante National Conservation Area and Wilderness. (John Salazar sponsored identical legislation in the House; their bills are currently under consideration by House and Senate committees.) He worked with Republicans and Democrats to renew the Patriot Act.

In December 2007 Salazar endorsed Senator Barack Obama's bid for the 2008 presidential nomination and campaigned for Obama in Colorado; in the general election Obama won the electoral college votes in that state, a former Republican stronghold. Obama's choice of Salazar to head the Department of the Interior drew a mixed response; even Salazar's stands on conservation issues, which are a matter of public record, earned both praise and condemnation. As quoted on motherjones.com (December 17, 2008), Kieran Suckling, for example, the executive director of the Center for Biological Diversity, described Salazar as "a right-of-center Democrat who often favors industry and big agriculture," and Daniel R. Patterson, the southwest regional director of Public Employees for Responsibility, charged that he had "a disturbingly weak conservation record, particularly on energy development, global warming, endangered wildlife and protecting scientific integrity." Josh Dorner, on the other hand, a spokesman for the Sierra Club, said, "He has been a very vocal critic of the Bush administration's reckless approach to rampant land development in the West," and Bill Meadows and David Albersworth of the Wilderness Society said, respectively, that Salazar is "going to be an honest broker" and has demonstrated "a genuine openness to . . . considering different ideas." An editorial in the *New York Times* (January 2, 2009) suggested that Salazar may be "too nice" to "bust heads when necessary and draw the line against the powerful commercial groups . . . that have long treated the [DOI] as a public extension of their private interests."

In his first several months in office, Salazar was "more active than any secretary in history in this early period," Charles Wilkinson, a University of Colorado professor of law and expert on Native American history, told Michael Riley for the *Denver Post* (May 3, 2009). According to various observers, one of Salazar's main challenges will be to forge a middle ground in the often polarizing debates over the use of public lands by industry and energy companies. In an early important decision, he canceled several controversial oil and gas leases awarded by the administration of George W. Bush, indicating that in the future commercial contracts would be awarded only after scientific experts reviewed their impacts on the environment. He also made clear that the Obama administration would be spending more time, resources, and energy on developing renewable-energy sources, and he emphasized that a new energy policy, based on the Obama administration's broad mandate of change and reform, would be the Department of the Interior's "signature issue."

Salazar's extracurricular civic activities include membership in the Israel Friendship League (1986–89), on an advisory committee for the Colorado University School of Law Natural Resources Law Center (1989–92), and on the board of directors of the human-services organization Servicios de la Raza's HUD 202 Project (1985–89), an effort, linked to the U.S. Department of Housing and Urban Development, to provide affordable housing for low-income elderly Hispanics and others. In 1986 and 1987 he worked on the American Bar Association's task force on opportunities for minorities in the legal profession. He served on the City and County of Denver Ethics Panel in 1993 and represented the Colorado government on the State Board on Property Tax Equalization from 1987 to 1991.

A former rancher who often sports a 10-gallon cowboy hat and bolo tie, Salazar has named basketball and outdoor activities among his interests. He married the former Esperanza "Hope" Hernandez in 1985. The couple have two daughters, Melinda and Andrea, and one granddaughter. Salazar and his wife have owned and operated several small, local businesses over the years, including a Dairy Queen franchise and several radio stations.

—M.M.

Suggested Reading: *Pueblo (Colorado) Chieftain* (on-line) Dec. 17, 2008; *Time* (on-line) Dec. 18, 2008; *Who's Who in America*

Courtesy of Dan Savage

Savage, Dan

Oct. 7, 1964– Advice columnist; editor

Address: The Stranger, *Third Fl., 1535 11th Ave., Seattle, WA 98122*

"Sex—abortion, birth control, divorce, AIDS, gay marriages—is the story of the millennium. But we get newspapers that write about sex in language that won't offend a 5-year-old," the openly gay sex columnist, author, and newspaper editorial director Dan Savage told Jim Simon for the *Seattle Times* (July 21, 1996). "Nobody talks about this stuff the way I do." Savage is best known as the outspoken figure behind the advice column "Savage Love," syndicated in more than 70 newspapers in the United States, Europe, Canada, and Asia and famous for its adult content, irreverence, humor, and attitude. Savage has spent much of his career generating controversy, criticizing both the gay community and conservative Republicans and engaging in political pranks that have offended many and nearly landed him in prison; in 2000, for example, the Washington State resident illegally voted in the Republican Iowa Caucuses for a candidate he believed would damage that party, and he mocked the antigay Republican U.S. senator Rick Santorum in 2003 by challenging readers to come up with a sex-related definition for "santorum" (not a real word). Savage has also written several books about his personal life, in which he has detailed the process of adopting a son with his partner; contemplated the issue of gay marriage; offered insight into his family and upbringing; and explored other topics related to gay life. From 1994 to 1997 he hosted the radio show *Savage Love Live*, and he has worked as contributing writer and pundit for numerous other publications and radio shows. Since 1991 Savage has also been associated with Seattle's alternative weekly paper the *Stranger*, becoming its editor in chief in 2001 and editorial director in 2007.

Daniel Keenan Savage was born on October 7, 1964 in the Rogers Park neighborhood of Chicago, Illinois, the third of the four children of William and Judy Savage. He has recalled that his family struggled to get by on his father's salary as a homicide detective. Savage was raised as a Catholic; his father was an ordained deacon and his mother a lay minister. For high school he attended Quigley Preparatory Seminary to train for the priesthood, before his discovery of his sexuality set him on a different path.

Two events significantly affected Savage's attitude toward marriage and monogamy: the death of his grandmother, in 1970, of natural causes or by suicide (the true cause has never been known, but she was reputedly an alcoholic who was unhappy in her marriage), and his parents' divorce, in 1984. In his 2005 book, *The Commitment: Love, Sex, Marriage, and My Family*, he wrote, "The instant my grandmother died, her marriage became a success. Death parted my grandparents, not divorce, and death is the sole measure of a successful marriage. When a marriage ends in divorce, we say that it's failed. . . . It doesn't matter if the parting is amicable, it doesn't matter if the exes are happier apart. . . . Only a marriage that ends with someone in the cooler down at [the funeral home] Maloney's is a success. . . . My parents' parting, finding new partners, and embarking on successful second marriages was a long, painful process, but it was preferable to one of them drinking themselves to death."

Savage knew by 15 that he was gay, but he was not yet ready to tell his family. In *The Commitment* he wrote that while he otherwise felt ready to begin exploring Chicago's gay haunts, the presence of his relatives in the city made him hesitant to do so. "If I walked around the gay neighborhood," he recalled, "one of my siblings might see me from a bus; if I snuck into a gay bar, one of my uncles might see me sneaking back out; if I stood in the gay section of a bookstore, a grandparent or a cousin or an aunt or a nephew or an uncle or—worst of all!—a parent might see me." He noted that he began to "associate the physical presence of . . . parents, siblings, grandparents, aunts, uncles, and cousins with a debilitating fear of discovery and rejection." Nonetheless, Savage "came out" to his family before leaving for college, recalling in his book that his family was, "after one rocky summer, aggressively supportive." Savage attended the University of Illinois at Champaign-Urbana, majoring in history and theater. Following his graduation, he lived in various places in the U.S. and Europe. He wrote, "Only by living far away from my family was I able to give myself permission to go places . . . and do things . . . that I couldn't bring myself to do in a city crawling with my relatives."

The advice column that would lead Savage to national fame came about through chance. In 1991 Savage was working at a video-rental store in Madison, Wisconsin, when he met Tim Keck, a cofounder of the now-popular satirical newspaper the *Onion*. Keck informed him that he was starting an alternative newspaper, the *Stranger*, in Seattle, Washington. Savage replied offhandedly, "Oh, have an advice column, everybody hates 'em, but everybody reads 'em," as he recalled to Tasha Robinson for the *Onion A.V. Club* (February 8, 2006, on-line). "And [Keck] thought that was good advice, and asked me to write it. It sounds so disingenuous all these many years later, but I wasn't trying to get the job. I'd never really written anything before in my life, except for student papers." He wrote a sample column, and Keck was sufficiently impressed by it to ask Savage to contribute to the paper. Savage soon moved to Seattle.

Savage told Robinson that he had "been a fan" of certain advice columns, citing Ann Landers's column and "Dear Abby" as influences on his own approach. He decided, however, to make his column more caustic than either of those models, writing from a gay perspective and addressing both homosexual and heterosexual issues with a sharp—and often profane—tongue. "Forever, I'd read letters that had been written to straight advice columnists from gay people," he said to Robinson. "Sometimes the advice was okay, but oftentimes it was clueless about gay issues or gay people or gay sex or gay rights. And I just thought it would be funny for once if there was an advice column written by a gay person where straight people had to get slapped around or treated with contempt. That was the agenda at first—I was just gonna be obnoxious and contemptuous about straight sex and straight relationships." The column, "Savage Love," appeared in the premiere issue of the *Stranger*, on September 23, 1991. In a controversial move, Savage added the salutation "Hey, Faggot," to each published letter written to him. (His editors had already rejected "Hey, Faggot" as the column's name.) As he later explained, his use of the phrase was an attempt to change the word "faggot" from a homophobic slur into an expression of gay pride.

Savage told Robinson that he was still honing his craft during the column's early years, saying, "If you read the first couple years of 'Savage Love,' it's pretty clear I'd never written anything before in my life." As Savage worked on improving his writing, he also began to address his readers in a somewhat more serious fashion, telling Robinson, "That humor vein lasted about a year, and then I realized that I was gonna actually have to give advice and learn a little about heterosexual life." When he began to offer gay and heterosexual readers serious advice, the column—and the *Stranger*—took off.

Savage's column was successful in part because it held appeal for heterosexual readers, for whom Savage "is a translator of gay culture," Jim Simon wrote. "At the same time, he delights in playing the outrageously out gay man ministering to and often magnifying the sexual anxieties of straight guys." William Grimes wrote for the *New York Times* (March 30, 1997), "'Savage Love' deals in sex and relationships, with side excursions. . . . Many of the questions, and answers, cannot be described in a family newspaper. The tone is lively, funny and confrontational, although Mr. Savage can be wise and kind."

In an example of that wisdom and kindness, in his column dated January 8, 2009, published in the *Chicago Reader* (on-line), Savage responded to a question from a woman who, out of fear of confrontation, had sex with her ex-boyfriend against her will. Savage wrote, "Your ex kept coming at you, and you were paralyzed by a set of inhibitions—a desire to avoid confrontation at all costs (even the cost of your own violation), a desire to avoid making your victimizer feel bad—that are pounded into the heads of girls and young women. Your ex exploited this vulnerability. Your ex may not think he raped you since you finally 'let him,' and perhaps he interprets that as consent. . . . But raped you were." Savage added, "He needs to hear from you that you regard—and, for what it's worth, I regard—what happened as rape. Tell him that he didn't get away with it—that he raped you, you know it, and now he knows it. Then tell him that if the circumstances were just a little less ambiguous . . . you would be going to the police."

In 1994, with his column rapidly growing in popularity and now syndicated in five alternative weeklies, Savage was given a radio show on Seattle's station KCMU-FM. The show, *Savage Love Live*, which ran until 1997, brought him almost instant notoriety. At the time Savage, who was concerned with protecting his identity, was noted for arriving at the radio station in drag. By 1996 Savage was receiving between 100 and 150 letters a week, and "Savage Love" was being syndicated in 15 weekly newspapers with a combined circulation of 725,000. An article in *Newsweek* (May 20, 1996) listed him as one of the top 30 "Movers, Shakers, and Coffee Makers" in Seattle and announced, "The far-out drag queen's unabashed sex-advice column in the free weekly the *Stranger* propelled that paper to must-read status." In 1998 *Savage Love: Straight Answers from America's Most Popular Sex Columnist*, a collection of Savage's columns, was published.

Savage has occasionally stirred controversy or worse. In December 1992 he said, during an interview on the Seattle radio station KNDD, that he would "kill" then-president-elect Bill Clinton if he did not follow through on his pledge to lift the ban on gays in the military. Though he later explained that he did not mean the word "kill" literally, the United States Secret Service branch in Seattle launched an investigation, treating Savage as a potential assassin. In 1993 Savage found himself the center of national media attention after he compared the look of a child's toy, "Earring Magic Ken," to that of a gay man, noting in his column that the ring necklace around the character's neck looked like a gay-sex device. Officials at Mattel Toys, the maker of Earring Magic Ken, said that any similarity was a coincidence; Savage argued that it was a sign that gay culture had seeped into mainstream thinking. The first of Savage's widely publicized political pranks occurred in 1996, when he managed to become a delegate for Patrick Buchanan at that years's King County, Washington, Republican Party convention. He wrote in the *Stranger* that he hoped to use his influence to either push the party to the left or steer it so far to the right that it would lose its appeal for mainstream America. He first received attention when he threatened to dress in drag for the event; he made further news when he held up the convention for a day by proposing a number of gay-rights planks to the GOP platform.

In 2000 Savage was involved in controversy that far surpassed any he had generated before. He was assigned by the publication *Salon.com* to cover the Iowa caucuses in Des Moines. Upon arriving, sick with the flu, Savage joined the presidential campaign of the conservative, antigay Republican Gary Bauer as a volunteer. According to his article in *Salon*, his idea was to infect Bauer with the flu, in order to "lay him flat" before the important New Hampshire primary. He would "go to Bauer's campaign office and cough on everything—phones and pens, staplers and staffers. I even hatched a plan to infect the candidate himself. I would keep the pen in my mouth until Bauer dropped by his offices to rally the troops. And when he did, I would approach him and ask for his autograph, handing him the pen from my flu-virus incubating mouth." Savage acknowledged that his plan "was a little malicious—even a little mean-spirited—but those same words describe the tactics used by Bauer and the rest of the religious right against gays and lesbians." Though Savage wrote in the piece that he did exactly as he had planned, he later admitted to fabricating his attempt at infecting the candidate. Nonetheless, once the piece was published (and before Savage admitted to exaggerating the events), it brought a torrent of criticism, especially from those working for Bauer. What landed Savage in more trouble was his lying about his state residency in order to vote in the Iowa caucuses for Bauer, the Republican candidate he believed could "most damage the Republican Party in the upcoming general election." Charged with voter fraud, in November 2000—on Election Day—Savage pleaded guilty to a misdemeanor and was sentenced to a year's probation, 50 hours of community service, and a $750 fine.

In 2003 Savage used his influence as a popular columnist to mock the Republican U.S. senator Rick Santorum of Pennsylvania, after being offended by comments about homosexuality the senator had made in interviews. In his column Savage announced a contest in which readers could suggest new meanings for "santorum." In January 2009, in response to Barack Obama's choice of the Saddleback Church pastor, Rick Warren—who has criticized homosexual behavior—to give the invocation at Obama's presidential inauguration, Savage invited his readers to come up with a sex-related meaning for another non-word, "saddlebacking."

Despite the popularity of "Savage Love," critics have argued that Savage's tone is often hostile to readers. Jennifer Knopf, a sex and marital therapist in Chicago, told Barbara Brotman for the *Chicago Tribune* (November 21, 1996), "There is an educational thread that runs through [the column], but he seems to treat the readers with some hostility and cynicism." Savage has also been noted for his fairly conservative advice and stance on sexual behavior. Malcolm McKay of the Seattle Institute for Sex Therapy said to Simon, "What really fascinates me about Dan is how moralistic he is. If you're really confused and looking for a place to turn for help, Dan's not the place to go." Brotman noted that Savage "is funny and fiercely opinionated, judging not the morality of sex acts, but the behavior of the people engaging in them. His most withering scorn is heaped on men who won't wear condoms and those who are sexually selfish." Discussing the advice he gives, Savage told Guy Trebay for the *Village Voice* (October 7–13, 1998), "What people don't always get, is, it's not binding arbitration.

You're free to ignore it. Sometimes I say things I don't mean. I say, 'Get drunk and drive fast.' I'm not unaware that that's bad 'advice.'" When one reader asked Savage in a letter what qualified him to advise heterosexuals on their love lives, he responded, as quoted by Simon, "Well, by simple virtue of being gay. To understand who I am and why I am, I've had to confront issues of sexuality—hetero and homo—on a level that you haven't. For straight people, sexuality is a simple matter of fact. But for queers, sexuality is the $ 64,000 question, the central question of our existence (beginning with 'Why me, God'), and thus our primary obsession. We have to find answers or go nuts."

Members of the gay community have expressed mixed feelings about Savage, in part because he has criticized certain gay-rights initiatives. In 1995, for example, a Seattle-based gay-rights organization, Hands Off Washington (HOW), pushed for a gay-rights referendum to be included on the state's general-election ballot. Savage opposed the measure, arguing that it would have to be passed by a popular vote—an unlikely outcome, in his view—and that its defeat would set back the cause of gay-rights legislation. His harshly worded position derailed the initiative, and some angry HOW leaders did not attend an annual gay political dinner that Savage later hosted.

In 1999 Savage published *The Kid: What Happened After My Boyfriend and I Decided to Go Get Pregnant*. The book chronicles his attempt to adopt a child with his partner, Terry Miller. The two went to Portland, Oregon, to pursue an "open adoption," in which the birth mother selected them as the child's parents and negotiated the terms of her visitation rights. Savage described his and Miller's surprise at the ease of the process and the absence of homophobia among the people they encountered as they adopted Daryl Jude "D. J." Pierce. ("Pierce" is the birth mother's surname.) He also wrote that it took time for him to form an emotional connection with his son, telling Daryl Lindsey for *Salon.com* (October 1, 1999), "In adoption, your parenthood is an act of will and it takes time. You have to perform these parent roles to feel like a parent. My boyfriend is the stay-at-home parent and has been more involved with the baby and still is. I'm on the book tour, he's home with the baby. It was only natural that I should not feel bonded." He said that the bonding "happened at about a year and it was powerful." Clarissa Cluz wrote for *Entertainment Weekly* (December 24, 1999), "Crammed with chokingly funny passages on everything from impressing a stone-faced birth mother to using a baby as an excuse to get fat, this account of gay adoption . . . is easily one of the most laugh-out-loud hilarious books of the year. But it's because *The Kid* doesn't remain a mere giggle-fest that it's also one of the best. Intelligent, provocative, and disarmingly honest, this is Savage's touching—and irreverent—love letter to his new son."

Savage's 2002 book, *Skipping Towards Gomorrah*, chronicles a road trip he took to prove that "sinners" are not inherently bad people. On the trip he committed each of the traditional "seven deadly sins"—lust, gluttony, greed, sloth, envy, anger, and pride—and met many people whose lives would be widely considered immoral, such as a married but "swinging" couple. Among other activities, he gambled, lay in bed while watching movies and smoking marijuana, fired a gun, attended a convention for obese people, and took part in the Gay Pride Parade in San Francisco, California. Reviewing the book for the Popmatters Web site (October 2002), Claire Zulkey wrote, "Savage's chapters vary in style from personal profile to personal essay to political rant, which keep them moving fast and generally avoid preachiness. And, let's face it, reading about sin and the practices we hear of yet perhaps do not perform is fascinating and voyeuristic. It's difficult to avoid thinking, however, about . . . Savage's selections for his investigations of the 'seven deadlies.' Is gun use the prototypical example of violence? Could he have attended an eating contest for gluttony? And does gay pride fall necessarily under 'pride,' or could that be 'lust'? Of course, though, [the] book is not a dissertation on what the seven deadly sins are: it's more of an examination of just how sinful the sinners actually are (i.e. he goes to great pains to display the swinging couple as being very upstanding, very religious and doting upon their children)."

The Commitment, Savage's 2005 book, continues his exploration of his new family and also deals with the issue of gay marriage. He revealed that his mother wanted him and Miller to marry; much to the couple's surprise, D.J., who at six learned about marriage in school, was initially opposed to the idea of his fathers' marrying. Savage and Miller were married in Vancouver, Canada, in 2005, because the state of Washington does not grant marriage licenses to same-sex couples. In March 2004 Savage had married his *Stranger* colleague Amy Jenniges, a lesbian, in Seattle. Even though Savage and Jenniges informed the clerk that they were not in love and that each had another partner, as a man and woman they were legally allowed to marry. According to Savage in the *Stranger* (March 11–17, 2004, on-line), the point of the marriage was to show the "absurdity of our marriage laws." "Amy can't marry [her girlfriend] Sonia, I can't marry Terry—why?" he wrote. "Because the sanctity of marriage must be protected from the queers! But Amy and I can get a marriage license—and into a sham marriage, if we care to, a joke marriage, one that I promise you won't produce children. And we can do this with the state's blessing—why? Because one of us is a man and one of us is a woman. Who cares that one of us is a gay man and one of us is a lesbian? So marriage is to be protected from the homos—unless the homos marry each other."

In *The Commitment* Savage recalled intimate conversations he had had with family members and included his analyses of contemporary politics and gay culture. Gayle Worland, reviewing the book for the *Wisconsin State Journal* (October 16, 2005), wrote, "Since *Commitment* is a Dan Savage work, it is relentlessly and understatedly funny. It is also an endearing memoir about family dynamics, a musing on the importance of lifelong vows and, at times, a sermon on the issue of same-sex marriage." Others felt that the book was not effective in addressing issues related to same-sex marriage. Carolyn See, writing for the *Miami Herald* (October 23, 2005), argued, "Savage fails to note any significant social progress or acknowledge the suffering of other repressed groups; he just drones on, preaching to the choir. And he can be mean-spirited, too. He makes fun of the 'morbidly obese.' . . . He crabs on and on about the wedding industry. When he accuses Terry of being a gold digger and not understanding the value of a dollar, I couldn't help but think Savage is a lucky man. Any woman worth her salt would have bopped him with a heavy vase."

Savage had become an associate editor of the *Stranger* in 1995; in April 2001, at 36, he became the publication's editor in chief. By 2002 the *Stranger* had become a serious competitor of the more established *Seattle Weekly*, with a circulation of 79,997—closing in on the *Seattle Weekly's* 104,397. At the time "Savage Love" was syndicated in 50 papers, and its author was receiving about 1,000 e-mail queries from readers every week. In 2007 Savage became the *Stranger's* editorial director, with Christopher Frizelle serving as editor in chief. In a post on the paper's blog, known as the Slog, Savage wrote that he would continue to work with Frizelle and others on the paper's content and would contribute heavily to the *Stranger's* Web presence. Recently Savage began responding via podcast to call-in questions about sex and relationships.

Savage has written several plays under the name Keenan Hollahan and is a founding member of Seattle's Greek Active Theatre, known for homosexual-themed takes on classic works. Savage is particularly known for his 2001 play *Egguus,* a parody of Peter Shaffer's *Equus.* In Shaffer's play, the main character is obsessed with horses; Savage's version replaces the horses with chickens. From 1998 to 2000 Savage wrote a biweekly, family-friendly advice column, "Dear Dan," for the ABC News Web site. He has served as a contributor to National Public Radio's program *This American Life* and written for *Out* magazine. In 2000 he won the prestigious PEN Center West award for creative nonfiction for *The Kid.* In 2009 Savage taped a pilot episode for a talk show based on his column. HBO expressed interest in picking it up but as of October 2009 had not announced whether it would. Savage lives in Seattle's Capital Hill district with Terry Miller and D.J.

—W.D.

Suggested Reading: *Onion* (on-line) Feb. 8, 2006; *Salon.com* Oct. 1 1999; *Seattle Times* p10 July 21, 1996; thestranger.com; *Washington Post* C p1 Feb. 3, 2000

Selected Books: *Savage Love: Straight Answers from America's Most Popular Sex Columnist,* 1998; *The Kid: What Happened After My Boyfriend and I Decided to Go Get Pregnant,* 1999; *Skipping Towards Gomorrah: The Seven Deadly Sins and the Pursuit of Happiness in America,* 2002; *The Commitment: Love, Sex, Marriage, and My Family,* 2005

Noel St. John

Schiller, Vivian

Sep. 13, 1961– President and CEO of National Public Radio

Address: National Public Radio, 635 Massachusetts Ave., N.W., Washington, DC 20001

"My whole career has been about taking advantage of opportunities that intrigue me," Vivian Schiller, the president and chief executive officer of National Public Radio, told Glynnis MacNicol for *mediabistro.com* (April 8, 2009). "Somewhere along the way, I realized the things I care about: journalism, media, quality content, a social mission. It sort of came into focus over time." Schiller also told MacNicol, "One impulse for me has always been the same, and that is curiosity . . . , which at the end of the day is sort of the fundamental quality of journalism. I realize that's what drives me." National

Public Radio (NPR) is a nonprofit organization that provides reports of news gathered by journalists based at 36 bureaus maintained by NPR worldwide; currently, about 28 million people tune in to one or another of its approximately 860 independent member radio stations. In addition to newscasts, NPR produces, acquires, and distributes commercial-free talk shows, music programs, and other types of broadcasts to its member stations. Schiller has never been a journalist, but "she's got a journalist's temperament," Michael Oreskes, the Associated Press managing editor for U.S. news, told Megan Miller for the *American Journalism Review* (February/March 2009, on-line). He added that Schiller understands "what it mean[s] to do good journalism." "She's been in complex companies, and she's always thrived . . . ," Colby Atlas, a former colleague of Schiller's, told Karen Everhart for *Current* (November 24, 2008, on-line). "[She] knows how to grow a business and how to build an audience. Plus, she understands technology."

Schiller's casual decision as an undergraduate to enroll in a course in Russian proved to be the crucial first step in the path that brought her to NPR. By the time she earned her college degree, in 1983, Schiller had become fluent in Russian; her skill with the language enabled her to become a tour guide for large groups of American professionals in what was then the Soviet Union. In that role she became adept at organizing, handling public-relations work, public speaking, troubleshooting, juggling multiple concurrent tasks, and crisis management. She also acquired what she described to Allison Romano for *Broadcasting & Cable* (October 20, 2003) as "cross-cultural skills." "I actually think that experience really laid the groundwork for me for a career in management," she told Megan Miller. "I think when I retire I'm going to write a book called *Everything I Know I Learned as a Tour Guide*." That occupation led directly to her next job, as a production assistant for Turner Broadcasting Systems (TBS) in the Soviet Union. In 1998, after a decade with TBS and increasingly responsible positions, she spent four years as an executive with CNN. Next, for half a dozen years beginning in 2002, she was associated with the *New York Times*, first as the general manager of Discovery Times, a TV channel, and then as the general manager of the newspaper's Internet operations. Schiller arrived at NPR on January 5, 2009. When Glynnis MacNicol interviewed her, four months later, she said, "I feel incredibly comfortable and at home there, because the fact is, at good news organizations, there's a certain commonality to the culture—people who are, for better or worse, very iconoclastic, very tough, very demanding about quality. That culture existed at *The New York Times* and it exists at NPR."

Vivian Luisa Schiller was born on September 13, 1961 in New York State. Her father, Ronald Schiller, an editor with *Reader's Digest*, and mother, Lillian Schiller, raised her in Larchmont, a suburb of New York City. After her high-school graduation, in 1979, Schiller entered Cornell University, in Ithaca, New York. Required to study a foreign language, she chose Russian, in part because the class did not meet too early in the day, as she recalled to Megan Miller. Under the enthusiastic tutelage of Kevin Moss, a teaching assistant in Russian literature, she grew to love the language and made it her major, along with Soviet studies. Moss, she told Robert Keren for a Middlebury College press release (November 24, 2008, on-line), "introduced me not just to the rules of grammar and syntax, but to the beauty and joy of Russian. And that made all the difference." After she earned a bachelor's degree, in 1983, she traveled to Moscow, Russia, where she completed a master's degree in 1985 in a graduate program in Russian studies maintained there by Middlebury College. While there she worked for a diplomat's family as an au pair and earned extra cash as an assistant in the nursery school run by the U.S. Embassy.

For four years beginning in 1985, Schiller worked as a tour guide and interpreter in the Soviet Union; her clients were American lawyers, doctors, and other professionals, sometimes in groups of as many as 200. At that time Ted Turner, who was then the president and chairman of the Turner Broadcasting Systems, was "in love with all things Russian," Schiller told Matt Kempner for the *Atlanta (Georgia) Journal-Constitution* (May 5, 2002). That is partly why, in 1988, TBS hired her as a production assistant; she also served as an interpreter, "fixer," and "go-to person to handle a lot of [TBS's] business," as she put it to Kempner. (She told Megan Miller that "in production terms," a fixer is "somebody in a foreign country who 'makes it happen.'") She worked with Soviet State Television as a negotiator regarding documentaries TBS wanted to produce; her responsibilities, she told Kempner, included "getting doors opened" and "arranging for us to see the right ministers and sub-ministers." "The cool thing was that because they were depending on me for my Russian skills, even though I was a flunky I got to travel and spend time with the highest-level executives in the company . . . ," she recalled to Miller. "So I was able to learn so much about the media business by sitting in with some of the most impressive people in media at the time."

By 1988 Schiller had returned to the U.S. and moved to Atlanta, Georgia, where, after a series of promotions, she had been named senior vice president and general manager of Turner Original Productions. In that post she managed the documentary division of Turner Entertainment Networks and produced documentaries that aired on TBS. Between 1991 and 1993 she also served as the executive producer of episodes of the animated children's series *Tom and Jerry Kids Show*. She was the supervising producer for the Emmy Award–nominated TV miniseries *A Century of Women* (1994), a documentary, with added fictional scenes, about the changing roles of women in the

20th-century U.S. She served in the same capacity for the National Aeronautics and Space Administration (NASA)–related documentary *Moon Shot* (1994). In 1995 she was the senior producer for *Hank Aaron: Chasing the Dream*, TBS's first film to earn an Oscar nomination, as best documentary. Schiller's filmography as a TBS senior producer includes *Hollywood's Amazing Animal Actors* (1996); *Biker Women* (1996); *Survivors of the Holocaust* (1996), which won an Emmy Award for outstanding informational special; *Animal ER* (1996); *Pirate Tales* (1997); and *Warner Bros. 75th Anniversary: No Guts, No Glory* (1998).

In 1998 Schiller joined the all-news cable-TV network CNN, founded by Ted Turner in 1980. As senior vice president for CNN Productions, she directed the CNN News Group's so-called long-form programming. She developed two acclaimed weekly series for CNN: *People in the News* (produced jointly with the magazine *People*) and the award-winning documentary series *CNN Presents*. For the latter, Schiller told Kempner, "I look for programs out in the world. . . . I negotiate the deals. I get the word out. I work very closely with the network. . . . I review every word of every script and every frame of every cut. . . . It's a three-ring circus around here most of the time. At any given time we have got 20 to 25 different documentaries in various stages of development or production. And another 20 . . . that we are trying to figure out if we should do them."

In 2002 Schiller left CNN to become general manager of the Discovery Times Channel, a joint venture of Discovery Communications Inc. and the New York Times Co.; based in Silver Spring, Maryland, it was the latest incarnation of what had begun, in 1996, as CBS Eye on People and was later renamed Discovery Civilization. Schiller scheduled documentaries and nightly and weekly shows devoted to reports on national and world affairs, with the aim of providing "a place where people can tune in anytime, day or night, and get smart, engaging television," she told David Bauder for the Associated Press State & Local Wire (March 23, 2003). The Discovery Times channel debuted in March 2003 with *Al Qaeda 2.0*. Other documentaries shown that year included *The American Car*, about the U.S. auto industry, and *Nowhere, Fast*, about the increasing prevalence of rush-hour traffic jams. The former *New York Times* Pulitzer Prize–winning journalist Sheryl WuDunn hosted the three-minute nightly segment *Page One*, about stories slated to appear in the next day's *New York Times*, and the paper's foreign-affairs columnist Thomas L. Friedman offered minute-long impressions of world events.

In 2005 the *Times* announced that Schiller had been appointed to a new position, that of senior vice president for TV and video. In addition to retaining responsibility for the Discovery Times Channel, she oversaw "continued efforts to extend the journalism of *The Times* beyond the printed page to media like television," according to a *Times* (May 20, 2005) notice. Toward that end she helped to launch the newspaper's podcast—an audio file that can be downloaded from a Web site onto a portable digital audio player, commonly known as an MP3 player. In April 2006 the Times Co. sold its share in the Discovery Times Channel to Discovery Communications. According to a writer for *Business Wire* (April 24, 2006, on-line), during her time with the channel, Schiller "led the network to early profitability and critical acclaim"—as reflected in such honors as three Emmy Awards, two Overseas Press Club Awards, and three National Headliner Awards—and its reach grew from 14 million households to more than 39 million.

In May 2006 Schiller assumed the job of senior vice president and general manager of the *New York Times*'s Web site, *nytimes.com*. (That promotion required her to commute weekly from her home in Bethesda, Maryland, to New York City.) She presided over the addition to the Web site of an increasing number of audio and video features, graphics, and photo slide shows. She also oversaw the abandonment of TimesSelect, an on-line system whereby, for a fee, *Times* subscribers could view op-ed columns, archived articles, and other materials not available to other Internet users. "TimesSelect brought new commentary and voices to the site, as well as an influx of subscription revenue," Schiller explained in an official statement, as quoted by John McCormick in *Baseline* (September 24, 2007). "But the increasing dominance of search and other forms of referral have changed the equation. Allowing unfettered, free access to our opinion content and recent archives should enable us to drive readership and advertising." Schiller supervised the introduction of blogs and interactive features, including "My Times," which allows users to compose a menu of what they prefer to read on the Web site; "City Room," about developments in New York City; and "The Board," written by members of the newspaper's editorial board. Other innovations included mobile news services; by 2008 users of Apple's iPhone could download items from the *New York Times*. On another front, nytimes.com and the business-networking site linkedin.com made it possible for LinkedIn users to view *New York Times* business stories. By October 2008 *nytimes.com* had significantly expanded business coverage, redesigned its technology section, and added a section devoted to the economy and a blog dedicated to energy and environmental issues. It had also added more than a dozen journalists to its staff, to write for the business and technology sections.

Schiller was among 50 people whom a search committee considered as the successor to Kenneth P. "Ken" Stern as head of NPR. NPR's mission, according to its Web site, is "to work in partnership with member stations to create a more informed public—one challenged and invigorated by a deeper understanding and appreciation of events, ideas and cultures." The organization is supported almost entirely by private funding, much of it from listeners. Schiller had not been looking to leave her post at the *Times*; rather, she told Karen Everhart for current.org (November 24, 2008) shortly after NPR announced that she had accepted the job, "This position pursued me." "I've been a listener for decades," she told Everhart. (Her favorite NPR programs are *Morning Edition*, *Car Talk*, *This American Life*, and *On the Media*.) During meetings with the search committee and others at NPR, she said, "as I got to know the people and hear their passion and the opportunities and even the challenges—which I find compelling—I really became very passionate about the opportunity. I'm going to the only other news organization"—besides the *New York Times*—"that I can think of that's passionate about the quality of the news brand."

According to Paul Farhi, writing for the *Washington Post* (March 7, 2008), Ken Stern had been forced to leave NPR in March 2008, after the organization's 17-member board of directors opted not to renew his contract. (The board's chairman, Dennis L. Haarsager, stepped down from that post to serve as interim CEO until Schiller took over, on January 5, 2009.) The board gave no reason for its decision, but others at NPR told Farhi that the 10 members of the board who represented NPR stations believed that the steps Stern had taken to expand into new media had come "at the expense of serving the hundreds of public stations that pay dues annually to NPR." Schiller told Leslie Cantu for *Public Broadcasting Report* (November 21, 2008) that she was "very sensitive" to the concerns of member stations. "I think we've got to find the right balance," she said, between activities aimed at enhancing content for radio listeners and those catering to people who prefer podcasts or other ways of receiving NPR content. "The entire media world is struggling with the digital future," Schiller told Everhart. "It's a very fast-moving, dynamic situation—and this is before you add in the complications caused by the economic situation." To increase traffic to npr.org and keep the organization relevant, Schiller pushed for "hyperlocal digital media"—NPR Web sites with local news. She told Everhart, "A lot of startups have tried this and failed because they didn't have the infrastructure and couldn't support it. Local newspapers are under such duress right now that they can't focus on it. NPR already has the infrastructure in every city, town, and campus. There's a level of trust in their communities that no other national or local organization has." She added that public radio has a "unique opportunity to create a digital town square." NPR provides local stations with technological innovations and other services. "The stations know their communities," Schiller told Glynnis MacNicol. "There's different demographics. There's different sensibilities. So we enable them and they provide [local news]." One of Schiller's biggest challenges will be to maintain and, ideally, increase donations to NPR and its member stations in a struggling economy. In October 2009 NPR announced the launch of an on-line journalism venture, the Local News Initiative. The project provides a dozen NPR stations with resources to expand local reporting on specialized topics relevant to each station's listeners. Schiller

Schiller has been married since 1992 to Phillip Frank, a freelance documentary producer. The couple's children, a daughter and a son, are young teenagers. The family live in Bethesda, close to Washington, D.C., where Schiller's NPR office is located.

—W.D.

Suggested Reading: *American Journalism Review* (on-line) Feb./Mar. 2009; *Atlanta Journal-Constitution* Q p2 May 5, 2002; *Business Wire* Apr. 24, 2006; *Current* (on-line) Nov. 24, 2008; *mediabistro.com* Apr. 8, 2009; npr.org; *Washington Post* C p7 Nov. 12, 2008

Selected Television Documentaries: as supervising producer—*A Century of Women*, 1994; *Moon Shot*, 1994; as senior producer—*Hank Aaron: Chasing the Dream*, 1995; *Hollywood's Amazing Animal Actors*, 1996; *Biker Women*, 1996; *Survivors of the Holocaust*, 1996; *Animal ER*, 1996; *Pirate Tales*, 1997; *Twin Stories*, 1997; *Warner Bros. 75th Anniversary: No Guts, No Glory*, 1998; *Dying to Tell the Story*, 1998

Schwartzman, Jason

June 26, 1980– Actor; musician

Address: c/o Sharon Sheinwold, United Talent Agency, 9560 Wilshire Blvd., Suite 500, Beverly Hills, CA 90212

Jason Schwartzman hails from a talented Hollywood family that includes the Academy Award–winning directors Francis Ford Coppola and Sofia Coppola and the actors Nicolas Cage and Talia Shire. Schwartzman himself was relatively unknown to the public, however, when he beat out more than 1,800 candidates to win the lead role—that of Max Fischer, an eccentric prep-school student who becomes entangled in a love triangle—in the big-screen comedy *Rushmore* (1998). Since his critically acclaimed debut in that film, which Wes Anderson directed, Schwartzman has become known for tackling offbeat roles in such pictures as *Slackers* (2002), *I Heart Huckabees* (2004), *Shopgirl* (2005), *The Darjeeling Limited* (2007), and *Funny People* (2009). Also an accomplished musician, he is a former member of the alternative-rock group Phantom Planet, whose song "California" was used as the theme for the Fox TV series *The O.C.*, and he is now recording as a solo artist.

Stephen Lovekin/Getty Images

Jason Schwartzman

Jason Francesco Schwartzman was born on June 26, 1980 in Los Angeles, California, to Jack Schwartzman and Talia (Coppola) Shire. His late father was a film producer whose credits include the Oscar-winning comedy *Being There* (1979) and the James Bond picture *Never Say Never Again* (1983). His mother is an actress best known for her performances as Adrian, the wife of the boxer Rocky Balboa (played by Sylvester Stallone), in the 1976 film *Rocky* and its sequels and as Connie Corleone, the daughter of Don Vito Corleone (Marlon Brando), in the *Godfather* film trilogy. The *Godfather* movies were directed by Schwartzman's uncle Francis Ford Coppola and scored by his grandfather Carmine Coppola.

As a boy Schwartzman idolized his cousin Nicolas Cage, a popular actor known for his roles in films including *Raising Arizona* (1987), *Moonstruck* (1987), *Leaving Las Vegas* (1995), *Con Air* (1997), and *Gone in Sixty Seconds* (2000). "He was a big influence," Schwartzman told Alexandra Jacobs for the *New York Times* (March 7, 2004, on-line). "But . . . I love [my whole family]. It really is a clan. We were all encouraged to pursue what made us happy, and it just so happens that [acting] is what makes me happy."

Determined to give her children a sense of normalcy, Talia Shire frequently turned down film roles to stay at home with Schwartzman and his siblings—his older half-brother, Matthew Shire, and younger brother, Robert Schwartzman, who is now a musician and actor. Schwartzman told Betsy Pickle for the *Knoxville (Tennessee) News-Sentinel* (February 1, 2002, on-line), "We were a very normal family. We all had dinner together and talked about stuff." Schwartzman attended private schools in Los Angeles. His father frequently attended his Little League games, cheering him on from the top bleachers.

Schwartzman's family also had loftier interests. "My earliest memories are of coming home and my mom being in the living room, reading Ibsen out loud," Schwartzman told a United Press International (October 15, 2006, on-line) interviewer. "There is a love of the arts that I've always kind of been around, but it wasn't [especially] encouraged, it was just presented." At age 10 he received a drum set for his birthday and began learning to play. He also started to pursue an acting career; he auditioned unsuccessfully for the role of Tom Hanks's son in the film *Sleepless in Seattle* (1993).

In early June 1994 Schwartzman's father died, of pancreatic cancer. That year Schwartzman, then 14, teamed up with the guitarist and vocalist Alex Greenwald, a former elementary-school classmate of his, to play cover songs by Nirvana and other bands. They were soon joined by the guitarists Darren Robinson and Jacques Brautbar and the bass player Sam Farrar, a son of the songwriter/producer John Farrar. They named the band Phantom Planet, after a 1961 science-fiction movie of the same name; they had been inspired by the film's theme song, which was included on the compilation album *Greatest Science Fiction Hits Volume 1* (1990). Phantom Planet rehearsed in the basement of Schwartzman's home, and in 1995 the band made their first public appearance, at the Dragonfly, a Los Angeles nightclub.

While attending Winward, a progressive private high school in Mar Vista, Schwartzman continued to drum with the group, which played gigs in and around Los Angeles on the weekends. Phantom Planet developed a loyal local following, and in 1997 the band signed with Geffen Records. The following year their debut album, *Phantom Planet Is Missing*, was released to a measure of critical acclaim. "For a debut album from a relatively young band (most of the members are still teenagers), *Phantom Planet Is Missing* is very accomplished and appealing," Jason Damas wrote for the All Music Guide (on-line). "While the hooks aren't particularly strong, the band makes up for it with youthful exuberance and colorful instrumentation—the music is upbeat and synthesized flourishes abound. . . . Phantom Planet walk the line between pop and alternative and manage to carve out their own unique sound—a rarity for younger alternative bands." A single from the album, "So I Fall Again," was featured on the soundtrack of the TV series *Sabrina the Teenage Witch*.

As a youngster Schwartzman often spent the summers with his cousins Roman and Sofia at his uncle Francis's wine estate in Napa Valley, California, where they performed one-act plays for neighbors. (The director ran informal "creativity camps," at which the younger members of the family were encouraged to write stories and plays, act, and draw.) When he was about 13, Schwartzman wrote and directed his first play, about a group of men who turn up at a bar on New Year's Eve and reminisce about a woman on the anniversary of her death: one of the men is her husband and another is the person responsible for causing her death.

One night in 1997 Schwartzman attended a dinner party held at his uncle's estate. During the festivities Sofia introduced him to the San Francisco–based casting director Davia Nelson, who had been frantically conducting a search for an actor to play Max Fischer, a gifted but underachieving 15-year-old student at an elite prep school, in the quirky comedy *Rushmore*. Fischer, in love with a first-grade teacher at the school, befriends a local business tycoon (played by Bill Murray), who becomes his romantic rival. Most of the other roles in the movie had already been cast, and the director and co-writer Wes Anderson, who had loosely based the story on his own prep-school years, was scheduled to begin filming in one month. "[Nelson] said: 'It's a story about this kid, he's eccentric, he writes plays, he's really horny and he likes older women.' I thought: 'Great, that sounds like me,'" Schwartzman told Paul Fischer for the Sydney, Australia, *Sunday Telegraph* (February 28, 1999). "So I gave her my number. When I got home that weekend, there was a script lying on the bed. I wasn't looking for anything, but I guess it was looking for me."

A week later Schwartzman met with Anderson. While many who auditioned for the role of Max had shown up wearing preppy, navy blazers, Schwartzman had gone one step further—he had designed a school patch for the fictional Rushmore Academy and affixed it to his lapel. Upon meeting Schwartzman the director immediately offered him the role. Anderson told Ruthe Stein for the *San Francisco Chronicle* (January 24, 1999, on-line), "Within 30 seconds of talking to him, I knew this was the kid."

Three weeks later Schwartzman flew to Houston, Texas, Anderson's hometown, where *Rushmore* was being filmed. To prepare for his role, he spent several weeks with Anderson, perfecting his character's hand gestures, body language, and deadpan way of speaking. Shortly after the camera started to roll for the first scene, Schwartzman recalled to Robert Hanks for the London *Independent* (May 10, 2002, on-line), Bill Murray, whom he greatly admired, "put his head in his hands, and I said, 'What's wrong?' He said, 'Maybe I made a mistake.' And I said, 'What do you mean?' He said: 'They said you were gonna be good. The movie's about you. You've gotta be good. [But] you suck.' . . . And he was thinking about quitting that night, because I was so bad." After a few rocky days of filming, Anderson invited Murray and Schwartzman to dinner so that they could get to know each other. The two talked for hours, and Murray later became a mentor to the newcomer.

Schwartzman earned raves for his performance in *Rushmore*. In a representative review, Julie Hinds wrote for the *San Jose (California) Mercury News* (February 5, 1999), "For an hour and a half, Schwartzman is in almost every scene, more than holding his own against Bill Murray. . . . It's hard to imagine *Rushmore* without him, just as it's difficult to picture another teenage actor with enough presence to carry off the part." Schwartzman earned best-actor honors at the Lone Star Film and Television Awards; the prize for best performance by a young actor in a comedy film at the YoungStar Awards; a citation as most promising actor at the Chicago Film Critics Association Awards; and nominations in two categories—breakout performance in a film and choice "hissy fit" in a film—at the 1999 Teen Choice Awards.

In 2000 Schwartzman guest-starred as a dealer in fake IDs in an episode of the short-lived NBC comedic series *Freaks and Geeks*. In early 2001 he and his bandmates returned to the studio to record Phantom Planet's sophomore album, *The Guest* (2002), their first release on the Epic Records label. The disc met with praise from reviewers, many of whom mentioned the band's infectious sound and the youth of its members.

After appearing in Roman Coppola's directorial debut, *CQ* (2001), Schwartzman had a small role in *Odessa or Bust* (2001), a little-seen picture starring the comedian Red Buttons. He provided the voice of the title character in the animated shorts *Julius and Friends: Hole in One* (2001) and *Julius and Friends: Yeti, Set, Go* (2002). He had a minor role in the mainstream Hollywood picture *S1m0ne* (2002), which starred Al Pacino.

While he had not landed another major acting role since *Rushmore*, Schwartzman was receiving increasing attention as a musician. "California," a song Schwartzman wrote for Phantom Planet, was included on the soundtrack of the Jack Black comedy *Orange County* (2002); the next year it became the theme song for the popular TV series *The O.C.* Phantom Planet served as the opening act for the rock band Incubus during a 2002 tour.

Also in 2002 Schwartzman appeared in *Slackers*, a campus comedy filmed two years earlier, whose release had been delayed by production issues. Most critics found the role unworthy of his talents. Schwartzman's next role, that of a young drug addict in *Spun* (2002), was widely regarded as far better. In a review for the *Chicago Sun-Times* (April 4, 2003, on-line), Roger Ebert wrote of the ensemble cast, which also included Mena Suvari, Patrick Fugit, and Brittany Murphy, who had appeared in *American Beauty*, *Almost Famous*, and *Just Married*, respectively: "Uncanny, in a way, how they all bring along some of the aura of their famous earlier characters, as if this were a [documentary] about Hollywood youth gone wrong." Ebert continued, "The film's charm, which is admittedly an acquired and elusive taste, comes from the fact that *Spun* does not romanticize its characters, does not enlarge or dramatize them, but seems to shake its head incredulously as these screw-ups persist in ruinous and insane behavior." Schwartzman next starred in *Just Like Mona* (2003), about a teenager living with his eccentric mother in the 1960s.

In August 2003, while Phantom Planet was recording a third album, Schwartzman announced that he was leaving the band. He explained to Betsy Pickle for the Scripps Howard News Service (October 19, 2004), "I didn't quit to make a movie, but I think it could come across that way. I just left because it was the right thing to do for me in that moment." Shortly afterward Schwartzman appeared as Albert Markovski opposite Jude Law and Naomi Watts in the philosophical comedy *I Heart Huckabees* (2004), directed by his friend David O. Russell, who also wrote the screenplay. The role of Markovski, a poet and environmental activist who hires a pair of "existential detectives" (played by Dustin Hoffman and Lily Tomlin) to investigate a rival, was written with Schwartzman in mind. Applauding Schwartzman's "most prominent role" since his cinema debut, David Rooney wrote for *Variety* (September 12, 2004, on-line), "The actor again is quick-witted and appealing here, playing an impassioned character who's far more neurotic and wired than his deadpan schoolboy in the earlier film."

Schwartzman was next cast as a college student living in Beverly Hills in the critically acclaimed but short-lived television sitcom *Cracking Up* (2004–06), for which he also composed the title song. In 2005 he had an uncredited role in the big-screen version of the 1960s TV comedy series *Bewitched*, and he portrayed a struggling musician caught in a complex love triangle in *Shopgirl*, a film adaptation of a novella by Steve Martin, who also co-starred. Following an uncredited role in *The Hitchhiker's Guide to the Galaxy* (2005), which starred his then-girlfriend, Zooey Deschanel, Schwartzman landed a lead part in the costume drama *Marie Antoinette* (2006), directed by Sofia Coppola. To portray King Louis XVI of France, the husband of the title character (played by Kirsten Dunst), he gained about 50 pounds and learned to ride a horse.

During the filming of *Marie Antoinette*, in Paris, France, Wes Anderson, whose press tour for his movie *The Life Aquatic* had concluded in that city, moved in with Schwartzman. The two collaborated with Roman Coppola on a screenplay about three estranged brothers who travel by train through India on the first anniversary of their father's death. In the fall of 2006, Schwartzman traveled to India with Anderson and his co-stars, Owen Wilson and Adrien Brody, to begin filming. A large portion of the shoot, which lasted five months, took place on a moving train that traveled for 12 hours each day across the Indian desert. The picture, *The Darjeeling Limited*, premiered at the Venice Film Festival, along with the Anderson-directed *Hotel Chevalier*, a 13-minute coda to the movie. "Wilson, Brody and Schwartzman are like a contemporary, depressive version of the Three Stooges, and there's something inspired about Anderson's decision to cast them as brothers," Carina Chocano wrote for the *Los Angeles Times* (October 5, 2007, on-line). "They are linked not only by their prodigious noses, but also by their air of melancholy." In a review for *Salon* (September 28, 2007, on-line), Stephanie Zacharek singled out Schwartzman for praise, writing: "Schwartzman . . . is finding ways to go deeper into characters that seem somewhat blank on the surface, and his timing just keeps getting better: He turns the intentionally awkward rhythms of the movie's dialogue into comically graceful, hippo-in-a-tutu pirouettes." *The Darjeeling Limited* attracted some unwelcome media attention when Wilson, suffering from clinical depression, attempted suicide a few weeks before its premiere. (He recovered and participated to a limited degree in the promotion of the movie.)

In December 2007 Schwartzman had a small part as the Beatles drummer Ringo Starr in the comedy *Walk Hard: The Dewey Cox Story*. He had a supporting role, as a shallow sitcom star, in *Funny People* (2009), written and directed by Judd Apatow. That film starred Adam Sandler as a terminally ill stand-up comic who hires a struggling fellow comic (played by Seth Rogen) to serve as his personal assistant. Critics focused on Sandler's nuanced performance and Rogen's newly slim physique, and most failed to mention Schwartzman. They noticed him in his next project, *The Marc Pease Experience* (2009), which starred Schwartzman as a former high-school drama student, now working as a limo driver. Directed by Todd Louiso, it drew universally dismal reviews. "*The Marc Pease Experience* is a cheerless and almost sullen experience," Roger Ebert wrote for the *Chicago Sun-Times* (August 19, 2009, on-line). "It's badly written and inertly directed, with actors who don't have a clue what drives their characters."

Schwartzman currently stars in a new HBO series, *Bored to Death*, in the role of Jonathan, a struggling Brooklyn-based writer with a drinking problem who decides to become a private eye after reading the stories of Raymond Chandler and Dashiell Hammett. The series premiered in September 2009. Schwartzman provided the voice of a character in the animated film *Fantastic Mr. Fox* (2009), a Wes Anderson–directed adaptation of the Roald Dahl children's book of the same name.

Schwartzman has continued to record music. In March 2007 he released the pop-rock album *Nighttiming*, his first solo effort. He uses the name Coconut Records for his solo projects, and the albums are distributed by Schwartzman's own company, Young Baby Records. "As evidenced by his debut *Nighttiming* Jason Schwartzman's Coconut Records is in the grand tradition of one-man band pop albums, a largely solitary affair in the spirit of Todd Rundgren, Stevie Wonder, and Prince that doesn't necessarily *sound* like any of those rockers yet shares a similar sense of eccentricity and, more importantly, melodicism," Stephen Thomas Erlewine wrote for the All Music Guide. "Schwartzman's gift for a persuasive hook is what ties *Nighttiming* together when it teeters between incandescent pop and halting introspection, but that flittering incoherence is its charm: *Nighttiming* has both sides of the one-man band mad genius, the pop maverick and the sensitive diarist spilling his soul onto the page." An equally well-received sophomore effort, *Davy*, was released in early 2009.

On July 11, 2009 Schwartzman married Brady Cunningham, a fashion designer, whom he dated for three years. The couple live in the San Fernando Valley, in California.

—B.M.

Suggested Reading: *Knoxville (Tennessee) News-Sentinel* (on-line) Feb. 1, 2002; (London) *Independent* (on-line) May 10, 2002; *New York Times* (on-line) Mar. 7, 2004; *Premiere* p72+ Feb. 2002; *San Francisco Chronicle* (on-line) Jan. 24, 1999; (Sydney, Australia) *Sunday Telegraph* p156 Feb. 28, 1999; United Press International Oct. 15, 2006; *Vanity Fair* p294 Mar. 2006

Selected Films: *Rushmore*, 1998; *CQ*, 2001; *Odessa or Bust*, 2001; *S1m0ne*, 2002; *Slackers*, 2002; *Spun*, 2002; *Just Like Mona*, 2003; *I Heart Huckabees*, 2004; *Bewitched*, 2005; *Shopgirl*, 2005; *The Hitchhiker's Guide to the Galaxy*, 2005; *Marie Antoinette*, 2006; *The Darjeeling Limited*, 2007; *Walk Hard: The Dewey Cox Story*, 2007; *Funny People*, 2009; *The Marc Pease Experience*, 2009; *Fantastic Mr. Fox*, 2009

Selected Television Shows: *Freeks and Geeks*, 2000; *Cracking Up*, 2004–06; *Bored to Death*, 2009–

Selected Recordings: with Phantom Planet—*Phantom Planet is Missing*, 1998; *The Guest*, 2002; as Coconut Records—*Nighttiming*, 2007; *Davy*, 2009

Frederick M. Brown/Getty Images

Seacrest, Ryan

Dec. 24, 1974– Host of American Idol

Address: Ryan Seacrest Productions Inc., 5750 Wilshire Blvd., Fourth Fl., Los Angeles, CA 90036

"As a kid I pretended to be a Personality," the television and radio host and producer—and personality—Ryan Seacrest told Allison Glock for the *New York Times Magazine* (May 23, 2004). Seacrest was still in elementary school when he came up with "a total, 100 percent strategy to be the Dick Clark for our generation, to be the Merv Griffin for our generation, to be the Larry King for our generation," he told Tom Shales for the *Washington Post* (March 23, 2008). "I knew exactly what my path was when I was 9 years old," he said. "Everything I did, every detail, every step I took I knew was a step closer to what I wanted. I knew there'd be about 3 million steps, but I also knew I had to get through them." Thanks to his single-minded determination, his willingness and even eagerness to work extremely hard, and his good looks, pleasing voice, charm, conversational gifts—and luck—the 34-year-old Seacrest has largely achieved his goals. Seacrest has often been compared to Clark, who built a media empire while serving for over three decades as the host of *American Bandstand*, a song-and-dance show for teenagers. The program that launched Seacrest to national prominence a dozen years into his career, and has served as the springboard for his own radio and television empire, is the phenomenally popular singing-contest show *American Idol*; described as a "cultural juggernaut" by Glock, *American Idol* has consistently ranked among the highest-rated shows on TV. Seacrest also hosts and produces *E! News*, on the E! Entertainment Television cable network, and two widely syndicated radio programs: *On Air with Ryan Seacrest*, a talk-and-music show that airs for four hours every weekday morning, and *American Top 40* (*AT40*), a weekend series whose co-founder Casey Kasem, Seacrest's predecessor on *AT40*, was another of his childhood idols, as was the TV personality Regis Philbin. In 2005 Seacrest signed a long-term agreement to executive-produce and co-host *Dick Clark's New Year's Rockin' Eve*; when Clark retires, Seacrest will get sole control of that long-running annual special. He has also formed his own company, Ryan Seacrest Productions, through which he has embarked on other ventures. "When you're hired to present a show or be on the show, you're hired help. How long can that really last? You never know . . . ," he told Lynn Elber for the Associated Press (January 24, 2006, on-line). "I want to build something I have for a long time."

In Judd Apatow's film comedy *Knocked Up* (2007), Seacrest appears in a scene-stealing cameo as a cantankerous version of himself at *E! News*. "It doesn't make any sense," he rages in the film, when a tabloid celebrity fails to arrive on time for an interview. "I got four jobs—hell, I'm more famous than half the people we talk to anyway!" While that statement may be an exaggeration, by 2004 Seacrest had become "perhaps one of the most ubiquitous Personalities pop culture has ever produced," Glock wrote. Seacrest is seen and heard by 10s of millions of people every week. "A lot of people are complacent," Seacrest told Tom Shales. "They're happy with their jobs and can make a good living doing that. I'm not like that. I have 10 jobs. I never want to lose one. I also run my organization like a general. I'm involved in every contract, I read every word. I do like that—I like the business."

Shales observed of Seacrest and his role on *American Idol*, "Although 'Seacrest' might sound like a waterfront retirement village, there's nothing remotely sleepy about him. It's not that he's multitalented; he's anti-talented, not a performer but a professional 'personality,' the latest variation on a type as old as broadcasting: the guy who stands there and introduces the acts. He's a low-key cheerleader who keeps the show moving and, with the judges as natural foils, allies himself with the audience and the contestants, never threatening to upstage the performers, even if he could." According to Glock, "A successful Personality attracts a large audience without challenging them. He lulls and coddles and strives not to alienate. He presents himself as likable, nonthreatening and, most important, reachable—never too handsome or too happening or too sharp. Theirs is not a world of superlatives but of glossy averageness. . . . A successful Personality never, not for a second, worries about being cool. . . . For his part, Seacrest has taken the art of the Personality and refined it to the level of German engineering. He is not simply the next Regis or Merv; he is a brand new model. Regis can be cranky; Merv is a business shark. Seacrest has willingly filed away any edges of himself, cast aside any ugly urges, embraced the manufactured self as actual self and been rewarded for his efforts with multiple, multiyear, [multimillion-dollar] contracts." The acid-tongued Simon Cowell, one of the *American Idol* judges, told Glock, "Ryan has the appeal of a dog that has been rescued from the pound. That is his secret. He's grateful. He's happy. Always, always. If he had a tail, he'd wag it. It kind of makes it difficult not to like him."

The first of the two children of Gary and Constance (née Zullinger) Seacrest, Ryan John Seacrest was born on December 24, 1974 in Dunwoody, Georgia, a town in the metropolitan Atlanta area, where he grew up. His father was an attorney, his mother a homemaker. Seacrest's sister, Meredith, is a publicist for the syndicated TV show *Entertainment Tonight*. As a boy Seacrest had dreams of hosting his own music-countdown radio show; he was overweight and thought that his chances of success would be greater on radio than on TV. "I always listened to the Top 10 songs of the day while doing my homework," he told Lola Ogunnaike for the *New York Times* (May 23, 2006). "I would call in and request songs. I would always try and get on the air." At age eight Seacrest began recording himself in his bedroom; he pretended to be a deejay, hoping to sound like Casey Kasem or another popular deejay, Rick Dees. His parents would play his audiotapes in their car.

As a freshman at Dunwoody High School, Seacrest won the job of reading announcements over the intercom and soon became known as "the voice of Dunwoody." He wrote for the student newspaper and was active on the model–United Nations club and captain of the swim team. At about 15 he started an internship at a local radio station, WSTR/Star 94, where for a year he trained under the deejay Tom Sullivan. Within another year he had become the host of his own show on WSTR, developing original segments and, as a deejay, handling call-in requests. The show aired from 7:00 p.m. to midnight on weekdays and became very popular. "I remember thinking, everything I do from this point on is a step," Seacrest told Katherine Wheelock for *Details* (April 2008, on-line). "If I'm scrubbing the break room, I'm closer to the studio room. And if I'm in the studio room, I'm closer to the microphone. If I'm closer to the microphone . . . I really got the psychology of it—that everything is connected."

After he graduated from high school, in 1993, Seacrest enrolled at the University of Georgia, where he studied journalism. As a freshman he was hired to host a half-hour children's TV game show called *Radical Outdoor Challenge*, which aired on ESPN. On weekends for a year, he worked both for ESPN and WSTR/Star 94. He dropped out of college and moved to the West Coast in 1994, having landed the job of co-host of a syndicated Saturday-morning children's TV show called *Gladiators 2000*, which was produced in Los Angeles, California. In 1995, after 13 episodes of *Gladiators 2000*, Seacrest left that series to start what turned out to be a six-year stint as a disc jockey on *Live from the Lounge*, on the Los Angeles radio station KYSR-FM/Star 98.7. That year, with the same station, he also became the deejay of *Ryan Seacrest for the Ride Home*, which soon became the top-rated show in the Los Angeles area for women in the 25-to-34 age bracket; he held that job for eight years. Concurrently, he hosted the TV series *Wild Animal Games*, in 1995; *The New Edge*, about technological advances, in 1996; and the Merv Griffin–produced *Click*, a game show for teens, which aired for two years beginning in September 1997. He learned a great deal by watching Griffin and occasionally sitting in on production meetings. Griffin later recalled to Lola Ogunnaike, "His energy just baffled me. I couldn't keep up with him." In 2000 he hosted *Disneyland 2000: 45 Years of Magic* and *NBC Saturday Night Movie.*

Seacrest's breakthrough in television came in 2002, when he was hired to co-host *American Idol*, a spin-off from the British show *Pop Idol*, which had premiered the previous year. *American Idol* debuted on the Fox TV network on June 11, 2002 and became an immediate success. With the exception of *American Idol*'s first season, when he shared hosting duties with the comedian Brian Dunkleman, Seacrest has hosted the show alone. Though he has admitted to being too "robotic" when the show first began, he quickly emerged as a personable, reliable master of ceremonies, and he has been widely credited with contributing to the show's success. He is known for creating a careful balance between the judges and the contestants, often coming to the defense of performers who have been attacked or demoralized by Cowell. (Seacrest and Cowell frequently engage in playful sparring with each other on the air.) Scott Raab, writing for *Esquire* (July 1, 2006), described Seacrest as "a perfect traffic cop, genial and efficient. Each ticking second pivots upon his glad-handing, bantering, and breaking for commercials while milking the 'drama'—and yet he seems not to be there at all." Amanda Cuda wrote for the *Connecticut Post Online* (August 24, 2007), "He's Robohost, a machine programmed to please, flatter and offer wild amusement. He's a blank slate, a hard worker who would show up on time, hit his marks, do everything he's supposed to and take no chances. With no risks, the odds for success are higher." Marc Hirsch offered the following assessment for MSNBC.com (February 13, 2007, on-line): "Nobody is ever going to confuse Seacrest with the Jon Stewarts, Charlie Roses or Johnny Carsons of the world. He's a little too smug and, perma-stubble notwithstanding, a little too smooth. But in the ocean of cheese that is *Idol*, he has capitalized on those qualities to become an effective captain, steering the performers and the audience capably around potential jarlsbergs that could sink the entire thing." Entertainers whose appearances on the show launched their careers include Kelly Clarkson, Clay Aiken, Fantasia Barrino, Jennifer Hudson, Carrie Underwood, Taylor Hicks, Chris Daughtry, Jordin Sparks, David Cook, David Archuleta, Kris Allen, and Adam Lambert. *American Idol* has consistently generated the highest ratings of any show on television. The show's ninth season is scheduled to begin in January 2010. Seacrest recently signed a contract to host it for three more years.

"Equity, ownership, production fees, license fees: those are the vocabulary words that are exciting to me," Seacrest said to Lola Ogunnaike. "If you really want to be in this business for a long time, you have to be more than just one moving part." In 2004 Seacrest took over as host of Casey Kasem's internationally syndicated countdown show, *American Top 40*, an institution in the radio world. Also that year he landed another coveted radio job when he succeeded Rick Dees as the host and executive producer of a popular morning radio show on the Los Angeles station KIIS-FM. The show, called *On Air with Ryan Seacrest*, went on the air at the same time that Seacrest's television show with the same name began broadcasting. The TV show was canceled after only one season due to low ratings, while the radio show has become the most-listened-to morning radio show in Los Angeles.

In 2005 Seacrest founded Ryan Seacrest Productions, an umbrella company for his investments in restaurants and nightclubs in Los Angeles and Las Vegas, Nevada, and a clothing venture called the R Line, in which he is collaborating with Jem Sportswear. With Regis Philbin and Kelly Ripa, he shared a Daytime Emmy Award for co-hosting the televised 2005 Walt Disney World Christmas Day Parade. In August of that year, Seacrest signed a lucrative deal with Dick Clark's eponymous production company to become executive producer and co-host of *Dick Clark's New Year's Rockin' Eve*; the deal stipulated that he would be Clark's eventual successor. Seacrest, who had hosted Fox's New Year coverage in 2005, when Clark was recuperating from a stroke, co-hosted the 2006 edition of the show with Clark and the actress and singer Hilary Duff.

In 2006 Seacrest signed a three-year, $21 million contract with the cable channel E! to host and produce programs through his company, with the option of selling shows to other networks or channels. That year he became the managing editor and lead anchor of the channel's nightly entertainment-news show *E! News* and began producing and hosting E!'s broadcasts of awards ceremonies. Seacrest has helped to develop and create the popular E! reality shows *Keeping Up with the Kardashians*, about the children and ex-wife and of the late attorney Robert Kardashian, and *Denise Richards: It's Complicated*, about the actress Richards in the wake of her much-publicized divorce from the actor Charlie Sheen. On average, the ratings for E! Channel shows have more than doubled since Seacrest's arrival. Ted Harbert, the president and CEO of Comcast Entertainment, which owns the E! Channel, told Scott Raab, "Seacrest wasn't the first person to think of doing a reality show with Denise Richards, but he was able to sign her. He wasn't the first person to think of doing a show with the Kardashians, but he was able to sign them. There have been a handful of people in television history who could do that. You put him in a room with somebody, and he can sign them."

Seacrest lives in a multimillion-dollar home in the Hollywood Hills section of Los Angeles. *People* named him among the world's 50 most beautiful people in 2003 and among the most eligible bachelors in 2005 and 2006. In 2005 Seacrest was honored with a star on the Hollywood Walk of Fame.

—C.C.

Suggested Reading: *Details* (on-line) Apr. 2008; *Entertainment Weekly* (on-line) Jan. 9, 2004; *Esquire* p120+ July 1, 2006; (London) *Guardian* p5 June 25, 2007; *Los Angeles Times* S p17 Sep. 12, 2007; (New Orleans, Louisiana) *Times-Picayune* p1 Jan. 16, 2007; *New York Times* p1 May 23, 2006; *Toronto Sun* S p3 Sep. 16, 2007; *Washington Post* M p1 Mar. 23, 2008

Selected Television Shows: as host—*Radical Outdoor Challenge*, 1993; *Gladiators 2000*, 1994; *Wild Animal Games*, 1995; *The New Edge*, 1996; *Click*, 1997–99; *Disneyland 2000: 45 Years of Magic*, 2000; *NBC Saturday Night Movie*, 2000; *On Air with Ryan Seacrest*, 2004; *Dick Clark's New Year's Rockin' Eve*, 2006– ; *American Idol*, 2002– ; as executive producer—*Keeping Up with the Kardashians*, 2007–09; *Denise Richards: It's Complicated*, 2008–09; *Bromance*, 2008–09; *Momma's Boys*, 2008–09

Selected Radio Shows: *Live from the Lounge*, 1995–2001; *Ryan Seacrest for the Ride Home*, 1995–2003; *American Top 40*, 2004– ; *On Air with Ryan Seacrest*, 2004–

Darryl James/Getty Images

Selick, Henry

Nov. 30, 1952– Filmmaker; animator

Address: c/o Gotham Group, 9255 Sunset Blvd., Los Angeles, CA 90069-9255

"For me, stop-motion is inherently magical, and if you make a movie with it, it just stands to reason that extraordinary things are going to happen," the filmmaker Henry Selick told Trevor Johnston for the *Sydney (Australia) Morning Herald* (April 4, 1997). Selick has directed seven full-length motion pictures made in whole or in part by means of stop-motion animation. The best known among them are *The Nightmare Before Christmas*, for which Tim Burton wrote the script; *James and the Giant Peach*, based on a story by Roald Dahl; and *Coraline*, an adaptation by Selick himself of a graphic novel by Neil Gaiman. In stop-motion animation, puppet-like figures are placed against painted backgrounds or miniature sets and filmed one frame at a time as their body parts are moved a little at a time. The projection of 24 frames of film per second creates an illusion of lifelike movement. In making *Coraline,* Selick and his team of 30 to 35 animators produced "about two minutes of finished footage a week over the course of almost two years," Neda Ulaby reported for National Public Radio (NPR, March 19, 2009, on-line). The earliest mass-market full-length animated cartoons, among them *Little Nemo* (1911), *Gertie the Dinosaur* (1914), and the Felix the Cat series of the 1920s, along with several decades' worth of Walt Disney films, relied on a series of images painstakingly hand-painted on thousands of individual sheets of paper or, later, cellophane. Selick himself contributed to such productions during several years of employment as a Disney Studios animator, after he completed an undergraduate program in animation, in the 1970s. He has worked as an independent filmmaker since 1981, when he began working on his short film *Seepage*. "I'm so tired of only the Disney model being the one that the public's supposed to want," he said to Johnston a dozen years ago. "Yes, it's hard to do, and I have a lot of respect for the people who can pull it off, but I wouldn't be doing animation if I had to follow that formula. I got into it so that I could do experimental work, and for me that's still the goal. Maybe they've gone as far as they can with cartoon animation, but stop-motion still leaves you so much room to create new worlds." It also "combines all of his favorite things—sculpture, drawing, photography, music and physics," Ulaby wrote. Selick has used computer graphics in his filmmaking, but only sparingly. In an earlier conversation with Ulaby for NPR (February 6, 2009, on-line), Tony Dalton, who co-wrote the book *A Century of Stop-Motion Animation: From Melies to Aardman* (2008) with the stop-motion pioneer Ray Harryhausen, described Selick as "one of the great innovators of today."

The second of the three children of Charles and Melanie Selick, Henry C. Selick was born on November 30, 1952 in Glen Ridge, New Jersey, and grew up in nearby Rumson. His father, who died several years ago, worked in food manufacturing and later started his own business selling parts for antique cars; his mother has owned and managed a consignment shop for four decades. His sister, Linda, is a writer; his brother, Barry, is a microbiologist and executive of a biotechnology firm. Selick began drawing at the age of three. Among his early influences were the local television show *The Terrytoon Circus*, which featured foreign cartoons, and several stop-motion classics, including the German animator Lotte Reiniger's *The Adventures of Prince Achmed* (1926). Considered by many to be the first animated feature film, *Achmed* used paper silhouettes to represent characters. Selick was also intrigued by the work of Harryhausen, who made models and created special effects for films including *The Seventh Voyage of Sinbad* (1958), *Jason and the Argonauts* (1963), and *Clash of the Titans* (1981). "I remember when I was 5, my mother took me to see *The Seventh Voyage of Sinbad*," Selick said in a speech at his induction into his high school's Hall of Fame, as quoted by Glenn Anton in the *Asbury Park (New Jersey) Press* (February 7, 2002). "At that age, it burned something into my consciousness. I totally believed those skeleton warriors were real."

When Selick was a student at Deane-Porter Elementary School, in Rumson, his prowess as an artist led the principal to tell a local artist, Stanley Meltzoff, about him. Meltzoff, who painted illustrations for *National Geographic* and other popular publications, took the boy under his wing and gave him weekly drawing lessons. "I was a snotty kid—highly emotional, anxious, and had a huge ego about my artwork," Selick recalled, as quoted by Anton. "I was a know-it-all." Nevertheless, by the time he reached adolescence, he had decided to drop drawing and concentrate on his other passion, music. He studied piano and clarinet and, as a teenager, played guitar and keyboards for amateur rock bands. "Music has always been interesting to me," Selick said. "With music, you're making art right then and there." His mother told *Current Biography* that he has also composed music.

Selick attended Rumson–Fair Haven Regional High School. "I wasn't very cool," he recalled, as quoted by Anton. "I was a geeky freshman, only 110 pounds. I had no school identity. I became invisible. I was cynical about everything that had to do with school." He graduated in 1970 and then enrolled at the New Brunswick, New Jersey, division of Rutgers University. After watching a public-television program about experimental animation, he decided to pursue a career in animation and transferred to Syracuse University, in Syracuse, New York, to study art. He soon received a scholarship to attend the California Institute of the Arts (CalArts), in Ventura. He was one of the first students in the school's experimental animation program, where he studied under its founder, Jules Engel, who had worked on the pioneering Disney animated films *Fantasia* (1940) and *Bambi* (1942). At CalArts Selick completed two student films, *Phases* and *Tube Tales*. He earned a bachelor's degree in 1977.

After his graduation Disney Studios hired Selick as an animator trainee and "in-betweener," someone who draws the many frames needed between the primary poses already drawn by the main animator, which all together will create smoothly flowing movement. Eric Larson, one of Disney's stable of nine core animators, mentored him. As an uncredited in-betweener, Selick worked on Disney's *Pete's Dragon* (1977), *The Small One* (1977), and *The Fox and the Hound* (1981). The studio also enlisted him to help design an alien for Disney's *The Watcher in the Woods* (1980). Concurrently, with a grant from the National Endowment of the Arts, Selick worked on a project of his own—the surreal, nine-minute, stop-motion animated film *Seepage*, for which he made flat, jointed, puppet-like characters and watercolored backgrounds. Released in 1981, *Seepage* won several top prizes on the animation circuit. In 1983 Selick worked as a sequence director on the film *Twice Upon a Time*, directed by John Korty and Charles Swenson, made for Lucasfilms. Its creators used an animation technique known as lumage, which makes use of two-dimensional translucent cutouts and a light table. The film was not widely released, but it sold well in video form and gained a cult following.

In 1986 Selick started his own production company, Selick Projects. He began producing a series of station IDs, brief on-the-hour segments, for the cable-television network MTV. Among his best known was the Clio Award–winning "Haircut M" ID, which showed an insect cutting the station logo into a woman's hairdo. "That is where I found myself—I had low budgets but freedom as long as I put the logo on at the end," Selick told Peter Sobczynski for the E-Film Critic Web site (February 6, 2009). In other commercial work from the late 1980s, Selick created TV animations for the Pillsbury Co. that starred the firm's symbol and mascot, the Pillsbury Doughboy. For an animation to advertise Nabisco's Ritz Bits crackers, he showed crackers searching for peanut butter and cheese. He also assisted with storyboard sequences for *Return to Oz* (1985) and *Nutcracker: The Motion Picture* (1986). In 1990 Selick's six-minute animated pilot for a TV series (never completed) called *Slow Bob in the Lower Dimensions* aired on MTV's animation show *Liquid Television*. It won first place at the 1992 Ottawa Animation Festival and a Silver Hugo at the Chicago Film Festival.

Selick's increasing prominence led Tim Burton to tap him to direct Disney's *The Nightmare Before Christmas*, after Burton, who had been slated to direct that film, had to bow out because of contractual obligations related to another motion picture. Burton and Selick had worked together at Disney, and both shared ideas far removed from those that prevailed there. Disney executives "didn't mind that we wanted to perform new tricks . . . just as long as they fit into their box," Selick told Jane Galbraith for the *Los Angeles Times* (November 18, 1993). "Nobody does animation better than Disney; it's just that some of us wanted out of the box. Burton was one. I was another." Adapted by Michael McDowell from a story by Burton, with a screenplay by Caroline Thompson, *The Nightmare Before Christmas* follows Jack Skellington, a living skeleton and resident of Halloween Town who, having overseen Halloween for many years, longs to do something new. By chance, he enters Christmas Town, where bright lights, cheerful decorations, gifts, and the benevolent persona of Santa Claus fascinate him. With the help of the ghoulish residents of his hometown, he has Santa Claus kidnaped and usurps Santa's role by delivering macabre and dangerous presents to humans on Christmas Eve. The recipients react with horror, and Skellington realizes that he has replaced the joy of Christmas with fear.

To make *The Nightmare Before Christmas*, Selick renamed his production company Skellington Productions, set up a specialized studio in San Francisco, California, and hired about 120 animators, puppeteers, art directors, camera operators, lighting designers, and editors. He chose San Francisco in part because, as he explained to Blaise Simpson for the *Los Angeles Times* (October 10, 1993), "it was important to me to stay away from Los Angeles. I think that if Disney and even Tim had too much access to us, they would have gotten too nervous and gummed up the works." Selick and his crew labored for three years to complete the film, painstakingly manipulating on 20 miniature sets the puppets that represented the characters. Selick supervised the animators, each of whom had his or her own character to work with. In his Rumson–Fair Haven speech, Selick said that he himself was the model for Jack. "I acted him out, every gesture Jack made I worked out with the character animator." The film's cinematographer, Pete Kozachik, invented many of the techniques used on the set, including a device that controlled the motion of the camera.

The Nightmare Before Christmas opened to critical and popular applause; it has become a holiday classic and cult hit and has spawned dozens of items of memorabilia and merchandise. It has also attracted a new generation of youthful fans. Clarke Fountain wrote for the All Movie Guide (on-line) that the film "was praised for its stunning originality and for the excellence of its execution. In addition, it was praised for being a completely absorbing fable that both grownups and children can enjoy, so long as the children are able to handle its scary bits." Roger Ebert wrote for the *Chicago Sun-Times* (October 22, 1993, on-line) that Selick's achievement was "enormous. Working with gifted artists and designers, he has made a world here that is as completely new as the worlds we saw for the first time in such films as *Metropolis*, *The Cabinet of Dr. Caligari* or *Star Wars*. What all of these films have in common is a visual richness, so abundant that they deserve more than one viewing. First, go for the story. Then go back just to look in the corners of the screen, and appreciate the little visual surprises and inspirations that are tucked into every nook and cranny." *The Nightmare Before Christmas* was nominated for an Academy Award for best visual effects and won the International Animated Film Society's Annie Award for best creative supervision.

Selick's growing reputation enabled him to gain from the family of the late British writer Roald Dahl the rights to his children's novel *James and the Giant Peach*. James is an orphan who lives with two extremely cruel aunts. He escapes from his virtual bondage by entering a magical, gigantic peach inhabited by friendly, human-size bugs. The peach rolls to the sea, squashing the aunts along the way, and carries James to freedom. Selick directed the film, which was made for Disney, from a screenplay by Karey Kirkpatrick, Jonathan Roberts, and Steve Bloom; performers including Susan Sarandon and Richard Dreyfuss provided the voices of the animated characters. The props included a specially built, 20-foot-high peach. Because of the studio's budgetary concerns, Selick was forced to use live action for a large part of the film—an approach that he felt diminished its quality significantly. For some of the special effects, he used computer graphics.

Released in 1996, *James and The Giant Peach* struck Janet Maslin, the reviewer for the *New York Times* (April 12, 1996), as "a technological marvel, arch and innovative with a daringly offbeat visual conception. But it's also a strenuously artful film with a macabre edge that may scare small children. And beyond that, it lacks a clear idea of who its audience might be." William Arnold wrote for the *Seattle Post-Intelligencer* (April 12, 1996), "Along the way, there are a few dull stretches. . . . But mostly this is a wonderfully weird visual journey that mixes period live-action (it's set in 1949), stop-action animation and computer special effects in a clever, funny, stylish way. It's a happy, almost psychedelic trip of a movie. *James* is both genuinely exciting as an adventure and genuinely charming as a fantasy."

Selick next directed *Monkeybone*, whose screenplay, by Sam Hamm, was based on *Dark Town* (1995), a graphic novel by Kaja Blackley. Another blend of live action and stop-motion animation, the film was made at Twitching Image, as Selick had renamed his studio. It starred Brendan Fraser as a cartoonist named Stu Miley, who is left in a coma after a car accident. While comatose he thinks he is entering a decaying urban purgatory, whose frightening denizens include a sinister version of Monkeybone, a character he had created before the accident. *Monkeybone* attracted few moviegoers; in the U.S. it grossed only $5 million, $70 million less than its cost to make. Among its few favorable reviews was that of A. O. Scott, who wrote for the *New York Times* (February 23, 2001) that *Monkeybone* was "a welcome antidote to the epidemic of witless, frenetic, secondhand low comedies that gnaw at our brains like antibody-resistant spirochetes." Scott also suggested that such a film might have resulted from a collaboration of the late surrealist filmmaker Luis Buñuel and the comedy specialists Peter and Bobby Farrelly, had they had "access to $50 million worth of foam rubber and modeling clay." "That's what dreams are made of," Scott remarked. Selick himself attributed the film's deficiencies to his limitations as a director of live action. "It's just not my forte," he told Sheila Roberts for the Web site Movies Online.

Selick's next foray into stop-motion animation was the creation of several underwater sequences for the director Wes Anderson's quirky comedy-drama *The Life Aquatic with Steve Zissou* (2004). Selick's cartoon-like, fictional sea creatures included the jaguar shark, the crayon ponyfish, and sugar crabs, which appeared as part of live-action shots of the title character, an oceanographer (played by Bill Murray), and his team during their explorations of the ocean's depths.

Earlier in 2004 Selick had joined Vinton Studios, in Portland, Oregon, as supervising director. He maintained that position when, soon afterward, Vinton was acquired by the entertainment studio Laika Entertainment and its sister division, Laika House, the former of which makes feature-length and short animated films and the latter of which specializes in commercials, music videos, and so-called branded entertainment. Selick's first creation for Laika was the eight-minute computer-generated short *Moongirl* (2005), about a boy who finds himself on the moon, where he meets the title character and must battle monsters. The short won the Ottawa International Animation Festival's Short Film Special Jury Prize.

Selick wrote the screenplay for and also directed the feature film *Coraline* (2009). Produced at Laika, *Coraline* is an adaptation of Neil Gaiman's multiple-award-winning, same-titled novella for young adults, published in 2002. The title character (voiced by Dakota Fanning) is an 11-year-old girl who has recently moved into an aging Victorian building with her parents, decent people who love her very much. After they are settled in their new apartment, her parents become preoccupied with their computer-related work and pay scant attention to her. In an attempt to allay her loneliness, Coraline explores the dark recesses of the house, discovering a secret door that leads to a parallel universe. A nameless black cat accompanies her. Initially, Coraline feels pleased with her new reality: her new parents dote on her, and her home contains many colorful amusements and surprises. Soon, however, Coraline discovers that all is not as it seems, and "Other Mother" and "Other Father"—who have buttons for eyes—attempt to keep her from returning to her real parents. When she succeeds in returning to her real home, she finds that her parents have disappeared. The story's fantastical premise and the original edition's gothic illustrations, by Dave McKean, instantly appealed to Selick. He told Sheila Roberts that several years ago, he persuaded his mother to read Gaiman's book. "When she finished, she said, 'You know, you used to sit in that chair in the kitchen in here when you were 4 or 5 and tell me about your other family in Africa and you would go on so convincingly that I started to worry maybe you had one.' So, I must have had some other connection there. The beautiful, strange details, this button-eyed image that's unnerving without necessarily knowing why, the delicious cat dialogue. . . . But, most of all, I loved the character of Coraline. I loved that she's ordinary, that she's very curious, but in the end she's an ordinary girl who lacks super powers or great fighting skills or weapons . . . and manages to defeat extraordinary evil."

More than 450 designers, camerapeople, and other specialists worked on *Coraline* in Laika's 140,000-square-foot warehouse in Hillsboro, Oregon. The production required 150 sets and, for Coraline's face alone, thousands of sculpted heads whose facial features depicted hundreds of expressions; a "face librarian" and an assistant face librarian handled the collection of heads. "We sort of split the lower and upper face, so the brows and eyes could act separately from [the] mouth," Selick explained to Neda Ulaby (March 19, 2009). Later, Ulaby reported, the "facial split" was "digitally erased." *Coraline* was the first feature-length animated film to make use of stereoscopic 3D, a technique in which each frame is recorded twice, from minutely different perspectives. When superimposed, the two images create the illusion of three dimensions to viewers wearing special glasses. Selick collaborated with the Japanese illustrator Tadahiro Uesugi to create *Coraline*'s otherworldly landscapes. He told Roberts, "From Tadahiro, we got our color palette, we got sort of a sense of shape, the fantastic garden, the way those flowers aren't all like things you know." Selick also said that he was particularly impressed with Uesugi's consistent ability to find ways to add "a touch of atmosphere" to every scene. Referring to the French artist Henri Matisse, Selick explained that Uesugi "would take almost like a Matisse world of 2D, but by putting a touch of atmosphere, the painting breathes. So I tried to put atmosphere everywhere in the movie."

Coraline was an immediate success; within three weeks of its release, in February 2009, its box-office receipts totaled more than $55 million. As of late October of that year, the film had earned $75 million in the U.S. and $47 million abroad. Reviews of *Coraline* were generally positive. Lisa Schwarzbaum wrote for *Entertainment Weekly* (February 4, 2009), "This thrilling stop-motion animated adventure is a high point in Selick's career of creating handcrafted wonderlands of beauty blended with deep, disconcerting creepiness." The *New York Times* (February 6, 2009) critic A. O. Scott wrote, "There are many scenes and images in *Coraline* that are likely to scare children. This is not a warning but rather a recommendation, since the cultivation of fright can be one of the great pleasures of youthful moviegoing. As long as it doesn't go too far toward violence or mortal dread, a film that elicits a tingle of unease or a tremor of spookiness can be a tonic to sensibilities dulled by wholesome, anodyne, school-approved entertainments." He continued, "Mr. Selick is hardly a doctrinaire Freudian, but he does grasp the intimate connection between fairy tales and the murky, occult power of longing, existential confusion and misplaced desire. *Coraline* explores the predatory implications of parental love—that other mother is a monster of misplaced maternal instinct—but is grounded in the pluck and common sense of its heroine, who is resilient, ingenious and magically real."

In October 2009 Selick left his job at Laika; his contract was about to expire, and he had not become involved in another project. He did not indicate publicly what he intended to work on next.

Selick's wife, Heather Ryan Selick, is a professional animator. The couple have two sons, Harry and George, who provided the voices for minor characters in *Coraline*. They maintain homes in Belvedere Tiburon, near San Francisco, and Lake Oswego, near Portland, Oregon.

—W.D.

Suggested Reading: *Asbury Park (New Jersey) Press* J p1+ Feb. 7, 2002; *Film Journal International* (on-line) Jan. 27, 2009; Laika.com; *Los Angeles Times* p5 Oct. 10, 1993, F p1 Nov. 8, 1993; MoviesOnline, 2009; NPR.org Feb. 6, 2009, Mar. 19, 2009

Selected Films: *Seepage*, 1981; *Slow Bob in the Lower Dimensions*, 1990; *The Nightmare Before Christmas*, 1993; *James and the Giant Peach*, 1996; *Monkeybone*, 2001; *Moongirl*, 2005; *Coraline*, 2009

Courtesy of the *Washington Post*

Shales, Tom

Nov. 3, 1944– Television and film critic

Address: Washington Post, *1150 15th St., N.W., Washington, DC 20071*

According to an unidentified writer widely quoted on the World Wide Web, the television critic Tom Shales "is generally credited for popularizing the idea of treating TV as seriously as theater or film from a critic's point of view." "I think a good critic is one who is willing to see the good in something that he or she doesn't personally enjoy . . . ," Shales told Richard Mahler, who interviewed him for *Electronic Media* (April 11, 1988), shortly after Shales won a Pulitzer Prize for criticism. "I certainly am often offended and irritated and provoked and angered. But I am also often delighted and thrilled and cheered and moved in a positive way." In 1977, six years after he joined the *Washington Post* as its Style editor, Shales was named that newspaper's chief television critic. Before the year was out, his column, "On the Air," was being syndicated through the Washington Post Writers Group. During the next few years, as Janice Castro reported for *Time* (June 8, 1981), he or his column was variously described as "brilliant, thoughtful, incisive and screamingly funny. Also, vicious, infuriating, cruel and unjust." By the late 1980s "On the Air" was appearing in 160 newspapers nationwide, and Shales had begun to wield enormous influence within the TV industry: As Mahler wrote, "The weight of a favorable Shales review has been known to skyrocket a struggling show to prominence, while his acid barbs have buried many a network project." The *Washingtonian*'s editor at large Garrett M. Graff wrote for that magazine's Web site (December 1, 2005), "The *Post* probably doesn't employ a sharper pen than the one belonging to its television critic—a man with the freedom to write on a presidential speech one day and the [television network] WB the next. Don't think, though, that the WB network executives read him any less carefully than the administration does."

Born during World War II, Shales was introduced to TV via his family's 14-inch RCA set, which, as was typical in the early days of television, was housed in a large mahogany console. "Always sort of a journalism nerd," as he described himself to Jody Temkin for the *Chicago Tribune* (October 22, 1995), he wrote for his high-school and college student newspapers and got a job as a journalist with the now-defunct *Washington Examiner*, a free daily newspaper in the Washington, D.C., area, as soon as he completed his undergraduate education, in 1968. (An unrelated *Washington Examiner* was launched in 2005.) In 1979 the *Washington Post* added "television editor" to Shales's titles. Shales provided film criticism for National Public Radio (NPR) from 1970 to 1979 and for the NPR program *Morning Edition* for the next quarter-century. "I think at some point television actually became a more interesting 'beat' for a critic [than film]—and besides, it's the medium I love most," he said during a chat conducted on the *Washington Post*'s Web site (September 19, 2007). Although Shales has often decried the quality of the fare offered on television, he has insisted that his criticisms are rooted in his love for the medium. "I still have a foolish faith that TV will get better before it gets worse, and then if it gets worse it will get better again," he said during the on-line chat. For the past eight years, Shales has written a column for *TelevisionWeek* (called *Electronic Media* until 2003). Shales has also written or co-written four books. "What makes Shales uniquely Shales is that the man is such a wonderful writer," Chuck Ross wrote for *Electronic Media* (April 24, 2000). "In these days of clichés and stillborn prose, Shales sings—with a sting."

Thomas William Shales was born to Clyde and Hulda (Reko) Shales on November 3, 1944 in Elgin, Illinois, 40 miles west of Chicago. He has a sister, Mary, and a brother, James. His father was mayor of the city for a short time in the 1960s; a four-lane road in Elgin is named for him. His mother, a pinochle enthusiast, worked for many years in a clothing store. As a child Shales loved radio and newspapers as well as television. At Elgin High School he served as co-editor of the school newspaper and created the job of house critic for himself. "I complained about things like the sticky floors at [the] movie theater. I thought I was very controversial," he told Temkin. In his senior year he also worked at the local radio station, WRMN, as a disc jockey, writer, and announcer.

After his high-school graduation, in 1962, Shales attended Elgin Community College before transferring to American University, in Washington, D.C. There, he wrote for the *Eagle*, the campus newspaper, as a self-proclaimed film critic and served as the editor in chief during the 1966–67 academic year. He helped pay his way through college by working at local public and commercial radio stations. "That was, without a doubt, the happiest time I've ever had at a job," he told Richard Mahler. Shales earned a B.A .degree in journalism in 1968 and then joined the *Washington Examiner* as the entertainment editor.

In 1971 the *Washington Post*, the capital's most widely circulated newspaper, hired Shales as a writer for its Style section, which had been launched three years earlier. For his first article, published on August 6, 1971, he interviewed the African-American actress Rosalind Cash, who had a small part in the recently released movie *Klute*. He was named the *Post*'s chief television critic in 1977. Concurrently in 1978 Shales worked part-time as an adjunct professor of film studies at American University. The *Post* appointed him television editor in 1979, and that year he became the resident film critic for the National Public Radio program *Morning Edition*.

In addition to reviews, Shales's "On the Air" column has included profiles of television stars and discussions of such television-related topics as trends in commercials, violence and sexual content in television programs, and the rise of "reality" television. In his critiques his opinions have run the gamut from gushingly enthusiastic to fiercely damning. In an example (March 19, 1977) of restrained praise for one program mixed with castigation of others, Shales commended *The Mary Tyler Moore Show* as the series drew to a close, in March 1977, writing that the sitcom "expanded the dimensions of the form and remained, for the most part, a model of civility in a medium that often seems populated largely by louts." In his September 12, 2006 review of the short-lived ABC sitcom *Men in Trees*, he declared that he would rather "relive my pimpliest week of puberty" than watch the show again. His column of March 26, 2005 disparaged ABC's medical drama *Grey's Anatomy*, which had debuted the night before, as "only nominally new" and as having "the audacity to stand there and restage . . . scenes from medical shows of the past already restaged ad infinitum and ad nauseam." *Planet Earth*, the 11-part nature documentary that first aired on the Discovery channel in March 2007, was, in his opinion (March 24, 2007), "breathtaking" and "so rich in spectacle that you won't want to take your eyes off the screen." In his January 6, 2008 "On the Air" column, he praised the HBO series *The Wire* as a "gruelingly edgy combination of complexity and clarity, written and acted to the highest standards of the best TV drama. It's not just good, it's passionately good." When asked on-line by a *Washington Post* reader what he believes constitutes a good television show, Shales replied, "I guess just that it succeed on its own terms, that it be true to some apparent purpose, have something unique to say or, I guess, just succeed as pleasantly frivolous escapism. I think I am capable of liking any kind of show—even if it's not my favorite type—as long as it's done well and with some attempt, however slight, at originality." In the same on-line chat, Shales said, "I think reality shows are now a fixture, the way we'll always have one-hour [scripted] dramas and half-hour sitcoms and such. Actually, one of the changes in TV is that we have hour-long sitcoms . . . or at least comedies . . . or at least dramas with high comedy content, like *Desperate [House]wives* and *Ugly Betty*. That it's harder to categorize shows is, I think, actually a good sign. Some of the old restrictive parameters have been trampled over—even the people who *make* TV shows are getting bored with the old formats and their rigidity. In that way, TV actually is improving."

In an essay for *Electronic Media* (February 4, 2002) entitled "I Take Most of It All Back," Shales wrote, "No one believes this when I tell them, but after writing a column that's been particularly mean to one poor helpless fabulously overpaid filthy-rich celebrity or another, I always ask editors if I've been 'too mean' and if the column should be 'toned down.' Nine times out of 10 over the years the answer has been along the lines of, 'No, it's not too mean. If anything, it's not mean enough.' I have almost always been encouraged to be meaner. See, it's really all the fault of editors." In the same essay, in an example of the lavish praise he sometimes bestows, he wrote, "I wish I hadn't been so critical of a TV movie Carroll O'Connor made of *The Last Hurrah*, a beloved book about politics, because Mr. O'Connor is gone now, and I am not sure I apologized while he was alive. I tried to make up for the review—which Mr. O'Connor carried around in his wallet for months, maybe years, so he could show friends what a monster I was—by properly praising Mr. O'Connor's amazing work as Archie Bunker on *All in the Family*. Even now I am often knocked for a loop when I see reruns of the show, at how forceful and yet subtle Mr. O'Connor could be." Also in that essay he wrote about Johnny Carson, the longtime host of *The Tonight Show*: "I think I even wrote unkind things about him at a certain point in his Herculean career as the nation's nightcap. . . . which in retrospect I thoroughly, absolutely and sheepishly regret. When you think of the hours he gave us, when you think of the depressions he cured, when you think of how effortlessly he was able to banish the blues in the night, to have carped or complained at any point seems the height of ingratitude."

Since the mid-1980s Shales has also covered political programming in his column. At the request of the *Post*'s then–Style editor, Shelby Coffey III, Shales reviewed one of President Ronald Reagan's State of the Union speeches "not for content and policy impact, but for the made-for-TV spectacle that it was," Alicia Mundy explained for *Mediaweek* (September 9, 1996). In that review (dated January 26, 1984), Shales wrote of Reagan's presentation, "No doubt it will be seen as the launching speech for Reagan's reelection campaign; he proclaimed most problems solved or manageable and then went back to his old campaign standbys: let's curtail abortions, let's put prayer back in the schools, and let's crack down on those child pornographers. Perhaps the president brings up these kinds of problems so people will forget about real problems. But in a TV age what he says may matter less than how he appears; facing Congress and the nation he seemed chipper, confident and robust, if not quite so much as he used to." Shales then added, referring to the many times Reagan had fumbled his words, "The bloopers are disconcerting because we've become accustomed to Reagan's professionalism. When the Great Communicator stumbles over words or loses his place, it's like seeing Mister Rogers open the door, trudge into the room, throw his sweater on the floor and groan, 'It's not such a hot day in the neighborhood.'"

Shales also offered his reactions to the opening day of the Democratic National Convention in Chicago, Illinois, in 1996, during which party members toasted the paralyzed actor Christopher Reeve and mourned the victims of a man who went on a shooting spree on the Long Island Rail Road in 1993. In Shales's view, those convention events had the "unsavory aura of blatant emotional manipulation, like a Jerry Lewis telethon." After watching ABC's coverage of the April 16, 2008 debate between two Democratic candidates for the presidency, U.S. senators Barack Obama and Hillary Clinton, Shales commented in "On the Air" (April 17, 2008), "For the first 52 minutes of the two-hour, commercial-crammed show," its moderators, Charles Gibson and George Stephanopoulos, "dwelled entirely on specious and gossipy trivia that already has been hashed and rehashed in the hope of getting the candidates to claw at one another over disputes that are no longer news." "The fact is, cable networks CNN and MSNBC both did better jobs with earlier candidate debates . . . ," he continued. "Cable news is indeed taking over from network news, and merely by being competent."

In an article called "Style-Section Politics" for the *New Criterion* (March 2005), the media critic James Bowman lamented what he termed "the blurring of the distinction between political reality and the movies"; he acknowledged that "presidents themselves have long been complicit" in that phenomenon, citing the practice, which began with Ronald Reagan, of introducing people in the audience during the presentation of the State of the Union address, as a way of including what he termed "uplifting made-for-TV Hallmark" moments. Nevertheless, he criticized Shales as "one of the Style section politicoes who have given up the task of pronouncing on the aesthetic artifacts thrown up by our politics in favor of what they take to be more substantive critiques, including inquiries into the genuineness of the emotions our political showmen put on display. . . . Neither Mr. Shales nor [his colleague Eugene] Robinson [a former assistant managing editor of the *Post*'s Style section] may have anything realistic to suggest, but both have learned to employ their critical talents in the higher cause of making their own insight or concern, and above all their own infinite superiority to those they criticize, the subject of every column. It's a critic's disease, and as a critic myself I know how easy it is to contract it. But the cure is to be subjected to criticism oneself, and that is what Style-section politics so rarely allows to happen." Shales has disputed such arguments; he told Mundy, "TV has made several defining moments in political history in the last 50 years—Nixon's Checkers speech; Joe McCarthy's hearings, when he looked so sinister; the Nixon-JFK debates; and the entire presidency of Ronald Reagan." He added, "Television is our national medium, our Hyde Park, our corner soapbox. Television and politics are one and the same in this country now."

Shales's first book, written with Kevin Brownlow and others, was *The American Film Heritage: Impressions from the American Film Institute Archives* (1972). The articles in it focus on a few of the thousands of films in that collection; pioneering filmmakers; other famous or little-known filmmakers; the treatment of minorities in cinema; and technical developments in moviemaking. Shales's next book, *On the Air!* (1982), is a collection of his television columns; for the third, *Legends: Remembering America's Greatest Stars* (1989), Shales compiled his profiles of entertainers. With the journalist James Andrew Miller, he put together *Live from New York: An Uncensored History of Saturday Night Live* (2002), which presents the reminiscences of former members of its cast and crew, celebrity hosts, writers, producers, and NBC executives, along with commentary by Miller and Shales.

Shales's honors include the American University's 1978 Distinguished Alumnus Award. In 1986 the *Washington Journalism Review* (now known as *American Journalism Review*) named him the "best critic writing for a newspaper." In 1988 he became the fourth television critic to win the Pulitzer Prize for outstanding criticism in journalism, and he was also honored that year with an American Society of Newspaper Editors Distinguished Writing Award for his obituaries of film and television personalities. Readers of the magazine the *Washingtonian* chose Shales as the city's best newspaper reporter in a poll conducted in 1990. In 2005 Shales received an award for his weekly *TelevisionWeek* column at the Los Angeles Press Club's Southern California Journalism Awards.

Shales, who has never married, lives in McLean, Virginia. He has named *I Love Lucy*, *All in the Family*, *The Twilight Zone*, and the 1981 miniseries *Brideshead Revisited* among his favorite television programs.

—M.A.S.

Suggested Reading: *Electronic Media* p3 Apr. 11, 1988, p12 Apr. 24, 2000; *Mediaweek* p23+ Sep. 9, 1996; *People* p18 Nov. 22, 1982; *Time* p52 June 8, 1981; Washington Post Writers Group Web site; *Who's Who in America* (on-line)

Selected Books: *The American Film Heritage: Impressions from the American Film Institute Archives* (with Kevin Brownlow and others), 1972; *On the Air!*, 1982; *Legends: Remembering America's Greatest Stars*, 1989; *Live from New York: An Uncensored History of Saturday Night Live* (with James Andrew Miller), 2002

Shamsie, Kamila

1973– Novelist; journalist

Address: c/o Bloomsbury Publishing, 38 Soho Sq., London W1D 3HB, England

In her first two novels, *In the City by the Sea* and *Salt and Saffron*, the Pakistani writer Kamila Shamsie did for her hometown of Karachi what the Indian writer Salman Rushdie did for his hometown, Bombay (now Mumbai): brought it to life, "warts and all," Ashok Chopra wrote for *India Today* (July 10, 2000). Since the publication of those novels, in 1998 and 2000, respectively, Shamsie has written three additional novels, which, like their predecessors, are set at least partly in Karachi: *Kartography*, *Broken Verses*, and *Burnt Shadows*. Internationally praised, her novels have been nominated for several prominent awards; the first two brought her the Pakistani Prime Minister's Award for Literature. *Salt and Saffron* earned Shamsie inclusion among "21 women writers to watch out for in the 21st century," a list compiled by Orange Futures, an offshoot of the Orange Prize for Fiction, which each year recognizes the best novel written in English by a woman of any nationality. In 2009 *Burnt Shadows* was shortlisted for the Orange Prize.

The lives and emotions of the characters in Shamsie's stories reflect the strained relationship that has existed between Pakistan and India for more than six decades. Pakistan did not exist until 1947, when Great Britain granted independence to India after nearly two centuries of British rule. The act that ended Britain's dominance over India, the birthplace of Hinduism, included a provision that created Pakistan from two widely separated parcels of Indian land where Muslims were in the majority. The emergence of India as a sovereign state and Pakistan as a new nation led to fierce fighting between Hindus and Muslims; at least a million people were killed, some 7.5 million Indian Muslims fled to Pakistan, and some 10 million Hindus left Pakistan for India. The repercussions from that human tragedy have continued to poison relations between Pakistan and India; at times their mutual distrust has flared into armed conflict. Shamsie grew up in the aftermath of the civil war that led to the end of East and West Pakistan as a single nation; the eastern part became a new country, Bangladesh, and the western part was renamed the Islamic Republic of Pakistan. That war, in which India sided militarily with East Pakistan, led in turn to the Indo-Pakistani war of 1971. Large and small skirmishes between India and Pakistan have occurred repeatedly since then, many over control of Jammu and Kashmir, whose status as an Indian

Shaun Curry/AFP/Getty Images

Kamila Shamsie

state Pakistan rejects. In explaining why she wove Pakistani-Indian affairs into her stories, Shamsie told Senay Boztas for the London *Sunday Times* (July 28, 2002), "There is a very peculiar relationship between Indians and Pakistanis. On one hand there is the constant threat of war, on the other hand there is this sense of shared history. It is difficult territory to navigate, even in friendships between people on both sides. You cannot do this warm, fuzzy glow of 'can't we get along: we are all nice people after all,' much as you would like to." She also told Boztas, "There are real issues between the two nations and a lot of profound misunderstanding. . . . You need to get a discourse going."

A descendant of several generations of writers, Kamila Naheed Shamsie was born to Saleem and Muneeza (Habibullah) Shamsie in 1973 in Karachi. Her great-grandmother Inam Habibullah was an advocate for women's rights at a time when most women in India were illiterate and led highly restricted lives; she wrote a book about her travels in Europe in the 1920s and served in the 1930s in a provisional Indian parliament as a member of the All-India Muslim League. Her grandmother Jahanara Habibullah wrote a memoir, called *Remembrance of Days Past: Glimpses of a Princely State During the Raj*, that was published by Oxford University Press in 2001, when she was 80. Shamsie's great-aunt Attia Hosain (also spelled Hussein) was one of the first Indian authors to write in English; her short-story collection, *Phoenix Fled* (1953), and her novel, *Sunlight on a Broken Column* (1961), were published by the well-respected London firm Chatto and Windus. Shamsie's mother was educated in British boarding schools; she is a renowned literary journalist, bibliographer, short-story writer, and editor. "I'm often told that there must be a writing gene passed on in my family," Kamila Shamsie wrote in an essay for the London *Guardian* (May 1, 2009). "I'm as inclined to think that I grew up in a writing atmosphere. Certainly it's impossible to [overestimate] the value of growing up the daughter of Muneeza Shamsie. My mother has always loved books, but for a long time thought her lack of university education meant she didn't have the qualifications to write or talk publicly about them. It was my father who first bought her a typewriter and encouraged her to write." Shamsie's granduncle Sahabzada Yaqub Khan was Pakistan's foreign minister from 1982 to 1991.

Kamila Shamsie grew up in Karachi with her older sister, Saman. Their family lived comfortably, vacationing in London, England, during summers. Shamsie was an avid reader throughout her adolescence, devouring her mother's unusually large collection of English-language books, which were difficult for Pakistanis to acquire then. She has said that she knew she wanted to become a writer at the age of nine. By 11 Shamsie had co-written a 40-page story with her best friend. "It was set in dog heaven, which was nice. But there was a feeling that the few published Pakistanis writing in English had filled the quota," she told Helen Brown for the London *Daily Telegraph* (April 9, 2005). "And it was hard to have heroes. The only writer we knew in Pakistan was Bapsi Sidhwa, who wrote *Ice-Candy-Man* [published in the early 1990s as *Cracking India*]. Then, when I was about 16, Sara Suleri published her memoir, *Meatless Days*, which seemed to proceed through metaphor rather than linear narrative. It also took in politics in Pakistan and the idea of women in Pakistan. I loved it. Salman Rushdie's *Midnight's Children* was also a really important book for me. I thought, 'Oh, you can do this, you can write about the world as you know it.'" Surrounded by female writers, Shamsie never felt her dream was unattainable. "While I grew up in the harsh world of a misogynist military government in 1980s Pakistan—where women's freedom was severely threatened—my familial legacy enabled me to imagine, without pressure or expectation, a life centred around writing," she explained in her *Guardian* reminiscence.

In 1990 Shamsie enrolled at Hamilton College, in Clinton, New York, where she studied creative writing. She was struck by the political differences between her homeland and the U.S. "If you grew up in Pakistan in the '70s and '80s, you always knew that what was happening politically had a very direct bearing on all kinds of aspects of individual lives," she told Vit Wagner for the *Toronto (Ontario, Canada) Star* (May 13, 2009). "One of the surprises for me of going to America for university was that people lived as if their lives had nothing to do with a grander, political narrative." Shamsie earned a B.A. degree in 1994 and entered the University of Massachusetts (UMass) at Amherst to pursue a master's degree. On the advice of a London literary agent to whom she had been introduced by her Hamilton adviser, the Indian writer Shona Ramaya, she began to write a novel; that novel, *In the City by the Sea*, became the thesis required for her M.F.A. degree. The London agent sent the manuscript to several publishers, and in December 1997 the London-based firm Granta Books accepted it. Six months later Shamsie graduated from UMass and immigrated to London.

In the City by the Sea (1998) follows Hasan, a privileged 11-year-old boy growing up in Karachi during the oppressive Pakistani military regimes of the 1970s. The book received positive critical notice. Writing for the London *Guardian Weekly* (December 13, 1998), Lewley McDowell described it as "an interesting and promising novel." "*In the City by the Sea* is full of fun, longing and wit," Ali Smith wrote for the *Scotsman* (December 12, 1998). "It's a debut of spirit and imagination loaded with intelligent charm." *In the City by the Sea* was short-listed for the annual John Llewellyn Rhys Prize, which honors the best work of literature by a writer 35 years old or younger from Britain or a British Commonwealth nation. In 1999 Shamsie earned Pakistan's Prime Minister's Award for Literature. On the day scheduled for the award ceremony, General Pervez Musharraf overthrew the nation's democratically elected prime minister, Nawaz Sharif. Shamsie later wrote about the incident, in an article for the magazine *Prospect* (November 22, 2001); in it she stated that although she is an ardent supporter of democracy, the military coup was not unwelcome, because Sharif "had been systematically undermining democracy," and Musharraf's more moderate political views had more supporters among Pakistanis.

Shamsie's second novel, *Salt and Saffron* (2000), received rave reviews. *Salt and Saffron* is about the Dard-e-Dil family, and in particular one of its members, a young woman named Aliya, who has finished up her studies at an American college and returned to Pakistan for the summer. Unlike most of her relatives, who look down on people who do not share their distinctive heritage, Aliya finds herself attracted to a man from a Karachi slum. Meanwhile, she begins to delve into her family's past and finds that all is not as it seems. In the London *Independent* (March 25, 2000), Geraldine Cooke described *Salt and Saffron* as "beautifully written in cunning, punning, glancing prose," and a *Publishers Weekly* (August 28, 2000) reviewer declared, "Clever, witty and inventive, this engaging novel tackles the challenges of reconciling one culture's progressive values with another's allegiance to family and tradition."

Kartography (2002) explores the relationships between members of two upper-class families living in Karachi during the 1970s and '80s. It focuses on a boy, Karim, from one of the families, and a girl, Raheen, from the other. Thirteen years old when the story begins, Karim and Raheen are best friends who have known each other since birth. As Raheen and Karim mature, and their relationship develops into a romance, they discover a secret that their parents had closely held: Raheen's father was once engaged to marry Karim's mother, and Raheen's mother was once betrothed to Karim's father. The swap of partners had resulted from the ethnic unrest that occurred during the 1971 civil war. Raheen and Karim's discovery threatens to uproot the bond between them. The title of the book refers to Karim's obsession with mapmaking—he hopes to make cartography his career—and it is spelled with a "K" in a play on "Karachi." "Shamsie's third novel is a strangely mixed affair: lively, engaging and sometimes funny, yet also at times gawky, unwieldy and occasionally even inept," Julie Myerson wrote in her review for the *Guardian* (August 3, 2002) "Considering Shamsie is not yet 30, this boundless narrative energy and confidence is impressive—this novel clearly believes itself to be funny and wise and true. Yet at times the plot—its setting up and, more especially, its later unravelling—seems forced and contrived, even its resolution oddly underwhelming." By contrast, a *Publishers Weekly* (July 14, 2003) assessment proclaimed, "Shamsie's cerebral, playful style sets her apart from most of her fellow subcontinental writers. Something of a cross between Arundhati Roy and Salman Rushdie, she deserves a larger readership in the U.S." For *Kartography*, Shamsie was again short-listed for the John Llewellyn Rhys Prize, and she won the Patras Bokhari Award from the Academy of Letters in Pakistan.

Broken Verses (2005) centers on Aasmaani, a 31-year-old woman who has been haunted by the murder of her mother's lover, "the Poet," and the disappearance of her mother, a feminist activist, 14 years earlier. When a letter surfaces with a secret code that only the three of them knew, Aasmaani begins to suspect that they may still be alive. "Wry, fetching and too clever for her own good, she is a captivating, unexpected heroine," a *Publishers Weekly* (March 21, 2005) critic wrote of Aasmaani. Deborah Donovan wrote in a review for *Booklist* (March 1, 2005), "Shamsie carries the reader along on Aasmaani's slow journey of discovery with magnetic and beguiling prose, intelligence and wit." Shamsie earned a second Patras Bokhari Award for *Broken Verses*.

Shamsie's most recent novel, *Burnt Shadows* (2009), examines identity and nationality against the backdrops of blood-drenched historic events of the past six decades: the atomic bombing of Nagasaki, Japan, by the U.S. in 1945; the partition of India and Pakistan; the Soviet Union's invasion of Afghanistan in 1979; and the consequences of the September 11, 2001 terrorist attacks in New York City. Hiroko, a 21-year-old Japanese woman, loses her German fiancé in the bombing of Nagasaki and moves to India, where she forms relationships with her fiancé's half-sister, the half-sister's English husband, and their Muslim servant, Sajjad. Hiroko and Sajjad fall in love and decide to move to the newly formed country of Pakistan to raise their young son. Later the characters find themselves in New York and Afghanistan, entangled with Islamic extremists and the CIA. "I was interested in what happens when people from different nations come together when those nations are at war . . . ," Shamsie told reporters for the British publication *Metro* (February 26, 2009). "And I've always been interested in national identity as something porous—half my family crossed over [to Pakistan] from India during Partition yet I grew up with India and Pakistan at war." In *Burnt Shadows* "Shamsie calls upon her considerable command of disciplined irony to examine how we arrived at where we are now, this beaten planet. . . ," Eileen Battersby wrote in a review for the *Irish Times* (February 28, 2009). "Although the hyper choreography of the plotting is too neat, almost clinically efficient, there is no doubting Shamsie's grasp of either the cultural and political chaos, or the unifying fear." *Burnt Shadows* was short-listed for the 2009 Orange Prize for Fiction.

Shamsie has written for publications including the *New York Times*, the *Times Literary Supplement*, *Index on Censorship*, *Prospect*, and *New Statesman*. She is currently a writer and reviewer for the *Guardian* and frequently contributes to BBC radio. Most of her nonfiction writing focuses on Pakistan and the Middle East. In one such article, written for the *Guardian* (November 1, 2001) and titled "After September 11: My Home Is Not the Place You See on TV," Shamsie criticized the U.S. media's depiction of Pakistan as a violent, ultra-religious nation. "Just as Pakistan looks like an extremist monolith if you watch news reports in the US, so the US looks like an arrogant nation baying for blood and willing to bypass due process if you watch news reports here [in Pakistan]," she wrote. "The interesting point is this: the same news channels which broadcast images of Pakistan to the US also broadcast images of the US to Pakistan. That is, we watch CNN and we think it's showing us a complete picture of America. But having lived in the US, having spoken to friends who've written articles criticising US policy for the print media in the US and found those pieces 'edited' or not published, I know that there is a voice of opposition within America which finds itself completely shut out by the mainstream media. Paradoxically, if the US media allowed those voices to come through to the rest of the world there might be less anger towards the US in places such as Pakistan."

In the early 2000s Shamsie spent various times of the year in Karachi, London, and Clinton, New York, where she taught creative writing at Hamilton. She now lives primarily in London, making occasional trips to Karachi to visit her family. Round-faced, with short, dark hair, Shamsie was described by Helen Brown as a "mature, cosmopolitan woman."

—M.A.S.

Suggested Reading: (Calcutta, India) *Telegraph* (on-line) Mar. 1, 2009; (Chennai, India) *Business Line* (on-line) July 2, 2004; (London) *Daily Telegraph* p12 Apr. 9, 2005; (London) *Guardian* Comment & Features p16 May 1, 2009; (London) *Metro* Books p30 Feb. 26, 2009

Selected Books: *In the City by the Sea*, 1998; *Salt and Saffron*, 2000; *Kartography*, 2002; *Broken Verses*, 2005; *Burnt Shadows*, 2009

Courtesy of Dash Shaw

Shaw, Dash

Apr. 6, 1983– Graphic novelist; comic-book artist

Address: c/o Fantagraphics Books, 7563 Lake City Way N.E., Seattle, WA 98115

"I want my comics to be an emotional experience," Dash Shaw told Tim Leong for *Comic Foundry* (April 27, 2005, on-line). "The main character in my comics is 'You' and the story is 'You're reading this comic.'" He continued, "Some people will relate to a character and others won't. I have no control over it. I could draw a character who looks like someone you hate, but to another person it could look like their sister or mother. It's all associative. But the emotions, the psychology of the drawings and sequences, is universal."

Shaw, whose comics have been praised for their eclectic style, innovative design, and emotional depth, has emerged from a growing breed of artists who maintain autonomy over their work. (By contrast, major comic-book publishing companies, such as Marvel and DC, employ an organized system of writers, who produce story lines and dialogue; pencillers, who are responsible for initial versions of the artwork; and inkers, who refine and complete the comics.) Shaw told *Current Biography*, "I want my comics to be beautiful. I want it to feel like you're transported to another place."

Shaw is the author of the critically acclaimed graphic novels *Love Eats Brains* (2004), published by Odd God Press; *The Mother's Mouth* (2006), published by Alternative Comics; and, most recently, *The Bottomless Belly Button* (2008), which was published by Fantagraphics Books. (Graphic novels, now widely recognized as a legitimate and respected format in literary circles, are novel-length tales in comics form.) In addition, he has produced a compilation of graphic-art short stories called *Goddess Head* (2005), and his work has appeared in numerous anthologies, newspapers, and magazines.

Dash Austin Shaw was born on April 6, 1983 in Los Angeles, California, to Monica Shaw, a child psychologist, and Daniel Shaw, a direct-mail copywriter. His parents moved to Richmond, Virginia, two years later, thinking that it would provide a better environment in which to raise a family. (Shaw has one younger brother, Nick.)

Daniel Shaw was a devoted comic-book aficionado. "My dad had a box of underground comics that I'd look through. He also had [the legendary artist] Will Eisner's *The Spirit* magazines," Shaw told *Current Biography*. When he was four years old, Shaw began creating his own comics by drawing the art for captions his father had written. Shaw told Sunyoung Lee for *Publishers Weekly* (December 5, 2006, on-line), "Luckily my dad . . . raised me with the idea that comics are a legitimate art form—not that I have a concern for being a 'legitimate artist.' But he encouraged me to make comics and continues to encourage me. It wasn't like I discovered *Maus* [a Pulitzer Prize–winning graphic novel about the Holocaust by Art Spiegelman] and it opened doors for me." Some of Shaw's early favorites included *The Teenage Mutant Ninja Turtles*, the crime-fighting stars of a wildly popular Saturday-morning TV cartoon, and the Japanese comics known as *manga*. He went on to be influenced by such luminaries as Chester Gould (best known as the creator of the *Dick Tracy* comic strip), the legendary Japanese manga artist Osamu Tezuka (the talent behind *Astro Boy* and *Kimba the White Lion*), the contemporary American cartoonist Chris Ware, and the influential illustrator and painter Gary Panter, among others.

Shaw attended high school in Richmond, going to morning classes at Godwin High School and spending the rest of the day at the Henrico High School Center for the Arts magnet program. He told *Current Biography*, "The Center for the Arts was a great program that allowed for hour-long arts classes every day and a budget for visiting teachers in different fields [and] mediums. An airbrush artist could come in for one class, and a digital artist for the next." When he was a freshman, Shaw started producing his own Xeroxed mini-comics, which included such titles as "Six Days," "Skylark," and "Shippori." Making roughly 50 or so copies of each, he distributed them to local comic-book stores. In addition, Shaw began providing illustrations for "InSync," a now-defunct youth supplement to the *Richmond Times-Dispatch*. At the *Times-Dispatch* he began experimenting with using such computer programs as Adobe Illustrator and Adobe Photoshop to manipulate images and fonts, and he tried out other methods, including watercolor painting. Describing that period to Leong as a kind of "illustration boot camp," he explained, "I was always attracted to artists who would juxtapose different kinds of drawings."

Shaw spent his junior year in Tatsumigaoka, Japan, as part of an exchange program. "There are so many kinds of comics in Japan," he told Lee. "You can pick up a weekly and find a comic that looks like *Astro Boy* in the front and something that looks like Panter's *Cola Madness* in the back. I'm skeptical of American artists who say they adopt manga into their work—which manga? Manga isn't a genre. It's a whole world of different artists and storytelling styles." Shaw explained to *Current Biography*, "The pace of manga has influenced a lot of my work. My comics don't look like manga on the surface, but they're manga underneath. This is something that a lot of other cartoonists notice about my work, people who think about structure and these things, but something that people outside of comics usually don't pick up on."

Upon graduating from high school, in 2001, Shaw moved to New York City and enrolled at the School of Visual Arts (SVA). As a freshman, he began self-publishing comics series. Thanks to a friend who worked the graveyard shift at the office-services chain Kinko's, the costs of the projects were kept at a minimum. Shaw's emotional stories and innovative design quickly started receiving attention from the comics cognoscenti, and at 19 he was named one of the top 10 artists to watch for at the Small Press Expo, an annual showcase for independent comic books.

Throughout college Shaw placed graphic-art short stories and illustrations in a variety of publications, including the SVA magazine *Visual Opinion*, the Belgian magazine *Front*, the now-defunct *Philadelphia Independent*, and anthologies from the artists' collective Meathaus. Many of the pieces were subsequently reprinted in Shaw's 2005 collection, *Goddess Head*, which was published by Hidden Agenda Press. In a review for *Afterimage* (May 1, 2006), Ariel Lin wrote, "Reading . . . *Goddess Head* is not a comfortable experience—[Shaw] seems to want you to feel uneasy. Unlike the common approach to comics, focusing on a conflict, structured with a beginning and an end, Shaw refuses to give you a straightforward, linear answer. . . . His drawings and texts turn blank pages into mirrors. Look into the mirrors and you can project an alter ego into his conflicting, contradictory, and sometimes compassionate short fantasies, and try to make sense of it for yourself."

Before *Goddess Head*, Shaw had published *Love Eats Brains*, which first appeared in comic-book form in September 2002. After publishing three issues, he decided to complete the series with the help of an assistant artist, who sabotaged the project by stealing the original prints. Shaw then opted to use the name and some of the themes of the series for a graphic novel, which was published in 2004 with the subtitle *A Zombie Romance*. The novel—which concerns a love triangle involving a photographer, his pregnant girlfriend, and a dead librarian—helped catapult Shaw to a degree of fame in the world of independent comics. In a review posted on the comics-oriented Little Terrors Web site, Sam Costello wrote, "*Love Eats Brains* is much more than a zombie story. In fact, it's not exactly a horror comic. Certainly there are zombies and murder. There's even necrophilia. But *Love Eats Brains* is, at its core, [a] comic about love that uses horror to illuminate deep human emotions. . . . Amid the murder and the zombies, there are touching human moments." In one portion of the novel, for example, two men who have been killed in a head-on car crash are reunited in a cemetery after their deaths and, instead of harboring ill will, become friends. Commenting on the passage, Costello explained, "This is a kind of acceptance and peace most horror work wouldn't ever think of, let alone include."

In 2005 Shaw graduated from the SVA, and the following year he published his senior thesis project, *The Mother's Mouth*. He had been supervised by one of his heroes, Gary Panter, an SVA instructor. Shaw told *Current Biography*, "What [Panter] taught me, in person, was how an artist should behave. He isn't stuck-up and he isn't annoyingly self-deprecating. He's casual, confident . . . perfect. It's important to have a teacher to act as a behavioral model." *The Mother's Mouth* tells the story of a young woman, Virginia, who travels to pre–Hurricane Katrina New Orleans, Louisiana, to look after her sick mother. There, she meets an aspiring musician named Dick, who bears some resemblance to her deceased childhood boyfriend, Richard. Shaw drew inspiration for the story from personal experience. He recalled to Lee, "The summer between junior and senior year [of college], I stayed at my parents' home in Richmond, Virginia, and started dating my high school girlfriend again, whom I hadn't spoken with for a few years. We would do the same things we did senior year of high school. If you have the opportunity to relive any time that you feel sentimental toward, and you seize that opportunity, you'll find that it's a creepy, unpleasant experience." *The Mother's Mouth* won praise for its exploration of sexuality and identity and its innovative design. In a review for *Booklist*, as posted on Amazon.com, Ray Olson wrote, "Shaw draws a bold but fragile line that allows his characters no beauty but forces consideration of their moral quality. Virginia and Dick emerge as decent, lonely thirtysomethings who deserve a good relationship. There is much more stylistically to Shaw's presentation, however: flashbacks to Richard, rendered in gray; interpolated photos of Virginia's mother and Richard's fatal therapy; drawn 'establishing shots' of settings; comic-strip-like scenes; typeset explanatory passages and notes; and more. Shaw adroitly uses this technical variety to give the simple story emotional, cultural, and psychological weight." In 2007 the novel was nominated for a Will Eisner Comic Industry Award.

In the fall of 2006, while attending the Small Press Expo, in Bethesda, Maryland, Shaw approached Gary Groth, the head of Fantagraphics Books and the editor of the *Comics Journal*, and gave him the first 300 pages of *The Bottomless Belly Button*. "While the comics business allows amateurs to submit their work directly to decision-makers in a manner unheard of in other media—no expo exists at which budding novelists hand manuscripts to Knopf's Sonny Mehta (Groth's closest analogue, if Mehta also edited a meaner version of *The New York Review of Books*)—it still took a striking confidence on Shaw's part to submit his book to Groth," Dan Kois wrote for *New York* (June 15, 2008, on-line). "The next day, back in his office in Seattle, Groth e-mailed Shaw to express his 'intense interest.' By May 2007, when Shaw sent Groth the last chapters of *Bottomless Belly Button*, a deal was struck, and now that enormous book—720 pages of knotty family drama, emotional teen angst, lyrical passages about nature, good jokes, bad parenting, architectural schematics, rudimentary codes, and explicit sex—has become the graphic novel of the year, combining youthful exuberance, sage storytelling, and visual experimentation."

The Bottomless Belly Button chronicles a week in the lives of Maggie and David Loony, who have called their three adult children home for a reunion at the family's old beach house, to announce that they are divorcing after 40 years of marriage. Dennis, the oldest of the children, responds by searching the house for love letters or other concrete evidence as to the nature of his parents' relationship. Claire, the middle child, who has been through a divorce herself, is more preoccupied with her own life and the difficulties of raising her teenage daughter. Peter, the youngest and the black sheep of the family, suffers from the others' lack of attention. Shaw told Matthew Shaer for the *Christian Science Monitor* (June 27, 2008), "I wanted to do a story that was about characters. With family stories, you don't have a lot to establish, in terms of background. These are people forced into a situation—forced into one space."

Shaw drew the three siblings as though each had come from a different graphic novel: Dennis is drawn in a childlike, cartoonish fashion; Claire is illustrated more realistically and is depicted with long gloves to symbolize her habit of keeping her loved ones at arm's length; and Peter, who tells his girlfriend that his family treats him "like I'm a big, dumb frog," is shown with the head of a frog for most of the book.

The Bottomless Belly Button received almost universally glowing notices. In a review for the Harrisburg, Pennsylvania, *Patriot News* (June 27, 2008), Chris Mautner called the book "an adventurous, admirable work, one that will further cement Shaw's growing reputation as a formidable author." In an assessment for *Booklist* (June 1, 2008), Ray Olson wrote, "Shaw [has created] situations and characters identical with those of mainstream realistic novels and movies and handles them with the sensitivity and humor of the best humanist novelists and filmmakers." George Gene Gustines wrote for the *New York Times* (August 1, 2008), "Most of Shaw's creative decisions simply leave the reader marveling at his work."

Shaw recently completed a science-fiction–inspired comic called *Bodyworld*, which was bought by Pantheon Books and was slated to be published in 2010. Earlier, he had serialized *Bodyworld* on his Web site. "I really like web comics and I like that they are free," he told David Paggi for the Wizard Universe Web site (July 6, 2008). "That is really moving to me. I know that most cartoonists don't make any money but for some reason the idea of spending twelve hours a day, or more, painting and putting together this thing where the end result is just posting it and not asking anybody for anything is just awesome!" Shaw does not, however, disparage commercially produced comics. He told Kois, "If Marvel called and asked if I wanted to do [the popular superhero series] *Ghost Rider*, I would be like, 'Hell, yeah.'" Shaw lives in the New York City borough of Brooklyn.

—C.C.

Suggested Reading: *Afterimage* p52 May 1, 2006; *Christian Science Monitor* p13 June 27, 2008; *Comic Foundry* (on-line) Apr. 27, 2005; *New York* (on-line) June 15, 2008; *New York Times* E p28 Aug. 1, 2008; *Publishers Weekly* (on-line) Dec. 5, 2006

Selected Books: *Love Eats Brains*, 2004; *Goddess Head*, 2005; *The Mother's Mouth*, 2006; *The Bottomless Belly Button*, 2008

Sheikh Hamad bin Khalifa al-Thani

1952– Emir of Qatar

Address: c/o Qatar Embassy, 2555 M St., N.W., Washington, DC 20037

Sheikh Hamad bin Khalifa al-Thani is the emir—ruler—of the small, oil- and natural-gas-rich state of Qatar, in the Persian Gulf. Since he ousted his father in a bloodless coup, in 1995, he has become one of the boldest of a new generation of Middle Eastern leaders, educated in the West and pursuing social and economic modernization and reform in a region often characterized by conservatism and autocracy. Sheikh Hamad's unconventional and outspoken manner has drawn many critics, particularly among the leadership of the neighboring countries Saudi Arabia, Bahrain, and Kuwait, who see his policies as a threat to their own regimes, prompting some observers to call Sheikh Hamad the "Young Turk of the Gulf" (*New York Times*, July 10, 1997) and the "Gulf's enfant terrible" (*Mideast Mirror*, June 27, 1995). Under Sheikh Hamad Qatar has brought in overseas investment; invited a U.S. military presence; made steps toward democracy; negotiated with both Israel and Iran, nations at opposite ends of the ongoing conflict in the region; relaxed laws on alcohol and censorship; and, perhaps most notably, launched the editorially independent TV station Al Jazeera, which has been celebrated for its unbiased and unfiltered reporting and analyses of developments in the Middle East. Hamad "has broken all the taboos," Riad Kahwaji, the chief executive of the Institute for Near East & Gulf Military Analysis, a Dubai-based think tank, told Laura Cohn for *Business Week* (March 24, 2003). "Sticking his neck out is nothing new . . . ," Scott MacLeod wrote for *Time* (November 4, 2002). "Balancing acts are Hamad's trademark." On the *Charlie Rose Show* (September 29, 2007, on-line), Rose asked the emir about the seeming contradictions in the policies of Qatar, which is a U.S. ally but allows Al Jazeera to criticize America and its regional allies, including Saudi Arabia; which conducts talks with Iran but

Karim Jaafar/AFP/Getty Images

trades with Israel; and which established a parliament but remains essentially an absolute monarchy. The sheikh responded, "Our policy is so clear. We would like to have friendship with everybody." He told Mary Anne Weaver for the *New Yorker* (November 20, 2000): "What I did was try to develop my country. I know that my time will not be that long, but I want to feel happy in the knowledge that I have put Qatar on the right path, and that those who come after me will continue, and correct the mistakes I have made. My hope is to see Qatar as a democracy before I leave; to have a well-educated generation that, in the smallest villages, can develop heavy industry. The challenge is how to build reserves so that, if the day comes when Qatar has no oil or gas, it can stand as a large nation and be proud of itself."

Born in 1952, the eldest of Sheikh Khalifa's five sons (some sources say there are seven), Sheikh Hamad attended school in Doha, the capital and largest city in Qatar. In his book *Al-Jazeera: The Inside Story of the Arab News Channel That Is Challenging the West* (2005), Hugh Miles wrote that the Sheikh's "first exposure to democracy was on a trip to London when he was still a boy and legend has it that the concept seemed so ridiculous to him that he had to be led in hysterical laughter from the balcony of the House of Commons after witnessing his first parliamentary debate." At the age of 17, as with many of the male members of Arab royal families, he was sent to the Sandhurst Royal Military Academy, in Great Britain, graduating in July 1971. In the same year Qatar, previously a British protectorate, attained independence, with one of Sheikh Khalifa's cousins assuming the position of emir. A year later Khalifa ousted his cousin in a coup. After completing his course work at Sandhurst, Hamad briefly extended his studies in Britain before returning to Qatar. There, he joined the army as a lieutenant colonel and was quickly promoted to the rank of major general and then appointed to the position of commander in chief of the armed forces. On May 31, 1977 he was named as his father's heir apparent and Qatar's first minister of defense. In the mid-to-late 1980s and early 1990s, Sheikh Hamad began to assume control of the Qatari state. In 1989 he created, then assumed, the position of chairman of the Higher Council for Planning, which, according to the Web site of the Qatari Embassy in the U.S., sets the country's economic and social policies and is "considered as the cornerstone in the building of the modern state." That move alienated his brother Sheikh Abdul Aziz, Sheikh Khalifa's second son, who was oil and finance minister and Hamad's chief rival; after the Persian Gulf War of 1991, Sheikh Hamad had his brother sacked, and Abdul Aziz subsequently settled in France.

Before the discovery in Qatar of oil (in 1939) and gas (in 1971), the nation (which is smaller than Connecticut) was known as a poor, barren British protectorate with resources for pearl fishing and an inhospitable populace. That small population (estimated to be between 800,000 and 1.4 million in 2008), which today is dwarfed by foreign workers and laborers brought in for the hydrocarbon-fueled building boom, was once made up largely of several connected ruling families, the biggest and most dominant of which was the al-Thani tribe. "In proportion to the country's small size, the Al Thani family is the largest of all the ruling families in the Middle East," Hugh Miles wrote. "It also has a reputation for being the most argumentative. Transition from one ruler to another has rarely been smooth and the family's propensity for spilling one another's blood won them the title 'the thugs of the Gulf' from one pre-independence British administrator." The al-Thanis had arrived in the mid-18th century from central Arabia and, through a combination of violence and negotiation, quickly assumed control of the region and its pearling industry. In 1916 Abdullah bin Mohammed al-Thani, like many of the rulers of the Arabian peninsula at the time, signed an agreement with the British ceding control of foreign affairs in exchange for security. In 1971, when the British withdrew from the region, Qatar, along with Bahrain, refused to join the federation that became the United Arab Emirates and instead declared independence, with Ahmed bin Ali al-Thani as the country's first emir. A year later Sheikh Khalifa, Hamad's father, ousted his cousin in a coup and today is seen as the father of the modern state. His rule is characterized as one in which power was retained through patronage; Qataris were provided with an all-encompassing welfare package and paid no taxes. But with that system came waste and stagnation; whereas other Gulf nations, such as the United Arab Emirates, were trading, diversifying, and reinvesting their oil wealth, the smaller Qatar, which deferred on all foreign-affairs issues to the larger kingdom of Saudi Arabia, lagged behind. "Khalifa wasn't a bad ruler," a Western diplomat told Weaver. "He was simply a seventeenth-century ruler. Everything stopped." Sheikh Khalifa's regime was also known for corruption.

In 1992 Khalifa made an extended visit to Europe, leaving Sheikh Hamad in charge. Hamad moved quickly "to purge the bureaucracy of the Old Guard and installed his own people—younger al-Thanis and members of other influential families—at all levels of the government," according to Weaver. "His advisers wanted to open the economy to foreign businessmen and to hasten development of the emirate's gas and oil reserves." In the early 1990s Sheikh Hamad began to invite foreign investment, particularly on the part of U.S. businesses, in order to develop the country's oil and natural-gas reserves on a much larger scale. In 1989 Hamad had been the first ruler of Qatar to grant by decree controversial production-sharing agreements (PSAs) to foreign companies in the hydrocarbon sector. According to the publication *APS Diplomat Operations in Oil Diplomacy* (October 30, 2000), "Shaikh Hamad's diwan [office] then became powerful in the lobbying for projects related to the North Field, the oil sector, the defence sector and other matters. His diwan also drew to its sphere of influence lobbyists working for Total, Technip, Elf Aquitaine and Italian contracting firms." By the mid-1990s Sheikh Hamad was in effect ruling Qatar. He had for the last several years abandoned his father's pro-Saudi, isolationist foreign policies and conservative economic policies, courting a U.S. military presence and signing energy-development deals with foreign multinational corporations. In early 1995 Khalifa returned to Doha and began reversing his son's policies, threatening to undermine Hamad's position and to bring Abdul Aziz back as prime minister. Khalifa then returned to Europe, paving the way for a coup.

On June 27, 1995, with Sheikh Khalifa in Switzerland, Sheikh Hamad sent troops to his father's palace, the Doha airport, and the Saudi border and in a bloodless coup declared himself emir. "I am not happy with what has happened but it had to be done and I had to do it," he said in a televised address hours after the coup, as quoted in the Toronto *Globe and Mail* (June 28, 1995). Three alleged countercoups followed, the most significant of which was foiled on February 14, 1996; the government arrested and condemned to death at least 20 defendants. Sheikh Hamad reached a compromise with his father, finalized in 1998, whereby the deposed emir would unfreeze state funds, estimated at around $2.5 billion, in exchange for a dropping of lawsuits pertaining to the countercoup and an annual stipend of an undisclosed amount. Sheikh Khalifa returned to Doha in 2004 to attend the funeral of his wife, with Sheikh Hamad formally greeting him upon his arrival, ending speculation of another countercoup. Another reason Sheikh Khalifa's position was weakened is the immense subsequent economic success of Hamad's rule.

Almost immediately upon assuming power, Sheikh Hamad undertook a series of controversial policy positions that would boost Qatar's international and regional profile to unprecedented levels. The first was to establish a site for the largest permanent U.S. military presence in the Middle East and a home to the U.S. headquarters in the region, known as Central Command (CENTCOM). "The emir's policy stems from Qatar's vulnerability in an unstable region," according to an article in the *Economist Intelligence Unit* (November 21, 2007). "As a geographically and demographically small country, Qatar is militarily too insignificant to protect its interests, and thus has chosen to shelter itself under the US security umbrella." Hamad's "national-security strategy, simply put, is that he wants to make himself crucial to the American presence in the Gulf," a top adviser to the emir told Weaver in 2000. "What do we get in exchange? We don't need to spend a lot of money on defense, we'll be attractive to American businessmen, and we'll get international status and prestige." In his interview with Charlie Rose, Sheikh Hamad addressed criticism of Qatar's relationship with the U.S., explaining his policy of separating business from politics: "If you are against the United States, OK, this is . . . a diplomatic [matter] . . . but you have to know how to make ties with the United States in energy, education, health—exactly what we're doing with the Americans." Shortly after the U.S. and its allies invaded Iraq, in 2003, using Qatar as a base, Sheikh Hamad was quoted by David R. Sands in the *Washington Times* (May 10, 2003) as saying, "If the United States managed to help establish democracy in Iraq, as it used to be in the 1920s, I think that would be the greatest step that could be taken both for America and for the whole Middle East. . . . When the United States was in need of [support] in its campaign against Iraq, we were the only country that would declare its position clearly regarding that subject." Observers began to predict that Qatar could become the target of terrorist attacks. In 2005 a bomb exploded outside a theater in Doha frequented by English-speaking expatriates, killing a British citizen and wounding more than a dozen others, in an act attributed to the terrorist group Al Qaeda. Journalists at the time wrote that the explosion might have been timed to coincide with the anniversary of the U.S. invasion of Iraq.

The most important, revolutionary, and visible of Sheikh Hamad's reforms has been the patronage of the Al Jazeera satellite news channel, a station "so provocative that almost every country in the Middle East has, at some point, banned it," Danna Harman wrote for the *Christian Science Monitor* (March 6, 2007). Jillian Schwedler and Maren Milligan, writing for the *Middle East Report* (June 20, 2004), called Al Jazeera "the most progressive development in the region in decades." One of Hamad's first moves after assuming power was to ease the press censorship laws in Qatar and abolish the Ministry of Information, whose counterparts in other countries in the region have operated as institutions of media control. Al Jazeera, established by decree with a roughly $150 million donation from the emir in February 1996, began operations in November of that year. The Saudi-owned Orbit network had recently dropped its sponsorship of BBC Arabic, by far the most popular network in the region, due to displeasure with the critical content of its reports. Al Jazeera immediately signed on more than 100 of BBC Arabic's former (overwhelmingly Arab) journalists and technicians. In a lecture at New York University on October 30, 2007, the Egyptian dissident, intellectual, and human-rights activist Saad Eddin Ibrahim recalled a conversation with Sheikh Hamad regarding the origin of Al Jazeera; he had asked the emir about the seeming contradiction that Qatar could have Al Jazeera, the first open, free, and critical news network in the region, at the same time that it housed the biggest U.S. military base in the Middle East, which implied shared interests with the U.S.—often a target of Al Jazeera's criticism. Sheikh Hamad, according to Ibrahim, had explained that the price for protection of Qatar was a military base, but the price the U.S. paid for the base was a media network that was free to report on issues, including U.S. involvement in the region, objectively and critically. "Al Jazeera was meant to pay its way by winning advertising, but this proved impossible, despite its 40 million viewership, because of the hostility of the Arab states towards the new channel—a hostility that extended to an undeclared threat to boycott any company that dared to advertise on it," John Gee wrote for the *Business Times Singapore* (June 22, 2005). "The very things that made it the object of anger on the part of Arab governments made Al Jazeera popular with the public across the Arab world: it gave a platform for a wide range of views to be expressed and for genuine debate to take place. The eagerness of some in Washington to have the channel closed down has enhanced its standing: most Arabs regard their position as a hypocritical attempt to deny to them the freedom of expression that the US officially holds sacred." Sheikh Hamad has argued that criticism of the station by both the U.S. and its enemies, and various contradictory claims by conspiracy theorists that Al Jazeera is run by the CIA, the terrorist Osama bin Laden, Israel, or, years ago, by the Iraqi dictator Saddam Hussein, prove that the network's reporting is objective. The network's success has led to the opening of stations in the Middle East that have modeled themselves on Al Jazeera. In 2006 Al Jazeera began operating a parallel station in English, Al Jazeera International.

While arguably its centerpiece, Al Jazeera is but part of a broader set of democratic reforms that Sheikh Hamad has instituted since the beginning of his reign. In an oft-quoted speech at Georgetown University in 1997, he quoted U.S. president John F. Kennedy's statement that the failure to empower peaceful revolutions results in the inevitability of violent ones; accordingly, he has said on numerous occasions that he intends to make the transition toward a parliamentary democracy in which the monarchy will be ceremonial. "We have simply got to reform ourselves. We're living in a modern age. People log on to the Internet. They watch cable TV. You cannot isolate yourself in today's world. And our reforms are progressing well. In a tribal country like Qatar, however, it could take time for everyone to accept what we've done. But change, more change, is coming," he told Weaver in 2000. "Democracy is not foreign to us. My grandfather and my great-grandfather used to have a shura [council] in their tents. All the people came and participated in it. And this is a form of democracy. But when oil came it introduced a whole new culture here. People suddenly found themselves so rich that they didn't know how to respond. Powerful countries came in to exploit the oil, and a lot of middlemen became involved. There was no control, no accountability. And, in the process, a gap developed between the old generation and the new, and the new generation forgot a lot about its traditions and culture. Now we are returning to the concept of the shura in a tent."

In 1999 Qatar held elections for a council that was intended to serve as a transition to a parliament, for whose members all Qataris over 18, male and female, would be allowed to vote. According to many observers, the council, which is limited to consultative duties and is elected every four years (elections took place again in 2003 and 2007), lacks power. Between 2003 and 2005 a far-reaching constitution was drafted; Jamal Yahya, an Egyptian constitutionalist involved in its creation, called the document "one of the most modern in the Arab world," according to *APS Review of Oil Market Trends* (September 17, 2007). "The new charter marks a new beginning for Qatar, as the country embraces democratic reform, gender equality and a new modern judiciary." The document calls for a Majlis al-Shura (consultative council or parliament), with two-thirds of members elected and one-third appointed. The initial election, originally expected in 2005, was delayed several times, and political parties are still outlawed. Critics point to several factors blocking the transition to democracy. One is that Hamad has not democratized the country's energy sector, which is controlled by the unelected government. Another is the reluctance of the influential al-Thani tribe to lose their traditional privileges, as they would in a democracy. Perhaps equally significant is political apathy in Qatar born of economic prosperity. Hamad is "giving the people the right to vote, but people are not asking for it," Abdelaziz Almahmoud, the chief editor of the Internet site of Al Jazeera, told Anthony Shadid for the *Boston Globe* (October 19, 2002). "We're the only people in history where the government is giving power which they hesitate to take." Similarly, Steven A. Cook wrote for the *Weekly Standard* (November 22, 2004), "How much does institutional liberalization really matter in a country with no politics? Competition over the control and distribution of resources is nonexistent. Qatar's wealth is spread liberally among . . . Qatari citizens, giving them the highest per capita income in the world. . . . As a result, most Qatari citizens are content."

Under Hamad Qatar has seen a marked push toward diversification, from oil to natural gas. While the emirate's oil supplies are predicted to be exhausted in the next several decades, it possesses 15 percent of the world's natural-gas reserves, and as the world's largest exporter of liquefied natural gas (LNG), Qatar is well-placed for extended economic prosperity. Doha has perhaps modeled its diversification on that of Dubai, Singapore, and Hong Kong, attempting to become a regional hub for transportation (with Qatar Airways); media (with Al Jazeera); and tourism (with international sporting events including the Asian Games of 2006 and, if Qatar's bid is successful, the 2022 Soccer World Cup). Doha also lifted its international profile by hosting such conferences as the World Trade Organization summit. On the global stage, in 2006 the country became a nonpermanent (two-year) member of the U.N. Security Council. In 2008 and 2009

Hamad again raised Qatar's profile as an emerging regional power broker and mediator. First, in May 2008, he hosted a meeting of Lebanon's bitterly divided politicians and produced an important power-sharing agreement for a country that had been on the brink of civil war. Then, in January 2009, as Israel carried out attacks on Gaza in response to rocket attacks by Hamas (the organization that serves as Gaza's government), Hamad tried to organize an emergency Arab League Summit. While the U.S. allies Egypt and Saudi Arabia boycotted the meeting and offered their own solutions, Hamad was seen as attempting to include all parties, even Hamas, Syria, and Iran. In the spring of 2009, Hamad hosted that year's Arab League Summit.

Central to Sheikh Hamad's long-term reforms, both economic and democratic, are his initiatives in the field of education. Doha's Education City—a tax- and tariff-free zone in Doha where private overseas universities can establish campuses—houses branches of Virginia Commonwealth University, Cornell University, Texas A&M University, Carnegie Mellon, and a think tank sponsored by the RAND Corp., among other institutions. Through the privately run Qatar Foundation, tuition for all Qataris is paid by the government in the hopes that a new, elite corps of citizens will replace the expatriates who, in large part, are overseeing the country's economy. The head of the Qatar Foundation is Hamad's high-profile and influential second wife, Sheikha Moza. "We believe that by encouraging critical thinking and processing of knowledge we are creating full, well-rounded human beings . . . that will enable Qatar to build up its society," Moza told Danna Harman. "You cannot build a healthy society without giving your citizens a sense of ownership. Otherwise, they will not share with you the responsibilities." As Danna Harman wrote, Sheikha Moza is "a royal wife the likes of which the conservative Arab region has never seen before. To begin with, she is seen . . . [and is thus] the first and only ruling spouse here to show herself in public." As Miles wrote, "The royal couple rule almost as a partnership: sometimes she speaks in public with complete authority while he sits in the audience and watches."

The issue of succession in Qatar has received a lot of attention, not least because of the al-Thanis' history of coups and Sheikh Hamad's poor health; chronically overweight, he suffers from diabetes and has undergone several kidney operations. In August 2003 Sheikh Hamad named his fourth son, Sheikh Tamim, as successor, replacing his third son, Sheikh Jassem. His eldest son, Sheikh Mishal, has never been regarded as a suitable heir, and his second, Sheikh Fahd, is believed to adhere to strict Islamist beliefs and is thus considered unable to continue the modernization and reform process. Sheikh Jassem, who made a televised appearance to reassure the public that he was stepping down as crown prince, is said to be uninterested in politics. Sheikh Tamim, on the other hand, is both politically active and strongly supportive of his father's reforms.

Sheikh Hamad bin Khalifa al-Thani, who lives in Doha, has three wives and a reported 27 children.

—M.M.

Suggested Reading: *Boston Globe* A p1 Oct. 19, 2002; *Business Times Singapore* June 22, 2005; *Charlie Rose Show* (on-line) Sep. 29, 2007; *Christian Science Monitor* Features p20 Mar. 6, 2007; *Mideast Mirror* Qatar June 27, 1995; *Middle East Policy* p88 June 2001; *New York Times* (on-line) July 10, 1997; *New Yorker* p54+ Nov. 20, 2000; *Philadelphia Inquirer* International News Mar. 14, 2000; Miles, Hugh. *Al-Jazeera: The Inside Story of the Arab News Channel That Is Challenging the West*, 2005

Ralf-Finn Hestoft-Pool/Getty Images

Shinseki, Eric K.

Nov. 28, 1942– Secretary of the U.S. Department of Veterans Affairs; retired four-star U.S. Army general

Address: Dept. of Veterans Affairs, 810 Vermont Ave., N.W., Washington, DC 20005

In December 2008 President-elect Barack Obama nominated the retired four-star U.S. Army general Eric K. Shinseki, the highest-ranking Asian-American in the history of the U.S. military, to head the U.S. Department of Veterans Affairs. The V.A., as it is often called, handles veterans' benefits, in areas including health care, vocational training, educational assistance, home loans, disability payments, pensions, life insurance, burial arrangements, and survivors' benefits. During the administration of President George W. Bush, Shinseki served as the U.S. Army's chief of staff, the highest-ranking officer, from 1999 until 2003. Many observers believe that Shinseki was forced to retire; in any case, it is clear that he had a different vision for the army than Bush or Donald Rumsfeld, who served as U.S. secretary of defense from 2001 to 2006. A 1965 graduate of the West Point Military Academy, Shinseki was seriously injured twice during the Vietnam War. In the 1970s he served at Fort Shafer in Hawaii, received a master's degree in English literature, and taught English at West Point. In the 1980s and early 1990s, he commanded U.S. forces in Europe and Texas. In 1997 and 1998, during the presidency of Bill Clinton and the armed conflict in the Balkans, Shinseki commanded U.S. forces in Europe and NATO peacekeeping forces. As the army's chief of staff, Peter J. Boyer wrote in a profile of him for the *New Yorker* (July 1, 2002), Shinseki "represented a rare form of the organizational man—the consummate careerist, wholly a product of his institution, yet able to perceive the organization's flaws with an outsider's clarity." During his confirmation hearing for the V.A., in January 2009, Shinseki said that his top priority will be to provide veterans of the wars in Iraq and Afghanistan with the support and services they need. He was sworn in as the nation's seventh secretary of veterans affairs on January 21, 2009.

Eric Ken Shinseki was born on November 28, 1942 in Lihue, on the Hawaiian island of Kauai. His paternal and maternal grandparents immigrated to the U.S. from Japan; his mother and father were native-born citizens of the United States. Not quite a year before Shinseki's birth, on December 7, 1941, the Japanese air force bombed Pearl Harbor, in Hawaii, prompting the United States to enter World War II. The Pearl Harbor attack also led the U.S. to imprison more than 100,000 Japanese men, women, and children who had been living in the United States—including many who were citizens, but apparently not Shinseki's immediate family—in detention camps in the United States for the duration of the war. Some of those Japanese-Americans had been drafted to fight with the U.S. military, but they were not allowed to do so until after the Pearl Harbor bombings. During the war nearly 20,000 Japanese-Americans enlisted. After the Japanese government surrendered, in August 1945, many Japanese-American veterans found themselves treated with respect—far different from the disdain that many non-Japanese had aimed at them after Pearl Harbor. Three of those veterans were Shinseki's uncles, all of whom shared war stories with their nephews. "They really believed in the United States," Shinseki's older brother, Paul, told Peter J. Boyer, "and they tried to explain to [young Eric] why they felt they were obligated to the United States." Those talks made a powerful and lasting impression on the boy.

As Boyer noted, Shinseki "embodied the nineteen-fifties ideal of the straight-arrow, all-American boy." As a Boy Scout he was awarded the God and Country emblem. At Kauai High School he performed well academically and was successful socially. He was elected student-body president, and his girlfriend (now his wife), Patty Yoshinobu, was homecoming queen at her high school. His excellent record enabled him to gain admission to the United States Military Academy, commonly referred to simply as West Point, the name of the town where it is located. Shinseki readily embraced the institution's motto, "Duty, Honor, Country."

After he graduated from West Point, in 1965, as a second lieutenant, Shinseki was sent to fight in Vietnam. "Shinseki's job as a forward observer was to 'hump the field' with his platoon"—that is, conduct reconnaissance missions—"until they encountered the enemy," according to Boyer, "and then to radio back the location coordinates to the artillery battery, which would deliver cannon fire from its howitzers"—short cannons used to fire projectiles. "It was meat-grinder duty." One night after he had been in Vietnam for three months, Shinseki and his infantry company were hit by mortar fire. Wounded in that attack, Shinseki was placed in a helicopter that was to fly him to a medical facility, but on the way it crashed, and he received additional injuries. Leslie Cotten, a sergeant who was also wounded, was with Shinseki during the mortar attack. After Cotten recovered he visited Shinseki in the hospital. "The injuries he'd had were pretty bad," Cotten told Boyer. "Head and chest. It was like the helicopter threw him out and rolled over on him. And the shape he was in, I didn't feel he would make it, and, if he did, he would be in bad shape the rest of his life." It took Shinseki seven months to recover. After attending an advanced armor school and being promoted to captain, Shinseki returned in 1970 to Vietnam, where he was placed in charge of an armored cavalry unit. Two months into his second deployment, Shinseki stepped on a land mine. As a result of the blast, he lost his right foot, among other injuries. This time his recovery, at Tripler Army Medical Center, in Hawaii, took one year.

During his recuperation Shinseki seriously considered leaving the military to pursue a career in law. His stay at the medical center coincided with a particularly difficult time for the military: disturbing, even horrific images of the war in Vietnam were broadcast on U.S. television news shows every day; by the end of 1970, the American death toll had climbed to more than 54,000. Moreover, soldiers were often snubbed or vilified when they returned to civilian life, and officers were leaving the military in large numbers. Shinseki applied to law school but then changed his mind about quitting the army. He served as a personnel staff officer at Fort Shafter, in Hawaii, from 1971 to 1974, then took time off to pursue a master's degree in English literature, from Duke University, in Durham, North

Carolina, which he received in 1976. He taught English at West Point from 1976 to 1978. In 1979 he studied at the Army Command and Staff College, in Fort Leavenworth, Kansas.

From May 1980 to June 1981, Shinseki served as regimental adjutant and then as executive officer of an armored cavalry regiment at Fort Bliss, Texas. Now a colonel, he was later stationed in Germany, where he helped command the American army that stood ready to attack in the event of an invasion by the Soviet Union. Beginning in June 1990 he was deputy chief of staff for support of the Allied Land Forces Southern Europe, in Verona, Italy. In 1992 he became the Third Infantry Division's assistant division commander in Germany. After a year he was named the commanding general of the First Cavalry Division in Fort Hood, Texas. Starting in July 1997 he served as the commanding general of U.S. Army Europe and as commander of Allied Land Forces Central Europe, in Germany. He commanded the NATO peacekeeping force in Bosnia-Herzegovina from 1997 to 1998. From 1998 to 1999 he served as the army's vice chief of staff. In June 1999, having been nominated by President Clinton, Shinseki, by then a four-star general, became the army's chief of staff, thus becoming the highest-ranking officer in the U.S. Army.

Speaking to reporters at the Pentagon on his second day in his new post, Shinseki, "acknowledging that the service was ill prepared to move 24 Apache helicopter gunships and artillery into Albania in the early stages of the Balkans air conflict," as Eric Schmitt wrote for the *New York Times* (June 24, 1999), vowed to "redouble the Army's efforts to become a more agile yet powerful force." His plan, Schmitt reported, was "to make the heavy forces more mobile and the lighter forces more lethal," with the aim of giving the army the ability to go anywhere in the world on short notice and achieve the desired results. During the Cold War—the political conflict between the United States and the Soviet Union that existed for much of the second half of the 20th century—the United States had had a clear idea of who its enemies were and how it would fight if a war were to break out. But with the dissolution of the Soviet Union and the collapse of Communist governments in Eastern Europe, the world had changed radically; the political and social conditions and prevailing ideologies in countries overseas as well as their fighting forces had become less predictable. For that reason it had become more important than ever to maintain a maximally flexible, mobile, and efficient army.

In October 2000 Shinseki unintentionally sparked a big controversy, when he announced that black berets, which until then had been worn only by the elite infantry unit known as the Rangers, would become standard headgear for all soldiers (including those working in such capacities as cooks, clerks, and drivers) starting in 2001. "It will be a symbol of unity, a symbol of Army excellence, a symbol of our values," he said, as quoted by Steven Lee Myers in the *New York Times* (October 22, 2000). Shinseki made that announcement in the course of giving the keynote address at the annual convention of the Association of the United States Army. While some agreed that his plan might promote unity among members of the army, others faulted the change as a superficial gesture that did nothing to ameliorate any of the real problems facing the army; active-duty and retired Rangers objected because the black beret had been something that had to be earned, and they argued that such a badge of honor would be meaningless if everyone had one. Still others complained that berets leave lines on their wearers' foreheads. The controversy was resolved in March 2001, when Shinseki, speaking at the Pentagon, announced that the black-beret plan would go through, but that Rangers would now wear tan berets.

Two months later Shinseki took on a more complicated, substantive problem: the departure from the service of many qualified men and women, even those on their way to higher leadership roles. In a survey of 13,000 soldiers and officers and their family members conducted before the start of the Iraq War, in 2003, two-thirds of the respondents rated as unacceptable the army's quality-of-life standards. Shinseki acknowledged that the army needed to improve the morale of its members and their families. He offered a few proposals, some of which he quickly implemented. The army would rotate its troops only in the summer, for example, so as to cause as little disruption as possible to families with school-age children, and personnel would receive at least six months' notice about upcoming transfers; orders for transfers in less than six months would be issued only after scrupulous review to ensure their necessity. Shinseki also said that he was going to instruct commanders to cut back on weekend training. The chief of staff could not on his own make changes regarding anything involving outlays of money—pay, health or education benefits, or housing, for instance—because they require the approval of Congress.

Among the ideological opponents with whom Shinseki had the most difficulty was Defense Secretary Donald Rumsfeld. Rumsfeld believed that future conflicts would be fought, as Boyer wrote, "mostly from the air and from space, with satellites, sensors, and precision weapons. Implicit in this thinking (though rarely expressed) is a diminished role in the future wars for ground troops." Shinseki did not question the significance of technology for intelligence gathering and other purposes, but he believed, in Boyer's words, that "no technological wizardry can eliminate the risks of close combat, and that even the new, unconventional conflicts that loom will ultimately hinge on the skill, commitment, and courage of the American soldier." Shinseki's ideal army—what he called the "Objective Force"—would be flexible enough to engage not only in conventional warfare but also in urban combat, peacekeeping missions, and operations undertaken on short notice. The appeal, to some, of Rumsfeld's theory, known as Revolution in Military Affairs (RMA), is that if fewer American troops are on the ground, there will be fewer American casualties. However, as Rumsfeld's critics pointed out, an ineffective RMA-style mission could lead to a great number of American casualties and many more casualties among civilians.

In February 2003, a few weeks before the U.S. invasion of Iraq, on March 20, General Shinseki told members of the House Appropriations Committee Subcommittee on Defense that the number of troops needed to stabilize Iraq after the anticipated invasion "could be as high as several hundred thousand." That statement received much media attention. Rumsfeld countered by dismissing Shinseki's estimate as "far off the mark"; he insisted that it was unreasonable to assume that more troops would be needed after the invasion than were used in the invasion itself. In June 2003 Shinseki retired. (In fact, a year earlier Shinseki had known that he would probably be replaced; Rumsfeld had hinted at it publicly.) In his last speech as army chief of staff, Shinseki did not mention Rumsfeld. "You must love those you lead before you can be an effective leader," he said, as quoted by Thom Shanker in the *New York Times* (June 12, 2003). "You can certainly command without that sense of commitment, but you cannot lead without it. And without leadership, command is a hollow experience, a vacuum often filled with mistrust and arrogance."

As the Iraq War dragged on, Shinseki began to be seen as something of a martyr. E. J. Dionne Jr., for example, wrote for his April 18, 2006 *Washington Post* op-ed column that Shinseki "bravely told the truth to Congress before the invasion about how many troops it would take to succeed in Iraq" and that Rumsfeld's treatment of Shinseki "was symptomatic of the contempt of [the Bush] administration toward anyone who dared question its approach." Many similar assessments had appeared in the media by that time.

On December 8, 2008, four weeks after Barack Obama was elected president of the United States, Obama nominated Shinseki to be secretary of the Department of Veterans Affairs. In addition to its traditional job of providing medical care and other benefits to former members of the armed services, the V.A. is currently trying to help the thousands of veterans who have suffered physical and psychological injuries in the Iraq and Afghanistan wars. After Obama announced his nomination of Shinseki, the general was again praised in the press for his foresight regarding Iraq. However, some journalists and military experts maintained that the image of Shinseki as a prophet, hero, or martyr was flawed. Among them was Jamie McIntyre, CNN's senior Pentagon correspondent, who wrote for the CNN Web site (December 8, 2008) that many "have elevated [Shinseki's] now-famous February 2003 testimony to the level of Scripture." McIntyre noted that before the invasion Shinseki had said that the number of mobilized forces was probably enough; that as the army's chief of staff, it was not his job to participate directly in planning for the war; that according to senior officers who were present in pre-war meetings, Shinseki never objected to the plans; and that he never spoke to the media about his concerns. Although Shinseki did not promote his admirers' depiction of him, his detractors pointed out that he had done nothing to squash it. Nevertheless, his critics acknowledged that Shinseki's many years of experience qualified him for the position of secretary of the Veterans Administration. Shinseki assumed his new post on January 21, 2009.

General Shinseki has received many honors, among them the U.S. Distinguished Service Medal, Legion of Merit (with oak-leaf cluster), Bronze Star "V" Device (with two oak-leaf clusters), two Purple Hearts (with oak-leaf cluster), and the NATO Service Medal; he has also been recognized for his service by the governments of Argentina, Brazil, Colombia, France, Germany, Japan, South Korea, Mexico, Poland, Portugal, and Thailand. He is a member of the advisory boards at the Center for Public Leadership at the John F. Kennedy School of Government, at Harvard University, in Cambridge, Massachusetts. He is a member of the Council on Foreign Relations, the Atlantic Council of the United States, and the Association of the United States Army. After 2003 he served as a director of Honeywell International and Ducommun Inc., both military contractors; DC Capital Partners; and BancWest Corp.

Shinseki and his wife, Patty, have a son, Ken, and a daughter, Lori, and five grandchildren.

—D.K.

Suggested Reading: CNN.com Dec. 8, 2008; *Fast Company* p72 Sep. 2004; *New York Times* A p32 June 12, 2003; *New Yorker* p54+ July 1, 2002; *Newsweek* p48 Nov. 22, 1999

Siemionow, Maria

(shem-YON-ov)

May 3, 1950– Microsurgeon

Address: Cleveland Clinic, Main Campus, Mail Code A60, 9500 Euclid Ave., Cleveland, OH 44195

In December 2008 Maria Siemionow led a medical team of 50 to carry out what one of the doctors involved called "the most complex surgical procedure ever performed"—a face transplant. The operation included removing a recently deceased donor's face—skin, eyelids, blood vessels, nerves, and muscles—and attaching it to a disfigured patient, an intricate process that is potentially life-threatening, as the patient's immune system might

J.D. Pooley/Getty Images

Maria Siemionow

reject the new tissue, among other possible complications. Before Siemionow and her team performed the operation, at Cleveland Clinic, in Ohio, only three partial face transplants had been carried out in the world, but none had been as complicated, controversial, or extensive (80 percent of the patient's face was replaced). Siemionow has been affiliated with the Cleveland Clinic since 1995; she is currently the clinic's director of plastic-surgery research and head of microsurgical training in its Department of Microsurgery, where she specializes in hand surgery, microsurgery, peripheral-nerve surgery, transplantation, and microcirculation. Her expressed goal in performing the face transplant was to further the cause of restoring a sense of normality to people whose lives have been marred by disfigurement.

The daughter of Bronislaw and Zofia Kusza, the surgeon was born Maria Kusza on May 3, 1950 in Poznan, Poland, located between the Polish capital, Warsaw, and the German capital, Berlin. She attended college and university in her hometown, graduating in 1974 from the Poznan Medical Academy. She served her residency at hospitals in Poznan and Finland.

During her residency in Finland, Siemionow had an experience that changed her life: she was asked to assist in an operation on a man who had accidentally cut off his hand with a circular saw. During the 15-hour operation, as Siemionow helped reattach the bone, vessels, tendons, and nerves of the hand to the arm, she saw the hand turn from white to pink, which indicated that blood was flowing into it again. "That you could restore to people a part of themselves that had been lost, and actually see it become vital again, was miraculous to me," Siemionow told Michael Mason for the *New York Times* (July 26, 2005). "I have never forgotten that day."

In 1978 Siemionow became the assistant clinical instructor at the Institute for Orthopaedics and Rehabilitation Medicine, in Poznan. Three years later she became a senior assistant lecturer at the institute, where she specialized in hand surgery. In 1985 Siemionow received a Ph.D. degree in microsurgery from the Poznan Medical Academy. She then went to the United States with a hand-surgery fellowship at the Christine Kleinert Institute for Hand and Microsurgery, in Louisville, Kentucky. "I got off the plane in Louisville at the end of June 1985," Siemionow wrote in her memoir, *Transplanting a Face: Notes on a Life in Medicine* (2007). "After hours of breathing the stale air-conditioning of planes and airports, I walked outside under the open sky of bluegrass country and felt as if I were diving into an aquarium left too long in the sun. I was prepared to learn medicine. I was prepared to spend the next several years of my life in America. I was prepared to meet new colleagues and make new friends. I was *not* prepared for a Kentucky summer. I was also unprepared for the pace of American life." Siemionow returned to Poland after completing the fellowship. The last position she held in her native country before immigrating to the U.S., in 1995, was in the Department of Hand and Microsurgery at the Institute for Orthopaedics and Rehabilitation Medicine. After a brief stint as a professor and research director at the University of Utah, in Salt Lake City, also in 1995, Siemionow moved on to the Cleveland Clinic.

In her book Siemionow pointed to the unusual opportunity she has to conduct research and practice medicine at the same time: "The great majority of practicing physicians have little opportunity to pursue research. They're simply too busy. They also lack the funding and facilities to conduct proper investigations. Laboratories and equipment are expensive." Most importantly, she wrote, research "taught me not only to always ask questions but to ask them in a way that suggests a path to an answer." The practical search for answers has defined the surgeon's research for over three decades. In 2004 she began to conduct research on animals in hopes of proving it possible to transplant hands, limbs, and faces without patients' having a permanent dependency on drugs that are meant to help the immune system adjust to the flesh, veins, nerves, skin, and tendons of new body parts. When the health reporter Harlan Spector, writing for the Cleveland *Plain Dealer* (October 31, 2004), visited Siemionow's animal-research lab at the Cleveland Clinic in the fall of 2004, he observed "white rats with brown faces and scalps. One with a half-brown, half-white face; another with a brown limb," which constituted "evidence of successful transplants of body parts. Using sutures one-third the thickness of human hair, Siemionow and the researchers who train under her stitch arteries under microscope[s], in experiments that one day could lead to routine human transplants of limbs, hands and faces." Siemionow "is essentially and uniquely a research worker," Graham Lister, one of Siemionow's mentors at the University of Louisville and the University of Utah, told Spector. "She's a workaholic," Lister added. "She's better now. But she used to be a bit uncomfortable if she wasn't doing three things at once."

Worldwide media reports about Siemionow's most ambitious—and controversial—undertaking began to emerge after late 2004. Siemionow and her team began planning what, as Mason put it, "may be the most shocking medical procedure to occur in decades." A face transplant would involve removing the facial skin, eyelids, blood vessels, nerves, and muscles from a recently deceased donor and connecting them to the skinless face of a patient who has a severe disfigurement. While there are no precise statistics as to how many people have facial disfigurements caused by disease, burns, trauma, accidents, or birth defects, medical experts maintain that the number is significant. Many people suffering from severe facial disfigurement become overwhelmingly self-conscious and sometimes receive harsh looks and comments when they are in public. Some feel so self-conscious, depressed, and defeated that they very rarely—if ever—leave their homes. Facial disfigurement also hampers communication. Even after standard reconstructive face surgery (with skin taken from the victim's own back, buttocks, or thighs), facial expressions such as slight smiles, raised eyebrows, narrowed eyelids, and dozens of others are either impossible to detect or barely discernible; and because body language is such an important element of communication, victims of facial disfigurement are at a further disadvantage. Human faces, Siemionow wrote in her book, "are essential to our communication with the world. It has been estimated that verbal communication conveys only 35 percent of the meaning we're expressing. Our looks, gestures, and body language carry 65 percent of the information received by the person at the other end of the conversation." For those reasons Siemionow worked passionately and diligently to make possible a successful face transplant that in time would look and feel relatively natural.

The world's first partial face transplant was performed in France in 2005 on a woman who lost her cheeks, nose, lips, and chin when she was attacked by her dog. (The operation, albeit controversial, was a success.) Because the operation being proposed by Siemionow was more complicated and risky than any other face transplant that had ever been attempted, she faced some opposition. Some objections were medical: the body's immune system can react violently to a transplanted organ, such as a kidney, and even more intensely to transplanted skin. That led to an ethical objection: is it right to perform an operation that will certainly endanger the health or life of a patient if it is not essential to saving that life? Siemionow and many doctors, nurses, ethicists, philosophers, and psychologists have argued that while a patient with severe facial deformities does not need a face transplant to preserve his or her life, such a patient needs the operation in order to have a quality of life others take for granted.

In December 2008 Siemionow and her team performed a 23-hour operation on a woman whose face had been disfigured by a shotgun blast that left her with only upper eyelids, one eye, forehead, lower lip, and chin and countless bits of shattered bone in her flesh. Siemionow, speaking at a press conference a few days after the operation, said that the woman—who had undergone more than two-dozen earlier, smaller surgeries involving skin grafts and other procedures to repair the damage to her face—had often been taunted and humiliated as a result of her injury. "She was called names," Siemionow said, as quoted by Spector in the *Plain Dealer* (December 18, 2008). "Children were afraid of her. They were running away." In contrast to characters in some Hollywood movies—most notably *Face/Off* (1997), starring John Travolta and Nicolas Cage—the patient did not end up resembling the donor of the facial tissue, because bone structure greatly determines one's appearance; nor did she look as she previously had. Rather, her features became something of a hybrid of two faces, the patient's and the cadaver's. In February 2009, about two months after the operation, the patient was released from the hospital. "She accepted her new face," Siemionow was quoted as saying in the *Los Angeles Times* (February 7, 2009), meaning that the patient's immune system did not reject the new skin, nerves, muscle tissue, and blood vessels. In fact, by February the patient could eat pizza, drink coffee, smell perfume, and purse her lips. The downside, however, is that for the rest of her life, the patient will have to take drugs that suppress her immune system, which, although necessary to prevent the body's rejection of the new tissue, increases risk of infection and cancer. In a prepared statement the woman's siblings thanked the donor, the hospital, and the surgical team led by Siemionow: "We never thought for a moment that our sister would ever have a chance at a normal life again." In May 2009 the patient, Connie Culp, appeared at a press conference; later she was interviewed on *Good Morning America*. The dosages of the immunosuppression drugs that she was taking had been greatly reduced by then. When the nerves and muscles of her new face develop sufficiently, she will undergo additional operations to remove excess tissue and add definition to her jawline.

Since February 2009 Siemionow and her colleagues at the Cleveland Clinic have been caring for a woman from Connecticut whose face and hands were severely damaged when her friend's pet chimpanzee attacked her. A facial transplant will be considered only after the woman undergoes other remedial surgeries, a process expected to take about two years.

Siemionow is currently the secretary of the American Society for Reconstructive Transplantation and the section coordinator of Research for the International Registry on Hand and Composite Tissue Transplantation. She has won numerous awards for her research and publications. In 2001 she received the Folkert Belzer Award in Transplantation, and in 2004 and 2007 she received the James Barrett Brown Award for the best publication in a plastic-surgery journal. She is a member of the American Society of Plastic Surgeons, the American Association of Plastic Surgeons, the American Association for Hand Surgery, the American Society for Reconstructive Microsurgery, the American Society for Peripheral Nerve, the American Society for Reconstructive Transplantation, and the Transplantation Society.

Siemionow and her husband, Wlodzimierz Siemionow, have a son, Krzysztof, a doctor who plans to specialize in spinal injuries.

—D.K.

Suggested Reading: clevelandclinic.org; *Los Angeles Times* A p14 Feb. 7, 2009; *New York Times* A p18 Dec. 18, 2008, (on-line) May 6, 2009; *Slate.com* Dec. 18, 2008; *USA Today* A p1 May 25, 2006; Siemionow, Maria. *Transplanting a Face: Notes on a Life in Medicine*, 2007

Selected Books: *Transplanting a Face: Notes on a Life in Medicine*, 2007

Courtesy of *Sports Illustrated*

Smith, Gary

Oct. 27, 1953– Sports journalist

Address: Sports Illustrated, *Time & Life Bldg., 1271 Ave. of the Americas, New York, NY 10020*

The acclaimed *Sports Illustrated* senior writer Gary Smith told Gary Mullinax for the Wilmington, Delaware, *News Journal* (January 6, 2001) that he does not think of his work as sportswriting. "It's just writing," he said. "Sports happens to be what these people do." Although often described as a sportswriter, Smith has dedicated his career to stories that have more in common with so-called human-interest pieces than with the brief, play-by-play accounts generally associated with sports journalism. Since 1982 he has produced award-winning stories for *Sports Illustrated* about not only the world's most famous athletes but unsung heroes and other obscure figures as well. He possesses an ability to immerse himself completely in his subjects' lives, relating their motivations, flaws, and fears to readers in detailed pieces of as many as 8,000 words—extremely long by today's journalistic standards. "Mr. Smith writes for *Sports Illustrated.* But his work is only tangentially about games, with great appeal for people who wouldn't know a nickel defense from a triangle offense," Richard Perez-Peña wrote for the *New York Times* (September 16, 2008). "Each year he produces four long, earnest feature articles that probe the psyches of wounded people, some of them famous but most obscure, from [the tennis player] Andre Agassi to high school basketball players on an Indian reservation." "Sports offer a fascinating laboratory that lets us see how human beings react," Smith told Bill Thompson for the Charleston, South Carolina, *Post and Courier* (November 11, 2000). "But that just happens to be the laboratory they're in. It wouldn't make much difference whether I was talking to politicians, construction workers or dentists. People have all these things going on in their lives and if you can get to them, that's where the story is."

Smith began his career in the 1970s, covering sporting events for the *Philadelphia Daily News*, the New York *Daily News*, and the short-lived magazine *Inside Sports*. He started contributing his signature stories to *Sports Illustrated* in 1982 and joined the magazine's staff in 1990. Smith produces four or five features a year and is a four-time winner of the National Magazine Award (NMA), often described as the Pulitzer Prize of the magazine industry. He has shed light on the troubled life of the controversial boxer Mike Tyson, explored the disgrace suffered by the college football coach George O'Leary, and revealed the personal struggles of the world-famous golfer Tiger Woods. Smith also profiles subjects outside the realm of mainstream sports; his 1991 piece on the struggle of a young Native American striving for a basketball career won him his first NMA. Other journalists have described Smith as one of the most talented sportswriters in America; Ben Yagoda wrote for slate.com (June 30, 2003), "Smith is not only the best sportswriter in America, he's the best magazine writer in America," and Richard Perez-Peña wrote, "His essays are genuine tear-jerkers and tales of redemption, utterly free of wry detachment. The people he profiles describe the experience as cathartic, some saying that Mr. Smith explains things about them that they had not understood themselves."

The fourth of the nine children of Harry and Jean Smith, Gary Smith was born on October 27, 1953. He was raised in the Heritage Park section of Milltown, Delaware, and attended Dickinson High School, in Wilmington, where his father was an assistant principal. He was a member of the school's basketball team, though not a particularly accomplished one; his coach, Don Albright, jokingly nicknamed him "Lightning." Early on, Smith had an interest in writing about sports, and he has credited his mother, a full-time homemaker when he was growing up, with motivating him and helping him to land his first newspaper job. He told Thompson that when he was 16, his mother called the editor of the Wilmington *News Journal* "to ask what college he would recommend to someone who had an interest in sportswriting, and he said he just happened to have an opening for a part-time clerk in the sports department. 'Send him in,' he told her." Once Smith began to learn the ropes at the paper, he knew that he wanted to pursue sportswriting professionally.

At the paper Smith compiled high-school sports scores and race results from the wire services and wrote stories about local Little League baseball games. Before long he was given his first major assignment for the newspaper—to test the security of area raceways. He did that by entering the Brandywine Raceway, in Pennsylvania, where he was able to roam the facilities and approach the horses, proving that it was possible to affect the outcome of a race by sneaking in to drug or otherwise abuse the animals. He also entered the Delaware Park Racetrack, in Stanton, and what was then Liberty Bell Park Racetrack, in Philadelphia, Pennsylvania. Smith's published stories on his findings caused a stir, and track owners responded by tightening security. Smith worked at the *News Journal* until he was 19, then moved to the *Philadelphia Daily News* to work as a sportswriter while taking classes at La Salle University, in Philadelphia. He graduated in 1975 with a degree in English.

Smith next went to work at the New York *Daily News*, writing for the paper's short-lived "Tonight" edition. "The *Daily News* was probably one of the five best sports sections in America," Smith told Bill Thompson. "There was a great crop of about a dozen guys and I swallowed it up every day. The creativity there was such that I quickly got into that frame of mind. You tried to do something different with it each time." In 1980 he accepted a job at *Inside Sports*, which was owned by *Newsweek*. He told Thompson, "I had two very good years there. [Editor John] Walsh let the writers spread their wings. I worked there until *Newsweek* pulled the plug on the magazine."

In 1982 Smith began to contribute to *Sports Illustrated*. The magazine's editors offered him a staff position; instead, Smith signed a contract to write four long stories per year. "I just wanted to travel, read, think and do a lot of fun stuff," Smith told Thompson. "I felt I could survive on that." His first two stories for the magazine demonstrated his ability to explore the psyches of his subjects and convey their motivations and shortcomings. The first, which appeared in the March 28, 1983 issue, was about the famously hard-working coach of the Philadelphia Eagles football team, Richard "Dick" Vermeil, who resigned from his post in 1982, claiming "burnout." (He later returned to coaching football, accepting posts with the St. Louis Rams and the Kansas City Chiefs.) In the article Smith described Vermeil's habits and idiosyncrasies, writing, "Every morning of his life as a football coach, Dick Vermeil would pull a yellow legal notepad from his office desk and make lists. With a first-grade teacher's neatness, he would write a number, circle it and then print the task to be performed. Exclamation points, as if by a zest all their own, would spring from his pencil at the end of his sentences. . . . It seemed all his life would be like this. List it. Do it. Check it off." Smith's next story, published on April 4, 1983, was on Calvin Griffith, then the owner of the Minnesota Twins baseball team. In the piece Smith noted that Griffith put his baseball team ahead of his family and, as a result—at the age of 71—was living alone. Smith wrote, "Griffith's life is no lonelier than those of many people his age in America. It's the way he combats his loneliness that marks him. . . . There's an American flag planted to the left of the desk and behind that is a statue of Babe Ruth. There are nine pictures of Griffith, including Richard Nixon with Calvin and Dwight Eisenhower with Calvin. Nowhere is there family with Calvin." In a letter from the publisher introducing Smith to the *Sports Illustrated* readership (April 4, 1983), Phillip G. Howlett noted, "Both of the stories Smith has done for us have dealt with . . . misplaced emphasis." Smith told Howlett, "Vermeil is obviously a guy who became consumed. He allowed his own dependence on sports to warp his values. Griffith is a man relying on sports to fill personal needs that should be fulfilled elsewhere: Sports replace family." Smith also said, "I worry when sports become all-consuming, when we begin to depend on them for our sense of community, when we use them as a substitute for real communication. I think sport should be an escape. For the participant, it's a physical canvas upon which one creates, but for the spectator it should be an escape."

In 1983 Smith traveled with the presidential hopeful and former vice president Walter Mondale for an article that was published in *Rolling Stone*. As he continued to write for *Sports Illustrated* during the 1980s, his interview subjects became more high-profile. For the June 23, 1986 issue, he wrote about Ted Turner, the media magnate best known for founding the Cable News Network (CNN). In an article published on March 21, 1988, Smith shed light on the controversial heavyweight boxing champion Mike Tyson, showing readers a side of the athlete usually eclipsed by his often-violent public outbursts. "Smith ended up with a story that uncovered a sensitivity underlying Tyson's public brutality both inside and outside the ring—a brutality that Smith discovers to be Tyson's way of forcing back the fear that comes from growing up poor and unloved on the mean streets of Brooklyn," Gary Mullinax wrote. "You can see Tyson's mixed emotions through the window Smith opens on his youth, when he kept vulnerable pigeons on a roof in Brooklyn." In the passage Mullinax referred to, Smith wrote, "One morning [Tyson] comes out to check his [pigeons]. For a moment their eyes meet, the hawk with its talons caught in the wire mesh of the pigeon coop, the man rigid with surprise. He reaches out, grabs its neck, tears its leg free of the mesh. At last he can mutilate it, cripple it, teach it justice. Instead his hands part. The hawk bursts into the sky."

Smith's April 25, 1988 story focused on the three-time world heavyweight boxing champion Muhammad Ali and the entourage—including his manager, doctor, and bodyguard—who had traveled with him during the height of his career. Smith interviewed each of those men to gain a deep insight into the fighter and paint a highly detailed picture of his life. In a passage on Ali's bodyguard, the former Chicago police officer Howard Patterson, Smith wrote, "Whenever they met, Ali made a game of guessing where Patterson's gun was hidden. One time it might be the Colt Diamondback strapped to his ankle, the next time, the 9-mm automatic tucked under his suit coat; then again, if it was cold enough for an overcoat, the Colt and a .38 would be buried in his pockets. . . . His protective instinct was fierce. At Yankee Stadium on the night of the fight against Ken Norton in 1976, he had a $400 leather suit ripped to shreds while fighting off a mob from the fender of Ali's limo. He turned down four-figure bribes from people desperate to get past his checkpoint in hotel hallways and see Ali. When Ali entered a public bathroom, Patterson went, too. 'If anything at all happened to Muhammad,' he said, 'I figured it would be my fault.'"

Smith is also highly regarded for his illuminating profiles of lesser-known sports figures. He told King Kaufman for Salon.com (September 25, 2008), "Usually it works out best with the unknown people because most of all they give you much more time and access. It's quite rare to get a celebrity to give you the kind of access and time to do what I do." His article from February 18, 1991 on Jonathan Takes Enemy, a Native American basketball player from the Crow tribe who struggled to escape the poverty of his reservation by playing professionally but succumbed to alcohol and depression, is regarded as one of the best examples of Smith's writing about those on the periphery of professional sports. Describing the cycle of alcohol abuse that often spelled disaster for Crow basketball players and derailed the once-promising career of Takes Enemy, Smith wrote, "There was weeping in the land that day. Sobs for . . . Crow stars of the past dead of cirrhosis and suicide and knife-stabbing and a liquor-fogged car wreck. Sobs for the slow deaths occurring every night a mile from Jonathan Takes Enemy's high school, where an entire squad of jump shooters and dunkers and power forwards from the past could be found huddling against the chill and sprawled upon the sidewalks outside the bars on the south side of Hardin [Montana]. Jonathan's predecessors. Jonathan's path-beaters." "Reading [the] story, it doesn't matter that you've never watched Jonathan Takes Enemy or [Crow player] Pretty Weasel on television," Gary Mullinax wrote. "What will matter is how young American Indians in Montana have tried—and too often failed—to use basketball as a way to escape the cycle of poverty." Smith won the first of his National Magazine Awards for the story.

In the January 11, 1993 issue of *Sports Illustrated*, Smith wrote about the North Carolina State University head basketball coach Jim Valvano's losing battle with cancer. His June 24, 1996 feature on the sexual-assault conviction of the star high-school basketball player Ritchie Parker won him his second NMA, and his profile on the acclaimed golfer Tiger Woods, published on December 23, 1996, was included in the anthology *The Best American Sports Writing of the Century* (1999), edited by David Halberstam and Glenn Stout. King Kaufman wrote that the story on Woods is not "so much about golf as it is about a young genius and his relationships, to the father who brought him this far and the world that awaits him." Smith's piece in the December 16, 1996 issue, on a high-school football coach who became the protector of a mentally disabled young man, was later adapted for the film *Radio* (2003), starring Cuba Gooding Jr. and Ed Harris. Smith won his third NMA for a detailed story in the July 26–August 2, 1999 issue on the Texas Christian University football team's 1957 Cotton Bowl victory. He received his fourth NMA for a story published on April 8, 2002 about George O'Leary, a skilled football coach who was hired by the University of Notre Dame but resigned—before he could coach a single game there—after the discovery of exaggerations on his résumé. In the piece Smith was able to re-create the moment of panic O'Leary suffered upon realizing that he had been caught. Smith wrote, "His hand began to work across his face. It was just after midnight. All the consequences, one horror and humiliation after the next, began to spread through him. The joke, the sick joke, was on him. Notre Dame hadn't cared whether he had a master's degree or whether he'd lettered in college football. The lies had been wasted. George O'Leary, the chipmunk trying to pass for a squirrel, when everyone saw him as a lion." Like that story, many of Smith's features have used sports as little more than a jumping-off point to shed light on contemporary issues and universal themes. For example, his story on the Arizona Cardinals football player Patrick Tillman, who was killed in 2004 by friendly fire while serving in the U.S. Army in Afghanistan, explored the mindset of people who are willing to sacrifice themselves for a cause.

"The only injustice," Yagoda wrote about Smith, "is that, outside the small world of editors who vote for the National Magazine Awards and the even smaller subset of *Sports Illustrated* readers who pay attention to bylines, he is a nobody." That assessment notwithstanding, journalists have championed Smith's writing. Bill Thompson wrote, "Of all the sportswriters who (try to) decipher the yin-yang, double-edged nature of sport under the modern media microscope, Smith is among the most respected. And he manages to reduce the whole kaleidoscopic tableau to human scale." Richard Perez-Peña wrote that if "the results [of Smith's work] are sometimes called melodrama, they have more often been praised as the work of perhaps the greatest American magazine writer currently working." Yagoda compared Smith's style to that of the New Journalists, a group of writers—Tom Wolfe and Gay Talese prominent among them—who gained attention beginning in the 1960s by infusing their nonfiction with literary techniques, such as adopting another's point of view. "Pulling that off requires prodigious reportorial stamina, capacious insight, and darned good literary chops," Yagoda noted. In a minor criticism of Smith's work, Yagoda observed that he "does tend to overuse a few devices, like rhetorical questions, deliberately repetitive phrasing, and direct address."

In his features Smith attempts to explore his subjects from multiple perspectives. He told Richard Perez-Peña, "The more they let you in, the more glimpses you get about why they are the way they are, the harder it is to see them all one way. Each person's life is a problem to be solved, and I try to get a grasp of what problem they're solving." He told Bill Thompson for the *Post and Courier* (September 14, 2008) that in order to represent both an objective point of view and the subject's, "You have to have some skills . . . I'm sure classical journalists who are trained by the book have questioned it. But to me it's closer to the truth than classic journalism is. To me, all of us live a subjective life in our head, and then there's the way in which others perceive us. If you don't find a subtle way to convey both in an in-depth story, you're losing truth. You come closer to reality when you have a finger in both those pies, the objective and the subjective. Not that what I'm doing is ultimate reality because we can never get there. But I think it gives me the chance to get closer."

Two collections of Smith's work have been published: *Beyond the Game: The Collected Sportswriting of Gary Smith* (2001) and *Sports Illustrated Going Deep: 20 Classic Sports Stories* (2008). He contributed to *Sports Illustrated: The Golf Book* (2009), a collection of essays and photographs about golf. Although he writes primarily for *Sports Illustrated*, Smith has written about nonathletes for other magazines. His profile of the actor Dustin Hoffman was published in *Rolling Stone*, and one on former U.S. president Jimmy Carter appeared in *Life*.

Smith lives in Charleston, South Carolina, with his wife, Sally, a psychiatrist. The couple have three children, all in college; they adopted the eldest, Gabriella, after a trip to Bolivia in the mid-1980s. Smith volunteers with the Big Brother program and dabbles in writing screenplays. He told Bill Thompson (September 14, 2008) that he writes about sports figures because athletics often brings out the essence of a person. "There are these incredibly revealing things about human nature that are bared by sports . . . ," he said. "The passions are all in play. There's not a lot of holding back. When you have people investing that much of their psychic and physical energy into something, figuring out why they are who they are is always intriguing. And each person really is different."

—W.D.

Suggested Reading: (Charleston, South Carolina) *Post and Courier* E p1 Sep. 14, 2008; *New York Times* (on-line) Sep.15, 2008; *Salon.com* Sep. 5, 2008; (Wilmington, Delaware) *News Journal* E p1 Jan. 6, 2001

Selected Books: *Beyond the Game: The Collected Sportswriting of Gary Smith*, 2001; *Sports Illustrated Going Deep: 20 Classic Sports Stories*, 2008

Soderberg, Alicia M.

Aug. 18, 1977– Astrophysicist

Address: Harvard–Smithsonian Center for Astrophysics, MS-51, 60 Garden St., Cambridge, MA 02138

"I truly won the astronomy lottery," the astrophysicist Alicia M. Soderberg said of the moment on January 9, 2008 when a star in a far-off galaxy exploded "right in front of my eyes." Soderberg, who said those words during an interview with Dennis Overbye for the *New York Times* (May 22, 2008), added, "We caught the whole thing on tape, so to speak." With an estimated 70,000 million million million (70 sextillion) stars in the observable uni-

Courtesy of Princeton University

Alicia M. Soderberg

verse—more than the number of grains of sand on our planet—the explosion of a star, known as a supernova, is not a rare event. But before January 9, 2008, it was unprecedented for anyone to witness such an explosion at the very moment when it could first be seen on Earth—when the light it created millions of light-years earlier reached telescopes on Earth; previously, astronomers had first noticed a new supernova days or weeks after the initial blast might have been visible. The supernova Soderberg observed was SN 2008D, in the constellation Lynx in the galaxy NGC 2770, whose distance from Earth is about 100 million light-years (one light-year is about 5.9 trillion miles). That Soderberg was the person who alerted other astronomers of the birth of that supernova was only partly due to luck; her coup can also be attributed to her expertise regarding supernovae and related phenomena known as X-ray flashes and gamma-ray bursts and, perhaps even more, to her unstinting devotion to unraveling the mysteries of the universe. During her undergraduate years, at Bates College, she secured funds from the National Science Foundation and the Howard Hughes Foundation and a scholarship from the Los Alamos National Laboratory to augment her studies and conduct research at institutions and observatories in Chile, Hawaii, and Puerto Rico, among other places. By the time she graduated from college, in 2000, Soderberg had identified nine new supernovae. When she detected SN 2008D, Soderberg was affiliated with both the Department of Astrophysical Sciences at Princeton University, in New Jersey, and the Carnegie Observatories of the Carnegie Institution for Science, in Pasadena, California. She has since joined the Harvard–Smithsonian Center for Astrophysics, in Cambridge, Massachusetts.

Astronomers have learned that the life spans of stars and the nature of their deaths depend upon their masses. About 99 percent of stars in the observable universe—that is, as much of the universe as we can detect with our most powerful instruments—are in the first size category, about eight times the mass of the sun or smaller. In the process of fusion that occurs in the cores of those and all other stars, hydrogen nuclei fuse into helium nuclei; after billions of years the helium nuclei fuse into carbon nuclei. The fusion process stops at that point in stars in the first size category: the stars die and become white dwarfs—lumps of carbon that are about the size of Earth (but far more dense); as the cores cool the stars get increasingly dim. (Theoretically, their luminosity will eventually end, and they will become black dwarfs. No black dwarf has been detected, because the universe has not existed long enough for a white dwarf to turn into a black dwarf.) Stars in the next size category are more than eight times but less than 40 times the mass of the sun. In such stars, not only the hydrogen and helium nuclei fuse; the carbon nuclei fuse, too, to become iron. That fusion process creates an insurmountable increase in the pull of gravity from the star's core, and it ends with the collapse of the core and then a tremendous shockwave that in turn sparks the enormous explosion that marks the start of the death of the star. The energy emitted in the explosion is equivalent to that of trillions of nuclear bombs set off simultaneously; it produces a blast of luminous X-rays and, an hour or two later, stupendously bright light rays, as pieces of the star shoot forth at speeds as great as 5,000 miles per second. When such stars die they generally become neutron stars. Stars in the third size category are at least 40 times the mass of the sun; their deaths generally result in black holes.

SN 2008D was a star in the second category. The blast of X-rays from SN 2008D was recorded by a satellite, sent into orbit by the National Aeronautics and Space Administration (NASA), that detects X-rays, gamma rays, and ultraviolet light in space. At Soderberg's request, in early January 2008 that satellite, called *Swift*, was aimed at a month-old supernova in NGC 2770 called SN 2007uy. The information about an X-ray blast from another part of that galaxy—which Soderberg, who was giving a lecture at that time, received in the form of an e-mail message—electrified her, partly because it is extremely unusual for one supernova to occur virtually on the heels of another in the same galaxy; on average, supernovae occur once every 100 years in any particular galaxy. The X-ray blast "flooded the satellite's instrument," Seth Borenstein wrote for the Associated Press (May 22, 2008, on-line), its exceptional brightness being similar to that of an image in a digital camera pointed at the sun. Soderberg immediately contacted many of her colleagues worldwide in the field of high-energy astrophysics, who in turn arranged to have both ground-based telescopes and satellites pointed at the site of the blast. Within two hours the supernova became visible as a brilliant light, some 100 billion times brighter than the sun, emitted from radioactive elements released during the explosion. Scientists continued to record data from the site continually for the next month, acquiring much new information about the death throes of a star. One reason why supernovae fascinate astronomers is that most of the chemical elements that are the building blocks of new stars and planets—and all the living organisms that inhabit Earth—are created by supernovae.

The paper in which SN 2008D was first described in the scientific literature, published in *Nature* (May 22, 2008) and titled "An Extremely Luminous X-ray Outburst at the Birth of a Supernova," lists as co-authors the names of 42 astronomers in addition to Soderberg. They include Edo Berger, a postdoctoral research associate at Princeton who was working with her at the time, as well as scientists from England, the Netherlands, Germany, Canada, South Africa, China, Taiwan, Israel, and 10 U.S. states. "It pays to be alert and to follow things up with energy," Robert Kirshner, a supernova specialist at Harvard University and onetime mentor of Soderberg's, observed, as quoted in a Princeton University news release (May 21, 2008, on-line). "Alicia has always been an energetic phenomenon: She has a keen sense of the possibility of finding something new by moving fast to get the data, and SN 2008D is just one more case where this has paid off." Soderberg's honors include the 2009 Annie Jump Cannon Award from the American Astronomical Society, which recognizes "outstanding research and promise for future research."

The only child of Nancy and Jon Soderberg, Alicia Margarita Soderberg was born on August 18, 1977 in Boston, Massachusetts. Raised in Falmouth, on Cape Cod, Alicia Soderberg was encouraged from an early age to explore the world of science. She told *Current Biography*, "My parents always emphasized science and academics in general. There was never an emphasis on social status, just a constant push to succeed academically. This was true not just of my parents but also of Falmouth in general. . . . There were always very bright professors teaching our physical science classes and lots of opportunity to do research in the summer months." As a high-school student, Soderberg spent her summers conducting research on water pollution affecting Cape Cod ponds.

After her graduation from Falmouth High School, in 1995, Soderberg enrolled at Bates College, in Lewiston, Maine, with the assumption that she would aim for a career in environmental science. Instead, she fell in love with astronomy while taking a basic course in that subject and pursued a double major in astronomy and physics. Because Bates College offered few additional astronomy classes, Soderberg spent three academic terms at other institutions, including the Harvard Smithsonian Center for Astrophysics; Kitt Peak National Observatory, in Tucson, Arizona; Cerro Tololo Inter-American Observatory, in Chile; Cornell University's Arecibo Observatory, in Puerto Rico; Los Alamos National Laboratory, in New Mexico; and the Canada-France Hawaii Telescope and the Keck Observatory, on Mauna Kea, Hawaii. She focused at various times on gamma-ray bursts and binary stars in globular clusters and searched for evidence of water in certain asteroids. Her studies at Harvard were funded by two consecutive grants from the National Science Foundation, in a program called Research Experience for Undergraduates; at Los Alamos a United States Department of Energy grant assisted her. Soderberg identified nine supernovae previously undetected by astronomers; as a college senior she became one of the first human beings to see the most distant supernova recorded up to that point. Her determination and perspicacity impressed the leader of the supernova research group, Brian Schmidt, who told Meredith Gold for the *Portland (Maine) Press Herald* (December 26, 1999), "Discovering supernovae requires one to remain organized and focused for several 20-hour work days in a row, something Alicia can do as well as any of the team's scientists. Very few students are given opportunities like this. Alicia has made the most of them by proving herself a hard worker, finding her own funding and asking the right questions of the right people." Guided by Eric R. Wollman, a Bates professor of physics and astronomy, Soderberg wrote a senior thesis entitled "The Efficiency Rate of Type Ia Supernova Searches." She earned a B.S. degree, magna cum laude, from Bates in 2000.

The following year Soderberg completed an M.S. degree in applied mathematics at Churchill College, the University of Cambridge, in England. She then entered a Ph.D. program in astrophysics at the California Institute of Technology (Caltech), in Pasadena. While there she helped to debunk the commonly held belief in the scientific community that X-ray flashes are ancient gamma-ray bursts or stars exploding in the early universe, detectable only in recent years because of their distance from Earth. She and her thesis adviser, Shrinivas R. Kulkarni, showed that the X-ray flashes originated in modern times in various galaxies. On December 3, 2003 Soderberg observed a cosmic explosion of a kind never before seen, one more powerful than a supernova but fainter than a gamma-ray burst. Until then supernovae and gamma-ray bursts were the only types of cosmic explosions known to accompany the deaths of stars. The burst observed by Soderberg, which became known as GRB031203, appeared in the constellation Puppis, approximately 1.6 billion light-years from Earth. Soderberg earned a Ph.D. degree in 2007. Her doctoral thesis, titled "The Many Facets of Cosmic Explosions," is available as a paperback from Universal Publishers and on-line booksellers.

Upon completion of her graduate studies, Soderberg won a NASA Hubble fellowship and the Carnegie-Princeton postdoctoral fellowship. (She won but declined to accept four others, as listed on her curriculum vitae.) She conducted research in association with the Princeton University Department of Astrophysics and the Carnegie Observatories of the Carnegie Institution for Science; the latter include, in California, the Giant Magellan telescope and two Magellan telescopes and, in Chile, the duPont and Swope telescopes. In addition to ground-based telescopes in several continents, she made use of NASA's *Swift* satellite: in January 2008 Neils Gehrels of NASA, who headed the team that managed *Swift*, agreed to Soderberg's request to focus the satellite's instruments on the month-old supernova SN 2007uy in the spiral galaxy NGC 2770. Edo Berger, whom Soderberg was supervising at Princeton, was monitoring the data from *Swift* on January 9, 2008 while Soderberg was giving a lecture when he suddenly noticed an X-ray burst in another part of the galaxy. Berger immediately notified Soderberg, who quickly informed many scientists in the U.S. and overseas. They in turn commandeered ground-based telescopes and the Hubble space telescope to focus on the new supernova, thus making possible recordings of the entire death of the star. "For years we have dreamed of seeing a star just as it was exploding," Soderberg said during a teleconference with media representatives, as widely quoted on the Internet, "but actually finding one is a once in a lifetime event. This newly born supernova is going to be the Rosetta stone of supernova studies for years to come." (The Rosetta stone made possible the interpretation of Egyptian hieroglyphics in the early 19th century.) "We were in the right place, at the right time, with the right telescope on January 9 and witnessed history," Soderberg said, as quoted in *Space Daily* (May 26, 2008, on-line). "Thanks to the unique capabilities of the *Swift* satellite and the rapid response of the Gemini telescope we were able to observe a star in the act of dying." Neil Gehrels told Lewis Smith for the London *Times* (May 22, 2008, on-line), "This first instance of catching the X-ray signature of stellar death is going to help us fill in a lot of gaps about the properties of massive stars, the birth of neutron stars and black holes, and the impact of supernovae on their environments. We also now know what X-ray pattern to look for. Hopefully we will be able to find many more supernovae at this critical moment" in their evolution.

Soderberg is currently a NASA Hubble postdoctoral fellow at the Institute of Theory and Computation at the Harvard–Smithsonian Center for Astrophysics. Her current work involves mapping the diversity of cataclysmic explosions in stars, discovering as rapidly as possible transient bursts of X-rays, radio waves, and light waves and studying their environments, and automating small telescopes. In 2010 she will join the faculty of Harvard University. In 2009 she earned the Annie Jump Cannon Award from the American Astronomical Society. Recipients of that honor, which is named for a 19th-century American astronomer, are North American female astronomers who earned their doctorates within the last five years.

Soderberg told *Current Biography* that on a typical workday, she analyzes data, writes proposals regarding the allocation of time for telescope use, and reads papers in professional journals. She travels often to use large telescopes, give lectures and seminars, and attend conferences. She lives in Cambridge. "I hope to emphasize that a bit of energy and ambition are the key to success in this field," she told *Current Biography*. "You have to be prepared 24 hours a day, seven days a week for the unexpected discovery of your career. My ultimate accomplishment would be to disprove the currently accepted notion of 'recipe for success.' A bit of hard work and quick thinking can actually be your winning ticket."

—T.O./M.H.

Suggested Reading: Associated Press Worldstream (on-line) May 21, 2008; Harvard-Smithsonian Center for Astrophysics Web site; *National Geographic News* (on-line) May 21, 2008; *New York Times* (on-line) June 2, 2008; *Portland (Maine) Press Herald* B p1 Dec. 26, 1999; Princeton University News (on-line) May 21, 2008; *Scientific American* (on-line) May 21, 2008; *Space Daily* (on-line) May 23, 2008

Solis, Hilda L.

Oct. 20, 1957– Secretary of the U.S. Department of Labor; former U.S. representative from California (Democrat)

Address: U.S. Dept. of Labor, 200 Constitution Ave., N.W., Washington, DC 20210

Hilda L. Solis was sworn into office as the secretary of the U.S. Department of Labor on February 24, 2009, one month after President Barack Obama entered the White House and two months after he nominated her for that position. Before she joined the Obama administration, Solis served for eight years (1992–2000) in the California state legislature and then another eight (2001–09) representing part of Los Angeles County, California, in the U.S. House of Representatives. Among the most liberal members of Congress, Solis was known for her strong support of labor unions and workers' rights. In a statement posted (December 19, 2008) on her now-defunct congressional Web site after her nomination as secretary of labor, Solis promised that, if confirmed, she would try to strengthen unions and expand training programs for workers, particularly in high-growth industries, including so-called green industries, which aim to conserve en-

Ann Ryan-Pool/Getty Images

Hilda L. Solis

ergy or develop energy-efficient products and processes. "We also must enforce federal labor laws and strengthen regulations to protect our nation's workers, such as wage and hour laws, and rules regarding overtime pay and pay discrimination," she said. In 2000 Solis became the first female recipient of the John F. Kennedy Profile in Courage Award, bestowed by the John F. Kennedy Library Foundation in recognition of her efforts to secure workers' rights, minority rights, women's rights, and environmental justice for Californians—that is, ensuring that their environment is free from pollution. "The extraordinary success of Hilda Solis in the California legislature shows the power of one person with vision, ability, dedication, and courage to overcome even the strongest forces of oppression and resistance," U.S. senator Edward M. Kennedy of Massachusetts said during the award ceremony, on May 22, 2000, as quoted on jfklibrary.org. In 2006 Solis was honored with the Walter Kaitz Foundation's Diversity Advocate Award for her advocacy on behalf of underserved and minority communities, and the next year she won the American Public Health Association's Distinguished Public Health Legislator of the Year Award.

The third of seven children—five girls and two boys—Hilda Lucia Solis was born on October 20, 1957 in Los Angeles, California, and grew up in the city of La Puente, in Los Angeles County. Earlier, in his native Mexico, her father, Raul Solis, had been a shop steward for a teamsters' union. After he settled in California, he became active with the International Brotherhood of Teamsters to secure better health-care benefits at the battery-recycling plant where he worked. Solis's mother, Juana (Sequiera) Solis, an immigrant from Nicaragua, worked for a time on an assembly line for the toy company Mattel and was a member of the United Rubber Workers Union. Solis's parents met in the U.S. in a citizenship class. Solis has credited their unions, and the benefits her parents received as members, with enabling her mother and father to enter and remain in the middle class.

From 1977 to 1979, while matriculated at California State Polytechnic University, in San Luis Obispo, Solis worked as an interpreter for the Immigration and Naturalization Service in Los Angeles. She earned a B.A. degree in political science in 1979, becoming the first member of her family to graduate from college. She received her master's degree in public administration from the University of Southern California, in Los Angeles, in 1981. During her graduate-student years, Solis moved to Washington, D.C., and worked (1980–81) as the editor in chief of a newsletter in the Office of Hispanic Affairs under President Jimmy Carter. She served (1981–82) as an analyst in the civil rights division of the Office of Management and Budget under Carter's successor, Ronald Reagan; when she realized the extent to which Carter's policies were being dismantled, she resigned. Back in California, she worked for a short while in 1982 as a field representative for Los Angeles assemblyman Art Torres. Before the end of that year, she became the director of the California Student Opportunity and Access Program, which aimed to help disadvantaged students prepare for college. In 1985 Solis was elected to the Rio Hondo Community College board of trustees, where she served two terms, until 1992, including a stint as president.

In 1992 Solis was elected to the California State Assembly as the representative of the state's 57th Assembly District. Two years later she won election to the California State Senate, becoming the first Hispanic woman to join that body. While representing the 24th Senate District, she was instrumental in the passage, in 1996, of a ballot initiative that raised the minimum wage in California from $4.25 to $5.75. (Earlier, the then-governor, Pete Wilson, had twice vetoed legislation to raise the minimum wage.) She also pushed successfully for legislation that aimed to reduce pollution in poor neighborhoods and wrote several bills designed to lower rates of domestic violence, define spousal rape, and improve women's health. She fought for greater enforcement of anti-sweatshop regulations and succeeded in getting federal funds to open a shelter for abused women in her district, which previously had shelters only for abused animals.

In 2000 Solis ran in the Democratic primary against the incumbent U.S. congressman Matthew G. Martinez, who had held his seat beginning in mid-1983. Since 1993 Martinez had represented California's 31st Congressional District, which lies entirely within the city of Los Angeles and is 70 percent Hispanic. Though Solis was criticized by some of her fellow Democrats for challenging a veteran congressman to further her political career,

Solis persisted in her quest. Among other issues, she attacked Martinez for voting against gun-control measures and for legislation that banned so-called partial-birth abortion (a rarely performed procedure known medically as intact dilation and extraction, or evacuation) even in cases in which the health of the mother was imperiled. Solis won the primary election with 62 percent of the vote. In the general election, she faced three minor-party candidates as well as Martinez, who had changed his registration to Republican; again she triumphed, this time with 79 percent of the ballots cast. (After the 2000 census and a subsequent redistricting, Solis's area became part of the 32d Congressional District.) Solis was reelected by large margins in 2002, 2004, and 2006; in 2008 she ran unopposed.

Solis often referred to her district as "the other Hollywood," far distant economically and socially from the glamorous, moneyed world of cinema. Its residents—Hispanics and Asians comprise 65 and 25 percent of its population, respectively—suffer from insufficient or inadequate housing, a high unemployment rate, and polluted water and air. A landfill 22 stories deep—the largest repository for solid waste west of the Mississippi River—lies directly over the water table in the district. With the White House in Republican hands during her eight years in Congress, and the Senate and House in Republican hands as well for six of those eight years, Solis was repeatedly rebuffed in many of her efforts to improve living and working conditions for her constituents. "I hear a lot about government being too large," she said on the PBS series *NewsHour with Jim Lehrer*, as quoted on pbs.org during Solis's freshman term. "I agree there are areas we can do a better job—make things simpler, eliminate redundancy—[but] sometimes the government has to be there to correct something that was wrong."

A close associate of House Speaker Nancy Pelosi, also of California, Solis served on the House Committee on Energy and Commerce and two of its subcommittees—the Environment and Hazardous Materials Subcommittee, and the Health and Telecommunications Subcommittee. In addition, she sat on the House Committee on Natural Resources and on the House Select Committee on Energy Independence and Global Warming. She was the vice chair of the Democratic Steering and Policy Committee and served as both a senior whip and a regional whip for Southern California. She also served on the Congressional Caucus for Women's Issues, the Democratic Women's Working Group, and the Congressional Hispanic Caucus and for several terms she chaired the last-named caucus's Task Force on Health and the Environment.

During her years in the House, Solis was the only member of Congress on the board of any actively pro-union, pro-labor group—namely, American Rights at Work. That nonprofit organization was devoted in part to pushing for passage of the Employee Free Choice Act, which would "amend the National Labor Relations Act to establish an efficient system to enable employees to form, join, or assist labor organizations [and] to provide for mandatory injunctions for unfair labor practices during organizing efforts," among other purposes, as quoted on-line on thomas.loc.gov, a Library of Congress Web site. The legislation, which Barack Obama sponsored in the U.S. Senate, is often referred to informally as the "card-check" bill, because workers could indicate their desire to join a union simply by filling out a card rather than having to wait for a special secret vote. Robert B. Reich, who served as the secretary of labor under President Bill Clinton, noted for the *Los Angeles Times* (January 26, 2009) that whereas in 1955, more than a third of working people in the U.S. belonged to unions, currently only 8 percent are members, and that workers who try to form a union have only a one in five chance of being successful. Moreover, typical union workers earn 20 percent more than comparable nonunion workers and "are 59% more likely to have employer-provided health insurance than their nonunion counterparts." "The way to get the economy back on track is to boost the purchasing power of the middle class," Reich wrote. "One major way to do this is to expand the percentage of working Americans in unions." In July 2009 several labor-friendly senators dropped the card-check provision of the bill in order to gain the support of moderate Democrats and make the bill filibuster-proof. That provision was replaced with one that banned prolonged unionization campaigns and required speedy union elections, so that management would have less time to pressure workers to vote against unionizing. Union leaders expressed disappointment with the loss of the card-check provision but noted that even without it, the bill included important provisions for labor. (As of late October the legislation had not yet become law.)

Solis was the author of the Green Jobs Act of 2007, which would allocate up to $125 million for new federal and state programs, administered by the U.S. Department of Labor, to train prospective workers for "green-collar" jobs in so-called green industries, which are geared toward greater energy efficiency and the creation of more renewable energy, for example in the construction of buildings and vehicles, the production of electric power, and the search for biofuels. (The act has not yet become law.) "Her work demonstrated her commitment to a socially responsible, clean-energy economy that will create millions of good-paying jobs and save our environment," Van Jones, the executive director of the Ella Baker Center for Human Rights and a founder of the organization Green For All, declared for the *Huffington Post* (December 19, 2008, on-line). Solis also pushed for health-care reforms, and she was staunchly pro-choice.

President-elect Obama's choice of Solis as secretary of the Department of Labor pleased people active in the labor movement, while some members of the business community and some Republican legislators criticized it. Ray Haynes, a Republican former California state senator, described Solis as being "in the pockets of labor," according to Dan Morain and Evelyn Larrubia, writing for the *Los Angeles Times* (January 9, 2009); Randel K. Johnson, a U.S. Chamber of Commerce vice president, remarked to those reporters, "She didn't win our Spirit of Enterprise Award." At her U.S. Senate confirmation hearing, on January 9, 2009, two Republican senators, Orrin G. Hatch of Utah and Johnny Isakson of Georgia, expressed their concern that Solis would favor labor in conflicts between labor and management and their skepticism of the "card-check" bill. Solis sidestepped that issue during the hearing by saying that since she had not discussed the bill with President-elect Obama and thus could not voice his coming administration's stand on it, she would not comment about it. In early February the Senate postponed a vote on Solis's nomination, after reports surfaced about tax liens against her husband's auto-repair business. Solis was confirmed as labor secretary on February 24, 2009, after Senate Republicans assured Democrats that they would not filibuster to prevent her nomination; she was sworn in that same evening.

In fiscal year 2008 the Department of Labor (DOL) had almost 17,000 full-time employees and a budget of $10.5 billion. According to its Web site, the DOL "fosters and promotes the welfare of the job seekers, wage earners, and retirees of the United States by improving their working conditions, advancing their opportunities for profitable employment, protecting their retirement and health care benefits, helping employers find workers, strengthening free collective bargaining, and tracking changes in employment, prices, and other national economic measurements. In carrying out this mission, the Department administers a variety of Federal labor laws including those that guarantee workers' rights to safe and healthful working conditions; a minimum hourly wage and overtime pay; freedom from employment discrimination; unemployment insurance; and other income support." Among its divisions are the Occupational Safety and Health Administration (commonly referred to as OSHA); the Women's Bureau; the Employment and Training Administration and another such administration specifically for veterans; the Office of Disability Employment Policy; the Mine Safety and Health Administration; and the Bureau of Labor Statistics.

Solis took office during a time of rising and widespread unemployment due to the worldwide financial crisis. In her first major speech as secretary, at the Greater Bethel AME Church in Miami, Florida, Solis announced that she intended to be more aggressive in enforcing workplace-protection laws than had the administration of President George W. Bush, declaring, "You can rest assured that there is a new sheriff in town," according to the *New York Times* (March 8, 2009, on-line). That same month the Government Accountability Office released a report that revealed widespread mishandling of cases by the Labor Department's Wage and Hour Division, which enforces laws regarding the minimum wage, overtime pay, and related matters. In response to that report, Solis announced plans to hire 250 additional labor and wage investigators—increasing the division's staff by about one-third—and to conduct a national outreach program to educate workers and employers about labor laws. In late May 2009, in an action applauded by the United Farm Workers union, she suspended regulations adopted by the Bush administration that placed restrictions on guest-worker programs for farms. In late June, after the Labor Department made public the information that 9.5 percent of the nation's workforce was unemployed, Solis noted that not all of the money allocated by Congress to stimulate the economy had been distributed yet. The stimulus bill, known formally as the American Recovery and Reinvestment Act of 2009, provided funds to extend the periods during which individuals can receive unemployment insurance, increased payments to the unemployed, and included other measures aimed at helping those who were out of work. A study of labor violations affecting low-wage workers (dated September 2009 and financed by the Ford, Joyce, Haynes and Russell Sage Foundations) found that in the first half of 2008, low-wage workers had frequently been paid less than the minimum wage, had often been denied overtime pay, and in many cases had been pressured by their employers to refrain from filing for worker's-compensation payments after they had been injured at work. "There is no excuse for the disregard of federal labor standards—especially those designated to protect the neediest among us," Solis declared in response to those findings, as quoted by the *New York Times* (September 2, 2009, on-line). "Today's report clearly shows we still have a major task before us."

Rob Hurtt, a Republican who served with Solis on the California State Senate Labor Committee, said of her to Dan Morain and Evelyn Larrubia, "We obviously didn't see eye to eye. But she was respectful. I'll give her credit; she was a very hard worker and she knew her stuff." Tom Hayden, another colleague of hers in the state Senate, told Morain and Larrubia that with her toughness and idealism, Solis "can get a lot done—with a smile." Described as genial and soft-spoken, Solis enjoys salsa dancing in her scarce leisure time. She has been married since 1982 to Sam H. Sayyad. The couple live in El Monte, in Los Angeles County. They have no children.

—M.E.R.

Suggested Reading: *California Journal Weekly* Jan. 23, 1995, Dec. 1, 2001; *Congressional Quarterly* (on-line) Dec. 18, 2008; *Los Angeles Times* A p1+ Jan. 9, 2009; *New York Times* (on-line) Dec. 19, 2008; *Who's Who in America*

Courtesy of Human Rights Campaign

Solmonese, Joe

Nov. 27, 1964– Gay-rights activist; president of Human Rights Campaign

Address: Human Rights Campaign, 1640 Rhode Island Ave., Washington, DC 20036

In 2005 Joe Solmonese became president of the Human Rights Campaign (HRC), an organization representing the lesbian, gay, bisexual, and transgender (LGBT) communities. He has since built that Washington, D.C.–based political action committee (PAC) into one of the largest and most successful lobbying groups in the U.S., one that has been at the forefront of the fight for legal recognition of same-sex marriage. "This is a long-term struggle," Solmonese told Don Aucoin for the *Boston Globe* (April 7, 2005). "It's going to take a lot of back and forth. We're going to take three steps forward and two steps back. A lot." HRC is the nation's largest LGBT-rights organization, with roughly 750,000 members and a budget of over $30 million. Since its formation, in 1980, it has invested in the campaigns of numerous pro-LGBT-rights politicians and spoken out against antigay discrimination in society and the workplace. Its efforts with regard to same-sex marriage have pitted the organization against religious groups and conservatives who believe that families with same-sex parents are damaging to children and an affront to the institution of marriage. According to the group's Web site, HRC "works to secure equal rights for LGBT individuals and families at the federal and state levels by lobbying elected officials, mobilizing grassroots supporters, educating Americans, investing strategically to elect fair-minded officials, and partnering with other LGBT organizations."

Mary Breslauer, a former board member of HRC, told Aucoin that Solmonese "has one of the greatest gifts you can have in politics, and that's understanding that it's all about relationships, that the conversation with the receptionist or the driver or the field director can be just as important as the conversation with the candidate. Because he really focuses on you, you really focus on him. It's a kind of contagious quality he has." Prior to his work with HRC, Solmonese was the chief executive officer of EMILY's List, a PAC dedicated to supporting the election of pro-choice female candidates to all levels of government. From 2006 to 2009 he hosted, with Breslauer, the XM Satellite Radio show *The Agenda with Joe Solmonese*, on which LGBT issues were discussed.

One of three children, Joe Solmonese was born on November 27, 1964 and grew up in the town of Attleboro, Massachusetts. His parents, both schoolteachers, inspired his interest in politics; in high school he served on the student council and became vice president of his class. (He also ran track.) Solmonese attended Boston University (BU), where he majored in communications. For several summers during his years there, he worked as an intern in the scheduling office of then–Massachusetts governor Michael Dukakis. (Dukakis, the 1988 Democratic presidential nominee, lost to the Republican George H. W. Bush in that year's general election.) After graduating with a B.S. degree, in 1987, Solmonese became a full-time staff member in Dukakis's office. Before leaving his job there, he was invited to a lunch with the governor, who advised him to remain in public service. "He is one of the most honest, decent people I know," Solmonese told Aucoin about Dukakis. "There are legions of people in my generation who are still in politics because he didn't just inspire us to stay in public service, he directed us to stay in public service, that was all you were supposed to do."

Solmonese came out as gay when he was in his early 20s. His decision to do so coincided with the height of the AIDS (Acquired Immune Deficiency Syndrome) epidemic; a sexually transmitted disease that severely weakens the body's immune system and leaves victims vulnerable to potentially fatal infections, AIDS proved devastating to the gay community. "There is that on your consciousness, and you're coming out," Solmonese told Aucoin. "It compounded everything that you experienced coming out." He told Aucoin that the AIDS epidemic brought the gay community closer together. In 1990 Solmonese joined the successful reelection campaign of U.S. representative Barney Frank of Massachusetts, one of the first openly gay members of Congress. In that capacity Solmonese learned the basics of campaigning—analyzing polls, building a donor base, finding supporters, and reaching out to voters.

Solmonese next worked as a strategist for a succession of political figures. In 1993 he served as a campaign worker for Dawn Clark Netsch, then a candidate for governor of Illinois. Solmonese was impressed by Netsch's well-financed campaign and learned that she had received a substantial amount of funding from EMILY's List. At the time the organization's executive director was Mary Beth Cahill, a former member of the Dukakis campaign, who had persuaded Solmonese to work for Frank; when Cahill learned of Solmonese's interest in EMILY's List, she invited him to join the group as deputy political director. In 1998 he became the group's chief of staff, and in 2003 he was named chief executive officer. ("EMILY" is an acronym for "Early Money Is Like Yeast," a reference to the fact that yeast makes bread rise; similarly, early funding of a political campaign raises a candidate's visibility and chances of victory.) The organization was founded by 25 women in 1985, at a time when there were few Democratic women in the U.S. House and Senate. The founders, including the current president, Ellen R. Malcolm, set up EMILY's List as a donor network through which members send campaign money to pro-choice candidates selected by the organization. Today EMILY's List boasts more than 100,000 members. According to its Web site, the organization "is committed to a three-pronged strategy to elect pro-choice Democratic women: recruiting and funding viable women candidates; helping them build and run effective campaign organizations; and mobilizing women voters to help elect progressive candidates across the nation."

Initially EMILY's List supported only candidates for the U.S. Congress. After Solmonese became chief of staff, the group shifted its approach. In 2000 the number of women serving in state legislatures declined for the first time in 30 years, and EMILY's List responded by launching its Political Opportunity Program (POP), which supports progressive female candidates on the state and local levels. Solmonese told Shaun Bugg for the Washington, D.C., *Metro Weekly* (May 12, 2005, on-line), "We realized that the work of electing a woman to the United States Senate has to begin long before the 24-month election cycle. So we went about electing women to the state senate or house, or the mayor's office, or the county commission. We strengthened them by building their political operation so that when a U.S. Senate seat opened up the powers that be in that state said 'She's the one who should go.' So when people asked, 'Is that a policy shift? Are you helping women get elected to the state legislature instead of the U.S. Senate?' No. It's just another way of getting women elected to the U.S. Senate."

Solmonese received mixed responses to his work as the CEO of EMILY's List. During his tenure, in which he emphasized outreach to "heartland and mainstream voters," as Aucoin reported, membership tripled and fund-raising records were broken. In 2003 EMILY's List had two noteworthy victories: Kamala Harris became the first African-American district attorney in California, and Annise Parker was the first openly gay candidate to win a city-wide election in Houston, Texas, where she was elected controller. EMILY's List was criticized, however, for supporting the Democrat Inez Tenenbaum for a seat in Congress in 2004 (she lost to the Republican Jim DeMint). Although pro-choice, Tenenbaum was opposed to same-sex marriage, and when EMILY's List recommended her as a choice to its membership, several gay-rights groups objected. In defense of his organization's support of Tenenbaum, Solmonese told Chad Graham for the *advocate.com* (March 10, 2005), "It's Emily's List's mission to elect pro-choice Democratic women. And I had been charged by the 100,000 members of Emily's List to uphold that mission." In 2004 results were mixed for candidates supported by the organization; many lost state Senate races in Florida, South Carolina, and Missouri. Still, out of the 225 candidates the organization endorsed that year, 140 won seats. All of the incumbents backed by the organization won reelection, including the U.S. senators Barbara Boxer of California, Patty Murray of Washington, and Barbara Mikulski of Maryland. Delaware's governor, Ruth Ann Minner, was reelected, and Christine Gregoire was elected to her first term as governor of Washington.

In the spring of 2005, after 12 years with EMILY's List, Solmonese was named president of the Human Rights Campaign, replacing another Massachusetts native, Cheryl Jacques. He took over the group at a tumultuous time in the gay-rights movement—when, as David Crary put it for the Associated Press (March 17, 2005), the same-sex-marriage debate rivaled the controversy over abortion "for volatility and virulence." The same-sex-marriage debate first came to widespread attention in the U.S. in 1993, with the case of *Baehr v. Lewin*, in which three homosexual couples challenged Hawaii's marriage law. The law had allowed only for heterosexual marriages, but the Supreme Court of Hawaii ruled that a compelling reason was needed to deny the extension of marriage rights to homosexual couples. The Hawaii state legislature soon overruled the court. In 1996 the U.S. Congress passed and President Bill Clinton signed the Defense of Marriage Act, which forbade the federal government from recognizing homosexual unions. (In 1998 Clinton signed an executive order banning the federal government from discriminating in employment on the basis of sexual orientation.) California passed a domestic-partnership policy in 1999, allowing homosexual couples to obtain many of the same benefits as married couples. In 2000 Vermont became the first state to allow civil unions, which grant same-sex partners the full legal benefits of marriage. Three years later the U.S. Supreme Court struck down all remaining laws barring gay sex, which was illegal in 13 states at the time. Massachusetts became the first state to legalize gay marriage, in 2004. Although the California

Supreme Court legalized same-sex marriage in May 2008, the ruling was overturned in November of that year when a majority of California voters favored a ballot measure known as Proposition 8.

Solmonese assumed his role as president of HRC in April 2005, with a salary of $225,000 per year. He began his tenure by traveling the country to meet with various community and religious leaders—gay and straight—to gauge how people felt about the gay-rights movement and same-sex marriage. He also spoke with corporate leaders from companies including Ford, Sprint, Hallmark, and Coca-Cola. At a news conference in June, Solmonese said of his travels, as quoted by Political Transcript Wire (June 6, 2005), "From Ford in Detroit to Sprint in Kansas City, it was reinforced to me that the American workplace is really a microcosm of America generally, because like no other part of American life, it's in the American workplace where strangers get to know each other and realize that we're united by our shared hopes and dreams and not divided by stereotypes and stigma." He noted that since 2002, when HRC began rating companies based on their LGBT policies, "over 8,000 employers now offer domestic partner benefits. That's a 13 percent increase from [2004]. Eighty-two percent of Fortune 500 companies include sexual orientation in their nondiscrimination policies. That's a 4 percent increase over [2004]." Nonetheless, he conceded that there was still much work to do. A year later Solmonese observed still more progress in HRC's efforts to affect the way corporations treat LGBT employees. He told Bugg in another article for the *Metro Weekly* (March 16, 2006), "A year ago we had 66 companies with a score of 100 [on HRC's corporate index]. This year we gave 104 companies a score of 100. That means that 5.6 million people are now working in a place where [everyone is] treated with the same benefits, same respect, same access to opportunity."

In 2006 HRC and XM Satellite Radio partnered to produce the show *The Agenda with Joe Solmonese*, which featured discussions of politics and culture, interviews with politicians and other celebrity guests, and calls from listeners. "This is a unique opportunity to engage millions of Americans in a real conversation about what it means to be gay, lesbian, bisexual, and transgender today," Solmonese said in a press release published by PR Newswire (June 8, 2006). The show was co-hosted by Mary Breslauer, a former HRC board member. Noteworthy guests included Democratic U.S. senator Edward M. Kennedy; Gene Robinson, an openly gay Episcopal bishop; and journalists from the *New York Times* and the *Washington Post*. The show proved so popular that by 2008 it had moved from Channel 120 on XM to Channel 155, a lifestyle XM channel that also features popular shows including *Good Morning America Radio* and *Dr. Laura Schlessinger*. The final installment of *The Agenda* aired on January 22, 2009.

In 2007 Solmonese announced further progress in HRC's work with corporations. "This year, more major American businesses received a perfect rating for equality and fairness than in any other year," he said, as quoted in *Health & Medicine Week* (February 12, 2007). "At an ever increasing pace, corporate executives understand that supporting their gay, lesbian, bisexual, and transgender employees is not only the right thing to do but it is also good for business. The findings in this year's report sends a clear message that the American workplace is rapidly becoming more inclusive of diversity." That year HRC also appointed its first chief diversity officer, Cuc Vu, whose mission is to establish relationships with LGBT communities of color; she reports directly to Solmonese. In August 2007 Solmonese served on a panel that questioned that year's Democratic presidential hopefuls on LGBT issues.

HRC suffered a blow in 2007 with regard to legislation targeting hate crimes against gay and transgender individuals—a proposed measure known informally as the Matthew Shepard Hate Crimes Prevention Act. HRC had been lobbying tirelessly for the measure, calling on organization members to encourage their congressional representatives to support it. Democrats in the Senate had hoped to pass the hate-crimes measure by attaching it to the National Defense Authorization Act (NDAA), which President George W. Bush was expected to sign. However, the hate-crimes component was abandoned when House Democrats threatened to vote against the bill because it lent support to Bush's policies regarding the war in Iraq. "Today's decision is deeply disappointing, especially given the historic passage of hate crimes legislation through both Houses of Congress this year," Solmonese said, as quoted by Lou Chibbaro Jr. for the *Washington Blade* (December 6, 2007, on-line). "However, we are not giving up on efforts to find another legislative vehicle, in the second half of this Congress, to move the Matthew Shepard Act." In 2008 President Barack Obama, Bush's successor, pledged to sign the act if Congress approved it. Congress did so the following year, and on October 28, 2009, Obama signed into law the renamed Matthew Shepard and James Byrd, Jr. Hate Crimes Prevention Act. Named for two victims of separate hate crimes, the act was appended to a $680 billion defense-spending bill (which was signed in a separate ceremony).

HRC has received criticism from the transgender community over its reluctance to support a provision for the protection of transgender individuals in the Employment Non-Discrimination Act (ENDA). Although HRC initially said that it would support the ENDA only if it included transgender protections, the organization continued to support the act after those protections were removed in 2007 by Democrats who were concerned that they would hamper ENDA's passage in the House. Solmonese told Cynthia Laird for the *Bay Area Reporter* (January 10, 2008) that HRC continued to support ENDA because abandoning it might have kept the measure from reaching a vote until 2011. "That's how I evaluated it," he said. "We are very much at the beginning of the ENDA process. In spite of all the criticism, we started a process. Now, we build on that in a more expeditious way than if we walked away." The bill has yet to pass the Senate, but if it does, Obama is expected to sign it. HRC has pledged to continue to fight for a bill protecting transgender individuals.

HRC endorsed Obama for president in 2008, citing his commitment to civil rights for the LGBT community. Solmonese said in a press release on the HRC Web site (June 6, 2008), "Senator Obama has consistently shown that he understands, as we do, that LGBT rights are civil rights, and human rights." Although he does not support same-sex marriage, Obama opposes a constitutional ban on it. He supports civil unions, hate-crimes legislation, the repeal of the military's controversial "Don't Ask, Don't Tell" policy, and expanded funding for HIV/AIDS research. In December 2008, the month after the election, HRC's support for the victorious Obama flagged, when the president-elect's team announced the selection of Rick Warren, pastor of the Saddleback Church in Lake Forest, California, to give the invocation at the presidential inauguration in January 2009. Warren, a vocal opponent of same-sex marriage, was a supporter of Proposition 8. Although Obama's team also chose the LGBT-friendly Reverend Joseph E. Lowery to close the ceremony, many in the LGBT community were offended. In an opinion piece in the *Washington Post* (December 19, 2008, on-line), Solmonese wrote, "It is difficult to comprehend how our president-elect, who has been so spot on in nearly every political move and gesture, could fail to grasp the symbolism of inviting an anti-gay theologian to deliver his inaugural invocation." On December 17 HRC sent a letter to Obama, signed by Solmonese and available on the HRC Web site, which read, "Our loss in California over the passage of Proposition 8, which stripped loving, committed same-sex couples of their given legal right to marry, is the greatest loss our community has faced in 40 years. And by inviting Rick Warren to your inauguration, you have tarnished the view that gay, lesbian, bisexual and transgender Americans have a place at your table."

Despite his criticism of Obama, Solmonese has continued to support the president and believes he will take the steps necessary to help the LGBT community achieve full equality. In an October 2009 message, Solmonese predicted to HRC supporters that on the last day of the president's term, the LGBT community would be proud of the accomplishments it had made under Obama. Some believed Solmonese meant that the LGBT should be content to wait for change; in response to that charge, Solmonese wrote, in an HRC weekly update on Facebook.com (October 18, 2009), "The fact is, we've got an agenda. It includes repealing Don't Ask, Don't Tell, passing an inclusive ENDA (Employment Non-Discrimination Act), repealing DOMA (Defense of Marriage Act), and getting real protections for families and people with HIV/AIDS. How do we make all this happen? We have to pass laws. When it comes to changing the lives of LGBT Americans, that's the name of the game. Whatever the president does or doesn't say, whatever I say and however anyone decides to read it, there is only one way to pass a law: secure a majority of votes in the House and a filibuster-proof 60 votes in the Senate." Solmonese added, correctly predicting that the Matthew Shepard and James Byrd, Jr. Hate Crimes Prevention Act would become law during the Obama administration, "This is a lot easier said than done, but one thing is certain: when an LGBT bill gets to the Oval Office, this president will sign it."

In 2005 Solmonese launched the Religion and Faith Program, which provides resources to religious LGBT individuals. He has overseen the Campaign College program, which selects 40 college-age individuals to attend a campaign-training seminar in Washington, D.C., and work with the HRC on a campaign. He is also credited with personally overseeing many efforts to support pro-gay congressional candidates, including the Democrat Bob Casey, who defeated the incumbent Republican senator Rick Santorum of Pennsylvania, a particularly outspoken opponent of gay rights, in 2006. HRC raised over $350,000 and committed over 200 volunteers to Casey's campaign.

Solmonese, who lives in Washington, D.C., told Graham about HRC, "You know, in everything that we do, we're working toward marriage. We're working toward equality and marriage. . . . It is a thread that runs through everything that we do."

—W.D.

Suggested Reading: Associated Press Online Mar. 17, 2005; *Boston Globe* D p1 Apr. 7, 2005; hrc.org; (Washington, D.C.) *Metro Weekly* (online) May 12, 2005

Sotomayor, Sonia

(soh-toh-my-YOHR, SOHN-yah)

June 25, 1954– U.S. Supreme Court justice

Address: U.S. Supreme Court, Washington, DC 20543

On May 26, 2009 President Barack Obama announced his nomination of the federal judge Sonia Sotomayor to the U.S. Supreme Court. Confirmed by the Senate in a 68–31 vote in August, Sotomayor is the first Hispanic member of the nation's highest judicial body. Born to Puerto Rican parents in the New York City borough of the Bronx, raised in low-income housing projects prior to her education at Princeton and Yale universities, Sotomayor has built a career that is inspiring to many Americans.

Jewel Samad/AFP/Getty Images

Sonia Sotomayor

The third woman to serve on the Supreme Court in its 220-year history, Sotomayor fills the vacancy left by Justice David Souter, whose retirement was effective at the end of the court's term on June 29, 2009. In his remarks regarding his selection of Sotomayor, President Obama spoke of her accomplishments and struggles. "Over a distinguished career that spans three decades, Judge Sotomayor has worked at almost every level of our judicial system, providing her with a depth of experience and a breadth of perspective that will be invaluable as a Supreme Court justice. . . . Along the way [Sotomayor has] faced down barriers, overcome the odds, lived out the American dream that brought her parents here so long ago," he said. "And even as she has accomplished so much in her life, she has never forgotten where she began, never lost touch with the community that supported her. What Sonia will bring to the Court, then, is not only the knowledge and experience acquired over [the] course of a brilliant legal career, but the wisdom accumulated from an inspiring life's journey."

Sonia Maria Sotomayor was born June 25, 1954 in the Bronx. She has a younger brother, Juan. Her parents, Juan Luis and Celina (Baez) Sotomayor, were from Puerto Rico. Celina had left that U.S. territory at 17, when she signed up with the Women's Army Corps (WAC), a branch of the U.S. Army, during World War II. After her discharge Celina arrived in New York City, where she met and married Juan Luis. The couple moved into the Bronxdale Houses, a public-housing complex in the East Bronx, home to a large Puerto Rican population. Juan Luis, who spoke only Spanish and had a third-grade education, went to work as a tool-and-die maker while Celina completed her graduate-equivalency diploma (G.E.D.). Celina later took a job as a telephone operator at Prospect Hospital, a private facility in the South Bronx.

When Sonia Sotomayor was eight years old, she was diagnosed with type I diabetes. The following year her father died of heart disease, leaving her mother to raise Sonia and her brother alone. Afterward Celina Sotomayor juggled child care, a full-time job, and college courses to become a registered nurse. She eventually got a job as a nurse at a methadone clinic. On a modest salary she sent Sotomayor and her brother to Catholic schools in hopes that they would receive a good education. "For my mother, as a single parent, education was paramount. We did without a lot of other things, clothing in particular," Sotomayor told M. P. McQueen for New York *Newsday* (May 31, 1992). "When you have a parent for whom education is a number one priority, it has an impact, certainly on my brother and [me]." (Her brother is now a doctor.) Sotomayor has been widely quoted as saying that her family, as far as she knew, was the only one in the neighborhood to own an *Encyclopaedia Britannica* set.

As a young girl Sotomayor was a fan of the *Nancy Drew* book series. She aspired to be a detective like the series' title character, but her doctor warned against a career as physically demanding as police or detective work, due to her diabetes. Sotomayor was also a fan of *Perry Mason*, a long-running television series following the cases of a fictional lawyer. An episode of the show inspired her career choice. "I watched how every time Perry wanted to do something, he had to ask the judge for permission," she told Joe Beck for the *Hispanic Outlook in Higher Education* (November 4, 2002). She recalled to Larry Neumeister, "I realized that the judge was the most important player in that room."

Sotomayor's family moved to Co-Op City, a cooperative housing development in the Bronx, in the late 1960s. She attended the School of the Blessed Sacrament on the Upper West Side of the New York City borough of Manhattan and later graduated as valedictorian of her class at Cardinal Spellman High School, in the Bronx, in 1972. She won a full scholarship to Princeton University, in Princeton, New Jersey, where she was a history major. Although academically gifted, Sotomayor—whose first language was Spanish— soon realized that she had to improve her English-writing skills significantly in order to pass her classes. "I had enough natural intelligence to get myself through my early education, but at Princeton I found out that my earlier education was not on par with that of many of my classmates," she told Joe Beck. "When my first mid-term paper came back to me in college, I found out that my Latina background had created difficulties in my writing that I needed to overcome."

Sotomayor, one of only a handful of Latino students at Princeton at the time (as well as one of the comparatively few female students), struggled with her new environment. "At that time in my life, as I was meeting all these new and very different people, taking reading classes, and relearning writing skills, Princeton was an alien land for me. I felt isolated from all I had ever known, and very unsure about how I would survive," she told Beck. "The Puerto Rican group on campus, Acción Puertorriqueña, and the Third World Center [now the Carl A. Fields Center for Equality and Cultural Understanding] provided me with an anchor I needed to ground myself in that new and different world." Sotomayor became co-chair of Acción Puertorriqueña, which, among other activities, sent a letter to the U.S. Department of Health, Education, and Welfare, accusing Princeton of discrimination in admissions and hiring.

In 1976 Sotomayor graduated from Princeton summa cum laude, with membership in Phi Beta Kappa. She also became the first Latina at the school to receive the M. Taylor Pyne Prize, the school's top academic award. The following August Sotomayor wed her high-school sweetheart, Kevin Edward Noonan, who later became a biologist and patent lawyer. During their seven-year marriage, the future judge went by the name Sonia Sotomayor de Noonan. The couple divorced in 1983.

Sotomayor went on to attend Yale Law School, in New Haven, Connecticut, where she edited the *Yale Law Journal* and was managing editor of *Yale Studies in World Public Order* (now the *Yale Journal of International Law*). Again she found herself among few Hispanic students; the law faculty was mostly male and nearly all white, with two women, one black professor, and no Hispanics. Sotomayor, passionate about minority representation, wrote a letter to the school newspaper complaining about the lack of Hispanic faculty members. She later filed a formal complaint against Shaw, Pittman, Potts & Trowbridge, a Washington, D.C., law firm, one of whose partners had suggested at a recruiting dinner that Sotomayor had been admitted to Yale only because of affirmative action. A faculty-student tribunal ruled in her favor, forcing the law firm to issue a formal apology to Sotomayor in 1978.

After graduating from Yale, in 1979, Sotomayor was hired as an assistant district attorney (ADA) in Manhattan under New York County district attorney Robert Morgenthau. (She was admitted to the New York Bar the following year.) Throughout her first year as an ADA, Sotomayor had misgivings about her work. Tasked with prosecuting such misdemeanors as shoplifting and prostitution, she often found her defendants to be minorities whose upbringing and economic hardships had contributed to their decisions to commit crimes. "There was a tremendous amount of pressure from my community, from the third-world community, at Yale. They could not understand why I was taking this job," she told Jonathan Barzilay for the *New York Times* (November 27, 1983), during her fourth year as an ADA. Once her work as an ADA involved prosecuting felonies, however, "it became less hard," as she told Barzilay. "No matter how liberal I am, I'm still outraged by crimes of violence. Regardless of whether I can sympathize with the causes that lead these individuals to do these crimes, the effects are outrageous." Still, Sotomayor added, "it pains me when I meet particularly bright defendants—and I've met quite a few of them—people who, if they had had the right guidance, the right education, the right breaks, could have been contributing members of our society. When they get convicted, there's a satisfaction, because they're doing things that are dangerous. But there are also nights when I sit back and say, 'My God, what a waste!'"

In 1984 Sotomayor joined the private Manhattan law firm of Pavia & Harcourt as an associate. There, she specialized in commercial litigation, representing such high-profile companies as the Italian automaker Ferrari and the Italian luxury-fashion house Fendi. Sotomayor won a series of lawsuits for Fendi against counterfeiters who imported and sold imitation Fendi products. She was made a partner of the firm in 1988. The previous year then–New York governor Mario M. Cuomo had appointed Sotomayor to an unpaid position on the board of the State of New York Mortgage Agency, which is dedicated to providing mortgage-insurance coverage to low-income families. When she left, in 1992, the board passed a resolution that honored her for defending the rights of the disadvantaged and for her unwavering stance regarding the negative effects of neighborhood gentrification.

On December 2, 1991, following the recommendation of Democratic U.S. senator Daniel Patrick Moynihan of New York, President George H. W. Bush announced his nomination of Sotomayor to fill one of seven vacancies on the U.S. District Court for the Southern District of New York, which covers Manhattan and the Bronx as well as Westchester, Putnam, Rockland, Orange, Dutchess, and Sullivan Counties. After a delay due to infighting between U.S. Senate Republicans and Democrats over a nominee to the federal appeals court in Florida, Sotomayor was unanimously confirmed as a U.S. district judge, in August 1992. She was the first Hispanic woman to sit on the federal court of the Southern District of New York, one of the most influential and important courts in the nation. The prospect of the pay cut Sotomayor would take upon leaving Pavia & Harcourt did not deter her. "I've never wanted to get adjusted to my income [at Pavia & Harcourt] because I knew I wanted to go back to public service," she told Jan Hoffman for the *New York Times* (September 25, 1992). "And in comparison to what my mother earns and how I was raised, it's not modest at all. . . . I have no right to complain." Due to rules stipulating that federal judges must live within the districts they serve, Sotomayor left her apartment in the Carroll

Gardens section of the borough of Brooklyn and moved back to the Bronx.

Of the roughly 450 cases Sotomayor presided over during her six-year tenure as a district-court judge, one of most widely discussed was that of *Silverman v. Major League Baseball Player Relations Committee, Inc.* in 1995. The lawsuit, filed during the Major League Baseball (MLB) strike of 1994–95, occurred after team owners, citing MLB's worsening financial situation, demanded the implementation of salary caps for players. Among other measures, the proposal set forth by the owners in 1994 would have also eliminated salary arbitration and decreased the amount of time before free agency began from six years to four years; owners would have retained the right to keep a four- or five-year player if they matched his best offer. The MLB Players Association leader, Donald Fehr, rejected the proposal. After owners and players failed to reach an agreement, the players went on strike in August 1994. After a salary cap and the use of replacement players were approved by baseball executives without the consent of players, Daniel Silverman, on behalf of the National Labor Relations Board, for which he served as the New York regional director, filed suit against MLB owners.

On March 31, 1995 Sotomayor issued a preliminary injunction against the owners, preventing them from implementing the new collective-bargaining agreement and using replacement players. The ruling, which restored 1994 rules with regard to free agency and salary arbitration, effectively ended the baseball strike the day before the 1995 season was scheduled to begin. (The strike had lasted 232 days and resulted in the cancellation of more than 900 games, including the entire 1994 postseason and that year's World Series.) Sotomayor's decision won her praise from sports fans, many of whom felt that she had "saved baseball."

In June 1997 President Bill Clinton nominated Sotomayor to serve on the U.S. Court of Appeals for the Second Circuit, in New York City. Republicans initially delayed her confirmation because they believed that Clinton, a Democrat, was grooming Sotomayor for a spot on the U.S. Supreme Court. The following year, in October, the Senate confirmed Sotomayor by a vote of 68–28. (Due to job requirements Sotomayor moved to the Manhattan neighborhood of Greenwich Village.) After her confirmation Sotomayor discussed the fears that she was "too liberal," telling Larry Neumeister for the Associated Press (November 9, 1998), "I don't think anybody looked at me as a woman or as a Hispanic and said, 'We're not going to appoint her because of those characteristics.' Clearly that's not what occurred. But I do believe there are gender and ethnic stereotypes that propel people to assumptions about what they expected me to be. . . . I obviously felt that any balanced view of my work would not support some of the allegations being made." In a speech she gave at her induction ceremony at the Ceremonial Courtroom in New York City in 1998, as quoted by Joe Beck, Sotomayor touched on how her past and heritage affected the way she viewed her success: "I do not live in the Latina world of my youth. Instead, I have a lovely apartment in a yuppie neighborhood of Manhattan. I have worked in job environments that have been challenging, stimulating, and engrossing, but none of them are controlled by Latinos. As accomplished as I have been in my professional settings, I am always looking over my shoulder wondering if I measure up and am always concerned that I have to work harder to succeed." She added, "This is the pathology of successful Latinos and other successful individuals who come from economically deprived populations. It is hard to enjoy your success and wear it comfortably when the world we have grown up in is filled with friends and sometimes relatives who don't make it in our society at all."

Sotomayor's influence within the law community continued to grow during her 11 years on the federal appeals bench. The more than 3,000 panel decisions and roughly 400 published opinions she authored included those for the cases *United States v. Santa* (1999) and *Hankins v. Lyght* (2006). In *United States v. Santa*, police had searched a suspect under the mistaken belief that there was a warrant out for his arrest and had found drugs in his possession. The case questioned whether evidence found during such a search should be suppressed. Sotomayor ruled that although the police had, in good faith, made an error, the evidence should not be suppressed. (The Supreme Court came to the same conclusion 10 years later, in *Herring v. United States.*) In *Hankins v. Lyght*, Sotomayor argued in dissent that, in accordance with the Constitution, the government cannot dictate whom a religious organization can hire or dismiss as a spiritual leader. For her work she was named in 2005 as one of *Latino Leaders* magazine's "101 most influential individuals in the [U.S] Latino community." For the magazine's December 1, 2005 issue, Jorge Ferraez, Kerri Allen, Francis Lora, and Lara Santiago Renta wrote, "Sotomayor is widely respected within and beyond the Second Circuit as a brilliant and formidable judge. She is lauded for her careful, fair and even-handed opinions." On October 1, 2008 Sotomayor was included on *Esquire*'s list of the "75 most influential people of the 21st century." The magazine designated her a "future Supreme Court justice," writing, "If Obama becomes president, his first nominee to the Supreme Court will likely be Sonia Sotomayor. As a Hispanic woman with 16 years of court experience, Sotomayor would slay two of the court's lack-of-diversity birds with one swift stone. . . . In her rulings, Sotomayor has often shown suspicion of bloated government and corporate power. She's offered a reinterpretation of copyright law, ruled in favor of public access to private information, and in her most famous decision, sided with labor in the Major League Baseball strike of 1995. More than anything else, she is seen as a realist."

Sotomayor faced a barrage of press coverage following her nomination to the Supreme Court, in May 2009. Conservative members of Congress scrutinized her record, searching for blemishes or hints as to how she would rule as a Supreme Court justice, while White House officials touted her rise from a humble upbringing and her three decades of experience. The nomination proved tricky for Republicans, who feared that Sotomayor, considered a moderate by many of her peers, would be an "activist judge," or one who would bring her personal biases to bear on rulings—thereby making, rather than interpreting, the nation's laws. Republicans were wary of coming down on her too harshly, however, for fear of alienating Hispanic and female voters, two groups that conservatives have worked to win over in recent years. Still, some conservatives attacked the nominee, in particular criticizing a remark Sotomayor made during a lecture at the University of California, Berkeley, School of Law in 2001, in which she stated, "I would hope that a wise Latina woman with the richness of her experiences would more often than not reach a better conclusion than a white male who hasn't lived that life." The remark sparked claims of racism from the conservative radio talk-show host Rush Limbaugh and former Speaker of the House Newt Gingrich. (Gingrich later apologized.) Sotomayor's supporters maintained that the comment—as they felt was made clear when the speech was read in its entirety—was merely intended to convey that a person's life experiences can influence the way he or she sees the world.

Of the rulings by Sotomayor that were cited in the period following her nomination, perhaps the most controversial was her decision in *Ricci v. DeStefano*, in 2008. The case involved reverse-discrimination charges brought by 20 New Haven, Connecticut, firefighters, all of whom were white (one was Hispanic), after the city tossed out their scores on an officer-candidate exam because no nonwhite candidates had scored high enough to qualify for promotion. City officials argued that they had thrown out the scores because they feared that minority firefighters would file lawsuits on the grounds that the test was unfair or had produced skewed results. (Other cities had abandoned that exam in favor of one viewed to be fairer.) A three-person panel of judges including Sotomayor ruled in the city's favor, stating that though "we are not unsympathetic to the plaintiffs' expression of frustration," the New Haven Civil Service Board had "found itself in the unfortunate position of having no good alternatives" and "was simply trying to fulfill its obligations" under Title VII of the Civil Rights Act of 1964, the federal law that prohibits employment discrimination based on race, "when confronted with test results that had a disproportionate racial impact." The judges ruled that the board's actions were protected under the Civil Rights Act. Sotomayor's role in the decision has led some conservatives to question her views on affirmative action and race. On June 29, 2009, by a 5–4 vote, the Supreme Court overturned the ruling, stating that New Haven officials' fear of litigation was not by itself a justifiable reason to throw out the test results.

The congressional hearings on Sotomayor's nomination began on July 13, 2009. For three days Sotomayor was questioned by members of the U.S. Senate about her judicial record and her personal views on the role of judges. Republicans were particularly adamant about questioning her on her "wise Latina" remark and her decision in *Ricci v. DeStefano*. When asked about the "wise Latina" comment, Sotomayor told the panel of senators, "I want to state upfront, unequivocally and without doubt: I do not believe that any racial, ethnic or gender group has an advantage in sound judging. I do believe that every person has an equal opportunity to be a good and wise judge, regardless of their background or life experiences." She later explained the intentions of the comment, saying, "I think life experiences generally, whether it's that I'm a Latina or was a state prosecutor or have been a commercial litigator or been a trial judge and an appellate judge, that the mixture of all of those things, the amalgam of them help me to listen and understand." "I stand by the words. It fell flat," she added. "And I understand that some people have understood them in a way that I never intended. And I would hope that, in the text of the speech, that they would be understood." As for *Ricci v. DeStefano*, Sotomayor affirmed that she and her colleagues were following precedent in their ruling. Sotomayor also distanced herself from a comment President Obama had made when he was a U.S. senator, to the effect that judges had to follow their hearts in deciding some cases. "I wouldn't approach the issue of judging the way the president does," she told the panel. "Judges can't rely on what's in their heart. They don't determine the law. Congress makes the laws. The job of the judge is to apply them." On August 6, Sotomayor was confirmed by a vote of 68 to 31. (Nine of the Senate's 40 Republicans voted for her confirmation.) She was sworn in by Chief Justice John Roberts on August 8. The Supreme Court convened early, on September 9, 2009, to hear a case on corporate campaign contributions. The regular court term began on October 5.

Sotomayor was an adjunct professor in trial and appellate advocacy at the New York University School of Law from 1998 to 2007 and a lecturer at Columbia Law School from 1999 to 2009. She also served on the board of the Puerto Rican Legal Defense and Education Fund from 1980 to 1992. Sotomayor maintains homes in both Washington, D.C., and Manhattan's Greenwich Village. In her leisure time she enjoys attending Broadway shows, the ballet, and New York Yankees baseball games.

—M.A.S.

Suggested Reading: Associated Press (on-line) Nov. 9, 1998; *Los Angeles Times* A p1 May 31, 2009; *New York Times* B p16 Sep. 25, 1992, A p1+ May 27, 2009; *Time* p24+ June 8, 2009; *Washington Post* A p1 June 1, 2009

Ron Sachs-Pool/Getty Images

Specter, Arlen

NOTE: An earlier article about Arlen Specter appeared in *Current Biography* in 1988.

Feb. 12, 1930– U.S. senator from Pennsylvania (Democrat)

Address: 711 Hart Senate Office Bldg., Washington, DC 20510

For nearly three decades Arlen Specter, the longest-serving U.S. senator in Pennsylvania's history, was one of Congress's moderate Republicans, priding himself on independent thinking with regard to such social issues as abortion and gay rights. It nonetheless came as a surprise when, on April 28, 2009, he announced his decision to become a Democrat, rejoining a party he had not belonged to since the mid-1960s. He did so, he said, because the Republicans had veered too far to the right. Specter's iconoclastic streak became apparent soon after he was first elected to the Senate, in 1980: during that decade he spoke in favor of curbing military spending and reducing subsidies to tobacco and corn farmers; he was also the only Republican on the Senate Judiciary Committee to vote against the conservative Supreme Court nominee Robert H. Bork, in 1987. Although a fiscal conservative, Specter repeatedly voted against Reagan administration proposals to trim social-welfare benefits. In 1991 he sparked much outrage among various liberal and women's-rights groups over the way he grilled the law professor Anita Hill during the Supreme Court confirmation hearings for Clarence Thomas, whom Hill had accused of sexual harassment. In 1998 he sided with Democrats in their opposition to the impeachment of President Bill Clinton. As the chairman of the Judiciary Committee, from 2005 to 2007, Specter oversaw the induction of two justices to the U.S. Supreme Court, John G. Roberts and Samuel Alito. Specter's passion for the law dates back to the 1950s, when he graduated from Yale Law School. From 1959 to 1964 he served as assistant district attorney of Philadelphia, Pennsylvania, and from 1966 to 1974 he served as the city's district attorney, after which he practiced law for six years before his first Senate race. The outspoken Specter has never been what might be called a "natural" politician. "I had a rocky road getting" to the Senate, he once admitted, "and I'm going to do my damnedest to stay here."

Arlen Specter was born on February 12, 1930 in Wichita, Kansas, to Harry and Lillie Specter, Russian-Jewish immigrants. He has two sisters, Hilda and Shirley. He was only a toddler when the family moved to Russell, Kansas. Specter enrolled at the University of Oklahoma in 1947, then transferred to the University of Pennsylvania during his sophomore year. He graduated with a B.A. degree in 1951 with membership in Phi Beta Kappa, then served in the U.S. Air Force from 1951 to 1953. He next earned an LL.B. degree at Yale Law School, in New Haven, Connecticut, where he edited the *Yale Law Journal*. Specter spent his first three years as an attorney in private practice in Philadelphia. Then, in 1959, he was appointed the city's assistant district attorney. During his four years in that position, he gained a reputation as a tough prosecutor by winning convictions against corrupt officials of the Teamsters Union.

In late 1963 Specter resigned from the district attorney's office to work as an assistant counsel to the Warren Commission, which was set up to investigate the assassination of President John F. Kennedy. He achieved national celebrity as the chief defender of the commission's controversial finding—the so-called single-bullet theory—that the same bullet killed the president and wounded Texas governor John B. Connally. After making an exhaustive investigation of the physical facts surrounding the Kennedy assassination, Specter told an interviewer from *U.S. News & World Report* (October 10, 1966): "The evidence is overwhelming that Lee Harvey Oswald was the assassin of President Kennedy."

After the Warren Commission's mandate was fulfilled, Specter took a job, in 1965, with the Pennsylvania Department of Justice as a special assistant attorney general in charge of an investigation of Philadelphia's magistrates. Later that year he sought the Democratic nomination for the job of Philadelphia's district attorney. Rebuffed by the Democratic Party machine, Specter, a registered

Democrat, accepted the invitation of the city's resurgent Republicans to run against his former boss, James C. Crumlish. In a city where Democrats far outnumbered Republicans, Specter defied the predictions of the pundits. With the backing of organizations such as Americans for Democratic Action and leading GOP politicians including Governor William W. Scranton and Senator Hugh Scott, he waged a determined campaign in which he portrayed himself as a reform candidate. The strategy paid off. Although his running mate failed to win the job of city controller, Specter defeated Crumlish by more than 36,000 votes, thus giving the Republicans their first victory in a citywide Philadelphia election since 1953.

Specter brought a new style to the district attorney's office. Outspoken and combative, he repeatedly crossed swords with Democratic mayor James H. Tate. According to Sandra Evans, Specter "soon acquired a reputation as a publicity-hungry official who launched numerous high-profile investigations and held frequent news conferences." But Dave Racher, a former City Hall reporter for the *Philadelphia Daily News*, disagreeing with such assessments, told Evans that Specter got a "bad rap" from the media. "I thought he was one of the best D.A.s we've ever had in this town. . . . He wasn't afraid to take on the heavyweights," Racher said.

Intent on using the district attorney's office as a steppingstone, Specter succeeded in gaining the nomination as the Republican candidate in the 1967 mayoral election. Although he portrayed himself as the logical heir to the liberal Democratic mayors Richardson Dilworth and Joseph C. Clark, who had presided over 11 years of reform at City Hall, Specter was, in the words of Douglas Bedell of the *Wall Street Journal* (October 25, 1967), "an upstart bucking Democratic control" in his bid to become Philadelphia's first Jewish mayor. On Election Day a strong Roman Catholic vote carried Tate to a razor-thin victory over Specter in the city's closest mayoral race in 32 years.

Undaunted by the defeat, Specter remained in the public eye as a result of his ongoing high-profile activities in the district attorney's office. Soon after he was reelected by a massive majority in the November 1969 election, Specter clashed with the feisty police commissioner, Frank Rizzo, and the following April he was at odds with Mayor Tate. In a controversial move he charged two white policemen with aggravated assault and battery following allegations of police brutality in the shooting death of a young black man.

The early 1970s were not kind to Republicans. The party was badly hurt by fallout from the Watergate scandal, which led President Richard Nixon to resign in disgrace, and by Vice President Spiro Agnew's political blunders. Specter became a victim of that fallout, and his reputation as the GOP's rising star in Pennsylvania politics suffered a serious setback when he was ousted from the district attorney's office in the November 1973 elections. He was beaten at the polls by the Democratic candidate, F. Emmett Fitzpatrick, a political newcomer.

Specter retreated to private legal practice with the Philadelphia firm of Dechert, Price & Rhoads and concurrently taught courses at Temple University Law School. He also remained active in Republican circles, and by 1976 he was again ready to enter the political arena. But Specter was unsuccessful in his party's Senate primaries that year. Similarly, in 1978 he failed in a bid to win the Republican gubernatorial nomination, despite his having been the early front-runner in the polls. In both cases, Specter's lack of support in the western part of the state proved to be his downfall.

When Senator Richard S. Schweiker announced his retirement in 1980, Specter sought, and this time won, his party's nomination for the United States Senate. With a major infusion of support and campaign contributions from Republicans who now rallied to his cause, Specter's ambitions were finally realized. He won the seat handily, defeating the Democratic candidate, Peter F. Flaherty, a former mayor of Pittsburgh, by campaigning on a cautious platform that called for tax cuts and reduced government regulation.

According to Martin Tolchin, writing for the *New York Times* (April 8, 1984), Specter spent much of his freshman term "seeking to balance the demands of his constituents in an older industrialized state with low per-capita income and high unemployment, against the demands of a conservative Republican president and the Senate conservative-dominated Republican majority." Unlike those senators who specialize in particular areas of committee activity, Specter seemed to be involved in everything at once. "The unifying thread is legal issues," he told Tolchin. "I have a deep interest in constitutional issues and law enforcement."

As a district attorney who had overseen the prosecution of more than 250,000 cases during his eight years in office, Specter had perfected his courtroom debating skills. Now, he consciously set out to tone down what Murray Waas, writing for the *New Republic* (September 30, 1985), called "his gangbusters prosecutor image." Nevertheless, it soon became apparent to political observers that Specter still thrived on confrontation. He often seemed most at home in the quasi-judicial setting of the committee hearing room, where Senate colleagues described him as "relentless."

As chairman of the Senate appropriations subcommittee that oversees the District of Columbia's budget—an appointment that many regard as being of minor importance—Specter had ample room for freewheeling. Declaring himself "a strong ally of the city," in 1983 he succeeded in securing $28 million in federal funding for new initiatives in the criminal justice system, including the hiring of seven new superior court judges needed to clear a backlog of cases.

Specter also began playing a pivotal role on the Senate Judiciary Committee, where Republicans held a slim majority, and he relished his chairmanship of that committee's subcommittee on juvenile justice. Murray Waas remarked that Specter often used the subcommittee's hearings as a high-profile forum in which to air his own views and to deal with his "big four" subjects—children, sex, drugs, and violence. Among the diverse witnesses whom Specter called to testify were the former porn-film star Linda Lovelace, the children's-television-show host Captain Kangaroo, and some of the jurors who had sat in judgment on John Hinckley Jr., who shot President Ronald Reagan. The media loved such sensational events; some of Specter's colleagues in the Senate clearly did not. "The subjects he chooses often are not even the remotest bit related to anything to do with juvenile justice," Waas quoted a senior Senate Judiciary Committee aide as saying. Senator Paul Simon of Illinois evidently agreed and even went so far as to breach Senate etiquette by chiding Specter in public.

Meanwhile, Specter's voting record puzzled some people. The *Washington Post* pointed out that Specter was among the few Senate Republicans who disagreed most often with President Reagan, voting against the administration more than 40 percent of the time. "I vote for the president as often as I can whenever he's not in conflict with Pennsylvania's interests," Specter explained. "People here [in Washington, D.C.] and my Senate colleagues understand that a Pennsylvania Republican can be reelected only if he shows some independence and pursues a moderate course."

A fiscal conservative with regard to the federal deficit, Specter raised the hackles of some senators on both sides of the floor when he called for a curb on defense spending as well as for a reevaluation of such "sacred cows" as government subsidies to the tobacco, sugar, and peanut industries. At the same time his liberal stands on some social and foreign-policy issues harkened back to his Democratic roots and also sparked criticism. Typically, he fought conservative efforts to disband the Civil Rights Commission, voted against the administration's nominee for assistant attorney general and against military aid to the Nicaraguan Contras, opposed the administration on school prayer and on cuts in funding for abortions, and sponsored a popular bill to scuttle a threatened relocation by the Philadelphia Eagles of the National Football League.

But Specter also incurred the wrath of civil libertarians with some of his controversial proposals for "law-and-order" bills. One called for a redefinition of the insanity defense in the wake of Hinckley's attempt on the life of President Reagan; another made it an offense for an attorney not to report a crime or fraud in which that attorney's services had been used. Still another, which received widespread support in Congress and the administration, was a seven-part omnibus crime bill that imposed stiff penalties on violent repeat offenders and persons involved in the sale and use of street drugs.

That Pennsylvania voters approved of Specter's performance was obvious from his 22-point lead in opinion polls as he headed into the 1986 elections. Although he shunned an endorsement from the president in a squabble over his vote on funding for the MX missile (which he backed after exchanging harsh words with White House aides), the lack of such support did not hurt his reelection campaign. Boosted by fund-raisers that were attended by such GOP luminaries as Vice President George H. W. Bush, Senator Barry M. Goldwater, and former secretary of state Henry Kissinger, a Specter victory seemed likely, but he left nothing to chance. Aware that Democrats led by Philadelphia mayor W. Wilson Goode could swing some of the crucial black vote over to the Democratic candidate, Representative Bob Edgar, Specter campaigned as if he were the challenger rather than the incumbent. "I run scared, that's accurate to say," he said, "but run hard is probably a better word." The effort paid off, and Specter was easily reelected.

Specter's second term on Capitol Hill continued the pattern he had established during his first six years. With the retirement of Senator Charles McC. Mathias Jr., Specter became one of the leaders of the moderate Republicans in Congress, particularly where social issues were concerned. Thus, in February 1987, he joined with other liberal and moderate senators in sponsoring a wide-ranging fair-housing bill. Later in the same year, he emerged as one of the key players in the Senate Judiciary Committee's hearings into President Reagan's nomination of the conservative judge Robert H. Bork to sit on the United States Supreme Court. Resisting the pressure exerted by a mass anti-Bork letter-writing campaign directed his way, Specter gave the nomination long and careful consideration before deciding to oppose it. "I reluctantly decided to vote against him because I had substantial doubts about what he would do with fundamental minority rights, about equal protection of the law, and freedom of speech," Specter explained. (He was the only Republican on the committee to vote against the nomination.)

Specter became involved in another of the important issues of 1987—the Iran-Contra scandal—as a result of his seat on the Senate Select Committee on Intelligence. (That scandal involved the government's sale of arms to Iran in exchange for the release of U.S. hostages there; funds from the sale were then illegally diverted to anti-Communist rebels in Nicaragua.) After attending hearings on the matter, he joined other senators in sponsoring a bill to bring about a radical reorganization of the nation's intelligence operations. The proposal called for a number of important changes, including presidential disclosure of covert activities, jail sentences for officials who lie to congressional committees, and a division of the powers of the director of the Central Intelligence Agency into two positions: one heading the CIA, the other acting as a presidential adviser. Specter told E. A. Wayne for the *Christian Science Monitor* (November 13,

1987) that the Iran-Contra affair had made clear the need to separate the gathering and analysis of intelligence information.

In 1991, as a member of the Senate Judiciary Committee, Specter again attracted controversy during hearings regarding President George H. W. Bush's nomination of Clarence Thomas to fill a vacancy on the U.S. Supreme Court. After the nomination Thomas was publicly accused of sexual harassment—inappropriate and suggestive comments—by a law professor, Anita Hill, who had worked as a legal adviser to Thomas at the U.S. Department of Education and then at the U.S. Equal Employment Opportunity Commission. Senator Specter grilled Hill during her testimony in front of the Senate, essentially accusing her of lying. He voted to confirm Thomas, whose nomination was approved in a 52–48 Senate vote. As a result of his hard-line questioning of Hill, various women's groups campaigned against his bid for reelection in 1992. Specter won that election, over the Democrat Lynn H. Yeakel, by only a few percentage points.

That election season also saw the Democrat Bill Clinton take the White House. Within a few months of being re-elected, Specter—seeking to emphasize his status as a moderate Republican—helped to found the Republican Majority Coalition, a group that sought to reclaim the political center for Republicans, taking no position on several hot-button social issues (most notably, abortion and gay rights) and expressing support for civil rights and fiscal responsibility; specifically, they aimed at reducing the deficit and lowering income taxes. In his failed bid for the 1996 Republican nomination for president, Specter campaigned on those issues, as well as health care for the poor, more stringent diplomacy with North Korea, and a flat income tax. He withdrew from campaigning for a variety of reasons, including lack of funding and strong opposition from socially conservative Republicans, whose main concern was abortion. Toward the end of his third term, Specter underwent brain surgery to get rid of a benign tumor. In 1998 he had double heart-bypass surgery.

Specter was reelected to his Senate seat in 1998. He continued to hold a moderate stance on many issues. He was one of the few Republicans to vote with Democrats against tax cuts, for a minimum-wage increase, for regulation of health-management organizations (HMOs), and for legislation that provided new regulations on overtime work. With regard to the impeachment of President Clinton (who had lied under oath about an extramarital affair), Specter did not toe the party line. Beginning in 1998 he openly criticized the Republican Party—and Senate Republicans in particular—for not treating President Clinton fairly. He urged his Senate colleagues to exercise restraint and not rush to judgment. In 2002 Specter, along with most members of the Senate (77 for, 23 against), voted to authorize the use of military force in Iraq. (In the spring of 2003, the United States invaded Iraq under the initial justification—later proven false—that Iraq had stockpiles of "weapons of mass destruction.") In 2006 and 2007 Specter voted against proposed timelines for troop withdrawal from Iraq.

Specter's relatively moderate stances and voting record made his 2004 reelection a challenge for him: he narrowly defeated Patrick J. Toomey, his challenger in the Pennsylvania Republican primary. That fall, however, Specter beat out his Democratic challenger, Joseph Hoeffel, by 11 percentage points in the general election. A few months later, in March 2005, Specter was diagnosed with Hodgkin's disease, a cancer of the lymph system. The senator underwent months of radiation therapy and recovered fully.

In December 2005 Specter played an important role in reapproving the Patriot Act, the national-security legislation that was passed after the September 11, 2001 terrorist attacks on the U.S. The original legislation had been controversial early on, with critics charging that lawmakers had failed to strike a balance between national security and individual liberties. During the debates over the new version of the Patriot Act, two of the biggest issues were the use of wiretaps and government access to library and business records. (The new version of the act allowed the government to use all of those methods, within limits and with justification.) During his fifth term as senator, Spector held the chairmanship of the Judiciary Committee from 2005 to 2007. During that time he oversaw the Senate's confirmation of two conservative Supreme Court nominees of President George W. Bush, John G. Roberts and Samuel Alito. The former was appointed chief justice. In the spring of 2008, Specter was again diagnosed with Hodgkin's disease; he again recovered and continued to work.

Meanwhile, Republicans—who had been dominant nationally since the younger Bush captured the White House, in 2000—suffered a reversal of fortunes in the 2006 elections, which returned control of the House and Senate to Democrats. (Many attributed that outcome to voter dissatisfaction over the course of the Iraq war.) The Democrats' success continued in 2008, with Barack Obama's election to the presidency. In February 2009 Specter was one of only a handful of Republicans to support Obama's $789 billion economic package, intended to stimulate the ailing economy. Specter's support for the stimulus package caused him to lose the support of many Pennsylvania Republicans and other fiscal conservatives. On April 28 the senator surprised many when he publicly announced his switch to the Democratic Party. One reason cited for the change was the opposition he encountered from Pennsylvania Republicans after his support for the stimulus. "I have been a Republican since 1966," he said in an official statement, quoted by the *New York Times* (April 28, 2009, online). "I have been working extremely hard for the Party, for its candidates and for the ideals of a Republican Party whose tent is big enough to welcome diverse points of view. While I have been comfortable being a Republican, my Party has not defined who I am. I have taken each issue one at a time and have exercised independent judgment to do what I thought was best for Pennsylvania and the nation. Since my election in 1980, as part of the Reagan Big Tent, the Republican Party has moved far to the right. Last year, more than 200,000 Republicans in Pennsylvania changed their registration to become Democrats. I now find my political philosophy more in line with Democrats than Republicans." Casting Specter's conversion in a different light, and echoing those who viewed it as an act of political expediency, the syndicated columnist E. J. Dionne wrote, as printed in the Portland *Oregonian* (April 29, 2009), "The raw political fact is that Specter was in grave danger of losing a Republican primary to former Rep. Pat Toomey, an anti-tax activist. One Democratic strategist reported seeing polling that showed Specter less popular among Pennsylvanian Republicans than President Obama. . . . At the instant of his conversion, Specter transformed himself from a political underdog into a favorite for reelection in 2010." On June 30, 2009 Specter's party switch took on new significance, after the Minnesota Supreme Court—following eight months of legal battles—ruled that the Democrat Al Franken had won his bid to succeed the state's senior U.S. senator, Norm Coleman. Specter's conversion and Franken's victory brought the number of Democrats in the Senate up to 60, a so-called supermajority. With 60 senators, Democrats—if they all voted the same way—could override a Republican filibuster.

In the fall of 2009, with the public and political debate over overhauling the health-care system in full swing, Specter sided mostly with the Senate's liberal Democrats in his support for a public-health-insurance option, which, he argued, would help keep the health-insurance industry honest. Critics of Specter have accused him of political opportunism, because earlier, in May 2009, he had been opposed to the so-called "public option." Others have suggested that perhaps his new party affiliation gave him the freedom to change his position.

The senator has written two books, *Passion for Truth: From Finding JFK's Single Bullet to Questioning Anita Hill to Impeaching Clinton* (2000), and *Never Give In: Battling Cancer in the Senate* (2008).

Specter and his wife, the former Joan Levy, have been married since 1953. The couple have two sons—Shanin, an attorney, and Stephen, a physician—and four granddaughters. Joan Specter served on the Philadelphia City Council for four terms; she founded both a pie company and a cooking school, has worked as a newspaper columnist and a consumer reporter on radio, and sits on the boards of directors of many educational and charitable organizations and businesses.

—D.K.

Suggested Reading: bioguide.congress.gov; *Economist* Oct. 17, 1992, May 2, 2009; *New Republic* p15+ Nov. 10, 1985; *New York Times* (on-line) Apr. 28, 2009; *New Yorker* p34+ Apr. 12, 2004; (Portland) *Oregonian* Editorial Apr. 29, 2009; specter.senate.gov; *Time* p29 Sep. 14, 1987, p8 Mar. 21, 2005; *U.S. News & World Report* p26 Apr. 29, 1985

Selected Books: *Passion for Truth: From Finding JFK's Single Bullet to Questioning Anita Hill to Impeaching Clinton*, 2000; *Never Give In: Battling Cancer in the Senate*, 2008

Courtesy of Rick Steves

Steves, Rick

May 10, 1955– Travel expert; writer; radio and television host; entrepreneur

Address: Europe Through the Back Door Inc., Box 2009, Edmonds, WA 98020-2009

Rick Steves's travel guidebooks have been praised for their upbeat tone and their emphasis on tourism that is economical, focused on out-of-the-way places, and aimed at learning rather than self-indulgence. Steves's advice to travelers, as he explained to Sara Corbett for the *New York Times* (July 4, 2004), is, "Stow your camera and be there. Pick grapes. Go to church. Buy something at the [local] market." He told Becky Emmons for the *South Bend (Indiana) Tribune* (December 11, 2005), "A lot of people's idea of travel is eating five meals a day and seeing if you can snorkel when you get into port. Don't call that travel. Call it hedonism."

Steves, who also hosts a long-running PBS travel program, *Rick Steves' Europe*, is perhaps best known for his quirky, personality-driven *Europe Through the Back Door* guide, first published in 1980. He told Corbett that the majority of his competitors in the guidebook market are "so dry they make your lips chap." His work, on the other hand, has inspired such devotion that his fans are often referred to in the travel industry as "Ricknikѕ."

Steves sees travel as more than mere recreation. He explained to Emmons, "Travel paints a human face on our globe [and] helps us celebrate differences and overcome misunderstandings between people." After the March 11, 2004 train bombings in Madrid, Spain, Steves said that the attacks, rather than discouraging people from traveling, should be viewed as a lesson in the importance of exploring other cultures. He told Harry Shattuck for the *Houston Chronicle* (March 21, 2004), "Tourism can be a vital force for peace. If we stop traveling, there will be more terrorism. I wish every American could travel before they voted. Our country would be smart to give every young person a stipend to travel."

Richard "Rick" Steves was born in Edmonds, Washington, on May 10, 1955. His mother was a homemaker, and his father ran a thriving piano-importing business. When he was 14 years old, Steves visited Europe for the first time, accompanying his parents on a trip to tour piano factories. He told Norma Libman for the *Chicago Tribune* (April 23, 1995), "I remember thinking, this is stupid, I haven't even seen my own country, I don't speak those people's languages, I'd rather be with my friends. But when I was at the airport in Oslo and I saw mothers taking care of their little children, it hit me like a bombshell that the world is filled with 5 billion equally precious people. This was a real enlightening sort of thing." Describing that trip to Emmons, he quipped, "I became enthralled. And there were these statuesque women with hairy armpits." Visiting such places as Ede, a town near Amsterdam, in the Netherlands, helped shape Steves's fascination with offbeat destinations, and after traveling to Europe with his father again at age 16, he decided to return there on his own. He recalled to Libman, "I was looking at a train schedule and all the backpackers at the Copenhagen train station, and suddenly it hit me: I could go to sleep on this train and wake up on the Rhine River or Amsterdam or Berlin or Stockholm. And I don't need my parents to do this."

In 1973, the day after he graduated from high school, Steves embarked on a backpacking trip across Europe with his best friend, Gene Openshaw. During the 10-week trip, which they have referred to as "Europe through the gutter," the two traveled with little money and were occasionally forced to sneak away without paying their hotel charges. Upon their return home, Steves studied European history and business at the University of Washington, in Seattle, graduating in 1978.

Steves had worked as a piano teacher to help pay his college tuition; recognizing the improbability of getting reluctant students to practice during the summer months, he spent each of his school breaks in Europe. After graduating and beginning to teach piano full-time, he maintained his summer ritual. He recalled to Kristin Jackson for the *Seattle Times* (February 11, 1996), "Each trip I made got so much easier. I was learning from what I did wrong." Citing as major influences Arthur Frommer's seminal *Europe on Five Dollars a Day* series and the guidebooks *The Art and Adventure of Traveling Cheaply*, by Rick Berg, and *Turn Right at the Fountain*, by George W. Oates, Steves made it his mission to behave and eat as much like a local as possible.

Once, in preparation for an overland trip from Europe to India, Steves signed up for a course called "Istanbul to Katmandu: An Independent Traveler's Guide" at the University of Washington's Experimental College. He recalled in his memoir, *Postcards from Europe* (1999), "When I signed up, I considered the class a godsend. But the teacher was unprepared, lazy, and disorganized. The room was filled with vagabonds about to embark on the trip of their lives. And the teacher didn't care. While he had the information we needed, he insulted us with pointless chatter. I learned nothing about travel to Katmandu, but the class taught me something far more important: I learned the value of well-presented travel information. And I realized that I could teach European travel."

In the late 1970s, Steves, who had developed the habit of taking detailed notes during his travels, began offering an eight-week course, "European Travel—Cheap," at the Experimental College. Although he expected, at most, a few dozen college students to sign up, the first course, which cost $8 per person, attracted 100 middle-aged adults seeking his advice. Steves realized that he had discovered a business niche. He wrote in his memoir, "At first I was happy to earn enough to pay for my annual plane ticket. But as enrollment grew, I began making more teaching travel than I did teaching piano."

In 1980 Steves rented an IBM Selectric typewriter and talked his girlfriend into typing a 256-page manuscript that he had written. Titled, at his father's suggestion, *Europe Through the Back Door*, the volume included illustrations by his college roommate. Steves used $3,000 to self-publish 2,500 copies of the book. He recalled in his memoir, "As if to sabotage my own work, I forgot to put on an ISBN number, which made it difficult for retailers to order the book. The first cover of the book was so basic that people in the media mistook it for a pre-publication edition."

That year Steves also organized his first tour, guiding seven women around Europe for three weeks and charging them only $350 each. Steves, who sometimes had to borrow money from his clients, took the women to places unknown to most tourists, including a tent at the Munich Botanical

Gardens, in Germany, in which people were allowed to sleep for 50 cents a night. The trip, which Steves recalled to Corbett as "a cross between Woodstock and a slumber party," was a huge success. Once word had spread about the women's adventures, Steves led numerous similar tour groups throughout the 1980s.

Steves received his big break after the travel editor of the *Seattle Post-Intelligencer* decided to serialize *Europe Through the Back Door* soon after its publication. The first edition of the book started selling in local stores, and Steves peddled the remaining copies through his travel classes. In 1981 he polished the prose for a second edition, which was published by Pacific Pipeline and distributed to bookstores throughout the Northwest. A third edition, even more polished than its predecessor, was professionally typeset but, Steves wrote on his Web site, "still looked so simple and amateurish that reviewers and talk show hosts repeatedly mistook it for a 'pre-publication edition.'"

By 1982 Steves had abandoned piano lessons altogether in order to focus on his travel business. In 1983 Carl Franz, who had written the highly acclaimed *People's Guide to Mexico*, helped Steves land a deal with John Muir Publications, which had been looking for other books similar to Franz's. The fourth edition of *Europe Through the Back Door*, published by Muir, quickly won a wide readership for its budget-conscious approach to travel and for its emphasis on unusual destinations. Other guidebooks of the time tended to concentrate on such mainstream attractions as the Roman Colosseum and the Tower of London. "You have to be more engaged—you have to figure out how to drive in a town, how to order a meal, how to use a phone booth," Steves explained to Joanne Blain for the Canwest News Service (May 10, 2008, on-line).

In 1984 Steves teamed up with his friend Gene Openshaw to write and self-publish the book *Europe 101: History and Art for Travelers*, which was aimed, according to Steves's Web site, at "smart people who slept through their art and history classes before they knew they were going to Europe." Steves and Openshaw followed up that volume in 1988 with *Mona Winks: Self-Guided Tours of Europe's Top Museums*, which covered such famed venues as the Louvre, in Paris, France; the Tate Gallery, in London, England; and the Uffizi Gallery, in Florence, Italy.

In the mid-1980s Steves wrote a rudimentary handbook to accompany his popular "Europe in 22 Days" tours. He displayed a sample of the book at his storefront business as a way to lure prospective travelers, but, as he noted on his Web site, the book started "driving decent people to theft. It needed to be available for sale." He self-published an expanded edition of the manual, which sold well and provided independent travelers with a blueprint for an efficient, economical 22-day tour. Muir subsequently expanded the guide into a series, each book detailing itineraries for two- to 22-day trips to Great Britain, Germany, Austria, Switzerland, Spain, Portugal, France, Scandinavia, and Italy. Steves told Blain, "I honestly wanted to put the information in my books so that I could drive myself out of business as a tour organizer. It didn't work, in a way, but I really wanted people to do the tours without me." (Muir has since been acquired by Avalon Travel Publishing, which continues to work with Steves.)

In 1990 Steves launched his own public-television program, *Travels in Europe with Rick Steves*, which airs across the country. Produced with his own funding and provided to public-television stations for free, the shows helped Steves become a nationally known figure. Thanks to the media exposure, his travel business, which had employed just five people until the show debuted, quickly became one of the leading private travel firms in the country. (Rick Steves' Europe Inc. now has more than 70 staff members and is among the leading sellers of Eurail Passes in the world.)

In 1993 Steves, who speaks no language other than English, began publishing phrase books; containing translations by native speakers, they are designed specifically for the independent budget traveler. The books have been lauded for their practicality and humor. Steves commented on his Web site, "Berlitz knew his languages but he never slept in a hotel where he had to ask 'At what time is the water hot?'"

By the mid-1990s Steves had some 20 books in print, many co-authored by Openshaw or another friend, Steve Smith. (Dave Hoerlein, an associate of Steves's and an architect by training, provided sketch-like, user-friendly maps for the volumes requiring them.) During the mid-1990s Steves also launched ricksteves.com, which quickly became one of the most popular European travel Web sites on the Internet.

While Steves made his name in the travel world by focusing on little-known destinations, treasured for their picturesque surroundings and lack of commercialism, he has been accused of single-handedly spoiling some of those locales, which are now visited by tens of thousands of tourists per year. One of the destinations he brought to prominence was Gimmelwald, a small village in the Swiss Alps accessible only by gondola or foot. Home to 140 dairy farmers, it had been known as one of the poorest places in Switzerland. While backpacking through the village during the late 1970s, Steves had become enamored with its quaint character and serene setting and featured it in the first edition of *Europe Through the Back Door*. Gimmelwald now draws an average of 20,000 visitors per year, and many of the town's farmers moonlight as innkeepers. The town of Rothenburg, Germany, has also undergone a major transformation since it was highlighted in Steves's guidebook. Steves wrote in his memoir, "Twenty years ago, I fell in love with a Rothenburg in the rough. At that time, the town still fed a few farm animals within its medieval walls. Today Rothenburg's barns are hotels and its livestock are tourists. Once the premier stop on a medieval trading route, Germany's best-preserved walled town survives today as a popular stop along the tourist trail called the Romantic Road. The English and German signs that long marked the entire route have been replaced by new ones—still bilingual, but in English and Japanese. And Mr. 'Off the Beaten Path' is right here with the camera-toting masses." The Rue Cler, a cobblestone pedestrian street in Paris known for its eclectic mix of cafés and markets, suffered a similar fate, after Steves called it the most Parisian of all Paris streets. (Parisians now jokingly refer to it as Rue Rick Steves.) Steves defended such changes to Blaine Greteman for *Time* (June 16, 2003): "Sure, there are places like Gimmelwald, or Cinque Terre in Italy, that I've promoted heavily and really had an impact on. They're now touristy, admittedly. And it's my fault, admittedly. But when I get back there, I check in with the locals and the tourists, and everybody's happy. The locals might be renting rooms and cooking nice meals instead of making wine—but they're also making money."

In contrast to other travel writers, who typically e-mail restaurants and hotels in order to update their guidebooks, Steves continues to travel for four months each year to discover new sights and attractions. While in the U.S., Steves tours the country, lecturing not only on travel but on other issues of importance to him. Along with the actor Woody Harrelson, he is one of the nation's most outspoken advocates for the legalization of marijuana; he currently serves on the advisory board of the National Organization for the Reform of Marijuana Laws (NORML). As noted by a writer for the *Contra Costa (California) Times* (April 10, 2008), Steves told the talk-show host Dave Ross, "The more I travel in Europe the more I realize how outdated and foolish our laws criminalizing marijuana are in this country." Referring to the period (1920–33) when the U.S. banned the manufacture, sale, and transportation of alcohol for drinking, he added, "Prohibition didn't work, and neither does this." He has also been outspoken in his opposition to the war in Iraq and about other foreign-policy issues.

Despite his sometimes controversial views, Steves is one of public television's top pledge-drive hosts, and he raises millions of dollars each year for stations across the country. His travel empire currently includes a variety of guidebooks, videos, downloadable audio tours, and a weekly public-radio program called *Travel with Rick Steves*, which features interviews with guest travel experts and listener call-in segments. His seminal book *Europe Through the Back Door* has expanded to almost 700 pages and is the number-one best-selling budget guidebook in the U.S. In January 2009 Steves appeared in an hourlong television special, *A Perspective on Iran*, which aired on public television stations. In that documentary, filmed during an 11-day visit to Iran in 2008, Steves addressed the country's reputation as a haven for terrorist organizations. Steves's book *Travel as a Political Act* (2009) includes field reports from Europe, Central America, Asia, and the Middle East.

Steves lives in Edmonds, Washington, with his wife, Anne, and their son, Andy, and daughter, Jackie. He has donated much of his multimillion-dollar fortune to various charities, and in 2005 he and his wife founded Trinity Place, a 24-unit apartment complex in Lynwood, Washington, which provides housing and other social services to homeless mothers and their children. In 2007 he spent $80,000 to plant trees, in an attempt to counteract, to a small degree, the air pollution caused by his European flights. Steves, a devout Lutheran, gives $30,000 a year to the Christian collective Bread for the World and is an avid supporter of the Mercy Corps. "I don't just want to leave a scrapbook of smiling faces and barbecues when I leave this planet," he told Christy Karras for the *Salt Lake Tribune* (October 31, 2004).

—C.C.

Suggested Reading: *Chicago Tribune* C p1+ Apr. 23, 1995; *Houston Chronicle* T p2 Mar. 21, 2004; *New York Times* p20+ July 4, 2004; *Publishers Weekly* (on-line) Jan. 30, 2006; *Seattle Post-Intelligencer* A p1+ Apr. 23, 2005, D p1 Aug. 17, 2007; *Seattle Times* K p1+ Feb. 11, 1996, F p8 Apr. 9, 2008; *South Bend (Indiana) Tribune* D p12 Dec. 11, 2005; *Time* p50+ June 16, 2003

Selected Books: *Europe Through the Back Door*, 1980; *Europe 101: History and Art for Travelers* (with Gene Openshaw), 1984; *Europe in 22 Days*, 1985; *Mona Winks: Self-Guided Tours of Europe's Top Museums* (with Gene Openshaw), 1988; *Rick Steves' Europe Through the Back Door*, 1995; *Postcards from Europe*, 1999; *Travel as a Political Act*, 2009

Selected Television Shows: *Travels in Europe with Rick Steves*, 1990–98; *Rick Steves' Europe*, 1999–

Taylor, Jill Bolte

May 1959– Neuroanatomist

Address: P.O. Box 1181, Bloomington, IN 47402

While all neuroanatomists study the structure of the brain and other parts of the nervous system, few can claim to have as deep and personal an understanding of the field as Jill Bolte Taylor. In 1996 Taylor, who had trained at Harvard Medical School's Department of Neuroscience, suffered a stroke that affected the left side of her brain, which largely controls logic, language, and calculation. Unlike other stroke victims, she has been able to

Courtesy of Jill Bolte Taylor

Jill Bolte Taylor

give a detailed and vivid explanation of her experience. "I think that I had an advantage because the brain was my area of expertise," she told Terry Gross for the National Public Radio program *Fresh Air* (June 25, 2008). "I do believe that it is unusual for someone to be so consciously tuned in to every step along the way during the process of cognitive degeneration."

In 2006, after years of recuperation, Taylor wrote a memoir, *My Stroke of Insight: A Brain Scientist's Personal Journey*, which became a bestseller when it was published by Viking in 2008. In it, she described the transformation she underwent in the wake of her medical emergency. She wrote: "I remember that first day of the stroke with terrific bitter-sweetness. In the absence of the normal functioning of my left orientation association area, my perception of my physical boundaries were no longer limited to where my skin met air. I felt like a genie liberated from its bottle. . . . It was obvious to me that I would never be able to squeeze the enormousness of my spirit back inside this tiny cellular matrix."

Taylor began spreading the word about the importance of tapping into the right side of the brain. In February 2008 she gave a speech at the annual Technology, Education, Design (TED) conference in Monterey, California, in which she passionately asserted, "We are the life force power of the universe, with manual dexterity and two cognitive minds. And we have the power to choose, moment by moment, who and how we want to be in this world. Right here, right now, I can step into the consciousness of my right hemisphere, where we are . . . at one with all that is. Or I can choose to step into the consciousness of my left hemisphere, where I become a single individual . . . separate from the flow, separate from you. I am Dr. Jill Bolte Taylor, intellectual, neuroanatomist." She concluded, "Which would you choose? Which do you choose? And when? I believe that the more time we spend choosing to run the deep inner peace circuitry of our right hemispheres, the more peace we will project into the world and the more peaceful our planet will be." The speech was posted on the TED Web site and quickly became an Internet sensation, with several million viewers to date.

Taylor, who was chosen as one of *Time* magazine's 100 most influential people in the world for 2008, acknowledges that she is lucky to have recuperated so fully—of the people who experience the same form of stroke, 10 percent die immediately, while half remain in a vegetative state. She does not, however, wish she had avoided the stroke. "It was one of the most fascinating experiences of my life," she told Rebecca Webber for *Psychology Today* (July/August 2008). "How many brain scientists have the opportunity to study their brains from the inside?"

Jill Bolte Taylor was born in May 1959 to Hal and Gladys (Gillman) Taylor. Her father was an Episcopal minister, and her mother taught math at a local college. (They later divorced.) Taylor was raised in Terre Haute, Indiana, with her older brother, who was diagnosed with schizophrenia as an adult. "During our childhood, he was very different from me in the way he experienced reality and chose to behave," Taylor wrote in *My Stroke of Insight*. "As a result I became fascinated with the brain at an early age." After graduating from Terre Haute South Vigo High School, in 1977, Taylor studied at Indiana University (IU), on the Bloomington campus. The school did not have a formal neuroscience program at the time, so she majored in human biology and physiological psychology. Taylor graduated in 1982 with a B.A. degree and was hired as a lab technician and teaching assistant at the Terre Haute Center for Medical Education (THCME), located on the campus of Indiana State University (ISU). Forgoing a master's degree, in 1984 Taylor enrolled in the ISU Department of Life Science Ph.D. program and spent the following years studying neuroanatomy. She also worked as a teaching assistant and later a visiting lecturer in gross human anatomy at the THCME.

Upon receiving her doctoral degree, in 1991, Taylor was offered a postdoctoral fellowship in the department of neuroscience at Harvard Medical School, in Boston, Massachusetts. She spent two years there working to locate Area MT, the part of the brain's visual cortex that controls a person's perception of motion. The project interested Taylor because many schizophrenia patients exhibit abnormal eye behavior while watching moving objects. In 1993 she became affiliated with Harvard Medical School's Department of Psychiatry, and she began conducting research in the Laboratory for Structural Neuroscience at the Harvard-affiliated McLean Hospital, in Belmont, Massachusetts, under the guidance of Francine M. Benes, an expert on postmortem investigation of the human brain as it relates to schizophrenia. During that time Taylor also taught human head-and-neck anatomy at the Harvard School of Dental Medicine.

McLean Hospital is home to the Harvard Brain Tissue Resource Center, known informally as the "Brain Bank." At the facility, donated postmortem brains are collected and distributed for the purpose of medical research. Taylor became a spokesperson for the center, lecturing all over the region and urging audience members to become brain donors upon their deaths and to inform their families accordingly.

At the age of 35, Taylor became the youngest person ever elected to the board of directors of the National Alliance on Mental Illness (NAMI), the country's largest grassroots organization dedicated to improving the quality of life for people with mental illness and their families. (From 1995 to 1996 she also served as a vice president of the organization.) Taylor had learned in the course of her own research that there was a shortage of donated brain tissue from people diagnosed with psychiatric illnesses. She explained in her memoir, "I decided this was merely a public awareness issue." In a link to her work with the Brain Bank, Taylor's NAMI platform focused on the need for brain donations from mentally ill patients, and she began to take her donation lecture across the country. At the end of each presentation, she brought out her guitar and sang a jingle she had written to lighten the mood: "Oh, I am a brain banker / Yes, banking brains is what I do / Oh, I am a brain banker / Asking for a deposit from you." Taylor was soon being billed on the lecture circuit as the "Singing Scientist," and thanks in large part to her efforts, an average of 30 brains from deceased psychiatric patients are now donated each year. (Taylor has stated that that figure is still inadequate.)

On December 10, 1996 Taylor awoke with a sharp pain behind her left eye. Thinking that it was just a headache, she continued with her normal morning routine of exercising and showering. Soon, however, she realized she was having trouble keeping her balance and began to feel detached from her body. "In addition to having problems with coordination and equilibrium, my ability to process incoming sound (auditory information) was erratic," Taylor wrote in *My Stroke of Insight*. "I understood neuroanatomically that coordination, equilibrium, audition and the action of inspirational breathing were processed through the pons of my brainstem. For the first time, I considered the possibility that I was perhaps having a major neurological malfunction that was life threatening."

Taylor was, in fact, suffering a hemorrhagic stroke caused by a birth defect known as arteriovenous malformation (AVM). As she explained in an essay for the London *Daily Mail* (July 22, 2008, online), "Normally, the heart pumps blood through the arteries with high pressure, while blood is retrieved through the veins, which are low pressure. A capillary bed acts as a buffering system between the two. But with AVM, an artery is connected to a vein with no buffering capillary bed in between. Over time, the vein can no longer handle the pressure and the connection between the artery and vein breaks, spilling blood into the brain."

In the human brain, the right and left sides have separate functions. The right side is the center of creativity and processes emotions, while the left side is more analytical, focusing on details, facts, calculations, and words. Because Taylor's hemorrhage was located on the left side of her brain, above her language center, Taylor began to lose all concept of language and numbers. The chatter she generally heard within her mind was silenced, and memories of her ill brother and demanding career faded. Taylor said at that point she experienced Nirvana, or a state of perfect peace. "As the language centers in my left hemisphere grew increasingly silent and I became detached from the memories of my life, I was comforted by an expanding sense of grace," she wrote in her memoir. "In this void of higher cognition and details pertaining to my normal life, my consciousness soared into an all-knowingness, a 'being at one' with the universe, if you will."

The moment Taylor's right arm became paralyzed, however, her euphoria was marred by the certainty that she was having a stroke. She told Terry Gross, "At this point people say, 'Well why didn't she just call 911?' Well, the group of cells in my left hemisphere that understood numbers, the group of cells that understood what 911 was, were swimming in a pool of blood and no longer functional." She continued, "So, eventually I did decide that I was going to call work and I had to locate a business card that had my phone number at work on it. And by the time I finally found my business card . . . I could not read. And eventually I had to match the shape of the squiggle of the number to the . . . squiggle on the telephone pad in order to get that phone number dialed." Once she had dialed successfully, Taylor could no longer speak but was able, by grunting, to make her co-worker understand that she needed help.

On her way to the emergency room at Massachusetts General Hospital, Taylor accepted the idea of her own death and was surprised to wake up in the hospital hours later. "I was not necessarily happy to find myself in that condition," she told Gross. "I really had to grieve the death of the woman whom I had been because I had none of her memories. I had none of her recollection of her life. And I was essentially now an infant." Two and a half weeks after she was admitted, Taylor had surgery to remove a golf ball–sized blood clot in her brain. When she was sent home, her mother moved in with her to help with her recovery.

Over the next eight years, Taylor was forced to relearn many everyday functions. "I had to learn to read again, wash dishes, do puzzles: I didn't know anything any more about edges, about how you use color as a clue when you're doing a puzzle. I had to start from scratch," she told Susan Schwartz for the Montreal, Quebec, *Gazette* (September 11, 1997). "Because I understood my brain so well, how it organizes information, it was probably easier for me: I believe in the ability of the brain to reroute itself." Aside from her regular visits to a speech therapist, Taylor did not follow conventional recovery methods, which dictate that a patient be roused from sleep early in the day, given amphetamines, and subjected to large doses of stimulation from television and radio. At first, Taylor slept most of the day, waking only to eat and use the bathroom. She never watched television and did not talk on the phone. Taylor used children's toys to master basic skills and also watched videotapes of herself giving lectures in order to imitate her own speech patterns. She ultimately regained the scientific knowledge she had lost and began giving lectures again, which she did at first by memorizing scripts and hoping no one would ask questions. "I had the advantage that I didn't lose my right hemisphere. . . . After enough time for the swelling in [my] brain to go down and after brain surgery, I had enough awareness that I still understood, for example, the head of the pancreas and how the duodenum fits around the head of the pancreas," she told Terry Gross. "I had the picture in my mind, but I didn't have any language. So I had to go back and re-learn all the terminology." Although many neurologists think that within six months of a stroke, the brain will have achieved whatever level of recovery is possible, Taylor believes that her eight years of steady improvement refute that. "I am living proof that you can lose your mind and get it back," she told Gina Barton for the *Indianapolis Star* (October 18, 2001).

Since her stroke, Taylor has said, she has become a more compassionate person, and she now makes time for such artistic endeavors as writing and playing music. "When I lost my left hemisphere I lost all of the normal 'in the box' thinking," she told Sandra Kiume for *Inkling* magazine (May 24, 2007, on-line). "When I lost the ability to define, organize and categorize information, I gained the ability to be intuitive and creative." Taylor also crafts anatomically correct depictions of brains in colorful stained glass, a hobby she began as part of her therapeutic regime. Her creations are sold on-line and can be seen on display at the National Institute of Mental Health, in Bethesda, Maryland, and the Harvard Brain Tissue Resource Center.

Taylor now lectures frequently about her belief that, as she said at the TED conference, "if I have found nirvana and I'm still alive, then everyone who is alive can find nirvana." Although some have tried to explain her experience in religious terms, Taylor asserts that the enlightenment she felt was scientifically based. "Religion is a story that the left brain tells the right brain," she told Leslie Kaufman for the *New York Times* (May 25, 2008).

Taylor, who hopes to one day open her own rehabilitation facility, continues to be a national spokesperson for the Harvard Brain Tissue Resource Center and now serves as president of the Greater Bloomington (Indiana) Area Affiliate for NAMI. She currently teaches part-time at the IU School of Medicine and works as a consulting neuroanatomist for the Midwest Proton Radiotherapy Institute, a cancer-treatment facility. She is the recipient of Harvard's Mysell Award, for scientific presentation, as well as several honors bestowed by NAMI.

Taylor, who frequently cites her mother as her dearest friend, currently lives in Bloomington. She has a dog and two cats.

—M.A.S.

Suggested Reading: *Fresh Air* (on-line) June 25, 2008; *Indianapolis Star* C p1 Oct. 18, 2001, A p1 May 1, 2008; *Inkling* (on-line) May 24, 2007; (London) *Daily Mail* (on-line) July 22, 2008; (Montreal, Quebec) *Gazette* E p1 Sep. 11, 1997; *New York Times* Style p1+ May 25, 2008; *Psychology Today* p41+ July/Aug. 2008

Selected Books: *My Stroke of Insight: A Brain Scientist's Personal Journey*, 2008

Thomson, David

1941– Film critic and historian; biographer; novelist

Address: c/o Random House Inc., 1745 Broadway, New York, NY 10019

Echoing a widely held view, Jeff Simon described the film historian David Thomson for the *Buffalo (New York) News* (November 23, 2008) as "one of the wonders of the English-speaking world—a critic of vast knowledge, great (though hardly infallible) taste, a habitually fresh perspective, a vehement candor and a stylistic elegance that makes just reading him a pleasure, even when you suspect (or are dead certain) his ideas are hooey." The most famous of Thomson's two-dozen-plus books of nonfiction and fiction is *A Biographical Dictionary of Film*; published in 1975, it has been updated four times, most recently in 2004. In 1983, at a time when relatively few had read Thomson's writing, the film theorist Raymond Carney wrote for the *Chicago Review* (Summer 1983) about *A Biographical Dictionary* and another of Thomson's early works, "Whether the rest of the world knows it or not, the history of film and film criticism is quietly being rewritten by this bright young critic. He is one of the few now practicing worthy of the company of the greatest film critics of our past—Robert Warshow, James Agee, and Manny Farber—and like theirs, his work has that rare depth and

Tim Mosenfelder/Getty Images

David Thomson

richness that can make one momentarily forget the artificial and destructive division between 'scholarship' and the general humane response any human being feels towards a film." Writing for the *Atlantic* (November 1, 2008) about *The New Biographical Dictionary of Film*, as the latest edition is titled, Benjamin Schwarz characterized it as "the most seductive, infuriating, and influential reference book ever written on the movies." The British-born Thomson, a film buff since his childhood, has analyzed the inner workings of Hollywood, deconstructed canonical films, and expounded on the careers of actors, actresses, directors, producers, television personalities, and his colleagues in the field of film criticism. He has been hailed not only for his insights and ideas but also for the literary merits of his prose. "So much writing about the movies is sub-literate piffle of either the academic or the journalistic kind," the film critic Richard Schickel wrote for the *Los Angeles Times* (August 10, 2002). "The sheen and sparkle of Thomson's prose, the way it gracefully asserts his particular sensibility, deserve celebration."

Thomson's books about cinema also include *Movie Man* (1967); *America in the Dark: Hollywood and the Gift of Unreality* (1978); *Beneath Mulholland: Thoughts on Hollywood and Its Ghosts* (1998); *The Alien Quartet: A Bloomsbury Movie Guide* (1999); *Hollywood: A Celebration* (2001); *The Whole Equation: A History of Hollywood* (2005); and *Have You Seen . . . ?: A Personal Introduction to 1,000 Films* (2008). He has written biographies of the writer Laurence Sterne, the polar explorer Robert Falcon Scott, the actor Marlon Brando, the actress Nicole Kidman, the actors and filmmakers Orson Welles and Warren Beatty, and the motion-picture producer David O. Selznick. He has also written several novels and has contributed articles to the *New York Times*, the *Nation*, the London *Guardian*, the London *Independent*, *Movieline*, the *New Republic*, and *Salon*. His memoir *4–2*, about his relationship with his father, was published in 1996; the title refers to the score of the 1966 World Cup soccer game, in which England trumped West Germany. His second memoir, *Try to Tell the Story*, reached bookstores in early 2009.

The only son of Nora Thomson and Kenneth "Tommy" Thomson, David Thomson was born in 1941 in Streatham, a suburb of London, England. World War II was raging, and London was repeatedly being bombed by German forces. As a child Thomson played with friends in buildings that had been reduced to empty shells or piles of rubble. He also talked to an imaginary sister, whom he named Sally. He had a strained relationship with his father, a former lightweight boxer who became an executive at Philco, a manufacturer of radios. "When my mother went into labor, my father chose that moment to leave her" for another woman, he told Emily Green for the *Los Angeles Times* (May 1, 2005). Thomson's father visited on weekends and would take his son to sports events; emotionally distant, he refused to acknowledge that he played only a minimal role in the boy's life. "It was the incredible attempt to act as if there was nothing untoward," Thomson told Green. "But you know, these things happen. It makes it sound as if I had a bad childhood. I didn't. My mother was devoted and I was raised in much happiness." Thomson's maternal grandmother, who lived with them, and a female neighbor contributed to his upbringing.

Young Thomson loved to listen to radio dramas and often watched movies at local theaters. He gained access to age-restricted films by asking strangers to accompany him. "There were old ladies who adored me, took me out for ice cream," he recalled to Green. By age 10, thanks to a scholarship, he had enrolled at a private boys' school called Dulwich College. When he was about 14, he became a member of the British Film Institute (BFI), "in order to see films at London's National Film Theater," he wrote for the *Los Angeles Weekly* (July 28, 2005, on-line). One of those films was Fritz Lang's *The Big Heat* (1953), which struck him as "extraordinary and beautiful in ways . . . I could not articulate." In an article about *The Big Heat* in the BFI quarterly *Sight & Sound*, which Thomson received as a BFI member, the screenwriter, biographer, and film critic Gavin Lambert expressed what Thomson had not been able to put into words. When he read Lambert's article, he recalled for the *Los Angeles Weekly*, "for the first time I felt there might be a useful future in writing about movies." At 19 Thomson turned down the chance to attend Oxford University; instead, he entered the London School of Film Technique (now called the London Film School). With a group of undergraduate friends, he made several 16mm films, for which he wrote the scripts. One film chronicled the emotional struggle of a recently released prison inmate; another was based on T. S. Eliot's poem "The Waste Land." By his own account, the discussions about film in which he and his friends frequently engaged strongly influenced his development as a critic. After he completed his studies at the film school, Thomson resolved to earn his living by writing about film. Through his father he got a job as a watchman at a factory that was being dismantled; with little to do there, he had time to write. During that time he met Anne Power, who had worked at the factory as a secretary and had a one-year-old daughter. Within a year the two were married; they later became the parents of a son and another daughter.

Thomson's first book, *Movie Man*, was published in 1967. Writing years later for the London *Independent* (November 27, 1994), Quentin Curtis described it as "quasi-academic" but added that "for all its stiffness, *Movie Man* is a remarkable debut. Its 26-year-old author had not only covered the canon of classic cinema, he had developed an original aesthetic, which remains the foundation of all his work." Thomson's next book was a novel, *A Bowl of Eggs* (1970). It was followed by *Wild Excursions: The Life and Fiction of Laurence Sterne* (1972), about the Irish-born British writer who, over a 10-year period (1759–69), wrote the pathbreaking comic novel *The Life and Opinions of Tristram Shandy, Gentleman*. Meanwhile, in the early 1970s Thomson was also working as a copy editor and teaching part-time at the Sussex, England, campus of the U.S.–based New England College.

In 1975 the famous London publishing firm Secker & Warburg published Thomson's 600-page *A Biographical Dictionary of Film*. In the introduction to the first edition, Thomson wrote, "Within nearly every entry there are things that may be startling in a biographical dictionary: the sharp expression of personal taste; jokes; digressions; insults and eulogies." The intended effect, he explained, is that "the reader who looks up Hawks, Renoir, Ford or Kubrick will be caught up in his own opinion by what I say. He will not placidly read through a list of irreproachable facts, but be jostled by agreement or scorn. He will begin to exercise his own critical faculties, . . . answer back, [or] throw down the book in exasperation." In a representative entry, Thomson wrote of the independent film pioneer John Cassavetes, who had been widely praised for his innovative style, "Cassevetes is earnest, obsessive but with a wildly variable talent. His supposed originality—of improvisation, handheld camera, rough editing and general graininess of cinéma vérité—is without intellectual or artistic substance." Thomson wrote of Cassevetes's debut film, *Shadows* (1959), which won the Critics Award at the 1960 Venice Film Festival, "It is a clumsy, callow film, struggling between the hope that improvisation will uncover truth and the imprint of Hollywood clichés. But worse than the film was the praise it received."

A Biographical Dictionary of Film was updated in 1981, 1994, 2002, and 2004. In an interview posted on the Web site of the New York State Writer's Institute, at the State University of New York, Thomson said, "The book just grew. On the first edition, . . . I never really knew where I was going until I had got there—and also I was younger and more innocent. The updates, especially those to make the 3rd and 4th editions, were actually more daunting. Because now I know how crazy and demanding the venture is. . . . As to where I draw the line, I do an instinctive interest test: does this person really grab me? If so, they're in." Among the numerous critics who differ decidedly with Thomson's opinions are many who have praised the dictionary as both thought-provoking and uncommonly well-written. Phillip Lopate wrote for the *New York Times* (June 30, 1985), "Among [Thomson's] many books, *A Biographical Dictionary of Film* remains the most addictive. It is impossible to read just one of its entries—they are so concise, informative and opinionated—without gobbling up a half-dozen more." An enthusiastic review of the dictionary that Gavin Lambert wrote for *Films and Filming* in late 1975 "helped launch the book," Thomson recalled for *Los Angeles Weekly* (July 28, 2005, on-line).

In 1975 Thomson moved with his family to New Hampshire, to teach at New England College's main campus, in Henniker. He later taught film studies at Dartmouth College, in Hanover. During that period he published *Scott's Men* (1977), about Robert Falcon Scott, the British Royal Navy officer who led two expeditions to Antarctica in the early 20th century. Scott hoped to become the first explorer to reach the South Pole; he succeeded in reaching the pole on his second trip (1910–13), only to find that the Norwegian explorer Roald Amundsen had arrived there a month earlier. On the return trip the ill-prepared and -provisioned Scott and his four crewmates succumbed to starvation, exhaustion, and hypothermia. In his book Thomson presented a psychological study of Scott as a bold but flawed leader. The book was reissued in 2003, with an expanded bibliography, as *Scott, Shackleton and Amundsen: Ambition and Leadership, Character and Tragedy in the Antarctic*.

In New Hampshire Thomson embarked on an affair with a student, Lucy Gray. His involvement with Gray led his wife to return to England with their children; the couple later divorced. In 1981 Thomson moved to San Francisco, California, where he married Gray. For his next book, his novel *Suspects* (1985), he re-created the family of George Bailey, the hero of the film *It's a Wonderful Life*, casting the title character of the film *Laura* as George's sister-in-law, the character Sally Bailey, from *Atlantic City*, as George's daughter, and Travis Bickle, from the film *Taxi Driver*, as his son. Other iconic characters from the silver screen, including Rick Blaine, Victor Laszlo, and Ilsa Lund from *Casablanca*, appear in situations far removed from those of their respective films. *Suspects* struck

Charles Champlin, writing for the *Los Angeles Times* (March 29, 1987), as "the wildest and most imaginative use of the movies as material that I had ever read."

In *America in the Dark: Hollywood and the Gift of Unreality* (1978), Thomson wrote about iconic and influential Hollywood figures, the studio system that reigned in Hollywood from the early 1920s through the 1950s, and the effects on audiences of that system and the films that emerged from it. His next book, *Overexposures: The Crisis in American Filmmaking* (1981), is a collection of his articles for such publications as *Film Comment*, *Sight & Sound*, and *American Film*. Raymond Carney summarized Thomson's view of the crisis referred to in the subtitle, as spelled out in two essays in *Overexposures*—"Alfred Hitchcock and the Prison of Mastery" and "*Psycho* and the Roller Coaster": Thomson, Carney wrote, had identified in the works of the director Hitchcock "not the genius, but the seeds of self-destruction in American film. As he argues . . . , it was as a result of Hitchcock and his strange blend of commercial and critical success that American film 'turned its back on human richness and enlightenment' in favor of anecdotal excerptibility, shallow manipulativeness, and impoverished inventiveness. It is, according to Thomson, Hitchcock's timid indifference to human motives and responsibilities, his 'fear of life, spontaneity, and the viewer's free mind,' his fear of failure, mistake, and human mystery that are his true legacy to contemporary film and film criticism. The wit, structural cleverness, and cinematic 'purity' of the Master are indeed seductive; but to David Thomson's credit and the great fortune of his readers, it is a seductiveness that this most humane, moral, and impure of critics is never taken in by."

Thomson's *Beneath Mulholland: Thoughts on Hollywood and Its Ghosts* (1998) is another collection of previously published essays. In *The Alien Quartet* (1999), written for the Bloomsbury Movie Guide Series, Thomson discussed the series of four blockbuster science-fiction cum horror films that began with *Alien* (1979) and ended with *Alien Resurrection* (1997). Thomson's comprehensive, leather-bound *Hollywood: A Celebration!* (2001) "would seem to be nothing but photos," Ty Burr wrote for *Entertainment Weekly* (November 7, 2001, on-line), but it "brings on David Thomson, . . . one of the most erudite critics around, to pen itty-bitty photo captions, which is like hiring James Agee to write fortune cookies. Against the odds, Thomson turns his captions into deft, analytic haiku. . . . The photos are not only glorious but unfamiliar enough to revivify American film history for even jaded movie fans."

Thomson's *The Whole Equation: A History of Hollywood* (2005) was followed by his *Have You Seen . . . ?: A Personal Introduction to 1,000 Films* (2008). "Thomson pros will have their usual supply of arguments, scoffs and sneers at both his entries and his choices but I can't imagine a better 1,000-page answer to a wanderer in the videoverse asking, 'what should I see?,'" Jeff Simon wrote of *The Whole Equation*. Benjamin Schwarz wrote, "It's impossible to read this book from cover to cover without being convinced that Hollywood's greatest achievements are not the monotonously important dramas that so often sucker in Academy voters but the stylish, highly polished entertainments, largely comedies, that endure even though they weren't made to be lasting. Above all, Thomson prizes wit, charm, and good-natured ease. He's reached an age . . . when he'd 'rather have a great screwball comedy than a profound tragedy. After all, tragedy is all around us and screwball is something only the movies can do.'"

Thomson's next work was about Warren Beatty, known for his leading roles in films including *Bonnie and Clyde* (1967) and *Shampoo* (1975) and as the director of movies including *Reds* (1981). Titled *Warren Beatty and Desert Eyes: A Life and Story* (1987), it presented in alternating chapters a biography and a novella, the latter based thematically on Beatty's films. Thomson's *Rosebud: The Story of Orson Welles* (1997) chronicled Welles's tumultuous career, beginning with the phenomenal success of *Citizen Kane*. Thomson wrote *Marlon Brando* (2003) to accompany a biography of the actor that aired on the A&E network. In his book *Nicole Kidman* (2006), Thomson "rewrites the celebrity biography into a savvy exploration of mythmaking," Cécile Alduy wrote for the *San Francisco Chronicle* (September 19, 2006). "As he proceeds to analyze Kidman's career film by film, he imagines alternative (and much more compelling) versions of each, relishing the new genre of film criticism he has invented for himself: the 'viewer's cut.'" Some reviewers accused Thomson of having a simple, undisguised crush on Kidman, pointing to his steamy descriptions of her and his fantastical, fictional interactions with her. According to Peter Conrad, writing for the London *Observer* (September 24, 2006), Thomson admitted that the Kidman biography was an idea "dreamt up by his agent and his editor." "Thomson's ardour," Conrad wrote, "will come as no surprise to anyone who knows his brilliant earlier work. His *Biographical Dictionary of Film* contains generous entries on a series of previous crushes: Donna Reed, Tuesday Weld and even Sharon Stone. . . . He risks embarrassment or absurdity in writing about these women because he believes that cinephilia is a state of erotic fixation." Thomson's memoir *Try to Tell the Story* (2009) was published to good reviews.

Thomson and his wife, Lucy Gray, live in San Francisco. The couple have two sons. Gray is a successful photographer and filmmaker. Her photos accompany the text of Thomson's book *In Nevada: The Land, the People, God, and Chance* (1999).

—W.D.

Suggested Reading: *Atlantic* p115 Nov. 1, 2008; New York State Writer's Institute Web site; (London) *Independent* p24 Nov. 27, 1994; *Los*

Angeles Times I p12 May 1, 2005; *New Statesman* p42+ Oct. 6, 2008; *Publishers Weekly* p29+ Dec. 2, 2002; Thomson, David. *4–2*, 1996, *Try to Tell the Story*, 2009

Selected Books: *Movie Man*, 1967; *A Bowl of Eggs*, 1970; *Wild Excursions: The Life and Fiction of Laurence Sterne*, 1972; *A Biographical Dictionary of Film*, 1975, (reissued) 1981, 1994, 2002; *Scott's Men*, 1977; *America in the Dark: Hollywood and the Gift of Unreality*, 1978; *Overexposures: The Crisis in American Filmmaking*, 1981; *Suspects*, 1985; *Warren Beatty and Desert Eyes*, 1987; *Silver Light*, 1990; *Showman: The Life of David O. Selznick*, 1992; *Rosebud: The Story of Orson Welles*, 1997; *Beneath Mulholland: Thoughts on Hollywood and Its Ghosts*, 1998; *The Alien Quartet: A Bloomsbury Movie Guide*, 1999; *In Nevada: the Land, the People, God, and Chance*, 1999; *Hollywood: A Celebration*, 2001; *Marlon Brando*, 2003; *The Whole Equation: A History of Hollywood*, 2005; *Nicole Kidman*, 2006; *Have You Seen . . . ?: A Personal Introduction to 1,000 Films*, 2008; *Try to Tell the Story*, 2009

Courtesy of the San Francisco Opera

Tian, Hao Jiang

1954– Opera singer

Address: c/o Zemsky/Green Artists Management Inc., 104 W. 73d St., Suite 1, New York, NY 10023

Since Hao Jiang Tian made his debut with the New York City Metropolitan Opera, in 1991, the renowned basso cantante has given more than 1,300 performances in upwards of 40 roles with companies in Italy, France, Portugal, Germany, Argentina, Holland, Japan, and China, among other countries, and has performed with such opera greats as Plácido Domingo, Luciano Pavarotti, and Kiri Te Kanawa. "If Tian's speaking voice is soft and buttery, his singing voice is molten chocolate," Chelsey Baker-Hauck wrote for the *University of Denver Magazine* (Fall 2007). "Critics consistently praise his rich, full, flexible voice, which can command or caress a note with equal acuity."

The Chinese-born singer entered his teens during Mao Zedong's Great Proletarian Cultural Revolution (1966–76), a political movement that sought to rid the nation of what was deemed to be educational and cultural elitism; only approved songs, plays, operas, and other items of entertainment could be performed, and everything representative of Western culture, from clothing to music, was forbidden. As a youth Tian bore the brunt of that and other forms of oppression: he was ordered to smash his father's collection of Western classical recordings to pieces and was present at the Tiananmen Incident in April 1976, in which citizens publicly mourning the death of the popular Chinese premier Zhou Enlai were beaten, some fatally, by government security forces in Tiananmen Square. "I'm glad I had that experience" of living through the Cultural Revolution, he told Marc Shulgold for the Denver, Colorado, *Rocky Mountain News* (December 13, 1998). "Most singers' lives are peaceful as they grow up. But not mine. Yet, whatever experiences I had from the past helped me to create a deeper feeling in my singing. You live, you have experiences—and that helps you express love, happiness, sadness."

As one of the first Chinese opera singers to have a lasting international career, Tian has experienced what he calls a prejudice against Asians in his chosen profession. "Especially when my career became global, I saw how great the disadvantages were for Chinese singers in the international opera world," he wrote in his autobiography, *Along the Roaring River: My Wild Ride from Mao to the Met* (written with Lois B. Morris, 2008). "There were so few of us singing at the highest levels in those days. . . . The odds were stacked against us for many reasons—and not all of them related to skill. Too many people in the business thought that Asian singers could not master this form or that audiences would not wish to see or hear Chinese people in Western roles."

Tian has nonetheless been celebrated and admired for his contributions to the opera world, in part for helping to create in the West "a new repertoire of Chinese opera—moving the field beyond stereotypes such as Timur [in Giacomo Puccini's *Turandot*] to authentic characters," as Andrew Druckenbrod noted for the *Pittsburgh Post-Gazette* (October 28, 2008). Tian has premiered the roles of Li Bai in Guo Wenjing's *Poet Li Bai*, Chang the Coffinmaker in Amy Tan and Stewart Wallace's *Bonesetter's Daughter*, and General Wang in Tan Dun's *The First Emperor*. After watching him perform in *Poet Li Bai*, the fine-arts critic Kyle McMillan wrote for the *Denver Post* (July 10, 2007, on-line), "[Tian] commands the stage from start to finish. Displaying amazing flexibility, he powerfully asserts his big, resonant voice and, a few moments later, caresses a phrase with supreme delicacy."

Hao Jiang Tian was born in Beijing, China, in the late summer of 1954. His mother's birth name was Du Li, "Li" meaning "beauty"; she changed her name during Mao's rule, during which vanity and femininity were looked down upon, to Lu Yuan, which translates as "big land." At the age of 13, she left her home to join what Tian described in his autobiography as a military propaganda entertainment troupe. In it she met Tian Xiaohai, who was a year older. He later changed his name to Tian Yun, which means "cultivate." The couple performed in the People's Liberation Army Zhongzheng Song and Dance Ensemble, Tian Yun as conductor and Lu Yuan as composer, and had three children, including Hao Jiang Tian's older brother, Hao Qian ("big road"), and younger sister, Lin. Hao Jiang Tian was not formally named until he had to enroll in middle school, at the age of 14. Up until that time his family had called him Xiao Lu ("little deer"), a feminine name that his parents had begun calling him before his birth in hopes of having a girl. They decided on the name Hao Jiang, which means "roaring river."

As a child Tian spent much of his time drawing and dreamed of becoming an artist. He hated his piano lessons, often crying during practice sessions. "So one happiest day came when I heard an announcement from the loudspeakers: My piano teacher was arrested as a counterrevolutionary . . . ," Tian told a reporter for New York's WNYC radio program *Soundcheck* (May 30, 2008, online). "I ran to the courtyard, screaming and jumping with joy. Thirty years later, actually, I went back to Beijing—I went to see him, and I told him I wanted to apologize to him because when he was arrested, I was so happy. And he laughed with tears in his eyes, and he said, 'Well, that was a crazy period, and it was so hard to figure out who was right and who was wrong.'"

Growing up under Mao's rule, Tian's parents were careful to maintain their allegiance to his Communist Party of China (CPC). Though they had both dedicated their lives to communism from a young age, their past came into question when it was discovered that they had once belonged to a propaganda performance troupe of the Kuomintang (KMT), also known as the Chinese Nationalist Party, a rival of the CPC. That discovery tarnished their names, and they were forced to leave Beijing. Tian—then 14—went with his sister to live for a period with his aunt on a farm; both later returned to the city to attend school. (Tian's brother, who was enrolled in the naval academy before authorities learned about his parents' past, was expelled afterward.) Tian's parents were banished to a "re-education" camp in 1969. They would not return to Beijing until 1981.

Years earlier Tian's father had ordered him to demolish the father's record collection, in order to spare the family embarrassment or worse if the records were found by authorities. As Tian was packing for his trip to the country, he discovered a single surviving record behind the phonograph. It was of Beethoven's Sixth Symphony, which his father had once conducted. Tian has said that on that occasion, when his father played the record for him, he came to understand the power of music. "My first impression of Western music was in my father's eyes," he told Robert Lipsyte and Lois B. Morris for the *New York Times* (October 22, 2002). "He was a remote man who did not show emotion. But his face became so human, so tender, as he told me this was an interlude, here is the first theme. The change in my father's face was the music lesson that changed my life."

With his newfound love of music, Tian began learning the accordion and joined his school's Mao Zedong Thought Propaganda Team. He was 15 when he graduated from the school in 1970 and went to work at the Beijing Boiler Factory, which manufactured electricity generators. For seven years he cut steel sheets for a living while continuing to play the accordion, composing for and conducting the factory's Thought Propaganda Team. One day in the summer of 1975, Tian rode his bicycle to a friend's house for a visit; too tired to climb the stairs to the fifth floor, he yelled up to his friend's window. The friend was not at home, but a man who lived next door overheard Tian and asked him if he was a singer. Telling Tian he had a "big voice," the man suggested that he find a singing teacher. Tian recalled the event in *Along the Roaring River*: "[The man] turned out to be a professional singer, perhaps about forty, and although I don't remember his name or his face, the five minutes I spent with him changed my life." Tian took the man's advice to heart and soon began taking voice lessons with a family friend. He often feigned illness in order to leave work and practice.

In 1973 Mao's wife, Jiang Qing, had ordered the recruitment of young musicians to be trained at the Central Conservatory of Music in order to join the Central Philharmonic Society, China's foremost state-sponsored performing group. Tian auditioned for a spot in 1976. Later that year, after Mao had died, Jiang Qing and her "Gang of Four" were arrested, and the Cultural Revolution came to an end. Nonetheless, the Central Conservatory continued the program long enough to train a last class of 30 musicians; Tian was the only singer from Beijing who was selected. From that point on, Tian, who had secretly gone against cultural norms by drinking, smoking, and dating girls, dedicated himself wholly to singing.

At the conservatory Tian studied several forms of music, including revolutionary songs, folk tunes, classical music, and Italian opera, even taking a master class with the Italian opera star Gino Bechi, and honed his solo-singing skills. He soon received a full scholarship to attend the University of Denver's Lamont School of Music, in Denver, Colorado, and became determined to immigrate to the United States, where he could have a more fulfilling career. With the help of Martha Liao, a Denver-based geneticist and pianist whom he had met in China a year earlier, when she was a visiting scholar, Tian obtained a visa and immigrated to the U.S. in 1983. During a layover in New York City, he used some of the little money he had to buy a standing-room ticket to see Luciano Pavarotti perform at the Metropolitan Opera. (Ten years later to the day, Tian performed alongside Pavarotti in a production of *I Lombardi* at the Met.) The opera, Verdi's *Ernani*, was the first Western opera Tian had seen. "Before the end of the second act, I knew I had to become an opera singer," he wrote in *Along the Roaring River*.

After graduating with a master's degree in vocal performance in 1987, Tian spent the subsequent three years auditioning, participating in local voice competitions, and working as a singer in a Chinese restaurant. He made his first stage appearances with Opera Colorado, and during the same period he won six international singing competitions. Determined to have a career in opera, he traveled to New York City frequently to find an agent and audition for roles. After being rejected by the New York City Opera, he was signed to become a resident singer with the Metropolitan Opera, starting in the 1991–92 season. He moved to New York and married Liao. (Tian and Liao had each had a previous marriage that ended in divorce.)

Tian has won acclaim for many of his roles, including Philip II in Verdi's *Don Carlos*, Procida in Verdi's *I Vespri Siciliani*, and Mephistopheles in Gounod's *Faust*. He has performed with Germany's Berlin State Opera; Teatro Comunale, in Florence, Italy; Arena di Verona, in Italy; Teatro Colon, in Buenos Aires, Argentina; the Chicago Lyric Opera; and the Washington National Opera, in Washington, D.C., among others. He has also appeared on the concert stage with orchestras around the world, including the Philadelphia Orchestra, the Colorado Symphony, London's Orchestra of St. Martin-in-the-Fields, and the Hong Kong Philharmonic. Discussing Tian's title role as the eighth-century Chinese poet in *Poet Li Bai*, performed with Colorado's Central City Opera, Bob Bows wrote for *Variety* (July 16–22, 2007), "Hao Jiang Tian . . . exudes jovial well-being as the gifted wordsmith blessed with Mozart-like spontaneity and a Taoist disposition. Hao's expressive basso cantante captures Li Bai's sensitivity and visionary phrasing, while his imposing stature argues for immortality." In reviewing the Baltimore Opera Company's 2008 production of Bellini's *Norma*, Tim Smith wrote for the *Baltimore Sun* (November 20, 2008), "As Oroveso, Norma's father and Druid elder, Hao Jiang Tian sang with admirable smoothness and solidity of tone and molded his phrases eloquently."

Tian has been a U.S. citizen since 1995. He appeared as the Devil in Fresno (California) Grand Opera's production of *Faust* in April 2009. The following September he taped a live performance of his autobiographical, one-man show *From Mao to the Met* at the Kaye Playhouse at New York City's Hunter College. (The performance was scheduled to air on PBS television stations in late 2009.) Tian expected to return to the Metropolitan Opera in January 2010 in the role of Timur in Franco Zeffirelli's production of *Turandot* and planned to present *From Mao to the Met* on April 11, 2010 at the Fresno Memorial Auditorium.

Tian's wife, Martha Liao, retired from her work as a genetic scientist to travel full-time with Tian. She serves as president of the Asian Performing Arts of Colorado, which she founded in 1987. She and Tian live in New York City with their English spaniel, Niu Niu, and their parrot, Luke. Though Tian intends to sing professionally for as long as he can, he has already planned on retiring to Colorado, where he hopes to spend his time exploring other art forms, such as writing poems and painting.

—M.A.S.

Suggested Reading: (Denver, Colorado) *Rocky Mountain News* D p25 Dec. 13, 1998; (Hong Kong) *South China Morning Post* p5 Sep. 24, 2003; *New York Times* E p1 Oct. 22, 2002; *Pittsburgh Post-Gazette* C p1 Oct. 28, 2008; TianHaoJiang.com

Selected Books: *Along the Roaring River: My Wild Ride from Mao to the Met* (with Lois B. Morris), 2008

Selected Recordings: *Operatic Arias*, 2006

Selected One-Man Shows: *From Mao to the Met*, 2009

Tonatto, Laura

1963– Perfumer; businesswoman

Address: Laura Tonatto profumi Italia, Strada Pecetto 154, 10131 Turin, Italy

The master perfumer Laura Tonatto "has for many years been resolutely fighting to compel us to take in the aromas of the world around us." So says the Web site of the State Hermitage Museum, in St. Petersburg, Russia, which included samples of

Courtesy of Laura Tonatto

Laura Tonatto

Tonatto's work in conjunction with an exhibition there in 2005. In the global fragrance industry, where perfumes bearing the names of celebrities have proliferated and 6,000 new scents are introduced each year, Tonatto is a member of a rare breed of artisans. Known in her field as the "Italian nose," she has produced a collection of distinctive perfumes, some based on ancient formulas, such as the orange-blossom water widely used among Muslims; others were inspired by literary classics, among them Marcel Proust's *Swann's Way* and Gustave Flaubert's *Madame Bovary*; and still others have links to films, paintings, or historical events. Tonatto, who as a young woman learned much about the art of perfumery in Cairo, Egypt, and Grasse, France (considered the perfume capital of the world), has flourished as a bespoke perfumer for more than 20 years; her clientele has included the fashion designer Giorgio Armani, the L'Oréal Group, noted entertainers, Swedish royalty, and Italian hotels including the San Clemente Palace, in Venice, and the Park Hyatt in Milan. In 2001 she launched the Laura Tonatto line of products, which range from bath oils and body sprays to scented candles and fragrances for linens, curtains, and upholstery. Her products are widely available in Europe and in specialty stores in a few American cities. In 2006, with Alessandra Montrucchio, Tonatto wrote *Storia di un naso* ("Story of a Nose"), a memoir cum discussion of perfumery. "My perfumes are compositions about places I've been, people I've met," she told Anne Boylan for the Dublin, Ireland, *Sunday Independent* (September 26, 2004). "They are entwined in personal experience. They are extremely personal. One's autograph, really."

"Our sense of smell, like our sense of taste, changes as we get older," Tonatto told a reporter for the *Irish Times* (January 10, 2004). "Whatever fragrance we choose to wear is an expression of oneself, it must speak about the person. It is a form of communication. God has given me a chance to have another view of life and creating fragrance comes completely naturally to me. No day of my life has ever been without it." Laura Tonatto was born in 1963 and raised in Turin, a city in northwestern Italy. Her keen sense of smell was evident early on. "If I went to a new house I could smell if there was an animal in the house, if they cooked, if they were clean," she recalled to the writer for the *Irish Times*. Her grandmother Ippolita, who owned many bottles of perfume, encouraged her to pursue her passion for scents. "I used to sneak up when she wasn't around and borrow a perfume," Tonatto told Boylan. "And she taught me to use my sense of smell for many other things—the smell of the sea, for instance. She could tell whether the sea was still or stormy just from its smell and I picked it up from her. When the sea was calm, the smell of seaweed was stronger. Using my sense of smell for everything became a game." An avid reader, as a child she "would read a book and be so overwhelmed by the aromas described," she recalled to Thomas Pettifor for the London *Independent* (September 16, 2004). She added, "Some books create such a strong reaction for me that if I hear the title mentioned, I will automatically smell it."

After she graduated from secondary school, in 1982, Tonatto enrolled at Turin University with the intention of studying law. She spent the summer before her freshman year in Cairo, where some of her relatives lived. There, she became a habitué of the Khan-El-Khalili, a district in Cairo's old city center known for its clothing boutiques, spice shops, and perfumeries. She befriended a young perfume vendor named Hassan, who began teaching her about traditional Asian formulations—how to extract and mix essences and how to find harmonies in perfumes' three notes: top notes, or scents perceived immediately upon application; middle notes, which are more mellow and "rounded" and comprise the "heart" of the perfume; and base notes, which give the perfume its solidity and depth and normally become apparent after the evaporation of the middle notes. Tonatto remained in Cairo three months longer than she had originally planned, then returned to Turin to attend college. Much to her parents' dismay, she dropped out a year and a half later to pursue her aspiration of becoming a perfumer.

For a short time Tonatto continued her education in perfume-making in Cairo. She next lived briefly in Singapore and then Sydney, Australia. In 1984 she moved to Naples, in southwestern Italy, and started working for the Ruocco Co., owned by a family of perfumers. For generations the Ruoccos, while living on the Italian island of Capri, had produced a small line of fragrances based on recipes that supposedly dated to the 13th century.

Commissioned to create four new perfumes that would capture the essence of the Italian island of Capri, Tonatto used a recipe found at Capri's Monastery of St. Giacomo to formulate Mediterraneo and Fiori di Capri. Ancient tales provided inspiration for her other two perfumes: Io Capri, whose name refers to the goddess to whom the Roman emperor Tiberius dedicated the largest royal palace on Capri, and Ligea La Sirena, named after the Greek sea nymph Ligea.

In the mid-1980s Tonatto left the Ruocco Co. and moved to Grasse, where she learned other methods of perfume-making under the tutelage of Serge Kalouguine, a celebrated French perfumer, at Fragonard, one of Grasse's most prestigious perfumeries. She and Kalouguine compiled an olfactory table containing information on the three notes of rare wines from the vineyards of Barolo, Italy; their compilation received widespread praise. In March 1986, at the age of 23, Tonatto started working as a bespoke perfumer in the Via Brera section of Milan. Within three days of the launch of her business, the pop and jazz singer Ornella Vanoni bought one of her personalized fragrances. Thanks to word of mouth, Tonatto's business flourished; she soon found herself making perfumes for other high-profile clients, among them the fashion mogul Elio Fiorucci and the soccer player Luca Bucci. Nevertheless, she grew unhappy with Milan's social atmosphere and closed her shop after a year. Later in the 1980s she opened a shop in Turin and over the next several years, she worked on freelance projects for upscale brands.

During the next decade Tonatto made several important contributions to her profession. In 1992 she produced her first assortment of custom-made cosmetics, for the actress Ornella Muti, and created for Tedeschi and Luciani perfumes for men and women that were the first made specifically to be worn with cashmere. Around that time Tonatto became deeply interested in the history of perfumery. In 1993 she curated a perfume exhibition at the Civic Museum in Turin. Guided by ancient texts and museum archives, she created a collection of new renditions of bygone compounds: Syrian Water (dating from the first century B.C.), based on formulas contained in the writings of Pliny the Elder; Aqua Admirabilis, a re-creation of a 16th-century perfume of the same name, made by the artist Paolo Farina and based on Farina's vision or olfactory memory of a spring morning after a rain; Fleur d'Oranger and Jonquille Composee, which were made from 18th-century recipes; and Parfumeur dell'Impereur, a perfume inspired by the French military and political leader Napoleon Bonaparte. In conjunction with the exhibition, Tonatto staged a series of workshops attended by more than 2,000 people, in which she provided a comprehensive history of perfume and information on basic methods of production. On commission in 1998 she created fragrances for youngsters for the children's-clothing designer Pupi Solari and a collection for the fashion designer Giorgio Armani. Also in 1998 she produced an exclusive fragrance and cosmetics collection for the downhill-skiing champion Isolde Kostner. The next year Tonatto produced a collection of perfumes to supplement the L'Oréal group's hair-care line Kerastase. (It has become customary for major designers and cosmetics companies to commission specialists to make haute-couture fragrances and signature scents.) When working for an individual, Tonatto starts by creating an "olfactory portrait" of the person. She explained to the *Irish Times* reporter, "I want to know their color preference, which perfumes they use and what they expect from a perfume. They usually want something special which expresses their style." "To go from inspiration to result can take months," she told Boylan.

In 2001 Tonatto launched her own brand of personal-care products and items for the home, the latter including Shanghai sticks (similar to incense); Notte, for spraying on bed linens, upholstery, and curtains; and Clou, a mild detergent for washing such delicate items as cashmere and baby blankets. The Laura Tonatto line of fragrances includes Ambrosia—its name refers to the food or drink of the gods in Greek mythology—and Fior d'Arancio, which is infused with orange blossom and was made in homage to the Luchino Visconti film *The Leopard* (1963). Visconti, Tonatto told Lucia Van der Post for the London *Times* (October 3, 2003), "was such a perfectionist that he insisted on perfuming the film set with orange blossom: he felt somehow that it would make a difference—even though clearly the audience wouldn't be able to smell it—that it would create the right atmosphere around [the actress] Claudia Cardinale" as Angelica. Later in 2001, for a science show in Turin, Tonatto designed an exhibit in which visitors were invited to experience various scents. She has since presented that exhibit at other events.

In 2002 Tonatto began marketing Oltre, "a whiff of the ocean," which won a major award in Paris that January after being selected from 2,500 entries from 45 countries. The fragrance was inspired in part by a passage in "On Contentment of the Mind" in the *Moralia*, a collection of essays by the first-century Greek philosopher and historian Plutarch: "When Alexander [the Great] saw the breadth of his domain, he wept for there were no more worlds to conquer." The next year Tonatto, on commission, created a perfume for guests at the San Clemente Palace that evoked the scent emanating from the lime tree in the hotel garden. For the same hotel she created a special fragrance for the paper on which visitors' bills were printed—to "sweeten the blow" presented by the high amounts due, Van der Post wrote. Tonatto also produced a collection of bath and beauty products for the Park Hyatt Hotel in Milan.

In 2004, as part of a promotion for Waterstone's, a chain of bookshops in Great Britain, Tonatto created five "literary" fragrances inspired by descriptions in the novels *Madame Bovary*, by Gustave Flaubert; *The Child of Pleasure*, by Gabriele

D'Annunzio; *Swann's Way*, by Marcel Proust; *The Picture of Dorian Gray*, by Oscar Wilde; and *Perfume: The Story of a Murderer*, by Patrick Süskind. The relevant passage in *Swann's Way* refers to a flood of memories triggered in the narrator by the taste of a tiny, shell-shaped cake called a madeleine, which led Tonatto to create an aroma containing essences of fresh pastry, vanilla, citrus, and tea. From Wilde's description of "violets that woke the memory of dead romances," she formulated what Ben McIntyre, writing for the London *Times* (September 18, 2004), described as "a thick, cloying fragrance, heady, headachy and voluptuous." In the selection from Flaubert's *Madame Bovary* (1857), the adulterous protagonist, Emma, enjoys sniffing the lining of her lover's cigar case, because the scent transports her to "a world of grandeur and glamour from which she is excluded," McIntyre noted. For that perfume, Tontatto blended chemicals whose smells were reminiscent of those of cigarette ashes and aftershave. Tonatto came up with an extremely odoriferous scent after reading *Perfume*, in which Süskind wrote that in 18th-century cities, residents were forced to live with the stench, "barely conceivable to us modern men and women," that wafted from rotting garbage, human waste thrown from windows, horse manure, and the entrails of animals butchered for meat, among other foul-smelling sources. "The resulting concoction," McIntyre wrote, "is, indeed, truly disgusting: part musketeer's jockstrap, part fish paste, all overlaid with odor of ancient abattoir."

In 2005 Tonatto created a collection of perfumed inks for use with Montegrappa fountain pens (Italian-made pens that in the U.S. cost hundreds of dollars apiece). That year also marked the debut of Tonatto's E. Duse, a violet-scented perfume made in honor of the great Italian actress Eleonora Duse (1858–1924). Tonatto's three years of study, with the art historian Alessandra Marini, of the *The Lute Player*, painted by Caravaggio (1571–1610), came to fruition in 2005 in an exhibition at the State Hermitage Museum, in St. Petersburg. In the Hermitage's *Lute Player*, one of three versions by Caravaggio of the same subject, a smooth-cheeked young boy strums a lute; lying on the table in front of him are a violin, sheet music ("You Know That I Love You," a madrigal by Jacoba Arcadelta), pieces of fruit, and a pitcher holding a bouquet. During the exhibition, according to the Hermitage Web site, 10 cylindrical vessels sat on a table near the painting; six held essences of the flowers in the pitcher, and three contained those of the fruits. In the 10th was a sample of Tonatto's perfume Caravaggio, a blend of the other scents. For the *New York Times* (December 4, 2005), Chandler Burr wrote that the perfume also evokes the scents of "the wood of the lute, the sheet music and the rich smell of cloth."

In the fall of 2006, in Florence, Italy, Tonatto took part in an acclaimed exhibition, titled Perfumes of Film: Beyond Taste and Smell, which ran in conjunction with the Rome Film Festival. In collaboration with Laura Delli Colli, the president of the Italian Union of Film Journalists, Tonatto re-created scents associated with scenes in several films: in *The Leopard*, that of the candied fruit in Sicilian ice cream; in Luis Buñuel's *Belle de Jour* (1967), that of cherries dipped in brandy, favored by Catherine Deneuve's character, Séverine; in *When Harry Met Sally . . .* (1989), the coconut cake served in a New York deli to Meg Ryan's character, Sally, before she loudly demonstrates the sound effects accompanying a faked orgasm; in *Runaway Bride* (1999), cinnamon rolls; in *Chocolat* (2000), the aroma of chocolate candies; in *Amélie* (2001), the vanilla of crème brûlée. In 2007, for an exhibition in Tokyo, Japan, that celebrated Italian culture, Tonatto produced an olfactory installation that evoked the atmosphere in which Botticelli painted *The Birth of Venus* (1482). Also in 2007 Tonatto's work was on exhibit at the National Museum of Riyadh, in Saudi Arabia. The following year she introduced the fragrance Profumi del lago Maggiore ("Scents of the lake Maggiore") at the World Expo in Saragossa, Spain. The perfume evokes the scents of flowers growing on the banks of the lake for which it was named.

Tonatto lives in Turin with her husband, Alberto; their son, Andrea, who is of elementary-school age; and their daughter, Diletta, who is about 20. Tonatto created the fragrances Anena for Andrea and 24.8 for Diletta. She seeks to awaken in her children an awareness of "how to experience the world around us through the nose—the odor of snow, for example, is fantastic," she told the *Irish Times* writer. Tonatto wears perfume, according to Boylan, only on occasions when she feels "good and happy and sexy." She advised placing perfume "where you have veins, behind the earlobes. Apply it from below, starting at the feet and move upwards, lightly perfuming the whole body," and she warned against applying it in the presence of food. Her favorite perfumes include Shalimar, by Guerlain, and Eau d'Orange Verte, by Hermès.

—C.C.

Suggested Reading: (Dublin, Ireland) *Sunday Independent* (on-line) Sep. 26, 2004; *Irish Times* p76 Jan. 10, 2004; Laura Tonatto Web site; Life in Italy Web site; (London) *Times* p10 Oct. 3, 2003, p26 Sep. 18, 2004

Selected Books: *Storia di un naso* (with Alessandra Montrucchio), 2006

Courtesy of J.D. Trout

Trout, J.D.

Dec. 28, 1959– Philosopher; educator; writer

Address: Philosophy Dept., Loyola University, 6525 Sheridan Rd., Chicago, IL 60626

J.D. Trout's work combines philosophy, science, psychology, and public policy. As a philosopher of science based at Loyola University in Chicago, Illinois, Trout espouses the view that philosophers should incorporate the empirical findings of psychologists and other social scientists in their theories; doing so, he feels, would make those theories more useful in helping individuals, governments, and organizations to overcome human biases and fallacies and improve the outcomes of decision-making. (In the social sciences, empirical findings, unlike theories, are based on experience and observation.) That view, known as philosophical naturalism, has made Trout controversial in philosophy circles—where theoretical and "inward-looking" analyses are the standard method of scrutiny—but popular with scholars in other disciplines, such as psychology, in which empirical research is standard practice. "Philosophers occasionally concede the importance of empirical research to their fields, but there isn't any professional expectation that philosophers should know about empirical findings," Trout wrote in the inaugural entry of his blog, *The Greater Good* (December 4, 2008). "So the standard philosophical approach is to try to move forward by cobbling together intuitions or generating proposals that feel coherent. And as a result, the influence of scientific evidence in these fields has been slow and uneven." Trout is the author or co-author of six books dealing with the philosophy of science, a field devoted to examining the assumptions, foundations, methods, and implications of scientific inquiry. His works include *Measuring the Intentional World: Realism, Naturalism, and Quantitative Methods in the Behavioral Sciences* and *Epistemology and the Psychology of Human Judgment* (written with Michael A. Bishop). In his most recent book, *The Empathy Gap: Building Bridges to the Good Life and the Good Society*, Trout argued that although people are neurologically wired with an instinct for empathy, that instinct is not evenly distributed or applied. For instance, people feel more empathy for those who are close and similar to them than for those who are a great distance away but are suffering greater hardships. Trout considers that "empathy gap" to be among the most socially debilitating aspects of human psychology, particualrly in American society. He advocates the creation of empathetic social policies, such as universal health insurance, that bridge the emotional gap and overcome cognitive biases. "No matter what your political attachments, a science-based government can be more efficient, more money saving," Trout told *Current Biography*, the source of quotes for this article unless otherwise noted. "And that is a consequence we can all embrace. But attention to science should not be left to the discretion of the person who happens to be living in the White House. It should be made a permanent feature of the legislative process."

The youngest of three children, John Dewain Trout was born in Cleveland, Ohio, on December 28, 1959. His father was a tile setter and his mother, who had been in the U.S. Navy, was a homemaker. When Trout was five years old, his father abandoned the family. Around that time Trout's mother was diagnosed with cancer, and the family moved to the Fairless Hills/Levittown area of Pennsylvania, to be closer to her relatives. Trout's mother died when he was 11 years old. She had "done her best to make sure my childhood was fun and carefree," Trout recalled. "And she succeeded. Apart from periods of adjustment and grieving, I had a happy childhood—fishing, playing sports, singing, and reading." Trout had long been interested in nature and fishing. "When I was eight and nine, I would take a fish book with me and read it while fishing in a local lake," he said. After his mother's death Trout moved in with his aunt and uncle. Deciding that he wanted to be on his own as soon as possible, he worked numerous jobs between the ages of 12 and 18, including "packing corn, clamming in Barnegat Bay, hauling auto parts at a junkyard, singing for hire at selected formal events, and driving a truck for a chicken hatchery," according to the biography posted on his Web site. A typical weekday in Trout's senior year of high school consisted of opening the doors of an exercise club from 6:00 to 7:30 a.m., then leaving school at 11:00 a.m. to work for 12 hours in the pantry of a restaurant. In high school Trout had a number of interests: he played soccer, lifted weights, and performed in choral groups, trading landscaping work for private voice lessons from a local teacher.

Trout's introduction to philosophy came when he took a newly offered course in the subject at his high school. "The topic gripped me," Trout said. He was intrigued by the ideas presented in Thomas Hobbes's classic work of political philosophy, *Leviathan* (1651), which argues for the establishment of a commonwealth whose rulers form a social contract with its citizens. Hobbes envisioned the commonwealth as being analogous to a person, with its citizens operating as body parts that allow society to function. Trout next picked up Immanuel Kant's *Critique of Practical Reason*, the 18th-century work that formed the basis for the study of ethics and moral philosophy. "I didn't understand much of it," Trout said, "but got the feeling the concepts were important." Trout attended Bucknell University, in Lewisburg, Pennsylvania, where he earned membership in the Phi Beta Kappa honor society and graduated with a B.A. degree in philosophy and history in 1982. Trout's honors thesis, which explored both philosophy and psychology, was titled "Einstein, Freud, and Marx: Some Epistemological Problems in the Philosophy of Science." In addition to his studies, he worked various jobs for 30 to 35 hours per week. "It was all easy work," Trout said, "and college felt like a vacation."

Trout was a National Science Foundation predoctoral fellow at Cornell University (1984–85), where he earned his Ph.D. degree in the philosophy of science. One of that field's main focuses is epistemology, the study of the nature, scope, and limitations of knowledge. For centuries traditional epistemology held that knowledge required three conditions to exist: truth, belief, and justification. In other words, the proposition being considered had to be true, the person had to believe the proposition, and that belief had to be justified. However, as Edmund Gettier pointed out in an influential three-page paper published in 1963, there are instances in which the meeting of the three requirements do not lead to knowledge. Those instances include situations in which a belief is true by chance and the evidence on which that belief hinges is not reliable. For example, if a man driving a car sees many barn façades along the side of the road and believes them to be actual barns, when he comes upon a real barn, he believes (correctly) that it is an actual barn. The man's justification is based on the false evidence that he has been seeing actual barns for the duration of his drive. In that situation justification, truth, and belief are present, but the justification is not reliable. Since the publication of Gettier's paper, epistemological discussions have typically revolved around questions of which processes or systems are sufficiently reliable to lead to actual justification. During his graduate studies Trout began to formulate his own ideas about the best methods of epistemological research; among the causes of his frustration with standard epistemology were that the contexts explored—such as the barns-along-the-road scenario—seemed unlikely to challenge people's real ideas of justification of belief. "These ordinary scenarios do not test our intuitions under theoretical or, more broadly, intellectual stress," Trout argued. "And the counterexamples used to test limits of epistemic theories of, say, justification, are too disrespectful of the standards normally imposed on thought experiments and idealizations in science to be truly probative."

While at Cornell Trout also studied psychology and became particularly captivated by spoken-language processing, or the cognitive processes used to interpret speech. "Spoken-language processing is so intimately related to [the cognitive process of] comprehension, a very flexible process, and yet so many of its functions are extremely automatic and well behaved . . . ," Trout said, explaining his interest in the subject. "Also, the study of language processing requires an unfamiliar way of conceptualizing the world, a fundamentally temporal rather than spatial representation of objects." In other words, cognitive psychology has revealed that language perception uses a process that is "unfamiliar" in that it relates more to time than to space. Trout's early academic papers focused on experimental psychology and the philosophy of the mind and science. What he learned about psychology fueled his frustration with the resistance of philosophers to the use of empirical findings of science and psychology in their study of knowledge. "When it comes to studying the nature and origin of empirical knowledge, science would seem to be a plausible place to start," Trout said. "So it is probably a bad sign that contemporary epistemology has so little to do with the philosophy of science." Trout spent a year (1988–89) as an Andrew W. Mellon postdoctoral fellow and lecturer at Bryn Mawr College. He was an assistant professor of philosophy at the Stevens Institute of Technology (1989–91) and at Virginia Polytechnic Institute and State University (1991–92) before joining the faculty of Loyola University's Philosophy Department, in 1992.

In 1991 Trout co-edited, with Richard Boyd and Philip Gasper, the anthology *The Philosophy of Science*. In 1995 Trout and Paul K. Moser edited a second anthology, *Contemporary Materialism: A Reader*. That book contains 16 articles exploring the major issues surrounding modern materialism and its effects on the fields of metaphysics, philosophy of language, philosophy of mind, and theories of value. In 1997 Trout published the epistemology textbook *The Theory of Knowledge: A Thematic Introduction*, which he co-wrote with Moser and Dwayne H. Mulder. That book focuses on the essential aspects of traditional epistemology and examines the major debates taking place in the field, leaving out esoteric arguments among its practitioners. The authors noted in the preface, "An overarching lesson of this book is that epistemology is alive and well, fortified by recent interaction with the cognitive sciences, decision theory, and cross-cultural studies."

In 1998 Trout published *Measuring the Intentional World*, which concerns scientific realism, the notion that the observable world is real and that the theories advanced by science continue to progress toward an ideal theory of reality. Trout wrote that while scientific realism forms the basis of inquiry in natural sciences, in the social sciences theories of scientific realism "don't inspire the same level of confidence." In other words, people do not view social or behavioral sciences to be as empirically driven as physical science. Trout argued that there are still certain legitimate quantitative methods used in social and behavioral science that yield uneven but indisputable progress; he dubbed that notion "measured realism." He also introduced a new theory of measurement to quantify progress in the social sciences, called "population-guided estimation," which connects scientific judgment to certain natural, psychological, and social features of a population. *Measuring the Intentional World* received an award in the category of outstanding academic book from *Choice*, a reviewer of academic titles. A critic for the *Philosophical Review* wrote in an excerpt that appeared on Trout's Web site: "The careful sorting out of often confused realist claims is welcome. [Trout's] recognition that the social sciences sometimes have measurement and testing procedures akin to those of the natural sciences is also a welcome antidote to the long tradition of arguing about their scientific status without looking at what they actually do."

Over the years Trout continued to formulate his objections to the conventional theories held by most English-speaking epistemologists, known as standard analytic epistemology (SAE). In 2005 Trout and Michael A. Bishop, a philosopher then at the University of California at San Diego, published *Epistemology and the Psychology of Human Judgment*. The authors attacked SAE on a number of grounds, chief among them its failure to offer guidance on how to seek ideal methods of decision-making in the real world. "Standard analytic epistemology gives pride of place to epistemic intuitions that English-speaking philosophers have reported in the last 50 years or so," Trout said. "Intuition-trading and clever counterexamples are still the method of content of graduate training in epistemology. Michael Bishop and I have argued that this reliance is wrong-headed." To replace SAE Trout and Bishop advanced a new epistemological theory, called strategic reliabilism, which argues for the use of "robustly reliable reasoning strategies" to analyze problems and act to solve them. Trout and Bishop incorporated findings from ameliorative psychology—a field of psychology focused on improving cognition—to create a framework to help determine the mental strategies that will improve reasoning skills and avoid the biases and fallacies that typically cloud human reasoning. An example of a common fallacy is the planning fallacy, in which people are unduly optimistic about how quickly tasks can be completed. "People have to learn to focus on the history of their own performance, for the most common biases of overconfidence and hindsight," Trout said. (Overconfidence is the tendency to overestimate the probability of being correct; hindsight bias is the tendency of a person to suppose, inaccurately, that he or she was correct all along.)

Trout and Bishop's ideas drew strong reactions from the academic community. In general, their arguments were embraced by psychologists and hotly debated among philosophers. Eldar Shafir, a professor of psychology and public affairs at Princeton University, wrote in a review quoted on Trout's Web site: "This book should be read by anyone interested in the foibles and fallibility of human reasoning, and in how an empirically informed view of human knowledge and understanding may help yield not only good philosophy, but also improved policy, better thinking and greater well being." In the *Notre Dame Philosophical Reviews* (June 4, 2006), Alan Goldman, a philosopher at the College of William and Mary, criticized Trout and Bishop's "uncritical confidence" in the studies used to justify their framework and dismissed their "persistent railing against more standard analytic epistemology" as a hollow exercise that fails to yield useful advice. "Their criticism is like blaming aestheticians for not providing formulas to artists or blaming ethicists . . . for not providing a fixed set of rules for the right behavior," Goldman wrote. In a review of the book posted on Arizona University's Web site, Jonathan M. Weinberg, a philosopher from Indiana University, found fault in what he saw as the "breezy" and simplified arguments used by Trout and Bishop. Weinberg also argued that strategic reliabilism should not be considered a rival to SAE because its tools can be used only when the outcomes of strategies and decisions can be measured. Weinberg ultimately credited Trout and Bishop, however, with offering valuable new ideas in the epistemological discussion, writing: "[Bishop and Trout's] frequent, easy, and exceptionally clear presentation of actual examples from the empirical literature is one of their book's chief pleasures, and in this regard is a model for empirically-engaged philosophizing."

In February 2009 Trout published *The Empathy Gap*, about what he sees as the ever-expanding emotional distances separating people in 21st-century society and how those gaps can be bridged, using science-based processes and policies. Trout cited psychological studies that show that humans are neurologically programmed to react sympathetically to other people's suffering, but that, because of bias, fallacies, and other cognitive factors, we typically tend to make selfish decisions. Among those biases is humans' tendency to feel more empathy for those who are closest and most culturally similar to them—typically friends, neighbors, and colleagues—while feeling much less empathy for those who are a great distance away and who are culturally different, even if the latter group's suffering is much more grave. For instance, people are more likely to feel empathy for a friend who recently broke her ankle than for one of the millions of Americans without health insurance. Trout explained to Deborah Solomon for the *New York Times Magazine* (February 1, 2009) that people are more likely to feel empathy for a puppy with a hurt paw than for a person without health insurance. "Part of the reason is banal," Trout told Deborah Solomon for the *New York Times* (February 1, 2009). "Ease of visualization. The person without health care is likely to appear as a statistic, one among 50 million others." Another bias is the tendency of people to feel that others bring problems on themselves but to attribute their own problems to bad luck. Trout described that and other cognitive failings in an interview with Neuronarrative.com as "deep, habitual, predictable, increasingly well-understood, and at least arguably, crucial to good economic theorizing about rationality." According to Trout, such biases are also shaped in part by a person's surroundings. He sees the American culture of individualism as being suppressive of the natural empathetic impulse; in his interview with Neuronarrative.com, Trout cited a study showing that Americans were more likely to attribute economic hardship to character, while citizens of European countries, many of whose policies protect the most vulnerable more than American policies do, were more likely to attribute such hardship to luck. Because empathy is generally an unreliable indicator of the need for help, Trout has called on the government to make changes in social policy that will bind people to empathic behavior. (An example of such a policy is the establishment of the U.S. Social Security program.) Trout sees government as the only way to address concerns of inequality in such areas as health care and education. "We *can* overcome our biases, but not in the way you might think," Trout told Neuronarrative.com. "Self-control doesn't work. Only policies that regulate our behavior from a distance and control our options will do the trick." Trout has received positive reviews for his most recent book. One reviewer wrote on the Barnes & Noble Web site, "With penetrating insight into our cognitive empathic limitations, Trout offers pragmatic political solutions to vault these crippling psychological barriers and outlines the best way to use our brains and our policies to improve society and the life of every individual."

After serving as an assistant professor (1992–95) and associate professor (1995–2003) at Loyola University, Trout obtained full professorship in 2003. He has also served as an adjunct professor at the Parmly Hearing Institute, Loyola's research institute for the study of sensory systems, since 1992. Trout's current courses at Loyola reflect his focus on interdisciplinary studies and include "Topics in Philosophy of Social Science: Philosophical Foundations of Narrative and Quantitative Methods in the Social Sciences"; "The Philosophy of Science"; "Epistemology: Rationality, Reasoning, and Judgment"; and "The Philosophy and Psychology of Decision-Making." Trout has served on a number of editorial boards, and since December 2008 he has kept a blog called *The Greater Good*, syndicated by *Psychology Today* (on-line), in which he discusses issues in psychology and public policy in practical and often controversial terms. In a recent entry, on March 31, 2009, Trout argued in favor of raising the estate tax for those in the highest income brackets to help reduce the ever-increasing national debt. He identified a common American argument against such a tax—that it would conflict with the notion of American individualism—as a fallacy that hides the otherwise naked self-interest people exhibit by holding onto money they have not earned. "Rather than re-experiencing a collective moral spasm every time we are reminded of the insensitivity of corporate leaders and arrogant wealth, we should craft a durable image of the America we want to occupy," Trout wrote. "We should take the moribund task of budget-balancing as an opportunity to redraw the frame that girds the rugged individualist, to redefine that image, now shapeless and undignified."

In response to President Barack Obama's statement (before he announced his nomination of Sonia Sotomayor to fill the seat on the Supreme Court being vacated by David Souter) that empathy was one of the qualities he was looking for in a prospective U.S. Supreme Court justice, Trout wrote an essay that appeared in the *Chicago Tribune* (May 5, 2009). In it he noted that personal experiences inevitably influence the decisions made by all Supreme Court justices; therefore, a Supreme Court that includes justices with diverse experiences is desirable. "An empathetic justice resists the easy fiction that his or her experiences are those of a normal U.S. citizen under ordinary stresses . . . ," he wrote. "As long as the justices use their own demographically insular experiences to base their judgments, it is worth appointing individuals who recognize the limits of this useful fiction. There is, after all, a profound civility in understanding how a teenager might feel deeply humiliated by being strip-searched at school or why a woman might feel she can't complain to a male boss about being paid less than male co-workers. It is easy to see the merits of diverse experiences. It is harder to appreciate that without them, the court is less likely to make decisions that are wise and fair."

Trout lives in Evanston, Illinois, with his wife, Janice Nadler, and their two children, Jack and Jessica. In his leisure time he enjoys fishing, working on his house, and spending time with friends and family. "It is a pretty idyllic existence," Trout said, "and one that I never expected." He told Neuronarrative.com that if he could redesign the human mind, he would make our sensory and perceptive powers more flexible, so that people could, for example, observe the progress of social movements over space and time. He said: "As a result, it would be much easier to isolate the causes of, and so to understand, labor struggles, speciation, demographic shifts, and so much more."

—M.E.R.

Suggested Reading: jdtrout.com; *New York Times* (on-line) Feb. 1, 2009; *Poughkeepsie (New York) Journal* I p5 Mar. 15, 2009; *The Greater Good* (on-line); (Toronto) *Globe and Mail* L p1 Feb. 17, 2009

Selected Books: *The Theory of Knowledge: A Thematic Introduction* (with Paul Moser and Dwayne Mulder), 1997; *Measuring the Intentional World: Realism, Naturalism, and Quantitative Methods in the Behavioral Sciences*, 1998; *Epistemology and the Psychology of Human Judgment* (with Michael A. Bishop), 2005; *The Empathy Gap: Building Bridges to the Good Life and the Good Society*, 2009

TV on the Radio

Music group

Sitek, David
1972– Guitarist; producer

Adebimpe, Tunde
1974– Singer; songwriter; actor

Malone, Kyp
1973(?)– Guitarist; singer; songwriter

Smith, Gerard
1974(?)– Bassist; keyboardist

Bunton, Jaleel
1975(?)– Drummer

Address: c/o Interscope Records, 40 W. 57th St., New York, NY 10019

"I was a lover, before this war." Those words, crooned in falsetto by Tunde Adebimpe on the rock group TV on the Radio's critically acclaimed album *Return to Cookie Mountain* (2006), represent the simultaneously personal and political nature of the group's songs—which have drawn comparisons to the works of artists as disparate as Brian Eno, Peter Gabriel, Prince, and 1950s-era doo-wop groups. The band formed in 2001, when Adebimpe and the producer/multi-instrumentalist David Sitek became roommates in Brooklyn, New York, and began experimenting with multilayered vocal and electronic tracks. The self-released *OK Calculator* (2002), of which Adebimpe admitted to Matt Bernstein for downhillbattle.org (May 12, 2004), "There's more hiss on some of those songs than there are songs," laid the groundwork for what would become some of the decade's most innovative music. Members of the emergent Brooklyn rock group the Yeah Yeah Yeahs joined Adebimpe and Sitek on the *Young Liars* EP (2003), released by the independent label Touch and Go Records. Though it had limited distribution, Internet buzz over its unique fusion of styles, including African vocal music, post-punk sounds, and electronica, helped garner a cult following. Shortly after its release the band added the guitarist/vocalist Kyp Malone, bassist Gerard Smith, and drummer Jaleel Bunton to the lineup, embarked on their first national tour, and recorded their debut full-length album, *Desperate Youth, Bloodthirsty Babes* (2004), for Touch and Go Records. Heather Phares, writing for the All Music Guide Web site, called that album "a deeper, darker, denser version of the band's already ambitious sound . . . an impressive expansion of TV on the Radio's fascinating music." The album won the 2004 Shortlist Music Prize, given by a panel of music-industry professionals to recognize accomplished recordings selling fewer than 100,000 copies. The group signed to a major label, Interscope, for *Return to Cookie Mountain*, which included contributions from the likes of the rock legend David Bowie. *Return* was widely hailed as one of the best albums of the year, with *Spin* magazine giving it the top spot and the *Village Voice* and *Pitchfork Media* placing it at number two. "Evoking *Fear of Music* Talking Heads, *Station to Station* David Bowie and *Sign O' the Times* Prince," Jonathan Ringen wrote for *Rolling Stone* (September 7, 2006), "the resulting disc might be the most oddly beautiful, psychedelic and ambitious of the year." The band duplicated their 2006 success with *Dear Science* (2008), which incorporates more pop influences and has received great acclaim. In support of their albums, TV on the Radio has toured with bands including Nine Inch Nails, Grizzly Bear, Celebration, and the Fall and has appeared on television shows including *The Tonight Show with Jay Leno* and *The Late Show with David Letterman*.

Adebimpe, whose full given name is Babatunde, was born in Nigeria in 1974 and grew up mainly in Pittsburgh, Pennsylvania; he also lived in Nigeria for several years. His father, Victor Adebimpe, who died in 2005, was a psychiatrist and social worker noted for battling racial prejudice on the part of mental-health-care providers; he was also a classical pianist, painter, and writer. Speaking with Lauren Mechling for the *Wall Street Journal* (September 20, 2008), Adebimpe described his mother, Folasade Oluremi Ogunlana, who worked as a pharmacist, as "one of the best storytellers I know." His sister is an opera and gospel singer, and his brother, now deceased, was a writer. When Adebimpe was young his parents listened to jazz and classical music as well as the work of Afrobeat artists such as Fela Kuti. As Adebimpe grew into a gawky, shy, and angst-ridden teenager, he found that he preferred music that expressed alienation and aggression. "When I was about 14, my friends introduced me to bands like Dead Kennedys, Bad Brains, The Pixies," he told Phil Meadley for the London *Independent* (July 19, 2006). "Everything else sounded stupid. Suddenly I'd found a vessel for how awkward I felt, and I met people who were

Courtesy of TV on the Radio
TV on the Radio (left to right): Gerard Smith, David Sitek, Kyp Malone, Tunde Adebimpe, Jaleel Bunton

in the same boat as me." Adebimpe's social anxiety has followed him to some degree into his adult life; at New York University, where he studied filmmaking, he changed his focus from live-action film to animation because he had trouble directing actors, and, as he told Theodore Hamm for the *Brooklyn Rail* (September 2008), it took him quite some time to introduce himself to band members Malone, Bunton, and Smith because he was intimidated by the thought that "that guy is way cooler than I am—I can't really talk to him." Despite his shyness, the tall, bespectacled Adebimpe has become something of a hipster heartthrob, appearing in half-joking projects such as the magazine *Venus Zine*'s "Sexbomb" issue.

After graduating from NYU, Adebimpe supported himself through freelance animation work, including a year-and-a-half-long stint as an animator for the MTV claymation show *Celebrity Deathwatch*. He later animated the video for the Yeah Yeah Yeahs' song "Pin." Adebimpe also won small-scale fame as an actor, starring in his NYU classmate Joel Hopkins's film *Jump Tomorrow* (2001), which received critical acclaim and rotation on the Independent Film Channel.

Like Adebimpe, David Sitek, born in 1972, had felt alienated as a young man growing up in Baltimore, Maryland. A visual artist, he moved to New York in 2000, hoping to sell some paintings and get a fresh start in life. He moved into a loft in the then-low-rent neighborhood of Williamsburg, Brooklyn, with his brother, Jason Sitek, and Adebimpe. Adebimpe and Sitek discovered a shared commitment to creative pursuits. While both men had been playing music for some time, neither had envisioned a career in it. Adebimpe had been in a noise-rock band, Strugglepuss, after finishing college. "Our main aim was to pretty much drive everyone out of the room," he told Phil Meadley. Adebimpe, Sitek, and their friends formed an artistic community of sorts, or what Sitek described to Meadley as "a karaoke vodka-energy-drink collective," and Sitek asked Adebimpe to help him experiment with a new multitracking software program, Pro-Tools, by singing on some tracks. "We'd be up way too late painting and drinking too much coffee," Adebimpe told Wayne Bledsoe for knoxnews.com (October 24, 2008). "The music making became an extension of that." Sitek described himself and Adebimpe to Steve Chick for *EQ* (2006) as having been "functionally unemployable" during that period, recalling that they would spend their time coming up with song ideas while hawking their paintings on the street. They recorded their songs at home, and as Sitek told Chick, "a couple came out way better than we imagined they would. It didn't seem like such a big joke anymore. . . . Finally, we decided, 'okay, we're a band.'" They began playing gigs at the Stinger Club and other local bars, took the name TV on the Radio (suggested by a friend), and continued experimenting with music software.

The duo's experimentation resulted in a self-released album, *OK Calculator* (2002), whose title is a reference to the electronic group Radiohead's *OK Computer* (1997). "We silk-screened the CD sleeves ourselves and left copies in coffeehouses and bookstores around Brooklyn with nothing more than an e-mail address on them," Adebimpe told Chris Riemenschneider for the *Minneapolis*

Star-Tribune (October 6, 2006). Despite its roughness, the homemade record contained the electronic soundscapes and melancholy vocals that would serve as the raw elements of TV on the Radio's later albums. Around that time Sitek also embarked on a parallel career as a producer and engineer, working at a feverish pace on other bands' albums. Chick described Sitek as "a jumble of restless, fitful energy, like he knows time spent talking is time not spent making music." "But he has so much to say," Chick continued, "like the ideas are percolating like lethally strong coffee in his head, and they're going to tumble out of him *somehow*."

Shortly after *OK Calculator* was completed, Sitek met David Caruso of the independent record label Touch and Go through his friends in the Yeah Yeah Yeahs. Caruso persuaded him and Adebimpe to let the label put out their next record. *The Young Liars* EP (2003) was a further exploration of the motifs of *OK Calculator*. Heather Phares wrote for the All Music Guide: "Elements of electronica, post-rock, film music, even spirituals and traditional African vocal music combine and recombine throughout *Young Liars*' five songs so organically that it's clear that TV on the Radio isn't striving to be 'eclectic' or 'atmospheric': the band is simply using their naturally diverse elements and influences to create something wholly distinctive." The buzz generated by the album, as well as Sitek's work as a producer for the Yeah Yeah Yeahs and other members of the exploding Williamsburg music scene, helped the band's star rise quickly. They recruited the guitarist/singer Kyp Malone, a Pittsburgh, Pennsylvania, native, noted for the political consciousness he brought to the band, as well as the drummer Jaleel Bunton, who had also worked as a scenic artist for movies including *Murder* (2000), and the bassist Gerard Smith, a visual artist from Long Island, New York.

TV on the Radio's full-length debut album was *Desperate Youth, Bloodthirsty Babes* (2004). Making use of harmonics and electronic textures, the record demonstrated the band's ever-changing nature. The Yeah Yeah Yeahs guitarist Nick Zinner and Celebration vocalist Katrina Ford also contributed to the album, which was recorded in Sitek's recently established Stay Gold studio. In reviews of the album, Adebimpe's soulful falsetto drew many comparisons to that of Peter Gabriel, but Chris Dahlen, writing for *Pitchfork Media* (March 8, 2004), was quick to point out the difference. Adebimpe "isn't a man who would go on stage dressed like a flower [as Gabriel did]," Dahlen wrote. "Instead, Adebimpe sounds like a superhero—a troubled, Batman-style superhero, who can rescue the girl but frets over whether to take the grateful French kiss when they hit safe ground. Nobody with his talents and forthrightness could also have insecurities, yet that was what the lyrics made us believe."

The album's lyrics also dealt with the issue of race. Although TV on the Radio has balked at being defined as a "black rock band," the Malone-penned lyrics to "The Wrong Way" comment on stereotypes of blacks in America. The song begins with a hypothetical situation: "Wake up in a magic nigger movie / With the bright lights pointed at me / As a metaphor / Teachin' folks the score / About patience, understanding, agape babe / And sweet sweet amour." Adebimpe then sings the question, "When I realized where I was / Did I stand up and testify / Oh, fist up signify / or did I show off my soft shoe?" He expresses regret that "no new Negro politician . . . is stirring inside me . . . there's nothing inside me / but an angry heartbeat," notes the irony of black entertainers' contributing to exploitation in Africa by supporting that continent's diamond trade ("the bling drips down"), and concludes with the album's titular line: "Hey, desperate youth! / Oh, bloodthirsty babes! / Your guns are pointed the wrong way." The band toured in support of the album, released the single "New Health Rock" (with "The Wrong Way" and a cover of the Yeah Yeah Yeahs' "Modern Romance" as B-sides), then returned to the studio to record *Return to Cookie Mountain* (2006). While recording, the band fielded many offers from major labels, ultimately agreeing to a deal with Interscope. Shortly before the release of *Return to Cookie Mountain*, the band put out a non-album single, "Dry Drunk Emperor," which was inspired by the George W. Bush administration's poor handling of the Hurricane Katrina disaster and the war in Iraq.

As with the band's previous albums, *Return to Cookie Mountain* both revisited previous themes and introduced new ones, employing many different styles in songs that combined the personal and political. The album included contributions from Katrina Ford, Kazu Makino of Blonde Redhead, the Antibalas Afrobeat Orchestra, and David Bowie, who had become a fan of TV on the Radio after Sitek gave recordings of the band's songs to Bowie's doorman to pass along to him. The album was widely hailed as one of the year's best. *Spin* named *Return to Cookie Mountain* album of the year, while the *Village Voice* and *Pitchfork Media* placed it second, and *Rolling Stone*, fourth. Jon Pareles wrote for the *New York Times* (September 11, 2006), "The second full-length album by Brooklyn's best band, it expands TV on the Radio's music in multiple directions. It's more experimental yet catchier, more introspective yet more assertive, by turns gloomier and funnier, and above all richer in both sound and implication. *Return to Cookie Mountain* is simply one of this year's best albums."

Following the release of *Return to Cookie Mountain*, the industrial rocker Trent Reznor invited TV on the Radio to accompany his band, Nine Inch Nails, and the post-punk band Bauhaus on a national tour. The tour, as well as Internet buzz and downloading of the band's songs, exposed TV on the Radio to a wider audience than ever before. By the time the band returned home, after nearly two years of touring, to record *Dear Science* (2008), they had the attention and anticipation of many. Adebimpe told Chris Martins for the *A.V. Club* (October 14, 2008, on-line) that the album's recording had gone more smoothly than sessions for previous efforts, which had found band members taking offense and sitting "depressed on a pier" when their ideas were not met with enthusiasm. With *Dear Science*, he said, "we all tried to keep in mind a kind of loving fast-forward button, where you're like, 'This isn't *really* important right now, so let's just skip to the part where you realize no one is trying to hurt you.'"

The album's name came from a note Sitek had jokingly tacked up in the studio, which read, "Dear Science, please fix all the things you keep talking about or shut . . . up." Adebimpe told Martins that the title also referred to "the questionable faith that we put in science. You know, we're allegedly able to live longer because of scientific advancement, but we're doing so in a world that might be getting hurt in the process. Or it's thinking about how quickly vessels for communication have progressed, but how genuine communication on a host of things that are still marring the human race hasn't advanced." The record continued the group's examination of complex issues such as race, technology, and liberalism in America. On the track "Red Dress," Adebimpe laments, "It's a stone cold shame / how they got you tame / and they got me tame," stating his opinion of how liberals (himself included) have behaved in the face of the Iraq war, the existence of prison camps at Guantánamo Bay, and other perceived injustices. However, the record's outlook also includes hope and optimism, especially on the disco-inflected single "Golden Age," written mainly by Malone. "I was trying consciously to create a utopian world inside a pop song," Malone told Jon Pareles for the *New York Times* (September 7, 2008). "I don't think that three minutes of music on a commercial record is going to bring paradise, but I feel like there is power in music and power in our words and power in what we put out into the world." Critics responded favorably to the album. *Rolling Stone*, *Spin*, and the *Village Voice* named *Dear Science* the best album of 2008.

In April 2009 the band released an EP, *Read Silence*, which consisted of other artists' remixes of three songs from *Dear Science*. In September of that year Adebimpe announced that TV on the Radio would be taking a break from their work together. He told James Montgomery and Kyle Anderson for MTV.com (September 3, 2009), "We've decided to take, well, the going theory is to take about a year off, because you have to go and live a life and change things up."

The members of TV on the Radio carry on numerous other projects. Sitek has produced records for bands including Liars, Foals, Dragons of Zynth, Celebration, and The Knife, as well as the actress Scarlett Johansson's record *Anywhere I Lay My Head* (2008). In 2008 Adebimpe returned to acting, with a role as the title character's fiancé in the family drama *Rachel Getting Married* (2008). He also released a seven-inch record as a solo act called *FMV* (Fake Male Voice) and has recently collaborated with Mike Patton of Faith No More and Mr. Bungle, among other acts. In 2009 Malone, calling himself Rain Machine, released a solo album on the Anti- label. The eponymously named album, according to the label's Web site, contains 10 "unflinchingly original and emotional songs mixing elements of modern jazz, blue-grass and blistering guitar driven rock."

TV on the Radio, meanwhile, has experienced a level of renown they never thought possible. "If you're going to reach for it, reach all the way for it," Sitek told Pareles in 2008 of the efforts that produced *Dear Science*. "Albums like *Purple Rain* and *Thriller* and those kind of records, you had to reach far above the din of cynicism and modern living to get to that place, against all the odds. The industry used to support that kind of record making, and just because the marketplace of the industry doesn't support it now doesn't mean you shouldn't still try for it."

—J.E.P.

Suggested Reading: All Music Web site; *Downhill Battle* (on-line) May 12, 2004; (London) *Independent* p15 July 19, 2006; *New York Times* Arts & Leisure p61 Sep. 7, 2008; *Salon.com* Sep. 30, 2008; *Washington Post* Weekend p6 Apr. 13, 2007

Selected Recordings: *OK Calculator*, 2002; *Desperate Youth, Bloodthirsty Babes*, 2004; *Return to Cookie Mountain*, 2006; *Dear Science*, 2008; *Read Silence*, 2009

Vanden Heuvel, Katrina

Oct. 7, 1959– Editor; publisher

Address: The Nation, *33 Irving Pl., New York, NY 10003*

Katrina vanden Heuvel is the editor, publisher, and part-owner of the *Nation* magazine, the oldest political-opinion weekly in the U.S., widely seen as the country's leading forum for progressive, leftist, dissident journalism. Vanden Heuvel has been associated with the iconic journal for her entire career, starting as an intern in 1980 before spending much of the next decade reporting from the Soviet Union on its reformist glasnost and perestroika movements. Taking the helm of the *Nation* in 1995, she became a rarity in the male-dominated field of political journalism. In a conversation with Ed Rampell for *LA City Beat* (July 1, 2004), vanden Heuvel described the *Nation*, founded by abolitionists in 1865, as an independent, "muckraking, troublemaking, idea-launching magazine of critical opinion." Over the years the magazine has provided a platform for the writings of such lumina-

Amanda Edwards/Getty Images

Katrina vanden Heuvel

ries as Martin Luther King Jr., Albert Einstein, H. L. Mencken, Gore Vidal, Arthur Miller, Hunter S. Thompson, Ralph Nader, James Baldwin, Jean-Paul Sartre, and, more recently, Christopher Hitchens, Toni Morrison, Calvin Trillin, Naomi Klein, Cornel West, Eric Alterman, and Katha Pollitt, among many other distinguished contributors. In addition to its traditional mission—to provide an incubator for solutions to what it views as social and political ills—the magazine has of late, under vanden Heuvel's stewardship, taken aim at the consolidation and corporatization of the mainstream media. It seeks to offer "an antidote to the suffocating consensus," vanden Heuvel told Owen Johnson in an interview for the program *Profiles* (January 6, 2008, on-line), broadcast in Indiana and on-line by the radio station WFIU. "The *Nation* exists to challenge the downsized politics of excluded alternatives." Ironically, the *Nation*'s fortunes seem to be closely correlated to the balance of power in the country: as with many political journals, its circulation almost always rises when it is in opposition to the policies of the current presidential administration. The *Nation*'s readership increased dramatically in the eras of Ronald Reagan, George H. W. Bush, and George W. Bush and fell in the Bill Clinton years (although they rose again with the ascendance of House Speaker Newt Gingrich during Clinton's first term). As Victor Navasky, vanden Heuvel's predecessor and mentor, famously noted, "What's bad for the country is good for the *Nation*." Vanden Heuvel told Tom Engelhardt for Tomdispatch.com (April 20, 2006) that in "bad" times "the core animating principles of [the] magazine just [come] into play: fierce independence, defense of the constitution, defense of democracy, first amendment rights, rule of law and of international law, civil rights, civil liberties, economic justice." The telegenic vanden Heuvel is known to many for her frequent appearances on cable-television news shows, on which she has often confronted her ideological opponents; such forums, she has said, allow her to discuss ideas that might not otherwise be represented in the mainstream media. She is the author, co-author, or editor of several books and anthologies published by the *Nation*.

Katrina vanden Heuvel was born in New York City on October 7, 1959 to Jean Stein, a writer and the editor of the literary journal *Grand Street*, and William vanden Heuvel, who served as a member of John F. Kennedy's presidential administration and as U.S. ambassador to the European office of the United Nations, among other prominent government posts. She has one sister and two step-siblings. Her maternal grandfather was Jules Stein, the Hollywood mogul and founder of the Music Corporation of America (MCA), an entertainment conglomerate. Growing up on New York City's Upper West Side, vanden Heuvel spent a lot of time with her grandfather in Los Angeles, California, and remembers meeting many movie celebrities. Stein—whose clients included Ronald Reagan during that politician's earlier career, as a movie actor—was a moderate Republican; his daughter Jean Stein "was very much the free radical spirit in the family," vanden Heuvel told Johnson. "I was the grownup. My mother . . . was always very loving but not your normal mother." Vanden Heuvel described her father to Johnson as "a populist, an unrepentant New Dealer but very pragmatic" and said that his proudest achievements included working to open up charter schools for black communities during segregation. She said to Mark F. Bernstein for the *Princeton Alumni Weekly* (February 11, 2004): "My father has been active in liberal Democratic politics for decades, so as someone who is both pragmatic and visionary, he had a strong influence on my political thinking." Vanden Heuvel told Johnson that her parents, who divorced when she was 10, were "passionate" about "doing good with government"; "I think I get a lot of my interest and fascination with politics from just absorbing it in my home." She added, "You absorb it all as a young person but then you find your own way." As a guest on the TV program *Charlie Rose* (July 24, 1995, on-line), she said, "One thing I've seen in my life is that the rich and powerful take care of themselves and that is something that we are seeing more and more of in this country. But for the poor, the weak, the working poor . . . for those people the government plays a role."

Vanden Heuvel attended the Trinity School, a private school on the Upper West Side, graduating in 1977. She then enrolled at Princeton University, in Princeton, New Jersey, where she studied politics and history. She told Bernstein, "I was . . . fortunate to work with some extraordinary professors, and through them became interested in those who challenged orthodoxy and consensus and came to value those Americans who had had the courage of their convictions. I also came to value the importance of studying historical and political alternatives. You could say I became an 'alternativist.'" She graduated summa cum laude in 1981, devoting her senior thesis to the political "witch hunts" of the 1950s, led by U.S. senator Joseph McCarthy and devoted to identifying people in government or the entertainment industry who were members of the Communist Party or communist sympathizers. "I learned how this country's politics were deformed by a fear of the Soviet Union," she told Charlie Rose. "The McCarthyist crusade was an attempt to root out ideas that didn't conform and it was done in the name of saving this country from un-Americanism when what was un-American was trying to root out dissident ideas." She said to Johnson that her study of the McCarthy era taught her that "if you don't challenge and dissent and speak your mind even in perilous times when you can be called un-American that you're abdicating the true American tradition." During her time at Princeton, she served as editor of the *Nassau Weekly*, a school publication, and had an internship at *National Lampoon* magazine in 1978. After taking a course at Princeton called "Politics and the Press," taught by Blair Clark, who had served as the *Nation*'s editor from 1976 to 1978, she got a nine-month internship at that magazine in her junior year. "To be at the *Nation* was kind of a second education for me," she told Robin Finn for the *New York Times* (November 11, 2005). She told Johnson, "The *Nation* was an important part [of my political formation] because to me, it's an alternative history of the United States. If you look at the 142 years of the *Nation*, you can see what was possible, the alternatives that were there, what was lost and what could still be retrieved." After graduating from Princeton vanden Heuvel worked as a production assistant at ABC Television. In 1984 she returned to the *Nation* as assistant editor for foreign affairs.

Vanden Heuvel had first visited the Soviet Union with a Princeton alumni group in 1978, her interest in the region growing out of her study of the McCarthy period. She met her future husband, Stephen F. Cohen, then a professor of Russian studies and Soviet politics at Princeton, in 1979, when he asked her to smuggle some manuscripts and documents from Russian dissidents to the U.S. The two traveled to the Soviet Union together in 1985, after Mikhail Gorbachev came to power. (Vanden Heuvel and Cohen later became friends with Gorbachev.) "To have that front row seat in the unfolding of Perestroika and Glasnost at a moment when I felt American politics was kind of stagnant, was extraordinary," she told Johnson. "For someone like me who missed the '60s in this country," she told Bill Hewitt for *People* (February 19, 1990), "it's like rediscovering intense political life." While working as a foreign correspondent, covering the Gorbachev years for the *Nation* and other publications, vanden Heuvel also worked at the *Moscow News* under Yegor Yakovlev, whom she described to Johnson as a "crusading Glasnost editor." In late 1989, the year after they were married, Cohen and vanden Heuvel published *Voices of Glasnost*, a collection of interviews conducted between June 1987 and May 1989 with 14 Soviet reformers. Also in 1989 vanden Heuvel was named editor-at-large of the *Nation*, responsible for the magazine's coverage of the Soviet Union. (Cohen penned a column called "Sovieticus" for the magazine in the 1980s.) The following year vanden Heuvel founded a quarterly Russian-language feminist journal based in Moscow and New York called *Vyi i Myi* ("You and We"), conceived to provide bridges between American and Russian women.

In 1994 vanden Heuvel took a leave of absence from *Vyi i Myi* to assume the post of acting editor of the *Nation*, while Victor Navasky went on leave to teach at Harvard University. In 1995 Navasky brought together a group of investors, including the actor and activist Paul Newman, Peter Norton of the Norton Software Co., Alan Sagner of the Corporation for Public Broadcasting, and several others, who bought the magazine—which was perennially operating at a loss—from the investment banker Arthur Carter. Later that year vanden Heuvel was officially named editor of the *Nation*, becoming one of very few women in the country to head a major political journal. (The trailblazing Freda Kirchwey had been editor and publisher of the *Nation* from 1933 to 1955.) While maintaining the standards and founding principles of the *Nation*, vanden Heuvel signaled changes aimed at making the publication more accessible and competitive. Pictures began to adorn what had been a very conservative cover, and over time the *Nation* expanded into different areas, such as book and anthology publications, radio, strategic partnerships involving content sharing, and the Internet.

Perhaps more than any publishing strategy, the presidency of George W. Bush gave a huge boost to the magazine, whose circulation increased by 70 percent during the years of his administration. While vanden Heuvel told Engelhardt that "we've been known for two things [since the magazine's founding], our ability to speak truth to power and our ability to not make a profit," the magazine began turning a modest profit in 2003. While the policies of the Bush administration, particularly with regard to civil liberties and foreign policy, were certainly a key factor in the magazine's recent success, the perceived failure of the corporate-owned media to maintain a proper skepticism toward government was at least as responsible in driving readers to see the *Nation* as a trusted source of critical information. Vanden Heuvel noted to Bernstein "the fact that the media have become so conglomeratized, corporatized, 'Murdoch-ized.' We are one of the few remaining independent publications, which I think gives us leeway to stand outside and raise larger questions." She also said, "If much of the media had been doing its job and not serving as stenographers to power, we might have been able to avert a war in Iraq." While many conservative critics of the *Nation* accused the magazine of being predictable, dogmatic, and "unpatriotic" after the attacks of September 11, 2001, vanden Heuvel has insisted that the *Nation* was just the opposite—that it gave a voice to alternative explanations, solutions, and opinions that were otherwise drowned out by the mainstream media. "How often do you see the idea of a living wage being addressed in the mainstream press?" she said to Bernstein in 2004. "How often do you see the media address the fact that universal health care is a core human right and not some wacky left-wing idea? How often do you see any questions raised about the folly of the militarization of our foreign policy? How often do you see real reporting on how the pharmaceutical companies are writing our drug bills, the oil and gas industry is writing our energy bills, or corporate media are writing telecommunications law? But often it's a matter of how the mainstream media address issues or a matter of who they use as sources, talking to corporate leaders, say, rather than workers." She told Engelhardt in 2006, "Our mainstream media does a real disservice to us all, because I do believe that this is a more progressive country than is understood. . . . I think people seek a saner, more decent country than our elected representatives offer and the mainstream media paint. And this blue/red divide they're always harping on, I don't like it. This is a much more complicated country than they imagine." Although the *Nation* and vanden Heuvel are often referred to as liberal, she has tried to include more viewpoints from progressives. Vanden Heuvel described the difference between the two approaches to Ed Rampell, arguing that "too often liberals construct a political system which involves top-down organization. Whereas progressives, more often, believe ordinary people have the right, wisdom, and good sense to organize their own politics, and build movements from the bottom up. It's more inclusive."

In 2005 vanden Heuvel became the *Nation*'s publisher and general partner as well as editor. Her daily activities include reading three to five newspapers by 8 a.m. and scanning international papers and the Internet. She is involved in every aspect of the *Nation*, including drafting editorials, vetting manuscripts, approving covers, recruiting and maintaining contact with writers, answering an average of 100 e-mail messages per day, and writing entries on her blog at the *Nation*'s Web site. Another part of vanden Heuvel's routine is writing op-ed pieces for such mainstream papers as the *Washington Post*, the *New York Times*, the *Boston Globe*, and the *Los Angeles Times*, as well as making appearances on TV news shows broadcast by MSNBC, CNN, and ABC. Given the comparatively limited reach of the *Nation*, vanden Heuvel has said that those appearances allow her both to boost the profile of the magazine and call attention to the issues it reports; Engelhardt called her "the branded face of her magazine." Vanden Heuvel is often paired on shows with conservative pundits such as Rich Lowry, editor of the right-wing *National Review*; her visibility in the mainstream media has drawn some criticism from some on the left, who see her as dignifying such programs with her presence. "I'll tell you why I do TV," she told Engelhardt. "Because there are very few opportunities for people on the left or progressives to speak to a broader audience, to reach people, and eighty percent of Americans still get their news from television. What's frustrating, of course, is how little time there is to say anything on TV. Still, as long as you come with the views you express in your real day job and you don't check your integrity at the door, it's an opportunity to say a few things you just don't hear in this mainstream media wasteland."

Vanden Heuvel has written or edited several books. In 1990 she edited *"The Nation", 1865–1990: Selections from the Independent Magazine of Politics and Culture*. In 2002 she co-edited, along with Jonathan Schell, *A Just Response: "The Nation" on Terrorism, Democracy and September 11, 2001*. In 2004 she collaborated with the *Nation* contributing editor Robert L. Borosage to edit *Taking Back America: And Taking Down the Radical Right*, which was conceived as a follow-up to a 2003 conference of progressives; the conference had been aimed at countering what vanden Heuvel and others viewed as the demonization of liberalism in the U.S. Taking part in a *New York Times* Roundtable discussion (March 6, 2005, on-line), vanden Heuvel said in response to the question, "Why has 'liberal' become a dirty word for so many Americans today?": "I would begin with the unrelenting assault on the term liberalism by the right wing. It has been a project over the last few decades. . . . Liberals have . . . paid a heavy price by allowing liberalism to be defined almost exclusively as social liberalism. So that you lost sight of economic rights, economic justice." In 2005 vanden Heuvel published the *Dictionary of Republicanisms*, a sometimes humorous take on the Republicans' use of language and semantics. For the book she solicited thousands of contributions from *Nation* readers to weigh in on what she told the *Hill* (December 7, 2005) is the American right wing's "well-funded and self-conscious program of Orwellian doublespeak, using the language to suit their ends." For example, Lawrence Sandek of Twin Peaks, California, defined "compassionate conservatism" as "poignant concern for the very wealthy"; Kevin Weaver of San Francisco, California, defined "pro-life" as "valuing human life up until birth"; Sue Bazy of Philadelphia, Pennsylvania, defined "voter fraud" as "a significant minority turnout"; and Denise Clay, also from Philadelphia, gave two definitions for "woman": "1. Person who can be trusted to bear a child but can't be trusted to decide whether or not she wishes to have the child. 2. Person who must have all decisions regarding her reproductive functions made by men with whom she wouldn't want to have sex in the first place." In 2009 vanden Heuvel edited a selection of the *Nation*'s best economic and financial coverage over the previous 20 years, entitled *Meltdown: How Greed and Corruption Shattered Our Financial System and How We Can Recover.* Vanden Heuvel and the *Nation*, while bitingly critical of George W. Bush, have been cautiously optimistic in the first months of the Barack Obama administration—particularly in regard to the economy. "Obama takes office at a time defined by hope and fear in equal measure," vanden Heuvel wrote on the *Nation*'s "Editor's Cut" blog the day after Obama was sworn in as president (January 21, 2009). "Fortunately, Obama has a mandate for change. . . . As the first Community-Organizer-in-Chief, Obama understands the power of change from below. He has oxygenated the grassroots and got people believing and dreaming again. But he will only be as brave as ordinary citizens move him to be. That's why independent small d- democratic movements, grassroots organizing, online and offline, will be vital to pushing the limit of Obama's own politics and countering the forces of money and establishment power which remain obstacles to meaningful reform."

In 1988 vanden Heuvel won an Olive Branch Award for work on "Gorbachev's Soviet Union," printed in a specially themed issue of the *Nation*. In 2003 she received the Maggie Award from Planned Parenthood for her article "Right-to-Lifers Hit Russia," a report on the antiabortion movement in that country. Vanden Heuvel has also received awards for public service from the Liberty Hill Foundation, the Correctional Association, the Association for American-Russian Women, the New York Civil Liberties Union, and the American-Arab Anti-discrimination Committee. She is a member of the Council on Foreign Relations and sits on the boards of the Nation Institute, the Institute for Women's Policy research, the Institute for Policy Studies, the World Policy Institute, and, with her father, the Correctional Association of New York and the Franklin and Eleanor Roosevelt Institute.

Vanden Heuvel and her husband, Stephen F. Cohen, two decades her senior, have a daughter, Nicola, born in 1991. Cohen also has a son and a daughter from a previous marriage. The family live on the Upper West Side of Manhattan.

—M.M.

Suggested Reading: *Charlie Rose* (on-line) July 24, 1995; *LA City Beat* (on-line) July 1, 2004; *New York Times* B p2 Nov. 11, 2005; *People* p58 Feb. 19, 1990; *Princeton Alumni Weekly* (on-line) Feb. 11, 2004; *Tomdispatch.com* Apr. 20, 2006

Selected Books: *Voices of Glastnost* (with Stephen Cohen), 1989; as editor—*"The Nation," 1865–1990: Selections from the Independent Magazine of Politics and Culture*, 1990; *A Just Response: "The Nation" on Terrorism, Democracy and September 11, 2001* (with Jonathan Schell), 2002; *Taking Back America: And Taking Down the Radical Right* (with Robert L. Borosage), 2004; *The Dictionary of Republicanisms*, 2005; *Meltdown: How Greed and Corruption Shattered Our Financial System and How We Can Recover*, 2009

Veneman, Ann M.

(VEN-eh-min)

June 29, 1949– Executive director of UNICEF

Address: UNICEF House, 3 U.N. Plaza, New York, NY 10017

Since 2005 Ann M. Veneman has been the executive director of the United Nations Children's Fund (UNICEF). Established as an arm of the United Nations in 1946, UNICEF works globally to improve conditions for children around the world, by trying to ensure that they get adequate nutrition and education; immunization against disease and proper care when they get sick; protection against violence in areas of civil or international strife; and protection from exploitation by their elders in the workplace. Earlier in her career Veneman practiced law in the private and public sectors and served in various capacities in the California and federal departments of agriculture. She was the secretary of the California Department of Food and Agriculture (CDFA) from 1995 to 1999, under Governor Pete Wilson, and secretary of the U.S. Department of Agriculture (USDA) from 2001 to 2005, under President George W. Bush. For six years beginning in 1963, the year Veneman turned 14, her father served in the California State Assembly. She shares many of the views held by her father, a Republican, who was a peach farmer until he entered politics. "My father was not a partisan person. He wanted to make things work better. He had friends on both sides," she told George Skelton for the *Los Angeles Times* (December 25, 2000). "It was a desire to do the right thing and make good public policy that drove him—rather than what we see today with all this partisan bickering." "[Ann Veneman's] got a lot of her daddy in her," Pete Wilson told Skelton. "Smart as a whip. Very conscientious and hard-working, but makes it look easy. Straightforward and gutsy, but not obnoxious. She has great charm."

Among many other honors, Veneman was named the Outstanding Woman of the Year by the Association of Women in International Trade (2001) and won the Sesame Workshop's Leadership Award for Children (2006). "I always like to say one of the reasons I was able to do all these

Scott Wintrow/Getty Images

Ann M. Veneman

things is because I didn't have real solid goals," Veneman told Jeff Jardine for the *Modesto (California) Bee* (April 10, 2008). "Setting goals blinds you from taking things that might come along the way. I couldn't have dreamed this whole thing."

The first of three siblings, Ann Margaret Veneman was born on June 29, 1949 in Modesto, California, a city about 80 miles east of San Francisco. Her parents, John G. "Jack" Veneman and Nita D. (Bomberger) Veneman, raised her and their other daughter, Jane, and their son, John, on a peach farm in that area. Jack Veneman made his living as a farmer until he was elected to the California State Assembly, in 1962. Later, from 1969 until 1973, he served as an undersecretary in the U.S. Department of Health, Education and Welfare, when Richard Nixon was in the White House. While a student at Thomas Downey High School, in Modesto, Ann Veneman was a page at the 1964 Republican National Convention, held in San Francisco. After her high-school graduation, in 1967, she attended the University of California (UC) at Davis and earned a B.A. degree in political science in 1970. Among other political activities during her college years, in 1969 Veneman interned in the office of Pete Wilson, a Republican who was then a California state assemblyman. She received an M.A. degree in public policy at UC–Berkeley in 1971 and a J.D. degree from the UC Hastings College of the Law, in San Francisco, in 1976. She is a member of the bar in both California and Washington, D.C.

After she earned a law degree, Veneman got a job as a staff attorney with the Bay Area Rapid Transit District (BART) in Oakland, California. Two years later she returned to Modesto to serve (1978–80) as a deputy public defender; concurrently, she joined the Modesto law firm of Damrell, Damrell & Nelson (now Damrell, Nelson, Schrimp, Pallios, Pacher & Silva) as an associate. Later she was made a partner. In 1986 Veneman moved to Washington, D.C., to become the associate administrator of the U.S. Department of Agriculture's Foreign Agriculture Service. Among other assignments, she worked on the Uruguay Round talks for the General Agreement on Tariffs and Trade, the North American Free Trade Agreement, and the U.S.–Canada Free Trade Agreement.

In 1989 Veneman was named the deputy undersecretary of agriculture for USDA's International Affairs and Commodity Programs. Her job involved such matters as international trade policies and negotiations and distribution of food aid. In 1991 Veneman was promoted to USDA deputy secretary, the second-highest position at the department. She remained the highest-ranking female in the department for two years before joining Patton Boggs, a general- and lobbying-law firm based in the nation's capital. During her time with Patton Boggs, she represented high-profile firms including the Dole Food Co.; she was also a member of the board of directors of Calgene, a biogenetics firm based in Davis, California.

Pete Wilson was California's governor when, in 1995, Veneman left Patton Boggs and the Calgene board to assume the job of secretary of California's Department of Food and Agriculture. She replaced Henry J. Voss, a lifelong farmer who had resigned after it was reported that he had failed to disclose income he had received from his farming businesses. (Although Veneman has been credited as the first woman to hold the position, another woman, Rose Bird, had served as secretary in the 1970s.) Wilson's choice of Veneman came as unwelcome news to many of the state's farm-group members, because traditionally only farmers had held that post. Bob Vice, for example, a former Farm Bureau president, declared, as quoted by Dan Morain in the *Los Angeles Times* (April 28, 1995), "The California Farm Bureau Federation continues to believe a farmer or rancher, someone who has experience with government regulation at the ground level, should serve as a secretary of food and agriculture." Others hailed Wilson's appointment of Veneman. "There is no question that the experience Ann Veneman brings to that position is going to benefit all of California agriculture," David Moore, the president of the Western Growers Association in Irvine, California, told Peter M. Tirshwell for the Newark, New Jersey, *Journal of Commerce* (August 21, 1995). Although Veneman understood her critics' desire to see a farmer in the position, she remained confident in her abilities. "I have been very involved with California agriculture. . . . I grew up on a farm and have been around it all my life, and [being a farmer] should not be a prerequisite for the job," she told Kathie A. Smith for the *Modesto Bee* (April 28, 1995).

For many years California's farmers have earned more money from sales of their crops and dairy products than farmers in any other state; they produce about half of the nation's fruits (including nuts) and vegetables. International trade was one of Veneman's top priorities as CDFA secretary, and during her tenure revenues from overseas sales grew dramatically. Another of her accomplishments was the "Taste the Sunshine" program, which successfully promoted California's crops. Veneman faced a crisis when, in 1996, hundreds of people across the nation were infected with the parasite *Cyclospora cayetanensis*. Many had reported eating strawberries, leading some to believe that strawberries from California, which at that time supplied 80 percent of the nation's crop, were to blame. To dispel those notions and quell growing public fears, Veneman held a press conference at which she ate strawberries. No link was ever found between the outbreak of the illness and California-grown strawberries.

In 1999 Veneman left the CDFA to become a partner at the law firm Nossaman, Guthner, Knox & Elliott (now Nossaman LLP) in Sacramento, California. She specialized in cases involving food, agriculture, the environment, technology, and trade-related issues. She also sat on the boards of several nonprofit organizations, including the Close-up Foundation, a group dedicated to educating young people on the democratic process, and ACDI/VOCA (the acronym stands for the names of two groups that merged in 1997—Agricultural Cooperative Development International and Volunteers in Overseas Cooperative Assistance), which promotes economic growth in developing countries. In 2000 she co-chaired the campaign in California of the Republican presidential nominee, George W. Bush. That December President-elect Bush announced that he had chosen Veneman to be secretary of the U.S. Department of Agriculture. The U.S. Senate unanimously confirmed her on January 20, 2001.

"Working in USDA wasn't some sort of life plan, but I was raised in a family that put a priority on public service," Veneman told Richard T. Estrada for the *Modesto Bee* (December 21, 2000). As USDA secretary Veneman was charged with overseeing the agency's operations, which include conserving natural resources, maintaining the safety of foods, ensuring the proper care of farm animals and plants, promoting good nutrition through education, managing school-lunch programs, issuing food stamps, distributing agricultural subsidies, and overseeing national and international agricultural trade. As with her appointment to CDFA, Bush's announcement prompted both praise and criticism. Bill Pauli, a former president of the California Farm Bureau, described Veneman to Michael Janofsky for the *New York Times* (December 21, 2000) as "a great choice." "She clearly knows and understands process and procedure of agriculture," he said. "Equally important, she understands the importance of good trade policy, relative to agriculture." Bruce Hamilton, then the conservation director for the environmental organization the Sierra Club, expressed concern. Citing instances in which Veneman had worked to gain access to public lands for corporate mineral extractors and drivers of off-road vehicles, he told Janofsky, "If that is the philosophy [Veneman] brings to the Department of Agriculture and the National Forest Service [an arm of the USDA], that is troubling."

After the outbreak of foot-and-mouth disease in European livestock in March 2001 and the terrorist attacks on the U.S. on September 11 of that year, Veneman spent much of her time focused on security, food-safety, and bioterrorism issues. On another front, in her September 2001 publication, "Food and Agricultural Policy: Taking Stock of the New Century," Veneman wrote that farm subsidies—money that the federal government gives to farmers to supplement their incomes and, indirectly, to affect production—were going predominantly to a small group of wealthy farmers. Her attempt to redirect the distribution of the $20 billion allocated for subsidies angered many farm-state lawmakers. Although Veneman said that she was simply trying to distribute the money more equitably, for the benefit of smaller farms, farm-state lawmakers maintained that she was planning to abolish subsidies altogether. The White House assigned a special assistant to help mediate between the two sides. In the end, Congress ignored her suggestions. Veneman was undaunted. "This is regular sport to beat up on the secretary of agriculture," she told Gebe Martinez for *Congressional Quarterly Weekly* (January 25, 2002).

In August 2002 Veneman learned that she had breast cancer; she successfully underwent six weeks of radiation treatment. The next month she disclosed her condition to the public. "It was a difficult thing to be diagnosed, and very difficult to lead up to going public about it," Veneman told Helen Rumbelow for the *Washington Post* (September 19, 2002). "I hope by doing so I can get a message out to both men and women about the importance of check-ups and a healthy lifestyle." Veneman remained committed to her job. "I think it's healthy to be engaged in your profession as long as it doesn't impact your overall well-being," she told Rumbelow.

In December 2003 the nation's first case of bovine spongiform encephalopathy (BSE), familiarly known as mad cow disease, was discovered in an animal at a farm in Mabton, Washington. The disease, which affects the nervous system, is invariably fatal, and many scientists believe it can spread to humans as well as cattle through the consumption of brain or spinal-cord tissue. (Manufacturers of animal feed typically use all parts of slaughtered animals in the manufacturing process.) The Mabton farm was immediately quarantined, the USDA launched an investigation, and Veneman immediately held a press conference to alert the public. "By far, it's the biggest food safety [and] animal disease crisis I've dealt with," she told Christopher Lee for the *Washington Post* (January 1, 2004). "Maybe this is my biggest experience, but over the years we've dealt with food safety crises. . . . And one of the things I've learned is that it's very important to be out there quickly, to tell the whole story as soon as possible." The outbreak was successfully contained. Veneman promptly announced new rules to increase the safety of the U.S. beef supply. Along with the implementation of a national identification system that can track cattle more efficiently, potentially ill cows must be held until test results clear them for slaughter, and "downer" cows (so-called because they are unable to walk due to illness) cannot be used for any purpose. Veneman was lauded for her quick and effective response to the crisis.

Among her other accomplishments at the USDA, Veneman reauthorized child-nutrition and food-stamp programs and completed the transition from paper food stamps to electronic debit cards, which has helped reduce fraud. She established the "Leaders of Tomorrow" initiative, which aims to inspire students to pursue careers in agriculture and public service. A financial audit of the USDA conducted in 2002 gave the department a clean bill of financial health—for the first time ever—and audits carried out during the next three years produced the same result. The nation's revenues from agricultural exports rose to a record $62.3 billion in 2004. In 2003 Veneman organized and hosted the first Ministerial Conference on Science and Technology; held in Sacramento, it brought together agriculture secretaries or ministers from 120 nations to discuss the roles of science and technology in reducing world hunger and poverty.

During her tenure at the USDA, Veneman was criticized regarding the influence on policymaking of lobbyists and others with ties to the meat industry. Veneman's chief of staff, Dale Moore, was the former head of legislative affairs at the National Cattlemen's Beef Association (NCBA), an advocacy group. Her director of communications, Alisa Harrison, and deputy undersecretary, Charles Lambert, had also previously worked for the NCBA. In 2004, following the detection of mad-cow disease in the U.S. and a Japanese ban on the import of U.S. beef, a Kansas beef producer requested permission to test all its cattle for the disease and thus convince the Japanese government of its safety. Representatives of the meatpacking industry, who feared that consumers would demand all beef producers to conduct such tests, opposed the request. Although the USDA had promised the nation's public to do everything in its power to detect any remaining cases of the disease in cattle, the agency took the lobbyists' position, calling such testing unwarranted; indeed, it forbade the Kansas producer from conducting the test. In another incident later that year, the USDA opposed mandatory country-of-origin labeling for meat, fruit, and vegetables, which some consumer groups have pushed for. The beef industry opposed labeling, citing added costs and burdensome paperwork; in addition, insiders feared that some consumers would balk at buying meat sold by American companies but imported from overseas. Although the labeling law had been introduced in 2002 and was due to take effect in 2004, meat-industry lobbyists successfully delayed its implementation for several years (except regarding fish and shellfish), and the USDA refused to enforce it. (The country-of-origin label law went into effect in March 2009.)

Veneman announced her resignation from the USDA on November 12, 2004, stating only that she was ready to move on to "new opportunities." On January 19, 2005 U.N. secretary-general Kofi Annan had named her the next executive director of UNICEF. "It is a great honor to have the opportunity to lead UNICEF, which is truly one of the world's great institutions," Veneman told reporters on May 2, 2005, the day after she assumed leadership. "Too many children in the world face hardships and challenges that should never be a part of childhood. I look forward to continuing UNICEF's mission of serving children around the globe."

In the four years since Veneman's appointment, UNICEF has continued its dedication to work toward the Millennium Development Goals set by the U.N. in 2000. Those goals, which the U.N. hopes to meet by 2015, include reducing by half the number of people living in extreme poverty, ensuring that all boys and girls complete primary schooling, eliminating inequalities in education between girls and boys, reducing the child mortality rate by two-thirds, and preventing the spread of HIV/AIDS, malaria, and other devastating diseases. Recently UNICEF reported progress in its efforts to protect children in the war-torn African nation of Sudan, where factions have forced youngsters to take up arms in their causes. In December 2008 UNICEF signed a Memorandum of Understanding with Sudan Armed Forces (SAF) and the National Council for Child Welfare. The memorandum contained provisions for the establishment of a Child Rights Unit in the SAF to enforce the 2007 Sudan People's Armed Forces Act, which specifies that no person under the age of 18 may be recruited for military purposes.

UNICEF has also been instrumental in aiding nations ravaged by natural disasters, disease, and war, including supplying medicine and clean water to Zimbabwe in the midst of the nation's cholera epidemic; providing the Chinese provinces devastated by the May 12, 2008 earthquake with $20 million in aid, to rebuild damaged and destroyed schools and for other purposes; and airlifting emergency-relief supplies to Sri Lankan families hurt by recent violence between the Tamil Tigers, a rebel organization, and the Sri Lankan military.

Veneman chaired the U.N.'s Standing Committee on Nutrition from 2006 to 2008. She currently co-chairs Mothers Day Every Day, a campaign that aims to provide access to basic health care and maternal services for women around the world. Since

2005 Veneman has traveled to more than 40 countries to visit sites of UNICEF's relief efforts. "It's difficult to see the poverty and suffering," she told Jeff Jardine. "But I've also seen so much hope in places UNICEF goes. I've heard people fill their difficult lives with music and singing."

Veneman is divorced and has no children.

—M.A.S.

Suggested Reading: *Lancet* p1061 Sep. 23–29, 2006; *Los Angeles Times* A p3 Apr. 28, 1995; *Modesto (California) Bee* A p1 Apr. 28, 1995; *New York Times* A p33 Dec. 21, 2000; UNICEF.org; *Washington Post* A p25 Sep. 19, 2002, A p23 Jan. 1, 2004

Jim Watson/AFP/Getty Images

Vilsack, Tom

Dec. 13, 1950– Secretary of the U.S. Department of Agriculture; former governor of Iowa (Democrat)

Address: U.S. Dept. of Agriculture, 1400 Independence Ave., S.W., Washington, DC 20250

Tom Vilsack, who was sworn in as secretary of the U.S. Department of Agriculture (USDA) on January 20, 2009, has never worked or lived on a farm. Rather, Vilsack, a native of Pittsburgh, Pennsylvania, who holds a degree in law, became an expert on farming, the concerns of farmers, and the role of agriculture in the U.S. as a resident since 1975 of Iowa—the nation's biggest grower of corn and a major producer of hogs, soybeans, oats, eggs, and dairy products. Vilsack served as a member of the Iowa state Senate for six years (1992–98) and as governor of that state for eight (1999–2007). The state's first Democratic governor in 30 years, he made a brief run for the 2008 Democratic presidential nomination during his second term, before his inability to raise much money for his campaign, even in Iowa, forced him to withdraw from the race. The announcement on December 18, 2008 that President-elect Barack Obama had selected Vilsack to head the USDA was generally greeted enthusiastically by those connected with commercial agriculture. The reaction was disappointment among many opponents of industrial farming, genetic bioengineering of plants and animals, and the federal government's large-scale subsidization of farms big and small—particularly critics of government-supported production of corn for the biofuel ethanol. Other detractors voiced the concern that Vilsack's ties to companies such as the multinational agricultural-biotechnology corporation Monsanto and his loyalty to Iowans might tip USDA policies in their favor. The writer Michael Pollan, who believes that cattle should eat grass rather than corn and who is a leader in the movement for what has become known as socially responsible eating, had a mixed response to Obama's choice of Vilsack. "It's hard to avoid the conclusion that this is agribusiness as usual," Pollan complained to an interviewer for National Public Radio (December 18, 2008, on-line), saying that Vilsack had "presided over the biggest expansion of feedlot agriculture in Iowa." But he also said, "There are reasons to be cautiously hopeful. Vilsack's spoken encouragingly about capping subsidies and using that money to drive a conservation agenda." If Pollan had been elected president, "I probably wouldn't be here right now," Vilsack joked to USDA employees on his second day in office, according to Philip Brasher, writing for the *Des Moines (Iowa) Register* (January 22, 2009, on-line). Vilsack also told the workers that the federal government must address the epidemic of obesity in the U.S. by encouraging Americans to eat more healthfully and that the U.S. must provide more food to people overseas who suffer from malnutrition. Vilsack has spoken publicly about the need to overhaul the U.S.'s multibillion-dollar farm-subsidy program and to curb global warming, in part by changing the agricultural practices that contribute to it. In an interview with Amanda Griscom Little for grist.org (February 23, 2007), Vilsack said, "My hope is that we transform from the traditional farm policy to a food-and-farm policy that encourages greater diversity in agriculture, including incentives for food production and enhanced conservation practices. I also think we ought to be looking at changing the way we subsidize agriculture generally, from a commodity-based process to a conservation-based process, which would benefit organic farms as well. I believe this type of transition in farm policy is key to developing opportunities in rural communities."

Thomas James Vilsack was born to an unwed mother on December 13, 1950 in Pittsburgh; shortly afterward he was placed in the Rosalia Foundling Home, a Roman Catholic orphanage. When he was a few months old, he was adopted by Bud and Dolly Vilsack, who had a six-year-old biological daughter, Alice. "My parents made sure that there was never, ever a distinction between myself and my sister," Vilsack told an interviewer, as quoted by James O'Toole in the *Pittsburgh Post-Gazette* (December 3, 2006). (His sister died in the mid-1980s.) One of Vilsack's great-grandfathers founded the still-operating Iron City Brewery, and relatives of his family owned Kennywood Park, a popular amusement park, both in Pittsburgh. Bud Vilsack was a commercial-real-estate agent and insurance salesman. In the 1960s his real-estate business foundered, and Vilsack's mother, a homemaker, began to drink to excess and became dependent on prescription drugs. She neglected her household responsibilities, and sometimes, according to James O'Toole, she would attack her son physically. When Vilsack was 13 she left the family; while on her own, she learned to drive, got a job, and gave up her addictions. Meanwhile, Vilsack's father had assumed the burdens of a single parent. He had also given up membership in an expensive private club in order to pay his son's tuition at a prestigious private school, the Shady Side Academy, in Pittsburgh. During his first two years there, Vilsack told O'Toole, he had "a very tough time," apparently because of his situation at home. "I know what it is to feel alone and forgotten . . . as if you do not belong," he said. His mother's return to the family, during his junior year of high school, was a turning point in his life. Not only did his grades improve markedly, but through her example he recognized the power of determination and hard work. "It's a fair observation that my mother was the most profound influence in my life," he told O'Toole. In his senior year of high school, Vilsack was elected vice president of the student body.

After his graduation from Shady Side, Vilsack enrolled at Hamilton College, in Clinton, New York, where he met his future wife, Ann Christine "Christie" Bell. After he earned a B.A. degree, in history, in 1972, he enrolled at the Albany Law School (affiliated with what is now Union University), in Albany, New York. He married in 1973 and received a J.D. degree in 1975. Vilsack then settled in his wife's hometown, Mount Pleasant, Iowa. There, he worked at his father-in-law's private law firm—its name was changed to Bell and Vilsack—and became a successful trial attorney. He won two high-profile class-action suits, one brought by a group of farmers and the other in behalf of thousands of insurance-policy holders. Vilsack remained associated with the firm until 1998.

Vilsack's political career was unexpectedly launched after Mount Pleasant's mayor, Edward King, was fatally shot by an angry constituent in December 1986, during a meeting of the town council. At the urging of King's father and others, in 1987 Vilsack ran to succeed King and won. After completing the remainder of King's term, he was reelected three times, serving as mayor until 1992. That year he made a successful bid for a seat in the Iowa Senate; he was reelected in 1994. During his tenure in the state Senate, he supported legislation requiring companies that received state tax breaks to offer better pay and benefits to their employees. Vilsack also sponsored a law permitting workers to retain their health coverage when changing jobs and another that required Iowa to contribute to the costs of mental-health treatment. Additionally, he helped redesign Iowa Workforce Development, which oversees both job placement and vocational training and regulates Iowa's health, safety, and employment laws.

In 1998 Vilsack ran for the gubernatorial seat vacated by the Republican Terry Branstad, who had announced that he would not seek a fifth term. After winning a three-way Democratic primary with 51 percent of the vote, Vilsack faced the Republican former Iowa congressman Jim Ross Lightfoot. He overcame a 20-point deficit in the polls to defeat Lightfoot by five percentage points—a victory that led a writer for the *Almanac of American Politics* to label him "probably the biggest upset winner of the year." Vilsack was the first Democrat to hold the governorship of Iowa since 1969.

As governor Vilsack increased education spending, reduced class sizes, and expanded health-insurance coverage to include 90,000 uninsured children; in time nearly all Iowan youngsters were covered. He also lowered state taxes for many families. He established Iowa as a national leader in renewable-energy programs, including those making use of wind energy, and helped create the Governors Biotechnology Partnership, a bipartisan coalition of governors that collects and distributes biotechnology information. In 2001 the Biotechnology Industry Organization named Vilsack governor of the year. He also created "a nationally recognized efficient and accountable state government," according to the Harvard University Institute of Politics Web site. In 2002 he won a second term and said that it would be his last as governor. His establishment in 2003 of the Grow Iowa Values Fund, a multimillion-dollar, 10-year appropriation that aimed to increase the number of higher-paying jobs in Iowa, aroused some controversy, with critics contending that there was no way of ensuring that businesses benefiting from tax breaks or cash incentives remained in the state; indeed, some such companies had already moved elsewhere.

In 2004 Vilsack was mentioned as a possible vice-presidential running mate for U.S. senator John Kerry of Massachusetts. (Kerry selected former U.S. senator John Edwards of North Carolina.) In 2005 Vilsack chaired the Democratic Governors Association's Democratic Leadership Council and set up the Heartland political action committee, whose aim was to fill governors' seats with Democrats. The next year Vilsack announced his candidacy for the presidency in 2008. Three months later, trailing far behind his major rivals in fund-raising, he ended his race. He served as the national campaign co-chairman for Senator Hillary Rodham Clinton of New York and later stumped for the Democratic nominee, Barack Obama.

Earlier, in May 2007, Vilsack had joined the Minneapolis-based law firm Dorsey & Whitney. He worked in its Des Moines office on a case-by-case basis, not as an associate or partner, on matters involving energy conservation, renewable energy, and agribusiness development. In September 2007 he was named a distinguished fellow at Iowa State University's Biosafety Institute for Genetically Modified Agricultural Products. In the fall of 2008, as a fellow at the John F. Kennedy School of Government at Harvard University, he led a study group that discussed "risk and responsibility in the big issues facing America today," according to the school's Web site. During that time, in an interview with Mark Nichols for the Organic Consumers Organization, as posted on Politicalbase.com (October 20, 2008), Vilsack said, "We're going to move from a commodity economy where you basically grow the same kind of crops—where a kernel of corn is a kernel of corn . . . —to an ingredient economy where there will be a kernel of corn that will be designed for fuel, there will be a kernel of corn designed for livestock, there will be kernels of corn that will be used to make paper or fabric for clothes."

As the secretary of the USDA since January 20, 2009, Vilsack oversees an agency with an annual budget of nearly $100 billion and more than 100,000 employees. Its "broad and sometimes competing mandates," in the words of Howard Berkes, a National Public Radio (December 17, 2008) commentator, include fostering rural economic development, conserving natural resources, maintaining the safety of foods (by inspection of meat, for example), ensuring the proper care of farm animals and plants (on megafarms and elsewhere), promoting good nutrition through education, managing school-lunch programs, issuing food stamps, distributing agricultural subsidies, overseeing national and international agricultural trade, conducting economic and agricultural research, and distributing and storing surplus foodstuffs. The mission of the USDA's Cooperative State Research, Education and Extension Service, its Web site states, is to "advance knowledge for agriculture, the environment, human health and well-being, and communities by supporting research, education, and extension programs in the Land-Grant University System and other partner organizations." The National Forest Service is also an arm of the USDA.

In his first 10 months in office, Vilsack surprised many of his critics by promoting local, organically grown produce and calling for a renewed focus on the restoration and conservation of the nation's forests. He said that his recent interest in organic foods was sparked in part by the impending arrival of his first grandson; Vilsack's own parents died before the birth of his children, and with the prospect of becoming a grandfather, he became committed to improving his eating habits. "I'm much more inclined to eat fresh fruits and vegetables [now]," Vilsack told Andrew Martin for the *New York Times* (March 22, 2009). "I had organic yogurt for breakfast. Trust me, I would have not have had that two years ago, or four years ago."

Among his top priorities, Vilsack is working to improve the USDA's record on civil rights (in the past, the USDA was known to discriminate against African-American farmers), to ensure the availability of safe and nutritious foods for all Americans, to end child hunger in the U.S. by 2015, and to expand economic opportunities for small farmers and ranchers. He hopes to improve the nutritional quality of school breakfasts and lunches, with small farmers and schools in their areas working together to accomplish that goal. In July 2009 a food-safety committee set up by President Obama and headed by Vilsack and Health and Human Services secretary Kathleen Sebelius announced stricter regulations for the production of certain foods, including eggs, poultry, beef, leafy greens, and tomatoes. The rules are aimed at preventing the spread of the E. coli and salmonella bacteria.

More recently, Vilsack, with Sebelius, launched the "Know Your Farmer, Know Your Food" initiative, which aims to educate the public on where food originates so they can make more-informed purchasing decisions. "There's a disconnect between the food that we eat and our awareness of where it comes from," Vilsack explained to Guy Raz for National Public Radio (October 4, 2009, online). "We think it comes from a grocery store. It doesn't. It comes from family farmers across the country working hard every day." As part of a pilot program, a handful of farmers' markets across the nation have begun to accept food stamps in an effort to provide lower-income families access to more-nutritious foods, which are often more expensive than so-called junk foods.

Vilsack and his wife, a former schoolteacher and newspaper columnist, have two adult sons—Jess and Douglas, both attorneys. The couple drive a hybrid car. One of Vilsack's most valued possessions is a Pittsburgh Pirates baseball jersey with the number 21 (that of the Pirates' star right-fielder Roberto Clemente) autographed by the team's longtime outfielder and first baseman Willie Stargell. "If I'm not buried in that jersey, I'm going to come back and find out why," he told James O'Toole. "I don't want my sons to fight over it."

—M.A.S.

Suggested Reading: *Des Moines (Iowa) Register* A p1+ July 26, 2004; (Dubuque, Iowa) *Telegraph Herald* A p6 May 31, 1998; *Los Angeles Times* A p15 Dec. 17, 2008; *New York Times* A p27 Dec. 17, 2008, Bus p1+ Mar. 22, 2009; *Pittsburgh Post-Gazette* (on-line) Dec. 3, 2006

Stephanie Rausser, courtesy of Ayelet Waldman

Waldman, Ayelet

(eye-YELL-it)

Dec. 11, 1964– Writer

Address: c/o Knopf Doubleday, 1745 Broadway, New York, NY 10019

Ayelet Waldman began publishing novels in the early 2000s, but she achieved widespread fame—some would say notoriety—when her essay "Motherlove" was adapted for the March 27, 2005 edition of the *New York Times.* Asked by the editors of the book *Because I Said So: 33 Mothers Write About Children, Sex, Men, Aging, Faith, Race, and Themselves* to write a chapter on the subject of sex, Waldman had decided to explore the question of why so few mothers she knew were enjoying sex with their husbands after having children. "My answer was that all of these women were good mothers," Waldman told Terry Gross in an interview for the National Public Radio program *Fresh Air* (May 5, 2009). "They had made this kind of erotic transference when they had children. They shifted all of their ardor and their passion and their devotion from their husbands to their children. The children had become the center of their passionate universes. And I'd never done that. I mean, I loved my kids like crazy. . . . But I had never sort of shifted that passionate focus." Waldman explained in the essay that she was not like those mothers because her husband, the Pulitzer Prize–winning novelist Michael Chabon, remained "the center of her passionate universe," and she went on to describe their sex life as "vital, even torrid." "If a good mother is one who loves her child more than anyone else in the world, I am not a good mother," Waldman wrote. "I am in fact a bad mother. I love my husband more than I love my children." Hundreds of women wrote to Waldman to thank her for expressing a sentiment that they shared, but the general public reaction was largely critical. Waldman found herself labeled as self-indulgent and as a "bad mother," and her comments were derided on television shows, such as *The View*, and on Web sites including Urbanbaby.com. In response she defended her ideas in a number of forums, even appearing as a guest on the *Oprah Winfrey Show.* Her arguments culminated in a full-length work: Waldman's 2009 book, *Bad Mother: A Chronicle of Maternal Crimes, Minor Calamities, and Occasional Moments of Grace,* contains 18 essays that challenge what she sees as the unreasonably high standards that society sets for mothers and that mothers set for themselves. Waldman explained in an interview with *Current Biography*, the source of quotes in this article unless otherwise noted: "What I'm arguing for is that we think of a good mother as a mother who sort of takes care of her children's needs and doesn't overidentify with them and manages to love them without making them feel like they're the most important people in the universe."

Waldman began her writing career after she quit her job as a public defender to become a stay-at-home mother and discovered that she felt unfulfilled in that role. "I was saying to [other full-time mothers], like, 'Doesn't this just suck? . . . aren't you bored out of your mind?' And the moms would be like, 'No I'm not bored, I'm completely happy. I've never been so happy,'" Waldman said. "And I would just be like, 'Oh, you know, that makes one of us.'" Her feelings about full-time parenting became the basis of the seven books in Waldman's Mommy Track mystery series, whose main character, a stay-at-home mom, moonlights as a private investigator. Waldman's feelings about motherhood also inform her later novels, *Daughter's Keeper* and *Love and Other Impossible Pursuits.* In addition, Waldman is a columnist for *Salon.com* and the author of numerous articles and essays on topics ranging from politics to Judaism.

Ayelet Waldman was born on December 11, 1964 in Israel. Her father, Leonard Waldman, an avid supporter of the formation of the Jewish state, had moved to Israel from Montreal, Canada, in the 1940s and fought in the early military conflicts between the newly established Israel and the surrounding Arab countries. He met Waldman's mother, Ricki, an American, in Montreal, when she was in graduate school studying art history; she left school to be married and became the stepmother to four children from her husband's previous marriage. Waldman's mother moved to Israel with her new family in the early 1960s before insisting that they return to Montreal. When Waldman was in the first grade, the family left Montreal, where they had moved in 1971, for New Jersey. Later she lived in Rhode Island before returning to New Jersey when she was in sixth grade. There, the family lived in what Waldman described as "the very definition of" suburbia. Waldman's father worked as a fundraiser for various Jewish organizations, while her mother raised the children, who by then included Waldman's younger brother, Paul. Waldman described her family as being "secular Zionist." Her mother was an ardent feminist who instilled in her daughter lessons about being independent and establishing her own career. "When she got married, that kind of derailed all those plans [for a career]," Waldman said, "and she wanted for me to not have to face that same conundrum, to be able to fulfill my ambitions without having to make any huge sacrifices."

In high school Waldman was a straight-A student. "It helps to be desperately unpopular," she said. "You know, when there's nothing else to do but do your schoolwork, you tend to do very well in school." With aspirations of becoming an actress, she performed in school plays. She spent her sophomore year of high school living on a kibbutz in Israel, "when I was in the thick of my sort of Zionist mania," she recalled. She attended Wesleyan University, in Connecticut, where she took many women's-studies classes and graduated early, with a B.A. degree in psychology. Waldman spent her junior year studying at Hebrew University, in Israel. After graduating she returned to Israel with the intention of living there indefinitely with her Israeli boyfriend. She was drafted into that country's army, but when she reported for duty, she learned that her entire group of women was being released from service. "It was like this epiphany that not only did I not want to go into the Israeli army, I didn't want to be in Israel," Waldman said. "I wanted to get the hell out of there."

Waldman moved with her boyfriend back to the U.S., where he got a job moving furniture. Figuring that she would need a high-paying job to support the family she expected to have with him, Waldman set her sights on becoming a psychotherapist. "Then I slept through the GREs so I couldn't go and do that," Waldman said. "Law seemed sort of a little bit like acting—you know, trial law—so I thought, all right, let's do that, that's a good idea." She and her boyfriend later broke up; Waldman applied and was accepted to Harvard Law School, in Cambridge, Massachusetts. "I was one of the few students who actually enjoyed law school," she said. "I thought it was pretty easy. That's the way I think. I think like a lawyer. I always have." She graduated from Harvard in 1991, in a class with future president Barack Obama. She then took a job at the New York City law firm Debevoice & Plimpton.

During those years Waldman's roommate set her up on a blind date. The date turned out to be with Michael Chabon, who had recently published his debut novel, the best-selling *The Mysteries of Pittsburgh* (1988), a coming-of-age tale that has a bisexual male as its protagonist and that earned Chabon a loyal gay following. "I said, 'Oh, great, another gay boyfriend,'" Waldman told Michael J. Ybarra for the *Los Angeles Times* (October 5, 2003). "When he showed up, I said, 'Thank you for the flowers, and are you gay?'" Three weeks later, according to Chabon, Waldman proposed marriage to him—in her sleep. "One morning I woke up and he said, 'So do you remember what you said last night?'" Waldman recalled. "And I said, 'No,' and he said, 'In the middle of the night you turned to me and you said, 'So Michael Chabon, are you going to marry me?' . . . I was completely humiliated and . . . blushed furiously and I said, 'Well what did you say?' and he said, 'I said yes.' And then that was the end of that."

Waldman and Chabon moved to California's San Francisco Bay Area and were married in 1993. They later moved to Los Angeles, where Waldman worked as a public defender during what she described as "the thick of the war on drugs." That "war" saw aggressive government policies aimed at reducing the sale and use of illegal drugs; those included federal laws, passed in 1986, requiring mandatory minimum sentencing for offenders who could not provide the court with information to help prosecute others. The vast majority of Waldman's clients were being prosecuted for drug-related crimes. "I thought I would be seeing kingpins going to jail, but the kingpins negotiate deals and go to jail for very little time," Waldman explained to Delia O'Hara for the *Chicago Sun-Times* (November 12, 2003). "It's the people who are on the lowest rungs on the ladder, and so have no information to sell, who go to prison for a long time—the guy who carries the box or the woman who takes a phone message." Waldman recalled that while almost all of her clients were guilty of the crimes with which they had been charged, they received disproportionately harsh sentences. Her work, which she found heartbreaking, led Waldman to believe that mandatory sentencing should be abolished. She believes that in the future, the untold numbers of drug-related convictions during the so-called war on drugs will be a "blight on American history."

Meanwhile, Waldman had given birth to a daughter, Sophie, and was working long hours while her husband stayed at home to write. Envious of the amount of time her husband spent with their daughter, Waldman decided to quit her job to become a stay-at-home mother. "It was lovely," she told Gross. "It was, you know, the baby pool and Mommy and Me [a mothers' group], and story time at the library, and that whole first day . . . it was awesome. And then the second day it was story time at the library, and the baby pool, and Mommy and Me; and then the third day and the fourth day and the fifth day. And really, within a week, I had started to completely lose my mind." Waldman turned to writing as a way to "find something in my life that my kids couldn't have access to," she told Gross. A mystery reader herself, she began writing a mystery novel about Juliet Applebaum, a fictional Jewish stay-at-home mother who moonlights as a private investigator. Waldman based the character on herself; Applebaum is a Harvard Law School graduate and former public defender who feels confined by the daily duties of motherhood. Waldman kept her writing a secret at first, having declared earlier in her relationship with Chabon that she would never become a writer. (Chabon had previously been married to an aspiring poet, and his literary success had been a source of tension between them.) When Waldman finally showed Chabon her writing, he advised her to "keep going." "I guess that was his way of saying it was good," she said. She submitted a draft of the novel to Chabon's agent, expecting it to be rejected, and was surprised when it was accepted for publication. *Nursery Crimes*, published in 2001, follows Applebaum, an eight-months-pregnant mother of a toddler and wife of a screenwriter; to escape the confines of motherhood, she takes up private investigating when the principal of an elite private school is killed in an apparent hit-and-run accident. Over the next several years, Waldman published six more novels in the Mommy Track series, which became known for its quirky sense of humor and Jewish themes: *The Big Nap* (2002), *A Playdate with Death* (2003), *Death Gets a Time-Out* (2004), *Murder Plays House* (2004), *The Cradle Robbers* (2005), and *Bye-Bye, Black Sheep* (2006).

In 2000 Waldman was four months pregnant with her third child (by that time she and Chabon also had a son, Ezekiel) when she learned, through a prenatal diagnostic procedure, that the unborn child had a genetic abnormality that might lead to severe mental retardation or to a predisposition to certain diseases. Waldman and Chabon made the decision to have the fetus aborted. She wrote eloquently about the difficulty of that decision in an essay entitled "Rocketship," included in *Bad Mother*. That experience had a profound effect on Waldman's writing. She felt compelled to write more-serious fiction and became focused on the subjects of troubled mother-child relationships and, as she put it, "dead babies." In her 2003 book, *Daughter's Keeper*, Waldman set out to write a polemic about the injustices of the war on drugs—incorporating her experiences as a public defender who had witnessed the unduly severe punishment of naïve drug criminals. The book, however, ended up focusing to a greater extent on the story of a mother who loses a daughter. The novel centers on the free-spirited 22-year-old Olivia Goodman's troubled relationship with her cold, aloof mother, Elaine. When Olivia becomes ensnared in a drug deal by a man she met while vacationing in Mexico, she and her mother are brought together and forced to face their past. The book received mostly favorable reviews.

Waldman was asked by the editors of *Because I Said So* to write a chapter about sex, because she seemed to be one of the few contributors who were having sex regularly. Her essay "Motherlove" sparked a fiery response when it was adapted for the *New York Times* under the title "Truly, Madly, Guiltily." The general public reacted with outrage and shock, and Waldman became the object of parody and criticism, some of it vicious. She was decried by many as an irresponsible mother; some went so far as to say that her children should be taken away from her. Others criticized her for being too candid about her personal life. Waldman did not expect the reaction the essay elicited. "I couldn't quite believe I was the first person who had ever said it because it was a saying—'the most important thing a man can do for his children is love their mother,'" Waldman said. "So I didn't think I was saying anything that transgressive, but it turns out that that was no longer part of the conversation about parenting. Now it is." Waldman said that she does not regret writing the article or framing her viewpoint so bluntly. "I had a period of wishing that, but you know if I had said it differently, the conversation wouldn't have happened," she said. "So I'm not sorry."

Waldman's novel *Love and Other Impossible Pursuits* was published in 2006. Set in Manhattan, in New York City, it focuses on Emilia Greenleaf, a Harvard-trained lawyer who met her husband, also a lawyer, when he was married to his first wife. Now Emilia must put up with her bright but obnoxious five-year-old stepson, William, whom she loathes, while struggling to deal with the recent death of her infant daughter. One of Waldman's aims when writing the book was to explore the idea of a woman's disliking a child, which she considers one of society's "great unmentionables." "When you have a lot of children like I do and you have a lot of play dates, you have kids come to your house," she said. "A lot of them you like and some of them—you know—kids are people. And some of them are awful." The book pointedly portrayed a culture of judgmental, perfectionist, upscale mothers who hold one another to unrealistic expectations. *Love and Other Impossible Pursuits* became a best-seller and a critical success. Shortly after its publication the book's movie rights were purchased by Disney. A film version of the novel, directed by Don Roos and starring Natalie Portman, Lisa Kudrow, and Scott Cohen, debuted at the Toronto Film Festival on September 16, 2009 and was set to be released nationally in the fall or winter of 2009.

In 2009 Waldman published her essay collection, *Bad Mother*, which focuses on the societal pressures to conform to what she believes is an unrealistic standard of motherhood. The topics of the chapters include Waldman's promiscuous teenage years, her painful decision to have an abortion, her struggle with her high standards for her children, and her secret hope that one of her sons grows up to be gay. She also discussed her experiences of living with a mild bipolar disorder, a diagnosis she received in her late 30s, and her decision to remain on medication for the disorder during her fourth pregnancy. Discussing why she wrote the book, Waldman explained on her Web site, "Because so many women I know are in real pain. They are so crippled by their guilt, by their unreasonable expectations, that they can't even allow themselves to celebrate the true joys of being a mom. When your little girl curls up in bed with you and says, 'Your hair always smells so good, Mama,' you should be able to melt with emotion without worrying about whether she's reading at grade level." *Bad Mother* has earned mainly positive reviews. In an assessment for the *New York Times* (May 10, 2009), Susan Dominus wrote, "Waldman doesn't always tie her essays up in a neat bow, which seems appropriately messy given the subject matter. They say that a good mother is one who doesn't need her kids to like her all the time. Of writers and their readers, Waldman's book leaves me thinking, the same might be true." Waldman's next book, *Red Hook Road*, a novel set in Maine, will be published in 2010.

The five-foot-tall Waldman lives in Berkeley, California, with Chabon and their four children: Sophie, Ezekiel (called Zeke), Ida-Rose (Rosie), and Abraham (Abe). Waldman described herself as a "happy mother" and her husband as "a superstar dad" and said her children are "very creative and they're very funny and they're very self-confident. And there's like a lot of personality in our house, which I think is a delight."

—M.E.R.

Suggested Reading: ayeletwaldman.com; *Chicago Sun-Times* Features p62 Nov. 12, 2003; (London) *Guardian* p17 Jan. 14, 2006; *Los Angeles Times* E p4 Oct. 5 2003; National Public Radio Web site May 5, 2009; *New York Observer* Culture p17 Jan. 30, 2006; *New York Times* (on-line) Mar. 27, 2005, Oct. 18, 2009

Selected Books: *Nursery Crimes*, 2001; *The Big Nap*, 2002; *A Playdate with Death*, 2003; *Daughter's Keeper*, 2003; *Death Gets a Time-Out*, 2004; *Murder Plays House*, 2004; *The Cradle Robbers*, 2005; *Bye-Bye, Black Sheep*, 2006; *Love and Other Impossible Pursuits*, 2006; *Bad Mother: A Chronicle of Maternal Crimes, Minor Calamaties, and Occasional Moments of Grace*, 2009

Wallerstein, Immanuel

Sep. 28, 1930– Sociologist; writer; educator

Address: P.O. Box 208265, New Haven, CT 06520-8265

The sociologist Immanuel Wallerstein is best known for his groundbreaking and hugely influential "world-systems" analysis of the global capitalist system, its origins, its evolution, and what he sees as its inherent inequalities. Published in 1974, the first volume of his *Modern World-System* was hailed as an instant classic and, along with subsequent volumes, has been called innovative, insightful, and provocative and been celebrated for constituting a new way of thinking about the world. To many, Wallerstein's work (along with that of Andre Gunder Frank, Samir Amin, Giovanni Arrighi, Christopher Chase-Dunn, and others) was pioneering in both its scope and purpose; influenced by several intellectual currents, Wallerstein achieved his greatest success by synthesizing those ideas into a grand theory that, unlike previous focal points of study, such as the nation-state, emphasized the interconnectedness of the world as well as of the ways we view it. "The world-systems paradigm offers linkages for previously unlinked studies and previously unaffiliated scholars . . . ," according to the citation that accompanied the Career of Distinguished Scholarship Award, presented to Wallerstein by the American Sociological Association in 2003. "His world-systems analysis . . . [brought] attention to interdependencies that had been largely ignored. . . . He has helped us to see that globalization is not merely

Courtesy of Immanuel Wallerstein

something that set in at the end of our century, but shaped the very character of the 'rise of the west' five centuries ago." While Wallerstein's "big-picture" approach might be said to suffer from the same deficiencies that plague any large-scale theory, its bulky and imperfect tools are nonetheless seen by many as useful in contextualizing historical developments and contemporary realities. In his review of Wallerstein's *Utopistics*, Dwight C. Kiel, writing for *Perspectives on Political Science*

(September 22, 1999), might have been referring to the sociologist's legacy: "This is not a book of detail or finesse, but rather of grand interpretation and acute vision."

Although Wallerstein has been most closely identified with world-systems analysis, his work can be seen as encompassing two other overlapping themes: African anticolonialism and Third World struggles for independence, and an effort to revolutionize social science and the academy in order to create a greater collective knowledge and foster more-critical thinking. "I have argued that world-systems analysis is not a theory but a protest against neglected issues and deceptive epistemologies. It is a call for intellectual change, indeed for 'unthinking' the premises of nineteenth-century social science . . . ," he wrote in *The Essential Wallterstein* (2000), as quoted on Yale University's Department of Sociology Web site. "It is an intellectual task that is and has to be a political task as well, because—I insist—the search for the true and the search for the good is but a single quest." Wallerstein's work has more recently brought him a reputation as one of the academic elder statesmen of the "alter-globalization" movement.

Immanuel Maurice Wallerstein was born to Lazar and Sally (Guensberg) Wallerstein on September 28, 1930 in New York City. In his introduction to *The Essential Wallerstein* (2000), as adapted for the Yale site, Wallerstein wrote, "My family was very politically conscious, and world affairs were always being discussed in our home. The fight against Nazism and fascism was our primary concern, and long before Pearl Harbor." As a teenager he became interested in India's struggle for independence from Great Britain, which it won officially in 1947, the year Wallerstein enrolled at Columbia University, in New York. There, as a result of political debates, relationships with other students, and his participation in an international youth congress, he switched his focus to Africa; during those years he studied colonialism on that continent at the École des Hautes Études en Sciences Sociales, in Paris, France. At the time Paris was a breeding ground for radical intellectual and political thought; the city, and the time he spent there, were formative for Wallerstein. One important influence on his early writing, among several others, was the French sociologist, anthropologist, and ethnologist Georges Balandier. Wallerstein has returned to Paris many times, teaching there regularly. At Columbia he earned his B.A. degree, in 1951. He served from that year until 1953 in the U.S. Army, then returned to Columbia to earn his M.A. (1954) and Ph.D. (1959) degrees. Having received a Ford Foundation African Fellowship, he conducted research for his doctoral thesis on the colonial systems and independence movements in Ghana and the Ivory Coast; at the time he was one of the only social scientists in his area of expertise to do his fieldwork in Africa. "It was Africa," he wrote, as quoted on the Yale site, "that was responsible for undoing the more stultifying parts of my educational heritage." His books *Africa: The Politics of Independence; The Road to Independence: Ghana and the Ivory Coast*; and *Africa: The Politics of Unity* appeared in 1961, 1964, and 1967, respectively. His study of colonialism and independence in Africa is seen by many as a precursor to his world-systems analysis of the global economy as well as his subsequent critique of globalization and U.S. hegemony. "Wallerstein's *Independence* and *Unity* are widely regarded as the first contemporary histories of African politics . . . ," Augustine Park wrote for the *Canadian Review of Sociology and Anthropology* (November 1, 2006), a year after Wallerstein's 1961 and 1967 volumes were reprinted in a single volume. "These texts should be 'required reading' for students of African politics . . . because Wallerstein wrote his histories as history was unfolding." Wallerstein quickly rose to prominence in the field of African studies, teaching a highly popular course on colonialism at Columbia and becoming president of the African Studies Association in 1973.

Earlier, in Ghana in 1960, Wallerstein had met and become a supporter of the anticolonial intellectual and writer Frantz Fanon, helping him to publish his classic *Wretched of the Earth* in the U.S. Walter L. Goldfrank wrote in an issue of the *Journal of World-Systems Research* (Summer/Fall 2000) devoted to Wallerstein's work that it was Fanon's "analysis of 'the pitfalls of national consciousness'—a savage critique of the post-colonial urban elite—that helped to propel Wallerstein in the direction of a world-systems perspective." Looking for explanations for the state of the Third World in the 1960s, Wallerstein had come to the conclusion that particular situations needed to be understood in the context of global economic, political, and historical forces and that the nation-state was not independent of the world. He came to view the geographical division between North and South as being based on the global division of labor.

At about the time that Wallerstein was forming those views, the antiestablishment protests of 1968 in the U.S., France, and elsewhere seized his attention and led him to identify with the politics they represented. He later described the movements that surfaced between 1966 and 1970 as sharing several fundamental characteristics; they were opposed to both U.S. hegemony and to the Old Left's proposed two-step strategy of gaining power and then changing the world. Disillusioned, the protestors saw leftists as having gained power in Eastern Europe and the Third World without following through on their promises. "The direct political consequences of the world revolutions of 1968 were minimal, but the geopolitical and intellectual repercussions were enormous and irrevocable," Wallerstein wrote for *Foreign Policy Magazine* (July/August 2002). One result, according to Wallerstein, was that "centrist liberalism tumbled from the throne it had occupied since the [multi-country] European revolutions of 1848 and that had enabled it to co-opt conservatives and radicals alike." Wallerstein's argument that even in failure the 1848 and 1968 movements were the "true" revolutions goes against the conventional wisdom that, for example, the French and Russian revolutions—of 1789 and 1917, respectively—were more significant; he maintained instead that the latter two revolutions did not challenge the dominant mode of production, as did the actions of 1848 and 1968. His interpretation of the impact and implications of developments in 1968 would influence his later analysis of globalization and the reactions to it.

"The 1968 student revolt at Columbia was a crucial turning point in Wallerstein's career," Goldfrank wrote. As Goldfrank noted, the protests at the school were focused on opposing the Vietnam War, protecting the mainly black neighborhood near Columbia from university expansion, and upholding the political rights of students. Wallerstein sided with the students at the cost of his standing among his colleagues, and in 1971 he moved to McGill University, in Montreal, Quebec, Canada, to teach sociology. Five years later he moved to the State University of New York (SUNY) at Binghamton, becoming a distinguished professor; he remained there until his retirement, in 1999. At Binghamton Wallerstein created an institutional backing for his work: the Fernand Braudel Center for the Study of Economies, Historical Systems and Civilizations (which he headed until 2005), a global center for world-systems analysis, which publishes the journal *Review*.

In 1974 Wallerstein published the first volume of *The Modern World-System*, creating an instant sensation. The book consisted of the work he had done with the assistance of Terence Hopkins and Michael Hechter from 1967 to 1974, focusing on transformations in early modern Europe, which, he argued, led to the birth of the capitalist system. Wallerstein's concept was groundbreaking because it saw not the nation-state but the global capitalist economy, according to Goldfrank, "as the basic unit of analysis for modern social change" and attacked "what he has called 'developmentalism,' the notion that each national society . . . passes through a similar set of stages, from tradition to modernity." The first volume is a study of the transition from feudalism to capitalism and of the subsequent expansion and supremacy of Western Europe from 1450 to 1640. Wallerstein argued that the move to capitalism was needed to protect and extend the power of the feudal ruling elites, which entailed territorial expansion and the development of a division of labor (which would then determine relationships and status in the system) and state machineries to enforce the new system. Wallerstein introduced a new "periodization" of history, based on his analysis of long waves of economic expansion and stagnation. In 1980 Volume II of *The Modern World-System* appeared, covering the period of stagnation between 1600 and 1750. Nine years later Volume III came out, covering the expansion from the mid-18th century to the 1840s. One of the key elements of the world-systems approach is its ability to synthesize various major strains of thought, among them Marxism and Third World radicalism, to produce a comprehensive alternative theory of how past events led to modern political and economic conditions. Wallerstein wrote in *The Modern World-System I* (1974): "The mark of the modern world is the imagination of its profiteers and the counter-assertiveness of the oppressed. Exploitation and the refusal to accept exploitation as either inevitable or just constitute the continuing antinomy of the modern era, joined together in a dialectic which has far from reached its climax in the twentieth century."

Wallerstein sees the world capitalist economy—whose predecessors, in his view, were empires—as being finite; he believes and hopes it will be followed by a transition to socialism. The basic idea behind Wallerstein's argument is that in the division of labor of the global capitalist system, there are two mutually dependent productive regions: the capital-intensive "core" in the Northern Hemisphere and the labor-intensive "periphery" to the South. Through the market the periphery provides cheap labor and cheap resources to the industrialized, technologically advanced core, which sells its finished products at high prices. That system, inherently unfair in Wallerstein's view, is self-reinforcing and designed to the advantage of the core, which has maintained and extended its advantages at the expense of the periphery. Higher standards of living in the core lead to greater technological advances, which in turn lead to even greater discrepancies between the core and periphery. Wallerstein's theory is that the system is unsustainable and will enter a crisis period from which it will not recover. "Periods of expansion come to an end when production outstrips the world distribution of income and hence effective demand," Goldfrank explained, and thus "capitalism is understood as a system in the process of slowly transforming itself in the direction of limits beyond which it cannot pass." Hegemonic states, such as the United States since World War II, enforce the status quo in the balance of power and economics, imposing free trade on an unfair playing field to their benefit, in Wallerstein's opinion. According to that theory, hegemony typically follows world wars but, like the capitalist system itself, is transitory—because, as Goldfrank wrote, "first, class struggles raise the wage level, lessening the competitive advantage, so that the hegemonic power can no longer undersell its rivals in the world market. Second, technical advantages are diffused through imitation, theft, or capital export. Third, world-wide technical advance makes possible the effectiveness of larger political units."

More recently Wallerstein has predicted the demise of U.S. hegemony and the capitalist system in general. In response to the financial crisis of 2008–09, Wallerstein explained why the capitalist system has moved in the last several decades from a production-oriented system to an unstable one based on financial speculation. "What has made the system move so far from equilibrium?" Wallerstein asked in an article entitled "The Depression: A Long-Term View," available on the Web site of the Fernand Braudel Center (October 15, 2008). "Because over 500 years the three basic costs of capitalist production—personnel, inputs, and taxation—have steadily risen as a percentage of possible sales price, such that today they make it impossible to obtain the large profits from quasi-monopolized production that have always been the basis of significant capital accumulation. It is not because capitalism is failing at what it does best. It is precisely because it has been doing it so well that it has finally undermined the basis of future accumulation." In a subsequent commentary, "The Politics of Economic Disaster," also available on the Fernand Braudel Center's Web site (February 15, 2009), Wallerstein looked ahead to how governments will deal with the capitalist crisis and how the world will emerge from it: "Protectionism and social-democratic welfare serve governments the way the cellar does during a tornado. The quasi-nationalization of banks is another way of taking shelter in the cellars. What we the people have to think about and prepare for is what we do when we emerge from the cellar, whenever that is. The fundamental question is how are we going to rebuild. That will be the real political battle. The landscape will be unfamiliar. And all our past rhetorics will be suspect. The key thing to realize is that rebuilding can take us into a far better world—but it can also take us into a far worse one. In either case, it will be a far different one."

Criticisms of Wallerstein's ideas have come from all sides. Some called his geographic area of analysis too narrow, others too wide; some complained that his time frame for the investigation of the development of the modern world-system began too late, while others claimed that it started too early. He is seen as too Marxist by some and as not Marxist enough by others. Some felt he assigned too much importance to the economy, others that he focused too little on it. His supporters felt that Wallerstein had been judged on an unfinished work, with the projected fourth and fifth volumes required to complete the expression of his theories.

Since the publication of Volume III, Wallerstein has spent much of his time attempting to revolutionize the social sciences, largely through his positions as president of the International Sociological Association and chair of the Gulbenkian Commission on the Restructuring of the Social Sciences in the 1990s. He has also been an outspoken critic of globalization, tracing it back through the postwar era to colonialism. In an oft-cited speech at Cornell University in 2004, entitled "After Developmentalism and Globalization, What?," he argued that during colonialism, "development" was understood as the exploitation of the non-European world by the European world. After 1945 and the anticolonial wars for independence, the rhetoric changed to focus on developmentalism: "The new assumption was that, if the countries of the South would only adopt the proper policies, they would one day, some time in the future, become as technologically modern and as wealthy as the countries of the North." Toward the latter stages of the postwar economic boom of 1945–70, developmentalism, specifically investments in infrastructure, became the U.N.-approved approach to solving the problems of the postcolonial South. But the stagflation—or inflation together with stagnant buyer demand and high unemployment—of the 1970s, Wallerstein argued, resulted in massive drops in the prices of the South's exports at the same time that prices of imports from the North increased, leading to significant payment imbalances. Meanwhile, the windfalls from OPEC (the Organization of Petroleum Exporting Countries) were being stored in banks in the developed world, which spent money on loans to the South, and by the end of the 1970s, a massive debt crisis had emerged. Developmentalism fell out of favor, and with the arrival of the 1980s, and the rise of conservatives led by U.S. president Ronald Reagan and British prime minister Margaret Thatcher, the dominant view came to be that there was "no alternative" to free trade, or the opening up of resources and markets of the South to the North. "Academic buzz words and fads are fickle and usually last but a decade or two," Wallerstein said. "Development was suddenly out. Globalization arrived in its wake." In an article for *Monthly Review* (January 2, 2008, on-line), he analyzed the performance of the "new dogmas" of the 1980s and '90s: "The only problem with this great political success was that it was not matched by economic success. The profit stagnation in industrial enterprises worldwide continued. The surge upward of the stock markets everywhere was based not on productive profits but largely on speculative financial manipulations. The distribution of income worldwide and within countries became very skewed—a massive increase in the income of the top 10% and especially of the top 1% of the world's populations, but a decline in real income of much of the rest of the world's populations." Beginning with the revolutionary activity in Mexico in 1994, through the 1999 protests at the World Trade Organization meeting in Seattle, Washington, and the World Social Forum in Porto Alegre, Brazil, Wallerstein identified a growing grassroots response to globalization, seeing it as an extension of a "lingering search" for a "better kind of antisystemic movement" that had begun with the disillusionment of 1968. Wallerstein said at Cornell, "All this and more leads one to suspect that globalization as rhetoric may be going quickly the way of developmentalism." Wallerstein has become a major voice in the "alter-globalization" movement, at the World Social Forum and elsewhere. His life's work has provided a framework of analysis for a new generation of activists and dissidents. "The whole discussion from 1945 to today has indeed been one long effort to take seriously the reality that the world-system is not only polarized but polarizing, and that this reality is both morally and politically intolerable," he said at Cornell. He believes that we are now in a 25- to 50-year period of transition to a new world-system and that we have a responsibility not only to analyze it, but also to participate in forging it by opposing commodification (particularly of public goods) and neoliberalism, or ideological economic policy that advocates laissez-faire capitalism, free-market fundamentalism, economic liberalization, the shrinking of government, deregulation, privatization, the unrestricted movement of capital, and low taxes.

Wallerstein is the author of dozens of other influential articles and books, the latter including *After Liberalism* (1995), *The Decline of American Power: The U.S. in a Chaotic World* (2003), *The Uncertainties of Knowledge* (2004), and *European Universalism: The Rhetoric of Power* (2006). For the past decade he has written widely read commentaries, published twice a month and syndicated (since 2005) by Agence Global. According to their tagline, the commentaries "are intended to be reflections on the contemporary world scene, as seen from the perspective not of the immediate headlines but of the long term." Wallerstein has received several prestigious awards. The American Sociological Association gave him its Sorokin Award in 1975 and formed a separate branch in 1980, the Section on the Political Economy of the World-System. He is currently a senior research scholar at Yale University, in New Haven, Connecticut. He and his wife, Beatrice Friedman, have one daughter, Katharine Wallerstein, who is a founding member and the executive director of the Global Commons Foundation. He also has two stepchildren, Susan and Robert.

—M.M.

Suggested Reading: *Journal of World-Systems Research* Summer/Fall 2000; Yale University Web site; Wallerstein, Immanuel. *The Essential Wallerstein*, 2000

Selected Books: *Africa: The Politics of Independence*, 1961; *The Road to Independence: Ghana and the Ivory Coast*, 1964; *Africa: The Politics of Unity*, 1967; *The Modern World-System, Volume I*, 1974; *The Modern World-System, Volume II*, 1980; *The Modern World-System, Volume III*, 1989; *After Liberalism*, 1995; *The Decline of American Power: The U.S. in a Chaotic World*, 2003; *The Uncertainties of Knowledge*, 2004; *European Universalism: The Rhetoric of Power*, 2006

Warner, Kurt

June 22, 1971– Football player

Address: Arizona Cardinals, P.O. Box 888, Phoenix, AZ 85001-0888

In his career Kurt Warner, a quarterback with the Arizona Cardinals, has journeyed from near-total obscurity to the top ranks of the National Football League (NFL) and from being seen as a has-been to giving a spectacular—if ultimately unsuccessful—performance in Super Bowl XLIII, in February 2009. Warner was a starting quarterback in just one out of his five years at Northern Iowa University, got passed over in the 1994 NFL draft, and was rejected by the Green Bay Packers after he attended their training camp. After such setbacks many would have given up dreams of playing in the NFL, but Warner remained confident that he had what it took to compete as a pro. After returning to his hometown of Cedar Rapids, Iowa, he took a job at a grocery store and continued to train and try out for teams. "'Kurt, are you sure you're that good?' I'd say that over and over," Warner's then-girlfriend and future wife, Brenda, told Vahe Gregorian for the St. Louis, Missouri, *Post-Dispatch* (January 13, 2002). "And he'd say, 'I really am.' . . . So I just had to trust." Later in the 1990s Warner played three seasons with the Iowa Barnstormers in the Arena Football League (AFL), becoming a two-time

Stephen Dunn/Getty Images

All-Star, before serving as a third-string quarterback with the struggling St. Louis Rams of the NFL and playing for the Amsterdam Admirals, a team in NFL Europe. In 1999, after the Rams' starting quarterback sustained a season-ending injury,

Warner embarked on his first starting season in the NFL, leading his team to a sensational season and a Super Bowl victory. Surpassing everyone's expectations, Warner posted record-breaking numbers and took home both the regular-season and Super Bowl Most Valuable Player (MVP) awards. In the next two seasons, he expertly led one of the most powerful offenses in the league (an offense that had become known as "the greatest show on turf"), won his second season MVP award, and earned the team its second Super Bowl spot in 2002. In 2004, after his play had begun to falter, Warner was released from the Rams and signed to the New York Giants for one season. He next joined the Cardinals, for the next three seasons sharing the starting-quarterback position with a younger player, Matt Leinart. Named the team's starter at the beginning of the 2008 season, Warner, at age 37, made a dramatic comeback: he posted his best statistics since 2001 and went for the third time to the Super Bowl, in which his team lost a close match against the Pittsburgh Steelers. Warner recently signed a two-year contract extension with the Cardinals and is widely considered a likely inductee into the Professional Football Hall of Fame.

The second son of Gene and Sue Warner, Kurtis Eugene Warner was born on June 22, 1971 in Burlington, Iowa, and grew up in Cedar Rapids. When he was four years old, his parents divorced; Kurt and his brother, Matt, lived with their mother during the week and spent time with their father and his second wife, Mimi, on weekends. With his father's second marriage the Warner brothers gained a stepbrother, Matt Post, with whom they became close. Raised as a Roman Catholic, Warner was taught from a young age to fear God and to respect and obey his elders. He was an energetic but well-behaved child. He and his brother attended parochial grade school and high school, which his mother paid for by working three jobs. At Regis High School Warner excelled at football, basketball, and baseball. Though he had wanted to be a receiver, he was asked by the football coach to play quarterback after he won an impromptu throwing contest. As the starting quarterback Warner led his high-school team to modest success; more importantly, he developed a love for the sport and confidence that he could one day play in the NFL.

Warner accepted a partial football scholarship to attend the University of Northern Iowa, a Division I-AA school. For four years he was the backup quarterback behind the team's starter, Jay Johnson; he grew so frustrated with his lack of playing time that at one point he almost quit the team (called the Panthers). When Warner finally got a chance to start, during his fifth and last year, he was named to the first team All-Gateway Football Conference and led the Panthers to the Division I-AA semifinals. Also that year Warner met his future wife, Brenda Meoni, at a country-western bar. Warner quickly fell in love with Meoni, a woman four years his senior, who was divorced and had two young children, one of whom was partially blind and mentally disabled as a result of an accident he had suffered as an infant. (The children's father was no longer involved in their lives.) When she met Warner Meoni was living with her parents and struggling to support her children. To her surprise, and unlike many men she had met, Warner was not intimidated by the challenges Meoni faced; rather, he was attracted to her strength and courage and soon grew close to her children. "I really saw a lot of my Mom in her," Warner told Tom Witosky for the *Des Moines Register* (December 5, 1999). "She was a strong woman who was doing the best she could in a difficult situation. She was terrific."

Though his college-football performance was less auspicious than that of most NFL draft prospects, Warner still thought himself good enough to play professionally. He was not drafted after his graduation, in 1994, but was invited to attend the training camp of the Green Bay Packers, to try out for the team. He knew his chances were slim, given that the team already had three talented quarterbacks in Bret Favre, Mark Brunell, and Ty Detmer. At the camp the quiet, introverted Warner was teased by the Packers players, who called him names including "Chachi" or "Potsie," references to characters from the TV sitcom *Happy Days.* After making 10 starts over six weeks of practice, Warner was cut from the roster. "I would have liked a better chance at it, but I also knew I wasn't strong enough or near ready," Warner told Witosky. "That was a very tough time for me." He returned to Cedar Rapids and moved in with Brenda's family, to save money and stay close to Brenda's children, to whom he had become a father figure. Warner also took a night job at a local grocery store, where he was paid minimum wage. During the days Warner spent time with Brenda's children while she attended nursing school; he also worked out and pored over football films in screening rooms at the University of Northern Iowa.

Around that time Warner received a call from John Gregory, the coach of a newly formed Arena Football League (AFL) team, the Iowa Barnstormers. Established in 1986, arena football uses eight players per team on fields measuring 50 yards in length and 85 feet in width, smaller than those in the NFL. That and other differences between arena and standard American football make the former a faster-moving game with higher scores. (The AFL, which is far less popular than the NFL, cancelled its 2009 season to develop a plan for increasing profits.) Warner joined the Barnstormers and played three seasons as the team's starting quarterback. Throwing 183 touchdowns and leading the team to compete in two championship games, he was named to the AFL All-Star team in 1996 and 1997. The experience Warner gained in the fast-paced game helped him develop a quick arm.

Al Luiginbill, the coach of the Amsterdam Admirals, a team in the NFL Europe league, heard of Warner's impressive AFL numbers but could not afford to sign him. (In existence from 1991 to 2007, NFL Europe was conceived by the American NFL as an opportunity for younger, developing players to gain experience. NFL Europe had a spring season, unlike the regular NFL.) Luiginbill shopped Warner to 12 American NFL coaches, so that he could be paid by the NFL while playing in Europe; finally, the St. Louis Rams agreed to sign him. Warner performed well in Europe in 1998, leading the league in passing yards, attempts, completions, and touchdowns. Later that year he became the third-string quarterback for the Rams, the NFL's least successful football club in the 1990s. His only playing time with the team came in the fourth quarter of the 1998 season's last game, a 19–38 loss to the San Francisco 49ers. The Rams offered Warner to the Cleveland Browns, which reentered the league in 1999, in the expansion draft that took place in the off-season, but the Browns did not select him.

In 1999 Warner was named the backup quarterback for the Rams' starter, Trent Green. Then, in a preseason game, Green sustained a season-ending injury when he tore the anterior cruciate ligament (ACL) in his knee, and Warner became the new starter. In his first starting game in the NFL, Warner surprised his coach and most of the league when he completed 28 out of 44 passes, passing for 316 yards, including two touchdowns, in the team's season-opening victory over the Baltimore Ravens. In the next game, a 35–7 victory over the Atlanta Falcons, he became the second NFL quarterback in history to throw a total of six touchdown passes in two starts. The rest of the season was equally triumphant; along with the star running back Marshall Faulk and the wide receivers Isaac Bruce, Torry Holt, Az-Zahir Hakim, and Ricky Proehl, Warner led the Rams to secure a play-off spot, with a 13–3 season record. Warner's statistics for the season included 4,353 passing yards, 41 touchdowns, a 65.1 completion percent, and a 131.4 quarterback rating. It was an astonishing performance for any player—his numbers were among the highest in history for any first-year quarterback—let alone one who had emerged from near-total obscurity. Named the NFL's Most Valuable Player, Warner became an overnight celebrity, and his fairy-tale journey from grocery-store employee to star quarterback was the talk of the NFL. He was a guest on the *Late Show with David Letterman*, and his picture appeared on the cover of *Sports Illustrated* (October 18, 1999), along with the words "Who IS This Guy?"

In the play-offs Warner led the Rams to defeat the Minnesota Vikings (49–37) in the first round, completing 27 out of 33 of his passes and setting a play-off record for passing yards (391). The Rams next bested the Tampa Bay Buccaneers (11–6), becoming the National Football Conference (NFC) Champions. Warner entered the Super Bowl having played in fewer NFL games than any other quarterback in the league. In that game, against the Tennessee Titans, Warner connected for two touchdowns and threw for 414 passing yards—the first 400-yard passing game of his career—including a 73-yard touchdown to Isaac Bruce when the game was tied with just over two minutes to play. He set a Super Bowl record for passing attempts (45) without a single interception. The Rams won the game, 23–16, and Warner was awarded the Super Bowl MVP award, making him the sixth player in NFL history to win both the regular-season and the Super Bowl MVP awards.

In July 2000 Warner signed a seven-year, $47 million deal that included $11.5 million as a signing bonus and $6 million in potential additional bonuses. (His highest-paying yearly contract with the AFL had been worth $65,000.) Warner racked up 2,260 passing yards in his first six games in the 2000 season, an NFL record, as well as 19 touchdowns. During a mid-season October game, however, he broke a finger of his throwing hand, leading him to miss four weeks of the season. Warner helped lead the team to a 10–6 season record but sustained a concussion during a December game that forced him to sit out for most of the last regular-season game, against the New Orleans Saints. The Rams lost, 31–28, in the wild-card play-off game against the Saints. The 2001 season witnessed Warner's return to full strength and high performance. Noted for his ability to drop back and release the ball quickly, Warner achieved a pass-completion percentage of 68.7 for the season. The Rams achieved a season record of 14–2, and Warner earned his second regular-season MVP award. After defeating the Packers in the divisional play-off game, Warner completed two-thirds of his passes for 212 yards and two touchdowns, to defeat the Philadelphia Eagles in the conference championship. In Super Bowl XXXVI the Rams faced the New England Patriots, helmed by quarterback Tom Brady and Head Coach Bill Belichick. Despite a valiant effort—Warner completed 28 of 44 passes for 365 yards, ran for one touchdown, and passed for another—the Rams lost to the Patriots, 20–17.

In the next two seasons, Warner faced trying times. During his first three games of 2002, he threw seven interceptions and only one touchdown. In the fourth game, against the Dallas Cowboys, he again broke a finger on his throwing hand, and he went on to miss all but two of the season's remaining games, both losses. Warner was replaced by Marc Bulger, and the Rams finished with a 7–9 record, failing to make the play-offs. Observers and fans wondered what had happened to the team's MVP quarterback. Warner performed well during the 2003 preseason practices, winning the starting position back from Bulger, and expressed his confidence that he had fully recuperated. He had a disastrous beginning, however; in the season's first game, against the New York Giants, he suffered a concussion during one of the six times he was sacked and fumbled the ball six times. Bulger replaced him for the rest of the season, leading the team to a 12–4 season record, the best in their division. The Rams, however, lost in the first round of the play-offs.

Warner was released from the Rams on June 1, 2004, becoming one of the biggest names to enter free agency. Three days later he was signed to the Giants, a team that had recently acquired the quarterback Eli Manning, a first-round draft pick from the University of Mississippi. It was widely assumed that New York had drafted Warner to fill the role of "caretaker quarterback"—an experienced quarterback who could start in the beginning of the season and mentor the young star, Manning, before his expected takeover at some point mid-season. Warner led the Giants to a record of 5–4, but after a few poor performances, he was replaced by Manning, who went 1–6 in the next seven games. Though by all accounts Warner was polite to Manning about the demotion, he was frustrated and disappointed with his experience in New York.

In early 2005 Warner signed a one-year contract worth $4 million with the Arizona Cardinals, a club that had not had a winning season in several years but had a roster of young receivers and running backs. He was immediately embraced by fans in Arizona; sales of Warner Arizona jerseys skyrocketed, outselling all jerseys of Rams players. Warner had a difficult start, leading the team to a 0–3 record, before sustaining a groin injury in September and being replaced by Josh McCown. Warner returned to the starting spot mid-season before injuring his knee. In 10 starts that season, Warner posted a record of 2–10, passed for 2,713 yards, 11 touchdowns, nine interceptions, and a 64.5 completion percentage. In February 2006 he signed a three-year contract with the Cardinals worth $18 million. The Cardinals drafted Matt Leinart, a young quarterback from the University of Southern California, who was predicted to be a starter later in the season. After throwing for 301 yards and three touchdowns in the season opener, against the San Francisco 49ers, Warner was named the NFC player of the week. In the third week Warner reached the 20,000-yards-passing milestone, in 76 games—two more than Dan Marino, the record-holder. Leinart replaced Warner mid-season and played for much of the rest of the year, until he injured his shoulder in the second-to-last game. In 2007 Leinart was the team's starting quarterback, but by the fourth game Warner returned to the starting position, after having successfully relieved Leinart on many occasions. Coupled with the team's fourth-year star wide receiver, Larry Fitzgerald, Warner led the team to an 8–8 record and finished the season with 27 touchdown passes in 14 games, just shy of the franchise record and one of the highest totals of his career.

In the spring of 2008, the Cardinals announced that Leinart would be the team's starting quarterback, but after his poor performance during the preseason—and in light of the strong play by Warner—in late August 2008 Head Coach Ken Whisenhunt announced that Warner would be the team's starter. That season was one of Warner's best; he notched 4,583 passing yards and 30 touchdowns and racked up an impressive completion rate of 67.1 percent. In December 2008 Warner was named the NFC's starting quarterback in the Pro Bowl. The Cardinals earned a 9–7 season record, winning their conference title and clinching their first play-off berth since 1998. In the play-offs Warner led the Cardinals to victory after victory, defeating the Atlanta Falcons (30–24) in the wild-card game, followed by the Carolina Panthers (33–13) and the Philadelphia Eagles (32–25). In the Super Bowl, which pitted the Cardinals against the Pittsburgh Steelers, Warner threw for 377 yards—the third-highest total in Super Bowl history—three touchdowns, and just one interception. Warner threw for more yards against the Steelers, whose defense was considered the best in the league, than had any quarterback that season. The Cardinals managed to take a three-point lead (23–20) with less than three minutes remaining, before the Steelers scored what would be the gaming-winning touchdown. The game gave Warner more career Super Bowl passing yards than any other quarterback in history. Warner received the NFL Walter Payton Man of the Year Award, which honors players for both their on-field excellence and community work. In the spring of 2009, after extensive negotiations that briefly resulted in Warner's becoming a free agent, the Cardinals signed him to a two-year contract worth a total of $23 million.

In the off-season Warner underwent arthroscopic surgery to repair a tear in his left hip. As of the sixth week of the 2009 season, the Cardinals were in second place in their division, with a record of 3–2. In a game on September 20, against the Carolina Panthers, Warner completed his first 15 passes and went on to break the NFL's single-game completion-percentage record, completing 14 of 26 passes for 243 yards and two touchdowns, with no turnovers or sacks. The Cardinals won that game, 31–17. On October 19, in a game against the Seattle Seahawks, Warner became one of only two quarterbacks in NFL history to pass for more than 30,000 yards in 114 games. (The other quarterback was Dan Marino.)

Warner married Brenda Meoni in 1997, having become, like her, a born-again Christian. They were wed the year after both of Brenda's parents were killed during a tornado. Warner legally adopted his wife's two children from her previous marriage, Zachary and Jesse, in 1998. In addition, the Warners have five children together: two sons (Elijah and Kade), a daughter (Jada), and twin girls (Sierra Rose and Sienna Rae). As "charismatic" Christians, Kurt and Brenda Warner often speak about their faith—in 1999 Warner spoke at a rally hosted by the Reverend Billy Graham—and take part in community-service activities. They run a foundation, First Things First, whose mission is to improve people's lives while promoting Christian values. With Jennifer Schuchmann they are the authors of the book *First Things First: The Rules of Being a Warner* (2009). Warner also published *All Things Possible: My Story of Faith, Football, and the First Miracle Season*, written with Michael Silver, in 2001. "Every time I put on my uniform, every time I throw a pass, every decision that I make, every time I speak to my children, every time I communicate with my wife, every time I go to church and pray—everything that I do, I want to be as close to perfect as I possibly can," Warner told Gregorian. "That's what motivates me more than anything."

—M.E.R.

Suggested Reading: *Des Moines Register* Sports D p1 Dec. 5, 1999, S p1 Jan. 29, 2000; (Mesa, Arizona) *East Valley Tribune* Sports Nov. 20, 2008; *New York Times* (on-line) Oct. 19, 2009; (Salt Lake City) *Deseret Morning News* Feb. 2, 2009; *St. Louis (Missouri) Post-Dispatch* Sports D p1 Jan. 13, 2002

Selected Books: *All Things Possible: My Story of Faith, Football, and the First Miracle Season* (with Michael Silver), 2001; *First Things First: The Rules of Being a Warner* (with Brenda Warner and Jennifer Schuchmann), 2009

Williams, Evan

Mar. 31, 1972– Co-founder and CEO of Twitter

Address: Twitter Inc., 539 Bryant St., San Francisco, CA 94107

"What are you doing right now?" That is the question millions of subscribers to the social-networking Web site Twitter are answering around the clock in sentence-long posts via cell phones and computers all over the world. Evan Williams, the company's co-founder and chief executive officer (CEO), has readily admitted that most Twitter posts are mundane. Yet the tool also has potential—some of it already evident, much still unknown—to convey important information. Big media companies including CNN and the *New York Times* have signed on as content providers, and even President Barack Obama had an account; when Obama won the presidential election, in November 2008, he sent out a Twitter message that read, "We just made history." Elsewhere on the spectrum, such celebrities as Britney Spears, Ashton Kutcher, and Shaquille O'Neal have become Twitter users, providing their many followers on the site with up-to-the-minute "tweets"—Twitter messages—about their everyday activities. If Twitter seems to be simply another form of blogging, though a very specific and limited one (a tweet contains a maximum of 140 characters and answers the question "What are you doing right now?"), there is a good reason. Before his work on Twitter, Williams, who coined the term "blogger," co-founded Blogger.com, the original blogging platform. He later sold the company to Google in a reportedly lucrative deal.

Williams and his small tech team at other companies he founded, Pyra Labs, Odeo Inc., and Obvious Corp., were initially working on Blogger.com and Twitter only as side projects. "Thinking with the left brain, most reasonable people seem to agree that this idea [Twitter] is hare-brained, frivolous, banal and ridiculous," a business journalist wrote for the *Economist* (December 22, 2007). "Indeed it is. And millions of people absolutely love it, twittering away throughout the day. Like all new and cool things, says Mr. Williams, it's 'experiential.' So it turns out that mums love to be notified on their mobile phones that their teenager is 'eating an orange.' Colleagues appreciate that you are 'running late' as they wait in the meeting room. Friends seeing that you are 'having an espresso at Starbucks' might stop by. And a lot of people simply feel more connected by scavenging for conversational scraps from their friends." Twitter has also demonstrated a capacity to help people communicate more important information—an outcome that Williams has admitted he did not predict. The site has allowed people to stay in touch and informed in the aftermaths of a number of disasters, such as the 2007 earthquake in the San Francisco Bay Area, the wildfires in Southern California in 2008, and the terrorist attack in Mumbai, India, the same year. As of June 2009 the number of Twitter users was reported to be between 10 million and 32 million. *Time* magazine recently named Evan Williams and the other two co-founders of Twitter, Biz Stone and Jack Dorsey—known collectively as the "Twitter guys"—among the world's 100 most influential people.

Evan ("Ev") Williams was born on March 31, 1972 outside Clarks, Nebraska, a town with a population of fewer than 400. He was raised on a soybean and corn farm. Evans attended a small public school, the only one in town, and took part in various extracurricular activities, such as band and sports. "But he was an indifferent student and felt like a black sheep at home, too," Michael S. Malone wrote for the *Wall Street Journal* (April 18, 2009). While his father and brother enjoyed farming and hunting, Williams—a vegetarian—preferred reading; he also dreamt of starting various enterprises. After high school he enrolled at the University of Nebraska at Lincoln. No more interested in his studies than he had been earlier, he never declared a major and left after a year and a half. "In some ways," he told Andy Boyle for the *Omaha World-Herald* (April 11, 2009), "I wish I would have finished my degree. I don't know why I was in such a hurry to work." He next went to Florida, where he found some copywriting work; then he spent some time in Texas, seeking employment in the technology sector. "Every time he got started on one idea," Malone wrote, "some new idea would pop into his head, luring him away and preventing him from ever following through on a project."

David Paul Morris/Getty Images

Evan Williams

At the age of 22, Williams moved back to Nebraska. Although he knew almost nothing about the Internet—except that it was "going to be a big deal," as he wrote in a personal essay for the *New York Times* (March 8, 2009, on-line)—Williams and his father started a company that made CD-ROMs and videos on how to use the World Wide Web. The company was by no means a success. "I had no business running a company at that time because I hadn't worked at a real company," Williams wrote for the *New York Times*. "I didn't know how to deal with people, I lacked focus, and I had no discipline. I'd start new projects without finishing old ones, and I didn't keep track of money. I lost a lot of it, including what my father had invested, and I ended up owing the I.R.S. because I hadn't paid payroll taxes. I made a lot of employees mad." Nonetheless, Williams remained optimistic. In the mid-1990s new technology and Internet companies were starting up on a regular basis, and Williams wanted to go to the center of the tech boom—the San Francisco Bay Area. He moved to California in 1997. "Unfortunately, my aim was a little off," Williams told Malone, referring to his decision to move to Marin County rather than Silicon Valley. After working for a year at what became O'Reilly Media, he became a freelance Web developer, most notably for Intel and Hewlett Packard. In 1999 he co-founded the company Pyra Labs, a maker of project-management programs.

While serving as that company's CEO, Williams was working on a side project—an on-line publishing tool he called Blogger. Williams created the company Blogger.com, which was the original model for blogs. (Most blogs, or Web logs, are personal Web sites on which users chronicle their lives and/or offer opinions on one or more of a great variety of topics, such as sports, celebrities, travel, electronics, or the media.) As the high-tech "bubble" burst in 2000 and 2001, and many Internet entrepreneurs went out of business, Williams and his new company managed to survive, with a workable idea and loyal investors. He eventually asked Biz Stone, a Web programmer and designer, to join Blogger. In 2003 Google bought the company, which brought Williams a lot of money. The deal also made him and Stone employees at Google. After two years Williams left, not wanting to work for a huge company and preferring to be in control of his own projects and ideas. In 2004 he co-founded Odeo Inc., a podcasting company. A year and a half later, he bought out his investors and transferred his assets to another company he co-founded, Obvious Corp., so named because Williams believes that the best ideas are always obvious in retrospect. (One of the main reasons that Odeo did not flourish was that Apple, a much bigger company, had added a podcasting function to iTunes.)

While at Odeo Williams had started Twitter. Like Blogger.com, Twitter had begun as a side project. Williams, Stone, and the engineer Jack Dorsey are the co-founders of Twitter; Dorsey is credited with creating its technology. (Tweets, or Twitter messages, are short instant messages that are sent out to people who "follow," or subscribe to, a user's account.) Williams appointed Dorsey as CEO but then, in the fall of 2008, made himself CEO and assigned Dorsey the position of company chairman. Twitter's rate of growth was impressive. In 2007 it had about 200,000 users; while that was a small number compared with those of other social-networking sites, big publications, such as *Time*, *Newsweek*, and the *New York Times*, were paying attention. They were also raising one essential question: how will Twitter make money? Williams and the other co-founders, however, were less concerned about developing a business plan than about increasing the number and loyalty of its subscribers. At the end of the year, the *Economist* (December 22, 2007) declared Twitter to be the third "next big thing" in Silicon Valley, after the social-networking site Facebook and Apple's new product, the iPhone. In 2008 Williams and his team still did not have a formal financial plan, at least not one they were willing to share with the media. That year, however, the company acquired more than two million users and rejected a reported $500 million buy-out offer from Facebook. By the end of the year, it had become clear that Twitter founders had no plans to make money from advertising. Instead, they were trying to figure out a way to charge businesses—Whole Foods, Jet Blue, Dell, Nike, Starbucks, and others—fees for using Twitter to communicate with consumers. But no specific plans were made. By the spring of 2009, Twitter had about 15 million users. It had also acquired more than $20 million in investments from venture capitalists. A profile in *New York* magazine (February 8, 2009) cited a report that estimated the value of the company to be $250 million.

Williams has acknowledged that technology giants such as Microsoft and Yahoo! will likely launch products similar to Twitter; in September 2009 Google launched Wave, its own multifunctional social-networking service. And, generally speaking, Internet entrepreneurs are concerned that their products will "jump the shark"—become overhyped, overexposed, or simply not cool. Although Twitter has been in the public eye only since 2007, in the age of instant communication—to which blogging and Twitter have greatly contributed—that is a very long time, certainly long enough for various Web sites and publications to claim that Twitter has jumped the shark. When the talk-show host Oprah Winfrey announced that she would join Twitter, in April 2009, Lance Ulanoff declared in *PC Magazine* (April 16, 2009), "Oprah joining the micro-blogging service and talking about it on her show is the beginning of the end." Williams later appeared on Winfrey's show to talk about Twitter.

With more exposure, Twitter encountered more problems: sometimes the site crashed, and at other times hackers broke in or people posed as celebrities when they created accounts. Despite the problems, the site grew in popularity. Accordingly, claims that Twitter had jumped the shark also increased. The commentator John Ridley said on the National Public Radio show *Morning Edition* (May 12, 2009), "At the risk of sounding like that old guy in *Gran Torino* telling those young punks to get off my lawn, it's gotten to the point whenever I hear somebody talking about Twitter or twittering or tweeting, it just makes my little tummy want to hurl. I haven't tweeted once in my life, but I'm sick of hearing about it already. What once may have been the cool way of letting a hundred people know you're about to go mow your lawn now has the feel of a used-to-be-fresh means of communication—so yesterday, like two-way pagers and AOL."

Two weeks later the Associated Press (May 26, 2009) reported that Twitter had teamed up with a production company, Reveille, to develop an unscripted TV show that would "harness Twitter to put players on the trail of celebrities in an interactive, competitive format." The reaction from users and critics was immediate: Twitter, some argued, should avoid distractions and stay focused on growing its social-networking community. Popular Twitter users such as Ashton Kutcher, who has more than one million followers on the site, threatened to quit if the TV-show deal went through. In an attempt at damage control, Williams sent out a Twitter message that read, according to *PC Magazine* (May 27, 2009), "There is a show in the works, but it's been mis-characterized." Twitter Inc., it turned out, had little to do with the show in development. While the details are not yet known, the uproar caused by the rumor showed that many people—whether they are critics or supporters—care about Twitter, and that Twitter users are very passionate about how their social network is used. What Williams and his team have yet to figure out is how to parlay that passion into profit.

Williams and his wife, Sara, live in the San Francisco Bay Area.

—D.K.

Suggested Reading: *Economist* Dec. 22, 2007; *Fast Company* (on-line) Mar. 7, 2008; *New York* (on-line) Feb. 8, 2009; *New York Times* (on-line) Mar. 8, 2009; *Portfolio* (on-line) Mar. 2009; *San Francisco Chronicle* K p1 Apr. 5, 2009

Alex Wong/Getty Images

Williams, Ronald A.

Nov. 11, 1949– Chairman and CEO of Aetna

Address: Aetna Inc., 151 Farmington Ave., Hartford, CT 06156

In 2001, when Ronald A. Williams joined the executive team of Aetna, the company was the largest health-insurance provider in the U.S., but it was itself in need of care. Aetna's financial condition was precarious, and it had lost its stellar reputation among policyholders, physicians, and shareholders. Currently, Aetna ranks third among American health-insurance companies in revenues, generating half as much as WellPoint, which is in second place, and less than 40 percent as much as United-Health Group, which ranks first, but it has regained a solid financial footing and has gone far toward repairing its good name. To a large degree that turnaround has been attributed to Williams, who became president of Aetna in 2002, added the positions of chairman and chief executive officer (CEO) in 2006, and since 2007 has served as chairman and CEO. During his first five years at Aetna, Williams worked closely and effectively with John W. "Jack" Rowe, Aetna's CEO and chairman from 2001 to 2006. Shortly before Rowe left Aetna, he told Jessi Hempel and Diane Brady for *BusinessWeek* (January 4, 2006) that Williams was "clearly recognized as the finest operating executive in the industry," and he noted his colleague's extraordinary "attention to detail," "great discipline," and "great technical proclivity." "While Rowe's vision and chutzpah were clearly critical to Aetna's success . . . ," Hempel and Brady wrote, Williams "took many of the ideas generated by his boss and turned them into reality."

Before he joined Aetna Williams worked for companies including Vista Health Corp., Blue Cross of California, and WellPoint Health Networks. The management consultant Jeff Weiss, the founder and director of the Center for Corporate Innovation, told Sonia Alleyne for *Black Enterprise* (September 2006) that thanks to Williams, WellPoint "went from near bankruptcy to just about being the best managed company in healthcare three or four years in a row." Weiss also said that at Aetna, Williams has inspired unshakable loyalty among employees. "The amount of work he gets out of people is ungodly," Weiss said. "He gets tens of thousands of people to put out 120%, and Ron does it by the quality of his thinking and the integrity of his actions." In a survey of hundreds of investment professionals conducted by *Institutional Investor* magazine in 2009, Williams was named the nation's best CEO in the managed-care category, in a list that recognized executives for being "forthright and transparent with shareholders and smart with their companies' balance sheets," and Aetna was named the country's most shareholder-friendly company. In another 2009 survey, conducted by *Fortune*, a panel of thousands of Wall Street research analysts and corporate executives and directors named Aetna the most admired company in the category "health care—insurance and managed care"; within that category, they ranked it first in quality of management, innovation, people management, quality of products or services, use of corporate assets, financial soundness, and long-term investment, and second in global competitiveness and social responsibility. In the ongoing national discussion about reform of the American health-care system, Williams has served as a public face of his industry, in appearances before congressional committees and in op-ed articles that he has written or co-written for newspapers including the *Wall Street Journal*, the *Washington Post*, the *Financial Times*, and the *Seattle Post-Intelligencer*.

Ronald A. Williams was born on November 11, 1949 in Chicago, Illinois. He grew up in a working-class neighborhood in South Chicago. His mother worked part-time as a manicurist; his father's jobs included parking-lot attendant, bus driver, and transit-union trustee. He got his first job at 14, painting details on cars at a car-wash. After he graduated from high school, Williams enrolled at Roosevelt University, in Chicago; he supported himself with a job as an administrative assistant and took classes at night. He earned a B.A. degree in psychology in 1970. Williams remained at Roosevelt to pursue a graduate degree in clinical psychology, then abandoned that goal after he realized that business appealed to him more. In 1984 he earned an M.S. degree in management from the Sloan School of Management at the Massachusetts Institute of Technology (MIT), in Cambridge. "There's just no substitute for the intellectual stimulation, analytical rigor, and global view of business you find at MIT Sloan," he has said, as quoted on the school's Web site. "It's the perfect environment for developing leadership skills." During the years 1970–87, Williams worked in the office of the governor of Illinois as an administrative assistant; co-founded Integrative Systems, a mid-career assessment and testing firm, where he was president; held the title of senior vice president of Vista Health Corp.; and served as a group marketing executive at Control Data Corp., a leading producer of supercomputers for some years.

In 1987 Williams was hired as vice president for corporate services for the health insurer Blue Cross of California, a WellPoint subsidiary. The company later promoted him, successively, to senior vice president of marketing and specialty products; executive vice president of group and network services; and, in 1995, president. He held that position until 1999, when he left to become president of the Large Group Division of WellPoint Health Networks Inc. In early 2001 he left WellPoint to join Aetna, with the titles of executive vice president and chief of health operations. "We needed a very senior operation executive who understood health insurance at the molecular level, somebody who could take apart the engine and put the 200 pieces on the garage floor, put it back together, turn the key, and it would start," John W. Rowe told Sonia Alleyne, in explaining why Aetna recruited Williams.

Named for Mount Etna ("Aetna" is the Latin name), an active volcano in Sicily, the firm grew out of the Aetna Insurance Co., established in 1850 in Hartford, Connecticut, where it still maintains its headquarters. By the end of the Civil War, in 1865, it had become one of the nation's biggest issuers of life-insurance policies. In subsequent years it lent money to farmers for mortgages and entered the accident-insurance business. The company began to offer health-insurance policies in 1899, but only to those who bought or already held other Aetna insurance. In the early 1900s Aetna expanded into the area of liability and casualty insurance, covering damages to automobiles and factory equipment as well as losses from burglaries. It paid out $3 million in claims related to the San Francisco, California, earthquake of 1906 and payments to family members of several people who died when the *Titanic* sank, in 1912. Aetna began selling surety bonds in 1911 and group life, accident, disability, and medical insurance in 1913, 1914, 1919, and 1936, respectively. Its surety bonds helped to finance construction of Hoover Dam; the National Archives Building; seven U.S. Navy aircraft carriers during World War II; and the United Nations headquarters. Also during World War II, Aetna provided insurance to cover aspects of the Manhattan Project, the U.S.'s secret program for building an atomic bomb. In 1930 Aetna entered the pension business, and in 1960 it began selling insurance internationally. The firm changed its name to Aetna Life & Casualty in 1965. In 1996 it left the property- and casualty-insurance businesses, selling those divisions to Travelers Insurance Group. That same year Aetna merged with U.S. Healthcare, creating Aetna U.S. Healthcare. For a total of $10 billion, it acquired NYLCare Health Plans in 1998 and Prudential HealthCare in 1999—years in which Richard L. Huber, a former banking executive, was Aetna's president and chairman—"making Aetna the country's largest provider of health benefits with more than 21 million members," according to its Web site.

Aetna's transformation "from a staid old-line insurance company to an aggressive managed care health insurer," as Milt Freudenheim described it for the *New York Times* (February 26, 2000), proved to be calamitous. The company's profits and stock value plummeted, and the firm was besieged by a rapidly increasing chorus of complaints from patients, physicians, and trial lawyers as well as shareholders. In February 2000 Huber was forced to resign; he was succeeded by William H. Donaldson, a former head of the New York Stock Exchange, whose expertise was in finance, not health care. Donaldson's efforts to remove some restrictions on patient care further increased Aetna's costs and reduced profits. In September 2000 Donaldson recruited Rowe, a physician specializing in geriatrics who had overseen the merger of two large New York City medical centers, as Aetna's president and chief executive officer; Donaldson retained the title of chairman. According to Jessi Hempel and Diane Brady, writing for *BusinessWeek* (January 16, 2006), Rowe "moved quickly to settle outstanding lawsuits with doctors and dentists, laid off 15,000 employees, and slashed the customer base" to 13 million, "in part by jettisoning half the counties in which Aetna offered Medicare," which were unprofitable. In December 2000 Aetna sold its financial services and international businesses to ING Group, a Dutch financial-services company, and spun off its health-care unit to shareholders as a separate company to be known as Aetna Inc.

Aetna was still on extremely shaky ground when, in March 2001, Williams joined the firm. (He started the job the day after his last day with WellPoint. "If I didn't show urgency in what I did, why should anyone else?" he remarked to Sonia Alleyne.) Aetna had ended the year 2000 in the red, and in 2001 its losses increased more than 10-fold, to nearly $280 million. Williams and Rowe agreed that "better profitability [would] come from improving the quality of Aetna's products rather than increasing the number of subscribers," Hempel and Brady wrote (January 16, 2006). Toward that end they initiated several important measures. One was the creation of the Executive Management Information System, which, according to the MIT Web site, is a "powerful data analysis and reporting system that gathers information from across the business to provide detailed reports on a wide variety of performance measures." Paraphrasing Williams, the MIT article explained that "the ability to capture information consistently and in real time allows leadership to spot trends early and manage Aetna's expansive business operations more effectively." Another important move was Aetna's promotion of consumer-driven health-care plans, which had low monthly payments and high deductibles. Aetna's primary goal in offering those plans, in addition to acquiring more customers, was to insure some of the many Americans who had no health insurance; the low monthly payments were the main selling point. The company also encouraged its members to set up so-called health savings accounts, under the name Aetna Health Fund, which permits visits to out-of-network physicians. Among many measures through which Aetna took advantage of technology to improve service and cut costs, the company began to provide members with on-line information about physicians' backgrounds and experience and assessments of their skills, in the belief that higher-quality medical care results in lower costs in the long run.

In April 2002 Donaldson left Aetna, and the following month Williams was promoted to president, with responsibility for Aetna's medical- and dental-insurance, life insurance, and disability and long-term care products; Rowe retained the post of CEO and became chairman. That September Williams was appointed to Aetna's board of directors. All the while Williams and Rowe had been working very closely "to transform Aetna from a lumbering symbol of all that was wrong with managed care into a nimble, well-respected industry leader," Laura B. Benko wrote for *Modern Healthcare* (January 9, 2006), noting that they "made an impressive team." Business journalists and insiders expressed the view that Williams's and Rowe's strong points were complementary, and that each man brought "critical skills to the operation," Lori Chordas wrote for *Best's Review* (July 2005), an insurance-industry magazine. Rowe was described as forthright, jolly, and magnetic, Williams as soft-spoken, pragmatic, uncommonly detail-oriented, and sensitive to employees' needs and as having at his fingertips a vast amount of information and a keen understanding of the complexities of the business. Williams also made it a point to interact with employees: he set up his office on the first floor of the company's headquarters rather than the executives' floor (the eighth), held quarterly meetings with 5,000 managers, held town-hall-style meetings with other employees, and invited workers to communicate with him via his Intranet column, "Ask Ron." "It's really to create an environment in which people know it's OK to ask the difficult, tough questions," he told Alleyne.

Making greater use of technology was one feature of a multipart strategy developed by Williams in the early 2000s that "created value for our customers and differentiated Aetna from our competitors," as he wrote for the company's 2008 annual report (on-line). A second aspect, known as segmentation, called for the pinpointing of specific populations—such as "public-sector industries with small and middle markets," in Williams's words—and designing products specifically for them. To achieve a third—"serving all of our constituents with a standard of operation excellence," Williams explained in the report—Aetna strived to "identify best practices," in part by heeding the voices of clients and making necessary improvements.

Another tactic that Aetna adopted was the purchase of insurance companies that catered to niche markets. In late 2003 Aetna acquired the Chickering Group, which provided health benefits to college students, and renamed it Aetna Student Health. The following year Aetna purchased the Strategic Resource Co. (SRC), which sells limited health-insurance policies to hourly, part-time, and seasonal workers. Both Aetna Student Health and SRC have come under attack from consumers. According to the business-news Web site TheStreet.com (December 6, 2006), in the fall of 2006, the labor and community coalition Citizens for Economic Opportunity sued Aetna regarding its marketing of the SRC plan. The coalition charged that Aetna's description of the plan in paperwork sent to buyers was designed to fool people into thinking that the coverage was greater than it actually was. The lawsuit was dropped in mid-2007, *Medical News Today* (August 14, 2007, on-line) reported, after a superior-court judge in Hartford ruled that limited-benefit health-plan policies and advertisements for them must include warnings regarding the limits of coverage in boldface capital letters printed in 12-point type—larger than the type commonly used in newspaper articles. In the case of the undergraduate plan, which covers students in more than 200 colleges, the attorney general of New York State, Andrew Cuomo, accused Aetna Student Health of using "outdated and inaccurate" data to "knowingly underpay" students and the physicians who provided care for them, according to Emily Berry, writing for *American Medical News* (February 23, 2009), published by the American Medical Association. In a settlement reached in February 2009, Aetna agreed to pay a total of $5.1 million plus interest and penalties to the students or their doctors.

In 2001 Aetna's revenues totaled $5.48 billion; by the end of December 2005, they had reached $22.885 billion. In 2006 revenues climbed to $25.145 billion; in 2007, to $27.673 billion; and in 2008, $31.606 billion. Meanwhile, during Williams's first five years with the company, the value of a share of Aetna stock had risen by about 600 percent, to about $30. Since then stock prices have fluctuated widely, reaching a high of more than $54 at the beginning of October 2007. To a great extent, the worldwide recession has been responsible for subsequent decreases, to about $25 at the end of October 2009. According to an article posted on the Web site of the *Wall Street Journal*, on June 3, 2009 the company "cut its 2009 profit forecast, citing higher-than-anticipated medical costs in its commercial plans and lower-than-expected revenue from its Medicare business. The surprise revision, announced after regular stock-market trading, triggered a 6% drop in Aetna shares in after-hours trading. Until recently, Aetna had been considered one of the best-performing companies of the country's major health insurers, and one of the only ones to see consistent increases in health-plan enrollment." Also as of early June 2009, Aetna reported that it was providing medical insurance to more than 19 million members, dental insurance to 14.5 million, and drug coverage to 11.2 million. Aetna is number 77 on the list of Fortune 500 companies, behind UnitedHealth Group (21) and WellPoint (32).

On March 24, 2009, in testimony presented before the Health, Education, Labor and Pensions Committee of the U.S. Senate, Williams talked about the need for reform of the health-care system. All Americans, he said, must be required to be covered by health insurance, regardless of the state of their health. Universal coverage can be accomplished, he explained, by means of subsidies from the federal government, to enable those with low incomes to buy it, and through tax credits for small businesses, to enable them to offer coverage to their employees. He also advocated "payment reform"—rewarding physicians and hospitals whose quality of care is above average—and measures to "engage consumers in their own health care by focusing on prevention and wellness," according to an Aetna news release (March 24, 2009, on-line). As he had in the past, Williams stated his opposition to national health insurance.

Williams is the chairman of the Council for Affordable Quality Healthcare and the vice chairman of the Business Council. He is a member of the board of directors of the American Express Co. His name was included on *Fortune*'s list of the top 50 most-powerful black executives in the U.S. in 2002, *Enterprise* magazine's list of the 75 most-powerful black leaders in corporate America in 2005, and *Ebony*'s "power 150" in 2008. He won the National Bridge Award from Chicago United Way in 2007 and received an honorary degree from Howard University in 2009.

According to Sonia Alleyne, Williams "is not a CEO driven by power, influence or celebrity. He makes few gestures when he speaks. His suits are not tailored; his shoes are soft-soled. He grants the press limited access and refuses to give details about his family life or offer any personal insight into what makes him tick. It's not eccentricity. He's an ultraprivate man focused on making Aetna bigger and better." Williams and his wife, Cynthia, have been married since about 1980. Their son, Christopher, is in his 20s. The couple live in Connecticut. In his leisure time Williams enjoys listening to jazz and watching movies.

—D.K.

Suggested Reading: aetna.com; *Black Enterprise* p96+ Sep. 2006; *BusinessWeek* p47+ Jan. 16, 2006, (on-line) Jan. 4, 2006; *Forbes.com* Mar. 6, 2000; *Hartford (Connecticut) Courant* A p1+ July 28, 2006; *Modern Healthcare* p10 Jan. 9, 2006; thestreet.com Dec. 6, 2006

Andrew H. Walker/Getty Images

Williams, Wendy

July 18, 1964– Television talk-show host; former radio talk-show host; writer

Address: The Wendy Williams Show, *433 W. 53d St., New York, NY 10019*

Called "a shock-jock diva," "the biggest mouth in New York," and "the urban celebrity gossip guru," the talk-show host Wendy Williams prefers the self-proclaimed title "queen of all media." Her most-recent radio show, *The Wendy Williams Experience*, which aired on the New York City radio station WBLS-FM and was syndicated nationally, was among the most popular offerings on American radio during the first decade of the 21st century, attracting some 12 million listeners every weekday by the time it went off the air, in July 2009. Its success was particularly noteworthy because talk radio, and in particular "shock-talk" radio, is dominated by male hosts, whose audiences are mostly men. The seven-year run of *The Wendy Williams Experience* ended, by her choice, three weeks after Williams launched her new weekday television program, *The Wendy Williams Show*, on July 13, 2009 on the Fox and BET networks.

"Virtually everything in my life I have plotted on to get it," Williams told Steve Fishman for *New York* (October 25, 2005). "Nothing has happened by fluke." Williams's career in radio began during her college days, 27 years ago; before her rise to fame on WBLS, she was heard on a series of eight other stations, in St. Croix; Washington, D.C.; Philadelphia, Pennsylvania; and New York City. "I always knew that if I was ever going to go into radio, I would have to carve my own niche and be different than every other woman out there," Williams wrote in her best-selling first memoir, *Wendy's Got the Heat* (2003). Toward that end she developed a blunt, confrontational style of interviewing and a knack for drawing from her celebrity guests revelations rarely disclosed in public. She also spread gossip, mostly about African-American or Hispanic entertainers or athletes; spoke with unusual candor about her private life, including her earlier cocaine addiction, plastic surgery, abortion, marriages, pregnancies, miscarriages, and her husband's infidelity; and shared her opinions on human relationships, dress, and similar topics deemed mainly of interest to women. Her highly publicized, on- and off-the-air spats with stars including Whitney Houston and Sean Combs reinforced her reputation for brashness and outrageousness and boosted her ratings. "My fans are first," Williams told a *Village Voice* (December 9, 1997) reporter. "I stopped caring about artists when I realized it's more lucrative to talk about them than with them." The terms "outsized" and "larger than life" have been applied to the nearly six-foot-tall Williams, whose work attire includes five-inch heels, a large variety of long-haired blond wigs, and plunging necklines that reveal much of her surgically augmented breasts—all of it part of her calculated effort to market herself. She told Gaby Wood for the London *Observer* (June 7, 2009), "I see myself as a product. . . . I am the product. I'm a good product." Williams's second memoir (co-written, like the first, with Karen Hunter) is *The Wendy Williams Experience* (2004). Williams has also co-written three novels, whose protagonist, Ritz Harper, a radio superstar, she modeled partly on herself: *Drama Is Her Middle Name* (2006) and *Is the Bitch Dead, Or What?* (2007), both co-written by Karen Hunter, and, with Zondra Hughes, *Ritz Harper Goes to Hollywood!* (2009).

The second of Thomas and Shirley Williams's three children, Wendy Williams was born on July 18, 1964 in New Jersey. Her older sister, Wanda, is an attorney; her brother, Tom, is a teacher. Her parents both earned postgraduate degrees; her mother was a schoolteacher, and her father was a school principal who later taught English literature at the college level. For her first five years, her family lived in Asbury Park, New Jersey. After that Williams was raised in Wayside, a predominantly white, upper-middle-class, conservative suburban community in Ocean Township, New Jersey. An overweight academic underachiever in a family of physically fit overachievers, Williams felt painfully conscious of falling short of her parents' expectations; in *Wendy's Got the Heat* she described herself as an "outcast" both at home and at school. Her brother, she wrote, was her best and only friend during her early years. In public her parents often judged her speech and actions to be unacceptable, and they would warn her to calm down by saying the letters "TMTLTF," which stood for "too much, too loud, too fast"—ways of behaving that she subsequently turned to her advantage, as she noted to Frazier Moore for the Associated Press (July 18, 2009). Williams ranked near the bottom of her class when she graduated from Ocean Township High School, in 1982, the same year her sister earned a law degree, with the help of a scholarship. "More was expected of my big sister than of me," Williams told Steve Fishman. "And while she's fabulous and she delivered all the goods, I ended up being fabulous, too, and delivering all the goods."

Despite her poor grades in high school, Williams, by her own account, won acceptance to all the colleges to which she applied; her parents, she wrote in her first memoir, sat on either side of her during all her college interviews. She enrolled at Northeastern University, in Boston, Massachusetts; with the goal of becoming a newscaster, she majored in communications and, to please her parents, minored in journalism. Her role model was Carol Ford, a black woman who had her own radio show in New York and, Williams wrote, "was big and loud. . . . She made radio fun and she seemed to be having fun doing it." At Northeastern's radio station, WRBB, Williams read news reports on air. One day the scheduled student disc jockey failed to show up, and she was asked to fill in. "I didn't think I was cool enough or had the voice for it," she recalled to Rita Charleston for the *Philadelphia Tribune* (September 10, 2004). "But, while I was scared to death, I agreed to do it and ended up loving it." She soon "became part of the lineup," she continued, "and got to know and love the lifestyle of the disc jockey rather than that of a newscaster, whose lifestyle was much more conservative and not really for me." Concurrently, Williams secured an internship with Matt Siegel, who had begun hosting *Matty in the Morning*, on the Boston radio station KISS 108, in 1981. (The show, which is still running, has long been the most popular in its time slot in Boston.) "I didn't want to be like all the other interns," Williams told Ivory M. Jones for *Billboard Radio Monitor* (July 8, 2005); "I wanted to be the queen of all interns." Williams would awaken at 3:00 a.m. and arrive at the station before Siegel went on the air, at 5:30 a.m., and she further attracted Siegel's attention by dressing in rhinestone-studded apparel of the sort that she had seen worn by characters on the TV show *Dynasty*. Soon, Siegel gave her the opportunity to gain on-air experience, as a reviewer of *Dynasty, Dallas*, and other TV shows. Williams graduated from Northeastern with a B.A. degree in 1986.

Two weeks later Williams won her first paying radio job, at WVIS, a pop-music station in St. Croix, in the U.S. Virgin Islands. She felt miserable during the eight months that she spent there, she told Farai Chideya for National Public Radio's *News and Notes* (April 9, 2007, on-line), because she felt like "a real outsider" in that environment and could barely support herself on her salary—\$3.25 per hour, the federal minimum wage at that time. She also believed that her parents disapproved of her decision to accept such a low-paying job and that her friends looked down on her for the same reason. "I hid all my feelings from everybody; I put on a brave face when I talk[ed] to people. I said it was glamorous and wonderful, and really it was torturous," she told Chideya. Having resolved not to quit and be forced to move back into her parents' home, she made a determined effort to get another job, mailing audiotapes and résumés to radio stations in the U.S. In early 1983 she landed a part-time job at WOL-AM in Washington, D.C., which at that time was changing its format from mostly R&B to talk, with a focus on African-American interests and issues.

While she was living in Washington, Williams began to use cocaine, and she soon became dependent on it. Nevertheless, she performed well at work. Within a year she had won another part-time radio job, on the night shift with the New York urban/hip-hop radio station WQHT (97.1 FM), known as Hot 97, and for a while she commuted between cities. She continued to commute to her next job, on the 10:00 p.m.–2:00 a.m. shift on the Top 40 New York station WPLJ. In 1989 she was hired as a fill-in and then as the full-time disc jockey on the morning show on WRKS, better known as 98.7 KISS FM, in New York. There, Williams displayed her knack for talking about the private lives of celebrities. The growing popularity of her show led to her promotion to more desirable time slots; in time she earned the coveted 6:00 p.m.–10 p.m. shift. In 1993 her show was rated number one in its time slot in the New York metropolitan area, and *Billboard* named her Radio Personality of the Year. Meanwhile, she had continued to abuse cocaine, underwent an abortion, and ended a five-month-long marriage.

In late 1994 Emmis Broadcasting, which owned WQHT, bought KISS FM, and Williams, along with other notable rap disc jockeys, moved from KISS to Hot 97. Heard in the afternoon on Hot 97, Williams began to dominate the competition in her time slot and became a fixture at the station, which is widely regarded as an icon of New York hip-hop music. As Gaby Wood noted, Williams's arrival occurred at a propitious moment, as rap was becoming a mainstream phenomenon: "At a time when hip-hop artists were going platinum, Williams went out at night and [then, in the afternoon,] reported back from the clubs; if a rapper dumped a woman, [Williams would] get her on the show; if a gossip item turned up, she'd add her own intelligence. Listeners loved to hate her, musicians sent her dead fish in the mail. Every day brought some new battle." The musical component of Williams's show shrank, and the talk increased. At one point Williams alleged or insinuated that Tupac Shakur, Sean Combs (who has used monikers including Puff Daddy and P. Diddy), and some other rappers were homosexuals—a hugely damaging label in the hip-hop community. Shakur and others responded by referring to her in insulting or angry lyrics in their songs. When Hot 97 executives pressured her to stop airing such allegations, she posted them on gowendy.com.

Earlier, in around 1994, Williams had become romantically involved with Kevin Hunter, a party promoter and former beauty-salon owner. (He is not related to Karen Hunter, the co-author of four of Williams's books.) Williams has said that Hunter, who soon became her manager, disapproved of her drug habit, so she stopped using cocaine, in about 1995. (Others have claimed that she continued to use it for several more years.) The addiction had kept her slender; without the drug, she gained a lot of unwanted weight, and she underwent liposuction treatments to improve her figure. She also had breast implants, to increase her bra size to a D, and had botox treatments to keep her facial skin smooth. Then, in 1997, just as her personal life seemed to be stabilizing, Hot 97 suspended Williams briefly, on the grounds that she had mentioned her Web site on the air and talked about a supposed relationship between the Hot 97 host Angie Martinez and the rapper Q-Tip. For her part, Williams has repeatedly said that Sean Combs pressured the station to suspend her because of his animosity toward her. After the station assigned her to voice commercials and other radio spots, Williams successfully sued Hot 97 to release her from her contract. Because of a noncompetition clause in the contract, she was barred from working in New York for a specified length of time.

Almost immediately, in 1998, after the lawsuit was settled, radio station WUSL-FM, called Power 99, in Philadelphia, hired Williams to co-host its popular morning show, *The Dream Team Show*, with Dee Lee and Smokin' Tony Richards. The following year she married Hunter, and in 2000 she gave birth to their son, Kevin Jr. During the last six months of her pregnancy, she had remained in bed, on doctor's orders; in broadcasts made from her bedroom, she talked about the miscarriages she had suffered earlier, the excess weight she was gaining, and her discovery that her husband had had an affair during her pregnancy. By 2001 the morning show had moved from 15th to first place in popularity among 18-to-34-year-olds in the Philadelphia area, and Williams's annual salary had reportedly risen to $275,000. That year she left WUSL for the New York City station WBLS—107.5 FM, a Hot 97 rival. "I reached a glass ceiling financially at Power 99, and that [show] should have been called *The Wendy Williams Show* from the moment I stepped foot on Philly soil," she told Richard Rys for the magazine *Philadelphia* (April 2003). "If I'm going to make your radio station all of this money, you're not going to treat me like some black woman with no backbone. I will forever feel burnt by it. But I've always believed success is the best revenge. And being in New York—I needed to be back where the moving and shaking and decision-making was going down." Williams's show, *The Wendy Williams Experience*, which aired from 2:00 to 6:00 p.m. on weekdays, went into national syndication via Superadio in 2003. "For a long time I've been faking the confidence that I finally own," Williams told Kenya N. Byrd for *Essence* (October 2004). "That confidence comes from being able to walk out tomorrow and leave it all and know that I'll get hired somewhere else. I'm fearless, not because I have a million dollars to sit back on, but because I finally believe in my own power and worth."

On *The Wendy Williams Experience*, Williams took calls from listeners, gave advice (usually about family or romantic relationships), interviewed celebrities, gossiped, talked about herself, and, sporadically, played a musical recording. (She was accompanied by a male sidekick known as Charlamagne Tha God until he was fired, in 2008, along with other members of her staff, reportedly for budgetary reasons.) "The show works best when its elements—confessional paired with snarkiness—are conflated, as they were during a phone interview with the singer Whitney Houston in 2003," according to Monica Drake. In that often-cited example of such fusion, Williams questioned the R&B/pop superstar Houston about her alleged drug abuse and her scandal-plagued marriage to the singer Bobby Brown, provoking Houston to utter threats and foul language (as well as some words of affection) in response. Williams described that interview to Gaby Wood as "the crowning jewel" of her career, while Kimberly C. Roberts, writing for the *Philadelphia Tribune* (October 20, 2006), characterized it as "a defining moment" in Williams's professional life.

In July 2008 a similar incident occurred, when Omarosa Manigault-Stallworth, a frequent participant on TV reality shows, appeared during what was termed a six-week, four-city "trial run" of a TV talk show Williams hosted. The two women traded insults in what Lola Ogunnaike, writing for CNN.com (July 24, 2008), called "a good catfight." (A video clip of their sparring match was viewed "hundreds of thousands of times" on the Internet, according to Ogunnaike, and as of mid-2009, the video could be seen or read about on more than 54,000 Web sites.) In a critique of the 2008 show for the *New York Times* (July 22, 2008), Alessandra Stanley wrote, "Williams . . . is a real-life scandal-monger, the kind of beauty-salon savant who wishes famous people the worst. She has a bawdy and arch side, but she can be startlingly mean-spirited. . . . She has a commanding and, at times, sassily comic stage presence, but so far her show is less a talk show than an alpha-female showcase, and Ms. Williams is careful to place herself on an equal footing with even her most famous guests." The trial run proved successful and led to the launch of *The Wendy Williams Show* on the Fox and BET networks on July 13, 2009. The show is executive-produced by Williams, Kevin Hunter, and Rob Dauber, who has worked with Oprah Winfrey, Rosie O'Donnell, and Martha Stewart. "This is such a great time for talk, especially with the economy still being so bad," Williams told Bill Zwecker for the *Chicago Sun-Times* (July 9, 2009), a week before it premiered. "Talk is cheap. Talk is free! This is such a great opportunity for all of us who have talk shows. There are now people home during daytime who normally would never have been home to catch any of the daytime talk shows. I'm very sorry that those people are out of work, or working less hours, but it does mean there are now millions of eyes out there able to catch me and everyone else doing talk shows."

Earlier, Williams had served as the host of *Wendy Williams Is on Fire*, which aired a handful of times on the VH1 TV network from 2003 to 2005 and offered a video of her radio show. Her autobiography *Wendy's Got the Heat: The Queen of Radio Bares All* (2003) appeared on the *New York Times* best-seller list for several weeks. As quoted on the Barnes & Noble Web site, the book got a mixed reception in *Publishers Weekly*, *Library Journal*, and *Kirkus Reviews*. The critic for *Publishers Weekly* wrote that "the story might be inspirational for some" and labeled it "a worthy tale . . . best suited to serious Williams fans." The *Library Journal* reviewer (Mark Bay) praised the book for its candor and "down-to-earth, casual style" and absence, for the most part, of "the hubris typical of celebrity autobiographies." The *Kirkus* writer dismissed the book as "tiresome" and "simple-minded," with "relationship rules and career advice" that seemed "embarrassingly simplistic" and a narrative presented "in the most casual of street slang," much of it peppered with obscenities. Williams's second memoir, *The Wendy Williams Experience: Queen of Radio*, was published in 2004. The following year saw the release on the Virgin Records label of the compilation R&B and hip-hop album *Wendy Williams Brings the Heat*, with tracks by artists including Nas, Jadakiss, and the Prodigy.

In 2008 Williams won the Thurgood Marshall Prestige Award, given by the Thurgood Marshall College Fund. In 2009, after she left her radio program to concentrate on her television show, she was inducted into the National Radio Hall of Fame. Williams has often said that when she returns to her home, in Montclair, New Jersey, she becomes Wendy Hunter, a traditional suburban housewife. "I have no regrets," she told Clane Cane for BET.com (July 13, 2009). "Everyday that I'm here it's just a glorious day because I'm painfully aware that the public is very fickle. They love you today and they hate you tomorrow. When they hate you, they leave you for dead."

—M.M.

Suggested Reading: *Essence* p266 Oct. 2004, p178+ June 2006; (London) *Observer* p34 June 7, 2009; *New York* p36+ Oct. 24, 2005; *New York Times* XIV NJ p1+ Sep. 28, 2003, (on-line) July 13, 2008, July 5, 2009; *Vibe* p160+ Oct. 2003; *Vibe Vixen Magazine* Apr./May 2007; Williams, Wendy, and Karen Hunter. *Wendy's Got the Heat: The Queen of Radio Bares All*, 2003, *The Wendy Williams Experience: Queen of Radio*, 2004

Selected Books: memoirs—with Karen Hunter: *Wendy's Got the Heat: The Queen of Radio Bares All*, 2003; *The Wendy Williams Experience: Queen of Radio*, 2004; novels—with Karen Hunter: *Drama Is Her Middle Name: The Ritz Harper Chronicles Vol. 1*, 2006; *Is the Bitch Dead, Or What?: The Ritz Harper Chronicles Book 2*, 2007; with Zondra Hughes: *Ritz Harper Goes to Hollywood*, 2009

Selected Radio Shows: *The Wendy Williams Experience*, 2002–09

Selected Television Shows: *The Wendy Williams Show*, 2009–

Wolfson, Evan

Feb. 4, 1957– Founder and executive director of Freedom to Marry; attorney; civil rights advocate

Address: Freedom to Marry, 116 W. 23d St., Suite 500, New York, NY 10011

Evan Wolfson, the founder (in 2001) and executive director of the organization Freedom to Marry, eschews the term "gay marriage." He believes that the term creates artificial distinctions and reinforces false perceptions regarding the marriages of men and women, on the one hand, and same-sex couples on the other. For the same reasons he does not accept the concept of civil unions, which offer same-sex couples only some of the rights that marriage confers. "Gay marriage is not what we're looking for," Wolfson explained to Robert Finn for the *New York Times* (February 18, 2007). "We're

Jeff Sheng, courtesy of Freedom to Marry
Evan Wolfson

looking for the legal right for gays to marry. You don't ask for half a loaf. We don't need two lines at the clerk's office when there's already an institution that works in this country, and it's called marriage. One of the main protections that come with marriage is inherent in the word: certainly in times of crisis any other word than marriage would not bring the same clarity or impart the same dignity." Wolfson considers the fight for same-sex marriage to be the most important civil rights battle at present. He also views it as the latest in a series of steps that have served not only to define marriage in contemporary society but also to determine the reach and limits of the law regarding marriage. Among those steps are the Supreme Court decision in 1967 to legalize interracial marriage and the ruling in 1984 that rapes that occur within marriage are illegal—that in the eyes of the law, the rape of a wife by a husband is no different from any other rape. "When we ended that legal subordination of women, we transformed marriage," Wolfson told Gary E. Nelson for *Masthead* (Winter 2005), "from a union based on domination to one based on love, commitment, and the choice of two equal partners." Wolfson, who revealed his homosexuality to his family when he was in his early 20s, has fought for equal rights for lesbians, gay men, bisexuals, and transgender people both as a lawyer and as a volunteer and then staff member of the Lambda Defense and Education Fund. In his book, *Why Marriage Matters* (2004), he offered a point-by-point argument for the legalization of same-sex marriage. As of October 2009 same-sex marriage was legal in four states—Massachusetts, Vermont, Connecticut, and Iowa—and it will become legal in New Hampshire on January 1, 2010. "The classic pattern for civil rights advancement in America is patchwork, but I see equal marriage rights for gays becoming a nationwide reality over the next 15 to 20 years," Wolfson told Finn. "I really believe it will happen in my lifetime."

One of the four children of Jerome H. "Jerry" Wolfson and Joan Wolfson, Evan Wolfson was born into a civic-minded Jewish family on February 4, 1957 in the New York City borough of Brooklyn. His father is a pediatrician; his mother was a full-time homemaker who later became a social worker. He has two brothers—David, a pediatrician, and Michael, a film producer and Internet entrepreneur—and one sister, Alison, a nonpracticing lawyer, who is gay. Wolfson was raised in the Squirrel Hill neighborhood of Pittsburgh, Pennsylvania, where his family attended a synagogue aligned with the Conservative branch of Judaism. He was a member of the Cub Scouts and then, briefly, the Boy Scouts. He attended Taylor Allderdice High School, the largest of Pittsburgh's public high schools, where his main interests were history, politics, and reading; the school's principal predicted to him that he would become the nation's first Jewish president. After his graduation, in 1974, Wolfson entered Yale University, in New Haven, Connecticut. "When he went to college, my husband and I couldn't get over how quiet the dinner table was," his mother told Mark S. Warnick for the *Pittsburgh Post-Gazette* (March 11, 1997). "He evoked a lot of ideas. He would often take the opposite side of something, just to get the discussion going."

At Yale Wolfson was elected speaker of the school's political union and was the campus coordinator for the 1976 campaign of the Democratic presidential and vice-presidential nominees, Governor Jimmy Carter of Georgia and U.S. senator Walter Mondale of Minnesota. During those years Wolfson had a couple of "intense crushes" on male classmates, as he told Joseph Hanania for the *Los Angeles Times* (August 26, 1996), and he came to the realization that he was gay. After he earned a B.A. degree in history, in 1978, Wolfson was accepted at Harvard Law School, in Cambridge, Massachusetts, but he did not enroll. Feeling that he needed a break from academia, he joined the Peace Corps. He spent two years in the tiny West African country of Togo, in the village of Pagouda, where he taught English and established the Pittsburgh-Pagouda Friendship Library. Wolfson told Hanania that in Togo he had a chance to "explore life free from everything that had gone on before. . . . It was the feeling of always being an alien, being alone. That made me think about sexual orientation. I realized that people can be gay on the inside, but how they build their life around that is shaped by society. I made [gay] friends in Africa who will undoubtedly marry women. They will never be as happy or as fulfilled as they would be were they able to do what their true heart wants."

When Wolfson returned from the Peace Corps, he told his parents that he was gay. "I think their main reaction was sadness," he told Warnick, "that I was not going to have the kind of life they expected and were familiar with. But they were always loving and supportive. They're very proud of what I do and they've always been there for me." Wolfson also reapplied to Harvard Law School, and when he was accepted again, he concluded that he was meant to be a lawyer. While at Harvard he read John Boswell's book *Christianity, Social Tolerance, and Homosexuality: Gay People in Western Europe from the Beginning of the Christian Era to the Fourteenth Century* (1980). "This book opened my eyes to the fact that being gay wasn't just about me personally," he told L. A. Johnson for the *Pittsburgh Post-Gazette* (July 26, 2004), "but had a political context that could change the way in which gay people are excluded from very important participation in society." In his last year at law school, Wolfson wrote a paper arguing in favor of the legalization of gay marriage, a subject not widely discussed at that time. After he earned a J.D. degree, in 1983, he taught political philosophy at Harvard College. He turned down lucrative job offers from law firms to work, from 1984 to 1988, as an assistant district attorney in Brooklyn.

Concurrently, beginning in 1985, Wolfson performed pro-bono work for the Lambda Defense and Education Fund; founded in 1973, Lambda is the nation's oldest and largest organization working to expand civil rights for lesbians, gay men, bisexuals, transgender people, and people infected with HIV (the virus that causes AIDS), through litigation, education, and public-policy efforts. In 1985 Wolfson wrote an amicus brief presented to the U.S. Supreme Court regarding *National Gay Task Force v. the Board of Education of Oklahoma City*. ("Amicus" means "friend" in Latin; an amicus brief is a document written by an individual or group not directly involved in the case at hand, filed to support the argument of the plaintiff or the defendant.) In his brief, which he filed as a "friend" of the National Gay Task Force, Wolfson argued against an Oklahoma state law that permitted the firing of teachers who "promote or support homosexuality." The National Gay Task Force won that case, and the law was overturned. Wolfson wrote another amicus brief for Michael Hardwick, the defendant in the closely watched 1986 Supreme Court case *Bowers v. Hardwick*. (The plaintiff was Michael Bowers, the attorney general of Georgia.) Hardwick and a gay friend of his had been arrested in their bedroom in Georgia on charges of sodomy; the police officer who made the arrest had been admitted into their home by another friend to deliver a summons for a lesser crime that Hardwick had committed. The case hinged on the notion of privacy, which is nowhere defined in the Constitution, as well as that of free association, which is protected by the Bill of Rights; the defense argued that the policeman had invaded Hardwick's privacy and that Georgia's anti-sodomy statute was unconstitutional. The Supreme Court ruled, 5–4, in favor of the state, arguing that historically, sodomy has long been reviled and forbidden, and therefore, in the words of Justice Byron White, who wrote the majority opinion, "to claim that a right to engage in such conduct is 'deeply rooted in this Nation's history and tradition' or 'implicit in the concept of ordered liberty' is, at best, facetious." Chief Justice Warren Burger, in a concurring opinion, wrote, "To hold that the act of homosexual sodomy is somehow protected as a fundamental right would be to cast aside millennia of moral teaching." Justice Lewis Powell, who cast the deciding vote, later said that his reasoning had been erroneous. (The Supreme Court struck down that ruling in 2003, in the case *Lawrence v. Texas*.)

Impressed by Wolfson's work with Lambda, his supervisor, Elizabeth Holtzman, the Brooklyn district attorney, asked him to write an amicus brief for *Batson v. Kentucky* (1986), which concerned racial discrimination in jury selection. In that case the U.S. Supreme Court ruled that it is illegal for prosecutors to exclude potential jurors based solely on their race. Wolfson also wrote a brief for a case—*People v. Liberta*—tried in 1984 in the New York State Court of Appeals that helped to eliminate the so-called marital-rape exemption, according to which the law in New York defined rape as forcible sexual intercourse with a female "who was not a spouse." In *People v. Liberta* the New York court ruled that marital rape is illegal. (Nebraska became the first state to abolish the marital-rape exemption, in 1976. Although marital rape is now illegal in every state, in some states the punishments for marital rape and other aspects of the law differ from those for other types of rape.)

In 1988 Wolfson was hired by Lawrence E. Walsh, the independent counsel, also known as the special prosecutor, appointed to investigate the Iran-Contra scandal, which involved weapons sold to Iran by members of the administration of President Ronald Reagan; those who participated in the sales then illegally directed the profits to anti-Communist rebels in Nicaragua. Walsh recalled to Hanania that Wolfson was "completely unafraid" when he drafted a brief challenging the refusal of the FBI and the CIA (backed by Attorney General Richard Thornburgh) to provide information about those activities.

In 1989 Wolfson took on a new job, as one of Lambda's four full-time attorneys and head of its marriage-equality division. The next year Lambda was approached by two women, Ninia Baehr and Genora Dancel, who had been denied a marriage license in Hawaii and wanted help in challenging legal restrictions to same-sex marriage in that state. Wolfson wanted to take on the case, but Lambda turned it down, sensing that the issue of same-sex marriage was not yet "ripe enough" for successful litigation. Wolfson provided Baehr and Dancel, along with two other same-sex couples who wanted to file a joint lawsuit, with informal advice and referred them to a civil rights lawyer, Dan Foley, who practiced in Hawaii. In 1993 the Hawaii Supreme Court ruled that legal barriers to same-sex marriage are discriminatory under the "equal protection" clause of the state constitution. Though the ruling did not technically strike down the law, it required Hawaii to show "compelling interest"—the strictest level of scrutiny required under judicial review—for the state to restrict same-sex marriage. (If the state could not demonstrate compelling interest, the restriction would be overturned.) The ruling sparked a national debate and led opponents of same-sex marriage to propose bills in state legislatures across the country that would ban it. Congress passed the Defense of Marriage Act, outlawing the federal recognition of gay marriage and allowing states to refuse to recognize same-sex marriages performed in other states. In September 1996 President Bill Clinton signed it into law.

At Foley's request Wolfson joined him as co-counsel in *Baehr v. Miike*, as the case was now known. At the trial hearing, in 1996, the state's witnesses relied on arguments related to parenting, presenting evidence that children were better off when raised by a married man and woman. The court found those arguments insufficient; it concluded that the key to good parenting was parents' ability to nurture, not their sexual orientation. That decision made Hawaii the first state to allow same-sex couples to marry. Much credit was given to Wolfson for his successful efforts to portray homosexual couples as no different from heterosexual couples. The landmark decision galvanized people on both sides of the argument; in subsequent years lawyers from the organization Gay and Lesbian Advocates and Defenders (GLAD) began to challenge laws in other states excluding gays from marriage, filing lawsuits in Vermont and Massachusetts, and state legislatures passed laws banning same-sex marriage. Hawaii was among the latter group; in 1998 the state's legislature amended the state's constitution to prohibit same-sex couples from marrying.

In 2000 Wolfson became the first Lambda attorney to argue before the U.S. Supreme Court. He represented James Dale, who in 1990, at 19 years of age, was dismissed from his position as assistant scoutmaster of a Boy Scout troop in Matawan, New Jersey, after being identified in a newspaper as the co-president of a campus lesbian and gay student group at Rutgers University (the state university of New Jersey). The Boy Scouts' Monmouth Council revoked Dale's registration as an adult leader, on the grounds that the organization did not allow openly gay members to lead troops. Dale sued, arguing that his ouster was illegal under New Jersey's antidiscrimination law. The New Jersey Supreme Court agreed with Dale and unanimously struck down the law. The Boy Scouts of America appealed, and the case eventually reached the U.S. Supreme Court. Among the issues the court considered were the right of public organizations to determine their own membership criteria and the right of individuals to join public organizations without being discriminated against. Wolfson argued that because the Scouts were not primarily an "anti-gay organization," Dale's sexual orientation did not interfere with the group's message. In June 2000 the Supreme Court ruled that the Boy Scouts could legally refuse to admit gay troop leaders under the First Amendment right of "expressive association." Although the ruling was a disappointment, Wolfson was pleased with the public attention that the case brought to the issue of discrimination against gay people. "We may have lost the case five to four, but we're winning the cause," he told John Tanasychuk for the Fort Lauderdale, Florida, *Sun-Sentinel* (October 30, 2000). "Non-gay people are now taking up their moral responsibility to speak out against discrimination and protect all kids, including gay kids. And their opinions are much more important than what five justices had to say."

Also in 2000 Wolfson submitted a brief to the Vermont Supreme Court arguing against the state's Defense of Marriage Act, which restricted marriage to one man and one woman. The court ruled that the act illegally discriminated against same-sex couples. In an effort to abide by the ruling, the Vermont legislature created the new category of "civil union," which provides gay and lesbian couples with the full range of legal rights and responsibilities awarded by the state to married couples, provided that they obtain a license and exchange vows in a civil-union ceremony. In no state do civil unions guarantee all of the federal benefits provided to married couples. Because the decision to legally recognize civil unions performed in other states is decided on a state-by-state basis, civil unions are not necessarily respected in states outside the ones in which they were performed.

Over the years other states—including Connecticut, New Jersey, and New Hampshire—allowed gay couples to form legally recognized civil unions. While Wolfson has acknowledged that the rights afforded by civil unions indicate progress, he has maintained that because civil unions—or domestic partnerships, another legal status—represent a separate status for gay couples, they are not sufficient. One reason stems from the use of language. "When you say, 'I'm married,' everyone knows who you are in relation to the primary person you're building your life with," Wolfson explained to Bill Hammond for the New York *Daily News* (April 21, 2009). "'Civil union' doesn't offer that clarity, that immediately understood respect." Wolfson told Hammond that opponents of same-sex marriage "can't have it both ways. Either civil union is the same as marriage—in which case, why do we need two lines at the clerk's office? Or it's not the same—in which case, what is the government withholding?"

In 2001 Wolfson left Lambda and founded Freedom to Marry, "a gay and non-gay partnership working to win marriage equality nationwide," according to the group's Web site. He spent much of his time delivering lectures, engaging in interviews and debates, and writing articles in support of the cause. In November 2003 the Massachusetts Supreme Court ruled that the state's constitution guaranteed equal marriage rights for gay couples, thereby legalizing same-sex marriage in that state. In many towns and cities across the country, mayors and county clerks began accepting marriage-license applications from same-sex couples illegally, prompting the launching of legal processes to challenge existing marriage laws. On January 20, 2004, in his State of the Union address, President George W. Bush declared that the U.S. needed to "defend the sanctity of marriage." By April 2005 18 states had approved amendments to their state constitutions banning same-sex marriage. In September 2005 the California legislature became the first state lawmaking body in the U.S. to pass a bill legalizing same-sex marriage without being forced to do so by court order, but Governor Arnold Schwarzenegger vetoed the bill.

Wolfson presented his case for legalizing same-sex marriage in his book, *Why Marriage Matters: America, Equality, and Gay People's Right to Marry*, published in 2004. Organized as a series of responses to the main arguments advanced by opponents of same-sex marriage, its chapters bear such titles as "Why Now?," "Isn't Marriage for Procreation?," and "Why Not Use Another Word?" Wolfson pointed out the areas in which only people who are legally married enjoy certain rights and privileges—among them family leave (which enables a spouse to take time off from work for particular family-related reasons, such as a spouse's illness), job-related health benefits, retirement benefits, adoption of children, visitation in hospital intensive-care units, and benefits related to death and inheritance. Wolfson responded to what he considers to be his opposition's weakest argument, that marriage be restricted to males and females in order to encourage childbearing, by noting that "no state requires that non-gay couples prove that they can procreate—or promise that they will procreate—before issuing them a marriage license." Wolfson also wrote, "There are at least a million kids being raised by gay and lesbian parents in this country who are indisputably disadvantaged by their families' inability to secure the legal protections and benefits that automatically accrue to heterosexual parents." He presented the finding of scientific studies that children raised by same-sex couples experienced no detectable disadvantages, countering the often-repeated claim that a male-female household is the optimal setting for child-rearing.

Wolfson's book was well received by gay-rights supporters, who judged it to be an important, lucidly written primer on the issue. In a representative review for the *Sunday Oregonian* (August 1, 2004), Kimberly Marlowe Hartnett wrote, "Wolfson adopts a patient tone and explains that marriage is a basic right and one that protects committed couples and their children without threatening heterosexual marriage or so-called traditional family values. He does so by reviewing the history of marriage, gathering points from relevant court cases at all levels and excerpting thoughtful commentators' work, then gluing it all together with common sense." Hartnett further noted: "Armed with Wolfson's arguments, you could sell anyone with an IQ over room temperature on the wisdom and humanity of marriage equality." The *Slate.com* columnist William Saletan, who has described himself as a liberal Republican and who supports same-sex marriage, nevertheless questioned some of Wolfson's reasoning; in an assessment of *Why Marriage Matters* for the *New York Times Book Review* (September 26, 2004), he took issue with Wolfson's argument that it is wrong to discriminate against those who are "different," noting that the term "different" "would apply even more clearly to polygamist and incestuous couples. Wolfson dismisses the idea that gay marriage will lead down this slippery slope, but his do-your-own-thing rationale invites it." The author, Saletan complained, had "fail[ed] to clarify how gays can be admitted to this institution [i.e., marriage] without spreading chaos."

Same-sex marriage continues to be a prime topic of national debate. During the 2008 presidential campaign, Wolfson commended the Democratic candidates' unanimous support for equal rights for committed gay and lesbian couples but criticized the failure of all of them—except Congressman Dennis Kucinich—to support the rights of gays and lesbians to marry. In May 2008 gay-rights advocates won a big victory in California, when that state's Supreme Court ruled that banning same-sex marriage was unconstitutional. That decision was overturned in November 2008, when California voters passed Proposition 8, amending the constitution to define marriage as between one man and one woman; in May 2009 the state Supreme Court upheld the legality of that vote. Earlier, in October 2008, same-sex marriage was made legal in Connecticut by that state's Supreme Court. In April 2009 two more states—Iowa and Vermont—legalized same-sex marriage; in Vermont, the first state in which a legislature did so, the law went into effect on September 1, 2009. In addition to those states where same-sex marriage is legal, three states, New York, Rhode Island, and California, as well as the District of Columbia, officially recognize same-sex marriage performed in other states. (According to the California bill signed into law in October 2009, the state will also recognize those marriages performed in California before the passage of Proposition 8.) On June 3, 2009 the governor of New Hampshire, John Lynch, signed into law a bill approving same-sex marriage, effective on January 1, 2010. On May 6, 2009 Maine's governor, John Baldacci, signed into law a bill allowing same-sex couples to marry. Before the law was to take effect, in mid-September, anti-same-sex-marriage protestors gathered more than the requisite 55,087 signatures to postpone the law's implementation and submit the matter to voters on Election Day, November 3, 2009. Supporters of same-sex marriage organized, under the name "No on 1/Protect Maine Equality," to mobilize voters to support the new law. Nonetheless, a majority of Maine's voters—53 percent—came out against same-sex marriage.

Still, Wolfson has credited the discriminatory rhetoric of anti-same-sex-marriage movements for spurring many people to support his side. "Any time people are prompted to push past their discomfort, the more fair minded people move to our side," he told Ruth Horowitz for the Burlington, Vermont, newspaper *Seven Days* (June 21–28, 2006). Polls have shown that the percentage of Americans who favor the legalization of same-sex marriage has grown from 20 to more than 30 in the last five years. Internationally same-sex marriage is legal in countries including the Netherlands, Spain, Norway, Sweden, Belgium, Canada, and South Africa.

Wolfson, who described himself to Finn as "portly, short, and baldish," has taught at Columbia Law School and Rutgers University and is a senior fellow at the Erwin and Rose Wolfson Center for National Affairs, a division of the New School, in New York City. (Erwin and Rose were not his grandparents.) He was named one of the most influential attorneys in America by the *National Law Journal* in 2000, one of the 100 most influential people in the world by *Time* magazine in 2004, and among the 100 most influential gay men and women in America by *Out Magazine* in 2008. A resident of New York City, he is in a long-term relationship with Cheng He, a Canadian who has a doctorate in molecular/cellular biology, whom he met via the Internet. The couple reportedly have no plans to marry, but Wolfson told Finn, "We would love the opportunity to have that choice."

—M.E.R.

Suggested Reading: (Fort Lauderdale, Florida) *Sun-Sentinel* E p1 Oct. 30, 2000; Freedom to Marry Web site; *Los Angeles Times* E p1 Aug. 26, 1996, R p3 Aug. 15, 2004; (New York) *Daily News* p21 Apr. 21, 2009; *New York Times* B p2 Feb. 16, 2007; *Pittsburgh Post-Gazette* F p1 Mar. 11, 1997; *Sunday Oregonian* D p7 Aug. 1, 2004

Selected Books: *Why Marriage Matters: America, Equality, and Gay People's Right to Marry*, 2004

Wood, Evan Rachel

Sep. 7, 1987– Actress

Address: c/o ICM, 8942 Wilshire Blvd., Beverly Hills, CA 90211

In 2003, at only 15 years of age, Evan Rachel Wood received the kind of praise generally reserved for long-established actresses when she turned in a breakthrough perfomance as a troubled, disaffected teen in the movie *Thirteen*. Writing for the Raleigh, North Carolina, *News & Observer* (September 19, 2003), Todd Lothery noted about Wood's performance in that shocking look at young-teen life, "She is called upon to register a range of emotions, and she nails every one. She's naive, tender, coquettish, jubilant, defiant, sullen, anguished, tempestuous, casually cruel, unbearably sad and much more. She's always convincing, frequently mesmerizing and never overstated. Her unguarded performance is a marvel of controlled ferocity, and her talents so far exceed those of her teen acting peers that it's almost ridiculous." While many young actors and actresses struggle to deal with celebrity, Wood appeared to maintain her humble demeanor after *Thirteen* and has continued to win ever-more-challenging roles. "Most teenage actors who got their start in the business as children are at best frighteningly precocious, at worst imbued with an inflated ego," Lesley O'Toole wrote for the London *Guardian Weekly* (June 24, 2006, on-line). "Wood, in contrast, seems wise beyond her years sometimes, still imbued with teen awkwardness at others, and not remotely arrogant or actressy."

Robyn Beck/AFP/Getty Images

Raised in North Carolina in a family of actors, Wood began her career with roles in plays directed by her father. She then appeared in small parts in television films before gaining attention as Jessie Sammler in the popular ABC television series *Once and Again* (1999–2002). After the unexpected success of *Thirteen*—a film about two female friends who sink into lives of drugs, petty crime, and sexual experimentation—Wood became one of Hollywood's top young actresses and gained a reputation for portraying "bad-girl" characters, with roles in *Pretty Persuasion* (2005), *Running with Scissors* (2006), *The Life Before Her Eyes* (2007), and *Whatever Works* (2009). Dubbing her the "distress princess," O'Toole noted that Wood "is famed in Hollywood for shocking antics but they are strictly isolated to moments between 'action' and 'cut.'" Wood has also won praise for less-controversial roles, in films including *The Upside of Anger* (2005), *Down in the Valley* (2006), and the Academy Award–nominated *The Wrestler* (2008). Discussing her penchant for playing misguided and morally ambiguous characters in dark films, she told Cindy Pearlman for the *Chicago Sun-Times* (August 28, 2005), "I love movies that leave you with question marks. I love sitting there in the dark not knowing if I'm supposed to laugh or cry."

Evan Rachel Wood was born on September 7, 1987 in Raleigh, North Carolina. Her father, Ira David Wood III, founded Theatre in the Park, an institution in Raleigh, and has served since the early 1970s as its executive director; he is also an actor and playwright. Her mother, Sara Lynne Moore, is an actress. Wood has two brothers—Ira David Wood IV, an actor, and Dana Wood—and all three children appeared in their father's musicals and other productions while growing up. Wood made her stage debut as an infant, in her father's adaptation of *A Christmas Carol*, and she later played Helen Keller in his production of *The Miracle Worker*. "When I was little I just assumed everybody acted," she said to O'Toole. During her childhood Wood took up ballet briefly before learning tae kwon do, eventually becoming a black belt. She told Lawrence Toppman for the North Carolina *Charlotte (North Carolina) Observer* (April 27, 2002) about that branch of martial arts, "It's more than self-defense skills; it's learning about meditation and having respect for your elders." (Her mother, too, is a black belt.)

After auditioning unsuccessfully for the feature film *Interview with the Vampire*, losing the role of a child vampire to Kirsten Dunst, Wood began at age seven to appear in made-for-TV movies, among them the crime film *In the Best of Families: Marriage, Pride, and Madness* (1994), *Search for Grace* (1994), *A Father for Charlie* (1995), and *Death in Small Doses* (1995). In 1995 she appeared in three episodes of the horror series *American Gothic*, which was produced by the future *Spider-Man* director Sam Raimi. Her parents divorced two years later, and Wood moved to Los Angeles, California, with her mother and brother Ira. Wood had her first feature-film roles in 1998, appearing alongside Nicole Kidman and Sandra Bullock in the romantic comedy *Practical Magic*, as part of a family of witches, and in *Digging to China*, in which she portrayed a lonely girl who finds a companion in a mentally handicapped adult played by Kevin Bacon. When she was 12 Wood asked to be removed from the public school she was attending in California's San Fernando Valley. "North Carolina schools were great," she told Susan King for the Fort Lauderdale, Florida, *Sun-Sentinel* (September 2, 2002), "but once I moved out here, I had a really bad experience. The kids were fine but the teachers were a nightmare. It was terrible." She told O'Toole that the teachers "just automatically throw a label on you when you're an actor and think you're spoiled. It was almost as if they had to put me in my place." Wood was home-schooled and received her high-school diploma when she was 15.

In 1999 Wood landed the role of the troubled teen Jessie Sammler in the critically praised ABC television drama *Once and Again*. The show followed the lives of two single parents, both divorced, who begin a relationship that brings their children and ex-spouses together. The role proved to be Wood's breakthrough, with television critics lauding her portrayal of Jessie. Kathleen Rizzo Young wrote for the New York *Buffalo News* (June 17, 2001), "Delicate and deep, [Wood] exudes angst beyond her years, holding her own in sessions with producer/director Ed Zwick playing her therapist. He is smitten with her and viewers are too." The show afforded Wood her first opportunity to portray a troubled character; in the first season, for example, Sammler struggles to hide her eating disorder from friends and family. "I had to put myself in that situation and imagine how it would feel if something like that was happening to me," she told Neal Justin for the Minneapolis *Star Tribune* (September 28, 2001). "It was difficult at first, a little overwhelming, because I wasn't sure how I was going to do it, but I put myself together." Around that time, on the big screen, she also appeared in the comedy *Little Secrets* (2001) and the science-fiction comedy *S1m0ne* (2002). She also appeared in the director Ron Howard's Western, *The Missing* (2002), as a young girl kidnapped by a Native American medicine man, and was cast in episodes of the television shows *The West Wing* (2002) and *CSI: Crime Scene Investigation* (2003).

It was Wood's role as Tracy Freeland in the controversial and shocking coming-of-age drama *Thirteen* (2003) that cemented her reputation as a capable actress. The screenplay for *Thirteen*, written by then-teenager Nikki Reed and the film's director, Catherine Hardwicke, was based on Reed's own struggles with self-destructive behavior while she was growing up in Los Angeles. In the film Wood played 13-year-old Tracy, an unpopular middle-school student often teased by her classmates. When she eventually wins the respect of the popular student Evie Zamora, played by Reed, the two become fast friends and descend into a life of shoplifting, drug abuse, and sexual experimentation. Describing the change Wood's character undergoes, Owen Gleiberman wrote for *Entertainment Weekly* (August 27, 2003, on-line) that she "begins to flaunt the porno fashion signifiers of a 21st-century trash princess. . . . Yet her baby-hooker-of-the-mall regalia is, in a sense, the least of her transformations. Tracy doesn't just look different.

She adopts a new attitude of tossed-off cruelty, a spiteful hauteur that cuts down everyone in her path." Despite the controversy over the film's content, in particular the sexual situations it depicted involving the underage actresses, *Thirteen* received widespread critical praise. Mike Clark described it for *USA Today* (August 19, 2003, on-line) as "the most powerful of all recent wayward-youth sagas; indeed, it's tough to recall the last such drama that packed as much emotional clout." Wood was lauded for her performance; Gleiberman wrote, "She makes Tracy defiant, cunning, morose, gleeful, and frightened, all at the same time; she's like a wobbly colt who grows up in an instant by harnessing her rage." Hardwicke won the directing award for *Thirteen* at the 2003 Sundance Film Festival, and in 2004 Wood was nominated for a Golden Globe Award for her performance in the film. She told Jason Dean for *h-monthly* (May 2008, on-line) about portraying Tracy, "That whole experience changed my life. Not just my career, but my life. I was the same age as my character. The scenes were shot [in sequence] and I went through the same arc without even realizing it at the time." She added, "It was the first time I'd gone so personal and it was nice 'cause no one was expecting it, including people who knew me. I was so much happier after that movie. It was like closing a chapter on the darkest period of my life."

Following the success of *Thirteen*, Wood became an in-demand actress for controversial and angst-ridden teen characters. In 2005 she played Kimberly Joyce in Marcos Siega's dark comedy *Pretty Persuasion*, a film described by Stephen Holden for the *New York Times* (August 12, 2005, on-line) as "an obscene, misanthropic go-for-broke satire" about an arrogant Beverly Hills teenager who maliciously and falsely accuses her drama teacher of sexual harassment. Roger Ebert wrote for the *Chicago Sun-Times* (August 26, 2005, on-line) that Wood "has emerged as a young actress who can bring an eerie conviction even to tricky and complex scenes. In *Thirteen* . . . she played a good girl who makes the mistake of friendship with a girl her age who introduces her to drugs, sex and lying. Here she essentially takes the other role and is just as convincing: She finds a coldness and heartlessness in Kimberly that moves beyond the high-school hellion category and into malevolence." While Kimberly's actions in the film are reprehensible, Wood tried to find a semblance of humanity at her core. "I figured this girl had been through a lot, which made it hard for me to play her as heartless," she told Pearlman. "She's a girl who just wants someone to love her because she feels so completely alone." Wood also appeared in the 2005 family drama the *The Upside of Anger*, as one of four sisters whose father has left their mother. The film starred Joan Allen as the mother and Kevin Costner as the single neighbor who pursues her.

In 2006 Wood acted in *Running with Scissors*, a film based on Augusten Burroughs's best-selling 2002 memoir of the same name. Directed by Ryan Murphy, the film—with Joseph Cross as the young Burroughs—focuses on the writer's childhood, when his mentally ill mother sent him to live with her eccentric psychiatrist, Dr. Finch. Wood played Natalie, Finch's similarly eccentric daughter, who befriends Burroughs and, in one memorable scene frequently mentioned in reviews, asks him to play "doctor" with her, using her father's electroshock-therapy equipment. The film received mixed reviews, as did Wood's performance.

That same year Wood also starred in David Jacobson's independent-film drama *Down in the Valley*. She played a rebellious young girl attracted to a polite older man, Harlan (played by Edward Norton), who shows hints of being something other than the former ranch hand he claims to be. Stephen Holden wrote for the *New York Times* (May 5, 2006, on-line), "Beautiful and rebellious, Ms. Wood's Tobe is almost as complex as Mr. Norton's Harlan. And as the cracks in his perfect image widen into crevices, we empathize with her reluctance to admit disenchantment." The next year Wood starred with Michael Douglas in Mike Cahill's *King of California* as Miranda, a girl who reluctantly embarks on a quest with her mentally ill father (Douglas) to find buried treasure. Wood also appeared in the musical *Across the Universe* (2007), directed by Julie Taymor and set in the turbulent 1960s to a soundtrack of songs by the Beatles. "I started out in musical theater and was dying to do a movie musical," Wood told Pearlman. "I heard about the Julie Taymor Beatles musical and auditioned." In the *San Francisco Chronicle* (September 14, 2007, on-line), Peter Hartlaub criticized Taymor for failing to direct her characters as believable 1960s youth, observing that "Wood is a particularly unconvincing 1960s radical." He nonetheless noted that "she sounds great, as does most of the cast, who were chosen for their theatrical talents over frequency of appearance on teen magazine covers."

In 2008 Wood co-starred with Uma Thurman in the drama *The Life Before Her Eyes*, directed by Vadim Perelman. The film focuses on the guilt felt by Diana McFee (Thurman), a mother and teacher who, in her high-school days, escaped a school shooting that took the life of her best friend. Wood played the younger, wilder version of Diana in flashback sequences. Despite few positive reviews for the film, the actresses received some praise. Michael Rechtshaffen wrote for the *Hollywood Reporter* (September 9, 2007, on-line), "For her part, Thurman convincingly pulls off a tricky part, while Wood also impresses as a bright, attractive young woman who is alternately hurt and emboldened by her 'loose' reputation."

Wood's already-high profile rose further when she co-starred in *The Wrestler* (2008), directed by Darren Aronofsky. In the film Mickey Rourke played Randy "The Ram" Robinson, a retired professional wrestler clinging to the memory of his 1980s stardom. Desperate to revive his past glory, Robinson fights his way through poorly attended, second-tier matches, hoping to make it to a final fight against his archrival, The Ayatollah. He must also contend with his failing health and the elements of his fractured personal life, including his relationship with his daughter, Stephanie (Wood), whom he abandoned and with whom he wants to reconcile. Critics and audiences alike celebrated the film. David Kronke wrote for the *San Gabriel (California) Valley Tribune* (December 16, 2008), "Easily the best scenes in the film are the confrontations between the contrite Ram and the justifiably bitter Stephanie. Rourke and Wood tear into these scenes with a heartbreaking rawness that elevates the melodramatic material." Leslie Adkins wrote for the *Dartmouth*, available on University Wire (March 2, 2009, on-line), "Wood's performance resonates . . . deeply. Every time Rourke looks at Wood, it seems as though he's on the edge of tears. Wood has the same effect on audiences—we sense the storm of emotions she feels when she looks at the man who has abandoned her multiple times, but still has the audacity to plead for her love." To add depth to her character, Wood recalled emotions she had felt during her parents' divorce. She told the *New Zealand Herald* (March 21, 2009), "My parents divorced when I was really young and it didn't help that I was in California and my father lived in North Carolina. Amidst all the family drama we were apart until recently. So I could completely relate to my character, to how she could be so sad and so angry at the same time."

In May 2009 Wood returned to her hometown to appear as the female lead in an adaptation of *Romeo and Juliet*, directed by her brother Ira at Theatre in the Park. The next month she was seen in Woody Allen's film *Whatever Works*, a romantic comedy also starring the comedian Larry David. Described by Scott Tobias for the *A.V. Club* (June 18, 2009, on-line) as a "wobbly odd-couple comedy," *Whatever Works* featured Wood as Melodie, a teenage runaway who is taken in by David's character, Boris, a grumpy, misanthropic former physics professor who lives in a dingy basement apartment. The two soon become lovers and get married; the arrival of Melodie's conservative mother shakes up the new arrangement. Most reviewers found serious flaws in the movie but praised Wood's performance: "Wood is totally beguiling in the role," Peter Travers wrote for *Rolling Stone* (June 18, 2009, on-line), while Kenneth Turan wrote for the *Los Angeles Times* (June 19, 2009, on-line) that Wood portrayed Melodie "with unexpected humor and style," and Stephanie Zacharek wrote for *Salon* (June 19, 2009, on-line), "Wood, doing less pouting and posturing than usual, is a relaxed, lively presence here."

Wood was cast as a vampire queen in two episodes of the popular HBO television drama series *True Blood* in August 2009. In 2010 she was to appear in the Broadway musical *Spider-Man, Turn Off the Dark*, a theatrical take on the story of the Marvel Comics superhero, and in two films, *The Conspirator* and *Flora Plum*.

For several years beginning in 2006, Wood was romantically linked with the shock-rocker Marilyn Manson. The two split up amicably in 2008, then got back together briefly in 2009 before separating again. Tabloid writers expressed amusement and surprise over the relationship, in part because Manson is 18 years older than Wood. "People would be surprised at the kind of healthy, loving relationship we have," Wood told Mark Kirby for *GQ* (September 2007, on-line) when she and Manson were together. "If it doesn't work out, I would never blame it on the fact that he's *Marilyn Manson*."

Wood is a self-described musical-theater "geek" and is passionate about singing. She counts Billie Holiday, Peggy Lee, and Judy Garland among her vocal influences. She told the *New Zealand Herald*, "I've been writing my own songs and singing on my own for a while, sort of enjoying it being just mine, my own private art form. I'm hoping that once I get comfortable enough with it that I can release it on my own." Despite her reputation for playing controversial characters, she told Dean that she does not intentionally seek out those roles. "I have a checklist I go by," she said. "Most important is the character."

—W.D.

Suggested Reading: *Charlotte Observer* E p1 Apr. 27, 2002; *h-monthly* (on-line) May 2008; (London) *Guardian* (on-line) June 24, 2006; (Raleigh, North Carolina) *News & Observer* E p1 Sep. 19, 2003

Selected Films: *In the Best of Families: Marriage, Pride, and Madness*, 1994; *Search for Grace*, 1994; *A Father for Charlie*, 1995; *Death in Small Doses*, 1995; *Practical Magic*, 1998; *Digging to China*, 1998; *Little Secrets*, 2001; *S1m0ne*, 2002; *The Missing*, 2002; *Thirteen*, 2003; *Pretty Persuasion*, 2005; *The Upside of Anger*, 2005; *Running with Scissors*, 2006; *Down in the Valley*, 2006; *King of California*, 2007; *Across the Universe*, 2007; *The Life Before Her Eyes*, 2008; *The Wrestler*, 2008; *Whatever Works*, 2009

Selected Television Shows: *Once and Again*, 1999–2002

Wright, David

Dec. 20, 1982– Baseball player

Address: New York Mets, Citi Field, 123-01 Roosevelt Ave., Flushing, NY 11368-1699

David Wright, the New York Mets' starting third baseman, "is not merely a player with the talent to anchor a team," according to David Amsden, writing for *New York* (April 9, 2007); "he is a star in the

Doug Benc/Getty Images

David Wright

old-school mold, a galvanizer, pure packaged Americana." A member of the Mets' farm system for three years beginning in 2001, the year he graduated from high school, Wright has established himself among the premier all-around players in Major League Baseball (MLB). His discipline at the plate, unusual consistency and power in batting, and solid base-running and defensive skills have earned him four appearances in All-Star Games, and his statistics in runs batted in (RBIs), stolen bases, and various other facets of individual achievement have placed him among the dozen top players in the National League (NL) virtually every year since his major-league debut. He has had hitting streaks of at least 15 games four times—more than any other Met, past or present—and in 2007 he became one of the youngest players in MLB history to join the so-called 30–30 club—players who have hit at least 30 home runs and stolen at least 30 bases in the same season. Wright is also outstanding for his enthusiasm, professionalism, graciousness toward fans, and selflessness as a player. The former Mets third baseman Howard Johnson told Franz Lidz for *Sports Illustrated* (May 29, 2006), "If you were going to start from scratch and design the perfect New York ballplayer, David is the kid you'd come up with." "David never looks for credit, and he never, ever seeks attention," Joe Hietpas, a minor-league Mets player and three-time roommate of Wright's, when both were members of the same farm teams, told Lidz. "Wherever he's played, he's been the most dedicated, the most motivated, the most enthusiastic." Josh Curtis wrote for the *New York Observer* (May 29, 2008), "He's not only the best player on the Mets, but also one of a scant few whose career remains on the ascent. . . . It is perhaps too obvious to say that the Mets need more players like David Wright; every team in baseball needs another David Wright." In 2005 Wright launched his own foundation, which raises money to assist children in need and organizations battling multiple sclerosis.

The oldest of four brothers, David Allen Wright was born on December 20, 1982 in Norfolk, Virginia, to Rhon and Elisa Wright. He grew up in Chesapeake, a Norfolk suburb, in a tight-knit family in which the importance of perseverance, honor, accepting responsibility, and other core values was stressed. His father works for the Norfolk Police Department; his latest promotion made him its assistant chief. His mother is a special-education teacher. He and his brothers—Stephen, Matthew, and Daniel—were extremely competitive with one another. "They even compete when they eat," his father told Kevin Kernan for the *New York Post* (January 8, 2006).

Wright's talents in baseball became apparent early on, when he played T-ball as a child. As a youngster he was a Mets fan and idolized the Baltimore Orioles' Cal Ripken Jr. and other baseball stars. He played in a Little League team whose head coach was his father. Although he was skilled enough to play shortstop, his father placed him in right field, a less flashy position, to prevent him from becoming cocky. Another Little League player, the Norfolk native and future MLB baseball star B.J. Upton, became his friend. He regularly attended games of the Orioles' top Triple-A club, the Tidewater Tides. As he got older he excelled in basketball and other sports as well as baseball. His parents insisted that he work equally hard in school. "If the best he could do was a 'B,' then we were OK with that," his father recalled to Scott Lauber for the *Binghamton (New York) Press & Sun-Bulletin* (May 23, 2004). "What would get David in hot water with me was if he wasn't putting forth the best effort he could."

Wright attended Hickory High School in Chesapeake. In the spring term of his freshman year, he played third base on the varsity baseball team. As a sophomore, under the team's head coach, Steve Gedro, he moved to shortstop and blossomed into an all-around player; with a batting average of .471, four homers, and 18 runs, he earned honorable-mention All-State honors. Throughout high school Wright worked diligently on his swing, using a wooden rather than an aluminum bat, and had his class schedule arranged so that he had an extra hour to practice hitting every afternoon. During summers he played on Amateur Athletic Union (AAU) teams that competed in tournaments throughout Virginia. B.J. Upton's brother, Justin, an Arizona Diamondbacks right fielder, told Dan Graziano for the *Newark (New Jersey) Star-Ledger* (June 11, 2008), "The rap on David was that he was the hardest-working high school player you ever saw. You couldn't get him out of the cage or off the field. He was always working to make himself better, and he was a great player—great hitter, great defense, he had everything." Wright said to Lauber, "In order to achieve a goal, you've got to make certain compromises. My friends and I did the normal going to football games on Friday nights. But I sacrificed a lot of summers. I love playing baseball, so that's what I had to do."

During his senior year Wright batted an astonishing .538, with six homers and 19 RBIs, and was named the Gatorade Virginia High School Player of the Year and the Virginia All-State Player of the Year. Overall while at Hickory he hit .438, with 13 home runs and 90 RBIs. Steve Gedro told Lauber that Wright was "the best student-athlete and citizen I've been associated with." Wright was also a perennial honor student and graduated with a high grade-point average. Earlier, following his junior year, in which his team fell one win short of the state championship, Wright had become one of the most heavily recruited shortstops in the United States. He signed a letter of intent to attend the Georgia Institute of Technology but then chose to forgo college to enter the Major League Baseball (MLB) draft, where he anticipated being a middle-round pick. In June 2001, in their supplemental first-round pick, the Mets selected Wright. (He was the 38th pick overall.) After negotiations that lasted a month, he agreed to a four-year contract, which included a $960,000 signing bonus.

Wright moved through the Mets farm system quickly. In July 2001 he joined the Kingsport Mets of the Appalachian League. Under their manager Joey Cora, a former MLB infielder, he played 36 games and batted .300. Around that time the Mets moved him to the third-base position. In 2002 he played for the Capital City Bombers of the Class-A South Atlantic League, where he tied for the team lead in homers and placed third in the league in RBIs, with 93, while stealing 21 bases. That year he was named the league's co-MVP. He spent the following season with the St. Lucie Mets of the more competitive Class-A Florida State League, under manager Ken Oberkfell. He struggled to maintain a batting average above .250 during the first half of the season; in the second half, he hit over .300. Before home games he would often show up hours ahead of time for extra batting practice. After the 2003 season Wright joined the Peoria Saguaros of the Arizona Fall League. Scouts noted not only Wright's ability to hit to every corner but also his ability to adapt to different pitchers and willingness to draw walks. He won that year's Sterling Award as the top player in the league.

By 2004 Wright was considered among the top five prospects in baseball and was ranked by the magazine *Baseball America* as the Mets' best position player (an infielder, outfielder, or catcher) in the Mets' farm system. That spring he was invited to the Mets' annual spring-training camp, despite the fact that the third baseman Ty Wigginton rather than Wright was expected to be invited to join the team. His performance earned him a promotion to the Class-AA Binghamton Mets. The former Mets third baseman Howard Johnson stepped in as Wright's mentor. During his 60 games with Binghamton, Wright batted .363, with 10 homers and 40 RBIs. When Wigginton went on the disabled list early in the season, members of the press and fans urged the team to have Wright replace him, but the organization sent him to the Class-AAA Norfolk Tides that June, as his last stop in preparation for the majors. While there he batted .298, with eight homers in 31 games. Johnson, then a hitting coach for the Tides, noted to Franz Lidz, "David is really the first legitimate third baseman the Mets ever developed."

Although Wigginton had performed well since his recovery and return to the team, in the summer of 2004 the Mets made Wright their starting third baseman. Wigginton took Wright under his wing but left the team weeks afterward, when he was traded to the Pittsburgh Pirates. The veteran catcher Mike Piazza soon became Wright's big-league mentor and began teaching him how to handle the on- and off-the-field pressures of playing in New York. Wright made his major-league debut on June 21, in a game against the Montreal Expos in which he went hitless. He collected his first and second major-league hits in his next contest, also against the Expos. Days later he hit his first home run and, with it, knocked in his first run, while facing the Expos pitcher John Patterson. In August, in a game against the Milwaukee Brewers, Wright belted a 445-foot homer and batted in six runs. The Mets, hampered by a larger-than-usual number of injured players, ended the season with a 71–91 record. Wright fared far better: he was named to *Baseball America*'s All-Rookie team, after finishing tied for first in batting average among NL rookies, second in slugging percentage (.525), tied for fourth in home runs (14) and stolen bases (six), tied for eighth in doubles (17), and ninth in extra-base hits (32).

Bent on a turnaround, during the 2004 off-season the team hired the Yankees' bench coach Willie Randolph as manager and then signed two of the year's most sought-after free agents, Pedro Martinez and Carlos Beltran. Thanks to the outfielder Cliff Floyd's power, the shortstop José Reyes's speed, and Wright's all-around offensive skills, along with the effective pitching of Martinez and Tom Glavine, the Mets improved their record to 83–79 during the 2005 season—the first time the team had more wins than losses since 2001. Wright emerged as the team's star player, tying a single-season club record for games played at third (160) and batting .306, with 27 home runs, 99 runs, 102 RBIs, 42 doubles, and 17 stolen bases. He led the team in batting average, on-base percentage, slugging percentage, RBIs, and numbers of runs and doubles, and he finished second in home runs to Floyd. Among NL players, he tied for eighth place in batting average, tied for seventh in doubles, placed 10th in hits and extra-base hits (70), tied for 10th in RBIs, and tied for seventh in total bases (301).

In 2006 Wright finished ninth in batting average (.311) in the NL and tied for seventh in RBIs, with a career-high 116. He thus became only the fourth player in Mets history (after Gary Carter, Darryl Strawberry, and Mike Piazza) to have consecutive 100-or-more-RBI seasons. He also became the seventh Met to have 20 or more stolen bases and 20 or more home runs in a single season, finishing with 20 and 26, respectively. He drove in 74 RBIs prior to the All-Star Game, breaking a franchise single-season record previously held by Piazza, who had 72 RBIs in 2000. That June Wright was named the NL Player of the Month, after hitting .327, with 20 runs, four doubles, a triple, 10 home runs, 29 RBIs, and three stolen bases, while collecting two home runs in two contests, against San Francisco and Cincinnati. In July he hit a dramatic three-run homer in the Mets' final game before the All-Star Game. The following day, July 12, Wright belted 16 home runs in the first round of the home-run derby—at that time, the third-highest total in any round in the history of the event—and reached the finals, where he lost to the Philadelphia Phillies' power hitter Ryan Howard. In the All-Star Game, which the NL lost, he hit a home run in his first at-bat, off the American League's starting pitcher, Kenny Rogers. Commenting on Wright's All-Star performance, Ryan Howard noted to Paul White for the Norfolk *Virginian-Pilot* (July 12, 2006), "He may have surprised a lot of people, but they won't be surprised anymore. The kid's for real." His overnight celebrity drew the interest of the late-night talk-show host David Letterman, who had Wright as a guest on his program the next day.

In 2006 Wright excelled in high-pressure situations, provided a number of game-winning hits, and shone for his defensive heroics. He also found himself being referred to as one of New York's most eligible bachelors for his clean-cut image and attractive smile. In addition, he gained a reputation as being one of the most accommodating players in the league, spending many minutes—sometimes hours—signing autographs before and after games. That August Wright signed a six-year contract extension with the Mets worth $55 million. (He had been earning $374,000 a year, $47,000 above the league minimum.) The Mets placed first in the NL East Division and finished the season with a league-best record of 97 wins and 65 losses. In the first game of the NL division series, against the Los Angeles Dodgers, Wright knocked in three runs in a Mets victory. The Mets went on to sweep the Dodgers. In the NL championship series, the Mets lost to the St. Louis Cardinals.

In the 2007 season Wright achieved career highs in batting average (.325), runs (113), home runs (30), and stolen bases (34) while leading the team in batting average, slugging percentage (.546), on-base percentage (.416), and total bases (330). He finished seventh in the NL in batting average, fifth in runs scored, fourth in hits (196), ninth in RBIs (107), fourth in on-base percentage, seventh in total bases, seventh in stolen bases, and tied for seventh in walks (115), and he made his second All-Star appearance. Between the end of the 2006 regular season and the beginning of the next, he made base hits in 26 successive games, and he had a 17-game hitting streak in May 2007, during which he batted .343 with nine runs scored, five doubles, four home runs, 11 RBIs, seven walks, and seven stolen bases. In September 2007 Wright became the 29th and one of the youngest players in MLB history to join the 30–30 club, while becoming only the third player to accomplish that feat before his 25th birthday. His team, by contrast, ended the season ingloriously. They had had an equal number of wins and losses at the end of the summer, with a seven-game lead over the Phillies, but then, in a stunning collapse, they lost 12 of their last 17 games, enabling the Phillies to win the the NL East Division title. Wright posted a 17-game hitting streak during that same stretch and batted .397. He also emerged as a team leader by taking on the responsibility of answering questions from reporters each night. "I wasn't up there during the rough times last year answering questions because I wanted to be considered a leader," he told Ben Shpigel for the *New York Times* (February 10, 2008) the following year. "I was up there because I'm as accountable as the 25th guy on the roster as to why we didn't get the job done. We're all in this together. We win as a team, we lose as a team." At the end of the season, Wright was honored with a Gold Glove and a Silver Slugger Award for his offensive and defensive successes at third base, and he finished fourth in the Baseball Writers' Association of America's MVP balloting. During the off-season, he told Shpigel, he "thought about what happened last year all the time. . . . I focused 100 percent on getting ready physically because I don't want to feel what I felt watching the playoffs from home."

During the 2008 season Wright batted .302 and set career highs in home runs (33), RBIs (124), and runs scored (115). That year he earned his third consecutive All-Star selection. Wright was the starting third baseman for Team USA in the 2009 World Baseball Classic. The U.S. lost in the semifinal round to the eventual champion, Japan.

The 2009 season was disappointing for the Mets. Injuries led 20 team members to the disabled list, among them Wright and other star players (Jose Reyes, Carlos Delgado, Carlos Beltran, Johan Santana, and Gary Sheffield). The Mets finished fourth in their division, with a record of 70–92, and missed the play-offs for the third straight year. Wright, however, continued to be a bright spot for the team and was among the league's batting leaders for most of the season. In August, in a game against the San Francisco Giants, he suffered a concussion when a 94-mile-per-hour fastball (thrown by Matt Cain) hit his head; he returned to the lineup two weeks later. That September he made his 836th career start at third base, the most starts at that position in franchise history, surpassing by one game the record set by Howard Johnson. While earning his fourth career All-Star selection and finishing the year with a .307 batting average, Wright saw a steep decline in his power numbers, posting a career low in home runs (10) and his lowest RBI total (72) since his rookie season. The decline was attributed in part to the difficulty of hitting homers in the Mets' new, state-of-the-art ballpark, Citi Field, which has an exceptionally large, asymmetric outfield and high outfield walls. (The Mets finished the season with a major-league low of 95 home runs.)

Wright has been romantically linked to Molly Beers, a model. He lives in a $6 million loft in the Flatiron district of New York City and maintains a summer home in Manalapan, New Jersey. He has founded his own charitable organization, the David Wright Foundation, whose mission, according to its Web site, is "to provide aid and assistance toward the health, emotional development, and education for children in need" in the New York and Norfolk, Virginia, metropolitan areas; driven by the illness of a friend of his who developed multiple sclerosis, he also supports efforts related to that disease. Recent beneficiaries of the David Wright Foundation's fund-raising activities include the Long Island chapter of the National Multiple Sclerosis Society, the Make-a-Wish Foundation of Metro New York, the United States Marine Corps Toys for Tots, and the New York City Patrolmen's Benevolent Association.

—C.C.

Suggested Reading: *Baseball Digest* p20+ July 1, 2006; *Binghamton (New York) Press & Sun-Bulletin* B p1+ May 23, 2004; *New York Magazine* Apr. 9, 2007; *New York Observer* May 29, 2008; *New York Post* p86 Jan. 8, 2006; *New York Times* A p1 Apr. 1, 2007, p1 Feb. 10, 2008; *Sports Illustrated* p44+ May 29, 2006

Aamir Qureshi/AFP/Getty Images

Zardari, Asif Ali

(zahr-DAH-ree, AH-sihf AH-lee)

July 26, 1955– President of Pakistan; interim chairman of the Pakistan People's Party

Address: Pakistan People's Party, H. No. 8, St. 19, Sector F-8/2, Islamabad, Pakistan

In September 2008 Asif Ali Zardari, one of the most controversial figures in Pakistan and the widower of the popular former prime minister Benazir Bhutto, was elected as the nation's 11th president. His win came as a surprise to many familiar with his past; during his wife's two terms as prime minister, he was charged with numerous counts of corruption, earning the nickname "Mr. Ten Percent" for the commissions and bribes he allegedly accepted in exchange for brokering government-related deals. Despite those allegations, some of which implicated his wife, Zardari has never been convicted of any crime, and as the current chairman of the center-left Pakistan People's Party (PPP), founded by Bhutto's assassinated father, Zalfikar Ali Bhutto, he has pledged to see his country through its current crises and unite its competing political factions. As Jason Burke wrote for the London *Guardian* (September 5, 2008), "To some, Asif Ali Khan Zardari is a corrupt, bullying chancer who was a political liability for his late wife. . . . To others, the 53-year-old politician is a likeable, experienced and sharp-witted middle-aged man who finally has his chance. For a few, he is all these things at once."

Zardari was thrust into the political spotlight when Bhutto, an iconic figure in Pakistan, was assassinated in December 2007, after having returned to Pakistan from her exile under Pervez Musharraf's rule to campaign for a third (nonconsecutive) term as prime minister. Following her death Zardari became PPP chairman. As president he is faced with a national economic crisis; opposition to his party from the Pakistan Muslim League (PML-N), led by Nawaz Sharif; and pressure to increase Pakistan's efforts to combat terrorists in the region, as part of the U.S.-led "war on terror." Between 1990 and 2004 Zardari spent a total of 11 years in prison awaiting trial on a variety of charges. Although his past activities have led his opponents to speculate that his presidency will be characterized by corruption, Zardari has not been implicated in any corruption scandals since he took office. Zardari's supporters believe that, despite many obstacles, he is pursuing a democratic agenda. After Zardari's election Peter Wonacott wrote for the *Wall Street Journal* (September 5, 2008), "In a matter of months, Mr. Zardari has emerged as a sort of accidental leader of a party that had long revolved around his wife. It now must embrace him, in spite of his past, and sell Mr. Zardari's presidency to the people of Pakistan and the outside world." At a February 2008 rally, commenting on Pakistan's political instability and its delicate relationship with the Western world, Zardari said, as quoted by the London *Sunday Times* (September 7, 2008, on-line), "We are not trying to become a problem for the world. We want to be part of the solution."

The contradictions in Pakistan's history and the presence of many rival factions have led to a turbulent political environment. After Pakistan became a state independent of India, in 1947 (the year India gained its independence from Britain), the country's early leaders attempted to combine the ideals of democracy and theocracy. When the country entered a period of economic hardship in 1954, Pakistani leaders dismissed the democratic government and declared a state of emergency, setting a precedent for the undermining of civilian governments in the name of national security. Religious, regional, and ethnic tensions also hurt the nation's stability, and Pakistan's first 10 years saw the fall of several civilian governments and seven prime ministers. That fragile state of affairs allowed General Ayub Khan to stage a coup in 1958 and begin over a decade of military rule. In 1971, following a war with India, a number of natural disasters, and a civil war that led to the secession of Bangladesh (formerly East Pakistan), civilian rule was restored and Ayub Khan's successor, General Yahya Khan, was replaced by the leader of the PPP, Zulfikar Ali Bhutto. General Zia ul-Haq deposed Bhutto in 1977 and had him hanged in 1979. During his tenure Zia declared martial law, moved the country away from secular politics, and increased presidential power. In 1988 Zia died in a mysterious plane crash. Ghulam Ishaq Khan succeeded him as president, and Zulfikar Ali Bhutto's daughter, Benazir, was elected prime minister. Throughout the 1990s power alternated between the PPP and Zia's protégé, Nawaz Sharif, of the PML-N. Bhutto and Sharif were each elected prime minister twice and voted out of office on allegations of corruption. In 1999 Sharif and the military leader Pervez Musharraf disagreed about policy regarding Pakistan's ongoing conflict with India over the Kashmir territory, and Musharraf was dismissed. He responded by staging a bloodless coup, and Bhutto and Sharif went into exile. Musharraf assumed the role of president in addition to head of the military and diminished the power of the prime minister, who, under the constitution, is designated as the nation's chief executive. After the 2001 terrorist attacks in New York City and Washington, D.C., Musharraf received substantial financial and political backing from the U.S., becoming an ally in the American-led "war on terror." He has been credited with managing Pakistan's economy successfully, but he became less popular during his presidency as he grew more autocratic. When Bhutto was assassinated during the run-up to the 2008 parliamentary elections, her supporters alleged that Musharraf had planned the murder. After the PPP and the PML-N won a majority in the 2008 parliamentary elections, their leaders attempted to impeach Musharraf, who then resigned, paving the way for Zardari's rise to power.

Asif Ali Khan Zardari was born on July 26, 1955 into a family from Nawabshah, in Sindh, a southern province of Pakistan from which the Bhutto family also hails. He was raised in Karachi, Pakistan's largest city, a few hours from Nawabshah. His father, Hakim Ali Zardari, was a Sindhi landlord, tribal leader, businessman, cinema owner, and politician. Zardari's mother, Bilquis Sultana (whose name has also been given as Zarrin Zardari), died in 2002; his sister, Faryal Talpur, is active in the PPP and is currently the nazim (a position similar to that of mayor) of Nawabshah. On his maternal side, Zardari is the great-grandson of Khan Bahadur Hassan Ali Effendi ("Afandi" in some sources), the founder of Sindh Madrasatul Islam, the first educational institution for Muslims in Sindh. By the 1970s Zardari's father had become wealthy and respected as the owner of the Bambina Cinema in Karachi, which was frequented by the city's elite class. Zardari's father built a private disco in the basement of the family home, and the frequent parties the young Zardari allegedly threw there earned him a reputation as a playboy and "party animal." He told Luke Harding in an interview for the London *Guardian* (September 29, 2000, on-line), "As a child I was spoilt by my parents as an only son. They indulged my every whim and I grew up in luxury." Zardari also earned a reputation for athleticism and aggressiveness; he broke several bones playing polo, and the rowdy boxing matches he held with friends were known to take place both inside and outside the ring. Zulfiqar Mirza, Sindh's interior minister and one of Zardari's childhood friends, told Wonacott, "We were very naughty. You can say, naughtier than others." Zardari has denied many of the descriptions of him as a youth, saying that they were put forth by his political opponents.

Zardari's education remains something of a mystery, and several journalists have revealed discrepancies in his academic record. (According to Wonacott, "Mr. Zardari didn't distinguish himself as a student.") An official biography on the PPP Web site claims that Zardari graduated in 1972 from Cadet College Petaro, a high school outside Karachi, and then attended St. Patrick's College, a prestigious Catholic secondary school in Karachi that Musharraf also attended. Wonacott learned through an interview with a St. Patrick's registration clerk that Zardari attended the school in 1973 and 1974 but failed his final examination, which barred him from attending college in Pakistan. Zardari's Web site biography also notes that he studied business and economics at the Pedinton School, in London, England, but Wonacott was unable to confirm the school's existence. Other journalists, including Jane Perlez, writing for the *New York Times* (March 11, 2008), similarly failed to find a record of the Pedinton School. In an interview with Perlez, Zardari said, "I do have a degree. That is not an issue," and noted that he attended the London School of Business Studies "much before I was married." He told Jane Perlez that he thinks the degree is a bachelor of education but that he had not "really looked at it." The PPP has not listed a college diploma among Zardari's credentials.

In any event, after leaving school Zardari tried his hand at local government. His first foray into politics, a 1983 bid for a seat on the district council of Nawabshah, was unsuccessful. He then tried to build a real-estate business, achieving only moderate success with the completion of a few projects. In the mid-1980s he began to pursue Benazir Bhutto romantically. Bhutto's career and background differed significantly from his; they were both raised in Karachi, but Bhutto was educated at Harvard University and Oxford University. After her father's execution, Bhutto became chairman of the PPP and protested Zia's rule. As a result she was repeatedly arrested and placed in detention—alternately in prison and under house arrest—until 1984. She was arrested again in 1985, following a trip to London for medical care, and released only when martial law was relaxed in December of that year. Once Bhutto was free, Zardari and his family made known their hopes of arranging a marriage. In her autobiography, quoted by Wonacott, Bhutto wrote that she and her family were usually able to put off her suitors until they "either lost interest or thought we were not interested." That tactic did not work in the case of the persistent Zardaris, however, and the two families eventually arranged for a wedding to be held in 1987.

Much speculation arose in Pakistan over the Bhutto family's choice of Zardari, who was virtually unknown in political circles. According to Raj Chengappa and Hasan Zaidi, writing for *India Today* (January 28, 2008), Zardari was "dashing and urbane," and after the execution of Zulfikar Ali Bhutto, Zardari's father had become part of the anti-Zia Movement for Restoration of Democracy, making the marriage a politically expedient arrangement in "a male-dominated society that may not have looked kindly upon a young, unmarried woman as a political leader." In marrying Bhutto, Zardari became "the designated fall guy," as a Zardari family friend told the BBC News (September 6, 2008, on-line). "Zardari knew this and accepted it. He walked into the marriage knowing it would always be about her, and never about him." When Zia died, in August 1988, and the military allowed free elections to be held, the PPP won a majority of seats in the Pakistani Parliament and chose Bhutto to serve as prime minister. Although Zardari held no official post in Bhutto's first administration, Chengappa and Zaidi noted that he "certainly helped her negotiate the largely male world of the bureaucracy and politicians. As a man, he was able to become part of the kind of back-slapping, old-boys backroom clubs that Bhutto could never have been part of." Zardari and Bhutto had three children—a son, Bilawal, and two daughters, Bakhtawar and Asifa. Per Bhutto's will, Bilawal is expected to become PPP chairman once he completes his education at Oxford University.

During Bhutto's first administration, Zardari's extravagant lifestyle and rumors of corruption soon began to tarnish his image and that of his wife, and he was seen as a political liability. The rumors included claims that Zardari had granted sugar-mill licenses and unsecured bank loans to friends, made illegal land deals, and taken government kickbacks for his role as an intermediary in government dealings. One of the most sensational allegations against Zardari was that he had tied a remote-controlled bomb to the leg of a businessman in 1990 and sent him into a bank to withdraw money.

Although Bhutto had campaigned on a platform of eradicating feudalism from Pakistani society, providing basic services for those in need, and increasing freedom for women, she had failed to deliver on many of those promises by 1990, when then-president Ghulam Ishaq Khan declared her administration corrupt and called for new elections. In fact, her administration had passed only one piece of legislation—for a budget—during its first 14 months in power, with much of that time spent feuding with the opposition party. Bhutto blamed conservatives in the Parliament and other opponents for blocking her administration's initiatives, but that argument was not enough to keep her from being voted out of office; the PPP lost to the PML-N, which was headed by Sharif, an opponent of Bhutto's. Once Sharif became prime minister, Zardari was arrested and imprisoned for 18 months after being charged in the bomb plot. Sharif's government was soon accused of corruption, however, and was dismissed by Khan in 1993. Bhutto was subsequently reelected, and Zardari was freed from prison. Upon taking office, Bhutto named Zardari as minister of investment, a move that generated controversy because of his reputation. In his position Zardari was credited with promoting private investment in Pakistan, but further allegations of his illegal transactions began to mount, and he acquired the nickname "Mr. Ten Percent."

Bhutto struggled through her second term, overseeing a fractious coalition. To help pay Pakistan's massive debt to the International Monetary Fund (IMF), Bhutto raised taxes, a move that angered citizens even as it failed to generate the necessary revenue. In an effort to placate the IMF, Bhutto gave up the finance portfolio she had held since her return to power. In 1996 then-president Farooq Leghari called for new elections, and the PPP government lost again to Sharif. Zardari was jailed again, this time on charges ranging from corruption to murder. He was accused of taking multimillion-dollar kickbacks in international contracts, using municipal funds for his own gain, amassing assets outside his known source of income, and drug trafficking. He was also charged with plotting the murders of Sindh High Court judge Nizam Ahmed; former federal secretary Alam Baloch; and Bhutto's estranged brother Murtaza Bhutto, whose party had opposed the PPP. Zardari remained in prison until 2004.

While in prison Zardari was elected PPP senator, retaining that title until the country's Parliament was dissolved during Musharraf's bloodless 1999 coup, which ousted Sharif. When Musharraf became president Bhutto fled the country and lived in London and Dubai, in part to escape corruption charges. Under Musharraf's regime the newly established National Accountability Commission further pursued corruption allegations against Bhutto and Zardari, even while Zardari was in prison, opening up international investigations into the couple's assets in Switzerland, Spain, Poland, and the United Kingdom. The couple were accused of maintaining offshore accounts, purchasing undeclared property and jewelry, and taking in roughly $1.5 billion in illegal transactions. They were convicted in Geneva, Switzerland, of taking bribes for granting two Swiss companies, SGS (Société Générale de Surveillance) and Cotecna, a Pakistani government contract for pre-shipment customs inspection of imports. The Swiss court sentenced the couple to six months in prison and forfeiture of their assets, but a mistrial was later declared and the convictions were suspended on appeal. Another investigation, on money laundering in the U.S. conducted by a Senate committee in 1999, cited allegations that Zardari's accounts with Citibank were used to hide $10 million in kickbacks from a gold company, which he denied. He told Harding in 2000, "Before my marriage I was a businessman in trading, construction, and hotelling. As the spouse of the prime minister, I refused even credit from public sector banks, borrowing instead from the markets. I had money and was more interested in the political success of the PPP. I may have behaved improperly in being extravagant or in allowing access to friends to the prime minister's house. However, I scrupulously adhered to the law of the land. In future, I will be more careful than in the past in allowing access as I have learnt many bitter lessons and realise that the prime minister's spouse must be above suspicion. Even if there isn't a fire, smoke makes people suspicious and I end up paying the price."

Zardari spent a total of 11 years in prison between 1990 and 2004, when he was freed after the PPP negotiated a deal with Musharraf's government. Zardari was said to endure his prison time bravely and philosophically; according to the BBC News, while in prison he "resolutely stood by his party as well as his wife—although at times he disagreed with the politics of both. His friends say this was entirely in character and that no-one can deny his personal courage." He told Harding in 2000, while still in prison, "The poor know that the PPP is their watchdog as do the discriminated classes. My wife has enormous stamina and a motivation to fight against injustice. She is intelligent and experienced, articulate and sensitive. She loves the poor people and the country. I know she will lead the PPP to victory because the PPP is the only national democratic and liberal party which has the programme to turn around the external and internal crisis and also has popular sanction. The support of the people for the PPP is evident in labour elections, bar elections, community meetings, and other forums. Its workers are battle hardened activists who have repeatedly faced tyranny with courage and are dedicated to the uplift of the common man." Although Zardari has said that he suffered various forms of torture while in prison, such as sleep deprivation and physical assault, he was also reportedly treated as an "A-class" prisoner with a number of privileges; Jane Perlez wrote that while in prison he had "a separate room from the main prison wing with an attached bathroom, air conditioning, and two servants."

Upon being released from prison, Zardari went into exile, living in New York City and London; he eventually joined Bhutto and their children in Dubai. Despite the numerous allegations against him, Zardari was never convicted of a crime, and in 2007 he was exonerated of all the charges through the passage of the National Reconciliation Ordinance, which instructed courts to dismiss any corruption charges brought against Pakistani politicians that predated Musharraf's 1999 coup. The ordinance was part of a deal made with Musharraf's government (brokered in part by the U.S. and Britain) to allow Bhutto to return to Pakistan. Zardari and his party maintain that the charges against him and Bhutto were false and politically motivated. In June 2008, for that reason, Pakistan's attorney general informed the Swiss government that he would discontinue the investigations of Zardari with regard to SGS and Cotecna. As a result the court dropped the money-laundering charges, although Daniel Devaud, the Swiss judge who originally investigated the case, told Soaud Mekhennet for the *New York Times* (August 28, 2008), "It would be very difficult to say that there is nothing in the files that shows there was possibly corruption going on after what I have seen in there." Meanwhile, in the U.K. Zardari faced a civil charge brought by the Pakistani government, alleging that he had purchased a 365-acre estate in Surrey, England, called the Rockwood Estate—known in Pakistan as the Surrey Palace—with illicitly obtained funds. In 2006 he put off the trial by filing affidavits from two doctors stating that he was mentally unhealthy as a result of his time in prison and thus incapable of assisting his lawyers. In October 2007 Bhutto returned to Pakistan to campaign in the 2008 elections for a third term as prime minister. In doing so she opposed the military regime of Musharraf, which had become unpopular due to his increasingly autocratic rule. With the backing of the U.S. and the U.K., Bhutto cast herself as a politician capable of taking a hardline stance against the region's terrorists. By returning to politics she was also accepting the possibility that her political opponents or members of extremist groups would attempt to assassinate her. Immediately after arriving in Pakistan, she narrowly survived a suicide-bomb attack that killed more than 130 of the supporters lining her motorcade route. She continued to campaign until late December 2007, when she died in a shooting and bombing attack as she was leaving a rally in Rawalpindi. After her death Bhutto was seen by her supporters as a martyr, and her assassination sent Pakistan into a political tailspin, with violent protests in the streets.

After Bhutto's assassination, Zardari and his son, Bilawal Bhutto Zardari, assumed joint chairmanship of the PPP. Zardari holds the position of interim chairman until his son, now 21, graduates from college, in 2010. In the parliamentary elections of February 2008, the PPP and Sharif's PML-N won the majority of the votes, with the PPP claiming 86 seats in the 342-seat National Assembly and the PML-N 66; Musharraf's PML-Q came away with only 40. Yousaf Raza Gilani of the PPP emerged as prime minister the following month. After the elections Zardari and Sharif announced that the two parties would form a coalition in Parliament. According to an article on the CNN Web site (February 20, 2008), Zardari said, "We are going to make a government of national consensus. . . . I think the democratic forces of the world will stand with Pakistan and democracy. The people of Pakistan have spoken and the parliament will be functional and every decision and every relationship will be according to the parliament and the democratic forces of Pakistan." The two parties soon began impeachment proceedings against Musharraf, who had said that he was going to remain in office and work with the new government. In August 2008, facing the threat of impeachment, Musharraf resigned from his post. (He had earlier stepped down as army chief.) That month the PPP announced that it had unanimously nominated Zardari as its presidential candidate. Sharif was not pleased with the decision, telling the press that he preferred a "consensus president." Tensions between Sharif and Zardari were also exacerbated when Sharif said that he would pull his party from the coalition government if the Supreme Court judges dismissed by Musharraf were not reinstated. The PPP was reluctant to reinstate the judges, including former chief justice Iftikhar Chaudhry, because they had the power to overturn the amnesty Musharraf had granted Zardari and Bhutto the year before. Sharif soon pulled his party from the coalition. Matters were worsened in early 2009, when the Supreme Court voted to disqualify Sharif's brother from his post as chief minister of the Punjab and to uphold a ban on Sharif's running for office (due to an earlier criminal conviction). In a major concession Zardari later reinstated some of the Supreme Court judges, including Chaudhry. Sharif's brother, too, was later allowed to return to his post.

In the presidential elections, held on September 6, 2008, Zardari won a majority of votes in the Parliament and the four provincial assemblies. The election was one of the few peaceful transitions of power in the country's history, with Zardari's two main opponents conceding without protest. As president Zardari is in command of Pakistan's military, which possesses nuclear-weapons capabilities. He faces several challenges, including an economic crisis that has led to increased food and fuel prices and a weakening rupee (the Pakistani unit of currency). Zardari has said that he is committed to assisting the U.S. in its efforts to rout members of the Taliban, an extremist Islamic organization, who occupy the semiautonomous tribal regions of Pakistan. The U.S. and the North Atlantic Treaty Organization (NATO) have been fighting the Taliban in Afghanistan since 2001. According to the transcript of an interview with Scott Simon for National Public Radio (August 23, 2008), Zardari said, "We need the support of the United States for our democracy, for our economy . . . to be regional friends in the region. There are lots of challenges this region is facing and the world is facing in our geographical surroundings. So we are hoping to work hand in hand with the United States to see a better tomorrow and a better region."

In November 2008 terrorists attacked hotels and other targets in the Indian financial capital of Mumbai, leaving 171 citizens and foreign visitors dead. Indian officials claimed that Pakistan supported the terrorists, which Zardari denied. India also pressured the Pakistani government to take action against those responsible, exacerbating tensions between the nuclear-armed countries, which have had a tumultuous relationship, including three wars over the territory of Kashmir and a 2001 attack on the Indian Parliament building in New Delhi by the militant Pakistan-based group Lashkar-e-Taiba (LeT).

When it was revealed in December 2008 that LeT was behind the Mumbai attacks, Zardari pledged to take action, and on December 7 Pakistani authorities arrested several members of the group. Two days later the *New York Times* (December 9, 2008) published an op-ed piece written by Zardari, in which he called on India to "pause and take a breath" before blaming Pakistan for the attacks. He wrote, "Pakistan is committed to the pursuit, arrest, trial and punishment of anyone involved in these heinous attacks. But we caution against hasty judgments and inflammatory statements. As was demonstrated in Sunday's raids, which resulted in the arrest of militants, Pakistan will take action against the non-state actors found within our territory, treating them as criminals, terrorists and murderers. Not only are the terrorists not linked to the government of Pakistan in any way, we are their targets and we continue to be their victims." He also wrote, "Benazir Bhutto once said that democracy is the best revenge against the abuses of dictatorship. In the current environment, reconciliation and rapprochement is the best revenge against the dark forces that are trying to provoke a confrontation between Pakistan and India, and ultimately a clash of civilizations." An article on cnn.com (no date/author) noted, however, that in the op-ed, "the Pakistani president never mentioned his country's past support of LeT, which Pakistan's intelligence agency, the ISI, helped create to fight against Indian rule in Kashmir in the 1990s."

In May 2009 Zardari met with President Barack Obama of the U.S. and President Hamid Karzai of Afghanistan to discuss the ongoing efforts to combat Taliban insurgents near Pakistan's border with Afghanistan. Although Pakistan had recently moved a large number of troops to the border, U.S. officials remained skeptical about its ability to end Taliban control of the Swat Valley region of the country. (As of October 2009 Pakistan's military was still engaged in operations against the Taliban there.) In August 2009 Zardari announced that he would lift a longstanding ban on political activity in the tribal areas in order to reduce the influence of the Taliban and other Islamic militants. A poll conducted two months later by the Washington-based International Republican Institute (a nonprofit, nonpartisan, prodemocracy organization that the U.S. government helps to support) revealed that Zardari's commitment to assisting the U.S. was unpopular with a huge majority of Pakistanis. That finding raised questions about the Obama administration's plans to boost financial aid to Pakistan. Kamran Khan, a Pakistani journalist, told Jane Perlez for the *New York Times* (October 1, 2009) that Pakistanis disapprove of the U.S. as a military partner because it "is seen as an occupying force and moving unilaterally against Muslim nations." Further complicating the situation was the U.S.'s insistence that the Pakistani government increase oversight of its military—one of several conditions included in a new, $7.5 billion U.S. aid package. (The U.S. had already sent more than $15 billion in aid to Pakistan since 2001.) Pakistani military officials accused the U.S. of threatening Pakistan's sovereignty, but Pakistani supporters of the package argued that the conditions were no different from those attached to other packages, and that the military was manufacturing a crisis in order to maintain its power.

In a move signaling Zardari's commitment to democratizing Pakistan, the president publicly acknowledged in July 2009 that the country's constitution contained undemocratic clauses, and he announced his intention of starting the process required for their removal. In addition to the Taliban, Zardari must also contend with insurgents in the province of Baluchistan who reject the Pakistani government. During Musharraf's rule many Baluch nationalists were tortured; some human-rights groups and Baluch activists have said that torture has continued under Zardari. The president visited Baluchistan in March 2009 and has pledged to work further to ease tensions there.

Although many are wary of Zardari's presidency, given his past, others believe he is a changed man capable of taking on Pakistan's national and international problems effectively. "He's an older and wiser man," a Pakistani political activist told Burke. "He's got health problems, he watches his diet, he doesn't drink any longer. He and Benazir were both very young when they came to power. They made mistakes." According to Burke, "Zardari is far from an intellectual and does not share his late wife's profound interest in geopolitics or economics, nor her education, eloquence or charisma." A Zardari associate told Burke, "He doesn't read much, it's true. But you don't necessarily need to be a bookworm type to be president of Pakistan." Zardari told Chengappa and Zaidi that his experience in prison "has taught me to live with myself, to look into myself and make my inner self as big as any problem is and confront it." He said about Bhutto, "We respected each other, we respected each other's space, we were an extension of each other. . . . By binding me to her legacy, she has shown the path for the future."

—W.D.

Suggested Reading: *Chicago Tribune* C p1+ Jan. 28, 2008; *India Today* p43+ Jan. 28, 2008; (London) *Guardian* (on-line) Sep. 5, 2008; *New York Times* A p4 Oct. 13, 2009, (on-line) Mar. 11, 2008; (Pakistan) *Nation* Sep. 5, 2008; *Wall Street Journal* (on-line) Sep. 5, 2008

Zell, Sam

Sep. 28, 1941– Chairman and CEO of the Tribune Co.; real-estate company executive; entrepreneur

Address: Tribune Co., 435 N. Michigan Ave., Chicago, IL 60611

A self-described "professional opportunist," "vulture capitalist," and "grave dancer," the multibillionaire real-estate and investment tycoon Sam Zell has bought many properties and businesses that were in serious or near-fatal difficulties and then turned them into highly profitable assets. "Grave dancing is an art that has many potential benefits," Zell wrote in 1976 in an article for *Real Estate Review*, as quoted by Emily Thornton and others in *BusinessWeek* (August 11, 2008). "But one must be careful while prancing around not to fall into the open pit and join the cadaver." Zell's carefulness has served him exceedingly well for over four decades. As an undergraduate, in the early 1960s, Zell embarked in business ventures with

Courtesy of the Tribune Company

Sam Zell

another student, Robert Lurie, and amassed a fortune by managing, renting, and buying houses and apartment buildings. After Lurie's death, in 1990, Zell increased his wealth exponentially by creating four real-estate investment trusts (REITs); one of them, Equity Residential Properties Trust, became the nation's largely publicly traded owner of apartments, and another, Equity Office Properties Trust (EOP), grew to be the country's largest office landlord, controlling close to 700 properties and 125 million square feet of office space in 24 states and the District of Columbia. In February 2007, in one of the largest leveraged buyouts in history, Zell sold EOP for $39 billion. Meanwhile, he had greatly diversified his portfolio: in March 2007 the Associated Press reported that real estate accounted for only about 25 percent of his businesses, with the other 75 percent involving cruise ships; barges; department stores; insurance; wiring systems, networking items, and other manufactured goods; oil and gas; wineries; and companies that convert waste products into energy. The mattress manufacturer Sealy and the drugstore chain Revco are among the firms Zell has bought, revived, and sold very profitably.

With his purchase, in April 2007, of the Tribune Co., Zell, who holds a degree in law, entered a field he knew little about: publishing. Since he officially took over that media conglomerate, the following December, his business skills have been sorely tested. Zell invested $315 million and amassed $8.4 billion worth of debt when he acquired Tribune, whose assets a year ago included nine daily English-language newspapers, among them the *Chicago Tribune*, the *Los Angeles Times*, the *Hartford Courant*, the *Orlando Sentinel*, *Newsday*, and the *Baltimore Sun*; three Spanish-language newspapers; 23 television stations; one television superstation, WGN America; seven Web-based classified advertising companies, among them ForSaleByOwner.com, Cars.com, and CareerBuilder.com; and the Chicago Cubs Major League Baseball franchise and its home stadium, Wrigley Field. In the exceedingly complicated megadeal in which he gained possession of Tribune, he bought back shares of the previously publicly traded company and created a private Subchapter S corporation, which, under federal law, is exempt from paying income tax. (Avoiding taxes has been cited as one of Zell's specialties.)

In his brief time as Tribune's owner, Zell has grappled with severe problems stemming from the company's steeply declining ad revenues, and his attempts to staunch the flow of red ink—including laying off many reporters and other workers, drastically decreasing the number of pages of hard news in his newspapers, and devoting more space to photos and graphics—have drawn the ire of the papers' staffs and others concerned about the decline of the print media in the U.S. "It's the deal from hell," Zell told Emily Thornton in August 2008. "And it will continue to be the deal from hell until we turn it around." Three months later, according to the *New York Times* blog DealBook (November 24, 2008), Tribune appeared to be in dire straits: "operating cash flow was down by 66 percent in the third quarter." "Tribune is on the cusp of breaching its debt covenants," the DealBook report continued, "and some of its bonds trade for as little as 9 cents on the dollar. With the advertising market deteriorating in line with the economy, Tribune has few easy options to stabilize its revenue." The company filed for bankruptcy in December 2008.

Samuel Zell was born on September 28, 1941 in Chicago, Illinois. He was the second child of Rochelle and Berek Zeilonka, Jewish natives of Poland who fled their home country in 1939, shortly before it was invaded by Nazi forces. According to various sources, Zell's parents and their first child, Julie (Sam was not yet born), crossed Russia to reach Japan and then sailed to Seattle, Washington. The family later settled in Chicago, where Berek Zeilonka changed his name to Bernard Zell and built a successful jewelry- and watchband-distribution business. After Sam a second daughter, Leah, was born in the U.S.; now Leah Zell Wanger, she was the lead portfolio manager of the Acorn International Fund and the head of international equities for the Liberty Wanger Asset Fund. The Zells raised their children in Highland Park, a suburb of Chicago. Robert Berger, a Chicago attorney who was a bunkmate of the 11-year-old Sam Zell at a summer camp, described him at that age to Katharine Q. Seelye and Terry Pristin for the *International Herald Tribune* (March 25, 2007) as "very smart, very savvy, very competitive, and very aggressive, whether on the sports field, playing a board game, or in anything else." As a student at Highland Park High School, Zell bought copies of *Playboy* from Chicago newsstands and sold them to his classmates for far more than the cover price. The caption under his photo in his 1959 high-school yearbook read, "I'm not asking you, I'm telling you."

Zell attended the University of Michigan in Ann Arbor, where he earned a B.A. degree in political science in 1963. He then entered the same university's law school. Earlier, during his last year as an undergraduate, Zell and his fraternity brother Robert Lurie had made their first foray into the real-estate business, managing dilapidated off-campus rental properties. Using their earnings they began to invest in houses—an activity that brought each of them profits of more than $50,000 a year. After Zell received a J.D. degree, in 1966, he worked for two years for the Chicago law firm Yates Holleb and Michelson. In 1968 he and Lurie formed Equity Financial & Management Co. and began buying apartment buildings in Rust Belt cities including Cleveland and Toledo, in Ohio, and in such other mid-size cities as Orlando, Florida, and Reno, Nevada. In the 1970s, as the national real-estate market entered a downturn, Zell added to his company's holdings by buying cheap properties from troubled REITs. (A REIT is analogous to a mutual fund, which pools money from many investors, or shareholders, and then invents the money in securities—stocks, bonds, and Treasury bills, for instance—with the aim of gaining more money. With the same aim, a REIT uses the pooled money from many investors, or shareholders, to purchase and manage income-producing property and/or mortgage loans. In general, REITS do not pay corporate income taxes. Instead, they must distribute at least 90 percent of their taxable earnings to their shareholders.)

In the early 1970s Zell was investigated by the Internal Revenue Service on suspicion of conspiring to avoid paying taxes on a 1969 Reno real-estate deal. The case went to trial in 1976, and Zell agreed to testify against Roger Baskes, his sister Julie's husband, who had also been involved in the transaction. The federal government ultimately dropped its charges against Zell, while Baskes was found guilty and sentenced to two years in prison. (Reportedly, Zell and Baskes have remained on good terms nevertheless.)

As changes in federal tax laws made the purchase of high-quality, undervalued buildings more difficult, Zell and Lurie expanded their operations to include corporate acquisitions. As with their real-estate ventures, they targeted companies that had fallen on hard times, such as Great American Management & Investment Inc. (GAMI), a REIT that, in 1980, was emerging from Chapter 11 bankruptcy. That year Zell and Lurie bought 3.5 percent of GAMI's stock; in 1981, with a 22.5 percent stake in the company, they refinanced the firm's debt and used money from property sales to fund the rapid acquisition of more than 80 companies. They pushed GAMI to diversify its interests, and by 1988 it was once again lucrative, earning $8.6 million in annual profits. Zell and Lurie applied the same approach with the Itel Corp., whose computer-leasing business had declined significantly beginning in 1979. Itel filed for bankruptcy soon afterward, and in 1984 Zell began buying shares in the firm. By the following year he had gained a seat on its board of directors, and he later became board chairman, president, and chief executive officer. "He became chairman because he's a forceful, articulate guy with ideas, and the board thought the best way to implement them was to make him chairman," the former Itel treasurer Richard Nevins told Paul Merrion for *Crane's Chicago Business* (March 10, 1986). (Some speculated that Zell used intimidation to force his way onto the board.) By 1988, thanks in part to the purchases of warehouses and railroad-related properties, Itel's annual profits had climbed to $24.8 million. Other companies Zell acquired included Midway Airlines Corp., Chart House restaurants, and the mattress manufacturer Sealy. "I have absolutely no line responsibility," he told Andy Serwer for *Fortune* (May 11, 1998), referring to his hands-off management style. He added, "I tell my people, 'Your job is to make me money.'"

In 1990 Lurie died, and without the man who had long been "the math whiz who crunched the numbers," according to David Barboza, writing for the *New York Times* (December 16, 2001, on-line), Zell felt compelled to reconfigure his real-estate business. In 1993 he launched his first two REITs: Equity Residential Properties Trust, an apartment-rental company, and Manufactured Home Communities, which dealt with mobile homes. He set up Equity Office Properties Trust (EOP), which became the largest owner of office buildings in the U.S., in 1997. "I didn't want to have extensive operations," Zell told Barboza. "By creating these public companies, each company has its own management team and balance sheet. I can be a strategic adviser, but I'm not in the day-to-day operations." Zell's decision to form REITs was also a response to the slowdown in the real-estate market in the late 1980s.

In September 1997 EOP announced that it would buy the Boston-based Beacon Properties Corp., the firm that had been its closest competitor. "We view ourselves as the dominant player in a gigantic industry," Zell told Barnaby J. Feder in an interview for the *New York Times* (September 16, 1997), shortly after the $2.9 billion deal became final. "Our scale will separate us from everyone else." By 2001 Zell had gained control of more than 700 office buildings—more than the number held by such big-name competitors as the Trump Organization and Leona Helmsley's companies. He began telling analysts that he planned to turn his REITs into "national brands" that could offer large companies "convenience and consistent quality," according to Feder. He envisioned a scenario whereby he could sell ad space in his buildings' elevators and parking lots, among other moneymaking devices. "There will be a concierge, selling telecommunications," he told Feder. "We'll create preferred services; we'll have software off the Web. We want to put the landlord where he ought to be—as the intermediary for delivering a number of services." For years Zell had been touting the so-called "economies of scale"—reduced painting and utility costs, for example—associated with owning a large number of buildings. "Concentration gives you pricing power," he told Catherine Wheatley for *Estates Gazette* (September 26, 1998). "To be successful, you have to be [ranked] one or two in the market."

In October 2001 EOP became the first REIT to gain entry into the Standard & Poor's 500 (commonly abbreviated as the S&P 500), an influential index of large stocks. Zell, who had long lobbied for REITs' inclusion in the S&P 500, told Suzanne Woolley for *Money* (December 2001), "It basically acknowledges the fact that over the past 10 years we've built an industry of operating companies that are part of the fabric of the U.S. economy." He added, "This inclusion says that anybody who wants to participate in the economy needs to participate in real estate. If you're an S&P index investor, S&P's job is to give you a slice of everything in the economy."

In the five years leading up to February 2007, when Zell sold EOP to the Blackstone Group for $39 billion, the average annual return of his REITs was 22.13 percent. While that figure was seen by many as respectable—on the whole, the REIT industry had posted an average return of 24.09 percent over the same period—many industry analysts felt that Zell had failed in his efforts to create a national brand. "It never became a truly well-oiled machine to correspond with the vision he laid out for creating a national office company," the Morgan Stanley analyst Matthew Ostrower told Katharine Q. Seelye and Terry Pristin. "He thought 'bigger was better,' but it didn't turn out to be." "We continuously and consistently told everybody that we—by virtue of going public and taking the public's money—had a responsibility both fiduciary and otherwise to protect them and recognize value," Zell told Janet Morrissey for *Time* (November 19, 2007, on-line), explaining his decision to sell EOP. "In the case of EOP, somebody made us an offer that was higher than our own internal assessment of the value, and under that set of circumstances, I had an absolute obligation to respond."

In April 2007 Zell outbid the billionaires Eli Broad and Ron Burkle to purchase the Tribune Co. for $8.2 billion. He put down $315 million and borrowed the rest, adding $8.4 billion to the company's existing debt of nearly $5 billion; the scheduled annual loan payments were to be about $1 billion. The deal, which was labeled "complicated" even by business specialists, involved creating an employee stock-ownership plan (ESOP) and turning the Tribune Co. into a Subchapter S corporation, a type of company that does not pay income taxes. When Zell entered the newspaper industry, it was on a downward slide—a phenomenon commonly attributed to the public's growing preference for free on-line news. In 2006 the Tribune Co. reported a net income of $594 million; within a year the corresponding figure had fallen to $87 million. Nevertheless, in an interview with the Associated Press, Zell said, as reported by Seelye and Pristin, "I probably am not as pessimistic about the future of the newspaper business as others might be."

By April 2008 Zell had cut more than 400 newspaper jobs, and in a memo to Tribune Co. staff members, he wrote, "I have discussed with many of you our mutual concern about the cyclical eroding of content quality to meet budgets manufactured in the corporate office," according to Richard Perez-Peña, writing for the *New York Times* (April 7, 2008). "I promise you, in time, we will end that downward spiral." In June 2008 Zell announced that the company's newspapers would trim a total of 500 pages of news each week, making way for a new format in which advertisements and editorial text would share equal space. "Management has to at least investigate which parts of the cost structure can be scaled back," Mick Simonton, a senior director at the Chicago company Fitch Ratings, told Perez-Peña for the *New York Times* (June 9, 2008, on-line), defending Zell's tactics. Others, among them the newspaper analyst John Morton, thought the move would only hasten readers' decisions to abandon newspapers for on-line news sources. "To the extent you diminish your product, I think you diminish your success, in print or online," Morton told Perez-Peña. "In the long run, it's going to be harmful to newspapers' brand names, which is the strongest thing they've got." In May 2008 Zell sold one of the company's newspapers, the Long Island–based *Newsday*, to Cablevision for $630 million. He created a so-called "leverage partnership" that allowed him to retain a 3 percent interest and thus avoid paying capital-gains taxes. In June 2008 Zell told Wall Street analysts that the company's newspapers would cut back on news and devote 50 percent of their page space to advertisements.

In an interview with Joanne Lipman, the editor in chief of *Condé Nast Portfolio*, held on November 12, 2008 at a media conference, Zell, "true to form, came out swinging against journalistic icons," according to portfolio.com (November 24, 2008). He declared that despite the advent of television and the Internet, newspapers have continued to operate as if they still have a monopoly on the dissemination of the news; thus, they have continued to offer what they consider most important rather than what, as determined by means of focus groups, consumers would prefer to read. "Every piece of a newspaper has to be economically evaluated, because, in the end, we're not an eleemosynary institution, even though most of the newspapers have been run as one," Zell said to Lipman. "I mean, how would I not challenge every cost, every decision, and basically look at the cost benefit, just like our government is supposed to do when it raises our taxes? I got to look at the cost benefit and say, 'What's the benefit? What's the cost? Does this make sense?'" When Lipman noted that the *Los Angeles Times*, a Tribune-owned newspaper, had won "quite a few Pulitzer Prizes and really put a lot of effort into pieces that may or may not pay off" and asked Zell, "Does that no longer make sense in the business model that we're talking about?," Zell answered, "I haven't figured out how to cash in a Pulitzer Prize. . . . We're not in the business of, in effect, underwriting writers for the future. We're a business that, in effect, has a bottom line. So as far as we're concerned, I think Pulitzers are terrific, but Pulitzers should be the cream on the top of the coffee. They shouldn't be the grounds. And I think there are a lot of scenarios in the newspaper industry where the entire focus is on Pulitzers."

In a response to that interview that appeared on NiemanWatchdog.org (December 1, 2008), James O'Shea, who left his job as editor of the *Los Angeles Times* soon after Zell purchased Tribune, wrote, "The real question is what kind of journalism will we have in the newspapers that manage to survive the current wave of circulation and advertising declines plaguing the industry. Will we have the rich, hard-hitting storytelling that gives the news its infrastructure of shoe-leather journalism from courthouses, police stations, legislatures and war zones, the kind of reporting that gives bloggers, broadcasters and others something to write and talk about? Or will the surviving newspapers become vessels for 'panderism' instead of journalism, flimsy content organized around the age-old principle of luring dog owners to stories in the paper so you can sell them some dog food? . . . The [*Los Angeles Times*] currently is in the throes of a massive redesign of its pages driven by people that Zell brought in from the radio industry to 'reinvent' the daily newspaper. Reporters and editors are being schooled in the art of marketing and packaging in an effort to reverse circulation declines at the paper and present 'content' in new and visually arresting ways. Instead of scanning the events, policies, tragedies and joys of the world and giving readers a balanced, in-depth, report on what is important, significant and interesting, editors now place a premium on stories that will appeal to 'frenzied families' or 'carefree couples.' These are categories of readers that the paper's marketing studies suggest are turned off by reports of war, corruption and complex issues like financial calamity. . . . I suspect that once again our future is at least in part in our past. To thrive and prosper, newspapers have to figure out how to deliver journalism that makes the public believe we once again are a public trust, something of value and something they won't hesitate to pay for. Instead many papers today are trying to give readers entertainment, without the drama and without the laughs."

When Zell purchased the Tribune Co., he also became owner of the Chicago Cubs and Wrigley Field, the team's iconic ballpark. He has said that he plans to sell both, as well as the company's 25 percent stake in the Comcast SportsNet Chicago cable channel. (Sold together, all three assets could once have commanded upward of $1 billion, experts speculated. Toward the end of 2008, the worsening economic situation in the U.S. led to lowered expectations.) In early 2008 it was reported that Zell intended to sell Wrigley Field for $1 to a state agency, which would then pay for extensive renovations, such as the addition of luxury boxes and a parking garage. (That deal would have been beneficial on two fronts: the stadium improvements would have made the team more valuable, and unloading the ballpark, even for $1, would have saved Zell and the Tribune Co. millions in property taxes.) On May 13, 2008 *Editor & Publisher* reported that Zell had abandoned that idea, since the only way the state could have avoided funding the renovations with taxpayer dollars—a strategy that was sure to have proved unpopular—would have been to sell individual seats in the stadium. That concept, known as "equity seat rights," was found to "violate both the Internal Revenue Service code and the rules of Major League Baseball," Fran Spielman and David Roeder reported in the *Chicago Sun-Times*, according to *Editor & Publisher.* In July 2008 investors submitted bids to purchase the Cubs; a second round of bids took place on December 1. In the summer of 2009, Zell completed a deal to sell the Cubs, Wrigley Field, and related assets to the family of J. Joseph "Joe" Ricketts, the founder of TD Ameritrade, for approximately $845 million.

On December 8, 2008, in a development that the *New York Times* DealBook blog called "only the latest—and biggest—sign of duress for the newspaper industry yet," the Tribune Co. filed for bankruptcy. The company's "most pressing problem," DealBook explained, "was a maintenance covenant on some of its debt that limits the company's borrowings to no more than nine times earnings before interest, depreciation and amortization." The Tribune Co. has sought the services of Alvarez & Marsal, a restructuring adviser.

Zell has long been labeled a free spirit and iconoclast, and when he began meeting with Tribune Co. employees, he delivered speeches "laced with profanity, political incorrectness, insults and self-deprecating humor," Perez-Peña wrote. He prefers blue jeans to business suits and often rides to work on his BMW motorcycle. Each year he and the "Zell's Angels," a group of a dozen friends, spend two weeks riding motorcycles in exotic locations, such as Vietnam. He also enjoys skiing and playing racquetball. To celebrate his 67th birthday, he hosted a party for 800 people, and every year, according to Seelye and Pristin, "he sends hundreds of friends and colleagues music boxes, with lyrics reflecting his latest insights about the real estate industry or the economy."

In 2009 Zell ranked 205th on *Forbes* magazine's list of the world's richest people. He has been divorced twice and has three children, one of whom, his son Matthew, has been the managing director of Equity Group Investments since 2001. Zell and his current wife, the former Helen Herzog, maintain four homes, three of them in Chicago, Malibu Beach, California, and Ketchum, Idaho; the couple own works of art by Joseph Cornell, David Hockney, and Frank Stella. Beneficiaries of the Zells' philanthropy include the University of Michigan, which opened the Samuel Zell and Robert H. Lurie Institute for Entrepreneurial Studies at the Ross School of Business in 1999. The couple also helped to fund a Holocaust memorial and study center at the Spertus Institute of Jewish Studies, in Chicago.

—K.J.P.

Suggested Reading: *Barron's* p221+ Mar. 12, 2007; *BusinessWeek* p88+ June 26, 1989, p84 May 11, 1998, p24 Apr. 16, 2007, p120+ Apr. 23, 2007, p34+ Aug. 11, 2008; *Chicago Reader* p7 Jan. 3, 2008; *Chicago Tribune* (on-line) June 12, 2008; *Crain's Chicago Business* p1 Mar. 10, 1986; *Estates Gazette* p67 Sep. 26, 1998; *Fortune* p203 May 11, 1998; *International Herald Tribune* (on-line) Mar. 25, 2007; *New York Times* III p1+ Dec. 16, 2001, C p1+ Mar. 26, 2007, C p1+ Apr. 7, 2008, C p12 June 9, 2008; *New Yorker* p52+ Nov. 12, 2007; *Time* (on-line) Nov. 19, 2007

Obituaries

AKSYONOV, VASSILY Aug. 20, 1932–July 6, 2009 Russian writer. Vassily Pavlovich Aksyonov first achieved prominence in the former Soviet Union during the 1960s, when his early novels thrust him into the role of spokesman for the disaffected Soviet generation that came of age during the period of de-Stalinization. That generation was sometimes referred to as the *Shestidesyatniki*, young Soviets who resisted Communist ideals and were inspired by American literature, jazz, and pop culture—elements that Aksyonov incorporated into his work. For nearly 20 years Aksyonov was the most popular living writer in the Soviet Union, until official harassment drove him from his native land in 1980. Along with a growing number of Russian émigré writers, he settled in the United States, where he taught literature and continued to write. Aksyonov's novels, short stories, and plays are notable for their clever use of modernist techniques, biting satire, and rollicking humor. His most popular and enduring novel, the surrealistic *The Burn* (1980), chronicles the lives of ambitious young Russians who suffer repression under their country's Communist regime. Aksyonov was born in the Russian city of Kazan, to parents who were active in the Communist Party. (Both his first and last names have been transliterated in various ways by the Western press; Vasilii or Vasily Aksenov are common variations.) When he was four, his parents, Pavel and Evgenia, were exiled to the gulag during one of many brutal Stalinist purges. He was sent to an orphanage, and he later lived with relatives. When Aksyonov was 16 he was allowed to join his mother in Magadan, Siberia, and his first sight of the labor camp, with its guards and dogs, made a lasting impression on him. (His mother's memoir of her time in the gulag, *Journey into the Whirlwind*, received international acclaim.) He spent eight years living in Magadan with his mother, during which time he graduated from high school. In 1956 he earned a degree from the First Leningrad Medical Institute; he then worked as a physician at Leningrad Hospital until 1960. He also began writing, and his first short stories were published in the popular literary magazine *Yunost* (Youth). Aksyonov's first novel, *The Colleagues* (1961), about a group of young doctors, had been originally published in *Yunost*. He quickly followed that with the highly successful novel *A Starry Ticket* (1962), which focused on a band of disillusioned teens who become attracted to Western values and reject the post-revolutionary ideals of their parents. Notable for its use of colloquial language, including American slang, the novel established Aksyonov's reputation worldwide as the literary spokesman for his generation. Aksyonov's next two novels, *Oranges from Morocco* (1963) and *It's Time, My Love, It's Time* (1963), dealt with similar youth-oriented themes. During that time he also began to write satirical plays, including *Always on Sale*, which was first performed in 1965 in Moscow, where it ran for eight years before being banned. From 1968 to 1980, despite his popularity as a writer, Aksyonov could not get his work published. In 1979, for example, he attempted to publish an experimental literary anthology titled *Metropol*, but Soviet authorities blocked his efforts. After suffering further government harassment for his subversive writing—especially after his inflammatory anti-Communist book *The Burn* was published in Italy—Aksyonov decided to immigrate to the U.S. As a result, he was stripped of his Soviet citizenship and would not regain it for a decade. In 1981 Aksyonov became a writer-in-residence at the University of Southern California, in Los Angeles, and in 1982 he accepted a similar position at George Washington University. *Metropol* was finally published in the U.S. in 1983, as was Aksyonov's fantasy novel *The Island of Crimea*. By 1984 Aksyonov was teaching seminars in Russian literature at Goucher College and Johns Hopkins University, both in Baltimore. He gradually adjusted to and embraced American culture—an experience he detailed in *In Search of Melancholy Baby* (1987). In 1987 Aksyonov was named the Clarence J. Robinson Professor of Russian Literature and Writing at George Mason University, in Fairfax, Virginia, a position he held until 2004. In 1994 he published *Moskovskaya Saga* (published in English as *Generations of Winter*), a trilogy that followed three generations of a family struggling to survive in the Soviet Union. In 2004 the book was made into a popular, 24-part Russian television series. That year Aksyonov won the Russian Booker Prize, considered that country's most prestigious literary award, for his historical novel *Voltairian Men and Women*. His final novels were *Moskva-kva-kva* (2006) and *Rare Earths* (2007). During the last few years of his life, he maintained apartments in both Moscow and France. Aksyonov died at a hospital in Moscow, where he was being treated after suffering a stroke while behind the wheel of his car. He is survived by his wife, Maya, and son, Aleksei. See *Current Biography* (1990). — W.D.

Obituary *New York Times* (on-line) July 8, 2009

ALEKSII II Feb. 23, 1929–Dec. 5, 2008 Russian church official. Patriarch Aleksii II took leadership of the Russian Orthodox Church, which had suffered intense persecution under Communist rule, shortly before the 1991 collapse of the Soviet Union. He was the first Russian Orthodox Church leader to be chosen without intervention from the state since the Bolshevik Revolution in 1917; his tenure was characterized by efforts to increase the church's role in the lives of Russians while adapting to the new government and the influences of Western capitalism. Aleksii II spearheaded efforts to erect and restore cathedrals that had been damaged and destroyed under Soviet rule, and he also introduced Orthodox religious education to the public schools. Aleksii II frequently spoke out on political and international issues, and when civil war threatened to break out in Russia in 1993, he mediated between the disputing parties. He also called for the restoration of peace during Russia's 2008 conflict with neighboring Georgia, citing the countries' shared Orthodox heritage. His tenure was not without its own conflicts; he had strained relationships with both the Roman Catholic Church and the Constantinople Patriarchate, traditionally considered the spiritual leader of all Orthodox Christians, and he was criticized by some for his close relationship with the Russian government and for involving the church in a number of businesses, including the oil giant Lukoil. Aleksii Mikhailovich Ridiger (whose name is sometimes transliterated as Aleksy or Alexy) was born in Tallinn, Estonia, to a Russian mother and a Baltic German father who was ordained a deacon and priest in 1940. The devout family regularly made religious pilgrimages. One particularly influential trip, to the Monastery of the Holy Transfiguration on the Valamo Island in Lake Ladoga, north of St. Petersburg, influenced Aleksii's own decision to enter religious life. He studied at the Leningrad Seminary, graduating with honors in 1949, and attended the theological school at the St. Petersburg Academy, where he was ordained a deacon in 1950. In August 1961 he was named bishop of Tallinn and Estonia. Continuing to rise through the church's hierarchy, he earned the rank of archbishop in 1964 and that of metropolitan (supervising bishop of a group of dioceses) in 1968. In 1986 he was named metropolitan of Leningrad and Novgorod and the administrator of the diocese of Tallinn. He was elected by the Local Council of the Russian Orthodox Church as Patriarchate of Moscow on June 7, 1990, and three days later he was enthroned as Patriarch Aleksii II. In 1950 he wed Vera Alekseyva, the daughter of a priest, prior to taking his own monastic vows, but that marriage was dissolved within a year. Aleksii II died at his country residence in Peredelkino, a small settlement outside Moscow. The cause of death was not reported, but the former patriarch was known to have myocardial ischemia, which affects oxygen flow to the heart. See *Current Biography International Yearbook* (2003). — M.E.R.

Obituary *New York Times* (on-line) Dec. 6, 2008

ALEXANDER, DONALD C. May 22, 1921–Feb. 2, 2009 Lawyer; government official. A commissioner of the Internal Revenue Service (IRS) during the 1970s, Donald C. Alexander made headlines during the Watergate scandal for resisting President Richard M. Nixon's attempts to use the agency to conduct tax audits and investigations against his political rivals. Donald Crichton Alexander was born in Pine Bluff, Arkansas, to William Crichton Alexander, a cotton grower, and the former Ella Temple Fox. Upon completing high school Alexander enrolled at Yale University, in New Haven, Connecticut, earning a B.A. degree with honors in 1942. Subsequently, he entered the U.S. Army and served in Europe during World War II. During his three-year tour of duty, Alexander, who saw combat in southern France, achieved the rank of major and received both the Silver Star and Bronze Star before being discharged in 1945. He then attended Harvard Law School, where he served as editor of the school's law review, and received his LL.B. degree magna cum laude in 1948. Alexander then began working for the Washington, D.C.–based law firm Covington & Burling as an associate, and remained there until 1954, when he joined Taft, Stettinius & Hollister, in Cincinnati, Ohio. Within two years Alexander, who specialized in tax law, was named partner, and in 1966 he became a partner at another Cincinnati law firm—Dinsmore, Shohl, Coates & Deupree (now called Dinsmore & Shohl). During his six-year stint at the latter firm, Alexander concurrently served as vice chairman of the American Bar Association's Tax Section (1968–69), a member of an advisory group to the commissioner of Internal Revenue (1969–70), and a consultant to the U.S. Treasury Department (1970-72). He also sat on the advisory boards of the New York University Tax Institute (1970–72) and Tax Management Inc. (1968–73). Alexander developed a reputation as one of the foremost experts on estate and gift taxation in the United States. On March 19, 1973 Nixon nominated Alexander to succeed Johnnie M. Walters as commissioner of the IRS, and the Senate confirmed him on May 17—the first day of the Watergate hearings. (Those publicly televised Senate hearings revolved around the break-in and wiretapping of the Democratic Party headquarters at Washington, D.C.'s Watergate hotel and office complex. A later investigation traced those illegal activities to members of Nixon's staff, and concluded that they had been authorized and carried out in an effort to learn the Democratic Party's strategy during the November 1972 presidential elections.) Alexander took office on May 29th, and in July 1973 he launched an inquiry in response to an allegation by John W. Dean III, Nixon's former counsel, who had testified before the Senate Watergate Committee that the administration had used the IRS to harass Nixon's political enemies. Alexander's investigation confirmed the Senate's findings: that his predecessors at the IRS had resisted the administration's pressure to use audits for political purposes. In August 1973 he closed down the agency's special service unit, whose original role had been to monitor extremist groups and who were charged with investigating critics of Nixon and the Vietnam War. That same night, Nixon made the first of three failed attempts to fire Alexander. Alexander made headlines again in the spring of 1974, when he audited Nixon's tax returns and uncovered that the disgraced president owed more than $400,000 in back taxes. During his tenure at the IRS, which ended in 1977, Alexander sought to improve compliance and taxpayer service. He is also credited with encouraging the 1976 congressional decision to strengthen taxpayer confidentiality laws. In addition to his other roles, Alexander sat on the Commission on Federal Paperwork (1975–77) and on the Interior Department's Coal Leasing Commission (1983–84). He served from 1984 to 1989 as the director of the U.S. Chamber of Commerce, and from 1987 to 1989 he chaired the Internal Revenue Service Exempt Organizations Advisory Group. In 1993 Alexander joined the law firm of Akin Gump Strauss Hauer & Feld, where he continued to work until two weeks before his death. From 1993 to 1996 he sat on the Martin Luther King Jr. Federal Holiday Commission. Alexander was predeceased by his wife of 52 years,

Margaret S. Alexander, who died in 1999, and his son Robert C. Alexander, who died in 2004. His survivors include his other son, James, and a granddaughter. See *Current Biography* (1974). — M.E.R.

Obituary *New York Times* (on-line) Feb. 8, 2009

ALFONSIN, RAUL Mar. 12, 1927–Mar. 31, 2009 Former president of Argentina. Raul Alfonsin's presidency, which lasted from 1983 to 1989, marked a transition to a renewed era of democracy and the end of one of the most violent and turbulent periods in Argentina's history. Alfonsin's father, a shopkeeper in Chascomus, in the province of Buenos Aires, had immigrated from Spain and was an ardent supporter of the loyalists in the Spanish Civil War. Alfonsin has credited his parents with stressing the value of ethical behavior and political liberty. He attended a military academy, where he earned a bachelor's degree and graduated with the rank of second lieutenant before entering the National University of La Plata to study law. There he became interested in politics and active in the Union Civica Radical (UCR). Argentina alternated between military and civilian rule after the exile of Juan Perón, in 1955, and Alfonsin held various local and provincial positions in the ensuing years. He won his first elected office at age 24, becoming a UCR representative on his town's council, and in 1958 he was elected to the Buenos Aires provincial legislature. In 1963 Alfonsin became a member of the national parliament. During that time he worked to remake the UCR, which he regarded as too conservative, into a democratic-reform movement capable of challenging the Perónist party, which wielded great influence over the masses. As the co-founder and co-president of the Permanent Assembly for Human Rights, Alfonsin was an outspoken critic of the Argentinean regimes responsible for thousands of murders, kidnappings, and disappearances of political dissidents, and as a lawyer, he defended many political prisoners. In 1982, following a failed invasion of the British-administered Falkland Islands, the Argentinean military, which had taken power in 1976 after overthrowing Isabel Perón, was forced to lift a ban on political parties and return the nation to civilian rule. Alfonsin campaigned energetically, staging rallies and signing up thousands of new UCR members. He was elected president on October 30, 1983. His surprise victory over Italo Luder of the Perónist Justice Liberation Front was celebrated by international human rights groups and leaders in Europe, the United States, and other Latin American countries as a new beginning for the region. Alfonsin embarked on an ambitious reform effort that included the prosecution of those guilty of human rights abuses, among them many high-ranking military officials and leftist guerrilla group members. Alfonsin's efforts improved Argentina's image in the eyes of the world and prompted the U.S. to lift a ban on sending military aid to the country. Alfonsin, however, encountered monumental economic challenges as soon as he took office. His budget plan included progressive taxation and spending reductions, but it proved no match for Argentina's rampant inflation. The failure of Alfonsin's economic policies led him to step down in 1989, before the end of his term. Alfonsin's passage of power to Carlos Saul Menem marked the first time in more than six decades that an elected Argentinean president had been succeeded by an elected president from a different political party. Alfonsin remained a highly regarded political figure in Argentina and an unofficial leader of the UCR. In later life he wrote frequent opinion articles and granted television interviews. His last public appearance came in October 2008, when President Cristina Fernandez de Kirchner unveiled a bust in his image. Alfonsin, who died of lung cancer at his home in Buenos Aires, is survived by his wife, Maria Lorenza Barrenechea, and their six children. See *Current Biography* (1984). — W.D.

Obituary *New York Times* (on-line) Apr. 1, 2009

ALLEN, BETTY Mar. 17, 1927–June 22, 2009 Opera singer; educator. Betty Allen was one of the first black women to gain renown on the opera stage. Arts journalists often commented that the life of the respected mezzo-soprano could itself have been the stuff of opera. Elizabeth Louise ("Betty Lou") Allen was born in Campbell, Ohio, a suburb near Youngstown, into the only family of blacks in that blue-collar community. From an early age she sang in her church choir and listened on Saturday afternoons to live radio broadcasts of the Metropolitan Opera, sponsored by Texaco. When Allen was 12, her mother died of lung cancer, and her father, a steel worker, began to drink heavily. The burden of running the household fell to the young girl. One day, fed up with her situation, she took a bus to the Youngstown courthouse, found a judge, and demanded to be adopted. Placed in the state's grim foster-care system, she endured a succession of homes in which she was forced to work as an unpaid maid or preyed upon by lecherous foster fathers. At age 16 Allen moved into the local Y.W.C.A., supported herself by cleaning houses, and worked hard enough in high school to earn a scholarship to Wilberforce University, a historically black institute of higher learning in Ohio. There she studied Latin and German and performed with the Wilberforce Singers and the women's glee club, among other groups. At Wilberforce University Allen met Theodor Heimann, a professor of German and voice who had been a tenor with the Berlin Opera. He introduced her to German lieder, and at his suggestion she undertook postgraduate work at the Hartford School of Music, in Connecticut. In the early 1950s Allen studied at Tanglewood, in Massachusetts, and one summer the famed conductor and composer Leonard Bernstein selected her to sing in his Symphony no. 1 (*Jeremiah*). While in New York City in 1952, she auditioned for Virgil Thomson, who was looking for singers for a revival of his opera *Four Saints in Three Acts.* She obtained the role of Saint Teresa II and continued to sing in *Four Saints in Three Acts* in all of its major revivals until 1982. In 1954 she made her debut as Queenie in the New York City Opera's revival of Jerome Kern's *Show Boat.* She made her New York solo recital debut at Town Hall in 1958. Following that performance Allen was invited to audition as a comprimario mezzo-soprano (assigned to secondary roles) for the Metropolitan Opera, but Max Rudolf, one of its conductors, told her at the time, "The voice is too good for comprimario, and the personality is too intrusive." Still, Allen went on to appear with various companies in *La Sonnambula*, *Oedipus Rex*, *Falstaff*, and *Treemonisha*, among other works, and maintained a close artistic affiliation with such composers as David Diamond, Ned Rorem, and Thomson. During the 1970s she began teaching and quickly developed a reputation as a stellar music educator and administrator. The executive director of the Harlem School of Arts from 1979 to 1992, she was ultimately named president emeritus of the institution. At the time of her death, from kidney disease, she was a faculty member of the Manhattan School of Music. Allen is survived by her husband, Ritten Edward Lee II; her daughter, Juliana; her son, Anthony; and her grandchildren. See *Current Biography* (1990). — D.K.

Obituary *New York Times* (on-line) June 25, 2009

ANDERSON, ROBERT Apr. 28, 1917–Feb. 9, 2009 Playwright. Robert Anderson was a contemporary of Tennessee Williams and Arthur Miller, and while he did not become a household name in the way that those playwrights did, he enjoyed a solid reputation on Broadway during the 1950s and 1960s. His first big hit, *Tea and Sympathy* (1953), starring Deborah Kerr in her Broadway debut, ran for nearly two years. The play, in which a sensitive young man at a New England school is taunted by his peers and criticized by his father because he would rather listen to classical music than participate in sports, ended with a line that became iconic. In the role of the seductive wife of the boy's housemaster, Kerr pulls the young man into her arms and says: "Years from now when you talk about this, and you will, be kind." Between 1953 and 1971 Anderson saw six of his plays staged on Broadway, and during that time he became known for his willingness to handle serious subject matter with emotional accuracy and sensitivity. Robert Woodruff Anderson was born in New York City. He attended Phillips Exeter Academy, in New Hampshire, where he played for the basketball and track teams, participated in musical clubs, and served on the student council. (Despite his extracurricular activities, he described his school years as lonely.) After graduating in 1935 he entered Harvard University, majoring in English. There, he joined the drama club, wrote musical shows, sang in the glee club, and was elected the class poet. He graduated with a bachelor's degree in 1939 and earned his M.A. degree in 1940. He was commissioned as an ensign in the U.S. Navy, and in 1945 his play *Come Marching Home* won $100 in a contest sponsored by the military for the best original drama by a man in uniform. (It was produced at the State University of Iowa in 1946.) After leaving the service Anderson taught playwriting at the American Theater Wing and continued to write. Apart from *Tea and Sympathy*, he is perhaps best known for *You Know I Can't Hear You When the Water's Running* (1967), which attracted enthusiastic reviews. Revolving around a playwright struggling to write honestly about sex despite his own prudishness, it was one of the first Broadway shows to feature on-stage nudity. Anderson's other plays included *All Summer Long* (1954), about a troubled family; *Silent Night, Lonely Night* (1959), about a pair of adulterers; *I Never Sang for My Father* (1968), inspired by his own difficult relationship with his father; and *Solitaire/Double Solitaire* (1970), his last Broadway production. Although he always considered himself primarily a playwright, to earn extra money Anderson also wrote screenplays, including the Audrey Hepburn vehicle *The Nun's Story* (1959) and *The Sand Pebbles* (1966), set in 1920s China. His television credits include the biopic *The Patricia Neal Story* (1981) and *Absolute Strangers* (1991), about a pregnant woman in a coma. Anderson, who suffered from Alzheimer's disease, died at his home in Manhattan. He was married twice, the first time to the director and agent Phyllis Stohl, who died in 1956. In 1959 he married the actress Teresa Wright, whom he divorced in 1978. Anderson had no children of his own but is survived by a stepson and stepdaughter. See *Current Biography* (1954). — D.K.

Obituary *New York Times* (on-line) Feb. 10, 2009

AQUINO, CORAZON Jan. 25, 1933–Aug. 1, 2009 Former president of the Philippines. Corazon "Cory" Aquino, Asia's first elected female head of state, assumed the presidency of the Philippines in the late 1980s, after inspiring a popular civilian uprising that led to the exile of longtime dictator Ferdinand E. Marcos. During her six-year term, she was relatively popular, but her indecisive leadership resulted in the failure of several attempts at social and political reform. Aquino, whose maiden name was Maria Corazon Cojuangco, was the sixth of eight children born to Demetria (Sumulong) and Jose Cojuangco, in Tarlac Province, north of Manila. Aquino hailed from one of the country's wealthiest and most prominent families; her parents ran a profitable sugar mill and later headed the country's first Filipino-owned bank, the Philippine Bank of Commerce. Following World War II, Aquino, who had attended a number of Catholic schools in Manila, studied abroad at Ravenhill Academy, a boarding school in Philadelphia, and Notre Dame Convent School (now Notre Dame School) in New York City. In 1953 she earned a bachelor's degree in French from Mount St. Vincent College, in the Riverdale section of the Bronx. Aquino subsequently returned to the Philippines, and while studying law at Far Eastern University, she met Benigno "Ninoy" S. Aquino Jr., a journalist and aspiring politician whom she married in 1954. Over the next two decades, Corazon Aquino took on the roles of mother to their five children and political spouse, as her husband, a member of the Liberal Party, became successively the youngest mayor, the youngest governor, and finally the youngest senator ever elected in the Philippines. In 1972 Benigno, who was mentioned as a possible presidential candidate, was imprisoned by President Ferdinand Marcos, who had declared martial law to enable him to prolong his presidency beyond two terms. After suffering a heart attack in 1980, Benigno was freed by Marcos, in response to increasing international pressure. Aquino and her family left the Philippines for Dallas, Texas, where her husband underwent successful heart-bypass surgery before settling in Newton, Massachusetts. During the family's three years in exile, Benigno held teaching posts at Harvard University and the Massachusetts Institute of Technology. Shortly after returning home in August 1983, Benigno was brutally assassinated at Manila's airport. Marcos was blamed for the assassination, although there was no proof of his involvement. Months later Aquino, who had vowed to continue her husband's work, called for Marcos's resignation. In the face of increasing international censure (which affected tourism) and economic decline (due in large part to the country's astronomical foreign debt, which totaled about $26 billion), Marcos scheduled a new presidential election for 1986. Despite her lack of political experience, Aquino decided to run after being presented with a petition containing one million signatures supporting her candidacy. During the campaign, Aquino, who frequently donned yellow dresses that eventually became her trademark, positioned herself as the antithesis of the corrupt and repressive Marcos regime. When rumors of fraud emerged during the February 7, 1986 election, both Aquino and Marcos claimed victory. The election stalemate was dramatically broken on February 22, 1986, when two Marcos allies, the defense minister, Juan Ponce Enrile, and the armed forces deputy chief of staff, Lieutenant General Fidel Ramos, defected to Aquino. On February 25, 1986 Marcos and Aquino held rival inaugurations, but after U.S. government officials advised him to quit, the dictator fled the country and Aquino became president. Shortly after taking office she authorized the release of several hundred political prisoners. In the interest of establishing a democratically operated government, she forced many judges and generals who had served under the previous regime to resign; she also supervised the enactment of a new Philippine constitution. Additionally, Aquino passed a reform bill authorizing the redistribution of agricultural lands, including sugar and coconut monopolies, to tenant farmers. Her administration also oversaw free elections and the appointment of an independent judiciary while championing the country's free press. However, Aquino also faced many challenges during her six years in office. She could not prevent the closure of two major U.S. military bases in the Philippines, which employed several thousand Filipinos and accounted for more than $2 billion in revenue. She also drew criticism for failing to put down the Communist insurgency. Although she remained a favorite of the people, Aquino faced a series of overthrow attempts from Marcos loyalists and disgruntled military officers during her tenure. After leaving the presidency in 1992, Aquino remained a visible political figure. She was instrumental in helping oust President Joseph Estrada in 2001, for example, and publicly appealed for Gloria Macapagal Arroyo to step down in 2005. Aquino, who was named Woman of the Year in 1986 by the editors of *Time* magazine, was nominated for the Nobel Peace Prize that same year. In March 2008 Aquino was diagnosed with advanced colon cancer and underwent chemotherapy. In July 2009, unable to eat and severely weakened, she was admitted to Manila's Makati Medical Center, where she remained until her death. Aquino is survived by her son and four daughters. See *Current Biography* (1986). — W.D.

Obituary *New York Times* (on-line) Aug. 1, 2009

ARTHUR, BEA May 13, 1922–Apr. 25, 2009 Actress. Although she spent many successful years on Broadway, Beatrice "Bea" Arthur did not become a household name until she was nearly in her 50s, when she played the title role on the groundbreaking CBS show *Maude* (1972–78). Maude Findlay, a brash and ardent feminist, was an unforgettable character thanks in large part to Arthur's deep voice, imposing stature, and acerbic wit, and the actress took home an Emmy Award in 1977 for her work on the program. Arthur won a second Emmy, in 1988, for the equally memorable role of Dorothy Zbornak in *The Golden Girls* (1985–92), a hit series revolving around the lives of four mature women sharing a home in Miami, Florida. Bruce Weber wrote for the *New York Times* (April 26, 2009, on-line), "With its emphasis on decidedly older characters, [*The Golden Girls*] ran counter to the conventional wisdom that youthful sex appeal was the key to ratings success." Arthur was born Bernice Frankel, one of the three daughters of Philip and Rebecca Frankel. She was always reluctant to disclose her date of birth, but since her death, a family spokesman has given it as May 13, 1922. During the Great Depression Arthur's family moved from New York to Cambridge, Maryland, where her father opened a clothing store. There Arthur attended high school and spent her free time at the movies, dreaming of becoming an actress. She studied for two years at the now-closed Blackstone College, in Blackstone, Virginia, before entering the Franklin Institute of Science and Arts, in Philadelphia, where she earned a degree as a medical laboratory technician. During World War II she served in the U.S. Marine Corps as a medical technician. After the war she enrolled in Erwin Piscator's celebrated Dramatic Workshop of the New School for Social Research, in New York City. She made her professional debut as a member of the speaking chorus in *The Dog Beneath the Skin*, at the Cherry Lane Theater, in New York's Greenwich Village, on July 21, 1947. Throughout the late 1940s Arthur appeared in a number of plays, including *The Taming of the Shrew* and *No Exit*, in small New York venues. The actor and director Gene Saks was one of her fellow students at the Dramatic Workshop, and the two performed in several plays together at the Cherry Lane Theater. Saks and Arthur married on May 28, 1950. They adopted two sons, Matthew and Daniel, but divorced in 1978. (Saks was not Arthur's first husband; she had been married previously to the screenwriter Robert Alan Aurther, whose name she kept, in a modified version.) In the early 1950s Arthur joined the stock company of the Circle Theatre, based in Atlantic City, New Jersey. Her profile was boosted when she received rave reviews in a 1954 adaptation of Kurt Weill's *The Threepenny Opera*. She also received praise for her performance in the 1955 musical *Shoestring Revue*. During that time she also sang in nightclubs and played parts in live television dramas. In 1959 she had her feature-film debut in *That Kind of Woman*. In 1964 she played the role of the matchmaker in a Broadway performance of *Fiddler on the Roof*. Arthur received the most acclaim of her Broadway career in 1966, for her performance as Vera Charles, the main character's drunken best friend, in the musical *Mame*. She won that year's Tony Award for best supporting actress in a musical comedy—and reprised her performance in a 1974 film version of *Mame.* (Her other big-screen credits include the 1971 film *Lovers and Other Strangers*, Mel Brooks's 1981 spoof *The History of the World: Part 1*, and the 1995 movie *For Better or Worse.*) In 1971 Arthur agreed to make a guest appearance on producer Norman Lear's sitcom *All in the Family.* Playing Maude Findlay, Arthur proved exceedingly popular with viewers, and a separate series starring her colorful, outspoken character was ordered by the network. *Maude* was as controversial as it was successful; although it was a comedy, the series addressed such serious contemporary issues as domestic violence, alcoholism, and abortion. From 1985 to 1992 Arthur received acclaim as Dorothy Zbornak, a divorcee who lived with her feisty mother and female friends, in the hit series *The Golden Girls*, which remains in syndication and still has a loyal following. In 2002 Arthur returned to her roots on the stage with *Bea Arthur on Broadway: Just Between Friends*, a one-woman show about her life. Arthur was a passionate crusader against cruelty to animals and an outspoken proponent of gay rights. She died of cancer at her home in Los Angeles. She is survived by her sons and two granddaughters. See *Current Biography* (1973). — W.D.

Obituary *New York Times* (on-line) Apr. 26, 2009

BALLARD, J.G. Nov. 15, 1930–Apr. 19, 2009 Writer. J.G. Ballard's dystopian novels and short stories "both expanded and defied the genre of science fiction," according to Bruce Weber, who wrote Ballard's obituary for the *New York Times* (April 21, 2009, on-line). Ballard first came to prominence with his controversial book *The Atrocity Exhibition* (1969), which examined society's obsession with sex, violence, and celebrity death—themes he explored again in the similarly provocative *Crash* (1973). *Empire of the Sun* (1984), based loosely on his boyhood experiences in Shanghai, China, during the Japanese occupation of the city in World War II, was short-listed for the Man Booker Prize and catapulted him from cult status to wide popularity on both sides of the Atlantic. In 1987, when Steven Spielberg adapted the novel for the screen, Ballard was introduced to an even broader audience. James Graham Ballard was born in Shanghai, where his father was an executive with a British textile manufacturer. When the Japanese occupied Shanghai early in World War II, he and his parents were sent to an internment camp outside the city, where they remained from 1942 to 1945. Settling in England as a teenager, Ballard completed his secondary education at the Leys School, in Cambridge. Intending to study medicine, he entered King's College, part of the University of Cambridge, in 1949. Ballard, who had been writing short stories for years, entered and won an annual writing competition at Cambridge. Emboldened, he dropped out of Cambridge in 1951 to devote himself to writing. He initially submitted stories of various genres to magazines but turned fully to science fiction in the mid-1950s. His first published story, "Prima Belladonna," published in 1956, included a character with bugs in place of her eyes. Ballard, who also served in the Royal Air Force during that decade, supported himself and his family by working on the staff of a science journal while amassing an audience for his fiction. His early stories, many about technology and nature gone awry, were collected in *The Voices of Time and Other Stories* (1962), *The Four-Dimensional Nightmare* (1963), *Passport to Eternity* (1963), and *The Terminal Beach* (1964). Ballard's early novels included *The Drowned World* (1962), in which the polar ice caps melt, causing catastrophic flooding; *The Wind from Nowhere* (1962), in which the planet is devastated by freak high-velocity winds; *The Drought* (1965), also published under the title *The Burning World*, in which industrial pollution causes the complete disruption of the world's water cycle; and *The Crystal World* (1966), in which an unexplained phenomenon is crystallizing the world's jungles and marshes, along with their inhabitants. Ballard's wife, Mary, died in 1964, leaving him to raise their three children, James, Fay, and Beatrice, alone. In the period following Mary's death, he began to write the short stories and experimental pieces that would be compiled into *The Atrocity Exhibition.* The first American edition of the book, scheduled to be published by Doubleday in June 1970, was pulped before being distributed because of its controversial nature. (It contained one piece titled "The Assassination of John Fitzgerald Kennedy Considered as a Downhill Motor Race," and another whose title included Ronald Reagan's name and an obscenity.) The book was published years later by Grove Press as *Love & Napalm: Export U.S.A.* Ballard also drew controversy with the novel *Crash*, which was partly inspired by the author's study of the medical textbook *Crash Injuries.* The protagonist of the novel, which was adapted to film by the iconoclastic director David Cronenberg in 1996, is a deviant who finds auto accidents erotic. "*Crash* would be a head-on charge into the arena, an open attack on all the conventional assumptions about our dislike of violence in general and sexual violence in particular," Ballard wrote for the London *Times* (January 27, 2008, online), explaining his motives for writing the book. "Human beings, I was sure, had far darker imaginations than we liked to believe. We were ruled by reason and self-interest, but only when it suited us, and much of the time we chose to be entertained by films, novels and comic strips that deployed horrific levels of cruelty and violence. . . . I have described the novel as a kind of psychopathic hymn, and it took an immense effort of will to enter the minds of the central characters. In an attempt to be faithful to my own imagination, I gave the narrator my own name, accepting all this entailed." Two weeks after finishing the book, Ballard was involved in a serious car accident. "Looking back, I suspect that if I had died, the accident might well have been judged deliberate, at least on the unconscious level," he wrote. "But I believe *Crash* is less a hymn to death than an attempt to buy off the executioner who waits for us all in a quiet garden nearby. *Crash* is set at a point where sex and death intersect, though the graph is difficult to read and is constantly recalibrating itself." Ballard's subsequent works included *Concrete Island* (1974), *High-Rise* (1975), *The Unlimited Dream Company* (1979), and *Hello America* (1981). Other notable books include *The Day of Creation* (1987), *Running*

Wild (1988), *The Kindness of Women* (1991), *Rushing to Paradise* (1994), *Cocaine Nights* (1996), *Super-Cannes* (2000), *Millennium People* (2003), and *Kingdom Come* (2006). In 2008 Ballard published a memoir, *Miracles of Life: Shanghai to Shepperton*. In a review for the London *Observer* (February 10, 2008, on-line), Robert McCrum called *Miracles of Life* a "brief, modest and occasionally shattering book," but noted that it "only glances at . . . the extraordinary body of work that has flowed from this remarkable life." Ballard died of cancer at his home in Shepperton, Surrey, England, where he had lived for some 50 years. He is survived by his three children and by his longtime companion, Claire Walsh. See *Current Biography* (1998). — D.K.

Obituary *New York Times* (on-line) Apr. 21, 2009

BARNES, CLIVE May 13, 1927–Nov. 19, 2008 Drama and dance critic. Armed with a nearly lifelong passion for, first-hand knowledge of, and extensive study of dance and dancers, as well as a colorful, witty, and sometimes sassy writing style and such traits as highly developed aesthetic sensitivity, open-mindedness, magnanimity, kindness, and humility, Clive Alexander Barnes was instrumental in significantly raising the quality of dance criticism in his native Great Britain and his adopted country, the United States; he also increased the public's awareness and appreciation of both up-and-coming and veteran dancers and choreographers. Beginning as an undergraduate in 1949 and continuing until just weeks before his death, Barnes provided criticism of or essays about dance and, in addition, sometimes for years at a stretch, wrote about drama, music, television, or film for periodicals including the London *Daily Express*, the London *Times*, the London *Evening Standard*, the *Spectator*, *Dance and Dancers*, *Dance Magazine*, the *New York Post*, and the *New York Times*. On many evenings in the early 1960s, he wrote reviews for five London dailies (without a byline for one, under his own name for another, and using pseudonyms for three). In an obituary of him for the *New York Times* (November 20, 2008), William Grimes wrote, "Barnes made dance an art for all, taking both dance criticism and American dance out of its specialized niche. His erudition, distilled into shrewdly pithy analysis, prompted not just readers but also choreographers and dancers to sit up and learn something new." "When it came to a challenging work, he would review not just the first performance, but the second performance and third performance, and then write an analytic piece, too," Lynn Garafola, a professor of dance at Barnard College, told Grimes. "He also had a remarkable visual memory. He wasn't just seeing the ballet in front of him. He had a bank of memories that went back half a century." Born in London, Barnes began attending theater performances at age eight and saw his first ballet at 10, thanks to the complimentary tickets his mother received through her job as secretary to a theatrical press agent. He attended the Kings College London School of Medicine on a scholarship until 1946, when he joined the Royal Air Force. He completed his military service two years later. Having decided to become a dance critic instead of a psychiatrist, he then enrolled at St. Catherine's College, Oxford University, also with a scholarship. As members of the school's ballet club, he and other like-minded students resolved to awaken newspaper and magazine editors to the idea that dance criticism should be a specialty of its own and not considered within the province of music critics, who, he told an interviewer for *McCall's* (March 1969), "didn't know a thing about dance." With a stream of freelance articles, he and his fellow balletomanes succeeded: within the next few years, all the major London newspapers had added dance critics to their staffs. Barnes wrote about ballet for the Oxford magazine *Isis* in 1949, then served as the co-editor of the school's dance magazine, *Arabesque*, in 1950. That same year he won an editorial position with the new international magazine *Dance and Dancers*; he became its executive editor in 1961 and from 1965 until it folded, in 1998, held the title of New York editor. In the early years of his association with *Dance and Dancers*, his name was also on the masthead of the magazine's sister publications *Plays and Players*, *Films and Filming*, and *Music and Musicians* (all issued by Hansom Books). Meanwhile, in 1951 he earned a B.A. degree with honors in English language and literature. That year he began a short stint as dance critic for the *New Statesman*. At the urging of his first wife, whom he had married at age 19, he also took a full-time day job as an administrative officer in the town planning section of the London County Council architect's department, writing about the arts freelance for the nine years he worked there. His first book, *Ballet in Britain Since the War*, was published in 1953. He began his association with *Dance Magazine* in 1955; his column "Attitudes" began appearing in that publication in 1989; he filed his final column on November 7, 2008. From 1956 to 1965 he wrote about music, dance, drama, and films for the London *Daily Express*; he wrote about dance, for half a dozen years beginning in 1959, for the British weekly the *Spectator* and for three years (1962–65) for the London *Times*. He also contributed articles for American publications, among them the *Nation*, the *Saturday Review*, the *Saturday Evening Post*, the *New Republic*, *Life*, *Vogue*, *Harper's*, *Opera News*, and *Holiday*. In 1965 Clifton Daniel, the managing editor of the *New York Times*, persuaded him to move to New York to become that paper's dance critic. He held the title of chief drama and dance critic at the *Times* from 1967 to 1977. "We want influence, not power," he told a reporter for *Newsweek* (March 20, 1967). "I'm terrified by the idea of the critic as a racing tipster." He also said, "The function of the critic is certainly not to lay down the law. His function is to stimulate thought and opinion . . . to help people make up their minds. He's sort of a catalyst or bridge between the artist and the audience." By his own account, he attempted to make clear in his writings that he was expressing only his own opinions. "This job's impossible," he once said, as quoted by Grimes, "and one must pray that one will be only moderately incompetent." In 1978 Barnes left the *Times*, which had decided to use separate reviewers for theater and dance, to become the chief drama and dance critic for the *New York Post*; beginning in 2002 he also assessed operatic performances for the *Post*. As a reviewer Barnes occasionally tangled with Broadway producers or directors, among them David Merrick and Joseph Papp. In June 1968, denouncing Barnes for "praising depravity," the conservative Republican U.S. senator from South Carolina Strom Thurmond read aloud into the *Congressional Record* Barnes's review of the musical *Hair*. In addition to his history of post-war dance in Great Britain, the immensely prolific Barnes wrote books including *Frederick Ashton and His Ballets* (1961), *Inside American Ballet Theatre* (1977), and *Nureyev* (1982). He co-wrote *Ballet Here and Now* (with A. V. Coton and Frank Jackson, 1961), *American Ballet Theatre: A 25 Year Retrospective* (with Elizabeth Kaye, 1999), and *Masters of Movement: Portraits of America's Great Choreographers* (with Rose Eichenbaum, 2004), and he contributed the text for *Dance Scene U.S.A.: America's Greatest Ballet and Modern Dance Companies in Photographs* (1967). He also edited or co-edited several collections of plays. Barnes was married four times and divorced three times. He was survived by his daughter and son from his second marriage, two grandchildren, and his fourth wife, Valerie Taylor Barnes. He died of complications of cancer in a hospital in New York City, where he lived. See *Current Biography* (1972). — M.H.

Obituary *New York Times* A p41 Nov. 20, 2008

BAUSCH, PINA July 27, 1940 – June 30, 2009 Dancer; choreographer. Widely regarded as a pioneer in the world of dance, Pina Bausch garnered a global reputation for her dynamic and innovative choreography, which incorporated classical and modern techniques and featured theatrical music, dialogue, and stage design. "More than any artist, she is credited with advancing the 'tanztheater,' or dance theater movement in Germany," Sarah Halzack once wrote for the *Washington Post*. Bausch was born to August and Anita Bausch in Solingen, an industrial German town. (She had two much older siblings.) A shy and lonely child, Bausch often entertained herself and the patrons at her parents' restaurant by dancing, doing handstands, and playing under the tables. After taking notice of Bausch's talent, her mother enrolled her in dance lessons. At age 14 Bausch attended the Folkwang Academy, a prestigious school for dance, music, and speech in Essen, Germany; there, she trained under the school's head, Kurt Jooss, a founding father of German expressionist dance or *ausdruckstanz*, which combines movement and music with elements of drama. After graduating in 1959, Bausch received a grant to attend the Juilliard School in New York City, and over the next three years she also performed with several modern dance troupes, including the Paul Sanasardo-Donya Feuer Dance Company, the New American Ballet, and the Metropolitan Opera's ballet company. In 1962 Bausch returned to Germany, subsequently joining Jooss's newly established Folkwang Ballett Essen as a principal dancer. Six years later Bausch choreographed *Fragment*, with Jooss's encouragement; her debut piece was set to music by Béla Bartók. In 1969 she entered a choreographic competition in Cologne, with the work *Im Winde der Zeit* (*In the Wind of Time*) and won first prize. Later that year Bausch succeeded Jooss as artistic director and chief choreographer of the Folkwang Ballett (later called the Folkwang Tanzstudio), a position she held until 1973, when she was appointed general director of the conservative Wuppertal Opera Ballet, which she subsequently renamed the Tanztheater Wuppertal Pina Bausch. In her new position, Bausch received criticism for eschewing the company's traditional ballets in favor of avant-garde performances. Many of her works during the 1970s were set to classical music and featured stunning lighting effects, daring staging, and outfits created by her frequent collaborator Rolf Borzik, a set and costume designer whom she later married. Bausch's productions that decade included *Fritz* (1974), a one-act homage to Jooss; *Adagio/Funf Lieder von Gustave Mahler* (1974); and the dance operas *Iphigenie Auf Tauris* (1974) and *Orpheus und Eurydike* (1975). Also in 1975, she attracted worldwide acclaim with her staging of *Le Sacre du Printemps* (*Rite of Spring*), one-third of the three-part piece *Fruhlingsofper*, which was based on Igor Stravinsky's work. In an interview with Sunil Kothari posted at narthaki.com, Bausch described *Rite of Spring* as "the ritualistic battle of sexes, sacrifice by symbolic use of red dress performed on layer of topsoil, incantory movements into dirt, panting audibly throughout." By the late 1970s Bausch's works were exploring the themes of physical and emotional violence as well as the power struggles between men and women. Those included her version of the Bertholt Brecht/Kurt Weill opera *Seven Deadly Sins* (1976); *Blaubart* (1977); *He Takes Her By the Hand and Leads Her into the Castle, the Others Follow* (1978), an adaptation of Shakespeare's *Macbeth*; *Cafe Muller* (1978), a childhood-inspired piece that featured Bausch flinging herself against a wall; *Kontakthof* (1978), a commentary on social rituals that featured male and female dancers playfully slapping and groping each other; and *Arien* (1979), which was set on a stage filled with ankle-deep water. By the next decade, Bausch, who had begun collaborating with the set designer Peter Pabst following Borzik's death in 1980, had established herself as an influential figure in European modern and expressionist dance. Her works were becoming increasingly lighter and more celebratory and optimistic, particularly after the birth of her son in 1981. Examples include *Nelken* (1982), in which the stage was covered with pink carnations, and *Danzon* (1995), which featured a cross-dressing man in red heels. The Tanztheater Wuppertal Pina Bausch troupe began touring widely in the 1980s. As a result of several extended residencies, Bausch started collaborating with theaters and festivals in several cities in the U.S. and around the world. Among her travelogue pieces were *Palermo, Palermo* (1989), her tribute to the Sicilian city; *Nur Do* (1996), Bausch's interpretation of the American West; *The Window Washer* (1997), a co-production with the Goethe-Institut Hong Kong and the Hong Kong Arts Festival Society; *Viktor* (1999), inspired by the city of Rome; *Masurca Fogo* (2001), inspired by a visit to Portugal; *Agua* (2001), her perspective on Brazil; *Nefes* (2003), a collaboration with the International Istanbul Theatre Festival and Istanbul Foundation for Culture and Arts; the Japan-inspired *Ten Chi* (2004); and *Bamboo Blues* (2007), Bausch's ode to India. Bausch's choreography has been featured in several films, including *E la Nava Va (And* *the Ship Sails On*, 1983) and *Hable con Ella (Talk to Her*, 2002). Her many honors include a 2006 Laurence Olivier Award and the 2007 Kyoto Prize. Bausch was diagnosed with cancer just five days before her death and had, as recently as late June 2009, appeared on stage following a performance of her newest work, which was untitled. Prior to her death, she had been collaborating with the director Wim Wenders on a 3-D cinema project, which was scheduled to start shooting in September. Bausch is survived by her companion, Ronald Kay, and her son, Salomon Bausch. See *Current Biography* (1986). — M.E.R.

Obituary *New York Times* (on-line) July 1, 2009

BEHRENS, HILDEGARD Feb. 9, 1937–Aug. 18, 2009 Opera singer. Hildegard Behrens was widely considered the leading Wagnerian soprano of her day. She became a fixture at New York City's Metropolitan Opera after her 1976 debut, and over the next 33 years she performed with that company more than 170 times. In addition to appearing frequently in Richard Wagner's Ring Cycle and *Tristan und Isolde*, she was noted for her roles in Wolfgang Amadeus Mozart's *Idomeneo* and *Don Giovanni*; Alban Berg's *Wozzeck*; and Richard Strauss's *Elektra*. Behrens was born in the small northern German town of Varel to parents who were physicians. Like her five older siblings, Behrens studied music as a child, but she attended the University of Freiburg with the aim of becoming a lawyer. There she joined the school chorus and found that she enjoyed it immensely. Her interest in singing ultimately grew to such an extent that she decided to take lessons. Although she passed her law exam, she worked as a substitute teacher to support herself while continuing her vocal studies at the Freiburg Conservatory. In 1972 Behrens joined the Deutsche Oper am Rhein in Dusseldorf, singing in small roles. It was with her triumphant debut at the Zurich Opera in October 1975 that Behrens first came to international attention. In a review for the British publication *Opera* (March 1976), Heinz Kern wrote that her performance as Leonore in Ludwig van Beethoven's sole operatic work, *Fidelio*, "caused a minor sensation." "Her powerful voice and completely unforced tone mastered this taxing soprano role with seemingly effortless accomplishment," Kern continued. "She also possesses such outstanding dramatic talent, that it almost places her among the ranks of the great tragediennes." In 1976 Behrens appeared for the first time at the Metropolitan Opera, singing the role of the adulterous Giorgetta in Giacomo Puccini's *Il Tabarro*. Over the years she was invited back repeatedly to perform with the company, receiving rhapsodic reviews from New York City critics whenever she appeared on the Met's stage. In 1977 Behrens was cast by the conductor Herbert von Karajan in a production of *Salome* at the Salzburg Festival in Austria. That role became something of a signature for her, as did Wagner's Brünnhilde, which she performed for the first time in 1983, at the Bayreuth Festival in Germany. As quoted on NPR.com (April 19, 2009), a critic once wrote: "There does not seem to be another Brunnhilde to match her vocal authority, expressivity and dramatic perception." In 1990, while performing at the Met in *Gotterdammerung*, one of the operas that comprise the cycle, Behrens was severely injured when a piece of scenery fell on her during the climactic scene. Behrens died unexpectedly from an aortic aneurysm while in Japan for the Kusatsu International Summer Music Festival. She is survived by a son, Philip, whose father was a musician she knew during her student days, and a daughter, Sara, whose father was the filmmaker Seth Schneidman, to whom Behrens was married for a time. See *Current Biography* (1985). — W.D.

Obituary *New York Times* (on-line) Aug. 20, 2009

BELL, GRIFFIN B. Oct. 31, 1918–Jan. 5, 2009 Judge; government official. Griffin Boyette Bell was a Southern judge known for the moderate decisions he made on civil rights cases that passed before the Fifth Circuit Court of Appeals during the tumultuous years of court-ordered desegregation. He was later credited for reforming the U.S. Justice Department during his time as President Jimmy Carter's attorney general. Bell was born to Adlai Cleveland Bell, a cotton farmer who later owned a handful of retail establishments, and Thelma Leola (Pilcher) Bell in Americus, Georgia, not far from Plains, Carter's hometown. Bell knew Carter as a boy and was a close friend of Carter's cousin Don Earl. In Americus, where he attended public schools and junior college, Bell worked part-time as a clerk in his father's service station and appliance store. In 1941 he joined the U.S. Army, and during his nearly five years of service in the transportation corps, he rose in rank from private to major. After World War II Bell enrolled in the Mercer University School of Law, in Macon, Georgia, with the help of the G.I. Bill. Upon earning his law degree in 1948, he worked for various firms around the state, and in 1953 he was asked to become a partner in the prestigious Atlanta-based practice King & Spalding. He remained associated with that firm, whose clients included Coca-Cola and the Catholic Archdiocese of Atlanta, for the rest of his life. From 1959 to 1961 Bell was Georgia governor Ernest Vandiver's chief of staff. During that time, Bell, who supported racial integration of the public schools while the governor did not, convened a commission that held statewide hearings on the matter. The Sibley Commission, as it was known, ultimately settled on a compromise policy of gradual integration. In 1960 Bell served as co-chairman for John F. Kennedy's presidential campaign in Georgia. In 1961 Kennedy, who won both the state and the presidency, appointed Bell to the U.S. Court of Appeals for the Fifth Circuit, which had jurisdiction over Alabama, Florida, Georgia, Louisiana, Mississippi, and Texas. Bell took a moderate position on the civil rights cases brought before the court. Although he supported integration efforts, he saw forced busing as a last resort, and while he opposed discrimination, he also opposed racial quotas. In 1976 Bell, citing his desire to earn a higher salary, resigned from the court and returned to King & Spalding as a managing partner. He did not stay away from government service for long, however. Later that year he was nominated to serve as Carter's attorney general. He was one of the president's more controversial cabinet picks because of his association with Vandiver and his membership in a handful of segregated Georgia private clubs. The controversy died down, however, after Bell quit the clubs and received public support from prominent black leaders in Georgia. Under Bell, more African-Americans and women were appointed to the federal bench, and he was considered a reformer in other respects as well. In 1978, for example, he supported the Foreign Intelligence Surveillance Act, which established restrictions on the government's ability to spy on its citizens. In 1979 Bell stepped down as attorney general and returned to King & Spalding, representing several major clients, including the corporate giant Dow Corning, which Bell helped defend against litigation concerning its silicone breast implants. In the early 1990s he represented President George H.W. Bush during an independent investigation into the Iran-Contra affair. Almost until the end of his life, Bell continued to serve on government panels. He served, for example, as chief judge of the U.S. Court of Military Commission Review, which is charged with hearing the appeals of military tribunal cases involving suspected terrorists. Bell co-wrote a book, *Taking Care of the Law* (1982), and was the subject of the Reg Murphy biography *Uncommon Sense* (1999). He died of cancer in an Atlanta hospital. His first wife, the former Mary Foy Powell, died in 2000. He is survived by his second wife, Nancy Duckworth Kinnebrew; a son from his first marriage; and three grandchildren. His son, Griffin Bell Jr., and a grandson, Griffin Bell III, are both lawyers. See *Current Biography* (1977). — W.D.

Obituary *New York Times* (on-line) Jan. 5, 2009

BELLMON, HENRY Sep. 3, 1921–Sep. 29, 2009 Politician; government official. Henry Bellmon was best known as the first Republican ever to hold the office of governor of Oklahoma. He also spent two terms in the U.S. Senate. Bellmon was born in Tonkawa, Oklahoma, the oldest of Edith (Caskey) and George D. Bellmon's four sons. (He also had nine half-siblings from his father's first marriage.) His mother was a teacher, and his father was a pioneer farmer on the Cherokee Strip, a 60-mile-wide stretch of land south of the Oklahoma-Kansas border. Bellmon, who spent his early childhood on a farm near Billings, in Noble County, graduated from high school in 1938 and enrolled at Oklahoma A & M (now Oklahoma State University) in Stillwater to study agronomy. While there he supported himself with odd jobs and graduated with a B.S. degree in 1942, finishing college in just three and a half years. Bellmon subsequently joined the U.S. Marines and served during World War II. He saw combat on Saipan and was awarded the Silver Star for bravery in action on Iwo Jima. Shortly after his discharge in 1946, Bellmon was elected to the Oklahoma House of Representatives. After serving a two-year term, he lost his reelection bid in the national Democratic tide of 1948. Bellmon then returned home and managed the family-owned farm with his brother Stephen. Bellmon remained politically active over the next decade, however. In 1958 he was named chair of the Noble County Republican Committee, and within two years he had become a well-known figure in state politics. In 1960 he assumed chairmanship of the Oklahoma Republican Party, and in that capacity he was instrumental in rallying support for Richard M. Nixon during the 1960 presidential election. Under Bellmon's direction, Oklahoma's Republican Party enjoyed a newfound resurgence, thanks to aggressive campaigning and to the recruitment of a younger crop of GOP leaders. In 1962 he entered the race for governor, handily winning the Republican primary and then narrowly defeating Democratic challenger Raymond Gary by a margin of about 77,000 votes in the general election. With that victory Bellmon became the state's first Republican governor. During his time in office he chaired the Interstate Oil Compact Commission, an oil regulatory committee, and was appointed to the executive committee of the National Governor's Association. Bellmon served as governor until 1967; under Oklahoma law at the time, he was prohibited from serving another term. Bellmon became the national chair of the Nixon for President campaign in 1967, and he returned to public office a year later, when he made a successful bid for the U.S. Senate, narrowly defeating three-term incumbent Mike Monroney by 55,000 votes. Bellmon drew criticism during his first Senate term for supporting a federal judge's ruling to integrate Oklahoma City's public schools. He barely won reelection in 1974 by a narrow margin of 3,000 votes against Democrat Ed Edmonson. As a U.S. senator, a post he held until 1980, Bellmon was known as a fiscal conservative who opposed new taxes. He held moderate stances on a number of social issues, which often put him at odds with Oklahoma's largely conservative base. After declining to run for reelection in 1980, Bellmon returned to work on the family farm, and three years later he was appointed interim director of the Oklahoma Department of Human Services. In 1986, following the removal of the term-limit provision, Bellmon ran for governor at the urging of Oklahoma Republican leaders. He was elected to a second term, and in an effort to revitalize the economy during the state's most severe economic crisis since the Dust Bowl years, he proposed increases in the state sales taxes, as well as taxes on liquor, cigarettes, and beer. He also sponsored a controversial school reform and tax act that called for compulsory kindergarten attendance, reduced class sizes, and financial incentives for teachers. Declining to run for reelection in 1990, Bellmon resumed his agriculture business interests and also held various teaching posts at Oklahoma City University, Central State University, Oklahoma State University, and the University of Oklahoma. Bellmon, who died of complications of Parkinson's disease at St. Mary's Mercy Hospital in Enid, Oklahoma, was predeceased in 2000 by his first wife, the former Shirley Osborn, to whom he was married for 53 years. He is survived by their three daughters, Patricia, Gail, and Ann; his second wife, Eloise; his brother George; and four grandchildren. See *Current Biography* (1963). — C.C.

Obituary *New York Times* (on-line) Oct. 1, 2009

BERRI, CLAUDE July 1, 1934–Jan. 12, 2009 French filmmaker. Widely regarded as one of his country's foremost filmmakers, Claude Berri earned international acclaim as the director of *Jean de Florette* and its sequel, *Manon des Sources*, which were both released in 1986. Berri was born Claude Berel Langmann in Paris, France, to Jewish parents. His father was of Polish descent, and his mother hailed from Romania. As a young boy Berri was sent away during the German occupation of France and returned following the end of World War II. He left school and briefly followed in his father's footsteps, working in the furrier business. He also studied film for a short time before pursuing an acting career. Berri, who adopted his mother's maiden name professionally, made his on-screen debut in *Le bon Dieu sans confession* (1953), and later in the decade, he appeared in the feature films *Le ble en herbe* (1954), *French Cancan* (1954), *Les jeux dangereux* (1958), *Asphalte* (1959), *J'irai cracher sur vos tombes* (1959), and the television movie *Cristobal de Lugo* (1959). Berri wrote the screenplay for Maurice Pialat's *Janine* (1961) and then stepped behind the camera for the first time to direct and produce the short, comedic film *Le Poulet* (1962), which earned him a prize at the Venice Film Festival and an Academy Award (1966). He followed that with the short films *Les Baisers* and *La Chance et l'Amour*, both released in the U.S. in 1967. A year later Berri made his feature-length directorial debut with the critically acclaimed *Le vieil homme et l'enfant* (1968), a semi-autobiographical tale of a Jewish boy living under the Nazi occupation of France. He also drew from personal experience for the coming-of-age *Le cinema de Papa*, which was released in the U.S. in 1970, the same year as the comedy *Le Pistonne*, another of Berri's hit films. Over the next decade Berri wrote and directed several comedies, most notably *Sex Shop* (1972), *La male du siecle* (1975), *La premiere fois* (1976), *Un moment d'egarement* (1977), and *Je vous aime* (1980). Although Berri largely devoted himself to producing films following the 1979 launch of his production company, Renn Films, he was praised for his screenwriting and directing work on the critically acclaimed films *Jean de Florette* and *Manon des Sources*, adaptations of works by the French author Marcel Pagnol. (Both pictures starred Daniel Auteuil, Yves Montand, and Gerard Depardieu.) For *Jean de Florette*, Berri won best adapted screenplay and best film prizes at the British Academy of Film and Television Arts (BAFTA) Awards and best-foreign-language film at the National Board of Review. He also earned a best-foreign-language film nomination from BAFTA for *Manon des Sources*. During that period Berri earned producing credits for Roman Polanski's *Tess* (1979), Philippe de Broca's *L'africain* (1983), Patrice Chereau's *Hotel de France* (1987), Jean-Jacques Annaud's *L'ours* (1992), and Chereau's *La Reine Margot* (1994). Berri returned to the director's chair with the Gerard Depardieu films *Uranus* (1990) and *Germinal* (1993). *Germinal*, an adaptation of Emile Zola's 1885 novel, earned Berri nods in the categories of best director and best writing (original or adaptation) at the 1994 Cesar Awards, which are regarded as the French equivalent of the Academy Awards. Berri then served as screenwriter and director for the biopic *Lucie Aubrac* (1997), the tale of a French Resistance fighter, and the comedy *La debandade* (1999). Berri next earned writing, directing, and producing credits for the films *Une femme de menage* (2002); *L'un reste, l'autre part* (2005); and *Ensemble, c'est tout* (2007). The following year Berri co-produced *Bienvenue chez les Ch'tis* (2008), which has since grossed nearly $200 million in France, making it the country's second-highest-grossing film to date. Also that year, he opened his own gallery in Paris to display artworks that he owned. Berri's personal life was marked by tragedy. His ex-wife, Anne Marie, committed suicide in 1995, and his son Julien followed suit in 2002. Prior to the stroke that led to his death, Berri was in the process of directing the film *Tresor*. He is survived by two sons, Thomas and Darius, and his sister, Arlette. See *Current Biography* (1989). — W.D.

Obituary *New York Times* (on-line) Jan. 13, 2009

BLANCHARD, FELIX A. Dec. 11, 1924–Apr. 19, 2009 Military officer; football player. Felix Anthony "Doc" Blanchard, who served in the U.S. Air Force for nearly a quarter-century, was perhaps best known as the first collegiate football player to win the Heisman Trophy during his junior year. Born in McColl, South Carolina, Blanchard was the older of two children in his family. He was raised in Bishopville, where his father, Felix A. "Doc" Blanchard Sr., worked as a physician. When Blanchard was young, his father, who had been an outstanding fullback at Tulane University, introduced him to football and other sports. As a result, he spent a good portion of his childhood carrying a football with him. Blanchard, who was nicknamed "Little Doc" by the local townspeople, attended St. Stanislaus Prep School in Bay St. Louis, Mississippi. In 1941, during his senior year, he helped the football team go undefeated and win the Gulf Coast Championship. Upon graduating from high school in 1942, Blanchard attended the University of North Carolina (UNC), where, as a fullback for the Tar Heels football squad, he honed his bone-crushing running style; it was not uncommon for him to barrel through several opponents at a time. At the end of his freshman year, he enlisted in the U.S. Army and spent time in New Mexico with a chemical-warfare unit. In 1944 Blanchard entered the U.S. Military Academy at West Point. (His father, who had helped him secure an appointment there, died shortly before he entered the academy.) During his three seasons as a football player at West Point (1944–46), Blanchard scored 38 touchdowns and was a three-time All-American. During that time he teamed up with speedy halfback Glenn Davis to form one of the most deadly backfield pairings in college football history, earning the nickname "the Touchdown Twins" and leading Army to a near-perfect 27–0–1 record. Blanchard's all-around athleticism also led him to serve as the team's punter and placekicker in addition to his primary roles as an offensive fullback and a linebacker on defense. Blanchard's best season came in 1945, when he averaged 7.1 yards a carry and scored 19 touchdowns, leading Army to a perfect 9–0 record. That year he became the first junior to garner the coveted Heisman Trophy (awarded to the nation's best college football player) and the first football player to win the Sullivan Award as the country's top amateur athlete. He was also the recipient of the Maxwell Award. Despite being selected third overall in the

1946 National Football League (NFL) draft by the Pittsburgh Steelers, Blanchard's request for a furlough to play in the NFL was ultimately turned down by the U.S. War Department. Blanchard went on to play himself in the movie *The Spirit of West Point*, which was filmed in the summer of 1947, before embarking on a 25-year career in the Air Force as a fighter pilot. In 1959 he was honored with an Air Force commendation for bravery, after deftly maneuvering his damaged plane to a safe landing spot in order to avoid crashing into a nearby village. A Vietnam War veteran, Blanchard piloted a fighter-bomber during a one-year tour of duty that ended in January 1969; he flew 113 missions from Thailand, 84 of them over North Vietnam. In 1971 he retired from the Air Force as a colonel. Blanchard, who also spent several years as the commandant of cadets at the New Mexico Military Institute, died of pneumonia at his home in Bulverde, Texas. At the time of his death, Blanchard, a member of the College Football Hall of Fame (1959) and a recipient of the Order of the Palmetto, the highest award given to a South Carolinian, was the oldest living Heisman Trophy winner. He is survived by his two daughters, Josephine and Mary Theresa; his son, Felix A. Blanchard III; seven grandchildren; and eight great-grandchildren. Blanchard was predeceased by his wife, Jody, in the early 1990s. See *Current Biography* (1946). — C.C.

Obituary *New York Times* B p11 Apr. 21, 2009

BORLAUG, NORMAN E. Mar. 25, 1914–Sep. 12, 2009 Agricultural scientist. Norman E. Borlaug bred many of the high-yielding crop varieties that helped avert predicted mass famines in developing Asian and Latin American countries in the latter half of the 20th century, thus saving millions of lives. The Nobel Prize–winning scientist was the son of Norwegian immigrants, Henry O. and Clara Borlaug, who owned a 56-acre farm in northeastern Iowa. The captain of his high-school football team, he graduated in 1932. Although many boys in his town dropped out of school to work on family farms, Borlaug's grandfather urged him to attend college. Borlaug worked his way through the University of Minnesota—an arduous undertaking during the Great Depression—and received a B.S. degree in forestry in 1937. As a graduate student of plant pathology, he divided his time between pursuing his studies and earning a living at forestry jobs. Borlaug earned his doctoral degree from the University of Minnesota in 1942, with a dissertation on a fungal disease of the flax plant. During World War II the U.S. government encouraged the development of herbicides, fungicides, and preservatives that might aid in the war effort, and from 1942 to 1944 Borlaug worked for E. I. du Pont de Nemours and Co., studying the effects of the new chemicals on plants and plant diseases. In 1944 the Rockefeller Foundation, at the request of the Mexican Ministry of Agriculture, sent a team of American agricultural scientists, including Borlaug, to address the severe crop failures then plaguing that country. Borlaug's development of high-yield, disease-resistant strains of wheat won him international acclaim. Within a few years Mexican wheat yields had increased dramatically, and the country was able to stop importing a large percentage of its needed grain. In the 1950s, when it was discovered that liberal fertilizer use was making the plants so tall that they were toppling over and failing, Borlaug began tinkering with the genetic composition of the wheat and found a way to breed a sturdy dwarf variety that produced a similarly high yield. A single field could thus be used to grow three or four times the grain than had previously been possible. That same principle was later applied to rice, a food staple in many countries. Borlaug, whose fame spread to India, Pakistan, Chile, Brazil, and the Philippines, among other countries, was widely lauded as the father of the so-called "Green Revolution," which allowed food production to keep pace with increased population growth. Despite his 1970 Nobel Peace Prize, his work eventually came under fire from activists who claimed that it relied too heavily on chemicals and set the stage for corporate control of agriculture, thus marginalizing small farmers. While Borlaug initially dismissed such criticisms as elitist rants from those who had never known hunger, he later called for a more measured use of pesticides and fertilizers. (He continued to argue, however, that the out-of-control population growth that had made his work neccessary in the first place was of greater concern.) Borlaug, who died of cancer, remained active into his 90s, researching a new variety of rust threatening the world's wheat crops, among other topics. Texas A&M University, where he had taught since 1984, is the site of the Norman Borlaug Institute for International Agriculture, which aims, according to its Web site, to "provide researchers, policymakers and university faculty from developing countries the ability to strengthen sustainable agricultural practices through scientific training and collaborative research opportunities." By some calculations, half of the world's population now consumes grain descended from one of the varieties developed by Borlaug and his colleagues. Borlaug was predeceased by his wife of nearly seven decades, Margaret. He is survived by his children, Jeanie and William, as well as several grandchildren and great-grandchildren. See *Current Biography* (1971). — D.K.

Obituary *New York Times* (on-line) Sep. 14, 2009

CALISHER, HORTENSE Dec. 20, 1911–Jan. 13, 2009 Hortense Calisher, whose fiction has drawn comparisons to that of Marcel Proust and Henry James, compiled an impressive body of work during her nearly six-decade career. In addition to being a four-time winner of the O. Henry Prize and a three-time nominee for the National Book Award, Calisher earned acclaim for several works, including the short story "In Greenwich There Are Many Gravelled Walks" and the novel *The New Yorkers*. The older of two children, Calisher was born into a middle-class Jewish family in New York City. Her father, Joseph Henry Calisher, was a perfume manufacturer who had come to the city from Richmond, Virginia, and her mother, Hedwig (Lichstern) Calisher, had immigrated from Germany. Calisher hailed from a family of storytellers. "At dinners, I would sit at the end of the table and I would listen. There were anecdotes and they [didn't] always run in a straight line," she told the Associated Press (January 16, 2009). At age seven

Calisher began keeping notebooks of her childhood experiences. Upon graduating from Hunter College High School in 1928, she remained in New York and enrolled at Barnard College, where she headed the drama club. After earning a B.A. degree in English in 1932, Calisher worked a variety of jobs, as a social worker with the New York Department of Public Welfare, a sales clerk, and a model. In 1935 she married Heaton Bennet Heffelfinger, an engineer with whom she had two children. The couple moved several times and eventually settled in Nyack, New York, where Calisher enrolled in a writing class taught by the novelist and literary critic Edmund Fuller. "I wrote a story that I had kept in my head while I was walking my little boy to nursery school, and I brought it to him and he said, 'That's publishable,'" she told the Associated Press interviewer. That autobiographical tale—"The Middle Drawer"—was published in *The New Yorker* in July 1948 and earned Calisher her first O. Henry Prize. "The Middle Drawer" was among the 15 short stories featured in her first book, *In the Absence of Angels* (1951), which also included "In Greenwich There Are Many Gravelled Walks," which has come to be regarded as a modern classic. Over the next four years, Calisher, the two-time recipient of a Guggenheim Fellowship (1952 and 1955), also won a 1955 O. Henry Prize for the short story "A Christmas Carillon." From 1956 to 1957 she worked as an adjunct English professor at her alma mater, Barnard College. Following her divorce from Heffelfinger in 1958, Calisher taught in Iowa, where she met fellow writer Curtis Harnack, whom she married a year later. She claimed her third O. Henry Prize in 1958, for the short story "What a Thing, to Keep a Wolf in a Cage!" During the rest of the decade, Calisher served as a visiting professor at Stanford University and again at the University of Iowa. In 1961 she published her well-received debut novel, *False Entry*, about the son of a London seamstress who grows up in the Southern U.S. and poses as a witness at a Ku Klux Klan murder trial. The next year Calisher was a finalist for the National Book Award for that volume. In the 1960s she also published the novels *Textures of Life* (1963), *Journal from Ellipsia* (1965), and *The New Yorkers* (1969); the novellas *The Railway Police* and *The Last Trolley Ride*, both published in 1966; and the short-story collections *Tale for the Mirror* (1962) and *Extreme Magic* (1964). Calisher earned her second and third National Book Award nominations for the memoir *Herself* (1972) and *The Collected Stories of Hortense Calisher* (1975). Among her notable works during the 1970s were the novels *Queenie* (1971) and *Eagle Eye* (1973), both coming-of-age tales, as well as *Standard Dreaming* (1972) and *On Keeping Women* (1977), both of which explored middle-aged identity crises. Calisher continued to write well into her 70s, producing three more novels—*Mysteries of Motion* (1983), *The Bobby-Soxer* (1986), and *Age* (1987); *Saratoga, Hot* (1985), another short-story collection; and her second memoir, *Kissing Cousins* (1988). Calisher, whose 1986 novel earned her the University of Rochester's Kafka Prize, served as president of the PEN American Center (1986–87) and of the American Academy and Institute of Arts and Letters (1987–90). While in the latter post, Calisher was the 1989 recipient of a lifetime achievement award from the National Endowment for the Arts. Under the pseudonym Jack Fenno, Calisher wrote her next book, *The Small Bang* (1992). She followed that with the politically themed novels *In the Palace of the Movie King* (1993), about a dissident filmmaker who flees Communist Albania for New York City, and *In the Slammer with Carol Smith* (1997), about a mentally ill 1960s radical. Also in 1997, Calisher published *The Novellas of Hortense Calisher*, which was followed by *Sunday Jews* (2002), her final novel, and *Tattoo for a Slave* (2004), a memoir and the last book of her career. Calisher died in Manhattan of natural causes. She is survived by her husband, Curtis Harnack, and Peter Heffelfinger, her son from her first marriage. She was predeceased by her daughter, Bennet Heffelfinger. See *Current Biography* (1973). — W.D.

Obituary *New York Times* (on-line) Jan. 15, 2009

CAMPBELL, DOUGLAS June 11, 1922–Oct. 6, 2009 Actor; theater director. During his lengthy career Douglas Campbell was both critically acclaimed and popular with audiences. Known primarily for his roles with the Stratford Shakespeare Festival in Ontario, he was also recognized by Canadian television fans for his starring role in the popular series *The Great Detective* (1979–82). "He had the gravitas needed to do Lear and the wit and sometimes silliness that Shakespeare demanded of his clowns," Antoni Cimolino, the general director of the Stratford Shakespeare Festival, told Dennis Hevesi for the *New York Times* (October 10, 2009, on-line). Campbell was born in Glasgow, Scotland, to Dugald Campbell, a postal inspector, and Ethel (Sloan) Campbell, a typist and amateur actress. His parents were progressive for the era, and Campbell grew up to become a pacifist, vegetarian, and socialist. When he was kicked out of high school for refusing to wear a gas mask during air-raid drills, he hitchhiked to London and found work as a truck driver and stagehand for the Old Vic theater company. Eventually the company's director, Tyrone Guthrie, began casting Campbell in bit parts. In 1941, when he was 19, Campbell appeared with Lewis Casson and Sybil Thorndike in the Old Vic's touring productions of *Medea* and *Jacob's Ladder*. He subsequently returned to Scotland to become a member of the Citizens Theater Company, and in 1947 he married the actress Ann Casson, the daughter of Lewis Casson and Sybil Thorndike. In 1948 Campbell appeared during the Edinburgh Festival in Guthrie's production of *The Three Estates*, and three years later he rejoined the Old Vic to star in its production of *Othello* at Glasgow's Theatre Royal. In 1953 Guthrie, who was in Canada to develop the Stratford Shakespeare Festival, invited Campbell to appear during the festival's inaugural season in *All's Well That Ends Well* and *Richard III*. Between 1953 and 2001 Campbell appeared in more than 50 roles with the festival, playing such classic characters as Othello, King Lear, Alfred P. Doolittle in *My Fair Lady*, and Falstaff in *Henry IV* (parts I and II). Along with Tom Patterson, Campbell co-founded the Canadian Players in 1954. The company, which offered actors off-season work, toured Canada performing a combination of Shakespearean and modern plays. Campbell served as the the Canadian Players' manager and director and also acted. The company found a permanent home in Toronto in the mid-1960s. In 1966 Campbell replaced Guthrie as the artistic director of the Guthrie Theater, in Minneapolis. He clashed regularly with management and the board, however, and left after a year. One of the more noteworthy of Campbell's productions with the Guthrie Theater was a 1967 version of Dominick Argento's *The Shoemaker's Holiday*, in which he also starred. Campbell next helped start the Heartland Players, based in Marshall, Minnesota, which toured the Midwest briefly. Among Campbell's Broadway roles were that of the title character in the Paddy Chayefsky play *Gideon* (1961–62) and the psychiatrist in the acclaimed drama *Equus* (which ran with a variety of actors from 1974 to 1977). From 1979 to 1982 Campbell appeared on Canadian television as Inspector Cameron in the popular series *The Great Detective*, about a 19th-century police inspector in Ontario. Campbell became a Canadian citizen in 1990, the year his first wife died. He later married another actress, Moira Wylie. Campbell died of heart failure in Montreal. He is survived by Wylie; four children from his first marriage, Dirk, Teresa, Tom, and Benedict; two children from his second marriage, Beatrice and Torquil; and eight grandchildren and two great-grandchildren. *See Current Biography* (1958). — W.D.

Obituary *New York Times* (on-line) Oct. 15, 2009

CAREY, RON Mar. 22, 1936–Dec. 11, 2008 Union official. During his tenure as president of the International Brotherhood of Teamsters (IBT), Ron Carey, who was sworn in to the post on February 1, 1992, emerged as one of the most effective labor leaders in the U.S. The Teamsters—then the largest private-sector union in the U.S., with 1.4 million members—had long been associated with corruption and Mafia connections, but Carey made great strides in reforming the organization. After he was reelected in 1996, Carey became embroiled in a campaign-finance scandal despite his sterling reputation, and he was banned from the union in 1998. Throughout the rest of his life, he maintained his innocence. Ronald Robert Carey was born in the New York City borough of Manhattan, the second of Joseph and Loretta Carey's five sons. His father, a driver for the United Parcel Service (UPS), was a member of the Teamsters. Raised in the New York City borough of Queens, Carey attended Long Island City High School. After graduating in 1953, he enlisted in the U.S. Marines. (A gifted athlete, he had been offered a swimming scholarship by St. John's University in Queens, but had turned it down.) Upon his discharge from the military in 1955, he joined his father at UPS as a driver at the Long Island City hub. Within two years he had been elected shop steward of Teamsters Local 804, and in his spare time, he began studying labor relations. Growing increasingly frustrated by the union leadership's unwillingness to take member complaints seriously, Carey ran for president of the Teamsters Local 804 in 1967. UPS officials, regarding him as a troublemaker, threatened to falsify evidence of marital infidelity and blackmail him into dropping out of the race. Carey secretly recorded the threats, however, and played the tape during his campaign rallies to demonstrate his opposition to such corrupt tactics and his ability to withstand bullying. He was easily elected and ultimately served eight successive three-year terms, often winning his races by landslide proportions. During his 24 years at the helm of Local 804, Carey worked hard to maintain relationships with its 7,000 members. Even though he was no longer a driver, he spent time at the garages to hear member grievances. Carey also barred union officers from putting relatives on the payroll and abolished union credit cards, which officers had commonly used for personal expenses. Known for his negotiating skills, Carey was one of the first local leaders to win pensions for members who had worked for at least 25 years, rather than 30, as had been the standard. In 1991 Carey made a run for national president of the IBT and won 48.5 percent of the vote over two "old guard" opponents. As president he sold off the union's two private jets, removed corrupt leaders, and drastically cut his own salary. In 1997 he led a 15-day national strike against UPS for its use of part-time workers. The strike resulted in one of the biggest victories for labor in decades, with UPS agreeing to wage increases, improved benefits, and the creation of 10,000 new full-time positions. For his 1996 reelection campaign, Carey hired a team of political consultants who diverted union money to several organizations. The organizations, in turn, donated some of those funds to Carey's campaign. Although he was not found guilty of participating in the illegal scheme, Carey was found to be at fault for failing to detect or stop it. As a result, in 1998 a court-appointed review board barred him from the union for life. In January 2001 federal prosecutors charged Carey with perjury for lying about his knowledge of the scheme; in October 2001 a jury found him to be not guilty. Carey died of lung cancer and is survived by Barbara, his wife of more than five decades; their five children; and more than a dozen grandchildren. See *Current Biography* (1992). — W.D.

Obituary *New York Times* (on-line) Dec. 13, 2008

CARROLL, JIM Aug. 1, 1949–Sep. 11, 2009 Poet; punk rocker. Jim Carroll, one of the most promising and celebrated poets and lyricists to emerge from New York City's literary scene in the 1960s, is best known for *The Basketball Diaries*, a journal he kept as an adolescent that chronicled his life as a high-school sports star and his descent into heroin addiction. First published in its entirety in 1978, the book inspired a 1995 film directed by Scott Kalvert and starring Leonardo DiCaprio. Born to Thomas Joseph Carroll, a World War II veteran and the owner of a New York City bar, and the former Agnes Coyle, James Dennis Carroll lived on the Lower East Side of Manhattan before moving to the neighborhood of Inwood, then an Irish-Catholic enclave on the borough's northern tip. Carroll's talents as an athlete and writer were apparent to his basketball coach, who arranged for him to receive a scholarship to the prestigious Trinity High School, where Carroll became the sports editor of the Trinity student newspaper. While attending poetry readings held at St. Mark's Church in New York City's East Village, Carroll became acquainted with such literary giants as Allen Ginsberg, Anne Waldman, and John Ashbery. In 1967, at the age of 16, Carroll published his first book of poetry, a 17-page collection called *Organic Trains*, which prompted established writer Ted Berrigan to declare him "the first truly new American poet." Carroll began publishing excerpts from his journal in obscure literary magazines, and the pieces became celebrated for their earnest documentation of his transformation from precocious child to drug-addicted, world-weary adolescent. Despite his growing heroin habit, Carroll continued to succeed as a high-school athlete, earning All-City honors in basketball. He briefly attended Wagner College, a small school in the New York City borough of Staten Island, and Columbia University, in Manhattan, before dropping out. By 1970, when a selection of his journal entries was published in the *Paris Review*, Carroll had become a well-known figure in New York's underground literary scene. He worked as an assistant for the artist Larry Rivers and was a frequent presence at pop artist Andy Warhol's studio and hangout, known as the "Factory." Carroll also earned money for heroin by prostituting himself in Times Square. In 1973 he published his first full-length book of poetry, *Living at the Movies*, to critical acclaim. That year, with his drug problem increasing in severity, Carroll left New York City and moved to California, where he joined an artists' colony in Bolinas and received treatment for his addiction. He met Rosemary Klemfuss, a law student who introduced him to the emerging punk-rock scene in San Francisco. The two married in 1978, the year *The Basketball Diaries* was published in full, and later divorced amicably. (She remained his friend and lawyer throughout his life.) Carroll, encouraged by the performer Patti Smith, a former girlfriend, began reading his poems at punk-rock shows in the late 1970s, and he soon decided to pursue a musical career of his own. In 1980 the Jim Carroll Band released its first album, *Catholic Boy*, which included the college radio hit and now iconic punk track "People Who Died." The song, which has been accused of glorifying early death, contained the lines: "Teddy, sniffing glue, he was 12 years old. / He fell from the roof on East Two-Nine. / Cathy was 11 when she pulled the plug / On 26 reds and a bottle of wine. / Bobby got leukemia, 14 years old. / He looked like 65 when he died. / He was a friend of mine." The Jim Carroll Band recorded two less successful albums, *Dry Dreams* (1982) and *I Write Your Name* (1984), and later released the greatest-hits album *A World Without Gravity: The Best of the Jim Carroll Band* (1993). His spoken-word recordings include *Praying Mantis* (1991) and *Pools of Mercury* (1998). In addition to *The Basketball Diaries*, Carroll published the poetry collections *The Book of Nods* (1986), *Fear of Dreaming* (1993), and *Void of Course: Poems 1994–1997* (1998), as well as *Forced Entries: The Downtown Diaries, 1971–1973* (1987), a memoir of his experiences in New York City. In the final years of his life, Carroll returned to Inwood. He suffered from numerous health problems, including hepatitis C, and faced continual financial difficulties. Increasingly remote and reclusive, he spent his time completing his first novel, tentatively titled "The Petting Zoo." Alex Williams wrote for the *New York Times* (September 27, 2009, on-line) that the book focused on "an art-world prodigy in the 1980s . . . who is driven by early fame into seclusion, where he suffers psychological and spiritual crises. It didn't take much to see the autobiographical thread." Carroll died from a heart attack, alone in his Inwood apartment. His novel is expected to be published in 2010. Carroll is survived by his older brother, Tom, and his former wife. See *Current Biography* (1995). — M.E.R.

Obituary *New York Times* (on-line) Sep. 14, 2009

CHAPIN, SCHUYLER G. Feb. 13, 1923–Mar. 7, 2009 Public and private arts administrator; college dean. Schuyler Garrison Chapin made a name for himself as one of New York City's most renowned arts administrators. From the early to the mid-1970s, Chapin worked as the general manager of the Metropolitan Opera (also known as the Met), and he was subsequently appointed the first dean of Columbia University's School of the Arts, a post he held for almost a dozen years. He next served a stint as the city's cultural affairs commissioner during the Rudy Giuliani administration (1994–2001). The eldest of three boys, Chapin was born in New York City to Leila Howard Burden Chapin and Lindley Hoffman "L.H." Paul Chapin. His parents named him after one of their ancestors: Philip Schuyler, a Revolutionary War general under George Washington and Alexander Hamilton's father-in-law. Chapin, who hailed from a prominent family on New York City's Upper East Side, grew up in an artistic environment. His father, a lawyer and investment counselor, was an opera lover who listened religiously to the Saturday afternoon broadcasts from the Metropolitan Opera, and his aunt, Katherine Garrison Chapin, was a respected poet. Chapin was a frequent visitor to his aunt's home, where he crossed paths with such luminaries as Edmund Wilson, T.S. Eliot, Archibald MacLeish, and Aaron Copland as well as numerous other writers, painters, statesmen, dancers, and musicians. Chapin, whose father died in 1938, developed a serious passion for the arts while taking a music appreciation class at the Millbrook School, an all-boys elementary school in New York. Upon leaving there in 1940, he began studying composition with Nadia Boulanger at the Longy School of Music in Cambridge, Massachusetts. When Boulanger suggested that Chapin had no musical talent and that he would fare better as an impresario, Chapin decided to pursue a career behind the scenes. He left the Longy School and briefly worked as a page at NBC before being called to serve during World War II. A decorated member of the U.S. Army Air Corps, Chapin made nearly 100 round-trip missions over the Himalayas from 1943 to 1946. In 1947 Chapin, who had achieved the rank of first lieutenant, returned to NBC, where he sold advertising space and then joined the staff of the Jinx Falkenburg and Tex McCrary radio and TV shows. In 1953 Chapin went to work for Columbia Artists Management, serving as the tour manager for Jascha Heifetz for several years before being promoted to booking director for the company's Midwest division. In 1959 Chapin joined Columbia Records as a vice president in charge of classical music and theater projects. There, he supervised the recordings of several notable artists, including Igor Stravinsky, Eugene Ormandy, and Rudolf Serkin. Dissatisfied with the business end of the musical profession, Chapin ultimately left that realm for New York City's Lincoln Center for the Performing Arts, where he was named vice president of programming in 1964. In that post he oversaw the first two Lincoln Center festivals, in 1967 and 1969, and helped launch the Mostly Mozart Festival and Great Performers series as well as the New York Film Festival. Chapin remained at Lincoln Center until 1969, when he joined Amberson Productions as an executive producer, supervising the recordings of the legendary conductor and composer Leonard Bernstein; he also helped produce several of Bernstein's recorded concerts, including the popular series called Young People's Concerts. In 1972 Chapin was named acting general manager of the Met, succeeding Goeran Gentele, who had died in a car accident before the opening of his first production. During his tenure at the Met, Chapin was credited with increasing box-office sales and attracting such notable talent as Beverly Sills. By the late 1970s Chapin had accepted a position as dean of Columbia University's Graduate School of the Arts, where he remained for almost a dozen years. (He was later conferred the title of dean emeritus by Columbia University officials.) In 1990 Chapin was named a vice president at Steinway & Sons, the premier piano-manufacturing company. Chapin's last major public position was as commissioner of cultural affairs for New York City, under Mayor Rudolph Giuliani, from 1994 to 2001. Chapin's term was marked by the controversial "Sensation" exhibition, which was held at the Brooklyn Museum of Art from October 1999 to January 2000. The exhibition was publicly denounced by Giuliani for its supposedly scandalous subject matter and blasphemous depictions of the Virgin Mary. In 2002 Chapin received France's prestigious Legion d'honneur, which had been awarded to his father 82 years earlier. Chapin, who authored three books, including *Musical Chairs: A Life in the Arts* (1977) and *Leonard Bernstein: Notes From a Friend* (1992), died of heart problems at his home in Manhattan. His first wife, Elizabeth Steinway, a member of the piano-making family, predeceased him in 1993. He is survived by his second wife, Catia; his sons, Henry, Theodore, Samuel, and Miles; eight grandchildren; two step-grandchildren; and one great-grandson. See *Current Biography* (1974). — C.C.

Obituary *New York Times* (on-line) Mar. 8, 2009

CHURCH, SAM JR. Sep. 20, 1936–July 14, 2009 Union official. From the late 1990s to the early 1980s, Sam Church Jr. served as president of the United Mine Workers of America (UMWA). In that role he lobbied for better mine-safety regulations, negotiated benefits for victims of black lung disease, and ended so-called wildcat strikes (strikes not sanctioned by the union). Samuel Morgan Church Jr. was born in the coal-mining town of Matewan, West Virginia. When he was eight years old, his family moved to Appalachia, Virginia. After graduating from Appalachia High School, Church enrolled at Berea College in Kentucky, but he dropped out in 1955, after less than two years of study. Since the era of cheap oil and the advent of the diesel locomotive had brought hard times to the coalfields, Church moved to Baltimore, where he took a job as a maintenance mechanic in a Domino Sugar Co. warehouse. He soon became active in the United Packing House Workers union, serving as a safety committeeman, a shop steward, and a reporter for his local's newspaper. In 1965 Church, by then married and the father of three children, found employment in the mines. He worked briefly for the Clinchfield Coal Co. and then obtained a job as an electrician-mechanic with the Westmoreland Coal Co. in southwestern Virginia, where he once again became engaged in union activities. Church served as a mine committeeman and a safety committeeman, and then rose to financial secretary, and later president, of his UMWA local. He made his first bid for statewide union office in 1973, just after he had been fired by the Westmoreland Coal Co. for allegedly hitting a foreman. He won election as a salaried field representative for UMWA District 28 and was later reinstated by the company. Church was victorious in over 70 percent of the arbitration cases he handled as field representative and won reelection in 1975. Later that year Arnold Miller, the UMWA president, asked Church to work at the union's national headquarters in Washington, D.C. There Church served as a troubleshooter, with the official title of international representative, until March 1976, when he became deputy director of the union's contract department. In October 1976 Miller, who had dismissed most of the young, college-educated staff of the union, named Church his executive assistant. About two months later the UMWA president, whose relations with many of his early allies had become badly strained, nominated Church to replace vice president Mike Trbovich on his ticket for the union's June 1977 presidential election. Miller and Church won a narrow victory in the hard-fought campaign and were sworn in for five-year terms on December 22, 1977. For the first three months of 1978, the union struggled through a strike, and twice during the stoppage the miners rejected pacts initially accepted by the leadership. Church blamed "Communists" for some of the dissension, but informed observers suggested that it had instead resulted largely from the bargaining team's willingness to accept medical-insurance provisions and other fringe benefits that many members found inadequate. As Miller, already chronically ill with black lung disease and arthritis, spent much of 1978 recuperating from two strokes, Church's responsibilities steadily increased. Although Miller was still making "the major decisions" and had no intention of resigning, Church and secretary-treasurer Bill Esselstyn ran the union on a day-to-day basis. Late in October 1979 Miller accused Church of trying to oust him and vowed to remove him as vice presidential candidate from the 1982 ticket. After Miller suffered a heart attack, the UMWA executive board unanimously elevated Church to the presidency, in November 1979. Most miners seemed willing to give Church a chance; they knew that the UMWA was almost bankrupt and that an epidemic of wildcat strikes under Miller had nearly ruined its credibility and capacity to recruit members. Although Church had some successes, he had failures as well: in 1981, for example, he negotiated a contract that ended up being rejected, and a 72-day strike resulted. In November 1982 his term as president ended, and his reelection bid failed. Church remained active with the union and returned to the mines, working as an underground electrician in Virginia. He died after a long illness and is survived by two sisters; one brother; his second wife, Patti; four children (three from his first marriage); and six grandchildren. See *Current Biography* (1981). — D.K.

Obituary *New York Times* (on-line) July 16, 2009

COWLES, FLEUR Jan. 20, 1908—June 5, 2009 Writer; editor; artist; socialite. Fleur Cowles was one of the leading socialites of the mid-20th century—hosting and visiting such luminaries as Queen Elizabeth II, Cary Grant, Marilyn Monroe, Pope John XXIII, and Judy Garland, among numerous others. She is known for her short-lived but influential magazine, *Flair*, which covered fashion, art, travel, and literature, and also broke new ground with innovative fold-outs, pop-ups, removable art reproductions, scents (several decades before scent strips became a frequent feature of glossy periodicals), and a variety of paper stocks. Featuring the writings of W.H. Auden and Tennessee Williams and paintings by Salvador Dali and other renowned artists, the magazine lasted only one year because of its high production costs, and copies are still prized as collectors' items. Cowles often gave her birthplace as either Boston, Massachusetts, or Montclair, New Jersey, and her year of birth as anywhere from 1910 to 1917, but her *New York Times* obituary reported that census records and relatives confirmed her birthplace to be New York City and the date of her birth to be January 20, 1908. Cowles had also told sources that her parents were named Matthew and Eleanor Pearl Fenton, but the *New York Times* reported them to be Morris and Lena Freidman. Her birth name was Florence, and she had a sister, Millicent. When she was young her family moved to Bloomfield, New Jersey, and she attended local public schools. Later, by her own account, she entered the now-defunct School of Fine and Applied Arts in New York City. Her father, who worked in the novelty business, abandoned the family while Cowles was still in school. Cowles has said she began her career at the age of 15, working as an advertising copywriter for the Gimbels Brothers department store. Later she was promoted to the rank of assistant advertising manager. Adept at devising slogans and promotional ideas, she ultimately left Gimbels to launch her own advertising agency in Boston. During that time Cowles also wrote a daily fashion and lifestyle column for the *New York World-Telegram*. While in Boston she married Bertram Klapper, a manufacturer of wooden heels. She stopped writing her column in 1934, at about the same time she divorced Klapper and married Atherton Pettingell, an advertising agency executive. Together they ran the Dorland International Pettingell and Fenton Advertising Agency, of which Cowles was vice president. The couple divorced in the mid-1940s. When the U.S. entered World War II, Cowles volunteered her services as a speechwriter for the War Production Board. Once the war was over, President Harry S. Truman appointed her to the Famine Emergency Committee. While working in Washington, D.C., she met Gardner "Mike" Cowles, who was then with the Office of War Information. He was also president of Cowles Magazines, Inc., the publishers of *Look*; president of the *Des Moines Register* and the *Des Moines Tribune*; president of the Cowles Broadcasting Co. (which operated radio stations); and chairman of the board of the Minneapolis Star and Tribune Co. The two married in December 1946. (It was during that period that Cowles changed her first name to Fleur.) The next year she became an associate editor at *Look* and, complaining that it was men's "barbershop reading," she added food and fashion sections to the magazine and redesigned it. From February 1950 to January 1951, Cowles published *Flair*. Although critically acclaimed, the magazine was too expensive to produce, and it ceased publication after only 12 issues. Nonetheless, many collectors still hold it in high regard, and in 1999 a lavish volume called *The Best of Flair* was published by HarperCollins and sold for $250. Cowles spent the late 1940s and early 1950s traveling the world and meeting with important political and cultural figures, including Winston Churchill and Eva Perón. Her meeting with Peron inspired her 1951 nonfiction book, *Bloody Precedent*. In 1952 she worked on the presidential campaign of Dwight D. Eisenhower, and a year later she was sent by the White House as a special envoy to the coronation of Queen Elizabeth II. In 1955 Cowles divorced her husband and married Tom Montague Meyer, a timber merchant. The newlyweds lived for part of the year in London; spent time in Sussex in an Elizabethan farmhouse (where many of her most famous guests visited); and restored a castle in Spain as a vacation home. Although she stopped working as an editor after marrying Meyer, Cowles continued to write books, including the authorized biography *The Case of Salvador Dali* (1959). Cowles was known for her own fantastical paintings and illustrations, which often included animals and other objects found in nature. Her work has been exhibited around the world, and in the early 1990s she was the subject of a one-woman show at the National Museum of Women's Art in Washington, D.C. A replica of her London study was created that year and put on display at the Harry Ransom Humanities Research Center at the University of Texas, Austin. The author of the autobiographies *Friends and Memories* (1975) and *She Made Friends and Kept Them* (1996), Cowles died at a nursing home in Sussex, England. She is survived by Meyer. See *Current Biography* (1952). — W.D.

Obituary *New York Times* (on-line) June 8, 2009

CRICHTON, MICHAEL Oct. 23, 1942–Nov. 4, 2008 Novelist; screenwriter; director. A student of anthropology and medicine (which he never practiced), Michael Crichton transmuted his learning into a rich oeuvre of popular thrillers, including a score of novels about science and technology gone awry, the most celebrated of which were *The Andromeda Strain* and *Jurassic Park*, both of which he co-adapted into screenplays. The motion picture *The Andromeda Strain*, released in 1971, was remade into a television miniseries in 2008. With its wondrous special effects, the director Steven Spielberg's film *Jurassic Park* shattered box-office records when it was released, in 1993. Crichton created for network television the extraordinarily successful medical drama *ER* (1994–2009). He had begun writing novels pseudonymously when he was a student at Harvard University, in the late 1960s. In 1969 he published his first novel under his own name, the best-seller *The Andromeda Strain*, the story of four scientists racing against time to save the world from a deadly alien microcosm inadvertently brought to Earth by an American space probe. He returned to the best-seller lists with *The Terminal Man* (1972), a novel in the *Frankenstein* tradition, about a brain-damaged automobile-accident victim who goes berserk after his computer implant fails; *Congo* (1980), about hunters for a rare diamond in Africa who are guided by a gorilla using sign language; *Jurassic Park* (1990), in which DNA bioengineers bring to life a horde of dinosaurs, who proceed to run amok in the theme park planned for them; *Rising Sun* (1992), a densely plotted murder mystery with a leitmotif alleging Japanese industrial imperialism; and *Timeline* (2000), about a group of time-traveling historians trapped in a parallel universe in medieval France with less than two days to escape. (*Timeline* was Crichton's first downloadable eBook, for Microsoft Reader on the Pocket PC.) In a $40 million deal in 2001, Crichton moved from the Alfred A. Knopf division of Random House to HarperCollins, after which his earnings per book rose above $20 million. He brought together nanotechnology and capitalistic greed in *Prey* (2002), a novel teeming with evil little robots. A skeptic regarding human-caused climate change, he stirred considerable controversy with his best-selling novel *State of Fear* (2004), in which the villains are a band of well-financed environmental lawyers who have an ulterior motive in fraudulently promoting a fear of global warming. In *Next* (2006) he presented imagined, frightening results of genetic and biotechnological experimentation. About half of Crichton's 22 novels were made into films, including *The Carey Treatment* (1972, originally titled *A Case of Need*), directed by Blake Edwards; *Disclosure* (1994), directed by Barry Levinson; and *Sphere*, directed by Levinson in 1998. Crichton's first Hollywood directorial effort was *Westworld* (1973), a film also scripted by him, about robots in an interactive virtual-reality theme park, including a gunslinger (Yul Brynner) who rejects his programmed code of behavior. (*Westworld* was the first theatrically released feature film to use two-dimensional computer-generated imagery [CGI].) Crichton next directed *Coma* (1978), adapted from a novel by Robin Cook, about a hospital where a group of surgeons are criminally harvesting body organs for transplants. Adapting a novel of his of the same title, he directed *The Great Train Robbery* (1979), about a historic Victorian locomotive heist, and from his own scripts he directed *Looker* (1981) and *Runaway* (1984). His sixth directorial project, *Physical Evidence* (1989), was from a screenplay by Bill Philips. He co-wrote the screenplay for the feature film *Twister* (1996). On television in 1973 he directed an adaptation of his novel *Pursuit*. Crichton's weekly hour-long television series *ER*, set in a fictional Chicago hospital, centered on the work and lives of an emergency-room staff. Running from September 1994 through the 2008–09 season, *ER* was the second-longest-lived show (after *Law and Order)* in television history. It and its cast drew 123 Emmy nominations and won 22 Emmy Awards. Crichton wrote three of *ER's* earliest episodes and was an executive producer of the show. His nonfiction books included a primer on computers, an insider's explanation of how a hospital works, and a biography of the painter Jasper Johns. A giant in personal physique was well as literary stature, Crichton stood six feet nine inches tall. He was married five times and divorced four. His survivors included his fifth wife, Sherri Alexander, and a daughter, Taylor Anne, from his marriage to his fourth wife, Anne-Marie Martin. He died of throat cancer in Los Angeles. See *Current Biography* (1993). — K.D.

Obituary *New York Times* A p31 Nov. 6, 2008

CRONKITE, WALTER Nov. 4, 1916–July 17, 2009 As the anchor of the *CBS Evening News* from 1962 to 1981, Walter Cronkite was a nightly fixture in millions of American homes. The pioneering television journalist covered wars, moonwalks, natural disasters, and national tragedies with a calm, authoritative delivery and reassuring on-screen presence that earned him the sobriquet "the most trusted man in America." Walter Leland Cronkite Jr. was born in St. Joseph, Missouri, the only child of Walter Leland Cronkite Sr., a dentist, and Helen Lena (Fritsche) Cronkite. When Cronkite was 10 the family moved to Houston, Texas, where his father had accepted a teaching post at the University of Texas Dental School. While still in high school, Cronkite got a job with the *Houston Post* as a junior reporter and copy boy. (He also had a paper route, making him, he joked, the only person delivering papers with his own writing inside.) He studied political science, economics, and journalism at the University of Texas at Austin, then left school during his junior year to work full-time for the Scripps-Howard–owned *Houston Press*, an afternoon daily for which he had sometimes written as a student. (The *Press* folded in 1964 and is unaffiliated with the news-and-entertainment weekly that now goes by the same name.) Cronkite next found a job reading the news and announcing football games at KCMO, a radio station in Kansas City, Missouri. (He was billed as Walter Wilcox, because radio stations then branded the names of their on-air talent, so that competitors could not use the same names.) Cronkite was fired from KCMO after he accused the station of shoddy journalistic standards. In the late 1930s he joined the United Press news agency (now United Press International). As one of the first journalists assigned to chronicle the actions of American forces after the U.S. entered World War II, he gained fame as a war correspondent and covered many of the conflict's major battles, including the Battle of the Bulge, in 1944. He flew on the first Flying Fortress bombing raids over Germany and gave eyewitness accounts of the invasion of Normandy. (He was part of a small group of journalists known as the "Writing 69th," which included Homer Bigart and Andy Rooney, among others.) Following the war Cronkite remained in Europe to work in United Press bureaus in Belgium, the Netherlands, and Luxembourg. He covered the Nuremberg trials and served as the United Press bureau chief in Moscow for two years (1946–48). Recruited by the famed journalist Edward R. Murrow, in 1950 Cronkite joined CBS News. He began appearing on several nationally broadcast public-affairs programs, including *Man of the Week, It's News to Me*, and *Pick the Winner*. In 1952, during the first nationally televised presidential campaign, Cronkite led CBS's coverage of the Democratic and Republican National Conventions, an assignment that set him on the road to stardom. With the exception of the 1964 Democratic National Convention, he covered every national political convention and national election between 1952 and 1980. (Cronkite expressed amazement that people were often more excited to see him than the politicians he was covering.) In February 1953 he narrated the first installment of the documentary series *You Are There*, which re-created historical events, such as the Battle of the Alamo, and reported them as if they were breaking news. Cronkite replaced Murrow as senior correspondent on the *CBS Evening News* in 1961, and on April 16, 1962 he succeeded Douglas Edwards as anchor. The show quickly became the top-rated news program on television, and Cronkite became a household name. He prided himself on his straightforward, unbiased delivery of the news. On only a few occasions did his emotions disturb his celebrated calm. When reporting the assassination of President John F. Kennedy, in 1963, for example, Cronkite blinked tears from his eyes and took a moment to regain his composure, and when the *Eagle* space capsule landed on the moon in 1969, he excitedly exclaimed, "Oh, boy!" While Cronkite rarely gave his own opinions on the air, in 1968, on camera, after visiting Vietnam, he declared the war there a bloody stalemate and called for peace negotiations. (The pronouncement reportedly swayed President Lyndon Johnson, who realized Cronkite's influence with the general public.) Cronkite retired from the *CBS Evening News* in 1981. Already the recipient of multiple Emmy, Peabody, and Golden Globe Awards, that year he received the Presidential Medal of Freedom. Cronkite continued to work after leaving the anchor desk, taking on the largely honorary title of CBS special correspondent, sitting on the network's board of directors, producing some 60 documentaries, presiding over the annual Kennedy Center Honors, publishing the best-selling autobiography *A Reporter's Life* (1996), and providing the voice for Benjamin Franklin on the PBS cartoon series *Liberty's Kids* in 2002, among other activities. Cronkite, who was inducted into the Academy of Television Arts & Sciences Hall of Fame in 1985, died from complications of dementia at his New York City home. His wife of 64 years, Mary Elizabeth, predeceased him in 2005. (During his final years the former opera singer Joanna Simon was his close companion.) Cronkite is survived by two daughters, Nancy Elizabeth and Mary Kathleen; a son, Walter Leland III, known as Chip; and four grandchildren. —M.A.S.

Obituary *New York Times* A p1+ July 18, 2009

CUNNINGHAM, MERCE Apr.16, 1919–July 26, 2009 Dancer; choreographer. Merce Cunningham was among the most influential figures in the dance world. He challenged many of the conventions of classical dance during his decades-long career; perhaps most notably he severed the assumed link between a dance piece and its musical accompaniment. With his numerous collaborators, including his longtime companion, the composer John Cage, Cunningham helped create performance pieces whose dance steps and music were independent of one another. In an effort to avoid dance clichés, Cunningham often used chance to determine the direction his dances would take. Influenced by such sources as zoology, anthropology, and Zen Buddhism, Cunningham created unconventional works that, though derided by some critics as self-indulgent, were eventually celebrated as beacons of a new form of classical dance. Cunningham was born in Centralia, Washington, the third of four children of Clifford Cunningham, a lawyer, and the former Mayme Joach. One of his brothers died in infancy, and his two other brothers followed in their father's footsteps, becoming lawyers. As a youth in Centralia, he studied piano and took dance classes from an eccentric former vaudeville performer. He attended George Washington University, in Washington, D.C., dropping out after a few months to enroll at the renowned Cornish School, an arts institution in Seattle, Washington. There, he pursued theater before switching his focus to modern dance, studying with the respected dance teacher Bonnie Bird. In 1938 Cunningham joined the Lester Horton Dance Theater and spent a summer at the Bennington School of Arts at Bennington College, in Vermont, where his talent was recognized by Martha Graham, a modern-dance pioneer, who invited him to join her company in New York City. Cunningham was a member of Graham's company from 1940 to 1945; he was only the second male to join the company. He appeared in the premieres of many of Graham's works, including *El Penitente* (1940), *Letter to the World* (1941), and *Appalachian Spring* (1944). Cunningham also studied intermittently at the School of American Ballet, where he later taught a weekly class. He began to present his own choreography in 1942. His early dances included *The Wind Remains* (1943), *Root of an Unfocus* (1944), and *Four Walls* (1944). His 1945 solo piece, *Mysterious Adventure*, introduced an element that would become a fixture of modern dance: the cessation of movement altogether. During that decade Cunningham met and began collaborating with Cage, who had recently moved to New York with his wife, Xenia (whom he eventually left for Cunningham). In 1947, inspired by the cyclical, disjointed structure of James Joyce's novel *Finnegan's Wake*, Cunningham worked with Cage to create *The Seasons*, a piece that lacked narrative altogether. Cunningham used "choreography by chance" for the first time in the pieces *Sixteen Dances for Soloist and Company of Three* (1951) and *Suite by Chance* (1952). (He sketched isolated body movements on pieces of paper, which he then shuffled in a random order to create the dance.) Cunningham founded his eponymous dance company in 1953 at Black Mountain College, in Asheville, North Carolina. There, he met the artist Robert Rauschenberg, who began working with Cunningham and Cage, designing sets for the dance performances on which they collaborated. While critics had harsh words for *Aeon* (1961) and *Winterbranch* (1964), both of which featured amplified, electronically produced abrasive noises composed by Cage, Cunningham achieved worldwide fame following an international tour in 1964. In later years Cunningham collaborated with such artists as Roy Lichtenstein, Bruce Nauman, Andy Warhol, and Jasper Johns. During the 1970s he produced several pieces that referred to places in his native Washington, including *Borst Park* (1972), *Solo* (1975), *Inlets* (1977), and *Inlets 2* (1983). Though he was noticeably aging, Cunningham performed in every one of his pieces up until 1989. Thereafter, he choreographed dances on his computer, creating such works as *Trackers* (1992) and *Biped* (1999). In 1999, at the age of 80, he danced a duet with Mikhail Baryshnikov at the New York State Theater at Lincoln Center. Following a performance of Cunningham's most recent piece, *Nearly Ninety* (2009), with music by the bassist John Paul Jones, the experimental composer Takehisa Kosugi, and the rock group Sonic Youth, which was performed at the Brooklyn Academy of Music, he appeared on stage in a wheelchair. Cunningham taught dance up until the time of his death, which occurred at his home in Manhattan. Cage, Cunningham's longtime romantic partner, had predeceased him in 1992. According to his *New York Times* obituary, Cunningham remarked to a friend that he was still creating dances in his head even as his health deteriorated. See *Current Biography* (1966). — M.E.R.

Obituary *New York Times* (on-line) July 27, 2009

DALY, CHUCK July 20, 1930–May 9, 2009 Basketball coach. Chuck Daly will be remembered in sports circles as the coach who led the Detroit Pistons to two consecutive National Basketball Association (NBA) championships, in 1989 and 1990, and as the coach of the formidable 1992 Olympic "Dream Team," which won the gold medal at the Games that year. "Daly was renowned for his ability to create harmony out of diverse personalities at all levels of the game, whether they were Ivy Leaguers at Pennsylvania, Dream Teamers Michael Jordan and [Charles] Barkley, or Pistons as dissimilar as Dennis Rodman and Joe Dumars," an Associated Press reporter wrote for the ESPN Web site. Daly was the first coach in basketball history to win both NBA and Olympic titles, and in 1994 he was inducted into the Basketball Hall of Fame. Two years later he was named one of the 10 greatest coaches in the first 50 years of the NBA, which had been founded in 1946. Charles Joseph Daly was born during the Great Depression in St. Mary's, Pennsylvania, but grew up in the hardscrabble western Pennsylvania town of Kane, some 90 miles from Pittsburgh. The two men who most influenced him when he was growing up were his father, Earl, and his Kane High School basketball coach, C. Stuart Edwards. Daly received a basketball scholarship to St. Bonaventure University, in New York State, but later transferred to Bloomsburg State College, a small school in Pennsylvania (now Bloomsburg State University). He graduated in 1953 and served for two years in the U.S. Army before becoming the basketball coach at Punxsutawney High, in Pennsylvania. In 1963 he moved up to college-level coaching when he began to work under Vic Bubas, the coach of the Duke University Blue Devils. In 1969 Daly was named the head coach at Boston College, and in 1971 he left for the Ivy League, to coach the University of Pennsylvania Quakers. The Quakers flourished under Daly, winning four consecutive titles during his six seasons at the school. Daly began to work in the NBA in 1978, as an assistant coach with the Philadelphia 76ers. He was head coach of the Cleveland Cavaliers for part of the 1980-81 season, and in 1983 he began to coach the Detroit Pistons, a team that had never had back-to-back winning seasons. Daly led the team's members—nicknamed the "Bad Boys" for their aggressive style of play and off-court antics—to the play-offs in each of the nine years he was coach, and they won two consecutive championships, in 1989 and 1990. "The Detroit Pistons made plenty of enemies while winning titles and throwing blows," the Associated Press reporter wrote. "Chuck Daly, though, was universally admired for his class and coaching acumen." Daly, who was also widely recognized for his elegant fashion sense and expensively tailored suits, left the Pistons after the 1991–92 season, and in 1992 he coached the U.S. Olympic Dream Team—which included such legendary players as Jordan, Barkley, Magic Johnson, and Larry Bird—to a gold-medal victory in Barcelona. From 1992 to 1994 Daly coached the New Jersey Nets, taking the team to the play-offs each season. After leaving the Nets Daly worked as a sports broadcaster, but in 1997 he left the booth to coach the Orlando Magic for two seasons. (That year the Pistons retired No. 2 to honor their former coach.) In March 2009 the Pistons announced that Daly was being treated for pancreatic cancer. He died at his home in Jupiter, Florida. He is survived by his wife, Terry, and his daughter, Cydney. See *Current Biography* (1991). — W.D.

Obituary *New York Times* (on-line) May 10, 2009

DAUSSET, JEAN Oct. 19, 1916–June 6, 2009 French medical scientist. Jean Dausset's scientific discoveries have allowed doctors to more effectively match compatible organ donors and recipients, thus considerably improving the overall success rate of transplant surgeries. Born in Toulouse, France, Dausset spent his early childhood in the luxurious resort town of Biarritz. His parents, Henri Pierre Jules Dausset, a pioneering rheumatologist, and the former Elisabeth Brullard, moved the family to Paris when Dausset was 11 years old. There he attended the Lycee Michelet, earning his undergraduate degree in mathematics. Wanting to emulate his father, he enrolled in medical school at the University of Paris in the late 1930s. His studies were interrupted in 1939, when he was drafted into the French medical corps. Upon returning to occupied France the following year, Dausset gave his identification papers to a Jewish friend, to help him avoid Nazi persecution, and then traveled to North Africa, where he joined the Forces Francaises Libres, which were continuing to fight, despite France's official surrender. While serving in Tunisia, Dausset performed blood transfusions on wounded servicemen and soon developed an interest in transfusion reactions. He went on to participate in the liberation of France in 1944 before being discharged from the military the following year as a second lieutenant. Dausset then received his medical degree from the University of Paris, and in 1946 he was appointed director of laboratories at the French National Blood Transfusion Center, a post he held until 1963. In 1948 Dausset was granted a leave from the center when he won a one-year fellowship in hematology to Harvard University. Over the next several decades, Dausset's experiments led to numerous breakthrough discoveries about the human immune system. Perhaps his most notable achievement was demonstrating that a person's immune response is determined by molecules on the surface of cells called human leukocyte antigens (HLA). The identification of those disease-fighting antigens eventually helped establish the system of tissue-compatibility typing between donors and recipients that revolutionized organ transplants. In 1980 Dausset and two of his fellow researchers, the American geneticist George Davis Snell and the American-Venezuelan immunologist Baruj Benacerraf, shared the Nobel Prize in Physiology or Medicine for their work. In 1984 Dausset established the Centre d'Etude du Polymorphisme Humain (CEPH or Human Polymorphism Study Centre), a genetic research laboratory in Paris that was responsible for creating the first comprehensive physical map of the human genome. In 1993 it became the Foundation Jean Dausset–CEPH. Dausset retired as president of the foundation in 2003. In addition to his tenure as head of the French National Transfusion Center, Dausset held a number of other prominent posts, including chief biologist for the Paris General Hospital System and director of research at the French National Institute of Health and Medical Research. He also chaired the immunology department at the University of Paris, where he taught for several years, and was a professor of experimental medicine at the College de France. A champion of human rights, Dausset served as chair of the Universal Movement of the Scientific Responsibility (MURS) for nearly 20 years and was a pivotal figure in the creation of the International Bioethics Committee. Dausset, who authored more than 400 scientific papers and several books, died of natural causes in Mallorca, Spain, where he had lived for the last two years of his life. He is survived by his wife, Rosita; his son, Henri; and his daughter, Irene. See *Current Biography* (1981). — C.C.

Obituary *New York Times* (on-line) June 23, 2009

DEARIE, BLOSSOM Apr. 28, 1924–Feb. 7, 2009 Musician. For more than half a century, Blossom Dearie, an acclaimed singer/songwriter and pianist, captivated audiences worldwide with her distinctive sound and voice. "Ms. Dearie pursued a singular career that blurred the line between jazz and cabaret," Stephen Holden noted in Dearie's *New York Times* obituary (February 9, 2009). He continued: "An interpretive minimalist with caviar taste in songs and musicians, she was a genre unto herself. Rarely raising her sly, kittenish voice, Ms. Dearie confided song lyrics in a playful style below whose surface layers of insinuation lurked." Blossom Margrete Dearie was born to a Scandinavian mother and an Irish-Scottish father in East Durham, in upstate New York. At age five she started learning to play the piano, and as a 10-year-old she was introduced to the works of classical composers Frédéric Chopin and Johann Sebastian Bach. She fell in love with jazz soon after joining her high-school band. Upon completing high school in the mid-1940s, Dearie moved to New York City to pursue a music career. She quickly became acquainted with several emerging jazz musicians, including Charlie Parker, Miles Davis, and Gerry Mulligan, while attending weekly gatherings at the Manhattan apartment of jazz pianist and composer Gil Evans. During the latter part of the decade, Dearie started singing with two vocal groups: the Blue Flames, part of conductor Woody Herman's band, and the Blue Reys, part of bandleader Alvino Rey's Blue Reys group. Dearie also performed solo at several New York City jazz venues, including the Chantilly Club. In 1952 Dearie moved from New York City to Paris, France, at the suggestion of one of the owners of the French-based label Barclay Records. There she founded the Blue Stars, a four-man, four-woman vocal group, whose 1954 recording of a French version of the George Shearing jazz standard *Lullaby of Birdland* was a hit in France and the U.S. Dearie also collaborated with singer Annie Ross as well as saxophonist Bobby Jaspar, her husband, whom she later divorced. During the mid-1950s Dearie met Norman Granz, the founder of the Verve record label, who signed her to a six-record deal. From 1956 to 1960 Dearie released the solo albums *Blossom Dearie* (1956), *Give Him the Ooh-La-La* (1957), *Once Upon a Summertime* (1958), *Blossom Dearie Sings Comden and Green* (1959), *My Gentleman Friend* (1959), and *Soubrette Sings Broadway Hit Songs* (1960)—her first record with orchestral arrangements. In the early 1960s Dearie recorded a radio commercial for a root beer brand; the ad grew so popular that it spawned the album *Blossom Dearie Sings Rootin' Songs* (1963), released on DIW Records. Next came *May I Come In?* (1964), a collection of pop songs that Dearie recorded for Capitol Records. In the late 1960s she traveled to London to record a group of albums for the Fontana Records label, including her first live album, *Blossom Time at Ronnie Scott's* (1966), and *Sweet Blossom Dearie* (1967). During the 1970s she performed at Carnegie Hall as part of a group called the Jazz Singers, which also featured Anita O'Day and Joe Williams. In 1974, as executives from major record labels began to lose interest in her particular style of music, Dearie decided to launch her own label, Daffodil Records. Over the next quarter-century she recorded several albums for her label, including *Blossom Dearie Sings* (1974), *My New Celebrity Is You* (1976), *Winchester in Apple Blossom Time* (1977), the live disc *Needlepoint Magic* (1979), *Positively* (1983), *Chez Wahlberg: Part One* (1985), and two collaborative discs with Mike Renzi (both 1991 releases)—*Tweedledum & Tweedledee (Two People Who Resemble Each Other, in this Case Musically)* and *Christmas Spice So Very Nice*. Other Daffodil recordings included the compilation albums *Our Favorite Songs* (1996) and *I'm Hip* (1998) as well as *Blossom's Planet* (2000). In 2003 Dearie recorded the song "It's All Right to Be Afraid," which she dedicated to the victims of 9/11. Beginning in the 1980s Dearie earned a loyal following among jazz enthusiasts with her live performances at several Manhattan clubs. Health issues forced her to retire in 2006. Dearie, who died of natural causes in her Greenwich Village apartment, is survived by her older brother, nephew, and niece. See *Current Biography* (1989). — W.D.

Obituary *New York Times* (on-line) Feb. 9, 2009

DECARAVA, ROY Dec. 9, 1919–Oct. 27, 2009 Photographer. Roy DeCarava, who grew up during the culturally rich period known as the Harlem Renaissance, was one of the most important and influential photographers of his day. Born in the historically black New York City neighborhood of Harlem, DeCarava was raised by his single mother, Elfreda, a Jamaican immigrant and amateur photographer who supplied her son with drawing materials and music lessons as he was growing up. One of only two black students at a public high school devoted to textile arts, DeCarava graduated in 1938 and won a scholarship to attend the Cooper Union, an arts and engineering school in Manhattan. Facing hostility from white students, he stayed at the school for only two years before entering the now-renowned Harlem Community Art Center, where he came into contact with a number of African-American cultural figures, including the writer Langston Hughes. DeCarava was hired to paint signs for the Work Projects Administration, a federally funded program created by New Deal legislation, and in 1943, during World War II, he served as a topographical draftsman in the U.S. Army. When he returned to New York City, he began to work as a commercial painter and silkscreen artist. DeCarava discovered his preferred medium after purchasing a handheld 35-mm camera to document images he wanted to paint and then made the life-changing decision to concentrate solely on photography. In 1950 DeCarava came to the attention of Edward Steichen, then the curator of photography at the Museum of Modern Art (MoMA), in New York City. Steichen purchased a few prints and advised DeCarava to apply for a Guggenheim Fellowship. DeCarava, who in 1952 became the first black photographer to win that prestigious fellowship, used money from it to shoot full-time in Harlem. The year 1955 was a watershed one for the photographer. Steichen used some of his pictures in the landmark Family of Man exhibit at MoMA, and he published *The Sweet Flypaper of Life*, a collection of photos—intimate, revealing snapshots of families at home and of life on the streets of Harlem—accompanied by Hughes's prose poetry. DeCarava began to win photojournalism assignments from such well-regarded magazines as *Fortune, Newsweek*, and *Time*. During the late 1950s and early 1960s, he photographed a number of legendary jazz musicians—among them Louis Armstrong, John Coltrane, Billie Holiday, Miles Davis, Duke Ellington, and Count Basie—in nightclubs around the city. Among the most celebrated works of his career, the jazz photos were lit only by the meager light available in the clubs, resulting in a distinctive look that reflected the emotional intensity of the music. During the civil rights movement of the 1960s, DeCarava photographed several marches and protests, including the famed 1963 March on Washington, and he later helped lead a protest against *Life* magazine, demanding that it hire more black photographers. In 1968 DeCarava became a contract photographer at *Sports Illustrated*, where he remained for 10 years. (He later referred to that period of relative commercial success as an irrelevant part of his career.) In 1969 the Studio Museum in Harlem hosted his first major solo exhibition. In 1975 DeCarava became an associate professor of photography at Hunter College, part of the City University of New York (CUNY) system, and three years later he was named a full professor. The organization Friends of Photography published a monograph in 1981 titled *Roy DeCarava: Photographs*, and an exhibition of his work with jazz musicians was held at the Studio Museum in Harlem in 1983. In 1996 DeCarava was honored at MoMA with a major, 200-print retrospective, which then traveled to other venues across the country. In 2006 DeCarava was the recipient of a National Medal of Arts for his body of work, which, as the prize citation stated, "seized the attention of our nation while displaying the dignity and determination of his subjects." DeCarava is survived by his wife, Sherry, an art historian, and three children, Susan, Wendy, and Laura. *See Current Biography* (2008). — D.K.

Obituary *New York Times* (on-line) Oct. 29, 2009

DEVI, GAYATRI, MAHARANI OF JAIPUR May 23, 1919–July 29, 2009 Indian stateswoman. Renowned for her beauty and elegance, Gayatri Devi helped her husband, the Maharajah of Jaipur, rule over a fiefdom in the northwest of India until the nation won its independence from Great Britain in 1947. Although India's princely states were abolished and Jaipur was integrated into the state of Rajasthan in the wake of independence, the maharani remained a popular figure, and she served as an elected member of the Parliament of India from 1962 to 1975. The fourth child of the Maharajah and Maharani of Cooch Behar, Gayatri Devi (known to her family and friends as Ayesha) was born in London, England. As described in her autobiography, *A Princess Remembers: The Memoirs of the Maharani of Jaipur* (1977), her childhood, spent on British estates and in Indian palaces, was one of fairy-tale luxury. In one telling segment of the book, she related that the family's pet turtles had emerald-encrusted shells. Devi, educated during her early years by governesses and tutors, attended Shantiniketan, the university established by the poet Tagore, in Bolpur, India. In 1936 she graduated from Shantiniketan and went abroad to complete her education at Brilliamount, a finishing school in Lausanne, Switzerland, and at the London College of Secretaries. On May 9, 1940 she married Sir Sawai Man Singh Bahadur, the Maharajah of Jaipur. Unlike the maharajah's first two wives, the new maharani refused to be subject to *purdah*, the practice in which women are shielded from public view. She served as hostess for numerous visiting dignitaries, including Queen Elizabeth II, First Lady Jacqueline Kennedy, and Franklin and Eleanor Roosevelt. Devi also traveled abroad frequently with her husband, accompanying him to polo tournaments and elite vacation resorts. She attracted attention in international high society for her exotic beauty and fashion sense. (Photographs of Devi donning her trademark strand of pearls and chiffon saris often appeared in high-profile magazines.) Devi had more serious interests as well and became known as a strong advocate of education for women. In 1943 she founded the Maharani Gayatri Devi Girls Public School. After India gained independence from Great Britain, in 1947, the city of Jaipur was designated the capital of the new state of Rajasthan. While the Maharajah of Jaipur served as the state's ceremonial head until 1956, the year the post was abolished, he and his wife lost their sovereignty, tax revenues, and several of their palaces. The couple received a stipend from the Indian government and supplemented that income by converting one of their remaining palaces into a luxury hotel. Devi, now unable to address the concerns of her former subjects, turned to politics, joining the right-wing Swatantra (Freedom) Party in 1961. She successfully ran for a seat in the *Lok Sabha*, the lower chamber of the Indian Parliament. She moved to Spain in 1965, when her husband was named an ambassador to that country, although she returned to India for parliamentary sessions. The couple also remained fixtures on the international polo circuit until 1970, when the former Maharajah collapsed and died while playing in a match. In 1975, after Prime Minister Indira Gandhi declared a state of emergency, Devi was among the many political opponents of the ruling Congress Party who were arrested, and she spent five months in prison. After her release she did not return to politics and lived instead in relative seclusion. During the late 1990s the Cooch Behar District Trinamul Congress nominated her as their candidate for the *Lok Sabha*, but she ultimately refused the nomination. Devi died at the Santokba Durlabhji Memorial Hospital in Jaipur, where she was being treated for respiratory and stomach problems. She is survived by two grandchildren, Devraj and Lalitya. (She and the maharajah had one son, Jagat, who died in 1997.) The Indian government abolished all princely titles in the early 1970s, and at the time of her death, the former maharani was known by the title of rajmata, which has been likened to the British title of queen mother. See *Current Biography* (1968). — D.K.

Obituary *New York Times* (on-line) July 31, 2009

DONALD, DAVID HERBERT Oct. 1, 1920–May 17, 2009 Historian; writer; educator. David Herbert Donald wrote several important books on Abraham Lincoln's life and presidency, the Civil War, and other historical topics. *Charles Sumner and the Coming of the Civil War* (1960), the first volume in his comprehensive biography of the abolitionist and statesman, and *Look Homeward: A Life of Thomas Wolfe* (1987), about the famed novelist, each won him a Pulitzer Prize. Donald was born in Goodman, Mississippi, to Ira Unger Donald, a farmer, and Sue Ella (Belford) Donald, a teacher. He had three brothers and two sisters. After graduating from high school in 1937 and from a local junior college in 1939, Donald finished his undergraduate work at Millsaps College, in Jackson, Mississippi, earning his bachelor's degree in history in 1941. He then entered the University of Illinois, where he studied under the Civil War scholar James G. Randall. Donald received a master's degree in 1942 and a doctoral degree in 1946. The following year he joined the faculty of Columbia University, and he later became a history professor at Princeton University. In 1973 he was named the Charles Warren Professor of American History at Harvard University, where he remained until his retirement from teaching in 1991. Donald's first book (and his doctoral thesis), *Lincoln's Herndon* (1948), was a biography of William Henry Herndon, Lincoln's friend and law partner. Critics noted the book's combination of scholarship and readability, praise that was regularly repeated in reviews of his subsequent work. In addition to the aforementioned Pulitzer Prize–winning volumes, that later work included *Inside Lincoln's Cabinet: The Civil War Diaries of Salmon P. Chase* (1954), a skillfully edited edition of the diaries of Lincoln's secretary of the treasury; *Lincoln Reconsidered: Essays on the Civil War Era* (1956), a volume widely considered seminal; *Why the North Won the Civil War* (1960); *The Politics of Reconstruction, 1863–1867* (1965), which reexamined the political dynamics of that period through a modern lens; *Charles Sumner and the Rights of Man* (1970), the second volume of his Sumner biography; and *Liberty and Union* (1978), a Civil War textbook. He also contributed to *The Great Republic: A History of the American People* (1977), a college text written by a group of prominent historians. (The others were Bernard Bailyn, Gordon Wood, David Brion Davis, Robert Wiebe, and John L. Thomas). In 1995 Donald published *Lincoln* (1995), which was praised by historians and critics as a masterful and insightful work. He followed that triumph with two more well-received volumes: *Lincoln at Home: Two Glimpses of Abraham Lincoln's Domestic Life* (1999) and *We Are Lincoln Men: Abraham Lincoln and His Friends* (2003). Donald frequently appeared on television documentaries and scholarly talk shows, and over the course of his career, he was occasionally invited to the White House to chat about his area of expertise. He lived, as journalists were quick to note, on Lincoln Road, in Lincoln, Massachusetts. At the time of his death, Donald was reportedly working on a biography of John Quincy Adams. He is survived by his wife, Aida, a fellow historian, and his son, Bruce. Since 2005 the Abraham Lincoln Presidential Library and Museum in Springfield, Illinois, has awarded the David Herbert Donald Prize for excellence in Lincoln studies. See *Current Biography* (1961). — D.K.

Obituary *New York Times* (on-line) May 19, 2009

DUNNE, DOMINICK Oct. 29, 1925–Aug. 26, 2009 Writer. Dominick Dunne, a former Hollywood producer and best-selling author, was one of the foremost chroniclers of crime and high society during the latter part of the 20th century. Born in Hartford, Connecticut, he was the second of six children in a well-to-do, Irish-Catholic family. One of his siblings was the writer John Gregory Dunne. Though Dunne enjoyed a privileged upbringing, he grew up feeling like an outsider in the predominantly Protestant circles in which he was raised. He also endured physical abuse from his father, Richard, a renowned heart surgeon, who mocked Dunne's lack of athleticism and disapproved of his artistic predilections; his father's displeasure sometimes escalated into beatings with a wooden coat hanger. Dunne attended Williams College, in Massachusetts. He took a hiatus from his studies to serve in the U.S. Army during World War II, winning some approval from his father after being awarded a Bronze Star for saving a wounded soldier at the Battle of the Bulge. After his military service was completed, Dunne resumed his studies at Williams College. Upon graduating in 1949, he moved to New York City, where he became a stage manager for television shows and later an assistant to the producer of *Playhouse 90.* In 1957 Dunne moved across the country, settling in Beverly Hills, California, where he became a producer at 20th Century Fox. He went on to produce several successful independent films, including *The Boys in the Band* (1970), *Panic in Needle Park* (1971), and *Play It As It Lays* (1972). After producing the widely panned feature film *Ash Wednesday* (1973), which starred Elizabeth Taylor, Dunne was forced back into unsatisfying television work. He began abusing drugs and alcohol and soon found it difficult to get any work at all. In 1979 Dunne left Los Angeles and moved to rural Oregon, where he overcame his addictions and began to write for the first time. In 1981 he returned to New York City to become a full-time writer. The following year he published his first novel, *The Winners*, which revolves around a group of decadent Hollywood insiders. Though the book was widely panned, Dunne was encouraged to continue writing by Michael Korda, then his editor. In 1982 Dunne's daughter, Dominique, an actress who had appeared in the hit horror film *Poltergeist*, was strangled to death by an ex-boyfriend, John Sweeney. Sweeney was convicted only of voluntary manslaughter, rather than murder, and was released from prison in 1986. In the wake of the murder, Dunne became dedicated to writing about the intersection of crime and wealth. He wrote an article about Sweeney's trial, "Justice: A Father's Account of the Trial of His Daughter's Killer," which was published in *Vanity Fair* in 1984. Dunne eventually rose to national prominence with his best-selling novels *The Two Mrs. Grenvilles* (1985) and *An Inconvenient Woman* (1990), both of which deal with murders in the upper strata of society. Dunne achieved success as a journalist as well, and he spent most of his later years writing about high-profile criminal trials for *Vanity Fair.* Among the notorious cases he covered for the publication were those of Claus von Bulow, William Kennedy Smith, the Menendez brothers, and Phil Spector. He was perhaps most noted for his around-the-clock coverage of the O.J. Simpson murder trial in 1994 and 1995, which ultimately led to his novel-cum-memoir about the case, *Another City, Not My Own* (1997). He subsequently served as the host of the television series *Dominick Dunne's Power, Privilege, and Justice*, which aired on Court TV (now known as truTV). A documentary of his life, *Dominick Dunne: After the Party*, premiered in 2008. Dunne, who authored several other best-selling novels and the memoir *The Way We Lived Then: Recollections of a Well-Known Name Dropper* (1999), died of bladder cancer at his home in Manhattan. He is survived by his sons, Griffin (an actor and director) and Alexander, as well as a granddaughter, Hannah. Ellen Griffin Dunne, to whom he was married from 1954 to 1965, died of bone cancer in 1997, and despite their divorce, he remained devoted to her until her death. Dunne's last book, *Too Much Money: A Novel*, was scheduled for publication in December 2009. See *Current Biography* (1999). — C.C.

Obituary *New York Times* (on-line) Aug. 27, 2009

ENDARA, GUILLERMO May 12, 1936–Sep. 28, 2009 Panamanian statesman. As the president of Panama from 1989 to 1994, Guillermo Endara is credited with leading the nation back to democracy after more than two decades of military rule. His ascent to power was not a smooth one, however. Although Endara had scored a decisive victory in the nation's May 1989 election, General Manuel Antonio Noriega, who had served as Panama's de facto leader throughout the 1980s, nullified the results and installed his own president. In December the U.S. invaded Panama to remove Noriega, and Endara was sworn in. Guillermo Endara Galimany was born in Panama City and attended schools in Argentina as well as a now-defunct military academy in Los Angeles. He graduated at the head of his law-school class at the University of Panama and studied briefly at New York University. Endara returned to Panama in 1963 and co-founded the law firm Solis, Endara, Delgado, and Guevara, where he specialized in labor law. A supporter of Arnulfo Arias Madrid, who had been president of Panama from 1940 to 1941 and from 1949 to 1951, Endara served two terms in the National Assembly under the Arias-led opposition. When Arias was voted into the presidency for the third time, in October 1968, Endara was named director general of planning and economic policy. He had served in the post for just 11 days when a military coup ousted Arias and his administration. Endara went into hiding but was captured and jailed briefly in 1971. He fled into exile but returned to help Arias rebuild his party after the ban on political activity was lifted. In 1989 Endara entered the presidential race against Carlos Duque, Noriega's hand-picked candidate. (Duque was the director of a reportedly shady military-owned company, and his running mate, Ramon Sieiro, was Noriega's brother-in-law.) After Noriega refused to recognize the results of the election, Endara organized a street protest in Panama City. During the demonstration Noriega-controlled military squads struck Endara over the head with a steel pipe, lacerating his scalp and causing a minor concussion. The incident did little to discourage Endara, who urged Panamanians to suspend payment of taxes and utility bills and launched a two-week hunger strike in September. Three months later the U.S. invaded Panama to oust Noriega. (The military dictator had been indicted in American courts for drug trafficking and had declared war on the U.S.) Although Endara had mixed feelings about U.S. intervention, he accepted the presidency. "It would have been easy for me to say, 'I'm not going to take this job under occupation by American forces.' But I knew that I couldn't do that. I had to assume the responsibility of government—the people chose me to be president," he explained to David E. Pitt for the *New York Times* (January 28, 1990). "I certainly knew that Latin Americans weren't going to be very fond of me. But morally, patriotically, civically, I had no other choice." During his presidency, Endara promoted freedom of speech, established a civilian-led police force, and instituted economic policies that resulted in an average annual economic growth rate of 8 percent. He lost the 1994 election to Ernesto Perez Balladares and made two more unsuccessful bids for the presidency. Endara, who suffered from diabetes and kidney ailments, died in his Panama City home. He was predeceased by his first wife, Marcela, and is survived by their daughter, Marcelita, and his second wife, Ana Mae Diaz. See *Current Biography* (1991). — M.A.S.

Obituary *New York Times* A p29 Sep. 30, 2009

FAWCETT, FARRAH Feb. 2, 1947–June 25, 2009 Actress. Farrah Fawcett became a symbol of 1970s America and an icon of wholesome American sexiness, openness, and fun the world over, thanks to her starring role in the TV series *Charlie's Angels*, which debuted in 1975, and a best-selling poster of her; in it, she is seen wearing a red bathing suit, her signature dazzling smile, and a hairdo later copied by millions of women. Born and raised in Corpus Christi, Texas, Fawcett worked as a model while enrolled at the University of Texas. She dropped out of college after her junior year and moved to Los Angeles, where she attracted notice as the "face" of various commercial promotions and ads. Her career took off after she met the actor Lee Majors, whom she married in 1973. The immediate success of *Charlie's Angels*, which aired on ABC, led to the so-called Farrah phenomenon, which saw voluminous fan mail sent to ABC, booming sales of Fawcett's bathing-suit poster, and articles about *Charlie's Angels* in *Time*, *People*, and scores of other magazines that placed Fawcett's image on their covers. After *Charlie's Angels'* first year, Fawcett left the show in a largely vain effort to build a film career. Nevertheless, she earned an Emmy Award nomination for her work in the made-for-TV movie *The Burning Bed* (1984) and a Golden Globe Award nomination for her role in the feature film *Extremities* (1986), and she won critical acclaim for her performances in the 1989 TV movies *Small Sacrifices* and *Margaret Bourke-White*. Her reputation suffered a severe blow when, in 1997, in conjunction with the making of a video for *Playboy* called *Farrah Fawcett: All of Me*, for which she had posed nude, she made a guest appearance on *The Late Show with David Letterman* and "came across dazed, confused, . . . and pretty much out of it," Ed Robertson wrote for *Media Life* (April 13, 2005, online). Her attempt to make a comeback by means of a "pseudo-reality" TV series, *Chasing Farrah* (2005), was unsuccessful. Fawcett's final movie, *Farrah's Story*, which documented her losing battle with cancer, aired on TV in May 2009 and generated a huge amount of media attention. Fawcett's survivors include Majors, from whom she was divorced in 1982, after becoming romantically involved with the actor Ryan O'Neal. Fawcett and O'Neal's tumultuous relationship continued until her death and produced one son, Redmond. See *Current Biography* (1978). — M.H.

Obituary *New York Times* A p21 June 26, 2009

FELT, W. MARK Aug. 17, 1913–Dec. 18, 2008 Government official. W. Mark Felt received national attention in 2005 when he revealed that he was the man known as Deep Throat, the mysterious informant who had helped *Washington Post* reporters Bob Woodward and Carl Bernstein shed light on President Richard M. Nixon's involvement in the Watergate scandal during the early 1970s. William Mark Felt was born in Twin Falls, Idaho, and attended the University of Idaho in Moscow. Upon graduating in 1935, he moved to Washington, D.C., to work for Democratic senator James P. Pope. Felt attended George Washington University Law School in the evenings and earned his J.D. degree in 1940. He was admitted to the D.C. bar the following year. After a brief stint at the Federal Trade Commission (FTC), Felt joined the Federal Bureau of Investigation in early 1942. He did field work in Texas for six months before being assigned to the agency's Espionage Section, where he spent much of World War II locating Nazi spies. After the war Felt was assigned to field offices in Seattle, New Orleans, and Los Angeles and then continued to climb the FBI ladder as a special agent in Salt Lake City and Kansas City. In 1962 Felt returned to FBI headquarters in Washington, D.C., to become one of the top officials at the agency's Training Division. Two years later he was promoted to chief of the Inspection Division. Reporting directly to FBI director J. Edgar Hoover, Felt oversaw internal compliance with the bureau's regulations and was responsible for conducting internal investigations. In 1971 he was named deputy associate director, the number-three position at bureau headquarters, under Hoover's second-in-command, Clive A. Tolson. Due to declining health on the part of both Hoover and Tolson, Felt was often left to carry out their daily duties. Hoover died in 1972, and, much to the ire of Felt, President Nixon appointed longtime supporter L. Patrick Gray to the director's post. Tolson resigned shortly thereafter, and Felt took over his duties as associate director. On June 17, 1972 five men were arrested when they attempted to break into the office of the Democratic National Committee at the Watergate complex in Washington, D.C. Despite attempts by Gray and the White House to thwart him, Felt, who suspected that White House officials had been involved in the incident, conducted an investigation into the case. Contacted by Bob Woodward, Felt agreed to provide the reporter with information on the condition that his identity not be revealed. Afraid their telephone conversations could be bugged, the two set up a system for contacting each other. Woodward moved a flowerpot on his apartment balcony to signal that he needed to meet with Felt; if Felt needed a meeting, he would draw a clock on page 20 of Woodward's home-delivered copy of the *New York Times*. Their meetings took place late at night in an underground parking garage in Arlington, Virginia. (The *Post*'s managing editor, Howard Simons, coined the famous pseudonym Deep Throat, inspired by the name of a well-known pornographic movie of the era.) Providing information directly from the FBI, Felt helped the *Post* reporters prove such abuses by the Nixon White House as illegal wiretapping, burglary, and money laundering. In June 1973 Felt retired from the FBI, and the following year Nixon, facing federal charges, resigned. In 1974 Woodward and Bernstein published the best-selling book *All the President's Men*, making Deep Throat a source of intense public fascination, which only increased when the movie version was released in 1976. (The informant was played by the popular actor Hal Holbrook.) For decades Felt, who in 1979 published a little-noticed autobiography, *The FBI Pyramid*, vehemently denied any suggestion that he had been Deep Throat. In 2005, however, after much prodding from family members, he allowed his identity to be revealed, with the publication of an article in *Vanity Fair*. Felt died of heart failure at his home in Santa Rosa, California. He was predeceased by his wife, Audrey Robinson, and is survived by a daughter and son. See *Current Biography* (2005). — M.A.S.

Obituary *New York Times* B p11 Dec. 19, 2008

FIDRYCH, MARK Aug. 14, 1954–Apr. 13, 2009 Baseball player. Mark Fidrych (pronounced FID-rich) burst onto the sports scene in 1976, winning the title of Major League Baseball (MLB) American League (AL) rookie of the year during his first season as a pitcher for the Detroit Tigers. Although his promising career was shortened by injuries, Fidrych became one of the most beloved figures in Tigers history. His gawky, school-boy manner and mop-top head of blond hair earned him the nickname "The Bird," inspired by the character Big Bird on the children's television program *Sesame Street*. Fidrych, who ended his career in 1985 with the Boston Red Sox, was also renowned for such colorful, endearing antics as talking to the ball to "psych himself up," smoothing the mound on his hands and knees between innings, and stomping around the infield to congratulate his teammates after they had recorded outs. Fidrych was born in Worcester, Massachusetts, and grew up in Northborough with his older sister, Paula, and two younger sisters, Carol Ann and Lorie Jean. Although the hyperactive and academically challenged Fidrych was forced to repeat first and second grades, he had a natural talent for sports. Fidrych played baseball, football, and basketball at Algonquin High School before transferring to the private Worcester Academy during his senior year. (Fidrych was not eligible to compete in the public-school system that year since he had already been held back twice.) After graduating from the Worcester Academy in 1974, Fidrych entered that year's MLB draft and was selected in the 10th round by the Detroit Tigers. He spent two seasons playing in the team's minor-league system before making his major-league debut on April 20, 1976. In his first game Fidrych was impressive, pitching seven innings without giving up a hit and leading the team to a 2–1 victory against the Cleveland Indians. Three months later he made headlines during a nationally televised contest against the New York Yankees. Fidrych's strong pitching performance, which propelled the Tigers to a 5–1 victory, prompted a curtain call from the enthusiastic fans. Fidrych returned to the field to take a bow, thereby initiating what became a major-league tradition. By the end of his rookie season, Fidrych, who was voted to the All-Star team, had compiled a win-loss record of 19–9, a major league–leading earned-run average (ERA) of 2.34, and 97 strikeouts. For his effort Fidrych was named the 1976 AL rookie of the year and was the second-place finisher in the voting for the AL Cy Young Award. He was among the league's leaders in several categories, including wins, win percentage (.679), and shutouts (4). His entertaining, charismatic on-the-mound performances made him a national icon; in May 1977 Fidrych, who had landed several endorsement deals, became the first player to grace the cover of *Rolling Stone*, and he was credited with attracting record-breaking crowds to the struggling franchise's home games. At the start of the 1977 season, Fidrych sustained two serious injuries, tearing cartilage in his knee and suffering damage to his rotator cuff, which would go undiagnosed for about eight years. Despite finishing the 1977 season with a 6–4 record and 2.89 ERA as well as his second consecutive All-Star Game appearance, Fidrych was demoted to the Tigers' minor-league system in 1980 and released by the team at the end of the 1981 season. A year later he signed with the Boston Red Sox but failed to make it back to the major leagues. Fidrych's career ended in 1985, after his torn rotator cuff, which had gone untreated for several years, was diagnosed. He retired from baseball with a 29–19 major-league record and a 3.10 ERA. Following his retirement Fidrych moved to Central Massachusetts, where he purchased a dump truck and became a licensed commercial truck driver. He later moved to Northborough, where his family owned a diner. A family friend discovered Fidrych's body beneath a dump truck, where he is presumed to have been working. A police investigation concluded that Fidrych had died accidentally of suffocation, when an article of his clothing got caught on the truck's spinning power-takeoff shaft. Fidrych is survived by his wife, Ann, whom he married in 1986, and his daughter, Jessica. See *Current Biography* (1978). — M.E.R.

Obituary *New York Times* (on-line) Apr. 14, 2009

FOOTE, HORTON Mar. 14, 1916–Mar. 4, 2009 Playwright; screenwriter. Often set in the small fictional town of Harrison, Texas, the works of the renowned American screenwriter and playwright Horton Foote chronicled the struggles of everyday people and have frequently drawn comparisons to the writing of the Russian dramatist Anton Chekhov. "I believe very deeply in the human spirit, and I have a sense of awe about it," Foote told Samuel G. Freedman for the *New York Times Magazine* (February 9, 1986, on-line). "Because I don't know how people carry on. I look around and I say . . . what makes the difference in people? What is it?" Albert Horton Foote Jr. was born to Albert Horton Sr., a haberdasher, and Hallie (Brooks) Foote, a piano teacher, in Wharton, a small town located about 50 miles outside Houston, Texas. At 12 Foote had aspirations to be an actor, and four years later he left home to pursue his dream. Foote had a two-year apprenticeship (1933–35) at the Pasadena Playhouse School of Theatre in California and then spent two years studying at Tamara Daykarhanova's Theatre School (1937–39). In 1939 Foote began appearing in Broadway productions and also co-founded the American Actors Company with famed Broadway producer Jerome Robbins and renowned dancer and choreographer Agnes DeMille, who suggested after hearing some of his childhood stories that he write about his experiences. His first produced play was *Wharton Dance* (1940), about the Friday night dances held in his hometown. He went on to write his first full-length play, *Texas Town*, in 1942. While serving as co-director of the King Smith School in Washington, D.C. (1944–49), Foote launched the school's theater—the first in the area to host integrated audiences. During that time he penned the Broadway production *Only the Heart* (1944), and following his return to New York, in 1950, he wrote several other Broadway productions, including *The Chase* (1952), *The Trip to Bountiful* (1953), and *The Traveling Lady* (1954). Foote also authored numerous one-hour teleplays for various live dramatic series, including *Gulf Playhouse*, *Philco Television Playhouse*, and *Playhouse 90*. He launched a screenwriting career in the mid-1950s, penning the screenplay for the Cornell Wilde film *Storm Fear*. He won his first Academy Award for the screenplay of *To Kill a Mockingbird* (1962), adapted from the classic Harper Lee novel. In 1984 Foote collected his second Academy Award for the original screenplay of his own play *Tender Mercies* (1983). (The film version starred Robert Duvall as an alcoholic country singer.) He also penned the screenplays for several other adaptations of his plays, including *Baby the Rain Must Fall* (1965)—an adaptation of *The Traveling Lady*—*The Chase* (1966), and *The Trip to Bountiful* (1985), for which he received an Academy Award nomination. Other notable achievements included winning the Pulitzer Prize for Drama in 1995 for the play *The Young Man from Atlanta*. Two years later he won an Emmy Award in the category of outstanding writing of a miniseries or special, for a 1997 television adaptation of William Faulkner's *Old Man*. For his body of work, Foote was presented with the National Medal of Arts in 2000. He was also honored with the Drama Desk Career Achievement Award in 2006. Foote died in Hartford, Connecticut, following a brief bout with an undisclosed illness. At the time of his death, he was adapting his nine-play *The Orphans' Home Cycle* into a three-part production. The project will debut in the fall of 2009 at the Hartford Stage Company in Connecticut and the Signature Theater in New York City. Foote was predeceased by his wife, Lillian Vallish Foote, and is survived by four children and two grandchildren. See *Current Biography* (1986). —M.A.S.

Obituary *New York Times* (on-line) Mar. 5, 2009

FORREST, VERNON Feb. 12, 1971–July 25, 2009 Boxer. Vernon Forrest, known as "the Viper" for his speed, held three boxing championships, and, in a major upset, defeated the welterweight titleholder "Sugar" Shane Mosley in 2002. The sixth of eight children, Forrest was born in Augusta, Georgia. Like many boys with brothers, he gained experience in fighting at an early age. He began his amateur boxing career when he was just nine years old and competed throughout his teens, compiling an impressive 225–16 record. Forrest won the U.S. junior welterweight national title in 1991 and the junior welterweight world amateur championship a year later. He received a scholarship to Northern Michigan University, in Marquette, where he studied business administration and trained under U.S. National Boxing Team head coach Al Mitchell. Forrest left school before graduating to pursue a spot on the U.S. Olympic Boxing Team, which would compete in the 1992 Olympic Games, in Barcelona, Spain. During the Olympic trials, Forrest fought Mosley in the light-welterweight semifinals, prevailing on points (24–15). Although considered the gold-medal favorite heading into the Olympics, Forrest lost his first-round fight, after suffering a bout of food poisoning the day before. After the Olympics he turned professional and moved to Atlanta, Georgia. In his first professional match, he scored a technical knockout (TKO) against Charles Hawkins, then proceeded to defeat four of his next five opponents by TKO before the end of the second round. Despite his undeniable talent, Forrest was not the kind of explosive or overwhelmingly powerful fighter who excited a lot of interest and demand. He was thus not matched with such big names in his division as Felix Trinidad and Oscar de la Hoya—contests that would have resulted in much greater media attention, televised bouts, and higher pay. While most members of the general public were unaware of Forrest, boxing insiders appreciated his willingness to train hard for his fights and to study his opponents' styles exhaustively before bouts. The six-foot-tall Forrest had a strong right hand and an arm reach of 73 inches, which enabled him to land punches from farther away than shorter opponents, a distinct advantage. Forrest won his first professional title in 1995, becoming the International Boxing Council (IBC) junior welterweight champion. Two years later he captured his second title, winning a unanimous decision in a 12-round match against Ray Oliveira to become the World Boxing Council (WBC) welterweight champion. Forrest relinquished his WBC title, however, so that he could fight Adrian Stone for the North American Boxing Federation welterweight title. (Professional boxing has many different governing bodies; there are rules regarding fighting outside the governing body in which one holds a title.) Forrest defeated Stone by TKO in the 11th round to take the champion's belt. In August 2000 Forrest took on Raul Frank for the International Boxing Federation (IBF) welterweight championship, but the match was stopped after Frank's head began to bleed. The two faced off again in May 2001 at Madison Square Garden, in New York City. This time, Forrest won a unanimous 12-round decision over Frank, becoming the new IBF welterweight champion. Forrest's victory accorded him world-champion status and greater visibility and recognition. In August 2001 he successfully defended his IBF title against Edgar Ruiz in a match that was the main event on the ESPN network's *Friday Night Fights* series. Forrest won in impressive fashion, knocking out Ruiz in the fourth round. Forrest's January 2002 fight at Madison Square Garden against Mosley was the most important of his career up to that time. He gave up his IBF title belt for the chance to fight Mosley for the WBC welterweight title. Despite being undefeated as a professional, just like Mosley, whose professional record was 38–0 at the time, and despite having beaten the other man as an amateur, Forrest, who had a 33–0 record, was a seven-to-one underdog going into the fight. Mosley won the first round of the bout, but in the second—during which the two boxers accidentally knocked heads—Forrest sent Mosley to the canvas twice, marking the first time Mosley had ever been knocked down in a professional fight. Forrest dominated most of the rest of the bout, knocking Mosley down again in the 10th round, before winning a unanimous decision—and the WBC welterweight title—after the 12th and final round. Forrest lost his title in 2003 to Ricardo Mayorga. In 2007 Forrest won the WBC light-middleweight title; he then lost the title to Sergio Mora but regained it in September 2008. In early 2009 Forrest was forced to vacate the WBC title after suffering a rib injury. Along with his girlfriend and her mother, Forrest established Destiny's Child Inc., a Georgia-based organization dedicated to providing housing and assistance to mentally disabled adults. He died after being shot multiple times in the course of an attempted robbery at a gas station in Atlanta. Shortly afterward three men were indicted for the crime. Forrest is survived by his son, Vernon Jr. See *Current Biography* (2002). — D.K.

Obituary *New York Times* July 27, 2009

FOSS, LUKAS Aug. 15, 1922–Feb. 1, 2009 Composer; conductor. Lukas Foss's compositions encompass an eclectic range of musical styles, including neoclassic, avant-garde, minimalist, and electronic. A composer of more than 100 works, including four symphonies and three string quartets as well as several choral, chamber, orchestral, and stage pieces, Foss also carved out a career as the music director and conductor of the Brooklyn Philharmonic and the Milwaukee Symphony. Foss, whose name at birth was Lukas Fuchs, was born in Berlin to Martin Fuchs, a philosophy professor, and Hilda (Schindler) Fuchs, a painter. When he was seven Foss began studying piano and music theory under Julius Goldstein, who introduced him to the music of the renowned classical masters Johann Sebastian Bach, Ludwig van Beethoven, and Wolfgang Mozart, whose compositions later inspired him. In 1933, following Hitler's rise to power, Foss and his family fled to Paris, where Foss attended the Lycee Pasteur and continued his musical training at the Paris Conservatory. Four years later they immigrated to the U.S., and the 15-year-old Foss studied with the conductor Fritz Reiner at the Curtis Institute of Music in Philadelphia. At age 17 Foss made his conducting debut, with the Pittsburgh Symphony, and after graduating from the Curtis Institute in 1940, he pursued further studies with classical music composer Paul Hindemith at Yale University and with conductor Serge Koussevitzky, also the longtime music director for the Boston Symphony. In 1944 Foss composed his first major work, *The Prairie*, a secular cantata inspired by the Carl Sandburg poem of the same name. For that effort, he received the New York Music Critics Circle Award (1944) and subsequently joined the Boston Symphony Orchestra as a pianist. During that period Foss's compositions displayed predominantly neo-classical and American folk elements and also reflected an appreciation for Igor Stravinsky and Bach. Allan Kozinn noted in Foss's *New York Times* obituary (February 2, 2009): "Works like *The Song of Songs* (1946) were dramatic and emotional; his *String Quartet No. 1* (1947) was more chromatic and abstract, and his first mature opera, *The Jumping Frog of Calaveras County* (1949), based on Mark Twain's story, was even folksier than *The Prairie*." After forming his own Improvisation Chamber Ensemble in 1957, Foss, then the head of the composition department at the University of California at Los Angeles, experimented with improvisation, serialism (music that uses a definite order of notes as a thematic basis for a musical composition), and aleatoric or chance music (music in which the composer has allowed chance to play a role either in the work's creation or its performance). Notable works from this period include *Time Cycle* (1960), a vocal and orchestral piece set to texts by W.H. Auden, A.E. Housman, Franz Kafka, and Friedrich Nietzsche, which earned him his second New York Music Critics Circle Award; *Baroque Variations* (1967), in which he deconstructed music by composers Bach, George Frideric Handel, and Domenico Scarlatti; *Paradigm* (1968), which referenced psychedelic rock music through the use of an electric guitar; and Symphony no. 3 (1975), a partly improvised deconstruction of works by Handel, Scarlatti, and Bach. Foss also gained prominence as a conductor. During his various stints with the Buffalo Philharmonic (1963–70), Brooklyn Philharmonic (1971–90), and Milwaukee Symphony (1981–86), Foss led several marathon concerts and was credited with incorporating contemporary compositions into the repertoire. Foss's later compositions were polystylistic, combining various past and present influences and techniques. Foss, who continued to compose well into his 80s, served as a guest conductor with several of the world's major orchestras, including the Chicago Symphony, Cleveland Orchestra, Los Angeles Philharmonic, New York Philharmonic, and San Francisco Symphony as well as the Berlin Philharmonic, the Leningrad Symphony, the London Symphony Orchestra, and the Tokyo Philharmonic, among others. Foss died at his home in New York City. He is survived by his wife, Cornelia; his son, Christopher; his daughter, Eliza; his brother, Oliver; and three grandchildren. See *Current Biography* (1966). — M.A.S.

Obituary *New York Times* (on-line) Feb. 2, 2009

FRANKLIN, JOHN HOPE Jan. 2, 1915–Mar. 25, 2009 Historian; educator; civil rights activist; consultant on social and legal matters; public intellectual. Some 120 honorary degrees awarded to him by U.S. colleges and universities indicate the extraordinary esteem in which John Hope Franklin was held in academia. His book *From Slavery to Freedom: A History of African Americans* and his other writings on the African-American experience—and particularly his demonstration that African-American history and American history are inseparable—were widely recognized as transformative, in part because they illuminated by means of a wealth of historical material the integral role of blacks in the development of the nation. The fact that Franklin and members of his family had lived through some of the events he described and had suffered for decades because of their color made his works all the more powerful. "Because of the life John Hope Franklin lived, the public service he rendered, and the scholarship that was the mark of his distinguished career, we all have a richer understanding of who we are as Americans and our journey as a people," President Barack Obama said in a White House press release (March 25, 2009, online). Franklin was born in Rentiesville, a small, all-black town in Oklahoma; his father was a lawyer, his mother a teacher. In what David Oshinsky characterized in the *New York Times* (November 27, 2005) as a "riveting and bitterly candid" memoir, *Mirror to America* (2005), Franklin described the horrific race riots in Tulsa, Oklahoma, in 1921, in which the law office his father had opened a few months earlier was destroyed. Four years passed before his father succeeded in opening another office in Tulsa, where Franklin spent the rest of his childhood. In *Mirror to America* Franklin wrote that while he was growing up, there "was never a moment in any contact I had with white people that I was not reminded that society as a whole had sentenced me to abject humiliation for the sole reason that I was not white." At age 11 he heard the historian, sociologist, and civil rights activist W. E. B. Du Bois speak in Tulsa; years later they became friends. At Fisk University, a traditionally black school where Franklin received an A.B. degree, in 1935, a young, white professor, Theodore S. Currier, inspired him to major in history and then borrowed $500 so that Franklin could pursue a graduate degree at Harvard University. There, in addition to hearing derogatory remarks and jokes about blacks, he witnessed putdowns of Harvard's few Jewish graduate students and realized, Oshinsky wrote, that prejudice "came in many forms." He earned a master's degree in 1936 and a Ph.D. in 1941. Earlier, in 1939, he had joined the History Department at St. Augustine's College. He later taught history (but never a course only on African-American history) at North Carolina College (1943–47); Howard University (1947–56); Brooklyn College (1956–64), which named him a full professor and chairman of the History Department—an event so unusual then that the *New York Times* announced it on its front page (February 15, 1956); the University of Chicago (1964–82, History Department chair, 1967–70), Duke University (1982–85, professor emeritus, 1985–2008); and Duke University Law School (1985–92). Franklin's best-known book, *From Slavery to Freedom* (1947), which has sold upwards of three million copies, "permanently altered the ways in which the American narrative was studied," Peter Applebome wrote for the *New York Times* (March 29, 2009). Referring to that volume, the historian David Leavering Lewis told Applebome, "What distinguishes [Franklin's] history or historiography is that he, like few other historians, wrote a book that transformed the way we understand a major social phenomenon. . . . Before him you had a field of study that had been feeble and marginalized, full of a pretty brutal discounting of the impact of people of color. And he moved it into the main American narrative. It empowered a whole new field of study." Among the many other books that he wrote, co-wrote, or edited are *The Militant South, 1800–1861* (1956) and *Runaway Slaves: Rebels on the Plantation* (co-written by Loren Schweninger, 1999). Background material regarding the Supreme Court's "separate but equal" decision of 1896 that Franklin compiled for Thurgood Marshall, the NAACP's national counsel, helped Marshall argue successfully for the plaintiffs in *Brown v. Board of Education* (1954), in which the Supreme Court unanimously ruled that segregated public schools are unconstitutional. Also in the public arena, Franklin participated in the march from Selma to Montgomery, Alabama, led by Martin Luther King Jr. in 1965, to protest race-based inequities in voting rights. In 1997 he headed President Bill Clinton's Initiative on Race. His many extracurricular activities also included service as the president of the American Historical Association, the Southern Historical Association, and the Organization of American Historians. Courtly and uncommonly generous as a mentor to students, Franklin was famous for the orchids he grew in the greenhouse behind his home in Durham, North Carolina, near Duke. He died in Duke University Hospital, in Durham. He was survived by his son, John Whittington Franklin, the director of partnerships and international programs at the National Museum of African American History and Culture, in Washington, D.C. His marriage in 1940 to the former Aurelia Whittington ended with her death, in 1999. See *Current Biography* (1963). — M.H.

Obituary *New York Times* B p13 Mar. 26, 2009

FRENCH, MARILYN Nov. 21, 1929–May 2, 2009 Writer. Marilyn French, who examined gender inequality and patriarchy in both her fiction and her nonfiction, was perhaps best known as the author of the feminist novel *The Women's Room* (1977). Born Martha Edwards in the New York City borough of Brooklyn, she was the older of two siblings. Her father, E. Charles Edwards, was an engineer, and her mother, Isabel Hazz Edwards, worked in a department store. French, a solitary child, was raised on Long Island, New York. By the age of 10, she was writing sonatas, stories, and poems; by 14, she was reading the works of Thomas Paine, Friedrich Nietzsche, and Arthur Schopenhauer. French attended Hofstra College (now University) in Hempstead, New York, where she received a bachelor's degree in English literature in 1951. She had married Robert M. French Jr. the previous year. During the 1950s and early 1960s, French worked at a series of office jobs to put her husband through law school; she also gave birth to two children and assumed the traditional role of a housewife. Wanting to escape from her cookie-cutter existence and craving intellectual stimulation, she found inspiration in Simone de Beauvoir's groundbreaking book *The Second Sex* (1949) and began rededicating herself to the practice of writing. Following several unsuccessful attempts to get her stories published, French returned to school, earning a master's degree in English from Hofstra in 1964. She remained at the school to teach for the next four years. Concurrently, her marriage deteriorated, and in 1967 she divorced her husband, who was unsupportive of her career. In 1968 French entered Harvard University on a full scholarship. After earning her doctoral degree in 1972, with a dissertation on James Joyce, she became an assistant professor of English at the College of the Holy Cross, in Worcester, Massachusetts. During her four-year tenure there, she began working in earnest on what would become her landmark novel, *The Women's Room*. The novel, about a group of submissive 1950s-era housewives who free themselves from their husbands' control and become independent women in the 1970s, quickly became a literary phenomenon. One of the most influential novels of the modern feminist movement, it sold more than 20 million copies and was translated into 20 languages. In 1980 the book was made into a television movie starring Lee Remick, Colleen Dewhurst, and Patty Duke. French subsequently wrote other novels as well as nonfiction works that challenged the system of patriarchy and traditional notions of femininity. They included *The Bleeding Heart* (1980), a novel about a female university professor and her dissatisfaction with her life and relationships; *Beyond Power: On Men, Women, and Morals* (1985), a historical survey; *Her Mother's Daughter* (1987), a novel about discontentment with motherhood; *The War Against Women* (1992), which examined the issues of rape, incest, female infanticide, and genital mutilation; and *Our Father* (1993), a novel about four half-sisters and their relationship with their dying father. In 1998 French, a longtime smoker, wrote *A Season in Hell: A Memoir*, which chronicled her battle in the early 1990s with and unexpected recovery from advanced esophageal cancer. Despite the undeniable physical toll the illness and its treatment took, she continued to write. Her most ambitious work in later years was arguably the four-volume *From Eve to Dawn: A History of Women in the World* (2008). French died of heart failure at a hospital in New York City. She is survived by her son, Robert, and her daughter, Jamie. See *Current Biography* (1992). — C.C.

Obituary *New York Times* B p11 May 4, 2009

FULLER, MILLARD Jan. 3, 1935–Feb. 3, 2009 Organization official. As the founder and president of Habitat for Humanity International, Millard Fuller led a massive effort to eliminate homelessness worldwide. The group, using donated materials and volunteer labor, has built more than 300,000 houses since its inception in 1976. "I see life as both a gift and a responsibility," Fuller once said, according to the organization's Web site. "My responsibility is to use what God has given me to help his people in need." Millard Dean Fuller was born in Lanett, a cotton-mill town in eastern Alabama. His mother, Estin (Cook) Fuller, died when he was just three years old. His father, Render Alexander Fuller, later remarried. Render and his new wife, Eunice, ran a grocery store together. When Fuller was 10, his father bought a large parcel of farmland. An elderly couple lived in a dilapidated shack on the land, and Render purchased lumber and helped them rebuild it—a kindness that set a powerful example for the young Fuller. In 1953 Fuller enrolled at Alabama's Auburn University, and after receiving a B.S. degree in economics, in 1957, he entered the School of Law at the University of Alabama, in Tuscaloosa. There he began collaborating with Morris S. Dees Jr., a fellow law student whose entrepreneurial instincts and aspirations closely matched his own. They started several businesses, including a direct-mail operation, a custom-cake delivery service, and various real-estate ventures. While still in law school, they were each soon making $25,000 a year. In 1960 Fuller, who served briefly in the U. S. Army, received his law degree and was admitted to the Alabama Bar. He and Dees opened a law office in Montgomery but continued to focus much of their energy on their commercial enterprises. The phenomenal success of a cookbook that they compiled and published themselves, *Favorite Recipes of Home Economics Teachers* (1963), prompted Fuller and Dees to publish other cookbooks. Abandoning their law practice, within two years they had become millionaires and the largest publishers of cookbooks in the country. In 1964 Fuller's wife, Linda, left him because of his frequent absences and single-minded pursuit of wealth. Fuller saved his marriage by agreeing to pastoral counseling. The couple decided to sell almost everything they owned and donate the proceeds to humanitarian and religious organizations. (Dees went on to co-found the Southern Poverty Law Center.) The Fullers moved to Koinonia Farm, a Christian community founded in 1942 to promote racial equality and the sharing of material possessions. In 1966 Fuller began working as a fundraiser for Tougaloo College, a small, church-supported institution in Mississippi. In 1968 the Fullers, gathering with a small group of like-minded people in a converted chicken barn at Koinonia Farm, created the Fund for Humanity. Their plan was to build simple houses on half-acre plots, to be sold interest-free to poor rural families. By 1972 almost 30 houses had been erected. That promising start awakened in the Fullers a desire to expand the program to other continents. As a representative of the National Stewardship Council of the United Church of Christ, Fuller had gone to Africa for two months and had been deeply disturbed by what he saw in the shantytowns of Zaire. In the summer of 1973, he and Linda traveled to Mbandaka, Zaire, with their four children: Christopher, Kimberly, Faith, and Georgia. There Fuller worked as the Church of Christ's director of development for the region, constructing numerous small cement-block homes and raising money for needed medical supplies. After returning to the U.S. in 1976, Fuller founded Habitat for Humanity International, which has since built homes for a reported 1.5 million people around the world. Habitat homes are sold to those living in substandard housing who do not earn enough to buy homes through other means. The small monthly mortgage payments go into a fund that keeps the program running. Additionally, each buyer is asked to help in some way with the construction, a requirement that Fuller felt contributed to a sense of pride and ownership. Former U.S. president Jimmy Carter has been a longtime volunteer, as has former president Bill Clinton, who presented Fuller with the Presidential Medal of Freedom in 1996. Fuller wrote several books about his work, among them *The Theology of the Hammer* (1994) and *More Than Houses* (1999). In 2009 he was stricken by a severe headache and chest pains and taken to a local hospital. He died while being transferred by ambulance to a larger regional facility. He is survived by his wife, four children, and several grandchildren. See *Current Biography* (1995). — D.K.

Obituary *New York Times* (on-line) Feb. 4, 2009

GAJDUSEK, D. CARLETON Sep. 9, 1923–Dec. 12, 2008 Scientist. D. Carleton Gajdusek (GUY-duh-shek), who headed the brain-studies laboratory at the National Institute of Neurological Disease and Stroke for nearly three decades, was the Nobel Prize–winning virologist responsible for identifying and describing kuru, a degenerative neurological disorder caused by a family of rogue proteins called prions. Born to a Slovakian father and Hungarian mother, he grew up in Yonkers, New York. Gajdusek's interest in science was sparked by an aunt who worked at the Boyce Thompson Institute for Plant Research in Yonkers. A frequent visitor to the institute as a child, Gajdusek worked there as a lab assistant during his teens. In 1939, after completing high school at the age of 16, Gajdusek entered the University of Rochester, graduating summa cum laude with a bachelor of science degree four years later. In 1946 Gajdusek earned a medical degree, with a specialty in pediatrics, from Harvard Medical School. He pursued postgraduate studies at Harvard, Columbia University, and the California Institute of Technology. In 1951 Gajdusek was drafted into the U.S. Army and sent to the Walter Reed Army Institute of Research, in Washington, D.C., where he studied viral and rickettsial diseases under Dr. Joseph Smadel. Gajdusek then spent time at the Institut Pasteur in Tehran, Iran, investigating the epidemic diseases of Iran, Afghanistan, and Turkey. Fascinated by mysterious medical problems in isolated populations, he traveled to such faraway lands as the Hindu Kush and the jungles of South America in search of remote tribes with unique diseases to study. In 1955, while performing postdoctoral work in Australia as a visiting professor, Gajdusek discovered the Fore tribe of New Guinea, whose members were suffering from a mysterious illness that they called kuru, the native word for tremors. He went on to classify the disease, which caused victims to suffer from severe bouts of trembling before descending into dementia and death, as a spongiform encephalopathy, after autopsies showed the victims' brains filled with gaping holes. Gajdusek then connected the prevalence of the disease to the tribe's former practice of consuming the bodies of their deceased. (The practice had been suppressed in the 1940s by missionaries and Australian law-enforcement officials.) After further investigating the disease in chimpanzees in the 1960s and 1970s, Gajdusek was able to demonstrate for the first time that a degenerative human brain disease could result from a slow-acting viral infection. (All the viruses, bacteria, and parasites studied up until that point had caused symptoms within weeks.) In 1976 Gajdusek was the co-recipient of the Nobel Prize in Physiology or Medicine for his work. (The American neurologist Stanley B. Prusiner later identified the cause of kuru and other similar diseases as a family of infectious proteins called prions; he was awarded his own Nobel Prize for that work in 1997.) Gajdusek, who worked at the National Institute of Neurological Disease and Stroke (part of the National Institutes of Health), in Bethesda, Maryland, for nearly three decades, is also credited with helping to establish the genetic basis of Huntington's disease and the causes of hermaphroditism. Despite his scientific achievements, Gajdusek's reputation was severely tarnished when he was charged with child molestation in 1997. Over the years he had adopted more than 50 children from New Guinea and Micronesia, and he was unrepentant about engaging in sexual relationships with some of his sons. Defending his behavior, he lambasted the prudery of Americans and argued that sex with young men was a common part of other cultures. Gajdusek ultimately served one year in prison and then left the United States. Reclusive and eccentric, he spent the remaining years of his life in Paris, Norway (where he wintered in Tromso, above the Arctic Circle, because of its isolation and perennial darkness during that season), and Amsterdam. Gajdusek died of congestive heart failure at a hotel in Tromso. He is survived by his many adopted children (some of whom testified against him in court) and two nephews. — See *Current Biography* (1981). — C.C.

Obituary *New York Times* (on-line) Dec. 15, 2008

GRANGER, CLIVE W. J. Sep. 4, 1934–May 27, 2009 Economist; educator. Clive William John Granger, who taught at the University of California at San Diego for three decades, was best known as the Nobel Prize–winning economist who made revolutionary use of statistics in studying the economy—a field that later came to be known as econometrics. He was born in Swansea, Wales, to Edward Granger and the former Evelyn Hessey, who returned to their native England when Granger was a year old. Granger spent his early childhood in the town of Lincoln, before moving with his mother to Cambridge at the outset of World War II. His father, who had worked for a fruit-preserves company, served in the Royal Air Force as a driver of large support vehicles until the end of the war. After the war, the reunited family moved to a middle-class suburb in West Bridgford. While Granger was, admittedly, an average student in most respects, he displayed an above-average aptitude for numbers and developed a strong interest in applied mathematics. He was accepted to the University of Nottingham, where he received a bachelor's degree in economics in 1955 and decided on a career in statistics. He remained at the school, earning a doctoral degree in statistics in 1959. Granger then received a fellowship to study at Princeton University, in New Jersey. Traveling to the U.S., he spent an academic year there and then returned to Great Britain to become a professor of economics and statistics at the University of Nottingham. In 1974 Granger left Nottingham to accept a professorship in the economics department of the University of California at San Diego (UCSD). There, he began working with fellow economist Robert F. Engle in developing what would become one of the most preeminent econometrics programs in the world. Over the next three decades, Granger conducted groundbreaking research on "methods of analyzing economic time series with common trends (co-integration)," as noted on the Nobel e-Museum Web site. (A time series, as the site also notes, is a "chronological sequence of observations.") Granger's scholarship applied mostly to time series that were nonstationary in nature. In econometrics, to say a statistic is nonstationary means that, despite periodic fluctuations, overall it follows a long-term trend of growth or diminution;

whereas such statistics as unemployment rate and interest rate remain, by and large, at or around a particular level, and can thus be described as stationary, nonstationary items increase or decrease in a specific direction over time. (The gross domestic product of the United States is an illustrative example of nonstationarity.) Granger's methods were subsequently applied to other fields as well, including biology and engineering. Following his retirement from UCSD, in the summer of 2003, Granger left San Diego for the University of Canterbury, in New Zealand. While serving as a visiting scholar there, he received a surprise 3 a.m. phone call from the Royal Swedish Academy of Sciences, informing him that he had been named the co-winner (along with Engle) of the 2003 Nobel Prize in Economics (more formally known as the Bank of Sweden Prize in Economic Sciences in Memory of Alfred Nobel). Peter Coy explained for *BusinessWeek* (October 10, 2003, on-line) that the laureate "helped build what might be described as the statistical plumbing of modern economics and finance. It may not be glamorous, but as the Nobel committee recognized, it's indispensable." Granger was later inducted into the Order of Knight Bachelor by Queen Elizabeth II, and a building at the University of Nottingham was named after him. Granger died of pneumonia at Scripps Memorial Hospital in La Jolla, California. He is survived by his wife, Patricia; his son, Mark; and his daughter, Claire. See *Current Biography International Yearbook* (2007). — C.C.

Obituary *New York Times* (on-line) May 31, 2009

GWATHMEY, CHARLES June 19, 1938–Aug. 3, 2009 Architect. Charles Gwathmey adhered to high Modernism, even when architectural trends shifted toward historicist and postmodern design. He was a member of a group of architects that emerged in the 1960s known as the "New York School" or the "White School" (a reference to the color of many of their buildings), who favored formal design over historical reference and embraced largely European aesthetic values. Gwathmey's work has been greatly influential, if sometimes controversial. Gwathmey was born in Charlotte, North Carolina, to Robert Gwathmey, an artist and teacher, and Rosalie Dean (Hook) Gwathmey, a textile designer and photographer. He attended the American School in Paris and traveled throughout Europe with his parents, visiting numerous museums and cathedrals. Gwathmey studied architecture at the University of Pennsylvania for three years before transferring to the Yale University School of Architecture, where he earned his master's degree in 1962 and was awarded the William Wirt Winchester fellowship. A Fulbright Scholar, he then studied proportional systems in architecture in Paris, where he became acquainted with the work of the French architect Le Corbusier. In 1964 Gwathmey joined a firm headed by Edward Larrabee Barnes and soon designed his first house, a residence on Fire Island. A year later he designed an ocean house and studio complex for his parents in Amagansett, Long Island, which were completed in 1967. The house's minimalist exterior was sheathed in vertical cedar planking. The large geometric forms—reminiscent of Le Corbusier—that comprise the project were rotated, cut, and punctuated with diagonal stairways and slanted roofs; the interior was open and full of light. The structure, which he later inherited, became one of the most influential of the modern era. Gwathmey followed that by designing several notable residential buildings in New York and elsewhere on the East Coast. In 1968 Robert Siegel joined the firm; two years later the pair formed Gwathmey Siegel & Associates. Designed in 1972, the Cogan residence, in East Hampton, New York, is considered among the firm's most successful residential projects; it features a rectangular pavilion, intersected by three ramps, and an elevated living area. Another notable work by the firm was the renovation of Princeton University's Whig Hall, which had been damaged in a fire. For that project they implanted a new structural system within the building's already existing neo-classical shell; the renovation, which received mixed reviews, was awarded a Progressive Architecture citation. In the 1970s the firm undertook work for several high-profile clients, including the actress Faye Dunaway and the hair-salon owner Vidal Sassoon. Later Gwathmey designed modern residences for the filmmaker Steven Spielberg, the producer Jeffrey Katzenberg, the comedian Jerry Seinfeld, and the entertainment executive David Geffen, among others. The firm was responsible for the Perinton housing project near Rochester, New York; an 800-student dormitory for the State University of New York at Purchase; the Playboy Hotel and Casino in Aruba; and the large-scale de Menil residence in East Hampton, which Gwathmey described as the "summation of the past [several] years," in which "every lesson learned finds expression or a conscious elimination." In 1973 Gwathmey's firm fought the constraints posed by an urban setting when it designed Columbia University's East Campus dormitory complex and the Heyman Center for the Humanities, which were widely praised. One of the firm's most controversial projects was a proposed 11-story addition to Frank Lloyd Wright's Guggenheim Museum, in Manhattan, whose intrusive design angered historical preservation groups and local residents. Gwathmey ultimately withdrew the proposal and reintroduced a new version in 1987 that was accepted and completed in 1992. During the last two decades of his career, Gwathmey continued to produce notable work, including designs for residences across the country as well as such urban institutions as the International Center of Photography, in Manhattan; the Museum of the Moving Image, in Astoria, Queens; an expansion of the Fogg Art Museum at Harvard University; the Basketball Hall of Fame in Springfield, Massachusetts; New York City's Science, Industry and Business Library; and the W Hotel in Hoboken, New Jersey. Gwathmey, who was known for his refined personal style, held faculty positions at the Pratt Institute, Princeton University, Columbia University, the University of Texas, Yale, and Harvard, among other institutions. He was the recipient of numerous awards, among them a 1990 Lifetime Achievement Award from the New York State Society of Architects. Gwathmey, who died of esophageal cancer in New York City, is survived by his second wife, the former Bette-Ann Damson, the vice president for corporate philanthropy at

Polo Ralph Lauren; Annie Gwathmey, his daughter from his first marriage; and his stepson Eric Steel. See *Current Biography* (1988). — M.E.R.

Obituary *New York Times* (on-line) Aug. 5, 2009

HALL, EDWARD T. May 16, 1914–July 20, 2009 Anthropologist. Edward T. Hall was widely recognized for his pioneering studies involving nonverbal modes of communication and intercultural relations. Hall, who was considered the father of intercultural communications as an academic discipline, studied the differences between cultures in order to facilitate international and universal communication, understanding, and cooperation. "Nothing is independent of anything else," Hall once said. "Yet in the U.S. we use a special-interest approach for solving political, economic, and environmental problems. . . . I feel strongly that there should be a few people at least whose task is synthesis—pulling things together. And that is impossible without a deep sense of context." Hall, who was known to friends as Ned, wrote in an accessible style, grounding his theories in practical, concrete examples. Although most celebrated for his academic work and writings, which included the seminal volume *The Silent Language* (1959), Hall also worked as a cultural consultant to the U.S. Department of State as well as in the private sector. Edward Twitchell Hall Jr. was born in Webster Groves, Missouri, and grew up in Santa Fe, New Mexico, an area with large Spanish-American and Native American populations. He initially aspired to be a biologist, but during college he was reluctant to dissect animal specimens as required by his lab instructors, and he switched his focus to anthropology. Hall graduated from the University of Denver in 1936 with a bachelor's degree in that field; two years later he earned a master's degree from the University of Arizona. While in Arizona, Hall lived and worked on Navajo and Hopi reservations, where he began developing the ideas for which he would become renowned. In 1942 Hall obtained his doctoral degree from Columbia University, in New York City. He served in the U.S. Army Corps of Engineers during World War II, as captain of a predominantly black regiment in Europe and then the Philippines. After the war, he spent time on the atoll of Truk, in Micronesia, serving as an intercultural liaison between the Trukese and the American Navy. From 1946 to 1948 he taught anthropology at the University of Denver and then joined the faculty of Bennington College, in Vermont, where he taught for three years. During the early 1950s he worked for the Foreign Service Institute at the U.S. Department of State, teaching communications skills to foreign-service personnel. In 1960, along with Mildred Reed Hall, whom he had married in 1946, he launched Edward T. Hall Associates, a consulting company focused on interpreting foreign cultures for both governmental and business clients. Despite running a well-regarded private enterprise, Hall did not abandon academia; he directed a communications research project at the Washington School of Psychiatry, and in 1962 he was the Leatherbee lecturer at the Harvard Business School. As a professor of anthropology at the Illinois Institute of Technology in Chicago (1963–67), he worked with design and architectural students and formulated his theories about space and time as components of communication. In studying space as a form of communication—a field he called proxemics—Hall examined territoriality among office workers and the cultural implications of architecture. He maintained that the use of time as a means of communication was exhibited, for example, by the business executive who kept each visitor waiting in an outer office for a specific number of minutes. From 1967 to 1977 Hall taught anthropology at Northwestern University, in Evanston, Illinois, where he was a hugely popular professor. After retiring from Northwestern he continued lecturing at colleges and universities around the globe. In addition to *The Silent Language*, Hall's influential books included *The Hidden Dimension* (1966), *Beyond Culture* (1976), *The Dance of Life: The Other Dimension of Time* (1983), *Hidden Differences: Doing Business with the Japanese* (1987), and *Understanding Cultural Differences: Germans, French, and Americans* (1990). (The latter two were co-written by his wife, Mildred.) In 1992 he published an autobiography, *An Anthropology of Everyday Life*. Mildred, with whom he had two children, Ellen and Eric, died in 1994. Hall suffered several strokes during his final years and died at his home in Santa Fe. He is survived by Karin Bergh, a longtime family friend whom he married in 2004; his son, Eric, now an attorney; and a grandson. (His daughter predeceased him.) See *Current Biography* (1992). — M.M.

Obituary *New York Times* (on-line) Aug. 4, 2009

HARRIS, E. LYNN June 20, 1955–July 23, 2009 Writer. E. Lynn Harris was renowned in urban-fiction circles for his groundbreaking novels, which exposed readers to a largely taboo subject—the subculture of publicly heterosexual black men who privately engage in gay sex. (In the black community the term "down low," or DL, refers to these seemingly straight men's hidden lifestyle.) "He was a pioneering voice within the black [lesbian, gay, bisexual, and transgender] community, but also resonated with mainstream communities, regardless of race and sexual orientation," Herndon Davis, a Los Angeles, California–based gay advocate and media consultant, told Errin Hayes for the Associated Press (July 24, 2009). "Harris painted with eloquent prose and revealing accuracy the lives of African American men and the many complicated struggles they faced reconciling their sexuality and spirituality while rising above societal taboos within the black community." The oldest of four children, Harris was born in Flint, Michigan. At age three he moved with his mother, Etta Mae Williams, and his three sisters to Little Rock, Arkansas, where he attended elementary and high schools. Harris's childhood was a painful one; he endured verbal and physical abuse at the hands of his stepfather, Ben Harris, whom he believed to be his biological father while growing up. (Harris discovered the truth at age 12, and three years later he met his birth father, James Jeter.) After high school Harris attended the University of Arkansas, in Fayetteville, where he achieved several firsts. Not only was he the school's first black male cheerleader, but he was also its first black yearbook editor. In 1977 Harris, who also served as president of the Alpha Phi Alpha fraternity and vice president of Black Americans for Democracy, graduated with honors with a B.A. degree in journalism. He spent the next 13 years working as a computer salesman for such companies as IBM, Hewlett-Packard, and AT&T and living in Dallas, Atlanta, and the District of Columbia. In his memoir *What Becomes of the Brokenhearted?* (2003), he recalled experiencing depression and self-hatred because of his closeted lifestyle. "There was no category for someone like me who wanted everything I saw on TV and who wanted everything I thought the world wanted for me—a relationship with someone, a home, to achieve a certain degree of the American dream," Bruce Weber quoted Harris as saying in the *New York Times* (July 25, 2009). Following an aborted suicide attempt in 1990, Harris quit his sales job and pursued a writing career. His first work, *Invisible Life*, a coming-of-age tale, centers on a black college senior who falls in love with another man. Harris was still not open about his own sexuality at the time. "People would often ask, 'Is this book about you?' I didn't want to talk about that," he was quoted as saying by Hayes. After receiving numerous rejections from mainstream publishers, Harris self-published *Invisible Life* in 1991 and sold all 5,000 copies of the book out of the trunk of his car to patrons of local black beauty parlors, book clubs, and black-owned independent bookstores in Atlanta, where he was then living. Harris's success attracted the attention of John Hawkins, a Doubleday sales representative who signed on as his agent and helped Harris sell the novel to Anchor Books, which published it as a trade paperback in 1994. Over the next 15 years, Harris achieved enviable commercial success, and 10 of his novels reached the *New York Times* best-seller list, including *Invisible Life*, *Just As I Am* (1995), *And This Too Shall Pass* (1997), *If This World Were Mine* (1998), *Abide With Me* (2000), *Not A Day Goes By* (2001), *Any Way the Wind Blows* (2002), *A Love of My Own* (2003), *I Say A Little Prayer* (2007), and *Just Too Good To Be True* (2008). *Basketball Jones*, the last of his books to be published during his lifetime, appeared on shelves in January 2009. That same year he signed a three-book deal with Karen Hunter Publishing, an imprint of Pocket Books/Simon & Schuster, which released *Mama Dearest*, posthumously, in September 2009. Among Harris's accolades are the James Baldwin Award for Literary Excellence (1998) and the Writers for Writing Award from *Poets & Writers* magazine (2002). Additionally, Harris was the first author to win the Novel of the Year Award from the Blackboard African American Bestsellers organization three times—in 1995 (for *Just As I Am*), 2002 (for *Any Way the Wind Blows*), and 2003 (for *A Love of My Own*). Harris, whose work has been featured in *American Visions*, *Essence*, the *Washington Post Sunday Magazine*, and the *Advocate*, among other publications, is the creator of an eponymous foundation that provides assistance to aspiring writers and artists. He died from complications of heart disease while on a book tour in Los Angeles and is survived by his mother and three sisters. At the time of his death, Harris was working on developing a play inspired by his debut book, *Invisible Life*. See *Current Biography* (1996). — M.M.

Obituary *New York Times* (on-line) July 24, 2009

HARTIGAN, GRACE Mar. 28, 1922–Nov. 15, 2008 Artist; educator. As a member of the so-called New York School in the 1950s, Grace Hartigan was arguably the most celebrated female artist in the United States. She was "one of the seminal figures of Abstract Expressionism, a real breakthrough artist," Robert Saltonstall Mattison, the author of *Grace Hartigan: A Painter's World* (1990), told Jacques Kelly for the *Baltimore Sun* (November 16, 2008, on-line). Hartigan's "influence as a painter is huge and widespread," Jay Fisher, the deputy director of curatorial affairs for the Baltimore Museum of Art, in Maryland, told Mary Carole McCauley for the *Baltimore Sun* (November 17, 2008). According to a biography of her on the Web site of the ACA Galleries, in New York City, "Her rich style, with its dynamic lines and sumptuous colors, fuses figuration and abstraction and often draws on elements of popular culture and art history." Hartigan once said of herself, according to Jacques Kelly, writing for the *Baltimore Sun* (November 16, 2008), "What I had, what was my gift, I was a colorist. You can't learn that from anyone. I have what might be called a startling virtuosity." Hartigan's father was an accountant, her mother a realtor. Hartigan had no formal education in art and never attended college. She began painting in the late 1940s, by which time she had married, given birth to a son, divorced, and left her son in the care of her in-laws. Within the next few years, her work attracted the attention of the influential art critics Meyer Shapiro and Clement Greenberg, and her paintings appeared in group and solo shows; she also joined a close-knit circle of artists and writers that included Jackson Pollock, Mark Rothko, Willem de Kooning, Frank O'Hara, Kenneth Koch, and John Ashbery. In 1953 the Museum of Modern Art (MoMA) in New York City bought Hartigan's painting *Persian Jacket* for its permanent collection, and by the end of the 1950s, other major museums, too, had acquired paintings by her.When, later, she incorporated representational images in her paintings, she lost favor with many of her admirers and before long fell into relative obscurity, only to be "discovered" again in the past decade or so. During her years outside the art world's spotlight, she continued to paint; she also embarked on what proved to be a long, fruitful career as an educator, teaching painting to several generations of graduate students at the Maryland Institute College of Art, in Baltimore, and, from 1965 until 2007, directing the Hoffberger School of Painting there. Works by her are in the permanent collections of museums including, in addition to MoMA, the Museum of Fine Arts in Boston; the National Museum of Women in the Arts, the National Museum of American Art, the Corcoran Gallery of Art, and the Hirshhorn Museum and Sculpture Garden, in Washington, D.C.; the Walker Art Center and the Minneapolis Institute of Arts, in Minneapolis, Minnesota; the Whitney Museum of American Art, the Metropolitan Museum of Art, and the Brooklyn Museum of Art, in New York City; and many university and private galleries. Her life and work are the subjects of Sharon L. Hirsh's book *Grace Hartigan: Painting Art History* (2003) and Murray Grigor's film *Shattering Boundaries: Grace Hartigan* (2008). *The Journals of Grace Hartigan, 1951–1955*, edited by William T. La Moy and Joseph

P. McCaffrey, was published in 2009. Hartigan's brief second and third marriages, to Harry Jackson, an artist, and Robert Keene, a gallery owner, respectively, ended in divorce. Her fourth marriage, in 1960, to Winston Price, an epidemiologist and collector of modern art, ended with his death, in 1981. Hartigan died in a nursing home in Baltimore. Her son, Jeffrey Jachens, died in 2006. She was survived by three grandchildren. See *Current Biography* (1962). — M.H.

Obituary *New York Times* B p14 Nov. 18, 2008

HARVEY, PAUL Sep. 4, 1918–Feb. 28, 2009 Radio and television commentator. At the height of his career, the radio pioneer Paul Harvey had 24 million listeners on more than 1,200 radio stations across the United States. His unmistakably resonant voice, which had been broadcast across the national airwaves since 1951, was known for its melodramatic inflection, courtly pacing, riveting pauses, and staccato riffs. Harvey maintained a unique editorial slant, a maverick conservatism that he called "political fundamentalism," and although he championed the old-fashioned values of God, country, family, hard work, and rugged individualism, Harvey could not safely be pigeonholed with the orthodox right. Paul Harvey Aurandt was born in Tulsa, Oklahoma. His father, who worked as an assistant to Tulsa's police and fire commissioner, was shot and killed when Harvey was a toddler. Harvey and his sister were raised by their mother, Anna, who rented out rooms in the family home to make ends meet. At an early age, Harvey developed an interest in radio, building his own cigar-box crystal sets. In high school he became a champion orator, with the help of an English teacher who encouraged him to pursue a career in broadcasting. When Harvey was 14, his high-school mentor took him to KVOO, a radio station in Tulsa, and requested that the management give the young man a chance to be on the air. Harvey helped with the cleaning and did other chores, and eventually he was allowed to fill in occasionally at the microphone, doing spot announcements, playing his guitar, and reading the wire-service news. Harvey worked as a staff announcer at KVOO while taking classes in speech and English at the University of Tulsa. He then became the station manager of KFBI in Abilene, Kansas, before moving on to posts as a newscaster at KOMA in Oklahoma City, Oklahoma, and news and special-events director at KXOK in St. Louis. In St. Louis he met Lynne, his future wife and professional collaborator. (He is said to have proposed marriage a few minutes into their first date.) From 1941 to 1943 Harvey was program director at WKZO in Kalamazoo, Michigan, and he worked concurrently as the Office of War Information's news director for Michigan and Indiana. In December 1943 Harvey enlisted in the U.S. Army Air Corps. In March 1944 he received an honorable medical discharge, after lacerating his heel on an obstacle course. Following his discharge, he dropped the surname Aurandt and moved to Chicago, where he provided twice-daily 15-minute news commentaries. In 1951 Harvey began broadcasting nationally with ABC Radio. (His critics often pointed out that in the 1950s he was a supporter of Senator Joseph McCarthy's crusade against alleged Communists.) In 1968 Harvey was seriously considered as a running mate of the unsuccessful third-party presidential candidate George C. Wallace. Along with his broadcasting colleague Walter Cronkite, Harvey was a runner-up as the 1969 Gallup Poll's most admired man in America. During the 1960s, Harvey editorialized against the government dole, leftist radicals, high taxes, forced school busing, and other federal initiatives. In 1970 he reversed his former support for the Vietnam War in what became an iconic broadcast, urging Richard Nixon to reverse his decision to expand into Cambodia and to withdraw from the war altogether. (He began the famed broadcast with the words, "Mr. President, I love you . . . but you're wrong.") In 1976 Harvey debuted *The Rest of the Story*, five-minute human-interest tales that took listeners behind the scenes in the lives of history makers, whose identities were not revealed until the end. (Those segments concluded with Harvey's voice booming, "And now you know . . . the rest of the story!") In 1979 Harvey, whose brief daily television commentaries were already in syndication at 120 stations, began to appear as a weekly contributor on the ABC show *Good Morning America*. In addition to his radio and television work, Harvey wrote weekly newspaper columns syndicated by the *Los Angeles Times*. In 2000, despite being more than 80 years old, he signed a new 10-year contract with ABC Radio. Harvey, who had been presented in 2005 with the Presidential Medal of Freedom, the nation's highest civilian honor, died at a hospital in Phoenix, Arizona, where he wintered. He is survived by his son, Paul Harvey Jr. His wife and longtime producer, Lynne, whom he often called "Angel" on the air, had died less than a year earlier. See *Current Biography* (1986). — D.K.

Obituary *New York Times* (on-line) Mar. 1, 2009

HEWITT, DON Dec. 14, 1922–Aug. 19, 2009 As the executive producer of the *CBS Evening News* in the 1960s and the creator and developer of the long-running CBS show *60 Minutes*, Don Hewitt helped redefine broadcast news. Donald Shepard Hewitt was born in New York City and raised in nearby New Rochelle, New York. At a young age he decided to become a reporter, and after graduating from high school, in 1940, he enrolled at New York University on an athletic scholarship. His grades were not good, however, and he dropped out after his freshman year. Still harboring ambitions for a career in journalism, he soon took a job as a copy boy at the now-defunct *New York Herald Tribune*. In 1943 Hewitt entered the United States Merchant Marine Academy in Kings Point, New York. He joined the staff of the *Stars and Stripes*, a daily newspaper published for the U.S. military, as a merchant marine correspondent and eventually became a war correspondent for the paper. After World War II ended, in 1945, Hewitt was hired as a night editor for the Associated Press bureau in Memphis, Tennessee. He moved back to New York the following year and became the editor of the *Pelham Sun*, a small, weekly newspaper in Westchester County, New York. After a year he was hired as the night telephoto editor for the photography division of the United Press. In

1948 CBS, then known for its radio broadcasts, was searching for new people to join its fledgling television network. Impressed by Hewitt's strong visual sense, CBS hired him as an associate director of their news program *CBS TV News*. By 1950 he had been promoted to producer and director of the program, which was renamed *Douglas Edwards with the News*. During his time working on the show, Hewitt introduced a number of innovations to televised news broadcasts, among them the use of still photos, charts, graphics, and maps to illustrate the day's top stories and the use of type on the lower third of the screen. He also developed several techniques that revolutionized the industry, arguably the most important of which was the double-projector system, which allowed a director to combine pictures and narration that had been recorded separately. Hewitt also introduced on-the-scene reporting, with a July 1956 broadcast during which he and anchor Douglas Edwards used an amphibious plane to fly to the mid-Atlantic site where the Italian luxury liner *Andrea Doria* was slowly sinking after its collision with a Swedish cruise ship. The incident marked the first time a network anchorman filmed an eyewitness account on location; the piece was later nominated for an Emmy Award. In 1962 Walter Cronkite replaced Edwards as lead anchor, and Hewitt became executive producer of the *CBS Evening News*. The following September the newscast became the first to expand to a 30-minute format. Although the *CBS Evening News* became the highest-rated news program on the air, some CBS executives were unhappy with the changes Hewitt had instituted, and he was fired in December 1964. Hewitt spent the next four years producing documentaries for the network. In 1968 he persuaded CBS to add *60 Minutes*, a show he had conceived, to its lineup. A fusion of investigative journalism, human-interest stories, and celebrity profiles, *60 Minutes* was unlike any other news program on television and ultimately spawned several competitors, including NBC's *Dateline* and ABC's *20/20*. At its peak, during the 1979-80 season, *60 Minutes* was seen in an estimated 28 million homes every Sunday evening. Hewitt served as executive producer of *60 Minutes* from its debut in 1968 until 2004, when he was pressured to relinquish his post. Up until his death, he remained with CBS as a consultant. Hewitt, who won multiple Emmy and Peabody Awards over the course of his distinguished career, is survived by his third wife, Marilyn Berger; two sons from his first marriage; two daughters from his second marriage; and three grandchildren. See *Current Biography* (1988). — M.A.S.

Obituary *New York Times* B p11 Aug. 20, 2009

HINGLE, PAT July 19, 1924–Jan. 3, 2009 Actor. A longtime character actor of film, television, and theater, with nearly 200 credits to his name, Pat Hingle is best known for his role as Commissioner Gordon in four of the *Batman* films. Martin Patterson Hingle was born in Miami, Florida. After his father, a building contractor, abandoned the family, six-year-old Hingle spent the next seven years traveling across the country with his sister and their mother, who found work where available. Upon graduating from high school, Hingle attended the University of Texas on a tuba scholarship but interrupted his studies to enlist in the Navy during World War II. When the war ended Hingle returned to the University of Texas and changed his major to radio broadcasting. He also joined the drama club, where he met his future wife, Alyce Dorsey. After earning his bachelor's degree in 1949, Hingle was recalled by the Navy to serve as a boilerman technician during the Korean War. In 1952 Hingle moved with his wife to New York City, where he trained with Uta Hagen and joined the renowned Actors Studio, which was founded by Elia Kazan. Hingle's big break came in 1953, when he landed his first starring role on Broadway, in the Calder Willingham play *End As a Man*, also appearing in the 1957 film adaptation. Throughout the rest of the decade, Hingle, whose film appearances included roles in Kazan's *On the Waterfront* (1954) and *No Down Payment* (1957), also starred in a series of Pulitzer Prize–winning plays including *Cat on a Hot Tin Roof* (1955), *The Dark at the Top of the Stairs* (1957), and Archibald MacLeish's *JB* (1958). While appearing in the latter production, Hingle fell 54 feet down an elevator shaft in his apartment building, sustaining a fractured hip and damaging a finger so badly it had to be amputated. Within a year Hingle recovered from his injuries and resumed his acting career. He went on to amass numerous big-screen credits, most notably in *Splendor in the Grass* (1961), *Invitation to a Gunfighter* (1964), *Hang 'Em High* (1968), *Bloody Mama* (1970), *WUSA* (1970), *Norma Rae* (1979), *Sudden Impact* (1983), *Brewster's Millions* (1985), *Baby Boom* (1987), and *The Grifters* (1990). Hingle had a successful run playing police commissioner James Gordon in *Batman* (1989) and the sequels *Batman Returns* (1992), *Batman Forever* (1995), and *Batman and Robin* (1997). Among his last film credits were *Shaft* (2000), *Talladega Nights: The Ballad of Ricky Bobby* (2006), *Waltzing Anna* (2006), *The List* (2007), and *Undoing Time* (2008). Hingle was also a fixture on the small screen, with roles in several television series, including *The Fugitive*, *The Loner*, *Gunsmoke*, *Medical Center*, *Hawaii Five-O*, *Stone*, *Hail to the Chief*, *Murder, She Wrote*, and *In the Heat of the Night*. Hingle, however, regarded his stage work as his greatest achievement, and he appeared in Broadway revivals of *Strange Interlude* (1965) and *The Glass Menagerie* (1965) as well as James Baldwin's *Blues for Mister Charlie* (1964) and Arthur Miller's *The Price* (1968-69). During the 1990s he had roles in revivals of *1776*, *Cat on a Hot Tin Roof*, and *The Last Hurrah*. Hingle died of myelodysplasia, a type of blood cancer, at his home in Carolina Beach, North Carolina. He is survived by his second wife, Julia, whom he married in 1979; two stepchildren; three children from his first marriage, to Alyce Faye Dorsey; and several grandchildren. See *Current Biography* (1965). — W.D.

Obituary *New York Times* B p7 Jan. 5, 2009

HUGHES, JOHN Feb. 18, 1950–Aug. 6, 2009 Filmmaker. In the 1980s John Hughes redefined the teen-film genre and significantly influenced pop culture with a string of hits, including *Sixteen Candles*, *Pretty in Pink*, *The Breakfast Club*, and *Ferris Bueller's Day Off*. Displaying what Thomas O'Connor, in a piece for the *New York Times* (March 9, 1986), called "a striking affinity for the nuances of contemporary adolescent style, speech, music, and, above all, emotional concerns," Hughes charted "the intricate, rigorously observed geography of high school caste systems." His films were praised for their well-developed characters, realistic conflicts, and depictions of sensitive, intelligent teens—a sharp contrast to the raunchier teen fare of the era. Although Hughes's 1980s films won him critical acclaim, his most commercially successful venture came in the 1990s, with the *Home Alone* film franchise, which he wrote and produced. John Wilden Hughes Jr. was born in Lansing, Michigan, and when he was 13, his family relocated to the middle-class North Shore suburbs of Chicago, which would later become the setting for many of his films. Following his graduation from high school, Hughes enrolled at the University of Arizona in Tucson, but he dropped out at age 20 and moved back to Chicago, where he found work as a copywriter at the Leo Burnett Agency. By the late 1970s Hughes had become a creative director at the agency, but he left when he was offered a chance to join the editorial staff of the *National Lampoon*, a popular humor magazine for which he had been freelancing. Hughes wrote the screenplay for the forgettable film *National Lampoon's Class Reunion* (1982), but he fared better the following year, penning the screenplays for *Mr. Mom* (1983), about the then-unusual phenomenon of stay-at-home dads, and the popular Chevy Chase film *National Lampoon's Vacation*, about a dysfunctional family's disastrous cross-country road trip. Hughes's string of acclaimed teen films began in 1984 with *Sixteen Candles*, a coming-of-age comedy starring Molly Ringwald as a high-school sophomore whose parents forget her 16th birthday in their preoccupation with her older sister's upcoming wedding. The film also features Anthony Michael Hall and John Cusack. *The Breakfast Club*, about a group of five vastly different high-school students who become friends while serving Saturday detention together, was released the following year. Along with Ringwald and Hall, the film starred Ally Sheedy, Judd Nelson, and Emilio Estevez—actors who were part of the "brat pack," a nickname given to the stars of several coming-of-age films of the era. Also in 1985, Hughes wrote and directed *Weird Science*, about two high-school "nerds" who use a computer to create the perfect woman. One of Hughes's most iconic films, *Ferris Bueller's Day Off*, was released in 1986. The picture starred Matthew Broderick as a slacker who cuts class for the day and persuades his best friend and girlfriend to accompany him on a trip to Chicago. The film was one of the year's biggest box-office hits and is now considered one of the top high-school movies of all time. Hughes next wrote the screenplay for the 1986 film *Pretty in Pink*, which was directed by Howard Deutch. It featured Ringwald as a high-school girl who falls for a boy in a different social clique. The perils of adolescent love also provided the subject matter for Hughes's next screenplay, the Deutch-directed *Some Kind of Wonderful* (1987). Hughes moved away from teen-oriented themes, however, with the 1987 comedy *Planes, Trains, and Automobiles*, which he directed, wrote, and produced. The film is about a pair of mismatched business travelers (Steve Martin and John Candy) on a disaster-plagued trip from New York to Chicago. Hughes also directed Candy in the 1989 comedy *Uncle Buck*. Hughes's last film as a director, *Curly Sue* (1991), about a pint-size grifter, was not as well received as his prior efforts. Still, Hughes enjoyed major success with *Home Alone* (1990), which he wrote and produced. The film, a blockbuster box-office hit, starred Macaulay Culkin as an eight-year-old boy accidentally abandoned by his vacationing family over the Christmas holiday. When the boy discovers two bungling burglars attempting to rob the family home, he sets up a series of clever traps and distractions to thwart their efforts. The film's success led Hughes to write and produce two sequels, *Home Alone 2: Lost in New York* (1992) and *Home Alone 3* (1997). (Hughes is also credited as a writer for the 2002 television movie *Home Alone 4*). In addition to the screenplays he wrote for films he directed, Hughes contributed to several other screenplays, sometimes under the pen name Edmond Dantes, a reference to the classic novel *The Count of Monte Cristo*. He is credited as a writer of the films *National Lampoon's Christmas Vacation* (1989), *Beethoven* (1992), *Dennis the Menace* (1993), *Baby's Day Out* (1994), *101 Dalmatians* (1995), *Flubber* (1997), and *Maid in Manhattan* (2002), among others. His last screen credit was as a co-writer, with Seth Rogen and Kristofor Brown, of the comedy *Drillbit Taylor* (2008). Hughes, who died of a heart attack, is survived by his wife, Nancy; his sons, John and James; and his grandchildren. "His death," Susan King wrote for the *Los Angeles Times* (October 1, 2009, on-line), "left his legion of fans feeling as if they'd lost a bit of their youth." See *Current Biography* (1991). — W.D.

Obituary *New York Times* (on-line) Aug. 7, 2009

JACKSON, MICHAEL Aug. 29, 1958–June 25, 2009 Pop musician. Known as the "King of Pop," Michael Jackson enjoyed a following few others in the history of recorded music could boast. He first made his mark during the late 1960s, as the youngest member and frontman of the R&B family singing group the Jackson 5. He had his greatest success, however, as a solo performer, most notably with the release of his breakthrough record *Off the Wall* (1979) and his soul/rock crossover *Thriller* (1982), the best-selling album of all time, according to the *Guinness Book of World Records*. He followed that with a series of multi-platinum solo records: *Bad* (1987), *Dangerous* (1991), *HIStory: Past, Present, and Future, Book I* (1995), and *Invincible* (2001), each of which reached the top of the *Billboard* album charts. During the course of his career, Jackson also had more than a dozen number-one hit singles, including "Rock with You," "Don't Stop 'til You Get Enough," "Billie Jean," "Beat It," and "Man in the Mirror," many of which merged soulful pop, disco, and R&B. He was widely credited with revolutionizing the music industry by creating big-budget music videos that were more like self-contained short films than mere promotional tools. He was hailed even more for his groundbreaking dance moves, including the now-iconic "moonwalk," as well as his signature fashion sense, most notably exemplified by his single sequined glove, fedora, and red leather jacket. A two-time Rock and Roll Hall of Fame inductee, he sold roughly 750 million records worldwide. His numerous honors include 19 Grammy Awards, 22 American Music Awards, and 12 World Music Awards. Despite his widely acknowledged contributions to pop music, Jackson's career was marred by lawsuits, allegations of child molestation, botched plastic surgery, and bizarre offstage behavior. Michael Joseph Jackson was born in Gary, Indiana, the fifth of the nine children of Joseph Jackson, a steel-mill crane operator, and Katherine Jackson, a Sears, Roebuck, and Co. employee. At age five Jackson made his performing debut at a Christmas recital, and three years later he joined the Jackson Brothers, an R&B group formed in 1964 by his older brothers Jackie, Tito, Marlon, and Jermaine (who left in 1976 and was replaced by another brother, Randy). Jackson started as a percussionist before being quickly promoted to vocals. "He was so energetic that at five years old he was like a leader," Jackie Jackson recalled to Gerri Hirshey for *Rolling Stone* (February 17, 1983). "We saw that. So we said, 'Hey, Michael, you be the lead guy.' The audience ate it up." Impressed by the group's performance during the famed amateur competition at Harlem's renowned Apollo Theater in 1967, the singer Gladys Knight and the pianist Billy Taylor alerted Berry Gordy, the founder of the Motown record label, who signed the Jacksons in 1968. The next year the newly renamed Jackson 5 released *Diana Ross Presents the Jackson 5*, which spawned the number-one single "I Want You Back." In 1970 the Jackson 5 had three consecutive number-one songs—"ABC," "The Love You Save," and "I'll Be There"—thus becoming the first group to have each of its first four major-label singles reach the top of the charts. The Jackson 5 quickly became a musical phenomenon, due in large part to the popular, prepubescent Jackson, who dazzled young female fans with his slick, James Brown–inspired dance moves and soulful soprano vocals. In an effort to capitalize on Jackson's appeal, Gordy began preparing him for a solo career. In the 1970s Michael Jackson released the solo albums *Got to Be There*, *Ben*, *Music & Me*, and *Forever Michael*. He continued to perform with the Jackson 5, who were the subjects of an eponymous Saturday-morning cartoon series and starred in two television specials between 1971 and 1973. The group went on to release several less successful albums—including *Lookin' Through the Windows* (1972) and *G.I.T.: Get It Together* (1974)—during the latter part of their Motown tenure, which ended in 1975, when the brothers signed with Epic Records. Over the next several years, the group, renamed the Jacksons due to a legal dispute with Motown, released a self-titled album (1976), which went gold, and the platinum-selling *Destiny* (1978), featuring the top-10 single "Shake Your Body (Down to the Ground)," which Jackson co-wrote. Also in 1978, Jackson made his movie debut, appearing as the Scarecrow in *The Wiz.* While shooting the movie, Jackson befriended the film's musical supervisor, Quincy Jones, who served as the producer for Jackson's fifth solo album, *Off the Wall* (1979), which spawned four top-10 singles, was certified platinum seven times in the U.S., and has since sold an estimated 20 million copies worldwide. Jackson and his brothers then released the platinum-selling *Triumph* (1980). A year later Jackson achieved even greater solo success with *Thriller* (1982), which became the best-selling record of 1983. *Thriller*'s meteoric rise to the top of the album charts was also credited to the popularity of Jackson's elaborate, narrative-driven, and intricately choreographed music videos for "Beat It" and "Billie Jean," which became staples on the MTV network. Jackson's nearly 14-minute video for the single "Thriller," directed by John Landis and featuring a troupe of zombies dancing in lockstep, is regarded as one of the most influential music videos of all time. Jackson took home eight Grammy Awards for the album. After reuniting with his brothers for the highly publicized and successful *Victory* album and tour, in 1984, Jackson collaborated with Lionel Richie to write the 1985 single "We Are the World," whose proceeds went to combat famine in Africa. Next came the solo album *Bad* (1987), which became Jackson's first disc to debut at number one. *Dangerous* (1991) also debuted at number one, where it remained for four weeks. During the 1990s Jackson's personal life became the subject of media frenzy. In 1993 he was accused of molesting a young boy at his Neverland Ranch home, in California, but he was not charged criminally due to a lack of evidence. Although he maintained his innocence, in 1994 he settled a civil suit with the boy's family. (In 2005 molestation charges were again brought against Jackson, and again he was acquitted.) In 1994 he also made headlines with his marriage to Lisa Marie Presley, the daughter of the music legend Elvis Presley. (Despite the marriage, rumors persisted about Jackson's possible homosexuality.) In 1995 Jackson released the double album *HIStory: Past, Present and Future, Book I.* Following his divorce from Presley, in January 1996, Jackson married Debbie Rowe in November of that year. The couple had two children: Michael Joseph Jackson Jr., born in 1997, and Paris Michael Katherine Jackson, born in 1998. Rowe and Jackson divorced a year later. (Since Jackson's death rumors have been rampant about the children's actual parentage.) Jackson had another son, Prince Michael Jackson II, in 2002, via a surrogate mother. Jackson was the subject of intense criticism following an incident in which he dangled his younger son, then 11 months old, from the window of a German hotel. By then Jackson had released his final solo disc, the double album *Invincible* (2001), which debuted at number one and has since sold 10 million copies worldwide. Jackson's physical appearance was the subject of much media fascination and ridicule, most notably for his numerous nose jobs and his skin, which he had lightened through undisclosed means. (Jackson claimed that he suffered from a condition called vitiligo, which caused the change in skin color.) Jackson was out of the public eye after he relocated to the Persian Gulf nation of Bahrain, in 2005, to work on his music. In 2009 he returned to California, where he began rehearsing for a series of 50 sold-out concerts to be held at the O2 arena in London, England. Jackson died of cardiac arrest at the University of California, Los Angeles (UCLA) Medical Center. An autopsy revealed that an overdose of painkillers and other prescription drugs caused his death. Jackson is survived by his parents, five brothers and three sisters, three children, and several nieces and nephews. See *Current Biography* (1983).—W.D.

Obituary *New York Times* (on-line) June 25, 2009

JOHANSSON, INGEMAR Sep. 22, 1932–Jan. 30, 2009 Boxer. In June 1959 Ingemar Johansson, nicknamed "The Hammer of Thor" and "Ingo's Bingo" for his ferocious right-hand punch, shocked the boxing world with his third-round technical knockout (TKO) of Floyd Patterson to win the world heavyweight championship title. (A technical knockout, or TKO, is declared when a referee judges one boxer to be unable to continue fighting.) With his upset victory Johansson became Sweden's first world heavyweight champion, and only the third European to win the title. Johansson and Patterson fought two more times, with Patterson winning both contests. Those losses were the only defeats that Johansson suffered during his professional career. Johansson was born in Gothenburg, Sweden's second-largest city. At age 13 he joined a boxing club, and two years later he left school to pursue a boxing career. Johansson, who developed his muscles by working as a dock laborer, had his first amateur bout when he was 16. Shortly afterward he began a 15-month stint in the Swedish navy. By age 19 Johansson was the Swedish heavyweight amateur champion, with a record of 80 wins and eight losses. In 1952 he represented his country at the Summer Olympic Games in Helsinki, Finland, and advanced to the gold-medal match, which consists of three rounds, each lasting three minutes. Johansson was disqualified in the second round for his lackluster effort against U.S. opponent Ed Sanders and labeled a national disgrace. (In 1982 the International Olympic Committee awarded him a silver medal after the fact.) After a six-month period of self-imposed seclusion, Johansson turned professional in December 1952. Managed by Eddie Ahlqvist, he won his first 21 professional fights and then captured the Scandinavian heavyweight title in 1953. Three years later Johansson added the European heavyweight title to his collection, following his 13th-round knockout of Italy's Franco Cavicchi. He successfully defended his European title in May 1957, with a five-round knockout of Britain's Henry Cooper, and in February 1958, with a 13th-round decision against Welsh opponent Joe Erskine. Johansson's first-round victory against U.S. fighter Eddie Machen in September 1958 raised his international profile. Johansson, who was named *Ring Magazine* fighter of the year for 1958, challenged Floyd Patterson for the world heavyweight title in 1959, in a match held at Yankee Stadium, in New York City. He began training at a resort in the Catskill Mountains and drew criticism in that more puritanical time for bringing his fiancée with him. Although boxing pundits predicted that Johansson would lose the fight, he pulled off a surprise upset in the third round, sending Patterson to the canvas seven times. Upon his return to Sweden, Johansson was greeted as a national hero. On June 20, 1960, Johansson and Patterson met for a rematch at the New York Polo Grounds, with much different results. Patterson regained his world heavyweight title, with a fifth-round knockout of Johansson. On March 13, 1961 the pair fought for a third and final time, at the Convention Hall in Miami Beach, Florida—a contest that Patterson won via a sixth-round TKO, despite being twice knocked down by Johansson in the first round. A year later Johansson regained the European heavyweight title, after an eighth-round knockout of Welsh fighter Dick Richardson. Also in 1962 Johansson had two other victories: a seventh-round TKO against Joe Bygraves and a fifth-round knockout of Wim Snoek. Johansson's last professional opponent was British boxer Brian London, whom he fought in a non-title, 12-round match in Stockholm, Sweden, on April 21, 1963. After winning the contest on points, Johansson announced his retirement from boxing and left the sport with a record of 26–2 and 17 knockouts. Johansson has been inducted into the World Boxing Hall of Fame (1988) and the International Boxing Hall of Fame (2002). He served as a boxing commentator and columnist and was also the owner of several business concerns, including a successful construction company, office suites in Stockholm, and a hotel in Florida. After living in Switzerland from 1959 to 1974, Johansson moved to Pompano Beach, Florida. Johansson, who was married and divorced three times, died from pneumonia-related complications at a nursing home in Kungsbucka, Sweden, a town near where he was raised. He is survived by four children: a son, Thomas, and a daughter, Jean, from his first marriage as well as a son, Patrick, and daughter, Maria, from his second marriage. See *Current Biography* (1959). — W.D.

Obituary *New York Times* (on-line) Feb. 1, 2009

JOHNSON, VAN Aug. 25, 1916–Dec. 12, 2008 Actor. Van Johnson was a film actor with "boy-next-door" looks who was best known for his affiliation with the Metro-Goldwyn-Mayer (MGM) studio during Hollywood's "golden age" in the 1940s and 1950s. Born Charles Van Dell Johnson in Newport, Rhode Island, he was the only child of Charles E. Johnson, a plumber turned real-estate salesman, and the former Loretta Snyder, who was of German-American and Pennsylvania Dutch ancestry. His mother, an alcoholic, left the family when Johnson was three, and he grew up under the watchful eye of his strict father, with whom he had a stormy relationship. In high school the star-struck Johnson juggled odd jobs to help support the family while also performing at local social clubs. Upon graduating from high school in 1935, Johnson moved to New York City, where he worked as a singer, dancer, and musician before landing a job as a substitute dancer in a touring New England theater troupe. His Broadway debut came in May 1936, when he appeared in the successful revue *The New Faces of 1936*. After the show closed, Johnson performed in Eight Young Men of Manhattan, a vaudeville act built around the stage and film actress Mary Martin at the swank New York City nightclub the Rainbow Room. His acting career received a much-needed boost in 1940, after he worked as an understudy to Desi Arnaz and Eddie Bracken in *Too Many Girls*. The Rodgers and Hammerstein musical comedy also starred Lucille Ball, who introduced Johnson to Billy Gould, a casting director at MGM; Gould signed Johnson to a contract in 1942. Johnson raised his visibility with his role as an aspiring doctor nicknamed "Red" in the medical drama *Dr. Gillespie's New Assistant* (1942), a continuation of the popular *Dr. Kildare* film franchise; he also reprised the role for *Dr. Gillespie's Criminal Case* (1943), *Three Men in White* (1944), and *Between Two Women* (1945). (The character Dr. Kildare was later featured in a radio serial and a popular TV series.) In 1943 Johnson's career was jeopardized by a car accident that left him with a metal plate in his forehead. He rebounded, however, with starring roles in the wartime films *A Guy Named Joe* (1943) and *The Human Comedy* (1943). During the rest of the 1940s and the early 1950s, he was cast in several other wartime dramas, including *Pilot #5* (1943), *The White Cliffs of Dover* (1944), *Thirty Seconds Over Tokyo* (1944), *Command Decision* (1948), *Battleground* (1949), and *Go For Broke!* (1951). Johnson also established himself as a romantic lead with starring roles in the musicals *Two Girls and a Sailor* (1944), *Thrill of a Romance* (1945), *Week-End at the Waldorf* (1945), *Till the Clouds Roll By* (1946), *In the Good Old Summertime* (1949), *Duchess of Idaho* (1950), *Grounds for Marriage* (1951), *Easy to Love* (1953), *Brigadoon* (1954), and *Men of the Fighting Lady* (1954). His other film credits of the period included the comedies *The Bride Goes Wild* (1948), *Mother Is a Freshman* (1949), *The Big Hangover* (1950), *Three Guys Named Mike* (1951), and *Confidentially Connie* (1953). After parting ways with MGM in 1954, Johnson freelanced for other movie studios, and during the latter part of the decade, he appeared on the big screen in such pictures as *The End of the Affair* (1955); *Slander* (1956); *23 Paces to Baker Place* (1956), in which he played a blind detective; *Action of the Tiger* (1957); and the mystery thriller *Beyond This Place* (1959). Also in 1959, the actor reportedly turned down the role of Eliot Ness in the blockbuster television series *The Untouchables*. During the early 1960s, Johnson struggled to land film roles and returned instead to the stage. In 1961 he played the title role in a London revival of *The Music Man*, and a year later he co-starred opposite Carroll Baker in the Broadway production *Come on Strong*, which had a short run. After undergoing treatment for skin cancer in 1963, Johnson resumed his acting career, and over the next decade, he appeared in numerous summer-stock and dinner-theater productions. He also made guest appearances on several television series, including *Batman*, *The Name of the Game*, *The Red Skelton Show*, *The Doris Day Show*, *Maude*, and *McMillan & Wife*. On the big screen Johnson had roles in the international co-productions *La Battaglia d'Inghilterra* and *Il Prezzo del Potere*, both 1969 releases. Johnson made headlines in the late 1970s, when his portrayal of Marsh Goodwin in the ABC miniseries *Rich Man, Poor Man* earned him an Emmy nomination (1976), in the category of outstanding single performance by a supporting actor in a comedy or drama series. He followed that with parts in the films *Superdome* (1978), *Glitter* (1984), and Woody Allen's *The Purple Rose of Cairo* (1985). Also in 1985, he replaced Gene Barry in a Broadway revival of *La Cage aux Folles*, and in the early 1990s he appeared in productions of *No, No Nanette* and *Showboat*. His career then slowed because of his failing health. Johnson, who overcame two separate bouts of cancer, died of natural causes at Tappan Zee Manor, an assisted-living facility in Nyack, New York, where he had resided for the last seven years of his life. Johnson is survived by Schuyler, his daughter from his marriage to the stage actress Eve Abbott, who died in 2004. He is also survived by two stepsons, Edmond and Tracy. See *Current Biography* (1945). — C.C.

Obituary *New York Times* A p4 Dec. 13, 2008

KANTROWITZ, ADRIAN Oct. 4, 1918–Nov. 14, 2008 Surgeon; biomedical engineer; educator. The inventor of two dozen devices and procedures that have significantly prolonged the lives of millions of cardiac patients and others with medical problems, Adrian Kantrowitz is probably best remembered as the first surgeon in the U.S. to perform a heart-transplant operation. Among those in his field, however, he is considered far more important for promoting ideas that were revolutionary when he began working in the 1950s: that the heart could be viewed "as yet another organ that could be fixed," in the words of Stephen J. Lahey, a thoracic surgeon, as quoted by Jascha Hoffman in the *New York Times* (November 19, 2008); and that supplementary or auxiliary devices could help the heart repair itself or keep it functioning. The surgeon was born Felix Adrian Kantrowitz in New York City. His father was an internist, his mother a Ziegfield Follies stage designer. As a youth he collaborated with his brother Arthur (who became an internationally renowned physicist) to build a crude electrocardiograph. He earned an A.B. degree in math from New York University in 1940. Thanks to an accelerated program aimed at producing new doctors for the military during World War II, he received an M.D. degree only three years later, from the Long Island College of Medicine (now the State University of New York Downstate Medical Center). He completed an internship at Brooklyn Jewish Hospital, in New York, before serving in the U.S. Army Medical Corps (1944–46) as a battalion surgeon. Back in New York he completed residencies in surgery and pathology. He worked at Montefiore Hospital, in New York (1951–55), and then at the Downstate Medical Center (1965–70). Simultaneously, at Maimonides Medical Center, in Brooklyn, he was the director of cardiovascular surgery (1955–64) and of surgery (1964–70). In 1970 he moved, with his entire team of surgeons, engineers, and nurses, to the Wayne State University School of Medicine and Sinai Hospital in Detroit, Michigan. (Very unusually, he received permission from the Heart Council of the National Heart Institute to transfer his multimillion-dollar grant, grant-purchased equipment, and patent rights from one institution to another.) He remained at the school until his death. Kantrowitz made his first, highly innovative contribution to medicine in 1950, when he filmed the inside of a beating animal heart. In 1954 he co-created a Teflon valve that enabled people with hardening of the arteries to pump significantly more blood to their legs and other body parts. To prevent patients undergoing cardiac surgery from suffering shock because of internal blood loss, in 1957 Kantrowitz built a machine that measured blood flow and indicated decreases in the flow; whenever the decrease became dangerous, his machine triggered a transfusion device to start replacing the lost blood.

Another of his major inventions was an improved automated heart-lung machine, for use with patients undergoing open-heart surgery. In 1958 he unveiled an auxiliary heart booster, the forerunner of his heart-assist pump; implanted in a dog, it was made of diaphragm muscle and a miniature radio and relieved a weakened heart of as much as 25 percent of its work. In 1961 he became the first person to use computer-controlled electrodes to stimulate the muscles of paraplegics and enable them to move their limbs. In 1962, in a joint effort with General Electric Co. engineers, he introduced an early version of an artificial heart pacemaker. In 1964, with Tetsuzo Akutsu and his brother Arthur, he designed a plastic pump that supplemented the work of the left ventricle. In the two patients in whom the pump was implanted in 1966, the first died of liver failure within a day. The second, who had been critically ill before the surgery, was repeatedly taken out of heart failure by the blood pump, went back into heart failure when the pump was stopped, and taken out of heart failure when the pump was activated, a dramatic demonstration that an assist device could be a treatment for heart failure. That patient lived for 12 days before a blood clot caused a fatal stroke. Kantrowitz then redesigned the blood pump and began testing the new version in animals. The U-shaped device used in the two patients had been implanted in the divided ascending aorta, rerouting the blood through the blood pump, which was connected to the aorta by means of two grafts. The redesign was implanted directly in the wall of the thoracic aorta, did not require grafts, and was called the "dynamic aortic patch." During that period Kantrowitz successfully demonstrated the use of another of his inventions, the intra-aortic balloon pump, which, when inserted after a heart attack, relieved strain on the heart, improving the chances for recovery. The balloon pump has now been used in more than three million patients worldwide. Meanwhile, Kantrowitz had also become interested in heart transplantation in infants. In 1967, after hundreds of experiments using puppies, Kantrowitz transplanted a heart from a two-day-old, brain-dead infant into a 19-day-old baby with a fatal heart defect. The recipient lived for six and one-half hours. (Three days earlier Christiaan Barnard had performed a similar operation on an adult in South Africa after far less preparation.) After the failure early the next year of a second transplant, in an adult, Kantrowitz turned away from that approach as premature, in light of the absence of adequate antirejection drugs. Continuing with the redesigned "dynamic aortic patch," he implanted the device in a third patient in terminal heart failure on September 18, 1971. That patient was the first person to be discharged from the hospital to home with an assist device intended for long-term, ambulatory use. Three months later he succumbed to infection originating at the site on the skin where he had placed the tube through which air was pumped from the drive unit to the aortic blood pump. Similarly, a second patient, also improved hemodynamically, succumbed to infection after three months. As an infection-resistant skin port was not commercially available, Kantrowitz turned his attention to developing one. He spent the next two decades developing and testing such a device. Later trademarked as the ViaDerm, it is precoated with the patient's skin cells, using a method that mimics normal wound healing. After the ViaDerm remained infection-free in animals for more than five years, Kantrowitz revived the aortic heart-assist system. To secure the funds for the extensive testing required by the FDA, in 1983 Kantrowitz, his wife, Jean, and the bioengineer Paul Free founded L.VAD Technology, to develop and make the intra-aortic–assist device available for treatment of advanced heart-failure patients. Recently the company's CardioPlus was approved for continued investigation as a treatment for chronic heart failure. Kantrowitz wrote well over 300 articles, professional abstracts, and book chapters. He died of heart failure in Ann Arbor, Michigan. His survivors include his wife; his daughters Niki, a cardiologist, and Lisa, a radiologist; his son, Allen, a neurosurgeon; and nine grandchildren. His death was followed 15 days later by that of his brother Arthur. See *Current Biography* (1967). — Jean Kantrowitz

Obituary *New York Times* A p33 Nov. 19, 2008

KANTROWITZ, ARTHUR Oct. 20, 1913–Nov. 29, 2008 Physicist. Arthur Robert Kantrowitz's pioneering physics research led directly to the invention of nose cones for rockets, making him a crucial contributor to American space flight. He was born in New York City to Bernard Kantrowitz, a physician, and Rose (Esserman) Kantrowitz, who designed costumes for the famed Ziegfield Follies. He had a sister and two brothers, one of whom became a prominent cardiac surgeon and biomedical engineer. A mediocre student, Kantrowitz was kicked out of his private school and did not perform measurably better at the public elementary school that he subsequently attended. Still, he was intensely interested in physics and other scientific topics, and he spent much of his spare time reading ham-radio magazines and stories about Thomas Edison and Albert Einstein. When the family moved to Connecticut, Kantrowitz concentrated on studying math books and conducting rudimentary electronic experiments. (He also started a small radio-repair business.) Kantrowitz attended Columbia University, in New York City, graduating with a bachelor's degree in physics in 1934 and a master's degree in 1936. He then went to Langley Field, in Virginia, to join the National Advisory Committee for Aeronautics (NACA), the forerunner of the national Aeronautics and Space Administration (NASA). In 1938 he and his supervisor at Langley, Eastman N. Jacobs, hit upon the idea of harnessing thermonuclear energy by heating hydrogen with radio waves. The Manhattan Project would not be initiated for another year, and no other scientists had attempted to create nuclear fusion. The two men, fearing that their superior would scoff at the notion of atomic energy, worked on the experiment in secret. The experiment failed, however, and before Kantrowitz and Jacobs could research further, their director discovered the project and called a halt to the work. (Physicists later revisited the idea of creating thermonuclear fusion in a magnetic bottle, and researchers continue to explore the topic.) In 1940 Kantrowitz took a leave of absence to complete his doctoral degree, but he interrupted his studies and returned to NACA when the U.S. entered World War II. During his second stint at NACA, Kantrowitz was assigned to study supersonic aerodynamics, and this research contributed significantly to the development of the supersonic diffuser and compressor for jet engines. He received his Ph.D. degree from Columbia University in 1947, by which time he was already teaching at Cornell University's School of Aeronautical Engineering. In 1954 he met Victor Emanuel, the chairman of the aeronautical corporation Avco, at a party. Emanuel mentioned to Kantrowitz the reentry problem that his company and the U.S. Air Force were having with the intercontinental ballistic missile. The nose cone of the missile, in the return from space to the atmosphere, had to withstand a reentry heat one and one-half times that of the sun. Such intense heat was not feasible for testing in a conventional wind tunnel, and it was therefore assumed that the problem would be solved only by four or more years of enormously expensive trial and error in actual flights. Kantrowitz confidently told Emanuel that he could come up with a solution in six months. "The conditions that will be encountered in the reentry phase can be duplicated with laboratory equipment, in shock tubes that are presently available at my laboratory at Cornell," Kantrowitz explained to Avco's chairman, according to Shirley Thomas in the third volume of *Men in Space* (1961). "When we can duplicate a condition, study it, and analyze its properties, the matter of dealing with it in practical terms cannot be difficult." (A shock tube was a strong metal pipe, divided by a thin copper diaphragm into two sections, one containing air at low pressure, and the other, light gas at high pressure. When the diaphragm was burst, a shock wave traversed the length of the tube.) In 1956 Kantrowitz left Cornell to devote himself exclusively to his work at the Avco Everett Research Laboratory, where he refined the design for a nose cone able to withstand the rigors of reentry. The first nose cone to be recovered after a space flight of intercontinental range was the Avcoite-coated RVX 1-5, which was carried into space on April 8, 1958 by a Thor Able rocket. After traveling at speeds of more than 15,000 mph and enduring air-friction heat greater than 12,000 degrees Fahrenheit, it was recovered near Ascension Island. "The recovery of that nose cone," Kantrowitz said, "gave the first really solid authentication of the shock-tube work that had been done several years before." The cone is now on display at the Smithsonian Institution. In the late 1960s, collaborating with his brother Adrian, Kantrowitz invented a heart pump to help circulate blood in cardiac patients, a device that has since been beneficial to millions of people. Later, Kantrowitz championed the need for a "science court," in which experts could weigh in on such controversies as the use of pesticides or the safety of nuclear reactors. (In 1975 he chaired a presidential task force on the idea.) In 1978 Kantrowitz left Avco and joined the faculty of Dartmouth University, where he attained the title of professor emeritus. Kantrowitz, who held more than 20 patents, was a fellow of the American Academy of Arts and Sciences, the American Physical Society, the American Association for the Advancement of Science, and the American Astronautical Society, among other organizations. The recipient of the Roosevelt Medal of Honor for Distinguished Service in Science, he sat on the advisory board of the PBS television program *Nova*. Kantrowitz died of heart failure and is survived by his second wife, Lee Stuart; his three daughters, Barbara, Lore, and Andrea; and his many grandchildren. See *Current Biography* (1966). — D.K.

Obituary *New York Times* (on-line) Dec. 9, 2008

KATZIR, EPHRAIM May 16, 1916–May 30, 2009 Israeli statesman; scientist. Although the post of Israeli president is largely ceremonial, Ephraim Katzir was nonetheless an influential national figure during his tenure, which lasted from 1973 to 1978, standing firm during the 1973 Arab-Israeli war and welcoming President Anwar el-Sadat of Egypt on his 1977 visit to Jerusalem. In addition to his political career, Katzir, who chaired the biophysics department at the renowned Weizmann Institute, was recognized as one of his country's most important scientists for his work on enzymes and synthetic proteins. Katzir, whose adopted Hebrew surname means "harvest," was born Ephraim Katchalski in Kiev, then part of Russia. He was the younger of the two sons of Yehuda Katchalski, a merchant, and Tsila (Suchowolski) Katchalski, both fervent Zionists. At the age of six, he moved with his parents and his brother, Aharon, to Palestine, then under British rule. After graduating from secondary school, Katzir entered the Hebrew University in Jerusalem, where he studied chemistry, bacteriology, and zoology. As a student, Katzir became active in Haganah, the Jewish underground army, and during the Jewish-Arab hostilities of the late 1930s, he helped to hide weapons under a lectern at the university. He obtained his M.Sc. degree summa cum laude in 1937 and his Ph.D. degree four years later. He remained at Hebrew University from 1941 to 1945 as a research assistant in the department of theoretical and macromolecular chemistry. In 1946 he came to the United States for a two-year stint as a research fellow at the Polytechnic Institute of Brooklyn and at Columbia University. During Israel's war for independence in 1948, Katzir and his brother, a molecular chemist, worked with Haganah in the development of explosives. In 1949 Katzir was named acting head of the department of biophysics at the newly created Weizmann Institute of Science, in Rehovot, Israel. Confirmed in 1951 as head of that department, a position he occupied until 1973, he also became the institute's senior researcher. As a scientist, Katzir contributed greatly to the understanding of the genetic code and the immune system's responses. He also developed a new method for binding enzymes to various surfaces and molecules, now an essential part of enzyme engineering, and he conducted groundbreaking work on synthetic protein models, ultimately creating a synthetic fiber that could be used to stitch internal wounds. In 1961 Katzir became a scientific adviser for Israel's Ministry of Defense. He was chief scientist at the ministry from 1966 to 1968. In 1973 Israeli prime minister Golda Meir asked Katzir to submit his name as a candidate for president. Meir's first choice had been Katzir's brother, Aharon, but he had been killed on May 30, 1972 by Japanese terrorists who shot passengers at what is now Ben-Gurion International Airport. Katzir was serving as president of Israel during the 1973 Arab-Israeli war, which began when Egypt and Syria unexpectedly attacked the nation on Yom Kippur, one of the holiest days on the Jewish calendar. Katzir helped to successfully lead the country through the war, which saw a high death toll, anti-government protests, and Meir's resignation. Four years later, in November 1977, Katzir famously welcomed Egyptian president Anwar el-Sadat on his visit to Jerusalem. Although he preferred to remain largely out of the spotlight, Katzir traveled the country pushing for the founding of Jewish studies departments in universities around the world and instituting awards for volunteerism. He turned down a second presidential term in 1978 and returned to the Weizmann Institute. He also worked to establish a biotechnology department at Tel Aviv University and wrote numerous academic papers. Katzir, who was awarded numerous honors over the course of his career, including the inaugural Japan Prize from the Science and Technology Foundation of Japan and an appointment to the French Legion of Honor, died at his home on the grounds of the Weizmann campus. He was predeceased by his wife, Nina, a Polish-born English teacher, and his two daughters, Nurit and Irit. He is survived by his son, Meir, and three grandchildren. Shortly before his death, Katzir completed an autobiography, *Sipur Chaim* ("A Life Story"). See *Current Biography* (1975). — W.D.

Obituary *New York Times* (on-line) June 4, 2009

KAUFMAN, MILLARD Mar. 12, 1917–Mar. 14, 2009 Screenwriter; novelist. Millard Kaufman came to prominence in the 1950s, after penning two Academy Award–nominated screenplays. More than five decades later, he became a first-time novelist at the age of 90. Born in Baltimore, Maryland, Kaufman developed an interest in cinema during his late teens. After completing high school he spent two years as a merchant seaman and then enrolled at Johns Hopkins University, in Baltimore, Maryland. He earned a B.A. degree in English literature in 1939 and then moved to New York City, where he worked as a copy boy for the *Daily News* and, later, as a reporter for *Newsday*. In 1942 he joined the Marines and fought in World War II. During his three-year stint, Kaufman contracted malaria and dengue fever while serving in the South Pacific. He saw combat at the Battle of Guadalcanal and fought in Guam and Okinawa. After the war Kaufman, whose heroic actions at Guadalcanal earned him a bronze star for bravery, moved to Los Angeles to pursue a screenwriting career. He was hired by Dore Schary, the chief of production at Metro Goldwyn Mayer (MGM), partly due to the film executive's stated fascination with the Marines. Kaufman's first screenplay was for the short cartoon *Ragtime Bear* (1949), which featured the debut of Mr. Magoo, a nearsighted, accident-prone animated character Kaufman created with John Hubley. Over the next two years, Kaufman amassed credits for *Punchy de Leon* (1950)—another Mr. Magoo cartoon—*Deadly Is the Female* (1950), *Unknown World* (1951), and *Aladdin and His Lamp* (1952). The following year Kaufman's screenplay for the war film *Take the High Ground!* (1953) earned him his first Academy Award nomination. Two years later Kaufman received a second Academy Award nod—this time for *Bad Day at Black Rock* (1955), another combat movie. Directed by John Sturges, *Bad Day* starred Spencer Tracy as a World War II veteran who visits a small Arizona town in search of the father of a fellow soldier. Kaufman's later screenplay credits included *Raintree County* (1957), a Civil War drama starring Elizabeth Taylor and Montgomery Clift that he also produced; *Never So Few* (1959), a World War II drama directed by John Sturges and starring Frank Sinatra and Steve McQueen; *Convicts 4* (1962), Kaufman's directorial debut; *The War Lord* (1965); *Living Free* (1972), an adaptation of Joy Adamson's novel of the same name about a lioness she raised in Africa; and *The Klansman* (1974), based on the novel by William Bradford Huie about racism in a small Alabama town in the 1960s, starring Lee Marvin and Richard Burton. Kaufman also penned scripts for the small screen, most notably the made-for-television movies *The Nativity* (1978) and *Enola Gay: The Men, the Mission, the Atomic Bomb* (1980). He also authored the book *Plots and Characters: A Screenwriter on Screenwriting* (1999). In 2003, when his screenplay for a project about Jack Johnson, the first black world heavyweight boxing champion, fell through, Kaufman, then in his 80s, launched a career as a novelist. "I decided, knowing that nobody my age gets work in movies, and that I had to do something, otherwise I'd get into terrible trouble, that I would try writing a novel," he told Steffie Nelson for the *Los Angeles Times* (October 31, 2007). The resulting book, *Bowl of Cherries* (2007), follows the comical journey of a 14-year-old prodigy who ends up in an Iraqi prison awaiting his execution. In a review for the *Washington Post* (September 23, 2007), William Booth wrote, "That weird incongruity between highbrow/lowbrow humor is only part of what makes *Bowl of Cherries* so irresistible. Kaufman's comic imagination, his ability to mix things scatological and historical, political and philosophical, reminds one of those young'uns Kurt Vonnegut and Joseph Heller." Kaufman, whose second novel, "Misadventure," was scheduled for publication in the fall of 2009, died of complications after open-heart surgery. He is survived by Lorraine, his wife of more than six decades; their three children, Frederick, Mary, and Amy; and several grandchildren. See *Current Biography* (2008). — D.K.

Obituary *New York Times* (on-line) Mar. 19, 2009

KEMP, JACK July 13, 1935–May 2, 2009 Former congressman; football player. "I think there is no doubt that [Jack Kemp] had a greater impact on conservative and Republican economic philosophy than anybody else. More than [economist Arthur] Laffer, more than [Ronald] Reagan," Norman J. Orstein, a scholar at the American Enterprise Institute, noted in the *New York Times* obituary (May 3, 2009, online) of Kemp. A former professional football quarterback and former Republican congressman, Kemp championed supply-side economics, a philosophy that embraced tax cuts as a way of promoting economic growth. Born in Los Angeles, California, Jack French Kemp was the third of four sons of Paul R.

Kemp, the owner of a Los Angeles–based trucking company, and Frances (Pope) Kemp, a social worker. Kemp played football while attending Fairfax High School, and following his graduation in 1953 he enrolled at Occidental College, where he served as captain and quarterback of the football team and also competed in track. While there, he met his future wife, Joanne Maine. After receiving a bachelor's degree in physical education in 1957, Kemp entered the National Football League (NFL) draft and was selected in the 17th round by the Detroit Lions, but failed to make the team. Over the next three years Kemp, who served in the U.S. Army Reserves from 1958 to 1962, had brief stints with a number of teams in the NFL and Canadian Football League (CFL), including the Pittsburgh Steelers, the New York Giants, and the Calgary Stampeders. In 1960 Kemp signed with the Los Angeles Chargers of the newly launched American Football League (AFL) as a quarterback. Following an injury to his passing hand, Kemp was placed on waivers in 1962 and picked up by the Buffalo Bills. As the Bills' starting quarterback, he led the team to three consecutive Eastern division titles and two consecutive AFL championships (1964–65) and was voted the AFL's most valuable player in 1965. During his stint with the Bills, Kemp co-founded the league's players association and also served as its president (1965–70). Kemp's involvement in politics began before his football career ended. He volunteered for Richard Nixon's unsuccessful gubernatorial campaign in 1962 and Senator Barry Goldwater's failed White House bid in 1964 and also served as an assistant chief of staff to Ronald Reagan, then governor of California, in 1968. In 1970, with the encouragement of several local Republicans, Kemp successfully campaigned for a seat in the U.S. House of Representatives, where he served from 1971 to 1989. During his nine terms in the U.S. House, Kemp represented New York's 39th Congressional District—which later was declared the 38th and then the 31st. (Concurrently, he held the post of Republican Conference chairman for seven years.) As a member of Congress, Kemp, influenced by existing theories of supply-side economics, developed a reputation as an advocate for tax cuts to stimulate the economy—a philosophy that ran counter to the Republican Party's traditional commitment to balanced budgets. He and Republican senator William Roth co-sponsored a bill (the Kemp-Roth Act) to cut personal income tax rates by 30 percent. The legislation became a talking point during Reagan's successful 1980 presidential campaign, and in 1981 the new president signed into law the Economic Recovery Tax Act, which was modeled after the Kemp-Roth Act. (Reagan's economic policies ultimately became known as "Reaganomics.") Kemp was also recognized for advocating political outreach by the Republican Party to minorities, particularly black and Hispanic voters. President George H.W. Bush appointed Kemp the secretary of the U.S. Department of Housing and Urban Development (HUD) in 1989. During his tenure as HUD secretary, which lasted until 1993, he supported tenant ownership programs and championed a program to create tax-free enterprise zones to attract businesses to inner-city neighborhoods. In 1996 Senator Bob Dole selected Kemp as his running mate during his failed presidential bid. Kemp founded the lobbying firm Kemp Partners, the public policy and advocacy group Empower America, and the Foundation for the Defense of Democracies, a non-profit think tank. He remained an influential figure in the Republican Party, endorsing and campaigning for Republican senator John McCain during the 2008 presidential election. Kemp died of cancer at his home in Bethesda, Maryland. He is survived by his wife, Joanne; four children; and several grandchildren. See *Current Biography* (1980). — M.E.R.

Obituary *New York Times* (on-line) May 3, 2009

KENNEDY, EDWARD M. Feb. 22, 1932–Aug. 25, 2009 U.S. senator. Edward Moore "Ted" Kennedy, who became known as the "lion of the Senate," was one of the most influential American statesmen in recent history. The last surviving brother of a famed political dynasty, he represented Massachusetts for 46 years, from 1963 until his death. Kennedy served under 10 presidents and was the third-longest-serving U.S. senator in history. A fierce champion of the poor and disadvantaged, he was admired for his masterful political strategizing and ability to shape national policy; although he was a staunch Democrat, he was genuinely bipartisan and enjoyed long friendships with some Republicans. He was largely responsible for the landmark 1990 Americans with Disabilities Act as well as bills providing health insurance to underprivileged children, access to safe abortion, and mandated family leave; his name appeared on nearly 1,000 measures. Kennedy's commitment to public service—which deepened after the assassinations of his brothers President John F. Kennedy and Senator Robert F. Kennedy—remained unwavering throughout his life. Despite his inarguable accomplishments, Kennedy had his share of detractors. Opponents sometimes characterized him as a classic example of a tax-and-spend liberal, and his personal failings were frequently seized upon by those wishing to discredit him. Kennedy was born in Brookline, Massachusetts, the last of the nine children of Joseph P. and Rose (Fitzgerald) Kennedy, third-generation Americans from prominent Irish-Catholic families involved in state Democratic politics. His father, a multimillionaire businessman, served in the administration of President Franklin D. Roosevelt, as chairman of the Securities and Exchange Commission and then as head of the Maritime Commission. Kennedy attended several boarding schools before enrolling at Milton Academy, in 1946. In 1950 he entered Harvard University, where he was expelled in his freshman year for cheating. Repentant, Kennedy enlisted in the U.S. Army and served for two years. After his discharge, in 1953, he returned to Harvard, graduating with a B.A. degree in history and government in 1956. He earned an LL.B. degree from the University of Virginia Law School in 1959 and was admitted to the Massachusetts bar. In 1958 he managed John F. Kennedy's successful campaign for reelection to the U.S. Senate. He coordinated his brother's presidential primary campaign in several western states in 1960. Following his brother's election to the presidency, Kennedy became an assistant to the district attorney of Suffolk County, Massachusetts. He was elected to the Senate in 1962 in a special election, taking his brother John's former seat. (The seat had been held for two years by a family friend, until Kennedy reached age 30, the minimum required.) Seven months after John Kennedy's assassination, on November 22, 1963, a plane carrying him crashed in Massachusetts. He recovered from serious spinal injuries and won reelection in 1964. After Robert Kennedy's assassination, on June 5, 1968, Kennedy withdrew from public life for 10 weeks. In 1969 he was elected Senate majority whip; he was the youngest majority whip in Senate history. Later that year, while driving home at night from a party on Chappaquiddick Island, Massachusetts, Kennedy accidentally drove his car off a bridge into water; his passenger, 28-year-old Mary Jo Kopechne, was trapped in the car and drowned. Kennedy, who failed to report the accident to police for 10 hours, pleaded guilty to leaving the scene of an accident, received a two-month suspended sentence, and lost his driver's license for a year. He denied allegations of drunk driving and won reelection in 1970. In 1979 Kennedy launched a bid for the Democratic presidential nomination. He ran what was generally described as a half-hearted race and lost to the incumbent, President Jimmy Carter. During the 1980s and 1990s, Kennedy played an integral role in the passage of many important pieces of legislation. However, his personal life often overshadowed his professional life in the media. After his divorce from Virginia Joan Bennett, in 1982, he had gained a reputation as an alcoholic and a womanizer. When his nephew William Kennedy Smith was charged with rape in Palm Beach, Florida, in 1991, after a night out with Kennedy, the senator's reputation suffered further damage. (Smith was later acquitted.) After that incident he changed his lifestyle. In 1992 he married Victoria Reggie, a lawyer. Kennedy was highly active during Bill Clinton's two presidential terms. In 1996 he saw the passage of the Kassebaum-Kennedy health-care bill, which allowed for portable health insurance, and in 1997 he helped push through the Children's Health Insurance Program (CHIP) legislation. While Kennedy often found himself in opposition to President George W. Bush, particularly on the issue of the war in Iraq, he worked on a slew of bipartisan bills related to defense, medical insurers, immigration, and more. In May 2008 he was diagnosed with a malignant brain tumor. An early supporter of Barack Obama for the presidency, he gave his last major speech at the 2008 Democratic National Convention, where he discussed the need for universal health care—as he had for decades. Even as cancer weakened him, he worked with the administration of President Obama on health-care reform. He died at his Cape Cod home. Kennedy wrote the books *Decisions for a Decade: Policies and Programs for the 1970s* (1968), *In Critical Condition: The Crisis in America's Health Care* (1972), *America Back on Track* (2006), and the children's book *My Senator and Me: A Dog's Eye View of Washington* (2006), told in the voice of one of his beloved Portuguese water dogs. His book *True Compass: A Memoir* (2009), which was published posthumously, became a *New York Times* best-seller. Kennedy was survived by his wife, Vicky; his children, Kara, Edward Jr., and Patrick (a congressman); his stepchildren, Curran and Caroline Raclin; four grandchildren, and one sibling, Jean Kennedy Smith. See *Current Biography* (1978). —W.D.

Obituary *New York Times* A p1+ Aug. 27, 2009

KIM DAE-JUNG Dec. 3, 1925–Aug. 18, 2009 Former president of South Korea. Kim Dae-jung, the president of South Korea from 1997 until 2003 and the first South Korean ever to win a Nobel Peace Prize, was often referred to as the "Nelson Mandela of Asia" for his lifelong efforts to promote democracy and cooperation on the Korean peninsula. Kim was the second of seven children born into a middle-class farming family on the island of Hayi-do (sometimes transliterated as Haeuido), off South Korea's Cholla Province. After graduating in 1943 from a vocational high school in the port city of Mokpo in Cholla, he began working as a clerk for a Japanese-owned shipping company. Within a few years, Kim, who later studied economics at Kyung Hee University in Seoul, was running his own shipping company with nine small freighters. Kim also enjoyed success in the newspaper business, publishing a provincial paper called the *Mokpo Daily News*. He entered politics shortly after the 1953 ceasefire agreement between North and South Korea. Kim, who had been arrested and narrowly escaped execution by a firing squad of North Korean forces during the conflict, was elected to the National Assembly in 1961. (He had been unsuccessful on three previous bids.) Within three days of his election, a military coup led by Major General Park Chung Hee overthrew the government and dissolved the legislature. When the electoral process was restored in 1963, Kim, who had been jailed briefly by the junta, was reelected to the National Assembly as a representative from the Mokpo district. Strongly opposed to Park's autocratic policies, he quickly emerged as an opposition leader and was chosen as the presidential candidate of the New Democratic Party in 1971. Despite losing to Park in the general election, which was tarnished by fraud according to most accounts, Kim still managed to garner more than 46 percent of the vote. His popularity continued to grow amid the increasingly dictatorial practices of Park's regime. Kim escaped a 1973 assassination attempt and spent several years in prison for anti-government actions. He reentered politics in 1979, after Park was assassinated by one of his close aides. However, in the wake of a coup led by General Chun Doo-hwan, in 1980, Kim was jailed again and sentenced to a 20-year prison term on charges of treason. In 1982, after the intervention of the U.S. government, his sentence was suspended, and he was granted permission to travel to the United States. During his three years in the U.S., he helped establish the Korean Institute for Human Rights and accepted a fellowship at the Center for International Affairs at Harvard University. Kim returned home in early 1985 and was immediately placed under house arrest. In 1987, however, he was officially cleared of all previous charges against him, and his civil and political rights were fully restored. Kim, who was defeated in the presidential elections of 1987 and 1992, won election to the South Korean presidency in 1997. His inauguration, in February 1998, marked the first time in Korean history that the ruling party had peacefully transferred power to a democratically elected opposition party. Kim dedicated himself to reviving South Korea's spiraling economy and led a series of reforms and restructuring plans that helped bring the country out of financial ruin. He also helped improve relations with North Korea and worked with North Korean leader Kim Jong-Il on a joint declaration that would pave the way for increased cooperation between the two countries. In 2000 Kim was awarded a Nobel Peace Prize for his efforts. He served as president of South Korea until 2003, when he was succeeded by Roh Moo-Hyun. Kim's final days were reportedly bleak; two of his three sons had been jailed for corruption, and a special investigator had found that Kim's administration had funneled $500 million to North Korea in a seeming attempt to buy Kim Jong-Il's cooperation. Furthermore, he was reportedly distressed by what he viewed as his flawed legacy: Despite his efforts, Kim Jong-Il had not dismantled his nuclear program and had never made a promised repeat visit to Seoul. Kim Dae-jung was being treated for pneumonia when he died. He is survived by his wife, former first lady Lee Hee-ho, and his sons, Hong-up, Hong-il, and Hong-gul. See *Current Biography* (1985). — C.C.

Obituary *New York Times* (on-line) Aug. 19, 2009

KIRCHNER, LEON Jan. 24, 1919–Sep. 17, 2009 Composer. Leon Kirchner was one of the most influential figures in contemporary classical music. He wrote numerous works for orchestra, chamber groups, and solo instruments as well as song-cycles for voice and one opera. Kirchner held numerous teaching posts, including a professorship at Harvard University, and was also a talented pianist and conductor. Among his many accolades were two New York Music Critics Circle Awards for his first two string quartets, in 1950 and 1960, respectively, and a Pulitzer Prize, in 1967, for his third. Despite a reputation for seriousness, Kirchner maintained that music was meant to bring people joy; one of his favorite quotes, by the 14th-century French composer Guillaume de Machaut, was, "Music is a science, but a science that must make people laugh and dance and sing." Kirchner was born in the New York City borough of Brooklyn and spent his early years in the Bronx. His father, Samuel, an embroidery manufacturer who had emigated from Odessa, and his mother, Pauline, moved the family to Los Angeles in 1928. Kirchner, who took piano lessons, showed remarkable talent as a young boy, and by the age of 14 he was performing publicly. In deference to his mother, however, he considered becoming a doctor and enrolled in a premedical program at Los Angeles City College. He spent his limited free time writing compositions of his own, and in 1937 some of his early works were performed at the college. Kirchner then transferred to the University of California at Los Angeles to take a course in composition with the famed Austrian composer Arnold Schoenberg. (Although Kirchner was influenced by Schoenberg, he never rigorously adopted the elder man's systematic 12-tone technique.) In 1938 Kirchner transferred to the University of California's Berkeley campus, where he studied theory and earned a B.A. degree in 1940. In 1942 he won the George Ladd Prix de Paris, but he was unable to travel to France to study because of World War II. In 1943 Kirchner was called from the reserves of the Army Signal Corps to active duty, and when he was discharged, three years later, he returned to Berkeley as a teaching assistant. In 1947 Kirchner was promoted to lecturer. He left Berkeley the following year to accept a Guggenheim Fellowship, which was renewed in 1949. During that period he wrote the first of his four famed string quartets and married the singer Gertrude Schoenberg, who was unrelated to the composer. In 1950 Kirchner joined the faculty of the University of Southern California, where he rose to the rank of associate professor. He composed four significant works during that time: the Sinfonia for Orchestra (1951), the Sonata Concertante for Violin and Piano (1952), Piano Concerto no. 1 (1953), and the Trio for Violin, Cello, and Piano (1954). In 1954 Kirchner became a professor at Mills College in Oakland, California. He joined Harvard's faculty in 1961 and soon introduced the popular course Music 180: Performance and Analysis, one of the few in the curriculum that allowed student musicians to receive academic credit for playing their instruments. Ultimately named the Walter Bigelow Rosen Professor of Music, Kirchner began directing the Harvard Chamber Players in 1973 and the Harvard Chamber Orchestra and Friends two years later. Before retiring from the university, in 1989, he taught such up-and-coming musicians and composers as Alan Gilbert, John Adams, and Yo-Yo Ma. Kirchner's Music for Cello and Orchestra (1996) was written for Ma and is considered one of the great works of the 1990s. Kirchner served as composer-in-residence at many prestigious venues, including Tanglewood in the U.S. and the Aldeburgh Festival in the U.K. He was a member of the National Institute of Arts and Letters and the American Academy of Arts and Sciences. Kirchner died from heart failure at his home in Manhattan. His wife, Gertrude, died in 1999. He is survived by his daughter, Lisa; a son, Paul; his brother, Julius; and his companion, Sally Wardwell. See *Current Biography* (1967). — W.D.

Obituary *New York Times* (on-line) Sep. 18, 2009

KITT, EARTHA Jan. 17, 1927–Dec. 25, 2008 During a career that spanned more than 60 years, Eartha Kitt, who became famous for her sultry persona and catlike purr, established a successful career as a dancer, actress, and singer. Eartha Mae Keith was born in rural South Carolina, the daughter of a black and Cherokee mother and a white father. Some sources state that she was sent to live with a black family after being rejected by her mother's new husband because of her light skin tone. According to other sources, at the age of eight she moved to the New York City neighborhood of Harlem to live with her aunt, who encouraged her to sing and take piano lessons. Kitt's life, according to most accounts, was far from ideal; she frequently ran away, claiming abuse at the hands of her aunt. At age 15 Kitt, who was attending the prestigious High School for the Performing Arts, dropped out and found work at a factory. A year later, with the help of a friend, she auditioned for choreographer Katherine Dunham, who offered her a dance training scholarship and later selected her to be one of the company's featured performers. As a member of the dance troupe, Kitt traveled worldwide and caught the eye of Orson Welles, who cast her as Helen of Troy in his 1950 production of *Dr. Faustus*. Kitt's breakthrough came with her yearlong run in the 1952 Broadway revue *New Faces of 1952*. (She also co-starred in the 1954 film adaptation, *New Faces*.) That led to roles in several films, including *The Mark of the Hawk* (1957), *St. Louis Blues* (1958), *Anna Lucasta* (1959), and *Uncle Tom's Cabin* (1965). The following year Kitt's guest performance opposite Bill Cosby in the series *I Spy* earned her an Emmy Award. During the late 1960s Kitt was picked to succeed the departing Julie Newmar as the sultry villain Catwoman in the television series *Batman*. In that role she became even more known for her distinctive voice, trademark growl, and sexy persona. In 1968 Kitt also received attention for anti–Vietnam War remarks she made at the White House, which led to an FBI investigation and her blacklisting by the Central Intelligence Agency (CIA). Unable to find work, Kitt moved to Europe, where she lived and performed for nearly a dozen years. In 1978 she made a triumphant return to Broadway in the musical *Timbuktu!*, for which she received her first Tony Award nomination. Kitt also had success with her music. Her 1953 rendition of "Santa Baby" remains one of her best-known songs. One of her most successful recordings was the 1984 disco hit "Where Is My Man," which achieved gold status and reached the Top 40 on the British singles chart and the Top 10 on the *Billboard* dance chart. Kitt also made her mark on the cabaret scene, performing in nightclubs across the U.S. and the United Kingdom. An advocate for gay rights and same-sex marriage, Kitt often performed at charity events to raise money for HIV/AIDS research. From the early 1990s to the late 2000s, Kitt had roles in several films, including *Boomerang* (1991), *Fatal Instinct* (1993), *Harriet the Spy* (1996), *I Woke Up Early the Day I Died* (1999), *Holes* (2003), and the limited theatrical release *And Then Came Love* (2007). She could be heard in the animated films *The Emperor's New Groove* (2000) and *Once Upon a Halloween* (2004) as well as the Disney TV series *The Emperor's New School*, for which she won Emmy Awards in 2007 and 2008. She also carved out a notable stage career later in life, earning both a Tony Award and a Drama Desk prize, in the best featured actress category, for George Wolfe's *The Wild Party* (2000). She appeared in a 2003 revival of the Broadway musical *Nine*, a 2004 New York City Opera production of *Cinderella*, and a 2006 Off-Broadway production of *Mimi Le Duck*. In 2007 a concert commemorating Kitt's 80th birthday was held at Carnegie Hall. She authored three autobiographies: *Thursday's Child* (1956), *Alone with Me* (1976), and *I'm Still Here: Confessions of a Sex Kitten* (1989). Kitt, who had been diagnosed with colon cancer in 2006, succumbed to the disease at her home in Weston, Connecticut. She is survived by her daughter, Kitt Shapiro, and two grandchildren. See *Current Biography* (1955). — D.K.

Obituary *New York Times* (on-line) Dec. 26, 2008

KLEIN, HERBERT G. Apr. 1, 1918–July 2, 2009 Political aide and newspaper editor. Herbert G. Klein was a pivotal figure in President Richard Nixon's administration but stepped down in 1973, a year before Nixon resigned in the midst of the Watergate scandal. A veteran newsman, after leaving the White House he took on a number of high-level jobs in the media. Klein was born in Los Angeles, California, and attended the University of Southern California (USC), where he became the sports editor of the student newspaper. He earned his B.A. degree in journalism in 1940 and then worked as a reporter for a succession of small papers. In 1942 Klein entered the U.S. Naval Reserve and was assigned to communications and public-relations posts. He ultimately rose to the rank of commander. In 1946 he went on inactive status and returned to the *Alhambra (California) Post-Advocate*, where he had previously worked as a copy boy and cub reporter. Assigned to a political beat, he covered Nixon's first bid for elective office, the race for California's 12th Congressional District seat in the U.S. House of Representatives. Klein and Nixon quickly bonded, and when Nixon, who won that 1946 race, ran for reelection in 1948, he persuaded Klein to act as an unpaid campaign publicist. In 1950 Klein joined the payroll as a publicist in Nixon's Senate race. When Nixon ran for vice president on General Dwight D. Eisenhower's ticket in 1952, Klein was publicity director of the Eisenhower-Nixon committee in California. In 1956, when Eisenhower and Nixon ran for reelection, Klein was assistant press secretary to the vice president, and at the January 1957 inauguration, he served as press secretary. According to *Time* (June 1, 1959), when he was carrying out those assignments, "Klein earned increasing respect from political reporters as a pressman's press secretary." Between election campaigns Klein continued to advance through the journalistic ranks. In 1950 he moved to the *San Diego Evening Tribune* as a feature writer, and he became an editorial writer in 1951. The following year he joined the *San Diego Union*, a staunchly Republican publication owned by Copley Newspapers, as chief editorial writer; he was promoted to editor in 1959. That year Klein took a leave of absence from the paper to join Nixon's staff as a special assistant. His first assignment was to accompany the vice president on his goodwill trip to Moscow during the summer of 1959. The trip was notable for the now famous "Kitchen Debate" between Nixon and Soviet Premier Nikita Khrushchev. During Nixon's unsuccessful 1960 presidential campaign against John F. Kennedy, Klein again served as his press secretary. Klein helped set the terms for Nixon's televised debate with Kennedy—an event said to have marked the start of a new, media-centered era in presidential politics. Nixon, up until then considered the front-runner, appeared unshaven and somewhat sinister next to his affable, telegenic challenger, and as a result, his campaign was badly damaged. Still, Klein was retained as Nixon's press secretary during his unsuccessful bid for the governorship of California in 1962 and for his victorious 1968 presidential campaign. After Nixon's win in that race, Klein agreed to remain on staff and was tasked with overseeing and coordinating press relations for the entire executive branch. In 1970 Nixon named Klein to the newly created post of director of communications. As one of several top assistants on the White House staff, Klein now formulated information policy for the executive branch and coordinated the public relations for the entire White House, the executive departments, and the Republican National Committee. Klein, who had remained loyal to Nixon for almost three decades, resigned in 1973, amidst the turmoil of the Watergate scandal and accusations by the president's inner circle that he was too friendly with the media. He joined Metromedia Inc., a national broadcasting group, and in 1980 he returned to Copley as editor in chief, guiding the entire chain's editorial policy. Klein died after suffering cardiac arrest. He is survived by his brother, Kenneth; daughter, Patricia; three grandsons; and two great-grandsons. His wife, the former Marjorie Galbraith, predeceased him in 2008. *See Current Biography* (1971). — D.K.

Obituary *New York Times* (on-line) July 3, 2009

KOLFF, WILLEM JOHAN Feb. 14, 1911–Feb. 11, 2009 Internist; biomedical engineer. Willem Johan Kolff, a pioneer in the field of biomedical engineering, was responsible for inventing the first artificial kidney (which evolved into the modern dialysis machine) and the first artificial heart, among other lifesaving innovations. Kolff was born in Leiden, a university town in the Netherlands. His father, Jacob, a physician, operated a tuberculosis sanatorium. After receiving his degree from the University of Leiden Medical School, in 1938, Kolff took a post at the University of Groningen. There, after watching a young patient die of kidney failure, he began experimenting with mechanical means of removing toxic waste products from the blood—in effect, doing the job that healthy kidneys perform naturally. When the Nazis invaded the Netherlands, in 1940, Kolff refused to work under the Nazi sympathizer who had been installed as head of the university's medical department and relocated to the small town of Kampen, to become a director of a small municipal hospital. There he set up the first blood bank in Europe and rescued a reported 800 people from the Nazis by hiding them in the hospital. He continued to work on his artificial kidney. "The device was an exemplar of Rube Goldberg ingenuity," Sandra Blakeslee wrote for the *New York Times* (February 12, 2009, on-line). "It consisted of 50 yards of sausage casing wrapped around a wooden drum set into a salt solution. The patient's blood was drawn from a wrist artery and fed into the casings. The drum was rotated, removing impurities. To get the blood safely back into the patient, Dr. Kolff copied the design of a water-pump coupling used in Ford motor engines. Later he used orange juice cans and a clothes washing machine to build his apparatuses." Following the end of the war, Kolff continued to improve upon his invention. When he discovered that no one had duplicated his revolutionary work, Kolff shipped machines to medical researchers and hospitals in England, Canada, and the U.S. In 1950 he was invited to join the research staff of the Ohio-based Cleveland Clinic Foundation, and he later became a naturalized American citizen. During his 17-year association with the clinic, Kolff developed a membrane oxygenator that is still used during open-heart surgery and the first artificial heart, which kept a dog alive for more than an hour during an experiment in 1957. A decade later Kolff, who founded the American Society of Artificial Internal Organs, moved to the University of Utah to head a large team of scientists and engineers. They continued to refine the mechanical heart, and in 1981 they received permission from the U.S. Food and Drug Administration to implant the device in a human. (The heart, first implanted in a patient named Barney Clark on December 2, 1981, was known as the Jarvik-7, after Robert Jarvik, a colleague of Kolff's who had made improvements to the model.) Kolff, who retired in 1997, was widely lauded throughout his career. His many accolades included the prestigious Albert Lasker Award for Clinical Medical Research and a dozen honorary doctoral degrees. He died of natural causes and is survived by his children—Therus, Jacob, Albert, Kees, and Adrie—as well as several grandchildren and great-grandchildren. He was predeceased in 2006 by his ex-wife, Janke Huidekoper, whom he had divorced in 2000, after more than six decades of marriage. See *Current Biography* (1983). — D.K.

Obituary *New York Times* (on-line) Feb. 12, 2009

KRAMER, JACK Aug. 1, 1921-Sep. 12, 2009 Tennis player. Jack Kramer was widely regarded as a pioneering figure in tennis, both on and off the court. From the late 1940s to the early 1950s he won singles titles at the U.S. Championships and Wimbledon, while also amassing seven other Grand Slam doubles titles. Following retirement he continued to make his mark in the sport as one of its more prominent promoters and as an advocate for players' rights. John Albert Kramer was born in Las Vegas, Nevada, and at age 13 he moved with his family to San Bernardino, California. (While sportswriters usually refer to him as Jack Kramer, he generally called himself Jake.) The athletically talented Kramer, whose father was a brakeman for the Union Pacific Railroad, was inspired to pick up a tennis racket after observing a match with Ellsworth Vines, one of the world's top-ranked players. "Up until that point, I was a pitcher on the baseball team, I was center on the basketball team. I took one look at Ellie and it made me give up all other sports," Kramer told David Allen for the Ontario, California, *Inland Valley Daily Bulletin* in 2000. When he was 14, Kramer was recruited into the Junior Development Program and trained under legendary tennis instructor Dick Skeen, with immediate success. In 1936 Kramer won the boys' singles and doubles titles at the 15-and-under National Championships, in Culver, Indiana, and two years later he was the winner of the National Juniors Interscholastics. In 1939 Kramer garnered international attention with his Davis Cup debut, partnering with Joseph Hunt to represent the U.S. in the men's doubles title match, which they ultimately lost to Australia's John Bromwich and Adrian Quist. Kramer left the University of Southern California (USC) after only one semester to focus on his burgeoning amateur tennis career. When he was 19 he and the 19-year-old Frederick "Ted" Schroeder teamed up to claim consecutive U.S. National Championship doubles titles (1940–41), becoming one of the youngest duos to win the event. Kramer was part of the pair that won the mixed doubles event at the 1941 U.S. Nationals. That same year Kramer landed a tennis scholarship to Rollins College, in Winter Park, Florida, where he played during the 1941 and 1942 seasons. Kramer continued to play even after enlisting in the U.S. Coast Guard in September 1942. Throughout his military service, Kramer was granted numerous leaves to compete in tournaments, with impressive results. In 1943 he won the men's singles crown at the Pacific Southwest Championships (now called the L.A. Tennis Open) and was a runner-up at the U.S. National Championships (the forerunner of the U.S. Open) at Forest Hills, where he captured another doubles title (with partner Frankie Parker). After his discharge, in January 1946, Kramer, who achieved the rank of lieutenant (junior grade), enjoyed continued success on the tennis court. He defeated Tom Brown Jr. to win the men's singles title at the 1946 U.S. National Championships and bested Schroeder to capture the singles title at the Pacific Southwest Championships (1946–47). In doubles competition Kramer reteamed with Schroeder to help the U.S. Davis Cup team garner consecutive championships (1946–47) and to claim the doubles title at the 1947 Pacific Southwest Championships. In 1947 Kramer faced Brown in the Wimbledon men's final and was again victorious. His winning ways continued at the 1947 U.S. National Championships, where he claimed the final three sets in the best-of-five final, after losing the first two against Parker. Because of economic considerations, Kramer turned professional that year and accepted an offer from promoter Jack Harris to join his roster of professional athletes. (Before 1968, professionals competed separately from amateurs; their events included tours involving head-to-head competition and annual matches called championship tournaments.) Kramer made his professional debut in December 1947, squaring off against Bobby Riggs in a widely publicized tournament at New York's Madison Square Garden. While Kramer lost that initial match, during their five-month nationwide tour, they played 89 games, 69 of which he won. In 1948 Kramer was victorious against Riggs at the U.S. Pro Tennis Championships. In 1952 Kramer became a promoter of the professional tour and was forced to retire from competitive tennis two years later due to an arthritic back. He continued to serve as a promoter until 1962, often advocating an open format for tournaments that would grant players greater freedom from the controls of national associations. He also helped usher in the Open era of tennis in 1968, marking the first time that amateurs and professionals competed together in tournaments for prize money. Kramer went on to develop the men's Grand Prix series of tournaments, which debuted in 1970 and lasted for two decades. In 1972 he helped found the Association of Tennis Professionals (ATP), serving as the union's first executive director. Kramer, who served for a time as a television commentator for the BBC, was also known for his wide range of business interests, which included a lucrative partnership with Wilson Sporting Goods and investments in several thoroughbred racehorses. In addition, he owned the Los Serranos Golf and Country Club near Chino Hills, California. Kramer, who was named to the International Tennis Hall of Fame in 1968 and penned a memoir, *The Game: My 40 Years in Tennis* (1979), with Frank Deford, died of soft-tissue sarcoma at his home in Los Angeles, California. He is survived by five sons—Bob, David, Michael, John, and Ron—and several grandchildren. Kramer's wife, Gloria, died in 2008. See *Current Biography* (1947). — C.C.

Obituary *New York Times* (on-line) Sep. 14, 2009

KRISTOL, IRVING Jan. 22, 1920–Sep. 18, 2009 Often called the father of neoconservatism, Irving Kristol was highly influential in U.S. politics as a writer, editor, publisher, and longtime fellow of the American Enterprise Institute. Kristol "helped revitalize the Republican Party in the late 1960s and early '70s, setting the stage for the Reagan presidency and years of conservative dominance," Barry Gewen wrote for the *New York Times* (September 19, 2009). Among Kristol's most widely quoted (and misquoted) assertions, from his book *Reflections of a Neoconservative*, is that a neoconservative is a liberal who has been "mugged by reality." Another of his well-known statements is from his book *Two Cheers for Capitalism*: "Neoconservatives are unlike old conservatives because they are utilitarians, not moralists, and because their aim is the prosperity of post-industrial society, not the recovery of a golden age." "More than anyone alive, perhaps, Irving Kristol can take the credit for reversing the direction of American political culture," Eric Alterman wrote for the *Nation* (November 22, 1999). Also in the *Nation* (September 23, 2009), Alterman wrote, "Far more important than [Kristol's] ideas themselves was the intellectual infrastructure—the think tanks, the magazines, the op-ed pages and the conferences—that Kristol helped build to provide support for arguments that otherwise would have been considered banal, dangerous or both." Kristol was born in New York City to Jewish immigrants from Europe. (There is some dispute as to whether January 20 or January 22 is his date of birth.) His father, a men's-clothing subcontractor, and mother raised Kristol and his sister in a working-class neighborhood of Brooklyn. Kristol attended the City College of New York, where he studied history, engaged in the heated political discussions common among CCNY's then–predominantly Jewish students, and briefly joined the Young People's Socialist League. Two years after he graduated, in 1940, he entered the U.S. Army; he saw combat in France and Germany. After his military discharge, in 1946, Kristol began writing for *Commentary*, an American Jewish Committee monthly journal of opinion; within a year he had become its managing editor. He remained at *Commentary* until 1952, when he co-founded the British-American intellectual magazine *Encounter*. (*Encounter* sparked controversy when it was revealed that the CIA—unbeknownst to him, according to Kristol—provided it with financial support.) He left *Encounter* in 1958 to become the editor of the liberal, anti-Communist publication the *Reporter*. Two years later he accepted an executive editorial position in the social-sciences division of Basic Books, a small but prestigious publishing firm. In 1965 he co-founded the *Public Interest*, a scholarly journal dealing with domestic affairs. From 1969 to 1988 he was a member of the New York University faculty, holding the title John M. Olin professor of social thought at NYU's Graduate School of Business for his last decade there. During the late 1960s he wrote a series of articles on such topics as urbanization, education, and the role of the historian that were collected in the book *On the Democratic Idea in America* (1972), which focused on the breakdown of American ideals, exacerbated, according to Kristol, by the "utopian" liberalism of the 1960s and the emergence of the New Left. Kristol's later books *Two Cheers for Capitalism* (1978), *Reflections of a Neoconservative* (1983), and *Neoconservatism: The Autobiography of an Idea* (1995) were also collections of previously published essays. In 1972 Kristol was appointed to the board of directors of the Corporation for Public Broadcasting, where he tried to counteract the actions of those at PBS who "sincerely believe[d] that they have the right—the responsibility, even—to use taxpayers' funds to excoriate the taxpayers' way of life," in his words. Kristol expressed extreme disillusionment with the domestic reform programs of the administrations of Presidents John F. Kennedy and Lyndon B. Johnson, which he believed were alien to the country's traditions, and by the mid-1970s he had switched his political affiliation from Democratic to Republican. In the 1970s he wrote an opinion column for the *Wall Street Journal*. In 1978 he co-founded the Institute for Educational Affairs, which channeled money to conservative causes. In 1985 Kristol established the *National Interest*, a magazine about foreign affairs, and two years later he became a distinguished fellow at the American Enterprise Institute, a conservative think tank. Kristol influenced, albeit indirectly, President Ronald Reagan's economic policies, collectively known as Reaganomics. Barry Gewen explained, "Behind-the-scenes maneuverings suited him. . . . Described by the economics writer Jude Wanniski as the 'hidden hand' of the conservative movement, he avoided television and other media spotlights; he was happier consulting with a congressman like Jack Kemp about the new notion of supply-side economics and then watching with satisfaction as Mr. Kemp converted . . . Reagan to the theory." In 2002 Kristol received the Presidential Medal of Freedom, one of the nation's highest honors, from George W. Bush. He died of lung cancer at a hospice in Arlington, Virginia. He is survived by his wife, Gertrude Himmelfarb, a renowned neoconservative historian, prolific writer, and educator; his daughter, Elizabeth Kristol Nelson, a writer and critic; his son, William Kristol, who edits the conservative magazine the *Weekly Standard*; and five grandchildren. See *Current Biography* (1974).— D.K.

Obituary *New York Times* (on-line) Sep. 19, 2009

LANG, PEARL May 29, 1921–Feb. 24, 2009 Dancer; choreographer. Pearl Lang, a modern dancer and choreographer, came to prominence for her work with the Martha Graham Dance Company. She was also the founder of her own modern-dance troupe, and many of the works she choreographed for the group reflected her Jewish heritage. The dancer was born to Freida (Feder) Lack, a seamstress, and Jacob Lack, a tailor, in Chicago, Illinois. (In the early 1940s, on the advice of a dance critic, she changed her name to Lang.) Her Yiddish-speaking parents greatly valued artistic and cultural accomplishments. Her father played the piano, and her mother wrote poetry and frequently took her to museums, theaters, operas, and ballets. Lang's interest in performing was sparked at age three, when she attended a performance at Chicago's Orchestra Hall by the Duncan Dancers. When she was 10, Lang choreographed her first dance for some of her classmates. During her teenage years she studied modern dance with Frances Allis. In 1938 Lang made her debut as a soloist with the Ukrainian Folk Dance Company at Chicago's Blackstone Theatre. Three years later Lang's mother allowed her to travel to New York City to study with Graham, a pioneering modern dancer, and shortly thereafter Lang joined Graham's company. During her decade-long stint (1942–52) as a member of the troupe, Lang originated roles in several of Graham's choreographed works, including the Woman in Red in *Diversion of Angels*. She also performed many of Graham's own roles in *El Penitente, Appalachian Spring, Letter to the World, Clytemnestra*, and *Primitive Mysteries*. Periodically, Lang worked as a featured dancer in Broadway musicals, including *One Touch of Venus* (1943), *Carousel* (1945), and *Touch and Go* (1949). Lang assisted the legendary Agnes de Mille in choreographing *Allegro* (1947) and replaced Anita Alvarez as Susan in *Finian's Rainbow* (1947). In a straight dramatic role, she played Solveig in Paul Green's version of Henrik Ibsen's *Peer Gynt* (1951). Shortly after leaving Graham's dance company in 1952, Lang—who remained affiliated with the group as a guest artist until the late 1970s—founded her own troupe. She created some 50 works, more than half of which contained Jewish themes. Among her notable works were the duet *Song of Deborah* (1949), commissioned by the Juilliard School of Music; *Legend* (1951), based on S. Ansky's *The Dybbuk*; *Falls the Shadow Between* (1957), later renamed *Persephone*; *Shirah* (1960); *Dismembered Fable* (1965); *The Possessed* (1974); *Icarus, Cantigas Ladino* (1978); *Notturno* (1980); *Tehillim* (1984); *Dance Panel #7* (2000); and *The Time Is Out of Joint* (2001). Over the course of her career, Lang also choreographed for several other dance companies, including the Dutch National Ballet, Boston Ballet, and Israel's Batsheva Dance Company. A dedicated dance instructor, she continued to teach until shortly before her death. (Lang suffered a heart attack while recuperating from hip surgery.) She is survived by her husband, the actor Joseph Wiseman. See *Current Biography* (1970). — D.K.

Obituary *New York Times* (on-line) Feb. 27, 2009

LARROCHA, ALICIA DE May 23, 1923–Sep. 25, 2009 Pianist. Alicia de Larrocha was considered one of the greatest pianists of the 20th century. Her interpretations and recordings of the works of several Spanish composers, including Isaac Albeniz and Enrique Granados, are considered definitive. (In addition to de Larrocha's reputation as an ambassador of Spanish composers, her repertoire included the works of Wolfgang Amadeus Mozart and Robert Schumann, among other mainstream composers.) "Her virtual monopoly on the works of the Spanish composers," according to a writer for the London *Telegraph* (September 27, 2009, on-line), "meant that few other pianists could go near them without drawing unfavourable comparisons. But it brought to those composers recognition and appreciation far beyond the Iberian peninsula." Known for her technical virtuosity, her perfect judgment of tempo and rhythm, and her subtle and graceful interpretations, de Larrocha stood well under five feet tall and possessed exceptionally small hands, making her gift all the more remarkable considering the physical demands of the pieces by such composers as Albeniz. According to Stuart Isacoff, writing for the *Wall Street Journal* (October 7, 2009, on-line), "She was forced to make unusual choices about where to place each finger, and her personal scores were cluttered with numbers written next to the notes." She was a humble and reluctant star. "She was not particularly glamorous, and she was rather shy," Herbert Breslin, her American publicist, said, as quoted in the *Telegraph* piece. "But by God she could play the piano." Alicia de Larrocha y de la Calle was born in Barcelona, Spain, to Eduardo Larrocha and Maria Teresa de la Calle. Both her mother and her aunt, who was a piano teacher, had been pupils of the great composer Granados. Neither her two sisters nor her brother took as serious an interest in the piano as de Larrocha; she was reportedly so determined to play that as a toddler, she banged her head on the floor until it bled after being refused a chance at the keyboard. When de Larrocha was three, her aunt took her to Frank Marshall, a former pupil of Granados who had taken over his mentor's legendary academy after his death. (Granados had been killed by a torpedo from a German U-boat in 1916, while on an ocean voyage from New York City to Spain.) While Marshall was reluctant to teach such a young child, he relented after seeing her determination. De Larrocha began performing compositions by Mozart and Johann Sebastian Bach at public concerts at age five, and by age nine she was recording Frédéric Chopin pieces. Marshall, a native of England, did not allow her to play Spanish music until she was 15, so that she could acquire a solid foundation in the classics first. "Spanish music is very, very, very hard," de Larrocha once said, as quoted by the BBC News (September 26, 2009, on-line). "Young people come to me and think they can play it right away. But Spanish music must have the right rhythm, just as Bach and Mozart must have the right rhythm. If you cannot play Bach and Mozart well, you cannot play Spanish music well." Marshall was forced to flee the country in 1936, due to the Spanish Civil War, but with her aunt's help, de Larrocha continued studying until he returned in 1939. (Like many families, de Larrocha's was forced to live in a state of deprivation during the conflict.) In 1947 de Larrocha embarked on a European tour that included dates in Paris and Geneva, among other cities, and she made her American debut with the Los Angeles Philharmonic in 1955. Later that same year she had her New York recital debut at Town Hall, performing works by Granados, Albeniz, and Schumann, among other composers. In 1958 de Larrocha married a fellow pianist and teacher, Juan Torra. After Marshall died, in 1959, de Larrocha and Torra became co-directors of his academy. De Larrocha began recording for the Hispavox label, and when the American concert manager Herbert Breslin heard some of those records, he persuaded her to return to America, where she played five hugely successful concerts with the New York Philharmonic in 1965. After those breakout performances, de Larrocha, then in her 40s, began spending much of her time on tour, and Breslin negotiated a record deal with Decca, a major label, taking her recording career to the international stage. In 2003 de Larrocha retired at the age of 80, after 75 years and several thousand live performances. (By then, she had shrunk several inches due to age, and her finger span was greatly reduced.) That year Decca reissued a comprehensive multi-disc set of her recordings. Larrocha was the first Spanish artist to win the Unesco Prize (1995), and her other honors included the Medalla de Oro al Merito de las Ballas Artes (1982), the Premio Principa de Asturias (1994), and multiple Grammy Awards. De Larrocha, whose husband died in 1982, broke her hip in 2007 and suffered steadily declining health until her own death. She is survived by their two children, Juan and Alicia. See *Current Biography* (1968). — M.M.

Obituary *New York Times* (on-line) Sep. 25, 2009

LEONARD, HUGH Nov. 9, 1926—Feb. 12, 2009– Irish dramatist. One of Ireland's most prolific playwrights, Hugh Leonard earned great acclaim for his play *Da*, winning both a Tony Award and a Drama Desk Award for the work in 1978. The writer was born John Joseph Byrne to a single mother, Annie Byrne, in Dublin, Ireland. Shortly after his birth, he was adopted by Nicholas Keys, a gardener, and Margaret (Doyle) Keys, a homemaker, who raised him in the coastal suburb of Dalkey. He began using the name John Keyes Byrne, changing the spelling of his adoptive family's surname for use as a middle name. He later took on the pen name Hugh Leonard, after one of his characters. (Throughout his life, however, he was known to those close to him as Jack.) Upon completing the Harold Boys' National School, he won a scholarship to attend Presentation College, a Roman Catholic school in Glasthule, from which he graduated in 1945. After working briefly for Columbia Pictures, he was hired as a clerical assistant by the Irish Land Commission, where he remained for 14 years. While there, he joined Lancos, the Commission's amateur dramatic society, and started writing plays under his pen name. Three of his plays—*The Big Birthday* (1956), *A Leap in the Dark* (1957), and *Madigan's Lock* (1958)—were produced at local theaters in Dublin. Encouraged, Leonard left the Land Commission in 1959 and wrote for several radio serials as well as the Dublin Theatre Festival. In 1961 he embarked on a two-year stint as a script editor for Granada Television in Manchester, England, and in 1963 he worked as a freelance writer in London. Over the next seven years, Leonard wrote television serials and film scripts; he also adapted several classic novels for British television during the latter part of the decade, including Charles Dickens's *Great Expectations* and *A Tale of Two Cities*, Wilkie Collins's

The Moonstone, Gustave Flaubert's *A Sentimental Education*, Emily Brontë's *Wuthering Heights*, and Fyodor Dostoyevsky's *The Possessed*. After returning to his hometown in Ireland in 1970, Leonard continued to write one or two television scripts a year while focusing on his playwriting. He made his Broadway debut in 1973 with *The Au Pair Man*, which starred Charles Durning and Julie Harris. Leonard's next play was the semi-autobiographical *Da*, in which a writer returns to his native Ireland following the death of his adoptive father and is visited by his ghost after the funeral. First produced in 1973 at the Olney Theater Center in Maryland, it appeared Off-Off-Broadway in early 1978 at the Hudson Guild Theatre in New York City and was then mounted at the Morosco Theatre, where it had a successful 20-month run (May 1978–January 1980) that included almost 700 performances. For his effort, Leonard received best-play honors at the 1978 Tony Awards. *Da* also earned the 1978 Drama Desk Award for outstanding new play. (Leonard subsequently wrote a screenplay for *Da*, which was adapted for the big screen in 1988.) During that period Leonard authored three books: two collections of essays—*Leonard's Last Book* (1978) and *A Peculiar People and Other Foibles* (1979)—and the autobiography *Home Before Night* (1979). He also became the program director of the Dublin Theatre Festival. Leonard's next play, *A Life* (1980), told the story of Desmond Drumm, a joyless, self-righteous civil servant who had been a secondary character in *Da*. In 1990, a year after the release of *Out After Dark* (1989), another autobiography, Leonard began writing "Curmudgeon," a weekly column that ran in the London *Sunday Independent* until 2006. In 2009 he was the subject of the documentary *Odd Man In*, which aired on the Irish channel RTE. Among other works written by Leonard are the novels *Parnell and the Englishwoman* (1992) and *The Offshore Island* (1993). Leonard died in Dalkey, after a lengthy battle with multiple illnesses. He is survived by his second wife, Katharine Hayes, and Danielle Byrne, his daughter with his late first wife, Paule Jacquet. See *Current Biography* (1983). — D.K.

Obituary *New York Times* (on-line) Feb. 13, 2009

LEVINE, IRVING R. Aug. 26, 1922–Mar. 27, 2009 Journalist. By making complicated economic matters accessible to the average viewer, Irving R. Levine helped establish the economy as a staple subject of television news. Before 1971, when NBC assigned him to be the network's first full-time reporter devoted to covering such topics as U.S. monetary policy, stock fluctuations, and the global financial system, Levine had enjoyed a decades-long career as a foreign correspondent. He broke boundaries as the first American television reporter accredited in the Soviet Union, and in 1959 he published *Main Street, U.S.S.R.*, an acclaimed depiction of daily life in the Soviet Union during the post-Stalin era. Levine was born in Pawtucket, Rhode Island. His parents, Ukrainian immigrants, owned a general store. From a young age Levine wanted to be a journalist, and he spent his high-school and college years working for local newspapers. He graduated from Brown University, where he was a member of the Phi Beta Kappa honors society, in 1944. Levine served as a lieutenant in the U.S. Army Signal Corps during World War II. After his discharge, he attended Columbia University's School of Journalism, graduating with a master's degree in 1947. The following year he was hired by the International News Service (INS). As the head of the INS bureau in Vienna, Austria, Levine covered events in several countries, including France, Italy, England, Ireland, and Germany, before being sent to Korea in the summer of 1950 to cover the war there. Later that year he joined NBC. In 1955 Levine traveled to the Soviet Union along with a group of American agricultural experts to conduct a five-week survey of farms, a rare instance of openness during the Cold War. (Over the next few years, Soviet censorship laws often hampered his reporting.) In 1959 Levine was transferred to NBC's Rome bureau, where he stayed for several years, eventually becoming bureau chief. In 1971 he returned to the U.S. to become the network's economics reporter and went on to cover such major stories as President Richard Nixon's decisions to combat out-of-control inflation with wage and price controls and to take the country off the gold standard. "As matters of money, trade and the budget grew in importance from then on, Mr. Levine, with his trademark bow tie, formal diction and decidedly unglamorous appearance, became the broadcast version of a favorite eccentric professor," Bruce Webber wrote in Levine's *New York Times* obituary. Levine retired from NBC in 1995 and became the dean of the College of International Communications at Lynn University, in Boca Raton, Florida. Levine died of complications from prostate cancer. He is survived by Nancy, his wife of more than five decades, and their three children: Daniel, Jeffrey, and Jennifer. See *Current Biography* (1959). — M.E.R.

Obituary *New York Times* (on-line) Mar. 28, 2009

MAKEBA, MIRIAM Mar. 4, 1932–Nov. 9, 2008 South African singer and social activist. Miriam Makeba helped to fuel the struggle against apartheid in South Africa through song, both while living in her native land during the first part of her career and then during her many years in exile. The first African vocalist who became an international celebrity, she served as an exponent of world music several decades before that genre was named. "Her haunting melodies gave voice to the pain of exile and dislocation which she felt for 31 long years," Nelson Mandela, South Africa's first postapartheid and first black president, stated in a tribute to her posted on the BBC News Web site (November 10, 2008). "At the same time, her music inspired a powerful sense of hope in all of us. . . . She was South Africa's first lady of song and so richly deserved the title of Mama Afrika. She was a mother to our struggle and to the young nation of ours." The singer was born Zenzile Miriam Makeba in a segregated shantytown on the outskirts of Johannesburg, South Africa, to a Xhosa father and a Swazi mother. (In some sources "Zenzile" appears as "Zenzi" or "Zensi," and it is sometimes listed as her middle name.) Starting at age 18 days, Makeba spent six months in jail with her mother, who had been convicted of brewing homemade beer. Her father died when she was six; afterward her mother moved with Miriam and her siblings to a black neighborhood in Pretoria. Makeba sang in a church choir and at 13 won a talent competition held at the Kilmerton Training Institute, a Methodist missionary school that she attended for eight years. During her teens she also entertained at weddings and other events and worked as a servant for white families, all the while witnessing, or experiencing firsthand, some of the many forms of the repression and brutalities of apartheid. In about 1949 she gave birth to a daughter; soon afterward her union with the child's father, James Kubali, ended. With her child in the care of Makeba's mother for the next 11 years, Makeba moved to Johannesburg, where she joined a cousin's band, the Cuban Boys. In about 1953 a far more popular group, the Manhattan Brothers, hired her as their sole female singer. For the next three years, she toured with them in Rhodesia (now Zimbabwe) and the Belgian Congo (now the Democratic Republic of the Congo) as well as South Africa. Makeba wrote the lyrics for the Manhattan Brothers' song "Laku Tshoni 'Ilanga," which became a hit recording. In 1956 Gallotone, a South African label, recruited her as the lead singer of a new female band, called the Sunbeams and, later, the Skylarks, with whom she made dozens of recordings. Concurrently, beginning in 1958, she toured with Alfred Herbert's group African Jazz and Variety, whose members included the singer Shunna Pillay, to whom she was briefly married, in about 1959–60, and the trumpeter Hugh Masekela, whom she later married (in 1963) and divorced (1965). In 1959 she won the lead role in *King Kong*, a jazz opera about an African boxer imprisoned for a crime of passion. The production enjoyed huge success in an eight-month tour of South Africa; when it was mounted in universities, blacks and whites—ignoring apartheid rules—sat side by side in the audiences. Also in about 1959 Makeba was filmed singing several songs for *Come Back, Africa*, an unauthorized motion picture about apartheid made in South Africa by the American independent filmmaker Lionel Rogosin under false pretenses. Partly a documentary and partly a re-creation of events, the film won the Critics Award at that year's Venice Film Festival and was widely discussed in Europe. With bribes, Rogosin succeeded in getting a passport for Makeba; according to Graeme Ewens, writing for the London *Guardian* (November 11, 2008, on-line), she became "an instant celebrity" when she appeared at the film festival. She then went to New York City, where, thanks to her appearance on *The Steve Allen Show* on TV on November 30, 1959, she "literally" became "an overnight sensation," according to Jon Lusk, writing for the London *Independent* (November 11, 2008). Mentored by the singer Harry Belafonte, she made solo recordings of traditional African songs, among them "Pata Pata" and "The Click Song" ("Qongqothwane" in the Xhosa language), and "Malaika" (long identified erroneously as traditional), which "formed the basis of her repertoire and remained the most popular songs through her career," Graeme Ewens wrote. *An Evening with Belafonte/Makeba* won the 1965 Grammy Award for best folk recording. Earlier, in 1960, Makeba was unable to return to South Africa to attend her mother's funeral, because the South African government had revoked her passport (the government also banned her records); for the next three decades, she remained in exile from South Africa. During those years she performed internationally, including in African countries, and enjoyed enormous success. In 1962 she performed at the celebration in Madison Square Garden, in New York City, of the 45th birthday of U.S. president John F. Kennedy (at which, more famously, the actress Marilyn Monroe also sang). In 1963 Makeba addressed the United Nations special committee on the evils of apartheid; she did so again in 1975 and 1976. In 1968, after her marriage to Stokely Carmichael, an American former civil rights activist who became a leader of the Black Panthers and the associated black-power movement, her record deals and concert engagements evaporated. In 1969 she moved to the West African nation of Guinea with Carmichael; there, her husband, who renamed himself Kwame Ture, rejected the Black Panthers and advocated Pan Africanism. Makeba's association with that movement led many Western nations to close their doors to her, officially or informally. She and Ture divorced in 1978; two years later she settled in Brussels, Belgium, and married Bageot Bah, an airline executive. In 1986 she performed with Paul Simon during his *Graceland* world tour. After the release from prison of Nelson Mandela, in 1990, she resumed concertizing in South Africa. By then, although she was held in high esteem, her music had lost much of its popularity. Nevertheless, she continued recording; her last album, *Reflections*, won three prizes at the South African Music Awards in 2004. Makeba had a leading role in the film *Sarafina!* (1992), appeared in the documentary *When We Were Kings* (1996), and played herself in the films *Sacred Sounds* (2000) and *Amandla! A Revolution in Four Part Harmony* (2002). Her many honors included the Dag Hammerskjöld Peace Prize (1986), a Lifetime Achievement Award from the South African Broadcasting Co. (1996), and honorary doctorates from three South African universities. She co-wrote the memoir *Makeba: My Story* (with James Hall), 1988; another book, *Makeba: The Miriam Makeba Story* (2004), was based on transcripts of her conversations with Nomsa Mwamuka. Beginning in 2005 she made a series of "farewell" concerts; she collapsed and died during one of them, in Campania, Italy. Makeba, whose daughter died in 1985, was unmarried at the time of her death. She is survived by a grandson and a granddaughter. See *Current Biography* (1965). — M.H.

Obituary *New York Times* B p13 Nov. 11, 2008

MALDEN, KARL Mar. 22, 1912–July 1, 2009 Actor. The Oscar-winning character actor Karl Malden enjoyed a decades-long career in theater, film, and television and served a lengthy tenure as an American Express pitchman. "In many ways, Mr. Malden was the ideal Everyman. He realized early on that he lacked the physical attributes of a leading man," Robert Berkvist wrote for the *New York Times* (July 1, 2009). "But he was determined 'to be No. 1 in the No. 2 parts I was destined to get,' he once said." Born Mladen Sekulovich in Chicago, Illinois, the actor was the son of a steel-mill worker who had immigrated from the Republic of Serbia and a homemaker from Bohemia, which later became part of the Czech Republic. Malden and his family moved to Gary, Indiana, when he was a young boy. As an athlete in high school, Malden broke his nose twice, resulting in the crooked, bulbous appendage that became one of his trademarks. He became interested in the theater during his early 20s and moved to Chicago to study acting at the Goodman Theatre. Upon graduating from the program, in 1937, he moved back to Gary and became a milk-truck driver. Robert Ardrey, a playwright he had met at Goodman, soon invited Malden to New York City to audition for his latest play. Though that show was never produced, Malden earned a small part in the Clifford Odets play *Golden Boy*. During the 1938 staging of *Golden Boy*, he met and befriended Elia Kazan, who would later direct several of Malden's most celebrated stage and film works. At about that time Malden had adopted his professional name, modifying his given name and taking Karl from one of his grandfathers. He served in the U.S. Army during World War II and returned to New York City in 1946 to perform alongside a then-unknown Marlon Brando in Maxwell Anderson's *Truckline Cafe*. Though the play was not a success, Malden received good reviews and went on to appear in the Broadway debut of Arthur Miller's *All My Sons* in 1947. Later that year he originated the role of Harold "Mitch" Mitchell in the first staging of Tennessee William's *A Streetcar Named Desire*, which was directed by Kazan and starred Brando, Kim Hunter, and Jessica Tandy. Malden reprised his role in the 1951 film version, also directed by Kazan, and won the 1952 Academy Award for best supporting actor. He was nominated for his second Academy Award three years later for his performance as Father Barry in Kazan's 1954 film *On the Waterfront*. In demand on both stage and screen throughout the 1950s, Malden appeared in Broadway revivals of Henrik Ibsen's *Peer Gynt* and Eugene O'Neill's *Desire Under the Elms*. Some of his most prominent film roles of the decade included well-reviewed turns in *Ruby Gentry* (1952), Alfred Hitchcock's *I Confess* (1953), and *Baby Doll* (1956). The 1960s saw him appear in *Gypsy* (1962), *Cheyenne Autumn* (1964), *Nevada Smith* (1966), and *The Adventures of Bullwhip Griffin* (1967), among other pictures. Malden won critical praise for his role in the 1970 war film *Patton*, and from 1972 to 1977 he starred in the television detective series *The Streets of San Francisco*—a role that earned him four Emmy nominations and a Golden Globe nod. In 1973 Malden began starring in a series of commercials for American Express travelers' checks. His gruff warning, "Don't leave home without them," became a national catch phrase during the two decades the spots appeared on the air. Malden, showing few signs of retiring, won an Emmy Award for his role in the NBC drama *Fatal Vision* (1984) and served as president of the Academy of Motion Picture Arts and Sciences from 1989 to 1992. In 2004 he received the Screen Actors Guild Life Achievement Award, which honors actors for both their careers and humanitarian achievements. Malden died of natural causes at his Los Angeles home. He is survived by his wife of 70 years, Mona; two daughters, Mila and Carla; three grandchildren; and four great-grandchildren. See *Current Biography* (1957). — M.A.S.

Obituary *New York Times* A p21 July 2, 2009

MCCOURT, FRANK Aug. 19, 1930–July 19, 2009 Writer; educator. Frank McCourt, who taught in the New York City public-school system for decades, was best known as the Pulitzer Prize–winning author of the phenomenally successful memoir *Angela's Ashes* (1996). Born in the New York City borough of Brooklyn, he was the first of seven children in his family. (Three of his six siblings died in early childhood.) Struggling to make ends meet in the depths of the Great Depression, his parents, Malachy McCourt and the former Angela Sheehan, returned to their native Ireland when McCourt was four years old. He spent his childhood years in Limerick, and he later recounted that hardscrabble existence in heartbreaking detail in *Angela's Ashes*. At the age of 11, McCourt was forced to become the family's primary breadwinner. (His alcoholic father frequently squandered his meager wages in pubs.) To feed his mother and siblings, McCourt regularly stole food from area shops. After dropping out of school entirely at the age of 13, he delivered telegrams and wrote letters for a local landlady to support the family, and at 16 he went to work for a newspaper distributor. In 1949 McCourt used his savings to board a ship to New York City. There, he worked at a series of menial jobs before being drafted into the U.S. Army during the Korean War. He served in what was then West Germany, working as a dog trainer and clerk. After completing his military service, McCourt persuaded officials at New York University to admit him, despite his lack of a high-school diploma. Thanks to the G.I. Bill, he earned a bachelor's degree in English education in 1957. (Later, in 1967, he earned a master's degree in English from Brooklyn College.) McCourt spent nearly three decades teaching in the New York City public-school system, beginning his career at McKee Vocational and Technical High School in Staten Island and retiring at the prestigious Stuyvesant High School in Manhattan. He was widely admired for his idiosyncratic style, humanity, and wide breadth of knowledge. Teaching English and creative writing, he captivated and inspired students with tales from his own life. After he retired from teaching, in 1987, McCourt, who had always encouraged his students to draw upon their own lives in their writing, began working in earnest on *Angela's Ashes*, which quickly became a literary phenomenon. It won many honors, among them the 1997 Pulitzer Prize for biography or autobiography, the National Book Critics Circle Award, and the *Los Angeles Times* Book Award. It was named one of the eight best books of 1996 by the *New York Times Book Review* and was ranked the number-one nonfiction book of 1996 by *Time* magazine. It also remained on the best-seller list for more than two years. Reportedly, the paperback rights sold for $1 million, and the Hollywood producers David Brown and Scott Rudin paid McCourt $1 million for the film rights. (The movie version, which was released in 1999, suffered from comparisons with the book and did not fare well at the box office.) In a speech to students at Bay Shore High School, in New York City, given soon after the announcement that he had won a Pulitzer Prize, McCourt revealed one of the major ways he benefited from *Angela's Ashes*: "I learned the significance of my own insignificant life." McCourt penned two additional memoirs, *'Tis*, about his life as a young adult, and *Teacher Man* (2005), about his career. (While neither received the rapturous praise the first had, they both landed on the best-seller list.) McCourt, who also wrote the plays *A Couple of Blaguards* (along with his brother Malachy) and *The Irish . . . and How They Got That Way*, died of metastatic melanoma at a hospice in Manhattan. He is survived by his third wife, Ellen; his daughter, Maggie; and three grandchildren. In addition to Malachy, he is also survived by his brothers Alphie and Mike. See *Current Biography* (1998). — C.C.

Obituary *New York Times* (on-line) July 20, 2009

MCMAHON, ED Mar. 6, 1923–June 23, 2009 Television personality. Ed McMahon was a familiar face to television audiences during his three-decade run on *The Tonight Show Starring Johnny Carson.* As Carson's sidekick (or second banana, as he was often described), he introduced his boss and crony each weeknight with the well-known catchphrase "Heeeeere's Johnny!" Edward Leo Peter McMahon Jr. was born in Detroit, Michigan. As a child he moved from city to city with his parents, who ran fortune wheels and bingo games for organizations that raised funds at carnival-like operations. After a stint selling bingo cards for his father, McMahon took a job "calling the ponies" in a pinball-type racing game outside Boston. Impressed by McMahon's voice, the concessionaire of the games sent him on the road as a bingo announcer. McMahon spent three summers working the carnival circuits in the Northeast, perfecting his skill as a bingo "mike man." At Boston College he majored in electrical engineering and enrolled in a U.S. Navy program that he hoped would allow him to become a fighter pilot. During World War II he remained stateside as an instructor and test pilot and received orders to ship out only at the war's end. After his discharge he enrolled at the Catholic University of America, in Washington, D.C. He had earned his tuition money by hawking vegetable slicers and juicers on the boardwalk in Atlantic City, a job that would become a key part of McMahon's lore when he became famous. McMahon earned his B.A. degree in 1949 and landed a job with WCAU, a Philadelphia radio station that was gradually venturing into television production. He was soon known locally as "Mr. Television," because at one point he was appearing concurrently on 13 TV programs, including the morning broadcast *Strictly for the Girls* and *The Big Top*, a circus-themed show that aired on Saturdays. Just as the network was about to show *Strictly for the Girls* regionally and *The Big Top* nationally, McMahon was called up to serve in the Korean War. Heavily decorated, he returned to Philadelphia, where he continued his work on *The Big Top* and introduced a new program called *Five Minutes More*, which he later described as a "five-minute *Tonight Show.*" He then began hosting his own late-night talk show, *McMahon and Company.* After the game show *Who Do You Trust?*, hosted by an up-and-coming Johnny Carson, lost its announcer in 1958, McMahon was selected as a replacement. He got along well with Carson, who insisted that McMahon accompany him when he moved to the NBC network in Los Angeles for his new talk show, *The Tonight Show Starring Johnny Carson*, in 1962. During his decades on the show, McMahon warmed up the audience, read commercials for several sponsors, bellowed his catchphrase, and served as Carson's straight man and foil. A running gag on the show portrayed McMahon as a heavy drinker who sometimes tippled on the set, but he was known throughout the industry as a hardworking professional and consummate entertainer. McMahon, who also acted in an occasional movie, including *The Incident* (1967) and *Fun with Dick and Jane* (1977), remained on *The Tonight Show* until Carson retired, in 1992. McMahon also hosted the talent show *Star Search* (1983–2003), co-hosted *TV's Bloopers and Practical Jokes* in the mid-1980s alongside Dick Clark, and appeared on Tom Arnold's short-lived sitcom *The Tom Show* (1997–98). Aside from his work with Carson, however, McMahon is perhaps best remembered as a pitchman. He taped commercials for Budweiser beer, Alpo dog food, Breck shampoo, and Sara Lee treats, among other products, and he was closely associated with American Family Publishers and its sweepstakes. He marketed his own brand of vodka, and, most recently, he promoted Cash4Gold, a gold-buying business. (In those commercials, he spoofed his own image by intoning, "Heeeeere's money!") McMahon was the author of several books, including *Here's Ed, or How to Be a Second Banana, From Midway to Midnight* (1976), *For Laughing Out Loud: My Life and Good Times* (1998), and *Here's Johnny! My Memories of Johnny Carson, the Tonight Show, and 46 Years of Friendship* (2005). McMahon, whose final years were marred by severe financial difficulties, died of bone cancer and pneumonia in Los Angeles. He is survived by his third wife, Pam Hurn, and six children. *See Current Biography* (1977). — D.K.

Obituary *New York Times* (on-line) June 24, 2009

MCNAIR, STEVE Feb. 14, 1973–July 4, 2009 Football player. Steve McNair was regarded as one of the top National Football League (NFL) quarterbacks of his day. During his decade-long tenure with the Tennessee Titans (formerly the Houston Oilers and then the Tennessee Oilers), he led the team to the 2000 Super Bowl and two additional postseason appearances (2002, 2003) while also earning most-valuable-player honors in 2003. McNair's career with the Titans came to an end two years later, when he was traded to the Baltimore Ravens. In 2006 he helped the team win a division title and play-off berth. When McNair, a three-time Pro Bowl candidate, retired from the sport the following year, he was one of only five players in NFL history to have passed for 20,000 yards and rushed for 3,000 yards. The fourth of five sons, Steve LaTreal McNair was born in the rural Mississippi town of Mount Olive. After his father, who worked on an offshore oil rig, abandoned the family when McNair was eight years old, his mother, Lucille, supported her five children by working 14-hour shifts at a chicken hatchery and, later, an electronic-component factory. During his teens, McNair attended Mount Olive High School, where he was a standout athlete in baseball, basketball, and football. During his junior year McNair, who earned All-America and All-State honors in football, helped lead Mount Olive to a 1989 Class-A state title. Despite being drafted by the Seattle Mariners in the 35th round of the 1991 Major League Baseball (MLB) Draft, he decided instead to pursue a football career, turning down scholarship offers from more prestigious schools to attend the predominantly black Alcorn State University (ASU), in Lorman, Mississippi—the only school to recruit him to play quarterback rather than defensive back. (ASU was also the alma mater of McNair's older brother Fred, a fellow quarterback who played briefly in the NFL before moving on to the Canadian Football League.) As a first-year player, McNair performed impressively in his debut game, coming off the bench to complete three touchdowns and single-handedly propel the Braves football squad to a 27–22 victory against the Grambling State University Tigers. McNair, who subsequently became the team's starting quarterback, was named the Southwestern Athletic Conference (SWAC) player of the year following his freshman season and led the nation in total offense as a sophomore. At his family's suggestion, McNair decided against turning pro after his junior year and completed his studies, earning his bachelor's degree in physical education in 1994. By the end of his senior year, McNair had shattered numerous game, season, and career passing and total-offense records at Alcorn. He had also claimed the National Collegiate Athletics Association (NCAA) records for total offense (16,823 yards) and average yardage per game (400.55). Equally impressive were his career passing statistics—928 completions on 1,673 attempts for a total of 14,496 yards, 119 touchdowns, and 58 interceptions—which earned him All-America honors. McNair's efforts also earned him third place in the voting for the 1994 Heisman Trophy. The following year he entered the 1995 NFL Draft, in which he was selected third overall by the Houston Oilers, who signed McNair to a seven-year contract reportedly worth $28.4 million—more than any of the team's other players at that time. He spent his first two seasons in the NFL (1995–96) as the backup to Chris Chandler before becoming a starter in 1997—the same year the team relocated to Tennessee. McNair, whose 2,665 passing yards were the most for the franchise since Warren Moon in 1993 and whose 13 interceptions were the fewest for a single season in the team's history, was also the team leader in rushing touchdowns (eight) and ranked second behind teammate and running back Eddie George with 674 yards on the ground—the third-highest total for a quarterback in the NFL's history. In 1998 McNair became the youngest quarterback in franchise history to reach 3,000 yards passing, amassing 3,228 yards for the season. He also continued to astound fans with his running prowess, leading all quarterbacks in rushing yards (559). Despite an injury-riddled 1999 season, McNair, who had missed several games after undergoing midseason back surgery, returned to guide the Titans to an NFL-best 13–3 regular-season record and their first-ever appearance in the Super Bowl, where they were defeated by the St. Louis Rams, 23–16. A year later Tennessee captured the American Football Conference (AFC) Central Division title and advanced to the AFC championship game, where the team lost to the Baltimore Ravens (24–10). McNair finished the regular season with 3,350 passing yards, 264 completions, 21 touchdowns, and a quarterback rating of 90.2—all career bests—and for the first time in his career, he was named to the Pro Bowl. (He did not play, however, due to a shoulder injury.) In July 2001 McNair was awarded a six-year, $47 million contract extension. After a disappointing 7–9 record in 2001, McNair overcame a series of nagging injuries to lead the team to an 11–2 regular-season record and another division title. The Titans then advanced to the AFC championships, in which they were bested by the Oakland Raiders. McNair, who had finished third in the MVP voting in 2002, shared MVP honors with Indianapolis Colts quarterback Peyton Manning following an impressive 2003 season in which he was the league leader in quarterback ratings and also had 3,215 passing yards, 24 touchdowns, and just seven interceptions. The Titans' 12–4 record led to another appearance in the AFC Divisional play-offs, which saw them suffer a 17–14 loss to the New England Patriots. Following sub-par seasons in 2004 and 2005, during which the Titans finished at the bottom of their division, McNair was traded to the Baltimore Ravens and paid immediate dividends for his new team. In 2006 he led the Ravens to a 13–3 record and an appearance in the divisional play-offs, which they lost to the Colts (15–6). McNair, who continued to be plagued by injuries, managed only six starts during the 2007 season, in which the Ravens had a record of 5–11. In April 2008 he announced his retirement from the NFL. During his professional football career, McNair was no stranger to off-the-field controversy. In 2003, for example, he was charged with drunk driving and possession of a handgun, although the charges were later dismissed. McNair found himself in trouble again in 2007, when he allowed his brother-in-law to drive his vehicle while intoxicated. On July 4, 2009 McNair and 20-year-old Sahel Kazemi, who was reported to be his mistress, were found dead of gunshot wounds in the football player's condominium in Nashville. A subsequent police investigation and autopsy revealed that the deaths were the result of a murder-suicide. Officials concluded that Kazemi, who feared that McNair was romantically involved with another woman, had shot him four times before turning the gun on herself. McNair is survived by his wife, Mechelle, and their sons, Tyler and Trenton, as well as Junior and Steven, McNair's sons from a previous relationship. See *Current Biography* (2005). —C.C.

Obituary *New York Times* (on-line) July 5, 2009

MCNAMARA, ROBERT S. June 9, 1916–July 6, 2009 Former government official; former businessman; former president of the World Bank. Robert S. McNamara was one of the most influential and controversial presidential cabinet members of the 20th century. As the defense secretary under John F. Kennedy and Lyndon B. Johnson from 1961 to 1968, he was responsible for crafting the policies that led the U.S.

into the long and bitter Vietnam War, which ultimately left more than 50,000 Americans dead and the country in turmoil. He was also an important player in the Bay of Pigs invasion and the Cuban Missile Crisis—two conflicts that came to define the Cold War era. Although McNamara served as president of the World Bank from 1968 to 1981, in the nation's collective consciousness he remained most closely associated with the Vietnam War. Robert Strange McNamara was born in San Francisco, California, the son of Robert James and Clara Nell (Strange) McNamara. He studied mathematics, economics, and philosophy at the University of California at Berkeley, earning a B.A. degree in 1937. After earning an M.B.A. degree at the Harvard University Graduate School of Business in 1939, McNamara worked briefly in the San Francisco branch of the accounting firm Price, Waterhouse & Co. before returning to Harvard as an assistant professor of business administration in 1940. Rejected for active military service because of his nearsightedness, when World War II started, McNamara remained at Harvard to teach practical statistics to Army Air Corps officers. He also helped devise a statistical system to control the flow of material, money, and personnel for the military. He was sent to England in 1943 to set up a statistical control system for the Eighth Air Force's B-17 bomber operations, and he helped to direct the logistics of the long-range B-29 bomber raids on Japan. Following the war McNamara began working at the Ford Motor Co., where he and a group of other young employees known as the "whiz kids" used statistical analysis to improve the company and measure trends. McNamara later served as general manager of the Ford automotive division and group executive of the car and truck divisions as a whole. In 1960 he was named the first company president from outside the Ford family. However, a short time later he was asked to work in the new Kennedy administration, and he accepted the post of defense secretary. McNamara assumed office in January 1961. One of his first tasks was to determine the extent of the so-called "missile gap." While Kennedy believed the Soviet Union had the advantage, McNamara discovered the opposite to be true—the U.S. had a much larger arsenal. One of McNamara's other early assignments was to devise a plan to help defend the weak South Vietnamese regime of Ngo Dinh Diem from the Communist state of North Vietnam. (His initial plan consisted of sending 400 Green Beret soldiers to train South Vietnamese troops, but by the time of Kennedy's assassination, in 1963, there would be 17,000 troops stationed in South Vietnam.) The year 1961 also saw the botched Bay of Pigs invasion, in which U.S.-trained Cuban exiles led an effort to overthrow the government of Fidel Castro. The invasion failed, and McNamara, who had encouraged Kennedy to go forward with the plan, later admitted that he regretted the incident. More satisfying was his key role in the Cuban Missile Crisis the following year, when he helped to open diplomatic talks with the Soviet Union, which had been shipping nuclear weapons to Cuba. Potential nuclear war was averted when the U.S. agreed to remove its missiles from Turkey, on the Russian border, if the Soviet Union removed its missiles from Cuba. After Kennedy's assassination, on November 22, 1963, McNamara was kept on staff by Kennedy's successor, Johnson. After reports of a skirmish in the Gulf of Tonkin between U.S. and North Vietnamese ships in 1964 (later proven to be false), McNamara persuaded Johnson to deploy ground troops to Vietnam. As the war pressed on, McNamara continued to add more troops—more than 150,000 by 1965. By 1966 McNamara was beginning to see no way out of the conflict. The following year, without alerting Johnson, he authorized a team of analysts to compile a report on the war, later known as the Pentagon Papers. McNamara sent a long letter to Johnson, advising him that the war was unpopular and impossible to win. Upon writing the missive, he realized that his tenure as defense secretary would be over shortly. On November 29, 1967 the White House announced that McNamara was leaving his defense post to become president of the World Bank. (McNamara later wrote that he was unsure if he had quit or been fired from his job.) McNamara oversaw the World Bank's growth into a major lending force, from $1 billion a year to $12 billion by the end of his tenure. (Some observers, however, were critical of the large debts poor countries amassed after borrowing from the bank.) McNamara resigned from the World Bank in 1981, still plagued by the Vietnam War. In his 1995 book, *In Retrospect: The Tragedy and Lessons of Vietnam*, he denounced the war and analyzed the mistakes he and other officials had made. (The public found it difficult to absolve him of his actions, despite his contrition.) McNamara reiterated his point of view in Errol Morris's 2003 documentary, *The Fog of War: Eleven Lessons from the Life of Robert S. McNamara*. McNamara, who was struggling with various health problems, died in his sleep. His survivors include his second wife, the former Diana Masieri Byfield, and three children from his first marriage to his childhood sweetheart, Margaret Craig, who predeceased him, in 1981. See *Current Biography* (1987). — W.D.

Obituary *New York Times* (on-line) July 7, 2009

MORTIMER, JOHN Apr. 21, 1923–Jan. 16, 2009 British writer; barrister. John Mortimer, an English barrister and writer of fiction, plays, and scripts for radio, television, and film, is best known to U.S. audiences for creating the character Horace Rumpole, the protagonist in the popular TV series *Rumpole of the Bailey*, which aired on the BBC and PBS for decades. Rumpole was also the focus of a 1978 novel that won Mortimer a writer-of-the-year award from the British Academy of Film and Television Arts, as well as numerous short stories. Supposedly based in part on Mortimer's father—a sharp-tongued barrister who specialized in divorce petitions and wills—Rumpole is an eccentric sherry-drinking defender of London's criminal classes. In the *New York Times* obituary of Mortimer, Helen Verongos described Rumpole as "an endearing and enduring relic of the British legal system who became a television hero of the courtroom comedy." She continued: "To read Rumpole or to watch the episodes of the popular television series . . . is to enter not only Rumpole's stuffy flat or crowded legal chambers but also to feel the itch of his yellowing court wig and the flapping of his disheveled, cigar-ash-dusted courtroom gown. Rumpole spends his days quoting Keats and his nights quaffing claret at Pommeroy's wine bar, putting off the time that he must return to his wife, Hilda, more commonly known as She Who Must Be Obeyed." While writing volumes of fiction and nonfiction, Mortimer spent his days defending human rights and free speech, representing such notable clients as the punk rock group the Sex Pistols and novelist Hubert Selby Jr., whose works were deemed unacceptable under England's 1959 Obscene Publications Act. In 1966 Mortimer became a Queen's Counsel, a title given to barristers who appear only on court cases of major importance. An only child, Mortimer was born to Clifford and Kathleen May (Smith) Mortimer, who had met in South Africa. (He had emigrated with his family from London, and she was working at an all-girls school.) When Mortimer was 13 his father went completely blind. His mother assisted the elder Mortimer, who refused to publicly admit to his blindness and continued to practice law. Mortimer received a traditional boarding-school education and sold his first short story for 10 shillings when he was still a child. Though he told his parents of his writing ambitions, they pressured him to become a lawyer. He found the field dull but studied law at Brasenose College, part of the University of Oxford, and earned his degree in 1947, the year he published his first novel, *Charade*. Prior to graduating he also studied art at the Slade School and worked as an assistant director and scriptwriter for the Ministry of Information, making propaganda films during World War II. Mortimer went on to develop a successful law practice in London while continuing to write. He often drew from his legal experiences in his novels, among them *Rumming Park* (1948), *Answer Yes or No* (1950), *Like Men Betrayed* (1953), and *The Narrowing Stream* (1954). He found great success writing scripts for radio dramas; his first, *The Dock Brief* (1957), won the Italia prize for radio drama in 1958, which led Mortimer to abandon writing novels for playwriting. His first full-length stage play was *The Wrong Side of the Park* (1960). Though most of Mortimer's plays were comedies, some critics included him with the "angry young men," a group of writers of that time who attacked British middle-class life. Mortimer also wrote a number of screenplays, including a script he adapted from a novel by Mervyn Jones for the film *John and Mary* (1970), which earned him a Golden Globe nod for best screenplay. Mortimer depicted his relationship with his father in the play *A Voyage Round My Father*, which was adapted for television in 1981. Mortimer, who often wrote articles for various magazines and newspapers, published two memoirs: *Clinging to the Wreckage* (1982) and *Murders and Other Friends of Life* (1994). Despite various illnesses, he remained a fixture on London's social scene until his death and was known for his prodigious drinking and great wit. Mortimer, who died at his home in Oxfordshire, England, is survived by his second wife, Penelope, and their two children, Rosamond and Emily. He is also survived by two children, Sally and Jeremy, from his first marriage, and a son, Ross Bentley, born of a liaison with the actress Wendy Craig. See *Current Biography* (1983). — M.E.R.

Obituary *New York Times* (on-line) Jan. 17, 2009

NEUHAUS, RICHARD JOHN May 14, 1936–Jan. 8, 2009 Canadian-born American priest. A former Lutheran pastor, Richard John Neuhaus was an influential Roman Catholic theologian and ecumenicist who characterized himself as "politically liberal but culturally conservative"; he was more widely viewed as a tough but nuanced traditionalist. Neuhaus was the founder of the Institute of Religion and Public Life, a Manhattan think tank, and its house organ, *First Things: The Journal of Religion, Culture, and Public Life*, whose self-described purpose is "to advance a religiously informed public policy for the ordering of society." (He had previously been director of the Lutheran-based Rockford Society's Center for Religion and Society.) To each issue of *First Things*, he contributed an essay reflecting his wide reading in Roman Catholicism and Protestantism. Edited by Joseph Buttom, the journal also contains essays by other Catholics and by Orthodox, Jewish, and Protestant intellectuals relating religious questions to popular culture and public policy. "Policy is chiefly the function of culture," Neuhaus wrote, "the heart of culture is morality, and the heart of morality is religion." As a Lutheran minister, Neuhaus was for many years the pastor of St. John the Evangelist Church, a poor black parish in Brooklyn, New York City. During the 1960s and early 1970s, he was prominently on the left in politics and a leader in the civil rights and anti–Vietnam War movements; by his own admission, he was "an unreliable leftist." Contributing to his political disillusionment were the stories brought back by refugees from Vietnam and Cambodia after the war, indicating that "by any calculation of pain and suffering" the situation was far worse in those nations than before the American withdrawal. His disillusionment was clinched when only half of the hundred prominent American liberals he approached agreed to sign a petition asking the Hanoi government to answer charges of human-rights violations. Politically, he definitively turned from left to right in response to the 1973 U.S. Supreme Court decision in favor of abortion rights, which stunned him, because in his view the "pro-life" movement was continuous with civil rights. With his "high-church" penchant and his love for the "adventure of orthodoxy," he long believed in a unification of the Christian church. Thus, his conversion to Roman Catholicism in 1990 was for him "just the completion and right ordering" of a vocation that had begun in the Lutheran ministry. Ordained a priest of the Roman Catholic Archdiocese of New York a year later, Neuhaus was assigned to Immaculate Conception parish in Manhattan. In 1994 he and Charles Colson, a specialist in a prison ministry, issued a manifesto called "Evangelicals and Catholics Together." The following year, despite his Roman Catholic affiliation, *Time* magazine listed Neuhaus as one of the "25 Most Influential Evangelicals in America." As a Lutheran, Neuhaus edited the liturgical publication *Una Sancta* and was an associate editor of *Worldview*. His first book was *Theology and the Kingdom of God* (1969). He and Peter Berger co-wrote *Movement and Revolution* (1970), an indictment of American domestic and international injustices and the necessity of reform to avert the possibility of revolution. Neuhaus's book *Defense of People: Ecology and The Seduction of*

Radicalism (1971) is an attack on what he regarded as the neo-Malthusian underside of the ecology movement, a concern about the growing world population to the neglect of attention to fairer world distribution of food. Among his best-known books are *The Naked Public Square: Religion and Democracy in America* (1984) and *The Catholic Moment: The Paradox of the Church in the Postmodern World* (1987). In the former he deplored religion's dispossession of what he saw as its rightful place in American public discourse by "judicial usurpation" and applauded the recent raising of the public voice (however strident) of the "religious right." In *The Catholic Moment* he carried forward the work of the the Jesuit theologian John Courtney Murray in looking to the Roman Catholic Church in the United States to assume "its rightful role in the culture-forming task of constructing a religiously informed philosophy for the American experiment in ordered liberty." Others among his books are *Doing Well and Good: The Challenge of the Christian Capitalist* (1992), *Catholic Matters* (2007), *American Babylon: Notes of a Christian Exile* (2009), a collection of essays, and a book of meditations on the death of Jesus Christ. In *As I Lay Dying: Meditations Upon Returning* (2002), he pondered his near-death experience, when a large tumor burst in his intestine in 1994. Neuhaus was a close adviser to President George W. Bush on such matters as bioethics (including stem-cell research) and the preservation of traditional marriage. He was the originator of Neuhaus's Law: "Where Orthodoxy is optional, Orthodoxy will sooner or later be prohibited." He died in Manhattan. See *Current Biography* (1988). — K.D.

Obituary *New York Times* B p9 Jan. 9, 2009

NIMEIRY, GAAFAR MUHAMMAD AL- Jan. 1, 1930–May 30, 2009 Former Sudanese head of state. Gaafar Muhammad al-Nimeiry, an army colonel, took control of Sudan in a bloodless coup in 1969 and served until another coup ousted him in 1985. (His name has been transliterated by the Western press in numerous ways; a common spelling of his first name is Jaafar, and his family name has appeared as Numayri, al-Nimeri, al-Numeiri, or an-Noumairy, among other variations.) He was born in Omdurman, in what was then the Anglo-Egyptian Sudan. (Sudan gained independence from England and Egypt in 1956.) Despite low grades, he gained entry into the Hantoub Secondary School, a government-run English-style boarding school for boys, and while there he developed an interest in politics and became an ardent nationalist. In 1949 Nimeiry enrolled at the Military College in Khartoum, graduating three years later as a second lieutenant. Inspired by his hero, Egyptian president Gamal Abdel Nasser, who had led the Egyptian Revolution of 1952 that removed King Farouk I from power, Nimeiry, along with some army colleagues, formed the Free Officers Organization, a nationalist group, in 1953. Four years later Nimeiry was among a number of officers arrested and accused of planning to orchestrate a military coup. He was dismissed from the army and placed under house arrest. He was permitted to rejoin the army in 1958, after a bloodless coup placed Lieutenant General Ibrahim Abboud in power. On May 25, 1969, Nimeiry, backed by 800 members of the Sudanese Army, seized power by arresting several politicians and top army generals. He changed the country's name to the Democratic Republic of the Sudan and sought to modernize the nation through socialism. Nimeiry survived four attempted coups during the 1970s, including one in 1971 during which he was held hostage for three days by Communist-leaning army officers. He escaped and subsequently executed the coup leaders. With Nimeiry emerging from the ordeal stronger than ever, the 10-member Revolutionary Command Council announced a plebiscite for September 30, 1971. Receiving 98.6 percent of the vote, Nimeiry became Sudan's first elected president. Soon thereafter, he dissolved the council; to provide himself with a broad base of popular support, he founded the Sudanese Socialist Union, which was patterned after Egypt's Arab Socialist Union. In 1972 Nimeiry brought an end to Sudan's civil war by signing a peace agreement granting the heavily Christian south regional autonomy from the Muslim majority. During that time Nimeiry enjoyed a close relationship with the U.S., which viewed him as an ally in its disputes with the Marxist government in neighboring Ethiopia and the increasingly hostile Libya. Nimeiry won reelection in 1977 but found that his opposition was gaining in popularity. In response, he jailed his detractors, and—seeking support from Muslim extremists—he imposed harsh *Sharia* law across Sudan in 1983. As a result, the civil war in the south resumed. The nation was also facing rising food and fuel prices and growing foreign debt. Nimeiry was ousted in April 1985, during an official visit to America. He lived in exile in Egypt until 1999, when Sudanese president Omar al-Bashir allowed him to return. Nimeiry died in Sudan of undisclosed causes. He is survived by his wife. See *Current Biography* (1977). — M.A.S.

Obituary *New York Times* B p15 June 12, 2009

NOLAN, CHRISTOPHER Sep. 6, 1965–Feb. 20, 2009 Irish writer. Christopher Nolan, mute and quadriplegic since birth, nonetheless became an award-winning author. His best-selling autobiography, *Under the Eye of the Clock* (1987), earned the prestigious Whitbread Prize, beating out works by such renowned competitors as Seamus Heaney and Richard Ellmann. Nolan, a native of Mullingar, Ireland, was deprived of oxygen for hours during his mother's difficult labor. His *Economist* obituary (February 26, 2009, on-line), which quoted Nolan's own words, described the resulting disabilities: "His two arms looked normal, but they would fly out randomly, like a clockwork doll's. 'Dreadful deadly spasms' of cerebral palsy shot their way from his cranium to his spine and into his feet. He needed carrying to the bath, to the toilet, to bed; his long legs were good for nothing, collapsing under him like a deck of cards. When he tried to talk, nothing came out but 'dull looks, dribbles and senseless sounds.' He could not even wipe the saliva from his own face." Nolan's parents owned a farm in Corcloon, a town 50 miles west of Dublin. Nolan credited his father, who earned extra money from a part-time position as a psychiatric nurse, with being a strong influence. In an interview with Ann Geracimos for *Publishers Weekly* (March 13, 2000), Nolan described him as someone who "always has been there talking and reminiscing and feeding me tidbits of [James] Joyce, [Samuel] Beckett, D.H. Lawrence. The real truth is I'm the writer he'd love to be or should be." To further stimulate Nolan's mind, his mother displayed the letters of the alphabet in the kitchen, and his older sister, Yvonne, sang songs and performed skits for him. Nolan devised a rudimentary form of communication, in which he would raise his eyes to indicate "yes" and lower them to say "no," among other simple signals. Although Nolan had been diagnosed at age six with the intellectual capacity of a baby, a subsequent test revealed what Nolan's parents already knew—that Nolan's mental faculties had remained intact despite his traumatic birth. In 1972 Nolan's parents sold their farm and moved the family to Dublin, so that he could attend the Central Remedial Clinic School. When he was 11 Nolan was prescribed a muscle relaxant that enabled him—with his mother's help—to write on a keyboard by lowering his head and striking selected keys with a stick that was strapped to his forehead. Nolan won his first literary award for poems he submitted to a 1977 contest sponsored by the British Spastics Society (now called Scope). In 1979, the year he won another prize, for his autobiographical essay "A Mammy Encomium," Nolan become the first severely disabled student to attend Mount Temple Comprehensive School. (His classmates included future members of the popular band U2, and Nolan later served as the inspiration for the group's song "Miracle Drug.") At age 15 Nolan published *Dam-Burst of Dreams* (1981), a book of poems, stories, and essays that received critical acclaim for his imaginative word play and skillful metaphors. In 1983 Nolan enrolled at Trinity College, where he received honors grades but left after a year to devote himself to *Under the Eye of the Clock.* Nolan turned down offers to adapt the memoir into a film, fearing that Hollyood might sentimentalize or cheapen his work. He noted in a letter to a prospective producer, as quoted by William Grimes in Nolan's *New York Time*s obituary (February 24, 2009, on-line): "I want to highlight the creativity within the brain of a cripple and while not attempting to hide the crippledom I want instead to filter all sob-storied sentiment from his portrait and dwell upon his life, his laughter, his vision, and his nervous normality." The following year Nolan adapted *Under the Eye of the Clock* for the stage, under the title *Torchlight and Laser Beams.* He then spent more than a decade writing his first novel, *The Banyan Tree* (1999), based on his family's history. Nolan was working on a second novel at the time of his death, which was the result of aspirating food into his airway. He is survived by his parents and his sister, who is now a freelance journalist. See *Current Biography* (1988). — M.E.R.

Obituary *New York Times* (on-line) Feb. 24, 2009

ODETTA Dec. 31, 1930–Dec. 2, 2008 Singer. Known professionally by her given name, Odetta was a highly influential musician who, through her performances and recordings of folk and traditional songs, gospels, spirituals, and blues, became an icon of the American civil rights movement; helped to spur the surge of interest in folk music in the 1960s; and significantly affected the careers of such artists as Bob Dylan, Joan Baez, Janis Joplin, and Tracy Chapman. "In her commanding presence, charismatic delivery and determination to sing black truth to white power, Odetta was the female Paul Robeson . . . ," Richard Corliss wrote for *Time* (December 3, 2008, on-line). "During the folk boom, each Odetta gig, in coffeehouse or concert hall, was a master class of work songs, folk songs, church songs, and an eloquent tutorial in raw American history. Identifiable from the first syllable, her voice fused the thrill of gospel, the techniques of art song—the wisdom that subtlety sometimes trumps volume—and the desperate wail of blues. If a line could be drawn from Bessie Smith to Janis Joplin, from Mahalia Jackson to Maria Callas, it would have to go through Odetta." "Her sensational voice could be a pure narrow flute in one phrase and a growly shout the next," Bruce Shapiro wrote for the *Nation* (December 4, 2008, on-line). In a review of a concert that Odetta gave at the Museum of Fine Arts in Boston in December 2006, just before her 76th birthday, James Reed wrote for the *Boston Globe* (December 22, 2006, on-line), "Odetta's voice is still a force of nature," and he described her as "a majestic figure in American music, a direct gateway to bygone generations." The singer was born Odetta Holmes in Birmingham, Alabama. Her father died a few years later, and when she was about six, her mother and stepfather (whose surname, Felious, became hers) settled in Los Angeles with Odetta and her two step-siblings. At home, guided by her parents, she listened to classical music and jazz, and at 13 began lessons in classical singing. While in junior high school, she performed with a group called the Madrigal Singers. Prevented by her color from attending a nearby high school, she rode a bus to a more distant school—one of the circumstances that later informed her interpretations of what she termed "liberation songs." After she graduated she worked as a domestic and, at night, took classes at Los Angeles City College, where she earned a bachelor's degree in music. Earlier, at 19, she was cast in the chorus of a West Coast production of the musical *Finian's Rainbow.* While on tour the company performed in San Francisco, and Odetta began to frequent bohemian coffeehouses. "It felt like home," she told an interviewer, as quoted by Tim Weiner in the *New York Times* (December 3, 2008). She taught herself to play guitar, left the theater troupe, and earned a gig at the Tin Angel, a San Francisco nightclub. The next year she landed a one-month engagement at the Blue Angel, in New York City, where she gained a fan base that grew to include the singers Harry Belafonte and Pete Seeger. In 1954 she and the erstwhile singer Larry Mohr, made two live and studio recordings for the Fantasy label; they contained traditional songs and blues covers, some of which were rereleased on the 1993 CD *The Tin Angel.* In *Cinerama Holiday* (1955), the first of a half-dozen films in which Odetta appeared as herself, she sang "Santy Anno". That song was among those on her debut solo album, *Odetta Sings Ballads and Blues* (1956). Reviewers of that LP took note of her "striking contralto voice" and her "electrifying sincerity."

With her next album, *Odetta at the Gate of Horn* (1957), her reputation greatly increased, and she secured engagements in big cities in Canada as well as the U.S. In 1959 she gave a sold-out concert in Town Hall, in New York City, impressing John Wilson, the reviewer for the *New York Times* (April 25, 1959), as "a highly cultivated singer . . . bringing to everything she sings the strong imprint of her warm, positive, and enormously skillful musical personality." Odetta won a Sylvania Award "for outstanding contribution to creative television technique" for her work on the 1959 TV special *Tonight with Belafonte*. Her debut recital at Carnegie Hall, in New York City, in 1960 earned glowing reviews, as did the vast majority of her subsequent concerts and her 1960s recordings. In 1963, during the March on Washington, she sang what she called her "Freedom Trilogy" at the Lincoln Memorial. Also in 1963 she performed at the White House for President John F. Kennedy. In 1965 she accompanied Martin Luther King Jr. on the civil-rights march in Selma, Alabama. She made two albums in 1973, but by that time her career, along with the popularity of folk and civil rights songs, had entered a decline. She continued to concertize, however, and in 1999 she received the National Endowment for the Arts Medal of the Arts and Humanities from President Bill Clinton. That year she recorded two albums; her most recent disks include *Absolutely the Best* (2000), *Looking for a Home* (2001), and *Gonna Let It Shine* (2005). Her first two marriages, to Don Gordon and Gary Shead, ended in divorce. According to many sources, in 1977 she married the singer Iverson Minter, known professionally as Louisiana Red, who moved to Germany in 1983. Her manager, Doug Yeager, told an Associated Press reporter (December 3, 2008, on-line) that she had divorced decades ago and never remarried. Odetta died in New York City of heart disease and kidney failure. Her survivors included a son and a daughter. See *Current Biography* (1960). — M.H.

Obituary *New York Times* A p24 Dec. 3, 2008

OHLIN, LLOYD E. Aug. 27, 1918–Dec. 6, 2008 Sociologist; criminologist. During his noteworthy career as a criminologist, Lloyd E. Ohlin explored the sociological factors, including poverty, that contribute to crime. Ohlin told a reporter for the *New York Post* (June 9, 1961), "In a democratic society such as ours, equal opportunity is expressed constantly. The myth of log-cabin-to-president and city-street-to-bank-president is deeply ingrained in us. . . . The trouble comes with the break between aspirations and opportunities. When we lead people to aspire to higher and higher standards and then fail to produce opportunities for them to do so, they are left with a sense of having been denied and they often become delinquents." An advocate of prison reform, Ohlin often criticized the methods used by correctional institutions. A past president of the American Society of Criminology, he had a long and distinguished teaching career and worked for government agencies related to criminal justice under three presidents: John F. Kennedy, Lyndon B. Johnson, and Jimmy Carter. Lloyd Edgar Ohlin was born in Belmont, Massachusetts. His family owned a chain of local bakeries. After graduating from Belmont High School, in 1936, Ohlin attended Brown University, where he studied sociology and psychology, earning a bachelor's degree with honors in 1940. After receiving his master's degree in sociology from Indiana University, in 1942, he served for three years in Europe with the counterintelligence corps of the U.S. Army. From 1947 to 1953 Ohlin was a sociologist-actuary with the Illinois People and Pardon Board at Joliet Penitentiary, a position that required him to interview inmates and prepare case materials for parole board dockets. From 1953 to 1956, as the director of the Center for Education and Research in Corrections at the University of Chicago, Ohlin conducted research on probation and parole organizations and analyzed correctional systems. In 1954 he received his Ph.D. degree in sociology from the University of Chicago, and two years later he became a professor of sociology at the New York School of Social Work, part of Columbia University. There he became a leading researcher in the field of corrections methods, specifically for juvenile offenders, and he conducted studies that revealed, among other findings, that workers were failing to provide young prisoners with adequate psychiatric treatment. In 1959 Ohlin was one of the main architects of an experimental anti-poverty program called Mobilization for Youth, which was implemented on New York City's then-gritty Lower East Side. The program included such services as job training, drug counseling, and legal help, and it later became a national model. In 1967 Ohlin became one of the few non-lawyers on the faculty of Harvard Law School, and he later worked as the research director of Harvard's Center for Criminal Justice. Ohlin retired from teaching in 1982, and Harvard named him a professor emeritus. Ohlin's death was the result of complications of Shy-Drager syndrome, a neurodegenerative disease. He was predeceased by his first wife, the former Helen Hunter, who died in 1990, as well as by two sons, Jor and Robert. He is survived by two daughters, Heather Nancy Ohlin and Janet McCandless, and his second wife, Elaine Cressey Ohlin, whom he married in 1993. See *Current Biography* (1963). — M.E.R.

Obituary *New York Times* (on-line) Jan. 4, 2009

O'HORGAN, TOM May 3, 1924–Jan. 11, 2009 Theater director. Tom O'Horgan has been called "the high priest of the American underground theater" and "the Busby Berkeley of the acid set." While he made his reputation in Off-Off-Broadway experimental theater, O'Horgan was best known to the general public as the innovative director of the influential Broadway musicals *Hair* and *Jesus Christ Superstar*. Known for his quest to liberate theater from the confines of 19th-century classicism, O'Hagan championed what has been dubbed "total theater," in which all aspects of expression, including music, dance, and pantomime, were fluidly integrated into highly visceral and participatory productions that encouraged spontaneity and improvisation. While some members of the theatrical establishment criticized his works as chaotic, his underground sensibilities seemed to resonate for a time with the public, and in 1971 four of his shows appeared concurrently on Broadway. A native of Chicago, Illinois, O'Horgan sang in his church choir and wrote plays from an early age. His father, a suburban-newspaper owner, encouraged his creative pursuits, taking him to shows and concerts and building a homemade wind machine and footlights for him. O'Horgan attended DePaul University, where he learned to play numerous musical instruments. After graduating he joined Chicago's Second City, the famed improvisational group, and then moved to New York City, where he began acting in experimental and improvisational productions, often at such now-renowned performance spaces as La MaMa in the East Village and the Judson Memorial Church in Greenwich Village. In the early 1960s he began directing plays and soon became a protégé of Ellen Stewart, who ran La MaMa. By the end of the decade, O'Horgan had directed more than 50 plays there. According to Michael Feingold, in a tribute for the *Village Voice* (January 21, 2009), O'Horgan "managed to create, for a few brief, dazzling years at La MaMa, something approaching the theater that he essentially dreamed of all his life: a troupe of infinite resource and pliancy, with a contemporary sensibility, equivalent to a medieval band of strolling players." In 1967 O'Horgan directed the Off-Broadway play *Futz!*, a controversial story of a farm boy who falls in love with a pig. *Futz!*, for which he also composed music, showcased O'Horgan's eclectic and energetic style and attracted the attention of James Rado and Gerome Ragni, the creators of the Off-Broadway hit *Hair*. O'Horgon agreed to help ready the musical for a Broadway run, which opened in April 1968 and went on to become, as Douglas Martin wrote for the *New York Times* (January 13, 2009), "perhaps more than any other play of the 1960s . . . the truest, most enduring expression of the hippie scene." (The entire cast appeared naked at the end of the first act—an innovation that was much imitated in subsequent Broadway shows.) O'Horgon was instantly catapulted to mainstream success. In 1971 Broadway theater fans could attend not only *Hair*, which garnered him a Tony Award nomination, but three other O'Horgan productions that were being staged at the same time: *Lenny*, about the controversial comedian Lenny Bruce; Andrew Lloyd Webber's *Jesus Christ Superstar*, another hugely popular musical that proved to be an enduring success; and *Inner City*, which was based on the politically charged poetry book *The Inner City Mother Goose* by Eve Merriam. After that flurry of activity in the limelight, O'Horgan drifted back into the underground theater scene and never repeated his success on Broadway. He later felt, as Martin wrote, that "he had been put on 'an enemies list' by critics and other members of the theatrical establishment." O'Horgan subsequently directed such productions as the Off-Broadway musical *Dude* (1972), created by Gerome Ragni; *The Leaf People* (1975), a Dennis Reardon play about the first contact between white men and a tribe of hostile Amazonians; and *I Won't Dance* (1981), a murder mystery, as well as several operas. O'Horgan also composed the music for *Alex in Wonderland* (1970), a Paul Mazursky film, and directed a movie version of Eugene Ionesco's absurdist play *Rhinoceros* (1974) starring Zero Mostel. Supported largely by royalties from his Broadway hits, for many years O'Horgan lived in a loft in downtown Manhattan, famous for housing his impressive collection of musical instruments and for its parties and salons, which were attended by some of New York's most prominent artistic figures, including Leonard Bernstein, Norman Mailer, and Gore Vidal. O'Horgan received numerous honors over the years, including three Drama Desk Awards (for *Tom Paine*, *Futz!*, and *Lenny*) and an Obie (as best director of 1967). In 1968 he was named theatrical director of the year by the editors of *Newsweek*, and in 2006 he was recognized for his lifetime achievements at the New York Innovative Theatre Awards, which celebrate Off-Off-Broadway works. Diagnosed with Alzheimer's disease in 2002, O'Horgan was forced in 2007 to sell his beloved loft and his collection of musical instruments. He died in the care of longtime friends in Florida, where he had moved after leaving New York City. See *Current Biography* (1970). — M.M.

Obituary *New York Times* (on-line) Jan. 13, 2009

PAUL, LES June 9, 1915–Aug. 13, 2009 Musician. Les Paul is widely acknowledged to have revolutionized 20th-century popular music. In addition to playing guitar with such iconic artists as Louis Armstrong and Bing Crosby and recording more than three dozen hits with Mary Ford, then his wife, Paul is perhaps best known for pioneering guitar amplification and for creating what was probably the first solid-bodied electric guitar. Prized for its clarity and tone, the Les Paul model, whose design has not been altered since 1958, is still produced by Gibson and continues to sell steadily. During his decades-long career, Paul also forged various innovations in the recording studio, experimenting with such techniques as overdubbing and multi-track recording. Paul, whose given name was Lester William Polsfuss, was born in Waukesha, Wisconsin. He had learned to play the guitar, banjo, and harmonica by ear by the time he was a teenager. His tinkering with musical production began early; at 10 he used a coat hanger to create his own harmonica holder, and a few years later he figured out how to amplify his guitar by connecting it to a phonograph needle that was wired to a radio speaker. Paul dropped out of high school to join a traveling cowboy band that was passing through his hometown. With that group he traveled to Chicago, Illinois, where he played on a local radio show called *Barn Dance*, achieving some success as a country musician. (He used the stage name Rhubarb Red during that period.) Aspiring next to be a jazz musician, Paul began rehearsing with the bassist Ernie Newton and vocalist and rhythm guitarist Jimmy Atkins, and in 1937 the Les Paul trio, as they were known, traveled to New York City and was discovered by Fred Waring, an orchestra and choral leader who featured the group on his NBC radio network for the next four years. During that time Paul gained experience performing on the New York City jazz circuit, with such notable frontmen as Art Tatum, Ben Webster, Louis Armstrong, Stuff Smith, and Charlie Christian. Meanwhile, Paul, who had been an unpaid consultant to the Gibson guitar company while in Chicago, began experimenting with creating an electric guitar that did not pick up feedback. He eventually settled on a solid-bodied design; the first model was made of an un-hollowed beam of wood known as the "log." It was not until 1952 that

Paul created a multi-pickup model that Gibson purchased and marketed. Paul left his trio and Waring's radio show in 1941 with the goal of playing with Bing Crosby in Hollywood. He traveled to Los Angeles with a new trio and managed to impress Crosby, who arranged a contract for him with Decca Records. The trio began to attract the attention of the jazz world with their recorded renditions of "Tiger Rag" and "Little Rock Getaway," among other tunes. After serving one year in the Armed Forces Radio Service during World War II, Paul toured with various artists, including Crosby, Nat King Cole, and the Andrews Sisters. In 1945 Paul stopped touring to build his own makeshift recording studio in his Hollywood garage. There he experimented with manipulating recordings by adjusting the microphone positioning and reverberation. He began making multilevel recordings using two disc machines; later he used magnetic tape to create the first eight-track recorder, which he sold to Ampex in 1954. Paul's first multi-track recordings included the 1948 instrumental solos "Lover" and "Brazil." That year, however, Paul shattered his right elbow in a car accident. After learning that it would be largely immovable upon healing, Paul asked the doctor to set it at a 90-degree angle so that he could continue playing guitar. In 1949 he married the vocalist Iris Colleen Summers (who changed her name to Mary Ford at his suggestion) and went on to produce a string of hit songs with her. Those multi-track recordings transformed Mary's voice into that of a female trio and Paul's guitar sound into that of a large rhythm section. Divorced from Ford in 1964, Paul began suffering from arthritis as well as a broken eardrum. He spent much of the 1960s designing guitars for Gibson; he also invented and patented a number of recording innovations, including an echo-repeat device called the Les Paulverizer, which reached the market in 1974. In 1981 he underwent quintuple-bypass surgery, and after recovering he returned to performing. For years he played weekly gigs at the Manhattan jazz club Fat Tuesdays. After that venue closed, in 1995, Paul played regular Monday-night shows at Iridium, another New York City venue, until a few months before his death. His last album, *American Made, World Played* (2005), won two Grammy Awards, for best pop instrumental performance and best rock instrumental performance. (He had received a Grammy Trustees Award for Lifetime Achievement in 1983; Trustees Awards are given to those who have made musical contributions outside of performing.) Paul was the subject of several documentaries, including *The Wizard of Waukesha*, which aired on British TV, and *Chasing Sound: Les Paul at 90*, which premiered in 2007 as part of the PBS *American Masters* series. A member of the Rock and Roll Hall of Fame, National Inventors Hall of Fame, and National Association of Broadcasters Hall of Fame, Paul died from complications of pneumonia in White Plains, New York. He is survived by his companion, Arlene Palmer; three sons; a daughter; five grandchildren; and five great-grandchildren. See *Current Biography* (1987). — M.E.R.

Obituary *New York Times* (on-line) Aug. 14, 2009

PELL, CLAIBORNE Nov. 22, 1918–Jan. 1, 2009 Former Democratic United States senator from Rhode Island; former diplomat. A blue-blooded patrician, Claiborne deBorda Pell was also unassuming, self-effacing, and invariably gracious and polite, and he often had the air of an absentminded professor; "his eccentricities"—among them, his habit of wearing a tweed suit jacket while jogging—"and his ability to laugh at himself endeared him to colleagues and constituents," William H. Honan wrote for the *New York Times* (January 2, 2009). Pell represented Rhode Island in the U.S. Senate for 36 years, from 1961 to 1997. His best-known contribution as a senator was his sponsorship of the legislation that created the Basic Educational Opportunity Grants (BEOGs), known familiarly, and since 1980 officially, as the Pell Grants, which helped to make it possible for millions of lower- and moderate-income students (more than 100 million, as of the end of 2008) to attend college. Pell also wrote the bills that established the National Endowment for the Arts and the National Endowment for the Humanities, and he helped to draft the legislation that led to the creation of Amtrak. An energetic supporter of the United Nations and advocate of ending the ostracism of Cuba, he was an equally outspoken opponent of the Vietnam War and, later, of American military intervention in Lebanon, El Salvador, and Bosnia and Herzegovina. He strongly supported unions, civil rights for homosexuals and abortion rights (despite the preponderance of Catholics in Rhode Island), arms control, and the rule of law in international affairs; also among his priorities was maintaining the environmental safety of the oceans, from the sea floor to the surface, and preventing the exploitation of the creatures that inhabit them. "Claiborne Pell was a gentleman and a gentle man," U.S. senator Edward M. Kennedy of Massachusetts said of him in a memorial service, as quoted by Eric Tucker for the Associated Press (January 5, 2009). "On the outside he was calm and composed, but deep down he was a real fighter." Pell was born in Manhattan into an extremely wealthy family that traced its arrival in the U.S. to colonial times and had once owned a huge swath of what became Westchester County, north of New York City, and parts of the city borough of the Bronx. One of his ancestors founded the Lorillard Tobacco Co. A great-great-granduncle of his, George Mifflin Dallas, held a seat from Pennsylvania in the U.S. Senate before becoming the country's 11th vice president, under President James M. Polk. Four other ancestors of his served in the U.S. Senate or House from other states—among them his father, Herbert Claiborne Pell, who represented the so-called Silk Stocking District of New York City in Congress for two years before holding ministerial posts in Portugal and Hungary under President Franklin Delano Roosevelt. Claiborne Pell earned a B.A. degree with honors in history from Princeton University in 1940. Immediately afterward he went to Europe to try to help people imprisoned in Nazi concentration camps; he was detained at least twice by Nazi authorities. Back in the U.S., he enlisted in the U.S. Coast Guard Reserve four months before the Japanese attack on Pearl Harbor, on December 7, 1941. In his first assignment he worked as a cook. He later served in the North Atlantic and the Mediterranean. Illness ended his active service in 1944. After his recovery and until the end of the war, Pell taught at the Navy School of Military Government, in Princeton. He retired from the Coast Guard Reserve as a captain several decades later. In 1945, as a U.S. State Department special assistant, he attended the conference in San Francisco whose participants set up the United Nations. (He often had a copy of the U.N. charter in a pocket.) The following year he earned an M.A. degree in international relations from Columbia University. In 1946–48, as a member of the Foreign Service, he worked in Czechoslovakia. He was a vice consul in Genoa, Italy, in 1949. From 1950 to 1952 he worked in the U.S. for the State Department. During the next eight years, he spent much of his time in the private sector. From 1956 until 1960 he was a vice president of the International Rescue Committee; he directed the committee's activities on the Hungarian border during and after the Hungarian Revolution of 1956. Meanwhile, Pell had become active in Democratic Party activities in Rhode Island and on the national level. Early in 1960, when Rhode Island's four-term senior senator, the 93-year-old Theodore F. Green, announced that he planned to retire, Pell took steps to win that seat and entered the Democratic primary. He won handily, with 61 percent of the vote, and defeated his Republican opponent in the general election with nearly 69 percent of the ballots cast. He won reelection five times. When Pell joined the Senate, in 1961, he got seats on both the Foreign Relations Committee and the Labor and Public Welfare Committee. He later also served on the Rules and Administration Committee and the Joint Committee on the Library (that is, the Library of Congress). On the Foreign Relations Committee, he served on the Terrorism, Narcotics, and International Operations Subcommittee, and on Labor, he chaired the Education, Arts, and Humanities Subcommittee and served on the Subcommittee on Aging and the Subcommittee on Children, Families, Drugs, and Alcoholism. In 1963 he urged the West to accept the separation of Germany into Communist and non-Communist sections and pushed for an international zone linking East and West Berlin, a proposal that gained the support of both the Soviet Union and the U.S. That year he signed a bipartisan report that warned the U.S. government not to exceed its advisory capacity in Vietnam. He later regretted, and labeled as one of his most serious errors as a senator, his approval of President Lyndon B. Johnson's Gulf of Tonkin Resolution (formally, the Southeast Asia Resolution of 1964), which gave the president the right to engage in warfare in Southeast Asia without congressional authorization and led to the escalation of the Vietnam War. Pell later vigorously opposed the support by the administration of President Ronald Reagan of the guerrilla groups—known as the Contras—that attempted to overthrow the elected government in Nicaragua. The passage in 1972 of the law that created the Pell Grants program is attributable largely to Pell's insistence that the grants go directly to students rather than to colleges. To date, according to the American Council on Education, the government has distributed about $250 billion in grants. During the administration of President George W. Bush, Pell fought unsuccessfully to increase funding for the grants to keep pace with inflation. During the civil wars in the Balkans in the 1990s, Pell pushed for sanctions against Serbia and for the establishment of war-crimes tribunals. In 1994, during a Senate debate in which the Republican senator Jesse Helms of North Carolina denounced the nomination of Roberta Achtenberg to be assistant secretary of the U.S. Department of Housing and Urban Development "because she's a damn lesbian," Pell revealed that his daughter Julia was a lesbian. "I would not want to see her barred from a government job because of her orientation," he declared. As the chairman of the Foreign Relations Committee for seven years beginning in 1987, Pell was faulted for lacking forcefulness and allowing the committee to lose much of its influence. In 1994 Pell was diagnosed with Parkinson's disease, which forced him to retire at the end of the 103rd Congress. In the *Providence Journal* (April 10, 2005, on-line), G. Wayne Miller wrote that in *The Pell Record* (1994), an update of a 1990 pamphlet that listed legislation the senator wrote or supported, four pages were devoted to bills on economic development, four pages each to energy, health care, and women's issues, and two pages each to veterans' affairs, the oceans and fishing, crime and drugs, and transportation. Pell wrote the book *Megalopolis Unbound: The Supercity and the Transportation of Tomorrow* and, with Harold Leland Goodwin, *Challenge of the Seven Seas*, both published in 1966. Pell was fluent in French, Spanish, and Portuguese as well as English. His honors included awards from a dozen European countries and 51 honorary degrees. Pell died in his home in Newport, Rhode Island, where he had lived for 82 years. His survivors included his wife of 64 years, the former Nuala O'Donnell, his son Christopher (called Toby), his daughter Nuala Dallas Yates, five grandchildren, and five great-grandchildren. He was predeceased by his daughter Julia and his son Herbert (known as Bertie). See *Current Biography* (1972). — M.H.

Obituary *New York Times* A p21 Jan. 2, 2009

PENN, IRVING June 16, 1917–Oct. 7, 2009 Photographer. Irving Penn's work set the aesthetic standards of fashion-magazine photography for a large part of the 20th century. He was one of the first to merge fashion photography and art successfully, beginning with his early assignments for *Vogue* in the 1940s, and his pictures are frequently compared to paintings. His photographs exhibited a sparse, studio-controlled style, with a given subject generally placed on a piece of carpet between two plain, intersecting walls. Such a minimalist approach set Penn's work apart from that of other photographers and gave the images a distinctive look that has led to their inclusion in museum collections worldwide. Penn was born in Plainfield, New Jersey, to Harry Penn, a watchmaker, and Sonia (Greenberg) Penn, a nurse. The family moved to Philadelphia in the early 1920s, before the birth of Penn's brother, Arthur Penn, now a noted film director. Penn prepared for a career in design at the Philadelphia Museum School of Industrial Art (now the University of the Arts) from 1934 to 1938, under the tutelage of Alexey Brodovitch, an art director at *Harper's Bazaar*. Penn then worked for a year as an assistant in the art department at *Harper's Bazaar*, and in 1940 he was hired as an art director at Saks Fifth Avenue, the famed New York City department store. Penn left New York City and journeyed to Mexico in 1942 to become a painter. Dissatisfied with the work he produced, he returned to the city the following year and took a job in *Vogue*'s art department, where he was assigned to come up with cover layouts. Because the magazine's photographers were unwilling to use his suggestions, Penn photographed one of his ideas himself. The resulting picture, a color still life of a woman's glove, pocketbook, belt, and other accessories, was published on the cover of the October 1943 issue. (Penn ultimately photographed more than 150 covers for *Vogue* over the next 50 years.) In late 1944, near the end of World War II, Penn left *Vogue* to join the American Field Service ambulance corps in Italy. Later, as an official photographer for the Field Service, he traveled throughout India with the British Army before returning to *Vogue* in 1946. During the 1950s, Penn refined his aesthetic, occasionally pushing simplification to the point of abstraction. This is perhaps best exemplified by his iconic cover photograph for *Vogue*'s April 1950 issue, which featured a model's face obscured by a black veil. In 1949 and 1950 Penn produced a series of photos of nude female torsos, stripped of skin tone. (The unsettling pictures were not exhibited or published until 1980.) In the 1960s and early 1970s, Penn traveled the world with a portable studio that allowed him to recreate the look of one of his studio shoots. His subjects ranged from hippies in San Francisco to the indigenous people of New Guinea. On the commercial end, in 1968 he began shooting crisp, minimalist ads for Clinique, photographing the company's skin-care products and cosmetics against clean, simple backgrounds. (The distinctive ads remain among Penn's most widely seen works.) By the 1980s Penn was photographing more frequently in color, choosing as subjects flowers and other objects instead of people. Many of his later photographs were concerned with the theme of decay, and his final work for *Vogue*, published in August 2009, consisted of a shot of aging bananas. Penn was the subject of a career retrospective at the Museum of Modern Art (MoMA) in New York City in 1984, and his work can be found in the permanent collections of the Smithsonian Institution in Washington, D.C, the Galleria Civica d'Arte Moderna e Contemporanea in Turin, the Stedelijk Museum in Amsterdam, and the Victoria and Albert Museum in London, among other institutions. His archives are held at the Art Institute of Chicago. Penn died at his Manhattan home. He is survived by his son, Tom; stepdaughter, Mia; and eight grandchildren. He was predeceased in 1992 by his wife of more than four decades, Lisa Fonssagrives, a prominent fashion model whom he often photographed. *See Current Biography* (1980). — W.D.

Obituary *New York Times* (on-line) Oct. 8, 2009

PICCARD, JACQUES July 28, 1922–Nov. 1, 2008 Oceanographer; oceanic engineer; economist. The pioneering deep-sea explorer and oceanographer Jacques Piccard is best known for traveling seven miles beneath the surface of the Pacific Ocean on January 23, 1960. The journey, made in a vessel he built with his father, the physicist and engineer Auguste Piccard, took him and his co-pilot, U.S. Navy Lieutenant Don Walsh, further into the depths of the sea than anyone had ever gone before—or has since. In the 1930s Piccard's father became the first person to take a balloon into the stratosphere, and in the 1990s his son Bertrand became the first man to fly a balloon around the world. (Auguste's twin brother, Jean-Felix, was also an aeronaut and balloonist; Gene Roddenberry, the creator of *Star Trek*, reportedly named his character Captain Jean-Luc Picard after the two brothers.) Born in Brussels, Belgium, Piccard was nine years old when his father flew a balloon with a pressurized aluminum cabin into the earth's stratosphere, setting a new altitude record of 51,961 feet. Piccard studied economics at the University of Geneva, taking a leave of absence to serve in the French military during World War II. After completing his formal education, he briefly taught college-level economics before abandoning his academic career to help his father design and build a bathyscaphe, a self-propelled deep-sea submersible modeled on the principles of a hot-air balloon. The bathyscaphe, which they christened the *Trieste*, featured a small, spherical crew cabin suspended below a cigar-shaped hull; it was the first deep-sea vessel that could operate independently, without being attached by cables to an overhead ship. In 1953—the same year Piccard married Marie-Claude Maillard, a pianist—father and son descended in the *Trieste* to a depth of 3,100 meters below the surface of the Mediterranean Sea. The U.S. Navy soon took an interest in their work, and in 1958 the military purchased the vessel, hiring the younger Piccard as a consultant. Navy officials proposed a dive into the Challenger Deep, the deepest known hole in the world's oceans, in the Marianas Trench, 250 miles southwest of the island of Guam. On January 23, 1960, Piccard, who stood six feet, six inches tall, and Walsh squeezed into the tiny cabin of the *Trieste* for the descent to the ocean floor. While an outer Plexiglass window cracked at 30,000 feet, the two continued to the bottom—35,838 feet below the surface. The trip had taken almost five hours and subjected the vessel to pressures of more than 16,000 pounds per square inch. For 20 minutes the pair remained at that depth—eating chocolate bars and watching the small, red shrimp-like creatures and the flat, white fish they had surprisingly discovered—before releasing two tons of ballast and returning to the surface. Piccard, along with co-writer Robert Dietz, chronicled his historic adventure in *Seven Miles Down: The Story of the Bathyscaphe Trieste* (1961). Today, the original *Trieste* can be seen in the Navy Museum in Washington, D.C. Piccard subsequently began building mesoscaphes (mid-depth submarines) to be used for research and education. In 1969 Piccard designed a mesoscaphe called the *Ben Franklin* for the U.S. Navy, and with five other crew members, he drifted some 1,500 miles in the Gulf Stream off the eastern U.S., in order to document both the oceanographic currents and the effects of prolonged isolation in contained environments. Piccard's account of the month-long voyage was published in *The Sun Beneath the Sea* (1971); the *Ben Franklin* is on display at the Vancouver Maritime Museum. In the 1970s Piccard established the

Foundation for the Study and Preservation of Seas and Lakes and became a staunch advocate of conservation, warning against the dangers of pollution and over-fishing. He began designing passenger submarines for tourist purposes, as a way of increasing awareness about environmental issues. "The more people discover the sea, the greater the chance of bringing marine issues into public view and the better off we will all be," Piccard was quoted as saying by Marcus Williams for the London *Independent* (November 5, 2008). While Piccard acknowledged in later interviews that funding for deep-sea research had been understandably diverted by the space race, he remained optimistic about the potential for deep-sea exploration. He made his last dive at the age of 82. In a statement made after his father's death at his Lake Geneva home, Bertrand Piccard said, as quoted by the Associated Press (November 2, 2008): "[He] passed on to me a sense of curiosity, a desire to mistrust dogmas and common assumptions, a belief in free will, and confidence in the face of the unknown." In addition to Bertrand, Piccard had two other children: Marie-Laure and Thierry. See *Current Biography* (1965). — M.M.

Obituary *New York Times* (on-line) Nov. 1, 2008

PINTER, HAROLD Oct. 10, 1930–Dec. 24, 2008 British playwright; screenwriter; director; actor; essayist; poet; political activist. In his 29 plays, the Swedish Academy stated in awarding him the Nobel Prize in literature in 2005, Harold Pinter "uncovers the precipice under everyday prattle and forces entry into oppression's closed rooms." The Nobel citation also read, "He restored theatre to its basic elements: an enclosed space and unpredictable dialogue where people are at the mercy of each other and pretence crumbles," and it described him as "generally seen as the foremost representative of British drama in the second half of the 20th century." Identified by the London *Telegraph* (December 26, 2008) as "the most original, stylish and enigmatic writer in post-war British theatre," Pinter was among the first of the British playwrights who revolutionized theater through unprecedented ways of examining the human condition. The word "Pinteresque" describes conversations, situations, and environments reminiscent of the cryptic, halting small talk, tension-filled silences, and air of menace that pervaded his plays, among them *The Room* (1957), *The Birthday Party* (1957), *The Caretaker* (1959), *The Homecoming* (1964), and *Betrayal* (1978), to cite five of the best known. "Though his plays deal with the slipperiness of memory and human character, they are also almost always about the struggle for power," according to a *New York Times* (December 26, 2008) obituary. *One for the Road* (1984), *Mountain Language* (1988), and others among his more recent plays are concerned, Pinter said, "not with ambiguities of power, but actual power." Martin Esslin wrote for his book *Pinter: The Playwright*, "Man's existential fear, not as an abstraction, but as something real, ordinary and acceptable as an everyday occurrence—here we have the core of Pinter's work." The playwright David Hare wrote for the book *Harold Pinter: A Celebration* (2000) that Pinter never offered audiences "the easy handhold with which they might be able to take some simplified view of the events on stage" and that it was his "willingness to say 'take it or leave it' which finally makes his work so inimitable." Descended, according to some sources, from Sephardic Jews surnamed da Pinta, Pinter was the grandchild of immigrants to England from Eastern Europe. His father was a tailor. He was raised in London's then–poverty-stricken, overcrowded East End; few Jewish families lived there—a circumstance that some have linked to the feelings of alienation that many of his characters display. Evacuated from London after the start of World War II, he was sent to live in Cornwall and Reading, where he felt lonely and isolated. He was back in London as a young teenager when his family's home was bombed; he succeeded in recovering from the wreckage a love poem he had written to a girlfriend and his cricket bat. (As an adult he listed cricket, love, and sex among his greatest passions.) Pinter attended the local Hackney Downs grammar and secondary schools; at the latter he enjoyed success in student productions and was inspired by his English teacher and mentor, Joseph Brearley, to pursue a career on the stage. In 1948 he enrolled at the Royal Academy of Dramatic Art; disgusted by what he described as "a terrible atmosphere of affectation and unreality," he dropped out in 1949. Earlier, he was fined for conscientious objection to service in the British military. For a few months in 1951, he attended the Central School of Speech and Drama, in London. Later that year he joined the first of a series of repertory companies, where for the next decade he performed two dozen roles, in plays ranging from Shakespearean comedies and dramas to contemporary works; his favorite roles were, in his words, "the sinister ones." He also narrated or had roles in several radio productions. Pinter wrote his first play in 1956 at the request of his friend Henry Woolf, who had to direct one for a postgraduate course at Bristol University. Completed in a few days, *The Room* was based on an event Pinter had witnessed in a kitchen while at a party. A one-act play, it ran for a few days in May 1957 at the university and opened again three years later—along with Pinter's second one-act play, *The Dumb Waiter* (or *Dumbwaiter*)—at the Hampstead Theater Club in London. Meanwhile, Pinter's full-length play *The Birthday Party*, the first of his to be performed professionally, had received a critical drubbing after its premiere, in London in 1958, and it closed after a week. In a glowing review for the London *Sunday Times* printed a day later, the critic Harold Hobson wrote, "Pinter, on the evidence of this work, possesses the most original, disturbing and arresting talent in theatrical London." Hobson's words gave newfound hope to Pinter, who—with a wife and infant son to support—had been about to set down his pen forever. A BBC commission for a radio play—the result was *A Slight Ache*, broadcast in 1959 and later adapted for the stage—and the popularity of sketches he wrote for two satirical reviews, *One to Another* and *Pieces of Eight*, further buoyed his spirits. Pinter's next full-length play, *The Caretaker*, earned rave reviews when it opened, in 1960; Michael Billington, writing for the *Guardian*, described it as "an austere masterpiece: a universally recognizable play about political maneuvering, fraternal love, spiritual isolation, language as a negotiating weapon or a form of cover-up"; according to the *Telegraph* in 2008, *The Caretaker* "sealed Pinter's reputation as a playwright who showed how speech was often used as a means of avoiding communication." Pinter invariably rejected the contention that his characters are unable to communicate. "I feel that instead of any inability to communicate there is a deliberate evasion of communication," he told Kenneth Tynan for the BBC (October 28, 1960). "Communication itself between people is so frightening that rather than do that there is continual crosstalk, a continual talking about other things rather than what is at the root of their relationship." Pinter's other plays include *The Collection* (1961); *The Lover* (1962); *The Basement* (1966); *Landscape* (1967); *Silence* (1968); *Victoria Station* and *A Kind of Alaska*, presented under the title *Other Places* (1982); *The New World Order* (1991); *Party Time* (1991); *Moonlight* (1993); *Ashes to Ashes* (1996); and *Celebration* (1999). He also wrote 15 dramatic sketches. Pinter made his debut in cinema in 1962, as the screenwriter for *The Caretaker*; he later wrote the screenplays for his plays *The Birthday Party* (1967), *The Homecoming* (1969), and *Betrayal* (1981), the last of which earned him an Academy Award nomination. His two dozen screenplays and scripts for film or television also include those for *The Pumpkin Eater* (1963), *The Servant* (1963), and, earning him another Oscar nomination, *The French Lieutenant's Woman* (1980). His more than three dozen directorial credits included works by Robert Shaw, James Joyce, Simon Gray, Noël Coward, Tennessee Williams, David Mamet, and Reginald Rose. His career as an actor after his years in repertory included work in film and television as well as theater and radio, in plays by others as well as himself. In his last appearance as an actor, in 2006, five years after he was diagnosed with esophageal cancer, he triumphed in a mounting of Samuel Beckett's *Krapp's Last Tape*, sitting on stage in a motorized wheelchair during the 10-performance run, in London. In recent decades Pinter often expressed publicly his opposition to human-rights abuses, his hatred of dictatorships, and his concern for the victims of wars and oppression. He devoted much of his Nobel lecture (which he gave via video, being too ill to travel to the awards ceremony, in Stockholm) to a diatribe against Great Britain and the U.S., for their launching of the war in Iraq in March 2003, and against the U.S. for what he viewed as the American government's "crimes" during the Cold War. "He could be dazzlingly charming to trusted friends and colleagues," according to the London *Times* (December 26, 2008, on-line). "But, like his plays, he often seemed exacting and rather alarming." In *Celebrating Pinter* the director Richard Eyre wrote that he was "sometimes pugnacious and occasionally splenetic" but "just as often droll and generous—particularly to actors, directors and (a rare quality this) other writers." In the 1980s Pinter and his second wife, the writer Antonia Fraser, formed a left-wing salon called the 20 June Group, but stormy confrontations with his compatriots led him to leave it a year later. He was active in organizations including the Campaign for Nuclear Disarmament, Amnesty International, and International PEN. Pinter, who turned down a knighthood, was named a Commander of the Order of the British Empire and a Companion of Honour. From 1962 to 1969, during his stormy first marriage, to the actress Vivien Merchant, Pinter had an affair with the British TV presenter Joan Bakewell; his play *Betrayal* mirrors the course of that affair. In 1975 Pinter became intimately involved with Fraser, who was then married to the conservative politician Hugh Fraser; in 1980 Pinter divorced Merchant and married Fraser. Merchant died of acute alcohol poisoning in 1982. Pinter and Merchant's son, Daniel, later changed his surname and ceased all contact with his father. His son survives him, as do Fraser, her three daughters and three sons, and their children. See *Current Biography* (1963). — M.H.

Obituary *New York Times* A p1+ Dec. 26, 2008

POWELL, JODY Sep. 30, 1943–Sep. 14, 2009 Former White House press secretary; businessman. Jody Powell served as Jimmy Carter's press secretary during both his gubernatorial and presidential administrations and was also one of Carter's most trusted companions. Upon learning of Powell's death, Carter released the statement: "Jody was beside me in every decision I made as a candidate, governor and president, and I could always depend on his advice and counsel being candid and direct. I will miss him dearly." Joseph Lester Powell was the older of Joseph and June Powell's two children. His nickname was derived from that of the young protagonist in Marjorie Kinnan Rawlings's iconic novel *The Yearling*. Like Carter, Powell was raised on a farm in a small Georgia community and attended a Baptist church. From his father, who grew cotton and peanuts, Powell learned how to "drink beer, drive a tractor, and shoot a gun" and "never to be ashamed of who you are or where you came from," as he once told an interviewer. From his mother, a high-school civics teacher, Powell gained an appetite for knowledge, becoming engrossed in books about the Civil War and the tales of King Arthur. A straight-A student, Powell was also a member of his high school's debate team and a quarterback on the football team. After graduating in 1961 he enrolled at the U.S. Air Force Academy, in Colorado Springs, Colorado, but during his final year he was expelled for cheating on an examination; he later stated that he viewed the incident as "a good lesson in learning to accept the consequences of your own actions." Powell completed his bachelor's degree at Georgia State University in 1966, and after briefly working for an insurance company, he enrolled in a graduate program at Emory University, in Atlanta. While researching his doctoral dissertation, which focused on populist political movements, Powell wrote to Carter—who was then running for governor of Georgia for the second time—and asked to work for his campaign. (Powell had met Carter at a mall during his first gubernatorial campaign, in 1966.) Impressed by Powell's enthusiasm and political knowledge, Carter hired him as a chauffeur. It was not long before Powell became Carter's confidant, adviser, speechwriter, and unofficial press secretary. Powell was appointed the official press secretary when Carter won the governor's office in 1970. Powell continued working for Carter during his presidential campaign in 1976, and he became one of Carter's first appointments, to the post of White House press secretary, in 1977. Powell strived for a more open relationship between the White House and the press, promising journalists access to Cabinet meetings, two formal press conferences per month, and the occasional one-on-one interview with the president. He established a positive rapport with members of the press and became known for his fierce loyalty to Carter as well as his extensive knowledge, quick wit, and earnestness. "If he wasn't going to tell you something he'd tell you," Jack Nelson, a former *Los Angeles Times* reporter and close friend, told David Stout for the *New York Times* (September 15, 2009, on-line). "But if he told you something, you could take it to the bank." (Powell was also, however, notoriously disorganized and bad at delegating duties to junior staff.) Upon leaving the White House, in 1981, Powell worked as a syndicated columnist and also wrote *The Other Side of the Story* (1984), a memoir about his years in the White House. In later years he was the chair of the influential Washington-based public-relations firm Powell Tate, which he ran with Sheila Tate, a former press aide to First Lady Nancy Reagan. Powell remained a history buff throughout his life and provided the voice of the Confederate general Stonewall Jackson in the public-television series *The Civil War* by Ken Burns. A longtime chain smoker, Powell died of a heart attack. He is survived by his wife, Nan, and his daughter, Emily, as well as three grandchildren. See *Current Biography* (1977). — M.E.R.

Obituary *New York Times* (on-line) Sep. 15, 2009

RAKOWSKI, MIECZYSLAW Dec. 1, 1926–Nov. 7, 2008 Polish statesman and journalist. Mieczyslaw Franciszek Rakowski played a key role in the history of Communist-era Poland, and he presided over the end of that era. After earning a doctorate in history, Rakowski was for 24 years (1958–82) the editor in chief of *Polityka,* a semi-satirical weekly newspaper that served as a safety valve for disaffected and dissenting Polish intellectuals. Having thus gained a reputation as a liberal reformist, in 1981 he was brought into the government as a deputy prime minister by General Wojciech Jaruzelski (who as chairman, or first secretary, of the Polish Communist Party was the de facto head of state). His job was to negotiate with the leaders of the newly formed and formidable workers' organization Solidarity, the Soviet bloc's first independent trade union, which was demanding the replacement of Marxist-Leninist socialism with what would be a Western-style democracy in Poland. The negotiations, held in the summer of 1981, ended in acrimony and mutual distrust. In December 1981 General Jaruzelski declared a state of martial law, under which Solidarity was banned, thousands of dissidents were arrested without charge, scores were killed, and press censorship was tightened. Rakowski defended the imposition of martial law (which lasted until December 1982) as necessary to avert a civil war and a Soviet invasion. As quoted in *Time* (January 25, 1982), Richard R. Davies, a former U.S. ambassador to Poland, explained that Rakowski "was sincere when he believed in democracy . . . as long as democracy was granted from on high, not from below, because that threatened the authorities." Rakowski served on the central committee of the Polish Communist Party from 1975 to 1990. He was the second-to-last prime minister of the People's Republic of Poland, serving from September 1988 to July 1989, the month following the first multiparty parliamentary elections. The last prime minister of the People's Republic of Poland was Czesław Kiszczak, who held office for less than a month before being succeeded by Tadeusz Mazowiecki, the leader among the Solidarity-endorsed candidates who had swept the June multiparty elections. After Wojciech Jaruzelski resigned as Communist Party leader, in June 1989, Rakowski replaced him long enough to preside over the party's last congress, in January 1990. After he retired from politics, Rakowski edited the monthly political journal *Dzis.* He published a number of books, including successive volumes of the daily diaries that he kept for 40 years. Rakowski died in a military hospital in Warsaw. His survivors include his second wife, the actress Elżbieta Kępińska, and two sons from his first marriage, to the violinist Wanda Wilkomirska. See *Current Biography* (1989). — K.D.

Obituary *New York Times* B p18 Nov. 12, 2008

RAMA RAU, SANTHA Jan. 24, 1923–Apr. 21, 2009 Indian-born writer. Santha Rama Rau was once one of the best-known Indian writers in America. Her work—which included *Home to India* (1945), *East of Home* (1950), *View to the Southeast* (1957), *This Is India* (1953), the autobiography *Gifts of Passage* (1961), and *The Cooking of India* (1970)—opened up new worlds to westerners. According to Bruce Weber, writing for the *New York Times* (April 24, 2009), her writing "helped demystify the Indian subcontinent for American readers in the decades after World War II and India's independence." After the publication of *This Is India*, Rama Rau told an interviewer for the *Wichita (Kansas) Beacon*, as quoted by Weber: "Our job—those of us lucky to have lived in these two countries—is to interpret them to one another. If we can make ourselves—the Indians—real people to the Americans, we shall have done more than our politicians are able to do." Vasanthi Rama Rau was born in Madras (now known as Chennai), India. Her father, Sir Benegal Rama Rau, was a high-ranking civil servant in India's department of finance. After the country gained its independence from Great Britain, in 1947, he served as an ambassador to Japan and the United States. Her mother, Dhanvanthi Rama Rau, a pioneer in the field of women's rights, was a founder and president of the Family Planning Association of India. She later headed the International Planned Parenthood Federation. Santha Rama Rau began her travels at the age of six, attending school in London, where her father was then stationed. Although her father was subsequently assigned to posts in other countries, she continued her education there for the next decade, joining her parents during her summer holidays. In 1939, while visiting South Africa, where her parents were living at the time, Rama Rau, then 16, was unable to return to England due to the outbreak of war. Instead, with her mother and sister, she returned to India. There she met Madame Sarojini Naidu, a poet and the first woman president of the Indian National Congress, who encouraged her to write. Rama Rau left India to attend Wellesley College, in Massachusetts, where she majored in English and served on the editorial board of the college magazine. She spent her vacations as a writer on the overseas program of the Office of War Information in New York and graduated with a B.A. degree in 1944. Returning to her native country, she published *Home to India*. "Though a youthful book, it immediately established the voice of an educated discoverer—observant, amused, self-deprecating, instructive without being pedantic—that would characterize her work even when she matured," Weber wrote. During that stay in India, Rama Rau wrote for several magazines and edited the periodical *Trend in Bombay*. When her father was named ambassador to Japan, in 1947, she joined him in Tokyo, where she served as his hostess and volunteered as an English teacher. The following year she traveled across China, Indochina, Siam, and Indonesia; she later published an account of those adventures, *East of Home*. In 1951 Rama Rau married Faubion Bowers, an American expert on Japanese Kabuki theater. Making their home in New York City, they traveled abroad extensively. She wrote numerous articles detailing their journeys through Asia, Africa, and Europe for such publications as the *New Yorker*, *Reader's Digest*, *Harper's*, and the *New York Times Magazine*; several of the pieces were later collected in book form, and Rama Rau became something of a literary celebrity. In 1962 she adapted E.M. Forster's classic 1924 novel about British colonialism in India, *A Passage to India*, for the stage, and the production became a critical and commercial success on both Broadway and London's West End. Divorced from Bowers in 1966, Rama Rau married Gurdon Wattles, a legal officer at the United Nations, in 1977. As Weber noted, "Both marriages afforded her the opportunity to travel widely." In 2007 the historian Antoinette Burton published *The Postcolonial Careers of Santha Rama Rau*, a book that examined Rama Rau's career as a cultural link between nations and touched upon such issues as imperialism, gender, celebrity, race, and cosmopolitanism in the postwar era. Santha Rama Rau died in Amenia, New York, of cardiopulmonary failure, at the age of 86. She is survived by her son, Jai Bowers, as well as four stepchildren, Stuart Scadron-Wattles, Joshua Wattles, Arabella Wattles Teal, and Katherine Wattles. See *Current Biography* (1959). — M.M.

Obituary *New York Times* (on-line) Apr. 24, 2009

REID, WHITELAW July 26, 1913–Apr. 18, 2009 Publisher; journalist; former diplomat. Whitelaw Reid, the scion of the wealthy and powerful New York publishing family who owned the *New York Herald Tribune*, joined the paper in the 1930s and worked as a war correspondent, among other posts, before becoming its editor, president, and chairman. Also known as an adventurer and avid sportsman, he played competitive tennis into his 90s. Reid was born at the family estate in Purchase, New York, the son of Ogden Mills Reid and Helen Rogers Reid. He was named after his grandfather Whitelaw Reid, who had become owner and editor of the conservative *New York Tribune* in the 1870s, succeeding the famed Horace Greeley. The elder Reid had also been a U.S. ambassador to France and Great Britain as well as a Republican vice-presidential nominee on the ticket of incumbent President Benjamin Harrison in 1892. His son—and Whitelaw Reid's father—merged the *Tribune* with the *Herald* in 1924 and served as its editor and publisher until his death, in 1947. (The paper's European edition, the *Paris Herald*, is now published as the *International Herald Tribune*.) The younger Whitelaw Reid was educated at the Lincoln School in New York City and St. Paul's School, in Concord, New Hampshire, before entering Yale University, where he was a member of the college's Conservative Party. Along with some classmates, he once sailed a schooner across the Atlantic Ocean. After graduating with a degree in sociology, in 1936, he received training in printing and machinery at the Rochester Institute of Technology. In 1938 he joined the *New York Herald Tribune*'s mechanical department. After working there and in the paper's business section, in 1940 he became a journalist and was sent to the London bureau. During his stint as a war reporter, from 1940 to 1941, he covered the Blitz of London and the shelling of Dover, flew on Royal Air Force missions over Europe, and patrolled the English Channel on a naval trawler. In 1941 Reid was commissioned as a U.S. Navy pilot, and in 1945 he was sent to the Pacific, joining a squadron on Iwo Jima that surveyed the Japanese coast for bombing raids. In 1946 Reid returned to the paper as an assistant to the editor, and after his father's death, in 1947, he was named editor and vice president. He became editor and president in 1953, and editor and chairman in 1955, succeeding his mother, a dominant and influential figure at the *New York Herald Tribune*, in those posts. (His brother, Ogden R. Reid, who was later a U.S. congressman and an ambassador to Israel, served as an editor and publisher of the family-run paper as well.) The paper had long had a reputation for Republican-leaning reportage and was often referred to as a "newspaperman's newspaper." But during Whitelaw Reid's tenure, its high journalistic standards gave way to gimmicky contests and puzzles that attracted more readers but gradually cost the publication its prestige. During his time at the helm of the *Herald Tribune*, Reid was president of the Fresh Air Fund, a charity run by the paper that helped send underprivileged New York children on summer holidays. (The charitable endeavor was later taken over by the *New York Times*.) The family sold the *Herald Tribune* in 1958 to the wealthy investor and U.S. ambassador to Great Britain John Hay Whitney, who redesigned it and hired new writers in an attempt to revive its flagging fortunes. After suffering a series of strikes and other setbacks, in 1966 the paper was merged with other faltering publications and renamed the *World Journal Tribune*, which folded the following year. After selling the paper, Whitelaw Reid established Reid Enterprises, a company that sold food and other products, which he ran until 1975. Reid enjoyed skiing, flying, sailing yachts, and horseback riding, as well as playing tennis. In 1998 he won a United States Tennis Association singles title in the over-85 category. In 2003, at the age of 90, he won a national doubles title. Reid had two sons, Brandon and Carson, from his first marriage, to the former Joan Brandon, which ended in divorce. In 1959 he married Elizabeth Ann Brooks, with whom he had two more children, Gina and John. Reid, who lived in Bedford Hills, New York, died of lung and heart failure. He is survived by his second wife, his brother, his four children, and several grandchildren and great-grandchildren. See *Current Biography* (1954). — M.M.

Obituary *New York Times* (on-line) Apr. 19, 2009

ROH MOO HYUN Aug. 6, 1946–May 23, 2009 South Korean statesman. Roh Moo Hyun (whose name is also transliterated as Roh Moo-hyun) served as president of South Korea from 2003 to 2008 and carefully cultivated a reputation as an upright and honest public servant. That image was tarnished in early 2009 by accusations of fraud and corruption, and Roh responded by committing suicide. He wrote a final posting on his Web site, quoted by Choe Sang-Hun in the *New York Times* (May 23, 2009), stating: "You should now discard me. . . . I no longer symbolize the values you pursue. I am no longer qualified to speak for such things as democracy, progressiveness and justice." Born in the farming village of Kimhae (sometimes spelled "Gimhae") in the South Korean province of Kyongsang-namdo, Roh, whose father was a poor farmer, earned a full scholarship to attend Pusan Commercial High School and graduated in 1966. With no money to attend college, he took on a series of odd jobs that included making fishing nets. He began his mandatory service in the South Korean army in 1968 and left the military in 1971, after attaining the rank of corporal. Roh dreamed of practicing law; with no funds for law school, he studied on his own for four years, and in 1975 he passed the bar exam. Following two years of formal training, Roh became a district court judge in Taejon but soon resigned to open his own office specializing in tax law. In 1980 he represented a group of college students who were accused of anti-government activities for reading books about Korean history and Chinese Communist leader Mao Zedong. The experience prompted Roh to become a human rights lawyer, and he went on to defend a number of pro-democracy and labor-rights activists. Following his nomination by the opposition Democratic Reunification Party, in 1988 Roh won a seat representing Pusan's Eastern District in the National Assembly. Three years later he joined forces with the New Democratic Party to form the United Democratic Party (UDP). Roh became the youngest member of the UDP's supreme council in 1993. After several failed elections and party changes, Roh won an assembly seat representing Seoul's Jongno District, this time as a candidate of the National Congress for New Politics (NCNP) Party. In 2000 he was appointed minister of maritime affairs and fisheries in the Kim Dae Jung administration. Roh, then a member of the Millennium Democratic Party (MDP), ran in the 2002 presidential elections, promising during his campaign to lessen Korean dependence on the U.S. Anti-American sentiment was then simmering in Korea, and the public was responsive to Roh's message. Defeating Lee Hoi Chang of the Grand National Party, he took office in February 2003. Within a year Roh and his supporters had formed the Uri Party (Our Party). In March 2004 Roh became the first South Korean president to be impeached after he was found guilty of disobeying the nation's voting rules by openly supporting Uri Party candidates in assembly elections. He was reinstated after two months, when the Constitutional Court of Korea overturned the verdict, stating that while Roh had violated the law, his offense was not serious enough to warrant impeachment. Though Roh had many supporters who had called for his reinstatement, his popularity began to diminish after a series of unpopular moves, including sending Korean troops to fight in the Iraq War, continuing a policy of engagement with North Korea, and making a failed attempt to move the capital from Seoul to Chungcheong. Following Roh's retirement in 2008—Korean presidents cannot run for a second five-year term—allegations of corruption involving his family began to surface. In April 2009 Roh was accused of having accepted $6 million in bribes during his rule as president. Though Roh admitted that his wife, his son, and his brother's son-in-law had received money from a wealthy businessman, he insisted that those funds were not bribes but rather payments to help settle a debt. His allies believed that the charges were politically motivated, and his friends spoke of the pain the accusations caused Roh, who had prided himself on his political reputation. Roh died after jumping off a cliff near the small South Korean hamlet of Bongha. He is survived by his wife, Kwon Yang-Suk (sometimes spelled "Kwon Ryang-Suk"), and their two children. — See *Current Biography International Yearbook* (2003). — M.A.S.

Obituary *New York Times* A p4 May 24, 2009

SAFIRE, WILLIAM Dec. 17, 1929–Sep. 27, 2009 Journalist; conservative pundit; former White House speechwriter; foundation administrator. William Safire was best known for his controversial columns in the *New York Times* and for his brilliant, cranky essays on etymology and semantics in that newspaper's Sunday magazine. Safire, who called himself a "libertarian conservative," advocating individual freedom and minimal government, relished his role as a maverick pundit and playful provocateur. Robert D. McFadden wrote for the *New York Times* (September 28, 2009) that Safire was "a pugnacious contrarian" as the often-lonely conservative voice on the *New York Times* editorial page, and in his celebrated "On Language" essays he was "a talented linguist with an addiction to alliterative allusions." William Lewis Safir was the youngest of three sons born to Oliver C. and Ida Panish Safir. (He later added the final vowel to his name to make the pronunciation more obvious.) His father, a successful thread manufacturer, died when Safire was a child, leaving the family somewhat strapped financially. Safire graduated from the highly competitive and rigorous Bronx High School of Science before attending Syracuse University on a scholarship. He dropped out after two years, however, and at the age of 19 he took a job as a legman, researcher, and writer for the *New York Herald Tribune* columnist and radio talk-show host Tex McCrary. Safire had decided, as quoted by Walter Shapiro for *Time* (February 12, 1990, on-line), that he "could get a better education interviewing

John Steinbeck than talking to an English professor about novels." McCrary, who dabbled in Republican politics, reportedly became something of a father figure to Safire. In 1951 Safire worked as a roving correspondent for WNBC radio and television in Europe and the Middle East, and the following year he made a foray into politics, organizing a successful campaign rally for Dwight D. Eisenhower at New York City's Madison Square Garden. That year he was inducted into the U.S. Army and was sent to work as a correspondent for the Armed Forces Network in Europe. In 1954, after leaving the military, he returned to NBC and produced a series of popular radio and TV shows featuring McCrary and his wife, Jinx Falkenburg. In 1955 McCrary named Safire vice president of Tex McCrary, Inc., a public relations firm. In 1959 All-State Properties, a client of the firm, built a model of the "typical American house," to be showcased at an exhibition in Moscow. The event was hosted by Richard Nixon, then the vice president, who ushered Soviet Premier Nikita Khrushchev around the exhibits. Safire managed to coax the two leaders to his client's "typical kitchen" for a photo-op, where the two engaged in a heated exchange on the virtues of capitalism versus communism, thereafter dubbed the "kitchen debate." After the encounter Nixon was portrayed by the media as a stalwart "cold warrior" who stood up admirably to the intimidating Khrushchev. Nixon was thrilled with the public-relations boost and hired Safire to work on his unsuccessful presidential bid against John F. Kennedy in 1960. The following year Safire established his own public-relations firm. He maintained a foothold in politics, continuing to take part in Republican electoral campaigns, mostly in New York, including Senator Jacob K. Javits's successful run for reelection in 1962, Governor Nelson A. Rockefeller's unsuccessful bid for the U.S. presidency in 1964, and John V. Lindsay's successful run for New York City mayor in 1965. After selling his agency, Safire returned to work for Nixon as a speechwriter during the 1968 presidential campaign; his belief in the candidate was such that he volunteered his services at no charge. Working with Nixon's other speechwriters, Patrick J. Buchanan and Raymond K. Price Jr., Safire became known for his powerful, catchy lines. After the Nixon victory, he became a senior White House speechwriter and was assigned to craft speeches for Vice President Spiro Agnew. Safire was credited with penning Agnew's memorable alliterative phrases "nattering nabobs of negativism," to describe those (especially in the press) who expressed doubts about the Vietnam War, and "hopeless, hysterical hypochondriacs of history." Safire resigned from his position in 1973 as the Watergate scandal broke, to accept a job as a Washington-based columnist for the *New York Times.* Liberal critics immediately pounced on the appointment, with one, according to Robert McFadden, likening it to "setting a hawk loose among the doves." In 1978 Safire won a Pulitzer Prize for his op-ed pieces on the shady personal finances of Bert Lance, the director of the Office of Management and the Budget under President Jimmy Carter. Although the articles led to Lance's resignation, he and Safire later became friends. Safire's twice-weekly political pieces ran in the paper until January 24, 2005, when his last column, "Never Retire," appeared. "The wonderful thing about being a *New York Times* columnist is that it's like a Supreme Court appointment—they're stuck with you for a long time," he told Howard Kurtz for the *Washington Post* (November 16, 2004). In 1979 Safire was also assigned a regular column in the newspaper's Sunday magazine. Entitled "On Language," it became a popular platform from which he could voice his scholarly and acerbic thoughts on such topics as the use of cliché (his advice was to "avoid it like the plague") and proper grammar (he ironically instructed his readers "to never split an infinitive"). "On Language" ran until shortly before his death from pancreatic cancer. Arthur Sulzberger Jr., the paper's publisher, wrote on November 15, 2004, "Whether you agreed with [Safire] or not was never the point. His writing is delightful, informed and engaging." Safire, who received the Presidential Medal of Freedom from George W. Bush in 2006, was also the author of a memoir, several books on language (mostly collections of his popular columns), and four novels, including the best-selling political thriller *Full Disclosure* (1977). He served on the Pulitzer Prize Board from 1995 to 2004 and later became the chair of the Dana Foundation, an organization that supports research in neuroscience, immunology, and brain disorders. Safire is survived by his wife of almost five decades, Helene; their children, Mark and Annabel; and a granddaughter, Lily. See *Current Biography* (1973). — M.M.

Obituary *New York Times* (on-line) Sep. 28, 2009

SALES, SOUPY Jan. 8, 1926–Oct. 22, 2009 Television and radio personality. Soupy Sales, whose slapstick pie-in-the-face routine became his signature during the 1950s and 1960s, was "a favorite of youngsters and an anarchic comedy hero for teenagers and college students," Richard Goldstein wrote for the *New York Times* (October 23, 2009). In an overview for the All Music Guide Web Site, Jason Ankeny asserted that Sales, who was also known for the popular novelty tunes "Do the Mouse" and "The Soupy Shuffle," was "the wildest, most innovative children's television host of the baby-boom era." While his shows were ostensibly aimed at children, and critics sometimes blasted them as unintelligent or mediocre, Sales became a cultural phenomenon with fans of all ages. As Michael Carlson wrote for the London *Independent* (October 31, 2009), "His slapstick brilliance should not overshadow his influence on a whole generation of Americans, including many notable comics who, as adolescents, teenagers, or even young adults in the late 1950s and early 1960s, were enthralled by the anarchic pleasures of Soupy's so-called 'children's' shows." Sales, who claimed to have received more than 20,000 pies in his face over the course of his career, was born Milton Supman, in Franklinton, North Carolina. His father, Irving, and mother, Sadie, owned a dry-goods store. The Supmans were the only Jewish family in town, and Sales later joked that local KKK members purchased the white sheets for their robes from his parents' store. Many stories have circulated about the derivation of his stage name. Reportedly, his older brothers had been affectionately called Hambone and Chickenbone, and he was referred to as Soupbone, which was then shortened to Soupy. (He later used the name Soupy Hines, but a radio-station manager asked him to change it because it too closely resembled the popular brand name Heinz, makers of ketchup, baked beans, and other products. The name Sales was apparently suggested by a colleague, in homage to a comedian known as Chic Sales.) Sales's father died when he was five, and the family moved to Huntington, West Virginia. In 1944 Sales graduated from Huntington High School, where he had been voted the most popular boy in his class. He then enlisted in the U.S. Navy and served in the South Pacific during the closing stages of World War II, assuming the unofficial role of entertainer and comic on his ship. Returning to West Virginia upon his discharge, he attended Marshall College and in 1949 earned a bachelor's degree in journalism. Sales then worked as a scriptwriter and deejay at a Huntington radio station before moving to Cincinnati. There he continued working in radio, performed stand-up comedy in nightclubs, and landed his first TV show, a dance program aimed at teens. He subsequently moved to Cleveland to work but left that city, as he often quipped, "due to illness. They got sick of me." Relocating to Detroit in 1953, Sales began hosting two enormously popular programs: an eponymous children's comedy show in which he introduced several recurring puppet characters and signature bits (including the pie-throwing); and a late-night show for adults, *Soupy's On.* Taking advantage of Detroit's rich music scene, Sales featured a guest artist each night; Duke Ellington, Ella Fitzgerald, Billie Holiday, Charlie Parker, Miles Davis, Stan Getz, and Clifford Brown all performed on the groundbreaking program. Sales moved to Los Angeles at the beginning of the 1960s to film his daytime show for ABC-TV, and even though it was billed as a children's program, he became even more of a cultural sensation there. "Entertainers who rose late became fans, prompting [a] call from [Frank] Sinatra, who asked to appear, but only if he could get hit with a pie," Carlson wrote. "Getting pied by Soupy became a mark of Hollywood hipness." Sales ultimately made the move to New York City, where his new daytime show debuted in 1964. One of his most memorable moments in show business took place during his New Year's Day broadcast in 1965, when he asked his young viewers to go through their sleeping parents' wallets and send him any little green pieces of paper with bearded men on them; in exchange, he promised to send them postcards from Puerto Rico. Several days and thousands of dollars (albeit mostly in Monopoly money) later, angry parents forced the station to suspend Sales. He returned to the air within a few weeks, however, and the episode served only to increase his popularity. Later that year, he recorded a Top 10 hit, "Do The Mouse," complete with its own comical dance. *The Soupy Sales Show* went into syndication in 1966, and Sales embarked on a new phase of his television career, appearing as a guest on such programs as *Vacation Playhouse, The Bob Hope Show,* and *The Beverly Hillbillies.* He soon became a fixture on such game shows as *What's My Line?, Hollywood Squares,* and *The Match Game* as well as the variety show *Sha Na Na,* on which he appeared from 1978 to 1981. A new version of his eponymous children's show was taped and syndicated in several markets during the mid-1970s. In the 1980s Sales hosted a midday variety and talk radio show on WNBC, his time slot sandwiched between those of the shock-jocks Howard Stern and Don Imus. Sales had two sons, Tony and Hunt, with his first wife, Barbara Fox. His union with Fox ended in divorce, and in 1980 he married the dancer Trudy Carson, whom he had met while appearing on *The Ed Sullivan Show.* After several years of declining health, Sales, who is survived by his second wife and his sons, died at a hospice in the New York City borough of the Bronx. *See Current Biography* (1967). — M.M.

Obituary *New York Times* (on-line) Oct. 23, 2009

SAULNIER, RAYMOND J. Sep. 20, 1908–Apr. 30, 2009 Economist; educator; former government official. Raymond Joseph Saulnier (pronounced SONE-yay), a longtime university professor and economist, was best known as the staunchly conservative chief economic adviser to U.S. president Dwight D. Eisenhower. A loyal Republican who later campaigned for Richard Nixon and Barry Goldwater, among others, Saulnier was a member of Eisenhower's Council of Economic Advisers (CEA) from 1956 to 1961, serving as chair for much of that time. He firmly believed in balanced budgets and earned the nickname "Dr. No" because of his resistance to using tax cuts as a solution to recessions. Saulnier, known to his friends as Steve, a name he felt better suited him than either Raymond or Joseph, was born in Hamilton, Massachusetts, to Philip Saulnier, a skilled factory mechanic from Canada, and the former Mary McArdle. Saulnier had a twin sister as well as two other siblings. In 1929 Saulnier, the president of his senior class, graduated from Middlebury College, in Vermont, with a B.S. degree in economics. Two years later he earned an M.A. degree in economics from Tufts College (later called Tufts University), in Massachusetts. As a George W. Ellis Fellow, Saulnier continued his education at Columbia University, in New York City, and was granted a Ph.D. degree in 1938. His doctoral thesis, entitled "Contemporary Monetary Theory: Studies of Some Recent Theories of Money, Prices, and Production," is an oft-cited critique of aspects of Keynesian theory. "At the time, the conventional wisdom was Keynesian, but I was persuaded that the great man overrated the antirecessionary effect (in the face of a downcast public confidence and a doggedly anti-inflationary money policy) of the government spending and tax cuts that he favored, and underestimated the capacity of an enterprise system to heal itself," Saulnier said, as quoted by Robert D. Hershey Jr. for the *New York Times* (May 8, 2009). After joining the faculty of Columbia University in 1934 as an instructor, he found that he disliked the core courses he was required to teach there, and in 1938 he transferred to Barnard, Columbia's sister school, where he taught finance and economics. He was named a full professor in 1949 and became chair of the economics department the following year. Saulnier, who remained in academia until 1993, also held other posts. He joined the National Bureau of Economic Research, a private, nonpartisan organization, as an associate after getting his doctoral degree, and in 1946 he was promoted to director of research. In 1952 he became a consultant to the CEA, and two years later he was appointed to the three-person council, which advises the president on the nation's economic policies. On November 13, 1956 Eisenhower named him chair of the council. After leaving office Saulnier held various posts, as the public governor of the American Stock Exchange (1965–75), a consultant to the U.S. Treasury Department (1969–77), a council member of the U.S. Federal Reserve (1976–79), the public governor of the American Commodities Exchange (1978–80), and a consultant and board member for several industrial and financial corporations. He also worked on the presidential campaigns of Richard Nixon and Barry Goldwater, among others. He continued to publicly comment on the economy well into his 90s. As the U.S. experienced severe recession in 2008 and 2009, Saulnier complained about the federal government's role in contributing to the crisis, and he expressed regret that he had not opposed the loosening of financial regulations that had begun in the early 1970s—during a period when he was a member of a commission tasked by President Nixon to find ways to ease Depression-era restrictions on financial institutions to make them more profitable. "I was not as vigorous pushing the minority view as I might have been," Saulnier once said, as quoted by Hershey. "I wish I had." Saulnier, the author of *Constructive Years: The U.S. Economy Under Eisenhower* (1991), moved into a retirement home in Chestertown, Maryland, the year after that book was published. He died there at the age of 100. He was predeceased in 1996 by his wife of more than six decades, the former Estelle Sydney. He is survived by their two children, Mark and Alice, as well as several grandchildren. See *Current Biography* (1957). — M.M.

Obituary *New York Times* (on-line) May 8, 2009

SCHULBERG, BUDD Mar. 27, 1914–Aug. 5, 2009 Screenwriter; novelist. Budd Schulberg was best known for penning the screenplay for the 1954 classic *On the Waterfront.* He also gained notoriety in Hollywood circles for his books, which offered satirical and scathing looks at the film industry, as well as for his testimony during the Communist witch hunt of the 1940s and 1950s. The oldest of three children, Seymour Wilson Schulberg, whose family nicknamed him Budd, was born in New York City, and at the age of eight, he moved to Los Angeles, after his father became head of production at the Paramount Pictures movie studio. His mother, the former Adeline Jaffe, was a famed literary agent whose brother, Sam, was a well-known agent and movie producer. Schulberg, who struggled with a childhood speech impediment, began writing poems and stories at an early age. While attending Los Angeles High School, from 1928 to 1931, Schulberg edited the school paper, for which he also wrote articles that attracted the attention of Random House publisher Bennett Cerf. From 1931 to 1932 Schulberg, whose parents had separated, attended Deerfield Academy, in Massachusetts, before enrolling at Dartmouth College. While there he joined the Communist Party of the United States, and after graduating cum laude with a B.A. degree in 1936, he married Virginia "Jigee" Ray, an actress and fellow Communist. In 1937 he was hired by Paramount Pictures as a reader and junior writer. Schulberg contributed to the screenplays for *A Star Is Born* (1937) and *Little Orphan Annie* (1938) while also penning short stories, some of which were published in major magazines, including *Liberty*, *Colliers*, and the *Saturday Evening Post.* He was fired from Paramount in 1939, following the box-office failure of the comedy *Winter Carnival*, for which he had co-authored the screenplay with an often-drunk F. Scott Fitzgerald. Taking Cerf's advice, Schulberg subsequently started working on turning one of his short stories into a novel. Published in 1941, *What Makes Sammy Run?* chronicled the rise of the ruthlessly ambitious Sammy Glick, the Jewish protagonist, who becomes a top Hollywood producer. Although Schulberg's debut novel became a critical and commercial success, he encountered backlash from prominent members of the movie community who were worried that the book presented anti-Semitic stereotypes based on such Hollywood studio heads as the Warner brothers, Harry Cohn of Columbia Pictures, and Louis B. Mayer of MGM. In 1943, a year after divorcing Ray, Schulberg wed the actress Victoria Anderson, to whom he remained married for 21 years. He also entered the U.S. Navy, and during his three-year stint (1943–46) he helped the filmmaker John Ford produce propaganda films for the Office of Strategic Services, a forerunner of the CIA. Following the war, Schulberg was entrusted with gathering photographic evidence for the Nuremberg trials, forcing Leni Riefenstahl, a German movie director and Nazi sympathizer, to identify war criminals in seized Nazi footage. In 1947 Schulberg published his second novel, the best-seller *The Harder They Fall*, a depiction of the world of professional boxing that was loosely based on the life of the champion Primo Carnera. The book inspired a 1955 film of the same name, which starred Humphrey Bogart in his last screen role. For Schulberg's next book, *The Disenchanted* (1950), about a young screenwriter who becomes disillusioned after collaborating with a once-famous and tragically flawed novelist, Schulberg drew upon his early experiences as a Hollywood scriptwriter. In 1951 Schulberg was called to appear before the notorious House Un-American Activities Committee (HUAC), which had launched a witch hunt against suspected Communists in the movie industry. Schulberg confessed to having been a member of the Communist Party until 1940, when he quit due both to Stalin's non-agression pact with Hitler and because he had felt pressured to advocate party doctrines in his novels. Schulberg was one of the HUAC's most prominent witnesses, and he exposed several Communist Party members who were eventually blacklisted and jailed. During the early 1950s he collaborated with the filmmaker Elia Kazan on the script for the drama *On the Waterfront*, which starred Marlon Brando. The film won eight Academy Awards, including one for Schulberg in the category of best writing, story and screenplay. He reunited with Kazan for *A Face in the Crowd* (1957), which was based on Schulberg's short story about a popular country singer who becomes megalomaniacal. In 1958 Schulberg, who also served as *Sports Illustrat-*

ed's first boxing editor, launched his own production company, and during the mid-1960s he established the Douglass House Watts Writers Workshop. In 1971 Schulberg founded the Frederick Douglass Creative Arts Center in New York City. Among his other books are the novel *Everything that Moves* (1980), the autobiography *Moving Pictures: Memories of a Hollywood Prince* (1981), and the nonfiction books *Sparring with Hemingway: And Other Legends of the Fight Game* (1995) and *Ringside: A Treasury of Boxing Reportage* (2006). Schulberg died of natural causes at his Westhampton Beach, New York, home. He is survived by his fourth wife, Betsy Ann Langman; their two children, Benjamin and Jessica; Virginia, his daughter from his first marriage; Stephen, his son from his second marriage; and his sister Sonia O'Sullivan. Schulberg was predeceased in 1977 by his third wife, the actress Geraldine Brooks, whom he married in 1964. See *Current Biography* (1951). — M.M.

Obituary *New York Times* (on-line) Aug. 6, 2009

SEIDMAN, L. WILLIAM Apr. 29, 1921–May 13, 2009 Economist; businessman; publisher; television commentator; former government official. Lewis William "Bill" Seidman (pronounced SEED-man) was an economic adviser who served under U.S. presidents Gerald Ford, Ronald Reagan, and George H.W. Bush. The role for which he became best known, however, was that of chairman of the Federal Deposit Insurance Corp. (FDIC), the federal-government entity that insures deposits in member banks. Seidman served in that post from 1985 to 1991, during a period of economic crisis that forced the FDIC to close hundreds of failed banks and savings institutions. In 1989 he was appointed the first chair of the Resolution Trust Corp., which was formed by the government to recover losses from the crisis. (The corporation was charged with liquidating the failed real-estate ventures and junk bonds left behind by the shuttered financial institutions.) A frequent bearer of bad economic news, Seidman managed to gain the admiration of lawmakers on both sides of the aisle with his honesty and quick wit. (His candor won him little praise, however, from Bush, who attempted unsuccessfully to push him out of office.) Lewis William Seidman was born in Grand Rapids, Michigan. His father, Frank E. Seidman, was a Jewish immigrant from Russia who worked as an accountant, auditor, and tax consultant. Seidman was a skilled athlete and student-council president at East Grand Rapids High School, from which he graduated in 1939. Four years later he received his bachelor's degree in economics from Dartmouth College, with Phi Beta Kappa honors. He subsequently served in the U.S. Navy during World War II, earning a bronze star and 11 battle stars in Pacific combat. In 1948 Seidman earned a law degree from Harvard University, and the following year he received an M.B.A. degree from the University of Michigan. He then joined his father's firm in an entry-level capacity, and within five years he was named a full partner. He ultimately oversaw the expansion of the company to 50 offices, making it one of the 10 largest certified public accounting firms in the United States. (In 1973 Seidman & Seidman came under investigation after one of the companies with which it had merged, the Equity Funding Corp. of America, was accused of fraud. Claiming that his involvement in the merger was incidental, Seidman emerged from the scandal with his reputation unscathed.) Seidman was also active in his Grand Rapids community. In 1958 he formed a committee to establish a four-year liberal-arts college in the area, eventually persuading the state legislature to charter what is now Grand Valley State University. After making an unsuccessful bid in 1962 to become Michigan's auditor general, Seidman went to work for the newly elected Republican governor George Romney as a special assistant for financial affairs. Seidman left his father's firm in 1974 to accept an assignment as management and budget consultant to Gerald Ford, then vice president. When Ford succeeded Richard Nixon as president later that year, Seidman was named executive director of the Economic Policy Board and also served as Ford's assistant for economic affairs. In 1977 Seidman left Washington to become the vice chairman and chief financial officer of the Phelps Dodge Corp., a large mining concern. He served as the dean of the business school at Arizona State University from 1982 to 1985, and from 1983 to 1985 he co-chaired Reagan's productivity commission. The latter position inspired Seidman to write the book *Productivity: The American Advantage* (1990). In 1993 he published *Full Faith and Credit*, which detailed his experiences as the head of the FDIC from 1985 to 1991. After leaving his post at the FDIC, Seidman became a chief commentator for the CNBC network and publisher of the magazine *Bank Director*. An artist at heart, he spent much of his free time creating mobiles. Seidman, who died following a bout with pneumonia, is survived by his wife, Sally; his five daughters, Tracy, Sarah, Carrie, Meg, and Robin; his son, Tom; and several grandchildren and great-grandchildren. See *Current Biography* (1976). — M.E.R.

Obituary *New York Times* (on-line) May 14, 2009

SHRIVER, EUNICE KENNEDY July 10, 1921–Aug. 11, 2009 Foundation administrator; social worker; volunteer. A member of one of the most respected families in American politics, Eunice Kennedy Shriver, the founder of the Special Olympics, used her stature to become an effective advocate for the developmentally disabled. Born Eunice Mary Kennedy in Brookline, Massachusetts, she was the fifth of nine children of Joseph P. and Rose Fitzgerald Kennedy, and a sister of President John F. Kennedy and Senators Robert F. Kennedy and Edward M. "Ted" Kennedy. Shriver attended Manhattanville College, in Purchase, New York, and later transferred to Stanford University in Palo Alto, California, where she received a bachelor's degree in sociology in 1943. Shriver subsequently moved to Washington, D.C., to work in the Special War Problems Division of the U.S. Department of State. In 1947 she became an executive secretary at a Department of Justice project on juvenile delinquency. Shriver went on to serve as a social worker at the Federal Penitentiary for Women in Alderson, West Virginia, and in 1951 she moved to Chicago, where she worked at a youth shelter and at the city's juvenile court. In 1956 Shriver became the executive vice president of the Joseph P. Kennedy Jr. Foundation, which her father had established in 1946 in honor of Shriver's eldest brother, who had been killed in World War II. The foundation had, up until that point, served largely as a source of funding for Catholic organizations and institutions for the mentally disabled. Under Shriver's leadership, the group began focusing on preventing mental retardation and improving the ways in which society dealt with the developmentally disabled. The foundation distributed millions of dollars in grants for research into the causes of retardation and helped establish a network of research centers as well as centers for the study of medical ethics at Harvard University and Georgetown University. Shriver pushed for the formation of President Kennedy's Panel on Mental Retardation in 1961 and the development of the National Institute of Child Health and Human Development (now named for Shriver) a year later. Shriver next established a summer camp for developmentally challenged children at her home in Maryland. In July 1968 she organized the first Special Olympics event in Chicago, bringing together 1,000 developmentally disabled athletes from the U.S. and Canada. That December Special Olympics Inc. became a nonprofit charitable organization, and it has since grown to include almost three million athletes in more than 180 countries. Shriver had been inspired, in part, by her older sister, Rosemary Kennedy, who had been born with a mild form of mental retardation. Throughout their childhood, she and Rosemary shared a close bond and often participated in athletic activities together. (In 1941, as Rosemary became moody and aggressive, her father secretly arranged for her to undergo a lobotomy. The procedure left her more disabled than before, and she was sent to live in an institution. Shriver was the first in her family to publicly speak about her sister.) In 1981 Shriver founded Community of Caring, a school-based program initially aimed at preventing teenage pregnancy, thus reducing the incidence of mental retardation, which is more often found in babies born to young mothers. The program now also focuses on the dangers of drug and alcohol abuse and dropping out of school. Over the course of her life, Shriver received numerous awards for her work on behalf of people with intellectual disabilities, including the Legion of Honor, the Albert Lasker Public Service Award, the National Recreation and Park Association National Voluntary Service Award, and the Order of the Smile of Polish Children. In 1984 she received the Presidential Medal of Freedom, the nation's highest civilian honor, from Ronald Reagan. After months of declining health following a series of strokes, Shriver died in Hyannis, Massachusetts. Her last surviving brother, Edward, died two weeks later. She is survived by her husband, Robert Sargent Shriver Jr.; her sister Jean Kennedy Smith; her children, Robert, Maria, Timothy, Mark, and Anthony; and 19 grandchildren. — See *Current Biography* (1996). — M.A.S.

Obituary *New York Times* A p23 Aug. 12, 2009

SINGH, VISHWANATH PRATAP June 25, 1931– Nov. 27, 2008 Indian statesman. Even before his short tenure as prime minister of India, Vishwanath Pratap Singh championed the rights of the country's poor and fought government corruption. Singh was born in Allahabad, in the Indian state of Uttar Pradesh. His father was the king of Daiya, a large feudal estate in northern India, and his mother was the second of the monarch's three wives. When Singh was five, his father allowed the childless ruler of the neighboring principality of Manda to adopt him. Cut off from his birth family, Singh had a privileged yet lonely childhood. His adoptive father died when Singh was 11. Because of conflicts among those seeking custody of him, Singh lived with armed bodyguards for several years. He studied law at Allahabad University and later took up physics at Fergusson College in Pune, India, hoping to join the country's atomic energy research center in Mumbai. Instead, Singh entered politics and joined the ruling Congress Party in the late 1960s. He was elected to the Uttar Pradesh state assembly in 1969 and to the Parliament of India in 1971. Three years later Prime Minister Indira Gandhi appointed Singh to her cabinet as deputy minister of commerce. She named him chief minister of Uttar Pradesh in 1980. When Rajiv Gandhi became prime minister, in 1984, Singh was appointed finance minister. In that post he initiated an aggressive campaign against tax evaders, ordering raids on several prominent industrialists—including supporters of the ruling party. When Singh began investigating the financial activities of close associates of the prime minister in 1987, Gandhi transferred him to the post of defense minister. Still determined to root out government corruption, Singh uncovered a military-contract scandal in which he believed the prime minister had been involved. Singh was soon dismissed from the cabinet, and he quit the Congress Party. He went on to form the National Front, a political coalition consisting of parties from all points on the political spectrum, united against the Congress Party. (He was often referred to as the father of coalition politics in India.) The National Front rose to power when it defeated the ruling party in the 1989 elections, and on December 2, 1989 Singh became the 10th prime minister of India. During his time in office, he attempted to implement the Mandal Commission recommendations, which reserved a fixed number of public sector jobs for the historically disadvantaged members of the lower classes, or "backward castes." Higher-caste youth retaliated with widespread protests across India. This, along with economic concerns and violent clashes between the nation's religious groups, diminished Singh's popularity, and he resigned from his duties as prime minister on November 7, 1990, after receiving a no-confidence vote from Parliament. Singh was instrumental in forming another political coalition group, the United Front, and when it defeated the Congress Party, in 1996, Singh was its first choice for prime minister. He declined the offer. Outside politics, Singh wrote poetry and painted. He died of blood cancer and renal failure in New Delhi and is survived by his wife, Sita Kumari, and two sons, Ajeya and Abhay. See *Current Biography* (1990). — M.A.S.

Obituary *New York Times* A p45 Nov. 30, 2008

SNODGRASS, W. D. Jan. 5, 1926–Jan. 13, 2009 Poet. Pulitzer Prize-winner William DeWitt (W.D.) Snodgrass was among the preeminent practitioners of the so-called "confessional" style of poetry. He wrote poems about his personal life and experiences, including the dissolution of his first marriage and feelings of alienation. Snodgrass was born in Wilkinsburg, Pennsylvania, and raised in Beaver Falls. He attended Geneva College for a brief time before enlisting in the U.S. Navy, where he served as a typist during World War II. Snodgrass was discharged after three years and went on to enroll in poetry-writing courses at the University of Iowa (then known as the State University of Iowa). As a graduate student, Snodgrass wrote several poems that were published throughout the early 1950s in various magazines and literary quarterlies, including the *Paris Review*, the *Hudson Review*, and the *New Yorker*. After obtaining his M.F.A. degree in 1953, Snodgrass embarked on a lengthy teaching career that included stints at Cornell University, the University of Rochester, Wayne State University, Syracuse University, and Old Dominion University. His first collection of poems, *Heart's Needle*, was published in 1959. For that volume, Snodgrass received the Pulitzer Prize for poetry in 1960, as well as several other awards, including a grant from the National Institute of Arts and a special citation from the Poetry Society of America. He went on to publish numerous other poetry collections, including *These Trees Stand* (1981), *Selected Poems: 1957–1987* (1987), *Each in His Season* (1993), and *Not for Specialists: New and Selected Poems* (2006). *The Führer Bunker: A Cycle of Poems in Progress* (1977), a controversial work that imagined a sequence of monologues by infamous Nazi figures during the last days of World War II, was nominated for the National Book Critics Circle Award for Poetry. Snodgrass adapted the work into a short-lived stage production for New York City's American Place Theater in 1981. Snodgrass also wrote books of literary criticism and translations, and his *Selected Translations* (1998) won the Academy of American Poets' Harold Morton Landon Award in 1999. Snodgrass retired from teaching in 1994, after 15 years as a professor of writing and contemporary poetry at the University of Delaware. He died of lung cancer in Erieville, New York, at the home in which he had lived for 40 years. Snodgrass is survived by his fourth wife, Kathleen Brown; a daughter from his first marriage; and a son from his second marriage. See *Current Biography* (1960). — M.A.S.

Obituary *New York Times* A p32 Jan. 15, 2009

SPRINKEL, BERYL Nov. 20, 1923–Aug. 22, 2009 Beryl Wayne Sprinkel, an undersecretary of monetary affairs and chairman of the Council of Economic Advisers (CEA) under President Ronald Reagan, played a key role in shaping the Reagan administration's economic policies. Born and raised in Richmond, Missouri, Sprinkel, a skilled singer, initially considered a career in music. Enlisting in the U.S. Army, he served as a tank gunner during World War II and subsequently attended the University of Missouri, in Columbia, where he earned a bachelor's degree in public administration in 1947. Sprinkel studied under Nobel Prize–winning economist Milton Friedman at the University of Chicago and received a master's degree in business administration in 1948 and a Ph.D. degree in economics four years later. He then spent almost three decades working for Harris Trust and Savings Bank, one of Chicago's largest financial institutions, rising through the ranks to become executive vice president. In 1981 Donald T. Regan, President Reagan's choice for treasury secretary, tapped Sprinkel to be his undersecretary for monetary affairs. In that role Sprinkel served as a tough principal negotiator on issues of Third World debt and the financing of such organizations as the International Monetary Fund. Sprinkel, a "monetarist," held that the nation's money supply was the chief determinant of economic growth and inflation, and his economic views often clashed with the Reagan administration's "supply-siders," who believed that tax cuts would lead to widespread financial prosperity. In 1985 Sprinkel was nominated as chairman of the three-person CEA, which provides policy advice to the president. In that capacity, he predicted the 1987 stock-market crash, warning in the months leading up to the event that the Federal Reserve's monetary policy was setting the stage for a financial crisis and advising the administration to permit negotiations with Congress on tax increases. In the fall of 1987, Sprinkel announced his resignation, ostensibly to deal with a family member's illness. Some observers suggested that his real reason for stepping down from the council was his disappointment that he had been passed over to succeed the departing Paul Volcker as chair of the Federal Reserve Board. (Alan Greenspan was appointed instead.) Whatever the actual reason, Reagan refused to accept the resignation and raised Sprinkel's post to cabinet level. Sprinkel, agreeing to stay, chaired the Council of Economic Advisers until 1989. He died on his way to a hospital in Chicago Heights, Illinois. The reported cause of death was Lambert-Eaton myasthenic syndrome, a rare neuromuscular disease. He was preceded in death by his first wife, Esther; his second wife, Barbara; and two sons, Dennis and Gary. He is survived by his third wife, Lory; a son, Kevin; two stepchildren, Janet and David; and 10 grandchildren. See *Current Biography* (1987). — M.A.S.

Obituary *New York Times* A p21 Sep. 2, 2009

SUZMAN, HELEN Nov. 17, 1917–Jan. 1, 2009 South African anti-apartheid activist; legislator. As a member of the South African Parliament (1953–89), where she was immune to prosecution for her utterance of anti-government sentiments, Helen Suzman fought relentlessly, vociferously, and for 13 years solitarily (and for six as the only woman) to end the discrimination against nonwhite South Africans and improve their living conditions; for many outside South Africa, she became the white face of the anti-apartheid struggle, acting as a spokesperson for all those denied the right to express openly their opposition to the government and their yearnings for other civil and human rights. For that reason she was reviled in her native land among whites and widely praised elsewhere. She continued her efforts to strengthen democracy in South Africa in the years following her departure from Parliament. She became a friend of Nelson Mandela's during his many years of imprisonment (as a member of Parliament, she was permitted to visit him), and after his release and his election as the first black leader of South Africa, she supported his policy of reconciliation with those who had carried out the oppressive policies of apartheid. In her final years she publicly condemned as "despicable" Mandela's successor, Thabo Mbeki, because of his willfully ignorant approach to the AIDS epidemic in South Africa, his anti-white rants, and his failure to confront Robert Mugabe, Zimbabwe's dictator, regarding policies that had caused widespread disease and destitution among black Zimbabweans. Suzman was born Helen Gavronsky in Germiston, near Johannesburg, to Jewish immigrants to South Africa from Lithuania. Although she was never religious, she embraced values associated with Judaism, including the imperative to treat others fairly and to pursue knowledge. To facilitate the latter, her father, who had prospered in business in Johannesburg, and her mother enrolled her in the Parktown Convent school, which offered a rigorous course of study. Years later, during an interview, she attributed her zeal in fighting apartheid to the mentoring of a teacher there: "When I shirk something I know I ought to do, the ghost of Sister Columba, the head nun, whispers in my ear 'Do it, child,' and I do." After she graduated, in 1934, she entered the University of Witwatersrand, in Johannesburg. In 1937 she married Moses Suzman (widely known by his nickname, Mosie or Mozie), a prominent neurosurgeon (or cardiologist, according to some sources) considerably older than she was, and withdrew from the school. After the births of their two daughters, she returned to the university; she always had helpers to care for the girls, and her husband always supported her activities outside their home. As an undergraduate, she told interviewers, she became aware of some of the indignities inflicted daily on nonwhite South Africans. She earned a B.Com. (bachelor of commerce) degree with first-class honors in economics and economic history in 1940. For the next four years, she served as a statistician with the South African War Supplies Board, a government agency. For eight years beginning in 1945, she lectured part-time on the South African economy at the University of Witwatersrand. In the mid-1940s, for a toothless commission of inquiry appointed by the administration of President Jan Christiaan Smuts, she gathered information about conditions endured by nonwhite laborers in the country, and she gained a newfound awareness of the deplorable circumstances under which many people worked—a state of affairs that she talked about during her university lectures. In 1953, with her husband's encouragement, Suzman ran successfully for a seat in Parliament as a United Party representative from Houghton, the Johannesburg district in which she lived. Six years later, fed up with the party's foot-dragging in opposing the government and fighting racial segregation, she co-founded the Progressive Party (later, the Progressive Federal Party). The Progs, as they became known informally, called for equal opportunity for all people and a bill of rights to guarantee basic freedoms. They made virtually no headway in achieving their goals, and in 1961 Suzman was the only one among 12 Progs who won election or reelection to Parliament—in her case, by a tiny margin. She thus became the sole member of the legislature, which then had 166 lawmakers, to speak out against apartheid and push for other unpopular causes, such as fair treatment of Communists and Jehovah's Witnesses. She never stopped doing so, despite total social ostracism by her fellow parliamentarians and denunciations by those who branded her with labels such as "tool of Communist agitators" or—though she never spoke in any official capacity as a Jew—directed anti-semitic remarks at her; death threats issued by phone and mail, too, failed to intimidate her. She also tried in vain to allocate part of the government's windfalls from sales of gold to improve black people's education, health care, housing, and transportation, and she pushed, equally unsuccessfully, for loosening government laws regarding peaceful assembly and censorship of films, publications, and advertisements. Among her few tangible achievements was the inclusion of identification numbers on police officers' badges. "It is useful to know who is hitting you on the head with a rubber truncheon," she observed, as quoted by Judy Rensberger in an Alicia Patterson Foundation newsletter in 1974, after Suzman had served in Parliament for two decades and had "finely honed" her skills as a legislator, in Rensberger's words. "She is a knowledgeable and effective speaker, a meticulous researcher and rarely, if ever, has she been caught with her facts wrong—a record that has won grudging respect even from bitter opponents," Rensberger wrote. When legislators accused her of deliberately asking "embarrassing" questions about, for example, the number of people being imprisoned without trial or the circumstances under which people had died while being detained, she would respond, "It is the answers, not the questions, that are embarrassing." The petite Suzman herself had a sharp tongue and a "waspish wit," according to the Helen Suzman Foundation; she was "a master of the pungent aside and cutting rejoinder," according to the *Australian* (January 3, 2009, on-line). She once recommended to B. J. "John" Vorster, South Africa's prime minister from 1966 to 1978, that he visit his district "heavily disguised as a human being," and she described a head of the Bureau of State Security as "South Africa's very own Heinrich Himmler"—a reference to the head of the police in Nazi Germany. Her reputation among many antiapartheid activists in the U.S. and Great Britain was dimmed to some degree when, to their surprise and dismay, Suzman voiced her opposition to economic sanctions against South Africa, boycotts of South African products or companies, and divestiture of stock in those firms, on the grounds that such tactics were completely ineffective. She maintained, rather, that more-rapid economic development and strikes by miners and other such internal economic pressures were more likely to weaken apartheid. Starting with the national elections of 1974, other Progressive politicians joined her in Parliament. She resigned her seat in 1989. In her last speech in Parliament, she proposed the censure of a judge who had merely slapped the wrists of two white farmers charged with beating a black laborer to death. (Although her motion failed, the judge was subsequently relieved of his court duties.) From 1991 to 1993 Suzman served as president of the South African Institute for Race Relations. Her autobiography, *In No Uncertain Terms: A South African Memoir*, came out in 1993. During her retirement she continued to give lectures; she also enjoyed playing golf and fly-fishing and spending time with her several dogs. Her many honors included the U.N. Human Rights Award (1978); the American Jewish Committee's American Liberties Medallion (1984); the Roger E. Joseph Award of Human Rights, from Hebrew Union College, New York (1986); the Moses Mendelssohn Prize, awarded by the West Berlin Senate (1988); the B'Nai B'Rith Dor L'Dor Award (1992), and more than two dozen honorary degrees. Suzman died at her home in Johannesburg. The hundreds of people who attended her funeral, which was private (her daughters, Patricia and Frances, turned down the government's request to hold a state funeral), included the former South African president F. W. de Klerk; Gwede Mantashe, the secretary general of the ruling African National Congress; and Winnie Madikizela-Mandela, the former wife of Nelson Mandela. The chief rabbi of South Africa, Warren Goldstein, eulogized Suzman, saying, "She concerned herself with the plight of individuals, following the Talmudic teaching that to save one life is to save a world. Suffering South Africans—black and white—turned to her for help. She . . . tried her best to solve each one of their problems, doing work which was nearly all unsung and unreported in the public domain. With kindness and compassion she visited prisoners to bring them comfort and to fight for ways of improving their conditions." On the day she was buried, South African flags flew at half-mast. In addition to her daughters, Suzman's survivors included the actress Janet Suzman, a niece by marriage. See *Current Biography* (1968). — M.H.

Obituary *New York Times* A p20 Jan. 2, 2009

SWAYZE, PATRICK Aug. 18, 1952–Sep. 14, 2009 Actor. With his rugged good looks, Patrick Swayze, a dancer turned actor, first rose to prominence during the early 1980s, after appearing in a series of teen films, including *The Outsiders*, *Red Dawn*, and *Youngblood*. He achieved romantic leading-man status with his roles in the breakthrough films *Dirty Dancing* (1987) and *Ghost* (1990). Although Swayze's popularity had waned by the late 1990s, he continued to work steadily in film and on television. In 2009 he starred as an undercover FBI agent in *The Beast*, which aired on A&E. Swayze was born in Houston, Texas, the second child of Jesse Wayne Swayze, an engineering draftsman for an oil company and rodeo champion, and Patsy Swayze, a choreographer and dance teacher who ran her own studio, the Houston Ballet Dance Company, where Swayze first studied. After attending Oak Forest Elementary School, Black Junior High, and Waltrip High School, Swayze accepted a gymnastics scholarship to Houston's San Jacinto College. He dropped out after two years to take part in the North American tour of the Disney on Parade ice show, after which the 20-year-old Swayze returned to Houston and became romantically involved with Lisa Niemi, one of his mother's pupils. Determined to pursue a career in dance, he moved to New York City in 1972. Swayze and Niemi married in 1975, when he joined the choreographer Eliott Feld's company as a principal dancer, but his ballet career ended prematurely after he experienced complications from knee surgery. Deciding instead to become an actor, Swayze appeared onstage in the musical *Goodtime Charley* in 1976. Two years later he landed the lead role of Danny Zuko in the long-running Broadway musical *Grease*. In 1979, the year that Swayze moved with his wife to Los Angeles, he made his feature-film debut in *Skatetown, U.S.A.*, a "roller-disco" movie starring Scott Baio. He followed that with roles in the made-for-television movies *The Comeback Kid* (1980) and *Return of the Rebels* (1981), as well as a guest appearance in the hit television comedy *M*A*S*H*. In 1982 Swayze starred in another television movie: *The Renegades*, in which he played Bandit, the leader of a street gang recruited by the police to do undercover work; he reprised the role a year later, in a short-lived ABC series. Swayze next co-starred opposite C. Thomas Howell, Tom Cruise, Rob Lowe, Emilio Estevez, and Matt Dillon in Francis Ford Coppola's 1983 adaptation of the S.E. Hinton novel *The Outsiders*. The following year he reunited with Howell in the post-apocalyptic drama *Red Dawn*, which also co-starred Jennifer Grey. In 1985 Swayze played a Southern soldier in the ABC miniseries *North and South*; he later reprised his role for the sequel in 1986, the same year that Swayze co-starred opposite Lowe in the teen drama *Youngblood*. He returned to his dancing roots in 1987, when he starred opposite Grey in the coming-of-age drama *Dirty Dancing*, in which he played Johnny Castle, an instructor at a Catskills resort. The film, which grossed more than $200 million worldwide, earned Swayze a legion of female fans and a Golden Globe Award nomination. Swayze also had a top-10 hit with the ballad "She's Like the Wind," which was featured on the film's soundtrack. He followed that blockbuster with a series of forgettable movies, including the science-fiction drama *Steel Dawn*, which co-starred his wife, and the action thrillers *Road House* (1989) and *Next of Kin* (1989). Swayze received his second Golden Globe nod for *Ghost* (1990), in which he played Sam Wheat, an investment banker who enlists a psychic (Whoopi Goldberg) to help solve his own murder. He then starred as a charismatic bank-robbing surfer in *Point Break* (1991) and as a doctor who travels to India in search of spiritual enlightenment in the 1992 adaptation of the Dominique Lapierre novel *City of Joy*. In 1996 Swayze earned his third Golden Globe nomination for playing a drag queen in *To Wong Foo, Thanks for Everything, Julie Newmar* (1995). Over the next decade Swayze amassed screen credits for his roles in several little-seen films, including *Three Wishes* (1995), *Black Dog* (1998), *Letters from a Killer* (1998), *Forever Lulu* (2000), and *Green Dragon* (2001). During that period the actor made tabloid headlines for his struggles with drugs and alcohol as well as his 1998 horseback-riding accident, which left him with two broken legs and a shattered left shoulder. Following a noteworthy performance in the cult film *Donnie Darko* (2001) as an overconfident motivational speaker, the actor appeared opposite his wife in the romantic drama *One Last Dance* (2003), also Niemi's directorial debut. The next year he had a brief cameo in the *Dirty Dancing* prequel, *Dirty Dancing: Havana Nights*, and also made a guest appearance in an episode of Whoopi Goldberg's eponymous sitcom. Then came roles in the television action films *George and the Dragon* (2004), *King Solomon's Mines* (2004), and *Icon* (2005). In 2006 Swayze appeared in a London theater production of the musical *Guys and Dolls*, and a year later he starred in the holiday caper *Christmas in Wonderland*. In March 2008 Swayze was diagnosed with an advanced form of pancreatic cancer, which was treated with chemotherapy. Early the following year, the actor gave an exclusive television interview to Barbara Walters, speaking publicly about his condition and prognosis, as well as denying media reports that he was close to death. Despite his frail appearance, Swayze continued to work. His final feature-film appearance came in the ensemble drama *Powder Blue* (2009), which co-starred Forrest Whitaker and Lisa Kudrow. Also in 2009 he starred in the acclaimed police drama *The Beast*, which was cancelled after one season due to declining ratings and Swayze's deteriorating health. Swayze died in Los Angeles, following his two-year battle with cancer, which was covered extensively by the entertainment and tabloid press. He is survived by his wife; his mother; his brothers, Donald and Sean; and a sister, Bambi. Another sister, Victoria, died in 1994. See *Current Biography* (1991). — W.D.

Obituary *New York Times* (on-line) Sep. 15, 2009

TAYLOR, KOKO Sep. 28, 1928–June 3, 2009 Singer. Koko Taylor, who was known for her brassy vocals and heartfelt performances, was often called the "Queen of the Blues." Born Cora Walton to a family of sharecroppers, she was raised in Memphis, Tennessee. (Her nickname, "Koko," stemmed from her love of chocolate.) Her parents, Annie Mae and William Walton, had died by the time she reached her teens, leaving her in the care of her older siblings. Together, they sang in the fields while picking cotton on the family farm and listened to the blues on a battery-operated radio. In the early 1950s Cora left Memphis and headed to Chicago with her boyfriend, Robert "Pops" Taylor, a truck driver. The two soon married. Finding work as a maid and babysitter in Chicago's wealthy northern suburbs, she accompanied her husband at night to the city's all-black juke joints. Taylor had given little thought to pursuing a career in music, but at her new husband's urging, she began joining the musicians on stage for impromptu performances. (Among those she sang with in those early days were the legendary Howlin' Wolf and Muddy Waters.) That eventually led to a meeting with the influential, Chicago-based bass player and composer Willie Dixon, who helped her land a contract with Chess Records. Dixon produced some of Taylor's earliest singles, including the 1965 hit "Wang Dang Doodle," which became her signature song. (The song included the suggestive lyrics: "We gonna romp and tromp till midnight/ We gonna fuss and fight till daylight/ We gonna pitch a wang dang doodle all night long.") Taylor steadily built her fan base, performing locally and touring the country. In 1972 she was featured at the Ann Arbor Blues and Jazz Festival, in Michigan, which attracted the attention of the record executive Bruce Iglauer. After signing to Iglauer's newly formed jazz label, Alligator Records, in 1975, Taylor enjoyed a surge in popularity. She went on to record several albums for the label, including *I Got What It Takes* (1975), *The Earthshaker* (1978), *From the Heart of a Woman* (1981), the Grammy Award–winning *Queen of the Blues* (1985), *Jump for Joy* (1990), *Force of Nature* (1993), *Royal Blue* (2000), *Deluxe Edition* (2002), and *Old School* (2007). Over the course of her recording career, Taylor won 29 Blues Music Awards—more than any other artist in the history of the prize. After being in a near-fatal car accident in 1988, Taylor recovered and made her movie debut in 1990, playing a lounge singer in the David Lynch film *Wild at Heart*. She also sang in the movies *Mercury Rising* (1998), *Blues Brothers 2000* (1998), *Big Momma's House* (2000), and *Shadowboxer* (2005). Taylor, a member of the Blues Foundation's Hall of Fame and the recipient of a 2003 Pioneer Award from the Rhythm & Blues Foundation, died of complications following surgery for gastrointestinal bleeding. (She had survived a similar surgery six years earlier.) She is survived by her second husband, Hays Harris, a tavern owner; her daughter, Joyce Threatt, known as Cookie; two grandchildren; and three great-grandchildren. Her first husband, Robert Taylor, died in 1989. See *Current Biography* (2002). — C.C.

Obituary *New York Times* B p12 June 4, 2009

TERKEL, STUDS May 16, 1912–Oct. 31, 2008 Pulitzer Prize winner Studs Terkel was one of the most influential and well-known broadcast figures of the 20th century. Best known for his long-running radio show *The Studs Terkel Program*, which aired on 98.7 WFMT in Chicago between 1952 and 1997, he was also widely credited with bringing American oral history into acceptance as a popular literary form. The third of four sons, Louis Terkel was born to Samuel and Anna (Finkelin) Terkel in the New York City borough of the Bronx. His parents, both of Russian Jewish origin, had immigrated to the U.S. in the early 1900s. When Terkel was about eight years old, he moved with his family to Chicago, where, he claimed, the winds from the stockyards cured his childhood asthma. Terkel's father, who suffered from chronic angina, worked as a tailor, and both of his parents managed the Wells-Grand Hotel, a men's rooming house located on the West Side that was frequented by the poor, working-class people who inspired Terkel's oral-history collections. (When Terkel was 19, his father died, and his mother continued to run the boarding house.) Upon completing high school, Terkel attended the University of Chicago, where he earned a bachelor's degree in philosophy in 1932 and a J.D. degree in 1934. After a failed first attempt at the bar exam, Terkel passed it on his second try, but instead of practicing law, he accepted a position with the Works Progress Administration's Federal Writers' Project. There, he presented shows of recorded music, wrote radio scripts and advertisements, and served as news and sports announcer. He also took on roles in various radio soap operas. After joining the Chicago Repertory Group in the late 1930s, Terkel, who appeared in the theater group's production of *Waiting for Lefty*, adopted the nickname "Studs," inspired by Studs Lonigan, the protagonist of James T. Farrell's novels about the Chicago proletarian Irish. While acting with the Chicago Repertory, Terkel met Ida Goldberg, whom he married in 1939. In 1942 Terkel joined the special services of the Army Air Forces as a speechwriter, but he was discharged a year later, due to perforated eardrums. He then found work on commercial radio stations in Chicago, where he read news, sports, and commentary. In 1945 Terkel was hired to host *The Wax Museum*, a jazz show. Four years later he began hosting *Studs's Place*. Initially a segment of the television variety series *Saturday Night Square*, it was spun-off into its own show in 1950. *Studs's Place*, which was set in a bar and featured songs and stories, was cancelled in 1952, because of Terkel's leftist leanings, which resulted in his being blacklisted during the early 1950s. Shortly after the cancellation of *Studs's Place*, Terkel was hired at the radio station WFMT, where he hosted several shows, including *The Studs Terkel Almanac* and *The Studs Terkel Show*. In 1954 he began hosting *The Studs Terkel Program*; originally a forum for music, the hourlong daily show later incorporated interviews, mostly improvisational, into its format. During its 23-year run, *The Studs Terkel Program* featured a variety of guests, including playwright Tennessee Williams, classical guitarist Andrés Segovia, and philosopher Bertrand Russell. In 1957 Terkel authored his first book, *Giants of Jazz*; a decade later his first oral history book, *Division Street: America* (1967), a collection of tape-recorded interviews that Terkel had conducted with citizens in the inner cities, was published to rave reviews. Terkel subsequently authored numerous other volumes of oral history on various subjects, including race, war, and employment. Those included *Hard Times: An Oral History of the Great Depression* (1970); *Working: People Talk About What They Do All Day and How They Feel About What They Do* (1974); *American Dreams: Lost and Found* (1983); and *The Good War: An Oral History of World War II* (1984). For *The Good War* he was awarded the 1985 Pulitzer Prize for nonfiction. He went on to write *The Great Divide: Second Thoughts on the American Dream* (1988); *Race: What Blacks and Whites Think and Feel About the American Obsession* (1992); *Coming of Age: The Story of Our Century by Those Who've Lived It* (1995); *The Spectator: Talk About Movies and Plays with Those Who Make Them* (1999); *Will the Circle Be Unbroken: Reflections on Death, Rebirth and Hunger for a Faith* (2001); *Hope Dies Last: Keeping the Faith in Difficult Times* (2003); and *And They All Sang: Adventures of an Eclectic Disc Jockey* (2005). Terkel also authored the autobiographical *Talking to Myself: A Memoir of My Times* (1977), *Touch and Go* (2007), and *P.S.: Further Thoughts from a Lifetime of Listening* (2008) and wrote a jazz column for the *Chicago Sun-Times*. Terkel's occasional screen credits included minor roles in the films *Beginning to Date* (1953) and *Eight Men Out* (1988) as well as the made-for-television movie *The Dollmaker* (1984). In addition to the Pulitzer Prize, his honors include a 1980 Peabody Award for excellence in journalism and a 1997 National Book Foundation Medal. Terkel suffered a fall, and a few weeks later he died at his home in Chicago. Before his accident he had been working on a catalogue of his 9,000 taped interviews. Terkel was predeceased by Ida, who died in 1999. He is survived by his son, Dan. See *Current Biography* (1974). — W.D.

Obituary *New York Times* Nov. 1, 2008

UNDERWOOD, CECIL H. Nov. 5, 1922–Nov. 24, 2008 Former governor of West Virginia. In 1956, when he was 34 years old, Cecil Harland Underwood became the youngest governor in West Virginia history. (At the time, he was also the youngest governor in the entire country.) Elected to a second term 40 years later, he became the oldest governor in the state's history. Born in Joseph Mills, West Virginia, Underwood attended Salem College (now Salem International University) in Salem, West Virginia, graduating in 1943. (In 1952 he would earn a master's degree in political science from West Virginia University.) Upon graduating from Salem, Underwood became a high-school biology teacher in St. Mary's, West Virginia, and in 1944 he successfully ran for a seat in West Virginia's State House. A Republican, he represented Tyler County for six terms and served as minority floor leader from 1949 to 1956. During his time in the State House, Underwood also worked as the assistant to the president of Marietta College, in Marietta, Ohio, and in 1950 he became vice president in charge of public relations for Salem College. In 1956 Underwood became the first Republican to be elected governor of West Virginia in nearly three decades. After his four-year term, he was unable to run for reelection due to term limits that existed in the state's Constitution at the time. Underwood went on to serve as president of Bethany College in Bethany, West Virginia, and held executive positions at the Island Creek Coal Co., the Monsanto Chemical Co., and the New York Life Insurance Co. In 1996 Underwood narrowly defeated Charlotte Pritt, an ex-teacher, to win his second term as state governor. He ran once more, in 2000, but lost to Democrat Bob Wise. Underwood died at the Charleston Area Medical Center's Memorial Hospital in Charleston, Virginia. He was predeceased in 2004 by his wife, Hovah. He is survived by a son (Craig), two daughters (Cecilia and Sharon), and several grandchildren. — See *Current Biography* (1958). — M.A.S.

Obituary *New York Times* D p8 Nov. 29, 2008

UPDIKE, JOHN Mar. 18, 1932–Jan. 27, 2009 Writer. John Updike is widely considered one of the most important writers of his time. In the many novels and short stories that make up his vast catalogue of fiction, Updike's preferred subjects were always ordinary people. "My subject is the American Protestant small-town middle class," Updike once said. "I like middles. It is in middles that extremes clash, where ambiguity restlessly lies." In Updike's *New York Times* obituary (January 28, 2009, on-line), Christopher Lehmann-Haupt noted that the late author "wrote about America with boundless curiosity and wit in prose so careful and attentive that it burnished the ordinary with a painterly gleam." Updike's novels featuring the now-iconic Harry "Rabbit" Angstrom, a restless, disillusioned family man, are among his most popular and acclaimed works. The first book, *Rabbit, Run* (1960), which finds Angstrom in a loveless marriage and a dead-end sales job, was followed by *Rabbit Redux* (1971), *Rabbit Is Rich* (1981), and *Rabbit at Rest* (1990). (The latter two won the Pulitzer Prize for fiction.) Updike's penchant for the small dramas of marriage, sex, and divorce was evident in his earliest works, many of which are set in the fictional small town of Olinger, Pennsylvania. Those include the novels *The Poorhouse Fair* (1959), *The Centaur* (1963), and *Of the Farm* (1965) and the short-story collections *The Same Door* (1959) and *Pigeon Feathers* (1962). In addition to the Rabbit novels, the best-selling novel *Couples* (1968), about the sexual escapades of several suburban couples, epitomized Updike's fondness for lengthy and detailed—even "clinical"—descriptions of sex. Updike also published three collections of short stories about his fictional alter ego, Henry Bech, an unprolific, celebrity-obsessed Jewish writer: *Bech: A Book* (1970), *Bech Is Back* (1982), and *Bech at Bay* (1998). Other Updike novels include *A Month of Sundays* (1975), *Roger's Version* (1986), and *S.* (1988), each of which was a response to Nathaniel Hawthorne's *The Scarlet Letter*. Over time the scope of Updike's novels broadened. His novel *The Coup* (1978), for example, was set in an imaginary African country; *Brazil* (1994) was an experiment in magical realism; *Gertrude and Claudius* (2000) focused on Hamlet's mother and uncle; and *Terrorist* (2006) followed an 18-year-old disciple of radical Islam who aims to blow up the Lincoln Tunnel. Along the way he published numerous acclaimed volumes of essays, including *Just Looking: Essays on Art* (1989) and *Golf Dreams: Writings on Golf* (1996). His poetry collections include *The Carpentered Hen and Other Tame Creatures* (1958), *Midpoint* (1969), and *Facing Nature* (1985). Born in Reading, Pennsylvania, Updike was the only child of Wesley Russell Updike, a math teacher, and Linda Grace (Hoyer) Updike, an aspiring writer. He spent his early years in the town of Shillington and on a family farm near Plowville. Updike attributes his "patience to sit down day after day and to whittle a fantasy out of paper" to both his loneliness as an only child and to his mother's fondness for writing. The co-valedictorian and senior-class president of his high school, Updike was a scholarship student at Harvard, where he majored in English and wrote for the *Harvard Lampoon*. He graduated summa cum laude in 1954. A longtime cartoonist who as a child envisioned a career working for Walt Disney, Updike next attended the Ruskin School of Drawing and Fine Arts in Oxford, England, before moving back to the United States. He published his first short story, *Friends from Philadelphia*, in the *New Yorker* and soon became a regular contributor to the magazine. He lived briefly in Manhattan before settling in Ipswich, Massachusetts, with his wife, Mary Entwistle Pennington, whom he married in 1953 and who bore him four children: Elizabeth, David, Michael, and Miranda. Updike, relishing small-town life, had by 1959 produced his first three books as well as more than 100 essays, articles, and poems for the *New Yorker*. Updike and his wife separated in 1974, at which point he moved to Boston and taught briefly at Boston University. His divorce was finalized in 1976, and the following year he married Martha Ruggles Bernhard, ultimately settling with her and her three children (John, Jason, and Frederic) in Beverly Farms, Massachusetts. A much-loved literary figure of immense personal charm, Updike, who died of cancer, published some 60 books over the course of his career. A collection of short fiction, *My Father's Tears and Other Stories*, and a collection of poetry written during the last few years of his life, *Endpoint and Other Poems*, were published posthumously. See *Current Biography* (1984).

Obituary *New York Times* (on-line) Jan. 28, 2009

UTZON, JORN Apr. 9, 1918–Nov. 29, 2008 The celebrated Danish architect Jorn Utzon is best known as the designer of one of the world's most recognizable buildings—the Sydney Opera House. The son of a naval architect, Utzon studied architecture at the Royal Academy of Fine Arts in Copenhagen. Upon graduation in 1942, he moved to Stockholm, where he worked with the Swedish architect Hakon Ahlberg. Utzon then worked for Finnish architect and designer Alvar Aalto in Helsinki before establishing his own architectural firm in Copenhagen in 1950. Six years later, Utzon entered a competition to design an opera house in Sydney, New South Wales, Australia. His submission, which involved a series of overlapping round shells, was declared the winner in January 1957. Construction began on the opera house in 1959. Utzon, who had up until that point worked on the project in Denmark, moved his family to Sydney in 1962. As the exterior of the building was completed, Utzon found himself in constant battle with the New South Wales minister for public works, Davis Hughes, over budget concerns and delays. A frustrated Utzon resigned from the project in 1966 and moved back to Copenhagen with his family. Australian architect Harry Seidler and others led protests and marches through Sydney, urging the government to reinstate Utzon to the project. Instead, a team of local architects was hired to complete the building. The Sydney Opera House opened in 1973 and was quickly hailed as one of the major architectural achievements of the 20th century. For his design, Utzon was awarded a Gold Medal by the Royal Australian Institute of Architecture in 1973. Though his reputation suffered due to the Sydney Opera House controversy, Utzon went on to design a number of respected projects, including the Bagsvaerd Community Church, Fredensborg Housing Development, and Skagen Odde Nature Center, all in Denmark, and a National Assembly building in Kuwait. Uzton later retired, dividing his time between Copenhagen and a home he had built on Majorca, an island off the coast of Spain. Various Australian organizations had sought to make amends with the architect in recent years, and he was invited to design interior renovations for the Sydney Opera House in 2002. (Utzon, who never saw the finished building, sent one of his sons to carry out the work.) In 2003 Utzon received the Pritzker Prize, considered to be architecture's highest honor. He died in Copenhagen in his sleep and is survived by his wife, Lis; two sons; a daughter; and several grandchildren and great-grandchildren. See *Current Biography International Yearbook* (2003). — M.A.S.

Obituary *New York Times* A p45 Nov. 30, 2008

WEYRICH, PAUL Oct. 7, 1942–Dec. 18, 2008 Conservative activist. Paul Michael Weyrich was a key architect of the Religious Right movement, which fuses deeply held religious beliefs and a sense of morality with politics. A small-government, free-market conservative, Weyrich is said to have coined the term "moral majority." He was born in Racine, Wisconsin, to a German immigrant father who instilled in him strong political and religious beliefs. Weyrich attended the University of Wisconsin, dropping out shortly after obtaining his associate's degree in 1962. He worked as a reporter at the *Milwaukee Sentinel* (now the *Milwaukee Journal Sentinel*) for a year and then took a job as a political reporter and newscaster for CBS in Milwaukee. In 1966 he became the news director of the radio station KQXI in Denver, Colorado. Weyrich then moved to Washington, D.C., where he served as an assistant to Republican senators Gordon Allott and Carl T. Curtis. In 1973 he helped establish the Heritage Foundation, a staunchly conservative public-policy research institute. In 1977 he started the Free Congress Foundation, to battle what had been termed the "culture war" between religious traditionalists and left-leaning secularists. A lifelong train enthusiast, Weyrich served on the board of Amtrak from 1987 to 1993. He made headlines in 1989 when he testified before the Senate Armed Services Committee that he had seen President George H.W. Bush's nominee for secretary of defense, John G. Tower, drink excessively and behave inappropriately with women. (The Senate later rejected Tower's nomination, and Bush went on to name Dick Cheney to the post.) In more recent years Weyrich accused President George W. Bush of extravagant domestic spending and criticized the war in Iraq. Raised a Roman Catholic, Weyrich left the church in the early 1960s because he felt that it had become too liberal after the reforms of Vatican II. He joined the ultra-conservative Melkite Greek Catholic Church and was ordained a deacon in 1990. Weyrich died at Inova Fair Oaks Hospital in Fairfax, Virginia. His cause of death was not released, but he had suffered a number of health problems during the last years of his life, including diabetes and the amputation of both legs. Weyrich is survived by his wife, Joyce, two daughters, three sons, and several grandchildren. See *Current Biography* (2005). — M.A.S.

Obituary *New York Times* B p11 Dec. 19, 2008

WHITCOMB, RICHARD T. Feb. 21, 1921–Oct. 13, 2009 Aeronautical engineer. A statement issued by the Smithsonian Institution's National Air and Space Museum deemed Richard T. Whitcomb "arguably the most influential aeronautical engineer/researcher of the jet age." Whitcomb's most celebrated design was that of the "wasp-waist" fuselage, which he developed in 1951. The design calls for a sloping indent in the plane's fuselage where the wings are attached. The innovative shape reduced drag on supersonic jets, increasing their speed by 25 percent without requiring additional engine power. Richard Travis Whitcomb was born in Evanston, Illinois. His father, an engineer who had flown balloons in World War I, moved the family to Worcester, Massachusetts, when Whitcomb was still a young boy. During his adolescence Whitcomb spent much of his time in his home's basement, tinkering with model planes. (He concentrated only on models that would actually fly.) As a teenager he developed a method for doubling the power ordinarily generated from the rubber bands used to turn the propellers and won several prizes for his models. Whitcomb graduated from the Worcester Polytechnic Institute in 1943 with a B.S. degree in mechanical engineering. He became a researcher with the National Advisory Committee for Aeronautics (NACA), a government agency that conducted aviation research at Langley Field, Virginia. (NACA was succeeded by the National Aeronautics and Space Administration, or NASA, in 1958.) At NACA Whitcomb discovered the "area rule": near the speed of sound the drag-rise of planes "is primarily dependent on the axial distribution of cross-sectional areas normal to the air stream," as an article in *Aviation Week* (September 19, 1955) explained. On the basis of the area rule, Whitcomb established the principle of narrowing the fuselage at the point where the wings are attached to it, in order to make room for the air waves. He also tapered and lengthened the nose of the supersonic design. Thus, the shock waves forming around the wasp-waist model flowed inward toward the body of the craft instead of being pushed outward against a solid mass of air. The area-rule formula was used successfully on two supersonic military jets that had been originally designed with bulging fuselages, the Convair F-102A Delta and the Grumman F11F-1 Tiger, to great success and was soon widely heralded. Following his discovery of the area rule, Whitcomb was selected by the aviation industry to receive the Collier Trophy in 1954. He was also honored with NACA's distinguished service medal in 1956. During the 1970s Whitcomb developed supercritical wings, which were far less curved on the top than conventional wings. The design reduced the size of shock waves over the wings, allowing high-speed planes to fly as much as 100 miles per hour faster. Supercritical wings are now a standard feature on all new commercial jets. Years later Whitcomb introduced winglets, the small, vertical panels that are attached to the tips of planes' wings. Providing another way to reduce drag, winglets increase fuel efficiency by as much as 7 percent. Whitcomb died of pneumonia in Newport News, Virginia. He never married and is survived by a sister, a brother, a stepbrother, and a nephew. See *Current Biography* (1956). — M.A.S.

Obituary *New York Times* A p21 Oct. 26, 2009

WHITMORE, JAMES Oct. 1, 1921–Feb. 6, 2009 Actor. James Whitmore, who is often described by journalists as "craggy," enjoyed a decades-long career on the stage and screen. Among his many film credits are John Huston's *Asphalt Jungle* (1950), *Kiss Me Kate* (1953), *Tora! Tora! Tora!* (1970), and *The Shawshank Redemption* (1994). In the 1970s he was also known for his traveling one-man shows; he portrayed the cowboy humorist Will Rogers in *Will Rogers' U.S.A.* and earned lavish praise for his portrayal of President Harry S. Truman in *Give 'Em Hell, Harry!*, which was later made into a movie. Born James Allen Whitmore Jr. in White Plains, New York, Whitmore enjoyed participating in school productions and hoped early on to become an actor. His mother, however, wanted him to become a lawyer. In 1939 he enrolled in the pre-law program at Yale University, in New Haven, Connecticut, on a football scholarship. During his senior year, in 1942, he enlisted in the U.S. Marines. He received his bachelor's degree from Yale during his service and was discharged in 1946. Whitmore then decided to pursue his dream of acting and joined the United Service Organizations (USO) as a performer. A year later he moved to New York City and studied at the Actors Studio and the American Theater Wing. Whitmore made his Broadway debut in 1947, as a wisecracking sergeant in the World War II play *Command Decision.* The play ran for more than 400 performances, and Whitmore received a Tony Award in the category of outstanding performance by a newcomer as well as a Theatre World Award. In 1950 Whitmore won a Golden Globe and was nominated for the best-supporting-actor Academy Award for only his second movie role, in the 1949 war picture *Battleground.* He went on to appear in dozens of films, including *Them!* (1954), *Oklahoma!* (1955), *Black Like Me* (1964), *Madigan* (1968), *Planet of the Apes* (1968), and *Where the Red Fern Grows* (1974). He earned a second Academy Award nomination, this time for best actor in a lead role, for the 1975 film version of his stage show *Give 'Em Hell, Harry!* Whitmore also appeared in several television series, including *Playhouse 90, The Twilight Zone, Gunsmoke,* and *CSI: Crime Scene Investigation.* He headlined his own series in 1960, the short-lived ABC drama *The Law and Mr. Jones.* For his guest appearance as a lawyer on the ABC series *The Practice,* Whitmore won the 2000 Emmy Award for outstanding guest actor in a drama series. Later in life he became a spokesman for Miracle-Gro plant foods; his TV commercials for the company ran from 1982 to 2002. Whitmore married his first wife, Nancy Mygatt, in 1947. Following their split, he married actress Audra Lindley in 1971. They too parted eventually, and Whitmore once again wed Mygatt, a reunion that ended in his third divorce. He married actress Noreen Nash in 2001. Whitmore, whose bushy eyebrows became something of a trademark during his career, died of lung cancer in his California home. He is survived by Noreen Nash, three sons from his first marriage (Daniel, Steven, and James), and several grandchildren. See *Current Biography* (1976).

Obituary *New York Times* A p19 Feb. 7, 2009

WILSON, MARGARET Jan. 30, 1919–Aug. 11, 2009 Organization official; lawyer. From the mid-1970s to the early 1980s, Margaret Wilson headed the board of directors of the National Association for the Advancement of Colored People (NAACP); she was the first woman to hold that post. During her tenure, Wilson worked to improve the organization's management and finances and addressed such issues as affirmative action and energy policy. She was ousted from her post after a contentious power struggle. She was born Margaret Berenice Bush in St. Louis, Missouri. Her mother, a teacher, occupied a seat on the NAACP's executive committee; her father, a railway postal clerk who later became a successful real-estate broker, was a longtime NAACP member and civil rights advocate. "In a literal sort of way, I was born and raised in the NAACP," Wilson told an *Ebony* (April 1975) interviewer, "and the issues that it faces have been a part of my life from my very earliest experiences." Wilson majored in economics (with a mathematics minor) at Talladega College, in Alabama, where she graduated cum laude in 1939 with a B.S. degree. Against the wishes of her father, who wanted her to become a nurse or teacher, she enrolled at the Lincoln University of Missouri School of Law, in Jefferson City. In 1943 she became one of the law school's first female graduates. She was the second black woman to pass the Missouri state bar exam. Wilson then worked in the legal division of the U.S. Department of Agriculture's Rural Electrification Administration, helping farmers create cooperatives. In 1945, a year after her marriage, she relocated to Chicago, where she volunteered at the Legal Aid Society while her husband completed his law-school studies. In 1946 the couple left Chicago and settled in St. Louis, where they founded a firm specializing in real-estate law. Wilson also served as legal counsel for the Real Estate Brokers Association of St. Louis; founded by her father, the organization figured in *Shelley v. Kraemer* (1948), a landmark case in which the U.S. Supreme Court ruled that racially restrictive covenants in real-estate contracts were unconstitutonal. Also in 1948 Wilson became the first black woman in Missouri to run for Congress. She ran on the Progressive Party ticket to represent Missouri's 11th Congressional District, losing to her Democratic opponent. In 1956 Wilson became actively involved with the St. Louis branch of the NAACP, working to encourage businesses to hire African-Americans. Within two years she was appointed head of the branch. In 1963, a year after serving as president of the Missouri State Conference of NAACP Branches, she was elected to the national board of the NAACP. During the 1960s she also held posts outside the organization. From 1961 to 1962 she was an assistant Missouri state attorney general, and in 1965 she began a two-year stint as a legal-services specialist with the State Technical Assistance Office, implementing the Lyndon B. Johnson administration's anti-poverty program. From 1967 to 1968 she worked for the Missouri Department of Community Affairs. Over the next decade Wilson continued to climb the ranks of the NAACP. In 1973 she became the permanent chair of the NAACP's national convention, also serving as the organization's chief parliamentarian for two years (1973–74). In 1974 Wilson was appointed head of the NAACP committee that lobbied for the impeachment of President Richard Nixon. The next year she won the position of board chair, which she held for nine years. Wilson's tenure as board chair was marked by controversy and a power struggle. Six months after Robert L. Hooks's appointment as NAACP's executive director, in 1977, Wilson, then a board member of the agricultural biotechnology company Monsanto Corp., shocked NAACP members and labor unions by supporting an oil policy that was in line with that of the oil industry. Her positions often frustrated Hooks, with whom she frequently clashed; their difficult relationship became fodder for the news media. In May 1983 Wilson suspended Hooks for managerial incompetence, citing a 25 percent decrease in membership, outstanding bills, and significant turnover of financial managers. The board, which had not been consulted on the firing, rehired Hooks eight days later, and Wilson retained only ceremonial power. After her dismissal Wilson argued that she had been the victim of sexism. After leaving the NAACP she moved back to St. Louis, where she resumed practicing law. She died at Barnes-Jewish Hospital in St. Louis. She was survived by her son, Robert, and two grandchildren. See *Current Biography* (1976).—W.D.

Obituary *New York Times* (on-line) Aug. 14, 2009

WYETH, ANDREW July 12, 1917–Jan. 16, 2009 Artist. Andrew Newell Wyeth was one of the most alternately celebrated and discredited artists of recent times. To some, the work of the magic-realist painter of rural landscapes, houses, and people was a welcome alternative to the abstractionist pieces prevalent throughout the 1940s, '50s, and '60s. To others, including many contemporary art critics, his paintings were uninspired and dull. Nevertheless, Wyeth was enormously popular, and his 1948 work *Christina's World*, in which a woman crippled by polio crawls through a grassy field towards her home, is considered one of the most iconic paintings of the 20th century. Andrew Wyeth was the youngest of five children. His father, N.C. Wyeth, was a popular artist who illustrated editions of such classics as *Treasure Island*, *Robin Hood*, and *The Last of the Mohicans*. A shut-in for most of his childhood due to illness, Wyeth was home-schooled and learned to draw and paint from his father. Born and raised in the small Pennsylvania town of Chadds Ford, Wyeth focused his early work on the landscapes of his rural surroundings as well as those of coastal Maine, where his family spent summers. His first solo exhibit, at New York City's William Macbeth Gallery in 1937, when he was only 20, was comprised of watercolors depicting Maine landscapes. In the late 1930s Wyeth began to work in egg tempera, a medium in which pigment is mixed with egg yolks. He married Betsy Merle James in 1940. She introduced him to her longtime friend Christina Olson, who lived in Cushing, Maine. Olson would later become Wyeth's most famous subject. The painter continued to live and work in Chadds Ford and kept a home in Cushing. In 1943 he was invited to participate in the Museum of Modern Art's "American Realists and Magic Realists" exhibition in New York City. Two years later his father and nephew died when their car stalled on a railroad track and was struck by a train. As a result of the tragedy, a sense of loneliness and melancholy informed Wyeth's subsequent work. He began to paint more portraits, enlisting neighbors as subjects—among them Karl and Anna Kuerner, a German couple who lived on a Chadds Ford farm; Helga Testorf, who worked as a housemaid for Wyeth's sister; and Olson, who is depicted in *Christina's World*. The Kuerners' expansive farm and Olson's weathered clapboard home provided the inspiration for many of his landscape and architectural paintings, including *Brown Swiss* (1957), *Groundhog Day* (1959), and *The End of Olsons* (1969). Wyeth's work has been exhibited in many of the nation's top museums, including the Pennsylvania Museum of Art, the Whitney Museum in New York City, and the Art Institute of Chicago. In 1976 Wyeth became the first living American artist to be the subject of a retrospective at the Metropolitan Museum of Art in New York City. In 1963 he became the first artist to receive the Presidential Medal of Freedom, the highest civilian honor in the U.S., and two years later he was awarded a gold medal from the National Institutes of Arts and Letters. In 2007 he was presented with the National Medal of Arts by President George W. Bush for his lifetime contributions to American arts and culture. Wyeth died quietly in his sleep at the age of 91 in Chadds Ford. He is survived by Betsy, known for her deep devotion to her husband and his work, and their two adult sons, Nicholas (an art dealer) and James (an artist). See *Current Biography* (1981). —M.A.S.

Obituary *New York Times* (on-line) Jan. 17, 2009

YORK, HERBERT F. Nov. 24, 1921–May 19, 2009 Physicist. As a participant in the Manhattan Project and a one-time director of the Lawrence Livermore Laboratory at the University of California, Herbert Frank York played a crucial part in the U.S. government's development of nuclear weapons. Later in life, however, he became a fierce advocate of arms control and an opponent of nuclear testing. He was born in Rochester, New York, to Herbert F. York, a railway worker, and Nelly Elizabeth (Lang) York. At the University of Rochester, York majored in physics and was a Phi Beta Kappa scholar. After earning bachelor's and master's degrees, in 1942 and 1943, respectively, he joined the staff of the Radiation Laboratory at the University of California at Berkeley. In 1944 he was recruited for the Manhattan Project and assigned to work on the electromagnetic separation of uranium 235. When World War II ended, he returned to the University of California to earn a doctoral degree in physics, completing the program in 1949. In 1951 UC Berkeley appointed York as an assistant professor of physics, and the following year he became director of the Livermore Laboratory, where he worked on developing the hydrogen bomb, among other projects sponsored by the Atomic Energy Commission. York took a leave of absence from the university in 1958 to become the chief scientist of the Advanced Research Projects Agency, established at the Pentagon. Serving as the director of space and antimissile research, he helped create a definite and cohesive space program. (Among the initiatives he championed was the development of the unmanned vehicles known as lunar probes.) While York often stated that the Manhattan Project could be credited with ending the war, his views on nuclear weapons and arms development changed during the next decades. In 1970 he published *Race to Oblivion: A Participant's View of the Arms Race*, and during the Jimmy Carter administration he was a delegate at several important nuclear-arms talks with the Soviet Union. (Known for his sense of humor and affability, York reportedly regaled the otherwise dour Soviet negotiators with jokes and anecdotes.) In 1983 he founded the Institute on Global Conflict and Cooperation, which was based at the University of California at San Diego, where he served as chancellor from 1961 to 1964 and again from 1970 to 1972. Lauded as a warm, enthusiastic instructor, he also chaired the school's physics department for a time and served as dean of graduate studies. York's other books include *Making Weapons, Talking Peace: A Physicist's Odyssey from Hiroshima to Geneva* (1987; also published with the subtitle *A Physicist's Journey from Hiroshima to Geneva*) and *Arms and the Physicist* (1995). York's many accolades included the E. O. Lawrence Prize (1964), a Guggenheim Fellowship (1972–73), the Leo Szilard Award for Physics in the Public Interest (1994), and the Enrico Fermi Award (2000). In 1991 York underwent radiation treatments for prostate cancer, and his death almost two decades later was reportedly related to the ill effects of that treatment. He is survived by his wife, Sybil; his three children, Rachel, Cynthia, and David; and his grandchildren. See *Current Biography* (1958). — D.K.

Obituary *New York Times* (on-line) May 25, 2009

CLASSIFICATION BY PROFESSION—2009

ACTIVISM
Ayers, William
Barlow, Maude
Cao, Anh "Joseph"
Clinton, Hillary Rodham
Doerr, John
Jealous, Benjamin Todd
Jones, Van
Maddow, Rachel
Mam, Somaly
Mortenson, Greg
Obama, Barack
Solis, Hilda L.
Solmonese, Joe
Steves, Rick
Taylor, Jill Bolte
Wolfson, Evan

AGRICULTURE
Vilsack, Tom

ARCHITECTURE
Donovan, Shaun
Mousavi, Mir Hossein

ART
Banksy
Bechdel, Alison
Emin, Tracey
Gallagher, Ellen
Gilbert and George
Hirschhorn, Thomas
Jacir, Emily
Knox, Simmie
M.I.A.
Mousavi, Mir Hossein
Neto, Ernesto
Otis, Clarence Jr.
Shaw, Dash

ASTRONOMY
McKay, Christopher P.
Soderberg, Alicia M.

BUSINESS
Ambani, Anil
Ambani, Mukesh
Baker, Mitchell
Boras, Scott
Charney, Dov
Clinton, Hillary Rodham
Doerr, John
Emanuel, Ari
Emanuel, Rahm
Greenwald, Julie
Iijima, Sumio
Jarrett, Valerie
Kilar, Jason
Mashouf, Manny
McCullough, Gary E.
Otis, Clarence Jr.
Plouffe, David
Salazar, Ken
Schiller, Vivian
Steves, Rick
Tonatto, Laura
Williams, Evan
Williams, Ronald A.
Zardari, Asif Ali
Zell, Sam

COMPUTERS
Baker, Mitchell

CONSERVATION
Jolly, Alison
Jones, Van
Layton, Jack
Mortenson, Greg

DANCE
Blankenbuehler, Andy
Elo, Jorma

ECONOMICS
Johnson, Simon

EDUCATION
Ayers, William
Cao, Anh "Joseph"
Chu, Steven
Cooper, Kyle
Duncan, Arne
Dutton, Denis
Gates, Robert M.
Gordon-Reed, Annette
Gordon, Wycliffe
Greenwald, Julie
Gunn, Tim
Higgs, Peter
Honderich, Ted
Iijima, Sumio
Jamison, Kay Redfield
Jarvis, Jeff
Johnson, Simon
Jones, Tayari
Kerlikowske, R. Gil
Knox, Simmie
LaHood, Ray
Layton, Jack
Llinás, Rodolfo R.
McCullough, Gary E.
McLachlin, Beverley
Mlodinow, Leonard
Mortenson, Greg
Mousavi, Mir Hossein
Nixon, Marni
Obama, Barack
Offit, Paul A.
Soderberg, Alicia M.
Sotomayor, Sonia
Thomson, David
Trout, J.D.
Wallerstein, Immanuel
Wolfson, Evan

FASHION
Charney, Dov
Gunn, Tim
M.I.A.
Mashouf, Manny
Odom, Lamar

FILM
Abrams, J.J.
Allen, Ray
Aronofsky, Darren
Cooper, Kyle
El-Tahri, Jihan
Emin, Tracey
Gordon, Wycliffe
Guggenheim, Davis
Hathaway, Anne

CUMULATED INDEX 2001–2009

This is the index to the January 2001–November 2009 issues. It also lists obituaries that appear only in yearbooks for the years 2001 to 2009. For the index to the 1940–2005 biographies, see Current Biography Cumulated Index 1940–2005.